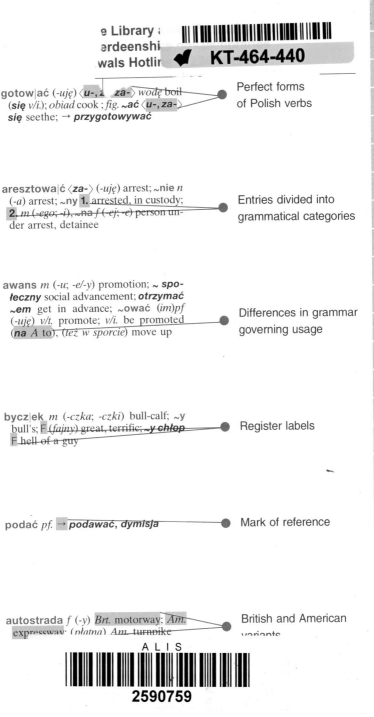

gotow|ać (*-uję*) ⟨**u-, z**... **za-**⟩ *wodę* boil (**się** *v/i.*); *obiad* cook ; *fig.* **~ać** ⟨**u-, za-**⟩ **się** seethe; → ***przygotowywać***

Perfect forms of Polish verbs

aresztowa|ć ⟨**za-**⟩ (*-uję*) arrest; **~nie** *n* (*-a*) arrest; **~ny 1.** arrested, in custody; **2.** *m* (*-ego*; *-i*), **~na** *f* (*-ej*; *-e*) person under arrest, detainee

Entries divided into grammatical categories

awans *m* (*-u*; *-e/-y*) promotion; ***~ społeczny*** social advancement; ***otrzymać ~em*** get in advance; **~ować** (*im*)*pf* (*-uję*) *v/t.* promote; *v/i.* be promoted (***na*** *A* to), (*też w sporcie*) move up

Differences in grammar governing usage

bycz|ek *m* (*-czka*; *-czki*) bull-calf; **~y** bull's; F (*fajny*) great, terrific; ***~y chłop*** F hell of a guy

Register labels

podać *pf.* → ***podawać, dymisja***

Mark of reference

autostrada *f* (*-y*) *Brt.* motorway; *Am.* expressway; (*płatna*) *Am.* turnpike

British and American variants

Berlitz®

Polish
Concise Dictionary

Polish – English
English – Polish

Berlitz Publishing
New York · Munich · Singapore

Edited by the Langenscheidt editorial staff

Based on a dictionary compiled by Prof. Tadeusz Piotrowski in collaboration with Dr. Adam Sumera

Book in cover photo: © Punchstock/Medioimages

Neither the presence nor the absence of a designation indicating that any entered word constitutes a trademark should be regarded as affecting the legal status thereof.

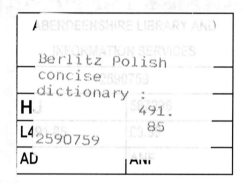

Berlitz Publishing
193 Morris Avenue
Springfield, NJ 07081
USA

Printed in Germany
ISBN 978-981-268-057-0

1. 2. 3. 4. 5. 11 10 09 08 07

Preface

This new dictionary of English and Polish is a tool with more than 50,000 references for learners of the Polish language at beginner's or intermediate level.

A large number of idiomatic expressions has been included. The user-friendly layout with all headwords in blue allows the user to have quick access to all the words, expressions and their translations.

Clarity of presentation has been a major objective. Is *flimsy* referring to furniture the same in Polish as *flimsy* referring to an excuse? This dictionary is rich in sense distinctions like this – and in translation options tied to specific, identified senses.

Vocabulary needs grammer to back it up. In this dictionary you will find irregular English verb and plural forms as well as inflectional endings of Polish verbs and nouns.

The additional activity section provides the user with an opportunity to develop language skills with a selection of engaging word puzzles. The games are designed specifically to improve vocabulary, spelling, grammar and comprehension in an enjoyable style.

Designed for a wide variety of uses, this dictionary will be of great value to those who wish to learn Polish and have fun at the same time.

Spis treści
Contents

Wskazówki dla użytkownika
Guide to Using the Dictionary

Porządek alfabetyczny i dobór haseł
Wszystkie wyrazy hasłowe podane są w porządku alfabetycznym. Do ich opisu stosowane są odpowiednie kwalifikatory dziedzinowe – przedstawiające ich przynależność do poszczególnych dziedzin oraz kwalifikatory stylistyczne – wskazujące na różne style danego wyrazu.

akuszer *m* (*-a*; *-rzy*) *med.* obstetrician; **~ka** *f* (*-i*; *G -rek*) midwife

Użycie tyldy (~) i dywizu
Tylda zastępuje cały wyraz hasłowy lub jego część, znajdującą się po lewej stronie kreski pionowej.

cierpliw|ość *f* (*-ści*; *0*) patience; ***uzbroić się w ~ość*** exercise one's patience; **~ie** patiently

bawić ⟨***po- za-***⟩ (*-ę*) v/i. stay; be on a visit (***u*** *G* to); *v/t.* entertain; amuse; ***~ się*** (*dobrze itp.*) have a good time; enjoy o.s.; ***~ się*** play (***z dziećmi*** with children, ***lalką*** with a doll); *fig.* ***nie ~ się w*** (*A*) not waste too much time on

W formach gramatycznych, podawanych w nawiasach okrągłych lub w nawiasach trójkątnych wyrazy hasłowe lub ekwiwalenty wyrazów hasłowych zastąpiono dywizem.

cierpliw|ość *f* (*-ści*; *0*) patience

Hasła mające kilka odpowiedników
Odpowiedniki bliskoznaczne wyrazu hasłowego podano obok siebie oddzielając je przecinkami.

administrować (*-uję*) (*I*) administer, manage

Jeżeli wyraz hasłowy ma kilka odpowiedników dalekoznacznych, w takim przypadku na pierwszym miejscu podano znaczenie bliższe lub pierwotne, a potem kolejno znaczenia dalsze lub pochodne, oddzielone średnikiem.
Różnice znaczeniowe objaśniane są za pomocą:
– kwalifikatorów działowych,
– poprzedzających synonimów, podawanych w nawiasach okrągłych,

Alphabetical order and the choice of entries
The entries are given in a strictly alphabetical order. Special labels are used to help to describe them. There are also labels for words that are restricted to specific fields of usage.

akuszer *m* (*-a*; *-rzy*) *med.* obstetrician; **~ka** *f* (*-i*; *G -rek*) midwife

The use of the swung dash (~) and the hyphen The swung dash replaces the headword or the part of it that appears to the left of the vertical bar.

cierpliw|ość *f* (*-ści*; *0*) patience; ***uzbroić się w ~ość*** exercise one's patience; **~ie** patiently

bawić ⟨***po- za-***⟩ (*-ę*) v/i. stay; be on a visit (***u*** *G* to); *v/t.* entertain; amuse; ***~ się*** (*dobrze itp.*) have a good time; enjoy o.s.; ***~ się*** play (***z dziećmi*** with children, ***lalką*** with a doll); *fig.* ***nie ~ się w*** (*A*) not waste too much time on

In grammatical forms given in round or angle brackets the entries or their equivalents are replaced with a hyphen.

cierpliw|ość *f* (*-ści*; *0*) patience

Entries with more than one meaning
Translations of the headword that are used synonymously are given next to each other and are separated by commas.

administrować (*-uję*) (*I*) administer, manage

If the Polish headword has more than one English equivalent, it is the basic or original meaning that is presented first. Further or derivative meanings come later and are separated by a semicolons.
Differences in meaning are explained by the use of:
– labels,
– preceding synonyms, given in round brackets,

– poprzedzających lub następujących po odpowiedniku dopełnień, podmiotów lub innych wskazówek objaśniających.

ciąć ⟨**ś-**⟩ *v/t.* cut; *impf. drzewa* fell; (*piłą*) saw; *v/i. deszcz wiatr*: lash

Jeżeli wyraz hasłowy należy do różnych kategorii gramatycznych, oddzielono je cyfrą arabską oraz oznaczono odpowiednim kwalifikatorem gramatycznym.

bez|ustanny 1. *adj.* incessant, unstopping; **2.** *adv.* **~*ustannie*** incessantly; **~usterkowy** (**-*wo***) trouble-free; **~użyteczny** useless

Homonimy podano w osobnych hasłach oznaczonych kolejnymi cyframi arabskimi, podanymi w indeksie.

ciepło[1] *n* (*-a*; *0*) warmth, heat
ciepło[2] *adv.* warm

Hasła rzeczownikowe
Hasła rzeczownikowe opatrzone są zawsze skrótem rodzaju gramatycznego *m, f, n*.
W nawiasach okrągłych podano końcówki drugiego przypadka l. poj., pierwszego przypadka l. mn. oraz sporadycznie drugiego przypadka l. mn.

cierń *m* (*-nia*; *-nie -ni*) thorn, spine

Hasła przymiotnikowe
Jako hasła główne występują przymiotniki w mianowniku liczby poj. w rodzaju męskim w stopniu równym. Przymiotniki występujące tylko w rodzaju żeńskim podane są jako oddzielne hasła. Formy stopnia wyższego i najwyższego przymiotników stopniowanych nieregularnie podawane są w nawiasach okrągłych. Dodatkowo formy te zostały ujęte w liście haseł.

ładny *adj.* (*comp. -niejszy*) pretty, nice

Hasła czasownikowe
Jako wyrazy hasłowe występują z reguły czasowniki niedokonane. Przy czasownikach niedokonanych, posiadających aspekt dokonany podano w nawiasach trójkątnych przedrostek lub przyrostek, za pomocą których tworzony jest ich aspekt dokonany. Czasowniki niedokonane, nieposiadające odpowiednika dokonanego pozostają nieoznaczone. Cza-

– objects, subjects or other explanatory notes preceding or following the translation.

ciąć ⟨**ś-**⟩ *v/t.* cut; *impf. drzewa* fell; (*piłą*) saw; *v/i. deszcz wiatr*: lash

If the Polish headword is used as more than one part of speech, it is separated by Arabic numerals and marked with a suitable grammatical label.

bez|ustanny 1. *adj.* incessant, unstopping; **2.** *adv.* **~*ustannie*** incessantly; **~usterkowy** (**-*wo***) trouble-free; **~użyteczny** useless

Homonyms are presented under separate entries marked with exponent numerals.

ciepło[1] *n* (*-a*; *0*) warmth, heat
ciepło[2] *adv.* warm

Nouns
Noun entries are always assigned an abbreviation of grammatical gender: *m, f* or *n*.
The endings of the second case singular, the first case plural and sometimes the second case plural are given in round brackets.

cierń *m* (*-nia*; *-nie -ni*) thorn, spine

Adjectives
Adjectives are given in the singular, masculine nominative of the simple form. Adjectives that are only feminine are given as separate entries. When the comparative and superlative forms of an adjective are irregular, these have been given in round brackets. Aditionally, these forms have been included in the list of entries.

ładny *adj.* (*comp. -niejszy*) pretty, nice

Verbs
As a rule imperfect verbs appear as entries. Imperfect verbs that have the perfect aspect are followed by angle brackets in which a prefix or a suffix that is used to form the perfect aspect of the verb is given. Imperfect verbs that do not have their perfect aspect are unmarked. Verbs that have only the perfect aspect are marked *pf.* Verbs that

sowniki, posiadające tylko aspekt dokonany opatrzone zostały kwalifikatorem *pf.* Czasowniki dwuaspektowe natomiast oznaczone kwalifikatorem *(im)pf.*

jechać (*-dę*) ⟨***po-***⟩ go (***koleją*** by train); ride (***rowerem*** (on) a bike, ***konno*** (on) a horse)
minąć *pf.* (*-nę -ń*) go by
kazać (*im*)*pf* (*każę każ!*) order, command

W nawiasach okrągłych z dywizem podano końcówki pierwszej osoby l. poj.

lamentować (*-uję*) lament (***nad*** *I* over)

can be used in both aspects are marked *(im)pf.*

jechać (*-dę*) ⟨***po-***⟩ go (***koleją*** by train); ride (***rowerem*** (on) a bike, ***konno*** (on) a horse)
minąć *pf.* (*-nę -ń*) go by
kazać (*im*)*pf* (*każę każ!*) order, command

The endings of the first person singular are given in round brackets with a hyphen.

lamentować (*-uję*) lament (***nad*** *I* over)

Skróty
Abbreviations

biernik	*A*	accusative
przymiotnik	*adj.*	adjective
przysłówek	*adv.*	adverb
rolnictwo	*agr.*	agriculture
amerykański angielski	*Am.*	American English
anatomia	*anat.*	anatomy
architektura	*arch.*	architecture
astronomia	*astr.*	astronomy
przydawka	*attr.*	attributive
lotnictwo	*aviat.*	aviation
bezokolicznik	*bezok.*	infinitive
biologia	*biol.*	biology
botanika	*bot.*	botany
brytyjski angielski	*Brt.*	British English
budownictwo	*bud.*	building
chemia	*chem.*	chemistry
spójnik	*cj.*	conjunction
stopień wyższy	*comp.*	comparative
pogardliwy	*cont.*	contemptuously
celownik	*D*	dative
dialekt	*dial.*	dialect
ekonomia	*econ.*	economics
elektronika	*electr.*	electrical engineering
rodzaj żeński	*f*	feminine
potoczny, pospolity	F	familiar, colloquial
przenośnie	*fig.*	figuratively

dopełniacz	*G*	genitive
gastronomia	*gastr.*	gastronomy
gerundium	*ger.*	gerund
gramatyka	*gr.*	grammar
historia	*hist.*	history
humorystyczny	*hum.*	humorous
łowiectwo	*hunt.*	hunting
narzędnik	*I*	instrumental
nieodmienny	*idkl*	indeclinable
aspekt niedokonany i dokonany	*(im)pf*	imperfective and perfective
wykrzyknik	*int.*	interjection
i tym podobnie	*itp.*	et cetera
prawniczy	*jur.*	legal
kogoś	*k-ś*	*somebody's*
miejscownik	*L*	locative
językoznawstwo	*ling.*	lingustics
literatura, literacki	*lit.*	literature, literary use
rodzaj męski	*m*	masculine
rodzaj męski lub rodzaj żeński	*m/f*	masculine or feminine
matematyka	*math.*	mathematics
medycyna	*med.*	medicine
meteorologia	*meteor.*	meteorology
wojskowość	*mil.*	military term
między innymi	*min.*	among other things
motoryzacja	*mot.*	motoring
muzyka	*mus.*	music
rodzaj nijaki	*n*	neuter
żeglarstwo	*naut.*	nautical
mianownik	*N*	nominative
ogólnie	*ogóln.*	generally
optyka	*opt.*	optics
parlamentarny	*parl.*	parliamentary term
partykuła	*part.*	particle
imiesłów czasu przeszłego	*p.p.*	past participle
pedagogika	*ped.*	pedagogy
pejoratywny	*pej.*	pejorative
farmacja	*pharm.*	pharmacy
fotografika	*phot.*	photography
fizyka	*phys.*	physics
fizjologia	*physiol.*	physiology
liczba mnoga	*pl.*	plural
poetycki	*poet.*	poetic
polityka	*pol.*	politics
czas przeszły	*pret.*	preterit(e)
drukarstwo	*print.*	printing
zaimek	*pron.*	pronoun
przyimek	*prp.*	preposition
przestarzały	*przest.*	obsolete
psychologia	*psych.*	psychology

kolejnictwo	*rail.*	railroad, railway
religia	*rel.*	religion
patrz	*see*	refer to
liczba pojedyncza	*sg.*	singular
slang	*sl.*	slang
sportowy	*sport.*	sports
stopień najwyższy	*sup.*	superlative
szkocki angielski	*Szkoc.*	Scottish
technika	*tech.*	technology
telekomunikacja	*teleph.*	telephony
zastrzeżony znak towarowy	*TM*	trademark
teatr	*theat.*	theatre
tylko	*t-ko*	only
uniwersytecki	*univ.*	university
wulgarny	V	vulgar
czasownik posiłkowy	*v/aux.*	auxiliary verb
czasownik nieprzechodni	*v/i.*	intransitive verb
czasownik momentalny	*v/s.*	instantaneous verb
czasownik przechodni	*v/t.*	transitive verb
weterynaria	*vet.*	veterinary medicine
w złożeniach	*w złoż.*	compound
wyraz zbiorowy	*zbior.*	collective noun
zoologia	*zo.*	zoology
zwykle	*zw.*	usually
zwłaszcza	*zwł.*	especially
patrz	→	see, refer to

Notes on Polish Pronunciation

Polish vowels

letter	sound	pronunciation	example
a	a	similar to English *a* in luck	mama
ą	ɔ̃	similar to English *ow*, in know	mąż
e	ɛ	between English *a* in man and *e* in men	chleb
ę	ɛ̃	similar to English *en* in ten	męski
i	i	as English *i* in he	mina
	ĭ	as English *y* in year	talia
o	ɔ	as English *o* in boy	okno
ó	u	as English *oo* in moon, but shorter	ósmy
u	u	as English *u* in put	suma
y	i	between English *i* in sit and *e* in set	syn

Pronunciation of nasalised vowels

1. When used at the end of a word the vowels **ą, ę** lose their nasality
ę → /e/, ą → /o/, e.g.:
daję → /daje/, gazetę → /gazete/, są → /so/, dają → /dajo/
2. Pronunciation of nasalised vowels **ą, ę** before consonants
before **p, b – ą, ę → /om/, /em/**, e.g.:
skąpy → /skompy/, kąpie → /kompie/, trąba → /tromba/
następny → /nastempny/, tępy → /tempy/, zęby → /zemby/
before **t, d, c, dz, cz – ą, ę → /on/, /en/**, e.g.:
piąty → /pionty/, kąty → /konty/, gorąco → /goronco/
piętro → /pientro/, chętnie → /chentnie/, więc → /wienc/
before **ć, dź – ą, ę → /oń/, /eń/**, e.g.:
płynąć → /płynońć/, bądź → /bońć/, mąci → /mońci/
pięć → /pieńć/, zdjęcie → /zdjeńcie/, wszędzie → /fszeńdzie/
before **k, g – ą, ę → /oŋ/, /eŋ/**, e.g.:
rąk → /roŋk/, strąk → /stroŋk/, drągiem → /droŋgiem/
ręka → /ręŋka/, węgiel → /weŋgiel/, tęgi → /teŋgi/
before **l, l, ł ą, ę → /o/, /e/**, e.g.:
zaczął → /zaczoł/, zaczęli → /zaczeli/
before **w, w, f, f, s, ś, z, ź, ż (rz), ch (h), ch, h – ą, ę** do not lose their nasality, e.g.:
wąs → /vąs/, kęs → /kęs/.

Polish consonants

letter	sound	pronunciation	example
c	ts	as English *ts* in its	cały
ch	x	as English *h* in hand	chyba
cz	tʃ	as English *tch* in itch	czas

ć (ci)	tç	as softly *tch*	bić, ciocia
dz	dz	as in English red zone	chodzę, dzwon
dź (dzi)	ðž	as softly *dz*	dźwig, działo
dż, drz	dʒ	as English *j* in just	dżem, drzwi
h	x	as English *h* in hand	herbata
ł	w	as English *w* in wet	stół, miło
ń (ni)	ŋ	as English *ni* in onion	koń, koniec
r	r	as English *r* in red	rak
rz	ʃ	as English *s* in ship	krzak
	ʒ	as English *s* in pleasure	rzeka
s	s	as English *s* in yes	sala
sz	ʃ	as English *sh* in show	szal
ś (si)	ç	as softly *s*	świt, siwy
w	v	as English *v* in voice	woda
z	z	as English *z* in zebra	zadanie
ź (zi)	ž	as softly *z*	późno, zimno
ż	ʒ	as English *s* in pleasure	żaba

Pronunciation of consonants

Most voiced consonants have voiceless equivalents, e.g. **b p**, **w f**, **d t**, **z s**, **dz c**, **ż sz**, **dż cz**, **ź ś**, **dź ć**, **g k**.

Voiced consonants become voiceless in the following contexts:

– at the end of a word, e.g.: *klub* → */klup/*, *bagaż* → */bagasz/*

– before voiceless consonants, e.g.: *babka* → */bapka/*, *brzydki* → */brzytki/*, *wszyscy* → */fszyscy/*

The consonant **ł** is not pronounced when situated between 2 consonants, e.g. *jabłko* → */japko/*.

on, **om**, **en**, **em** are pronounced **ą**, **ę**, before the following consonants: **f, w, s, z, t, d, dz, n, ł,** *e.g.*: *sens* → */sęs/*, *konsul* → */kąsul/*, *komfort* → */kąfort/*.

Stress in Polish

Stress in Polish is regular and usually falls on the penultimate syllable, e.g.: *gotowanie, przemówienie, robotnik, klasówka*. Stressed syllables are pronounced longer than unstressed syllables.

Exceptions:

a) The third syllable from the end is stressed in the first and second person plural, e.g: *czytaliśmy, zwiedzaliście*, as well as in all singular forms and third person plural of the conditional, e.g.: *zrobiłabym, widzieliby*.

b) The third syllable from the end is stressed in nouns ending in *-yka*, *-ika*, e.g.: *matematyka, turystyka, polemika*.

c) The fourth syllable from the end is stressed in the first and second person plural of the conditional, e.g.: *zrobilibyśmy, widzielibyście*.

Zestawienie symboli fonetycznych w języku angielskim

Samogłoski i dwugłoski

znak fonetyczny	zbliżony polski odpowiednik	przykłady
iː	*i*	see, read
ɪ	*y*	in, chips
e	*e*	bed, head
ɜː	*e (długie)*	first, nurse
ə	*a (zanikowe)*	about, butter
æ	*a*	bad, cat
ʌ	*a (krótkie)*	much, love
ɑː	*a (długie)*	father, start
uː	*u (długie)*	too, two
ʊ	*u (krótkie)*	good, put
ɔː	*o (długie)*	door, law
ɒ	*o (krótkie)*	shop, lot
aɪ	*ay (łączne)*	ride, try
eɪ	*ey (łączne)*	day, face
ɔɪ	*oy (łączne)*	boy, choice
ɪə	*ya (łączne)*	here, beer
eə	*ea (łączne)*	hair, pear
ʊə	*ua (łączne)*	poor tour
aʊ	*au (łączne)*	now, mouth
əʊ	*ou (łączne)*	home, no

Spółgłoski

znak fonetyczny	zbliżony polski odpowiednik	przykłady
p	*p*	pen, happen
b	*b (rozdźwięcznione)*	body, job
t	*t*	toy, better
d	*d (rozdźwięcznione)*	odd, day
k	*k*	key, school
g	*g (rozdźwięcznione)*	ghost, go
f	*f*	coffee, physics

v	*w*	heavy, very
θ	*f (wymawiane międzyzębowo)*	think, path
ð	*z (wymawiane międzyzębowo)*	this, other
s	*s lub z (po dźwięcznej spółgłosce)*	sister, glass, dogs
z	*z (rozdźwięcznione)*	zero
ʃ	*sz*	shop, fish
ʒ	*ż (rozdźwięcznione)*	pleasure, television
tʃ	*cz*	church, much
dʒ	*dż (rozdźwięcznione)*	age, just
h	*h (wymawiane wydechowo)*	hot, whole
m	*m*	more, hammer
n	*n*	nice, sun
ŋ	*n (jak np. w bank)*	thing, long
l	*l*	light, feel
r	*r (bryt. ang. wymawiane tylko przed samogłoskami)*	right, hurry
j	*j*	yes, use
w	*ł*	one, when

Alfabet angielski

	wymowa		wymowa
a	[eɪ]	**n**	[en]
b	[biː]	**o**	[əʊ]
c	[siː]	**p**	[piː]
d	[diː]	**q**	[kjuː]
e	[iː]	**r**	[ɑː]
f	[ef]	**s**	[es]
g	[dʒiː]	**t**	[tiː]
h	[eɪtʃ]	**u**	[juː]
i	[ai]	**v**	[viː]
j	[dʒeɪ]	**w**	['dʌbljuː]
k	[keɪ]	**x**	[eks]
l	[el]	**y**	[waɪ]
m	[em]	**z**	[zed]

The Polish Alphabet

	Pronunciation
a	[a]
ą	[ɔ̃]
b	[bɛ]
c	[tsɛ]
ć	[tɕɛ]
d	[dɛ]
e	[ɛ]
ę	[ɛ̃]
f	[ɛf]
g	[gɛ]
h	[xa]
i	[i]
j	[jɔt]
k	[ka]
l	[ɛl]
ł	[ɛw]
m	[ɛm]
n	[ɛn]
ń	[ɛɳ]
o	[ɔ]
ó	[ɔ kreskovanɛ]

	Pronunciation
p	[pɛ]
r	[ɛr]
s	[ɛs]
ś	[ɛɕ]
t	[tɛ]
u	[u]
w	[vu]
x	[iks]
y	[i grɛk]
z	[zɛt]
ź	[ɛt]
ż	[ʒet]

Compound letters

ch	[xa]
cz	[tʃɛ]
dz	[dzɛ]
dź	[dʑɛ]
dż	[dʒɛ]
rz	[ɛrzɛt]
sz	[ɛʃ]

Polish – English

A

a *cj.*, *part* and; **~!** *int.* oh!, ah!; ***nic ~ nic*** nothing at all
a. *skrót pisany*: ***albo*** or
abażur *m* (*-u/-a*; *-y*) lampshade
abdykacja *f* (*-i*; *-e*) abdication
abecadło *n* (*-a*; *G -deł*) alphabet; (*podstawy*) the ABC
abonament *m* (*-u*; *-y*) (*teatralny itp.*) season ticket; *tel.* rental charge; *RTV*: *Brt.* licence (*Am.* license) fee
abonent *m* (*-a*; *-ci*), **~ka** *f* (*-i*; *G -tek*) *tel. itp.* subscriber
abonować (*-uję*) subscribe to
aborcja *f* (*-i*; *-e*) abortion
abp *skrót pisany*: ***arcybiskup*** Abp, Arch. (*Archbishop*)
absencja *f* (*-i*; *-e*) absence; (*chorobowa*) absenteeism
absolutny absolute; *cisza* complete
absolwent *m* (*-a*; *-ci*), **~ka** *f* (*-i*; *G -tek*) graduate, school-leaver
absorbować ⟨**za-**⟩ (*-uję*) absorb (*też fig.*)
abstrahować (*-uję*): **~ *od*** (*G*) ignore, take no notice of
absurd *m* (*-u*; *-y*) absurdity
absurdalny absurd
aby *cj.* (in order) to, in order that; ***~ tylko*** let's (just) hope (that)
acetylen *m* (*-u*; *0*) acetylene
ach *int.* oh
aczkolwiek although
adamaszek *m* (*-szku*; *-szki*) damask
adaptacja *f* (*-i*; *-e*) adaptation; *bud.* conversion (***na biuro*** into offices)
adapt|er *m* (*-a/-u*; *-y*) F record-player; **~ować** (*im*)*pf* (*-uję*) *dzieło* adapt; *bud.* convert (***na*** *A* into); ***~ować się*** adapt (o.s.) (***do*** to)
adekwatny (***do*** *G*) commensurate (with *lub* to), adequate (to)
adidasy F *m/pl.* (*-ów*) sports shoes *pl.*, *Brt.* trainers *pl.*
adiunkt *m* (*-a*; *-nci*) (senior) lecturer
adiutant *m* (*-a*; *-nci*) aide-de-camp
administra|cja *f* (*-i*; *-e*) administration; **~cyjny** administrative; ***kara ~cyjna*** penalty for contempt of court; **~tor** *m* (*-a*; *-rzy*), **~torka** *f* (*-i*; *G -rek*) administrator
administrować (*-uję*) (*I*) administer, manage
admirał *m* (*-a*; *-owie*) admiral
adnotacja *f* (*-i*; *-e*) note
adoptować ⟨**za-**⟩ (*-uję*) adopt
adorator *m* (*-a*; *-rzy/-owie*), **~ka** *f* (*-i*; *G -rek*) admirer
adres *m* (*-u*; *-y*) address; ***pod jej ~em*** to her address; *fig.* to her; **~at** *m* (*-a*; *-ci*), **~atka** *f* (*-i*) addressee; *fig.* receiver; ***~at nieznany*** address unknown
adresować ⟨**za-**⟩ (*-uję*) address; (***do*** *G*) address (to); *fig.* direct (at)
Adriatyk *m* (*-u*; *0*) Adriatic Sea
adwent *m* (*-u*; *-y*) Advent; **~owy**: ***okres ~owy*** time of Advent
adwoka|cki lawyer's; ***zespół ~cki*** lawyer's office; **~t** *m* (*-a*; *-ci*), **~tka** *f* (*-i*; *G -tek*) lawyer; *Brt.* solicitor, *Am.* attorney; (*przed sądem*) *Brt.* barrister, *Am.* attorney(-at-law); **~tura** *f* (*-y*; *0*) legal profession
aero|- aero-, air-; **~bik** *m* (*-u*; *-i*) aerobics *sg.*; **~dynamiczny** aerodynamic; **~zol** *m* (*-u*; *-e*) aerosol, spray
afektowany affected
afera *f* (*-y*) scandal
aferzyst|a *m* (*-y*; *-ści*, *-ów*), **~ka** *f* (*-i*; *G -tek*) confidence trickster; F con-man
afgański Afghan
afisz *m* (*-a*; *-e*) poster; ***zejść z ~a*** *theat.* not to be performed any longer; **~ować się** (*-uję*) (*I*, ***z*** *I*) make a show (of), parade (s.th.)
Afryka *f* (*-i*) Africa
Afrykan|in *m* (*-a*; *-anie*; *-ów*), **~ka** *f* (*-i*; *G -nek*) African
afrykański African
agat *m* (*-u*; *-y*) agate
agen|cja *f* (*-i*; *-e*) agency; ***~cja towarzyska*** escort agency; **~cyjny** agency; **~da** *f* (*-y*) branch; (*terminarz*) agenda; **~t** *m* (*-a*; *-ci*), **~tka** *f* (*-i*; *G -tek*) agent; **~tura** *f* (*-y*) → ***agencja***; *coll.* agents *m/pl.*
agitac|ja *f* (*-i*; *zw. 0*) agitation; *pol.* can-

vassing; **~ja wyborcza** election propaganda; **~yjny** propaganda
aglomeracja *f* (*-i*; *-e*) conurbation
agonia *f* (*GDL -ii*; *0*) agony
agrafka *f* (*-i*; *G -fek*) safety pin
agrarny agrarian, agricultural
agresja *f* (*-i*; *-e*) aggression
agresor *m* (*-a*; *-rzy/-owie*) aggressor
agrest *m* (*-u*; *zw. 0*) *bot.* gooseberry
agresywny aggressive
agro|nom *m* (*-a*; *-owie/-i*) agronomist; **~technika** *f* agricultural technology
AIDS *m* (*idkl.*) AIDS; ***chory na ~*** person suffering from AIDS
airbus *m* (*-a*; *-y*) *aviat.* airbus
akacja *f* (*-i*; *-e*) *bot.* acacia; F robinia
akademia *f* (*GDL -ii*; *-e*) academy; (*zebranie*) ceremony
akademick|i academic; student; ***dom ~i*** student hostel; students' (hall of) residence; ***młodzież ~a*** students *pl.*; student body; ***rok ~i*** academic year
akademik *m* **1.** (*-a*; *-i*) F student hostel; students' (hall of) residence; **2.** (*-a*; *-cy*) (*członek akademii*) academic
akcent *m* (*-u*; *-y*) accent; stress; **~ować** ⟨**za-**⟩ (*-uję*) accent, stress; *fig.* emphasize
akcept *m* (*-u*; *-y*) *econ.* acceptance
akceptować ⟨**za-**⟩ (*-uję*) accept
akces *m* (*-u*; *zw. 0*) accession; ***zgłaszać ~ do*** (*G*) affirm one's wish to become
akcesoria *n/pl.* accessories *pl.*
akcj|a *f* (*-i*; *-e*) action; *econ.* campaign; ***~a powieści*** plot of the novel; ***~a wyborcza*** canvassing; ***~a policyjna*** police operation; ***wprowadzić do ~i*** put into action; ***miejsce ~i*** scene; **~e** *pl.* shares *pl.*
akcjonariusz *m* (*-a*; *-e*), **~ka** *f* (*-i*; *G -szek*) shareholder
akcyjn|y unsystematic; *econ.* share; ***spółka ~a*** *econ.* joint-stock company; ***kapitał ~y*** *econ.* share capital
aklamacj|a *f* (*-i*; *0*): ***przez ~ę*** by acclamation
akompani|ament *m* (*-u*; *zw. 0*) (*fortepianowy*) (piano) accompaniment; **~ować** accompany
akord *m* (*-u*; *-y*) *econ.* piece-work; *mus.* chord; ***pracować na ~*** be on piece-work
akordeon *m* (*-u*; *-y*) accordion
akordow|o *adv*: ***pracować ~o*** be on piece-work; **~y** piece-work; ***robotnik ~y*** pieceworker
akredytować (*-uję*) accredit
akredytywa *f* (*-y*) *econ.* letter of credit
akrobat|a *m* (*-y*; *-ci*), **~ka** *f* (*-i*; *G -tek*) acrobat; ***~(k)a na trapezie*** trapeze artist
akrylow|y acrylic; ***żywica ~a*** acrylic resin
aksamit *m* (*-u*; *-y*) velvet; **~ka** *f* (*-i*; *G -tek*) velvet ribbon; *bot.* marigold; **~ny** velvet; *głos itp.* velvety
akt *m* **1.** (*-u*; *-y*) act (*też jur.*); (*uroczystość*) ceremony; (*dokument*) act, deed; (*malarstwo*) nude; **2.** (*pl. -a*) file; ***~ kupna*** bill of sale; (*domu*) title deed; ***~ oskarżenia*** indictment; ***~ otwarcia*** opening ceremony; ***~ zgonu*** death certificate; ***~a*** *pl.* ***osobowe*** personal file *lub* dossier; ***odkładać do ~*** file away; *fig.* lay to rest
aktor *m* (*-a*; *-rzy*), **~ka** *f* (*-i*; *G -rek*) actor; **~ski** acting; **~sko** like an actor; **~stwo** *n* (*-a*; *0*) acting; (*sztuka*) dramatic art
aktówka *f* (*-i*; *G -wek*) briefcase, attaché case
aktual|izować (*-uję*) update; **~nie** *adv.* at present, currently; **~ność** *f* (*-ści*) relevance (to the present); (*wiadomości itp.*) topicality; **~ny** current; *problemy* topical
aktywizować (*-uję*) activate; *ludzi* mobilize
aktywn|ość *f* (*-ści*) activity; **~y** active
akumu|lacja *f* (*-i*; *0*) accumulation; **~lator** *m* (*-a*; *-y*) *Brt.* accumulator, *Am.* storage battery; **~lować** ⟨**z-**⟩ (*-uję*) accumulate
akupunktura *f* (*-y*; *0*) acupuncture
akurat *adv.* (*teraz*) at this very moment; (*dokładnie*) exactly; ***~!*** no way!
akustyczny acoustic(al)
akuszer *m* (*-a*; *-rzy*) *med.* obstetrician; **~ka** *f* (*-i*; *G -rek*) midwife
akwa|planacja *f* (*-i*; *-e*) aquaplaning; **~rela** *f* (*-i*; *-e*) water-colo(u)r; **~rium** *n* (*idkl.*; *-ia*, *-ów*) aquarium
al. *skrót pisany*: **aleja** Ave. (*Avenue*)
alarm *m* (*-u*; *-y*) alarm; (*stan*) alert; ***bić na ~*** sound the alarm; **~ować** ⟨**za-**⟩ (*-uję*) alarm; *policję itp.* call out; **~owy** alarm
Alaska *f* (*-i*; *0*) Alaska

Alban|ia *f* (*-ii*; *0*) Albania; **~ka** *f* (*-i*; *G* *-nek*) Albanian

Albań|czyk *m* (*-a*; *-cy*) Albanian; **²ski** Albanian; ***mówić po ²sku*** speak Albanian

albatros *m* (*-a*; *-y*) albatross

albinos *m* (*-a*; *-y/m-os -i*) albino

albo *cj.* or; **~ ..., ~ ...** either ... or ...; **~-~** alternative; **~ *też*** or else; **~wiem** *cj.* because, for

album *m* (*-u*; *-y*) album

ale *cj.* but; however; **~ *jesteś duży!*** aren't you tall!; **~ *gdzie tam!*** of course not!; ***bez żadnego*** **~** no ifs and buts

alegoria *f* (*-ii*; *-e*) allegory

alegoryczny allegoric

aleja *f* (*-ei*; *-e*, *-ei/-ej*) alley; (*droga*) avenue

alergi|a *f* (*GDL* *-ii*; *zw.* *0*) allergy; **~czny** allergic (***na*** *A* to)

ależ *part.* but; **~ *tak!*** why, yes!

alfabet *m* (*-u*; *-y*) alphabet; **~ *Braille'a*** Braille

alfabetyczny alphabetic(al)

alfons F *m* (*-a*; *-i/-y*) pimp

algebra *f* (*-y*; *0*) algebra

Algier|ia *f* (*-ii*; *0*) Algeria; **~czyk** *m* (*-a*; *-cy*), **~ka** *f* (*-i*; *G* *-rek*) Algerian; **²ski** Algerian

alian|cki allied; **~t** *m* (*-a*; *-ci*) ally

alibi *n* (*idkl.*) alibi

alienacja *f* (*-i*; *0*) alienation

aligator *m* (*-a*; *-y*) *zo.* alligator

alimenty *pl.* (*-ów*) (*po rozwodzie*) maintenance payment *sg.*; (*w separacji*) alimony *sg.*

alkaliczny alkaline

alkohol *m* (*-u*; *-e*) alcohol; (*napój*) (alcoholic) drink; **~ik** *m* (*-a*; *-cy*), **~iczka** *f* (*-i*; *G* *-czek*) alcoholic; **~owy** alcoholic

alleluja *n* (*idkl.*) hallelujah; ***Wesołego ²!*** Happy Easter!

alpejski Alpine

alpinist|a *m* (*-y*; *-ści*, *-ów*), **~ka** *f* (*-i*; *G* *-tek*) mountaineer, climber

Alpy *pl.* (*G* -) the Alps

alt *m* (*-u*; *-y*) alto

altan|a *f* (*-y*), **~ka** *f* (*-i*; *G* *-tek*) arbo(u)r; summerhouse

alternat|or *m* (*-a*; *-y*) *mot.* alternator; **~ywa** (*-y*) alternative; **~ywny** alternative

altowiolist|a *m* (*-y*; *-ści*), **~ka** *f* (*-i*; *-ki*) viola player

altówka *f* (*-i*; *G* *-wek*) *mus.* viola

alumini|owy *Brt.* aluminium, *Am.* aluminum; **~um** *n* (*idkl.*) *Brt.* aluminium, *Am.* aluminum

aluzj|a *f* (*-i*; *e*) allusion, hint; ***czynić ~e*** (***do*** *G*) hint (at)

aluzyjnie *adv.* in the form of a hint

alzacki Alsatian

ałun *m* (*-u*; *-y*) alum

AM *skrót pisany*: ***Akademia Medyczna*** Medical Academy

amalgamat *m* (*-u*; *-y*) amalgam (*też fig.*)

amant *m* (*-a*; *-ci*), **~ka** *f* (*-i*; *G* *-tek*) *theat.* lover

amarantowy amaranthine

amator *m* (*-a*; *-rzy*), **~ka** *f* (*-i*; *G* *-rek*) amateur (*też sport.*); lover; (*reflektujący*) potential buyer (***na*** *A* of); **~ski** amateurish; ***teatr ~ski*** amateur *Brt.* theatre (*Am.* theater) group; **~sko** *adv.* in an amateurish way

ambasa|da *f* (*-y*) *pol.* embassy; **~dor** *m* (*-a*; *-rzy*) ambassador

ambicja *f* (*-i*; *-e*) *też pej.* ambition; (*poczucie godności*) sense of hono(u)r

ambitny ambitious

ambona *f* (*-y*) *rel.* pulpit

ambulans *m* (*-u*; *-e*) ambulance; **~ *pocztowy*** mail coach

ambula'to|rium *n* (*idkl.*; *-ia*, *-ów*) *med.* out-patient(s') department; **~ryjny** *med.* out-patient

amen *n* (*idkl.*) amen; ***pewne jak ~ w pacierzu*** you can bet your bottom dollar on it; ***na ~*** totally, utterly

Ameryka *f* (*-i*; *G* -) America; **~nin** *m* (*-a*; *-anie*, *-ów*), **~nka** *f* (*-i*; *G* *-nek*) American; **²nka** sofa, bed; **²ński** American; ***po ²ńsku*** like an American

ametyst *m* (*-u*; *-y*) amethyst

amfibia *f* (*GDL* *-ii*; *-e*) *tech.* amphibious vehicle; *zo.* amphibian

aminokwas *m* (*-u*; *-y*) amino acid

amne|stia *f* (*GDL* *-ii*; *-e*) amnesty; **~zja** *f* (*-i*; *0*) amnesia

amoniak *m* (*-u*; *0*) ammonia

amoralny amoral

amorty|zacja *f* (*-i*; *0*) *econ.* (*maszyn*) depreciation; (*aktywów*) amortization; *tech.* shock absorption; **~zator** *m* (*-a*; *-y*) shock absorber; **~zować** (*-uję*) *wstrząsy* cushion, absorb; *econ.* amortize, depreciate (*też* ***się***)

ampero|godzina *f* ampere-hour; **~mierz** *m* (*-a*; *-e*) ammeter
ampułka *f* (*-i*; *G -łek*) ampoule
amputować (*im*)*pf* (*-uję*) amputate
amunicja *f* (*-i*; *0*) ammunition, F ammo
anabolicz|ny: **~ne** anabolic drugs *pl.*
anachroniczny anachronic
analfabet|a *m* (*-y*; *-ci*), **~ka** *f* (*-i*; *G -tek*) illiterate (person); **~yzm** *m* illiteracy
analiz|a *f* (*-y*) analysis; *med.* test; → ***badanie***; **~ować** ⟨**prze-**⟩ (*-uję*) analyze
analogiczny analogical
analogowy analog(ue)
ananas *m* (*-a*; *-y*) pineapple; *fig.* good-for-nothing; **~owy** pineapple
anarchia *f* (*-i*; *0*) anarchy
anarchi|czny anarchic; **~sta** *m* (*-y*; *-ści*, *-ów*), **~stka** *f* (*-i*; *G -tek*) anarchist; **~styczny** anarchistic
anatomi|a *f* (*GDL -ii*; *0*) anatomy; **~czny** anatomic(al)
androny *pl.* (*-ów*) rubbish, nonsense; ***pleść ~*** F drivel
andrut *m* (*-a*; *-y*) waffle
anegdota *f* (*-y*) anecdote
anek|s *m* (*-u*; *-y*) supplement, *Brt.* annexe, *Am.* annex; *bud.* extension; **~tować** ⟨**za-**⟩ (*-uję*) annex
anemiczny an(a)emic
aneste|tyk *m* (*-u*; *-i*) anesthetic, *Brt.* anaesthetic; **~zja** *f* (*-i*; *-e*) anesthesia, *Brt.* anaesthesia; **~zjolog** *m* (*-a*; *-dzy*/*-owie*) *Brt.* anaesthetist, *Am.* anesthesiologist
ang. *skrót pisany*: ***angielski*** Eng. (*English*)
angażować ⟨**za-**⟩ (*-uję*) take on, employ; *theat.* engage; → ***wplątywać***; **~** ⟨**za-**⟩ ***się*** become involved (***w*** *A*/*I* in)
Angiel|ka *f* (*-i*; *G -lek*) Englishwoman, English girl; **⁀ski** English; ***mówić po ⁀sku*** speak English; ***ziele ⁀skie*** *bot.* allspice; **⁀szczyzna** F *f* (*-y*; *0*) English
angina *f* (*-y*; *0*) throat infection; **~ *pectoris*** angina (pectoris)
Anglia *f* (*-ii*; *0*) England
Anglik *m* (*-a*; *-cy*) Englishman, English boy
anglikański Anglican
anglistyka *f* (*-i*; *0*) (*studia*) English studies *pl.*; (*instytut*) English department
anglo|języczny English-speaking; **~saski** Anglo-Saxon
angorski *zo.*, *włók.* angora
ani 1. *cj.*: ***~ … ~, nie … ~ nie*** neither … nor …; **2.** *part.* not a; ***~ chybi*** without fail; ***~ razu*** not once; ***~ rusz*** not at all; ***~ kropli*** not a (single) drop; ***~ odrobiny*** not a bit; ***~ śladu*** (*G*) not a trace (of)
aniels|ki angelic; **~ko** angelically
animowany: ***film ~*** (animated) cartoon
anioł *m* (*-a*; *aniele!*; *-y*/*-owie*/*anieli*) angel; ***~ stróż*** guardian angel
aniżeli *cj.* than
ankiet|a *f* (*-y*) questionnaire; (*akcja*) survey; **~owany** *m* (*-ego*; *-i*), **~owana** *f* (*-ej*; *-e*) person questioned
ano *part.* well
anonim *m* **1.** (*-a*; *-owie*) anonymous person; **2.** (*-u*; *-y*) anonymous letter; **~owo** anonymously; **~owy** anonymous
anons *m* (*-u*; *-e*) advertisement, F ad; (*ogłoszenie*) announcement; **~ować** ⟨**za-**⟩ (*-uję*) advertise; announce
ans|a: ***mieć ~ę do kogoś*** bear s.o. ill will
antagonistyczny antagonistic
antałek *m* (*-łka*; *-łki*) small barrell
Antarkty|da *f* (*-y*; *0*) Antarctica; **⁀czny** Antarctic
antena *f* (*-y*) aerial, antenna
antenat *m* (*-a*; *-ci*), **~ka** *f* (*-i*; *G -tek*) forefather, ancestor
antenowy aerial; ***czas ~*** broadcasting time
antologia *f* (*-ii*; *-e*) anthology
antrakt *m* (*-u*; *-y*) (*przerwa*) intermission
antresola *f* (*-i*; *-e*) mezzanine
antropologiczny anthropological
antrykot *m* (*-u*; *-y*) *gastr.* entrecôte
anty- *w złoż.* anti-
antyaborcyjn|y: ***ustawa ~a*** anti-abortion law
anty|biotyk *m* (*-u*; *-i*) antibiotic; **~cyklon** *m* anticyclon, F high
antyczny antique
anty|datować (*-uję*) antedate; **~demokratyczny** anti-democratic; **~dopingowy**: ***kontrola ~dopingowa*** doping control
antyk *m* (*-u*; *-i*) (*okres*) classical antiquity; (*rzecz*) antique
antykoncepcyjny: ***środek ~*** *med.* contraceptive
antykwa|riat *m* (*-u*; *-y*) (*z książkami*) second-hand bookshop; (*z antykami*) antique shop; **~riusz** *m* (*-a*; *-e*) sec-

ond-hand bookseller; **~rski, ~ryczny** second-hand; (*cenny*) antiquarian
antylopa *f* (*-y*) antelope
anty|narkotykowy: ***wydział służb ~narkotykowych*** narcotics squad; **~naukowy** unscientific; **~niemiecki** anti-German; **~patia** *f* (*-i*; *-e*) antipathy; **~patyczny** antipathetic(al); **~polski** anti-Polish; **~semicki** anti-Semitic; **~septyczny** antiseptic; **~wojenny** anti-war, antimilitaristic
anulowa|ć (*-uję*) annul; *dokument* cancel; **~nie** *n* (*-a*) annulment
anyż *m* (*-u*; *-e*) aniseed; **~owy** aniseed
Apacz *m* (*-a*; *-e*) Apache
aparat *m* (*-u*; *-y*) (*techniczny*, *państwowy*) apparatus; (*w domu*) appliance; (*radiowy*) radio; (*telewizyjny*) TV set; (*telefoniczny*) phone; **~ura** *f* (*-y*) apparatus (*też fig.*); (*sprzęt*) equipment
apartament *m* (*-u*; *-y*) apartment; (*hotelowy*) suite
apaszka *f* (*-i*; *G -szek*) scarf
apatyczny apathetic
apel *m* (*-u*; *-e*, *-i/-ów*) roll call; (*odezwa*) appeal (***o*** *A* for)
apelacj|a *f* (*-i*; *-e*) *jur.* appeal; ***wnosić ~ę*** appeal, lodge an appeal
apel|acyjny *jur.* of appeal; **~ować** ⟨***za-***⟩ (*-uję*) appeal (***do*** *G* to)
apety|czny appetizing; **~t** *m* (*-u*; *-y*) appetite (*też fig.* ***na*** *A* for); ***pobudzać ~t*** stimulate the appetite
aplauz *m* (*-u*; *-e*) applause, cheer
aplika|cja *f* (*-i*; *-e*) *jur.* (practical) training for the bar; **~nt** *m* (*-a*; *-ci*), **~ntka** *f* (*-i*; *G -tek*) *jur.* trainee lawyer, *Brt.* articled clerk; **~ntura** *f* (*-y*) → ***aplikacja***
aplikować ⟨***za-***⟩ (*-uję*) administer
apoplektyczny apoplectic; ***atak ~*** stroke
aposto|lski apostolic; **~ł** *m* (*-a*; *-owie*) apostle (*też fig.*), disciple
apostrof *m* (*-u*; *-y*) apostrophe
Appalachy *pl.* (*G -ów*) Appalachian Mountains *pl.*
aprob|ata *f* (*-y*; *0/-y*) approval; **~ować** ⟨***za-***⟩ (*-uję*) approve of
aprowizac|ja *f* (*-i*; *0*) food supply; **~yjny** food
aptecz|ka *f* (*-i*; *G -czek*) (*w domu*) medicine cabinet; first-aid kit (*pierwszej pomocy*); **~ny** pharmaceutical
apteka *f* (*-i*) *Brt.* chemist's (shop), *Am.* drugstore; (*szpitalna*) dispensary; **~rka** *f* (*-i*; *G -rek*), **~rz** *m* (*-a*; *e*, *G -y*) *Brt.* (dispensing) chemist, *Am.* druggist
Arab *m* (*-a*; *-owie*) Arab; **♀** (*pl. -y*) (*koń*) Arab; **~ia** *f* (*-ii*; *0*) Arabia; **~ka** *f* (*-i*; *G -bek*) Arab; ***♀ka*** (*koń*) Arab; **♀ski 1.** (*narody itp.*) Arab; (*półwysep itp.*) Arabian; (*język*, *cyfra itp.*) Arabic; ***mówić po ♀sku*** speak Arabic; **2.** *m* (*-ego*; *0*) Arabic
aranż|er *m* (*-a*; *-owie/-rzy*) organizer; *mus.* arranger; **~ować** ⟨***za-***⟩ (*-uję*) arrange (***na*** *A* for)
arbitraż *m* (*-u*; *-e*, *y/-ów*) arbitration
arbitrażow|y: ***sąd ~y*** arbitration tribunal; ***wyrok sądu ~ego*** verdict of the arbitration tribunal
arbuz *m* (*-a*; *-y*) watermelon
archanioł *m* (*-a*; *-y*) archangel
archeologi|a *f* (*GDL -i*; *0/-ie*) arch(a)eology; **~czny** arch(a)eological
archipelag *m* (*-u*; *-i*) archipelago
architekt *m* (*-a*; *-ci*), **~ka** *f* (*-i*; *G -tek*) architect; **~oniczny** architectural; **~ura** *f* architecture
archiwum *n* (*idkl.*; *-wa*; *G -wów*) archives *pl.*
arcy|biskup *m* archbishop; **~ciekawy** fascinating; **~dzieło** *n* masterpiece; **~nudny** extremely boring, F deadly; **~zabawny** hilarious
areał *m* (*-u*; *-y*) area
arena *f* (*-y*) (*sportowa*) arena; (*w cyrku*) ring
areszt *m* (*-u*; *-y*) arrest; (*budynek*) prison; **~ *śledczy*** (*stan*) detention while awaiting trial; (*budynek*) prison (for people awaiting trial); → *jur.* ***zajęcie***
aresztowa|ć ⟨***za-***⟩ (*-uję*) arrest; **~nie** *n* (*-a*) arrest; **~ny 1.** arrested, in custody; **2.** *m* (*-ego*; *-i*), **~na** *f* (*-ej*; *-e*) person under arrest, detainee
Argent|yna *f* (*-y*) Argentina; **~ynka** *f* (*-i*; *G -nek*), **~yńczyk** *m* (*-a*; *-cy*) Argentinian; **♀yński** Argentinian, Argentine
argumentować (*-uję*) argue; → ***uzasadniać***
aria *f* (*GDL -ii*; *-e*) aria
ark. *skrót pisany*: **arkusz** sht (*sheet*)
arka *f* (*-i*; *G ark*) ark; ***~ przymierza*** *rel.* Ark of the Covenant
arkada *f* (*-y*) arcade
arktyczny Arctic
arkusz *m* (*-a*; *-e*, *-y*) sheet

armat|a *f* (*-y*) gun, *hist.* cannon; **~ni** gun, cannon
armator *m* (*-ra*, *-rzy*) shipowner
armatura *f* (*-y*) fittings *pl.*
armeńs|ki Armenian; ***mówić po ~ku*** speak Armenian
armia *f* (*GDL -ii*; *-e*) army; ♀ ***Zbawienia*** Salvation Army
aroganc|ki arrogant; **~ko** arrogantly
aromat *m* (*-u*; *-y*) aroma, scent; (*przyprawa*) flavo(u)ring
aromatyczny aromatic
arras *m* (*-u*; *-y*) tapestry
arsenał *m* (*-u*; *-y*) arsenal
arszenik *m* (*-u*; *0*) arsenic
arteri|a *f* (*GDL -ii*; *-e*) artery (*med.*, *mot.*); *fig.* vein; **~o-** arterio-
artretyzm *m* (*-u*; *-y/0*) arthritis
artykuł *m* (*-u*; *-y*) article; (*w gazecie też*) piece; ***~ wstępny*** editorial; ***~y pl. spożywcze*** food (stuffs *pl.*), (*w sklepie*) groceries *pl.*
artyle|ria *f* (*GDL -ii*; *0*) artillery; **~ryjski** artillery
artyst|a *m* (*-y*; *-ści*, *-ów*), **~ka** *f* (*-i*; *G -tek*) artist; ***~a malarz*** painter
artystyczn|y artistic; (*harmonijny*) exquisite; ***rzemiosło ~e*** arts and crafts *pl.*
artyzm *m* (*-u*; *-y*) artistic skill, artistry
arystokrat|a *m* (*-y*; *-ci*), **~ka** *f* (*-i*) aristocrat
arystokratyczny aristocratic
arytmety|czny arithmetic(al); ***działanie ~czne*** arithmetical operation; **~ka** *f* (*-i*; *0*) arithmetic
as *m* (*-a*; *-y*) ace (*też fig.*)
ascetyczny ascetic
asekurac|ja *f* (*-i*; *-e*) (*zabezpieczenie*) safeguard (**przeciw**(**ko**) against); (*ubezpieczenie*) insurance; **~yjny** security; insurance
asekurować się ⟨***za- się***⟩ (*-uję*) protect o.s.; *fig.* cover o.s. (two ways)
asesor *m* (*-a*; *-rzy*, *-ów*) assistant judge
asfaltowy asphalt
askorbinowy: ***kwas ~*** ascorbic acid
asocjacja *f* (*-i*; *-e*) association
asortyment *m* (*-u*; *-y*) range
ASP *skrót*: ***Akademia Sztuk Pięknych*** Academy of Fine Arts
aspekt *m* (*-u*; *-y*) aspect
aspiracje *f/pl* (*-ji*) aspirations *pl*; → ***ambicja***
aspołeczny antisocial, asocial

astma *f* (*-y*; *0*) asthma; **~tyczny** asthmatic
astro|logia *f* (*GDL -ii*; *0*) astrology; **~nauta** *m* (*-y*; *-ci*), **~nautka** *f* (*-i*; *G -tek*) astronaut; **~nautyka** *f* (*-i*; *0*) astronautics; **~nomia** *f* (*GDL -ii*; *0*) astronomy; **~nomiczny** astronomical
asygnować ⟨**wy-**⟩ (*-uję*) *sumę* allocate; *środki* award (**na** *A* for)
asyst|a *f* (*-y*) company; **~ent** *m* (*-a*; *-ci*), **~entka** *f* (*-i*; *G -tek*) assistant; **~ować** (*-uję*) (*pomagać*) assist (**przy** *L* with); (*towarzyszyć*) accompany
atak *m* (*-u*; *-i*) attack (*też fig.*); *mil.* assault; (*w sporcie*) forward line; *med.* attack, fit
atakować ⟨**za-**⟩ (*-uję*) attack; *mil.* assault
ateistyczny atheistic
atelier *n* (*idkl.*) studio; ***~ filmowe*** film studio
Ateny *pl.* (*G -*) Athens *sg.*
atest *m* (*-u*; *-y*) certificate
atlantycki Atlantic
Atlantyk *m* (*-u*; *0*) (the) Atlantic
atlas *m* (*-u*; *-y*) atlas
atlet|a *m* (*-y*; *-ci*), **~ka** *f* (*-i*; *G -tek*) athlete; (*w cyrku*) strongman; **~yczny** athletic; **~yka** *f* (*-i*; *0*) athletics; ***lekka ~yka*** track-and-field events
atłas *m* (*-u*; *-y*) satin; ***jak ~*** velvety; **~owy** of satin; *fig.* velvety
atmosfer|a *f* (*-y*) atmosphere (*też fig.*); **~yczny** atmospheric
atol *m* (*-u*; *-e*) atoll
atom *m* (*-u*; *-y*) atom; **~owy** atomic; *okręt itp.* nuclear; ***energia ~owa*** nuclear energy
atrakc|ja *f* (*-e*; *-i*) attraction; **~yjny** attractive
atrament *m* (*-u*; *-y*) ink; ***~ do stempli*** stamp-pad ink; **~owy** ink
atut *m* (*-u*; *-y*) trump (card) (*też fig.*)
audiowizualny audio-visual
audycj|a *f* (*-i*; *-e*) *RTV*: programme; broadcast; ***cykl ~i*** series (of programmes)
audytorium *n* (*idkl.*; *-ria*, *-ów*) (*pomieäszczenie*) auditorium; (*słuchacze*) audience
aukcja *f* (*-i*; *-je*) auction
aura *f* (*-y*; *0*) weather; *fig.* aura
auspicj|e *pl*: ***pod ~ami*** (*G*) under the auspices (of)

Australia *f* (*-ii*; *0*) Australia
Australij|czyk *m* (*-a*; *-cy*), **~ka** *f* (*-i*; *G -jek*) Australian; **Ꙩski** Australian
Austria *f* (*G -ii*; *0*)Austria; **Ꙩcki** Austrian; **~czka** *f* (*-i*; *-czek*), **~k** *m* (*-a*; *-cy*) Austrian
aut *m* (*-u*; *-y*) (*w sporcie*) out
autentyczny authentic
auto *n* (*-a*; *G aut*) *Brt.* car, *Am.* automobile; ***autem*** by car; **~alarm** *m mot.* alarm (device)
autobiograficzny autobiographic(al)
autobus *m* (*-a*; *-y*) bus; coach; ***~em*** by bus, (*między miastami*) by coach
autocasco (*idkl.*) → ***casco***
autochton *m* (*-a*; *-ni*), **~ka** *f* (*-ki*; *G -nek*) native
auto|geniczny: ***trening ~geniczny*** autogenic training; autogenics; **~graf** *m* (*-u*; *-y*) autograph; **~kar** coach; **~mat** *m* (*-u*; *-y*) automatic (*też mil.*); (*sprzedający*) vending machine; ***~mat telefoniczny*** *Brt.* pay phone, *Am.* pay station; **~matyczny** automatic
automatyz|acja *f* (*-i*; *0*) automatization; **~ować** ⟨**z-**⟩ (*-uję*) automatize, automate
autonomi|a *f* (*-ii*; *0*) autonomy; **~czny** autonomous
autoportret *m* self-portrait
autopsj|a *f* (*-i*; *-e*) *med.* autopsy; post-mortem (examination); ***z ~i*** from experience
autor *m* (*-a*; *-rzy*), **~ka** *f* (*-i*; *G - rek*) author; (*pisarz*) writer; (*sprawca*) originator; **~ski** authorial; author's; **~stwo** *n* (*-a*; *0*) authorship
autory|tatywny authoritative; **~tet** *m* (*-u*; *-y*) authority; prestige; **~zowany** authorized
auto|sanie *pl.* motorized sledge; **~serwis** *m* service station
autostop *m*: ***jechać ~em*** hitch-hike
autostopowicz F *m*, **~ka** *f* (*-i*; *G -czek*) hitch-hiker
autostrada *f* (*-y*) *Brt.* motorway; *Am.* expressway; (*płatna*) *Am.* turnpike
autowy: ***sędzia ~*** linesman
awangarda *f* (*-y*) avant-garde
awans *m* (*-u*; *-e*/*-y*) promotion; ***~ społeczny*** social advancement; ***otrzymać ~em*** get in advance; **~ować** (*im*)*pf* (*-uję*) *v/t.* promote; *v/i.* be promoted (**na** *A* to), (*też w sporcie*) move up
awantur|a *f* (*-y*) row, fracas; **~niczo** adventurously; **~niczy** adventure; adventurous; (*kłótliwy*) quarrelsome; **~nica** *f* (*-y*; *-e*) quarrelsome woman; **~nik** *m* (*-a*; *-cy*) rowdy, troublemaker; **~ować się** (*-uję*) make a row; cause trouble (**z** *I* with)
awar|ia *f* (*GDL -ii*; *-e*) (*zwł. mot.*) breakdown; **~yjny** emergency; ***wyjście ~yjne*** emergency exit
awers *m* (*-u*; *-y*) obverse; **~ja** *f* (*-i*; *0*) aversion
AWF *skrót*: ***Akademia Wychowania Fizycznego*** Academy of Physical Education
awizować ⟨**za-**⟩ (*-uję*) send notification (*A* of)
azalia *f* (*GDL -ii*; *-e*) azalea
azbest *m* (*-u*; *0*) asbestos; **~owy** asbestos
Azja *f* (*-i*; *0*) Asia; **~ta** *m* (*-y*; *-ci*), **~tka** *f* (*-i*; *G -tek*) Asian; **Ꙩtycki** Asian
azot *m* (*-u*; *0*) nitrogen; **~owy** nitrogen, nitrogenous, nitric; ***kwas ~owy*** nitric acid
azyl *m* (*-u*; *-e*) asylum; ***prawo ~u*** right of asylum; ***udzielić ~u*** grant asylum
azylant *m* (*-a*; *-ci*), **~ka** *f* (*-i*; *G -tek*) (*mający azyl*) person granted asylum; (*szukający azylu*) person seeking asylum
aż *cj.*, *part.* till, until; ***~ do*** (*G*) till, up to; ***~ do wczoraj*** until yesterday; ***~ po kolana*** up to the knees; ***~ pięć*** as many as five; ***~ miło słuchać*** it is nice to hear of it; ***~ nadto*** more than enough; ***~ strach pomyśleć*** one shudders to think of it
ażeby → ***aby***
ażurowy open-work

B

b. *skrót pisany*: **były** former; **bardzo** very

bab|a *f* (*-y*; *G -*) (old, peasant *itp.*) woman; **~cia** *f* (*-i*; *-e*) grandmother, F granny; **~i**: **~ie lato** (*pora*) Indian summer; **~ka** → **babcia**; *gastr.* (ring) cake; F chick

babrać się (*-rzę*; *-am*) slosh about, *fig.* dirty one's hands

bab|ski female; **~unia** *f*, **~usia** *f* (*-i*; *-iu!/-e*) → **babcia**

bachor *m* (*-a*; *-y*) brat

baczki *m/pl.* (*-ków*) whiskers *pl.*

baczn|ość *f* (*-ści*; *0*): **stać na ~ość** stand at attention; **mieć się na ~ości** stand at one's guard, look out; **~y** vigilant, attentive

bacz|yć: **nie ~ąc na** (*A*) regardless of

bać się be afraid, be worried (**o** *A* about)

bada|cz *m* (*-a*; *-e*), **~czka** *f* (*-ki*; *G -czek*) researcher, student; **~ć** ⟨**z-**⟩ (*-am*) (*przestudiować*) research, study; *chorych* examine; *świadka* interrogate; *puls* feel; **~nie** *n* (*-a*) study, examination; interrogation; (**opinii publicznej** public) opinion poll; **~wczo** inquisitively; **~wczy** searching; **pracownik ~wczy** researcher

bagatela *f* (*-i*; *-e*) trifle

bagaż *m* (*-u*; *-e*) *Brt.* luggage, *Am.* baggage; **~nik** *m* (*-a*; *-i*) *mot. Brt.* boot, *Am.* trunk; (*dachowy*) (roof) rack; **~owy 1.** luggage, baggage; **2.** *m* (*-ego*; *-i*) porter

bagnet *m* (*-u*; *-y*) bayonet

bagnisty swampy, marshy

bagno *n* (*-a*; *G -gien*) swamp, marshes *pl.*

bajeczny fairy-story, magical

bajka *f* (*-i*; *G -jek*) fairy tale

bajoro *n* (*-a*) muddy pool

bak *m* (*-u*; *-i*) tank

bakalie *pl.* (*-ii*) nuts and raisins *pl.*

bakier: **na ~** at a slant

bakłażan *m* (*-u*; *-y*) *bot. Brt.* aubergine, *Am.* eggplant

bakterio|bójczy (**-czo**) germicidal; **~logiczny** bacteriological

bal[1] *m* (*-a*; *-e*, *-i*) balk

bal[2] *m* (*-u*; *-e*, *-ów*) (**maskowy** masked) ball

balast *m* (*-u*; *-y*) ballast

baleron *m* (*-u*; *-y*) rolled smoked ham

balet *m* (*-u*; *-y*) ballet; **~nica** *f* (*-y*; *-e*), **~nik** *m* (*-a*; *-cy*) ballet-dancer; **~owy** ballet

balkon *m* (*-u*; *-y*) balcony; *theat.* gallery

balon *m* (*-u*; *-y*), **~ik** *m* (*-a*; *-i*) balloon

balowy ball

balustrada *f* (*-y*) balustrade

bała|gan F *m* (*-u*; *-y*) muddle; mess; **narobić ~ganu** (**w** *L*) mess up (in); **~mucić** ⟨**z-**⟩ (*-cę*) *v/t.* chat up

Bałka|ny *pl.* (*G -ów*) the Balkans *pl.*; **≈ński** Balkan

Bałty|k *m* (*-u*; *0*) (the) Baltic Sea; **≈cki** Baltic

bałwan *m* (*-a*; *-y*) F dimwit; (*bożek*) idol; (*śniegowy*) snowman; **~y** *pl. też* breakers *pl.*, whitecaps *pl.*

bambosz *m* (*-a*; *-y/-ów*) slipper

bambus *m* (*-a*; *-y*) bamboo; **~owy** bamboo

banalny banal; (*trywialny*) trivial

banał *m* (*-u*; *-y*) banality; commonplace

banan *m* (*-a/-u*; *-y*) banana

banda *f* (*-y*) gang

bandaż *m* (*-a*; *-e*) *med.* bandage; **~ować** ⟨**o-**⟩ (*-uję*) bandage

bandera *f* (*-y*) *naut.* flag

bandy|cki vicious; **~ta** *m* (*-y*; *-ci*, *-ów*) bandit, robber; **~tyzm** *m* (*-u*; *0*) crime

bank *m* (*-u*; *-i*) bank

bankiet *m* (*-u*; *-y*) banquet

bank|not *m* (*-u*; *-y*) *zwł. Brt.* banknote, *Am.* bill; **~omat** cash dispenser; **~ructwo** *n* (*-a*) bankruptcy; **~rutować** ⟨**z-**⟩ (*-uję*) go bankrupt

bańka *f* (*-i*; *G -niek*) (**mydlana** soap) bubble; (*naczynie*) can; *med.* cuppping glass

bar[1] *m* (*-u*; *-y*) bar; **~ samoobsługowy** snack bar

bar[2] *m* (*-u*; *0*) *chem.* barium

barak *m* (*-u*; *-i*) shack; (*na budowie itp.*) hut

baran *m* (*-a*; *-y*) ram; F **nosić kogoś na ~a** carry s.o. piggyback; ≈ *znak Zodia-*

ku: Aries; ***on(a) jest spod znaku Barana*** he/she is (an) Aries; **~ek** *m* (*-nka*; *-nki*) lamb (*też rel.*); **~i** mutton; **~ina** *f* (*-y*; *0*) mutton

barbarzyńca *m* (*-y*; *G -ów*) barbarian

barczysty broad-shouldered

bardz|iej more; ***coraz ~iej*** more and more; ***tym ~iej że*** the more so that; ***tym ~iej nie*** all the more not; **~o** *adv.* very; ***nie ~o*** not much

bariera *f* (*-y*) barrier; ***~ dźwiękowa*** sound barrier; ***~ ochronna*** (*przy drodze*) crash barrier

bark *m* (*-u*; *-i*) *anat.* shoulder

barka *f* (*-i*; *G -rek*) barge

barłóg *m* (*-ogu*; *-ogi*) (*dla zwierzęcia*) litter; (*dla człowieka*) pallet

barman *m* (*-a*; *-i*) *Brt.* barman, bartender, *Am.* barkeeper; **~ka** *f* (*-i*; *G -nek*) barmaid

barokowy Baroque

barometr *m* (*-u*; *-y*) barometer

barowy bar; *chem.* barium, baric

barszcz *m* (*-u*; *-e*) *Brt.* beetroot soup, *Am.* beet soup, bortsch (borsch)

barw|a *f* (*-y*) colo(u)r; ***~ głosu*** timbre; **~ić** ⟨***u-, za-***⟩ colo(u)r (***na czerwono*** red); *też* ***się*** dye; **~inek** *m* (*-nka*; *-nki*) periwinkle; **~nik** *m* (*-a*; *-i*) dye; pigment; **~ny** (*oddający kolory*) colo(u)r; (*barwny*) colourful

barykad|a *f* (*-y*) barricade; **~ować** ⟨***za-***⟩ barricade

baryłka *f* (*-i*; *G -łek*) (*piwa itp.*) keg; (*ropy*) barrel

baryton *m* (*-u/os. -a*; *-y*) baritone

bas *m* (*-u/os. -a*; *-y*) bass

basen *m* (*-u*; *-y*) (***pływacki*** swimming) pool; (*dla chorych*) bedpan

baskij|ka *f* (*-i*; *G -jek*) beret; **~ski** Basque; ***mówić po ~sku*** speak Basque

baszta *f* (*-y*) tower

baśniowy fairy-tale, fable

baśń *f* (*-ni*; *-nie*) fable

bat *m* (*-a*; *D -owi*; *-y*) whip; ***dostać ~y*** get a hiding

bateria *f* (*GDL -ii*; *-e*) *electr.* battery

bateryjka *f* (*-i*; *G -jek*) *electr.* battery

batut|a *f* (*-y*) baton; ***pod ~ą*** (*G*) *mus.* conducted by

batyst *m* (*-u*; *-y*) batiste

Bawar|czyk *m* (*-a*; *-cy*), **~ka** *f* (*-i*; *G -rek*) Bavarian; **≈ski** Bavarian; ***po ≈sku*** like a Bavarian

baweł|na *f* cotton; **~niany** cotton

bawić ⟨***po-, za-***⟩ (*-ę*) *v/i.* stay; be on a visit (***u*** *G* to); *v/t.* entertain; amuse; **~** ⟨***po-, za-***⟩ ***się*** (*dobrze itp.*) have a good time; enjoy o.s.; ***~ się z dziećmi*** play with children; ***~ się lalką*** play with a doll; *fig.* ***nie ~ się w*** (*A*) not waste too much time on

baw|oli buffalo; **~ół** *m* (*-ołu*; *-oły*) buffalo

baza *f* (*-y*) base; (*podstawa*) basis; (*transportowa itp.*) depot; ***~ danych*** database; ***~ pływająca*** mother ship

bazar *m* (*-u*; *-y*) bazaar; (*targ*) market-place

bazgrać (*-rzę*; *-rz/-raj!*) ⟨***na-***⟩ scribble, scrawl; ⟨***po-***⟩ scribble on

bazgranina *f* (*-y*) scribble, scrawl

bazia *f* (*-i*; *- e*, *-i*) willow catkin

bazować (*-uję*) base (***na*** *L* on)

Bazylea *f* (*-i*; *-0*) Basle, Basel

bazylia *f* (*GDL -ii*; *-e*) *bot.* (sweet) basil

bazylika *f* (*-i*) *arch.* basilica

bażant *m* (*-a*; *-y*) pheasant

bąbe|l *m* (*-bla*; *-ble*) (*na pięcie itp.*) blister; (*na wodzie*) bubble; **~lek** *m* (*-lka*; *-lki*) (small) blister; (small) bubble

bądź *cj.* or; ***~ ... ~ ...*** either … or …; ***~ co ~*** after all; ***co ~*** anything; ***kto ~*** anybody; → ***być***

bąk *m* (*-a*; *-i*) *zo.* (*owad bydlęcy*) horse-fly, (*trzmiel*) bumble-bee, (*ptak*) bittern; (*zabawka*) top; F (*dziecko*) toddler, tot; ***zbijać ~i*** hang around the streets; **~ać** (*-am*) mumble, mutter; (*czytać*) read in a halting way; (*napomykać*) hint

beatyfikacja *f* (*-i*; *-e*) beatification

beczeć ⟨***za-***⟩ (*-ę*) *owca, koza*: bleat; F (*płakać*) whinge, whimper

beczk|a *f* (*-i*; *G -czek*) barrel; (*drewniana, na wino*) cask; *aviat.* roll; **~owy** barrell, cask; ***piwo ~owe*** draught beer

beczułka *f* (*-i*; *G -łek*) (small) barrel, (small) cask

bednarz *m* (*-a*; *-e*) cooper

befsztyk *m* (*-a*; *-i*) beefsteak; ***~ po tatarsku*** steak tartar(e)

bejc|a *f* (*-y*; *-e*, *-y*) wood-stain; **~ować** (*-uję*) stain

bek *m* (*-u*; *-i*) bleat; blubber, whimper; → ***beczeć***

bekas *m* (*-a*; *-y*) *zo.* snipe

bekhend *m* (*-u*; *-y*) (*w sporcie*) backhand

B

beknąć *v/s.* (*-nę*) → ***beczeć***
bekon *m* (*-u*; *-y*) (*wędzonka*) bacon
beksa F *f/m* (*-y*; *G -/-ów*) cry-baby
bela *f* (*-i*; *-e*) (*drewniana*) beam; (*materiału*) bale; ***pijany jak ~*** blind drunk
belfer F *m* (*-fra*; *-frowie/-frzy*), **~ka** *f* (*-rek*; *-rki*) teacher
Belg *m* (*-a*; *-owie*, *-ów*) Belgian; **~ia** *f* (*-ii*; *0*) Belgium; **~ijka** *f* (*-i*; *G -jek*) Belgian; **≗ijski** Belgian
belka *f* (*-i*; *G -lek*) beam; F *mil.* stripe; ***~ nośna*** supporting beam
bełkot *m* (*-u*; *-y*) gibberish, babble; **~ać** ⟨**wy-**⟩ gibber, babble
bełtać ⟨**z-**⟩ (*-am*) stir up
beniaminek *m* (*-nka*; *-nki/-nkowie*) darling, pet
benzoesowy: ***kwas ~*** benzoic acid
benzyn|a *f* (*-y*) *Brt.* petrol, *Am.* gasoline, *Am.* F gas; **~owy** *Brt.* petrol, *Am.* gas; ***stacja ~owa*** filling station
berbeć F *m* (*-cia*; *-cie*, *-ci/-ciów*) tot
beret *m* (*-u*; *-y*) beret
Berl|in *m* (*-a*; *0*) Berlin; **≗iński** Berlin
berło *n* (*-ła*; *G -reł*) *Brt.* sceptre, *Am.* scepter
bernardyn *m* (*-a*; *-y*) (*pies*) St. Bernard (dog)
Berno *n* (*-a*; *0*) Bern(e)
bessa *f* (*-y*) *econ.* fall (*na giełdzie*) bear
besti|a *f* (*GDL -ii*; *-e*) beast; **~alski** bestial, savage; **~alsko** bestially, savagely
besztać ⟨**z-**⟩ (*-am*) tell off, scold
Betlejem *n* (*idkl.*) Bethlehem
beton *m* (*-u*; *-y*) concrete; **~ować** ⟨**za-**⟩ (*-uję*) concrete; *drogę* surface with concrete; **~owy** concrete
bez[1] *m* (*bzu*; *bzy*) lilac; ***czarny ~*** elder
bez[2] *prp.* without; ***~ potrzeby*** unnecessarily; ***~ ustanku*** incessantly; ***~ wad*** faultless
beza *f* (*-y*) meringue
bez|alkoholowy non-alcoholic, alcohol-free; *napój* soft; **~awaryjny** trouble-free; **~barwny** colo(u)rless; **~błędny** perfect, faultless; **~bolesny** painless; **~bronny** defenceless; **~brzeżny** boundless (*też fig.*); **~celowość** pointlessness; **~celowy** pointless
bezcen: ***za ~*** dirt cheap; **~ny** invaluable, priceless
bez|ceremonialny unceremonious; **~chmurny** cloudless; **~czelność** impudence; **~czelny** impudent; **~czynność** inactivity; idleness; **~czynny** inactive; idle; **~darny**, **~denny** bottomless; *fig.* incredible; **~domny 1.** homeless; **2.** (*m-os -ni*) vagrant; ***bezdomni*** the homeless; **~droże** *n* (*-a*; *G -y*): *zwł. pl.* ***~droża*** wilderness
bez|drzewny treeless; *papier* woodfree; **~duszny** heartless; soulless; **~dzietność** *f* (*-i*; *0*) childlessness; **~dzietny** childless; **~dźwięczny** soundless; *jęz.* voiceless
beze → ***bez***; **~cny** *lit.* heinous
bez|gorączkowy free from fever; **~gotówkowo** without cash; **~gotówkowy** cashless; **~graniczny** boundless; **~imienny** nameless; **~interesowny** unselfish, selfless; **~karny** unpunished; with impunity; **~kofeinowy** decaffeinated; **~kompromisowy** uncompromising; **~konkurencyjny** unrivalled; **~kresny** limitless; **~krwawo** bloodlessly; **~krwawy** bloodless; **~krwisty** bloodless; **~krytyczny** uncritical; **~kształtny** shapeless; **~leśny** unwooded
bez liku *adv.* countless, innumerable
bez|litosny merciless; **~litośnie** mercilessly; **~ludny** desolate; *wyspa* uninhabited, desert; **~ład** disorder, F mess; **~ładny** disorderly
bez mała almost, nearly
bez|miar *m* (*-u*; *-y*) huge expanse; **~mierny** immeasurable, immense; **~mięsny** *gastr.* without meat; **~miłosierny** → ***bezlitosny***; **~myślny** thoughtless; **~nadziejny** hopeless; **~namiętny** dispassionate, detached; **~nogi** (*bez jednej*) one-legged; (*bez obu*) legless; **~objawowy** (**-wo**) *med.* without symptoms, asymptomatic(ally); **~oki** eyeless
bezokolicznik *m* (*-a*; *-i*) *jęz.* infinitive
bez|ołowiowy unleaded, lead-free; **~osobowo** impersonally; **~osobowy** impersonal; **~owocny** fruitless; **~pański** abandoned; *pies* stray; **~partyjny** independent; **~pestkowy** *bot.* seedless
bezpieczeństw|o *n* (*-a*; *0*) security, safety; ***~o i higiena pracy*** protection of health and safety standards at work; ***~o ruchu*** road safety; ***pas ~a*** safety belt, seat belt; ***Rada ≗a*** Security Council
bezpiecz|nik *m* (*-a*; *-i*) *electr.* fuse; (*ka-*

rabinu) safety-catch; **~ny** safe; ***~ny w użyciu*** (operationally) safe
bez|planowo aimlessly, unsystematically; **~planowy** aimless, unsystematic; **~płatny** free (of charge); **~płciowy** sexless; (*roślina itp.*) asexual; **~płodność** bareness, sterility; **~płodny** bare, sterile; *fig.* → ***bezowocny***
bez|podstawny baseless; **~pośredni** direct, immediate; just (***po*** *L* after); **~pośrednio** directly, immediately; **~powrotny** irretrievable
bezpraw|ie *n* (*-a*; *0*) lawlessness; illegality; **~ny** lawless; illegal
bez|precedensowy unprecedented; **~problemowy** unproblematic; **~procentowy** (*kredyt itp.*) interest-free; **~przedmiotowo** baselessly; **~przedmiotowy** unfounded, baseless; **~przewodowy** cordless; **~przykładny** unparalleled, outrageous; **~radny** helpless
bezręki (*bez jednej*) one-armed; (*bez obu*) armless
bezrobo|cie *n* (*-a*) unemployment; **~tny 1.** unemployed; **2.** *m* (*-ego*; *-ni*), **~tna** *f* (*-ej*; *-e*) unemployed person; ***bezrobotni*** *pl.* the unemployed *pl.*; ***zasiłek dla ~tnych*** unemployment benefit, F dole
bezrolny landless
bezruch *m* (*0*): ***w ~u*** immobility, stillness
bez|senność *f* sleeplessness; **~senny** sleepless; **~sens** *m* senselessness; **~sensowny** senseless; **~silny** powerless (***wobec*** *G* in the face of)
bezskutecz|nie *adv.* vainly; **~ny** vain, futile
bez|słoneczny sunless; **~sporny** doubtless; **~sprzeczny** unquestionable; **~stronny** impartial; **~szelestnie** *adv.* noiselessly; **~śnieżny** snowless; **~terminowy** (**-wo**) for an unlimited period; **~treściowy** empty
beztros|ka *f* (*-i*; *0*) carelessness, carefreeness; **~ki** careless, carefree; **~ko** carelessly
bez|ustanny 1. *adj.* incessant, unstopping; **2.** *adv.*: ***~ustannie*** incessantly; **~usterkowy** (**-wo**) trouble-free; **~użyteczny** useless
bez|wartościowy valueless; **~warunkowo** unconditionally; **~warunkowy** unconditional; **~wiedny** unconscious; (*niezamierzony*) unintentional; **~wizowy** without a visa
bezwład *m* (*-u*; *0*) inertia; (*kończyny itp.*) paralysis; **~ność** *f* (*-ci*; *0*) inertia, inactivity; ***siła ~ności*** *phys.* inertia; **~ny** inert, inactive
bez|włosy hairless; **~wodny** waterless; **~wolny** passive, without will; **~wonny** odo(u)rless
bezwstyd *m* (*-u*; *0*) shamelessness, impudence; **~ny** shameless, impudent
bez|wyznaniowy non-denominational, not belonging to any denomination; **~względność** *f* ruthlessness; **~względny** ruthless; absolute; **~zakłóceniowy** trouble-free; **~załogowy** unmanned; **~zasadny** groundless; unfounded; **~zębny** toothless; **~zwłoczny** immediate; **~zwrotny** non-returnable; **~żenny** celibate
beż *m* (*idkl.*), **~owy** (**-wo**) beige
bęb|en *m* (*-bna*; *-bny*) drum; ***grać na ~nie*** play the drum; **~enek** *m* (*-nka*; *-nki*) drum; *anat.* ear-drum; **~nić** (*-ę*; *-nij!*) drum
bęcwał *m* (*-a*; *-y*) → ***próżniak***
będę, będzie → ***być***
bękart *m* (*-a*; *-y*) bastard (*też fig.*)
BHP *skrót pisany*: ***bezpieczeństwo i higiena pracy*** protection of health and safety standards at work
biad|a! woe betide you/him *itp.*; **~ać** (*-am*), **~olić** (*-lę*) lament (***nad czymś*** s.th.)
biała|czka *f* (*-i*; *0*) *Brt.* leukaemia, *Am.* leukemia; **~wy** (**-wo**) whitish
białko *n* (*-a*; *G -łek*) (*jajka, oka itp.*) white; *biol.*, *chem.* protein
biało *adv.* white; ***ubrany na ~*** dressed in white; **~-czerwony** white-red; **~rusin** *m* (*-a*; *-i*), **~rusinka** *f* (*-i*; *G - nek*) B(y)elorussian; **~ruski** B(y)elorussian; ***mówić po ~rusku*** speak B(y)elorussian; **~ruś** *f* (*-si*; *0*) B(y)elarus; **~ść** *f* (*-i*; *0*) whiteness
biał|y white; ***~a kawa*** *Brt.* white coffee, coffee with milk; ***w ~y dzień*** in broad daylight; ***czarno na ~ym*** in black and white
bibka F *f* (*-i*) party, F bash
biblia *f* (*GDL -ii*; *-e*) (the) Bible
biblijny Biblical
bibliotecz|ka *f* (*-i*; *G -czek*) (*zwł. podręczna*) reference library; (*mebel*) bookcase; **~ny** library

B

biblioteka *f* library; **~rka** *f* (*-ki*; *G -rek*), **~rz** *m* (*-a*; *-e*, *-y*) librarian; **~rski** library
bibuł|a *f* (*-y*) blotting paper; ***~a filtracyjna*** filter paper; **~ka** *f* (*-i*; *G -łek*) tissue paper; cigarette-paper
bicie *n* (*-a*) striking (***zegara*** of the clock); ringing (***w dzwony*** of the bells); (*pobicie*) beating; ***z ~m serca*** with a pounding heart
bicz *m* (*-a*; *-e*) whip; *fig.* scourge; ***jak zá~aátrzasł*** in no time
bić (*-ję*; *bij!*) *v/t.* hit (***po twarzy, w twarz*** in the face), beat; *rywala*, *rekord itp.* beat; *drób* slaughter; *kartę* take; *medal* strike; ***~ brawo*** applaud; *v/i. zegar*: strike; *serce*: beat; *źródło*: gush; *działo*: shoot; ***~ w dzwony*** ring the bells; ***to bije w oczy*** it is as clear as daylight; ***~ásię*** fight, beat; ***~ się z myślami*** be in two minds; → ***uderzać***
biec ⟨**po-**⟩ (→***biegnąć***) run; *fig.* (*życie itp.*) pass
bied|a *f* (*-y*) poverty; *fig.* trouble; (*nieszczęście*) bad luck; ***~a z nędzą*** abject poverty; ***klepać ~ę*** suffer poverty; ***zá~ą, od ~y*** with difficulty; ***pół ~y*** it's not as bad as all that; ***mieć ~ę*** have great difficulty (***z*** *I* in); **~actwo** *n* (*-a*) poor thing; **~aczka** *f* (*-i*; *G -czek*) poor woman; **~aczysko** *m/n* (*-a*) poor devil; **~ak** *m* (*-a*; *-cy*) poor (wo)man; ***biedacy*** *pl.* the poor *pl.*; **~nieć** ⟨**z-**⟩ (*-eję*) become poor; **~ny 1.** poor (*też fig.*); (*nędzny*) poor, shabby; **2.** → ***biedak***; **~ota** *f* (*-y*) *zbior.* the poor *pl.*; **~ować** (*-uję*) suffer poverty
biedronka *f* (*-i*; *G -nek*) *zo. Brt.* ladybird, *Am.* ladybug
biedzić się ⟨***na- się***⟩ (*-dzę*) slave away (***z, nad*** *I* at)
bieg *m* (*-u*; *i*) run (*też fig., hunt.*); (*pociągu itp.*) motion; *mot.* gear; (*w sporcie*) race; ***~ krótkodystansowy*** short-distance race; ***~ zjazdowy*** downhill racing; ***~ przełajowy*** cross-country; ***w pełnym ~u*** at full speed; ***dolny/górny ~*** lower/upper reaches *pl.*; ***z ~iem rzeki*** downstream; ***z ~iem czasu/lat*** in the course of time; ***zmiana ~ów*** gear change; **~acz** *m* (*-a*; *-e*), **~aczka** *f* (*-i*; *G -czek*) runner
biega|ć (*-am*) run; ***~ć po sklepach*** doáthe rounds of all the shops; ***~ć za*** (*D*) run *lub* chase after; **~nina** *f* (*-y*) running around
bieg|le *adv. mówić*: fluently; **~ły 1.** *adj.* (*comp. -lejszy*) skilful (**w** *L* at); **2.** *m* (*-ego*; *-li*) expert; **~nąć** ⟨**po-**⟩ (*-nę*, *-ł*) run; → ***biec***; **~owy** (*narty*) cross-country; **~un** *m* (*-a*; *-y*) *phys.*, *geogr.* pole; ***koń na ~unach*** rocking horse
biegunka *f* (*-i*; *G -nek*) *Brt.* diarrhoea, *Am.* diarrhea
biegunow|o diametrally; **~y** Polar; ***koło ~e*** polar circle
biel *f* (*-i*; *-e*) (***cynkowa*** Chinese) white; ***w ~i*** in white; **~eć** (*-eję*) ⟨**po-, z-**⟩ whiten, go white; **~ej** *comp. od adv.* → ***biało***; **~ić** ⟨**po-, wy-**⟩ *ściany* whitewash; *materiał* bleach; ⟨**za-**⟩ make white; *zupę* add cream to
bielizna *f* (*-y*) (***pościelowa, stołowa*** bed-, table-) linen; ***~ osobista*** underwear
bieliźnia|ny linen; **~rka** *f* (*-i*; *G -rek*) chest of drawers
biel|mo *n* (*-a*) *med.* leukoma; film (*też fig.*); **~ony** whitewashed; **~szy** *adj. comp. od* → ***biały***
bielutki F quite white, white all over
bier|nik *m* (*-a*; *-i*) *gr.* accusative; **~ność** *f* (*-ści*; *0*) passivity; **~ny** passive (*też chem.*); ***strona ~na*** the passive (voice)
bierzmowanie *n* (*-a*) *rel.* confirmation
bies *m* (*-a*; *-y*) devil
biesiada *m* (*-y*) banquet
bież. *skrót pisany*: ***bieżący*** ct (*current*)
bież|ąco: ***prowadzić na ~ąco*** (***A***) keep up-to-date; **~ący** running; actual, current; ***rachunek ~ący*** current account; **~nia** *f* (*-i*; *-e*) (*w sporcie*) track; **~nik** *m* (*-a*; *-i*) (*na stół*) runner; *mot.* tread
bigamista *m* (*-y*; *-ci*) bigamist
bigos *m* (*-u*; *y*) bigos (*stew made with meat and cabbage*); F *fig.* ***narobić ~u*** make a mess
bijak *m* (*-a*; *-i*) (*w sporcie*) batter
bijatyka *f* (*-i*) brawl
bila *f* (*-i*; *-e*, *-/-i*) *sport*: billiard-ball
bilans *m* (*-u*; *-e*) balance (*też fig.*); **~ować** ⟨**z-**⟩ (*-uję*) balance
bilard *m* (*-u*; *-e*) billiards
bile|t *m* (*-u*; *-y*) (***powrotny, lotniczy*** return, plane) ticket; ***~t miesięczny*** monthly season-ticket; ***~t wstępu*** entrance ticket; ***~t do teatru*** *Brt.* theatre (*Am.* theater) ticket; **~ter** *m* (*-a*; *-rzy*)

usher; **-rka** *f* (*-i*; *G -rek*) usherette; **~towy**: ***kasa ~towa*** ticket window; (*w teatrze, kinie*) box office
bilon *m* (*-u*; *0*) coins *pl.*; small change
bimber *m* (*-bru*; *0*) *Brt.* poteen, *zwł. Am.* moonshine
biochemia *f* biochemistry
biodro *n* (*-a*) hip; **~wy** hip
bio|'grafia *f* (*GDL -ii*; *-e*) biography; **~'logia** *f* (*GDL -ii*; *e*) biology; **~logiczny** biological; **~technologia** *f* biotechnology
biorą(c) → ***brać***
biorca *m* (*-y*; *G -ów*) recipient
biorę → ***brać***
biret *m* (*-u*; *-y*) (*duchownego itp.*) biretta; (*profesora, prawnika*) cap
bis *m* (*-u*; *-y*) *theat.* encore
biskup *m* (*-a*; *-i*) bishop; **~i** bishop's, episcopal; **~stwo** *n* (*-a*) bishopric
biskwit *m* (*-u*; *-y*) *gastr.* biscuit
biszkopt *m* (*-u*; *-y*) *gastr.* sponge biscuit; **~owy** sponge-biscuit; ***tort ~owy*** sponge-biscuit gateau
bit *m* (*-u*; *-y*) *komp.* bit
bitka *f* (*-i*) brawl, fight; *zwł. pl.* ***bitki*** chops *pl.*
bit|ny brave, courageous; **~wa** *f* (*-y*) battle; **~y** (*szlak itp.*) beaten; (*drób*) slaughtered; ***~a godzina*** a whole hour; ***~a śmietana*** whipped cream
biuletyn *m* (*-u*; *-y*) bulletin
biurko *n* (*-a*) desk
biuro *n* (*-a*) office; (*podróży itp.*) agency; (*matrymonialne itp.*) bureau; ***~ meldunkowe*** local government office for registration of residents; F ***po biurze*** after office hours; **~kracja** *f* (*-i*; *-e*) bureaucracy; **~kratyczny** bureaucratic; **~wiec** *m* (*-wca*; *-wce*) office building; **~wość** *f* (*-ści*; *0*) office work; **~wy** office
biust *m* (*-u*; *-y*) bust, bosom; → ***popiersie***; **~onosz** *m* (*-a*; *-e*) bra, brassière
biwak *m* (*-u*; *-i*) bivouac, camp; **~ować** (*-uję*) bivouac, camp
bizmut *m* (*-u*; *0*) *chem.* bismuth
biznes *m* (*-u*; *y*) business; **~men** *m* (*-a*; *-i*) businessman; **~menka** *f* (*-i*) businesswoman
bizon *m* (*-a*; *-y*) buffalo; bison
biżuteria *f* (*GDL -ii*; *0*) (***sztuczna*** costume) jewellery
blacha *f* (*-y*) sheet metal; (*do ciasta*) baking tray; (*kuchenna, węglowa*) top, (*elektryczna*) hotplate; **~rka** *f* (*-ki*) metalwork; **~rski** tin; **~rz** *m* (*-a*; *-e*) tinsmith
blad|ł(a, -o) → ***blednąć***; **~o** *adv.* pale(ly); *w złoż.* pale-; **~ość** *f* (*-i*; *0*) paleness, pallor
blady (***jak trup*** deathly) pale; white
blag|a F *f* (*-i*) tall story, hoax; **~ier** *m* (*-a*; *-rzy*), **-rka** *f* (*-i*; *G -rek*) hoaxer; **~ować** F (*-uję*) talk rubbish, humbug
blaknąć ⟨**wy-**⟩ (*-nę*; *-kł/-nął*) fade, pale (*też fig.*)
blamować się ⟨***z- się***⟩ (*-uję*) make a fool of o.s.
blankiet *m* (*-u*; *-y*) form
blanszować (*-uję*) *gastr.* blanch
blask *m* (*-u*; *-i*) (*rażący*) glare; (*nie rażący*) shine, (*klejnotów*) sparkle
blaszan|ka *f* (*-i*; *G -nek*) can, *Brt.* tin; **~y** tin, metal
blaszka *f* (*-i*; *G-szek*) a piece of metal
blat *m* (*-u*; *-y*) (table-)top
blednąć ⟨**z-**⟩ (*-nę*; *-nął/bladł*) go *lub* turn pale; *fig.* pale, fade
blef *m* (*-u*; *0*) bluff; **~ować** (*-uję*) bluff
blenda *f* (*-y*) *arch.* blind window; *chem.* blende
blezer *m* (*-a/-u*; *-y*) blazer
blichtr *m* (*-u*; *0*) gaudiness, tawdriness
blisk|i 1. near; close (*też fig.*); → ***pobliski, bliższy***; ***~a przyjaźń*** close friendship; **2.** (*m-os -scy*) relative, member of one's family; **~o** *adv.* near, close (*G*, **od** *G* to) (*też w czasie*); (*prawie*) almost; ***z ~a*** at close quarters; from a short distance; → ***bliżej***
bliskość *f* (*-ści*; *0*) closeness (*też fig.*); proximity
blisko|wschodni Middle-Eastern; **~znaczny** synonymous
blizna *f* (*-y*) scar
bliź|ni *m* (*-ego*; *i*) fellow human being; *rel.* neighbo(u)r; **~niaczka** *f* (*-i*; *G -czek*) twin sister; **~niaczo**: ***być ~niaczo podobnym do*** (*G*) be the spitting image of; **~niaczy** twin; **~niak** *m* (*-a*; *-i*) twin brother; **~nięta** *n/pl.* (*-niąt*) twins *pl.*; *znak Zodiaku:* ***♊nięta*** Gemini; ***on(a) jest spod znaku ♊niąt*** he/she is (a) Gemini
bliż|ej *adv.* (*comp. od* → ***blisko***) nearer; ***~ej nieznany*** little known; **~szy** *adj.* (*comp. od* → ***najbliższy***) nearer,

closer; ***~sze dane*** more precise information
bloczek *m* (*-czka*; *-czki*) notepad
blok *m* (*-u*; *-i*) block; *tech.* ***~ rysunkowy*** sketch-pad; ***~ mieszkalny*** block (of flats); ***~ cylindrów*** cylinder block; **~ada** *f* (*-y*) blockade; (*w sporcie*) blocking; **~ować** ⟨**za-**⟩ (*-uję*) block; *państwo itp.* blockade; *ruch* stop; **~owisko** *n* (*-a*) prefab housing estate
blond *idkl.* blond(e); ***włosy ~*** (***mężczyzny***) blond, (*kobiety*) blonde; **~yn** *m* (*-a*; *-i*) fair-haired *lub* blond man; **~ynka** *f* (*-i*; *G -nek*) blonde
bluszcz *m* (*-u*; *-e*) *bot.* ivy
bluz|a *f* (*-y*) (*żołnierza itp.*) tunic; (*sportowca itp.*) sweatshirt; **~ka** (*-i*) blouse
bluz|gać (*-am*) ⟨**~nąć**⟩ (*-nę*) *błoto, itp.*: spout, splash; F (*przekleństwami itp.*) hurl
bluźnierstwo *n* (*-a*) blasphemy
błaga|ć (*-am*) plead, implore; **~lny** imploring; **~nie** *n* (*-a*) plea, entreaty
błah|ostka *f* (*-i*; *G -tek*) trifle; **~y** trivial; unimportant
bławatek *m* (*-tka*; *-tki*) *bot.* cornflower, bluebottle
błaz|en *m* (*-na*; *-zny/-źni*) clown; *fig.* fool; **~eński** foolish; **~eńsko** foolishly; **~eństwo** *n* (*-a*) folly; stupidity; **~nować** (*-uję*) F fool (around)
błaźnić się ⟨***z- się***⟩ (*-nę*, *-nij!*) make a fool of o.s.
błą|d *m* (*błędu*; *błędy*) mistake, error; ***~d maszynowy*** typing error, F typo; ***~d w rachunku*** arithmetical error; ***być w błędzie*** be wrong *lub* mistaken; ***wprowadzić w ~d*** mislead, deceive; **~dzić** (*-dzę*) wander (***po*** *L*, ***wśród*** *G* around); ⟨**po-**, **z-**⟩ go wrong (***w*** *L* with); *tylko pf* lose one's way; **~kać się** (*-am*) wander about *lub* around
błęd|nie *adv.* mistakenly; **~ny** mistaken; *wzrok itp.* vague; ***~ne koło*** vicious circle; **~y** *pl.* → ***błąd***
błękit *m* (*-u*; *-y*) blue; **~nooki** blue-eyed; **~ny** blue
błocić ⟨**na-**, **za-**⟩ (*-cę*) get dirty (with mud)
bło|gi blissful, delightful; **~go** blissfully, delightfully
błogosła|wić ⟨**po-**⟩ (*-ę*) bless; **~wieństwo** *n* (*-a*) blessing (*też iron.*); **~wiony** blessed
błon|a *f* (*-y*) membrane; *phot.* film; ***~a śluzowa*** mucous membrane; ***~a dziewicza*** hymen; **~ica** *f* (*-y*; *-0*) diphtheria
błonka *f* (*-i*; *G -nek*) membrane
błot|nik *m* (*-a*; *-i*) *Am.* fender, *Brt. mot.* wing, (*rowerowy*) mudguard; **~nisty** muddy; **~ny** muddy, marshy; (*roślina itp.*) marsh; **~o** *n* (*-a*) mud, dirt; *fig.* dirt, filth, F muck; **~a** *pl.* swamp; ***zmieszać z ~em*** *fig.* drag through the mud
błysk *m* (*-u*; *-i*) flash; **~ać** (*-am*) flash, sparkle; ***błysnęło*** there was a flash of lightning; ***~a się*** there are flashes of lightning
błyskawi|ca *f* (*-y*; *-e*) lightning; ***jak ~ca*** as fast as lightning; **~czny** (*szybki*) lightning; (*zupa*) instant; → ***zamek***
błyskot|ka *f* (*-i*; *G -tek*) trinket; ***~ki*** *pl.* tinsel; **~liwie** glitteringly; *fig.* brilliantly; **~liwy** glittering; *fig.* brilliant
błys|kowy flash; **~nąć** *v/s.* (*-nę*) → ***błyskać***
błyszcz|ący shining, shiny; *papier itp.* glossy; ***wypolerować coś na ~ąco*** polish s.th. until it shines; **~eć** (*-ę*) shine (*też fig.*); glitter, sparkle; **~ka** *f* (*-i*; *G -czek*) (*na ryby*) spoon(-bait)
błyśnięcie *n* (*-a*) → ***błysk***
bm. *skrót pisany*: ***bieżącego miesiąca*** inst. (*instant*: *this month*)
bo *cj.* because, or (else)
boazeria *f* (*GDL -ii*; *-e*) wainscoting, wood panelling
bobas F *m* (*-a*; *-y*) baby
bobkowy: ***listek ~*** bay leaf
bobslej *m* (*-a*; *-e*) bobsleigh; **~owy**: ***tor ~owy*** bobsleigh run
bochen *m* (*-chna*; *-chny*), **~ek** *m* (*-nka*; *-nki*) loaf (of bread)
bocian *m* (*-a*; *-y*) *zo.* stork; **~i** stork
bocz|ek *m* (*-czku*; *-czki*) *gastr.* bacon; **~nica** *f* (*-y*; *-e*) *rail.* siding; (*ulica*) side-street; **~ny** side
boczyć się (*-ę*) (***na*** *A*) be cross with
boćwina *f* (*-y*; *0*) → ***botwina***
bodaj, **~że** *part.* at least; perhaps; → ***chyba***, ***pewnie***
bodziec *m* (*-dźca*; *-dźce*) stimulus; (*też materialny*) incentive
boga|cić ⟨**wz-**⟩ (*-cę*) enrich; ***~cić*** ⟨**wz-**⟩ ***się*** get rich; **~ctwo** *n* (*-a*) wealth, riches *pl.*
bogacz *m* (*-a*; *-e*) rich man; **~ka** *f* (*-i*; *G -czek*) rich woman

Bogarodzica *f* (*-y*; *0*) Mother of God
bogat|o richly, *fig.* abundantly; **~y** rich, *fig.* abundant (**w** *A* in)
bogini *f* (*GDL -ni*; *-e*, *-iń*) goddess
boginka *f* (*-ki*; *G -nek*) goddess, nymph
bogobojny god-fearing
bohater *m* (*-a*; *-erzy*/*-owie*) hero; **~ka** *f* (*-i*; *G -rek*) heroine; **~ski** heroic; **~sko** heroically; **~stwo** *n* (*-a*; *0*) heroism
bohomaz *m* (*-u*/*-a*; *-y*) *fig.* F daub; (*na papierze*) doodle
boi się → ***bać się***
boisko *n* (*-a*) sports field; ***~ do piłki nożnej*** football ground *lub* field
boja *f* (*GDL boi*; *-e*) *naut.* buoy
bojaź|liwie timidly; **~liwy** timid, fearful, fainthearted; **~ń** *f* (*-ni*; *0*) fear; ***z ~ni*** (*G*) for fear of
boj|ą, ~ę się → ***bać się***
bojkot *m* (*-u*; *-y*) boycott
bojkotować ⟨**z-**⟩ (*-uję*) boycott
bojler *m* (*-a*; *-y*) boiler; (*w domu*) (electric) water heater
bojow|niczka *f* (*-i*; *G- czek*), **~nik** *m* (*-a*; *-cy*) fighter; (***o prawa człowieka*** for human rights); **~o** (*zaczepnie*) belligerently; **~y** fighting, (*patrol itp.*) battle; (*buty itp.*) combat; (*zaczepny*) belligerent; ***organizacja ~a*** military organization
bojówka *f* (*-ki*; *G -wek*) raiding part; (*partyjna itp.*) hit-squad
bok *m* (*-u*; *-i*) side; ***na ~*** to one side; ***na ~u*** at the side; (*w odległości*) away; ***przy/u ~u*** (*G*) at the side (of); ***w ~*** in the side; away; ***z ~u*** at the side; ***pod ~iem*** near (at hand); ***robić ~ami*** *fig.* (*z wysiłku*) slave away; ***zarabiać na ~u*** earn on the side; ***zrywać ~i ze śmiechu*** split one's sides; **~ami, ~iem** *adv.* sidewise; ***~iem*** (*G*) sideways; **~obrody** *pl.* (*-ów*) (side) whiskers *pl.*; *Brt.* sideboards *pl.*, *Am.* sideburns *pl.*
boks[1] *m* (*-u*; *-y*) (*dla koni*) loosebox; (*w garażu*) (partitioned off) (parking-)space
boks[2] *m* (*-u*; *0*) boxing; ***uprawiać ~*** practise boxing; **~er** *m* (*-a*; *-rzy*) boxer; **~erski** boxing; **~ować** (*-uję*) fight (**się** *v/i.*)
bolą|cy → ***bolesny***; **~czka** *f* (*-i*; *G -czek*) *fig.* difficulty, problem
bolec *m* (*-lca*; *-lce*) pin, bolt
bole|ć[1] *też fig.* hurt, ache; ***boli mnie ząb*** I have a toothache; my tooth hurts me; ***nie mogę na to patrzeć*** *fig.* I am not able to stand the sight of it any more
bole|ć[2] (*-eję*) (**nad** *I*) lament; **~sny** (**-śnie**) painful (*też fig.*), aching; F sore; **~ści** *f/pl.* (*G -ści*) pain (*zwł.* abdominal)
Boliw|ia *f* (*GDL -ii*) Bolivia; **≈ijski** Bolivian
bom|ba *f* (*-y*) bomb; *fig.* sensation, bombshell; **~bardować** (*-uję*) bomb; (*silnie*) blitz; **~bastyczny** bombastic; **~bka** *f* (*-i*; *G -bek*) glass ball
bombow|iec *m* (*-wca*; *-wce*) *aviat.* bomber; **~y** bomb; F (*kapitalny*) super
bon *m* (*-u*; *-y*) coupon
bonifikata *f* (*-y*) price reduction, discount; *sport*: handicap
boraks *m* (*-u*; *0*) borax
bordo[1] *n*, *też* ***Bordeaux*** (*idkl.*) *wino*: Bordeaux
bordo[2] *adj.* (*idkl.*), **~wy** (**-wo**) wine-red
borny: ***kwas ~*** boric acid
borowik *m* (*-a*; *-i*) cep
borowin|a *f* (*-y*; *G -in*) mud; **~owy**: ***kąpiel ~owa*** mud bath
borowy → ***borny***
borówka *f* (*-i*; *G -wek*): ***~ brusznica*** cowberry; ***~ czernica*** bilberry, blueberry, whortleberry
borsu|czy badger; **~k** *m* (*-a*; *-i*) badger
borykać się (*-am*) contend (**z** *I* with)
bosak[1]: ***na ~a*** barefoot
bosak[2] *m* (*-a*; *-i*) boat-hook
bosk|i God's, divine; ***na litość ~ą*** for God's sake; ***rany ~ie!*** for heaven's sake
bosko *adv. fig.* heavenly
bosman *m* (*-a*; *-i*) *naut.* boatswain
boso *adv.* barefoot; **~nogi, bosy** barefoot
Bośnia *f* (*-i*; *0*) Bosnia; **≈cki** Bosnian
bot *m* (*-a*; *-y*) → ***boty***
botani|czny botanic(al); **~ka** *f* (*-i*; *0*) botany
botwin|a *f* (*-y*), **~ka** *f* (*-i*; *G -nek*) beetroot leaves *pl.*; (*soup from beetroot leaves*)
boty *m/pl.* (*-ów*) snow-boots *pl.*
bowiem *cj.* as, since; → ***bo***
boy *m* (*-a*; *-e. -ów*) (*w hotelu*) *Brt.* page, *Am.* bellboy
Bozia *f* F (*-i*; *0*) sweet God
Boż|e → ***bóg***; **≈ek** *m* (*-ka*; *-ki*) god, idol; **≈onarodzeniowy** Christmas; **≈y**

B

God's; ***Boże Narodzenie*** Christmas; ***Boże Ciało*** Corpus Christi
bożyszcze *n* (*-a*) idol
bób *m* (*bobu*; *boby*) *bot.* broad bean
bóbr *m* (*bobra*; *bobry*) *zo.* beaver
bóg *m* (*boga*, *bogu*, *boże!*; *bogowie/bogi*, *rel.* **Bóg**) god, *rel.* God; ~ ***wojny*** god of war; ***jak Boga kocham!*** I swear on God!; ***broń Boże, Boże uchowaj*** Heaven forbid; ***jak*** ♀ ***da*** God willing; ***Bogu ducha winien/winna*** innocent; ***szczęść Boże!*** God bless you!
bójka *f* (*-i*; *G -jek*) skirmish, fight
ból *m* (*-u*, *-e*; *-ów*) (***głowy, zęba*** head-, tooth-) ache; ~ ***gardła*** sore throat; ***~e porodowe*** *pl.* labo(u)r pains *pl.*; ***z ~em serca*** with a heavy heart
bór *m* (*boru*; *bory*) forest
bóstwo *n* (*-a*; *G -*) deity; *fig.* good-looker
bóść *v/i.* gore
bóżnica *f* (*-y*; *-e*) *rel.* (*żydowska*) synagogue
bp *skrót pisany*: **biskup** Bp (*Bishop*)
br. *skrót pisany*: ***bieżącego roku*** ha (*of/in this year*)
brac|ia → ***brat***; (*firma*) brothers *pl.* (*skrót*: **Bros**); **~iszek** *m* (*-szka*; *-szkowie*) little brother; (*zakonny*) brother; **~two** *n* (*-a*) brotherhood
brać *v/t.* take; ~ ***kogoś do wojska*** call s.o. up; ~ ***na serio*** take seriously; ~ ***na siebie*** take on; ~ ***ze sobą*** take with o.s.; → ***rachuba, uwaga, zły*** *itp.*; ~ ***się*** (***do*** (***robienia***) ***czegoś***) set about ((doing) s.th.); *v/i. ryba*: bite
brak[1] *m* (*-u*; *-i*) lack; (*niedostatek*, *wada*) shortcoming; (*produkt*) reject; ***z ~u czasu*** owing to lack of time; ***~i w wykształceniu*** gaps *pl.* in education; ***~i w kasie*** cash deficit; ***cierpieć na*** ~ (*G*) suffer for lack of; ***odczuwać*** ~ (*G*) (*czegoś*) lack, (*zwł. kogoś*) miss
brak[2] *pred. s.o./s.th.* lacks *s.o./s.th.*; ~ ***mi ciebie*** I miss you; ~ ***mi słów*** I am lost for words; ***nie ~ mu odwagi*** he does not lack courage; **~nąć** (*-nę*) → ***brakować***[1]; **~oróbstwo** *n* (*-a*; *0*) slipshod work, sloppiness
brakow|ać[1] (*-uję*) (*G*) lack; *komuś* ***brakuje ...*** *s.o.* lacks…; ***tego tylko ~ało*** that was all we needed; → ***brak***[2]
brakować[2] (*-uję*) → ***wybrakowywać***
bram|a *f* (*-y*) gate, (*do garażu itp.*) door; (*przejazdowa, też fig.*) gateway; **~ka** *f* (*-i*; *G -mek*) little gate/door; (*w sporcie*) goal; ***strzał w ~kę*** shot (at goal); **~karz** *m* (*-a*; *-e*) (*w sporcie*) goalkeeper; (*przy drzwiach*) F bouncer, chucker-out; **~kowy** (*w sporcie*) goal
bramofon *m* (*-u*; *-y*) intercom, *Brt.* entryphone
Brandenbur|gia *f* (*-ii*; *0*) Brandenburg; ♀**ski** Brandenburg
bransoletka *f* (*-i*; *G - tek*) bracelet
branż|a *f* (*-y*; *-e*) (*przemysłowa*) (branch of) industry; (*biznesu*) line (of business); **~owy** trade; ***sklep ~owy*** specialist shop
brat *m* (*-a*; *D -tu*, *L -cie*; *-cia*, *-ci*, *I -ćmi*) brother (*też rel.*); ***być za pan*** ~ be close friends (***z*** *I* with); → ***cioteczny***
bratan|ek *m* (*-nka*; *-nki/-nkowie*) nephew; **~ica** *f* (*-y*; *-e*), **~ka** *f* (*-i*; *G -nek*) niece
bratek *m* (*-tka*; *-tki*) *bot.* pansy
braters|ki brotherly, fraternal; ***po ~ku*** like brothers; **~two** *n* (*-a*; *0*) (*broni*) brotherhood (-in-arms)
bratni brotherly, fraternal
bratobój|czy: ***wojna ~cza*** fratricidal war; **~stwo** *n* (*-a*) fratricide
bratowa *f* (*-wej*, *-wo!*; *-e*) sister-in-law
Bratysława *f* (*-y*; *0*) Bratislava
brawo *n* (*-a*) cheer(ing); ***~!*** bravo!; → ***bić***
brawurow|o daringly, courageously; **~y** daring, courageous
Brazyli|a *f* (*-ii*) Brazil; **~jczyk** *m* (*-a*; *-ycy*), **~jka** *f* (*-i*) Brazilian; ♀**jski** Brazilian
brąz *m* (*-u*; *-y*) brown; (*metal*) bronze; ***opalić się na*** ~ be sun-tanned; **~owy** (**-wo**) brown; (*z metalu*) bronze
bre|dnie *f/pl.* (*-i*) nonsense, F balderdash; **~dzić** (*-dzę*) (*w gorączce*) rave; babble
breja *f* (*brei*; *0*) mush
brew *f* (*brwi*; *brwi*) (eye-)brow
brewerie *f/pl.* (*-ii*) row, fuss; ***wyprawiać*** ~ scrap
brewiarz *m* (*-a*; *-e*) breviary
brezent *m* (*-u*; *-y*) canvas
brnąć (*-nę*) tramp, plod (***przez błoto*** through mud; ***w śniegu*** through the snow)
broczyć (*-czę*): ~ ***krwią*** bleed
broda *f* (*-y*; *G bród*) chin; (*zarost*)

beard; ***zapuścić brodę*** grow a beard; **~ty** bearded; **~wka** *f* (*-i*; *G -wek*) *med.*, *bot.* wart

brodz|ić (*-dzę*) wade; **~ik** *m* (*-a*; *-i*) (*basen dla dzieci*) paddling-pool; (*w łazience*) shower base

broić ⟨**na-, z-**⟩ (*-ję*; *-isz*, *brój!*) act up, frolic

brona *f* (*-y*) harrow

bronchit *m* (*-u*; *-y*) bronchitis

bronić (*-ę*) ⟨**o-**⟩ (*G*) defend (*A*; ***się*** o.s.); protect, guard (***przed*** *I* against); ***~ się*** *też* defend o.s. (***przed*** *I* against); ⟨**za-**⟩ (*G*) prevent, prohibit

bronować ⟨**za-**⟩ (*-uję*) harrow

broń[1] → ***bronić, bóg***

broń[2] *f* (*-ni*; *-ie*) weapon, arms *pl.*; ***~ krótka*** small arms *pl.*; ***~ masowego rażenia*** weapon(s *pl.*) of mass destruction; ***~ biała*** cutting weapon(s *pl.*); ***powołać pod ~*** call to arms; ***złożyć ~*** lay down one's arms

broszka *f* (*-i*; *G -szek*) brooch

broszura *f* (*-y*) brochure, leaflet

browar *m* (*-u*; *-y*) brewery

bród *m* (*-odu*; *-ody*) ford; ***przejść w ~*** ford, wade; *fig.* ***w ~*** in abundance

bródka *f* (*-i*; *G -dek*) (*zarost*) (little) beard

brud *m* (*-u*; *-y*) dirt; → ***brudy***; ***... od ~u ...*** with dirt; **~as** *m* (*-a*; *-y*) F (dirty) pig; (*dziecko*) dirty brat; **~no** *adv.* → ***brudny***; ***pisać na ~no*** make a rough copy; **~nopis** *m* (*-u*; *-y*) rough copy; **~ny** dirty (*też fig.*); **~y** *m/pl.* (*-ów*) (dirty) laundry; *fig.* dirty linen; → ***brud***

brudzić ⟨**po-, za-**⟩ (*-dzę*) make dirty, dirty; **~** ⟨**po-, za-**⟩ ***się*** get dirty

bruk *m* (*-u*; *-i*) paving; ***wyrzucić kogoś na ~*** (*z pracy*) give s.o. the sack; (*z mieszkania*) turn s.o. out on to the street

brukać (*-am*) *lit.* defile

brukiew *f* (*-kwi*; *-kwie*) swede

brukow|ać ⟨**wy-**⟩ (*-uję*) surface; **~iec** *m* (*nieregularny*) cobble(stone); (*czworokątny*) set(t); **~y** paving; ***prasa ~a*** gutter press

Bruksel|a *f* (*-i*; *0*) Brussels; **2ka** *f* (*-i*) Brussels sprout(s *pl.*); **2ski** Brussels

brulion *m* (*-u*; *-y*) notebook

brunatny (***-no***) dark brown

brunet *m* (*-a*; *-ci*) dark-haired man; **~ka** *f* (*-i*; *G -tek*) brunette

brusznica *f* (*-y*; *-e*) *bot.* cowberry

brutal *m* (*-a*; *-e*, *-i/-ów*) brute, brutal person; **~ność** *f* (*-ści*; *0*) brutality; **~ny** brutal

brutto (*idkl.*) gross

bruzda *f* (*-y*) (*zwł. w ziemi*) furrow; groove

bruździć (*-żdżę*; *-isz*) furrow; *fig.* make difficulties (***w*** *I* in), put obstacles in *s.o.'s* way

brwi → ***brew***; **~owy** brow

bryczesy *pl.* (*-ów*) (riding) breeches *pl.*

brydż *m* (*-a*; *0*) bridge

brygada *f* (*-y*) *mil.* brigade; (***pracowników*** work) team

brygadzist|a *m* (*-y*; *-ści*) foreman; **~ka** *f* (*-i*; *G -tek*) forewoman

bryk F *m* (*-a*; *-i*) crib

brykać (*-am*) romp about

brykiet *m* (*-u*; *-y*) briquette

bryknąć *pf* (*-nę*) F (*zwiać*) scram; scarper

brylant *m* (*-u*; *-y*) diamond

brył|a *f* (*-y*) (*ziemi itp.*) lump, clod; **~ka** *f* (*-i*) (*złota itp.*) nugget

brył(k)owaty lumpy

bryndza *f* (*-y*; *-e*) sheep's cheese

brytan *m* (*-a*; *-y*) mastiff

Brytania *f* (*-ii*; *0*) Britain; ***Wielka ~*** Great Britain

brytfanna *f* (*-y*) baking pan

Brytyj|czyk *m* (*-a*; *-ycy*) Briton; **~czycy** *pl.* the British *pl.*; **~ka** *f* (*-i*; *G -jek*) Briton; **2ski** British

bryza *f* (*-y*) breeze

bryz|g *m* (*-u*; *-i*) splash; **~gać** (*-am*) ⟨**~nąć**⟩ (*-nę*) splash, splatter

bryzol *m* (*-u*; *-e*, *-i/-ów*) *gastr.* (fried) piece of loin

brzask *m* (*-u*; *-i*) dawn; ***o ~u, z ~iem*** at dawn

brzdąc *m* (*-a*; *-e*) *Brt.* nipper, kid

brzd|ąkać, ~ękać (*-am*) *v/t. melodię* plunk out; *v/i.* strum (***na gitarze*** (on) the guitar); **~ąkanie, ~ękanie** *n* (*-a*) plunking

brzeg *m* (*-u*; *-i*) edge; (*naczynia itp.*) rim; (*rzeki itp.*) bank; (*morza*) coast; ***na ~u*** *fig.* on the verge; ***po ~i*** (*naczynie*) brimfull; (*sala itp.*) chock-full; ***nad ~iem morza*** by the sea; ***wystąpić z ~ów*** overflow

brzemienny pregnant; ***~ w skutki*** fateful

brzemię *n* (*-enia*; *-iona*) burden (*też fig.*)

B

brzezina *f* (*-y*) (*drewno*) birch(wood); (*zagajnik*) birch grove
brzeżek *m* (*-żka*; *-żki*) edge, rim
brzę|czeć ⟨**za-**⟩ (*-ę*, *-y*) *mucha*, *dzwonek*: buzz; *szkło*, *szyba*: ring; *naczynia*: clink; **~czyk** *m* (*-a*; *-i*) buzzer; **~k** *m* (*-u*; *-i*) buzz; ringing; clinking
brzmie|ć (*-ę*; *-mij!*) sound; *słowa itp.*: read; **~nie** *n* (*-a*) sound
brzoskwinia *f* (*-i*; *-e*) *bot.* peach
brzoz|a *f* (*-y*) *bot.* birch; **~owy** birch
brzuch *m* (*-a*; *-y*) stomach, F belly; ***na ~u*** on one's stomach; ***taniec ~a*** belly dance; **~acz** F *m* (*-a*; *-e*) potbelly, F fatso; **~aty** potbellied; (*dzbanek*) bulbous
brzuchomów|ca *m* (*-y*;*-y*), **~czyni** *f* (*-yni*; *-ynie*) ventriloquist
brzuszny belly; *ból itp.* abdominal; ***dur ~*** typhus
brzyd|actwo *n* (*-a*) fright, frump; **~al** *m* (*-a*; *-e*) ugly man; **~ki** (*m-os -dsi*) ugly; **~ko** in an ugly way; **~nąć** ⟨**z-**⟩ (*-nę*, *-ł/-nął*) become ugly; **~ota** *f* (*-y*) ugliness; **~ula** *f* (*-i*; *-e*) ugly woman
brzydzić się (*-dzę*) (*I*) find *s.th.* repulsive
brzydziej *adv. comp. od* → ***brzydki***
brzytwa *f* (*-y*; *G -tew*) razor
bubek *m* (*-bka*; *-bki*) *pej.* (*modniś*) dandy; (*głupek*) *Am.* jerk, *Brt.* twit
buble F *m/pl.* (*-i*) trash *sg.*, inferior merchandise *sg.*
buchać (*-am*) *v/i. płomienie*, *dym*: belch (out); *krew*, *woda*: gush; *v/t. smrodem*, *zapachem*: give off; ***~ żarem*** → ***buchnąć***
buchalteria *f* (*GDL -ii*; *-e*) accountancy
buchnąć *v/s.* (*-nę*) *v/i.* → ***buchać***; *v/t.* F pilfer, snitch
buci|k *m* (*-a*; *-i*) shoe; **~or** *m* (*-a*; *-y*) heavy shoe *lub* boot
bucze|ć (*-ę*) *syrena*: sound; *dziecko*: blubber; **~k** *m* (*-czka*; *-czki*) siren; buzzer
buczyna *f* (*-y*; *0*) (*drewno*) beech(wood), (*drzewa*) beech wood
buda *f* (*-y*) shed; (*na targu*) booth, stall; *mot.* canvas cover; F (*szkoła*) school; ***psia ~*** kennel
Budapeszt *m* (*-u*; *0*) Budapest
buddyjski Buddhist
budka *f* (*-i*; *G -dek*) kiosk; small shed; (*schronienie*) shelter; *tel.* (tele)phone booth, *Brt.* (tele)phone box
budow|a *f* (*-y*) building; (*czynność*) construction; ***plac/teren ~y*** construction/building site; **~ać** ⟨**po-, wy-, z-**⟩ (*-uję*) build; *fig.* construct, create; ***~ać*** ⟨**po-**⟩ ***się*** be under construction; (*dla siebie*) be building a house for o.s.; **~la** *f* (*-i*; *-e*) building, structure; **~lany** **1.** building, construction; **2.** *m/zbior.*: ***~lani*** *pl.* construction workers; *pl.*; **~nictwo** *n* (*-a*; *0*) building and construction industry; ***~nictwo mieszkaniowe*** housing construction; **~niczy** *m* (*-ego*; *-czowie*) builder
budu|jący edifying; **~lec** *m* (*-lca*; *0*) building material(s *pl.*)
budynek *m* (*-nku*; *-nki*) building, house; ***~ mieszkalny*** dwelling house
budyń *m* (*-nia*; *-nie*, *-ni/-niów*) pudding
budzi|ć ⟨**o-, z-**⟩ (*-dzę*) wake; *fig.* ⟨**o-, roz-**⟩ arouse; ***~ć*** ⟨**o-, roz-**⟩ ***się*** wake up; **~k** *m* (*-a*; *-i*) alarm clock
budżet *m* (*-u*; *-y*) budget; **~owy** budget, budgetary
bufet *m* (*-u*; *-y*) buffet; (*na dworcu itp.*) (station) bar; ***zimny ~*** cold buffet
bufiasty (*rękaw itp.*) puff
bufonada *f* (*-y*) bragging
bufor *m* (*-u/-a*; *-y*) buffer; **~owy** buffer
buhaj *m* (*-a*; *-e*, *-ów*) breeding bull
buja|ć (*-am*) *v/i.* fly, hover (*też fig.*); (*wędrować*) romp about (***po*** *L* in); ⟨**z-**⟩ (*kłamać*) fib, tell fibs; *v/t.* ⟨**po-**⟩ rock (***się*** *v/t.*); **~k** *m* (*-a*; *-i*) rocking-chair
bujda *f* (*-y*) (*kłamstwo*) fib; (*oszustwo*) humbug
bujn|y *roślinność* luxuriant; *włosy* thick; *życie* eventful; ***~a fantazja*** lively imagination
buk *m* (*-a/-u*; *-i*) *bot.* beech
bukiet *m* (*-u*; *-y*) (*kwiaty*) bunch, (*oficjalny*) bouquet; (*aromat*) bouquet
bukiew *f* (*-kwi*; *0*) beech-nut(s)
bukinista *m* (*-y*; *-ści*, *-stów*) second-hand bookseller
bukmacher *m* (*-a*; *-rzy*) bookmaker, F bookie
bukowy beech
buksować (*-uję*) *v/i. koło*: spin
bukszpan *m* (*-u*; *-y*) box(-tree)
bulaj *m* (*-a/-u*; *-e*) *naut.* (circular) porthole
buldog *m* (*-a*; *-i*) bulldog

B

buldożer *m* (*-a*; *-y*) bulldozer
bulgotać (*-czę/-ocę*) *strumień itp.*: gurgle; (*w czajniku*) bubble
bulić F ⟨**wy-**⟩ (*-lę*) cough up
bulion *m* (*-u*; *-y*) stock; (*zupa*) broth; **~ *w kostkach*** stock cube(s *pl.*)
bulwa *m* (*-y*) tuber
bulwar *m* (*-u*; *-y*) boulevard; **~owy** boulevard; *prasa itp.* gutter
bulwersować ⟨**z-**⟩ (*-uję*) shock
bulwiasty bulbous
buława *f* (*-y*): **~ *marszałkowska*** marshal's baton (*też fig.*)
bułeczka *f* (*-i*; *G -czek*) → ***bułka***
Bułgar *m* (*-a*; *-rzy*) Bulgarian; **~ia** *f* (*-ii*; *0*) Bulgaria; **~ka** *f* (*-i*; *G- rek*) Bulgarian; **ꝏski** Bulgarian; ***mówić po ꝏsku*** speak Bulgarian
bułka *f* (*-i*; *G -łek*) (bread) roll
bumel|anctwo *n* (*-a*; *0*) dawdling; **~ować** (*-uję*) dawdle
bumerang *m* (*-u*; *-i*) boomerang
bunkier *m* (*-kra*; *-kry*) *mil.* bunker; (*dla cywilów*) shelter; **~*przeciwlotniczy*** air-raid shelter
bunt *m* (*-u*; *-y*) revolt, rebellion (*też fig.*); (*na statku*) mutiny
buntow|ać ⟨**pod-, z-**⟩ (*-uję*) incite to rebel; ***~ać*** ⟨**z-**⟩ ***się*** rebel *lub* revolt; **~niczo** rebelliously; **~niczy** rebellious; **~nik** *m* (*-a*; *-cy*) rebel
buńczuczny cheeky, impertinent
bura *f* (*-y*) bawling-out
bura|czany beet(root); **~czki** *m/pl.* (*-ów*) boiled beetroots; **~k** *m* (*-a*; *-i*) beet; (*ćwikłowy*) beetroot
burczeć (*-czę*) mumble, mutter; *żołądek*: rumble
burda *f* (*-y*) row
burdel *m* (*-u*; *-e*, *G -i*) F brothel; *fig.* (*bałagan*) mess
burgund *m* (*-a*; *-y*) burgundy
burkliwy sullen, sulky
burmistrz *m* (*-a*; *-e*) mayor
buro *adv.* → ***bury***
bursztyn *m* (*-u*; *-y*) amber; **~owy** amber
burt|a *f naut.*: ***lewa ~a*** port; ***prawa ~a*** starboard; ***wyrzucić za ~ę*** throw overboard
bury (***-ro***) mousy
burz|a *f* (*-y*; *-e*) storm (*też fig.*); (*z piorunami*) thunderstorm; **~liwie** *fig.* tempestuously; **~liwy** stormy; *fig.* tempestuous; **~yć** (*-ę*) ⟨**z-**⟩ destroy; *dom, mur, też* pull down; ⟨**wz-**⟩ *wodę* churn up; ***~yć*** ⟨**z-**⟩ ***się*** seethe, churn
burżuaz|ja *f* (*-i*; *0*) bourgeoisie; **~yjny** bourgeois
burżuj *m* (*-a*; *-e*) bourgeois
busola *f* (*-i*; *-e*) compass
buszować (*-uję*) rummage (**po** *L* through, around)
but *m* (*-a*; *-y*) shoe; (*z cholewką*) boot; ***takie ~y*** that's the way things stand; ***głupi jak ~*** as thick as two short planks
butan *m* (*-u*; *0*) → ***propan***
butelk|a *f* (*-i*) bottle; ***~a od wina, po winie*** wine bottle; ***~a wina*** bottle of wine; **~owy** bottle; ***piwo ~owe*** bottled beer
butik *m* (*-u*; *-i*) boutique
butla *f* (*-i*; *-e*) large bottle; (*na wino*) flask; **~ *tlenowa*** oxygen cylinder
butny overbearing; imperious
butonierka *f* (*-i*; *G -rek*) buttonhole
butwieć ⟨**z-**⟩ (*-eję*) rot, decay
buzia F *f* (*-i*; *-e*, *-ź/-i*) face; (*usta*) mouth; **~k** *m* (*-a*; *-i*) (*całus*) little kiss, F peck
by 1. *cj.* (in order) to, in order that; **2.** *part.*: (*trybu warunkowego*) ***napisałbym to*** I would write it
by|cie *n* (*-a*; *0*): ***sposób ~cia*** manner
bycz|ek *m* (*-czka*; *-czki*) bull-calf; **~y** bull's; F (*fajny*) great, terrific; ***~y chłop*** F hell of a guy
być be; (*istnieć też*) exist; **~ *może*** perhaps, maybe; ***nie może ~!*** this cannot be!; ***bądź zdrów!*** farewell!; ***będę pamiętać*** I will remember; ***był naprawiony ...*** it has been repaired; ***było już późno*** it was already late; ***niech i tak będzie*** let it be so; F if you like; ***co z nim będzie?*** what will happen with him?; ***jest mu zimno*** he is cold; → ***jest, są***
bydlę *n* (*-ęcia*; *-ęta*) cow, bull, calf; **~ta** *pl.* cattle *pl.*; (*człowiek*) beast, animal; **~cy** cattle; *fig.* animal, savage
bydło *n* (*-a*; *0*) *zbior.* cattle *pl.*
byk *m* (*-a*; *-i*) bull; ꝏ *znak Zodiaku:* Taurus; ***on(a) jest spod znaku ꝏa*** he/she is (a) Taurus; F (*gafa*) goof; ***strzelić ~a*** *Brt. sl.* boob; *Am. sl.* make a boo-boo
byle *adv.* any-; **~ *co*** anything; **~ *gdzie***

C

anywhere; **~jak** anyhow; **~jaki** any; (*lichy*) shoddy; **~ kto** anybody, anyone; **~by** *cj.* in order to, in order that
byli → **być, były**
bylina *f* (*-y*) *bot.* herbaceous perennial
były (*m-os byli*) former; ex-; **mój ~** my ex; → **być**
bynajmniej (**nie**) not at all, not in the least; **~!** not in the slightest!
bystr|ość *f* (*-ści*; *0*) rapidity; speed; **~ość umysłu** astuteness; **~y** *adj.* (*comp. -rzejszy*), **~o** *adv.* (*comp. -rzej*) *adv.* fast; *nurt itp.* swift; *człowiek, uczeń* bright, sharp
byt *m* (*-u*; *-y*) (*istnienie*) existence; (*istota*) being; **~ność** *f* (*-ści*; *0*) presence; (*odwiedziny*) stay; **~owy** social; **warunki ~owe** living conditions, conditions of life
bywa|ć (*-am*) visit (**u kogoś** s.o., **w czymś** s.th.); **bywa**(**, że**) it happens (that); **~lczyni** *f* (*-ni*; *-nie*, *G -ń*), **~lec** *m* (*-lca*; *-lcy*) regular visitor, (*w sklepie itp.*) regular customer; **~ły** experienced
b.z. *skrót pisany*: **bez zmian** no changes; *med.* NAD (*no abnormality detected*; *no appreciable difference*)
bzdet F *m* (*-u*; *-y*) rubbish
bzdur|a *f* (*-y*) nonsense; **~ny** nonsensical, absurd
bzik F *m* (*-a*; *0*) fad; **mieć ~a** be mad about *s.th.*
bzów, bzu, bzy → **bez²**
bzykać (*-am*) hum, buzz

C

cack|ać się F (*-am*) fuss (**z** *I* over); **~o** *n* (*-a*; *G -cek*) *fig.* trinket, knick-knack
cal *m* (*-a*; *-e*, *-i*) inch; **w każdym ~u** every inch
calówka *f* (*-i*; *G -wek*) folding rule
cał|ka *f* (*-i*; *G -łek*) *math.* integral; **~kiem** *adv.* quite, wholly, completely
całkow|icie entirely, completely; wholly; **~ity** complete; (*suma też*) total; whole; (*liczba*) integral; **~y**: **rachunek ~y** *math.* integral calculus
cało *adv.* (*niezraniony*) undamaged, unhurt
cało|dobowy round the clock, twenty-four-hour; **~dzienny** all-day; (*praca itp.*) full-time; **~kształt** *m* the whole; general picture; **~nocny** all-night; **~roczny** yearlong, all the year round; (*dochód*) full year's
całoś|ciowo completely, in an integrated way; **~ciowy** complete, integrated; **~ć** *f* (*-ści*) whole; completeness; **w ~ci** as a whole; entirely, in its entirety
całotygodniowy all-week, for the whole week
całować ⟨**po-**⟩ (*-uję*) kiss (**się** *też* each other)
całus *m* (*-a*; *-y*) kiss
cał|y *adj.* whole; (*kompletny*) complete; (*zdrowy*) unhurt; → **cało**; **z ~ej siły** with full force; with all one's might; **~ymi godzinami** for hours
camping → **kemping**
Cambridge (*idkl.*) Cambridge
cap *m* (*-a*; *-y*) *zo.* (billy)goat
capnąć *pf.* (*-nę*) F grab; (*aresztować*) nab
capstrzyk *m* (*-a*; *-i*) tattoo
car *m* (*-a*; *-owie*) tsar; **~owa** → **caryca**; **~ski** tsar; **~yca** *f* (*-y*; *-e*) tsarina
casco *n* (*idkl.*) vehicle insurance, *naut.* hull insurance
cążki *pl.* (*-ów*) clippers *pl.*, F clips *pl.*
CBOS *skrót pisany*: **Centrum Badania Opinii Społecznej** Public Opinion Research Centre
cdn., c.d.n. *skrót*: **ciąg dalszy nastąpi** to be continued
ceb|er *m* (*-bra*; *-bry*) tub; **leje jak z ~ra** it's raining cats and dogs
cebul|a *f* (*-i*; *-e*) *bot.* onion; **~ka** *f* (*-i*; *G -lek*) *bot.* onion; (*tulipana itp.*) bulb; **~(k)owaty** bulbous, bulb-shaped; **~owy** onion; **wzór ~owy** onion pattern
cech *m* (*-u*; *-y*) guild, fraternity
cecha *f* (*-y*) feature; characteristic; (*znak*) mark; (*probiercza*) hallmark; **~ charakteru** characteristic
cechować (*-uję*) mark; label; *obrączkę itp.* hallmark; *przyrząd* standardize; **~ się** be marked (*I* by)
cedować ⟨**s-**⟩ (*-uję*) *jur.* cede

cedr *m* (*-u*; *-y*) cedar
ceduła *f* (*-y*) *fin.*: **~ giełdowa** exchange list
cedz|ak *m* (*-a*; *-i*) colander, strainer; **~ić** (*-dzę*) ⟨**prze-**⟩ strain; ⟨**wy-**⟩ *napój* sip; *słowa* drawl, mince
ceg|ielnia *f* (*-i*; *-e*) brickworks *sg.*; **~iełka** *f* (*-i*) (small) brick; *fig.* contribution; **~lasty** (**-to**) brick-red; **~ła** *f* (*-y*; *G* *-gieł*) brick
cekaem *m* (*-u*; *-y*) machine gun
cel *m* (*-u*; *-e*, *-ów*) aim, goal; (*tarcza*, *obiekt*, *też fig.*) target; (*podróży*) destination; **bez ~u** aimlessly; **do ~u** to the target/aim; **u ~u** at the end; **na ten ~, w tym ~u** for this purpose; **w ~u** for the purpose of; **wziąć na ~** take aim; **mieć na ~u/za ~** aim at, aim to achieve; → **celem**
cela *f* (*-i*; *-e*) (**klasztorna, więzienna** monastery, prison) cell
celibat *m* (*-u*; *-0*) celibacy
celni|czka *f* (*-i*; *G* *-czek*), **~k** *m* (*-a*; *-cy*) customs officer
celn|ość *f* (*-ści*; *0*) (*strzału*) accuracy; (*uwagi itp.*) relevance, aptitude; **~y**[1] *strzał*, *strzelec* accurate; *uwaga* relevant, apt
celn|y[2] customs; **opłata ~a** (customs) duty; **urząd ~y** customs office
celny[3] *proza* eminent, distinguished
celow|ać[1] ⟨**wy-**⟩ (*-uję*) aim (**do** *G* to, **w** *A* at)
celow|ać[2] (*-uję*) distinguish o.s. (**w** *L* in); **~nik** *m* (*-a*; *-i*) backsight; *phot.* viewfinder; *gr.* dative; **~nik lunetowy** telescopic sight; **~ość** *f* (*-ości*; *0*) appropriateness; **~o** appropriately, relevantly; **~y** appropriate, relevant
celując|o excellent; **~y** eminent, distinguished; (*ocena*) excellent
celuloza *f* (*-y*; *0*) cellulose
cement *m* (*-u*; *-y*) cement; **~ownia** *f* (*-i*; *-e*) cement plant; **~owy** cement
cen|a *f* (*-y*) price; **po tej ~ie** at this price; **za wszelką ~ę** at any price; **~ić** (*-ę*) *fig.* value; **~nik** *m* (*-a*; *-i*) price list; **~ny** valuable; **~owy** price
centnar → **cetnar**
central|a *f* (*-i*; *-e*) head/central office; (*policji*, *partii*) headquarters *sg./pl.*; (*sterowania*) control room; *tel.* **~a międzymiastowa** telephone exchange; (*w biurze itp.*) switchboard; **~izacja** *f* (*-i*; *-e*) centralization; **~ny** central
centrum *n* (*idkl.*; *-ra*. *-ów*) *Brt.* centre, *Am.* center; **~ handlowe** shopping centre/center; **~ obliczeniowe** computer centre/center
centymetr *m Brt.* centimetre, *Am.* centimeter; (*taśma*) (centimetre) measuring-tape
cenzur|a *f* (*-y*) censorship; **~ować** (*-uję*) censor; object to
cep *m* (*-u/-a*; *-y*) flail
cera[1] *f* (*-y*; *0*) complexion
cera[2] *f* (*-y*) (*w tkaninie*) darn
cerami|czny ceramic; **~ka** *f* (*-i*) ceramics *pl.*; pottery; **~ka szlachetna** ceramic whiteware
cerata *f* (*-y*) oilcloth
ceregiel|e F *pl.* (*-i*) fuss; **bez ~i** without ceremony
cere'monia *f* (*GDL* *-ii*; *-e*) ceremony; F *pl.* fuss
cerkiew *f* (*-kwi*; *-kwie*, *-kwi*) (*wyznanie*) the Orthodox Church; (*budynek*) orthodox church; **~ny** orthodox
cerować ⟨**za-**⟩ (*-uję*) darn
certować się (*-uję*) make a fuss (**z** *I* about)
certyfikat *m* (*-u*; *-y*) certificate; **~ pochodzenia** certificate of birth
cesa|rski imperial; **~rstwo** *n* (*-a*; *G* *-*) empire; **~rz** *m* (*-a*; *-e/-owie*) emperor; **~rzowa** *f* (*-wej*, *-wo!*; *-we*) empress
cesja *f* (*-i*; *-e*) *jur.* cession
cetnar *m* (*-a*; *-y*) centner; metric hundredweight
cewka *f* (*-i*; *G* *-wek*) *tech.* coil; *anat.* **~ moczowa** urethra; *electr.* **~ zapłonowa** spark coil
cez *m* (*-u*; *0*) *chem.* caesium
cęgi *pl.* (*-ów*) pliers *pl.*, pincers *pl.*
cętk|a *f* (*-i*; *G* *-tek*) dot, (*większa*) spot; **~owany** mottled; speckled
chaber *m* (*-bra*; *-bry*) *bot.* cornflower
chadec|ja *f* (*-i*; *-e*) Christian Democratic Party, Christian Democratics; **~ki** Christian Democratic
chała *f* (*-y*) *fig.* trash
chałka *f* (*-i*; *G* *-łek*) F (*bułka*) plait
chałupa *f* (*-y*) hut; (*biedna*) shack; (*z drewna*) (log) cabin
chałupni|ctwo *n* (*-a*; *0*) outwork, home work; **~czka** *f* (*-i*; *G* *-czek*), **~k** *m* (*-a*; *-cy*) outworker, home worker
cham *m* (*-a*; *-y*) lout, boor; **~ka** *f* (*-i*)

C

loutish woman; **~ski** loutish
chao|s *m* (*-u*; *0*) chaos; **~tyczny** chaotic
charakte|r *m* (*-u*; *y*): ***~r pisma*** handwriting; ***bez ~ru*** unprincipled; (*miasto itp.*) characterless; ***w ~rze gościa*** as a guest; **~rystyczny** characteristic (***dla*** *G* of); **~'rystyka** *f* (*-i*) characterization; **~ryzacja** *f* (*-i*) *theat.* make-up; **~ryzator** *m* (*-a*; *-rzy*), **-rka** *f* (*-i*) make-up artist
charakteryzować (*-uję*) ⟨**s-**⟩ characterize; **~** ⟨**s-**⟩ ***się*** be characterized by (*I*); ⟨**u-**⟩ make up; **~** ***się*** put make-up
char|czeć (*-czę*, *-y*) rasp; **~kać** (*-am*) ⟨***~knąć***⟩ spew
charkot *m* (*-u*; *-y*) rattle; *med.* stertor
chart *m* (*-a*; *-y*) *zo.* greyhound; ***~ afgański*** Afghan hound
charter *m* (*-u*; *-y*) charter; **~owy** charter(ed)
charytatywny charitable
chaszcze *pl.* (*-y*/*-ów*) thicket, (*w lesie*) dense undergrowth
chata *f* (*-y*) → ***chałupa***
chcieć ⟨**ze-**⟩ want; (***nie***) ***chce mi się czegoś zrobić*** I (don't) feel like doing s.th.; ***nie chce mi się*** *też* I can't be bothered; ***chciał(a)bym*** I would like
chciw|ie *adv.* → ***chciwy***; **~iec** *m* (*-wca*; *-wcy*) miser, niggard; **~ość** *f* (*-ści*; *0*) greed, avarice; **~y** greedy, avaricious; ***~y wiedzy*** eager for knowledge; *dziecko* eager to learn
chełbia *f* (*-i*; *-e*) aurelia
chełp|ić się (*-ę*) boast, brag (*I* about); **~liwość** *f* (*-ści*; *0*) boastfulness; **~liwie** boastfully; **~liwy** boastful
chemi|a *f* (*GDL -ii*; *0*) chemistry; **~czka** *f* (*-i*) chemist; **~czny** chemical; ***ołówek ~czny*** indelible pencil; **~k** *m* (*-a*; *-cy*) chemist
cherlawy frail, sickly
cherubinek *m* (*-a*; *-i*) putto; (*dziecko*) cherub
chę|ć *f* (*-i*) desire; (*zamiar*) intention; ***mieć ~ć*** feel like (***do zrobienia*** doing, ***na coś*** s.th.); ***dobre ~ci*** goodwill; ***z miłą ~cią*** with pleasure
chęt|ka *f* (*-i*; *G -tek*) desire; ***mieć ~kę*** F be really keen (***na*** *A* on); **~nie** *adv.* willingly; **~ny** willing; ***on jest ~ny do nauki*** he is an eager student
chichot *m* (*-u*; *-y*) giggle; **~ać** (*-czę*/*-ocę*) giggle
Chil|e *n* (*idkl.*) Chile; **~ijczyk** *m* (*-a*; *-ycy*), **~ijka** *f* (*-i*) Chilean; **ᘓijski** Chilean
chimer|a *f* (*-y*) *fig.* chimera, illusion; **~y** *pl.* moods *pl.*
chinina *f* (*-y*; *0*) quinine
Chin|ka *f* (*-i*; *G -nek*) Chinese; **~y** *pl.* (*G -*) China
Chiń|czyk *m* (*-a*; *-cy*) Chinese; **ᘓski 1.** Chinese; ***mówić po ᘓsku*** speak Chinese; **2.** *m* (*-ego*) Chinese (language); **ᘓszczyzna** *f* (*-y*; *0*) Chinese; *fig.* double Dutch
chiromancja *f* (*-i*; *0*) palmistry
chirurg *m* (*-a*; *-dzy*/*-owie*) surgeon; **~ia** (*GDL -ii*; *0*) surgery; **~iczny** surgical
chlać (*-am*/*-eję*) F booze
chlap|a *f* (*-y*) slush; (*pogoda*) slushy weather; **~ać** (*-ię*) *v/i.* splash (***po*** *L* about); *v/t.* ⟨*też* ***~nąć***⟩ (*-nę*) splay; *głupstwo itp.* babble
chlas|tać (*-am*/*-szczę*) *v/i.* *deszcz*: beat; *v/t.* ⟨*też* ***~nąć***⟩ whip
chleb *m* (*-a*, *-y*) bread (*też fig.*); ***~ z masłem*** bread and butter; ***zarabiać na ~*** earn one's daily bread; **~odawca** *m* (*-y*) employer; **~owy** bread
chlew *m* (*-a*/*-u*; *-y*) pigsty; **~ny**: ***trzoda ~na*** *zbior* pigs *pl.*, swine *pl.*
chlipać (*-pię*) sob, whimper
chlor *m* (*-u*; *0*) chlorine; **~ek** *m* (*-rku*; *-rki*): ***~ek*** (***bielący***) bleaching powder; *tech.* chloride of lime; **~owodór** *m* hydrogen chloride; **~owy** chloric
chlub|a *f* (*-y*; *0*) fame, esteem; (*pl. -y*) pride; **~ić się** pride o.s. (*I* on); **~ny** glorious; (*świadectwo*) outstanding, excellent
chlup|ać (*-ię*) *v/i.* splash; *rzeka itp.*: bubble, gurgle; ***~ać się*** splash about; ***~nąć do*** *v/s.* (*-nę*) splash into
chlus|tać (*-am*) ⟨***~nąć***⟩ gush, spurt; → ***chlastać, chlupnąć***
chłam F *m* (*-u*; *0*) trash, rubbish
chłeptać (*-czę*/*-cę*) *kot*: lap
chłod|ek *m* (*-dku*; *-dki*) cool, coolness; **~nia** *f* (*-i*; *-e*) refrigerator, cool store; ***wagon ~nia*** refrigerator car *lub Brt.* wagon; **~nica** *f* (*-y*; *-e*) *mot.* radiator; **~niczy** refrigeration; **~nieć** ⟨**po-**⟩ (*-eję*) get colder; **~nik** *m* (*-a*; *-i*) (*cold beetroot soup*); **~no** coldly; ***jest ~no*** it is cold; **~ny** cold (*też fig.*)
chłodz|iarka refrigerator, F fridge; **~ić**

⟨**o-**⟩ (*-dzę*) cool (down); ***~ić*** ⟨**o-**⟩ ***się*** cool; ***~ony wodą*** water-cooled
chłon|ąć ⟨**w-**⟩ (*-nę*) absorb; **~ka** *f* (*-i*) → ***limfa***; **~ny** absorptive, absorbent; *fig.* receptive, responsive; ***węzeł ~ny*** *anat.* lymphatic node
chłop *m* (*-a, -u; -i*) peasant; F (*pl. -y*) guy, chap; **~ak** *m* (*-a; -cy/-i*) boy; **~czyk** *m* (*-a; -i*) (young) boy
chłopiec *m* (*-pca, -pcy*) → ***chłopak***; (*adorator*) boyfriend; ***~ do wszystkiego***, ***~ na posyłki*** errand boy
chłop|ięco boyishly; **~ięcy** boyish; *odzież itp.* boy('s); **~ka** *f* (*-i; G -pek*) peasant woman; **~ski** peasant; ***po ~sku*** in a peasant way; **~stwo** *n* (*-a; 0*) *zbior.* peasantry
chłost|a *f* (*-y*) whipping, lashing; ***kara ~y*** corporal punishment; **~ać** (*-szczę*) whip, lash; *fig.* castigate
chłód *m* (*-odu; -ody*) cold; chill
chmara *f* (*-y*) (*owadów*) swarm; (*ludzi*) crowd
chmiel *m* (*-u; 0*) *bot.* hop; (*kwiatostan*) hops *pl.*
chmur|a *f* (*-y*), **~ka** *f* (*-i; G -rek*) cloud; **~nie** with clouds; *fig.* sullenly, gloomily; **~ny** cloudy; *fig.* sullen, gloomy
chmurzyć (*-ę*) ⟨**na-**⟩ *czoło* frown; *brwi* knit; ***~ się*** cloud over; *fig.* darken
chochla *f* (*-i; -e, -i/-chel*) soup-ladle
chochlik *m* (*-a; -i*) brownie, sprite
cho|ciaż, ~ć *cj.* although; though; → **~cby 1.** *cj.* even if; **2.** *part.* at least
chod|ak *m* (*-a; -i*) clog; **~nik** *m* (*-a; -i*) *Brt.* pavement, *Am.* sidewalk; (*dywan*) (long narrow) carpet; (*w kopalni*) gallery, gangway; **~y** *pl* → ***chód***
chodzić (*-dzę*) walk, go; *pociąg*: run; *maszyna*: work, run; look after (***koło czegoś*** s.th.); ***~ do szkoły*** go to school; ***~ o lasce*** walk with a stick; ***~ o kulach*** go about on crutches; ***~ w sukni*** wear a dress; ***chodzi o …*** it is about …; ***nie chodzi o …*** the point is not that …; ***o co chodzi?*** what is the matter?; ***o ile o mnie chodzi*** as far as I am concerned; ***~ z*** (*narzeczonym itp.*) go out with, go steady
choink|a *f* (*-i; -nek*) Christmas tree; (*zabawa*) Christmas party; ***dostać pod ~ę*** to get as a Christmas present; **~owy**: ***zabawki*** *f/pl.* ***~owe*** Christmas-tree ornaments
cholera *f* (*-y; 0*) *med.* cholera; F ***~!*** damn!
cholerny F damned
cholesterol *m* (*-u; -e*) cholesterol
cholewa *f* (*-y*) boot-leg; ***buty*** *m/pl.* ***z ~mi*** high boots
chomąto *n* (*-a*) (horse-)collar
chomik *m* (*-a; -i*) *zo.* hamster
chorą|giew *f* (*-gwi; -gwie*) flag, banner; *hist.* cavalry company; (*harcerzy*) troop; **~giewka** *f* (*-i; -wek*) (little) flag; ***~giewka na dachu*** (weather-)vane; **~ży** *m* (*-ego; -owie*) standard-bearer, ensign
choro|ba *f* (*-y*) disease, illness; ***~ba morska*** seasickness; ***~ba zawodowa*** occupational disease; ***~ba Heinego-Medina*** poliomyelitis, polio; ***~ba!*** damn!, shit!; **~bliwie** morbidly (*też fig.*); **~bliwy** morbid (*też fig.*); **~botwórczy** pathogenic; **~bowy 1.** *adj.* disease; **2.** ***~bowe*** *n* F (*-ego; -owe*) sickness benefit; **~wać** (*-uję*) be ill, *Am.* be sick; (***na*** *A*) suffer (from); ***~wać na serce*** have a heart condition
chorowity sickly
Chorwa|cja *f* (*-i; 0*) Croatia; **≈cki** Croatian; ***mówić po ≈cku*** speak Croatian; **~t** *m* (*-a; -ci*), **~tka** *f* (*-i*) Croatian
chor|y 1. ill, sick; *organ itp.* bad, diseased; *fig.* sick, ailing; ***~y na wątrobę*** suffering from a liver complaint; ***~y umysłowo*** mentally ill; **2.** *m* (*-ego, -rzy*), **~a** *f* (*-ej; -e*) patient; sick person
chować (*-am*) ⟨**s-**⟩ (*ukrywać*) hide (*też* ***się***); conceal; → ***wkładać***; ⟨**po-**⟩ bury; ⟨**wy-**⟩ bring up; *impf* (*hodować*) raise; ***zdrowo się ~*** flourish, prosper
chowan|y *m* (*-ego; 0*) *podwozie itp.* retractable; ***bawić się w ~ego*** play hide and seek
chód *m* (*-odu; -ody*) walk, gait; (*chód sportowy*) walking; F ***mieć chody*** have connections
chór *m* (*-u; -y*) choir, (*w operze itp.*) chorus; ***~em*** *adv.* in chorus
chórzyst|a *m* (*-y; -ści, -stów*), **~ka** *f* (*-i; G -tek*) member of the choir/chorus
chów *m* (*-owu; 0*) breeding, raising
chrabąszcz *m* (*-a; -e*) *zo.* cockchafer; ***~ majowy*** May beetle, May bug
chrapać (*-pię*) snore; → ***charczeć***
chrapliwy hoarse
chrapy *f/pl.* (*-[ów]*) nostrils
chrobotać (*-czę/-cę*) *v/i.* grate, scratch
chrobry brave, heroic

C

chrom *m* (*-u*; *0*) *chem.* chromium; **~owy** chromium
chroniczny chronic
chronić (*-ę*) ⟨**u-**⟩ protect (**się** o.s., **od** *G* from, **przed** *I* against); **~** ⟨**s-**⟩ **się** take shelter (**przed** *I* against)
chroniony protected
chronometraż *m* timekeeping
chrop|awo roughly; *głos* hoarsely; **~awy** rough; *głos* hoarse; **~owato** roughly; *głos* hoarsely; **~owaty** rough; *głos* hoarse
chrup|ać ⟨**s-**⟩ (*-ię*) crunch; **~ki** crunchy; ***~ki chleb*** crispbread
chrust *m* (*-u*; *0*) brushwood
chryja F *f* (*-yi*; *-e*) trouble
chryp|a *f* (*-a*; *-y*), **~ka** *f* (*-i*; *G -pek*) hoarseness; huskiness; **~liwie** hoarsely, huskily; **~liwy** hoarse, husky; **~nąć** ⟨**o-**⟩ get *lub* become hoarse
Chrystus *m* (*-a*, *-sie/Chryste!*; *0*) Christ; ***przed ~em, przed narodzeniem ~a*** before Christ (*skrót*: BC)
chrzan *m* (*-u*; *0*) horse-radish
chrząk|ać (*-am*) ⟨**~nąć**⟩ clear one's throat; *zwł. zwierzęta*: grunt; **~anie** *n* (*-a*), **~nięcie** *n* (*-a*) grunting
chrząstka *f* (*-i*; *G -tek*) *anat.* cartilage; (*w jedzeniu*) gristle
chrząszcz *m* (*-a*; *-e*) *zo.* beetle
chrzcić ⟨**o-**⟩ (*-czę*) *rel.* christen, baptize
chrzcielnica *f* (*-y*; *-e*) *rel.* font
chrzciny *pl.* (*chrzcin*) *rel.* christening, baptism
chrzest *m* (*chrztu*; *chrzty*) baptism; **~ny** **1.** baptismal; **2.** *m* (*-ego*, *-i*) godparent; (*mężczyzna*) godfather; **~na** *f* (*-ej*; *-e*) godmother; ***rodzice*** *m/pl.* **~ni** godparents *pl.*; ***~ny syn*** *f* godson; ***~na córka*** *f* goddaughter
chrześcijan|in *m* (*-a*; *-anie*, *-*), **~ka** *f* (*-i*; *G -nek*) Christian
chrześcijańs|ki Christian; ***po ~ku*** in a Christian way, like a Christian; **~two** *n* (*-a*; *0*) Christianity
chrześnia|czka *f* (*-i*; *G -czek*), **~k** *m* (*-a*; *-cy*) godchild
chrzę|st *m* (*-u*; *-y*) crunching; scraping, grating; **~ścić** (*-szczę*) rustle; crunch; scrape, grate
chuch|ać (*-am*) ⟨**~nąć**⟩ (*-nę*) breathe, blow; ***~ać na*** (*A*) breathe on
chu|derlawy slight; **~dnąć** ⟨**s-**⟩ (*-nę*, *-dł*) become thin, lose weight; (*celowo*) slim; **~dość** *f* (*-ści*; *0*) thinness; **~dy** thin; *fig. Brt.* meagre, *Am.* meager; *mięso itp.* lean; **~dzielec** F *m* (*-lca*; *-lcy*; *-lce*) bag of bones
chuligan *m* (*-a*; *-i*) hooligan
chuligaństwo *n* (*-a*) hooliganism
chust|a *f* (*-y*) shawl; **~eczka** *f* (*-i*; *G -czek*) handkerchief, F hanky; ***~eczka higieniczna*** tissue, Kleenex *TM*; → **~ka** *f* (*-i*; *G -tek*): ***~ka do nosa*** handkerchief; ***~ka na głowę*** headscarf
chwa|lebny praiseworthy; laudable; **~lić** ⟨**po-**⟩ (*-lę*) praise; laud; ***~lić*** ⟨***po-***⟩ ***się*** (*I*) boast (about), brag (about); **~ła** *f* (*-y*; *0*) glory; ***~ła Bogu*** thank goodness
chwast *m* (*-u*; *-y*) (*zielsko*) weed
chwiać (*-eję*) rock; sway; **~ się** sway; (*jak pijany*) totter; *ząb*: be loose
chwiejn|ość *f* (*-ści*; *0*) instability; *fig.* inconstancy, fickleness; **~y** instable; *fig.* inconstant, fickle
chwil|a *f* (*-i*; *-e*) moment, instant; while; **~e** *pl. też* time; ***~a wytchnienia*** breathing space; ***~ami*** from time to time, occasionally; ***co ~a*** all the time; ***lada ~a*** any moment; ***na ~ę*** for a moment; ***od tej ~i*** from this moment, from now on; ***po ~i*** after a while; ***przed ~ą*** a minute ago; ***przez ~ę*** for a moment or so; ***w danej ~i*** in this very moment; ***w tej ~i*** instantly; immediately; at once; ***za ~ę*** in a minute; in a short while; ***z ~ą*** the moment
chwilow|o momentarily; temporarily; **~y** momentary; temporary; short-lived
chwy|cić *pf* (*-cę*) → ***chwytać***; **~t** *m* (*-u*; *-y*) hold; grip, grasp; → ***uchwyt***; **~tać** (*-am*) *v/t.* grasp, grip (**za** *A*); take hold (**za** *A* of); *piłkę itp.* catch; *żal, gniew* seize; ***~tać powietrze*** gasp for breath *lub* air; ***~tać za pióro*** take up one's pen; ***mróz ~ta*** it is freezing; ***~tać się*** catch; ***~tać*** *się* ***za głowę*** throw up one's hands in despair
chyba **1.** *part.* maybe, probably; **2.** *cj.*: ***~ że*** unless; ***~ nie*** hardly
chybi|ać (*-am*) ⟨**~ć**⟩ (*-ę*) miss (**celu** the target); ***na ~ł trafił*** at random; **~ony** missed; *fig.* ineffective
chylić ⟨**po-, s-**⟩ (*-lę*) (**się**) lean, bend
chyłkiem *adv.* furtively; surreptitiously
chytro *adv.* → ***chytry***; **~ść** *f* (*-ści*) shrewdness, cunning

chytry clever, shrewd, cunning; → ***chciwy***
chytrzej(szy) *adv.* (*adj.*), *comp. od* → ***chytro, chytry***
ci *m-os* → ***ten***
ciałko *n* (*-a*; *G -łek*) *biol.* corpuscle; ***czerwone ~ krwi*** erythrocyte; ***białe ~ krwi*** leucocyte
ciał|o *n* (*-a*) body (*też fig.*); (*tkanka*) flesh; (*zwłoki*) corpse; ***~o pedagogiczne*** teachers, teaching staff; ***spaść z ~a*** F waste away; → ***boży***
ciarki *f/pl.* (*-rek*) creeps; ***przeszły mnie ~*** cold shivers ran down my spine
ciasn|ota *f* (*-y*; *0*) lack of space; *fig.* narrow-mindedness; **~o** tightly; narrowly; **~y** *ubranie* tight, close-fitting; *pomieszczenie* cramped, restricted; narrow (*też fig.*)
ciast|ko *n* (*-a*; *G -tek*) cake; (*suche*) *Brt.* biscuit, *Am.* cookie; (*nadziewane*) tartlet; **~o** *n* (*-a*, *L cieście*; *-a*) cake; (*do nadziewania*) pastry; ***~o francuskie*** puff pastry
ciaśniej(szy) *adv.* (*adj.*) *comp. od* → ***ciasno, ciasny***
ciąć ⟨**ś-**⟩ *v/t.* cut; *impf. drzewa* fell; (*piłą*) saw; *v/i. deszcz, wiatr*: lash; ⟨**po-**⟩ *komary*: sting
ciąg *m* (*-u*; *-i*) pull, *tech.* traction; ***~ powietrza*** draught; ***~ uliczny*** street; (*czasu*) course; ***~ dalszy*** continuation; (*odcinek*) instalment; ***w ~u*** (*G*) (*za*) within, in; (*w trakcie*) in the course (*of*); ***w dalszym ~u*** still; **~le** *adv.* constantly, permanently; continuously; **~łość** *f* (*-ści*; *0*) continuity; **~ły** continuous, constant; → ***stały, ustawiczny***; **~nąć** (*-nę*) pull (*też* ***za*** *A* at, ***do*** *G* to); (*wlec*) drag; *samochód itp.* tow; → ***pociągać***; *v/t.* pull; ***~nąć dalej*** continue, go on; ***tu ~nie*** there is a draught here; ***~nąć się*** drag, (*w czasie*) go on and on; **~nienie** *n* (*-a*) (*loterii*) draw; *tech.* drawing; **~nik** *m* (*-a*; *-i*) tractor
ciąż|a *f* (*-y*) pregnancy; ***być w ~y*** be pregnant; ***zajść w ~ę*** become pregnant; **~enie** *n* (*-a*; *0*) gravity; **~yć** (*-ę*) be a burden; weigh heavily (***na*** *L* on); tend (***ku*** *D* towards)
cichaczem *adv.* secretly, in secret
cich|nąć ⟨**u-**⟩ (*-nę*; *też -ł*) fall silent; (*stopniowo*) die away; *wiatr*: die down; **~o** (**po -chu, z -cha**) silently, quietly; ***bądź ~o!*** be quiet!; **~y** silent, quiet; *partner itp.* sleeping
ciebie (*GA* → ***ty***) you; ***u ~*** with you, at your place
ciec → ***ciekną***
ciecz *f* (*-y*; *-e*) fluid
ciekaw|ić (*-ę*) interest; **~ie** *adv.* → ***ciekawy***; **~ostka** *f* (*-i*; *G -tek*) (*przedmiot*) curio; (*fakt*) interesting fact; **~ość** *f* (*-ści*; *0*) curiosity; ***przez ~ość, z ~ości*** out of curiosity; **~ie** curiously; interestingly, excitingly; **~y** curious (*G* of); interesting, exciting; ***~(a) jestem, czy ...*** I am keen to know whether…
ciek|ły fluid; **~nąć** (*-nę*; *też -ł*) flow; *rura itp.* leak; → ***przeciekać***
cielesny (**-śnie**) bodily
cielę *n* (*-ęcia*; *-ęta*) calf; **~cina** *f* (*-y*; *0*) veal; **~cy** *skóra itp.* calf; *mięso itp.* veal
cieliczka *f* (*-i*; *G -czek*) (young) heifer
cielić się ⟨**o- się**⟩ (*-lę*) calf
cielisty flesh-colo(u)red
ciem *G/pl.* → ***ćma***
ciemię *n* (*-enia*; *-iona*) *anat.* top of one's head
ciemku: ***po ~*** in the dark
ciemni|a *f* (*-i*; *-e*) darkroom; **~eć** ⟨**po-**⟩ (*-eję*) get dark; darken
ciemno → ***ciemny***; ***robi się ~*** it is getting dark; **~blond** light brown; **~czerwony** dark red; **~granatowy** dark blue; **~skóry** dark-skinned
ciemność *f* (*-ści*) darkness
ciemn|o dark; **~y** dark; *pokój, zarys itp.* dim; (*zacofany*) outdated; antiquated
cieniej *adv. comp. od* → ***cienko***
cienist|o *adv.* shadily; **~y** shady
cien|iutki *materiał itp.* gossamer-thin; *plasterek* paper-thin; **~ki** thin; *książka itp.* slim; *herbata itp.* weak; **~ko** thinly; **~kość** *f* (*-ści*; *0*) thinness
cień *m* (*-niu*; *-nie*) shadow; (*miejsce zacienione*) shade
cieńszy → ***cienki***
ciepl|arnia *f* (*-i*; *-e*, *-i/-ń*) greenhouse; **~eć** ⟨**po-**⟩ (*-eję*) get warm; **~ej(szy)** *adv.* (*adj.*) *comp. od* → ***ciepło, ciepły***; **~ica** *f* (*-y*; *-e*) thermal spring; **~ny** heat
ciep|ławo tepidly; **~ławy** lukewarm, tepid
ciepło[1] *n* (*-a*; *0*) warmth, heat
ciep|ło[2] *adv.* warm; ***robi się ~ło*** it is getting warm; **~łownia** *f* (*-i*; *-e*) heat-generating plant; **~ły** *adj.* warm (*też fig.*)

C

cierni|owy, ~sty thorny
cierń *m* (*-nia*; *-nie*, *-ni*) thorn, spine
cierpiący suffering (**na** *A* from)
cierpie|ć (*-ę*, *-i*) suffer; (**głód** hunger; **z powodu** *G* because of; **na** *A* from); (*znosić*) tolerate; put up with; **nie ~ć** (*G*) hate; **~nie** *n* (*-a*) suffering
cierpk|i sour → **kwaśny**; **~o** sourly → **kwaśny**
cierpliw|ość *f* (*-ści*; *0*) patience; **uzbroić się w ~ość** exercise one's patience; **~ie** patiently; **~y** patient
cierpn|ąć ⟨**ś-**⟩ (*-nę*; *też -ł*) (*drętwieć*) become numb, go to sleep; **aż skóra ~ie** so that a cold shiver runs down one's spine
ciesielski carpenter
cieszyć ⟨**u-**⟩ (*-ę*) please; **~** ⟨**u-**⟩ **się** be pleased (**z** *G*, **na** *A* with), take pleasure in, enjoy; **~ zdrowiem** enjoy the best of health
cieśla *m* (*-li*; *-le*) carpenter
cieśnina *f* (*-y*) straits *pl.*; ♀ **Kaletańska** Strait of Dover
cietrzew *m* (*-wia*; *-wie*) black grouse
cię (*A* → **ty**) you; *por.* **ciebie**
cię|cie *n* (*-a*) cut, (*też czynność*) cutting; *med.* incision; (*cios*) blow; **~ciwa** *f* (*-y*) (*łuku*) bow; *math.* chord
cięgi *pl.* (*-ów*) beating, hiding
cięty cut; *fig.* incisive; *uwaga* biting, cutting
ciężar *m* (*-u*; *-y*) weight; (*też fig.*) burden; **być ~em** be a burden (**dla** *G* on); **podnoszenie ~ów** weight-lifting; **~ek** *m* (*-rka*; *-rki*) weight; **~na 1.** *adj.* pregnant; **2.** *f* (*-nej*; *-ne*) pregnant woman, expectant mother; **~owy** (*transport*) *zwł. Brt.* goods, freight; (*w sporcie*) weightlifting
ciężarówka *f* (*-i*; *G -wek*) *mot. Brt.* lorry, *Am.* truck
cięż|ej *adv. comp. od* → **ciężko**; **~ki** *adj.* heavy (*też fig.*); (*trudny*) difficult, hard; *szok*, *sztorm itp.* severe; *choroba itp.* serious
ciężko *adv.* heavily; (*trudno*) hard; **~ chory** seriously ill; **~ ranny** badly wounded
ciężkoś|ć *f* (*-ści*; *0*) weight; *phys.* gravity; **punkt/środek ~ci** *Brt.* centre (*Am.* center) of gravity; *fig.* main focus
ciocia *f* (*-i*; *-e*) aunt, F auntie
cios *m* (*-u*; *-y*) blow (*też fig.*); (*pięścią*) punch
ciosać ⟨**o-**⟩ (*-am*) hew
ciota *f* (*-y*) F queen, queer
cioteczn|y: **brat ~y, siostra ~a** cousin
ciotka *f* (*-i*; *G -tek*) aunt
cis *m* (*-u/a*; *-y*) yew(-tree)
ciskać (*-am*) fling, hurl; **~ obelgi na** *A* hurl insults at
cisnąć[1] *pf* (*-nę*) → **ciskać**
cisną|ć[2] (*-nę*) press; *ubranie* pinch; **~ć się** press, push (forward)
cisz|a *f* (*-y*; *0*) silence; calm (*też naut.*); *fig.* quiet, calm; **proszę o ~ę!** silence, please!; **~ej** *adv. comp. od* → **cicho**; **~kiem** → **cichaczem**
ciśnienie *n* (*-a*) (**powietrza** air, **krwi** blood) pressure
ciuchy F *m/pl.* (*-ów*) togs *pl.*, clobber
ciuciubabk|a *f*: **bawić się w ~ę** play blind man's buff
ciułać ⟨**u-**⟩ (*-am*) save up, salt away
ciupaga *f* (*-i*) alpenstock
ciurkiem: **płynąć ~** dribble, trickle
ciż *m-os* → **tenże**
ciżba *f* (*-y*) crowd, throng
ckliw|ie maudlinly; **~y** maudlin, F tear-jerking; **robi mi się ~ie** I am getting sick → **mdły**
clić ⟨**o-**⟩ (*-lę*; *clij!*) pay duty on; clear (*s.th.* through) customs
cło *n* (*cła*; *G ceł*) duty; **wolny od cła** duty-free; **podlegający cłu** dutiable
cmenta|rny cemetery, graveyard; **~rz** *m* (*-a*; *-e*) cemetery, (*przy kościele*) graveyard
cmentarzysko *n* (*-a*) (large) cemetery; **~ starych samochodów** car dump
cmok|ać (*-am*) ⟨**~nąć**⟩ smack one's lips; (*całować*) smack; *fajkę*, *palec* suck
cnot|a *f* (*-y*) virtue; **~liwie** virtuously; righteously; **~liwy** virtuous; (*pełen cnót też*) righteous
c.o. *skrót pisany*: **centralne ogrzewanie** c.h. (*central heating*)
co *pron.* (*G czego*, *D czemu*, *I czym*; *0*) what; (*który*) that; **~ za …** what (a)…; **~ innego** something else; **~ do** as to; **~ do mnie** as for me; **~ mu jest?** what is the matter with him?; **~ to jest?** what is this?; **czego chcesz?** what do you want?; **w razie czego** if need be, if necessary; **czym mogę służyć?** what can I do for you?; **~ gorsza** what is worse; **o czym** about what; **po czym** after which; (*idkl.*) **~** (**drugi**) **tydzień**

every (second) week; ~ ***krok*** every step; → ***czas, bądź***
codzien|nie *adv.* everyday; **~ny** *adj.* everyday; *gazeta* daily; (*nie świąteczny*) everyday, workaday
cof|ać (*-am*) ⟨**~nąć**⟩ (*-nę*) *rękę, wojska itp.* pull back; *samochód* move back; reverse; back; *zegar* put back; *słowo, obietnicę* take back; *zlecenie, zamówienie* cancel, withdraw; ***~ać*** ⟨***~nąć***⟩ ***się*** retreat, move back (***przed*** *I* against)
co|godzinny hourly; **~kolwiek** (*G czego-, D czemu-, I czymkolwiek; 0*) anything; (*nieco*) some, a little
cokół *m* (*-ołu; -oły*) plinth, pedestal
comber *m* (*-bra; -bry*) *gastr.* saddle
conocny nightly, every night
coraz more and more; ~ ***cieplej*** warmer and warmer; ~ ***więcej*** more and more; ~ ***to*** again and again
coroczny yearly, annual
coś *pron.* (*G czegoś, D czemuś, I czymś; 0*) something, anything; ~ ***takiego!*** would you believe it!; **~kolwiek** → ***cokolwiek***
cotygodniowy weekly
córka *f* (*-i; G -rek*) daughter
cóż *pron.* (*G czegoż, D czemuż, I czymże; 0*) → **co**; well; ***no i ~?*** so what? ***~ dopiero*** let alone
cuchnąć (*-nę*) stink
cucić ⟨**o-**⟩ (*-cę*) revive, bring round
cud *m* (*-u; -a/-y, -ów*) wonder; *rel.* miracle; ***~em*** by a miracle; **~aczny** → ***dziwaczny***; **~ny** pleasing; beautiful
cudo *n* (*-a*) marvel; **~twórca** *m*, **~twórczyni** *f* wonder-worker; **~wnie** *adv.* → ***cudem***; *też* **~wny** wonderful; (*piękny*) exquisite, marvellous
cudzo|łóstwo *n* (*-a; 0*) adultery; **~ziemiec** *m* (*-mca; -mcy*), **~ziemka** *f* (*-i; G -mek*) foreigner; **~ziemski** foreign; ***po ~ziemsku, z ~ziemska*** in a foreign way/manner
cudzy foreign; (*nie mój*) other people's; of others; (*nieznany*) strange; **~słów** *m* (*-owu; -owy, -owów*) quotation marks *pl.*, inverted commas *pl.*
cugle *pl.* (*-i*) reins *pl.*
cukier *m* (*-kru; -kry*) sugar; **~ek** *m* (*-rka; -rki*) sweet, *Am.* candy; **~nia** *f* (*-i; -e, -i*) cake-shop; (*lokal*) café; **~nica** *f* (*-y; -e*) sugar bowl; **~nik** *m* (*-a; -cy*) confectioner, pastry cook
cu'kinia *f* (*GDL -ii; -e*) *Brt.* courgette; *Am.* zucchini
cukrownia *f* (*-i; -e*) sugar factory
cukrzyca *f* (*-y; 0*) diabetes
cukrzyć ⟨**o-, po-**⟩ (*-ę*) sugar
cumować (*-uję*) *naut.* moor
cwał *m* (*-u; 0*) gallop; ***~em, w ~*** at a gallop; **~ować** ⟨**po-**⟩ gallop
cwan|iaczka F *f* (*-i; G -czek*), **~iak** F *m* (*-a; -cy/-i*) sly *lub* cunning person; **~y** cunning, sly
cycek *m* (*-cka, -cki*) teat; **cycki** *pl. pej.* tits *pl.*
cyfr|a *f* (*-y*) digit, figure; **~owy** digital
Cygan *m* (*-a; -anie*), **~ka** *f* (*-i; G -nek*) Gypsy; **ℒić** F (*-ę*) cheat, fib
cygańs|ki: ***po ~ku*** Gypsy; (*język*) Romany
cygar|niczka *f* (*-i; G -czek*) cigarette-holder; **~o** *n* (*-a*) cigar
cyjanek *m* (*-nka; -nki*) cyanide
cykać (*-am*) tick; *świerszcz*: chirp
cykata *f* (*-y; 0*) candied lemon-peel
cykl *m* (*-u; -e*) cycle
cyklamen *m* (*-u; -y*) cyclamen
cykliczny cyclic, periodic
cyklistówka *f* (*-i; G -wek*) baseball cap
cyklon *m* (*-u; -y*) cyclone, hurricane
cykuta *f* (*-y*) *bot.* hemlock
cylinder *m* (*-dra; -dry*) cylinder; (*kapelusz*) top hat
cymbał *m* (*-a; -y*) F fool; ***cymbały*** *pl.* dulcimer, (*węgierskie*) cimbalom
cyna *f* (*-y; 0*) *chem.* tin
cynaderki *f/pl.* (*-rek*) *gastr.* kidneys *pl.*
cynamon *m* (*-u; 0*) cinnamon; **~owy** cinnamon
cynfolia *f* (*GDL -ii; 0*) tinfoil
cyniczny cynical
cynk *m* (*-u; 0*) zinc; F tip; **~ować** ⟨**o-**⟩ (*-uję*) galvanize; **~owy** zinc
cynować ⟨**o-**⟩ (*-uję*) tin, plate with tin
cypel *m* (*-pla; -ple*) headland, spit
Cypr *m* (*-u*) Cyprus; **ℒyjski** Cyprus
cyprys *m* (*-a; -y*) cypress
cyrk *m* (*-u; -i*) circus (*też fig.*)
cyrkiel *m* (*-kla; -kle*) compasses *pl.*
cyrk|owiec *m* (*-wca; -wce*); **~ówka** *f* (*-i; G -wek*) circus artist; **~owy** circus
cyrkul|acja *f* (*-i; -e*) circulation; **~ować** (*-uję*) circulate
cysterna *f* (*-y*) tank, cistern
cysterski Cistercian
cytadela *f* (*-i; -e*) citadel

C

cytat *m* (*-u*; *-y*), **~a** *f* (*-y*) quotation, citation
cytować ⟨**za-**⟩ (*-uję*) quote
cyt|rusowy: ***owoce*** *m/pl.* ***~owe*** citrus fruit; **~ryna** *f* (*-y*) lemon; **~rynowy** lemon
cyw. *skrót pisany*: **cywilny** civ. (*civil*)
cywil *m* (*-a*; *-e*, *-ów*): ***w ~u*** civilian; ***w ~u*** (*ubraniu*) in civilian clothes, F in mufti; (*w życiu*) F in civilian life; **~izacja** *f* (*-i*; *-e*) civilisation; **~noprawny** civil law, of civil law; **~ny** civilian; civil; ***stan ~ny*** marital status; → ***urząd***
cz. *skrót pisany*: **część** pt (*part*)
czad *m* (*-u*; *-y*) carbon monoxide; (*woń spalenizny*) smell of burning
czaić się ⟨**przy-**, **za- się**⟩ (*-ję*) lie in wait
czajnik *m* (*-a*; *-i*) kettle
czambuł *m*: ***w ~*** wholesale, without exception
czap|eczka *f* (*-i*; *G -czek*) (little) cap; **~ka** *f* (*-i*; *G -pek*) cap
czapla *f* (*-i*; *-e*) *zo.* heron
czaprak *m* (*-a*; *-i*) saddle-cloth
czar *m* (*-u*; *-y*) magic; (*oczarowanie*) magic spell; (*urok*) charm; ***~y*** *pl.* magic
czarno *adv.*: ***na ~*** black; → ***biały***; **~-biały** black and white; **℞góra** *f* (*-y*; *0*) Montenegro; **~księżnik** *m* (*-a*; *-cy*) sorcerer; **~oki** black-eyed; **~rynkowy** black-market; **~skóry** black; **~włosy** black-haired
czarn|y black; *fig.* gloomy; ***~a jagoda*** bilberry, blueberry; ***pół ~ej, mała ~a*** a cup of black coffee; ***na ~ą godzinę*** in case of emergency
czarodziej *m* (*-a*; *-e*, *-i/-ów*), **~ka** *f* (*-i*) magician; **~ski** magic, magical; **~stwo** *n* (*-a*) magic
czarow|ać (*-uję*) do *lub* work magic, *fig.* ⟨**o-**⟩ bewitch, enchant; **~nica** *f* (*-y*; *-e*) witch; **~nik** *m* (*-a*; *-cy*) wizard; **~ny** enchanting, charming
czart *m* (*-a*, *D -u/-rcie*; *-y*) devil
czarter *m* (*-u*; *-y*) charter; **~ować** (*-uję*) charter; **~owy** charter
czar|ująco charmingly; **~ujący** charming; **~y** → ***czar***
czas *m* (*-u*; *-y*) time; ***~ odjazdu*** time of departure; ***~ pracy*** working time; working hours *pl.*; ***już ~*** (*+bezok.*) it is (high) time we went; ***mieć ~ na*** (*A*) to have time to; ***~ przeszły*** *gr.* the past tense; ***~ przyszły*** *gr.* the future tense; ***~ teraźniejszy*** *gr.* the present tense; (***przez***) ***jakiś ~*** for some time; ***co jakiś ~, od ~u do ~u*** from time to time; ***do tego ~u*** until then; ***na ~*** in time; ***na ~ie*** up to the minute, topical; ***od ~u*** (***jak***) since the time (when); ***od tego ~u*** from that time on, since then; ***po ~ie*** too late; ***przed ~em*** too early, (*przedwcześnie*) prematurely; ***w ~ie*** (*G*) when; ***w krótkim ~ie*** shortly, soon; ***swego ~u*** at that time; in those days; ***w sam ~*** just in time; ***z ~em*** with time; ***za moich ~ów*** in my times; **~ami** now and again; at times; **~em** → ***czasami***; (*przypadkiem*) perhaps
czaso|chłonny time-consuming; **~pismo** *n* periodical; (*zwł. codzienne*) newspaper; **~wnik** *m* (*-a*; *-i*) *gr.* verb; **~wo** *adv.* temporarily; **~wy** temporal, temporary
czaszka *f* (*-i*; *G -szek*) *anat.* skull; ***trupia ~*** (*jako symbol*) death's head
czat|ować (*-uję*) lie in wait (***na*** *A* for); **~y** *f/pl.* (-) lookout; ***stać na ~ach*** be on the lookout
cząst|eczka *f* (*-i*; *G -czek*) *phys.* molecule; **~ka** *f* (*-i*; *G -tek*) particle; small part; **~kowy** partial
czci → ***cześć, czcić***; **~ciel** *m* (*-a*; *-e*), **~cielka** *f* (*-i*; *G -lek*) worshipper, adorer; **~ć** worship, adore; **~godny** venerable, esteemed
czcionka *f* (*-i*; *G -nek*) type; font, *Brt.* fount
czcz|ą, ~ę → ***czcić***; **~o** *adv.* → ***czczy***; ***na ~o*** on an empty stomach; **~y** (*płonny, pusty*) idle, futile; *żołądek, też fig.* empty
Czech *m* (*-a*; *-si*) Czech; **~y** *pl.* (*G -*) (*region*) Bohemia; (*państwo*) Czech Republic
czego, ~kolwiek, ~ś → **co**(***kolwiek***)
czek *m* (*-u*; *i*) *Brt.* cheque, *Am.* check; ***~ gotówkowy*** open *lub* uncrossed cheque/check; ***~ podróżny*** *Brt.* traveller's cheque, *Am.* traveler's check; ***~iem*** by checque/check
czekać ⟨**po-**, **za-**⟩ (*-am*) wait (*G*, ***na*** *A* for; *impf. też być udziałem*) expect
czekolad|a *f* (*-y*) chocolate; **~ka** *f* (*-i*; *G -dek*) chocolate; ***~ka nadziewana*** filled chocolate; **~owy** chocolate
czekowy *Brt.* cheque, *Am.* check
czeladnik *m* (*-a*; *-cy*) journeyman

czel|e → ***czoło***; **~ny** arrogant
czeluść *f* (*-ści*; *-ście*) abyss, chasm
czemu → ***co***; (*dlaczego*) why; F ***po ~*** how much; **~kolwiek, ~ś**; **~ż** → ***cokolwiek, coś, cóż***
czepek *m* (*-pka*; *-pki*) (*pielęgniarki, dziecka itp.*) cap; (*dawniej*) bonnet; **~ *kąpielowy*** swimming *lub* bathing cap
czepi|ać się (*-am*) ⟨***~ć się***⟩ (*-ę*) cling (*G* to), hang (*G* to); *fig.* (*G*) find fault (with), carp (at)
czepiec *m* (*-pca*; *-pce*) cap
czeremcha *f* (*-y*) *bot.* bird cherry
czerep *m* (*-u*; *-y*) head; (*odłamek*) piece, fragment
czereśnia *f* (*-i*; *-e*) *bot.* sweet cherry
czerni|ak *m* (*-a*; *-i*) *med.* melanoma; **~ca** *f* (*-y*; *-e*) → ***borówka***; **~ć** (*-ę*, *-ń/-nij!*) blacken; **~eć** (*-eję*) appear in black; ⟨**po-, s-**⟩ get *lub* become black, turn black
czernina *f* (*-y*) *gastr.* (*soup made of blood*)
czerń *f* (*-ni*) black; blackness
czerp|ać (*-ię*) *wodę, zasoby, fig. itp.* draw; (*czerpakiem*) scoop (up); **~ak** *m* (*-a*; *-i*) scoop; *tech.* dredge, bucket
czerstw|o *adv.* robustly; **~y** *chleb itp.* stale; *fig.* hale (and hearty), robust
czerw *m* (*-wia*; *-wie*, *-wi*) maggot
czerw|cowy June; **~iec** June; **~ienić się** ⟨***za- się***⟩ (*-ę*), **~ienieć** ⟨***po-***⟩ (*-eję*) redden (*na twarzy*), become red
czerwonka *f* (*-i*; *0*) *med.* dysentery
czerwono *adv.*: ***na ~*** red; **~skóry** *pej.* redskin; **~ść** *f* (*-ści*; *0*) red, redness, blush
czerwony *adj.* red
czesać ⟨**u-**⟩ (*-szę*) comb (***się*** *też* one's hair)
czesankow|y: ***wełna ~a*** worsted
czeski (***po -ku***) Czech
Czeszka *f* (*-i*; *G -szek*) Czech
cześć *f* (*czci*, *czcią*; *0*) deference, hono(u)r; ***otaczać czcią*** venerate; revere; (*zmarłego*) hono(u)r s.o.'s memory; ***na ~, ku czci*** (*G*) in hono(u)r of; ***~!*** bye!, so long!
często *adv.*, **~kroć** *adv.* often, frequently
częstotliwość *f* (*-ści*) frequency
częstować ⟨**po-**⟩ (*-uję*) offer (*I* to), treat (*I* to); **~** ⟨**po-**⟩ ***się*** help o.s. (*I* to)
częsty *adj.* (*m-os części, comp. -tszy*) often

częś|ciej *adv.* more often; **~ciowo** *adv.* partly; **~ciowy** partial; **~ć** *f* (*-ci*) part; ***~ć składowa*** component, element; ***większa ~ć*** larger part; ***lwia ~ć*** lion's share; ***~ć mowy*** *gr.* part of speech; ***po/w ~ci*** partly
czka|ć (*-m*) hiccup; **~wka** *f* (*-i*; *G -wek*) hiccup
człapać (*-pię*) clump, trudge
człek *m* (*-a*, *-owi/-u*, *-u/-ecze!*, *I -kiem*; *0*) → ***człowiek***
człon *m* (*-a/-u*; *-y*) section, part
członek[1] *m* (*-nka*; *-nki*) *anat.* (*penis*) penis; (*kończyna*) limb
człon|ek[2] *m* (*-nka*; *-nkowie*), **~kini** *f* (*-*; *-inie*) member; ***być ~kiem komitetu*** sit on a committee; **~kostwo** *n* (*-a*) membership; **~kowski** member('s)
człowie|czeństwo *n* (*-a*; *0*) humanity; **~k** *m* (*-a*; *ludzie*) human being, (*zwł. mężczyzna*) man; (*bezosobowo*) one; ***szary ~k*** the man in the street; ***~k interesu*** (*zwł. mężczyzna*) businessman, (*kobieta*) businesswoman; → ***czyn***
czmychać (*-am*) make off
czołg *m* (*-u*; *-i*) tank
czołgać się (*-am*) crawl, creep
czoł|o *n* (*-a*, *L -czele*; *-a*, *czół*) *anat.* forehead; (*przód*) front; (*pochodu*) head; (*burzy*) front(line); ***stawić ~o*** stand *lub* face up to; ***na czele*** at the head; ***~em!*** hallo!
czołowy forehead; *med.* frontal; *zderzenie itp.* head-on; *fig.* foremost
czołówka *f* (*-i*; *G -wek*) forefront; (*artykuł*) leading article; (*na filmie*) opening credits *pl.*; *sport*: lead, top
czop *m* (*-a*; *-y*) bung; **~ek** *m* (*-pka*; *-pki*) plug; *med.* suppository
czosn|ek *m* (*-nku*; *0*) garlic; **~kowy** garlic
czół|enka *n/pl.* (*-nek*) pumps *pl.*; **~no** *n* (*-na*; *G -łen*) boat, canoe; (*z pnia*) dug-out
czterdzie|stka *f* (*-i*; *G -tek*) forty; **~stoletni** forty-year-long, -old; **~stu** *m-s*, **~sty**, **~ści**(***oro***) → ***715***
czter|ech (*też w zł.*); **~ej** four; **~nastka** *f* (*-i*; *G -tek*) fourteen; (*linia*) number fourteen; **~nastu** *m-os*, **~nasty, ~naście, ~naścioro** → ***715***
cztero|- *w zł.* four; **~krotny** fourfold; **~letni** four-year-long, -old; **~motoro-**

C

wy four-engine; **~osobowy** for four persons; **~pasmowy** *droga* four-lane; **~suwowy** *Brt.* four-stroke, *Am.* four-cycle; **~ścieżkowy** *zapis* (*na ścieżce*) four-track
cztery four; **~sta, ~stu** *m-os* four hundred
czub *m* (*-a*; *-y*) (*włosów*) shock of hair; (*piór*) crest; ***z ~em*** heaped; *fig.* with interest; **~ato** *adv.* with a heap; **~aty** *zo.* crested; **~ek** *m* (*-bka*; *-bki*) tip; (*szczyt*) top; ***~ek głowy*** top of one's head; ***~ek palca*** fingertip
czu|cie *n* (*-a*; *-a*) feeling; ***bez ~cia*** (*odrętwiały*) numb, insensitive; (*nieprzytomny*) unconscious; **~ć** ⟨**po-, u-**⟩ (*-uję*) feel (**się** *też* o.s.; **dobrze** good; **Polakiem** o.s. to be a Pole); ***~ć miłość do*** (*G*) feel love for; *impf.* (*I*) smell (of)
czuj|ka *f* (*-i*; *G -jek*) *tech.* detector; **~nik** *m* (*-a*; *-i*) *tech.* sensor; **~ny** watchful, vigilant, alert; *sen* light
czule *adv.* → ***czuły***
czuło|stkowo (over-)sentimentally; **~stkowy** (over-)sentimental; **~ść** *f* (*-ści*) tenderness; affection; (*pieszczota*) *zwł. pl.* caress(es *pl.*); (*wagi, instrumentu*) sensitivity; (*filmu*) speed
czuły tender, affectionate; (*uczulony*) sensitive (*też przyrząd itp.*); *słuch* acute; ***~ na światło*** sensitive to light; *tech.* photosensitive
czupiradło *n* (*-a*; *G -deł*) *fig.* scarecrow
czupryna *f* (*-y*) hair
czuwać (*-am*) be awake, sit up (***przy*** *I* at); (*pilnować*) watch (***nad*** *I* over)
czw. *skrót pisany*: **czwartek** Thur(s). (*Thursday*)
czwart|ek *m* (*-tku*; *-tki*) Thursday; **~kowy** Thursday; **~y** fourth; ***~a godzina*** four o'clock; ***po ~e*** fourthly
czwora|czki *m/pl.* (*-ów*) quadruplets *pl.*, F quads *pl.*; **~ki** four-fold; ***na ~kach*** on all fours
czworo four; ***we ~*** in a foursome, in a group of four; ***złożyć we ~*** fold in four; **~bok** *m* (*-u*; *-i*), **~kąt** *m* (*-a*; *-y*) quadrangle; **~nożny** four-legged
czwórk|a *f* (*-i*; *G -rek*) four; (*linia*) number four; *szkoła*: *jakby*: B; ***we ~ę*** in a foursome, in a group of four; ***~ami*** in fours
czy 1. *part.* if, whether; ***~ to prawda?*** is it true?; ***~ wierzysz w to?*** do you believe in this?; ***nie wiem ~ to dobrze*** I don't know if it is OK; **2.** *cj.* or; ***tak ~ inaczej*** one way or the other
czyhać (*-am*) lie in wait (***na*** *A* for)
czyj *m*, **~a** *f*, **~e** *n* whose; **~kolwiek** anyone's, anybody's; **~ś** someone's, somebody's
czyli that is
czym → ***co***; ***~ … tym*** the … the …; ***~prędzej*** as soon as possible; **~kolwiek** → ***cokolwiek***; **~ś** → ***coś***; **~że** → ***cóż***
czyn *m* (*-u*; *-y*) act, deed, action; ***człowiek ~u*** man/woman of action; **~ić** ⟨**u-**⟩ (*-ę*) do; *postępy, ustępstwa* make; *cuda* work; (*wynosić*) constitute, make; **~nie** → ***czynny***; **~nik** *m* (*-a*; *-i*) factor; *zwł. pl.* organ(s *pl.*); **~ność** *f* (*-ści*) activity; action; (*organu itp.*) function; **~ny** active; *mechanizm* operating, functioning; *sklep* open; *napad* physical; ***~ny zawodowo*** working, in paid employment; *gr.* ***strona ~na*** the active voice
czynsz *m* (*-u*; *-y*) rent
czyrak *m* (*-a*; *-i*) *med.* boil, *med.* furuncle
czyst|a 1. *f* (*-ej*; *-e*) F (clear) vodka; **2.** *adj. f* → ***czysty***; **~o** *adv.* clean(ly); (*bez domieszek*) purely; (*schludnie*) tidily, neatly; *śpiewać* in tune; ***przepisać na ~o*** make a fair copy; ***wyjść na ~ o*** break even
czystość *f* (*-ści*; *0*) tidiness, cleanness; (*chemikalia itp.*) purity; (*skóry*) clearness
czyst|y clean, tidy, neat; (*bez domieszek*) pure; *dochód* net(t); *niebo* clear; *przyjemność itp.* sheer; ***do ~a*** completely, entirely
czyszczenie *n* (*-a*) cleaning, cleansing; (*w pralni chemicznej*) dry-cleaning
czyś|cibut *m* shoe-cleaner; **~cić** ⟨**o-, wy-**⟩ (*-szczę*) clean, cleanse, tidy; ***~cić szczotką*** brush; **~ciej(szy)** *adv.* (*adj.*) *comp. od* → ***czysto, czysty***
czytać (*-am*) read (***głośno*** aloud)
czytan|ie *n* (*-a*) reading; ***do ~ia*** to be read; **~ka** *f* (*-i*) reader
czyteln|ia *f* (*-i*; *-ie*) reading room; (*wypożyczalnia*) (lending) library; **~iczka** *f* (*-i*; *G -czek*), **~ik** *m* (*-a*; *-cy*) reader; **~y** readable, legible
czytnik *m* (*-a*; *-i*) *komp.* reader
czyż → ***czy***
czyżyk *m* (*-a*; *-i*) siskin

Ć

ćma *f* (*-y*; *G ciem*) *zo.* moth
ćmić (*-ę*; *ćmij!*) *v/i.* (*boleć*) ache; (*też* **się**) smo(u)lder, burn without fire; *v/t.* (*palić*) F puff (away) at; → ***przy-ćmiewać***
ćpać F (*-am*) (*brać*) take, F do; (*regularnie*) be an addict
ćpun F *m* (*-a*; *-y*) drug addict, F junkie
ćwiartka *f* (*-i*; *G -tek*) quarter; F quarter *Brt.* litre (*Am.* liter); (*butelka*) *Brt.* quarter-liter, *Am.* liter bottle; ***~ papieru*** slip of paper
ćwicze|bny drill, practice; (*ubiór*) training; **~nie** *n* (*-a*) exercise; ***~nie domowe*** homework; ***~nia*** *pl. mil.* exercise(s *pl.*); ***~nia*** *pl.* (*na uniwersytecie itp.*) classes
ćwiczyć (*-ę*) ⟨**wy-**⟩ train; drill; *opanowanie itp.* exercise; *pamięć* practise; **~** ⟨**wy-**⟩ **się** (**w** *L*) practise; ⟨**o-**⟩ flog
ćwiek *m* (*-a*; *-i*) tack
ćwierć *f* (*-ci*; *-ci*) quarter; **~finałowy** quarterfinal; **~litrowy** *Brt.* quarter-litre (*Am.* -liter); **~nuta** *f mus. Brt.* crotchet, *Am.* quarter note; **~wiecze** *n* (*-a*) quarter of a century
ćwierkać (*-am*) chirp
ćwikł|a *f* (*-y*; *G -kieł*) red-beet salad; **~owy**: ***burak ~owy*** *Brt.* beetroot, *Am.* red beet

D

da → ***dać***
dach *m* (*-u*; *-y*) roof; ***bez ~u nad głową*** homeless; **~ówka** *f* (*-i*) (roof) tile
dać *pf* (*dam, dadzą, daj!*) → ***dawać***; **~ się** (*być możliwym*) be possible; ***da się zrobić*** it can be done; ***co się da*** whatever is possible; ***gdzie się da(ło)*** somewhere, anywhere; ***jak się da*** somehow or other; ***dajmy na to*** let's say; ***daj spokój!*** come off it!
daktyl *m* (*-a*; *-e*) date
dal *f* (*-i*; *-e*) distance; ***w ~i*** in the distance; ***z ~a*** at a distance (***od*** *G* from)
dale|ce *adv.*: ***jak ~ce*** to what extent, how far; ***tak ~ce*** so much (***że*** that); **~j** *adv.* (*comp. od* → ***daleko***) further; farther; ***i tak ~j*** and so on; ***nie ~j jak tydzień temu*** a week or so ago; **~ki** distant (*też fig.*); far-off, faraway; ***z ~ka*** from a distance; **~ko** *adv.* far; ***~ko idący*** far reaching; ***~ko lepiej*** far better; ***~ko więcej*** far more
daleko|bieżny *rail.* long-distance; **~morski** *statek* oceangoing; *połowy* deep-sea; **~pis** telex; **~siężny** far-reaching; **~wzroczność** *f* (*-ści*; *0*) long-sightedness; *fig.* far-sightedness
dalia *f* (*GDL -ii*; *-e*) dahlia
dal|mierz *m* (-a; -e) range-finder; **~szy** *adj.* (*comp. od* → ***daleki***) farther, further; ***~szy plan*** background; → ***ciąg***
dam → ***dać***
dam|a *f* (*-y*) lady; (*szlachcianka*) Dame; (*w kartach*) queen; **~ski** lady('s), women('s), female, feminine
dan|e¹ → ***dany***; **~e²** *pl.* (*-ych*) data *sg./pl.*; ***baza ~ych*** data base; ***przetwarzanie ~ych*** data processing; **~ie** *n* (*-a*; *0*) giving; (*pl. -a, G -ń*) *gastr.* dish, meal; ***bez ~ia racji*** without an explanation
Dania *f* (*-ii*; *0*) Denmark
daniel *m* (*-a*; *-e*) *zo.* fallow deer *sg./pl.*
danina *f* (*-y*) *hist. fig.* tribute
dansing *m* (*-u*; *-i*) dancing; (*lokal*) café/restaurant with dancing
dany given; ***w ~m razie*** in this case; ***w ~ch warunkach*** given these circumstances
dar *m* (*-u*; *-y*) gift (*też fig.*), present
daremny futile, vain
darmo *adv.* free; (*bezpłatnie*) free of charge; ***za pół ~*** for a song; **~wy** free; **~zjad** *m* (*-a*; *-y*) sponger, scrounger
dar|nina *f* (*-y*), **~ń** *f* (*-ni*; *-nie*) sod, turf
darow|ać *pf* (*-uję*) ⟨*też* **po-**⟩ give, present; *karę* remit; *winy, urazę* forgive;

D

~izna *f* (*-y*) donation, gift; ***akt ~izny*** deed of gift
da|rzyć ⟨***ob-***⟩ (*-ę*) give, favo(u)r; **~sz** → ***dać***
daszek *m* (*-szka*; *-szki*) (small) roof; (*nad drzwiami itp.*) canopy; (*czapki*) peak
dat|a *f* (*-y*) date; F ***pod dobrą ~ą*** tipsy
datek *m* (*-tka*; *-tki*) donation, contribution
datow|ać (*-uję*) date; (***się***) be dated; **~nik** *m* (*-a*; *-i*) date-stamp; ***~nik okolicznościowy*** special postmark
dawać (*-ję*) give; *podarunek też* present; *dowód* provide; *okazję* offer, give; *zysk* bring in; *zezwolenie* grant; *cień* afford, give; ***~ coś do naprawy*** have s.th. repaired; ***~ k-ś spokój*** let s.o. alone; ***~ się słyszeć*** could be heard; ***tego nie da się otworzyć*** it cannot be opened; → ***dać***
daw|ca *m* (*-y*; *G -ów*), **~czyni** *f* (*-i*; *-e*) donor; ***~ca, ~czyni krwi*** blood-donor; **~ka** *f* (*-i*; *G -wek*) dose; **~kować** (*-uję*) dose; *fig. uczucia itp.* dispense in small doses
dawn|iej *adv.* (*comp. od* → ***dawno***); earlier; formerly; **~o** *adv.* a long time ago; ***jak ~o*** how long; **~y** (*były*) former; earlier; ***od ~a*** for a long time; ***po ~emu*** (the same) as before
dąb *m* (*dębu*; *dęby*) *bot.* oak; ***stawać dęba*** *koń*: rear up; *włosy*: stand on end
dąć (*dmę*) blow; ⟨***na-***⟩ *też* ***się*** puff up
dąs|ać się (*-am*) sulk, be cross (***na*** *A* with); **~y** *pl.* (*-ów*) sulk
dąż|enie *n* (*-a*) aspiration; **~ność** *f* (*-ści*) effort, attempt; tendency; **~yć** (*-ę*) (***do*** *G*) strive (for), aspire (to), (*do celu*) pursue, ⟨*też* ***po-***⟩ make (for), go (to)
dba|ć (*-am*) (***o*** *A*) *chorego* care (for), nurse; *wygląd* take care (of), *maszynę itp.* look after; **~le** *adv.* carefully; considerately, thoughtfully; **~łość** *f* (*-ści*; *0*) care (for, of); **~ły** careful; considerate, thoughtful
dealer *m* (*-a*; *-rzy*) dealer; (*też sprzedawca*) retailer
debat|a *f* (*-y*) debate, discussion; **~ować** (*-uję*) debate (***nad*** *I*)
debel *m* (*-bla*; *-ble*) (*w sporcie*) double
debil *m* (*-a*; *-e*), **~ka** *f* (*-i*; *G -lek*) moron (*też med.*); **~ny** moronic
debiut *m* (*-u*; *-y*) debut, first appearance; **~ować** ⟨***za-***⟩ (*-uję*) debut, make a debut
decentraliz|acja *f* (*-i*; *-e*) decentralisation; **~ować** (*-uję*) decentralize
dech *m* (*tchu*, *tchowi*, *dech*, *tchem*, *tchu*; *0*) breath; (*powiew*) breeze; ***nabrać tchu*** take *lub* draw a breath; ***bez tchu*** breathless; ***co/ile tchu*** F for all one's worth; ***jednym tchem*** at once
decy- *w złoż.* deci-
decyd|ent *m* (*-a*; *-ci*) decision-maker; **~ować** ⟨***za-***⟩ (*-uję*) decide; make decisions (***o*** *L* about); ***~ować*** ⟨***z-***⟩ ***się*** (***na*** *A*, *bezok.*) decide (on, *bezok.*), settle (on)
decy|dująco decisively; **~dujący** decisive; **~zja** *f* (*-i*; *-e*) decision; (*sędziego itp.*) ruling, verdict; ***powziąć ~zję*** make a decision
dedyk|acja *f* (*-i*; *-e*) dedication; **~ować** ⟨***za-***⟩ (*-uję*) dedicate
defekt *m* (*-u*; *-y*) defect, fault; (*usterka*) breakdown, malfunction; ***z ~em*** faulty; defective
defensyw|a *f* (*-y*) defensive; **~ny** defensive
deficyt *m* (*-u*; *-y*) deficit; (*niedobór*) shortage, lack; **~owy**: ***towar ~owy*** (*brakujący*) product in short supply, (*niezyskowny*) unprofitable product
defil|ada *f* (*-y*) parade, march; **~ować** ⟨***prze-***⟩ parade, march
defini|cja *f* (*-i*; *-e*) definition; **~tywny** definitive, definite, conclusive
deformować ⟨***z-***⟩ (*-uję*) deform; ***~ się*** become deformed
de|fraudacja *f* (*-i*; *-e*) embezzlement; **~generacja** *f* (*-i*; *0*) degeneration; **~generować się** (*-uję*) degenerate; (*w pracy*) degrade
degradacja *f* (*-i*; *0*) degradation; (*w pracy*) demotion; ***~ środowiska*** environmental degradation; *med.*, *chem.* breakdown; *fig.* decline, deterioration
deka F *n* (*-idkl.*) decagram; *w zł.* deca; **~da** *f* (*-y*) decade
dekarstwo *n* (*-a*; *0*) roofwork
dekarz *m* (*-a*; *-e*) roofer
dekla|mator *m* (*-a*; *-rzy*) reciter; **~mować** (*-uję*) recite, declaim
deklaracja *f* (*-i*; *-e*) declaration; ***~ celna*** customs declaration; (*blankiet*) form; ***~ podatkowa*** tax return

deklarować ⟨**za-**⟩ (*-uję*) declare; state
deklin|acja *f* (*-i*; *-e*) *gr.* declension; **~ować** (*-uję*) decline
dekolt *m* (*-u*; *-y*) low(-cut) neckline; ***sukienka z dużym ~em*** very low-cut dress; **~ować się** (*-uję*) wear low-cut dresses; put on a low-cut dress
dekora|cja *f* (*-i*; *-e*) decoration; (*wystawa*) window-dressing; (*w teatrze, filmie*) set, scenery; **~cyjny** (**-*nie***) decorative; **~tor** *m* (*-a*; *-rzy*), **~torka** *f* (*-i*; *G -rek*) (*wystaw*) window-dresser; (*wnętrz*) interior decorator; *teatr.* scene-painter; **~tywny** decorative
dekorować ⟨**u-**⟩ (*-uję*) decorate (*też odznaczeniem*); *wystawę* dress
dekować F (*-uję*) cover up for; **~ *się*** dodge (service), shirk
dekret *m* (*-u*; *-y*) decree; **~ować** ⟨**za-**⟩ (*-uję*) decree
delega|cja *f* (*-i*; *-e*) (*wysłannicy*) delegation; (*wyjazd służbowy*) business trip; **~t** *m* (*-a*; *-ci*), **~tka** *f* (*-i*; *G- tek*) delegate; **~tura** *f* (*-y*) agency, branch
delegować ⟨**wy-**⟩ (*-uję*) send as a delegate/delegates; (*służbowo*) send on a business trip; *odpowiedzialność* delegate
delektować się (*-uję*) savo(u)r
delfin *m* (*-a*; *-y*) *zo.* dolphin; (*w sporcie*) (*pływanie*) butterfly (stroke)
delicje *f/pl.* (*-i/-cyj*) delicacy
delikatesy *m/pl.* (*-ów*) (*sklep*) delicatessen, F deli
delikatn|ość *f* (*-ści*; *0*) delicacy; (*skóry*) softness; (*porcelany*) fragility; (*zdrowia, dziecka*) frailty; **~y** delicate; soft; fragile
delikwent *m* (*-a*; *-ci*), **~ka** *f* (*-i*; *G -tek*) offender
demaskować ⟨**z-**⟩ (*-uję*) expose; **~** ⟨**z-**⟩ ***się*** give o.s. away
demen|tować ⟨**z-**⟩ (*-uję*) deny; **~ti** *n* (*idkl.*) denial
demilitaryzacja *f* (*-i*; *0*) demilitarisation
demobilizować (*-uję*) demobilize
demokra|cja *f* (*-i*; *-e*) democracy; **~ta** *m* (*-y*; *-ci*), **~tka** *f* (*-i*; *G -tek*) democrat (*też pol.*); **~tyczny** democratic
demolować ⟨**z-**⟩ (*-uję*) wreck, smash up
demonstra|cja *f* (*-i*; *-e*) demonstration, manifestation; (*manifestacja itp.*) demonstration, F demo; **~cyjny** demonstrative
demon|strować (*-uję*) demonstrate; **~tować** ⟨**z-**⟩ (*-uję*) take apart, dismantle, disassemble
demoralizować ⟨**z-**⟩ (*-uję*) deprave, debase; **~** ⟨**z-**⟩ ***się*** become depraved *lub* debased
den → ***dno***
denat *m* (*-a*; *-ci*), **~ka** *f* (*-i*; *G -tek*) victim, casualty; (*samobójca*) suicide
denaturat *m* (*-u*; *0*) methylated spirits
denerwować ⟨**z-**⟩ (*-uję*) irritate, annoy; **~** ⟨**z-**⟩ ***się*** get excited, get worked up
denerwująco: ***działać ~ na kogoś*** get on s.o.'s nerves
den|ko *n* (*-a*) bottom; **~ny** bottom
dentyst|a, *m* (*-y*; *-ści*); **~ka** *f* (*-i*; *-tek*) dentist; **~yczny** dentist; **~yka** *f* (*-i*; *0*) dentistry
de|nuklearyzacja *f* (*-i*; *-e*) denuclearisation; **~nuncjator** *m* (*-a*; *-rzy*), **-rka** *f* (*-i*; *G-rek*) informer
denuncjować ⟨**za-**⟩ (*-uję*) inform (***kogoś*** on s.o.)
departament *m* (*-u*; *-y*) department, (*ministerialny Brt. też*) office; **♀ *stanu*** *Am.* Department of State
depesza *f* (*-y*; *-e*) telegram, *Brt.* Telemessage; (*kablem podmorskim*) cable
deponować ⟨**z-**⟩ (*-uję*) deposit (***u*** *A* with)
deport|acja *f* (*-i*; *-e*) deportation; **~ować** (*-uję*) deport
depozyt *m* (*-u*; *-y*) deposit; ***oddać do ~u u*** deposit with
de|prawować ⟨**z-**⟩ (*-uję*) deprave, corrupt, debase; **~precjacja** *f* (*-i*; *-e*) depreciation; **~presja** *f* (*-i*; *-e*) depression (*też fin., psych.*); **~prymować** ⟨**z-**⟩ (*-uję*) depress; **~prymująco** depressingly, dishearteningly; **~prymujący** depressing, disheartening
depta|ć ⟨**po-, roz-**⟩ (*-pczę/-cę*) (*A*, ***po*** *L*) (*nieumyślnie*) step (on), tread (on); (*umyślnie*) stamp (on); *też fig.* trample (on); *impf.* ***~ć komuś po piętach*** follow at s.o.'s heels; **~k** *m* (*-a*; *-i*) promenade, public walk
deput|at *m* (*-u*; *-y*) payment in kind; **~owany** *m* (*-ego*, *-i*), **~owana** *f* (*-ej*; *-e*) delegate, deputy
derka *f* (*-i*; *G -rek*) (horse-) blanket
dermatolog *m* (*-a*; *-dzy*) dermatologist

D

desant *m* (*-u*; *-y*) landing; **~ *powietrzny*** air landing operation; **~owiec** *m* (*-wca*; *-wce*) (*urządzenie*) landing craft
deseń *m* (*-niu/-nia*; *-nie*) pattern
deser *m* (*-u*; *-y*) dessert, *Brt.* F afters; ***na ~*** as a *lub* for dessert; **~owy** dessert
desk|a *f* (*-i*; *G -sek*) board; (*długa, gruba*) plank; *pl.* ***deski*** (*narty*) skis; ***~a do prasowania*** ironing board; ***ostatnia ~a ratunku*** the last hope; ***od ~i do ~i*** from cover to cover; → ***tablica***
desko|rolka *f* (*-i*) skateboard; **~wanie** *n* (*-a*) *bud.* formwork, *Brt.* shuttering; (*deski*) boarding
desperac|ki desperate; **~ko** *adv.* desperately
despotyczny despotic
destruk|cyjny, ~tywny destructive
de|stylacja *f* (*-i*; *-e*) destilation; **~stylować** ⟨***prze-***⟩ (*-uję*) destilate; **~sygnować** (*-uję*) designate (***na*** *A* as)
deszcz *m* (*-u/rzadk. dżdżu*; *-e*) rain; ***drobny ~*** drizzle, fine rain; ***ulewny ~*** downpour; → ***padać***; **~ownia** *f* (*-i*; *-e*) sprinkler; **~owy** rainy; **~ówka** *f* (*-i*; *0*) rainwater
deszczułka *f* (*-i*; *G -łek*) board
deszczyk *m* (*-u*; *-i*) light rain
detal *m* (*-u*; *-e*) detail; (*szczegół*) particular; F *econ.* retail (trade); ***nie wchodząc w ~e*** without going into (the) details; **~iczny** retail; ***cena ~iczna*** retail price
detektyw *m* (*-a*; *-i*) detective; (*prywatny*) private detective/investigator; **~istyczny** detective
deton|ator *m* (*-a*; *-y*) detonator; **~ować** ⟨***z-***⟩ (*-uję*) *bombę* detonate, explode; *kogoś* confuse, disconcert
dewaluacja f (*-i*; *-e*) devaluation
dewast|acja *f* (*-i*; *-e*) vandalism, destruction; **~ować** ⟨***z-***⟩ (*-uję*) vandalize
dewiz|a *f* (*-*; *-y*) motto, maxim; → ***dewizy***; **~ka** *f* (*-i*; *G -zek*) watch-chain; **~y** *pl.* (-) foreign currrency
dewocjonalia *pl.* (*-ów*) devotional objects *pl.*
dezaprobata *f* (*-y*; *0*) disapproval
dezer|cja *f* (*-i*; *-e*) desertion; **~terować** ⟨***z-***⟩ (*-uję*) desert
dezodorant *m* (*-u*; *-y*) deodorant; ***~ do pach*** underarm deodorant; ***~ w sprayu/kulce*** spray/roll-on deodorant
dezodoryzator *m* (*-a*; *-y*) (*do pomieszczeń*) deodorant
dezorganiz|acja *f* (*-i*; *-e*) lack of organisation; **~ować** ⟨***z-***⟩ (*-uję*) disorganize
dezorientować ⟨***z-***⟩ (*-uję*) confuse, disorientate; **~** ⟨***z-***⟩ ***się*** get confused
dezyderat *m* (*-u*; *-y*) claim
dezynfekcja *f* (*-i*; *-e*) disinfection
dęb|ina *f* (*-y*) (*drewno*) oak(-wood); **~owy** oak(en); **~y** → ***dąb***
dęt|ka *f* (*-i*; *G -tek*) *mot.* inner tube; **~y** wind; ***orkiestra ~a*** brass band
dia|belny F damned; **~belski** diabolic(al); fiendish, devilish; **~belsko** fiendishly, devilishly; **~beł** *m* (*-bła*, *D -błu*, *-ble*; *-bły/-bli*, *-ów*) devil; ***do ~bła!*** damn it!
diab|lica *f* (*-y*; *-e*) she-devil; **~oliczny** diabolical
dia|gnoza *f* (*-y*) diagnosis; **~gnozować** (*-uję*) diagnose; **~gonalny** diagonal; **~gram** *m* (*-u*; *-y*) diagram; **~lekt** *m* (*-u*; *-y*) *gr.* dialect; **~lektyczny** dialectical; *gr.* dialectal
dializacyjny dialysis; ***ośrodek ~*** *med.* dialysis *Brt.* centre (*Am.* center)
di'alog *m* (*-u*; *-i*) *Brt.* dialogue, *Am.* dialog
di'ament *m* (*-u*; *-y*) diamond; **~owy** diamond
diecezja *f* (*-i*; *-e*) diocese; **~lny** diocesan
dies|el *m* (*-sla*; *-sle*) diesel (engine); **~lowski** diesel
di'e|ta *f* (*-y*) diet; ***~ty*** *pl.* (*parlamentarzysty*) parliamentary allowance; (*na delegacji*) travelling (traveling *Am.*) expenses *pl.*; ***być na ~cie*** diet; **~tetyczny** diet; dietary; ***napój ~tetyczny*** diet drink
dla *prp.* (*G*) for; ***~ dorosłych*** for adults; ***miły ~ rąk*** kind to the hands; ***przyjazny ~ zwierząt*** animal-friendly; ***~ nabrania tchu*** in order to take a breath of air; **~czego** why; **~ń** = ***dla niego***; **~tego** for that reason; because of that; ***~tego, że*** because
dł. *skrót pisany*: ***długość*** (*length*)
dławić ⟨***z-***⟩ (*-ę*) choke, strangle; *fig.* sup press, hold back; **~** ⟨***z-***⟩ ***się*** (*I*) choke (on)
dławik *m* (*-a*; *-i*) *electr.* choking coil
dło|ń *f* (*-ni*; *-nie*) palm; hand; ***jasne jak na ~ni*** it is obvious
dłubać (*mieszać się*) fiddle (***przy*** *L* with); **~** ⟨***wy-***⟩ (*-bię*) (*w nosie, zębach*)

pick; (*w jedzeniu*) pick (**w** *L* at)
dług *m* (*-u*; *-i*) debt, (*też moralny*) obligation
długawy longish; **~i** long; **~o** long; ***jak ~o?*** how long?; ***na ~o*** for a long time; ***tak ~o aż*** so/as long that
długodystansowiec *m* (*-wca*; *-wcy*) long-distance runner; **~falowy** long-term; ***~falowo*** on a long-term basis, in the long term; **~letni** long-standing; of many years' standing; **~pis** *m* (*-u*; *-y*) ball-point (pen); **~ść** *f* (*-ci*) length; (*okres też*) duration; **~terminowo** long-term; **~terminowy** long-term; **~trwały** long-lasting; *choroba itp.* lengthy, prolonged; **~wieczny** long-lived; **~włosy** long-haired
dłuto *n* (*-a*) chisel
dłużej *adv.* (*comp. od* → ***długo***); ***~ nie*** no longer
dłużniczka *f* (*-i*; *G -czek*), **~ik** *m* (*-a*; *-cy*) debtor; **~y**: ***być ~ym*** owe to
dłuższy *adj.* (*comp. od* → ***długi***); ***na ~szy czas, od ~szego czasu*** for a longer time; **~yć się** (*-ę*) drag
dmą, dmę → ***dąć***
dmuchać (*-am*) blow; **~awa** *f* (*-y*) blower; **~awiec** *m* (*-wca*; *-wce*) *bot.* dandelion; **~nąć** → ***dmuchać*** F (*ukraść*) pinch, swipe
dn. *skrót pisany*: ***dnia*** on; *też* **d.n.** ***dokończenie nastąpi*** to be cont'd (*to be continued*)
dna, dnem → ***dno***
dni, ~a, ~e → ***dzień***; **~eć**: ***~eje*** it is dawning; ***~ało*** the day broke
dniówka *f* (*-i*; *G -wek*) working day; (*zapłata*) daily *lub* day's wage(s *pl.*); ***pracować na ~ę*** work as a day-labo(u)rer
dniu → ***dzień***
dno *n* (*-a*; *G den*) bottom; ***pójść na ~*** go down; ***do góry dnem*** bottom up
do *prp.* (*G*) to; till, until; into ; ***~ niego*** to him; ***~ szkoły*** to school; ***~ piątku*** until Friday; **(*aż*)** ***~ rana*** until the morning; ***~ pudła*** into the box; ***pół ~ drugiej*** half past one ***od ... ~ ...*** from ... to ...; (*często nie tłumaczy się, zwłaszcza w złożeniach*); ***łańcuch ~ drzwi*** door chain; ***beczka ~ wina*** wine barrel; ***lekki ~ strawienia*** easily digestible
doba *f* (*-y*; *G dób*) day (and night); 24 hours; *fig.* age; ***przez całą ~ę*** round the clock
dobić *pf.* → ***dobijać, targ***
dobiegać ⟨***~c, ~gnąć***⟩ (*-gam*) (**do** *G*) run (to); (*do celu*) reach; (*o dźwiękach*) reach, come; ***~ga godzina ...*** it is almost ... o'clock; ***to ~ga końca*** it is drawing to an end
dobierać (*-am*) take more; (*wybierać*) choose, select; ***~ się*** get (**do** *G* at); (*majstrować*) fiddle (**do** *G* with)
dobijać (*-am*) *v/t.* deal the final blow to; finish off (*też fig.*); *fig.* destroy, ruin; *v/i.* ***~ do celu*** reach the goal; ***~ do brzegu*** reach the shore; ***~ się do drzwi*** rap at the door
dobitek: ***na ~ek***, **~ka**: ***na ~kę*** on top of that; **~ny** *głos* stentorian, resonant; *żądanie* insistent, urgent
doborowy excellent; *oddziały* elite
dobosz *m* (*-a*; *-e*) drummer
dobowy day-and-night; → ***doba***
dobór *m* (*-boru*; *0*) selection
dobrać *pf.* → ***dobierać* (*się*)**; ***~ się*** (*pasować*) make a good match
dobranoc (*idkl.*) good night; **~ka** *f* (*-i*)- (*bedtime TV feature for children*)
dobrany *adj.* well-matched
dobre *n* (*-ego*; *0*) → ***dobro, dobry***; ***na ~*** for good; ***po ~mu*** in an amicable way; ***wszystkiego ~go!*** all the best!
dobrnąć *pf.* (**do** *G*) get (to), reach (with difficulty)
dobro *n* (*-a*; *G dóbr*) good; ***~o społeczne*** public *lub* common good; ***~a*** *pl.* ***rodzinne*** (*majątek*) property; ***~a*** *pl.* ***kulturalne*** cultural possessions *pl.*; ***dla ~a*** (*G*) for the good (of); ***na ~o*** in favo(u)r of; ***zapisać*** (*A*) ***na ~o k-ś/rachunku*** *econ.* credit s.o./s.o.'s account with
dobrobyt *m* (*-u*) prosperity, affluence; **~czynność** *f* charity; **~czynny** *skutek itp.* beneficial, agreeable; *akcja itp.* charitable
dobroć *f* (*-ci*; *0*) goodness, kindness; ***po ~ci*** amicably; **~duszny** good-natured; **~dziejstwo** good deed, favo(u)r; *pl. rel.* blessings *pl.*; **~tliwość** *f* (*-ści*) goodness, kindness; **~tliwie** kindly, good-naturedly; **~tliwy** good, kind, good-natured; *med.* benign; **~wolnie** voluntarily, of one's own will; **~wolny** voluntary
dobry good; (***na*** *A*, ***do*** *G*) good (for); (*w L*) good (at); ***~ra!*** OK!; ***a to ~re!*** I like that!; ***na ~rą sprawę*** actually;

D

na ~rej drodze on the right track; *przez ~re dwie godziny* for two solid hours, F for two hours solid; → *dobre*
dobrze well; *wyglądać, czuć się* good; *~ ubrany* well-dressed; *~ wychowany* well brought-up; *on ma się ~* he is fine; *~ mu tak!* (it) serves him right!
dobudow(yw)ać (-[*w*]*uję*) *skrzydło* build on, add
dobudówka *f* (-*i*; *G* -*wek*) extension
doby|ć *pf.* → *dobywać*; **~tek** *m* (-*tku*; *0*) possessions *pl.*, belongings *pl.*; (*bydło*) cattle; **~wać** (*G*) draw; (*wytężyć*) exert, call on; *~wać się* appear
docelowy destination; *port ~* destination
doceni|ać (-*am*) ⟨*~ć*⟩ appreciate, acknowledge; *nie ~ć* underestimate
docent *m* (-*a*; -*ci*) lecturer
dochodow|ość *f* (-*ści*; *0*) profitability; **~y** profitable; → *podatek*
dochodz|enie *n* (-*a*) investigation; *jur. też* assertion; *~enie sądowe jur.* preliminary inquiry; **~ić** (**do** *G*) approach, come up (to); (*nadchodzić*) come; (*sięgać*) (**do** *G*) reach (to), get (to); (*dociekać*) investigate; *prawa* claim; *gastr.* be coming along; *owoce*: ripen; *~ić swego* assert one's rights; *~ić do głosu* get a chance to speak; *fig.* come to the fore; *~i ósma* it is almost eight (o'clock); → *dojść*
dochow|ywać (-*wuję*) ⟨*~ać*⟩ (*G*) preserve; *~ać słowa* keep one's word; *~(yw)ać się* remain in good condition; *~ać się* manage to bring up
dochód *m* (-*chodu*; -*chody*) income; *czysty ~* net income; *dochody pl.* returns *pl.*
docią|ć → *docinać*; **~gać** (-*am*) ⟨*~gnąć*⟩ draw (**do** *G* as far as); *pas, śrubę* tighten
docie|kać (-*am*) ⟨*~c*⟩ *fig.* (*G*) make inquiries about; **~kliwie** inquisitively; **~kliwy** inquisitive; **~rać** (-*am*) *v/i.* (**do**) get as far as (to), reach; *v/t. mot.* run in
docin|ać (-*am*) *fig.* (*D*) tease, gibe (at); **~ek** *m* (-*nka*; -*nki*) gibe, dig
docis|kać ⟨*~nąć*⟩ (-*am*) tighten; *~kać* ⟨*~nąć*⟩ *się* force one's way through
do cna completely
doczekać (**się**) *pf.* (*G*) wait until; live to; *~ się* receive at last; *nie móc się ~* be impatient for
doczepi(a)ć attach
doczesny earthly, worldly
dod. *skrót pisany*: *dodatek* sup. (*supplement*)
dodać *pf.* → *dodawać*
dodat|ek *m* (-*tku*; -*tki*) addition; (*budynek*) annex, extension; (*do pensji*) extra pay, additional allowance; (*do gazety*) supplement; (*do książki*) supplement, appendix; *~ek mieszkaniowy* housing benefit; *~ek nadzwyczajny* special edition, extra; *z ~kiem* (*G*) with; *na ~ek, w ~ku* in addition, additionally; *~ki pl.* ingredients *pl.*
dodatkow|o *adv.* additionally; **~y** additional; *wartość ~a* value added
doda|tni positive; *fig.* advantageous, beneficial; *znak ~tni* plus (sign); *bilans* favourable; **~nio** *adv.* positively; *fig.* advantageously, beneficially; **~(wa)ć** (-*ję*) (**do** G) add (to); *fig.* give, lend; *math.* add (up); *~ć otuchy* (*D*) encourage; *~ć gazu* F step on it; **~wanie** addition
dodzwonić się *pf* (**do** *G*) get through (to); *nie mogę się ~* nobody answers
doga|dać się *pf* (**z** *I*) (*porozumieć się*) make o.s. understood (to); (*uzgodnić*) come to terms (with); **~dywać** (-*uję*) → *docinać*; **~dzać** (-*am*) (*D*) pamper; coddle; satisfy (*zachciankom* whims); *to mu nie ~dza* that does not appeal to him; **~niać** catch up with; **~snąć** go out
doglądać (-*am*) (*G*) supervize, care for; look after
dogmat *m* (-*u*; -*y*) dogma
dogo|dny convenient; *na ~dnych warunkach* on favo(u)rable conditions; **~dzić** *pf.* → *dogadzać*; **~nić** *pf.* → *doganiać*; **~rywać** (-*am*) be in agony; **~towywać się** (-*wuję*) ⟨*~tować się*⟩ finish cooking
do|grywać (-*am*) ⟨*~grać*⟩ (*mecz*) play extra time; **~grywka** (-*i*; -*wek*) extra time; **~gryzać** (-*am*) ⟨*~gryźć*⟩; *fig.* (*D*) tease; **~grzewać** (-*am*) warm (up)
doić ⟨**wy-**⟩ (-*ję*; *dój!*) milk
dojadać finish eating; *resztki* finish; *nie ~* not eat enough
dojarka *f* (-*i*; *G* -*rek*) milkmaid; *~ mechaniczna* milking machine
dojazd *m* (-*u*; -*y*) journey, way; (*droga*) approach, drive; **~owy** *droga* access; *kolejka ~owa rail.* local (train)

do|jąć *pf* (*-jmę*) → ***dojmować***; **~jechać** *pf.* (**do** *G*) arrive (at, in), reach; **~jeść** → ***dojadać***; **~jeżdżać** (*-am*): ***~jeżdżać do pracy*** commute (to work)
dojm|ować (*-uję*) *v/t.* get through to, pierce; **~ujący** piercing; acute
dojn|y: ***krowa ~a*** dairy cow
dojrzale *adv.* in a mature way, *owoc itp.* ripely
dojrzał|ość *f* (*-ści*; *0*) maturity; (*owocu itp.*) ripeness; ***egzamin ~ości*** *jakby*: *Brt.* GCSE, *Am.* high school diploma; **~y** mature, *owoc itp.* ripe
dojrze|ć[1] *pf* (*-ę*; *-y*) catch sight of, see; **~wać** ⟨**~ć**[2]⟩ (*-eję*) *człowiek*: mature, *ser*, *owoc*: ripen
dojście *n* (*-a*) way, approach (**do** *G* to); ***~ do skutku*** coming into effect
dojść *pf.* (*-dę*) → ***dochodzić***; *fig.* (**do** *G*) come to, approach; ***~ do zdrowia*** regain one's health; ***~ do skutku*** come into being *lub* effect; ***~ do władzy*** come to power
dok *m* (*-u*; *-i*) *naut.* dock
dokańczać (*-am*) finish, complete, bring to an end
dokazywać[1] (*-uję*) romp around
doka|zywać[2] accomplish, achieve; ⟨**~zać**⟩ ***~ywać swego*** assert o.s.
dokąd where; (*czas*) as long as; ***~ bądź*** → ***bądź***; **~kolwiek, ~ś** anywhere
doker *m* (*-a*; *-rzy*) dock-worker; docker
dokład|ać (*-am*) add; (*szczodrobliwie*) throw in; **~ność** *f* (*-ci*; *0*) precision; **~ny** precise, exact, accurate
dokoła *adv.* all around; *prp.* (*G*) (a)round; ***~ siebie*** (a)round o.s.
dokon|any finished, accomplished; *gr.* perfect, perfective; **~ywać** (*-uję*) ⟨**~ać**⟩ *wyczynu itp.* accomplish; *zbrodni* commit; *wyboru* make; ***~(yw)ać się*** take place, occur
dokończenie *n* (*-a*) ending; end; ***~ nastąpi*** to be continued
dokończyć *pf.* → ***dokańczać***
dokształcać (*-am*) ⟨**-ić**⟩ provide further education; ***~ się*** continue one's education
dokształcający further education
doktor *m* (*-a*; *-rzy/-owie*) doctor; (*lekarz też*) medical doctor; **~ant** *m* (*-a*; *-nci*) post-graduate student; **~at** *m* (*-u*; *-y*) doctorate; **~ski** doctor's, doctoral; **~yzować się** (*-uję*) obtain a/one's doctorate (**z** *G* in)
dokucz|ać (*-am*) ⟨**~yć**⟩ (*D*) tease, annoy; *ból*, *głód*: torment, plague; **~liwie** *adv.* pesteringly, tiresomely; plaguingly; **~liwy** pestering, tiresome; plaguing
dokument *m* (*-u*; *-y*) document; **~y** *pl. też* F (identity) papers; **~acja** *f* (*-i*; *-e*) documentation; **~alny, ~arny** documentary; **~ować** ⟨**u-**⟩ (*-uję*) document
dokup|ywać (*-uję*) ⟨**~ić**⟩ buy additionally
dola *f* (*-i*; *zw. 0*) fate, destiny
do|lać → ***dolewać***; **~latywać** (*-uję*) ⟨**~lecieć**⟩ (**do** *G*) approach (by plane) (to); *pf.* reach; *fig.* get through (to), come through (to) (**z** *G* from)
doleg|ać (*-am*; *t-ko bezok. i 3. os.*) (*D*) trouble, bother; (*boleć*) hurt; ***co ci/Panu ~a?*** what seems to be the matter?; **~liwość** *f* (*-ści*) trouble; (*ból*) pain
dolewać (*-am*) (*G*) fill up
dolicz|ać (*-am*) ⟨**~yć**⟩ add; ***~yć się*** count (up); ***nie ~yć się*** be … short
dolin|a *f* (*-y*) valley; ***dno ~y*** valley floor
doliniarz *m* (*-a*; *-e*) pickpocket
dolno- *w zł.* lower, low
dolnoniemiecki Low German
doln|y lower, bottom; ***~a część*** lower part
dołącz|ać (*-am*) ⟨**~yć**⟩ (**do** *G*) add (to); (*z listem*) enclose; join (**się** to)
doł|ek *m* (*-łka*, *-łki*) hole; *med.* pit; (*w brodzie*) dimple; *fig.* F ***być w ~ku*** have a crisis, be depressed; **~em** below, underneath
do|łożyć *pf.* → ***dokładać***; **~ły** *pl.* → ***dół***
dom *m* (*-u*; *-y*) (*budynek*) house; (*rodzinny*) *fig.* home; ***~ dziecka*** children's home; ***do ~u*** home; ***w ~u*** at home; ***z ~u*** *kobieta*: née; ***czuć się jak u siebie w ~u*** feel like at home; ***pan(i) ~u*** host
domagać się (*-am*) (*G*) demand
domek *m* (*-mku*; *-mki*) (small) house; ***~ letniskowy*** (summer) holiday house; ***~ jednorodzinny*** (one-family) house
domiar *m* (*-u*; *-y*) *econ.* back tax; ***na ~ złego*** to make matters worse
domiesz|ać *pf.* (*G* **do** *G*) add (to); **~ka** *f* (*-i*; *G -szek*) addition
domięśniow|o *adv. med.* intramuscularly; **~y** *med.* intramuscular
domin|ować (*-uję*) (**nad** *I*) dominate

D

(over); **~ujący** dominating
domknąć *pf.* → ***domykać***
domniemany alleged, purported
domo|fon *m* (*-u*; *-y*) intercom, *Brt.* entryphone; **~krążca** *m* (*-y*; *G -ów*) pedlar, hawker; **~stwo** *n* (*-a*) (*rolne*) farmstead; house; **~wnik** *m* (*-a*; *-cy*) member of the household; **~wy** home; domestic; household; ***porządki*** *m/pl.* ***~we*** clean-out, (*wiosenne*) spring-clean; ***~wej produkcji*** domestic
domy|kać (*-am*) shut, push to; ***drzwi nie ~kają się*** the door won't shut; **~sł** *m* (*-u*; *-y*) supposition, conjecture; **~ślać się** (*-am*) 〈**~ślić się**〉 (*-lę*) (*G*) suspect, presume; *pf.* guess, find out (**że** that); **~ślny** perceptive, shrewd
doni|ca *f* (*-y*; *-e*) (*na kwiaty*) large flowerpot; (*kuchenna*) pot; **~czka** *f* (*-i*; *G -czek*) flowerpot; **~czkowy**: ***kwiaty*** *m/pl.* ***~czkowe*** potted flowers
donie|sienie *n* (*-a*; *G -ń*) report; → ***donos***; **~ść** *pf.* → ***donosić***
donikąd nowhere
doniosł|ość *f* (*-ści*; *0*), significance, importance, moment; **~y** significant, important, momentous
donos *m* (*-u*; *-y*) denunciation; **~iciel** *m* (*-a*; *-e*), **-lka** *f* (*-i*) informer; **~ić** (*-szę*) (**na** *A*) report (against, on); (**o** *L*) report (about)
donośny stentorian, resonant
doń = ***do niego***; → ***on***
dookoła → ***dokoła***
dopa|dać (**do** *G*) lay hands (on), seize; *smutek itp.*: come over; → ***dopaść***; **~lać** (*-am*) 〈**~lić**〉 *cygaro* finish (smoking); *węgiel* burn; ***~lać się*** *ogień*: burn low; *budynek*: burn down
dopa|sow(yw)ać (*-[w]uję*) fit; (*do otoczenia*) adapt (**się** o.s.; **do** *G* to); **~ść** *pf.* → ***dopadać***; (*dogonić*) catch (up with); **~trywać się** (*-uję*) 〈**~trzyć się**〉 (**w kimś** *G*) see (in s.o.)
dopełni|acz *m* (*-a*; *-e*) *gr.* genitive; **~ać** (*-am*) 〈**~ć**〉 fill up, refill; (*uzupełnić*) complete; *fig.* fulfill; **~ający** completing; **~enie** *n* (*-a*) completion; *gr.* object
dopędz|ać (*-am*) 〈**~ić**〉 catch up with
dopiąć *pf. fig.* (*G*) achieve; ***~ swego*** have one's will; → ***dopinać***
do|pić *pf.* → ***dopijać***; **~piekać** (*-am*) 〈**~piec**〉 *v/i. słońce*: be scorching, be burning down; *fig.* (*D*) nettle, sting
dopiero only, just; ***~ co*** just now; ***a to ~!*** well, well!
dopi|jać (*-am*) drink up; **~lnować** *pf.* (*G*, **aby**) look (to it that); **~nać** (*-am*) button up, *też fig.*; → ***dopiąć***
dopingować (*-uję*) spur on, encourage, cheer
doping|owy, ~ujący: ***środek ~owy***/***~ujący*** stimulant drug
dopis|ek *m* (*-sku*; *-ski*) comment, note; ***~ek na marginesie*** marginal note *lub* comment; **~ywać** (*-uję*) 〈**~ać**〉 *v/t.* add (in writing); *v/i.* (*-3. os.*) be good, be favourable; ***pogoda ~uje*** the weather is fine; ***zdrowie mu nie ~uje*** he is in poor health; ***szczęście mu nie ~ało*** he had bad luck
dopła|cać (*-am*) 〈**~cić**〉 (**do** *G*); pay extra (to), pay an additional sum (to); *porto* pay additionally (to); **~ta** *f* (*-y*) additional payment; extra payment; (*w pociągu*) excess (fare)
dopły|nąć *pf.* → ***dopływać***; **~w** *m* (*-u*; *0*) (*energii*) supply, (*kabel*) line; *fig.* influx; (*pl. -y*) feeder stream; (*rzeka*) tributary
dopływ|ać (*-am*) (**do** *G*) reach; *statek, łódź*: approach; **~owy** *kabel itp.* supply; *rzeka itp.* tributary, feeder
dopo|magać (*-m*) (**w** *L*) help out (with), be helpful (with); **~minać się** (*-am*) 〈**~mnieć się**〉 (*-nę, -nij!*) (**o coś** (*A*) **u kogoś**) claim (s.th. from s.o.), demand (s.th. from s.o.); ask (for)
dopó|ki *cj.* as/so long as; **~ty**: ***~ty ... aż***, ***~ty ... dopóki*** as long as
doprawdy *adv.* really
doprowadz|ać (*-am*) 〈**~ić**〉 (**do** *G*) lead (to), result (in); *tech.* convey (to), supply (to); *prąd, gaz* connect (to); ***~ić do końca*** bring to an end; ***~ić do ruiny*** ruin; **~enie** *n* supply; connection; *electr.* lead
dopuszcza|ć (*-m*) (**do** *G*) allow, permit; ***nie możemy do tego ~ć*** we cannot let it happen; ***~ć się*** (*G*) commit, make; **~lny** permissible
dopuścić *pf.* → ***dopuszczać***; ***~ do głosu*** let s.o. speak
dopyt|ywać się (*-uję*) 〈**~ać się**〉 (*G*, **o** *A*) ask (about), inquire (about)
dorabiać (*-am*) prepare; *klucz* duplicate; *też* ***~ sobie*** (*I*) earn on the side, earn extra; ***~ się*** (*G*) make one's way;

(*wzbogacać*) get rich, do all right for o.s.

dorad|ca *m* (*-y*; *-y*), **~czyni** *f* (*-*; *-e*, *-yń*) advisor *lub* adviser; consultant; **~czy** advisory, consultative

doradz|ać (*-am*) ⟨**~ić**⟩ advise; **~two** *n* (*-a*; *0*) consultation; (*usługi*) consultancy (services *pl.*)

dorasta|ć (*-am*) grow up (*też fig.*) (**do** *G* (in)to); → ***dorównywać***; **~jący** growing up

doraźn|ie *adv.* (*na razie*) for the time being; temporarily; (*karać*) summarily; **~y** summary; temporary; ***pomoc ~a*** emergency relief; (*medyczna*) first aid; ***sąd ~y*** summary court

doręcz|ać (*-am*) ⟨**~yć**⟩ hand over; *list itp.* deliver; **~enie** *n* (*-a*) delivery

dorob|ek *m* (*-bku*; *0*) (*niematerialny*) achievements *pl.*, (*materialny*) property; (*utwory itp.*) work; ***~ek kulturalny*** cultural possessions *pl.*; ***być na ~ku*** make one's way; **~ić** *pf.* → ***dorabiać***

doroczny annual

dorodny well-built, good-looking; *zboże itp.* ripe

doros|ły 1. *adj.* adult, grown-up; **2.** *m* (*-ego*; *-śli*) adult, grown-up; **~nąć** → ***dorastać***

do|rożka *f* (*-i*; *G -żek*) cab; **~róść** *pf.* → ***dorastać***

dorówn|ywać (*-uję*) ⟨**~ać**⟩ (*D*) equal, match; ***~ywać komuś*** be s.o.'s equal/ match

dorsz *m* (*-a*; *-e*) *zo.* cod

dorysow(yw)ać (*-*[*w*]*uję*) finish drawing; (*dodać*) add

dorywcz|o *adv.* occasionally, from time to time, incidentally; **~y** occasional, incidental; *praca* odd

dorzecze *m* (*-a*) *geogr.* basin

dorzeczny reasonable

dorzuc|ać ⟨**~ić**⟩ (**do** *G*) throw (as far as); add (*też fig.*); *węgla itp.* put more

dosadny *dowcip itp.* earthy, crude

do|salać (*-am*) add salt; **~siadać** ⟨**~siąść**⟩ mount (**konia** the horse), get on; ***~siąść się*** (**do k-ś**) join (s.o.)

do siego: ***~ roku!*** happy New Year!

dosięg|ać ⟨**~nąć**⟩ (*G*, **do** *G*) reach (to) (*też fig.*)

doskona|le *adv.* → ***doskonały***; **~lenie (się)** *n* (*-a*; *0*) perfecting; (*nauka*) further education; **~lić** ⟨**u-**⟩ (*-lę*) perfect; ***~lić się*** improve; **~łość** *f* (*-ci*; *0*) perfection; **~ły** *adj.* perfect; (*znakomity*) excellent, first-rate

do|słać → ***dosyłać***; **~słowny** literal; **~słyszeć** *pf.* hear; ***on nie ~słyszy*** he is hard of hearing; **~solić** *pf.* → ***dosalać***; **~spać** *pf.* → ***dosypiać***; **~stać** *pf.* → ***dostawać***

dostarcz|ać ⟨**~yć**⟩ (*A*, *G*) deliver (to), supply (with); *świadka, dowody* produce; *fig.* (*dawać*) provide

dostat|ecznie *adv.* sufficiently, (*dobry itp.*) acceptably; **~eczny** sufficient, acceptable; *ocena* fair; **~ek** *m* (*-tku*; *0*) prosperity; ***pod ~kiem*** in abundance, in plenty; **~ni** prosperous, comfortable; **~nio** *adv.* prosperously, comfortably

dostaw|a *f* (*-y*) delivery, supply; ***termin ~y*** delivery time; **~ać** get, obtain, receive; (*wyjmować*) take out; (*dosięgać*) get, reach (**do** *G* to); ***~ać się*** (**do** *G*) get (to, into); ***~ać się w ... ręce*** get into the hands of …; ***nagroda dostała się*** (*D*) the price was given to; **~ca** *m* (*-y*; *G -ów*) supplier; (*bezpośredni*) delivery man; **~czy** delivery; **~i(a)ć** *stół itp.* add; *więźnia itp.* deliver, bring; → ***przystawiać, dostarczać***

dostąpić *pf.* (*-ę*) → ***dostępować***

dostęp *m* (*-u*; zw. 0) admission; *też fig.* access; **~ny** accessible; *cena też* reasonable; *tekst też* clear; **~ować** (*-uję*) (*dochodzić*) (**do** *G*) approach, go up (to); *fig.* → ***dostąpić***

dostoj|eństwo *n* (*-a*) dignity; **~nik** *m* (*-a*; *-cy*) dignitary; **~ny** dignified; → ***czcigodny***

dostosow|anie *n* (*-a*; *0*) adaptation, adjustment; **~(yw)ać** adapt, adjust (**do** *G* to; **się** o.s.); **~awczy** adaptative

do|strajać (*-am*) ⟨**~stroić**⟩ *mus.*, *RTV*: tune; *fig.* adjust (**się do** o.s. to); **~strzegać** (*-am*) ⟨**~strzec**⟩ notice

dostrzegalny noticeable; ***~ ledwo*** hardly noticeable

dosu|wać ⟨**~nąć**⟩ move up closer, push (**do** *G* to)

dosyć *adv.* quite, fairly; ***~ dobrze*** quite good; ***mieć ~*** (*G*) be sick *lub* tired of

dosy|łać (*-am*) send on, send after; **~piać** (*-am*): ***nie ~piać*** sleep too little; **~pywać** (*-uję*) ⟨**~pać**⟩ (**do** *G*) pour in more, *węgla itp.* put on more

D

do|szczętny (*adv. też* ***do szczętu***) complete, total; **~szkalać** (*-am*) ⟨***~szkolić***⟩ → ***dokształcać***; **~sztukow(yw)ać** (*-[w]uję*) (**do** *G*) *dywanu itp.* add a piece to; *sukienkę itp.* lengthen

doszuk|ać się *pf.* (*G*) find, come across; **~iwać się** (*-uję*) (*G*) suspect

dościg|ać ⟨***~nąć***⟩ (*-am*) catch up with

dość → ***dosyć***; ***~ na tym, że ...*** in a word; ***od ~ dawna*** for quite a long time

dośpiewać *pf.*: ***~ sobie*** guess

dośrodkow|(yw)ać (*-[w]uję*) (*w sporcie*) *Brt.* centre, *Am.* center; **~o** *adv.* centripetally; **~y** centripetal

doświadcz|ać (*-am*) (*G*) experience; *bólu itp.* go through, endure; ***los go ciężko ~ył*** fate has been very unkind to him; **~alny** experimental; **~enie** *m* (*-a*) experiment (***na zwierzętach*** on animals), (*próba też*) test; experience; ***brak ~enia*** lack of experience; ***z ~enia*** from experience; **~ony** experienced; (*wypróbowany*) (tried and) tested; **~yć** *pf.* → ***doświadczać***

dot. *skrót pisany*: ***dotyczy*** Re:

dotacja *f* (*-i*; *-e*) subvention

dotąd (*w czasie*) until now; up to now; (*w przestrzeni*) so far; → ***dopóty***

dotk|liwie *adv.* sharply, severely; **~liwy** sharp, severe; **~nąć** *pf.* → ***dotykać***; *fig.* hurt, wound; **~nięcie (się)** *n* (*-a*) touch, contact; **~nięty** (*I*) (*urażony*) upset, hurt; (*spustoszony itp.*) stricken

dotować (*-uję*) subsidize

do|trwać *pf.* (**do** *G*) remain (until), hold out (until), last (until); **~trzeć** *pf.* → ***docierać***; **~trzymywać** (*-uję*) ⟨***~trzymać***⟩ *słowa, kroku, towarzystwa* keep; *warunków* keep to

dotychczas *adv.* until now; **~owy** previous

doty|czyć (*G*) concern, apply to; ***co ~czy ...*** as to *lub* for; ***to mnie nie ~czy*** that does not concern me; ***~czące ciebie ...*** concerning you; **~k** *m* (*-u*; *-i*) touch; ***na ~k*** to the touch; ***być szorstkim w ~ku*** be rough to the touch; ***zmysł ~ku*** sense of touch; **~kać** (*-am*) (*G*) touch (***się*** o.s., each other); **~kalny** palpable, tangible; **~kowy** touch

doucz|ać (*-am*) ⟨***~yć***⟩ continue (***się*** one's) education; ***~yć się*** learn

doustny oral

doważać (*-am*) ⟨***doważyć***⟩: ***nie ~*** cheat on the weight

dowcip *m* (*-u*; *-y*) joke; **~kować** (*-uję*) joke; **~ny** witty

dowiadywać się (*-uję*) enquire (**o** *A* about); → ***dowiedzieć się***

dowidzieć: ***nie~*** have poor eyesight

dowie|dzieć się *pf.* learn, hear (**o** *A* about); **~dziony** proved, proven; **~rzać** (*-am*) trust; ***nie~rzać*** mistrust; **~ść** *pf.* → ***dowodzić***; **~źć** *pf.* → ***dowozić***

dowlec *pf.* drag (**się** o.s.)

dowodow|y: *jur.* ***wartość ~a*** value as evidence; ***postępowanie ~e*** *jur.* hearing of evidence

dowodz|enie *n* (*-a*) command; (*wykazywanie*) argumentation, reasoning; *jur.* presentation of the case; **~ić** (*-dzę*) argue (for), prove; *mil.* have command of, be in command of

dowoln|y free; ***ćwiczenia ~e*** (*w sporcie*) free *Brt.* programme (*Am.* program), optional exercises

dowozić *v/t.* (**do** G) bring (to), drive (to), *rzeczy* transport (to); (*dostarczać*) supply

dowód *m* (*-odu*; *-ody*) (*też jur.*) proof, evidence; (*dokument*) certificate, receipt; ***~ osobisty*** identity card; ***~ nadania*** certificate of posting; ***~ rzeczowy*** *jur.* (piece of) material evidence; ***na/w ~*** (*G*) in token of; **~ca** *m* (*-y*; *G -ów*) commander; *mil.* commanding officer; ***~ca plutonu*** *mil.* platoon commander

dowództwo *n* (*-a*) command; (*miejsce*) command post; (*siedziba*) headquarters *sg./pl.*

dowóz *m* supply

doza *f* (*-y*) dose

dozbr|ajać (*-am*) ⟨***~oić***⟩ rearm

dozgonny lifelong, for life

dozna|wać (*-ję*) ⟨***~ć***⟩ (*G*) feel; *złego* experience; *straty, kontuzji* suffer; ***~ć zawodu*** feel disappointment; ***~ć wrażenia*** get an impression

dozor|ca *m* (*-y*; *-y*, *G -ów*), **~czyni** *f* (*-ni*; *-e*, *G -yń*) (*domu*) caretaker, janitor (*zwł. Am.*); (*w więzieniu*) *Brt.* warder, *Am.* (prison) guard; **~ować** (*-uję*) (*G*) supervize, oversee

dozować (*-uję*) dose, measure out (a dose)

dozór *m* (*-oru*; *0*) supervision; **~ techniczny** technical inspection/supervision
dozw|alać (*-am*) ⟨**~olić**⟩ (*-lę*; *-wól!*) allow; permit; **~olony dla młodzieży** suitable for persons under 18
dożyć *pf.* (*G*) live (to); **~ stu lat** live to be a hundred; **~ późnego wieku** live to a ripe old age
dożylny *med.* intravenous
dożynki *pl.* (*-nek*) harvest festival
doży|wać (*-am*) → **dożyć**; **~wać swoich dni** reach the twilight of one's life; **~wiać się** (*-am*) take additional food; **~wotni** lifelong; *jur.* life; **~wotnio** *adv.* lifelong; for life
dójka *f* (*-i*; *G -jek*) milkmaid; (*cycek*) teat
dób *G pl.* → **doba**; **~r** *G pl.* → **dobro**
dół *m* (*dołu*; *doły*) hole, pit; (*dolna część*) bottom part; under-side; bottom; **w/na ~** down; **na ~** (*domu*) downstairs; **iść w ~** *fig.* go down; **w ~ rzeki** downstream; **z/od dołu** from below; **w/na dole, u dołu** (down) below; **płatny z dołu** payment on delivery
dr *skrót pisany*: **doktor** Dr, PhD, MedD
drab F *m* (*-a*; *-y*) ruffian, thug
drabin|a *f* (*-y*) ladder; **~iasty**: **wóz ~iasty** open-frame wooden cart; **~ka** *f* (*-i*) ladder; **~ka linowa, sznurowa** rope ladder; **~ka szwedzka** (*w sporcie*) wall bars *pl.*
dragi *f/pl. sl.* (*narkotyki*) drugs
draka *f* (*-i*) F row
drakoński draconian
dramat *m* (*-u*; *-y*) drama (*też fig.*)
drama|topisarz *m* (*-a*; *-e*), **-rka** *f* (*-i*) playwright; **~tyczny** dramatic
drań *m* (*-nia*; *-nie*, *-ni*[*ów*]) *pej.* scoundrel, swine; **~stwo** *n* (*-a*) meanness; nastiness
drapa|cz *m* (*-a*; *-e*): **~cz chmur** skyscraper; **~ć** ⟨**po-**⟩ (*-ię*) scratch (**się** (o.s.), **w** *A* on); **~ć się pod górę** clamber up; **~k** *m* (*-a*; *-i*) old comb; **dać ~ka** → **drapnąć**
drapieżn|ik *m* (*-a*; *-i*) predator (*też fig.*), (*ptak*) bird of prey, (*ssak*) beast of prey; **~ość** *f* (*-ci*; *0*) rapacity; **~y** predacious, predaceous
drapn|ąć *v/s.* (*-nę*) scratch; F make o.s. scarce; **~ięcie** *n* (*-a*; *G -ć*) scratch
drapować ⟨**u-**⟩ (*-uję*) drape
drasnąć *v/s.* (*-nę*) scratch, scrape; *kula*: graze; *fig.* hurt, wound
drastyczny drastic
draśnięcie *n* (*-a*; *G -ć*) scratch
drażetka *f* (*-i*; *G -tek*) *med.* dragée
draż|liwość *f* (*-ści*; *0*) irritability; **~liwie** *adv.* irritably; **~liwy** irritable; touchy; *sytuacja* risky; **~niąco** *adv.*: **działać ~niąco** →; **~nić** (*-ę*, *-ń/-nij!*) irritate
drą → **drzeć**
drą|g *m* (*-a*; *-i*) pole, rod; **~żek** *m* (*-żka*; *-żki*) (*w sporcie*) horizontal bar, high bar; **na ~żkach ...** on the horizontal bar; **~żyć** ⟨**wy-**⟩ (*-żę*) hollow out; *tunel* bore
drelować → **drylować**
drelich *m* (*-u*; *-y*) drill, (*dżins*) denim; (*ubranie*) overalls *pl.*
dren *m* (*-u*;*-y*) *tech.* drain pipe; *med.* drain; **~ować** (*-uję*) drain
dreptać ⟨**po-**⟩ (*-czę/-cę*) toddle, patter
dres *m* (*-u*; *-y*) sweat suit, (*cieplejszy*) tracksuit
dreszcz *m* (*-u*; *-e*) shudder, shiver; **~e** *pl.* shivers; *fig.* F kick, buzz; **~yk** *m* (*-u*; *-i*) shiver, shudder; *fig.* F kick, buzz; **opowieść z ~ykiem** horror story
drew|niak *m* (*-a*; *-i*) timber house; (*but*) clog; **~niany** wooden (*też fig.*); **~nieć** ⟨**z-**⟩ (*-eję*) *fig.* stiffen; **~no** *n* (*-a*; *0*) wood; (*kawałek*) piece of wood
drę → **drzeć**; **~czący** tormenting, torturing; **~czyć** (*-ę*) torment, torture; **~czyć się** worry, agonize (*I* about)
drętw|ieć ⟨**o-, z-**⟩ (*-eję*) stiffen (**z zimna** from cold); *noga, ręka*: go numb, go to sleep; be paralysed (**na myśl** by the thought of); **~o** *adv. fig.* drearily, boringly; **~y** (*ścierpnięty*) numb; *fig.* dreary, dull
drg|ać (*-am*) tremble, shiver; (*nerwowo*) twitter, jerk; *urządzenie*: vibrate; **~ania** *n/pl.* (*-ń*) *phys.* vibrations *pl.*; **~awki** *f/pl.* (*-wek*) spasms *pl.*, convulsions *pl.*; **~nąć** *v/s.* (*-nę*) → **drgać**; **ani** (**nie**) **~nąć** not budge
drobiazg *m* (*-u*; *-i*) trifle; small thing, minor detail; **to ~!** don't mention it!; **~owość** *f* (*-ści*, *0*) pedantry, punctiliousness, **~owo** *adv.* pedantically, punctiliously; **~owy** pedantic, punctilious
drobi|ć ⟨**roz-**⟩ (*-ę*) *chleb* crumble, break into crumbs; (*nogami*) toddle; **~na** *f*

(*-y*) particle; *chem.*, *phys.* molecule
drobn|e *pl.* (*-ych*) small change; **~ica** *f* (*-y*; *0*) *econ.* general cargo; **~icowiec** *m* (*-wca*; *-wce*) *econ.* general cargo ship
D **drobno** *adv.* → **drobny**; **~mieszczański** petit(e) bourgeois; **~stka** *f* (*-i*; *G -tek*) trifle; small thing, minor detail; **~stkowy** pernickety, small-minded; **~ustrój** *m* microorganism; **~ziarnisty** fine, fine-grained
drobny small; petty; *szczegół* petty; (*miałki*) fine; (*delikatny*) delicate; → ***drobne, deszcz***
droczyć się F (*-ę*) (***z*** *I*) tease
droga¹ *adj. f* → **drogi**
drog|a² *f* (*-i*; *G dróg*) way (*też fig.*); (*szosa*) road; (*podróż*) journey; ***~a szybkiego ruchu*** expressway; ***~a startowa*** (take-off) runway; ***wybrać się w ~ę*** set off; ***zejść k-ś z ~i*** get out of s.o.'s way; ***~ą urzędową*** through the official channels; ***swoją ~ą*** at any rate, anyhow; ***po/w drodze*** on one's way; ***szczęśliwej ~i!*** have a good journey!
dro'geria *f* (*GDL -ii*; *-e*) *Brt.* chemist's (shop), *Am.* drugstore
drogi expensive; *fig. też* dear; *pl.* → **droga²**
drogo *adv.* expensively, dearly; **~cenny** precious, valuable
drogo|wskaz *m* (*-u*; *-y*) signpost; **~wy** road; traffic; ***kodeks ~wy*** rules of the road, *Brt.* Highway Code
drogówka F *f* (*-i*; *0*) traffic police
drozd *m* (*-a*; *-y*) *zo.* thrush
drożdż|e *pl.* (*-y*) yeast; **~owy** yeast
droż|eć ⟨**po-, z-**⟩ (*-eję*) get more expensive, go up; **~ej** *adv.* (*comp. od* → **drogo**), **~szy** *adj.* (*comp. od* → **drogi**) more expensive; **~yzna** *f* (*-y*; *0*) high prices *pl.*
drób *m* (*drobiu*; *0*) poultry
dró|g *G pl.* → **droga²**; **~żka** *f* (*-i*; *G -żek*) path; **~żnik** *m* (*-a*; *-cy*) *rail. Brt.* linesman, *Am.* trackman
druci|any wire; **~k** *f* (*-a*; *-i*) little wire
druczek *m* (*-czka*; *-czki*) form
drugi second; (*inny*) (the) other; (*z dwóch*) (the) latter; ***~e danie*** main course; ***co ~*** every second; ***po ~e*** secondly; ***~e tyle*** twice as much; ***jeden po/za ~m*** one after the other; ***po ~ej stronie*** on the other side; ***z ~ej strony*** on the other hand; ***z ~ej ręki*** second-hand; ***druga*** (***godzina***) two o'clock
drugo|planowy secondary; **~rzędny** second-rate;
druh *m* (*-a*; *-owie/-y*) friend; (*harcerz*) scout; **~na** *f* (*-y*; *G -hen*) (*na weselu*) bridesmaid; (*harcerka*) *jakby*: *Brt.* (Girl) Guide, *Am.* Girl Scout
druk *m* (*-u*; *0*) print; (*pl. -i*) form; (*na poczcie*) printed matter; ***wyjść ~iem*** appear in print
drukar|ka *f* (*-i*) printer; ***~ka igłowa/laserowa/atramentowa*** dot-matrix/laser/ink-jet printer; **~nia** *f* (*-ni*; *-e*) printing-works; (*firma*) printing-house; printer's; **~ski** print; ***błąd ~ski*** misprint
druk|arz *m* (*-a*; *-e*) printer; **~ować** (*-uję*) print
drut *m* (*-u*; *-y*) wire; **~y** *pl. też* knitting-needles *pl.*; ***robić na ~ach*** knit
druzgotać ⟨**z-**⟩ (*-czę/-cę*) crush, smash
druż|ba *m* (*-y*; *-owie*) best man; **~ka** *f* (*-i*; *G -żek*) bridesmaid
drużyn|a *f* (*-y*) (*w sporcie*) team; *mil.* squad; (*harcerzy*) troop; **~owo** *adv.* in a group, together; **~owy 1.** group, team; **2.** *m* (*-ego*; *-i*), **~owa** *f* (*-ej*; *-e*) Scouter, scout leader
drwa *pl.* (*drew*) wood
drwalnia *f* (*-i*; *-e*) wood-shed
drwi|ąco *adv.* sneeringly, mockingly; **~ący** sneering, mocking; **~ć** (*-ę*; *-ij!*) (***z*** *G*) sneer (at), mock (at); **~ny** *f/pl.* (-) sneer(ing), mocking
dryblas F *m* (*-a*; *-y*) beanpole, strapper
dryblować (*-uję*) (*w sporcie*) dribble (the ball)
dryfować (*-uję*) *v/i.* drift
dryl *m* (*-u*; *0*) *mil. zwł. pej.* drill, training
drylować (*-uję*) stone
drzazg|a *f* (*-i*) splinter; ***rozbić na/w ~i*** splinter, shatter
drzeć ⟨**po-**⟩ *v/t.* tear (to pieces); *ubranie* wear out; **~ się** *ubranie*: wear out; (*krzyczeć*) shout
drzem|ać (*-mię*) doze, snooze, nap; *fig.* lie dormant; **~ka** *f* (*-i*; *G -mek*) nap, snooze; ***~ka poobiednia*** after-lunch nap
drzew|ce *n* (*-a*) shaft; (*flagi*) pole, staff; **~ko** *n* (*-a*; *G -wek*) small tree; (*młode*) young tree; **~ny** tree, timber; **~o** *n* (*-a*) *bot.* tree; ***~o iglaste/liściaste/owocowe*** deciduous/coniferous/fruit tree; (*drewno*) wood; **~oryt** *m* (*-u*; *-y*): ***~oryt***

wzdłużny woodcut; **~*oryt sztorcowy*** wood engraving
drzwi *pl.* (*drzwi*) door; ***rozsuwane ~*** sliding door; **~ *oszklone/przeszklone*** French window; **~*ami*** through the door; ***przy ~ach zamkniętych*** *jur.* in camera; *fig.* behind closed doors; **~czki** *pl.* (*-czek*) (small) door; (*klapa*) (hinged) lid; **~owy** door
drże|ć (*-ę*) tremble, shiver, shake; **~nie** *n* (*-a*; *zw. 0*) tremble, shiver, shaking; *med.* tremor
d/s, d.s. *skrót pisany*: ***do spraw*** for
dubbing *m* (*-u*; *0*) dubbing; **~ować** (*-uję*) dub
dubeltówka *m* (*-i*; *G -wek*) double-barrelled shotgun
dubler *m* (*-a*; *-rzy*), **~ka** *f* (*-i*; *G -rek*) stand-in, (*w filmie też*) double
Dublin *m* (*-a/-u*; *0*) Dublin
dublować ⟨**z-**⟩ (*-uję*) double; *kogoś* stand in for; (*w sporcie*) lap
duch *m* (*-a*; *-y*) spirit, (*też zjawa*) ghost; (*odwaga*) spirit, mettle; **~ *czasu*** spirit of the age; ***wierzyć w ~y*** believe in ghosts; ***w ~u*** in spirit; ***nabrać ~a*** cheer up; ***podnieść k-ś na ~u*** cheer s.o. up
duchow|ieństwo *n* (*-a*; *0*) clergy; **~ny** **1.** spiritual, religious; **2.** *m* (*-ego*; *-i*) clergyman; **~o** *adv.* mentally, intellectually; **~y** mental, intellectual
dud|ka *f* (*-i*; *G -dek*) → ***fujarka***; **~nić** (*-ę*) *deszcz*: drum, batter; *grzmot*, *czołg*: rumble, grumble; **~y** *pl.* (*dud/dudów*) *mus.* bagpipes *pl.*
duet *m* (*-u*; *-y*) (*wokalny*) duet; (*instrumentalny*) duo
dum|a *f* (*-y 0*) pride; (*w Rosji*) duma; **~ać** (*-am*) (**o** *L*) think (of, about), muse (on), ponder (on); **~ka** *f* (*-i*; *G -mek*) (*romantic Ukrainian folk song*); **~ny** proud (**z** *G* of)
Du|naj *m* (*-u*; *0*) Danube; **~nka** *f* (*-i*; *G -nek*), **~ńczyk** *m* (*-a*; *-cy*) Dane; **≗ński** Danish; ***mówić po ≗ńsku*** speak Danish
dup|a V *f* (*-y*) *Brt.* arse, *Am.* ass; ***do ~y*** lousy, shitty
dur¹ *m* (*-u*; *0*) *med.* typhus; **~ *plamisty*** typhoid fever
dur² (*idkl.*) major; ***C-dur*** C major
dur|eń *m* (*-rnia*; *-rnie*, *-rni*[*ów*]) fool; **~ny** foolish, dense
durszlak *m* (*-a*; *-i*) → ***cedzak***
du|rzyć się (*-ę*) F have a crush (***w*** *L* on); **~sić** (*-szę*) ⟨**u-, za-**⟩ strangle, choke; *fig.* suppress, quell; *gastr.* ⟨**u-**⟩ stew; **~*sić się*** suffocate; *gastr.* stew
dusz|a *f* (*-y*; *-e*) soul (*też fig.*); *tech.* core; ***zrobiło jej się lekko na ~y*** a weight was lifted from her heart; ***czego ~a zapragnie*** everything one's heart desires; **~kiem** *adv.* *wypić* at one gulp; **~nica** *f* (*-y*; *-e*): **~*nica bolesna*** angina pectoris; **~ność** *f* (*-ści*) shortness of breath; **~ny** (*parny*) sultry, close; **~pasterski** pastoral; **~pasterz** *m* (*-a*; *-e*) priest
duż|o *adv.* much; many; **~y** big, large; *deszcz, mróz, zachmurzenie* heavy
dw. *skrót pisany*: ***dworzec*** Stn (*Station*)
dwa two; **~ *słowa*** a word or two; → ***715***; **~dzieścia** twenty; **~j** *m-os* two; **~naście** twelve
dwie *f/pl.* two; **~ście** two hundred
dwo|ić się (*-ję*; *dwój!*) → ***podwajać***; **~*i mi się w oczach*** I see everything double; **~isty** dual, double; **~jaczki** *m/pl.* (*-ów*) twins *pl.*; **~jaki** double, two different; **~jako** *adv.* doubly; **~je** two; ***jedno z ~jga*** one of the two; ***na ~je*** in two; ***za ~je*** for two
dwom *D* → ***dwa***
dwo|rcowy (railway) station; **~rski** court, courtly; **~ry, ~rze** → ***dwór***; **~rzec** *m* (*-rca*; *-rce*) station; **~*rzec lotniczy*** airport
dwóch *m-os* two
dwójk|a *f* (*-i*; *G -jek*) two; (*linia*) number two; (*łódź*) pair-oar, double-scull; (*ocena*) unsatisfactory; ***we ~ę*** in two; **~*ami*** two by two
dwójnasób: ***w ~*** doubly
dwóm *D* → ***dwa***
dwór *m* (*-oru*; *-ory*) (*królewski*) court, (*magnacki*) manor; ***na ~*** out, outdoors; ***na dworze*** in the open
dwu **1.** *m-os* two; **2.** *w zł.* two, double; **~aktówka** *f* (*-i*) two-act play; **~bój** *m* (*-boju*; *-boje*) biathlon; **~cyfrowy** two-figure, two-digit; **~częściowy** two-part; *ubiór* two-piece; **~daniowy** two-course; **~dniowy** two-day
dwudziest|ka (*-i*; *G -tek*) twenty; (*banknot*) twenty-zloty *itp.* note; (*linia*) number twenty; **~o-** *w zł.* twenty-; **~y**

twentieth; ***lata ~e*** the twenties
dwu|głoska *f* (*-i*) *gr.* diphthong; **~godzinny** two-hour (long); **~języczny** bilingual; **~kierunkowy** bidirectional; two-way; **~kropek** *m* (*-pka*; *-pki*) colon
dwukrotn|ie *adv.* twice, ***wzrosnąć ~ie*** grow twice as much; **~y** twofold
dwu|letni two-year-long, -old; ***roślina ~letnia*** biennial; **~licowy** duplicitous; **~mian** *m* (*-u*; *-y*) *math.* binomial; **~miejscowy** two-seat, for two people; **~miesięcznik** *m* (*-a*; *-i*) bimonthly; **~miesięczny** bimonthly
dwunast|ka *f* (*-i*; *G- tek*) twelve; (*linia*) number twelve; **~nica** *f* (*-y*; *-e*) duodenum; **~o-** *w zł.* twelve; **~y** twelfth; ***~a*** twelve (o'clock); → ***715***
dwu|nogi, ~nożny bipedal; **~osobowy** two-person; double; **~piętrowy** two-floor, two-stor(e)y; **~pokojowy** two-room
dwu|rodzinny two-family; **~rzędowy** double-breasted; **~rzędówka** F *f* (*-i*) double-breasted suit/coat/jacket; **~setny** two-hundredth; **~silnikowy** two-engine; **~stopniowy** two-stage; **~stronny** bilateral; two-sided; **~suwowy** *Brt.* two-stroke, *Am.* two-cycle; **~szereg** *m* (*-u*; *-i*) double-line; **~tlenek** *m* (*-nku*; *-nki*) dioxide; ***~tlenek węgla*** carbon dioxide; **~tomowy** two-volume; **~torowy** double-track, double-line; **~tygodnik** *m* (*-a*; *-i*) biweekly; **~tygodniowy** biweekly
dwuwęglan *m*: ***~ sodu*** sodium bicarbonate, bicarbonate of soda
dwu|wymiarowy two-dimensional; **~zakresowy** *RTV*: with two wavebands; **~zmianowy** two-shift; **~znaczny** ambiguous, equivocal; **~żeństwo** *n* (*-a*; *0*) bigamy
dybel *m* (*-bla*; *-ble*) dowel
dychawica *f* (*-y*; *-e*) asthma
dydaktyczny didactic
dyfteryt *m* (*-u*; *-y*) diphtheria
dygnitarz *m* (*-a*; *-e*) dignitary
dygotać (*-czę*/*-cę*) tremble, shiver (***z*** *G* from)
dykcja *f* (*-i*; *-e*) pronunciation
dykta *f* (*-y*) plywood
dykta|fon *m* (*-u*; *-y*) Dictaphone *TM*, dictating machine; **~ndo** *n* (*-a*; *G -nd*) dictation; ***pisać pod ~ndo*** take dictation; **~tor** *m* (*-a*; *-rzy*/*-owie*) dictator; **~tura** *f* (*-y*) dictatorship
dyktować (*-uję*) dictate
dyl *m* (*-a*; *-e*, *-i*/*ów*) floor-board; thick plank
dylemat *m* (*-u*; *-y*) dilemma
dyletanck|i dilettant, amateurish; ***po ~u*** in an amateurish way
dym *m* (*-u*; *-y*) smoke; ***pójść z ~em*** go up in smoke; ***puścić z ~em*** lay in ashes; ***rozwiać się jak ~*** *fig.* go up in smoke; **~ić** (*-ę*) smoke; ***~ić się*** be smoking
dymisj|a *f* (*-i*; *-e*) *komuś* dismissal; (*własna*) resignation; ***udzielić ~i*** (*D*) dismiss; ***podać się do ~i z*** resign from; **~onować** dismiss; **~onowany** retired, in retirement
dymny smoke
dynamiczny dynamic
dy'nastia *f* (*GDL -ii*; *-e*) dynasty; house
dynia *f* (*-i*; *-e*) *bot.* pumpkin
dyplom *m* (*-u*; *-y*) diploma, certificate; (*wyższej szkoły*) degree; **~acja** *f* (*-i*; *0*) diplomacy; **~ata** *m* (*-y*; *-ci*), **~atka** *f* (*-i*) diplomat; **~atyczny** diplomatic; **~owany** qualified; **~owy** degree, diploma
dyr. *skrót pisany*: ***dyrektor*** dir. (*director*)
dyrek|cja *f* (*-i*; *-e*) management, administration; **~tor** *m* (*-a*; *-rzy*/*-owie*), **~torka** *f* (*-i*) director, manager; (*szkoły*) head teacher; **~torski** director's; **~tywa** *f* (*-y*) directive, instruction
dyrygent *m* (*-a*; *-ci*) conductor
dyrygować (*-uję*) conduct
dyscyplina *f* (*-y*) discipline; **~rny** disciplinary
dysertacja *f* (*-i*; *-e*) dissertation, thesis
dysfunkcja *f* (*-i*; *-e*) malfunction
dysk *m* (*-u*; *-i*) *Brt.* disc, *Am.* disk; ***~ twardy*** *komp.* hard disk; (*w sporcie*) discus; ***rzut ~iem*** the discus
dyskietka *f* (*-i*; *G -tek*) floppy disk, diskette
dyskobol *m* (*-a*; *-e*), **~ka** *f* (*-i*) discus thrower
dys|komfort *m* (*-u*; *0*) discomfort, uneasiness; **~konto** *n* (*-a*) discount; **~kontowy** discount
dyskotek|a *f* (*-i*) discotheque, F disco; **~owy**: ***muzyka ~owa*** disco music
dyskre|cja *f* (*-i*; *0*) discretion; **~dytować** ⟨**z-**⟩ (*-uję*) discredit

dyskrymin|acja *f* (*-i*; *0*) discrimination; **~ować** (*-uję*) discriminate
dysku|sja *f* (*-i*; *-e*) discussion, debate; ***poddać ~sji/pod ~się*** put forward to discussion; **~syjny** controversial, debatable; **~tować** ⟨***prze-***⟩ (*-uję*) discuss
dyskwalifik|acja *f* (*-i*; *-e*) disqualification; **~ować** ⟨***z-***⟩ (*-uję*) disqualify
dysponować (*-uję*) have at one's disposal
dyspozy|cja *f* (*-i*; *-e*) right of disposal; ***mieć do ~cji*** have at one's disposal
dysproporcja *f* (*-i*; *-e*) disproportion, disparity
dystans *m* (*-u*; *-e*) distance; ***trzymać na ~*** keep at long range
dystrybu|cja *f* (*-i*; *0*) distribution; **~tor** *m* (*-a*; *-y*) *mot. Brt.* petrol-pump, *Am.* gas(oline) pump
dystynkcje *f/pl.* (*-i*) insignia (of rank)
dysydent *m* (*-a*; *-ci*), **~ka** *f* (*-i*) dissident
dysz|a *f* (*-y*; *-e*) nozzle, jet; **~eć** (*-ę*, *-y*) pant, puff
dyszel *m* (*-szla*, *-szle*) pole
dywan *m* (*-u*; *-y*) carpet
dywersja *f* (*-i*; *-e*) sabotage
dywidenda *f* (*-y*) dividend
dywiz|ja *f* (*-i*; *-e*) *mil.* division; **~jon** *m* (*-u*; *-y*) *aviat.*, *naut.* squadron
dyżur *m* (*-u*; *-y*) duty; ***~ nocny*** night duty; **~ny 1.** *adj.* duty; on duty; ***~na zupa*** soup of the day; ***~ny temat*** current topic; **2.** *m* (*-ego*; *-i*), **~na** *f* (*-ej*; *-e*) duty officer, (*w szkole*) monitor; ***~ny ruchu*** *rail.* train controller; **~ować** (*-uję*) be on duty
dz. *skrót pisany*: ***dzień*** d. (*day*); ***dziennie*** dly (*daily*); ***dziennik*** J. (*journal*)
dzban *m* (*-a*; *-y*) jug, (*wiekszy lub Am.*) pitcher; ***~ gliniany*** clay jug; **~ek** *m* (*-nka*; *-nki*) pot, jug
dziać[1] (*dzieję*; *dział*) knit
dziać[2] **się** (*t-ko 3. os. dzieje*, *działo się*) go on, happen, be; be the matter (***z*** *I* with); ***co się tu dzieje?*** what's going on here?
dziad *m* (*-a*, *-dzie/-du!*; *-y*) beggar; (*starzec*) old man; *pej.* chap, bloke; (*pl. -owie*) → **~ek** *m* (*-dka*; *-dkowie*) grandfather; F grandpa; *pl.* grandfathers *pl.*, grandparents *pl.*; ***~ek do orzechów*** nutcracker; **~owski** trashy, poor; (*nędzny*) pitiful; dreadful, appalling; **~y** *pl.* (*-ów*) *hist.* memorial service
dział *m* (*-u*; *-y*) department, section (*też część czasopisma*); (*część własności*) share; ***~ kadr*** personnel department; ***~ wód*** watershed
działacz *m* (*-a*; *-e*) activist; ***~ partyjny*** cadre-party member; ***~ polityczny*** politician; ***~ rewolucyjny*** professional revolutionist; ***~ ruchu robotniczego*** workers' leader; **~ka** *f* (*-i*) activist; → ***działacz***; ***~ka społeczna*** socially committed woman; ***~ka podziemia*** underground fighter
działa|ć (*-am*) function, work, operate; (*oddziaływać*) act; ⟨***po-***⟩ have an effect; ***~ć na nerwy*** get on one's nerves; **~lność** *f* (*-ci*; *0*) activity; **~nie** *n* (*-a*) operating, functioning, working; effect; *mil.* operation; → ***arytmetyczny***
działk|a *f* (*-i*; *G -łek*) plot (of land); (*ogródek*) small garden, *Brt.* allotment; **~owicz** *m* (*-a*; *-e*), **~owiczka** *f* (*-i*) allotment-holder
działo[1] *n* (*-a*) gun
działo[2] **się** → ***dziać się***
działow|y: ***ścianka ~a*** partition
dzia|nina *f* (*-y*) (*tkanina*) jersey; (*ubiór*) jersey clothes *pl.*; **~ny** knitted
dziarsk|i hale (and hearty); robust, vigorous; **~o** *adv.* robustly, vigorously
dziąsło *m* (*-a*) *anat.* gum
dzicz *f* (*-y*; *0*) (*miejsce*) wilderness, back country; *fig. zbior.* (*ludzie*) mob, rabble; **~eć** ⟨***z-***⟩ (*-eję*) go wild; *fig.* brutalize; **~yzna** *f* (*-y*; *0*) venison, game
dzida *f* (*-y*) spear
dzie|ci *pl.* → ***dziecko***; **~ciak** *m* (*-a*; *-i*) child, F kid; **~ciarnia** *f* (*-i*; *0*) *zbior.* children *pl.*; **~ciątko** *n* (*-a*; *G -tek*) baby; ***Ƨciątko Jezus*** Baby Jesus; **~cięco** like a child; **~cięcy** children's; childlike; **~cinada** *f* (*-y*; *0*) childish behavio(u)r; **~cinny** → ***dziecięcy***; *fig.* childish; ***po ~cinnemu*** like a child; **~ciństwo** *n* (*-a*; *0*) childhood; **~ciobójstwo** *n* (*-a*) child murder, (*własnego*) infanticide; **~ciuch** F *m* (*-a*; *-y*) child; **~cko** *n* (*-a*; *dzieci*, *I*) child; ***od ~cka*** from childhood
dziedzi|c *m* (*-a*; *-e*) heir; *hist.* squire; **~ctwo** *n* (*-a*; *0*) heritage, inheritance; **~czka** *f* (*-i*; *G -czek*) heiress; *hist.* lady of the manor; **~czny** hereditary; **~czyć** ⟨***o-***⟩ (*-czę*) inherit (***po*** *L* from)
dziedzina *f* (*-y*) domain, area, field
dziedziniec *m* (*-ńca*; *-ńce*) courtyard

dziegieć *m* (*-gciu*; *0*) tar
dzieje *pl.* (*-ów*) history, *fig.* story; **~ się** → **dziać się**
dziejowy historical, (*przełomowy*) historic
D
dziekan *n* (*-a*; *-i*) dean; (*dyplomatów*) doyen; **~at** *m* (*-u*; *-y*) dean's office
dziel|enie *n* (*-a*; *0*) division (*też math.*); **~ić** ⟨**po-, roz-**⟩ (*-lę*) divide (*też math.* **przez** by, **się**); share (out) (**między** *A* among, between); (*rozdzielać*) separate; **~ić** ⟨**po-**⟩ **się** (*I*) share; (*sekretami*) confide (**z kimś** in s.o.); *math.* be divisible; **~na 1.** *f* (*-ej*; *-e*) *math.* dividend; **2.** → **dzielny**
dziel|nica *f* (*-y*; *-e*) region, province; (*miasta*) district, part; **~nicowy** regional, provincial; district; **~nie** → **dzielny**; **~nik** *m* (*-a*; *-i*) *math.* divisor; **~ność** *f* (*-ści*; *0*) bravery, boldness; **~ny** brave, bold
dzieł|o *n* (*-a*) work; ⟨**za**⟩**brać się/przystąpić do ~a** set to work
dzien|nie daily; (*na dzień*) a day; **~nik** *m* (*-a*; *-i*) (*gazeta*) daily; (*pamiętnik*) diary; (*wiadomości*) news; **~nik urzędowy** official gazette; **~nik klasowy** *jakby*: class-register; **~nikarka** *f* (*-i*; *G -rek*), **~nikarz** *m* (*-a*; *-e*, *-y*) journalist; **~ny** daily; (*w ciągu dnia*) daytime
dzień *m* (*dnia*; *dni/dnie*, *G dni*) day; **~ świąteczny** holiday, (*religijny*) feast-day; **~ dobry!** hello!; **~ w ~, ~ po dniu** day after day; **za dnia** in daylight; **z dnia na ~** from one day to the next; **w ciągu dnia** during the day (time); **co** (**drugi**) **~** every other day; **na drugi ~** next day; **do dziś dnia** until today
dzierżaw|a *f* (*-y*) lease, tenancy; **~ca** *f* (*-y*) leaseholder, tenant; **~czy** leasing; *gr.* possessive; **~czyni** *f* (*-*, *-e*) leaseholder, tenant; **~ić** ⟨**wy-**⟩ (*-ę*) lease, rent; **~ne** *n* (*-ego*; *0*) rent; **~ny**: **czynsz ~ny** rent; **umowa ~na** lease contract
dzierżyć (*-ę*) wield, hold
dziesiąt|ek *m* (*-tka*; *-tki*) decade; *też* → **~ka** *f* (*-tki*; *G -tek*) ten; (*linia*) number ten; (*banknot itp.*) F tenner; **~kować** ⟨**z-**⟩ (*-uję*) decimate; **~y** tenth; **jedna ~a** a tenth
dziesięcio|- *w zł.* deca-, ten-; **~boista** *m* (*-y*; *-ści*, *-ów*) decathlete; **~krotny** tenfold; **~lecie** *n* (*-a*) tenth anniversary
dziesię|ć, *m-os* **~ciu** ten → **715**; **~ćkroć** *adv.* tenfold; **~tnik** *m* (*-a*; *-cy*) *hist.* decurion; **~tny** decimal
dziewcz|ę *n* (*-ęcia*; *-ęta*) girl; **~ęco** *adv.* girlishly; **~ęcy** girlish; **~yna** *f* (*-y*) girl; **~czynka** *f* (*-i*) little girl
dziewiąt|ka *f* (*-i*; *G -tek*) nine; (*linia*) number nine; **~y** ninth → **715**
dziewica *f* (*-y*; *-e*) virgin
dziewiczy virginal, virgin (*też fig.*)
dziewięcio|- *w zł.* nine, **~krotny** ninefold; **~letni** nine-year-long, -old
dziewię|ć *m-os*; **~ciu** nine → **715**; **~ćdziesiąt** ninety; **~ćset** nine hundred; **~tnastka** *f* (*-i*; *G -tek*) nineteen; (*linia*) number nineteen; **~tnasto-** *w zł.* nineteen; **~tnaście** nineteen → **715**
dziewucha *f* (*-y*) girl, *żart.* wench
dzieża *f* (*-y*; *-e*) kneading trough
dzięcioł *m* (*-a*; *-y*) *zo.* woodpecker
dzięk|czynny thankful, thank-you; **~i 1.** *pl.* thanks *pl.* (**za** *A* for); **2.** *prp.* thanks (to); **~i Bogu** thank God!; **~ować** ⟨**po-**⟩ (*-uję*) thank (**k-u za** *A* s.o. for)
dzik *m* (*-a*; *-i*) *zo.* wild boar (*też odyniec*); **~i** wild; *fig.* (*dziwny*) odd, peculiar; **~o** *adv.* wildly; *fig.* (*dziwnie*) oddly, peculiarly; **~us** *m* (*-a*; *-y*), **-ska** *f* (*-i*; *G -sek*) savage
dziob|ać (*-ię*), ⟨**~nąć**⟩ (*-nę*) peck; **~aty** pock-marked; **~y** *pl.* → **dziób**
dziób *m* (*-obu/-oba*; *-oby*) bill; (*drapieżcy*) beak; (*statku*) bow, (*samolotu*) nose; F gob; **dzioby** *pl.* (*na twarzy*) pock-marks
dzi|siaj → **dziś**; **~siejszy** today's; contemporary; **po dzień ~siejszy** until the present day; **~ś 1.** *adv.* today; **2.** *n* (*idkl.*) today; **~ś rano** this morning; **od ~ś** from now on; **na ~ś** for today
dziupla *f* (*-i*; *-e*) hollow
dziura *f* (*-y*) hole; (*w zębie*) cavity; F (*miejsce*) dump, hole; **~wić** ⟨**prze-**⟩ (*-ę*) puncture, pierce, perforate; **~wy** full of holes (*też fig.*); *garnek* broken
dziur|ka *f* (*-i*; *G -rek*) hole; **~ka od klucza** keyhole; **~ka na guzik** buttonhole; **~kacz** *m* (*-a*; *-e*) punch; **~kować** (*-uję*) punch; perforate
dziw *m* (*-u*; *-y*) wonder, (*natury itp.*) curio; **nie ~** no wonder; **~actwo** *n* (*-a*) oddity; **~aczeć** ⟨**z-**⟩ (*-eję*) become odd; **~aczka** *f* (*-i*; *G -czek*) eccentric,

F oddity; **~aczny** odd, eccentric; **~ak** *m* (*-a*; *-cy*/*-i*) eccentric, F oddity; **~ić** ⟨**z-**, **za-**⟩ (*-ę*) surprise, astonish; ***~ić*** ⟨**z-**⟩ **się** (*D*) be surprised (**z** *A* at)
dziwka *f* (*-i*; *G -wek*) *pej.* slut
dziwn|y strange, odd; ***~a rzecz*** strangely enough; ***nic ~ego, że*** no wonder that
dziwo *n* (*-a*) → ***dziw***; **~ląg** *m* (*-a*; *-i*) freak, curiosity
DzU, Dz.U *skrót pisany*: ***Dziennik Urzędowy*** (*law gazette*)
dzwon *m* (*-u*; *-y*) bell; **~ek** *m* (*-nka*; *-nki*) bell; (*dźwięk*) ringing; *bot.* bellflower, campanula; **~ić** ⟨***za-***⟩ (*-ę*) ring (the bell); (*szkłem itp.*) clink; F (**do** *G*) call, *Brt.* ring up; **~ko** *n* (*-a*; *G -nek*) slice (***śledzia*** of herring); **~nica** *f* (*-y*; *-e*) belfry
dźwię|czeć ⟨***za-***⟩ (*-czę*) sound; ring; **~czny** *głos* sonorous; *gr.* voiced; **~k** *m* (*-u*; *-i*) sound; *mus.* tone; ***barwa ~ku*** tone colo(u)r; ***zapis ~ku*** sound recording; **~koszczelny** soundproof; **~kowy** *ścieżka*, *film*: sound
dźwig *m* (*-u*; *-i*) (*winda*) *Brt.* lift, *Am.* elevator; *tech.* crane; **~ać** (*-am*) *impf.* lift up; (*nosić*) carry; **~ar** *m* (*-a*/*-u*; *-y*) supporting beam; **~nąć** *pf.* lift (up); ***~nąć z gruzów*** rebuild; ***~nąć się*** rise up; **~nia** *f* (*-i*; *-e*) *tech.* lever; **~owy 1.** *adj.* crane; lift, elevator; **2.** *m* (*-ego*; *-i*), **~owa** *f* (*-ej*; *-e*) crane-operator
dżdż|ownica *f* (*-y*; *-e*) *zo.* earthworm; **~u** → ***deszcz***; **~ysty** rainy
dżem *m* (*-u*; *-y*) jam; (*z cytrusów*) marmalade
dżentelmen *m* (*-a*; *-i*) gentleman
dżersej *m* (*-u*; *-e*) jersey
dżez → ***jazz***
dżins|owy denim, jean; **~y** *pl.* (*-ów*) jeans
dżokej *m* (*-a*; *-e*) jockey
dżul *m* (*-a*; *-e*) *phys.* joule
dżuma *f* (*-y*; *0*) *med.* (bubonic) plague
dżungla *f* (*-i*; *-e*) jungle

E

echo *f* (*-a*) echo; *fig.* response, repercussions *pl.*; **~sonda** *f* (*-y*) echo-sounder; sonic depth finder
Edynburg *m* (*-a*; *0*) Edinburgh
edukac|ja *f* (*-i*; *0*) education; **~cyjny** educational
edycja *f* (*-i*; *-e*) edition
efek|ciarstwo *f* (*-a*; *0*) showiness, flashiness; **~t** *m* (*-u*; *-y*) effect; (*skutek*) result, outcome; ***zrobić wielki ~t na*** leave a great impression on; **~towny** effective; **~tywny** efficient, effective
egi|da *f* (*-y*; *0*): ***pod ~dą*** (*G*) under the auspices of
Egipcjan|in *m* (*-a*; *-nie*, *-*), **~ka** *f* (*-i*) Egyptian
egipski (***po -ku***) Egyptian
Egipt *m* (*-u*; *0*) Egypt
egoist|a *m* (*-y*; *-ści*), **~ka** *f* (*-i*) egoist; **~yczny** egoistic(al)
egz. *skrót pisany*: ***egzemplarz*** co. (*copy*)
egzaltowany affected, pretentious
egzamin *m* (*-u*; *-y*) examination, F exam; ***~ z polskiego*** examination in Polish, ***~ na prawo jazdy*** driving test; ***~ wstępny*** entrance examination; → ***zda***(***wa***)***ć***; **~acyjny** examination; **~ować** (*-uję*) examine
egzekuc|ja *f* (*-i*; *-e*) execution; **~yjny** *nakaz itp.* enforcement; ***pluton ~yjny*** firing squad
egzekwować ⟨***wy-***⟩ (*-uję*) (*wymagać*) demand, insist on; (*wykonywać*) extort, exact
egzema (*-y*) *med.* eczema
egzemplarz *m* (*-a*; *-e*) copy; ***w trzech ~ach*** in three copies
egzotyczny exotic
egzys|tencja *f* (*-i*; *-e*) existence; ***minimum ~tencji*** subsistence level; **~tować** (*-uję*) (*istnieć*) exist; (*utrzymywać się*) subsist
ekierka *f* (*-i*; *G -rek*) set square
ekipa *f* (*-y*) team; (*pracowników*) crew
ekler *m* (*-a*; *-y*) *gastr.* éclair; (*zamek*) zip (fastener); **~ka** *f* (*-i*) *gastr.* éclair
ekologi|a *f* (*GDL -ii*; *0*) ecology; **~czny** ecological
ekonomi|a *f* (*GDL -ii*; *0*) economy; (*nauka*) economics; → ***oszczędność***; **~czny** economic; (*oszczędny*) economical; **~ka** *f* (*-i*; *0*) economics; manage-

ment; **~ka przedsiębiorstwa** business management
ekonomist|a *m* (*-y*; *-ści*), **~ka** *f* (*-i*) economist
eko|system *m* (*-u*; *-y*) ecosystem; **~turystyka** *f* ecotourism
ekran *m* (*-u*; *-y*) screen (*też RTV*); *tech.* shield; **~ kinowy** cinema screen; **szeroki ~** wide screen; **~izacja** *f* (*-i*; *-e*) filming (**powieści** of a novel)
eks|- *w zł.* ex-, former; **~centryczny** eccentric; **~cesy** *m/pl.* (*-ów*) act of violence *pl.*, disturbances *pl.*; **~humacja** *f* (*-i*; *-e*) exhumation, disinterment; **~kluzywny** exclusive; (*luksusowy*) luxurious; **~komunikować** (*-uję*) excommunicate; **~misja** *f* (*-i*; *-e*) eviction; **~mitować** (*-uję*) evict; **~pansja** *f* (*-i*; *0*) expansion; **~patriacja** *f* (*-i*; *-e*) expatriation; **~patriować** (*-uję*) expatriate
ekspedient *m* (*-a*; *-ci*), **~ka** *f* (*-i*) (shop) assistant
eksped|iować ⟨**wy-**⟩ (*-uję*) ship, dispatch, forward; **~ycja** *f* (*-i*; *-e*) expedition; (*towar*) shipment; **~ycja bagażowa** dispatch office; **~ycyjny** expeditionary; dispatch
ekspert *m* (*-a*; *-ci*) expert, specialist, authority; **~yza** *f* (*-y*) expert opinion, expert's report
eksperyment|alny experimental; **~ować** (*-uję*) experiment
eksploat|acja *f* (*-i*; *-e*) use; utilisation; exploitation; *górnictwo*: mining; **być w ~acji** be in use; **oddać do ~acji** put into service; **~ować** (*-uję*) use; utilize; *ludzi* exploit
eksplozja *f* (*-i*; *-e*) explosion
ekspon|at *m* (*-u*; *-y*) exhibit, display item; **~ować** ⟨**wy-**⟩ (*-uję*) display, exhibit; (*podkreślać*) make prominent
eksport *m* (*-u*; *0*) export; **na ~** to be exported; **~ować** ⟨**wy-**⟩ (*-uję*) export; **~owy** export
ekspozy|cja *f* (*-y*; *-e*) exposition, display; **~tura** *f* (*-y*) branch office, agency
ekspres *m* (*-u*; *-y*) (*pociąg itp.*) express; (*pocztowy*) special delivery; **~ do kawy** coffee-maker; **~owy** express; **herbata ~owa** tea bags
ekstaza *f* (*-y*) ecstasy, rapture
eksterminacja *f* (*-i*; *0*) extermination
ekstra (*idkl.*) extra; F first-class, great; **~dycja** *f* (*-i*; *-e*) extradition
ekstrakt *m* (*-u*; *-y*) extract
ekstrawagancki extravagant
ekstrem|alny extreme; **~ista** *m* (*-y*; *-ści*), **~istka** *f* (*-i*) extremist
ekwi|punek *m* (*-nku*; *0*) equipment, gear, outfit; **~walent** *f* (*-u*; *-y*) equivalent
elastyczn|ość *f* (*-ci*; *0*) elasticity; *fig.* flexibility; **~y** elastic; *fig.* flexible
elegan|cki elegant; **~tować się** ⟨**wy-się**⟩ F (*-uję*) doll up, dress up
elektor *m* (*-a*; *-rzy*) elector (*też hist.*); **~at** *m* (*-u*; *zw. 0*) electorate; voters *pl.*; **~ski** electoral
elektro|ciepłownia *f* (*-i*; *-e*) heat and power plant; **~da** *f* (*-y*) electrode; **~kardiogram** *m* (*-u*; *-y*) electrocardiogram; **~liza** *f* (*-y*; *0*) electrolysis; **~magnes** *m* (*-u*; *-y*) electromagnet; **~mechanik** *m* (*-a*; *-cy*) electrical engineer; **~monter** *m* (*-a*; *-rzy*) electrician; **~niczny** electronic; **poczta ~niczna** e-mail, email; **~nowy** electron, electronic; **~technika** *f* (*-i*; *0*) electrical engineering
elektrownia *f* (*-i*; *-e*) power station; **~ cieplna/wodna** thermal/hydroelectric power station
elektrowóz *m* (*-wozu*; *-wozy*) electric locomotive
elektry|czność *f* (*-ci*; *0*) electricity; **~czny** electric; **~k** *m* electrician; **inżynier ~k** electrical engineer; **~zować** ⟨**na-, z-**⟩ (*-uję*) electrify
element *m* (*-u*; *-y*) element, component; F shady elements *pl.*; **~y** *pl.* elements *pl.*, rudiments *pl.*
elementarz *m* (*-a*; *-e*) primer
elewa|cja *f* (*-i*; *-e*) façade, frontage; **~tor** *m* (*-a*; *-y*) elevator (*zwł. Am.*), grain silo
eliminac|ja *f* (*-i*; *-e*) elimination; (*w sporcie*) qualifier, qualifying round; **~yjny** qualifying
eliminować ⟨**wy-**⟩ (*-uję*) eliminate; (*wyłączać*) exclude
elip|sa *f* (*-y*) ellipsis; **~tyczny** elliptical
elita *f* (*-y*) élite; **~rny** elitist, select
emali|a *f* (*GDL -ii*; *-e*) enamel; **~owany** enamel(l)ed
emancyp|antka *f* (*-i*) woman emancipation activist, suffragist; **~ować się** ⟨**wy- się**⟩ (*-uję*) emancipate o.s.
emblemat *m* (*-u*; *-y*) emblem
embrion *m* (*-a/-u*; *-y*) embryo

ementalski: ***ser ~*** Emmenthal(er)
emeryt *m* (*-a*; *-ci*), **~ka** *f* (*-i*) old-age pensioner; retired person; **~owany** retired; **~ura** *f* (*-y*) retirement; (*pieniądze*) pension; ***wcześniejsza ~ura*** early retirement; ***przejść na ~urę*** retire; ***pobierać ~urę*** receive pension
emigr|acja *f* (*-i*; *-e*) emigration; ***na ~acji*** in exile; **~acyjny** émigré; in exile; **~ować** (*im*)*pf* ⟨**wy-**⟩ (*-uję*) emigrate
emi|sja *f* (*-i*; *-e*) (*znaczków itp.*) issue; (*gazów itp.*) emission; (*radiowa lub telewizyjna* broadcast; **~tować** (*-uję*) emit
emocja *f* (*-i*; *-e*) emotion
emocjonalny emotional
emocjonujący (**-*co***) exciting
emulsja *f* (*-i*; *-e*) emulsion; (*kosmetyk*) lotion
encyklika *f* (*-i*) *rel.* encyclical
encykloped|ia *f* (*GDL -ii*; *-e*) *Brt.* encyclopaedia, *Am.* encyclopedia; **~yczny** encyclopedic
energety|czny energy; ***surowce*** *m/pl.* ***~czne*** energy sources *pl.*; **~ka** *f* (*-i*; *0*) energy sector; (*przemysł*) power industry
energi|a *f* (*GDL -ii*; *0*) energy; power; **~czny** energetic
energo|chłonny energy-consuming; **~oszczędny** energy-saving
entuzja|styczny enthusiastic; **~zmować się** (*-uję*) (*I*) be enthusiastic about
epatować (*-uję*) impress, amaze
epi|cki (**-*ko***), **~czny** epic
epi|demia *f* (*GDL -ii*; *-e*) epidemic; **~lepsja** *f* (*-i*; *-e*) epilepsy
episkopat *m* (*-u*; *-y*) episcopate
epi|tafium *n* (*pl. -fia*, *-fiów*) epitaph; memorial plaque; **~tet** *m* (*-u*; *-y*) epithet; F epithet, abusive word
epizod *m* (*-u*; *-y*) episode
epo|ka *f* (*-i*) epoch, age, time; ***~ka kamienna*** Stone Age; **~kowy** historic, epoch-making; **~peja** *f* (*-ei*; *-e*, *-ei*) epic, epos
era *f* (*-y*) era; ***naszej ery*** AD, ***przed naszą erą*** BC
erekcja *f* (*-i*; *-e*) erection
eremita *m* (*-y*; *-ci*) hermit
erka F *f* (*-i*; *-rek*) emergency ambulance
eroty|ka *f* (*-i*; *0*) eroticism; **~czny** erotic
erudycja *f* (*-i*; *0*) erudition
erupcja *f* (*-i*; *-e*) eruption
esej *m* (*-u*; *-e*, *-ów*) essay
esencja *f* (*-i*; *-e*) essence; (*herbaciana*) brew
eskadra *f* (*-y*) *aviat.* flight; *naut.* squadron
eskalacja *f* (*-i*; *0*) escalation
Eskimos *m* (*-a*; *-i*), **~ka** *f* (*-i*) Eskimo; **&ki** Eskimo
eskort|a *f* (*-y*) escort; ***pod ~ą*** under escort; **~ować** (*-uję*) escort
estetyczny esthetic, *Brt.* aesthetic
Esto|nia *f* (*GDL -ii*; *0*) Estonia; **~nka** *f* (*-i*); **~ńczyk** *m* (*-a*; *-cy*) Estonian; **&ński** (***po -ku***) Estonian
estrad|a *f* (*-y*) platform, podium, dais; **~owy** cabaret
etap *m* (*-u*; *-y*) stage; (*podróży*) leg; **~owo** by stages
eta|t *m* (*-u*; *-y*) permanent position, full-time job; ***pracować na pół ~tu*** work part-time; ***być na ~cie*** have a full-time job; have a permanent position; **~towy** permanent, regular
etażerka *f* (*-i*; *G -rek*) shelf unit
eter *m* (*-u*; *0*) *chem.*, *phys.* ether; ***na falach ~u*** on the air
Etiop|czyk *m* (*-a*; *-cy*) Ethiopian; **~ia** *f* (*GDL -ii*) Ethiopia; **&ski** Ethiopian
etiuda *f* (*-y*) *mus.* etude
etniczny ethnic
ety|czny ethical; **~kieta** *f* (*-y*), **~kietka** *f* (*-i*; *G -tek*) label
etylina *f* (*-y*) *Brt.* leaded petrol, *Am.* ethyl gasoline
eukaliptus *m* (*-a*; *-y*) *bot.* eucalyptus; **~owy** eucalyptus
euroczek *m* (*-u*; *-i*) *Brt.* Eurocheque, *Am.* Eurocheck
Europa *f* (*-y*; *0*) Europe
Europej|czyk *m* (*-a*; *-cy*), **~ka** *f* (*-i*) European; **&ski** European
ewakuac|ja *f* (*-i*; *-e*) evacuation; **~yjny** evacuation
ewakuować (*-uuję*) evacuate
ewan'geli|a *f* (*GDl -ii*; *-e*) (*rel.* &) Gospel; **~cki** Protestant
ewenement *m* (*-u*; *-y*) sensation
ew(ent). *skrót pisany*: ***ewentualnie*** alternatively
ewentual|ność *f* (*-ci*; *0*) eventuality; **~ny** possible; ***~nie*** *adv. też* if applicable, if possible
ewidencja *f* (*-i*; *-e*) registration; (*wykaz*) record(s *pl.*)
ewidencjonować (*-uję*)register;record
ewolucja *f* (*-i*; *-e*) evolution

E

F

fabryczny factory
'fabryka *f* (*-i*) factory; works *sg.*
fabrykować (*-uję*) fabricate
fabularny: ***film ~*** feature film
facet F *m* (*-a*; *-ci*) guy, fellow; **~ka** *f* (*-i*) *pej.* female
fach *m* (*-u*; *-y*) trade; ***kolega po ~u*** fellow-worker by trade; professional colleague; **~owiec** *m* (*-wca*; *-wcy*) F fixer, repairman; (*ekspert*) specialist, expert; **~owy** professional; expert
facjata *f* (*-y*) attic (room); F (*twarz*) gob
faja F *f* (*GDL -fai*; *-e*, *-*) pipe
fajansowy faience; earthenware
fajdać F ⟨**za-**⟩ (*-am*) shit
fajerwerk *m* (*-u*; *-i*) firework; **~i** *pl.* (*pokaz*) fireworks *pl.*
fajk|a *f* (*-i*) pipe; F (*papieros*) fag; (*znaczek*) *Brt.* tick, *Am.* check; **~owy** pipe
fajny F (**-no, -nie**) super, great
fajtłapa *m/f* (*-y*; *G f*: *-/m*: *-ów*) bungler, duffer
faks *m* (*-u*; *-y*) fax; **~ować** fax
fak|t *m* (*-u*; *-y*) fact; ***~t ~tem*** it is true; ***po ~cie*** afterwards, belatedly; **~tura** *f* (*-y*) *econ.* invoice, bill; **~tyczny** actual; ***stan ~tyczny*** facts of the matter
fakultatywny optional
fakultet *m* (*-u*; *-y*) faculty
fal|a *f* (*-i*; *-e*) wave (*też phys.*, *fig.*); *fig.* flood; ***~a zimna*** cold wave; ***~e*** *pl.* ***średnie*** medium waves *pl.*; ***~ami*** in waves
falban|a *f* (*-y*), **~ka** *f* (*-i*; *G -nek*) frill
falisty *ruch*, *linia*, *włosy* wavy; (**-ście, -to**) *ruch* wavelike
falo|chron *m* (*-u*; *-y*) breakwater; **~wać** (*-uję*) *morze*, *tłum*: surge; *zboże*: wave; **~wanie** *n* (*-a*) surge, waving
falstart *m* (*-u*; *-y*) (*w sporcie*) false start
falsyfikat *m* (*-u*; *-y*) fake, forgery
fałd *m* (*-u*; *-y*), **~a** *f* (*-y*) fold; **~ować** ⟨**po-, s-**⟩ (*-uję*) fold
fałsz *m* (*-u*; *-e*) (*kłamstwo*) falsity, falsehood; (*obłuda*) falseness; **~erka** *f* (*-i*; *G -rek*) forger; counterfeiter; **~erstwo** *n* (*-a*; *G -tw*) forgery; **~erz** *m* (*-a*; *-e*) forger; counterfeiter
fałszowa|ć ⟨**s-**⟩ (*-uję*) forge, counterfeit; *fakty* falsify; *melodię* sing/play out of tune; **~ny** counterfeit, forged
fałszyw|ość *f* (*-ci*; *0*) (*cecha*) duplicity; (*stan*) falseness; **~y** (**-wie**) false
fanaty|czny fanatic(al); **~czka** *f* (*-i*; *G -czek*), **~k** *m* (*-a*; *-cy*) fanatic
fanfara *f* (*-y*) fanfare; flourish
fant *m* (*-u/-a*; *-y*) (*na loterii*) prize; (*w zabawie*) forfeit; ***gra w ~y*** (game of) forfeits
fantastyczny fantastic
fantaz|ja *f* (*-i*; *-e*) fantasy; (*wymysł*) fancy; (*animusz*) panache, flair; *mus.* fantasia; **~jować** (*-uję*) fantasize; **~yjny** imaginative
fantow|y: ***loteria ~a*** prize lottery
faraon *m* (*-a*; *-i/-owie*) pharaoh
farb|a *f* (*-y*) paint; ***~a kryjąca*** hiding paint; ***~a olejna*** oil paint; **~ować** ⟨**po-, u-**⟩ (*-uję*) dye
farma *f* (*-y*) farm
farma|ceutyczny pharmaceutical; **~cja** *f* (*-i*; *0*) pharmacy
farmer *m* (*-a*; *-rzy*) farmer
farsa *f* (*-y*) farce, burlesque
farsz *m* (*-u*; *-e*) *gastr.* stuffing, (*mięsny*) forcemeat
fart F *m* (*-u*; *0*) luck, break
fartu|ch *m* (*-a*; *-y*) apron; (*mechanika*) overall; (*lekarza*) white coat; **~szek** *m* (*-szka*; *-szki*) apron
fasada *f* (*-y*) façade; *fig.* front
fascyn|ować ⟨**za-**⟩ (*-uję*) fascinate; **~ujący** (**-co**) fascinating
fasol|a *f* (*-i*; *-e*) *bot.* bean(s *pl.*); **~owy** bean; ***zupa ~owa*** bean soup; **~ka** *f* (*-i*; *G -lek*) *bot.* bean; ***~ka szparagowa*** string bean; ***~ka po bretońsku*** baked beans *pl.*
fason *m* (*-u*; *-y*) pattern, cut; *fig.* style; F ***trzymać ~*** stand fast
fastryg|a *f* (*-i*) tack; **~ować** ⟨**s-**⟩ (*-uję*) baste, tack
faszerowa|ć ⟨**na-**⟩ (*-uję*) *gastr.* stuff; **~ć** (**się**) ⟨**na-**⟩ pump (o.s.) full of; **~ny** stuffed; *warzywa* filled
faszystowski Fascist
fatalny *skutki itp.* unfortunate, fatal; *pogoda* awful

fatałaszki *m/pl.* (*-ów*) frippery, finery
fatyg|a *m* (*-i*) trouble, bother; (*zmęczenie*) fatigue; ***nie żałować ~i*** spare no effort; ***szkoda ~i*** it is not worth the trouble; **~ować** ⟨***po-***⟩ (*-uję*) trouble; ***~ować*** ⟨***po-***⟩ ***się*** (*bezok.*) make an effort (to do)
faul *m* (*-a*; *-e*) (*w sporcie*) foul
fawo|ryt *m* (*-a*; *-ci*), **-tka** *f* (*-i*; *G -tek*) favo(u)rite; **~ryzować** (*-uję*) favo(u)r
faza *f* (*-y*) stage, phase
febra *f* (*-y*) *med.* fever
federa|cja *f* (*-i*; *-e*) federation; **~cyjny, ~lny** federal
feler F *m* (*-u*; *-y*) fault, flaw, defect
felieton *m* (*-u*; *-y*) column
feministka *f* (*-i*) feminist, F libber
fenig *m* (*-a*; *-i*) pfennig
fenol *m* (*-u*; *-e*) *chem.* phenol
fenomenalny phenomenal, extraordinary
feralny unlucky, fatal
ferie *pl.* vacation (*zwł. Am.*), *Brt.* holiday
ferma *f* (*-y*) farm
fermentować (*-uje*) ferment
fertyczny spry
festiwal *m* (*-u*; *-e*) festival
festyn *m* (*-u*; *-y*) feast, festival; ***~ ludowy*** public festival; (*w ogrodzie*) garden party
fetor *m* (*-u*; *-y*) stink, fetor
fetyszyst|a *m* (*-y*, *-ści*), **~ka** *f* (*-i*) fetishist
feudalny feudal
fig|a *f* (*-i*) fig; ***~i*** *pl.* (*majtki*) panties *pl.*
fig|iel *m* (*-gla*; *-gle*) joke; ***~le*** *pl.* fooling around; ***o mały ~iel*** almost, nearly; **~larka** *f* (*-i*) → ***~larz***; **~larny** playful; *uśmiech też.* coquettish; **~larz** *m* (*-a*; *-e*) trickster, prankster; **~lować** (*-uję*) play jokes; (*wygłupiać się*) fool around
figow|iec *m* (*-wca*; *-wce*) fig tree; **~y** fig; ***listek ~y*** fig leaf (*też fig.*)
figur|a *f* (*-y*) figure; (*postać też*) form; *szachowa*: piece; *iron.* sort, character; ***~a myślowa*** hypothesis; F ***do ~y*** without a coat; **~ować** (*-uję*) figure; (*na spisie*) be, appear; **~owy**: ***jazda ~owa na lodzie*** figure skating
fikać (*-am*): ***~ nogami*** kick one's feet; → ***koziołek***
fikcyjny fictional
fikus *m* (*-a*; *-y*) *bot.* rubber plant
Filadelfia *f* (*-ii*; *0*) Philadelphia
filar *m* (*-a*/*-u*; *-y*) pillar (*też fig.*); (*mostu*) pier
filatelistyka *f* (*-i*; *0*) philately, stamp collecting
filcowy felt
filet *m* (*-u*; *-y*) fillet; ***~ rybny*** fish fillet
filharmoni|a *f* (*GDL -ii*; *-e*) (*budynek*) (philharmonic) concert hall; (*instytucja*) philharmonic society; **~czny** philharmonic
filia *f* (*GDL -ii*; *-e*) branch
Filipi|ny *pl.* (*G* -) Philippines; **~ńczyk** *m* (*-a*; *-cy*), **~nka** *f* (*-i*; *-nek*) Filipino
filiżanka *f* (*-i*) cup
film *m* (*-u*; *-y*) film; ***~ oświatowy*** documentary film; → ***animowany, fabularny, błona***; **~ować** ⟨***s-***⟩ (*-uję*) film, shoot; **~owy** film
filologi|a *f* (*GDL -ii*; *-e*) philology; ***~a angielska*** English department; **~czny** philological; ***studia*** *pl.* ***~czne*** foreign language studies *pl.*
filozof *m* (*-a*; *-owie*) philosopher; **~ia** *f* (*GDL -ii*; *-e*) philosophy; **~iczny** philosophical; **~ka** *f* (*-i*) philosopher; **~ować** (*-uję*) philosophize
filtr *m* (*-a*/*-u*; *-y*) filter; **~ować** (*-uję*) filter
filuterny roguish; mischievous
Fin *m* (*-a*; *-owie*) Finn
finali|sta *m* (*-y*; *-ści*), **~stka** *f* (*-i*; *G -tek*) finalist; **~zować** ⟨***s-***⟩ (*-uję*) finalize, complete, make final
finał *m* (*-u*; *-y*) ending; (*w sporcie*) final; *mus.* finale; **~owy** final
finans|e *pl.* (*-ów*) finances *pl.*; funds *pl.*; **~ować** ⟨***s-***⟩ (*-uję*) finance; **~owy** financial
fingować ⟨***s-***⟩ (*-uję*) fake
Finka *f* (*-i*; *G -nek*) Finn; 𝔰 (*nóż*) sheath knife
Finlandia *f* (*GDL -ii*) Finland
fińsk|i Finnish; ***mówić po ~u*** speak Finnish
fioletowy (**-wo**) purple; violet
fioł|ek *m* (*-łka*; *-łki*) violet; ***~ek alpejski*** cyclamen; ***~ek trójbarwny*** pansy; **~kowy** (**-wo**) violet
firanka *f* (*-i*; *G -nek*) (net) curtain
fircyk *m* (*-y*; *-i*) dandy, fop
firm|a *f* (*-y*) firm, business; **~owy** company; ***danie ~owe*** *Brt.* speciality, *Am.* specialty; ***papier ~owy*** letterhead
fiskalny fiscal
fistuła *f* (*-y*) *med.* → ***przetoka***

fito- *w zł.* phyto
fizjologi|a *f* (*GDL -ii; 0*) physiology; **~czny** physiological
fizjonomia *f* (*GDL -ii; -e*) physiognomy, countenance
fizyczn|y physical; corporal; (*ręczny*) manual; ***wychowanie ~e*** (*skrót* ***WF***) physical education
fizyk *m* (*-a; -cy*) physicist; **~a** *f* (*-i; 0*) physics

F

f-ka *skrót pisany*: ***fabryka*** factory
flaczki *m/pl.* (*-ów*) *gastr.* tripe
flag|a *f* (*-i*) flag; **~owy** flag
flaki *m/pl.* (*-ów*) intestines, F guts; *gastr.* → ***flaczki***
flakon *m* (*-u; -y*), **~ik** *m* (*-a; -i*) bottle; (*na kwiaty*) vase
Flaman|d *m* (*-a; -owie*), **~dka** *f* (*-i*) Fleming; **ƀdzki** (***po -ku***) Flemish
flamaster *m* (*-a; -y*) felt-tip pen
flaming *m* (*-a; -i*) *zo.* flamingo
flanca *f* (*-y; -e*) seedling
flanel|a *f* (*-i; -e*) flannel; **~owy** flannel
flanka *f* (*-i; G flank*) flank
flaszka *f* (*-i*) bottle
flądra *f* (*-y*) *zo.* flounder
flecist|a *m* (*-y; -ści*), **~ka** *f* (*-i*) flutist
flegma *f* (*-y; 0*) phlegm; (*opanowanie też*) sluggishness; **~tyczny** phlegmatic
flejtuchowaty (***-to***) slobbish
flesz *m* (*-a; -e*) *phot.* flash
flet *m* (*-u; -y*) (*poprzeczny*) flute; (*prosty*) recorder
flirtować (*-uję*) flirt
flisak *m* (*-a; -cy*) raftsman
florecist|a *m* (*-y; -ści*); **~ka** *f* (*-i*) foil fencer
Florencja *f* (*-i; 0*) Florence
floret *m* (*-u; -y*) foil
Floryda *f* (*-y; 0*) Florida
flota *f* (*-y*) fleet; ***~a dalekomorska*** deep-sea fleet; ***~a wojenna*** navy
flower *m* (*-u; -y*) small-bore rifle
fluktuacja *f* (*-i; -e*) fluctuation
fluor *m* (*-u; 0*) *chem.* fluorine
fochy F *pl.*(*-ów*) whims *pl.*
fok|a *f* (*-i*) seal; ***~i*** *pl.* (*futro*) sealskin
fokstrot *m* (*-a; -y*) foxtrot
folgować (*-uję*) (*D*) be lenient; ***~ sobie*** take it easy; indulge (***w*** in)
foli|a *f* (*GDL -ii; -e*) (*z metalu*) foil; (*plastik*) plastic; **~owy** foil; plastic
folwark *m* (*-u; -i*) estate
fon|etyczny phonetic; **~etyka** *f* (*-i*) phonetics; **~ia** *f* (*-i; 0*) sound; **~o-** *w zł.* phono-
fonoteka *f* (*-i*) sound archive
fontanna *f* (*-y*) fountain
for *m* (*-a; -y*) handicap; ***mieć ~y u*** find favo(u)r with
foremka *f* (*-i*) (*do ciasta*) (baking) tin; (*do zabawy*) *Brt.* mould, *Am.* mold; → ***forma***
foremny shapely
form|a *f* (*-y; G form*) shape, form; ***nie być w ~ie*** be out of form, ***być w ~ie*** be in (good) form; ***~y towarzyskie*** good manners; → ***foremka***
forma|cja *f* (*-i; -e*) formation; **~listyczny** formal; **~lność** *f* (*-ci*) formality; **~lny** formal; ***w kwestii ~lnej*** point of order; **~t** *m* (*-u; -y*) format (*też komp.*); (*rozmiar*) size; **~tować** ⟨**s-**⟩ (*-uję*) *komp.* format
formować ⟨**u-**⟩ (*też* ***się*** *v/i.*) form, build up; ⟨**s-**⟩ form, group
formu|larz *m* (*-a; -e*) form; **~ła** *f* (*-y*), **~łka** *f* (*-i*) formula; **~łować** ⟨**s-**⟩ (*-uję*) formulate, express
fornir *m* (*-u; -y*) veneer
forsa F *f* (*-y; 0*) dough
forsow|ać (*-uję*) force (*też mil*), step up; ⟨**s-**⟩ strain; ***~ać się*** overstrain; **~ny** forced, intensive
forteca *f* (*-y; -e*) fortress
fortel *m* (*-u; -e*) trick, scheme
fortepian *m* (*-u; -y*) piano; ***na ~*** for the piano; *też.* → **~owy** piano
fortun|a *f* (*-y; 0*) fortune; ***koło ~y*** wheel of fortune
fortyfikacja *f* (*-i; -e*) fortifications *pl.*
fosa *f* (*-y*) moat
fosfor *m* (*-u; 0*) *chem.* phosphorus; **~yzować** (*-uję*) phosphoresce
fotel *m* (*-a; -e*) armchair; ***~ wyrzucany*** ejector seat
fotka *f* (*-i; G -tek*) snapshot
fotogeniczny photogenic
fotogra|f *m* (*-a; -owie*) photographer; **~fia** *f* (*GDL -ii; -e*) (*sztuka*) photography; (*zdjęcie*) photo(graph); **~ficzny** photographic; **~fować** ⟨**s-**⟩ (*-uję*) photograph
foto|komórka *f* photo-electric cell; **~kopia** *f* photocopy; **~montaż** *m* photomontage; **~reporter(ka** *f*) *m* news reporter
fotos F *m* (*-u; -y*) still; (*zdjęcie*) snapshot

fracht *m* (*-u*; *-y*) freight; **~owiec** *m* (*-wca*; *-wce*) freighter; **~owy** freight
fragment *m* (*-u*; *-y*) fragment; (*tekstu*) excerpt
frajda *f* (*-y*) fun
frajer *m* (*-a*; *-rzy*/*-y*) nincompoop; ***zrobić ~a*** (***z k-ś***) take (s.o.) for a ride; **~ka** *f* (*-i*; *G -rek*) silly goose
frak *m* (*-a*; *-i*) tail coat, F tails *pl.*
frakcja *f* (*-i*; *-e*) fraction; *pol.* faction
Fran|cja *f* (*-i*; *0*) France; **⁓cuski** (***po -ku***) French; **⁓cuszczyzna** *f* (*-y*; *0*) French language; **~cuz** *m* (*-a*; *-i*) Frenchman; **~zi** the French; **~cuzka** *f* (*-i*) Frenchwoman
frank *m* (*-a*; *-i*) franc
frankować ⟨**o-**⟩ (*-uję*) frank
frapujący (***-co***) astonishing
fraszka *f* (*-i*; *G -szek*) trifle; (*wiersz*) epigram
frazes *m* (*-u*; *-y*) phrase, hackneyed phrase
frekwencj|a *f* (*-i*; *0*) attendance; turnout; ***cieszyć się ~ą*** be popular
fresk *m* (*-u*; *-i*) fresco
frez *m* (*-u*; *-y*) cutter; **~arka** *f* (*-i*; *G -rek*) (*do drewna*) mo(u)lding machine; (*do metalu*) milling machine
frędzla *f* (*-i*; *-e*) tassel; ***frędzle*** *pl.* fringe
fron|t *m* (*-u*; *-y*): ***na ~cie*** at the front; **~towy** front
froterować ⟨**wy-**⟩ (*-uję*) polish
frotté *n* (*idkl.*) terry (towel(l)ing); ***ręcznik ~*** terry towel
frunąć *pf.* (*-nę*) → ***fruwać***
frustrować (*-uję*) frustrate; ⟨**s-**⟩ ***~ się*** get frustrated
fruwać (*-am*) fly
frycowe F *n* (*-wego*; *0*): ***płacić ~*** learn the hard way
frykasy *m/pl.* (*-ów*) titbits *pl.*, *zwł. Am.* tidbits *pl.*
frytki *f/pl. Brt.* chips, *Am.* (French) fries
fryzjer *m* (*-a*; *-rzy*) hairdresser, (*męski*) barber; **~ka** *f* (*-i*; *G -rek*) → ***fryzjer***; **~ski**: ***zakład ~ski*** hairdresser's
fryzura *f* (*-y*) hairstyle
fujarka *f* (*-i*; *G -rek*) pipe
fund|acja *f* (*-i*; *-e*) foundation; **~ament** *m* (*-u*; *-y*) foundation(s); **~ować** (*-uję*) ⟨**u-**⟩ found, grant; ⟨**za-**⟩ *napój itp.* stand; **~usz** *m* (*-u*; *-e*) fund(s *pl.*); ***~usz powierniczy*** trust fund
funkc|ja *f* (*-i*; *-e*) function; **~jonalny** functional; **~jonariusz** *m* (*-a*; *-e*), **~jonariuszka** *f* (*-i*) functionary, officer
funkcjonować (*-uję*) function
funt *m* (*-a*; *-y*) pound
fura *f* (*-y*) cart; F (*G*) a heap of
furgonetka *f* (*-i*) van
furi|a *f* (*GDl -ii*; *-e*) fury, rage; ***wpaść w ~ę*** fly into a rage
furkotać (*-czę*/*-cę*) *Brt.* whirr, *Am.* whir
furman *m* (*-a*; *-i*) carter, driver; **~ka** *f* (*-i*; *G -nek*) cart
furt|a *f* (*-y*), **~ka** *f* (*-i*; *G -tek*) gate, door
fusy *m/pl.* dregs *pl.*; (*kawy też*) grounds *pl.*; (*herbaty*) tea leaves
fuszer|ka *f* (*-i*) botch, bungle; **~ować** → ***partaczyć***
futbolowy soccer, football
futerał *m* (*-u*; *-y*) case; étui
futerkow|y fur; ***zwierzę ~e*** fur-bearing animal
futro *f* (*-a*) fur
futryna *f* (*-y*): ***~ drzwiowa/okienna*** door/window frame
futrzany fur
fuzja[1] *f* (*-i*; *-e*) (*strzelba*) shotgun
fuzja[2] *f* (*-i*; *-e*) *econ.* fusion, merger

G

g. *skrót pisany*: ***godzina*** hr (*hour*)
gabinet *m* (*-u*, *y*) office; (*pokój w domu*) study; *pol.* cabinet; ***~ lekarski*** consulting-room; ***~ kosmetyczny*** beauty salon; **~owy** cabinet
gablotka *f* (*-i*; *G -tek*) display case; show-case
gad *m* (*-a*; *-y*) *zo.* reptile
gada|ć (*-am*) talk, chat, chatter; **~nie** *n* (*-a*), **~nina** *f* (*-y*) chatter; **~tliwy** (***-wie***) talkative
gadzina *f* (*-y*) *pej. fig.* reptile
gaf|a *f* (*-y*) faux pas; gaffe; ***popełnić ~ę*** make a gaffe
gaj *m* (*-u*; *-e*) grove
gajowy *m* (*-ego*, *-i*) forester

gala *f* (*-i*; *-e*) gala
galaktyka *f* (*-i*; *G* -) galaxy
galanteria *f* (*GDL -ii*; *0*) gallantry; *zbior.* fashion accessories *pl.*
galare|ta *f* (*-y*) jelly; (*do ryby, mięsa*) aspic; ***w ~cie*** in aspic; **~tka** *f* (*-i*) jelly
galeria *f* (*GDl -ii*; *-e*) gallery
galimatias *m* (*-u*; *0*) → ***bałagan***
galon[1] *m* (*-u*; *-y*) (*miara*) gallon
galon[2] *m* (*-u*; *-y*) braid; (*na mundurze*) stripe
galop *m* (*-u*; *0*) gallop; ***~em*** at a gallop; **~ować** (*-uję*) gallop
galowy gala; ***w stroju ~m*** in gala dress; (*wojskowy*) in full uniform
gałą|zka *f* (*-i*) twig; **~ź** *f* (*-ęzi*) branch
gałgan *m* (*-a*; *-y*) rag; *fig.* (*pl. -i/-*) (*łobuz*) scamp
gałka *f* (*-i*; *G -łek*) ball; (*do drzwi itp.*, *w radiu itp.*) knob; ***~ oczna*** eyeball
gama *f* (*-y*) *mus.* scale; (*zakres*) range
gamoń *m* (*-nia*; *-nie*) nitwit
ganek *m* (*-nku*; *-nki*) veranda, porch
gang *m* (*-u*; *-i*) gang; ***~ samochodowy*** gang of car thieves; **~sterski** criminal, gangster
gani|ać (*-am*) run around/about; (***za*** *I*) run after; **~ć** ⟨***z-***⟩ criticize (***za*** *A* for)
gap *m* (*gapia*; *-pie*, *-piów*) onlooker; bystander; **~a** F *m/f* (*-y*; *G* -) scatterbrain; → ***oferma***; ***jechać na ~ę*** dodge paying the fare; **~ić się** ⟨***za- się***⟩ (*-ię*) gape (***na*** *A* at); **~iostwo** *n* (*-a*; *0*) absent-mindedness; **~iowaty** (***-to***) foolish, simple-minded
garaż *m* (*-u*; *-e*) garage
garb *m* (*-u*; *-y*) hunchback, hump (*też zo.*)
garbarnia *f* (*-i*, *-e*) tannery
garb|aty (***-to***) hunchbacked; **~ić się** (*-ię*) stoop
garbować ⟨***wy-***⟩ tan; *fig.* ***~ komuś skórę*** tan s.o's hide
garbus *m* (*-a*; *-i/-y*) hunchback; F (*samochód*) beetle; **~ka** *f* (*-i*) hunchback
garderoba *f* (*-y*) (*pokój*) dressing-room; (*szatnia*) *Am.* check-room, *Brt.* cloak-room; (*ubrania*) clothes *pl.*, wardrobe
gard|ło *n* (*-a*, *L -dle*; *G -deł*) throat; ***wąskie ~ło*** bottleneck; ***ból ~ła*** sore throat; ***na całe ~ło*** at the top of one's voice; **~łować** (*-uję*) clamo(u)r; **~łowy** *głos* throaty
gardzić ⟨***po-, wz-***⟩ (*I*) (*-dzę*) despise
gardziel *f* (*-i*; *-e*) → ***gardło***; *fig.* bottleneck
garkuchnia *f* soup kitchen
garmaże|ria *f* (*GDl -ii*; *-e*) delicatessen *pl.*; **~ryjny** delicatessen *pl.*
garnąć ⟨***przy-***⟩ (*-nę*): ***~ się*** cuddle up (***do*** *G* to); ***~ się do nauki*** be eager to learn
garn|carnia *f* (*-i*; *-e*) pottery, potter's workshop; **~carz** *m* (*-a*; *-e*) potter
garnek *m* (*-nka*; *-nki*) pot
garnirować (*-uję*) *gastr.* garnish
garnitur *m* (*-u*; *-y*) suit; (*komplet*) set, (*mebli*) suite
garnuszek *m* (*-szka*; *-szki*) small pot; (*kubek*) mug
garsonka *f* (*-i*; *G -nek*) woman's suit
gar|stka *f* (*-i*; *G -tek*) *fig.* handful; **~ść** *f* (*-ści*; *-ście*) hand; (*ilość*) handful; ***wziąć się w ~ść*** pull o.s. together
gas|ić ⟨***wy-, z-***⟩ (*-szę*) put out, extinguish; *światło* turn off; *silnik* switch off; ⟨***u-***⟩ *pragnienie* quench; *zapał* kill; **~nąć** ⟨***z-***⟩ (*-nę*) go out; *silnik*: stall
gastro'nomi|a *f* (*GDL -ii*; *0*) gastronomy; (*restauracje*) restaurant trade; **~czny** gastronomic; restaurant
gaszenie *n* (*-a*) extinguishing
gaśnica *f* (*-y*; *-e*) fire-extinguisher
gatun|ek *m* (*-nku*; *-nki*) sort, type, brand; *biol.* species; (*jakość*) high quality; **~kowy** high-quality; select
gawęda *f* (*-y*) tale, chat
gawędzić ⟨***po-***⟩ (*-ę*) chat
gaworzyć (*-rzę*) *niemowlę*: babble
gawron *m* (*-a*; *-y*) *zo.* rook
gaz *m* (*-u*; *-y*) gas; ***~ łzawiący*** tear gas; ***~ rozweselający*** laughing gas; ***~ ziemny*** natural gas; ***pełnym ~em, na pełnym ~ie*** at full speed; ***pod ~em*** drunk; ***~y*** *pl.* (*jelitowe*) wind
gaza *f* (*-y*) gauze
gazda *m* (*-y*; *-owie*) *jakby*: mountain farmer
gaze|ciarka *f* (*-i*), **~ciarz** *m* (*-a*; *-e*) (*sprzedawca*) newspaper-seller, (*roznosiciel*) newspaper-deliverer; **~ta** *f* (*-y*) newspaper, paper; **~towy** newspaper
gazo|ciąg *m* (*-u*; *-i*) gas pipeline; **~mierz** *m* (*-a*; *-e*) gas meter; **~wany** *napój* sparkling; **~wnia** *f* (*-i*; *-e*) gasworks *sg.*; **~wy** gas; *chem.*, *phys.* gaseous
gaździna *f* (*-y*) *jakby*: mountain farmer
gaźnik *m* (*-a*; *-i*) carburettor, *Am.* carburetor

gaża *f* (*-y*; *-e*) fee, honorarium
gąb|czasty (**-*to***) spongy; **~ka** *f* (*-i*) sponge (*też zo.*)
gąsienic|a *f* (*-y*; *-e*) *zo.*, *tech.* caterpillar; *tech.* caterpillar (track); **~owy** caterpillar
gąsior *m* (*-a*; *-y*) *zo.* gander; (*naczynie*) demijohn
gąska *f* (*-i*; *-sek*) *zo.* young goose; gosling; *bot.* blewits *sg.*; ***głupia* ~** a silly goose
gąszcz *m* (*-u*; *-e*) thicket; dense undergrowth; *fig.* tangle
gbur *m* (*-a*; *-y*) oaf; **~owaty** (**-*to***) oafish
gdakać (*-czę*) *kura*: cackle
gderać (*-am*) grumble, carp
gdy *cj.* when; as; **~ *tylko*** as soon as; ***podczas* ~** when, during; **~by** *cj.* if
gdynki
gdyż *cj.* because
gdzie where; **~ *indziej*** somewhere else; → ***bądź***; **~'kolwiek** anywhere; **~'niegdzie** here and there; **~ś** some place (or other); **~ż** where else
gej F *m* (*-a*; *-e*) gay
gem *m* (*-a*; *-e*) (*w sporcie*) game
gen *m* (*-u*; *-y*) gene
gencjana *f* (*-y*) gentian
genealogiczn|y: ***drzewo* ~*e*** family tree
genera|cja *f* (*-i*; *-e*) generation; **~lny** general, overall; **~*lne porządki*** thorough cleaning
generał *m* (*-a*; *-owie*) general
gene|tyczny genetic; **~tyka** *f* (*-i*; *0*) genetics *sg.*; **~za** *f* (*-y*; *0*) genesis
geni|alny brilliant; of genius; **~usz** *m* (*-a*; *-e*) genius
genowy *biol.* gene
geo|'grafia *f* (*GDL -ii*; *0*) geography; **~graficzny** geographical; **~logia** *f* (*GDL -ii*; *0*) geology; **~logiczny** geological; **~metria** *f* (*GDL -ii*; *-e*) geometry; **~metryczny** geometrical
germa'nistyka *f* (*-i*) (*studia*) German studies *pl.*; (*instytut*) German department
gest *m* (*-u*; *-y*) gesture (*też fig.*)
getto *n* (*-a*) ghetto
gęb|a F *f* (*-y*; *G gąb/gęb*) (*usta*) trap, *Brt.* gob; (*twarz*) mug; *zo.* mouth; ***zamknij* ~*ę!*** shut your trap!; ***dać w* ~*ę*** smack in the gob; **~owy** oral
gę|gać (*-am*) gaggle; **~si** goose; **~*siego*** in single *lub* Indian file; **~si-na** *f* (*-y*; *0*) goose
gęst|nieć ⟨**z-**⟩ (*-eję*) *ciecz*, *mgła*: thicken, get thicker; *tłum*: become more dense; **~ość** *f* (*-ści*) thickness; density; **~wina** *f* (*-y*) thicket, dense undergrowth; **~y** (**-*to***) thick; dense
gęś *f* (*-si*; *I -siami/-śmi*) goose
giąć (*gnę*) (**się** *v/i.*) bend
gibki (**-*ko***) lithe, supple
gicz *f* (*-y*; *-e*): **~ *cielęca*** knuckle of veal
gieł|da *f* (*-y*) *econ.* exchange; **~dowy** exchange; **~dziarz** *m* (*-a*; *-e*) stock-market speculator
giemza *f* (*-y*; *0*) kid
gier *G pl.* → ***gra***
giermek *m* (*-mka*; *-mkowie*) *hist.* shield-bearer
giętk|i elastic; *fig.* flexible; **~ość** (*-ści*; *0*) elasticity; flexibility
gigantyczny gigantic
gil *m* (*-a*; *-e*) *zo.* bullfinch
gimnasty|czny gymnastic; **~k** *m* (*-a*; *-cy*), **~czka** *f* (*-i*; *G -czek*) gymnast; (*nauczyciel*) PE teacher; **~ka** *f* (*-i*; *0*) gymnastics *sg.*; (*ćwiczenia*) gymnastics *pl.*; **~kować się** (*-uję*) do gymnastics, exercise
gimna|zjalny *Brt.* grammar-school, *Am.* high-school; **~zjum** *n* (*idkl.*; *-a*, *-ów*) *Brt.* (*a three-year school between primary school and secondary school*)
ginąć (*-nę*) ⟨**z-**⟩ die (*też fig.* **z** *G* of), perish; (*niknąć*) disappear, vanish; (*gubić się*) ⟨***też* za-**⟩ get lost
ginekolog *m* (*-a*; *-owie/-dzy*) gynecologist, *Brt.* gynaecologist; **~ia** *f* (*GDl -ii*; *0*) gynecology, Brt. gynaecology
gips *m* (*-u*; *-y*) plaster; *chem.* gypsum; **~owy** plaster; gypsum
girlsa *f* (*-y*) chorus-girl
giro- *w zł.* → ***żyro-***
gisernia *f* (*-i*; *-e*) *tech.* foundry
gita|ra *f* (*-y*) *mus.* guitar; **~rzysta** *m* (*-y*; *-ści*), **~rzystka** *f* (*-i*) guitar player, guitarist
glansowany shining, gleaming, polished
glazur|a *f* (*-y*) glaze, glazing; (*kafelki*) tiling; **~ować** ⟨**po-**⟩ (*-uję*) glaze; (*kafelkami*) tile
gleba *f* (*-y*) soil; *fig.* ground
ględzić F (*-dzę*) blather, *zwł. Am.* blether; prattle
gliceryna *f* (*-y*; *0*) glycerine

G

glin *m* (*-u*; *-0*) *chem. Brt.* aluminium, *Am.* aluminum
glina *f* (*-y*) clay
glinian|ka *f* (*-i*; *G -nek*) (*zagłębienie*) clay-pit; **~y** clay; (*naczynie itp.*) earthen
gliniarz *m* (*-a*; *-e*) F cop
gliniasty clayey
glinka *f* (*-i*; *G -nek*) clay; ***~ kaolinowa*** kaolin
glista *f* (*-y*; *-y*, *glist*) ascarid; F earthworm
glob *m* (*-u*; *-y*) globe; **~alny** global; (*suma itp.*) total
globus *m* (*-a/-u*; *-y*) globe
glon *m* (*-u*; *-y*) *bot.* alga
glosa *f* (*-y*) gloss
gł. *skrót pisany*: ***główny*** main
gładk|i smooth (*też fig.*); (*bez ozdób*) simple; ***~o wygolony*** clean-shaven; **~ość** *f* (*-ci*; *0*) smoothness; simplicity
gładzić (*-dzę*) ⟨**wy-**⟩ smooth out/down; ⟨**po-**⟩ → ***głaskać***
głaskać ⟨**po-**⟩ (*-szczę/-am*) stroke; ***~ się*** stroke o.s.
głaz *m* (*-u*; *-y*) boulder
głąb[1] *m* (*-a*; *-y*) (*kapusty*) heart; F *fig.* fool
głąb[2] *f* (*głębi*; *-ębie*) interior; ***w ~ kraju*** inland, toward the interior
głęb|ia *f* (*-i*; *-e*) depth; *phot.* ***~ia ostrości*** depth of focus; ***w ~i*** inside; ***do ~i*** deeply, profoundly; ***z ~i serca*** from the bottom of the heart; **~iej** *adv.* (*comp. od* → ***głęboki***) deeper; **~inowy** abyssal; ***studnia ~inowa*** deep well; **~oki** deep; profound (*też fig.*); *głos* low; *sen* sound; **~oko** deep(ly); ***~oko idący*** far-reaching; **~okość** *f* (*-ści*) depth; **~szy** *adj. comp. od* → ***głęboki***
głodny (**-no**) hungry; F ***strasznie ~ jestem*** I'm famished
głodow|ać (*-uję*) starve; **~y** hunger; *dieta itp.* starvation; ***umrzeć śmiercią ~ą*** starve to death
głodówka *f* (*-i*) (*leczenie*) starvation diet; (*strajk*) hunger strike
głodzić ⟨**wy-**⟩ (*-dzę*) starve; ***~ się*** go hungry, starve
głos *m* (*-u*; *-y*) voice; (*ptaka*) call; (*prawo głosu*) say; (*w wyborach*) vote; *mus.* part; ***prosić o ~*** ask to speak; ***zabrać ~*** take the floor; ***na cały ~*** loud(ly); **~ić** (*-szę*) preach; **~ka** *f* (*-i*; *G -sek*) *gr.* sound
głosow|ać (*-uję*) vote (***nad*** *I* on; ***za*** *I*, ***na*** *A* for; ***przeciwko*** *D* against); **~anie** *n* (*-a*) voting; **~y** (**-wo**) vocal; *gr.* sound
głoś|nik *m* (*-a*; *-i*) loudspeaker; **~ność** *f* (*-ci*; *0*) loudness; **~ny** (**-no**) loud; (*sławny*) famous
głow|a *f* (*-y*) head; ***~a państwa/rodziny*** head of state/the family; ***bez ~y*** *fig.* panic-stricken; ***na ~ę, od ~y*** per head/capita; ***uderzyć k-ś do ~y*** go to s.o.'s head; ***strzelić do ~y*** suddenly occur to, come to mind; ***łamać ~ę, zachodzić w ~ę*** rack one's brains; ***chodzić komu po ~ie*** have *s.th.* on the brain; ***wbić sobie do ~y*** get it into one's head; ***mieć ~ę na karku*** have one's head screwed on; ***włos mu z ~y nie spadnie*** (*D*) nobody will harm a hair on his head; ***to stoi na ~ie*** it is wrong side up; ***~ą w dół*** headlong; ***~a do góry!*** cheer up!; ***od stóp do głów*** from head to toe
głowiasty *bot.* head
głowi|ca *f* (*-y*; *-e*) *tech.*, *mil.* head; *arch.* capital; **~ć się** (*-ię*; *głów!*) rack one's brains (***nad*** *I* over); **~zna** *f* (*-y*) pig's head
głód *m* (*-łodu*; *0*) hunger; ***~ mieszkaniowy*** housing crisis; ***klęska głodu*** famine
głóg *m* (*-ogu*; *-ogi*) *bot.* hawthorn
głów|ka *f* (*-i*) (*fajki*) bowl; (*młotka*) head; (*w sporcie*) header; ***~ka maku*** poppyhead; ***~ka czosnku*** bulb of garlic
główn|ie *adv.* mainly, chiefly; **~odowodzący** *m* (*-ego*; *-y*) commander in chief; **~y** main, chief
głuchnąć (*-nę*) ⟨**o-**⟩ go deaf; (*cichnąć*) die away
głucho *adv.* hollowly, dully; quietly; ***zamknięty na ~*** locked up; **~niemy** deaf-mute, *pej.* deaf and dumb; **~ta** *f* (*-y*; *0*) deafness
głuchy **1.** deaf (*też fig.* ***na*** *A* to); (*dźwięki*) hollow; (*cisza*, *prowincja*) deep; ***~ jak pień*** stone-deaf; **2.** *m* (*-ego*; *-si*) deaf; ***głusi*** the deaf *pl.*
głupi **1.** foolish, stupid; ***udawać ~ego*** act stupid; **2.** *m* (*-ego*; *-*) → fool; **~ec** *m* (*-pca*; *-pcy*) fool; **~eć** ⟨**z-**⟩ (*-eję*) go stupid, get daft
głup|io *adv.* stupidly; foolishly; ***czuć się ~io*** feel stupid; **~ota** *f* (*-y*; *0*) foolishness, stupidity; **~stwo** *n* (*-a*) nonsense; (*drobnostka*) trifle, nothing

głusz|a *f* (*-y*; *-e*) wilderness; **~ec** *m* (*-szca*; *-szce*) *zo.* capercaillie, wood grouse; **~yć** (*-szę*) ⟨**o-**⟩ stun; ⟨**za-**⟩ drown out; (*chwasty*) overgrow

gm. *skrót pisany*: *gmina* commune

gmach *m* (*-u*; *-y*) building, edifice

gmatwać ⟨**po-**⟩ tangle; (*też* ⟨**za-**⟩) (*-am*) confuse; **~ *się*** get confused

gmatwanina *f* (*-y*) tangle

gmerać (*-am*) rummage around/about

gmin|a *f* (*-y*) commune; **~ny** communal

gnać (*gnam*) rush

gnat F *m* (*-a*; *-y*) bone

gną, gnę → ***giąć***

gnębić (*-ę*) suppress, oppress; *fig.* worry, pester

gniazd|ko *n* (*-a*) *electr.* socket, *Am.* outlet; → **~o** *n* (*-a*) nest; → ***wtyczkowy***

gnicie *n* (*-a*; *0*) decay, rotting

gnić ⟨**z-**⟩ (*-ję*) decay, rot

gnida *f* (*-y*) *zo.* nit; *fig. pej.* blighter

gnie|sz → ***giąć***; **~ść** press; *gastr.* mash, *ciasto* knead; *fig.* weigh on; → ***miąć***; ***~ść się*** crowd, throng

gniew *m* anger; ***wpaść w ~*** get angry; **~ać** (*-am*) anger, enrage; ***~ać*** ⟨**po-**⟩ ***się*** get angry (**na** *A* with); **~ny** angry, cross

gnieździć się (*-żdżę*) nest *fig.* live (in a cramped space)

gnij → ***giąć, gnić***

gno|ić (*-ję*) fertilize; (*upokarzać*) F slag off, put down; **~jowisko** *n* (*-a*) manure heap; **~jówka** *f* (*-i*; *G -wek*) liquid manure

gnój *m* (*gnoju*; *0*) manure, dung; (*gnoju*; *-e*) V asshole

gnuśn|ieć ⟨**z-**⟩ (*-eję*) get sluggish; **~y** sluggish

go *pron.* (*ściągn. jego*) → ***on***

godło *n* (*-a*; *G -deł*) emblem; ***~ państwowe*** national emblem

godn|ie *adv.* fittingly; (*z godnością*) with dignity; **~ość** *f* (*-ci*; *0*) dignity; (*pl. -ści*) high position/rank; ***jak Pana/Pani ~ość?*** what is your name?; **~y** worthy; suitable; ***podziwu ~y*** admirable; ***~y zaufania*** trustworthy; ***~y pogardy*** despicable; ***~y polecenia*** recommendable; ***nic ~ego uwagi*** nothing noteworthy

gody *pl.* (*-ów*) *biol.* mating period; ***weselne ~*** wedding; ***złote ~*** golden wedding (anniversary)

godz. *skrót pisany*: ***godzina*** hr (*hour*)

godzi|ć (*-dzę, gódź!*) *v/t.* ⟨**po-**⟩ reconcile, conciliate; ***~ć się*** become reconciled; *v/i.* (**w** *A*) aim (at); *v/r.* ***~ć*** ⟨**po-**⟩ ***się*** (**z** *I*) agree (to); resign o.s. (to); → ***zgadzać się, przystawać***[1]; **~en** *pred.* → ***godny***

godzin|a *f* (*-y*) hour; ***która ~a?*** what time is it? ***jest*** (***~a***) ***druga*** it is two (o'clock); ***o której ~ie?*** at what time?; ***za ~ę*** in an hour; ***z ~y na ~ę*** from hour to hour, hourly; ***~ami*** for hours and hours; ***~y otwarcia*** opening hours; → ***przyjęcie, nadliczbowy***; **~ny** one-hour; **~owy** (**-wo**) hour(ly)

gogle *pl.*(*-i*) (protective) goggles *pl.*

goić ⟨**wy-, za-**⟩ (*-ję, gój!*) heal; **~** ⟨**wy-, za-**⟩ ***się*** heal up/over

golarka *f* (*-i*; *G -rek*) shaver

goleni|e (**się**) *n* (*-a*) shaving, shave; ***maszynka do ~a*** electric shaver; ***płyn po ~u*** shaving lotion

goleń *f* (*-ni*; *-nie*) shank

golf[1] *m* (*-a*; *0*) golf

golf[2] *m* (*-u*; *-y*) polo neck, turtleneck; **~y** *pl.* (*spodnie*) knickerbockers *pl.*

golić ⟨**o-**⟩ (*-lę, gól!*) (**się** *v/i.*) shave

golonka *f* (*-i*; *G -nek*) *gastr.* knuckle of pork

gołąb *m* (*-ębia*; *-ębie*, *-bi*) pigeon, dove; ***~ pocztowy*** carrier pigeon; **~ki** *m/pl.* (*-bków*) *gastr.* stuffed cabbage

gołęb|i pigeon; *fig.* dovelike; **~iarz** *m* (*-a*; *-e*) pigeon keeper; **~ica** *f* (*-y*; *-e*) pigeon; **~nik** *m* (*-a*; *-i*) pigeon-loft

goło *adv.* → ***goły***; **~ledź** *f* (*-dzi*; *-dzie*) black ice; **~słowny** groundless; **~wąs** F *m* callow youth

goły naked, bare; *drut*, *ręce*, *drzewa* bare; ***pod ~m niebem*** in the open (air); ***~mi rękoma*** with bare hands; ***~m okiem*** with the naked eye

gondola *f* (*-i*; *-e*) gondola

goni|ć (*-ę*) (*A*, **za** *I*) chase (after); → ***poganiać***; *v/i.* hurry, hasten; ***~ć się*** race; **~ec** *m* (*-ńca*; *-ńcy*, *-ńców*) office boy, (*dziewczyna*) office girl; (*pl. -ńce*) *szachy*: bishop; **~twa** *f* (*-y*; *G -*) race; chase

gont *m* (*-a/-u*; *-y*) shingle

gończy (*pies*) hunting; ***list ~*** 'wanted' poster

GOPR *skrót*: ***Górskie Ochotnicze Pogotowie Ratunkowe*** mountain rescue service

gorąco[1] *n* (*-a*; *0*) heat
gorąc|o[2] *adv*. warmly; hot; **~o** (**jest**) it is hot; ***na ~o*** *fig*. live; ***parówki*** *f/pl*. ***na ~o*** sausages served hot
gorącokrwisty warm-blooded
gorący hot; *fig*. hot-blooded; ***złapać k-ś na ~m uczynku*** catch s.o. red-handed
gorączk|a *f* (*-i*) fever (*też fig*.); *fig*. excitement; F (*człowiek*) hothead; ***biała ~a*** delirium tremens; **~ować** (*-uję*) run a fever; ***~ować się*** get excited; **~owy** feverish (*też fig*.)
gorczyca *f* (*-y*; *0*) *bot*. mustard
goręcej *adv*. *comp*. *od* → **gorąco**; **~tszy** *adj*. *comp*. *od* → **gorący**
gorliw|iec *m* (*-wca*; *-wcy*) zealot, fanatic; **~ość** *f* (*-ci*; *0*) zeal, enthusiasm; **~y** (**-*wie***) zealous
gors *m* (*-u*; *-y*) bust; (*koszuli*) shirtfront; **~et** *m* (*-u*; *-y*) corset
gorsz|ący (**-co**) offensive, objectionable; **~y** *adj*. (*comp*. *od* → **zły**); ***co ~a*** what is worse; **~yć** ⟨**z-**⟩ (*-ę*) give offence (***k-o*** to s.o.), scandalize (*I* with); ***~yć*** ⟨**z-**⟩ ***się*** (*I*) be offended (at), be scandalized (at)
gorycz *f* (*-y*; *0*) bitterness (*też fig*.); **~ka** *f* (*-i*; *G -czek*) bitter taste; *bot*. gentian
goryl *m* (*-a*; *-e*) *zo*. gorilla
gorzej *adv*., *adv*. (*comp*. *od* → **źle**) worse
gorzelnia *f* (*-i*; *-e*) distillery
gorzk|i (**-*ko***) bitter (*też fig*.); **~nąć** (*-nę*), **~nieć** ⟨**z-**⟩ (*-eję*) grow bitter, *fig*. become embittered
gospoda *f* (*-y*) inn, restaurant
gospodar|czy (**-*czo***) economic; **~ka** *f* (*-i*; *G -rek*) economy; (*rolna*) farm, farming; (*zarządzanie*) management; ***zła ~ka*** mismanagement; **~ny** economical; **~ować** (*-uję*) (*I*) manage; (***na*** *L*) farm; **~ski** economic; **~stwo** *n* (*-a*) farm; ***~stwo domowe*** household
gospo|darz *m* (*-a*; *-e*) farmer; (*pan domu*) host; (*wynajmujący*) landlord; ***~darz schroniska*** warden; **~dyni** *f* (*-i*; *-e*, *-ń*) (*pani domu*) hostess; (*wynajmująca*) landlady; → **~sia** *f* (*-i*; *-e*) housekeeper
gościć (*-szczę*) *v/t*. be host to, entertain; *v/i*. stay (***u*** *G* with); ***zbyt długo u k-ś ~*** overstay one's welcome
gościec *m* (*-śćca*; *0*) *med*. rheumatism; F rheumatics *pl*.
gościn|a *f* (*-y*; *0*) visit; ***w ~ie***/***~ę*** on a visit; **~iec** *m* (*-ńca*; *-ńce*) (*droga*) country road; **~ność** *f* (*-ści*; *0*) hospitality; **~ny** hospitable; ***pokój ~ny*** guest *lub* spare room
gość *m* (*-ścia*; *-ście*, *ści*, *I -śćmi*) guest; visitor; F guy, chap; → ***facet, klient***; ***mieć ~ci*** have visitors
gotow|ać (*-uję*) ⟨**u-, z-, za-**⟩ *wodę* boil (***się*** *v/i*.); *obiad* cook ; *fig*. **~ać** ⟨**u-, za-**⟩ ***się*** seethe; → ***przygotowywać***; **~any** boiled; **~ość** *f* (*-ści*; *0*) readiness; **~y** ready (**do** *G* for; ***na*** *A* to do); ***~y do użycia*** ready to be used; ***~e ubrania*** ready-made clothes
gotów *pred*. → **gotowy**; **~ka** *f* (*-i*; *0*) cash; ***zapłacić ~ką*** pay cash; ***za ~kę*** for cash; **~kowy** cash
goty|cki Gothic; **~k** *m* (*-u*; *i*) Gothic
goździk *m* (*-a*; *-i*) *bot*. (*kwiat*) pink, carnation; (*przyprawa*) clove; **~owy** pink, carnation; clove
gór|a *f* (*-y*) mountain; (*sukni*) top; (*fartucha*) bib; (*budynku*) (the) upstairs; ***do ~y, na***/***w ~ę*** up(wards), (*budynku*) upstairs; ***na górze*** up (here/there), (*budynku*) upstairs; ***od ~y do dołu*** from top to bottom; ***pod ~ę*** uphill; ***u ~y*** at the top; ***z ~y*** from above; *fig*. condescendingly; (*płacić*) in advance; ***z ~ą*** (*ponad*) with interest; ***iść w ~ę*** *fig*. go up; ***brać ~ę*** gain the upper hand
góral *m* (*-a*; *-e*), **~ka** *f* (*-a*; *-i*) highlander
górka *f* (*-i*; *G -rek*) mountain
górni|ctwo *n* (*-a*; *0*) mining; **~czy** mining; **~k** *m* (*-a*; *-cy*) miner
gór|nolotny high-flown; **~ny** upper; high; ***2ny Śląsk*** Upper Silesia; **~ować** (*-uję*) (***nad*** *I*) dominate, overlook; be superior (***~ować siłą nad*** in power to); → ***dominować, przodować***; **~ski** mountain; ***choroba ~ska*** *med*. mountain sickness
Góry Skaliste *pl*. Rocky Mountains *pl*., Rockies *pl*.
górzysty mountainous
gówniarz *m* (*-a*; *-e*) F squirt
gówno V *n* (*-a*; *G -wien*) shit; ***~ prawda*** bullshit
gr *skrót pisany*: **grosz**(**y**) gr (*grosze*)
gra *f* (*gry*; *G gier*) play (*też fig*.); *mus*. playing, performance; (*w sporcie*) game; (*aktora*) acting, performance; ***~ na fortepianie*** piano performance; ***~ w kar-***

ty card game, ***nie wchodzić w grę*** be out of the question
grab *m* (*-u/-a*; *-y*) *bot.* hornbeam
grabarz *m* (*-a*; *-e*) grave-digger
grabi|ć (*-ę*) rake; ⟨***o-***⟩ (*łupić*) rob; **~e** *pl.* (*-i*) rake; **~eć** ⟨***z-***⟩ (*-eję*) grow numb (***z zimna*** from cold)
grabież *f* (*-y*; *-e*) robbery, plunder; **~ca** *m* (*-y*; *G -ów*) robber; plunderer
grabina *f* (*-y*) hornbeam (wood)
graca *f* (*-y*; *-e*) hoe
gracj|a *f* (*-i*; *-e*) grace; ***z ~ą*** gracefully
gracować (*-uję*) hoe
gracz *m* (*-a*; *-e*) player
grać (*-am*) ⟨***za-***⟩ play (***na flecie*** the flute; ***w koszykówkę*** play basketball); → ***gra***; ***~ na nerwach*** get on *s.o.'s* nerves; ***~ na zwłokę*** play for time; ***co grają w kinie?*** what's on at the cinema?
grad *m* (*-u*; *0*) hail; *fig.* storm; ***pada ~*** it is hailing; **~obicie** *n* (*-a*) hailstorm
gradzina *f* (*-y*) hailstone
grafi|czny graphic; ***karta ~czna*** *komp.* graphics card; **~k** *m* (*-a*; *-cy*) graphic designer; **~ka** *f* (*-i*; *0*) graphics *sg.*
grafit *m* (*-u*; *0*) *chem.* graphite; (*-u*; *-y*) (*do ołówka*) lead
grafologiczny graphologic(al)
graham *m* (*-a*; *-y*) whole-wheat bread
grajek *m* (*-jka*; *-jki*, *-jkowie*) player
gram *m* (*-a*; *-y*) gram
gramaty|czny grammatical; **~ka** *f* (*-i*) grammar
granat *m* (*-u*; *-y*) *bot.* pomegranate; (*minerał*) garnet; (*kolor*) navy blue; *mil.* grenade; ***~ ręczny*** hand grenade; **~owy** (***-wo***) navy blue
grand|a *f* (*-y*) row; ***na ~ę*** by force, unceremoniously
graniastosłup *m* (*-a*; *-y*) prism
graniasty sharp-edged, angular
grani|ca *f* (*-y*; *-e*) (*państwowa*) border, frontier; (*majątku itp.*) boundary; (*rozgraniczenie*) borderline; (*zakres*) limit; ***za ~cą/za ~cę*** abroad; ***na ~cy*** at the border; **~czny** border, frontier; **~czyć** (*-ę*) border (***z*** *A* on); *fig.* verge (***z*** *A* on)
granit *m* (*-u*; *-y*) granite; **~owy** granite
granulowany granulated
grań *f* (*-ni*; *-nie*, *-ni*) ridge
grasica *f* (*-y*; *-e*) *anat.* thymus (gland)
grasować (*-uję*) stalk, prowl; *choroba*: rage
grat *m* (*-a*; *-y*) a piece of junk; (*pojazd*) F heap; ***~y*** *pl.* junk, trash
gratis(owy) free, complimentary
gratka *f* (*-i*) (dead) bargain; windfall
gratul|acje *pl.* (*-i*) congratulations *pl.*; **~ować** ⟨***po-***⟩ congratulate (***czegoś*** on s.th.)
gratyfikacja *f* (*-i*; *-e*) gratuity, bonus
grawerować ⟨***wy-***⟩ (*-uję*) engrave
grawerunek *m* (*-nku*; *-nki*) engraving
grążel *m* (*-a*; *-e*) *bot.* water-lily
grdyka *f* (*-i*) Adam's apple
Gre|cja *f* (*-i*; *0*) Greece; **&cki** (***po -cku***) Greek; **~czynka** *f* (*-i*; *G -nek*), **~k** *m* (*-a*; *-cy*) Greek; **&ka** *f* (*-i*; *0*) Greek (language)
gremi|alnie *adv.* in a body, en masse; **~alny** joint, unified
Grenlandia *f* (*-ii*; *0*) Greenland
grobla *f* (*-i*; *-e*, *G -el*) dike, embankment
grobow|iec *m* (*-wca*; *-wce*) tomb; ***~iec rodzinny*** family vault; **~o** gravely; gloomily; **~y** grave; sepulchral; (*ponury*) gloomy; *cisza* dead; ***do ~ej deski*** till death
groch *m* (*-u*; *0*) *bot.* pea(s *pl.*); ***~ z kapustą*** mishmash; **~owy** pea; **~ówka** *f* (*-i*, *G -wek*) *gastr.* pea soup
grodzi|ć (*-dzę*) → ***ogradzać, zagradzać***; **~sko** *n* (*-a*) castle
grodzki municipal, city, town
grom *m* (*-u*; *-y*) thunder; ***jak ~ z jasnego nieba*** like a bolt from the blue
gromad|a *f* (*-y*) crowd, group; **~nie** *adv.* in a group, in droves; **~ny** group, (*liczny*) numerous
gromadz|ić ⟨***na-, z-***⟩ (*-dzę*) accumulate (*też* ***się*** *v/i.*); (*o ludziach*) group together, gather (*też* ***się*** *v/i.*)
gromić ⟨***z-***⟩ (*-ę*) rebuke, scold
gromki loud; *oklaski itp.* thunderous
gromni|ca *f* (*-y*; *-e*) votive candle; **~czny**: (***dzień***) ***Matki Boskiej &cznej*** Candlemas
gron|kowce *m/pl.* (*-ów*) staphylococci; **~o** *f* (*-a*; *G -*) (*winne*) bunch, (*porzeczek itp.*) cluster; (*grupa*) bunch
gronostaj *m* (*-u*; *-e*) *zo.* stoat; **~e** *pl.* (*futro*) ermine
gronowy grape
grosz *m* (*-a*; *-e*) grosz; (*austriacki*) groschen; *fig.* penny; F (*pieniądze*) *zbior.* money, F dough; ***bez ~a*** without a penny; ***co do ~a*** down to a penny
grosz|ek *m* (*-szku*; *-szki*) green pea-

(s *pl.*); (*deseń*) polka-dot; ***w ~ki*** polka-dot
groszowy grosz, *fig.* penny
grot *m* (*-u*; *-y*) head; ***~ strzały*** arrowhead
grota *f* (*-y*) cave
groteskowy grotesque; (*śmieszny*) ridiculous
grotołaz *m* (*-a*; *-i/-y*) speleologist; (*sportowy*) caver
groz|a *f* (*-y*) awe; terror; ***zdjęty ~ą*** overawed, intimidated; **~ić** (*-żę*) terrify (*I* with); endanger; ***za … ~i mu więzienie*** he is liable to imprisonment for …
groź|ba *f* (*-y*; *G gróźb*) threat; danger; ***~ba pożaru*** danger of fire; ***pod ~bą*** (*G*) under threat of; **~ny** dangerous; *mina itp.* threatening
grożący impending, threatening: ***~ śmiercią*** mortally dangerous; ***~ zawaleniem*** in imminent danger of collapsing
grób *m* (*-obu*; *-oby*) grave
gród *m* (*-odu*; *-ody*) castle; town
grub|as *m* (*-a*; *-y*), **~aska** *f* (*-i*) fatty, F fatso; **~ieć** ⟨**po-, z-**⟩ (*-eję*) grow fat; *głos*: become lower; **~iej** *adv. comp. od* → ***grubo***
grubo *adv.* thickly; (*z miarami*) thick; *podkreślać* heavily; (*mało subtelnie*) coarsely, roughly; → ***gruby***; **~skórny** *fig.* thick-skinned; **~ść** *f* (*-ści*; *0*) thickness; (*ludzi*) fatness; **~ziarnisty** coarse
grub|y thick; *człowiek* fat; *płótno*, *ziarno* coarse; *głos* deep; ***~e pieniądze*** F heaps of money; ***z ~sza*** roughly; ***w ~szych zarysach*** in rough outline
gruch|ać (*-am*) coo; *fig.* bill and coo; **~nąć** *v/s.* (*-chnę*) *v/i.* crash; *wieść*: break; → ***grzmotnąć*** (**się** *v/i.*); **~ot** *m* (*-u*; *-y*) rattle; F (*rzecz*) museum-piece, (*samochód*) heap; **~otać** (*-oczę/-cę*) *v/i.* rattle, clatter; ⟨**po-, z-**⟩ shatter, smash
gruczoł *m* (*-u*; *-y*) *anat.* gland; ***~ dokrewny*** endocrine gland; **~owy** glandular
gru|da *f* (*-y*; *G -*) clod, clump; ***jak po ~dzie*** with great difficulty; **~dka** *f* (*-i*; *G -dek*) small clod; **~dniowy** December; **~dzień** *m* (*-dnia*; *-dnie*) December
grunt *m* (*-u*; *-y*) ground; soil; land; F ***~ to …*** the main thing is …; ***do ~u*** totally, utterly; ***z ~u*** at heart; in fact; ***w gruncie rzeczy*** in fact, at bottom
gruntow|ać ⟨**za-**⟩ (*-uję*) prime; (*zmierzyć*) *też fig.* fathom; **~ny** fundamental; basic; **~y** soil; *warzywa* outdoor
grup|a *f* (*-y*) group; **~ować** ⟨**z-**⟩ (*-uję*) group, gather (*też* **się** *v/i.*); **~owo** in a group; **~owy** group
grusz|a *f* (*-y*; *-e*) *anat.* pear (tree) → **~ka** *f* (*-i*; *G -szek*) pear; **~(k)owy** pear
gruz *m* (*-u*; *-y*) rubble; ***~y*** *pl.* ruins *pl.*; ***zamienić w ~y*** devastate, ravage
gruzeł *m* (*-zła*; *-zły*) lump
Gruz|ja *f* (*-i*; *0*) Georgia; **~in** *m* (*-a*; *-i*), **~inka** *f* (*-i*; *G -nek*) Georgian; **ﾠ~iński** (***po -ku***) Georgian
gruzowisko *n* (*-a*) heap of rubble
gruźli|ca *f* (*-y*; *-e*) *med.* tuberculosis, TB; **~czy** tubercular; **~k** *m* (*-a*; *-cy*), **~czka** *f* (*-i*; *G -czek*) tubercular
gry *G pl.* → ***gra***
gryczan|y buckwheat; ***kasza ~a*** buckwheat (grits)
gryf *m* (*-a*; *-y*) griffin; (*-u*; *-y*) (*gitary itp.*) neck
gryka *f* (*-i*) buckwheat
gryma|s *m* (*-u*; *-y*) grimace; ***~sy*** *pl.* whims *pl.*; **~sić** (*-szę*) be finicky; *dziecko*: give trouble, *Brt.* play up; **~śny** capricious, whimsical
gryp|a *f* (*-y*) influenza, F flu; **~owy** influenza, F flu
gryps F *m* (*-u*; *-y*) secret message
grysik *m* (*-u*; *0*) semolina
grywać (*-am*) play occasionally
gryzący biting (*też fig.*); *zapach* sharp; *dym* acrid
gryzmolić (*-lę*) scrawl, scribble
gryzoń *m* (*-nia*; *-nie*) rodent
gryźć bite; *kość* gnaw (at); *orzechy* crack; *dym*, *osy*: sting; *pchły*, *komary*: bite; *sumienie*: gnaw at; **~ się** *kolory*: clash; (*martwić się*) worry (*I* about); F be at loggerheads (***z*** *I* with)
grza|ć (*-eję*) heat, warm; *słońce itp.*: beat down; F (*bić*) belt; ***~ć się*** warm o.s.; warm up; → ***ogrzewać***; **~łka** *f* (*-i*; *G -łek*) heater; ***~łka nurkowa*** immersion heater; **~nka** *f* (*-i*; *G -nek*) toast; (*w zupie*) crouton
grządka *f* (*-i*; *G -dek*) (*kwiatów*) bed, (*warzyw*) patch, plot
grząski marshy
grzbiet *m* (*-u*; *-y*) back; (*górski*) ridge
grzebać (*-ię*) (***w*** *L*) (*w ziemi*) root (in); *fig.* rummage (in); *kury*: scratch; F **~ się** (***z*** *I*) dawdle (over); → ***pogrzebać***

grzebień *m* (*-nia*; *-nie*) comb; (*zwierząt*) crest
grzebyk *m* (*-a*; *-i*) comb
grzech *m* (*-u*; *-y*) sin
grzechot|ać (*-czę/-cę*) rattle; **~ka** *f* (*-i*; *G -tek*) rattle; **~nik** *m* (*-a*; *-i*) rattlesnake
grzeczn|ościowy courtesy; **~ość** *f* (*-ci*; *0*) politeness, courtesy; (*przysługa*) favo(u)r, courtesy; ***z ~ości, przez ~ość*** out of kindness; **~ny** polite, courteous
grzej|nik *m* (*-a*; *-i*) heater; (*kaloryfer*) radiator; ***~nik elektryczny*** electric heater, *Brt.* electric fire; ***~nik wody*** hot-water heater, *Brt.* geyser; **~ny** heating
grzesz|nica *f* (*-y*; *-e*), **~nik** *m* (*-a*; *-cy*) sinner; **~ny** sinful; **~yć** ⟨**z-**⟩ (*-ę*) sin
grzę|da *f* (*-y*) patch, plot, bed; (*dla kur*) roost, perch; **~znąć** ⟨**u-**⟩ (*-nę*, *grzązł*) sink, swamp; *pf. też* get stuck
grzmi|ąco *adv.* boomingly; **~eć** (*-ę*; *-mij!*) thunder; *głos*: boom; ***grzmi*** *nieos* it is thundering
grzmo|cić (*-cę*) beat, belt; **~t** *m* (*-u*; *-y*) thunder; **~tnąć** *v/s.* (*-nę*) *v/t.* F clout *s.o. one*; (*rzucić*) smash; F ***~tnąć się*** (**o** *A*) bump o.s. (on)
grzyb *m* (*-a*; *-y*) *bot.*, *med.* fungus; *bot.* (*z kapeluszem*) mushroom; (*na ścianie*) mould; ***~ trujący*** toadstool; **~ica** *f* (*-y*; *-e*) *med.* mycosis; **~owy** mushroom
grzywa *f* (*-y*; *G -*) mane
grzywna *f* (*-y*; *G -wien*) fine
gubern|ator *m* (*-a*; *-rzy*) governor; **~ia** *f* (*-i*; *-nie*) province
gubić ⟨**z-**⟩ (*-ę*) lose; **~** ⟨**z-**⟩ ***się*** get lost; lose one's way
guma *f* (*-y*) rubber; gum; ***~ do żucia*** chewing gum; F (*prezerwatywa*) rubber
gumisie *m/pl.* jelly babies
gumka *f* (*-i*; *G -mek*) (*do ubrania*) elastic; (*do wycierania*) eraser, *Brt.* rubber
gumowy rubber; *fig.* rubbery
GUS *skrót pisany*: ***Główny Urząd Statystyczny*** Main Statistical Organization
gusła *n/pl.* (*-seł*) sorcery; superstition
gust *m* (*-u*; *-y/-a*) taste; ***w tym guście*** of this type; **~ować** (*-uję*) (**w** *L*) take pleasure (in); **~owny** tasteful, in good taste
guz *m* (*-a*; *-y*) bump; knob; *med.* tumo(u)r
guzdrać się F (*-am*) dawdle
guzik *m* (*-a*; *-i*) button
gwał|cić (*-cę*) ⟨**po-**⟩ *prawo* violate; ⟨**z-**⟩ *kobietę* rape; **~t** *m* (*-u*; *-y*) violation; rape; (*przemoc*) force; ***zadać ~t*** force; ***~tem*** by force; ***na ~t*** immediately, at once; **~towny** violent; (*nagły*) abrupt
gwar *m* (*-u*; *0*) clatter, hum
gwara *f* (*-y*; *G -*) *gr.* dialect
gwaran|cja *f* (*-i*; *-e*) guarantee; (*zwł. na towar*) warranty; **~cyjny** guarantee; warranty; **~tować** ⟨**za-**⟩ (*-uję*) guarantee, warrant
gwardia *f* (*GDl -ii*; *-e*) guard; ***♀ Narodowa*** *Am.* National Guard
gwarny noisy
gwiazd|a *f* (*-y*) star; **~ka** *f* (*-i*; *D -dek*) star; (*znak*) asterisk; (*aktorka*) starlet; (*24-26.XII*) Christmas; **~kowy**: ***podarunek ~kowy*** Christmas gift; **~or** *m* (*-a*; *-rzy*) star; **~ozbiór** *m* (*-oru*; *-ory*) constellation
gwiaździsty (**-ście**) starry; *kształt* star-shaped
gwiezdny stellar, star
gwint *m* (*-u*; *-y*) thread
gwizd *m* (*-u*; *-y*) whistle; **~ać** (*-żdżę*) whistle; **~ek** *m* (*-dka*; *-dki*) whistle; **~nąć** *v/s.* (*-nę*) whistle; F (*ukraść*) pinch
gwóźdź *m* (*gwoździa*; *-oździe*, *I -oździami/-oźdźmi*) nail
gzyms *m* (*-u*; *-y*) *arch.* cornice; → ***karnisz***

H

H

habit *m* (*-u*; *-y*) habit
haczyk *m* (*-a*; *-i*) hook
hafciarka *f* (*-i*; *G -rek*) embroiderer
haft *m* (*-u*; *-y*) embroidery; **~ka** *f* (*-i*; *G -tek*) hook and eye; **~ować** ⟨**wy-**⟩ (*-uję*) embroider; F (*wymiotować*) puke
Haga *f* (*-i*) The Hague
hak *m* (*-u*; *-i*) hook
hala[1] *f* (*-i*; *-e*) hall; (*w fabryce*) workshop; ***~ targowa*** covered market
hala[2] *f* (*-i*; *-e*) mountain pasture
halibut *m* (*-a*; *-y*) *zo.* halibut
halka *f* (*-i*; *G -lek*) slip
halogenowy halogen

halowy indoor
hałas *m* (*-u*; *-y*) noise; **~ować** (*-uję*) make a noise, be noisy
hałaśliwy (**-*wie***) noisy
hałda *f* (*-y*; *G hałd*) slag-heap; *fig.* heap
hamak *m* (*-a*; *-i*) hammock
hamować (*-uję*) ⟨**za-**⟩ brake; *fig. też* hinder, hamper; ⟨**po-**⟩ *łzy* hold back, keep in; *gniew itp.* curb, restrain; **~ *się*** control o.s.
hamul|cowy brake, braking; **~ec** *m* (*-ca*; *-e*, *-ów*) brake; *fig.* inhibition
hand|el *m* (*-dlu*; *-0*) trade, commerce; ***prowadzić ~el, zajmować się ~lem*** (*I*) trade (in), deal (in); do business; **~larz** *m* (*-a*; *-e*) (***używanymi samochodami, narkotykami*** used-car, drug) dealer, (***uliczny*** street) vendor; **~larka** *f* (*-i*; *G -rek*) dealer, vendor
handlow|ać (*-uję*) (*I*) trade (in), deal (in); **~iec** *m* (*-wca*; *-wcy*) trader; salesperson; **~y** trade, commercial
hangar *m* (*-u*; *-y*) hangar
haniebny disgraceful, disreputable
hańb|a *f* (*-y*; *0*) dishono(u)r, disgrace; **~ić** ⟨**z-**⟩ (*-ę*) dishono(u)r, disgrace
haracz *m* (*-u*; *-e*) tribute; (*okup*) ransom
haratać F ⟨**po-**⟩ (*-am/-czę*) mangle, cut up (***się*** o.s.)
harce|rka *f* (*-i*; *G -rek*) *Brt.* (Girl) Guide, *Am.* Girl Scout; **~rz** *m* (*-a*; *-e*) Scout; **~rski** Scouting, Scout(s *pl.*); **~rstwo** *n* (*-a*; *0*) Scouting
hard|ość *f* (*-ści*; *0*) imperiousness; (*dziecko itp.*) unruliness; **~y** (**-*do***) overbearing; imperious; *dziecko itp.* unruly
harfa *f* (*-y*; *G -*) *mus.* harp
har'mo|nia *f* (*GDL -ii*; *0*) harmony; (*GDL -ii*; *-e*) *mus.* (*ręczna*) concertina; **~nijka** *f* (*-i*; *G -jek*) *mus.* harmonica, mouth organ; **~nijny** harmonious; **~nizować** (*-uję*) ⟨**z-**⟩ *też mus.* harmonize (***z** I* with); **~nogram** *m* (*-u*; *-y*) chart, diagram
harować F (*-uję*) slave, slog away
harówka *f* (*-i*; *G -wek*) slaving away; slog
harpun *m* (*-a*; *-y*) harpoon
hart *m* (*-u*; *0*) power, strength; **~ *ducha*** will-power; **~ *fizyczny*** stamina, staying-power; **~ować** ⟨**za-**⟩ (*-uję*) *stal* temper; *plastik* cure; *fig.* harden (***się*** o.s.); **~ow(a)ny** tempered; cured; hardened
haski Hague
hasło *n* (*-a*; *G -seł*) motto, slogan; *mil.*, *komp.* password; (*w słowniku*) entry
haszysz *m* (*-u*; *0*) hashish
haust *m* (*-u*; *-y*) swallow, (*duży*) gulp; ***jednym ~em*** at a gulp
Hawaje *pl.* (*G -ów*) Hawaii
hazardow|y gambling; ***gra ~a*** gambling; ***grać ~o w karty*** gamble at cards
heban *m* (*-u*; *0*) ebony
heb|el *m* (*-bla*, *-ble*) plane; **~lować** (*-uję*) plane
hebrajski (**po -ku**) Hebrew
Hebrydy *pl.* (*G -ów*) Hebrides *pl.*
hec|a *f* (*-y*; *-e*) farce, fuss; ***urządzić ~ę*** make a fuss; ***to ci ~a!*** what a farce!
hejnał *m* (*-u*; *-y*) bugle-call
hektar *m* (*-a*; *-y*) hectare
hel *m* (*-u*; *0*) *chem.* helium
helikopter *m* (*-a*; *-y*) helicopter
hełm *m* (*-u*; *-y*) helmet; (*na wieży*) steeple
hemo|filik *m* (*-a*; *-cy*) *med. Brt.* haemophiliac, *Am.* hemophiliac; F bleeder; **~roidy** *pl.* (*-ów*) *med. Brt.* haemorrhoids *pl.*, *Am.* hemorrhoids *pl.*, F piles *pl.*
hen: ***~daleko*** far away; ***~wysoko*** high up
hera *f* (*-y*; *0*) *sl.* (*heroina*) junk
herb *m* (*-u*; *-y*) coat of arms; **~ *rodowy*** family coat of arms
herba|ciany tea; **~ciarnia** *f* (*-i*; *-e*) teashop, tearoom; **~ta** *f* (*-y*) tea; ***~ta ekspresowa*** tea bag; **~tniki** *pl.* (*-ów*) *Brt.* biscuits, *Am.* cookies
herbowy armorial
herc *m* (*-a*; *-e*) *phys.* hertz
here|tycki heretic; **~zja** *f* (*-i*; *-e*) heresy
hermetycz|ny hermetic; *fig.* opaque, dense; **~nie** air-tight
herod-baba F *f* (*-y*) dragon
heroi|czny heroic, valiant; **~na** *f* (*-y*; *0*) *chem.* heroin; **~nowy** heroin
herszt *m* (*-a*; *-ci/-y*) ringleader
heteroseksualny heterosexual
hetman *m* (*-a*; *-i/-owie*) *hist.* hetman; (*w szachach*) queen
hiena *f* (*-y*) *zo.* hyena
hieroglif *m* (*-u*; *-y*) hieroglyph (*też fig.*)
higi'ena *f* (*-y*; *0*) hygiene; **~ *osobista***, **~ *ciała*** personal hygiene
higieniczny hygienic, healthy
higroskopijny hygroscopic
Himalaje *pl.* (*G -jów/-ai*) Himalayas *pl.*
Hindus *m* (*-a*; *-si*), **~ka** *f* (*-i*; *G -sek*) (*narodowość*) Indian, Hindu; **~m**, **~ka** *f* (*przynależność do religii*) Hindu; **♀ki** Indian

hiobow|y: ***wieść ~a*** dismal news
hipiczny: ***konkurs ~*** riding event
hipis *m* (*-a*; *-i*), **~ka** *f* (*-i*) hippie *lub* hippy
hipno|tyzować ⟨***za-***⟩ (*-uję*) hypnotize; **~za** *f* (*-y*; *0*) hypnosis
hipopotam *m* (*-a*; *-y*) *zo.* hippopotamus
hipo|teczny hypothetical; **~teka** *f* (*-i*) mortgage; **~teza** *f* (*-y*) hypothesis
histeryczny hysterical
hi'stor|ia *f* (*GDL -ii*; *-e*) history; **~yk** *m* (*-a*; *-cy*) historian; (*nauczyciel*) history teacher; **~yczny** historical; (*przełomowy*) historic
Hiszpan *m* (*-a*; *-ie*) Spaniard; **~ia** *f* (*GDl - ii*; *0*) Spain; **~ka** *f* (*-i*; *G -nek*) Spaniard
hiszpańsk|i Spanish; ***mówić po ~u*** speak Spanish
hodow|ać (*-uję*) breed; *rośliny* cultivate, grow; ⟨**wy-**⟩ bring up; raise; rear; **~ca** *m* (*-y*; *G -ów*), **~czyni** *f* (*-*; *-e*) breeder; (*roślin*) grower; **~la** *f* (*-i*; *-e*) breeding; growing; **~lany** breeding
hojn|ie *adv.* generously, copiously; **~y** generous, copious
hokej *m* (*-a*; *0*) hockey; ***~ na lodzie*** ice hockey
hol[1] *m* (*-u*; *-e*, *-ów/-i*) foyer, hall, entrance
hol[2] *m* (*-u*; *-e*, *-ów*) tow; ***brać na ~*** take in tow
Holandia *f* (*-ii*; *0*) Holland
Holender *m* (*-dra*; *-drzy*, *-rów*), Dutchman; ***Holendrzy*** *pl.* the Dutch *pl.*; **~ka** *f* (*-i*; *G -rek*) Dutch woman; **ˆski** (***po -ku***) Dutch
holow|ać (*-uję*) ⟨**od-**⟩ tow; **~niczy** towing; ***lina ~nicza*** towrope; **~nik** *m* (*-a*; *-i*) tug(boat)
hołd *m* (*-u*; *-y*) tribute, homage; ***złożyć ~ pamięci*** (*G*) commemorate; **~ować** (*-uję*) *fig.* (*D*) indulge in
hołota *f* (*-y*) mob, rabble
homar *m* (*-a*; *-y*) *zo.* lobster
homeopatyczny homeopathic
homoseksual|ny homosexual; **~ista** *m* (*-y*; *-ści*) homosexual
honor *m* (*-u*) hono(u)r; ***słowo ~u*** word of hono(u)r; → ***honory***; **~arium** *n* (*-a*; *G -ów*) (*adwokata itp.*) fee; (*autorskie*) royalty; **~ować** (*-uję*) hono(u)r; **~owy** hono(u)rable; *pozycja itp.* honorary; **~y** *pl.* (*-ów*) salute; ***~y domu*** the hono(u)rs *pl.*
hormon *m* (*-u*; *-y*) hormone; **~alny** hormonal
horyzont *m* (*-u*; *-y*) horizon (*też fig.*)
hossa *f* (*-y*) *econ.* boom; (*na giełdzie*) bull market
hostia *f* (*GDL -ii*; *-e*) the Host
hotel *m* (*-u*; *-e*) hotel; ***~ robotniczy*** workers' hostel; **~owy** hotel
hoży (**-** ***żo***) well-built; *cera itp.* fine
hrabi|a *m* (*GA -ego/-i*, *D -iemu/-i*, *V -io!*, *I -ią/-im*, *L -i*; *-iowie*, *GA -iów*, *D -iom*, *I -iami*, *L -iach*) count; **~anka** (*-i*; *G -nek*) count's (unmarried) daughter; **~na** *f* (*-y*) countess; **~owski** count's, of the count
hreczka *f* (*-i*; *G -czek*) → ***gryka***
hucz|eć (*-ę*, *-y*) boom; *morze*, *wiatr*, *maszyna*: roar; **~nie** *adv.* loud(ly); **~ny** *impreza* lively, exuberant; *oklaski* thunderous; *śmiech* booming
hufiec *m* (*-fca*; *-fce*): ***~ harcerski*** troop unit
huk *m* (*-u*; *-i*) boom; roar
hulać (*-am*) F live it up
hulajnoga *f* scooter
hulanka *f* (*-i*; *G -nek*) booze-up
humanitarny humanitarian; (*ludzki*) humane
humo|r *m* (*-u*; *0*) humo(u)r; (*-u*; *-y*) (*nastrój*) mood; whim; ***w złym ~rze*** in a bad mood; **~rystyczny** humorous, comic(al)
huragan *m* (*-u*; *-y*) hurricane; (*wiatr*) gale; **~owy** hurricane; *fig.* thunderous
hurt *m* (*-u*; *0*) *econ.* wholesale; ***~em*** wholesale; F en bloc
hurtow|nia *f* (*-i*; *-e*) wholesale business; **~nik** *m* (*-a*; *-cy*) wholesaler; **~o** *adv.* wholesale; **~y** wholesale
huśtać ⟨**po-**⟩ (*-am*) swing; (*w krześle*) rock; (***się*** *v/i.*)
huśtawka *f* (*-i*; *G -wek*) swing; (*pozioma*) seesaw
hut|a *f* (*-t*) works *sg./pl.*; ***~a stali*** iron (and steel) works; ***~a szkła*** glassworks; **~nictwo** *n* (*-a*; *0*) iron and steel industry; **~nik** *m* (*-a*; *-cy*) ironworker, steelworker
hydrauli|czny hydraulic; **~k** *m* (*-a*; *-cy*) plumber
hydro|elektrownia *f* water power station; **~energia** *f* water power; **~plan** *m* hydroplane; **~terapia** *f* hydrotherapy
hymn *m* (*-u*; *-y*) (*kościelny*) hymn; (*państwowy*) anthem

H

I

i *cj.* and; **~ … ~ …** both … and …, … as well as …; **~ *tak*** anyway

ich 1. *pron. D* → ***one***, *G, A* → ***oni***; **2.** *poss.* **~ *rzeczy*** their things

idą *3. os. pl* → ***iść***

ide|a *f* (*GDL idei*; *-ee*, *-ei*, *-eom*) idea; **~alny** ideal; **~ał** *m* (*-u*; *-y*) ideal

identy|czny identical, the same; **~fikować** (*-uję*) identify (***się*** *v/i.* ***z*** with)

ideo|logiczny ideological; **~wy** ideological

idę *1. os. sg.* → ***iść***

idiot|a *m* (*-y*; *-ci*), **~ka** *f* (*-i*; *G -tek*) idiot (*też med.*), fool; **~yczny** foolish, stupid; **~yzm** *m* (*-u*; *-y*) stupidity, idiocy; nonsense

idyll|a *f* (*-i*; *-e*) idyll; **~iczny** idyllic

idzie|my, ~sz, idź → ***iść***

igie|lny needle; **~łka** *f* (*-i*; *G -łek*) (little) needle; **~łkowy** needle(-shaped)

iglast|y coniferous; ***drzewo ~e*** conifer

ig|lica *f* (*-y*; *-e*) *tech.* pin; (*w broni*) firing pin; (*na wieży*) spire; **~liwie** *n* (*-a*; *0*) needles *pl.*; **~ła** *f* (*-y*; *G -ieł*) needle; (*kaktusa itp.*) spine; ***~ła do szycia*** sewing needle; ***jak z ~ły*** spick and span

ignorować ⟨**z-**⟩ (*-uję*) ignore

igra|ć (*-m*) play (**z** *I* with); **~szka** *f* (*-i*; *G -szek*) plaything

igrzyska *n/pl.* games *pl.*; **♀ *Olimpijskie*** the Olympic Games

i in. *skrót pisany*: ***i inni, i inne*** et al. (*and others*)

ikr|a *f* (*-y*; *0*) roe, spawn; ***składać ~ę*** spawn; ***z ~ą*** with nerve, with guts

ile (*m-os ilu*, *I iloma*) (*niepoliczalne*) how much, (*policzalne*) how many; **~ *razy*** how often; **~ *masz lat?*** how old are you?; ***o ~ bardziej*** how much more; ***o ~ wiem*** as far as I know; ***o ~ … o tyle …*** in so far as; ***o ~ nie*** unless; **~kroć** whenever; **~ś** (*m-os iluś*) some; ***~ś lat temu*** some years ago

ilo|czyn *m* (*-u*; *-y*) *math.* product; **~ma** → ***ile***; **~raz** *m* (*-u*; *-y*) *math.* quotient; **~ściowy** quantitative; **~ść** *f* (*-ci*) quantity

ilu *m-os* → ***ile***

ilumina|cja *f* (*-i*; *-e*) illumination; (festive) illuminations *pl.*; **~tor** *m* (*-a*; *-y*) (circular) porthole

ilustracja *f* (*-i*; *-e*) illustration; (*obrazek*) picture

ilustrowany illustrated; ***magazyn ~*** glossy

iluz|ja *f* (*-i*; *-e*) illusion; **~jonista** *m* (*-y*; *-ści*), **-tka** *f* (*-i*) conjurer; **~oryczny** illusory; pointless

ił *m* (*-u*; *-y*) clay; **~owaty** clay, clayey

im. *skrót pisany*: ***imię*** n. (*name*)

im 1. *pron.* (*D* → ***one, oni***) **2.** *adv.* the; **~ *prędzej, tym lepiej*** the sooner the better

imadło *n* (*-a*) vice

imaginac|ja *f* (*-i*; *0*) imagination; **~yjny** imaginary

imbir *m* (*-u*; *0*) ginger; **~owy** ginger

imbryk *m* (*-a*; *-i*) kettle

imien|iny *pl.* (*-in*) name-day; **~niczka** *f* (*-i*; *G -czek*), **~nik** *m* (*-a*; *-cy*) namesake; **~ny** name; *gr.* nominal; (***-nie***) by name

imiesłów *m* (*-u*; *-y*) *gr.* participle

imię *n* name; *gr.* noun; *fig. też* ***dobre ~*** good reputation; ***mieć na ~*** be called; ***jak ci na ~?*** what is your name?; ***po imieniu*** by name; ***w ~*** (*G*), ***w imieniu*** (*G*) in the name of, on behalf of; ***szkoła imienia NN*** NN school

imigracja *f* (*-i*; *-e*) immigration

imiona *pl.* → ***imię***

imit|acja *f* (*-i*; *-cje*) imitation; **~ować** (*-uję*) imitate

im|matrykulacja (*-i*; *-e*) matriculation; **~munizować** (*-uję*) immunize

impas *m* (*-u*; *-y*) *fig.* impasse, stalemate

imperialistyczny imperialistic

imperium *n* (*-a*; *G -ów*) empire

impertynen|cja *f* (*-i*; *-e*) impertinence, impudence; (*wyzwisko*) a piece of impertinence; **~cki** impertinent, impudent; **~t** *m* (*-a*; *-ci*), **~tka** *f* (*-i*; *G -tek*) impertinent *lub* impudent person

impet *m* (*-u*; *0*) momentum, impetus, drive

impon|ować ⟨**za-**⟩ (*-uję*) impress (***czymś*** with s.th.); **~ujący** (**-co**) impressive, imposing

import *m* (*-u*; *-y*) import; **~ować** (*-uję*)

import; **~owy** imported
impotencj|a *f* (*-i*; *0*) *med.* impotence; ***cierpieć na ~ę*** be impotent
im|pregnować (*-uję*) impregnate, waterproof; **~preza** *f* (*-y*) (***sportowa*** sporting) event; (*przyjęcie*) party; **~prowizować** (*-uję*) improvize; **~pulsywny** impulsive, impetuous
in. *skrót pisany*: ***inaczej*** differently
inaczej differently (***niż*** than); (*w przeciwnym razie*) otherwise; ***tak czy ~*** either way; ***jakże ~*** how else
inaugur|acja *f* (*-i*; *-cje*) inauguration; opening; **~acyjny** inaugural; inauguration; **~ować** ⟨***za-***⟩ (*-uję*) inaugurate; open
incydent *m* (*-u*; *-y*) incident, event
indagować (*-uję*) ask (***o*** *A* about)
indeks *m* (*-u*; *-y*) index; (*studenta*) student's credit book; ***~ rzeczowy*** subject index
indeksacja *f* (*-i*; *-e*) *econ.* indexation, index-linking
Indi'a|nin *m* (*-a*; *-ie*), **~nka** *f* (*-i*; *G -nek*) Indian; **♀ński** Indian
Indie *pl.* (*GDL -ii*; *0*) India
Indonez|ja *f* (*-i*; *0*) Indonesia; **♀yjski** Indonesian
indor *m* (*-a*; *-y*) turkey (cock)
indos *m* (*-a*; *-y*) *econ.* endorsement
indosować (*-uję*) endorse
indukc|ja *f* (*-i*; *-e*) induction; **~yjny** inductive
indycz|ka *f* (*-i*; *G -czek*) turkey (hen); **~y** turkey; **~yć się** F (*-ę*) get annoyed
indyjs|ki (***po -ku***) Indian
indyk *m* (*-a*; *-i*) turkey
indywidu|alność *f* (*-ści*; *0*) individuality; **~alny** individual; personal; single; **~um** *n* (*idkl.*; *-ua*, *-duów*) individual; character
indziej → ***gdzie, kiedy, nigdzie***
inercj|a *f* (*-i*; *0*) inertia; ***siła ~i*** inertia
infekcja *f* (*-i*; *-e*) infection
inflacja *f* (*-i*; *-e*) inflation
informa|cja *f* (*-i*; *-e*) information; (*jedna*) piece of information; (*okienko itp.*) information desk/office *etc.*; **~cyjny** information; **~tor** *m* (*-a*; *-ry*) (*książka*) guide (***po*** *L* to); (*pl. -rzy*) informer **~tyka** *f* (*-i*; *0*) computer science
informować ⟨***po-***⟩ (*-uję*) inform; ***~ się*** inquire (***o*** *L*, ***w sprawie*** G about); ask (***u*** *G* s.o.)
infuła *f* (*-y*) *Brt.* mitre, *Am.* miter
ingerować ⟨***za-***⟩ (*-uję*) interfere, intervene
inhalować (*-uję*) inhale
inicjator *m* (*-a*; *-rzy*), **~ka** *f* (*-i*; *G -rek*) initiator, originator
inicjatyw|a *f* (*-y*) initiative; ***z ~y*** on s.o.'s own initiative
inicjować ⟨***za-***⟩ (*-uję*) initiate, originate
iniekcja *f* (*-i*; *-e*) *med.* injection
inkas|ent *m* (*-a*; *-ci*) collector; ***~ent gazowni*** gas-meter reader; **~o** *n* (*-a*) *econ.* collection
inkrustowany inlaid
inkubacyjny: ***okres ~*** *med.* incubation period
inkubator *m* (*-a*; *-y*) incubator
in|na, ~ne, ~ni → ***inny***; **~no-** *w zł.* differently
innowacja *f* (*-i*; *-e*) innovation
inny another, other; ***co innego*** something else; ***kto ~*** someone else; → ***między***
inscenizacja *f* (*-i*; *-e*) *theat.* staging
inspek|cja *f* (*-i*; *-e*) inspection, checking; **~tor** *m* (*-a*; *-rzy*), inspector; superintendent; ***~tor szkolny*** schools inspector; **~torat** *m* (*-u*; *-y*) inspectorate; **~towy** hothouse; **~ty** *m/pl.* (*-ów*) (cold) frame
instal|acja *f* (*-i*; *-e*) installation; (*zakładanie*) fitting; (*urządzenia*) *zw. pl.* installations *pl.*, facilities *pl.*; **~ować** ⟨***za-***⟩ (*-uję*) install; put in, put up, fit in; ***~ować się*** make o.s. at home
instruk|cja *f* (*-i*; *-e*) instruction; ***~cja obsługi*** operating instructions *pl.*; **~tor** *m* (*-a*; *-rzy*), **-rka** *f* (*-i*; *G -rek*) (***jazdy, pilotażu*** driving, flying) instructor; **~tywny** instructive
instrument *m* (*-u*; *-y*) instrument
instynktowny instinctive
instytucja *f* (*-i*; *-e*) institution
instytut *m* (*-u*; *-y*) institute; department
insynuacja *f* (*-i*; *-e*) insinuation
insynuować (*-uję*) insinuate
integra|cja *f* (*-i*; *0*) integration; **~lny** integral
integrować ⟨***z-***⟩ (*-uję*) integrate
intelektual|ista *m* (*-y*; *-ści*), **~istka** *f* (*-i*; *G -tek*) intellectual; **~ny** intellectual
inteligen|cja *f* (*-i*; *0*) intelligence; (*klasa*) intelligentsia; **~cki** of intelligentsia; **~tny** intelligent

intencj|a *f* (*-i*; *-e*) intention; plan; ***w ~i*** on behalf of

intencyjny: ***list ~*** letter of intent

intensyfikować ⟨**z-**⟩ (*-uję*) intensify

intensywn|ość *f* (*-ci*; *0*) intensity; **~y** intensive; *światło, kolor itp.* intense

intonacja *f* (*-i*; *-e*) intonation

interes *m* (*-u*; *-y*) business; (*sprawa*) interest; (*transakcja*) dealings *pl.*; ***nie twój ~*** none of your business; ***w twoim ~ie*** in your (best) interest(s *pl.*); ***ładny ~!*** a pretty kettle of fish!

interesant *m* (*-a*; *-ci*), **~ka** *f* (*-i*; *G -tek*) client, customer; *econ.* potential buyer

interesow|ać ⟨**za-**⟩ (*-uję*) *v/t.* interest; *v/i.* (***~ać się***) be interested (*I* in); **~ny** self-interested, selfish

interesujący (**-co**) interesting

inter|na F *f* (*-y*; *0*) internal medicine; **~nat** *m* (*-u*; *-y*) dormitory bloc; (***prywatna***) ***szkoła z ~natem*** boarding school; **~nować** (*-uję*) intern; **~pretować** (*-uję*) interpret; **~punkcja** *f* (*-i*; *0*) punctuation

interwen|cja *f* (*-i*; *-e*) intervention; **~cyjny**: ***prace*** *f/pl.* ***~cyjne*** job-creation measures; **~iować** (*-uję*) intervene; F step in

intonować ⟨**za-**⟩ (*-uję*) *pieśń* start singing

intratny lucrative, profitable

introligatornia *f* (*-i*; *-e*) bindery

intruz *m* (*-a*; *-i/-y*) intruder

intry|ga *f* (*-i*) intrigue, scheme; **~gancki** scheming; **~gować** ⟨**za-**⟩ (*-uję*) scheme; **~gujący** intriguing

intymn|ość *f* (*-ci*; *0*) intimacy; (*odosobnienie*) privacy; **~y** intimate; (*osobny*) private

inwali|da *m* (*-y*; *-dzi*), **~dka** *f* (*-i*; *G -dek*) invalid; ***~da wojenny*** war invalid; **~dzki** invalid; ***wózek ~dzki*** wheelchair

in|wazja *f* (*-i*; *-e*) invasion; **~wentaryzacja** *f* (*-i*; *-e*) stock-taking; **~wentarz** *m* (*-a*; *-e*) stock, inventory

inwersyjny: ***film ~*** *phot.* reversal film

inwestor *m* (*-a*; *-rzy*) investor

inwestować ⟨**za-**⟩ (*-uję*) invest

inwestyc|ja *f* (*-i*; *-e*) (*działalność*) investment; (*przedsięwzięcie*) investment project; **~yjny** investment

inwigilacja *f* (*-i*; *-e*) surveillance

inż. *skrót pisany*: ***inżynier*** Eng., Engr. (*Engineer*)

inżynie|r *m* (*-a*; *-owie*) engineer; **~ria** *f* (*GDL -ii*; *0*) engineering; ***~ria genetyczna*** genetic engineering; ***~ria lądowa*** (building) construction and civil engineering

ira|cki Iraqi; **≈k** (*-u*; *0*) Iraq; **≈kijczyk** *m* (*-a*; *-cy*), **≈kijka** *f* (*-i*; *G -jek*) Iraqi; **≈n** (*-u*; *0*) Iran; **≈nka** *f* (*-i*; *G -nek*), **≈ńczyk** *m* (*-a*; *-cy*) Iranian; **~ński** Iranian

Irlan|dczyk *m* (*-a*; *-cy*) Irishman; ***~dczycy*** *pl.* the Irish; **~dia** *f* (*GDL -ii*; *0*) Ireland; **~dka** *f* (*-i*; *G -dek*) Irishwoman; **≈dzki** Irish

ironiczny ironic

irygacyjny irrigation

irys *m* (*-a*; *-y*) *bot.* iris

iryt|acja *f* (*-i*; *0*) annoyance, irritation; **~ować** ⟨**po-, z-**⟩ (*-uję*) annoy; ***~ować*** ⟨**z-**⟩ ***się*** get annoyed

isk|ra *f* (*-y*; *G -kier*) spark; **~rzyć** (*-ę*) spark (***się*** *v/i.*)

islam *m* (*-u*; *0*) Islam; **~ski** Islamic

Islan|dia *f* (*GDL -ii*; *0*) Iceland; **~dczyk** *m* (*-a*; *-cy*), **~dka** *f* (*-i*; *G -dek*) Icelander; **≈dzki** Icelandic

istnie|ć (*-eję*) exist; be; → ***być, trwać***; **~nie** *n* (*-a*) existence, being

istny veritable, virtual

isto|ta *f* (*-y*) creature, being; (*sedno*) essence; ***w ~cie*** in fact; **~tny** essential, fundamental

iść go, (**do** *G* to); (*pieszo*) walk; (*pojazdy*) run; ***~ po*** fetch, get; ***~ za*** (*I*) follow; ***~ za mąż*** (**za** *I*) get married (to); ***~ dalej*** go on, continue; ***idzie o …*** all this is about…, what is at stake is…; ***co za tym idzie*** what follows from this is …; → (***przy***)***chodzić, pójść***

itd. *skrót*: ***i tak dalej*** etc. (*and so on*)

itp. *skrót*: ***i tym podobne*** etc. (*and so on*)

izba *f* (*-y*) room; (instytucja *itp.*) chamber; *pol.* house; ***≈ Gmin*** the House of Commons; ***~ przyjęć*** (*w szpitalu*) admissions office

izola|cja *f* (*-i*) isolation; (*kabla, pokoju itp.*) insulating, insulation; **~cyjny** isolating; insulating; **~tka** *f* (*-i*; *G -tek*) (*dla chorego*) isolation ward; (*w szkole itp.*) sickbay

izolować ⟨**za-, od-**⟩ (*-uję*) isolate; *kabel itp.* insulate

Izrael *m* (*-a*; *0*) Israel; **~czyk** *m* (*-a*; *-cy*), **~ka** *f* (*-i*; *G -lek*) Israeli; **≈ski** Israeli

iż *cj.* that; → ***że***

J

ja *pron.* I; ***kto tam? to ~*** who is it? - that's me; ***własne ~*** one's own self
jabłeczn|ik *m* apple pie; (*wino*) cider; **~y** apple
jabłko *n* (*-a*; *G -łek*) apple
jabło|ń *f* (*-ni*, *-nie*) apple-tree; ***kwiat ~ni*** apple blossom
jacht *m* (*-u*; *-y*) yacht; ***~ kabinowy*** cabin cruiser
jacy *m-os* → ***jaki***
jad *m* (*-u*; *-y*) venom (*też fig.*); (*trucizna*) poison; ***~ kiełbasiany*** botulin
jada|ć (*-am*) → ***jeść***; **~lnia** *f* (*-i*; *-e*, *-i*) dining-room; (*meble*) dining-room suite; **~lny** edible, eatable; ***sala ~lna*** dining-room
ja|dą, ~dę → ***jechać***; **~dł(a)** → ***jeść***
jadło|dajnia (*-i*; *-e*, *-i*) restaurant, *Am.* diner; **~spis** *m* (*-u*; *-y*) menu
jado|wity venomous (*też fig.*), poisonous; **~wy** *zo.* venomous
jaglan|y: ***kasza ~a*** millet gruel
jagły *f/pl.* (*-gieł*) millet; millet gruel
jagnię *n* (*-cia*; *-ta*, *G -niąt*) lamb
jagnięcy lamb
jagod|a *f* (*-y*; *G -gód*) *bot.* berry; ***czarna ~a*** → ***borówka brusznica***; **~y** *pl.* *też* soft fruit; **~owy** bilberry, blueberry, whortleberry
jajeczkowanie *n* (*-a*) *biol.* ovulation
jajecznica *f* (*-y*; *-ce*) scrambled eggs *pl.*
jaj|ko *n* (*-a*; *G -jek*) egg; ***~ka*** *pl.* ***sadzone*** fried eggs *pl.*; **~nik** *m* (*-a*;*-i*) *anat.* ovary
jajo egg; *biol.* ovum; **~waty** egg-shaped; *biol.* ovoid
jak 1. *pron.* how; as; ***~ się masz?*** how are you?; **2.** *cj.* as; like; ***~ gdyby*** as if; ***~ na owe czasy*** for those times; **3.** *part.* as; ***nic innego ~*** nothing else but; ***~ najwięcej*** as much as possible; ***~ najlepszy*** best of all; → ***byle, tylko***
jakby as if, as though; F something like; → ***gdyby***
jaki (*m-os jacy*) what; which; how; ***~ bądź*** whichever; ***~ taki*** so so; ***~m prawem*** by what right; ***~m cudem*** by a miracle or what; ***za ~ rok*** in a year or so; F ***po ~emu*** how, in what language; **~'kolwiek** any; **~ś** some; about; ***~eś trzy metry*** about three meters; ***~ś dziwny*** sort of strange
jak'kolwiek however; (*chociaż*) although
jako as; ***~ taki*** as such; ***~ tako*** to some extent, F a bit; ***~ że*** because, as; **~by** *adv.* supposedly, allegedly; **~ś** somehow
jakoś|ciowy (***-wo***) qualitative; **~ć** *f* (*-ci*; *0*) quality
jakże how; → ***jak***
jałmużna *f* (*-y*; *zw. 0*) alms *pl.*; *fig.* pittance
jałow|cowy juniper; **~iec** *m* (*-wca/-wcu*; *-wce*) juniper
jałowy arid, barren; *biol.* infertile, barren; *electr.*, *tech.* neutral; *tech.* idle; ***bieg ~*** neutral
jałówka *f* (*-i*; *G -wek*) heifer
jama *f* (*-y*) pit, hole; *anat.* cavity
jamnik *m* (*-a*; *-i*) *zo.* dachshund
janowiec *m* (*-wca*; *-wce*) broom
Japo|nia *f* (*GDL -ii*; *0*) Japan; **~nka** *f* (*-i*; *G -nek*), **~ńczyk** *m* (*-a*; *-cy*) Japanese; **♀ński** (***po -ku***) Japanese
jarmar|czny fair, market; *fig.* cheapjack; **~k** *m* (*-u*; *-i*) fair, market
jarosz *m* (*-a*; *-e*) vegetarian
jar|ski vegetarian; **~y** *agr.* spring
jarząb *m* (*-rzębu/-ęba*; *-rzęby/-ębie*, *-ębiów*) *bot.* mountain ash; **~ek** *m* (*-bka*; *-bki*) *zo.* hazelhen
jarzeniówka *f* (*-i*; *G -wek*) strip light
jarzębina *f* (*-y*) *bot.* rowan, European mountain ash
jarzmo *n* (*-a*; *G -/-rzem*) yoke
jarzyć się (*-ę*) glow; (*lśnić*) glisten
jarzyn|a *f* (*-y*) vegetable; **~owy** vegetable
jasełka *n/pl.* (*-łek*) *rel.* nativity play
jasiek *m* (*-śka*; *-śki*) little pillow; *bot.* (*type of large white bean*)
jaski|nia *f* (*-i*; *-e*) cave, cavern; **~niowiec** *m* (*-wca*; *-wcy*) caveman (*też fig.*); **~niowy** cave
jaskół|czy swallow; **~ka** *f* (*-i*; *G -łek*) *zo.* swallow; (*w sporcie*) arabesque
jaskra *f* (*-y*; *0*) *med.* glaucoma
jaskraw|o- glaringly; bright; **~y** (***-wo***) glaring (*też fig.*); bright

jasno light; **~blond** (*idkl.*) very fair; (*o kobiecie*) light blonde, **~ść** *f* (*-ści*; *0*) brightness; *fig.* clarity, lucidity; **~widz** *m* (*-a*; *-e*) clairvoyant; **~żółty** light yellow
jasn|y light; *fig.* clear, lucid; ***rzecz ~a***, F ***~e*** it is clear; ***w ~y dzień*** in broad daylight
jastrząb *m* (*-rzębia*; *-ębie*, *-ębi*) hawk (*też pol.*)
jaszczur *m* (*-a*; *-y*) *zo.* reptile; **~ka** *f* (*-i*; *G -rek*) *zo.* lizard
jaśmin *m* (*-u*; *-y*) *bot.* jasmine
jaśnie|ć (*-eję*) be shining (*też fig.* with); glow; ⟨**po-**⟩ brighten, become lighter; **~j**(**szy**) *adv.* (*adj.*) *comp. od* → ***jasno, jasny***
jatka *f* (*-i*; *G -tek*) slaughter house; *fig.* slaughter, butchery
jaw: ***wyjść na ~*** come to light; ***wydobyć na ~*** bring to light; **~ić się** (*im*)*pf* (*-ę*) appear (***k-ś*** to s.o.); **~nie** *adv.* openly, in the open; **~ny** open; undisguised
jawor *m* (*-a*; *-y*) *bot.* sycamore (maple)
jaz *m* (*-u*; *-y*) dam, *Brt.* weir
jazda *f* (*-y*) travel, journey; ***~ koleją*** journey by train; ***~ na rowerze*** bike ride; ***~ na nartach*** skiing; ***~ konna*** → ***prawo, rozkład***
jazz *m* (*-u*; *0*) *mus.* jazz; **~ować** (*-uję*) play jazz; **~owy** jazz, F jazzy
jaź|ń *f* (*-ni*; *-nie*) ego, the I; ***rozdwojenie ~ni*** split personality
ją *pron.* → ***ona***
jąd|ro *f* (*-a*; *G -der*) core; nucleus (*też phys., biol., fig.*); (*orzecha*) kernel; *anat.* testicle; **~rowy** nuclear;
jąkać się (*-am*) stutter, stammer
jątrzyć (*-ę*) foment, stir up; ***~ się*** fester, ulcerate
je *pron. A*; → ***one, ono***; *v/t.*, *v/i.* → ***jeść***
jechać (*-dę*) ⟨**po-**⟩ go (***koleją*** by train); ride (***rowerem*** (on) a bike; ***konno*** (on) a horse); (*samochodem*) *kierowca*: drive, *pasażer*: ride in; travel; *windą* take; → ***jeździć***
jeden → ***715***; one; ***~ raz*** once; ***~drugiego/drugiemu*** one another; ***~ do zera*** one-nil; ***ani ~*** not a single one; ***sam ~*** all alone; ***~ i ten sam*** the same; ***jednym słowem*** in a word; ***z jednej strony*** on the one hand; ***co to za ~?*** who is he?
jedena|stka *f* (*-i*; *G -tek*) eleven; (*w sporcie*) penalty kick; (*drużyna*) team; **~sty** eleventh; **~ście**, **~stu** *m-os* eleven
jedlina *f* (*-y*) → ***jodła***; fir sprigs *pl.*
jedn. *skrót pisany* ***jednostka*** unit
jedna *f* → ***jeden***; **~ć** ⟨**z-**⟩ (*-am*) gain, win (*też* ***sobie***); → ***pojednać***; **~k** nevertheless, however; **~kowo** *adv.* identically; in the same way; equally; **~kowy** identical
jedni *m-os pl.* → ***jeden***
jedno *n* (*jednego*; *jedni*) one; the same; → ***jeden***; **~barwny** unicolo(u)r; monochromatic; **~brzmiący** identical (in sound); **~czesny** (***-śnie***) simultaneous; **~czyć** ⟨**z-**⟩ (*-ę*) unite (***się*** *v/i.*); **~dniowy** one-day; **~głośnie** unanimously; **~imienny** of the same name
jednokierunkow|y one-way; ***ruch ~y*** one-way traffic; ***ulica ~a*** one-way street
jedno|kondygnacyjny one-stor(e)y, single-stor(e)y; **~konny** one-horse; **~krotny** single; **~lity** uniform; homogeneous; **~myślny** unanimous; **~oki** one-eyed; **~osobowy** single; single-person; **~piętrowy** two-stor(e)y; **~pokojowy** one-room
jednoraz|owy single; ***do ~owego użycia*** disposable; **~ówka** *f* (*-i*; *G -wek*) disposable
jedno|ręki one-handed; **~roczny** one-year; **~rodny** homogeneous; **~rodzinny** one-family, single-family; **~rzędowy** *marynarka* single-breasted; **~silnikowy** one-engine; **~stajny** monotonous
jednost|ka *f* (*-i*; *G -tek*) unit; (*osobnik*) individual; ***~ka miary*** unit of measure; ***~ka wojskowa*** army unit (*też math.*); **~kowy** unique; individual, single
jednostronny one-sided, unilateral
jedność *f* (*-ci*; *0*) unity; unit
jedno|tlenek *m* monoxide; **~torowy** one-track; **~zgłoskowy** *gr.* monosyllabic; **~znaczny** unambiguous, unequivocal
jedwab *m* (*-iu*; *-ie*) silk; **~isty** silky, silken; **~ny** silk, silken, silky
jedyna|czka *f* (*-i*; *G -czek*) only daughter; **~k** *f* (*-a*; *-i*) only son
jedyn|ie *adv.* only, merely; **~ka** *f* (*-i*; *G -nek*) one; (*linia*) number one; *szkoła*: *jakby*: F, failing; **~y** only, single; ***~y w swoim rodzaju*** unique

jedz|(ą) → ***jeść***; **~enie** *n* (*-a*; *0*) food; eating
jedzie(cie, -sz), jedź → ***jechać***
je|go 1. *pron.* (*GA* → ***on***) him; (*G* → ***ono***) it; **2.** *poss.* his; **~j** *pron.* (*GD* → ***ona***) her; *poss.* her, hers
jeleń *m* (*-nia*, *-nie*) *zo.* deer, (*samiec*) stag
jelito *n* (*-a*) *anat.* intestine, bowel; **~ *grube*** large intestine; **~wy** intestinal
jełczeć ⟨***z-***⟩ (*-eję*) grow rancid, go bad
jem *1. os. sg.* → ***jeść***
jemioła *f* (*-y*) *bot.* mistletoe
jemu *pron.* (*D* → ***on, ono***) him
jeniec *m* (*-ńca*; *-ńcy*) prisoner; **~ki** prisoner
Jerozolima *f* (*-y*; *0*) Jerusalem
jesie|nny autumn(al); fall; **~ń** *f* (*-ni*; *-nie*) *Brt.* autumn, *Am.* fall; ***~nią*** in autumn/fall
jesion *m* (*-u*; *-y*) *bot.* ash
jesionka *f* (*-i*; *G -nek*) coat
jesiotr *m* (*-a*; *-y*) *zo.* sturgeon
jest (he, she, it) is; ***~em*** (I) am; ***~eś*** (you) are; ***~eśmy*** (we) are; ***~eście*** (you) are; → ***być***
jesz *2. os. sg.* → ***jeść***
jeszcze yet, still; ***~ jak!*** and how!; ***~ nie*** not yet; ***~ dłuższy*** even longer
jeść ⟨***z-***⟩ eat; have; ***~ c-ś*** have s.th. to eat; ***~ śniadanie*** have breakfast; ***dać c-ś ~*** give s.th. to eat; ***chce mi się ~*** I am hungry
jeśli *cj.* if, when
jez. *skrót pisany*: ***jezioro*** L., *lub* l. (*lake*)
jezdnia *f* (*-i*; *-e*) roadway
jezioro *n* (*-a*) lake; ***~ sztuczne*** artificial lake
jezuicki Jesuit
jeździć (*-żdzę*) go (***na urlop*** on holiday); travel (***po kraju*** all over the country); *autobus*, *pociąg*: run; ***~ na nartach*** ski; ***~ samochodem*** *kierowca*: drive; → ***jechać***
jeździec *m* (*-dźca -dźcy*, *jeźdźcze!*) rider; **~ki** riding; **~two** *n* (*-a*; *0*) riding
jeż *m* (*-a*; *-e*) *zo.* hedgehog; ***włosy*** *m/pl.* ***na ~a*** crew-cut
jeżeli → ***jeśli***
jeżyć ⟨***na-***⟩ (*-ę*) bristle (***się*** *v/i.*)
jeżyna *f* (*-y*) *bot.* blackberry, bramble
jęczeć (*-ę*, *-y*) moan, groan
jęczmie|nny barley; **~ń** *m* (*-nia*; *-nie*) barley; *med.* sty(e)
jędrny husky; *styl* expressive
jędza *f* (*-y*; *-e*) termagant, shrew; (*czarownica*) witch
jęk *m* (*-u*; *-i*) moan, groan; **~liwy (*-wie*)** moaning; **~nąć** *v/s.* (*-nę*) give a groan
jęzor *m* (*-a*; *-y*) tongue
języ|czek *m* (*-czka*; *-czki*) tongue; *anat.* uvula; **~k** *m anat.* tongue (*też fig.*); ***~k ojczysty*** mother tongue; ***kaleczyć ~k polski*** speak broken Polish; ***mleć ~kiem*** waffle about; **~kowy** linguistic; **~koznawstwo** *n* (*-a*; *0*) linguistics
jidysz *m* (*-u*; *0*) Yiddish
j.n. *skrót pisany*: ***jak niżej*** as below
jod *m* (*-u*; *0*) *chem.* iodine
jod|ełka *f* (*-i*; *G -łek*): ***garnitur w ~ełkę*** a herringbone suit; **~ła** *f* (*-y*; *G -deł*) *bot.* fir
jodyna *f* (*-y*; *0*) iodine
jogurt *m* (*-u*; *-y*) yoghurt
jonowy ionic
Jowisz *m.* (*-a*; *0*) *astr.* Jupiter
jubilat *m* (*-a*; *-ci*), (*man celebrating his anniversary/birthday*); **~ka** *f* (*-i*; *G -tek*) (*woman celebrating her anniversary/birthday*)
jubiler *m* (*-a*; *-ów*) jeweller; **~ka** F *f* (*-i*; *0*) (*rzemiosło*) jewellery; **~ski** jeweller's
jubileusz *m* (*-u*; *-e*) anniversary
juczny *zwierzę* pack
juda|istyczny Judaistic; **~izm** *m* (*-u*) Judaism
judasz *m* (*-a*; *-e*) *fig.* Judas; (*w drzwiach*) peep-hole, judas; **~owski, ~owy** judas
judzić (*-dzę*) goad (***do*** *G* into)
juhas *m* (*-a*; *-i*) junior sheep herder (*in the Tatras*); **~ka** *f* (*-i*; *G -sek*) junior sheep woman herder (*in the Tatras*)
junacki daring, audacious
junior *m* (*-a*; *-rzy*), **~ka** *f* (*-i*; *G -rek*) junior
juror *m* (*-a*; *-rzy*) juryman; **~ka** *f* (*-i*; *G -rek*) jurywoman, juryperson
jutr|o 1. *adv.* tomorrow; **2.** *n* (*-a*; *0*) tomorrow; ***od ~a*** from/since tomorrow
jutrze|jszy tomorrow; **~nka** *f* (*-i*; *G -nek*) dawn; ***Ωnka*** Morning Star
już already; yet; ***~ nie*** no longer; ***~ nigdy*** never again; ***~!*** OK; (I'm) coming
jw. *skrót pisany*: ***jak wyżej*** as above

J

K

kabaczek *m* (*-czka*; *-czki*) *Brt.* marrow, *Am.* squash

kabał|a *f* (*-y*; *G -*) cabbala; ***stawiać ~ę*** tell fortunes (from the cards); ***wpaść w ~ę*** F get into a mess

kabaret *m* (*-u*; *-y*) cabaret

ka|bel *m* (*-bla*; *-ble*, *-bli*) cable; **~bina** cabin; *tel.* phone booth; (*przepierzenie*) cubicle; *lotn.* ***~bina pilota*** cockpit; **~blowy**: ***telewizja ~blowa*** cable TV

kabłąk *m* (*-u*; *-i*) bow; bail; *tech.* pantograph, bow; **~owaty** (**-*to***) bent

kabura *f* (*-y*) holster

kabz|a *f*: F ***nabić ~ę*** make a pile

kac F *m* (*-a*; *-e*) hangover; ***mieć ~a*** be hung over

kacyk *m* (*-a*; *-i*) chieftain

kaczan *m* → ***głąb***[1]; corncob

kacz|ka *f* (*-i*; *G -czek*) *zo.* duck; ***~ka pieczona*** roast duck; **~or** *m* (*-a*; *-y*) *zo.* drake; **~y** duck

kadencja *f* (*-i*; *-e*) term (of office); *parl.* legislative period; *mus.* cadence

kadłub *m* (*-a*; *-y*) body; (*samolotu*) fuselage; (*statku*) hull

kadr *m* (*-u*; *-y*) frame

kadr|a *f* (*-y*; *G -*) personnel, staff, cadre; ***~y kierownicze*** management; **~owy** **1.** (*zawodowy*) cadre; (*personalny*) personnel; **2.** *m* (*-ego*; *-wi*), ***~owa*** *f* (*-wej*; *-we*) personnel officer

kadzi|ć (*-dzę*) incense; *fig.* honey up; **~dło** *n* (*-a*; *G -deł*) incense

kadź *f* (*-dzi*; *-dzie*) tub

kafar *m* (*-u*) *bud.* pile-driver

kafejka *f* (*-ki*; *G -jek*) cafe/café

kafel *m* (*-fla*; *-fle*, *-fli*), **~ek** *m* (*-ka*; *-ki*) tile

kaflowy tile, tiled

kaftan *m* (*-a*; *-y*): ***~ bezpieczeństwa*** strait-jacket; **~ik** *m* (*-a*; *-i*) (*niemowlęcia*) shirt, *Brt.* vest

kaganiec *m* (*-ńca*; *-ńce*) muzzle

Kair *m* (*-u*; *0*) Cairo

kajak *m* (*-a*; *-i*) kayak, canoe; ***~ składany*** collapsible kayak/canoe; **~arstwo** *n* (*-a*) canoeing

kajdan|ki *pl.* (*-nek*/*-nków*) handcuffs *pl.*; **~y** *pl.* (-) fetters *pl.*, shackles *pl.*

kajuta *f* (*-y*) cabin

kajzerka *f* (*-i*; *G -rek*) bread roll

kakao *n* (*idkl.*) cocoa

kaktus *m* (*-a*; *-y*) cactus

kalać ⟨**po-, s-**⟩ (*-am*) defile

kalafior *m* (*-a*; *-y*) *bot.* cauliflower

kalambur *m* (*-a*; *-y*) pun

kalarepa *f* (*-y*) kohlrabi

kale|ctwo *n* (*-a*) disability; **~czyć** ⟨**po-, s-**⟩ (*-ę*) cut (**się** o.s.; ***sobie rękę*** one's hand); → ***język***; **~ka** *m/f* (*-i*; *-i*/*-cy*, *G -/-ów*) disabled person, *pej.* cripple (*też fig.*); **~ki** disabled, cripple(d)

kalendarz *m* (*-a*; *-e*) calendar; (*podręczny*) *Brt.* diary, *Am.* (pocket) calendar

kalenica *f* (*-y*; *-e*) (roof-)ridge

kalesony *pl.* (*-ów*) underpants; (*długie*) long underwear, F long johns *pl.*

kaliber *m* (*-bru*; *-y*) *Brt.* calibre, *Am.* caliber (*też fig.*)

Kalifornia *f* (*-ii*; *0*) California

kalina *f* (*-y*) *bot.* snowball

kalk|a *f* (*-i*; *G -/-lek*) carbon paper; **~omania** *m* (*GDL -ii*; *-e*) *Brt.* transfer, *Am.* decalc(omania)

kalkula|cja *f* (*-i*; *-e*) calculation; **~cyjny**: ***arkusz ~cyjny*** spreadsheet; **~tor** *m* (*-a*; *-y*), **~torek** *m* (*-rka*; *-rki*) calculator

kalkulować ⟨**s-, wy-**⟩ (*-uję*) calculate; ***~ się*** F pay, pay off

kaloryczny caloric; (*pożywny*) high-calorie

kaloryfer *m* (*-u*; *-y*) radiator

kalosz *m* (*-a*; *-e*) *Brt.* wellington (boot), *Am.* rubber (boot)

kal'waria (*GDL -ii*; *-e*) calvary (*też fig.*)

kalwiński Calvinist

kał *m* (*-u*; *0*) *Brt.* faeces *pl.*, *Am.* feces

kałamarz *m* (*-a*; *-e*) ink-pot

kałuża *f* (*-y*, *-e*) puddle; (*krwi*, *oleju*) pool

kambuz *m* (*-a*; *-y*) *naut.* galley

kameleon *m* (*-a*; *-y*) *zo.* chameleon

kamer|a *f* (*-y*) camera; **~alny** *mus.* chamber; **~ton** *m* (*-u*; *-y*) tuning fork

kamerzysta *m* (*-y*; *-ści*) cameraman

kamfora *f* (*-y*; *0*) camphor

kamica *m* (*-y*; *-e*) *med.* lithiasis; ***~ nerkowa*** *med.* urolithiasis

K

kamieni|arka *f* (*-i*) masonry; stonework; **~arski**: ***zakład ~arski*** (*nagrobkowy*) monumental mason's workshop; marble mason's workshop; **~arz** marble mason; (*nagrobków*) monumental mason; **~ca** *f* (*-y*; *-e*) house; ***~ca czynszowa*** block of (rented) *Brt.* flats *lub Am.* apartments; **~eć** ⟨**s-**⟩ (*-eję*) turn to stone, petrify (*też fig.*); **~ołom** *m* (*-u*; *-y*) quarry; **~sty** (**-*ście***) stony
kamie|nny stone; **~ń** *m* (*-nia*; *-nie*) stone; (*pojedynczy też*) pebble; (*kotłowy*) scale, *Brt.* fur; ***~ń węgielny*** corner-stone (*też fig.*); ***~ń do zapalniczki*** flint; ***~ń obrazy*** a bone of contention; ***jak ~ń w wodę*** without a trace; F ***jak z ~nia*** with a difficulty
kamionkowy stoneware
kamizelka *f* (*-i*; *G -lek*) *Brt.* waistcoat, *Am.* vest
kam'pania *f* (*GDL -ii*; *-e*) campaign; ***~ promocyjna*** advertising *lub* promotion campaign; ***~ wyborcza*** election campaign
kamrat *m* (*-a*; *-ci*) pal, mate, buddy
kamy|czek *m* (*-czka*; *-czki*), **~k** *m* (*-ka*; *-ki*) stone; pebble
Kanad|a *f* (*-y*) Canada; **~yjczyk** *m* (*-a*; *-cy*), **~yjka** *f* (*-i*; *G -jek*) Canadian; ***♀yjka*** (*kajak*) Canadian canoe; **♀yjski** Canadian
kanaliza|cja *f* (*-i*; *-e*) (*urządzenia*) sewage system; (*kanalizowanie*) installation of a sewage system; **~cyjny** sewage
kanał *m* (*-u*; *-y*) *naturalny* channel; *sztuczny* canal; *ściekowy* sewer; (*rów*) ditch; *TV*: channel; ***♀ La Manche*** English Channel; **~owy**: ***leczenie ~owe*** *med.* root(-canal) therapy
kanap|a *f* (*-y*) sofa, couch; **~ka** *f* (*-i*; *G -pek*) settee, sofa; (*przekąska*) sandwich
kanarek *m* (*-rka*; *-rki*) *zo.* canary
kance'la|ria *f* (*GDL -ii*; *-e*) office; **~ryjny** office; ***papier ~ryjny*** (large-size) writing paper
kancia|rstwo F *n* (*-a*) swindling; **~rka** *f* (*-i*; *G -rek*), **~rz** *m* (*-a*, *-e*) swindler
kanciasty (**-*to***) angular
kanc|lerski chancellor's; **~lerz** *m* (*-a*; *-e*) chancellor
kand. *skrót pisany*: **kandydat** cand. (*candidate*)
kandy|dat *m* (*-a*; *-ci*), **~datka** *f* (*-i*; *G -tek*) candidate (***na*** *A*, ***do*** *G* to); **~dować** (*-uję*) apply (***na*** *A* for), stand (as a candidate) (***na*** *A* for)
kandyzowany glacé, candied
kangur *m* (*-a*; *-y*) *zo.* kangaroo
kanikuła *f* (*-y*) dog days *pl.*; (*upał*) heat wave
kanonada *f* (*-y*) bombardment, cannonade
kanoni|k *m* (*-a*; *-cy*) canon; **~zować** (*-uję*) canonize
kant *m* (*-u*; *-y*) edge; (*po zaprasowaniu*) crease; F swindle
kantor¹ *m* (*-u*; *-y*) office; ***~ walutowy*** exchange office
kantor² *m* (*-a*; *-rzy*) cantor
kantować F ⟨**o-**⟩ (*-uję*) swindle, cheat
kantówka *m* (*-i*; *G -wek*) *bud.* square timber; ruler
kantyna *f* (*-y*) (*sklep*) canteen
kapa *f* (*-a*; *-y*) bedspread; *rel.* cope
kapać (*-ię*) drop, drip
kapary *m/pl.* (*-ów*) capers *pl.*
kapeć *m* (*-pcia*; *-pcie*, *-pci*[*ów*]) slipper; (*stary but*) old worn-out slipper/shoe
kapela *f* (*-i*; *-e*) *mus.* F band; (*ludowa*) folk group
kapel|an *m* (*-a*; *-i/-owie*) *rel.* chaplain; *mil.* army chaplain; **~mistrz** *m* (*-a*; *-e/-owie*) *mus.* bandmaster, band leader; (*dyrygent*) conductor
kapelusz *m* (*-a*; *-e*) hat
kaper|ować ⟨**s-**⟩ (*-uję*) capture, seize; (*w sporcie*) entice; **~unek** *m* (*-nku*; *-nki*) capturing; enticing
kapiszon *m* (*-a*; *-y*) → ***kaptur***, ***spłonka***
kapitali|sta *m* (*-y*; *-ści*) capitalist; **~styczny** capitalist; **~zm** *m* (*-u*; *-y*) capitalism
kapita|lny F splendid, wonderful; ***remont ~lny*** general overhaul; **~ł** *m* (*-u*; *-y*) capital; ***~ł zakładowy*** registered *lub* nominal capital; ***~ł akcyjny*** joint stock
kapitan *m* (*-a*; *-owie*) *mil.*, *naut.*, (*w sporcie*) captain; **~at** *m* (*-u*; *-y*) *naut.* port authority
kapitański: ***mostek ~*** bridge
kapitu|lacja *f* (*-i*; *-e*) capitulation, surrender; **~lować** ⟨**s-**⟩ (*-uję*) capitulate, surrender; *fig.* give up
kapituła *f* (*-y*) *rel.* chapter
kapli|ca *f* (*-y*; *-e*, *G -czek*), **~czka** *rel.* chapel; wayside shrine
kapła|n *m* (*-a*; *-i*) priest; **~nka** *f* (*-i*; *G*

K

-nek) priestess; **~ński** clerical, priestly, sacerdotal
kapnąć *v/s.* (*-nę*) drip
kapota *f* (*-y*) coat, jacket
kapować ⟨**s-**⟩ F (*-uję*) get, understand
kapral *m* (*-a*; *-e*) corporal
kapry|s *m* (*-u*; *-y*) whim; caprice; *mus.* capriccio; **~sić** → ***grymasić***; **~śny** capricious, whimsical
kapsel *m* (*-sla*; *-sle*, *-sli*) (crown) cap
kapsuł|a *f* (*-y*; *G -*) capsule; *astr.* (space) capsule; **~ka** *f* (*-i*; *G -łek*) *med.* capsule
Kapsztad *m* (*-u*; *0*) Cape Town
kaptować ⟨**s-**⟩ (*-uję*) entice; buy
kaptur *m* (*-a*; *-y*) hood; *tech.* cover
kapucyn *m* (*-a*; *-i*) *rel.* Capuchin (friar)
kapu|sta *f* (*-y*; *G -*) *bot.* cabbage; ***biała ~sta*** white cabbage; ***głowiasta ~sta*** headed cabbage; ***włoska ~sta*** savoy cabbage; **~ściany** cabbage; **~śniak** *m* (*-a*; *-i*) *gastr.* cabbage soup; (*deszcz*) drizzle
kar|a *f* (*-y*; *G -*) punishment (***za*** *A* for); penalty; ***~a pozbawienia wolności*** imprisonment; ***pod ~ą więzienia*** punishable by prison; ***za ~ę*** as a punishment
karabin *m* (*-u*; *-y*) gun, *mil. zwł.* rifle; **~ek** *m* (*-nka*; *-nki*) small-bore rifle; snap hook, karabiner, **~owy** rifle, gun
karać ⟨**u-**⟩ (*-rzę*) punish (***za*** *A* for; ***więzieniem*** with imprisonment)
karafka *f* (*-i*; *G -fek*) decanter
karakułowy astrakhan
karalny punishable; ***czyn ~*** *jur.* criminal offence
karaluch *m* (*-a*; *-y*) *zo.* cockroach
karambol *m* (*-u*; *-e*) *mot.* pile-up
karaś *m* (*-sia*; *-sie*) *zo.* crucian
karawan *m* (*-u*; *-y*) hearse; **~a** *f* (*-y*; *G -*) caravan
karb *m* (*-u*; *-y*) notch, score; ***kłaść na ~*** (*G*) put down to, set down to; ***trzymać w ~ach*** curb, restrain
karbidówka *f* (*-i*; *G -wek*) carbide lamp
karbowa|ć (*-uje*) notch, score; *włosy* → ***kręcić***; **~ny** notched, scored
karcąco *adv.* reproachfully
karciany card
karcić ⟨**s-**⟩ (*-cę*) rebuke; → ***ganić***
karczma *f* (*-y*; *G -czem*) inn
karczoch *m* (*-a*; *-y*) *bot.* artichoke
karczow|ać ⟨**wy-**⟩ (*-uję*) grub; **~isko** *n* (*-a*) clearance
kardio|gram *m* (*-u*; *-y*) *med.* cardiogram; **~stymulator** *m* (*-a*; *-y*) *med.* pace-maker
kardynalny fundamental, basic, cardinal
kardynał *m* (*-a*; *-owie*) *rel.* cardinal
karet|a *f* (*-y*) carriage, coach; **~ka** *f* (*-i*; *G -tek*): ***~ka pogotowia*** (***ratunkowego***) ambulance; ***~ka więzienna*** *Brt.* prison van, *Am.* patrol wagon
kariera *f* (*-y*) career; success
kark *m* (*-u*; *-i*) *anat.* neck; ***nadstawiać ~u*** risk one's neck; ***zima na ~u*** the winter is approaching; **~ołomny** breakneck, headlong
karłowaty dwarfish, dwarf
karmazyn *m* (*-a*; *-y*) zo. rose-fish; **~owy** crimson
karmel *m* (*-u*; *-e*) caramel; **~ek** *m* (*-ka*; *-ki*) caramel (toffee)
karmelicki Carmelite
karmi|ć ⟨**na-**⟩ give food to; *niemowlę* breast-feed; *zwł. zwierzę* feed; ***~ się*** live on; **~enie** *n* (*-a*) feeding
karnawał *m* (*-u*; *-y*) carnival
karn|ość *f* (*-ści*; *0*) discipline; **~y** disciplined
karo *n* (*-a lub idkl.*; *-a*) *gra w karty*: diamond(s *pl.*); ***as ~*** ace of diamonds; ***wyjść w ~*** play diamonds
karoseria *f* (*GDL -ii*; *-e*) *mot.* bodywork
karowy *gra w karty*: diamond
karp *m* (*-ia*; *-ie*) *zo.* carp
kart|a *f* (*-y*; *G -*) (*kredytowa*, *do gry*) card; (*papieru*) sheet; *komp.* expansion card; ***~a tytułowa*** title page; ***~a łowiecka*** game licence; ***~a wyborcza*** ballot-paper; ***~a telefoniczna*** *zwł. Brt.* phonecard; ***zielona ~a*** *Brt.* green card, certificate of motor insurance; ***grać w*** (***otwarte***) ***~y*** put one's cards on the table; ***z ~y*** à la carte; **~ka** *f* (*-i*; *G -tek*) (*w książce*) leaf; (*luzem*) sheet; ***~ka pocztowa*** postcard
kartof|el *m* (*-fla*; *-fle*) potato; **~lanka** *m* (*-i*; *G -nek*) potato soup
karton *m* (*-u*; *-y*) cardboard; (*pudło*) box; **~owy** cardboard
kartoteka *f* card file *lub* index
karuzela *f* (*-i -e*) *Brt.* merry-go-round, *Am.* carousel
karygodny criminal
karykatu|ra *f* (*-y*) cartoon; (*portret*) caricature; **~rować** ⟨**s-**⟩ (*-uję*) caricature;

~rzysta *m* (*-y*; *-ści*), **~rzystka** *f* (*-i*; *G -tek*) cartoonist, caricaturist
karzeł *m* (*-rła*; *-rły*) dwarf
kasa *f* (*-y*) cash-box, (*urządzenie*) cash register; (*miejsce*) pay desk, (*w supermarkecie*) check-out; (*w teatrze itp.*) box-office; F (*pieniądze*) money; **~ pancerna** safe, strongbox
kasacja *f* (*-i*; *-e*) *jur.* annulment, cassation
kaset|a *f* (*-y*; *G -*) (*na pieniądze*) cash-box; *RTV*: cassette, tape; *phot.* cartridge; **~ka** *f* (*-i*; *G -tek*) box; **~owy** cassette
kasjer *m* (*-a*; *-rzy*), **~ka** *f* (*-i*; *G -rek*) cashier, teller
kask *m* (*-u*; *-i*) (*motocyklisty itp.*) helmet, (*robotnika itp.*) hard-hat
kaskader *m* (*-a*; *-rzy*) stuntman
kasłać (*-am*) → ***kaszlać***
kasow|ać ⟨**s-**⟩ (*-uję*) *wyrok* annul; *zapis* cancel; *bilet* cancel, punch; *nagranie* erase; *komp.* delete, erase; **~ość** *f* (*-ści*; *0*) success at the box-office; **~y** *wpływy* cash; *sukces* box-office
kastet *m* (*-u*; *-y*) *Brt.* knuckle-duster, *Am.* brass knuckles *pl.*
kastrować ⟨**wy-**⟩ (*-uję*) *samca* castrate; *samicę* spay
kasyno *n* (*-a*) casino; *mil.* mess
kasza *f* (*-y*; *-e*) (*sypka*) groats *pl.*; (*przyrządzona*) gruel; **~nka** *f* (*-i*; *G -nek*) *Brt.* black pudding, *Am.* blood sausage
kaszel *m* (*-szlu*; *-szle*) cough
kaszkiet *m* (*-u*; *-y*) peaked cap
kaszl|ać, ~eć (*-lę*, *-l!*) ⟨**~nąć**⟩ *v/s.* (*-nę*) cough
kasztan *m* (*-a*; *-y*) (*jadalny*) chestnut; (*kasztanowiec*) horse chestnut, (*owoc*) conker; (*koń*) chestnut; **~owy** chestnut
kat *m* (*-a*; *-ci/-y*) hangman, executioner
kata|klizm *m* (*-u*; *-y*) cataclysm, catastrophe, (natural) disaster; **~lizator** *m* (*-a*; *-y*) *chem.*, *mot.* catalyst; **~log** *m* (*-u*; *-i*) catalog(ue); *komp.* directory; **~logować** ⟨**s-**⟩ (*-uję*) catalog(ue)
katar *m* (*-u*; *-y*) cold (in the head), catarrh
katarakta *f* (*-y*) cataract (*też med.*)
katarynka *f* (*-i*; *G -nek*) barrel organ
katastrofa *f* (*-y*) catastrophe; **~ *kolejowa*/*lotnicza*** train/air crash; **~ *samochodowa*** car accident
katechizm *m* (*-u*; *-y*) catechism
katedra *f* (*-y*) cathedral; (*uczelnia*) chair (***historii*** of history); **~lny** cathedral
kategor|ia *f* (*GDL -ii*; *-e*) category; **~yczny** categorical; **~yzować** (*-uję*) categorize
katoli|cki (***po -ku***) (Roman) Catholic; **~cyzm** (Roman) Catholicism; **~czka** *f* (*-i*; *G -czek*), **~k** *m* (*-a*; *-cy*) (Roman) Catholic
katować (*-uję*) torment, torture
kaucja *f* (*-i*; *-e*) (*w sklepie itp.*) deposit; *jur.* bail
kauczukowy caoutchouc, rubber
Kauk|az *m* (*-u*; *0*) the Caucasus; **~aski** Caucasus, Caucasian
kawa *f* (*-y*) coffee; **~ *naturalna*** real coffee; → ***biały, zbożowy***
kawalarz F *m* (*-a*; *-e*) joker
kawaler *m* (*-a*; *-rzy/-owie*) bachelor, unmarried man; (*amant*) boyfriend, beau; (*pl. -owie*) Knight (***Orderu …*** of the Order…); (*na dworze*) chevalier; **~ia** *f* (*GDL -ii*; *-e*) *mil.* cavalry; **~ka** *f* (*-i*; *0*) *Brt.* bachelor flat, *Am.* studio apartment; **~ski** bachelor; **~yjski** cavalry
kawał *m* (*-u*; *-y*) lump, chunk; F joke; **~ *drogi*** a long way; **~ *chłopa*** a fine figure of a man; ***zrobić komuś ~*** play a joke on s.o.; **~eczek** *m* (*-czka*; *-czki*) a little bit, piece; **~ek** *m* (*-ka*; *-ki*) a bit, piece; ***na ~ki*** to pieces
kawiarnia *f* (*-i*; *-e*) café/cafe, coffee shop
kawior *m* (*-u*; *0*) caviar(e)
kawka *f* (*-i*; *G -wek*) jackdaw
kawowy coffee
kaza|ć (*im*)*pf* (*każę*, *każ!*) order, command; ***~ł mi na siebie czekać*** he made me wait for him, he kept me waiting; **~lnica** *f* (*-y*; *-e*) *rel.* pulpit; **~nie** *n* (*-a*) *rel.* sermon; *fig.* lecture
kazirodztwo *n* (*-a*; *0*) incest
kaznodzieja *m* (*-i*; *-e*, *G -jów*) *rel.* preacher
kaźń *f* (*-ni*; *0*) torture
każdorazowo *adv.* each/every time
każd|y (***~a, ~e***) every, each; everybody, everyone; ***w ~ej chwili*** (at) any moment; ***o ~ej porze*** (at) any time; ***za ~ym razem*** every time; ***na ~ym kroku*** at every step
kącik *m* (*-a*; *-i*) → **kąt**; (*zakątek*) nook
kąpać ⟨**wy-**⟩ (*-ię*) *v/t. Brt.* bath, *Am.* bathe; **~** ⟨**wy-**⟩ **się** *v/i.*; (*myć*) take *lub* have a bath; (*pływać*) swim; ***~ się w słońcu*** soak up the sun

K

kąpiel *f* (*-i*; *-e*) (*mycie*) bath; (*pływanie*) swim; **~isko** *n* (*-a*) bathing place; bathing beach; ***~isko morskie*** seaside resort; **~owy** bathing; ***strój ~owy*** bathing suit; **~ówki** *f/pl.* (*-wek*) bathing trunks *pl.*

kąs|ać (*-am*) bite; **~ek** *m* (*-ska*; *-ski*) morsel, bit, chunk

kąśliwy (**-*wie***) biting, sharp

kąt *m* (*-a*; *-y*) *math.* angle; (*pokoju itp.*) corner; F place to stay; ***~ widzenia*** point of view; ***pod ostrym ~em*** at an acute angle; ***pod ~em*** at an angle; (*G*) from the point of; ***po ~ach*** secretly; **~omierz** *m* (*-a*; *-e*) protractor; **~ownik** *m* (*-a*; *-i*) *tech.* angle (iron), angle (bar); **~owy** angle, angular

kc *skrót pisany*: ***kodeks cywilny*** civil code

kciuk *m* (*-a*; *-i*) thumb

keczup *m* (*-a*; *0*) ketchup

kefir *m* (*-u*; *-y*) kefir

keks *m* (*-u*; *-y*) fruit cake

kelner *m* (*-a*; *-rzy*) waiter; **~ka** *f* (*-i*; *G -rek*) waitress

kemping *m* (*-u*; *-i*) camping site; **~owy** camping; ***przyczepa ~owa*** *Brt.* caravan, *Am.* trailer

kędzierzawy curly, curling

kędzior *m* (*-a*; *-y*) lock

kęp|a *f* (*-y*) (*drzew*) clump, cluster; (*trawy*) tuft, bunch; (*wyspa*) islet, *Brt.* holm; **~ka** *f* (*-i*; *G -pek*) little cluster

kęs *m* (*-a*; *-y*), **~ek** (*-ska*; *-ski*) bite, mouthful

kibel F *m* (*-bla*; *-ble*) (*toaleta*) *Brt.* loo, *Am.* john

kibic *m* (*-a*; *-e*) fan, supporter

kibuc *m* (*-a*; *-e*) kibbutz

kich|ać (*-am*) 〈***~nąć***〉 (*-chnę*) sneeze; *fig.* think nothing (***na*** *A* of)

kicia *m* (*-i*; *-e*) F pussy

kiczowaty (**-*to***) kitschy, trashy, cheap

kić F (*-cia*, *-cie*; *-ciów*) *Brt.* nick, *zwł. Am.* slammer

kiecka *f* (*-i*; *G -cek*) skirt; ***kiecki*** *pl.* F togs *pl.*

kiedy 1. *pron.* when; **2.** *cj.* when; as; ***~ indziej*** another time; **~'kolwiek** whenever; at any time; **~ś** sometime, (at) some time (or other); **~ż** when at last

kielich *m* (*-a*; *-y*) goblet; *rel.* chalice; *bot.* calyx; ***iść na ~a*** go for a drink

kieliszek *m* (*-a*; *-szki*) glass; ***~ do wódki*** vodka glas; ***~ do jaj*** egg cup

kielnia *f* (*-i*; *-e*) *bud.* trowel

kieł *m* (*kła*; *kły*) canine tooth; (*drapieżcy*) fang; (*słonia*, *dzika*) tusk

kiełbas|a *f* (*-y*; *G* -) sausage; **~iany** sausage; ***jad ~iany*** botulin, **~ka** *f* (*-i*; *G -sek*) sausage; frankfurter

kiełkować 〈**wy-**〉 (*-uję*) germinate; sprout; *fig.* stir, awaken

kiepski bad; poor

kier. *skrót pisany*: ***kierownik*** man., mngr (*manager*); ***kierunek*** dir. (*direction*)

kier *m* (*-a*; *-y*) *gra w karty*: heart(s *pl.*); ***as ~*** ace of hearts; → *też* ***kra***; ***wyjść w ~y*** play hearts

kierat *m* (*-u*; *-y*) treadmill (*też fig.*); *fig.* drudgery, dreary routine

kiermasz *m* (*-u*; *-e*) fair, bazaar

kierować (*-uję*) 〈**s-**〉 (**do** *G*, **na** *A*) direct (to, towards, *też fig.*), aim (at); *spojrzenie* turn (towards); *broń* point (at); 〈**po-**〉 (*I*) (*autem itp.*) drive (*też v/i.*); (*zakładem*) manage, run; ***~ się*** (*I*) be guided (by)

kierow|ca *m* (*-cy*; *G -ów*) driver; **~nica** *m* (*-y*; *-e*) steering wheel; (*roweru*) handlebars *pl.*

kierowni|ctwo *n* (*-a*) management; supervision; **~czka** *f* (*-i*; *G -czek*) manager, director, head; (*szkoły*) headmistress; **~czy** managerial, executive; **~k** *m* (*-a*; *-cy*) manager, director, head; (*szkoły*) headmaster

kierowy heart(s)

kierun|ek *m* (*-nku*; *-nki*) direction; ***pod ~kiem*** under the direction *lub* supervision of; **~kowskaz** *m* (*-y*; *G -ów*) (*drogowskaz*) signpost; *mot. Brt.* indicator, *Am.* turn signal; **~kowy** directional; ***numer ~kowy*** *tel.* dialling code, *Am.* area code

kieszeń *f* (*-ni*; *-nie*) (***spodni, wewnętrzna*** trouser, inside) pocket

kieszonkow|e *n* (*-ego*) pocket money; **~iec** *m* (*-wca*; *-wcy*) pickpocket; (*pl. -wce*) (*książka*) pocket book; **~y** pocket

kij *m* (*-a*; *-e*, *-ów*) stick; ***~ golfowy*** golf club; F ***~e*** *pl.* beating, caning, hiding

kijanka *f* (*-i*; *G -nek*) tadpole

Kijów *m* (*-jowa*; *0*) Kiev

kikut *m* (*-a*; *-y*) stump, stub

kilim *m* (*-a*; *-y*) kilim

kilka (*m-os kilku*) several, some; F a

couple (of); **~dziesiąt** a few dozen; **~krotny** repeated; ***-nie*** *adv.* repeatedly; **~naście** a dozen or so; **~set** several hundred
kilk|oro, ~u *m-os* → ***kilka***
kilku|dniowy lasting several days; several days long; **~godzinny** lasting several hours, of several hours; **~letni** lasting several years, of several years; **~miesięczny** lasting several months, of several months; **~nasto-** *w zł.* → ***kilkanaście***; **~nastoletni** lasting over ten years; in one's teens; **~osobowy** for several people; **~rodzinny** for several families; multifamily; **~set** → ***kilkaset***; **~tysięczny** of several thousand
kilof *m* (*-a*; *-y*) pick mattock, *Brt.* pickaxe, *Am.* pickax
kilo|gram *m* kilogram; **~metr** *m Brt.* kilometre, *Am.* kilometer; **~wy** one-kilogram; *naut.* keel
kiła *m* (*-y*; *0*) *med.* syphilis
kim(że) (*IL* → ***kto, któż***): ***z ~*** with who(m); ***o ~*** about who(m)
kimać (*-am*) F nap, doze off
kinkiet *m* (*-u*; *-y*) wall lamp
kino *n* (*-a*) (*budynek*) *Brt.* cinema, *Am.* movie theater; (*seans*) *Brt.* the cinema, *Am.* the movies; (*sztuka*) cinema; **~operator** *m* (*-a*; *-rzy*) projectionist; **~wy** cinema
kiosk *m* (*-u*; *-i*) kiosk; newsagent('s); **~arka** *f* (*-i*; *G -rek*), **~arz** *m* (*-a*; *-e*) newsagent
kipi|ący boiling, seething; **~eć** (*-ę*, *-i*) boil, seethe (*też fig.* ***z*** *G* with)
kir *m* (*-u*; *-y*) crepe; *fig.* mourning
kis|ić ⟨**za-**⟩ (*-szę*, *-ś!*) pickle; ***~ić się*** pickle; *fig.* ferment; **~iel** *m* (*-ślu*; *-śle*) jelly-like dessert; **~nąć** ⟨**s-**⟩ (*-nę*, *-[ną]ł*) turn sour
kiszka *f* (*-i*; *G -szek*) F gut, bowel; ***ślepa ~*** F *med.* appendix; ***~ pasztetowa*** *gastr.* liver sausage
kiszon|ka *f* (*-G -nek*) *agr.* silage; **~y**: ***~a kapusta*** sauerkraut; ***~y ogórek*** pickled cucumber/gherkin
kiść *f* (*-ci*; *-cie*) bunch
kit *m* (*-u*; *-y*) putty; **~a** *f* (*-y*) plume, (*ogon*) brush, brushy tail
kitel *m* (*-tla*; *-tle*) overall; (*lekarza itp.*) white coat
kitować (*-uję*) ⟨**za-**⟩ putty, fix with putty; ⟨**wy-**⟩ F *Brt.* croak, peg out
kiw|ać (*-am*) ⟨**~nąć**⟩ (*-nę*) (*głową*) nod (one's head); (*ręką*) wave (***na k-oś*** to s.o.); ***~ać się*** move about, be loose; *meble*: be rickety; → ***kołysać się***
kiwi *n* (*idkl.*) *zo.*, *bot.* kiwi
kk *skrót pisany*: **kodeks karny** criminal code
kl. *skrót pisany*: **klasa** cl. *lub* Cl. (*class*)
klacz *f* (*-y*; *-e*) mare
klajster *m* (*-tra*; *-try*) paste; (*paćka*) goo
klakson *m* (*-u*; *-y*) *mot.* horn
klam|ka *f* (*-i*; *G -mek*) door-handle, (*gałka*) doorknob; **~ra** *f* (*-y*; *G -mer*) clasp; buckle
klap|a *f* (*-y*; *-*) hinged lid, trapdoor; (*marynarki*) lapel; ***~a bezpieczeństwa*** safety valve; ***zrobić ~ę*** fall flat; **~ać** (*-ię*) *chodaki*: click; *kapcie*: pad; *deska*: rattle; **~nąć** *v/s.* (*-nę*) fall *lub* sit with a bump
klarnet *m* (*-u*; *-y*) *mus.* clarinet
klarow|ać ⟨**wy-**⟩ (*-uję*) *wino* clear; clarify, make clear; **~ny** clear
klas|a *f* (*-y*; *G -*) class (*też uczniów*); (*oddział uczniów w szkole*) *Brt.* form, *Am.* grade, (*sala*) classroom; **~kać** (*-szczę/-kam*) ⟨**~nąć**⟩ (*-nę*) clap (one's hands), applaud; **~owy** class; classroom; **~ówka** *f* (*-i*; *G -wek*) test; **~yczny** classical, classic
klasy|fikować ⟨**za-**⟩ (*-uję*) classify; ***~fikować się*** be classified, be grouped; **~ka** *f* (*-i*; *0*) classics *pl.*
klasztor *m* (*-u*; *-y*) *rel.* (*męski*) monastery, (*żeński*) convent; **~ny** monastery, monastic; convent, conventual
klatka *f* (*-i*; *G -tek*) cage; (*zdjęciowa*) frame; ***~ piersiowa*** chest, *med.* thorax; ***~ schodowa*** staircase
klauzula *f* (*-i*; *-le*) *jur.* clause
klawiatura *f* (*-y*) keyboard
klawisz *m* (*-a*; *-e*) key; **~owy** *instrument* keyboard
klą|ć (*klnę*) (**na** *A*) swear (at), curse; **~twa** *f* (*-y*; *G -*) curse
klecić ⟨**s-**⟩ (*-cę*) *meble itp.* knock together; *wypracowanie itp.* knock off
kleić ⟨**s-, za-**⟩ (*-ję*) glue (together), stick (together); ***~ się*** be sticky; stick; (*do kogoś*) cling (**do** G to); F *fig.* ***nie ~ się*** not work out (all right)
kle|ik *m* (*-u*; *-i*) gruel; **~isty** sticky; *ręce itp.* clammy
klej *m* (*-u*; *-e*) glue; paste

K

klejnot *m* (*-u*; *-y*) jewel
klekotać (*-cę/-czę*) rattle, clatter; → ***paplać***
klep|ać (*-ię*) 〈**po-**〉 slap, pat (**się** o.s., each other); 〈**wy-**〉 (*mówić*) patter; *kosę* strickle; *metal* chase; **~isko** *n* (*-a*) (*w stodole*) thrashing floor; **~ka** *f* (*-i*; *G -pek*) (*w beczce*) stave; (*na podłodze*) flooring strip *lub* block; F ***brak mu piątej ~ki*** he has got a screw loose; **~nąć** → ***klepać***
klepsydra *f* (*-y*; *G -*) hourglass; (*nekrolog*) obituary (notice)
kler *m* (*-u*; *0*) (the) clergy; **~ykalny** clerical
kleszcz *m* (*-a*; *-e*) *zo.* tick; **~e** *m/pl.* (*-y/-ów*) *tech.* pliers *pl.* pincers *pl.*; *med.* forceps *pl.*; *zo.* pincers *pl.*; **~owy**: ***poród ~owy*** *med.* forceps delivery
klęcz|eć (*-ę*) kneel; **~ki** *pl.*: ***na ~kach*** on knees; **~nik** *m* (*-a*; *-i*) prie-dieu
K
klęk|ać (*-am*) 〈***~nąć***〉 (*-nę*, *też -kła*, *-kli*) kneel down
klę|li, ~łam → ***kląć***
klęsk|a *f* (*-i*; *G -*) defeat; disaster, catastrophe; ***~a pożaru*** fire, conflagration, ***~a głodu*** hunger, famine; ***ponieść ~ę*** suffer defeat
klient *m* (*-a*; *-ci*) client; customer; **~ela** *f* (*-i*; *G -el*) clientele, customers *pl.*; **~ka** *f* (*-i*; *G -tek*) client; customer
klika *f* (*-i*; *G -*) clique
klikać (*-nę*) *komp.* (*A*) click (on)
klimat *m* (*-u*; *-y*) climate; **~yczny** climatic; ***stacja ~yczna*** climatic health resort; **~yzacja** *f* (*-i*; *0*) air-conditioning; **~yzator** air-conditioner
klin *m* (*-a*; *-y*) wedge; (*w ubraniu*) (wedge-shaped) gusset; ***zabić ~(a) między*** drive a wedge between
klinga *f* (*-i*; *G -*) blade
klini|czny clinical; **~ka** *f* (*-i*) teaching hospital; clinic
klinow|aty wedge-shaped; **~y**: ***pas ~y*** *tech.* V-belt; ***pismo ~e*** cuneiform writing
klisza *f* (*-y*; *-e*) plate; film
kln|ą, ~ę, ~iecie, ~iesz → ***kląć***
kloc *m* (*-a*; *-e*) block, (*pień*) log; **~ek** *m* (*-cka*; *-cki*) block
klomb *m* (*-u*; *-y*) flowerbed
klon *m* (*-u*; *-y*) *bot.* maple; *biol.* clone; **~ować** (*-uję*) clone
klops *m* (*-a*; *-y*) meat loaf; (*mały*) meatball; F washout; **~ik** *m* (*-a*; *-i*) meatball, rissole
klosz *m* (*-a*; *-e*) lampshade; (*na ser itp.*) bell-shaped cover; (*na rośliny*) cloche; **w ~** → **~owy** (widely) flared
klown *m* (*-a*; *-y/-i*) clown
klozet *m* (*-u*; *-y*) WC, toilet; **~owy** toilet
klub *m* (*-u*; *-y*) club; ***~ poselski*** parliamentary group; **~owy** club
klucz *m* (*-a*; *-e*) key (*też fig.*); *mus.* clef; *tech. Brt.* spanner, *Am.* wrench; ***pod ~em*** under lock and key; (*w więzieniu*) behind bars; **~owy** key
kluć się (*-ję*) hatch
klusk|a *f* (*-i*; *G -sek*) dumpling; ***~i*** *pl. też* pasta
kła → ***kieł***
kłaczkowaty fluffy
kła|dą, ~dę → ***kłaść***; **~dka** (*-i*; *G -dek*) foot-bridge, *naut.* gangplank; **~dziesz** → ***kłaść***
kłak *m* (*-a*; *-i*) flock, tuft; ***~i*** *pl. pej.* shock, mop
kłam *m* (*-u*; *0*): ***zadać ~*** (*D*) give the lie to; **~ać** 〈**s-**〉 (*-ię*) lie; **~ca** *m* (*-y*; *G -ów*) lier; **~liwy** (***-wie***) lying; **~stwo** *n* (*-a*) lie
kłania|ć się (*-am*) bow; nod (***znajomym*** to acquaintances); ***~j się im od nas*** remember us to them
kłaść lay; (*do łóżka*) lay down; put (***do kieszeni*** (in)to the pocket); ***~ się*** lie down; → ***wkładać***
kłąb *m* (*kłębu*; *kłęby*) ball, tangle; *zo.* withers *pl.*; ***kłęby*** clouds (***dymu, kurzu*** of smoke, of dust)
kłęb|ek *m* (*-ka*; *-ki*) ball, tangle; *fig.* ***~ek nerwów*** a bundle of nerves; ***zwinąć się w ~ek*** curl up; **~ić się** (*-ę*) get up (in clouds), hang (in clouds); mill about
kłoda *m* (*-y*; *G kłód*) log
kłonić 〈**s-, po-**〉 bow down (**się** *v/i.*)
kłopot *m* (*-u*; *-y*) trouble, problem, worry; ***~y pieniężne*** financial difficulties *pl.*; ***~y z sercem*** heart trouble; ***wprawić w ~*** embarrass; **~ać się** (*-czę/-cę*) worry (***o*** *A* about); **~liwy** troublesome, difficult
kłos *m* (*-a*; *-y*) ear
kłócić się (*-cę*) quarrel, argue (***o*** *A* about); *kolory*: clash
kłódka *m* (*-i*; *G -dek*) padlock
kłót|liwy (***-wie***) quarrelsome; **~nia** *f* (*-i*; *-e*) quarrel, argument
kłu|ć (*-ję/kolę*, *kolesz*, *kole*, *kłuj!*) prick;

ból: stab; **~jący** prickling; stabbing
kłus *m* (*-a*; *0*) trot; **~*em*** at a trot; **~ak** *m* (*-a*; *-i*) trotter
kłusować[1] (*-uję*) trot
kłusow|ać[2] (*-uję*) poach; **~nictwo** *n* (*-a*; *0*) poaching; **~nik** *m* (*-a*; *-cy*) poacher
kły *pl.* → ***kieł***
KM *skrót pisany*: ***koń mechaniczny*** HP (*horse power*)
kminek *m* (*-nku*; *0*) caraway (seed)
knajpa F *f* (*-y*) joint, *Brt.* dive, boozer, *Am.* beanery
knedle *m/pl.* dumplings
knocić F ⟨***na-, s-***⟩ (*-cę*) → ***partaczyć***
knot *m* (*-a*; *-y*) wick; F (*partactwo*) botch-up
knowania *pl.* (*-ń*) intrigues *pl.*
knuć ⟨***u-***⟩ (*-ję*) scheme, intrigue
koalic|ja *f* (*-i -e*) coalition; **~yjny** coalition
kobiałka *f* (*-i*; *G -łek*) basket
kobie|ciarz *m* (*-a*; *-e*) womanizer; **~cy** (***-co, po -cemu***) feminine; female; **~ta** *f* (*-y*) woman
kobyła *f* (*-y*) mare
koc *m* (*-a*; *-e*) blanket; ***wełniany ~*** woollen blanket
kocha|ć (*-am*) love (***się*** o.s.); ***~ć się*** (***w*** *I*) be in love (with); (***z*** *I*) make love (to); ***~m cię*** I love you; ***jak mamę ~m*** cross my heart; **~nek** *m* (*-nka*; *-nkowie*) lover; **~nka** *f* (*-i*; *G -nek*) mistress; **~ny** dear
kocher *m* (*-u*; *-y*) stove
koci catty, catlike; *biol.* feline; **~ak** *m* (*-a*; *-i*), **~ę** *n* (*-ęcia*; *-ęta*) kitten, kitty
kocioł *m* (*kotła*; *-tły*) vat, pot, cauldron; *tech.* boiler; ***kotły*** *pl.* *mus.* (kettle)-drums *pl.*
kocur *m* (*-a*; *-y*) tom(cat)
koczow|ać (*-uję*) lead a nomadic existence; F squat, park (o.s.); **~nik** *m* (*-a*; *-cy*) nomad
kod *m* (*-u*; *-y*) code; ***~ banku*** sorting code number; ***~ pocztowy*** *Brt.* postcode, *Am.* zip code
kodeks *m* (*-u*; *-y*) code; ***~ karny*** criminal code; ***~ postępowania cywilnego*** civil procedure
kodować ⟨***za-***⟩ (*-uję*) code
kogo(ż) (*GA* → ***kto, któż***) who(m); ***do ~*** to who(m); ***od ~*** from who(m)
kogu|ci: ***waga ~cia*** bantam weight; **~t** *m* (*-a*; *-y*) cock, *zwł. Am.* rooster
koić ⟨***u-***⟩ (*-ję*) soothe, comfort, calm
kojarzyć ⟨***s-***⟩ (*-ę*) associate; ***~ się*** be associated (***z*** *I* with)
kojący (***-co***) soothing, calming
kojec *m* (*-jca*; *-jce*) (*dla kur*) coop; (*dla dziecka*) playpen
kok *m* (*-a*; *-i*) bun
kokain|a *f* (*-y*; *0*) cocaine; **~izować się** (*-uję*) take cocaine, snort (cocaine)
kokarda *f* (*-y*) bow
kokiet|eryjny coquettish, flirtatious; **~ować** (*-uję*) flirt (*A* with)
koklusz *m* (*-u*; *0*) *med.* whopping cough
kokos *m* (*-a*; *-y*) *bot.* coconut; **~owy** coconut; ***~owy interes*** gold mine
kokoszka *f* (*-i*; *G -szek*) brood-hen
koks *m* (*-u*; *0*) coke; ***na ~ie*** F doped
koksownia *f* (*-i*; *-e*) coking plant
koktajl *m* (*-u*; *-e*) (*alkohol*) cocktail; (*mleczny*) milk shake
kol. *skrót pisany*: ***kolega, koleżanka*** colleague; ***kolejowy*** rail. (*railway*); ***kolegium*** college
kolacj|a *f* (*-i*; *-e*) supper; (*późny obiad*) dinner; ***jeść ~ę*** have supper/dinner
kolano *n* (*-a*) knee; **~wy** knee, *med.* genual
kola|rski cycle; **~rstwo** *n* (*-a*; *0*) cycling; **~rz** *m* (*-a*; *-e*) cyclist
kolaż *m* (*-u*; *-e*) collage
kolą → ***kłuć***; **~cy** → ***kłujący***
kolba *f* (*-y*; *G -*) *mil.* butt; *bot.* cob
kol|ce → ***kolec***; **~czasty** (***-to***) prickly, **~czyk** *m* (*-a*; *-i*) earring; *agr.* earmark
kolebka *f* (*-i*; *G -bek*) cradle (*też fig.*)
kol|e → ***kłuć***; **~ec** *m* (*-lca*, *-lce*) thorn, spine; **~ce** *pl.* (*w sporcie*) spikes *pl.*
kolega *m* (*-i*; *-dzy*) colleague, friend; ***~ z pracy*** workmate, fellow worker; ***~ szkolny*** schoolmate; → ***fach***
kole|gialny collective; **~giata** *f* (*-y*) *rel.* collegiate church; **~gować** (*-uję*) be friends (***z*** with)
kole'ina *f* (*-y*) rut
kole|j *f* (*GDl -i*; *-e*, *-ei*) *rail. Brt.* railway, *Am.* railroad; order, sequence; ***~j rzeczy*** course of events; ***pracować na ~i*** work on the railway; ***spóźnić się na ~j*** miss the train; ***po ~i*** one by one, by turns; ***~j na mnie*** it is my turn; ***z ~i*** in turn
kolejarz *m* (*-a*; *-e*, *-y*) *Brt.* railwayman, *Am.* railroader
kolej|ka *f* (*-i*; *G -jek*) train; (*do skle-*

K

pu) *Brt.* queue, *Am.* line; **~ka górska** mountain railway/railroad; **stać w ~ce** queue up (**po** *A* for); **wejść poza ~kę** jump the queue; **stawiać ~kę** (*G*) buy a round of …
kolej|nictwo *n* (*-a*; *0*) railway/railroad system; **~no** in turn; **~ność** *f* (*-ci*; *0*) sequence, order; **według ~ności** one after the other; **~ny** next
kolejowy *Brt.* railway, *Am.* railroad
kolek|cjonować (*-uję*) collect; **~tura** *f* (*-y*) lottery-ticket selling point
kolektyw *m* (*-u*; *-y*) collective, body; **~ny** collective
koleż|anka *f* (*-i*; *G -nek*) → **kolega**; **~eński** comradely; **~eństwo** *n* (*-a*; *0*) friendship, comradeship
kolę *1. os. sg.* → **kłuć**
kolęda *f* (*-y*) carol
kolidować (*-uję*) clash (**z** *I* with)
kolisty (**-to**) circular
kolizja *f* (*-i*; *-e*) collision; → **zderzenie**
kolka *f* (*-i*; *G -lek*) stitch; *med.*, *wet.* colic
kolokwium *n* (*idkl.*; *-a*, *G -ów*) test
koloni|a *f* (*GDL -ii*; *-e*) colony; **~e** (**letnie**) *pl.* holiday camp; **~zować** ⟨**s-**⟩ (*-uję*) colonize
koloński|i: **woda ~a** (eau de) cologne
kolor *m* (*-u*; *-y*) colo(u)r; (*w grze w karty*) suit; **pod ~** colo(u)r-coordinated; **~y** *pl.* colo(u)reds *pl.*; → **barwa, barwnik**; **~owy** colo(u)red, colo(u)rful
koloryzować (*-uję*) embellish, whitewash
kolos *m* (*-a*; *-y*) colossus; **~alny** colossal
kolpor|taż *m* (*-u*; *0*) distribution; **~ter** *m* (*-a*; *-rzy*), **-rka** *f* (*-i*; *G -rek*) distributor; **~tować** (*-uję*) distribute
kolumna *m* (*-y*) column; (*głośnik*) loudspeaker; **~da** *f* (*-y*) colonnade
kołatać (*-czę*) knock (**do** *G* on); beat; **~ się** shake, rattle *v/i.*
kołczan *m* (*-u*; *-y*) quiver
kołdra *f* (*-y*; *G -der*) blanket, quilt
kołduny *m/pl.* (*-ów*) meat-filled dumplings *pl.*
kołek *m* (*-łka*; *-łki*) peg
kołnierz *m* (*-a*; *-e*), **~yk** *m* (*-a*; *-i*) collar; **~yk koszuli** shirt collar
koł|o¹ *n* (*-a*; *G kół*) circle (*też fig.*, *math.*); (*pojazdu*) wheel; **~em, w ~o** all around; → **grono, kółko**
koło² *prp.* (*G*) near, close to, next to; **~ Wrocławia** near Wroclaw; → **niedaleko, około**
kołow|acizna *f* (*-y*; *0*) *wet.* staggers *sg./pl.*; F confusion; **~ać** (*-uję*) circle; (*po lotnisku*) taxi; **~rotek** *m* (*-tka*; *-tki*) spinning-wheel; *wędkarstwo*: reel; **~rót** *m* (*-rotu*; *-roty*) winch; (*przy wejściu itp.*) turnstile; (*w sporcie*) circle; **~y** circular; *pojazd* wheeled
kołpak *m* (*-a*; *-i*) cap, helmet; *mot.* hubcap
kołtun *m* (*-a*; *-y*) *fig.* bourgeois, philistine; **~y** *pl.* matted hair *sg.*
koły|sać (*-szę*) rock, (*biodrami itp.*) sway; **~sać się** rock; sway; → **bujać** (**się**); **~sanka** *f* (*-i*; *G -nek*) lullaby; **~ska** *f* (*-ski*; *G -sek*) cradle
koman|dorski: **Krzyż ~dorski** Grand Cross; **~dos** *m* (*-a*; *-i*) commando
komandytow|y: **spółka ~a** limited partnership
komar *m* (*-a*; *-y*) mosquito, gnat
kombajn *m* (*-u*; *-y*) *agr.* combine harvester; (*górniczy*) cutter loader
kombina|cja *f* (*-i*; *-e*) combination; *fig.* **~cje** *pl.* wheeling and dealing; **~tor** *m* (*-a*; *-rzy*), **~torka** *f* (*-i*; *G -rek*) swindler
kombi|nerki *pl.* *tech.* (a pair of) combination pliers *pl.*; **~nezon** *m* (*-u*; *-y*) *Brt.* overalls, *Am.* coveralls; jump suit; (*astronauty*) space suit; **~nować** (*-uję*) combine, join together; F think; **~nować jak** *inf.* how to *bezok.*; F be up to
ko'media *f* (*GDL -ii*; *-e*) comedy; **~nt** *m* (*-a*; *-ci*), **~ntka** *f* (*-i*; *G -tek*) comedian, comic
komediowy comedy
komenda *f* (*-y*) command; **~ policji/straży pożarnej** police/fire brigade headquarters *pl.*; **~nt** *m* (*-a*; *-ci*) commandant; *mil.* commander, commanding officer
komenderować (*-uję*) command, be in command of
komentarz *m* (*-a*; *-e*) commentary
komentować ⟨**s-**⟩ (*-uję*) comment
komercyjny commercial
komet|a *f* (*-y*; *G -*) comet; **~ka** *f* (*-i*; *G -tek*) *sport*: badminton
komfortowy comfortable
komi|czny comical, funny; **~k** *m* (*-a*; *-cy*) comic, comedian; **~ks** *m* (*-u*; *-y*) comic strip; (*książeczka*) comic
komin *m* (*-a*; *-y*) chimney, (*wysoki*)

smokestack; (*statku*) funnel; **~ek** *m* (*-nka*; *-nki*) (*w pokoju*) fireplace; **~iarz** *m* (*-a*; *-e*) chimney sweep; **~kowy** fireplace

komis F *m* (*-u*; *-y*) commission shop

komi|'sariat *m* (*-u*; *-y*) police station; **~saryczny**: ***zarząd ~saryczny*** receivership; **~sarz** *m* (*-a*; *-e*) commissioner; (*policji*) *Brt.* superintendent, *Am.* captain; (*komunistyczny*) commissar; **~sja** *f* (*-i*) committee, commission; board; **~tet** *m* (*-u*; *-y*) committee

komityw|a *f* (*-y*; *0*): ***żyć w ~ie*** be good friends (***z*** *I* with); ***wejść w ~ę*** become good friends (***z*** *I* with)

komiwojażer *m* (*-a*; *-owie/-rzy*) (travelling) salesman/saleswoman, commercial travel(l)er

komnata *f* (*-y*) chamber

komoda *f* (*-y*) chest of drawers

komor|a *f* (*-y*) *biol.*, *med.*, *tech.* chamber; *anat.* ventricle; **~ne** *n* (*-ego*; *0*) rent; **~nik** *m* (*-a*; *-cy*) *jur.* bailiff; **~owy** *tech.* chamber

komórk|a *f* (*-i*; *G -rek*) *biol.*, *tech.* cell; (*pomieszczenie*) closet; F (*telefon komórkowy*) mobile; **~owiec** mobile; **~owy** cellular; → ***telefon***

kompakt *m* (*-u*; *-y*) CD, *Brt.* compact disc, *Am.* compact disk; CD player; **~owy** CD, compact

kompan *m* (*-a*; *-i*) mate, buddy

kom'pania *f* (*GDL -ii*; *-e*) *mil.*, *econ.* company

kompas *m* (*-u*; *-y*) compass

kompatybilny compatible

kompensa|cyjny compensatory; **~ta** *f* (*-i*; *-e*) compensation

kompensować (*-uję*) compensate

kompeten|cja *f* (*-i*; *-e*) competence; **~tny** competent

kompleks *m* (*-u*; *-y*) complex

komplement *m* (*-u*; *-y*) compliment

komple|t *m* (*-u*; *-y*) set; (*mebli itp.*) suite; ***~t widzów*** full house; ***w ~cie*** in full force; ***do ~tu*** to make complete

komplet|ny complete; F utter; **~ować** ⟨**s-**⟩ (*-uję*) complete, make complete

komplik|acja *f* (*-i*; *-e*) complication; **~ować** ⟨**s-**⟩ (*-uję*) complicate

kompo|nent *m* (*-u*; *-y*) component, constituent; **~nować** ⟨**s-**⟩ (*-uję*) compose

kompost *m* (*-u*; *0*) *agr.* compost; **~ować** ⟨**za-**⟩ (*-uję*) compost

kompot *m* (*-u*; *-y*) stewed fruit; compote

kompozy|cja *f* (*-i*; *-e*) composition; **~tor** *m* (*-a*; *-rzy*), **~torka** *f* (*-i G -rek*) composer

kompres *m* (*-u*; *-y*) compress; **~ja** *f* (*-i*; *-e*) compression

kompromi|s *m* (*-u*; *-y*) compromise; **~tacja** *f* (*-i*; *-e*) discredit; **~tować** ⟨**s-**⟩ (*-uję*) discredit, compromise; **~tujący** discrediting, compromising

komputer *m* (*-a*; *-y*) computer; ***~ osobisty*** personal computer (*skrót*: **PC**); **~owy** computer; **~owiec** F *m* (*-wca*; *-wcy*) computer wizard; **~ować** ⟨**s-**⟩ (*-uję*) computerize

komu (*D* → ***kto***) to whom

komuch F *m* (*-a*; *-y*) commie

komu|na *f* (*-y*) *hist.* commune; *pej.* communist system, commies *pl.*; **~nalny** municipal; *bud. Brt.* council, *Am.* low-cost; **~nał** *m* (*-u*; *-y*) commonplace; **~nia** *f* (*GDl -ii*; *-e*) communion; **~nikacja** *f* (*-i*; *0*) communication; (*transport*) communications *pl.*, *Brt.* transport, *Am.* transportation; **~nikacyjny** communication; *Brt.* transport, *Am.* transportation; **~nikat** *m* (*-u*; *-y*) (*rządowy itp.*) communiqué; announcement; (***o stanie pogody***, ***radiowy*** weather, radio) report

komunikować (*-uję*) ⟨***za-***⟩ communicate, announce; ***~ się*** *t-ko impf.* be in touch; ⟨**s-**⟩ get in touch

komunistyczny Communist

komuż (*D* → ***któż***) to who(m)

komża *f* (*-y*; *-e*, *-y/-meż*) surplice

kona|ć (*-am*) be dying; ***~ć ze śmiechu*** die laughing; **~jący** dying

konar *m* (*-a*; *-y*) bough

koncentra|cja *f* (*-i*; *0*) concentration; **~cyjny** concentration

koncentrować ⟨**s-**⟩ (*-uję*) concentrate, focus (***się na*** *L* on)

koncep|cja *f* (*-i*; *-e*) idea, conception; **~t** *m* (*-u*; *-y*) idea; ***ruszyć ~tem*** think of s.th.

koncern *m* (*-u*; *-y*) concern

koncert *m* (*-u*; *-y*) performance, concert

konces|ja *m* (*-i*; *-e*) *Brt.* licence, *Am.* license; **~jonować** (*-uję*) license

koncha *f* (*-y*; *G -*) conch

kondensowa|ć (*-uję*) condense; ***mleko ~ne*** (*słodzone*) condensed milk, (*niesłodzone*) evaporated milk

K

kondolenc|je *f/pl.* (*-i*)*:* ***składać ~je*** offer one's condolences (*D* to); **~yjny** condolence
kondom *m* (*-u*; *-y*) condom, F rubber
kondukt *m* (*-u*; *-y*): ***~ żałobny*** funeral procession
konduktor *m* (*-a*; *-rzy*), **~ka** *f* (*-i*; *G -rek*) (*w autobusie*) conductor; *rail. Brt.* guard, *Am.* conductor; ***~ka*** *też* satchel
kondy|cja *f* (*-i*; *-e*) condition, fitness; **~cyjny** fitness; **~gnacja** *f* (*-i*; *-e*) stor(e)y, level
konewka *f* (*-i*; *G -wek*) watering-can
konfederacja *f* (*-i*; *-e*) confederation
konfekcyjny ready-made
konfe|ransjer *m* (*-a*; *-rzy*),**~ransjerka** *f* (*-i*; *G -rek*) *Brt.* compère, master of ceremonies (*skrót*: ***MC***); **~rencja** *f*(*-i*; *-e*) conference; **~rować** (*-uję*) confer
konfesjonał *m* (*-u*; *-y*) *rel.* confessional
konfiden|cjonalny confidential; **~t** *m* (*-a*; *-ci*), **~tka** *f* (*-i*; *G -tek*) informer
konfirmacja *f* (*-i*; *-e*) confirmation (*też rel.*)
konfisk|ata *f* (*-y*) confiscation; **~ować** ⟨**s-**⟩ (*-uję*) confiscate
konfitury *f/pl.* (-) jam
konfliktowy provocative
konfront|acja *f* (*-i*; *-e*) confrontation; comparison; **~ować** ⟨**s-**⟩ (*-uję*) (***z*** *I*) confront (with), compare (with)
kongres *m* (*-u*; *-y*) congress
koniak *m* (*-u*; *-i*) *gastr.* brandy, (*francuski*) cognac
koniczyna *f* (*-y*) clover
koniec *m* (*-ńca*; *-ńce*) ending, end; (*szpic też*) tip; ***~ świata*** end of the world; ***i na tym ~*** and that will do; ***bez końca*** infinite, interminable; ***do*** (***samego***) ***końca*** to the very end; ***na/w końcu*** in the end, finally; ***od końca*** from the end, from back; ***pod ~*** at the end; ***~ końców*** in the end, finally; → ***kres, dobiegać***
koniecz|nie *adv.* absolutely; necessarily; **~ność** *f* (*-ści*; *0*) necessity; ***z ~ności*** of necessity; **~ny** necessary, obligatory
koni|k *m* (*-a*; *-i*) pony; *fig.* hobby; (*w szachach*) knight; ***~k polny*** grasshopper; **~na** *f* (*-y*) horse-meat; **~okrad** *m* (*-a*; *-y*) horse thief; **~uch** *m* (*-a*; *-y/-owie*) groom, stableman
kon|iugacja *f* (*-i*; *-e*) *gr.* conjugation; **~iunktura** *f* (*-y*) economic trend; (*dobra*) economic boom
koniuszek *m* (*-szka*; *-szki*) tip
konkluzja *f* (*-i*; *-e*) conclusion
konkret|ny concrete; specific; *człowiek* practical, down-to-earth; **~yzować** ⟨**s-**⟩ (*-uję*) put in concrete terms
konkubina *f* (*-y*) *jur.* concubine; cohabitant
konkur|encja *f* (*-i*) competition; (*w sporcie*) event; **~encyjny** competitive; **~ent** *m* (*-a*; *-ci*), **~entka** *f* (*-i*; *G -tek*) competitor, rival; **~ować** (*-uję*) compete (***o*** for)
konkurs *m* (*-u*; *-y*) competition, contest; ***otwarty ~*** open competition (***na*** *A* for); ***brać udział poza ~em*** take part as an unofficial competitor; **~owy** competition, contest
kon|no *adv.* on horseback; → ***jechać***; **~ny** horse; horse-drawn; mounted
konopie *f/pl.* (*-pi*) *bot.* hemp, cannabis
konosament *m* (*-u*; *-y*) *econ.* bill of lading
konował *f* (*-a*; *-y*) *pej.* quack
konsekwen|cja *f* (*-i*; *-e*) consequence; logicality, consistency; **~tny** consequent; consistent, logical
konserwa *f* (*-y*) *Brt.* tinned food, *Am.* canned food; **~cja** *f* (*-i*; *-e*) maintenance; conservation; **~'torium** *n* (*idkl.*; *-ia*, *-iów*) conservatory, music school; **~tysta** *m* (*-y*; *-ści*), **~tystka** *f* (*-i*; *G -tek*) conservative; **~tywny** conservative
konserwo|wać ⟨**za-**⟩ (*-uję*) preserve, conserve; maintain; **~wy** *Brt.* tinned, *Am.* canned
kon|solidacja *f* (*-i*; *-e*) consolidation; **~sorcjum** *n* (*idkl.*; *-ja*, *-ów*) consortium; **~spekt** *m* (*-u*; *-y*) outline, draft
konspira|cja *f* (*-i*; *-e*) conspiracy; underground movement; underground organisation; **~cyjny** conspiratorial; underground
kon|spirować (*-uję*) conspire; ⟨**za-**⟩ hide, camouflage (***się*** o.s.); **~statować** ⟨**s-**⟩ (*-uję*) state
konsternacja *f* (*-i*; *0*) consternation, dismay
konstru|kcja *f* (*-i*; *-e*) construction; structure; **~kcyjny** constructional; structural; **~ktor** *m* (*-a*; *-rzy*), **~ktorka** *f* (*-i*; *G -rek*) constructor; designer; **~ktywny** constructive; **~ować** ⟨**s-**⟩ (*-uję*) construct, design

konsty|tucja *f* (*-i*; *-e*) constitution; **~tucyjny** constitutional; **~tuować** ⟨**u-**⟩ (*-uję*) constitute
konsul *m* (*-a*; *-owie*, *-ów*) consul; **~at** *m* (*-u*; *-y*) consulate
konsul|tacja *f* (*-i*; *-e*) consultation; **~tant** *m* (*-a*; *-nci*), **~tantka** *f* (*-i*; *G -tek*) consultant; specialist; **~tingowy** consulting; *firma* consultancy; **~tować** (*-uję*) consult; discuss; give advice; ***~tować się*** (***u*** *A*) consult (with), take advice (from)
konsum|encki consumer; **~ent** *m* (*-a*; *-nci*), **~entka** *f* (*-i*; *G -tek*) consumer; **~ować** ⟨**s-**⟩ (*-uję*) consume; **~pcja** *f* (*-i*; *0*) consumption; **~pcyjny** consumer; ***artykuły*** *pl.* ***~pcyjne*** consumer goods *pl.*
konsygnacja *f* (*-i*; *-e*) *econ.* delivery note
konsystorz *m* (*-a*; *-e*) *rel.* consistory
konszachty *pl.* (*-ów*) underhand dealings *pl.*
kontakt *m* (*-u*; *-y*) contact; *electr.* (*przełącznik*) switch, (*gniazdko*) socket, *Am.* outlet; **~ować** ⟨**s-**⟩ (*-uję*) bring into contact (***k-o z*** *I* s.o. with); ***~ować*** ⟨**s-**⟩ ***się*** (***z*** *I*) come into contact (with); stay in contact; **~owy** friendly, approachable
kontener *m* (*-a*; *-y*) container; **~owiec** *m* (*-wca*; *-wce*) *naut.* container ship
konto *n* (*-a*; *G* -) account; ***na ~*** on account
kontra[1] *f* (*-y*) (*w kartach*) double; (*boks*) counter-blow
kontra[2] against; versus; **~banda** *f* contraband → ***przemyt***
kontrahent *m* (*-a*; *-nci*), **~ka** *f* (*-i*; *G -tek*) *econ.* contractor
kontrakt *m* (*-u*; *-y*) contract; **~owy** contractual
kontrargument *m* (*-u*; *-y*) counter-argument
kontrast *m* (*-u*; *-y*) contrast; **~owy** full of contrasts; *med.* contrast
kontr|asygnować (*-uję*) countersign; **~atak** *m* counterattack; **~kandydat** *m*, **~kandydatka** *f* opponent; **~ofensywa** *f* counteroffensive
kontrol|a *f* (*-i*; *-e*) control; inspection, check; (*punkt*) checkpoint; **~er** *m* (*-a*; *-rzy*), **~erka** *f* (*-i*; *G -rek*) inspector; **~ny** controlling; check; **~ować** ⟨**s-**⟩ (*-uję*) control; inspect, check
kontro|wać (*-uję*) counter; (*w kartach*) double; **~wersyjny** controversial
kontr|propozycja *f* counterproposal; **~rewolucja** *f* counterrevolution; **~uderzenie** *n* counterstroke; counterattack; **~wywiad** *m* counterintelligence
kontuar *m* (*-u*; *-y*) counter
kon|tur *m* (*-u*; *-y*) outline, conto(u)r; **~tuzja** *f* (*-i*; *-e*) *med.* contusion; F injury
konty|nent *m* (*-u*; *-y*) continent; **~nentalny** continental, mainland; **~ngent** *m* (*-u*; *-y*) quota; *mil.* contingent; **~nuacja** *f* (*-i*; *0*) continuation; **~nuować** (*-uuję*) continue
kon'walia *f* (*GDL -ii*; *-e*) *bot.* lily of the valley
konwen|anse *m/pl.* (*-ów*) conventions *pl.*, propriety; **~cja** *f* (*-i*; *-e*) convention; **~cjonalny** conventional; **~t** *m* (*-u*; *-y*) council of elders; ***~t seniorów*** *parl.* advisory parliamentary committee
konwersacja *f* (*-i*; *-e*) conversation
konwersja *f* (*-i*; *-e*) conversion
konwo|jent *m* (*-a*; *-nci*) escort; **~jować** (*-uję*) escort; convoy
konw|ój *m* (*-oju*; *-oje*) convoy; ***pod ~ojem*** *też* under guard
konwuls|je *f/pl.* (*-i*) convulsions *pl.*; **~yjny** convulsive
koń *m* (*-nia*; *-nie*, *I -ńmi*) *zo.* horse; (*w szachach*) knight; ***~ mechaniczny*** *tech.* horsepower; ***na koniu*** on horseback
końc|a *G*, **~e** *pl.* → ***koniec***; **~owy** final, end; **~ówka** *f* (*-i*; *G -wek*) ending (*też gr.*); (*reszta*) remainder; (*w sporcie*) final; (*w szachach*) endgame; *tech.* tip, end, terminal
kończy|ć (*-ę*) ⟨**s-, u-**⟩ end, finish, complete; *v/i.* stop (***z czymś*** s.th.); ***~ć*** ⟨**s-**⟩ ***się*** end; (*zużywać się*) come to an end; run out; (*kończyć ważność*) expire; **~na** *f anat.* limb, extremity
koński horse; *biol.* equine
kooper|acja *f* (*-i*; *-e*) co-operation; **~ant** *m* (*-a*; *-ci*) co-operating partner; **~ować** (*-uję*) co-operate
koordynować ⟨**s-**⟩ (*-uję*) co-ordinate
kopa|czka *f* (*-i*; *G -czek*) *agr.* digger; **~ć** (*-pię*) *piłkę itp.* kick; ⟨**wy-**⟩ *dół* dig out/up; *studnię* sink; *ziemniaki* lift; *węgiel* excavate; **~lnia** *f* (*-ni*; *-nie*) mine (*też fig.*), pit; **~lniany** mine; **~lny** fossil; **~nie** *n* (*-a*; *0*) digging; kicking; excavating; **~rka** *f* (*-i*; *G -rek*) excavator; digger

K

kop|cić (*-cę, ć!*) give off clouds of smoke; F *papierosy* puff away (at); **~eć** *f* (*-pcia/-pciu; 0*) soot
Kopenhaga *f* (*-i; 0*) Copenhagen
koper *m* (*-pru; -pry*), **~ek** (*-rku; -rki*) *bot.* dill; **~kowy** dill
koperta *f* (*-y; G -*) envelope
kopi|a *f* (*GDL -ii; -e*) copy; duplicate; **~ał** *m* (*-u; -y*) duplicate pad; **~arka** *f* (*-i; G -rek*) copier; (*kserograficzna*) photocopier
kopiec *m* (*-pca; -pce*) heap; **~ *mogilny*** grave mound; *agr.* clamp
kopiow|ać (*-uję*) ⟨**s-**⟩ copy, duplicate; ⟨**prze-**⟩ trace; **~y**: ***ołówek ~y*** indelible pencil
kopn|ąć *v/s.* (*-nę*) → ***kopać***; **~iak** *m* (*-a; -i*) kick
kopu|lacja *f* (*-i; -e*) copulation; **~lacyjny** copulative; **~lować** (*-uję*) copulate; **~ła** *f* (*-y; G -*) cupola, dome
kopyto *n* (*-a; G -*) hoof
kora *f* (*-y; G -*) bark
koral *m* (*-a; -e*) *zo.* coral; ***~e szklane*** glass beads; **~owy** coral
korb|a *f* (*-y; G -*) crank (handle), handle; **~owód** *m* (*-odu; -ody*) connecting-rod
korci|ć (*t-ko 3.os.*) tempt, attract; ***~ło go/ją, by*** he/she was tempted to
kordon *m* (*-u; -y*) cordon
Korea *f* (*-ei; 0*) Korea; **~nka** *f* (*-i; G -nek*), **~ńczyk** *m* (*-a; -cy*) Korean; **♀ński** (***po -ku***) Korean
kor|ek *m* (*-rka; -rki*) *bot.* cork; (*do butelki itp.*) cork, stopper; (*do wanny itp.*) plug; F *electr.* fuse; F (*na jezdni*) jam, *Brt.* tailback, *Am.* backup; ***~ek wlewu paliwa*** filler cap; ***~ki*** *pl.* cork heels *pl.*
kore|kta *f* (*-y; G -*) correction; revision; (*publikacji itp.*) proof-reading; F (*materiał do korekty*) the proofs; **~petycje** *f/pl.* (*-i; G -cji*) private lessons *pl.*
koresponden|cja *f* (*-i; 0*) correspondence; letters *pl.*, *Brt.* post, *Am.* mail; **~cyjny** correspondence; ***studia*** *pl.* ***~cyjne*** correspondence course, *Brt.* Open University course; **~t** *m* (*-a; -ci*), **~tka** *f* (*-i; G -tek*) correspondent
korespondować (*-uję*) correspond
korko|ciąg *m* (*-u; -i*) corkscrew; **~wać** ⟨**za-**⟩ (*-uję*) cork
kornet *m* (*-u; -y*) *mus.* cornet
kornik *m* (*-a; -i*) *zo.* bark beetle
korniszon *m* (*-a; -y*) gherkin
Kornwalia *f* (*-ii; 0*) Cornwall
koron|a *f* (*-y; G -*) crown; **~acja** *f* (*-i; -e*) crowning; **~ka** *f* (*-i; G -nek*) *med.* tooth cap; lace; **~kowy** lace; **~ować** ⟨**u-**⟩ (*-uję*) crown (***kogoś na króla*** s.o. king)
korozja *f* (*-i; 0*) corrosion
korowód *m* (*-wodu; -wody*) round dance
korporacja *f* (*-i; -e*) corporation, corporate body
korpu|lentny corpulent, obese; **~s** *m* (*-u; -y*) trunk; *mil.* corps *sg.*
Korsyka *f* (*-i; 0*) Corsica; **~ńczyk** *m* (*-a; -cy*) Corsican; **♀ński** Corsican
kort *m* (*-u; -y*) (*w sporcie*) court
korup|cja *f* (*-i; -e*) corruption; **~cyjny** corrupt
korygować ⟨**s-**⟩ (*-uję*) correct, revise
koryntka *f* (*-i; G -tek*) *bot.* currant
koryt|arz *m* (*-a; -e*) hall, hallway, corridor; **~o** *n* (*-a; G -*) (*rzeki*) bed; (*świni*) trough
korze|nić się (*-nię*) take root; **~nny** spicy; **~ń** *m* (*-nia; -nie*) root; ***~nie*** *pl.* (*przyprawa*) spices *pl.*
korzon|ek *m* (*-nka, -nki*) *med.* radicle; ***zapalenie ~ków*** *med.* radiculitis; → ***korzeń***
korzyst|ać ⟨**s-**⟩ (*-am*) (**z** *G*) use; make use (of); take advantage (of); **~ny** useful; favo(u)rable; profitable
korzyść *f* (*-ści*) advantage; profit; ***na twoją ~*** in your favo(u)r, to your benefit
kos *m* (*-a; -y*) *zo.* blackbird
ko|sa *f* (*-y; G -*) *agr.* scythe (*też fig.*); **~siarka** *f* (*-i; G -rek*) mower; **~sić** ⟨**s-**⟩ (*-szę*) mow
kosmaty (***-to***) shaggy; hirsute
kosmety|czka *f* (*-i; G -czek*) beautician, cosmetician; (*torebka*) vanity bag, *Brt.* sponge bag; **~czny** cosmetic (*też fig.*); **~k** *m* (*-u; -i*) cosmetic; **~ka** *f* (*-i; 0*) *fig.* cosmetic procedures *pl.*
kosm|iczny cosmic; **~os** *m* (*-u; -y*) cosmos
kosmyk *m* (*-a; -i*) wisp, stray lock
koso: ***patrzeć ~*** (***na*** *A*) look askance (at); **~drzewina** *f* (*-y; 0*) *bot.* (*sosna*) dwarf pine; **~oki** slit-eyed; → ***zezowaty***
kostium *m* (*-u; -y*) costume; → ***kąpielowy***
kost|ka *f* (*-i; G -tek*) small bone; *anat.* ankle; (*cukru*) lump; (*brukowa*) cobble

(stone); (*do gry*) die, *pl.* dice; ***krajać w ~kę*** *gastr.* dice; ***po ~ki*** ankle-deep; **~nica** *f* (*-y*; *-e*) mortuary, morgue; **~nieć** ⟨**s-**⟩ (*-eję*) grow stiff (***z zimna*** with cold); **~ny** bone

kosy slanting; scowling

kosz *m* (*-a*; *-e*) basket; F (*w sporcie*) basketball; *mot.* sidecar

koszar|owy barrack(s); **~y** *pl.* barracks *sg.*

koszerny kosher

koszmar *m* (*-u*; *-y*) nightmare; horror; **~ny** nightmarish; horrible

koszt *f* (*-u*; *-y*) cost, expense; (*rozchody*) *pl.* expenses *pl.*; ***~em*** (*G*) at the cost (of); ***narazić na ~y*** put s.o. to expense

koszto|rys *m* (*-u*; *-y*) cost estimate; **~wać** (*-uję*) cost; **~wności** *pl.* precious objects *pl.*, jewel(le)ry; **~wny** expensive

koszul|a *f* (*-i*; *-e*) shirt; ***~a nocna*** nightdress; **~ka** *f* (*-i*; *G -lek*) singlet, T-shirt; *tech.* mantel; → ***podkoszulek***

koszyk *m* (*-a*; *-i*) basket; **~arka** *f* (*-i*; *G -rek*), **~arz** *m* (*-a*; *-e*) basketball player; **~ówka** *f* (*-i*; *0*) basketball

kościec *m* (*-ścca*; *- ścce*) bone structure; *fig.* backbone

kościelny 1. church; **2.** *m* (*-nego*; *-ni*) sexton

kościotrup *m* (*-a*; *-y*) skeleton

kościół *m* (*-cioła*; *-cioły*) church

koś|cisty bony; **~ć** *f* (*-ści*; *-ści*, *I śćmi*) bone; ***kości*** *pl. do gry* dice; ***~ć słoniowa*** ivory; ***~ć strzałkowa*** *anat.* fibula; ***~ć niezgody*** a bone of contention; ***do*** (***szpiku***) ***~ci*** to the bone; **~lawy** crooked, lopsided; *meble* wobbly; *styl* halting

kot *m* (*-a*; *-y*) *zo.* cat

kotara *f* (*-y*; *G -*) curtain, drape

ko'teria *f* (*GDL -ii*; *-e*) coterie, clique

kotka *f* (*-i*; *G -tek*) *zo.* (she-)cat, tabby

kotlet *m* (*-a*; *-y*) cutlet, chop; ***~ mielony*** hamburger, beefburger; ***~ siekany*** rissole

kotlina *f* (*-y*; *G -*) valley

kotł|a, ~em → ***kocioł***; **~ować się** (*-uję*) churn, seethe; **~ownia** *f* (*-i*; *-e*) boiler room; boiler-house; **~owy** boiler; ***kamień ~owy*** fur; **~y** *pl.* → ***kocioł***

kotny pregnant

kotwi|ca *f* (*-y*; *-e*) *naut.* anchor; ***rzucać ~cę*** anchor, drop anchor; **~czny** anchor

kowa|dło *n* (*-a*) anvil; **~l** *m* (*-a*; *-e*) blacksmith; **~lik** *m* (*-a*; *-i*) *zo.* nuthatch; **~lski** blacksmith

kowboj *m* (*-a*; *-e*) cowboy

koz|a *f* (*-y*; *G kóz*) *zo.* goat, (*samica*) nanny-goat; ***siedzieć w ~ie*** *przest.* be in clink

kozetka *f* (*-i*; *G -tek*) couch, day bed

kozi goat, *biol.* caprine; **~ca** *f* (*-y*; *-e*) chamois; **~na** *f* (*-y*; *0*) goat (meat)

kozioł *m* (*-zła*; *-zły*) *zo.* buck; (*kozy*) billy goat; ***~ ofiarny*** scapegoat; **~ek** *m* (*-łka*; *-łki*): ***fikać ~ki*** turn somersaults

koziorożec *m* (*-żca*; *-żce*) *zo.* ibex; **♀ec** *znak Zodiaku:* Capricorn; ***on***(***a***) ***jest spod znaku ♀ca*** he/she is (a) Capricorn

koźl|ątko *n* (*-a*; *G -tek*), **~ę** *n* (*-ecia*; *-ęta*) kid

kożuch *m* (*-a*; *-y*) sheepskin; (*do ubrania*) sheepskin coat; (*na mleku*) skin

kół *m* (*kołu*; *koły*) stake; → ***koło***

kółko *n* (*-a*; *G -łek*) ring; circle (*też fig.*); ***~ do kluczy*** key-ring; ***w ~*** in a circle, in circles; *fig.* over and over; → ***koło***

k.p.a. *skrót pisany*: ***kodeks postępowania administracyjnego*** code of administrative proceedings

kpi|ąco mockingly; **~ć** (*-ę*; *kpij!*) (***z*** *G*) mock, ridicule, poke fun (at); **~na** *f* (*-y*) jeer; *zwł. pl.* ***~ny*** mockery, ridicule

kpt. *skrót pisany*: ***kapitan*** Capt. (*captain*)

kra *f* (*-y*; *G kier*) ice floe

krab *m* (*-a*; *-y*) *zo.* crab

krach *m* (*-u*; *-y*) collapse; (*giełdowy*) crash

kraciasty checked, *Am.* checkered

kra|dli, ~dł *itp.* → ***kraść***; **~dzież** *f* (*-y*; *-e*) theft; (*z włamaniem*) robbery; (*w sklepie*) shoplifting; **~dziony** stolen

kraj *m* (*-u*; *-e*) country; ***~ rodzinny*** homeland; ***tęsknota za ~em*** homesickness; ***do ~u*** home

krajać ⟨***na-, po-***⟩ (*-ę*) cut; *mięso* carve

krajo|braz *m* (*-u*; *-y*) landscape, scenery; ***~braz miejski*** cityscape; **~wiec** *m* (*-wca*; *-wcy*) native; **~wy** native; *produkt* domestic; **~znawczy** sightseeing

krakać (*-czę*) caw; *fig.* croak

Krak|ów *m* (*-owa*; *0*) Cracow, Krakow; **♀owski** Cracow

krakers *m* (*-a*; *-y*) cracker

kraksa *f* (*-y*; *G -*) collision, crash, smash

K

kram *m* (*-u*; *-y*) stall; (*rzeczy*) stuff, junk; → ***kłopot***
kran *m* (*-u*; *-y*) (*kurek*) *Brt.* tap, *Am.* faucet; ***woda z ~u*** tap-water; → ***żuraw***
kra|niec *m* (*-ńca*; *-ńce*) end; ***na ~ńcu*** at the end; ***~ńce*** *pl.* ***miasta*** outskirts; **~ńcowy** extreme
krasić ⟨**o-**⟩ (*-szę*) *gastr.* add fat to
kras|nal *m* (*-a*; *-e*), **~noludek** *m* (*-dka*; *-dki*) dwarf, brownie; gnome; **~omówca** *m* (*-y*) orator
kraszanka *f* (*-i*; *G -nek*) → ***pisanka***
kraść ⟨**s-, u-**⟩ (*-dnę*) steal
krat|a *f* (*-y*; *G* -) grating, bars *pl.*; (*deseń*) check; **~ka**: ***za ~kami*** behind bars; ***w ~kę*** checked; **~kowany** checked; *papier* squared; **~kować** (*-uję*) square
kraul *m* (*-u*; *-e*) (*w sporcie*) crawl
krawat *m* (*-a*; *-y*) neck-tie
kra|wcowa *f* (*-wej*; *-e*) (*damski*) dressmaker; → ***~wiec***; **~wędź** *f* (*-dzi*; *-dzie*) edge, brink; (*łyżki*) rim; (*filiżanki*) lip; **~wężnik** *m* (*-a*; *-i*) *Brt.* kerb, *Am.* curb; **~wiec** *m* (*-wca*; *-wcy*) dressmaker, (*męski*) tailor; **~wiectwo** *n* (*-a*; *0*) dressmaking; tailoring
krą|g *m* (*kręgu*; *kręgi*) circle (*też fig.*); ring; **~żek** *m* (*-żka*; *-żki*) *Brt.* disc, *Am.* disk; (*w hokeju*) puck; *tech.* roller; **~żenie** *n* (*-a*) (*też med.*) circulation; **~żownik** *m* (*-a*; *-i*) *naut.* cruiser; **~żyć** (*-żę*) go (***dokoła*** (a)round), circle; circulate
krea|cja *f* (*-i*; *-e*) creation; **~tura** *f* (*-y*; *G* -) *pej.* wretch; **~tywny** creative
kreci mole; ***~a robota*** ruse, scheme
kreda *f* (*-y*) chalk
kredens *m* (*-u*; *-y*) dresser, sideboard
kredka *f* (*-i*; *G -dek*) crayon; (*rodzaj ołówka*) colo(u)red pencil; ***~ do ust*** lipstick
kredow|o- *w zł.* chalk; ***~o-biały*** as white as sheet; **~y** chalk
kredyt *m* (*-u*; *-y*) credit, loan; ***na ~*** on credit; **~ować** (*-uję*) credit, extend credit to; **~owy** credit
krem *m* (*-u*; *-y*) cream
kremacja *f* (*-i*; *-e*) cremation
kremowy (***-wo***) cream, creamy
kreować (*-uję*) create; perform
krepa *f* (*-y*) crepe
kres *m* (*-u*; *-y*) limit; end; ***być u ~u*** (*G*) be at the end of; ***położyć ~*** (*D*) put an end (to)
kresk|a *f* (*-i*; *G -sek*) line; (*w rysunku*) stroke; (*na skali*) mark; **~ować** (*-uję*) shade; **~owany** shaded; **~owy** line; **~ówka** *f* (*-i*; *G -wek*) (animated) cartoon
kreśl|arka *f* (*-i*; *G -rek*) *Brt.* draughtswoman, *Am.* draftswoman; **~arz** *m* (*-a*; *-e*) *Brt.* draughtsman, *Am.* draftsman; **~enie** *n* (*-a*) *tech.* drawing; **~ić** (*-lę*) ⟨**na-**⟩ draw; ⟨**s-, wy-**⟩ cross out, strike out
kret *m* (*-a*; *-y*) *zo.* mole; **~owisko** *n* (*-a*) molehill
kret|yn *m* (*-a*; *-i/-y*) moron, cretin (*też med.*); **~yński** moronic
krew *f* (*krwi*; *0*) blood; ***~ go zalała na to*** it made him see red; ***z krwi i kości*** flesh and blood; ***czystej krwi*** purebred, pure-blooded; ***z zimną krwią*** in cold blood
krewet|ka *f* (*-i*; *G -tek*) *zo.*, *gastr.* shrimp, prawn; ***~ki panierowane*** scampi *pl.*
krew|ki hot-blooded, rash; **~na** *f* (*-nej*; *-ne*), **~ny** *m* (*-nego*; *-ni*) relative, relation; ***najbliższy ~ny*** next of kin
kręc|ić (*-cę*) turn; *włosy* curl; *wąsa* twirl; F (*kłamać*) tell fibs; ***~ić głową*** shake one's head; ***~ić nosem na*** turn up one's nose at; ***~ić się*** spin; turn; *włosy* curl; twitch, fidget; ***~ić się koło*** (*G*) hover about; ***w głowie jej się ~i*** her head is spinning; **~ony** *włosy* curly; ***schody ~one*** spiral staircase
kręg *m* (*-u*; *-i*) *anat.* vertebra; → ***krąg***; **~arstwo** *n* (*-a*; *0*) chiropractic; **~ielnia** *f* (*-i*; *-e*) bowling alley; **~le** *m/pl.* (*-i*) skittles *pl.*; ***grać w ~le*** bowl
kręgo|słup *m* (*-a*; *-y*) *anat.* spinal column; backbone; spine (*też fig.*); **~wce** *m/pl.* (*-wców*) vertebrates *pl.*
krępować ⟨**s-**⟩ (*-uję*) tie up; *fig.* limit; (*żenować*) embarrass; ***~⟨s-⟩ się*** be ashamed
krępujący (***-co***) embarrassing; awkward
krępy stocky
kręta|ctwo *n* (*-a*; *G* -) crookedness, guile; **~cz** *m* (*-a*; *-e*), **~czka** *f* (*-i*; *G -czek*) crook
kręty (***-to***) *droga* winding; *wyjaśnienie* devious
krnąbrny unruly
krochmal *m* (*-u*; *0*) starch; **~ić** ⟨**na-, wy-**⟩ (*-ę*) starch
krocze *n* (*-a*) *anat.* crotch, *med.* perineum

kroczyć (*-ę*) pace, (*dużymi krokami*) stride; (*dumnie*) strut
kroić (*-ję, krój!; -ją*) ⟨**po-**⟩ cut, slice; ⟨**s-**⟩ cut out
krok *m* (*-u; -i*) step (*też fig.*); (*krocze*) crotch; **~i** *pl.* measures *pl.*; **~ za ~iem** step by step; **podejmować ~i, aby** take steps to; **na każdym ~u** at everystep
krokiet *m* (*-a; -y*) *gastr.* croquet
krokodyl *m* (*-a; -e*) *zo.* crocodile
kromka *f* (*-i; -mek*) slice (of bread)
kronika *f* (*-i; G -*) chronicle; **~ filmowa** newsreel
krop|elka *f* (*-i; G -lek*) → **kropla**; **~ić** ⟨**po-, s-**⟩ (*-ę*) sprinkle; **~i** it is spitting; **~idło** *n* (*-a; G -deł*) aspersorium, aspergillum; **~ielnica** *f* (*-y; -e*) aspersorium; **~ka** *f* (*-i; G -pek*) dot, spot; (*w interpunkcji*) *Brt.* full stop, *Am.* period; **w ~ki** dotted; **~kowany** dotted; **~la** *f* (*-i; -e, -i/-pel*) drop; (*potu*) bead; **~lówka** *f* (*-i; G -wek*) *med.* drip (infusion)
krosno *n* (*-a; G -sen*) loom
krosta *f* (*-y*) spot, pimple; *med.* pustule
krotochwila *f* (*-i; -e*) farce
krow|a *f* (*-y; G krów*) *zo.* cow; **~i** cow(s')
króc|ej *adv.* (*comp. od* → **krótki**) shorter; **~iutki** very short
krój *m* (*-oju; -oje, -ojów*) cut
król *m* (*-a; -owie*) king; **Święto Trzech ♀li** *rel.* Epiphany
królestwo *n* (*-wa; G -tw*) kingdom
królew|na *f* (*-ny; G -wien*) princess; **~ski** royal, regal
królik *m* (*-a; -i*) *zo.* rabbit; **~arnia** *f* (*-i; -e*) rabbit hutch
królowa *f* (*-ej, -wo!; -e*) queen; **~ć** (*-uję*) reign, rule (**nad** *I* over); *fig. też* predominate
krótki short; brief; *rozmowa tel., spacer* quick
krótko *adv.* briefly; **~dystansowiec** *m* (*-wca; -wcy*) short (film); **~falowy** short-wave; **~metrażówka** *f* (*-i; G -wek*) (*w sporcie*) sprint; **~ść** *f* (*-ści; 0*) brevity; shortness; **~terminowy** short-term; **~trwały** short-lived; **~widz** *m* (*-a; -e*) short-sighted person; **~wzroczny** short-sighted
krótszy *adj.* (*comp. od* → **krótko** shorter (**od** *G* than, from)
krówka *f* (*-i; G -wek*) → **krowa**; fudge; **boża ~** *Brt.* ladybird, *Am.* ladybug
krta|ń *f* (*-ni; -nie*) *anat.* larynx; **zapalenie ~ni** *med.* laryngitis
krucho *adv.* → **kruchy**; F terribly, badly
kruchta *f* (*-y; G -*) porch
kruch|y fragile (*też fig.*), brittle; *mięso* tender; *ciastko, sałata* crisp; **~e ciasto** short pastry
krucjata *f* (*-y; G -*) crusade
krucyfiks *m* (*-u; -y*) crucifix
kruczek *m* (*-czka; -czki*) snag, catch
kru|czy raven; **~k** *m* (*-a; -i*) *zo.* raven
krup *m* (*-u; -0*) *med.* croup; **~a** *f* (*y*), *zwł. pl.* **~y** grains *pl.*; *meteo.* soft hail pellet, graupel; **~nik** *m* (*-u; -i*) *gastr.* barley soup
krusz|ec *m* (*-szca; -szce*) ore; precious metal; **~eć** ⟨**s-**⟩ (*-eję*) become brittle; *mięso*: become tender; **~on** *m* (*-u; -y*) *gastr.* punch; **~onka** *f* (*-i; G -nek*) *gastr.* crumbly topping, *Am.* streusel
kruszy|ć ⟨**po-, s-**⟩ (*-ę*) crumble (**się** *v/i.*); → **drobić**; **~na** *f* (*-y; G -*) crumb; (*dziecko*) a little one; **~wo** *n* (*-a; G -*) *bud.* aggregate, ballast
krużganek *m* (*-nka; -nki*) cloister
krwawią|cy bleeding; **~czka** *f* (*-i; 0*) h(a)emophilia
krwawi|ca *f* (*-y; -e*) back-breaking work; hard-earned money; **~ć** (*-wię*) bleed
krwa|woczerwony blood-red; **~wy** bloody, bloodstained; *praca* hard
krwi|ak *m* (*-a; -i*) *med.* h(a)ematoma; **~ą** → **krew**; **~nka** *f* (*-ki; G -nek*) *med.* blood cell; **czerwona ~nka** erythrocyte
krwio|bieg *m* (*-u; -i*) blood circulation, bloodstream; **~dawca** *m* (*-y*), **~dawczyni** *f* (*-; G -yń*) blood donor; **~nośny**: **naczynie ~nośne** blood vessel; **~żerczy** bloodthirsty
krwisty *oczy itp.* bloodshot; *kiszka* blood; *befsztyk* rare; *rumieniec* ruddy
krwotok *m* (*-u; -i*) h(a)emorrhage
kry|ć (*-ję*) ⟨**u-**⟩ conceal, hide (*też* **się** *v/i.*); (*tuszować*) cover up; (*w sporcie*) cover, mark; ⟨**po-**⟩ cover (**się** o.s.); **~jówka** *f* (*-i; G -wek*) hiding place, hideaway
Krym *m* (*-u; 0*) the Crimea
kryminal|ista *m* (*-y; -ści*), **~istka** *f* (*-i; G -tek*) criminal; **~ny** criminal; **policja ~na** criminal police
kryminał F *m* (*-u; -y*) nick; (*utwór*) thriller, detective story; (*czyn*) criminal activity
krynica *f* (*-y; -e*) fount

krystali|czny crystal; *fig.* crystal clear; **~zować się** (*-uję*) crystallize
kryształ *m* (*-u*; *-y*) crystal; **~owy** (**-wo**) crystal
kryterium *n* (*idkl.*; *-a*) criterion
kryty covered; roofed
kryty|czny critical; **~k** *m* (*-a*; *-cy*) critic; reviewer; **~ka** *f* (*-i*; *G* -) criticism; critique; **~kować** ⟨**s-**⟩ (*-uję*) criticize (**za** *A* for)
kryzys *m* (*-u*; *-e*) crisis; **~owy** crisis
krza|czasty (**-to**) bushy; **~k** *m* (*-a*; *-i*) bush, shrub
krząta|ć się bustle (**koło** *G*, **przy** *L* about); **~nina** *f* (*-y*; *0*) bustle
krze|m *m* (*-u*; *0*) *chem.* silicon; **~mian** *m* (*-u* *-y*) silicate; **~mień** *m* (*-nia*; *-nie*) flint; **~mionka** *f* (*-i*; *G* *-nek*) siliceous earth
krzep|ić ⟨**po-**⟩ (*-ę*) fortify; refresh (**się** o.s.); **~ki** robust, vigorous; (*silny*) hefty; **~nąć** ⟨**s-**, **za-**⟩ (*-ę*; *-[ną]ł*, *-pła*) set, solidify; *krew*: coagulate, congeal
krzesać ⟨**wy-**⟩ (*-szę*) *iskry* strike
krzesełkowy: **wyciąg ~** chair lift
krzesło *n* (*-ła*; *G* *-seł*) chair
krzew *m* (*-u*; *-y*) shrub
krzewić (*-ę*) spread (**się** *v/i.*)
krzt|a: **ani ~y** not an ounce
krztusić się ⟨**za- się**⟩ (*-szę*) choke (*I* on); → **dławić się**
krztusiec *m* (*-śca*; *0*) *med.* whooping cough
krzy|czący (**-co**) crying; **~czeć** (*-ę*) cry (**z** *G* with); shout (**na kogoś** at s.o.); scream; **~k** *m* (*-u*; *-i*) cry, shout; scream; **~kliwy** noisy; loud (*też fig.*); *kolory* garish, lurid; (**-wie**) **~kliwy dzieciak** bawler
krzywa *f* (*-wej*; *-e*) *math.* curve
krzyw|da *f* (*-y*; *G* -) harm, injustice; wrong; **~dzić** ⟨**po-**, **s-**⟩ (*-dzę*) harm, hurt; do injustice to, do *s.o.* wrong
krzywi|ca *f* (*-y*; *0*) *med.* rickets *pl.*; **~ć** ⟨**s-**, **wy-**⟩ (*-ę*) bend (**się** *v/i.*); **~ć** ⟨**s-**⟩ **się** make faces (**na** *A* at); (*z bólu*) wince; **~zna** *f* (*-y*; *G* -) curvature
krzywo *adv.* not straight, crookedly; **spojrzeć ~** frown (**na** *A* on); **~nogi** bandy-legged; **~przysięstwo** *n* (*-a*) *jur.* perjury
krzywy bent; crooked; uneven; *uśmiech* wry; **w ~m zwierciadle** distorted; → **krzywo**
krzyż *m* (*-a*; *-e*) cross (*też rel.*); *anat.* small of the back; **na ~** across, crosswise; **bóle w ~u** pain in the small of the back; **~ak** *m* (*-a*; *-i*) *tech.* cross; *zo.* cross spider; **Ꝍak** (*-a*; *-cy*) knight of the Teutonic Order; **~ować** (*-uję*) ⟨**u-**⟩ cross; *rel.* crucify; ⟨**u-**⟩ upset; ⟨**s-**⟩ cross (**się** *v/i.*); **~ować się** intersect; **~owy** cruciform; *anat.* sacral; **wojny ~owe** Crusades; **wziąć w ~owy ogień pytań** cross-examine; **~ówka** *f* (*-i*; *G* *-wek*) intersection; (*w gazecie*) crossword (puzzle); **~yk** *m* (*-a*; *-i*) cross; **oznaczyć ~ykiem** cross; *mus.* sharp
ks. *skrót pisany*: **książę** duke, prince, **ksiądz** the Rev. (*reverend*)
kserokopia *f* photocopy; **~rka** *f* (*-i*; *G* *-rek*) photocopier
ksiądz *m* (*księdza*, *-ędzu*, *-ęże!*; *księża*, *-ęży*, *-ężom*; *I* *-ężmi*) priest; (*tytuł*) Father (*skrót*: the Rev.)
książeczka *f* (*-i*; *G* *-czek*) book, booklet; **~ oszczędnościowa** saving book; **~ czekowa** *Brt.* chequebook, *Am.* checkbook
książę *m* (*GA księcia*, *DL księciu*, *I księciem*, *książę!*; *książęta*, *-ząt*) prince, duke; **~cy** ducal, princely
książk|a *f* (*-i*; *G* *-żek*) book; **~owy** book; **mól ~owy** bookworm
księ|cia, ~dza → **książę, ksiądz**
księga *f* (*-i*; *G* *ksiąg*) book; **księgi** *pl.* (*rachunkowe*) the books; **~rnia** *f* (*-i*; *-e*) *Brt.* bookshop, *Am.* bookstore; **~rz** *f* (*-a*; *-e*) bookseller
księgo|susz *m* (*-u*; *0*) *wet.* rinder pest; **~wa** *f* (*-ej*; *-e*) accountant; **~wać** ⟨**za-**⟩ (*-uję*) enter; **~wość** *f* (*-ci*; *0*) accountancy, bookkeeping; **~wy** *m* (*-ego*; *-i*) accountant; **~zbiór** *m* (*-oru*; *-ory*) library
księ|stwo *n* (*-a*; *G* -) dukedom, duchy; **~żna** *f* (*-nej/-ny*; *DL nej/-nie*, *A* *-nę/-ną*, *-no!/*; *-ne*, *-nych*, *-nym/-nom*) duchess, princess; **~żniczka** *f* (*-i*) princess
księżyc *m* (*-a*; *-e*) moon; **światło ~a** moonlight; **~owy** moon(lit), lunar
ksylofon *m* (*-u*; *-y*) xylophone
ksywa F *f* (*-y*) nickname, F moniker
kształc|enie *n* (*-a*; *0*) education; → **doskonalenie**; **~ić** ⟨**wy-**⟩ (*-cę*) educate; *umysł itp.* train, discipline, develop; **~ić się** learn, study; **~ić się** study (**na** *A* to be)

kształt *m* (*-u*; *-y*) shape, form; ***coś na ~*** (*G*) something like; **~ny** shapely; **~ować** ⟨**u-**⟩ shape; form; ***~ować się*** *ceny, liczby*: be established, stand
kto *pron.* who; → ***bądź***; **~'kolwiek** anyone, anybody; whoever; **~ś** someone, somebody
któr|ędy where, which way; **~y** *pron.* which, that, who; what; → ***godzina***; ***~ego dziś mamy?*** what day is it today?; ***dom, w ~ym …*** the house in which…; ***ludzie, ~zy …*** the people who/that
który|'kolwiek, ~ś any, either (***z was*** of you)
któż who; ***kogóż ja widzę?*** who do I see here?
ku *prp.* (*D*) to, towards; for, → ***cześć***
Kuba *f* (*-y*; *0*) Cuba; **℞ński** Cuban; **~ńczyk** *m* (*-a*; *-cy*), **~nka** *f* (*-i*; *G -nek*) Cuban
kubatura *f* (*-y*; *G -*) cubature, capacity
kubek *m* (*-bka*; *-bki*) mug
kubeł *m* (*-bła*; *-bły*) bucket, pail; (*na śmieci*) *Brt.* dustbin, *Am.* trash can
kubiczny cubic
kucha|rka *f* (*-i*; *G -rek*) cook; **~rski** cookery, cooking; ***książka ~rska*** *Brt.* cookery book, *Am.* cookbook; **~rz** *m* (*-a*; *-e*) cook
kuchen|ka *f* (*-i*; *G -nek*) cooker, stove; **~ny** kitchen
kuchmistrz *m* (*-a*; *-e*), **~yni** *f* (*-*; *G -yń*) chef
kuchnia *f* (*-i*; *-e*, *-i/-chen*) kitchen; (*styl*) cookery
kuc|ać (*-am*) ⟨***~nąć***⟩ squat, croach; **~ki** *pl.* (*-cek*): ***siedzieć w ~ki*** squat, crouch; **~nąć** (*-nę*) → ***kucać***
kucyk *m* (*-a*; *-i*) pony
kuć (*kuję*, *kuj!*, *kuł*) *metal* forge, hammer; *dziurę* chisel; F *Brt.* cram, *Am.* bone up on; → ***podkuwać, w(y)kuwać***
kudłaty shaggy
kufel *m* (*-fla*; *-fle*) mug
kufer *m* (*-fra*; *-fry*) trunk; → ***bagażnik***
kuglarz *m* (*-a*; *-e*) conjurer
kuk *m* (*-a*; *-owie*) *naut.* cook
kukanie *n* (*-a*) cuckooing
kuk|iełka *f* (*-i*; *G -łek*) puppet; **~iełkowy** puppet; **~ła** *f* (*-y*; *G -kieł*) dummy
kukuł|czy cuckoo; **~ka** *f* (*-i*; *G -łek*) *zo.* cuckoo; ***zegar z ~ką*** cuckoo clock
kukurydza *f* (*-y*; *-e*) *Brt.* maize, *Am.* corn; ***~ prażona*** popcorn
KUL *skrót pisany*: ***Katolicki Uniwersytet Lubelski*** Lublin Catholic University
kul|a¹ *f* (*-i*; *-e*) ball; *math.* sphere; (*nabój*) bullet; ***pchnięcie ~ą*** (*w sporcie*) shot put
kul|a² *f* (*-i*; *-e*) crutch; ***chodzić o ~ach*** walk on crutches; **~awy** lame
kule|czka *f* (*-i*; *G -czek*) → ***kulka, kula***; **~ć** (*-ję*) limp, hobble; *fig.* ail
kulić (*-lę*) *nogi itp.* curl up; **~** ⟨**s-**⟩ ***się*** huddle, curl up; (*ze strachu*) cower
kulig *m* (*-u*; *-i*) sleigh ride
kuli|s *m* (*-a*; *-i*) coolie; **~sty** spherical; **~sy** *pl.* (*-*) wings *pl.*
kulk|a *f* (*-i*; *G -lek*) → ***kula***; ***~a szklana*** marble; **~owy** ball
kuloodporny bullet-proof
kulszowy: ***nerw ~*** schiatic nerve
kult *m* (*-u*; *-y*) cult; ***~ jednostki*** personality cult
kultur|a *f* (*-y*; *G -*) culture; (*osobista*) good manners; **~alny** cultural; polite; **~owy** cultural, culture; **~ystyka** *f* (*-i*; *0*) body-building
kultywować (*-uję*) cultivate, nourish
kuluary *m/pl.* (*-ów*) lobby
kułak *m* (*-a*; *-i*) fist
kum *m* (*-a*; *-y/-owie*) godfather; **~a** *f* (*-y*; *G -*) godmother; **~kać** (*-am*) croak
kumo|szka *f* (*-i*; *G -szek*) gossip; **~ter** *m* (*-tra*; *-trzy/-trowie*) mate; **~terstwo** *m* (*-a*; *0*) nepotism
kumpel F *m* (*-pla*; *-ple*) pal, buddy, mate
kuna *f* (*-y*; *G -*) *zo.* marten
kundel *m* (*-dla*; *-dle*) mongrel
kunsztowny ornate, elaborate
kup|a *f* (*-y*; *G -*) heap, pile (*też fig.*); F (*odchody*) turd; ***do ~y, na ~ę, na ~ie*** together; ***trzymać się ~y*** stick together
kuper *m* (*-pra*; *-pry*) rump (*też* F)
kupić *pf* (*-ę*) → ***kupować***
kupiec *m* (*-pca*, *-pcze/-pcu!*; *-pcy*) trader, merchant; (*w sklepiku*) shopkeeper; (*nabywca*) buyer, purchaser; **~ki** (***po -ku***) businesslike
kupka *f* (*-i*; *G -pek*) → ***kupa***
kupn|o *n* (*-pna*; *0*) purchase, buying; **~y** F bought
kupon *m* (*-a*; *-y*) coupon; national-lottery coupon; voucher
kup|ować (*-uję*) buy; purchase; **~ujący**

K

m (*-ego*; *-y*), **-ca** *f* (*-ej*; *-e*) buyer, purchaser

kur *m* (*-a*; *-y*): ***czerwony ~*** fire; **~a** *f* (*-y*; *G -*) hen

kurac|ja *f* (*-i*; *-e*) cure, treatment; ***na ~ji, na ~ję*** on a cure, to a health resort; **~jusz** *m* (*-a*; *-e*), **-szka** *f* (*-i*; *G -szek*) visitor, patient; **~yjny** health

kuranty *m/pl.* (*-ów*) *mus.* glockenspiel

kurat|ela *f* (*-i*; *-e*) *jur.* guardianship; **~or** *m* (*-a*; *-rzy*), **-rka** *f* (*-i*; *G -rek*) guardian; (*szkolny*) superintendent of schools; **~orium** *n* (*idkl.*; *-ia*, *-iów*) education authority

kurcz *m* (*-a*; *-e*) spasm, cramp

kurcz|ak *m* (*-a*; *-i*), **~ę** *n* (*-cia*; *-ta*) chicken

kurcz|owy spasmodic, convulsive; **~yć się** ⟨**s- się**⟩ (*-ę*) *muskuł*: contract; *materiał*: shrink

kurek *m* (*-rka*; *-rki*) *tech.*, *mil.* cock; (*z wodą*) *Brt.* tap, *Am.* faucet

kurenda *f* (*-y*; *G -*) circular (letter)

kurewski V whorish, whore, bitch

kuria *f* (*GDL -ii*; *-e*) *rel.* curia

kurier *m* (*-a*; *-rzy*) courier, messenger; **~ski** courier

kuriozalny odd

kurnik *m* (*-a*; *-i*) *agr.* hen house

kuropatwa *f* (*-y*; *G -*) *zo.* partridge

kurs *m* (*-u*; *-y*) course (*też fig.*); *econ.* rate, price; (*wykład*) course, class; (*jazda*) ride; → ***obieg***; **~ant** *m* (*-a*; *-ci*), **-tka** *f* (*-i*; *G -tek*) course participant; **~ować** (*-uję*) run

kursywa *f* (*-y*; *G -*) italics *pl.*

kurtka *f* (*-i*; *G -tek*) jacket

kurtuazyjny courteous

kurtyna *f* (*-y*; *G -*) curtain

kurwa V *f* (*-y*; *G -*) whore, bitch, hooker

kurz *m* (*-u*; *-e*) dust; **~ajka** *f* (*-i*; *G -jek*) flat wart, *med.* verruca; **~awa** *f* (*-y*; *G -*) cloud of dust

kurz|y hen, chicken; ***~e łapki*** crow's feet

kurzyć (*-ę*) dust; raise dust; ***kurzy się*** there is a lot of dust; ***kurzy się z*** (*G*) there is smoke from

kusi|ciel *m* (*-a*; *-e*), **~cielka** *f* (*-i*; *G -lek*) temptress; **~ć** ⟨**s-**⟩ (*-szę*) tempt; lure

kustosz *m* (*-a*; *-e*) curator

kusy (**-*so***) short; skimpy, scanty

kusza *f* (*-y*; *G -*) crossbow

kuszący (**-*co***) tempting, alluring

kuszetka *f* (*-i*; *G -tek*) couchette

kuśnierz *m* (*-a*; *-e*) furrier

kuśtykać ⟨***po-***⟩ (*-am*) limp, walk with a limp

kutas V *m* (*-a*; *-y*) prick, cock

kuter *m* (*-tra*; *-try*) fishing boat, cutter

kutia *f* (*GDL-ii*;*-e*) (*Christmas sweet dish*)

kutwa *m/f* (*-y*; *-ów/-*) skinflint

kuty wrought; *koń* shod

kuzyn *m* (*-a*; *-i*), **~ka** *f* (*-i*; *G -nek*) cousin; **~ostwo** *n* (*-a*) cousin with his wife

kuźnia *f* (*-ni*; *-nie*) smithy

kw. *skrót pisany*: ***kwadratowy*** sq. (*square*); ***kwartał*** q. (*quarter*)

kwadra *f* (*-y*; *G -*) *astr.* quarter; **~ns** *m* (*-u*; *-e*) quarter; ***za ~ns druga*** a quarter to two; ***~ns po drugiej*** a quarter *Brt.* past two *lub Am.* after two; **~t** *m* (*-u*; *-y*) *math.* square; **~towy** square; ***metr ~towy*** square *Brt.* metre (*Am.* meter) (*skrót*: **sq. m**)

kwakać (*-czę*) quack

kwakier *m* (*-a*; *-rzy*), **~ka** *f* (*-i*; *G -rek*) Quaker

kwalifikacja *f* (*-i*; *-e*) qualification

kwalifikowa|ć ⟨**za-**⟩ (*-uję*) qualify; **~ć** ⟨**za-**⟩ **się** (**na** *A*) be suitable (as); qualify (as); **~ny** qualified

kwantowy quantum

kwapić się (*-ę*): ***nie ~*** (***z*** *I*) not be in any hurry (with)

kwarantanna *f* (*-y*; *G -*) quarantine

kwarc *m* (*-u*; *-e*) *chem.* quartz; **~ówka** *f* (*-i*; *G -wek*) sun lamp

kwart|a *f* (*-y*; *G -*) quart; ***pół ~y piwa*** pint of beer

kwarta|lnik *m* (*-a*; *-i*) quarterly; **~lny** quarterly; **~ł** *m* (*-u*; *-y*) quarter

kwartet *m* (*-u*; *-y*) *mus.* quartet

kwas *m* (*-u*; *-y*) *chem.* acid; (*zaczyn*) leaven; ***~y*** *pl.* quarrels *pl.*, arguments *pl.*; **~ić** (*-szę*) → ***kisić***; **~kowaty** (**-*to***) sharp

kwa|soodporny acid-resistant; **~sowy** acid; **~szony** → ***kiszony***; **~śnieć** ⟨**s-**⟩ (*-ję*) turn acid, turn sour; **~śno** *fig.* sourly, wryly; **~śnosłodki** sweet and sour; **~śny** acid, sour

kwater|a *f* (*-y*; *G -*) *mil.* quarters *pl.*; accommodation(s *pl.*); lodgings *pl.*; ***~a główna*** headquarters (*skrót*: HQ); **~ować** (*-uję*) house, take lodgings; **~unkowy** *Brt.* municipal

kwes|ta *f* (*-y*) collection; **~tia** *f* (*GDl -ii*; *-e*) question; **~tionariusz** *m* (*-a*; *-e*) questionnaire; **~tionować** ⟨***za-***⟩

K

(*-uję*) question, challenge, dispute
kwestować (*-uję*) collect
kwękać (*-am*) be ailing
kwiacia|rka *f* (*-i*; *G -rek*) flower girl, florist; **~rnia** *f* (*-i*; *-e*) florist('s), flower shop; **~sty** → ***kwiecisty***
kwiat *m* (*-u*, *L kwiecie*; *-y*) flower (*też fig.*), bloom, blossom; **~ek** *m* (*-tka*; *-tki*) → ***kwiat***; **~owy** *bot.* flowering; flowery
kwiczeć (*-czę*) squeal
kwie|cień *m* (*-tnia*; *-tnie*) April; **~cisty** (***-to, -ście***) flowery; flowered; **~tnik** *m* (*-a*; *-i*) flower bed; **~tniowy** April
kwik *m* (*-u*; *-i*) squeal
kwilić (*-ę*) whimper
kwint|al *m* (*-a*; *-e*) quintal; **~et** *m* (*-u*; *-y*) *mus.* quintet
kwit *m* (*-u*; *-y*) receipt; **~ *bagażowy*** *Brt.* luggage ticket, *Am.* baggage check; **~ *zastawny*** pawn ticket; **~a** F (*idkl.*): ***być ~a z kimś*** be quits with s.o.; **~ariusz** *m* (*-a*; *-e*) receipt block
kwitnąć (*-nę*) flower, bloom, blossom; *fig.* flourish
kwitować ⟨**po-**⟩ (*-uję*) acknowledge receipt of
kwiz *m* (*-u*; *-y*) quiz
kwoka *f* (*-i*; *G -*) hen
kworum *n* (*idkl.*) quorum
kwota *f* (*-y*; *G -*) amount, sum

L

laborato|rium *n* (*idkl.*; *-ia*, *-iów*) laboratory, F lab; **~ryjny** laboratory
l. *skrót pisany*: **liczba** n. (*number*)
lać (*leję*) pour; F (*bić*) shower blows (on), hit; **~ *się*** pour; stream; run; ***leje*** (***jak z cebra***) it's pouring buckets; → ***nalewać***, ***rozlewać***, ***wylewać***
lada¹ *f* (*-y*; *G -*) counter; **~ *chłodnicza*** cold shelves *pl.*
lada² *part.*(+ *rzecz.*): **~ *trudność*** any (small) difficulty; **~ *chwila*** any moment; (+ *pron.*) → ***byle***; ***nie ~*** not to be scoffed at
lafirynda *f* (*-y*; *G -*) *pej.* slut
lai|cki lay; **~k** *m* (*-a*; *-cy*) lay person, layman
lak *m* (*-u*; *-i*) sealing wax; *bot.* wall flower
lakier *m* (*-u*; *-y*) varnish, lacquer; **~ *do paznokci*** nail polish; **~ować** ⟨**po-**⟩ (*-uję*) varnish; polish; **~owany** varnished; lacquered; *skóra* patent
lakować ⟨**za-**⟩ (*-uję*) seal
lal|a *f* (*-i*; *-e*), **~ka** *f* (*-i*; *G -lek*) doll; ***teatr ~ek*** puppet *Brt.* theatre (*Am.* theater)
lamentować (*-uję*) lament (***nad*** *I* over)
lamówka *f* (*-i*; *G -wek*) binding
lampa *f* (*-y*; *G -*) lamp; → ***błyskowy***
lampart *m* (*-a*; *-y*) *zo.* leopard
lampka *f* (*-i*; *G -pek*) lamp; **~ *nocna*** bedside lamp; **~ *kontrolna*** control lamp; **~ *wina*** a glass of wine
lamus *m* (*-a*; *-y*) junk room; ***złożyć do ~a*** discard, scrap
landrynk|a *f* (*-i*; *G -nek*) fruit drop; **~owy** sweet
lan|ie *n* (*-a*; *G lań*) pouring; (*bicie*) beating, hiding; ***~e wody*** *fig.* waffle; **~y** poured; *metal* cast
Lap|onia *f* (*GDL -ii*; *0*) Lapland; **~ończyk** *m* (*-a*; *-cy*), **~oka** *f* (*-i*; *G -nek*) Lapp; **²oński** Lapp
larwa *f* (*-y*; *G -*) *zo.* larva
laryngolog *m* (*-a*; *-owie/-dzy*) laryngologist, ENT specialist
las *m* (*-u*; *-y*) wood, forest
lase|cznik *m.* (*-a*; *-i*) *biol.* bacillus; **~k** *m* (*-sku*; *-ski*) → ***las***
laser *m* (*-a*; *-y*) laser; **~owy** laser
lask|a *f* (*-i*; *G -sek*) walking stick, cane; F chick, *Brt.* bird; *tech.* rod; **~owy** stick; ***orzech ~y*** hazelnut
lasować (*-uję*) slake
lata *pl.* years *pl.*; → ***lato***; *1. sg. od* **latać**; ***ile masz lat?*** how old are you?; **~ *dziewięćdziesiąte*** the 1990's; ***sto lat!*** many happy returns!; ***na swoje ~*** for his/her age
lata|ć (*-am*) fly; F (*biegać*) run (***do*** *G* to); (***za*** *I*) run (after); ***~ć po zakupy*** go shopping in a hurry; **~nina** *f* (*-y*; *G -*) running around
latar|ka *f* (*-i*; *G -rek*) *Brt.* torch, *Am.* flashlight; **~nia** *f* (*-i*; *-e*) lamp, *naut.* lantern; ***~nia morska*** lighthouse; **~niowiec** *m* (*-wca*; *-wce*) lightship
latawiec *m* (*-wca*; *-wce*) kite

L

lato *n* (*-a*; *G -*) summer; ***latem, w lecie*** in summer; ***na ~*** for the summer; **~rośl** *f* (*-i*; *-e*) offspring
lau|r *m* (*-u*; *-y*) laurel; **~reat** *m* (*-a*; *-ci*), **~reatka** *f* (*-i*; *G -tek*) laureate; **~rowy** laurel, bay
lawa *f* (*-y*) lava
lawenda *f* (*-y*) *zo.* lavender
lawin|a *f* (*-y*; *G -*) avalanche (*też fig.*); **~owy (*-wo*)** like an avalanche
lawirować (*-uję*) *Brt.* manoeuvre, *Am.* manoeuver
laz|ł(a), ~łam, ~łem → ***leźć***
lazurowy (*-wo*) azure
ląd *m* (*-u*; *-y*) land; ***~ stały*** mainland, dry land; ***~em*** overland; ***zejść na ~*** go on shore; **~ować** ⟨***wy-***⟩ (*-uję*) land; *samolot*: touch down; **~owanie** *n* (*-a*; *G -ń*) landing; (*samolotu*) touchdown; **~owisko** *n* (*-a*; *G -*) airfield, landing strip; (*helikoptera*) pad; **~owy** land; *przesyłka* overland; *biol.* terrestrial; ***poczta ~owa*** surface mail
lecieć ⟨***po-***⟩ (*-cę, -ci, leć!*) fly; *ciecz*: run; F run, hurry; → ***przelatywać***; ***jak leci?*** how are you?; ***co leci w telewizji wieczorem?*** what's on TV tonight?
leciutki lightweight
leciwy aged
lecz but; yet; ***nie tylko …, ~ także …*** not only … but also …
lecz|enie *n* (*-a*) treatment; **~nica** *f* (*-y*; *G -*) hospital, clinic; **~nictwo** *n* (*-a*; *0*) health care; **~niczy** therapeutic; *kosmetyk* medicated; **~yć** (*-czę*) treat, cure; ***~yć się*** be under medical treatment; *rana itp.*: heal
ledw|ie, ~o hardly, scarcely; ***~ie/~o nie*** almost, nearly; ***~ie żywy*** nearly dead
legal|izować ⟨***za-***⟩ (*-uję*) legalize; **~ny** legal, lawful
legawy: ***pies ~*** pointer
legenda *f* (*-y*; *G -*) legend; (*mapy*) key
legi|a *f* (*GDL -ii*; *-e*) legion; **~onista** *m* (*-y*; *-ści*) legionnaire
leginsy *pl.* (*-ów*) leggings *pl.*
legislacyjny legislative
legitym|acja *f* (*-y*; *-e*) identification, identity card; (*członkowska*) membership card; **~ować** (*-uję*) ask to see identification; ***~ować*** ⟨***wy-***⟩ ***się*** establish one's identity (*I* by); hold, have
legowisko *n* (*-a*; *G -*) bedding; → ***barłóg***
legumina *f* (*-y*; *G -*) pudding
lej *m* (*-a*; *-e*) crater; → ***lać***
lejce *pl.* (*-y/-ów*) reins *pl.*
lejek *m* (*-ka*; *-ki*) funnel
lek. *skrót pisany*: ***lekarz*** MD (*Doctor of Medicine*)
lek *m* (*-u*; *-i*) *med.* medicine, drug; *fig.* cure
lekar|ka *f* (*-i*; *G -rek*) doctor, physician; **~ski** medical; doctor's; **~stwo** *n* (*-a*; *G -*) → ***lek***
lekarz doctor, physician; ***~ specjalista*** consultant
lekceważ|ący (*-co*) disdainful, disrespectful; neglecting (*obowiązków*); **~enie** *n* (*-a*; *0*) disdain, disrespect; **~yć** ⟨***z-***⟩ disdain, disrespect; *obowiązki* neglect
lekcj|a *f* (*-i*) lesson, class; (*godzina*) period; ***prowadzić ~e*** teach; ***odrabiać ~e*** do homework
lekk|i light (*też fig.*); slight; *herbata* weak; *szum* faint; ***z ~a*** lightly; **~o** *adv.* light; lightly; slightly
lekko|atletyczny track; **~myślny** careless; irresponsible; **~ść** *f* (*-ści*; *0*) lightness; → ***łatwość***; **~strawny** light, easily digestible
lekooporny *med.* drug-resistant
lek|sykon *m* (*-u*; *-y*) lexicon; **~tor** *m* (*-a*; *-rzy*) instructor; **~tura** *f* (*-y*; *G -*) reading; text; ***~tura obowiązkowa*** set book
lemiesz *m* (*-a*; *-e*) *agr. Brt.* ploughshare, *Am.* plowshare
lemoniada *f* (*-y*; *G -*) lemonade
len *m* (*lnu*, *G lnie*; *lny*) *bot.* flax; (*materiał*) linen
leni|ć się (*-ę*) be lazy (**do** *G* to, ***z*** *I* with); → ***linieć***; **~stwo** *n* (*-a*; *0*) laziness
leniuch *m* (*-a*; *-y*) layabout; idler; **~ować** (*-uję*) laze (away)
leniw|iec *m* (*-wca*; *-wce*) *zo.* sloth; (*-wcy*) → ***leniuch***; **~y** lazy, idle
leń *m* (*-nia*; *-nie*, *-ni/-niów*); → ***leniuch***
lep *m* (*-u*; *-y*) glue; ***~ na muchy*** fly paper; **~ić** (*-pię*) ⟨***u-***⟩ shape, model; ⟨***przy-***⟩ stick, glue; ***~ić się*** (*być lepkim*) be sticky
lepiej *adv.* (*comp. od* → ***najlepiej***) better
lepki sticky, tacky
lepsz|y *adj.* (*comp. od* → ***dobry***; *m-os lepsi*) better; ***zmienić się na ~e*** turn for the better
lesbijka *f* (*-i*; *G -jek*) Lesbian
lesisty woody
leszcz *m* (*-a*; *-e*) *zo.* bream

L

leszczyna *f (-y; G -) bot.* hazel
leśni|ctwo *n (-a; G -)* forestry; **~czówka** *f (-i; G -wek)* forester's house; **~czy** *m (-ego; G -ych)* forester
leśn|ik *m (-a; -cy)* forester; **~y** woodland, forest
letni tepid, lukewarm; summer, summery; **~czka** *f (-i; G -czek)*, **~k** *m (-a; -cy)* holiday-maker; **~o** *adv.* → ***letni***; **~sko** *n (-a; G -)* summer resort
lew *m (lwa; lwy, G lwów) zo.* lion; Ω *znak Zodiaku:* Leo; ***on(a) jest spod znaku Lwa*** he/she is (a) Leo
lew|a *f (-y) (w kartach)* trick; **~acki** leftist
lewar|ek *m (-rka; -rki)* jack; ***podnosić ~kiem*** jack up
lewatywa *f (-y; G -) med.* enema
lewic|a *f (-y; -e) zwł. pol.* left; left wing; **~owy** left, leftist
lew'konia *f (GDL -ii; -e) bot.* stock
lewo *adv.*: ***na ~, w ~*** to the left, left; ***na ~*** under the table, on the sly; **~ręczny** left-handed
lewostronny: ***ruch ~*** driving on the left
lew|y left; F *fig. też* fake, pseudo; ***po ~ej (stronie)*** on the left; ***z ~a*** from the left; → ***lewo***
leźć F climb; (***do*** *G*) get (into)
leż|ak *m (-a; -i)* deck-chair; **~anka** *f (-i; G -nek)* couch; **~ąco**: ***na ~ąco*** when lying, lying down; **~eć** *(-żę, -y)* lie *(też fig.); suknia:* fit
lędźwie *pl. (-dźwi)* loins *pl.*
lęgnąć się ⟨***wy- się***⟩ *(-nę, lągł) (z jaja)* hatch; *fig.* breed
lęk *m (-u; -i)* fear, anxiety; **~ać się** *(-am)* fear, dread; **~liwy** fearful, apprehensive
lgnąć *(-nę)* (***do*** *G*) cling (to)
libacja *f (-i; -e)* binge, F booze-up
Liba|n *m (-u; 0)* Lebanon; **~ńczyk** *m (-a; -cy)* Lebanese; Ω**ński** Lebanese
libera|lizować *(-uję)* liberalize; **~lny** liberal; **~ł** *m (-a; -owie)* liberal
Libi|a *f (GDL -ii; 0)* Libya; **~jczyk** *m (-a; -cy)*; **~jka** *f (-i; G -jek)* Libyan; Ω**jski** Libyan
licealist|a *m (-y; -ści)*, **~ka** *f (-i; G -tek)* secondary-school student
licenc|ja *f (-i; -e) Brt.* licence, *Am.* license; **~jat** *m (-u; -y)* Bachelor's degree
liceum *n (idkl.; -a, -ów) Brt.* grammar school, *Am.* high school, lycée; ***~ zawodowe*** vocational secondary school
licho[1] *adv.* → ***lichy***
lich|o[2] *n (-a)* devil; ***~o wie*** God knows; ***co u ~a*** what on earth; ***mieć do ~a*** *(G)* have in plenty
lichota *f (-y; G -)* trash
lichtarz *m (-a; -e)* candlestick
lichwia|rski extortionate; **~rstwo** *n (-a)* usury; **~rz** *m (-a; -e)* usurer
lichy crummy, paltry, poor
lico *n (-a; G lic) lit.* face, countenance; **~wać** *(-uję)* (***z*** *I*) *v/i.* fit, be suitable, be appropriate; *v/t. arch.* face; **~wy** facing
licyt|acja *f (-i; -e)* auction; *(w kartach)* bidding; **~ator** *m (-a; -rzy)* auctioneer; **~ować** *(-uję)* auction; *(w kartach)* bid
liczb|a *f (-y; G -)* number; ***~a mnoga*** the plural; ***~a pojedyncza*** the singular; ***w ~ie gości*** among the guests; ***przeważać ~ą*** outnumber, exceed in number; ***~a ofiar śmiertelnych*** death toll; **~owo** *adv.* numerically; in numbers; **~owy** numerical
licze|bnik *m (-a; -i) gr.* numeral; ***~bnik porządkowy*** ordinal; ***~bnik główny*** cardinal; **~bny** numerical; ***stan ~bny*** number, size; **~nie** *n (-a; 0)* counting
licz|nik *m (-a; -i)* meter, *(w taksówce)* clock; *tech.* counter; *math.* numerator; ***~nik gazowy*** gas meter; **~ny** numerous
liczy|ć ⟨***po-***⟩ *(-ę)* count *(impf też v/i.);* calculate; number; → ***obliczać, wyliczać***; *fig.* (***na*** *A*) depend (on), rely (on); ***on ~ł sobie … lat*** he was … years old; ***~ć się*** count *v/i.*; (***z*** *I*) reckon (with), take *s.o./s.th.* into account; ***to się nie ~*** it does not count; **~dło** *n (-a; G -deł)* abacus
lider *m (-a; -rzy)* leader
liga *f (-i; G -)* league
lignina *f (-y; G -) med.* wood-wool
ligow|iec *m (-wca; -wcy)* league player; **~y** league
likier *m (-u; -y)* liqueur
likwid|acja *f (-i; -e)* liquidation; elimination; **~ować** ⟨***z-***⟩ *(-uję)* liquidate; eliminate
lili|a *f (GDL -ii; -e)* lily; **~owy** lilac
liliput *m (-a; -ci)*, **~ka** *f (-i; G -tek)* Lilliputian
limfa *f (-y; 0)* lymph; **~tyczny** lymphatic
limit *m (-u; -y)* limit; **~ować** *(-uję)* limit, restrict
lin *m (-a; -y) zo.* tench
lina *f (-y; G -)* rope, line; *(w cyrku)* tightrope

linczować ⟨**z-**⟩ (*-uję*) lynch
lingwistyczny linguistic
lini|a *f* (*GDL -ii*; *-e*) line (*też fig.*); **~a polityczna** platform; **dbać o ~ę** watch one's weight; → **kreska**; **~ał** *m* (*-u*; *-y*) ruler
linieć (*-eję*) *Brt.* moult, *Am.* molt
lini|jka *f* (*-i*; *G -jek*) ruler; **~owany** ruled; **~owy** linear
linka *f* (*-i*; *G -nek*) →**lina**
lino|leum *n* (*idkl.*) linoleum; **~ryt** *m* (*-u*; *-y*) linocut
lino|skoczek *m* (*-czka*; *-czkowie/-czki*) tightrope-walker; **~wy** rope, cable
lip|a *f* (*-y*; *G -*) lime, linden; **~cowy** July; **~iec** *m* (*-pca*; *-pce*) July; **~ny** F fake; → **lichy**; **~owy** lime, linden
liry|czny lyrical; lyric; **~ka** *f* (*-i*; *G -*) lyric poetry
lis *m* (*-a*; *-y*) *zo.* fox
lisi fox; foxlike; **~ca** *f* (*-y*; *G -*) *zo.* vixen; *bot.* chanterelle
list *m* (*-u*; *-y*) letter; **~a** *f* (*-y*; *G -*) list, register; **~ek** *m* (*-tka*; *-tki*) → **liść**
listonosz *m* (*-a*; *-e*) *Brt.* postman, *Am.* mailman, mail carrier; **~ka** *f* (*-i*; *G -szek*) *Brt.* postwoman, *Am.* mail carrier
listo|pad *m* (*-a*; *-y*) November; **~padowy** November; **~wie** *n* (*-wia*; *0*) leaves *pl.*, foliage
listow|ny, ~y letter
listwa *f* (*-y*; *G -tew*) strip; batten, slat; **~ zasilająca** power strip
liszaj *m* (*-a*; *-e*) *med.* lichen
liszka *f* (*-i*; *G -szek*) *zo.* caterpillar
liś|ciasty deciduous; **~ć** *m* (*-cia*; *-cie*) leaf
lit *m* (*-u*; *0*) *chem.* lithium
li'tania *f* (*GDL -ii*; *-e*) litany
litera *f* (*-y*; *G -*) letter; **~cki** (**-ko, po -ku**) literary; **~lny** literal; **~t** *m* (*-a*; *-ci*); **~tka** *f* (*-i*; *G -tek*) writer; **~tura** *f* (*-y*; *G -*) literature
literować ⟨**prze-**⟩ (*-uję*) spell
litewski (**po -ku**) Lithuanian
litoś|ciwy merciful, compassionate; **~ć** *f* (*-ści*; *0*) mercy, pity
litować się ⟨**u-, z- się**⟩ (*-uję*) have mercy (**nad** *I* on), pity
litr *m* (*-a*; *-y*) *Brt.* litre, *Am.* liter; **~aż** *m* (*-u*; *0*) *mot.* cubic capacity; **~owy** *Brt.* litre, *Am.* liter
li'turgia *f* (*GDL -ii*; *-e*) liturgy
Lit|wa *f* (*-y*; *0*) Lithuania; **~win** *m* (*-a*; *-i*), **~winka** *f* (*-i*; *G -nek*) Lithuanian

lity solid
liz|ać (*-żę*, *liż!*) lick; **~ak** *m* (*-a*; *-i*) lollipop
Lizbona *f* (*-y*; *0*) Lisbon
liznąć *v/s.* (*-nę*) → **lizać**
lizus *m* (*-a*; *-y*) *pej.* bootlicker, toady, creep; **~owski** toady
lm *skrót pisany:* **liczba mnoga** pl. (*plural*)
ln|iany *bot.* flaxen; linen; **~u, ~y** → **len**
loch *m* (*-u*; *-y*) dungeon
locha *f* (*-y*; *G -*) *zo.* wild sow; (*młoda*) gilt
loczek *m* (*-czka*; *-czki*) → **lok**
lodo|łamacz *m* (*-a*; *-e*) *naut.* icebreaker; **~waty** (**-to**) icy; glacial, ice-cold; **~wiec** *m* (*-wca*; *-wce*) glacier; **~wisko** *n* (*-a*; *G -*) ice rink; **~wnia** *f* (*-i*; *-e*) cold room
lo|dowy ice; ice-cream; **~dówka** *f* (*-i*; *G -wek*) fridge; **~dy** *m/pl.* (*-ów*) ice-cream; → **lód**; **~dziarnia** *f* (*-i*; *-e*) ice-cream parlo(u)r; **~dziarka** *f* (*-i*; *G -rek*), **~dziarz** *m* (*-a*; *-e*) ice-cream seller, *Am.* iceman
logarytm *m* (*-u*; *-y*) logarithm
logi|czny logical, coherent; **~ka** *f* (*-i*; *-*) logic; coherence
logować się (*-uję*) *komp.* log in
lojaln|ość *f* (*-ści*; *0*) loyalty; **~y** loyal
lok *m* (*-a*; *-i*) curl, lock
lokaj *m* (*-a*; *-e*) lackey (*też fig.*), valet
lokal *m* (*-u*; *-e*) place; accommodation; restaurant; **~ nocny** night club; **~ wyborczy** polling station; **~izować** ⟨**z-**⟩ (*-uję*) localize, locate; **~ny** local
lokata *f* (*-y*; *G -*) place, position; (*w banku*) deposit; (*kapitału*) investment
lokator *m* (*-a*; *-rzy*), **~ka** *f* (*-i*; *G -rek*) lodger, tenant, occupant
lokaut *m* (*-u*; *-y*) *econ.* lockout
lokomo|cja *f* (*-i*): **środek ~cji** vehicle, means of *Brt.* transport, *Am.* transportation; **~tywa** *f* (*-y*; *G -*) locomotive, engine
lokować ⟨**u-**⟩ (*-uję*) place, position (**się** o.s.); *econ.* invest
lokówka *f* (*-i*; *G -wek*) curler
lombard *m* (*-u*; *-y*) pawnshop
Londyn *m* (*-u*; *0*) London; **~ńczyk** Londoner; **⁓ński** London
lont *m* (*-u*; *-y*) fuse
lord *m* (*-a*; *-owie*) Lord, lord
lornetka *f* (*-i*; *G -tek*) binoculars *pl.*, glasses *pl.*; **~ teatralna** opera-glasses *pl.*
los *m* (*-u*; *-y*) fate, lot; (*w grze*) ticket; **dobry ~** good luck; **~ loteryjny** lottery ticket; **rzucać ~y** cast lots; **na ~ szczęścia** hit-or-miss

losow|ać (*-uję*) draw (lots *v/i.*); **~anie** *n* (*-a*; *G -ań*) drawing; **~y** random; ***wybrany ~owo*** chosen at random
lot *m* (*-u*; *-y*) flight; ***w ~*** immediately, at once; → ***ptak***; ***~em błyskawicy*** like lightning
lo'ter|ia *f* (*GDL -ii*; *-e*) lottery; ***~ia fantowa*** raffle
lot|ka *f* (*-i*; *G -tek*) *zo.* flight feather; (*w sporcie*) shuttlecock; **~nia** *f* (*-i*; *-e*) hang-glider; **~niarz** *m* (*-a*; *-e*) hang-glider; **~nictwo** *n* (*-a*; *0*) aviation; (*wojskowe*) air force; **~niczy** air, aerial; **~nik** *m* (*-a*; *-cy*) aviator, airman; **~nisko** *n* (*-a*; *G -*) airport; (*małe*) airfield; **~niskowiec** *m* (*-wca*; *-wce*) *mil.* aircraft carrier; **~niskowy** airport
lotn. *skrót pisany*: ***lotniczy*** airline
lotny airborne; *ciecz* volatile; *człowiek* quick, alert
loża *f* (*-y*; *G lóż*) *theat.* box
lód (*lodu*; *lody*) ice; → ***lody***
lp. ***liczba porządkowa*** No. (*number*); ***liczba pojedyncza*** sing. (*singular*)
lśni|ący (**-*co***) glistening, glittering; **~ć** (**się**) (*-ę*) glisten, glitter
lub *cj.* or
lubić (*-ę*) like, enjoy
lubieżny lewd, lascivious; ***czyn ~*** *jur.* immoral act
lubować się (*-uję*) (*I*) take pleasure (in)
lud *m* (*-u*, *-u/-dzie!*; *-y*) people, nation; **~ność** *f* (*-ści*; *0*) population, inhabitants *pl.*; **~ny** populated
ludo|bójstwo *n* (*-a*; *G -*) genocide; **~wy** folk; (*wiejski*) rural, peasant; *pol.* people's; **~znawczy** ethnographic; **~żerca** *m* (*-y*) cannibal
ludz|ie *pl.* (*-i*, *I -dźmi*) people; **~ki** (***po -ku***) human; (*dobry*) humane; **~kość** *f* (*-ści*; *0*) humanity, mankind, humankind
lufa *f* (*-y*; *G -*) barrel
lufcik *m* (*-a*; *-i*) air vent (in a window)
luft: F ***do ~u*** good-for-nothing
luk *m* (*-u*; *-i*) hatch; **~a** *f* (*-i*; *G -*) gap
lukier *m* (*-kru*; *0*) icing
lukrecja *f* (*-i*; *-e*) *bot.* liquorice
lukrować ⟨**po-**⟩ ice
luksusowy (**-*wo***) luxurious
lunaty|czka *f* (*-i*; *G -czek*), **~k** *m* (*-a*; *-cy*) sleepwalker
lunąć *pf.* (*-nę*, *-ń!*) *v/i.* beat down, pelt down
luneta *f* (*-y*; *G -*) telescope
lupa *f* (*-y*; *G -*) magnifying glass
lust|erko *n* (*-rka*; *G -rek*) pocket mirror; **~racja** *f* (*-i*; *-e*) inspection, review; **~ro** *n* (*-a*; *G -ter*) mirror; **~rować** ⟨**z-**⟩ (*-uję*) inspect, review
lustrzan|ka *f* (*-i*; *G -nek*) reflex camera; **~y** mirror
lut *m* (*-u*; *-y*) solder
Lutera|nin *m* (*-a*; *-e*), **~nka** *f* (*-i*; *G -nek*) Lutheran; **~nizm** *m* (*-u*; *0*) Lutheranism; **ℒński** Lutheran
lutnia *f* (*-i*; *-e*) *mus.* lute
lutow|ać (*-uję*) solder; **~nica** *f* (*-y*; *-e*) soldering iron; **~niczy** soldering
lut|owy February; **~y** *m* (*-ego*; *0*) February
luz *m* (*-u*; *-y*) room; *tech.* play, slackness; *mot.* neutral (gear); F ***~em*** loose; *wóz* empty; *fig.* free; ***na ~ie*** *mot.* in neutral; ***na*** (***pełnym***) ***~ie*** *fig.* easygoing, carefree; **~ować** ⟨**z-**⟩ (*-uję*) relieve, take over from (**się** *v/i.*); ⟨**ob-, po-**⟩ loosen
luźny (**-*no***) loose; *lina* slack; *sweter* baggy
lw|a → ***lew***; **~i** lion; **~ica** *f* (*-y*; *-e*) *zo.* lioness; **~y** *pl.* → ***lew***
lżej(**szy**) *adv.* (*adj.*) *comp. od* → ***lekki, lekko***
lżyć ⟨**ze-**⟩ (*-ę*, *lżyj!*) scold, abuse

Ł

Łaba *f* (*-y*; *0*) Elbe
łabę|dzi swan; **~dź** *m* (*-dzia*; *-dzie*, *-dzi*) *zo.* swan
łach(**man**) *m* (*-a*; *-y*) rag; ***~y*** *pl.* *też* F togs *pl.*, things *pl.*
łachudra *f/m* (*-y*; *G -der/-drów*) *pej.* sloven, bum; → ***szubrawiec***
łaciaty *koń* roan
łaci|na *f* (*-y*; *0*) Latin; **~ński** Latin
ład *m* (*-u*; *0*) order; ***dojść do ~u*** straighten out (***z*** *I*)
ładny *adj.* (*comp. -niejszy*) pretty, nice

Ł

ładow|ać (*-uję*) ⟨**za-, wy-**⟩ load; ⟨**na-**⟩ *broń* load; *akumulator* charge; **~nia** *f* (*-i*; *-e*) hold; **~ność** *f* (*-ści*; *0*) load capacity; **~ny** → ***pakowny***

ładunek *m* (*-nku*; *-nki*) load, cargo; *electr.* charge; ***~ wybuchowy*** (explosive) charge

łago|dnieć ⟨**z-**⟩ (*-ję*) soften; *ból, wiatr*: subside; **~dność** *f* (*-ści*; *0*) gentleness, mildness; **~dny** gentle, mild, soft; *med.* benign; **~dzić** (*-dzę*) ⟨**z-**⟩ ease, appease; relieve; ***okoliczności*** *f/pl.* ***~dzące*** mitigating (*lub* extenuating) circumstances *pl.*

łajać ⟨**z-**⟩ (*-am*) scold, rap

łajda|cki villainous; **~ctwo** *n* (*-a*; *G -*) rascality, villainy; **~czka** *f* (*-i*; *G -czek*), **~k** *m* (*-a*; *-i/-cy*) scoundrel

łajno *n* (*-a*; *G -jen*) dung; F turd, crap

łakocie *pl.* (*-i*) *Brt.* sweets *pl.*, *Am.* candy

łakom|ić się ⟨**po- się**⟩ (*-ę*) (**na** *A*) crave (for); be greedy (for); **~y** greedy (*też* **na** *A* for); (*na słodycze*) sweet-toothed

łam *m* (*-u*; *-y*) *print.* column; **~ać** (*-ię*) ⟨**po-, z-**⟩ break; ***~ać*** ⟨**po-**⟩ ***się*** break, give way; *fig.* crack up; **~anie** *n* (*-a*; *G -ń*) *med.* pains *pl.*; **~any** broken

łami|główka *f* (*-i*; *G -wek*) puzzle; **~strajk** *m* (*-a*; *-i*) strike-breaker, scab

łamliwy fragile, breakable

łan *m* (*-u*; *-y*) field

łania *f* (*-ni*; *-e*) *zo.* doe

łańcu|ch *m* (*-a*; *-y*) chain; (*gór*) ridge; ***przykuwać ~chem*** chain; **~chowy** chain; ***pies ~chowy*** watchdog; **~szek** *m* (*-szka*; *-szki*) chain

łapa *f* (*-y*; *G -*) paw (*też fig.*)

łapa|ć ⟨**z-**⟩ (*-pię*) catch (*też fig.*); get hold of; get; (*nagle*) grab; ***~ć się na cz-ś*** catch o.s. doing s.th.; **~nka** *f* (*-i*; *G -nek*) raid

łap|czywy greedy, avid; **~ka** *f* (*-i*; *G -pek*) (***na myszy*** mouse)trap

łapówk|a *f* (*-i*; *G -wek*) bribe; ***dawać ~kę*** bribe; **~arski** bribery; **~arstwo** *n* (*-a*; *0*) bribery

łasica *f* (*-y*; *G -*) *zo.* weasel

łasić się (*-szę*) fawn (**do** *G* on)

łas|ka *f* (*-i*; *G -*) favo(u)r; mercy, clemency; *rel.* grace; ***prawo ~ki*** the right of reprieve; ***niech pan z ~ki swojej*** would you be so kind as to; ***z ~ki*** condescendingly; **~kawy** gracious; favo(u)rable; kind; ***bądź ~kaw*** be so kind

łaskot|ać ⟨**po-**⟩ (*-am*) tickle; **~ki** *f/pl.*: ***mieć ~tki*** be ticklish; **~liwy** ticklish

łas|ować (*-uję*) treat o.s. to; **~y** → ***łakomy***

łata[1] *f* (*-y*; *G -*) slat

łata[2] *f* (*-y*; *G -*) patch; **~ć** ⟨**za-**⟩ (*-am*) patch (up); **~nina** *f* (*-y*) botch, patchwork

łatka *f* (*-i*; *G -tek*) → ***łata***

łatwo *adv.* (*comp. -wiej*) easily; readily; **~ść** *f* (*-ści*; *0*) easiness, ease; readiness; **~wierny** credulous, gullible

łatwy *adj.* (*comp. -wiejszy*) easy; simple

ław|a *f* (*-y*; *G -*) bench; coffee table; ***~a oskarżonych*** dock; ***~a przysięgłych*** jury; **~ica** *f* (*-y*; *G -*) school; (*piasku*) drift, shoal; **~ka** *f* (*-i*; *G -wek*) bench; (*w kościele*) pew; **~niczka** *f* (*-i*; *G -czek*), **~nik** *m* (*-a*; *-cy*) juror

łazanki *f/pl.* *jakby*: lasagne

łazić (*-żę*) (**po** *I*) F trudge, walk; climb

łazienka *f* (*-i*; *G -nek*) bathroom

łazik *m* (*-a*; *-i*) *Brt.* tramp, *Am.* hobo; *mot.* jeep; **~ować** (*-uję*) roam, hang around (***po ulicach*** the streets)

łaźnia *f* (*-i*; *-e*) baths *sg./pl.*

łącz|nica *f* (*-y*; *G -*) *tel.* switchboard; **~niczka** *f* (*-i*; *G -czek*) courier, messenger; **~nie** together (**z** *I* with); including; **~nik** *m* (*-a*; *-cy*) courier, messenger; *mil.* liaison officer; *print.* hyphen; *tech.* coupling; **~ność** *f* (*-ści*; *0*) connection (*też tel.*), contact; *tel.* (tele)communications *pl.*; *fig.* (sense of) community; **~ny** all-in, inclusive; joint; **~yć** ⟨**po-, z-**⟩ (*-czę*) (**się**) connect, link; join; combine, merge; unite; *tel.* put through; ***~ymy się z*** (*I*) we are going over to

łąk|a *f* (*-i*; *G -*) meadow; **~owy** meadow

łeb *m* (*łba*; *łby*) head, F nut; ***na ~, na szyję*** headlong; ***kocie łby*** *pl.* cobbles *pl.*; **~ek** *m* (*-bka*; *-bki*) head (***gwoździa*** of the nail); ***od ~ka*** per head; ***po ~kach*** cursorily, slapdash

łechta|czka *f* (*-i*; F *-czek*) *anat.* clitoris; **~ć** (*-am*) tickle

łga|ć F lie; tell fibs; **~rz** *m* (*-a*; *-e*) liar

łkać (*-am*) sob

łobuz *m* (*-a*; *-y/-i*) hooligan, yob; (*chłopiec*) rascal; **~erski** roguish; *spojrzenie* arch; **~ować** (*-uję*) go wild, charge about

łodyga *f* (*-i*; *G -*) stalk, stem
łodzi *G* → **łódź**
łojo|tok *m* (*-u*; *0*) seborrh(o)ea; **~wy** seborrh(o)eal, seborrh(o)eic
łok|ciowy elbow; **~ieć** *m* (*-kcia*; *-kcie*) elbow
łom *m* (*-u*; *-y*) crowbar
łomot *m* (*-u*; *-y*) thud, bang, crash; **~ać** (*-czę/-cę*) crash, bang, thud
łon|o *n* (*-a*; *G -*) womb; (*piersi*) bosom (*też fig.*); *anat.* pubis; *fig.* **w ~ie** (*G*) inside; in the bosom of; **~owy** pubic
łopat|a *f* (*-y*; *G -*) shovel; (*śmigła*) blade; **~ka** *f* (*-i*; *G -tek*) (small) shovel; *anat.* (shoulder) blade; *gastr.* (*przyrząd*) spatula; (*potrawa*) shoulder of ham
łopian *m* (*-u*; *-y*) *bot.* burdock
łopotać (*-czę/-cę*) flutter, flap
łosi|ca *f* (*-y*; *-e*, *G -*) *zo.* elk; **~ca amerykańska** moose
łoskot *m* (*-u*; *-y*) din; bang, crash
łoso|siowy salmon; **~ś** *m* (*-sia*; *-sie*) *zo.* salmon
łoś *m* (*-a*; *G łosi*) *zo.* elk; **~ amerykański** moose
Łot|wa *f* (*-y*; *0*) Latvia; **≗ewski** (**po -ku**) Latvian; **~ysz** *m* (*-a*; *-e*), **-szka** *f* (*-i*; *G -szek*) Latvian
łot|r *m* (*-a*; *-y/-trzy*), **~rzyca** *f* (*-y*; *G -*) villain, scoundrel
łow|ca *m* (*-y*; *-cy*), **~czyni** *f* (*-ń*, *-nie*) hunter; **~czy 1.** hunting; **2.** *m* (*-ego*; *-owie*) master of the hunt; **~ić** ⟨**z-**⟩ (*-ię*) catch; hunt; **~ić ryby** fish; **~iecki** hunting; **~ny**: **zwierzyna ~na** game; **~y** *pl.* (*-ów*) hunt
łoza *f* (*-y*; *łóz*) *bot.* willow
łoże *n* (*-a*; *G łóż*) (**małżeńskie, śmierci** marital, death) bed
łoży|ć (*-żę*) (**na** *A*) finance, pay (for); **~sko** *n* (*-a*; *G -*) (**kulkowe** ball) bearing
łó|dka *f* (*-i*; *G -dek*), **~dź** *f* (*łodzi*; *łodzie*, *-dzi*) boat
łój *m* (*łoju*; *0*) (*jadalny*) suet, (*na mydło itp.*) tallow
łóż|eczko *n* (*-a*; *G -czek*): **~eczko dziecięce** *zwł. Brt.* cot, crib; → **kołyska**; **~ko** *n* (*-a*; *G -żek*) bed; **do ~ka** to bed; **~kowy** bed
łubin *m* (*-u*; *-y*) *bot.* lupin
łuczni|ctwo *n* (*-a*; *0*) archery; **~czka** *f* (*-i*; *G -czek*), **~k** *m* (*-a*; *-cy*) archer
łudz|ący (**-co**) *podobieństwo* remarkable, striking; **~ić** ⟨**z-**⟩ (*-dzę*) deceive, delude; (**nie**) **~ić się, że** (not) be under the illusion that; **~ić się nadzieją** entertain the hope
ług *m* (*-u*; *-i*) *chem.* lye
łuk *m* (*-u*; *-i*) curve; *math.* arc; *arch.* arch; (*broń*) bow; **~owy** *tech.* arc; *arch.* arch
łuna *f* (*-y*; *G -*) glow
łup *m* (*-u*; *-y*) loot, plunder; **paść ~em** (*D*) fall prey (to)
łup|acz *m* (*-a*; *-e*) *zo.* haddock; **~ać** ⟨**roz-**⟩ (*-pię*) split; *orzech* crack; **~ek** *m* (*-pka*; *-pki*) slate; **~ić** (*-pię*) loot, plunder
łupież *m* (*-u*; *0*) dandruff
łupin|a *f* (*-y*; *G -*) (*owoców*) skin, (*ziemniaków*) peel; (*orzecha*, *też arch.*) shell; **~owy** *arch.* shell
łupnąć F *v/s.* (*-nę*) hit, smash
łuska *f* (*-i*; *G -sek*) scale; (*grochu itp.*) pod, hull; *mil.* shell; → **łupina**; **~ć** (*-am*) shell
łuszczy|ca *f* (*-y*; *0*) *med.* psoriasis; **~ć** (*-szczę*) → **łuskać**; **~ć się** peel, flake
łut *m* (*-u*; *-y*): **~ szczęścia** a piece of luck
Łużyc|e *pl.* (*-c*) Lusatia; **≗ki** Lusatian
łydk|a *f* (*-i*; *G -dek*) calf
łyk *m* (*-a/-u*; *-i*) swallow, mouthful; **~ać** (*-am*) swallow; **~nąć** *v/s.* (*-nę*) (*G*) take a swallow
łyko *n* (*-a*) *bot.* phloem; **~waty** *gastr.* stringy
łys|ieć ⟨**wy-**⟩ (*-eję*) bald, go bald; **~ina** *f* (*-y*; *G -*) bald patch; (*cała głowa*) bald head; **~y** bald
łyż|eczka *f* (*-i*; *G -czek*) (tea)spoon; **~ka** *f* (*-i*; *G -żek*) (**stołowa** soup-)-spoon; **~ka do nabierania** table-spoon
łyżwa *f* (*-y*; *G -żew*) skate
łyżwia|rstwo *n* (*-a*; *0*) skating; **~rka** *f* (*-i*; *G -rek*), **~rz** *m* (*-a*; *-e*) skater
łyżworolki *f/pl.* (*G -lek*) Rollerblades *pl.*, in-line skates *pl.*
łza *f* (*łzy*; *łzy*, *G łez*) tear; **śmiać się do łez** laugh till the tears come; **przez łzy** through tears; **~wiący** *oczy* watering; **gaz ~wiący** teargas; **~wić** (*-wię*) water; **~wy** tear-jerking, maudlin
łzowy *anat.* lachrymal, lacrimal
łżą, łże(sz) → **łgać**

Ł

M

m. *skrót pisany*: ***miasto*** town; ***miesiąc*** month; ***mieszkanie*** flat; apt. (*apartment*)
ma¹ *3. os. sg.* → ***mieć***; *econ.* credit
ma² *pron.* (*ściągn.* ***moja***) → ***mój***
macać ⟨**po-**⟩ (*-am*) feel, finger; feel up
Macedo|nia *f* (*GDL -ii*; *0*) Macedonia; **~nka** *f* (*-i*; *G -nek*), **~ńczyk** *m* (*-a*; *-cy*) Macedonian; **ℒński** Macedonian
machać (*-am*) wave (**do** *G* to); (*skrzydłami*) flap; **~ *ogonem*** wag
machin|a *f* (*-y*; *G -*) machine; *fig.* machinery; **~acje** *f/pl.* (*G -i*) machinations *pl.*
machlojka F *f* (*-i*; *G -jek*) fraud, *Brt.* fiddle, wangle
machnąć *v/s.* (*-nę*) → ***machać***; **~ *ręką*** (***na*** *A*) give up
maci|ca *f* (*-y*; *-e*, *G -*) *anat.* uterus; ***~ca perłowa*** mother of pearl; **~czny** uterine
macie *2. os. pl.* → ***mieć***
macierz *f* (*-y*; *-e*) *math.* matrix
macierzanka *f* (*-i*; *G -nek*) *bot.* thyme
macierzy|ński maternal; motherly; ***urlop ~ński*** maternity leave; **~ństwo** *n* (*-a*; *G -*) maternity, motherhood; **~sty** native, indigenous
maciora *f* (*-y*; *G -*) sow
mac|ka *f* (*-i*; *G -cek*) feeler, tentacle; **~nąć** *v/s.* (*-nę*) → ***macać***
maco|cha *f* (*-y*; *G -*) stepmother; **~szy** (***po -szemu***) *fig.* unfeeling, uncompassionate
maczać (*-czam*) dip
mać V: ***psia ~!*** shit!, *Brt.* bloody hell!; ***kurwa ~!*** fucking hell!
madera *f* (*-y*) Madeira
Madryt *m* (*-u*; *0*) Madrid
mafia *f* (*GDL -ii*; *-e*) the Mafia
mag *m* (*-a*; *-owie*) magician
magazy|n *m* (*-u*; *-y*) store(-room), warehouse; (*pismo*) magazine; **~nek** *m* (*-nku*; *-nki*) *mil.* magazine; **~nier** *m* (*-a*; *-rzy*) warehouseman; **~nować** ⟨**z-**⟩ (*-uję*) store (up)
magi|a *f* (*GDL -ii*; *-e*) magic; **~czny** magic(al)
magiel *m* (*-gla*; *-gle*) mangle; **~ *elektryczny*** electric ironer
magik *m* (*-a*; *-cy*) magician; conjurer
magi|ster *m* (*-a*; *-trzy*) person with a Master's degree; **~stracki** municipal; **~strala** *f* (*-i*; *-e*) main road; *rail.* main line; (*gazowa itp.*) main; *komp.* bus
maglować ⟨**wy-**⟩ (*-uję*) mangle, iron, press; *fig.* mangle
magnes *m* (*-u*; *-y*) magnet (*też fig.*)
magnetofon *m* (*-u*; *-y*) tape-recorder; (*bez wzmacniacza*) tape deck; **~ *kasetowy*** cassette recorder; **~owy** tape-recorder
magne|towid *m* (*-u*; *-y*) videocassette recorder (*skrót*: VCR); **~tyczny** magnetic
magnez *m* (*-u*; *-y*) *chem.* magnesium
mahometa|nizm *m* (*-u*; *0*) Islam; **~ański** Islamic, Muslim; **ℒanin** *m* (*-a*; *-e*), **ℒanka** *f* (*-i*; *G -nek*) Muslim
maho|ń *m* (*-niu*; *-nie*) *bot.* mahogany; **~niowy** mahogany
maj *m* (*-a*; *-e*) May; ***1 ℒa*** May Day
majacz|enie *n* (*-a*; *G -ń*) delirium; **~yć** (*-ę*) be delirious, rave; → ***bredzić***; (***się***) appear, loom
mają *3. os. sg.* → ***mieć***; **~tek** *m* (*-tku*; *-tki*) fortune, possessions *pl.*; (*ziemski*) landed property; **~tkowy** financial
majeranek *m* (*-nku*; *-nki*) *bot.* marjoram
majestat *m* (*-u*; *0*) majesty
majętny wealthy, affluent
majonez *m* (*-u*; *-y*) *gastr.* mayonnaise
major *m* (*-a*; *-rzy*) *mil.* major
majowy May
majster *m* (*-tra*; *-trzy*, *-trowie*) (*w fabryce*) foreman; (*rzemieślnik*) master craftsman; (*mistrz*) master; **~ *do wszystkiego*** handyman
majsterkow|ać (*-uję*) *Brt.* do DIY, *Am.* fix things; **~anie** *n* (*-a*) DIY; **~icz** *m* (*-a*; *-e*) *Brt.* DIY enthusiast, *Am.* do-it-yourselfer
majstrować (*-uję*) tinker (***przy*** *I* with); ⟨**z-**⟩ build, make; *fig.* tinker
majtać (*-am*) nogami dangle; ogonem wag
majt|eczki *pl.* (*-czek*) → ***majtki***; **~ki** *pl.* (*-tek*) briefs *pl.*, (*damskie*) panties *pl.*
mak *m* (*-u*; *-i*) *bot.* poppy

makabryczny ghastly, grusome
makaron *m* (*-u*; *-y*) pasta; **~ *nitki*** vermicelli *pl.*; **~ *paski*** noodles *pl.*; **~ *rurki*** macaroni; **~owy** pasta
makata *f* (*-y*; *G -*) wall-hanging
makieta *f* (*-y*; *G -*) model; *tech.* mock-up; *print.* dummy
makijaż *m* (*-u*; *-e*) make-up
makler *m* (*-a*; *-rzy*) *econ.* stock-broker
makow|iec *m* (*-wca*; *-wce*), **~nik** *m* (*-a*; *-i*) poppyseed cake; **~y** poppyseed
makówka *f* (*-i*; *G -wek*) poppy-head
maksyma *f* (*-y*; *G -*) maxime, saying; **~lny** maximum, maximal
Malaj *m* (*-a*; *-e*) Malay; **2ski** Malay
malaria *f* (*GDL -ii*; *-e*) *med.* malaria
malar|ka *f* (*-i*; *G -rek*) painter; **~ski** painting; painter's; ***sztuka ~ska*** painting; **~stwo** *n* (*-a*; *0*) painting
malarz *m* (*-a*; *-e*) painter
male|c *m* (*-lca*; *-lce*) little one, F kid; **~ć** ⟨**z-**⟩ (*-eję*) diminish; *siły*: decline; **~ńki** tiny; **~ństwo** *n* (*-a*; *G -*) baby
Malezja *f* (*-i*; *0*) Malaysia
mali *m-os pl.* → ***mały***
malign|a *f* (*-y*; *0*): ***w ~ie*** in fever
malin|a *f* (*-y*; *G -*) raspberry; **~owy** raspberry
malkontenctwo *n* (*-a*; *G -*) grumbling
malow|ać (*-uję*) ⟨**na-, po-**⟩ paint (**się** o.s.; ***na biało*** white); ⟨**u-, po-**⟩ **~ać się** make up; **~anki** *f/pl.* (*-nek*) colo(u)ring-book; **~idło** *n* (*-a*; *G -deł*) painting; **~niczy** (**-czo**) picturesque; scenic
maltańs|ki (***po -ku***) Maltese
maltretować (*-uję*) maltreat, ill-treat; (*bić*) batter
malu|ch *m* (*-a*; *-y*) kid, toddler; **~tki** tiny
malwa *f* (*-y*; *G -*) *bot.* mallow
malwersacja *f* (*-i*; *-e*) embezzlement
mała, małe → ***mały***
mało *adv.* little, few; ***~ kto*** few people; ***~ co, o ~ nie*** nearly, almost; ***~ kiedy*** hardly ever; ***~ tego*** that's not all; ***~ ważny*** insignificant; **~duszny** mean; **~kaloryczny** low-calorie; **~lat** *m* (*-a*; *-y*) F teenager; **~letni** teenage; *jur.* juvenile; **~mówny** taciturn; **~obrazkowy** 35 mm; **~rolny**: ***chłop ~rolny*** smallholder; **~stkowy** mean, petty; **~wartościowy** low-quality, inferior
małp|a *f* (*-y*; *G -*) monkey; (*człekokształtna*) ape; **~i** (***-pio***) monkey; ape; **~ować** (*-uję*) ape

mał|y **1.** small, little; ***bez ~a*** almost, nearly; ***od ~ego*** from childhood; **2.** *m* (*-ego*, *-li*), **~a** *f* (*-ej*; *-e*), **~e** *n* (*-ego*; *-e*) baby, little one
małż *m* (*-a*; *-e*) *zo.* clam; (*jadalny*) mussel
małżeńs|ki marital, matrimonial, married; **~two** *n* (*-a*; *G -*) (*związek*) marriage; (*mąż i żona*) couple
małżon|ek *m* (*-ka*; *-kowie*) spouse, partner; (*mąż*) husband; **~ka** *f* (*-i*; *G -nek*) wife
małżowina *f* (*-y*; *G -*) *anat.* external ear, auricle
mam *1. os. sg. pres.* → ***mieć***
mama *f* (*-y*; *G -*) mother, mum
mamer F *m* (*-mra*; *-mry*) clink
mamić ⟨**z-**⟩ (*-ę*) → ***wabić, zwodzić***
maminsynek *m* (*-a*; *-i*) mother's boy
mam|lać, ~leć (*-ę*, *-i*), **~rotać** (*-czę/ -cę*) ⟨**wy-**⟩ mumble, mutter
mamy *1. os. pl. pres.* → ***mieć***
manatki F (*-tków*) stuff
mandarynka *f* (*-i*; *G -nek*) mandarin, tangerine
mandat *m* (*-u*; *-y*) fine, ticket; (*parlamentarny*) seat
manekin *m* (*-a*; *-y*) dummy
manewr *m* (*-u*; *-y*) *Brt.* manoeuvre, *Am.* maneuver; **~ować** (*-uję*) *Brt.* manoeuvre, *Am.* maneuver
mango *n* (*-a*) *bot.* mango
mania *f* (*GDl -ii*; *-e*) mania; ***~ prześladowcza*** persecution mania; **~cki** maniac(al); **~czka** *f* (*-i*; *G -czek*), **~k** *m* (*-a*; *-cy*) maniac
manicurzystka *f* (*-i*; *G -tek*) → **manikiurzystka**
maniera *f* (*-y*; *G -*) manner; mannerism
manierka *f* (*-i*; *G -rek*) canteen
manifest|acja *f* (*-i*; *G -e*) demonstration; rally; manifestation; **~ować** (*-uję*) demonstrate (***na rzecz*** *G* in support of)
manikiurzystka *f* (*-i*; *G -tek*) manicurist
manipul|acja *f* (*-i*; *-e*) manipulation; **~ować** (*-uję*) manipulate; handle; *niepotrzebnie* tamper
mankament *m* (*-u*; *-y*) defect, shortcoming
mankiet *m* (*-u*; *-y*) cuff; ***~ u spodni*** *Brt.* turn-up, *Am.* cuff
manna *f* (*-y*; *0*) *fig.* manna; ***kasza ~*** semolina
manowce *m/pl.* (*-ów*) wrong track; ***zejść na ~*** go astray

M

mańkut *m* (*-a*; *-ci/-y*) left-hander
mapa *f* (*-y*; *G -*) map
mara|tończyk *m* (*-a*; *-cy*) marathon runner; **~toński**: ***bieg ~toński*** marathon (race)
marc|a *G*, **~e** *pl.* → ***marzec***
marcepan *m* (*-a*; *-y*) marzipan
marchew *f* (*-wi*; *-wie*), **~ka** *f* (*-i*; *G -wek*) carrot
marc|owy March; **~u** *DL* → ***marzec***
margaryna *f* (*-y*; *G -*) margarine, F marge
margines *m* (*-u*; *-y*) margin; ***uwaga na ~ie*** marginal note, comment in passing; **~owy** marginal
marihuana *f* (*-y*; *0*) marijuana *lub* marihuana
marionetka *f* (*-i*; *G -tek*) marionette; *fig.* puppet
marka¹ *f* (*-i*; *G -rek*) mark
marka² (*-i*; *G -rek*) brand, make
marketingowy marketing
marko|tny (***-nie***, ***-no***) glum, morose; **~wać** (*-uję*) feign, pretend
marmolada *f* (*-y*; *G -*) jam, (*z cytrusów*) marmalade
marmur *m* (*-u*; *-y*) marble; **~owy** marble
marnie *adv.* → ***marny***; **~ć** ⟨**z-**⟩ (*-ję*) wither, wilt, fade
marnotraw|ić ⟨**z-**⟩ (*-ię*) squander, waste; **~stwo** *n* (*-a*; *G -*) waste
marnować ⟨**z-**⟩ (*-uję*) waste; *okazję* lose; **~** ⟨**z-**⟩ ***się*** go to waste
marn|y poor; bad; worthless; ***pójść na ~e*** go to waste
marskość *f* (*-ci*; *0*) *med.* cirrhosis
marsz *m* (*-u/mus. -a*; *-e*) march; ***~ stąd!***, ***~ za drzwi!*** out you go!
marszałek *m* (*-łka*; *-łkowie*) *mil.* marshal; ***~ sejmu*** speaker
marszczyć ⟨***na-***, ***z-***⟩ (*-czę*) wrinkle (***się*** *v/i.*); *woda*: ripple; **~ *się*** shrivel; crease
marszruta *f* (*-y*; *G -*) itinerary
martwi|ca *f* (*-y*; *0*) *med.* necrosis; **~ć** ⟨**z-**⟩ (*-ę*) trouble, worry; ***~ć się*** worry (**o** *A* about); **~eć** ⟨**z-**⟩ (*-eję*) *fig.* be paralysed (**z** *G* by)
martw|y dead; ***~a natura*** still life; ***utknąć w ~ym punkcie*** come to a standstill
martyro'logia *f* (*GDL -ii*; *0*) martyrdom
maru|dny peevish, sulky; **~dzić** (*-dzę*) dawdle; → ***guzdrać się***
maryjny *rel.* Marian, Lady
maryna|rka *f* (*-i*; *G -rek*) jacket; (*-i*; *0*) *naut.* (*wojenna*) navy, (*handlowa też*) marine; **~rski** nautical, naval; **~rz** *m* (*-a*; *-e*) *naut.* sailor, seaman
mary|nata *f* (*-y*; *G -*) marinade, pickle; **~nować** ⟨***za-***⟩ (*-uję*) pickle, marinade
marzec March
marzenie *n* (*-a*; *G -eń*) dream, day-dream
marznąć [-r·z-] (*-nę*, *-ł*) ⟨**z-**⟩ freeze; ⟨***za-***⟩ freeze to death; *roślina*: be damaged by frost
marzyciel *m* (*-a*; *-e*), **~ka** *f* (*-i*; *G -lek*) dreamer; **~ski** dreaming; **~stwo** *n* (*-a*; *0*) dreaming
marzyć (*-ę*) dream (**o** *L* about); *fig.* be dying (**o** *L* for)
marża *f* (*-y*; *G -*) *econ.* margin
masa *f* (*-y*; *0*) *phys.* mass; *fig.* F heaps *pl.*; (*do ciasta*) paste
masakra *f* (*-y*; *G -kr*) massacre, slaughter
masarski meat, butcher
masaż *m* (*-u*; *-e*) massage; ***salon ~u*** massage parlo(u)r; **~ysta** *m* (*-y*; *-ści*), **~ystka** *f* (*-i*; *-tek*) masseur
maselniczka *f* (*-i*; *G -czek*) butter dish
maska *f* (*-i*; *G -sek*) mask; *mot. Brt.* bonnet, *Am.* hood; **~rada** *f* (*-y*; *G -*) masquerade
maskotka *f* (*-i*; *G -tek*) mascot, charm
maskow|ać ⟨***za-***⟩ (*-uję*) mask, *mil.* camouflage; ***~ać*** ⟨***za-***⟩ ***się*** disguise o.s.; **~y** mask
masło *n* (*-a*; *G -seł*) butter; ***~ maślane*** tautology
mason *m* (*-a*; *-i*) Freemason
masować ⟨***po-***, ***wy-***⟩ (*-uję*) massage
masow|o *adv.* in masses; **~y** mass
mass 'media *pl.* (*G -ów*) mass media *pl.*, the media *pl.*
masturb|acja *f* (*-i*; *-e*) masturbation; **~ować się** (*-uję*) masturbate
masyw *m* (*-u*; *-y*) massif; **~ny** massive, solid
masz *2. os. sg. pres.* → ***mieć***
maszerować (*-uję*) march
maszkara *f* (*-y*; *G -*) nightmare
maszt *m* (*-u*; *-y*) mast
maszy|na *f* (*-y*; *G -*) machine, device; ***~na do pisania*** typewriter; ***~na do szycia*** sewing-machine; **~nista** *m* (*-y*; *-ści*) *rail. Brt.* engine-driver, *Am.* engineer; **~nistka** *f* (*-i*; *G -stek*) typist
maszynka *f* (*-i*; *G -nek*): ***~ do kawy***

M

coffee-maker; ~ ***do mięsa*** mincer; ~ ***spirytusowa*** spiritus stove
maszyno|pis *m* (*-u*; *-y*) typescript, manuscript; **~wy** machine; automatic
maść *f* (*-ci*) ointment
maśla|k *m* (*-a*; *-i*) boletus luteus; **~nka** *f* (*-i*; *-nek*) buttermilk; **~ny** butter
mat *m* (*-u*; *0*) matt; (*-a*; *0*) (*w szachach*) checkmate; ***dać ~a*** checkmate
mata *f* (*-y*; *G -*) mat
matactwo *n* (*-a*; *G -*) cheating, fraud
matczyn(y) motherly
matema|tyczny mathematical; **~tyk** *m* (*-a*; *-cy*) mathematician; **~tyka** *f* (*-i*) mathematics *sg.*
materac *m* (*-a*; *-e*) mattress
ma'teri|a *m* (*GDL -ii*; *0*) matter; **~alny** material; **~ał** *m* (*-u*; *-y*) fabric, textile; (*surowiec*) material
matka *f* (*-i*; *G -tek*) mother; ≗ ***Boska*** Mother of God; ~ ***chrzestna*** godmother; ~ ***zastępcza*** surrogate mother
matnia *f* (*-i*; *-e*) *fig.* trap
matołek *m* (*-łka*; *-łki*) simpleton, dimwit
matowy (**-wo**) matt; frosted
matryca *f* (*-y*; *G -*) *Brt.* mould, *Am.* mold; pattern
matrymonialny matrimonial
matu|ra *f* (*-y*; *G -*) (*secondary-school leaving examination*; *secondary-school examination certificate*); **~rzysta** *m* (*-y*; *-ści*), **~rzystka** *f* (*-i*; *G -tek*) *Brt.* (*secondary school leaver*); *Am.* graduate
mawiać (*-am*) say
maza|ć (*-żę*) smear; **~k** *m* (*-a*; *-i*) felt-tip pen; **~nina** *f* (*-y*; *G -*) scribble
mazgaj *m* (*-a*; *-e*) cry-baby
maznąć *v/s.* (*-nę*) → ***mazać***
Mazowsze *n* (*-a*; *0*) Mazovia
mazurek *m* (*-rka*; *-rki*) *mus.* mazurka; *gastr.* Easter cake
Mazury *pl.* (*G -*) Masuria
maź *f* (*-zi*; *-zie*) grease; F gook, goo
mącić ⟨**z-**⟩ (*-cę*) make cloudy, cloud; ~ ***się*** become cloudy; *fig.* get confused
mącz|ka *f* (*-i*; *G -czek*) flour; **~ny** flour; **~ysty** (**-to**) powdery
mąd|rość *f* (*-ci*; *0*) wisdom; **~ry** (**-rze**) wise; **~rzeć** ⟨**z-**⟩ (*-ję*) become wiser; **~rzej(szy)** *adv.* (*adj.*) (*comp. od* → ***mądrze***, ***mądry***) wiser
mąka *f* (*-i*; *G -*) flour; ~ ***ziemniaczana*** potato starch
mątwa *f* (*-y*; *G -*) *zo.* cuttlefish
mąż *m* (*męża*, *mężowie*, *mężów*) husband; ***wyjść za ~*** (***za*** *A*) marry, get married (to); ***wydać za ~*** marry; ~ ***stanu*** statesman
m.b. *skrót pisany*: ***metr bieżący*** m. (*metre*)
m-c *skrót pisany*: ***miesiąc*** m. (*month*)
mchu *DL*, **mchy** *pl.* → ***mech***
mdleć ⟨**ze-**⟩ (*-ję*) faint, pass out
mdlić: ***k-ś mdli*** s.o. feels sick
mdł|ości *pl.* (-) nausea; ***mieć ~ości*** feel sick; **~y** (**-ło**) bland, tasteless
me *pron.* (*ściągn.* ***moje***) → ***mój***
mebel *m* (*-bla*; *-ble*, *-bli*) piece of furniture; ***meble*** *pl.* furniture
meblo|wać ⟨**u-**⟩ (*-uję*) furnish; **~wóz** *m* furniture van
mecenas *m* (*-a*; *-si*) Maecenas; (*adwokat*) lawyer
mech *m* (*mchu*; *mchy*) moss
mechani|czny mechanical; **~k** *m* (*-a*; *-cy*) mechanic; **~zm** *m* (*-u*; *-y*) mechanism; ***~zm zegara*** clockwork; **~zować** ⟨**z-**⟩ (*-uję*) mechanize
mecz *m* (*-u*; *-e*) match, game
meczet *m* (*-u*; *-y*) *rel.* mosque
meda|l *m* (*-a*; *-e*) medal; **~lik** *m* (*-a*; *-i*) locket; **~lista** *m* (*-y*; *-ści*), **~listka** *f* (*-i*; *G -tek*) (*w sporcie*) medal winner, medallist, title holder
medi'ator *m* (*-a*; *-rzy*) mediator
Mediolan *m* (*-u*; *0*) Milan
meduza *f* (*-y*; *G -*) *zo.* jellyfish
medy|cyna *f* (*-y*; *0*) medicine; **~czny** medical
medytować (*-uję*) meditate
mega|bajt *m* (*-u*; *-y*) megabyte (*skrót*: MB); **~lo'mania** *f* (*GDL -ii*; *0*) megalomania; **~tona** *f* megaton
mego *pron.* (*ściągn.* ***mojego***), **mej** *pron.* (*ściągn.* ***mojej***) → ***mój***
Meksy|k *m* (*-u*; *0*) Mexico; **~kanka** *f* (*-i*; *G -nek*), **~kańczyk** *m* (*-a*; *-cy*) Mexican; **≗kański** Mexican
melancholijny melancholic
meld|ować ⟨**za-**⟩ (*-uję*) report (***się*** *v/i.*); *zamieszkanie* register (***się*** *v/i.*); **~unek** *m* (*-nku*; *-nki*) report; **~unkowy** registration
melin|a F *f* (*-y*; *G -*) hide-out; den; *z alkoholem* after-hours joint; **~ować** ⟨**za-**⟩ (*-uję*) F hide (*też* ***się*** *v/i.*)
melioracja *f* (*-i*; *-e*) *agr.* melioration
me'lodia *f* (*GDL -ii*; *-e*) melody

melo|dyjny melodious; musical, tuneful; **~man** *m* (*-a*; *-i*); **~manka** *f* (*-i*; *G -nek*) music-lover
melon *m* (*-a*; *-y*) *bot.* melon; **~ik** *m* (*-a*; *-i*) bowler (hat)
mel|li, ~ł(am, -em) → ***mielić***
me'moriał *m* (*-u*; *-y*) memorandum; F (*w sporcie*) memorial contest
Men *m* (*-u*; *0*) Main
menażka *f* (*-i*; *G -żek*) *Brt.* mess tin, *Am.* mess kit
menedżer *m* (*-a*; *-rzy*) manager
mennica *f* (*-y*; *G -*) mint
mentalność *f* (*-ci*; *0*) mentality
mentolowy menthol
menu *n* (*idkl.*) menu
merdać ⟨**po-**⟩ (*-am*) wag
mereżka *f* (*-i*; *G -żek*) hem-stitch
merla *f* gauze
merynos *m* (*-a*; *-y*) *zo.* merino
merytoryczn|y substantial; ***w sprawie ~ej*** to the point
Mesjasz *m* (*-a*) *rel.* Messiah
meszek *m* (*-szka*; *-szki*) down
met|a *f* (*-y*; *G -*) finish; ***na bliższą/dalszą ~ę*** in the short/long run
meta|l *m* (*-u*; *-e*) metal; *mus.* heavy-metal; **~liczny** metallic; **~lowiec** *m* (*-wca*; *-wcy*) metalworker; **~lowy** metal
metan *m* (*-u*; *-y*) methane
meteorologiczny meteorologic(al)
meteor *m* (*-u*; *-y*) meteor; **~yt** *m* (*-u*; *-y*) meteorite
metka[1] *f* (*-i*; *G -tek*) (soft) sausage
metka[2] *f* (*-i*; *G -tek*) label, tag
meto|da *f* (*-y*; *G -*) method; **~dyczny** methodical; **~dysta** *m* (*-y*; *-ów*), **~dystka** *f* (*-i*; *G -tek*) *rel.* Methodist
metr *m* (*-a*; *-y*) *Brt.* metre, *Am.* meter
metraż *m* (*-u*; *-e*) area (in metres); ***krótki ~*** *zbior.* short film
metro *n* (*-a, 0*) *Brt.* underground, *Am.* subway
metrowy *Brt.* metre, *Am.* meter
metryka *f* (*-i*; *G -*) (**ślubu, urodzenia, zgonu, chrztu** wedding, birth, death, baptismal) certificate
metylowy methyl
Metys *m* (*-a*; *-i*) mestizo; **~ka** *f* (-i) mestiza
mewa *f* (*-y*; *G -*) gull; ***~ śmieszka*** black-headed gull
męcz|arnia *f* (*-i*; *-e*) agony, torment, torture; **~ący** (***-co***) tiring; *fig.* trying; **~ennik** *m* (*-a*; *-cy*), **~ennica** *f* (*-e*; *G-*) martyr (*też rel.*); **~eński** martyr's; **~yć** (*-ę*) torment; ***~yć się*** suffer; ⟨**z-**⟩ tire, make tired; *oczy itp.*: strain; ***~yć się*** get tired; *też* ***~yć się*** slave away (***nad*** *I* over)
męd|rek *m* (*-rka*; *-rki/-rkowie*) F smart aleck; **~rzec** *m* (*-drca*; *-drcy/-drcowie*) sage, savant
męka *f* (*-i*; *G mąk*) torment, torture, agony
męs|ki male; masculine, manly; *gr.* masculine; ***po ~ku*** like a man; **~kość** *f* (*-ci*; *0*) masculinity, manhood, virility; **~two** *n* (*-a*; *0*) bravery, valo(u)r
męt|lik *m* (*-a*; *-i*) confusion, mess; **~nieć** ⟨**z-**⟩ (*-eję*) become cloudy/opaque, cloud; **~ny** cloudy; opaque; **~y** *pl.* (*-ów*) dregs *pl.*
mężatk|a *f* (*-i*; *G -tek*) married woman; ***ona jest ~ą*** she is married
męż|czyzna *m* (*-y*; *G -*) man, male; **~ny** brave, valiant, valorous; **~owski** husband's
mglisty (***-ście***) foggy, misty; *fig.* vague, hazy
mgła *f* (*-y*, *DL mgle*; *-y*, *G mgieł*) fog, mist; ***zajść mgłą*** mist up; **~wica** *f* (*-y*; *G -wic*) nebula
mgnieni|e *n* (*-a*; *G -eń*): ***na ~e*** for a moment; ***w ~u oka*** in no time
mgr *skrót pisany*: ***magister*** MA (*Master of Arts*)
mi *pron.* (*ściągn. D*) → ***mnie***
miał[1]**, ~a, ~o** → ***mieć***
miał[2] *m* (*-u*; *-y*) dust, powder; **~ki** fine
miano *n* (*-a*; *G -*) *lit.* name; → ***nazwa***; **~wać** (*-uję*) appoint (*I* as), nominate; **~wicie** namely; ***a ~wicie*** to be precise; **~wnik** *m* (*-a*; *-i*) *gr.* nominative; *math.* denominator
miar|a *f* (*-y*; *G -*) measurement, measure; ***bez ~y*** boundless; ***szyty na ~ę*** made to measure; ***nad ~ę*** beyond measure; ***w ~ę*** moderately; ***w ~ę jak*** as; ***w ~ę możliwości/potrzeby*** as the need arises; ***w pewnej mierze*** to some extent; ***w dużej mierze*** to a great extent; ***ze wszech miar*** by all means; ***żadną ~ą*** by no means; **~ka** *f* (*-i*; *G -rek*) measure
miarkować (*-uję*) (**się**) contain (o.s.), restrain (o.s.), control (o.s.)
miaro|dajny authoritative; **~wy** rhythmic

miasteczko *n* (*-a*; *G -czek*) → **miasto**; ***wesołe ~*** amusement park, *Brt.* funfair

miast|o *n* (*-a*, *L mieście*; *G -*) town, city; ***jechać do ~a*** go to town; ***~o portowe*** port

miauczeć (*-czę*) meow

miazga *f* (*-i*; *G -*) pulp

miażdży|ca *f* (*-y*; *0*) *med.* sclerosis, *zwł.* arteriosclerosis; **~ć** ⟨**z-**⟩ (*-ę*) crush, squash; *fig.* overwhelm

miąć ⟨**wy-, z-**⟩ (*mnę*) crumple, crease (**się** *v/i.*)

miąższ *m* (*-u*; *0*) pulp, flesh

miech *m* (*-u*; *-y*) bellows *sg. lub pl.*

miecz *m* (*-a*; *-e*) sword; *naut. Brt.* centreboard, *Am.* centerboard; **~nik** *m* (*-a*; *-i*) *zo.* swordfish; (*orka*) orc, killer whale; **~yk** *m* (*-a*; *-i*) *bot.* gladiolus

mieć have, possess; (+ *bezok.*) be going to; (**tu**) ***masz, macie ...*** here is, here are ...; ***nie ma*** there is not; ***~ na sobie*** have on, wear; ***~ 40 lat*** be 40 years old; ***nie ma za co*** you are welcome; ***~ miejsce*** take place; ***~ za złe*** take amiss; ***masz ci los!*** there we are!; ***ja miałbym to zrobić?*** I am supposed to do it?; ***miano tu budować dom*** a house was to be built here; ***nie ma jak ...*** there is nothing like...; ***on ma się dobrze*** he is fine; ***jak się masz?*** how are you?; ***nie ma się czego wstydzić*** there is nothing to be ashamed of; ***ma się na deszcz*** it looks like rain; ***on ma się za artystę*** he considers himself an artist; ***~ się ku*** it is going to; → ***baczność, lata***

miednic|a *f* (*-y*; *G -*) bowl; *anat.* pelvis; **~owy** *anat.* pelvic

miedza *f* (*-y*; *G -*) balk

miedziany copper

miedzioryt *m* (*-u*; *-y*) copperplate engraving

miedź *f* (*-dzi*; *0*) *chem.* copper

miej(cie) → ***mieć***

miejsc|e *n* (*-a*; *G -*) place (**na** *A*, **do** *G* for); position, location; space, room; seat (*też fig.*); ***~e pracy*** workplace; ***~e zbrodni*** scene of the crime; ***~e spotkania*** meeting place, rendezvous; ***na ~u*** there and then; on the spot; ***na twoim ~u*** if I were you; ***w ~e*** in place of; ***w tym ~u*** at this place; ***z ~a*** at once; ***ustąpić ~a*** make room; *fig.* give way; → ***pobyt, przeznaczenie***; **~ami** in place

miejscownik *m* (*-a*; *-i*) *gr.* locative

miejscow|ość *f* (*-ści*) locality, place; **~y** local; (*w sporcie*) home

miejs|cówka *f* (*-i*; *G -wek*) *rail.* seat reservation (ticket); **~ki** urban, municipal; (**po -ku**) town; ***rada ~ka*** town council

miel|ą, ~e(sz), ~ę, ~i → ***mleć***

mieliś|cie, ~my → ***mieć***

mieli|zna *f* (*-y*; *G -*) shallow; ***osiąść na ~źnie*** run aground

mielon|y minced; ***mięso ~e*** minced meat, *Brt.* mince

mienić się (*-nię*) shimmer

mienie *n* (*-a*; *0*) property; ***~ społeczne*** common property

miern|iczy **1.** measuring; **2.** *m* (*-ego*; *-owie*) land surveyor; **~ik** *m* (*-a*; *-i*) measure; *tech.* measuring instrument; *fig.* yardstick; ***~ik wartości*** standard; **~ość** *f* (*-ści*; *0*) mediocrity; **~y** mediocre

mierz·eja *f* (*-i*; *-e*) sandbar

mierzić [-r·z-] (*t-ko 3. os. -i*) feel with digust

mierzwić ⟨**z-**⟩ (*-wię*) tousle, ruffle

mierzyć ⟨**z-**⟩ (*-ę*) measure; *suknię* try on; ***~ wzrokiem*** eye; ***nie móc się ~ z*** be no match for; *v/i.* take aim (**do** *G* at)

mies. *skrót pisany:* **miesiąc** m. (*month*); ***miesięczny*** monthly; ***miesięcznik*** monthly

miesiąc *m* (*-a*; *-e*) month; ***raz na ~*** once a month; ***za ~*** in a month; **~ami** for months on end

miesiączk|a *f* (*-i*; *G -czek*) menstruation, period; ***mieć ~ę*** have a period, menstruate

miesić ⟨**wy-**⟩ (*-szę*) knead

miesięczn|ik *m* (*-a*; *-i*) monthly; **~y** monthly

miesza|ć (*-am*) ⟨**za-**⟩ stir; ⟨**z-**⟩ mix together, blend; ⟨**w-**⟩ add (**do** *G* to); *fig.* drag into, involve; ***~ć się*** interfere (**do** *G* in), intervene; **~dło** *n* (*-a*; *G -deł*) mixer; **~niec** *m* (*-ńca*; *-ńce/-ńcy*) mongrel; (*też -ńcy*) half-caste; **~nina** *f* (*-y*; *G -*) mixture; **~nka** *f* (*-i*; *G -nek*) mixture; blend, assortment

mieszczań|ski middle-class; **~stwo** *n* (*-a*; *G -*) middle class, bourgeoisie

mieszka|ć (*-am*) live; inhabit; **~lny** inhabitable, habitable; **~nie** *n* (*-a*; *G -ań*) *Brt.* flat, *Am.* apartment; home; **~niec** *m* (*-ńca*; *-ńcy*), **~nka** *f* (*-nki*; *G -nek*) inhabitant, resident; **~niowy** housing;

dzielnica residential; → ***głód***
mieści|ć (*-szczę*) contain, hold; accommodate; ***~ć się*** fit; 〈***po-, z-***〉 fit in; *budynek*: house; **~na** *f* (*-y; G -*) little town
miewać (*-am*) have from time to time
mię (*ściągn. GA*) → ***mnie***
mięczak *m* (*-a; -i*) *pej.* softy, pushover; *zo. Brt.* mollusc, *Am.* mollusk
międlić F (*-lę*) → ***miąć, ględzić***
między *prp.* (*I, A*) between, among; ***~innymi*** among other things; **~czas** *m*: ***w ~czasie*** in the meantime; **~kontynentalny** intercontinental; **~ludzki** interpersonal; **~miastowy**: ***rozmowa ~miastowa*** long-distance call, trunk call; **~narodowy** international; **~wojenny** interwar
mięk|czyć 〈***z-***〉 (*-ę*) make soft; soften (*też fig.*); *gr.* palatalize; **~isz** *m* (*-a; -e*) (bread)crumb; *biol.* parenchyma; **~ki** (*m-os -kcy*) soft; *mięso* tender; *fig.* wet; *gr.* palatalized; ***jajko na ~ko*** soft-boiled egg; **~kość** *f* (*-ści; 0*) softness; **~nąć** 〈***z-***〉 (*-nę*) become soft, soften
mię|sień *m* (*-śnia; -śnie*) muscle; **~sisty** meaty; *fig.* brawny; **~sny** meat; **~so** *n* (*-a; G mięs*) meat, flesh; **~sożerny** carnivorous; **~śniowy** muscular
mię|ta *f* (*-y; G mięt*) mint, (*zwł. pieprzowa*) peppermint; **~tosić** (*-szę*) → ***miąć***; **~towy** mint, peppermint
mig *m* (*-u; -i*): ***na ~i*** by signs, in sign language; ***w ~*** in an instant; **~acz** *mot. Brt.* indicator, *Am.* turn signal; **~ać** (*-am*) flash; *lampa*: flicker; → ***przemykać***
migawk|a *f* (*-i; G -wek*) *phot.* shutter; *fig.* ***~i*** *pl.* scenes *pl.*; **~owy** shutter
migdał *m* (*-a; -y*) *bot.* almond; **~ek** *m* → **migdał**; *anat.* tonsil; **~owy** almond
mig|nąć *v/s.* (*-nę*) → ***migać***; **~otać** (*-czę/-cę*) flicker, waver; **~owy** sign
migracja *f* (*-i; -e*) migration
migrena *f* (*-y; G -*) migraine
mija|ć (*-am*) *v/t.* pass; *v/i.* pass by, go by; ***~ć się*** pass each other; *listy*: cross; *fig.* (***z*** *I*) miss; ***~ć się z prawdą*** depart from the truth; ***... go nie minie*** he will not escape ...; **~nka** *f* (*-i; G -nek*) passing place; *rail., mot.* turnout
mika *f* (*-i; 0*) mica
Mikołaj *m* (*-a; -e*) *też* ***św****(****ięty****)* ***~*** *jakby*: Santa Claus, Father Christmas
mikro|bus *m* (*-u; -y*) minibus; **~element** *m* (*-u; -y*) trace element; **~fala** *f* (*-i; -e*) microwave; **~falowy** microwave; **~falówka** *f* (*-i*) F microwave (oven); **~fon** *m* (*-u; -y*) microphone; **~komputer** *m* (*-a; -y*) *komp.* microcomputer; **~procesor** *m* (*-a; -y*) *komp.* microprocessor; **~skop** *m* (*-u; -y*) microscope; **~skopijny, ~skopowy** microscopic
mikrus *m* (*-a; -y*) little one
mikser *m* (*-a; -y*) mixer; *gastr. też* liquidizer; *Brt.* blender; *RTV*: mixing desk
mila *f* (*-i; -e*) mile; ***~ morska*** nautical mile
milcz|ący silent; implicit; **~eć** (*-czę*) be silent; **~enie** *n* (*-a; 0*) silence; ***chwila ~enia*** minute's silence; ***pominąć ~eniem*** pass over in silence; **~kiem** *adv.* stealthily, secretively
mile *adv.* kindly; (*ładnie*) pretty; ***~ widziany*** welcome
miliard *m* (*-a; -y*) billion, *Brt. też* milliard; **~owy** billionth; ***jedna ~owa*** one billionth
milicja *f* (*-i; 0*) (Communist) police; **~nt** *m* (*-a; -nci*) policeman
mili|gram *m* (*-u; -y*) milligram; **~metr** *m* (*-a; -y*)*Brt.* millimetre, *Am.* millimeter; **~on** *m* (*-a; -y*) million; **~oner** *m* (*-a; -rzy*), **~onerka** *f* (*-i; G -rek*) millionaire; **~onowy** millionth ***jedna ~onowa*** one millionth
militarystyczny militaristic
milknąć 〈***za-***〉 (*-nę, -[ną]ł*) fall silent; *fig.* calm down
milowy mile
mi|lszy *adv. comp. od* → ***miły***; **~luchny, ~lutki** nice
miło *adv.* pleasantly, agreeably; kind(ly); ***~ mi*** pleased to meet you; **~sierdzie** *n* (*-a; 0*) mercy, charity; **~sierny** merciful, charitable; **~sny** love; **~stka** *f* (*-i; G -tek*) (love) affair; **~ść** *f* (*-ści*) love; **~śniczka** *f* (*-i; G -czek*), **~śnik** *m* (*-a; -cy*) (*sztuki*) lover; (*sportu*) fan; **~wać** (*-uję*) *lit.* love
miły (***-le, -ło***) kind; pleasant, agreeable; (*drogi*) dear
mimo *cj.* (*G*) in spite of; despite; ***~ to*** nevertheless; ***~ wszystko*** all the same; ***~ że, ~ iż*** though, although; → ***pomimo, wola***; **~chodem** *adv.* in passing; **~wolny** involuntary
m.in. *skrót pisany*: ***między innymi*** among others
mina[1] *f* (*-y; G -*) face

mina² *f* (*-y*; *G -*) *mil.* mine
minąć *pf.* (*-nę*, *-ń*) go by, pass by → ***mijać***
minera|lny mineral; **~ł** *m* (*-u.* *-y*) mineral
mini *f* (*idkl.*) *w złoż.* mini; F mini(skirt); **~aturowy** (**-wo**) miniature; **~malny** minimum, minimal; **~mum** **1.** *n* (*idkl.*; *-a*, *-mów*) minimum; **2.** *adv.* at least
miniony last; past
mini|ówa F *f* (*-wy*) mini; **~spódniczka** *f* (*-i*; *G -czek*) miniskirt
minister *m* (*-tra*; *-trowie*) minister, secretary; ***rada ministrów*** Council of Ministers; **~ialny** ministerial; **~stwo** *n* (*-a*; *G -*) (***sprawiedliwości***) ministry (of justice)
minorowy *mus.* minor; (**-wo**) gloomy
minować ⟨**za-**⟩ (*-nuję*) *mil.* mine
minus *m* (*-a*; *-y*) *math.* minus (sign); (*-u*; *-y*) minus; ***plus ~*** give or take; ***2 ~ 1*** 2 minus/less 1; **~owy** minus; negative; below zero
minut|a *f* (*-y*; *G -*) minute; ***za ~ę*** in a minute; ***co do ~y*** to a minute; **~owy** minute; *wskazówka* big
miodow|nik *m* (*-a*; *-i*) *gastr.* honey cake; **~y** honey; ***miesiąc ~y*** honeymoon
miot *m* (*-u*; *-y*) *zo.* litter; **~acz** *m* (*-a*; *-e*), **~aczka** *f* (*-i*; *G -czek*) thrower; ***~acz kulą*** (*w sporcie*) shot putter; ***~acz gazu*** (Chemical) Mace; ***~acz płomieni*** flame thrower; **~ać** (*-am*) hurl, throw; **~ła** *f* (*-y*; *G -teł*) broom, brush
miód *m* (*miodu*; *miody*) honey; ***~ pitny*** mead
miraż *m* (*-u*; *-e*) mirage; *fig.* illusion
mirt *m* (*-u*; *-y*) *bot.* myrtle
misja *f* (*-i*; *-e*) mission
miska *f* (*-i*; *G -sek*) bowl; ***~ klozetowa*** toilet bowl
Missisipi (*idkl.*) Mississippi
misterny elaborate, delicate
mistrz *m* (*-a*; *-owie*, *-ów*) master; (*w sporcie*) champion; ***~ Polski*** Polish champion
mistrzo|stwo *n* (*-a*; *G -*) mastery; (*w sporcie*) championship; **~wski** masterful, masterly; champion; ***po ~wsku*** expertly
mistrzyni *f* (*-ni*; *-nie*, *-ń*) master; (*w sporcie*) champion
misty|fikować (*-uję*) deceive; mystify; **~czka** *f* (*-i*; *G -czek*), **~k** *m* (*-a*; *-cy*) mystic; **~ka** *f* (*-i*; *0*) mysticism
misyjny missionary
miś *m* (*-sia*; *-sie*) (*zabawka*) teddy-bear; (*w bajkach*) bruin
mit *m* (*-u*; *-y*) myth; **~ologiczny** mythological
mitręga *f* (*-i*; *G -*) waste of time
mityczny mythical
mitygować (*-uję*) calm, mollify
mizdrzyć się F (*-rzę*) (**do** *G*) letch after
mi'zer|ia *f* (*GDL -ii*; *-e*) *gastr.* cucumber salad; **~nieć** ⟨**z-**⟩ (*-nię*) waste away; grow thin; **~ny** poor; paltry
m-ka *skrót pisany*: ***marka*** make; mark
mknąć (*-knę*) hurry (along)
MKOl *skrót pisany*: ***Międzynarodowy Komitet Olimpijski*** IOC (*International Olympic Committee*)
mkw. *skrót pisany*: ***metr kwadratowy*** sq. m. (*square metre*)
mlas|kać (*-skam*) F slurp; ⟨***~nąć***⟩ (*-nę*) click one's tongue
mld *skrót pisany*: ***miliard*** billion
mlecz *m* (*-a*; *-e*) *bot.* sow-thistle; F (*mniszek*) dandelion; *zo.* milt, soft roe; **~arnia** *f* (*-i*; *-e*) dairy; **~arstwo** *n* (*-a*; *0*) dairy industry; dairying; **~arz** *m* (*-a*; *-e*) milkman; **~ko** *n* (*-a*; *G -czek*) milk; **~ny** milk; milky
mleć ⟨**ze-**⟩, **mielić** grind, mill; ***~ językiem*** chatter
mleko *n* (*-a*; *0*) milk; ***~ pełne*** full-cream milk; ***~ w proszku*** powdered milk; ***na mleku*** *gastr.* milk; **~dajny** dairy
mln *skrót pisany*: ***milion*** m (*million*)
mł. *skrót pisany*: ***młodszy*** the younger
młocarnia *f* (*-i*; *-e*) threshing machine
młocka *f* (*-i*; *G -cek*) threshing
młod|e *n* (*-ego*; *-e*) young, baby; → ***młody***; **~nieć** (*-eję*) get younger
młodo *adv.* young; **~ciany** *jur.* **1.** juvenile; **2.** *m* (*-nego*; *-ni*), **~ciana** *f* (*-nej*; *-ne*) juvenile; **~ść** *f* (*-ci*; *0*) youth; ***nie pierwszej ~ści*** not young any more
młod|szy *adj.* (*comp. od* → **młody**; *m-os -dsi*) younger; **~y** young; *ziemniak*, *wino* new; *mięso* tender; ***pan ~y*** (bride)groom; ***panna ~a*** bride; ***za ~u*** in one's youth
młodzie|j *adv. comp. od* → **młodo**; **~niec** *m* (*-ńca*; *-ńcy*) youth, boy, young man, adolescent; **~ńczy** (**-czo, po -czemu**) youthful; **~ż** *f* (*-y*; *0*) the young *pl.*; ***~ż szkolna*** school children; **~żowy** youth
młodzik *m* (*-a*;*- i*) youngster

M

młodziutki very young
młokos *m* (*-a*; *-y*) *pej. Brt.* pup
młot *m* (*-a*; *-y*) hammer; **~ *pneumatyczny*** pneumatic drill; ***walić jak ~em*** pound; **~ek** *m* (*-tka*; *-tki*) hammer
młócić ⟨**wy-**⟩ (*-cę*) thresh
młyn *m* (*-a*; *-y*) mill; **~arka** *f* (*-i*; *G -rek*), **~arz** *m* (*-a*; *-e*) miller; **~ek** *m* (*-nka*; *-nki*) mill; ***~ek do kawy*** coffee grinder
młyński mill; ***koło ~e*** millstone
mną¹ *pron.* (*I* → ***ja***); ***ze ~*** with me
mną² *3. os. pl. pres.* → ***miąć***
mnich *m* (*-a*; *-si*) monk
mnie¹ *pron.* (*GA* → ***ja***) me; (*DL* → ***ja***) me; ***o ~*** about me; ***u ~*** with me
mnie² *3. os. pl. sg.* → ***miąć***
mniej *adv.* (*comp. od* → ***mało***) less, fewer; ***~ więcej*** more or less; **~szość** *f* (*-ści*) minority; **~szy** *adj.* (*comp. od* → ***mały***) smaller (***od*** *G* than); lesser; ***~sza o to/z tym*** never mind
mniema|ć (*-am*) believe; **~nie** *n* (*-a*) belief; ***w ~niu*** *też* on the assumption
mni|si → ***mnich***; *adj.* monastic; **~szek** *m* (*-szka*; *-szki*) *bot.* dandelion; **~szka** *f* (*-i*; *G -szek*) nun; *zo.* nun moth
mnog|i (*m-os mnodzy*) numerous; → ***liczba***; **~ość** *f* (*-ści*; *0*) multitude
mnoż|enie *n* (*-a*) reproduction; *math.* multiplication; **~na** *f* (*-nej*; *-ne*) *math.* multiplicand; **~nik** *m* (*-a*; *-i*) *math.* multiplier; **~yć** ⟨**po-**⟩ (*-żę*) multiply (*też math.*; **się** *v/i.*)
mnóstwo *n* (*-a*; *0*) lots of
mobil|izacja *f* (*-i*; *-e*) mobilisation; **~izować** ⟨**z-**⟩ mobilize; **~ny** mobile
moc *f* (*-y*; *-e*) power; *jur.* force; F lots of; ***nabierać ~y*** take effect; ***wszystko, co w jego ~y*** all in his power; ***na ~y*** (*G*) on the strength (of), in virtue (of); ***~ą*** (*G*) by virtue (of); ***~ alkoholu*** proof; **~arstwo** *n* (*-a*; *G -*) power; ***wielkie ~arstwo*** superpower; **~niej(szy)** *adv.* (*adj.*) (*comp. od* → ***mocno, mocny***) more powerful, stronger; **~no** *adv.* very, hard; **~ny** powerful, strong; *ból* sharp; *chwyt itp.* firm, tight
mocować ⟨**przy-, u-**⟩ (*-uję*) attach, fix (**do** *G* to); ***~ się*** wrestle (*też fig.*)
mocz *m* (*-u*; *-e*) urine
moczary *m/pl.* (*-ów*) marsh, swamp
mocznik *m* (*-a*; *0*) *chem.* urea
moczo|pędny diuretic; **~wód** *m* (*-odu*; *-ody*) *anat.* ureter; **~wy** uretic
moczyć (*-czę*) ⟨**z-**⟩ wet; ⟨**za-**⟩ soak; water; *impf.* ***~ się*** soak; (*moczem*) water
mod|a *f* (*-y*; *G mód*) fashion, vogue; ***wyjść z ~y*** go out of fashion
model *m* (*-u*; *-e*) model; *tech.* mock-up; **~arstwo** *n* (*-a*; *G -*) model making; **~ka** *f* (*-i*; *G -lek*) model; **~ować** (*-uję*) model; *włosy* style
modem *m* (*-u*; *-y*) modem; **~owy** modem
moderni|zacja *f* (*-i*; *-e*) modernisation; **~zować** ⟨**z-**⟩ (*-uję*) modernize, update
modli|ć się ⟨**po- się**⟩ (*-ę*; *módl!*) pray (**do** *G* to); **~twa** *f* (*-y*; *G -*) prayer
modł|a *f* (*-y*; *-deł*): ***na ~ę*** (*G*) after the fashion (of); **~y** *pl.* (*-ów*) prayers *pl.*
modrzew *m* (*-ia*; *-ie*) *bot.* larch; **~iowy** larch
moduł *m* (*-u*; *-y*) module (*też math.*); unit; *phys.* modulus; **~owy** modular
modyfik|acja *f* (*-i*; *-e*) modification; **~ować** ⟨**z-**⟩ (*-uję*) modify
modzel *m* (*-a*; *-e*) *med.* callus
mogiła *f* (*-y*; *G -*) grave; ***~ wspólna*** mass grave
mog|ą, ~ę, ~li, ~łam, ~łem → ***móc***
mohair, moher *m* (*-u*; *0*) mohair
moi, moja, moje → ***mój***
mojżeszowy Mosaic
mok|nąć ⟨**z-**⟩ (*-nę*, *nął/mókł*) get wet; *impf.* soak; **~ry** (**-ro**) wet
moll *m* (*idkl.*) *mus.* minor; ***c-moll*** C-minor
molo *n* (*idkl./-a*; *G mol*) pier, jetty
moloodporny moth-resistant
moment *m* (*-u*; *-y*) moment; ***za ~*** in a moment; **~alnie** at once, immediately, instantaneously; **~alny** immediate, instantaneous
Monachium *n* (*idkl.*) Munich
monarch|a *m* (*-y*; *-owie*) monarch; **~ia** *f* (*GDL -ii*; *-e*) monarchy; **~istyczny** monarchist
monet|a *f* (*-y*; *G -*) coin; ***brać coś za dobrą ~ę*** take s.th. at its face value
Mongo|lia *f* (*GDL -ii*; *0*) Mongolia; **~lski** Mongolian
monit *m* (*-u*; *-y*) reminder; **~ować** (*-uję*) remind
mono (*idkl.*) mono, *w złoż.* mono-; **~'grafia** *f* (*GDl -ii*; *-e*) monograph; **~gram** *m* (*-u*; *-y*) monogram; **~partyjny** mono-party; **~pol** *m* (*-u*; *-e*) *econ.*, *pol.* monopoly; **~polowy**: ***sklep ~polowy*** *Brt.* off-licence, *Am.* liquor store;

M

~tonny monotonous
monstrualny monstrous
monsun *m* (*-u*; *-y*) monsoon
montaż *m* (*-u*; *-e*) *tech.* assembly, installation; *phot.* editing; **~owy** editing; assembly; **~ysta** *m* (*-y*; *-ści*), **~ystka** *f* (*-y*; *G -tek*) *phot.*, *RTV*: editor
monter *m* (*-a*; *-rzy*) mechanic; fitter; ***~ instalacji wodociągowych*** plumber
montować (*-uję*) ⟨**z-**⟩ assemble; install; erect; *phot.*, *RTV*: edit; ⟨**za-**⟩ fix, put up, build in
mora|lność *f* (*-ci*; *0*) morality; **~lny** moral; **~ł** *m* (*-u*; *-y*) moral, maxim
mord *m* (*-u*; *-y*) murder
morda *f* (*G -*; *-y*) muzzle; F gob, mug
morder|ca *m* (*-y*; *G -ów*), **~czyni** *f* (*-i*; *-nie*, *-ń*) murderer; **~czy** (**-czo**) murderous; **~stwo** *n* (*-a*; *G -*) murder
mordęga F *f* (*-i G -*) toil; drudgery
mordować (*-uję*) ⟨***po-, za-***⟩ murder; ⟨**z-**⟩ exhaust, tire, strain; **~** ⟨***na-, z-***⟩ ***się*** get tired; struggle (***z** I*, ***przy** I* with); ⟨**z-**⟩ *pf. też* be dead tired
morel|a *f* (*-i*; *-e*) *bot.* apricot; **~owy** apricot
morfin|a *f* (*-y*; *0*) morphine; **~izować się** (*-uję*) take morphine
morfo'logia *f* (*GDl -ii*; *0*) *bot.*, *gr.* morphology
morowy pestilential; ***~ chłop*** *Brt.* great bloke, *Am.* great chap
mors *m* (*-a*; *-y*) *bot.* walrus
mor|ski sea; naval; maritime; marine; ***drogą ~ską*** by sea; **~szczuk** *m* (*-a*; *-i*) *zo.* hake; **~świn** *m* (*-a*; *-y*) *zo.* porpoise
morwa *f* (*-y*; *G morw*) *bot.* mulberry
morz|e *n* (*-a*; *G mórz*) sea; ***pełne ~e*** the high seas; ***nad ~em*** (*wakacje itp.*) at the seaside; ***wyjść w ~e*** put to sea; ***na ~u*** at sea; → ***poziom***
Morze Karaibskie *n* the Caribbean Sea
Morze Śródziemne *n* the Mediterranean Sea
morzyć (*-ę*) *v/i.* ⟨**z-**⟩ *sen*: overcome; *v/t.* ***~ głodem*** ⟨***za-***⟩ starve
mosiądz *m* (*-u*; *0*) brass
mosiężny brass
moskit *m* (*-a*; *-y*) mosquito; **~iera** *f* (*-y*; *G -*) mosquito net
Moskwa *f* (*-y*; *0*) Moscow
most *m* (*-u*; *-y*) bridge; ***~ zwodzony*** drawbridge; ***prosto z ~u*** without beating about the bush; **~ek** *m* (*-ku*; *-tki*) bridge; → ***kapitański***; **~owy** bridge
moszcz *m* (*-u*; *0*) new wine
moszn|a *f* (*-y*; *G -*) *anat.* scrotum; **~owy** scrotal
mot|ać (*-am*) wind, entangle; ***~ać się*** get entangled; **~ek** *m* (*-tka*; *-tki*) skein
motel *m* (*-u*; *-e*) motel
motłoch *m* (*-u*; *-y*) mob, rabble
motocykl *m* (*-a*; *-e*) motorcycle; **~ista** *m* (*-y*; *-ści*), **~istka** *f* (*-i*; *G -tek*) motorcyclist; **~owy** motorcycle
motor *m* (*-u*; *-y*) engine, motor; F cycle, bike; **~niczy** *m* (*-ego*; *-owie*), **-cza** *f* (*-ej*; *-e*) tram-driver
motorow|er *m* (*-u*; *-y*) moped, light motorcycle; **~iec** *m* (*-wca*; *-wce*) motor ship; **~y** motor, engine
motorówka *f* (*-i*; *G -wek*) motor boat
motory|zacyjny motor, automobile, automotive; **~zować** ⟨**z-**⟩ (*-uję*) motorize; ***być zmotoryzowanym*** have a car, have wheels; ***~zować się*** get a car, get o.s. wheels
motyka *f* (*-i*; *G -*) hoe
motyl *m* (*-a*; *-e*) butterfly
motyw *m* (*-u*; *-y*) (*postępku*) motive; (*literacki*) motif; theme; **~ować** ⟨**u-**⟩ (*-uję*) *coś* give a reason for; *kogoś* motivate
mow|a *f* (*-y*; *G mów*) speech; language, tongue; ***wygłosić ~ę*** deliver a speech; ***~a ojczysta*** mother tongue; ***w ~ie*** orally; ***nie ma ~y!*** F no way!
mozaika *f* (*-i*; *G -*) mosaic; *fig.* patchwork
mozol|ić się (*-lę*, *-zól!*) (***nad** I*) labo(u)r (over), toil (over); **~ny** laborious
moździerz *m* (*-a*; *-e*) *mil.*, *gastr.* mortar
może *3. os. sg. pres.* → ***móc***; *adv.* maybe; ***być ~*** perhaps; ***~ byśmy usiedli*** why don't we sit down?; **~cie, ~my, ~sz** → ***móc***
możliw|ie *adv.* possibly; **~ość** *f* (*-ści*; *0*) possibility, chance; **~y** possible, likely; F not too bad, fair enough; ***~y do*** (*G*) -able; ***~y do realizacji*** implementable, realisable; ***robić wszystko co ~e*** do whatever is possible
można one can/may…; ***nie ~*** one must not…, one cannot…; ***~ by*** one could…; ***jak ~ najlepiej*** as good as possible
możność *f* (*-ci*; *0*) possibility, opportunity, chance
możny affluent, opulent
móc can, may; be able to; be allowed to

mój (*moja f, moje n, moi m-os/pl., moje f/pl.*) my, mine; ***to moje*** that's mine; ***moi*** my family
mól *m* (*mola; mole*) moth
mów|ca *m* (*-y; G -ów*), **~czyni** *f* (*-i; -e*) speaker; **~ić** (*-ę*) speak, say; talk, tell; ***~ić po angielsku*** speak English; ***~ią, że*** they say that, it is said that; ***szczerze ~iąc*** to be frank; ***szkoda ~ić*** it is not even worth talking about; ***nie ma o czym ~ić*** don't mention it; ***to ~i samo za siebie*** it speaks for itself; **~ienie** *n* (*-a; 0*) speaking; **~nica** *f* (*-y; -e*) rostrum, platform
mózg *m* (*-u; -i*) brain (*też fig.*); F ***padło mu na ~*** he is off his rocker; **~owy** cerebral (*też fig.*)
MPK *skrót*: ***Miejskie Przedsiębiorstwo Komunikacyjne*** Municipal Transport Company
mro|czny (***-no***) dark; *fig.* gloomy; **~k** *m* (*-u; -i*) dark, darkness; *fig.* gloom; ***zapada ~k*** dusk is falling
mrowi|ć się (*-ę*) swarm, teem; **~e** *n* (*-a; 0*) → ***mnóstwo***; **~sko** *n* (*-a; G -*) ant-hill
mrozić (*-żę*) ⟨**z-**⟩ freeze (*też fig.*), chill
mrozoodporny frost-resistant
mroźn|o *adv.*: ***jest ~o*** it is freezing; **~y** frosty, icy
mrożon|ki *f/pl.* (*-nek*) frozen food; ***~ka warzywna*** frozen vegetables *pl.*; **~y** frozen, deep-frozen
mrówk|a *f* (*-i; G -wek*) *zo.* ant; **~owiec** *m* (*-wca; -wce*) F high-rise block
mróz *m* (*-ozu; -y*) frost
mru|czeć (*-ę, -y*) murmur; mutter; *kot*: purr; **~gać** (*-am*) ⟨***~gnąć***⟩ blink; *gwiazda*: twinkle; (**do** *G*, **na** *A*) wink (to, at); **~k** *m* (*-a; -i*) grouch, grumbler; **~kliwy** (***-wie***) grumpy, grouchy; **~knąć** *v/s.* (*-nę*) → ***mruczeć***
mrużyć (*-żę*) ⟨**z-**⟩: ***~ oczy*** squint
mrzonka *f* (*-i; G -nek*) pipe-dream, daydream
m.st. *skrót pisany*: ***miasto stołeczne*** capital city
MSW *skrót pisany*: ***Ministerstwo Spraw Wewnętrznych*** Ministry of Interior; *Brt.* HO (*Home Office*)
MSZ *skrót pisany*: ***Ministerstwo Spraw Zagranicznych*** Ministry of Foreign Affairs; *Brt.* FO (*Foreign Office*)
msz|a *f* (*-y; msze*) *rel.* Mass, service; ***służyć do ~y*** serve at Mass; ***dać na ~ę*** have a Mass said; ***iść na ~ę*** go to Mass; **~ał** *m* (*-u; -y*) *rel.* missal
mszcz|ą, ~ę → ***mścić***
mszyca *f* (*-y; -e*) *zo.* aphid, greenfly
mści|ciel *m* (*-a; -e*), **-lka** *f* (*-i; G -lek*) avenger; **~ć** ⟨**po-**⟩ avenge, take revenge for; ***~ć się*** take one's revenge (***za*** *A* for); **~wość** *f* (*-ci; -*) revengefulness, vindictiveness; **~wy** (***-wie***) revengeful, vindictive
MTP *skrót pisany*: ***Międzynarodowe Targi Poznańskie*** International Poznan Fair
mu *pron.* (*ściągn.* ***jemu***) → ***on***
much|a *f* (*-y; G -*) *zo.* fly; bow-tie; ***~a nie siada*** tip-top; ***być pod ~ą*** be tipsy
muchomór *m* (*-ora; -ory*) toadstool
mularski → ***murarski***
mulisty muddy, slimy
multimedialny multimedia
muł[1] *m* (*-a; -y*) *zo.* mule
muł[2] *m* (*-u; -y*) mud, slime
mumia *f* (*-i; -e*) mummy
mundur *m* (*-u; -y*) uniform; **~owy** uniform
mur *m* (*-u; -y*) wall (*też fig.*); ***~ pruski*** half-timbering; ***na ~*** F for sure; **~arski** mason's; **~arstwo** *n* (*-a; 0*) bricklaying, masonry; **~arz** *m* (*-a; -e*) mason, bricklayer; **~ować** ⟨**wy-**⟩ (*-uję*) lay bricks; *budynek* build; **~owany** brick, stone; F dead-certain
Murzy|n *m* (*-a; -i*), **~nka** *f* (*-i; G -nek*) African; (*w USA*) Afro-American, Black; **♀ński** Black
mus[1] *m* (*-u; -y*) *gastr.* mousse
mus[2] *m* (*-u; 0*) necessity; ***z ~u*** out of necessity; **~ieć** (*-szę*) have to, must
muskać (*-am*) brush
muskularny muscular
musnąć *v/s.* (*-nę*) → ***muskać***
mus|ować (*-uję*) effervesce, fizz; **~ujący** effervescent, fizzy; *wino* sparkling
muszk|a *f* (*-i; G -szek*) → ***mucha***; *mil.* foresight; ***wziąć na ~ę*** take aim at
muszkat *m* (*-u; -y*) nutmeg; **~ołowy**: ***gałka ~ołowa*** nutmeg
muszla *m* (*-i; -e, -i/-szel*) shell; ***~ klozetowa*** toilet bowl
musztard|a *f* (*-y; G -*) mustard; **~owy** mustard
musztr|a *f* (*-y; G -*) drill; **~ować** (*-uję*) drill
musz|y fly; ***waga ~a*** flyweight; ***~e śla-***

dy fly droppings *pl.*
muśnięcie *n* (*-a*; *G -ęć*) brushing
muza *f* (*-y*) muse
muze|um *n* (*idkl.*; *-a*, *-ów*) museum; **~alny** museum
muzułma|nin *m* (*-a*; *-anie*, *-ów*), **~nka** *f* (*-i*; *G -nek*) Muslim; **~ński** Muslim
muzy|czny music(al), melodious; **~k** *m* (*-a*; *-cy*) musician; **~ka** *f* (*-i*; *0*) music; **~kalny** musical; **~kować** (*-uję*) play music, make music; ***~kować na ulicy*** *Brt.* busk
my *pron.* (*GAL* **nas**, *D* **nam**, *I* **nami**) we; ***o nas*** about us; ***z nami*** with us
myć (*-ję*) ⟨**u-**⟩ wash (**się** *v/i. lub* o.s.); *warzywa, kafelki* clean
myd|lany soap; **~lić** ⟨**na-**⟩ (*-lę*) soap (**się** o.s.); *mydło*: lather; ***~lić oczy*** dupe; **~liny** *pl.* (*G -*) suds *pl.*; **~ło** *n* (*-a*; *G -deł*) soap
myjnia *f* (*-i*; *-e*) car wash
myl|ić (*-lę*) ⟨**po-, z-**⟩ confuse, mix; ***~ić*** ⟨**o-, po-**⟩ ***się*** get confused, go wrong; be wrong; **~ny** mistaken, wrong
mysi mouse; *fig.* mousy
mysz *f* (*-y*), **~ka** *f* (*-i*; *G -szek*) mouse; **~kować** (*-uję*) snoop about, nose about
myśl *f* (*-i*) thought; idea; ***w ~*** according to; ***mieć na ~i*** have in mind; ***w ~i*** in mind; ***wpaść na ~*** hit on an idea; ***przyjść na ~*** come to mind; ***być dobrej ~i*** be in good spirits; **~ący** thinking; **~eć** ⟨**po-**⟩ (*-lę*, *-i*) think (**o** *L* of, about); ***niewiele ~ąc*** without thinking too much; **~enie** *n* (*-a*; *0*) thinking; ***sposób ~enia*** way of thinking, mentality; **~iciel** *m* (*-a*; *-e*) thinker
myśli|stwo *n* (*-a*; *0*) hunting; **~wiec** *m* (*-wca*; *-wce*) *mil.* fighter; (*-wca*; *-wcy*) hunter; **~wski** hunting; *mil.* fighter; **~wy** hunting
myśl|nik *m* (*-a*; *-i*) dash; **~owy** intellectual
MZK *skrót*: ***Miejskie Zakłady Komunikacyjne*** Municipal Transport Company
mżawka *f* (*-i*; *G -wek*) drizzle
mżyć: (***deszcz***) ***mży*** it is drizzling

N

n. *skrót pisany*: **nad** over, above
na *prp.* (*L*) *pozycja* on (***~ półce*** on the shelf); in (***~ łóżku*** in bed; ***~ Litwie*** in Lithuania); *istnienie* in (***~ piśmie*** in writing); (*A*) *ruch*: on(to), on (***~ łóżko*** on the bed), to (***~ Ukrainę*** to (the) Ukraine); *okres, termin* in (***~ wiosnę*** in spring), for (***~ Wielkanoc*** for Easter; ***~ dwa dni*** for two days), on (***~ drugi dzień*** on the next day); *miara* per (***raz ~ miesiąc*** once a/per month); *cel* to, on, for (***iść ~ spacer*** go for a walk); *skutek, przyczyna* at, with, about (***zachorować ~*** be taken ill with; ***skarżyć się ~*** complain about); *przeznaczenie* for (***lekarstwo ~ kaszel*** medicine for coughing); *rezultat* into (***dzielić ~ części*** divide into parts); ***~ końcu …*** in the end; finally; **…**; *często nie tłumaczy się*: *miara* ***głęboki ~ dwa metry*** two metres deep; ***~ dole*** downstairs; *gra* ***grać ~ flecie*** play the flute; *przeznaczenie* ***pojemnik ~ chleb*** bread-bin; ***złapać ~ kradzieży*** catch stealing; → *odnośne rzeczowniki i czasowniki*
nabawi|ać się (*-am*) ⟨***~ć się***⟩ (*G*) catch, contract
nabiał *m* (*-u*; *0*) dairy products *pl.*; **~owy** dairy
na|bić → ***bić, nabijać***; **~biegać** ⟨***~biec, ~biegnąć***⟩ (*I*) *łzy*: well up; *rumieniec*: spread
nabierać (*-am*) (*G, A*) take; *powietrza, tchu* take in; F (*oszukiwać*) take in, kid; ***~ znaczenia*** gain importance; → ***nabrać, siła***
nabijać (*-am*) (*wypełniać*) stuff full; *broń* load; ***~ gwoździami*** stud with nails; ***~ się*** (***z*** *G*) → ***drwić***
naboż|eństwo *n* (*-a*; *G -w*) divine service; **~ny** pious
nabój *m* (*-boju*; *-boje*, *-boi*) charge; (*kula*) bullet; ***ślepy ~*** blank
nabrać *pf.* → ***nabierać***; F ***~ na kawał*** take in; ***dać się ~*** fall for
nabrzeże *n* (*-a*; *G -y*) quay, wharf; embankment

na|brzmiały swollen; **~brzmiewać** ⟨**~mieć**⟩ (*-am*) swell

naby|tek *m* (*-tku*; *-tki*) purchase, acquisition; **~wać** ⟨**~ć**⟩ (*-am*) buy, purchase, acquire; **~wca** *m* (*-y*) buyer, purchaser; **~wczy**: ***siła ~wcza*** *econ.* purchasing power

na|chalny F cheeky, brazen; **~chmurzony** frowning, grim

nachodzić (*opanować*) overcome; (*odwiedzać*) descend (up)on; **~ *się*** tire o.s. by walking

nachy|lać (*-am*) ⟨**~lić**⟩ bend (**się** down); **~lony** bent

nacią|ć → ***nacinać***; **~gać** (*-am*) ⟨**~gnąć**⟩ *v/t.* draw *lub* pull tight; *koszulę itp.* pull on; *mięsień* strain; F *fig.* → ***nabierać***; *v/i.* *herbata* draw, brew

nacie|k *m* (*-u*; *-i*) *med.* (o)edema; **~kać** (*-am*) ⟨**~c, ~knąć**⟩ leak in(to), flow in(to); **~rać** (*-am*) *v/t.* run in; *v/i.* (**na** *A*) attack, assault

na|cięcie *n* (*-a*; *G -ęć*) score, notch, incision; **~cinać** (*-am*) cut, incise

nacis|k *m* (*-u*; *-i*) pressure (*też fig.*); *gr.* stress; *fig.* ***z ~kiem*** with emphasis; **~kać** ⟨**~nąć**⟩ press; *guzik* push; *fig.* pressurize

nacjonali|styczny nationalistic; **~zować** (*-uję*) nationalize

nacz. *skrót pisany*: ***naczelny*** chief

naczeln|ik *m* (*-a*; *-cy*) head; chief; ***~ik urzędu pocztowego*** postmaster; ***~ik stacji*** stationmaster; ***~ik urzędu policyjnego*** *Am.* marshal; **~y** head; chief, foremost; supreme

naczyni|e *n* (*-a*; *G -yń*) vessel (*też anat.*); dish; ***~a*** *pl.* crockery

nać *f* (*-ci*; *-cie*) tops *pl.*

naćpany F high (*I* on)

nad *prp.* (*I*) *miejsce* over, above; (*przy*) on, by (***~ Wisłą*** on the Vistula, ***~ morzem*** by the sea); ***~ ranem*** towards morning; (*A*) *kierunek* to; ***~ podziw*** astonishingly; → ***miara, wyraz, wszystko***

nad. *skrót pisany*: ***nadawca*** sender

nada|ć *pf.* → ***nadawać***; **~jnik** *m* (*-a*; *-i*) transmitter

nadal *adv.* still

nada|remnie *adv.* to no effect, fruitlessly; **~remny** futile, fruitless; **~rzać się** (*-am*) ⟨**~rzyć się**⟩ *okazja*: occur

nadaw|ać *list* send; *imię, kształt* give; *tytuł* confer, bestow; *RTV*: broadcast; ***~ać się*** (**do** *G*, **na** *A*) be fit (for), be suitable (for, to); **~anie** *n* (*-a*; *G -ań*) *RTV*: broadcast; (*tytułu*) conferral; **~ca** *m* (*-y*; *G -ców*), **~czyni** *f* (*-i*; *-e*) sender; **~czy**: ***zespół ~czy*** transmitter unit

nadą|ć *pf.* → ***nadymać***; **~sany** sulky; **~żać** (*-am*) ⟨**~żyć**⟩ (**za** *I*) keep pace (with); ***nie ~żać*** *też* fall behind; *fig.* not be with s.o.

nad|bagaż *m* excess baggage; **~bałtycki** Baltic; **~biegać** ⟨**~biec, ~biegnąć**⟩ come running up; **~bity** *talerz* chipped; **~brzeże** *n* (*-a*; *G -y*) seafront

nadbudow|a *f* superstructure; **~(yw)ać** (*-uję*) build on

nadchodz|ący approaching; **~ić** (*-dzę*) approach, come up

nad|ciąć *pf.* → ***nacinać***; **~ciągać** (*-am*) ⟨**~ciągnąć**⟩ *v/i.* arrive; come up; *burza*: approach; **~cięcie** *n* (*-a*; *G -ć*) incision, cut; **~cinać** (*-am*) → ***nacinać***; **~ciśnienie** *m* (*-a*; *G -ń*) excess pressure; *med.* hypertension; **~czuły** hypersensitive; **~czynność** *f* (*-ści*; *0*) *med.* hyperfunction; **~dzierać** (*-am*) → ***nadrywać***; **~dźwiękowy** supersonic

nade → ***nad***; **~drzeć** *pf.*, **~rwać** → ***nadrywać***

nadejś|cie *n* (*-a*) approach, coming; oncoming; **~ć** *pf.* come, approach; → ***nadchodzić***

na|depnąć *pf.* (**na** *A*) tread (on), *niechcący* step (on); **~der** *adv.* extremely, very, greatly; **~derwać** *pf.* → ***nadrywać***; F ***~derwać się*** overstrain, sprain; **~desłać** *pf.* → ***nadsyłać***

nadetatowy supernumerary

nadęty → ***nadąsany, napuszony***

nad|fioletowy ultraviolet; **~garstek** *m* (*-tka*; *-tki*) wrist; **~godzina** *f* (*-y*; *G -*) one hour's overtime; ***~godziny*** *pl.* overtime; **~gorliwy** officious; **~graniczny** border, frontier; **~gryzać** (*-am*) ⟨**~gryźć**⟩ bite into, take a bite of; **~jeżdżać** (*-am*) ⟨**~jechać**⟩ come, arrive; **~latywać** (*-uję*) ⟨**~lecieć**⟩ come flying up, arrive

nadleśni|ctwo *n* (*-a*; *G -*) forestry administration (office); **~czy** *m* senior forestry officer

nadliczbow|y overtime; ***godziny*** *f/pl.* ***~e*** overtime

nad|ludzki superhuman; **~łamywać** (*-uję*) ⟨**~łamać**⟩ *v/t.* crack; **~miar** *m*

(*-u*; *0*) (*G*) excess; surplus; ***w ~miarze*** in excess
nadmie|niać (*-am*) 〈**~nić**〉 mention
nadmierny excessive, surplus
nadmorski seaside
nadmuch|iwać (*-uję*) 〈**~ać**〉 blow up, inflate; **~iwany** inflated
nad|naturalny supernatural; **~obowiązkowy** optional; **~palać** (*-am*) 〈***~palić***〉 singe; **~pijać** (*-am*) 〈***~pić***〉 start drinking; **~piłow(yw)ać** (*-*[*w*]*uję*) start to saw; **~płacać** (*-am*) 〈***~płacić***〉 overpay; **~pływać** (*-am*) 〈***~płynąć***〉 → ***przypływać***; **~produkcja** *f* (*-i*; *0*) overproduction, surplus
nadprogram *m* supporting program(me); **~owy** additional, surplus
nad|przyrodzony supernatural; → ***nadnaturalny***; **~psuty** slightly spoiled; *mięso* bad; **~rabiać** (*-am*) 〈***~robić***〉 *czas* make up; *zaległości* catch up on, make up for; ***~rabiać miną*** put on a show of bravery; ***~robić drogi*** go a long way round
nadruk *m* (*-u*; *-i*) imprint
nad|rywać (*-am*) rip, tear; ***~rywać się*** strain o.s., overstrain; **~rzędny** overriding; higher; **~skakiwać** (*-uję*) (*D*) pay court to, toady; **~słuchiwać** (*-uję*) listen out for; **~spodziewany** surprise, startling, unanticipated; **~stawi(a)ć** (*-am*) hold out, *uszy* prick up (*też fig.*); ***~stawi(a)ć głowy*** take risks; **~stawka** *f* (*-i*; *G -wek*) top *lub* upper part; **~syłać** (*-am*) send in; **~szarpnąć** *pf. fig.* shatter; *zdrowie* ruin; **~tlenek** *m chem.* peroxide
nadto *adv.* moreover
nadużу|cie *n* (*-cia*; *G -ć*) abuse, misuse; *jur.* embezzlement; ***~cie podatkowe*** tax evasion; **~(wa)ć** (*G*) abuse; ***~wać alkoholu*** drink too much
nad|waga *f* overweight, excess weight; **~wątlony** impaired, weakened
nadwerężać (*-am*) 〈***~yć***〉 (*-ę*) impair, weaken
nadwodny aquatic; above water level
nadworny court
nadwozie *n* (*-a*; *G -i*) *mot.* body
nad|wrażliwy hypersensitive; **~wyżka** *f* (*-i*; *G -żek*) surplus
na|dymać (*-am*) inflate, blow up; ***~dymać się*** puff o.s. up; **~dziać** *pf.* → ***nadziewać*** (*-am*)
nadzie|ja *f* (*-ei*; *-e*, *-ei*) hope; ***mieć ~ję*** hope; ***w ~i/z ~ją, że*** in the hope that; ***przy ~i*** with child
nadziemny above ground, overhead
nadziemski ethereal; supernatural
nadzie|nie *n* (*-a*; *G -ń*) *gastr.* filling, stuffing; **~wać** (*-am*) *gastr.* (*nadzieniem*) fill, stuff (*I* with); impale (***się na*** o.s. on); **~wany** filled
nadzor|ca *m* (*-y*; *GA -ców*), **~czyni** *f* (*-i*; *-nie*, *-ń*) warder, supervisor; **~czy** supervising, supervisory; **~ować** (*-uję*) supervize, oversee, control
nadzór *m* (*-oru*; *0*) supervision, overseeing, control
nadzwyczaj(nie) *adv.* unusually, remarkably; **~ny** unusual, remarkable; *profesor* extraordinary; extra
nadzy *m-os pl.* → ***nagi***
naft|a *f* (*-y*; *0*) *Brt.* paraffin (oil), *Am.* kerosene; **~owy** paraffin, kerosene; → ***ropa***
nagab|ywać (*-uję*) 〈***~nąć***〉 (*-nę*), pester, solicit; bother (***o*** *A* about)
nagana *f* (*-y*; *G -*) rebuke, reprimand
nag|i (***-go***) naked, *też drzewo itp.* bare; ***do ~a*** naked
na|ginać (*-am*) 〈***~giąć***〉 bend (down), bow; ***~ginać się*** bend; → ***chylić***; **~glący** urgent, pressing; **~gle** suddenly; abruptly, all at once; → ***nagły***; **~glić** (*-lę*) → ***przynaglać***; ***czas ~gli*** time presses; **~głaśniać** (*-am*) 〈***~głośnić***〉 (*-ę*, *-nij!*) *fig.* make public; **~głość** *f* (*-ści*; *0*) suddenness, urgency; **~główek** *m* (*-wka*; *-wki*) headline; letter-heading; **~gły** sudden, abrupt; **~gminny** common, wide-spread; **~gniotek** *m* (*-tka*; *-tki*) corn
nago *adv.* → ***nagi***
nagonka *f* (*-ki*; *-G -nek*) battue; *fig.* witch-hunt
nagość *f* (*-ści*; *0*) nudity, nakedness, bareness
nagra|ć *pf.* → ***nagrywać***; **~dzać** (*-am*) reward; **~nie** *n* (*-a*; *G -ań*) recording
nagrob|ek *m* (*-bka*; *-bki*) tomb; tombstone, gravestone; **~kowy, ~ny** tombstone, gravestone
nagro|da *f* (*-y*; *G -ród*) award, reward; prize; ***~da pocieszenia*** consolation prize; ***w ~dę za*** (*A*) in reward for; **~dzić** *pf.* → ***nagradzać***; **~dzony** awarded
nagromadz|enie *n* (*-a*) accumulation,

N

amassing; **~ać** (*-am*) → ***gromadzić***
na|grywać (*-am*) record; ***~grywać na taśmę*** tape, put on tape; **~grzewać** (*-am*) ⟨**~grzać**⟩ (*-eję*) heat, warm (**się** *v/i.*)
nagusieńki stark-naked, F starkers
naigrawać się (*-am*) → ***kpić, drwić***
naiwn|ość *f* (*-ci*; *0*) naivety *lub* naïveté, ingenuousness; **~y** naive *lub* naïve, ingenuous
najadać się (*-am*) eat one's fill
najazd *m* (*-u*; *-y*) invasion; raid
nająć *pf.* (*-jmę*) → ***najmować***
naj|bardziej *adv.* (*sup. od* → ***bardzo***) most; **~bliższy** (***~bliżej***) (*sup. od* → ***bliski***); nearest, closest; *czas* next; ***~bliższa rodzina*** next of kin; **~częściej** *adv.* (*sup. od* → ***często***); most frequently, most often; mostly; **~dalej** *adv.* (*sup. od* → ***daleki***) farthest, furthest; *czas* at the latest; **~dalszy** *adv.* (*sup. od* → ***daleko***) farthest, furthest; **~dłużej** *adv.* (*sup. od* → ***długo***) longest; *fig.* at the most; **~dłuższy** *adj.* (*sup. od* → ***długi***) longest
najechać *pf.* → ***najeżdżać***
najem *m* (*-jmu*; *0*) hire, lease; ***umowa o ~*** tenancy agreement; **~ca** *m* (*-y*; *GA -ów*), **~czyni** *f* (*-ń*; *-nie*) tenant; **~nik** *m* (*-a*; *-cy*) *mil.* mercenary; **~ny** hired; ***praca ~na*** hired labo(u)r; ***wojsko ~ne*** mercenary troops *pl.*
naje|ść się *pf.* → ***najadać się***; **~źdźca** *m* (*-cy*; *GA -ców*) invader, aggressor; **~żać** (*-am*) → ***jeżyć***; **~żdżać** (*-am*) (**na** *A*) drive (into), run (into); (*na kraj*) invade; **~żony** (*I*) bristling (with)
naj|gorszy *adj.* (*sup. od* → ***zły***) worst; ***w ~gorszym razie*** at (the) worst; **~gorzej** *adv.* (*sup. od* → ***źle***) worst
naj|lepiej *adv.* (*sup. od* → ***dobrze***) best; **~lepszy** *adj.* (*sup. od* → ***dobry***) best; ***w ~lepszym razie*** at best, at most; ***wszystkiego ~lepszego!*** all the best!
najmniej *adv.* (*sup. od* → ***mało***) least, smallest; ***co ~*** at least; ***jak ~*** as little as possible; **~szy** *adj.* (*sup. od* → ***mały***) least, smallest; ***w ~szym stopniu*** not in the least
najmować (*-uję*) hire, rent; *osobę* engage, hire; **~ się** become engaged, get a job
naj|niżej *adv.* (*sup.* → ***nisko***) lowest; right at the bottom; **~niższy** *adj.* (*sup. od* → ***nisko***) lowest; **~nowszy** *adj.* (*sup. od* → ***nowy***) latest, most recent; **~pierw** *adv.* at first; first; to begin with; **~prawdopodobniej** *adv.* (*sup. od* → ***prawdopodobnie***) most probably; **~prędzej** *adv.* (*sup. od* → ***prędko***) at the earliest; ***jak ~prędzej*** as soon as possible; **~starszy** *adj.* (*sup. od* → ***stary***) oldest, eldest; **~ście** *n* (*-a*) intrusion, trespass; **~ść** *pf.* (→ **-jść**) → ***nachodzić***; **~ważniejszy** *adj.* (*sup. od* → ***ważny***) most important; uppermost, paramount; **~wcześniej** *adv.* (*sup. od* → ***wcześnie***) earliest; ***jak ~wcześniej*** as soon as; **~wyżej** *adv.* (*sup.* → ***wysoko***) highest; (***co - żej***) at (the) most; **~wyższy** *adj.* (*sup. od* → ***wysoki***) highest, tallest; *sąd itp.* supreme; ***stopień ~wyższy*** *gr.* (the) superlative; **~zupełniej** *adj.* (*sup. od* → ***zupełny***) totally, utterly
nakarmić *pf.* → ***karmić***
nakaz *m* (*-u*; *-y*) order; *fig.* dictate; *jur.* warrant; *jur.* **~ sądowy** writ, injunction; **~ywać** (*-uję*) ⟨**~ać**⟩ order, impose; *dietę itp.* prescribe; *szacunek* command
nakle|jać (*-am*) ⟨**~ić**⟩ stick on, paste on; **~jka** *f* (*-i*; *G -jek*) sticker
nakład *m* (*-u*; *-y*) expenditure, expense; *print.* print run, circulation; ***~em*** (*G*) published by; **~ać** (*-am*) put on; *krem, lekarstwo* apply; *obowiązek, podatek, karę itp.* impose; *podatek też* levy; **~any:** ***kieszeń ~ana*** patch-pocket
nakł|aniać ⟨**~onić**⟩ → ***skłaniać***
nakra|- *pf.* → ***kra-***, **~piany** speckled
nakre- *pf.* → ***kre-***
nakrę|cać (*-am*) ⟨**~cić**⟩ *zegarek* wind up; *numer* dial; *film* shoot, tape; **~tka** *f* (*-i*; *G -tek*) *tech.* nut; (*butelki*) cap
nakry|cie *n* (*-a*; *G -yć*) cover; ***~cie głowy*** headgear, head covering; **~wać** (*-am*) ⟨**~ć**⟩ cover (**się** o.s.); ***~wać stół, ~wać do stołu*** lay the table; ***~wać się nogami*** do a head over heels
nakup|ować ⟨**~ić**⟩ buy a lot of things
nalać *pf.* → ***nalewać***
nale|gać (*-am*) (**na** *A*) insist (on), demand; **~piać** (*-am*) ⟨**~pić**⟩ stick on, paste on; **~pka** *f* (*-i*; *G -pek*) sticker; **~śnik** *m* (*-a*; *-i*) pancake; **~wać** (*-am*) pour; **~wka** *f* (*-i*; *G -wek*) fruit liqueur
należ|eć (**do** *G*) belong (to); ***~eć się*** (*D*) be due (to); ***~y*** (***się***)**...** one should..., it is necessary to...; ***~ałoby...*** it would be necessary to...; ***jak ~y*** correctly,

N

properly; ***ile się panu/pani ~y?*** how much do I owe you?; **~ność** *f* (*-ści*) charge, amount due, outstanding amount; **~ny** due; *zapłata* outstanding; **~y** → ***należeć***; **~yty** appropriate
nalot *m* (*-u*; *-y*) raid; *med.* coating, (*na języku*) fur; **~ *bombowy*** *mil.* bomb attack, bombing raid
nała|- *pf.* → ***ła-***; **~dowany** loaded (*też* F)
nałogow|iec *m* (*-wca*; *-wcy*) addict; **~y** *palacz* habitual; *pijak* compulsive
nałożyć *pf.* → ***nakładać***
nałóg *m* (*-łogu*; *-łogi*) addiction; *fig.* (bad) habit
nam *pron.* (*D pl.* → ***my***) us
namaca|ć *pf.* make out by touch; *drogę* feel one's way; **~lny** tangible; *med.* palpable
namal-, namar- *pf.* → ***mal-, mar-***
namaszczenie *n* (*-a*; *G -eń*) *rel.* unction; ***z ~m*** solemnly; ***ostatnie ~*** *rel.* anointing of the sick, extreme unction
namawiać (*-am*) persuade (***do kupna*** *G* to buy; ***kogoś na spacer*** s.o. to go for a walk)
nami *pron.* (*I pl.* → ***my***); ***z ~*** with us
namiastka *f* (*-i*; *G -tek*) substitute, surrogate
namięk|ać (*-am*) ⟨**~nąć**⟩ become soft
namiętn|ość *f* (*-ści*) passion; **~y** passionate
namiot *m* (*-u*; *-y*) tent
namo|- *pf.* → ***mo-***; **~knąć** *pf.* become soft; soak through; **~wa** *f* (*-y*; *G -mów*) persuasion, instigation; ***za jego ~wą*** at his instigation
namówić → ***namawiać***
namy|dlać (*-am*) → ***mydlić***; **~sł** *m* (*-u*; *0*) reflection, consideration; ***bez ~słu*** without thinking; (*od razu*) without a moment's thought; ***po ~śle*** on reflection; ***czas do ~słu*** time for reflection; **~ślać się** (*-am*) ⟨**~ślić się**⟩ reflect, think (***nad*** *I* about)
na|nosić (*im*)*pf* ⟨**~nieść**⟩ (*G*) *błota itp.* track; *wiatr*: drift; *woda*: wash up; na mapę plot; ***~nosić poprawki*** make corrections
naoczn|ie *adv.* with one's own eyes; **~y** visible *fig.* apparent, obvious; → ***świadek***
naokoło *prp.* (*G*) (a)round
naówczas *lit.* at that time
napad *m* (*-u*; *-y*) attack, assault; (*na państwo*) invasion; (*kradzież*) robbery; *med. fig.* attack, fit; **~ać** (*-am*) (***na*** *A*) attack, assault; ***~ało dużo śniegu*** there has been a heavy snowfall
napalić *pf.* (***w*** *L*) heat, stoke; ***~ się na*** (*A*) F get hooked on
na|par *m* (*-u*; *-y*) infusion; **~parstek** *m* (*-tka*; *-tki*) thimble; **~parzać** (*-am*) → ***parzyć***; **~paskudzić** F *pf.* (*-dzę*) mess up, make filthy
napast|liwy (***-wie***) aggressive; → ***złośliwy***; **~nik** *m* (*-a*; *-cy*) attacker, assailant; (*w sporcie*) forward, striker; **~ować** (*-uję*) bother, pester; (*seksualnie*) molest; *owady*: plague
na|paść[1] (*paść*[1]) → ***napadać***; **~paść**[2] → ***paść***[2]; *f* (*-ści*; *-ści*) attack, assault; → ***napad***; **~pawać** (*-am*) fill with (***dumą*** pride); ***~pawać się*** (*I*) feast (on), delight (in); **~pchać** *pf.* → ***napychać***; ***~pchać się*** (***do*** *G*) push one's way (into)
napełni|ać (*-am*) ⟨**~ć**⟩ fill up (*I* with; ***się*** *v/i.*); *fig.* fill (*I* with)
napę|d *m* (*-u*; *-y*) drive (*też mot., komp.*); *mot.* transmission; **~dowy** driving, drive; **~dzać** (*-am*) *tech.* drive, propel; *też* ⟨**~dzić**⟩ (*G*) herd into; ***~dzać do*** *fig.* set to; ***~dzać komuś strachu*** give s.o. a fright
na|piąć *pf.* → ***napinać***; **~pić się** *pf.* (*G*) drink, have a drink; **~piec** *pf.* → ***piec***[2]; **~pierać** (*-am*) (***na*** *A*) press (against); *fig.* assail (with)
napię|cie *n* (*-a*; *G -ęć*) tension, strain; suspense; *electr.* voltage; **~tek** *m* (*-tka*; *-tki*) (*buta*) heel; **~tnować** *f* → ***piętnować***; **~ty** tense (*też fig.*); *uwaga* close; *nerwy* taut; *sytuacja* fraught
napinać (*-am*) tighten, tauten; *muskuły* tense, flex; ***~ się*** become *lub* go taut; *muskuły* tense
napis *m* (*-u*; *-y*) inscription; (*kwestii na filmie*) subtitles *pl.*, (*na zakończenie*) credits *pl.*; **~ać** *pf.* → ***pisać***
napiwek *m* (*-wku*; *-wki*) tip
napletek *m* (*-tka*; *-tki*) *anat.* prepuce, foreskin
napływ *m* (*-u*; *-y*) flow, inflow; (*też fig.*) influx, rush; *med.* inflow, afflux; **~ać** ⟨**napłynąć**⟩ flow in; (*w dużych ilościach*) flood in; *ludzie*: come in crowds, (*na stałe*) immigrate; **~owy** immigrational

N

napo|cić się *pf.* sweat (*też fig.* ***przy** I* over); **~czynać** ⟨**~cząć**⟩ *chleb* start (eating); *butelkę* open; **~minać** (*-am*) admonish, reprimand; **~mknąć** *pf.* → ***napomykać***; **~mnienie** *n* (*-a*) admonition, reprimand; **~mnieć** *pf.* (*-nę; -nij*) → ***napominać***; **~mykać** (*-am*) (**o** *L*) mention, hint; **~t(y)kać** (*-am*) encounter; come across

na|pój *m* (*-poju; -poje*) beverage, drink; ***~pój bezalkoholowy*** soft drink; ***~pój gazowany*** pop; **~pór** *m* (*-poru; 0*) pressure; *fig.* power, weight

napraw|a *f* (*-y; G -*) repair; renovation; *fig.* recovery; ***dać do ~y*** have repaired; **~czy** repair; *fig.* recovery

naprawdę *adv.* really, actually

napraw|iać (*-am*) ⟨**~ić**⟩ repair, renovate; *fig.* improve (**się** *v/i.*); *zło, krzywdę* right, undo

naprędce *adv.* hastily, rashly

napręż|ać (*-am*) ⟨**~yć**⟩ (*-ę*) (**się** *v/i.*) tighten, tauten; tense; *mięśnie* flex; **~enie** *n* (*-a*) tension; *fig.* strain, stress; **~ony** → ***napięty***

napro|mieniować (*-uję*) *phys.* irradiate; **~mieniowanie** *n* (*-a; G -ań*) irradiation, exposure; **~wadzać** (*-am*) ⟨**~wadzić**⟩ guide; direct; ***~wadzać na właściwy ślad*** put on the right track

naprze|ciw **1.** *prp.* (*G*) against, opposite (to); in front of; **2.** *adv.* towards; ***wyjść ~ciw*** (*D*) *fig.* meet halfway; **~ć** *pf.* → ***napierać***

naprzód *adv.* forward(s), ahead

naprzykrz|ać się (*-am*) ⟨**~yć się**⟩ (*D*) bother, hassle

na|pso- *pf.* → ***pso-***; **~puchnięty** swollen; **~puszony** pompous; **~pychać** (*-am*) (**do** *G*) stuff (into); → ***napchać***

nara|da *f* (*-y; G -*) meeting, conference; **~dzać się** (*-am*) ⟨**~dzić się**⟩ discuss, consult, confer

naramien|nik *m* (*-a; -i*) shoulder-strap; **~ny** shoulder

narastać (*-am*) grow, mount up

naraz *adv.* at once, suddenly

nara|żać (*-am*) ⟨**~zić**⟩ risk, jeopardize; (***na** A*) subject (to) **~zić się** (*D*) run the risk of; F displease; **~żenie** *n* (*-a; 0*): ***z ~żeniem życia*** at the risk of one's life

narcia|rka *f* (*-i; G -rek*) skier; **~rski** ski, skiing; **~rstwo** *n* (*-a; 0*) skiing; **~rz** *m* (*-a; -e*) skier

narcyz *m* (*-a; -y*) *bot.* narcissus, daffodil

nareszcie *adv.* at last, finally

naręcze *n* (*-a; G -y*) bunch, armful

narko|man *m* (*-a; -i*), **~manka** *f* (*-i; G -nek*) drug addict; F junkie; **~mania** *f* (*GDL -ii; 0*) drug addiction; **~tyk** *m* (*-u; -i*) (hard) drug; narcotic; **~tyzować się** (*-uję*) take drugs; **~za** *f* (*-y; G -*) sedation, an(a)esthesia

narobić *pf.* (*G*) make, do, cause

narodow|ość *f* (*-ci; 0*) nationality; **~y** national

naro|dzenie (się) *n* (*-a; G -eń*) birth; ***Boże* ꝶ*dzenie*** Christmas; **~dziny** *pl.* (-) birth; **~snąć** *pf.* → ***narastać***; **~śl** *f* (*-i; -e*) growth; *med.* excrescence, tumo(u)r; **~wisty** *koń* vicious

naroż|nik *m* (*-a; -i*) corner; **~ny** corner; ***dom ~ny*** house on the corner

naród *m* (*-odu; -ody*) nation

narta *f* (*-y; G -*) ski; ***jeździć na ~ch*** ski

narusz|ać *prawo, granicę* violate; *umowę* breach; *słowo* break; *równowagę* upset; *zapasy, kapitał* make inroads in; *prywatność* trespass on; **~enie** *n* (*-a; G -ń*) (*też prawa*) violation, breach, infringement

narwany F *fig.* crazy

narybek *m* (*-bku; -bki*) *zo.* fry; *fig.* new blood, new recruits *pl.*

narząd *m* (*-u; -y*) organ

narzecze *n* (*-a; G -y*) dialect

narzeczon|a *f* (*-ej; -e*) fiancee *lub* fiancée; **~y** *m* (*-ego; -czeni*) fiancé

na|rzekać (*-am*) complain (***na** A* about); **~rzędnik** *m* (*-a; -i*) *gr.* instrumental; **~rzędzie** *n* (*-a; G -*) tool, implement

narznąć *pf.* → ***narzynać***

narzu|cać ⟨**~cić**⟩ *płaszcz* throw on *lub* over; *fig.* force (**na** *A* on); ***~cać się*** impose o.s. on (*A*); **~t** *m* (*-u; -y*) *econ.* mark-up; **~ta** *f* (*-y; G -*) bedspread; **~tka** *f* (*-i; G -tek*) cape

narżnąć *pf.* → ***narzynać***

nas *pron.* (*GA* → ***my***) us

nasa|da *f* (*-y; G -*) butt, handle; *anat.*, *bot.* base; ***~da włosów*** hairline; **~dka** *f* (*-i; G -dek*) cap; **~dzać** ⟨**~dzić**⟩ put on, pin on

nasenny: ***środek ~*** soporific; sleeping pill

nasercowy: ***środek ~*** cardiac, F heart pill

nasi *pron. m-os* → ***nasz***

nasiadówka *f* (*-i; G -wek*) hip-bath

nasiąk|ać (*-am*) 〈**~nąć**〉 (*-nę*) (*I*) soak through, absorb
nasien|ie *n* (*-a*; *-siona*, *-sion*) *bot.* seed; *zo.* sperm, semen; **~ny** seed
nasilenie *n* (*-a*; *G -eń*) intensification; escalation
nasiona *pl.* → ***nasienie***
na|skoczyć *pf.* → ***naskakiwać***; **~skórek** *m* (*-rka*; *-rki*) *anat.* cuticle; **~słać** *pf.* → ***nasyłać***; **~słuchiwać** (*-uję*) listen in; **~sma-** *pf.* → ***sma-***; **~so-** *pf.* → ***so-***; **~srożony** angry; **~stać** *pf.* → ***nastawać***; **~stanie** *n* (*-a*; *0*) start, onset; **~starczyć** *pf.*: ***nie móc ~starczyć*** (*G*) not be able to satisfy the needs (of)
nasta|wać come; (**po** *L*) follow (after); ***~wać na czyjeś życie*** threaten s.o.'s life; **~wiać** *budzik* set; *mechanizm* adjust, regulate; *RTV*: tune in; *uszy* cock; *med.* set; ***~wiać wodę na herbatę*** put the kettle on; **~wienie** *n* (*-a*; *G -eń*) setting (*też med.*); (*umysłowe*) attitude; **~wnia** *f* (*-i*; *-e*) *rail. Brt.* signal box, *Am.* switch tower
nastąpić *pf.* → ***następować***
następ|ca *m* (*-y*; *G -ców*) successor; ***~ca tronu*** crown prince; **~czyni** *f* (*-i*; *-nie*, *-ń*) successor; **~nie** *adv.* next, then; **~ny** next, following; ***~nego dnia*** next day; **~ować** (*-uję*) step (**na** *A* on); follow (***po sobie*** one after the other); ***jak ~uje*** as follows; → ***nastawać***; **~stwo** *n* (*-a*; *G -*) succession; consequence, after-effect; **~ująco** *adv.* as follows, in the following way; **~ujący** following
nastolat|ek *m* (*-tka*; *G -tków*), **~ka** *f* (*-i*; *G -tek*) teenager
nastoletni teenage
nastra|jać (*-am*) → ***stroić***; **~szyć** *pf.* → (***prze***)***straszyć***
nastręcz|ać (*-am*) 〈***~yć***〉 present, offer (***się*** o.s.)
nastro|ić *pf.* → ***stroić***; **~jowy** atmospheric; **~szony** bristled; *ptak*, *pióra*: ruffled up; → ***stroszyć***
nastr|ój *m* (*-oju*; *-oje*, *-ojów*) spirit, mood; atmosphere, climate; ***w dobrym ~oju*** in good spirits
nasturcja *f* (*-i*; *-e*) nasturtium
nasu|wać 〈**~nąć**〉 *czapkę* pull (***na oczy*** over one's eyes); draw (**na** *A* on); *fig.* *wątpliwości*: give rise to; *pomysł* suggest; ***~wać*** 〈***na-***〉 ***się*** arise, occur, *pomysł*: come

nasy|cać (*-am*) → ***sycić***; **~cony** *chem.* saturated; satiated, satisfied; **~łać** (*-am*) F put *s.o.* on (to)
nasyp *m* (*-u*; *-y*) embankment; **~ywać** (*-uję*) 〈***~ać***〉 pour (***do*** *G* into)
nasz *pron.* (*m-os nasi*) our, ours; F ***po ~emu*** like we do; like we speak
na|szki- *pf.* → ***szki-***; **~szukać się** search for hours
naszy|ć *pf.* → ***naszywać***; **~jnik** *m* (*-a*; *-i*) necklace; **~wka** *f* (*-i*; *G -wek*) *mil.* stripe; **~wać** (*-am*) sew on(to)
naśladow|ać (*-uję*) imitate, copy; mimic; **~ca** *m* (*-y*; *G -ów*), **~czyni** *f* (*-i*; *-nie*, *-ń*) imitator; mimic; **~czy** imitative; **~nictwo** *n* (*-a*; *G -*) imitation
na|śmiewać się (*-am*) (***z*** *G*) mock, ridicule; **~świetlać** (*-am*) 〈***~świetlić***〉 (*-lę*) *phys.* irradiate; *med.* use radiation treatment; *phot*, expose (*też fig.*)
natar|cie *n* (*-a*; *G -ć*) *mil.*, (*w sporcie*) attack; *mil.* advance; **~czywy** (***-wie***) insistent
natchn|ąć *pf.* inspire (***do*** *G* to); **~ienie** *n* (*-a*; *G -ń*) inspiration
natęż|ać (*-am*) 〈***~yć***〉 (*-ę*) *wzrok itp.* strain, exert; **~enie** *n* (*-a*; *G -eń*) intensity (*też phys.*); (*dźwięku*) volume
na|tknąć się *pf.* → ***natykać się***; **~tłoczony** crowded, packed; **~tłok** *m* (*-u*; *0*) crowd, crush; *fig.* flood, influx
natomiast *adv.* however
natrafi(a)ć (***na*** *A*) encounter, come across; (*na złoto*) strike
natręctwo *n* (*-a*; *G -w*) pushiness, insistence; *med.* compulsion, obsession; **~tny** pushy, insistent
natrysk *m* (*-u*; *-i*) shower; **~iwać** (*-uję*) spray, sprinkle; **~owy** shower
na|trząsać się (*-am*) (***z*** *G*) mock, ridicule; **~trzeć** *pf.* → ***nacierać***
natu|ra *f* (*-y*; *G -*) nature; ***z ~ry*** by nature; ***w ~rze*** in nature; **~ralizacja** *f* (*-i*; *-e*) naturalisation; **~ralny** natural
natychmiast *adv.* immediately, instantly; **~owy** immediate, instant
natykać się (*-am*) (***na*** *A*) meet, come across
naucz|ać (*-am*) teach; **~anie** *n* (*-a*; *G -ń*) teaching, instruction; **~ka** *f* (*-i*; *G -czek*) *fig.* lesson; ***dać k-ś ~kę*** give s.o. a lesson
nauczyciel *m* (*-a*; *-e*), **~ka** *f* (*-i*; *G -lek*) teacher; **~ski** teacher

N

nau|czyć *pf.* → **nauczać, uczyć**; **~czyć się** (*G*) teach; **~ka** *f* (*-i*; *G* -) (*przyrodnicza*) science, (*humanistyczna*) scholarship; (*szkolna*) teaching; (*teoria*) teaching(s *pl.*); (*morał*) lesson; (*nauczanie zawodu*) apprenticeship; **~kowiec** *m* (*-wca*; *-wcy*) (*przyrodnik*) scientist, (*humanista*) scholar; **~kowy** academic, scientific, scholarly

naumyślnie *adv.* on purpose

nausznik *m* (*-a*; *-i*) ear-flap

nawa *f* (*-y*; *G* -): **~ *główna*** nave; **~ *boczna*** aisle

nawadniać (*-am*) irrigate

nawa|lać (*-am*) 〈**~lić**〉 *v/t.* pile up, heap up; *v/i.* F fail, crash; *pf. też* be broken down

nawał *m* (*-u*; *0*) barrage, spate; **~a** *f* (*-y*; *G* -) *mil.* barrage; **~nica** *f* (*-y*; *-e*) thunderstorm

nawet *adv.* even; **~ *gdyby*** even if; **~ *nie*** not even

nawia|ć *pf.* → **nawiewać**; **~s** *m* (*-u*; *-y*) parenthesis, (*zwł. kwadratowy*) bracket; ***~sem mówiąc*** incidentally; ***wyłączyć poza ~s*** exclude; **~sowy** parenthetic(al), bracket

nawiąz|ywać (*-uję*) 〈**~ać**〉 *kontakty*, establish; *negocjacje* open, start; *stosunki* form; *znajomość* strike up; take (**do** *G* up); **~ując do** (*G*) with reference (to), referring (to)

nawiedz|ać (*-am*) 〈**~ić**〉 (*-dzę*) *nieszczęście* afflict, strike, plague; (*we śnie*) appear; *duch*, *wspomnienia*: haunt

nawierzchnia *f* (*-i*; *-e*, *-i*) surface

nawietrzn|y: ***strona ~a*** windward

na|wiewać (*-am*) 〈**~wiać**〉 (*-eję*) blow (in); F scram

nawi|jać (*-am*) wind up, reel up, roll up (**się** *v/i.*); **~jać się** *fig. okazja* come up, crop up; **~nąć** *pf.* (*-nę*; *-ń!*) → **nawijać**

na|wlekać (*-am*) 〈**~wlec**〉 *igłę* thread; *paciorki* string; **~wodnić** *pf.* (*-ę*, *-nij!*) → **nawadniać**; **~wodny**: ***budowla ~wodna*** lacustrine dwelling

nawoływać (*-uję*) call; *fig.* call (**do** *G* up(on))

na|wozić fertilize; **~wóz** *m* (*-ozu*; *-ozy*) dung, manure; ***~wóz sztuczny*** fertilizer

na|wracać (*-am*) 〈**~wrócić**〉 *v/i. mot.* do an about-turn; → **wracać**; *v/t. mot.* turn; *rel.* convert (**na** *A* to); **~wracać** 〈**~wrócić**〉 **się** become converted (**na** *A* to); **~wrócenie** *n* (*-a*; *G -eń*) *rel.* conversion; **~wrót** *m* (*-otu*; *-oty*) return, recurrence; *med.* relapse

nawyk *m* (*-u*; *-i*) habit; **~ać** (*-am*) 〈**~nąć**〉 (*-nę*) (**do** *G*) get used (to), get accustomed (to)

nawzajem *adv.* each other, one another; ***dziękuję, ~!*** thank you, the same to you!

nazajutrz *adv.* (on) the next day

nazbyt *adv.* too, excessively

na|zębny dental; ***kamień ~zębny*** dental plaque; **~ziemny** *zo.* terrestrial; *astr.*, *aviat.* ground

naznacz|ać (*-am*) 〈**~yć**〉 mark; *termin* fix, establish

nazw. *skrót pisany*: **nazwisko** n. (*name*)

nazwa *f* (*-y*; *G* -) name; **~ć** *pf.* → **nazywać**

nazwisk|o *n* (*-a*) (family) name, surname; ***~iem, o ~u …*** by name; ***znać z ~a*** know by name

nazyw|ać (*-am*) call, name; ***~ać się*** be called; ***to się ~a …!*** that's what I call…; ***jak się to ~a?*** what's its name?; ***jak się ~asz?*** what's your name?

nażreć się *pf.* (*fig.*) stuff o.s.

NBP *skrót*: ***Narodowy Bank Polski*** Polish National Bank

n.e. *skrót pisany*: ***naszej ery*** AD (*Anno Domini*)

Neapol *m* (*-u*; *0*) Naples

negatyw *m* (*-u*; *-y*) negative; **~ny** negative

negliż *m* (*-u*; *-e*, *-y*) undress; ***w ~u*** in a state of undress

negocja|cje *f/pl.* (*-i*) negotiations *pl.*; **~tor** *m* (*-a*; *-rzy*), **~torka** (*-i*; *G -rek*) negotiator

ne|gocjować (*-uję*) negotiate; **~gować** (*-uję*) negate; **~krolog** *m* (*-u*; *-i*) obituary; (*w gazecie*) death notice

nenufar *m* (*-u/-a*; *-y*) *bot.* water lily, (*zwł.*) yellow water lily

neo- *w zł.* neo-

neon *m* (*-u*; *0*) *chem.* neon; (*-u*; *-y*) neon light; **~ówka** *f* (*-i*; *G -wek*) strip light

nerk|a *f* (*-i*;*G -rek*) *anat.*, *gastr.* kidney; **~owaty** kidney-shaped, reniform; **~owy** kidney; renal

nerw *m* (*-u*; *-y*) *anat.* nerve; ***działać na ~y*** get on nerves; **~ica** *f* (*-y*; *G* -) *med.* neurosis; ***~ica lękowa*** anxiety neurosis; **~oból** *m med.* neuralgia; **~owy** nerv-

N

ous; nerve; **~owo chory** mentally ill
neseser *m* (*-u, -y*) *Brt.* sponge-bag, *Am.* toilet bag; *też* briefcase, attaché case
neska F *f* (*-i; 0*) instant (coffee)
netto (*idkl.*) net
neuro- *w zł.* neuro-
neutral|izować ⟨**z-**⟩ (*-uję*) neutralize; **~ny** neutral
newralgiczny sore, touchy
nęc|ący tempting, enticing; **~ić** ⟨**z-**⟩ (*-cę*) tempt, entice
nędz|a *f* (*-y; -e*) poverty; misery, destitution; ***cierpieć ~ę*** suffer poverty; **~arka** *f* (*-i; G -rek*), **~arz** *m* (*-a; -e*) pauper; **~ny** poor, destitute, miserable; → ***nikczemny***
nękać ⟨**z-**⟩ (*-am*) plague; *fig.* pester
ni *cj.* → ***ani***; ***~ stąd, ~ zowąd*** without reason; ***~ to ..., ~ owo ...*** neither fish nor fowl; ***~ w pięć, ~ w dziewięć*** without rhyme or reason
niań|czyć (*-ę*) nurse; **~ka** *f* (*-i; G -niek*) nurse
nią *pron.* (*AI* → ***ona***); ***z ~*** with her
niby 1. *part.* (*A*) as though, as it were; of a kind; ***małżeństwo na ~*** sham marriage; ***~ śpi ...*** he is apparently sleeping; **2.** *w złoż.* pseudo-, quasi-, sham
nic *pron.* nothing; ***~ a ~*** not a thing; ***jak gdyby ~*** as if nothing (had) happened; ***na ~*** for nothing; a waste of time; ***~ z tego*** (***nie będzie***) nothing will come of it; ***tyle co ~*** next to nothing; ***~ ci do tego*** that's none of your business; ***za ~ w świecie*** not for anything; ***niczego nie brakuje*** there's nothing missing; ***być do niczego*** be of no use; ***zostać bez niczego*** be left with nothing; ***z niczym*** empty-handed; ***na niczym mu nie zależy*** he doesn't care about anything; ***skończyć się na niczym*** come to nothing; ***w niczym*** not at all
nich *pron.* (*GL* → ***oni, one***; *A* → ***oni***); ***o ~*** about them
nici *pl.* → ***nić***
nicować ⟨**prze-**⟩ (*-uję*) *ubranie* turn over
nicpoń *m* (*-nia; -nie, -i/-ów*) god-for--nothing
nicz|ego (*G*) → ***nic***; F **~ego sobie** not bad; **~emu** (*D*) → ***nic***; **~yj** no-one's; ***ziemia ~yja*** no man's land; ***bez ~yjej pomocy*** on one's own; **~ym** (*IL* → ***nic***) *prp. lit.* (*A*) like

nić *f* (*-ci; -ci, I -ćmi*) thread; *med.* suture
niderlandzki Netherlandic, Netherlandian
nie 1. *part.* no; (+ *verb*) not; ***jeszcze ~*** not yet; ***to ~ żarty*** no joking; ***~ płacąc*** without paying; ***~ zapytany*** not asked; ***no ~?*** isn't it so?; ***~ ma*** there isn't; → ***już, mieć, nic***; **2.** *w złoż.* un-, in-, non-
nie|aktualny out of date; invalid; **~apetyczny** unappetizing; **~baczny** careless, inconsiderate; **~bawem** soon, before long
niebezpiecz|eństwo *n* (*-a; G -*) danger; threat; **~ny** dangerous, hazardous; perilous
niebiesk|awy (**-*wo***) bluish; **~i**[1] (**-*ko***) blue; **~i**[2] heavenly; ***Królestwo ~ie*** Kingdom of Heaven; **~ooki** blue-eyed
niebiosa *pl.* (*-os, L -osach*) heavens *pl.*
nieb|o *n* (*-a; -a,* → ***niebiosa***) sky; *rel.* heaven; ***na ~ie*** in the sky; ***w ~ie*** *rel.* in heaven
niebora|czka *f* (*-i; G -czek*) → ***biedaczka***; **~k** *m* (*-a; -cy/-i*) → ***biedak***
nieboszcz|ka *f* (*-i; G -czek*), **~yk** *m* (*-a; -cy/-i*) the deceased; ***moja babka ~ka*** my late lamented Grandmother
niebotyczny sky-high, lofty
nie|brzydki not bad; **~bywały** unbelievable, unheard-of; **~całkowity** incomplete, not complete; **~cały** not quite; ***~cały tydzień*** less than a week, under a week; **~celny** imprecise; **~celowy** inadvisable; **~cenzuralny** indecent, obscene; unprintable
niech *part.* let; ***~ zaczeka*** let him wait; ***~ sobie jadą*** let them go; ***~ pan(i) pozwoli*** allow me; ***~ żyje demokracja!*** long live democracy; ***~ żyje Jan!*** hurray for John!; **~by** suppose; even though
niechcący unwittingly, incidentally
niechę|ć *f* (*-ci*) dislike (***do*** *G* towards); reluctance; **~tnie** *adv.* reluctantly; **~tny** reluctant; averse (***do*** *G* to); hostile
nie|chlujny untidy, squalid, sloppy; **~chlujstwo** *n* (*-a; G -*) squalor, sloppiness; **~chodliwy** *econ.* unattractive, hardly saleable; **~chybny** inevitable; **~ciekawy** unattractive, uninteresting; *człowiek* uninterested (*G* in)
niecierpliw|ić ⟨**z-**⟩ (*-ę*) *v/t.* make impatient; ***~ić*** ⟨**z-**⟩ ***się*** be impatient, grow impatient; **~ość** *f* (*-ci*) impatience; **~y** impatient

niecka *f* (*-i*; *G -cek*) trough; *geol.* hollow
niecny dastardly, heinous
nieco *adv.* somewhat; **~ za mały** on the small side; **~dzienny** unusual; **~ś** → **nieco**; **coś ~ś** a little bit
nie|często *adv.* infrequently, now and then; **~czuły** insensitive (**na** *A* to); **~czynny** inactive; out of order; *zakład* closed; *wulkan* extinct; *chem.* inert; **~czysto** *adv.* → **nieczysty**
nieczyst|ość (*-ści*; *0*) untidiness; *tylko pl.* **~ości** waste; *Brt.* refuse, *Am.* garbage; **~y** (**-to**) untidy, unclean; *chem.* impure (*też fig.*); dirty; **~e sumienie** guilty conscience
nie|czytelny illegible; **~daleki** → **pobliski**; (**od** *G*) near (to), not far (from); (*w czasie*) at hand; **~daleko** *adv.* (*G*, **od** *G*) not far (from)
niedawn|o *adv.* recently; **~o temu** not long ago; **~y** recent; **od ~a** for a short time; **do ~a** until recently
niedba|lstwo *n* (*-a*; *0*) carelessness, negligence; **~ły** careless, negligent
nie|delikatny indelicate; tactless; **~długo** *adv.* before long; (*wkrótce*) soon
niedo|bór *m* (*-boru*; *-ory*) lack, shortage; deficiency; **~brany** ill-matched, mismatched; **~bry** bad; wrong; *czyn* bad, wicked, nasty; *smak*, *pogoda* bad, foul, nasty; (*niezdrowy*) unwell; **niedobrze mi** I feel sick; **~ciągnięcie** *n* (*-a*) shortcoming; **~czas** *m* (*-u*; *-y*): **być w ~czasie** be pressed for time
niedogod|ność *f* (*-ści*) inconvenience; **~ny** inconvenient
niedojadanie *n* (*-a*) malnutrition
niedojrzały immature
niedo|kładny imprecise, inaccurate; **~konany** *gr.* imperfect(ive); **~krwistość** *f* (*-ści*; *0*) *med.* an(a)emia; **~kształcony** half-educated
niedola *f* (*-i*; *-e*) adversity, misfortune
niedołę|ga *f/m* (*-i*; *G -/-ów*) failure; → **niezdara**; **~stwo** *n* (*-a*; *0*) infirmity, frailty; **~żny** infirm, frail
niedomag|ać (*-am*) be ailing; be ill (**na** *A* with); **~anie** *n* (*-a*) illness, complaint; *fig.* shortcoming; defect
niedo|moga *f* (*-i*; *G -móg*) *med.* insufficiency; *fig.* shortcoming; **~mówienie** *n* (*-a*; *G -eń*) hint, suggestion; vague hint; **~myślny** slow to understand; **~pałek** *m* (*-ałka*; *-ałki*, *-ałków*) butt, stub; **~patrzenie** *n* (*-a*; *-eń*) inattentiveness, carelessness; **przez ~patrzenie** by oversight; **~płata** *f* (*-y*; *G -*) underpayment; **~powiedzenie** *n* (*-a*; *G -eń*) → **niedomówienie**; **~puszczalny** inadmissible
niedorajda *f/m* (*-y*; *G -*) bungler; → **niedołęga**
niedoręczeni|e *n* (*-a*; *G -eń*): **w razie ~a …** if undelivered …
niedo|rosły immature; **~rostek** *m* (*-tka*; *-tki*) adolescent, teenager; **~rozwinięty** retarded, (**umysłowo** mentally-)handicapped; **~rozwój** underdevelopment; (*psychiczny*) mental deficiency; **~rzeczny** absurd, ridiculous; **~sięgły** unattainable, beyond grasp; **~skonały** (*m-os -li*) imperfect
niedosłysz|alny inaudible; **~eć** (*-ę*) be hard of hearing; **~enie** *n* (*-a*; *0*) hardness of hearing
niedo|smażony underdone; **~solony** insufficiently salted; **~spać** *pf.* → **niedosypiać**; **~stateczny** insufficient, *ocena* unsatisfactory; **~statek** *m* (*-tku*; *-tki*) shortage, lack; **~stępny** inaccessible, unattainable; **~strzegalny** indiscernible, imperceptible; **~sypiać** (*-am*) sleep too short *lub* too little; **~szły** would-be, potential, unfulfilled
niedo|ścigły, ~ścigniony unequalled; unmatched; **~świadczony** inexperienced; **~trzymanie** *n* (*-a*) non-compliance, breach; **~tykalny** untouchable; **~uczony** half-educated; → **niedokształcony**; **~waga** *f* underweight; **~warzony** *fig.* unripe, immature; **~wiarek** *m* (*-rka*; *-rki/-rkowie*) sceptic, disbeliever; **~widzieć** (*-dzę*) be short-sighted
niedowierza|jąco disbelievingly, incredulously; **~nie** *n* (*-a*) disbelief, doubt
nie|dowład *m* (*-u*; *-y*) *med.* paresis; **~dozwolony** forbidden, prohibited; **~dożywiony** undernourished; **~drogi** (**-go**) inexpensive, low-priced; **~dużo** *adv.* not much, little; not many, few; **~duży** small; **~dwuznaczny** unambiguous, unequivocal; **~dyskrecja** *f* indiscretion; **~dysponowany** unwell; **~dyspozycja** *f* indisposition
niedz. *skrót pisany*: **niedziela** Sun. (*Sunday*)
niedziel|a *f* (*-i*; *-e*) Sunday; **~ny** Sunday
niedźwiadek *m* (*-dka*; *-dki*) *zo.* → **miś**, **niedźwiedź**

N

niedźwiedzi bear, *biol.* ursine; **~ca** *f* (*-y*; *-e*, *-*) *zo.* she-bear; ***Wielka Ꝍca*** Ursa Major, (Great) Bear

niedźwiedź *m* (*-dzia*; *-dzie*) *zo.* (***biały, brunatny*** polar, brown) bear

nie|efektowny unattractive; **~ekonomiczny** uneconomical; **~estetyczny** unsightly, disagreeable; **~efektywny** ineffective

nie|fachowy unprofessional, incompetent; **~foremny** ungainly, shapeless; **~formalny** informal; **~fortunny** unfortunate; luckless, unhappy; **~frasobliwy** (***-wie***) carefree, free and easy; **~gazowany** still; **~głęboki** shallow, superficial; **~głupi** clever, sensible

niego *pron.* (*GA* → **on**; *G* → **ono**); **dla/ /od/do/u ~** for/from/to/with him

niego|dny, *pred.* **~dzien** (*G*) unworthy, undeserving; **~dziwy** (***-wie***) → ***nieczny***

nie|gospodarny uneconomic; **~gościnny** inhospitable; **~gotowy, ~gotów** *pred.* unfinished, not ready; **~groźny** harmless; **~grzeczność** *f* impoliteness, unkindness, rudeness; **~grzeczny** impolite, unkind, rude; **~gustowny** tasteless; **~higieniczny** insanitary, unhealthy; **~ingerencja** non-intervention; **~istotny** insignificant, inconsiderable

niej *pron.* (*GDL* → **ona**); **dla/od/do/u ~** for/from/to/with her

nieja|dalny inedible; **~dowity** non-poisonous

nieja|ki certain; some; ***od ~kiego czasu*** for some time; ***~ki pan ...*** a certain Mr; **~ko** *adv.* as it were; **~sny** (***-no***) unclear, vague; **~wny** closed, classified

niejed|en, ~na, ~no[1] many a, many; ***~na kobieta*** many a woman, many women

niejedno[2] all kinds of, all sorts of; ***przeżył ~*** he has seen a lot of life; **~krotnie** *adv.* several times, repeatedly; **~krotny** repeated; **~lity** non-uniform; **~znaczny** ambiguous

niekar|alny exempt from punishment; **~ność** *f* (*-ści*) exemption from punishment; **~ny 1.** without criminal record; **2.** *m* (*-ego*) person without criminal record

niekiedy sometimes, occasionally; ***kiedy ~*** now and then

nie|kłamany sincere, honest; **~koleżeński** unhelpful to one's colleagues; **~kompetentny** incompetent; **~kompletny** incomplete; **~koniecznie** *adv.* not necessarily; **~konsekwentny** inconsistent

niekorzy|stny unfavo(u)rable; **~ść** *f*: ***na ~ść*** (*G*) to disadvantage, to detriment

nie|kształtny shapeless, ungainly; **~którzy** *pl.*, ***~które*** *f/pl.* some; ***~którzy z nich*** some of them; **~kulturalny** uncultured, uncultivated; **~legalny** illegal; **~letni** under age; **~liczny**: ***~liczni, ~liczne*** few; **~litościwy** unmerciful; **~logiczny** illogical; **~lojalny** disloyal; **~ludzki** inhuman

niеła|d *m* (*-u*; *0*) disorder, disarray, mess; ***w ~dzie*** disordered

nie|ładny plain; wrong; **~łamliwy** unbreakable; **~łaska** (*-i*; *0*): ***być w ~łasce*** be out of favo(u)r; **~łatwy** not easy; ***~łatwe zadanie*** not an easy task

nie|mal(że) *adv.* almost, nearly; **~mało** *adv.* quite a lot; **~mały** quite big; **~mądry** (***-rze***) unwise

niemczyzna *f* (*-y*; *0*) German, the German language

nie|męski unmanly; effeminate; **~miara** *f* F: ***co ~miara*** a heap of

Niemcy *pl.* (*-iec*) Germany

Niemiec *m* (*-mca*; *-mcy*, *-mców*) German; **Ꝍki** (***po -ku***) German

nie|mieszkalny non-residential; **~mile** *adv.*; **~miło** *adv.* → ***niemiły***; **~miłosierny** unmerciful; F terrible, awful; **~miły** unkind, unpleasant

Niemka *f* (*-i*; *G -mek*) German (woman/girl *itp.*)

niemnący non-crease

niemniej nevertheless, even so

niemo *adv.* silently, speechlessly

niemoc *f* (*-y*; *0*) weakness; ***~ płciowa*** impotence; **~ny** weak (*też* F *fig.*)

nie|modny unfashionable; **~moralny** immoral; ***czyn ~moralny*** *jur.* sexual *Brt.* offence (*Am.* offence); **~mowa** *f/m.* (*-y*; *G -mów/-owów*) mute

niemowlę *n* (*-cia*; *-ta*, *G -ląt*) baby, infant; **~ctwo** *n* (*-a*; *0*) infancy; **~cy** infant, baby

niemoż|liwie *adv.* F impossibly, awfully, terribly; **~liwy** impossible; awful, terrible; ***to ~liwe*** that's impossible; ***~liwy do opisania*** indescribable, beyond

N

description; **~ność** *f* (*-ci*; *0*) lack of ability, impossibility
niemrawy sluggish, languid
niemu *pron.* → ***jemu***; ***ku ~*** to him
niemy mute, dumb; *fig.* speechless,-wordless; → ***niemowa***
niena|ganny beyond reproach; **~prawialny** irreparable, beyond repair; **~ruszalny** inviolable, sacred; **~ruszony** intact; **~sycony** insatiable, quenchless; **~turalny** unnatural; **~umyślnie** *adv.* unintentionally
nienawi|dzić (*-dzę*) hate, detest (***się*** each other); **~stny** hateful, detestable; **~ść** *f* (*-ści*; *0*) hatred, hate, loathing
nie|nawykły unaccustomed (***do*** *G* to); **~normalny** abnormal; **~nowy** not new, used; **~obcy** not strange
nieobecn|ość *f* (*-ści*; *0*) absence; ***pod ~ość*** (*G*) in the absence (of); **~y** absent; ***być ~ym*** be absent (***na*** *L* at)
nie|obliczalny incalculable; *fig.* unpredictable; **~obowiązkowy** *osoba* negligent; **~obrobiony** rough; untreated; **~obsadzony** vacant; **~obywatelski** unsocial, antisocial; **~oceniony** inestimable; **~oczekiwany** unexpected; **~odczuwalny** indiscernible, imperceptible
nieod|gadniony inscrutable; **~łączny** inseparable; **~mienny** unalterable, unchangeable; *gr.* uninflected; **~party** irresistible; *chęć* irrepressible; *argument* irrefutable; **~płatny** free (of charge); **~powiedni** inappropriate, inadequate, improper; **~powiedzialny** irresponsible; **~stępny** → ***nieodłączny***; **~wołalny** irrevocable, **~wracalny** irreversible; **~zowny** indispensable, essential; **~żałowany** *strata* irretrievable, irrecoverable
nie|oficjalny unofficial; **~oględny** careless, rash; **~ograniczony** (***-czenie***) unlimited; limitless; **~okiełznany** *fig.* rampant, uncontrolled; **~określony** indefinite (*też gr.*), nondescript; **~okrzesany** *fig.* loutish; **~omal** → ***niemal***; **~omylny** infallible, unerring; **~opanowany** uncontrollable, unruly; **~opatrzny** unguarded; **~opisany** indescribable; **~opłacalny** unprofitable, uneconomic; **~organiczny** inorganic; **~osiągalny** unattainable, beyond reach; **~osobowy** impersonal
nieostrożn|ość *f* (*-ści*; *0*) carelessness, rashness; **~y** careless, rash
nie|ostry not sharp, blunt; *phot.* out of focus; *zdjęcie* fuzzy; *zima* mild; **~oświecony** unenlightened, backward; **~ożywiony** inanimate
niepaląc|y 1. non-smoking; **2.** *m* (*-ego*; *-y*), **~a** *f* (*-ej*; *-e*) non-smoker; ***jestem ~y*** I don't smoke; ***wagon dla ~ych*** non-smoker
niepalny non-flammable, not flammable
niepamię|ć *f*: ***puścić w ~ć*** forgive and forget; ***wydobyć z ~ci*** rescue from oblivion; **~tliwy** forgiving, relenting; **~tny**: ***od ~tnych czasów*** from time immemorial
nieparzysty odd
niepełno|letni 1. under age; **2.** *m* (*-ego*; *-ni*), **~letnia** *f* (*-ej*; *-e*) minor; **~prawny** without full legal capacity; **~sprawny** disabled
nie|pełny incomplete; deficient; **~pewność** uncertainty, incertitude; **~pewny** uncertain, doubtful; **~pijący** *m* (*-ego*; *-y*) non-drinker; **~piśmienny** illiterate; **~planowy** unplanned; unscheduled; **~płodny** sterile; fruitless; **~pochlebny** unfavo(u)rable; **~pocieszony** disconsolate, inconsolable; **~poczytalny** not responsible for one's actions, of unsound mind
niepodległ|ość *f* (*-ci*; *0*) independence; **~y** independent
niepodob|ieństwo *n* imposibility; **~na** (*nieos.*) it is impossible; **~ny** (***do*** *G*) unlike
niepo|dzielny indivisible; *fig.* absolute; **~goda** (*-y*; *0*) bad weather; **~hamowany** unrestrained, uncontrollable; **~jętny** untalented, ungifted; **~jęty** incomprehensible; **~kalany** *rel.* immaculate; **~kaźny** inconspicuous; **~koić** ⟨***za-***⟩ (*-ję*) bother, worry, disturb; ***~koić się*** worry (***o*** *A* about); **~kojący** (***-co***) worrying; disturbing; **~konany** invincible, unconquered; **~kój** *m* (*-koju*; *-koje*) anxiety, worry, disquiet; **~liczalny** uncountable
nie|pomierny excessive; **~pomny** (*G*) forgetful (of), unmindful (of); **~pomyślny** unfavo(u)rable, adverse; **~popłatny** unprofitable; **~poprawny** incorrect, inaccurate; *winowajca* incorri-

gible; **~popularny** unpopular; **~poradny** → ***niezaradny***; **~poręczny** unwieldy, cumbersome; **~porozumienie** *n* (*-a*; *G -eń*) misunderstanding; *zw. pl.* (*spory*) difference of opinion
nieporów|nany incomparable, inimitable; **~nywalny** incomparable
niepo|ruszony immovable, still; *spojrzenie* fixed; **~rządek** *m* → ***nieład***; **~rządny** → ***niechlujny***; **~skromiony** → ***niepohamowany***
nieposłusz|eństwo *n* disobedience, insubordination; **~ny** disobedient, insubordinate
niepo|spolity uncommon; **~strzeżenie** unnoticed; **~szanowanie** disrespectfulness; lack of respect; ***~szanowanie prawa*** disregard for law; **~szlakowany** impeccable, irreproachable; **~trzebny** unnecessary, needless
niepo|ważny frivolous, flippant; **~wetowany** irreparable, irrecoverable; **~wodzenie** *n* failure, misadventure; **~wołany** unauthorized; **~wstrzymany** irrepressible, unrestrained; **~wszedni** not everyday; → ***niepospolity***; **~wtarzalny** unique, single, one-off; **~znawalny** *fig.* unfathomable; **~zorny** inconspicuous; **~żądany** undesirable
niepraktyczny impractical, unpractical
niepraw|da *f* untruth, untruthfulness; ***to ~da*** that's not true; ***jest duży, ~da?*** it is big, isn't it?, ***był duży, ~da?*** it was big, wasn't it?; **~dopodobny** improbable; **~dziwy** (***-wie***) untrue; (*sztuczny*) false
nieprawidłow|ość *f* (*-ści*) irregularity; **~y** incorrect, wrong, improper
niepra|wny unlawful, illegal; **~womocny** *jur.* not final; invalid; **~wowity** unlawful, illegal
nie|prędko *adv.* not soon; **~produktywny** unproductive; **~profesjonalny** unprofessional, amateur
nieproliferacj|a *f* (*-i*; *0*): ***układ o ~i*** nonproliferation treaty
nie|proporcjonalny disproportionate (**do** *G* to); **~proszony** uninvited, unwelcome, unbidden
nieprze|brany innumerable; immeasurable; **~byty** impassable, impenetrable; **~chodni** *gr.* intransitive; **~ciętny** uncommon, above average; **~jednany** irreconcilable; **~jezdny** impassable
nieprzejrzany *tłum* enormous, immense; *mrok* impenetrable
nieprze|konujący, ~konywujący unconvincing; **~kraczalny** impassable; *termin* latest possible; **~kupny** incorruptible; **~makalny** waterproof; **~mijający** *piękno* unchanging; *sława* immortal; **~nikniony** impenetrable; **~pisowy** (***-wo***) against the rules; **~puszczalny** impermeable, impervious
nieprzerwany incessant, ceaseless
nieprze|ścigniony unsurpassable; **~tłumaczalny** untranslatable; **~widziany** unforeseen; **~zorny** careless; inadvertent; **~zroczysty** opaque; **~zwyciężony** insurmountable
nieprzy|chylny unfavo(u)rable; **~datny** useless (**do** *G*, **na** *A* to, for); → ***bezużyteczny***; **~jaciel** *m* (*-a*; *-e*, *G -ciół*), **~jaciółka** *f* (*-i*; *G -łek*) enemy; **~jacielski** enemy, hostile; **~jazny** unfriendly, inimical; **~jemność** *f* trouble; **~jemny** unpleasant; **~padkowy** not accidental; purposeful, deliberate; **~stępny** unapproachable; *cena* prohibitive; **~tomny** unconscious; *wzrok* absent-minded; ***~tomny ze strachu*** frightened out of one's wits; **~tulny** cheerless, unfriendly; **~zwoity** indecent; *wyrazy* obscene
nie|punktualny unpunctual; **~racjonalny** irrational
nierad (*m-os -dzi*) (*D*) unwilling; ***rad ~*** willy-nilly
nieraz *adv.* frequently; sometimes
nierdzewny stainless
nie|realny unreal; **~regularny** irregular; **~rentowny** unprofitable; **~rogacizna** (*-y*; *0*) *zbior.* swine; **~rozdzielny** inseparable; **~rozerwalny** indissoluble
nieroz|garnięty slow-witted; **~łączka** *f* (*-i*; *G -czek*) *zo.* budgerigar, F budgie; **~łączny** inseparable; **~poznawalny** unrecognizable; **~puszczalny** insoluble; **~sądny** unreasonable; thoughtless; **~strzygalny** unsolvable, insoluble; **~tropny** → ***nierozsądny***; *czyn* unthinking, ill-considered, rash
nierozumny irrational
nierozwa|ga *f* (*-i*; *0*) thoughtlessness; rashness; **~żny** thoughtless, rash
nieroz|wiązalny insoluble, insurmountable; **~winięty** undeveloped; immature; *pąk* unopened
nieróbstwo *n* (*-a*; *0*) idleness

nierów|no *adv.* → ***nierówny***; **~nomierny** uneven; **~ność** *f* (*-ści*) inequality; **~ny** (*statusem*) unequal; *powierzchnia, droga* uneven; *teren* rough

nieruch|awy, ~liwy slow, lethargic; **~omo** → ***nieruchomy***; **~omość** *f*(*-ści*) *Brt.* real property, *Am.* real estate; **~omy** motionless, immobile, immovable

nierzadk|i frequent, often; **~o** *adv.* frequently, often

nierząd *m* (*-u*; *0*) prostitution; **~ny**: ***czyn ~ny*** *jur.* indecent assault

nierze|czowy pointless, futile; **~czywisty** unreal; **~telny** dishonest, unreliable

nie|samowity weird, uncanny; **~sforny** unruly; **~skalany, ~skazitelny** impeccable *fig.* immaculate; **~skłonny** (***do*** *G*) averse (to), unwilling (to); **~skomplikowany** uncomplicated, simple; **~skończony** (**-*czenie***) infinite, endless; **~skromny** immodest; indecent; **~skuteczny** ineffective, inefficient; **~sławny** inglorious, obscure; **~słony** unsalted; **~słowny** unreliable; **~słusznie** *adv.* unjustly; **~słuszny** unjust (*też jur.*); unfair; **~słychany** unheard of; unbelievable; **~smaczny** tasteless (*też fig.*); **~smak** *m* (*-u*; *0*) nasty after-taste

niesnaski *f/pl.* (*-sek*) quarrelling, disputes *pl.*

N

nie|solidny unreliable; **~specjalnie** *adv.* not really; **~spełna** less than; ***~spełna rozumu*** out of one's mind; **~spodzianka** *f* (*-i*; *G -nek*) surprise; **~spodzi(ew)any** unexpected; **~spokojny** uneasy; *wzrok itp.* restless; **~sporo** *adv.* slowly, slow; **~spożyty** robust, vigorous

niesprawiedliw|ość *f* (*-ści*; *0*) unjustness, injustice; **~y** unjust, unfair (***wobec, dla*** *G* on)

niesprawny *urządzenie* out of order

niesta|ły unstable; changeable, variable; **~ranny** careless; slapdash; messy; **~stateczny** fickle, unstable

niestety *adv.* unfortunately, regrettably

nie|stosowny inappropriate; unsuitable; **~strawność** *f* (*-ści*; *0*) *med.* indigestion, dyspepsia; **~strawny** indigestible; **~strudzony** restless, tireless, unflagging; **~stworzony** F incredible; **~sumienny** → ***nierzetelny, niestaranny***; **~swojo** *adv.* uneasily, uncomfortably; **~swój** (→ ***swój***) unwell

nie|symetryczny asymmetric(al); **~sympatyczny** disagreeable, unpleasant; **~systematyczny** unsystematic, haphazard; **~syty** insatiable; **~szablonowy** → ***niepospolity***; **~szczególny** insignificant, nondescript, uninteresting; **~szczelny** leaky; **~szczery** insincere

nieszczę|sny unfortunate; F wretched; **~ście** *n* (*-cia*; *G -ść*) bad luck; ***na ~ście*** unfortunately; **~śliwy** unlucky; unhappy

nieszkodliwy safe; harmless (***dla zdrowia*** to health); ***~ dla środowiska*** environment-friendly

nieszpory *pl.* (*-ów*) *rel.* vespers *pl.*

nieścisł|ość *f* (*-ci*; *0*) inaccuracy, imprecision; **~y** inaccurate, imprecise

nieść *v/t.* carry; bring (*też sprawiać*); *jaja* lay; **~ się** *dźwięki, woń*: carry; *kura*: lay eggs

nie|ślubny *dziecko* illegitimate; **~śmiały** timid, shy; **~śmiertelny** immortal

nieświado|mość *f* unawareness, unconsciousness; ignorance; **~my** (*pred. m* ***~m***) unaware; unconscious; ignorant

nie|świeży off, not fresh; **~takt** *m* tactlessness; discourtesy; **~taktowny** tactless; discourteous; **~terminowy** (**-*wo***) after the closing date; **~tęgi** (**-*go***) F weak; **~tknięty** → ***nienaruszony***; **~tłukący** unbreakable; **~tolerancyjny** intolerant

nietoperz *m* (*-a*; *-e*) *zo.* bat

nie|towarzyski unsociable; **~trafny** → ***chybiony***; **~trudny** easy, effortless; **~trwały** non-durable, short-lived; *kolor* not fast, fast-fading; **~trzeźwość** *f* insobriety, intoxication; **~trzeźwy** intoxicated, drunk; **~tutejszy** strange, not local

nietykaln|ość *f* (*-ści*; *0*) inviolability; *pol.* immunity; **~y** inviolable; *pol.* possessing immunity

nie|typowy atypical; **~ubłagany** implacable; **~uchronny** inevitable; **~uchwytny** difficult to catch; *fig.* imperceptible; ***~uchwytny dla ucha*** inaudible; **~uctwo** *n* (*-a*; *0*) ignorance; **~uczciwy** dishonest, fraudulent; **~udany** unsuccessful, failed

nieudoln|ość *f* (*-ści*; *0*) incompetence, ineptitude; **~y** incompetent, inept

nie|ufność *f* distrust, mistrust; **~ufny** distrustful, mistrustful, suspicious; **~ugaszony** inextinguishable, *fig.* unquenchable; **~ugięty** unyielding
nieuk *m* (*-a*; *-cy*) ignorant
nie|ukojony inconsolable; **~uleczalny** incurable; **~ulękły** intrepid, fearless; **~umiarkowany** intemperate; unrestrained; **~umiejętny** inept, incompetent; **~umyślny** unintentional; **~uniknionу** unavoidable; **~uprzedzony** unbiased; **~uprzejmy** unkind, impolite
nieurodzaj *m* (*-u*; *-e*) bad harvest; **~ny** *ziemia* infertile, barren; ***~ny rok*** bad year
nieusta|jący, ~nny incessant, ceaseless
nie|ustępliwy (**-*wie***) unyielding; **~ustraszony** intrepid, fearless; **~usuwalny** *plama* indelible; **~uwaga** *f* inattentiveness, carelessness; ***przez ~uwagę*** because of carelessness; **~uważny** inattentive; **~uzasadniony** unfounded, groundless; **~użyteczny** useless; **~użytki** *m/pl.* (*-ów*) *agr.* fallow land, uncultivated land
niewart (*m-os -rci*) not worth; ***nic ~ …*** worth nothing
nieważ|kość *f* (*-ści*; *0*) weightlessness; **~ny** unimportant, insignificant
niewątpliw|ie *adv.* undoubtedly, without doubt; **~y** undoubted, certain
nie|wczas *m*: ***po ~wczasie*** afterwards, after the event; **~wdzięczny** unthankful, ungrateful; **~wesoły** (**-*ło***) joyless, sad
niewiadom|y unknown; **~a** *f* (*-ej*; *-e*) *math.* unknown; ***w ~e*** to nowhere in particular
niewiar|a *f* (*-y*; *0*) disbelief, unbelief; **~ogodny, ~ygodny** incredible, unreliable
niewiasta *f* (*-y*; *G -*) woman, fair
niewido|czny invisible; **~my 1.** blind, visually impaired; **2.** *m* (*-ego*; *-mi*), **~ma** *f* (*-ej*; *-e*) blind person; ***~mi*** the blind
nie|widzialny invisible; **~wiedza** *f* ignorance
niewiel|e 1. (*m-os -lu*) not much, little; not many, few; **2.** *adv.* little; ***~e brakowało*** all but, nearly; → ***myśleć***; **~ki** small, little, low
niewie|rność *f* infidelity, unfaithfulness; **~rny** unfaithful; **~rzący 1.** unbelieving; **2.** *m* (*-ego*; *-cy*), ***~rząca*** *f* (*-ej*; *-e*) unbeliever
niewin|iątko *n* (*-a*; *G -tek*) *iron.* innocent; **~ność** *f* (*-ści*; *0*) innocence; **~ny** innocent
niewłaściwy (**-*wie***) improper, inappropriate
niewol|a *f* (*-i*; *-e*) captivity, slavery; **~nica** *f* (*-y*; *-e*) slave; **~nictwo** *n* (*-a*; *G -*) slavery; **~niczy** (**-*czo***) slavish, servile; **~nik** *m* (*-a*; *-cy*) slave
niewód *m* (*-wodu*; *-wody*) dragnet
nie|wprawny unskilful; **~wrażliwy** (***na*** *A*) insensitive (to); insensible (to); **~wskazany** inadvisable; **~współmierny** disproportionate, incommensurate; **~wybaczalny** inexcusable, unforgivable; **~wybredny** undemanding, not fussy; *iron.* tasteless; **~wybuch** *m* blind, F dud; **~wyczerpany** inexhaustible; **~wydolny** *med.* insufficient
niewy|goda *f* discomfort, inconvenience; **~godny** uncomfortable, inconvenient; **~konalny** impracticable; **~kwalifikowany** unqualified, unskilled; **~magający** undemanding; **~mierny** immeasurable; **~mowny** unspeakable; **~muszony** natural, unaffected; **~myślny** simple, plain
niewy|pał *m* misfired shell, F dud; F fiasco, flop; **~płacalny** insolvent, bankrupt; **~powiedziany** unuttered, unspoken; **~raźny** indistinct; *kształt* blurred; *mowa* inarticulate; F *mina itp.* strange; **~robiony** unpractised; inexperienced; **~spany**: ***być ~spanym*** be sleepy; **~starczająco** *adv.* insufficiently; inadequately; **~szukany** homely, plain; **~tłumaczalny** inexplicable; **~tłumaczony** unexplained; **~trzymały** (***na*** *A*) not resistant (to), sensitive (to); **~żyty** unsated, unsatisfied
nie|wzruszony (**-*szenie***) adamant, imperturbable; **~zaangażowany** *pol.* non-aligned; **~zachwiany** unshaken, steadfast; **~zadługo** *adv.* shortly, soon; **~zadowolenie** *n* discontent, displeasure; **~zadowolony** discontented, displeased (***z*** *G* with)
niezależn|ość *f* independence; **~y** independent (***od*** *G* of); ***mowa ~a*** *gr.* direct speech; → ***samodzielny***
nieza|mącony imperturbable, unruffled; **~mężny** single, unmarried; **~możny** impecunious; **~pominajka** *f*

N

(*-i*; *G -jek*) *bot.* forget-me-not; **~pomniany** unforgettable; **~przeczalny** undeniable, indisputable; **~radny** helpless, unenterprising; **~służenie** *adv.* unjustly, undeservedly; **~stąpiony** irreplaceable; **~tarty** indelible; **~uważalny** inconspicuous; **~uważony** unnoticed

niezawisł|ość *f* (*-ści*; *0*) independence; **~y** (**-śle**) independent

niezawodn|ie *adv.* without fail; reliably; **~ość** *f* (*-ści*; *0*) reliability, dependability; **~y** reliable, dependable

nie|zbadany unstudied, unexplored; *fig.* unfathomable; **~zbędny** indispensable, necessary; **~zbity** irrefutable

niezbyt *adv.* not very (much)

nie|zdarny clumsy, awkward; **~zdatny** (**do** *G*, **na** *A*) unfit (to); → ***niezdolny***

niezdecydowa|nie¹ *n* indecision, hesitation; **~nie²** *adv.*, **~ny** undecided, indecisive, hesitant

niezdoln|ość *f* (*-ści*; *0*) inability, incompetence; **~y** (**do** *G*) unable (to), incapable (of), unfit (for); ***~y do służby wojskowej*** unfit for military service; ***~y do pracy*** unable to work

nie|zdrowy unwell, indisposed; **~zdyscyplinowany** undisciplined; **~zgłębiony** unfathomed

niezgod|a *f* (*-y*; *0*) discord; **~ność** *f* incompatibility, conflict; **~ny** incompatible, inconsistent; ***~ny z przepisami*** against the regulations, irregular

nie|zgrabny ungainly, shapeless; → ***niezdarny***; **~ziszczalny** unrealizable; **~zliczony** innumerable; **~złomny** steadfast, inflexible; unbroken; **~zły** not bad; **~zmienny** unchangeable, immutable; **~zmiernie** *adv.* extremely, exceedingly; **~zmierny** immense; **~zmordowany** indefatigable, untiring; **~zmywalny** indelible

niezna|czny slight; **~jomość** *f* (*-ści*; *0*) ignorance; **~jomy** **1.** *adj.* unfamiliar, unknown; **2.** *m* (*-ego*; *-i*), **~joma** *f* (*-ej*; *-e*) stranger; **~ny** unknown; ***w ~ne*** to nowhere in particular

nie|znośny unbearable; **~zręczny** clumsy, awkward; → ***niezdarny***; **~zrozumiały** incomprehensible; **~zrozumienie** *n* (*-a*; *0*) incomprehension; **~zrównany** unmatched, unequalled; **~zupełnie** *adv.* not quite; incompletely; **~zupełny** incomplete; **~zwłoczny** prompt, immediate; **~zwyciężony** unconquerable, invincible; **~zwykły** uncommon, unusual; extraordinary

nieźle *adv.* not bad

nie|żonaty single, unmarried; **~życiowy** unrealistic; **~życzliwy** (**-wie**) unkind; **~żyjący** dead; the late

nieżyt *m* (*-u*; *-y*) *med.* infection, inflammation; ***~ żołądka*** gastritis

nieżyw|otny inanimate; **~y** dead

nigdy never; ***~ więcej*** never more *lub* again; ***jak ~*** as never before

nigdzie nowhere, anywhere; ***~ indziej*** nowhere else

nijak F in no way, nowise; **~i** nondescript, commonplace; *gr.* neuter; **~o** *adv.* indefinably, F awkward; ***czuć się ~o*** feel unpleasant

NIK *skrót*: ***Najwyższa Izba Kontroli*** Supreme Chamber of Control

nikczemny vile, mean, wicked

nikiel *m* (*-klu*; *0*) *chem.* nickel

nikim (*IL* → ***nikt***); ***z ~ innym*** with nobody else

niklow|ać ⟨**po-**⟩ (*-uję*) nickel, plate with nickel; **~any** nickel-plated; **~y** nickel

nik|ły (**-le, -ło**) faint; **~nąć** (*-nę*) fade, die away

niko|go (*G* → ***nikt***); ***~go tam nie ma*** there's no-one there, there isn't anyone there; **~mu** (*D* → ***nikt***): ***nie ufam ~mu*** I do not trust anybody

nikotyna *f* (*-y*; *0*) nicotine

nikt *pron.* nobody, no-one; anyone, anybody; → ***nikim, nikogo, nikomu***

nim¹ *cj.* before

nim² (*IL* → ***on*[*o*]**); ***z ~*** with him; (*D* → ***oni, one***); ***dzięki ~*** thanks to them; **~i** (*I* → ***oni, one***); ***z ~i*** with them

nin. *skrót pisany*: ***niniejszy*** this

niniejszy present; ***~m*** hereby; ***wraz z ~m*** enclosed

nisk|i low; *wzrost* short; *głos, ukłon* deep; → ***niższy***; **~o** *adv.* low; deep; → ***niżej***

nisko|gatunkowy low-quality, low-grade; **~kaloryczny** low-calorie

nisza *f* (*-y*; *G -*) niche

niszcz|ący (**-co**) destructive; **~eć** ⟨**z-**⟩ (*-eję*) decay, become ruined; fall to pieces; **~yciel** *m* (*-a*; *-e*) *mil.* destroyer; **~yć** ⟨**z-**⟩ (*-ę*) destroy, ruin; ***~yć się*** → ***niszczeć***

N

nit *m* (*-u*; *-y*) rivet; **~ka** *f* (*-i*; *G -tek*) thread; **~ować** (*-uję*) rivet
niuans *m* (*-u*; *-e*) nuance, subtlety
niuch *m* (*-a*; *-y*) pinch of snuff; F smell; **~ać** (*-am*): ***~ać tabakę*** snuff
niwa *f* (*-y*; *G -*) *lit.* field; *fig.* area, field
niweczyć ⟨**z-**⟩ (*-ę*) thwart, shatter; → ***niszczyć, udaremniać***
niwelować ⟨**z-**⟩ (*-uję*) level
nizać ⟨**na-**⟩ (*-żę*) thread
nizin|a *f* (*-y*; *G -*) lowland; **~ny** lowland
niziutki → ***niski***
niż¹ *cj.* than; ***więcej ~*** more than
niż² *m* (*-u*; *-e*) → ***nizina***; *meteo.* depression; **~ej** *adv.* (*comp. od* → ***nisko***); lower, below; ***~ej podpisany*** the undersigned; **~owy**: ***zatoka ~owa*** *meteo.* trough; **~szość** *f* (*-ści*; *0*) inferiority; **~szy** *adj.* (*comp. od* → ***niski***); lower; *fig.* inferior; junior
no *part.* well; now; ***patrz ~!*** well, I never!; ***~ proszę!*** well, well!; ***~ dobrze*** well, all right; ***~, mówże!*** fire away!
noc *f* (*-y*; *-e*) night; ***po ~y, w ~y*** by night; ***~ w ~, całymi ~ami*** night after night; ***do późna w ~y*** until late at night; ***przez ~, na ~*** overnight; **~leg** *m* (*-u*; *-i*) accommodation for the night; **~legowy**: ***dom ~legowy*** hostel; ***miejsce ~legowe*** place to sleep; **~nik** *m* (*-a*; *-i*) chamber pot, F potty; **~ny** night, nightly; **~ować** ⟨**prze-, za-**⟩ (*-uję*) spend the night; *kogoś* put up
nog|a *f* (*-i*; *G nóg*) leg; (*stopa*) foot; ***zerwać się na równe ~i*** jump up; ***walić się z nóg*** hardly stand up; ***wstawać lewą ~ą*** get out on the wrong side of the bed; ***do góry ~ami*** upside down, head over heels; ***stanąć na ~i*** find one's feet; ***do ~i!*** heel!; ***w ~i!*** F let's hop it!
nogawka *f* (*-i*; *G -wek*) (trouser *itp.*) leg
nokaut *m* (*-u*; *-y*) knockout, k.o.; **~ować** ⟨**z-**⟩ (*-uję*) knock out
nomada *m* (*-y*; *-dzi/-owie*, *-ów*) nomad
nomina|cja *f* (*-i*; *-e*) nomination, appointment; **~cyjny** appointment; **~lny** nominal; **~ł** *m* (*-u*; *-y*) denomination
nonsens *m* (*-u*; *-y*) nonsense, absurd; **~owny** nonsensical
nora *f* (*-y*; *G -*) (*lisia*) burrow; (*mysia*) hole; *fig.* hole
nork|a *f* (*-i*; *G -rek*) → ***nora***; *zo.* mink; ***~i*** *pl.* mink coat
norma *f* (*-y*; *G -*) norm; ***~ prawna*** legal norm; **~lizować** (*-uję*) normalize (***się*** *v/i.*); **~lny** normal
normować ⟨**u-**⟩ standardize; **~** ⟨**u-**⟩ ***się*** be standardized
Norwe|gia *f* (*-ii*) Norway; **~g** *m* (*-a*; *-dzy/-owie*), **~żka** *f* (*-ki*; *G -żek*) Norwegian; **ˆski** (**po -ku**) Norwegian
nos *m* (*-a*; *-y*) nose (*też fig.*); ***przez ~*** through the nose; F ***mieć w ~ie*** (*A*) not care (about); → ***kręcić, sprzątnąć, wodzić***; **~acizna** *f* (*-y*; *0*) *wet.* glanders *sg.*; **~ek** *m* (*-ska*; *-ski*) → ***nos***; (*buta*) toe
nosi|ciel *m* (*-a*; *-e*), **~cielka** *f* (*-i*; *G -lek*) carrier; **~ć** (*-szę*) carry (***przy sobie*** on o.s.); bear; *ubranie* wear; ***~ć się*** dress; be contemplating, think (***z*** *I* of)
noso|rożec *m* (*-żca*; *-żce*) *zo.* rhinoceros, F rhino; **~wy** nasal, nose
nostalgiczny nostalgic, romantic
nosze *pl.* (*-y*) stretcher; **~nie** *n* (*-a*; *0*) carrying, bearing; ***~nie się*** style of dress
nośn|ik *m* (*-a*; *-i*) *tech.*, *econ.* medium; vehicle; **~ość** *f* (*-ści*; *0*) capacity; (*broni*) range; **~y** carrying; *bud.* load-carrying; ***kura ~a*** laying hen; ***rakieta ~a*** carrier vehicle
nota *f* (*-y*; *G -*) note; memorandum, F memo; **~bene** (*idkl.*) incidentally, by the way
notari|alny notarial; notarized; **~usz** *m* (*-a*; *-e*) notary
notat|ka *f* (*-i*; *G -tek*) note; **~nik** *m* (*-a*; *-i*) notepad
notes *m* (*-u*; *-y*) notebook
notoryczny notorious
notowa|ć ⟨**za-**⟩ (*-uję*) take down, take notes; *fig.* note, notice; ***być źle ~nym u kogoś*** be in s.o.'s bad books; **~nie** *n* (*-a*; *G -ań*) *econ.* quotation
nowa|lie *pl.* (*-ii/-ij*), **~lijki** *pl.* (*-jek*) early vegetables *pl.*; **~tor** *m* (*-a*; *-rzy*), **~torka** *f* (*-i*; *G -rek*) innovator; **~torski** innovative
Nowa Zelandia *f* New Zealand
nowela *f* (*-i*; *-e*) short story
nowelizacja *f* (*-i*; *-e*) *jur.* amendment
nowicjusz *m* (*-a*; *-e*), **~ka** *f* (*-i*; *G -szek*) novice, recruit
nowin|a *f* (*-y*; *G -*) piece of news; ***~y*** *pl.* news *sg.*; ***to nie ~a*** that is nothing new; **~ka** (*-i*; *G -nek*) → ***nowina***
nowiut(eń)ki brand new

N

nowo|czesny (**-śnie**) modern; **~modny** newfangled; **~roczny** New Year's; **~rodek** *m* (*-dka*; *-dki*) newborn baby
nowość *f* (*-ści*) novelty
nowo|twór *m* (*-woru*; *-wory*) *med.* tumo(u)r; **~żeniec** *m* (*-ńca*; *-ńcy*) newlywed; **~żytny** modern
now|y new; ***~y Rok*** New Year; ***od ~a, na ~o*** anew, afresh; ***po ~emu*** in a new way; ***~e*** *n* (*-ego*; *0*) the latest; ***co ~ego?*** what's new?
Nowy Jork *m* New York
Nowy Orlean *m* New Orleans
nozdrze *n* (*-a*; *-y*) nostril
noż|e *pl.* → ***nóż***; **~ny** foot; **~ownik** *m* (*-a*; *-cy*) knifeman; **~yce** *f/pl.* (-), **~yczki** *f/pl.* (*-czek*) scissors *pl.*
nów *m* (*GL nowiu*; *0*) new moon
nóż *m* (*noża*; *noże*, *noży*) knife; ***~ do*** (***otwierania***) ***konserw*** *Brt.* tin opener, *Am.* can opener; ***być na noże*** (***z*** *I*) be in conflict (with), fight (with *lub* against); ***mieć ~ na gardle*** be pinned into a tight corner
nóżka *f* (*-i*; *G -żek*) → ***noga***; (*grzyba*, *kieliszka*) stem
np. *skrót pisany*: ***na przykład*** e.g. (*for example*)
n.p.m. *skrót pisany*: ***nad poziomem morza*** a.s.l. (*above sea level*)
nr *skrót pisany*: ***numer*** No (*number*)
NSA *skrót pisany*: ***Naczelny Sąd Administracyjny*** Chief Administrative Court
nucić (*-cę*) hum
nud|a *f* (*-y*; *-y*, *-ów*) boredom; ***z ~ów*** out of boredom; **~ności** *f/pl.* nausea; **~ny** boring, dull
nudyst|a *m* (*-y*; *-yści*), **~ka** *f* (*-i*; *G -tek*) nudist; **~yczny** nudist
nudzi|ara *f* (*-y*; *G* -), **~arz** *m* (*-a*; *-e*) bore, nuisance; **~ć** (*-dzę*) bore; ***~ć się*** be bored; → ***mdlić***
numer *m* (*-u*; *-y*) number (*skrót*: No.); (*butów itp.*) size; (*czasopisma*) issue; (*w kabarecie*) act; ***~ rejestracyjny*** *mot.* registration number; **~ować** ⟨**po-**⟩ (*-uję*) number;
nuncjusz *m* (*-a*; *-e*) *rel.* nuncio
nur *m* (*-a*; *-y*): ***dać ~a*** dive; **~ek** *m* (*-rka*; *-rkowie*) diver; ***dać ~ka*** → ***nur***; **~ka** *f* (*-i*; *G -rek*) → ***norka***
nurkow|ać (*-uję*) dive; **~y** diving; ***lot ~y*** nose-dive
nurt *m* (*-u*; *-y*) current; trend; ***~y*** *pl. też* waters *pl.*; **~ować** (*-uję*; *t-ko 3. os.*) be on *s.o.'s* mind; (*dręczyć*) torment
nurzać (*-am*) immerse; dip; ***~ się*** (***w*** *L*) wallow (in); revel (in)
nut|a *f* (*-y*; *G* -) *mus.* note (*też fig.*); ***cała ~a*** *Brt.* semibreve, *Am.* whole note; **~owy** note
nuż: ***a ~*** what if
nuż|ący (**-co**) tiring, tiresome; **~yć** ⟨**z-**⟩ (*-ę*) tire, exhaust
nygus F *m* (*-a*; *-i*) loafer
nylon *m* (*-u*; *-y*) nylon; **~owy** nylon

O

O

o[1] *prp.* (*L*, *A*) about, on; ***mówił ~ tobie*** he was talking about you; ***niepokoić się ~ dzieci*** worry about the children; ***pytać ~ drogę*** ask about the way; *godzina, pora*: at; ***~ świcie*** at dawn; *cecha*: with; ***~ jasnych włosach*** with fair hair; *styczność*: against; ***oprzeć ~ ścianę*** lean against the wall; *sposób*: on, with; ***chodzić ~ lasce*** walk with a stick; ***~ kulach*** on crutches; ***~ własnych siłach*** by one's own efforts; *może być tłumaczony przez złożenie*: ***~ napędzie silnikowym*** motor-driven
o[2] *int.* oh; ***~ tak!*** oh, yes!
oaza *f* (*-y*; *G* -) oasis
ob. *skrót pisany*: ***obywatel***(***ka***) citizen
oba, ~j *num.* both
obal|ać (*-am*)⟨**~ić**⟩(*-lę*) *v/t.* knock down; *władzę* overthrow; *prawo*, *zwyczaje* abolish; *teorię* disprove; **~enie** *n* (*-a*; *G -ń*) *fig.* overturn, overthrow; *jur.* abolition
obandażowany *med.* bandaged
obarcz|ać (*-am*) ⟨**~yć**⟩ (*-ę*) (**k-o** *I*) burden (with), overburden (with); ***~ać*** ⟨**~yć**⟩ ***się*** (*I*) burden (o.s.); ***~ony rodziną*** with a family
obaw|a *f* (*-y*; *G* -) fear, anxiety; *pl. też* doubt; ***z ~y przed*** (*I*) for fear of; ***mieć***

lub **żywić ~y** fear, be afraid; **~iać się** (*-am*) (*G*) be afraid (of); (**o** *A*) be worried (about)
obcas *m* (*-a*; *-y*) heel
obcesow|o brusquely, bluntly; **~y** brusque, blunt
obcęgi *pl.* pincers *pl.*
obcho|dzenie się *n* (*-a*; *0*) (**z** *I*) handling (of); dealing (with); **~dzić** pace out, walk around; *przeszkodę*, *prawo* go round; (*interesować się*) concern, interest, care; *rocznicę* celebrate, commemorate; ***~dzić sklepy*** do the rounds of the shops; ***~dzić się*** (**z** *I*) treat, handle; use, operate; (**bez** *G*) go (without), do (without)
obchód *m* round; patrol; ***obchody*** *pl.* celebrations *pl.*, festivities *pl.*
obcią|ć *pf.* → ***obcinać***; **~gać** (*-am*) ⟨***~gnąć***⟩ (*I*) cover (with); *suknię itp.* straighten; **~żać** (*-am*) ⟨***~żyć***⟩ load (*I* with; **się** o.s.); weight, weigh down; *fig.* burden; (*też fin.*, *jur.*) charge; *jur.* incriminate; → ***obarczać***; **~żenie** *n* (*-a*; *G -eń*) load; drain; *electr.* load; *tech.* ballast; ***~żenie dziedziczne*** inherited susceptibility to a disease
ob|cierać (*-am*) wipe off/away; rub; ***~cierać się*** wipe; **~cięcie** *n* cutting; clipping; (*zarobków*) (*G*) cut (in); **~cinać** (*-am*) cut off; clip; *fig.* restrict; F (*na egzaminie*) fail, *Am.* flunk; **~ciosywać** (*-uję*) → ***ciosać***; **~cisły** skin-tight
obco *adv.* (*czuć się*) foreign, strange; **~języczny** foreign-language; **~krajowiec** *m* foreigner; **~ść** *f* (*-ści*; *0*) strangeness, foreignness; **~wać** (*-uję*) (**z** *I*) associate (with); mix (with); **~wanie** *n* (*-a*; *0*) (**z** *I*) association (with), mixing (with); dealings *pl.* (with)
ob|cy 1. somebody else's, other people's; strange; foreign; **2.** *m* (*-ego*; *-cy*), **~ca** *f* (*-ej*; *-ce*) stranger; outsider; **~czyzna** *f* (*-y*; *0*) foreign lands *pl.*; ***na ~czyźnie*** in exile
obdarow(yw)ać (*-[w]uję*) present
obdarty shabby, ragged
obdarzać (*-am*) → ***darzyć***
obdrapany scratched
obdukcja *f* (*-i*; *-e*) *jur.* autopsy, post-mortem
obdzie|lać (*-am*)⟨***~lić***⟩(***k-o*** *I*) distribute (to); hand out (to); **~rać** (*-am*) (*ze skóry*) skin; *skórę* graze; *korę* bark; *fig.* (***k-o*** **z** *G*) rob (of); F ***~rać ze skóry*** (*A*) fleece
obecn|ie *adv.* at present, now; **~ość** *f* (*-ści*; *0*) presence; ***lista ~ości*** attendance list; **~y** present (**przy** *L* at; **na** *L* in); current; ***~i*** *pl.* those *pl.* present
obedrzeć *pf.* → ***obdzierać***
obejmować (*-uję*) embrace, hug (**się** *v/i.*); (*zawierać*, *włączać*) include; *urząd*, *rządy* take; *okres* span; *lęk*: overcome; *płomienie*: catch; *umysłem* grasp; *wzrokiem* take in
obej|rzeć *pf.* → ***oglądać***; **~rzenie** *n*: ***do ~rzenia*** for inspection; **~ście** *n* **1.** (*-a*; *G -ść*) *dom* farmstead; **2.** (*-a*; *0*) manner *pl.*; ***miły w ~ściu*** charming, pleasant; **~ść** *pf.* (→ ***-jść***) → ***obchodzić***
obel|ga *f* (*-i*; *G-*) insult, ***~gi*** *pl.* abuse; **~żywie** *adv.* insultingly; offensively; abusively; **~żywy** insulting; offensive; abusive
oberwa|ć *pf.* → ***obrywać***; **~nie** *n*: ***~nie*** (***się***) ***chmury*** cloudburst; **~ny** ragged; → ***obdarty***
oberża *f* (*-y*; *G -*) inn
oberżnąć *pf.* → ***obrzynać***
oberżyna *f* (*-y*; *G -*) → ***bakłażan***
obe|schnąć *pf.* → ***obsychać***; **~trzeć** *pf.* → ***obcierać***; **~znany** familiar (**z** *I* with)
obezwładni|ać (*-am*) ⟨**~ć**⟩ (*-ę*, *-nij!*) overpower; *uczucie*: overwhelm, overcome
obeżreć *pf.* → ***obżerać***
obfi|cie *adv.* → ***obfity***; **~tość** *f* (*-ści*; *0*) abundance; ***róg ~tości*** horn of plenty, *fig.* cornucopia; **~tować** (*-uję*) (**w** *A*) abound (with), teem (with); **~ty** abundant; plentiful; *porcja* generous
obgry|zać ⟨***~źć***⟩ → ***ogryzać***
obiad *m* (*-u*; *-y*) (*wieczorem*) dinner; (*w południe*) lunch; ***jeść ~*** have dinner/lunch; **~owy** dinner, lunch
obibok *m* (*-a*; *-i*) loafer
obi|cie *n* (*-a*; *G -ć*) upholstery; **~ć** *pf.* → ***obijać***; **~e** *num. f/pl.* → ***oba***
obiec|ać *pf.* (*-am*) → ***obiecywać***; **~anka** *f* (*-i*; *G -nek*) empty promise; **~ująco** promisingly; **~ujący** promising; **~ywać** (*-uję*) promise; ***~ywać sobie po*** (*L*) hope for
obieg *m* (*-u*; *0*) *astr.*, *phys.* rotation, revolution; (***krwi*** blood) circulation; ***czas ~u*** *astr.* period; ***puścić w ~*** circulate; ***wycofać z ~u*** withdraw from circulation; **~ać** ⟨***~nąć***⟩ (*-am*) circulate,

go (a)round; *astr.* revolve; *sklepy itp.* do the rounds of; **~owy** current; ***pieniądz ~owy*** currency
obiek|cja *f* (*-i*; *-e*) objection; reservation; **~tyw** *m* (*-u*; *-y*) *phot.* lens *sg.*; **~tywny** objective
obie|rać (*-am*) *warzywa* peel; *owoce* skin; *os., zawód* go into; (*na stanowisko*) choose, appoint; **~ralny** elected; **~rki** *f/pl.* (*-rek*), **~rzyny** *f/pl.* (-) peelings *pl.*
obietnica *f* (*-y*; *G* -) promise
obieżyświat F *m* (*-a*; *-y*) globetrotter
obijać (*-am*) (*młotkiem itp.*) knock off; *kubek itp.* chip; *krzesło* upholster; ***~ się o uszy*** come to one's ears; ***~ się*** F loaf about/around
objadać się F gorge o.s., stuff o.s.
objaśni|ać (*-am*) 〈***~ć***〉 (*-ę*, *nij!*) explain; **~enie** *n* (*-a*) explanation
obja|w *m* (*-u*; *-y*) symptom (*też med.*); **~wiać** (*-am*) 〈***~wić***〉 manifest; show, reveal (***się*** o.s.); **~wienie** *n* (*-a*; *G -eń*) revelation (*też rel.*)
objazd *m* (*-u*; *-y*) detour; diversion; (*artystyczny*) tour; **~owy** itinerant; *wystawa itp.* touring; ***droga ~owa*** bypass
ob|jąć *pf.* (*-ejmę*) → ***obejmować***; **~jeść** *pf.* → ***objadać***; **~jeżdżać** (*-am*) 〈***~jechać***〉 *przeszkodę*, *plac* go round; *kraj* travel around; **~jęcie** *n* (*-a*; *G -ęć*) embrace, hug; beginning; taking over; takeover; ***w ~jęciach*** (*G*) in the arms (of); → ***obejmować***
objętość *f* (*-ści*; *0*) volume; capacity; size
ob|juczony (*I*) loaded (with), laden (with); **~kła-**, **~ko-**, **~kra-** → ***okła-***, ***oko-***, ***okra-***; **~lać** *pf.* → ***oblewać***; **~latany** F *fig.* knowledgeable, well-versed; **~latywać** (*-uję*) 〈***~lecieć***〉 *v/t.* fly (a)round; (*wypróbować samolot*) test-fly; ***~latywać sklepy*** F do the rounds of the shops; **~legać** (*-am*) 〈***~lec***, ***~legnąć***〉 besiege
oble|piać (*-am*) 〈***~pić***〉 stick all over (*ścianę itp.*); **~śny** lecherous; lascivious; **~wać** (*-am*) douse; *wody*: wash; *fig.* (*ogarnąć*) flood; F *egzamin* fail; ***~wać się potem*** be bathed in sweat; **~wanie** *n* (*mieszkania*) house-warming (party); **~źć** *pf.* → ***obłazić***
oblężenie *n* (*-a*) siege
obli|cow(yw)ać (*-[w]uję*) *bud.* face; **~czać** (*-am*) count; calculate; **~czalny** calculable
oblicz|e *n* (*-a*; *G* -) *lit.* countenance, face; ***w ~u*** (*G*) in the face (of), in view (of); **~enie** *n* (*-a*) calculation; count; **~eniowy** computational; **~yć** *pf.* → ***obliczać***
obligacja *f* (*-i*; *-e*) *econ.* bond, stock
obliz|ywać (*-uję*) 〈***~ać***〉 lick
ob|lodzić (*-dzę*) ice up; **~lodzony** icy; **~luzowany** loose
obła|dow(yw)ać (*-[w]uję*) load, weigh; **~mywać** (*-uję*) 〈***~mać***〉 break (***się*** *v/i.*); **~piać** F (*-am*) 〈***~pić***〉 (*-ę*) neck; **~skawiony** tame(d); **~wa** *f* (*-y*; *G* -) hunt; (*na człowieka*) manhunt; **~zić** *robaki*: cover (with); *farba*: peel off
obłąka|nie *n* (*-a*; *0*) → ***obłęd***; **~niec** F (*-ńca*; *-ńcy*) madman *m*, madwoman *f*; **~ny**, **~ńczy** mad, insane
obłęd *m* (*-u*; *-y*) madness, insanity; **~ny** F terrific
obłok *m* (*-u*; *-i*) cloud
obło|wić się *pf.* F (***na*** *L*) make a profit (from); **~żny**: ***~żna choroba*** serious illness; ***~żnie chory*** bed-ridden; **~żyć** *pf.* → ***okładać***
obłożony: ***~ język*** coated tongue
obłud|a *f* (*-y*; *0*) hypocrisy; **~nica** *f* (*-y*; *G* -), **~nik** *m* (*-a*; *-cy*) hypocrite; **~ny** hypocritical, false
obłu|pywać (*-uję*) 〈***~pać***〉 peel; *jajko* shell; **~skiwać** (*-uję*) shell; → ***łuskać***
obły oval
obmac|ywać (*-uję*) 〈***~ać***〉 → ***macać***
obmarz|ać [-r·z-] (*-am*) 〈***~nąć***〉 ice up; freeze over
ob|mawiać (*-am*) slander, backbite; **~mierzać** (*-am*) 〈***~mierzyć***〉 measure; **~mierzły** [-r·z-] nasty; **~mowa** *f* (*-y*; *G -mów*) slander, backbiting; **~mówić** *pf.* → ***obmawiać***; **~murow(yw)ać** (*-[w]uję*) wall, surround with a wall; **~myć** *pf.* → ***obmywać***; **~myślać** (*-am*) 〈***~myślić***〉 devise, think out; **~mywać** (*-am*) bathe, wash; *fale*: wash
obnaż|ać (*-am*) 〈***~yć***〉 (*-ę*) bare, uncover; *fig.* reveal; ***~ać się*** take one's clothes off; *fig.* expose o.s.; **~ony** bare; naked; *fig.* reveal
obniż|ać (*-am*) 〈***~yć***〉 lower; *econ. też* reduce; ***~ać się*** sink, come down; subside; **~ka** *f* (*-i*; *G -żek*) (***cen***, ***kosztów*** price, cost) reduction; ***~ka płac*** wage cut
obnosić pass round, show round
obojczyk *m* (*-a*; *-i*) *anat.* collar-bone, clavicle

oboje → ***obaj***
obojętn|ieć ⟨**z-**⟩ (*-eję*) become indifferent (***na*** *A* to); **~ość** *f* (*-ści*; *0*) indifference; **~y** indifferent; (*nijaki*) bland; ***to mi ~e*** I do not care
obojnak *m* (*-a*; *-i*) hermaphrodite
obok 1. *adv.* nearby, next to, past; ***tuż ~***, ***~ siebie*** side by side; **2.** *prp.* beside, by, near
obolały sore, painful, aching
OBOP *skrót*: ***Ośrodek Badania Opinii Publicznej*** Centre for Research of Public Opinion
obopólny mutual, reciprocal
obor|a *f* (*-y*; *G obór*) cowshed, *Am.* barn; **~nik** *m* (*-a*; *0*) manure
obosieczny double-edged
obostrz|ać (*-am*) ⟨***~yć***⟩ make more severe, tighten; **~enie** *n* (*-a*; *G -eń*) tightening; greater severity
obowiąz|any obliged (***do*** *G* to); **~ek** *m* (*-zku*; *-zki*) obligation; ***poczuwać się do ~ku*** feel obliged; ***pełniący ~ki*** (*G*) acting, deputy; **~kowo** *adv.* obligatorily; → ***obowiązkowy***; **~kowość** *f* (*-ści*; *0*) sense of duty; **~kowy** obligatory, compulsory; *człowiek* conscientious; **~ujący** valid, in force, binding; ***nadać moc ~ującą*** bring into force; **~ywać** (*-uję*, *t-ko 3. os.*) be in force, hold
obozow|ać (*-uję*) camp (out); **~isko** *n* (*-a*; *G -*) camping site, campsite; **~y** camp, camping
obój *m* (*-boju*; *-boje*) *mus.* oboe
obóz *m* (*-bozu*; *-bozy*) camp; ***stanąć obozem*** set up camp
obrabia|ć (*-am*) work; machine; *ziemię* cultivate, till; *brzeg* hem; **~rka** *f* (*-i*; *G -rek*) machine tool
obra|bow(yw)ać (*-[w]uję*) rob; **~cać** (*-am*) turn; use; ***~cać na kupno*** use for buying; reduce ***~cać w gruzy*** reduce to rabble; ***~cać się*** turn, rotate, spin; revolve; **~chow(yw)ać** (*-[w]uję*) → ***obliczać***; **~chunek** *m* reckoning
obrać *pf.* → ***obierać***
obrad|y *pl.* (*G -*) proceedings *pl.*, debate; **~ować** (*-uję*) (***nad*** *I*) debate
obra|dzać (*-am*) *roślina*: produce a good crop; **~mow(yw)ać** (*-[w]uję*) border; frame; **~stać** (*-am*) (*I*) grow over (with); be overgrown (with)
obraz *m* (*-u*; *-y*) picture; painting; film, *Am.* movie
obraza *f* (*-y*; *zw. 0*) offence, *Am.* offense; outrage; ***~ moralności publicznej*** indecency
obrazek *m* (*-zka*; *-zki*) → ***obraz***
obrazić *pf.* → ***obrażać***
obraz|kowy picture; **~ować** ⟨**z-**⟩ (*-uję*) portray; depict; **~owo** graphically, vividly; **~owy** graphic, vivid
obra|źliwie *adv.* offensively, insultingly; **~źliwy** offensive, insulting; **~żać** (*-am*) offend, insult; **~żenie** *n* (*-a*; *G -eń*) injury; **~żony** offended, insulted
obrąb|ywać (*-uję*) ⟨***~ać***⟩ chop off
obrączka *f* (*-i*; *G -czek*) (*ślubna*) ring; → ***obręcz***
obręb *m* (*-u*; *-y*) area; ***w ~ie*** within, inside; ***poza ~em*** outside; **~ek** *m* (*-bka*; *-bki*) hem; **~iać** (*-am*) ⟨***~ić***⟩ (*-ę*) hem
obręcz *f* (*-y*; *-e*, *-y*) hoop, ring; (*koła*) (wheel) rim
obr/min *skrót pisany*: ***obrotów na minutę*** rpm (*revolutions per minute*)
obro|bić *pf.* → ***obrabiać***; **~dzić** *pf.* → ***obradzać***; **~k** *m* (*-u*; *-i*) horse feed, provender
obro|na *f* (*-y*; *G -*) defence, *Am.* defense; ***~na własna*** self-defence; ***stawać w ~nie*** (*G*) stand up (for); → ***bronić***; **~nny** defence; **~ńca** *m* (*-y*; *G -ów*); **~ńczyni** *f* (*-ni*; *-e*, *G -yń*) defender (*też sport*); *fig.* protector; **~ńcy** *pl.* (*w sporcie*) defence; **~ńczy** *jur.*: ***mowa ~ńcza*** final speech, speech for the defence
obro|snąć *pf.* → ***obrastać***; **~śnięty** (*I*) overgrown (with)
obrotn|ość *f* (*-ści*; *0*) resourcefulness, ingenuity; **~y** resourceful, ingenuous
obrotomierz *m* (*-a*; *-e*) *mot.* tachometer, rev counter
obrotow|y revolving; *krzesło* swivel; *econ.* sales, turnover; ***środki*** *pl.* ***~e*** active assets *pl.*
obroża *f* (*-y*; *-e*) collar
obróbka *f* (*-i*; *G -bek*) processing; *tech.* working
obró|cić *pf.* → ***obracać***; **~t** *m* (*-rotu*; *-roty*) turn; revolution; rotation; *econ.* turnover; *fig.* turn (***na*** *A* for); ***wziąć w obroty*** (*A*) F give a talking-to
obrumieni|ać (*-am*) ⟨***~ć***⟩ *gastr.* brown
obrus *m* (*-a*; *-y*) tablecloth
obrys *m* (*-u*; *-y*) outline
obrywać (*-am*) tear down; *owoce* pick; ***~ się*** come off

obryzgiwać (*-uję*) ⟨**~ać**⟩ splash
obrządek *m* (*-dku*; *-dki*) ritual; rite
obrzez|ać (*-am*) circumcise; **~anie** *n* (*-a*; *G -ań*) circumcision
obrzeże *n* (*-a*; *G -y*) edge
obrzęd *m* (*-u*; *-y*) ceremony; → ***obrządek***; **~owy** ceremonial; ritual
obrzęk *m* (*-u*; *-i*) *med.* (o)edema; **~ać** (*-am*) ⟨**~nąć**⟩ (*-nę*) *med.* swell (up); **~ły** swollen
obrzmi|ałość *f* (*-ści*), **~enie** *n* (*-a*; *-eń*) swelling; **~ały** bloated; → ***obrzękły***
obrzuc|ać (*-am*) ⟨**~ić**⟩ throw; pelt (**się** at each other); ***~ić wzrokiem*** (*A*) cast a glance (at)
obrzyd|listwo *n* (*-a*; *G -*) disgusting thing; repulsiveness; **~liwiec** *m* (*-wca*; *-wcy*) scoundrel; **~liwość** *n* (*-ści*; *0*) abomination; **~liwy** (**-*wie***), **~ły** disgusting, repulsive; **~nąć** (*-nę*) *pf.*: ***~ł(a)/~ło mi ...*** I am sick of…; → ***brzydnąć***
obrzydz|ać (*-am*) ⟨**~ić**⟩ spoil, put off; **~enie** *n* (*-a*; *0*) disgust; loathing; revulsion; ***do ~enia*** until one has wearied
obrzynać (*-am*) cut off
obsa|da *f* (*-y*; *G -*) *theat.* cast, casting; (*załoga*) crew; personnel; *tech.* holder, mounting; **~dka** *f* (*-i*; *G -dek*) holder; **~dzać** (*-am*) ⟨**~dzić**⟩ (*I*) plant (with); *fig.* fill, cast; → ***osadzać***
obserwa|cja *f* (*-i*; *-e*) observation; **~cyjny** observational; **~tor** *m* (*-a*; *-rzy*) observer; **~torium** *n* (*idkl.*; *-ia*, *-iów*) observatory; **~torka** *f* (*-i*) observer
obserwować (*-uję*) ⟨**za-**⟩ watch; observe
obsług|a *f* (*-i*; *G -*) service; handling; (*personel*) staff; **~iwać** (*-uję*) serve, deal with
obstaw|a *f* (*-y*; *G -*) *zbior.* F guard; **~ać** (*-ję*) (***przy*** *L*) insist (on), persist (in); **~i(a)ć** (*I*) surround; *pieniądze* bet (on), stake (on)
obst|ępować (*-uję*) ⟨**~ąpić**⟩ surround, ring
obstrukcja *f* (*-i*; *-e*) obstruction; *med.* constipation
obstrz|ał *m* (*-u*; *-y*) shelling, shooting; **~eliwać** (*-wuję*) ⟨**~elać**⟩ (*A*) shoot (at), fire (at)
obsu|wać się ⟨**~nąć się**⟩ slip
obsy|chać (*-am*) dry; **~pywać** (*-uję*) ⟨**~pać**⟩ scatter, sprinkle; *fig.* heap, shower; ***~p(yw)ać się*** crumble away
obszar *m* (*-u*; *-y*) area, region; territory; **~nik** *m* (*-a*; *-cy*) big landowner
obszarpany ragged
obszerny large, extensive; *ubranie* loose
obszy|cie *n* (*-a*; *G -yć*) trimming, edging; **~wać** (*-am*) ⟨**~ć**⟩ (*I*) trim (with), edge (with)
obt|aczać ⟨**~oczyć**⟩ roll; ***~aczać w mące*** toss in flour; *tech.* turn
obtarcie *n* (*-a*; *G -rć*) *med.* abrasion, graze; (*szmatą itp.*) wipe
obu *num.* → ***oba***; *w złoż.* bi-, di-, two-
obuch *m* (*-a*; *-y*) poll
obudow|a *f* (*-y*; *G -dów*) casing, housing; **~(yw)ać** (*-[w]uję*) (*I*) build up; encase
obudzić *pf.* → ***budzić***
obukierunkowy two-way
ob|umarły dead; **~umierać** ⟨**~umrzeć**⟩ die; *fig.* die out
oburącz *adv.* with both hands
oburz|ać (*-am*) ⟨**~yć**⟩ outrage, incense; ***~ać się*** become outraged *lub* indignant (***na*** *A* about); **~ająco** *adv.* outrageously; **~ający** outrageous; **~enie** *n* (*-a*; *0*) outrage; indignation; **~ony** indignant, incensed
obustron|nie *adv.* mutually; bilaterally; **~ny** mutual; bilateral
obuwie *n* (*-a*; *0*) shoes *pl.*, footgear; ***sklep z ~m*** shoe shop/store
obwa|łow(yw)ać (*-[w]uję*) *rzekę* embank; **~rowanie** *n* (*-a*; *G -ań*) embankment
obwarzanek *m* (*-nka*; *-nki*) pretzel
obwąch|iwać (*-uję*) ⟨**~ać**⟩ sniff
obwiąz|ywać (*-uję*) ⟨**~ać**⟩ (*I*) tie up (with); wrap (with)
obwie|szczać (*-am*) ⟨**~ścić**⟩ announce; make public; **~szczenie** *n* (*-a*; *G -eń*) announcement; public notice; **~źć** *pf.* → ***obwozić***
obwi|jać → ***owijać***; **~niać** (*-am*) ⟨**~nić**⟩ (***k-o o*** *A*) blame (s.o. for); **~sać** (*-am*) ⟨**~snąć**⟩ droop, sag
obwo|dnica *f* (*-y*; *-e*) *Brt.* ring road; bypass, *Am.* belt(way); **~dowy** peripheral; district; **~luta** *f* (*-y*; *G -*) dust jacket; **~ływać** (*-uję*) ⟨**~łać**⟩ (*I*) proclaim; **~zić** drive round (***po mieście*** the town)
obwód *m* (*-odu*; *-ody*) perimeter; *math.* circumference; (*obszar*) district; *electr.* circuit; ***~ scalony*** integrated circuit; **~ka** *f* (*-i*; *G -dek*) border, edge

oby *part.* may it be so; **~ był szczęśliwy!** may he be happy!
obycie *n* (-*a*; *0*) good manners *pl.*; **~ w świecie** worldliness
obyczaj *m* (-*u*; -*e*, -*ów*) custom; *pl. też* morals *pl.*; **starym ~em** in accordance with an old custom; **zepsucie ~ów** moral decline; **~owość** *f* (-*ści*; *0*) custom, customs *pl.*; morals *pl.*; **~owy** moral; *policja*: vice
obyć się *pf.* → **obywać się**
obydw|a(j), ~ie, ~oje → **oba, oboje**
oby|ty polite, well-bred; (**z** *I*) experienced (with), familiar (with); **~wać się** (**bez** *G*) do without, go without; (*I*) make do (without), content o.s. (with)
obywatel *m* (-*a*; -*e*), **~ka** *f* (-*i*; *G* -*lek*) citizen; national; **~ski** civic; civil; **~stwo** *n* (-*a*; *G* -) citizenship; nationality
obżar|stwo *f* (-*a*; *0*) gluttony; **~tuch** *m* (-*a*; -*y*) F pig, glutton
OC *skrót pisany*: **ubezpieczenie OC** (**odpowiedzialności cywilnej**) *mot* third party insurance
ocal|ać (-*am*) → **ocalić**; **~eć** (-*eję*) (**z** *G*) survive (from); **~eć od śmierci** escape death; **~enie** *n* (-*a*) rescue; salvation; saving; **~ić** *pf.* (-*ę*) (**od** *G*) save (from)
ocean *m* (-*u*; -*y*) ocean
ocen|a *f* (-*y*; *G* -) assessment, valuation; estimate; (*w szkole*) *Brt.* mark, *Am.* grade; **~iać** (-*am*) ⟨**~ić**⟩ assess, evaluate; estimate; *Brt.* mark, *Am.* grade
ocet *m* (*octu*; *octy*) vinegar
ochładzać (-*am*) → **chłodzić**
ochłap *m* (-*u*; -*y*) scrap of meat
ochł|odzenie *n* (-*a*; *G* -*eń*) cooling; **~onąć** *pf.* cool down; calm down; **~onąć z szoku** recover from shock
ocho|czo *adv.* willingly; eagerly; **~czy** eager; cheerful; (**do** *G*) → **chętny**; **~ta** *f* (-*y*; *0*) desire, willingness; **mieć ~tę na** (*A*) feel like doing; → **chęć**
ochotni|czka *f* (-*i*; *G* -*czek*) volunteer; **~czo** *adv.* voluntarily; **~czy** voluntary; **~k** *m* (-*a*; -*cy*) volunteer
ochra *f* (-*y*; *0*) ochre
ochrania|cz *m* (-*a*; -*e*) guard; pad; **~ć** (-*am*) protect, shelter (**od** *G* from, against)
ochron|a *f* (-*y*; *G* -) protection; (*osoba*) bodyguard; **~a środowiska naturalnego** conservation; **~iarz** *m* (-*a*; -*e*) F bodyguard; **~ić** *pf.* (-*nię*) → **ochraniać, chronić**; **~ny** protective
ochryp|le hoarsely; **~ły** hoarse, husky; → **chrypnąć**
ochrzanić F *pf.* (-*ę*) rap
ociągać się (-*am*) (**z** *I*) dawdle (over)
ocie|kać (-*am*) (*I*) be dripping wet; drip (with); **~lić się** *pf.* calf
ociemniały (*m-os* -*li*) blind; **związek ~ch** organization of the blind
ocieplać (-*am*) ⟨**~ić**⟩ (-*lę*) warm; *budynek itp.* insulate; **~ać się** get warm; **~enie** *n* (-*a*; *0*) warming up; insulation
ocierać (-*am*) → **obcierać**; *skórę* chafe
ociąża|le heavily; **~ły** heavy
ocios|ywać (-*uję*) ⟨**~ać**⟩ hew
ocknąć się *pf.* (-*nę*) wake up; (*po omdleniu itp.*) come round
ocleni|e *n* payment of duty; **podlegający ~u** dutiable; **nie mieć nic do ~a** have nothing to declare
oclić *pf.* → **clić**
oct|an *m* (-*u*; -*y*) *chem.* acetate; **~owy** vinegar
o|cukrzyć *pf.* → **cukrzyć**; **~cyganić** F *pf.* con, diddle; **~czarow(yw)ać** (-[*w*]*uję*) charm, enthral(l)
oczekiw|ać (-*uję*) expect (**po kimś** from s.o.); wait (**na** *A* for); **~anie** *n* (-*a*) expectation; waiting; **wbrew ~aniom** contrary to expectation
oczerni|ać (-*am*) ⟨**~ć**⟩ *fig.* blacken; defame
ocz|ko *n* (-*a*; *G* -*czek*) → **oko**; (*na karcie*) pip; (*gra w karty*) blackjack; (*w pończosze*) *Brt.* ladder, *Am.* run; (*przy dzierganiu*) stitch; (*w pierścionku*) stone; (*w sieci*) mesh; **~ny** eye; *anat.* ocular; optic; **~odół** *m anat.* eye-socket, orbit; **~y** *pl.* → **oko**
oczyszcza|ć (-*am*) (**z** *G*) clean (from/off), clear (from), *fig.* exonerate (from); *por.* **czyścić**; **~lnia** *f* (-*i*; -*e*) (*ścieków*) sewage treatment plant; **~nie** *n* (-*a*; *G* -*ań*) cleaning; clearing
oczy|tany well-read; **~wisty** obvious, evident; **~wiście** *adv.* obviously, evidently
od *prp.* (*G*) from; (*czasu*) since, for; (*niż*) than; (*przeciw*) against, for; **~ morza** from the sea; **~ rana** since the morning; **~ 2 godzin** for 2 hours; **starszy ~e mnie** older than me; **~ kaszlu** for coughing, against coughing; *często nie*

tłumaczy się: ***dziurka ~ klucza*** keyhole; ***~ ręki*** right away; *por.* ***dla, do***

odb. *skrót pisany*: **odbiorca** addressee

odbarwi|ać (*-am*) ⟨**~ć**⟩ discolo(u)r (**się** *v/i.*)

odbezpiecz|ać (*-am*) ⟨**~yć**⟩ (*-ę*) *broń* release the safety catch

odbi|cie *n* reflection; image; (*piłki*) hitting off; (*kraju*) reconquest; (*uwolnienie*) release; ***~cie od brzegu*** *naut.* cast-off; ***kąt ~cia*** angle of reflection; **~ć** *pf.* → ***odbijać***

odbie|c *pf.*, **~gać** ⟨**~gnąć**⟩ (**od** *A*) run away (from); *fig.* differ (from), deviate (from); ***~gł go sen*** he was unable to sleep; ***~gła ją chęć na to*** she no longer took pleasure in it; **~rać** (*-am*) (**od** *G*) take away (from); *paczkę* collect (from), reclaim; *dziecko* pick up; *przysięgę, towar, RTV*: receive (from); *telefon* answer; → ***odebrać***

odbijać (*-am*) *v/t. światło* reflect, throw back; *pieczęć* imprint; *deseń* print; (*na kopiarce*) run off; *tynk itp.* knock off; *atak* fend off; *piłkę* return; *jeńców* rescue; *miasto itp.* win back; (*w tańcu*) cut in; *sympatię* steal; *v/i. łódź*: cast off; ***~ się*** be reflected; *głos*: echo, resound; *piłka*: bounce; *narciarz*: push off; *ślad*: leave marks; *fig.* have an effect (**na** *A* on); F (*po jedzeniu*) belch, *dziecko*: burp

odbior|ca *m* (*-y*; *G -ców*), **~czyni** *f* (*-i*; *-e*) receiver; recipient; **~czy** receiving; **~nik** *m* (*-a*; *-i*) *RTV*: receiver, set

od|biór *m* (*-oru*; *0*) reception; **~bitka** *f* (*-i*; *G -tek*) *phot.*, *print.* copy; **~bity** *światło* reflected; **~blask** *m* reflection; **~blaskowy** *tech.* reflective; **~błyśnik** *m* (*-a*; *-i*) reflector

odbudo|wa *f* restoration; re-building; **~w(yw)ać** (*-[w]uję*) restore, re-build

odby|cie *n* (*-a*; *0*): ***~cie kary*** serving of sentence; ***w celu ~cia rozmów*** to carry out negotiations; **~ć** *pf.* → ***odbywać***

odbytnica *f* (*-y*; *-e*, *G -*) *anat.* rectum

odbywać *zebranie* hold; *studia* pursue; *służbę*, *karę* serve, go through; *podróż* make; **~ się** take place

odc. *skrót pisany*: **odcinek** sector

odcho|dy *pl.* (*-ów*) excrements *pl.*, f(a)eces *pl.*; **~dzić** go away; *pociąg itp.*: leave, depart; *ulica*: branch (off), diverge; (*z pracy*) (**z** *G*) quit, leave; (**od** *G*) leave; (*umrzeć*) depart from this world; *fig.* leave; ***~dzić od zmysłów*** be out of one's senses

od|chrząknąć *pf.* clear one's throat; → ***chrząkać***; **~chudzać się** (*-am*) slim

odchyl|ać (*-am*) ⟨**~ić**⟩ deflect (**się** *v/i.*); (**do tyłu**) bend back (**się** *v/i.*); *firankę* draw back; ***~ać się*** deflect; deviate (**od** *G* from); **~enie** *n* (*-a*) deviation; departure

odcią|ć *pf.* → ***odcinać***; **~gać** (*-am*) ⟨**~gnąć**⟩ *v/t.* draw back; pull away; *fig.* dissuade (**od** *G* from); *uwagę* divert; ***mleko ~gane*** *Brt.* skimmed milk, *Am.* skim milk; **~żać** (*-am*) ⟨**~żyć**⟩ lighten, relieve

odcie|kać (*-am*) ⟨**~c**⟩ drain away

od|cień *m* (*-nia*; *-nie*) shade; tone; nuance; **~cierpieć** *pf.* (**za** *A*) suffer (for); *rel.* atone (for)

odcię|cie *n* (*-a*; *G -ęć*) cutting off; *med.* amputation; **~ty** cut off; **~ta** *f* (*-ej*; *-e*) *math.* abscissa

odcin|ać (*-am*) cut (off); *med.* amputate; *dostęp* seal off; *gaz* disconnect; *połączenia* sever (*też fig.*); ***~ać się*** answer back; (**od** *G*) separate (from), distance (from); stand out, contrast (***na tle*** against); **~ek** *m* (*-nka*; *-nki*) section; *math.* segment; stub, (*biletu itp.*) counterfoil; (*podróży*) leg; (*filmu*) episode; ***~ek czasu*** period; ***powieść w ~kach*** serialized novel

odcis|k *m* (*-u*; *-i*) impression, imprint; (*stopy*) print; *med.* corn; ***~k palca*** fingerprint; **~kać** (*-am*) ⟨**~nąć**⟩ *pieczęć* impress; *ser* squeeze; *ślad* make; ***~nąć się*** leave an imprint

od|cyfrować *pf.* (*-uję*) decode; decipher; **~czekać** *pf.* wait; **~czepi(a)ć** (*-am*) detach, remove; unfasten, undo; ***~czepić się*** lay off (**od** *G*)

odczu|(wa)ć feel; (*wyczuwać*) sense; perceive; ***dać się ~ć*** be felt; **~walny** perceivable, perceptible

odczyn *m* (*-u*; *-y*) *chem.* reaction; *med.* ***~ Biernackiego*** (*skrót*: OB) erythrocyte sedimentation rate (*skrót*: ESR); **~nik** *m* (*-a*; *-i*) *chem.* reagent

odczyt *m* (*-u*; *-y*) lecture, talk; **~ywać** (*-uję*) ⟨**~ać**⟩ read out

oddać *pf.* → ***oddawać***

odda|lać (*-am*) ⟨**~lić**⟩ (*-lę*) drive away; (*ze szkoły*) expel; *wniosek* reject; *jur.* dismiss; ***~lać*** ⟨**~lić**⟩ ***się*** go away; (**z** *G*) leave; **~lenie** *n* (*-a*; *-leń*) distance; *jur.* rejection, dismissal; (*ze szkoły*) expulsion; **~lony** distant, remote; **~nie** *n* (*-a*; *G -ń*) return; *fig.* devotion, dedication; ***~nie do eksploatacji*** bringing into service; **~ny** devoted, dedicated

oddaw|ać (*-ję*) give back, return; give; *cześć* pay; *usługę* do; *ukłony* return; (*do instytucji*) send; *broń*, *miasto* surrender; ***~ać mocz*** pass water; ***~ać pod sąd*** bring to court; ***~ać się*** give o.s. up; *komuś* give o.s. to; **~ca** *m* (*-y*), **~czyni** *f* (*-i*; *-e*) bearer

oddech *m* (*-u*; *-y*) breath; **~owy** breathing

oddolny *fig.* grass-roots

oddycha|ć (*-am*) breathe; **~nie** *n* (*-a*; *0*) breathing, respiration; ***sztuczne ~nie*** artificial respiration, resuscitation

oddz. *skrót pisany*: ***oddział*** department

oddział *m* (*-u*; *-y*) department, section; *mil.* troop, unit; *med.* ward; **~owy** departmental; *med.* ward; **~ywać** (*-uję/-am*) ⟨**~ać**⟩ (**na** *A*) affect, act (on)

oddziel|ać (*-am*) ⟨**~ić**⟩ separate (***się*** *v/i.*); **~ny** separate

oddzwaniać (*-niam*) ⟨***-dzwonić***⟩ (*-nię*) (***do k-ś***) call back s.o.

oddźwięk *m* (*-u*; *-i*) repercussion; *fig.* response, reaction

ode *pf.* → ***od***; **~brać** *pf.* → ***odbierać***

ode|chcie(wa)ć się: ***~chciewa*** ⟨***~chciało***⟩ ***mu się*** (*G*, *bezok.*) he is not eager (to *bezok.*) any more; **~gnać** *pf.* → ***odganiać***; **~grać** *pf.* → ***odgrywać***

odejmowa|ć (*-uję*) *math.* subtract; (*zabierać*) deduct; (*odłączać*) take away; **~nie** *n* (*-a*; *0*) *math.* subtraction

odejś|cie *n* (*-a*; *G -ść*) departure; **~ć** *pf.* → (***-jść***) → ***odchodzić***

ode|mknąć → ***odmykać***; **~pchnąć** *pf.* → ***odpychać***; **~przeć** *pf.* → ***odpierać***; *v/i.* retort, reply; **~rwać** *pf.* → ***odrywać***; **~rwanie** *n* (*-a*; *0*) detachment; ***w ~rwaniu*** (***od*** *G*) in isolation (from); **~rznąć** *pf.*, **~rżnąć** *pf.* → ***odrzynać***; **~słać** *pf.* → ***odsyłać***; **~tchnąć** *pf.* breathe (***swobodnie*** freely); *fig.* have a breather; **~tkać** *pf.* (*-am*) → ***odtykać***; **~zwa** *f* (*-y*; *G -dezw*) proclamation; **~zwać się** *pf.* (*-ę*, *-ie*, *-wij!*) → ***odzywać się***

odęty puffed up; grumpy, surly; → ***nadąsany***

odfajkow(yw)ać (*-[w]uję*) *Brt.* tick off, *Am.* check off

odfru|wać (*-am*) ⟨**~nąć**⟩ (*-nę*) fly away, take flight

odga|dywać (*-uję*) ⟨**~dnąć**⟩ (*-nę*) guess; **~łęziać się** (*-am*) ⟨**~łęzić się**⟩ (*-żę*) branch off; **~łęzienie** *f* (*-a*; *G -eń*) branching, forking; **~niać** → ***odpędzać***; **~rniać** (*-am*) ⟨**~rnąć**⟩ rake aside, push aside; *śnieg* scrape away

od|ginać (*-am*) ⟨**~giąć**⟩ (*-egnę*) bend (up, back *itp.*); **~głos** *m* (*-u*; *-y*) echo; *zw. pl.* sound, noise; **~gniatać** (*-am*) ⟨**~gnieść**⟩ mark; ***~gniatać się*** make marks; **~gonić** *pf.* → ***odpędzić***; **~gradzać** (*-am*) fence off

odgranicz|ać (*-am*) ⟨**~yć**⟩ bound, enclose

od|grażać się (*-am*) threaten; **~grodzić** *pf.* → ***odgradzać***; **~gruzow(yw)ać** (*-[w]uję*) remove the rubble; **~grywać** (*-am*) play; *głupiego* play, act; ***~grywać się*** get one's revenge; **~gryzać** (*-am*) ⟨**~gryźć**⟩ bite off; ***~gryzać się*** hit back; **~grzać** *pf.* → ***odgrzewać***

odgrze|bywać (*-uję*) ⟨**~bać**⟩ dig up; *fig.* rake up; **~wać** (*-am*) re-warm, warm up

od|gwizdać *pf.* whistle; blow the whistle; **~holować** *pf.* tow away; **~izolowywać** (*-wuję*) → ***izolować***

od|jazd *m* (*-u*; *-y*) departure; **~jąć** *pf.* (*-ejmę*) → ***odejmować***; **~jemna** *f* (*-ej*; *-e*) *math.* minuend; **~jemnik** *m* (*-a*; *-i*) *math.* subtrahend; **~jeżdżać** (*-am*) ⟨**~jechać**⟩ (*I*, **na** *L*) depart (in/on), drive off (in/on); leave (**do** *G* for); **~karmiony** well-fed; **~każać** (*-am*) ⟨**~kazić**⟩ (*-żę*) disinfect, *teren* decontaminate; **~każający** disinfecting, antiseptic

odkąd *pron.* from/since when; since, from; (from) where

odkła|dać (*-am*) put away, put back, replace; *słuchawkę* hang up; (*oszczędzać*) put aside, put by; (*odraczać*) put off, postpone; ***~dać się*** deposit, be deposited; **~niać się** ⟨***odkłonić się***⟩ (*D*) return s.o.'s greetings

odkodować (*-uję*) *szyfrogram* decode; *RTV*: unscramble

od|komenderować *pf.* send, detail (**do** *G* to/for); **~kopywać** (*-uję*) ⟨**~kopać**⟩ dig up; **~korkow(yw)ać** (*-[w]uję*) uncork; **~krajać**, **~krawać** (*-am*) cut off; **~kręcać** (*-am*) ⟨**~kręcić**⟩ unscrew; twist off; *kurek* turn on; **~kroić** *pf.* → ***odkrajać***

O

odkry|cie *n* (*-a*; *G -yć*) discovery; **~wać** (*-am*) ⟨**~ć**⟩ *ląd* discover; *ramię, twarz* uncover; *fig.* reveal, expose; ***~wać*** ⟨***~ć***⟩ ***się*** throw off one's covers; **~ty** uncovered; *ląd* discovered; **~wca** *m* (*-y*; *G -ów*), **~wczyni** *f* (*-i*; *G -yń*) discoverer; **~wczy** of discovery; *fig.* revealing; **~wka** *f* (*-i*; *G -wek*) *Brt.* opencast mine, *Am.* strip mine

odkup|iciel *m* (*-a*; *-e*) *rel.* redeemer; **~ywać** (*-uję*)⟨**~ić**⟩ (**od** *G*) buy back (from), repurchase (from); *winę* compensate, expiate; *rel.* redeem; → ***okupywać***

odkurz|acz *m* (*-a*; *-e*) vacuum, vacuum cleaner, *Brt.* Hoover; **~ać** (*-am*) ⟨**~yć**⟩ vacuum

od|lać *pf.* → ***odlewać***; **~latywać** (*-uję*) ⟨***~lecieć***⟩ fly away; *samolot*: depart; *obcas itp.*: come off

odległ|ość *f* (*-ści*) distance; range; **~y** *adj.* (*comp. -glejszy*) remote; distant; far-away; ***~y o pięć kroków*** 5 steps away

odlepi|ać (*-am*) ⟨**~ć**⟩ remove, unstick

odlew *m* (*-u*; *-y*) cast; **~ać** (*-am*) pour off; *tech.* cast; ***~ać się*** V take a leak; **~nia** *f* (*-i*; *-e*) foundry

odleż|eć się *pf.* *owoce*: mature; *fig.* wait one's turn; **~yny** *pl.* (*G -yn*) *med.* bedsores

odlicz|ać (*-am*) ⟨**~yć**⟩ count (out); (*odjąć*) deduct; **~enie** *n* (*-a*) count; deduction; (*czasu*) countdown

odlot *m* departure; ***czas ~u*** departure time

odludny secluded, isolated

odłam *m* (*-u*; *-y*) *fig.* fraction; *pol.* faction; **~ek** *m* (*-mka*; *-mki*) splinter; chip; fragment; **~ywać** (*-uję*) ⟨***~ać***⟩ break (off) (**się** *v/i.*)

od|łączać (*-am*) ⟨***~łączyć***⟩ disconnect; isolate (**się** *v/i.*); → ***odczepiać***; **~łożyć** *pf.* → ***odkładać***; **~łóg** *m* (*-ogu*; *-ogi*) fallow land; ***leżeć ~łogiem*** lie fallow; **~łupywać** (*-uję*)⟨***~łupać***⟩ chip off, split off

odma|czać soak off; **~low(yw)ać** (*-[w]uję*) repaint; *fig.* depict; → ***malować***; **~rzać** [-r·z-] (*-am*) ⟨***~rznąć***⟩ thaw out (*v/i.*); defrost; **~wiać** (*G*) refuse, deny (**sobie** o.s.), (**k-o od** *G*) talk s.o. out of s.th.; (*A*) *pacierz* say; *wizytę* cancel; ***~wiać przyjęcia*** reject; ***~wiać wstępu*** turn away

odmęt *m* (*-u*; *-y*) *lit.* *zw. pl.* waters *pl.*, *fig.* whirls *pl.*

odmian|a *f* (*-y*; *G -*) change; *agr.*, *biol.* variety; (*odmianka*) variant; *gr.* inflection; ***dla ~y, na ~ę*** for a change

odmien|iać (*-am*)⟨~ić⟩ change (**się** *v/i.*); transform; *gr.* inflect; ***~ić się*** change; **~ność** *f* (*-ści*; *0*) difference; different nature; **~ny** different; *gr.* inflectional

od|mierzać (*-am*)⟨***~mierzyć***⟩ measure; **~mładzać** (*-am*) ⟨***~młodzić***⟩ rejuvenate, make younger; ***~mładzać*** ⟨***~młodzić***⟩ ***się*** become younger; grow young again; **~młodnieć** *pf.* → ***młodnieć***; **~moczyć** *pf.* → ***odmaczać***; **~mowa** *f* (*-y*; *G -mów*) refusal, denial; **~mowny** negative; **~mówić** *pf.* → ***odmawiać***; **~mrażać** (*-am*) ⟨***~mrozić***⟩ defrost, de-ice; ***~mrażać sobie uszy*** lose ears through frostbite; **~mrożenie** *n* (*-a*; *G -eń*) frostbite; **~myć** *pf.* → ***odmywać***; **~mykać** *pf.* (*-am*) open, unlock; **~mywać** (*-am*) wash off; *naczynia* wash up

odna|jdować, ~jdywać (*-uję*) find again (**się** each other); *fig.* regain; **~jmować** ⟨***~jąć***⟩ hire, rent; **~leźć** *pf.* (→ *-naleźć*) → ***odnajdować***; **~wiać** (*-am*) renovate; ***~wiać się*** renew itself

odnie|sienie *n* (*-a*): ***w ~sieniu do*** (*G*) with reference to; **~ść** *pf.* → ***odnosić***

odno|ga *f* → ***odgałęzienie***; arm, branch; (*górska*) offset, spur; (***rzeki*** river) arm, branch; **~sić** (*-szę*) carry back, take back; *wrażenie* form; *sukces, zwycięstwo* achieve; *korzyść* reap; *szkodę, rany* suffer; ***~sić się*** (**do** *G*) apply (to), refer (to); relate (to); feel (about); **~śnie**: ***~śnie do*** (*G*) with respect to; **~śny** concerning, appropriate

odno|tow(yw)ać (*-[w]ję*) take down; *fig.* note; **~wić** *pf.* (*-ę, -nów!*) → ***odnawiać***

odos|abniać (*-am*) ⟨***~obnić***⟩ (*-ę, -nij!*) isolate (**się** *v/i.*); **~obnienie** *n* (*-a*; *0*) isolation; (*zamknięcie*) confinement; **~obniony** isolated; confined

odór *m* (*-oru*; *-ory*) bad smell, stench

odpad|ać (*-am*) fall off, come off; *fig.* be inapplicable, be inappropriate; *sport*: be eliminated; **~ek** *m* (*-dka*; *-dki*) *zw. pl.* ***~ki*** refuse, *Brt.* rubbish, *Am.* garbage; (*na ulicy*) litter; **~(k)owy** waste; **~y** *m/pl.* (*G -ów*) (*przemysłowe*) waste

odpa|rcie *n* (*-a*; *0*) (*ataku*) repulsion; (*zarzutu*) refutation, rebuttal; **~row(yw)ać** (*-[w]uję*) evaporate; *fig.*

parry, fend off; **~rzać** (*-am*) ⟨**~rzyć**⟩ chafe; **~ść** *pf.* → **odpadać**
od|pędzać (*-am*) ⟨**~pędzić**⟩ chase away; ward off; **~piąć** *pf.* (*-epnę*) → **odpinać**; **~pić** *pf.* → **odpijać**; **~pieczętow(yw)ać** (*-[w]uję*) unseal; **~pierać** (*-am*) *atak*, *wroga* repel, drive back; *cios* parry, ward off; *zarzut* refute, disprove
odpi|jać (*-am*) drink off; **~łow(yw)ać** (*-[w]uję*) saw off; **~nać** (*-am*) undo, unfasten; *guzik* unbutton; **~nać** ⟨**~ąć**⟩ **się** get undone
odpis *m* (*-u*; *-y*) copy; *econ.* deduction; **~ywać** (*-uję*) ⟨**~ać**⟩ copy; *econ.* write off; deduct
odpła|cać (*-am*) ⟨**~cić**⟩ (**za** *A*) pay back (*też fig.*), repay; **~ta** *f* (*-y*; *G* -) repayment (*też fig.*); **~tny** paid
odpły|nąć *pf.* → **odpływać**; **~w** *m* (*-u*; *-y*) outlet; (*morza*) ebb, low tide; *fig.* migration, departure; **~wać** (*-am*) *ludzie*: swim away; *statek*: sail out; *ciecz*: flow away; *ludność*: emigrate; **~wowy** *kratka* drain
odpocz|ynek *m* (*-nku*; *-nki*) rest; peace; **~ywać** (*-am*) ⟨**~ąć**⟩ rest, have a rest
odpo|kutow(yw)ać (*-[w]uję*) atone for; *rel.* redeem; **~mpow(yw)ać** (*-[w]uję*) pump out
odporn|ość *f* (*-ści*) resistance; resilience (*też biol.*); *med.* immunity, resistance; **~y** (**na** *A*) resistant (to); **~y na wpływy atmosferyczne** weather-resistant
odpowi|adać (*-am*) answer (**na** *A* to; **za** *A* for); reply, respond; (*być odpowiednim*) be appropriate, be suitable; match; **~edni** (**do** *G*) appropriate (to), suitable (to); adequate (to); **~ednik** *m* (*-a*; *-i*) counterpart, equivalent; **~ednio** *adv.* appropriately, suitably
odpowiedzialn|ość *f* (*-ści*; *0*) responsibility; accountability; *econ.* liability; **spółka z ograniczoną ~ością** limited liability company; **~y** responsible (**za** *A* for)
od|powiedzieć *pf.* → **odpowiadać**; **~powiedź** *f* (*-dzi*) answer, reply; response
odpowietrzyć *pf.* (*-ę*) bleed
odpór *m* (*-poru*; *0*) resistance
odpra|cow(yw)ać (*-[w]uję*) work out; **~wa** *f* (*-y*; *G* -) briefing; (*odmowa*) rebuff; (*zapłata*) compensation; *aviat.* check-in; **~wa celna** customs *pl.*; **~wiać** (*-am*) ⟨**~wić**⟩ *towar* dispatch; *rel.* celebrate, officiate; → **odsyłać**
odpręż|ać (*-am*) ⟨**~yć**⟩ (*-ę*) relax (**się** *v/i.*); **~enie** *n* (*-a*; *G -eń*) relaxation; *pol.* détente
odprowadz|ać (*-am*) ⟨**~ić**⟩ accomany, escort; *ścieki itp.* carry (away); **~ać do drzwi** show to the door; **~ać do domu** see home; **~ać na dworzec** see off
odpru|wać (*-am*) ⟨**~ć**⟩ unseam, rip
odprys|kiwać (*-uję*) ⟨**~nąć**⟩ flake off
odprzeda|wać (*-ję*) ⟨**~ć**⟩ (*-am*) resell
odpu|st *m* (*-u*; *-y*) *rel.* indulgence; (*festyn*) fête; **~szczać** (*-am*) ⟨**~ścić**⟩ pardon, forgive
odpycha|ć (*-am*) push away, shove away; *fig.*, *phys.* repel; **~jąco** *adv.* repulsively; **~jący** repulsive
odpyl|ać (*-am*) ⟨**~ić**⟩ dust
odra *f* (*-y*; *0*) *med.* measles *sg.*;lemma⟩/ lemma⟩ *f* (*-y*; *0*) (the) Oder, Odra
odra|biać (*-am*) *dług* work off; *lekcje* do; *zaległości*, *błędy* make up for; *zaległości też* catch up with; **~czać** (*-am*) put off, postpone; *jur.* suspend; **~dzać**[1] (*-am*) ⟨**~dzić**⟩ (*A*) advise (against)
odra|dzać[2] → **odrodzić**; **~pywać** (*-uję*) ⟨**~pać**⟩ scratch; **~stać** (*-am*) grow again; → **podrastać**; **~tow(yw)ać** (*-[w]uję*) rescue; *fig.* revive; **~za** *f* (*-y*; *0*) repulsion, aversion; **~żająco** *adv.* repulsively, disgustingly; **~żający** repulsive, disgusting
odrąb|ywać (*-uję*) ⟨**~ać**⟩ chop off
odre- *pf.* → **re-**
odrę|bny different; distinct, special; **~czny** hand-written; *rysunek* free-hand; *naprawa* on the spot, immediate
odrętwie|ć *pf.* → **drętwieć**; **~nie** *n* (*-a*) numbness; *fig.* lethargy
odro|bić *pf.* → **odrabiać**; **~bina** *f* (*-y*; *G* -) particle; (*G*) a bit (of); **~czenie** *n* (*-a*; *G -eń*) postponement, adjournment; (*wyroku*) reprieve; **~czyć** *pf.* → **odraczać**; **~dzenie** *n* (*-a*; *0*) renascence, rebirth, renaissance; **≈dzenie** Renaissance; **~dzić** *pf.* revive, renew; **~dzić się** revive; **~snąć** *pf.* → **odrastać**
odróżni|ać (*-am*) ⟨**~ć**⟩ distinguish (**od** *G* from); **~ać się** differ (**od** *G* from); **~enie** *n* (*-a*; *0*) distinction; **w ~eniu** (**od** *G*) in contrast (to), unlike; **nie do ~enia** indistinguishable

odruch *m* (*-u*; *-y*) *biol.* reflex; *fig.* emotion, prompting; **~owo** *adv.* involuntarily; **~owy** involuntary
odry|glow(yw)ać (-[*w*]*uję*) unbolt; **~wać** (*-am*) tear off; *wzrok* turn away; ***~wać się*** come off, break off; *fig.* wrench o.s. away (**od** *G* from)
odrzec *pf.* say
odrzu|cać ⟨***~cić***⟩ discard, cast off; *prośbę* turn down; (*w głosowaniu*) overrule; *skargę, warunki* reject; **~t** *m mil.* recoil; *econ.* reject; **~towiec** *m* (*-wca*; *-wce*) jet (plane); **~towy** jet
odrzwia *pl.* door frame
od|rzynać (*-am*) cut off; **~salanie** *n* (*-a*; *0*) desalination; **~salutować** (*-uję*) salute; **~sapnąć** (*-nę*) have a breather; **~sądzać** (*-am*) ⟨***~sądzić***⟩ (***kogoś od*** *G*) deny
odset|ek *m* (*-tka*; *-tki*) percentage; ***~ki*** *pl.* interest (***za zwłokę*** for late payment)
odsia|ć *pf.* → ***odsiewać***; **~dywać** (*-uję*) sit out, F *wyrok* do
odsie|cz *f* (*-y*; *-e*) *mil.* relief; **~dzieć** *pf.* → ***odsiadywać***; **~wać** (*-am*) sift; *fig.* sift through
od|skakiwać (*-uję*) ⟨***~skoczyć***⟩ (***od*** *G*) jump aside/back; *piłka*: bounce (off); **~skocznia** *f* (*-i*; *-e*) springboard; **~słaniać** (*-am*) uncover; *pomnik* unveil; *prawdę* reveal; *głowę* bare; *zasłonę* draw (back); ***~słaniać się*** appear; **~słona** *f* (*-y*; *G -*) *theat.* act; **~słonić** *pf.* → ***odsłaniać***; **~słonięcie** *n* (*-a*; *G -ęć*) unveiling; revelation
odsprzedawać → ***odprzedawać***
odsta|wać ⟨***~ć***⟩ (→ *stać*[2]) come off; *uszy*: stick out; (*wyróżniać się*) stand out; **~wi(a)ć** put away, put aside; deliver; *lekarstwo* stop taking; ***~wiać dziecko od piersi*** wean the baby
odstąpi|ć *pf.* → ***odstępować***; **~enie** *n* (*-a*) (*praw, ziemi*) cession; relinquishment, renunciation (**od** *G* of)
odstęp *m* (*-u*; *-y*) interval, distance; space, gap; **~ne** *n* (*-ego*; *-e*) compensation; **~nik** *m* (*-a*; *-i*) space-bar; **~ować** (*-uję*) *v/i.* step aside; cede; waive; *econ.* dispose; transfer; withdraw (***od umowy*** from the agreement); *mil.* retreat, move away (**od** *G* from); *v/t.* cede, transfer; **~stwo** *n* (*-a*; *G -*) departure; *rel.* dissent
odstrasz|ać (*-am*) ⟨***~yć***⟩ scare away (**od** *G* from); deter; **~ająco** *adv.* frighteningly; **~ający** deterrent; frightening
odstręcz|ać (*-am*) ⟨***~yć***⟩ (*-ę*) *fig.* repel, put off; (*zniechęcać*) (**od** *G*) prevent (from)
odstrzał *m* (*-u*; *-y*) *hunt.* shooting down
odsuwać (*-am*) ⟨***odsunąć***⟩ push away, move away; *zasuwę, firankę* draw back; ***~ od władzy*** remove from power; **~** ⟨***odsunąć***⟩ ***się*** move away; *fig.* withdraw, retire
odsyła|cz *m* (*-a*; *-e*) reference; **~ć** (*-am*) (***do*** *G*) send back (to), return (to); refer (to)
odsyp|ywać (*-uję*) ⟨***~ać***⟩ pour away
odszkodowani|e *n* (*-a*; *G -ań*) compensation, recompense; *jur.* damages *pl.*; ***~a wojenne*** reparations *pl.*
od|szraniać (*-am*) ⟨***~szronić***⟩ (*-ę*) defrost; **~szukać** (*-am*) trace, find (again) (***się*** *v/i.*); **~szyfrow(yw)ać** (-[*w*]*uję*) decipher, decode; **~śpiewać** *pf.* sing; **~środkowy** centrifugal
odśwież|ać (*-am*) ⟨***~yć***⟩ (*-ę*) refresh; *mieszkanie* renew; *fig.* brush up on; ***~yć się*** freshen o.s. up, refresh o.s.
od|świętny festive; **~tajać** *pf.* thaw
odtąd since; from… on…; *przestrzeń*: from here
odtłuszczon|y: ***mleko ~e*** skimmed milk
od|transportować *pf.* take away, remove; **~trącać** (*-am*) ⟨***~trącić***⟩ push away, shove away; *fig.* reject; → ***potrącać***; **~trutka** *f* (*-i*; *G -tek*) antidote (*też fig.*); **~twarzacz** *m* (*-a*; *-e*): ***~twarzacz płyt kompaktowych*** CD player; **~twarzać** (*-am*) ⟨***~tworzyć***⟩ reconstruct, reproduce; *taśmę* play; *rolę* play, act; ***~twarzać się*** *biol.* regenerate
odtwór|ca *m* (*-y*; *G -ców*), **~czyni** *f* (*-i*; *-e*) interpreter, performer
od|tykać (*-am*) unblock, unstop; **~uczać** (*-am*) ⟨***~uczyć***⟩: ***~uczać kogoś od*** (*G*) teach s.o. not to; (*zwyczaju*) break s.o. of; ***~uczać się*** unlearn
odurz|ać (*-am*) ⟨***~yć***⟩ intoxicate; ***~ać*** ⟨***~yć***⟩ ***się*** become intoxicated; *fig.* become carried away; **~ająco** *adv.* intoxicatingly; **~ający** intoxicating, heady; **~enie** *n* (*-a*; *G -eń*) intoxication
odwadniać (*-am*) drain
odwag|a *f* (*-i*; *0*) courage; ***~a cywilna***

O

courage of one's convictions; ***nabrać ~i, zebrać się na ~ę*** muster up courage; ***dodać ~i*** encourage

odwal|ać (*-am*)⟨**~ić**⟩ remove; F (*wykonać*) get *s.th.* over and done with; (*wykonać źle*) bungle; ***zostać ~onym*** be given the brush-off; F ***~ się!*** get lost!

odwar *m* (*-u*; *-y*) *med.* decoction

odważ|ać (*-am*) weigh out; ***~ać się → odważyć***; **~nik** *m* (*-a*; *-i*) weight; **~ny** courageous; brave; **~yć** *pf.* → ***odważać***; ***~yć się*** (***na*** *A*) dare (to); have the courage (to)

odwdzięcz|ać się (*-am*) ⟨***~yć się***⟩ (*-ę*) (***za*** *A*) repay (for), return (for)

odwet *m* (*-u*; *0*) retaliation, reprisal; ***w ~ za*** in reprisal/retaliation for; **~owiec** *m* (*-wca*; *-wcy*) revanchist

od|wiązywać (*-uję*) ⟨***~wiązać***⟩ untie, undo; ***~wiązać się*** get untied, get undone; **~wieczny** perennial

odwiedz|ać (*-am*) ⟨***~ić***⟩ (*-dzę*) visit; **~iny** *pl.* (-) visit; ***przyjść w ~iny*** (***do*** *G*) visit, come to visit

odwiert *m* (*-u*; *-y*) *tech.* well

od|wieść *pf.* → ***odwodzić***; **~wieźć** *pf.* → ***odwozić***; **~wijać** (*-am*) unwind, reel off; *rękaw* turn up; ***~wijać się*** unwind o.s.; **~wilż** *f* (*-y*; *-e*) thaw (*też fig.*); **~winąć** *pf.* → ***odwijać***

od|wirow(yw)ać (*-[w]uję*) spin; *pranie też.* spin-dry; **~wlekać** (*-am*) ⟨***~wlec***⟩ drag away, pull away; *fig.* put off, delay; **~wodnić** *pf.* (*-ę*, *-nij!*) → ***odwadniać***; **~wodzić** lead away, take away; *kurek* cock; ***~wodzić od*** (*G*) dissuade from

odwoła|ć *pf.* → ***odwoływać***; **~nie** *n* cancellation; *jur.* repeal; ***aż do ~nia*** until further notice; ***~nie alarmu*** all-clear (signal); ***~nie się*** (***do*** *G*) call (to), appeal (to); **~wczy** *jur.* appeal

odwoływać (*-uję*) call off, cancel; *urzędnika* recall, call back; *rozkaz, zamówienie* cancel, revoke; ***~ się*** (***do*** *G*) turn (to), appeal (to)

odwozić (*samochodem*) drive off; cart away

odwraca|ć turn (round) (***się*** *v/i.*); *głowę, klęskę* turn away; ***~ć uwagę*** distract; **~lny** reversible; ***film ~lny*** reversal film

odwrot|nie *adv.* conversely, vice versa; inversely; the other way round; **~ność** *f* (*-ści*; *0*) the opposite; reversal; *math.* reciprocal; **~ny** opposite; reverse; ***~na strona*** back, reverse, the other side

odwró|cenie *n* (*-a*; *0*) reversal; **~cić** *pf.* → ***odwracać***; **~t** *m* (*-otu*; *-oty*) *mil.*, *fig.* retreat; withdrawal; ***na ~t → odwrotnie***; ***na odwrocie*** (*strony*) overleaf

odwyk|ać (*-am*) ⟨***~nąć***⟩ (*-nę*) (***od*** *G*) lose the habit (of); **~owy** withdrawal

odwzajemni|ać (*-am*)⟨**~ć**⟩(*-ę*, *-nij!*) return; ***~(a)ć się*** repay (***k-u za*** *A* s.o. for)

odyniec *m* (*-ńca*; *-ńce*) wild boar

odzew *m* (*-u*; *-y*) *mil.* password; *fig.* response

odziedziczony inherited

odzież *f* (*-y*; *0*) clothing, clothes *pl.*; **~owy** clothing, clothes

odzna|czać (*-am*) (*orderem*) decorate; single out, distinguish; ***~czać się*** stand out; **~czenie** *n* (*-a*; *G -eń*) decoration; (*wyróżnienie*) award; **~czyć** *pf.* → ***odznaczać***; **~ka** *f* (*-i*; *G* -) badge

odzwierciedl|ać (*-am*) ⟨***~ić***⟩ (*-lę*, *-lij!*) reflect, mirror; ***~ać się*** be reflected; **~enie** *n* (*-a*; *G -eń*) reflection

odzwyczа|jać (*-am*) ⟨***~ić***⟩ (*-ję*, *-j!*) break (***k-o od*** *G* s.o. of) a habit, wean (***od*** *G* from); ***~jać*** ⟨***~ić***⟩ ***się*** (***od*** *G*) lose the habit (of)

odzysk|anie *n* (*-a*; *0*) recovery, recuperation; **~(iw)ać** (*-[w]uję*) recover; regain; *zdrowie* recuperate; *surowce* recycle; ***~ać przytomność*** regain consciousness

odzyw|ać się (*-am*) say, speak; *dzwonek*: sound, be heard; *gry w karty*: bid; (***do*** *G*) speak (to); ***nikt się nie odzywa*** *tel.* nobody answers; F ***nie odezwał się jeszcze*** we haven't heard from him yet; **~ka** *f* (*-i*) *gry w karty*: bid

odźwierny *m* (*-ego*; *-ni*) porter, doorman, gatekeeper

odżałować *pf.* get over

odżyw|ać (*-ję*)⟨***odżyć***⟩ come (back) to life; *fig.* revive, rejuvenate; **~czo** *adv.* nutritiously; **~czy** nutritious, nourishing; **~iać** (*-am*) ⟨***~ić***⟩ feed; nourish ***~iać się*** *zw. zwierzęta*: feed (on); live on; **~ianie** nutrition, nourishment; **~ka** *f* (*-i*; *G -wek*) nutrient; (*do włosów*) conditioner; ***~ka dla dzieci*** formula feed, baby food

ofensyw|a *f* (*-y*; *G* -) offensive; *sport*: attack; **~ny** offensive

ofer|ent *m* (*-a*; *-ci*) bidder; **~ować** (*-uję*)

O

⟨**za-**⟩ (*-uję*) offer; **~ta** *f* (*-y*; *G* -) offer; ***złożyć ~tę*** make an offer
ofiar|a *f* (*-y*, *DL ofierze*; *-y*, *G* -) sacrifice; *osoba itp.*: victim; casualty (*wypadku*); *datek*: offering, donation; F *oferma*: loss-loser; ***paść ~ą*** (*G*) fall victim (to); **~ność** *f* devotion; **~ny** devoted; **~odawca** *m*, **~odawczyni** *f* contributor, donor, donator; **~ow(yw)ać** (*-*[*w*]*uję*) give, *też* (**się z** *I*) offer; donate, (*poświęcać*) sacrifice
ofi|cer *m* (*-a*; *-owie*) officer; **~cerski** officer; **~cjalny** official, formal
oficyna *f* (*-y*; *G* -) (building) wing; *wydawnicza* publishing house
ofsajd *m* (*-u*; *-y*) (*w sporcie*) offside
ofuk|iwać (*-uję*) ⟨***~nąć***⟩ (*-nę*) snub
oganiać (się) → ***opędzać* (*się*)**
ogarek *m* (*-rka*; *-rki*) stump
ogarn|iać (*-am*) ⟨***~ąć***⟩ take in, include; (*pojąć*) grasp, catch; *por.* ***obejmować, otaczać***
og|ień *m* (*ognia*; *ognie*, *-ni*) fire; ***w ~niu*** on fire; ***puścić z ~niem*** set on fire; ***otwierać ~ień*** (**na** *A*) open fire (at)
ogier *m* (*-a*; *-y*) *zo.* stallion
oglądać (*-am*) watch (**się** o.s.; **w** *I* in); view, see; ***~ się*** look round (**na** *A* at)
oglę|dność *f* (*-ści*; *0*) prudence; **~dny** cautious, guarded; ***~dnie mówiąc*** putting it mildly; **~dziny** *pl.* (-) inspection; ***~dziny zwłok*** post-mortem, autopsy
ogład|a *f* (*-y*; *0*) polish, politeness; ***bez ~y*** unrefined, uncouth; → ***obycie***
ogłaszać (*-am*) announce, make public; ***~ drukiem*** publish; ***~ się*** advertise
ogło|sić *pf.* → ***ogłaszać***; **~szenie** *n* (*-a*; *G -eń*) announcement; notice; advertisement; **~szeniowy** notice
ogłuchnąć *pf.* grow deaf
ogłupi|ały stupefied; **~eć** *pf.* lose one's head; go soft in the head
ogłusz|ać (*-am*) → ***głuszyć***; **~ająco** *adv.* deafeningly
ogni|e *pl.* → ***ogień***; ***sztuczne ~e*** *pl.* fireworks *pl.*; ***zimne ~e*** *pl.* sparklers *pl.*; **~k** *m* (*-a*; *-i*) flame; ***błędny ~k*** will o' the wisp; jack o' lantern
ognio|odporny, ~trwały fire-proof; **~wy** fire; ***straż ~wa*** *Brt.* fire brigade, *Am.* fire department
ognisko *n* (*-a*; *G* -) (bon)fire; *fig. Brt.* centre, *Am.* center; *phys.*, *phot.* focus; ***~ domowe*** hearth (and home); **~wa** *f* (*-ej*; *-e*) *phys.* focal length; **~wać** (*-uję*) ⟨**z-**⟩ (*-uję*) focus (**się** *v/i.*)
ogni|sto- *w złoż.* fire; **~ście** *adv.* passionately; **~sty** fiery; *fig.* fiery, passionate; flaming red
ogniwo *n* (*-a*; *G* -) link; *electr.* cell
ogołoc|ić *pf.* (*-cę*) denude; take away (***z pieniędzy*** one's money); ***~ony z liści*** bare, without leaves
ogon *m* (*-a*; *-y*) tail; ***wlec się w ~ie*** bring up the rear; **~ek** *m* (*-nka*; *-nki*) → ***ogon***; (*kucyk*) ponytail; (*kolejka*) *Brt.* queue, *Am.* line; ***ustawić się w ~ku*** *Brt.* queue up, *Am.* line up; **~owy** tail; *biol.* caudal
ogorzały tanned
ogólni|e *adv.* generally; **~k** *m* (*-a*; *-i*) → ***komunał***; **~kowo** *adv.* generally, vaguely; **~kowy** general, vague
ogólno|europejski European, pan-European; **~kształcący** all-round education; **~polski** Polish, all-Polish; **~światowy** world-wide, world
ogólny general
ogół *m* (*-u*; *0*) general public, public at large; ***dobro ~u*** public welfare *lub* good; **~em** in all; ***na ~*** usually; on the whole; ***w ogóle*** by and large; ***w ogóle nie*** not at all
ogór|ek *m* (*-rka*; *-rki*) *bot.* cucumber; **~kowy** cucumber; ***sezon ~kowy*** the silly season
ogra|biać (*-am*) → ***grabić***; **~ć** *pf.* → ***ogrywać***; **~dzać** (*-am*) fence off/in
ogranicz|ać (*-am*) limit, restrict; ***~ać się*** (**do** *G*) restrict o.s. (to), confine o.s.(to); **~enie** *n* (*-a*; *G -eń*) restriction, limit; **~oność** *f* (*-ści*; *0*) limited intelligence; **~ony** limited, restricted; *fig.* dull-witted, narrow-minded; **~yć** *pf.* → ***ograniczać***
ograny *dowcip itp.* hackneyed, trite
ogrod|nictwo *n* (*-a*; *0*) gardening; horticulture; **~niczka** *f* (*-ki*; *G -czek*), **~nik** *m* (*-a*; *-icy*) gardener; **~owy** garden, gardening; horticultural
ogrodz|enie *n* (*-a*; *G -eń*) fence; **~ić** *pf.* → ***ogradzać***
ogrom *m* (*-u*; *0*) enormity; immensity; magnitude; **~ny** enormous; immense; magnitude
ogród *m* (*-odu*; *-ody*) garden; ***~ owocowy*** orchard; **~ek** *m.* → ***ogród***; (*działka*) *Brt.* allotment; ***~ek przed domem*** front garden

ogród|ka *f*: ***bez ~ek*** without beating about the bush
ogry|wać (*-am*) win all *s.o.'s* money (***w pokera*** at poker); beat (***w*** *A* at); **~zać** (*-am*) ⟨***~źć***⟩ gnaw at; **~zek** *m* (*-zka*; *-zki*) (*owocu*) core
ogrzewa|ć (*-am*)⟨***ogrzać***⟩ heat, warm; ***~ć*** ⟨***ogrzać***⟩ ***się*** get warm; **~nie** *n* (*-a*; *G -ń*) (***centralne*** central) heating
ogumienie *n* (*-a*; *G -eń*) *mot.* set of *Brt.* tyres, *Am.* tires
ohydny hideous
OI *skrót pisany*: ***Ośrodek Informacyjny*** information centre
oj oh
ojciec *m* (*-jca*; *-jców*) father; ***~ chrzestny*** godfather; ***po ojcu*** paternal; ***bez ojca*** fatherless
ojco|stwo *n* (*-a*; *G -tw*) fatherhood, paternity; **~wizna** *f* (*-y*; *G -zn*) patrimony; **~wski** fatherly, paternal; ***po ~wsku*** like a father
ojczy|m *m* (*-a*; *-y*) stepfather; **~sty** native; → ***język***; **~zna** *f* (*-y*; *G -zn*) homeland, motherland, mother country
ok. *skrót pisany*: ***około*** c. (*around*)
okalać (*-am*) surround, encircle
okalecz|enie *n* (*-a*; *G -eń*) injury; **~yć** (*-ę*) injure, hurt
okamgnieni|e *n* (*-a*): ***w ~u*** in a flash
okap *m* (*-u*; *-y*) *bud.* eaves *pl.*; (*wyciąg*) hood
okaz *m* (*-u*; *-y*) specimen; **~ać się** *pf.* → ***okazywać się***; **~ale** *adv.* spectacularly; **~ały** spectacular, impressive; **~anie** *n* (*-a*; *0*) (*dowodu*) production, demonstration; ***~anie pomocy*** assistance; ***za ~aniem*** on production *lub* presentation; **~iciel** *m* (*-a*; *-e*), **~icielka** *f* (*-i*; *G -lek*) bearer; ***czek na ~iciela*** *Brt.* bearer cheque, *Am.* bearer check
okazj|a *f* (*-i*; *-e*) occasion; (*kupna*) bargain, good buy; ***przy ~i, z ~i*** (*G*) on the occasion (of)
okaz|owy specimen; **~yjny** bargain; ***~yjna cena*** special price; **~ywać** (*-uję*) present, demonstrate; (*dać wyraz*) express; ***~ywać pomoc*** help; ***~ywać się*** (*I*) turn out, prove; ***jak się ~ało*** as it turned out
okien|ko *n* (*-nka*; *G -nek*) window; (*w urzędzie też*) counter; **~nica** *f* (*-y*; *-e*) shutter; **~ny** window
oklapnąć *pf.* F *fig.* wilt, sag
oklaski *m/pl.* (*-ów*) applause; **~wać** (*-uję*) applaud
okle|ina *f* (*-y*; *G -*) veneer; **~jać** (*-am*) ⟨***~ić***⟩ stick (all over s.th.)
oklepany hackneyed, trite
okład *m* (*-u*; *-y*) *med.* compress, (*ciepły*) poultice; F ***sto ... z ~em*** a good hundred ...; **~ać** (*-am*) cover; (*kompresem*) apply; *tech.* face, (*metalem*) clad; ***~ać kijem*** thrash with a stick; **~ka** *f* (*-i*; *G -dek*) (*książki*) cover; (*na książkę*) jacket; (*płyty*) sleeve
okładzina *f* (*-y*; *G -*) overing, lining; facing
okłam|ywać (*-uję*) ⟨***~ać***⟩ lie (*A* to)
okno *n* (*-a*; *G okien*) window; ***~ wystawowe*** shop window; ***przez ~, z okna, oknem*** out of the window
oko *n* (*oka*; *oczy*, *oczu*, *oczom*, *oczami/oczyma*, *o oczach*) *anat.* eye; (*oka*; *oka*, *ok*, *okami*) mesh; → ***oczko***; ***mieć ~ na*** (*A*) have an eye (on); ***nie rzucać się w oczy*** keep a low profile; ***~ za ~*** eye for eye; ***na ~*** approximately; ***na oczach*** in full view; ***w cztery oczy*** face to face; ***na własne oczy*** with one's own eyes; ***w oczach*** visibly
okolic|a *f* (*-y*; *G -*) area; neighbo(u)rhood; ***w ~y*** round about
okolicz|nik *m* (*-a*; *-i*) *gr.* adverbial; **~nościowy** occasional; **~ność** *f* (*-ści*) *zw. pl.* circumstances *pl.*, conditions *pl.*; ***w tych ~nościach*** under these circumstances; **~ny** local; neighbo(u)ring; ***~ni mieszkańcy*** *pl.* locals *pl.*
oko|lić *pf.* (*-lę*) → ***okalać***; **~ło** *prp.* (*G*) about, around
okoń *m* (*-nia*; *-nie*) *zo.* perch
okop *m* (*-u*; *-y*) trench; **~ywać** (*-uję*) ⟨***~ać***⟩ *agr.* earth up
oko|stna *f* (*-nej*; *0*) *anat.* periosteum; **~wy** *f/pl.* (*-wów*) fetters *pl.*, chains *pl.*
okóln|ik *m* (*-a*; *-i*) circular; **~y** circular; → ***okrężny***
ok|piwać (*-am*) ⟨***~pić***⟩ F lead on
okradać (*-am*) rob
okra|jać → ***okrawać***; **~kiem** astride; **~sa** *f* (*-y*; *-*) fat; **~szać** (*-am*) → ***krasić***; **~ść** *pf.* → ***okradać***; **~tować** (*-uję*) put bars over; **~wać** (*-am*) trim, cut; *fig.* shorten; **~wek** *m* (*-wka*; *-wki*) paring, scrap
okrąg *m* (*okręgu*; *okręgi*) *math.* circle; **~lak** (*-a*; *-i*) round timber; **~ły** round; circular

okrąż|ać (*-am*) go round; enclose; surround; **~enie** *n* (*-a*; *G -eń*) circuit; (*w sporcie*) lap; **~yć** *pf.* → **okrążać**
okres *m* (*-u*; *-y*) (**próbny, ochronny** trial, close) period; *szkoła*: term; (*u kobiety*) period, menstruation; season (*świąt itp.*); **~owo** *adv.* periodically; **~owy** periodic; *tymczasowy* temporary; **bilet ~owy** season ticket
określ|ać (*-am*) ⟨**~ić**⟩ determine, define; (*nazywać*) call, describe; **~enie** *n* (*-a*; *G -eń*) determination, definition; description, label; **~ony** specific; *gr.* definite
okręc|ać (*-am*) ⟨**~ić**⟩ (*I*) bind (with), wind (with), wrap (with); (*obracać*) twist; **~ać** ⟨**~ić**⟩ **się** (**wokół**) coil (around); (*obracać się*) turn (a)round
okręg *m* (*-u*; *-i*) district, region; **~owy** district; regional
okręt *m* (*-u*; *-y*) *naut.* warship; **~ownictwo** *n* (*-a*; *0*) shipbuilding; **~ować** ⟨**za-**⟩ (*-uję*) embark; **~owy** ship, naval, marine; **linia ~owa** shipping line; **dziennik ~owy** log
okrężn|y roundabout; circular; **droga ~a** roundabout way, detour; **drogą ~ą** *fig.* indirectly; → **skrzyżowanie**
okroić *pf.* → **okrawać**
okrop|ieństwo *n* (*-a*; *G -*) horror, atrocity; **~ność** *f* (*-ści*; *0*) horror; **~ny** horrible, atrocious; *ból itp.* awful, terrible
okruch *m* (*-a*; *-y*) crumb; *fig.* piece, bit
okrucieństwo *n* (*-a*; *G -*) cruelty
okruszyna *f* (*-y*; *G -*) crumb; → **okruch**
okrutny cruel
okry|cie *n* (*-a*; *G -yć*) cover; (*płaszcz*) coat; **~wać** (*-am*) ⟨**~ć**⟩ (*-ję*) cover (**się** o.s.; *I* with); envelop (*też fig.*)
okrzepnąć *pf.* → **krzepnąć**
okrzy|czany famous; (*złej sławy*) notorious; **~k** *m* (*-u*; *-i*) shout, cry; **~ki radości** shouts of joy
Oksford *m* (*-u*; *0*) Oxford
oktawa *f* (*-y*; *G -*) *mus.* octave
oku|cie *n* (*-a*; *G -uć*) fitting; (*laski itp.*) ferrule; **~ć** *pf.* → **okuwać**; **~lary** *pl.* (*-ów*) glasses *pl.*; (*końskie*) blinkers *pl.*; **on nosi ~lary** he wears glasses
okulist|a *m* (*-y*; *-ów*), **~ka** *f* (*-i*; *G -tek*) *med.* eye doctor; ophthalmologist; **~yczny** ophthalmological
okup *m* (*-u*; *-y*) ransom; **~acja** *f* (*-i*; *-e*) occupation; **~acyjny** occupation; **~ant** *m* (*-a*; *-nci*) occupant; **~ować** (*-uję*) *kraj* occupy; *fig.* hog, monopolize; **~ywać** (*-uję*) pay (**życiem** with one's life); *krzywdę* redeem; **~ywać się** buy o.s. off, buy one's freedom
okuwać (*-am*) fit; *konia* shoe
olbrzym *m* (*-a*; *-i/-y*) giant; **~i** giant, colossal; **~ka** *f* (*-i*; *G -ek*) giant
olch|a *f* (*-y*; *G -*) *bot.* alder; **~owy** alder
ole|isty oily; **~j** *m* (*-u*; *-e*) (**jadalny, opałowy, napędowy** cooking, heating, diesel) oil; **~jarka** *f* (*-i*; *G -jek*) oiler, oilcan; **~jarnia** *f* (*-i*; *-e*) oil-mill; **~jek** *m* (*-jku*; *-jki*) (**do opalania** suntan) oil; **~jny, ~jowy** oil; **~odruk** *m* (*-u*; *-i*) oleograph
olicowanie *n* (*-a*) *bud.* facing
olimpi|ada *f* (*-y*; *G -*) Olympics *pl.*; **~jczyk** *m* (*-a*; *-cy*), **~jka** *f* (*-i*; *G -jek*) Olympic competitor, *Am.* Olympian; **~jski** Olympic
oliw|a *f* (*-y*; *zw. 0*) (olive) oil; **~ić** ⟨**na-**⟩ (*-ę*) oil, lubricate; **~ka** *f* (*-i*; *G -wek*) olive; **~kowy** olive; *kolor* olive-green; **~ny** olive; **gałązka ~na** *też fig.* olive branch
olsz|a *f* (*-y*; *G -*) *bot.*, **~yna** *f* (*-y*; *G -*) → **olcha**
olśnić *pf.* → **olśniewać**
olśnie|nie *n* (*-a*; *G -eń*) *fig.* flash of inspiration, brain wave; **~wać** (*-am*) dazzle (*też fig.*); **~wająco** *adv.* stunningly, brilliantly; **~wający** stunning, glamorous, brilliant
ołowi|any, ~owy lead; *fig.* leaden
ołów *m* (*-łowiu*; *0*) *chem.* lead; **~ek** *m* (*-wka*; *-wki*) pencil; **~ek do brwi** eyebrow pencil; **~ek kolorowy** colo(u)red pencil; **~ek automatyczny** *Brt.* propelling pencil, *Am.* mechanical pencil
ołtarz *m* (*-a*; *-e*) *rel.* altar; **wielki ~** high altar
omac|ek: **iść po ~ku, ~kiem** grope one's way; **szukać po ~ku** grope for; **~ywać** (*-uję*) → **macać**
omal: **~ (że) nie** almost, nearly
omam *m* (*-u*; *-y*) delusion, illusion; **~iać** (*-iam*) ⟨**~ić**⟩ (*-ię*) beguile, deceive
omawiać go over, discuss; treat
omdl|ały faint, limp; **~enie** *n* (*-a*; *G -eń*) faint; **~ewać** (*-am*) ⟨**~eć**⟩ faint, pass out
omiatać (*-am*) sweep
omieszkać (*-am*): **nie ~** not fail, not forget
omi|eść *pf.* → **omiatać**; **~jać** ⟨**~nąć**⟩ *v/t.* go round, bypass; *trudność, prob-*

lem, zakaz get round; (*t-ko impf.*) avoid; ***nie ~nie go kara*** he will not escape punishment; ***~nął ją awans*** she was passed over for promotion; → ***mijać***
omlet *m* (*-u*; *-y*) *gastr.* omelette
omłot *m* (*-u*; *-y*) *agr.* threshing; **~owy** threshing
omomierz *m* (*-a*; *-e*) *tech.* ohmmeter
omot|ywać (*-uję*) 〈***~ać***〉 wrap (*I* with); *fig.* ensnare (***w*** *A* in)
omówi|ć *pf.* → ***omawiać***; **~enie** *n* (*-a*; *G -eń*) discussion, treatment; ***bez ~eń*** openly
omszały mossy
omułek *m* (*-łka*; *-łki*) *zo.* (edible) mussel
omy|ć *pf.* → ***omywać***; **~lić** *pf.* → ***mylić***; **~lny** fallible; **~łka** *f* (*-i*; *G -łek*) error, mistake; → ***błąd, pomyłka***; **~łkowo** *adv.* erroneously; **~łkowy** erroneous
on *pron.* (*G* [*je*]*go*, *D* [*je*]*mu*, *A* [*je*]*go*, *IL nim*) he; *rzecz*: it; **~a** *pron.* (*GD jej*, *A ją*, *I nią*, *L niej*) she; *rzecz*: it
onanizować się (*-uję*) masturbate
ondulacja *f* (*-i*; *-e*): ***trwała ~*** perm
on|e *pron. ż-rzecz* (*G* [*n*]*ich*, *D* [*n*]*im*, *A je*, *nie*, *I nimi*, *L nich*), **~i** *pron. m-os* (*A* [*n*]*ich*; → ***one***) they
oniemiały (***z*** *G*) dumbfounded, speechless (with)
onieśmiel|ać (*-am*) 〈***~ić***〉 (*-lę*) discourage, overawe
ono *pron.* (*A je*; → ***on***) it
ONZ *skrót pisany*: ***Organizacja Narodów Zjednoczonych*** UN (*United Nations*)
opactwo *n* (*-a*; *G -w*) abbey
opaczn|ie *adv.* wrong, falsely; **~y** wrong, false
opad *m* (*-u*; *-y*) fall; (*w sporcie*) bend from the hips; ***~ krwi*** F *med.* EST, sedimentation test; *zw. pl.* ***~y*** *meteo.* showers *pl.*; ***~y śnieżne*** snowfall; **~ać** *v/i.* fall, drop (*też fig.*); *głowa, głos itp.*: droop; *teren*: sink down; *gorączka*: subside; (*ze zmęczenia*) collapse; *v/t. owady itp.* besiege, swarm around; *fig.* plague, persecute; ***on ~a z sił*** he is losing his strength
opak: ***na ~*** the other way round, amiss
opakow|anie *n* (*-a*; *G -ań*) packaging, wrapping, packet; ***w ładnym ~aniu*** *fig.* in nice packaging; ***w*** (***próżniowym***) ***~aniu*** vacuum-packed; **~ywać** (*-uję*) → ***pakować***
opala|cz *m* (*-a*; *-e*) bikini top; **~ć** (*-am*) *pokój* heat; *sierść* singe; (*część ciała*) tan; ***~ć się*** tan, sunbathe
opal|enizna *f* (*-y*; *G -zn*) suntan; **~ić** *pf.* → ***opalać***; **~ony** (sun)tanned
opał *m* (*-u*; *-y*) fuel; ***skład ~u*** coal merchant's; **~owy**: ***drewno ~owe*** firewood
opamięt|ywać się (*-uję*) 〈***~ać się***〉 come to one's senses
opancerzony armo(u)red; → ***pancerny***
opanow|anie *n* composure; calmness; **~any** calm, self-controlled; **~(yw)ać** (*-*[*w*]*uję*) control (***się*** o.s.); *pożar, sytuację* bring under control; (*o uczuciach*) overcome, seize
opar *m* (*-u*; *-y*) veil of mist; ***~y*** *pl.* fumes *pl.*, vapo(u)rs *pl.*; → ***wyziewy***
opar|cie *m* (*-a*; *G -rć*) (*krzesła itp.*) back; support; *fig.* reliance; ***~cie dla głowy*** headrest; ***punkt ~cia*** hold; **~ty** based (***na*** *L* on)
oparz|elina *f* (*-y*; *G -in*) *med.* scalding; **~enie** *n* (*-a*; *G -eń*) burning; **~yć** *pf.* → ***parzyć***
opas|ać *pf.* → ***opasywać***; **~ka** *f* (*-i*; *G -sek*) band; ***~ka żałobna*** mourning-band; **~ły** obese; **~ywać** (*-uję*) (*I*) belt (with), bind (with), gird (with); ***~ywać się*** gird
opaść *pf.* → ***paść***[1]***, opadać***
opat *m* (*-a*; *-ci*) abbot
opatentować *pf.* (*-uję*) patent
opatrun|ek *m* (*-nku*; *-nki*) *med.* dressing; **~kowy** dressing
opatrywać (*-uję*) get ready; *ranę* dress; (*pieczęcią, kratą*) (*D*) provide (with); ***~ datą*** date
opatrznoś|ciowy providential; **~ć** *f* (*-ści*; *0*) providence
opa|trzyć *pf.* → ***opatrywać***; **~tulać** (*-am*) 〈***~tulić***〉 (*-lę*) wrap up
opcja *f* (*-i*; *-e*) option
opera *f* (*-y*; *G -er*) opera; (*budynek*) opera house
opera|cja *f* (*-i*; *-e*) operation (*też mil.*, *med.*); *med.* surgery; ***~cja handlowa*** transaction; **~cyjny** operating; surgical; ***system ~cyjny*** *komp.* operating system; **~tor** *m* (*-a*; *-rzy*), **~torka** *f* (*-i*; *G -rek*) operator; **~tywny** efficient
operetk|a *f* (*-i*; *G -tek*) operetta; **~owy** operetta
operować (*-uję*) (*-uję*) 〈***z-***〉 *v/i.* operate; *v/t. med.* operate on; manipulate

O

operowy opera, operatic

opędz|ać (*-am*) ⟨**~ić**⟩ (*też* ***się od*** *G*) chase away; *wydatki* meet; *potrzeby* satisfy; ***nie móc się ~ić*** not be able to get rid of

opęt|ać *pf.* → ***opętywać***; **~anie** *n* (*-a*) possession; *fig.* obsession; **~ańczy** like one possessed; **~ywać** (*-uję*) possess; ***być ~anym przez*** (*A*) be possessed by, *fig.* be obsessed with

opić *pf.* → ***opijać***

opie|c *pf.* → ***opiekać***; **~czę-** *pf.* → ***pieczę-***; **~ka** *f* (*-i*; *G* -) care; ***~ka społeczna*** social security, welfare; ***~ka lekarska*** medical care; ***~ka nad zabytkami*** preservation of historic monuments; ***być pod ~ką*** (*G*) be under the care (of)

opieka|cz *m* (*-a*; *-e*) toaster; **~ć** (*-am*) *chleb* toast; (*na ruszcie*) grill; (*w tłuszczu*) braise

opiek|ować ⟨***za-***⟩ **się** (*-uję*) (*I*) look (after), take care (of); (*chorym*) nurse; (*dziećmi dorywczo*) baby-sit; **~un** *m* (*-a*; *-owie/-i*), **~unka** *f* (*-i*; *G -nek*) (*starszych itp.*) social worker; (*dzieci*, *stały*) (child) minder, (*dorywczy*) baby-sitter; (*studentów*) tutor; *jur.* guardian; **~uńczo** protectively; **~uńczy** protective, caring; ***państwo ~uńcze*** welfare state

opieprz|ać (*-am*) ⟨**~yć**⟩ F *Brt.* tear a strip, *Am.* chew out

opierać (*-am*) (**o** *A*) lean (against) (**się** *v/i.*), prop (against); rest (on) (**się** *v/i.*); (**na** *A*) *fig.* base (on); **~ się** *fig.* resist, withstand

opiesza|le *adv.* negligently, inertly; **~łość** *f* (*-ści*; *0*) negligence; **~ły** slow-moving, negligent, inert

opiewać (*-am*) extol, glorify; (**na** *A*) amount to; *wyrok* come to

opięty tight, close-fitting

opi|jać (*-am*) celebrate with a drink; ***~jać się*** (*I*) drink too much, F sink; **~lstwo** *n* (*-a*; *0*) alcoholism; ***w stanie ~lstwa*** when drunk

opił|ki *m/pl.* filings *pl.*; **~ow(yw)ać** (*-[w]uję*) file

opini|a *f* (*GDl -ii*; *-e*) opinion, view, belief; (*sława*) reputation; *szkoła*: school report; → ***ocena***; **~ować** ⟨***za-***⟩ (*-uję*) (*A*, **o** *L*) express opinion (about)

opis *m* (*-u*; *-y*) description; **~ywać** (*-uję*) ⟨**~ać**⟩ describe

o|platać (*-am*) entwine (**się** *v/i.*); fold around; **~plątywać** (*-uję*) ⟨~plątać⟩ entangle (*też fig.*); **~pleść** *pf.* → ***oplatać***; **~pluwać** (*-am*) ⟨**~pluć**⟩ (**na** *A*) spit (at)

opłac|ać (*-am*) pay; ***~ać się*** pay (*też fig.*); *szantażyście* pay off; ***nie opłaca się*** it's no use; **~alny** profitable, lucrative; *fig.* worthwhile, rewarding; **~ić** *pf.* → ***opłacać***; **~ony** paid; *koperta* stamped

opłak|any sorry, pitiful; **~iwać** (*-uję*) lament, mourn (*też fig.*)

opłata *f* (*-y*; *G* -) charge, fee; (*opłacenie*) payment; ***~ za przejazd*** fare; ***~ pocztowa*** postage

opłatek *m* (*-tka*; *-tki*) *rel.* wafer

opłucna *f* (*-ej*; *-e*) *anat.* pleura

opłuk|iwać (*-uję*) ⟨**~ać**⟩ rinse, flush

opły|wać ⟨**~nąć**⟩ *v/t.* *człowiek*: swim round; *okręt*: sail round; *woda*: wash round; ***~wać w dostatki*** be rolling in money; **~wowy** streamlined

opodal **1.** *adv.* (*też* ***nie ~***) nearby; **2.** *prp.* (*G*) nearby

opodatkow|anie *n* (*-a*; *G -ań*) taxation; **~(yw)ać** (*-[w]uję*) tax

opona *f* (*-y*; *G* -) *mot. Brt.* tyre, *Am.* tire; *anat.* ***~ mózgowa*** meninx

oponować ⟨***za-***⟩ (*-uję*) (***przeciw*** *D*) protest, oppose

opończa *f* (*-y*; *G -cz*) cape

opor|nie *adv.* *robić* reluctantly; *przesuwać* with difficulty; **~nik** *m* (*-a*; *-i*) *electr.* resistor; **~ność** *f* (*-ści*; *0*) *electr.* resistance; **~ny** (*niegrzeczny*) disobedient; resistant

oportunistyczny opportunistic

oporządz|ać (*-am*) ⟨**~ić**⟩ *bydło* look after; *gastr.* gut

opowiada|ć (*-am*) narrate, tell; ***~ć się*** (***za*** *I*) declare o.s. in favo(u)r (of); **~nie** *n* (*-a*; *G -ań*) tale; story

opowie|dzieć *pf.* → ***opowiadać***; **~ść** *f* tale

opozyc|ja *f* (*-i*; *-e*) opposition; **~yjny** opposition

opór *m* (*-oru*; *-ory*) resistance; opposition; ***ruch oporu*** the Resistance

opóźni|ać (*-am*) ⟨**~ć**⟩ delay, hold up; ***~ać*** ⟨**~ć**⟩ ***się*** be late (***z*** *I* with); **~enie** *n* (*-a*; *G -eń*) delay; hold-up; **~ony** late, delayed; *fig.* retarded (***w*** *I* in)

opracow|anie *n* (*dzieło*) treatise, study; working out; **~(yw)ać** (*-[w]uję*) work out, develop, prepare; *dzieło* prepare, make up

opraw|a *f* (*-y*; *G* -) setting (*też theat.*, *fig.*); *print.* binding; ***w ~ie*** *print.* bound; ***w twardej ~ie*** hardback; → ***oprawka***; **~iać** (*-am*) ⟨**~ić**⟩ bind; *obraz* frame; *klejnot* set, mount; *tuszę* dress, skin; **~ka** *f* (*-i*; *G -wek*) → ***oprawa***; *okularów* frame, rim; *żarówki* socket; *tech.* holder; **~ny** bound; framed; set, mounted

opresj|a *f* (*-i*; *-e*) predicament, F fix; ***w ~i*** in dire straits

oprocentowanie *n* (*-a*; *G -ań*) interest

oprogramowanie *n* (*-a*; *G -ań*) *komp.* software

opromieniony *fig.* bright

oprowadz|ać (*-am*) ⟨**~ić**⟩ show around

oprócz *prp.* (*G*) besides, aside from

opróżni|ać (*-am*) ⟨**~ć**⟩ (*-ę*, *-nij!*) empty (***się*** *v/i.*); *pokój* vacate, move out of; *teren* evacuate; ***~ać*** ⟨***~ć***⟩ ***się*** become empty

oprysk|iwać (*-uję*) ⟨**~ać**⟩ sprinkle, spatter; **~liwie** *adv.* gruffly, brusquely; **~liwy** gruff, brusque

opryszczka *f* (*-i*; *G -ek*) *med.* herpes

opryszek *m* (*-szka*; *-szki/-szkowie*) thug, mugger, hudlum

oprzeć *pf.* → ***opierać***

oprzęd *m* (*-u*; *-y*) cocoon shell, floss

oprzytomnieć *pf.* (*-eję*) regain consciousness; collect o.s.; → ***opamiętywać się***

optować (*-uję*) opt (***na rzecz*** *G* in favo(u)r of, for)

opty|czny optical; **~k** *m* (*-a*; *-ycy*) optician; **~ka** *f* (*-i*; *0*) optics *sg.*

opty|malizować (*-uję*) optimize; **~malny** optimal, optimum; **~mista** *m* (*-y*; *G -tów*), **~mistka** *f* (*-i*; *G -tek*) optimist; **~mistyczny** optimistic

opuch|li(z)na *f* (*-y*; *G -(z)n*) swelling; **~ły**, **~nięty** swollen; → ***puchnąć***

opuk|iwać (*-uję*) ⟨**~ać**⟩ tap; *med.* percuss

opust *econ.* → ***upust***

opustosz|ały deserted, empty; **~eć** *pf.* (*-eję*) become deserted; **~yć** *pf.* → ***pustoszyć***

opuszcz|ać leave; *wyraz* omit, skip; *wykład* miss, skip; *rodzinę* desert; *por.* ***spuszczać***; ***~ać się*** come down; (*w pracy*) become disorderly/untidy; **~enie** *n* (*-a*; *0*) desolation; neglect; (*rodziny itp.*) desertion; (*pl. -a*) (*tekstu*) omission; **~ony** left; deserted; omitted; skipped

opuszka *f* (*-i*; *G -szek*) fingertip

opuścić *pf.* → ***opuszczać***

opyl|ać (*-am*) ⟨**~ić**⟩ dust; F sell

orać ⟨**z-, za-**⟩ *Brt.* plough, *Am.* plow; (*t-ko impf.*) F *fig.* work like hell

oranżada *f* (*-y*; *G -ad*) orangeade

oraz *cj.* and

orbi|ta *f* (*-y*; *G* -) orbit; ***na ~cie*** in orbit

orchidea *f* (*-dei*; *-dee*) *bot.* orchid

orczyk *m* (*-a*; *-i*) swingletree, *Am.* whiffletree; *aviat.* rudder bar; (*w sporcie*) tow bar; **~owy**: ***wyciąg ~owy*** tow lift

order *m* (*-u*; *-y*) medal, decoration

ordy|nacja *f*: ***~nacja wyborcza*** voting regulations *pl.*; **~nans** *m* (*-a*; *-i*) *mil.* orderly; **~narny** vulgar, gross; **~nator** *m* (*-a*; *-rzy*) consultant; **~nować** (*-uję*) administer, prescribe

orędowni|czka *f* (*-i*; *G -czek*), **~k** *m* (*-a*; *-cy*) advocate, champion

orędzie *n* (*-a*; *G* -) speech, address

oręż *m* (*-a*; *zw. 0*) weapons *pl.*

organ *m* (*-u*; *-y*) organ; ***~y*** *pl. mus.* organ; **~iczny** organic; **~ista** *m* (*-y*; *-ści*, *-stów*), **~istka** *f* (*-i*; *G -tek*) organist

organiza|cja *f* (*-i*; *-e*) organization; institution; **~cyjny** organizational; **~tor** *m* (*-a*; *-rzy*), **~torka** *f* (*-i*; *G -rek*) organizer

organizm *m* (*-y*) organism

organizować ⟨**z-**⟩ (*-uję*) organize; *spotkanie* arrange; *przyjęcie* hold

organ|ki *pl.* (*-ków*) *mus.* mouth organ; **~owy** organ; **~y** *pl.* → ***organ***

orgazm *m* (*-u*; *-y*) orgasm

orgia *f* (*GDl -ii*; *-e*) orgy

orienta|cja *f* (*-i*; *-e*) orientation; *fig.* view; ***zmysł ~cji*** sense of direction; ***~cja seksualna*** sexuality; **~cyjny** guiding; (*przybliżony*) approximate; **~lny** Oriental

orientować ⟨**z-**⟩ (*-uję*) inform; (*w terenie*, *kościół*) orient, orientate; ***~ się*** orientate o.s.; be familiar (***w*** *L* with); understand

orka *f* (*-i*; *0*) *Brt.* ploughing, *Am.* plowing

Orkady *pl.* (*G -ów*) Orkneys *pl.*

orkiestra *f* (*-y*; *G* -) orchestra; ***~ symfoniczna*** symphony orchestra

orli aquiline

Ormianin *m* (*-a*; *-nie*), **~ka** *f* (*-i*; *G -nek*) Armenian

ormiańs|ki Armenian; ***mówić po ~ku*** speak Armenian

ornament *m* (*-u*; *-y*) ornament

ornat *m* (*-u*; *-y*) *rel.* chasuble

ornitologi|a *f* (*GDL -ii*; *0*) ornithology; **~czny** ornithological
orny arable; ***grunt ~*** arable land
orszak *m* (*-u*; *-i*) entourage; (***ślubny, żałobny*** wedding, funeral) procession
ortodoksyjny orthodox
ortograficzny spelling
ortodontyczny orthodontic
ortopedyczny orthop(a)edic
oryginaln|ie originally; **~y** original
oryginał *m* (*-u*; *-y*) original, (*m-os a*; *-y/-owie*) original, nonconformist
orzec *pf.* → ***orzekać***
orzech *m* (*-a*; *-y*) *bot.* nut; ***~ włoski*** walnut; **~owy** nut; *zapach* nutty; *kolor* hazel
orzecz|enie *n* (*-a*; *G -eń*) decision; *jur.* judg(e)ment, verdict, ruling; *gr.* predicate; *med.* expert (medical) opinion
orzeka|ć (*-am*) decide, judge; *jur.* rule, adjudicate; **~jący**: ***tryb ~jący*** indicative mood
orzeł *m* (*orła*; *orły*) eagle; → ***reszka***
orzeszek *m* (*-szka*; *-szki*) → ***orzech***
orzeźwi|ać (*-am*) 〈**~ć**〉 refresh (**się** o.s.); **~ająco** *adv.* refreshingly; **~ający** refreshing; *fig.* invigorating; ***napoje*** *pl.* ***~ające*** refreshments *pl.*
os. *skrót pisany*: ***osoba, osób*** person; ***osiedle*** estate, settlement
osa *f* (*-y*; *G os*) *zo.* wasp
osacz|ać (*-am*) 〈**~yć**〉 encircle, beset
osad *m* (*-u*; *-y*) sediment, deposit; **~a** *f* (*-y*; *G -*) settlement; **~niczka** *f* (*-i*; *G -czek*), **~nik** *m* (*-a*; *-cy*) settler; **~owy** sedimentation, sedimentary
osadz|ać (*-am*) 〈**~ić**〉 (*w miejscu, też osad*) settle (**się** *v/i.*); *łopatę* fix; mount; *fig.* establish; ***~ić w areszcie*** put under arrest
osamotni|eć *pf.* (*-eję*) become lonely; **~enie** *n* (*-a*; *G -eń*) loneliness, solitude; **~ony** lonely
osącz|ać (*-am*) 〈**~yć**〉 drip off
osą|d *m* (*-u*; *-y*) estimation; judg(e)ment; **~dzać** (*-am*) 〈**~dzić**〉 estimate; *czyny* adjudge
osch|le *adv.* stiffly, crisply; **~łość** *f* (*-ści*; *0*) stiffness; **~ły** stiff, crisp
oscyla-, oscylo- *w złoż.* oscilla-, oscillo-
osełka *f* (*-i*; *G -łek*) whetstone
oset *m* (*ostu*; *osty*) *bot.* thistle
osiad|ać settle down; *budynek, teren* subside, sink; *osad* settle, deposit (***na*** *L* on); → ***osadzać się***; **~ły** settled
osiąg|ać (*-am*) 〈**~nąć**〉 (*-nę*) reach, achieve; *cenę* fetch; **~alny** within reach; available, attainable; **~i** *m/pl.* (*-ów*) *tech.* performance; **~nięcie** *n* (*-a*) achievement, attainment; accomplishment
osiąść → ***osiadać, mielizna***
osie *pl.* → ***oś***
osiedl|ać (*-am*) settle (**się** *v/i.*); **~e** *n* (*-a*; *G -i*) *Brt.* housing estate, *Am.* housing development; **~eńczy** settling; **~ić** *pf.* (*-lę*) → ***osiedlać***; **~owy** estate
osiem eight; **~dziesiąt** eighty; → ***715***; **~nasto-** *w złoż.* eighteen-; **~nastka** *f* (*-i*; *G -tek*) eighteen; (*linia*) number eighteen; **~nasty** eighteenth; **~naście** eighteen; → ***715***; **~set** eight hundred; → ***715***; **~setny** eight hundredth
osierdzie *n* (*-a*; *G -dź*) *anat.* pericardium
osieroc|ać (*-am*) 〈**~ić**〉 orphan
osi|ka *f* (*-i*; *G -*) *bot.* aspen; **~na** *f* (*-y*; *G -*) aspen wood
osioł *m* (*osła*; *osły*) *zo.* donkey, ass (*też fig.*)
osiow|y axial; **~e** *n* (*-ego*; *0*) *rail.* stall fee
oskarż|ać (*-am*) accuse (**o** *A* of); *jur. też.* impeach, charge (**o** *A* with); ***~ać przed sądem*** sue, take to court; **~enie** *n* (*-a*; *G -eń*) accusation; charge; ***wnieść ~enie*** (***przeciw*** *D*) sue (against); ***akt ~enia*** indictment; **~ony** *m* (*-ego*; *-żeni*, *G -żonych*), **~ona** *f* (*-ej*; *G -ych*) *jur.* the accused, defendant; ***ława ~onych*** the dock; **~yciel** *m* (*-a*; *-e*), **~cielka** *f* (*-i*; *G -lek*) *jur.* prosecutor; **~yć** *pf.* (*-am*) → ***oskarżać***
oskrob|ywać (*-uję*) 〈**~ać**〉 scrape; (*z łusek*) scale
oskrzel|e *n* (*-a*; *G -i*) *anat.* bronchus, bronchial tube; ***zapalenie/nieżyt ~i*** bronchitis
oskubywać (*-uję*) pluck; → ***skubać***
osłabi|ać (*-am*) 〈**~ć**〉 (*-ę*) lessen, weaken; *krytykę, argumenty* tone down, moderate; **~enie** *n* (*-a*; *0*) weakening, lessening; moderation; **~ony** weakened; moderated
osła|bnąć *pf.* → ***słabnąć***; **~dzać** (*-am*) sweeten, sugar (*też fig.*); **~niać** (*-am*) cover; protect; (*przed światłem*) shade; *fig.* shield; **~wiony** notorious
osło|dzić *pf.* → ***osładzać***; **~na** *f* (*-y*; *G -*) cover, shield; shelter; *fig.* protec-

O

tion; *mil.* covering (fire); (*w sporcie*) covering, guard; **~nić** *pf.* → **osłaniać**; **~nka** *f* (-; *G -nek*) (*kiełbasy*) skin; ***bez ~nek*** openly
osłuch|iwać (*-uję*) ⟨**~ać**⟩ listen to; *med.* auscultate
osłupie|ć *pf.* (*-eję*) be flabbergasted; **~nie** *n* (*-a*; *0*) amazement, bewilderment; ***wprawić w ~nie*** amaze, bewilder
osma|lać (*-am*) → **smalić**; **~row(yw)ać** (*-[w]uję*) daub; besmear (*też fig.*); **~żać** (*-am*) ⟨**~żyć**⟩ brown
osnowa *f* (*-y*; *G -nów*) *włók.* warp; *fig.* fabric
osob|a *f* (*-y*; *G osób*): ***~a fizyczna/prawna*** natural/legal person; individual; ***na ~ę, od ~y*** per person; ***starsza ~a*** older person; **~istość** *f* (*-ści*) personage, notable; **~isty** personal; individual; → **dowód**; **~iście** in person, personally, individually
osobliw|ie *adv.* peculiarly; unusually; **~ość** *f* (*-ści*) curiosity; rarity; peculiarity; **~y** peculiar; unusual; ***nic ~ego*** nothing peculiar
osobn|ik *m* (*-a*; *-i*; *m-os pl. -cy*) individual; **~o** *adv.* separately, individually; **~y** separate, individual; → **oddzielny, odrębny**; ***każdy z ~a*** each individual
osobow|ość *f* (*-ści*) personality; ***~ość prawna*** *jur.* legal capacity; **~y** personal; ***akta*** *pl.* **~e** personal files/dossiers *pl.*; ***pociąg ~y*** slow train
osowia|le *adv.* dejectedly; **~ły** depressed, downcast
ospa *f* (*-y*; 0) *med.* smallpox, variola; ***~ wietrzna*** chickenpox
ospa|le *adv.* sluggishly; lethargically; **~ły** sluggish; lethargic
ospowaty pock-marked
osprzęt *m* (*-u*; *-y*) equipment; *zwł. komp.* hardware
ostateczn|ie *adv.* finally, after all; **~ość** *f* (*-ści*) extremity; finality; ***w ~ości*** as a last resort; in an emergency; **~y** final; extreme → **sąd**
ostat|ek *m* (*-tku*; *-tki*) rest; *t-ko pl.* **~ki** Shrovetide, Mardi Gras; ***do ~ka*** to the end; ***na ~ek*** at the end; **~ni** last; final; (*najnowszy*) latest; ***~nimi czasy*** → **~nio** *adv.* recently, lately; → **namaszczenie**
ostentacyjny ostentatious, F splashy
ostoja *f* (*-oi*; *-oje*, *-oi*) *fig.* bastion, mainstay
ostro *adv.* sharply, sharp; keenly; → **ostry**; **~ga** *f* (*-i*; *G ostróg*) spur; **~kątny** acute-angled; **~słup** *math.* pyramid; **~ść** *f* (*-ści*; *0*) sharpness; *phot.* focus; (*nauczyciela itp.*) harshness
ostrożn|ie carefully; cautiously; **~ość** *f* (*-ści*; *0*) care, caution; carefulness; ***środki*** *pl.* ***~ości*** precautions *pl.*, precautionary measures *pl.*; **~y** careful, cautious; *wyliczenia* conservative
ostr|y sharp; *światło* dazzling; *głos* shrill; *nauczyciel itp.* harsh; *zdjęcie* in focus; *zapach* pungent; *jedzenie* hot; *med.* acute; ***~e pogotowie*** alert; ***~y dyżur*** *med.* emergency service, emergency *Brt.* centre (*Am.* center)
ostryga *f* (*-i*; *G -*) *zo.* oyster
ostrze *n* (*-a*; *G -y*) blade
ostrze|gać (*-am*) ⟨**~c**⟩ warn (**przed** *I* against); **~gawczy** warning; **~liwać** (*-wuję*) ⟨**~lać**⟩ shell, bombard; **~żenie** *n* (*-a*; *G -eń*) warning
o|strzyc *pf.* → **strzyc**; **~strzyć** ⟨**na-**⟩ (*-ę*) sharpen, (*na szlifierce*) grind; *fig.* whet; **~studzać** (*-am*) cool; **~stygać** (*-am*) → **stygnąć**; **~sunąć się** *pf.* → **osuwać**
osusz|ać (*-am*) ⟨**~yć**⟩ dry; *bagno itp.* drain; F *butelkę* empty
osuw|ać się slip, slip off; *ziemia*: give way, slide; *ktoś*: sink (down); **~isko** *n* (*-a*; *G -*) landslide, landslip
oswa|badzać (*-am*) → **oswobadzać**; **~jać** (*-am*) (**się z** *I*) get used (to), get accustomed (to); *zwierzę* tame
oswo|badzać (*-am*) ⟨**~bodzić**⟩ (*-dzę*; *też -bódź!*) free (**się** o.s.; **od** *G* from), liberate; **~bodzenie** *n* (*-a*; *0*) freeing; liberating; **~ić** *pf.* → **oswajać**; **~ić się** *zwierzę*: become tame; **~jony** tame
osyp(yw)ać → **obsypywać**
osza|cować *pf.* → **szacować**; **~leć** go mad
oszałamia|ć (*-am*) stun; *fig.* daze, dazzle; **~jąco** *adv.* stunningly; bewilderingly; **~jący** stunning; dazzling, bewildering
oszczep *m* (*-u*; *-y*) (*w sporcie*) javelin
oszczepni|ctwo *n* (*-a*; *0*) (*w sporcie*) javelin-throwing; **~czka** *f* (*-i*; *G -czek*), **~k** *m* (*-a*; *-cy*) *sport*: javelin-thrower
oszczer|ca *m* (*-y*; *G -ców*) slanderer; **~czo** *adv.* slanderously; libellously; **~czy** slanderous; libellous; **~stwo** *n* (*-a*; *G -*) slander; libel

oszczę|dnościowy *rachunek itp.* savings; *poczynania* economy; **~dność** *f* (*-ści*; *0*) economy; thriftiness; (*pl.* **~dności**) savings *pl.*; **~dny** economical; sparing; *osoba* thrifty; **~dzać** (*-am*) ⟨**~dzić**⟩ (**na** *A*) save (up for); (**na** *L*) be sparing (with); *światło*, *materiały* save, economize on; *k-uś* save, spare; (*żyć oszczędnie*) economize

oszk|- *fig.* → **szk-**; **~lony** glazed

oszołomi|ć *pf.* → **oszałamiać**; **~enie** *n* (*-a*; *0*) daze; *fig.* bewilderment

oszpecać *pf.* → **szpecić**

oszroniony frosted

oszuka|ć *pf.* → **oszukiwać**; **~ńczo** *adv.* deceitfully; **~ńczy** deceitful; deceptive; **~ństwo** *n* (*-a*; *G -*) deceit; deceptiveness

oszukiwać (*-uję*) deceive; *v/i.* cheat; **~ się** deceive o.s.

oszust *m* (*-a*; *-ści*), **~ka** *f* (*-i*; *G -tek*) cheat, fraud, impostor; **~wo** *n* (*-a*; *G -*) deceit, deception; fraud

oś *f* (*osi*; *osie*) *mot.* axle; *math. itp.* axis

ościenny neighbo(u)ring

oścież: **na ~** wide open

ość *f* (*ości*) fishbone

oślep: **na ~** blindly, blind; **~iać** (*-am*) ⟨**~ić**⟩ (*-ę*) blind; (*światłem*) daze; **~iająco** *adv.* dazzlingly; **~iający** dazzling; **~nąć** (*-nę*) *pf.* go blind

ośl|i donkey; asinine (*też fig.*); **~e uszy** *fig.* dog ears; **~ica** *f* (*-y*; *G -*) *zo.* she-donkey; jenny-ass

ośliz(g)ły slimy

ośmie|lać (*-am*) ⟨**~lić**⟩ (*-lę*) encourage; **~lić się** take heart; dare; **~szać** (*-am*) ⟨**~szyć**⟩ (*-szę*) ridicule; **~szać** ⟨**~szyć**⟩ **się** make a fool of o.s.

ośmio|- *w złoż.* eight-; *math.*, *chem. itp.* octo-, octa-; **~bok** *m* (*-u*; *-i*) *math.* octagon; **~dniowy** eight-day(-long); **~krotny** eightfold; **~letni** eight-year-long, -old

ośmiornica *f* (*-y*; *G -*) *zo.* octopus

ośmi|oro, ~u *m-os* eight → **715**

ośnieżony snow-covered

ośr. *skrót pisany*: **ośrodek** *Brt.* centre, *Am.* center

ośrodek *m* (*-dka*; *-dki*) *Brt.* centre, *Am.* center

oświadcz|ać (*-am*) ⟨**~yć**⟩ state, declare; **~yć się** (*D*) propose (to); **~enie** *n* (*-a*; *G -eń*) statement, declaration; **~yny** *pl.* (*-*) proposal

oświat|a *f* (*-y*; *0*) education; **~owy** educational; **film ~owy** educational film

oświec|ać (*-am*) ⟨**~ić**⟩ *zwł. fig.* enlighten; **~enie** *n* (*-a*; *0*) enlightenment; **Ꙍenie** Enlightenment; **~ony** enlighted

oświetl|ać (*-am*) ⟨**~ić**⟩ (*-lę*) light, light up; illuminate; **~enie** *n* light (*s pl.*); lighting; illumination; **~eniowy** lighting

Oświęcim *m* (*-ia*) (*miejsce obozu koncentracyjnego*) Auschwitz; **Ꙍski** Auschwitz

otaczać (*-am*) surround, encircle; **~ się** (*I*) surround o.s. (with)

otchłań *f* (*-ni*; *-nie*) abyss, chasm

otępi|ały stupefied, torpid; *wzrok* vacant; **~eć** (*-eję*) deaden, become stupefied; **~enie** *n* (*-a*; *0*) stupefaction; *med.* dementia

oto here, there; **~ wszystko** that's all; **~ nasz dom** here is our house; **~ oni/one** here they are

otocz|ak *m* (*-a*; *-i*) pebble; **~enie** *n* (*-a*; *G -eń*) surrounding(s *pl.*); environment; **w ~eniu** (*G*) surrounded (by); **~yć** *pf.* → **otaczać**

otok *m* (*-u*; *-i*) round; **~ czapki** cap band

otomana *f* (*-y*; *G -*) ottoman

otóż → **oto**; **~ to** that is it

otręby *pl.* (*-rąb*/*-bów*) bran

otru|cie *n* (*-a*; *G -uć*) poisoning; **~ć** *pf.* poison; **~ty** poisoned

otrzaska|ć się F *pf.* (**z** *I*) get the knack (of); **~ny** F → **obyty**

otrząs|ać (*-am*) ⟨**~nąć**⟩ (*-nę*) (*też* **się z** *G*) shake off; **~ać** ⟨**~nąć**⟩ **się** shake o.s.; *fig.* recover (**po** *I* after)

otrze|ć *fig.* → **ocierać**; **~pywać** (*-uję*) ⟨**~pać**⟩ knock off, tap off

otrzewna *f* (*-ej*; *-e*) *anat.* peritoneum

otrzeźwi|ać (*-am*) ⟨**~ć**⟩ (*-ę*) refresh (**się** o.s.); *fig.* sober up

otrzym|anie *n* (*-a*; *0*) receipt; reception; **~ywać** (*-uję*) ⟨**~ać**⟩ receive, get, obtain; *tech.* produce

otuch|a *f* (*-y*; *0*) comfort; **pełen ~y** confident

otul|ać (*-am*) ⟨**~ić**⟩ (*I*) wrap (with); *v/i. fig.* shroud

otumaniać (*-am*) → **tumanić**

otwar|cie 1. *adv.* openly; **2.** *n* (*-a*; *G -rć*) opening; → **godzina**; **~tość** *f* (*-ści*; *0*) openness; cando(u)r; **~ty** open; *ktoś* candid, frank

otwier|acz *m* (*-a*; *-e*) opener; **~ać** (*-am*) open; (*zaczynać*) open, start; *parasol* put up; ***~ać się*** open
otwo|rek *m* (*-rka*; *-rki*) → ***otwór***; **~rem**: ***stać ~rem*** be open; **~rzyć** *pf.* → ***otwierać***
otwór *m* (*-woru*; *-wory*) opening; hole; gap
otyłość *f* (*-ści*; *0*) obesity
otyły obese
owa *f* → ***ów***; **~cja** *f* (*-i*; *-e*) ovation, applause; **~cyjny** enthusiastic
owad *m* (*-a*; *-y*) *zo.* insect
owado|bójczy: ***środek ~bójczy*** insecticide, insect poison; **~żerny** insectivore
owak(i) → ***tak(i)***
owal *m* (*-u*; *-e*) oval; **~ny** oval
owca *f* (*-y*; *-e*, *G -wiec*) *zo.* sheep *sg./pl.*
owcza|rek *m* (*-rka*; *-rki*) sheepdog, shepherd dog; ***~rek niemiecki*** Alsatian; ***~rek szkocki*** collie; **~rnia** *f* (*-i*; *-e*, *-i/-ń*) sheep-fold; **~rstwo** *f* (*-a*; *0*) sheep-breeding; **~rz** *m* (*-a*; *-e*) shepherd
owczy sheep; ***~ pęd*** herd instinct
owdowi|eć (*-eję*) *kobieta*: become a widow; *mężczyzna*: become a widower; ***~ały*** widowed
owdzie → ***ówdzie***
owe *ż-rzecz* → ***ów***
owędy: ***tędy i ~*** here and there
owi *pl. m-os* → ***ów***
owieczka *f* (*-i*; *G -czek*) *zo.* → ***owca***
owies *m* (*-wsa*; *-wsy*) *bot.* oat, (*nasiona*) oats *pl.*
owi|ewać (*-am*) blow on; *fig.* envelope; **~jać** (*-am*) ⟨***~nąć***⟩ (*-nę*, *-ń!*) wrap (round), bind (round); ***~jać*** ⟨~nąć⟩ ***się*** wind o.s., wrap o.s. (***wokół*** *G* round)
owładnąć *pf* (*-nę*) → ***zawładnąć***
owłosiony hairy
owo *n* → ***ów***
owoc *m* (*-u*; *-e*) *bot.* fruit (*też fig.*); **~arski** fruit; **~ny** fruitful; **~ować** fruit; **~owy** fruit
owrzodz|enie *n* (*-a*; *G -eń*) *med.* ulceration; **~ony** ulcerated
owsian|ka *f* (*-i*; *G -nek*) porridge; **~y** oat
owszem *adv.* of course, without a doubt; on the contrary
ozdabiać (*-am*) decorate, embellish; → ***zdobić***
ozdob|a *f* (*-y*; *G -dób*) decoration, ornament; **~ić** *pf.* → ***ozdabiać***; **~ny** ornamental, decorative; (*przeładowany*) ornate
ozdrowie|niec *m* (*-a*; *-y*) convalescent; **~ńczy** convalescent; *econ.* redevelopment, rehabilitation
oziębi|ać (*-am*) ⟨***~ć***⟩ cool down (***się*** *v/i.*); **~enie** *n* (*-a*; *G -eń*) cooling
oziębł|le *adv.* coldly; **~ły** cold; chilly; (*seksualnie*) frigid
ozim|ina *f* (*-y*; *G -*) *agr.* winter seed; winter grain; **~y** *agr.* winter
oznacz|ać (*-am*) mean, signify; symbolize, represent; ⟨***~yć***⟩ *też* mark, label
oznajmi|ać (*-am*) ⟨***~ć***⟩ (*-ę*, *-mij!*) declare, state, announce; **~enie** *n* (*-a*) announcement; → ***obwieszczenie***
oznajmujący: ***tryb ~*** *gr.* indicative mood
oznaka *f* (*-i*; *G -*) symptom, sign, indication; (*znaczek*) badge
ozon *m* (*-u*; *0*) *chem.* ozone; **~owy** ozone; ***warstwa ~owa*** ozone layer
ozór *m* (*-zoru*; *-zory*) tongue (*też gastr.*)
ożaglowanie *n* (*-a*; *G -ań*) *naut.* rig
ożen|ek *m* (*-nku*; *-nki*) marriage; **~ić się** → ***żenić się***; **~iony** married (***z*** *I* to)
oży|wać (*-am*) ⟨***~ć***⟩ come alive; *fig.* revive; **~wczo** *adv.* in a stimulating way; **~wczy** stimulating, invigorating; **~wiać** (*-am*) ⟨***~wić***⟩ enliven, F liven up; stimulate; ***~wiać*** ⟨***~wić***⟩ ***się*** *oczy*: light up; *gospodarka*: revive; **~wiony** lively, animated

Ó

ósemka *f* (*-i*; *G -mek*) eight; (*linia itp.*) number eight; *mus. Brt.* quaver, *Am.* eighth note
ósm|y eighth; ***~a*** eight (o'clock); → ***715***
ów (***owa*** *f*, ***owo*** *n*, ***owe*** *ż-rzecz*, ***owi*** *m-os*) this; ***to i owo*** this and that; ***ni z tego ni z owego*** out of the blue
ów|czesny the then; **~dzie**: ***tu i ~dzie*** here and there

P

p. *skrót pisany*: ***pan*** Mr; ***pani*** Mrs, Ms; ***panna*** Miss; ***patrz*** see; ***piętro*** floor; ***porównaj*** cf. (*compare*); ***punkt*** point; ***po*** after

pach|a *f* (*-y*) armpit; (*w ubraniu*) armhole; ***pod ~ą*** under the arm

pach|nąco *adv.* fragrantly; **~nący** fragrant, scented; **~nieć** (*-nę*; *-nij!*) smell; (*I*) smell, pick up the scent

pachołek *m* (*-łka*; *-łki/-łkowie*) (*słupek*) *naut.* bollard

pachwina *f* (*-y*; *G -*) *anat.* groin

pacierz *m* (*-a*; *-e*, *-y*) prayer; ***odmawiać ~*** pray, say prayers

paciorek *m* (*-rka*; *-rki*) bead

pacjent *m* (*-a*; *-nci*), **~ka** *f* (*-i*; *G -tek*) patient

packa *f* (*-i*; *G -cek*) fly swat

Pacyfik *m* (*-u*; *0*) the Pacific Ocean

pacz|ka *f* (*-i*; *G -czek*) parcel; packet; (*papierosów*) *Brt.* packet, *Am.* package; F (*ludzi*) bunch, crowd; **~kowany** packaged; **~yć** ⟨**s-, wy-**⟩ (*-ę*): ***~yć*** ⟨***s-, wy-***⟩ ***się*** warp

padaczka *f* (*-i*; *0*) epilepsy

padać (*-am*) fall, drop; ***pada deszcz/śnieg*** it is raining/snowing

padalec *m* (*-lca*; *-lce*) *zo.* slow-worm

padlina *f* (*-y*; 0) rotten carcass; (*mięso*) carrion

pagaj *m* (*-a*; *-e*) paddle

pagór|ek *m* (*-rka*; *-rki*) hillock; **~kowaty** hilly

pajacyk *m* (*-a*; *-i*) (*zabawka*) jumping jack; (*ubranie*) rompers *pl.*, play-suit

pa|jąk *m* (*-a*; *-i*) *zo.* spider; **~jęczyna** *f* (*-y*; *G -*) cobweb

paka *f* (*-i*; *G -*) box, chest; → ***paczka***; F (*więzienie*) clink

pakie|cik *m* (*-a*; *-i*) → ***pakiet***; **~t** *m* (*-u*; *-y*) packet

pakow|ać (*-uję*) ⟨**za-**⟩ pack; ⟨**o-**⟩ wrap (up); ⟨**w-**⟩ put into; (*siłą*) cram into; ***~ać*** ⟨***s-***⟩ ***się*** pack up; **~ny** roomy; **~y**: ***papier ~y*** manila paper, wrapping paper

paktować (*-uję*) pact

pakunek *m* (*-nku*; *-nki*) package; bundle; *tech.* packing

pal *m* (*-a*; *-e*, *-i/-ów*) stake, post; *bud.* pile

palacz *m* (*-a*; *-e*), (*w piecu*) stoker; (*papierosów*) smoker; **~ka** *f* (*-i*; *G -czek*) smoker

palarnia *f* (*-i*; *-e*) smoking room

palący burning (*też fig.*); smoking; *słońce* scorching; ***dla ~ch*** smoker

pal|ec *m* (*-lca*; *-lce*) (*ręki*) finger, (*stopy*) toe; *anat.* digit; ***~ec wskazujący*** index finger; ***~ec serdeczny*** ring finger; ***duży ~ec*** big toe; ***na ~cach*** tip-toe; ***sam jak ~ec*** all alone

pale|nie *n* (*-a*; *G -eń*) burning; (*w piecu*) heating; (*tytoniu*) smoking; (*kawy*) roasting; **~nisko** *n* (*-a*; *G -*) hearth

Palestyna *f* (*-y*; *0*) Palestine

paleta *f* (*-y*; *G -*) (*malarza*) palette; *tech.* pallet

pali|ć (*-lę*) *v/i.* (*w piecu*) heat, stove; (*rana, w gardle*) burn; *papierosy* smoke; *papiery* burn; *lampę* have on, keep on; ⟨**s-**⟩ burn; ***~ć się*** burn; *budynek*: be on fire; *lampa*: be on; F be burning to do; **~wo** *n* (*-a*; *G -*) fuel

palm|a *f* (*-y*; *G -*) *bot.* palm (tree); **~owy** palm

paln|ąć F *v/s* (*-nę*) (*trzasnąć*) bash; ***~ąć sobie w łeb*** blow one's brains out; **~ik** *m* (*-a*; *-i*) burner; **~y** inflammable, combustible; ***broń ~a*** firearm

palto *n* (*-a*; *G -*) overcoat

palu|ch *m* (*-a*; *-y*) *anat.* big toe; **~szek** *m* (*-szka*; *-szki*) → ***palec***; ***~szki*** *pl.* ***rybne*** *gastr.* fish fingers *pl.*

pałac *m* (*-u*; *-e*) palace

pałać (*-am*) *oczy*: blaze; ***~ nienawiścią*** be burning with hatred

pał|ąk *m* (*-a*; *-i*) bail; bow; **~eczka** *f* (*-i*; *G -czek*) → ***pałka***; *gastr.* chopstick; **~ka** *f* (*-i*; *G -łek*) stick; (*policjanta*) club, *Brt.* truncheon, *Am.* night stick

pamiątk|a *f* (*-i*; *G -tek*) memento, souvenir (***~a po matce*** of the mother); (*z wczasów*) souvenir; ***na ~ę*** to remember; **~owy** commemorative

pamię|ć *f* (*-ci*; *0*) memory (*też komp.*); (*wspomnienie*) remembrance; ***na ~ć*** by heart; ***świętej ~ci*** of blessed memory; ***ku ~ci*** (*G*) in memory (of); **~tać** (*-am*) (*A*) remember; (**o** *L*) not forget (about);

~tnik *m* (*-a*; *-i*) diary; *pl.* **~tniki** memoirs *pl.*; **~tny** memorable, unforgettable
PAN *skrót pisany*: **Polska Akademia Nauk** Polish Academy of Sciences
pan *m* (*-a*; *DL -u*; *-owie*) gentleman; (*psa itp.*) master; (*przy zwracaniu się*: *z nazwiskiem*) Mr, (*bez nazwiska*) sir; **~ Nowak** Mr Nowak; **~ie doktorze** Doctor (*skrót*: Dr); **czy ~ ma ...?** do you have...?; **~ domu** (*gospodarz*) host, landlord; **~ młody** bridegroom
pan|cernik *m* (*-a*; *-i*) battleship; *zo.* armadillo; **~cerny** armo(u)red; **~cerz** *m* (*-a*; *-e*) armo(u)r
panel *m* (*-a*; *-e*) panel; (*dyskusja*) panel discussion
pani *f* (*A -ą*, *G -*; *-e*) woman, lady; (*psa, władczyni*) mistress; (*przy zwracaniu się*, *z nazwiskiem*) Ms, *zamężna* Mrs, *niezamężna* Miss; (*bez nazwiska*) madam; **czy ~ ma ...?** do you have...?; **~ domu** hostess, landlady
paniczny panic
panienka *f* (*-i*; *G -nek*) young woman, young lady; (*przy zwracaniu się*) Miss
panień|ski: **nazwisko ~skie** maiden name
panierować ⟨**o-**⟩ (*-uję*) bread
panika *f* (*-i*; *0*) panic
pann|a *f* (*-y*; *G -nien*) girl, maiden; (*w dowodzie*) unmarried woman; (*przy zwracaniu się*) Miss; **♍a** *znak Zodiaku:* Virgo; **on(a) jest spod znaku ♍y** (s)he is (a) Virgo; **stara ~a** spinster; **~a młoda** bride; → **pani**
panowa|ć (*-uję*) rule, reign (*też* **nad** *I* over); ⟨**za-**⟩ (**nad sobą**) control (o.s.), be in control of (o.s.); **panuje ...** there is ...; **~nie** *n* (*-a*; *0*) rule, ruling, mastery; control (**nad sobą** of o.s.)
pantera *f* (*-y*; *G -*) *zo.* panther
panterka *f* (*-i*; *G -rek*) camouflage jacket
pantof|el *m* (*-fla*; *-fle*, *-fli*) shoe; **~le** *pl.* **damskie** ladies' shoes *pl.*; **~le** *pl.* **domowe** slippers *pl.*; **~larz** F *m* (*-a*; *-e*) henpecked husband
pantomima *f* (*-y*; *G -*) mime
pańsk|i *gest* lordly, grand; your, yours; **~i list** your letter; **po pańsku** gentlemanly
państw|o *n* (*-a*; *G -*) (*kraj*) country, state; you, (*z nazwiskiem*) Mr and Mrs; **proszę ~a ...** Ladies and Gentleman; **~o pozwolą** please allow me; **~o młodzi** *pl.* the newlyweds *pl.*
państwowy state
PAP *skrót pisany:* **Polska Agencja Prasowa** Polish Press Agency
papa *f* (*-y*; *G -*): **~ dachowa** roofing-felt
papier *m* (*-u*; *-y*) (**maszynowy, toaletowy** typing, toilet) paper; F **~y** *pl.* documents *pl.*, identity papers *pl.*; **~ek** *m* (*-rka*; *-rki*) a piece of paper
papiero|s *m* (*-a*; *-y*) cigarette; **~śnica** *f* (*-y*; *G -*) cigarette-case; **~wy** paper
papieski papal
papież *m* (*-a*; *-e*) *rel.* pope
papk|a *f* (*-i*; *G -ek*) mash, pap; **~owaty** mashy
paplanina *f* (*-y*; *G -*) chatter
paprać (*-przę*) smear; **~ się** *rana*: fester
paproć *f* (*-oci*; *-ocie*) *bot.* fern
papryka *f* (*-i*; *G -*) *bot.* (*w strączkach*) pepper, (*proszek*) paprika
papuć *m* (*-cia*; *-cie*) F slipper
papu|ga *f* (*-i*; *G -*) *zo.* parrot; **~żka** *f* (*-i G -żek*): **~żka falista** *zo.* budgie, budgerigar
par *m* (*-a*; *-owie*) *Brt.* peer
para[1] *f* (*-y*; *0*) steam, vapo(u)r; (*na szybie*) mist
par|a[2] *f* (*-y*; *G -*) pair; couple; **~a zakochanych** (pair of) lovers; **~a małżonków** married couple; **w ~y, ~ami** in pairs; **nie do ~y** odd; **iść w parze** go hand in hand
parad|a *f* (*-y*; *G -*) parade; *piłka nożna*: save; **wejść komuś w ~ę** get in s.o.'s way
paradoksalny paradoxical
parafia *f* (*GDL -ii*; *-e*) *rel.* parish; **~lny** parish, parochial; **~nin** *m* (*-a*; *-anie*,*-*), **~nka** *f* (*-i*; *G -nek*) parishioner
parafinowy paraffin
para|gon *m* (*-u*; *-y*) sales slip, receipt; **~graf** *m* (*-u*; *-y*) clause
paraliż *m* (*-u*; *-y*) *med.* paralysis; **~ dziecięcy** polio; **~ować** ⟨**s-**⟩ (*-uję*) paralyse (*też fig.*)
para|pet *m* (*-u*; *-y*) windowsill; **~sol** *m* (*-a*; *-e*), **~solka** *f* (*-i*; *G -lek*) umbrella; (*od słońca*) parasol; **~wan** *m* (*-u*; *-y*) (folding)screen
parcela *f* (*-i*; *-e*) plot, lot
parciany sacking
parcie *n* (*-a*; *0*) pressure; *med.* pushing
parę (*GDL -ru*, *I -roma*; *m-os NA -ru*) (*G*) a couple (of), a few; **~ razy** several times; **~set** several hundred

park *m* (*-u*; *-i*) park

parkan *m* (*-u*; *-y*) fence

parkiet *m* (*-u*; *-y*) parquet

park|ing *m* (*-u*; *-i*) *Brt.* car park, *Am.* parking lot; **~ometr** *m* parking-meter

parkow|ać ⟨***za-***⟩ (*-uję*) park; **~anie** *n* (*-a*; *G -ań*) parking; **~y** park

parlament *m* (*-u*; *-y*) parliament

parlamenta|rny parliamentary; **~rzysta** *m* (*-y*; *-ści*, *-tów*) *Brt.* Member of Parliament, *Am.* Congressman

parn|o *adv.* close, sultry; **~y** close, sultry

parodia *f* (*GDl -ii*; *-e*) parody

paro|godzinny of several hours; **~konny** drawn by two horses; **~krotnie** *adv.* several times; repeatedly; **~krotny** repeated, multiple

paroksyzm *m* (*-u*; *-y*) paroxysm, fit

paro|letni several years old; several yearslong; **~miesięczny** severalmonths long; **~statek** *m* (*-tka*; *-tki*) → ***parowiec***; **~tygodniowy** several weeks long

parować¹ (*-uję*) *cios* parry, ward off

paro|wać² (*-uję*) *v/i.* evaporate; vaporize; *v/t.* steam; **~wiec** *m* (*-wca*; *-wce*) *naut.* steamship (*skrót*: SS); **~wóz** *m* (*-wozu*; *-wozy*) *rail.* steam engine; **~wy** steam

parów *m* (*-rowu*; *-rowy*) ravine, gorge

parówka *f* (*-i*; *G -wek*) frankfurter, *Am.* wiener

parsk|ać (*-am*) ⟨***~nąć***⟩ (*-nę*) snort; ***~nąć śmiechem*** snort with laughter

parszywy *pies* mangy; *fig.* rotten

parta|cki botched, bungled; **~ctwo** *n* (*-a*; *G -*) botching, botched-up job; **~czyć** ⟨**s-** ⟩ (*-ę*) botch, bungle

parter *m* (*-u*; *-y*) *Brt.* ground floor, *Am.* first floor; *teatr.* stalls *pl.*; **~owy** *Brt.* ground-floor, *Am.* first-floor; one-stor(e)y

partia *m* (*GDl -ii*; *-e*) *pol.* party; (*towaru itp.*) shipment, lot; (*w sporcie*) game, round; (*do małżeństwa*) match; *teatr itp.* part

partner *m* (*-a*; *-rzy*), **~ka** *f* (*-i*; *G -rek*) partner; **~stwo** *n* (*-a*; *G -*) partnership

partolić F ⟨**s-**⟩ (*-lę*) → ***partaczyć***

party|jny party; **~kuła** *f* (*-y*; *G -*) *gr.* particle; **~tura** *f* (*-y*; *G -*) *mus.* score

partyza|ncki guerrilla; **~nt** *f* (*-a*; *-nci*) guerrilla; **~ntka** *f* (*walka*) guerrilla war; (*kobieta*) guerilla

paru(-) → ***paro***(-)

paryski Paris

Paryż *m* (*-a*; *0*) Paris

parytet *m* (*-u*; *-y*) *econ.* parity

parzyć (*-ę*) *v/t.* (*zaparzać*) brew; *zwierzęta* mate; ⟨**o-, po-, s-**⟩ burn (**sobie usta** one's lips); (*mocno*) scald; ***~ się*** burn (*też* o.s.), get burnt; *herbata*: draw; *zwierzęta*: mate

parzysty even

pas *m* (*-a*; *-y*) band; (*do ubrania*) belt; (*część ciała, sukni*) waist; ***~ ratunkowy*** life belt; ***~ startowy*** runway; ***~ ruchu*** lane; ***w ~y*** striped; ***po ~*** waist-high, -deep; scald; → ***klinowy***; **~ać** (*-am*) → ***paść²***

pasaż *m* (*-u*; *-e*) (*sklepowy*) shopping arcade; *mus. itp.* passage

pasażer *m* (*-a*; *-owie*), **~ka** *f* (*-i*; *G -rek*) passenger

pasek *m* (*-ska*; *-ski*) → ***pas***; ***~ do zegarka*** watchband

paser *m* fence, receiver of stolen goods; **~stwo** *n* (*-a*; *0*) receiving (stolen goods)

pasieka *f* (*-i*; *G -*) apiary

pasierb *m* (*-a*; *-owie*) stepson; **~ica** *f* (*-y*; *-e*) stepdaughter

pas|ja *f* (*-i*; *-e*) passion; ***wpaść w ~ję*** get furious; **~jonująco** *adv.* excitingly; **~jonujący** exciting

paska|rstwo *n* (*-a*; *0*) profiteering; **~rka** *f* (*-i*; *G -rek*), **~rz** *m* (*-a*; *-e*) profiteer

paskudny terrible, dreadful

pasmo *n* (*-a*; *G -/-sem*) strip, strand; *RTV*: band; (*górskie*) range, chain; (*ruchu*) lane, (*na autostradzie*) *Brt.* carriageway

pasować¹ (*-uję*) *v/i.* be suitable, be appropriate (**do** *G* to); *v/t.* ⟨**do-**⟩ fit (**do** *G* to); *kolory itp.*: match

pasować² (*-uję*) (*w grze w karty*) pass

pasożyt *m* (*-a*; *-y*) *biol.*, *fig.* parasite; *fig.* sponger; **~ować** (*-uję*) parasitize (**na** *L* on); *fig.* sponge

pasta *f* (*-y*; *G -*) paste; ***~ do butów*** shoe polish; ***~ do zębów*** tooth paste; ***~ do podłogi*** floor polish

paster|ka *f* (*-i*; *G -rek*) → ***pastuszka***; *rel.* midnight mass (at Christmas); **~ski** shepherd; *rel.* pastoral

pasteryzowany pasteurized

pasterz *m* (*-a*; *-e*) → ***pastuch***

pastewny fodder

pastor *m* (*-a*; *-orzy/-owie*) pastor, (*anglikański*) vicar

pastorał *m* (*-u*; *-y*) *rel.* crosier
pastować ⟨***na-***⟩ (*-uję*) *parkiet* polish
pastu|ch *m* (*-a*; *-y/-si/-owie*) shepherd; **~szka** *f* (*-i*; *G -szek*) shepherdess
past|wa: ***stać się, paść ~wą*** (*G*) fall prey (to); **~wisko** *n* (*-a*; *G -*) pasture
pastylka *f* (*-i*; *G -lek*) *med.* pill, dragée
pasywny passive
pasza *f* (*-y*;*-e*) *agr.* (***zielona*** green) fodder
paszcza *f* (*-y*; *G -*) mouth, *fig.* jaws *pl.*
paszport *m* (*-u*; *-y*) passport; **~owy** passport; ***biuro ~owe*** passport office
paszte|cik *m* (*-a*; *-i*) *gastr.* pie, patty; **~t** *m* (*-u*; *-y*) *gastr.* pâté
paść[1] *pf.* fall (down) → ***padać***
paść[2] *bydło* graze; (*karmić*) feed; ***~ się*** graze
patałach *m* (*-a*; *-y*) F botcher, bungler
patelnia *f* (*-i*; *G -e*) frying-pan
pa|tentowany patented; **~tetyczny** pathetic; **~tologiczny** pathological
patriot|a *m* (*-y*; *-ci*), **~ka** *f* (*-i*) patriot; **~yczny** patriotic
patrol *m* (*-u*; *-e*) patrol; **~ować** (*-uję*) patrol
patron *m* (*-a*; *-i*); **~ka** *f* (*-i*; *G -nek*) patron; *rel.* patron saint
patroszyć ⟨***wy-***⟩ (*-ę*) *gastr.* gut
patrz|eć, ~yć ⟨***po-***⟩ (*-ę*) look (***przez okno*** out of the window; ***na*** *A* at); ***jak się ~y*** comme il faut, as it should be; ***patrz*** look
patyk *m* (*-a*; *-i*) stick
pauza *f* (*-y*; *G -*) break; (*przy mówieniu itp.*) pause; *mus.* rest
paw *m* (*-ia*; *-ie*) *zo.* peacock; **~i** peacock
pawian *m* (*-a*; *-y*) *zo.* baboon
pawilon *m* (*-u*; *-y*) (*sklep*) shop; *bud.* pavilion
pawlacz *m* (*-a*; *-e*) shallow mezzanine
pazerny greedy
paznok|ieć *m* (*-kcia*; *-kcie*) *anat.* nail; ***do ~ci*** nail
pazur *m* (*-a*; *-y*) claw, talon
październik *m* (*-a*; *-i*) October; **~owy** October
pączek *m* (*-czka*; *-czki*) *bot.* → ***pąk***; *gastr.* doughnut
pąk *bot.* bud; ***wypuszczać ~i*** bud
pąsowy crimson
pchać (*-am*) push, (*mocno*) shove; thrust (***do*** *G* into); ***~ się*** crowd, throng; (***przez*** *A*) push one's way (through); → ***pchnąć***
pch|ełka *f* (*-i*; *G -łek*) (*do gry*) tiddlywink; ***~ełki*** *pl. gra*: tiddlywinks; **~ła** *f* (*-y*; *G pcheł*) *zo.* flea; **~li** flea; ***~li targ*** flea market
pchn|ąć *pf* (*-nę*) → ***pchać***; (*nożem*) stab; **~ięcie** *n* (*-a*; *G -ęć*) thrust; (*w sporcie*) put; ***~ięcie nożem*** stab
PCK *skrót pisany:* ***Polski Czerwony Krzyż*** Polish Red Cross
pech *m* (*-a*; *0*) bad luck, misfortune; ***mieć ~a*** be unlucky; **~owiec** *m* (*-wca*; *-wcy*) unfortunate
pe|dagogiczny pedagogic(al); **~dał** *m* **1.** (*-u*; *-y*) pedal; **2.** (*-a*; *-y*) V (*homoseksualista*) queer; **~dantyczny** pedantic
pedi'kiur *m* (*-u*; *0*) pedicure
pejcz *m* (*-a*; *-e*) whip
pejzaż *m* (*-u*; *-e*) landscape
Pekin *m* (*-u*; *0*) Peking, Beiging
peklowany corned
pelargonia *f* (*-ii*; *-e*) geranium
peleryna *f* (*-y*; *G -*) cape
pelisa *f* (*-y*; *G -*) fur coat
peł|en → ***pełny***; **~nia** *f* (*-i*; *-e*) full moon; (*szczyt*) heyday, peak; ***~nia życia*** the prime of life; ***w ~ni lata*** in high summer; ***w całej ~ni*** completely; **~nić** (*-ę*, *-ń/-nij!*) *obowiązki* fulfil; *wartę* keep; ***~nić służbę*** serve
pełno *adv.* (*G*) a lot (of); **~letni** of age; **~metrażowy** full-length
pełnomocn|ictwo *n* (*-a*; *G -*) proxy; *jur.* power of attorney; **~ik** *m* (*-a*; *-cy*) authorized representative; *jur.* proxy, plenipotentiary; **~y** plenipotentiary, authorized
pełno|morski *flota* deep-sea; *jacht* ocean-going; **~prawny** rightful; **~wartościowy** fully adequate
peł|ny full; complete; whole; ***~ne mleko*** full-cream milk; ***na ~nym morzu*** on the high seas; ***~en nadziei*** hopeful; ***~en energii*** vigorous; ***do ~na*** to the brim; ***napełnić do ~na*** fill up
pełz|ać (*-am*), **~nąć** (*-nę*) crawl
penicylina *f* (*-y*; *G -*) *med.* penicillin
pens *m* (*-a*; *-y*) penny, *pl.* pennies *lub* pence
pensja *f* (*-i*; *-e*) salary, (*robotnika, cotygodniowa*) wages *pl.*; (*dla panien*) boarding school
pensjonat *m* (*-u*; *-y*) guest-house
pepegi *pl.* (*-ów*) tennis-shoes *pl.*
pepitka *f* (*-i*; *G -tek*) shepherd's check

perfidny perfidious
perfum|eria *f* (*GDL -ii*; *-e*) perfumery; **~y** *pl.* (-) perfume, scent
pergamin *m* (*-u*; *-y*) parchment; parchment paper
periody|czny periodic(al); **~k** *m* (*-u*; *-i*) periodical
perkaty F: **~ nos** snub nose
perku|sista *m* (*-y*; *-ści*) *mus.* drummer; percussionist; **~sja** *f* (*-i*; *0*) *mus.* drums; percussion
per|lić się (*-lę*) pearl; *śmiech*: ripple; **~listy** beady, pearly; **~ła** *f* (*-y*; *G -reł*) pearl; **~łowy** pearly; *kolor* pearl-grey
peron *m* (*-u*; *-y*) *rail.* platform; **~ówka** *f* (*-i*; *G -wek*) platform ticket
perski Persian; **~e oko** wink
perso|nalny personal; (*dotyczący pracowników*) personnel; **~nel** *m* (*-u*; *0*) personnel, staff
perspektyw|a *m* (*-y*; *G -*) perspective; **~y** *pl.* (*szanse*) prospects *pl.*
perswazja *f* (*-i*; *-e*) persuasion
pertrakt|acje *pl.* (*-i*) negotiations *pl.*; **~ować** (*-uję*) negotiate
peruka *f* (*-i*; *G -*) wig
perwers|ja *f* (*-i*; *-e*) perversion; **~yjny** perverse, perverted
peryferie *f/pl.* (*GDL -ii*) periphery; **~ miasta** outskirts *pl.*
peryskop *m* (*-u*; *-y*) periscope
pestka *f* (*-i*; *G -tek*) stone, (*mała*) pit
pesymist|yczny pessimistic; **~a** *m* (*-y*; *-ści*), **~ka** *f* (*-i*; *-tek*) pessimist
peszyć ⟨**s-**⟩ (*-ę*) put out, disturb
petarda *f* (*-y*; *G -*) banger
petent *m* (*-a*; *-ci*), **~ka** *f* (*-i*; *G -tek*) applicant
petycja *f* (*-i*; *-e*) petition
pew|ien[1] (*-wna*, *-wne*, *m-os -wni*) (*niejaki*) a certain; a, one; **~na ilość** a certain amount; **co ~ien czas** from time to time; **~nego dnia** one day; **po ~nym czasie** after some time
pew|ien[2] → **pewny**; **~nie** *adv.* surely; reliably; stać firmly; **~nie!** sure!; **~no** *adv.*: **na ~no** for certain, sure; **~ność** *f* (*-ści*; *0*) certainty; (*niezawodność*) reliability; (*zaufanie*) confidence; **~ność siebie** self-confidence; **z całą ~nością** surely; **~ny** certain, sure; *oparcie*, *krok* firm; *ręka*, *cięcie* steady; (*niezawodny*) confident; **nic ~nego** nothing definite
pęcherz *m* (*-a*; *-e*) (*z odparzenia*) blister; *anat.* bladder; **~yk** *m* (*-a*; *-i*) → **pęcherz**; *anat.* bladder
pęczak *m* (*-u*; *0*) *gastr.* pearl barley
pęcz|ek *m* (*-czka*; *-czki*) bunch; (*mały*) wisp; **~nieć** ⟨**na-**⟩ (*-eję*) swell
pęd rush; shoot, sprout; **~ do wiedzy** thirst for knowledge; **biec ~em** dash
pędny *tech.* driving, propellent
pędzel *m* (*-dzla*; *-dzle*) brush
pędzić (*-dzę*) *v/i.* dash, rush, race; *v/t.* drive; → **spędzać, wypędzać**
pędzlować (*-uję*) *med.* paint (*D* with)
pęk *m* (**kluczy** key) bunch; (*chrustu*) armful
pęk|ać (*-am*) ⟨**~nąć**⟩ (*-nę*) burst; *lina itp.*: break; *szkło*: crack; *wargi*: crack, chap; **~ać ze śmiechu** laugh one's head off; **~aty** squat; (*wypchany*) bulging; **~nięcie** *n* (*-a*; *G -ęć*) (*szczelina*) crack; (**rury** pipe) burst; (*kości*) fracture
pęp|ek *m* (*-pka*; *-pki*) *anat.* navel; **~owina** *f* (*-y*; *G -*) *anat.* umbilical cord
pęseta *f* (*-y*; *G -*) tweezers *pl.*
pęt|ak *m* F (*-a*; *-i*) sprog; **~elka** *f* (*-i*; *G -lek*) loop; **~la** *f* (*-i*; *-e*) loop; (*na linie*) noose; (*tramwaju itp.*) terminus
piach *m* (*-u*; *-y*) → **piasek**
piać ⟨**za-**⟩ (*-eję*) crow
piana *f* (*-y*; *G -*) foam; (*z mydła*) lather; (*na napoju*) froth
piani|no *n* (*-a*; *G -*) *mus.* (upright) piano; **~sta** *m* (*-y*; *-ści*) pianist
pianka *f* (*-i*; *G -nek*) → **piana**
piano|guma *f* (*-y*; *G -*) foam rubber; **~wy**: **gaśnica ~wa** foam extinguisher
pias|ek *m* (*-ku*; *-ki*) sand; **~kowiec** *m* (*-wca*; *-wce*) sandstone; **~kownica** *f* (*-y*; *G -*) *Brt.* sand-pit, *Am.* sand-box
piasta *f* (*-y*; *G -*) hub
piastować (*-uję*) hold
piaszczysty sandy, sand
piąć się (*pnę*, *piął*) climb
piąt. *skrót pisany*: **piątek** Fri. (*Friday*)
piąt|ek *m* (*-tku*; *-tki*) Friday; **Wielki ~ek** *rel.* Good Friday; **~ka** *f* (*-i*; *G -tek*) five; (*linia*) number five; *szkoła*: *jakby*: A; **w ~kę**; in a group of five; **~kowy** Friday; **~y** fifth; **o ~ej** at five (o'clock)
pici|e *n* (*-a*; *-*) drinking; (*napój*) drink; **do ~a** to drink
pić (*piję*) drink; **chce mi się ~** I am thirsty; → **zdrowie**
piec[1] *m* (*-a*; *-e*) stove; *tech.* furnace, kiln; **~ kuchenny** range

piec² ⟨**na-**, **u-**, **wy-**⟩ *v/t. ciasto* bake (**się** *v/i.*); *mięso* roast (**się** *v/i.*); *v/t. impf. słońce* beat down; *oczy itp.*: smart, sting
piechot|a *f* (*-y*; *G -*) *mil.* infantry; ***~ą, na ~ę*** on foot
piecyk *m* (*-a*; *-i*) → **piec²**; (*do wody itp.*) heater
piecz|a *f* (*-y*; *-e*) care; ***on sprawuje ~ę nad*** he takes care of
piecza|ra *f* (*-y*; *G -*) cave; **~rka** *f* (*-i*; *G -rek*) *bot.* meadow mushroom
pieczątka *f* (*-i*; *G -tek*) (rubber) stamp
pieczeń *f* (*-eni*; *-nie*) roast meat; ***~ z sarny*** roast venison
pieczę|ć *f* (*-ci*; *-cie*) seal; stamp; **~tować** ⟨**o-**⟩ (*-uję*) seal; stamp
pieczołowi|tość *f* (*-ści*; *0*) care; **~cie** *adv.* carefully; **~ty** careful
piecz|ony roast; **~yste** *n* (*-go*) roast meat; **~ywo** *n* (*-a*; *0*) bread, cakes, and pastries
piedestał *m* (*-u*; *-y*) pedestal; *arch.* plinth
pieg|i *m/pl.* (*-ów*) freckles *pl.*; **~owaty** freckled
piek|arnia *f* (*-i*; *-e*) bakery; **~arnik** *m* (*-a*; *-i*) oven; **~arz** *m* (*-a*; *-e*) baker; **~ący** *ból* stinging; **~ielny** hellish; **~ło** *n* (*-a*; *G -kieł*) hell
pielęgnacja *f* (*-i*; *0*) care; (*urządzenia*) maintenance
pielęgnia|rka *f* (*-i*; *G -rek*) nurse; **~rz** *m* (*-a*; *-e*) (male) nurse
pielęgnować (*-uję*) look after; *ludzi* care for; *zęby* take care of; *ogródek* look after
pielgrzym *m* (*-a*; *-i*) pilgrim; **~ka** *f* (*-i*; *G -mek*) pilgrimage
pielić ⟨**wy-**⟩ (*-lę*) weed
pielu|chomajtki *pl.* nappy pants *pl.*; **~szka** *f* (*-i*; *G -szek*) (***do jednorazowego użytku*** disposable) *Brt.* nappy, *Am.* diaper
pieniądz *m* (*-a*; *-e*, *-iędzy*, *I -iędzmi*) coin; *zbior.* → **pieniądze**; **~e** *m/pl.* money; ***przy ~ach*** in the money
pienić się (*-ę*, *-ń!*) foam, froth; *mydło*: lather
pieniężn|y money; ***kara ~a*** fine
pienisty foaming, frothing; → ***musujący***
pień *m* (*pnia*; *pnie*, *pni*) trunk; (*pniak*) tree-stump
pie|prz *m* (*-u*; *0*) *bot.*, *gastr.* pepper; **~przny** hot, peppery; *kawał* dirty; **~rnik** *m* (*-a*; *-i*) *gastr.* ginger bread
pierogi *pl.* (*-gów*) dumplings *pl.*
pier|siowy chest; *anat.* pectoral; **~ś** *f* (*-si*) (*kobieca*, *też gastr.*) breast; **~si** *pl.* (*klatka piersiowa*) chest; ***pełną ~sią*** lustily
pierście|niowy ring (*też fig.*); **~ń** *m* (*-nia*; *-nie*, *-ni*) ring
pier|ścionek *m* → **pierścień**; **~wiastek** *m* (*-stka*; *-stki*) *chem.* element; *math.* root, radical; ***~wiastek kwadratowy*** square root; **~wiosnek** *m* (*-snka*; *-snki*) *bot.* primrose
pierwo|rodny first-born; **~tny** (*nieskażony*) prim(a)eval; (*prymitywny*) primitive; (*pierwszy*) original; **~wzór** *m* (*-oru*; *-ory*) prototype, archetype
pierwszeństwo *n* (*-a*; *0*) priority; ***~ przejazdu*** right of way; ***dać ~*** (*D*) give precedence (to)
pierwszo|planowy foreground; **~rzędny** first-class
pierwsz|y first; ***~a godzina*** one o'clock; ***~ego maja*** first of May; ***po ~e*** first(ly); ***po raz ~y*** for the first time
pierzch|ać (*-am*) ⟨**~nąć¹**⟩ (*-nę*) run away; *ptaki*: fly away; *nastrój*: disappear; **~nąć²** (*-nę*) *skóra*: chap
pierze *n* (*-a*; *0*) *zbior.* feathers *pl.*
pierzyna *f* (*-y*; *G -*) duvet, *Brt.* continental quilt, *Am.* stuffed quilt
pies *m* (*psa*, *psu*, *L psie*; *psy*) *zo.* dog; (*myśliwski*) hound; ***pod psem*** under the weather; **~ek** *m* (*-ska*; *-ski*) → **pies**
pieszczot|a *f* (*-y*; *G -*) caress; ***~y*** *pl.* petting; **~liwy** gentle; ***~liwe imię*** pet name
piesz|o on foot; **~y** foot, pedestrian; ***~a wycieczka*** hike; ***przejście dla ~ych*** pedestrian crossing
pieścić (*-szczę*) caress, pet
pieś|niarka *f* (*-ki*; *G -rek*), **~niarz** *m* (*-a*; *-e*) singer
pieśń *f* (*-ni*) song; ***~ ludowa*** folk song
pietruszka *f* (*-i*; *G -szek*) *bot.* parsley
pięcio|bok *m* pentagon; **~bój** *m* (*w sporcie*) pentathlon; **~krotny** fivefold; **~letni** five-year-long, -old; **~linia** *f* (*-ii*; *-e*) staff, stave; **~raczki** *pl.* (*-ów*) quintuplets *pl.*; **~ro** five → ***715***
pięć five; **~dziesiąt** fifty; **~dziesiątka** *f* (*-i*; *G -tek*) fifty; **~set** five hundred; → ***715***
piękn|ie *adv.* prettily, beautifully; **~o** *n*

(*-a; 0*), **~ość** *f* (*-ci*) beauty; **~y** beautiful

pięś|ciarstwo *n* (*-a; 0*) (*w sporcie*) boxing; **~ciarz** *m* (*-a; -e*) (*w sporcie*) boxer

pięść *f* (*-ci*) *anat.* fist

pięta *f* (*-y; G -*) *anat.* heel

piętna|sto- *w złoż.* fifteen; **~stka** *f* (*-i; G -tek*) fifteen; (*linia*) number fifteen; **~ście** fifteen; → ***715***

pięt|no *n* (*-a, L -nie; G -tn*) brand; mark, mole; *fig.* ***wyciskać swoje ~no*** (na *I*) take its toll (on); **~nować** ⟨***na-***⟩ (*-uję*) brand; **~ro** *n* (*-a; G -ter*) floor, storey; ***na drugim ~rze*** *Brt.* on the second floor, *Am.* on the third floor

piętrzyć się (*-ę*) be piled up

pigułka *f* (*-i; G -łek*) pill (*też fig.*)

pija|czka *f* (*-i; G -czek*), **~k** *m* (*-a; -i*) drunk, drunkard; **~ny** drunk; ***po ~nemu*** when drunk; **~ństwo** *n* (*-a; G -*) alcoholism, drunkenness; **~tyka** *f* (*-i; G -*) binge, spree

pijawka *f* (*-i; G -wek*) *zo.* leech (*też fig.*)

pik *m* (*-a; -i*) *gra w karty*: spade(s *pl.*); ***as ~*** ace of spades; ***wyjść w ~i*** play spades

pikantny hot, piquant; *fig.* juicy

pikle *m/pl.* (*-i*) *gastr.* pickles *pl.*

pikling *m* (*-a; -i*) *gastr.* smoked herring

pilniczek *m* (*-czka; -czki*) file

pilno|ść *f* (*-ści; 0*) diligence; hard work; **~wać** (*-uję*) (*G*) guard, keep watch (on); ***~wać się*** take care, be careful; watch each other

pilny urgent, immediate; *ktoś* diligent, conscientious

pilot *m* (*-a; -ci*) *aviat.* pilot; (*przewodnik, też fig.*) guide; *RTV*: remote control; **~ować** (*-uję*) navigate; *aviat.* pilot

pilśniow|y felt; ***płyta ~a*** *bud.* hardboard

piła *f* (*-y; G -*) saw; *fig.* pain in the neck

piłka[1] *f* (*-i; G -łek*) → ***piła***

piłka[2] *f* (*-i; G -łek*) (*w sporcie*) ball; ***~ nożna*** football, soccer; ***grać w piłkę*** play ball; **~rski** football; **~rz** *m* (*-a; -e*) (*w sporcie*) footballer, football player

piłować (*-uję*) saw

pinceta *f* (*-y; G -*) tweezers *pl.*

pineska (*-i; G -sek*), **pinezka** (*-i; G -zek*) *Brt.* drawing pin, *Am.* thumbtack

ping-pong *m* (*-a; -i*) table tennis

pingwin *m* (*-a; -y*) penguin

piołun *m* (*-u; -y*) *bot.* wormwood, mugwort

pion *m* (*-u; -y*) (*narzędzie*) plumb (line); (*kierunek*) perpendicular, verticality; *fig.* area of responsibility; **~ek** *m* (*-nka; -nki*) (*w grze w szachy*) pawn; (*w grze w warcaby*) piece, counter

pi'onier *m* (*-a; -rzy*) pioneer

piono|wo *adv.* vertically; (*w krzyżówce*) down; **~wy** vertical, perpendicular; **~wzlot** *m* (*-u; -y*) *aviat.* VTOL

piorun *m* (*-a; -y*) lightning; ***huk ~a*** thunder; ***~em*** like lightning; ***do ~a!*** damn it!

piorunochron *m* (*-u; -y*) lightning rod

piosenka *f* (*-i; G -nek*) song; **~rka** *f* (*-i; G -rek*), **~rz** *m* (*-a; -e*) singer

piórnik *m* (*-a; -i*) pen-case

pióro *n* (*-a; G -*) (*ptaka*) feather; (***wieczne*** fountain) pen; ***~ kulkowe*** rollerball (pen), ballpoint (pen)

pira|cki pirate; ***~ckie wydanie*** pirated edition; **~mida** *f* (*-y; G -*) pyramid; **~t** *m* (*-a; -ci*) pirate; (*drogowy*) F speeder

piro- *w złoż. zwł.* pyro-

pisa|ć ⟨***na-***⟩ (*-szę*) write; ***~ć na maszynie*** type; **~nka** *f* (*-ki; G -nek*) Easter egg; **~k** *m* (*-a; -i*) felt-tip pen; **~rka** *f* (*-i; G -rek*), **~rz** *m* (*-a; -e*) writer, author

pisemn|ie *adv.* in writing; **~y** written

pisk *m* (*-u; -i*) squeal; (*człowieka*) shriek; (*opon*) screech; **~lę** *n* (*-cia; -ta, G -ląt*) nestling, fledgling; **~liwy** shrill, squeaky

pism|o *n* (*-a; G -sem*) writing; (*list*) letter; → ***charakter***; ***Ⓢo Święte*** the Scriptures *pl.*; ***na piśmie*** in writing

pisnąć *pf.* → ***piszczeć***; F ***nie ~ ani słówka*** not utter a single word

pisownia *f* (*-i; 0*) writing, spelling

pistolet *m* (*-u; -y*) pistol

piszcz|ałka *f* (*-i; G -łek*) *mus.* (*w organach*) pipe; (*w orkiestrze*) fife; **~eć** (*-ę, -y*) *mysz, urządzenie*: squeal; *koła*: screech; **~el** *f* (*-i; -e*) *anat.* tibia

piśmien|nictwo *n* (*-a; G -*) literature; **~ny** writing; *człowiek* literate; ***artykuły*** *pl.* ***~ne*** stationery, writing materials *pl.*

pitny drinking; ***miód ~*** mead

piw|iarnia *f* (*-i; -e*) *Brt.* pub, *Am.* beer bar; **~nica** *f* (*-y; -e, G -*) cellar; **~ny** beer; *oczy* light brown, hazel; **~o** *n* (*-a; G -*) (***z beczki*** draught) beer; ***małe ~o*** *fig.* small beer

piwonia *f* (*GDl -ii; -e*) *bot.* peony

pizz|a *f* (*-y ; G -*) *gastr.* pizza; **~eria** *f* (*GDl -ii; -e*) pizzeria

piżama *f* (*-y*; *G* *-*) *Brt.* pyjamas *pl.*, *Am.* pajamas *pl.*
piżmak *m* (*-a*; *-i*) *zo.* muskrat
piżmo *n* (*-a*; *0*) musk
p-ko *skrót pisany*: ***przeciwko*** agst., ver. (*against*)
PKOl *skrót pisany*: ***Polski Komitet Olimpijski*** Polish Olympic Committee
PKP *skrót pisany*: ***Polskie Koleje Państwowe*** Polish State Railways
PKS *skrót pisany*: ***Państwowa Komunikacja Samochodowa*** Polish State Coach Company
pkt *skrót pisany*: ***punkt*** p. (*point*)
pl. *skrót pisany*: ***plac*** Sq. (*Square*)
plac *m* (*-u*; *-e*) square; ***~ zabaw*** playground; ***~ targowy*** market square; ***~ budowy*** construction site
plac|ek *m* (*-ka*; *-ki*) (***śliwkowy, z serem*** plum, cheese) cake; ***~ki*** *pl.* ***kartoflane*** potato pancakes; ***~ek nadziewany*** pie; **~ówka** *f* (*-i*; *G* *-wek*) outpost, post
plaga *f* (*-i*; *G* *-*) plague (*też fig.*)
plagiat *m* (*-u*; *-y*) plagiarism
plajtować ⟨**s-**⟩ (*-uję*) go bankrupt, go bust
plakat *m* (*-u*; *-y*) poster
plakietka *f* (*-i*; *G* *-tek*) badge
plam|a *f* (*-y*; *G* *-*) stain, smudge; blot; **~ić** ⟨***po-, s-, za-***⟩ (*-ię*) stain, smudge; blot
plan *m* (*-u*; *-y*) plan; (*zajęć itp.*) schedule; (*lekcji*) timetable; (*mapa*) map; ***na pierwszym ~ie*** in the foreground
planeta *f* (*-y*; *G* *-*) planet
planow|ać ⟨***za-***⟩ (*-uję*) plan; **~anie** *n* (*-a*; *G* *-ań*) planning; **~y** planned, scheduled
plansza *f* (*-y*; *-e*, *G* *-*) (*do gry*) board
plantacja *f* (*-i*; *-e*) plantation
planty *f/pl.* (*-*) green space
plas|kać (*-am*) ⟨***~nąć***⟩ (*-nę*) slap
plaster *m* (*-tra*; *-try*) (***przylepny*** sticking) plaster; ***~ miodu*** honeycomb; **~ek** *m* (*-rka*, *-rki*) slice
plastik(owy) → ***plastyk²***, ***plastykowy***
plastycz|ka *f* (*-i*; *G* *-czek*) artist; **~ny** plastic; *opis* graphic, vivid; ***sztuki*** *pl.* ***~ne*** fine arts *pl.*
plastyk¹ *m* (*-a*; *-cy*) artist
plastyk² *m* (*-u*; *-i*) plastic; **~owy** plastic
platyn|a *f* (*-y*; *0*) *chem.* platinum; **~owy** platinum
plaż|a *f* (*-y*; *G* *-*) beach; ***na ~y*** on the beach; **~ować** (*-uję*) sunbathe; **~owy** beach
plądrować ⟨**s-**⟩ (*-uję*) loot, plunder
pląta|ć ⟨***po-, s-, za-***⟩ (*-czę*) tangle up, entangle; *fig.* confuse; ***~ć*** ⟨***po-, za-***⟩ ***się*** get tangled; *fig.* get confused; (*łazić*) loaf around; **~nina** *f* (*-y*; *G* *-*) tangle; *fig.* confusion
plebania *f* (*GDL* *-ii*; *-e*) (*katolicka*) presbytery, (*protestancka*) vicarage
plecak *m* (*-a*; *-i*) rucksack; (*turystyczny*) backpack
pleciony plaited, woven
plec|y *pl.* (*-ców*) back; ***za moimi ~ami*** behind my back; ***stać ~ami*** (***do*** *G*) have one's back (to); ***szeroki w ~ach*** broad-shouldered
pleć ⟨***wy-***⟩ → ***pielić***
plem|ię *n* (*-ienia*; -iona, *G* *-ion*) tribe; **~nik** *m* (*-a*; *-i*) sperm
plenarny plenary
plene|r *m* (*-u*; *-y*) outdoors, open air; ***w ~rze*** on location
plenić się (*-ę*) reproduce, spread
plenum *n* (*idkl.*; *-na*; *-nów*) plenary session
pleść ⟨**s-**⟩ weave, plait; F ⟨***na-***⟩ natter
pleś|nieć ⟨**s-**⟩ (*-eję*) *Brt.* mould, *Am.* mold; **~ń** *f* (*-ni*; *-nie*) *Brt.* mould, *Am.* mold
plewa *f* (*-y*; *G* *-*) husk
plik *m* (*-u*; *-i*) pile, stack; *komp.* file
plisowany pleated
pliszka *f* (*-i*; *G* *-szek*) *zo.* wagtail
PLN *skrót pisany*: ***polski nowy złoty*** new Polish zloty
plomb|a *f* (*-y*; *G* *-*) seal; *med.* filling; *bud.* infilling building; **~ować** ⟨***za-***⟩ (*-uję*) seal; *med.* fill; **~owy**: ***budownictwo ~owe*** infilling
plon *m* (*-u*; *-y*) harvest (*też fig.*); ***święto ~ów*** harvest festival
plotk|a *f* (*-i*; *G* *-tek*) rumo(u)r, gossip; ***~i*** *pl.* gossip; **~ować** (*-uję*) gossip
plucha *f* (*-y*; *G* *-*) wet weather
pluć (*-uję*) spit
plugaw|ić ⟨**s-**⟩ (*-ię*) defile; **~y** foul, filthy → ***obrzydliwy***
plunąć *pf.* → ***pluć***
plus *m* (*-a*; *-y*) *math.* plus; ***~ minus*** *fig.* give or take
pluskać (*-am/-szczę*) splash (***o*** *A* against); ***~ się*** splash about
pluskiewka *m* (*-i*; *G* *-wek*) → ***pinezka***

P

pluskwa *f* (*-y*; *G -kiew*) *zo.* bedbug; F (*urządzenie podsłuchowe*) bug
plusnąć *v/s.* (*-nę*) → **pluskać**; **~ do wody** plop into the water
plusz *m* (*-u*; *-e*) plush
pluton¹ *m* (*-u*; *0*) *chem.* plutonium
pluton² *m* (*-u*; *-y*) *mil.* platoon; **~owy** *m* (*-ego*; *-wi*) platoon leader
plwocina *f* (*-y*; *G -*) *med.* spit, spittle
płaca *f* (*-y*; *-e*, *G -*) payment, pay; **~ za urlop** holiday pay
płachta *f* (*-y*; *G -*) tarpaulin; (*papieru*) sheet; **~ ratownicza** safety blanket
płacić ⟨**o-, za-**⟩ (*-cę*) pay
płacowy pay, payment
pła|cz *m* (*-u*; *-e*) weeping, cry; **~czliwy** weepy, tearful; **~czliwie** *adv.* tearfully; **~kać** (*-czę*) cry, weep
płaski flat
płasko *adv.* flatly, flat; **~rzeźba** *f* (*-y*; *G -*) bas-relief; **~stopie** *n* (*-a*; *0*) flat feet *pl.*, *med.* platypodia; **~wzgórze** *n* (*-a*; *G -*) plateau
płaszcz *m* (*-a*; *-e*) coat; *biol.* mantle
płaszczyć ⟨**s-**⟩ (*-ę*) flatten; **~ się** *fig. pej.* crawl, grovel
płaszczyzna *f* (*-y*; *G -*) *math.* plane; *fig.* ground
płat *m* (*-a*; *-y*) (*kawał*) piece; (*mięsa itp.*) cut, slice; *anat.* lobe; **~ek** *m* (*-tka*; *-tki*) flake; *bot.* petal; **~ki** *pl.* **owsiane** oatmeal; **~ki** *pl.* **kukurydziane** cornflakes *pl.*; F **jak z ~ka** without a hitch
płatn|iczy payment, of payment; **~ik** *m* (*-a*; *-nicy*) payer; **~ik podatku** taxpayer; **~ość** *f* (*-ści*; *0*) payment; **warunki** *pl.* **~ości** terms *pl.* of payment; **~y** paid
pława *f* (*-y*; *G -*) *naut.* beacon
płaz *m* **1.** (*-a*; *-y*) *zo.* reptile; **2.** (*-u*; *-y*) (*klingi*) flat; **puścić ~em** (*A*) let get away (with)
płciowy sexual
płd. *skrót pisany*: **południe** S (*south*); **południowy** S (*southern*)
płeć *f* (*płci*; *płcie*) sex, gender
płet|wa *f* (*-y*; *G -*) (*ryby*) fin; (*nurka, foki itp.*) flipper; **~wonurek** *m* (*-rka*; *-rkowie*/*-rki*) diver; *mil.* frogman
płochliw|ie *adv.* shyly; **~y** shy
płoć *f* (*-ci*; *-cie*) *zo.* roach
płodność *f* (*-ści*; *0*) fertility
płod|ny fertile; **~y** *pl.* → **płód**
płodzić ⟨**s-**⟩ (*-dzę*, *płódź!*) beget, engender
płomie|nny flaming; *fig.* fiery; **~ń** *m* (*-nia*; *-nie*) flame
płomyk *m* (*-a*; *-i*) flame
płoną|cy burning; **~ć** (*-nę*; *-ń!*) burn; *twarz*: glow
płonica *f* (*-y*; *0*) *med.* scarlet fever
płonny vain, futile
płoszyć ⟨**s-, wy-**⟩ (*-ę*) shoo, scare; **~ się** shy
płot *m* (*-u*; *-y*) fence; **~ek** *m* (*-tka*; *-tki*) → **płot**; (*w sporcie*) hurdle; **bieg przez ~ki** hurdle race
płow|ieć ⟨**s-, wy-**⟩ (*-eję*) fade; **~y** fawn
płoza *f* (*-y*; *G płóz*) runner
płócienny linen
płód *m* (*-łodu*; *-łody*) *med.* fo(e)tus; **płody ziemi** agricultural produce
płótno *n* (*-a*; *G -cien*) linen; *mal.* canvas
płuc|ny pulmonary; **~o** *n* (*-a*; *G -*) *anat.* *zw.* **~a** *pl.* lungs *pl.*; **zapalenie ~** pneumonia
pług *m* (*-a*; *-i*) *Brt.* plough, *Am.* plow
płukać ⟨**prze-, wy-**⟩ (*-czę*) rinse; **~ gardło** gargle
płycizna *f* (*-y*; *G -*) shallow
płyn *m* (*-u*; *-y*) liquid, fluid; **w ~ie** liquid; **~ do włosów** hair lotion; **~ąć** (*-nę*, *-ń!*) swim; *statek*: sail; *patyk itp.*: float; **~ność** *f* (*-ści*; *0*) fluidity, liquidity; **~ność płatnicza** cash liquidity; **~ny** liquid, fluid
płyt|a *f* (*-y*; *G -*) (*kamienna*) slab; (*metalowa*) plate; *bud.* tile; (*dźwiękowa*) record, (*zwł. kompakt*) disk; **~a pamiątkowa** commemorative plaque; **muzyka z ~** canned music
płytk|i shallow; *fig.* superficial; **~o** *adv.* shallowly; *fig.* superficially
pływa|czka *f* (*-i*; *G -czek*) swimmer; **~ć** (*-am*) swim; (*statkiem*) sail; **~k** *m* (*-a*; *-cy*) swimmer; (*-a*; *-i*) *tech.* float; **~lnia** *f* (*-i*; *-e*) swimming pool; **~nie** *n* (*-a*; *0*) swimming; sailing
pływy *m/pl.* (*-ów*) tides *pl.*
p.n.e. *skrót pisany*: **przed naszą erą** BC (*before Christ*)
pneumatyczny pneumatic; inflatable
p.o. *skrót pisany*: **pełniący obowiązki** acting
po *prp.* (*L*) after; by, from; on; **odziedziczyć ~ ojcu** inherit after the father; **~ wojnie** after the war; **pięć ~ piątej** five minutes past five (o'clock); **~ ramieniu** on the shoulder; **~ stole** on

P

the table; **~ pokoju** in the room; **~ głosie** by the voice; **wędrować ~ kraju** wander all over the country; **~ kolei** in succession; **~ całych nocach** night after night; (*A*) to; for; per; **~ co?** what for?; **~ ... złotych za funta** ... zlotys per pound; *często nie tłumaczy się*: **~ kolana** knee-deep; **puszka ~ konserwach** *Am.* can, *Brt.* tin; **~ pierwsze** firstly; **~ bohatersku** valiantly; **~ niemiecku** (in) German

poba-, pobe- *pf.* → **ba-, be-**

pobi|cie *n* beating; *fig.* **nie do ~cia** unbeatable; **~ć** *pf.* → **bić**

pobie|- → **bie-**; **~lany** *rondel* tin; *fig.* whited; **~rać** (*-am*) *pensję* draw; *lekcje*, *próbki* take; *podatki* levy; *opłaty* collect; **~rać się** get married

pobieżny superficial, cursory

pobli|ski nearby; **~że** *n*: **w ~żu** (*G*) nearby, in the vicinity (of)

pobłaż|ać (*-am*) (*D*) indulge, be lenient (towards); **~liwie** *adv.* leniently; **~liwy** lenient, permissive

po|bła-, ~błą-, ~bły- *pf.* → **bła-, błą-, bły-**; **~bocze** *n* (*-a*; *G -y*) (*drogi*) *mot.* hard houlder; (*trawiaste*) verge; **~boczny** collateral

pobo|jowisko *n* (*-a*; *G -*) battlefield; **~rca** *m* (*-y*; *G -ców*): **~rca podatków** tax collector; **~rowy 1.** military; recruitment; **2.** *m* (*-ego*; *-wi*) recruit; **~ry** *m/pl.* (*-ów*) → **pobór**; (*pensja*) pay, salary, wages *pl.*

po|bożność *f* (*-ści*; *0*) *rel.* piety; **~bożny** pious; **~bór** *m* (*-boru*; *-bory*) *mil.* *Brt.* conscription, *Am.* draft; *econ.* collection; (*wody*) consumption; **~brać** *pf.* → **pobierać**

pobranie *n* (*-a*): **za ~m** cash on delivery

pobru- *pf.* → **bru-**

pobrzeż|e *n* (*-a*; *-y*) coast, riverside; (*skraj*) edge; **na ~u** on the edge

pobu|- → **bu-**; **~dka** *f* (*-i*; *G -dek*) motive, impulse; *mil.* reveille; **~dliwy** impetuous, impulsive

pobudz|ać (*-am*) ⟨**~ić**⟩ (*-ę*) stimulate (**do** *G* to); **~ająco** *adv.* stimulatingly; **~ający** stimulating; **środek ~ający** stimulant

poby|ć *pf.* stay; **~t** *m* (*-u*; *-y*) stay; **miejsce stałego ~tu** place of residence, domicile

pocałunek *m* (*-nku*; *-nki*) kiss

pochleb|ca *m* (*-y*; *G -ców*), **~czyni** *f* (*-yni*; *G -yń*) flatterer, sycophant; **~czy** flattering, cajoling; **~iać** (*-am*) flatter; **~ny** flattering; **~stwo** *n* (*-a*; *G -*) flattery; compliment

pochł|aniać (*-am*) ⟨**~onąć**⟩ → **chłonąć**; absorb; *ofiary* claim; **~onięty** (*I*) absorbed (in)

pochmurny cloudy; *fig.* gloomy, dismal

pochodn|ia *f* (*-i*; *-e*) torch; **~y** derivative; (*wtórny*) secondary

pochodz|enie *n* (*-a*; *0*) descent; origin(s *pl.*); **~ić** (**z** *G*) come (from); be descended (**z** *G*, **od** *G* from); (*wynikać*) (**z** *G*) stem (from), result (from); date (**z** *G* from); → **chodzić**

po|chopny rash, impulsive; **~chować** *pf.* → **chować**; **~chód** *m* (*-chodu*; *-chody*) procession, parade; **~chwa** *f* (*-y*; *G -*) (*kabura*) holster; (*na miecz itp.*) sheath; *anat.* vagina

pochwa|lać (*-am*) → **chwalić**; **~lnie** *adv.* approvingly; **~lny** commendatory; approving; **~ła** *f* (*-y*; *G -*) praise (**za** *A* for)

pochwy- *pl.* → **chwy-**

pochy|lać (*-am*) ⟨**~lić**⟩ → **chylić**; **~lony** sloping; bent (**nad** *I* over); **~łość** *f* (*-ści*) inclination, slope; **~ło** *adv.* at an angle, slopingly; **~ły** sloping, slanted, oblique

pociąg *m* (*-u*; *-i*) *rail.* train; (*skłonność*) attraction (**do** *G* to); **~ drogowy** *mot.* road train; **~iem** by rail; **~ać** (*-am*) ⟨**~nąć**⟩ draw (**do** *G* to), pull (**za** *A* after); (*farbą itp.*) cover; (*nęcić*) attract; **~ać za sobą** result in; **~ająco** *adv.* attractively; **~ający** attractive; **~ły** *twarz* oval; **~nięcie** *n* (*-a*; *G -ęć*) pull

po cichu *adv.* quietly, softly; *fig.* in silence, quietly

pocić się (*-cę*) sweat; *metal*, *szkło*: mist, steam up

pocie|cha *f* (*-y*; *G -*) comfort; (*dziecko*) offspring; **~m-** *pf.* → **ciem-**

po ciemku *adv.* in dark

pocierać (*-am*) rub (**o** *A* on, *I* with)

pociesza|ć (*-am*) comfort, console; **~ć się** take comfort (*I* in); **~jący** comforting, consoling

pociesz|enie *n* (*-a*; *0*) comfort, consolation; **na ~enie** by way of consolation; **~ny** funny; **~yć** *pf.* → **pocieszać**

pocisk *m* (*-u*; *-i*) *karabinowy itp.* bullet; (*artyleryjski itp.*) shell; **~ kierowany** guided missile

P

po co/cóż what for
pocu-, pocwa- *pf.* → ***cu-, cwa-***
pocz|ąć *pf.* → ***poczynać***
począt|ek *m* (*-tku*; *-tki*) start, beginning; (*choroby itp.*) onset; **~ki** *pl.* rudiments *pl.*; ***na ~ek / ~ku*** at the beginning; ***od ~ku*** from the start; **~kowo** *adv.* initially, at first; **~kowy** initial; **~kujący 1.** beginning; **2.** *m* (*-ego*; *-y*, *G -ych*) beginner; ***dla ~kujących*** for beginners
poczciw|ie *adv.* kindly; **~y** kind; good
po|czekalnia *f* (*-i*; *-e*) waiting room; **~czesny** hono(u)rable; **~częcie** *n* (*-a*; *G -ęć*) conception; **~częstunek** *m* (*-nku*; *-nki*) treat
po części *adv.* partly
pocz|ęty *dziecko* conceived; ***życie ~ęte*** unborn children *pl.*
poczt|a *f* (*-y*; *G -*) *Brt.* post, *Am.* mail; (*placówka, instytucja*) post office; ***~a lotnicza*** airmail; ***~ą*** by post/mail; → ***elektroniczny***; **~owy** post; postal; **~ówka** *f* (*-i*; *G -wek*) postcard
poczu|cie *n* (*-a*; *0*) sense; ***~cie czasu, honoru, winy, humoru*** sense of time, hono(u)r, guilt, humo(u)r; **~ć** *pf.* → ***czuć***; **~wać się** feel; ***~wać się do winy*** feel guilty
poczwarka *f* (*-i*; *G -rek*) *zo.* chrysalis
poczwórny fourfold; quadruple
poczyna|ć (*-am*) (*-cznę*) do; *dziecko* conceive; **~nia** *n/pl.* (*-ń*) deeds *pl.*, actions *pl.*
poczyt|ać *pf.* (*-am*) read; → ***poczytywać***; **~alny** sound of mind, responsible; **~ny** best-selling, widely read; **~ywać** (*-uję*) consider (***coś za dobre*** s.th. good; ***sobie za obowiązek*** it one's duty)
poćw- *pf.* → ***ćw-***
pod *prp.* (*A*) *kierunek* under; below; ***~ okno*** under the window; *czas* towards; ***~ wieczór*** towards the evening; ***~ sam(o) …*** up to; ***~ dyskusję*** for discussion; ***~ światło*** to the light; (*I*) *miejsce* under; below; beneath, underneath; ***~ oknem*** under the window; ***~ warunkiem*** under the condition; *bliskość* near, by; ***~ Warszawą*** near Warsaw; ***~ ścianą*** by the wall; ***~ karą*** (*G*) on the penalty (of); ***~ postacią*** (*G*) in the shape/form (of)
podać *pf.* → ***podawać, dymisja***
podagra *f* (*-y*; *0*) *med.* gout
podajnik *m* (*-a*; *-i*) *tech.* feeder
podanie *n* (*-a*; *G -ań*) (*pismo*) application; (*legenda*) legend; (*w sporcie*) pass; ***~ do wiadomości*** announcement; ***~ ręki*** handshake
podarować *pf.* → ***darować***
podarty ragged
podat|ek *m* (*-tku*; *-tki*) (***dochodowy, obrotowy*** income, sales) tax; ***~ek od wartości dodanej*** VAT; ***wolny od ~ku*** tax-free, exempt from taxation; **~kowy** tax; ***urząd ~kowy*** *Brt.* Inland Revenue; **~nik** *m* (*-a*; *-cy*) taxpayer; **~ny** susceptible (***na*** *A* to); ***~ny grunt*** *fig.* hotbed
podawać (*wręczyć*) pass; *prośbę, skargę* submit, hand in; *adres* give; *obiad* serve (up); *lekarstwo* administer; (*w sporcie*) *piłkę* pass; *rękę* hold out; ***~ do sądu*** sue; ***~ do wiadomości*** announce; ***~ się za*** (*A*) pass o.s. off (as); ***~ sobie ręce*** shake hands
podaż *f* (*-y*; *0*) *econ.* supply
podąż|ać (*-am*) ⟨**~yć**⟩ go; ***~ać za*** (*I*) follow, go after; ***~yć z pomocą*** rush to s.o.'s aid
pod|bicie *n* (*-a*; *G -ić*) *anat.* instep; *kraw.* lining; **~bić** *pf.* → ***podbijać***; **~biegać** ⟨**~biec, ~biegnąć**⟩ run up (***do*** *G* to); **~biegunowy** *geogr.* polar; **~bijać** (*-am*) *kraj* conquer; *piłkę* flick (up), (*wysoko*) loft; *oko* black; *cenę* push up; *buty* sole; *kraw.* line; **~bój** *m* (*-boju*; *-boje*) conquest (*też fig.*); **~bródek** *m* (*-a*; *-i*) *anat.* chin; **~budowa** *f* foundation, basis
pod|burzać (*-am*) ⟨**~burzyć**⟩ incite, stir up; **~chmielony** F tipsy; **~chodzić** approach (***do*** *G*), come up (***do*** *G* to); **~chorąży** *m mil.* officer cadet
podchwy|tywać (*-uję*) ⟨**~cić**⟩ catch; *melodię* pick up
podcią|ć *pf.* → ***podcinać***; **~gać** (*-am*) ⟨**~gnąć**⟩ pull up (***się*** o.s.); pull, draw up (***do*** *G* towards)
podci|nać (*-am*) cut; *krzaki* lop; (*w baseballu*) curve; (*w tenisie*) slice; **~śnienie** *n tech.* low pressure; *med.* hypotension
podczas *prp.* (*G*) during; ***~ gdy*** while
podczerwony infrared
podda|ć *pf.* → ***poddawać***; **~sze** *n* (*-a*; *G -y*) attic (storey); **~wać** (*-ję*) surrender (***się*** *v/i.*); *myśl* suggest; ***~wać próbie*** try out; ***~wać się*** give up; (*operacji*) undergo; (*żądaniom itp.*) give way

poddostawca *m* subcontractor
pode → ***pod***; ~ ***mną*** under me
podejmować (*-uję*) take, take up; (*wznosić*) lift up; *pieniądze* draw, withdraw; *decyzję* take; *walkę* take up; *podróż* make, undertake; *gości* receive, entertain; ~ ***się*** (*G*) undertake
podejrz|any 1. suspicious, suspect; **2.** *m* (*-ego*; *-ych*), **~ana** *f* (*-ej*; *-e*) suspect; **~enie** *n* (*-a*; *G -eń*) suspicion; **~ewać** (*-am*) suspect (**o** *A* of); (*przypuszczać*) suspect, believe, suppose; **~liwość** *f* (*-ści*; *0*) mistrust, distrust; **~liwie** *adv.* suspiciously; **~liwy** suspicious
podejś|cie *n* (*-a*; *G -jść*) approach (*też fig.* **do** *G* to); (*pod górę*) climb; *fig.* treatment; **~ć** *pf.* (→ ***-jść***) → ***podchodzić***; *fig.* approach
podekscytowany excited
pode|przeć *pf.* → ***podpierać***; **~rwać** *pf.* → ***podrywać***; **~słać** *pf.* → ***podścielić***; **~szły** *wiek* advanced
podeszwa *f* (*-y*; *G -szew*) sole
pod|galać (*-am*) ⟨**~*golić***⟩ shave
podglląda|cz *m* (*-a*; *-e*) peeper; voyeur; **~ć** (*-am*) peep (*A* at)
pod|główek *m* (*-wka*; *-wki*) head-rest; **~górze** *n* (*-a*) foothills *pl.*; **~grzewać** (*-am*) ⟨**~*grzać***⟩ warm up; **~jazd** *m* (*-u*; *-y*) drive; **~jąć** *pf.* → ***podejmować***; **~jeżdżać** (*-am*) ⟨**~*jechać***⟩ drive up, draw up; **~jęcie** *n* (*-a*; *0*) *fig.* start(ing); *por.* **podejmować**; **~judzać** (*-am*) ⟨**~*judzić***⟩ incite; **~klejać** (*-am*) ⟨**~*kleić***⟩ glue, paste
podkład *m* (*-u*; *-y*) (*o farbie*) undercoat; *rail. Brt.* sleeper, *Am.* tie; *med.* absorbent pad; **~ać** (*-am*) put under; *fig.* plant; **~ka** *f* (*-i*; *G -dek*) mat, pad; *tech.* washer
podkop|ywać (*-uję*) ⟨**~*ać***⟩ dig in; *fig.* undermine, erode
podko|szulek *m* (*-lka*; *-lki*), **~szulka** *f* (*-lki*; *G -lek*) *Brt.* vest, *Am.* undershirt; **~wa** *f* (*-y*; *G -ków*) horse-shoe
podkra|dać się (*-am*) ⟨**~*ść się***⟩ sneak up
podkreś|lać (*-am*) ⟨**~*lić***⟩ underline; *fig. też* emphasize
pod|kusić *pf.* → ***kusić***; **~kuwać** (*-am*) ⟨**~*kuć***⟩ shoe; **~lać** *pf.* → ***podlewać***; **~latywać** (*-uję*) ⟨**~*lecieć***⟩ (*w górę*) fly up; **~le** *adv.* despicably, basely; **~legać** (*-am*) ⟨**~*lec***⟩ (→ ***lec***) be subordinate (*D* to); *podatkowi* be subject (*D* to); **~legły 1.** subordinate; subject; **2.** *m* (*-ego*; *-li*) subordinate
pod|lewać (*-am*) water; **~liczać** (*-am*) ⟨**~*liczyć***⟩ count up, add up; **~lotek** *m* (*-tka*; *-tki*) teenager; **~łączać** (*-am*) ⟨**~*łączyć***⟩ (**do** *G*) connect (to), hook up (to); **~łoga** *f* (*-i*; *G -łóg*) floor; **~łość** *f* (*-ści*; *0*) meanness; nastiness; **~łoże** *n* (*-a*; *G -ży*) foundation, base; **~łożyć** *pf.* → ***podkładać***
podłuż|nie *adv.* longitudinally; lengthways; **~ny** longitudinal; oblong
podły mean; base, despicable
podma|kać (*-am*) get damp; **~lowywać** (*-uję*) ⟨**~*lować***⟩ paint
pod|miejski suburban; **~miot** *m* (*-u*; *-y*) subject (*też gr.*); **~moknąć** *pf.* → ***podmakać***; **~morski** submarine
podmuch *m* (*-u*; *-y*) gust
pod|mywać (*-am*) ⟨**~*myć***⟩ *brzeg* undermine, underwash; **~najemca** *m* (*-y*; *G -ców*) subtenant
podniebienie *n* (*-a*; *G -eń*) *anat.* palate
podnie|cać (*-am*) ⟨**~*cić***⟩ excite; (*podsycać*) stimulate; **~*cać się*** get excited; **~cenie** *n* (*-a*; *G -eń*) excitement; stimulation; **~ść** *pf.* → ***podnosić***; **~ta** *f* (*-y*; *G -*) incentive
pod|niosły lofty, elevated; **~nosić** raise (*też fig., math.*); pick up; *flagę* hoist up, run up; *kotwicę* weigh; *kołnierz* turn up; *cenę też* put up; **~*nosić się*** rise; get up, stand; (*w łóżku*) sit up; *mgła*: lift up; **~nośnik** *m* (*-a*; *-i*) jack
podnóż|e *n* (*-a*; *G -y*) foot; ***u ~a*** (*G*) at the foot of (of); **~ek** *m* (*-ka*; *-ki*) footstool
podob|ać się (*-am*) like, enjoy; ***nie ~ać się*** *też* dislike; ***jak ci się to ~a?*** how do you like it?; ***ile ci się ~a*** as much as you like it; **~ieństwo** *n* (*-a*; *G -w*) similarity; **~nie** *adv.* similarly (***jak*** to), likewise; **~no** *adv.* supposedly; ***on ~no wyjechał*** they say he has gone; **~ny** like, similar (**do** *G* to); ***i tym*/*temu ~ne*** and the like
podoficer *m* (*-a*; *-owie*) non-commissioned officer
podokiennik *m* (*-a*; *-i*) → ***parapet***
podołać (*-am*) (*D*) cope (with), manage
podomka *f* (*-i*; *G -mek*) housecoat
podpa|dać (***pod*** *A*) come under, fall into; (*D*) get into trouble (with); **~lacz** *m* (*-a*; *-e*) arsonist; **~lać** (*-am*) ⟨**~*lić***⟩ (*A*) set fire (to); **~ska** (*-i*; *G -sek*) *Brt.* san-

itary towel, *Am.* sanitary napkin; **~ść** *pf.* → ***podpadać***; **~trywać** (*-uję*) ⟨***~trzyć***⟩ spy, peep

podpełz|ać (*-am*) ⟨***~nąć***⟩ crawl, creep (***pod*** *A* to)

pod|piąć *pf.* → ***podpinać***; **~pić**: ***~pić sobie*** get tipsy, get o.s. Dutch courage; **~pierać** (*-am*) support, prop up; ***~pierać się*** lean, support o.s.; **~pinać** (*-am*) (***do*** *G*) pin up (to); *papier* attach (to)

podpis *m* (*-u*; *-y*) signature; (*pod rysunkiem*) caption; **~ywać** (*-uję*) ⟨***~ać***⟩ (*też* ***się***) sign

pod|pity tipsy; **~pływać** ⟨***~płynąć***⟩ (***do*** *G*) *pływak*: swim up (to); *wioślarz*: row up (to); *statek*: sail up (to); **~pora** *f* (*-y*) support; **~porucznik** *m* second lieutenant

podpo|rządkow(yw)ać (*-[w]uję*) subordinate; ***~rządkow(yw)ać się*** conform to *s.th.*; comply with *s.th.*; defer to *s.o.*; **~wiadać** (*-am*) ⟨***~wiedzieć***⟩ prompt; suggest

podpórka *f* (*-i*; *G -rek*) support

podpułkownik *m* lieutenant colonel

podra|biać (*-am*) forge; **~pać** *pf.* scratch; **~stać** (*-am*) grow; **~żać** (*-am*) raise the cost of

podrażnienie *n* (*-a*) irritation (*też med.*)

podreperować *pf.* repair, mend; patch up

podręczn|ik *m* manual; ***~ik szkolny*** textbook, handbook; **~y** hand

pod|robić *pf.* → ***podrabiać, drobić***; **~rosnąć** *pf.* → ***podrastać***; **~rostek** *m* (*-tka*; *-tki*) teenager; juvenile

podroż|eć *pf.*, **~yć** *pf.* (*-ę*) → ***drożeć, podrażać***

podróż *f* (*-y*; *-e*) (*krótka*) trip; (*długa*) journey; voyage; ***biuro ~y*** travel agency; **~ny** **1.** travel(l)ing, travel(l)er's; **2.** *m* (*-ego*; *-i*), **~na** *f* (*-ej*; *-e*) travel(l)er; **~ować** travel; ***~ować koleją*** travel by train) (***po*** *L* in)

podrumienić *pf.* roast/bake slightly brown

podrywać (*-am*) raise; snatch; *fig.* undermine; F *dziewczynę* pick up; ***~ się*** start; jump to one's feet; *ptak*: take wing

podrzeć *pf.* tear up; tear *s.th.* to pieces; *ubranie też* wear out

podrzędny inferior; (*mierny*) second-rate; *gr.* subordinate

podrzu|cać ⟨***~cić***⟩ toss/throw into the air; *dziecko* expose; F (*dostarczyć*) deliver; let *s.o.* have *s.th.*; (*kogoś*) give *s.o.* a lift; **~tek** *m* (*-tka*; *-tki*) foundling

pod|sadzać ⟨***~sadzić***⟩ help up; **~sądny** *m* (*-ego*; *-i*), **-na** *f* (*-ej*; *-e*) defendant; **~skakiwać** (*-uję*) jump up; *piłka*: bounce; F *ceny*: shoot up; soar; ***~skakiwać z radości*** jump for joy; **~skok** *m* jump; leap; **~skórny** *med.* subcutaneous; *zastrzyk*: hypodermic

podsłuch *m* (*-u*) bug; tap; ***założyć ~*** bug (s.o.'s room); tap (s.o.'s phone); **~iwać** (*-uję*) ⟨***~ać***⟩ *v/i.* eavesdrop; (*pod drzwiami*) overhear; **~owy** tapping; (*urządzenie*) device

podsmaż|ać (*-am*) ⟨***~yć***⟩ fry

podstarzały elderly

podstaw|a *f* (*-y*) base; basis; foundation; *tech.* mount, pedestal; *mat.* base; ***na ~ie czegoś*** on the ground of sth; ***mieć ~ę*** (do *G*) to have good reason for doing sth; ***mieć ~ę*** have good reason for; ***na ~ie*** (*G*) on the basis of; **~i(a)ć** put *s.th.* under *s.th.*; substitute; *samochód* to bring round; **~ka** *f* (*-i*; *G -wek*) support; (*spodek*) saucer; **~owy** basic; fundamental; ***szkoła ~owa*** *Brt.* primary school, *Am.* elementary school

podstęp *m* (*-u*; *-y*) trick; ruse; **~ny** deceitful; scheming; tricky; *plan* insidious

pod|strzygać (*-am*) ⟨***~strzyc***⟩ trim; **~sumow(yw)ać** (*-[w]uję*) add up; *fig.* sum up; **~suwać** ⟨~sunąć⟩ push; shove; draw; *myśl* suggest; **~sycać** (*-am*) ⟨~sycić⟩ *nienawiść* hatred; **~szeptywać** (*-uję*) ⟨***~szepnąć***⟩ *fig.* prompt; hint; insinuate; **~szewka** *f* (*-i*; *G -wek*) *kraw.* lining

podszy|wać (*-am*) ⟨***~ć***⟩ line; ***~ć się*** impersonate; pretend to be (***pod*** *s.o.*)

pod|ścielić *pf.* (*-lę*) *koc* spread; **~ściółka** *f* (*-i*; *G -łek*) bed; (*słoma itp.*) litter; **~śpiewywać** (*-uję*) hum; **~świadomy** subconscious; **~tytuł** *m* (*-u*; *-y*) subtitle; (*w gazecie*) subheading

podtrzym|ywać (*-uję*) ⟨***~ać***⟩ support; hold up; *fig.* support; uphold; keep up; *żądania, stosunki itp.* maintain; ***~ywać ogień*** keep the fire burning

pod|udzie *n* (*-a*) shank; **~upadać** ⟨***~upaść***⟩ (→***paść***[2]) deteriorate; fall into decline; fall into poverty

poduszk|a *f* (*-i*; *G -szek*) pillow; cushion; *tech.* cushion, pad; **~owiec** *m*

P

(*-wca*; *-wce*) hovercraft
podwajać (*-am*) double
pod|walina *f* (*-y*) *fig.* foundations *pl*; **~ważać** (*-am*) ⟨**~ważyć**⟩ lever up; prize upon; *fig.* undermine; challenge
podwiąz|ka *f* (*-i*; *G -zek*) garter; suspender; **~ywać** (*-uję*) ⟨**~zać**⟩ tie; bind up; *med.* ligate
pod|wieczorek *m* (*-rku*; *-rki*) tea; **~wieźć** *pf* → **podwozić**; **~wijać**(*-am*) ⟨**~winąć**⟩ (*-nę*, *-ń!*) *rękawy* roll up; *nogi* draw up; **z ~winiętym ogonem** with the tail between the legs; **~władny** subordinate; inferior; → **podległy**; **~wodny** underwater; **okręt ~ny** submarine
podwo|ić *pf.* → **podwajać**; **~zić** give *s.o.* a lift; **~zie** *n* (*-a*; *G -zi*) *mot.* chassis; *aviat.* undercarriage
podwój|nie *adv.* double; doubly; (*dwukrotnie*) twice; **~ny** double; **gra ~na** (*w sporcie*) doubles; *fig.* **~na gra** double-dealing
podwó|rko *n* (*-a*; *G -rek*), **~rze** *n* (*-a*) court, (back) yard
podwyż|ka *f* (*-i*; *G -żek*) rise, increase; **~ka płac** *Brt.* rise, *Am.* raise; **~ka cen** increase in prices; **~szać** (*-am*) ⟨**~szyć**⟩ (*-ę*) raise, increase; **~szać się** rise; **~szenie** *n* (*-a*) rise; platform
podzelować [-d·z-] *pf.* re-sole
po|dziać *pf.* → **podziewać**; **~dział** *m* division; **~działka** *f* scale; **~dzielić** *pf.* → **dzielić**; **~dzielnik** *math.* divisor
podziem|ie[-d·ź-] *n* (*-a*; *G -i*) basement; *fig.* underground; **~ny** underground
podziewać (*-am*) (*zgubić*) to get lost, to vanish; (*znaleźć schronienie*) **~ się** to find shelter
podziękowanie *n* (*-a*) thanks
podziurawiony full of holes, in holes
podziw *m* (*-u*; *0*) admiration; → **nad**; **~iać** (*-am*) admire
podzwrotnikowy [-d·z-] subtropical
podźwignąć *pf.* raise, lift; *fig.* restore; **~ się** pull oneself up
podżegać [-d·ʒ-] (*-am*) incite (**przeciw** *D* against; **do** *G* to)
poe|mat *m* (*-u*; *-y*) poem; **~ta** *m* (*-y*; *-ci*), **~tka** *f* (*-i*; *G -tek*) poet; **~tycki** (**-ko**), **~tyczny** poetic; **~zja** *f* (*-i*; *0*) poetry; (*pl. -e*) poems
po|fa-, ~fi-, ~fo- *pf.* → **fa-, fi-, fo-**
poga|danka *f* (*-i*; *G -nek*) talk; **~niać** drive; urge; **~nin** *m* (*-a*; *-anie*, *-*), **~nka** *f* (*-i*; *G -nek*) pagan, heathen; **~ński** pagan, heathen
pogar|da *f* (*-y*; *0*) contempt; disdain; scorn; **godny ~dy** contemptible; despicable; **mieć w ~dzie** hold in contempt; **~dliwy** (**-wie**) contemptuous; disdainful; scornful; **~dzać** (*-am*) ⟨**~dzić**⟩ (*I*) despise; scorn; hold in contempt; (*czymś też*) renounce *s.th.*
pogarszać (*-am*) worsen; make *s.th.* worse; **~ się** deteriorate
pogawędka *f* (*-i*; *G -dek*) chat
pogląd *m* (*-u*; *-y*) view; opinion; **~ na świat** outlook; **wymiana ~ów** exchange of ideas; **~owy** visual
po|głębiać (*-am*) ⟨**~głębić**⟩ deepen; *fig.* intensify; **~głębiarka** *f* (*-i*) dredger; **~głos** *m* (*-u*; *0*) reverberation; **~głoska** *f* rumo(u)r; hearsay; **~gmatwany** entangled; intricate; **~gnać** *pf.* → **poganiać**; *v/i.* rush, speed off
pogod|a *f* (*-y*) weather; **będzie ~a** we're going to have fine weather; **~ny** bright; fine; clear; *fig.* cheerful
pogodzeni|e *n* (*-a*) reconciliation; **niemożliwy do ~a** irreconcilable
pogo|nić *pf.* → **poganiać, pognać**; **~ń** *f* (*-ni*; *-nie*) chase; pursuit
pogorsz|enie (się) *n* (*-a*) deterioration; **~yć** *pf.* → **pogarszać**
pogorzelisko *n* (*-a*) site of a fire
pogotowi|e *n* (*-a*; *0*) alert; (*karetka*) ambulance; **~e górskie** mountain rescue team; **~e awaryjne/techniczne** public utilities emergency service; **~e górskie** mountain rescue service; **w ~u** in readiness; on the alert
pogranicz|e *n* (*-a*) borderland; **na ~u** on borderline; **~ny** frontier; *fig.* borderline
pogrąż|ać (*-am*) ⟨**~yć**⟩ (*-ę*) sink; plunge; *fig.* crash, destroy; **~yć się** sink, become immersed
pogrom *m* (*-u*; *-y*) rout; *hist.* pogrom; **~ca** *m* (*-y*; *G -ów*), **~czyni** *f* (*-i*) conqueror; **~ca zwierząt** tamer
pogróżka *f* (*-i*; *G -żek*) threat
pogru-, pogry- *pf.* → **gru-, gry-**
pogrzeb *m* (*-u*; *-y*) funeral; (*kondukt*) funeral procession; **~acz** *m* (*-a*; *-e*) poker; **~ać** *pf.* → **grzebać**; *ciało* bury (*też fig.*); **~owy** funeral; **zakład ~owy** undertaker's; funeral parlour
pogu- *pf.* → **gu-**

P

pogwałc|ać (*-am*) 〈**~ić**〉 *uczucia* violate, transgress; *prawo* break
pogwizdywać (*-uję*) whistle
pohamowa|ć się *pf.* control o.s.; check o.s.; **~nie** *n* restraint, self-control
po|ić 〈**na-**〉 (*-ję, -isz, pój!*) *v/t.* give *s.th.* to drink; *konie* water; F (*upijać*) ply *s.o.* with drink; **~in-** *pf.* → **in-**; **~jawiać się** (*-am*) 〈**~jawić się**〉 appear; emerge; become visible; **~jazd** *m* (*-u; -y*) (*mechaniczny* motor) vehicle; **~jazd kosmiczny** spacecraft; **~jąć** *pf.* → **pojmować**; **~je-** *pf.* → **je-**
pojedna|nie *n* (*-a*) reconciliation; **~wczy** conciliatory
pojedyn|czy individual; (*nie podwójny*) single; **gra ~cza** (*w sporcie*) singles; **liczba ~cza** *gr.* singular; **~ek** *m* (*-nku; -nki*) duel (*też fig.*)
pojemn|ik *m* (*-a; -i*) container; **~ość** *f* (*-ści; 0*) capacity (*też phys.*); *mar.* tonnage; **~ość skokowa** cubic capacity; **~y** capacious; roomy
pojezierze *n* (*-a; G -rzy*) lake district
pojęci|e *n* (*-a*) notion; F (*pl. 0*) idea; **nie do ~a** incomprehensible; **nie mam ~a** I have no idea
pojętny intelligent; clever
pojmować (*-uję*) understand; comprehend
pojutrze the day after tomorow
po|ka- *pf.* → **ka-**
pokarm *m* (*-u; -y*) food; **~owy**: **przewód ~owy** alimentary canal
pokaz *m* (*-u; -y*) (*mody* fashion) show; demonstration; **na ~** for show; **~ywać** (*-uję*) 〈**~ać**〉 show; **~ywać się** turn up; show up
po|kaźny sizeable; considerable; **~kątny** illegal; *transakcja* under the table
poklask *m* (*-u; 0*) applause (*też fig.*)
poklep|ywać (*-uję*) 〈**~ać**〉 → **klepać**
pokła|d *m* (*-u; -y*) *mar* deck; (*warstwa*) layer; stratum; (*w górnictwie*) seam; **na ~dzie** (**statku**) on board (a ship); **~dać** (*-am*) *nadzieję itp.* put (one's hopes) (**w** *L* in); **~dowy** deck
pokłosie *n* (*-a; G -si*) *fig.* aftermath
po|kłócić *pf.* turn *s.o.* against *s.o.*; **~kłócić się** quarrel (with); **~kochać** *pf. v/t.* fall in love (with); come to love
poko|jowy[1] peacuful; peace; **~jowy**[2] room; **~jówka** *f* (*-i; G -wek*) (chamber)maid
pokolenie *n* (*-a*) generation
poko|nywać (*-uję*) 〈**~nać**〉 defeat; beat; *fig.* overcome; **~nany** beaten; conquered; **~ra** *f* (*-y; 0*) humility; **~rny** humble
pokost *m* (*-u; -y*) varnish
po|kój[1] *m* (*-oju; 0*) peace; **~kój**[2] *m* (*-oju; -oje*) (**hotelowy, stołowy** hotel, dining) room
pokra- *pf.* → **kra-**
pokrew|ieństwo *n* (*-a*) kinship; **~ny** related (*D* to)
pokro|- *pf.* → **kro-**; **~wiec** *m* (*-wca; -wce*) cover
pokrój *m* (*-oju; 0*) type; sort
pokrótce *adv.* briefly
pokry|cie *n* (*-a*) covering; *tech.* (roof) cover; *fin., econ.* cover, backing; **wystawić czek bez ~cia** bounce a cheque; **słowa bez ~cia** empty words; **~ć** *pf.* → **pokrywać, kryć**
po kryjomu *adv.* secretly
pokryw|a *f* (*-y*) cover; *tech.* bonnet; **~ać** (*-am*) be covered (with); **~ać się z** (*I*) agree with; **~ka** *f* (*-i; G -wek*) lid
pokrzepi|ać (*-am*) 〈**~ć**〉 strengthen; fortify; **~ć na duchu** comfort; cheer; **~ający** strengthening; fortifying
pokrzywa *f* (*-y*) nettle
pokrzywdzony deprived, disadvantaged, harmed
pokrzywk|a *f* (*-i; 0*) *med.* rash, hives
pokupny *towar* sal(e)able; in demand
pokus|a *f* (*-y*) temptation; **~ić się** (*o* A) attempt to *inf.*
pokut|a *f* (*-y*) penance; **~ować** (*-uję*) to do penance (**za** A for); *fig.* pay for *s.th.*
pokwa-, pokwę- *pf.* → **kwa-, kwę-**
pokwitowanie *f* (*-a*) receipt; **za ~m** against receipt
pola|- *pf.* → **la-**; **~ć** *pf.* → **polewać**
Polak *m* (*-a; -cy*) Pole
pola|na *f* (*-y*) clearing; **~no** *n* (*-a*) log
polarny polar; → **zorza**
pole *n* (*-a; G pól*) field (*też fig.*); *mat.* area; **wywieść w ~** hoodwink *s.o.*
pole|c *pf.* fall; be killed; **~c za ojczyznę** be killed for *one's* country; **~cać** (*-am*) 〈**~cić**〉 (*-cę*) command; (*powierzać*) entrust; (*doradzać*) recommend; **list ~cający** letter of recommendation; **list ~cony** registered letter; **~cenie** *n* (*-a*) (*zlecenie*) command, order; **z ~cenia** on *s.o.'s* recommendation;

P

~gać (*-am*) (**na** *L*) depend, rely (on); (*zasadzać się*) consist (in); **~gły** killed; *m* (*-ego*; *-li*) casualty
polemiczny polemic
polepsz|ać (*-am*) ⟨**~yć**⟩ (*-ę*) improve (*też* **się**); **~enie** *n* (*-a*) improvement
polerować ⟨**wy-**⟩ (*-uję*) polish
polew|a *f* (*-y*) glaze; (*na cieście*) icing; **~aczka** *f* (*-i*; *G -czek*) → **konewka**; **~ać** (*-am*) pour water on; *tech.* glaze; **~ka** *f* (*-i*; *G -wek*) soup
poleżeć *pf.* lie (some time)
polędwica *f* (*-y*; *-e*) fillet, loin
polichlorek *m* (*-rku*; *-rki*): **~ winylu** polyvinyl chloride
polic|ja *f* (*-i*; *0*) (**drogowa** traffic) police; **~ja śledcza** criminal investigation department, CID; **~jant** *m* (*-a*; *-ci*) policeman; **~jantka** *f* (*-i*; *G -tek*) policewoman; **~yjny** police
policz|ek *m* (*-czka*; *-czki*) cheek; slap in the face; **~kować** ⟨**s-**⟩ (*-uję*) slap *s.o.'s* face; **~yć** *pf.* → **liczyć**
poli|etylenowy polythene; **~gon** *m* (*-u*; *-y*) *mil.* military training ground; **~'grafia** *f* (*GDL -ii*; *0*) typography, printing
polisa *f* (*-y*) policy
politechnika *f* politechnic
politowanie *n* (*-a*; *0*) pity, compassion; **z ~m** pitifully, with compassion
politur|a *f* (*-y*) French polish; **~ować** (*-uję*) French-polish
polity|czny political; **~k** *m* (*-a*; *-cy*) politician; **~ka** [-'li-] *f* (*-i*) politics; policy
polka *f* (*-i*; *G -lek*) (*taniec*) polka
Polka *f* (*-i*; *G -lek*) Pole; Polish girl *lub* woman
polny field; **konik ~** grasshopper
polonez *m* (*-a*; *-y*) polonaise
polonijny: **ośrodek ~** Polish community centre
polonistyka *f* (*-i*; *0*) Polish studies
polot *m* (*-u*; *0*) inspiration
polowa|ć (*-uję*) (**na** *A*) hunt; *zwierzę*: prey; **~nie** *n* (*-a*) (**na lisa** fox) hunting; hunt
Polska *f* (*-i*; *0*) Poland
pols|ki Polish; **po ~ku** Polish
polszczyzna *f* (*-y*; *0*) Polish (language)
polub|ić *pf.* become fond (of); come to like; **~owny** conciliatory; **sąd ~owny** court of conciliation
poła *f* (*-y*; *G pół*) tail
poła|- *pf.* → **ła-**; **~many** broken
połącz|enie *n* (*-a*) combination; joint; *kolej*, *tel. Brt.* connection, *Am.* connexion; (*firm itp.*) merger; **~ony** joint; *fig.* connected (**z** *I* with); **~yć** *pf.* → **łączyć**
połknąć *pf.* (*-nę*) swallow
połow|a *f* (*-y*) (*część*) half; (*środek*) middle; **do ~y** half-…; **w ~ie maja** in the middle of May; **w ~owie drogi** halfway; **podzielić na ~ę** halve; **~iczny**: **środki ~iczne** half measures
położ|enie *n* (*-a*) location; position, situation; **~na** *f* (*-ej*; *-e*) midwife; **~nictwo** *n* (*-a*; *0*) obstetrics; **~yć** *pf.* → **kłaść**
połóg *m* (*-ogu*; *-ogi*) *med.* puerperium
połów *m* (*-owu*; *-owy*) fishing; (*złowione ryby*) catch
połówka *f* (*-i*; *G -wek*) half
południ|e *n* (*-a*) noon; midday; *geogr.* south; **po ~u** in the afternoon; **przed ~em** in the morning; **w ~e** at noon, at midday; **na ~e od** (*G*) south of; **~k** *m* (*-a*; *-i*) *geogr.* meridian
południo|wo-wschodni south-east(ern); **~wo-zachodni** south-west(ern); **~wy** southern; south
połykać (*-am*) swallow
połysk *m* (*-u*; *0*) polish; gloss; lustre/luster
połyskiwać (*-uję*) glitter; glisten
poma|- *pf.* → **ma-**; **~dka** *f* (*-i*; *G -dek*): **~dka do ust** lipstick; **~gać** (*-am*) help; assist (**przy, w** *L*) with; **~gać na** (*A*) *kaszel itp.* relieve; **~lo-** *pf.* → **malo-**; **~łu** *adv.* slowly; F *fig.* slow down!
pomarańcz|a *f* (*-y*; *-e*) orange; **~owy** (**-wo**) orange
pomarszczony wrinkled
pomawiać (**k-o o** *A*) unjustly accuse (s.o. of s.th.)
po|mazać *pf.* smear; **~mą-**, **~me-**, **~mę-** *pf.* → **mą-, me-, mę-**
pomiar *m* (*-u*; *-y*) measurement; **~owy** measuring
pomi(ą)- *pf.* → **mi(ą)-**
pomidor *m* (*-a*; *-y*) tomato; **~owy** tomato; *kolor*: tomato-red
pomie|- *pf.* → **mie-**; **~szanie** *n* (*-a*; *0*): **~szanie zmysłów** insanity; **~szczenie** *n* (**-a**) room; **~ścić** *pf.* hold; find room for; **~ścić się** find room
pomię|- *pf.* → **mię-**; **~ty** crumpled
pomi|jać ⟨**~nąć**⟩ (*opuścić*) omit; (*nie uwzględnić*) pass over; **~jając** (*A*) ex-

P

cepted; **~mo** *prp.* (*G*) in spite of, despite
pomnażać (*-am*) → ***mnożyć***
pomniejsz|ać (*-am*) ⟨**~yć**⟩ (*-ę*) diminish; lessen; *fig.* diminish, belittle; **~y** smaller; lesser
pomnik *m* (*-a*; *-i*) monument
pomoc *f* (*-y*; *0*) help; assistance; aid; (*pl.* *-e*) help, aid; (*w sporcie*) midfield; ***~e naukowe*** teaching aids; ***przyjść z ~ą*** come to s.o.'s help; ***wzywać na ~*** call for help; ***przy ~y, za ~ą*** by means of; **~nica** *f* (*-y*; *-e*) helper; **~nictwo** *n* (*-a*) *jur.* abetting; **~niczy** auxiliary; **~nik** *m* (*-a*; *-cy*) helper; assistant; **~ny** helpful; ***być ~nym*** (***w*** *L*) be helpful in
pomor|- *pf.* → ***mor-***; **~ski** Pomeranian
pomost *m* (*-u*; *-y*) pier; platform; *tech*; ***~ wieńcowy*** bypass
pomóc *pf.* (*-móż!*) → ***pomagać***
pomór *m* (*-oru*; *0*) plague, pest
pomówić *pf.* → ***pomawiać***
pomp|a[1] *f* (*-y*) pump; **~a**[2] *f* (*-y*, *0*) pomp; **~atyczny** pompous; bombastic; **~ka** *f* (*-i*) (*do roweru itp.*) pump; (*ćwiczenie*) *Brt.* press-up, *Am.* push-up; **~ować** (*-uję*) ⟨**na-**⟩ pump (up); *powietrze* inflate
pomruk *m* (*-u*; *-i*) murmur; rumble
po|mstować (*-uję*) execrate; **~mścić** *pf.* (*-mszczę*) avenge; **~myje** *pl.* (-) swill
pomy|lić *pf.* mistake; confuse; mix up; ***~lić się*** → ***mylić***; **~lony** F crazy, loony; **~łka** *f* (*-i*; *G -łek*) mistake, error; ***przez ~łkę*** by mistake; ***~łka!*** wrong number
pomysł *m* (*-u*; *-y*) idea; **~odawca** *m* (*-y*) originator; **~owy** ingenious; inventive
pomyśleni|e: ***nie do ~a*** unthinkable, inconceivable
pomyśln|ość *f* (*-ści*) prosperity; success; ***życzyć wszelkiej ~ości*** wish *s.o.* the best of luck; **~y** favo(u)rable
pona- *pf.* → ***na-***
ponad *prp.* (*A I*) above, over; beyond; ***~ miarę*** beyond measure, excessively; ***to jest ~ moje siły*** it is beyond me; **~dźwiękowy** supersonic; **~to** *adv.* besides; moreover
pona|glać (*-am*) rush, press; → ***naglić***; **~glenie** *n* (*-a*) (*pismo*) reminder; **~wiać** (*-am*) renew; repeat
poncz *m* (*-u*; *-e*) punch
ponętny tempting
poniedział|ek *m* (*-łku*; *-łki*) Monday; **~kowy** Monday
ponie|kąd *adv.* in a way; **~ść** *pf.* → ***ponosić***; **~waż** *cj.* because; as; since; **~wczasie** *adv.* too late; tardily
poniewierać (*-am*) (*A*, *I*) hold in contempt, treat *s.o.* badly; ***~ się*** (*o rzeczach*) lie about
poniż|ać (*-am*) humiliate; ***~ać się*** stoop, demean o.s.; **~ej** *prp.* (*G*) below; beneath; *adv.* below; **~enie** *n* (*-a*) humiliation; **~szy** the following; **~yć** *pf.* (*-ę*) → ***poniżać***
ponosić (*-szę*) ⟨**ponieść**⟩ *v/t.* bear (*też fig. koszty*); *ryzyko* incur, *klęskę* suffer; *karę* undergo a punishment; *v/i. konie*: bolt; ***~*** ⟨***ponieść***⟩ ***winę*** (***za*** A) take blame for; ***ponieść śmierć*** meet one's death; ***poniosło go*** he got carried away
ponow|ić *pf.* (*-ę*) → ***ponawiać***; **~nie** *adv.* again **~ny** renewed, repeated
ponton *m* (*-u*; *-y*) pontoon
pontyfikat *m* (*-u*; *-y*) *rel.* pontificate
ponu|- *pf.* → ***nu-***; **~ry** gloomy; bleak; dismal
pończocha *f* (*-y*) stocking
po|ob- *pf.* → ***ob-***; **~obiedni** after-dinner; **~od-** *pf.* → ***od-***
po omacku *adv.* gropingly
po|op- *pf.* → ***op-***; **~operacyjny** postoperative; **~os-**, **~ot-** *pf.* → ***os-, ot-***; **~padać** fall (into); **~pamiętać** *pf.*: ***popamiętasz mnie!*** I'll show you!; **~parcie** *n* (*-a*) support; **~parzenie** *n* (*-a*) burn; **~paść** *pf.* → ***popadać, paść***[2]; ***brać co ~padnie*** take whatever turns up; **~pchnąć** *pf.* → ***popychać***
popelinowy poplin
popełni|ać (*-am*) ⟨**~ć**⟩ commit; make
popę|d *m* (*-u*; *-y*) impulse, urge; inclination; **~dliwy** impetuous; **~dzać** (*-am*) ⟨**~dzić**⟩ rush; hurry; → ***pędzić***; **~kany** cracked
popić *pf.* → ***popijać***
popiel|aty (***-to***) grey, *Am.* gray; **♀ec** *m* (*-lca*; *-lce*) Ash Wednesday; **~niczka** *f* (*-i*; *G -czek*) ashtray
popierać (*-am*) support, back
popiersie *n* (*-a*; *G -i*) bust
popijać (*-am*) *v/t.* sip; *jedzenie* wash down
popiół *m* (*-ołu*, *L -iele*; *-oły*) ash
popis *m* (*-u*; *-y*) show; **~owy** spectacular; **~ywać się** (*-uję*) ⟨**~ać się**⟩ (*I*) show off
po|pl- *pf.* → ***pl-***; **~plecznik** *m* (*-a*; *-cy*) partisan, supporter; **~płacać** (*-am*) pay; **~płatny** well-paid; profitable; **~płoch**

P

m (*-u*; *0*) panic; ***w ~płochu*** in panic
popołudni|e *n* (*-a*) afternoon; → ***południe***; **~owy** afternoon
popra- *pf.* → ***pra-***
popraw|a *f* (*-y*) improvement; (*poprawienie*) correction; **~czy**: ***zakład ~czy*** *Brt.* borstal, *Am.* reformatory; **~iać** (*-am*) ⟨***~ić***⟩ correct; adjust; improve; ***~i(a)ć się*** correct o.s.; *v/i* improve; **~ka** *f* (*-i*; *G -wek*) correction; (*o sukni*) alteration; (*do ustawy*) amendment; F (*egzamin*) repeat an exam; **~ność** *f* (*-ści*; *0*) correctness; **~ny** correct
popro- *pf.* → ***pro-***
po prostu *adv.* simply; → ***prosty***
po|pró-, ~pru- *pf.* → ***pró-, pru-***
poprzecz|ka *f* (*-i*; *G -czek*) cross-beam; (*w sporcie*) crossbar; **~ny** transversal
poprzeć *pf.* → ***popierać***
poprzedni previous; ***~ego dnia*** the day before; **~czka** *f* (*-i*; *G -czek*), **~k** *m* (*-a*; *-cy*) predecessor; **~o** *adv.* previously
poprzedz|ać (*-am*) ⟨***~ić***⟩ (*-dzę*) *v/t.* precede
poprze|k: ***na*** *lub* ***w ~k*** crosswise; **~sta(wa)ć** content o.s. (***na*** *L* with s.th.)
poprzez *prp.* through; across
po|przy- *pf.* → ***przy-***; **~psu-** *pf.* → ***psu-***
popular|ność *f* (*-ści*; *0*) popularity; **~ny** popular; **~yzować** ⟨**s-**⟩ (*-uję*) popularize
popu|szczać ⟨***~ścić***⟩ *v/t.* loosen; slacken; *fig. v/i* relent
popycha|ć (*-am*) → ***pchać***; *fig.* ill-treat; **~dło** *n* (*-a*; *G -deł*) *fig.* drudge
popyt *m* (*-u*; *0*) *econ.* demand
por *m* (*-u*; *-y*) *anat.* pore; (*-a*) (*warzywo*) leek
por. *skrót pisany*: ***porównaj*** cf. (compare); *skrót pisany*: ***porucznik*** Lt. (lieutenant)
po|ra *f* (*-y*; *G pór*) time; hour; ***~ra roku*** season; ***w ~rę*** at the right moment, in time; ***nie w ~rę*** ill-timed; ***do tej ~ry*** until now; so far; ***o tej ~rze*** at this time; ***o każdej ~rze*** at any time
porabia|ć (*-am*): ***co ~sz?*** what are you up to?; how are you getting on?
porachunki *m/pl. fig.* accounts
porad|a *f* advice; ***za ~ą*** (*G*) on s.o.'s advice; **~nia** *f* (*-i*; *-e*): ***~nia lekarska*** outpatient clinic; **~nik** *m* (*-a*; *-i*) guide
poran|ek *m* morning; (*impreza*) matinée; **~ny** morning
pora|stać (*-am*) *v/t* overgrow: *v/i* become overgrown; **~żać** (*-am*) ⟨***~zić***⟩ *med.*, *fig. Brt.* paralyse, *Am.* paralyze; *agr.* attack; **~żenie** *n* (*-a*) paralysis; ***~żenie słoneczne*** sunstroke; ***~żenie prądem*** electric shock; **~żka** *f* (*-i*; *G -żek*) defeat
porcelana *f* (*-y*) china, porcelain
porcja *f* (*-i*; *-e*) portion, helping; ***żelazna ~*** emergency ration
pore- *pf.* → ***re-***
poręcz *f* (*-y*; *-e*, *-y*) banister; handrail; (*oparcie*) arm; ***~e*** *pl.* (*w sporcie*) parallel bars; **~ać** (*-am*) → ***ręczyć***; **~enie** *n* (*-a*) guarantee; **~ny** handy; **~yciel** *m* (*-a*; *-e*, *-i*), **~ycielka** *f* (*-i*; *G -lek*) guarantor
poręka *f* (*-i*; *0*) guarantee
porno F, **~graficzny** porno(graphic)
poro|- *pf.* → ***ro-***; **~dowy**: ***izba ~dowa*** delivery room **~nienie** *n* (*-a*) miscarriage; abortion; **~niony** F *fig.* silly, foolish
poros|nąć *pf.* → ***porastać***; **~t** *m* (*-u*; *0*) growth; ***~ty*** *pl. bot.* lichen(s)
porowaty porous
poroz- *pf.* → ***roz-***
porozumie|nie *n* (*-a*) understanding, agreement; (*układ*) agreement; ***dojść do ~nia*** come to an agreement; **~wać się** (*-am*) ⟨***~ć się***⟩ communicate (***z*** *I* with); (*dojść do zgody*) come to an agreement (***co do*** *G* about s.th.); **~wawczy** knowing
poród *m* (*-odu*; *-ody*) (child)birth, delivery
porówn|anie *n* (*-a*) comparison; **~awczy** comparative; **~ywać** (*-uję*) ⟨***~ać***⟩ compare
poróżnić *pf.* set *s.o.* against *s.o.*; ***~ się*** fall out with *s.o.*
port *m* (*-u*; *-y*) port, harbo(u)r; *fig.* haven; ***~ lotniczy*** airport
portfel *m* (*-a*; *-e*) wallet
portier *m* (*-a*; *-rzy*) porter, doorman; **~a** *f* (*-y*) portière; **~nia** *f* (*-ni*; *-nie*) porter's lodge
portki F *pl.* (*-tek*) *Brt.* trousers, *Am.* pants
portmonetka *f* (*-i*; *G -tek*) purse
porto *n* (*idkl./-a*; *0*) (*wino*) port; (*opłata*) postage
portowy port; dock
portret *m* (*-u*; *-y*) portrait
Portugalia *f* (*-ii*; *0*) Portugal

P

Portugal|czyk *m* (*-a*; *-cy*), **~ka** *f* (*-i*; *G -lek*) Portuguese; **ℒski** (**po -ku**) Portuguese

porucznik *m* (*-a*; *-cy*) lieutenant

porusz|ać ⟨**~yć**⟩ (*I*, *fig. A*) move; *tech.* drive, propel; *temat itp.* touch (up)on; **~ać** ⟨**~yć**⟩ **się** move; **~enie** *n* (*-a*) *fig.* agitation

porwa|ć *pf.* → ***porywać, rwać***; **~nie** *n* (*-a*) kidnapping; (*samolotu*) hijacking

poryw *m* (*-u*; *-y*) gust; *fig.* outburst; **~acz** *m* (*-a*; *-e*) kidnapper; (*samolotu*) hijacker; **~ać** (*-am*) kidnap; *samolot* hijack; (*unieść*) sweep away, carry away; (*chwycić*) snatch, grab; *fig.* (*ogarnąć*) carry away; (*pociągać*) ravish, enrapture; **~ać się** (*z miejsca*) jump to one's feet; (**na** *A*) fall (on s.o.); (*podjąć się*) attempt *s.th.*; ***~ać się z motyką na słońce*** attempt the impossible; **~ający** ravishing; **~czy** impetuous, hot-tempered

porząd|ek *m* (*-dku*; *-dki*) order (*też ciąg*); ***w ~ku*** in good order; ***w ~ku!*** all right!, OK!; ***~ek dzienny*** order of the day; ***robić ~ki*** clean up; **~kować** ⟨**u-**⟩ order; tidy; **~ny** tidy; *fig.* respectable; proper

porzeczka *f* (*-i*; *G -czek*) currant

porzuc|ać ⟨**~ić**⟩ leave, abandon; → ***rzucać***

posa|- *pf.* → **sa-**; **~da** *f* (*-y*) job; ***bez ~dy*** out of work

posadzka *f* (*-i*; *G -dzek*) floor

posag *m* (*-u*; *-i*) dowry

posądz|ać (*-am*) ⟨**~ić**⟩ (**k-o o** *A*) suspect (s.o. of s.th.)

posąg *m* (*-u*; *-i*) statue

pose|lski parliamentary; → ***klub***; **~lstwo** *n* (*-a*) *pol.* legation; mission; **~ł** *m* (*-sła*; *-słowie*) envoy; *pol.* member of parliament

posesja *f* (*-i*; *-e*) estate; property

posępny gloomy, *Brt.* sombre, *Am.* somber

posiadacz *m* (*-a*; *-e*), **~ka** *f* (*-i*; *G -czek*) owner

posiad|ać own; possess; ***nie ~ać się*** (**z** *G*) be beside o.s. (with); **~łość** *f* (*-ci*) estate, property

po|siąść *pf.* acquire; **~siedzenie** *n* sitting, session; meeting

posi|lać się (*-am*) have a meal, take some refreshment; **~łek** *m* (*-łku*; *-łki*) meal; *pl. mil.* reinforcements *pl.*; **~łkowy** *gr.* auxiliary

po|sk- *pf.* → **sk-**; **~skramiać** (*-am*) ⟨***~skromić***⟩ (*-ę*) tame; *fig.* restrain

posła|ć *pf.* → ***słać, posyłać***; **~nie**[1] *n* (*-a*; *0*) message; **~nie**[2] *n* (*-a*) (*do spania*) bedding; **~niec** *m* (*-ńca*; *-ńcy*) messenger; **~nka** *f* (*-i*; *G -nek*) *pol.* member of parliament

posłowie *n* (*-a*) afterword; → ***poseł***

posłuch *m* obedience, discipline; ***dawać ~*** (*D*) give s.o. a hearing; **~ać** *pf.* → ***słuchać***

posługacz *m* (*-a*; *-e*) attendant; **~ka** *f* (*-i*; *G -czek*) charwoman

posługiwać się (*-uję*) (*I*) use, employ

posłusz|eństwo *n* (*-a*; *0*) obedience; ***odmówić ~eństwa*** refuse obedience; (*o przedmiocie*) ***odmawia ~eństwa*** it won't work; **~ny** obedient

po|służyć się *pf.* → ***posługiwać się***; **~smak** *m* aftertaste; **~spa-** *pf.* → ***spa-***; **~spiech** *m* → ***pośpiech***; **~spolity** (**-cie**) common, ordinary; **~sprzeczać się** *pf.* quarrel; fall out

posrebrzany silver-plated

post *m* (*-u*; *-y*) fast; *rel.* ***Wielki ℒ*** Lent; ***zachowywać ~*** observe fast

posta|ć *f* (*-ci*; *-cie/-ci*) (*sylwetka*) figure; (*w książce*) character; (*forma*) form, shape; **~nawiać** (*-am*) ⟨***~nowić***⟩ decide; **~nowienie** *n* (*-a*) decision; (*uchwała*) resolution; **~rzać** (*-am*) age; **~wa** *f* (*-y*) bearing; posture; *fig.* attitude; **~wić** *pf.* → ***stawiać***; **~wny** portly

postąpić *pf.* → ***postępować***

posterunek *m* (*-nku*; *-nki*) post

postęp *m* (*-u*; *-y*) progress; **~ek** *m* (*-pku*; *-pki*) deed; (*zły*) misdeed; **~ować** (*-uję*) proceed; ***~ować za*** (*I*) follow; *praca, choroba*: progress; (*czynić*) act, behave; ***~ować z*** (*I*) treat s.o.; **~owanie** *n* (*-a*) conduct, behavio(u)r; *jur.* legal action; **~owy** progressive; **~ujący** progressive

postny fast(-day); → ***bezmięsny***

po|stojowy: ***światła*** *n/pl* ***~stojowe*** *mot.* parking lights; **~stój** *m* (*-oju*; *-oje*, *-ojów/-oi*) (*odpoczynek*) halt, stop; *tech.* stoppage; ***~stój taksówek*** taxi rank

postrach *m* (*-u*; *0*) terror

postradać *pf.* (*-am*) lose

postronny: ***~ widz*** outsider, stranger

postrzał *m* gunshot wound; *med.* lumbago

postrze|gać (*-am*) ⟨**~c**⟩ perceive; **~lić** *pf.* shoot; **~lony** wounded; F *fig.* crazy, wacky; **~żenie** *n* (*-a*) perception
postrzępiony *ubranie* ragged; *kontury* jagged, rugged
postu|lat *m* (*-u*; *-y*) postulate; **~lować** (*-uję*) postulate, stipulate; **~ment** *m* (*-u*; *-y*) pedestal
posucha *f* (-y) drought; *fig.* lack (**na** *A* of)
posu|nąć *pf.* → ***posuwać, sunąć***; **~nięcie** *n* (*-a*) (*w grze*) move (*też fig.*); **~wać** *v/t.* move forward, advance; ***~wać się*** move, advance, progress (*też fig.*); ***~wać się za daleko*** go too far; → ***suwać***
posy|łać (*-am*) *v/t.*send; *v/i.* (**po** *A*) send (for s.th.); **~łka** *f* (*-i*; *G -łek*) errand; **~pywać** (*-uję*) ⟨**~pać**⟩ ***sprinkle***; → ***sypać***
po|sza- → ***sza-***; **~nowanie** *n* (*-a*) respect; **~szarpany** *ubranie* torn, ragged; *kontury* jagged, rugged; **~szczególny** individual, particular
poszerz|ać (*-am*) ⟨**~yć**⟩ widen; broaden (*też* **się**); *ubranie* let out; **~ać** ⟨**~yć**⟩ **się** *fig.* spread
poszewka *f* (*-i*; *G -wek*) pillow case
poszkodowany injured; *jur.* injured person; ***być ~m*** be injured, suffer damage
poszlak|a *f* (*-i*) circumstancial evidence; **~owy** circumstancial
poszukiw|acz *m* (*-a*; *-e*), **~czka** *f* (*-i*; *G -czek*) searcher; ***~acz przygód*** adventurer; **~ać** (*-uję*) search (*G* for s.th.); **~anie** *n* (*-a*) search; quest; hunt; *pl. też* investigation, inquiries; (*naukowe*) research; **~any** sought after; *przestępca* wanted; **~awczy** exploratory
poszwa *f* (*-y*) quilt cover
pościć (*-szczę, pość!*) fast
pościel *f* (*-i*; *0*) bedclothes, bedding; **~ić** → **słać²**; **~owy**: ***bielizna ~owa*** bedlinen
pościg *m* (*-u*; *-i*) chase; pursuit
poślad|ek *m* (*-dka*; *-dki*) buttock; ***~ki*** *pl. med.* nates; F bottom
pośledni mediocre, second-rate; *fig.* delay
poślizg *m* (*-u*) skid; ***wpaść w ~*** *mot.* go into a skid
pośliznąć się *pf.* (*-nę*) slip
po|ślubny: ***podróż ~ślubna*** honeymoon; **~śmiertny** posthumous
pośmiewisko *n* (*-a*; *0*) laughing-stock
pośpie|ch *m* (*-u*; *0*) hurry, haste; **~szać** (*-am*) ⟨**~szyć**⟩ hasten, hurry, be quick (**z** *I* in); **~sznie** *adv.* hurriedly, in a hurry; **~szny** hasty; ***pociąg ~szny*** fast train; → ***pochopny***
pośredni indirect; (*stadium*) intermediate; **~ctwo** *n* (*-a*) mediation; ***za ~ctwem*** (G) throgh the medium; ***biuro ~ctwa pracy*** employment agency; **~czka** *f* (*-i*; *G -czek*) → ***pośrednik***; **~czyć** (*-ę*) mediate, be instrumental (**w** *L* in); **~k** *m* (*-a*; *-cy*) intermediary; mediator; agent
po|środku *adv.* in the middle; **~śród** *prp.* (*G*) among(st)
poświadcz|ać (*-am*) ⟨**~yć**⟩ certify; **~enie** *n* (*-a*) certificate; certification
poświęc|ać (*-am*) ⟨**~ić**⟩ sacrifice, devote (**się** oneself); (*składać w ofierze*) sacrifice; *kościół* consecrate; **~enie** *n* (*-a*) sacrifice; devotion; consecration; ***z ~eniem*** with devotion
poświst *m* (*-u*; *-y*) whistle; whizz
pot *m* (*-u*; *-y*) sweat, perspiration; ***mokry od ~u, zlany ~em*** in a sweat; ***na ~y*** sudorific
potajemny secret; clandestine; underhand
potakiwać (*-uję*) assent
potańcówka F *f* (*-i*; *G -wek*) dance
po|tar- *pf.* → ***tar-***; **~tas** *m* (*-u*; *0*) *chem.* potassium; **~taż** *m* (*-u*; *-e*) potash
po|tąd up to here; **~tem** then; afterwards, later; ***na ~tem*** for a future occasion
potencjał *m* (*-u*; *-y*) potential
potęg|a *f* (*-a*; *0*) might; force; power; *mat.* power; ***druga ~a*** square; ***trzecia ~a*** cube; **~ować** ⟨**s-**⟩ (*-uję*) increase, intensify; *mat.* raise to a power; ***~ować*** ⟨**s-**⟩ **się** be intensified
potępi|ać (*-am*) ⟨**~ć**⟩ damn; (*ganić*) condemn; disapprove (of); **~enie** *n* (*-a*) condemnation; disapproval; *rel.* damnation; ***godny ~enia*** codemnable; blameworthy
potężny powerful; mighty
potkn|ąć się *pf.* (*-nę*) → ***potykać się***; **~ięcie** *n* (*-a*) stumble; *fig.* slip; lapse
potłuczenie *n* (*-a*) bruise
poto|czny everyday; common; ordinary; ***język ~czny*** colloquial speech; **~czysty** fluent; well-turned; **~czyście**

fluently; glibly; **~k** *m* (*-u*; *-i*) stream, brook; (*nurt*) stream, torrent; ***~k słów*** deluge of words; ***lać się ~kiem*** gush
potom|ek *m* (*-mka*; *-mkowie*), **~kini** *f* (*-i*; *-e*, *-ń*) descendant; **~ność** *f* (*-ci*; *0*) posterity; **~stwo** *n* (*-a*; *0*) offspring; progeny; (*o zwierzętach*) breed, young
po|to- *pf.* → ***to-***; **~top** *m* (*-u*; *0*) deluge; flood; **~tra** *pf.* → ***tra-***; **~trafić** *pf.* be able (to), be capable (of), manage (to); **~trajać** → ***troić***
potraw|a *f* (*-y*) dish; ***spis potraw*** menu; **~ka** *f* (*-i*; *G -wek*) ragout; fricassee
potrąc|ać ⟨***~ić***⟩ jostle; push; (*autem*) run *s.o.* down; **~enia** *n/pl.* (*-ń*) deduction
po|trójny threefold; triple; treble; **~tru-**, **~trw-** *pf.* → ***tru-***, ***trw-***; **~trzask** *m* (*-u*; *-i*) trap (*też fig.*); **~trzaskać** *pf.* smash, shatter, break (to pieces); *v/i.* crack; **~trząsać** (*-am*) shake
potrzeb|a [-t·ʃ-] *f* (*-y*) need; ***~y*** *pl.* needs; ***bez ~y*** needlessly; ***w razie ~y*** if necessary; *pred.* → ***trzeba***; **~ny** necessary, needed; ***to jest mi ~ne*** I need that; **~ować** (*-uję*) (*G*) need; require; **~ujący** (*G*) in need (of)
po|trzeć *pf.* → ***pocierać***; **~tulny** submissive; meek; **~turbować** *pf.* beat; batter; **~twarca** *m* (*-y*; *G -ów*) calumniator; slanderer; **~twarz** *f* (*-y*; *-e*) (*ustna*) slander; (*na piśmie*) libel
potwierdz|ać (*-am*) ⟨***~ić***⟩ confirm; corroborate; ***~ać*** ⟨***~ić***⟩ ***się*** be confirmed; **~ająco** *adv.* affirmatively; **~enie** *n* (*-a*) confirmation; **~ony** confirmed
potworn|ość *f* (*-ści*) monstrosity; *pl.* (*postępki*) atrocities *pl.*; **~y** monstrous; horrible
potwór *m* (*-a*; *-y*) monster
poty|czka *f* (*-i*) skirmish; **~kać się** (*-am*) trip (up), stumble (***o*** *A* against)
potylica *f* (*-y*; *-e*) occiput
poucz|ać (*-am*) ⟨***~yć***⟩ instruct; advise; (*strofować*) admonish; **~ający** instructive; edifying; **~enie** *n* (*-a*) instruction(s)
poufa|le *adv.* informally; **~łość** *f* (*-ści*) familiarity; **~ły** familiar; unceremonious
po|ufny confidential; secret; ***informacja ~ufna*** inside information; **~uk-**, **~um-**, **~un-**, **~us-**, **~ut-** *pf.* → ***uk-***, ***um-***, ***un-***, ***us-***, ***ut-***
powabny charming; attractive; alluring
powag|a *f* (*-i*; *0*) seriousness; dignity; authority; ***cieszyć się ~ą*** enjoy high reputation (***u*** *G* among); ***zachować ~ę*** keep one's countenance, keep serious
powalać *pf.* (*-am*) strike down; → ***walać, walić***
poważ|ać (*-am*) esteem; respect; **~anie** *n* (*-a*; *0*) respect; regard; esteem; ***z ~aniem*** (*w listach*) yours sincerely *lub* faithfully; **~nie** *adv.* seriously; in earnest; **~ny** serious; grave; solemn; *wiek* old; (*wybitny*) respectable; (*znaczny*) considerable; ***w ~nym stanie*** in the family way; ***muzyka ~na*** classical music
powątpiewa|ć (*-am*) doubt (***o*** *L* s.th.); be dubious (about s.th.); **~nie** *n* (*-a*) doubt(s); ***z ~niem*** doubtfully; dubiously
powetować *pf.* (*-uję*): ***~ sobie*** retrieve (***stratę*** one's losses); ***~ sobie stracony czas*** make up for the lost time
powia|ć *pf.* → ***wiać***, ***powiewać***; **~damiać** (*-am*) ⟨***~domić***⟩ (*-ę*) inform, notify (***o*** *L* of)
powiat *m* (*-u*; *-y*) administrative district; **~owy** district
powiąza|ć *pf.* tie; bind; *fig.* connect; join; **~nie** *n fig.* connection, connexion
powidła *n/pl.* (*-deł*) plum jam
powiedz|enie *n* (*-a*): ***mieć dużo*** (***nie mieć nic***) ***do ~enia*** have a lot (nothing) to say; **~ieć** *pf.* say; tell; ***że tak powiem*** so to say; **~onko** *n* (*-a*; *G -nek*) stock phrase
powieka *f* (*-i*) eyelid
powie|lacz *m* (*-a*; *-e*) duplicator; duplicating machine; **~lać** (*-am*) ⟨***~lić***⟩ (*-ę*) copy; duplicate
powierni|ca *f* (*-y*; *-e*) confidante; **~ctwo** *n* (*-a*) trusteeship; **~czy**: ***fundusz ~czy*** trust fund; **~k** *m* (*-a*; *-cy*) confidant
powierzać (*-am*) entrust (***komuś*** *A* s.o. with s.th.)
powierzch|nia *f* (*-i*; *-e*) surface; (*obszar*) area; **~niowy** surface **~owność** *f* (*-ści*) (outward) appearance; *fig.* superficiality; **~owny** superficial; shallow
powie|rzyć *pf.* → ***powierzać***; **~sić** *pf.* (*-szę*) → ***wieszać***; ***~sić się*** hang oneself
powieścio|pisarka *f*, **~pisarz** *m* novelist; **~wy** novel
powieść[1] *f* (*-ści*) novel
powieść[2] *pf.* → ***wieść***[2]; ***~ się*** succeed, be successful; ***powiodło mi się*** I made

it; ***nie powiodło mi się*** I was unsuccessful *lub* I failed
powietrz|e [-t·ʃ-] *n* (*-a*; *0*) air; ***na wolnym ~u*** outdoors; outside; in the open; **~ny** air; ***trąba ~na*** whirlwind; ***poduszka ~na*** *mot.* airbag
powiew *m* (*-u*; *-y*) puff of air, waft of air; **~ać** (*-am*) flutter; ***~ać na wietrze*** flutter in the wind; (*machać*) wave
powiększ|ać (*-am*) increase (*też* **się**); enlarge; ***szkło ~ające*** magnifying glass; **~alnik** *m* (*-a*; *-i*) *phot.* enlarger; **~enie** *n* (*-a*) *phot.* enlargement, F blow-up; *opt.* magnification; **~yć** *pf.* (*-ę*) → ***powiększać***
powikłan|ie *n* (*-a*) complication (*też med.*); **~y** complicated
powinien (*m-os powinni*) *pred.* should, ought; ***~em to zrobić*** I should do it; ***~em był to zrobić*** I should have done it
powin|na (*pl. powinny*), **~no** *pred.* should, ought
powinność *f* (*-ści*) *lit.* duty, obligation
powinowaty related, akin
powinszowanie *n* (*-a*) congratulations
powita|lny welcoming; **~nie** *n* (*-a*) greeting, welcome; ***na ~nie*** by way of greeting; **~ć** *pf.* → ***witać***
powk- *pf.* → ***wk-***
powle|kać (*-am*) ⟨**~c**⟩ coat (*I* with); ***~kać pościel*** put on fresh bed-linen; ***~kać się*** become overcast
powło|czka *f* (*-czki*; *G -czek*) pillowcase; **~ka** *f* (*-i*) cover; (*warstwa*) coat; (*osłona*) shelter
powodować ⟨**s-**⟩ (*-uję*) cause; bring about; *impf.* **~ się** (*I*) be motivated, be prompted (by)
powodzeni|e *n* (*-a*) success; well-being; prosperity; (*popularność*) popularity; ***cieszyć się ~em*** be successful; prosper; ***~a!*** good luck
powodz|ić: ***dobrze mu się ~i*** he is well off, he is thriving; ***jak ci się ~i?*** how are you?
powodziowy inundation, flood
po|wojenny post-war; **~woli** *adv.* slowly; (*stopniowo*) gradually; **~wolny** slow; leisurely
powoł|anie *n* appointment; *mil.* call-up; **~ywać** (*-uję*) ⟨**~ać**⟩ appoint (**na** *A* s.o. *lub* to); ***~ać do życia*** bring *s.th.* into being; ***~ać do wojska*** call up, conscript; ***~ać się*** refer, quote
powonienie *n* (*-a*; *0*) (sense of) smell
powozić (*I*) drive
po|wód¹ *m* (*-odu*; *-ody*) (*G*, **do** *G*) reason for, cause; ***z ~wodu*** due to; ***bez żadnego ~wodu*** for no reason
powó|d² *m* (*-oda*; *-owie*), **~dka** *f* (*-i*; *G -dek*) *jur.* plaintiff; **~dztwo** *n* (*-a*) complaint
powódź *f* (*-odzi*; *-odzie*) flood (*też fig.*); inundation
powóz *m* (*-ozu*; *-ozy*) carriage, coach
powr|acać ⟨**~ócić**⟩ → ***wracać***; **~otny** return; **~ót** *m* (*-otu*; *-oty*) return; ***~ót do domu*** homecoming; ***~ót do zdrowia*** recovery; ***z ~otem*** back; *ponownie* again; ***tam i z ~otem*** to and fro, back and forth
powróz *m* (*-ozu*; *-ozy*) rope
powsta|ć *pf.* → (**po**)***wstawać***; **~nie** *n* (*-a*) rise; origin; *zbrojne* (up)rising; **~niec** *m* (*-ńca*; *-ńcy*) insurgent; **~ńczy** insurgent; **~wać** (*stać*) get up; rise; *fig.* revolt (**przeciw** *D* against); (*utworzyć się*) come into being; originate
powstrzym(yw)ać → ***wstrzymywać***
powszechn|ie *adv.* universally; generally; **~y** (**-*nie***) universal; general; public; widespread
powszedni everyday; commonplace; ***chleb ~*** daily bread, *fig.* everyday occurrence; ***dzień ~*** weekday
powściągliw|ość *f* (*-ści*; *0*) moderation; restraint; **~y** moderate; reticent; reserved
powtarzać (*-am*) repeat; **~ *się*** *człowiek*: repeat o.s.; *zjawisko*: happen again, recur
powtór|ka *f* (*-i*; *G -rek*) repetition; **~kowy** repeat; **~nie** *adv.* once more; **~ny** second
po|wtórzyć *pf.* (*-ę*) → ***powtarzać***; **~wy-** *pf.* → ***wy-***; **~wyżej** *prp.* (*G*) above, over; *adv.* above; **~wyższy** above-mentioned, the above; **~wziąć** *pf. decyzję* take, make; *podejrzenie* conceive
poza¹ *f* (*-y*; *G póz*) attitude
poza² *prp.* (*A*, *I*) behind, beyond; (*I*) outside, beside; ***~ tym*** besides; furthermore; ***nikt ~ tym*** nobody else
poza|- *prp.* → ***za-***; **~czasowy** beyond the limits of time, eternal; **~grobowy** afterlife; **~małżeński** extramarital; *dziecko* illegitimate; **~ziemski** extraterrestrial

P

pozawałowy post-infractional
pozaziemski extraterrestrial
pozbawi|ać (*-am*)⟨**~ć**⟩ deprive (***kogoś*** *G* s.o. of s.th.); **~(a)ć się** (*G*) deprive o.s (of);**~ony** (*G*) deprived (of); devoid (of)
po|zbierać *pf.* gather, collect; **~zby-(wa)ć się** (*G*) get rid (of)
pozdr|awiać (*-am*) ⟨**~owić**⟩ (*-ę, -rów!*) greet; ***~awiać*** ⟨***~owić***⟩ ***się*** exchange greetings; ***kazał cię ~owić*** he sends his love *lub* regards; **~owienie** *n* (*-a*) greetings; regards
pozew *m* (*-zwu; -zwy*) *jur.* citation, summons; ***wnieść ~*** file a suit *lub* petition
pozie- *pf.* → ***zie-***
poziom *m* (*-u; -y*) level; *fig.* standard; ***~ morza*** sea level; ***na ~ie*** up to the mark; **~ka** *f* (*-i; G -mek*) wild strawberry; **~o** *adv.* horizontally; (*w krzyżówce*) across; **~y** horizontal
pozł|acać (*-am*) → ***złocić***;**~acany** gilt, gilded; **~ota** *f* (*-y*) gilding
pozna|ć *pf.* → ***poznawać***;**~nie** *n* (*-a; 0*) knowledge; (*kogoś*) meeting; *filoz.* cognition; ***nie do ~nia*** unrecognizable; **~wać** (*-ję*) get to know; recognize (**po** *L* by); ***~wać się*** become acquainted; ***~ć się*** see the value (**na** *L* of)
pozor|ny apparent; seeming; **~ować** ⟨**u-**⟩ (*-uję*) simulate; feign
pozosta|ć *pf.* → ***pozostawać***;**~łość** *f* (*-ści*) remainder, remains *pl.*; *fig.* relic; **~ły** remaining; ***~ły przy życiu*** surviving; **~wać** stay, remain; ***~wać w tyle*** lag behind; ***nie ~je mi nic innego*** nothing remains for me to do but; **~wi(a)ć** leave behind; *decyzję itp.* leave; → ***zostawiać***
pozować (*-uję*) sit, pose; *fig.* show off; ***~ na*** (*A*) affect
poz|ór *m* (*-oru; -ory*) appearance; ***na ~ór*** seemingly; ***pod ~orem*** (*G*) under a pretence of *s.th.*; ***pod żadnym ~orem*** on no account; ***zachowywać ~ory*** keep up appearances; ***~ory mylą*** appearances are deceptive
pozwa|ć *pf.* (*-ę*) → ***pozywać***; **~lać** (*-am*) permit, allow; ***~lać sobie*** (**na** *A*) be able to afford; ***~lam sobie zauważyć ...*** allow me to say that ...; → ***pozwolić***; **~na** *f* (*-ej; -e*), **~ny** *m* (*-ego; -ni*) *jur.* defendant
pozwol|enie *n* (*-a*) permission; permit; → ***zezwolenie***; **~ić** *pf.* (*-lę, -wól!*) → ***pozwalać***; ***pan(i) ~i*** let me ...
pozy|cja *f* (*-i; -e*) position (*też mil.*); (*w spisie*) item;**~sk(iw)ać** (*sobie*) gain, win (**do** *G* to); **~tyw** *m* (*-u; -y*) *fot.* positive; **~tywny** *odpowiedź* affirmative; *korzystny* favo(u)rable; **~wać** (*-am*) *jur.* sue
pożałowani|e *n*: ***godny ~a*** (*przykry*) regrettable, (*żałosny*) lamentable, pitiful
pożar *m* (*-u; -y*) fire; **~ny**: ***straż ~na*** *Brt.* fire brigade, *Am.* fire department; **~owy** fire
pożąd|ać (*G*) desire; **~anie** *n* (*-a*) desire; lust; **~any** (much-)desired; desirable; *gość itp.*: welcome; **~liwie** *adv.* greedily; lustfully; **~liwy** greedy; lustful; lewd
poże|- *pf.* → ***że-***;**~gnalny** parting; farewell; **~gnanie** *n* (*-a*) farewell; good-bye; ***ucałować na ~gnanie*** kiss s.o. good-bye
pożerać (*-am*) devour
pożoga *f* (*-i; G -żóg*) conflagration
po|żółkły yellow(ed); **~żreć** *pf.* → ***pożerać***
pożycie *n* life; ***~ małżeńskie*** married life; ***~ seksualne*** sexual relationship
pożycz|ać (*-am*) lend (**k-u** *A* s.o. s.th.); borrow (**od, u** *G* from); **~ka** *f* (*-i; G -czek*) loan; **~kobiorca** *m* borrower; **~yć** *pf.* → ***pożyczać***
pożyt|eczny useful; **~ek** *m* (*-tku; -tki*) advantage, benefit; ***z ~kiem*** profitably; ***z ~kiem dla kogoś*** to s.o.'s advantage
pożyw|iać się (*-am*) ⟨***~ić się***⟩ have some food, have a bite; **~ienie** *n* (*-a; 0*) food, nourishment; **~ny** nutritious
pójść *pf.* → ***iść***
póki *cj* till, until; as long as; → ***póty***
pół (*idkl.*) half; ***~ godziny*** half an hour; ***~ do drugiej*** half past one; ***~ na ~*** half-and-half; ***w ~ drogi*** half-way; midway; ***za ~ ceny*** at half price; ***~ na ~*** fifty-fifty; **~automatyczny** semi-automatic; **~buty** *m/pl.* low shoes; **~etatowy** half-time, part-time; **~fabrykat** *m* semi-finished product; **~finał** *m* semifinal; **~głosem** *adv.* in an undertone; under one's breath; **~główek** *m* (*-wka;-wki*) halfwit: **~godzinny** half-an-hour's, thirty minutes'
półka *f* (*-i; G -łek*) shelf; ***~ na bagaż*** rack

P

pół|kole *n* (*-a*; *G -i*) semicircle; **~kolisty** semicircular; **~księżyc** *m* half-moon; crescent; **~kula** *f* hemisphere; **~litrówka** *f* (*-i*; *G -wek*) half-litre bottle; **~metek** *m* (*-tka*; *-tki*) halfway mark; *fig.* halfway; **~metrowy** half-a-metre long; **~misek** *m* (*-ska*; *-ski*) *gastr.* dish
północ *f* (*-y*; *0*) midnight; *geogr.* north; ***o ~y*** at midnight; ***na ~y*** in the north; ***na ~ od*** (*G*) north of; **~ny** northern, north
pół|okrągły semicircular; **~piętro** *n* landing; **~przewodnik** *m* semiconductor; **~rocze** *n* (*-a*) half-year; **~słodki** *wino* demi-sec; **~szlachetny**: ***kamień ~szlachetny*** semi-precious stone; **~tora** (*m/n*), **~torej** (*f*) *num.* (*idkl.*) one and a half; **~wiecze** *n* (*-a*) half-century; **~wysep** *m* (*-spu*; *-spy*) peninsula; **~żartem** *adv.* half-jokingly
póty: ***~ ... aż, ~ ... póki*** till, until
późn|ić się (*o zegarku*) be slow; **~iej** *adv. comp.* later; **~iejszy** *adj. comp.* later; subsequent; **~o** *adv.*, **~y** late
prababka *f* great-grandmother
prac|a *f* (*-y*; *-e*) work, labour; (*zajęcie*) occupation; (*dzieło*) work; ***~a zawodowa*** employment; ***zwolnić z ~y*** dismiss, fire; ***iść do ~y*** go to work
praco|biorca *m* (*-y*) worker, employee; **~dawca** *m* employer; **~holik** *m* (*-a*; *-cy*) workaholic
pracow|ać ⟨**po-**⟩ (*-uję*) work (**na** *A* for; ***u*** *G* by; ***nad*** *I* on); **~icie** *adv.* industriously; **~itość** *f* (*-ści*; *0*) diligence; **~ity** hard-working; diligent; **~nia** *f*(*-i*; *-e*) (*artysty*) studio; (*fizyczna*, *chemiczna*) laboratory; (*rzemieślnicza*) workshop; **~nica** *f* (*-y*; *-e*) worker, employee; →***pracownik***; **~niczy** workers'; **~nik** *m* (*-a*; *-y*) worker, employee; ***~nik fizyczny*** manual worker, labo(u)rer, blue-collar worker; ***~nik naukowy*** research worker; ***~nik umysłowy*** office worker, white-collar worker
prać ⟨**u-, wy-**⟩ wash, launder; (*chemicznie*) dry-clean
pra|dawny prim(a)eval; **~dziad(ek)** *m* great-grandfather; **~dzieje** *pl.* prim(a)eval history
Praga *f* (*-i*; *0*) Prague
pragn|ąć ⟨**za-**⟩ (*-nę*) (*G*) desire; long (for); be anxious (to do *s.th.*); **~ienie** *n* (*-a*) thirst; *fig.* desire; longing
prakty|czny practical; **~ka** ['pra-] *f* (*-i*) *Brt.* practice, *Am.* practise; training; ***~ki*** *pl.* practices *pl.*; **~kant** *m* (*-a*; *-ci*), **-tka** *f* (*-i*; *G -tek*) trainee; apprentice; **~kować** (*-uję*) *Brt.* practise, *Am.* practice; carry on
pralinka *f* (*-i*; *G -nek*) chocolate cream
pral|ka *f* (*-i*; *G -lek*) washing machine; **~nia** *f* (*-i*; *-e*) laundry; ***~nia chemiczna*** (dry-)cleaner's
prałat *m* (*-a*; *-ci*) prelate
prani|e *n* (*-a*) washing; (*prana bielizna*) laundry
pras|a *f* **1.** (*-y*) *tech.* press; printing press; **2.** (*0*) press; ***na łamach ~y, w ~ie*** in the press; **~ować** ⟨**s-**⟩ press; ⟨**wy-**⟩ *suknię* iron; **~owy** press
prastary prim(a)eval; ancient
prawd|a *f* (*-y*) truth; ***czy to ~a?*** is that true?
prawdo|mówny truthful; **~podobieństwo** *n* (*-a*) probability; likelihood; **~podobnie** *adv.* probably
prawdziw|ie *adv.* truly; really; indeed; **~ość** *f* (*-ści*; *0*) truth; veracity; **~y** (*nie zmyślony*) true; (*realny*, *niefałszywy*) real; genuine; authentic; (*typowy*) regular
prawi|ca *f* (*-y*; *-e*) right hand; *pol.* the right; **~cowy** *pol.* right-wing; **~ć** (*-ę*) talk; say; ***~ć komplementy*** pay compliments
prawidło *n* (*-a*; *G -deł*) rule; (*do butów*) foot-tree; **~wo** *adv.* properly; correctly; **~wy** proper; correct; (*regularny*) regular
prawie *adv.* almost; nearly; ***~ nie*** hardly; ***~ nikt/nic*** hardly anybody/anything
prawnicz|ka *f* (*-i*; *G -czek*) lawyer; **~y** legal
praw|nie *adv.* legally; legitimately; **~nik** *m* (*-a*; *-cy*) lawyer
prawnu|czka *f* great-granddaughter; **~k** *m* great-grandson
praw|ny legal; lawful; *akt* legislative; ***środki ~ne*** *pl.* legal measures *pl.*; ***osobowość ~na*** legal personality; **~o**[1] *n* (*-a*) law; ***~o autorskie*** copyright; ***~o głosowania*** voting rights *pl.*; ***~o karne*** criminal law; ***~o natury*** law of nature; ***~a człowieka*** *pl.* human rights *pl.*; F ***~o jazdy*** *Brt.* driving licence, *Am.* driver's license; ***mieć ~o*** be entitled (**do** *G* to); ***studiować ~o*** study law
prawo[2]: ***na ~, w ~*** right, to the right
prawo|dawca *m* legislator; lawmaker;

P

~mocny legally valid; **~ręczny** right-handed; **~rządność** *f* (*-ści*; *0*) law and order; **~rządny** law-abiding; **~sławny** Orthodox; **~stronny**: ***ruch ~stronny*** right-hand traffic; **~wierny** orthodox; **~wity** legal; lawful; legitimate; **~znawstwo** *n* (*-a*; *0*) jurisprudence
praw|y right, right-handed; *fig.* hono(u)rable; honest; ***po ~ej stronie*** on the right side; ***z ~a*** on the right
prawzór *m* prototype
praży|ć (*-ę*) *v/t.* roast; *v/i. słońce*: beat down, scorch; **~nki** *f/pl.* (*-nek*) *Brt.* crisps, *Am.* chips
prącie *n* (*-a*; *G -i*) *anat.* penis
prąd *m* (*-u*; *-y*) current (*też elektryczny*); stream; ***~ stały*** direct current; ***~ zmienny*** alternating current; ***pod ~*** upstream; against the stream; ***z ~em czasu*** with time; **~nica** *f* (*-y*; *-e*) generator
prąż|ek *m* (*-żka*; *-żki*) line; stripe; ***w ~ki*** → **~kowany** striped
precedens *m* (*-u*; *-y*) precedent; ***bez ~u*** unprecedented
precy|zować ⟨**s-**⟩ (*-uję*) specify; state precisely; **~zyjny** precise; exact; *tech.* precision
precz *adv.* away; ***~ z nim*** down with him; ***~ stąd!*** go away!, off with you
pre|destynowany predestined (***do*** *G*, ***na*** *A* to); **~fabrykat** *m* prefabricated element; **~fabrykowany** prefabricated; **~ferencyjny** preferential; **~historyczny** prehistoric(al); **~kursor** *m* (*-a*; *-rzy*), **~kursorka** *f* (*-i*; *G -rek*) forerunner; **~legent** *m* (*-a*; *-ci*), **~legentka** *f* (*-i*; *G -tek*) lecturer; **~lekcja** *f* lecture; talk
prelimin|arz *m* (*-a*; *-e*) budget estimate; **~ować** (*-uję*) assign (***na*** *A* for)
preludium *n* (*idkl*; *-ia*, *-iów*) prelude
premedytacj|a *f* (*-i*; *0*) *jur.* premeditation; ***z ~ą*** with malice aforethought
premi|a *f* (*GDL-ii*; *-e*) bonus; **~er** *m* (*-a*; *-rzy*) prime minister; **~era** *f* (*-y*) première, first night; **~ować** (*-uję*) award a bonus; **~owy** bonus; premium
prenume|rata *f* (*-y*) subscription; **~rator** *m* (*-a*; *-rzy*), **~ratorka** *f* (*-i*; *G -rek*) subscriber; **~rować** ⟨**za-**⟩ (*-uję*) subscribe (to *s.th.*)
preparat *m* (*-u*; *-y*) *chem.* preparation; *biol.* specimen
preria *f* (*-i*; *-e*) prairie
prerogatywy *f/pl.* (-) prerogatives
presja *f* (*-i*; *-e*) pressure
prestiż *m* (*-u*; *0*) prestige
pretekst *m* (*-u*; *-y*) pretext
preten|dent *m* (*-a*; *-ci*), **~dentka** *f* (*-i*; *G -tek*) pretender; **~dować** (*-uję*) (*do urzędu*) run for (*an office*); **~sja** *f* (*-i*; *-e*) claim; (*uraza*) grudge; (*żal*) resentment; ***nie mam do niej ~sji*** I hold no grudge against her; **~sjonalny** pretentious; affected
prewencyjny preventive
prezent *m* (*-u*; *-y*) present, gift; **~er** *m* (*-a*; *-rzy*), **~erka** *f* (*-i*; *G -rek*) *RTV*: presenter; **~ować** ⟨**za-**⟩ (*-uję*) show; ***~ować się*** look
prezerwatywa *f* (*-y*) condom, sheath, F French letter
prezes *m* (*-a*; *-i*) president; chairman, chairperson
prezy|dent *m* (*-a*; *-nci*) president; (*miasta*) mayor; **~dium** *n* (*idkl.*; *-ia*, *-ów*) presidium; **~dować** (*-uję*) (*D*) preside
pręcik *m* (*-a*; *-i*) *bot.* stamen
pręd|ki fast, quick, swift; **~ko** *adv.* quickly; → ***rychło***; **~kościomierz** *m* (*-a*; *-e*) speedometer; **~kość** *f* (*-ści*) speed; velocity; ***~kość dźwięku*** speed of sound; → ***szybkość***; **~szy** faster
prędzej *adv.* faster; (*rychlej*) sooner; ***czym ~*** as quickly as possible; ***~ czy później*** sooner or later
pręg|a *f* (*-i*) streak; **~ierz** *m* (*-a*; *-e*) pillory
pręt *m* (*-a*; *-y*) rod; *tech.* bar, rod
prężn|ość *f* (*-ści*; *0*) (*działania*) vigo(u)r; **~y** *ciało* supple; *krok* springy; *fig.* resilient, buoyant, energetic
prima aprilis *n* (*idkl.*) April Fool's Day
priorytetowy priority
probierczy: ***urząd ~*** assay office; ***kamień ~*** touchstone
problem *m* (*-u*; *-y*) problem, issue
problematyczny questionable
probo|stwo *n* (*-a*) (*katolickie*) presbytery; (*anglikańskie*) rectory; **~szcz** *m* (*-a*; *-owie/-e*) parish priest; rector
probówk|a *f* (*-i*; *G -wek*) test tube; F ***dziecko z ~i*** test-tube baby
proca *f* (*-y*) sling; *hist.* catapult
proce|der *m* (*-u*; *0*) (underhand) dealings *pl.*; shady business; **~dura** *f* (*-y*) procedure, practice
procent *m* (*-u*; *-y*) *Brt.* per cent, *Am.* percent; (*odsetki*) interest; ***w stu ~ach***

P

one hundred per cent; **~owo** *adv.* in proportion; **~owy** proportional; ***stopa ~owa*** interest rate
proces *m* (*-u*; *-y*) process (*też tech.*); *jur.* (law)suit, case, trial; **~ja** *f* (*-i*; *-e*) procession; **~or** *m* (*-a*; *-y*) *tech.* processor; **~ować się** (*-uję*) take legal action (***z** I* against), sue
proch *m* (*-u*; *-y*) gunpowder; (*pył*) dust; ***~y*** *pl.* remains, (*popioły*) ashes; F dope; **~owy** powder
producent *m* (*-a*; *-nci*) producer (*też filmowy*), manufacturer
produk|cja *f* (*-i*; *0*) production, manufacture; **~cyjność** *f* (*-ści*; *0*) productivness, productivity; **~ować** ⟨**wy-**⟩ (*-uję*) produce, manufacture, make; **~t** *m* (*-u*; *-y*) product; produce; **~tywny** productive
proekologiczny environmentally friendly, green
prof. *skrót pisany*: ***profesor*** Prof. (*Professor*)
profanacja *f* (*-i*; *0*) profanation, desecration
profes|jonalny professional; **~or**[1] *m* (*-a*; *-owie/-orzy*) professor; (*nauczyciel*) teacher; **~or**[2] *f* (*idkl.*) professor; teacher; → **~orka** F *f* (*-i*; *G -rek*) teacher
profil *m* (*-u*; *-e*) profile; (*zarys*) outline
profilaktyczny prophylactic, preventive
progi *pl.* → ***próg***
prognoz|a *f* (*-y*) prognosis; ***~a pogody*** weather forecast; **~ować** (*-uję*) forecast
program *m* (*-u*; *-y*) *Brt.* programme, *Am.* program; (*wyborczy*) manifesto; ***~ nauczania*** curriculum, syllabus; **~ista** *m* (*-y*; *-ści*), **~istka** *f* (*-i*; *G -tek*) programmer; **~ować** ⟨**za-**⟩ (*-uję*) *Brt.* programme, *Am.* program; **~owy** manifesto
pro|gresywny progressive; **~jekcja** *f* (*-i*; *-e*) projection; **~jekcyjny** projection
projekt *m* (*-u*; *-y*) plan; design; (*szkic*) draft; (*zamierzenie*) project; ***~ ustawy*** bill; **~ant** *m* (*-a*; *-ci*) designer; **~or** *m* (*-a*; *-y*) projektor; **~ować** ⟨**za-**⟩ (*-uję*) plan; *arch.*, *tech.* design; **~owy** design(ing)
prokurator *m* (*-a*; *-rzy*), **~ka** F *f* (*-i*; *G -rek*) prosecutor, prosecuting attorney
prokuratura *f* (*-y*) public prosecutor's office
proletariacki proletarian
proletariusz *m* (*-a*; *-e*), **~ka** *f* (*-i*; *G -szek*) proletarian
prolong|ata *f* (*-y*) prolongation; extension; **~ować** ⟨**s-**⟩ (*-uję*) prolong
prom *m* (*-u*; *-y*) ferry; ***~ kosmiczny*** space shuttle
promienio|twórczy radioactive; **~wać** (*-uję*) radiate; *fig.* (*I*) beam (with); **~wanie** *n* (*-a*) radiation
promienny beaming, radiant
promie|ń *m* (*-nia*; *-nie*) ray; *mat.* radius; ***~ń słońca*** sunbeam; ***w ~niu*** (*G*) within a radius (of)
promil *m* (*-a*; *-e*) per mil
prominentny prominent
promo|cja *f* (*-i*; *-e*) promotion (*też ucznia*); **~cyjny**: ***sprzedaż ~cyjna*** promotion; **~wać** (*-uję*) promote (*też ucznia*)
promyk *m* (*-a*; *-i*) ray
proniemiecki pro-German
propag|anda *f* (*-y*) propaganda; **~ować** (*-uję*) popularize
proponować ⟨**za-**⟩ (*-uję*) suggest, propose; *towar, zakąskę* offer
proporcj|a *f* (*-i*; *-e*) proportion, ratio; **~onalny** (***odwrotnie*** inversely) proportional (to)
propo|rczyk *m* (*-a*; *-i*) banner; **~rzec** *m* (*-rca*; *-rce*) banner
propozycj|a *f* (*-i*; *-e*) suggestion, proposal, offer; ***zgodzić się na ~ę*** accept a proposal
proro|ctwo *n* (*-a*) prophecy; **~czy** prophetic; **~k** *m* (*-a*; *-cy*), **~kini** *f* (*-i*; *-e*) prophet(ess); **~kować** (*-uję*) prophesy
pro|sić ⟨**po-**⟩ (*-szę*) ask (***o** A* for; ***na** A* to); (*urzędowo, formalnie*) request; ***~szę!*** come in!; ***~szę bardzo*** (*odpowiedź na „dziękuję"*) you're welcome; ***~szę pana/pani***, … sir/madam …
prosię *n* (*-ięcia*; *-ięta*, *G -siąt*) piglet; ***~ pieczone*** *gastr.* roast pig
proso *n* (*-a*) millet
prospekt *m* (*-u*; *-y*) brochure, prospectus
prosperować (*-uję*) prosper, thrive
prosta *f* (*-tej*; *-te*) straight line; **~cki** coarse, boorish; **~cko, po ~cku** coarsely, boorishly; **~k** *m* (*-a*, *-cy*) boor
prosto *adv.* straight; (*niezawile*) clearly **~duszny** simple-hearted, guileless; **~kąt** *m* rectangle; **~kątny** rectangular; **~linijny** *fig.* straightforward; **~liniowy** (***-wo***) rectilinear; **~padłościan** *m* (*-u*; *-y*) cuboid; **~padły** (***-le***) perpendicular;

P

(*liniowo*) square (to); **~ta** *f* (*-y*; *0*) simplicity; **~wać** (*-uję*) ⟨**wy-**⟩ straighten; *prąd* rectify; ⟨**s-**⟩ *błąd itp.* rectify, correct; **~wnik** *m* (*-a*; *-i*) *anat.* extensor; *electr.* rectifier
prost|y[1] *adj.* (*m-os -ści*; *comp. -tszy*) (*nie wygięty*) straight; (*zwykły*) simple; (*skromny*) plain; ***kąt ~y*** right angle; ***po ~u*** simply; (*bez ceremonii*) unceremoniously; **~y**[2] *m* (*-ego*; *-e*) (*cios*) straight
prostytutka *f* (*-i*; *G -tek*) prostitute
prosz|ek *m* (*-szku*; *-szki*) (***do prania, do pieczenia*** washing, baking) powder; ***mleko w ~ku*** powdered milk; ***utrzeć na ~ek*** pulverize; **~kowy** powder
prośb|a *f* (*-y*; *G próśb*) request; (*podanie*) application; ***mam do ciebie ~ę*** I have a favo(u)r to ask of you; → ***prosić***
proś|ciej *comp.* → ***prosto***; **~ciutki** (**-*ko***) perfectly straight; → ***prosty***
protegować (*-uję*) pull strings for *s.o.*, open doors for *s.o.*
protek|cja *f* (*-i*; *-e*) favo(u)ritism; **~cjonalny** patronizing, condescending; **~tor**[1] *m* (*-a*; *-y*) (tyre) tread; **~tor**[2] *m* (*-a*; *-rzy/-owie*), **~torka** *f* (*-i*; *G -rek*) protector; **~torat** *m* (*-u*; *0*) patronage; *pol.* protectorate
protest *m* (*-u*; *-y*) protest; ***na znak ~u*** in protest; **~acyjny** protest
protestan|cki Protestant; **~t** *m* (*-a*; *-nci*), **~tka** *f* (*-i*; *G -tek*) Protestant
protestować ⟨**za-**⟩ (*-uję*) protest (against *lub* about)
proteza *f* (*-y*) (*ortopedyczna*) artificial limb; (*dentystyczna*) dentures *pl.*
protoko|lant *m* (*-a*; *-nci*), **~lantka** *f* (*-i*; *G -tek*) recorder; *jur.* clerk of the court; **~łować** ⟨**za-**⟩ (*-uję*) record, (*zebranie*) keep the minutes
protokół *m* (*-ołu*; *-oły*) report; minutes; ***sporządzić ~*** take the minutes
prototyp *m* (*-u*; *-y*) prototype
prowadz|ąca *f* (*-ej*; *-e*), **~ący** *m* (*-ego*; *-y*) *RTV*: host; **~enie** *n* (*-a*) (*domu*) running; (*samochodu*) driving; ***objąć ~enie*** be in the lead; **~ić** ⟨**po-**⟩(*-dzę*) *v/t.* lead; conduct; *pojazd* drive; *zakład* run; *rozmowę* carry on; *wojnę* wage; → ***kierować***; *v/i.* lead; ⟨**do-, za-**⟩ lead (**do** *G* to); ***~ić się*** conduct oneself, behave
prowiant *m* (*-u*; *-y*) provisions *pl.*, victuals *pl.*
prowi|ncja *f* (*-i*; *-e*) province; (*obszar poza stolicą*) provinces; **~ncjonalny** provincial; **~zja** *f* (*-i*; *-e*) commission; **~zorka** *f* (*-i*; *G -rek*) makeshift, improvisation; **~zoryczny** makeshift, rough-and-ready
prowodyr *m* (*-a*; *-rzy/-owie*) ringleader
prowo|kacja *f* (*-i*; *-e*) provocation; instigation; **~kacyjny** provocative; **~kować** ⟨**s-**⟩ (*-uję*) provoke; **~kujący** (*-co*) provocative; (*spojrzenie, uśmiech*) lascivious
proza *f* (*-y*; *0*) prose; **~iczny** prose; *fig.* prosaic; **~ik** *m* (*-a*; *-cy*) prose writer
prób|a *f* (*-y*) test; (*w teatrze*) rehearsal; (*usiłowanie*) attempt; ***na ~ę, dla ~y*** on a trial basis; **~ka** *f* (*-i*; *G -bek*) sample, specimen; **~ny**: ***lot ~ny*** test flight; ***zdjęcia ~ne*** screen test; ***okres ~ny*** trial period; **~ować** (*-uję*) try; attempt; ⟨**po-, s-**⟩ *potrawy* taste; ⟨**wy-**⟩ test, put *s.th.* to the test
próch|nica *f* (*-y*; *0*) *med.* caries; *agr.* humus; **~nieć** ⟨**s-**⟩ (*-eję*) rot; *ząb*: decay; **~no** *n* (*-a*; *0*) rotten wood
prócz *prp.* (*G*) apart from; beside(s); except; ***~ tego*** except
próg *m* (*-ogu*; *-ogi*) threshold (*też fig.*), doorstep; ***zima za progiem*** winter is near; ***u progu*** *fig.* on the doorstep
prósz|yć (*-szę*): ***śnieg ~y*** it is snowing lightly
próżnia *f* (*-i*; *-e*) void; *phys.* vacuum; **~ctwo** *n* (*-a*; *0*) idleness; **~k** *m* (*-a*; *-cy*) idler
próżn|o: ***na ~o*** in vain; **~ość** *f* (*-ści*; *0*) vanity; **~ować** (*-uję*) loaf; **~y** empty; *fig.* vain; (*daremny*) futile
pruć ⟨**po-, s-**⟩ (*-ję*) *kraw.* undo, unravel; *suknię* unpick
pruderyjny prudish
prus|ak *m* (*-a*; *-i*) *zo.* cockroach; **~ki** Prussian; ***kwas ~ki*** prussic acid
prych|ać (*-am*) ⟨***~nąć***⟩ (*-nę*) snort; → ***parskać***
prycza *f* (*-y*; *-e*) bunk
pry|mas *m* (*-a*; *-i/-owie*) primate; **~mitywny** primitive; **~mula** *f* (*-i*; *-e*) primrose; **~mus** *m* (*-a*; *-i/-y*), **~muska** *f* (*-i*; *G -sek*) top student
prys|kać (*-am*) ⟨***~nąć***⟩ (*-nę*) splash; spray; *szkło*: burst; *fig.* vanish; F (*uciec*) scram, hop it
pryszcz *m* (*-a*; *-e*) spot, pimple; **~yca** *f* (*-y*; *0*) *vet.* foot-and-mouth disease

prysznic *m* (*-a*; *-e*) shower
prywat|ka *f* (*-i*; *G -tek*) party; **~nie** *adv.* privately; **~ność** *f* (*-ści*; *0*) privacy; **~ny** private; personal
prywatyz|acja *f* (*-i*; *0*) privatization; **~ować** ⟨**s-**⟩ (*-uję*) privatize
pryzmat *m* (*-u*; *-y*) prism
przaśny *chleb* unleavened
prząść ⟨**u-**⟩ spin
przebacz|ać (*-am*) ⟨**~yć**⟩ (*-ę*) forgive; **~enie** *n* (*-a*) forgiveness
przebi|cie *f electr.* breakdown; **~ć** *pf.* → ***przebijać***
przebie|c *pf.* → ***przebiegać***; **~g** *m* course; mil(e)age **~gać** run, rush, dash (***przez*** *A* across); *droga*: go, run; *sprawa*: proceed; ***~c wzrokiem*** run one's eyes over *s.th.*; **~gły** cunning, shrewd
przebiera|ć (*-am*) be fussy; (*sortować*) sift; ***~ się*** disguise o.s. (***za*** *A* as); (*zmienić ubranie*) change one's clothes; ***~ć nogami*** hop from one leg to the other; **~lnia** *f* (*-i*; *-e*) dressing-room
przebijać (*-am*) pierce; puncture; *tunel* dig up, drill; *barwa*: show through; (*w kartach*) beat
przebiśnieg *m* (*-u*; *-i*) snowdrop
przebitk|a *f* (*-i*; *G -tek*) copy, duplicate, carbon copy; **~owy**: ***papier ~owy*** copying paper
przebłysk *m* glimmer, flash
prze|boleć *pf.* (*-eję*) get over; **~bój** *m* hit
przebra|ć *pf.* → ***przebierać***; ***~ć miarę*** go too far; **~nie** *n* (*-a*) disguise; **~ny** disguised
prze|brnąć *pf.* wade; struggle (***przez*** *A* through *lub* across); → ***brnąć***; **~brzmiały** out-of-date
przebudow|a *f* conversion; rebuilding; **~(yw)ać** (*-*[*w*]*uję*) convert; rebuild
przebudzenie (się) *n* (*-a*) awakening
przeby(wa)ć *drogę* travel, cover; *granicę* cross; *chorobę itp.* suffer (from); (*zostawać*) stay
przecedzać (*-am*) ⟨**~ić**⟩ strain
przecen|a *f* (*-y*; *0*) repricing, sale; **~iać** (*-am*), ⟨**~ić**⟩ overestimate; *hdl.* reduce the price
przechadz|ać się (*-am*) stroll; ***~ać się tam i z powrotem*** walk up and down; **~ka** *f* (*-i*; *G -dzek*) stroll; ***iść na ~kę*** go for a walk
przecho|dni *gr.* transitive; ***puchar ~dni*** challenge cup; ***pokój ~dni*** passage-room; **~dzić**[1] *v/i.* go, get (***do*** *G* to); (*przebyć*) go, come; *światło*, *kula*: go *lub* pass through; *droga itp.*: run; *zima*, *deszcz*: be over; *ból*: pass, ease; *czas*: pass; *v/t. biedę*, *chorobę* suffer; *wyobraźnię* be beyond; *oczekiwania* surpass; *samego siebie* excel o.s.; *kurs* go (through); **~dzić**[2] *pf.* pass (by), cross, go over; **~dzień** *m* (*-dnia*; *-dnie*, *-dniów*) passer-by
przechow|ać *pf.* → ***przechowywać***; **~alnia** *f* (*-i*; *-e*) *kolej*: *Brt.* left-luggage office, *Am.* checkroom; **~anie** *n* (*-a*; *0*) preservation, storage; ***na ~anie*** for safekeeping; **~ywać** (*-wuję*) keep; store; hold; *zbiega* hide
prze|chwalać się (*-am*) boast (*I* of *lub* about); **~chwytywać** (*-uję*) ⟨**~chwycić**⟩ intercept; **~chylać** (*-am*) ⟨**~chylić**⟩ tilt; ***~chylać się*** lean over; **~ciąć** *pf.* → ***przecinać***
przeciąg *m Brt.* draught, *Am.* draft; ***w ~u tygodnia*** in the course of a week; **~ać** (*-am*)⟨**~nąć**⟩ *v/t.* pull; thread (***przez*** *A* through); (*w czasie*) prolong, protract; *v/i.* ***~ać ręką po*** (*L*) run one's hand across *s.th.*; ***~ać się*** stretch out; drag on; *człowiek*: stretch o.s.; **~ły** *dźwięk* drawn-out; *spojrzenie* lingering
przeciąż|ać (*-am*) ⟨**~yć**⟩ overload; overburden
przecie|kać (*-am*) ⟨**~c, ~knąć**⟩ *beczka*, *łódź*: leak; *płyn*: leak through, (*też fig.*) leak out
przecier *m* (*-u*; *-y*) paste, purée; **~ać** (*-am*) sieve, *Am.* rice; ***~ać się*** *spodnie*: wear through
przecierpieć *pf.* suffer, endure; undergo *s.th.*
przecież *adv.* but, yet
przecię|cie *n* cut; intersection; **~tna** *f* (*-ej*; *-e*) average; **~tnie** *adv.* on (the) average; **~tny** average; mean; (*mierny*) mediocre
przecin|ać (*-am*) cut; *drogę*, *odwrót* block one's way; *rozmowę itp.* cut short; ***~ać się*** intersect; **~ak** *m* (*-a*; *-i*) cutter; **~ek** *m* (*-nka*; *-nki*) comma; *mat.* point
przecis|kać ⟨**~nąć**⟩ squeeze through, force through; ***~kać*** ⟨***~nąć***⟩ ***się*** squeeze o.s. (under *lub* through)
przeciw *prp.* (*D*) against; *w złoż.* anti-, counter-; **~bólowy** analgesic; ***środek ~bólowy*** painkiller; **~ciała** *n/pl.* anti-

P

bodies; ~**deszczowy**: ***płaszcz ~deszczowy*** raincoat; ~**działać** (*D*) counteract
przeciwgrypowy against flu
przeciwieństw|o *n* (*-a*) contrast; contradiction; the opposite of; ***w ~ie do*** (*G*) in contrast to, unlike
przeciw|jad *m* counterpoison, antidote; ~**ko** → ***przeciw***; ~**kurczowy** (*-wo*) antispasmodic; ~**legły** opposite; ~**lotniczy** anti-aircraft; ***schron ~lotniczy*** air-raid shelter; ~**mgłowy**: ***reflektor ~mgłowy*** fog-lamp; ~**niczka** *f* (*-i*; *G -czek*) adversary; opponent; ~**nie** *adv.* in reverse; on the contrary; ~**nik** *m* (*-a*; *-cy*) adversary; opponent; ~**ność** *f* (*-ści*) reverse (of fortune); *pl.* adversities; ~**ny** opposite; opposed to; (*odwrotny*) contrary; ***być ~nym*** (*D*) oppose s.th., be against s.th.; ***wiatr ~ny*** headwind, opposing wind; ***w ~nym razie*** otherwise; or else
przeciw|odblaskowy anti-dazzle; ~**pożarowy** fire
przeciwsłonecz|ny: ***okulary ~ne*** sunglasses, F shades
przeciwstaw|i(a)ć (*D*) contrast (s.th. with s.th.); ***~ić się*** oppose; ~**ienie** *n* (*-a*) contrast; → ***przeciwieństwo***; ~**ny** opposing
przeciw|tężcowy antitetanic; ~**waga** *f* counterweight, counterbalance; ~**wskazany** *med.* contraindicated; ~**zapalny** *med.* antiphlogistic
przeczący negative
przeczekać *pf.* wait for the end (of)
przeczenie *n* (*-a*) negative
przecznica *f* (*-y*; *-e*) cross-street
przeczu|cie *f* intuition; ***złe ~cie*** premonition; ~**ć** *pf.* → ***przeczuwać***; ~**lenie** *n* (*-a*; *0*) oversensitiveness; ~**wać** sense; have an inkling of
przeczyć (*-ę*) deny
przeczyszcza|ć (*-am*) → ***czyścić***; ~**jący**: ***środek ~jący*** laxative, purgative
przeć push (*też med.*)
przed *prp.* (*I*, *A*) (*miejsce*) in front of; (*czas*) before; (*obrona*) against; ***~ laty*** years ago; ***żalić się ~ matką*** open one's heart to one's mother, complain to one's mother
przedawkować *pf.* overdose
przedawni|enie *n* (*-a*) *jur.* limitation, prescription; ~**ony** prescribed
przeddzień *m*: ***w ~*** on the day before; on the eve of
przed|e → ***przed***; ***~e wszystkim*** first of all; ~**emerytalny** before retirement; ***w wieku ~emerytalnym*** heading for retirement; ~**gwiazdkowy** Christmas (sale *itp.*); ~**imek** *m* (*-mka*; *-mki*) *gr.* article; ~**kładać** (*-am*) (*woleć*) prefer (*s.th.* to *s.th.*); ⟨***~łożyć***⟩ submit, present
przedłuż|acz *m* (*-a*; *-e*) *electr. Brt.* extension lead, *Am.* extension cord; ~**ać** (*-am*) ⟨***~yć***⟩ extend; prolong; ~**enie** *n* (*-a*) extension
przed|małżeński premarital; ~**miejski** suburban; ~**mieście** *n* (*-a*) suburb(s); ~**miot** *m* (*rzecz*) object; (*temat*) topic, subject; ~**miotowy** topical; ~**mowa** *f* foreword, preface; ~**mówca** *m*, ~**mówczyni** *f* the preceding speaker
przedmuch|iwać (*-uję*) ⟨***~ać***⟩ blow; blow air (through)
przed|ni front; *fig.* exquisite, outstanding; ~**nówek** *m* time before the harvest; ~**obiedni** before the dinner; ~**ostatni** penultimate; *Brt.* last but one, *Am.* next to last
przedosta(wa)ć się get through
przed|płata *f* advance payment; ~**pokój** *m* hall; ~**południe** *n* morning; ~**potopowy** *fig.* obsolete; ~**ramię** *n* forearm; ~**rostek** *m* (*-tka*; *-tki*) *gr.* prefix
przedruk *m* reprint; ~**ow(yw)ać** (*-[w]uję*) reprint
przedrze|ć *pf.* → ***przedzierać***; ~**źniać** (*-am*) mock
przedsię|biorca *m* (*-y*) entrepreneur; ***~biorca budowlany*** building contractor; ***~biorca pogrzebowy*** undertaker; ~**biorczość** *f* (*-ści*; *0*) enterprise; ~**biorczy** enterprising; ~**biorstwo** *n* (*-a*) enterprise, company; ~**brać** ⟨***~wziąć***⟩ undertake; ~**wzięcie** *n* undertaking, venture
przed|sionek *m* (*-nka*; *-nki*) vestibule; ~**smak** *m* foretaste; ~**sprzedaż** *f* advance sale, pre-booking
przedstawiać introduce (*s.o.*); *sprawę*, *plan itp.* present; *wniosek* bring forward; *dowód* produce, submit; (*zgłosić*) put forward; (*na scenie*) act; ***~ się*** *os.* introduce o.s., *widok*: present itself, *sprawa*: stand
przedstawi|ciel *m* (*-a*; *-e*, *-i*), ~**cielka** *f* (*-i*; *G -lek*) representative, agent; ~**ciel-**

P

stwo *n* (*-a*) agency; sales *lub* branch office; *pol.* diplomatic post; **~ć** *pf.* → ***przedstawiać***; **~enie** *n* (*-a*) show; *theatr.* spectacle, performance; play
przedszkol|e *f* (*-a*) *Brt.* nursery school, *Am.* kindergarten; **~ny** *Brt.* nursery school, *Am.* kindergarten
przed|śmiertny deathbed; **~świąteczny** preceding a holiday; **~świt** *m* (*-u*; *-y*) daybreak; dawn; *fig.* harbinger
przedtem *adv.* earlier; before
przed|terminowy early; executed ahead of time; **~wczesny** premature, untimely; **~wcześnie** *adv.* prematurely **~wczoraj** the day before yesterday; **~wczorajszy** of the day before yesterday; **~wieczorny** (of) late afternoon; **~wiośnie** *n* (*-a*) early spring; **~wojenny** pre-war; **~wyborczy** *spotkanie* election; pre-election
przedział *m* range; (*kolejowy*) compartment; **~ek** *m* (*-łka*; *-łki*) parting
przedzie|lać (*-am*) ⟨**~lić**⟩ divide; **~rać** (*-am*) tear (*też* **się**); ***~rać się*** struggle (***przez*** *A* through)
prze|dziurawiać (*-am*) → ***dziurawić***; **~faksować** *pf.* (*-uję*) fax; **~forsować** *pf.* (*postawić na swoim*) carry; **~ganiać** (*-am*) ⟨**~gonić**⟩ (*przepędzić*) chase away; (*być szybszym*) outrun; **~gapiać** (*-am*) ⟨**~gapić**⟩ overlook; *okazję* miss; **~ginać** (*-am*) ⟨**~giąć**⟩ bend; ***~ginać*** ⟨***~giąć***⟩ **się** bend over
przegląd *m* (*-u*; *-y*) inspection; review; survey; **~ *lekarski*** medical examination; **~ *prasy*** review of the press; **~ać** (*-am*) look through; (*sprawdzać*) check; ***~ać się*** examine o.s. in the mirror; **~arka** *f* (*-i*) *komp.* browser
przegłos *m* (*-u*; *0*) *gr.* vowel change; **~ować** *pf.* outvote; vote down; → ***głosować***
przegotow(yw)ać (*-[w]uję*) boil; (*za długo gotować*) overboil; **~ się** boil too much *v/i.*
prze|grać *pf.* → ***przegrywać***; **~gradzać** (*-am*) partition, divide; **~grana** *f* (*-ej*; *-e*) loss; (*porażka*) defeat; **~groda** *f* (*-y*) partition; division; (*kojec, przedział*) stall; **~grodzić** *pf.* → ***przegradzać***; **~gródka** *f* (*-i*; *G -dek*) compartment; pigeon-hole
prze|grupow(yw)ać (*-[w]uję*) redeploy; **~grywać** (*-am*) lose (*też pieniądze*); *kasetę* copy; **~gryzać** (*-am*) ⟨***~gryźć***⟩ bite through; F *rdza*: eat; **~gryźć coś** F have a bite to eat; **~grzewać** (*-am*) ⟨***~grzać***⟩ overheat; ***~grzewać*** ⟨***~grzać***⟩ **się** become overheated
przegub *m* (*-u*; *-y*) wrist; *tech.* joint
prze|holow(yw)ać (*-[w]uję*) F *fig.* go too far; **~inaczać** (*-am*) ⟨**-czyć**⟩ (*-czę*) misrepresent; **~istoczenie** *n* (*-a*) transformation; *rel.* transubstantiation; **~jadać** spend on food; **~jaskrawiać** (*-am*) ⟨***~jaskrawić***⟩ exaggerate
przejaśni|ać się (*-am*) ⟨***~ć się***⟩ clear up; **~enie** *n* (*-a*): ***~enia*** *pl.* sunny intervals *pl.*
przejaw *m* (*-u*; *-y*) manifestation; (*choroby*) symptom; (*wyraz*) expression, sign; **~iać** (*-am*) ⟨**~ić**⟩ display; ***~iać się*** manifest itself (in *s.th.*)
przejazd *m* (*-u*; *-y*) (*samochodem*) drive; (*koleją*) ride; **~ *kolejowy*** *Brt.* level crossing, *Am.* grade crossing; ***~em*** passing through
przejażdżka *f* (*-i*; *G -dżek*) ride
prze|jąć *pf.* (*-jmę*) → ***przejmować***; **~jechać** *pf.* → ***przejeżdżać***; (*rozjechać*) run over; ***~jechać się*** go for a ride; **~jeść** *pf.* → ***przejadać***; **~jeździć** *pf.* *czas, pieniądze* spend on travel; **~jeżdżać** (*-am*) (*A*, ***przez*** *A*) cross, pass; drive, ride (***przez*** *A* through, **po** *L* in, **koło** *G* past, by)
przejęcie *n* (*-a*) taking over; (*wzruszenie*) excitement, emotion; ***z ~m*** with excitement
przejęzyczenie *n* (*-a*) slip of the tongue
przejm|ować (*-uję*) take over; adopt; *strach itp.*: seize; *zimno itp.*: penetrate; ***~ować się*** (*I*) be concerned (about *s.th.*); **~ujący** (**-co**) piercing; *głos* shrill; *widok* impressive, moving; *smutek* deep
przejrzały overripe
przejrz|eć *pf.* (*-ę*, *-y*, *-yj!*) *v/t.* → ***przeglądać***; *fig.* see through; *v/i.* recover one's sight; *fig.* become conscious of; **~ysty** transparent; *fig.* clear, lucid **~yście** *adv.* clearly
przejś|cie *n* (*-a*) passage; gangway; (*w sporcie*) transfer; (*doznanie*) ordeal; ***~cie dla pieszych*** pedestrian crossing; ***~cie podziemne*** *Brt.* subway, *Am.* underpass; **~ciowo** *adv.* temporarily; **~ciowy** passing, transitory, temporary;

P

(*pośredni*) transitional; **~ć** *pf.* → ***przechodzić***; ***~ć się*** take a walk (**po** *L* in)

przekaz *m* (*-u*; *-y*) (*za pośrednictwem banku*) transfer; ***~ pocztowy*** postal order; ***środki*** *m/pl.* ***~u*** mass media; **~anie** *n* (*-a*) (*paczki*) delivery; (*wiadomości*) transmission; (*własności*) transferrence; **~ywać** (*-uję*) ⟨***~ać***⟩ pass; hand over; *prawo* transfer; ***~ywać komuś pozdrowienia*** give one's regards to s.o.

przekąs *m*: ***z ~em*** sneeringly; **~ić** *pf.* (*-szę*) have a bite to eat; **~ka** *f* (*-i*; *G -sek*) snack

przekątna *f* (*-ej*; *-e*) diagonal

prze|kląć *pf.* → ***przeklinać*** *v/t.*; **~kleństwo** *n* (*-a*) swear-word; **~klęty** damned; **~klinać** (*-am*) *v/t.* curse; *v/i.* swear

przekład *m* (*-u*; *-y*) translation; **~ać** (*-am*) ⟨***-żyć***⟩ (*-ę*) rearrange; (*tłumaczyć*) translate; *termin* reschedule; **~nia** *f* (*-i*; *-e*) *tech.* transmission (gear)

przekłamanie *n* (*-a*) distortion

przekłu|wać (*-am*) ⟨***~ć***⟩ *balon* prick; *uszy* pierce

przekon|anie *n* (*-a*) conviction, belief; ***nie mieć ~ania do*** (*G*) be wary of, be sceptical about; **~ywać** (*-uję*) ⟨***~ać***⟩ convince (*s.o.* of *s.th.*); ***~ywać*** ⟨***~ać***⟩ ***się*** become convinced; **~ywujący** (**-*co***) convincing

przekop *m* (*-u*; *-y*) ditch, excavation; **~ywać** (*-uję*) ⟨***~ać***⟩ dig

przekor|a *f* (*-y*; *0*) perversity; **~ny** perverse, contrary

przekór *m*: ***na ~*** in defiance of

przekra|czać (*-am*) *v/t.* cross; exceed; *prawo* transgress; ***~czać stan konta*** overdraw one's account; **~dać się** (*-am*) ⟨***~ść się***⟩ slip through *lub* across; **~wać** (*-am*) cut (***na pół*** in two)

prze|kreślać (*-am*) ⟨***~kreślić***⟩ cross out; **~kręcać** (*-am*) ⟨***~kręcić***⟩ turn; *fakty* twist; *sprężynę* overwind

przekro|czenie *n* (*-a*) transgression; (*przepisów*) infringement; *granicy* crossing; ***~czenie salda*** overdraft; ***~czenie szybkości*** speeding; **~czyć** *pf.* → ***przekraczać***; **~ić** *pf.* → ***przekrawać***

przekrój *m* (*-roju*; *-roje*) section; ***~ podłużny*** longitudinal section; ***~ poprzeczny*** cross section

przekrzywiony tilted, askew

przekształc|ać (*-am*) ⟨***~ić***⟩ convert; reshape; transform; ***~ać się*** evolve; **~enie** *n* conversion; transformation

przekup|ić *pf.* → ***przekupywać***; **~ka** *f* (*-i*; *G -pek*) tradeswoman, vendor; **~ny** corruptible; **~stwo** *n* (*-a*) bribery, corruption; **~ywać** (*-uję*) bribe

prze|kwalifikować *pf.* retrain; **~kwaterować** *pf.* change housing *lub* lodging; **~kwitać** (*-am*) ⟨***~kwitnąć***⟩ wither; **~kwitanie** *n med.* menopause; **~lać** *pf.* → ***przelewać***; **~latywać** (*-uję*) ⟨***~lecieć***⟩ fly (***z*** from ***do/na*** to, ***nad*** *I* over, ***koło*** *G* past); *czas* fly (by)

przelew *m* (*-u*; *-y*) *fin.*, *jur.* transfer; ***~ krwi*** bloodshed; **~ać** (*-am*) *płyn* pour; *prawa* transfer; ***~ać krew*** shed blood; ***~ać się*** overflow

prze|leźć *pf.* → ***przełazić***; **~lęknąć się** *pf.* (*-nę*) take fright at

przelicz|ać (*-am*) ⟨***~yć***⟩ (*zliczać*) count; convert; **~enie** *n* conversion; ***w ~eniu*** in conversion

przelot *m* flight; ***~ ptaków*** passage; **~nie** *adv.* fleetingly; **~ny** fleeting, occasional; ***deszcz ~ny*** shower; ***ptaki ~ne*** birds of passage

przeludni|enie *n* (*-a*; *0*) overpopulation; **~ony** overpopulated

przeład|ow(yw)ać (*-[w]uję*) reload; (*przeciążyć*) overburden, overload; **~unek** *m* reloading; **~unkowy** reloading

przełaj *m*(*-u*; *-e*) cross; ***bieg na ~*** cross-country race; ***droga na ~*** short cut

przełam|ywać (*-uję*) ⟨***~ać***⟩ (*-ię*) break; *fig.* overcome

przełazić (***przez*** *A*) get through *lub* over *lub* across

przełącz|ać (*-am*) ⟨***~yć***⟩ (*-ę*) switch (over); **~nik** *m* (*-a*; *-i*) switch

przełęcz *f* (*-y*; *-e*) *geogr.* pass

przełknąć *pf.* (*-nę*) swallow, swallow down

przełom *m* fracture; *geol.* gorge; *fig.* breakthrough, turning point; ***na ~ie wieków*** on the turn of the centuries; **~owy** crucial, critical

przełoż|ona *f* (*-ej*; *-e*), **~ony** *m* (*-ego*; *-żeni*) superior; *pl. też* the people overhead *lub* in command; **~yć** *pf.* → ***przekładać***

przełyk *m* gullet, oesophagus; **~ać** → ***łykać***

P

prze|maczać ⟨**~moczyć**⟩ wet, drench; ***~moczyć sobie nogi*** get one's feet wet; **~magać** (*-am*) ⟨**~móc**⟩ *v/t* overcome; *v/i* prevail; ***~móc się*** conquer one's fears; **~makać** (*-am*) ⟨**~moknąć**⟩ get soaked, get drenched; **~marzać** [-r·z-] ⟨**~marznąć**⟩ freeze; **~maszerować** *pf. v/i.* march by; **~mawiać** give *lub* make a speech; speak (**do** *G* to; **za** *I* in *s.o.'s* favour)
przemądrzały bigheaded
przemeldow(yw)ać (-[*w*]*uję*) report *s.o.'s* change of address
przemęcz|ać (*-am*) ⟨**~yć**⟩ (over)strain; ***~yć się*** overexert o.s.; → ***męczyć się***; **~enie** *n* (*-a*; *0*) exhaustion, fatigue; **~ony** (*pracą*) exhausted, fatigued
przemian: ***na ~*** alternately; **~a** *f* (*-y*) transformation; ***~a materii*** metabolism; **~owanie** *n* renaming
przemie|ni(a)ć transform, change; ***~nić się*** change (**w** *A* into); **~szać** *pf.* mix (thoroughly); **~szczać** (*-am*) move
przemi|jać ⟨**~nąć**⟩ pass, go by; come to an end; *uroda*: fade; **~lczać** (*-am*) ⟨**~lczeć**⟩ *v/t.* pass over (in silence); leave unsaid
przemknąć *pf.* → ***przemykać***
przemoc *f* (*-y*; *0*) violence; ***akt ~y*** act of violence; ***~ą*** through violence, forcibly
przemo|czyć *pf.* → ***przemaczać***; **~knąć** *pf.* → ***przemakać***; **~knięty** soaked, drenched
prze|mowa *f* → ***przemówienie***; **~móc** *pf.* → ***przemagać***; **~mówić** *pf.* → ***przemawiać***; **~mówienie** *n* speech; **~mycać** (*-am*) ⟨**~mycić**⟩ smuggle; **~myć** *pf.* → ***przemywać***; **~mykać** (*-am*) steal; *myśli*: flit; ***~mykać się*** steal
przemysł *m* (*-u*; *-y*) industry; F ***własnym ~em*** oneself, by one's own means
przemysłow|iec *m* (*-wca*; *-wcy*) industrialist; **~y** industrial
przemyśl|any well-thought-out, deliberate; **~eć** *pf.* think *s.th.* over; **~iwać** (*-am*) ponder (**o** *L* upon) **~ny** clever; *urządzenie* ingenious
prze|myt *m* (*-u*; *0*) smuggling; **~mytniczka** *f* (*-czek*; *-czki*), **~mytnik** *m* (*-a*; *-cy*) smuggler; **~mywać** (*-am*) wash, bathe; **~nicować** *pf.* → ***nicować***
przeniesieni|e *n* (*-a*) transfer (*też służbowe*); ***z ~a*** *fin.* brought forward
przenieść *pf.* → ***przenosić***
przenik|ać (*-am*) penetrate (**do** *G* s.th. *lub* into s.th.) **~liwość** *f* (*-ści*; *0*) *fig.* perspicacity; **~liwy** penetrating; *fig.* keen, searching; **~nąć** *pf.* → ***przenikać***
przeno|cować *pf. v/i.* → ***nocować***; *v/t.* put up; **~sić** move, carry; *słowo* hyphenate; ***~sić na emeryturę*** pension s.o.; ***~sić się*** move (**do** *G* to), *ogień*: spread **~śnia** *f* (*-i*; *-e*) metaphor; **~śnie** *adv.* figuratively; **~śnik** *m* (*-a*; *-i*) *tech.* conveyor; **~śny** portable; *fig.* figurative, metaphorical
przeobra|żać ⟨**~zić**⟩ transform; ***~żać*** ⟨**~zić**⟩ ***się*** be transformed, turn; **~żenie** *n* (*-a*) transformation, change
przeocz|ać (*-am*) ⟨**~yć**⟩ (*-czę*) overlook; **~enie** *n* oversight; ***przez ~enie*** by an oversight
przeor *m* (*-a*; *-rzy/-owie*) prior
prze|orać *pf.* plough; *fig.* furrow; **~organizować** *pf.* reorganize
przeorysza *f* (*-y*; *-e*) prioress
przepa|dać disappear; ***~dać za*** (*I*) be very fond of → ***przepaść²***; **~dły** missing; **~jać** (*-am*) fill (*I* with); permeate; **~kow(yw)ać** (-[*w*]*uję*) repack; **~lać** (*-am*) ⟨**~lić**⟩ *v/t.* burn (through); ***~lić dziurę*** burn a hole; ***~lić się*** *żarówka*: blow; **~lony** blown
przepas|ka *f* (*-i*; *G -sek*) sweatband; (*na oczy*) blindfold; **~ywać** (*-uję*) ⟨**~ać**⟩ (*-szę*) tie *s.th.* around one's waist
przepa|ść¹ *f* (*-ści*; *-ści/-ście*) precipice; *fig.* gap, gulf; **~ść²** *pf.* → ***przepadać***; (*na egzaminie itp.*) fail; ***~ść bez wieści*** he is missing; **~trywać** (*-uję*) ⟨**~trzyć, ~trzeć**⟩ examine, study
przepchnąć *pf.* → ***przepychać***
przepełni|enie *n* (*-a*; *0*) crowd; excess; **~ony** overcrowded; (*wodą*) overflowing
przepędz|ać (*-am*) ⟨**~ić**⟩ drive; *ludzi* drive away *lub* out of
prze|pić *pf.* → ***przepijać***; **~pierać** (*-am*) launder; **~pierzenie** *n* partition; **~piękny** most beautiful, exquisite; **~pijać** (*-am*) *v/t.* spend on drink; *v/i.* (**do** *G*) drink to; **~piłow(yw)ać** (-[*w*]*uję*) saw through
przepiórka *f* (*-i*; *G -rek*) quail
przepis *m* (*-u*; *-y*) regulation; ***~y bezpieczeństwa*** safety code; ***~ kucharski*** recipe; ***~y ruchu drogowego*** highway code; ***~y drogowe*** traffic regula-

P

tions, Highway Code; **~ać** *pf.* → ***przepisywać***; **~owy** regulation; **~ywać** (*-uję*) copy out; type out; *med.* prescribe

przepity *głos* hoarse from drinking; *człowiek* hung over

przeplatać (*-am*) interlace, interweave; **~ się** alternate with *s.th.*

prze|płacać (*-am*) ⟨**~płacić**⟩ pay too much; **~płaszać** (*-am*) ⟨**~płoszyć**⟩ frighten away; **~płukiwać** (*-uję*) ⟨**~płukać**⟩ rinse; → ***płukać***; **~pływać** ⟨**~płynąć**⟩ *v/t człowiek*: swim; *statek*: sail (***przez*** *A* across); (*łodzią*) row; *woda*: flow; **~pocić** *pf.* sweat; **~poić** *pf.* → ***przepajać***; **~pona** *f* (*-y*) *anat.* diaphragm; *tech.* diaphragm, membrane

przepowi|adać (*-am*) ⟨**~edzieć**⟩ prophesy; foretell; *pogodę* predict; **~ednia** *f* (*-i*; *-e*) prophecy

prze|pracow(yw)ać (-[*w*]*uję*): ***~pracować trzy dni*** work three days; (*na nowo*) do *s.th.* over again; ***~pracować się*** overstrain o.s. **~prać** *pf.* → ***przepierać***; **~praszać** (*-am*) apologize (***kogoś za*** *A* to s.o. for s.th.); ***~praszam!*** (I'm) sorry!

przepraw|a *f* (*-y*) crossing; (*bród*) ford; **~iać** (*-am*) ⟨**~ić**⟩ (*-ę*) ferry; ***~ić się na drugi brzeg*** get to the other side; ***~ić się*** (***przez*** *A*) get across (*a river itp.*)

przepro|sić *pf.* → ***przepraszać***; ***~sić się*** make friends again; **~szenie** *n* (*-a*) apology

przeprowadz|ać (*-am*) ⟨**~ić**⟩ take (***przez*** *A* across *lub* through); (*realizować*) carry out; *szosę* build; ***~ić się*** move; **~ka** *f* (*-i*; *G -dzek*) move

przepuklina *f* (*-y*) *med.* hernia, rupture

przepu|st *m* (*-u*; *-y*) (*śluza*) sluice (-gate); **~stka** *f* (*-i*; *G -tek*) pass; **~szczać** ⟨**~ścić**⟩ let through; F *zw. pf.* → ***pominąć, przeoczyć***; **~szczalny** penetrable, permeable

przepych *m* (*-u*; *0*) *Brt.* splendour, *Am.* splendor

przepychać (*-am*) *v/t.* shove (through); *rurę* unclog; **~ się** elbow one's way

przera|biać (*-am*) alter; (*opracować na nowo*) rewrite; (*przetworzyć*) process; *lekcję* do; **~chow(yw)ać** (-[*w*]*uję*) → ***przeliczać***; **~dzać się** (*-am*) turn into; **~stać** (*-am*) *v/t.* outgrow; *fig.* surpass; **~zić** *pf.* → ***przerażać***; **~źliwy** frightful; *krzyk*: ear-piercing; **~żać** (*-am*) terrify, horrify; ***~żać się*** be terrified; **~żający** terrifying, horrifying; **~żony** terrified

prze|rdzewieć *pf.* be eaten up with rust; **~robić** *pf.* → ***przerabiać***; **~rodzić się** *pf.* → ***przeradzać się***; **~rosnąć** *pf.* → ***przerastać***; **~rób** *m* (*-obu*; *0*) processing; **~róbka** *f* (*-i*; *G -bek*) alteration; adaptation

przerw|a *f* (*-y*) break; *teatr.* interval; (*luka*) gap; ***bez ~y*** without a break; **~ać** *pf.* → ***przerywać***; ***~ać się*** break; **~anie** *n* (*-a*) break; disconnection; ***~anie ciąży*** abortion

przerywa|cz *m* (*-a*; *-e*) *tech.* interrupter, breaker; **~ć** (*-am*) break, interrupt; discontinue; (*nie skończyć*) break off; ***~ć ciążę*** have an abortion; **~ny** *oddech, głos* broken

przerzedz|ać (*-am*) ⟨**~ić**⟩ (*-dzę*) thin (*też agr.*)

przerzuc|ać ⟨**~ić**⟩ throw (***przez*** *A* over); ***~ić most*** bridge a river; ***~ić bieg*** *Brt.* change gear, *Am.* shift gear; ***~ać kartki*** (*G*) leaf through; → ***przetrząsać***; ***~ić się*** (***na*** *A*) pass over (to)

prze|rzynać (*-am*) ⟨**~rżnąć**⟩ cut; (*przepiłować*) saw; F (*przegrać*) lose

przesa|da *f* (*-y*) exaggeration; **~dnie** *adv.* excessively; **~dny** exaggerated; **~dzać** ⟨**~dzić**⟩ *ucznia* move (to another seat); *agr.* transplant; *v/i. fig.* exaggerate

przesalać (*-am*) → ***przesolić***

przesącz|ać ⟨**~yć**⟩ filter, percolate

przesą|d *m* superstition; (*uprzedzenie*) prejudice; **~dny** superstitious; **~dzać** (*-am*) ⟨**~dzić**⟩ determine; ***niczego nie ~dzając*** without prejudice

przesia|ć *pf.* → ***przesiewać***; **~dać się** move to another seat; (*w podróży*) change; **~dka** *f* (*-i*; *G -dek*) change

przesią|kać (*-am*) ⟨**~knąć**⟩ (*-nę*) soak (through); *pf.* → ***nasiąkać***; **~ść się** *pf.* → ***przesiadać się***

przesiedl|ać (*-am*) displace; rehouse; ***~ać się*** migrate (***do*** *G* to); **~enie** *n* (*-a*) displacement; rehousing; ***~enie się*** migration; **~eniec** *m* (*-ńca*; *-ńcy*) emigrant; displaced person; **~ić** *pf.* (*-ę*) → ***przesiedlać***

przesieka *f* (*-i*) cutting

przesiewać (*-am*) sift

przesilenie *n* (*-a*) turning point; *med.*

crisis; ~ ***letnie*** solstice

przesk|akiwać (*-uję*) ⟨**~*oczyć***⟩ *v/t.* jump (over); *fig.* skip (***przez*** *A* over, ***z ... na ...*** from ... to ...); **~ok** *m* jump

przeskrobać F *pf.* (*zawinić*) perpetrate; (*spsocić*) be up to (some mischief)

przesła|ć *pf.* → ***przesyłać, prześcielać***; **~niać** (*-am*) conceal; **~nie** *n* (*-a*) message; **~nka** *f* (*-i*; *G -nek*) circumstance; *filoz.* premise

przesło|dzić *pf.* make too sweet; **~na** *f* (*-y*) screen; *phot.* aperture; **~nić** *pf.* → ***przesłaniać***

przesłuch|anie *n* (*-a*) *jur.* interrogation, questioning; (*świadków*) examination; **~iwać** (*-uję*) ⟨**~*ać***⟩ *artystę* audition; *jur.* interrogate, examine

prze|smyk *m* (*-u*; *-i*) pass; *geogr.* isthmus; **~solić** put too much salt in; F *fig.* overdo; **~spać** *pf.* → ***przesypiać***

przestać¹ *pf.* (*stać*¹) stand

przesta|ć² *pf.* (*stać*²) → ***przestawać***; **~nkowy**: ***znaki*** *m/pl.* **~*nkowe*** punctuation marks; **~rzały** obsolete; **~wać** (*-ję*): **~*wać coś robić*** stop doing s.th.; **~*wać z kimś*** associate with s.o.; **~wi(a)ć** move, rearrange; **~*wi(a)ć się na coś*** switch (over) to s.th.

przestąpić *pf.* → ***przestępować***

przestęp|ca *m* (*-y*; *G -ów*) criminal; **~czość** *f* (*-ści*; *0*) crime; **~czy** criminal; **~czyni** *f* (*-i*; *-nie*, *G -ń*) criminal; **~ny** *jur.* criminal, felonious; ***rok*** **~*ny*** leap year; **~ować** (*-uję*) cross (***przez*** *A* s.th.); **~stwo** *n* (*-a*) crime; ***popełnić*** **~*stwo*** commit a crime

przestój *m* (*-oju*; *-oje*) stoppage

przestra|ch *m* fright; **~szony** frightened; **~szyć** *pf.* frighten, scare; **~*szyć się*** be frightened, take fright

przestroga *f* (*-i*; *G -óg*) admonition, (fore)warning

przestronny spacious

przestrze|gać¹ (*-am*) (*G*) obey; abide by; observe; (*o tajemnicach*) keep; **~gać**² ⟨**~*c***⟩ (***przed*** *I*) warn (of *lub* against)

przestrze|nny three-dimensional; spatial; **~ń** *f* (*-ni*; *-nie*, *-ni*) (***życiowa*** living) space; (*powierzchnia*) expanse; (*dystans*) distance; **~*ń kosmiczna*** (outer) space

przestudiować *pf.* *v/t.* make a thorough study; examine

przesu|nięcie *n* (*-a*) shift; displacement; **~wać** ⟨**~*nąć***⟩ move, shift; **~*wać*** ⟨**~*nąć***⟩ ***się*** shift, *człowiek*: move over; **~*nąć się do przodu*** move forward; **~wny** mov(e)able, slidable

przesy|cać (*-am*) ⟨**~*cić***⟩ saturate; **~cony** permeated with *s.th.*; **~łać** (*-am*) send; **~*łać dalej*** forward; **~łka** *f* (*-i*; *G -łek*) mail; (*przesyłanie*) sending, dispatch; **~pać** *pf.* → ***przesypywać***; **~piać** (*-am*) sleep through; (*przepuścić*) *fig.* let slip; **~pywać** (*-uję*) pour

przesyt *m* (*-u*; *0*) surfeit

przeszczep *m* (*-u*; *-y*) *med.* transplant, graft; **~iać** (*-am*) ⟨**~*ić***⟩ transplant, graft

przeszka|dzać (*-am*) disturb; interfere; ***proszę sobie nie*** **~*dzać*** don't let me disturb you; → ***przeszkodzić***; **~lać** (*-am*) train, instruct

przeszko|da *f* (*-y*) obstruction; obstacle; ***stać na*** **~*dzie*** stand in *s.o.'s* way; **~dzić** *pf.* → ***przeszkadzać***; **~lenie** *n* training; **~lić** *pf.* → ***przeszkalać***

przesz|ło *adv.* more than, over; **~łość** *f* (*-ści*; *0*) past; **~ły** past

przeszuk|iwać (*-uję*) ⟨**~*ać***⟩ search; *teren* scour, comb

przeszy|wać (*-am*) ⟨**~*ć***⟩ stitch; (*przebić*) pierce; *fig.* penetrate

przeście|łać (*-am*) *łóżko* rearrange; **~radło** *n* (*-a*; *G -deł*) sheet; **~*radło kąpielowe*** bath towel

prześcig|ać (*-am*) ⟨**~*gnąć***⟩ (*-nę*) outrun; *fig.* beat *s.o.* at *s.th*; **~*ać się*** *fig.* try to outdo one another (***w*** *L* at)

prześladow|ać (*-uję*) persecute; *fig.* haunt; (*dręczyć*) pester; **~anie** *n* (*-a*) persecution; **~any** persecuted, oppressed; **~ca** *m* (*-y*) persecutor; **~czy**: ***mania*** **~*cza*** persecution mania *lub* complex

prześliczny lovely

prześliz|giwać się (*-uję*) ⟨**~*(g)nąć się***⟩ (*-nę*) steal through *lub* past; *fig.* skate (over *s.th.*)

prześmie|szny extremely funny

przeświadcz|enie *n* conviction; **~ony** (***o*** *L*) convinced (of)

prześwie|cać (*-am*) show (through); shine (***przez*** *A* through); **~tlać** (*-am*) ⟨**~*tlić***⟩ (*-lę*) X-ray; *pf. phot.* overexpose; **~tlenie** *n* (*-a*) X-ray

prześwit *m* (*-u*; *-y*) gap, clearance

przeta|czać (*-am*) roll; *wagony* strunt;

P

płyn decant; *krew* give a blood transfusion; **~czać się** roll by; **~piać** (*-am*) melt down; *gastr.* melt
przetarg *m* (*wybór ofert*) tender; (*licytacja*) auction
prze|tarty frayed; **~tasow(yw)ać** (-[*w*]*uję*) shuffle; **~terminowany** expired; **~tkać** *pf.* → ***przetykać***
przeto *cj.* therefore; ***niemniej ~*** nevertheless; **~ka** *f* (*-i*) *med.* fistula; **~czyć** *pf.* → ***przetaczać***; **~pić** *pf.* → ***przetapiać***
przetraw|iać (*-am*) ⟨**~ić**⟩ digest; *fig.* mull over
prze|trącić F *pf.* break; have a snack; **~trenowany** stale; **~trwać** *pf.* survive
przetrząs|ać [-t·ʃ-] (*-am*) ⟨**~nąć**⟩ (*-nę*) (*szukać*) scour
przetrze|biać [-t·ʃe-] (*-am*) ⟨**~bić**⟩ (*-bię*) fig. thin, make thin; **~ć** *pf.* → ***przecierać***
przetrzym|ywać [-t·ʃ-] (*-uję*) ⟨**~ać**⟩ keep; hold; detain; (*ukrywać*) conceal, hide; (*znieść*) endure
przetwarza|ć (*-am*) ⟨**-rzyć**⟩ process; *electr.* convert; *fig.* convert; **~nie** *n* (*-a*; *0*): ***~nie danych*** data processing
przetwór *m* product; ***przetwory*** *pl.* preserves; **~czy** processing; **~nia** *f* (*-i*; *-e*) food processing plant
przetykać *v/t. rurę, fajkę* clear, clean out; *tkaninę* interweave, interlace
przewag|a *f* superiority; (*w tenisie*) advantage; ***mieć ~ę nad kimś*** have the upper hand over s.o; ***uzyskać ~ę*** get the upper hand
P
przeważ|ać (*-am*) *v/i.* overweigh; *fig.* prevail, predominate; **~ający** *siła*: overwhelming; (*dominujący*) predominant, prevailing; **~nie** *adv.* mostly; **~yć** *pf.* → ***przeważać***
przewąch|iwać (*-uję*)⟨**~ać**⟩ F *v/t.* scent
przewiąz|ywać (*-uję*) ⟨**~ać**⟩ tie; *ranę* tie up
przewi|dujący foreseeing; far-sighted; **~dywać** (*-uję*) foresee, predict; *pogodę* forecast; (*planować*) anticipate
przewidywa|nie *n* (*-a*) expectation; ***~nie pogody*** weather forecast; ***w ~niu*** in anticipation (of); ***według wszelkich ~ń*** according to expectation; **~ny** expected
przewidz|enie *n*: ***to było do ~enia*** it was predictable *lub* foreseeable; **~iany, ~ieć** *pf.* → ***przewidywany, przewidywać***
przewie|rcać (*-am*) ⟨**~rcić**⟩ drill through; *fig.* pierce; **~szać** ⟨**~sić**⟩ *v/t.* (***przez*** *A*) hang, sling (over)
przewietrz|ać (*-am*)⟨**~yć**⟩ air, ventilate
przewiew *m* (*-u*; *-y*) *Brt.* draught, *Am.* draft; **~ny** *ubiór* cool; *budynek* airy
prze|wieźć *pf.* → ***przewozić***; **~wijać** (*-am*) ⟨**~winąć**⟩ (*-nę*) rewind; *dziecko* change; *ranę* put a new dressing on; **~winienie** *n* (*-a*) *Brt.* offence, *Am.* offense; (*w sporcie*) foul; **~wlekać** (*-am*) ⟨**~wlec**⟩ pass (*s.th.* through *s.th.*); *fig.* protract; ***~wlekać się*** drag on; **~wlekły** protracted; *med.* chronic
przewodni leading; ***motyw ~*** leitmotiv; **~ctwo** *n* (*-a*; *0*) leadership; (*obrad*) chairmanship; *phys.* conduction, conductance (of); **~czący** *m* (*-ego*; *-y*), **~cząca** *f* (*-ej*; *-e*) chair, chairperson; **~czka** *f* (*-i*; *G -czek*) guide; **~czyć** (*-ę*) be in the chair; (*D*) chair (a meeting); **~k** *m* (*-a*; *-cy*) (*osoba*) guide; (*książka*) guidebook; *phys.* conductor
przewo|dowy wire; **~dzić** (*D*) lead; (*A*) *phys.* conduct **~zić** *v/t.* transport; take; **~zowy** transport; ***list ~zowy*** bill of lading, consignment note; **~źnik** *m* (*-a*; *-cy*) carrier; *Brt.* haulier, *Am.* hauler; (*na promie*) ferryman; **~źny** mobile
przewód *m* (*-odu*; *-ody*) (*gazowy* gas) pipe; *electr.* wire; ***~ pokarmowy*** alimentary canal; ***~ słuchowy*** accoustic duct; ***~ sądowy*** legal proceedings; ***pod przewodem*** under *s.o.'s* leadership
przewóz *m* transport; (*samochodowy*) haulage, trucking
przewracać ⟨**po-**⟩ *v/t.* overturn; knock over; *kartki* turn; (*obracać*) turn round; *v/i* (*szperać*) rummage; ***~ się*** fall over; turn over, roll over; ***~ się do góry dnem*** *łódź*: capsize
przewrażliwiony → ***przeczulony***
przewrotny perverse
przewró|cić *pf.* → ***przewracać***; **~t** *m* (*-otu*; *-oty*) revolution; *pol.* coup (d'état); (*w sporcie*) somersault
przewyższ|ać (*-am*) ⟨**~yć**⟩ outstrip, surpass; be better than; (*liczebnie*) outnumber
przez *prp.* (*A*) across; through; over; ***~ radio*** over *lub* on the radio; ***~ przypadek*** by accident; ***~ telefon*** over *lub* on the

phone; ~ ***cały rok*** all year; ~ ***sekundę*** for a second; ***~e mnie*** because of me
przeziębi|ać (*-am*) ⟨***~ć***⟩ catch (a) cold; **~enie** *n* (*-a*) cold; **~ony**: ***jestem przeziębiony*** have a cold
przeznacz|ać (*-am*) ⟨***~yć***⟩ intend, destine; assign (***na*** *A*, ***do*** *G* for); **~enie** *n* (*-a*) use, purpose; (*los*) destiny, fate; ***miejsce ~enia*** destination
przezorn|ie *adv*. providently, far-sightedly; **~y** foreseeing, far-sighted; (*ostrożny*) circumspect
przezrocz|e *n* (*-a*) slide; **~ysty** transparent; *materiał*: see-through; *płyn*: clear
prze|zwać *pf.* → ***przezywać***; **~zwisko** *n* (*-a*) nickname; → ***wyzwisko***; **~zwyciężać** ⟨***~zwyciężyć***⟩ overcome; ***~zwyciężyć się*** control o.s., overcome a feeling; **~zywać** (*-am*) *v/t.* nickname; (*ubliżać*) call *s.o.* names
prze|źrocz- → ***przezrocz-***; **~żegnać się** *pf.* cross o.s.; **~żerać** (*-am*) ⟨***~żreć***⟩ eat away; **~żuwać** (*-am*) *krowa*: ruminate; ⟨***~żuć***⟩ chew
przeży|cie *n* survival; (*doznanie*) experience; **~tek** *m* (*-u*; *-i*) anachronism; **~wać** (*-am*) ⟨***~ć***⟩ ***experience, go through***; ***~wać*** ⟨***~ć***⟩ ***się*** become outdated
przędza *f* (*-y*) yarn; **~lnia** *f* (*-i*; *-e*) spinning room; spinning mill
przęsło *n* (*-a*; *G -seł*) *arch.* span
przodek *m* (*-dka*; *-dki*) *górn.* coalface; (*pl. -dkowie*) ancestor, forefather
przodow|ać (*-uję*) (***w*** *L*) excel (in *lub* at) **~nica** *f* (*-y*; *-e*), **~nik** *m* (*-a*; *-cy*) leader
przodujący leading
przód *m* (*-odu*; *-ody*) front; ***w ~, do przodu*** forward; ***z przodu*** in front; ***przodem, na przedzie*** in front
przy *prp* (*L*) by; at; ~ ***stole*** at the table; ***mieć coś ~ sobie*** have s.th. on *lub* about one; ***~ pracy*** at work; ~ ***czym*** *lub* ~ ***tym*** at the same time; ~ ***ulicy*** on the street; **~bić** *pf.* → ***przybijać***; **~biegać** ⟨***~biec***⟩ come running; **~bierać** (*-am*) *v/t.* assume; (*zdobić*) decorate, *potrawę* garnish; *v/i. rzeka*: rise; ***~bierać na wadze*** put on weight; **~bijać** (*-am*) *v/t. gwóźdź* hammer, drive; *deskę* nail; *pieczęć* set; *v/i.* ***~bijać do brzegu*** reach the shore, land
przybliż|ać ⟨***~yć***⟩ bring closer, bring nearer; *lornetka*: magnify; ***~ać*** ⟨***~yć***⟩ ***się*** come closer, approach; **~enie** *n* (*-a*) approximation; ***w ~eniu*** approximately, roughly; **~ony** approximate
przy|błąkany *pies*: stray; **~boczny**: ***straż przyboczna*** bodyguard; **~bój** surf; **~bory** *m/pl.* (*-ów*) accessories *pl.*; gear; ***~bory do golenia*** shaving gear; ***~bory toaletowe*** toilet set; **~brać** *pf.* → ***przybierać***; **~brany** → ***przybierać***; ***~brane dziecko*** foster child; ***~brane nazwisko*** assumed name; ***~brani rodzice*** *pl.* foster parents *pl.*; **~brudzony** (slightly) soiled; **~brzeżny** coastal
przybudówka *f* (*-i*; *G -wek*) *Brt.* annexe, *Am.* annex
przyby|cie *n* (*-a*) arrival; **~ć** *pf.* → ***przybywać***; **~sz** *m* (*-a*; *-e*) newcomer; **~tek** *m* (*-tku*; *-tki*) gain; (*świątynia*) shrine; **~wać** arrive, come; ***~wa*** (*G*): ***dnia ~wa*** the days are getting longer; ***~ło mu pięć lat*** he is five years older
przycho|dnia *f* (*-i*; *-e*) out-patient clinic; **~dzić** come; arrive; *fig.* ***~dzić do siebie*** recover; ***~dzić na myśl*** enter s.o.'s mind; ***~dzić po*** (*A*) fetch, collect; ***to ~dzi mu z trudem*** he has difficulty in doing that
przychód *m* income; (*zysk*) profit
przychyl|ać (*-am*) ⟨***~ić***⟩ bend, incline; *fig.* ***~ić się do*** (*G*) consent to; **~ność** *f* (*-ści*; *0*) *Brt.* favour, *Am.* favor; **~ny** *Brt.* favourable, *Am.* favorable
przyciąć *pf.* → ***przycinać***
przyciąg|ać (*-am*) ⟨***~nąć***⟩ pull closer; *zwł. impf. phys.* attract; *fig.* attract; ***~ać się*** attract one another; **~anie** *n* (*-a*; *0*): ***~anie ziemskie*** gravity
przyciemni|ać (*-am*) ⟨***~ć***⟩ (*-ę*) darken; *światło* dim
przycinać (*-am*) *v/t.* cut (to size); *włosy itp.* clip, trim; *v/i. fig*, gibe at s.o.
przycis|k *m* (*-u*; *-i*) (paper-)weight; (*dzwonka itp.*) button; *fig.* emphasis; **~kać** ⟨***~nąć***⟩ *v/t.* press (*też fig.*)
przycisz|ać (*-am*) ⟨***~yć***⟩ (*-ę*) *głos* subdue; *radio* turn down
przyczajony lurking, hidden
przyczep|a *f* (*-y*) *mot.* trailer; *motocyklowa* sidecar; **~i(a)ć** attach, fasten; *fig.* ***~i(a)ć się*** (***do*** *G*) pick on s.o., find fault (with) → ***czepiać się***; **~ka** *f* (*-i*; *G -pek*) (*motocykla*) sidecar; **~ny** adhesive; attachable
przyczołgać się *pf.* crawl up, creep up

P

przyczyn|a *f* (*-y*) reason, cause; ***z tej ~y*** for that reason; **~ek** *m* (*-nku*; *-nki*) contribution; **~iać się** (*-am*) ⟨**~ić się**⟩ (**do** *G*) contribute (to); **~owy** causal
przyćm|iewać (*-am*) ⟨**~ić**⟩ *niebo* darken; *światło*, *pamięć* dim; *fig.* outshine; **~iony** dim
przyda|ć *pf.* → ***przydawać***; **~tność** *f* (*-ści*; *0*) usefulness, utility; **~tny** useful, helpful; **~wać** add; ***~wać się*** (**do** *G*, ***na*** *A*) come in useful, be of use (for s.o.); ***~łby mi się ...*** I could do with ...; ***to na nic się nie ~*** it's no use; **~wka** *f* (*-i*; *G -wek*) *gr.* attribute
przydept|ywać (*-uję*) ⟨**~ać**⟩ *v/t.* tread, step (on *s.th.*)
przydługi F longish; lengthy
przydo|mek *m* (*-mka*; *-mki*) nickname; **~mowy** adjacent (to the house)
przydrożny wayside
przydu|szać (*-am*) ⟨**~sić**⟩ *v/t.* smother; suppress; (*ciężarem*) press down
przyduży F somewhat too large
przydzi|ał *m* allowance; ration; (*dokument*) order of allocation; **~elać** (*-am*) ⟨**~elić**⟩ allocate; assign
przyganiać (*D*) reprimand, rebuke
przygar|biony stooping; → ***garbić się***; **~niać** (*-am*) ⟨**~nąć**⟩ take in one's arms, (*dać przytułek*) take in, take under one's roof; ***~nąć się do kogoś*** nestle close to s.o.
przy|gasać (*-am*) ⟨**~gasnąć**⟩ *ogień*: be going out; **~gaszać** (*-am*) ⟨**~gasić**⟩ stifle; *światło* dim, turn down; **~glądać się** (*-am*) (*D*) watch, observe; **~gładzać** (*-am*) ⟨**~gładzić**⟩ smooth
przygłu|chy hard of hearing; **~szać** (*-am*) ⟨**~szyć**⟩ muffle; stifle, smother
przygnębi|ać (*-am*) ⟨**~ić**⟩ depress; **~ający** depressing; **~enie** *n* (*-a*; *0*) depression; **~ony** depressed
przy|gniatać (*-am*) ⟨**~gnieść**⟩ crush, squash; overwhelm; → ***przyduszać***, ***przytłaczać***; **~gniatający** *większość* overwhelming; *cisza* oppressive
przygod|a *f* (*-y*) adventure; ***~a miłosna*** love affair; **~ny** accidental, chance; **~owy** adventure
przygotow|ać *pf.* → ***przygotowywać***; **~anie** *n* preparation; **~awczy** preparatory; **~ywać** (*-wuję*) prepare; ***~ywać się*** (**do** *G*) get ready (for); → ***przyrządzać***

przy|graniczny border; **~gruby** F thickish; *człowiek* stoutish; **~grywka** *f* (*-i*; *G -wek*) prelude (*też fig.*); **~grzewać** (*-am*) ⟨**~grzać**⟩ *v/t.* warm up; *v/i.* *słońce*: swelter
przyimek *m* (*-mka*; *-mki*) preposition
przyjaciel *m* (*-a*; *-e*, *-ciół*, *-ciołom*, *-ciółmi*, *-ciołach*) friend; **~ski** friendly; ***~sko, po ~sku*** in a friendly manner
przyjaciółka *f* (*-i*; *G -łek*) (girl)friend
przyjazd *m* (*-u*; *-y*) arrival
przyja|zny friendly; **~źnić się** (*-ę*, *-nij!*) be friends (**z** *I* with); **~źń** *f* (*-źni*; *-źnie*) friendship
przy|jąć *pf.* (*-jmę*) → ***przyjmować***; **~jechać** *pf.* → ***przyjeżdżać***
przyjemn|ie *adv.* pleasantly; **~ość** *f* (*-ści*) pleasure; **~y** pleasant; (*miły*) nice; ***~ej zabawy!*** have a good time!
przyje|zdny visiting; ***dla ~zdnych*** for visitors; **~żdżać** (*-am*) arrive, come
przyję|cie *n* (*-a*) acceptance; reception; party; (*gości*) reception; (*do szkoły itp.*) admission; (*do pracy*) engagement; **~ty** established
przyjmować (*-uję*) *v/t.* accept; admit; *pokarm*, *lek* take; *pracownika* engage; *gościa*, *interesanta* receive; ***~ coś na siebie*** undertake s.th.; ***~ do wiadomości*** take note of; *v/i.* receive; ***~ się*** *moda*: catch on; *roślina*: take root; *fig.* take on, become generally accepted
przyj|rzeć się *pf.* (*-ę*, *-rzyj!*) → ***przyglądać się***; **~ście** *n* (*-a*) coming, arrival; ***~ście do zdrowia*** recovery; **~ść** *pf.* → ***przychodzić***
przykaz|anie *n* *rel.* commandment; **~ywać** (*-uję*) ⟨**~ać**⟩ tell, enjoin
przyklas|kiwać (*-uję*) ⟨**~nąć**⟩ (*D*) applaud, praise
przykle|jać (*-am*) ⟨**~ić**⟩ stick
przyklęknąć *pf.* bend the knee
przykład *m* (*-u*; *-y*) example; ***na ~*** for example, for instance; ***iść za ~em, brać ~*** follow *s.o.'s* example; **~ać** (*-am*) (**do** *G*) put *s.th.* (against); **~ny** exemplary; **~owo** for example, for instance; **~owy** hypothetical, exemplary
przykręc|ać (*-am*) ⟨**~ić**⟩ screw in; screw; *gaz itp.* turn down
przykro *adv.*: ***~ mi*** I'm sorry; **~ść** *f* (*-ści*) distress; unpleasantness; ***sprawić ~ść*** distress; annoy; ***z ~ścią coś robić*** regret to do s.th.

P

przykrótki F shortish
przykry unpleasant, nasty; *misja itp.* awkward; *wspomnienia itp.* bad; *człowiek* tiresome
przykry|cie *n* cover(ing); **~wać** (*-am*) ⟨**~ć**⟩ cover (up); **~wać** ⟨**~ć**⟩ **się** be covered; **~wka** *f* (*-i*; *G -wek*) lid, cover
przykrz|yć się (*-ę*): **~y mi się** (**bez** *G*) I'm longing (for)
przykuc|ać ⟨**~nąć**⟩ squat, crouch
przy|kuwać (*-am*) ⟨**~kuć**⟩ *fig.* rivet; catch; **~latywać** (*-uję*) fly in; *aviat.* arrive; F *fig.* come running; **~lądek** *m* (*-dka*; *-dki*) cape; **~lecieć** *pf.* → **przylatywać**
przyleg|ać (*-am*) (**do** *G*) stick (to *s.th.*); (*stykać się*) border (on *s.th.*); **~ać do siebie** lie close together, meet; **~ły** adjoining; adjacent
przylepi|ać (*-am*) ⟨**~ć**⟩ stick, glue; **~ć się** stick (**do** *G* to *s.th.*); **~ec** *m* (*-pca*; *-pce*) *Brt.* (sticking) plaster, *Am.* Band-Aid *TM*
przy|leźć *pf.* → **przyłazić**; **~lgnąć** *pf.* (**do** *G*) cling (to) **~lot** *m zo.* coming, return; *aviat.* arrival; **~łapywać** (*-uję*) ⟨**~łapać**⟩ catch; **~łapywać się na** (*L*) find o.s. doing s.th.; **~łazić** F come
przyłącz|ać (*-am*) ⟨**~yć**⟩ (**do** *G*) attach; *electr.* connect; **~yć się** join in; **~enie** *n* annexation; *electr.* connection; **~eniowy** additive
przyłbica *f* (*-y*; *-e*) *hist.* visor
przy|łożyć *pf.* → **przykładać**; **~marzać** [-r·z-] (*-am*) ⟨**~marznąć**⟩ freeze; freeze on (to *s.th.*); **~mglony** hazy, misty; **~miarka** *f* F fitting
przymie|rać (*-am*): **~rać głodem** starve; **~rzać** (*-am*) ⟨**~rzyć**⟩ try on; **~rze** *n* (*-a*) alliance
przymilny cajoling, ingratiating
przymiot *m* attribute, quality; **~nik** *m* (*-a*; *-i*) *gr.* adjective
przy|mknąć *pf.* → **przymykać**; **~mocow(yw)ać** (*-[w]uję*) fasten, fix; **~mówka** *f* (*-i*; *G -wek*) gibe; (*aluzja*) hint; **~mrozek** *m* (*-zka*; *-zki*) ground frost
przymruż|ać (*-am*) ⟨**~yć**⟩ *oczy* screw up one's eyes; **z ~eniem oka** with tongue in cheek
przymus *m* (*-u*; *0*) compulsion; **pod ~em, z ~u** under compulsion; *jur.* under duress; **~ić** (*-szę*) *pf.* → **przymuszać**; **~owy** compulsory; **lądowanie ~owe** forced landing
przymuszać (*-am*) force *s.o.* (**do** *G* to)
przymykać (*-am*) cover up; *drzwi, okno* push to, set ajar; F *os.* arrest, lock *s.o.* up; **~ oko** *fig.* turn a blind eye (**na** *A* to *s.th.*)
przyna|glać (*-am*) ⟨**~glić**⟩ rush *s.o.*; **~jmniej** at least
przynależność *f* membership; **~ państwowa** nationality
przy|nęcać (*-am*) → **nęcić**; **~nęta** *f* (*-y*) bait; *fig.* decoy; **~nosić** ⟨**~nieść**⟩ bring (*też fig.*); **~obiec(yw)ać** promise; **~padać** ⟨**~paść**⟩ fall (**do** *G* to); **~paść komuś do gustu** to take s.o.'s fancy
przypad|ek *m* (*-dku*; *-dki*) coincidence, chance; *med.* case; *gr.* (*-dka*) case; **~kiem** by chance, by accident; **~kowo** *adv.* accidentally; **~kowy** accidental
przypal|ać (*-am*) ⟨**~ić**⟩ singe; *pieczeń* burn; *papierosa* light; **~ić się** burn
przypas|ywać (*-uję*) ⟨**~ać**⟩ (*-szę*) buckle on; *fartuch* fasten on; **~ać się** fasten one's seat belt
przy|patrywać się (*-uję*) ⟨**~patrzyć się**⟩ → **przyglądać się**; **~pełzać** ⟨**~pełznąć**⟩ creep up, crawl up; **~pędzać** (*-am*) ⟨**~pędzić**⟩ *v/t.* drive; *v/i.* run up; **~piąć** *pf.* → **przypinać**; **~piec** *pf.* → **przypiekać**; **~pieczętować** *pf.* seal; *fig.* confirm; **~piekać** (*-am*) *v/t.* brown; *v/i.* *słońce*: beat down; **~pierać** (*-am*) press, push (**do** *G* against); **~pinać** (*-am*) pin, strap; *narty* put on
przypis *m* (*-u*; *-y*) note; (*u dołu strony*) footnote; (*na końcu tekstu*) endnote; **~ywać** (*-uję*) ⟨**~ać**⟩ ascribe; attribute
przypłac|ać (*-am*) ⟨**~ić**⟩ *fig.* pay for *s.th.* with *s.th.*
przypły|nąć *pf.* → **przypływać**; **~w** *m* (*-u*; *-y*) high tide; **w ~wie** (*G*) in a flash of; **~wać** (*-am*) swim up; *łódź, statek*: arrive, come in
przypo|minać (*-am*) ⟨**~mnieć**⟩ (*być podobnym*) resemble; **~minać** ⟨**~mnieć**⟩ **komuś o czymś** remind s.o. of s.th.; **~minać** ⟨**~mnieć**⟩ **sobie** (*A*) recall; **~minać** ⟨**~mnieć**⟩ **się** come back, (*o potrawie*) lie on *s.o.'s* stomach; **~mnienie** *n* (*-a*) reminder; **~wiastka** *f* (*-i*; *G -tek*) anecdote
przypraw|a *f* (*-y*) spice, seasoning; **~iać** (*-am*) ⟨**~ić**⟩ *gastr.* spice (up), season;

~iać ⟨~ić⟩ kogoś o coś give s.th. to s.o.
przyprostokątna *f* (*-ej*; *-e*) leg (of a right-angled triangle)
przyprowadz|ać (*-am*) ⟨**~ić**⟩ → **doprowadzać**
przyprzeć *pf.* → **przypierać**
przypuszcz|ać *fig.* suppose; **~ający**: **tryb ~ający** conditional; **~alny** presumable; **~enie** *n* (*-a*) presumption, supposition
przy|puścić *pf.* → **przypuszczać**; **~rastać** (*-am*) increase
przyro|da *f* (*-y*) nature; **~dni** half-; **~dniczy** nature; *nauki* natural; **~dnik** *m* (*-a*; *-cy*) naturalist; **~dzony** inborn, innate; **~snąć** *pf.* → **przyrastać**; **~st** *m* (*-u*; *-y*) increase, growth; **~st naturalny** population growth, population rate, birth rate; **~stek** *m* (*-stka*; *-stki*) suffix
przyrówn|ywać (*-uję*) ⟨**~ać**⟩ compare (**do** *G* to), equate
przyrzą|d *m* instrument, device, appliance; **~dzać** (*-am*) ⟨**~dzić**⟩ prepare
przyrze|c *pf.* → **przyrzekać**; **~czenie** *n* promise; **~kać** (*-am*) promise
przysadzisty squat
przysądz|ać (*-am*) ⟨**~ić**⟩ *jur.* award
przysiad *m* knee bend; **~ać** sit down; (*kucnąć*) crouch; **~ać się** (**do** *G*) join s.o.
przy|siąc *pf.* (→ *-siąc*) → **przysięgać**; **~siąść** *pf.* → **przysiadać**
przysięg|a *f* (*-i*; *G -siąg*) oath; **pod ~ą** under oath; **składać ~ę** take *lub* swear an oath; **~ać** ⟨**~nąć**⟩ swear (**na** *A* by); **~ły** sworn; **ława ~łych** *zbior.* jury
przy|skakiwać (*-uję*) ⟨**~skoczyć**⟩ jump up, spring up (**do** *G* to); **~słać** → **przysyłać**; **~słaniać** (*-am*) cover up; obscure; *lampę* shade; **~słona** *f* (*-y*) aperture; **~słonić** *pf.* (*-ę*) → **przysłaniać**; **~słowie** *n* (*-a*; *G -słów*) proverb; **~słowiowy** proverbial; **~słówek** *m* (*-wka*; *-wki*) adverb
przysłu|chiwać się (*-uję*) listen in (to); **~ga** *f* (*-i*) favo(u)r; **~giwać** (*-uję*): **~guje mi ...** I am entitled to ...; **~żyć się** *pf.* do *s.o.* a service
przysmak *m* delicacy
przysmaż|ać (*-am*) ⟨**~yć**⟩ fry, brown
przyspa|rzać (*-am*) (*G*) (*o troskach itp.*) cause *s.o.* trouble; **~wać** *pf.* (*-am*) *tech.* weld on
przyspiesz|ać (*-am*) ⟨**~yć**⟩ speed up; accelerate; **~ony** accelerated
przyspo|rzyć *pf.* (*-ę*) → **przysparzać**; **~sabiać** (*-am*) ⟨**~sobić**⟩ (*-ę*) prepare; train; **~sabiać się do czegoś** prepare o.s. for s.th.; *dziecko* adopt; **~sobienie** *n* (*-a*) preparation, training; *jur.* adoption
przysta|ć *pf.* → **przystawać**[1]; **~nąć** *pf.* → **przystawać**[2]; **~nek** *m* (*-nku*; *-nki*) stop; **~ń** *f* (*-ni*; *-nie*, *-ni*) harbo(u)r, port; (*jachtowa*) marina; *fig.* haven; **~wać**[1] (*zgodzić się*) (**na** *A*); → **przylegać**; (**na** *A*); **jak ~ło/jak przystoi** as befits s.o./s.th.; **~wać**[2] stop, pause; **~wi(a)ć** (**do** G) put s.th. against s.th.; **~wka** *f* (*-wki*; *G -wek*) *gastr. Brt.* starter, hors d'oeuvre, *Am.* appetizer
przystąpić *pf.* → **przystępować**
przystęp *m* (*-u*; *-y*) access, approach; **~ny** approachable; *wykład* accessible, clear; *cena* affordable, moderate; **~ować** (*-uję*) (**do** *G*) (*zaczynać*) begin, start; (*przyłączyć się*) join
przystoi → **przystawać**[2]
przystojny handsome
przystoso|wanie *n* adaptation; adjustment; **~w(yw)ać** (*-[w]uję*) adapt *s.th.* to *s.th.*; **~w(yw)ać się** adapt to *s.th.*
przy|strajać (*-am*) ⟨**~stroić**⟩ (*I*) adorn (with); **~strzygać** (*-am*) ⟨**~strzyc**⟩ trim; **~suwać** ⟨**~sunąć**⟩ (**do** *G*) bring *s.th.* nearer to *s.th.*; **~suwać** ⟨**~sunąć**⟩ **się** move closer; **~swajać** (*-am*) ⟨**~swoić**⟩ (*-ję*) *sobie* acquire; learn; *metodę* adopt; **~syłać** (*-am*) send, send in; **~sypywać** (*-uję*) ⟨**~sypać**⟩ (*I*) cover *s.th.* up (with); **~szkolny** school
przyszł|ość *f* (*-ści*; *0*) future; **w ~ości** in future; **~y** future; next; prospective
przy|sztukować *pf.* tie on; stick on; sew on; nail on; **~szywać** (*-am*) ⟨**~szyć**⟩ sew (on); **~śnić się** *pf.*: **~śniło mi się ...** I had a dream about ...; **~śpie-** → **przyspie-**; **~śrubowywać** (*-uję*) ⟨**~śrubować**⟩ screw on; **~świecać** (*-am*) *słońce*: shine; *fig.* (*D*) be s.o.'s guiding principle; **~taczać** (*-am*) roll up; (*wymienić*) quote
przytak|iwać (*-uję*) ⟨**~nąć**⟩ (*-nę*) nod
przytęp|iać (*-am*) ⟨**~ić**⟩ dull, deaden; **~i(a)ć się** deaden, become dull; **~iony** *słuch*, *umysł* dull; *wzrok* dim
przytknąć *pf.* → **przytykać**

P

przytłacza|ć (*-am*) ⟨**~przytłoczyć**⟩ overwhelm; (*ciężarem*) crush; **~jący** *fig.* overwhelming

przy|tłumiony muffled; **~toczyć** *pf.* → ***przytaczać***

przytomn|ie *adv.* consciously; (*rozsądnie*) sensibly; **~ość** *f* (*-ści; 0*) consciousness; ***~ość umysłu*** presence of mind; **~y** conscious; (*bystry*) astute

przy|trafi(a)ć się happen to *s.o.*; **~trzymywać** (*-uję*) ⟨**~trzymać**⟩ support, hold; (*zatrzymać*) hold back

przytu|lać (*-am*) ⟨**~lić**⟩ hug, give a hug *lub* cuddle; **~lny** cosy, *Am.* cozy; **~łek** *m* (*-łku; -łki*) shelter

przytwierdz|ać (*-am*) ⟨**~ić**⟩ attach, affix; → ***przytakiwać***

przytyk *m* (*-u; -i*) hint, allusion; **~ać** *v/t.* (**do** *G*) put *s.th.* (against s.th.); *v/i.* meet, abut

przyucz|ać (*-am*) ⟨**~yć**⟩ (**kogoś do** *G*) train (s.o. in s.th.)

przywal|ać (*-am*) ⟨**~ić**⟩ → ***przytłaczać***

przywara *f* (*-y*) vice

przywiąz|anie *n fig.* attachment; **~ywać** (*-uję*) ⟨**~ać**⟩ tie, attach; *fig. wagę* attach importance (to *s.th.*); **~(yw)ać się** (**do** *G*) become attached (to)

przy|widzieć się *pf.*: ***coś ci się przywidziało*** you must have been seeing things; **~wieść** *pf.* → ***przywodzić***; **~wieźć** *pf.* → ***przywozić***; **~więdnąć** *pf.* wither

przywilej *m* (*-u; -e*) privilege

przywitanie *n* greeting, welcome

przywle|kać (*-am*) ⟨**~c**⟩ drag up

przywłaszcz|ać (*-am*) ⟨**~yć**⟩ (*sobie*) appropriate *s.th.*; *władzę, tytuł* usurp

przywo|dzić bring (**do** *G* to); → ***przyprowadzać***; **~ływać** (*-uję*) ⟨**~łać**⟩ call; **~zić** *v/t.* bring; (*importować*) import; **~zowy** import

przywódca *m* (*-y; G -ów*) leader

przywóz *m* delivery; (*z zagranicy*) importation

przywr|acać ⟨**~ócić**⟩ restore

przywyk|ać (*-am*) ⟨**~nąć**⟩ (*-ę*) get used *lub* accustomed (**do** *G* to)

przyzna|nie *n* (*-a*) admission, recognition; ***~nie się*** confession; **~wać** (*-ję*) ⟨**~ć**⟩ admit, acknowledge; *kredyt* grant; *nagrodę* award; *tytuł* confer; (*uznać*) acknowledge; ***~ć się do winy*** confess one's guilt, *jur.* plead guilty

przyzwoi|tość *f* (*-ści; 0*) decency; **~ty** decent

przyzwycza|jać (*-am*) ⟨**~ić**⟩ (*-ję*) accustom; ***~jać*** ⟨***~ić***⟩ ***się*** get accustomed *lub* used (**do** *G* to); **~jenie** *n* (*-a*) habit; **~jony** accustomed (to), used (to)

psa (*G*) → ***pies***

psalm *m* (*-u; -y*) psalm

pseudonim *m* (*-u; -y*) pseudonym; (*literacki*) pen name

psi canine, dog's; ***~e życie*** dog's life; F ***za ~ grosz*** dog-cheap

psia|kość!, ~krew! F damnation!; **~rnia** *f* (*-i; -e*) kennel; F ***zimno jak w ~rni*** it's icy cold

psikus (*-a; -y*) prank

psioczyć F (*-czę*) gripe (**na** *A* about *lub* at s.o./s.th.)

psisko *n* (*-a*) big dog

pso|cić (*-cę*) ⟨**na-**⟩ play tricks, be up to mischief; **~ta** *f* (*-y*) → ***psikus***; **~tnica** *f* (*-y; -e*), **~tnik** *m* (*-a; -cy*) prankster

pstrąg *m* (*-a; -i*) trout

pstry (**-o**) gaudy

pstryk|ać (*-am*) ⟨**~nąć**⟩ click; ***~ać palcami*** snap one's fingers

psu (*DL*) → ***pies***; **~ć** ⟨**po-, ze-**⟩ (*-ję*) break; ruin; *nastrój itp.* spoil; ***~ć*** ⟨**po-, ze-**⟩ **się** break down; (*gnić*) go bad; *pogoda itp.*: get worse

psy *pl.* → ***pies***

psychi|atra *m* (*-y; -rzy, -ów*) psychiatrist; **~czny** mental; psychic; **~ka** *f* (*-i; 0*) psyche

psycho|analiza *f* psychoanalysis; **~log** *m* (*-a; -dzy/-owie*) psychologist; **~logiczny** psychological; **~patyczny** psychopathic; **~te'rapia** *f* psychotherapy; **~za** *f* (*-y*) psychosis

pszczela|rstwo *n* (*-a; 0*) bee-keeping; **~rz** *m* (*-a; -e*) bee-keeper

pszczoła *f* (*-y, G -czół*) bee

pszen|ica *f* (*-y; -e*) wheat; **~iczny, ~ny** wheat

pta|ctwo *n* (*-a; 0*) *zbior.* birds, fowl; ***~ctwo domowe*** domestic fowl, poultry; **~k** *m* (*-a; -i*) ptak; ***widok z lotu ~a*** bird's eye view; **~si** bird('s); **~szek** *m* (*-szka; -szki*) bird; F *Brt.* tick, *Am.* check

ptyś *m* (*-ysia; -ysie*) *gastr.* cream puff

publiczn|ość *f* (*-ści; 0*) audience, public; **~y** public; ***dobro ~e*** common good; ***dom ~y*** brothel

publikować ⟨**o-**⟩ (*-uję*) publish
puch *m* (*-u*; *-y*) down; fluff
puchacz *m* (*-a*; *-e*) eagle owl
puchar *m* (*-u*; *-y*) cup
puch|lina *f* (*-y*): **~lina wodna** *med.* dropsy, hydropsy; **~nąć** ⟨**s-**⟩ swell; **~owy** down, down-filled
pucołowaty chubby
pucybut *m* (*-a*; *-ci/-y*) shoeblack, bootblack
pucz *m* (*-u*; *-e*) coup (d'état)
pudełko *n* (*-a*; *G -łek*) box; **~ od zapałek** matchbox
puder *m* (*-dru*; *-dry*) powder; **~niczka** *f* (*-i*; *G -czek*) (powder) compact
pudło *m* (*-a*; *G -deł*) box; F *fig.* miss; (*więzienie*) pen; **~wać** (*-uję*) ⟨**s-**⟩ miss
pudrować ⟨**przy-**⟩ (*-uję*) powder
puenta *f* (*-y*; *G -*) punchline
puka|ć (*-am*) knock; F (*strzelać*) pop; **~nina** F *f* (*-y*) gun-fire
pukiel *m* (*-kla*; *-kle*) lock
puknięty F nuts, tonto, crazy
pula *f* (*-i*; *-e*) (*w kartach*) pool, kitty
pularda *f* (*-y*) poulard
pulchny *ciasto* spongy; *ciało* plump; *grunt* loose
pulower *m* (*-u*; *-y*) pullover, *Brt.* jumper
pulpet *m* (*-a/-u*; *-y*) meat ball
pulpit *m* (*-u*; *-y*) music stand; desk top; **~ sterowniczy** console
puls *m* (*-u*; *-y*) pulse; **~ować** (-uję) pulsate (*też fig.*)
pulweryzator *m* (*-a*; *-y*) atomizer
pułap *m* (*-u*; *-y*) *bud.* ceiling (*też aviat.*, *fig.*)
pułapka *f* (*-i*; *G -pek*) trap (*też fig.*)
pułk *m* (*-u*; *-i*) regiment
pułkownik *m* (*-a*; *-cy*) colonel
pumeks *m* (*-u*; *-y*) pumice (stone)
punk|t *m* (*-u*; *-y*) point; (*programu*) item; **~t widzenia** viewpoint, point of view; **w dobrym ~cie** well-situated; **na ~cie** (*G*) about; **~t zwrotny** turning-point; **~towiec** *m* (*-wca*; *-wce*) block of flats; **~tualny** punctual
pupa F *f* (*-y*) bottom
pupil *m* (*-a*; *-e*) teacher's pet
purpurowy purplish red
Purym *m* (*idkl.*) *rel.* Purim
purytański puritan; *fig.* puritanical
pust|ak *m* (*-a*; *-i*) *bud.* hollow block; **~elnia** *f* (*-i*; *-e*) hermitage; **~elnik** *m* (*-a*; *-cy*) hermit; **~ka** *f* (*-i*; *G -tek*) emptiness; **świecić ~kami** be (half-)empty; **~kowie** *n* (*-a*) waste
pusto *adv.*: **było ~ na ulicach** the streets were deserted; **~słowie** *n* verbosity, empty talk; **~szyć** ⟨**s-**⟩ (*-ę*) ravage
pusty empty; *fig.* empty, hollow; **~nia** *f* (*-i*; *-e*) desert; **~nny** desert
puszcza *f* (*-y*; *-e*) (primeval) forest
puszczać (*-am*) *v/t.* release; let go; → **w(y)puszczać**; *liście*, *korzenie* send out; *maszynę* run; *latawca* fly; *v/i. mróz*: break; *oczko*: wink; *farba*: come off; **~ się** (*wyruszać*) set out; F (*o kobiecie*) sleep around
pusz|czyk *m* (*-a*; *-i*) tawny owl; **~ek** *m* (*-szku*; *-szki*) (*na policzkach*) down; (*do pudru*) powder puff; **~ka** *f* (*-i*; *G -szek*) *Brt.* tin, *Am.* can
puszy|ć ⟨**na-**⟩ **się** (*-ę*) *ptak*: fluff the feathers; *człowiek*: swager, give oneself airs **~sty** fluffy; *dywan*: nappy; *śnieg*, *ciasto*: flaky; *ogon*: furry
puścić *pf.* (*-szczę*) → **puszczać**
puzon *m* (*-u*; *-y*) trombone
pycha *f* (*-y*; *0*) pride; F **~!** yum-yum!
py|kać (*-am*) puff; **~lić** (*-lę*) dust; *bot.* pollen;
pył *m* (*-u*; *-y*) dust; **~ek** *m* (*-łku*; *-łki*) speck of dust, mote; *bot.* pollen
pysk *m* (*-a*; *-i*) mouth, snout, muzzle; *fig.* F mug, gob; **~aty** F cheeky; **~ować** F (*-uję*) talk back
pyszałkowaty conceited, prancing
pyszn|ić się (*-ię*, *-nij!*) boast; **~y** proud; (*smaczny*) delicious; (*doskonały*) excellent
pyta|ć (się) (*-am*) ask, inquire (**o** *A* about); **~jący** questioning; *gr.* interrogative; **~jnik** *m* (*-a*; *-i*) question mark; **~jny** *gr.* interrogative; **~nie** *n* (*-a*) question
pytlowy: **chleb ~** whole meal bread
pyza *f* (*-y*) dumpling; **~ty** chubby

P

R

r. *skrót pisany*: **rok** y. (*year*)
raban *m* (*-u*; *-y*) (*hałas*) din; (*protesty*) fuss
rabarbar *m* (*-u*; *-y*) *bot.* rhubarb
rabat *m* (*-u*; *-y*) *econ.* discount; **~a** *f* (*-y*; *G* -) flower-bed
rabin *m* (*-a*; *-i*) *rel.* rabbi
rabować ⟨**ob-, z-**⟩ (*-uję*) rob
rabun|ek *m* (*-nku*; *-nki*) robbery; **~kowy** predatory; ***napad ~kowy*** robbery
raca *f* (*-y*; *G* -) flare
rachmistrz *m* accountant
rachować *v/t.* ⟨**ob-**⟩ calculate; ⟨**po-**⟩ add up; *v/i.* (**na** *A*) count (on)
rachu|ba *f* (*-y*; *G* -) calculation; ***brać w ~bę*** take into account; ***nie wchodzić w ~bę*** be out of the question; ***stracić ~bę*** (*G*) lose count (of); **~nek** *m* (*-nku*; *-nki*) calculation; (*do zapłacenia*) bill; (*konto*) account; ***~nki*** *pl. szkoła*: *Brt.* maths *sg.*, *Am.* math
rachunkow|ość *f* (*-ści*; *0*) accountancy, bookkeeping; **~o** *adv.* by calculation, mathematically; **~y** arithmetical; *wartość* in figures
racica *f* (*-y*; *-e*, *G* -) *zo.* hoof
racj|a *f* (*-i*; *-e*) reason; (*do jedzenia*) ration; ***~a stanu*** reasons of state; ***mieć ~ę*** be right; ***nie mieć ~i*** be wrong; ***nie bez ~i*** not without reason; ***z jakiej ~i*** for what reason?; ***z ~i*** (*G*) by virtue (of), for reasons (of)
racjona|lizacja *f* (*-i*; *-e*) rationalization; **~lizować** ⟨***z-***⟩ rationalize; **~lny** rational
racjonować ⟨***z-***⟩ ration
raczej *adv.* rather, fairly
raczkować (*-uję*) *dziecko*: crawl
raczyć (*-ę*) condescend, deign; ⟨**u-**⟩ (*I*) treat (to), help (to); **~** ⟨**u-**⟩ ***się*** (*I*) treat o.s. to, help o.s. to
rad[1] *m* (*-u*; *0*) *chem.* radium
rad[2] *adj.* (*D*, **z** *G*): ***być ~*** be glad (to); ***~(a) bym*** I would be glad (to); ***~ nierad*** willy-nilly, nolens volens
rada[1] *adj. f* → ***rad***[2]
rad|a[2] *f* (*-y*; *G* -) a piece of advice; (*grupa ludzi*) council; (***nadzorcza*** supervisory) board; ***pójść za ~ą*** (*G*) follow *s.o.'s* advice; ***dać sobie ~ę*** (**z** *I*) → ***radzić sobie***; ***dawać sobie ~ę bez*** (*G*) manage without, do without; ***na to nie ma ~y*** there is nothing one can do about it
radar *m* (*-u*; *-y*) radar; **~owy** radar
radca *m* (*-y*; *-y*, *G -ców*) *hist.* councillor; ***~ prawny*** legal advisor
radio *n* (*-a*, *L -u*/*-o*, *0 lub -a*) radio; **~aktywność** *f* radioactivity; **~aktywny** radioactive; **~amator** *m* radio ham; **~'fonia** *f* (*GDL -ii*; *0*) radio; radio communication; **~komunikacja** *f* radio communication; **~lokacja** *f* radio position-finding; **~magnetofon** *m* radio-cassette recorder *lub* player, **~odbiornik** *m* radio; **~pajęczarz** *m* (*-a*; *-e*) radio licence dodger
radio|słuchacz(ka *f*) *m* listener; **~stacja** *f* (*-i*; *-e*) radio station; **~telefon** *m* radiotelephone, radiophone; **~telegram** *m* radiotelegram, radiogram; **~terapia** *f med.* radiotherapy; **~wóz** *m* radio patrol car; **~wy** radio
radn|a *f* (*-nej*; *-e*), **~y** *m* (*-ego*; *-i*) councillor; ***~y miejski*** city councillor
rado|sny joyful, happy, joyous; **~ść** *f* (*-ści*) joy, happiness; ***z ~ści*** for *lub* with joy; ***nie posiadać się z ~ści*** be overjoyed; **~śnie** *adv.* joyfully, happily; **~wać** ⟨**po-, u-**⟩ (*-uję*) gladden, delight; ***~wać się*** rejoice
radykaln|ie *adv.* radically; **~y** radical
radzi *m-os* → ***rad***[2]
radzić (*-dzę*) (**nad** *I*) discuss; ⟨**po-**⟩ advise; ⟨**po-, za-**⟩ (**na** *A*) remedy; ***~ sobie*** (**z** *I*) manage (with), cope (with); **~** ⟨**po-**⟩ ***się*** (*G*) consult, ask advice
radziecki *hist.* Soviet; ***Związek*** ♎ Soviet Union
rafa *f* (*-y*; *G* -) reef
rafi'neria *f* (*GDL -ii*; *-e*) refinery
raj *m* (*-u*; *-e*) paradise; *rel.* Eden
rajd *m* (*-u*; *-y*) (*turystyczny*) trip, hike; *mot.* rally; *mil.* raid
rajski paradisiacal
rajstopy *f/pl. Brt.* tights *pl.*, *Am.* pantyhose
rak *m* (*-a*; *-i*) *zo.* crayfish; *med.* cancer; ♎ *znak Zodiaku:* Cancer; ***on(a) jest***

spod znaku* ♋*a he/she is (a) Cancer; ***spiec ~a*** flush, turn as red as a beetroot
rakarz *m* (*-a*; *-e*) dog-catcher
rakiet|a¹ *f* (*-y*; *G* -) (*w tenisie*) racket
rakiet|a² *f* (*-y*; *G* -) rocket; *mil.* missile; ***~a świetlna*** flare; **~ka** *f* (*-i*; *G -tek*) (*w sporcie*) bat; **~nica** *f* (*- y*; *-e*, *G* -) flare pistol; **~owy** rocket; missile
rakotwórczy carcinogenic
rakowy crayfish
ram|a *f* (*-y*; *G* -) frame; *fig. tylko* ***~y*** *pl.* framework
ramiączko *n* (*-a*; *G -czek*) (shoulder) strap
rami|ę *n* (*-enia*; *-ona*) arm (*też fig.*, *tech.*); (*bark*) shoulder; ***~ę w ~ę*** arm in arm, shoulder to shoulder; ***z ~enia*** (*G*) on behalf (of); ***wzruszyć ~onami*** shrug (one's shoulders)
ramka *f* (*-i*; *G -mek*) frame; (*w formularzu*) box
ramol F *m* (*-a*; *-e*) old geezer
ramowy framework
rampa *f* (*-y*; *G* -) loading platform; → ***szlaban***
rana *f* (*-y*; *G* -) (***kłuta*** stab) wound
randka F *f* (*-i*; *G -dek*) date
ran|ek *m* (*-nka*; *-nki*) morning; ***~kiem*** in the morning
ranga *f* (*-i*; *G* -) rank, status
ran|ić (*-ę*) wound, injure (*też fig.*); *fig.* hurt; **~iony** wounded; *fig.* hurt
ranking *m* (*-u*; *-i*) rating, ranking; (*lista*) ranking list
ran|ny¹ **1.** wounded; **2.** *m* (*-ego*; *-i*), **~na** *f* (*-ej*; *-e*, *G -ych*) wounded person, casualty; ***~ni*** *pl.* the wounded
ranny² morning
ran|o¹ *adv.* (early) in the morning; ***dziś ~o*** this morning
ran|o² *n* (*-a*; *G* -) morning; ***nad ~em*** in the morning; ***od razu z ~a*** first thing in the morning
raport *m* (*-u*; *-y*) report; **~ować** ⟨**za-**⟩ (*-uję*) report
rap'sodia (*GDL -ii*; *-e*) rhapsody
rapt|em *adv.* all of a sudden; **~owny** sudden, unexpected
ras|a *f* (*-y*; *G* -) race; (*psa*) breed; **~istowski** racist; **~owy** racial; *pies* pedigree
rat|a *f* (*-y*; *G* -) instal(l)ment; ***~ami, na ~y*** by instal(l)ments; **~alny**: ***sprzedaż ~alna*** *Brt.* hire purchase (*skrót*: HP), *Am.* instalment plan
ratow|ać ⟨**po-, u-, wy-**⟩ (*-uję*) save, rescue (***od*** *G* from); *przedmioty* salvage; ***~ać się*** escape; **~niczy** rescue; **~niczka** *f* (*-i*; *G -czek*), **~nik** *m* (*-a*; *-cy*) rescuer; (*na plaży itp.*) life-guard
ratun|ek *m* (*-nku*; *0*) rescue, help; ***~ku!*** help!; **~kowy** rescue
ratusz *m* (*-a*; *-e*) town hall
ratyfikować (*-uję*) ratify
raut *m* (*-u*; *-y*) evening party
raz¹ *m* (*-u*; *-y*, *-ów*) blow; (*G/pl. -y*) time; ***dwa ~y*** twice, two times; ***dwa ~y dwa*** two times two; ***ile ~y*** how many times; ***jeszcze ~*** once again; ***~ po ~, ~ za ~em*** time and again; ***~ na zawsze*** once and for all; ***za każdym ~em*** every time; ***pewnego ~u*** once upon a time; ***tym ~em*** this time; ***w obu ~ach*** in both cases; ***w ~ie*** (*G*) in case (of); in the event (of); ***w każdym ~ie*** in any case; ***w takim ~ie*** in this case; ***w przeciwnym ~ie*** otherwise; ***na przyszły ~*** next time; ***na ~ie*** for the time being; ***od ~u*** at once; *por.* ***wypadek***
raz² **1.** *num.* (*idkl.*) one; **2.** *adv.* once; **3.** *cj.*, *part.* **~ … ~ …** now …now …
razem *adv.* together; (*w sumie*) altogether
razić (*-żę*) annoy, make hostile; *światło*: dazzle; (*im*)*pf.* strike, hit; → ***rażony***
razowy: ***chleb ~*** *Brt.* wholemeal (*Am.* wholewheat) bread
raźn|ie *adv.* in a lively way; cheerfully; **~y** lively
rażąc|o *adv.* dazzlingly; *fig.* glaringly; **~y** *kolor* gaudy, garish; *światło* dazzling; *błąd* glaring
rażony (*I*) *chorobą itp.* stricken (with)
rąb|ać (*-ię*) ⟨**po-, na-**⟩ chop; ⟨**wy-**⟩ *las* fell, cut down; F → ***rąbnąć***; **~ek** *m* (*-bka*; *-bki*) hem; **~nąć** F *v/s.* (*-nę*) *v/t.* clout *s.o.* one; ***~nąć się*** F bum o.s., knock o.s.
rą|czka *f* (*-i*; *G -czek*) → ***ręka***; (*uchwyt*) handle; → ***rękojeść***; **~k** *G pl.* → ***ręka***
rdza *f* (*-y*; *0*) rust (*też bot.*); **~wy** rusty, rust-colo(u)red
rdzen|iowy *anat.* spinal; *tech.* core; **~ny** indigenous; *gr.* stem
rdzeń *m* (*-nia*; *-nie*) core (*też tech.*); *anat.* medulla; ***~ kręgowy*** spinal cord
rdzewieć ⟨**za-**⟩ (*-wieję*) rust

reagować ⟨**za-**⟩ (*-uję*) react, respond (**na** *A* to)
reak|cja *f* (*-i*; *-e*) reaction, response; **~cjonista** *m* (*-y*; *-ści*), **~cjonistka** *f* (*-i*; *G -tek*) reactionary; **~cyjny** reactionary; **~tor** *m* (*-a*; *-y*) *tech.* reactor
reali|sta *m* (*-y*; *-ści*), **~stka** *f* (*-i*; *G -tek*) realist; **~styczny** realistic
realiza|cja *f* (*-i*; *-e*) realization; (*projektu itp.*) execution; *econ.* cashing; *theat.* staging, production; **~tor** *m* (*-a*; *-rzy*), **~torka** *f* (*-i*; *G -rek*) producer (*filmu*); ***~torem projektu jest …*** the project will be executed by …
rea|lizm *m* (*-u*; *0*) realism; **~lizować** ⟨**z-**⟩ realize; *econ.* cash; **~lność** *f* (*-ści*; *0*) reality; **~lny** real; genuine
reasekuracja *f* (*-i*; *-e*) reassurance, reinsurance
reasumować ⟨**z-**⟩ (*-uję*) summarize, recapitulate
rebus *m* (*-u*; *-y*) rebus
recenzja *f* (*-i*; *-e*) review
recep|cja *f* (*-i*; *-e*) reception; **~cjonista** receptionist; **~cyjny** reception; ***sala ~cyjna*** banqueting hall; **~ta** *f* (*-y*; *G -*) remedy; *med.* prescription
recesja *f* (*-i*; *-e*) *econ.* recession
rechot *m* (*-u*; *-y*) croak; **~ać** (*-am*) croak
recydyw|a *f* (*-y*; *G -yw*) relapse; **~ista** *m* (*-y*; *-ści*), **~istka** *f* (*-i*; *-tek*) habitual offender
recytować (*-uję*) recite
red. *skrót pisany*: ***redaktor*** ed. (*editor*); ***redakcja*** editorial office
redagować ⟨**z-**⟩ (*-uję*) edit
redak|cja *f* (*-i*; *G -e*) editing; (*pomieszczenie*) editorial department; (*redaktorzy*) editorial staff; **~cyjny** editorial; **~tor** *m* (*-a*; *-rzy*), **~torka** *f* (*-i*; *G -rek*) editor
reduk|cja *f* (*-i*; *-e*) reduction (***personelu*** in staff); cutback; ***~cja płac*** wage cut; **~ować** ⟨**z-**⟩ (*-uję*) reduce; *personel* make redundant
reedukacja *f* (*-i*; *-e*) re-education; (*przestępcy*) rehabilitation
refektarz *m* (*-a*; *-e*) refectory
refe|rat *m* (*-u*; *-y*) paper; **~rencja** *f* (*-i*; *-e*) reference; **~rent** *m* (*-a*; *-ci*), **-tka** *f* (*-i*; *G -tek*) speaker; (*urzędnik*) clerk; **~rować** ⟨**z-**⟩ (*-uję*) give a paper (on *v/i.*)
refleks *m* (*-u*; *-y*) reflex; reflection, reflexion
reflekt|ant *m* (*-a*; *-ci*), **~antka** *f* (*-i*; *-tek*) customer; **~or** *m* (*-a*; *-y*) flood light; *mot.* light; **~ować** (*-uję*) *v/i.* (**na** *A*) be interested (in)
reform|a *f* (*-y*; *G -*) reform; **~acja** *f* (*-i*; *0*) *rel.* reformation; **~ować** ⟨**z-**⟩ (*-uję*) reform
refren *m* (*-u*; *-y*) chorus, refrain
regał *m* (*-u*; *-y*) (set of) shelves *pl.*
regaty *f/pl.* (*-*) regatta
re|generować ⟨**z-**⟩ (*-uję*) regenerate (**się** *v/i.*); **~gion** *m* (*-u*; *-y*) region; **~gionalny** regional
reglament|acja *f* (*-i*; *-e*) rationing; **~ować** (*-uję*) ration
regresowy *math.* regressive
regula|cja *f* (*-i*; *-e*) regulation; adjustment; (*zapłacenie*) settlement; **~min** *m* (*-u*; *-y*) regulations *pl.*; **~minowy** regulation; **~rnie** *adv.* regularly; **~rny** regular; **~tor** *m* (*-a*; *-ry*) control
regu|lować (*-uję*) regulate; ⟨**na-**⟩ adjust, set; ⟨**u-**⟩ *rachunek* settle, pay; **~ła** *f* (*-y*; *G -*) rule; ***z ~ły*** as a rule, usually
rehabilit|acja *f* (*-i*; *-e*) rehabilitation; **~ować** ⟨**z-**⟩ (*-uję*) rehabilitate
rej: ***wodzić ~*** set the tone
reja *f* (*-ei*; *-je*) *naut.* yard
rejestr *m* (*-u*; *-y*) register
rejestrac|ja *f* (*-i*; *-e*) registration; (*dźwięku itp.*) recording; **~yjny**: *mot.* ***tablica ~yjna*** number plate
rejestrow|ać ⟨**za-**⟩ (*-uję*) register (**się** *v/i.*); *tech. też* record; **~y** register
rejon *m* (*-u*; *-y*) district, region; **~owy** district, regional
rejs *m* (*-u*; *-y*) *naut.* cruise, voyage; *aviat.* flight
rekcja *f* (*-i*; *-e*) *gr.* rection, government
rekin *m* (*-a*; *-y*) *zo.* shark
reklam|a *f* (*-y*; *G -*) advertisement, F ad; *RTV*: commercial; **~acja** *f* (*-i*; *-e*) complaint; **~ować** ⟨**za-**⟩ (*-uję*) advertise; lodge a complaint about; **~owy** advertising; **~ówka** *f* (*-i*; *G -wek*) commercial; (*torba*) carrier-bag
rekolekcje *f/pl.* (*-i*) *rel.* spiritual exercises *pl.*
rekomendacja *f* (*-i*; *-e*) recommendation
rekompen|sata *f* (*-y*; *G -*) compensation; **~sować** ⟨**z-**⟩ (*-uję*) (*A*) compensate (for)
rekonesans *m* (*-u*; *-e*) reconnaissance

rekonstruować ⟨**z-**⟩ (*-uję*) reconstruct, rebuild
rekord *m* (*-u*; *-y*) (**świata** world) record; *komp.* record; **bić ~** beat a record; **~owy** record
rekordzist|a *m* (*-y*; *-ści*), **~ka** *f* (*-i*; *G -tek*) record holder; **~(k)a świata** world-record holder
rekreacyjny recreational
rekrut *m* (*-a*; *-ci*) *mil.* recruit, conscript; **~ować** (*-uję*) recruit; **~ować się** come from
rektor *m* (*-a*; *-rzy*) rector, *Brt.* vice-chancellor, *Am.* president
rekultywacja *f* (*-i*; *-e*) *agr.* land reclamation
rekwiem *n* (*idkl.*) *rel.*, *mus.* requiem
rekwirować ⟨**za-**⟩ (*-uję*) requisition
rekwizyt *m* (*-u*; *-y*) prop
relacj|a *f* (*-i*; *-e*) relation; (**o** *L*) account (of), relation (about); **zdać ~ę** (**z** *G*) → **relacjonować**; **~onować** ⟨**z-**⟩ (*-uję*) relate
relaks *m* (*-u*; *0*) relaxation; **~ować się** (*-uję*) relax
relatywn|ie *adv.* relatively; **~y** relative
relief *m* (*-u*; *-y*) relief
re'ligi|a *f* (*GDl -ii*; *-e*) religion; **nauka ~i** religious instruction
religijny religious
re'likwia *f* (*GDl -ii*; *-e*) relic
remanent *m* (*-u*; *-y*) stock-taking; (*stan*) stock; **~owy** stock-taking
remis *m* (*-u*; *-y*) (*w sporcie*) draw, tie; **~ować** (*-uję*) draw, tie; **~owo** *adv.* in a draw *lub* tie; **~owy** drawn
remiza *f* (*-y*; *G -*), depot; **~ strażacka** fire station
remont *m* (*-u*; *-y*) renovation; repair; (re)decoration; **~ować** ⟨**od-**, **wy-**⟩ (*-uję*) renovate; repair; (re)decorate; **~owy** repairing
ren *m* (*-a*; *-y*) *zo.* → **renifer**
Ren *m* (*-u*; *0*) Rhine
rencist|a *m* (*-y*; *-ści*), **~ka** *f* (*-i*; *G -tek*) (old-age) pensioner
renesans *m* (*-u*; *-y*) renaissance; *2 hist.* the Renaissance
renifer *m* (*-a*; *-y*) *zo.* reindeer
renom|a *f* (*-y*) renown; **~owany** renowned
renowacja *f* (*-i*; *-e*) renovation, redecoration
renta *f* (*-y*; *G -*) pension; **~ starcza** old-age pension; **~ inwalidzka** disability pension; **być na rencie** receive a pension
rentgen *m* (*-a*; *-y*) (*zdjęcie*) X-ray; (*urządzenie*) X-ray machine; **zrobić ~** (*G*) X-ray
rentgeno|gram *m* (*-u*; *-y*) x-ray photograph; **~wski** x-ray
rentowność *f* (*-ści*) profitability
rentowny profitable
reorganizować ⟨**z-**⟩ reorganize
repa|tri'acja *f* (*-i*; *0*) repatriation; **~triant** *m* (*-a*; *-ci*), **~triantka** *f* (*-i*; *G -tek*) repatriate
reperacja *f* (*-i*; *-e*) repair
reperować ⟨**z-**⟩ (*-uję*) repair
repertuar *m* (*-u*; *-y*) repertoire
repet|a *f* (*-y*; *G -*) second helping, F seconds; **~ować** (*-uję*) (*w szkole*) repeat; *mil.* cock
replika *f* (*-i*; *G -*) replica; *theat.* cue
repor|taż *m* (*-u*; *-e*) report; **~tażysta** *m* (*-y*; *-ści*), **~tażystka** *f* (*-i*; *G -tek*) reporter, correspondent; **~ter** *m* (*-a*; *-rzy*), **~terka** *f* (*-i*; *G -rek*) reporter, journalist
repres|ja *f* (*-i*; *-e*) repression; **~yjny** repressive
reprezent|acja *f* (*-i*; *-e*) representation; (*w sporcie*) selected team; **~acyjny** representative; (*elegancki*) imposing; **~ować** (*-uję*) represent
reproduk|cja *f* (*-i*; *-e*) reproduction; **~ować** (*-uję*) reproduce, copy
reprywatyz|acja *f* (*-i*; *-e*) re-privatization; **~ować** (*-uję*) re-privatize
re'publika *f* (*-i*; *G -*) republic; **~nin** *m* (*-a*; *-nie*, *-*), **~nka** *f* (*-i*; *G -nek*) republican; **~ński** republican
reputacja *f* (*-i*; *-e*) reputation
resocjaliz|acja *f* (*-i*; *0*) rehabilitation; **~ować** (*-uję*) rehabilitate
resor *m* (*-u*; *-y*) *tech.* spring
resort *m* (*-u*; *-y*) department
respekt *m* (*-u*; *0*) respect, deference; **~ować** (*-uję*) respect
respirator *m* (*-a*; *-y*) respirator
respondent *m* (*-a*; *-ci*), **~ka** *f* (*-i*; *G -tek*) respondent
restaura|cja *f* (*-i*; *-e*) restaurant; (*odnowienie*) restoration; **~cyjny** restaurant; **wagon ~cyjny** *rail.* dining car; **~tor** *m* (*-a*; *-rzy*), **~torka** *f* (*-i*; *G -rek*) restaurateur
re|staurować ⟨**od-**⟩ (*-uję*) restore;

R

~strukturyzować (*-uję*) restructure; **~strykcja** *f* (*-i*; *-e*) restriction
reszka *f* (*-i*): ***orzeł czy ~?*** heads or tails?
reszt|a *f* (*-y*; *G -*) rest; (*pieniądze*) change; ***bez ~y*** completely, totally; ***do ~y*** completely; **~ka** *f* (*-i*; *G -tek*) rest; ***~ki*** *pl.* remains *pl.*, (*jedzenia*) leftovers *pl.*
retoryczny rhetoric
retransmisja *f* (*-i*; *-e*) *RTV* broadcast, transmission
retuszować (*-uję*) retouch; *fig.* gloss over
reumaty|czny rheumatic; **~zm** *m* (*-u*; *0*) *med.* rheumatism
rewaloryzacja *f* (*-i*; *-e*) revaluation
rewanż *m* (*-u*; *-e*) revenge; (*w sporcie*) return match *lub* game; **~ować** ⟨**z-**⟩ **się** (*-uję*) settle accounts (***za*** *A* for); **~owy** (*w sporcie*) return
rewelac|ja *f* (*-i*; *-e*) revelation, sensation; **~yjny** sensational
rewia *f* (*GDL -ii*; *-e*) revue
rewid|ent *m* (*-a*; *-ci*), **~entka** *f* (*-i*; *-tek*) *econ.* auditor; **~ować** ⟨**z-**⟩ (*-uję*) *tekst* revise; *bagaż* search; *econ.* audit
rewiowy revue
rewiz|ja *f* (*-i*; *-e*) (*tekstu*) review; ***~ja osobista*** body search; ***nakaz dokonania ~ji*** search warrant; **~jonistyczny** revisionist; **~yjny** review; ***komisja ~yjna*** committee of auditors
rewizyta *f* (*-y*; *G -*) return visit
rewoluc|ja *f* (*-i*; *-e*) revolution; **~jonista** *m* (*-y*; *-ści*), **~jonistka** *f* (*-i*; *-tek*) revolutionary; **~yjny** revolutionary
rewolwer *m* (*-u*; *-y*) revolver
rezerw|a *f* (*-y*; *G -*) reserve; *mil.*, (*w sporcie*) reserves *pl.*; ***mieć/trzymać w ~ie*** have in reserve; **~acja** *f* (*-i*; *-e*) reservation, *Brt.* booking; **~at** *m* (*-u*; *-y*) reserve; (*Indian*) reservation; ***~at przyrody*** nature reserve; **~ować** ⟨**za-**⟩ reserve, *Brt.* book; **~owy** reserve
rezolu|cja *f* (*-i*; *-e*) resolution; **~tność** *f* (*-ści*; *0*) resoluteness; ingenuity; **~tny** resolute; ingenious
rezonans *m* (*-u*; *-e*) resonance; *fig.* response
rezultat *m* (*-u*; *-y*) result
rezurekc|ja *f* (*-i*; *-e*) *rel.* Resurrection service
rezy|dencja *f* (*-i*; *-e*) residence; **~dować** (*-uję*) reside; **~gnacja** *f* (*-i*; *-e*) resignation; (***z*** *A*) renunciation; **~gnować** ⟨**z-**⟩ (*-uję*) (***z*** *A*) give up; (*z jedzenia*) do without; (*z planu*) abandon; (*z pracy*) resign (from)
rezyst|ancja *f* (*-i*; *0*) *electr.* resistance; **~or** *m* (*-a*; *-y*) *electr.* resistor
reż. *skrót pisany*: ***reżyser*** dir. (*director*)
reżim *m*, **reżym** *m* (*-u*; *-y*) regime
reżyser *m* (*-a*; *-rzy/-owie*) director; **~ia** *f* (*GDL -ii*; *0*) direction; **~ka** *f* (*-i*; *G -rek*) director; F direction; **~ować** ⟨**wy-**⟩ (*-uję*) direct
rębacz *m* (*-a*; *-e*) *górnictwo*: face-worker
ręce *pl.* → ***ręka***
ręczn|ie *adv.* manually; by hand; ***pisany ~ie*** handwritten; **~ik** *m* (*-a*; *-i*) towel; ***~ik kąpielowy*** bath towel; **~y** manual; *bagaż itp.* hand; hand-made; ***hamulec ~y*** *mot.* hand brake; emergency brake
ręczyć ⟨**po-, za-**⟩ (*-ę*) (***za*** *A*) guarantee (for), vouch (for)
ręk|a *f* (*-i*, *L ręce*; *ręce*, *rąk*, *rękami/-koma*, *L -kach/-ku*) hand; ***~a w ~ę*** hand in hand; ***za ~ę*** by the hand; ***przechodzić z rąk do rąk*** change hands; ***od ~i*** on the spot; ***pod ~ę*** arm in arm, with linked arms; ***być na ~ę*** (*D*) be convenient (for); ***mieć pod ~ą*** have *s.th.* at hand; ***iść na ~ę*** play ball; ***dać/mieć wolną ~ę*** have carte blanche; ***na własną ~ę*** on one's own initiative, F off one's own bat; ***podać/wyciągnąć ~ę*** stretch a hand; ***uścisnąć ~ę*** shake *s.o.'s* hand; ***z pierwszej*** (***drugiej***) ***~i*** at first (second) hand
rękaw *m* (*-a*; *-y*) sleeve; **~ica** *f* (*-y*; *-e*), **~iczka** *f* (*-i*; *G -czek*) glove
rękoczyn *m* (*-u*; *-y*) manhandling; ***posunąć się do ~u*** start using one's fists
rękodzieł|o *n* (*-a*; *0*) handicraft; ***~a*** *pl.* arts and crafts *pl.*
ręko|jeść *f* (*-ści*; *-e*) handle; (*łopaty*) stick; **~jmia** *f* (*-i*; *-e*) guarantee, security; **~pis** *m* (*-u*; *-y*) manuscript
ring *m* (*-u*; *-i*) *sport*: ring; **~owy** ring
r-k *skrót pisany*: ***rachunek*** inv. (*invoice*)
robactwo *n* (*-a*; *G -*) *zbior.* vermin
robacz|ek *m* (*-czka*; *-czki*) → ***robak***; ***~ek świętojański*** glow-worm; **~kowy** *biol.* vermiform; ***wyrostek ~kowy*** *anat.* appendix; **~ywy** worm-eaten
robak *m* (*-a*; *-i*) worm; F insect

R

rober *m* (*-bra*; *-bry*) rubber

robić⟨**z-**⟩ (*-ę*, *rób!*) do, make; ***co on robi?*** what is he doing?; ***co ~*** (**z** I) what to do (with); **~ *się*** become, get; *nieos.* it is getting (***ciemno*** dark; ***gorąco*** hot); F ***już się robi!*** will do!

robiony *fig.* artificial; forced

robocizna *f* (*-y*; *0*) labo(u)r; (*koszt pracy też*) wage costs *pl.*

robocz|y labo(u)r; working; ***siła ~a*** labo(u)r force; ***dzień ~y*** work day

robot *m* (*-a*; *-y*) robot; ***~ kuchenny*** food-processor; **~a** *f* (*-y*; *G robót*) work, (*ciężka*) labo(u)r; ***krecia ~a*** *pej.* subversive activities *pl.*; *zw. pl.* ***~y na drodze*** men at work; *zw. pl.* ***~y przymusowe*** forced labo(u)r; ***po robocie*** after work; ***własnej/swojej ~y*** home-made; ***nie mieć nic do ~y*** have nothing to do; **~nica** *f* (*-y*; *-e*) worker; **~niczy** working; **~nik** *m* (*-a*; *-cy*) worker

robótka *f* (*-i*; *G -tek*) (*na drutach*) needlework

rockowy *mus.* rock

roczni|ca *f* (*-y*; *G -*) anniversary; ***setna ~ca*** centenary; **~e** *adv.* annually; **~k** *m* (*-a*; *-i*) year; (*wina itp.*) vintage; (*czasopism*) volume; (*książka*) year-book

roczny annual, yearly

roda|czka *f* (*-i*; *G -czek*), **~k** *m* (*-a*; *-cy*) compatriot

rodo|wity indigenous, native; ***~wity Polak*** a Pole by birth; **~wód** *m* (*-wodu*; *-wody*) (*człowieka*) family tree; (*zwierzęcia*) pedigree; **~wy** pedigree; ***szlachta ~wa*** ancient nobility

rody *pl.* → ***ród***

rodzaj *m* (*-u*; *-e*) type, kind; *biol.* species; *gr.* genus; *sztuka*: genre; ***~ ludzki*** humankind, mankind; ***coś w ~u*** (*G*) s.th. like; ***jedyny w swoim ~u*** unique; **~nik** *m* (*-a*; *-i*) *gr.* article; **~owy** generic; ***malarstwo ~owe*** genre painting

rodzeństwo *n* (*-a*; *G -*) brothers and sisters *pl.*; *biol.* siblings *pl.*

rodzi|c *m* (*-a*; *-e*) parent; **~ce** *pl.* (*-ów*) parents *pl.*; **~cielski** parent(al)

rodzić (*-dzę*, *też ródź!*) ⟨**na-**, **u-**⟩ give birth to, bear; ⟨**ob-**, **u-**⟩ *agr.* bear, produce; *fig.* produce, generate; **~** ⟨**na-**, **u-**⟩ ***się*** be born

rodzi|my native, indigenous; **~na** *f* (*-y*; *G -*) family; ***ojciec ~ny*** paterfamilias; ***bez ~ny*** no family *lub* dependants; **~nny** family; ***dom ~nny*** (parental) home

rodzony *dziecko*, *brat itp.* one's own

rodzyn|ek *m* (*-nka*, *-nki*), **~ka** *f* (*-nki*; *-nek*) raisin

roga|cz *m* (*-a*; *-e*) *zo.* deer; *iron.* cuckold; **~l** *m* (*-a*; *-e*), **~lik** *m* (*-a*; *-i*) croissant; **~tka** *f* (*-i*; *G -tek*) barrier; bar, toll-house ***za ~tkami miasta*** outside the city limits; **~ty** horned, antlered

rogi *pl.* → ***róg***

rogow|acieć⟨**z-**⟩ (*-eję*) become horny; **~aty** hornlike; **~y** horn

rogoża *f* (*-y*; *-e*) bast mat

rogówka *f* (*-i*; *G -wek*) *anat.* cornea

ro|ić (*-ję*; *rój!*) (**o** *L*) dream (of), fantasize (about); ***~ić się*** *muchy*: swarm, teem; ***~i się*** (**od** *G*) it is crawling (with); ***~i mu się*** (*A*) he fancies; **~je** *pl.* → ***rój***

rojn|y busy, bustling; ***na ulicach było ~o*** the streets were crowded

rok *m* (*-u*; *lata*) year; ***od ~u*** for a year; ***raz do ~u*** once a year; ***z ~u na ~*** every year; ***~ w ~*** year in, year out; → ***nowy, lata, przestępny***

rokowa|ć (*-uję*) *v/i.* negotiate (**o** *A* about; **z** *I* with); *v/t.* hope (***sobie*** for); ***~ć nadzieje*** promise well; **~nie** *n* (*-a*; *G -ań*) *med.* prognosis; *t-ko pl.* ***~nia*** negotiations *pl.*

rokrocznie *adv.* annually, every year

rola[1] *f* (*-i*; *-e*, *ról*) soil; → ***gleba***

rola[2] *f* (*-i*; *-e*, *ról*) *theat. fig.* role, part

rolada *f* (*-y*; *G -*) *gastr.* (*mięsna*) roulade

roleta *f* (*-y*; *G -*) (roller) shutter, (roller) blind

rolka *f* (*-i*; *G -lek*) roll, reel; ***~ papieru*** paper roll; ***~ nici*** thread reel

rolni|ctwo *f* (*-a*; *0*) agriculture; **~czka** *f* (*-i*; *-czek*), **~k** *m* (*-a*; *-cy*) farmer; **~czo** *adv.* agriculturally; **~czy** agricultural

roln|y agricultural; ***gospodarstwo ~e*** farm; ***produkty*** *pl.* ***~e*** produce

roma'nistyka *f* (*-i*) (*studia*) French studies *pl.*; (*instytut*) French department

roman|s *m* (*-u*; *-y*) (*literatura*, *mus.*, *fig.*) romance; (*miłostka*) love affair; **~sik** *m* (*-u*; *-i*) flirtation, casual affair; **~tyczny** romantic; *hist.* Romantic; **~tyczka** *f* (*-i*; *-czek*), **~tyk** (*-a*; *- cy*) romantic; **~tyzm** *m* (*-u*; *-y*) *hist.* Romanticism

romański Romanesque

romb *m* (*-u*; *-y*) *math.* diamond, rhombus

rondel *m* (*-dla*; *-dle*) pan

R

rond|o[1] *n* (*-a*; *G -*) (hat) brim; *mus.* rondo; *lit.* rondeau
rond|o[2] *n* (*-a*; *G -*) *Brt.* roundabout, *Am.* traffic circle
ronić (*-ę*) *lit.*: **~ łzy** shed tears; ⟨**po-**⟩ *med.* miscarry
rop|a *f* (*-y*; *0*) *med.* pus; (*naftowa*) oil; **~ieć** (*-eję*) suppurate, fester; **~ień** *m* (*-pnia*; *-pnie*) abscess; **~ny** *mot.* Diesel; *med.* purulent
ropucha *f* (*-y*; *G -*) *zo.* toad
rosa *f* (*-y*; *0*) dew
Rosja *f* (*-i*; *0*) Russia; **~nin** *m* (*-a*; *-anie*, *-*), **~nka** *f* (*-i*; *G -nek*) Russian
ros|ły tall, big; **~nąć** ⟨**u-, wy-**⟩ grow (*też fig.*); *ciasto*, *ceny*: rise
rosochaty forked, branching
ros|ołowy broth; **~ół** *m* (*-ołu*; *-oły*) stock, broth, clear soup; ***~ół z kury*** consommé
rostbef *m* (*-u*; *-y*) roast beef
rosyjs|ki Russian; ***mówić po ~ku*** speak Russian
roszczenie *n* (*-a*; *G -eń*) claim; ***wysunąć ~*** (**o** *A*) make a claim (for)
rościć (*-szczę*) claim; **~** (***sobie***) ***prawo*** (**do** *G*) lay claim (to); ***~ pretensje*** (**do** *G*) pretend (to)
rośl|lejszy *adj. comp. od* → **rosły**; **~lina** *f* (***lekarska, ogrodowa, użytkowa*** medicinal, garden, economically useful) plant; **~linność** *f* (*-ści*; *0*) vegetation; flora; **~linny** plant; **~linożerny** herbivorous
rota *f* (*-y*; *G -*) (***przysięgi*** oath) formula
rotacja *f* (*-i*; *-e*) rotation
rowek *m* (*-wka*; *-wki*) (*na płycie itp.*) groove; furrow; → ***rów***
rowe|r *m* (*-ru*; *-y*) bicycle, F bike; ***jeździć na ~rze*** ride a bike, cycle; **~rowy** bicycle, bike; **~rzysta** *m* (*-y*; *-ści*), **~rzystka** *f* (*-i*; *-tek*) cyclist
rowy *pl.* → ***rów***
roz|bawiony amused; **~bełtywać** (*-uję*) → ***bełtać***; **~bestwiony** (*wściekły*) raging, mad; (*nieposłuszny*) unruly, wild
rozbi|cie *n* (*-a*; *G -ić*) breaking, crashing, breakage; ***~cie okrętu*** shipwreck; ***ulec ~ciu*** be broken; **~ć** *pf.* → ***rozbijać***
rozbie|g *m* (*w sporcie*) run-up; **~gać się** ⟨***~c się***⟩ *tłum*: scatter, disperse; take a run-up; **~gany** *oczy* restless; **~rać** (*-am*) undress (***się*** *v/i.*); *aparat* take to pieces, dismantle; *budynek* demolish, take down; **~ralnia** *f* (*-i*; *-e*) changing-cubicle
rozbieżn|ość *f* (*-ści*) divergence, discrepancy; **~y** divergent, different, differing
rozbijać (*-am*) break, smash (***się*** *v/i.*; ***o*** *A* against); *samochód itp.* wreck; *obóz*, *namiot* set up, pitch; *kolano itp.* injure; *kraj* divide up (***na*** *A* into); ***~ bank*** break a bank; ***~ się*** F move about the world
rozbiór *m* (*-bioru*; *-biory*) analysis; (*państwa*) partition; **~ka** *f* (*-i*; *G -rek*) (*domu*) demolition; (*maszyny*) dismantling; **~kowy** demolition
rozbit|ek *m* (*-tka*; *-tkowie/-tki*) castaway (*też fig.*); *fig.* wreck; **~y** broken, smashed
rozbój *m* robbery; **~niczka** *f* (*-i*; *G -czek*), **~nik** *m* (*-a*; *-cy*) robber; ***~nik morski*** pirate
rozbraja|ć (*-am*) disarm (*też fig.*; ***się*** *v/i.*); **~jąco** *adv.* disarmingly; **~jący** disarming
rozbratel *m* (*-tla*; *-tle*) rump steak
rozbro|ić *pf.* → ***rozbrajać***; **~jenie** *n* (*-a*; *0*) disarmament
roz|bryzgiwać (*-uję*) ⟨***~bryzgać, ~bryznąć***⟩ spray; **~brzmiewać** (*-am*) ⟨***~brzmieć***⟩ resound, ring out; **~budowa** *f* (*-y*; *G -dów*) extension; **~budow(yw)ać** (*-[w]uję*) extend; ***~budow(yw)ać się*** expand; **~budzać** (*-am*) → ***budzić***; **~charakteryzow(yw)ać** (*-[w]uję*) remove make-up; ***~charakteryzow(yw)ać się*** remove one's make-up; **~chmurzać się** (*-am*) ⟨***~chmurzyć się***⟩ clear
roz|chodowy expenditure; **~chodzić się** disperse; *drogi*: fork; *fig.* drift apart; *wieść*, *ciepło*: spread; *wiadomość*: get around; *pieniądze*: be spent; *małżeństwo*: break up, split up; **~chorować się** *pf.* be taken ill, fall ill; **~chód** *m econ.* expenditure; **~chwiać** *pf.* set *s.th.* swinging, work *s.th.* loose
rozchwyt|ywać (*-uję*) ⟨***~ać***⟩ buy up; ***być ~ywanym*** be much sought-after; **~ywany** in demand
rozchy|botany loose; *krzesło itp.* rickety, wobbly; **~lać** (*-am*) ⟨***~lić***⟩ part (***się*** *v/i.*); **~lony** parted
rozciąć *pf.* → ***rozcinać***;
rozciąg|ać (*-am*) ⟨***~nąć***⟩ stretch (***się*** *v/i.*); extend (***się*** *v/i.*); *sznury* put up;

R

→ ***rozpościerać***; **~liwy** stretchy, stretch, elastic; **~łość** *f* (*-ści*) extent, extension; ***w całej ~łości*** completely, to the full extent
rozcieńcz|ać (*-am*) ⟨**~yć**⟩ (*-ę*) dilute, thin, (*wodą*) water down; **~alnik** *m* (*-a*; *-i*) thinner
roz|cierać (*-am*) rub; *maść* rub in; *żółtka* beat; crush (***na proch*** to a powder); **~cięcie** *n* (*-a*; *G -ęć*) slit; cut; **~cinać** (*-am*) slit, cut
rozcza|pierzać (*-am*) ⟨**~pierzyć**⟩ (*-ę*) spread; **~rowanie** *n* (*-a*; *0*) disappointment; **~row(yw)ać** (*-[w]uję*) disappoint; ***~row(yw)ać się*** become disappointed
rozcze|pi(a)ć separate; *tech.* uncouple; **~sywać** (*-uję*) ⟨**~czesać**⟩ comb through
roz|członkow(yw)ać (*-[w]uję*) dismember; **~czochrany** unkempt, dishevel(l)ed
rozczul|ać (*-am*) ⟨**~ić**⟩ (*-lę*) move (***do łez*** to tears); ***~ić się nad*** melt over; **~ająco** *adv.* touchingly; **~ający** touching; **~enie** *n* (*-a*; *0*) emotion
rozczyn *m* (*-u*; *-y*) *chem.* solution; *gastr.* leaven; **~iać** (*-am*) ⟨**~ić**⟩ (*-ę*) *ciasto* mix (***na*** *A* for)
rozda|ć *pf.* → ***rozdawać***; **~rcie** *n* (*-a*; *G -rć*) tear; *fig.* inner turmoil; **~wać** ⟨**po-**⟩ (*D*) give out (to), give away (to), distribute (to)
rozdąć *pf.* → ***rozdymać***
rozdept|ywać (*-uję*) ⟨**~ać**⟩ stamp on, crush; *nowe buty* break in
rozdmuch|iwać (*-uję*) ⟨**~ać**⟩ *ogień* fan; *fig.* blow up, exaggerate
rozdrabniać (*-am*) break into small pieces, fritter; **~ się** *fig.* try to do too many things at once
rozdrap|ywać (*-uję*) ⟨**~ać**⟩ scratch
rozdrażn|iać (*-am*) ⟨**~ić**⟩ annoy, irritate; **~ienie** *n* (*-a*; *G -eń*) annoyance, irritation; **~iony** annoyed, irritated
roz|drobnić *pf.* (*-ę*, *nij!*) → ***rozdrabniać***; **~droże** *n* (*-a*; *G -y*) crossroads *sg.*; ***na ~drożu*** *fig.* at the crossroads
rozdw|ajać (*-am*) ⟨**~oić**⟩ split, divide; ***~ajać*** ⟨**~oić**⟩ ***się*** split; *droga, konar*: fork; **~ojenie** *n* (*-a*; *G -eń*) → ***jaźń***
roz|dymać (*-am*) *żagiel, ubranie* billow (***się*** *v/i.*); *fig.* blow up; **~dział** *m* (*-u*; *-y*) (*funduszy itp.*) distribution, allocation; (*rozdzielenie*) separation (***od*** *G* from); (*w książce*) chapter
rozdziawi|ać (*-am*) ⟨**~ć**⟩ (*-ę*) open wide
rozdziel|ać (*-am*) ⟨**~ić**⟩ distribute, allocate; separate; → ***dzielić, rozdawać***; **~czy** distributive; ***tablica ~cza*** *tech.* control panel; **~nia** *f* (*-i*; *-e*) *electr.* switching station; **~nik** *m* (*-a*; *-i*) distribution list; **~ny** separate
rozdziera|ć (*-am*) tear, rip (***się*** *v/i.*); **~jąco** *adv.* piercingly; **~jący** *krzyk* piercing; *ból* excruciating
rozdźwięk *m* dissonance, discord
roze|brać *pf.* → ***rozbierać***; **~brany** undressed; **~drzeć** *pf.* → ***rozdzierać***; **~gnać** *pf.* → ***rozganiać***; **~grać** *pf.* → ***rozgrywać***
rozejm *m* (*-u*; *-y*) truce, armistice
roze|jrzeć się *pf.* → ***rozglądać się***; **~jść** (*-dę*) **się** (→***-jść***) → ***rozchodzić się***; **~pchać**, **~pchnąć** *pf.* → ***rozpychać***
rozerwa|ć *pf.* → ***rozrywać***; *fig.* entertain, amuse; ***~ć się*** have fun; **~ny** torn
roze|rżnąć *pf.* → ***rozrzynać***; **~słać** *pf.* →***rozsyłać, rozściełać***; **~spany** drowsy; **~śmiać się** *pf.* laugh, burst into laughter; **~trzeć** *pf.* → ***rozcierać***; **~wrzeć** *pf.* (→ ***-wrzeć***) → ***rozwierać***
rozezna|nie *n* (*-a*; *0*) knowledge, information; ***mieć ~nie w sytuacji*** be in the know; **~wać** (*-ję*) ⟨**~ć**⟩ distinguish; ***~(wa)ć się*** know what's what
rozga|łęziać się (*-am*) branch out; **~łęzienie** *n* (*-a*; *G -eń*) branching; (*dróg*) crossroads *sg.*; **~niać** disperse
roz'gar|diasz *m* (*-u*; *0*) mess, confusion; **~niać** (*-am*) ⟨**~nąć**⟩ move apart; *popiół* rake aside; **~'nięty** brainy
roz|ginać (*-am*) ⟨**~giąć**⟩ unbend; bend apart; **~glądać się** (*-am*) look around; (***za*** *I*) *fig.* look for; **~głaszać** (*-am*) publicize, make public
rozgło|s *m* (*-u*; *0*) publicity; fame; ***sprawa nabrała ~su*** it has become public knowledge; ***bez ~su*** in quiet; **~sić** *pf.* → ***rozgłaszać***; **~śnia** *f* (*-i*; *-e*) broadcasting station; **~śny** loud
rozgni|atać (*-am*) ⟨**~eść**⟩ mash; *muchę* squash
rozgniewa|ć *pf.* → ***gniewać***; **~ny** angry, enraged
roz|gonić *pf.* → ***rozganiać***; **~gorączkować się** *pf.* become frantic; **~gorączkowany** feverish, frantic (*też fig.*)

R

rozgoryczony embittered, bitter
rozgotować się *pf.* get overcooked
rozgra|biać (*-am*) ⟨**~bić**⟩ plunder; **~miać** (*-am*) crush, rout; **~niczać** (*-am*) ⟨**~niczyć**⟩ demarcate, delimit
rozgromić *pf.* → **rozgramiać**
rozgry|wać (*-am*) *mecz*, *partię* play; **~wać się** take place; **~wka** *f* (*-i*; *G -wek*) (*w sporcie*) game; **~wki** *pl.* games *pl.*, tournament; **~zać** ⟨**~źć**⟩ bit in two, crack; *fig.* solve
rozgrzać *pf.* → **rozgrzewać**
rozgrze|bywać (*-uję*) ⟨**~bać**⟩ rake aside *lub* up; *fig.* rake up; **~szać** (*-ę*) ⟨**~szyć**⟩ *v/t. rel.* absolve; *fig.* (**z** *I*) forgive; **~szenie** *n* (*-a*; *G -eń*) *rel.* absolution; **~wać** (*-am*) (*też sport*, *mot.*) warm up (**się** *v/i.*); **~wka** *f* (*-i*; *G -wek*) warm-up
roz|gwiazda *f zo.* starfish; **~hermetyzowanie** *n* (*-a*; *G -ań*) depressurization; **~hukany** unruly, wild; **~huśtać** *pf.* → **rozkołysać**; **~jarzony** *pred.* ablaze; bright; **~jaśniacz** *m* (*-a*; *-e*) *chem.* bleach; **~jaśniać** (*-am*) ⟨**~jaśnić**⟩ (*-ę*; *-nij!*) make lighter; lighten; *twarz* light up; *włosy*, *oczy* brighten (**się** *v/i.*); **~jazd** *m* (*-u*; *-y*) junction; **być w ~jazdach** travel much; **~jątrzać** *pf.* → **jątrzyć**; **~jechać** *pf.* → **rozjeżdżać**
rozjem|ca *m* (*-y*; *G -ów*) arbitrator; **~czy** arbitration; **~czyni** *f* (*-*; *G -yń*) arbitrator
rozjeżdżać (*-am*) travel much; *coś* knock down; **~ się** part, go one's separate ways
rozjuszony enraged
rozkaz *m* (*-u*; *-y*) order, command; **być pod ~ami** (*G*) be under *s.o.'s* command; **~ać** *pf.* → **rozkazywać**; **~ująco** *adv.* commandingly; **~ujący** commanding; **tryb ~ujący** *gr.* imperative; **~ywać** (*-uję*) *v/t.* command, order; *v/i.* be in command
rozkaźnik *m* (*-a*; *-i*) *gr.* imperative
roz|kiełznać *pf.* (*-am*) unbridle; **~klejać** (*-am*) ⟨**~kleić**⟩ *plakaty* stick up, post; *kopertę* undo, unstick; **~klejać się** come undone; **~kleić się** *fig.* go to pieces; **~klekotany** rickety; **~kloszowany** *suknia* (widely-)flared
rozkład *m* (*-u*; *-y*) arrangement; **~ jazdy** *Brt.* timetable, *Am.* schedule; **~ lekcji** schedule; *biol.* rot; *chem.* breakdown, disintegration; *fig.* decline, collapse; *math.* distribution; **~ać** (*-am*) spread (out), unfold; *gazetę* open up; *łóżko* fold out; *pracę* assign; *maszynę* dismantle; *biol.*, *chem.* decompose; *fig.* undermine; **~ać się** unfold; stretch (o.s.) up; (**z** *I*) spread out; *chem.* break down; *biol.* *też* decompose, decay; **~any** *łóżko* collapsible
rozkoch|iwać (*-uję*) ⟨**~ać**⟩ make enamo(u)red; inspire with love (**w sztuce** towards art); **~ać się** fall in love
rozkojarzony absent-minded
rozkołysać *pf. v/t.* (*-am*) sway (to and fro) (**się** *v/i.*)
rozkop|ywać (*-uję*) ⟨**~ać**⟩ dig over
rozkosz *f* (*-y*; *-e*) delight, joy; pleasure; **~e** *pl.* pleasures *pl.*, delights *pl.*; **~ny** delightful; sweet; **~ować się** (*-uję*) (*I*) delight (in), feast (on)
roz|kręcać (*-am*) ⟨**~kręcić**⟩ unscrew; *maszynę* take apart; *fig. gospodarkę itp.* boost up; **~kręcić się** bloom, burgeon; **~krok** *m* straddle; **~kruszać** (*-am*) → **kruszyć**; **~krwawić** *pf.* make bleed; **~krzewiać** (*-am*) → **krzewić**; **~kupywać** (*-uję*) ⟨**~kupić**⟩ buy up; **~kurczać** (*-am*) ⟨**~kurczyć**⟩ *mięsień* relax; **~kurczowy** *med.* diastolic
rozkwit *m* (*-u*; *0*) bloom, flowering, blossoming (*też fig.*); **w pełni ~u** in full bloom; **~ać** (*-am*) ⟨**~nąć**⟩ bloom, flower, blossom
roz|lać *pf.* → **rozlewać**; **~latywać się** (*-uję*) ⟨**~lecieć się**⟩ fall apart, go to pieces; → **rozbijać się**
rozleg|ać się (*-am*) ⟨**rozlec się**⟩ (→ **lec**) ring out; *echo*: resound, reverberate; *protest*: be vociferous; **~le** *adv.* extensively, widely; substantially; **~łość** *f* (*-ści*; *0*) spaciousness; extensiveness; **~ły** extensive, wide; substantial; widespread
rozleniwi|ać (*-am*) ⟨**~ć**⟩ (*-ę*) make lazy; **~(a)ć się** grow lazy
rozlepi|ać (*-am*) ⟨**~ć**⟩ → **rozklejać**
rozlew *m* (*-u*; *0*) filling, (*do butelek itp.*) bottling; **~ krwi** bloodshed; **~ać** (*-am*) *v/t.* spill; *herbatę itp.* pour out; *krew* shed; fill (**do kieliszków** the glasses); **~ać do butelek** bottle; *v/i. rzeka*: overflow; **~ać się** spill
rozleźć się *pf.* → **rozłazić się**
rozlicz|ać (*-am*) ⟨**~yć**⟩ *wydatki* account for; *czek* clear; **~ać** ⟨**~yć**⟩ **się** (**z** *I*) settle

R

(accounts) (with); **~enie** *n* (*-a*; *G -eń*) settlement, clearing
rozlokow(yw)ać (-[*w*]*uję*) put up; *mil.* quarter; **~ *się*** find accommodation
rozlosow(yw)ać (-[*w*]*uję*) raffle
rozluźni|ać (*-am*) ⟨**~ć**⟩ (*-ę*, *-nij!*) loosen; ***~ać*** ⟨**~ć**⟩ ***się*** work o.s. loose; **~ony** loosened
rozładow(yw)ać (-[*w*]*uję*) unload (***się*** *v/i.*); **~ *napięcie*** relax the tension
roz|ładunek *m* (*-nku*; *-nki*) unloading; **~łam** *m* (*-u*; *-y*) split, division; **~łamywać** (*-uję*) ⟨***~łamać***⟩ break (***się*** *v/i.*). break (into pieces); *fig.* break up; **~łazić się** F (***po*** *L*) spread; *ludzie*: disperse; *buty*: fall apart
rozłą|czać (*-am*) disconnect, cut off; part (***się*** *v/i.*); **~ka** *f* (*-i*; *G -*) separation
rozłoży|ć *pf.* → ***rozkładać***; **~sty** spreading
rozłupywać (*-uję*) → ***łupać***
rozmach *m* (*-u*; *0*) swing; *fig.* drive, energy; **~iwać** (*-uję*) (*I*) → ***machać***
rozma|czać soak; **~gnesow(yw)ać** (-[*w*]*uję*) demagnetize
rozmai|cie *adv.* variously; **~tość** *f* (*-ści*; *0*) diversity, variety; ***~tości*** *pl.* sundries *pl.*, bits and pieces *pl.*; **~ty** diverse, various
rozmaryn *m* (*-u*; *-y*) *bot.* rosemary
roz|marzać [-r·z-] *v/i.* thaw; **~marzony** dreamy; **~mawiać** speak (***o*** *L* about); talk (***z*** *I* to, with); **~miar** *m* (*-u*; *-y*) size; dimension
rozmie|niać (*-am*) ⟨***~nić***⟩ *banknot* change; **~szać** (*-am*) *pf.* mix; **~szczać** ⟨***po-***⟩ (*-am*) ⟨***~ścić***⟩ place, situate, position; → ***rozlokowywać***; ***~ścić się*** take places; **~szczenie** *n* (*-a*; *G -eń*) placement, situation
rozmięk|ać (*-am*) *v/i.* get *lub* become soft; soften (up); **~czać** (*-am*) ⟨***~czyć***⟩ *v/i.* soften; **~nąć** *pf* → ***rozmiękać***
rozmiłowany: ***być ~m*** (***w*** *L*) be in love (with)
rozminąć się *pf.* → ***mijać się***
rozmnaża|ć (*-am*) reproduce (***się*** *v/i. lub* o.s.), *bakterie itp.* multiply; **~nie** *n* (*-a*; *0*) reproduction
roz|mnożyć *pf.* → ***rozmnażać***; **~moczyć** *pf.* → ***rozmaczać***; **~moknąć** *pf.* → ***rozmiękać***; **~montow(yw)ać** (-[*w*]*uję*) disassemble, take apart; **~mowa** *f* (*-y*; *G -mów*) talk, conversation; ***~mowy*** *pl. pol.* negotiations *pl.*; *tel.* call; **~mowny** talkative
rozmów|ca *m* (*-y*; *G -ów*), **~czyni** *f* (*-i*; *-e*) interlocutor; **~ić się** *pf.* talk (***na temat*** *G* on, about), come to an understanding; **~nica** *f* (*-y*; *-e*) *tel.* (post office) telephone booth
roz|mrażać (*-am*) ⟨***~mrozić***⟩ defrost
rozmyć *pf.* → ***rozmywać***
rozmy|sł *m* (*-u*; *-y*) deliberation; ***z ~słem*** intentionally, deliberately; **~ślać** (*-am*) think, ponder (***nad*** *I* on); **~ślić się** *pf.* (*-lę*) change one's mind, think better of; **~ślny** deliberate, intentional
rozmywać (*-am*) undermine and wash away
roznamiętni|ać (*-am*) ⟨**~ć**⟩ (*-ę*, *-nij!*) incense (***się*** *v/i.*); ***~ać się*** *iron.* become amorous; **~ony** incensed, enflamed; amorous, passionate
roz|negliżowany undressed; **~niecać** (*-am*) ⟨***~niecić***⟩ (*-cę*) kindle (*też fig.*); *fig.* provoke; **~nieść** *pf.* → ***roznosić***; **~nosiciel** *m* (*-a*; *-e*), **~nosicielka** *f* (*-i*; *G -lek*) delivery person; **~nosić** (*-szę*) deliver, distribute; *wieści, chorobę itp.* spread (***się*** *v/i.*; ***po*** *L* around); → ***rozbijać, rozrywać***; **~ochocić się** (*-cę*) *pf.* liven up; (***do*** *G*) get excited (about); **~ogniony** inflamed; *fig.* heated
rozpacz *f* (*-y*; *0*) despair; ***doprowadzić do ~y*** drive to despair; ***szaleć z ~y*** be frantic; **~ać** (*-am*) despair (***nad*** *I* at, of); **~liwie** *adv.* desperately; **~liwy** desperate
rozpad *m* (*-u*; *0*) disintegration, breakup; **~ać się** (*-am*) disintegrate, break apart *lub* up, disunite; ***~ało się*** it has begun to rain steadily; **~lina** *f* (*-y*; *G -*) crack, crevice
rozpakow(yw)ać (-[*w*]*uję*) unpack
rozpal|ać (*-am*) ⟨***~ić***⟩ *ogień* kindle; *kominek* light; *piec, kocioł* fire up; *fig.* arouse, kindle; ***~ić się*** start burning; catch fire
roz|paplać *pf.* let out, blab; **~parcelow(yw)ać** (-[*w*]*uję*) divide into plots; **~pasany** rampant, unbridled; **~paść się** *pf.* → ***rozpadać się***
rozpatrywać (*-uję*) ⟨***rozpatrzyć***⟩ examine, investigate; *jur.* hear; **~** ⟨***rozpatrzyć***⟩ ***się*** (***w*** *L*) get acquainted (with)
rozpęd *m* (*-u*; *0*) momentum, impetus;

R

nabierać ~u gain momentum; **~owy:** ***koło ~owe*** *tech.* flywheel
rozpędz|ać (*-am*) ⟨**~ić**⟩ *tłum, chmury* disperse, scatter; *pojazd* accelerate, speed up; *fig.* drive away; ***~ać*** ⟨***~ić***⟩ ***się*** speed up; (*w sporcie*) take a run-up; *fig.* gain momentum
rozpęt|ywać (*-uję*) ⟨**~ać**⟩ (*-am*) *fig.* foment, stir up; ***~ać się*** break off
rozpiąć *pf.* → ***rozpinać***
rozpie|czętow(yw)ać (*-*[*w*]*uję*) unseal; *list* open; **~rać** (*-am*) distend, expand; *tech.* strut; ***~rać się*** lounge; **~rzchnąć się** *pf.* (*-nę*) scatter, disperse; **~szczać** (*-am*) ⟨**~ścić**⟩ spoil; **~szczony** *dziecko* spoiled
rozpiętość *f* (*-ści; 0*) span; *fig.* range, scope
rozpi|jaczony F boozy; **~łow(yw)ać** (*-*[*w*]*uję*) saw up; **~nać** (*-am*) undo, unbutton; *płótno itp.* stretch; ***~nać się*** come undone
rozpis|ywać (*-uję*) ⟨**~ać**⟩ *wybory* call, announce; ***~ywać konkurs na coś*** open s.th. to competition
rozpląt|ywać (*-uję*) ⟨**~ać**⟩ disentangle, untangle
rozpleni|ać się (*-am*) ⟨**~ć się**⟩ (*-ę*) multiply
rozpłakać się *pf.* burst into tears
rozpła|szczać (*-am*) → ***płaszczyć***; **~tać** *pf.* (*-am*) slit open, slash open
rozpłodowy foetal; *agr.* breeding
rozpły|wać się ⟨**~nąć się**⟩ melt away
rozpocz|ynać ⟨**~ąć**⟩ start, begin; ***~ynać*** ⟨***~ąć***⟩ ***się*** start
rozpo|gadzać (*-am*) ⟨**~godzić**⟩ brighten (**się** *v/i.*); **~godzenie** *n* (*-a; G -eń*) (*w pogodzie*) bright period
rozporek *m* (*-rka; -rki*) fly, flies *pl.*
rozporządz|ać (*-am*) ⟨**~ić**⟩ (*nakazywać*) order, decree; (*dysponować*) have at one's disposal; **~enie** *n* (*-a; G -eń*) order, decree
rozpo|ścierać (*-am*) *papier* spread (**się** *v/t.*); ***~ścierać się*** extend, stretch (out); **~wiadać** (*-am*) ⟨**~wiedzieć**⟩ tell; *pogłoski* spread
rozpowszechni|ać (*-am*) ⟨**~ć**⟩ (*-ę, -nij!*) spread (**się** *v/i.*); (*popularyzować*) popularize; *doktrynę* disseminate; **~enie** *n* (*-a; 0*) spreading; popularization; dissemination; **~ony** widespread
rozpozna|ć *pf.* → ***rozpoznawać***; **~nie** *n* (*-a; G -ań*) identification, recognition; *mil.* reconnaissance; *med.* diagnosis; *jur.* examination, cognizance; **~wać** recognize, identify (**się** o.s.); *med.* diagnose; *jur.* examine; **~wczy** *mil.* reconnaissance
rozpra|szać (*-am*) scatter, disperse (**się** *v/i.*); *kogoś, uwagę* distract; **~wa** *f* (*-y; G -*) debate; *jur.* hearing; (*traktat*) treatise, dissertation; (*walka*) fight, struggle; ***~wa doktorska*** doctoral *lub* PhD dissertation
rozpra|wiać[1] (*-am*) discourse, hold forth (***o*** *L* on, about)
rozpra|wiaćl'2É się (*-am*) ⟨**~wić się**⟩ (***z*** *I*) settle matters (with); (*zabić*) dispose (of); ***szybko się ~wić*** make short shrift (***z*** *I* with)
rozpręż|ać (*-am*) ⟨**~yć**⟩ (*-ę*) *ramiona* strech out; *tech.* expand (**się** *v/i.*); ***~yć się*** *fig.* relax
rozpromieniony *fig.* beaming, radiant
rozpro|stow(yw)ać (*-*[*w*]*uję*) *drut itp.* straighten out; *ramiona* stretch out (**się** *v/i.*); **~szyć** *pf.* → ***rozpraszać***; **~szony** scattered; *ktoś* distracted; **~wadzać** (*-am*) ⟨**~wadzić**⟩ distribute; *farbę* spread; (*rozcieńczać*) thin down, dilute; *posterunki* station
rozpruwać (*-am*) → ***pruć***; *brzuch* slash open; *kasę* rip open
rozprysk|iwać (*-uję*) ⟨**~ać**⟩ spray; ***pryskać***
rozprząc (→ *-prząc*) → ***rozprzęgać***
rozprzeda(wa)ć → ***wyprzedawać***
rozprzestrzeni|ać (*-am*) ⟨**~ć**⟩ → ***rozpowszechniać***; **~(a)ć się** spread
rozprzę|gać (*-am*) ⟨**~gnąć**⟩ (*-nę*) *konia* unharness, unhitch; *fig.* disarrange
rozprzężenie *n* (*-a; 0*) *fig.* disorder, confusion; anarchy; ***~ obyczajów*** dissoluteness
rozpust|a *f* (*-y; 0*) debauchery; *fig.* self-indulgence; **~ny** dissipated, dissolute; *fig.* self-indulgent
rozpuszcz|ać (*-am*) dissolve (**się** *v/i.*); (*topić*) melt (**się** *v/i.*); *załogę* dismiss; *plotkę* spread; *dziecko* spoil; **~alnik** *m* (*-a; -i*) solvent; **~alny** (**łatwo** readily) soluble; ***kawa ~alna*** instant coffee
rozpuścić *pf.* → ***rozpuszczać***
rozpy|chać (*-am*) *kieszeń* make baggy; push (**się** one's way); **~lacz** *m* (*-a; -e*) spray, atomizer; **~lać** (*-am*)⟨**~lić**⟩(*-lę*)

R

spray; **~tywać** (*-uję*) ⟨**~tać**⟩ question; enquire (**się** *v/i.*; **o** *A* about)
rozrabia|ctwo *n* (*-a*; *0*) hooliganism, vandalism; **~cz** *m* (*-a*; *-e*), **~czka** (*-i*; *G -czek*) *pej.* stirrer; **~ć** (*-am*) *farbę* mix; *v/i.* stir up trouble
rozrachun|ek *m* → ***rozliczenie***; ***~ek z przeszłością*** getting over the past; **~kowy** *econ.* clearing
rozra|dowany overjoyed; **~dzać się** (*-am*) multiply; **~rastać się** (*-am*) increase, grow
roz|rąbać *pf.* chop up; **~regulow(yw)ać** (*-[w]uję*) deregulate; adjust wrongly; ***~regulow(yw)ać się*** go out of adjustment; **~robić** *pf.* → ***rozrabiać***; **~rodczy** reproductive; **~rodzić się** *pf.* → ***rozradzać się***; **~rosnąć, ~róść się** *pf.* → ***rozrastać się***
rozróżni|ać (*-am*) ⟨**~ć**⟩ distinguish
rozruch *m* start(ing); *mot.* start-up; ***~ próbny*** test run; *t-ko pl.* ***~y*** riots *pl.*; **~owy** starting, launching
rozrusz|ać *pf.* set in motion; cheer up (**się** *v/i.*); **~nik** *m* (*-a*; *-i*) *mot.* starter
rozryw|ać (*-am*) tear (**się** *v/i.*); *fig.* break; → ***rozerwać***; **~ka** *f* (*-i*; *G -wek*) entertainment; **~kowy** entertainment
rozrze|dzać (*-am*) ⟨**~dzić**⟩ (*-dzę*) thin (down) (**się** *v/i.*); **~wniająco** *adv.* pathetically; **~wniający** moving, pathetic; **~wnienie** (*-a*; *0*) emotion
rozrzu|cać ⟨**~cić**⟩ scatter; *fig.* waste
rozrzutn|ość *f* (*-ści*; *0*) wastefulness, extravagance; **~y** wasteful, extravagant
rozrzynać (*-am*) cut open, slit open
rozsa|da *f* (*-y*; *G -*) *agr.* seedling; **~dnik** *m* (*-a*; *-i*) *agr.* seed-plot, nursery plot; **~dzać** ⟨**~dzić**⟩ place, seat; *uczniów* separate; *skałę itp.* blow up; *agr.* plant; → ***sadzić***
rozsąd|ek *m* (*-dku*; *0*) reason; ***zdrowy ~ek*** common sense; **~ny** reasonable, sensible
rozsądz|ać (*-am*) ⟨**~ić**⟩ decide (on), arbitrate
rozsi|ewać (*-am*) ⟨**~ać**⟩ sow (*też fig.*); *fig.* scatter, spread; ***~any*** *też* scattered over
rozsiodł|ywać (*-uję*) ⟨**~ać**⟩ unsaddle
roz|sławiać (*-am*) glorify, extol; **~smarow(yw)ać** (*-[w]uję*) spread
rozsta|ć się *pf.* → ***rozstawać się***; **~j** *m* (*-u/-a*; *-e*, *-ai/-ów*) crossroads *sg.*; **~nie** *n* (*-a*; *G -ań*) parting; **~w** *m* (*-u*; *-y*): ***rozstaw osi*** *mot.* wheelbase; **~wać się** (*-ję*) (**z** *I*) part (with), part company (with); **~wi(a)ć** place; *mil.* post, station; position (**się** o.s.); *palce* spread; **~wienie** *n* (*-a*; *G -eń*) (*w sporcie*) line-up (*też mil.*); *mil.* deployment
roz|stępować się (*-uję*) ⟨***~stąpić się***⟩ part, divide; *ziemia*: open up, split; **~strajać** (*-am*) ⟨***~stroić***⟩ *mus.* put out of tune; *nerwy* upset; **~strój** *m* (*-roju*; *-roje*) shattering; ***~strój żołądka*** stomach upset;
rozstrzel|iwać (*-uję*) ⟨***~ać***⟩ execute (by firing squad); **~ić** *print.* space out
rozstrzyg|ać (*-am*) ⟨***~nąć***⟩ (*-nę*) decide (*też v/i.* **się**; **o** *L* on); turn the scales; **~ająco** *adv.* conclusively; **~ający** conclusive, final; **~nięcie** *n* (*-a*; *G -ęć*) decision
rozsu|nąć *pf.* → ***rozsuwać***; **~pływać** (*-uję*) ⟨***~płać***⟩ (*-am*) untangle, undo, unravel; **~wać** part; *stół* extend; ***~wać się*** *kurtyna*: go up; → ***rozstępować się***
rozsy|łać (*-am*) send out; **~pywać** (*-uję*) ⟨***~pać***⟩ scatter (**się** *v/i.*)
rozszarp|ywać (*-uję*) ⟨***~ać***⟩ tear apart; *ciało itp.* tear limb from limb
rozszczep|iać (*-am*) ⟨**~ić**⟩ split up; *światło* disperse; *atom* split; **~ialny** fissionable; **~ienie** *n* (*-a*; *0*) *phys.* fission
rozszerz|ać (*-am*) ⟨**~yć**⟩ (**się**) widen; extend (*też fig.*); *źrenice itp.* dilate; **~enie** *n* (*-a*; *G -eń*) widening; extension
roz|sznurow(yw)ać (*-[w]uję*) undo, untie; **~szyfrow(yw)ać** (*-[w]uję*) decipher, decode; **~ścielać** (*-am*) spread (**się** *v/i.*); **~śmieszać** (*-am*) ⟨***~śmieszyć***⟩ make *s.o.* laugh, amuse; **~świetlać** (*-am*) ⟨***~świetlić***⟩ (*-lę*) light up; ***~świetlać*** ⟨***~świetlić***⟩ **się** brighten
rozta|czać (*-am*) unfold; *zapach* give off; *fig.* display; ***~czać opiekę*** (***nad** I*) take care (of); ***~czać się*** spread, extend; **~piać** (*-am*) melt (**się** *v/i.*)
roztargni|enie *n* (*-a*; *0*) absent-mindedness; ***przez ~enie*** absent-mindedly; ***w ~eniu*** → ***przez roztargnienie***; **~ony** absent-minded, distracted
rozter|ka *f* (*-i*; *0*) dilemma; ***w ~ce*** in a dilemma
roztkliwi|ać (*-am*) ⟨**~ć**⟩ (*-ę*) move, touch; ***~(a)ć się*** be moved; (***nad sobą***) feel sorry (for o.s.)

R

roztłuc smash, crush
rozto|cza *n/pl.* (*-y*) *zo.* mite; **~czyć** *pf.* → ***roztaczać***; **~pić** *pf.* → ***roztapiać***; **~py** *m/pl.* (*-ów*) slush; ***okres ~pów*** thaw
roz|tratować *pf.* trample all over; **~trąbić** *pf.* tell the whole world about; **~trącać** ⟨***~trącić***⟩ push aside
roztropny reasonable, sound
roz|trwonić *pf.* → ***trwonić***; **~trzaskać** *pf.* smash, shatter; → ***rozbijać***; **~trząsać** (*-am*) *fig.* discuss
roztrzep|any *fig.* absent-minded, distracted; **~ywać** (*-uję*) ⟨***~ać***⟩ *włosy* ruffle; *gastr.* beat
roz|trzęsiony rickety, wobbly; *fig.* worried, excited; **~twór** *m* (***soli*** salt) solution
rozum *m* (*-u*; *-y*) reason; ***odchodzić od ~u*** (***z*** *G*) go out of one's mind (because of); ***brać na ~*** consider; ***mieć swój ~*** have a mind of one's own; ***ruszyć ~em*** think hard; ***uczyć ~u*** teach *s.o.* a lesson; **~ieć** ⟨***z-***⟩ understand (***się*** each other); ***co przez to ~iesz?*** what do you mean by that?; ***to się ~ie samo przez się*** that goes without saying; ***ma się ~ieć*** naturally, of course; **~ny** reasonable; wise
rozumow|ać (*-uję*) consider, think; conclude; **~anie** *n* (*-a*; *G -ań*) thinking; reasoning; ***tok ~ania*** train of thought; ***sposób ~ania*** way of thinking; mental attitude; **~o** *adv.* rationally; **~y** rational
roz|wadniać (*-am*) water down; **~waga** *f* (*-i*; *0*) caution, carefulness; ***brać pod ~wagę*** take into consideration
rozwal|ać ⟨***~ić***⟩ destroy, demolish; *dom też* pull down; ***~ić się*** break down; fall apart; (*na krześle*) lounge
rozwalniający *med.* laxative
rozwałkow(yw)ać (*-[w]uję*) *ciasto* roll out; *fig.* go on about
rozwarty open; ***kąt ~*** *math.* obtuse angle
rozważ|ać (*-am*) ⟨***~yć***⟩ *fig.* consider; weigh (up); **~ny** considerate, thoughtful
rozwesel|ać (*-am*) ⟨***~ić***⟩ cheer up, brighten up; ***~ać*** ⟨***~ić***⟩ ***się*** brighten; ***gaz ~ający*** laughing gas; **~ony** cheerful, happy
rozwiać *pf.* → ***rozwiewać***
rozwiąz|ać *pf.* → ***rozwiązywać***; **~alny** soluble; **~anie** *n* (*-a*; *G -ań*) (*problemu, zadania, zagadki*) solution; (*umowy*) termination, cancellation; (*poród*) delivery; **~ły** dissipated, licentious; **~ywać** (*-uję*) *supeł* undo, untie; *problem* solve; *zgromadzenie, firmę* dissolve; *por.* ***rozwiązanie***
rozwid|lać się (*-am*) ⟨***~lić się***⟩ (*-lę*) fork; **~lenie** *n* (*-a*; *G -eń*) forking; **~niać się**: ***~nia się*** day is breaking
rozwie|dziony divorced; **~rać** (*-am*) open (wide) (***się*** *v/i.*); *ramiona* spread, stretch; **~szać** (*-am*) ⟨***~sić***⟩ (*-szę*) hang up; **~ść** *pf.* → ***rozwodzić***; **~wać** (*-am*) *v/t.* blow away; *włosy* ruffle; *obawy* dispel; *marzenia* dash; ***~wać się*** *mgła*: clear, lift; *fig.* vanish, disappear; **~źć** *pf.* → ***rozwozić***
rozwi|jać (*-am*) unwind, unfold; *zwój* unroll; *sztandar, parasol* unfurl; *cechy, działalność, plany, kraj itp.* develop; *temat* expand on; ***~jać się*** unfold; *fig.* develop, evolve; **~kływać** (*-uję*) ⟨***~kłać***⟩ (*-am*) unravel (***się*** *v/i.*); **~nąć** *pf.* → ***rozwijać***; **~nięty** (***w pełni, słabo*** fully, poorly) developed
rozwlek|le *adv.* in a lengthy way; **~ły** long-winded, lengthy
rozwo|dnić *pf.* (*-ę*) → ***rozwadniać***; **~dnik** *m* (*-a*; *-cy*) divorcé; **~dowy** divorce; **~dzić** (*-dzę*) divorce; ***~dzić się*** get divorced; divorce (***z k-ś*** s.o.); dwell (***nad*** *I* on); **~jowy** developmental
rozwolnienie *n* (*-a*) *med.* diarrh(o)ea
roz|wozić *towar* deliver (***po domach*** home); **~wód** *m* (*-odu*; *-ody*) divorce; **~wódka** *f* (*-i*; *G -dek*) divorcée; **~wój** *m* (*-woju*; *0*) development; *por.* ***rozwijać***; **~wścieczony** enraged; **~wydrzony** impertinent; **~złoszczony** furious, angry; *por.* ***złościć***
rozzuchwa|lać się (*-am*) ⟨***~lić się***⟩ (*-lę*) grow insolent
rozża|lony embittered; morose, resentful; **~rzać** (*-am*) ⟨***~rzyć***⟩ enflame; ***~rzyć się*** heat until red-hot
roż|ek *m* (*-żka*; *-żki*) (*na lody*) cone; **~en** *m* (*-żna*; *-żny*) spit; **~ny**: ***rzut ~ny*** corner (kick)
ród *m* (*rodu*; *rody*) family, stock; ***ona jest rodem z …*** she comes from…
różdżkarz *m* (*-a*; *-e*) water diviner, water finder
róg *m* (*rogu*; *rogi*) *biol.* horn; (*kąt, zbieg ulic*) corner; *mus.* horn, *zwł.* French horn; ***w/na rogu*** on/at the corner; ***za rogiem*** round the corner

rój *m* (*roju*; *roje*) swarm
róść → ***rosnąć***
rów *m* (*rowu*; *rowy*) ditch; (*oceaniczny*) trench
rówie|śnica *f* (*-y*; *G* -), **~śnik** *m* (*-a*; *-cy*) one's contemporary; ***jest moim ~śnikiem*** he is my age
równ|ać (*-am*) ⟨**wy-**⟩ level; straighten (out); ⟨**z-**⟩ (**z** *I*) make similar (to), bring into line (with); **~ać się** *mil.* dress ranks, line up; equal; match; *math.* **~a się** equals, is; **~anie** *n* (*-a*; *G -ań*) *math.* equation; **~ia** *f* (*-i*; *-e*, *-i*) *tech.* plane; **na ~i** (**z** *I*) on a par (with); **~ie** *adv.* equally; just as; exactly (the same); **~ież** *adv.* also, too, as well
równi|k *m* (*-a*; *-i*) equator; **~kowy** equatorial; **~na** *f* (*-y*; *G* -) plain, lowland
równo *adv.* evenly, equally; **~boczny** *math.* equilateral; **~brzmiący** identical; **~czesny** simultaneous, coincidental; **~legły** parallel; **~leżnik** *m* (*-a*; *-i*) parallel; **~mierny** even, regular; **~prawny** with equal rights; **~ramienny** *math.* isosceles; **~rzędny** of the same value; *chem.* equivalent; *fig.* equal
równoś|ć *f* (*-ści*; *0*) equality; ***znak ~ci*** equals sign
równo|uprawnienie *n* equality, equal rights *pl.*; **~waga** *f* balance (*też fig.*); ***wyprowadzić z ~wagi*** throw off balance; **~wartościowy** of the same value; **~ważyć** ⟨**z-**⟩ (*-ę*) balance (**się** out); equate, equalize; **~ważnia** *f* (*-i*; *-e*) (*w sporcie*) balance beam; **~ważnik** *m* (*-a*; *-i*) equivalent; **~znaczny** synonymous
równy (*gładki*) even, smooth; (*płaski*) level, flat; (*prosty*) straight; *oddech*, *krok* regular, even; (*spokojny*) balanced; F *kwota* round; (*jednakowy*) (*D*, **z** *I*) equal (to); *gr.* ***stopień ~*** positive; ***w ~m wieku*** of the same age
rózga *f* (*-i*; *G -z[e]g*) rod, cane
róż *m* (*-u*; *-e*) rouge, pink
róża *f* (*-y*; *G* -) rose; **~niec** *m* (*-ńca*; *-ńce*) *rel.* rosary; **~ny** rosy, rose
różdżka *f* (*-i*; *G -dżek*) divining rod; ***~ czarodziejska*** magic wand
różni|ca *f* (*-y*; *G* -) difference (*też math.*); **~cować** (*-uję*) differentiate; **~czkowy**: *math.* ***rachunek ~czkowy*** differential calculus; **~ć** (*-ę*; *-nij!*) differ (**się** *v/i.*; *I*, ***pod względem*** *G* in; **od** *G* from); **~e** *adv.* differently
różno|barwny multicolo(u)red; **~języczny** multilingual; **~raki** → ***~rodny*** (**-ko**) *adv.* in a multifarious way; **~rodny** multifarious, diverse; **~ść** *f* (*0*) diversity; *zwł. pl.* (**różne**) **~ści** all sorts
różny → ***rozmaity***; (*odmienny*) different (**od** *G* from)
różow|ić ⟨**za-**⟩ (*-ę*) become pink *lub* rosy; **~ić** ⟨**za-**⟩ **się** → **~ieć** ⟨**po-**⟩ (*-eję*) become pink *lub* rosy; **~o** *adv. fig.* in an optimistic way; **~y** pink; *wino*, *fig.* rosy
różyczka (*-i*; *0*) *med.* German measles *sg.*
RP *skrót pisany*: ***Rzeczpospolita Polska*** Republic of Poland
RPA *skrót pisany*: ***Republika Południowej Afryki*** Republic of South Africa
rtęć *f* (*-ci*; *0*) *chem.* mercury
rubaszny ribald, bawdy
rubin *m* (*-u*; *-y*) ruby; **~owy** ruby
rubryka *f* (*-i*; *G* -) column
ruch *m* (*-u*; *-y*) movement (*też fig.*, *pol.*); (*statku*, *ręki*) motion; (*drogowy*) traffic; (*w grach*) move; (*maszyny*) operation; ***bez ~u*** motionless; ***wprawić w ~*** set in motion; ***zażywać ~u*** exercise
ruchliw|ość *f* (*-ści*; *0*) mobility; **~ie** *adv.* busily; restlessly; **~y** busy; (*bez przerwy*) restless
rucho|mo *adv.* movably; movingly; **~mości** *f/pl.* *jur.* movables *pl.*; **~my** movable; moving
ruda *f* (*-y*; *G* -) (***żelaza*** iron) ore
rudera *f* (*-y*; *G* -) hovel, dump
rudobrody with a red beard, red-bearded
rudowiec *m* (*-wca*; *-wce*) *naut.* ore carrier
rudy red
rudzik *m* (*-a*; *-i*) *zo.* robin
ruf|a *f* (*-y*; *G* -) *naut.* stern; ***na ~ie*** astern, aft
rugować ⟨**wy-**⟩ (*-uję*) drive out; oust
ru'ina *f* (*-y*; *G* -) ruin
rujnować ⟨**z-**⟩ (*-uję*) ruin (**się** o.s.)
rulet|a *f* (*-y*; *G* -), **~ka** *f* (*-i*; *G -tek*) roulette; ***~ka*** *też tech.* measuring tape
rulon *m* (*-u*; *-y*) roll
rum *m* (*-u*; *-y*) rum
rumian|ek *m* (*-nku*; *-nki*) *bot.* camomile, chamomile; **~y** ruddy
rumie|nić *gastr.* ⟨**ob-**, **przy-**⟩ brown; ***~nić*** ⟨**za-**⟩ **się** blush, flush; **~niec** *m* (*-ńca*; *-ńce*) blush, flush; ***nabrać***

R

~ńców gain colo(u)r; *fig.* take shape
rumor *m* (*-u*; *-y*) racket, din
rumowisko *n* (*-a*; *G -*) debris
rumsztyk *m* (*-u*; *-i*) *gastr.* rump steak
Rumu|nia *f* (*-ii*; *0*) Romania; **~n** *m* (*-a*; *-i*), **~nka** *f* (*-i*; *G -nek*) Romanian; **2ński** Romanian; ***mówić po 2ńsku*** speak Romanian
runąć *pf.* (*-nę*, *-ń!*) fall, collapse; *plany*: fail
runda *f* (*-y*; *G -*) (*w sporcie*) round, bout
rupieciarnia *f* (*-i*; *-e*) junk-room
rupiecie *m/pl.* (*-ci*) junk
rur|a *f* (*-y*; *G -*) pipe; **~ka** *f* (*-i*; *G -rek*) tube; ***~ka do picia*** straw
rurociąg *m* pipeline; ***~ gazowy*** gas pipe
rusałka *f* (*-i*; *G -łek*) nymph
ruski F Russian
rusy'cystyka *f* (*-i*) (*studia*) Russian studies *pl.*; (*instytut*) Russian department
ruszać (*-am*) *v/t.* move (***ręką*** the hand; ***się*** *v/t.*); touch; *v/i. pojazd*: pull out; (*w podróż*) set off; *silnik*: start; ***~ się*** move; stir
ruszt *m* (*-u*; *-y*) (*pieca*) grate; (*do pieczenia*) grill
rusztowanie *n* (*-a*; *G -ań*) scaffolding
ruszyć *pf.* → ***ruszać***; ***nie ~ palcem*** not lift a finger
rutynow|any experienced; **~y** routine
rwać ⟨**po-**⟩ tear (***się*** *v/i.*); ⟨**wy-**⟩ tear out; *ząb* pull out; ⟨**ze-**⟩ *plakat itp.* tear off, tear down; *kwiaty itp.* pick; *v/i. impf.* (*t-ko 3. os.*) ache; ***~*** ⟨**po-**⟩ ***się*** break; *fig.* ***~ się*** (***do*** *G*) be dying (to *bezok.*), be keen (on)
rwący *potok* raging; *ból* stabbing
rwetes *m* (*-u*; *0*) hubbub, turmoil
ryb|a *f* (*-y*; *G -*) *zo.* fish; ***gruba ~a*** *fig.* big noise; ***iść na ~y*** go fishing; **2y** *pl. znak Zodiaku*: Pisces; ***on/ona jest spod znaku*** 2 he/she is (a) Pisces
ryb|acki fishing; **~aczka** *m* (*-i*; *G -czek*), fisher; ***~aczki*** *pl.* (*spodnie*) dungarees *pl.*; **~ak** *m* (*-a*; *-cy*) fisher; **~ka** *f* (*-i*; *G -bek*) → ***ryba***; ***złota ~ka*** goldfish; **~ny** fish
rybołówstwo *n* (*-a*; *0*) fishery, fishing
ryc. *skrót pisany*: ***rycina*** fig. (*figure*)
rycerski knightly; (*też uprzejmy*) chivalrous
rycerz *m* (*-a*; *-e*) *hist.* knight
rychł|o *adv.* shortly; ***~o patrzeć jak*** at any moment; **~y** early
rycina *f* (*-y*; *G -*) figure
rycyna *f* (*-y*; *0*) *med.* castor oil
ryczałt *m* (*-u*; *-y*) flat-rate payment; ***~em*** by flat-rate payment; **~owy** flat-rate, lump
ryczeć (*-ę*, *-y*) roar; *syrena*: wail
ry|ć (*-ję*, *ryj!*; *rył*, *ryty*) burrow; *napis* inscribe; **~del** *m* (*-dla*; *-dle*) spade
rydz *m* (*-a*; *-e*) *bot.* saffron milk cap
ryg|iel *m* (*-gla*; *-gle*) bolt; **~lować** ⟨**za-**⟩ (*-uję*) bolt
rygor *m* (*-u*; *-y*) discipline; *jur.* ***pod ~em*** (*G*) under the penalty (of); **~ystyczny** rigorous
ryj 1. *m* (*-a*; *-e*) snout; V mug; **2.** → ***ryć***
ryk *m* (*-u*; *-i*) roar, bellow, yell; **~nąć** *v/s.* (*-nę*) → ***ryczeć***
rym *m* (*-u*; *-y*) rhyme
rymarz *m* (*-a*; *-e*) leather-worker
rymować (*-uję*) rhyme (***się*** *v/s.*)
rynek *m* (*-nku*; *-nki*) market(place); *econ.* (***krajowy*** domestic) market; ***wypuścić na ~*** launch; ***~ papierów wartościowych*** stock exchange
rynkowy market
ryn|na *f* (*-y*; *G -nien*) gutter; drainpipe; **~sztok** *m* (*-u*; *-i*) gutter
rynsztunek *m* (*-nku*; *-nki*) gear; *hist.* suit of armo(u)r
rypsowy *włok.* rep
rys. *skrót pisany*: ***rysunek*** fig. (*figure*)
rys *m* (*-u*; *-y*) feature; ***~ charakteru*** trait; ***~y twarzy*** facial features; **~a** *f* (*-y*; *G -*) crack; scratch; *fig.* flaw; **~ik** *m* (*-a*; *-i*) lead
ryso|pis *m* (*-u*; *-y*) personal description; **~wać** ⟨**na-**⟩ (*-uję*) draw; ⟨**po-**⟩ scratch; ***~wać*** ⟨**za-**⟩ ***się*** begin to emerge; ⟨**po-**⟩ become scratched; **~wnica** *f* (*-y*; *G -*) drawing-board; **~wniczka** *f* (*-i*; *G -czek*) draughtswoman; **~wnik** *m* (*-a*; *-cy*) draughtsman
rysun|ek *m* (*-nku*; *-nki*) (***w ołówku, węglem*** pencil, charcoal) drawing; ***nauka ~ku*** drawing lessons *pl.*; **~ki** *pl. szkoła*: drawing class; **~kowy** drawing; ***film ~kowy*** (animated) cartoon
ryś *m* (*-sia*; *-sie*) *zo.* lynx
rytm *m* (*-u*; *-y*) rhythm; **~iczny** rhythmic(al)
rytować ⟨**wy-**⟩ engrave
rytualny ritual
rywal *m* (*-a*; *-e*) rival, competitor; **~izacja** *f* (*-i*; *-e*) rivalry; competition; **~izo-**

R

wać (*-uję*) compete (**z** *I* with; **o** *L* for); **~ka** *f* (*-i*; *G -lek*) rival, competitor
ryzykancki risky; reckless
ryzyko *n* (*-a*; *0*) risk; **~wać** (*-uję*) risk; **~wny** risky
ryż *m* (*-u*; *0*) *bot.*, *gastr.* rice; **~owy** rice
ryży → **rudy**
rzadk|i rare; uncommon; infrequent; *płyn*, *włosy itp.* thin; **z ~a** rarely, once in a while; **~o** *adv.* rarely; uncommonly; thinly; sparsely; **~o zaludniony** sparsely populated; **~o kto** hardly anyone; **~ość** *f* (*-ści*; *0*) rarity
rzadziej *adv. comp. od* → **rzadko**
rząd[1] *m* (*rzędu*; *rzędy*) line, row; *biol*, *math.* order; **z rzędu, pod ~** in a row; in succession; **drugi z rzędu** next; **w pierwszym rzędzie** above all, in the first place; **wydatki rzędu …** expenses in the order of …
rząd[2] (*-u*; *-y*) government; **~y** *pl.* rule, regime; **związek ~u** *gr.* agreement, concord; **~ca** *m* (*-y*; *G -ów*) administrator, manager
rządek *m* (*-dka*; *-dki*) row, line
rzą|dowy government(al); **~dzić** (*-dzę*) (*I*) govern (*też gr.*); *fig.* order about; **~dzić się** give the orders
rzec say; **jak się rzekło** as I've said; **~ można** one can say
rzecz *f* (*-y*) thing; (*sprawa*) matter; **~ sama przez się zrozumiała** self-evident thing; **ogólnie ~ biorąc** in general; (**cała**) **~ w tym, że** the matter is (that); **ściśle ~ biorąc** to be precise; **na ~** (*G*) in favo(u)r (of); **od ~y** irrelevant(ly); **jak ~y stoją, jak się ~ ma** as things stand (at the moment); **mówić od ~y** wander; (**przystąpić**) **do ~y** come to the point; **co to ma do ~y?** what has that got to do with it?; **niestworzone ~y** nonsense
rzeczka *f* (*-i*; *G -czek*) → **rzeka**
rzeczni|czka *f* (*-i*; *G -czek*), **~k** *m* (*-a*; *-cy*) (**rządu** government's) spokesperson; **~k patentowy** patent agent; **~k praw obywatelskich** ombudsman, ombudswoman
rzeczny river
rzeczo|wnik *m* (*-a*; *-i*) *gr.* noun; **~wo** *adv.* to the point; **~wość** *f* (*-ści*; *0*) matter-of-factness; **~wy** matter-of-fact; businesslike; **~znawca** *m* (*-y*; *G -ców*) expert
rzeczpospolita *f* [-'pOli-] (*rzecz[y]…'litej*, *…'litą itp.*; *'lite*, *-'litych -itp.*) republic; **♀ Polska** the Republic of Poland
rzeczywist|ość *f* (*-ści*; *0*) reality; **w ~ości** in reality; as a matter of fact; **~y** real; **~y członek** full member
rzeczywiście *adv.* really
rzednąć ⟨**z-**⟩ (*-nę*, *-nął/-dł!*) thin, become thin
rzek|a *f* (*-i*; *G -*) river; *fig.* stream; **w górę ~i** upstream
rzek|li, ~ł(a, -o) → **rzec**; **~omo** *adv.* allegedly; **~omy** alleged
rzekotka *f* (*-i*; *G -tek*) *zo.* tree frog
rzemie|nny leather; **~ń** *m* (*-nia*; *-nie*) (leather) belt, (leather) strap
rzemieślni|czy craft guild; **~k** *m* (*-a*; *-cy*) craftsman, tradesman
rzemiosło *n* (*-a*; *G -*) craft, trade; **~ artystyczne** arts and crafts *pl.*
rzemyk *m* (*-a*; *-i*) strap
rzep *m* (*-a*; *-y*) burr; (*zapięcie*) *TM* Velcro ; **~a** *f* (*-y*; *G -*) *bot.* turnip; **~ak** *m* (*-a*; *-i*) *bot.* rape
rzepka *f* (*-i*; *G -pek*) → **rzepa**; *anat.* kneecap
rzesz|a *f* (*-y*; *G -e*) throng, crowd; **~e** *pl.* masses *pl.*; **♀a** *hist.* Third Reich
rześk|i fresh; brisk; **~o** *adv.* briskly
rzetelny upright; credible
rzewny sentimental, mawkish, maudlin
rzeź *f* (*-zi*; *-zie*) slaughter (*też fig.*); **bydło na ~** animals for slaughter
rzeźba *f* (*-y*; *G -*) (**w brązie** bronze) sculpture; *geol.* relief
rzeźbi|arka *f* (*-i*; *G -rek*) sculptor; **~arstwo** *n* (*-a*; *0*) sculpture; **~arz** *m* (*-a*; *-e*) sculptor; **~ć** ⟨**wy-**⟩ (*-bię*) sculpture, sculpt
rzeźni|a *f* (*-i*; *-e*) slaughterhouse, abattoir; **~k** *m* (*-a*; *-cy*) butcher
rzeźw|iąco *adv.*, **~ić** (*-ę*) → **orzeźwiać**; **~y** (**-wo** *adv.*) → **raźny, rześki**
rzeżączka *f* (*-i*; *0*) gonorrh(o)ea
rzęd|na *f* (*-nej*; *-ne*) *math.* ordinate; **~owy**: **siew ~owy** drilling; **silnik ~owy** in-line engine; **~y** *pl.* → **rząd**[1]
rzęsa *f* (*-y*; *G -*) eyelash
rzęsist|ek *m* (*-tka*; *-tki*) *med.* trichomonad; **~y** *deszcz* heavy; *brawa* thunderous; **~e łzy** a flood of tears
rzęsiście *adv.* heavily; thunderously
rzężenie *n* (*-a*; *G -eń*) *med.* death-rattle

rznąć → ***rżnąć***
rzodkiew *f* (*-kwi*; *-kwie*), **~ka** *f* (*-i*; *G -wek*) radish
rzuc|ać (*-am*) ⟨**~ić**⟩ (*-cę*) *v/t.* throw (*też fig.*); → **ciskać**; *dom* abandon; *palenie* give up; *uwagę* drop; *kogoś* walk out on; ***~ać*** ⟨***~ić***⟩ ***się*** (**na** *A*) fall (on), pounce (on); (**do** *G*) rush (to *bezok.*); ***~ać się do ucieczki*** take (to) flight; ***~ać się na szyję*** fling one's arms around s.o.'s neck; ***~ać się w oczy*** stand out
rzut *m* (*-u*; *-y*) throw (*też sport*); *math.*, *tech.* projection; ***~ karny*** penalty; ***na pierwszy ~ oka*** at first glance; (*w piłce nożnej*) ***~ rożny*** corner (kick); ***~ wolny*** free kick; **~ki** dynamic, go-ahead; enterprising; **~kość** *f* (*-ści*; *0*) spirit of enterprise; **~nik** *m* (*-a*; *-i*) projector; **~ować** (*-uję*) project
rzygać (*-am*) V puke
rzym. kat. *skrót pisany*: ***rzymskokatolicki*** RC (*Roman Catholic*)
Rzym *m* (*-u*; *0*) Rome; **~ianin** *m* (*-a*; *-anie*, *-*), **~ianka** *f* (*-i*; *G -nek*) Roman; **♀ski** Roman; **♀skokatolicki** Roman Catholic
rżeć (*-ę*, *-y*) neigh
rżnąć (*im*)*pf* (*-nę*) saw; cut; *bydło* slaughter; (*grać*) blare out; V *kogoś* screw; ***~ w karty*** play cards
rżysko *n* (*-a*) stubble

S

s *skrót pisany*: ***strona*** p. (*page*); ***siostra*** s. (*sister*); ***sekunda*** s (*second*)
sabot|aż *m* (*-u*; *-e*) sabotage, subversion; **~ażysta** *m* (*-y*; *-ści*, *-ów*), **-tka** *f* (*-i*; *G -tek*) saboteur; **~ować** (*-uję*) sabotage
sacharyna *f* (*-y*; *0*) saccharine
sad *m* (*-u*; *-y*) orchard
sadło *n* (*-a*; *0*) fat
sadowić się ⟨**u- się**⟩ (*-ę*, *-ów!*) settle (o.s.)
sadownictwo *n* (*-a*; *0*) fruit-growing
sadyst|a *m* (*-y*; *-ści*), **~ka** *f* (*-i*; *G -tek*) sadist; **~yczny** sadistic
sadza *f* (*-y*; *-e*) soot
sadz|ać (*-am*) seat, put; **~awka** *f* (*-i*; *G -wek*) pond; **~ić** ⟨**po-**⟩ (*-dzę*) *agr.* plant; **~onka** *f* (*-i*; *G -nek*) seedling; **~ony**: *gastr.* ***jajko ~one*** fried egg
sadź *f* (*-dzi*; *0*) hoarfrost, white frost
sakiewka *f* (*-i*; *G -wek*) purse
sakrament *m* (*-u*; *-y*) *rel.* sacrament; ***ostatnie ~y*** extreme unction
saksofon *m* (*-u*; *-y*) *mus.* saxophone
saksoński Saxon
sala *f* (*-i*; *-e*) room, hall; (*w szpitalu*) ward; ***~ gimnastyczna*** gym(nasium); ***~ operacyjna*** *Brt.* operating theatre, *Am.* operating room
salaterka *f* (*-i*; *G -rek*) salad-bowl
salceson *m* (*-u*; *-y*) *gastr.* *Brt.* brawn, *Am.* head cheese
saldo *n* (*-a*) balance
saletra *f* (*-y*; *G -*) *chem.* *Brt.* saltpetre, *Am.* saltpeter
salomonowy Solomon's; ***wyrok ~*** a judgement of Solomon
salon *m* (*-u*; *-y*) drawing-room; (*w hotelu*) salon (*też fryzjerski itp.*); (*ze sprzętem*) showroom; **~owy** drawing-room
salowa *f* (*-ej*; *-e*) ward maid
salutować ⟨**za-**⟩ (*-uję*) salute
salwa *f* (*-y*; *G -*) salvo, volley; (*śmiechu*) peal, burst
sałat|a *f* (*-y*; *G -*) *bot.*, *gastr.* (***głowiasta*** head) lettuce; **~ka** *f* (*-i*; *G -tek*) (***śledziowa, jarzynowa*** herring, vegetable) salad
sam **1.** *pron.*, oneself; *m* himself, ***~a*** *f* herself; ***~o*** *n* itself, ***~e*** *pl.*, ***~i*** *m-os* themselves; (*samotny*) alone; (*bez pomocy*) by himself *etc.*; ***~ sobie*** to himself *etc.*; ***~ w sobie*** in itself; as such; ***~ jeden*** all alone; ***do ~ej góry*** to the very top; ***nad ~ym brzegiem*** just on the shore; ***~e fakty*** only the facts; ***z ~ego rana*** first thing in the morning; ***w ~ą porę*** just in time; ***ten ~, ta ~a, to ~o*** the same; ***tym ~ym*** by the same token; ***~ na ~*** in private; *n* (*idkl.*) tête-à-tête; → ***tak, tyle***; **2.** *m* (*-u*; *-y*) self-service shop
sami|ca *f* (*-y*; *-e*, *G -*), **~czka** *f* (*-i*; *G -czek*) *zo.* female; *w złoż.* she-; **~ec** *m* (*-mca*; *-mce*) *zo.* male; *w złoż.* he-

S

samobój|ca *m* (*-y*; *G -ców*) suicide; **~czo** *adv.* suicidally; **~czyni** *f* (*-yń*; *-ynie*) suicide; **~czy** suicidal; ***gol ~czy*** own goal; **~stwo** *n* (*-a*; *G -*) suicide
samo|chodowy (motor)car, automobile; motoring; **~chód** *m* (*-chodu*; *-chody*) *mot.* car, *zwł. Am.* automobile; ***~chodem*** by car; **~chwalstwo** *n* (*-a*; *0*) self-praise; **~czynny** automatic; **~dział** *m* (*-u*; *-y*) homespun; **~dzielność** *f* (*-ści*; *0*) independency; **~dzielny** independent; **~głoska** *f gr.* vowel; **~gon** *m* (*-u*; *0*) *Brt.* poteen, *zwł. Am.* moonshine; **~istny** spontaneous; **~krytyczny** self-critical; **~krytyka** *f* self-criticism; **~kształcenie** *n* self-education
samolot *m* (*-u*; *-y*) *aviat. Brt.* (aero)-plane, *Am.* (air)plane, aircraft; ***~em*** by plane; **~owy** plane, aircraft
samo|lub *m* (*-a*; *-y/-i*) egoist; **~lubny** egoistic, selfish; **~naprowadzający się** *mil.* homing; **~obrona** *f* self-defence; **~obsługa** *f* self-service; **~obsługowy** self-service; **~pał** *m* (*-u*; *-y*) spring gun; *hist.* arquebus; **~poczucie** *n* feeling; **~pomoc** *f* self-help, mutual aid; **~przylepny** self-adhesive; **~rodny** self-generated; self-produced; autogenous
samorząd *m* self-government; local government; **~ny** self-governing; independent; **~owy** self-governing, local-government
samo|rzutny spontaneous; **~sąd** *m* self-administered justice; **~spalenie** *n* self-immolation by burning; **~stanowienie** *n* (*-a*; *0*) *pol.* self-determination; **~tnica** *f* (*-y*; *-e*) solitary, recluse; **~tnie** *adv.* alone; **~tnik** *m* (*-a*; *-cy*) solitary, recluse; **~tność** *f* (*-ści*, *0*) loneliness; solitude; **~tny** solitary, lonely; *rodzic* single
samo|uczek *m* (*-czka*; *-czki*) self-study textbook; **~uk** *m* (*-a*; *-cy/-ki*) autodidact; ***on jest ~ukiem*** he is self-taught; **~wola** *f* wil(l)fulness; arbitrariness; **~wolny** wil(l)ful; arbitrary; **~wystarczalny** self-sufficient; *pol.* autarkic; **~wyzwalacz** *m phot.* delayed-action shutter release; self-timer; **~zachowawczy**: ***instynkt ~zachowawczy*** survival instinct; **~zaparcie** *n* self-denial; **~zapłon** *m tech.* spontaneous ignition
samozwańczy self-assumed, self-styled

sanatorium *n* (*idkl.*; *-a*, *-iów*) sanatorium
sandacz *m* (*-a*; *-e*) *zo.* zander
sandał *m* (*-a*; *-y*) sandal; **~ek** *m* (*-łka*; *-łki*) → ***sandał***
sandałowy sandal
saneczk|i *pl.* (*-czek*) sledge
sanie *pl.* (*-sań*) sledge; (*konne*) sleigh
sanitar|iusz *m* (*-a*; *-e*) male nurse; *mil.* medical orderly; **~iuszka** *f* (*-szki*; *-szek*) *mil.* nurse; **~ka** F *f* (*-i*; *G -rek*) ambulance; **~ny** sanitary
sankcj|a *f* (*-i*; *-e*) sanction; **~onować** (*-uję*) sanction
san|ki *pl.* (*-nek*) sledge, *zwł. Am.* sled; *sport*: toboggan; **~na** *f* (*-y*; *0*) sleigh ride
sapać (*-ię*) pant, gasp
saper *m* (*-a*; *-rzy*) *mil.* engineer
sardela *f* (*-i*; *-e*) *zo.* anchovy
sardynka *f* (*-i*; *-nek*) *zo.* sardine
sarkać (*-am*) grumble, complain
sarkastyczny sarcastic
sarn|a *f* (*-y*; *G -ren*) *zo.* deer; **~ina** *f* (*-y*; *0*) venison; *gastr.* roast venison
sasanka *f* (*-i*; *G -nek*) *bot.* anemone
saski Saxon
saszetka *f* (*-i*; *G -tek*) sachet
sateli|ta *m* (*-y*; *G -tów*) satellite; **~tarny** satellite; ***antena ~tarna*** satellite dish
satyna *f* (*-y*; *G -*) satin
satynow|any *papier* supercalendered; **~y** satin; *fig.* satiny
satyr|a *f* (*-y*; *G -*) satire; **~yczny** satirical
satysfakcj|a *f* (*-i*; *0*) satisfaction; gratification; **~onować** (*-uję*) satisfy; **~onujący** *też* rewarding
są *3. os. pl. pres.* → ***być***
sącz|ek *m* (*-czka*; *-czki*) filter; *tech.*, *med.* drain; **~yć** (*-ę*) filter; *napój* sip; ***~yć się*** seep, trickle
sąd *m* (*-u*; *-y*) *jur.* court; (*ocena*) judg(e)-ment, verdict; ***~ ostateczny*** Last Judgement; ***≈ Najwyższy*** Supreme Court; ***podawać do ~u*** go to court, sue; ***wyrobić sobie ~*** (***o*** *L*) form an opinion (about); **~ownictwo** *n* (*-a*; *0*) jurisdiction; **~ownie** *adv.* legally; **~owy** judicial; *medycyna* forensic; ***w drodze ~owej*** through legal action
sądzić (*-dzę*) *v/i.* (*oceniać*) evaluate, judge; have an opinion (***o*** *L* about); form an opinion (***po*** *L*; ***z*** *G* by, from); *v/t. jur.* try (***za*** *A* for); (***nie***) ***sądzę, że*** I (don't) think that

S

sąg *m* (*-a/-u*; *-i*) cord
sąsiad *m* (*-a*; *sąsiedzi*, *-adów*), **~ka** *f* (*-i*; *G -dek*) neighbo(u)r; **~ować** (*-uję*) (**z** *I*) live next door (to); *państwo*: border (on)
sąsie|dni neighbo(u)ring; next door (to); **~dzki** neighbo(u)rly; ***mieszkać po ~dzku*** live next door to; **~dztwo** *n* (*-a*; *0*) neighbo(u)rhood; vicinity
sążnisty very long
scalony *obwód* integrated
scen|a *f* (*-y*; *G -*) scene; *theat.*, *fig.* stage; *pol.* arena; **~ariusz** *m* (*-a*; *-e*) script, scenario (*też fig.*); **~arzysta** *m* (*-y*; *-ści*) scriptwriter; **~eria** *f* (*GDL -rii*; *-e*) scenery; setting; **~iczny** stage
scenograf *m* (*-a*; *-owie*) set designer
sceptyczny sceptic
schab *m* (*-u*; *-y*) *gastr.* pork loin; **~owy**: ***kotlet ~owy*** pork chop
schadzka *f* (*-i*; *G -dzek*) date, tryst
schemat *m* (*-u*; *-y*) pattern; (*działania*) routine; *tech.* circuit diagram; **~yczny** *działanie* routine; *wykres* schematic
schlany F blind drunk
schlebiać (*-am*) flatter
schludn|ie *adv.* tidily, neatly; **~y** tidy, neat
schnąć (*-nę*, *-nął/sechł*, *schła*) dry; *roślina*: wither; *fig.* pine away (**z** *G* for)
schod|ek *m* (*-dka*; *-dki*) stair, step; **~owy** staircase; → ***klatka***; **~y** *pl.* (*-ów*) stairs *pl.*; ***ruchome ~y*** escalator; ***zejść po ~ach*** go down the stairs
schodzić (*-dzę*) go down, descend; move (***na bok*** aside); get (***z drogi*** out of one's way); *farba*, *skóra*: peel; *plama*: come out; ***~ na ląd*** go ashore; ***~ z konia*** dismount; → ***zejść***; ***~ się*** get together, meet; assemble
scho|rowany emaciated; **~rzenie** *n* (*-a*; *G -eń*) disorder; (***serca*** heart) condition
schow|ać *pf.* → ***chować***; **~ek** *m* (*-wka*; *-wki*) → ***skrytka***
schron *m* (*-u*; *-y*) shelter
schroni|ć się *pf.* → ***chronić***; **~enie** *n* (*-a*; *0*) shelter; **~sko** *n* (*-a*; *G -sk*) youth hostel; mountain hut; ***~sko dla zwierząt*** shelter
schrypnięty hoarse
schwy|cić *pf.* → ***chwytać***; **~tać** *pf.* grab, seize, grasp; catch (**na** *L* at)
schy|lać (*-am*) → ***chylić***; **~łek** *m* (*-łku*; *0*) end(ing); ***u ~łku*** at the end; ***~łek życia*** autumn of one's life; **~łkowy** decadent
scysja *f* (*-i*; *-e*) argument, row
scyzoryk *m* (*-a*; *-i*) pocket-knife
seans *m* (*-u*; *-e*) *kino*: show(ing); presentation; seance
secesyjny: ***styl ~*** Art Nouveau
sedes *m* (*-u*; *-y*) toilet-seat
sedno *n* (*-a*; *0*) heart (***sprawy, rzeczy*** of the matter); ***trafić w ~*** hit the nail on the head
segreg|ator *m* (*-a*; *-y*) file binder; **~ować** ⟨**po-**⟩ (*-uję*) sort (out)
sejf *m* (*-u*; *-y*) safe
Sejm *m* (*-u*; *0*) *parl.* the Sejm
sekc|iarski sectarian; **~ja** *f* (*-i*; *-e*) section; ***~ja zwłok*** *med.* post-mortem (examination), autopsy
sekr *skrót pisany*: **sekretarz** S(ec.) (*secretary*)
sekre|t *m* (*-u*; *-y*) secret; ***pod ~tem, w ~cie*** in secret, confidentially; **~tariat** *m* (*-u*; *-y*) secretary's office; **~tarka** *f* (*-i*; *G -rek*), secretary; ***automatyczna ~tarka*** answering machine; **~tarz** *m* (*-a*; *-e*) secretary; **~tny** secret
seks *m* (*-u*; *0*) sex; **~owny** sexy; **~ualny** sexual
sekt|a *f* (*-y*; *G -*) sect; **~or** *m* (*-a*; *-y*) sector
sekund|a *f* (*-y*; *G -*) second; ***chodzić co do ~y*** keep perfect time; **~nik** *m* (*-a*; *-i*) second hand
Sekwana *f* (*-y*; *0*) Seine
sekwencja *f* (*-i*; *-e*) sequence
seledyn *m* (*-u*; *0*) celadon, greyish-green; **~owy** celadon, greyish-green
selek|cja *f* (*-i*; *-e*) selection; **~tywność** *f* (*-ści*; *0*) *RTV*: selectivity
seler *m* (*-a*; *-y*) *bot.* celeriac; (*nać*) celery
se|mafor *m* (*-a*; *-y*) *rail.* semaphore
semestr *m* (*-u*; *-y*) semester, term
semi'narium *n* (*idkl.*; *-a*, *-ów*) seminar; *rel.* seminary
sen. *skrót pisany*: **senator** Sen. (*Senator*)
sen *m* (*snu*; *sny*) sleep; (*marzenie*) dream; ***kłaść się do snu*** go to sleep; ***ujrzeć we śnie*** see in a dream
sena|cki Senate; **~t** *m* (*-u*; *-y*) *parl.* Senate
senior *m* (*-a*; *-rzy/-owie*), **~ka** *f* (*-i*; *G -rek*) senior
sen|ność *f* (*-ści*; *0*) sleepiness, drowsiness; **~ny** sleepy, drowsy
sens *m* (*-u*; *-y*) sense; meaning; ***z ~em*** sensibly; ***co za ~ …*** what point there is

S

…; ***bez ~u*** meaningless
sensac|ja *f* (*-i*; *-e*) sensation; **~yjny** sensational; ***film ~yjny*** thriller
sensowny sensible; meaningful
sentencja *f* (*-i*; *-e*) aphorism, maxim; *jur.* tenor
sentyment *m* (*-u*; *-y*) feeling; sentiment; liking; **~alny** sentimental
separ|acja *f* (*-i*; *-e*) *jur.* separation; **~atka** *f* (*-i*; *G -tek*) *med.* isolation room; **~ować** (*-uję*) separate
seplenić (*-ę*) lisp
ser *m* (*-a*; *-y*) cheese; ***~ topiony*** processed cheese; ***biały ~*** cottage cheese
Serb *m* (*-a*; *-owie*) Serb; **~ia** *f* (*GDL -ii*; *0*) Serbia; **~ka** *f* (*-i*; *G -bek*) Serb; **°ski** Serbian; ***mówić po °sku*** speak Serbian
serc|e *n* (*-a*; *G -*) heart (*też fig.*); (*dzwonu*) clapper; ***chory na ~e*** suffering from a heart condition; ***brak ~a*** heartlessness; ***brać do ~a*** take to heart; ***przypaść do ~a*** grow fond (of); ***z całego ~a*** whole-heartedly; ***w głębi ~a*** at heart; **~owy** *med.* cardiac; romantic
serdeczn|ość *f* (*-ści*; *0*) kindness; warmth; **~y** kind; warm; ***~y palec*** ring finger; ***~y przyjaciel*** bosom friend
serdel|ek *m* (*-lka*; *-lki*) frankfurter; **~owy**: ***kiełbasa ~owa*** pork sausage
serduszko *f n* (*-a*; *G -szek*) → ***serce***
seria *f* (*GDL -ii*; *-e*) series; (*znaczków*) set; (*zastrzyków*) course; *mil.* burst; **~l** *m* (*-a*; *-e*) *RTV*: serial, series
serio: ***na ~*** seriously, in earnest
sernik *m* (*-a*; *-i*) *gastr.* cheesecake
serwantka *f* (*-i*; *G -tek*) display cabinet
serwatka *f* (*-i*; *G -tek*) whey
serwet|a *f* (*-y*; *G -*) tablecloth; **~ka** *f* (*-i*; *G -tek*) (***bibułkowa*** paper) napkin; → ***serweta***
serwis *m* (*-u*; *-y*) (***do kawy*** coffee) set; (*obsługa*) service; (*w tenisie*) serve
serwować (*-uję*) serve
seryjny serial; mass-produced
sesja *f* (*-i*; *-e*) session
set *m* (*-a*; *-y*) *sport*: set
seter *m* (*-a*; *-y*) *zo.* setter
set|ka *f* (*-i*; *G -tek*) hundred; F (*w sporcie*) hundred *Brt.* metres, *Am.* meters; F double vodka 100 *Brt.* gramme, *Am.* gram; F pure wool; **~ny** hundredth; ***jedna ~na*** one hundredth
Seul *m* (*-u*; *0*) Seoul
sezon *m* (*-u*; *-y*) season
sędzia *m* (*-i*[*ego*], *i*[*emu*], *-iego*, *-io!*, *-ią*, *i*[*m*]; *-owie*, *-ów*) *jur.* judge; (*w sporcie*) judge, referee, umpire
sędziowski judicial
sędziwy aged, advanced in years
sęk *m* (*-a*; *-i*) knot; F ***w tym ~, że*** the snag is; **~aty** gnarled
sęp *m* (*-a*; *-y*) *zo.* vulture
sfał-, sfas- *pf.* → ***fał-, fas-***
sfer|a *f* (*-y*; *G -*) sphere (*też fig.*); (*w społeczeństwie*) class; *fig.* area; **~yczny** spherical
sfi- *pf.* → ***fi-***
sfor- *pf.* → ***for-***; **~mułowanie** *n* (*-a*; *G -ań*) formulation, wording
sfru- *pf.* → ***fru-***
siać ⟨***po-, za-***⟩ (*-eję*) sow (*też fig.*)
siad *m* (*-u*; *-y*) *sport*: seat, (*kucnięcie*) squat; **~ać** (*-am*) sit (down) (**do** *G*, **przy** *I* at); *aviat.* land
siano *n* (*-a*; *0*) hay; **~kosy** *pl.* (*-ów*) hay harvest, haymaking
siarcz|an *m* (*-u*; *-y*) *chem. Brt.* sulphate, *Am.* sulfate; **~any** *Brt.* sulphurous, *Am.* sulfurous; **~yn** *m* (*-u*; *-y*) *Brt.* sulphite, *Am.* sulfite; **~ysty** (*mocny*) powerful; *mróz* biting
siark|a *f* (*-i*; *0*) *chem. Brt.* sulphur, *Am.* sulfur; **~owodór** *m chem.* hydrogen *Brt.* sulphide, *Am.* sulfide; **~owy** *Brt.* sulphur, *Am.* sulfur
siatk|a *f* (*-i*; *G -tek*) net (*też fig.*); *tech.*, *el.* grid; *chem.* lattice; ***~a na zakupy*** carrier bag, *zwł.* string bag; **~ówka** *f* (*-i*; *G -wek*) *anat.* retina; (*w sporcie*) volleyball
sią|pić (*-ę*): ***siąpi*** it is drizzling; **~ść** *pf.* → ***siadać***
sidła *n/pl.* (*-deł*) snare, trap (*też fig.*)
siebie *pron.* (*GDL* ***sobie***, *A* ***siebie*** *lub* ***się***, *I* ***sobą***) oneself; each other, one another; ***dla/do/od ~*** for/to/from oneself; ***przy/w sobie*** with/in oneself; ***po sobie*** after oneself; ***z sobą*** with oneself; ***blisko ~*** nearby, close at hand; ***u ~*** at home; ***pewny ~*** self-assured
siec *v/t.* chop, hack; *deszcz*: lash
sieciowy net, network
siecz|ka *f* (*-i*; *G -czek*) *agr.* chaff (*też fig.*); *fig.* jumble; **~na** *f* (*-ej*; *-e*) *math.* secant; **~ny** *broń* cutting
sieć *f* (*-ci*; *-ci*) net; (*komputerowa itp.*) network; (*pająka*) web

S

siedem seven; → ***715***; **~dziesiąt** seventy; **~dziesiąty** seventieth; **~dziesięcio-** *w złoż.* seventy; **~nasto-** *w złoż.* seventeen; **~nasty** seventeenth; **~naście** seventeen

siedlisko *n* (*-a*; *G -*) seat; *fig.* breeding ground, hotbed; *biol.* habitat; **~ *choroby*** site of the disease

siedmi|o- *w złoż.* seven; **~okrotny** sevenfold; seven-times; **~oletni** seven-year-old; **~oro, ~u** *m-os* seven → **715**

siedz|enie *n* (*-a*; *G -dzeń*) seat; sitting; F (*pupa*) bottom, behind; **~iba** *f* (*-y*; *G -*) seat; **~ieć** (*-dzę*, *-i*) sit (*też fig.*); F (*w więzieniu*) do time

sieka|cz *m* (*-a*; *-e*) *anat.* incisor; chopper; **~ć** ⟨**po-**⟩ (*-am*) chop, hack; → ***siec***; ***mięso ~ne*** minced meat

siekiera *f* (*-y*; *G -*) ax(e)

sielank|a *f* (*-i*; *G -nek*) idyl(l); **~owy** idyllic

siemię *n* (*-ienia*; *0*) seed

sien|nik *m* (*-a*; *-i*) palliasse, *zwł. Am.* paillasse, pallet; **~ny**: ***katar ~ny*** hay fever

sień *f* (*-ni*; *-nie*) hall-way, entrance-hall

siero|cy orphan; **~ta** *f/m* (*-y*; *G -*) orphan

sierp *m* (*-a*; *-y*) sickle; (*cios*) hook; **~ień** *m* (*-pnia*; *-pnie*) August; **~niowy** August; **~owy** *m* (*-ego*; *-e*) (*w sporcie*) hook

sierść *f* (*-ści*; *0*) fur, coat

sierżant *m* (*-a*; *-ci*) *mil.* sergeant

siew *m* (*-u*; *-y*) sowing; **~nik** *m* (*-a*; *-i*) *agr.* seeder, seed-drill; **~ny** seed

się *pron.* oneself; *nieos.* one, *Brt.* you; ***on ~ myje*** he washes himself; ***myj ~*** wash yourself; ***jeśli ~ chce*** if one *lub* *Brt.* you want it; ***nigdy ~ nie wie*** one never knows; → ***czasowniki + się***

sięg|ać (*-am*) ⟨**~*nąć***⟩ (*-nę*) reach (**po** *A* for; **do** *G* to); *impf.* reach, extend (*G*, [**aż**] **do** *G* as far as); ***jak okiem ~nąć*** as far as the eye can see

sik|ać F (*-am*) ⟨**~*nąć***⟩ (*-nę*) squirt, spray; F *impf.* pee; **~awka** *f* (*-i*; *G -wek*) fire hose

sikor|a *f* (*-y*; *G -*), **~ka** *f* (*-i*; *G -rek*) *zo.* tit

silić się (*-lę*) make an effort, exert o.s.; try (**na** *A* to be)

siln|ie *adv.* strongly; powerfully; **~iej(szy)** *adv.* (*adj*). (*comp. od* → ***silnie, silny***) stronger; more powerful; **~ik** *m* (*-a*; *-i*) engine; **~ikowy** engine; **~y** strong; powerful

silos [s·i-] *m* (*-a*; *-y*) *agr.*, *mil.* silo; storage bin; **~ować** ⟨**za-**⟩ (*-uję*) ensile

siła *f* (*-y*; *G -*) (***fizyczna*** physical) strength; power; force; violence; *mil. pl.* forces *pl.*; **~ *ciężkości*** gravity; **~ *dźwięku*** volume; **~ *robocza*** workforce; **~ *wyższa*** act of God; ***nabierać sił*** recover; ***czuć się na ~ch*** feel up to; ***co sił(y)*** with all one's strength; ***w sile wieku*** in one's prime; ***siłą*** by force; ***siłą rzeczy*** inevitably; → ***opadać, wola***; **~cz** *m* (*-a*; *-e*), **~czka** *f* (*-i*; *G -czek*) athlete

siłownia *f* (*-i*; *-e*) *electr.* power station; (*w sporcie*) fitness *Brt.* centre (*Am.* center)

singel *m* (*-gla*; *-gle*) *mus.* single

sini|ak *m* (*-a*; *-i*), **~ec** *m* (*-ńca*; *-ńce*) bruise; **~eć** ⟨**po-**⟩ (*-eję*) go *lub* turn blue

sin|o *w złoż.* blue-; **~y** *adj.* (*comp. -ńszy*) blue; livid

siod|ełko *n* (*-a*; *G -łek*) (*roweru itp.*) saddle; **~ło** *n* (*-a*; *G -deł*) saddle; **~łać** ⟨**o-**⟩ (*-am*) saddle

siorbać (*-ię*) slurp

siost|ra *f* (*-y*; *G sióstr*) sister; (*zakonnica*) nun; (*pielęgniarka*) nurse; **~rzenica** *f* (*-y*; *-e*, *G -*) niece; **~rzeniec** *m* (*-ńca*; *-ńcy*) nephew

siód|emka *f* (*-i*; *G -mek*) seven; (*linia itp.*) number seven; **~my** seventh; → ***715***

sit|ko *n* (*-a*; *G -tek*) (*kuchenne*) strainer; → **~o** *n* (*-a*; *G -*) sieve; **~owie** (*a*; *0*) *bot.* bulrush

siusiu F: ⟨***z***⟩***robić ~*** pee, wee

siw|ieć ⟨**o-, po-**⟩ (*-eję*) go *Brt.* grey, *Am.* gray; **~izna** *f* (*-y*; *G -*) *Brt.* grey, *Am.* gray, hair; **~owłosy** *Brt.* grey-haired, *Am.* gray-haired; **~y** *Brt.* grey, *Am.* gray

ska, s-ka *skrót pisany*: *spółka* partnership

skafander *m* (*-dra*; *-dry*) parka; *Brt.* wind-cheater, *Am.* windbreaker; *astr.* spacesuit; *aviat.* pressure suit; *naut.* diving suit

skaka|ć (*-czę*) jump, leap; *ptak itp.*: hop; F (*do sklepu itp.*) pop; (*do wody*) dive; (*w sporcie*) hurdle; **~nka** *f* (*-i*; *G -nek*) skipping rope; ***skakać przez ~nkę*** skip

skal|a *f* (*-i*; *-e*, *-i/-*) scale (*też fig.*); ***w ~i 1:100*** to a scale of 1:100; ***na dużą/wielką ~ę*** on a large-scale

S

skalecz|enie *n* (*-a*; *G -eń*) injury; **~ony** injured; **~yć** *pf.* → ***kaleczyć***
ska|listy rocky; **~lny** rocky
skała *f* (*-y*; *G -*) rock
skamieniały petrified (*też fig.*)
skandal *m* (*-u*; *-e*) scandal, disgrace; **~iczny** scandalous, disgraceful
Skandynaw *m* (*-a*; *-owie*) Scandinavian; **~ia** *f* (*GDl -ii*) Scandinavia; **②istyka** *f* (*studia*) Scandinavian studies *pl.*; (*instytut*) department of Scandinavian studies; **~ka** *f* (*-i*; *G -wek*) Scandinavian; **②ski** Scandinavian
skan|er *m* (*-a*; *-y*) *komp.* scanner; **~ować** (*-uję*) scan
skansen *m* (*-u*; *-y*) outdoor museum; *zwł.* museum of traditional architecture
skap-, skar- *pf.* → ***kap-, kar-***
skarb *m* (*-u*; *-y*) treasure; **~ *państwa*** the Treasury, public purse; **~iec** *m* (*-bca*; *-bce*) safe; (*w banku*) strong-room; *hist.* treasure-chamber; **~nica** *f* (*-y*; *-e*, *G -*) *fig.* treasure; **~niczka** *f* (*-i*; *G -czek*), **~nik** *m* (*-a*; *-cy*) treasurer; **~onka** *f* (*-i*; *G -nek*) money-box; (*dziecka*) piggy bank; **~owy** fiscal; ***opłata ~owa*** stamp duty; ***urząd ~owy*** *Brt.* Inland Revenue, *Am.* Internal Revenue Service
skarga *f* (*-i*; *G -*) complaint (**na** *A*, **przeciw** *D* against)
skarpa *f* (*-y*; *G -*) *bud.* slope
skarpet|a *f* (*-y*; *G -*), **~ka** *f* (*-i*; *G -tek*) sock
skarżyć (*-ę*) 〈**za-**〉 sue (**o** *A* for); 〈**na-**〉 inform (**na** *A* against); **~ *się*** complain (**na** *A* about)
skas-, skat- *pf.* → ***kas-, kat-***
skaut *m* (*-a*; *-ci*) scout; **~ka** *f* (*-i*; *G -tek*) *Brt.* girl guide, *Am.* girl scout; **~owski** scout
skaza *f* (*-y*; *G -*) flaw, defect
skaz|ać *pf.* → ***skazywać***; **~anie** *n* (*-a*; *G -ań*) *jur.* conviction; **~any** **1.** convicted; **2.** *m* **~any** (*-ego*; *-ni*), *f* **~ana** (*-ej*; *-e*) convict; **~ić** *pf.* → ***skażać***; **~ywać** (*-uję*) sentence (**na** *A* to)
skażać (*-am*) contaminate
skąd *adv.* from where; **~ *jesteś?*** where are you from?; **~'inąd** *pron.* from elsewhere; **~'kolwiek, ~ś** *pron.* from anywhere
skąp|ić 〈**po-**〉 (*-ę*) (**na** *L*) be mean (with); (***k-u*** *G*) skimp (s.o. s.th.); **~o** *adv.* sparingly; scantily; **~iec** *m* (*-pca*; *-pcy*) miser; **~stwo** *n* (*-a*; *0*) miserliness; **~y** miserly, stingy
skierowa|ć *pf.* → ***kierować***; **~ć *się*** (**do** *G*, **ku** *D*) turn (to); **~nie** *n* (*-a*; *G -ań*) pass, authorization
skin *m* (*-a*; *-i*/*-owie*) skinhead
skinąć *pf.* (*-nę*, *-ń!*) (**na** *A*) beckon (to); **~ *głową*** nod
skinienie *n* (*-a*; *G -eń*) sign (with one's hand); (*głową*) nod
skisły sour, fermented; → ***kisnąć***
skle|jać (*-am*) 〈**~ić**〉 cement (together), paste (together), glue (together)
sklejka *f* (*-i*; *G -jek*) plywood
sklep *m* (*-u*; *-y*) *zwł. Brt.* shop, *zwł. Am.* store
sklepienie *n* (*-a*; *G -eń*) vault
sklepika|rka *f* (*-i*; *G -rek*), **~rz** *m* (*-a*; *-e*) *Brt.* shopkeeper, *Am.* storekeeper
sklep|iony vaulted; **~owy** *Brt.* shop, *Am.* store
skleroza *f* (*-y*) sclerosis
skład *m* (*-u*; *-y*) composition (*też chem.*); (*magazyn*) store, warehouse; *print.* setting; (*w sporcie*) lineup; ***wchodzić w ~*** (*G*) be included (in), be a member (of); ***w pełnym składzie*** complete, in full strength
składać (*-am*) (*zestawiać*) put together, assemble; *papier* fold; *jaja*, *wieniec* lay; *broń*, *obowiązki* lay down, resign from; *przysięgę* swear; *egzamin* sit; *podpis* put, affix; *wizytę* pay; *podanie* submit; *sprawozdanie* present, submit; *oświadczenie*, *ofiarę* make; *zeznanie*, *zastaw* give; *życzenia*, *dzięki* express; *wiersze* write; *pieniądze* save; *print.* set; → ***wkładać, złożyć***; **~ *się*** (**z** *G*) be made up (of), be composed (of); (**na** *A*) form; (*dać składkę*) club together (for)
skład|ak *m* (*-a*; *-i*) (*łódka*) collapsible boat; (*rower*) folding bike; **~anka** *f* (*-i*; *G -nek*) compilation; **~any** collapsible; folding; **~ka** *f* (*-i*; *G -dek*) collection; (***członkowska*** membership) fee; **~nia** *f* (*-i*; *-e*, *-i*) *gr.* syntax; **~nica** *f* (*-y*; *-e*) warehouse; **~nik** *m* (*-a*; *-i*) ingredient; component, element; *math.* summand; **~niowy** *gr.* syntactical; **~ny** *mowa* fluent; *robota* orderly
składow|ać (*-uję*) store; **~isko** *n* (*-a*; *G -*) storage place *lub* yard; ***~isko odpadów*** waste dump; **~y** storage; component
skła|m- *pf.* → ***kłam-***; **~niać** (*-am*) per-

suade (***k-o do*** *G* s.o. to *bezok.*); → ***kłonić***; ***~niać się*** (***do*** *G*) be inclined (to); (***ku*** *D*) tend (towards)
skłon *m* (*-u*; *-y*) nod; (*w sporcie*) bend; (*góry*) slope; **~ić** *pf.* → ***skłaniać***; **~ność** *f* (*-ści*) inclination (***do*** *G* to); susceptibility; *med.* predisposition; **~ny** (***do*** *G*) inclined (to); prone (to); susceptible (to)
skłóc|ać (*-am*) ⟨***~ić***⟩ → ***pokłócić***
sknera *f/m* (*-y*; *G -/-ów*) skinflint
skobel *m* (*-bla*; *-ble*, *-bli*) staple
skocz|ek *m* (*-czka*; *-czkowie*) jumper; (*pl. -i*) (*w szachach*) knight; **~nia** *f* (*-i*; *-e*, *-i*) ski jump; **~ny** *rytm* lively; **~yć** *pf. v/s.* (*-ę*) → ***skakać***; ***~yć na równe nogi*** jump up
skojarzenie *n* (*-a*; *G -eń*) association
skok *m* (*-u*; *-i*) (***w dal, wzwyż*** long, high) jump; ***~ o tyczce*** pole-vault; *mot.* (***tłoka*** piston) stroke; *fig.* jump; **~owy** *anat.* ankle; *mot.* cubic
skoligacony (***z*** *I*) related (to)
sko|łatany confused; troubled; **~łowany** confused
skom|en- *pf.* → ***komen-***; **~leć** (*-ę*, *-/-lij!*), **~lić** (*-lę*, *-lij!*) whine, whimper; **~ple-** *pf.* → ***komple-***; **~plikowany** complex, complicated; **~p(r)o-**, **~u-** *pf.* → ***komp(r)o-, komu-***
skon|- *pf.* → ***kon-***; **~ać** (*-am*) *pf.* die; **~any** F dead tired; **~sternowany** dumbfounded
skończ|ony finished (*też fig.*); completed; **~yć** *pf.* → ***kończyć***; ***~ywszy na*** (*L*) down to…
sko|o-, **~p-** *pf.* → ***koo-, kop-***; **~ro** *cj.* (*jak tylko*) as soon as; (*jeśli*) if; as **~roszyt** *m* (*-u*; *-y*) loose-leaf binder; **~rowidz** *m* (*-u*; *-e*) index
skorpion *m* (*-a*; *-y*) *zo.* scorpion; ♏ *znak Zodiaku:* Scorpio; ***on(a) jest spod znaku*** ***♏a*** he/she is (a) Scorpio
skorumpowany corrupt
skorup|a *f* (*-y*; *G -*) shell; (*raka*) carapace; (*gliniana*) potsherd; ***~a ziemska*** earth's crust; ***~a ślimaka*** snail shell; **~iak** *m* (*-a*; *-i*) *zo.* crustacean; **~ka** *f* (*-i*) shell; ***~ka jajka*** eggshell
sko|ry (*m-os skorzy*) → ***chętny, skłonny***; **~ry-** *pf.* → ***kory-***; **~rzy-** *pf.* → ***korzy-***
skos *m*: ***na ~, w ~*** obliquely, slantwise
skostniały numb
skośny oblique, slanting
skowronek *m* (*-nka*; *-nki*) *zo.* lark
skowyczeć (*-am*) howl
skór|a *f* (*-y*; *G -*) skin; (*wyprawiona*) leather; (*niewyprawiona*) hide (*też fig.*); F ***dostać w ~ę*** get a thrashing; **~ka** *f* (*-i*; *G -rek*) → ***skóra***; (*przy paznokciu*) cuticle; (*sera*) rind; (*banana*) skin; ***~ka chleba*** crust; ***~ka cytryny*** lemon peel; ***gęsia ~ka*** goose flesh; **~kowy** leather; **~ny** skin
skórzany leather
skra|cać (*-am*) shorten, abbreviate; ***~cać się*** be short; ***~dać się*** (*-am*) sneak (***do*** *G* up to; ***przez*** *A* through)
skraj *m* (*-u*; *-e*) edge; (*przepaści, tez fig.*) brink; ***na ~u*** (*G*) on the brink (of); **~ność** *f* (*-ści*) extreme; **~ny** extreme
skra|piać (*-am*) sprinkle; ***~piać wodą*** sprinkle with water; **~plać** (*-am*) condense (***się*** *v/i.*); *chem.* liquefy (***się*** *v/i.*); **~ść** *pf.* → ***kraść***; **~wać** (*-am*) cut away; **~wek** *m* (*-wka*; *-wki*) snippet; scrap
skreśl|ać (*-am*) ⟨***~ić***⟩ → ***kreślić***; *list* write
skrę|cać (*-am*) ⟨***~cić***⟩ *v/t. papierosa* roll; (*wygiąć, też linę*) twist; (*zwijać*) roll up (***się*** *v/i.*); *nogę* sprain; F ***~cić kark*** break one's neck; *v/i. os., pojazd*: turn; *rzeka, droga*: turn, bend; ***~cać się*** writhe (***z bólu*** in pain); **~powanie** *n* (*-a*; *0*) discomfort, unease; **~powany** *fig.* → ***krępować***
skręt *m* (*-u*; *-y*) twist; turning; (*zakręt*) turn; bend; *med.* torsion, twisting
skroba|czka *f* (*-i*; *G -czek*) scraper; **~ć** (*-ię*) scrape (***się*** o.s.); **~ć** ⟨***o-***⟩ scrape off *lub* clean; *rybę* scale; **~nka** F *f* (*-nki*; *-nek*) (*zabieg*) curettage; (*rezultat*) abortion
skrobi|a *f* (*GDL -bi*; *0*) starch; **~owy** starch
skroić *pf.* → ***skrawać***
skromn|ie *adv.* modestly; **~ość** *f* (*-ści*; *0*) modesty; **~y** modest
skroń *f* (*-ni*; *-nie*) *anat.* temple
skrop|ić *pf.* → ***skrapiać***; **~lić** *pf.* → ***skraplać***; **~lina** *f* (*-y*; *G -*) condensate
skró|cenie *n* (*-a*; *G -eń*) shortening; reduction; abbreviation; abridgement; **~cić** *pf.* → ***skracać***; **~cony** shortened; abbreviated, abridged; **~t** *m* (*-u*; *-y*) abbreviation; abridgement; summary; (*drogi, też fig.*) shortcut; ***w ~cie*** in short *lub* brief; **~towiec** *m* (*-wca*; *-wce*) *gr.* acronym; **~towo** *adv.* in an abbreviated form; **~towy** shortened; abbreviated

S

skruch|a *f* (*-y; 0*) *rel.* repentance; remorse; ***okazywać ~ę*** repent
skru|pić się *pf.*: ***~pi(ło) się na mnie*** I had to suffer the consequences (for it); **~pulatny** scrupulous, meticulous; **~puł** *m* (*-u; -y*) scruple(s *pl.*); ***bez ~pułów*** unscrupulous
skrusz|- *pf.* → ***krusz-***; **~ony** repentant, penitent
skrutacyjn|y: ***komisja ~a*** tellers *pl.*, *Brt.* scrutineers
skrwawiony bloody
skry|cie *adv.* in secret, secretly; **~ć** *pf.* → ***skrywać***
skrypt *m* (*-u; -y*) (university) textbook; ***~ dłużny*** promissory note
skry|tka *f* (*-i; G -tek*) secret compartment; ***~tka pocztowa*** post-office box; **~tobójstwo** *n* (*-a; G -stw*) treacherous murder; **~tość** *f* (*-ści; 0*) reserve; secretiveness; **~ty** reserved; secretive; (*tajemny*) hidden; **~wać** (*-am*) hide (***się*** *v/i.*), conceal; *uczucia* harbo(u)r
skrzat *m* (*-a; -y*) kobold, goblin; F nipper
skrze|czeć (*-ę, -y*) screech, squawk; **~k** *m* (*-u; -i*) screech, squawk; (*jaja*) spawn; **~kliwie** *adv.* in a rasping *lub* screeching way; **~kliwy** rasping, screeching
skrzel|a *n/pl.* (*G -li*) *anat.* gills *pl.*
skrzep *m* (*-u; -y*) *med.* clot; **~nięty** coagulated, clotted; **~owy** clot
skrzętny assiduous, diligent
skrzyć (się) (*-ę*) glitter, sparkle
skrzyd|laty winged; **~ło** *n* (*-a; G -deł*) *anat.*, *aviat.* wing; *mil. Brt.* wing, *Am.* group
skrzyn|ia *f* (*-i; -e*) box, chest; ***~ia biegów*** gearbox; **~ka** *f* (*-i; G -nek*) → ***skrzynia***; (*piwa itp.*) crate
skrzyp *m* (*-u; -y*) creak; *bot.* horsetail; **~aczka** *f* (*-i; G -czek*) violinist; **~ce** *pl.* (*-piec*) *mus.* violin; **~ek** *m* (*-pka; -pkowie*) violinist; **~ieć** (*-ę, -i*) ⟨**~nąć**⟩ (*-nę*) creak; *śnieg*: crunch
skrzyżowani|e *n* (*-a; G -ań*) crossing, crossroad(s *sg.*); ***na ~u*** at the crossroad(s *sg.*); ***~e okrężne*** *Brt.* roundabout, *Am.* traffic circle; ***~e na autostradzie*** interchange
skubać (*-ę*) *jedzenie* nibble; *trawę* browse, graze; *drób* pluck; ⟨**o-**⟩ *kogoś* fleece
sku|ć *pf.* → ***skuwać***; **~lić** *pf.* → ***kulić***
skup *m* (*-u; -y*) purchase, buying
skupi|ać (*-am*) ⟨**~ć**[1]⟩ ***assemble, gather together***; focus; concentrate (***się*** *v/i.*)
skupi|ć[2] *pf.* → ***skupować***; **~enie** *n* (*-a; G -eń*) concentration; *chem.* ***stan ~enia*** state; ***w ~eniu*** with rapt attention, raptly; **~ony** concentrated; focused; **~sko** *n* (*-a; G -*) accumulation; cluster
skupować (*-uję*) buy up
skurcz *m* (*-u; -e*) cramp; *med.* contraction; **~ać** *pf.* → ***kurczyć***
skurwysyn *m* (*-a; -y*) V son of a bitch, bastard
sku|sić *pf.* → ***kusić***; **~teczny** effective, efficient; **~tek** *m* (*-tku; -tki*) effect, result, consequence; ***~tek prawny*** legal effect; ***~tek uboczny*** side effect; ***nie odnieść ~tku*** have no effect; ***~tkiem/na ~tek*** (*G*) as a result (of)
skuter *m* (*-a; -y*) motor scooter
skutkować ⟨**po-**⟩ (*-uję*) take effect, be effective
skwapliw|ie *adv.* eagerly; **~y** eager
skwar *m* (*-u; -y*) heat; **~ki** *m/f/pl.* (*G - ków/-rek*) cracklings *pl.*, greaves *pl.*
skwaśnieć *pf.* → ***kwaśnieć***
skwer *m* (*-u; -y*) green space
slajd *m* (*-u; -y*) *phot.* slide, transparency
slalomowy slalom
slipy *pl.* (*-ów*) briefs, underpants; (*kąpielówki*) bathing trunks *pl.*
slogan *m* (*-u; -y*) slogan; (*hasło*) catchword
słab|iej *adj. comp. od* ***słaby***; **~nąć** ⟨**o-**⟩ (*-ę*) get weaker; **~o** *adv.* weakly; ***czuć się ~o*** feel unwell; **~ostka** *f* (*-i; G -tek*) soft spot; **~ość** *f* (*-ści; 0*) weakness; **~owity** weak; (*chorowity*) sickly, feeble; **~y** weak; poor; ***~y punkt*** flaw
słać[1] ⟨**po-**⟩ send, forward
słać[2] ⟨**po-**⟩: ***~ łóżko*** make the bed; → ***rozściełać***; *impf.* ***~ się*** stretch, spread
słaniać się (*-am*) stagger, wobble
sław|a *f* (*-y; 0*) fame; ***światowej ~y*** world-famous; ***cieszyć się złą ~ą*** have a bad reputation; **~ić** (*-ę*) praise, exalt; **~ny** famous, eminent
słod|kawy sweetish; slightly sweet; **~ko** *adv.* sweetly; **~ki** sweet (*też fig.*); **~kowodny** freshwater; **~ycz** *f* (*-y; 0*) sweetness; ***~ycze*** *pl. Brt.* sweets *pl.*, *Am.* candy
słodzi|ć ⟨**o-**⟩ (*-dzę, też słódź!*) sweeten; **~k** *m* (*-a; -i*) sweetener
słoik *m* (*-a; -i*) jar

S

słom|a *f* (*-y*; *G* -) straw; **~iany** straw; **~ka** *f* (*-i*; *G -mek*) straw; **~kowy** straw
słoneczn|ik *m* (*-a*; *-i*) *bot.* sunflower; **~y** sunny; sun; *tech.* solar; ***udar ~y*** sun stroke
słonica *f* (*-y*; *G* -) *zo.* she-elephant, cow
słonina *f* (*-y*; *G* -) pork fat
słoniowy elephant; → ***kość***
słono *adv.* saltily; **~wodny** salt-water
słony salty; ***za ~*** too salty
słoń *m* (*-nia*; *-nie*) *zo.* elephant
słońc|e *n* (*-a*; *G* -) sun; (*światło*) sunshine; ***leżeć na ~u*** lie in the sun; ***jasne jak ~e*** crystal clear; ***mieć słońce prosto w oczy*** have the sun in one's eyes
słot|a *f* (*-y*; *G* -) rainy weather; continuous rain; **~ny** rainy
Sło|wacja *f* (*-i*; *0*) Slovakia; Slovak Republic; **♀wacki** Slovak; ***mówić po ♀wacku*** speak Slovak; **~waczka** *f* (*-i*; *G -czek*), **~wak** *m* (*-a*; *-cy*) Slovak
Sło|wenia *f* (*GDL -ii*; -) Slovenia; **~weniec** *m* (*-ńca*; *-ńcy*), **~wenka** *f* (*-i*; *G -nek*) Slovene; **♀weński** Slovenian; (*język*) Slovene; **~wianin** *m* (*-a*; *-anie*, -), **~wianka** *f* (*-i*; *G -nek*) Slav; **~wiański** Slavonic, Slavic
słowik *m* (*-a*; *-i*) *zo.* nightingale
słow|nie *adv.* verbally; in words; **~nik** *m* (*-a*; *-i*) dictionary; (*zasób słów*) vocabulary; **~ny** verbal; *człowiek* reliable
słow|o *n* (*-a*; *G -łów*, *I -wami/-wy*) word; ***~o w ~o*** word for word, literally; ***co do ~a*** to the word; ***dojść do ~a*** get a word in; ***w całym tego ~a znaczeniu*** in the truest sense of the word; ***ani ~a*** not a word; ***łapać za ~o, trzymać za ~o*** take *s.o.* at one's word; ***dać ~o*** give *s.o.* one's word; ***liczyć się ze ~ami*** watch one's tongue; ***swoimi ~ami*** in one's own words; ***innymi ~y*** in other words; ***w krótkich ~ach*** briefly, in a few brief words; ***~em*** in a word; ***brak mi słów*** I'm lost for words; ***być po ~ie*** (***z*** *I*) be engaged (to)
słowotwórczy word-building
słód *m* (*-łodu*;*0*) malt
słój *m* (*-łoju*; *-oje*, *-oi/-ojów*) → **słoik**; *bot.* annual ring
słówk|o *n* (*-a*; *G -wek*) word; *zwł. pl.* **~a** vocabulary
słuch *m* (*-u*; *0*) hearing; ***zamienić się w ~*** be all ears; ***w zasięgu ~u*** within hearing; ***~ zaginął o nim*** he was not heard from any more; **~y** *m/pl.* (*-ów*) rumo(u)r; ***chodzą ~y*** there is a rumo(u)r; **~acz** *m* (*-a*; *-e*, *-y/-ów*), **~aczka** *f* (*-i*; *G -czek*) listener; **~ać** ⟨**po-**⟩ (*-am*) (*G*) listen (to); follow (***rady*** the advice); (*też* **się**) obey
słuchawk|a *f* (*-i*; *G -wek*) *tel.* receiver; *med.* stethoscope; **~i** *pl.* headphones *pl.*
słuchow|isko *n* (*-a*; *G* -) radio play; **~y** hearing
sługa *m* (*-i*; *G -/-dzy*, -) servant
słup *m* (*-a*; *-y*) pillar; (*latarni*) post; *tel.* pole; *electr.* pylon; **~ek** *m* (*-pka*; *-pki*) post; *sport*: goal-post; *bot.* pistil; ***~ek drogowy*** bollard; ***~ek rtęci*** column of mercury; ***~ek startowy*** starting-block
słuszn|ie *adv.* justly, deservedly; rightly; **~ość** *f* (*-ści*; *0*) rightness; validity; correctness; ***mieć ~ość*** be right; ***nie mieć ~ości*** be wrong; **~y** right, correct; valid; → ***sprawiedliwy***
służalcz|o in a servile manner; **~y** servile
służąc|a *f* (*-ej*; *-e*), **~y** (*-ego*; -) servant
służb|a *f* (*-y*; *G* -) service; ***pełniący ~ę*** (on) duty; ***na ~ie*** on duty; ***po ~ie*** free, in free time; ***zdolny do ~y*** fit for service; **~owo** *adv.* on business; **~owy** business; official
służ|yć ⟨**po-**⟩ (*-żę*) serve (**w** *L*, **u** *G*, *D* in; **do** *G* for; **za** *A*, **jako** as); ***zdrowie mu ~y*** he enjoys good health; ***czym mogę pani ~yć?*** can I help you, Madam?; ***to mi nie ~y*** it does not agree with me
słychać (*t-ko bezok.*) be heard; ***co ~?*** what's new?
słyn|ąć (*-nę*, *-ń!*) (**z** *G*, **jako**) be famous (for, as); **~ny** famous
słysz|alny audible; **~eć** ⟨**po-, u-**⟩ (*-ę*, *-y*) hear
smaczn|y tasty; ***~ego!*** enjoy your meal!
smagać (*-am*) lash (*też fig.*)
smagły dark-skinned
smak *m* (*-u*; *-i*) taste (*też fig.*); (*potrawy*) flavo(u)r; ***ze ~iem*** *fig.* tasteful; ***bez ~u***, *fig.* ***w złym ~u*** tasteless; ***przypaść do ~u*** be to one's liking
smako|łyk *m* (*-u*; *-i*) delicacy; **~sz** *m* (*-a*; *-e*) gourmet; **~wać** (*-uję*) taste; **~wicie** *adv.* deliciously; **~wity** tasty, delicious
smalec *m* (*-lca*; *0*) *gastr.* lard
smalić ⟨**o-**⟩ (*-lę*) singe off

S

smar *m* (*-u*; *-y*) grease, lubricant; **~ *do nart*** ski-wax

smark F *m* (*-u*; *-i*) snot; **~acz** *m* F (*-a*; *-e*) snotty brat; **~ać** F (*-am*) blow one's nose; **~aty** F *fig.* wet behind the ears; **~ula** F *f* (*-i*; *-e*) snotty brat

smarow|ać ⟨**na-, po-**⟩ (*-uję*) spread; (*maść*) apply; *tech.* grease, lubricate; **~idło** *n* (*-a*; *G -deł*) grease

smaż|ony fried; **~yć** ⟨**u-**⟩ (*-ę*) fry (***się*** *v/i.*); roast (***na słońcu*** in the sun)

smętny gloomy

smoczek *m* (*-czka*; *-czki*) *Brt.* dummy, *Am.* pacifier

smok *m* (*-a*; *-i*) dragon

smoking *m* (*-u*; *-i*) *Brt.* dinner jacket, *Am.* tuxedo

smo|lić ⟨**u-**⟩ (*-lę*, *smol/smól!*) smear; **~listy, ~lny** pitchy; **~ła** *f* (*-y*; *0*) tar; **~łować** (*-uję*) tar

smro|dliwy stinky; **~dzić** ⟨**na-**⟩ (*-dzę*) break wind

smród *m* (*-rodu*; *-rody*) stink, stench

smucić ⟨**za-**⟩ (*-cę*) sadden; **~** ⟨**za-**⟩ ***się*** become sad

smuga *f* (*-i*; *G -*) streak; (*brudu*) smudge; (*samolotu*) trail

smukł|o *adv.* in a slim way; **~y** slender, slim

smut|ek *m* (*-tku*; *-tki*) sorrow; sadness; **~no** *adv.* sadly; with sorrow; **~ny** sad; sorrowful; ***~no mi*** I am sad

smycz *f* (*-y*; *-e*) leash; **~ek** *m* (*-czka*; *-czki*) *mus.* bow; **~kowy** *instrument* string

smyk *m* F (*-a*; *-i*) nipper

sna|ch, ~mi → ***sen***

snajper *m* (*-a*; *-rzy*) sniper

snem → ***sen***

snop *m* (*-u*; *-y*) sheaf; **~ *światła*** beam of light; **~owiązałka** *f* (*-i*; *G -łek*) *agr.* sheaf-binder

snów, snu → ***sen***

snuć (*-ję*) *przędzę* spin; **~ *domysły*** speculate; **~ *marzenia*** dream; **~ *się*** *dym itp.*: hang; *myśli*: buzz through (***po głowie*** one's head)

sny → ***sen***

snycerstwo *n* (*-a*; *0*) wood-carving

sob. *skrót pisany*: **sobota** Sat. (*Saturday*)

sob|ą → ***siebie***; **~ie** → ***siebie***; ***był ~ie*** there was; **~kostwo** *n* (*-a*; *G -*) egoism

sobot|a *f* (*-y*; *G -bót*) Saturday; ***w ~ę*** on Saturday

sobowtór *m* (*-a*; *-y*) double

soból *m* (*-bola*; *-bole*) *zo.* sable

sobór *m* (*-boru*; *-bory*) *rel.* council; cathedral

sobótk|a *f* (*-i*; *G -tek*) Saint John's fire; *też* ***~i*** *pl.* Midsummer's night

socjal|demokratyczny social democratic; **~istyczny** socialist; **~ny** social

socjolog *m* (*-a*; *-dzy*) sociologist; **~ia** *f* (*GDL -gii*; *0*) sociology

soczew|ica *f* (*-y*; *G -*) *bot.* lentil; **~ka** *f* (*-i*; *G -wek*) *phot.*, *phys.* lens *sg.*

soczysty juicy; *kolor*, *barwa itp.* rich; *język* earthy; *zieleń* lush

sod|a *f* (*-y*; *0*) *chem.* soda; ***~a oczyszczona*** bicarbonate of soda; F bicarb; ***~a żrąca*** caustic soda; **~owy**: ***woda ~owa*** soda (water)

sofa *f* (*-y*; *G -*) sofa

soj|a *f* (*GDL soi*; *0*) *agr.* soy(a) bean; **~owy** soy(a)

sojusz *m* (*-u*; *-e*) alliance; **~niczy** allied; **~niczka** *f* (*-i*; *G -czek*), **~nik** *m* (*-a*; *-cy*) ally

sok *m* (*-u*; *-i*) juice

sokol|i falcon; **~nik** *m* (*-a*; *-cy*) falconer

sokół *m* (*-koła*; *-koły*) *zo.* falcon

sola *f* (*-i*; *-e*) *zo.* sole

sol|anka *f* (*-i*; *G -nek*) salt water, brine; (*źródło*) salt-water *lub* brine spring; **~ankowy** salt-water, brine

solarium *n* (*idkl.*; *-a*, *-iów*) solarium

sole *pl.* → ***sól***

solenizant *m* (*-a*; *-ci*), **~ka** *f* (*-i*; *G -tek*) (*person celebrating his/her name-day*)

solenny solemn, festive

solić ⟨**o-, po-**; **na-, za-**⟩ salt

solidar|ność *f* (*-ści*; *0*) solidarity; **~ny** cooperative; ***być ~nym*** show one's solidarity; **~yzować się** (*-uję*) show one's solidarity

solidny solid; *fig.* reliable, dependable

soli|sta *m* (*-y*; *-ści*), **~stka** *f* (*-i*; *G -tek*) soloist; **~ter** *m* (*-a*; *-y*) *zo.* tapeworm

sol|niczka *f* (*-i*; *G -czek*) salt sprinkler, *Am.* salt-shaker; **~ny** salt; *chem.*, *geol.* saline; ***kwas ~ny*** *chem.* hydrochloric acid

solowy solo

sołtys *m* (*-a*; *-i*) president of the village council

sond|a *f* (*-y*; *G -*) probe; → **~aż** *m* (*-a*; *-e*) sounding out; (***opinii publicznej*** public opinion) poll; **~ować** (*-uję*) sound

out; *med.* probe; *naut.* sound, plumb
sopel *m* (*-pla*; *-ple*) icicle
sopran *m* (*-u*; *-y*) soprano; **~owy** soprano
sortować (*-uję*) sort
sos *m* (*-u*; *-y*) sauce; gravy
sosn|a *f* (*-y*; *G -sen*) *bot.* pine; **~owy** pine
sow|a *f* (*-y*; *G sów*) *zo.* owl; **~i** owl
sowiecki *pej.* Soviet
sowi|cie *adv.* generously; **~ty** generous
sód *m* (*sodu*; *0*) *chem.* sodium
sójka *f* (*-i*; *G -jek*) *zo.* jay
sól *f* (*soli*; *0*) (**kuchenna** common) salt; *chem.* (*pl. sole*) salt; **być solą w oku** be a thorn in s.o.'s side
spacer *m* (*-u*; *-y*) walk; **iść na ~** go for a walk; **~niak** F *m* (*-a*; *-i*) prison yard; **~ować** (*-uję*) walk, stroll (**po** *L* around)
spacz|enie *n* (*-a*; *G -eń*) warp(ing); **~ony** warped
spać sleep (*też fig.*)
spad (*-y*; *-u*) slope, incline; **~y** *pl.* (*owoce*) windfalls *pl.*; **~ać** (*-am*) fall, drop (**z** *G* from, off); *teren*: slope; *ceny*: go down, fall; (**na** *A*) *cios*: hit; *wina*: fall (**na** *A* on); *obowiązki*: fall (**na** *A* to)
spad|ek[1] *m* (*-dku*; *-dki*) decrease, fall; **~ek ciśnienia** drop in pressure; → **spad**
spad|ek[2] *m* (*-dku*; *-dki*) heritage, legacy, inheritance (*też fig.*); **otrzymać w ~ku** (**po** *L*) inherit (from); **zostawić w ~ku** leave, bequeath
spadko|bierca *m* (*-y*; *G -ów*), **~bierczyni** *f* (*-i*; *-ie*, *G -yń*) heir; **~dawca** *m* (*-y*; *G -ców*), **~dawczyni** *f* (*-i*; *-ie*, *G -yń*) *jur.* testator; **~wy** decreasing, on the wane; *jur.* hereditary
spadochro|n *m* (*-u*; *-y*) parachute; **~niarka** *f* (*-i*; *G -rek*), **~niarz** *m* (*-a*; *-e*) parachutist; **~niarstwo** *n* (*-a*; *0*) parachuting; **~nowy** parachute
spadzi|sto *adv.* steeply; **~sty** steep; **~ście** *adv.* → **spadzisto**
spa|jać[1] (*-am*) join, connect; *fig.* unite
spa|jać[2] (*-am*) make drunk; **~kować** *pf.* pack (**się** *v/i.*); **~lać** (*-am*) burn (**się** *v/i.*); **~lanie** *n* (*-a*; *G -ań*) burning; *tech.* combustion; **~lenie** *n* (*-a*; *G -eń*) burning; **~larnia** *f* (*-i*; *-e*) (*odpadków*) incinerating plant; **~lić** *pf.* → **spalać**; **~linowy**: **silnik ~linowy** internal-combustion engine; **~liny** *f/pl.* *mot.* exhaust (fumes *pl.*); *tech.* waste gases *pl.*; **~lony** **1.** burnt; *fig.* uncovered, disclosed; **2.** *m* (*-ego*; *-e*) (*w sporcie*) offside
spani|e *n* (*-a*; *0*) sleeping; **miejsce do ~a** sleeping place
sparaliżowany paralysed (*też fig.*)
spa|r- *pf.* → **par-**; **~rz-** *pf.* → **parz-**
spas|iony, ~ły obese, fat
spastyczny *med.* spastic
spaść[1] *pf.* → **spadać**
spawa|cz *m* (*-a*; *-e*) *tech.* welder; **~ć** (*-am*) *tech.* weld; **~rka** *f* (*-i*; *G -rek*) *tech.* welder, welding machine
spazm *m* (*-u*; *-y*) spasm
spec *m* F (*-a*; *-e*) expert
specjali|sta *m* (*-y*; *-ści*, *G -ów*), **~stka** *f* (*-i*; *G -tek*) specialist; **lekarz ~sta** consultant, specialist; **~styczny** specialist, specialized; **~zować się** ⟨**wy- się**⟩ (*-uję*) specialize (**w** *L* in)
specjaln|ie *adv.* peculiarly, (e)specially; **~ość** *f* (*-ści*) speciality (*też gastr.*); **~y** special
specyficzny specific, peculiar
spedycyjny shipping, forwarding
spektrum *n* (*idkl.*; *-a*; *-ów*) spectrum; range
spektakl *m* (*-u*; *-e*) *theat.* performance
spekul|acja *f* (*-i*; *-e*) speculation; **~ant** *m* (*-a*; *-ci*), **~antka** *f* (*-i*; *G -tek*) speculator; **~ować** (*-uję*) speculate
spełn|iać (*-am*) ⟨**~nić**⟩ *warunek itp.* meet; *prośbę itp.* grant; *postanowienia* fulfil(l); *funkcję* serve, perform; **~niać się** *życzenie*: come true; **~nienie** *n* (*-a*; *G -eń*) granting, meeting; performance; realization; **~zać** (*-am*) ⟨**~znąć**⟩ fail, end in failure; *pf.* (*kolor*) → **płowieć**
sperma *f* (*-y*; *G -*) sperm, semen
speszony mixed-up, confused; → **peszyć**
spędz|ać (*-am*) ⟨**~ić**⟩ *bydło* round up, gather; *czas* spend; *płód* abort
spiąć *pf.* → **spinać**
spi|czasto *adv.* pointedly, sharply; **~czasty** pointed, sharp; **~ć** *pf.* → **spijać**
spie|kać (*-am*) ⟨**~c**⟩ bake, burn; *tech.* sinter; **~c się na słońcu** sun-burn
spienięż|ać (*-am*) ⟨**~yć**⟩ (*-ę*) sell, cash in
spie|niony foamy, frothy, bubbly
spie|rać się[1] (*-am*) argue (**o** *A* about)
spie|rać[2] (*-am*) *plamę* wash up; **~rzchnięty** parched; *wargi też* chapped
spiesz|ny, ~yć → **śpiesz-**

S

spięcie *n* (*-a*; *G -ęć*) *electr.* short-circuit; *fig.* clash
spiętrz|ać (*-am*) ⟨**~yć**⟩ tower up, pile up; *wodę* dam up
spijać (*-am*) drink off; F get drunk; ***spić się*** *pf.* get drunk
spiker *m* (*-a*; *-rzy*), **~ka** *f* (*-i*; *G -rek*) announcer; newscaster
spilśniony → ***pilśniowy***
spiłow(yw)ać (*-*[*w*]*uję*) saw off; (*pilnikiem*) file off
spin|acz *m* (*-a*; *-e*) paper-clip; **~ać** (*-am*) staple together; **~ka** *f* (*-i*; *G -nek*) cuff(-link); ***~ka do włosów*** *Brt.* hair-grip, *Am.* bobby pin
spirala *f* (*-i*; *-e*) spiral; *med.* (*domaciczna*) loop
spiry|tus *m* (*-u*; *0*) spirit, ethyl alcohol; **~tusowy** spirit; **~tystyczny** spiritualist(ic)
spis *m* (*-u*; *-y*) list; ***~ rzeczy*** table of contents; ***~ ludności*** census; ***~ potraw*** menu
spis|ać *pf.* → ***spisywać***; **~ek** *m* (*-sku*; *-ski*) plot; scheme; conspiracy; **~kować** (*-uję*) plot, conspire; **~kowiec** *m* (*-wca*; *-wcy*) conspirator; **~ywać** (*-uję*) *v/t.* make a list of; list; ***~ać na straty*** write off; ***~ywać się*** behave (o.s.); ***~ać się*** distinguish o.s., do well
spiżar|ka *f* (*-i*; *G -rek*), **~nia** *f* (*-i*; *-e*) pantry, larder
spiżowy bronze
spla|- *pf.* → ***pla-***; **~tać** *pf.* (*-am*) → ***pleść***
spleśniały mo(u)ldy
splot *m* (*-u*; *-y*) tangle, twist; *włók.* weave; *anat.* plexus; ***~ okoliczności*** set of coincidences
splu|- *pf.* → ***plu-*** **~nąć** *pf.* → ***pluć, spluwać***; **~wa** *f* (*-y*; *G -*) F shooting-iron; **~waczka** *f* (*-i*; *G -czek*) spittoon; **~wać** (*-am*) spit
spłac|ać (*-am*) ⟨**~ić**⟩ pay off, pay back
spłakany tear-stained
spła|szczać (*-am*) → ***płaszczyć***; **~ta** *f* (*-y*; *G -*) payment; repayment; **~tać** (*-am*): ***~tać figla*** (*D*) play a trick (on)
spław *m* (*-u*; *-0*) rafting, floating; **~iać** (*-am*) ⟨**~ić**⟩ float, raft; *fig.* get rid of; **~ny** navigable
spłon|ąć *pf.* get burnt; **~ka** *f* (*-i*; *G -nek*) detonator
spłowiały faded
spłu|czka *f* (*-i*; *-czek*) (*w toalecie*) flush; **~kiwać** (*-uję*) ⟨**~kać**⟩ rinse (off); *toaletę* flush
spły|nąć *pf.* → ***spływać***; **~w** *m* (*-u*; *-y*) drain; outlet; ***~w tratwą*** voyage by raft; **~wać** (*-am*) drain away; flow off *lub* away; *pot*, *łzy*: run; *tratwa*: float downstream; ***~wać krwią*** be stained with blood; F ***~waj!*** get lost!
spocony sweaty
spocz|ąć *pf.* → ***spoczywać***; **~ynek** *m* (*-nku*; *0*) rest; ***miejsce ostatniego ~ynku*** last resting-place; ***w stanie ~ynku*** retired; **~ywać** (*-am*) rest; *fig.* lie
spod *prp.* (*G*) from under
spod|ek *m* (*-dka*; *-dki*) saucer; **~em** *adv.* below, underneath; **~enki** *pl.* (*-nek*) shorts *pl.*; **~ni** bottom; **~nie** *pl.* (*-i*) *zwł. Brt.* trousers *pl.*, *zwł. Am.* pants *pl.*; **~nium** *n* (*-u*; *-y lub idkl.*) *Brt.* trouser suit, *Am.* pant suit
spodoba|ć się *pf.*: ***to ci się ~*** you will like it, you will enjoy it; → ***podobać się***
spody *pl.* → ***spód***
spodziewa|ć się (*-am*) (*G*) expect; hope; ***nie ~ł się niczego złego*** he was unsuspecting
spoglądać (*-am*) (***na*** *A*) look (at), glance (at)
spo|ić *pf.* → ***spajać¹, spajać²***; **~ina** *f* (*-y*; *G -*) weld; joint; **~isty** compact; *fig.* coherent; **~iwo** *n* (*-a*; *G -*) binder, binding material
spojó|wka *f* (*-i*; *G -wek*) *anat.* conjunctiva; ***zapalenie ~wek*** conjunctivitis
spojrze|ć *pf.* → ***spoglądać***; **~nie** *n* (*-a*; *G -eń*) look, glance
spo|kojny calm, peaceful; **~kój** *m* (*-koju*) peace, calm; ***daj mi ~kój*** leave me alone
spokrewniony related (***z*** *I* to)
spolszcz|ać (*-am*) ⟨**~yć**⟩ (*-ę*) translate into Polish; polonize
społecz|eństwo *n* (*-a*; *G -*) society, community; **~ność** *f* (*-ści*) community; **~ny** social; (*dla społeczeństwa*) community
społem *adv.* together
spo|między *prp.* (*G*) from among; **~nad** *prp.* (*G*) from above
sponsorować (*-uję*) sponsor
spontaniczny spontaneous, impulsive
spo|pielały burnt to ashes; **~pu-** *pf.* → ***popu-***; **~radycznie** *adv.* sporadically,

occasionally; **~radyczny** sporadic, occasional
spor|ny disputable, questionable; **~o** *adv.* a lot of, plenty of
sport *m* (*-u*; *-y*) sport; ***~y** pl.* ***zimowe*** winter sports *pl.*; **~owiec** *m* (*-wca*; *-wcy*) sportsman; **~owo** *adv.* in a sporty manner; **~owy** sport, sporting, sports; **~smen** *m* (*-a*; *-i*) sportsman; **~smenka** *f* (*-i*; *G -nek*) sportswoman
spory 1. big, large; fair; **2.** *pl.* → ***spór***
sporysz *m* (*-u*; *-e*) *bot.* ergot
sporządz|ać (*-am*) ⟨**~*ić***⟩ *pismo*, make; *testament jur.* draw up; → ***przyrządzać***
sposobność *f* (*-ści*) opportunity
sposób *m* (*-sobu*; *-soby*) way, manner; means *sg.*; ***~ użycia*** instructions *pl.* for use; ***w ten ~*** (in) this way; ***w następujący ~*** in the following way; ***jakimś sposobem*** in some way, somehow; ***w istotny ~*** significantly; ***wszelkimi sposobami*** by hook or by crook; ***w żaden ~, żadnym sposobem*** by no means; ***nie ~*** (***jest***) it is impossible
spostrze|gać (*-am*) ⟨**~*c***⟩ perceive, sight; (*też odczuwać*) notice; **~żenie** *n* (*-a*; *G -eń*) observation
spośród *prp.* (*G*) → ***spomiędzy***
spot|ę- *pf.* → ***potę-***; **~kać** *pf.* → ***spotykać***; **~kanie** *n* (*-a*; *G -ań*) meeting, encounter; *sport*: match; (*umówione*) appointment
spotnieć *pf.* → ***pocić się, potnieć***
spotwarz|ać (*-am*) ⟨**~*yć***⟩ (*-ę*) slander, libel
spotyka|ć (*-am*) *v/t.* meet, encounter; *Nowy Rok* greet; (*t-ko 3. os.*) *bieda*: happen to; *kara, nieszczęście*: befall to; ***~ć się*** meet (***z*** *I v/i.*); *fig.* (***z*** *I*) meet (with); ***to się często ~*** you can often see this
spowiadać ⟨***wy-***⟩ (*-am*) *rel.* hear *s.o.'s* confession; ***~*** ⟨***wy-***⟩ ***się*** go to confession; (***z*** *I*) confess
spowiednik *m* (*-a*; *-cy*) *rel.* confessor
spowiedź *f* (*-dzi*) *rel.* confession
spo|winowacony related; **~wodowany** caused (***przez*** *A* by)
spowszedniały commonplace, ordinary
spoza *prp.* (*G*) from; from outside; from behind
spoży|cie *n* (*-a*; *0*) consumption; use; **~wać** (*-am*) ⟨**~*ć***⟩ consume, use up; eat; **~wca** *m* (*-y*; *G -ców*) consumer, user; **~wczy** food; ***sklep ~wczy*** grocer('s), food shop
spód *m* (*spodu*; *spody*) bottom; (*listy, strony*) foot; (*podeszwa*) sole; ***na spodzie, u spodu*** at the bottom; ***pod spodem*** underneath; ***od spodu*** from below; **~nica** *f* (*-y*; *G -*), **~niczka** *f* (*-i*; *G -czek*) skirt
spój|nik *m* (*-a*; *-i*) *gr.* conjunction; **~ność** *f* (*-ści*; *0*) coherence, cohesion
spół|dzielczy cooperative; **~dzielnia** *f* (*-i*; *-e*) cooperative; **~głoska** *f* (*-i*; *G -sek*) *gr.* consonant; **~ka** *f* (*-i*; *G -łek*) *econ.* partnership; company; ***do ~ki*** (***z*** *I*) together (with); **~kować** (*-uję*) copulate
spór *m* (*sporu*; *spory*) argument, quarrel (***z powodu*** *G* about)
spóźni|ać się (*-am*) ⟨**~*ć się***⟩ be late; *impf. zegar*: be slow; ***~ć się na pociąg*** miss the train; **~enie n** (*-a*; *G -eń*) delay, hold-up; **~ony** late, delayed
spra|cowany worn out; **~ć** *pf.* → ***spierać***² F give s.o. a thrashing; **~gniony** thirsty (*też fig.*)
spraw|a *f* (*-y*; *G -*) business, matter; question; cause; *jur.* case, proceedings *pl.*; ***gorsza ~a, że*** what is worse; ***na dobrą ~ę*** after all; ***zdać ~ę*** (***z*** *G*) account (for); ***zdawać sobie ~ę*** (***z*** *G*) realize, be aware (of); ***za jej ~ą*** at her instigation, because of her; ***pokpił ~ę*** F he botched it; **~ca** *m* (*-y*; *G -ców*), **~czyni** *f* (*-i*; *-e, -yń*) perpetrator; ***przeciw(ko) nieznanemu ~cy*** against person(s *pl.*) unknown
sprawdz|ać (*-am*) ⟨**~*ić***⟩ (*-dzę*) check, verify; examine; (*w słowniku*) look up; ***~ić się*** realize, come true; → ***spełniać się***
sprawdzian *m* (*-u*; *-y*) *szkoła*: test; *fig.* lesson
spraw|iać (*-am*) ⟨**~*ić***⟩ (*-dzę*) cause, give; → ***wywierać***; ***~ić sobie*** (*A*) buy, get o.s. s.th.
sprawiedliw|ie *adv.* fairly, justly; **~ość** *f* (*-ści*) justice; → ***wymiar***; ***Ministerstwo ℒości*** Ministry of Justice; **~y** fair, just
spraw|ka *f* (*-i*; *G -wek*) doing; **~ność** *f* (*-ści*; *0*) skill; ability, capability; **~ny** skil(l)ful, able, capable
sprawo|wać (*-uję*) *władzę* exercise;

S

urząd hold; **~wać nadzór** (**nad** *I*) watch (over); **~wać się** *urządzenie*: function; *ktoś*: behave; **~wanie (się)** *n* (*-a*; *0*) functioning; behavio(u)r
sprawozda|nie *n* (*-a*; *G -ań*) report; **~wca** *m* (*-y*; *G -ców*), **~wczyni** *f* (*-i*; *-e*) reporter; commentator; **~wczy**: ***referat ~wczy*** report
sprawun|ek *m* (*-nku*; *-nki*) purchase; ***załatwić ~ki*** do the shopping
Sprewa *f* (*-y*; *0*) Spree
spręż|arka *f* (*-i*; *G -rek*) compressor; **~ony** compressed; *bud.* prestressed; *fig.* tense; **~yna** *f* (*-y*; *G -*) spring; **~ysty** springy; elastic; *fig. też* energetic; → ***sprawny***
sprint *m* (*-u*; *-y*) *sport*: sprint; **~er** *m* (*-a*; *-rzy*), **~erka** *f* (*-i*; *G -rek*) (*w sporcie*) sprinter
spro|- *pf.* → ***pro-***; **~stać** (*-am*) (*D*) be equal (to), to match
sprostowa|ć *pf.* → ***prostować***; **~nie** *n* (*-a*; *G -ań*) correction; denial
sproszkowany powdered
sprośny bawdy, ribald
sprowadz|ać (*-am*) ⟨**~ić**⟩ *v/t.* bring, get; *Brt.* fetch; *lekarza itp.* send for; *towar* obtain; *fig.* lead (**na** *A* to); (**do** *G*) reduce (to); (**z** *G*) import (from), get (from); *v/i.* ***co cię ~a?*** what brings you here?; ***~ać się*** (**do** *G*) be reduced (to); ***~ić się*** (**do** *G*) (*do miejscowości*) move in
spró|- *pf.* → ***pró-***; **~chniały** rotten; *ząb* decayed; *med.* carious
sprysk|iwać (*-uję*) ⟨**~ać**⟩ sprinkle
spryt *m* (*-u*; *0*) cleverness; cunning; shrewdness; **~ny** clever; cunning; shrewd
sprzą|c *pf.* (→ *-prząc*) → ***sprzęgać***; **~czka** *f* (*-i*; *G -czek*) buckle
sprząt|aczka *f* (*-i*; *G -czek*) cleaner; *Brt.* char(lady); **~ać** ⟨**po-**⟩ (*-am*) ⟨**~nąć**⟩ (*-nę*) clear up, tidy up (*też v/i.*); (*usunąć*) remove, get rid of; *zboże* gather in; *fig.* (*zabić*) eliminate; ***~nąć sprzed nosa*** F snatch away from under *s.o.'s* nose; ***~nąć ze stołu*** clear; **~anie** *n* (*-a*; *G -ań*) cleaning up, tidying up
sprzeciw *m* (*-u*; *-y*) protest; opposition; ***bez ~u*** without objecting; **~iać się** (*-am*) ⟨**~ić się**⟩ (*-ę*) (*D*) oppose; be opposed (to)
sprzecz|ać się ⟨**po- się**⟩ (*-am*) argue, quarrel (**o** *A* about); **~ka** *f* (*-i*; *G -czek*) argument, quarrel; **~ność** *f* (*-ści*) (*logiczna itp.*) contradiction; (*konflikt*) conflict; **~ny** contradictory; (**z** *I*) incompatible (with); conflicting
sprzed *prp.* (*G*) (from) before
sprzeda|ć *pf.* → ***sprzedawać***; **~jący** *m* (*-ego*; *-y*) seller; **~jny** mercenary, venal; **~nie** *n* (*-a*; *0*) selling; sale; ***do ~nia*** for sale; **~wać** (*-ję*) sell; **~wca** *m* (*-y*; *G -ów*), **~wczyni** *f* (*-i*; *G -yń*) *econ.* sales assistant, salesperson; **~ż** *f* (*-y*; *-e*) sale; ***na ~ż*** for sale; **~żny** sale(s)
sprzeniewierz|ać (*-am*) ⟨**~yć**⟩ embezzle; **~yć się** (*D*) betray; **~enie** *n* (*-a*; *G -eń*) embezzlement; ***~enie się*** betrayal
sprzę|gać (*-am*) couple; interconnect; **~gło** *n* (*-a*; *G -gieł*) *mot.* clutch; ***włączyć ~gło*** clutch; ***wyłączyć ~gło*** declutch; **~t** *m* (*-u*; *-y*) equipment (*też RTV*); gear; *agr.* harvest; **~ty** *pl.* furniture; fittings *pl.*; ***~t komputerowy*** hardware; **~żony** *m* coupled
sprzy|jać (*-am*) favo(u)r; encourage, further; **~jający** favo(u)rable; auspicious
sprzykrzy|ć się *pf.* (*t-ko pret.*): **~ł** (**a, -o, -y**) ***mi się*** I am tired of *lub* F fed up with it (him, her, them)
sprzymierz|eniec *m* (*-ńca*; *-ńcy*) ally; **~ony** allied
sprzysi|ęgać się (*-am*) ⟨**~ąc się**⟩ conspire (***przeciwko*** *D* against)
spuchnięty swollen
spulchni|ać (*-am*) ⟨**~ć**⟩ (*-ę*, *-nij!*) *glebę itp.* break up, loosen
spust *m* (*-u*; *-y*) *tech. itp.* outlet; *phot.* shutter release; (*broni*, *tez fig.*) trigger; F ***mieć ~*** eat like a horse; ***zamknąć na cztery ~y*** lock up
spustoszenie *n* (*-a*; *G -eń*) devastation
spuszczać (*-am*) let down; *głowę*, *oczy*, *flagę* lower (**się** *v/i.*); *płyn* let out; *psa* let go, ***~ na wodę*** put out, launch; ***~ cenę*** lower the price; ***nie ~ oczu z kogoś*** not take one's eyes off s.o.; ***~ się*** come down; F come, come off
spuści|ć *pf.* → ***spuszczać***; **~zna** *f* (*-y*; *G -*) legacy; (*pisarska*) output, work
spycha|cz *m* (*-a*; *-e*) bulldozer; **~ć** (*-am*) push, shove (***w bok*** aside); **~rka** *f* (*-i*; *G -rek*) → ***spychacz***
sp. z o.o. *skrót pisany*: ***spółka z ograniczoną odpowiedzialnością*** limited liability company; (*prywatna*) Ltd., plc (*publiczna*)

S

srać V (*-am*) shit
sreb|rnoszary silver-grey, *Am.* -gray; **~rny** silver, silvery; **~ro** *n* (*-a*; *0*) *chem.* silver; (*naczynia*) (*pl. G -ber*) silver(ware); **~rzyć** ⟨**po-**⟩ (*-ę*) silver-plate; **~rzysty** silvery (*też fig.*)
sro|czy magpie; **~gi** strict, severe; *mróz* severe, sharp; **~go** *adv.* strictly, severely; **~gość** *f* (*-ści*; *0*) strictness, severity
sroka *f* (*-i*; *G -*) *zo.* magpie; **~ty** piebald
srom *m* (*-u*; *-y*) *anat.* vulva; **~otny** shameful; **~owy** vulval, vulvar; ***wargi*** *pl.* ***~owe*** *anat.* labia *pl.*
sroż|ej, ~szy *adj. comp. od* → ***srogo, srogi***; **~yć się** (*-ę*) rage
ssa|ć suck; **~k** *m* (*-a*; *-i*) *biol.* mammal; **~nie** *n* (*-a*; *G -ań*) *tech.* suction; **~wka** *f* (*-i*; *G -wek*) (suction) nozzle
st. *skrót pisany*: ***stacja*** railway station; ***starszy*** senior
stabil|izować ⟨**u-**⟩ (*-uję*) stabilize; ***~izować*** ⟨**u-**⟩ ***się*** stabilize, become stabilized; **~ny** stable
stacja *f* (*-i*; *-e*) station (*też mot., rail.*); ***~ benzynowa*** *Brt.* petrol station, filling station, *Am.* gas station; ***~ nadawcza*** broadcasting station; (*urządzenie*) transmitter
stacyjka *f* (*-i*; *G -jek*) → ***stacja***; *mot.* ignition (lock)
staczać (*-am*) roll down (***się*** *v/i.*); ***~ się na dno*** *fig.* sink low
stać[1] stand; *fabryka, maszyna*: be idle; ***~!, stój!*** halt!; ***~ na straży*** be on guard; (***nie***) ***~ go na to*** he can(not) afford it
sta|ć[2] ***się*** *pf.* (*zajść*) become, get; ***co się ~ło?*** what has happened?; ***co się z nim ~ło?*** what has happened to him?; ***dobrze się ~ło, że*** it is good that; → ***stawać się***
stadion *m* (*-u*; *-y*) *sport*: stadium
stad|ło *n* (*-a*; *G -deł*) (married) couple; **~nina** *f* (*-y*; *G -*) stud(-farm); **~ny** herd; **~o** *n* (*-a*; *G -*) herd; (*wilków, psów*) pack; (*lwów*) pride; (*ptaków*) flock
sta|jać *pf.* (*-ję*) thaw, melt; **~je** → ***stawać***
stajnia *f* (*-i*; *-e*, *-i/-jen*) stable
stal *f* (*-i*; *-e*) steel
stal|e *adv.* steadily, constantly; **~i** → ***stały***
stalinowski Stalinist
stalo|wnia *f* (*-i*; *-e*) *tech.* steelworks; **~woszary** steel-grey, *Am.* -gray; **~wy** steel
stalówka *f* (*-i*; *G -wek*) nib
stał|a się, ~o się → ***stawać się***
sta|łocieplny *zo.* warm-blooded; **~łość** *f* (*-ści*; *0*) constancy, permanence
stał|y 1. (*m-os stali*) steady; regular; *phys., chem.* solid; *członek, korespondent* permanent; *komisja* standing; *math., koszty* constant; ***~y gość*** regular (visitor); ***na ~e*** for ever; **2.** ***~a*** *f* (*-ej*; *-e*, *G -ych*) *math.* constant
stamtąd *adv.* from there
stan *m* (*-u*; *-y*) condition; state; status; (*jednostka administracyjna*) state; ***~ dróg*** road conditions *pl.*; ***~ wojny*** state of war; ***~ zdrowia*** state of health; ***~ pogody*** weather situation; ***~ wody*** water level; ***~ kasy*** cash (at hand); ***~ rzeczy*** state of affairs; ***~ wojenny*** martial law; ***~ wyjątkowy*** state of emergency; ***Sy Zjednoczone*** (***Ameryki***) the United States (of America); ***w … ~ie*** in … form, in …state; ***być w ~ie*** be able to do, be capable of; ***żyć ponad ~*** live beyond one's means; → ***cywilny, liczebny, poważny***
stan|ąć *pf.* (*-nę*, *-ń!*) → ***stawać***; *rzeka*: freeze over; *dom*: be erected; ***~ęło na tym*** it was agreed that
stancja *f* (*-i*; *-e*) lodgings *pl.*
standaryzować (*-uję*) standardize
stanica *f* (*-u*; *-e*, *G -*) *jakby*: boat harbo(u)r (*with on-site facilities*)
stanieć *pf.* become cheaper
stanik *m* (*-a*; *-i*) bra
staniol (*-u*; *-e*) tin foil
stanow|czo *adv.* decidedly; decisively; **~czość** *f* (*-ści*; *0*) decisiveness; finality; **~czy** decisive, definitive, final
stanowi|ć (*-ię*, *-nów!*) *v/i.* (**o** *L*) be decisive (in), determine; *v/t.* constitute, form; **~sko** *n* (*-a*; *G -*) position (*też mil.*); (*wykopalisk itp.*) site; (*posada też*) post, appointment; (*pogląd*) viewpoint, stance; ***~sko pracy*** work-place; ***zająć ~sko*** take a stand (***w sprawie*** on)
stanowy *pol.* state
stapiać (*-am*) fuse; alloy
stara|ć się ⟨***po- się***⟩ (*-am*) (**o** *A*) try (to obtain); apply (for); *pf. też* get, gain; **~nie** *n* (*-a*; *G -ań*): *zwł. pl.* **~nia** efforts *pl.*; ***dołożyć ~ń*** (**do** *G*) take pains (to do); ***poczynić ~nia*** → ***starać się***; **~nność** *f* (*-ści*; *0*) care; **~nny** careful
star|cie *n* (*-a*; *G -rć*) *mil.* engagement,

S

battle; *fig.* clash; (*w sporcie*) round; *med.* → **obtarcie**; **~cy** *pl.* → **starzec**; **~czać** (*-am*) ⟨**~czyć**⟩ (*-ę*) be enough *lub* sufficient (**na** *A* for); **~czy** *adj.* senile
staro *adv. czuć się* old; **~cie** *n* (*-a*; *G -i*) jumble, junk; **~dawny** ancient; **~miejski** old town; **~modny** old-fashioned; **~polski** Old Polish; (*tradycje*) traditional; **~sta** *m* (*-y*; *-towie*, *G -tów*), **~ścina** *f* (*-y*; *G -*) *szkoła*: form captain; *hist.* starosta
starość *f* (*-ści*; *0*) old age; **na~** for old age
staro|świecki old-fashioned; **~świecko** *adv.* in an old-fashioned way; **~żytność** *f* (*-ści*; *0*) antiquity; → **antyk**; **~żytny** antique
star|si → **starszy**; **~szawy** oldish
starszeństw|o *n* (*-a*; *0*) seniority
starszy 1. *adj.* (*comp. od* → **stary**; *m-os -rsi*); older, elder; (*w hierarchii*) senior; **2.** (*-rszego*;*-rsi*) adult; elder; **~zna** *f* (*-y*; *G -*) elders *pl.*
start *m* (*-u*; *-y*) start; beginning; *aviat.* take-off; *astronautyka*: lift-off; **~er** *m* **1.** (*-a*; *-rzy*) (*w sporcie*) starter; **2.** (*-u*; *-ry*) *mot.* starter; **~ować** ⟨**wy-**⟩ (*-uję*) start, take part; *aviat.* take off; *astronautyka*: lift off; **~owy** starting
starty *adj. gastr.* grated
starusz|ek *m* (*-ka*; *-kowie*) old man; **~ka** *f* (*-i*; *G -szek*) old woman
star|y 1. (*m-os -rzy*) old; **2.** *m* (*-ego*, *-rzy*), **~a** *f* (*-ej*; *-e*), **~e** *n* (*-ego*; *-rzy*) the old, the past; **po ~emu** as before; as it was
starze|c *m* (*-rca*; *-rcy*) old man; **~ć** ⟨**po-, ze-**⟩ **się** (*-ję*) grow old; **~j** *adv.* (*comp. od* → **stary**) older
starzyzna *f* (*-y*; *0*) junk
stateczny stable; *ktoś* sedate, staid
stat|ek *m* (*-tku*; *-tki*) (**handlowy, spacerowy, kosmiczny** merchant, excursion, space) ship; **na ~ku**/**~ek** on board; **~kiem** by ship
statut *m* (*-u*; *-y*) statute(s *pl.*); **~owy** statutory
statyczny static
statyst|a *m* (*-y*; *-ści*, *-ów*), **~ka** *f* (*-i*; *G -tek*) extra; *fig.* bystander; **~yczny** statistic(al); **~yka** *f* (*-i*; *0*) statistics *sg./pl.*
statyw *m* (*-u*; *-y*) tripod
staw *m* (*-u*; *-y*) pond; *med.* joint
stawać (*-ję*) stand (**na** *A*, *L* on; **za** *I* behind; **przed** *I* in front of); (*zatrzymać się*) stop, halt; (*zgłaszać się*) report (**do** *G*, **przed** to); (*zaczynać*) go (**do** *G* to); → **dąb, stanąć**
stawać się (*-ję*) become; → **stać²**
staw|iać (*-am*) stand, put; *fig. zwł.* place; *pomnik* erect; *namiot* pitch; *płot* put up; *pytanie* ask; (*w grze*) bet; **~iać opór** put up resistance; **~iać się** appear; report (**do** *G* to); F get tough; **~ić** (*-im*) *pf.* (*-ę*) → **czoło**; **~ić się** → **stawiać się**; **~iennictwo** *n* (*-a*; *0*) appearance; **~ka** *f* (*-i*; *G -wek*) (**dzienna, podatkowa** daily, tax) rate; (*w grze*) stake
staż *m* (*-u*; *-e*) (practical) training; **~ pracy** seniority; **trzyletni ~ pracy** three years' service; **~ysta** *m* (*-y*; *G -tów*), **~ystka** *f* (*-i*; *G -tek*) trainee
stąd from here; (*dlatego*) therefore
stąp|ać (*-am*) ⟨**~nąć**⟩ (*-nę*) tread, stamp
stchórzyć *pf.* (*-ę*) back out, F chicken out
stek¹ *m* (*-u*; *-i*) (*wyzwisk itp.*) heap, pack
stek² *m* (*-u*; *-i*) *gastr.* steak
stek³ *m* (*-u*; *-i*) *biol.* cloaca; **~owiec** *m* (*-wca*; *-wce*) *zo.* monotreme
stempel *m* (*-pla*; *-ple*) (rubber) stamp
stemplow|ać ⟨**o-**⟩ (*-uję*) stamp; **~y** stamp; **znaczek ~y** postage mark
stenograf|ia *f* (*GDL -ii*; *0*) shorthand; **~ować** (*-uję*) record in shorthand
step *m* (*-u*; *-y*) steppe; **~owy** steppe
ster *m* (-u; -y) rudder; *fig.* helm
sterburta *f* (*-y*; *G -*) starboard
stercz *m* (*-a*; *-e*) *anat.* prostate (gland); **~ący** sticking out; **~eć** (*-ę*) stick out, jut out, project; F stand around *lub* about
stereo (*idkl.*) stereo; stereophonic; **~foniczny** stereophonic
stereotypow|o *adv.* in a stereotyped way; **~y** stereotyped, stock
sternik *m* (*-a*; *-cy*) *naut.* helmsman, steersman; *sport*: cox(swain)
sterow|ać (*-uję*) steer; control; **~anie** *n* (*-a*; *G -ań*) control; **zdalne ~anie** remote control; **~y** steering
sterta *f* (*-y*; *G -*) heap, pile, stack
sterujący steering
sterydy *m/pl.* (*-ów*): *pharm.* **~ anaboliczne** anabolic steroids *pl.*
steryl|izować (*-uję*) sterilize; **~ny** sterile
steward *m* (*-da*; *-dzi*) *aviat.* flight attendant; *naut.* steward; **~essa** *f* (*-y*; *G -*) *aviat.* air hostess, flight attendant; *naut.* stewardess

S

stębnować (*-uję*) backstitch
stęch|lizna *f* (*-y*; *0*) musty smell; **~ły** musty
stękać (*-am*) ⟨**~nąć**⟩ (*-nę*) moan, groan
stępi|ać (*-am*)⟨**~ć**⟩ blunt; **~ony** blunted
stępka *f* (*-i*; *G -pek*) keel
stęskniony nostalgic; longing (**za** *I* for); **~ za ojczyzną** homesick; → **tęskny**
stęż|ać (*-am*) ⟨**~yć**⟩ (*-ę*) *chem.* concentrate; *bud.* brace; **~enie** *n* (*-a*; *-eń*) *chem.* concentration; *bud.* bracing; **~enie pośmiertne** rigor mortis; **~ony** concentrated; *bud.* braced
stłoczony crowded
stłu|c *pf.* → **tłuc**; **~czenie** *n* (*-a*; *G -eń*) *med.* bruise, contusion; **~miony** muted
sto (*m-os stu*) hundred; → **715**
stocznia *f* (*-i*; *-e*) shipyard
sto|czyć *pf.* → **staczać**; **~doła** *f* (*-y*; *G -dół*) barn; **~gi** *pl.* → **stóg**
sto|i → **stać¹**; **~isko** *n* (*-a*; *G -*) stand, stall; (*w dużym sklepie*: *półki*) gondola, shelves *pl.*, (*lada*) counter; **~jak** *m* (*-a*; *-i*) stand; (*na płyty*) rack; **~jący** standing; **miejsce ~jące** standing place, standing room
stok *m* (*-u*; *-i*) slope
stokrot|ka *f* (*-i*; *G -tek*) *bot.* daisy; **~ny** hundredfold
stola|rnia *f* (*-i*; *-e*) carpenter's/cabinet--maker's (workshop); **~rz** *m* (*-a*; *-e*) carpenter; (*meblowy*) cabinet-maker
stol|ec *m* (*-lca*; *-lce*) *med.* stool; **~ica** *f* (*-y*; *G -*) capital (city); (*biskupstwa itp.*) see; **℃ica Apostolska** Holy See; **~ik** *m* (*-a*; *-i*) → **stół**; **~nica** *f* (*-y*; *-e*, *G -*) (pastry) board
stoł|eczny capital; **~ek** *m* (*-łka*; *-łki*) stool; **~ować** (*-uję*) cater for; **~ować się** dine (**u** with)
stołowni|czka *f* (*-i*; *G -czek*), **~k** *m* (*-a*; *-cy*) diner
sto|łowy table; **~łówka** *f* (*-i*; *G -wek*) canteen; **~łówkowy** canteen; **~ły** *pl.* → **stół**
stomatologiczny dental, dentist's; **fotel ~** dentist's chair
stonka *f* (*-i*; *G -nek*) *zo.* Colorado beetle
stonoga *f* (*-i*; *G -nóg*) *zo.* centipede
stop *m* (*-u*; *-y*) *tech.* alloy
stop|a *f* (*-y*; *G stóp*) foot (*też fig.*); (*buta*) sole; (*jednostka miary*) foot (= *0,30 m*); *econ.* rate; **~a życiowa** standard of living; **u stóp** (*G*) at the foot (of); **od stóp do głów** from head to foot; → **procentowy**
stoper *m* (*-a*; *-y*) stopwatch
stop|ić *pf.* → **stapiać**; **~ień** *m* (*-pnia*; *-pnie*) step (*też fig.*), stair; degree (*też math.*, *geogr.*, *fig.*); *mil.* rank; (*w szkole*) *Brt.* mark, *Am.* grade; **~ień wyższy, najwyższy** *gr.* comparative, superlative degree; **do tego ~nia, że** to such an extent that; **w mniejszym ~niu** to a lesser extent; **w wysokim ~niu** to a high degree
stop-klatka *f* (*-i*) freeze-frame
stopniały melted
stopniow|ać (*-uję*) grade, change by degrees; *gr.* compare; **~o** *adv.* gradually; **~y** gradual, by degrees
stopować (*-uję*) stop, halt
storczyk *m* (*-a*; *-i*) *bot.* orchid
stornia *f* (*-i*; *-e*) *zo.* flounder
stornować ⟨**wy-**⟩ (*-uję*) *econ.* reverse
stos *m* (*-u*; *-y*) pile, stack; (*dla czarownicy*) stake; **ułożyć w ~** stack, pile
stosow|ać ⟨**za-**⟩ (*-uję*) use, apply; **~ać się** (**do** *G*) apply (to); conform (to); comply (with), be appropriate (for); → **dostosowywać się**; **~any** *nauka itp.* applied; **~nie** *adv.* appropriately (**do** *G* to); **~ny** appropriate, suitable; **w ~nej chwili** in the appropriate moment; **uważać za ~ne** (*A*) think it fit (to)
stosun|ek *m* (*-nku*; *-nki*) *math.* ratio; (*kontakt*) relation, relationship; (*płciowy*) intercourse; **w ~ku do** (*G*) in relation (to); **być w dobrych ~kach** (**z** *I*) have good relations (with); **~kowo** *adv.* relatively; **~kowy** relative
stow. *skrót pisany*: **stowarzyszenie** association
stowarzysz|enie *n* (*-a*; *G -eń*) association; **~ony** associated
stoż|ek *m* (*-żka*; *-żki*) cone (*też math.*); **~kowato** *adv.* conically; **~kowaty** conical
stóg *m* (*stogu*; *stogi*) haystack
stół *m* (*stołu*; *stoły*) table; (*posiłki*) board; **przy stole** at the table; **nakryć ~** lay the table
stówka F *f* (*-i*; *G -wek*) one hundred
str. *skrót pisany*: **strona** p. (*page*)
straceni|e *n* (*-a*; *G -eń*) (*więźnia*) execution; loss; **nie mieć nic do ~a** have nothing to lose
strach *m* (*-u*; *-y*) fear, fright, dread;

S

(*zjawa*) nightmare, *Brt.* spectre, *Am.* specter; ***ze ~u*** (***przed*** *I*) for fear (of); ***aż ~*** awfully; ***~ na wróble*** scarecrow
strac|ić (*-ę*) *pf.* → ***tracić***; *skazańca* execute; **~ony** executed; (*zgubiony*) lost
stragan *m* (*-u*; *-y*) stall; **~iarka** *f* (*-i*; *G -rek*), **~iarz** *m* (*-a*; *-e*) stall-holder
strajk *m* (*-u*; *-i*) (***powszechny, okupacyjny*** general, sit-down/sit-in) strike; **~ować** (*-uję*) strike; go on strike; **~owy** striking; **~ujący 1.** striking; **2.** *m* (*-ego*; *-y*), **~ująca** *f* (*-ej*; *-e*) striker
strapi|enie *n* (*-a*; *G -eń*) trouble, problem, worry; **~ony** troubled, dejected
strasz|ak *m* (*-a*; *-i*) toy gun; → ***straszydło***; **~liwie** *adv.* frightfully, horribly; **~liwy** frightful, horrible; **~ny** terrible; **~yć** *v/t.* ⟨***na-, prze-***⟩ frighten, scare; **~yć**⟨***wy-***⟩ ***się*** get a fright; *v/i.* haunt; ***tu ~y*** this place is haunted; **~ydło** *n* (*-a*; *-deł*) nightmare; *fig.* scarecrow, frump
strat|a *f* (*-y*; *G -*) loss (*też econ.*); ***ze ~ą*** at a loss; ***narazić się na ~ę*** suffer losses
strategiczny strategic
stratny: ***być ~m*** suffer a loss
straw|a *f* (*-y*; *G -*) food; **~ić** *pf.* → ***trawić***; **~ny** digestible
straż *f* (*-y*; *-e*) (***przyboczna, przednia*** body, advance) guard; ***trzymać pod ~ą*** keep under guard; → ***pożarny***; **~acki** fire; fireman's; **~ak** *m* (*-a*; *-cy*) fireman; **~nica** *f* (*-y*; *G -*) watchtower; **~niczka** *f* (*-i*; *G -czek*) guard, warder; **~nik** *m* (*-a*; *-cy*) watchman, guard, warder
strąc|ać ⟨***~ić***⟩ knock off; precipitate (*też ze szczytu itp.*)
strą|czek *m* (*-czka*; *-czki*), **~k** *m* (*-a*; *-i*) pod
stref|a *f* (*-y*; *G -*) zone, area, region; **~owy** zone, zonal
stremowany nervous
stres *m* (*-u*; *-y*) stress; **~owy** stressing
streszcz|ać (*-am*) ⟨***streścić***⟩ (*-szczę*) abbreviate, summarize; ***~ać się*** be brief; **~enie** *n* (*-a*; *G -eń*) abbreviation, summary
stręczy|cielstwo *n* (*-a*; *0*) procurement; **~ć** procure; → ***nastręczać***
striptizerka *f* (*-i*; *G -rek*) striptease artist, stripper
strofa *f* (*-y*; *G -*) stanza
strofować (*-uję*) criticize, reprimand
stroić (*-ję*, *strój*) ⟨***u-, wy-***⟩ decorate; ***~*** ⟨***wy-***⟩ ***się*** dress up; ⟨***na-***⟩ *mus.*, *tech.* tune; (*t-ko impf.*) *figle* play, make; *miny* make
stroj|e *pl.* → ***strój***; **~ny** decorated, ornamented; *ktoś* dressed up
strom|o *adv.* steeply; **~y** steep, precipitous
stron|a *f* (*-y*; *G -*) side (*też fig.*); (*książki*) page; *jur.* party (***w*** *L* to); ***cztery ~y świata*** the four points of the compass; ***na ~ę*** aside; ***ze ~y*** (*G*) *fig.* on the part of; ***w ~ę*** (*G*) in the direction (of); ***z jednej ~y ... z drugiej ~y ...*** on the one hand … on the other (hand) …; ***~a tytułowa*** title page
stronica *f* (*-y*; *G -*) page
stronić (*-ę*) (***od*** *G*) avoid, escape (from)
stronni|ctwo *n* (*-a*; *G -*) *pol.* party; **~czka** *f* (*-i*; *G -czek*) supporter, adherent, follower; **~czo** *adv.* in a biased way; **~czy** biased, prejudiced; **~k** *m* (*-a*; *-cy*) supporter, adherent, follower
stront *m* (*-u*; *0*) *chem.* strontium
strop *m* (*-u*; *-y*) ceiling, ceiling; *górnictwo*: roof
stroskany anxious, careworn
stroszyć ⟨***na-***⟩ (*-ę*) ruffle (up), bristle; ***~*** ⟨***na-***⟩ ***się*** become ruffled, bristle
strój *m* (*stroju*; *stroje*, *strojów*) dress, costume; → ***adamowy***
stróż *m* (*-a*; *-e*) watchman, caretaker; → **~ka** *f* (*-i*; *G -żek*) caretaker; → ***anioł***
stru|- *pf.* → ***tru-***; **~dzony** weary, fatigued
strug *m* (*-a*; *-i*) *tech.* plane; **~a** *f* (*-i*; *G -*) stream, brook; (*wody*) gush, jet; **~ać** ⟨***o-***⟩ (*-am*) *figurkę* carve; *tech.* plane; F *fig.* play, act
struktura *f* (*-y*; *G -*) structure
strumie|ń *m* (*-nia*; *-nie*) stream; *fig. też* torrent; ***padać ~niem, ~niami*** pour with rain
strumyk *m* (*-a*; *-i*) → ***strumień***; trickle
strun|a *f* (*-y*; *G -*) string; *anat.* chord; ***~y*** *pl.* ***głosowe*** vocal chords *pl.*; **~owy** string
strup *m* (*-a*; *-y*) *med.* scab
strusi ostrich
struś *m* (*-sia*; *-sie*) *zo.* ostrich
strwożony frightened
strych *m* (*-u*; *-y*) loft, attic
stryczek *m* (*-czka*, *-czki*) halter (*też fig.*)
stry|j *m* (*-a*; *-owie*) uncle; **~jeczny**: ***brat ~jeczny, siostra ~jeczna*** cousin; **~jenka** *f* (*-i*; *G -nek*) aunt; **~jostwo** *n*

(*-a*; *G -*) uncle and aunt
strzał *m* (*-u*; *-y*) shot; **~a** *f* (*-y*; *G -*) arrow; **~ka** *f* (*-i*; *G -łek*) arrow; (*w sporcie*) dart; *anat.* fibula; **~kowy** *anat.* fibular
strząs|ać (*-am*) ⟨**~nąć**⟩ (*-nę*) shake down
strzec (*G*) guard, keep watch (over); **~ się** be on one's guard; look out for
strzecha *f* (*-y*; *G -*) thatch
strzel|ać (*-am*) (**do** *G*) shoot (to) (*też sport*), fire (at); (*trzaskać*) snap, click; **~ać bramkę** score; **~anina** *f* (*-y*; *G -*) shooting; **~ba** *f* (*-y*; *G -*) shotgun; **~ec** *m* (*-lca*; *G -lców*) shot; **~ec wyborowy** marksman; **≗ec** *znak Zodiaku:* Sagittarius; **on(a) jest spod znaku ≗ca** he/she is (a) Sagittarius **~ectwo** *n* (*-a*; *0*) *sport*: shooting; **~ić** *pf.* (*-lę*) → **strzelać**; **~isty** slender, soaring; *fig.* lofty; **~nica** *f* (*-y*; *G -*) shooting range
strzem|iączko *n* (*-a*; *G -czek*) strap; **~ienny** *m* (*-ego*; *0*) stirrup cup; **~ię** *n* (*-enia*; *-iona*, *G -ion*) stirrup
strzep|ywać (*-uję*) ⟨**~nąć**⟩ (*-nę*) shake off, shake down
strzeżony guarded
strzęp *m* (*-u*; *-y*) shred, scrap; *fig.* bit, piece; **~ić** ⟨**wy-**⟩ (*-ę*) fringe; **~ić się** fray
strzyc ⟨**o-**⟩ *włosy* cut, crop; *trawę* mow, cut; *owce* shear; **~ się** have a haircut; *impf.* **~ uszami** prick one's ears
strzyk|ać (*-am*) squirt, spurt; *med.* have a stabbing pain; **~awka** *f* (*-i*; *G -wek*) syringe; **~nąć** *pf.* → **strzykać**
strzyż|enie *n* (*-a*; *G -eń*) cutting, shearing; mowing; **~ony** shorn
stu *m-os* → **sto**; → **715**
studen|cki student(s'); **dom ~cki** *Brt.* hall of residence, *Am.* dormitory; **~t** *m* (*-a*; *-ci*), **~tka** *f* (*-i*; *G -tek*) student
studi|a *pl.* (**medyczne** medical) studies *pl.* (**na, w** *L* at); **~ować** (*-uję*) study; **~um** *n* (*idkl.*; *-a*; *-iów*) study; college
studnia *f* (*-i*; *-e*) well
studniówka *f* (*-i*; *G -wek*) graduation ball (*in secondary schools, traditionally 100 days before the final exams*)
studzić ⟨**o-**⟩ (*-dzę*) cool down
studzienny well
stuk *m* (*-u*; *-i*) knocking; **~ać** ⟨**~nąć**⟩ knock (**do** *G*, **w** *A* on, at); *serce*: pound; *silnik*: knock, pink; **~nięty** F loony, *Brt.* barmy
stu|lecie *n* (*-a*; *G -eci*) century; (*rocznica*) centenary; **~letni** a hundred years old; **~metrówka** *f* (*-i*; *G -wek*) hundred metres *sg.*; **~procentowy** (one-)hundred per cent
stwardni|ały hardened; **~enie** *n* (*-a*; *G -eń*) hardening; **~enie rozsiane** *med.* multiple sclerosis
stwarzać (*-am*) create
stwierdz|ać (*-am*) ⟨**~ić**⟩ find, establish, state; **~enie** *n* (*-a*; *G -eń*) finding; statement
stworz|enie *n* (*-a*; *0*) creation, *rel.* the Creation; (*pl. -a*) creature; **~yć** *pf.* → **stwarzać**
stwórca *m* (*-y*; *G -ców*) creator
styczeń *m* (*-cznia*; *-cznie*) January
styczna *f* (*-ej*; *G -ych*) *math.* tangent
styczniowy January
styczn|ość *f* (*-ści*; *0*) contact; **wejść w ~ość** (**z** *I*) get in touch *lub* contact (with); **~y**: **punkt ~y** point of contact
stygnąć ⟨**o-, wy-**⟩ (*-nę*) cool (*też fig.*); ⟨**za-**⟩ set; *krew*: congeal
styk *m* (*-u*; *-i*) touch, contact; (*miejsce*) joint; **na ~** edge to edge; *fig.* by a narrow margin; **~ać** (*-am*) bring into contact, bring together; **~ać się** touch (**z** *I* to); **~owy** contact; *złącze* butt
styl *m* (*-u*; *-e*) style; **~istyczny** stylistic; **~owo** *adv.* stylishly, elegantly; **~owy** stylish, elegant
stymul|ator *m* (*-a*; *-y*): *med.* **~ator serca** pace maker; **~ować** (*-uję*) stimulate
stypa *f* (*-y*; *G -*) (funeral) wake
stypend|ium *n* (*idkl.*; *-ia*, *-iów*) scholarship, grant; **~ysta** *m* (*-y*; *-ści*), **~ystka** *f* (*-i*; *-tek*) scholar, grantee, scholarship holder
styropian *m* (*-u*; *-y*) polystyrene (foam)
subiektywn|ie *adv.* subjectively; **~y** subjective
sub|lokator(ka *f*) *m* subtenant, lodger; **~lokatorski**: **pokój ~lokatorski** subleased room; **~ordynacja** *f* obedience; **~skrybować** (*-uję*) subscribe (*A* to), take out; **~skrypcja** *f* (*-i*; *-e*) subscription (**na** *A* to); **~stancja** *f* (*-i*; *-e*) substance
sub|sydiować (*-uję*) subsidize, support; **~telny** subtle; **~wencjonować** (*-uję*) subsidize
such|arek *m* (*-rka*; *-rki*) (*dla dzieci*) rusk, biscuit; **~o** *adv.* dryly; **~ość** *f* (*-ści*; *0*) dryness

suchoty *hist. pl.* (-) consumption, tuberculosis
such|y (*m-os susi*) dry (*też fig.*); (*wyschnięty*) withered, dried up; *osoba* gaunt; ***wytrzeć do ~a*** wipe dry
Sudety *pl.* the Sudety *pl.*, the Sudeten *pl.*
sufit *m* (*-u*; *-y*) *bud.* ceiling
suflet *m* (*-u*; *-y*) *gastr.* soufflé
sufragan *m* (*-a*; *-i*) *rel.* suffragan (bishop)
suge|rować ⟨**za-**⟩ (*-uję*) suggest, propose; **~stia** *f* (*GDL -ii*;*-e*) suggestion
suita *f* (*-y*; *G* -) *mus.* suite
suka *f* (*-i*; *G* -) bitch (*też pej.*); she-dog
sukces *m* (*-y*; *-u*) success; ***odnosić ~*** succeed; **~ja** *f* (*-i*; *G -e*) succession; **~ywny** successive
sukien|ka *f* (*-i*; *G -nek*) dress; **~nice** *f/pl.* (*G* -) cloth hall; **~ny** cloth
sukinsyn *m* (*-a*; *-y*) V son of a bitch
sukn|ia *f* (*-i*; *-e*, *-i/-ien*) (*zwł.* evening) dress; **~o** *n* (*-a*; *G sukien*) cloth
sułtan *m* (*-a*; *-i*) sultan; **~ka** *f* (*-i*; *G -nek*) *bot.* sultana
sum|a *f* (*-y*; *G* -) sum; (*kwota też*) amount; *rel.* high mass; ***w ~ie*** in all, *lub* altogether
sumien|ie *n* (*-a*; *G -eń*) conscience; **~ny** conscientious
sumow|ać (*-uję*) add up (**się** *v/i.*); **~anie** *n* (*-a*; *G -ań*) addition
sunąć (*-nę*, *-ń!*) glide; (*na kółkach, piłka*) roll
supeł *m* (*-pła*; *-pły*) knot
super super; *w złoż.* super-, ultra-; **~nowoczesny** ultra-modern; **~sam** *m* (*-u*; *-y*) (*zwł.* self-service) supermarket
surfing *m* (*-u*; *-i*) *sport*: surfing; **~owy** surfing; ***deska ~owa*** surf-board
surogat *m* (*-u*; *-y*) surrogate, substitute
surow|cowy raw material; **~ica** *f* (*-y*; *-e*, *G* -) serum; **~iec** *m* (*-wca*; *-wce*) raw material; ***~ce** pl.* ***naturalne*** natural resources *pl.*; **~o** *adv.* severely; harshly; ***na ~o*** raw; **~ość** *f* (*-ści*; *0*) severity, harshness; **~y** raw; severe; harsh; ***w stan ~y zakończony*** *bud.* structurally complete
surówka *f* (*-i*; *G -wek*) (*zwł.* raw vegetable) salad; *tech.* pig-iron
sus *m* (*-a*; *-y*) jump, leap, bound
susi *m-os* → ***suchy***
susza *f* (*-y*; *G* -) drought; **~rka** *f* (*-i*; *G -rek*) dryer; (*na naczynia*) *Brt.* draining rack, *Am.* (dish) drainer; **~rnia** *f* (*-i*; *-e*) drying room
susz|enie *n* (*-a*; *G -eń*) drying; **~ony** dried; **~yć** ⟨**wy-**⟩ (*-ę*) dry; ***~yć sobie głowę*** (***nad*** *I*) rack one's brains (over)
sutanna *f* (*-y*; *G* -) *rel.* cassock
sutek *m* (*-tka*; *-tki*) *anat.* nipple
sutenerstwo *n* (*-a*; *0*) pimping
suterena *f* (*-y*; *G* -) basement
suty generous; opulent
suw *m* (*-u*; *-y*) *tech.*, *mot.* stroke; **~ać** (*-am*) *v/t.* slide; ***~ać nogami*** shuffle; **~ak** *m* (*-a*; *-i*) (***logarytmiczny*** slide-)-rule; → ***zamek błyskawiczny***
suwerenn|ość *f* (*-ści*; *0*) sovereignty; **~y** sovereign
suwnica *f* (*-y*; *G* -) *tech.* (overhead) crane
swa (*ściągn.* **swoja**) → ***swój***
swar|liwie *adv.* quarrelsomely; contentiously; **~liwy** quarrelsome, contentious; **~y** *m/pl.* (*-ów*) quarrels *pl.*, quarrelling
swastyka *f* (*-i*; *G* -) swastika
swat *m* (*-a*; *-owie/-ci*), **~ka** *f* (*-i*; *G -tek*) matchmaker; **~y** *m/pl.* (*G -ów*) matchmaking
swawol|a *f* (*-i*; *-e*) frolic, prank; **~ić** (*-ę*) frolic; **~ny** playful; → ***figlarny***
swąd *m* (*swędu*; *0*) smell of burning
swe (*ściągn.* **swoje**) → ***swój***
sweter *m* (*-tra*; *-try*) sweater
swędz|enie *n* (*-a*; *0*) itching; **~i(e)ć** (*-ę*) itch
swobod|a *f* (*-y*; *G -bód*) freedom; liberty; **~nie** *adv.* freely; **~ny** free
swo|i *m-s* → ***swój***; **~isty** specific; characteristic; **~iście** *adv.* specifically; characteristically; **~ja**, **~je** **1.** → ***swój***; **2. *~je*** *n* (*-ego*; *0*) one's own; ***obstawać przy ~im*** stand up to one's opinion; ***postawić na ~im*** get one's own way; ***robić ~je*** do one's job; → ***czas, dopiąć***; **~jski** familiar; home-made
swój *poss.* (**swoja** *f*, **swoje** *n i pl.*, **swoi** *m-os*) my, your, his, her, our, your, their (*często* + *own*); ***wziął swoje rzeczy*** he took his things; ***swoimi słowami*** in your own words; ***chodzić swoimi drogami*** walk by oneself; ***na ~ sposób*** in one's own way; → ***krewny, rodaczka, rodak, swoje***
Syberia *f* (*GDl -ii*; *0*) Siberia

S

sycić ⟨**na-**⟩ (*-cę*) satiate; *fig.* satisfy
Sycylia *f* (*GDL -ii; 0*) Sicily
syczeć (*-ę*) hiss
syfon *m* (*-u; -y*) siphon
sygnalizator *m* (*-a; -y*) (**pożarowy** fire) alarm; **~ alarmowy** alarm system
sygnał *m* (*-u; -y*) signal; **~ świetlny** headlight flasher; **~ wzywania pomocy** *naut.* Mayday call
sygnatura *f* (*-y*) (*w bibliotece*) catalogue number
sygnet *m* (*-u; -y*) signet-ring
syjonistyczny Zionistic
syk *m* (*-u; -i*) hiss; **~ać** (*-am*), **~nąć** *v/s.* hiss
sylab|a *f* (*-y; G -*) syllable; **~izować** (*-uję*) read letter by letter
syl|wester *m* (*-a; -y*) New Year's Eve; ***obchodzić ~westra*** see the New Year in; **~westrowy** New Year's; **~wetka** *f* (*-i; G -tek*) silhouette; *fig.* portrait
symbol *m* (*-u; -e*) symbol; **~iczny** symbolic
symetr|ia *f* (*GDL -ii; -e*) symmetry; **~yczny** symmetric(al)
symfoni|a *f* (*GDL -ii; -e*) *mus.* symphony; **~czny** symphony; ***poemat ~czny*** symphonic poem
sympat|ia *f* (*GDl -ii; -e*) liking, affection; F (*dziewczyna*) girlfriend, (*chłopak*) boyfriend; **czuć ~ię** (**do** *G*) feel attracted (to); **~yczny** likeable; **~yk** *m* (*-a; -cy*) (*G*) sympathizer
symptom *m* (*-u; -y*) symptom
symul|ować (*-uję*) simulate; *chorobę* fake; **~taniczny** simultaneous
syn *m* (*-a; -owie*) son
synagoga *f* (*-i; G -*) *rel.* synagogue
synchro|niczny synchronic; **~nizować** ⟨**z-**⟩ (*-uję*) synchronize
syndyk *m* (*-a; -cy/-owie*) receiver
synek *m* (*-nka; -nkowie*) son
syno|d *m* (*-u; -y*) synod; **~nim** *m* (*-u; -y*) synonym; **~nimiczny** synonymous
synoptyczny synoptic
synow|a *f* (*-ej; -e*) daughter-in-law; **~ski** filial; ***po ~sku*** like a son
syntetyczny synthetic; (*plastikowy*) plastic
sypać (*-ię*) *v/t. mąkę itp.* pour (**się** *v/i.*); sprinkle; *wał* build; *fig.* reel off; F *kogoś* split on; *v/i. śnieg*: snow; **~ się** *tynk itp.*: crumble off *lub* away (**z** *G* from); *wąsy*: sprout; *fig.* rain down; *iskry*: fly
sypial|nia *f* (*-i; -e*) bedroom; (*w internacie itp.*) dormitory; **~ny** bedroom
syp|ki loose; **~nąć** *pf.* → ***sypać***
syrena *f* (*-y; G -*) *tech.* siren; *zo.* sea cow; (*w mitologii*) mermaid, siren
syrop (*-u; -y*) syrup
Syria *f* (*GDL -ii; 0*) Syria
syryj|ski Syrian; **♀czyk** *m* (*-a; -cy*), **♀ka** (*-i; G -jek*) Syrian
system *m* (*-u; -y*) system; **~atyczny** systematic
syt|ny filling; **~ość** *f* (*-ści; 0*) satiety, repleteness
sytuac|ja (*-i; -e*) situation; **~yjny** situational
sytuowa|ć ⟨**u-**⟩ (*-uuję*) locate, situate; ***dobrze ~ny*** well-to-do
syty (*pred.* **do syta**) full-up
szabas *m* (*-u; -y*), **szabat** *m* (*-u; -y*) *rel.* Sabbath
szabl|a *f* (*-i; -e*) *Brt.* sabre, *Am.* saber; **~ista** *m* (*-y; -ści*) *Brt.* sabre (*Am.* saber) fencer
szablon *m m* pattern; (*językowy*) cliché; **~owo** *adv.* in a clichéd *lub* stereotyped manner; **~owy** clichéd, stereotyped
szach *m* (*-a; -owie*) shah; (*-u/-a; -y*) check (*też fig.*); **dać ~a** (give) check; **~ mat** checkmate; *t-ko pl.* **~y** (*-ów*) chess; **~ista** *m* (*-y; -ści, G -tów*), **~istka** *f* (*-i; G -tek*) chess-player; **~ownica** *f* (*-y; -e, G -*) chessboard; *fig.* patchwork
szachr|aj *m* (*-a; -e*), **~ajka** *f* (*-i; G -jek*) swindler; **~ajstwo** *n* (*-a; G -*) swindle; **~ować** (*-uję*) swindle
szachy *pl.* → ***szach***
szacować ⟨**o-**⟩ (*-uję*) estimate
szacun|ek *m* (*-nku; 0*) esteem, respect; (*ocena*) estimate, estimation; → ***wyraz***; **~kowo** *adv.* approximately
szafa *f* (*-y; G -*) wardrobe, cupboard; ***~ grająca*** jukebox
szafir *m* (*-u; -y*) sapphire; **~owy** sapphire
szafk|a *f* (*-i; G -fek*) cabinet; locker; ***~a nocna*** bedside table; **~owy** cabinet
szafować (*-uję*) (*I*) be wasteful (with)
szafran *m* (*-u; -y*) *bot.*, *gastr.* saffron
szajka *f* (*-i; G -jek*) gang
szal *m* (*-a; -e*) shawl, scarf
szala *f* (*-i; -e*) scale (pan)
szalbierstwo *n* (*-a; G -*) imposition

S

szale|ć (*-eję*) go wild, rage; be beside o.s. (**z** *G* with); be mad (**za** *I* about); **~niec** *m* (*-ńca*; *-ńcy*) madman, maniac, lunatic; **~ńczo** *adv.* madly, crazily; **~ńczy** mad, crazy; lunatic; **~ństwo** *n* (*-a*; *G* -) madness, craziness, craze
szalet *m* (*-u*; *-y*) public convenience
szalik *m* (*-a*; *-i*) scarf
szalony mad, crazy
szalować ⟨**o-**⟩ (*-uję*) board, shutter
szalunek *m* (*-nku*; *-nki*) boarding, shuttering
szalupa *f* (*-y*; *G* -) *naut.* launch; lifeboat
szał *m* (*-u*; *0*) rage, frenzy; craze; ***wpaść w ~*** go mad; → ***furia***
szałas *m* (*-u*; *-y*) shanty, shed, hut
szałowy great, fantastic
szałwia *f* (*GDL -ii*; *-e*) *bot.* sage
szamotać (*-czę/-cę*): ***~ się*** struggle
szampa|n *m* (*-a*; *-y*) *gastr.* champagne; **~ński** champagne; *fig.* wonderful
szampon *m* (*-u*; *-y*) shampoo
szaniec *m* (*-ńca*; *-ńce*) entrenchment
szanow|ać (*-uję*) respect, esteem; *prawo* respect, observe; *ubranie* treat with care; **~ny** respected; (*w listach*) Dear
szansa *f* (*-y*; *G* -) chance, prospect
szantaż *m* (*-u*; *-e*) blackmail; **~ować** (*-uję*) blackmail; **~ysta** *m* (*-y*; *G -stów*), **~ystka** *f* (*-i*; *G -tek*) blackmailer
szarak *m* (*-a*; *-i*) *zo.* hare
szarańcza *f* (*-y*; *-e*, *-y*) *zo.* locust
szarfa *f* (*-y*; *G* -) sash
szarlata|n *m* (*-a*; *-i*) charlatan; **~neria** *f* (*GDL -ii*; *0*) charlatanism
szarlotka *f* (*-i*; *G -tek*) apple-pie
szaro *adv. w złoż. Brt.* grey, *Am.* gray; **~tka** *f* (*-i*; *G -tek*) *bot.* edelweiss; **~zielony** grey-green
szarówka *f* (*-i*; *G -wek*) twilight, dusk
szarp|ać *v/i.* tug, yank (**za** *A* at); *pojazd*: jerk, jolt; ⟨**po-, roz-**⟩ *v/t.* tear up; ***~ać się*** struggle; (**na** *A*) lash out (on); **~nąć** *v/s.* (*-nę*) → ***szarpać***; **~nięcie** *n* (*-a*; *G -ęć*) jolt, jerk
szaruga *f* (*-i*; *G* -) rainy weather
szary (*m-os -rzy*) *Brt.* grey, *Am.* gray; *fig.* drab; ***na ~m końcu*** at the very end
szarz|eć ⟨**po-**⟩ (*-eję*) grow dusky; grow *Brt.* grey, *Am.* gray; ***~eje*** it is getting dark; **~y** *pl.* → ***szary***; **~yzna** *f* (*-y*; *0*) *fig.* monotony, tediousness
szastać (*-am*) → ***szafować***

S

szata *f* (*-y*; *G* -) dress, garment; *print.* layout
szata|n *m* (*-a*; *-i/-y*) satan; **~ński** satanic
szatkować (*-uję*) *gastr.* shred
szatnia *f* (*-i*; *-e*) *Brt.* cloakroom, *Am.* checkroom; (*do przebrania się*) changing room; **~rka** *f* (*-i*; *G -rek*), **~rz** *m* (*-a*; *-e*) cloakroom attendant
szatyn *m* (*-a*; *-i*), **~ka** *f* (*-i*; *G -nek*) dark-haired/brown-haired person
szczać V (*-ę*) piss
szczapa *f* (*-y*; *G* -) piece of wood
szczaw *m* (*-wiu*; *-wie*, *-wi*) *bot.* sorrel; **~iowy** sorrel
szczęt|ek *m* (*-tka*; *-tki*) fragment; *przew.* ***~ki*** *pl.* remains *pl.*; (*po katastrofie*) debris; **~kowy** residual
szczeb|el *m* (*-bla*; *-ble*) rung; *fig.* rank, level; *pol.* ***na … ~lu*** at the … level
szczebiot *m* (*-u*; *-y*) twittering; chirping; **~ać** (*-czę/-cę*) twitter; chirp
szczecina *f* (*-y*; *G* -) bristle; (*na brodzie*) stubble
szczególn|ie *adv.* particularly, in particular; especially, specially; **~ość** (*-ści*; *0*): ***w ~ości*** in particular; **~y** particular; especial, special
szczegół *m* (*-u*; *-y*) detail; **~owo** *adv.* in detail; **~owy** detailed
szczekać (*-am*) bark
szczel|ina *f* (*-y*; *G* -) split, crevice; **~ny** air-tight, water-tight
szczeni|ak *m* (*-a*; *-i*) *fig. pej.* whippersnapper; → **~ę** *n* (*-cia*; *-nięta*, *G -niąt*) puppy
szczep *m* (*-u*; *-y*) tribe; *biol.*, *med.* strain; *agr.* scion, graft; **~ić** (*-ę*) ⟨**za-**⟩ *med.* vaccinate; ⟨**prze-**⟩ *med.* graft; **~ienie** *n* (*-a*; *G -eń*) *med.* vaccination; *agr.* grafting; **~ionka** *f* (*-i*; *G -nek*) vaccine
szczerba *f* (*-y*; *G* -) chip, nick; (*między zębami*) gap (in one's teeth); **~ty** gap-toothed; → ***wyszczerbiony***
szczero|ść *f* (*-ści*; *0*) frankness, openness, sincerity; **~ry** frank, open, sincere; **~rze** *adv.* frankly, openly, sincerely
szczerzyć ⟨**wy-**⟩ (*-ę*): ***~ zęby*** bare one's teeth; *fig.* give a friendly smile (**do** *G* to)
szczędzić (*-ę*): ***nie ~*** (*G*) not spare, be generous
szczęk *m* (*-u*; *-i*) clank, clink; **~a** *f* (*-i*; *G* -) *anat.* jaw; ***sztuczna ~a*** false teeth *pl.*, denture; **~ać** (*-am*) clink, clank

szczęś|ciara *f* (*-y*; *G -*), **~ciarz** *m* (*-a*; *-e*) lucky person; **~cić się**: ***~ci mu się*** he is lucky; **~cie** *n* (*-a*; *0*) (good) luck, fortune; ***~ciem, na ~cie*** fortunately; luckily; **~liwie** *adv.* fortunately; luckily; happily; **~liwy** fortunate; lucky; happy
szczod|ry generous; **~rze** *adv.* generously
szczot|eczka *f* (*-i*; *G -czek*) (**do zębów** tooth) brush; **~ka** *f* (*-i*; *G -tek*) brush; ***~ka do zamiatania*** broom; ***~ka mechaniczna*** carpet sweeper; **~kować** ⟨**wy-**⟩ (*-uję*) brush
szczuć ⟨**po-**⟩ (*-ję*) set the dog(s) on
szczudło *n* (*-a*; *G -deł*) stilt; → ***kula²***
szczupak *m* (*-a*; *-i*) *zo.* pike
szczup|leć ⟨**ze-**⟩ (*-eję*) slim down, get slimmer; **~ły** slim, slender
szczu|r *m* (*-a*; *-y*) *zo.* rat (*też fig.*); **~rzy** rat
szczwany shrewd, crafty
szczycić się (*-cę*) (*I*) boast, be proud (of)
szczygieł *m* (*-gła*, *-gły*) *zo.* goldfinch
szczy|pać (*-pię*) pinch; *trawę* nip; *dym*: sting, be stinging; **~pce** *pl.* (*-piec/-pców*) → ***kleszcze***; **~piorek** *m* (*-rku*; *0*) chives *pl.*; **~pta** *f* (*-y*; *G -*) pinch
szczyt *m* (*-u*; *-y*) top (*też fig.*); (*góry*) peak, summit; *bud.* gable; (*łóżka, stołu*) head; ***godziny*** *pl.* ***~u*** rush hours *pl.*; ***spotkanie na szczycie*** summit meeting; **~ny** noble; **~ować** (*-uję*) climax; **~owanie** *n* (*-a*; *G -ań*) climax; **~owy** summit; climax; peak
szedł(em) *3.* (*1.*) *os. pret. sg.* → ***iść***
szef *m* (*-a*; *-owie*) boss, chief; (*kuchni*) chef; **~owa** *f* (*-ej*; *-e*) boss, chief
szejk *m* (*-a*; *-owie*) sheikh
szele|st *m* (*-u*; *-y*) rustle; **~ścić** (*-ę*) rustle
szelki *pl.* (*G -lek*) *Brt.* braces *pl.*, *Am.* suspenders *pl.*
szelma *f/m* (*-y*; *G -/ów*) rogue
szemrać (*-rzę*) *deszcz, drzewa*: whisper; *strumyk*: babble; *fig.* grumble, murmur
szep|nąć *v/s* (*-nę*) whisper; **~t** *m* (*-u*; *-y*) whisper; **~tać** (*-czę/-cę*) whisper; **~tany** whispered
szer. *skrót pisany*: **szerokość** w. (*width*); **szeregowiec** Pvt. (*private*)
szereg *m* (*-u*; *-i*) row; line; series; (*wydarzeń*) chain
szeregow|ać ⟨**u-**⟩ (*-uję*) line up; **~iec** *m* (*-wca*; *-wcy*) *mil.* private; **~y** **1.** ordinary; **2.** *m* (*-ego*; *-wi*) *mil.* private; ***~i*** *pl.* *mil.* the ranks; ***~i członkowie*** *pl.* rank and file
szermie|rka *f* (*-i*; *0*) *sport*: fencing; **~rz** *m* (*-a*; *-e*) (*w sporcie*) fencer
szerok|i wide, broad; **~o** *adv.* widely, broadly
szeroko|kątny *phot.* wide-angle; **~ść** *f* (*-ści*) breadth, width; ***~ść torów*** *rail.* gauge; **~torowy** *rail.* broad-gauge
szerszeń *m* (*-nia*; *-nie*) *zo.* hornet
sze|rszy, ~rzej *adj./adv. comp. od* → ***szeroki, -ko***
szerzyć (*-ę*) spread (**się** *v/i.*)
szesna|stka *mus. Brt.* semiquaver, *Am.* sixteenth note; **~sto-** *w złoż.* sixteen; **~sty** sixteenth; **~ście** sixteen; → ***715***
sześc. *skrót pisany*: **sześcienny** c (*cubic*)
sześci|an *m* (*-u*; *-y*) *math.* cube; ***podnieść do ~anu*** cube; **~enny** *math.* cubic; *kształt* cubical
sześ|cio- *w złoż.* six; **~ciokąt** *m* (*-a*; *-y*) hexagon; **~ciokrotny** sixfold; **~cioletni** six-year-long, -old; **~ciu** *m-os*, **~ć** six → ***715***
sześć|dziesiąt sixty; → ***715***; **~dziesiąty** sixtieth; **~set** six hundred; → ***715***; **~setny** six hundredth
Szetlandy *pl.* (*G -ów*) Shetland Islands *pl.*, Shetlands *pl.*
szew *m* (*szwu*; *szwy*) seam; *med.* suture; ***zdjąć szwy*** remove the stitches; ***bez szwu*** seamless
szew|c *m* (*-a*; *-y*) shoemaker; **~ski** shoemaker's
szkalować ⟨**o-**⟩ (*-uję*) malign
szkapa *f* (*-y*; *G -*) nag, hack
szkaradny hideous
szkarlatyna *f* (*-y*; *0*) *med.* scarlet fever
szkatułka *f* (*-i*; *G -łek*) box
szkic *m* (*-u*; *-e*) sketch; **~ować** ⟨**na-**⟩ (*-uję*) sketch; **~owo** *adv.* sketchily; in rough; **~owy** sketchy
szkielet *m* (*-u*; *-y*) *anat.* skeleton (*też fig.*)
szkiełko *n* (*-a*; *G -łek*) glass; (*zegarka*) crystal
szkla|nka *f* (*-i*; *G -nek*) glass; **~ny** glass; **~rnia** *f* (*-i*; *-e*) greenhouse, *Brt.* glasshouse; **~rski** glazier's; **~rz** *m* (*-a*; *-e*) glazier
szkli|ć ⟨**o-**⟩ (*-lę*; *-lij!*) glaze; **~sty** glassy; **~ście** *adv.* in a glassy manner; **~wo** *n* (*-a*; *G -*) *anat.* enamel; *tech.* glaze
szkło *n* (*-a*; *G szkieł*) glass

S

Szko|cja *f* (*-i*; *0*) Scotland; **2cki** Scots, Scottish
szkod|a¹ *f* (*-y*; *G szkód*) damage, harm; mischief; ***na ~ę, ze ~ą dla*** (*G*) to the detriment (of)
szkod|a² *adv.* pity; ***~a, że*** a pity that; ***jaka ~a!*** what a pity!; **~liwość** *f* (*-ści*; *0*) harmfulness; **~liwie** *adv.* harmfully; **~liwy** harmful; (*niezdrowy*) unhealthy; **~nik** *m* (*-a*; *-i*) pest
szkodz|ić (*-dzę*) damage, harm; ***co to ~i?*** what harm does it do?; ***nie ~i*** not at all
szkol|enie *n* (*-a*; *G -eń*) training; **~ić** ⟨**wy-**⟩ (*-lę*) train; **~nictwo** *n* (*-a*; *G -*) educational system; **~ny** school
szkoła *f* (*-y*; *G szkół*) school (*też fig.*); ***~ wyższa*** higher education institution
szkopuł *m* (*-u*; *-y*) hitch, difficulty
Szkot *m* (*-a*; *-ci*), **~ka** *f* (*-i*; *G -tek*) Scot
szkółka *f* (*-i*; *G -łek*) → **szkoła**; course for beginners; *agr.* nursery
szkuner *m* (*-a*; *-y*) schooner
szkwał *m* (*-u*; *-y*) squall
szlaban *m* (*-u*; *-y*) gate, barrier
szlach|cianka *f* (*-i*; *G -nek*) noblewoman; **~cic** *m* (*-a*; *-e*) nobleman; **~ecki** noble
szlachetn|ość *f* (*-ści*; *0*) nobility; **~y** noble
szlachta *f* (*-y*; *G -*) nobility
szlafrok *m* (*-a*; *-i*) dressing-gown, *Am.* bath robe
szlak *m* (*-u*; *-i*) route, track; (*turystyczny*) trail
szlam *m* (*-u*; *0*) mire, sludge
szli *3. os. pret. pl.* → **iść**
szlifować ⟨**o-**⟩ (*-uję*) grind
szlochać (*-am*) sob
szła(m) *3.* (*1.*) *os. pret. pl.* → **iść**
szmacia|ny rag; ***lalka ~na*** rag doll; **~rz** *m* (*-a*; *-e*) rag-and-bone man; *fig.* bum
szmaragd *m* (*-u*; *-y*) emerald; **~owy** emerald
szmat *m*: ***~ drogi*** a long way; ***~ czasu*** a long time; **~a** *f* (*-y*; *G -*) rag; → **~ka** *f* (*-i*; *G -tek*) cloth; rag
szmelc *m* (*-u*; *0*) junk, rubbish
szmer *m* (*-u*; *-y*) noise, sound
szminka *f* (*-i*; *G -nek*) (*do ust*) lipstick; (*do charakteryzacji*) make-up
szmira *f* (*-y*) trash, rubbish
szmuglować (*-uję*) smuggle
sznur *m* (*-a*; *-y*) string (*też fig.*); cord (*też electr.*); ***~ do bielizny*** clothes-line; **~ek** *m* (*-rka*; *-rki*) string, line; **~owadło** *n* (*-a*; *G -deł*) lace
sznycel *m* (*-cla*; *-cle*) *gastr.* schnitzel
szofer *m* (*-a*; *-rzy*) driver; **~ka** *f* (*-i*; *G -rek*) cab
szok *m* (*-u*; *-i*) shock; **~ować** ⟨**za-**⟩ shock; **~owy** shock
szop *m* (*-a*; *-y*) *zo.* racoon
szop|a *f* (*-y*; *G szop*) shed; **~ka** *f* (*-i*; *G -pek*) *rel.* crib
szorować ⟨**wy-**⟩ (*-uję*) scrub, scour
szorstk|o *adv.* roughly; coarsely; **~i** rough; *ktoś* coarse, abrupt
szorty *pl.* (*G -tów*) shorts *pl.*
szosa *f* (*-y*; *G szos*) high road, highway
szowinistyczny chauvinist
szóst|ka *f* (*-i*; *G -tek*) six; (*linia itp.*) number six; **~y** sixth; → ***715***
szpachl|a *f* (*-i*; *-e*) spatula; **~ować** (*-uję*) stop, fill
szpa|da *f* (*-y*; *G -*) épée; **~del** *m* (*-dla*; *-dle*) spade; **~dzista** *m* (*-y*; *G -tów*), **~dzistka** *f* (*-i*; *G -tek*) épéeist
szpa|gat *m* (*-u*; *-y*) splits *pl.*; (*sznurek*) string; **~k** *m* (*-a*; *-i*) *zo.* starling; **~kowaty** *Brt.* greying, *Am.* graying; *koń* roan; **~ler** *m* (*-u*; *-y*) line; **~ra** *f* (*-y*; *G -*) slit, cleft; crack
szparag *m* (*-u*; *-i*) *bot.*: *zw.* ***~i*** *pl.* asparagus
szpargał *m* (*-u*; *-y*) bit of paper; ***~y*** *pl.* useless papers
szpecić (*-cę*) mar; ⟨**o-, ze-**⟩ disfigure
szperać (*-am*) rummage about *lub* through
szpetny ugly, unsightly
szpic *m* (*-a*; *-e*) point, tip; *zo.* spitz; **~el** *m* (*-cla*; *-cle*) *pej.* informer; **~ruta** *f* (*-y*; *G -*) riding whip
szpieg *m* (*-a*; *-dzy*) spy
szpiego|stwo *n* (*-a*; *G -*) spying, espionage; **~wać** (*-uję*) spy; **~wski** spy
szpik *m* (*-u*; *0*) *anat.* marrow; → ***kość***
szpilk|a *f* (*-i*; *G -lek*) pin; (*do włosów*) hairpin; (*obcas*) stiletto; **~owy** *bot.* coniferous
szpinak *m* (*-u*; *-i*) *bot.* spinach
szpital *m* (*-a*; *-e*) hospital; **~ny** hospital
szpon *m* (*-a*/*-u*; *-y*) claw, talon
szprotka *f* (*-i*; *G -tek*) *zo.* sprat
szprycha *f* (*-y*; *G -*) spoke

szpul|a *f* (*-i*; *-e*) reel, spool; **~ka** *f* (*-i*; *G -lek*) reel, spool
szrama *f* (*-y*; *G -*) scar
szreń *f* (*-ni*; *0*) firn, névé
szron *m* (*-u*; *0*) frost
szt. *skrót pisany*: ***sztuk(a)*** pc. (*piece*)
sztab *m* (*-u*; *-y*) staff; ***~ główny*** headquarters *pl.*
sztab|a *f* (*-y*; *G -*) bar; ***~a złota*** gold bar *lub* ingot
sztabowy staff
sztacheta *f* (*-y*; *G -*) pale
sztafet|a *f* (*-y*; *G -*) *sport*: relay; **~owy**: ***bieg ~owy*** relay race
sztalug|a *f* (*-i*; *G -*): *zw.* ***~i*** easel
sztandar *m* (*-u*; *-y*) flag, standard; **~owy** flag, standard
sztang|a *f* (*-i*; *G -*) (*w sporcie*) weight; **~ista** *m* (*-y*; *G -ów*) (*w sporcie*) weightlifter
sztolnia *f* (*-i*; *-e*) (*w górnictwie*) gallery
szton *m* (*-u*; *-y*) chip
sztorc: ***na ~*** on end
sztorm *m* (*-u*; *-y*) storm; **~owy** storm
sztruks|owy corduroy; **~y** *pl.* cords *pl.*
sztucz|ka *f* (*-i*; *G -czek*) trick; **~ny** artificial, *biżuteria itp.* imitation
sztućce *m/pl.* (*-ćców*) cutlery
sztufada *f* (*-y*; *G -*) *gastr.* marinated roast beef
sztuk|a *f* (*-i*; *G -*) art; (*jednostka*) piece; *theat.* play; (*umiejętność*) artistry; (*robienia czegoś*) knack; ***historia ~i*** history of art; ***~a mięsa*** boiled beef; **~ować** ⟨**nad-**⟩ (*-uję*) piece together
szturch|ać ⟨**~nąć**⟩ nudge, elbow
szturm *m* (*-u*; *-y*) *mil.* assault, storm; **~ować** (*-uję*) *mil.* storm; **~owy** *mil.* assault
sztych *m* (*-u*; *-y*) stab; (*rycina*) engraving
sztygar *m* (*-a*; *-rzy*) (*w górnictwie*) pit foreman
sztylet *m* (*-u*; *-y*) dagger
sztywn|ieć ⟨**ze-**⟩ (*-eję*) stiffen; grow stiff; **~o** *adv.* stiffly; **~y** stiff
szubienica *f* (*-y*; *G -*) gallows
szubrawiec *m* (*-wca*; *-wcy*) *pej.* scoundrel
szuf|elka *f* (*-i*; *G -lek*) (*do zamiatania*) dustpan; **~la** *f* (*-i*; *-e*) shovel; **~lada** *f* (*-y*; *G -*) drawer; **~lować** (*-uję*) shovel
szukać (*-am*) ⟨**po-**⟩ look for, search
szuler *m* (*-a*; *-rzy*) card-sharper
szum *m* (*-u*; *-y*) noise; (*fal*) hum; (*wody, drzew*) rustle; F *fig.* fuss
szumieć[1] (*-ę*, *-i*) be noisy; rustle
szum|ieć[2] (*-ę*, *-i*) effervesce; ***~i mu w głowie*** his head is buzzing; **~ny** noisy; *fig.* high-flown; **~owiny** *f/pl.* (-) scum (*też fig.*)
szur|ać (*-am*) scrape (***nogami*** one's feet)
szus *m* (*-u/-a*; *-y*) (*w sporcie*) schuss
szuter *m* (*-tru*; *0*) gravel
szuwary *m/pl.* (*-ów*) reeds *pl.*
szwaczka *f* (*-i*; *G -czek*) needlewoman, seamstress
szwagier *m* (*-gra*; *-growie*) brother-in-law; **~ka** *f* (*-i*; *G -rek*) sister-in-law
Szwajcar *m* (*-a*; *-rzy*) Swiss; **~ia** *f* (*GDL -ii*) Switzerland; **~ka** Swiss; **&ski** Swiss
szwalnia *f* (*-i*; *-e*) sewing workshop
szwank *m* (*-u*; *0*): ***bez ~u*** unscathed; **~ować** (*-uję*) go wrong, malfunction
Szwecja *f* (*-i*; *0*) Sweden
Szwed *m* (*-a*; *-dzi*), **~ka** *f* (*-i*; *G -dek*) Swede
szwedz|ki Swedish; ***mówić po ~ku*** speak Swedish
szwu, szwy → ***szew***
szyb *m* (*-u*; *-y*) shaft; ***~ naftowy*** oil well; **~a** *f* (*-y*; *G -*) (window) pane
szyb|ciej *adv. comp. od* → **~ki** fast, quick, swift; **~ko** *adv.* fast, quickly, swiftly
szyberdach *m mot.* sunroof, sliding roof
szybko|strzelny *mil.* quick-fire, quick-firing; **~ściomierz** speedometer; **~ściowy** high-speed; **~ść** *f* (*-ści*) speed, rapidity; *tech., phys.* velocity; **~war** *m* (*-u*; *-y*) *gastr.* pressure cooker
szybow|ać (*-uję*) glide; **~iec** *m* (*-wca*; *-wce*) glider; **~nictwo** *n* (*-a*; *0*) gliding; **~nik** *m* (*-a*; *-cy*) glider pilot; **~y** gliding
szybszy *adj.* (*m-os -bsi*) *comp. od* → ***szybki***
szyci|e *n* (*-a*; *G -yć*) sewing; ***do ~a*** sewing
szyć ⟨**u-**⟩ (*szyję*) sew
szydełko *n* (*-a*; *G -łek*) crochet hook; **~wać** (*-uję*) crochet
szyder|czo *adv.* derisively; **~czy** derisive; **~stwo** *n* (*-a*; *G -*) derisiveness
szydło *n* (*-a*; *G -deł*) awl
szydzić (*-dzę*) (***z*** *G*) ridicule, mock, deride

S

szyfr *m* (*-u*; *-y*) cipher, code; **~ować** ⟨**za-**⟩ (*-uję*) cipher, code, encode
szyj|a *f* (*szyi*; *-e*, *szyj*) *anat.* neck; **po ~ę** up to one's neck; **~ka** *f* (*-i*; *G -jek*) neck; *anat.* **~ka macicy** cervix; **~ny** neck
szyk[1] *m* (*-u*; *0*) chic, stylish
szyk[2] *m* (*-u*; *0*) order; formation; *gr.* (word) order; *t-ko pl.* **~i** *pl.* (*-ów*) ranks *pl.*; *fig.* **pomieszać ~i** (*D*) thwart, frustrate
szykować ⟨**na-, przy-**⟩ (*-uję*) prepare; **~** ⟨**na-, przy-**⟩ **się** get prepared, get ready (**do** *G* for)
szyl|d *m* (*-u*; *-y*), **~dzik** *m* (*-u*; *-i*) sign
szyling *m* (*-a*; *-i*) shilling
szympans *m* (*-a*; *-y*) *zo.* chimpanzee
szyna *f* (*-y*; *G -*) *rail.* rail; *med.* splint
szynel *m* (*-a*; *-e*) *mil.* overcoat
szynka *f* (*-i*; *G -nek*) ham
szynowy rail
szyper *m* (*-pra*; *-prowie*) skipper
szyszka *f* (*-i*; *G -szek*) cone

Ś

ścian|a *f* (*-y*; *G -*) wall; ***mieszkać przez ~ę*** (**z** *I*) live next door (to); **~ka** *f* (*-i*; *G -nek*) wall (*też biol.*, *anat.*)
ściąć *pf.* → **ścinać**
ściąg|a *f* (*-i*; *G -*) *szkoła*: F crib; **~acz** *m* (*-a*; *-e*) (knitted) welt; **~ać** (*-am*) ⟨**~nąć**⟩ *v/t.* pull down; *skórę* peel off; *pierścionek* pull off; *wino* bottle; *buty*, *ubranie* take off; *uwagę* draw (**na siebie** to o.s.); *podatki* levy; *wojska* move together; *brwi* knit; F (*w szkole*) copy, crib; *zw. pf.* (*ukraść*) pinch, swipe; *v./i. ludzie*: gather, congregate
ściec *pf.* → **ściekać**
ścieg *m* (*-u*; *-i*) stitch
ściek *m* (*-u*; *-i*) sewer; **~i** *pl.* sewage, sewerage; **~ać** (*-am*) ⟨**~nąć**⟩ flow off *lub* away
ściemni|ać (*-am*) ⟨**~ć**⟩ (*-ę*, *-nij!*) → **przyciemniać**; **~a się** it is getting dark; **~eć** *pf.* grow dark
ście|nny wall; **~rać** (*-am*) *skórę* rub off (**się** *v/i.*) *gastr.* grate; (*gumką*) erase, rub out; (*gąbką*, *kurz*) wipe off; **~rka** *f* (*-i*; *G -rek*) cloth; (*do wycierania naczyń*) *Brt.* drying-up cloth, *Am.* dish towel
ścier|nisko *f* (*-a*; *G -*) stubble field; **~ny** *tech.* abrasive; **~pieć** (*-ę*) *pf.* bear, tolerate; **~pnąć** *pf.* → **cierpnąć**
ścieśni|ać (*-am*) ⟨**~ć**⟩ (*-ę*, *-nij!*) (**się**) narrow, become narrow; contract; crowd together; **~ć szeregi** close ranks
ścieżka *f* (*-i*; *G -żek*) (foot)path; track **~ dźwiękowa** sound track; **~ zdrowia** keep-fit trail
ścięgno *n* (*-a*; *G -gien*) *anat.* tendon
ścięty cut off; *białko* stiff; **stożek ~** truncated cone; **~ skośnie** bevelled
ściga|cz *m* (*-a*; *-e*) speedboat; **~ć** (*-am*) chase, pursue; *zbrodniarza* hunt; **~ć się** race; *fig.* compete
ścinać (*-am*) cut (*też zakręt*); (*piłą*) saw off; (*w sporcie*) smash; *hist.* behead; **~ się** coagulate, clot; *mleko*: curdle
ścis|k *m* (*-u*; *0*) crowd; **~kać** *v/t.* (*w objęciach*) squeeze, hug; *rękę* press, squeeze; compress; clasp; *fig.* **coś ~ka mnie w gardle** I have a lump in my throat; → **uściskać**; **zaciskać**; **~kać się** crowd, throng; move together
ści|słość *f* (*-ści*; *0*) precision; **dla ~słości** to be precise; **~sły** (*m-os -śli*) precise; *więzi* close; *dieta* strict; *przepis* exact, strict; **nauki ~słe** the sciences; **~snąć** *pf.* → **ściskać**; **~szać** (*-am*) → **przyciszać**; **~śle** *adv.*, **~ślejszy** *adj.* (*comp. od* → **ścisły**); **~śle biorąc** to be precise
ślad *m* (*-u*; *-y*) (*pojedynczy*) print; (*ciąg*) trail; (*pozostałość*) trace; **bez ~u** without trace; **ani ~u** (*G*) not a trace (of); **iść ~em, iść w ~y** (*G*) follow in s.o.'s footsteps
ślamazarny sluggish, slothful
ślaz *m* (*-u*; *-y*) *bot.* mallow
Śląsk *m* (*-a*; *0*) Silesia; **♀ski** Silesian; **~zaczka** *f* (*-i*; *G -czek*), **~zak** *m* (*-a*; *-cy*) Silesian
śledczy *jur.* investigating
śledzić (*-dzę*) *v/t.* follow, trail; *por.* **tropić**
śledzio|na *f* (*-y*; *G -*) *anat.* spleen; **~wy** herring
śledztwo *n* (*-a*; *G -*) investigation

śledź *m* (*-dzia*; *-dzie*) *zo.* herring; **~ wędzony** bloater, smoked herring
ślep|ia *n/pl.* eyes *pl.*; **~iec** *m* (*-pca, -cze!*; *-pcy, -pców*) blind person; **~nąć** ⟨**o-**⟩ (*-nę*) go blind; lose one's sight; **~o** *adv.* blindly; ***na ~o*** blindly; **~ota** *f* (*-y*; *0*) blindness; **~y 1.** blind (*też fig.*; ***na*** *A* to); → ***uliczka, tor***; **2.** *m* (*-ego*; *-i*), **~a** *f* (*-ej*; *-e*) blind person
ślęczeć (*-ę, -y*) (***nad*** *I*) pore (over)
śliczny beautiful, lovely
ślima|czy sluggish; **~k** *m* (*-a*; *-i*) *zo.* (*skorupkowy*) snail, (*nagi*) slug; *anat.* cochlea; *tech.* worm, screw; **~kowaty** helical, helicoid
ślin|a *f* (*-y*; *0*) saliva, (*wypluta*) spit; **~ić** (*-ę*) ⟨**po-**⟩ moisten; ***~ić się*** dribble, drool; ⟨**za-**⟩ slobber; **~ka** *f* (*-i*; *G -nek*) → ***ślina***; ***~ka mi do ust idzie*** my mouth waters
ślisk|i slippery; *fig.* tricky; **~o** *adv.*: ***jest ~o*** it is slippery
śliw|a *f* (*-y*; *G -*) *bot.* plum tree; **~ka** *f* (*-i*; *G -wek*) plum; ***~ka suszona*** prune; **~kowy** plum
ślizg *m* (*-u*; *-i*) chute; (*łódka*) → **~acz** *m* (*-a*; *-e*) hydroplane boat; **~ać się** (*-am*) slide, glide (***po*** *I* on); ***~ać się na łyżwach*** skate; **~awica** *f* (*-y*; *G -*) black ice; **~awka** *f* (*-i*; *G -wek*) ice-rink
ślub *m* (*-u*; *-y*) (***cywilny, kościelny*** registry office, church) wedding; ***brać ~*** be married; ***dawać ~, udzielić ~u*** marry; *rel.* ***~y*** *pl.* ***zakonne*** vows *pl.*; **~ny** wedding; marriage; **~ować** (*im*)*pf.* (*-uję*) vow, promise solemnly; **~owanie** *n* (*-a*; *G -ań*) vow
ślusa|rnia *f* (*-i*; *-e*) locksmith's workshop; **~rz** *m* (*-a*; *-e*) locksmith
śluz *m* (*-u*; *-y*) *med.* mucus; *biol.* slime
śluz|a *f* (*-y*; *G -*) sluice(way), lock
śluz|owy[1] sluice, lock
śluz|owy[2] *biol.*, *med.* mucous; **~ówka** *f* (*-i*; *G -wek*) mucous membrane
śmiać się ⟨***za- się***⟩ (*-eję*) laugh (***z*** *G* at)
śmiał|ek *m* (*-łka*; *-łkowie*) daredevil; **~o** *adv.* bravely, boldly **~ość** *f* (*-ści*; *0*) bravery, daring, boldness; **~y** brave, daring
śmiech *m* (*-u*; *-y*) laughter ***pokładać się ze ~u*** double up with laughter; ***ze ~em*** with laughter
śmie|ciarka *f* (*-i*; *G -rek*) *Brt.* dust-cart; *Am.* garbage truck; **~cić** ⟨**na-**⟩ (*-cę*) dirty, soil; litter; **~ci(e)** *pl.* (*-i*) litter, refuse, *Brt.* rubbish; *Am.* garbage
śmie|ć 1. dare; **2.** *m* (*-cia*; *-ci(e)*) → ***śmieci***; **~lej** *adv. comp. od* → ***śmiało***; **~lszy** *adj. comp. od* → ***śmiały***
śmier|ć *f* (*-ci*; *0*) death; ***ponieść ~ć*** die; ***na ~ć*** to death; *jur.* ***wyrok ~ci*** death sentence
śmierdz|ący stinking; **~ieć** (*-ę*; *-i*) stink; *fig.* smell; ***tu ~i*** it stinks here
śmierteln|iczka *f* (*-i*; *G -czek*), **~ik** *m* (*-a*; *-cy*) mortal; **~ość** *f* (*-ści*; *0*) mortality; **~y** *człowiek* mortal *wypadek* fatal; *dawka* lethal
śmieszn|ie *adv.* funnily; ***~ie niska cena*** ridiculously low price; **~ość** *f* (*-ści*; *0*) ridiculousness; ludicrousness; **~y** funny; ridiculous; ludicrous
śmietan|a *f* (*-y*; *0*) cream; **~ka** *f* (*-i*; *G -nek*) cream (*też fig.*); **~kowy** cream
śmietni|czka *f* (*-i*; *G -czek*) dustpan; **~k** *m* (*-a*; *-i*) *Brt.* dustbin, *Am.* garbage can, trash can; *fig.* mess; **~sko** *n* (*-a*; *G -*) *Brt.* tip; rubbish dump
śmig|ać (*-am*) ⟨***~nąć***⟩ (*-nąć*) *v/i.* flick; flit, dart; **~ło** *n* (*-a*; *G -gieł*) *aviat.* propeller; **~łowiec** *m* (*-wca*; *-wce*) *aviat.* helicopter; **~łowy** *aviat.* propeller-driven
śniadani|e *n* (*-a*; *-G -ań*) breakfast; ***jeść ~e*** have breakfast; **~owy** breakfast
śniady dark-skinned
śni|ć (*-ę, -nij!*) dream (***o*** *L* about); ***~ł(a) mu się*** (*A*) he dreamt (about); ***ani mi się ~!*** I can't be bothered!
śniedź *f* (*-dzi*; *0*) verdigris
śnieg *m* (*-u*; *-i*) snow; ***biały jak ~*** snow--white; **~owce** *m/pl.* (*-ów*) overshoes *pl.*; **~owy** snow
śnież|ka *f* (*-i*; *G -żek*) snowball; **~ny** snow; **~yca** *f* (*-y*; *G -*) snowstorm; **~yczka** *f* (*-i*; *-czek*) *bot.* snowdrop
śp. *skrót pisany*: ***świętej pamięci*** the late
śpią|cy sleepy, drowsy; **~czka** *f* (*-i*; *G -czek*) coma
śpiesz|ny hurried; **~yć się** (*-ę*) hurry; *zegar*: be fast; (***z*** *I*) hurry up (with)
śpiew *m* (*-u*; *-y*) *mus.* song, singing; **~aczka** *f* (*-i*; *G -czek*) *mus.* singer; **~aczy** singing; **~ać** (*-am*) sing; **~ak** *m* (*-a*; *-cy*) *mus.* singer; **~anie** *n* (*-a*; *0*) singing; **~ka** *f* (*-i*; *G -wek*) → ***śpiew***; **~nik** *m* (*-a*; *-i*) songbook; **~ny** melodious; *akcent* singsong

śpio|ch *m* (*-a*; *-y*) late riser; → **~szki** *m/pl.* (*-ków*) playsuit, rompers *pl.*
śpiwór *m* (*-woru*; *-wory*) sleeping-bag
śr. *skrót pisany*: ***średni(o)*** on average; ***środa*** Wed.; ***średnica*** diameter
średni medium; average, mean, moderate; **~a** *f* (*-ej*; *-e*) mean (value); ***~a roczna*** annual average; **~ca** *f* (*-y*; *-e*) diameter; **~k** *m* (*-a*; *-i*) semicolon; **~o** *adv.* on (an) average; moderately
średnio|terminowy medium-term; **~wiecze** *n* (*-a*; *0*) the Middle Ages *pl.*; **~wieczny** medi(a)eval
środ|a *f* (*-y*; *G śród*) Wednesday; **~ek** *m* (*-dka*; *-dki*) middle, *Brt.* centre, *Am.* center; inside; agent; *fig.* means *sg/.pl.*, measures *pl.*; ***~ek leczniczy*** remedy; ***~ek płatniczy*** means of payment; *jur.* ***~ek prawny*** appeal; ***~ki** pl.* ***trwałe*** fixed assets *pl.*; → ***ciężkość, przekaz*** *itp.*; ***do ~ka*** inside; ***od ~ka*** from within; ***bez ~ków*** without means; ***wszelkimi ~kami*** by all means; **~kowy** central, middle
środowisk|o *n* (*-a*; *G -*) environment; surroundings *pl.*; ***zanieczyszczenie ~a*** environmental pollution; **~owy** environmental
środowy Wednesday
śród|mieście *n* (*-a*; *G -ść*) centre, *Am.* downtown; inner city; **~ziemnomorski** Mediterranean; **~ziemny**: ***Morze* Śziemne** the Mediterranean (Sea)
śruba *f* (*-y*; *G -*) screw; *naut.* propeller
śrubo|kręt *m* (*-u*; *-y*) screwdriver; **~wy** screw
śrut *m* (*-u*; *-y*) shot; **~a** *f* (*-y*; *G -*) crushed grain, groats *pl.*; **~owy** shot; *agr.* groats; **~ówka** *f* (*-i*; *G -wek*) shotgun
św. *skrót pisany*: ***święty*** St. (*saint*); ***świadek*** witness
świadcz|enie *n* (*-a*; *G -eń*), *zw. pl.* ***~enia*** benefits *pl.*; **~yć** (*-ę*) (**o** *L*) testify (to); testify (***w sądzie*** in court); *usługi* provide, render
świad|ectwo *n* (*-a*; *G -ectw*) (*dokument*) certificate; (*stwierdzenie*) testimony; (*w szkole*) *Brt.* school report, *Am.* report card; ***~ectwo urodzenia*** birth certificate; **~ek** *m* (*-dka*; *-dkowie*) *jur.* (***naoczny*** eye)witness
świadom|ość *f* (*-ści*; *0*) consciousness; **~y** (*nie nieprzytomny*) conscious; (*zamierzony*) deliberate, intentional; ***być ~(ym)*** (*G*) (*zdający sobie sprawę*) be aware (of)
świat *m* (*-a*; *-y*) world; *fig.* realm; ***za nic w świecie*** not for anything in the world
światł|o *n* (*-a*; *G -teł*) (***dzienne*** day)-light; *mot.* ***~a** pl.* ***długie/drogowe*** full beam; ***~a** pl.* ***krótkie/mijania*** *Brt.* dipped, *Am.* dimmed, beam; ***pod ~o*** to the light
światło|czuły photosensitive; **~mierz** *m* (*-a*; *-e*) *phot.* exposure meter; **~odporny** light-fast
światopogląd *m* (*-u*; *-y*) outlook, viewpoint; **~wy** *ktoś* worldly; (*na całym świecie*) worldwide
świąd *m* (*-u*; *0*) *med.* itch
świąt|eczny festive, holiday; *ubranie itp.* Sunday; **~ek** *m* (*-tka*; *-tki*) *rel.* holy figure; ***Zielone* Śki** *pl.* Whitsuntide; **~ynia** *f* (*-i*; *-e*) temple; (*kościół*) church
świd|er *m* (*-dra*; *-dry*) *tech.* bit; *górnictwo*: drill, bore; **~rować** (*-uję*) drill; *fig.* bore; **~rujący** piercing
świec|a *f* (*-y*; *G -*) candle; *mot.* spark--plug; **~ący** shiny, luminous; **~ić** (*-cę*) (*też* ***się***) shine, glow; ***~ić pustkami*** be deserted
świecki lay
świecz|ka *f* (*-i*; *G -czek*) → ***świeca***; **~nik** *m* (*-a*; *-i*) candlestick, candle holder
świergot *m* (*-u*; *-y*) chirp, twitter; **~ać** (*-am*) chirp, twitter
świerk *m* (*-u*; *-i*) *bot.* spruce; **~owy** spruce
świerszcz *m* (*-a*; *-e*) *zo.* cricket
świerzb *m* (*-u*; *-y*) *med.* itch; **~ić**, **~ieć** (*-ę*, *-i*) itch
świet|lany shining, luminous; *fig.* bright, rosy; **~lica** *f* (*-y*; *G -*) day-room; community-room; **~lik** *m* (*-a*; *-i*) *zo.* glow-worm; *bud.* skylight; *naut.* porthole; **~lny** light; **~lówka** *f* (*-i*; *G -wek*) fluorescent lamp
świetny splendid, magnificent
śwież|o *adv.* freshly; newly; **~ość** *f* (*-ści*; *0*) freshness; newness; **~y** fresh; new
święc|ić (*-cę*) celebrate; ⟨**po-**⟩ *rel.* consecrate; *dzień* keep, observe; **~ie** *adv.* faithfully, solemnly; **~ony** **1.** consecrated; sanctified; **2.** ***~one*** *n* (*-ego*; *0*) Easter meal; (*food blessed in church at Easter*)

Ś

święto *n* (*-a*; *G świąt*) holiday; feast-day; special day; ♀ ***Matki*** Mother's Day; **~jański** St. John's; **~kradztwo** *n* (*-a*; *G -*) sacrilege, profanation, desecration; **~szek** *m* (*-szka*; *-szki/-szkowie*) hypocrite, prude; **~ść** *f* (*-ści*) holiness; sanctity, sacredness; **~wać** (*-uję*) celebrate; keep, observe
święty holy, blessed; ***Wszystkich ♀ch*** All Saints' Day
świn|ia *f* (*-i*; *-e*) *zo.* pig; *fig.* swine; **~ka** *f* (*-i*; *G -nek*) → ***świnia***; ***~ka morska*** *zo.* guinea pig; *med.* mumps *sg.*; **~tuch** *m* (*-a*; *-y*) *fig. pej.* (*brudas*) slob, pig; (*bezecny*) dirty old man
świńs|ki piggish; *fig.* filthy; **~two** *n* (*-a*; *G -*) (*brud*) mess; (*jedzenie*) nasty stuff; (*postępek*) dirty trick
świr *m* (*-a*; *-y*) F nut
świs|nąć *v/s.* (*-nę*) whistle; F pinch; **~t** *m* (*-u*; *-y*) whistle; **~tać** (*-am*) whistle; **~tak** *m* (*-a*; *-i*) *zo.* marmot; **~tek** *m* (*-stka*; *-stki*) slip of paper
świt *m* (*-u*; *-y*) dawn; ***o świcie*** at dawn; **~a** *f* (*-y*; *G -*) entourage, retinue; **~ać** (*-am*) dawn; *fig.* ⟨***za-***⟩ cross one's mind; ***~a*** it dawns; the day breaks

T

ta *pron. f* → ***ten***
t. *skrót pisany*: ***tom*** vol. (*volume*)
tabaka *f* (*-i*; *G -*) snuff
tabela *f* (*-i*; *G -*) table; chart; ***~ wygranych*** list of winners; **~ryczny** tabular
tabletka *f* (*-i*; *G -tek*) tablet
tablica *f* (*-y*; *G -*) plate; *szkoła*: blackboard; *baseball*: backboard; → ***rejestracyjny, rozdzielczy***
tabliczka *f* (*-i*; *G -czek*) → ***tablica***; (*z numerem*) number-plate, (*z nazwiskiem*) name-plate; ***~ czekolady*** bar of chocolate; ***~ mnożenia*** multiplication tables *pl.*
tabor *m* (*-u*; *-y*) transport fleet; *rail.* rolling stock; (**cygański** Gypsy) camp
taboret *m* (*-u*; *-y*) stool
taca *f* (*-y*; *G -*) plate (*też rel.*); tray
tacy *pl.* → ***taki***
taczać (*-am*) roll (***się*** *v/i.*)
taczk|a *f* (*-i*), **~i** *f/pl.* (*G -czek*) wheelbarrow
tafla *f* (*-i*; *-e*, *-i/ -fel*) sheet; expanse
taić ⟨***za-***⟩ (*-ję*) hide, conceal (***przed*** *I* against); *poglądy też* keep secret, suppress
tajać (*-ję*) melt
tajemni|ca *f* (*-y*; *-e*, *-*) secret; ***w ~cy*** in secret; ***trzymać w ~cy*** keep secret; **~czo** *adv.* secretly; **~czy** secretive, enigmatic
taj|emny secret; underhand; **~niak** F *m* (*-a*; *-cy*) secret agent; **~nie** *adv.* secretly; underhand; **~nik** *m* (*-a*; *-i*): *zw. pl.* ***~niki*** secrets *pl.*; **~ność** *f* (*-ści*; *0*) secrecy; **~ny** secret; ***ściśle ~ne*** top secret
tak yes; (*dla wzmocnienia znaczenia następującego wyrazu*) so; ***~ jak on*** like he (does *itp.*); ***~ że*** so that; ***~ żeby*** in such a way that; ***i ~*** anyway; ***~ samo*** just as, ***~ sobie*** so-so, not too bad; ***~ … jak i …*** … as well as …; ***~ czy owak/siak*** one way or the other; *mil.* ***~ jest!*** yes, sir!
tak|i *pron. m* (*m-os tacy*) such; so; → ***jaki, jako, raz***[1]; ***~i sam*** the same, identical; ***~i sobie*** so-so; ***nic ~iego*** nothing special; ***~i czy owaki/siaki*** it makes no odds; ***coś ~iego*** something like, a thing like that; **~iż** → ***taki*** (***sam***); **~o** → ***jako***
tak|sa *f* (*-y*; *G -*): ***~sa klimatyczna*** visitors' tax; **~siarz** *m* (*-a*; *-e*) F → ***taksówkarz***; **~sować**⟨***o-***⟩(*-uję*) estimate; **~sówka** *f* (*-i*; *G -wek*) taxi, cab; **~sówkarz** *m* (*-a*; *-e*) taxi-driver, cab-driver
takt *m* (*-u*; *-y*) *mus.* bar; (*poczucie*) time, rhythm; *fig.* tact; **~owny** tactful
taktyczny tactical
taktyka *f* (*-i*; *G -*) tactics *sg.*
także also
talarek *m* (*-rka*; *-rki*) *gastr.* slice
talent *m* (*-u*; *-y*) (**do** *G*) talent (to), gift (to)
talerz *m* (*-a*; *-e*), **~yk** *m* (*-a*; *-i*) plate
tali|a *f* (*GDL -ii*; *-e*) waist; ***~a kart*** pack, *Am.* deck; ***wcięty w ~i*** *ubranie* fit at the waist

talk *m* (*-u*; *-0*) talcum (powder)
talon *m* (*-u*; *-y*) coupon
tam (over) there; ***kto ~?*** who's there?; ***tu i ~*** here and there; ***gdzie ~!*** nothing of the kind!; ***co mi ~!*** what do I care!; ***jakiś ~ …*** some …; → ***powrót***
tam|a *f* (*-y*; *G -*) dam; *fig.* ***położyć ~ę*** (*D*) check, stem
tamci *pl.* → ***tamten***
Tamiza *f* (*-y*; *0*) the Thames
tamować ⟨**za-**⟩ (*-uję*) stop; *krwotok* stanch
tam|ta *f*, **~te** *f/pl.* → ***tamten***; **~tejszy** local; **~ten** that; ***ani ten, ani ~ten*** neither; ***po ~tej stronie*** on the other side; ***na ~tym świecie*** hereafter; **~tędy** that way; **~to** → ***tamten***; ***to i ~to*** this and that; **~że** in the same place
tance|rka *f* (*-i*; *G -rek*), **~rz** *m* (*-a*; *-e*) dancer
tande|ciarnia *f* (*-i*; *-e*) junk shop; **~ta** *f* (*-y*; *zw. 0*) trashy goods *pl.*, junk; **~tnie** *adv.* trashily, shoddily; **~tny** trashy, shoddy
taneczny dancing
tani cheap (*też fig.*); ***za ~e pieniądze*** dirt cheap
taniec *m* (*-ńca*; *-ńce*) dance
tanieć ⟨**po-, s-**⟩ get cheaper
tanio *adv.* cheaply; **~cha** F *f* (*-y*; *G -*) low price
tankow|ać ⟨**za-**⟩ (*-uję*) *v/t.* fill up; *v/i.* put *Brt.* petrol (*Am.* gas) in; **~iec** *m* (*-wca*; *-wce*) *naut.* tanker
tań|ce *pl.* → ***taniec***; **~czyć** ⟨**po-, za-**⟩ (*-ę*) dance (*też fig.*)
tapczan *m* (*-u*; *-y*) divan
tapet|a *f* (*-y*; *G -*) wallpaper; **~ować** ⟨**wy-**⟩ (*-uję*) wallpaper, paper
tapicer *m* (*-a*; *-rzy*) upholsterer; **~ka** *f* (*-i*; *G -rek*) upholstery
tapirować ⟨**u-**⟩ (*-uję*) backcomb
tarapaty *pl.* (*-ów*) trouble; ***wpaść w ~*** get in trouble
taras *m* (*-u*; *-y*) terrace; **~ować** ⟨**za-**⟩ (*-uję*) block; *drzwi* barricade
tarci|ca *f* (*-y*; *-e*) cut timber; **~e** *n* (*-a*; *G -rć*) friction (*też tech.*); ***~a*** *pl.* friction
tarcz|a *f* (*-y*; *-e*, *G -*) shield; *Brt.* disc, *Am.* disk; (*do strzelania*) target; *tel.* dial; ***~a zegara*** clock/watch face; **~owy** *tech.* disc/disk, circular; ***piła ~owa*** circular saw; ***hamulce ~owe*** disk brakes; **~yca** *f* (*-y*; *-e*) *anat.* thyroid (gland)
targ *m* (*-u*; *-i*) market; ***~i*** *pl. econ.* fair; ***dobić ~u*** (***z*** *I*) come to an agreement (with); ***po długich ~ach*** after lengthy haggling
targ|ać (*-am*) ruffle one's hair; pull; → ***szarpać***; **~nąć się** *pf.* (*-nę*) make an attempt (**na** *A* on); ***~nąć się na życie*** (attempt to) commit a suicide
targow|ać (*-uję*) (*I*) trade (with), deal (with); ***~ać się*** haggle (**o** *A* over); **~isko** *n* (*-a*; *G -*) market(-place); **~y** market, fair
tar|ka *f* (*-i*; *G -rek*) grater; **~lisko** *n* (*-a*; *G -*) spawning-ground; **~mosić** (*-szę*) → ***targać, szarpać***; **~nik** *n* (*-a*; *-i*) *tech.* rasp; **~nina** *f* (*-y*; *G -*) *bot.* blackthorn
tart|ak *m* (*-u*; *-i*) sawmill; **~y** grated; ***bułka ~a*** breadcrumbs *pl.*
taryf|a *f* (*-y*; *G -*) (*opłaty*) rates *pl.*; (*opłaty za przejazd*) fares *pl.*; F (*taksówka*) cab; **~owy** *tabela* rate, fare
tarzać (*-am*) roll; ***~ się*** roll about
tasak *m* (*-a*; *-i*) chopper, cleaver
tasiem|iec *m* (*-mca*; *-mce*) *zo.* tapeworm; **~ka** *f* (*-i*; *G -mek*) tape
tasować ⟨**prze-**⟩ (*-uję*) *karty* shuffle
taśm|a *f* (*-y*; *G -*) tape; (*montażowa*) assembly line; ***~a samoklejąca*** adhesive tape, *Brt.* Sellotape, *Am.* Scotch tape; ***~a maszynowa*** typewriter ribbon; ***~a filmowa*** film; *mil.* cartridge-belt; ***przy ~ie*** *tech.* on the assembly line; **~owy** tape
tata *m* (*-y*; *DL tacie*; *-owie*, *-ów*) → ***tatuś***
Tatar *m* **1.** (*-a*; *-rzy*) Tartar; **2.** ♀ F (*-a*; *-y*) *gastr.* steak tartar(e); **♀ak** *m* (*-a*; *-i*) *bot.* sweet flag, calamus; **♀ski** Tartar; ***sos ♀ski*** tartar(e) sauce
taterni|czka *f* (*-i*; *G -czek*), **~k** *m* (*-a*; *-cy*) mountaineer
tato *m* (*-y*; *DL tacie*; *-owie*, *-ów*) → ***tatuś***
Tatry *pl.* (*G Tatr*) the Tatra Mountains *pl.*
tatrzański Tatra
tatuaż *m* (*-u*; *-e*) tattoo
tatuś *m* (*-sia*; *-siowie*) F dad
taż *pron. f* → ***tenże***
tą *pron.* (*I/sg*, F *A/sg.* → ***ta***) → ***ten***
tch|awica *f* (*-y*; *G -*) *anat.* windpipe, trachea; **~em** → ***dech***; **~nąć** (*-nę*) (*im*)*pf.* *v/i* smell (*I* of); *v/t. pf. pf.* breathe (into); **~nienie** *n* (*-a*; *G -eń*) breath
tchórz *m* (*-a*; *-e*) coward; **~liwie** *adv.* in a cowardly manner; **~liwy** cowardly;

T

~ostwo *n* (*-a*; *G -stw*) cowardliness; **~yć** ⟨**s-**⟩ (*-ę*) back out
tchu → ***dech***
te *pron. pl. f* → ***ten***
teatr *m* (*-u*; *-y*) *Brt.* theatre, *Am.* theater; **~alny** theatrical
tech|niczny technical; **~nik** *m* (*-a*; *-i*) technician; **~nika** *f* (*-i*; *G -*) technology; (*sposób*) technique; **~nikum** *n* (*idkl.*; *-a*, *-ów*) technical secondary school; **~nokracja** *f* (*-i*; *-e*) technocracy; **~nologia** *f* (*GDl -ii*; *-e*) technology
teczka *f* (*-i*; *G -czek*) briefcase; (*do akt*) folder; ***~ szkolna*** school-bag, satchel
teflonowy Teflon *TM*, non stick
tego *pron. GA* → ***ten*** *G*; → ***to***[1]; **~roczny** this year('s)
tej *pron.* (*GDL/sg.* → ***ta***) → ***ten***
teka *f* (*-i*; *G -*) portfolio
tekowy teak
Teksas *m* (*-u*; *0*) Texas
tekst *m* (*-u*; *-y*) text
tekstylia *pl.* (*-ów*) textile goods *pl.*
tekściarz F *m* (*-a*; *-e*) songwriter; (*reklam*) copywriter
tektur|a *f* (*-y*; *G -*) cardboard; **~owy** cardboard
telefaks → ***faks***
telefon *m* (*-u*; *-y*) (tele)phone; ***~ komórkowy*** mobile (phone); ***przez ~*** on the phone; **~iczny** (tele)phone; ***rozmowa ~iczna*** phone call; ***książka ~iczna*** (phone) directory; ***karta ~iczna*** phonecard; **~ować** ⟨**za-**⟩ (**do** *G*) call, phone
telegazeta *f* (*-y*; *G -*) *TV*: teletext
telegraf *m* (*-u*; *-y*) telegraph; **~iczny** telegraphic; ***w stylu ~icznym*** in telegraphese; **~ować** ⟨**za-**⟩ (*-uję*) (**do** *G*) cable, telegraph
tele|gram *m* (*-u*; *-y*) telegram, cable; **~komunikacja** *f* telecommunications *sg.*; **~ks** *m* (*-u*; *-y*) telex; **~ksować** ⟨**za-**⟩ (*-uję*) (**do** *G*) telex (to); **~ksowy** telex; **~obiektyw** *m* (*-u*; *-y*) *phot.* telephoto lens; **~pajęczarz** F *m* (*-a*; *-e*) licence dodger; **~patyczny** telepathic; **~skop** *m* (*-u*; *-y*) telescope; **~transmisja** *f* television broadcast; **~turniej** *m* quiz show; **~widz** *m* viewer
telewiz|ja *f* (*-i*; *-e*) television; ***oglądać ~ję*** watch TV; **~or** *m* (*-a*; *-y*) TV set; **~yjny** television, TV
temat *m* (*-u*; *-y*) subject (matter); topic, theme; *gr.* stem; ***~ do rozmowy*** subject of conversation; **~yczny** thematic, topical
temblak *m* (*-a*; *-i*) *med.* sling; ***na ~u*** in a sling
tempe|rament *m* (*-u*; *-y*) temperament; **~ratura** *f* (*-y*; *G -*) temperature; **~rować** ⟨**za-**⟩ (*-uję*) *ołówek* sharpen; **~rówka** *f* (*-i*; *G -wek*) sharpener
temp|o *n* (*-a*; *G -*) speed; ***dobrym ~em*** at a good speed
temu **1.** *pron. D* → ***ten, to***[1]; **2.** *adv.*: ***rok ~*** a year ago; ***dawno ~*** a long time ago
ten *pron. m* (*f* ***ta***, *n* ***to***, *pl.* ***te, ci***) this; → ***chwila, czas, sam***
tenden|cja *f* (*-i*; *-e*) trend, tendency; **~cyjny** tendentious, biased
tenis *m* (*-a*; *0*): ***~ stołowy*** table tennis; **~ówki** *f/pl.* (*-wek*) tennis shoes, *Am.* sneakers; **~ista** *m* (*-y*; *-ści*), **~istka** *f* (*-i*; *G -tek*) tennis-player; **~owy** tennis
tenor *m* (*-u/os. -a*; *-y/os. -rzy*) *mus.* tenor
tenże *pron. m* (***taż*** *f*, ***toż*** *n*, *pl.* ***też, ciż***) the same; *por.* ***ten***
teo|logiczny theological; **~retyczny** theoretical; **~ria** *f* (*GDL -ii*; *-e*) theory
terapeu|ta *m* (*-y*; *-ci*) therapist; **~tyczny** therapeutic
te'rapia *f* (*GDL -ii*; *-e*) therapy
teraz now; ***od ~*** from now on
teraźniejsz|ość *f* (*-ści*; *0*) the present; **~y** present; → ***czas***
tercja *f* (*-i*; *-e*) *mus.* third; *szermierka*: tierce; (*w hokeju*) (*część meczu*) period, (*część boiska*) zone
teren *m* (*-u*; *-y*) area; ground, terrain; ***~y*** *pl.* ***zielone*** green spaces *pl.*; ***w ~ie*** (*badania*) in the field; (*urzędowanie*) out of the office; **~owy** field; (*lokalny*) local; ***samochód ~owy*** all-terrain car
terkotać (*-czę/-cę*) *maszyna*: clutter; *budzik*: rattle; (*mówić*) jabber, chatter
termin *m* (*-u*; *-y*) time-limit; (*data*) date; (*wyrażenie, też med.*) term; ***przed ~em*** ahead of schedule; ***po ~ie*** behind schedule; ***na ~*** on time, to schedule; ***~ ostateczny*** deadline; → ***terminowy***
terminal *m* (*-u/-a*; *-e*) terminal
termin|arz *m* (*-a*; *-e*) schedule; (*kalendarz*) diary; **~ować** (*-uję*) be apprenticed (***u*** *G* to); **~owo** *adv.* on time, to schedule; **~owy** with a deadline
termit *m* (*-a*; *-y*) *zo.* termite
termo|- *w złoż.* thermo-; **~jądrowy** thermonuclear; **~metr** *m* (*-u*; *-y*) thermo-

meter; **~s** *m* (*-u*; *-y*) thermos *TM* flask, vacuum flask
terrory|sta *m* (*-y*; *-ści*), **~stka** *f* (*-y*; *G -tek*) terrorist; **~styczny** terrorist **~zm** *m* (*-u*; *0*) terrorism; ***akt ~zmu*** act of terrorism; **~zować** (*-uję*) terrorize
terytorium *n* (*idkl.*; *-a*) territory
test *m* (*-u*; *-y*) test
testament *m* (*-u*; *-y*) will; *rel.* testament; *fig.* legacy; **~owy** testamentary
testow|ać (*-uję*) test; **~y** test
teś|ciowa *f* (*-wej*; *-we*) mother-in-law; **~ć** *m* (*-ścia*; *-ściowie*, *-ściów*) father-in-law
teza *f* (*-y*; *G -*) thesis
też[1] *adv.*, *part.* also
też[2] *pron. f* → ***tenże***
tę *pron.* (*A/sg.* → ***ta***) → ***ten***
tęcz|a *f* (*-y*; *G -*) rainbow; **~ówka** *f* (*-i*; *G -wek*) *anat.* iris
tędy *adv.* this way
tęg|i stout; (*dobry*) efficient, good; (*mocny*) strong; **~o** *adv.* strongly
tęp|ić ⟨**wy-**⟩ (*-ię*) eradicate, exterminate; ***~ić się*** → **~ieć** ⟨**s-**⟩ (*-eję*) blunt; *słuch*: deteriorate; **~y** blunt; *fig.* dull; *człowiek* thick-headed; *wzrok* vacant; apathetic
tęskn|ić ⟨**s- się**⟩ (*-ę*, *-nij!*) (**za** *I*) long (for); (**do** *I*) miss; ***~ić za krajem/domem*** be homesick; **~o** *adv.* nostalgically; ***jest mu ~o do*** he is longing for; **~ota** *f* (*-y*; *G -*) longing; homesickness; **~y** longing; homesick
tęt|ent *m* (*-u*; *0*) hoofbeats *pl.*, clatter; **~nica** *f* (*-y*; *G -*) *anat.* artery (*też fig.*); **~niczy** arterial; **~nić** (*-ę*, *nij!*) pulsate, throb; **~no** *n* (*-a*; *G -*) pulse
tęż|ec *m* (*-żca*; *-żce*) *med.* tetanus; **~eć** ⟨**s-**⟩ (*-ę*) set; *mróz itp.*: grow stronger; **~yzna** *f* (*-y*; *0*) strength
tj. *skrót pisany*: ***to jest*** i.e. (*that is*)
tka|ctwo *n* (*-a*; *0*) weaving; **~cz** *m* (*-a*; *-e*), **~czka** *f* (*-i*; *G -czek*) weaver; **~ć** ⟨**u-**⟩ (*-am*) weave
tkan|ina *f* (*-y*; *G -*) fabric; *fig.* tissue; **~ka** *f* (*-i*; *G -nek*) *biol.* tissue (*też fig.*); **~y** woven
tkliw|ość *f* (*-ści*; *0*) tenderness; **~ie** *adv.* tenderly; **~y** tender
tknąć *pf.* (*-nę*) → (**do**)***tykać***
tkwić ⟨**u-**⟩ (*-ę*, *-wij!*) stick (*fig.* around)
tlejący *Brt.* smouldering, *Am.* smoldering; glowing; → ***tlić***
tlen *m* (*-u*; *0*) *chem.* oxygen; **~ek** *m* (*-nku*; *-nki*) *chem.* oxide; **~ić** (*-ę*) → ***u-tleniać***; **~owy** oxygen
tlić się *Brt.* smoulder, *Am.* smolder; *fig.* glow
tłamsić ⟨ **s-**⟩ (*-szę*) suppress
tło *n* (*-a*; *G teł*) background; ***na białym tle*** against a white background; ***w tle*** in the background
tłocz|nia *f* (*-i*; *-e*) *tech.* stamping press; **~no** *adv.*: ***jest ~no tu*** it is overcrowded here; **~ny** crowded; *ulica* busy; **~yć** (*-ę*) ⟨**wy-**⟩ press out, squeeze out; *tech.* stamp; ⟨**prze-**⟩ *płyn* pump; ***~yć*** ⟨**s-**⟩ ***się*** crowd, throng
tłok *m* (*-u*; *0*) crowd; (*-a*; *-i*) *tech.* piston
tłuc ⟨**po-, roz-, s-**⟩ smash, crush; ⟨**na-, u-**⟩ *ziemniaki* mash; *przyprawy* crush; ⟨**s-, wy-**⟩ *kogoś* beat up, clobber; ⟨**s-**⟩ bump (**o** *A* against); ***~ się*** *szkło*: break; *fale itp.*: pound (**o** *A* on); *serce*: pound, thump; (*robić hałas*) make a noise; F travel a long distance
tłucz|ek *m* (*-czka*; *-czki*) pestle, (***do kartofli*** potato) masher; **~eń** *m* (*-nia*; *0*) broken stone
tłum *m* (*-u*; *-y*) crowd; **~em** → ***tłumnie***
tłumacz *m* (*-a*; *-e*) translator; (*ustny*) interpreter; **~enie** *n* (*-a*; *G -eń*) translation; (*ustny*) interpreting; **~ka** *f* (*-i*; *G -czek*) translator; (*ustny*) interpreter; **~yć** (*-ę*) ⟨**wy-**⟩ explain; ***~yć się*** excuse o.s.; ⟨**prze-**⟩ translate (***na polski*** into Polish); ***~yć się jako*** be translated as
tłum|ić ⟨**s-**⟩ (*-ę*) *płomienie* smother; *bunt*, *uczucie* suppress; *odgłos* muffle; **~ik** *m* (*-a*; *-i*) *mot. Brt.* silence, *Am.* muffler; (*broni*) silencer; *mus.* mute
tłumn|ie *adv.* in huge numbers; **~y** numerous
tłumok *m* (*-a*;*-i*) bundle, pack
tłust|o *adv.*: ***jeść ~o*** eat fatty things; **~y** *ktoś* fat; *jedzenie* fatty; (*zatłuszczony*) greased
tłuszcz *m* (*-u*; *-e*) fat; **~owy** *biol.* adipose, fatty
tłuści|ć ⟨**na-**⟩ (*-szczę*) grease; (*kremem*) rub *cream* into; **~eć** F ⟨**po-**⟩ (*-eję*) become fat; **~och** *m* (*-a*; *-y*) fatso, fatty
tną *3. os. pl. pres.*, **tnę** *1. os. sg. pres.* → ***ciąć***
tnący cutting
to[1] *pron. n* this, that; → ***ten***; ***do tego*** moreover; ***na tym, na ~*** for it; ***w tym***

T

in it; **za ~** behind it; **z tego** from that; **z tym, że** provided that; **~ jest** that is
to² *part.* (*idkl.*) this, that, it; **kto ~?** who is there?; **~ fakt** this is a fact; **~ ..., ~ ...** now ... now ...; **no ~ co?** so what?; **a ~ ... !** what (a) ...!
toalet|a *f* (*-y*; *G* -) toilet; **~owy** toilet
toast *m* (*-u*; *-y*) toast
tobą (*I/sg.* → **ty**); **z ~** with you
tobie (*DL/sg.* → **ty**); **o ~** about you
tobół *m* (*-bołu*; *-boły*) → **tłumok**
tocz|ony *tech.* turned; **~yć** (*-ę*) ⟨**po-**⟩ *kulę itp.* roll (**się** *v/i.*); ⟨**s-**⟩ *bój* fight out; ⟨**na-**⟩ *impf. płyn* fill in; ⟨**wy-**⟩ *tech.* turn; *impf. płyn*: draw off, tap; *spór* have; *drewno* live on; *rokowania* carry out; **~yć się** roll; *łzy*: roll down, flow down; *czas*, *życie*: go, pass; *dyskusja*, *walka*: go on; *akcja*: take place; *rozmowa*: be (**o** *L* about); **~ydło** *n* (*-a*; *G -deł*) grindstone
toga *f* (*-i*; *G tóg*) toga; *jur.* robe
tok *m* (*-u*; *0*) course; process; **być w ~u** be under way; **w ~u** (*G*) in the course (of)
toka|rka *f* (*-i*; *G -rek*) *tech.* (turning) lathe; **~rz** *m* (*-a*; *-e*) *tech.* turner
tokować (*-uję*) *zo.* display (in courtship)
toksyczny toxic
toler|ancyjny tolerant; **~ować** (*-uję*) tolerate
tom *m* (*-u*; *-y*) volume
tomo'grafia *f* (*GDL -ii*; *-e*) tomography; **~komputerowa** *Brt.* computerized (*Am.* computer) tomography
ton *m* (*-u*; *-y*) tone
tona *f* (*-y*; *G ton*) ton; (*metryczna*) tonne, metric ton
tonacja *f* (*-i*; *-e*) *mus.* key; *fig.* tone
tonaż *m* (*-u*; *0*) *naut.* tonnage
toną|cy *m* (*-ego*; *-cy*), **~ca** *f* (*-ej*; *-e*) drowning person; **~ć** (*-ę*, *toń!*) *fig.* be up to (**w** *L* in); ⟨**u-**⟩ drown; ⟨**za-**⟩ *statek*: sink, go down
tonować (*-uję*) tone down
toń *f* (*GDL -ni*; *-nie*, *-ni*, *-ńmi*) *lit.* depth
topić (*-ę*) ⟨**po-, u-**⟩ drown; ⟨**za-**⟩ sink; ⟨**roz-**⟩ melt (**się** *v/i.*); **~ się** → **tonąć**
topiel *f* (*-i*; *-e*) whirlpool (*też fig.*); **~ec** *m* (*-lca*; *-lcy*), **~ica** *f* (*-cy*; *-ce*) drowned person
topik *m* (*-a*; *-i*) *electr.* fusible-element; **~owy** fuse
toples(s) topless
top|liwy fusible; **~nieć** ⟨**s-**⟩ (*-eję*) melt; *tech.* fuse
topola *f* (*-i*; *-e*) *bot.* poplar
topo|rny ungainly, coarse; **~rzysko** *n* (*-a*; *G* -) helve, handle
topór *m* (*-pora*; *-pory*) ax(e)
tor *m* (*-u*; *-y*) path; *rail.* track, line; (*w sporcie*) track, (*bobslejowy itp.*) run, (*koni*) course; **~ wodny** *naut.* fairway; *fig.* **ślepy ~** blind alley
Tora *f* (*-y*; *0*) *rel.* the Torah
tor|ba *f* (*-y*; *G -reb*) bag; *biol.* pouch; **~ba na zakupy** shopping bag; → **~ebka** *f* (*-i*; *G -bek*) bag; (*kobieca*) handbag
torf *m* (*-u*; *-y*) peat; **~owisko** *n* (*-a*; *G* -) peat bog; **~owy** peat
tornister *m* (*-tra*; *-try*) satchel
torow|ać ⟨**u-**⟩ (*-uję*): **~ać (sobie) drogę** clear a path; pave the way; **~y** rail
torpedo|wać ⟨**s-**⟩ (*-uję*) *mil.* torpedo (*też fig.*); **~wiec** *m* (*-wca*; *-wce*) *mil.* torpedo boat
tors *m* (*-u*; *-y*) trunk, torso
torsje *pl.* (*-ji*) vomiting
tort *m* (*-u*; *-y*) layer cake, gateau *lub* gâteau; **~owy** gateau *lub* gâteau
tortu|ra *f* (*-y*; *G* -) torture (*też fig.*); **narzędzie ~r** instrument of torture; **~rować** (*-uję*) torture
Toskania *f* (*-ii*; *0*) Tuscany
tost *m* (*-u*; *-y*) toast
total|itarny totalitarian; **~ny** total
toteż *cj.* that is why
totolotek *m* (*-tka*; *0*) lottery
tow. *skrót pisany*: **towarzystwo** ass. (*association*)
towar *m* (*-u*; *-y*) article, commodity; goods *pl.*
towaro|wy commodity; trade; *rail. Brt.* goods, *Am.* freight; **dom ~wy** department store
towarzys|ki (*m-os -scy*) sociable, social; **formy** *pl.* **~kie** good manners *pl.*; (*w sporcie*) **spotkanie ~kie** friendly meeting; **agencja ~ka** escort agency; **~two** *n* (*-a*; *G -tw*) company; (*stowarzyszenie*) association, society; *econ.* company
towarzysz *m* (*-a*; *-e*), **~ka** *f* (*-i*; *G -szek*) companion; (*partyjny*) comrade; **~(ka) niedoli** fellow-sufferer; **~(ka) zabaw** playmate; **~yć** (*-ę*) (*D*) accompany; (*czemuś*) go with
toż¹ *pron.* → **tenże**

tożž[2] *part.* (*idkl.*) → ***przecież***
tożsamość *f* (*-ści*; *0*) identity
tracić ⟨**s-, u-**⟩ (*-cę*) lose (*też fig.*) miss; *pieniądze*, *czas* lose (**na** *L*) lose out (on); *prawo* forfeit
trady|cja *f* (*-i*; *-e*) tradition; **~cyjny** traditional
traf *m* (*-u*; *-y*) chance; ***szczęśliwym ~em*** by a fluke; **~iać** (*-am*) ⟨**~ić**⟩ (*-ę*) hit; find one's way (**do** *G* to); find o.s. (**do** *G* in); ***nie ~ić*** miss; ***~iać się*** *okazja*: come up; **~ienie** *n* (*-a*; *G -eń*) hit; ***sześć ~ień*** six right ones; **~ność** *f* (*-ści*; *0*) accuracy; (*uwagi*) relevance; **~nie** *adv.* accurately; relevantly; aptly; **~ny** accurate; relevant; apt
tragarz *m* (*-a*; *-e*) porter
tra'gedia *f* (*GDL -ii*; *-e*) tragedy (*też fig.*)
tragiczny tragic(al)
trajkotać (*-czę/-cę*) → ***terkotać***
trak|t *m* (*-u*; *-y*) country road; *bud.* section, wing; ***w ~cie*** (*G*) in the course (of)
traktat *m* (*-u*; *-y*) treatise, dissertation
trakto|r *m* (*-a*; *-y*) tractor; **~rzysta** *m* (*-y*; *-ści*), **-tka** *f* (*-i*; *G -tek*) tractor-driver
traktowa|ć (*-uję*) *v/t.* ⟨**po-**⟩ treat (**się** each other); ***źle ~ć*** maltreat; *v/i.* (**o** *L*) treat (of), deal (with); **~nie** *n* (*-a*; *G -ań*) treatment
trał *m* (*-u*; *-y*) *naut.*, *mil.* sweep
trampki *m/pl.* (*-pek*) sports shoes *pl.*
trampolina *f* (*-y*; *G -*) (*w sporcie*) springboard; (*przy basenie*) diving board
tramwaj *m* (*-u*; *-e*) *Brt.* tram(way), *Am.* streetcar; **~owy** tramway, streetcar
tran *m* (*-u*; *0*) cod-liver oil
trans *m* (*-u*; *-y*) trance
trans|akcja *f* (*-i*; *-e*) transaction; ***~akcje*** *pl.* dealings *pl.*; **~fer** *m* (*-u*; *-y*) *econ.*, (*też w sporcie*) transfer; **~formator** *m* (*-a*; *-y*) transformer; **~fuzja** *f* (*-i*; *-e*) *med.* transfusion; **~kontynentalny** transcontinental; **~misja** *f* (*-i*; *-e*) transmission, broadcast; **~mitować** (*-uję*) transmit, broadcast; **~parent** *m* (*-u*; *-y*) banner; **~plantacja** *f* (*-i*; *-e*) transplantation
transport *m* (*-u*; *-y*) *Brt.* transport, *Am.* transportation; (*ładunek*) consignment, shipment; **~ować** ⟨**od-, prze-**⟩ (*-uję*) transport, ship; **~owy** transport
transwestyta *m* (*-y*; *-yci*) transvestite
tranzystor *m* (*-a*; *-y*) *electr.* transistor
tranzytowy transit
trapez *m* (*-u*; *-y*) *math. Brt.* trapezium, *Am.* trapezoid; (*w cyrku itp.*) trapeze
trapić (*-ę*) (*I*) plague (with); → ***martwić*** (***się***)
trasa *f* (*-y*; *G -*) route; way
trasowany *econ. weksel* drawn
trata *f* (*-y*; *G -*) *econ.* bill of exchange
tratować ⟨**s-**⟩ (*-uję*) trample
tratwa *f* (*-y*; *G -*) raft
traumatyczny traumatic
trawa *f* (*-y*; *G -*) grass
trawestacja *f* (*-i*; *-e*) travesty
trawiasty grass(y)
trawi|ć (*-ę*) ⟨**s-**⟩ *biol.* digest; (*o ogniu itp.*) consume; *czas* waste (**na** *L* for); ⟨**wy-**⟩ *tech.*, *chem.* etch; **~enie** *n* (*-a*; *G -eń*) digestion; *chem.*, *tech.* etching
trawler *m* (*-a*; *-y*) *naut.* trawler; ***~-przetwórnia*** *naut.* factory *lub* processing trawler
trawnik *m* (*-a*; *-i*) lawn
trąb|a *f* (*-y*; *G -*) *mus.* trumpet; *zo.* trunk; *meteo.* (*powietrzna*) whirlwind; (*wodna*) waterspout; F (*ktoś*) fool; **~ić** (*-ę*) (**w** *A*) blow; *słoń*: trumpet; *mil.* sound (***na alarm*** the alarm); *mot.* hoot, sound the horn; **~ka** *f* (*-i*; *G -bek*) *mus.* trumpet; *mil.* bugle
trąc|ać (*-am*) ⟨**~ić**⟩ (*-cę*) knock (*A* against); (*łokciem itp.*) nudge, elbow; ***~ać się kieliszkami*** clink glasses
trącić[2] (*-cę*; *nieos.*) (*I*) smell (of), smack (of)
trą|d *m* (*-u*; *-0*) *med.* leprosy; **~dzik** *m* (*-a*; *-i*) *med.* acne
trefl *m* (*-a*; *-e*) (*w kartach*) club(s *pl.*); ***as ~*** ace of clubs; ***wyjść w ~e*** play clubs
trefny tref, not kosher
trema *f* (*-y*; *G -*) stage fright
tren[1] *m* (*-u*; *-y*) threnody
tren[2] *m* (*-u*; *-y*) train
tren|er *m* (*-a*; *-rzy*) trainer, coach; **~ing** *m* (*-u*; *-i*) training; **~ować** ⟨**wy-**⟩ (*-uję*) *v/t.* train, coach; *v/i. Brt.* practise, *Am.* practice; train
trep|ki *m/pl.*, **~y** *m/pl.* (*-ów*) sandals
tresować ⟨**wy-**⟩ (*-uję*) train
treś|ciwie *adv.* succinctly; nutritiously; **~ciwy** rich in substance; *jedzenie* nutritious, nourishing; *tekst* succinct; **~ć** *f* (*-ści*; *0*) content; meaning
trębacz *m* (*-a*; *-e*) trumpeter
trędowat|y **1.** leprous; **2.** *m* (*-ego*; *-ci*), **~a** *f* (*-ej*; *-e*) leper

T

trik *m* (*-u*; *-i*) trick; play; **~owy** trick
triumf *m* (*-u*; *-y*) triumph; **~ować** ⟨**za-**⟩ (*-uję*) triumph (***nad*** *I* over)
trochę a bit, a little; somewhat; ***ani ~*** not a bit; not at all
trociny *pl.* (-) wood shavings *pl.*
troć *f* (*-ci*; *-cie*) *zo.* brown trout
trofeum *n* (*idkl.*; *-ea*, *-eów*) trophy
tro|ić się (*-ję*, *trój!*) treble, triple; **~jaczki** *m/pl.* (*-ków*) triplets *pl.*; **~jaki** threefold; **~je** three; ***we ~je*** in three
trolejbus *m* (*-u*; *-y*) trolleybus
tron *m* (*-u*; *-y*) throne; **~owy** throne
trop *m* (*-y*; *G -ów*) trail, scent; ***być na czyimś ~ie*** be on s.o.'s trail; **~ić** (*-ę*) track, trail
tropikalny tropical
tro|ska *f* (*-i*; *G* -) care; **~skliwie** *adv.* carefully; **~skliwy** careful; **~szczyć się** ⟨**za- się**⟩ (*-ę*) (***o*** *A*) look (after), take care (of); → ***niepokoić się***
trosz|eczkę, ~kę → ***trochę***
trój|- *w złoż.* three-, tri-; **~ca** *f* (*-y*; *G* -): *rel.* ***Ⓢca Święta*** the Holy Trinity; **~drożny** *tech.* three-way; **~ka** *f* (*-i*; *G -jek*) three; (*linia*) number three; (*w szkole*) *jakby*: C; ***we ~kę*** in a group of three; ***~kami*** in threes
trójkąt *m* (*-a*; *-y*) *math.* triangle (*też fig.*); **~ny** triangular
trój|niak *m* (*-a*; *-i*) (*type of*) mead; **~nóg** *m* (*-noga*; *-nogi*) tripod; **~pasmowy** three-band; **~skok** *m* (*-u*; *0*) triple jump; **~stronny** tripartite; **~wymiarowy** three-dimensional; **~ząb** *m* trident
truchle|ć (*-eję*) be terrified; ***~ję na myśl o*** (*I*) I tremble at the thought of
trucht *m* (*-u*; *0*) trot; **~ać** (*-am*) trot
tru|cizna *f* (*-y*; *G* -) poison; **~ć** ⟨**o-**⟩ (*-ję*) poison (***się*** o.s.)
trud *m* (*-u*; *-y*) trouble; ***zadać sobie ~ z*** (*I*) go to a lot of trouble over; ***nie szczędzić ~ów*** spare no efforts; ***z ~em*** with difficulty; **~nić się** (*-ę*, *-nij!*) (*I*) occupy o.s. (with); be engaged (in); **~no** *adv.* with difficulty; ***~no mi powiedzieć*** it is hard for me to say; ***~no o*** (*A*) it is hard to get; (***no to***) ***~no!*** there's nothing I can do (about it)!; **~ność** *f* (*-ści*; *0*) difficulty; ***bez ~ności*** without trouble; **~ny** difficult, hard; ***~ny w pożyciu*** difficult to get along with
trudzić (*-dzę*) trouble; ***~ się*** try; (***nad*** *I*) struggle (with)
trujący poisonous
trumna *f* (*-y*; *G -mien*) coffin, *Am. też* casket
trun|ek *m* (*-nku*; *-nki*) (alcoholic) drink; **~kowy** F fond of drinking
trup *m* (*-a*; *-y*) corpse, (dead) body; ***paść ~em*** fall down dead; ***iść po ~ach*** stoop to anything, be ruthless; **~i** deathly; ***~ia czaszka*** skull and crossbones; **~io** *adv.* deathly; ***~io blady*** deathly pale
truskawk|a *f* (*-i*; *G -wek*) *bot.* raspberry; **~owy** raspberry
truteń *m* (*-tnia*; *-tnie*) *zo.* drone (*też Brt. fig.*); *fig.* parasite
trutka *f* (*-i*; *G -tek*) (***na szczury*** rat) poison
trwa|ć (*-am*) last; (***długo***) take (long); (***w*** *L*, ***przy*** *I*) persist (in); *rozmowa*: go on, continue; **~le** *adv.* long-lasting; **~łość** *f* (*-ści*; *0*) durability; **~ły** long-lasting; *produkt* durable
trwog|a *f* (*-i*; *G trwóg*) fright, fear; horror; ***bić na ~ę*** sound the alarm
trwonić (*-ę*) waste; squander
trwożyć (*-ę*) frighten, worry; ***~się*** (***o*** *A*) be frightened (about); be worried (about)
tryb *m* (*-u*; *-y*) course, mode; *tech.* cogwheel, gear; *gr.* mood; ***iść swoim ~em*** go on as usual; *jur.* ***~ przyspieszony*** summary proceedings *pl.*; ***w ~ie przyspieszonym*** *fig.* in a rush
trybu|na *f* (*-y*; *G* -) (grand)stand; **~nał** *m* (*-u*; *-y*) *jur.* tribunal
tryk *m* (*-a*; *-i*) *zo.* ram
trykot *m* (*-u*; *-y*) (*materiał*) cotton jersey; (*ubranie*) leotard; **~owy** cotton knitted
try'logia *f* (*GDL -ii*; *-e*) trilogy
trymestr *m* (*-u*; *-y*) trimester
trys|kać (*-am*) ⟨***~nąć***⟩ (*-nę*) spurt, squirt, gush; *iskry*: fly; *fig.* sparkle (*I* with) ***~kać zdrowiem*** be bursting with health
tryumf *m* → ***triumf***
trzas|k *m* (*-u*; *-i*) crack, snap; *por.* ***trzeszczeć***; **~kać** (*-am*) crack, snap; F *zdjęcia* snap; (*drzwiami*) slam; **~kający** *mróz* sharp; **~nąć** *pf.* → ***trzaskać***
trząść ⟨**po-, za-**⟩ (*A*, *I*) shake; *pojazd*: jerk; ***~ się*** shake, shiver (***z zimna*** with cold); quiver (***ze strachu*** with fear)
trzcin|a *f* (*-y*; *G* -) *bot.* reed; ***~a cukrowa*** sugar cane; **~owy** reed, cane
trzeba (*nieos.*) one needs (***na to*** to do it); it is necessary to; ***~ to zrobić*** it needs to be done; ***ile ~*** as much/many

T

as necessary; ***jak ~*** if necessary; ***nie ~*** it is not necessary

trzebić ⟨**wy-**⟩ (*-ę*) *zwierzę* neuter; *fig.* eradicate

trzech *m-os* three; ***Święto*** ⚲ ***Króli*** Epiphany; → ***715***

trzeci third; ***po ~e*** thirdly; ***jedna ~a, ~a część*** one third

trzeciorzędny third-class, third-rate

trzeć ⟨**po-**⟩ rub (**się** o.s.); *gastr.* grate

trzej *m-os* three; → ***715***

trzep|aczka *f* (*-i*; *G -czek*) (*do dywanów*) carpet-beater; (*do piany itp.*) whisk; **~ać** (*-ię*) beat (*I* with) (*też dywan* ⟨**wy-**⟩); ***~ać językiem*** blab, babble; **~nąć** *v/s.* (*-nę*) hit; **~otać** (*-czę/-cę*) flutter; flap (***na wietrze*** in the wind); ***~otać się*** flutter; *ryba*: flounder

trzeszczeć (*-ę, -y*) *deski*: creak; (*w ogniu*) crackle; *lód*: crack; ***~ w szwach*** be bursting at the seams

trzewi|a *pl.* (*-i*) entrails *pl.*, insides *pl.*; *med.* viscera; **~owy** visceral

trzewik *m* (*-a*; *-i*) shoe

trzeźw|ić ⟨**o-**⟩ (*-ę, -wij!*) sober up; *fig.* bring back to earth; **~ieć** ⟨**o-, wy-**⟩ sober up; come to one's senses; **~o** *adv.* soberly; **~y** sober

trzęsawisko *n* (*-a*; *G -*) bog, marsh

trzęsienie *n* (*-a*; *G -eń*) shaking; ***~ ziemi*** earthquake

trzmiel *m* (*-a*; *-e*) *zo.* bumble bee

trzoda *f* (*-y*; *G trzód*) → ***chlewny***

trzon *m* (*-u*; *-y*) core; nucleus; *tech.* shank, stem, shaft; → **~ek** *m* (*-nka*; *-nki*) handle; **~owy**: ***ząb ~owy*** *anat.* molar

trzpień *m* (*-enia*; *-enie*) pin, bolt

trzustka *f* (*-i*; *G -tek*) *anat.* pancreas

trzy three; → ***trój- i 715***; **~cyfrowy** three-figure; **~częściowy** three-piece; **~drzwiowy** three-door; **~dziestka** *f* (*-ki*; *G -tek*) thirty; **~dziesty** thirtieth; **~dzieści** thirty; → ***715***; **~krotnie** *adv.* threefold, three times; **~krotny** threefold; **~letni** three-year-long, -old

trzyma|ć (*-am*) hold; keep; ***~ć się*** hold on (***za*** *A*, *G* to); (*G*) keep (to); ***~ć się razem*** stick together; ***~ć się z dala*** (***od*** *G*) keep away (from); ***~j się!*** so long!, take care!

trzyna|stka *f* (*-i*; *G -tek*) thirteen; **~sto-** *w złoż.* thirteen-; **~stu** *m-os* thirteen; **~sty** thirteenth; **~ście, ~ścioro** *m-os* thirteen; → ***715***

trzy|osobowy for three persons; **~pokojowy** three-room; **~sta, ~stu** *m-os* three hundred; → ***715***

tu here; → ***tam***

tub|a *f* (*-y*; *G -*) *mus.* tuba; *fig.* spokesperson, mouthpiece; → **~ka** *f* (*-i*; *G -bek*) tube

tubyl|czy native; indigenous; **~ec** *m* (*-ca*; *-cy*) native

tucz|nik *m* (*-a*; *-i*) fattening pig; **~ny** fattening; **~yć** ⟨**u-**⟩ (*-ę*) fatten

tulej|a *f* (*GDl -ei*; *-eje*), **~ka** *f* (*-i*; *G -jek*) *tech.* sleeve, bush

tulić ⟨**przy-**⟩ (*-lę*) hug, cuddle; **~** ⟨**przy-**⟩ **się** (**do** *G*) nestle close (to), snuggle up (to)

tulipan *m* (*-a*; *-y*) *bot.* tulip

tułacz *m* (*-a*; *-e*) wanderer; **~ka** *f* (*-i*; *-czek*) wandering; **~y** wandering

tułać się (*-am*) wander

tułów *m* (*-łowia*; *-łowie*) trunk

tuman *m* (*-u*; *-y*) cloud (***kurzu*** of dust); *pej.* (*-a*; *-i*) dunce, fool

tunel *m* (*-u*; *-e*) tunnel

Tunez|ja *f* (*-i*; *0*) Tunisia; **~yjczyk** *m* (*-a*; *-cy*), **~yjka** *f* (*-i*; *G -jek*) Tunisian; **⚲yjski** Tunisian

tuńczyk *m* (*-a*; *-i*) *zo.* tuna

tupać (*-pię*) stamp

tupet *m* (*-u*; *-y*) nerve, cheek

tup|nąć *v/s.* (*-nę*) stamp; **~ot** *m* (*-u*; *-y*) patter, clatter

tura *f* (*-y*; *G -*) round

turbo|sprężarka *f tech.* turbo-compressor; **~śmigłowy** turbo-prop

Tur|cja *f* (*-i*; *0*) Turkey; **~czynka** *f* (*-i*; *G -nek*) Turk; **⚲ecki** Turkish; ***mówić po ~ecku*** speak Turkish; **~ek** *m* (*-rka*; *-rcy*) Turk

turkot *m* (*-u*; *-y*) rattle; **~ać** (*-cę/-czę*) rattle

turkus *m* (*-a*; *-y*) turquoise; **~owy** turquoise

turniej *m* (*-u*; *-e*) tournament

turnus *m* (*-u*; *-y*) period

turyst|a *m* (*-y*; *G -tów*), **~ka** *f* (*-i*; *G -tek*) tourist; **~yczny** tourist; ***ruch ~yczny*** tourism

tusz *m* (*-u*; *-e*) (*do pisania itp.*) India(n) ink; (*prysznic*) shower; *mus.* flourish; ***~ do rzęs*** mascara

tusza *f* (*-y*; *0*) obesity; (*pl. -e*) (*zwierzęcia*) carcass

tut|aj → ***tu***; **~ejszy** local

tuzin *m* (*-a*; *-y*) dozen
tuż *adv.* immediately; **~ przy** right to; **~ za** right behind
twa *pron f* (*ściągn.* **twoja**) → **twój**
tward|nieć ⟨**s-**⟩ (*-ję*) harden; **~o** *adv.* firmly; **jajko na ~o** hard-boiled egg; **~ość** *f* (*-ści*; *0*) hardness; **~y** hard, firm; *sen* sound; *mięso* tough
twaróg *m* (*-rogu*; *-rogi*) cottage cheese
twarz *f* (*-y*; *-e*) face; **stać ~ą do** (*G*) face; **być do ~y** (*D*) suit; **~ą w ~** (**z** *I*) face to face (with); **~owy** becoming, suitable; *anat.* facial
twe *pron. f, n/pl.* (*ściągn.* **twoje**) → **twój**
twierdz|a *f* (*-y*; *-e*) fortress; **~ąco** *adv.* affirmatively; **~ący** affirmative; **~enie** *n* (*-a*; *G -eń*) claim; *math.* proposition; **bezpodstawne ~enie** allegation; **~ić** (*-ę*) claim, maintain
two|i *m-os pl.*, **~ja**, **~je** → **twój**
tworzy|ć (*-ę*, *twórz!*) ⟨**s-**⟩ create; *całość* constitute, make up; ⟨**u-**⟩ form (**się** *v/i.*); **~ć się** *też* be formed, be created **~wo** *n* (*-a*; *G -*) material, substance; **sztuczne ~wo** plastic
twój *pron. m* (*f* **twoja**/**twa**, *n* **twoje**/**twe**; *pl.* **twoi**/**twoje**/**twe**) your, yours
twór *m* (*tworu*; *twory*) creation; **~ca** *m* (*-y*; *G -ów*) creator; **~czo** *adv.* creatively; **~czość** *f* (*-ści*; *0*) creativity; output; **~czy** creative; **~czyni** *f* (*-yni*; *-ynie*, *-yń*) creator
tw. szt. *skrót pisany*: **tworzywo sztuczne** plastic
ty *pron.* (*GA ciebie/cię*, *D tobie/ci*, *I tobą*, *L tobie*) you; **być na ~** (**z** *I*) be on first name terms (with)
tych *pron. GL/pl.* → **ten, to**[1]
tyczka *f* (*-i*; *G -czek*) pole (*też sport*); **~rz** *m* (*-a*; *-e*) (*w sporcie*) pole-vaulter
tycz|yć się (*-ę*, *t-ko 3. os. lub bezok.*) relate to, concern; **co się ~y** (*G*) as to
tyć ⟨**u-**⟩ (*-ję*) grow fat, put on weight
tydzień *m* (*tygodnia*; *tygodnie*) week; **za ~** in a week; **~ temu** a week ago; **całymi tygodniami** for weeks on end
tyfus *m* (*-a*; *-y*) *med.* typhoid fever; → **dur**[1]
tygodni|e *pl.* → **tydzień**; **~k** *m* (*-a*; *-i*) weekly; **~owo** *adv.* weekly; **dwu ~owo** two a/every week; **~owy** weekly
tygrys *m* (*-a*; *-y*) *zo.* tiger; **~ica** *f* (*-y*; *-e*) *zo.* tigress (*też fig.*)
tyka *f* (*-i*; *G -*) pole, stick
tykać[1] (*-am*) *zegar*: tick
tykać[2] (*-am*) touch; (*zwracać się*) be on first-name terms
tyle[1] (*m-os GAL tylu*, *I tyloma*) so much, so many; → **ile**; **~ czasu** so much time; **~ ... co ...** as much/many ... as ...; **drugie ~** twice as much/many; **nie ~ ..., ile ...** not so much, ... as ...; **~ samo**, **~ż** just as much/many
tyle[2] → **tył**
tylko *adv.* only; merely; **jak ~** as soon as
tyln|y back; *tech.* rear; *zo.* hind; **~e światło** rear-light
tylu → **tyle**[1]
tył *m* (*-u*; *-y*) back; rear; **~em, do ~u, w ~** backwards; **w tyle** behind; **z ~u** in the back; **obrócić się ~em** turn backwards (**do** *G* to); *mil. pl.* **~y** rear; **~ na przód** back to front; **pozostawać w tyle** drop behind; **~ek** F *m* (*-łka*; *-łki*) behind, bottom
tym **1.** *DIL/pl.* → **ten, to**[1]; **2.** *part.* (+ *comp.*) the; → **im, bardziej**
tymczas|em *adv.* (in the) meanwhile; **~owość** *f* (*-ści*; *0*) temporariness; **~owo** *adv.* temporarily; provisionally; **~owy** temporary; provisional
tymi → **ten, to**[1]
tymianek *m* (*-nku*; *-nki*) *bot.* thyme
tynk *m* (*-u*; *-y*) plaster; **~ować** ⟨**o-**⟩ (*-uję*) plaster
typ *m* (*-u*; *-y*) type, sort; (*-a*; *-y*) *pej.* character
typow|ać (*-uję*) tip; (*w loterii*) do the lottery; ⟨**wy-**⟩ select, pick; **~o** *adv.* typically; **~y** typical
tyranizować bully, tyrannize
tys. *skrót pisany*: **tysiąc(e)** thou. (*thousand*)
tysiąc (*G/pl. tysięcy*) thousand; → **715**; **~ami** by the thousands; **~krotny** thousandfold; **~lecie** *n* (*-a*; *G -ci*) millennium; **~letni** thousand-year-long, -old
tysięczn|y thousandth; **jedna ~a** one thousandth; → **715**
tyto|niowy tobacco; **~ń** *m* (*-niu*; *-nie*) *bot.* (**fajkowy** pipe) tobacco
tytuł *m* (*-u*; *-y*) title; **~em** (*G*) as, by way (of)
tytułow|ać (*-uję*) address; **~ać się** (*I*) use the title; ⟨**za-**⟩ *książkę* entitle; **~y** title
tzn. *skrót pisany*: **to znaczy** i.e. (*that is*)
tzw. *skrót pisany*: **tak zwany** so-called

U

u *prp.* (*G*) at; with; **~ ciebie** with you, at your place; **~ brzegu** on the shore; *często nie tłumaczy się*: **klamka ~ drzwi** door handle; → **dół, góra**

uak|tualniać (*-am*) ⟨**~tualnić**⟩ (*-ę, -nij!*) update, bring up to date; **~tywniać** (*-am*) ⟨**~tywnić**⟩ (*-ę, -nij!*) activate, make active; **~tywniać** ⟨**~tywnić**⟩ **się** become active

ub. *skrót pisany*: **ubiegły** last

ubarwienie *n* (*-a; G -eń*) coloration; → **barwa**

ubezpiecz|ać (*-am*) insure (**się** o.s.; **od** *G* against); *mil.*, (*w sporcie*) cover; **~alnia** *f* (*-i; -e*) insurance company; **~enie** *n* (*-a; G -eń*) insurance, cover; **~enie od odpowiedzialności cywilnej** *mot.* third-party insurance; **~enie na życie** life insurance; **~eniowy** insurance; **~ony** *m* (*-ego; -eni*), **~ona** *f* (*-nej; -ne*) insured person; **~yciel** *m* (*-a; -e*) insurer; **~yć** *pf.* → **ubezpieczać**

ubić *pf.* → **ubijać**; *hunt.* shoot; **~ interes** strike a bargain

ubie|c *pf. v/t.* (*przebiec*) cover; *kogoś* beat *s.o.* to *s.th.*; *v/i.* → **~gać** (*-am*) *czas*: pass, go by; **~gać się** (**o** *A*) apply (for), try to obtain; **~gły** last, previous; **~gnąć** *pf.* → **ubiec**; **~rać** (*-am*) dress (**k-o w** *A* s.o. in); *choinkę itp.* decorate; **~rać się** dress, get dressed; **~rać się w** (*A*) put on

ubija|ć (*-am*) *ziemię* stamp; *gastr.* beat, whip; **~k** *m* (*-a; -i*) tamper, pestle

ubikacja *f* (*-i; -e*) toilet

ubiór *m* (*-bioru; -biory*) dress; costume

ubliż|ać (*-am*) ⟨**~yć**⟩ (*-ę*) insult; **~ająco** *adv.* insultingly; **~ający** insulting

ubocz|e *n*: **na ~u** out of the way; **~nie** *adv.* incidentally; **~ny** incidental; **działanie ~ne** side effect

ubog|i **1.** poor; **2.** *m* (*-ego; -odzy*), **~a** *f* (*-iej; -ie*) poor man/woman, pauper; **ubodzy** *pl.* the poor *pl.*; **~o** *adv.* poorly

ubolewa|ć (*-am*) (**nad** *I*) regret, deplore; **~nie** *n* (*-a; -ań*) regret; **godny ~nia** regrettable

uboż|eć ⟨**z-**⟩ (*-eję*) become impoverished; **~ej** *adv. comp. od* → **ubogo**; **~szy** *adj. comp. od* → **ubogi**

ubój *m* (*-boju; -boje*) slaughter

ubóstwiać (*-am*) adore

ubóstwo *n* (*-a; 0*) poverty

ubra|ć *pf.* → **ubierać**; **~nie** *n* (*-a; G -ań*) dress; **~nie ochronne** protective clothing; **~ny** dressed; **być ~nym w** be dressed in …, wear …

uby|ć *pf.* → **ubywać**; **~tek** *m* (*-tku; -tki*) loss; *med.* cavity; **~wać** (*-am*) (*D*) decrease, be on the decrease; *księżyc*: wane; **dnia ~wa** the days are getting shorter

ucałowa|ć *pf.* kiss; **~nie** *n* (*-a; G -ań*) kiss

uchlany F blind drunk

ucho *n* **1.** (*-a; uszy, uszu, uszom, uszami, uszach*) *anat.* ear; **2.** (*pl. -a, uch*) handle; eye; **na własne uszy** with one's own ears; **obijać się o uszy** (*D*) come to one's ears; **szepnąć na ~** whisper in s.o.'s ears; **po uszy** up to one's ears

uchodz|ić escape (**cało** unhurt), fly; *gaz, woda*: leak, escape; **~ić za** (*A*) pass (as); **to nie ~i** it is not done; → **ujść**

uchodź|ca *m* (*-y; G -ców*) refugee; **~stwo** *n* (*-a; 0*) emigration

uchować *pf.* protect, preserve (**przed** *I* against); **~ się** survive

uchronić *pf.* protect (**od** *G* against)

uchwa|lać (*-am*) ⟨**~lić**⟩ *ustawę* pass; *wniosek* adopt; **~ła** *f* (*-y; G -*) resolution, decision

uchwy|cić *pf.* → **chwytać**; **~t** *m* grip, grasp, hold; (*rączka*) handle; **~tny** tangible, concrete; *ktoś* available

uchybi|(a)ć (*D*) insult; **~enie** *n* (*-a; G -eń*) insult

uchyl|ać (*-am*) ⟨**~ić**⟩ *drzwi* open slightly (**się** *v/i.*); *kotarę* draw aside; *decyzję itp.* cancel, annul; **~ić kapelusza** raise the hat; **~ić rąbka tajemnicy** reveal a secret; **~ać** ⟨**~ić**⟩ **się** (**od** *G*) shirk, evade, F dodge

uciąć *pf.* → **ucinać**

uciążliw|ie *adv.* arduously; **~y** arduous; burdensome, troublesome; **~y dla środowiska naturalnego** ecologically undesirable

ucichnąć *pf.* → **cichnąć**
ucie|c *pf.* (*ucieknę, -kniesz, -kł*) → **uciekać**; **~cha** *f* (*-y; G -*) fun, enjoyment; **~czka** *f* (*-i; G -czek*) flight, escape; (*zwł. z więzienia*) break-out; ***zmusić do ~czki*** put to flight; **~kać** (*-am*) (**od** *G*) escape (from), run away (from), flee; *gaz*: escape; (*z więzienia*) break out; ***~kać się*** (**do** *G*) resort (to); ***~kać po wypadku*** *mot.* fail to stop after an accident; commit a hit-and-run offence; **~kinier** *m* (*-a; -rzy*), **~kinierka** *f* (*-i; G -rek*) fugitive, runaway
ucieleśni|ać (*-am*) ⟨**~ć**⟩ (*-ę, -nij!*) embody; ***~(a)ć się*** be realized
ucier|ać (*-am*) *gastr.* grate; (*rozmieszać*) stir; *ziarno* grind; **~pieć** *pf.* suffer
uciesz|ny comical, amusing; **~yć** *pf.* → **cieszyć**
ucinać (*-am*) cut (off); cut short, curtail; → **ciąć**
ucisk *m* (*-u; -i*) pressure; *fig.* oppression, suppression; **~ać** (*-am*) press; *fig.* oppress, suppress
ucisz|ać (*-am*) ⟨**~yć**⟩ (*-ę*) calm (down) (**się** *v/i.*)
uciśniony suppressed
ucywilizować *pf.* (*-uję*) civilize
uczci|ć *pf.* → **czcić**; *rocznicę* celebrate; **~wość** *f* (*-ści; 0*) honesty, integrity; **~wie** *adv.* honestly; **~wy** honest
uczelnia *f* (*-i; -e*) college; ***~ wyższa*** university
ucze|nie się[1] *n* (*-a; 0*) learning, study
ucze|nie[2] *adv.* learnedly, eruditely; **~nnica** *f* (*-y; G -*), **~ń** *m* (*ucznia; uczniowie*) pupil, student
ucze|pić się *pf.* → **czepiać się**; **~rnić** *pf.* (*-ę, ń/-nij!*) blacken (*też fig.*); **~sać** *pf.* → **czesać**; **~sanie** *n* (*-a; G -ań*) hairdo, hairstyle
uczestni|ctwo *n* (*-a; 0*), **~czenie** *n* (*-a; 0*) participation; **~czka** *f* (*-i; G -czek*), **~k** *m* (*-a; -cy*) participant (*G* in); ***~k wypadku*** person involved in an accident; **~czyć** (*-ę*) participate, take part (**w** *L* in)
uczęszcza|ć (*-am*) (**do** *G*, **na** *A*) attend, take part (in); **~ny** well-attended, much-frequented
uczniowski student, pupil
uczon|ość *f* (*-ści; 0*) erudition; scholarship; **~y** **1.** scholarly, scientific; learned, erudite; **2.** *m* (*-ego, uczeni*), **~a** *f* (*-ej; -e*) scholar; (*przyrodnik*) scientist
uczt|a *f* (*-y; G -*) feast; **~ować** (*-uję*) feast
uczuci|e *n* (*-a; G -*) feeling; emotion; **~owość** *f* (*-ści; 0*) sensitivity; **~owo** *adv.* with feeling; sentimentally; affectionately; **~owy** affectionate; emotional
uczu|ć *pf.* → **uczuwać, czuć**; **~lać** (*-am*) ⟨**~lić**⟩ (*-lę*) make sensitive (**na** *A* to); *chem.*, *biol.* make allergic (**na** *A* to); ***~lić się*** (**na** *A*) become allergic (to); *fig.* be susceptible (to); **~lenie** *n* (*-a*) *med.* allergy
uczyć ⟨**na-**⟩ (*-ę*) (**k-o** *G*) teach (s.o. s.th., *bezok.*); **~ się** (*G*) learn, study
uczyn|ek *m* (*-nku; -nki*) act, deed; → **gorący**; **~ny** helpful, accommodating
uda|ć (się) *pf.* → **udawać (się)**; **~ny** successful; *dzieci* fine; (*nieszczery*) pretended; simulated
udar *m* (*-u; -y*) *med.* (**cieplny** heat-)stroke; ***~ słoneczny*** sunstroke
udaremni|ać (*-am*) ⟨**~ć**⟩ (*-ę, -nij!*) upset, thwart, frustrate
uda|(wa)ć (*-ję*) *v/t. chorobę* feign; pretend (**głuchego** to be deaf), pose (**głuchego** as a deaf person); *v/i.* pretend, pose; ***~(wa)ć się*** succeed, be successful; (**do** *G*, **na** *A*) *doktora*, *miejsce* go (to); *miejsce* make one's way (to)
uderz|ać (*-am*) *v/t.* hit, strike; *fig.* strike, fascinate; *v/i.* (**o** *A*) (*też* **się**) knock (against, on), hit; bump (against, on); **~ająco** *adv.* strikingly; **~ający** striking; **~enie** *n* (*-a; G -eń*) hit, knock, bang; strike (*też mil.*); **~eniowy** *mil.* assault; *med.* shock; **~yć** *pf.* (*-ę*) → **uderzać, bić**
udławić się *pf.* choke (*I* on)
udo *n* (*-a; G ud*) *anat.* thigh
udobruchać *pf.* (*-am*) placate, pacify, mollify
udogodni|ć *pf.* (*-ę, -nij!*) make (more) convenient; make easier; **~enie** *n* (*-a; G -eń*) convenience
udoskonal|ać (*-am*) ⟨**~ić**⟩ perfect, improve; **~enie** *n* (*-a; G -eń*) improvement, refinement
udostępni|ać (*-am*) ⟨**~ć**⟩ (*-ę, -nij!*) make accessible *lub* available
udow|adniać (*-am*) ⟨**~odnić**⟩ (*-ę, -nij!*) prove; substantiate
udowy thigh; *med.* femoral
udrę|czenie *n* (*-a; G -eń*), **~ka** *f* (*-i; G -*) agony, torment
udu|sić *pf.* choke, strangle; ***~sić się*** (*I*)

choke (on); *por.* **dusić**; **~szenie** *n* (*-a*; *G -eń*) strangling; choking; ***śmierć od ~szenia*** death by strangling
udział *m* (*-u*; *-y*) participation; (*wkład*, *też econ.*) share; ***~ w zbrodni*** participation in a crime; ***brać ~*** → ***uczestniczyć***; **~owiec** *m* (*-wca*; *-wcy*) *econ.* shareholder; **~owy** share
udziec *m* (*udźca*; *udźce*) *gastr.* leg
udziel|ać (*-am*) (*G*) offer; *pomocy, pożyczki* grant; *rady, słowa* give; ***~ać się*** *choroba itp.*: spread; *komuś* rub off (*D* on); **~enie** *n* (*-a*; *0*) granting, giving; ***~enie pomocy*** assistance; **~ić** *pf.* → ***udzielać***
udziesięciokrotni|ać (*-am*) ⟨**~ć**⟩ (*-ę*, *-nij!*) increase tenfold (**się** *v/i.*)
udźwiękowi|ać (*-am*) ⟨**~ć**⟩ (*-ę*, *-wij!*) add sound to; *film*: add sound-track to
UE *skrót pisany*: ***Unia Europejska*** EC (*European Community*)
uf|ać (*-am*) ⟨**za-**⟩ (*-am*) trust (*D*; *impf.* **że** that); hope (*impf.* **że** that); ***nie ~ać*** distrust, mistrust; **~ność** *f* (*-ści*; *0*) trust; **~ny** trusting; (**w** *A*) confident (in)
uga|niać się → ***ganiać***; **~sić** *pf.* → ***gasić***; **~szczać** (*-am*) (*D*) give; entertain
ugi|nać się (*-am*) ⟨***~ąć się***⟩ bend, bow; sag (under the weight)
ugłaskać *pf. fig.* mollify, appease
ugni|atać (*-am*) *v/i. but*: pinch; *v/t.* ⟨**~eść**⟩ *ciasto* knead
ugo|da *f* (*-y*; *G ugód*) agreement, settlement; **~dowy** conciliatory; willing to compromise; **~dzić** *pf.* hit; F (*do pracy*) sign on; **~ścić** *pf.* → ***ugaszczać***
ugór *m* (*ugoru*; *ugory*) wasteland; fallow land; ***leżeć ugorem*** lie fallow
ugruntow(yw)ać (*-[w]uję*) substantiate, ground
ugrupowanie *n* (*-a*; *G -ań*) group
ugryźć *pf.* bite; *komar*: sting
ugrząźć *pf.* → ***grzęznąć***
ui|szczać (*-am*) ⟨**~ścić**⟩ (*-szczę*) pay (***z góry*** in advance)
UJ *skrót pisany*: ***Uniwersytet Jagielloński*** Jagiellonian University
ujadać bark (**na** *A* at)
ujarzmi|ać (*-am*) ⟨**~ć**⟩ (*-ę*, *-mij!*) subjugate, enslave; *rzekę* master, control
ujawni|ać (*-am*) ⟨**~ć**⟩ (*-ę*, *-nij!*) reveal, expose; ***~(a)ć się*** manifest o.s.; *usterka itp.*: develop; *pol.* reveal o.s.
ująć *pf.* → ***ujmować***
ujednolic|ać (*-am*) ⟨**~ić**⟩ (*-cę*) make uniform, standardize
ujemny negative
ujeżdża|ć (*-am*) ⟨***ujeździć***⟩ *konia* break in; **~lnia** *f* (*-i*; *-e*, *-i*) riding school
ujęcie *n* (*-a*; *G -jęć*) capture; seizure; *fig.* point of view; *phot.* shot; (*wody itp.*) intake
ujm|a *f* (*-y*; *G ujm*) disgrace, discredit; ***przynosić ~ę*** (*D*) bring discredit (on); **~ować** (*-uję*) grab, seize (**za** *A* at); (*w słowa*) phrase, formulate; *fig. kogoś* enchant; (*odejmować, G*) take away; ***~ować się*** (**za** *I*) support; **~ujący** enchanting
ujrzeć *pf.* (*-ę*, *-y*, *-yj!*) catch sight of, see
ujś|cie *n* (*-a*; *G ujść*) mouth; *fig.* outlet; → ***wylot***; **~ć** (*-jść*) → ***uchodzić***
ukartowany pre-arranged
ukatrupić F *pf.* (*-ę*) do in, bump off
ukaz|ywać (*-uję*) ⟨**~ać**⟩ reveal (**się** o.s.); ***~(yw)ać się*** appear
uką|sić *pf.* (*-szę*) → ***kąsać***; **~szenie** *n* (*-a*; *G -eń*) bite; (*skorpiona*) sting
UKF *skrót pisany*: ***ultrakrótkie fale*** VHF (*ultrashort waves*)
układ *m* (*-u*; *-y*) arrangement; system; (*kontrakt*) contract, agreement; *pol.* treaty; ***zbiorowy ~ pracy*** framework collective agreement; ***≈ Słoneczny*** solar system; *t-ko pl.* ***~y*** negotiations *pl.*; F connections; **~ać** (*-am*) arrange, lay out; *tekst* compose; *plan* work out; *listę* make out; *sprawozdanie* compile; *melodię* compose; ***~ać się*** lie down (***do snu*** to sleep); *stosunki*: turn out (***dobrze*** all right); ***~ać się wygodnie*** snuggle, cuddle; ***~ać się w fałdy*** fall into folds; **~anka** *f* (*-i*; *G -nek*) jigsaw puzzle; **~ny** kind, charming; **~owy** system; contractual
ukłon *m* (*-u*; *-y*) bow; ***~y*** *pl. też* greetings; regards (**dla** *G* to); **~ić się** *pf.* bow; *por.* ***kłaniać się***
ukłucie *n* (*-a*; *G -łuć*) prick (*też fig.*); sting
ukochan|a *f* (*-ej*; *-e*), **~y** **1.** *m* (*-ego*; *-ani*) darling; **2.** beloved, loved
ukon- *pf.* → ***kon-***
ukończ|enie *n* (*-a*; *G -eń*) ending, conclusion; (*budowy itp.*) completion; (***szkoły*** school-leaving) qualification; **~yć** *pf.* → ***kończyć***
ukoronowanie *n* (*-a*; *G -ań*) crowning (*też fig.*)

ukorzeni|ać się (*-am*) ⟨**~ć się**⟩ take root; **~ony** rooted
ukos *m* (*-a*; *-y*) slant; *tech.* bevel; ***na ~, z ~a, ~em*** at a slant; obliquely; ***patrzeć z ~a*** look askance (***na*** *A* at)
ukośny slanting; oblique
ukradkiem *adv.* stealthily, furtively
Ukra'i|na *f* (*-y*; *0*) (the) Ukraine; **~niec** *m* (*-ńca*; *-ńcy*), **~nka** *f* (*-i*; *G -nek*) Ukrainian; **♀ński** Ukrainian; ***mówić po ~ńsku*** speak Ukrainian
u|krajać (*-am*) cut off; **~kręcić** *pf. powróz* twist; (*oderwać*) twist off; *gastr.* mix; **~kroić** *pf.* → ***ukrajać***
ukrop *m* (*-u*; *0*) boiling water
ukry|cie *n* (*-a*; *G -yć*) hiding place; *fig.* concealment; → ***kryjówka***; ***z ~cia*** from hiding; **~ty** concealed, hidden; *choroba* latent; **~wać** (*-am*) → ***kryć***; *plany itp.* conceal, hide
ukrzyżowanie *n* (*-a*; *G -ań*) crucifixion; *rel.* the Crucifixion
ukształtowanie *n* (*-a*; *G -ań*) shape, shaping
ukuć *pf.* forge; *fig.* hatch
ukwiecony flower-bedecked, flowery
ul. *skrót pisany*: ***ulica*** St. (*street*)
ul *m* (*-a*; *-e*) beehive
ula|ć *pf.* → ***ulewać***; ***jak ~ł*** fit like a glove; **~tniać się** (*-am*) evaporate; *zapach, nastrój*: disappear; F *fig.* clear off; **~tywać** (*-uję*) fly away/off; *woń*: disappear; → ***uchodzić***
ule|c *pf.* → ***ulegać***; **~cieć** *pf.* → ***ulatywać***; **~czalny** curable; **~gać** (*-am*) (*D*) yield, submit; lose, give in; agree to (***prośbie*** a request); ***~gać woli*** (*G*) bow to the will (of); ***~gać wpływom*** come under influence; ***~c zmianie*** undergo a change; ***~c wypadkowi*** have an accident; ***~c zapomnieniu*** fall into oblivion; *jur.* ***~c przedawnieniu*** be subject to prescription; → ***wątpliwość***; ***~gający zepsuciu*** highly perishable
uleg|le *adv.* submissively; **~łość** *f* (*-ści*; *0*) submission; **~ły** submissive, meek
ulepsz|ać (*-am*) ⟨**~yć**⟩ (*-ę*) improve; **~enie** *n* (*-a*; *G -eń*) improvement
ulewa *f* (*-y*; *G -*) downpour, heavy rain; **~ć** (*-am*) pour away; *niemowlę*: spit; **~ny** *deszcz* heavy
uleżeć *pf.*: **~ *się*** mellow, mature
ulg|a *f* (*-i*; *G -*) relief; (*zniżka*) discount, reduction; ***~a podatkowa*** *Brt.* tax allowance, *Am.* tax deduction; **~owo** *adv. traktować* preferentially; **~owy** with a discount, reduced; *traktowanie* preferential
uli|ca *f* (*-y*; *G -*) street; ***na/przy ~cy*** *Brt.* in (*Am.* on) the street; **~czka** *f* (*-czki*; *G -czek*) street; ***ślepa ~czka*** blind alley (*też fig.*); **~cznik** *m* (*-a*; *-cy*) waif, street urchin; **~czny** street
ulokowa|ć *pf.* → ***lokować***; **~nie** *n* (*-a*; *G -ań*) accommodation; location
ulot|ka *f* (*-i*; *G -tek*) leaflet; *reklamowa* prospectus, advertising brochure; ***~ka z instrukcją*** instruction leaflet; **~nić się** *pf.* (*-ę*, *-nij!*) → ***ulatniać się***
ultra|dźwiękowy ultrasonic, ultrasound; **~fioletowy** ultraviolet; **~krótkofalowy** very high frequency; VHF; **~nowoczesny** ultramodern; **~sonograf** *m* (*-u*; *-y*) *med.* ultrasound scanner; **~sonograficzny** *med.* ultrasound
ulubi|enica *f* (*-y*; *G -*), **~eniec** *m* (*-ńca*; *-ńcy*) darling, pet; favo(u)rite; **~ony** favo(u)rite, pet
ulży|ć (*-ę*) *pf.* (*D*, ***k-u w*** *L*) relieve (s.o. of), make easier (s.o. with); ***~ć sobie*** (*w toalecie*) relieve o.s.; *fig.* get *s.th.* off one's chest; ***~ło mi*** (***na sercu***) that came as a relief to me
ułam|ać *pf.* → ***ułamywać***; **~ek** *m* (*-mka*; *-mki*) *math.* fraction; piece; ***w ~ku sekundy*** in a split second; **~kowy** fraction; **~ywać** (*-uję*) break (off) (***się*** *v/i.*)
ułaskawi|ać (*-am*) ⟨**~ć**⟩ (*-ę*) *jur.* pardon; **~enie** *n* (*-a*; *G -eń*) *jur.* pardon
ułatwi|ać (*-am*) ⟨**~ć**⟩ (*-ę*) simplify, make easier; facilitate; **~enie** *n* (*-a*; *G -eń*) simplification
ułom|ek *m* (*-mka*; *-mki*) fragment, piece; **~ność** *f* (*-ści*; *0*) → ***kalectwo***; **~ny** disabled, physically handicapped
ułoż|enie *n* (*-a*; *G -eń*) arrangement; **~yć** *pf.* → ***układać***; ***~yć się*** *fig.* come to an agreement
ułuda *f* (*-y*; *G -*) illusion, hallucination
umacniać (*-am*) strengthen; *mil.* fortify; *fig.* consolidate; **~ *się*** become stronger; **~ *się w*** (*L*) make one's intentions stronger
umarł|y **1.** dead; **2.** *m* (*-ego*; *-rli*), **~a** *f* (*-ej*; *-e*) dead person; ***umarli*** *pl.* the dead *pl.*
umarzać (*-am*) *econ. środek* amortize;

U

dług write off; *jur. rozprawę* abandon; *dochodzenie* stop
umawiać arrange (*też* **się** *v/i.*); agree; **~ się** (**co do** *G*) agree (on), reach an agreement (about); (**z** *I*) make an appointment (with)
umeblowanie *f* (*-a*; *0*) furniture
umiar *m* (*-u*; *0*) moderation; **z ~em** moderately, in moderation; **zachować ~** be moderate; **~kowanie** *n* (*-a*; *0*) temperance (*też w piciu*), restraint → **~kowany** temperate; *poglądy, kierunek* moderate
umie|ć (*-em*) be able to, can; **czy ~sz ...?** can you...?; **on ~ sobie poradzić** he can manage (it) on his own; **~jętność** *f* (*-ści*) skill; ability, capability; **~jętny** skilful
umiejs|cawiać (*-am*) ⟨**~cowić**⟩ (*-ę, -ców!*) locate; (*w klasyfikacji*) classify
umiera|ć (*-am*) die **~ć na raka** die of cancer, *fig.* **~ć ze strachu** die of fear; **~jący** dying
umie|szczać (*-am*) ⟨**~ścić**⟩ put, locate; place (**się** o.s.); (*publikować*) publish; *pieniądze* deposit
umięśniony muscular
umi|lać (*-am*) ⟨**~lić**⟩ (*-ę*) make more agreeable; brighten up; **~lknąć** (*-nę*) *pf.* fall silent; *muzyka, rozmowa*: stop; **~łowanie** *n* (*-a*) fondness (*G* for)
umizg|ać się (*-am*) (**do** *G*) flirt (with), make passes (to); (**o** *A*) woo, curry favo(u)r (with); **~i** *pl.* flirting; wooing
umknąć *pf.* → **umykać**
umniejsz|ać (*-am*) ⟨**~yć**⟩ (*-ę*) decrease, diminish
umocn|ić pp → **umacniać**; **~ienie** *n* (*-a*; *G -eń*) fortification; *fig.* strengthening, consolidation
umo|cow(yw)ać (*-*[*w*]*uję*) (*I*) fix (with), fasten (with); **~czyć** *pf.* → **maczać**; **~rusać** *pf.* (*-am*) smear; **~rusać się** get dirty; **~rzyć** *pf.* → **umarzać**; **~tywowanie** *n* (*-a*; *G -ań*) reason, grounds *pl.*
umow|a *f* (*-y*; *G umów*) agreement; contract; **~a kupna** contract of sale; **~a o pracę** contract of employment; **zgodnie z ~ą** as stipulated in the contract; **~ny** contractual; *econ.* **kara ~na** liquidated damages *pl.*
umożliwi|ać (*-am*) ⟨**~ć**⟩ (*-ę*) make possible, enable
umówi|ć *pf.* → **umawiać**; **~ony** *spotkanie* appointed
umrzeć *pf.* → **umierać**
umundurowa|ć *pf.* (*-uję*) uniform; **~nie** *n* (*-a*; *G -ań*) uniform
umy|ć *pf.* → **umywać, myć**; **~kać** (*-am*) escape, run away/off
umy|sł *m* (*-u*; *-y*) mind; intellect; **zdrowy na ~śle** of sound mind; → **przytomność**; **~słowo** *adv.* mentally; intellectually; → **chory**; **~słowość** *f* (*-ści*) mentality; **~słowy** mental; intellectual; → **pracownik**
umyślny intentional, on purpose, deliberate
umywa|ć (*-am*) wash (**się** o.s./*v/i.*); *naczynia* wash up; **~lka** *f* (*-i*; *G -lek*) washbasin; **~lnia** *f* (*-i*; *-e*) washing-room
unaoczni|ać (*-am*) ⟨**~ć**⟩ (*-ę, -nij!*) reveal, show
unia *f* (*GDl -ii*; *-e*) union
uncja *f* (*-i*; *-e*) ounce
unicestwi|ać (*-am*) ⟨**~ć**⟩ (*-ę*) destroy, exterminate; *plany* wreck; *nadzieje* dash
uniemożliwi|ać (*-am*) ⟨**~ć**⟩ (*-ę*) prevent, frustrate; make impossible
unieru|chamiać (*-am*) ⟨**~chomić**⟩ (*-ę*) immobilize; *aviat.* ground; *tech.* lock; *kapitał* tie; *med.* set
uniesieni|e *n* (*-a*; *G -eń*) rapture, elation; **w ~u** (*w zachwycie*) in rapture(s); (*w gniewie*) in anger
unieszkodliwi|ać (*-am*) ⟨**~ć**⟩ (*-ę*) neutralize; *śmieci* dispose of
unieść *pf.* → **unosić**
unieważni|ać (*-am*) ⟨**~ć**⟩ (*-ę, -nij!*) *legitymację, kontrakt* invalidate; *jur.* void, nullify, annul; **~enie** *n* (*-a*; *G -eń*) voidance, nullification, annulment, invalidation
uniewinni|ać (*-am*) ⟨**~ć**⟩ (*-ę*) (**z** *G*) exonerate (from); *jur.* acquit (of); **~enie** *n* (*-a*; *G -eń*) exoneration; *jur.* acquittal
uniezależni|ać (*-am*) ⟨**~ć**⟩ (*-ę, -nij!*) make independent; **~(a)ć się** become independent (**od** *G* from)
unik *m* (*-u*; *-i*) dodge, duck; **zrobić ~** dodge, duck; **~ać** (*-am*) (*G*) avoid
unika|lny, ~towy unique, only
uniknąć *pf.* → **unikać**; (*G*) escape, avoid
uniknięci|e *n* (*-a*; *G -ęć*) avoidance, escape; **nie do ~a** unavoidable
uniwer|salny universal; **~sytecki** university; academic; **~sytet** *m* (*-u*; *-y*) university
uniżony humble, servile

U

unosić raise; *rzeka*: carry away; ***uniesiony*** (*D*) in a fit (of); **~ się** rise; *w powietrzu, na wodzie* float; *na falach* drift
unowocześni|ać (*-am*) ⟨**~ć**⟩ (*-ę, -nij!*) modernize
uodporni|ać (*-am*) ⟨**~ć**⟩ (*-ę, -nij!*) immunize (**na** *A* against); **~ć się** (**na** *A*) become immune (to)
u|ogólniać (*-am*) ⟨**~ogólnić**⟩ (*-ę, -nij!*) generalize; **~osabiać** (*-am*) ⟨**~osobić**⟩ (*-ę, -nij!*) personify; **~osobienie** *n* (*-a; G -eń*) personification
upad|ać fall; *fig.* (*niszczeć*) decline, deteriorate; *pol.* fall, collapse; *econ.* go bankrupt; ***~ać na duchu*** lose heart; **~ek** *m* (*-dku; -dki*) fall; *fig.* decline, deterioration; *pol.* collapse; **~łość** *f* (*-ści; 0*) *econ.* bankruptcy, insolvency; **~ły** fallen; *fig.* sunk (low); ***do ~łego*** to the point of exhaustion
upa|jać (*-am*) (*alkoholem*) intoxicate, inebriate; *fig.* make euphoric, exhilarate; ***~jać się*** become intoxicated; become euphoric; **~lny** hot; **~ł** *m* (*-u; -y*) heat
upamiętni|ać (*-am*) ⟨**~ć**⟩ (*-ę, -nij!*) memorialize, commemorate; **~(a)ć się** be remembered, remain in memory
upaństw|awiać (*-am*) ⟨**~owić**⟩ (*-ę, -wów!*) nationalize
upar|cie *adv.* stubbornly, obstinately; **~ty** stubborn, obstinate
upa|ść[1] *pf.* (*paść*[1]) → (**u**)**padać**
upa|ść[2] *pf.* (*paść*[2]) fatten; **~trywać** (*-uję*) ⟨**~trzyć**⟩ → ***wypatrywać, wypatrzyć***; ***~trywać stosownej chwili*** wait for the suitable time
upch|ać *pf.*, **~nąć** *pf.* → **upychać**
upełnomocni|ać (*-am*) ⟨**~ć**⟩ (*-ę, -nij!*) authorize (**do** *G* to)
uperfumowany scented, perfumed
upewni|ać (*-am*) assure (**k-o o** s.o. of); ***~ć się*** make sure (**co do** of)
upi|ąć *pf.* → **upinać**; **~ć** *pf.* → **upijać**
upie|c *pf.* bake; *mięso* roast; ***świeżo ~czony*** *fig.* new, newly-qualified
upierać się (*-am*) insist (**przy** *L* on), persist (**przy** *L* in)
upierzenie *n* (*-a; G -eń*) plumage
upiększ|ać (*-am*) ⟨**~yć**⟩ (*-ę*) decorate, deck out; *fig.* embellish
upi|jać (*-am*) (*G*) make drunk, inebriate, intoxicate; ***~jać się*** get drunk; **~nać** (*-am*) *włosy* pin up
u|piorny ghastly; **~piór** *m* (*-piora; -piory*) ghost
upły|nąć *pf.* → **upływać**; **~w** *m* (*-u; 0*) (*czasu*) passage, passing; ***z ~wem lat*** with years; ***~w krwi*** loss of blood; **~wać** *czas*: go by, fly; *termin*: expire, lapse
upodoba|ć (*-am*): ***~ć sobie*** (*A*) take a liking (to); **~nie** *n* (*-a; G -ań*) liking, fondness (**do** *G* for); ***z ~niem*** with pleasure; ***według ~nia*** to one's liking
upo|ić *pf.* → **upajać**; **~jenie** *n* (*-a; G -eń*) inebriation, intoxication (*też fig.*); **~karzać** (*-am*) ⟨**~korzyć**⟩ (*-ę, -kórz!*) humble (**się** o.s.)
upomin|ać (*-am*) admonish, rebuke; ***~ać się*** (**o** *A*) demand, insist (on); **~ek** *m* (*-nka; -nki*) souvenir, keepsake
upomnie|ć *pf.* → **upominać**; **~nie** *n* (*-a; G -eń*) (*na piśmie*) reminder; reprimand, rebuke
upor|ać się *pf.* (*-am*) (**z** *I*) get ready (with); clear (up); **~czywy** unrelenting; tenacious; *wzrok* insistent; *ból* persistent
uporządkow(yw)ać (*-[w]uję*) tidy up; *fig.* straighten out, sort out
uposażeni|e *n* (*-a; G -eń*) pay, salary; **~owy** pay, salary
upośledz|ać (*-am*) ⟨**~ić**⟩ handicap, impair; **~enie** *n* (*-a; G -eń*) disability; handicap; **~ony** disabled; underprivileged
upoważni|ać (*-am*) ⟨**~ć**⟩ (*-ę*) authorize, empower (**do** *G* to); **~enie** *n* (*-a; G -eń*) authorization, authority; *jur.* power of attorney; ***z ~enia*** by proxy
upowszechni|ać (*-am*) ⟨**~ć**⟩ (*-ę, -nij!*) spread, disseminate
upozorowanie *n* (*-a; G -ań*) simulation, feigning
upór *m* (*uporu; 0*) stubbornness, obstinacy
upragnienie *n*: ***z ~m*** longingly
upragniony longed for
uprasz|ać (*-am*) request; ***~a się o ciszę!*** silence, please!; **~czać** (*-am*) simplify; *ułamek* cancel
upraw|a *f* (*-y; G -*) *agr.* tillage, cultivation; growing; crop; **~iać** (*-am*) ⟨**~ić**⟩ *ziemię* cultivate; *t-ko impf. rośliny* grow; *sport itp.* go in for, *Brt.* practise, *Am.* practice; **~niać** (*-am*) ⟨**~nić**⟩ (*-ę, -nij!*) (**do** *G*) entitle (to); **~nienie** *n* (*-a; G -eń*) entitlement, right; **~niony** entitled (**do głosowania** to vote); eligible (**do** *G* for); **~ny** *agr.* arable

uprawomocnić się *pf.* (*-ę, -nij!*) come into force
upro|sić *pf.* → ***upraszać***; **~szczenie** *n* (*-a; G -eń*) simplification; **~ścić** *pf.* → ***upraszczać***; **~wadzać** (*-am*) ⟨**~wadzić**⟩ (*-ę*) hijack; *samolot* skyjack; **~wadzenie** *n* (*-a; G -eń*) hijacking; (*samolotu*) skyjacking
u|prząż *f* (*uprzęży; uprzęże*) harness; **~przeć się** *pf.* → ***upierać się***; **~przednio** *adv.* previously, before
uprzedz|ać (*-am*) *v/t.* forestall, anticipate; (*przestrzegać*) (**o** *L*) forewarn, warn (of); ***~ać się*** (**do** *G*) become prejudiced (against); **~ająco** *adv.* obligingly; **~ający** obliging; **~enie** *n* (*-a; G -eń*) prejudice, bias; ***bez ~enia*** unbiased, open-minded; (*nagle*) without warning; **~ić** (*-am*) *v/t. pf.* → ***uprzedzać***; **~ony** prejudiced, biased
uprzejm|ość *f* (*-ści; 0*) kindness, politeness; **~ie** *adv.*: ***dziękuję ~ie*** thank you very much; **~y** (***dla*** *G*, ***wobec*** *A*) polite (for), kind (for); ***bądź tak ~y*** (***i***) be so kind as to
uprzemysło|wienie *n* (*-a; 0*) industrialization; **~wiony** industrialized
uprzyjemni|ać (*-am*) ⟨**~ć**⟩ (*-ę, -nij!*) make nicer, make enjoyable
uprzykrz|ać (*-am*) ⟨**~yć**⟩ spoil; make miserable; ***~yć sobie*** (*A*) grow tired (of); ***~ać się*** be a nuisance; **~ony** tiresome
uprzy|stępniać (*-am*) ⟨**~stępnić**⟩ (*-ę, -nij!*) → ***udostępniać***; **~tamniać, ~tomniać** (*-am*) ⟨**~tomnić**⟩ (*-ę, -nij!*) (*też* ***sobie***) realize; **~wilejowany** privileged
upu|st *m* (*-u; -y*) *tech.* bleed(ing); (*śluza*) sluice; ***dać ~st*** (*D*) *fig.* give vent (to); **~szczać** (*-am*) ⟨**~ścić**⟩ drop; ***~szczać krew*** bleed, draw blood
upychać (*-am*) stuff
ura|biać (*-am*) form (***się*** *v/i.*); (*w górnictwie*) mine, *kamień* quarry; F *kogoś* work on; **~czać** (*-am*) → ***raczyć***; **~dowany** delighted, joyful; *por.* ***radować***; **~dzać** (*-am*) ⟨**~dzić**⟩ agree on; conclude
uran *m* (*-u; 0*) *chem.* uranium
Uran *m* (*-a; 0*) *astr.* Uranus
uranowy uranium
ura|stać (*-am*) grow, increase; (**do** *G*) take on the proportions (of); **~tować** *pf.* save
uraz *m* (*-u; -y*) trauma, injury; **~a** *f* (*-y; G -*) resentment, offence; grudge; ***mieć ~ę*** *Brt.* bear (*Am.* hold) a grudge (**do** *G* against); **~ić** *pf.* → ***urażać***; **~owy** traumatic
urażać (*-am*) hurt, wound (*też fig.*)
urąg|ać (*-am*) defy; *lit. komuś* insult; → ***wymyślać***; **~owisko** *n* (*-a; 0*) laughingstock
urbanistyczny urbanistic, town-planning
uregulowanie *n* (*-a; G -ań*) regulation
urlop *m* (*-u; -y*) (***macierzyński*** maternity) leave, (*wypoczynkowy*) holiday, *zwł. Am.* vacation; ***być na ~ie, korzystać z ~u*** be on *Brt.* holidays (*Am.* vacation); **~ować** (*im*)*pf.* (*-uję*) give *s.o.* leave (of absence); **~owy** holiday, vacation
urna *f* (*-y; G urn*) (*wyborcza*) ballot-box
uro|bić *pf.* → ***urabiać***; **~czo** *adv.* charmingly; **~czy** charming, lovely; **~czystość** *f* (*-ści*) ceremony; festivity, celebration; **~czysty** solemn, ceremonial; **~czyście** *adv.* solemnly; ceremonially; **~da** *f* (*-y; 0*) beauty; looks *pl.*
urodz|aj *m* (*-u; -e*) good harvest/crop; ***~aj na owoce*** a good year for fruit; **~ajny** fertile; **~enie** *n* (*-a; G -eń*) birth; ***miejsce ~enia*** birthplace; ***rok ~enia*** year of birth; ***Polak z ~enia*** a Pole by birth; **~ić** *pf.* → ***rodzić***; **~inowy** birthday; **~iny** *pl.* (*-*) birthday (party)
uro|jenie *n* (*-a; -eń*) illusion, hallucination; **~jony** imaginary
urok *m* (*-u; -i*) charm; ***pełen ~u*** charming; ***na psa ~!*** touch wood!
urosnąć *pf.* → ***urastać***
urozmaic|ać (*-am*) ⟨**~ić**⟩ (*-ę*) vary, diversify; **~enie** *n* (*-a; G -eń*) variety, diversity; **~ony** varied, diversified
uruch|amiać (*-am*) ⟨**~omić**⟩ (*-ę*) set in motion; turn on; *silnik* start up
urwać *pf.* → ***urywać, rwać***
urwis *m* (*-a; -y*) young rascal
urwis|ko *n* (*-a; G -*) precipice, bluff **~ty** → ***stromy***
uryw|ać (*-am*) *v/t.* cut short; tear off; *v/i.* ***~ać się*** come off; break off; F *ktoś*: slip away; **~any** interrupted; **~ek** *m* (*-wka; -wki*) bit, snatch, snippet; **~kowy** fragmentary, incomplete
urząd *m* (*-rzędu; -rzędy*) (***pocztowy, stanu cywilnego*** post, registry) office;

authorities *pl.*; ***z urzędu*** because of one's profession; *jur.* assigned (by court)
urządz|ać (*-am*) arrange; *mieszkanie* furnish; *przyjęcie* give; ***~ać się*** furnish, make o.s. at home; **~enie** *n* (*-a*; *G -eń*) appliance, device; facility; ***~enie sanitarne*** sanitary facilities *pl.*; **~ić** *pf.* → ***urządzać***
urze|c *pf.* → ***urzekać***; **~czony** bewitched; ***jak ~czony*** like one bewitched
urzeczywistni|ać (*-am*) ⟨**~ć**⟩ (*-ę, -nij!*) realize, put into practice; ***~ać*** ⟨**~ć**⟩ ***się*** be realized, be fulfilled
urzeka|ć (*-am*) enchant, bewitch; *fig.* (*I*) win, captivate; **~jąco** *adv.* enchantingly; captivatingly; **~jący** enchanting; captivating
urzędni|czka *f* (*-i*; *G -czek*), **~k** *m* (*-a*; *-cy*) clerk, official
urzędow|ać (*-uję*) work (in an office); **~anie** *n* (*-a*; *0*) discharge of one's duties; ***godziny*** *pl.* ***~ania*** office hours *pl.*; **~o** *adv.* officially; **~y** official
urzynać (*-am*) ⟨**urznąć, urżnąć**⟩ cut off; F **~** ⟨**urżnąć**⟩ ***się*** get drunk
usamodzielni|ać się (*-am*) ⟨**~ć się**⟩ (*-ę, -nij!*) become independent
USC *skrót pisany*: ***Urząd Stanu Cywilnego*** registry office
uschnąć *pf.* → ***usychać***
USG *n skrót*: *med.* ***ultrasonografia*** F ultrasound scan; ***zrobił sobie ~*** he was given an ultrasound scan
usiany studded
usi|ąść *pf.* → ***siadać***; **~edzieć** *pf.*: ***nie móc ~edzieć*** be on edge
usi|lny *prośba* insistent, urgent; *praca, starania* concentrated; **~łować** (*-uję*) (+ *bezok.*) try (to *bezok.*), endeavo(u)r (to *bezok.*); (*bardzo*) struggle (to *bezok.*); **~łowanie** *n* (*-a*; *G -ań*) endeavo(u)r; attempt
uskakiwać (*-uję*) jump aside
uskarżać się (*-am*) complain (***na*** *A* about)
u|składać *pf.* (*-am*) save (***na*** *A* for); **~skoczyć** *pf.* → ***uskakiwać***; **~słany** (*I*) covered (with); **~słuchać** *pf.* (*G*) respond (to); (*być posłusznym*) listen (to)
usłu|ga *f* (*-i*; *G -*) service; (*grzeczność*) favo(u)r; → ***przysługa***; **~giwać** (*-uję*) serve (***gościom*** the guests; ***przy stole*** at table); **~gowy** service; **~żność** *f* (*-ści*; *0*) willingness to help; **~żny** → ***uczynny***; **~żyć** *pf.* → ***usługiwać***
usłyszeć *pf.* → ***słyszeć***
usnąć *pf.* (*-nę*) fall asleep; *lit.* ***~ na wieki*** die
uspo|kajać (*-am*) ⟨**~koić**⟩ (*-ję*) calm down (***się*** *v/i.*); ***~koić się*** *wiatr, burza*: die down; *morze*: become calm; **~kajająco** *adv.* soothingly; **~kajający** soothing; *med.* sedative
uspołeczni|ać (*-am*) ⟨**~ć**⟩ socialize; *econ.* nationalize
uspos|abiać (*-am*) ⟨**~obić**⟩ (*-ę, -sób!*) set (***przeciw*** against); (***do*** *G*) dispose (toward(s)); ***nie być ~obionym*** not feel like (***do czegoś*** doing s.th.); **~obienie** *n* (*-a*; *G -eń*) nature, character
usprawiedliwi|ać (*-am*) ⟨**~ć**⟩ (*-ę*) excuse (***się*** o.s.); (*wytłumaczyć*) justify; **~enie** *n* (*-a*; *G -eń*) excuse; (*wytłumaczenie*) justification
usprawni|ać (*-am*) ⟨**~ć**⟩ (*-ę, -nij!*) improve (on), make more efficient
ust. *skrót pisany*: ***ustawa*** act; ***ustęp*** paragraph, passage
usta *pl.* (*ust*) mouth, lips *pl.*
usta|ć[1] *pf.* (*stać*[2]) stop, end
usta|ć[2] *pf.* (*stać*[1]) stand, keep standing; ***~ć się*** *płyn*: clear; **~lać** (*-am*) ⟨**~lić**⟩ (*-ę*) stabilize (***się*** *v/i.*); *warunki, termin itp.* fix, determine; *fakt* establish; **~nawiać** (*-am*) ⟨**~nowić**⟩ *zwyczaj itp.* introduce; *rekord* establish; *spadkobiercę* appoint, name; **~wa** *f* (*-y*; *G -*) rule, law; **~wać** (*-ję*) stop, end
ustawi|(a)ć się put up, set up; ***~(a)ć się*** place o.s.; (*w szeregu itp.*) line up; **~czny** continual, incessant
ustawodaw|ca *m* (*-y*; *G -ców*) law-maker, legislator; **~czy** legislative; ***władza ~cza*** legislative power; **~stwo** *n* (*-a*; *G -*) legislation
ustawow|o *adv.* by law *lub* statute; **~y** legal, statutory
ustąpi|ć *pf.* (*-ę*) → ***ustępować***; **~enie** *n* (*-a*; *G -eń*) withdrawal, resignation
uster|ka *f* (*-i*; *G -rek*) defect, fault; ***bez ~ek*** faultless
ustęp *m* (*-u*; *-y*) excerpt; passage; → ***klozet***; **~liwie** *adv.* yieldingly; compliantly; **~liwy** yielding; compliant; **~ować** (*-uję*) *v/i.* (*przed siłą itp.*) yield; give in; (*pod naciskiem*) give; (*z funkcji*) step down, resign; *pierwszeństwa itp.*,

U

też fig. give way; (**k-u w** *L*) be inferior (to s.o. in); *wróg*: retreat (**wobec** *A* against); *ból itp.*: subside, die away; **~ować z ceny** lower the price; *v/t.* let have, leave; **~stwo** *n* (*-a*; *G* -) concession
ustn|ie *adv.* orally; **~ik** *m* (*-a*; *-i*) mouthpiece; **~y** oral
ustokrotni|ać (*-am*) 〈**~ć**〉 (*-ę*, *-nij!*) increase a hundredfold (**się** *v/i.*)
ustosunkow(yw)ać się (-[*w*]*uję*) (**do** *G*) react (to), respond (to); take a position (to)
ustrojowy *biol.* body, organic; *pol.* political, constitutional
ustronny remote, out-of-the-way
ustrój *m* (*-roju*; *-roje*) system; *biol.* organism; **~ państwowy** state system
ustrzec *pf.* preserve (**przed** *I*, **od** *G* from); **~ się** (**przed** *I*) avoid
usu|nąć *pf.* → **usuwać**; **~nięcie** *n* (*-a*; *G -ęć*) removal; elimination; **~wać** (*-am*) remove; (*z grupy itp.*) get rid of, eliminate; *med.* take out (**z** *G* from); **~wać się** withdraw (**od** *G* from); move (**na bok** aside)
usychać (*-am*) dry
usynowienie *n* (*-a*; *G -eń*) adoption
usy|pać *pf.* → **usypywać**; **~piać** (*-am*) fall asleep, doze off; **~piająco** *adv.* soporifically; **~piający** soporific
usy|pisko *n* (*-a*; *G* -) (*śmieci*) dump, *Brt.* tip; (*piasku itp.*) pile; **~pywać** (*-uję*) pile (up)
usytuowanie *n* (*-a*; *G -ań*) localization, location
uszanowani|e *n* (*-a*; *G -ań*) → **poszanowanie, szacunek**; **brak ~a** lack of respect
uszczel|ka *f* (*-i*; *G -lek*) seal; washer; **~niać** (*-am*) 〈**~nić**〉 (*-ę*, *-nij!*) make tight; seal, stop
uszczerb|ek *m* (*-bku*; *0*) damage; **z ~kiem** (**dla**) **zdrowia** to the detriment of health
uszczęśliwi|ać (*-am*) 〈**~ć**〉 (*-ę*) make happy
uszczupl|ać (*-am*) 〈**~ić**〉 (*-lę*, *-lij!*) reduce, deplete
uszczyp|liwie *adv.* caustically, stingingly; **~liwy** caustic, stinging; **~nąć** *v/s.* (*-ę*) pinch
uszkadzać (*-am*) damage
uszko *n* (*-a*; *G -szek*) → **ucho**; (*igły*) ear; (*filiżanki*) handle
uszkodz|enie *n* (*-a*; *G -eń*) damage; injury; **~enie ciała** bodily harm; **~ony** damaged; broken-down; **~ić** *pf.* → **uszkadzać**
uszlachetni|ać (*-am*) 〈**~ć**〉 (*-ę*, *-nij!*) ennoble; *tech.* enrich, refine
usz|ny ear; *med.* aural; **~y** *pl.* → **ucho**
uszy|ć *pf.* → **szyć**; **~kować** (*-uję*) prepare, make ready
uścis|k *m* (*-u*; *-i*) (*ramionami*) embrace; hug; (*ręką*) grip; **~k dłoni** handshake; **~kać** 〈**~nąć**〉 embrace, hug; grip; *dłoń* shake
uśmiać się laugh (**do łez, serdecznie** to tears, heartily; **z** *G* at)
uśmiech *m* (*-u*; *-y*) smile; **szyderczy ~** smirk, grin; **~ać się** (*-am*) 〈**~nąć się**〉 (*-nę*) smile; (**z** *G*) grin (at), smirk (at); (**do** *G*) give a smile (to), smile (at); **~nięty** smiling
uśmierc|ać (*-am*) 〈**~ić**〉 (*-cę*) kill; *zwł. zwierzę* put to death
uśmierz|ać (*-am*) 〈**~yć**〉 (*-ę*) *ból* alleviate, soothe; *bunt* suppress
u|śmieszek *m* (*-szka*; *-szki*) grin; **~śpić** *pf.* → **usypiać**
uświad|amiać (*-am*) 〈**~omić**〉 (*-ę*) educate; tell, inform (**co do** *G* about); **~omić sobie** realize; **~omienie** *n* (*-a*; *0*) education; realization
uświęcony sanctified; traditional
uta|jniony secret; classified; **~jony** secret; latent, dormant; **~lentowany** talented, gifted
utarczka *f* (*-i*; *G -czek*) *mil.* skirmish; **~ słowna** battle of words, clash
utarg *m* (*-u*; *-i*) (**dzienny** daily) proceeds *pl.*; **~ować** *pf.* take, earn, make
utarty *fig.* commonplace, stock; **~m zwyczajem** traditionally; **~ zwrot** platitude
utęsknienie *n*: **z ~m** longingly; yearningly
utknąć (*-nę*) get stuck
utkwić *pf. v/s.* fix; stick; **~ w pamięci** stick in the memory
utleni|ać (*-am*) 〈**~ć**〉 (*-ę*) oxydize (**się** *v/i.*); *włosy* bleach; **~ony** oxydized; **woda ~ona** hydrogen peroxide
utonąć *pf.* drown; *por.* **tonąć**
utopić *pf.* sink; drown; **~ się** be drowned
utopijny utopian
utożsami|ać (*-am*) 〈**~ć**〉 (*-ę*) identify (**się** *v/i.*; **z** *I* with)
utra|cać (*-am*) → **tracić**; **~pienie** *n* (*-a*;

G -eń) sorrow, grief; **~ta** *f* (*-y*; *G -*) loss
utrącić *pf.* knock off; *fig.* kill
utrudni|ać (*-am*) ⟨**~ć**⟩ (*-ę*) make difficult; impede; **~enie** *n* (*-a*; *G -eń*) impediment, handicap
utrwal|acz *m* (*-a*; *-e*) *phot.* fixer, F hypo; (*do włosów*) setting lotion; **~ać** (*-am*) ⟨**~ić**⟩ (*-lę*) strengthen; *fig.* cement, consolidate; record (***na taśmie filmowej*** on film); preserve (***w pamięci*** in memory); *phot.* fix; ***~ać*** ⟨***~ić***⟩ ***się*** become stronger
utrzeć *pf.* → ***ucierać***
utrzyma|ć *pf.* → ***utrzymywać***; **~nie** *n* (*-a*; *0*) keep, living; (*maszyny*) maintenance; ***nie do ~nia*** not to be supported; ***mieć na ~niu*** (*A*) support; ***całodzienne ~nie*** full board
utrzymywać (*-uję*) *v/t.* support, bear; *rodzinę* support, provide for; *kochankę, spokój* keep; ***~ przy życiu*** keep alive; *v/i.* claim; ***~ się*** (***z*** *G*) support o.s. (by), earn one's living (by)
utwardz|acz *m* (*-a*; *-e*) *chem.* hardener; **~ać** (*-am*) ⟨***~ić***⟩ (*-dzę*) harden; *fig. związki* strengthen, consolidate; *postawę* toughen
utwierdz|ać (*-am*) ⟨***~ić***⟩ (*-ę*) *fig.* confirm; ***~ić się w przekonaniu, że*** become convinced that
utwór *m* (*-woru*; *-wory*) piece, work; composition
utycie *n* (*-a*; *0*) increase in weight
utykać (*-am*) limp, walk with a limp; → ***utknąć***
utylizacja *f* (*-i*; *0*) *tech.* utilization
utyskiwać (*-uję*) complain (***na*** *A* about)
uwag|a *f* (*-i*; *0*) attention; (*pl. -i*) remark, comment; ***~a!*** look out!; ***brać pod ~ę*** take into attention; ***skupić ~ę*** (***na*** *L*) concentrate (on); ***zwrócić ~ę k-u*** (***na*** *A*) draw s.o.'s attention (to); ***zwrócić ~ę*** (***na*** *A*) pay attention (to); ***zwrócić na siebie ~ę*** catch s.o.'s attention; ***nie zwracać ~i*** not pay attention (***na*** *A* to); ***z ~i na*** (*A*) because (of), considering; ***mieć na uwadze*** take into consideration
uwalniać (*-am*) free (***od*** *G* from, of)
uwarunkow(yw)ać (*-[w]uję*) condition
uważ|ać (*-am*) *v/i.* look out; take care (***na siebie*** of o.s.); (***z*** *I*) be careful (with); (***za*** *A*) consider (to be), regard (as); ***~am, że …*** I think that …; ***jak pan ~a*** as you wish; **~nie** *adv.* carefully, cautiously; **~ny** careful, cautious
uwertura *f* (*-y*; *G -*) *mus.* overture (*też fig.*)
uwiąz(yw)ać *pf.* → ***przywiązywać***
uwidaczniać (*-am*) ⟨***uwidocznić***⟩ (*-ę*, *-nij!*) show; ***~ się*** manifest, be manifested
uwielbi|ać (*-am*) adore, worship; **~enie** *n* (*-a*; *0*) adoration, worship
uwielokrotni|ać (*-am*) ⟨**~ć**⟩ (*-ę*, *-nij!*) multiply
uwieńczać *pf.* → ***wieńczyć***
uwierać (*-am*) press, pinch
uwierz|enie *n*: ***nie do ~enia*** unbelievable, beyond belief; **~yć** *pf.* believe; *por.* ***wierzyć***
uwierzytelni|ać (*-am*) ⟨**~ć**⟩ (*-ę*, *-nij!*) authenticate; **~enie** *n* (*-a*) authentication
uwie|sić *pf.* (*-szę*) hang; **~ść** *pf.* → ***uwodzić***; **~źć** *pf.* → ***uwozić***
uwięz|ić *pf.* (*-żę*) imprison; **~nąć** *pf.* (*-nę*) get stuck
uwię|ź *f* (*-zi*; *-zie*, *-zi*): ***na ~zi*** *balon* tethered; *fig.* tied down
uwijać się (*-am*) bustle (***koło*** *G* about)
uwikłać *pf. v/t.* involve; *v/i.* ***~ się*** be involved, be entangled
uwłaczający derogatory
uwłosienie *n* (*-a*; *0*) hair, hair cover
uwodziciel *m* (*-a*; *-e*), **~ka** *f* (*-i*; *G -lek*) seducer; **~sko** *adv.* seductively; **~ski** seductive
uwo|dzić (*-dzę*) seduce; **~lnić** *pf.* (*-ę*, *-nij!*) → ***uwalniać***; **~lnienie** *n* (*-a*; *G -eń*) freeing, liberation; **~zić** carry away
uwspółcześniony modernized, updated
uwsteczniony *fig.* retarded, degenerated
uwydatni|ać (*-am*) ⟨**~ć**⟩ (*-ę*, *-nij!*) emphasize, enhance; ***~(a)ć się*** be prominent, stand out
uwypukl|ać (*-am*) ⟨***~ić***⟩ (*-lę*, *-lij!*) *fig.* emphasize; → ***uwydatniać***
uwzględni|ać (*-am*) ⟨**~ć**⟩ (*-ę*, *-nij!*) *v/t.* take into consideration *lub* account; ***nie ~ć*** (*G*) ignore; **~enie** *n* (*-a*; *0*) taking into account *lub* consideration
uwziąć się → ***zawziąć się***
uzależni|ać (*-am*) ⟨**~ć**⟩ (*-ę*, *-nij!*) (***od*** *G*) make dependent (on); ***~ć się*** become dependent (on); (*od narkotyków*)

become addicted (to); **~enie** *n* (*-a*; *G -eń*) addiction; **~ony** (*od papierosów itp.*) addicted; **być ~onym** be addicted (**od** *G* to)
uzasadni|ać (*-am*) ⟨**~ć**⟩ (*-ę, -nij!*) justify, give reasons for; **~enie** *n* (*-a*; *G -eń*) justification; **~ony** justified
uzbierać *pf.* (*-am*) gather (**się** *v/i.*; *też* together)
uzbr|ajać (*-am*) ⟨**~oić**⟩ arm (*fig.* **się** o.s.; **w** *A* with); *tech.* (**w** *A*) equip (with), fit (with); *bud.* develop; → **zbroić**; **~ojenie** *n* (*-a*; *G -eń*) armament; *tech.* armo(u)r; *bud.* **~ojenie terenu** territorial development
uzda *f* (*-y*; *G -*) bridle
u|zdatniać (*-am*) ⟨**~zdatnić**⟩ (*-ę, -nij!*) *tech.* treat, condition; **~zdolnienie** *n* (*-a*; *-eń*) talent, gift; **~zdolniony** talented, gifted
uzdrawia|ć (*-am*) heal, cure; *fig.* improve, repair; **~jąco** *adv.* in a healing way; **~jący** healing
uzdrowi|ciel *m* (*-a*; *-e*), **~cielka** *f* (*-i*; *G -lek*) healer; **~ć** (*-ę*; *-ów!*) *pf.* → **uzdrawiać**; **~enie** *n* (*-a*; *G -eń*) healing; **~sko** *n* (*-a*; *G -*) spa, health resort
uzewnętrzni|ać się (*-am*) ⟨**~ć się**⟩ (*-ę, -nij!*) manifest o.s., be expressed
uzębienie *n* (*-a*; *0*) (set of) teeth *pl.*
uzgadniać (*-am*) ⟨**uzgodnić**⟩ (*-ę, -nij!*) agree on
uziemienie *n* (*-a*; *G -eń*) *electr. Brt.* earth, *Am.* ground
uzmysł|awiać (*-am*) ⟨**~owić**⟩ (*-ę, -łów!*) make *s.o.* realize; **~owić sobie** realize
uzna|ć *pf.* → **uznawać**; **~nie** *n* (*-a*; *G -ań*) acknowledg(e)ment; (*szacunek*) respect; **zależeć od ~nia** be at *s.o.'s* discretion; **według … ~nia** at *s.o.'s* discretion; **spotkać się z ~niem** be appreciated; **~wać** (*-ję*) recognize; *błąd, winę* admit, *dług* acknowledge; (**za** *A*) accept (as), regard (as), consider (**się** o.s. to be); **~ć za zmarłego** pronounce dead; **~ć kogoś winnym** admit one's guilt
uzupeł|niać (*-am*) ⟨**~nić**⟩ (*-ę, -nij!*) complete; supplement; **~niać się** be complementary; **~niający** supplementary; *pol.* **wybory** *pl.* **~niające** by(e)-election
uzwojenie *n* (*-a*; *-eń*) *electr.* winding
uzysk|anie *n* (*-a*; *0*) attainment; **~(iw)ać** (*-uję*) obtain, get; attain
użal|ać się (*-am*) ⟨**~ić się**⟩ (**na** *A*) complain (about); (**nad** *I*) feel sorry (for), pity
użądlić *pf.* (*-ę*) sting
uży|cie *n* (*-a*; *G -yć*) use; **sposób ~cia** instructions *pl.* for use; **gotowy do ~cia** ready for use; **~ć** *pf.* → **używać**
użyteczn|ość *f* (*-ści*; *0*) usefulness; **przedsiębiorstwo ~ości publicznej** public utility; **~y** useful
użyt|ek *m* (*-tku*; *-tki*) use, application; **do ~ku domowego** for home use; **~ki** *pl.* **rolne** *agr.* arable land
użytkowa|ć (*-uję*) use; ⟨**z-**⟩ use up; **~nie** *n* (*-a*; *G -ań*) use
użytkow|niczka *f* (*-i*; *G -czek*), **~nik** *m* (*-a*; *-cy*) user; (*języka*) speaker; **~y** utilitarian; *lokal* for commercial purposes; **powierzchnia ~a** usable (floor) area
używ|ać (*-am*) use, make use of, employ; *swobody* enjoy; *med.* take; **~any** used; **~ka** *f* (*-i*; *G -wek*) stimulant
użyźni|ać (*-am*) ⟨**~ć**⟩ (*-ę, -nij!*) fertilize

W

w *prp.* (*L*) *pozycja, stan, czas*: in; **~ lesie** in the forest; (*A*) *ruch, kierunek*: in(to); **~ pole** to the field; **~e wszystkie strony** in all directions; **~ czasie rozmowy** during the talk; **~ dzień** (*G*) on the day (of); **~ odwiedziny** for a visit **dzień ~ dzień** day after day; **~ paski** striped; *tłumaczony też bez przyimka*: **~ poprzek** crosswise; → *odnośne rzeczowniki i czasowniki*
w. *skrót pisany*: **wyspa** isl. (*island*); **wiek** c. (*century*); **wieś** v., vil. (*village*)
wabi|ć (*-ę*) ⟨**z-**⟩ lure; *fig.* attract; **~ć się** *pies*: be called; **~k** *m* (*-a*; *-i*) *hunt.* decoy; *fig.* enticement
wach|larz *m* (*-a*; *-e*) fan; *fig.* range, spectrum; **~lować** (*-uję*) fan
wach|ta *f* (*-y*; *G -*) watch; **~towy** watch

wada *f* (*-y*; *G -*) shortcoming, disadvantage, fault, defect
wadium *n* (*-idkl.*; *-ia*, *-iów*) *econ.* deposit
wadliw|ie *adv.* defectively; **~y** defective, faulty
wafel *m* (*-fla*; *-fle*) wafer; (*do lodów*) cone
wag|a *f* (*-i*; *G -*) weight (*też sport*); (*przyrząd*) scales *pl.*; (*aptekarska itp.*) balance; (*ważność*) importance; ***na ~ę*** by weight; ***zrzucić ~ę*** lose weight; ***najwyższej ~i*** of the utmost importance; **≈a** *znak Zodiaku:* Libra; ***on*(*a*) *jest spod znaku* ≈*i*** he/she is (a) Libra
wagarować (*-uję*) play *Brt.* truant (*Am.* hookey)
wagon *m* (*-u*; *-y*) *rail. Brt.* carriage, *Am.* car; ***~ sypialny*** sleeping car; ***~ restauracyjny*** dining car
waha|ć się (*-am*) swing; *temperatura, ceny*: fluctuate, vary; ⟨**za-**⟩ hesitate; **~dło** *n* (*-a*; *G -deł*) pendulum; **~dłowiec** *m* (*-wca*; *-wce*) space shuttle; **~dłowo** *adv.* as a shuttle; **~dłowy** *zegar* pendulum; *drzwi* swing; *autobus itp.* shuttle; **~nie** *n* (*-a*; *G -ań*) *fig.* hesitation, indecision; ***bez ~nia*** without hesitation
wakac|je *pl.* (*-i*) *Brt.* holidays *pl.*, *Am.* vacation; **~yjny** *Brt.* holiday, *Am.* vacation
wakować (*-uję*) be vacant
walać ⟨**po-, u-, za-**⟩ (*-am*) → ***brudzić***; ***~ się*** F *impf.* be scattered about
walc *m* (*-a*; *-e*) *mus.* waltz
walcow|ać (*-uję*) roll; (*tańczyć*) waltz; **~nia** *f* (*-i*; *-e*, *-i*) rolling mill; **~y** cylindrical
walczyć (*-ę*) struggle (***o*** *A* for), fight (***z*** *I* (with); ***o*** *A* for)
walec *m* (*-lca*; *-lce*, *-lców*) roller; *math.* cylinder
waleczn|ość *f* (*-ści*; *0*) courage, bravery; **~y** brave, courageous; valiant
walentynka *f* (*-i*; *G -nek*) Valentine
walerianow|y: ***krople*** *pl.* ***~e*** valerian drops *pl.*
walet *m* (*-a*; *-y*) *gra w karty*: knave, jack
Wali|a *f* (*GDL -ii*; *0*) Wales; **~jczyk** *m* (*-a*; *-cy*), **~jka** *f* (*-i*; *G -jek*) Welsh; ***Walijczycy*** *pl.* the Welsh *pl.*; **≈jski** Welsh; ***mówić po ≈jsku*** speak Welsh
walić (*-lę*) *v/i.* (*uderzać*) bang, pound; *lit. dym, ludzie*: stream; *v/t.* ⟨**z-**⟩ *mur* pull down; ***~*** ⟨**po-, z-**⟩ ***z nóg knock*** over *lub* down; ***~*** ⟨**za-**⟩ ***się*** come down, collapse (*też fig.*); (*bić się*) fight; ***~ się z nóg*** be dead tired
waliz|a *f* (*-y*; *G -*), **~ka** *f* (*-i*; *G -zek*) suitcase; **~kowy** suitcase
walka *f* (*-i*; *G -*) fight (*też sport, mil.*); *fig.* struggle
walnąć *v/s.* (*-nę*) strike, hit
walny general, plenary
walor *m* (*-u*; *-y*) value; ***~y*** *pl. też* assets *pl.*, holdings *pl.*
walut|a *f* (*-y*; *G -*) currency; (*dewizy*) foreign currency; **~owy** currency, foreign currency
wał *m* (*-u*; *-y*) (*rzeczny*) embankment, bank; *tech.* shaft; **~ek** *m* roll; (*-łka*; *-łki*) (*do włosów itp.*) roller; (*maszyny do pisania, drukarki*) platen; ***~ek do ciasta*** rolling-pin; ***zwinąć w ~ek*** roll up
wałęsać się (*-am*) hang around, loiter
wałkoń *m* (*-nia*; *-nie*, *-ni*[*ów*]) lazy-bones *sg.*
wam (*D* → ***wy***) you; ***z ~i*** with you
wampir *m* (*-a*; *-y*) vampire
wanienka *f* (*-i*; *G -nek*) *chem.*, *phot.* dish, tray
waniliowy vanilla
wanna *f* (*-y*; *G wanien*) (bath)tub, *Brt.* bath
wap|ienny lime; limy; *chem.* calcareous; **~ień** *m* (*-enia*; *-enie*) limestone; **~no** *n* (*-a*; *0*) lime; **~ń** (*-nia*; *0*) *chem.* calcium
warcaby *pl.* (*-ów*) *Brt.* draughts *pl.*, *Am.* checkers *pl.* ***grać w ~*** play draughts *lub* checkers
warchoł *m* (*-a*; *-y*) troublemaker
warczeć ⟨**za-**⟩ (*-ę*, *-y*) growl, gnarl; ***~ na siebie*** growl at each other; → ***warkotać***
warga *f* (*-i*; *G -*) (***górna, dolna*** upper, lower) lip; ***zajęcza ~*** *med.* harelip
wariack|i crazy; ***po ~u*** like crazy
wariant *m* (*-u*; *-y*) variant
wariat *m* (*-a*; *-ci*) madman, loony, lunatic; **~ka** *f* (*-i*; *G -tek*) madwoman, loony, lunatic
wariować ⟨**z-**⟩ (*-uję*) go mad *lub* mad; *fig. ktoś*: act crazy; *coś*: play up
warknąć *v/s.* (*-nę*) → ***warczeć***
warkocz *m* (*-a*; *-e*) plait, braid
warkot *m* (*-u*; *-y*) whirr; **~ać** (*-am*) whirr

warown|ia *f* (*-i-*; *-e*) stronghold; **~y** fortified
warstwa *f* (*-y*; *G* -) layer, stratum; (*społeczna*) class
Warszaw|a *f* (*-y*; *0*) Warsaw; **≗ski** Warsaw; **~wiak** *m* (*-a*; *-cy*) → **~wianin** *m* (*-a*; *-anie*), **~wianka** *f* (*-i*; *G -nek*) Varsovian
warsztat *m* (*-u*; *-y*) workshop; shop; **~owy** workshop
wart (**-ta** *f*, **-te** *n*, *pl. m-os* ***warci***) worth; ***to nic nie ~e*** it is worth nothing *lub* worthless; ***śmiechu ~e*** ridiculous, laughable
war|ta *f* (*-y*; *G* -) guard (duty); ***stać na ~cie*** keep guard; ***zmiana ~y*** changing of the guard
warto (*nieos.*): ***~ by było*** it would be worth it
wartościow|o *adv.* valuably; **~y** valuable
wartoś|ć *f* (*-ści*) value; ***podanie ~ci*** declaration of value; ***bez ~ci*** worthless; ***~ć dodatkowa*** *econ.* value added
wartowni|a *f* (*-i*; *-e*) guardroom, guardhouse; **~k** *m* (*-a*; *-cy*) guard, sentry
warun|ek *m* (*-nku*; *-nki*) condition; ***~ki*** (*umowy*) *pl. też* terms *pl.*; ***pod żadnym ~kiem*** on no account; **~kowo** *adv.* conditionally; **~kowy** conditional
warzyw|niczy, **~ny** vegetable; **~o** *n* (*-a*; *G* -) vegetable
was (*AL* → ***wy***) you
wasz **1.** (*m-os* ***wasi***) your(s); **2.** ***wasi*** *pl. też* your people
Waszyngton *m* (*-u*; *0*) Washington
waśń *f* (*-śni*; *-śnie*, *-śni*) feud
wat|a *f* (*-y*; *G* -) *Brt.* cotton wool, *Am.* absorbent cotton; **~owany** padded
Watyka|n *m* (*-u*; *0*) Vatican (City); **≗ński** Vatican
wawrzyn *m* (*-u*; *-y*) laurel
waza *f* (*-y*; *G* -) tureen
wazeli|na *f* (*-y*; *G* -) vaseline *TM*, petrolatum; **~niarstwo** *n* (*-a*; *0*) soft-soap
wazon *m* (*-u*; *-y*) vase
ważka *f* (*-i*; *G -żek*) *zo.* dragonfly
waż|ki important, significant; **~niactwo** *n* (*-a*; *0*) self-importance; pomposity; **~niejszy** *adj.* (*comp. od* → ***ważny***) more important; **~ność** *f* (*-ści*; *0*) importance, significance; ***stracić ~ność*** expire; ***data ~ności*** expiry date; **~ny** important, significant; ***~ny do …*** valid until …; **~yć** (*-ę*) *v/t.* ⟨**z-**⟩ weigh (*też fig.*); *v/i.* weigh; *v/i.* ***~yć się*** weigh o.s.; (***na*** *A*) dare, risk
wąchać ⟨**po-**⟩ (*-am*) smell; *pies*: scent
wąg|ier *m* (*-gra*; *-gry*) blackhead; *biol.*, *med.* cysticercus
wąs *m* (*-a*; *-y*): *zw.* ***~y*** *pl.* m(o)ustache, m(o)ustaches *pl.*; **~aty** moustached, mustached
wąsk|o *adv.* narrowly; tightly; **~i** narrow; tight
wąskotorow|y: ***kolejka ~a*** narrow-gauge railway
wątek *m* (*-tku*; *-tki*) *włók.* weft, woof; *bud.* bond; *fig.* thread; (*sztuki*) plot
wątł|o *adv.* delicately; frailly; **~y** delicate; frail
wątp|ić ⟨**z-**⟩ (*-ę*) doubt (***w*** *A*, ***o*** *L* in); **~ienie** *n*: ***bez ~ienia*** no doubt; doubtless; **~liwie** *adv.* doubtfully, dubiously; **~liwość** *f* (*-ści*) doubt; ***nie ulega ~liwości, że*** there is no doubt that; **~liwy** doubtful, dubious
wątrob|a *f* (*-y*; *G -rób*) *anat.*, *gastr.* liver; **~ianka** *f* (*-i*; *G -nek*) liver sausage; **~owy** liver
wąwóz *m* (*-wozu*; *-wozy*) ravine, gorge
wąż *m* (*węża*; *węże*) *zo.* snake; (***gumowy*** rubber) hose
wbić *pf.* → ***wbijać***
wbie|gać ⟨***~c, ~gnąć***⟩ run in; run (***do pokoju*** into the room; ***na piętro*** upstairs)
wbijać (*-am*) *gwóźdź itp.* hammer in; *pal* ram into; *igłę*, *nóż* plunge in; *gola* shoot; *klin* drive into
wbrew *prp.* (*D*) against, contrary to
w bród → ***bród***
wbudow(yw)ać (-[*w*]*uję*) build in, fit; *tech.* install
wcale *adv.*: ***~ nie*** not at all, not a bit
wchł|aniać (*-am*) ⟨***~onąć***⟩ (*-nę*) absorb; *zapach* breathe in
wchodzić (***do*** *G*, ***w*** *A*) come (in), get (in), enter; get on (***do wagonu*** the carriage); (***na*** *A*) *trawnik itp.* walk (on), step (on); *drzewo itp.* climb, go (up); (***do*** *G*) (*być w składzie*) be included (in); ***~ na górę*** go up (***w domu*** the stairs); ***~ w położenie*** (*G*) put o.s. in *s.o.'s* position; ***~ na ekrany*** *film*: go on release; → ***wejść***
wcią|ć *pf.* → ***wcinać***; **~gać** (*-am*) ⟨***~gnąć***⟩ (***do*** *G*) draw (in, into), pull

(in, into); (**na** *A*) pull (up); **~gnąć się** (**do** *G*) *fig.* get used (to), get accustomed (to)
wciąż *adv.* ever, always
wciel|ać (*-am*)⟨**~ić**⟩ (*-lę*) (**do** *G*) incorporate (into), integrate (into); **~ać w życie** bring into effect, put into practice; **~ić w czyn** put into action *lub* effect; **~enie** *n* (*-a*; *G -eń*) integration; incorporation; **~ony** incarnate, embodied
wcierać (*-am*) rub in
wcięcie *n* (*-a*; *G -ęć*) notch, indentation; (*linii*) indentation, indention
wcinać (*-am*) make a cut; F (*jeść*) tuck in; **~ się** cut into
wcis|kać ⟨**~nąć**⟩ press into; **~nąć się** (**do** *G*) push one's way (into)
wczasowicz *m* (*-a*; *-e*), **~ka** *f* (*-i*; *G -czek*) holiday-maker
wczas|owy holiday; **~y** *pl. Brt.* holiday, *Am.* vacation; **~y lecznicze** rest cure
wczepi(a)ć się (*-am*) (**do** *G*) cling (to)
wcze|sno- *w złoż.* early; **~sny** early; **~śnie** *adv.* early; **~śniejszy** *adj.* (*comp. od* → **wczesny**) earlier
wczoraj yesterday; **~szy** yesterday
wczu(wa)ć się identify with
wda(wa)ć: **~ się w coś** get involved in; F **~ się w kogoś** take after
wdech *m* (*-u*; *-y*) inspiration; **~owy** → **kapitalny**
wdow|a *f* (*-y*; *G wdów*) widow; **~i** widow's; **~iec** *m* (*-wca*; *-wcy*) widower; **słomiany ~iec** grass widower
wdrażać (*-am*) ⟨**wdrożyć**⟩ (*-ę*) implement, introduce; **~ kogoś do** (*G*) bring s.o. up to; **~ się do pracy** be training for the job
wdychać (*-am*) breathe in
wdzia|ć *pf.* → **wdziewać**; **~nko** *n* (*-a*; *G -nek*) jacket
wdzierać się (*-am*) (**do** *G*) *ktoś*: burst (into); *coś*: penetrate; climb (**na szczyt** the peak)
wdziewać (*-am*) put on
wdzięczn|ość *f* (*-ści*; *0*) gratitude, thankfulness; **dług ~ości** indebtedness; **~y** (**za** *A*) grateful (for), thankful (for); (*zgrabny*) graceful
wdzięk *m* (*-u*; *-i*) grace; gracefulness; *t-ko pl.* **~i kobiece** female charms *pl.*
we *prp.* → **w**
według *prp.* (*G*) according to
wedrzeć się *pf.* → **wdzierać się**
wegetaria|nin *m* (*-a*; *-e*), **~nka** *f* (*-i*; *G -nek*) vegetarian; **~ński** vegetarian
wegetować (*-uję*) vegetate
wejrze|ć *pf.* → **wglądać**; **~nie** *n* (*-a*; *G -eń*): **od pierwszego ~nia** at first glance *lub* sight
wejś|cie *n* (*-a*; *G -ejść*) entrance; entry; **~ciowy** entrance; **~ć** *pf.* → **wchodzić**
wek *m* (*-u*; *-i*) food preserve; **~ować** ⟨**za-**⟩ (*-uję*) preserve
weksel *m* (*-sla*; *-sle*) bill of exchange
welon *m* (*-u*; *-y*) veil
welurowy suede
wełn|a *f* (*-y*; *G -łen*) wool; **~iany** wool(en)
Wene|cja *f* (*-i*; *0*) Venice; **♀cki** Venetian
weneryczn|y: *med.* **choroba ~a** venereal disease
wentyl *m* (*-a*; *-e*) *tech.* valve; *fig.* outlet
wentyla|cyjny ventilation; **~tor** *m* (*-a*; *-y*) fan; (*w murze*) ventilator
wepchnąć (się) *pf.* → **wpychać**
werbel *m* (*-bla*; *-ble*) *mus.* drum; (*dźwięk*) drum-roll
werb|ować ⟨**z-**⟩ (*-uję*) recruit (*też mil.*); **~unek** *m* (*-nku*; *-nki*) recruitment
wersalka *f* (*-i*; *G -lek*) bed-settee
wersja *f* (*-i*; *-e*) version
wertować (*-uję*) leaf through, look through
werwa *f* (*-y*; *0*) enthusiasm, verve
weryfikować ⟨**z-**⟩ (*-uję*) verify
werżnąć się *pf.* → **wrzynać się**
wesel|e *n* (*-a*; *G -*) wedding; (*przyjęcie*) wedding party; **~ny** wedding; **~ej** *com. adv.*, **~szy** *com. adj.* → **wesoło, wesoły**
wesoł|o *adv.* (*pred.* **wesół**) cheerfully; merrily; **~ość** *f* (*-ści*; *0*) cheerfulness; mirth, merriment; **~y** cheerful; merry
wes|przeć *pf.* → **wspierać**; **~sać** *pf.* → **wsysać**; **~tchnąć** *pf.* → **wzdychać**; **~tchnienie** *n* (*-a*; *G -eń*) sigh
wesz *f* (*wszy*; *N, G wszy*) *zo.* louse
wetery|'naria *f* (*GDL -ii*; *0*) veterinary medicine; **~narz** *m* (*-a*; *-e*) *Brt.* vet(erinary surgeon), *Am.* veterinarian
wetknąć *pf.* → **wtykać**
wetować ⟨**za-**⟩ (*-uję*) veto
we|trzeć *pf.* → **wcierać**; **~wnątrz** *adv.* inside; **do ~wnątrz** inward; **od ~wnątrz** from the inside; **~wnątrz-** *w złoż.* inside; **~wnętrzny** inner; *kieszeń* inside; *med., psych., struktura itp.* internal; inward; *rynek itp.* home, domestic; **nu-**

W

mer ~wnętrzny *tel.* extension; **~zbrać** *pf.* → **wzbierać**; **~zgłowie** *n* (*-a*; *G -wi*) head end; (*podgłówek*) headrest
wezwa|ć *pf.* → **wzywać**; **~nie** *n* (*-a*; *G -ań*) summons *sg.*; (*monit*) demand; (*apel*) call, appeal; **kościół pod ~niem św. Piotra** St. Peter's Church
węch *m* (*-u*; *0*) smell; *fig.* nose
wędka *f* (*-i*; *G -dek*) angling rod; **~rski** fishing; **~rstwo** *n* (*-a*; *0*) fishing, angling; **~rz** *m* (*-a*; *-e*) angler
wędlin|a *f* (*-y*; *G -*): *zw. pl.* **~y** cured meat products *pl.*; **~iarnia** *f* (*-i*; *-e*) retailer of sausages
wędrow|ać (*-uję*) wander (**po** *L* around); **~iec** *m* (*-wca*; *-wcy*) wanderer; **~ny** wandering; *biol.* migrating, migratory; **ptak ~ny** migratory bird, bird of passage
wędrówka *f* (*-i*; *G -wek*) wandering; travel; *biol.* migration
wędz|ić ⟨**u-**⟩ (*-ę*) smoke, cure; **~onka** *f* (*-i*; *G -nek*) *gastr.* smoked bacon; **~ony** smoked, cured
węgiel *m* (*-gla*; *-gle*) *chem.* coal; **~ brunatny** lignite, brown coal; **~ kamienny** anthracite, hard coal; **~ drzewny** charcoal; **~ny** → **kamień**
węgieł *m* (*-gła*; *-gły*) corner
Węg|ier *m* (*-gra*; *-grzy*), **~ierka** *f* (*-i*; *G -rek*) Hungarian; **♀ierka** *bot.* garden plum; **♀ierski** Hungarian; **mówić po ♀iersku** speak Hungarian
węg|lan *m* (*-u*; *-y*) *chem.* carbonate; **~lowodór** *m chem.* hydrocarbon; **~lowy** coal; carbon
węgorz *m* (*-a*; *-e*) *zo.* eel
Węgry *pl.* (*G -gier*) Hungary
węszyć (*-ę*) sniff; *fig.* sniff about
węz|eł *m* (*-zła*; *-zły*) knot; (*transportowy*) hub; *med., anat.* node; **~łowato** *adv.*: **krótko i ~łowato** in brief, in a nutshell; **~łowaty** knobbly; **~łowy** hub; *fig.* central, crucial
węże *pl.* → **wąż**
wężow|nica *f* (*-y*; *G -*) *tech.* coil; **~y** serpentine
węższy *adj. comp. od* → **wąski**
wf. *skrót pisany*: **wychowanie fizyczne** PE (*physical education*)
wg *skrót pisany*: **według** according to
wgięcie *n* (*-a*; *G -ęć*) dent
wgląd *m* (*-u*; *0*) view; insight; **do ~u** for inspection
wgłębienie *n* (*-a*; *G -eń*) indentation
wgniatać (*-am*) ⟨**wgnieść**⟩ dent, depress
wgry|zać się (*-am*) ⟨**~źć się**⟩ bite into; *fig.* get stuck into; (*wżerać się*) eat into
wiać (*-eję*) *v/i.* ⟨**po-**⟩ blow; F ⟨**z-**⟩ take o.s. off; **wieje tu** there is a draught here
wiadomo *nieos.* it is known; **nigdy nie ~** you never know; **jak ~** as is known; **o ile mi ~** as far as I know; **~ść** *f* (*-ści*) information; **do twojej ~ści** for your knowledge
wiadomy known
wiadro *n* (*-a*; *G -der*) bucket, pail
wiadukt *m* (*-u*; *-y*) *mot. Brt.* flyover, *Am.* overpass
wianek *m* (*-nka*; *-nki*) wreath, garland; *fig.* hymen
wiar|a *f* (*-y*; *G -*) belief (**w** *A* in); faith (*też rel.*); (**w siebie** self-)confidence; **nie do ~y** unbelievable; **w dobrej wierze** in good faith
wiarołomny unfaithful
wiarygodny reliable, dependable, credible
wiat|r *m* (*-u*, *L wietrze*; *-y*) wind; **pod ~r** against the wind; **na ~r** to the wind; **~rak** *m* (*-a*; *-i*) windmill; **~rówka** *f* (*-i*; *G -wek*) (*ubranie*) *Brt.* wind-cheater, *Am.* wind-breaker; (*broń*) airgun
wiąz *m* (*-u*; *-y*) *bot.* elm
wiąz|ać (*-żę*) bind (*też fig., chem.*); *jeńca itp.* tie (up); *fig.* relate (**z** *I* to); **~ać się** (**z** *I*) be associated (with); **~anie** *n* (*-a*; *G -ań*) *sport*: binding; *chem.* bond; **~anka** *f* (*-i*; *G -nek*) bunch, bouquet; *mus.* potpourri, medley; **~ka** *f* (*-i*; *G -zek*) bundle; (*światła itp.*) beam
wiążąc|o *adv.* definitely; **~y** binding; definite
wice|- *w złoż.* vice-, deputy; **~dyrektor** deputy director *lub* manager; **~mistrz** *sport*: runner-up
wicher *m* (*-chru*; *-chry*) gale
wichrzy|ciel *m* (*-a*; *-e*), **~cielka** *f* (*-i*; *G -lek*) trouble-maker; **~ć** (*-ę*) *v/t.* ⟨**z-**⟩ *włosy* ruffle, tousle; *v/i.* make trouble; stir up
wić¹ *f* (*-ci*; *NG -ci*) *biol.* tendril; *zo.* flagellum
wić² (*-ję*) ⟨**u-**⟩ *wianek* wreathe; *gniazdo* build; *t-ko impf.* **~ się** wind, meander
widać (*t-ko bezok.*) can be seen; **jak ~** as can be seen; **to ~ po nim** he shows it
wide|lec *m* (*-lca*; *-lce*) fork; **~łki** *pl.* (*-łek*) *tech.* fork

wideo video; ***film ~*** video (film); ***wypożyczalnia ~*** video hire (shop); **~kaseta** *f* (*-y*; *G -*) video (cassette)
widły *pl.* (*-deł*) pitchfork, fork
widmo *n* (*-a*; *G -*) *Brt.* spectre, *Am.* specter; *phys.* spectrum; **~wy** spectral
wid|nieć (*-eję*) appear, be visible; **~no** *adv.*: ***robi się ~no*** it is getting light; **~nokrąg** *m* horizon; ***na ~nokręgu*** on the horizon; **~ny** *pokój* light
widoczn|ie *adv.* apparently, clearly; visibly; **~ość** *f* (*-ści*; *0*) visibility; **~y** visible
wido|k *m* (*-u*; *-i*) (***na*** *G*) view (of) (*też fig.*); (*wygląd*) appearance; (*co widać*) scene; *fig.* prospect, chance; ***na ~k*** (*G*) by the appearance (of), outwardly; ***pokój z ~kiem na morze*** a room overlooking the sea; ***na ~ku*** at sight; ***mieć na ~ku*** have in prospect; **~kówka** *f* (*-i*; *G -wek*) picture postcard; **~wisko** *n* (*-a*; *G -*) show, spectacle; *fig.* exhibition; **~wnia** *f* (*-i*; *-e*) (*ludzie*) audience, spectators *pl.*; (*pomieszczenie*) auditorium; house
widywać (*-uję*) see
widz *m* (*-a*; *-owie*) spectator, viewer; (***kinowy*** *Brt.* cinema-, *Am.* movie-)goer
widzeni|e *n* (*-a*; *G -eń*) sight, seeing; (*więźnia*) visit; ***z ~a*** by sight; ***do ~a*** goodbye; ***zezwolenie na ~e*** visiting permit; → ***punkt***
widzia|dło *n* (*-a*; *G -deł*) → ***widmo***; **~lność** *f* (*-ści*; *0*) visibility; **~lny** visible
widzieć (*-dzę*, *-i*) see; (***się*** o.s., each other); ***~ się z kimś*** → ***zobaczyć***
wiec *m* (*-u*; *-e*) rally
wiech|a *f* (*-y*; *G -*) *bud.* wreath (*used in the topping-out ceremony*); ***uroczystość zawieszenia ~y*** topping-out ceremony
wiecowy rally
wieczerza *f* (*-y*; *-e*) *lit.* supper
wieczn|ość *f* (*-ści*; *0*) eternity; **~y** eternal
wieczor|ek *m* (*-rku*; *-rki*): ***~ek taneczny*** dancing party; **~em** in the evening; at night; ***jutro ~em*** tomorrow evening; **~ny** evening, night; **~owy**: ***suknia ~owa*** evening dress
wieczór *m* (*-u*; *-czory*) evening, night; ***dobry ~*** good evening
Wiedeń *m* (*-dnia*; *0*) Vienna; **♀ński** Viennese
wiedz|a *f* (*-y*; *0*) knowledge; (*uczoność*) learning, scholarship; (*wyspecjalizowana*) know-how; ***bez jego ~y*** without his knowledge; **~ieć** know (***o*** *L* about); ***o ile wiem*** as far as I know
wiedźma *f* (*-y*; *G -*) witch
wiejski rural; country; village
wiek *m* (*-u*; *0*) (***starczy*** old) age; ***dziecięcy ~*** childhood; (*pl. -i*) century; *fig.* age; ***~i*** *pl.* ***średnie*** the Middle Ages *pl.*
wieko *n* (*-a*; *G -*) lid; cover
wiekowy centuries-old
wiekuisty eternal
wielbiciel *m* (*-a*; *-e*), **~ka** *f* (*-i*; *G -lek*) admirer; worshipper; enthusiast, buff
wielbić (*-ę*, *-bij!*) → ***uwielbiać***
wielbłą|d *m* (*-a*; *-y*) *zo.* camel; **~dzi** camel
wiel|ce *adv.* much; **~cy** *m-os* → ***wielki***; **~e** a lot of; many, much; ***o ~e*** (by) far; ***o ~e za dużo*** far too much
Wielkanoc *f* (*-y/Wielkiejnocy*, *I -ą/Wielkąnocą*; *-e*) *rel.* Easter; ***na ~*** at Easter
wielkanocny easter
wielki big, large; *fig.* great; ***już ~ czas*** it is high time; ***Kazimierz ♀*** Casimir the Great; ***nic ~ego*** nothing much
wielko|duszny magnanimous; **~lud** *m* (*-a*; *-y*) giant; **~miejski** metropolitan; **~ść** *f* (*-ści*) size; (*problemu itp.*) magnitude; (*znaczenie*) greatness; *math.*, *phys.* quantity; ***~ści grochu*** pea-sized; the size of a pea; ***jednakowej ~ści*** the same in size
wielo|barwny multicolo(u)red; **~bój** *m* (*w sporcie*) multi-discipline event; **~dniowy** lasting several days; **~dzietny** with many children; *rodzina* large
wielokropek *m* (*-pka*; *-pki*) suspension points *pl.*
wielokrotn|ie *adv.* repeatedly; **~y** repeated, multiple
wielo|milionowy million; **~narodowy** multinational; **~piętrowy** multi-stor(e)y; **~raki** multiple; **~rako** *adv.* in many different ways
wieloryb *m* (*-a*; *-y*) *zo.* whale
wielo|stopniowy multistage; **~stronny** multilateral; **~znaczny** ambiguous; **~żeństwo** *n* (*-a*; *G -stw*) polygamy
wielu *m-os* → ***wiele***
wieniec *m* (*-ńca*; *-ńce*) garland; wreath (*też na pogrzeb*)
wień|cowy *med.* coronary; **~czyć** ⟨***u-***⟩ crown

wieprz *m* (*-a*; *-e*) hog; **~owina** *f* (*-y*) pork; **~owy** pork
wiercić (*-cę*) drill; **~ się** fidget
wiern|ość *f* (*-ści*; *0*) fidelity, faithfulness; **~y** **1.** faithful, **2.** **~i** *m/pl.* the faithful
wiersz *m* (*-a*; *-e*) (*utwór*) poem; (*linijka*) line; **~owy** line
wiertarka *f* (*-i*; *G -rek*) drill
wiertło *n* (*-a*; *G -teł*) drill, bit
wierzba *f* (*-y*; *G -*) *bot.*: **~ płacząca** weeping willow
wierzch *m* (*-u*; *-y*) top; upper side; outside; (*buta*) upper; **na ~** on top; **do ~u, po ~u** to the top; **~em** on horseback; **~ni** outer, top; **~ołek** *m* (*-łka*; *-łki*) summit (*też fig.*), peak; *math.* apex, vertex; **~owiec** *m* (*-wca*; *-wce*) saddle-horse; **~owy** saddle
wierzy|ciel *m* (*-a*; *-e*), **~cielka** *f* (*-i*; *G -lek*) *econ.* creditor; **~ć** (*-ę*) (**w** *A*) believe (in); (*ufać*) trust, have faith (in); **~telność** *f* (*-ści*) *econ.* liability, claim
wiesza|ć (*-am*) hang (**na** *A* on; **się** o.s.); **~k** *m* (*-a*; *-i*) hanger
wieś *f* (*wsi*; *wsie*, *wsi*) village; (*region*) country; **na ~** to the country; **na wsi** in the country
wieść[1] *f* (*-ści*) news *sg.*, information; → **przepaść**[2]
wieść[2] lead; → **prowadzić**
wieśnia|czka *f* (*-i*; *G -czek*) countrywoman; peasant; **~k** *m* (*-a*; *-cy*) countryman; peasant
wietrz|eć (*-eję*) ⟨**wy-**⟩ *zapach*: fade, disappear; *geol.* erode; ⟨**z-**⟩ *wino*: become stale; **~nie** *adv.*: **jest ~nie** it is windy; **~ny** windy; **~yć** (*-ę*) air; ⟨**z-**⟩ scent, get wind of
wiewiórka *f* (*-i*; *G -rek*) *zo.* squirrel
wieźć ⟨**po-**⟩ carry, transport; *kogoś* drive
wież|a *f* (*-y*; *-e*) tower; (*w szachach*) castle, rook; *mil.* turret; **~owiec** *m* (*-wca*; *-wce*) high-rise
więc so; **a ~** well; **tak ~** thus
więcej *adv.* (*comp. od* → **dużo, wiele**); **co ~** moreover; → **mniej**
więdnąć ⟨**z-**⟩ (*-nę*, *też zwiądł*) fade, wither
większ|ość *f* (*-ści*; *0*) majority; **~ością głosów** by the majority; **stanowić ~ość** be in the majority; **~y** *adj.* (*comp. od* → **duży, wielki**) larger, bigger
więzić (*-żę*) keep in prison
więzie|nie *n* (*-a*; *G -eń*) prison; **~nny** prison; **~ń** *m* (*-nia*; *-niowie*) prisoner
więź *f* (*-zi*; *-zie*) bond; **~niarka** *f* (*-rki*; *G -rek*) → **więzień**
wi'gilia *f* (*GDl -ii*; *-e*) eve; ♀ Christmas Eve
wigor *m* (*-u*; *0*) vigo(u)r
wiklina *f* (*-y*; *G -*) *bot.* oasier
wikłać ⟨**po-**⟩ (*-am*) *fig.* complicate; **~ się** become complicated; → **plątać**
wikt *m* (*-u*; *0*) fare
wilcz|ur *m* (*-a*; *-y*) *zo.* Alsatian; **~y** wolfish
wilgo|ć *f* (*-ci*; *0*) humidity; damp(ness); moisture; **~tno** *adv.*, **~tny** *ściana*, *ubranie* damp; *klimat* humid; *wargi* moist
wilia *f* (*GDL -ii*; *-e*) → **wigilia**
wilk *m* (*-a*; *-i*) *zo.* wolf; **~ morski** sea dog
will|a *f* (*GDL -ii*) F (semi-)detached house; villa; **~owy** residential
win|a *f* (*-y*; *G -*) fault; blame; *jur.* guilt; **ponosić ~ę** (**za** *A*) be to blame (for); **z ~y** (*G*) because of; **z własnej ~y** because of one's own fault; (**nie**) **przyznawać się do ~y** plead (not) guilty
winda *f* (*-y*; *G -*) *Brt.* lift, *Am.* elevator
winia|k *m* (*-a*; *-i*) brandy; **~rnia** *f* (*-i*; *-e*) wine bar
wini|ć (*-ę*) (**k-o o** *A*) blame (s.o. for); **~en** (*f* **-nna**, *n* **-nno**, *ż-rzecz.* **-nne**, *m-os* **-nni**) *pred.* guilty; **kto temu ~en?** who is to blame for it?; **jestem mu ~en ...** I owe him; → **powinien, powinna**
winni|ca *f* (*-y*; *G -*) vineyard; **~czek** *m* (*-czka*; *-czki*) *zo.* European edible snail
winno → **winien, powinno**
winny[1] wine; (*kwaśny*) tart; **~ krzew** grapevine
winn|y[2] guilty; **uznać za ~ego** consider guilty; → **winien**
wino *n* (*-a*; *G -*) wine; **~branie** *n* (*-a*; *G -ań*) grape picking; **~grono** *n* (*-a*; *G -*) grape; **~rośl** *f* (*-i*; *-e*) vine
winowaj|ca *m* (*-y*; *G -ców*), **~czyni** *f* (*-i*; *-e*) culprit
winszować (*-uję*) (**k-u** *G*) congratulate (s.o. on)
wiod|ą, ~ę → **wieść**[2]; **~ący** leading
wiolonczela *f* (*-i*; *-e*) *mus.* cello
wiosenny spring
wiosło *n* (*-a*, *L -śle*; *G -seł*) oar; paddle; **~wać** (*-uję*) row, paddle
wiosn|a *f* (*-y*; *G -sen*) spring; **~ą, na ~ę** in spring

W

wioślar|ka *f* (*-i*; *G -rek*) rower; oarswoman; **~stwo** *n* (*-a*; *0*) rowing
wioślarz *m* (*-a*; *-e*) rower; oarsman
wiotki limp; frail; (*szczupły*) thin
wioz|ą, ~ę → ***wieźć***
wiór *m* (*-u*; *-y*) shaving; (*metalu*) swarf
wir *m* (*-u*; *-y*) whirl; (*wody*) eddy, whirlpool
wiraż *m* (*-u*; *-e*) sharp bend, curve
wirnik *m* (*-a*; *-i*) *tech.*, *aviat.* rotor
wirować (*-uję*) spin, whirl; (*przed oczyma*) swim; ⟨**od-**⟩ *pranie* spin-dry
wirówka *f* (*-i*; *G -wek*) spin-drier; *tech.* centrifuge
wirus *m* (*-a*; *-y*) *biol.* virus; **~owy** virus; viral
wi|sieć (*-szę*) hang (**na** *L* on; **nad** *I* over); *owad itp.*: hover (**nad** *I* over, above); **~sielec** *m* (*-lca*; *-lcy*, *-lców*) hanged person; **~siorek** *m* (*-rka*; *-rki*, *-rków*) pendant; **~szący** hanging
Wisła *f* (*-y*; *0*) the Vistula
wiśni|a *f* (*-i*; *-e*) *bot.* sour cherry; **~owy** (sour) cherry
witać (*-am*) ⟨**po-**⟩ greet; *fig.* welcome; **~** ⟨**przy-**⟩ **się** (**z** *I*) greet, exchange greetings (with)
witamina *f* (*-y*; *G -*) vitamin
witraż *m* (*-a*; *-e*) stained-glass window
witryna *f* (*-y*; *G -*) shop-window; *komp.* web site; **~ *internetowa*** *komp.* web site
wiwat: **~ ...!** long live ...!; **~ować** (*-uję*) cheer (***na cześć k-o*** s.o.)
wiza *f* (*-y*; *G -*) visa
wizerunek *m* (*-nku*; *-nki*) picture
wiz|ja *f* (*-i*; *-e*) vision (*też RTV*); *jur.* inspection; **~jer** *m* (*-a*; *-y*) peephole; **~owy** visa
wizyt|a *f* (*-y*; *G -*) visit; ***składać ~ę*** → **~ować** (*-uję*) pay a visit; visit; **~ówka** *f* (*-i*; *G -wek*) visiting card
wjazd *m* (*-u*; *-y*) entry; entrance; ***~ na autostradę*** *Brt.* slip road, *Am.* ramp; **~owy** entry
wje|żdżać (*-am*) ⟨**~chać**⟩ (**do** *G*) come (in), *mot.* drive (in); (**do** *G*, **na** *A*) *rail.* pull (in(to)); (*najeżdżać*) (**w** *A*) drive (into)
wkle|jać (*-am*) ⟨**~ić**⟩ paste
wklęsł|o *adv.* concavely; **~y** concave
wkład *m* (*-u*; *-y*) (*pieniężny itp.*) contribution; *fig.* input; *econ.* deposit; *tech.* inset, cartridge; ***~ do długopisu*** refill; **~ać** (*-am*) put (**do** *G* into); insert; *ubranie itp.* put on; *nabój itp.* load; *kapitał, czas* invest; **~ka** *f* (*-i*; *G -dek*) inset; *tech.* cartridge; *med.* intrauterine device (*skrót*: ***IUD***)
wkoło *prp.* (a)round
wkop|ywać (*-uję*) ⟨**~ać**⟩ (**do** *G*; **w** *A*) dig (into); *tyczkę* sink (into); ***~ywać się*** bury o.s.
wkra|czać (*-am*) (**do** *G*) enter, step (in); (*na czyjś teren*) encroach; (*z interwencją*) step (in); *mil.* invade; ***~czać nielegalnie*** trespass; **~dać się** (*-am*) sneak in; *fig.* creep in; **~plać** (*-am*) put drops (in one's eyes); **~ść się** *pf.* → ***wkradać się***
wkrę|cać (*-am*) ⟨**~cić**⟩ screw in
wkręt *m* (*-u*; *-y*) screw
wkro|czyć *pf.* → ***wkraczać***; **~plić** *pf.* (*-lę*) → ***wkraplać***
wkrótce soon
wkurzony F annoyed, peeved
wkuwać (*-am*) cram, *Brt.* swot (up)
wlać *pf.* → ***wlewać***; **~ *się*** F get completely canned; ***wlany*** F canned, pissed
wlatywać ⟨***wlecieć***⟩ (*-uję*) → ***wpadać***
wle|c drag (**się** o.s.); ***~c się*** *czas*: wear on; draw out, drag out; **~cieć** *pf.* → ***wlatywać***; **~piać** (*-am*) ⟨**~pić**⟩ stick in(to); F *fig.* (*klepnąć*) slap, (*wcisnąć*) give; ***~pić oczy*** (**w** *A*) stare at
wlew *m* (*-u*; *-y*) *med.* infusion; **~ać** (*-am*) pour (in); ***~ać się*** flow in (**do** *G* to)
wleźć *pf.* → ***włazić***
wlicz|ać (*-am*) ⟨**~yć**⟩ (**do** *G*) include (in); *kogoś* involve
wlotowy *tech.* inlet
wład|ać (*-am*) (*I*) rule; (*językiem*) speak; (*bronią*) wield; (*nogą itp.*) be able to move; **~ca** *m* (*-y*; *G -ców*) ruler; **~czo** *adv.* imperiously; **~czy** imperious; overbearing; **~czyni** *f* (*-i*; *-e*) ruler
władz|a *f* (*-y*; *0*) power; rule, control; (*pl. -e*) authority; ***dojść do ~y*** come to power; ***stracić ~ę nad*** (*I*) lose control (over); ***stracić ~ę w*** (*I*) lose the use (of)
włam|ać się *pf.* → ***włamywać się***; **~anie** *n* (*-a*; *G -ań*) burglary; **~ywacz** *m* (*-a*; *-e*) burglar; **~ywać się** (*-uję*) break (**do** *G* into); *Brt.* burglarize, *Am.* burgle
własno|ręczny personal; **~ściowy** *mieszkanie Brt.* owner-occupied, *Am.* condominium, co-op; **~ść** *f* (*-ści*; *0*) property; ***mieć na ~ść*** own

własn|y (one's) own; ***z ~ej woli*** of one's own free will; → ***ręka***
właści|ciel *m* (*-a*; *-e*), **~cielka** *f* (*-i*; *G -lek*) owner; proprietor; holder; **~wie** *adv.* actually, in (actual) fact; **~wość** *f* (*-ści*) property, peculiarity; (*odpowiedniość*) appropriateness; **~wy** proper; correct; appropriate
właśnie *part.* just; (*akurat*) exactly, precisely; ***no ~*** quite
właz *m* (*-u*; *-y*) *mil.* hatch; (*do kanału itp.*) manhole; **~ić** (*-żę*) climb, get
włącz|ać (*-am*) ⟨**~yć**⟩ include; *electr.* turn on, switch on; ***~ać*** ⟨***~yć***⟩ ***się*** *electr.* go on; *ktoś*: join; (*do ruchu*) pull out; → ***przyłączać***; **~nie** *adv.* inclusive
Włoch *m* (*-a*; *-si*) Italian
włochaty hairy; shaggy
Włochy *pl.* (*G Włoch*) Italy
włos *m* (*-a*; *-y*) hair; ***~y*** *pl.* hair; ***nie odstąpić ani na ~ od*** (*G*) not to budge an inch from; ***o*** (***mały***) ***~*** by a hair's breadth; ***do ~ów*** hair; **~ek** *m* (*-ska*; *-ski*) → ***włos***; **~ie** *n* (*-a*; *0*) horsehair; **~ień** *m* (*-nia*/*-śnia*; *-nie*/*-śnie*) *zo.*, *med.* trichina
włosk|i Italian; ***mówić po ~u*** speak Italian; → ***kapusta***
włoszczyzna *f* (*-y*; *G -*) mixed vegetables (*for soup*)
Włoszka *f* (*-i*; *G -szek*) Italian
włożyć *pf.* → ***wkładać***
włóczęga[1] *f* (*-i*; *G -*) wandering
włóczęga[2] *m* (*-i*; *-dzy*/*-i*, *-ów*/*-*) tramp, vagrant
włóczka *f* (*-i*; *G -czek*) yarn
włóczyć się (*-ę*) wander, roam
włókiennictwo *n* (*-a*; *G -*) textile industry
włók|nisty stringy; **~no** *n* (*-a*; *G -kien*) *Brt.* fibre, *Am.* fiber
w|mawiać (*-am*) persuade (***komuś*** s.o.); **~mieszać** *pf.* → ***mieszać***; **~montow(yw)ać** (*-[w]uję*) fit in, equip; **~mówić** *pf.* → ***wmawiać***
wmurow(yw)ać (*-[w]uję*) set into the wall, build into
wnet soon
wnęka *f* (*-i*; *G -*) bay, recess, niche
wnętrz|e *n* (*-a*; *G -*) interior, inside; *bud.* interior; ***do***/***od ~a*** within, inward/from within; **~ności** *pl.* (*-ci*) entrails *pl.*; *gastr.* offal
Wniebo|wstąpienie *n rel.* the Ascension; **~wzięcie** *n rel.* the Assumption
wnieść *pf.* → ***wnosić***
wnik|ać (*-am*) ⟨**~nąć**⟩ penetrate; inquire; **~liwie** *adv.* penetratingly; in depth; **~liwy** penetrating; → ***dociekliwy***
wnios|ek *m* (*-sku*; *-ski*) conclusion; (*propozycja*) motion, proposition; ***dojść do ~ku*** come to the conclusion; ***wystąpić z ~kiem, żeby*** move that; **~kodawca** *m* (*-y*; *G -ców*), **~kodawczyni** *f* (*-i*; *-ie*, *G -yń*) mover; **~kować** ⟨**wy-**⟩ (*-uję*) conclude (***z*** *G* from)
wnosić *v/t.* carry in, bring (into), get (into); *wkład* make; *skargę*, *protest* lodge, make; *prośbę* make; *sprawę jur.* bring; *v/i.* conclude; (***z*** *G*) deduce (from), infer (from); *jur.* (***o*** *A*) propose
wnu|czka *m* (*-i*; *G -czek*) granddaughter; **~k** *m* (*-a*; *-i*) grandson
woalka *f* (*-i*; *G -lek*) veil
wobec *prp.* (*G*) in the face (of), in view (of); ***~ czego*** consequently; ***~ tego, że*** in view of the fact that
wod|a *f* (*-y*; *G wód*) water; ***z ~y*** *gastr.* boiled
w oddali in the distance
wod|niak *m* (*-a*; *-cy*) water-sports enthusiast; **♒nik** *m* (*-a*; *0*) *znak Zodiaku:* Aquarius; ***on***(***a***) ***jest spod znaku ♒nika*** he/she is (an) Aquarius; **~nisty** watery; **~nosamolot** *m* seaplane; **~ny** water
wodociąg *m* water-pipe, (*główny*) water-main; ***~i*** *pl.* waterworks *sg.*; **~owy** *woda* tap
wodo|lecznictwo *n med.* hydrotherapy; **~lot** *m naut.* hydrofoil; **~pój** *m* (*-oju*; *-oje*) watering-place; **~rost** *m* (*-u*; *-y*) *bot.* seaweed; **~rowy** hydrogen; **~spad** *m* waterfall, falls *pl.*; **~szczelny** water-tight; **~trysk** *m* (*-u*; *-i*) fountain; F *fig.* frill(s *pl.*); **~wać** (*-uję*) *v/t. naut.* launch; *v/i.* (*w astronautyce*) splashdown
wodór *m* (*-doru*) *chem.* hydrogen
wodz|a *f* (*-y*; *-e*) *zw. pl.* rein; ***trzymać*** (***się***) ***na ~y*** restrain o.s., control o.s.; ***puszczać ~e*** (*D*) *fig.* give rein (to); ***pod ~ą*** (*G*) under s.o.'s command
wodz|ić (*-dzę*, *wódź!*) lead; *fig.* ***~ić za nos*** *fig.* lead by the nose; **~owie** *pl.* → ***wódz***
woj. *skrót pisany*: ***województwo*** province; ***wojewódzki*** provincial
wojaż *m* (*-u*; *-e*) *żart.*, *iron.* journey, voyage, trip

wojenn|y war; military; *jur.* martial; ***być na stopie ~ej*** (***z*** *I*) be on a war footing (with)

woje|woda *m* (*-y*; *G -dów*) (*chief officer in the province*); **~wódzki** provincial; **~wództwo** *n* (*-a*; *G -*) province

wojłok *m* (*-u*; *-i*) felt

wojn|a *f* (*-y*; *G -jen*) (***domowa*** civil) war; ***iść na ~ę*** go to war; ***na ~ie*** at war

wojow|ać (*-uję*) fight (***z*** *I* with; ***o*** *A* for); wage war; **~niczo** *adv.* militantly, belligerently; **~niczy** militant, belligerent; **~nik** *m* (*-a*; *-cy*) warrior

wojsk|o *n* (*-a*; *G -*) army; troops *pl.*; ***zaciągnąć się do ~a, iść do ~a*** join up; ***on po ~u*** he was in the army; **~owy 1.** military; ***służba ~owa*** military service; ***odmowa służby ~owej*** conscientious objection; ***po ~owemu*** in a military way; (*ubrany*) in uniform; **2.** *m* (*-ego*; *-i*) military man, soldier

wokalist|a *m*, **~ka** *f* vocalist

wokalny vocal

wokanda *f* (*-y*; *G -*) *jur.* (court) calendar

wokoło, wokół *prp.* (a)round

wol|a *f* (*-i*; *0*) will; ***do ~i*** at will; ***mimo ~i*** involuntarily; ***dobra ~a*** goodwill; ***z własnej ~i*** of one's own accord

wole *n* (*-a*; *G -i*) *med.* goitre; *zo.* crop

wol|eć (*-ę*, *-i*) prefer; ***wolę ... niż/od ...*** I prefer ... to ...; ***~ał(a)bym*** I would rather; **~ne** *n* (*-ego*; *-e*): ***mieć ~ne*** have a day off; ***~nego!*** just a minute!; **~niutki** very slow; **~niutko** *adv.* very slowly

wolno[1] *prp.* one can, it is allowed; ***czy ~ zapytać*** may I ask; ***nie ~ mi*** I must not; ***nikomu nie ~*** nobody is allowed to

wolno[2] *adv.* slowly; (*swobodnie*) freely; **~cłowy** duty-free; **~mularstwo** *n* (*-a*; *0*) Freemasonry; **~myśliciel** *m* free thinker; **~rynkowy**: ***cena ~rynkowa*** free-market price

wolnoś|ciowy liberation; **~ć** *f* (*-ści*; *0*) freedom, liberty; ***~ć słowa*** freedom of speech; ***na ~ci*** at liberty; free; ***wypuścić na ~ć*** set free

wolny free (***od*** *G* from); (*powolny*) slow; ***~ od opłaty*** free (of charge); ***dzień ~ od pracy*** day off, holiday; ***na ~m powietrzu*** in the open; ***na ~m ogniu*** at a simmer; ***wstęp ~*** admission free

woltomierz *m* (*-a*; *-e*) *electr.* voltmeter

woła|cz *m* (*-a*; *-e*) *gr.* the Vocative; **~ć** ⟨**za-**⟩ (*-am*) call; **~nie** *n* (*-a*; *G -ań*) call (***o pomoc*** for help)

Wołga *f* (*-i*; *0*) the Volga

woło|wina *f* (*-y*; *G -*) beef; **~wy** *gastr.* beef

woły *pl.* → ***wół***

wonny fragrant, aromatic

woń *f* (*woni*; *wonie*, *woni*) smell; ***przykra ~*** odo(u)r; ***przyjemna ~*** fragrance, aroma

woreczek *m* → ***worek***; *anat.* bladder; ***~ żółciowy*** *anat.* gall bladder

wor|ek *m* (*-rka*; *-rki*) bag; (*duży*) sac; ***~ki pod oczami*** bags under the eyes; **~y** *pl.* → ***wór***

wosk *m* (*-u*; *-i*) wax; **~owy** wax

wotum *n* (*idkl.*; *-a*; *-ów*) vote (***zaufania, nieufności*** of confidence, of no confidence); *rel.* votive offering

woz|ić (*-żę*, *woź/wóź!*) carry; transport; *kogoś* drive; **~y** *pl.* → ***wóz***

woźn|a *f* (*-ej*; *-e*) *Brt.* janitor, *Am.* caretaker; **~ica** *m* (*-y*; *-e*) coachman; **~y** *m* (*-ego*; *-i*) *Brt.* janitor, *Am.* caretaker; *jur.* court usher

wódka *f* (*-i*; *G -dek*) vodka

wódz *m* (*wodza*; *wodzowie*) leader; chief; ***~ naczelny*** commander-in-chief; → ***dowódca, przywódca***

wójt *m* (*-a*; *-owie*) chairman of the village council

wół *m* (*wołu*; *woły*) ox

wór *m* (*wora*; *wory*) sack, bag

wówczas *lit. adv.* then, at that time

wóz *m* (*wozu*; *wozy*) cart; *mot.* car; **~ek** *m* (*-zka*; *-zki*) cart; (*dziecięcy*) *Brt.* pram, *Am.* baby carriage, (*spacerowy*) *Brt.* pushchair; *Am.* stroller; ***~ek inwalidzki*** wheelchair

W.P. *skrót pisany*: ***Wielmożny Pan*** Esq.

WP *skrót pisany*: ***Wojsko Polskie*** Polish Army

wpadać (*-am*) fall; *rzeka*: flow into; *policzki*: sink; (*wbiec*) rush into; (***na*** *A*, ***w*** *A*) collide (with), bang (into); ***~ w oczy*** catch s.o.'s eye; (*zajść*) drop in (***do*** *G* on); ***~ w objęcia*** fall into s.o.'s arms; ***~ na pomysł*** hit on an idea; ***~ w złość*** fly into a rage; ***~ do rąk/w ręce*** fall into s.o.'s hands; ***~ w kłopoty*** get into trouble; → ***wpaść***

wpajać (*-am*) instil

wpakow(yw)ać (*-[w]uję*) pack, cram; ***~ się*** (*na przyjęcie*) gate crash; ***~ się w kłopoty*** get into trouble

wpaść → ***wpadać***; (***na*** *A*) bump into

W

wpatrywać się (*-uję*) (**w** *A*) stare (at)
wpędz|ać (*-am*) ⟨**~ić**⟩ (**w** *A*) drive into
wpić *pf.* → **wpijać**
wpierw *adv.* first
wpijać (*-am*) *paznokcie* dig; **~ się** (*cisnąć*) cut (**w** *A* into); *kleszcz itp.*: attach o.s.; **~ (się) zębami** sink o.s. teeth (**w** *A* into)
wpis *m* (*-u*; *-y*) entry; (*opłata*) fee; **~owy** admission; **~ywać** (*-uję*) ⟨**~ać**⟩ enrol(l) (**się** *v/i.*; **do** *A* in, for); write in
wpląt|ywać (*-uję*) ⟨**~ać**⟩ entangle, involve; **~ywać** ⟨**~ać**⟩ **się** get involved *lub* entangled (**w** *L* in)
wpła|cać (*-am*) ⟨**~cić**⟩ pay in, deposit; **~ta** *f* (*-y*; *G* -) payment, deposit
wpław *adv.* by swimming
wpły|nąć *pf.* → **wpływać**; **~w** *m* (*-u*; *-y*) influence; *tech.* inflow; **~wy** *pl. econ.* receipts *pl.*, revenue; **mieć ~wy** have connections; **~wać** (*-am*) *okręt*: come in, make port (**do** *G* to); *zapach itp.*: waft in; *kwota, listy*: come in; *rzeka*: flow in (to); (**na** *A*) have an influence (on); **~wowy** influential
wpoić *pf.* → **wpajać**
wpół *adv.* half; **~ do drugiej** half past one; **na ~** half-; *w złoż.* → **pół-**; **~darmo** *adv.* dirt cheap; **~żywy** dead tired
wpraw|a *f* (*-y*; *0*) *Brt.* practice, *Am.* practise, skill, mastery; **wyjść z ~y** be out of practice
wprawdzie *part.* though
wprawi|ać (*-am*) ⟨**~ć**⟩ *szybę* fit, put in; *obraz* frame; make (**w podziw** astonished); **~ać** ⟨**~ć**⟩ **w ruch** set in motion; **~ać** ⟨**~ć**⟩ **się** get practice (**w** *I* in)
wpraw|nie *adv.* skil(l)fully, skilled; **~ny** skil(l)ful, skilled
wprost *adv.* straight; *fig.* directly
wprowadz|ać (*-am*) ⟨**~ić**⟩ (**do** *G*) show (into); (*przedstawić, zaprowadzić*) introduce (to, into); **~ać w zakłopotanie** embarrass; **~ić się** move in (**do** *G* to); **~enie** *n* (*-a*; *G -eń*) introduction; **~enie się** move
wprzęg|ać (*-am*) ⟨ **~nąć**⟩ (*-nę*) harness
wprzód *adv. lit.* first
wpust *m* (*-u*; *-y*) *tech.* inlet; (*w drewnie*) groove; **~ ściekowy** drain
wpu|szczać ⟨**~ścić**⟩ let in
wpychać (*-am*) cram in, pack in; shove in; *fig.* palm off; **~ się** (**do** *G*) push in (to)
wracać (*-am*) return, come back (**do** *G* to); **~ z drogi** turn back; **~ do zdrowia** recover; → **zwracać**
wrak *m* (*-a*/*-u*; *-i*) wreck
wrastać (*-am*) grow in
wraz (**z** *I*) *adv.* (together) with
wrażenie *n* (*-a*; *G -eń*) impression; feeling; **odnieść ~** get an impression
wrażliw|ość *f* (*-ści*; *0*) sensibility; (*też tech.*) sensitivity; **~y** sensitive (**na** *A* to)
wre → **wrzeć**
wreszcie *adv.* at last
wręcz *adv.* straight, directly; **walka ~** *mil.* close combat; **~ać** (*-am*) ⟨**~yć**⟩ (*-ę*) hand in, hand over; present
wrodzony inborn; *med.* congenital
wrog|i hostile; **~o** *adv.* in a hostile manner; **~ość** *f* (*-ści*; *0*) hostility, enmity; **~owie** *pl.* → **wróg**
wrona *f* (*-y*; *G* -) *zo.* crow
wrosnąć *pf.* → **wrastać**
wrota *pl.* (*wrót*) gate, door (*też fig.* **do** *G* to)
wrotka *f* (*-i*; *G -tek*) (*w sporcie*) roller skate
wróbel *m* (*-bla*; *-ble*) *zo.* sparrow
wrócić *pf.* (*-cę*) → **wracać, zwracać**
wróg *m* (*wroga*; *wrogowie*) enemy
wró|ść *pf.* → **wrastać**; **~t** *G* → **wrota**
wróż|ba *f* (*-y*; *G* -) omen; prediction; **~biarstwo** (*-a*; *0*) fortune-telling; **~bita** *m* (*-y*; *-ci*) fortune-teller; **~ka** *f* (*-i*; *G -ek*) fortune-teller; (*w baśni*) fairy; **~yć** ⟨**po-**⟩ (*-ę*) *v/i.* tell fortunes; read fortune (**z kart, z ręki** from the cards, from the hand); *v/t.* predict
wryć *pf.*: *fig.* **~ się w pamięć** be imprinted on one's memory
wrzas|k *m* (*-u*; *-i*) shout, shriek, scream; **~kliwy** noisy, tumultuous; **~nąć** *pf.* → **wrzeszczeć**
wrzawa *f* (*-y*; *G* -) uproar, clamo(u)r
wrzą|cy boiling; **~tek** *m* (*-tku*) boiling water (milk *etc.*)
wrzeciono *n* (*-a*; *G* -) spindle
wrze|ć boil; *fig.* seethe; *pol.* ferment; **praca wre** the work is in full swing; **~nie** *n* (*-a*; *0*) boiling; ferment
wrzesień *m* (*-śnia*; *-śnie*) September
wrzeszczeć (*-ę*) yell, shriek
wrześniowy September
wrzodow|y: **choroba ~a** *med.* chronic peptic ulcer disease
wrzos *m* (*-u*; *-y*) *bot.* heather; **~owisko** *n* (*-a*; *G* -) heath
wrzód *m* (*-rzodu*; *-rzody*) *med.* ulcer;

(*czyrak*) abscess, boil
wrzu|cać (*-am*) ⟨**~cić**⟩ throw in (**do** *G* to); *mot. bieg* engage; **~t** *m* (*-u*; *-y*) *sport*: throw(-in)
wrzynać się (*-am*) cut into
wsadz|ać (*-am*) ⟨**~ić**⟩ put (**do auta, do kieszeni**, into the car, into the pocket); *ubranie*, *okulary* put on; **~ać za kraty** lock up
wsch. *skrót pisany*: **wschód** E (*East*); **wschodni** E (*Eastern*)
wschodni Eastern
wschodzić (*-dzę*) rise, get up
wschód *m* (*-chodu*; *0*) east; (*pl. -chody*) **~ słońca** sunrise, sunup; **ze wschodu** from the east; **na ~ od** (*G*) east of
wsi → **wieś**
wsiadać (*-am*) get in (**do** *G*); get on, board (**na** *A*); **~ na statek** embark
wsiąkać (*-am*) seep in, soak up
wsiąść *pf.* → **wsiadać**
wsie *pl.* → **wieś**
wskakiwać (*-uję*) jump (on); (**do** *G*) jump (into), plunge (into)
wskaz|ać *pf.* → **wskazywać**; **~any** shown; (*zalecany*) advisable; **~ówka** *m* (*-i*; *G -wek*) (*zegara*) hand; (*wskaźnik*) pointer; (*sugestia*) hint; → **oznaka**; **~ujący** pointing; *anat.* index; **~ywać** (*-uję*) point (**na** *A* at, *fig.* to)
wskaźnik *m* (*-a*; *-i*) *tech.* indicator, gauge; pointer; (**cen** price) index; **~ benzyny** *mot.* fuel gauge
wskoczyć *pf.* → **wskakiwać**
wskórać *pf.* (*-am*) accomplish, achieve
wskroś: **na ~** through (and through)
wskrze|szać (*-am*) ⟨**~sić**⟩ (*-szę*) raise *s.o.* from the dead
wskutek *prp.* because of
wsławi|ać się (*-am*) ⟨**~ć się**⟩ become famous (**jako** as)
wsłuch|iwać się (*-uję*) ⟨**~ać się**⟩ listen; (**w** *A*) listen (to)
wspak: **na ~** *adv.* backwards
wspaniale *adv.* magnificently
wspaniał|omyślny magnanimous; generous; **~y** magnificent; splendid, grand
wsparcie *n* (*-a*; *G -rć*) support, backing
wspiąć się *pf.* → **wspinać się**
wspierać (*-am*) support; *fig.* back
wspina|czka *f* (*-i*; *G -czek*) mountaineering; **~ć się** (*-am*) climb
wspomag|ać help, assist; **~anie** *n* (*-a*; *0*): **~anie kierownicy** *mot.* power steering
wspom|inać (*-am*) ⟨**~nieć**⟩ (*-nę*, *-nij!*) (*A*) recall, remember; (**o** *L*) mention; **~nienie** *n* (*-a*; *G -eń*) remembrance, memory; **~nienie pośmiertne** obituary; **na samo ~nienie** at the very thought; **~óc** *pf.* → **wspomagać**
wspóln|iczka *f* (*-i*; *G -czek*), **~ik** *m* (*-a*; *-cy*) partner; *jur.* (*w zbrodni*) accomplice; **~ota** *f* (*-y*; *G-*) community; **℘ota Narodów** the Commonwealth of Nations; **℘ota Niepodległych Państw** Commonwealth of Independent States; **~y** common; mutual; **~ymi siłami** with combined efforts; **~a mogiła** mass grave; **nie mieć nic ~ego** (**z** *I*) have nothing in common (with)
współczes|ność *f* (*-ści*; *0*) presence; contemporaneity; **~ny** contemporary; **historia ~na** contemporary history
współczu|cie *n* (*-a*; *0*) compassion; sympathy; **złożyć wyrazy ~cia** (*D*) offer one's condolences (to); **~ć** (*-uję*) (*D*) sympathize (with), pity; feel sorry (for); **~jąco** *adv.* with sympathy
współ|czynnik *m* (*-a*; *-i*) factor, coefficient; **~decydować** (*-uję*) have a say (**przy** *L* in); **~działać** (*-am*) cooperate, collaborate, work together (**przy** *L* with); **~istnienie** *n* (*-a*; *G -eń*) coexistence; **~małżonek** *m* spouse, marriage partner; **~mierny** (**do** *G*) appropriate (to); adequate (to); **~mieszkaniec** *m* (*-ńca*; *-ńcy*), **~mieszkanka** *f* (*-i*; *G -nek*) fellow occupant; (*pokoju*) roommate **~obywatel** (**ka** *f*) *m* fellow citizen; **~oskarżony** *m*, **~oskarżona** *f* co-defendant
współprac|a *f* cooperation, collaboration; **~ować** (**przy** *L*, **w** *L*) work together (on), collaborate (on), cooperate (on); **~owniczka** *f*, **~ownik** *m* co-worker, collaborator
współ|rządzić to control jointly; **~rzędna** *f* (*-ej*; *-e*) *math.* coordinate
współspraw|ca *m*, **~czyni** *f jur.* accomplice, accessory
współuczestni|ctwo *n* participation; **~czyć** (*-ę*) participate (**w** *L* in); *jur.* aid and abet; **~czka** *f*, **~k** *m* participant
współ|udział *m* participation; involvement; *jur.* complicity; **~więzień** *m*, **~więźniarka** *f* fellow prisoner; **~właściciel** (**ka** *f*) *m* co-owner, joint owner; **~wyznawca** *m rel.* fellow-believer

współzawodni|ctwo *n* (*-a*; *0*) competition, rivalry; **~czka** *f* (*w sporcie*) competitor, contestant; **~czyć** (*-ę*) compete (***z** I* with); **~k** *m* competitor, contestant
współży|cie *n* living together; *zwł.* married life; ***trudny we ~ciu*** difficult to get along with; **~ć** live together; *biol.* live in symbiosis
wsta|wać ⟨***wstać***⟩ (*stać²*) get up, rise; stand; **~wi(a)ć** put in, insert; ***~wi(a)ć się*** (***za** I*) intercede (on *s.o.'s* behalf), put in a good word (for); **~wiennictwo** *n* (*-a*; *0*) intercession; **~wka** *f* (*-i*; *G -wek*) insertion; *theat.* interlude
wstąpić *pf.* (*-ę*) → ***wstępować***
wstąpienie *n* (*-a*) entry, joining; ***~ na tron*** ascension to the throne
wstążka *f* (*-i*; *G -żek*) ribbon
wstecz *adv.* back(wards); **~nictwo** *n* (*-a*; *0*) backwardness; **~ny** *jur.* retrospective; *fig.* reactionary, retrograde; ***bieg ~ny*** *mot.* reverse (gear); ***lusterko ~ne*** *mot.* rear-view mirror
wstęga *f* (*-i*; *G -*) band, ribbon
wstęp *m* (*-u*; *-y*) entry, entrance; (*do książki*) introduction (*też fig.*); ***na ~ie*** at the beginning; to begin with; **~nie** *adv.* initially; **~ny** introductory; preliminary; initial; ***słowo ~ne*** foreword; → ***egzamin***; **~ować** (*-uję*) (***do** G*) enter, join; (*zajść*) drop in (at); (***na** A*) enter; (*na tron*) ascend (to)
wstręt *m* (*-u*; *-y*) disgust, repulsion, revulsion; **~ny** disgusting, repulsive
wstrząs *m* (*-u*; *-y*) (*pojazdu itp.*) jolt; *fig.* shock (*też med.*); *geol.* tremor; **~ać** (*-am*) (*I*) shake (*też fig.*); *pojazd itp.*: jolt; ***~ać się*** (***z** G*) shake (with), convulse (with); **~ająco** *adv.* shockingly; **~ający** shocking; **~nąć** *pf.* → ***wstrząsać***; **~owy** shock
wstrzemięźliw|ie *adv.* temperately, abstemiously, abstinently; **~y** temperate, abstemious, abstinent
wstrzy|kiwać (*-uję*) ⟨***~knąć***⟩ *med.* inject; **~mywać** (*-uję*) ⟨***~mać***⟩ stop, hold up; *fig.* impede, inhibit; ***~mać się*** suppress, hold back (***od łez*** tears); ***~mać się od głosu*** abstain; (***z** I*) put off, delay
wstyd *m* (*-u*; *0*) shame; (*zakłopotanie*) embarrassment; ***~ mi*** (*G*) I am ashamed (of); ***ze ~u*** with shame *lub* embarrassment; **~liwie** *adv.* timidly; with shame; **~liwy** timid, embarrassed; → ***nieśmiały, żenujący***
wsty|dzić ⟨***za-***⟩ (*-dzę*) put to shame; ***~dzić*** ⟨***za-***⟩ ***się*** (*G*; *bezok.*) be ashamed (of; to *bezok.*); ***~dź się*** shame on you
wsu|wać (*-am*) ⟨***~nąć***⟩ (*-nę*) insert, slide in(to); (*jeść*) tuck in; ***~nąć się*** (***do** G*, ***pod** A*) slip (into, under); **~wka** *f* (*-i*; *G -wek*) (*do włosów*) hairgrip
wsyp|ywać (*-uję*) ⟨***~ać***⟩ pour (***do** G* into); ***~ać się*** *fig.* F get caught
wsysać (*-am*) suck into
wszakże *lit.* however, anyhow
wszcząć *pf.* → ***wszczynać***
wszczepi|ać (*-am*) ⟨***~ć***⟩ *med.* implant; *fig.* instil(l)
wszczynać (*-am*) instigate; *śledztwo, negocjacje* open; ***~ kłótnię*** brawl
wszech|mocny almighty; **~obecny** omnipresent; **~stronny** versatile; **~świat** *m* (*-a*; *-y*) universe; **~światowy** world-wide; **~władny** omnipotent
wszelk|i every, any; ***za ~ą cenę*** at any price; ***na ~i wypadek*** just in case
wszerz *adv.* across; → ***wzdłuż***
wszędzie *adv.* everywhere
wszy *pl.* → ***wesz***; **~ć** *pf.* → ***wszywać***
wszys|cy *m-os* everybody, all; **~tek** *m* (*f* ***~tka***, *n* ***~tko***, *pl.* ***~tkie***) all; ***~tko jedno*** all the same; ***nade ~tko*** above all; ***~tkiego najlepszego!*** all the best!
wszywać (*-am*) sew in(to)
wścibski snooping; F nosy
wściec się *pf.* (*o psie, fig.*) go mad; → ***wściekać się***
wściek|ać się (*-am*) *fig.* F rage, fume, seethe; **~le** *adv.* furiously, madly; **~lizna** *f* (*-y*; *0*) *med.* rabies *sg.*; **~łość** *f* (*-ści*; *0*) rage, madness, fury; **~ły** *med.* rabid; *fig.* mad, furious
wśliz|giwać się (*-uję*) ⟨***~(g)nąć się***⟩ (*-nę*) (***do** G*) slip in(to)
wśród *prp.* (*G*) among, between
wt. *skrót pisany*: ***wtorek*** Tue(s). (*Tuesday*)
wtaczać roll (***się*** *v/i.*; ***do** G* into)
wtajemnicz|ać (*-am*) ⟨***~yć***⟩ let *s.o.* in (***w** A* on); **~ony** initiated
wtargnąć *pf.* (***do** G*) invade; *fig.* burst in (on)
wte|dy *adv.* then; at that time; **~m** *adv.* suddenly; abruptly; **~nczas** *adv.* → ***wtedy***
wtłaczać (*-am*) ⟨***wtłoczyć***⟩ stuff, cram;

W

~ się push (one's way) (**do** *G* into)
wtoczyć *pf.* → **wtaczać**
wtor|ek *m* (*-rku*; *-rki*) Tuesday; **~kowy** Tuesday
wtór|nik *m* (*-a*; *-i*) duplicate, copy; **~ny** secondary; **~ować** *mus.*, *fig.* (*D*) accompany; **~y**: **po ~e** secondly
wtrąc|ać ⟨**~ić**⟩ *v/t. uwagę* throw in; **~ić do więzienia** put in prison; *v/i.* interject, remark; **~ać** ⟨**~ić**⟩ **się** interfere (**w** *A*, **do** *A* in), *fig.* butt in
wtrys|kiwać (*-uję*) ⟨**~nąć**⟩ inject
wtyczk|a *f* (*-i*; *G -czek*) *electr.* plug; F informer, plug; **~owy** *electr.*: **gniazd(k)o ~owe** power point, socket outlet
wtykać (*-am*) insert, put into
wuj *m* (*-a*; *-owie*, *-ów*), **~ek** *m* (*-ka*; *-kowie*) uncle; **~enka** *f* (*-i*; *G -nek*) aunt
wulgarny vulgar; gross
wulkan *m* (*-u*; *-y*) volcano; **~iczny** volcanic; **~izować** (*-uję*) vulcanize
ww. *skrót pisany*: **wyżej wymieniony** above-mentioned
Wwa, W-wa *skrót pisany*: **Warszawa** Warsaw
wwozić ⟨**wwieźć**⟩ bring in; import (**do** *G* into)
wy *pron.* (*GAL was*, *D wam*, *I wami*) you
wybacz|ać (*-am*) forgive; **~alny** forgivable, excusable; **~enie** *n* (*-a*; *G -eń*) forgiveness; **nie do ~enia** unforgivable, inexcusable; **~yć** *pf.* → **wybaczać**
wybaw|ca *m* (*-y*; *G -ców*), **~czyni** *f* (*-i*; *-e*) rescuer; savio(u)r (*też rel.*); **~iać** (*-am*) ⟨**~ić**⟩ rescue, save (**z** *G* from)
wybić *pf.* → **wybijać**; (*wygubić*) eradicate; *drób itp.* kill off; (*zbić*) beat up; **~ sobie z głowy** get *s.th.* out of one's head; **~ się ze snu** be unable to fall asleep again
wybie|g *m* (*-u*; *-i*) (*drobiu*) run; (*koni*) paddock; (*dla modelek*) *Brt.* catwalk, *Am.* runway; *fig.* device, trick; **~gać** ⟨**~c, ~gnąć**⟩ run out (**z** *G* of); **~lać** (*-am*) ⟨**~lić**⟩ make white, whiten; *fig.* clear; → **bielić**
wybierać (*-am*) (*dokonywać wyboru*) choose, select; (*w wyborach*) elect; *numer* dial; (*wyjmować*) take out; **~ się** (**do** *G*) be going (to); **~ się do teatru** go to the *Brt.* theatre (*Am.* theater); **~ się w podróż** get ready for the journey
wybi|jać (*-am*) *dno*, *ząb*, *oko* knock out; *szybę* break, smash; *medal* strike, mint; (*obić ścianę itp.*) line (*I* with); *takt* beat; *godzinę* strike; **~jać się** distinguish o.s.; excel (**w** *L* in); → **wybić**; **~tnie** *adv.* eminently; **~tny** eminent, distinguished
wyblakły faded
wyboisty uneven, bumpy
wybor|ca *m* (*-y*; *G -ów*) voter; **~czy** electoral, election; **~ny** excellent; → **wyśmienity**; **~owy** elite; **strzelec ~owy** marksman; **~y** *pl.* → **wybór**
wybój *m* (*-boju*; *-boje*, *G -boi*/*-bojów*) pothole
wybór *m* (*-boru*; *-bory*) selection, choice; (*mianowanie*) appointment (**na** *A* to); *pol.* **wybory** *pl.* elections *pl.* (**do parlamentu** to Parliament); **do wyboru** to choose from
wybra|ć *pf.* → **wybierać**; **~kow(yw)ać** (*-[w]uję*) sort out; **~kowany towar** rejects *pl.*; **~ny** elected; chosen
wybredny fastidious, choosy
wybrnąć *pf.* (**z** *G*) work one's way out (of) (*też fig.*); *fig.* get out (**z długów** of one's debt)
wybro- *pf.*, **wybru-** *pf.* → **bro-, bru-**
wybryk *m* (*-u*; *-i*) trick, prank; **~ natury** freak of nature
wybrzeż|e *n* (*-a*; *G -y*) coast; (*morza*) seaside; **na ~e** to the coast; **na ~u** on the coast
wybrzuszenie *n* (*-a*; *G -eń*) bulge
wy|brzydzać F (*-am*) (**na** *A*) fuss (about); **~bu-** *pf.* → **bu-**
wybuch *m* (*-u*; *-y*) explosion; (*wulkanu*) eruption (*też fig.*); (*wojny*, *epidemii*) outbreak; (*gniewu*) outburst; **~ać** (*-am*) ⟨**~nąć**⟩ explode; *wulkan*: erupt; *wojna*, *panika*: break out; burst out (**śmiechem, płaczem** laughing, crying); (*gniewem*) blow up; **~owy** explosive; *fig.* bad-tempered
wybujały → **bujny**; tall
wyca-, wyce- *pf.* → **ca-, ce-**
wycena *f* (*-y*; *G -*) estimate, valuation
wychł|adzać (*-am*) ⟨**~odzić**⟩ cool down; → **ochładzać, oziębiać**
wychodn|e *n* (*-ego*; *0*) day off; F **być na ~ym** be just about to leave
wychodzić (**z** *G*) go out (of), leave; (**na** *A*) look out on (to); (**na** *L*) profit (from); *książka*, *zdjęcie itp.*: come out, appear; *praca itp.*: work; **~ na pierwsze miejsce** take the lead; **~ na wolność** be released; **~ z mody** go out of

fashion; ~ ***w morze*** put to sea; ***nie ~ z głowy*** haunt; ~ ***dobrze na*** (*L*) profit (from); ~ ***na swoje*** break even; → ***iść, wyjść***
wychodź|ca *m* (*-y*; *G -ów*) emigrant; ~**stwo** *n* (*-a*; *0*) emigration
wychowa|ć (*-am*) → ***wychowywać***; ~**nek** *m* (*-nka*; *-nkowie*) foster-child; (*były uczeń*) graduate; ~**nie** *n* (*-a*; *0*) upbringing, education; ***dobre ~nie*** good manners *pl.*; ~**nka** *f* (*-i*; *G -nek*) → ***wychowanek***; ~**wca** *m* (*-cy*; *G -ców*), ~**wczyni** *f* (*-ni*; *-ie*, *-yń*) caregiver; ~**wczo** *adv.* educationally; ~**wczy** educational
wychowywać (*-uję*) *dziecko* bring up; *ucznia* educate; ~ ***się*** grow up (***u*** *G* with); be brought up
wychudły emaciated, drawn
wychwalać (*-am*) praise
wychyl|ać (*-am*) ⟨***~ić***⟩ *kieliszek* empty, drain; ***~ać głowę z okna*** put one's head out of the window; ***~ać się*** *wskazówka*: swing; look out (***zza*** *G* from behind); ***~ić się do przodu*** bend *lub* lean forward
wyciąć *pf.* → ***wycinać***
wyciąg *m* (*-u*; *-i*) *med. itp.* extract; (*kuchenny, tech.*) hood; *tech.* hoist; (*winda*) *Brt.* lift, *Am.* elevator; (*narciarski*) (ski)lift
wyciąg|ać (*-am*) ⟨***~nąć***⟩ pull out; *gumę, rękę itp.* stretch; *ręce, nogi* extend, stretch out; *fig. wnioski*, draw; *math. pierwiastek* extract; ***~nąć się*** stretch out
wycie *n* (*-a*; *G wyć*) howl
wyciec *pf.* → ***wyciekać***
wycieczk|a *f* (*-i*; *G -czek*) outing, (*zorganizowana, też fig.*) excursion; trip; ~**owy** excursion
wyciekać (*-am*) leak out
wycieńcz|ać (*-am*) ⟨***~yć***⟩ (*-ę*) weaken, exhaust
wyciera|czka *f* (*-i*; *G -czek*) (*przy drzwiach*) doormat; *mot.* screen wiper; ~**ć** (*-am*) wipe; (*osuszyć*) dry; ***~ć gumką*** erase, rub out; ***~ć się*** dry o.s.; (*ręcznikiem*) towel o.s.; *ubranie* wear (out)
wycięcie *n* (*-a*; *G -ęć*) opening; (*ubrania*) neckline
wycin|ać (*-am*) cut (out); *drzewa* fell; ~**anka** *f* (*-i*; *G -nek*) silhouette, cutout; ~**ek** *m* (*-nka*; *-nki*) clipping; *med.* specimen; *math.* segment
wycis|kać ⟨***~nąć***⟩ *sok* press out, squeeze out; *ubranie* wring (out); *pieczęć* impress
wycisz|ać (*-am*) ⟨***~yć***⟩ (*-ę*) silence
wycof|ywać (*-uję*) ⟨***~ać***⟩ withdraw, pull out (***się*** *v/i.*; ***z*** *G* from); → ***cofać***
wyczek|ać *pf.* (*G*, *A*), ~**iwać** (*-uję*) (***na*** *A*) wait (for)
wyczerp|ać *pf.* → ***wyczerpywać***; ~**any** exhausted; *towar* out of stock; ~**ujący** exhaustive; ~**ywać** (*-ać*) exhaust; *kogoś* wear out; *zapasy* deplete; ***~ywać się*** get tired; *zasoby*: become depleted
wyczu|cie *n* (*-a*; *0*) sensation; (*G*); feeling (of); ~(**wa**)**ć** (*-*[*w*]*am*) sense; feel; *zapach* smell; ~**walny** perceptible
wyczyn *m* outstanding performance; ~**owy** (*w sporcie*) competitive
wyć (*wyję*) howl
wyćwiczony practised, mastered
wyda|ć *pf.* → ***wydawać***; ~**jność** *f* (*-ści*; *0*) efficiency, effectiveness; productivity; *agr.* fertility; ~**jny** efficient, effective; productive; ~**lać** (*-am*) ⟨***~lić***⟩ (*-lę*) (*z kraju*) exile; (*z pracy*) dismiss; (*ze szkoły*) expel; *biol.* secrete; ~**lenie** *n* (*-a*; *G -leń*) exile; dismissal; expulsion; ~**nie** *n* (*-a*; *G -ań*) issuing; *print.* edition; *jur.* handing over, extradition; (*zdrada*) betrayal
wydarz|enie *n* (*-a*; *G -eń*) event; ~**yć się** (*t-ko 3. os.*) occur, happen
wydat|ek *m* (*-tku*; *-tki*) expenditure; expense; ~**kować** (*imp*)*pf.* (*-uję*) expend, pay; ~**ny** prominent, protuberant; *fig.* considerable, significant
wydaw|ać *pieniądze* spend; *rzeczy* give out; *dokument, dekret* issue; *książkę* publish; *woń* give off; *dźwięk* make; *przyjęcie, rozkaz* give; *zbiega* give over; *sekret* reveal; *córkę* marry (***za*** *A* to); *jur. wyrok* pronounce; ***~ać się*** seem, appear; *sekret*: be revealed, come out; get married (***za*** *A* to); ~**ca** *m* (*-y*; *G -ców*), ~**czyni** *f* (*-i*; *-e*) publisher; ~**nictwo** *n* (*-a*; *G -ctw*) publishing house
wy|dąć *pf.* → ***wydymać***; ~**dech** *m* (*-u*; *-y*) exhalation; ~**dechowy**: ***rura ~dechowa*** *mot.* exhaust pipe
wydekoltowany *suknia* low-cut
wydept|ywać (*-uję*) ⟨***~ać***⟩ *trawnik* stamp on, tread; *ścieżkę* tread out
wydęty *usta* pouted
wydłub|ywać (*-uję*) ⟨***~ać***⟩ pick out
wydłuż|ać (*-am*) ⟨***~yć***⟩ extend, leng-

W

then; *okres* prolong; **~ony** elongated
wydma *f* (*-y*; *G* -) dune
wydmuch|iwać (*-uję*) 〈**~ać**〉 blow out
wydoby|wać 〈**~ć**〉 get (**z** *A* out of); *rudę* extract, mine; *informacje* elicit; **~(wa)ć się** escape; → **wydostawać (się)**; **~wczy** *przemysł* mining
wydolny efficient
wydoskonalać (*-am*) → **doskonalić**
wydosta(wa)ć get (**z** *A* out of); (*uzyskać*) receive, get; **~ się** come out, get out
wydra *f* (*-y*; *G -der/-*) *zo.* otter
wydrap|ywać (*-uję*) 〈**~ać**〉 (*usuwać*) scrape out; *słowa* scratch
wydrążony hollow
wydruk *m* (*-u*; *-i*) *komp.* printout; **~ować** (*-uję*) *komp.* print out
wydrwigrosz *m* (*-a*; *-e*) con man
wy|drzeć *pf.* → **wydzierać**; **~dusić** *pf. fig.* squeeze out, wring out; **~dychać** (*-am*) breathe out; **~dymać** (*-am*) *policzki* puff out; *brzuch* distend; **~dział** *m* (*-u*; *-y*) uniwersytet: faculty; department, section
wydziedzicz|ać (*-am*) 〈**~yć**〉 disinherit
wydziel|ać (*-am*) *biol.* excrete; *promieniowanie* radiate; *chem., med. itp.* emit, release; *zapach* give off; *biol.* be excreted; *chem.* be emitted; 〈*też* **~ić**〉 ration, divide, distribute; destine, intend (**na, pod** *A* for); **~ina** *f* (*-y*; *G* -) secretion; **~ony**: **miasto ~one** (*a town that is an administrative district in its own right*)
wydzierać (*-am*) tear out/away; *fig.* rescue, save; F **~ się** roar, shout; → **wyrywać**
wydzierżawi|ać (*-am*) 〈**~ć**〉 rent; (*wziąć w dzierżawę*) lease
wydźwięk *m* implication(s)
wy|egz-, ~eks-, ~el-, ~em-, ~fro- *pf.* → **egz-, eks-, el-, em-, fro-**
wyga|dać F *pf.* spill the beans; **~dany** F glib; **~dywać** F (*-uję*) blab; find fault (**na** *A* with); **~lać** (*-am*) shave off; **~niać** → **wypędzać**; **~rniać** (*-am*) 〈**~rnąć**〉 *popiół* remove; F *fig.* make *s.th.* clear *lub* plain; **~sać** (*-am*) 〈**~snąć**〉 go out
wy|giąć *pf.* → **wyginać**; **~gięcie** *n* (*-a*; *G -ęć*) curvature, curve; bend; **~ginać** (*-am*) bend, bow; *w łuk* arch; **~ginąć** *pf.* die out; *zwł. biol.* become extinct
wygląd *m* (*-u*; *0*) appearance, look; **~ać** (*-am*) look (**oknem** out of the window; **młodo** young; **na artystę** like an artist; **na szczęśliwego** happy); *sprawy*: stand; (**spod, zza** *G*) appear (from behind, beneath); (*G*) look forward (to)
wygładz|ać (*-am*) 〈**~ić**〉 smooth out
wygłodzony famished, starving
wygł|aszać (*-am*) 〈**~osić**〉 *mowę* give, deliver
wygłupia|ć się (*-am*) fool about; **nie ~j się!** stop messing about!, (*bądź poważny*) stop joking!
wygna|ć *pf.* → **wypędzać**; **~nie** *n* (*-a*; *G -ań*) exile; **na ~niu** in exile; **~niec** *m* (*-ńca*; *-ńcy*) exile
wygni|atać (*-am*) 〈**~eść**〉 *ciasto* knead; *pf.* crease, rumple; → **miąć**
wygod|a *f* (*-y*; *G -gód*) comfort, convenience; **z ~ami** *mieszkanie* with all modern conveniences *pl.*; **~ny** comfortable; convenient; → **dogodny**
wygo|lić *pf.* → **wygalać**; **~nić** *pf.* → **wypędzać**; **~spodarować** *pf.* obtain through careful management; **~tow(yw)ać** (*-[w]uję*) boil out
wygórowany exorbitant, extravagant
wygra|ć *pf.* → **wygrywać**; **~na** *f* (*-ej*; *-e*) win, victory; **dać za ~ną** give up; **łatwa ~na** walk-over; **~ny** won
wygr|ywać (*-am*) (*A*, **w**) win; **~ać na loterii** win (on) the lottery; *fig.* have good luck; **~yzać** (*-am*) 〈**~źć**〉 *dziurę* eat through
wygrzeb|ywać (*-uję*) 〈**~ać**〉 dig out; *fig.* dig up, unearth
wygrzewać się (*-am*) warm o.s., sun
wygwizd|ywać (*-uję*) 〈**~ać**〉 *melodię* whistle; *zwł. pf. aktora* hiss
wy|ha-, ~ho- *pf.* → **ha-, ho-**; **~imaginowany** imaginary
wyja|dać eat up; **~ławiać** (*-am*) 〈**~łowić**〉 (*-ę*) exhaust, drain; *med.* sterilize; **~śniać** (*-am*) 〈**~śnić**〉 (*-ę*, *-nij!*) explain; **~śniać** 〈**~śnić**〉 **się** be explained, make clear; **~śnienie** *n* (*-a*; *G -eń*) explanation; **~wiać** (*-am*) 〈**~wić**〉 reveal; *skandal* expose
wyjazd *m* (*-u*; *-y*) exit, departure; (*podróż*) journey, travel
wyjąć *pf.* → **wyjmować**
wyjąt|ek *m* (*-tku*; *-tki*) exception; **bez ~ku** without exception; **z ~kiem** (*G*) with the exception (of); **w drodze ~ku** → **~kowo** *adv.* exceptionally, by way of exception; **~kowy** exceptional

wyje|chać *pf.* → ***wyjeżdżać***; **~dnać** *pf.* obtain; **~ść** *pf.* → ***wyjadać***
wyjezdn|e: ***na ~ym*** just before leaving
wyjeżdżać (*-am*) leave, go away/out; drive (***z*** *G* out of, from; ***po zakupy*** to do the shopping); ***~ na urlop*** go on a holiday (***do*** *A* to); ***~ za granicę*** go abroad; → ***odjeżdżać***
wyj|mować (*-uję*) get out, take out; **~rzeć** *pf.* (*-ę; -y*) → ***wyglądać***
wyjś|cie *n* (*-a; G -jść*) leaving, departure; (*drzwi itp.*) exit, way out; (*na lotnisku*) gate; *fig.* solution; *tech.* output; ***~cie za mąż*** marriage; ***położenie bez ~cia*** deadlock, stalemate; **~ciowy** *drzwi itp.* exit; (*początkowy*) starting; *tech.* output; **~ć** *pf.* → ***wychodzić***; F ***nie wyszło*** it did not work out
wy|kałaczka *f* (*-i; G -czek*) toothpick; **~kantować** F *pf.* swindle; **~kańczać** (*-am*) finish; F *fig.* finish off
wykapan|y: ***~y ojciec*** the spitting image of the father
wykarmi|ać (*-am*) 〈**~ć**〉 feed
wykaz *m* (*-u; -y*) list; **~ywać** 〈**~ać**〉 (*udowodnić*) prove; (*przejawić*) show; (*ujawnić*) reveal; ***~ać się*** prove o.s.
wykidajło F *m* (*-u; -ów*) bouncer, chucker-out
wy|kipieć *pf.* boil out; **~kitować** F (*-uję*) pop off, snuff it; **~kiwać** F (*-am*) fool, con; **~kląć** *pf.* → ***wyklinać***; **~klejać** (*-am*) 〈**~kleić**〉 (*I*) line (with); **~klinać** (*-am*) *dziecko* curse; *grzesznika* excommunicate
wyklucz|ać (*-am*) 〈**~yć**〉 (*-ę*) exclude, rule out; ***~ać się*** be mutually exclusive; **~ony** excluded; ***to jest ~one*** it's out of the question
wyklu|wać (*-am*) 〈**~ć**〉 (*-ję*) ***się*** → ***kluć***
wykład *m* (*-u; -y*) lecture, talk
wykładać[1] (*-am*) *v/t.* lecture; (*uczyć*) teach, *zwł. Brt.* read
wykład|ać[2] (*-am*) lay out; *kołnierz* turn down; (*płytami itp.*) pave; *myśl* elucidate; **~any** *mebel* inlaid; **~nik** *m* (*-a; -i*) *math.* exponent; **~owca** *m* (*-y; G -ców*) lecturer, reader; **~owy** lecture
wykładzina *f* (*-y; G -*) lining, coating; (*na podłogę*) linoleum, *Brt.* lino; ***~ dywanowa*** fitted carpet
wykłu|wać (*-am*) 〈**~ć**〉 put out, gouge out
wykole|jać się (*-am*) 〈***~ić się***〉 (*-ję*) *pociąg*: derail; *fig.* go astray; **~jeniec** *m* (*-ńca; -ńcy*) social misfit
wykomb- *pf.* → ***komb-***
wykona|ć *pf.* → ***wykonywać***; **~lny** practicable, feasible, workable; **~nie** *n* (*-a; G -ań*) execution; production; performance; playing; *por.* ***wykonywać***; **~wca** *m* (*-y; G -ców*), **~wczyni** *f* (*-i; -e*) performer; *jur.* executor; *econ.* contractor; *por.* ***wykonywać***; **~wczy** executive
wykonywać (*-uję*) *pracę* do, execute; *rzecz* make, produce; *zamiar, zadanie, wyrok* carry out; *piosenkę, sztukę* perform; *rolę* play; *zawód* work
wykończyć *pf.* → ***wykańczać, kończyć***
wykop *m* (*-u; -y*) excavation; trench; **~ywać** (*-uję*) 〈**~ać**〉 *dół itp.* dig (out)
wykorzyst|ywać (*-uję*) 〈**~ać**〉 use; employ; → ***wyzyskiwać***
wykpi|wać (*-am*) 〈**~ć**〉 *v/t.* make fun of, mock
wykra|czać (*-am*) (***poza*** *A*) go beyond; (***przeciw*** *D*) infringe, contravene; **~dać** (*-am*) steal; *kogoś* kidnap, abduct; ***~dać się*** steal out *lub* away; **~jać** (*-am*) cut out; **~ść** *pf.* → ***wykradać***; **~wać** (*-am*) *pf.* → ***wykrajać***
wykre|s *m* (*-u; -y*) diagram; chart; **~ślać** (*-am*) 〈**~ślić**〉 cross *lub* strike out; *tech.* plot, draw; **~ślny** graphical; diagrammatic
wykrę|cać (*-am*) 〈**~cić**〉 *żarówkę* screw out, unscrew; *bieliznę* wring; *szyję* crick; *rękę* twist; F *numer* dial; ***~cać się*** turn; *fig.* wriggle out (***od*** *G* of); **~t** *m* (*-u; -y*) (*ustny*) excuse; dodge; **~tny** evasive
wykro|czenie *n* (*-a; G -eń*) *jur. Brt.* offence, *Am.* offense; **~czyć** *pf.* → ***wykraczać***; **~ić** *pf.* → ***wykrajać***
wykrój *m* (*-kroju; -kroje*) pattern
wykrusz|ać się (*-am*) 〈***~yć się***〉 crumble away (***z*** *G* from); *fig.* decrease
wykrwawić się *pf.* bleed to death
wykry|cie *n* (*-a; G -yć*) detection; uncovering, exposure; **~ć** *pf.* → ***wykrywać***; **~wacz** *m* detector; ***~wacz kłamstw*** lie detector; **~wać** (*-am*) detect; *zbrodnię* find; (*odkryć*) discover
wykrzyk|iwać (*-uję*) shout, cry out; **~nąć** *v/s.* call out, exclaim; **~nik** *m* (*-a; -i*) *print.* exclamation mark; *gr.* interjection

W

wykrzywi|ać (*-am*) ⟨**~ć**⟩ contort, distort; bend; *usta* screw out; **z twarzą ~oną bólem** with the face twisted with pain

wykształceni|e *n* (*-a*; *0*) education; (**zawodowe** vocational) training; **wyższe ~e** higher education; **z ~a …** … by profession

wykształcony educated

wyku|ć *pf.* → **wykuwać**; **~pywać** (*-uję*) ⟨**~pić**⟩ buy up; *zastaw*, *jeńca* redeem; *zastaw itp.* buy back; **~rzać** (*-am*) ⟨**~rzyć**⟩ smoke out

wykusz *m* (*-a*; *-e*) bay window

wykuwać (*-am*) forge; *posąg* carve, chisel; F (*w szkole*) cram

wykwalifikowany qualified, skilled

wykwintny elegant

wyla|ć *pf.* → **wylewać**; **~nie** *n* F (*z pracy*) boot; throw-out; **~tywać** (*-uję*) *samolot*, *ptak*: fly off; *samolot kursowy*: leave; (*jako pasażer*) leave (by plane); F (*z pracy*) get the boot; *dym itp.*: go up; → **wyskakiwać, wylecieć, wypadać**

wylądować *pf. aviat.* touch down; *astr.* (*na morzu*) splash down; (*na księżycu*) land

wyle|cieć *pf.* → **wylatywać**; **~cieć w powietrze** blow up; **~czyć** *pf.* cure; heal; **~czyć się** recover (**z** *G* from); **~giwać się** (*-uję*) lie around; loll; (*w łóżku*) lie in; **~w** *m* (*-u*; *-y*) (*rzeki*) flood, overflow; *med.* h(a)emorrhage; **~w krwi do mózgu** apoplexy, stroke; **~wać** (*-am*) *v/t.* pour out; F *kogoś z pracy* give the boot; *v/i. rzeka*: overflow; **~wać się** spill; **~źć** *pf.* → **wyłazić**

wylęga|ć się (*-am*) → **lęgnąć się**; **~nie** *n* (*-a*; *0*) incubation; hatching; **~rnia** *f* (*-i*; *-e*) *agr.* hatchery; *fig.* hotbed

wylęk|ły, ~niony frightened, scared

wylicz|ać (*-am*) ⟨**~yć**⟩ enumerate, list; (*obliczyć*) calculate, count; *sport*: count out; **~yć się** (**z** *G*) account (for)

wylosow(yw)ać (*-[w]uję*) draw out

wylot *m* (*-u*; *-y*) (*otwór*) outlet, vent; (*rury*) nozzle; (*lufy*) muzzle; (*ulicy itp.*) end, exit; (*odlot*) departure; **na ~** through and through

wyludniony desolate, depopulated

wyład|ow(yw)ać (*-[w]uję*) unload; *naut.* land; *fig. złość* vent (**na** *L* on); **~ow(yw)ać się** *electr.* run down; *fig.* take it out (**na** *L* on); **~owanie** *n* (*-a*; *G -ań*) *electr.* discharge; **~unek** *m* (*-nku*; *-nki*) unloading

wyłam|ywać (*-uję*) ⟨**~ać**⟩ break (**się** *v/i.*); *zamek* force; **~ywać** ⟨**~ać**⟩ **się** (**z** *G*) *fig.* break away (from)

wyłaniać (*-am*) *komisję* form; **~ się** emerge, appear

wyłazić (*-żę*) (**z** *G*) climb out (of), get out (of)

wyłącz|ać (*-am*) switch off, turn off (**się** *v/i.*); (*pomijać*) exclude; *tech.* disengage, disconnect; **~ać się** go off; **~enie** *n* (*-a*; *G -eń*) switching off; (*pominięcie*) exclusion; **~nie** *adv.* exclusively; **~nik** *m* (*-a*; *-i*) switch; **~ny** exclusive, sole

wyłogi *m/pl.* (*-ów*) lapels *pl.*

wyło|m *m* (*-u*; *-y*) breach, break; **~nić** *pf.* (*-ę*) → **wyłaniać**; **~żyć** *pf.* → **wykładać**; **~żyć się** (**na** *L*) trip up (on, over)

wyłudz|ać (*-am*) ⟨**~ić**⟩ swindle (**coś od k-o** s.o. out of s.th.)

wyłusk|iwać (*-uję*) ⟨**~ać**⟩ → **łuskać**

wyłuszcz|ać (*-am*) ⟨**~yć**⟩ → **łuszczyć**; *fig.* explain, set forth

wyłysiały bald

wymaga|ć (*-am*) (*G*) require; (*potrzebować też*) need, necessitate; **~jący** *adj. szef* demanding, exacting; **~nie** *n* (*-a*; *G -ań*) *zw. pl.* demands *pl.*, requirements *pl.*; **~ny** required, needed

wymar|cie *n* (*-a*; *0*): **być na ~ciu** be threatened with extinction; **~ły** extinct

wymarsz *m* (*-u*; *-e*) departure, marching off

wymarzony ideal

wymawiać *słowa* pronounce; *umowę* terminate; **~ sobie** reproach o.s.; **~ się** be pronounced; → **wykręcać się, wytykać**

wymaz|ywać (*-uję*) ⟨**~ać**⟩ (*farbą*) smear, daub; (*usuwać*) rub out

wymeldow(yw)ać (*-[w]uję*) report moving away (**się** *v/i.*); (*w hotelu*) check out (**się** *v/i.*)

wymian|a *f* (*-y*; *G -*) exchange (*też waluty*); (*kogoś*, *rury*) replacement; → **wymieniać**

wymiar *m* (*-u*; *-y*) dimension (*też math.*, *phys.*); size; **~ kary** sentence; **~ sprawiedliwości** administration of justice; **~ podatku** assessment; **~ godzin** teaching load

wy|miatać (*-am*) sweep out; **~mie-**

W

ni(a)ć (*-am*) exchange; *część itp.* replace; *pieniądze* change; (*wspominać*) mention, name; **~mienialny** *waluta* convertible; **~mieniony** mentioned, named; **~mienny** replaceable; interchangeable

wymie|rać (*-am*) die out; **~rny** measurable; *math.* rational; **~rzać** (*-am*) ⟨**~rzyć**⟩ measure; *karę* (*D*) mete out (to); *podatek* assess; *sprawiedliwość* administer; (*skierować*) direct, aim (**przeciwko** *D* at); → ***mierzyć***; **~ść** *pf.* → ***wymiatać***

wymię *n* (*-ienia*; *-iona*) udder

wymi|jać (*-am*) ⟨**~nąć**⟩ pass, go past; ***~jać się*** meet and pass, cross; → **(*o*)*mijać***; **~jająco** *adv.* evasively; **~jający** evasive

wymiot|ować (*-uję*) ⟨**z-**⟩ vomit; **~y** *pl.* (*-ów*) vomiting

wymknąć się *pf.* → ***wymykać się***

wymogi *m/pl.* (*-ogów*) requirements *pl.*

wymontow(yw)ać (*-[w]uję*) remove, dismount

wymow|a *f* (*-y*; *0*) pronunciation; **~ny** eloquent, outspoken

wymóc *pf.* (**na** *L*) wrest (from), extort (from)

wymów|ić *pf.* → ***wymawiać***; **~ienie** *n* (*-a*) → ***wymawianie***; **~ka** *f* (*-i*; *G -wek*) excuse; (*wyrzut*) reproach

wymrzeć *pf.* → ***wymierać***

wymu|szać (*-am*) ⟨**~sić**⟩ (*-szę*) (**z** *G*) force (from, out of), extract (from); (**na** *L*) extort (from); **~szenie** *n* (*-a*; *G -eń*) extortion; extraction; **~szony** *fig.* half-hearted

wymykać się (*-am*) slip away; *fig.* slip out

wymy|sł *m* (*-u*; *-y*) invention; (*przekleństwa*) *zw. pl.* insults *pl*; **~ślać** (*-am*) ⟨**~ślić**⟩ (*-lę*) invent, make up; *t-ko impf.* (*D*) insult; **~ślny** intricate, fancy

wynagr|adzać (*-am*) ⟨**~odzić**⟩ (*-ę*) reward, award; *krzywdy itp.* compensate, recompense

wynagrodzenie *n* (*-a*; *G -eń*) payment, pay; compensation

wyna|jąć *pf.* → **(*wy*)*najmować***; **~jdywać** (*-uję*) find; → ***wynaleźć***; **~jem** *m* (*-jmu*; *0*), **~jęcie** renting; ***~jem samochodu*** car rental *lub Brt.* hire; ***biuro ~jmu samochodów*** car rental *lub Brt.* hire car rental (firm); **~jmować** (*-uję*) rent, hire; *mieszkanie* let; (*oddać w najem*) rent out, let out; **~lazca** *m* (*-y*; *G -ców*) inventor; **~lazek** *m* (*-zku*; *-zki*) invention; **~leźć** invent; → ***wyszukać***

wynaturzenie *n* (*-a*; *G -eń*) degeneration

wynegocjować *pf.* (*-uję*) negotiate

wynieść *pf.* → ***wynosić***

wynik *m* (*-u*; *-i*) result (*też med.*); finding; (*w sporcie*) score; ***~i*** *pl. też* achievements *pl.*; ***w ~u*** (*G*) as a result (of); **~ać** (*-am*) ⟨**~nąć**⟩ (**z** *G*) result (from); *zw. impf.* follow, ensue

wynio|sły haughty, proud; **~śle** *adv.* haughtily, proudly

wyniszcz|ać (*-am*) ⟨**~yć**⟩ destroy; *kogoś* emaciate, weaken

wynos: ***na ~*** *Brt.* take-away, *Am.* take-out; **~ić** take *lub* carry away (**z** *G* from); carry up (**na** *A* to); *sumę, ilość* amount to; ***~ić się*** F leave; (*z dumą*) turn one's nose up; ***wynoś się!*** get away!

wynurz|ać (*-am*) ⟨**~yć**⟩ put *lub* stick out (***z wody*** of the water); ***~yć się*** emerge, appear

wyobcowany alienated (**z** *G* from)

wyobra|źnia *f* (*-i*; *0*) imagination; **~żać** ⟨**~zić**⟩ represent; ***~żać sobie*** imagine; ***~ź sobie***(**, *że***) just imagine (that); **~żenie** *n* (*-a*; *G -eń*) idea, notion; representation, picture

wyodrębni|ać (*-am*) ⟨**~ć**⟩ (*-ę*, *-nij!*) isolate, detach (***się*** o.s.); ***~*(*a*)*ć się*** (*I*) differ (from), stand out (from)

wyolbrzymi|ać (*-am*)⟨~ć⟩(*-ę*) exaggerate, overestimate

wypacz|ać (*-am*) ⟨**~yć**⟩ *fig.* distort

wypad *m* (*-u*; *-y*) trip; (*w szermierce*) lunge; (*w piłce nożnej*) attack; *mil.* foray; **~ać** fall out; (*wybiec*) rush out; fall (***w niedzielę*** on Sunday); do, turn out (***dobrze, źle*** well, badly); (*nagle zaistnieć*) pop up; ***~a*(*ło*)** it is (was) proper, it is (was) in order; (***nie***) ***~a*** one should not, it is not fitting; *fig.* ***~ać na kogoś*** be s.o.'s turn; ***~ać z pamięci*** escape s.o.'s mind; **~ek** *m* (*-dku*; *-dki*) event, case; (***drogowy, przy pracy***, road, industrial) accident; ***na ~ek*** (*G*) in case (of); ***w najlepszym ~ku*** at best; ***w żadnym ~ku*** in no case, on no account; **~kowy** accident

wypal|ać (*-am*) ⟨**~ić**⟩ burn out; *cegły itp.* fire; ***~ić się*** burn out

W

wypa|row(yw)ać (-[*w*]*uję*) evaporate; *fig.* vanish **~siony** well-fed; **~ść** *pf.* → ***wypadać***; **~trywać** (*-uję*) (*G*) look out (for); **~trzyć** *pf.* catch sight of; *fig.* spot

wypch|ać, ~nąć *pf.* → ***wypychać***

wypeł|niać (*-am*) ⟨**~nić**⟩ → ***spełniać***; fill (**się** *v/i.*); *blankiet* fill in, complete; *zadanie* carry out; **~niony** full; *formularz* completed; **~zać** ⟨**~znąć**⟩ (**z** *G*) crawl out (of)

wypędz|ać (*-am*) ⟨**~ić**⟩ drive (***na pastwisko*** to the pasture); drive out; (*z kraju itp.*) expel; **~ony** expelled

wypi|ąć *pf.* → ***wypinać***; **~ć** *pf.* → ***wypijać***

wypiek *m* (*-u*; *-i*) baking; (*pieczywo*) baked product; **~i** *pl.* flush, blush; **~ać** (*-am*) → **piec²**

wypierać (*-am*) *konkurenta* oust; (*z miejsca*) dislodge; *phys.* displace; **~ się** (*G*) deny; *kogoś* disown

wypi|jać (*-am*) drink up; **~nać** (*-am*) push out; *tyłek itp.* stick out

wypis *m* (*-u*; *-y*) extract; **~y** *pl.* anthology; **~ywać** (*-uję*) ⟨**~ać**⟩ *czek*, *receptę* write *lub* make out; take notes (**sobie** for o.s.); (*ze szkoły itp.*) strike off the list; (*ze szpitala*) discharge; **~ać się** (**z** *G*) withdraw (from); *pióro itp.*: run out

wypitka *f* (*-i*; *G -tek*) drink

wypląt|ywać (*-uję*) ⟨**~ać**⟩ disentangle (**się** *v/i.*); **~ywać** ⟨**~ać**⟩ **się** *fig.* free o.s. (**z** *G* from)

wypleni|ać (*-am*) ⟨**~ć**⟩ eradicate

wyplu|wać (*-am*) ⟨**~(ną)ć**⟩ spit out

wypła|cać (*-am*) ⟨**~cić**⟩ pay; **~calny** solvent; **~szać** *pf.* → **płoszyć**; **~ta** *f* (*-y*; *G -*) payment, pay; ***dzień ~ty*** payday

wypłoszyć *pf.* → **płoszyć**

wypłowiały faded

wypłuk|iwać (*-uję*) ⟨**~ać**⟩ wash out *lub* away

wypły|wać ⟨**~nąć**⟩ swim out; (*łódką*) sail out; *płyn*: flow out; → ***wynurzać się, wynikać***

wypocz|ąć *pf.* → ***wypoczywać***; **~ęty** rested; **~ynek** *m* (*-nku*; *-nki*) rest; **~ynkowy** holiday; ***meble*** *pl.* ***~ynkowe*** suite; **~ywać** (*-am*) rest (**po** *L* after)

wypo|gadzać się (*-am*) ⟨**~godzić się**⟩ clear up, brighten up; **~minać** (*-am*) ⟨**~mnieć**⟩ (*-nę*, *-nij!*) reproach (**k-u** *A* s.o. for); **~mpow(yw)ać** (-[*w*]*uję*) pump out

wyporność *f* (*-ści*; *0*) *naut.* draught

wyposaż|ać (*-am*) ⟨**~yć**⟩ (*-ę*) fit (**w** *A* with); equip; **~enie** *n* (*-a*; *G -eń*) furnishing *pl.*; (*urządzenia*) fittings *pl.*; equipment

wypowi|adać (*-am*) utter; *pracę*, *mieszkanie* give notice; *wojnę* declare; *posłuszeństwo* renounce; **~adać się** (***za*** *I*, ***przeciwko*** *D*) declare *lub* pronounce o.s. (for, against); **~edzenie** *n* (*-a*; *G -eń*) utterance; notice; declaration; **~edzieć** *pf.* → ***wypowiadać***; **~edź** *f* (*-dzi*) statement; utterance

wypożycz|alnia *f* (*-i*; *-e*) (*sprzętu itp.*) hire firm; (*książek*, *płyt*) (lending) library; **~yć** *pf.* *komuś* lend, *od kogoś* borrow; → ***pożyczać***

wypracow|anie *n* (*-a*; *G -ań*) essay, composition; **~(yw)ać** (-[*w*]*uję*) work out, develop

wypra|ć *pf.* → ***prać***; **~szać** (*-am*) beg for; *natręta* show the door

wyprawa *f* (*-y*; *G -*) expedition; ***~ krzyżowa*** crusade; (*ślubna*) trousseau; → ***wycieczka***

wypraw|iać (*-am*) ⟨**~ić**⟩ send (**do** *G*, **na** *A* to; **po** *A* for); (*robić*) do; *wesele* make; *skóry* dress; **~ka** *f* (*-i*; *G -wek*) layette

wypręż|ać (*-am*) ⟨**~yć**⟩ (*-ę*) stretch (**się** *v/i.*); tense; **~ony** tight, taut

wypro|sić *pf.* → ***wypraszać***; **~stowywać** (*-wuję*) → ***prostować***

wyprowadz|ać (*-am*) ⟨**~ić**⟩ lead out; *auto itp.* drive out; *fig.* *wniosek* draw; *math.* *wzór* derive; *psa* walk, take out; ***~ić z równowagi*** unnerve; ***~ić się*** move out

wy|próbowany tested; **~próbow(yw)ać** (-[*w*]*uję*) test, try out; **~próżni(a)ć** → ***opróżniać***; **~prysk** *m* (*-u*; *-i*) *med.* eczema; **~prysnąć** *pf.* dash; **~prząc** *pf.* → ***wyprzęgać***; **~przeć** *pf.* → ***wypierać***

wyprzedany sold out

wyprzeda|wać (*-ję*) ⟨**~ć**⟩ (*-am*) sell off, clear; **~ż** *f* (*-y*; *-e*) sale(s *pl.*)

wyprzedz|ać (*-am*) ⟨**~ić**⟩ (*-dzę*) *mot.* *Brt.* overtake, *Am.* pass; ***~ać epokę*** *fig.* be ahead of one's times

wyprzęgać (*-am*) unharness

wypukł|ość *f* (*-ści*; *0*) bulge; *tech.* convexity; **~o** *adv.* convexly; **~y** convex

wypu|szczać (*-am*) ⟨**~ścić**⟩ set free; *film*, *więźnia*, release; (*upuszczać*)

drop, let drop; *znaczek itp.* issue; *econ.* put on the market; *tech.* discharge
wypychać (*-am*) pack (up), fill (up); *zwierzę* stuff
wypyt|ywać (*-uję*) ⟨**~ać**⟩ question
wyrabiać (*-am*) make, produce; *sąd* form; *paszport* obtain; *język itp.* develop; **~ się** develop, evolve
wyrachowan|ie *n* (*-a*; *0*) deliberation, calculation; **~y** calculating, mercenary
wyra|dzać się (*-am*) degenerate; **~finowany** sophisticated; **~stać** (*-am*) grow; → ***rosnąć***
wyraz *m* (*-u*; *-y*) expression; (*słowo*) word; ***dać ~*** (*D*) voice; ***bez ~u*** expressionless, bland; ***nad ~*** decidedly; ***z ~ami szacunku*** yours faithfully; **~ić** *pf.* → ***wyrażać***; **~isty** expressive; distinct; **~iście** *adv.* expressively; distinct
wyra|źny distinct; clear; **~żać** (*-am*) express (***się*** o.s.); ***~żać się*** *też* be expressed (***w*** *L* by); **~żenie** *n* (*-a*) expression; ***~żenie zgody*** consent, approval
wy|rąbywać (*-uję*) ⟨**~rąbać**⟩ *drzewa* fell; *polanę* clear (of trees); *otwór* hack; **~re-** *pf.* → ***re-***
wyręcz|ać (*-am*) ⟨**~yć**⟩ (***kogoś w*** *L*) stand in (for s.o. in); (***on***) ***w tych sprawach ~a się synem*** these things are done by his son
wyrob|ić (*-ę*) *pf.* → ***wyrabiać***; **~ienie** *n* (*-a*; *0*) skill; expertness; ***~ienie życiowe*** experience of life; **~y** *pl.* → ***wyrób***
wyrocznia *f* (*-i*; *G -e*) oracle
wyro|dek *m* (*-dka*; *-dki*) monster; **~dnieć** ⟨**z-**⟩ (*-eję*) degenerate; **~dny** prodigal, profligate; ***~dna matka*** uncaring mother; **~dzić się** *pf.* → ***wyradzać się***
wyrok *m* (*-u*; *-i*) *jur.* judg(e)ment, sentence, verdict; ***~ skazujący*** conviction; **~ować** ⟨**za-**⟩ (*-uję*) decide
wyros|nąć *pf.* → ***wyrastać***; **~t**: ***na ~t*** a size larger; **~tek** *m* (*-tka*; *-tki*) adolescent, teenager; *anat.* ***~tek robaczkowy*** (vermiform) appendix
wyrozumia|le *adv.* forbearingly; understandingly; **~ły** forbearing; understanding
wyrób *m* (*-robu*; *-roby*) production, manufacture; ***wyroby*** *pl. econ.* goods *pl.*, products *pl.*
wyrówn|ać *pf.* → ***wyrównywać***; **~anie** *n* (*-a*; *G -ań*) evening out; (*płaca*) additional payment; (*zadośćuczynienie*) compensation; (*w sporcie*) equalizer; **~any** balanced; *pogoda* equable; **~awczy** compensation; **~ywać** (*-uję*) *wyniki* bring into line; *wynik*, *powierzchnię* level; *dług* settle; *zaległości* make up for; (*w sporcie*) level, equalize; ***~ywać się*** balance out; level out; → ***równać***
wyróżni|ać (*-am*) ⟨**~ć**⟩ favo(u)r; (*A*) give preferential treatment (to); (*wyodrębniać*) distinguish; ***~ać się*** distinguish o.s.; **~enie** *n* (*-a*; *G -eń*) distinction; award; ***z ~eniem*** with merit *lub* distinction
wyru|gować (*-uję*) *pf.* drive out, oust; **~szać** ⟨**~szyć**⟩ set off, start out; ***~szyć w podróż*** set out on a journey
wyrwa *f* (*-y*; *G -*) gap; **~ć** *pf.* → ***wyrywać***; ***~ć się*** blurt out (***z czymś*** s.th.)
wyryw|ać (*-am*) snatch; *ząb*, *korzenie* pull out; *fig.* (***z*** *G*) arouse (from); ***~ać się*** blurt out (***z czymś*** s.th.); → ***wyrwać***; **~kowo** *adv.* randomly; **~kowy** random
wyrządz|ać (*-am*) ⟨**~ić**⟩ *szkody* cause; *krzywdę* do
wyrze|c *pf.* → ***wyrzekać***; **~czenie** *n* (*-a*; *G -eń*) sacrifice; ***~czenie się*** renunciation; **~kać** (*-am*) complain (***na*** *A* about); ***~kać się*** (*G*) give up, renounce
wyrznąć *pf.* → ***wyrzynać***
wyrzu|cać (*-am*) ⟨**~cić**⟩ throw out *lub* away; (*z pracy*) F give the boot, fire; **~t** *m* (*-u*; *-y*) reproach; ***~y*** *pl.* ***sumienia*** remorses *pl.*; **~tnia** *f* (*-i*; *-e*) *astr.*, *mil.* launch(ing) pad; launcher
wyrzyna|ć (*-am*) ⟨***wyrznąć***⟩ cut out; ***jemu ~ją się ząbki*** he is teething
wys. *skrót pisany*: ***wysokość***
wysadz|ać (*-am*) ⟨**~ić**⟩ blow up; (*z autobusu*) put down; (*z auta*) drop off; ***~ić na ląd*** disembark, put ashore; ***~ić w powietrze*** blow up
wyschnąć *pf.* → ***wysychać***
wysepka *f* (*-pki*; *G -pek*) → ***wyspa***; islet; ***~ na jezdni*** traffic island
wysia|ć *pf.* → ***wysiewać***; **~dać** ⟨***wysiąść***⟩ get off; disembark
wysiedl|ać (*-am*) ⟨**~ić**⟩ (*-lę*) evacuate
wysiedlenie *n* (*-a*; *G -eń*) evacuation; displacement; **~c** *m* (*-a*; *-y*) displaced person
wy|siewać (*-am*) sow; **~silać** (*-am*) ⟨**~silić**⟩ *oczy itp.* strain; ***~silać się*** exert o.s.; **~siłek** *m* (*-łku*; *-łki*) effort;

W

~skakiwać⟨***~skoczyć***⟩ jump *lub* leap out; **~skok** *m* excess; → ***wypad***; **~skokowy** alcoholic; **~skrobywać** (*-uję*) ⟨***~skrobać***⟩ scrape out; **~skubywać** (*-uję*) → ***skubać***; **~słać** *pf.* → ***wysyłać, wyściełać***
wysłanni|czka *f* (*-i*; *G -czek*), **~k** *m* (*-a*; *-cy*) messenger
wysławiać[1] (*-am*) extol(l)
wysł|awiać[2] (*-am*) ⟨***~owić***⟩ (**się**) express (o.s.) (in words)
wysłuch|iwać (*-uję*) ⟨***~ać***⟩ (*G*, *A*) listen (to)
wysłu|giwać się (*-uję*) (*D*) *pej.* grovel (to); (*I*) use; **~żyć się** *pf.*: ***~żył się*** it has seen service, it has worn out
wy|sma- *pf.* → ***sma-***; **~smukły** slender
wysnu|wać (*-am*) ⟨***~ć***⟩ *wniosek* draw
wyso|ce *adv.* highly; **~ki** high; *człowiek* tall; *electr.* ***~kie napięcie*** high-voltage current; ***~ki na 10 m*** 10 *Brt.* metres high (*Am.* meters)
wysoko *adv.* highly; **~gatunkowy** high-quality; **~górski** alpine
wysokoś|ciomierz *m* (*-a*; *-e*) altimeter; **~ciowiec** *m* (*-wca*; *-wce*) high-rise; **~ć** *f* (*-ści*) height; altitude; (*na poziomem morza*) elevation; ***na dużej ~ci*** at a high altitude; ***o ~ci …*** … high; *kwota itp.*: ***w ~ci …*** in the amount (of) …; ***nabierać ~ci*** gain height
wysoko|wartościowy high-quality; **~wydajny** highly efficient; *drukarka itp.* heavy-duty
wysp|a *f* (*-y*; *G -*) island (*też fig.*), isle; ***&y Brytyjskie*** *pl.* British Isles *pl.*; ***&y Normandzkie*** *pl.* Channel Islands *pl.*
wyspać się *pf.* get enough sleep
wyspia|rka *f* (*-i*; *G -rek*), **~rz** *m* (*-a*; *-e*) islander
wysportowany athletic
wy|ssać *pf.* (*-ę*) → ***wysysać***; **~stający** protruding, projecting; **~starać się** (***o*** *A*) arrange, get
wystarcz|ać (*-am*) ⟨***~yć***⟩ be sufficient; ***~yło …*** it was enough …; **~ająco** *adv.* sufficiently; **~ający** sufficient
wystaw|a *f* (*-y*; *G -*) exhibition, display, show; (*witryna*) shop-window; **~ać** (*-ję*) protrude, jut out, stick out; (*stać*) stand (for a long time); **~ca** *m* (*-y*; *G -ców*) exhibitor
wystawi(a)ć put out; *obraz, towar* display; *czek* make out; *produkty itp.* offer (***na*** *A* for); *wartę* post; *kandydata* put up; *theat.* stage; *pomnik* erect; *dom* build; (*narażać*) expose; (***na*** *A* to); ***~ na próbę*** test; ***~ się*** (***na*** *A* to) be exposed (to), risk
wystaw|ny sumptuous; **~owy** exhibition, display
wystąpi|ć *pf.* → ***występować***; **~enie** *n* (*-a*; *G -eń*) appearance; presentation; speech
występ *m* (*-u*; *-y*) (*muru*) projection; *theat. itp.* appearance; **~ek** *m* (*-pku*; *-pki*) vice; *jur.* felony; **~ny** criminal; punishable; **~ować** (*-uję*) come out; (*istnieć*) occur; (*ukazać się*) appear, make an appearance (***w, na*** *L* in, at); act (***jako*** as); give (***z mową*** a speech; ***z koncertem*** a concert); come out (***w obronie*** *G* in support of); be (***przeciwko*** *D* against); put forward (***z wnioskiem*** a proposition); make (***z prośbą*** a request); (*opuścić*) (***z*** *A*) leave; *rzeka*: burst (***z brzegów*** the banks)
wy|stosować *pf.* address; **~straszyć** *pf.* → (***prze***)***straszyć***; **~strojony** decked out; **~strzał** *m* shot
wystrze|gać się (*-am*) (*G*) be wary (of); avoid, shun; **~lać** *pf.* shoot dead; *amunicję* use up; **~lić** *pf.* (***z*** *G*) fire; *astr.* launch
wystrzępiony frayed
wystu-, wysty- *pf.* → ***stu-, sty-***
wysu|wać ⟨***~nąć***⟩ pull out (**się** *v/i.*); *nogę* stick out; *żądanie* make, put forward; (*proponować*) suggest, propose; → ***wymykać się***
wyswo|badzać (*-am*) ⟨***~bodzić***⟩ (*-dzę, -bódź*) free (**się** o.s.)
wysy|chać (*-am*) dry up; **~łać** (*-am*) send; **~łka** *f* (*-i*; *G -łek*) dispatch; (*czynność*) shipping; **~pać** *pf.* → ***wysypywać***; **~pisko** *n* (*-a*; *G -*) (***śmieci*** refuse) dump (*Brt.* tip); **~pka** *f* (*-i*; *G -pek*) *med.* rash; **~pywać** (*-uję*) tip out; scatter (***piaskiem*** sand); ***~pywać się*** spill; **~sać** (*-am*) suck out
wyszarp|ywać (*-uję*) ⟨***~ać, ~nąć***⟩ → ***wydzierać, wyrywać***
wyszczególni|ać (*-am*) ⟨***~ć***⟩ (*-ę, -nij!*) list, cite; specify
wyszcze|rbiony jagged; *talerz* chipped **~rzać** *pf.* → ***szczerzyć***
wysz|czo-, ~czu-, ~k-, ~l-, ~o- *pf.* → ***szczo-, szczu-, szk-, szl-, szo-***

W

wyszpiegować *pf.* spy out
wyszuka|ć *pf.* find; choose, pick; **~ny** → ***wykwintny, wytworny***
wyszukiwarka *f* (*-i*) *komp.* search engine
wyszy|ć *pf.* → ***wyszywać***; **~dzać** (*-am*) ⟨***~dzić***⟩ mock, deride, ridicule
wyszynk *m* (*-u*; *0*) liquor *Brt.* licence, *Am.* license; ***z ~iem*** selling liquor
wyszywać (*-am*) sew; *zwł.* embroider
wyście|lać (*-am*), **~łać** *kurtkę* pad; *meble* upholster
wyścig *m* (*-u*; *-i*) race (*też fig.*); ***~ zbrojeń*** arms race; ***~i*** *pl. też* racing; ***na ~i*** racing one another; *fig.* vying with one another; **~owiec** *m* (*-wca*; *-wcy*) racehorse; **~owy** racing, race; **~ówka** *f* (*-i*; *G -wek*) (*rower*) racing bike; (*łyżwa*) speed skate
wyśledzić *pf.* spy out
wyśliz|giwać się (*-uję*) ⟨***~(g)nąć się***⟩ (*-nę*) slip (***z ręki*** out of the hand; ***z sukienki*** out of the dress)
wyś|miać *pf.* → ***wyśmiewać***; **~mienicie** *adv.* exquisitely; **~mienity** exquisite; **~piewywać** (*-uję*) sing
wyświadcz|ać (*-am*) ⟨***~yć***⟩ do
wyświechtany well-worn, threadbare
wyświetl|ać (*-am*) ⟨***~ić***⟩ (*-lę*) *film* show; *sprawę* clear up; (*na ekranie*) display; **~acz** *m* (*-a*; *-e*) *komp.* display
wyświę|cać (*-am*)⟨***~cić***⟩(*-ę*) *rel.* ordain
wyta|czać *pf.* → ***(wy)toczyć***; **~piać** (*-am*) *metal* melt; **~rty** threadbare; → ***wyświechtany***
wytchnieni|e *n* (*-a*; *0*) rest; respite; ***bez ~a*** without intermission *lub* rest; ***chwila ~a*** breather
wytę|- *pf.* → ***tę-***; **~pienie** *n* (*-a*; *0*) extermination; eradication; **~żać** (*-am*) ⟨***~żyć***⟩ (*-ę*) strain; ***~żać się*** exert o.s.; **~żony** intense, concentrated
wy|tknąć *pf.* → ***wytykać***; **~tłaczać** (*-am*) ⟨***~tłoczyć***⟩ press *lub* squeeze out; → ***tłoczyć***
wytłumaczenie *n* (*-a*; *G -eń*) explanation
wy|tnę, ~tnie(sz) → ***wycinać***; **~toczyć** *pf. proces* institute; → ***toczyć***; **~topić** *pf.* → ***wytapiać***; **~tra-** *pf.* → ***tra-***; **~trawny** *podróżnik* seasoned; *wino* dry; **~trącać** (*-am*)⟨***~trącić***⟩ knock out (***z ręki*** of the hand); wake (***ze snu*** *s.o.* from the sleep); ***~trącić z równowagi*** upset (*też fig.*); *chem.* precipitate; **~tropić** *pf.* track down
wytrwa|ć *pf.* stand, withstand; persevere (***w swoim zamiarze*** in one's intention); **~łość** *f* (*-ści*; *0*) (*duchowa*) perseverance; (*fizyczna*) stamina; **~le** *adv.* persistently; **~ły** persistent
wytrych *m* (*-u*; *-y*) passkey
wytrys|k *m* (*-u*; *-i*) jet; (*nasienia*) ejaculation; **~kiwać** (*-uję*) ⟨***~kać, ~nąć***⟩ (*nasieniem*) ejaculate; → ***tryskać***
wytrzą|sać (*-am*) ⟨***~snąć, ~ść***⟩ shake out; ***~ść się*** be shaken
wytrze|ć *pf.* → ***wycierać***; **~pywać** (*-uję*) → ***trzepać***
wytrzeszczać (*-am*) ⟨***wytrzeszczyć***⟩: ***~ oczy*** goggle (***na*** *A* at)
wytrzeźwieć *pf.* sober up
wytrzyma|ć *pf.* → ***wytrzymywać*** **~łość** *f* (*-ści*; *0*) strength, resistance (*też tech.*); (*kogoś*) endurance, stamina; *tech.* durability; **~ły** strong; durable; (***na*** *A*) resistant (to); **~nie** *n*: ***nie do ~nia*** unbearable, unendurable
wytrzymywać (*-uję*) stand, bear, endure; *atak* withstand; *próbę* pass; *krytykę* stand up to
wytwarzać (*-am*) produce, manufacture; *fig.* create; ***~ się*** be formed; be produced
wytwo|rny refined, classy; **~rzyć** *pf.* → ***wytwarzać***
wytwór *m* (*-woru*; *-wory*) product; **~ca** *m* (*-y*; *G -ców*) producer; **~czość** *f* (*-ści*; *0*) production; **~czy** productive; **~nia** *f* (*-i*; *-e*) factory; ***~nia filmowa*** film company; (*miejsce*) film studios *pl.*
wytycz|ać (*-am*) *trasę* mark out; *fig.* lay down; **~na** *f* (*-ej*; *-e*) directive, guideline; **~yć** *pf.* → ***wytyczać***
wyty|kać reproach (***komuś coś*** s.o. for s.th.); F *głowę* stick out; **~po-** *pf.* → ***typo-***
wyucz|ać (*-am*) ⟨***~yć***⟩ (***k-o*** *G*) teach (s.th. to s.o.), educate (s.o. in s.th.)
wyuzdany unrestrained, unbridled
wywa|biacz *m* (*-a*; *-e*) (***plam*** stain) remover; **~biać** (*-am*) ⟨***~bić***⟩ *plamę* remove; **~lać** (*-am*) throw out; (*z pracy*) fire; *drzwi* force; **~lczyć** *pf.* win; **~lić** *pf.* → ***wywalać***; ***~lić się*** F fall (down)
wywar *m* (*-u*; *-y*): ***~ z mięsa*** meat stock
wyważ|ać (*-am*)⟨***~yć***⟩(*-ę*) *drzwi* force; *wieko* pry open; *tech.* balance; **~ony** balanced

wywąch|iwać (*-uję*) ⟨**~ać, wywęszyć**⟩ scent; *fig.* sense
wywiad *m* (*-u*; *-y*) interview; *med.* case history, anamnesis; *mil.*, *pol.* intelligence; **~owca** *m* (*-y*; *G -ców*) secret agent; (*w policji itp.*) detective; **~ówka** *f* (*-i*; *G -wek*) parents' meeting; **~ywać się** (*-uję*) enquire (**o** *A* about)
wywiąz|ywać się (*-uję*) ⟨**~ać się**⟩ (**z** *G*) result (from), ensue (from); discharge, perform (**z zadań** one's duties)
wy|wichnąć *pf.* (*-nę*) → **zwichnąć**; **~wiedzieć się** *pf.* → **wywiadywać się**; **~wierać** (*-am*) *nacisk*, *wpływ* exert; *wrażenie* make; *skutek* produce
wywie|rcać (*-am*) ⟨**~rcić**⟩ bore (out), drill (out); **~szać** ⟨**~sić**⟩ (*-szę*) hang out; **~szka** *f* (*-i*; *G -szek*) sign; notice; **~ść** *pf.* → **wywodzić**; **~trzeć** *pf.* → **wietrzeć**; **~trznik** *m* (*-a*; *-i*) ventilator; **~źć** *pf.* → **wywozić**
wywi|jać (*-am*) ⟨**~nąć**⟩ (*-nę*) *rękaw* roll up; (*I*) brandish (with), flourish (with); **~nąć się** (**z**, *fig.* **od** *G*) evade, wriggle (out of); **~kłać** (**się**) (*-am*) *pf.* → **wyplątywać** (**się**)
wy|wlekać (*-am*) ⟨**~wlec**⟩ pull out; drag out; *fig.* draw up; **~właszczać** (*-am*) ⟨**~właszczyć**⟩ (*-szczę*) expropriate; **~wnętrzać się** (*-am*) (**przed** *I*) pour out one's heart (to); **~wnio-** *pf.* → **wnio-**
wywo|dy *pf.* → **wywód**; **~dzić** (*-dzę*) lead out (**z** *G* of); *fig.* derive (**z** *G* from); set forth; **~dzić się** (**z** *G*) be descended (from), come (from); **~łać** *pf.* → **wywoływać**
wywoły|wacz *m* (*-a*; *-e*) *phot.* developer; **~wać** (*-uję*) call out (**do** *G* to); call (up)on (**do odpowiedzi** for an answer); *uczucie* evoke; *panikę itp.* cause; *dyskusję* provoke; *phot.* develop; → **powodować**
wy|wozić take away; F (*za granicę*) take abroad; (*eksportować*) export; **~wód** *m* (*-odu*; *-ody*) argument; exposition; deduction; **~wóz** *m* (*-ozu*; *0*) export; transport; → **~wózka** *f* (*-i*; *G -zek*) deportation; **~wracać** (*-am*) knock over; (*do góry nogami*) overturn; *łódź* capsize (**się** *v/i.*); *kieszeń* turn inside out; **~wracać się** fall down; *coś*: overturn; **~wrotny** unbalanced; *naut.* crank(y), tender; **~wrotowy** subversive; **działalność ~wrotowa** subversion; **~wrócić** *pf.* → **wywracać**; **~wróżyć** *pf.* → **wróżyć**; **~wrzeć** *pf.* (→ *-wrzeć*) → **wywierać**; **~zbywać się** ⟨**~zbyć się**⟩ (*G*) dispose (of), get rid (of); *nawyku* give up
wyzdrowie|ć *pf.* (*-eję*) recover; **~nie** *n* (*-a*; *G -en*) recovery
wyziewy *m/pl.* (*-ów*) fumes *pl.*
wyziębi|ać (*-am*) ⟨**~ć**⟩ chill
wyzna|ć *pf.* → **wyznawać**; **~czać** (*-am*) ⟨**~czyć**⟩ mark; *fig.* (*określać*) name; *cenę* fix; appoint (**kogoś na kierownika** s.o. manager); **~nie** *n* (*-a*; *G -ań*) confession (*też rel.*); **~nie miłosne** declaration of love; **wolność ~nia** freedom of worship; **~niowy** confessional; **~wać** (*-ję*) *grzech*, *winę* confess; *winę też* own up to; *rel. impf.* declare one's faith
wyznaw|ca *m* (*-y*; *G -ców*), **~czyni** *f* (*-i*; *-e*) believer (**buddyzmu, chrześcijaństwa** of Buddhism, Christianity); worshipper; → **zwolennik** (**-iczka**)
wyzwa|ć *pf.* → **wyzywać**; **~lacz** *m* (*-a*; *-e*) *phot.* shutter release; **~lać** (*-am*) free (**się** o.s.; **od, z** *G* from, of), *kraj itp.* liberate; *energię* release; **~lać się** *też* release o.s.; **~nie** *n* (*-a*; *G -ań*) challenge
wyzwisko *n* (*-a*; *G -*) insult, abuse
wyzwol|enie *n* (*-a*; *G -eń*) liberation; **~eńczy** liberating; **~ić** *pf.* (*-lę*, *-wól!*) → **wyzwalać**
wyzysk *m* (*-u*; *0*) exploitation; **~(iw)ać** exploit
wyzywa|ć (*-am*) challenge (**na** *A*, **do** *G* to); F abuse, insult; **~jąco** *adv.* provocatively **~jący** provocative
wyż *m* (*-u*; *-e*) *meteor.* high (pressure); **~ demograficzny** population boom
wy|żąć *pf.* (*-żmę/-żnę*) → **wyżymać, wyżynać**; **~żebrać** *pf.* get by begging; **~żej** *adv.* (*comp. od* → **wysoki**) higher
wyżeł *m* (*-żła*; *-żły*) *zo.* pointer
wy|żerać (*-am*) *wszystko* eat up; *dziurę itp.* eat away; **~żłabiać** *pf.* → **żłobić**; **~żłobienie** *n* (*-a*; *G -eń*) groove; **~żowy** *meteor.* high-pressure **~żreć** *pf.* → **wyżerać**
wyższ|ość *f* (*-ści*; *0*) superiority; **z ~ością** in a patronizing manner, condescendingly; **~y** *adj.* (*comp. od* → **wysoki**) higher; **siła ~a** act of God
wyży|ć *pf.* survive; (**na** *L*) live (on); **~mać** (*-am*) wring; **~na** *f* (*-y*) plateau; **~ny** *pl.* uplands *pl.*; *fig.* height; **~nać** *pf.* → **żąć**; **~nny** highland

W

wyżywi|ać (*-am*) ⟨**~ć**⟩ feed; *rodzinę* keep
wyżywienie (*-a*; *0*) food; ***całodzienne ~*** full board; ***pokój z ~m*** board and lodging
wz. *skrót pisany*: ***w zastępstwie*** pp. (*by delegation to*)
wzajemn|ie *adv.* mutually, reciprocally; each other; (*dziękując*) the same to you; **~ość** *f* (*-ści*; *0*) mutuality; ***miłość bez ~ości*** unrequited love; **~y** mutual, reciprocal
wzbi|erać (*-am*) swell up; *rzeka*: rise; **~jać się** (*-am*) ⟨**~ć się**⟩ climb; rise
wzbogac|ać (*-am*) ⟨**~ić**⟩ enrich; ***~ać*** ⟨**~ić**⟩ **się** get rich; **~enie** *n* (*-a*; *G-eń*) enrichment
wzbr|aniać (*-am*) ⟨**~onić**⟩ prohibit, forbid; ***~aniać się*** (***przed*** *I*) shrink (from)
wzbudz|ać (*-am*) ⟨**~ić**⟩ *uczucie* wake, arouse; *tech.* induce; → ***wywoływać***; **~enie** *n* (*-a*; *0*) excitement; *tech.* induction
wzburz|ać (*-am*) ⟨**~yć**⟩ annoy, irritate; ***~ać*** ⟨**~yć**⟩ ***się*** get annoyed; → ***burzyć***; **~enie** *n* (*-a*; *G -eń*) annoyance, irritation; **~ony** annoyed; *morze* choppy
wzdąć *pf.* → ***wzdymać***
wzdęcie *n* (*-a*) *med.* flatulence
wzdłuż **1.** *prp.* (*G*) along; **2.** *adv.* lengthways; ***~ i wszerz*** all over
wzdryg|ać się (*-am*) ⟨**~nąć się**⟩ (*-nę*) shudder, start
wzdy|chać (*-am*) sigh; **~mać** (*-am*) distend; *policzki* puff out; *żagiel* billow (**się** *v/i.*)
wzejść (*-jść*) *pf.* → ***wschodzić***
wzgard|a *f* (*-y*; *0*) disdain, contempt; **~liwie** *adv.* disdainfully; **~liwy** disdainful
wzgardzić *pf.* (*I*) spurn
wzgl. *skrót pisany*: ***względnie*** or
wzgl|ąd *m* (*-lędu*; *-lędy*) respect; consideration; ***mieć na ~ędzie*** take into consideration; ***ze ~ędu*** (***na*** *A*) in view (of); ***pod tym ~ędem*** in this respect; ***~ędy*** *pl.* favo(u)rs *pl.*; grounds *pl.*, reasons *pl.*; → ***względem***
względ|em *prp.* (*G*) in relation (to); ***~em siebie*** to one another; **~nie** *adv.* relatively; or; **~ny** relative
wzgórek *m* (*-rka*; *-rki*) hill, hillock
wziąć *pf.* → ***brać***
wzię|cie *n* (*-a*; *0*) taking; popularity; ***~cie do niewoli*** capture; ***do ~cia*** to be taken; **~ty** popular, in demand
wzlatywać (*-uję*) ⟨**wzlecieć**⟩ fly up, soar (*też fig.*)
wzma|cniacz *m* (*-a*; *-e*) *tech.* amplifier; **~cniać** (*-am*) strengthen; *tech.* amplify; ***~cniać się*** get stronger; **~gać** (*-am*) intensify, strengthen, increase (**się** *v/i.*)
wzmianka *f* (*-i*; *G -nek*) mention (**o** *L* of)
wzmo|cnić *pf.* → ***wzmacniać***; **~cnienie** *n* (*-a*; *G -eń*) strengthening, intensification; *tech.* increase; **~żony** increased
wzmóc (**się**) *pf.* → ***wzmagać*** (**się**)
wznak *m*: ***na ~*** on one's back, supine
wznawiać (*-am*) *pracę* renew; *książkę* republish; *sztukę* revive; *film* rerun
wznie|cać (*-am*) ⟨**~cić**⟩ (*-cę*) *fig.* provoke, start, incite; **~sienie** *n* (*-a*; *G -eń*) hill; **~ść** *pf.* → ***wznosić***
wzniosły lofty; **~śle** *adv.* loftily
wzno|sić raise; *toast* propose; *dom*, *pomnik* build, erect; ***~sić się*** rise; **~wić** *pf.* → ***wznawiać***; **~wienie** *n* (*-a*; *G -eń*) renewal; *theat.* revival; *print.* new impression
wzor|cowy model; **~ować się** (*-uję*) (***na*** *L*) model (on); copy (after); **~owo** *adv.* perfectly; exemplarily; in a model manner; **~owy** exemplary; perfect; model; **~y** *pl.* → ***wzór***
wzorz|ec *m* (*-rca*; *-rce*) model; pattern; **~ysty** colo(u)red, colo(u)rful
wzór *m* (*-oru*; *-ory*) model; pattern; (*na tapecie*) design; *math.*, *chem.* formula
wzrastać (*-am*) grow, increase
wzrok *m* (*-u*; *0*) sight; eye(s *pl.*), look; **~owo** *adv.* visually; **~owy** visual; *anat.* optic
wzros|nąć *pf.* → ***wzrastać***; **~t** *m* (*-u*; *-y*) (*rośliny itp.*) growth; (*człowieka*) height; *fig.* increase; ***wysokiego ~tu*** tall; ***mieć … ~tu*** be … tall
wzróść *pf.* → ***wzrastać***
wzrusz|ać (*-am*) ⟨**~yć**⟩ *fig.* move, stir, touch; **~ająco** *adv.* movingly, touchingly; **~ający** moving, touching; **~enie** *n* (*-a*; *G -eń*) *fig.* emotion; **~ony** moved, touched
wzwód *m* (*-wodu*; *-wody*) *anat.* erection
wzwyż *adv.* up(wards); *sport*: ***skok ~*** high-jump
wzywać (*-am*) (***do*** *G*) call; *jur.* summon; (***kogoś do*** *G*) call (on s.o. to *bezok.*)

Z

z 1. *prp.* (*G*) from; of; at; out of; (*I*) with; of; **~ *domu*** from home; (*o nazwisku panieńskim*) née; ***każdy ~ nas*** each of us; ***~e srebra*** of silver; ***drżeć ~ zimna*** shake with cold; **~ *ciekawości*** out of curiosity; ***~e śmiechem*** with laughter; ***cieszyć się ~ prezentu*** be pleased with the present; ***razem ~ nami*** with us; **~ *początkiem roku*** at the beginning of the year; ***dobry ~*** good at; **~ *nazwiska*** by name; *często nie tłumaczy się*: ***~e śpiewem*** singing; **~ *nagła*** suddenly; ***zegar ~ kukułką*** cuckoo clock; **2.** *adv.* about, around, approximately; **~ *pięć*** around five

z. *skrót pisany*: **zobacz** see

za 1. *prp.* (*A*) *miejsce, następowanie*: behind, after; *cel*: for; with; *czas*: in; by; *funkcja*: as; (*I*) *miejsce*: behind, at; **~ *drzewo*/*drzewem*** behind the tree; ***walczyć ~ wolność*** fight for freedom; **~ *rok*** in a year; ***trzymać ~ rękę*** hold by the hand; **~ *stołem*** at the table; ***jeden ~ drugim*** one behind *lub* after the other; **~ *rogiem*** round the corner; **~ *gotówkę*** for cash; **~ *pomocą*** with the help; **~ *panowania Stuartów*** under the Stuarts; **~ *moich czasów*** in my day; ***przebrać się ~ …*** dress as …; ***służyć ~ …*** serve as …; ***mieć ~ …*** consider to be …, regard as …; **2.** *adv.* (+ *adv.*, *adj.*) too; **~ *ciężki*** too heavy; **~ *dużo*** too much; → ***co***

za|a- *pf.* → **a-**; **~aferowany** preoccupied, absorbed; **~awansowany** advanced; **~ba-** *pf.* → **ba-**; **~barwienie** *n* (*-a*; *G -eń*) coloration; *fig.* slant

zabaw|a *f* (*-y*; *G -*) play; festival; party; ***~a taneczna*** dance; ***przyjemnej*/*wesołej ~y!*** enjoy yourself (-selves *pl.*); ***dla ~y*** for fun; **~iać** (*-am*) → ***bawić***; **~ka** *f* (*-i*; *G -wek*) toy; *fig.* plaything; **~ny** funny, amusing

zabe- *pf.* → **be-**

zabezpiecz|ać (*-am*) ⟨**~yć**⟩ (*-ę*) protect, safeguard (**się** o.s.; **od** *G* against); (*łańcuchem itp.*, *jur.*) secure (**od** *G*, **przed** *I* against); **~enie** *n* (*-a*; *G -eń*) protection; *econ.* security, cover; ***~enie na starość*** provision for one's old age; **~ony** protected

zabi|cie *n* (*-a*; *0*) killing; **~ć** *pf.* → ***zabijać***

zabie|c *pf.* → ***zabiegać***; **~g** *m* (*-u*; *-i*) *med.* procedure, operation; ***~gi*** *pl.* endeavo(u)rs *pl.*, attempts *pl.*; **~gać** ⟨**~c**⟩: ***~gać drogę*** block the way; *t-ko impf.* (**o** *A*) strive for, solicit; → ***starać się***; **~gany** F busy

zabierać (*-am*) take, bring; (**z** *I*) take (with); *czas* take; (*na kolację*) take out; (*samochodem*) pick up; **~ *głos*** take the floor; **~ *się*** get away; (**do** *G*) get down (to), be about (to); F (*I*, **z** *I*) come (with)

zabi|jać (*-am*) kill (**się** o.s.; *też fig.* *czas*); *bydło* slaughter; (*gwoździami*) nail up; → ***wbijać***; F ***~jać się*** work o.s. to death

zabliźni|ać się (*-am*) ⟨**~ć się**⟩ (*-ę*, *-nij!*) (form a) scar, *med.* cicatrize

zabłą|dzić (*-ę*) *pf.*, **~kać się** *pf.* lose one's way, get lost

zabłocony F soiled; *por.* ***błocić***

zabobon *m* (*-u*; *-y*) superstition; **~ny** superstitious

zabor|ca *m* (*-y*; *G -ców*) occupant, partitioning country; **~czo** *adv.* possessively; **~czy** possessive

zabój|ca *m* (*-y*; *G -ców*), **~czyni** *f* (*-i*; *-e*) killer; **~czo** *adv.* fatally; *fig.* irresistibly; **~czy** lethal, deadly; fatal; *uśmiech itp.* irresistible; **~stwo** *n* (*-a*; *G -*) killing

zabór *m* (*-boru*; *-bory*) (*mienia itp.*) seizure; *hist.* partition, annexation

zabra|ć *pf.* → ***zabierać***; **~knąć** *pf.* → ***brakować*[1]**; ***~kło nam pieniędzy*** we are short of money; **~niać** (*-am*) (*G*) prohibit, forbid; ***~nia się …*** it is prohibited to (*bezok.*), … is not allowed

zabroni|ć *pf.* → ***zabraniać***, ***bronić***; ***~ony*** forbidden, prohibited

za|brudzony dirty; **~bryzgać** *pf.* splash

zabudow|a *f* (*-y*; *G -dów*) development; buildings *pl.*; **~ania** *pl.* buildings *pl.*; **~(yw)ać** (*-[w]uję*) build up; develop

zaburz|ać (*-am*) disturb; **~enie** *n* (*-a*; *G -eń*) disturbance

zabyt|ek *m* (*-tku*; *-tki*) (*architektonicz-*

ny) historic monument; (*przedmiot*) period piece; **~kowy** historic; period
zace- *pf.* → **ce-**
zach. *skrót pisany*: **zachód** W (*west*); **zachodni** W (*western*)
za|chcianka *f* (*-i*; *G -nek*) whim, caprice; → **chętka**; **~chęcać** (*-am*) ⟨**~chęcić**⟩ (*-cę*) (**do** *G*) encourage (to); **~chęta** *f* (*-y*; *G -*) incentive, encouragement; **~chlany** F blind drunk; **~chłanność** *f* (*-ści*; *0*) greed(iness); **~chłanny** greedy; **~chłysnąć się** (*-nę*) choke
zachmurz|ać się (*-am*) → **chmurzyć się**; **~enie** *n* (*-a*; *0*) cloud; **~ony** cloudy, overcast; *fig.* gloomy, dismal
zachodni western, west
zachodnioeuropejski West European
zachodzić arrive; reach ([**aż**] **do** as far as); (*wstępować*) drop in (**do** *G* on); *słońce*: set; *okoliczności*: arise; *pomyłka*: occur; *wypadek*: take place, happen; *zmiany*: take place; *oczy*: fill (**łzami** with tears); **~ parą** mist *lub* steam up; → **ciąża, głowa**
zacho|rować *pf.* fall ill; be taken ill (**na** *A* with); **~wać** *pf.* → **zachowywać**; **~wanie** *n* (*-a*; *G -ań*) behavio(u)r, conduct; *phys.* conservation; keeping; **~wywać** (*-wuję*) keep, retain; *dietę* keep to; *zwyczaj*, *miarę* preserve; *ostrożność* exercise; *pozory* keep up; **~wać przy sobie** keep to o.s.; **~wywać się** behave; (*trwać*) survive; act
zachód *m* (*-chodu*; *0*) west; **na ~** to the west; **na ~ od** west of; **~ słońca** sunset; F (*pl. -ody*) → **fatyga, trud**
za|chrypły, ~chrypnięty husky, hoarse; **~chwalać** (*-am*) praise; **~chwaszczony** weedy; **~chwiać** (*I*) sway, upset; *fig.* shake
zachwy|cać (*-am*) ⟨**~cić**⟩ delight; **~cać się** (*I*) go into raptures (over); **~cająco** *adv.* delightfully; **~cający** delightful; **~cenie** *n* (*-a*; *G -eń*) → **zachwyt**; **w ~ceniu** in rapture, enraptured; **~t** *m* (*-u*; *-y*) delight, fascination
zaciąć *pf.* → **zacinać**
zaciąg *m* (*-u*; *-i*) recruitment; **~ać** (*-am*) ⟨**~nąć**⟩ drag, haul (**do** *G* to); *zasłonę* draw; *pas* pull tight; *pożyczkę* raise, take out; (*mówiąc*) drawl; **~ać** ⟨**~nąć**⟩ **się papierosem** take a drag; (*do wojska itp.*) get enlisted (**do** *G* to); *niebo*: overcast
zacie|c *pf.* → **zaciekać**; **~k** *m* (*-u*; *-i*) water stain; **~kać** (*-am*) leak through; (*o deszczu*) come in
zaciekawi|ać *pf.* → **ciekawić**; **~enie** *n* (*-a*; *0*) curiosity
zaciek|le *adv.* ferociously; fiercely; **~ły** ferocious; fierce
zacie|knąć *pf.* → **zaciekać**; **~mniać** (*-am*) ⟨**~mnić**⟩ (*-ę*, *-nij!*) arken, black out
zacier *m* (*-u*; *-y*) mash; **~ać** (*-am*) smudge; *ślady*, *też fig.* cover up; *ręce* rub; **~ać się** *pamięć*: fade away; *tech.* seize up; **~ki** *pl.* (*-rek*) *type of noodles*
zacieśni|ać (*-am*) ⟨**~ć**⟩ (*-ę*, *-nij!*) *fig.* tighten (**się** *v/i.*)
zacietrzewi|ać się (*-am*) ⟨**~ć się**⟩ (*-ę*) get worked up
zacięcie[1] *n* (*-a*; *G -ęć*) cut; *fig.* verve; (*w drewnie*) notch
zacię|cie[2] *adv.* determinedly; doggedly; **~ty** determined; dogged
zacinać (*-am*) *v/t.* cut; *drewno* notch; *zęby* clench together; *v/i.* *deszcz*: lash; **~ się** cut o.s.; *tech.* jam; → **jąkać się**
zacis|k *m* (*-u*; *-i*) clamp; clip; *electr.* terminal; **~kać** ⟨**~nąć**⟩ press; clench; *pętlę* pull tight; **~kać się** get tight; **~nąć pasa** tighten one's belt
zacisz|e *n* (*-a*; *G -szy*) privacy; retreat; **~ny** secluded
zacny good
zacofan|ie *n* (*-a*; *0*) backwardness; **~y** backward, old-fashioned
zaczadzieć *pf.* (*-eję*) get poisoned with carbon monoxide
zacza|jać się (*-am*) ⟨**~ić się**⟩ lie in wait; **~rowany** bewitched; magic
zacząć *pf.* (*-nę*) → **zaczynać**
zacze|kać *pf.* → **czekać**; **~pi(a)ć** catch, hook; F *fig.* accost; **~pić się** (**o** *L*) catch (on); get stuck; **~pka** *f* (*-i*; *G -pek*) provocation; **szukać ~pki** look for trouble; **~pny** aggressive; *mil.* offensive
zaczerwieniony reddened; *por.* **czerwienić się**
zaczyn *m* (*-u*; *-y*) *gastr.* leaven; **~ać** (*-am*) *v/t.* start, begin (**się** *v/i.*); *paczkę*, *butelkę* open; F **~a się** it's starting
zaćmi|enie *n* (*-a*; *G -eń*) *astr.* eclipse; **~ewać** (*-am*) ⟨**~ć**⟩ darken (**się** *v/i.*); *astr.* obscure; *fig.* (*I*) overshadow, outshine
zad *m* (*-u*; *-y*) *zo.* rump (*też kogoś*)
zada|ć *pf.* → **zadawać**; **~nie** *n* (*-a*; *G*

-*ań*) problem; (*w szkole*) exercise; **~rty** snub, upturned; **~tek** *m* (*-tku*; *-tki*) down payment, deposit; ***mieć ~tki na*** have the makings of; **~tkować** (*-uję*) deposit; **~wać** *pytanie* ask; *zadanie domowe Brt.* set, *Am.* assign; *zagadkę* give; *cios* deliver; *ból* inflict; ***~wać klęskę*** defeat; → ***trud***; ***~wać się*** (***z*** *I*) go round (with)

za|dawniony *choroba* inveterate; **~dbany** tidy; neat; **~de-** *pf.* → ***de-***

zadek *m* (*-dka*; *-dki*) bottom; → ***zad***

zadłuż|enie *n* (*-a*; *G -eń*) debt; **~ony** in debt

zado|kumentować *pf. fig.* show; **~mowić się** *pf.* (*-ę*, *-ów!*) make o.s. at home; get settled

zadośćuczyni|ć *pf.* (*D*) satisfy; **~enie** *n* (*-a*; *G -eń*) satisfaction

zadowala|ć (*-am*) satisfy; ***~ć się*** (*I*) be satisfied (with); **~jąco** *adv.* satisfactorily; **~jący** satisfactory

zadowol|enie *n* (*-a*; *0*) satisfaction; **~ić** *pf.* (*-lę*, *-wól!*) → ***zadowalać***; **~ony** satisfied, pleased (***z*** *G* with); ***~ony z siebie*** complacent

zadra|pać ⟨***~pnąć***⟩ scratch; → ***drasnąć***; **~żnienia** *n/pl.* (*-ń*) frictions *pl.*; **~żniony** *stosunki* strained, tense

zadrzeć *pf.* → ***zadzierać***

zadrzewi|ać (*-am*) ⟨***~ć***⟩ (*-ę*) afforest; **~ony** wooded

zaduch *m* (*-u*; *0*) stale air, *Brt. zwł.* fug

zadufany overconfident

zaduma *f* (*-y*; *0*) deep thought; **~ny** thoughtful

zadurzony infatuated

zadusić *pf.* → (***u***)***dusić***

Zaduszki *pf.* (*-szek*) *rel.* All Souls' Day

zadym|a *f* F row, racket; **~iać** (*-am*) ⟨***~ić***⟩ fill with smoke; **~ka** *f* (*-i*; *G -mek*) driving snow, snowstorm

zadysz|any breathless, short-winded; **~ka** *f* (*-i*; *G -szek*) breathlessness, shortness of breath

zadzierać (*-am*) *v/t. głowę* throw back; *spódnicę* pull up; *naskórek* tear; *ogon* raise; ***~ nosa*** look down one's nose (at), put on airs; *v/i.* (***z*** *I*) get in trouble (with); ***~ się*** pull up

zadzierzysty defiant

zadziwi|ać (*-am*) ⟨***~ć***⟩ astonish, amaze; **~ająco** *adv.* amazingly; **~ający** amazing

za|dzwo- *pf.* → ***dzwo-***; **~dźgać** (*-am*) stab (to death); **~fascynowany** fascinated; **~frapować** *pf.* (*-uję*) strike; **~frasowany** worried

zagad|ka *f* (*-i*; *G -dek*) riddle, puzzle (*też fig.*); **~kowo** *adv.* enigmatically; **~kowy** enigmatic, puzzling; **~nąć** *pf.* (*-nę*) speak (***kogoś o*** *A* to s.o. about); **~nienie** *n* (*-a*; *G -eń*) problem, question

zaga|jać (*-am*) ⟨***~ić***⟩ (*-ję*) open; **~jenie** *n* (*-a*; *G -eń*) opening

zagajnik *m* (*-a*; *-i*) copse, wood

zagalopować się *pf.* go too far

zaganiać (*-am*) drive (***do*** *G* to)

zagarn|iać (*-am*) ⟨***~ąć***⟩ *fig.* seize, grab

zagazować *pf.* (*-uję*) gas

zagę|szczać (*-am*) ⟨***~ścić***⟩ (*-szczę*) thicken; ***~ścić się*** become thicker

zagi|ęcie *n* (*-a*; *G -ęć*) bend; **~nać** (*-am*) ⟨***~ąć***⟩ bend (***się*** *v/i.*); fold; **~nąć** *pf.* → ***ginąć***; **~niony** missing

zaglądać (*-am*) (***do*** *G*) look (into); (*z wizytą*) drop in (on); consult (***do książki*** a book)

zagłada *f* (*-y*; *0*) extermination

zagłębi|ać (*-am*) ⟨***~ć***⟩ (*-ę*) immerse (***się*** o.s.); *rękę* sink; ***~ć się*** *fig.* (***w*** *L*) become absorbed (in); **~e** *n* (*-a*; *G -i*) *górnictwo*: coalfields *pl.*; **~enie** *n* (*-a*; *G -eń*) hollow

za|głodzić *pf.* (*-ę*) starve; **~główek** *m* (*-wka*; *-wki*) headrest; **~głuszać** (*-am*) → ***głuszyć***; **~gmatwany** tangled, complicated; **~gnać** *pf.* → ***zaganiać***; **~gniewany** angry; **~gnieżdżać się** (*-am*) ⟨***~gnieździć się***⟩ nest; *med.* be implanted

zagon *m* (*-u*; *-y*) field; *hist.* incursion; **~ić** *pf.* → ***zaganiać***; **~iony** exhausted

zagorzały fanatic, fervent

zagospodarow(yw)ać (*-*[*w*]*uję*) *teren* develop; ***~się*** furnish, make o.s. at home

zagotować *pf.* boil

zagra|ć *pf.* → ***grać***; **~bić** *pf.* plunder; **~dzać** (*-am*) (*płotem*) fence off; *ulicę* bar; block (***k-u drogę*** s.o.'s path)

zagrani|ca *f* (*-y*; *0*) foreign countries *pl.*; **~czny** foreign

zagraż|ać (*-am*) threaten; jeopardize, endanger ***~ać zdrowiu*** be a threat to one's health; ***~a głód*** hunger is threatening

zagroda *f* (*-y*; *G -ód*) farmstead

zagro|dzić *pf.* → ***zagradzać***; **~zić** *pf.* → ***grozić, zagrażać***; **~żenie** *n* (*-a*; *G*

-eń) threat (*G* to); ***stan ~żenia*** state of emergency; **~żony** threatened

zagry|piony F down with flu; **~wka** *f* (*w sporcie*) serve; **~zać** (*-am*) ⟨**~źć**⟩ (*I*) have a snack; *pf.* bite to death; ***~źć usta do krwi*** bite one's lips till they bleed; **~zka** *f* (*-i*; *G -zek*) snack

za|grzać *pf.* → ***zagrzewać***

Zagrzeb *m* (*-bia*; *0*) Zagreb

za|grzebywać (*-uję*) ⟨**~grzebać**⟩ bury (**się** o.s.; *też fig.*), **~grzewać** (*-am*) *gastr.* heat, warm up; *fig.* (**do** *G*) spur on (to); ***~grzać się*** warm up, heat up

zagubion|y lost; ***rzeczy*** *pl.* ***~e*** lost property

zahacz|ać (*-am*) ⟨**~yć**⟩ (*-ę*) hook up (**się** *v/i.*); get *s.th.* caught (**o** *A* on); F ask (**kogoś o** *A* to s.o. about)

zahamowa|nie *n* (*-a*; *G -ań*) braking; *psych.* inhibition; **~ć** *pf.* → ***hamować***

zahar|owany overworked; **~towany** hardened; seasoned; → ***hartować***

za|hipnotyzowany under hypnosis; **~hukany** meek, intimidated

zaimek *m* (*-mka*; *-mki*) *gr.* pronoun

za|improwizowany improvised; impromptu; **~ini-**, **~ink-**, **~ins-** *pf.* → ***in-***

zainteresowan|ie *n* (*-a*; *G -ań*) interest; **~y** (**w** *L* in) interested

zaiste *przest.* indeed

zaistnieć *pf.* come into being; appear

zajad|ać (*-am*) F eat heartily, *zwł. Brt.* tuck in; **~le** *adv.* fiercely; **~ły** fierce; *zwolennik* staunch, stout

zajazd *m* (*-u*; *-y*) inn

zając *m* (*-a*; *-e*) *zo.* hare

zają|ć *pf.* (*-jmę*) → ***zajmować***; **~knąć się** *pf.* (*-nę*) stammer; ***nie ~knąć się*** (**o** *L*) not say a word (about)

zaje|chać *pf.* → ***zajeżdżać***; **~zdnia** *f* (*-i*; *-e*) terminus, *Brt.* depot; **~żdżać** (*-am*) (**do** *G*) arrive (to); stop (at); (**przed** *A*) drive up (outside, in front of); ***~żdżać drogę*** *mot.* cut in

zajęcie *n* (*-a*; *G -ęć*) taking; (*siłą itp.*) capture; *jur.* seizure; (*praca*) occupation, job; (*w szkole zw. pl.*) classes *pl.*; lectures *pl.*; ***z ~m*** interested

zajęczy hare('s), *biol.* leporine; → ***warga***

zajęty busy (*też Am. tel.*), *tel. Brt.* engaged; *stół* occupied

zajmować (*-uję*) *postawę* take; *miasto* capture; *przestrzeń, miejsce, kraj* occupy; *jur.* seize; (*zużyć czas*) take up; *pokój* live in; *stanowisko* take, adopt; occupy (**się** o.s.; *I* with); (*budzić ciekawość*) interest

zajmując|o *adv.* interestingly; fascinatingly; **~y** interesting; fascinating

zajrzeć *pf.* (*-ę*, *-y*) → ***zaglądać***

zajś|cie *n* (*-a*; *G -jść*) incident, occurrence; → ***zatarg***; **~ć** *pf.* (*-dę*) → ***zachodzić***

zakamarek *m* (*-rka*; *-rki*) *fig.* corner, spot

za|kamuflowany disguised; **~kańczać** *pf.* → ***kończyć***; **~kasywać** (*-uję*) ⟨**~kasać**⟩ (*-szę*) roll up; **~katarzony** suffering from a cold; **~katrupić** *pf.* (*-ę*) do in

zaka|z *m* (*-u*; *-y*) ban, prohibition; **~zać** *pf.* → ***zakazywać***; **~zany** prohibited, forbidden; **~zić** *pf.* (*-żę*) → ***zakażać***; **~zywać** (*-uję*) forbid, prohibit; **~kaźny** infectious; contagious; **~żać** (*-am*) *med.* infect; **~żenie** *n* (*-a*; *G -eń*) infection

zakąs|ić *pf.* (*-szę*) → ***przekąsić***; **~ka** *f* (*-i*; *G -sek*) hors d'oeuvre, appetizer; ***na ~kę*** for a starter

zakątek *m* (*-tku*; *-tki*) → ***zakamarek***

za|ki-, **~kla-** *pf.* → ***ki-***, ***kla-***; **~kląć** *pf.* → ***kląć***; ***zaklinać***; **~kle-** *pf.* → ***kle-***; **~klęcie** *n* (*-a*; *G -ęć*) spell; *fig.* magic formula

zaklinać (*-am*) bewitch; *fig.* beg, beseech; **~ się** swear (**na** *A* by)

zakład *m* (*-u*; *-y*) firm, business; (*fabryka*) works *sg.*; (*instytucja*) institution; (*założenie się*) bet; ***~ pracy*** place of work; ***iść o ~*** bet; **~ać** (*-am*) *rodzinę* start; *firmę* set up, establish; *miasto* found; *okulary* put on; (*w ubraniu*) tuck; *opatrunek* apply, put on; *gaz, prąd* lay; ***~ać nogę na nogę*** cross legs; ***~ać, że …*** assume that …; *v/i.* ***~ać się*** (**o** *A*) bet (on); **~ka** *f* (*-i*; *G -dek*) (*w książce*) bookmark; (*ubrania*) tuck

zakład|niczka *f* (*-i*; *G -czek*), **~nik** *m* (*-a*; *-cy*) hostage; ***wzięcie ~ników*** taking of hostages; **~owy** company; staff

zakłaman|ie *n* (*-a*; *0*) hypocrisy; **~y** hypocritical

zakłopotan|ie *n* (*-a*; *0*) embarrassment; **~y** embarrassed, perplexed

zakłóc|ać (*-am*) ⟨**~ić**⟩ disturb; **~enie** *n* (*-a*; *G -eń*) disturbance; *RTV*: static

zakoch|iwać się (*-uję*) ⟨**~ać się**⟩ fall in love (**w** *L* with); **~any** **1.** in love (**w** *L* with), infatuated; **2.** *m* (*-ego*; *-ni*), **~ana** *f* (*-ej*; *-e*) lover

zako|do- *pf.* → ***kodo-*** **~mu-** *pf.* → ***komu-***

zakon *m* (*-u*; *-y*) *rel.* order; **~nica** *f* (*-y*; *G* -) nun; **~nik** *m* (*-a*; *-cy*) monk; brother; **~ny** monastic

za|kons- *pf.* → ***kons-***; **~kończenie** *n* (*-a*; *G -eń*) ending, conclusion; (*palce itp.*) tip; **~kończyć** *pf.* → ***kończyć***; **~kopać** *pf.* → ***zakopywać***; **~kopcony** covered in soot; **~kopywać** (*-uję*) bury; **~korkowany** corked; F blocked; **~korzenić się** (*-ę*) take root; **~kotwiczać** (*-am*) ⟨***~kotwiczyć***⟩ (*-ę*) *v/t. naut.* anchor; *v/i.* drop anchor

zakra|dać się (*-am*) ⟨***~ść się***⟩ steal in, sneak in; **~plać** (*-am*) put drops in one's eye(s *pl.*); **~towany** barred; **~wać** (*-am*) (**na** *A*) look (like)

zakres *m* (*-u*; *-y*) range, scope; ***we własnym ~ie*** on one's own

zakreśl|ać (*-am*) ⟨***~ić***⟩ (*-ę*) (*w tekście*) highlight, mark; *koło* describe

zakręc|ać (*-am*) ⟨***~ić***⟩ *włosy* curl; *kran* turn off; *zawór* screw shut; *t-ko pf.* turn (*I*; **się** *v/i.*); *v/i.* turn round; ***~ić się*** (***koło*** *G*) busy o.s. (about)

zakręt *m* (*-u*; *-y*) bend, curve; **~as** *m* (*-a*; *-y*) flourish; **~ka** *f* (*-i*; *G -tek*) cap, lid

za|kroplić *pf.* → ***zakraplać***; **~krwawić** bleed; **~kryć** *pf.* → ***zakrywać***

za'krystia *f* (*GDL -ii*; *-e*) *rel.* vestry, sacristy

za|krywać (*-am*) hide, conceal; *widok* block; **~krzątnąć się** *pf.* (*-nę*) → ***krzątać się***

zakrzep *m* (*-u*; *-y*) *med.* thrombus; **~ica** *f* (*-y*; *0*) *med.* thrombosis; **~ły** clotted; set

za|krzt- *pf.* → ***krzt-*** ; **~krzywiony** bent, crooked; **~księ-** *pf.* → ***księ-***

zaktualizowany updated, modernized

zakuć *pf.* → ***zakuwać***

zakulisowy *fig.* behind the scenes

zakup *m* (*-u*; *-y*) purchase, buy; ***na ~y*** shopping; ***iść po ~y*** go shopping

zakurzony dusty, covered in dust

zaku|ty F *fig.*: ***~ty łeb*** blockhead; **~wać** (*-am*): ***~wać w kajdany*** put in chains

za|kwaterow(yw)ać (*-[w]uję*) *mil.* quarter, billet; **~kwitnąć** (*-nę*) blossom, bloom; **~lać** *pf.* → ***zalewać***; **~lany** flooded; V *fig.* pissed; **~lążek** *m* (*-żka*; *-żki*) *bot.* bud; *fig.* bud, germ

zale|c *pf.* → ***zalegać***; **~cać** (*-am*) ⟨***~cić***⟩ (*-cę*) recommend; ***~cać się*** (**do** G) woo, court; **~cenie** *n* (*-a*; *G -eń*) recommendation; *med.* order

zaledwie *part.*, *cj.* hardly, scarcely

zaleg|ać (*-am*) *v/i. geol.* occur, be found; *milczenie*: descend; *ciemność*: set in; (**z** *I*) be behind (with), (*z opłatą*) be in arrears (with); **~łość** *f* (*-ści*; *0*) *zw. pl.* (*płatnicze*) arrears *pl.*; (*w pracy*) backlog; **~ły** outstanding, due

zale|piać (*-am*) ⟨***~pić***⟩ (*-ę*) stick down; *dziurę* seal up; **~siać** (*-am*) ⟨***~sić***⟩ (*-ę*) afforest

zaleta *f* (*-y*; *G* -) advantage, value

zalew *m* (*-u*; *-y*) flooding; *geogr.* bay; **~ać** (*-am*) *v/t.* flood; *fig.* swamp; (*uszczelniać*) seal; *v/i.* F tell stories; ***~ać robaka*** drown one's sorrows (in drink)

zależ|eć (***od*** *G*) depend (on); be dependent (on); ***~y mi na tym*** it matters much to me; ***to ~y*** it depends; **~nie** *adv.*: ***~nie od*** (*G*) depending on; **~ność** *f* (*-ści*) relationship; **~ny** dependent; *gr.* indirect

zalicz|ać (*-am*) (**do** *G*) include (to); ***~ać się*** be included (with); (*w szkole*) pass; **~enie** *n* (*-a*; *G -eń*) (*w szkole*) pass, (*podpis*) credit; ***za ~eniem*** (**pocztowym**) cash on delivery; **~ka** *f* (*-i*; *G -ek*) advance payment; **~kowo** *adv.* as an advance payment

zalot|ny flirtatious; coy; **~y** *pl.* courtship; → ***umizgi***

zaludni|ać (*-am*) ⟨***~ć***⟩ (*-ę*, *-nij!*) populate; ***~(a)ć się*** fill in

zał. *skrót pisany*: ***załącznik*** enc. (*enclosure*)

zała|dowczy loading; **~dow(yw)ać** (*-uję*) load; **~dunek** *m* (*-nku*; *-nki*) loading; **~dunkowy** loading; **~godzić** *pf.* soothe; *karę* mitigate; *spór* settle

załama|ć *pf.* → ***załamywać***; **~ny** desolate; crestfallen; **~nie** *n* (*-a*; *G -ań*) *phys.* refraction; *fig.* breakdown, collapse

załamywać (*-uję*) bend; *papier* fold; *ręce* wring; *phys.* refract; ***~ się*** break; *sufit*, *też fig.*: collapse; *phys.* be refracted; *głos*: fail

załatwi|ać (*-am*) ⟨***~ć***⟩ (*-ę*) deal with, settle; *klienta* serve; *komuś* fix up; F ***~ć się*** (***z*** *I*) finish (with); (*w toalecie*) relieve o.s.; **~enie** *n* (*-a*; *G -eń*) completion, settling

załącz|ać (*-am*) enclose; *ukłony* send; **~enie** *n*: ***w ~eniu*** enclosed; **~nik** *m* (*-a*; *-i*) enclosure

załoga *f* (*-i*; *G -łóg*) crew; (*fabryki*) staff, workforce

załom *m* (*-u*; *-y*) fold, crease
założeni|e *n* (*-a*; *G -eń*) establishment, foundation; (*teza*) assumption; **~a** *pl.* basic conceptions; ***wychodzić z ~a*** start from the assumption
założyciel *m* (*-a*; *-e*), **~ka** *f* (*-i*; *G -lek*) founder; **~ski** founding
założyć *pf.* → ***zakładać***
załzawiony runny, watery
zamach *m* (*-u*; *-y*) (***na życie*** assassination) attempt; (*ruch*) stroke, swing; ***~ stanu*** coup d'état; (***wojskowy*** military) putsch; ***za jednym ~em*** at one stroke; **~nąć się** (*-nę*) take a swing (***na*** *A* at); **~owiec** *m* (*-wca*; *-wcy*) assassin; **~owy**: ***koło ~owe*** flywheel
zama|czać *pf.* → ***moczyć***; **~low(yw)ać** (*-[w]uję*) paint over
za|martwiać się (*-am*) → ***martwić się***; **~marzać** (*-am*) → ***morzyć***; **~marzać** [-r·z-] (*-am*) *jezioro itp.*: freeze solid; → ***marznąć***; **~maskowany** masked, disguised
zamaszy|sty sweeping; *pismo* bold; **~ście** *adv.* sweepingly
zama|wiać (*-am*) order; *symfonię itp.* commission; *tel.*, *miejsce* book; **~zywać** (*-uję*) 〈**~zać**〉 smear, daub
zamącić *pf.* *wodę* make cloudy, cloud; *fig.* → ***zakłócić***
zamążpójście *n* (*-ą*) marriage
zamczysko *n* (*-a*; *G -*) → ***zamek***
zamek *m* (*-mku*; *-mki*) lock; (*obronny*) castle; ***~ błyskawiczny*** zip (fastener); ***~ centralny*** central locking
zameldowa|ć *pf.* → ***meldować***; **~nie** *n* (*-a*; *G -ań*) registration
zamę|czać (*-am*) → ***męczyć***; **~t** *m* (*-u*; *0*) muddle, confusion
zamężna married
zamgl|enie *n* (*-a*; *G -eń*) fog, mist; **~ony** foggy, misty
zamian: ***w ~*** (***za*** *A*) in exchange (for); **~a** *f* (*-y*; *G -*) exchange (***mieszkania*** of flats, *Am.* apartments), swap; (*jednostek*) conversion
zamiar *m* (*-u*; *-y*) intention; ***nosić się z ~em***, ***mieć ~*** intend, plan
zamiast 1. *prp.* (*G*) instead (of); **2.** *adv.* instead of
zamiata|ć (*-am*) sweep; **~rka** *f* (*-i*; *G -rek*) *Brt.* road-sweeper, *Am.* street-sweeper
zamieć *f* (*-ci*; *-cie*) blizzard
zamiejscow|y non-local; visiting; ***rozmowa ~a*** long-distance call
zamien|iać (*-am*) 〈**~ić**〉 *v/t.* exchange (***na*** *A* for); *miejsca* change, swap; (*przeobrażać*) convert; **~i(a)ć się** turn, change (***w*** *A* into); (***na*** *A*) change, swap; **~ny** interchangeable; ***część ~na*** spare part
zamierać (*-am*) die; *fig. głos itp.*: die away; *śmiech, ktoś*: freeze; be paralyzed (***ze strachu*** with fear)
zamierzać (*-am*) intend, plan; ***~ się*** raise one's hand (***na*** *A* against)
zamie|rzchły ancient; *czasy* remote; **~rzenie** *n* (*-a*; *G -eń*) intention; **~rzony** intended; **~szać** *pf.* → ***mieszać***; **~szanie** *n* (*-a*; *0*) confusion; → ***zamęt***; **~szany** *fig.* involved (***w*** *A* in); **~szczać** (*-am*) → ***umieszczać***
zamieszka|ć *pf.* inhabit; occupy; settle; **~ły** occupied, inhabited; (***w*** *L*) resident (in); **~nie** *n* (*-a*; *G -ań*) living; ***miejsce ~nia*** residence, *jur.* abode
zamieszki *pl.* (*-szek*) riot, disturbance
zamieszkiwać (*-uję*) live, inhabit
za|mieścić *pf.* → ***umieścić***; **~mieść** → ***zamiatać***; **~milczeć** *pf.* pass over in silence; **~milknąć** *pf.* → ***milknąć***
zamiłowan|ie *n* (*-a*; *G -ań*) (***do*** *G*) passion (for), enthusiasm (for); ***z ~iem*** with passion; **~y** keen
zaminowany mined; → ***minować***
zamkn|ąć *pf.* → ***zamykać***; **~ięcie** *n* (*-a*; *G -ęć*) closure; closing; locking; (*zamek*) lock; (*ksiąg*) balancing; ***w ~ięciu*** under lock and key; **~ięty** closed; *fig.* withdrawn
zamkowy castle
za|mocow(yw)ać → ***przymocowywać, mocować***; **~moczyć** *pf.* → ***moczyć***; **~montowywać** (*-uję*) → ***montować***
zamordowan|ie *n* (*-a*; *G -ań*) assassination, murdering; **~y** assassinated, murdered; → ***mordować***
zamorski overseas
zamożny affluent, prosperous
zamówi|ć *pf.* → ***zamawiać***; **~enie** *n* (*-a*; *G -eń*) order, commission
zamraczać (*-am*) daze
zamraża|ć (*-am*) freeze; **~lnik** *m* (*-a*; *-i*) freezing compartment; **~rka** *f* (*-i*; *G -rek*) freezer, deep freeze
zamrocz|enie *n* (*-a*; *G -eń*) daze; ***stan***

Z

~enia (*alkoholowego*) state of drunkenness; **~ony** dazed; (*alkoholem*) intoxicated; **~yć** (*-ę*) → ***zamraczać***
zamrozić *pf.* → ***zamrażać***
zamrzeć *pf.* → ***zamierać***
zamsz *m* (*-u*; *-e*) suede
zamulony muddy
zamurow(yw)ać (*-[w]uję*) wall up
zamykać (*-am*) close, shut (**się** *v/i.*); *kogoś w pokoju itp.* lock in (**się** *v/i.*); *mieszkanie* lock up; *ulicę* close, block; *fabrykę* close down; *komp.* quit, exit; *econ.* balance; **~ gaz** turn off the gas; **~ na klucz** lock; **~ pochód** bring up the rear; **~ się w sobie** clam up; **zamknij się!** shut up!
zamyś|lać (*-am*) ⟨**~lić**⟩ (*-lę*) plan, intend; **~lić się** fall into thought; (**nad** *I*) reflect (about), muse (on, about); **~lony** thoughtful, pensive
zanadto *adv.* too, exceedingly
zaniecha|ć *pf.* (*-am*) give up, abandon; **~nie** *n* (*-a*; *0*) *jur.* omission
zanieczy|szczać (*-am*) ⟨**~ścić**⟩ (*-ę*) make dirty; *środowisko* pollute; *wodę* contaminate; **~szczenie** *n* (*-a*; *G -eń*) soiling; (**środowiska** environmental) pollution; **~szczenia** *pl.* impurities *pl.*
zaniedba|ć (*-am*) → ***zaniedbywać***; **~nie** *n* (*-a*; *G -ań*) neglect, negligence; **~ny** neglected; (*brudny*) untidy; (*podniszczony*) run-down
zaniedbywać (*-uję*) neglect; **~ się** be negligent (**w** *L* in); become untidy, let o.s. go
zanie|móc *pf.* fall ill; **~mówić** *pf.* become dumb (**z** *G* with); **~pokojenie** *n* (*-a*; *G -eń*) concern, worry; → ***niepokój, niepokoić***; **~pokojony** worried, anxious; alarmed
zanie|ść → ***zanosić***; **~widzieć** *pf.* become blind
zanik *m* (*-u*; *-i*) decrease; (*zainteresowania*) waning; *med.* atrophy; **~ać** (*-am*) ⟨**~nąć**⟩ disappear, vanish; fade, die out; *zw. impf.* decrease
zanim *cj.* before
zaniż|ać (*-am*) ⟨**~yć**⟩ (*-ę*) lower; *liczbę* understate
zano|- *pf.* → **no-**; **~sić** *v/t.* take; carry; cover (**śniegiem** with snow); **~sić się** look like (**na deszcz** rain); **~sić się od płaczu** cry uncontrollably; **~sić się od śmiechu** be in hysterics
zanu|dzać (*-am*) (*I*) bore (with); → ***nudzić***; **~rzać** (*-am*) ⟨**~rzyć**⟩ (*-ę*) immerse (**w** *I* in; **po szyję** to the neck; **się** *v/i.*); *pędzel itp.* dip; **~rzenie** *n* (*-a*; *G -eń*) immersion
zaoczn|ie *adv.* in one's absence; *jur.* in default; **~y**: ***studia ~e*** extramural studies
za|of- *pf.* → **of-**; **~ogniać** (*-am*) ⟨**~ognić**⟩ (*-ę*, *-nij!*) (**się**) inflame (*też fig.*); *fig.* aggravate
zaokrągl|ać (*-am*) ⟨**~ić**⟩ (*-lę*, *-lij!*) round (**w górę, w dół** up, down); *rogi* round off
zaokrętować *pf.* (*-uję*) embark (**się** *v/i.*)
zaopatrywać (*-uję*) (**w** *A*) supply (with), provide (with); (*wyposażać*) equip (with); **~ się** (**w** *A*) provide o.s. (with)
zaopatrz|enie *n* (*-a*; *0*) supply; *econ.* provision; (*na ekspedycję*) provisions *pl.*; (*dostarczenie*) delivery; **~yć** *pf.* (*-ę*) → ***zaopatrywać***
za|opi- *pf.* → **opi-**; **~orywać** (*-uję*) **~orać**; **~ostrzać** (*-am*) *fig.* aggravate; → ***ostrzyć***; **~oszczę-** *pf.* → **oszczę-**
zapach *m* (*-u*; *-y*) smell
zapad|ać (*-am*) *kurtyna, cisza, ciemność*: fall; *oczy*: sink in; *policzki*: sag; *wyrok*: be pronounced; **~ać na zdrowiu** be in poor health; **~ać w sen** sink into a sleep; **~ać się** cave in, sink; **~ły** sunken, sagged; **~ły kąt, ~ła dziura** godforsaken place
zapako- *pf.* → **pako-**
zapala|ć (*-am*) light; *światło* turn on; *ogień* kindle; *zapałkę* strike; *silnik* start; **~ć się** light; catch fire; *światło, silnik*: go on; *oczy*: light up; (**do** *G*) become enthusiastic (over); **~jący** *mil.* incendiary
zapalczyw|ie *adv.* impetuously; impulsively; **~ość** *f* (*-ści*; *0*) impetuousness; **~y** impetuous, impulsive
zapal|enie *n* (*-a*; *G -eń*) *med.* inflammation; **~eniec** *m* (*-ńca*; *-ńcy*) enthusiast; **~ić** *pf.* → ***zapalać*** **~niczka** *f* (*-i*; *G -czek*) lighter; **~nik** *m* (*-a*; *-i*) *mil.* fuse; **~ny** inflammable (*też fig.*); *med.* inflammatory; **punkt ~ny** hotspot; **~ony** enthusiastic, avid
zapał *m* (*-u*; *0*) fervo(u)r; zeal; enthusiasm; **~czany** match; **~ka** *f* (*-i*; *G -ek*) match
zapamięt|ać *pf.* remember; *komp.* save; **~ać się** (**w** *I*) become engrossed

(in); ~ały obsessive; → ***zagorzały, zapalony***; ~anie *n* (*-a*; *0*) obsessiveness; ***łatwy do ~ania*** easy to remember; ~ywać (*-uję*) → ***zapamiętać***
zapanować *pf.* → ***panować***; *fig.* prevail
zapar|- *pf.* → ***par-***; ~cie *n* (*-a*; *G -rć*) *med.* constipation; ~ty: ***z ~tym tchem*** with bated breath
zaparz|ać (*-am*) ⟨***~yć***⟩ brew
zapas *m* (*-u*; *-y*) supply, stock; ***w ~ie*** in reserve; ***~y*** *pl.* provisions *pl.*; *t-ko pl.* (*w sporcie*) wrestling; ~owy reserve; replacement; *część* spare; ***wyjście ~owe*** emergency exit
zapaś|ć[1] *pf.* → ***zapadać***
zapaś|ć[2] *f* (*-ści*; *0*) *med. fig.* collapse; ~niczy (*w sporcie*) wrestling; ~nik *m* (*-a*; *-cy*) *sport:* wrestler
zapatrywa|ć się (*-uję*) (**na** *A*) regard (as), view (as) ***jak się na to zapatrujesz?*** what is your opinion about it?; ~nie *n* (*-a*; *G -ań*) view, opinion
zapatrzyć się *pf.* → ***wpatrywać się***
zapchać *pf.* → ***zapychać***
zapełni|ać (*-am*) ⟨***~ć***⟩ fill (**się** *v/i.*)
zaperzony irritable, touchy
zapewn|e *adv.* surely; ~iać (*-am*) ⟨***~ić***⟩ (*-ę, -nij!*) assure (**kogoś o** *L* s.o. of); (*gwarantować*) ensure, guarantee; ~ienie *n* (*-a*; *G -eń*) assurance
zapę|dy *m/pl.* (*-ów*) efforts *pl.*, attempts *pl.*; ~dzać (*-am*) ⟨***~dzić***⟩ drive (**do** *G* to); ***~dzić się*** *fig.* go too far
zapiąć *pf.* → ***zapinać***
zapie|czętować *pf.* seal (*też fig.*); ~kać (*-am*) ⟨***~c***⟩ *gastr.* bake (*zwł.* in a casserole); ~kanka *f* (*-i*; *G -nek*) casserole; ~rać (*-am*) *dech* take away; → ***zaparty***; ***~rać się*** (*G*) deny, disown
za|pięcie *n* (*-a*; *G -ęć*) (*zamek*) fastener; ~pinać (*-am*) *guzik, bluzkę* do up; *pasy* fasten; *zamek błysk.* zip up
zapis *m* (*-u*; *-y*) (*wpis*) entry; record; (***na taśmie*** tape) recording; *jur.* bequest; → ***dźwięk***; ~ek *m* (*-sku*; *-ski*) *zw. pl.* note; ~ywać (*-uję*) ⟨***~ać***⟩ take down, note down; *stronę* fill with writing; *dźwięk* record; *econ.* (**na** *A*) credit; *lek.* prescribe; *komp.* save; leave, bequeath (***w testamencie*** in one's last will); → ***wpisywać***
zapity besotted; *głos* boozy
zapla|nowany planned; → ***planować***; ~tać (*-am*) weave
zapląt|ywać (*-uję*) ⟨***~ać***⟩ → ***plątać***; ***~ać się*** get involved (**w** *A* in)
zaplecze *n* (*-a*; *G -y*) *mil.* back area
za|pleść *pf.* → ***zaplatać***; ~pleśniały mo(u)ldy; ~plombowany sealed; → ***plombować***
zapła|cenie *n* (*-a*; *0*) payment; ~cić *pf.* → ***płacić***; *dług, rachunek* settle; ~dniać (*-am*) *kobietę, samicę* impregnate; *jajko* fertilize; ~kany weeping; tear-stained; ~ta *f* (*-y*; *G -*) payment
zapłodni|ć *pf.* → ***zapładniać***; ~enie *n* (*-a*; *G -eń*) fertilisation; ***sztuczne ~enie*** artificial insemination
zapłon *m* (*-u*; *-y*) *mot.* ignition; detonation; ***włącznik ~u*** ignition lock; ~ąć *pf.* kindle (*też fig.*); ~owy ignition
zapobieg|ać (*-am*) ⟨**zapobiec**⟩ (*D*) prevent; ~anie *n* (*-a*; *0*) prevention; ~awczo *adv.* preventively; ~awczy preventive; ~liwie *adv.* providently; ~liwy provident; → ***przezorny, przewidujący***
zapo|cony sweated; *szyba* misted-up, fogged-up; → ***pocić się***; ~czątkow(yw)ać (*-[w]uję*) start; ~dziać (się) *pf.* → ***podziewać***; ~minać (*-am*) ⟨***~mnieć***⟩ (*A*, **o** *L*) forget (about); ~mnienie *n* (*-a*; *0*) oblivion; forgetfulness; ***pójść w ~mnienie*** fall into oblivion; ~moga *f* (*-i*; *G -móg*) benefit
zapor|a *f* (*-y*; *G -pór*) barrier (*też rail.*); ***~a wodna*** dam; ~owy *mil.* barrage
zapotrzebowa|ć *pf.* order; ~nie *n* (*-a*; *G -ań*) *econ.* demand (**na** *A* for)
zapowi|adać (*-am*) ⟨***~edzieć***⟩ announce; *występ* introduce; ***~adać się*** (*z wizytą*) say one is coming; ***~adać się*** (**na** *A*) promise (to be); ~edź *f* (*-dzi*; *-e*) announcement; (*oznaka*) sign, prognostic; ***dać na ~edzi*** put up the banns
zapozna|ny misunderstood, disregarded; ~(wa)ć (**z** *L*) acquaint (**z** *I* with; **się** o.s.); ***~(wa)ć się*** get to know
zapożycz|ać (*-am*) ⟨***~yć***⟩ (*-ę*) (**od, z** *G*) borrow (from); ~enie *n* (*-a*; *G -eń*) borrowing
zapra|cowany *ktoś* overworked; *pieniądz* earned; ~cow(yw)ać (*-[w]uję*) earn, make; ***~cow(yw)ać się*** overwork; ~gn- *pf.* → ***pragn-***; ~szać (*-am*) (**na** *A*, **do** *G*) invite (to); ~wa *f* (*-y*; *G -*) training, exercise; *bud.* mortar; → ***przyprawa***; ~wiać (*-am*) ⟨***~wić***⟩ train (**się** *v/i.*;

do *G* for); **~wiać się** practise (for)
za|pre-, ~pro- *pf.* → **pre-, pro-**
zapro|sić *pf.* → **zapraszać**; **~szenie** *n* (*-a*; *G -eń*) invitation; **~wadzać** (*-am*) ⟨**~wadzić**⟩ lead; *zwyczaj, modę* introduce; → **zakładać**
zaprzą|c *pf.* → **zaprzęgać**; **~tać** (*-am*) ⟨**~tnąć**⟩ (*-nę, -nij!*) *czas* take up; *kogoś czymś* busy (with)
zaprzecz|ać (*-am*) ⟨**~yć**⟩ (*D*) deny; *doświadczeniu, komuś* contradict; → **przeczyć**; **~enie** *n* (*-a*; *G -eń*) denial, contradiction
zaprze|ć *pf.* → **zapierać**; **~da(wa)ć** betray; **~paszczać** (*-am*) ⟨**~paścić**⟩ (*-szczę*) ruin; *szansę* squander; **~stawać** (*-ję*) ⟨**~stać**⟩ (*G*) stop, cease; *produkcję* discontinue
zaprzęg *m* (*-u*; *-i*) team; **~ać** (*-am*) ⟨**~nąć**⟩ (*-nę*) harness
zaprzyjaź|niać się (*-am*) ⟨**~nić się**⟩ (**z** *I*) make friends (with); **~niony** friendly
zaprzy|sięgać (*-am*) ⟨**~sięgnąć, ~siąc**⟩ *jur.* swear in; swear (**komuś/sobie** to s.o./o.s.); **~siężenie** *n* (*-a*; *G -eń*) swearing in
zapuchnięty swollen
zapu|sty *pl.* (*-tów*) Shrovetide, *w szer. zn.* carnival; **~puszczać** (*-am*) ⟨**~ścić**⟩ *włosy* grow; *korzenie* take; F *silnik* start; *ogród itp.* neglect; **~szczony** neglected, run-down
zapychać (*-am*) block (**się** *v/i.*)
zapylony dusty
zapyt|anie *n* (*-a*; *G -ań*) question; inquiry; **znak ~ania** question mark; **~ywać** (*-uję*) → **pytać**
zarabiać (*-am*) earn (**na** *L* for)
zara|dczy: **środki** *m/pl.* **~dcze** remedies *pl.*; **~dny** resourceful; **~dzać** (*-am*) ⟨**~dzić**⟩ (*D*) remedy
zarastać (*-am*) overgrow
zaraz *adv.* at once, immediately
zaraz|a *f* (*-y*; *G -*) plague, *fig.* plague, pest; **~ek** *m* (*-zka*; *-zki*) germ
zarazem *adv.* at the same time
zara|zić *pf.* → **zarażać**; **~źliwy** infectious, contagious; **~żać** (*-am*) infect; **~żać się** become infected
zardzewiały rusty; → **rdzewieć**
zare- *pf.* → **re-**
zaręcz|ać (*-am*) ⟨**~yć**⟩ (*-ę*) → **ręczyć, zapewniać**; **~yć się** become engaged (**z** *I* to); **~yny** *pl.* (*-*) engagement
zarob|ek *m* (*-bku*; *-bki*) earnings *pl.*, wages *pl.*; **~ić** (*-ę*) → **zarabiać**; **~kowy** working; **pracować ~kowo** work for payment; have a job
zarod|ek *m* (*-dka*; *-dki*) germ; embryo; **~nik** *m* (*-a*; *-i*) spore
zaro|snąć *pf.* → **zarastać**; **~st** *m* (*-u*; *0*) growth of hair; **~śla** *n/pl.* thicket; **~śnięty** overgrown; (*zarośnięty*) unshaven, unshaved
zarozumia|lec *m* (*-lca*; *-lcy*) show-off, boaster; **~łość** *f* (*-ści*; *0*) conceit; vanity; **~ły** conceited, vain
zarówno: **~ ... jak ...** both … and …
zaróżowiony rosy
zarumieniony flushed; → **rumiany, rumienić**
zaryglowany bolted; → **ryglować**
zarys *m* (*-u*; *-y*) outline; **w głównych ~ach** in broad outline
zarysow(yw)ać (*-[w]uję*) *arkusz* cover with drawings; *lakier* scratch; *fig.* outline; **~ się** get scratched; *fig.* stand out
zarz. *skrót pisany*: **zarząd** board
zarzą|d *m* (*-u*; *-y*) board; (*dyrekcja*) management, administration; **~dzać** (*-am*) (*I*) manage, administer; (*krajem*) govern; (*hotelem*) run; ⟨**~dzić**⟩ order; decree; **~dzenie** *n* (*-a*; *G -eń*) order, decree; instruction
zarzu|cać (*-am*) ⟨**~cić**⟩ *v/t. szal itp.* throw on; *sieć* cast; *dół* fill up; *rynek* flood (*I* with); (*obwiniać*) accuse (*A* of), reproach (*A* with); *palenie itp.* give up; *v/i. pojazd*: skid; **~t** *m* (*-u*; *-y*) reproach; accusation; **bez ~tu** faultless
za|rzynać (*-am*) ⟨**~rżnąć**⟩ slaughter
zasad|a *f* (*-y*; *G -*) principle; rule; basis; *chem.* base; **z ~y** on principle; **~niczo** *adv.* principally; **~niczy** principal; **ustawa ~nicza** constitution; **~owy** *chem.* basic, alkaline
zasa|dzać (*-am*) ⟨**~dzić**⟩ plant; **~dzać** ⟨**~dzić**⟩ **się** (**na** *L*) be based on; (*w zasadzce*) lie in wait; **~dzka** *f* (*-i*; *G -dzek*) ambush; **~lać** → **zasolić**; **~pać się** *pf.* lose one's breath
zasądz|ać (*-am*) ⟨**~ić**⟩ *jur. odszkodowanie* award; (*skazać*) sentence (**na** *A* for)
zaschnięty dried (up); withered
zasępiony gloomy
zasia|ć *pf.* → **zasiewać**; **~dać** (*-am*) ⟨**zasiąść**⟩ sit down (**do** *G*, **za** *I* to); (*w komisji itp.*) sit (**w** *L* on)

Z

zasiedl|ać (*-am*) ⟨**~ić**⟩ (*-lę*) settle
zasięg *m* (*-u*; *0*) range, scope; **~ *widzenia*** visibility; ***dalekiego ~u*** long-range; ***w ~u*** within reach;**~ać** ⟨**~nąć**⟩ *rady* seek, take; *informacji* get, gather
zasi|lać (*-am*) ⟨**~lić**⟩ supply (***w*** *A* with); (*prądem*) power; (*wzmagać*) boost
zasiłek *m* (*-łku*; *-łki*) benefit, allowance; **~ *chorobowy*** sickness benefit; **~ *rodzinny*** family allowance; **~ *dla bezrobotnych*** unemployment benefit, F dole
zaska|kiwać (*-uję*) *v/t.* surprise; *v/i.* click to;**~kująco** *adv.* surprisingly;**~kujący** surprising; **~rżać** (*-am*) ⟨**~rżyć**⟩ *v/t. kogoś* sue; *wyrok* sue against, challenge; ***~rżać do sądu*** prosecute
zasko|czenie *n* (*-a*; *G -eń*) surprise; **~czony** surprised;**~czyć** *pf.* → ***zaskakiwać***
zaskórny *geol.* → ***podskórny***
zasła|bnąć *pf.* faint; **~ć** (*słać*) → ***zaścielać***;**~niać** (***się*** *v/i.*) *widok* obstruct; *twarz, okno* cover
zasłon|a *f* (*-y*; *G* -) curtain; (*osłona*) screen; *szermierka*: parry; **~ić** *pf.* (*-ę*) → ***zasłaniać***
zasłu|ga *f* (*-i*; *G* -) merit, credit; ***położyć ~gi*** (***dla*** *G*) make contribution (to); **~giwać** (*-uję*) (***na*** *A*) deserve, merit; be worthy (***na uwagę*** of attention); **~żenie** *adv.* deservedly;**~żony** of outstanding merit; well-deserved;**~żyć** *pf.* → ***zasługiwać***; ***~żyć się*** (*D*) render outstanding services (to)
za|słynąć *pf.* (***z*** *G*) become famous (for);**~smakować** *pf.* (***w*** *L*) take a liking (to);**~smarkany** snotty;**~smarow(yw)ać** (*-[w]uję*) smear; **~smucony** sad; → ***smucić***
zasnąć *pf.* (*-nę*) → ***zasypiać***
zasobn|ik *m* (*-a*; *-i*) container; holder; **~y** prosperous; (*obfitujący*) (***w*** *A*) abundant (in), rich (in)
zasolić *pf.* salt
za|sób *m* (*-sobu*; *-soby*) stock, reserve; ***~soby*** *pl.* resources *pl.*; ***~sób wyrazów*** vocabulary
zaspa *f* (*-y*; *G* -) snowdrift;**~ć** *pf.* oversleep;**~ny** half-asleep; (*gnuśny*) sleepy
zaspok|ajać (*-am*) ⟨**~oić**⟩ (*-ję*) *głód, ciekawość itp.* satisfy; *potrzeby* meet
zasrany V *fig. Brt.* shitty, crap(py)
zastać *pf.* (*stać*²) → ***zastawać***
zastanawiać (*-am*) *v/t.* puzzle; **~ *się*** (***nad*** *I*) think (about), consider
zastanowi|ć (**się**) *pf.* → ***zastanawiać***; **~enie** *n* (*-a*; *0*) thought, reflection
zastarzały old; *med.* inveterate
zastaw *m* (*-u*; *-y*) deposit; *econ.* security, collateral; ***dać w ~*** pawn;**~a** *f* (*-y*; *G* -) (***stołowa*** dinner) service; **~ać** (***przy*** *L*) meet (at);**~i(a)ć** block, obstruct; *pułapkę* set; (*dać w zastaw*) pawn; (*zagracać*) (*I*) clutter (with);**~ka** *f* (*-i*; *G -wek*) *anat.* valve
zastąpi|ć *pf.* (*-ę*) → ***zastępować***; ***~ć drogę*** bar s.o.'s way;**~enie** *n*: ***nie do ~enia*** irreplaceable
zastęp *m* (*-u*; *-y*) (*harcerzy*) patrol; **~y** *pl.* (*aniołów*) hosts *pl.*
zastęp|ca *m* (*-y*; *G -ów*),**~czyni** *f* (*-i*; *-e*) deputy, assistant; ***~ca dyrektora*** deputy manager;**~czo** *adv. ktoś* as a deputy; *coś* as a substitute;**~czy** substitute; ***~cza matka*** *med.* surrogate mother; **~ować** (*-uję*) *coś* substitute, replace; *kogoś* deputize (*A* for); (*czasowo*) stand in (*A* for);**~stwo** *n* (*-a*; *G* -) substitution
zastopować (*-uję*) stop
zastosowanie *n* (*-a*; *G -ań*) use, application; → ***stosować***
zastój *m* (*-toju*; *-toje*) stagnation
zastrasz|ający intimidating; **~yć** *pf.* intimidate, overawe
zastrze|gać (*-am*) ⟨**~c**⟩ *sobie prawo* reserve, *jur.* stipulate; ***~c się*** specify one's position;**~żenie** *n* (*-a*; *G -eń*) reservation;**~żony** reserved; *tel. Brt.* ex-directory, *Am.* unlisted
zastrzyk *m* (*-u*; *-i*) *med.* injection; *fig.* boost; ***dawać ~*** inject
zastyg|ać (*-am*) ⟨**~nąć**⟩ set; *fig.* be paralysed
zasu|- *pf.* → **su-**;**~nąć** *pf.* → ***zasuwać***; **~szać** (*-am*) ⟨**~szyć**⟩ *liść* dry;**~wa** *f* (*-y*; *G* -) bolt;**~wać** *zasuwę* bolt; *firankę* draw; (*pracować*) *fig.* be on the go
zasy|chać (*-am*) → ***schnąć***;**~łać** (*-am*) send; **~pać** *pf.* → ***zasypywać***; **~piać** (*-am*) fall asleep; **~pka** *f* (*-i*; *G -pek*) *med.* dusting powder; **~pywać** (*-uję*) *dół* fill in; *ludzi* bury (alive); *fig.* shower (*I* with); → ***obsypywać***
zaszczepiać (*-am*) → ***szczepić***
zaszczy|cać (*-am*) ⟨**~cić**⟩ (*I*) hono(u)r (with);**~t** *m* (*-u*; *-y*) hono(u)r; ***~ty*** *pl.* hono(u)rs *pl.*;**~tny** hono(u)rable

Z

za|szeregow(yw)ać (-[*w*]*uję*) classify; *pracownika* put (**do wyższej kategorii** in a higher income bracket); **~szkodzić** *pf.* damage, harm; → **szkodzić**; **~szo-** *pf.* → **szo-**; **~sztyletować** (-*uję*) stab to death; **~szywać** (-*am*) ⟨**~szyć**⟩ sew up; → **szyć**
zaś 1. *cj.* whereas; **2.** *part.* however, yet
zaściankowy parochial
zaściełać (-*am*) *łóżko* make; → **słać²**
zaślepi|ać (-*am*) ⟨**~ć**⟩ (-*ę*) *fig.* blind; **~enie** *n* (-*a*; *G* -*eń*) blindness
zaśmiec|ać (-*am*) ⟨**~ić**⟩ litter
zaśnieżony snow-covered, covered with snow
zaświadcz|ać (-*am*) ⟨**~yć**⟩ certify; **~enie** *n* (-*a*; *G* -*eń*) certificate
zaświecić *pf. v/t.* light; *lampę* turn on; **~ się** *lampa*: go on; *fig.* light up
zata|czać (-*am*) *krąg* describe; **~czać się** stagger, reel; **~jać** *pf.* → **taić**; **~m-, ~n-, ~ń-** *pf.* → **tam-, tan-, tań-**; **~piać** (-*am*) sink; *pola* flood; → **topić**; **~rasowywać** (-*wuję*) → **tarasować**
zatarg *m* (-*u*; -*i*) conflict, friction
za|tel-, ~tem- *pf.* → **tel-, tem-**; **~tem** (*też* **a ~tem**) *cj.* as a result; so; that is; **~tęchły** musty; **~tkać** *pf.*, **~tknąć** *pf.* → **zatykać**; **~tłoczony** crowded; **~tłuc** *pf.* beat to death; **~tłuszczony** greasy; **~tłuścić** *pf.* (-*szczę*) make greasy
zato|ka *f* (-*i*; *G* -) bay; *anat.* (**czołowa** frontal) sinus; *meteo.* **~ka wyżowa** ridge; **~nąć** *pf.* → **tonąć**; **~nięcie** *n* (-*a*; *G* -*ęć*) drowning; *naut.* sinking; **~pić** *pf.* → **zatapiać, topić**
zator *m* (-*u*; -*y*) traffic jam, *Brt.* tailback, *Am.* backup; *med.* embolism
zatrac|ać (-*am*) ⟨**~ić**⟩ *fig.* lose; **~ony** F damned
za|trącać (-*am*) → **trącić²**; **~troskany** worried, concerned, anxious; **~trucie** *n* (-*a*; *G* -*uć*) poisoning; **~truć** *pf.* → **zatruwać**
zatrudni|ać (-*am*) ⟨**~ć**⟩ employ; **~enie** *n* (-*a*; *G* -*eń*) employment; **~ony** (**w** *L*) employed (by)
zatru|ty poisoned; **~wać** (-*am*) poison
zatrważa|ć (-*am*) → **trwożyć**; **~jąco** *adv.* frighteningly; **~jący** frightening
zatrzask *m* (-*u*; -*i*) spring lock; (*do zapinania*) *Brt.* press-stud, snap-fastener; **~iwać** (-*uję*) shut, close (**się** *v/i.*)
za|trząść *pf.* → **trząść**; **~trzeć** *pf.* → **zacierać**
zatrzym|ywać (-*uję*) ⟨**~ać**⟩ *v/t.* stop (**się** *v/i.*); (*nie puszczać*) halt, check; *ciepło* retain, keep; *złodziej* arrest; (*zachować*) keep (**dla siebie** for o.s.); **~ać się** come to a stop; stay (**w hotelu** at a hotel); *mot.* pull up
zatuszow(yw)ać (-[*w*]*uję*) hush up
zatwardz|enie *n* (-*a*; *G* -*eń*) *med.* constipation; **~iały** inveterate
zatwierdz|ać (-*am*) ⟨**~ić**⟩ confirm, endorse; *plan itp.* approve
zaty|czka *f* (-*i*; *G* -*czek*) plug; **~kać** (-*am*) *zlew* block; *butelkę* cork; *uszy*, *dziurę* plug; **~kać się** get blocked; → **wtykać**
zaufani|e *n* (-*a*; *0*) trust; confidence (**do** *G* in); **brak ~a** mistrust; **w ~u** confidentially
zaufany trusted
zaułek *m* (-*łka*; -*łki*) lane
zautomatyzowany automated; *też fig.* mechanized
zauważ|ać ⟨**~yć**⟩ (-*ę*) notice; (*mówić*) mention
zawadia|cki spirited, flamboyant; **~ka** *m* (-*a*; *G* -*ów*) daredevil
zawadz|ać (-*am*) ⟨**~ić**⟩ (**o** *A*) knock, bump (against, on); get caught (on); *t-ko impf.* be in the way
zawa|hać się *pf.* → **wahać**
zawalać¹ *pf.* → **walać**
zawa|lać² ⟨**~lić**⟩ *pokój* clutter (up); *drogę* block, obstruct; F mess up; **~lić się** collapse; **~lony** F (*pracą*) snowed under
zawał *m* (-*u*; -*y*) (**serca** heart) attack, *med.* cardiac infarction
zawart|ość *f* (-*ści*; *0*) (*paczki*) contents *pl.*; (*książki*) content(s *pl.*); **~y** *umowa* concluded
za|ważyć *pf.* (**na** *L*) weigh (on); **~wczasu** *adv.* in good time; **~wdzięczać** (-*am*) owe; **~wezwać** *pf.* → **wzywać**; **~wiać** *pf.* → **zawiewać**
zawiad|amiać (-*am*) ⟨**~omić**⟩ (**o** *L*) inform (about), notify (about); **~omienie** *n* (-*a*; *G* -*eń*) notice, notification; announcement
zawiadowca *m* (-*y*; *G* -*ców*): **~ stacji** *rail.* station master
zawiany F tipsy
zawias *m* (-*u*; -*y*) hinge
zawiąz|ywać ⟨**~ać**⟩ tie; *supeł też* knot;

chustę itp. put on; *oczy* blindfold; *fig. spółkę* establish, form; **~(yw)ać się** *bot. owoc*: form; *fig.* become established
zawiedziony (*m-os. -dzeni*) disappointed
zawie|ja *f* (*-ei*; *-e*, *-ei*) blizzard; **~rać** (*-am*) contain; include; *kontrakt* conclude; *znajomość* make; **~rucha** *f* (*-y*; *G -*) gale; *fig.* turmoil; **~ruszyć się** F *pf.* (*-ę*) get lost; **~sić** *pf.* (*-szę*) → **zawieszać**; **~sisty** thick
zawiesz|ać (*-am*) *v/t.* hang (*też ściany itp. I* with); *fig. obrady* suspend; *karę jur.* defer; **~ać w czynnościach** suspend from one's post; **~enie** *n* (*-a*; *G -eń*) suspension (*też mot.*); deferment; **~enie broni** cease-fire; **z ~eniem** *jur.* on probation
zawie|ść *pf. v/t.* disappoint; *nadzieje* deceive; *v/i. głos*: fail; **~ść się** (**na, w** *L*) become disappointed (with)
zawietrzn|y: **strona ~a** lee
zawiewać (*-am*) *drogę* cover
zawieźć *pf.* → **zawozić**
zawi|jać (*-am*) *v/t.* fold; wrap (up); *rękawy* roll up; *v/i.* **~jać do portu** put in at a port; **~kłany** → **zawiły**; **~le** *adv.* in a complex way; intricately; **~lgnąć** *pf.* (*-nę*, *też -ł*) become damp; **~ły** complex, complicated; intricate; **~nąć** *pf.* → **zawijać**; **~niątko** *n* (*-a*; *G -tek*) bundle; parcel; **~nić** *pf.* be guilty, be at fault (*I* for); **w czym on ci ~nił?** what did he do to you?; **~niony**: **nie ~niony** through no fault of one's own
zawis|ać (*-am*) *v/i.* hang; hover; **~ać w powietrzu** hover in the air; **~ły** dependent; **~nąć** *pf.* (*-nę*) → **zawisać**
zawi|stny envious, jealous; **~ść** *f* (*-ści*; *0*) envy, jealousy
za|witać *pf.* (**do** *G*) come (to), pay a visit (to); **~wlec** *pf.* drag (**się** o.s.); *chorobę* bring in; **~władnąć** *pf.* (*-nę*) (*I*) possess, seize
zawod|niczka *f* (*-i*; *G -czek*), **~nik** *m* (*-a*; *-cy*) (*w sporcie*) contestant; competitor; player; **~ny** unreliable; *nadzieje* deceptive; **~owiec** *m* (*-wca*; *-wcy*) professional, F pro; (*sport*) professional sportsman; **~owo** *adv.* professionally; **~owy** professional; **~ówka** *f* (*-i*; *G -wek*) F trade school; **~y** *m/pl.* (*-dów*) competition, contest; **~y międzynarodowe** international competition
zawodzić wail; → **zawieść**
zawojow(yw)ać (*-[w]uję*) win, conquer
zawołanie *n* call; **jak na ~** on cue; **na każde ~** at s.o.'s beck and call
zawozić drive, carry
zawód *m* (*-wodu*; *-wody*) profession, occupation; (*rozczarowanie*) disappointment; **z zawodu** by profession; **spotkał go ~** it was a disappointment to him; **sprawić ~** disappoint
zawór *m* (*-woru*, *-wory*) *tech.* valve **~ bezpieczeństwa** safety valve
zawracać *v/i.* turn back; *mot.* make a U-turn; **~ komuś w głowie** turn s.o.'s head; *v/t.* **~ głowę** (*D*) bother, hassle
za|wrotny vertiginous, dizzying; **~wrócić** *pf.* → **zawracać**; **~wrót** *m* (*-otu*; *-oty*): **~wrót głowy** dizziness, vertigo; **~wrzeć** *pf.* → **zawierać, wrzeć**; **~wstydzać** (*-am*) → **wstydzić**; **~wstydzony** ashamed
zawsze 1. *adv.* ever; **na ~** for ever; **2.** *part.* yet, after all
zawy|- *pf.* → **wy-**; **~żać** (*-am*) ⟨**~żyć**⟩ (*-ę*) *poziom* make too high
za|wziąć się *pf.* be determined (**że** to *bezok.*); (**na** *A*) harass; **~wzięty** fierce
zazdro|sny jealous, envious (**o** *A* of); **~ścić** ⟨**po-**⟩ (*-szczę*) (**k-u** *G*) envy (s.o. s.th.); **~ść** *f* (*-ści*; *0*) envy; jealousy; **~śnie** *adv.* jealously, enviously
zazębi|ać się (*-am*) ⟨**~ć się**⟩ (*-ę*) mesh, engage; **~ony** meshed together
zazieleni|ać (*-am*) ⟨**~ć**⟩ make green; **~ać się** become green
zaziębi(a)ć się *pf.* → **przeziębi(a)ć się**
zaznacz|ać (*-am*) ⟨**~yć**⟩ (*-ę*) mark, highlight; (*występować*) emphasize; **~ać się** be marked; (*pojawiać się*) appear
zazna|ć *pf.* → **zaznawać**; **~jamiać** (*-am*) ⟨**~jomić**⟩ (*-ę*) → **zapoznawać**; **~wać** (*-ję*) → **doświadczać**; **nie ~ć spokoju** have no peace
zazwyczaj *adv.* usually
zażalenie *n* (*-a*; *G -eń*) complaint, grievance
za|żarcie *adv.* vehemently; fiercely; **~żarty** vehement; fierce; **~żą-** *pf.* → **żą-**; **~żegnywać** (*-uję*) ⟨**~żegnać**⟩ (*zapobiec*) prevent, forestall; *kłótni, rebelii* head off
zażenowan|ie *n* (*-a*; *0*) embarrassment; **~y** embarrassed, ashamed
zaży|ć *pf.* → **zażywać**; **~łość** *f* (*-ści*; *0*)

closeness, intimacy; **~ły** close, intimate; **~wać** (*-am*) *lek* take; *spokoju itp.* enjoy; **~wny** corpulent
ząb *m* (*zęba*; *zęby*) (***mądrości, mleczny*** wisdom, milk) tooth; (***jadowy*** poison) fang; ***do zębów*** dental, tooth; **~ek** *m* (*-bka*; *-bki*) → **ząb**; ***~ek czosnku*** clove of garlic; **~kować** (*-uję*) teethe, cut teeth; **~kowany** serrated
zba- *pf.* → ***ba-***
zbaczać (*-am*) turn off (***z głównej drogi*** the main road); *fig.* deviate
zbankrutowany bankrupt
zbaw|ca *m* (*-y*; *G -ców*), **~czyni** *f* (*-i*; *-e*) savio(u)r; **~iać** (*-am*) ⟨**~ić**⟩ (*-ę*) save; **Ƨiciel** *m* (*-a*; *-e*) *rel.* Savio(u)r
zbawien|ie *n* (*-a*; *0*) salvation, redemption; **~ny** salutary, beneficial
zbe- *pf.* → **be-**
zbędny needless; → ***niepotrzebny***
zbić *pf.* beat up; *szybę* break; → ***zbijać***
zbiec *pf.* (→ *biegnąć*) (**z** *G*) flee, run away (from); → ***zbiegać***
zbieg *m* **1.** (*-a*; *-owie*) fugitive, runaway; **2.** (*-u*; *-i*): ***~ ulic*** junction of the streets; ***~ okoliczności*** coincidence; **~ać** (*-am*) run down (***po schodach*** the stairs); ***~ać się*** *ludzie*: gather; *materiał*: shrink; (*w czasie*) coincide; **~owisko** *n* (*-a*; *G -*) mixed lot
zbiera|cz *m* (*-a*; *-e*), **~czka** *f* (*-i*; *G -czek*) collector; **~ć** (*-am*) *fig. siły* summon; ***~ć się*** *coś*: accumulate; *ktoś*: gather, assemble; ***~ mi się na*** (*A*) I am going to …; ***~ć obfite żniwo*** *fig.* take one's toll; ⟨**na-, po-**⟩ (*do kolekcji*) collect; *agr. kwiaty* pick, (*z pola*) harvest; **~nina** *f* (*-y*; *G -*) jumble, hotchpotch; (*ludzi*) ill-assorted group
zbieżn|ość *f* (*-ści*; *0*) convergence; (*opinii itp.*) concurrence; ***~ość kół*** *mot.* toe-in; **~y** convergent; concurrent
zbijać (*-am*) *skrzynię* make; *deski* nail together; *argumenty* disprove; ***~ z tropu*** disconcert, put off; → ***zbić, bąk***
zbiorni|ca *f* (*-y*; *G -*) collecting point; **~k** *m* (*-a*; *-i*) tank; container; (*jezioro*) reservoir; **~kowiec** *m* (*-wca*; *-wce*) *naut.* tanker
zbiorow|isko *n* (*-a*; *G -*) collection; (*ludzi*) crowd; **~o** *adv.* collectively; **~y** collective; → ***układ***
zbiór *m* (*zbioru*, *zbiory*) collection; *math.* set; *zw. agr.* harvest, crop; **~ka** *f* (*-i*; *G -rek*) *mil.* roll-call, muster; (*pieniędzy*) collection
zbity beaten; ***~ z tropu*** baffled; *por.* ***zbić***
zbla|- *pf.* → ***bla-***; **~zowany** blasé
zbliż|ać (*-am*) bring nearer *lub* closer, move closer (**do** *G* to); (***do siebie***) bring (closer) together; ***~ać się*** get closer, approach; *data też*: be forthcoming; *ludzie*: be drawn together; **~enie** *n* (*-a*; *G -eń*) approach; *phot.* close-up; (*stosunek*) intimacy; **~ony** close (**do** *G* to); **~yć** *pf.* (*-ę*) → ***zbliżać***
zbłąkany lost, stray; → ***błądzić***
zbocz|e *n* (*-a*; *-y*) slope; **~enie** *n* (*-a*; *G -eń*) deviation, perversion; **~eniec** *m* (*-ńca*; *-ńcy*) pervert; **~yć** *pf.* → ***zbaczać***
zbolały hurt, painful (*też fig.*)
zboż|e *n* (*-a*; *G zbóż*) *bot.* cereal, grain, *Brt.* corn; **~owy** grain, cereal; ***kawa ~owa*** coffee substitute (*from barley*)
zbór *m* (*zboru*; *zbory*) (Protestant) church; (Protestant church) community
zbroczony: ***~ krwią*** bloodstained
zbrodni|a *f* (*-i*; *-e*) crime; **~arka** *f* (*-i*; *G -rek*), **~arz** *m* (*-a*; *-e*) criminal; **~czy** criminal
zbro|ić[1] ⟨**u-**⟩ (*-ę*, *zbrój!*) arm (**się** o.s.); supply new weapons; *beton itp.* reinforce; *teren* develop
zbro|ić[2] *pf.* → **broić**; **~ja** *f* (*-oi*; *-e*, *-oi/-ój*) *hist.* (suit of) armo(u)r; **~jenia** *n/pl.* (*-ń*) armament; (*betonu itp.*) reinforcement; → ***wyścig***; **~jeniowy** arms; **~jnie** *adv.* militarily; **~jny** armed; military; ***siły*** *f/pl.* ***~jne*** armed forces *pl.*; **~jony**: ***beton ~jony*** reinforced concrete
zbrzyd|nąć *pf.* → ***brzydnąć***; ***~ło mi ...*** I am sick of …
zbudzić *pf.* → ***budzić***
zbulwersowany indignant
zbutwiały rotten, decayed
zby|cie *n* (*-a*; *0*) sale; **~ć** *pf.* → ***zbywać***
zbyt[1] *adv.* too, over…
zbyt[2] *m* (*-u*; *0*) sale; ***cena ~u*** selling price, retail price
zby|teczny superfluous; excessive; **~tek** *m* (*-tku*; *0*) excess; (*-tku*; *-tki*) luxury; opulence; ***~tki*** *pl.* → ***figiel***
zbyt|kowny luxurious, sumptuous; **~ni** excessive, exceeding; **~nio** *adv.* excessively, exceedingly
zbywać (*-am*) sell; *fig. kogoś* put off, get rid of; ***nie zbywa mu na*** (*L*) he has enough of everything

Z

zca, z-ca *skrót pisany*: ***zastępca*** Dep. (*deputy*)

z.d. *skrót pisany*: ***z domu*** née

zda|ć *pf.* → ***zdawać***; *egzamin* pass; *szkoła*: (*do wyższej klasy*) be promoted; ***nie ~ć*** fail; F ***~ć się*** → ***przydawać się***; ***być ~nym*** (***na*** *A*) be at the mercy (of); depend (on); **~lny**: ***~lnie kierowany*** remote-controlled; *mil.* guided

zdanie *n* (*-a*; *G -ań*) sentence; (***podrzędne, główne*** subordinate, main) clause; (*pogląd*) view, opinion; ***moim ~m*** in my view

zdarz|ać się (*-am*) ⟨***~yć się***⟩ happen, occur; **~enie** *n* (*-a*; *G -eń*) event; occurrence

zdatny fit (***do*** *G* to)

zdawać (*przekazywać*) transfer, make over; *raport* hand over; ***~ bagaż*** *aviat.* check in; *rail.* deposit; ***~ egzamin*** take (*Brt.* sit) an exam(ination); ***~ się*** (***na*** *A*) rely (on), depend (on); ***zdaje się, że*** it seems/appears that; → ***przydawać się***

zdawkowy trivial, insignificant

zdąż|ać (*-am*) ⟨***~yć***⟩ → ***dążyć, nadążać***; ***nie ~yć*** be late, miss *s.th.*

zdech|ły dead; **~nąć** *pf.* → ***zdychać***

zdecydowanie[1] *n* (*-a*; *0*) determination; decisiveness

zdecydowan|ie[2] *adv.* decisively; **~y** determined, decisive; *por.* ***decydować***

zdegustowany displeased,

zdejmować (*-uję*) remove (*też ze stanowiska*); *ubranie* take off; *słuchawkę* pick up; (*z porządku dnia*) delete

zde|ma-, ~me-, ~mo- *pf.* → ***ma-, me-, mo-***; **~nerwowany** upset, irritated; **~po-** *pf.* → ***po-***; **~prymowany** depressed, dejected

zderz|ać się (*-am*) (***z*** *I*) collide (with), crash (into); **~ak** *m* (*-a*; *-i*) *mot.* bumper; *rail.* buffer; **~enie** *n* (*-a*; *G -eń*) collision, crash; **~yć się** *pf.* (*-ę*) → ***zderzać się***

zde|terminowany determined; intent (***co do*** *G* on); **~tonowany** confused, bewildered; **~wastowany** damaged; ravaged; **~ze-, ~zo-** *pf.* → ***deze-, dezo-***

zdjąć *pf.* → ***zdejmować***

zdjęcie *n* (*-a*; *G -ęć*) removal; *phot.* photograph, F snap(shot); *też* picture

zdła|- *pf.* → ***dła-***; **~wiony** muted, choked

zdmuch|iwać (*-uję*) ⟨***~nąć***⟩ blow away

zdob|ić ⟨***o-***⟩ (*-ę, -ób!*) decorate; **~niczy** decorative

zdoby|cie *n* (*-a*; *G -yć*) conquest; **~ć** *pf.* → ***zdobywać***; **~cz** *f* (*-y*) haul, loot; capture; **~czny** captured; **~wać** (*-am*) get, obtain; *kraj* conquer; *wiedzę* gain; *bramkę* score; *rezultat* achieve; capture; **~wca** *m* (*-y*; *G -ców*), **~wczyni** *f* (*-i*; *-nie*, *G -yń*) conqueror; (***medalu*** medal) winner

zdoln|ość *f* (*-ści*) ability; *zw. pl.* ***~ości*** (***do*** *G*) talent, gift; **~y** talented, gifted; (***do*** *G*) fit (for); ***~y do pracy*** fit for work

zdołać *pf.* (*-am*) be able to

zdra|da *f* (*-y*; *G -*) betrayal, treachery; (*państwa*) treason; ***~da małżeńska*** infidelity; **~dliwy** (***-wie***) treacherous; **~dzać** (*-am*) ⟨***~dzić***⟩ (*-ę*) betray (***się*** o.s.); be unfaithful (***żonę*** to the wife); **~dziecki** treacherous; **~dziecko** *adv.* treacherously; **~jca** *m* (*-y*; *G -ców*), **~jczyni** *f* (*-i*; *-nie*, *G -yń*) traitor

zdrap|ywać (*-uję*) ⟨***~ać***⟩ scrape off

zdrętwiały numb; → ***drętwieć***

zdrobnienie *n* (*-a*; *G -eń*) pet-name; *gr.* diminutive

zdro|je *pl.* → ***zdrój***; **~jowisko** *n* (*-a*; *G -*) spa; **~jowy** spa

zdrow|ie *n* (*-a*; *0*) health; ***on zapadł na ~iu*** his health deteriorated; (***za***) ***~ie twoje!*** your health!; ***na ~ie!*** bless you!; **~o** *adv.* healthily; **~otny** sanitary; healthy; **~y** healthy (*też fig.*); ***~y rozsądek*** common sense

zdrój *m* (*-oju*; *-oje*) spring; *lit.* fount

zdrów *pred.* → ***zdrowy***; ***bądź ~!*** farewell!, good-bye!; ***cały i ~*** safe and well

zdruzgotany shattered (*też fig.*)

zdrzemnąć się *pf.* (*-nę*) drowse; nod off

zdumi|enie *n* (*-a*; *0*) astonishment; **~ewać się** (*-am*) ⟨***~eć się***⟩ (*-eję*) (*I*) be astonished *lub* amazed (at); **~ewająco** *adv.* amazingly; **~ewający** astonishing, amazing; **~ony** astonished

zdun *m* (*-a*; *-i*) stove-builder

zduszony choked; → ***dusić***

zdwajać (*-am*) double; → ***podwajać***

zdy|- *pf.* → ***dy-***; **~chać** (*-am*) die; **~szany** out of breath;

zdziecinniały infantile

zdzier|ać (*-am*) tear off *lub* down; *odzież* wear out; ***~ać skórę*** (*zwierzęcia*) skin; (*na kolanach itp.*) chafe the

skin; F rip off; **~stwo** *n* (*-a*; *G* -) F rip-off
zdzira *f* (*-y*; *G* -) *pej.* bitch
zdziwi|ć *pf.* → ***dziwić***; **~enie** *n* (*-a*; *0*) astonishment
ze *prp.* → ***z***
zebra *m* (*-y*; *G* -) *zo.* zebra; *mot. Brt.* zebra (crossing), *Am.* crosswalk
zebra|ć *pf.* → ***zbierać***; **~nie** *n* (*-a*; *G -ań*) (***wyborcze*** election) meeting
zecernia *f* (*-i*; *-e*) *print.* composing room
zedrzeć *pf.* → ***zdzierać***
zegar *m* (*-a*; *-y*) clock; **~ek** *m* (*-rka*; *-rki*) watch; **~mistrz** *m* watchmaker; **~ynka** *f* (*-i*; *G -nek*) *tel.* speaking clock
ze|gnać *pf.* → ***zganiać***; **~jście** *n* (*-a*; *G -jść*) way down, descent; **~jść** *pf.* (*-jść*) → ***schodzić***
zelować ⟨***pod-***⟩ (*-uję*) sole
zelówka *f* (*-i*; *G -wek*) sole
ze|lżeć *pf.* (*-eję*) let up; *ból*, *wiatr*: ease; *burza*, *gniew*: die down; *gorączka*: go down; **~mdlenie** *n* (*-a*; *G -eń*) faint; **~mdlony** fainted; **~mknąć** → ***zmykać***
zemsta *f* (*-y*; *0*) revenge
zepchnąć *pf.* → ***spychać***
zepsu|cie *n* (*-a*; *0*) decay; *fig.* corruptness, depravity; ***ulegać ~ciu*** decay; → ***psuć się***; **~ty** broken; *mięso* off, bad;
zerk|ać (*-am*) ⟨***~nąć***⟩ (*-nę*) take a glance (***na*** *A* at)
zer|o *n* (*-a*; *G* -) zero; nought; ***poniżej/powyżej ~a*** below/above zero; ***dwa ~o*** two to nil
ze|rwać *pf.* → ***zrywać***; **~rznąć, ~rżnąć** *pf.* → ***zrzynać***; **~schnąć się** *pf.* → ***zsychać się***; **~skakiwać** (*-uję*) ⟨***~skoczyć***⟩ (***z*** *G*) jump (down); (*z roweru*) jump (off); **~skrobywać** (*-uję*) ⟨***~skrobać***⟩ scrape off; **~słać** *pf.* (*słać*1) → ***zsyłać***; **~słanie** *n* (*-a*; *G -ań*) deportation
ze|spalać (*-am*) unite (***się*** *v/i.*); **~spawać** *pf. tech.* weld together; **~spolić** *pf.* (*-lę*, *-ól!*) → ***zespalać***; **~społowy** group, collective; **~spół** *m* (*-połu*; *-poły*) group (*też mus.*); team; *tech.* unit, set; *med.* syndrome
zestaw *m* (*-u*; *-y*) set; kit; ***~ stereo*** stereo; **~iać** ⟨***~ić***⟩ put together (***z*** *I* with); **~ienie** *n* (*-a*; *G -eń*) combination, comparison; compilation (*danych*); ***w ~ieniu z*** (*I*) in comparison with
zestrzelić *pf.* shoot down
zeszlifow(yw)ać (*-[w]uję*) grind down *lub* off
zesz|łoroczny of the previous year; **~ły** last; ***w ~łym roku*** last *lub* previous year
zeszpecony disfigured; → ***szpecić***
zeszyt *m* (*-u*; *-y*) exercise-book; (*czasopisma*) issue
ześliz|giwać się (*-uję*) ⟨***~(g)nąć się***⟩ (*-nę*) slide off; slip off *lub* down
ze|śrubow(yw)ać (*-[w]uję*) screw together; **~tknąć** *pf.* → ***stykać***; **~trzeć** *pf.* → ***ścierać***
zewnątrz: *adv.* ***na ~*** outside; ***z ~*** from the outside
ze|wnętrzny outside; external; outer; **~wrzeć** *pf.* (*-wrzeć*) → ***zwierać***; **~wsząd** *adv.* from everywhere
zez *m* (*-a*; *0*) squint; ***mieć ~a*** squint, have a squint
zezna|nie *n* (*-a*; *G -ań*) *jur.* statement; **~wać** (*-ję*) ⟨***~ć***⟩ state, testify
zezowa|ć (*-uję*) squint, have a squint; **~ty** cross-eyed
zezw|alać (*-am*) ⟨***~olić***⟩ (*-ę*, *-ól!*) (***na*** *A*) allow (to *bezok.*), permit; **~olenie** *n* (*-a*; *G -eń*) permission
zeżreć *pf.* → ***zżerać***
zęb|aty toothed; *tech.* cog; **~owy** dental, tooth; **~y** *pl.* → ***ząb***
ZG *skrót pisany*: ***Zarząd Główny*** head office
zgad|ywać (*-uję*) ⟨***~nąć***⟩ (*-nę*) guess; *zagadkę* solve; ***~nij*** (have a) guess; **~ywanka** *f* (*-i*; *G -nek*) guessing game
zgadzać się (*-am*) (***na*** *A*, ***z*** *I*) agree (to, with); *rachunek*: be correct
zgaga *f* (*-i*; *G* -) *med.* heartburn
zga|lać (*-am*) shave off; **~niać** herd together; → ***odganiać***; **~rniać** (*-am*) ⟨***~rnąć***⟩ sweep; rake together; → ***zgrabiać, odgarniać***; **~sły** *ogień* extinguished; extinct
zgęszczać (*-am*) → ***zagęszczać***
zgiąć *pf.* → ***zginać, giąć***
zgiełk *m* (*-u*; *0*) noise; din; **~liwy** noisy
zgię|cie *n* (*-a*; *G -ęć*) bend; crook; **~ty** bent
zgin|ać (*-am*) (**się**) bend; ***~ać się*** double up; **~ąć** *pf.* → ***ginąć***
zgliszcza *pl.* (-) smouldering ruins *pl.*
zgładzić *pf.* slay
zgłaszać (*-am*) *kradzież itp.* report; *wniosek* put forward, submit; *protest* lodge; *akces*, *do oclenia* declare; ***~ się***

(**u, do** *G*) report (to); (**do** *G*) enter
zgłębiać (*-am*) fathom, penetrate
zgłodniały hungry, famished
zgło|sić *pf.* → ***zgłaszać***; **~ska** *f* (*-i*; *G -sek*) syllable; **~szenie** *n* (*-a*; *G -eń*) report; declaration; application; entry
z|głu- *pf.* → ***głu-***; **~gnębiony** harassed
zgniat|ać (*-am*) ⟨***zgnieść***⟩ squash; mash; **~anie** *n* (*-a*; *G -eń*): ***strefa ~ania*** → ***zgniot***
zgni|ć *pf.* → ***gnić***; **~lizna** (*-y*; *0*) *fig.* decadence, decay; **~ły** rotten, decayed
zgniot *m* (*-u*; *-y*): ***strefa ~u*** *mot.* crumple zone
zgod|a *f* (*-y*; *0*) agreement, consent; ***wyrazić ~ę*** (**na** *A*) agree (to); ***dojść do ~y*** come to an agreement; ***~a!*** OK!, (*przy kupowaniu*) done; → ***~ność***; **~nie** *adv.* in harmony; ***~nie z*** according to; **~ność** *f* (*-ści*) agreement; unanimity; **~ny** agreeable; *decyzja* unanimous; (**z** *I*) compatible (with); consistent (with); ***~ny z prawem*** lawful
zgo|dzić się *pf.* → ***zgadzać się***; **~lić** *pf.* → ***zgalać***; **~ła** *adv.* quite, completely
zgon *m* (*-u*; *-y*) death; **~ić** *pf.* → ***zganiać***
zgorsz|enie *n* (*-a*; *G -eń*) scandal, outrage; ***wywołać ~enie*** cause offence; **~ony** offended, shocked
zgorzel *f* (*-i*; *0*) *med.* gangrene
zgorzkniały embittered, bitter
zgotować *pf.* → ***gotować, przygotowywać***
zgrabi|ać (*-am*) ⟨***~ć***⟩ rake together
zgrabiały numb (with cold)
zgrabny deft, adroit; (*kształtny*) shapely; (*zręczny*) nimble
zgraja *f* (*-ai*; *-e*) (*wilków*) pack; *fig.* gang
zgrany harmonious
zgromadz|ać *pf.* → ***gromadzić***; **~enie** *n* (*-a*; *G -eń*) assembly, gathering
zgroza *f* (*-y*; *0*) horror
zgru|biały thickened, swollen; **~bienie** *n* (*-a*; *G -eń*) thickening; swelling; *gr.* augmentative; **~bny** rough; **~cho-** *pf.* → ***grucho-***
zgrupowanie *n* (*-a*; *G -ań*) group(ing)
zgry|wać (*-am*) harmonize; ***~wać się*** overact; (**na** *A*) play; **~zać** (*-am*) bite; **~ziony** sorrowful; **~zota** *f* (*-y*; *G -*) worry, anxiety; ***~źć*** *pf.* → ***zgryzać***; **~źliwie** *adv.* caustically, bitingly; **~źliwy** caustic, biting
zgrza|ć (*-eję*) *pf.* → ***zgrzewać***; ***~łem się*** I am hot
zgrzebło *n* (*-a*; *G -beł*) curry-comb
zgrzewa|ć (*-am*) *folię* seal; *tech.* weld (together); **~rka** *f* (*-i*; *G -rek*) (*do folii*) (bag) sealer
zgrzybiały decrepit
zgrzyt *m* (*-u*; *-y*) screech, jar; *fig.* hitch; **~ać** (*-am*) screech, grate; jar; (*zębami*) grind
zgub|a *f* (*-y*; *G -*) loss; (*-y*; *0*) undoing; doom; **~ić** *pf.* → ***gubić***; **~iony** lost; *fig.* doomed; **~ny** pernicious
zgwałcenie *n* (*-a*; *G -eń*) raping, rape
zhań- *pf.* → ***hań-***
ZHP *skrót pisany*: ***Związek Harcerstwa Polskiego*** Polish Scouts Organization
ziać (*zieję*) yawn; *otchłań*: gape; ***~ stęchlizną*** have a musty smell; ***~ ogniem*** belch fire
ziar|(e)nko *n* (*-a*; *G -nek*) → ***ziarno***; (*kawy itp.*) bean; *fig.* germ, seed; **~nisty** grainy; ***kawa ~nista*** whole-bean coffee; **~no** *n* (*-a*; *G -ren*) grain; (*nasienie*) seed
ziele *n* (*-a*; *zioła*, *G ziół*) herb; **~niak** *m* (*-a*; *-i*) F greengrocer('s); **~nić** ⟨***za-***⟩ **się** (*-ę*) turn green; **~niec** *m* (*-ńca*; *-ńce*) green space; **~nieć** (*-eję*) look green; **~nina** *n* (*-y*; *G -*) greens *pl.*; **~ń** *f* (*-ni*; *-nie*) green
zielon|o- *w złoż.* green-; **~y** green
zielsko *n* (*-a*; *G -*) weed
ziem|ia *f* (*-i*; *0*) earth; soil, ground; land; ***Źia*** *astr.* (*pl. 0*) Earth; ***nad Źią*** above ground; **~iopłody** *m/pl.* (*-dów*) agricultural products *pl.*; produce; **~niaczany** potato; **~niak** (*-a*; *-i*) potato; **~ny** ground; ***orzeszek ~ny*** peanut; **~ski** earthly, worldly; Earth('s); *posiadłość* landed
ziew|ać (*-am*) ⟨***~nąć***⟩ (*-nę*) yawn
zięb|a *f* (*-y*; *G -*) *zo.* chaffinch; **~ić** (*-ę*) chill, cool; **~nąć** (*-nę*, *też ziąbł*) be *lub* feel cold
zięć *m* (*-cia*; *-ciowie*) son-in-law
zim|a *f* (*-y*; *G -*) winter; ***~ą*** in winter; **~niej(szy)** *adv.* (*adj.*) (*comp. od* → ***cold***) colder
zimno[1] *n* (*-a*; *0*) cold, chill
zim|no[2] *adv.* cold; *fig.* coldly; ***~no mi*** I am cold; **~ny** cold; chilly; **~orodek** *m* (*-dka*; *-dki*) *zo.* kingfisher; **~ować** ⟨***prze-***⟩ (*-uję*) winter; **~owy** winter

ziół|a *pl.* → ***ziele***; **~olecznictwo** *n* phytotherapy; **~owy** herbal
ziomek *m* (*-mka*; *-mkowie*) fellow-countryman
zionąć (*im*)*pf.* (*-nę*, *-ń!*) → ***ziać***
ziółk|o *n* (*-a*; *G -łek*) *fig.* good-for-nothing; **~a** *pl.* herb tea; → ***ziele***
zirytowany irritated, annoyed
ziszczać (*-am*) ⟨***ziścić***⟩ (*-szczę*) realize, fulfill; **~ *się*** come true
zjad|ać (*-am*) eat up; **~liwie** *adv.* viciously; **~liwy** vicious, scathing; *med.* virulent;
zjaw|a *f* (*-y*; *G -*) apparition; phantom; **~iać się** (*-am*) ⟨***~ić się***⟩ appear; **~isko** *n* (*-a*; *G -*) phenomenon
zjazd *m* (*-u*; *-y*) (*samochodem*) downhill drive; (*spotkanie*) assembly, meeting; *sport*: downhill racing; *mot.* exit; **~owy** *narty*: downhill
zje|chać *pf.* → ***zjeżdżać***; **~d-** *pf.* → ***jed-***
zjednocz|enie *n* (*-a*; *G -eń*) unification, union; **~ony** unified, united; ***2one Królestwo*** United Kingdom; **~yć** *pf.* → ***jednoczyć***
zje|dnywać *pf.* → ***jednać***; **~łczały** rancid; **~ść** *pf.* → ***zjadać***; **~żdżać** (*-am*) drive down; (*na nartach*) go down; turn off (***z drogi*** the road); slip down; ***~żdżaj!*** hop it!; ***~żdżać się*** come together; arrive; **~żdżalnia** *f* (*-i*; *-e*) slide
zla|ć *pf.* → ***zlewać***; **~tywać** (*-uję*) fly down; (*spadać*) fall down; ***~tywać się*** come flying up; come together
zląc się *pf.* → ***zlęknąć się***
zlec|ać (*-am*) (***k-u*** *A*) commission (s.o. to do s.th.); **~enie** *n* (*-a*; *G -eń*) order, commission; (***wypłaty*** payment) order; → ***polecenie***; **~eniodawca** *m* client, customer; **~ić** *pf.* (*-cę*) → ***zlecać***
zlecieć *pf.* → ***zlatywać***
zlep|ek *m* (*-pku*; *-pki*) conglomeration, aggregate; **~iać** (*-am*) ⟨***~ić***⟩ glue (***się*** together)
zlew *m* (*-u*; *-y*) (***kuchenny*** kitchen) sink; **~ać** (*-am*) pour away; ***~ać się*** run together; *dźwięki*: blend together; **~isko** *n* (*-a*) *geogr.* basin; **~ki** *m/pl.* swill, slops *pl.*; **~ozmywak** *m* (*-a*; *-i*) sink
zleźć *pf.* → ***złazić***
zlęknąć się become frightened
zli|czać ⟨***~czyć***⟩ total, add up; **~kwi-**, **~to-** *pf.* → ***likwi-***, ***lito-***; **~zywać** (*-uję*) ⟨***~ać***⟩ lick off

zlodowaciały iced up; (*też fig.*) icy
zlot *m* (*-u*; *-y*) meeting, reunion
ZLP *skrót pisany*: ***Związek Literatów Polskich*** Polish Writers' Association
zlustr-, **zluz-** *pf.* → ***lustr-***, ***luz-***
zł *skrót pisany*: ***złoty*** zloty
zła → ***zło***, ***zły***; **~go-** *pf.* → ***łago-***; **~godzenie** *n* (*-a*; *G -eń*) alleviation; moderation; *jur.* mitigation
zła|mać *pf.* → ***łamać***; **~manie** *n* (*-a*; *G -ań*) breaking; break; *med.* fracture; **~many** broken; **~zić** (*-żę*) (***z*** *G*) climb (down); *farba*: flake off
złącz|ać *pf.* → ***łączyć***; **~e** *n* (*-a*; *G -y*) *tech.* joint, connection; **~ka** *f* (*-i*; *G -czek*) *tech.* coupling
zł|e → ***zły***; **~o** *n* (*-a*; *DL złu*; *0*) (***mniejsze*** lesser) evil; → ***zły***
złoci *m-os* → ***złoty***; **~ć** ⟨***po-***⟩ (*-ę*) gild; **~sty** golden
złoczyńca *m* (*-y*; *G -ców*) lawbreaker, criminal
złodziej *m* (*-a*; *-e*), **~ka** *f* (*-i*; *G jek*) thief; (*w sklepie*) shop-lifter; ***~ka*** F *electr.* adapter; **~ski** thievish; **~stwo** *n* (*-a*; *G -*) thieving
złom *m* (*-u*; *0*) scrap metal; **~ować** (*-uję*) scrap
złorzeczyć (*-ę*) (*D*) curse
złoś|cić ⟨***roz-***⟩ (*-szczę*) make angry; irritate; ***~cić się*** get angry (***na*** *A* at; ***z powodu*** *G*, ***o*** *A* about); get cross (***na*** *A* with); **~ć** *f* (*-ści*; *0*) anger; irritation; ***na ~ć*** (*G*) in defiance (of); **~liwie** *adv.* maliciously; **~liwość** *f* (*-ści*; *0*) malice; maliciousness; **~liwy** malicious
złot|(aw)obrązowy golden brown; **~nictwo** *n* (*-a*; *0*) goldsmithery; **~nik** *m* (*-a*; *-cy*) goldsmith; **~o** *n* (*-a*; *0*) *chem.* gold; **~ówka** *f* (*-i*; *G -wek*) one zloty coin; **~y** **1.** gold; golden; **2.** *m* (*-ego*; *-e*) zloty
zło|wieszczo *adv.* ominously; **~wieszczy** ominous; **~wrogi** sinister; **~wrogo** *adv.* in a sinister manner
złoż|e *n* (*-a*; *G złóż*) *geol.* deposit; **~enie** *n* submission; resignation; laying; saving; *gr.* compound; *por.* ***składać***; **~ony** composed (***z*** *G* of); complicated; **~yć** *pf.* → ***składać***
złu|dny illusory; deceptive; **~dzenie** *n* (*-a*; *G -eń*) illusion, delusion; deception; ***być do ~dzenia podobnym do kogoś*** be s.o.'s spit(ting) image

zły 1. (*comp.* **gorszy**) bad; evil; *odpowiedź też* wrong; *uczony* poor; **2. złe** *n* (*-ego*; *0*) evil; **brać/mieć za złe** take amiss; → **zło**

zm. *skrót pisany*: **zmarł(a)** died

zma|- *pf.* → **ma-**; **~gać się** (*-am*) (**z** *I*) struggle (with); **~gania** *n/pl.* (*-ań*) struggle

zmar|ły dead, deceased; **~n-** *pf.* → **marn-**

zmarszcz|ka *f* (*-i*; *G -szczek*) wrinkle; **~ony** wrinkled

zmartwi|enie *n* (*-a*; *G -eń*) worry; **~ony** worried

zmartwychwsta|(wa)ć rise from the dead; **~nie** *n* (*-a*; *G -ań*) resurrection

zmarznięty [-r·z-] cold

zmaz|ywać (*-uję*) ⟨**~ać**⟩ wipe away *lub* off; *fig. winę* expiate

zmą-, zme-, zmę- *pf.* → **mą-, me-, mę-**

zmęcz|enie *n* (*-a*; *0*) exhaustion; weariness; **~ony** tired, weary, exhausted

zmia|- *pf.* → **mia-**; **~na** *f* (*-y*; *G -*) change; transformation; shift; (**nocna** night) duty; **na ~nę** interchangeably; **bez ~n** unchanged; *med.* no abnormality detected (*skrót*: **NAD**); **~tać** (*-am*) sweep away

zmiażdżenie *n* (*-a*; *G -eń*) *med.* crush

zmien|iać (*-am*) ⟨**~ić**⟩ change, alter (**się** *v/i.*); **~iać się** vary; (*przy pracy*) take turns; (**w** *A*) change over (to); **~ny 1.** changing; *tech.* alternating → **prąd**; **2. ~na** *f* (*-ej*; *-e*) *math.* variable

zmierz|- *pf.* → **mierz-**; **~ać** (*-am*) (**ku** *D*, **do** *G*) head (for); *fig.* be driving (**do** *G* at); → **podążać**

zmierzch *m* (*-u*; *-y*) twilight, dusk; **~ać (się)** (*-am*) ⟨**~nąć (się)**⟩ (*-nę*, *-ł*) grow dark

zmierzwiony ruffled; matted

zmiesza|ć *pf.* → **mieszać, peszyć**; **~ć się** get confused; **~nie** *n* (*-a*; *0*) confusion

zmieść *pf.* → **zmiatać**

zmiękcz|acz *m* (*-a*; *-e*) softener; *chem.* plasticizer; **~ać** (*-am*) → **miękczyć**

zmiłowa|ć się *pf.* (**nad** *I*) have mercy (on); **~nie** *n* (*-a*; *0*) mercy

zmizerowany → **mizerny**

zmniejsz|ać (*-am*) decrease, diminish (**się** *v/i.*); reduce; *ból też* alleviate; **~enie** *n* (*-a*; *G -eń*) decrease; reduction

zmo|- *pf.* → **mo-**; **~kły** wet

zmora *f* (*-y*; *G zmór*) nightmare (*też fig.*)

zmordowany dead tired

zmotoryzowany *mil.* motorized; with a car

zmowa *f* (*-y*; *G zmów*) conspiracy; *jur.* collusion

zmó|c *pf. sen*: overcome; *choroba*: lay low; **~wić** *pf. pacierz* say; **~wić się** → **umawiać**

zmrok *m* (*-u*; *0*) darkness; → **mrok, zmierzch**

zmurszały rotten, decayed

zmu|szać (*-am*) ⟨**~sić**⟩ (*-szę*) force (**do** *G* to); **~szać się** force o.s. (**do** *G*); **~szony** forced; **być ~szonym** be forced (**do** *G* to)

zmy|ć *pf.* → **zmywać**; **~kać** (*-am*) → **umykać**; **~lić** *pf.* → **mylić**

zmysł *m* (*-u*; *-y*) sense, faculty; (**do** *G*) instinct (for); **postradać ~y** be out of one's mind; **~owo** *adv.* sensuously; **~owość** *f* (*-ści*; *0*) sensuousness, sensuality; **~owy** sensual, sensuous

zmyśl|ać (*-am*) ⟨**~ić**⟩ (*-ę*) make up, fib; **~ony** made-up, fictional

zmywa|ć (*-am*) wash up; **~lny** washable; **~rka** *f* (*-i*; *G -rek*) dishwasher

znachor *m* (*-a*; *-rzy*), **~ka** *f* (*-i*; *G -rek*) quack

znacz|ąco *adv.* significantly; **~ący** significant; meaningful; **~ek** *m* (*-czka*; *-czki*) (**stemplowy, pocztowy** fiscal, postage) stamp; (*oznaka*) badge; **~enie** *n* (*-a*; *G -eń*) meaning; significance, importance; **mieć ~enie dla** mean for; **~ny** considerable, substantial; significant; **~ony** marked; **~yć** (*-ę*) mean; **to ~y** that means *lub* is (*skrót*: i.e.); → **oznaczać**

znać (*-am*) know; **dać ~** (*D*) let know; **~ po niej, że …** one can see that she…; **~ się** be acquainted; (*nawzajem*) know each other; **~ się** (**na** *L*) know (about); be familiar (with)

znad *prep.* (*G*) from above; **~ morza** from the seaside

znajdować (*-uję*) find; **~ się** be; *dom, wieś*: be situated *lub* located; (*po zgubieniu*) be found; (*zjawiać się*) turn up

znajom|ość *f* (*-ści*) acquaintance; (*przedmiotu*) (*G*) familiarity (with); **po ~ości** through connections *pl.*; **~y** *m* (*-ego*; *-i*), **~a** *f* (*-ej*; *-e*) acquaintance

znak *m* (*-u*; *-i*) (**drogowy** road) sign; (*oznaka*) symbol; (*przestankowy*) mark; **~ firmowy** logo; trademark; **~ życia**

sign of life; ***na ~*** (*G*) as a sign that; ***~i*** *pl.* ***szczególne*** distinguishing features *pl.*; ***dawać się we ~i*** (*D*) plague; (*wydarzenie*) be a heavy blow (for)
znakomi|cie *adv.* eminently, outstandingly; **~tość** *f* (*-ści*) (*ktoś*) celebrity; **~ty** eminent, outstanding
znakować ⟨**o-**⟩ (*-uję*) mark
znalaz|ca *m* (*-y*; *G -ców*), **~czyni** *f* (*-ni*; *-nie*, *-yń*) founder
znale|ziony found; ***biuro rzeczy ~zionych*** *Brt.* lost property office, *Am.* lost and found office; **~zisko** *n* (*-a*; *G -*) finding; **~źć** *pf.* → ***znajdować***; **~źne** *n* (*-ego*; *-e*) reward
zna|mienity outstanding; **~mienny** symptomatic (***dla*** *G* of); **~mię** *n* (*-mienia*; *-miona*) birthmark; (*cecha*) characteristic
znany known (***z tego, że*** from)
znaw|ca *m* (*-y*; *G -ców*), **~czyni** *f* (*-ni*; *-nie*, *-yń*) expert; ***okiem ~cy*** with an expert eye
znę|cać się (*-am*) (***nad*** *I*) abuse, maltreat; **~cić** *pf.* → ***nęcić***; **~kany** (*I*) exhausted (with)
znicz *m* (*-a*; *-e*) grave-light; (*w kościele*) sanctuary lamp; ***~ olimpijski*** the Olympic torch
zniechęc|ać (*-am*) ⟨***~ić***⟩ (*-cę*) (***do*** *G*) discourage (from); ***~ić się*** (***do*** *G*) become discouraged; **~ający** discouraging; **~enie** *n* (*-a*; *0*) discouragement
zniecierpliwi|enie *n* (*-a*; *0*) impatience; **~ony** impatient; → ***niecierpliwić***
znieczu|lać (*-am*) ⟨***~ić***⟩ (*-lę*) *med.* an(a)esthetize; (*miejscowo*) give a local an(a)esthetic; **~lający** an(a)esthetic; **~lenie** *n* (*-a*; *G -eń*) *med.* an(a)esthesia
zniedołężniały infirm, frail
zniekształc|ać (*-am*) ⟨***~ić***⟩ (*-ę*) *informacje* distort; *palce itp.* deform, disfigure
znie|nacka *adv.* suddenly; out of the blue; **~nawidzony** hated; → ***nienawidzić***; **~sienie** *n* (*-a*; *0*) *jur.* abolition; ***nie do ~sienia*** unbearable
zniesławi|ać (*-am*) ⟨***~ć***⟩ (*-ę*) slander; libel; **~enie** *n* (*-a*; *G -eń*) slander; libel;
znieść *pf.* → ***znosić***[1]
zniewa|ga *f* (*-i*; *G -*) insult; **~żać** (*-am*) ⟨***~żyć***⟩ insult
zniewieściały effeminate
znikać (*-am*) → ***niknąć***
znikąd *adv.* from nowhere
znik|nąć *pf.* → ***znikać***; **~nięcie** *n* (*-a*; *G -ęć*) disappearance; **~omy** slight, small, trivial; ***~omo krótki/mało*** very short/little
zniszcz|ały dilapidated; → ***niszczeć***; **~enie** *n* (*-a*; *G -eń*) damage; **~ony** broken, damaged
zni|we- *pf.* → ***niwe-***; **~żać** (*-am*) lower; let down, take down; ***~żać się*** go down; *teren*: drop away, slope
zniżk|a *f* (*-i*; *G -żek*) reduction; discount; **~ować** (*-uję*) *econ.* go down, sink; **~owy** reduced; *trend* downhill; ***po cenie ~owej*** at a discount price;
zno|- *pf.* → ***no-***
znosić[1] carry; *prawo* abolish, repeal; *jajka* lay; *dom* demolish; *most* wash away; *łódź* drift (***z kursu*** off the course); *zakaz* lift; *przykrość*, *ból* bear, endure; *klimat* tolerate; *kogoś* stand; ***~ się*** (***z*** *I*) get on *lub* along (with);
zno|sić[2] *pf.* *ubranie* wear out; **~śny** bearable; passable, *Brt.* not (so) bad
znowu, ~ż, znów 1. *adv.* again; once again; **2.** *part.* so
znudz|enie *n* (*-a*; *0*) boredom, dullness, tedium; ***do ~enia*** ad nauseam; ***ze ~eniem*** bored; **~ić** *pf.* bore; pall on; ***~ić się*** (*I*) be bored (with); **~ony** bored
znuż|enie *n* (*-a*; *0*) exhaustion; weariness; **~yć się** (*I*) become exhausted; → ***nużyć***
zob. *skrót pisany*: ***zobacz*** see
zobacz|enie *n*: ***do ~enia!*** good-bye!; **~yć** *pf.* (*-ę*) see; ***~yć się*** meet, see each other; ***~ymy*** we'll see
zobo|- *pf.* → ***obo-***; **~jętniały** indifferent
zobowiąz|ać *pf.* → ***zobowiązywać***; **~anie** *n* (*-a*; *G -ań*) obligation, commitment; *econ.* liability; **~ywać** (*-uję*) oblige (***do*** *G* to); ***~ywać się*** commit o.s. (***do*** *G* to)
zodiak *m* (*-u*; *0*) zodiac
zohydz|ać (*-am*) ⟨***~ić***⟩ (*-dzę*) make *s.o.* loathe *s.th.*
zoolog *m* (*-a*; *-dzy*) zoologist; **~iczny** zoological
zop-, zor- *pf.* → ***op-, or-***
zorza *f* (*-y*; *-e*, *G zórz*) dawn; ***~ polarna*** aurora, polar lights *pl.*
zosta|(wa)ć stay; remain, be (***przy*** *I* with); *t-ko pf.* become (***uszkodzonym*** damaged; ***ojcem*** a father); **~wi(a)ć** → ***pozostawiać***

ZOZ *skrót pisany*: ***Zespół Opieki Zdrowotnej*** health-care centre
zra|- *pf.* → ***ra-***; **~stać się** (*-am*) *kości*: knit together; **~szać** (*-am*) spray; water
zraz *m* (*-u*; *-y*) *gastr.* steak
zrażać (*-am*) ⟨**zrazić**⟩: ***~ do siebie, ~ sobie*** (*A*) set s.o. against; prejudice against; ***nie ~ się*** (*I*) not be put off
zrąb *m* (*zrębu*; *zręby*) log framing; *pl. fig.* foundations *pl.*; **~ać** *pf. drzewo* fell; hew down
zre|- *pf.* → ***re-***; **~formowany** reformed; **~organizowany** re-organized
zresztą *adv.* incidentally
zrezygnowany resigned
zręby *pl.* → ***zrąb***
zręczn|ość *f* (*-ści*; *0*) dexterity, deftness; **~y** deft, dexterous, skil(l)ful
zro|dzić (*-ę*) → ***rodzić***; **~gowacenie** *n* (*-a*; *G -eń*) callosity; **~sić** *pf.* → ***zraszać***; **~snąć się** *pf.* → ***zrastać się***; **~st** *m* (*-u*; *-y*) *med.* adhesion; **~śnięty** grown together; knitted together
zrozpaczony despairing
zrozumi|ale *adv.* understandably; comprehensibly; **~ały** understandable; comprehensible; ***~ały sam przez się*** natural; self-evident; **~enie** *n* (*-a*; *G -eń*) understanding; comprehension; ***nie do ~enia*** beyond comprehension; ***dać do ~enia*** give to understand; hint; **~eć** *pf.* → ***rozumieć***
zróść się *pf.* → ***zrastać się***
zrówn|ać *pf.* → ***równać, zrównywać***; **~anie** *n* (*-a*; *G -ań*) equalization; parity; *astr.* equinox
zrównoważony balanced
zrównywać (*-uję*) *teren* level, even out; (**z** *I*) equate (with); ***~ z ziemią*** raze to the ground
zróżnicowany varied, differentiated
zrujnowany ruined; → ***rujnować***
zryć *pf.* → ***ryć***
zryw *m* (*-u*; *-y*) spurt; *mot.* acceleration; → ***poryw***; **~ać** (*-am*) *v/t.* tear off *lub* down; *agr.* pick; *stosunki*, *zaręczyny* break off; *umowę* cancel, terminate; *głos* strain; *v/i.* (**z** *I*) break up (with); part (with); (*ukochanym*) walk out (on); ***~ać się*** break; (*ruszyć*) rush off; *ptak*: fly up; *wiatr*: spring up; → ***rwać***
zrządz|ać (*-am*) ⟨**~ić**⟩ bring about
zrze|czenie (**się**) *n* (*-a*; *G -eń*) renunciation, relinquishment; **~kać się** (*-am*) ⟨**~c się**⟩ renounce, relinquish; *tronu, funkcji* abdicate; **~szać** (*-am*) ⟨**~szyć**⟩ bring together; unite; ***~szać się*** be associated; organize; **~szenie** *n* (*-a*; *G -eń*) association; **~szony** unionized (**w** *L* in)
zrzę|da *m/f* (*-y*; *G -*) grumbler, faultfinder; **~dzić** (*-ę*) (**na** *A*) grumble (at), find fault (with)
zrzu|cać (*-am*) ⟨**~cić**⟩ *v/t.* drop; *rogi, liście* shed; *ubranie, maskę* throw off; *winę* shift; **~t** *m* (*-u*; *-y*) *aviat.* (air)drop; **~tka** *f* (*-i*; *G -tek*) collection, *Brt.* F whip-round
zrzynać (*-am*) F copy (**od** *G* from)
zsadz|ać (*-am*) ⟨**~ić**⟩ help down; get down
zsiad|ać (*-am*) ⟨**zsiąść**⟩ (**z** *G*) get off; → ***wysiadać***; ***~ać się*** curdle, set; ***~łe mleko*** sour milk
zstąpić *pf.* → ***zstępować***
zstęp|ny *jur.* descending; **~ować** (*-uję*) descend (***po schodach*** down the stairs); come down
zsu|wać (*-am*) ⟨**~nąć**⟩ (**z** *G*) slide (down); *stoły* push together; ***~nąć się*** (**z** *G*) slide (off), slip (off)
zsy|chać się (*-am*) dry up; wither; **~łać** (*-am*) deport, expel; **~p** *m* (*-u*; *-y*): ***~p do śmieci*** (*Brt.* garbage, *Am.* rubbish) chute; **~pywać** (*-uję*) ⟨**~pać**⟩ (**do** *G*) tip, pour off
zszy|wacz *m* (*-a*; *-e*) stapler; **~wać** (*-am*) ⟨**~ć**⟩ sew together; **~wka** *f* (*-i*; *G -wek*) staple
zubożały impoverished
zuch *m* (*-a*; *-y*) Cub; ***~!*** nice show!; **~owaty** daring, bold
zuchwa|le *adv.* audaciously; **~lstwo** *n* (*-a*; *G -*) impudence, impertinence; nerve; audacity; **~ły** bold; impudent, impertinent; audacious
zupa *f* (*-y*; *G -*) soup; ***~ w proszku*** instant soup
zupełn|ie *adv.* completely, entirely, wholly; **~y** complete, entire, whole; *por.* ***całkowity***
Zurych *m* (*-u*; *0*) Zurich
ZUS *skrót pisany*: ***Zakład Ubezpieczeń Społecznych*** state social insurance company
zuży|cie *n* use; (*paliwa itp.*) consumption; **~ć** *pf.* → ***zużywać***; *też* → **~tkow(yw)ać** (*-[w]uję*) exploit, utilize, make

use of; **~ty** used; **~wać** use up; use (**na** *A* for); ***~wać się*** wear out, become used
zw. *skrót pisany*: ***zwany*** called; ***zwyczajny*** ordinary
zwać call (***się*** o.s.)
zwal|ać pile up, heap up; (**z** *G*) unload (off, from); *winę, obowiązek* shift; *drzewo* fell; ***~ać z nóg*** knock out; ***~ać się*** fall down; → ***walić***; **~czać** (*-am*) ⟨***~czyć***⟩ combat; fight (***się*** each other); *pf. fig.* overcome, get over; **~ić** *pf.* → ***zwalać, walić***; **~niać** (*-am*) *bieg, tempo* reduce, slow down; (*z lekcji*) dismiss, send out; *hamulec* release; *pokój* vacate; *przejście* clear; (*z wojska*) discharge; *kogoś z pracy* lay off, dismiss; *kogoś* set free; liberate (**od** *G* from; ***się*** o.s.); *v/i.* slow down; ***~niać się*** (*z pracy*) give notice; → ***zwolnić***
zwał *m* (*-u*; *-y*) *górnictwo*: slag-heap; ***~y*** *pl. fig.* heap, pile; mountains *pl.*
zwany → ***zwać***; ***tak ~*** so-called
zwapnienie *n* (*-a*; *G -eń*) calcification
zwarcie[1] *n* (*-a*; *G -rć*) *electr.* short circuit; *sport*: clinch; *gr.* stop
zwarcie[2] *adv.* densely, tightly
zwariowany crazy; → ***wariować***
zwarty compact; *tłum* thick; dense, tight; *gr.* stop
zwarzyć się *pf.* (*-ę*) curdle; go sour
zważ|ać (*-am*) ⟨***~yć***⟩ (**na** *A*) pay attention (to), allow (for); ***nie ~ając na*** notwithstanding, despite; ***~ywszy, że*** in view of the fact that; → ***ważyć***
zwątpi|ć *pf.* (**w** *A*) doubt (in); **~enie** *n* (*-a*; *G -eń*) doubt
z|we- *pf.* → ***we-***; **~wędzić** F *pf.* pinch
zwę|glony charred; **~szyć** *pf.* scent, get wind of; **~żać** (*-am*) ⟨***~zić***⟩ (*-żę*) narrow (***się*** *v/i.*); *źrenice itp.* constrict; *suknię* take in; **~żenie** *n* (*-a*; *G -eń*) narrowing; constriction
zwia|ć *pf.* → ***zwiewać***; **~d** *m* (*-u*; *-y*) *mil.* reconnaissance; (*patrol*) scouting patrol; **~dowca** *m* (*-y*; *G -ców*) *mil.* scout
zwiastowa|ć (*-uję*) announce; *fig.* herald; **℞nie** *n* (*-a*; *G -ań*) *rel.* the Annunciation
zwiastun *m* (*-a*; *-i/-owie*) harbinger; *med.* symptom; (*-a*; *-y*) trailer (*filmu*)
związ|ać *pf.* → ***związywać***; **~ek** *m* (*-zku*; *-zki*) connection; relation; relationship; ***~ek zawodowy*** trade union; ***wstąpić w ~ki małżeńskie*** enter into the bond of marriage; ***w ~ku z*** in relation to; **~kowiec** *m* (*-wca*; *-wcy*) (trade) unionist; **~kowy** trade-union; **~ywać** (*-uję*) tie together, tie up; associate; ***~ywać się*** (***z*** *I*) associate (with), be joined together (with)
zwichn|ąć (*-nę*) sprain, wrench, dislocate; **~ięcie** *n* (*-a*; *G -ęć*) *med.* dislocation
zwiedz|ać (*-am*) visit; *miasto* see the sights, see; **~ający** *m* (*-ego*; *G -ych*), **~ająca** *f* (*-ej*; *-e*) visitor; **~anie** *n* (*-a*; *G -ań*) (*G*) visit (to); sightseeing; **~ić** *pf.* → ***zwiedzać***
zwierać (*-am*) *electr.* short-circuit; ***~ się*** clinch
zwierciadło *n* (*-a*; *G -deł*) looking-glass
zwierzać (*-am*) confide; ***~ się*** (***k-o***) unburden o.s. (to s.o.), confide (in s.o.)
zwierzątko *n* (*-a*; *G -tek*) (small) animal
zwierzchni superior; **~czka** *f* (*-i*; *G -czek*), **~k** *m* (*-a*; *-cy*) superior
zwierzenie *n* (*-a*; *G -eń*) confession
zwierzę *n* (*-ęcia*; *-ęta*, *G -rząt*) animal; **~cy** animal
zwie|rzyna *f* (*-y*; *G -*) *zbior.* animals; *hunt.*(***gruba*** big) game; (***płowa*** red) deer; **~szać** (*-am*) ⟨***~sić***⟩ droop; **~ść** *pf.* → ***zwodzić***; **~trzały** stale, flat; *geol.* eroded; **~wać** (*-am*) *v/t.* blow away; *v/i.* F clear off; **~wny** flimsy, gossamer
zwieźć *pf.* → ***zwozić***
zwiędnięty wilted; → ***więdnąć***
zwiększ|ać (*-am*) ⟨***~yć***⟩ (*-ę*) increase (***się*** *v/i.*) → ***mnożyć***
zwię|zły concise; **~źle** *adv.* concisely
zwijać (*-am*) wind up; roll up (***się*** *v/i.*); *obóz* break, strike; *interes* wind up; F ***~ się*** *fig.* → ***uwijać się***
zwil|gotnieć *pf.* (*-eję*) become damp; **~żać** (*-am*) ⟨***~żyć***⟩ (*-ę*) dampen, wet; *wargi* moisten
zwin|ąć *pf.* → ***zwijać***; **~ny** nimble, agile
zwiotczały flaccid, flabby
zwi|sać (*-am*) ⟨***~snąć***⟩ (*-nę*, *-ł*) droop, sag; **~tek** *m* (*-tka*; *-tki*) roll (***papieru*** of paper)
zwlekać (*-am*) *v/i.* (***z***) linger (with)
zwłaszcza *adv.* especially
zwłok|a *f* (*-i*; *G -*) delay; ***kara za ~ę*** *econ.* interest for late payment; ***nie cierpiący ~i*** imperative, urgent
zwłoki *pl.* (*-*) corpse, dead body

zwodniczy misleading
zwodz|ić (*-ę*) mislead, deceive; **~ony** → ***most***
zwolenni|czka *f* (*-i*; *G -czek*), **~k** *m* (*-a*; *-cy*) supporter; adherent
zwolni|ć *pf.* → ***zwalniać***; **~ć się** *lokal*: become vacant; (*z pracy*) give notice, leave; **~enie** *n* (*-a*; *G -eń*) reduction, slow-down; dismissal, redundancy; release; vacating; clearing; discharge; liberation; (*z obowiązku, podatku itp.*) exemption; *por.* ***zwalniać***; ***~enie lekarskie*** sick leave; *szkoła*: *Brt.* doctor's note, *Am.* doctor's excuse; **~ony** (*z pracy*) redundant, dismissed; (*z obowiązku, płacenia*) exempt; (*z lekcji*) excused
zwoł|ywać (*-uję*) 〈***~ać***〉 call together; *zebranie* call for, convene
zwozić (*-żę*) deliver, bring
zwój *m* (*zwoju*; *zwoje*) (*drutu itp.*) coil; (*papieru*) roll; (*pergaminu*) scroll
zwracać return, take back, give back; *pieniądze* repay; (*kierować*) direct (**do** *G* to); *twarz*, *wzrok* turn (**do** *G* to); (*wymiotować*) vomit, bring up; ***~ koszty*** reimburse; → ***uwaga***; **~ się** turn (**do** *G* to, **ku** *D* towards); (*być opłacalnym*) pay
zwrot *m* (*-u*; *-y*) turn; (*zwrócenie*) return; repayment; (*wyrażenie*) expression; ***~ w tył*** *mil. Brt.* about-turn, *Am.* about-face; ***~ kosztów*** reimbursement; **~ka** *f* (*-i*; *G -tek*) stanza; **~nica** *f* (*-y*; *-e*, *G -*) *rail. Brt.* points, *Am.* switch; **~nik** *m* (*-a*; *-i*) *geogr.* tropic; **~nikowy** tropical; **~ność** *f* (*-ści*; *0*) *mot. Brt.* manoeuvrability, *Am.* maneuverability; **~ny** *mot. Brt.* manoeuvrable, *Am.* maneuverable; *econ.* repayable; *gr.* reflexive
zwrócić *pf.* → ***zwracać***
zwycię|ski victorious; **~sko** *adv.* victoriously; **~stwo** *n* (*-a*; *G -*) victory; **~zca** *m* (*-y*; *G -ców*) victor, (*w konkursie itp.*) winner **~żać** (*-am*) 〈***~żyć***〉 (*-ę*) *v/i.* win; *v/t.* defeat; *fig.* overcome; **~żony** defeated; overcome
zwyczaj *m* (*-u*; *-e*) habit; (***ludowy*** popular) custom; ***starym ~em*** in the traditional way; ***wejść w ~*** become a habit; **~ny** ordinary, normal; *profesor, członek* full; **~owo** *adv.* customarily; **~owy** customary
zwyk|le *adv.* usually; ***jak ~le*** as usual; **~ły** usual; regular; normal
zwymyślać (*-am*) *pf.* insult, abuse
zwyrodniały degenerate
zwyżk|a *f* (*-i*; *G -żek*) increase; rise; **~ować** (*-uję*) be on the increase; rise
zygzak *m* (*-a*; *-i*) zigzag; **~owaty** zigzag
zysk *m* (*-u*; *-i*) profit; *fig.* gain, benefit; **~iwać** (*-uję*) 〈***~ać***〉 (*-am*) (**na** *L*) profit (by, from); gain (***na czasie*** time; ***na wartości*** in value); *sławę* acquire; **~owny** profitable
z.z. *skrót pisany*: ***za zgodność*** (*G*) for the correctness of
zza *prp.* (*G*) from behind, from beyond
zziajany out of breath; *pies* panting
zzielenieć *pf.* become green; turn green
zziębnięty chilled, cold
zżerać (*-am*) eat; *rdza też*: corrode
zżół|kły, ~nięty yellow; (*ze starości*) discolo(u)red
zży|ć się *pf.* → ***zżywać się***; **~mać się** (*-am*) wince (**na** *A* at); ***~mał się na myśl*** (**o** *L*) he was annoyed at the thought (of); **~wać się** (*-am*) (**z** *I*) get accustomed (to), get familiar (with); (*z kimś*) get close (to)

Ź

ździebko F a little bit
źdźbło *n* (*-a*, *L źdźble*; *G źdźbeł*) blade
źl|e *adv.* (*comp. gorzej*) badly, poorly; (*ze złym wynikiem*) wrongly; ***~e, że ...*** it's bad that; ***~e się czuć*** feel bad; **~i** *m-os pl.* → ***zły***
źreb|ak *m* (*-a*; *-i*) *zo.* colt; **~ić** 〈**o-**〉 **się** (*-ę*) foal; **~ię** *n* (*-ęcia*; *-ęta*) foal
źrenic|a *f* (*-y*; *G -*) *anat.* pupil; ***pilnować jak ~y oka*** cherish *s.th.* like life itself
źródlan|y: ***woda ~a*** spring water
źródło *n* (*-a*; *G -deł*) (***mineralne, gorące*** mineral, thermal) spring (*też fig.*); *lit., fig.* fount; **~wy** source

Ź

Ż

-ż *part.* → **-że**

żab|a *f* (*-y*; *G* -) *zo.* frog; **~i** frog('s); *fig.* froggy; **~ka** *f* (*-i*; *G -bek*) → **żaba**; (*drzewna*) arboreal frog, *zwł.* tree frog; *tech.* pipe wrench; *sport*: breaststroke; **~karka** *f* (*-i*; *G -rek*), **~karz** *m* (*-a*; *-e*) F *sport*: breaststroke swimmer

żad|en (*f* **~na**, *n/pl.* **~ne**) no, none; no one, nobody; (*z przeczeniem*) any, anybody; **w ~en sposób** in no way; → **wypadek**

żag|iel *m* (*-gla*; *-gle*) *naut.* sail; **~lowiec** *m* (*-wca*; *-wce*) *naut.* sailing ship; **~lowy** sailing; **~lówka** *f* (*-i*; *G -wek*) *naut. Brt.* sailing boat, *Am.* sailboat

żakie|cik *m* (*-a*; *-i*) → **~t** *m* (*-u*; *-y*) jacket

żal[1] *m* (*-u*; *-e*) sorrow, regret; (*uraza*) grudge; (*skrucha*) remorse; *rel.* penitence; **~e** *pl.* complaints *pl.*

żal[2] *pred.*: **~(, że)** it is a pity (that); **~ mi go** I am sorry for him; **było jej ~** (*G*) she felt sorry (for); **czuć ~** (**do** *G*) bear a grudge (against); **~ić się** (*-lę*) complain (**na** *A* about)

żaluzja *f* (*-i*; *-e*) (*listwowa*) venetian blind; (*roleta*) *Brt.* roller blind, *Am.* roller window shade

żałob|a *f* (*-y*; *0*) mourning; **nosić ~ę, chodzić w ~ie** be in mourning; **~ny** mourning; **msza ~na** requiem (mass)

żało|sny pitiful; pathetic; **~śnie** *adv.* pitifully; pathetically; **~wać** ⟨**po-**⟩ (*G*) feel sorry (for); pity (*skąpić*) begrudge, deny; **nie ~wać sobie** (*G*) not deny o.s., allow o.s.; **nie ~wać** (*G*) not spare; **bardzo żałuję** I am very sorry

żar *m* (*-u*; *0*) heat; glow; *fig.* fervo(u)r

żarcie *f* (*-a*; *0*) F grub

żargon *m* (*-u*; *-y*) jargon, slang

żarliw|ie *adv.* fervently, ardently; **~y** fervent, *miłość* ardent; → **gorliwy**

żarłoczn|ość *f* (*-ści*; *0*) gluttony (*też rel.*), greed; **~ie** *adv.* greedily; **~y** greedy

żarłok *m* (*-a*; *-i*) glutton, overeater

żaroodporny heat-resistant

żarówka *f* (*-i*; *G -wek*) *electr.* bulb

żart *m* (*-u*; *-y*) joke; prank, trick; **~em, dla ~u** for fun; **z nim nie ma ~ów …** he is not to be trifled with

żarto|bliwie *adv.* jokingly; **~bliwy** joking; **~wać** ⟨**za-**⟩ (*-uję*) joke

żartowni|sia *f* (*-i*; *-e*), **~ś** *m* (*-sia*; *-sie*) joker; prankster

żarzyć się (*-ę*) glow (*też fig.*)

żąć ⟨**z-**⟩ (*żnę*) reap

żąda|ć ⟨**za-**⟩ (*-am*) demand; **~nie** *n* (*-a*; *G -ań*) demand; **na ~nie** on demand

żądło *n* (*-a*; *G -deł*) sting

żą|dny (*G*) craving (for); avid (for, of); **~dny wiedzy** thirsty for knowledge; **~dza** *f* (*-y*; *G* -) (*G*) desire (for); (*pożądanie*) lust (for); **~dza wiedzy** thirst for knowledge

że 1. *cj.* that; **2.** *part.*: **ledwo ~** hardly, scarcely; **tyle ~** only; → **dlatego, mimo, omal**

-że *part.* (*wzmacniająca*) **siadajże!** do sit down!

żeberka *m/pl. gastr.* spare ribs *pl.*

żebra|czka *f* (*-i*; *G -czek*) beggar; **~ć** (*-am*) beg (**o** *A* for); **~k** *m* (*-a*; *-cy*) beggar; **~nina** *f* (*-y*; *0*) begging

żebro *n* (*-a*; *G -ber*) *anat.* rib

żeby 1. *cj.* (in order) to, in order that; **nie ~** not that; **2.** → **oby, chyba**

żegla|rka *f* (*-o*; *G -rek*) *naut.* yachtswoman; sailor; **~rski** sailing; **~rstwo** *n* (*-a*; *0*) *naut.* sailing; **~rz** *m* (*-a*; *-e*) *naut.* yachtsman; sailor

żeg|lować (*-uję*) sail; **~lowny** navigable; **~luga** *f* (*-i*; *G* -) navigation

żegnać (*-am*) ⟨**po-**⟩ *v/t.* say goodbye (**się** *v/i.*; **z** *I* to); **~j!** farewell!; **~** ⟨**prze-**⟩ **cross** (**się** o.s.)

żel *m* (*-u*; *-e*) gel (*też chem.*)

żelatyna *f* (*-y*; *G* -) gelatine

żela|zisty *geol.* ferruginous; *woda* tasting of iron; **~zko** *n* (*-a*; *G -zek*) iron; **~zny** iron; **~zo** *n* (*-a*; *0*) *chem.* iron

żelbet *m* (*-u*; *-y*) reinforced concrete, ferroconcrete

żeliw|ny cast-iron; **~o** *n* (*-a*; *0*) cast iron

żeni|aczka *f* (*-i*; *G -czek*) marriage; **~ć** ⟨**o-**⟩ (*-ę*) marry; **~ć** ⟨**o-**⟩ **się** (**z** *I*) get married (to)

żen|ować (się) ⟨**za-**⟩ (*-uję*) → **krępować**; **~ująco** *adv.* embarrassingly, awkwardly; **~ujący** embarrassing, awkward

żeński female; *gr.* feminine
żeń-szeń *m* (*-nia*; *-nie*) *bot.* ginseng
żer *m* (*-u*; *0*) prey
żerdź *f* (*-dzi*; *-dzie*) pole
żerować (*-uję*) (*też fig.*) prey (**na** *L* on)
żeton *m* (*-u*; *-y*) token; chip; → ***szton***
żg|ać (*-am*) ⟨**~nąć**⟩ (*-nę*) stab, prick
żleb *m* (*-u*; *-y*) gully
żłob|ek *m* (*-bka*; *-bki*) day nursery; *Brt.* crèche; (*rowek*) groove; **~ić** ⟨**wy-**⟩ (*-ę*) groove; **~kowy** day nursery
żłopać (*-ię*) guzzle, swill
żłób *m* (*-łobu*; *-łoby*) manger
żmija *f* (*GDL - ii*; *-e*) viper; ***~ zygzakowata*** adder
żmudny strenuous
żniw|a *n/pl.* (-) → ***żniwo***; **~iarka** *f* (*-i*; *G -rek*) (*też maszyna*), **~iarz** *m* (*-a*; *-e*) reaper; **~ny** harvesting; **~o** *n* (*-a*; *G* -) harvest
żołąd|ek *m* (*-dka*; *-dki*) *anat.* stomach; **~kowy** stomach
żołądź *f* (F *m*) (*-ędzi*; *-ędzie*) *bot.* acorn; *anat.* glans penis
żoł|d *m* (*-u*; *zw. 0*) pay; **~dak** *m* (*-a*; *-cy*) *pej.* mercenary, soldier; **~nierski** soldier('s), military; ***po ~niersku*** like a soldier; **~nierz** *m* (*-a*; *-e*) *mil.* soldier
żona *f* (*-y*; *G* -) wife; **~ty** married
żonglować (*-uję*) (*I*) juggle (with)
żół|cić ⟨**po-**⟩ make yellow; **~ciowy** bilious; **~ć** *f anat.* bile; (*kolor*) yellow; **~knąć** ⟨**po-, z-**⟩ (*-nę*, *-ł*) turn yellow; (*ze starości*) discolo(u)r; **~taczka** *f* (*-i*; *G -czek*) *med.* jaundice; (*wirusowa*) hepatitis; **~tawo** *adv.* sallowly; **~tawy** yellowish; *skóra* sallow; **~tko** *n* (*-a*; *G -tek*) yolk
żółto *adv.* (*comp. żółciej*) yellow; **~ść** *f* (*-ści*; *0*) yellow; **~zielony** yellowish-green
żółty yellow; (*niezdrowa skóra*) sallow; (*w sygnalizacji*) amber; (*z zazdrości*) green
żółw *m* (*-wia*; *-wie*, *-wi*) *zo.* turtle; tortoise; **~i** turtle; ***~im krokiem*** at a snail's pace
żrąc|y corrosive; **~o** *adv.* corrosively
żreć ⟨**po-, ze-**⟩ F devour; eat, corrode
żubr *m* (*-a*; *-y*) *zo.* wisent, European bison
żu|chwa *f* (*-y*; *G* -) *anat.* mandible, lower jaw; **~ć** (*-ję*) chew; → ***przeżuwać***
żuk *m* (*-a*; *-i*) *zo.* beetle
żuławy *f/pl.* (*G* -) marshland
żur *m* (*-u*; *-y*) *type of Polish soup*
żuraw *m* (*-wia*; *-wie*) *zo.*, *tech.* crane; **~i** crane; **~ina** *f* (*-y*; *G* -) *bot.* cranberry
żurnal *m* (*-a/-u*; *-e*) fashion magazine, glossy
żuż|el *m* (*-żla*; *-żle*) cinders *pl.*, (*większy*) clinker; *sport*: ***wyścigi*** *m/pl.* ***na ~lu*** speedway; **~lowy** cinder; *sport*: speedway
żwaw|o *adv.* briskly; **~y** brisk
żwir *m* (*-u*; *-y*) gravel; **~ownia** *f* (*-i*; *-e*) gravel pit; **~owy** gravel
życi|e *n* (*-a*; *0*) life; ***przy ~u*** living; ***bez ~a*** lifeless; ***za mego ~a*** in my lifetime; ***powołać do ~a*** bring into life; ***wejść w ~e*** *ustawa*: come into force; ***zarabiać na ~e*** earn one's living
życio|rys *m* (*-u*; *-y*) c.v., curriculum vitae; *Am.* résumé; **~wo** *adv.* practically, realistically; **~wy** vital; F practical, realistic
życz|enie *n* (*-a*; *G -eń*) wish, desire; **~enia** *pl.* (*świąteczne itp.*) greetings *pl.*; ***pozostawiać wiele do ~enia*** leave much to be desired; ***na ~enie*** on request; **~liwie** *adv.* kindly; **~liwość** *f* (*-ści*; *0*) kindness, friendliness; **~liwy** kind, friendly; **~yć** (*-ę*) wish (***szczęścia*** (***dobrze***) ***k-u*** s.o. good luck (well)); (*sobie*) desire
żyć (*-ję*) live (**z** *I* with; **z** *G* on, by); ***niech żyje …!*** long live …!
Żyd *m* (*-a*; *-dzi*) Jew; **℞owski** Jewish; ***po ℞owsku*** like a Jew; **~ówka** *f* (*-i*; *G -wek*) Jewess
żyją|cy living, alive; **~tko** *n* (*-a*; *G -tek*) living being, creature
żyla|k *m* (*-a*; *-i*) *med.* varicose vein; **~sty** *mięso* stringy, wiry; *ramiona* sinewy
żyletka *f* (*-i*; *G -tek*) razor-blade
ży|lny venous; **~ła** *f* (*-y*; *G* -) *anat.* vein; **~łka** *f* (*-i*; *G -łek*) *anat.*, *bot.* → ***żyła***; (*wędki*) fishing-line; *fig.* ***mieć ~łkę*** (**do** *G*) have a flair (to); **~łowaty** *mięso* → ***żylasty***
żyrafa *f* (*-y*; *G* -) *zo.* giraffe
żyrandol *m* (*-a*; *-e*) chandelier
żyro *n* (*-a*;) *econ.* endorsement **~kompas** *m* gyro compass; **~wać** (*-uję*) endorse
żyt|ni rye; **~o** *n* (*-a*; *G* -) *bot.* rye

żywcem *adv.* → ***żywiec***
żywica *f* (*-y*; *-e*) resin (*też chem.*)
żywiciel *m* (*-a*; *-e*) *biol.* host; **~ka** *f* (*-i*; *G -lek*) breadwinner
żywiczny resinous
żyw|ić (*-ę*) feed; nourish; *rodzinę* keep; *fig.* cherish; ***~ić się*** *ktoś*: live on, *zwierzę*: feed on; **~iec** *m* **1.** (*-wca*; *-wce*) *wędkowanie*: live-bait; **2.** (*-wca*; *0*) livestock on the hoof; ***~cem*** alive, living
żywienie *n* (*-a*; *0*) nourishment; feeding
żywioł *m* (*-u*; *-y*) element; **~owo** *adv.* vigorously; spontaneously; **~owy** vigorous; spontaneous; *klęska* natural
żywnoś|ciowy food; **~ć** *f* (*-ści*; *0*) food
żywo *adv.* vividly; ***na ~*** live; **~płot** *m* hedge; **~t** *m* (*-a*; *-y*) life; **~tność** *f* (*-ści*; *0*) vitality; (*urządzenia*) life; **~tny** vital
żywy living; *pred.* alive; (*ruchliwy*) lively, vivacious; *światło*, *barwa* vivid; ***handel ~m towarem*** trade in human beings; ***jak ~*** lifelike
żyzny fertile

Ż

Activity Section

The following section contains **games and puzzles** to help you learn how to use this dictionary and practice your Polish language skills. You'll learn about the different features of this dictionary and how to look something up effectively.

Also, you will be provided with some important **grammatical information** where necessary.

Using Your Dictionary

The proper use of a bilingual dictionary is important if you want to speak, read, or write in a foreign language. By understanding the symbols in your dictionary or the structure of the entries, you will save time and avoid making errors.

Perhaps the most common mistake in dictionary use is the confusion of words that look or sound alike but have different meanings. For example, think about the word band. How many meanings can you think of for the word band? Try to list at least three:

a. ______________________________

b. ______________________________

c. ______________________________

Now look up *band* in the English side of the dictionary. There are several Polish words and expressions that correspond to the single English word *band*. Some of these Polish words are listed below in scrambled form.

Unscramble the Polish words, then draw a line connecting each Polish word or expression with the appropriate English meaning.

Polish jumble	***English meaning***
1. tęwsga	a. a conveyor belt
2. daban	b. a musical group
3. pagru	c. a ribbon
4. mataś	d. a criminal group

With several Polish definitions to choose from, each meaning something different, you must be careful to choose the right one that matches the sense of the word you are looking for. The wrong word can make it, at the least, hard for other people to understand you. If you never looked beyond the first translation, you might create a sentence that makes absolutely no sense.

For example

Jane bought tickets to see her favorite ribbon.

We should be careful. Our enemies have decided to conveyor belt together.

When you unjumbled the example words above, you probably noticed that two of them resemble English words. However, even in cases such as this it is better to look up the word if there is any doubt as to its meaning, as the definition will not always be the same in both languages. A Polish word might be either broader or more restricted in meaning than its English counterpart, or it may have a different meaning altogether. This is what is known as a false friend.

For example

Windy in Polish has nothing to do with the weather. It means *elevators*, and is a common sign in office buildings.

Aktualny doesn't mean *actual* but *current*.

Ordynarny might seem something unexceptional, but it means *vulgar* or *rude*.

Kielbasa in English refers to a specific kind of Polish sausage. In Polish, **kiełbasa** is simply the word for *sausage* and can mean any kind.

Look up the English meaning of the following Polish words. Do they mean what you think they do?

on________________________

spacer________________________

but________________________

nowela________________________

okazja________________________

lunatyk________________________

szef________________________

hazard________________________

dres________________________

pupil________________________

Another potential problem in finding a correct translation from English to Polish lies with irregular verbs. The past tense of some irregular verbs in English looks and sounds identical to other words (nouns, adverbs, etc.) that have completely different meanings.

For example, writing a sentence with the past tense of the verb *to bear* might seem straightforward: *He bore a heavy burden*. But problems arise if, instead of converting the past form of the verb to its infinitive *to bear*, you look up the word *bore*. The dictionary does not give you a direct translation of verbs in their past tense form, but it does direct you to the infinitive form. The third headword entry under *bore* states that it is a past form of the verb *to bear*. But the word bore has several other meanings. The first entry provides a translation for the noun, meaning a *cylinder size*, or *caliber*. Translate a sentence carelessly with the first word you find and you get: *He* ***cylinder*** *a heavy burden*.

Below you'll find several phrases that contain irregular verbs in the past tense. Find Polish translations of those verbs by looking up their infinitive forms. Write out the Polish infinitives in the spaces provided.

1. I **thought** it was you. ____________________

2. I **felt** like crying. ____________________

3. The celebrity has **left** the building. __________________

4. That poem **spoke** to me. ______________________

5. The antenna was **bent** out of shape. ______________________

Now find the direct translations for the words in bold (i.e., without going to the infinitive form).

1. _______________________

2. _______________________

3. _______________________

4. _______________________

5. _______________________

Now translate the five Polish words you just found back into English.

1. _____________________

2. _____________________

3. _____________________

4. _____________________

5. _____________________

As you can see, mistakes like these are not a beginner's slight misunderstandings; they simply won't be understood. However, knowing the basics of dictionary use, as well as having an understanding of Polish and English grammar, will help you avoid these kinds of errors. The following pages will review the structure of your dictionary and show you how to pick the right word when you use it. Read the guidelines; then complete the puzzles and exercises to practice what you have learned.

Pronunciation and Spelling

To an English-speaker, the Polish language may at first appear very hard to pronounce, with unfamiliar chains of consonants presenting the most difficulty. However, the good news is, Polish spelling is far more consistent than English, and words are pronounced as they are written. What's more, with very few exceptions, the stress falls on the second-last syllable. You can usually look a Polish word up in the dictionary without difficulty.

However, correct spelling and pronunciation are important if you want others to understand what you are saying. This is especially true in a language like Polish, which uses several sounds that are not commonly found in English. Pages 12 and 13 of your dictionary show you some of the basic pronunciation rules of the Polish language and provide examples of equivalent sounds in English.

Most letters produce only one sound. There are, however, some groups of consonants that combine to produce a single sound:

Letter combination	*Pronounced as*	*Example*
rz	final *g* in *garage*	**rzeka** *(river)*
cz	*ch* in *check*	**czek** *(bank check)*
sz	*sh* in *shop*	**szary** *(grey)*
dz	*ds* in *needs*	**dzwonek** *(bell)*
dż	*j* in *jam*	**dżem** *(jam)*
dź	*j* in *jeans*	**dźwig** *(crane)*

These are often found together with other consonants to produce combinations that do not appear in English. Looking through the dictionary, we can see, for example, that many words begin with **prz**, but while this combination may look daunting, it is pronounced almost the same as *psh* in English. Other unpronounceable-looking combinations include **rz**, as in **krz** (pronounced *ksh*), **chrz** (*hsh*), or **trz** (*tsh*). **Szcz**, as in the city of Szczecin, looks like a tongue-twister, yet the same sound appears in English phrases such as *fresh cheese*.

There are also some single letters that are pronounced differently from English. Most of these are accented letters. Again, you can find more about them on pages 12 and 13 of the dictionary.

Certain consonant combinations are pronounced in exactly the same way as some single letters. This does not present any problem in reading Polish, but knowing how these sounds are written will help you find unfamiliar words in the dictionary.

When the letter **i** is combined with certain letters, it produces a softer sound equivalent to that of another Polish letter:

Letter combination	***Example***
si is pronounced as **ś**	**siostra / ślad** *(sister/footstep)*
ci = ć	**cieć / dać** *(shadow/to give)*
zi = ź	**zima / źle** *(winter/badly)*
ni = ń	**nigdy / koń** *(never/horse)*
dzi = dź	**dzień / niedźwiedź** *(day/bear)*

Other letter combinations also sound the same as single letters:

rz = ż	**rzadki / żywy** *(rare/alive)*
ó = u	**ósmy / uwaga** *(eighth/warning)*
ch = h	**Chiny / halo** *(China/hello)*

These letter combinations can make Polish look difficult at first. But as Polish spelling and stress are very regular, once you have learned the pronunciation, looking up words you have heard should present no further problems. And as you will soon discover, when you talk to people in Polish, you will be able to communicate without requiring perfect pronunciation.

And now, let's practice pronouncing these words!

szynka	czas	osiem	ktoś
chwila	herbata	nić	ojciec
dzień	nikt	do widzenia	wieś
ciocia	rzecz	każdy	róża
ziemia	zimny	niedziela	czarny
szansa	źródło	koniak	słoń
środa	morze	pieniądze	dżentelmen
kaczka	żołnierz	grzyb	dżungla
córka	ogród	mąż	dlaczego

Many of these are common words that are useful to know. Use your dictionary to look up their meanings.

Next, try to read the following sentences:

Szczecin to* duże miasto.

To jest Łukasz, mój bardzo dobry przyjaciel.

Nasz pies jest czarny.

Naleśniki to polskie danie.

Pan Lech jest przystojny.

To jest nowoczesna kuchnia.

What do the sentences mean? Use the dictionary to find out.

* **to** is often said to mean **to jest** (*this is*)

Identifying Headwords

If you are looking for a single word in the dictionary, you simply look for that word's location in alphabetical order. However, if you are looking for a phrase, or an object that is described by several words, you will have to decide which word to look up.

Two-word terms are listed by their first word. If you are looking for the Polish equivalent of *civil servant*, you will find it under *civil*.

The so-called phrasal verbs in English are found in a block under the main verb. The phrasal verbs *get ahead*, *get along*, *get about*, and *get over* are all found in a block after *get*.

Idiomatic expressions are found under the key word in the expression. The phrase *be full of beans*, meaning to have a lot of energy and enthusiasm, is found under the entry for bean.

Polish is a language with grammatical gender. This means there are three categories for words, masculine, feminine, and neuter. While gender is discussed at greater length later, it is important to remember the role it plays when looking at headwords. Nouns will be marked *m*, *f*, or *n*, depending on gender. Feminine headwords that are variants of a masculine headword and share a meaning with that word are listed in alphabetical order with their masculine counterpart. Such feminine headwords are easily identified by their endings – almost always **-a** or **-i**. Thus in Polish, a male teacher is called **nauczyciel** and a female teacher is **nauczycielka**. The masculine form, **nauczyciel** is listed as the headword in the dictionary, and the feminine suffix **~ka** is shown following it, showing that it can be added to the headword to create **nauczycielka**.

Besides suffixes like **-ka**, there are numerous grammatical word endings, but the stem of a word is usually clear. For example, the noun form **mężczyzny**, which means *of a man*, is not found in the dictionary, but finding the headword **mężczyzna** (*man*) presents no difficulty.

Verbs can be trickier, because the verb suffix can also change. If, for instance, you want to discover the meaning of **pracuje** you should look for the stem **prac-**, because **-uj-** is the suffix and **-e** is the third person singular ending (*he/she/it works*). The verb ending **-ować** produces **pracować** (*to work*).

Find the following words in your dictionary. Identify the headword that each is found under and write it next to each word.

1. domu ___dom___
2. książką ___książka___
3. koleżance ______________
4. uważam ______________
5. przyjacielem ______________
6. łóżku ______________
7. maluje ______________
8. gazecie ______________
9. mieszkaniach ______________
10. samochodzie ______________
11. dziewczynami ______________
12. ścianie ______________
13. owoców ______________
14. żyją ______________
15. lekarzowi ______________
16. włoskiego ______________

Now try to find all of these headwords in the following word-search puzzle.

a	d	ł	u	r	z	j	s	a	m	o	c	h	ó	d
k	w	o	g	a	z	e	t	a	s	t	ą	d	i	z
l	k	o	l	e	ż	a	n	k	a	h	c	ó	w	ę
y	t	m	a	e	p	s	k	l	u	w	a	ż	a	ć
d	o	m	r	y	j	b	e	ś	c	i	a	n	a	j
n	s	z	i	b	k	s	i	ą	ż	k	a	r	z	o
c	ę	ż	y	ć	ą	ś	ć	y	b	a	t	s	z	i
ó	h	e	l	w	t	u	b	a	ł	ó	ż	k	o	z
r	b	ą	w	p	r	z	y	j	a	c	i	e	l	ą
u	m	i	e	s	z	k	a	n	i	e	p	r	z	w
k	i	r	c	o	w	o	c	t	ą	p	r	y	i	e
w	l	e	k	a	r	z	u	w	k	k	r	y	w	a
a	e	w	a	ł	m	a	l	o	w	a	ć	ę	l	s
l	r	a	d	z	i	e	w	c	z	y	n	a	ę	ł
m	z	n	r	s	z	i	l	o	w	c	z	y	r	z
o	i	y	g	w	ł	o	s	k	i	t	a	r	j	u

Other letter combinations

As you become familiar with the Polish language, you will see that certain combinations of letters do not occur. For example, the consonants with an accent over them (**ś**, **ć**, **ź**, **ń**, and **dź**) are not followed by a vowel. To write these sounds followed by a vowel, an unaccented consonant and **i** (**si**, **ci**, **zi**, **ni** and **dzi**) are used instead. Another example: No Polish word begins with the letters **y**, **ą**, or **ę**. Knowing these rules will make looking up words in the dictionary much easier.

Most of these letter combinations are easy to learn, and as Polish becomes better known to you, it will be simpler to determine what "looks Polish" and what does not. There are some other matters that present more of a challenge, such as the pairs of letters **ó** and **u**, **rz** and **ż**, and **ch** and **h**, which are pronounced the same. But with a little practice you will notice, for example, that the ending **-ów** is always written with **ó**, while the common verb suffix **-uj** and its derivative forms are always written with **u**.

Practice checking your spelling using the words on the list. Each group includes one correct spelling and two incorrect ones. Look up the words and cross out the misspelled ones. Rewrite the correct spelling in the blanks on the next page.

1.	Krakuw	Kraków	Krakóf
2.	yak	iak	jak
3.	przygoda	pszygoda	pżygoda
4.	tżysta	tszysta	trzysta
5.	krzyk	kszyk	kżyk
6.	zirebak	źrebak	źirebak
7.	wszos	wżos	wrzos
8.	niedziela	ńedźela	ńiedziela

When you have filled in all of the blanks, use the circled letters to build a hidden word below.

1. ___ ___ ___ ___ ___ (___)
   1 2 3 4 5 6

2. ___ (___) ___
   1 2 3

3. ___ (___) ___ ___ ___ ___ ___ ___
   1 2 3 4 5 6 7 8

4. ___ ___ ___ ___ (___) ___ ___
   1 2 3 4 5 6 7

5. ___ ___ (___) ___ ___
   1 2 3 4 5

6. ___ ___ ___ ___ (___) ___
   1 2 3 4 5 6

7. (___) ___ ___ ___ ___
   1 2 3 4 5

8. ___ ___ ___ ___ ___ ___ ___ ___ (___)
   1 2 3 4 5 6 7 8 9

And the hidden word is:

___ ___ ___ ___ ___ ___ ___ ___

Parts of Speech

In English and Polish, words are categorized into different **parts of speech**. These labels tell us what function a word performs in a sentence.

Nouns are things. (Hint: On the Polish side of your dictionary, all nouns are followed by the letters *m*, *f*, or *n*, which indicate their gender. Thus if you see any of those letters following an entry in the vocabulary, you can assume that it is a noun.) *Flower*, *people*, *book*, *doctor*, and *tiger* are all nouns.

Verbs describe actions. *Eat*, *go*, *observe*, and *build* are all verbs.

Adjectives describe nouns in sentences. For example, the adjective *pretty* tells us about the noun *girl* in the phrase *a pretty girl*. *Happy*, *new*, *ugly*, *blue*, and *excellent* are all adjectives.

Adverbs also describe, but they modify verbs, adjectives, and other adverbs. The adverb *quickly* tells you more about how the action is carried out in the phrase *ran quickly*. *Well*, *happily*, *newly*, *critically*, and *theoretically* are all adverbs.

Prepositions specify relationships in time and space. They are words such as *in*, *on*, *before*, or *with*.

Articles are words that accompany nouns. Words like *the* and *a* or *an* modify the noun, marking it as specific or general, and known or unknown. There are no articles in Polish, so **jabłko** can mean *apple*, *an apple*, or *the apple*, depending on context.

Conjunctions are words like *and*, *but*, and *if* that join phrases and sentences together.

Pronouns take the place of nouns in a sentence, such as *it*, *me*, and *they*.

Below is a list of nouns, adjectives, adverbs, and verbs. Look up each word to find out what part of speech it represents and then classify them according to their part of speech into one of the four columns provided below.

stół, ludzie, piękny, nowo, szczęśliwy, dobrze, lekarz, książka, budować, niebieski, krytycznie, ludzie, jeść, nowy, szybko, kwiat, brzydki, tygrys, oglądać, wspaniały, teoretycznie, iść, szczęśliwie, telewizor, spać, źle, być, dom, cicho, solidarność.

Nouns	***Adjectives***	***Verbs***	***Adverbs***
stół	**piękny**		

Nouns

Polish nouns are divided into three gender categories: masculine, feminine, and neuter. Gender plays an important role in the inflection, or changing of word endings according to context, of nouns, as well as adjectives, pronouns, adjectival participles, and verbs. A noun's gender is indicated in the dictionary after the headword with *m* for masculine, *f* for feminine, and *n* for neuter. Note that the grammatical gender of a noun does not necessarily correspond to any natural gender; therefore, a *table* (**stół**) is masculine and the *post office* (**poczta**) is feminine, while a *child* (**dziecko**) is neuter.

Unlike in languages such as French or German, it is usually easy to determine the gender of a Polish noun by looking at the nominative form (i.e., the way the word is given to you in the dictionary). In general, masculine nouns end with a consonant, feminine nouns end with **-a** or **-i**, and neuter words end with **-e**, **-o**, **-ę**, or **-um**.

Masculine	***Feminine***	***Neuter***
brat	kobieta	radio
pokój	lampa	centrum
długopis	pani	ramię
sok	herbata	ubranie
samochód	sprzedawczyni	metro

There are, however, some other endings that are less common, although these, too, follow regular patterns. Some feminine nouns have consonant endings (usually **-c**, **-ść**, **-ź**, **-ż**, **-ń**, **-szcz**, or **-l**, as in **noc**, **miłość**, **sól**), and a few masculine words end in **-a** or **-o**, such as **kolega**, **poeta**, **dentysta**, and diminutives like **Jasio**. Although these masculine words behave like feminine or neuter nouns, they are easy to spot, as they refer to male people.

As in English, there are also a certain number of nouns that exist only in the plural (e.g., **spodnie**, **drzwi**). They are indicated after the headword with *pl.*

Look up the words in the table below. Put an **X** in the right field corresponding to their gender.

Noun	*Masculine*	*Feminine*	*Neuter*	*Plural*
jesień				
mężczyzna				
dziewczyna				
liceum				
zegar				
gospodyni				
okulary				
mieszkanie				
imię				
kość				

Below you will find a set of words with a dot next to each one of them. Look up these words in your dictionary. First, underline all feminine words. Then draw lines to connect all the dots that belong to feminine words (make sure to draw your lines moving from word to word in a clockwise direction, starting from the top).

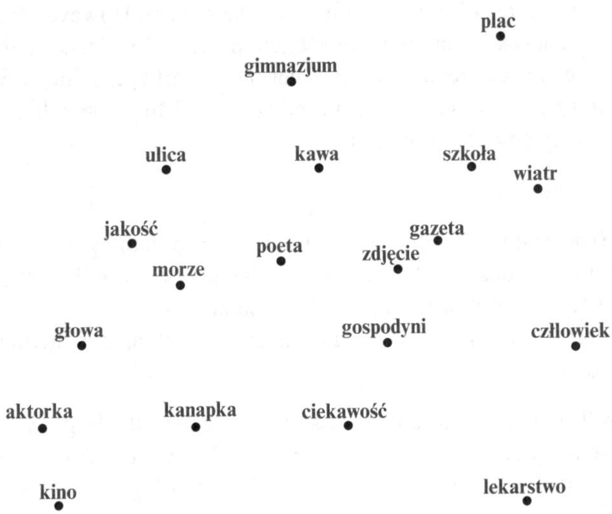

What geometric figure do you see?
Now do the same for all the masculine nouns you find. And then do the same for all the neuter ones.

Declension of Nouns

Polish is an inflected language. This means that a word's ending will change according to its function in a sentence. In Polish, nouns change endings to reflect their position in a sentence (or what is known as a **case**). Your dictionary gives you a declension table for nouns on pages 704–709. That table shows you the changes that a noun goes through from the nominative to the prepositional case. (Note that case endings are different for each gender.)

In the English language, there are no cases, and nouns do not change; the possessive form -*'s* is the closest thing we have to a case. In English, word order determines what is happening. Thus in the phrases *Peter sees a bird* and *A bird sees Peter* neither *Peter* nor *a bird* look any different despite the change in their position in the phrase.

That is not the case in Polish, where the first phrase would look like this: **Piotr widzi ptaka**; and the second phrase would look like this: **Ptak widzi Piotra**. In English, the word order shows who does what; in Polish also the endings (cases) show the word's function.

Beginners are often a little scared by the case system. However, the word endings are consistent and the word function is usually clear. Languages without cases instead tend to use a larger number of prepositions (words such as *in*, *upon*, *through*, *inside*) to indicate word function, which are not necessarily any easier to learn.

The Polish cases are:

Nominative. The nominative case is used when something is the subject of a sentence. Nouns are always listed in the dictionary in the nominative case (and are thus not inflected). In the sentence **Pies ugryzł mężczyznę** (*The dog bit the man*) – **pies** (*the dog*) is the subject, as it is the thing doing something.

Genitive. The genitive describes possession, much as the English possessive form does: **To jest pies Barbary** (*That is Barbara's dog*) – **Barbary** is the genitive form of **Barbara**. The Polish genitive case is also used to refer to things that are lacking: **Barbara nie ma psa** (*Barbara doesn't have a dog*) – here, **psa** is the genitive form of **pies** (*dog*).

Dative. The dative case refers to an indirect object. In **Mężczyzna oddał psa przyjacielowi** (*The man gave the dog to his friend*) the indirect object is **przyjacielowi** (*the friend*).

Accusative. The accusative describes the direct object in a sentence. In **Pies ugryzł mężczyznę** (*The dog bit the man*) – **mężczyznę** (*the man*) is the direct object of the action. (Ouch!)

Instrumental. The instrumental is used when a noun is being used to do something; in other words, if it is functioning as an instrument. If we translated **Pies ugryzł mężczyznę ostrymi zębami** (*The dog bit the man with its sharp teeth*) into Polish, the **ostrymi zębami** (*sharp teeth*) would be in the instrumental case. The instrumental is also used with the verb *to be* when we say something is the same as something else: **Barbara jest inżynierem** (*Barbara is an engineer*).

Locative. As you probably guessed, the locative indicates the location of an action. **W Warszawie pies ugryzł mężczyznę ostrymi zębami w nogę** (*In Warsaw, the dog bit the man in the leg with its sharp teeth*).
In Polish, there would be two locative nouns here, **Warszawie** (*Warsaw*) and **nogę** (*leg*).

Vocative. The vocative is the least common Polish case, and only applies to some words in the singular (although it is often ignored and the nominative used instead). It is used to address someone or something, calling out its name. **Psie, dlaczego mnie ugryzłeś?** (*Oh dog, why did you bite me?*)

Putting these examples together, try to find all of the cases in the following:

> In Warsaw, Barbara's dog bit the man in the leg with its sharp teeth.
> He gave the dog back to her, saying "Barbara, you can keep it!"

It should be noted that the cases are used for almost all nouns, even numbers and proper names. For instance, **pan Kowalski** (Mr. Kowalski) will be **z panem Kowalskim** (*with Mr. Kowalski,* instrumental) or **panu Kowalskiemu** (*to Mr. Kowalski*, dative) and sometimes **pana Kowalskiego** (*Mr. Kowalski's*, genitive). As you can see, there is no escaping the cases, and understanding how they work will make finding headwords, which are always written in the nominative, easier.

In the following set of sentences the word *son* is placed in different positions to show the different cases. The Polish word **syn** is written next to each sentence, but it is missing the ending. The endings are listed in the grammar tables on page 704 of your dictionary. For each sentence look up the ending for a masculine noun for the case that is written in parentheses and write the appropriate ending to the Polish word in the space provided.

1. My **son** is left-handed. (Nominative) **syn__**
2. I was at my **son's** house. (Genitive) **(u) syn__**
3. I lent a book <u>to</u> my **son**. (Dative) **syn__**
4. I see my **son**. (Accusative) **syn__**
5. I am going shopping <u>with</u> my **son**. (Instrumental) **(z) syn__**
6. I am thinking <u>about</u> my **son**. (Locative) **(o) syn__**
7. Come here, my **son**! (Vocative) **Syn__!**

When looking this up, you may have noticed that there are two kinds of masculine nouns: animate and inanimate. Animate nouns refer to animals and people, while inanimate nouns refer to everything else, including plants. The only difference is that the accusative form of animate nouns is the same as the genitive case. For inanimate nouns, it is the same as the nominative.

Now let's try a few sentences with nouns of different genders and numbers and in different cases. As before, the noun will be given to you without the ending. You will need to look up the correct ending and write it in.

1. There is an oak tree outside the **window**. (Inst., neuter, singular) **(za) okn____**
2. We enjoy swimming in the **sea**. (Loc., neuter, singular) **(w) mor___**
3. He last saw his **sister** a year ago. (Acc., feminine, singular) **siostr___**
4. The teacher gave the results to her **students**. (Dat., masculine, plural) **student_____**
5. I don't own a **bicycle**. (Gen., masculine, singular) **rower_____**

Using the dictionary to decipher nouns

The dictionary cannot list every single word ending; if it did, you would need to carry it around in a wheelbarrow. Since Polish nouns follow fairly regular patterns of declension, the dictionary provides hints as to how the word can be used.

For example, we'll look at the entry for the Polish word *heart*, **serce**:

serc|e, *n* (*-a*, *G* -) heart

The first thing in the dictionary after the headword is the letter *n*, indicating that **serce** is a neuter noun (which you knew already, because it ends with the letter **-e**). What is listed in parenthesis requires a more detailed explanation; there are three entries:

The first is the genitive singular ending (**-a**), which means that to build the genitive singular you drop the **-e** ending and put an **-a** instead: **serca**, thus *heartless* is **bez serca**.

The second entry refers to the genitive plural ending. In this case *G* - means that the genitive plural has no ending: **serc**. *Lonely hearts club*, which uses the genitive in Polish, would thus be **klub samotnych serc**. Not every headword will include the genitive plural entry if it isn't likely to be used. Irregular words will be written in full.

Now that we have explained how the cases work, we'll use the dictionary to look up some genitive endings.

Remember that the genitive case is the equivalent of the English possessive (**Dom Jana**, *Jan's house*). It is also used with negatives (**Nie piję kawy**, *I don't drink coffee*), and streets, places, and buildings that are named for people take the genitive form: **Plac Jerzego Waszyngtona** (*George Washington Place*); **Ulica Marii Skłodowskiej-Curie** (*Maria Skłodowska-Curie Street*); **Liceum imienia Tadeusza Kościuszki** (*Thaddeus Kosciusko High School*).

Look up the words in brackets in the dictionary and build the genitive singular forms filling the gaps below. We've supplied the first couple of headwords as examples.

1. To jest córka **przyjaciółki**. (**przyjaciółka** = female friend)
2. On nie ma **czasu**. (**czas** = time)
3. Ja piję dużo ___ ___ ___ ___ ___ ___ ___. (**herbata** = tea)
4. Chętnie uczę się ___ ___ ___ ___ ___ ___ ___ ___ polskiego. (**język** = language)
5. Dzieci chodzą do ___ ___ ___ ___ ___ ___ ___. (school)
6. Mój mąż pochodzi z ___ ___ ___ ___ ___ ___ ___. (Poland)
7. Nie lubię ___ ___ ___ ___ ___. (meat)
8. To zdjęcie mojej ___ ___ ___ ___ ___ ___. (mother)
9. To prezent dla twojego ___ ___ ___ ___ ___ ___. (brother)
10. Restauracja jest niedaleko ___ ___ ___ ___ ___ ___ ___. (post office)
11. Jutro mamy wizytę u ___ ___ ___ ___ ___ ___ ___ ___. (doctor)
12. Chcę herbatę bez ___ ___ ___ ___ ___ ___ ___ ___. (lemon)

Now that you know to form the genitive singular, we can form other cases as well. The accusative case is used to indicate the direct object:

> Peter sees the bird. (*The bird* is the direct object.)
> The dog bit the man. (*The man* is the direct object.)

For neuter nouns, the accusative is the same as the nominative (headword) form. It is also the same as the nominative for most masculine nouns. However, the accusative form of masculine nouns referring to people and animals is the same as the genitive. As mentioned earlier, these are known as masculine animate nouns:

> Jerzy ma kwiat. (*George has a flower*; here **kwiat** is the same in nominative or accusative.)
>
> but
>
> Jerzy ma kota. (*George has a cat*; the nominative is **kot**, genitive and accusative are **kota**.)

Feminine nouns have different accusative endings from either the nominative or genitive. However, these are relatively simple: The vast majority of feminine nouns ending in **-a** drop the **-a** and take **-ę** in the accusative (**kobieta** becomes **kobietę**), and the others end with **-ą** (**pani** becomes **panią**). The accusative endings are shown in the declension tables in the grammar summary on pages 704–709 of the dictionary.

Below are some examples of phrases where the accusative is required. Fill in the missing forms and then put them in the crossword spaces provided. The first letters of each answer placed together form a word. What is it?

1. Mam dobrego _ _ _ _ _ _ _ _ _ _ _. (friend)
2. Jestem głodny. Co jest na _ _ _ _ _? (dinner)
3. Piszę _ _ _ _ od córki. (letter)
4. Muszę kupić _ _ _ _ _ _. (ham)
5. Sąsiadka ma _ _ _ _ _ _ _ w pracy. (troubles)
6. Od wczoraj mamy _ _ _ _ _ _ prądu. (break down)

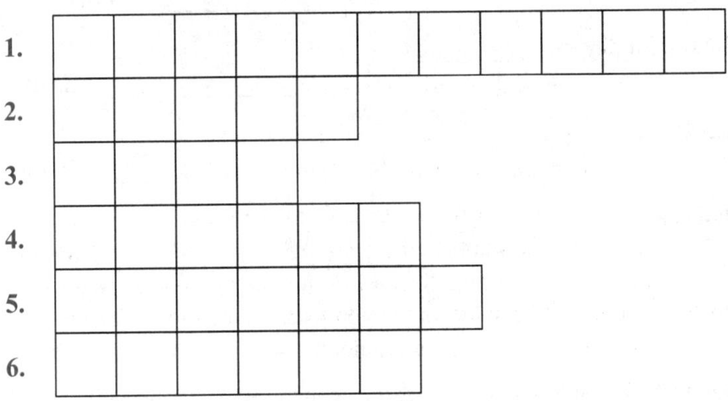

_ _ _ _ _ _

Adjectives

Adjectives in Polish change endings to agree in gender, number, and cases with the noun they modify. In the nominative singular form, masculine adjectives have the endings **-y** or **-i**, and this is the form that is given in the dictionary. To build adjectives for other forms, it is necessary to drop these endings and add those that are appropriate. In the nominative singular, feminine adjectives have the ending **-a**, and neuter adjectives have the ending **-e**.

Use the dictionary to determine whether the nouns in the following phrases are feminine, masculine, or neuter. Look up the Polish translations of the English adjectives and write them next to the English phrases. Then write in the correct forms of the adjectives to complete the phrase.

1. a **blue** sky = ________________

________________ niebo

2. an **interesting** person = ________________

________________ osoba

3. a **small** car = ________________

________________ samochód

4. a **new** apartment = ________________

________________ mieszkanie

5. a **beautiful** day = ________________

________________ dzień

6. a **dark** color = ________________

________________ kolor

7. a **hot** tea = ________________

________________ herbata

8. a **difficult** question = ________________

________________ pytanie

9. an **urgent** message = ________________

________________ wiadomość

10. a **sad** story = ________________

________________ historia

Some nouns take the form of adjectives. For example, many Polish family names are actually adjectives. The well-known **-ski** (or **-dzki** or **-cki**) ending is used only by men, as it is masculine gender; women are **-ska** (or **-dzka** or **-cka**), e.g., **Jan Kwiatkowski**, **Roman Domaniewski**, **Piotr Górski**, **Lech Brodzki**, **Andrzej Łęcki** and **Barbara Kwiatkowska**, **Joanna Domaniewska**, **Halina Brodzka**, **Ewa Łęcka**. As mentioned earlier, these names also change according to case and whether they are singular or plural. Learning how to look up dictionary headwords might therefore also help you make sense of a social invitation (**Kowalscy** are the people we might call *the Kowalskis* in English; **u Podolskich** means *at the Podolskis' place*).

Some street names are adjectives too, such as **ulica Piękna** (*Beautiful Street*), **ulica Długa** (*Wide Street*), or **ulica Prosta** (*Straight Street*). This means they are also declined as adjectives when they appear in a sentence. Therefore, **to jest ulica Długa** (*this is Wide Street*) but **mieszkam na ulicy Długiej** (*I live on Wide Street*).

Have a look at the adjective endings in the grammar summary on pages 708 and 709 of your dictionary. Describe each noun on the left using an appropriate adjective from the list on the right.

1. Pies jest ______________________.	**a.** duży
2. Spodnie są ______________________.	**b.** zielone
3. Zupa jest ______________________.	**c.** zdrowy
4. Pacjent jest już ______________________.	**d.** czyste
5. Ulica jest ______________________.	**e.** smaczna
6. Biurko jest ______________________.	**f.** głodny
7. Róża jest ______________________.	**g.** długie
8. Pokój jest ______________________.	**h.** czerwona
9. Lustro jest ______________________.	**i.** nowe
10. Drzewo jest ______________________.	**j.** szeroka

In the plural, adjectives have only two forms: masculine (sometimes called masculine personal) and non-masculine (sometimes called common or neuter).

The masculine form refers only to male human beings, or to groups including them (thus **polscy profesorowie**, *Polish professors*; **młodzi lekarze**, *young doctors*). All other nouns, regardless of what gender they are in the singular (also female human beings), are described using non-masculine adjectives (**kolorowe ptaki**, *colorful birds*, **polskie gazety**, *Polish newspapers* and **historiczne muzea**, *historical museums*).

Have a look at the adjective endings in plural in the grammar summary. Connect the plural nouns on the left hand side with the corresponding adjectives on the right.

1. dzieci	**a.** atrakcyjne
2. książki	**b.** wymagający
3. budynki	**c.** czarne
4. nauczyciele	**d.** historyczne
5. samochody	**e.** inteligentni
6. koty	**f.** grube
7. studenci	**g.** brudne
8. sekretarki	**h.** wysokie
9. muzea	**i.** małe
10. okna	**j.** wyścigowe

Below you can see some common Polish abbreviations. What are their full names? Fill in the spaces with the missing adjectives.

polska, elektroniczny, społecznych, polski, narodowy, powszechny, polskie, prasowa, państwowe

PKP (Polish National Railways) = __________ Koleje ____________

NBP (National Bank of Poland) = __________ Bank ____________

PAP (Polish Press Agency) = __________ Agencja ___________

PESEL (Universal Electronic System for Registration of the Population, national identification number) = __________ __________ System Ewidencji Ludności

ZUS (Social Insurance Company) = Zakład Ubezpieczeń ___________

Verbs

Verbs in the dictionary are presented in their infinitive form. To use the verb in a sentence, you must conjugate it and use the form that agrees with that verb's subject. Unlike English, verbal endings change depending on the person and tense. When you are reading Polish, you face a different challenge. You see a conjugated verb in context and you need to determine what its infinitive is in order to understand its meaning.

For example, one person says *thank you* as **dziękuję** (*I thank you*), while a group of people say **dziękujemy** (*we thank you*). The dictionary gives only the infinitive form of the verb, in this case **dziękować** (*to thank*), as well as the ending of the first-person present-tense form. This shows which pattern a verb follows, so that we can know the endings for the other persons.

You will notice that most of the time personal pronouns (*I*, *you*, *they*, etc.) are not used in Polish. This is because the ending makes it clear who is performing the action. The second-person *you* forms, **ty** and **wy**, are only used with friends, children, or animals; formal address is described in detail later.

Using the dictionary, see if you can understand what is being said in the dialog below. Look up the infinitive forms of verbs. To find them you have to identify the stem of the word, which in the dictionary is usually separated from the changeable ending. If a conjugated form is very different from the infinitive, the dictionary will direct you to the main form.

– Dzień dobry, pani! Nazywam się Kowalski, a to jest moja współpracowniczka, pani Zaręba. Szukamy pana Nowaka.

– Witam państwa. Miło mi, Podolska. Pan Nowak ma teraz zebranie. Wróci za pięć minut. Proszę siadać.

– Dobrze. Dziękujemy. Poczekamy.

1. nazywam się	**nazyw|ać się**	**5.** ma	____________
2. jest	____________	**6.** wróci	____________
3. szukamy	____________	**7.** dziękujemy	____________
4. witam	____________	**8.** poczekamy	____________

For the next puzzle, you will see conjugated verbs in the sentences. Figure out which verbs the conjugated forms are and write the infinitive (the headword form) for each one in the crossword puzzle.

Across

2. Niemowlę dużo **śpi**. (*The newborn sleeps a lot.*)
4. Na obiad **jemy** zupę. (*We eat soup for dinner.*)
6. Syn **chodzi** do szkoły.
8. Chyba nie **zdążę** na pociąg.
10. One **przygotowują się** do egzaminu.
12. Wczoraj **zarezerwowałem** pokój w hotelu.
13. Nie **mamy** dużo pieniędzy.
14. Czy **możesz** tu przyjść?
15. Gdzie **mieszkacie**?

Down

1. Kuzynka **studiuje** na uniwersytecie. (*My cousin studies at the university.*)
3. Jutro **jadę** na wakacje. (*Tomorrow I'm going on vacation.*)
5. W królestwie **rządzi** król.
7. Malarz **maluje** portret.
9. Rodzice ciężko **pracują.**
11. Sportowiec codziennie **ćwiczy.**

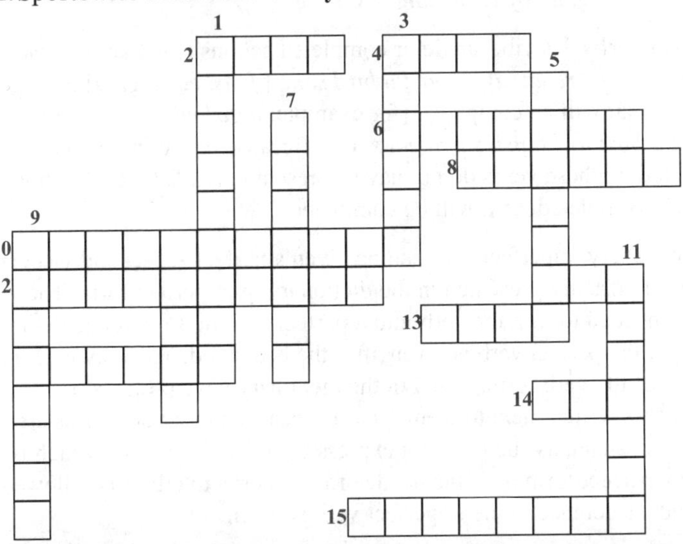

Reflexive verbs

Some of the verbs in the Polish language are called **reflexive verbs**. The subject of a reflexive verb is the same as its direct object – in other words, the action of the verb action is reflected back to its subject. A common example is the verb **nazywać się**, which means *to be called*. Here the object of the verb, which literally means *to call oneself*, is the same as its subject; for example, **Nazywam się Barbara Nowak**, My *name is Barbara Nowak.*

In English, such reflection is accomplished by reflexive pronouns, such as *myself, herself, yourself*, etc. The matter is simpler in Polish, where the reflexive pronoun is always **się**.

Perfect and imperfect verbs

You will notice that some verb entries in your dictionary are followed by letters *(im)pf.* or *pf.* Those stand for **imperfect** and **perfect verb aspects**. This is one of the more challenging elements of the Polish language, and learning it can take a great deal of effort. However, it is important to know the difference when looking up verbs in the dictionary, because a change in aspect can mean a significantly different occurrence, such as between an action now and one that will take place in the future.

Imperfect verbs describe actions that are continuous, habitual, or repeated in nature or where the conclusion is not emphasized (such as a *bird is singing, a boy is reading*, etc.).

Perfect verbs describe single or completed actions (for example: *the girl read* [*finished reading*] *a book*; *a bird sang* [*finished singing*] *a song*, etc.) or that will be completed (for example: *a girl will finish reading a book*; *a bird will finish singing a song*). Because of the importance of completion, these verbs do not have a present tense. Either the action has already completed, or it will be completed.

Almost every imperfect verb can be given a perfect aspect and viceversa. Verbs are usually presented in the dictionary in imperfect form. The prefix needed to turn the verb into a perfect verb or a reference to the entry of the perfect verb is given after the headword. You may notice that not all of the verb forms listed in the dictionary have prefixes or references written next to them. That is because those verb forms are continuous and, as such, cannot express completed actions – which is what a perfect form is. If the headword is a perfect verb, it is followed by *pf.* and a reference to the imperfect verb is given.

The examples of conjugation in the back of your dictionary on pages 713 and 714 show how imperfect verbs can become perfect by adding a prefix in front of the verb. Thus the verb **czytać** (*to read*), which is an imperfect verb, becomes perfect when given the prefix **prze-**. So the statement **Czytam książkę**, meaning *I am reading a book*, becomes *I will read* (or *will have read*) *a book* in the following case: **Przeczytam książkę**.

Below you will find several sentences that contain imperfect verbs. Put those sentences in the future by looking in the dictionary and adding the prefixes listed next to those verbs, making them perfective verbs. Bear in mind that verbs in the dictionary are listed in the infinitive form.

1. **Piszę** list.____

2. **Gotuję** obiad. ______________________________________

3. **Uczę się** polskiego.__________________________________

4. **Jadę** do domu. ______________________________________

5. **Robię** śniadanie. ____________________________________

Now translate the new sentences that you have created into English.

1. ____

2. ____

3. ____

4. ____

5. ____

Formality

Like most European languages, Polish has different ways of addressing people, depending on formality and the number of people we are talking to. While a close friend, a child, or an animal is **ty** (*thou*) and more than one is **wy** (think of the plural form *y'all*), people we do not know as well are addressed in the third person (using the same verb forms as *he*, *she*, or *they*).

We have already seen that **pan** means *sir* and **pani** means *madam*. To address someone politely, these terms are also used along with a third-person singular verb to address someone formally.

Czy **Pan** jest z Warszawy?

(*Are you from Warsaw?* Literally, *Is the gentleman from Warsaw?*)

Czy może mi **Pani** pomóc?

(*Can you help me?* Literally, *Can the lady help me?*)

Niestety, spóźnił się **Pan**.

(*Unfortunately, you were late*. Literally, *Unfortunately, the gentleman was late*.)

In the plural, men are **panowie** (*gentlemen*), women are **panie** (*ladies*), and a mixed group is **państwo** (*ladies and gentlemen*); here, a third-person plural verb (*they*) is used. Remember that pronouns such as **ty**, **wy**, **ja** (*I*), or **my** (*we*), are not always used in Polish. On the other hand, **pan**, **państwo**, etc., are always used if the polite address.

Czy **Państwo** mają dzieci?

(*Do you have children?* Literally, *Do the lady and the gentleman have children?*)

Panie muszą poczekać.

(*You'll have to wait*. Literally, *The ladies will have to wait*.)

Panowie pozwolą ze mną.

(*Follow me*. Literally, *The gentlemen should follow me*.)

In fact, a similar, highly formal equivalent exists in English although we might hear it only from a butler (*Would the gentleman care for coffee? How is the lady feeling today?*). Even so, if we translate these Polish forms back into English, we generally use *you* when they are used in this manner.

Note the use of formal address in the following exchange:

– Proszę **Pana!**
– Słucham **Panią!**
– Czy może mi **Pan** powiedzieć, gdzie jest ulica Sienkiewicza?
– To daleko. Powinna **Pani** jechać prosto a potem skręcić w lewo na skrzyżowaniu.

Unscramble the jumbled words from the dialog.

1. CHAMSŁU ____________________

2. OSZPRĘ ____________________

3. WIEPODZIEĆ ____________________

4. EIZDG ____________________

5. KOLEDA ____________________

6. ECHJĆA ____________________

7. CIĆSKRĘ ____________________

8. ŻOSKNIUWARZY ____________________

Entries in Context

In this dictionary, in addition to the literal translation of each headword, entries sometimes include phrases using that word. When the headword is repeated within an English-Polish entry, a symbol called a tilde (~) takes the place of the paragraph's first headword. For example, the phrase *within reach*, which is listed under the headword *reach*, in your dictionary looks like this: ***within ~***.

On the Polish-English side, some headwords are split by a vertical bar, which serves as a mark of repetition. The tilde replaces only the part of the headword that precedes the vertical bar. For example, when the headword **godzin|a** (*hour*) is used in a question **która godzina?** (*what's the time?*), in your dictionary it looks like this: ***która ~a?***.

Fill in the expressions below, using the correct word in context. Then find those words in the puzzle that follows.

Hint: Each clue contains key words that will help you find the answer. Look up the bold words in each clue. You will find the answers in expressions within each entry.

1. it isn't worth the trouble

   _______________ fatygi

2. amusement park

   _______________ miasteczko

3. to teach somebody a lesson

   _______________ rozumu

4. friendly meeting

   _______________ towarzyskie

5. embarrass

   wprowadzać ______ _____________________

6. thirst for knowledge

   żądza ___________________

7. to offer one's condolences

_______________ ________________ współczucia

8. sick leave

zwolnienie ___________________

9. in one's prime

_______ sile ________________

10. student hostel

________________ akademicki

K	R	W	I	C	S	Z	K	O	D	A	P	U	J	Ą	W	G	Y	L	Ą
I	N	A	C	O	B	Ń	R	I	W	E	S	O	Ł	E	Ż	A	F	S	Z
L	Ó	C	M	A	J	D	A	P	Y	W	Ą	D	U	C	Z	Y	Ć	I	Ę
P	Ą	S	P	O	T	K	A	N	I	E	T	R	A	L	O	J	Ą	C	Z
Z	A	K	Ł	O	P	O	T	A	N	I	E	W	I	Y	Z	D	O	K	D
L	U	M	P	S	Z	I	W	T	A	G	B	E	C	W	I	E	D	Z	Y
Y	Z	Ł	O	Ż	Y	Ć	J	Ó	D	Ź	W	Y	R	A	Z	Y	Ą	C	I
W	Ę	H	L	E	K	A	R	S	K	I	E	Ć	W	Ó	K	O	Ż	U	Ł
Ł	U	R	E	Ś	Z	Y	Ź	M	Y	C	I	W	I	E	K	U	H	U	J
A	C	H	I	P	Ń	D	O	M	A	U	Ż	E	R	Z	I	S	Z	Ę	C

Running Heads

Running heads are words printed at the top of each page. The running head on the left tells you the first headword on the left-hand page. The running head on the right tells you the last headword on the right-hand page. All the words that fall in alphabetical order between the two running heads appear on those two dictionary pages.

Look up the running head on the page where each headword appears and write it in the space provided. Then unscramble the jumbled running heads and match them with what you wrote.

Headword	***Running head***	***Jumbled running head***
1. kelner	KĄPIEL	NOŚĆPIĘK
2. lek	______________	BATRZE
3. niewiele	______________	PISPRZE
4. piosenka	______________	SŁANYW
5. przemysł	______________	TAFERO
6. stokrotka	______________	YNTNEGILETNI
7. truskawka	______________	TOLA
8. woda	______________	CORĄGO
9. ogród	______________	ZAMINIENAJPOKA
10. instytucja	______________	EICYŁP
11. góra	______________	PIELKĄ
12. ciastko	______________	HCARTS

Riddles

Solve the following riddles in English. Then write the Polish translation of the answer on the lines. You will need the numbers below the lines for the activity "Cryptogram."

1. A large fortified building where a king lives.

___ ___ ___ ___ ___
4 3 18 8 22

2. The direction opposite of South.

___ ___ ___ ___ ___ ___
14 39 19 27 26 10

3. Made from fermented milk, this is something a mouse likes to eat.

___ ___ ___
42 8 28

4. A rodent that carries disease.

___ ___ ___ ___ ___ ___
42 4 10 4 51 28

5. A device to talk to people far away using wires.

___ ___ ___ ___ ___ ___ ___
34 8 33 8 32 26 27

6. This is the biggest planet in the solar system.

___ ___ ___ ___ ___ ___
11 26 15 21 42 4

7. A baby horse.

___ ___ ___ ___ ___ ___
2 28 8 9 3 22

8. You study it if you want to be a doctor.

____ ____ ____ ____ ____ ____ ____ ____
18 8 30 5 10 5 27 3

9. People first visited this celestial object in 1969.

____ ____ ____ ____ ____ ____ ____
22 42 21 16 1 5 10

10. A story children like to hear.

____ ____ ____ ____ ____
9 3 11 22 3

11. A small timepiece worn on the wrist.

____ ____ ____ ____ ____ ____ ____
4 8 7 3 28 8 22

12. An animal that moves by hopping and carries her babies in a small pouch.

____ ____ ____ ____ ____ ____
22 3 27 7 51 28

13. Someone who does not eat meat.

____ ____ ____ ____ ____ ____
11 3 28 26 42 4

14. A long green vegetable suitable for making Polish pickles.

____ ____ ____ ____ ____ ____
26 7 39 28 8 22

15. A place where flowers grow, usually with a lawn.

____ ____ ____ ____ ____
26 7 28 39 30

Cryptogram

Write the letter that corresponds to each number (refer to the previous activity "Riddles") in the spaces. When you are done, you will discover a famous expression in Polish. What does it say? Do you know what it is? Try your best to translate it into English.

11	8	42	4	10	4	8		14	26	33	42	22	3	
27	21	8		4	7	21	27	16	19	3				
22	21	8	30	5		18	5		1	5	11	8	18	5

Answer Key

Using Your Dictionary

a.-c. *Answers will vary*

Polish word jumble

1. wstęga, **c**
2. banda, **d**
3. grupa, **b**
4. taśma, **a**

False friends

on = *he*
spacer = *a walk*
but = *shoe*
nowela = *short story*
okazja = *bargain* (but also *occasion*)
lunatyk = *sleepwalker*
szef = *boss*
hazard = *gambling*
dres = *tracksuit*
pupil = *teacher's pet*

Polish verbs infinitives

1. myśleć
2. czuć się
3. opuścić
4. mówić
5. wyginać

Direct translations of words in bold

1. myśl
2. filc
3. lewy
4. szprycha
5. skłonność

Translation back into English

1. *thought, idea*
2. *felt*
3. *left*
4. *spoke*
5. *inclination*

Pronunciation and Spelling

Szczecin is a big city.
This is Lukas, my very good friend.
Our dog is black.
Pancakes are a Polish dish.
Mr. Lech is handsome.
This is a modern kitchen.

Identifying Headwords

1. dom
2. książka
3. koleżanka
4. uważać
5. przyjaciel
6. łóżko
7. malować
8. gazeta
9. mieszkanie
10. samochód
11. dziewczyna
12. ściana
13. owoc
14. żyć
15. lekarz
16. włoski

a	d	ł	u	r	z	j	s	a	m	o	c	h	ó	d
k	w	o	g	a	z	e	t	a	s	t	ą	d	i	z
l	k	o	l	e	ż	a	n	k	a	h	c	ó	w	ę
y	t	m	a	e	p	s	k	l	u	w	a	ż	a	ç
d	o	m	r	y	j	b	e	ś	c	i	a	n	a	j
n	s	z	i	b	k	s	i	ą	ż	k	a	r	z	o
c	ę	ż	y	ç	ą	ś	ć	y	b	a	t	s	z	i
ó	h	e	l	w	t	u	b	a	ł	ó	ż	k	o	z
r	b	ą	w	p	r	z	y	j	a	c	i	e	l	ą
u	m	i	e	s	z	k	a	n	i	e	p	r	z	w
k	i	r	c	o	w	o	c	t	ą	p	r	y	i	e
w	l	e	k	a	r	z	u	w	k	k	r	y	w	a
a	e	w	a	ł	m	a	l	o	w	a	ç	ę	l	s
l	r	a	d	z	i	e	w	c	z	y	n	a	ę	ł
m	z	n	r	s	z	i	l	o	w	c	z	y	r	z
o	i	y	g	w	ł	o	s	k	i	t	a	r	j	u

Other letter combinations

1. Kraków
2. jak
3. przygoda
4. trzysta
5. krzyk
6. źrebak
7. wrzos
8. niedziela

Hidden word: **WARSZAWA**

Parts of Speech

Nouns	Adjectives	Verbs	Adverbs
stół	piękny	budować	nowo
ludzie	szczęśliwy	jeść	dobrze
lekarz	niebieski	oglądać	krytycznie
książka	nowy	iść	szybko
kwiat	brzydki	spać	teoretycznie
tygrys	wspaniały	być	szczęśliwie
telewizor			źle
dom			cicho
solidarność			

Nouns

Noun	Masculine	Feminine	Neuter	Plural
jesień		X		
mężczyzna	X			
dziewczyna		X		
liceum			X	
zegar	X			
gospodyni		X		
okulary				X
mieszkanie			X	
imię			X	
kość		X		

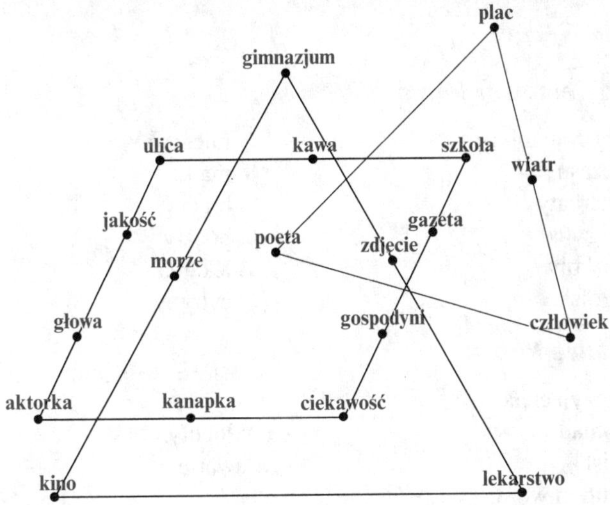

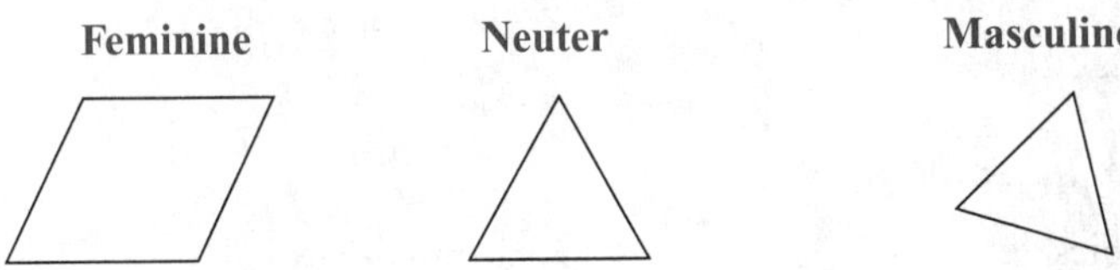

Declension of Nouns

Declension

1. (Nominative)	syn
2. (Genitive)	(u) syna
3. (Dative)	synowi
4. (Accusative)	syna
5. (Instrumental)	(z) synem
6. (Locative)	(o) synu
7. (Vocative)	Synu!

Nouns of different gender and number

1. (Inst., neuter, singular)	(za) oknem
2. (Loc, neuter, singular)	(w) morzu
3. (Acc., feminine, singular)	siostrę
4. (Dat., masculine, plural)	studentowi
5. (Gen., masculine, singular)	rower

Genitive singular forms

1. przyjaciółki
2. czasu
3. herbaty
4. języka
5. szkoły
6. Polski
7. mięsa
8. matki
9. brata
10. poczty
11. lekarza
12. cytryny

Accusative forms

1. przyjaciela
2. obiad
3. list
4. szynkę
5. kłopoty
6. awarię

Solution word: POLSKA

Adjectives

Gender of adjectives

1. niebieskie
2. interesująca
3. mały
4. nowe
5. piękny
6. ciemny
7. gorąca
8. trudne
9. pilna
10. smutna

Declension of adjectives

1. głodny, f
2. długie, g
3. smaczna, e
4. zdrowy, c
5. szeroka, j
6. nowe, i
7. czerwona, h
8. duży, a
9. czyste, d
10. zielone, b

Plural adjectives

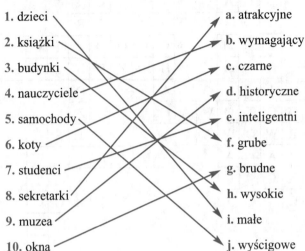

1. dzieci	a. atrakcyjne
2. książki	b. wymagający
3. budynki	c. czarne
4. nauczyciele	d. historyczne
5. samochody	e. inteligentni
6. koty	f. grube
7. studenci	g. brudne
8. sekretarki	h. wysokie
9. muzea	i. małe
10. okna	j. wyścigowe

Polish abbreviations

PKP	= Polskie Koleje Państwowe
NBP	= Narodowy Bank Polski
PAP	= Polska Agencja Prasowa
PESEL	= Powszechny Elektroniczny System Ewidencji Ludności
ZUS	= Zakład Ubezpieczeń Społecznych

Verbs

Infinitives

1. nazyw|ać się
2. być
3. szukać
4. witać
5. mieć
6. wrócić
7. dzięk|ować
8. po|czekać

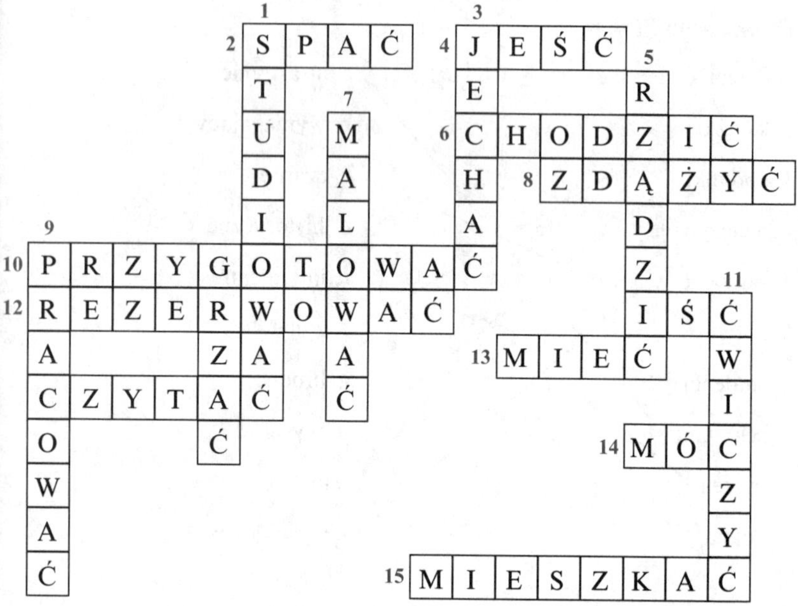

Perfect and imperfect verbs

1. Napiszę list. = *I will write a letter. (I will have written a letter.)*
2. Ugotuję obiad. = *I will cook dinner. (I will have cooked dinner.)*
3. Nauczę się polskiego. = *I will learn Polish. (I will have learned Polish.)*
4. Pojadę do domu. = *I will go home. (I will have gone home.)*
5. Zrobię śniadanie. = *I will prepare breakfast. (I will have prepared breakfast.)*

Formality

1. SŁUCHAM
2. PROSZĘ
3. POWIEDZIEĆ
4. GDZIE
5. DALEKO
6. JECHAĆ
7. SKRĘCIĆ
8. SKRZYŻOWANIU

Entries in Context

1. szkoda fatygi
2. wesołe miasteczko
3. nauczyć rozumu
4. spotkanie towarzyskie
5. wprowadzać w zakłopotanie
6. żądza wiedzy
7. złożyć wyrazy współczucia
8. zwolnienie lekarskie
9. w sile wieku
10. dom akademicki

K	R	W	I	C	S	Z	K	O	D	A	P	U	J	Ą	W	G	Y	L	Ą
I	N	A	C	O	B	Ń	R	I	W	E	S	O	Ł	E	Ż	A	F	S	Z
L	Ó	C	M	A	J	D	A	P	Y	W	Ą	D	U	C	Z	Y	Ć	I	Ę
P	Ą	S	P	O	T	K	A	N	I	E	T	R	A	L	O	J	Ą	C	Z
Z	A	K	Ł	O	P	O	T	A	N	I	E	W	I	Y	Z	D	O	K	D
L	U	M	P	S	Z	I	W	T	A	G	B	E	C	W	I	E	D	Z	Y
Y	Z	Ł	O	Ż	Y	Ć	J	Ó	D	Ź	W	Y	R	A	Z	Y	Ą	C	I
W	Ę	H	L	E	K	A	R	S	K	I	E	Ć	W	Ó	K	O	Ż	U	Ł
Ł	U	R	E	Ś	Z	Y	Ź	M	Y	C	I	W	I	E	K	U	H	U	J
A	C	H	I	P	Ń	D	O	M	A	U	Ż	E	R	Z	I	S	Z	Ę	C

Running Heads

Headword	Running head	Jumbled running head
1. kelner	KĄPIEL	NOŚĆPIĘK
2. lek	LATO	BATRZE
3. niewiele	NIEZAPOMINAJKA	PISPRZE
4. piosenka	PIĘKNOŚĆ	SŁANYW
5. przemysł	PRZEPIS	TAFERO
6. stokrotka	STRACH	YNTNEGILETNI
7. truskawka	TRZEBA	TOLA
8. woda	WŁASNY	CORĄGO
9. ogród	OFERTA	ZAMINIENAJPOKA
10. instytucja	INTELIGENTNY	EICYŁP
11. góra	GORĄCO	PIELKĄ
12. ciastko	CIEPŁY	HCARTS

Riddles

1. zamek
2. północ
3. ser
4. szczur
5. telefon
6. Jowisz
7. źrebak
8. medycyna
9. księżyc
10. bajka
11. zegarek
12. kangur
13. jarosz
14. ogórek
15. ogród

Cryptogram

11 J	8 E	42 S	4 Z	10 C	4 Z	8 E		14 P	26 O	33 L	42 S	22 K	3 A	
27 N	21 I	8 E		4 Z	7 G	21 I	27 N	16 Ę	19 Ł	3 A				
22 K	21 I	8 E	30 D	5 Y		18 M	5 Y		1 Ż	5 Y	11 J	8 E	18 M	5 Y

Jeszcze Polska nie zginęła kiedy my żyjemy.
(Beginning of Polish national anthem: *Poland is not yet lost so long as we still live.*)

Wskazówki dla użytkownika
Guide to Using the Dictionary

Porządek alfabetyczny i dobór haseł
Wszystkie wyrazy hasłowe podane są w porządku alfabetycznym. Do ich opisu stosowane są odpowiednie kwalifikatory gramatyczne – ilustrujące kategorię gramatyczną, do której należą, kwalifikatory działowe – przedstawiające ich przynależność do poszczególnych dziedzin oraz kwalifikatory stylistyczne – wskazujące na różne style danego wyrazu. W liście haseł podane są także nieregularne formy stopniowania przymiotników i przysłówków.

Użycie tyldy (~) i dywizu
Tylda zastępuje cały wyraz hasłowy lub jego część, znajdującą się po lewej stronie kreski pionowej.

a·lone [ə'ləʊn] **1.** *adj.* sam; **2.** *adv.* samotnie; ***let ~*** zostawiać ⟨-wić⟩ w spokoju; ***let ~ ...*** nie mówiąc już o (*L*)

W formach gramatycznych, podawanych w nawiasach okrągłych lub w nawiasach trójkątnych wyrazy hasłowe lub ekwiwalenty wyrazów hasłowych zastąpiono dywizem.

gor·y ['gɔːrɪ] F (***-ier, -iest***) zakrwawiony; *fig.* krwawy

gorge [gɔːdʒ] **1.** wąwóz *m*; gardziel *f*; **2.** pochłaniać ⟨-łonąć⟩ napychać ⟨-pchać⟩ (się)

Hasła mające kilka odpowiedników
Odpowiedniki bliskoznaczne wyrazu hasłowego podano obok siebie oddzielając je przecinkami.

chip [tʃɪp] **1.** wiór *m*, drzazga *f*

Jeżeli wyraz hasłowy ma kilka odpowiedników dalekoznacznych, w takim przypadku na pierwszym miejscu podano znaczenie bliższe lub pierwotne, a potem kolejno znaczenia dalsze lub pochodne, oddzielone średnikiem.

a·buse 1. [ə'bjuːs] znęcanie *n* się; nadużywanie *n*; nadużycie *n*; wymysły *pl.*

Jeżeli wyraz hasłowy występuje w chara-

Alphabetical order and the choice of entries
The entries are given in a strictly alphabetical order. Special labels are used to help to describe them. Grammatical labels indicate their grammatical category. Stylistic labels show the register to which the entry belongs. There are also labels for words that are restricted to specific fields of usage.
Irregular forms of adjectives and adverbs are also listed as entries.

The use of the swung dash (~) and the hyphen The swung dash replaces the headword or the part of it that appears to the left of the vertical bar.

a·lone [ə'ləʊn] **1.** *adj.* sam; **2.** *adv.* samotnie; ***let ~*** zostawiać ⟨-wić⟩ w spokoju; ***let ~ ...*** nie mówiąc już o (*L*)

In grammatical forms given in round or angle brackets the entries or their equivalents are replaced with a hyphen.

gor·y ['gɔːrɪ] F (***-ier, -iest***) zakrwawiony; *fig.* krwawy

gorge [gɔːdʒ] **1.** wąwóz *m*; gardziel *f*; **2.** pochłaniać ⟨-łonąć⟩ napychać ⟨-pchać⟩ (się)

Entries with more than one meaning
Translations of the headword which are used synonymously are given next to each other and are separated by commas.

chip [tʃɪp] **1.** wiór *m*, drzazga *f*

If the English headword has more than one Polish equivalent, it is the basic or original meaning that is presented first. Further or derivative meanings come later and are separated by a semicolons.

a·buse 1. [ə'bjuːs] znęcanie *n* się; nadużywanie *n*; nadużycie *n*; wymysły *pl.*

If the English headword is used as more

kterze różnych części mowy, identycznych pod względem formy, to w takim przypadku podano go w jednym artykule hasłowym z jego odpowiednikami w języku polskim, uszeregowanymi według ustalonej w gramatyce kolejności. Poszczególne znaczenia zostały wyróżnione cyframi arabskimi i oddzielone średnikiem.

ab•stract **1.** ['æbstrækt] abstrakcyjny; **2.** ['æbstrækt] abstrakt *m*; **3.** [æb'strækt] abstrahować

Homonimy podano w osobnych hasłach oznaczonych kolejnymi cyframi arabskimi, podanymi w górnym indeksie.

air[1] [eə] powietrze *n*
air[2] [eə] *mus.* aria *f*

Hasła rzeczownikowe

Przy polskich odpowiednikach angielskich haseł rzeczownikowych podano za pomocą skrótów *m*, *f*, *n* ich rodzaj gramatyczny.
Regularne formy liczby mnogiej zostały pominięte, natomiast formy nieregularne lub nasuwające wątpliwości podano w nawiasach okrągłych.

leaf [li:f] (*pl.* ***leaves*** [li:vz]) liść *m*; *drzwi itp.*: skrzydło *n*

Hasła przymiotnikowe

Przy przymiotnikach stopniowanych nieregularnie podano w nawiasach okrągłych formy stopnia wyższego i najwyższego. Dodatkowo formy te zostały także ujęte w liście haseł.

good [gʊd] **1.** (***better, best***) dobry; grzeczny

Hasła czasownikowe

W słowniku nie uwzględniono form podstawowych czasowników regularnych, tworzonych za pomocą końcówki *-ed*. Przy hasłach podano natomiast w nawiasach okrągłych formy czasowników nieregularnych. Jako odpowiedniki podano polskie czasowniki niedokonane. W nawiasy trójkątne ujęto przedrostki lub przyrostki, za pomocą których tworzone są ich formy dokonane.

come [kʌm] (***came, come***) przychodzić ⟨przyjść⟩ przyjeżdżać ⟨przyjechać⟩
re•sign [rɪ'zaɪn] *v/i.* ⟨z⟩rezygnować

Różnice w rekcji angielskich i polskich czasowników zaznaczane są za pomocą

than one part of speech, then it appears under one entry together with its Polish equivalents arranged according to the accepted grammar order. Separate meanings have been marked with Arabic numerals and separated by semicolons.

ab•stract **1.** ['æbstrækt] abstrakcyjny; **2.** ['æbstrækt] abstrakt *m*; **3.** [æb'strækt] abstrahować

Homonyms are presented under separate entries marked with exponent numerals.

air[1] [eə] powietrze *n*
air[2] [eə] *mus.* aria *f*

Nouns

Polish equivalents are always accompanied by an abbreviation of the grammatical gender: *m*, *f* or *n*.

Plurals formed regularly have been omitted. Irregular or problematic forms are given in round brackets.

leaf [li:f] (*pl.* ***leaves*** [li:vz]) liść *m*; *drzwi itp.*: skrzydło *n*

Adjectives

When the comparative and superlative forms of an adjective are irregular, these have been given in round brackets. Additionally, these forms have been included in the list of entries.

good [gʊd] **1.** (***better, best***) dobry; grzeczny

Verbs

The endings of regular verbs have been omitted, while those of irregular verbs have been included in round brackets. For their equivalents imperfect Polish verbs have been supplied. Prefixes and suffixes which are used to make perfect forms of verbs are given in angle brackets.

come [kʌm] (***came, come***) przychodzić ⟨przyjść⟩ przyjeżdżać ⟨przyjechać⟩
re•sign [rɪ'zaɪn] *v/i.* ⟨z⟩rezygnować

The differences in grammar governing usage are marked by means of special

odpowiednich zaimków i skrótów przypadków, podawanych w nawiasach okrągłych, zaraz po polskim odpowiedniku.

ag·i|·tate ['ædʒɪteɪt] *v/t.* poruszać ⟨-ruszyć⟩; *płyn* wstrząsać ⟨-snąć⟩; *v/i.* agitować (***for*** za *I*, ***against*** przeciw *D*)

Transkrypcja
Przy wyrazach hasłowych podano w nawiasach kwadratowych transkrypcję fonetyczną. W słowniku zastosowano międzynarodową transkrypcję fonetyczną.

Fałszywi przyjaciele
Symbol ⚠ ostrzega przed fałszywymi przyjaciółmi tłumacza

ru·mo(u)r ['ruːmə] **1.** pogłoska *f*, plotka *f*; ***~ has it that*** wieść niesie że; ***he is ~ed to be*** mówi się że on; ⚠ *nie* ***rumor***

pronouns and shortened forms of cases given in round brackets following their Polish equivalent.

ag·i|·tate ['ædʒɪteɪt] *v/t.* poruszać ⟨-ruszyć⟩; *płyn* wstrząsać ⟨-snąć⟩; *v/i.* agitować (***for*** za *I*, ***against*** przeciw *D*)

Phonetic transcription
Dictionary entries are accompanied by phonetic transcriptions. The symbols used are those of the International Phonetic Association.

False friends
The sign ⚠ warns of false friends.

ru·mo(u)r ['ruːmə] **1.** pogłoska *f*, plotka *f*; ***~ has it that*** wieść niesie że; ***he is ~ed to be*** mówi się że on; ⚠ *nie* ***rumor***

English – Polish

A

A, a [eɪ] A, a; ***from A to B*** od A do B

A [eɪ] *ocena*: celujący; bardzo dobry

a [ə, *akcentowane*: eɪ], *przed samogłoską*: **an** [ən, *akcentowane*: æn] *rodzajnik nieokreślony*: jeden; na; za; ***a horse*** koń; ***not a*(*n*)** żaden, ani jeden; ***all of a size*** wszyscy (wszystkie) tego samego rozmiaru; ***£10 a year*** dziesięć funtów na rok; ***twice a week*** dwa razy na tydzień

a·back [ə'bæk]: ***taken ~*** zaskoczony

a·ban·don [ə'bændən] opuszczać ⟨-ścić⟩; porzucać ⟨-cić⟩; poniechać; **~ed**: ***be found ~ed*** *samochód itp.*: zostać znalezionym po porzuceniu

a·base [ə'beɪs] poniżać ⟨-yć⟩; upokarzać ⟨-orzyć⟩; **~·ment** poniżenie *n*, upokorzenie *n*

a·bashed [ə'bæʃt] speszony

ab·at·toir ['æbətwɑː] rzeźnia *f*

ab·bess ['æbɪs] przeorysza *f*

ab·bey ['æbɪ] opactwo *n*

ab·bot ['æbət] przeor *m*, opat *m*

ab·bre·vi|·ate [ə'briːvɪeɪt] skracać ⟨-rócić⟩; **~·a·tion** [əbriːvɪ'eɪʃn] skrót *m*

ABC[1] [eɪ biː 'siː] abecadło *n*, alfabet *m*

ABC[2] [eɪ biː 'siː] *skrót*: ***American Broadcasting Company*** (*amerykańska firma telewizyjna i radiowa*)

ab·di|·cate ['æbdɪkeɪt] *prawo, władza itp.*: zrzekać ⟨-ec⟩ się; ***~cate from*** (***the***) ***throne*** abdykować; **~·ca·tion** [æbdɪ'keɪʃn] zrzeczenie się *n*, abdykacja *f*

ab·do·men ['æbdəmən] *anat.* brzuch *m*; **ab·dom·i·nal** [æb'dɒmɪnl] *anat.* brzuszny

ab·duct [əb'dʌkt] *kogoś* porywać ⟨-rwać⟩

a·bet [ə'bet] → ***aid***

ab·hor [əb'hɔː] odczuwać ⟨-czuć⟩ wstręt; **~·rence** [əb'hɒrəns] wstręt *m* (***of*** do *D*); **~·rent** [əb'hɒrənt] odrażający (***to*** dla *D*); wstrętny

a·bide [ə'baɪd] *v/i.*: ***~ by the law*** *itp.* przestrzegać prawa *itp.*; *v/t.* ***I can't ~ him*** nie mogę go znieść

a·bil·i·ty [ə'bɪlətɪ] umiejętność *f*, zdolność *f*

ab·ject ['æbdʒekt] uniżony; ***in ~ poverty*** w skrajnej nędzy

ab·jure [əb'dʒʊə] odwoływać ⟨-łać⟩ publicznie

a·blaze [ə'bleɪz] w płomieniach; rozjarzony, rozświetlony (***with*** *L*)

a·ble ['eɪbl] zdolny; ***be ~ to*** móc, potrafić; **~-'bod·ied** *fizycznie* krzepki, zdrowy

ab·norm·al [æb'nɔːml] nienormalny

a·board [ə'bɔːd] na pokładzie; ***all ~!*** *naut.* wszyscy na pokład!, *rail.* proszę wsiadać!; ***~ a bus*** w autobusie; ***go ~ a train*** wsiadać ⟨wsiąść⟩ do pociągu

a·bode [ə'bəʊd] *też* ***place of ~*** miejsce zamieszkania; ***of*** *lub* ***with no fixed ~*** bez stałego miejsca zamieszkania

a·bol·ish [ə'bɒlɪʃ] obalać ⟨-lić⟩

ab·o·li·tion [æbə'lɪʃn] obalenie *n*

A-bomb ['eɪbɒm] → ***atom*(*ic*) *bomb***

a·bom·i|·na·ble [ə'bɒmɪnəbl] odrażający, wstrętny; **~·nate** [ə'bɒmɪneɪt] czuć wstręt; **~·na·tion** [əbɒmɪ'neɪʃn] wstręt *m*, odraza *f*

ab·o·rig·i·nal [æbə'rɪdʒənl] **1.** pierwotny; **2.** aborygen(ka *f*) *m*

ab·o·rig·i·ne [æbə'rɪdʒəniː] aborygen(ka *f*) *m* (*zwł. w Australii*)

a·bort [ə'bɔːt] *med. ciążę* przerwać (*A*); *płód* usunąć (*A*); *dziecka* pozbyć się (*G*); przerwać (*też komp.*); *v/i.* dokonać aborcji; *fig.* nie powieść się; **a·bor·tion** [ə'bɔːʃn] *med.* aborcja *f*; poronienie *n*, przerwanie *n* ciąży; ***have an ~*** przerwać ciążę, dokonać aborcji; **a·bor·tive** [ə'bɔːtɪv] nieudany

a·bound [ə'baʊnd] mnożyć się; obfitować (***in*** w *A*); być wypełnionym

a·bout [ə'baʊt] **1.** *prp.* o (*L*); po (*L*); przy (*L*); ***I had no money ~ me*** nie miałem pieniędzy przy sobie; ***what ~ going to the cinema?*** może byśmy poszli do kina?; **2.** *adv.* około (*G*); w przybliżeniu; dookoła (*G*)

a·bove [ə'bʌv] **1.** *prp.* nad (*I*); ponad (*I*); *fig.* ponad; ***~ all*** ponad wszystko; **2.** *adv.* (po)wyżej (*G*); **3.** *adj.* powyższy, (wyżej) wspomniany

a·breast [ə'brest] obok siebie; ***keep ~***

of, be ~ of *fig.* być na bieżąco z (*I*)
a·bridge [ə'brɪdʒ] skracać ⟨-rócić⟩; **a'bridg(e)·ment** skrót *m*
a·broad [ə'brɔːd] za granicę, za granicą; wszędzie; ***the news soon spread ~*** wieści szybko się rozniosły
a·brupt [ə'brʌpt] nagły; stromy
ab·scess ['æbsɪs] ropień *m*
ab·sence ['æbsəns] nieobecność *f*; brak *m*
ab·sent 1. ['æbsənt] nieobecny; ***be ~*** być nieobecnym (***from school*** w szkole); **2.** [æb'sent]: ***~ o.s. from school*** być nieobecnym w szkole; **~-mind·ed** [æbsənt'maɪndid] roztargniony
ab·so·lute ['æbsəluːt] absolutny; *chem.* czysty
ab·so·lu·tion [æbsə'luːʃn] rozgrzeszenie *n*
ab·solve [əb'zɒlv] grzechy odpuszczać; oczyszczać (*z winy*)
ab·sorb [əb'sɔːb] absorbować; wchłaniać (*też fig.*); **~·ing** absorbujący
ab·stain [əb'steɪn] powstrzymywać ⟨-mać⟩ się (***from*** od *A*)
ab·ste·mi·ous [æb'stiːmɪəs] wstrzemięźliwy
ab·sten·tion [əb'stenʃn] powstrzymanie *n* się; *pol.* głos wstrzymujący się
ab·sti|·nence ['æbstɪnəns] abstynencja *f*; wstrzemięźliwość *f*
ab·stract 1. ['æbstrækt] abstrakcyjny; **2.** ['æbstrækt] abstrakt *m*; **3.** [æb'strækt] abstrahować; *najważniejsze punkty z artykułu* streszczać ⟨streścić⟩; **ab·stract·ed** [əb'stræktɪd] zatopiony w myślach; **ab·strac·tion** [əb'strækʃn] abstrakcja *f*; pojęcie *n* abstrakcyjne
ab·surd [əb'sɜːd] absurdalny; groteskowy
a·bun|·dance [ə'bʌndəns] obfitość *f*; nadmiar *m*; mnóstwo *n*; **~·dant** obfity
a·buse 1. [ə'bjuːs] znęcanie *n* się; nadużywanie *n*; nadużycie *n*; wymysły *pl.*; ***~ of drugs*** nadużywanie narkotyków; ***~ of power*** nadużycie *n* władzy; **2.** [ə'bjuːz] znęcać się; nadużywać; **a·bu·sive**[ə'bjuːsɪv]obelżywy;obraźliwy
a·but [ə'bʌt] (***-tt-***) graniczyć (***on*** z *L*)
a·byss [ə'bɪs] otchłań *f* (*też fig.*)
a/c, A/C [eɪ 'siː] *skrót:* ***account*** konto *m* bankowe
AC [eɪ 'siː] *skrót:* ***alternating current*** prąd *m* zmienny
ac·a·dem·ic [ækə'demɪk] **1.** nauczyciel(ka *f*) *m* akademicki (-ka); **2.** (***~ally***) akademicki; uniwersytecki;
a·cad·e·mi·cian [əkædə'mɪʃn] członek *m* akademii (*nauk*)
a·cad·e·my [ə'kædəmɪ] akademia *f*; ***~ of music*** wyższa szkoła muzyczna, akademia muzyczna
ac·cede [æk'siːd]: ***~ to*** zgadzać ⟨-dzić⟩ się na (*A*); *urząd* obejmować ⟨-jąć⟩; wstępować ⟨wstąpić⟩ na (*L*) (*tron*)
ac·cel·e|·rate [ək'seləreɪt] przyspieszać ⟨-szyć⟩; **~·ra·tion** [əkselə'reɪʃn] przyspieszenie *n*; **~·ra·tor** [ək'seləreɪtə] pedał *m* gazu, gaz *m* F
ac·cent ['æksənt] akcent *m*; **ac·cen·tu·ate** [æk'sentjʊeɪt] ⟨za⟩akcentować, podkreślić
ac·cept [ək'sept] przyjmować ⟨-jąć⟩; ⟨za⟩akceptować; **ac'cep·ta·ble** (*możliwy*) do przyjęcia; **ac'cept·ance** przyjęcie *n*; akceptacja *f*
ac·cess ['ækses] dojście *n* (***to*** do *G*); dostęp (*też komp.*); ***~ code*** *komp.* kod *m* dostępu; ***~ road*** droga *f* dojazdowa; ***~ time*** *komp.*, (*odtwarzacz CD*) czas *m* dostępu
ac·ces·sa·ry [ək'sesərɪ] → ***accessory***
ac·ces|·si·ble [ək'sesəbl] *łatwo* dostępny; **~·sion** [ək'seʃn] objęcie *n* (*urzędu*); ***~sion to power*** przejęcie *n* władzy; ***~sion to the throne*** objęcie *n* tronu
ac·ces·so·ry [ək'sesərɪ] *jur.* współsprawca *m* (-wczyni *f*) przestępstwa; *zw.* ***accessories*** *pl.* dodatki *pl.*, *tech.* akcesoria *pl.*
ac·ci|·dent ['æksɪdənt] przypadek *m*; *samochodowy* wypadek *m*; ***by ~dent*** przypadkiem; **~·den·tal** [æksɪ'dentl] przypadkowy
ac·claim [ə'kleɪm] zdobyć uznanie (***as*** jako)
ac·cla·ma·tion [æklə'meɪʃn] aklamacja *f*, aplauz *m*
ac·cli·ma·tize [ə'klaɪmətaɪz] ⟨za⟩aklimatyzować się; przyzwyczaić ⟨-ajać się⟩
ac·com·mo|·date [ə'kɒmədeɪt] (*w domu*) przyjmować ⟨-jąć⟩; (*w hotelu*) ⟨po⟩mieścić; wyświadczać ⟨-czyć⟩ przysługę; dostosowywać ⟨-ować⟩ się (***to*** do *G*); **~·da·tion** [əkɒmə'deɪʃn] (*Am. zw. pl.*) miejsce *n*; zakwaterowanie *n*

ac·com·pa|·ni·ment [ə'kʌmpənɪmənt] akompaniament *m*; **~·ny** [ə'kʌmpənɪ] towarzyszyć (*też muz.*)
ac·com·plice [ə'kʌmplɪs] współsprawca *m*, współsprawczyni *f*
ac·com·plish [ə'kʌmplɪʃ] osiągać ⟨-gnąć⟩; **~ed** znakomity; **~·ment** osiągnięcie *n*; (*w pracy*) osiągnięcia *pl.*
ac·cord [ə'kɔːd] **1.** uznanie *n*; ***of one's own ~*** z własnej woli; ***with one ~*** jednogłośnie; ⚠ *nie* ***akord***; **2.** przyznawać ⟨-nać⟩; **~·ance**: ***in ~ance with*** zgodnie z (*L*); **~·ing**: ***~ing to*** według (*G*); zgodnie z (*L*); **~·ing·ly** stosownie, odpowiednio
ac·cost [ə'kɒst] *kogoś na ulicy* zaczepiać ⟨-pić⟩
ac·count [ə'kaʊnt] **1.** *econ.* rachunek *m*; *econ.* konto *n*; sprawozdanie *n*; ***by all ~s*** podobno; ***of no ~*** bez znaczenia; ***on no ~*** w żadnym wypadku; ***on ~ of*** w przypadku (*G*); ***take into ~, take ~ of*** brać ⟨wziąć⟩ (*A*) pod uwagę; ***turn s.th. to*** (***good***) ***~*** coś dobrze wykorzystywać ⟨-stać⟩; ***keep ~s*** prowadzić księgi *pl.* rachunkowe; ***call to ~*** pociągać ⟨-gnąć⟩ do odpowiedzialności; ***give*** (***an***) ***~ of s.th.*** wyjaśniać ⟨-nić⟩; ***give an ~ of s.th*** składać ⟨złożyć⟩ sprawozdanie z czegoś, opisywać ⟨-sać⟩ coś; **2.** *v/i.* ***~ for*** wyjaśniać ⟨-nić⟩; (*w liczbie*) stanowić; **ac'coun·ta·ble** odpowiedzialny; **ac'coun·tant** księgowy *m* (-wa *f*); **ac'count·ing** księgowość *f*
acct *skrót pisany*: ***account*** konto *n*
ac·cu·mu|·late [ə'kjuːmjʊleɪt] ⟨na-, z⟩gromadzić (się); **~·la·tion** [əkjuːmjʊ'leɪʃn] nagromadzenie *n*; **~·la·tor** *electr.* [ə'kjuːmjʊleɪtə] akumulator *m*
ac·cu|·ra·cy ['ækjʊrəsɪ] dokładność *f*; precyzja *f*; **~·rate** ['ækjʊrət] dokładny
ac·cu·sa·tion [ækjuː'zeɪʃn] oskarżenie *n*
ac·cu·sa·tive [ə'kjuːzətɪv] *też* ***~ case*** biernik *m*
ac·cuse [ə'kjuːz] oskarżać ⟨-żyć⟩; ***the ~d*** oskarżony *m* (-na *f*); **ac'cus·er** oskarżyciel(ka *f*) *m*; **ac'cus·ing** oskarżycielski
ac·cus·tom [ə'kʌstəm] przyzwyczajać (***to*** do *G*); **~ed** przyzwyczajony (***to*** do *G*), przywykły
AC/DC [eɪ siː 'diː siː] → ***bisexual***
ace [eɪs] as *m* (*też fig.*); ***have an ~ up one's sleeve***, *Am.* ***have an ~ in the hole*** *fig.* mieć asa w rękawie; ***within an ~*** o włosek
ache [eɪk] **1.** czuć ból; ***my stomach ~s*** brzuch mnie boli; **2.** *ciągły* ból *m*
a·chieve [ə'tʃiːv] osiągać ⟨-gnąć⟩; **~·ment** osiągnięcie *n*
ac·id ['æsɪd] **1.** kwaśny (*też fig.*); skwaśniały (*też fig.*); **2.** *chem.* kwas *m*; ***~ rain*** kwaśny deszcz *m*; **a·cid·i·ty** [ə'sɪdətɪ] kwasowość *f*
ac·knowl·edge [ək'nɒlɪdʒ] potwierdzać ⟨-dzić⟩ (*przyjęcie*); przyznawać ⟨-znać⟩; **ac'knowl·edg(e)·ment** potwierdzenie *n* (*przyjęcia*); przyznanie *n*
a·corn ['eɪkɔːn] żołądź *f*
a·cous·tics [ə'kuːstɪks] *pl.* akustyka *f* (*pomieszczenia*)
ac·quaint [ə'kweɪnt] zaznajamiać ⟨-jomić⟩; ***~ s.o. with s.th.*** zaznajamiać ⟨-jomić⟩ kogoś z czymś; ***be ~ed with*** znać (*A*); **~·ance** znajomość *f*; znajomy *m* (-ma *f*)
ac·quire [ə'kwaɪə] nabywać ⟨-yć⟩ (*też umiejętność*)
ac·qui·si·tion [ækwɪ'zɪʃn] nabycie *n*; nabytek *m*; *umiejętność*: przyswojenie *n*
ac·quit [ə'kwɪt] (***-tt-***) *jur.* uniewinniać ⟨-nić⟩ (***of*** z *G*); ***~ o.s. well*** dobrze się spisać; **~·tal** [ə'kwɪtl] *jur.* uniewinnienie *n*
a·cre ['eɪkə] akr *m* (*4047 m²*)
ac·rid ['ækrɪd] ostry, gryzący
ac·ro·bat ['ækrəbæt] akrobata *m* (-tka *f*); **~·ic** [ækrə'bætɪk] akrobatyczny
a·cross [ə'krɒs] **1.** *adv.* na szerokość, o szerokości; na krzyż; (*w krzyżówce*) poziomo; **2.** *prp.* w poprzek (*G*); na drugą stronę (*G*), po drugiej stronie (*G*); przez (*A*); ***come ~, run ~*** przebiegać ⟨-biec⟩
act [ækt] **1.** *v/i.* działać; funkcjonować; zachowywać ⟨-ować⟩ się; (za)grać; *v/t.* *theat.* (za)grać (*też fig.*); *sztukę* wystawiać ⟨-wić⟩; ***~ as*** funkcjonować jako; **2.** czyn *m*; uczynek *m*; postępek *m*; *jur.* ustawa *f*; *theat.* akt *m*; '**~·ing 1.** *theat.* gra *f*; aktorstwo *n*; **2.** pełniący obowiązki (*dyrektora*)
ac·tion ['ækʃn] akcja *f* (*też mil., theat.*); działanie *n*; funkcjonowanie *n*; uczynek *m*, czyn *m*; *jur.* powództwo *n*, sprawa *f* sądowa; *mil.* działania *pl.*; ***take ~*** podejmować ⟨-jąć⟩ działanie

ac·tive ['æktɪv] aktywny; czynny; ożywiony (*też econ.*); rzutki
ac·tiv·ist ['æktɪvɪst] *zwł. pol.* działacz(ka *f*) *m*
ac·tiv·i·ty [æk'tɪvətɪ] działalność *f*; działanie *n*; zajęcie *n*; ~ ***hol·i·day*** czynny urlop *m*; czynne wakacje *pl.*
ac·tor ['æktə] aktor *m*; **actress** ['æktrɪs] aktorka *f*
ac·tu·al ['æktʃʊəl] faktyczny, rzeczywisty; sam; ⚠ *nie* ***aktualny***
ac·u·punc·ture ['ækjʊpʌŋktʃə] akupunktura *f*
a·cute [ə'kjuːt] (***~r, ~est***) ostry (*też med.*); przenikliwy; silny; *trudności*: zaostrzony
ad [æd] → ***advertisement***
ad·a·mant ['ædəmənt] *fig.* nieugięty
a·dapt [ə'dæpt] *v/i.* ⟨za⟩adaptować się (***to*** do *G*); dostosowywać ⟨-ować⟩ się; *v/t.* ⟨za⟩adaptować; *tekst* dostosowywać ⟨-ować⟩; *tech.* przystosowywać ⟨-ować⟩; **a·dap·ta·ble** [ə'dæptəbl] *ktoś* łatwo się przystosowujący; *coś* dające się dostosować; **ad·ap·ta·tion** [ædæp'teɪʃn] adaptacja *f*; przystosowanie *n*; **a·dapt·er, a·dapt·or** *electr.* [ə'dæptə] rozgałęziacz *m*; ⚠ *nie* ***adapter***
add [æd] *v/t.* dodawać ⟨-dać⟩; ~ ***up*** ⟨z⟩sumować, podliczać ⟨-czyć⟩; *v/i.* ~ ***to*** powiększać ⟨-szyć⟩; ~ ***up*** *fig.* F mieć sens, zgadzać się
ad·der ['ædə] *zo.* żmija *f*
ad·dict ['ædɪkt] osoba *f* uzależniona; ***alcohol ~*** alkoholik *m* (-iczka *f*); ***drug ~*** narkoman(ka *f*) *m*; entuzjasta *m* (-tka *f*) (*sportu, filmu itp.*), fanatyk *m* (-yczka *f*); **ad·dic·ted** [ə'dɪktɪd] uzależniony (***to*** od); ***be ~ to alcohol*** *lub* ***drugs*** być uzależnionym od alkoholu *lub* narkotyków; **ad·dic·tion** [ə'dɪkʃn] uzależnienie *n*, ***alcohol ~*** alkoholizm *m*; ***drug ~*** narkomania *f*
ad·di·tion [ə'dɪʃn] dodanie *n*; dodatek *m*; *math.* dodawanie *n*; sumowanie *n*; ***in ~*** w dodatku; ***in ~ to*** oprócz (*G*); **~·al** [ə'dɪʃənl] dodatkowy
ad·dress [ə'dres] **1.** *słowa* kierować; (*do kogoś*) zwracać ⟨-rócić⟩ się do (*G*); przemawiać ⟨-mówić⟩ do (*G*); *przesyłkę* ⟨za⟩adresować (*A*); **2.** adres *m*; przemowa *f*; **~·ee** [ædre'siː] adresat(ka *f*) *m*
ad·ept ['ædept] biegły (***at, in*** w *L*)
ad·e|·qua·cy ['ædɪkwəsɪ] adekwatność *f*; dostateczność *f*; **~·quate** ['ædɪkwət] odpowiedni; dostateczny
ad·here [əd'hɪə] (***to***) przylegać ⟨-lgnąć⟩ do (*G*); ⟨za⟩stosować się do (*G*); *fig.* obstawać (przy *L*); **ad·her·ence** [əd'hɪərəns] przyleganie *n* (***to*** do *G*); *prawa* stosowanie *n* się (***to*** do *G*); *fig.* obstawanie *n* (***to*** przy *L*); **ad·her·ent** [əd'hɪərənt] stronnik *m* (-niczka *f*)
ad·he·sive [əd'hiːsɪv] **1.** klejący (się); **2.** klej *m*; ~ **'plas·ter** plaster *m*, przylepiec *m*; ~ **'tape** taśma *f* klejąca; *Am.* plaster *m*, przylepiec *m*
ad·ja·cent [ə'dʒeɪsnt] przyległy (***to*** do *G*); sąsiadujący (***to*** z *I*)
ad·jec·tive ['ædʒɪktɪv] *gr.* przymiotnik *m*
ad·join [ə'dʒɔɪn] przylegać do (*G*)
ad·journ [ə'dʒɜːn] *v/t.* odraczać ⟨-roczyć⟩; *v/i.* zostawać ⟨-stać⟩ odroczonym; **~·ment** odroczenie *n*; zawieszenie *n* (*obrad*)
ad·just [ə'dʒʌst] poprawiać ⟨-wić⟩; *tech.* ⟨wy⟩regulować; nastawiać ⟨-wić⟩; **~·a·ble** [ə'dʒʌstəbl] *tech.* nastawny; regulowany; **~·ment** regulacja *f*; nastawienie *n*
ad·min·is|·ter [əd'mɪnɪstə] zarządzać, administrować; *lekarstwo* podawać ⟨-dać⟩; ***~ter justice*** wymierzać ⟨-rzyć⟩ sprawiedliwość; **~·tra·tion** [ədmɪnɪ'streɪʃn] administracja *f*; *zwł. Am. pol.* rząd *m*; *zwł. Am.* kadencja *f* (*prezydenta*); **~·tra·tive** [əd'mɪnɪstrətɪv] administracyjny; **~·tra·tor** [əd'mɪnɪstreɪtə] administrator(ka *f*) *m*
ad·mi·ra·ble ['ædmərəbl] wspaniały, godny podziwu
ad·mi·ral ['ædmərəl] admirał *m*
ad·mi·ra·tion [ædmə'reɪʃn] podziw *m*
ad·mire [əd'maɪə] podziwiać; **ad·mir·er** [əd'maɪərə] wielbiciel(ka *f*) *m*
ad·mis|·si·ble [əd'mɪsəbl] dopuszczalny; **~·sion** [əd'mɪʃn] wstęp *m*; opłata *f* za wstęp; przyjęcie *n*; ***~sion free*** wstęp wolny
ad·mit [əd'mɪt] (***-tt-***) *v/t.* przyznawać ⟨-nać⟩ się do (*G*); wpuszczać ⟨-uścić⟩ (***to, into*** do *G*); przyjmować ⟨-jąć⟩ (***to*** do *G*); dopuszczać ⟨-uścić⟩; **~·tance** [əd'mɪtəns] wstęp *m*; przyjęcie *n*; dopuszczenie *n*; ***no ~tance*** wstęp wzbroniony

ad•mon•ish [əd'mɒnɪʃ] upominać ⟨-mnieć⟩; przestrzegać ⟨-rzec⟩ (***of, against*** przed *I*)

a•do [ə'duː] (*pl.* ***-dos***) zamieszanie *n*; ***without more*** *lub* ***further ~*** bez dalszych ceregieli

ad•o•les|•cence [ædə'lesns] okres *m* dojrzewania; **~•cent** [ædə'lesnt] **1.** nastoletni; młodociany; **2.** nastolatek *m* (-tka *f*); *jur.* młodociany *m* (-na *f*)

a•dopt [ə'dɒpt] ⟨za⟩adoptować; przyjmować ⟨przyjąć⟩; ***~ed child*** przybrane dziecko *n*; **a•dop•tion** [ə'dɒpʃn] adopcja *f*; **a'dop•tive**: ***~ child*** przybrane dziecko *n*; ***~ par•ents*** *pl.* przybrani rodzice *pl.*

a•dor•a•ble [ə'dɔːrəbl] F cudowny, wspaniały; **ad•o•ra•tion** [ædə'reɪʃn] uwielbienie *n*, adoracja *f*; **a•dore** [ə'dɔː] uwielbiać ⟨-bić⟩; adorować

a•dorn [ə'dɔːn] ozdabiać ⟨ozdobić⟩; upiększać ⟨-szyć⟩; **~•ment** ozdobienie *n*; upiększenie *n*

A•dri•at•ic Sea Adriatyk *m*

a•droit [ə'drɔɪt] zręczny

ad•ult ['ædʌlt] **1.** dorosły; **2.** dorosły *m* (-sła *f*); ***~s only*** tylko dla dorosłych; **~ ed•u'ca•tion** kształcenie *n* dorosłych

a•dul•ter|•ate [ə'dʌltəreɪt] ⟨s⟩fałszować; *wino* rozcieńczać ⟨-czyć⟩, ⟨o⟩chrzcić; **~•er** [ə'dʌltərə] cudzołożnik *m*; **~•ess** [ə'dʌltərɪs] cudzołożnica *f*; **~•ous** [ə'dʌltərəs] cudzołożny; **~•y** [ə'dʌltərɪ] cudzołóstwo *n*

ad•vance [əd'vɑːns] **1.** *v/i.* posuwać ⟨-unąć⟩ się (*do przodu*), iść ⟨pójść⟩ do przodu (*też o czasie*); ⟨po⟩czynić postępy *pl.*; nadchodzić ⟨-dejść⟩; *v/t. pieniądze* wypłacać ⟨-cić⟩ z góry; *cenę* zwiększać ⟨-szyć⟩; *argument* przedstawiać ⟨-wić⟩; *wzrost* przyspieszać ⟨-szyć⟩; *pracownika* awansować; **2.** posuwanie *n* się; postęp *m*; zwiększenie *n*; zaliczka *f*; ***in ~*** z góry; **~d** zaawansowany; *kraj*: rozwinięty; ***~d for one's years*** dobrze rozwinięty jak na swój wiek; **~•ment** postęp *m*; awans *m*

ad•van|•tage [əd'vɑːntɪdʒ] korzyść *f*; zaleta *f*; (*w sporcie*) przewaga *f*; ***~tage rule*** reguła *f* przewagi; ***take ~tage of*** wykorzystywać ⟨-tać⟩; **~•ta•geous** [ædvən'teɪdʒəs] korzystny

ad•ven|•ture [əd'ventʃə] przygoda *f*; ryzykowne przedsięwzięcie *n*; **~•tur•er** [əd'ventʃərə] poszukiwacz *m* przygód; spekulant *m*; **~•tur•ess** [əd'ventʃərɪs] poszukiwaczka *f* przygód; spekulantka *f*; **~•tur•ous** [əd'ventʃərəs] śmiały; ryzykowny; *życie*: pełen przygód

ad•verb ['ædvɜːb] przysłówek *m*

ad•ver•sa•ry ['ædvəsərɪ] przeciwnik *m* (-niczka *f*)

ad•ver|•tise ['ædvətaɪz] ⟨za⟩reklamować (się); ogłaszać ⟨-łosić⟩ (się); **~•tise•ment** [əd'vɜːtɪsmənt] ogłoszenie *n*; reklama *f*; **~•tis•ing** ['ædvətaɪzɪŋ] **1.** reklama *f*; reklamowanie *n*; **2.** reklamowy; ***~tising agency*** agencja *f* reklamowa

ad•vice [əd'vaɪs] rada *f*; porada *f*; *econ.* zawiadomienie *n*; ***a piece of ~*** rada *f*; ***take medical ~*** zasięgać ⟨-gnąć⟩ porady lekarskiej; ***take my ~*** proszę mnie posłuchać; **~ cen•tre** *Brt.* poradnia *f*

ad•vi•sab•le [əd'vaɪzəbl] wskazany, celowy; **ad•vise** [əd'vaɪz] *v/t. komuś* ⟨po⟩radzić; *zwł. econ.* zawiadamiać ⟨-domić⟩, awizować; *v/i.* radzić się; **ad•vis•er** *zwł. Brt.*, **ad•vis•or** *Am.* [əd'vaɪzə] doradca *m*; **ad•vi•so•ry** [əd'vaɪzərɪ] doradczy

aer•i•al ['eərɪəl] **1.** powietrzny; lotniczy; **2.** antena *f*; **~ 'pho•to•graph** zdjęcie *n* z lotu ptaka *lub* lotnicze; **~ 'view** widok *m* z lotu ptaka

ae•ro... ['eərəʊ] aero...

aer•o|•bics [eə'rəʊbɪks] (*sg. w sporcie*) aerobik *m*; **~•drome** ['eərədrəʊm] *zwł. Brt.* lotnisko *n*; **~•dy•nam•ic** [eərəʊdaɪ'næmɪk] (***-ally***) aerodynamiczny; **~•dy'nam•ics** *sg.* aerodynamika *f*; **~•nau•tics** [eərə'nɔːtɪks] *sg.* aeronautyka *f*; **~•plane** *Brt.* ['eərəpleɪn] samolot *m*; **~•sol** ['eərəsɒl] aerozol *m*

aes•thet•ic [iːs'θetɪk] estetyczny; **~s** *sg.* estetyka *f*

a•far [ə'fɑː]: ***from ~*** z oddali

af•fair [ə'feə] sprawa *f*; F rzecz *f*, urządzenie *n*; romans *m*

af•fect [ə'fekt] mieć wpływ na (*A*), wpływać ⟨-łynąć⟩; *med.* ⟨za⟩atakować; oddziaływać na (*A*); mieć oddziaływanie na (*A*); wzruszać ⟨-szyć⟩, poruszać ⟨-szyć⟩

af•fec•tion [ə'fekʃn] uczucie *n*; **~•ate** [ə'fekʃnət] czuły; uczuciowy

af•fil•i•ate [ə'fɪlɪeɪt] stowarzyszać ⟨-szyć⟩ (*jako członek*); zrzeszać ⟨-szyć⟩;

af·fin·i·ty [ə'fɪnətɪ] podobieństwo *n*; *duchowe* pokrewieństwo *n*; sympatia *f* (**for, to** do *G*)
af·firm [ə'fɜːm] potwierdzać ⟨-dzić⟩; zapewniać ⟨-nić⟩; ⟨s⟩twierdzić, stwierdzać ⟨-dzić⟩; **af·fir·ma·tion** [æfə'meɪʃn] potwierdzenie *n*; zapewnienie *n*; stwierdzenie *n*; **af·fir·ma·tive** [ə'fɜːmətɪv] **1.** twierdzący; **2.** ***answer in the ~*** odpowiadać ⟨-wiedzieć⟩ twierdząco; potwierdzać ⟨-dzić⟩
af·fix [ə'fɪks] (**to**) przyklejać ⟨-leić⟩ (do *A*); przytwierdzać ⟨-dzić⟩ (do *A*)
af·flict [ə'flɪkt] dotykać ⟨-tknąć⟩; ***~ed with*** dotknięty (*I*), cierpiący na (*A*); **af·flic·tion** [ə'flɪkʃn] przypadłość *f*; nieszczęście *n*
af·flu|·ence ['æflʊəns] dostatek *m*; bogactwo *n*; **'~·ent** dostatni; zamożny; **'~·ent so·ci·e·ty** społeczeństwo *n* dobrobytu
af·ford [ə'fɔːd] pozwalać sobie na (*A*); *czas* mieć; ***I cannot ~ it*** nie stać mnie na to
af·front [ə'frʌnt] **1.** znieważać ⟨-żyć⟩; **2.** zniewaga *f*
a·float [ə'fləʊt] unosząc(y) się na wodzie, pływając(y); ***set ~*** *naut.* puszczać ⟨puścić⟩ na wodę; puszczać ⟨puścić⟩ w obieg (*plotkę*)
a·fraid [ə'freɪd]: ***be ~ of*** bać się, obawiać się; ***I'm ~ she won't be coming*** obawiam się, że nie przyjdzie; ***I'm ~ I have to go now*** niestety muszę już iść
a·fresh [ə'freʃ] od nowa
Af·ric·a ['æfrɪkə] Afryka *f*; **Af·ri·can** ['æfrɪkən] **1.** afrykański; **2.** Afrykańczyk *m*, Afrykanka *f*; Murzyn(ka *f*) *m*
af·ter ['ɑːftə] **1.** *adv.* potem; później; **2.** *prp.* po (*L*); za (*I*); ***~ all*** przecież; mimo wszystko; ostatecznie; **3.** *cj.* gdy; po (*tym, jak*); **4.** *adj.* późniejszy; tylny; **'~·ef·fect** *med.* następstwo *n*; efekt *m*; **'~·glow** zorza *f* (*wieczorna*); **~·math** ['ɑːftəmæθ] pokłosie *n*; następstwa *pl.*; **~'noon** popołudnie *n*; ***this ~noon*** dzisiaj po południu; ***good ~noon!*** dzień dobry!; **'~·taste** posmak *m*; **'~·thought** zastanowienie *n* się; refleksja *f*; **~·ward** *Am.*, **~·wards** *Brt.* ['ɑːftəwəd(z)] później, następnie
a·gain [ə'gen] znowu, znów, ponownie; jeszcze raz; ***~ and ~, time and ~*** ciągle; ***as much ~*** drugie tyle; ***never ~*** nigdy więcej
a·gainst [ə'genst] przeciw(ko) (*D*); o (*A*); ***as ~*** w porównaniu z (*I*); ***she was ~ it*** była temu przeciwna
age [eɪdʒ] **1.** wiek *m*; ***old ~*** zaawansowany wiek *m*, starość *f*; ***at the ~ of*** w wieku (*G*); ***your ~*** w twoim wieku; ***come of ~*** stać się pełnoletnim, osiągnąć pełnoletniość; ***be over ~*** przekroczyć (*właściwy*) wiek; ***be under ~*** być niepełnoletnim; ***wait for ~s*** F czekać wieki całe; **2.** postarzeć się; **~d** ['eɪdʒɪd] stary, w podeszłym wieku; [eɪdʒd]: ***~d 20*** w wieku 20 lat; **'~·less** wieczny; wiecznie młody
a·gen·cy ['eɪdʒənsɪ] agencja *f*; urząd *m*, biuro *n*
a·gen·da [ə'dʒendə] porządek *m* dnia; ***be on the ~*** być w programie; ⚠ *nie agenda*
a·gent ['eɪdʒənt] agent(ka *f*) *m* (*też pol.*); przedstawiciel(ka *f*) *m*; ajent(ka *f*) *m*; makler *m*; środek *m*, czynnik *m*
ag·glom·er·ate [ə'glɒməreɪt] skupiać ⟨-pić⟩ się
ag·gra·vate ['ægrəveɪt] pogarszać ⟨-szyć⟩; zaostrzać ⟨-rzyć⟩; F ⟨z⟩irytować
ag·gre·gate **1.** ['ægrɪgeɪt] skupiać ⟨skupić⟩ (się); ⟨po⟩łączyć (się) (**to** z); wynosić ⟨-nieść⟩ łącznie **2.** ['ægrɪgət] łączny; globalny; **3.** ['ægrɪgət] całość *f*; suma *f* ogólna
ag·gres|·sion [ə'greʃn] agresja *f*; **~·sive** [ə'gresɪv] agresywny; *fig.* intensywny, energiczny; **~·sor** [ə'gresə] agresor *m*
ag·grieved [ə'griːvd] dotknięty; pokrzywdzony
a·ghast [ə'gɑːst] wstrząśnięty; przerażony
ag·ile ['ædʒaɪl] zwinny, zręczny; **a·gil·i·ty** [ə'dʒɪlətɪ] zręczność *f*
ag·i|·tate ['ædʒɪteɪt] *v/t.* poruszać ⟨-ruszyć⟩; *płyn* wstrząsać ⟨-snąć⟩; *v/i.* agitować (**for** za *I*, **against** przeciw *D*); **~·ta·tion** [ædʒɪ'teɪʃn] poruszenie *n*; agitacja *f*; **~·ta·tor** ['ædʒɪteɪtə] agitator(ka *f*) *m*
a·glow [ə'gləʊ]: ***be ~*** jarzyć się (**with** od *G*)
a·go [ə'gəʊ]: ***a year/month ~*** rok/miesiąc temu

ag·o·ny ['ægənɪ] *wielki* ból *m*; męczarnia *f*
a·gree [ə'griː] *v/i.* zgadzać ⟨-godzić⟩ się; uzgadniać ⟨-godnić⟩; porozumiewać ⟨-mieć⟩ się; **~ *to*** przystawać ⟨-rzystać⟩ na (*A*); być zgodnym (***with*** z *I*); **~ *with*** *jedzenie*: ⟨po⟩służyć (*D*); **~·a·ble** [ə'grɪəbl] zgodny; chętny; ***be ~able to*** zgadzać ⟨-godzić⟩ się na (*A*); **~·ment** [ə'griːmənt] zgoda *f*; porozumienie *n*; umowa *f*
ag·ri·cul·tur|·al [ægrɪ'kʌltʃərəl] rolniczy; **~e** ['ægrɪkʌltʃə] rolnictwo *n*
a·ground [ə'graʊnd] *naut.* na mieliźnie; ***run ~*** osiadać ⟨osiąść⟩ na mieliźnie
a·head [ə'hed] z przodu; na przedzie; naprzód; do przodu; **~ *of*** przed (*I*); ***go ~!*** proszę bardzo!; ***straight ~*** prosto
aid [eɪd] **1.** wspierać ⟨wesprzeć⟩; *komuś* pomagać ⟨pomóc⟩ (***in*** przy *L*); ***he was accused of ~ing and abetting*** *jur.* oskarżony został o pomoc w dokonaniu przestępstwa; **2.** pomoc *f*; wsparcie *n*
AIDS, **Aids** [eɪdz] AIDS *m*; ***person with ~*** chory na AIDS
ail [eɪl] niedomagać; '**~·ment** dolegliwość *f*
aim [eɪm] **1.** *v/i.* ⟨wy⟩celować (***at*** do *G*); **~ *at*** *fig.* dążyć do (*G*), mieć na celu; ***be ~ing to do s.th.*** mieć zamiar coś zrobić; *v/t.* **~ *at*** *broń itp.*: celować do (*G*); kierować w stronę (*G*); **2.** cel *m* (*też fig.*); ***take ~ at*** mierzyć do (*G*); '**~·less** bezcelowy
air[1] [eə] powietrze *n*; *fig.* atmosfera *f*; wygląd *m*; ***by ~*** powietrzem, samolotem; ***in the open ~*** na powietrzu, na dworze; ***on the ~*** na wizji *lub* fonii; ***be on the ~*** *program*: być na antenie; *stacja*: nadawać; ***go off the ~*** ⟨s⟩kończyć program; *stacja*: przestawać ⟨-stać⟩ nadawać; ***give o.s. ~s, put on ~s*** zadzierać ⟨-drzeć⟩ nosa; **2.** ⟨wy⟩wietrzyć; przewietrzać ⟨-wietrzyć⟩; *fig.* przedstawiać ⟨-wić⟩; wygłaszać ⟨-głosić⟩
air[2] [eə] *mus.* aria *f*; melodia *f*
'**air|·bag** poduszka *f* powietrzna; '**~·base** baza *f* powietrzna; '**~·bed** materac *m* dmuchany; '**~·borne** *samolot*: lecący, w powietrzu; *mil.* powietrznodesantowy; '**~·brake** *mot.* hamulec *m* penumatyczny; '**~·bus** *aviat.* aerobus *m*, airbus *m*; '**~con·di·tioned** klimatyzowany; '**~con·di·tion·ing** klimatyzacja *f*; '**~·craft car·ri·er** *mil.* lotniskowiec *m*; '**~·field** lotnisko *n*; '**~·force** *mil.* siły *pl.* powietrzne; '**~·host·ess** *aviat.* stewardessa *f*; '**~ jack·et** kamizelka *f* ratunkowa; '**~·lift** *aviat.* most *m* powietrzny; '**~·line** *aviat.* linia *f* lotnicza; '**~·lin·er** *aviat.* samolot *m* pasażerski; '**~·mail** poczta *f* lotnicza; ***by ~mail*** pocztą lotniczą; '**~·man** (*pl.* **-*men***) *wojskowy* lotnik *m*; '**~·plane** *Am.* samolot *m*; '**~·pock·et** *aviat.* dziura *f* powietrzna; '**~ pol·lu·tion** zanieczyszczenia *pl.* powietrza; '**~·port** port *m* lotniczy, lotnisko *n*; **~ raid** nalot *m*; **~-raid pre'cau·tions** *pl.* obrona *f* przeciwlotnicza; **~-raid-shel·ter** schron *m* przeciwlotniczy; '**~ route** *aviat.* trasa *f* przelotu; '**~·sick**: ***be ~sick*** mieć mdłości, czuć się niedobrze; '**~·space** przestrzeń *f* powietrzna; '**~·strip** *aviat.* pas startowy *lub* lądowania; '**~ ter·mi·nal** *aviat.* terminal *m* lotów; '**~·tight** hermetyczny, szczelny; '**~ traf·fic** *aviat.* ruch *m* lotniczy; **~-'traf·fic con·trol** *aviat.* kontrola *f* ruchu lotniczego; **~-'traf·fic con·trol·ler** *aviat.* kontroler *m* ruchu lotniczego; '**~·way** *aviat.* trasa *f* lotnicza; '**~·wor·thy** zdatny do lotu
air·y ['eərɪ] (**-*ier*, -*iest***) przewiewny, przestronny
aisle [aɪl] *arch.* nawa *f* boczna; przejście *n*
a·jar [ə'dʒɑː] uchylony
a·kin [ə'kɪn] pokrewny (***to*** *D*)
a·lac·ri·ty [ə'lækrətɪ] ochota *f*; ochoczość *f*
a·larm [ə'lɑːm] **1.** alarm *m*; sygnał *m* alarmowy; urządzenie *n* alarmowe; budzik *m*; niepokój *m*; **2.** ⟨za⟩alarmować; ⟨za⟩niepokoić; **~ clock** budzik *m*
A·las·ka Alaska *f*
Al·ba·ni·a Albania *f*
al·bum ['ælbəm] album *m* (*też płytowy*)
al·bu·mi·nous [æl'bjuːmɪnəs] białkowy; zawierający białko
al·co·hol ['ælkəhɒl] alkohol *m*; **~·ic** [ælkə'hɒlɪk] **1.** alkoholowy; **2.** alkoholik *m* (-liczka *f*)
ale [eɪl] ale *m* (*piwo jasne, mocno chmielone*)
a·lert [ə'lɜːrt] **1.** czujny; **2.** stan *m* pogotowia; pogotowie *n*; ***on the ~*** w stanie gotowości; w pogotowiu; **3.** ⟨za⟩alarmować; ostrzegać ⟨-rzec⟩ (***to*** przed *I*)

alga ['ælgə] (*pl.* ***algae*** ['ældʒiː]) glon *m*, alga *f*
al·ge·bra ['ældʒɪbrə] *math.* algebra *f*
al·i·bi ['ælɪbaɪ] alibi *n*
a·li·en ['eɪljən] **1.** obcy, odmienny; cudzoziemski; **2.** cudzoziemiec *m* (-mka *f*); **~·ate** ['eɪljəneɪt] odpychać ⟨odepchnąć⟩; zrażać ⟨zrazić⟩
a·light [ə'laɪt] **1.** płonący; **2.** (***alighted*** *lub* ***alit***) *ptak:* siadać ⟨usiąść⟩; wysiadać ⟨-siąść⟩
a·lign [ə'laɪn] wyrównywać ⟨-nać⟩ (***with*** w stosunku do *G*)
a·like [ə'laɪk] **1.** *adj.* podobny; **2.** *adv.* podobnie, jednakowo
al·i·men·ta·ry [ælɪ'mentərɪ] pokarmowy; odżywczy; **~ ca·nal** przewód *m* pokarmowy
al·i·mo·ny ['ælɪmənɪ] *jur.* alimenty *pl.*
alive [ə'laɪv] żywy, żyjący; pełen życia; ***~ and kicking*** w świetnym stanie; ***be ~ with*** pełen (*G*), wypełniony (*I*)
all [ɔːl] **1.** *adj.* wszyscy *pl.* wszystkie *pl.*; cały; wszystek; **2.** *pron.* wszystko; wszystkie *pl.*, wszyscy *pl.*; **3.** *adv.* zupełnie, całkowicie; ***~ at once*** nagle; ***~ the better*** tym lepiej; ***~ but*** prawie, niemalże; ***~ in*** *Am.* F wykończony; ***~ in ~*** ogółem; ***~ right*** w porządku; dobrze; ***for ~ that*** mimo tego; ***for ~ I know*** na ile mi wiadomo; ***at ~*** wcale, w ogóle; ***not at ~*** bynajmniej; ani trochę; nie ma za co; ***the score was two ~*** wynik był dwa dwa
all-A·mer·i·can [ɔːlə'merɪkən] ogólnoamerykański; typowo amerykański
al·lay [ə'leɪ] rozpraszać ⟨-szyć⟩; zmniejszać ⟨-szyć⟩
al·le·ga·tion [ælɪ'geɪʃn] *bezpodstawne* twierdzenie *n*
al·lege [ə'ledʒ] ⟨s⟩twierdzić; **~d** rzekomy; domniemany
al·le·giance [ə'liːdʒəns] lojalność *f*; wierność *f*
al·ler|·gic [ə'lɜːdʒɪk] alergiczny (***to*** na *A*); **~·gy** ['ælədʒɪ] alergia *f*
al·le·vi·ate [ə'liːvɪeɪt] zmniejszać ⟨-szyć⟩; ⟨z⟩łagodzić
al·ley ['ælɪ] aleja *f*; (*w parku, ogrodzie*) alejka *f*, dróżka *f*, ścieżka *f*; tor (*do gry w kręgle*) *m*
al·li|·ance [ə'laɪəns] przymierze *n*, sojusz *m*; **~ed** [ə'laɪd] sprzymierzony
al·li·ga·tor ['ælɪgeɪtə] *zo.* aligator *m*
al·lo|·cate ['æləkeɪt] przydzielać ⟨-lić⟩; ⟨wy⟩asygnować; **~·ca·tion** [ælə'keɪʃn] przydział *m*
al·lot [ə'lɒt] (**-*tt*-**) przeznaczać ⟨-czyć⟩; przydzielać ⟨-lić⟩; rozdzielać ⟨-lić⟩; **~·ment** przydział *m*; działka *f*
al·low [ə'laʊ] pozwalać ⟨-wolić⟩; dopuszczać ⟨-puścić⟩; dawać ⟨dać⟩; udzielać ⟨udzielić⟩; ***~ for*** uwzględniać ⟨-nić⟩ (*A*); **~·a·ble** dopuszczalny; **~·ance** (*w delegacji*) dieta *f*; zasiłek *m*; stypendium *m*; odpis *m* podatkowy; *fig.* uwzględnienie; ***make ~ance(s) for s.th.*** uwzględniać ⟨-nić⟩ coś
al·loy 1. ['ælɔɪ] stop *m*; **2.** [ə'lɔɪ] ⟨s⟩tworzyć stop
all-round ['ɔːlraʊnd] wszechstronny; **~·er** [ɔːl'raʊndə] osoba *f* wszechstronna; wszechstronny sportowiec *m*
al·lude [ə'luːd] ⟨z⟩robić aluzje *pl.* (***to*** do *G*)
al·lure [ə'ljʊə] ⟨z-, przy⟩nęcić; **~·ment** atrakcja *f*, przynęta *f*
al·lu·sion [ə'luːʒn] aluzja *f*
all-wheel 'drive *mot.* napęd *m* na wszystkie koła
al·ly 1. [ə'laɪ] sprzymierzać ⟨-rzyć⟩ się (***to, with*** z *I*); ['ælaɪ] sojusznik *m*; sprzymierzeniec *m*; ***the Allies*** *pl.* państwa sprzymierzone *pl.*, alianci *pl.*
al·might·y [ɔːl'maɪtɪ] wszechmocny; ***the*** ♀ Bóg *m* Wszechmogący
al·mond ['ɑːmənd] *bot.* migdał *m*; *attr.* migdałowy
al·most ['ɔːlməʊst] prawie, niemal
alms [ɑːmz] *pl.* jałmużna *f*
a·loft [ə'lɒft] w górę, w górze
a·lone [ə'ləʊn] **1.** *adj.* sam; **2.** *adv.* samotnie; ***let ~*** zostawiać ⟨-wić⟩ w spokoju; ***let ~ ...*** nie mówiąc już o (*L*)
a·long [ə'lɒŋ] **1.** *adv.* naprzód, w przód; ***all ~*** (przez) cały czas; ***come ~ with s.o.*** iść ⟨pójść⟩ z kimś; ***get ~*** dawać ⟨dać⟩ sobie radę; ⟨po⟩radzić sobie; być w dobrych stosunkach (***with*** z *I*); dobrze się porozumiewać ⟨-mieć⟩; ***take ~*** brać ⟨wziąć⟩ z (*I*); **2.** *prp.* wzdłuż (*G*); **~'side** obok (*G*); wzdłuż (*G*)
a·loof [ə'luːf] powściągliwy; pełen rezerwy
a·loud [ə'laʊd] na głos, głośno
al·pha·bet ['ælfəbet] alfabet *m*
al·pine ['ælpaɪn] alpejski, wysokogórski
Alps *pl.* Alpy *pl.*

al·read·y [ɔːl'redɪ] już
al·right [ɔːl'raɪt] → ***all right***
Al·sa·tian [æl'seɪʃən] *zwł. Brt.* owczarek *m* alzacki *lub* niemiecki, F wilczur *m*
al·so ['ɔːlsəʊ] też, także
al·tar ['ɔːltə] ołtarz *m*
al·ter ['ɔːltə] zmieniać ⟨-nić⟩ (się); *ubranie* przerabiać ⟨-robić⟩; **~·a·tion** [ɔːltə'reɪʃn] zmiana *f* (***to*** na *A*); przemiana *f*; przeróbka *f* (*ubrania*)
al·ter|·nate **1.** ['ɔːltəneɪt] następować ⟨-tąpić⟩ na zmianę; **2.** [ɔːl'tɜːnət] naprzemienny; **~·nat·ing cur·rent** ['ɔːltəneɪtɪŋ -] prąd *m* zmienny; **~·na·tion** [ɔːltə'neɪʃn] zmiana *f*; przemiana *f*; **~·na·tive** [ɔːl'tɜːnətɪv] **1.** alternatywny; **2.** alternatywa *f*; wybór *m*
al·though [ɔːl'ðəʊ] choć, chociaż
al·ti·tude ['æltɪtjuːd] wysokość *f*; ***at an ~ of*** na wysokości (*G*)
al·to·geth·er [ɔːltə'geðə] ogólnie; ogółem; zupełnie, całkowicie
al·u·min·i·um [æljʊ'mɪnjəm] *Brt.*, **a·lu·mi·num** [ə'luːmɪnəm] *Am. chem.* aluminium *n*, glin *m*; *attr.* aluminiowy
al·ways ['ɔːlweɪz] zawsze
am [æm; *we frazie* əm] *1. os. poj. ter. od* ***be*** jestem
am, **AM** [eɪ 'em] *skrót*: ***before noon*** (*łacińskie* ***ante meridiem***) przed południem
a·mal·gam·ate [ə'mælgəmeɪt] *też econ.* ⟨po-, z⟩łączyć się; *econ.* dokonywać ⟨-nać⟩ fuzji
a·mass [ə'mæs] ⟨na-, z⟩gromadzić
am·a·teur ['æmətə] **1.** amator(ka *f*); **2.** amatorski
a·maze [ə'meɪz] zdumiewać ⟨-mieć⟩; **a'maze·ment** zdumienie *n*; **a'maz·ing** zdumiewający
am·bas·sa|·dor [æm'bæsədə] ambasador (***to*** w *L*); *fig.* przedstawiciel(ka *f*) *m*; **~·dress** [æm'bæsədrɪs] kobieta *f* ambasador; *fig.* przestawicielka *f*
am·ber ['æmbə] bursztyn *m*; bursztynowy
am·bi·gu·i·ty [æmbɪ'gjuːɪtɪ] dwuznaczność *f*; wieloznaczność *f*; niejasność *f*; **am·big·u·ous** [æm'bɪgjʊəs] dwuznaczny; wieloznaczny; niejasny
am·bi|·tion [æm'bɪʃn] ambicja *f*; **~·tious** [æm'bɪʃəs] ambitny
am·ble ['æmbl] **1.** przechadzka *f*; spokojny chód *m*; **2.** przechadzać ⟨przejść⟩ się; spokojnie iść ⟨pójść⟩;
am·bu·lance ['æmbjʊləns] karetka *f* (*pogotowia*)
am·bush ['æmbʊʃ] **1.** zasadzka *f*; ***be*** *lub* ***lie in ~ for s.o.*** czekać w zasadzce na kogoś; czatować na kogoś; **2.** wciągać ⟨-gnąć⟩ w zasadzkę
a·men [ɑː'men] *int.* amen; niech tak będzie
a·mend [ə'mend] poprawiać ⟨-wić⟩; ⟨z⟩modyfikować; *prawo* wnosić ⟨wnieść⟩ poprawki; **~·ment** poprawka *f* (*też parl., Am. do konstytucji*); modyfikacja *f*; zmiana *f*; **~s** *pl.* rekompensata *f*; ***make ~s*** ⟨z⟩rekompensować; naprawiać ⟨-wić⟩ szkody; ***make ~s to s.o. for s.th.*** wynagradzać coś komuś, rekompensować coś komuś
a·men·i·ty [ə'miːnətɪ] *często* ***amenities*** *pl.* wygody *pl.*; urządzenia *pl.* ułatwiające życie
A·mer·i·ca [ə'merɪkə] Ameryka *f*; **A·mer·i·can** [ə'merɪkən] **1.** amerykański; **~' *plan*** pełne utrzymanie *n*; **2.** Amerykanin *m* (-nka *f*)
A·mer·i·can|·is·m [ə'merɪkənɪzəm] amerykanizm *m*; **~·ize** [ə'merɪkənaɪz] ⟨z⟩amerykanizować (się)
a·mi·a·ble ['eɪmjəbl] przyjazny; miły
am·i·ca·ble ['æmɪkəbl] przyjacielski; *jur.* polubowny, ugodowy
a·mid(st) [ə'mɪd(st)] wśród (*G*); (po)między (*I*)
a·miss [ə'mɪs] źle, błędnie; ***take ~*** ⟨po⟩czuć się urażonym
am·mo·ni·a [ə'məʊnjə] amoniak *m*
am·mu·ni·tion [æmjʊ'nɪʃn] amunicja *f*
am·nes·ty ['æmnɪstɪ] **1.** amnestia *f*; **2.** ułaskawiać ⟨-wić⟩
a·mok [ə'mɒk] amok *m*; ***run ~*** dostawać ⟨-tać⟩ amoku
a·mong(st) [ə'mʌŋ(st)] (po)między
am·o·rous ['æmərəs] rozkochany (***of*** w *L*)
a·mount [ə'maʊnt] **1.** (***to***) wynosić ⟨-nieść⟩ (*A*); stanowić (*A*); sprowadzać ⟨-dzić⟩ się do (*G*); **2.** kwota *f*; liczba *f*; suma *f*
am·ple ['æmpl] (***~r, ~st***) obfity; pokaźny; dostateczny
am·pli|·fi·ca·tion [æmplɪfɪ'keɪʃn] zwiększenie *n*; *electr.* wzmocnienie *n*; **~·fi·er** *electr.* ['æmplɪfaɪə] wzmacniacz

m; ~·**fy** ['æmplɪfaɪ] zwiększać ⟨-szyć⟩; *electr.* wzmacniać ⟨-nić⟩; ~·**tude** ['æmplɪtjuːd] zasięg; amplituda
am·pu·tate ['æmpjʊteɪt] ⟨z⟩amputować
a·muck [ə'mʌk] → ***amok***
a·muse [ə'mjuːz] (***o.s.*** się) ⟨roz⟩bawić, zabawiać ⟨-wić⟩; ~·**ment** rozrywka *f*; zabawa *f*; radość *f*; ~·**ment arcade** salon *m* gier automatycznych *lub* komputerowych; ~·**ment park** wesołe miasteczko *n*; **a'mus·ing** zabawny
an [æn, ən] → ***a***
an·a·bol·ic ster·oid [ænəbɒlɪk 'stɪərɔɪd] *pharm.* steryd *m* anaboliczny
a·nae·mi·a [ə'niːmjə] anemia *f*
an·aes·thet·ic [ænɪs'θetɪk] *med.* **1.** (~***ally***) znieczulający; **2.** środek *m* znieczulający
a·nal ['eɪnl] *anat.* odbytniczy; analny
a·nal·o|·gous [ə'næləgəs] analogiczny, podobny; ~·**gy** [ə'nælədʒɪ] analogia *f*
an·a·lyse *zwł. Brt.*, **an·a·lyze** *Am.* ['ænəlaɪz] ⟨prze-, z⟩analizować; przeprowadzać ⟨-dzić⟩ analizę; **a·nal·y·sis** [ə'næləsɪs] (*pl.* ***-ses*** [-siːz]) analiza *f*
an·arch·y ['ænəkɪ] anarchia *f*
a·nat·o|·mize [ə'nætəmaɪz] *med.* przeprowadzać ⟨-dzić⟩ sekcję; *fig.* ⟨prze-, z⟩analizować; ~·**my** [ə'nætəmɪ] anatomia *f*; analiza *f*
an·ces|·tor ['ænsestə] przodek *m*; protoplasta *m*; ~·**tress** ['ænsestrɪs] protoplastka *f*
an·chor ['æŋkə] **1.** kotwica *f*; ***at*** ~ na kotwicy; **2.** zakotwiczać ⟨-czyć⟩
an·chor|·man ['æŋkəmæn] *Am. TV* (*pl.* ***-men***) prowadzący *m* (*wiadomości*); '~·**wom·an** *Am. TV* (*pl.* ***-women***) prowadząca *f* (*wiadomości*)
an·cho·vy ['æntʃəvɪ] sardela *f*
an·cient ['eɪnʃənt] **1.** starożytny; prastary; **2.** ***the*** ~***s*** *pl. hist.* starożytni *pl.*
and [ænd, ənd] i; a
an·ec·dote ['ænɪkdəʊt] anegdota *f*
a·ne·mi·a [ə'niːmjə] *Am.* → ***anaemia***
an·es·thet·ic [ænɪs'θetɪk] *Am.* → ***anesthetic***
an·gel ['eɪndʒəl] anioł *m*
an·ger ['æŋgə] **1.** gniew *m* (***at*** z powodu *G*); **2.** rozgniewać
an·gi·na (pec·to·ris) [æn'dʒaɪnə('pektərɪs)] *med.* dusznica *f* bolesna, angina *f* pectoris; ⚠ *nie* ***angina***
an·gle[1] ['æŋgl] kąt *m*; róg *m*
an·gle[2] ['æŋgl] ⟨z⟩łowić; '~**r** wędkarz *m*
An·gli·can ['æŋglɪkən] **1.** anglikański; **2.** anglikanin *m*, anglikanka *f*
An·glo-Sax·on [æŋgləʊ'sæksən] **1.** anglosaski; **2.** Anglosas *m*
an·gry ['æŋgrɪ] (***-ier, -iest***) zły, rozgniewany (***at, with*** na *A*)
an·guish ['æŋgwɪʃ] cierpienie *n*
an·gu·lar ['æŋgjʊlə] kanciasty
an·i·mal ['ænɪml] **1.** zwierzę *n*; **2.** zwierzęcy; '~ **lov·er** miłośnik *m* (-niczka *f*) zwierząt
an·i|·mate ['ænɪmeɪt] ożywiać ⟨-wić⟩; pobudzać ⟨-dzić⟩; '~·**ma·ted** ożywiony; pobudzony; ~·**ma·ted car'toon** film *m* animowany; ~·**ma·tion** [ænɪ'meɪʃn] ożywienie *n*; pobudzenie *n*; animacja *f*; *komp.* grafika *f* animowana
an·i·mos·i·ty [ænɪ'mɒsətɪ] wrogość *f*; wrogie nastawienie *n*
an·kle ['æŋkl] *anat.* kostka
an·nals ['ænlz] *pl.* roczniki *pl.*; annały *pl.*
an·nex **1.** [ə'neks] dołączać ⟨-czyć⟩; ⟨za⟩anektować; **2.** ['æneks] aneks *m*, dodatek *m*; przybudówka *f*
an·ni·ver·sa·ry [ænɪ'vɜːsərɪ] rocznica *f*
an·no·tate ['ænəʊteɪt] zaopatrywać ⟨-trzyć⟩ w adnotacje *lub* przypisy
an·nounce [ə'naʊns] ogłaszać ⟨ogłosić⟩; oświadczać ⟨-czyć⟩; *radio*, *TV*: zapowiadać ⟨-wiedzieć⟩; ⚠ *nie* anonsować; ~·**ment** zapowiedź *f* (*też radio*, *TV*); ogłoszenie *n*; komunikat *m*; **an'nounc·er** spiker(ka *f*) *m*
an·noy [ə'nɔɪ] ⟨z⟩irytować; ~·**ance** irytacja *f*; poirytowanie *n*; ~·**ing** irytujący
an·nu·al ['ænjʊəl] **1.** roczny; coroczny; doroczny; **2.** *bot.* roślina *f* jednoroczna; rocznik *m*
an·nu·i·ty [ə'njuːɪtɪ] renta *f* (roczna)
an·nul [ə'nʌl] (***-ll-***) anulować; unieważniać ⟨-nić⟩; ~·**ment** anulowanie *n*; unieważnienie *n*
an·o·dyne ['ænəʊdaɪn] *med.* **1.** uśmierzający bóle; **2.** środek *m* uśmierzający bóle
a·noint [ə'nɔɪnt] namaszczać ⟨-maścić⟩
a·nom·a·lous [ə'nɒmələs] nieprawidłowy; nieregularny
a·non·y·mous [ə'nɒnɪməs] anonimowy

an·o·rak ['ænəræk] skafander *m* (*z kapturem*); kurtka *f*
an·oth·er [ə'nʌðə] inny; jeszcze jeden
ANSI ['ænsɪ] *skrót*: ***American National Standards Institute*** Amerykański Urząd Norm
an·swer ['ɑːnsə] **1.** *v/t.* odpowiadać ⟨-wiedzieć⟩; *cel* spełniać ⟨-nić⟩; *problem* rozwiązywać ⟨-zać⟩; *opis* odpowiadać; ~ ***the bell*** *lub* ***door*** otworzyć drzwi; ~ ***the telephone*** odbierać ⟨-debrać⟩ telefon; *v/i.* odpowiadać ⟨-wiedzieć⟩; podnosić ⟨-nieść⟩ słuchawkę; ~ ***back*** odpyskowywać ⟨-ować⟩, odcinać ⟨-ciąć⟩ się; ~ ***for*** ponosić ⟨-nieść⟩ odpowiedzialność za (*G*); **2.** odpowiedź *f* (***to*** na *A*); ~**·a·ble** ['ɑːnsərəbl] odpowiedzialny (***for*** za *A*); ~**·ing machine** *tel.* ['ɑːnsərɪŋ -] automatyczna sekretarka *f*
ant [ænt] *zo.* mrówka *f*
an·tag·o|·nis·m [æn'tægənɪzəm] antagonizm *m*; wrogość *f*; ~**·nist** [æn'tægənɪst] przeciwnik *m* (-niczka *f*); ~**·nize** [æn'tægənaɪz] zrażać ⟨zrazić⟩; wzbudzać ⟨-dzić⟩ wrogość
Ant·arc·tic [æn'tɑːktɪk] antarktyczny
Ant·arc·tica [æn'tɑːktɪkə] Antarktyda *f*
an·te·ced·ent [æntɪ'siːdənt] poprzedni, uprzedni
an·te·lope ['æntɪləʊp] *zo.* (*pl.* ***-lopes, -lope***) antylopa *f*
an·ten·na[1] [æn'tenə] *zo.* (*pl.* ***-nae*** [-niː]) czułek *m*
an·ten·na[2] [æn'tenə] *Am.* antena *f*
an·te·ri·or [æn'tɪərɪə] poprzedni; wcześniejszy (***to*** niż)
an·them ['ænθəm] hymn *m*
an·ti... ['æntɪ] anty..., przeciw...; ~**'air·craft** *mil.* przeciwlotniczy; ~**·bi·ot·ic** [æntɪbaɪ'ɒtɪk] *pharm.* antybiotyk *m*; '~**·bod·y** *biol.* przeciwciało *n*
an·tic·i|·pate [æn'tɪsɪpeɪt] przewidywać ⟨-widzieć⟩; oczekiwać, wyczekiwać; ~**·pa·tion** [æntɪsɪ'peɪʃn] oczekiwanie *n*; przewidywanie *n*; ***in ~pation*** z góry, naprzód
an·ti·clock·wise [æntɪ'klɒkwaɪz] *Brt.* w kierunku odwrotnym do ruchu wskazówek zegara
an·tics ['æntɪks] *pl.* błazeństwa *pl.*, wygłupy *pl.*; ⚠ *nie* ***antyk***
an·ti|·dote ['æntɪdəʊt] antidotum *n*, odtrutka *f*; '~**·freeze** płyn *m* nie zamarzający; ~**'lock braking sys·tem** *mot.* (system) ABS *m* (*przeciwdziałający blokadzie hamulców*); ~**'mis·sile** przeciwrakietowy; ~**'nu·cle·ar ac·tiv·ist** działacz(ka *f*) *m* ruchu przeciw broni nuklearnej
an·tip·a·thy [æn'tɪpəθɪ] antypatia
an·ti·quat·ed ['æntɪkweɪtɪd] przestarzały, staroświecki; ⚠ *nie* ***antykwaryczny***
an·tique [æn'tiːk] **1.** antyczny; starożytny; **2.** antyk *m*, zabytek *m*; ~ ***deal·er*** antykwariusz *m*; ~ ***shop*** *zwł. Brt.*, ~ ***store*** *Am.* sklep *m* z antykami
an·tiq·ui·ty [æn'tɪkwətɪ] starożytność *f*
an·ti·sep·tic [æntɪ'septɪk] **1.** antyseptyczny, odkażający; **2.** środek antyseptyczny *lub* odkażający
ant·lers ['æntləz] *pl.* rogi *pl.*, poroże *n*
a·nus ['eɪnəs] *anat.* odbyt *m*
an·vil ['ænvɪl] kowadło *n*
anx·i·e·ty [æŋ'zaɪətɪ] lęk *m*; niepokój *m*, obawa *f*; troska *f*
anx·ious ['æŋkʃəs] zatroskany; zaniepokojony; wyczekujący; ***he is ~ about you*** niepokoi się o ciebie; ***he is ~ to do s.th.*** zależy mu, by coś zrobić
an·y ['enɪ] **1.** *adj. i pron.* jakiś, trochę; jakikolwiek; którykolwiek; każdy; *z przeczeniem*: żaden; ***not ~*** w ogóle; żaden; **2.** trochę, nieco; '~**·bod·y** ktokolwiek; każdy; *z przeczeniem*: nikt; '~**·how** jakkolwiek; byle jak; '~**·one** → ***anybody***; '~**·thing** cokolwiek; coś; cokolwiek; *z przeczeniem*: nic; ***~thing but*** w ogóle; wcale; ani trochę; ***~thing else?*** czy coś jeszcze?; '~**·way** → ***anyhow***; '~**·where** gdziekolwiek; gdzieś; *z przeczeniem*: nigdzie
AP [eɪ 'piː] *skrót*: ***Associated Press*** (*amerykańska agencja prasowa*)
a·part [ə'pɑːt] osobno, na boku; od siebie; ~ ***from*** oprócz
a·part·heid [ə'pɑːtheɪt] apartheid *m*, polityka *f* segregacji rasowej
a·part·ment [ə'pɑːtmənt] *Am.* mieszkanie *n*; ⚠ *nie* ***apartament***; ~ ***building*** *zwł. Brt.*, ~ ***house*** *Am.* blok *m* mieszkaniowy, kamienica *f*
ap·a|·thet·ic [æpə'θetɪk] (***-ally***) apatyczny, obojętny, zobojętniały; ~**·thy** ['æpəθɪ] apatia *f*, obojętność *f*, zobojętnienie *n*

ape [eɪp] *zo.* małpa *f* człekokształtna
ap·er·ture ['æpətjʊə] otwór *m*; szczelina *f*
a·pi·a·ry ['eɪpjərɪ] pasieka *f*
a·piece [ə'pi:s] za sztukę; na głowę, na osobę
a·pol·o|·gize [ə'pɒlədʒaɪz] przepraszać ⟨-prosić⟩; **~·gy** [ə'pɒlədʒɪ] przeprosiny *pl.*; ***make an ~gy*** (***for s.th.***) przepraszać ⟨-prosić⟩ (za coś)
ap·o·plex·y ['æpəpleksɪ] apopleksja *f*, udar *m*
a·pos·tle [ə'pɒsl] *rel.* apostoł *m* (*też fig.*)
a·pos·tro·phe [ə'pɒstrəfɪ] apostrof *m*
ap·pal(l) [ə'pɔ:l] (***-ll-***) przerażać ⟨-razić⟩; trwożyć ⟨zatrważać⟩
Ap·pa·la·chians *pl.* Appalachy *pl.*
ap'pal·ling przerażający; zatrważający
ap·pa·ra·tus [æpə'reɪtəs] aparat *m*; aparatura *f*; urządzenie *n*; przyrząd *m*
ap·par·ent [ə'pærənt] pozorny; widoczny
ap·pa·ri·tion [æpə'rɪʃn] widmo *n*, zjawa *f*
ap·peal [ə'pi:l] **1.** *jur.* składać ⟨złożyć⟩ odwołanie, odwoływać ⟨odwołać⟩ się; ⟨za⟩apelować (***for*** o *A*); wzywać ⟨wezwać⟩ (***to*** do *G*); **~ *to*** odwoływać ⟨odwołać⟩ się do (*G*), przemawiać ⟨-mówić⟩ do (*G*); *kogoś* pociągać (***to*** *A*), ⟨s⟩podobać się; **2.** *jur.* apelacja *f*, odwołanie *n* się; urok *m*, powab *m*; prośba *f* (***to*** do *G*, ***for*** o *A*), apel *m*; ***~ for mercy*** *jur.* prośba *f* o łaskę; ***sex ~*** seksapil *m*, atrakcyjność *f*; **~·ing** pociągający; błagalny
ap·pear [ə'pɪə] ukazywać ⟨-zać⟩ się; pojawiać ⟨-wić⟩ się; *publicznie* występować ⟨-stąpić⟩; wydawać się; **~·ance** [ə'pɪərəns] pojawienie *n* się; wygląd *m*; wystąpienie *n*; ***keep up ~ances*** zachowywać ⟨-chować⟩ pozory; ***to*** *lub* ***by all ~ances*** pozornie, na pozór
ap·pease [ə'pi:z] uspokajać ⟨-koić⟩; *pragnienie itp.* zaspokajać ⟨-koić⟩
ap·pend [ə'pend] dołączać ⟨-czyć⟩, przyłączać ⟨-łączyć⟩; **~·age** [ə'pendɪdʒ] dodatek *m*; uzupełnienie *n*
ap·pen|·di·ci·tis [əpendɪ'saɪtɪs] *med.* zapalenie *n* wyrostka robaczkowego; **~·dix** [ə'pendɪks] (*pl.* ***-dixes, -dices*** [-dɪsi:z]) dodatek *m*, suplement *m*; *też* ***vermiform ~dix*** *anat.* wyrostek *m* robaczkowy, ślepa kiszka *f*
ap·pe|·tite ['æpɪtaɪt] apetyt *m*; *fig.* chęć *f*, chętka *f* (***for*** na *L*); **~·tiz·er** ['æpɪtaɪzə] przystawka *f*, zakąska *f*; aperitif *m*; **~·tiz·ing** ['æpɪtaɪzɪŋ] apetyczny, smakowity
ap·plaud [ə'plɔ:d] *v/t.* oklaskiwać; *v/i.* ⟨za⟩klaskać; **ap·plause** [ə'plɔ:z] aplauz *m*, brawa *pl.*
ap·ple ['æpl] jabłko *n*; **'~ cart**: ***upset s.o.'s ~cart*** F ⟨po⟩psuć komuś szyki; **~ 'pie** szarlotka *f*; ***in ~pie order*** F w porządku, jak z pudełka; **~ 'sauce** przecier *m* jabłkowy; *Am. sl.* bzdury *pl.*, banialuki *pl.*; **~ 'tree** *bot.* jabłoń *f*
ap·pli·ance [ə'plaɪəns] urządzenie *n*; przyrząd *m*
ap·plic·a·ble ['æplɪkəbl] mający zastosowanie (***to*** do *G*)
ap·pli|·cant ['æplɪkənt] kandydat(ka *f*) *m* (***for*** do *G*), aplikant(ka *f*) *m*; **~·ca·tion** [æplɪ'keɪʃn] zastosowanie *n*; podanie *n* (***to*** do *G*); ubieganie *n* się (***for*** o *A*); nałożenie *n* (*kremu*)
ap·ply [ə'plaɪ] *v/t.* (***to***) ⟨za⟩stosować (do *G*); nakładać ⟨nałożyć⟩ (na *L*); ***~ o.s. to*** przykładać ⟨-łożyć⟩ się (do *G*); *v/i.* (***to***) stosować się (do *G*), mieć zastosowanie (do *G*); zgłaszać ⟨zgłosić⟩ się (***for*** do *G*), składać ⟨złożyć⟩ podanie (***for*** na *A*)
ap·point [ə'pɔɪnt] wyznaczać ⟨-czyć⟩; mianować (***s.o. director*** kogoś *I*), powołać (***s.o. director*** kogoś na *A*); **~·ment** mianowanie *n*, nominacja *f*; stanowisko *n*; (*z lekarzem itp.*) *umówione* spotkanie *n*; termin *m* (*wizyty*); ***by ~ment*** po uzgodnieniu terminu; ***~ment book*** terminarz *m*
ap·por·tion [ə'pɔ:ʃn] przydzielać ⟨-dzielić⟩
ap·prais|·al [ə'preɪzl] oszacowanie *n*, ocena *f*; **~e** [ə'preɪz] oszacowywać ⟨-wać⟩, oceniać ⟨-nić⟩
ap·pre|·cia·ble [ə'pri:ʃəbl] znaczny, dostrzegalny; **~·ci·ate** [ə'pri:ʃɪeɪt] *v/t.* doceniać ⟨-nić⟩; cenić sobie; uznać ⟨-wać⟩; *v/i.* wzrastać ⟨wzrosnąc⟩ na wartości; **~·ci·a·tion** [əpri:ʃɪ'eɪʃn] uznanie *n*; wzrost *m* wartości *lub* ceny; uznanie *n*, wdzięczność *f*
ap·pre|·hend [æprɪ'hend] pojmować ⟨-jąć⟩, ⟨z⟩rozumieć; ⟨za⟩aresztować;

obawiać się; **~·hen·sion** [æprɪ'henʃn] obawa *f*; aresztowanie *n*; pojmowanie *n*, zrozumienie *n*; **~·hen·sive** [æprɪ'hensɪv] pełen obaw (***for*** o *A*, ***that*** że); bojaźliwy
ap·pren·tice [ə'prentɪs] **1.** praktykant(ka *f*) *m*; terminator *m*; **2.** ⟨od⟩dawać w termin; **~·ship** praktyka *f*; termin *m*
ap·proach [ə'prəʊtʃ] **1.** *v/i.* zbliżać ⟨zbliżyć⟩ się, przybliżać ⟨przybliżyć⟩ się, nadchodzić ⟨nadejść⟩; *v/t.* zbliżać ⟨zbliżyć⟩ się do (*G*), przybliżać ⟨przybliżyć⟩ się do (*G*); podchodzić ⟨podejść⟩ do (*G*); zwracać ⟨zwrócić⟩ się do (*G*); **2.** nadejście *n*; podejście *n*; dostęp *m*; zbliżanie *n* się
ap·pro·ba·tion [æprə'beɪʃn] aprobata *f*; akceptacja *f*
ap·pro·pri·ate 1. [ə'prəʊprɪeɪt] przywłaszczać ⟨-łaścić⟩ sobie; ⟨wy⟩asygnować, przeznaczać ⟨-czyć⟩; **2.** [ə'prəʊprɪɪt] (***for, to***) właściwy (do *G*); odpowiedni (do *G*)
ap·prov|·al [ə'pru:vl] aprobata *f*; zgoda *f*; **~e**[ə'pru:v] ⟨za⟩aprobować; uznawać ⟨-nać⟩; zatwierdzać ⟨-dzić⟩; **~ed** zatwierdzony, zaaprobowany
ap·prox·i·mate [ə'prɒksɪmət] przybliżony
Apr *skrót pisany*: ***April*** kw., kwiecień *m*
a·pri·cot ['eɪprɪkɒt] morela *f*
A·pril ['eɪprəl] (*skrót*: ***Apr***) kwiecień *m*; *attr.* kwietniowy
a·pron ['eɪprən] fartuch *m*; **'~ strings** *pl.* tasiemki *pl.* fartucha; ***be tied to one's mother's ~ strings*** trzymać się maminego fartucha
apt [æpt] trafny, celny; zdatny, nadający się; zdolny; ***be ~ to do s.th.*** mieć skłonności do robienia czegoś; **ap·ti·tude** ['æptɪtju:d] (***for***) zdatność *f* (do *G*); talent *m*; **'~ *test*** test *m* zdolności
aq·ua·plan·ing ['ækwəpleɪnɪŋ] *Brt. mot.* akwaplanacja *f*; *tech.* poślizg hydrodynamiczny *m*
a·quar·i·um [ə'kweərɪəm] (*pl.* ***-iums, -ia*** [-ɪə]) akwarium *n*
A·quar·i·us [ə'kweərɪəs] *znak Zodiaku*: Wodnik *m*; ***he/she is*** (***an***) **~** on(a) jest spod znaku Wodnika
a·quat·ic [ə'kwætɪk] wodny; **~ *plant*** *bot.* roślina *f* wodna; **~s** *sg.*: **~ *sports*** *pl.* sporty *pl.* wodne
aq·ue·duct ['ækwɪdʌkt] akwedukt *m*
aq·ui·line ['ækwɪlaɪn] *nos*: orli; **'~ *nose*** orli *lub* rzymski nos *m*
Ar·ab ['ærəb] **1.** Arab(ka *f*) *m*; **2.** *kraj* arabski; **A·ra·bi·a** [ə'reɪbjə] Arabia *f*; **Ar·a·bic** ['ærəbɪk] **1.** arabski; **2.** język *m* arabski
ar·a·ble ['ærəbl] orny; uprawny
ar·bi|·tra·ry ['ɑ:bɪtrərɪ] arbitralny; przypadkowy; **~·trate** ['ɑ:bɪtreɪt] rozstrzygać ⟨-gnąć⟩ w arbitrażu; ‘0s⟩pełnić rolę arbitra; **~·tra·tion** [ɑ:bɪ'treɪʃn] arbitraż *m*; **~·tra·tor** ['ɑ:bɪtreɪtə] arbiter *m*, rozjemca *m* (-czyni *f*)
ar·bo(u)r ['ɑ:bə] altana *f*
arc [ɑ:k] łuk *m* (*electr.* elektryczny); **ar·cade** [ɑ:'keɪd] arkada *f*; pasaż *m*
ARC [eɪ ɑ: 'si:] *skrót*: ***American Red Cross*** Amerykański Czerwony Krzyż
arch¹ [ɑ:tʃ] **1.** łuk *m*; sklepienie *n*; przęsło *n* (*mostu*); **2.** wyginać ⟨-giąć⟩ (się) w łuk
arch² [ɑ:tʃ] arcy...; arch...
arch³ [ɑ:tʃ] psotny, figlarny
ar·cha·ic [ɑ:'keɪɪk] (***~ally***) archaiczny
arch|·an·gel ['ɑ:keɪndʒəl] archanioł *m*; **~·bish·op** ['ɑ:tʃbɪʃəp] arcybiskup *m*
ar·cher ['ɑ:tʃə] łucznik *m*, (-niczka *f*); **~·y** ['ɑ:tʃərɪ] łucznictwo *n*
ar·chi|·tect ['ɑ:kɪtekt] architekt *m*; **~·tec·ture** ['ɑ:kɪtektʃə] architektura *f*
ar·chives ['ɑ:kaɪvz] *pl.* archiwum *n*, archiwa *pl.*
'arch·way pasaż *m*, *sklepione* przejście *n*
arc·tic ['ɑ:ktɪk] arktyczny
ar·dent ['ɑ:dənt] płonący, rozżarzony; *fig.* gorliwy, ożywiony
ar·do(u)r ['ɑ:də] żar *m*; gorliwość *f*
are [ɑ:] *2. os. ter. poj. i 1., 2., 3. mn. od* ***be***; *ty* jesteś, *my* jesteśmy, *wy* jesteście, *oni, one* są
ar·e·a ['eərɪə] powierzchnia *f*; obszar *m*; miejsce *n*; dziedzina *f*; rejon *m*, strefa *f*; **'~ *code*** *Am. tel.* numer *m* kierunkowy
Ar·gen|·ti·na [ɑ:dʒən'ti:nə] Argentyna *f*; **~·tine** ['ɑ:dʒəntaɪn] **1.** argentyński; **2.** Argentyńczyk *m*, Argentynka *f*
a·re·na [ə'ri:nə] arena *f*; miejsce *n*
ar·gue ['ɑ:gju:] spierać się, ⟨po⟩sprzeczać się; argumentować, wysuwać ⟨-nąć⟩ argumenty; utrzymywać (***that*** że)
ar·gu·ment ['ɑ:gjʊmənt] sprzeczka *f*,

spór *m*; argument *m*; dyskusja *f*
ar·id ['ærɪd] suchy, jałowy
Ar·ies ['eəri:z] *znak Zodiaku*: Baran *m*; ***he/she is (an) ~*** on(a) jest spod znaku Barana
a·rise [ə'raɪz] (***arose, arisen***) powstawać ⟨-stać⟩, pojawiać ⟨-wić⟩ się; wynikać ⟨-knąć⟩; **a·ris·en** [ə'rɪzn] *p.p. od* ***arise***
ar·is|·toc·ra·cy [ærɪ'stɒkrəsɪ] arystokracja *f*; **~·to·crat** ['ærɪstəkræt] arystokrata *m* (-tka *f*)
a·rith·me·tic[1] [ə'rɪθmətɪk] *math.* arytmetyka *f*; obliczenia *pl.*, wyliczenia *pl.*
ar·ith·met·ic[2] [ærɪθ'metɪk] arytmetyczny, rachunkowy; **~ 'u·nit** *komp.* arytmometr *m*, jednostka *f* arytmetyczno-logiczna
ark [ɑ:k] arka *f*
arm[1] [ɑ:m] ramię *n*; ręka *f*; poręcz *f*; ***keep s.o. at ~'s length*** trzymać kogoś na dystans
arm[2] [ɑ:m] ⟨u⟩zbroić (się)
ar·ma·ment ['ɑ:məmənt] zbrojenie *n* się; zbrojenia *pl.*
'arm·chair fotel *m*
ar·mi·stice ['ɑ:mɪstɪs] zawieszenie *n* broni
ar·mo(u)r ['ɑ:mə] **1.** *mil.* pancerz *m* (*też fig.*, *zo.*); opancerzenie *n*; wojska *pl.* pancerne; zbroja *f*; **2.** opancerzać ⟨-rzyć⟩; ***~ed 'car*** wóz *m* opancerzony, samochód *m* pancerny
'arm·pit pacha *f*
arms [ɑ:mz] *pl.* broń *f*, uzbrojenie; ***'~ control*** kontrola *f* zbrojeń; ***'~ race*** wyścig *m* zbrojeń
ar·my ['ɑ:mɪ] wojsko *n*, armia *f*
a·ro·ma [ə'rəʊmə] aromat *m*, woń *f*; **ar·o·mat·ic** [ærə'mætɪk] aromatyczny, wonny
a·rose [ə'rəʊz] *pret. od* ***arise***
a·round [ə'raʊnd] **1.** *adv.* dookoła, wokoło; w pobliżu; **2.** *prp.* wokół (*G*), dookoła (*G*), koło (*G*); około (*G*)
a·rouse [ə'raʊz] ⟨z⟩budzić; *fig.* pobudzać ⟨-dzić⟩; rozbudzać ⟨-dzić⟩
ar·range [ə'reɪndʒ] układać ⟨ułożyć⟩, ustawiać ⟨-wić⟩, rozmieszczać ⟨-ścić⟩, ⟨z⟩organizować, załatwiać ⟨-wić⟩; *muz.* aranżować, opracowywać ⟨-ować⟩ (*też theat.*); **~·ment** ułożenie *n*, ustawienie *n*, rozłożenie *n*; załatwienie *n*, zorganizowanie *n*; *muz.* aranżacja *f*, opracowanie *n* (*też theat.*)
ar·rears [ə'rɪəz] *pl.* zaległości *pl.*; ***be in ~ with*** zalegać z (*I*)
ar·rest [ə'rest] **1.** *jur.* aresztowanie *n*, zatrzymanie *n*; **2.** *jur.* ⟨za⟩aresztować, zatrzymywać ⟨-ymać⟩
ar·riv·al [ə'raɪvl] przybycie *n*, przyjazd *m*, przylot *m*; *fig.* przybycie *n*, nadejście *n*; ***~s*** *pl.* przyjazdy (*przyloty itp. - informacja*); **ar·rive** [ə'raɪv] przybywać ⟨-być⟩, przyjeżdżać ⟨-jechać⟩, przylatywać ⟨-lecieć⟩; *fig.* nadchodzić ⟨-dejść⟩; ***~ at*** przybywać ⟨-być⟩ do (*G*), *fig.* dochodzić ⟨dojść⟩ do (*G*)
ar·ro|·gance ['ærəgəns] arogancja *f*; **'~·gant** arogancki
ar·row ['ærəʊ] strzała *f*, strzałka *f*; **'~·head** grot *m* (*strzały*)
ar·se·nic ['ɑ:snɪk] *chem.* arsen *m*; arszenik *m*
ar·son ['ɑ:sn] *jur.* podpalenie *n*
art [ɑ:t] sztuka *f*
ar·ter·i·al [ɑ:'tɪərɪəl] *anat.* tętniczy; ***~ road*** droga *f* przelotowa; **ar·te·ry** ['ɑ:tərɪ] *anat.* tętnica *f*, arteria *f*; arteria *f* komunikacyjna
ar·ter·i·o·scle·ro·sis [ɑ:tɪərɪəʊsklɪə'rəʊsɪs] *med.* stwardnienie *n* tętnic
'art·ful chytry, przemyślny
'art gal·le·ry galeria *f* sztuki
ar·thri·tis [ɑ:'θraɪtɪs] *med.* artretyzm *m*
ar·ti·choke ['ɑ:tɪtʃəʊk] *bot.* karczoch *m*
ar·ti·cle ['ɑ:tɪkl] artykuł *m*; *gr.* rodzajnik *m*, przedimek *m*
ar·tic·u|·late **1.** [ɑ:'tɪkjʊleɪt] wyraźnie mówiący; wyraźny; **2.** [ɑ:'tɪkjʊlət] wymawiać ⟨-mówić⟩, ⟨wy⟩artykułować; **~·lat·ed** [ɑ:'tɪkjʊleɪtɪd] przegubowy; ***~lated lorry*** *Brt. mot.* ciągnik *m* *lub* ciężarówka *f* z naczepą; **~·la·tion** [ɑ:tɪkjʊ'leɪʃn] *wyraźna* wymowa *f*; przegub *m*
ar·ti·fi·cial [ɑ:tɪ'fɪʃl] sztuczny; ***~ person*** *jur.* osoba *f* prawna
ar·til·le·ry [ɑ:'tɪlərɪ] *mil.* artyleria *f*
ar·ti·san [ɑ:tɪ'zæn] rzemieślnik *m*
art·ist ['ɑ:tɪst] artysta *m* (*-tka f*); **ar·tis·tic** [ɑ:'tɪstɪk] (***~ally***) artystyczny
'art·less naturalny, bezpretensjonalny
arts [ɑ:ts] *pl.* nauki *pl.* humanistyczne; ***Faculty of ♀, Am. ♀ Department*** wydział *m* nauk humanistycznych
as [æz] **1.** *adv.* (tak) jak, równie, tak sa-

mo jak; **2.** *cj.* gdy, kiedy; ponieważ, jako że; jako; **~ ... ~ ...** tak ... jak ...; **~ for, ~ to** co do, co się tyczy; **~ from** począwszy od; **~ it were** jak gdyby; **~ Hamlet** jako Hamlet; **~ usual** jak zwykle

as·bes·tos [æs'bestəs] azbest *m*

as·cend [ə'send] iść ⟨pójść⟩ do góry; wspinać ⟨wspiąć⟩ się (na *L*); (*na tron*) wstępować (*L*)

as·cen|·dan·cy, ~·den·cy [ə'sendənsɪ] przewaga *f*, dominacja *f*; **~·sion** [ə'senʃn] wznoszenie *n* się (*balonu itp.*); wschodzenie *n* (*zwł. astr.*); **ꕔ·sion** (**Day**) *rel.* Wniebowstąpienie *n*; **~t** [ə'sent] wznoszenie *n* się; wspinanie *n* się; wzlot *m*

as·cet·ic [ə'setɪk] (**~ally**) ascetyczny

ASCII ['æskɪ] *skrót: komp.* **American Standard Code for Information Interchange** (kod *m*) ASCII (*standardowy kod do reprezentacji znaków alfanumerycznych*)

a·sep·tic [æ'septɪk] **1.** aseptyczny; **2.** środek *m* aseptyczny

ash[1] [æʃ] *bot.* jesion *m*; drewno *n* jesionowe

ash[2] [æʃ] *też* **~es** *pl.* popiół *m*; prochy *pl.*

a·shamed [ə'ʃeɪmd] zawstydzony; **be ~ of s.th.** wstydzić się (*G*)

'ash can *Am.* → **dustbin**

ash·en ['æʃn] popielaty, zszarzały

a·shore [ə'ʃɔː] na brzeg *lub* brzegu

'ash|·tray popielniczka *f*; **ꕔ 'Wednesday** *rel.* Popielec *m*, środa *f* popielcowa

A·sia ['eɪʃə] Azja *f*; **A·sian** ['eɪʃn, 'eɪʒn]; **A·si·at·ic** [eɪʃɪ'ætɪk] **1.** azjatycki; **2.** Azjata *m*, Azjatka *f*

a·side [ə'saɪd] **1.** *adv.* na bok; na stronę; **~ from** *Am.* oprócz, z wyjątkiem; **2.** uwaga *f* na stronie *lub* marginesie

ask [ɑːsk] *v/t.* pytać (**s.th.** o *A*, **s.o. about** kogoś o *A*); prosić (**of, from s.o.** kogoś, **s.o.** (**for**) **s.th.** kogoś o coś, **that** o *A*); **~ s.o. a question** zadawać komuś pytanie; *v/i.* **~ for** prosić o (*A*); **he ~ed for it** *lub* **for trouble** sam się o to prosił; **to be had for the ~ing** do otrzymania za darmo

a·skance [ə'skæns]: **look ~ at s.o.** krzywo na kogoś ⟨po⟩patrzeć

a·skew [ə'skjuː] krzywy, przekrzywiony

a·sleep [ə'sliːp] śpiący; **be** (**fast, sound**) **~** spać (twardo); **fall ~** zasnąć

as·par·a·gus [ə'spærəgəs] *bot.* szparag *m*; asparagus *m*

as·pect ['æspekt] aspekt *m*; strona *f*; wygląd *m*; widok *m*

as·phalt ['æsfælt] **1.** asfalt *m*; **2.** ⟨wy⟩-asfaltować

as·pic ['æspɪk] galareta *f* (*np. z nóżek*)

as·pi|·rant [ə'spaɪərənt] kandydat(ka *f*) *m*, reflektant *m*; **~·ra·tion** [æspə'reɪʃn] ambicja *f*, aspiracje *pl.*

as·pire [ə'spaɪə] mieć ambicję, aspirować (**to, for** do *G*)

ass [æs] *zo.* osioł *m*

as·sail [ə'seɪl] napadać ⟨-paść⟩; **be ~ed with doubts** być owładniętym wątpliwościami; **as·sai·lant** [ə'seɪlənt] napastnik *m* (-iczka *f*)

as·sas·sin [ə'sæsɪn] morderca *m*, (-czyni *f*) (*zwł. z przyczyn politycznych*), zamachowiec *m*; **~·ate** *zwł. pol.* [ə'sæsɪneɪt] ⟨za⟩mordować, dokonywać ⟨-nać⟩ zamachu; **~·a·tion** [əsæsɪ'neɪʃn] (*zwł.* polityczne) morderstwo *n*, zamach *m*

as·sault [ə'sɔːlt] **1.** napad *m*; napaść *f*; **2.** napadać ⟨-paść⟩

as·sem|·blage [ə'semblɪdʒ] zgromadzenie *n*; zbiór *m*; *tech.* montaż; **~·ble** [ə'sembl] zbierać (się); ⟨z⟩montować; **~·bler** [ə'semblə] *komp.* (*język programowania; program tłumaczący na kod maszynowy*) asembler *m*; **~·bly** [ə'semblɪ] zgromadzenie *n*, zebranie *n*; *tech.* montaż *m*; **~·bly line** *tech.* linia *f* montażowa

as·sent [ə'sent] **1.** zgoda *f*; **2.** zgadzać ⟨-odzić⟩ się (**to** na *A*)

as·sert [ə'sɜːt] ⟨s⟩twierdzić; zapewniać ⟨-nić⟩; *autorytet* utwierdzać ⟨-dzić⟩; **~ o.s.** przebijać ⟨-bić⟩ się; **as·ser·tion** [ə'sɜːʃn] stwierdzenie *n*; zapewnienie *n*

as·sess [ə'ses] *koszty* ⟨o⟩szacować (*też fig.*); *podatku* ustalić ⟨-lać⟩ wysokość (**at** na *A*); **~·ment** oszacowanie *n* (*też fig.*); ustalenie *n* wysokości (*podatku*)

as·set ['æset] *econ.* rzecz *f* wartościowa; *fig.* zaleta *f*, plus *m*; **~s** *pl. jur.* majątek *m*; stan *m* posiadania; *econ.* aktywa *pl.*, środki *pl.* finansowe

as·sid·u·ous [ə'sɪdjʊəs] skrzętny, pracowity

as·sign [ə'saɪn] wyznaczać ⟨-czyć⟩; przydzielać ⟨-lić⟩; przeznaczać ⟨-czyć⟩;

~·ment wyznaczenie *n*; przydział *m*; zadanie *n* (*do wykonania*); *jur.* cesja *f*, przeniesienie *n* (*własności*)

as·sim·i|·late [ə'sɪmɪleɪt] przyswajać ⟨-woić⟩; ⟨z⟩asymilować (się) (***to, with*** z *I*); **~·la·tion** [əsɪmɪ'leɪʃn] asymilacja *f*; przyswojenie *n*

as·sist [ə'sɪst] pomagać ⟨-móc⟩; wspierać ⟨wesprzeć⟩; **~·ance** pomoc *f*; wsparcie *n*; **as·sis·tant** **1.** zastępca *m*, (-czyni *f*); asystent(ka *f*) *m*; pomocnik *m*, (-ica *f*); *Brt.* (***shop***) **~** ekspedient(ka *f*) *m*; **2.** pomocny; zastępujący

as·so·ci|·ate **1.** [ə'səʊʃɪeɪt] zrzeszać ⟨-szyć⟩ (się), stowarzyszać ⟨-szyć⟩(się); ⟨z⟩łączyć (się); ***~ate with*** obcować z (*I*), przestawać z (*I*); **2.** [ə'səʊʃɪət] partner(ka *f*) *m*; **~·a·tion** [əsəʊsɪ'eɪʃn] stowarzyszenie *n*, towarzystwo *n*; asocjacja *f*

as·sort [ə'sɔːt] ⟨po⟩segregować, ⟨po⟩sortować; **~·ment** *econ.* (***of***) asortyment *m* (*G*), wybór *m* (*G*)

as·sume [ə'sjuːm] przyjmować ⟨-jąć⟩, zakładać ⟨założyć⟩; *władzę* przejmować ⟨-jąć⟩; **as·sump·tion** [ə'sʌmpʃn] założenie *n*, przypuszczenie *n*; przejęcie *n* (*władzy*); ***the*** ♀ *rel.* Wniebowzięcie *n* (*Matki Boskiej*)

as·sur|·ance [ə'ʃɔːrəns] pewność *f*; zapewnienie *n*; *zwł. Brt.* ubezpieczenie *n* (*na życie*); **~e** [ə'ʃɔː] upewniać ⟨-nić⟩, zapewniać ⟨-nić⟩; *zwł. Brt. czyjeś życie* ubezpieczać ⟨-czyć⟩; **~ed** **1.** pewny; **2.** *zwł. Brt.* ubezpieczony *m* (-na *f*); **~·ed·ly** [ə'ʃɔːrɪdlɪ] z całkowitą pewnością

as·te·risk ['æstərɪsk] gwiazdka *f*

asth·ma ['æsmə] *med.* astma *f*, dychawica *f*

as·ton·ish [ə'stɒnɪʃ] zadziwiać ⟨-wić⟩, zdumiewać ⟨-mieć⟩; ***be ~ed*** zdumiewać ⟨-mieć⟩ się; **~·ing** zadziwiający, zdumiewający; **~·ment** zdumienie *n*

as·tound [ə'staʊnd] zdumiewać ⟨-mieć⟩

a·stray [ə'streɪ]: ***go ~*** schodzić ⟨zejść⟩ z drogi; *fig.* schodzić ⟨zejść⟩ na manowce; ***lead ~*** ⟨po⟩prowadzić na manowce

a·stride [ə'straɪd] okrakiem (***of*** na *L*)

as·trin·gent [ə'strɪndʒənt] *med.* **1.** ściągający; **2.** środek *m* ściągający

as·trol·o·gy [ə'strɒlədʒɪ] astrologia *f*

as·tro·naut ['æstrənɔːt] astronauta *m* (-tka *f*), kosmonauta *m* (-tka *f*)

as·tron·o·my [ə'strɒnəmɪ] astronomia *f*

as·tute [ə'stjuːt] bystry, sprytny

a·sun·der [ə'sʌndə] na kawałki

a·sy·lum [ə'saɪləm] azyl *m*; ***right of ~*** prawo *n* azylu; **~ *seek·er*** azylant(ka *f*) *m*

at [æt] *prp. miejsce*: przy (*L*), na (*L*), w (*L*); *kierunek*: na (*L*), w (*A*), do (*G*); *zajęcie*: przy (*L*); *czas*: o; *okres*: w; *cena*: po; **~ *the baker's*** u piekarza, w piekarni; **~ *the door*** przy drzwiach; **~ *school*** w szkole, na zajęciach; **~ *10 pounds*** po 10 funtów; **~ *the age of*** w wieku (*G*); **~ *8 o'clock*** o ósmej

ate [et] *pret. od* ***eat***

Ath·ens *pl.* Ateny *pl.*

a·the·is·m ['eɪθɪɪzəm] ateizm *m*

ath|·lete ['æθliːt] (*zwł.* lekko)atleta *m*; **~·let·ic** [æθ'letɪk] (***-ally***) atletyczny; **~'let·ics** *sg. lub pl.* (*zwł.* lekka) atletyka *f*

At·lan·tic [ət'læntɪk] **1.** *też* **~ *Ocean*** Ocean *m* Atlantycki, Atlantyk *m*; **2.** atlantycki

ATM [eɪ tiː 'em] *Am. skrót*: ***automatic teller machine*** → ***cash dispenser***

at·mo|·sphere ['ætməsfɪə] atmosfera *f* (*też fig.*); **~·spher·ic** [ætməs'ferɪk] (***-ally***) atmosferyczny

at·oll ['ætɒl] atol *m*

at·om ['ætəm] atom *m* (*też fig.*); **'~ *bomb*** bomba *f* atomowa

a·tom·ic [ə'tɒmɪk] (***~ally***) atomowy, jądrowy, nuklearny; **~ *'age*** era *f* nuklearna, okres *m* panowania atomu; **~ *'bomb*** bomba *f* atomowa; **~ *'en·er·gy*** energia *f* nuklearna *lub* jądrowa; **~ *'pile*** reaktor *m* atomowy, stos *m* atomowy; **~ *'pow·er*** energia *f* atomowa; ***~-'pow·ered*** zasilany energią nuklearną *lub* jądrową; **~ *'waste*** odpady *pl.* radioaktywne

at·om|·ize ['ætəmaɪz] rozbijać ⟨-bić⟩ w drobne cząstki; *płyn, proszek* rozpylać ⟨-lić⟩; **'~·iz·er** rozpylacz *m*, atomizer *m*

a·tone [ə'təʊn]: **~ *for*** odpokutowywać ⟨-wać⟩ za *A*; **~·ment** odpokutowanie *n*, zadośćuczynienie *n*

a·tro|·cious [ə'trəʊʃəs] okropny, odrażający; **~c·i·ty** [ə'trɒsətɪ] okrucieństwo *n*, czyn *m* nieludzki

at·tach [ə'tætʃ] *v/t.* (**to**) przytwierdzać ⟨-dzić⟩ (do *G*), przyklejać ⟨-leić⟩ (do *G*), przymocowywać ⟨-wać⟩ (do *G*); *znaczenie* przywiązywać ⟨-zać⟩ (do *G*); ***be ~ed to*** *fig.* być przywiązanym do (*G*); **~·ment** przytwierdzenie *n* (do *G*), przywiązanie *n* (do *G*)
at·tack [ə'tæk] **1.** ⟨za⟩atakować, napadać ⟨-paść⟩; **2.** *też med.* atak *m*, napad *m*
at·tempt [ə'tempt] **1.** usiłować, ⟨s⟩próbować; **2.** próba *f*; ***an ~ on s.o.'s life*** zamach *m* na kogoś
at·tend [ə'tend] *v/t. chorego* doglądać ⟨-dnąć⟩, pielęgnować; *lekarz*: zajmować ⟨zająć⟩ się; (*do szkoły itp.*) uczęszczać (*G*), chodzić ⟨pójść⟩ (*G*); (*na zajęcia*) uczęszczać (*A*); *fig.* towarzyszyć; *v/i.* być obecnym; **~ *to*** (*w sklepie*) obsługiwać ⟨obsłużyć⟩ (*A*), ***are you being ~ed to?*** czy jest pan(i) obsługiwany (-na)?; **~ *to*** załatwiać ⟨-wić⟩ (*A*); **~·ance** opieka *f*, pielęgnacja *f*; obecność *f*; obecni *pl.*, publiczność *f*; liczba *f* obecnych, frekwencja *f*; **~·ant** pomocnik *m* (-ica *f*); osoba *f* dozorująca; pracownik *m* stacji benzynowej
at·ten|·tion [ə'tenʃn] uwaga (*też fig.*); troska *f*; ***~tion!*** *mil.* baczność!; **~·tive** [ə'tentɪv] uważny, gorliwy, troskliwy
at·tic ['ætɪk] strych *m*, poddasze *n*
at·ti·tude ['ætɪtjuːd] postawa *f*
at·tor·ney [ə'tɜːnɪ] *jur.* pełnomocnik *m*; *Am. jur.* adwokat *m*, obrońca *m*; ***power of ~*** pełnomocnictwo *n*; **♀ 'Gen·e·ral** *Brt. jur.* Prokurator *m* Generalny; *Am. jur.* Minister *m* Sprawiedliwości
at·tract [ə'trækt] przyciągać ⟨przyciągnąć⟩; *uwagę* skupiać ⟨-pić⟩; *fig.* pociągać, ⟨z⟩nęcić; **at·trac·tion** [ə'trækʃn] urok *m*, atrakcyjność *f*; atrakcja *f*; przyciąganie *n*; **at·trac·tive** [ə'træktɪv] atrakcyjny
at·trib·ute[1] [ə'trɪbjuːt] przypisywać ⟨-sać⟩
at·tri·bute[2] ['ætrɪbjuːt] cecha *f*; atrybut *m*
at·tune [ə'tjuːn]: **~ *to*** *fig.* dostrajać ⟨-troić⟩ się do (*G*), dostosowywać ⟨-sować⟩ się do (*G*)
au·ber·gine ['əʊbəʒiːn] *bot.* bakłażan *m*
au·burn ['ɔːbən] *włosy*: kasztanowy
auc|·tion ['ɔːkʃn] **1.** aukcja *f*, przetarg *m*; **2.** *zw.* ***~tion off*** licytować, wystawiać na aukcji *lub* przetargu; **~·tio·neer** [ɔːkʃə'nɪə] licytator(ka *f*) *m*
au·da|·cious [ɔː'deɪʃəs] śmiały, zuchwały; **~c·i·ty** [ɔː'dæsətɪ] śmiałość *f*, zuchwałość *f*
au·di·ble ['ɔːdəbl] słyszalny
au·di·ence ['ɔːdjəns] publiczność *f*, widownia *f*; widzowie *pl.*, słuchacze *pl.*; audiencja *f*
au·di·o... ['ɔːdɪəʊ] audio...; **'~ cassette** kaseta *f* audio *lub* magnetofonowa; **~-vis·u·al** ***~visual 'aids*** *pl.* pomoce *pl.* audiowizualne
au·dit ['ɔːdɪt] *econ.* **1.** rewizja *f* ksiąg; **2.** dokonywać ⟨-nać⟩ rewizji ksiąg
au·di·tion [ɔː'dɪʃn] *mus.*, *theat.* przesłuchanie *n*; ⚠ *nie* ***audycja***
au·di·tor ['ɔːdɪtə] *econ.* rewident *m*, audytor *m*
au·di·to·ri·um [ɔːdɪ'tɔːrɪəm] widownia *f.*; *Am.* sala *f* zebrań *lub* koncertowa
Aug *skrót pisany*: ***August*** sierp., sierpień *m*
au·ger ['ɔːgə] *tech.* wiertło *n* kręte; świder *m* ziemny
Au·gust ['ɔːgəst] (*skrót*: ***Aug***) sierpień *m*; *attr.* sierpniowy
aunt [ɑːnt] ciotka *f*; **~·ie**, **~·y** ['ɑːntɪ] ciocia *f*
au pair (girl) [əʊ 'peə gɜːl] *Brt.* (*młoda cudzoziemka poznająca angielski zamieszkując z rodziną angielską w zamian za swą pomoc*)
aus·pic·es ['ɔːspɪsɪz] *pl.*: ***under the ~ of*** pod auspicjami (*G*)
aus·tere [ɒ'stɪə] oschły, surowy
Aus·tra·li·a [ɒ'streɪljə] Australia *f*; **Aus·tra·li·an** [ɒ'streɪljən] **1.** australijski; **2.** Australijczyk *m* (-jka *f*)
Aus·tri·a ['ɒstrɪə] Austria *f*; **Aus·tri·an** ['ɒstrɪən] **1.** austriacki; **2.** Austriak *m* (-aczka *f*)
au·then·tic [ɔː'θentɪk] (***~ally***) autentyczny; prawdziwy
au·thor ['ɔːθə] autor(ka *f*) *m*; pisarz *m*, pisarka *f*; **~·ess** ['ɔːθərɪs] autorka *f*; pisarka *f*
au·thor·i|·ta·tive [ɔː'θɒrɪtətɪv] autorytatywny, władczy, apodyktyczny; miarodajny; **~·ty** [ɔː'θɒrətɪ] autorytet *m*; znaczenie *n*; zaświadczenie *n*, pozwo-

lenie *n*; wpływ *m* (***over*** na *A*); *zw.* ***authorities*** *pl.* władze *pl.*, urząd *m*
au·thor·ize ['ɔːθəraɪz] autoryzować, upoważniać ⟨-nić⟩
'au·thor·ship autorstwo *n*
au·to ['ɔːtəʊ] *Am.* (*pl.* ***-tos***) auto *n*, samochód *m*
au·to... ['ɔːtəʊ] auto..., samo...
au·to·bi·og·ra·phy [ɔːtəbaɪ'ɒgrəfɪ] autobiografia *f*
au·to·graph ['ɔːtəgrɑːf] autograf *m*
au·to·mat ['ɔːtəmæt] *TM Am.* zautomatyzowana restauracja *f*
au·to·mate ['ɔːtəmeɪt] ⟨z⟩automatyzować
au·to·mat·ic [ɔːtə'mætɪk] **1.** (***~ally***) automatyczny; **2.** (*broń itp.*) automat *m*; **~ tel·ler ma·chine** *Am.* (*skrót*: ***ATM***) → ***cash dispenser***
au·to·ma·tion [ɔːtə'meɪʃn] automatyzacja *f*
au·tom·a·ton [ɔː'tɒmətən] *fig.* (*pl.* ***-ta*** [-tə], ***-tons***) automat *m*, robot *m*
au·to·mo·bile ['ɔːtəməbiːl] *zwł. Am.* auto *n*, samochód *m*
au·ton·o·my [ɔː'tɒnəmɪ] autonomia *f*
'au·to·tel·ler *Am.* → ***cash dispenser***
au·tumn ['ɔːtəm] jesień *f*; **au·tum·nal** [ɔː'tʌmnəl] jesienny
aux·il·i·a·ry [ɔːg'zɪljərɪ] pomocniczy
a·vail [ə'veɪl]: ***to no ~*** bezskutecznie, daremnie; **a'vai·la·ble** dostępny, osiągalny; wolny; *econ.* do nabycia
av·a·lanche ['ævəlɑːnʃ] lawina *f*
av·a|·rice ['ævərɪs] skąpstwo *n*; **~·ri·cious** [ævə'rɪʃəs] skąpy
Ave *skrót pisany*: ***Avenue*** aleja
a·venge [ə'vendʒ] ⟨ze-, po⟩mścić; **a'veng·er** mściciel
av·e·nue ['ævənjuː] aleja *f*; bulwar *m*
av·e·rage ['ævərɪdʒ] **1.** przeciętna *f*, średnia *f*; **2.** przeciętny, średni
a·verse [ə'vɜːs] niechętny; **a·ver·sion** [ə'vɜːʃn] niechęć *f*, awersja *f*
a·vert [ə'vɜːt] *nieszczęściu* zapobiegać ⟨-biec⟩, *oczy* odwracać ⟨-wrócić⟩
a·vi·a·ry ['eɪvɪərɪ] ptaszarnia *f*
a·vi·a|·tion [eɪvɪ'eɪʃn] *aviat.* lotnictwo *n*; **~·tor** ['eɪvɪeɪtə] lotnik *m*
av·id ['ævɪd] entuzjastyczny; żądny
av·o·ca·do [ævə'kɑːdəʊ] *bot.* awokado *n*
a·void [ə'vɔɪd] unikać ⟨-knąć⟩ (*G*); wymijać; **~·ance** unikanie *n*
a·vow·al [ə'vaʊəl] przyznanie *n* się
AWACS ['eɪwæks] *skrót*: ***Airborne Warning and Control System*** (system *m*) AWACS (*lotniczy system kontroli radarowej*)
a·wait [ə'weɪt] oczekiwać na (*A*)
a·wake [ə'weɪk] **1.** nie śpiący; ***be ~*** nie spać; **2.** *też* **a·wak·en** [ə'weɪkən] (***awoke*** *lub* ***awoken, awoken*** *lub* ***awaked***) *v/t.* ⟨z⟩budzić; *v/i.* ⟨z⟩budzić się; **a·wak·en·ing** [ə'weɪkənɪŋ] *też fig.* obudzenie *n*, przebudzenie *n*
a·ward [ə'wɔːd] **1.** nagroda *f*, odznaczenie *n*, wyróżnienie *n*; **2.** nagradzać ⟨-grodzić⟩, *odznaczenie itp.* przyznawać ⟨-znać⟩
a·ware [ə'weə]: ***be ~ of s.th.*** zdawać sobie sprawę z czegoś, uświadamiać sobie coś; ***become ~ of s.th.*** zdać sobie sprawę z czegoś, uświadomić sobie coś
a·way [ə'weɪ] **1.** *adv.* z dala, w oddaleniu; nieobecny; ***far ~*** daleko; ***5 kilometres ~*** w odległości 5 km; **2.** *adj.* (*w sporcie*) na wyjeździe; ***~ match*** mecz *m* na wyjeździe
awe [ɔː] **1.** cześć *f*, głębokie poważanie *n*; **2.** wzbudzać ⟨-dzić⟩ głębokie poważanie *lub* cześć
aw·ful ['ɔːfl] (***~ly***) straszny, okropny
awk·ward ['ɔːkwəd] niezręczny, niezdarny; niewygodny, nieporęczny; niedogodny
aw·ning ['ɔːnɪŋ] (*nad sklepem*) markiza *f*, daszek *m*
a·woke [ə'wəuk] *pret. od* ***awake*** 2; *też* **a·wok·en** [ə'wəukən] *p.p. od* ***awake*** 2
A.W.O.L. [eɪ dʌbljuː əʊ 'el, 'eɪwɒl] *skrót*: ***absent without leave*** nieobecny nieusprawiedliwiony
a·wry [ə'raɪ] krzywy, skośny; ***be ~*** leżeć krzywo
ax(e) [æks] topór *m*, siekiera *f*
ax·is ['æksɪs] (*pl.* ***-es*** [-siːz]) oś *f*
ax·le ['æksl] *tech.* oś *f*
ay(e) [aɪ] *parl.* głos *m* za
A-Z [eɪ tə 'zed] *Brt.* plan *m* miasta
az·ure ['æʒə] lazurowy

B

B, **b** [biː] b *n*; *mus*. H, h
b *skrót pisany*: ***born*** ur., urodzony
BA [biː 'eɪ] **1.** *skrót*: ***Bachelor of Arts*** (*niższy stopień naukowy*) licencjat *m*, bakalaureat *m*; **2.** ***British Airways*** (*brytyjskie linie lotnicze*)
bab•ble ['bæbl] **1.** ⟨za⟩bełkotać; ⟨po⟩paplać; *dziecko*: ⟨za⟩gaworzyć; *potok*: ⟨za⟩szemrać; **2.** bełkot *m*; paplanina *f*; gaworzenie *n*; szemranie *n*
babe [beɪb] dziecinka *f*, dziecko *n*; *Am*. F dziewczyna *f*
ba•boon [bə'buːn] *zo*. pawian *m*
ba•by ['beɪbɪ] **1.** niemowlę *n*, dziecko *n*; osesek *m*; *Am*. F dziewczyna *f*; **2.** dziecięcy, dla dzieci; mały; '**~ boom** wyż *m* demograficzny; '**~ bug•gy** *Am*., '**~ car•riage** *Am*. wózek *m* dla dziecka; **~•hood** ['beɪbɪhʊd] dzieciństwo *n*; **~•ish** ['beɪbɪɪʃ] *pej*. dziecinny; **~-mind•er** ['beɪbɪmaɪndə] *Brt*. opiekun(ka *f*) *m* (do) dzieci (*zwykle do południa*); '**~-sit** (***-tt, -sat***) opiekować się dzieckiem; '**~-sit•ter** opiekun(ka *f*) *m* (do) dzieci (*zwykle po południu*)
bach•e•lor ['bætʃələ] kawaler *m*; *univ*. bakałarz *m*, licencjat *m* (*posiadacz niższego stopnia naukowego*)
back [bæk] **1.** plecy *pl*., grzbiet *m*; tył *m*; tylna *lub* odwrotna strona *f*; oparcie *n*; *sport*: obrońca *m*; **2.** *adj*. tylny; grzbietowy; *opłata*: zaległy; *podwórko*: za domem; *czasopismo*: nieaktualny; ***be ~*** wrócić; **3.** *adv*. do tyłu, w tył; **4.** *v/t*. ⟨wy⟩cofać; wspierać ⟨wesprzeć⟩; *też* ***~ up*** popierać ⟨poprzeć⟩; ***~ up*** *komp*. (z)robić kopię bezpieczeństwa z (*G*); *v/i*. *często* ***~ up*** cofać ⟨wycofywać⟩ się; *mot*. cofać się; ***~ in*****(*****to a parking space*****)** ⟨za⟩parkować tyłem; ***~ up*** *komp*. ⟨z⟩robić kopię bezpieczeństwa; '**~•ache** ból(e *pl*.) *m* pleców; '**~•bite** (***-bit, bitten***) obgadywać ⟨-gadać⟩ (*za plecami*); '**~•bone** kręgosłup *m*; *fig*. kościec *m*; '**~-break•ing** *praca*: morderczy, wykańczający '**~•chat** *Brt*. pyskowanie *n*; '**~•comb** *włosy* ⟨na⟩tapirować; **~ 'door** tylne drzwi *pl*., *fig*. ukryty, nieoficjalny; '**~•er** sponsor(ka *f*) *m*, inwestor(ka *f*) *m*; **~'fire** *mot*. zapłon *m* przedwczesny; '**~•ground** tło *n*; *fig*. sytuacja *f*; '**~•hand** *sport*: bekhend *m*; '**~•ing** wsparcie *n*, pomoc *f*; **~ 'number** stary numer (*czasopisma*) *m*; '**~•pack** duży plecak *m*; '**~•pack•er** turysta *m* (-tka *f*) pieszy (-sza) (*z plecakiem*); '**~•pack•ing** turystyka *f* piesza (*z plecakiem*); **~ 'seat** siedzenie *n lub* miejsce *n* z tyłu; '**~•side** tyłek *m*; '**~•space** (**key**) *komp*. *itp*.: klawisz *m* Backspace (*cofania lub kasowania*); '**~ stairs** *pl*. tylne schody *pl*.; **~ street** boczna uliczka *f*; '**~•stroke** *sport*: styl *m* grzbietowy; '**~ talk** *Am*. pyskowanie *n*; '**~•track** *fig*. wycofywać ⟨-fać⟩ się; '**~•up** wsparcie *n*, pomoc *f*; *komp*. *itp*.: kopia *f* zapasowa *lub* bezpieczeństwa; *Am*. *mot*. nagromadzenie *n*, zatkanie *n* się; **~•ward** ['bækwəd] **1.** *adj*. wsteczny; zmierzający do tyłu; zacofany; **2.** *adv*. (*też* '**~•wards**) do tyłu, w tył; **~'yard** *Brt*. (*z tyłu domu*) podwórko *n*; *Am*. (*z tyłu domu*) ogród *m*
ba•con ['beɪkən] boczek *m*, bekon *m*
bac•te•ri•a [bæk'tɪərɪə] *biol*. *pl*. bakterie *pl*.
bad [bæd] (***worse, worst***) zły, niedobry; niewłaściwy, niepoprawny; niegrzeczny; ***go ~*** ⟨ze⟩psuć się; ***he is in a ~ way*** źle mu idzie, niedobrze z nim; (***-ly***) ***he is ~ly off*** źle mu się powodzi; ***~ly wounded*** ciężko ranny; ***want ~ly*** F bardzo chcieć
bade [beɪd] *pret*. *od* ***bid*** 1
badge [bædʒ] odznaka *f*, plakietka *f*
bad•ger ['bædʒə] **1.** *zo*. borsuk *m*; **2.** ⟨u⟩dręczyć
bad•min•ton ['bædmɪntən] badminton *m*, kometka *f*
bad-'tempered o przykrym usposobieniu
baf•fle ['bæfl] zdumiewać ⟨-mieć⟩; *plan itp*. ⟨po⟩krzyżować, udaremniać ⟨-nić⟩
bag [bæg] **1.** worek *m*; torba *f*; torebka *f* (*damska, z cukrem*); ***~ and baggage*** ze wszystkimi rzeczami, z całym dobytkiem; **2.** (***-gg-***) ⟨za⟩pakować do worka

B

lub worków; *hunt.* upolować; *też* **~ out** wybrzuszać ⟨-szyć⟩ się
bag·gage ['bægɪdʒ] *zwł. Am.* bagaż *m*; '**~ car** *Am. rail.* wagon *m* bagażowy; '**~ check** *Am.* kwit *m* na bagaż; '**~ claim** *aviat.* odbiór *m* bagażu; '**~ room** *Am.* przechowalnia *f* bagażu
bag·gy ['bægɪ] F (**-ier, -iest**) wypchany; *spodnie*: workowaty
'**bag·pipes** *pl.* dudy *pl.*, F kobza *m*
bail [baɪl] *jur.* **1.** kaucja *f*; ***be out on ~*** być zwolnionym za kaucją; ***go*** *lub* ***stand ~ for s.o.*** (za)płacić kaucję za kogoś; **2. *~ out*** zwalniać ⟨zwolnić⟩ za kaucją; *Am. aviat.* → ***bale²***
bai·liff ['beɪlɪf] *Brt. zwł. jur.* urzędnik *m* sądowy (*rodzaj komornika*)
bait [beɪt] **1.** przynęta *f* (*też fig.*); **2.** zakładać przynętę na (*A*); *fig.* ⟨z⟩nęcić (*A*)
bake [beɪk] ⟨u⟩piec; wypiekać ⟨-piec⟩; *cegły* wypalać ⟨-lić⟩; suszyć (*w piecu*); ***~d 'beans*** *pl. puszkowana* fasolka *f* po bretońsku; **~d po'ta·toes** *pl.* pieczone ziemniaki *pl.* (*w piekarniku*); '**bak·er** piekarz *m*; **bak·er·y** ['beɪkərɪ] piekarnia *f*; '**bak·ing-pow·der** proszek *m* do pieczenia
bal·ance ['bæləns] **1.** waga *f*; równowaga *f* (*też econ.*); *econ.* bilans *m*; *econ.* saldo *n*, stan *m* konta; *econ.* reszta *f*, pozostałość *f*; ***keep one's ~*** utrzymywać ⟨-mać⟩ równowagę; ***lose one's ~*** ⟨s⟩tracić równowagę (*też fig.*); ***~ of payments*** *econ.* bilans *m* płatniczy; ***~ of power*** *pol.* równowaga *f* sił; ***~ of trade*** *econ.* bilans *m* handlowy; **2.** *v/t.* utrzymywać ⟨-mać⟩ w równowadze, ⟨z⟩balansować; *konta itp.* utrzymywać ⟨-mać⟩ w równowadze, uzgadniać; *v/i.* utrzymywać ⟨-mać⟩ się w równowadze; '**~ sheet** *econ.* zestawienie *n* bilansowe, bilans *m*
bal·co·ny ['bælkənɪ] balkon *m* (*też theat.*)
bald [bɔːld] łysy
bale¹ [beɪl] *econ.* bela *f*
bale² [beɪl] *Brt. aviat.*: ***~ out*** wyskakiwać ⟨-skoczyć⟩ (*ze spadochronem*)
bale·ful ['beɪlfl] złowrogi, złowieszczy
balk [bɔːk] **1.** belka *f*; **2.** wzdragać się, lękać się
Bal·kans *pl.* Bałkany *pl.*
ball¹ [bɔːl] **1.** kula *f*; piłka *f*; *anat.* kłąb *m*; kłębek *m*; bryła *f*; ***keep the ~ rolling*** podtrzymywać ⟨-trzymać⟩ rozmowę; ***play ~*** F iść na rękę
ball² [bɔːl] bal *m*
bal·lad ['bæləd] ballada *f*
bal·last ['bæləst] **1.** balast *m*; **2.** obciążać ⟨-żyć⟩ balastem
ball 'bear·ing *tech.* łożysko *n* kulkowe
bal·let ['bæleɪ] balet *m*
bal·lis·tics [bə'lɪstɪks] *mil., phys., sg.* balistyka *f*
bal·loon [bə'luːn] **1.** balon *m*; dymek (*w komiksie*); **2.** wydymać ⟨-dąć⟩ się (*jak balon*)
bal·lot ['bælət] **1.** głos *m*, kartka *f* z głosem; głosowanie *n* (*zwł. tajne*); **2.** ⟨za⟩głosować (**for** na *A*), wybierać ⟨-brać⟩ (*A*) (*zwł. w tajnym głosowaniu*); '**~ box** urna *f* wyborcza; '**~ pa·per** kartka *f* z głosem
'**ball·point**, **~ 'pen** długopis *m*
'**ball·room** sala *f* balowa
balls [bɔːlz] V *pl.* jaja *pl.*(*jądra*)
balm [bɑːm] balsam *m* (*też fig.*)
balm·y ['bɑːmɪ] (**-ier, -iest**) łagodny
ba·lo·ney [bə'ləʊnɪ] *Am. sl.* bzdury *pl.*, brednie *pl.*
Bal·tic Sea Bałtyk *m*
bal·us·trade [bælə'streɪd] balustrada *f*
bam·boo [bæm'buː] *bot.* (*pl.* **-oos**) bambus *m*; pęd *m* bambusa; *attr.* bambusowy
bam·boo·zle [bæm'buːzl] F oszukiwać ⟨-szukać⟩, ⟨o-, wy⟩kantować
ban [bæn] **1.** *oficjalny* zakaz *m*; *rel.* klątwa *f*, interdykt *m*; **2.** (**-nn-**) zakazywać ⟨-zać⟩
ba·nal [bə'nɑːl] banalny; nieistotny
ba·na·na [bə'nɑːnə] *bot.* banan *m*; *attr.* bananowy
band [bænd] **1.** taśma *f*, wstęga *f*; opaska *f*; *kryminalna* banda *f*; kapela *f muzyczna*, grupa *f*, orkiestra *f* (*do tańca*); pasmo *n* (*częstotliwości*); **2. *~ together*** skupiać ⟨-pić⟩ się, zbierać ⟨zebrać⟩ się razem
ban·dage ['bændɪdʒ] **1.** bandaż *m*; opatrunek *m*; opaska *f*; *Am.* przylepiec *m*, plaster *m*; **2.** ⟨za-, o⟩bandażować
'**Band-Aid** *TM Am.* przylepiec *m*, plaster *m*
b & b, B & B [biː ənd 'biː] *skrót*: ***bed and breakfast*** nocleg ze śniadaniem
ban·dit ['bændɪt] bandyta *m*

'band|·lead·er *mus.* kierownik *m* orkiestry (*zwł. jazzowej*), bandleader *m*; **'~·mas·ter** dyrygent *m*

ban·dy ['bændɪ] (**-ier, -iest**) krzywy; **~-'legged** krzywonogi

bang [bæŋ] **1.** *silne* uderzenie *n*, walnięcie *n*; wrzawa *f*; *zw.* **~s** *pl.* grzywka; **2.** uderzać ⟨-rzyć⟩, walić ⟨walnąć⟩; V ⟨po-, wy⟩dupczyć; **~ (away)** walić ⟨walnąć⟩

ban·gle ['bæŋgl] bransoletka *f* (*na ramię, nogę*)

ban·ish ['bænɪʃ] wypędzać ⟨-pędzić⟩ z kraju, skazywać ⟨-zać⟩ na banicję; **'~·ment** banicja *f*, wygnanie *n*

ban·is·ter ['bænɪstə] *też* **~s** *pl.* poręcz *f*, bariera *f*

ban·jo ['bændʒəʊ] *mus.* (*pl.* **-jos, joes**) bandżo *n*

bank[1] [bæŋk] **1.** *econ.* bank *m* (*też krwi itp.*); **2.** *v/t. pieniądze* wpłacać ⟨-cić⟩ do banku; *v/i.* mieć konto bankowe (**with** w *L*)

bank[2] [bæŋk] brzeg *m*; *ziemna* skarpa *f*, nasyp *m*; nagromadzenie *n* (*chmur, piasku*)

'bank| ac·count konto *n* bankowe; **'~ bill** *Am.* → **bank note**; **'~·book** książeczka *f* oszczędnościowa; **'~ code** *też* **~ sorting code** *econ.* numer *m* banku; **'~·er** bankier *m*, bankowiec *m*; **'~·er's card** karta *f* bankowa; **~ 'hol·i·day** *Brt.* święto *n* państwowe (*gdy banki są nieczynne*); **'~·ing** bankowość *f*; bankowy; **'~ note** banknot *m*; **'~ rate** bankowa stopa *f*

bank·rupt ['bæŋkrʌpt] *jur.* **1.** dłużnik *m* niewypłacalny, bankrut *m*; **2.** ⟨z⟩bankrutować; *kogoś* doprowadzać ⟨-dzić⟩ do bankructwa; **~·cy** ['bæŋkrʌptsɪ] upadłość *f*, bankructwo *n*

ban·ner ['bænə] transparent *m*

banns [bænz] *pl.* zapowiedzi *pl.*

ban·quet ['bæŋkwɪt] bankiet *m*

ban·ter ['bæntə] przekomarzać się

bap|·tis·m ['bæptɪzəm] chrzest *m*; **~·tize** [bæp'taɪz] ⟨o⟩chrzcić

bar [bɑː] **1.** sztaba *f*, zasuwa *f*, rygiel *m*; poprzeczka *f*; zapora *f*, bariera *f*; *fig.* przeszkoda *f*; bar *m*, lokal *m*; kontuar *m*; gruba kreska *f*; *jur.* sąd *m*; *jur.* ława *f* oskarżonych; *jur.* adwokatura *f*; *mus.* kreska *f* taktowa, takt *m*; **a ~ of chocolate** tabliczka *f* czekolady, baton *m* czekoladowy; **a ~ of soap** kostka *f* mydła; **~s** *pl.* kraty *pl.*; **2.** zamykać ⟨-knąć⟩ na zasuwę, ⟨za⟩ryglować; ⟨za⟩tarasować, zagradzać ⟨-dzić⟩; zabraniać ⟨-bronić⟩

barb [bɑːb] kolec *m*, zadzior *m*

bar·bar·i·an [bɑː'beərɪən] **1.** barbarzyński; **2.** barbarzyńca *m*

bar·be·cue ['bɑːbɪkjuː] **1.** grill *m*; barbecue *n*; przyjęcie *n* z grillem; **2.** ⟨u⟩piec na grillu

barbed wire [bɑːbd 'waɪə] drut *m* kolczasty

bar·ber ['bɑːbə] fryzjer *m* (*męski*)

'bar code kod *m* paskowy

bare [beə] **1.** (**~r, ~st**) goły, nagi; bosy; nieosłonięty; **2.** obnażać ⟨-żyć⟩; odsłaniać ⟨-słonić⟩; **'~·faced** bezwstydny, bezczelny; **'~·foot, ~'footed** bosą stopą, na bosaka; **~'head·ed** z gołą głową; **'~·ly** ledwie, ledwo

bar·gain ['bɑːgɪn] **1.** interes *m*, transakcja *f*; okazja *f* (*kupna*); **a (dead) ~** świetna okazja *f*; **make a ~** dochodzić ⟨dojść⟩ do porozumienia; **it's a ~!** zgoda!; **into the ~** w dodatku; **2.** ⟨wy-, u⟩targować się; **'~ sale** wyprzedaż *f* po obniżonych cenach

barge [bɑːdʒ] **1.** barka *f*; **2. ~ in** wpychać ⟨wepchnąć⟩ się, wtrącać ⟨wtrącić⟩ się

bark[1] [bɑːk] kora *f*

bark[2] [bɑːk] **1.** ⟨za⟩szczekać; **~ up the wrong tree** F kierować *coś* pod niewłaściwym adresem; **2.** szczekanie *n*

bar·ley ['bɑːlɪ] *bot.* jęczmień *m*

barn [bɑːn] stodoła *f*, obora *f*

ba·rom·e·ter [bə'rɒmɪtə] barometr *m*

bar·on ['bærən] baron *m*; **~·ess** ['bærənɪs] baronowa *f*

bar·racks ['bærəks] *sg., mil.* koszary *pl.*, *pej.* kamienica *f*; ⚠ *nie* **baraki**

bar·rage ['bærɑːʒ] zapora *f*; *mil.* ogień *m* zaporowy; potok *m* (*słów*)

bar·rel ['bærəl] beczka *f*, baryłka *f*; lufa *f*; *tech.* bęben *m*, tuleja *f*; **'~ or·gan** *mus.* katarynka *f*

bar·ren ['bærən] jałowy, niepłodny

bar·ri·cade [bærɪ'keɪd] **1.** barykada *f*; **2.** ⟨za⟩barykadować (się)

bar·ri·er ['bærɪə] bariera *f*, przegroda *f* (*też fig.*); ogrodzenie *n*

bar·ris·ter ['bærɪstə] *Brt. jur.* adwokat *m* (-ka *f*) (*uprawniony do występowania przed sądami wyższej instancji*)

bar·row ['bærəʊ] taczka *f*; wózek *m*

bar·ter ['bɑːtə] **1.** handel *m* wymienny; *econ. attr.* barterowy; **2.** prowadzić handel wymienny, wymieniać ⟨-nić⟩ się (***for*** na *A*)
base1 [beɪs] (***~r, -est***) podły, nikczemny
base2 [beɪs] **1.** podstawa *f*; baza *f*; fundament *m*; *mil.* stanowisko *n*, pozycja; *mil.* baza; **2.** opierać ⟨-przeć⟩ się (***on*** na *L*), bazować
base3 [beɪs] *chem.* zasada *f*
'base|·ball (*w sporcie*) baseball *m*; **'~·board** *Am.* listwa przypodłogowa; **'~·less** bezpodstawny; **'~·line** (*w tenisie itp.*) linia *f* główna; **'~·ment** suterena *f*, przyziemie *n*
bash·ful ['bæʃfl] wstydliwy, płochliwy
ba·sic1 ['beɪsɪk] **1.** podstawowy, zasadniczy; **2. *~s*** *pl.* podstawy *pl.*
ba·sic2 ['beɪsɪk] *chem.* zasadowy, alkaliczny
BA·SIC ['beɪsɪk] *komp.* (*język programowania*) BASIC *m*
ba·sic·al·ly ['beɪsɪkəlɪ] zasadniczo
ba·sin ['beɪsn] misa *f*, miska *f*; miednica *f*; zbiornik *m*; *sportowy* basen *m*; *geogr.* dorzecze *n*, zlewisko *n*;
ba·sis ['beɪsɪs] (*pl.* ***-ses*** [-siːz]) podstawa *f*, baza *f*; zasada *f*
bask [bɑːsk] grzać ⟨pogrzać⟩ się; *fig.* pławić się
bas·ket ['bɑːskɪt] kosz(yk) *m*; **'~·ball** *sport:* koszykówka *f*
Basle Bazylea *f*
bass1 [beɪs] *mus.* bas *m*; *attr.* basowy
bass2 [bæs] *zo.* (*pl.* ***bass, basses***) okoń *m*
bas·tard ['bɑːstəd] bękart *m*, bastard *m*; F świnia *f*, gnój *m*
baste1 [beɪst] *pieczeń* polewać ⟨-lać⟩ tłuszczem
baste2 [beɪst] ⟨przy⟩fastrygować
bat1 [bæt] *zo.* nietoperz *m*; ***as blind as a ~*** ślepy jak kret; ***be*** *lub* ***have ~s in the belfry*** F mieć nierówno pod sufitem
bat2 [bæt] (*w baseballu, krykiecie*) kij *m*; *Brt.* (*w ping-pongu*) rakietka *f*
batch [bætʃ] partia *f*, grupa *f*, wsad *m*; **~ 'file** *komp.* plik *m* typu batch, plik *m* wsadowy
bate [beɪt]: ***with ~d breath*** z zapartym tchem
bath [bɑːθ] **1.** (*pl.* ***baths*** [bɑːðz]) wanna *f*; kąpiel *f* (*w wannie*); ***have a ~*** *Brt.*, ***take a ~*** *Am.* ⟨wy⟩kąpać się, brać ⟨wziąć⟩ kąpiel; ***~s*** *pl.* kąpielisko *n*, pływalnia *f*; uzdrowisko *n*; **2.** *Brt. v/t. dziecko itp.* ⟨wy⟩kąpać; *v/i.* ⟨wy⟩kąpać się, brać ⟨wziąć⟩ kąpiel
bathe [beɪð] *v/t. dziecko, zwł. Am.* ⟨wy⟩kąpać; *ranę* obmywać ⟨-myć⟩; *v/i.* ⟨wy⟩kąpać się, ⟨po⟩pływać; *zwł. Am.* ⟨wy⟩kąpać się, brać ⟨wziąć⟩ kąpiel
bath·ing ['beɪðɪŋ] kąpiel *f*; *attr.* kąpielowy, do kąpieli; **'~ cos·tume**, **'~ suit** → ***swimsuit***
'bath|·robe płaszcz *m* kąpielowy; *Am.* szlafrok *m*; **'~·room** łazienka *f*; **'~·tub** wanna *f*
bat·on ['bætən] pałeczka *f*; *mus.* batuta *f*; pałka *f* (policyjna); ⚠ *nie* ***baton***
bat·tal·i·on [bə'tæljən] *mil.* batalion *m*
bat·ten ['bætn] listwa *f*; łata *f*
bat·ter1 ['bætə] walić, ⟨po⟩bić; *żonę, dziecko* ⟨z⟩maltretować; ⟨po⟩giąć; ***~ down, ~ in*** *drzwi* wyłamywać ⟨-mać⟩
bat·ter2 ['bætə] *gastr.* ciasto *n* (*na naleśniki*); panier *m*, panierka *f*
bat·ter3 ['bætə] (*w baseballu, krykiecie*) gracz *m* przy piłce
bat·ter·y ['bætərɪ] *mil.* bateria *f*; *electr.* bateria *f*, akumulator *m*; *jur.* pobicie *n*, naruszenie *n* nietykalności cielesnej; ***assault and ~*** *jur.* napad z pobiciem; **'~ charg·er** *electr.* ładowarka *f* do baterii *lub* akumulatorów; **'~-op·e·rat·ed** na baterie
bat·tle ['bætl] **1.** bitwa *f* (***of*** pod *I*), *fig.* walka *f* (***for*** o *A*); **2.** walczyć; **'~·field, '~·ground** pole *m* bitwy; **~·ments** ['bætlmənts] *pl.* blanki *pl.*; **'~·ship** *mil.* pancernik *m*
baulk [bɔːk] → ***balk***
Ba·va·ri·a [bə'veərɪə] Bawaria *f*; **Ba·var·i·an** [bə'veərɪən] **1.** bawarski; **2.** Bawarczyk *m*, Bawarka *f*
bawd·y ['bɔːdɪ] (***-ier, -iest***) sprośny
bawl [bɔːl] ryczeć ⟨ryknąć⟩, wrzeszczeć ⟨wrzasnąć⟩
bay1 [beɪ] zatoka *f*; *arch.* wykusz
bay2 [beɪ] *bot. też* ***~ tree*** laur *m*, drzewo *n* laurowe, wawrzyn *m*
bay3 [beɪ] **1.** ryczeć ⟨ryknąć⟩; *psy:* ujadać; **2. *hold*** *lub* ***keep at ~*** *kogoś* trzymać w szachu, trzymać na dystans
bay4 [beɪ] **1.** gniady, kasztanowaty; **2.** kasztanek *m*, gniady *m*
bay·o·net ['beɪənɪt] *mil.* bagnet *m*
bay·ou ['baɪuː] *Am.* leniwy dopływ *m*

bay 'win•dow wykusz *m*
ba•zaar [bə'zɑː] bazar *m*, targ *m*
BBC [biː biː 'siː] *skrót*: ***British Broadcasting Corporation*** BBC *n* (*brytyjska radiofonia*)
BC [biː 'siː] *skrót*: ***before Christ*** p.n.e., przed naszą erą, przed narodzeniem Chrystusa
be [biː] (***was*** *lub* ***were, been***) być; istnieć; znajdować się; stawać się; ***he wants to ~ ...*** chce zostać ...; ***how much are the shoes?*** ile kosztują te buty?; ***that's five pounds*** (kosztuje) pięć funtów; ***she is reading*** właśnie czyta; ***there is*** jest; ***there are*** są; ***there isn't*** nie ma
B/E *skrót pisany*: ***bill of exchange*** *econ.* weksel *m*
beach [biːtʃ] plaża *f*; **'~ ball** piłka *f* plażowa; **'~ bug•gy** buggy *m* (*pojazd do jazdy po wydmach dla przyjemności*); **'~•wear** strój *m* plażowy
bea•con ['biːkən] światło *n* sygnalne; *naut.* latarnia *n* kierunkowa
bead [biːd] paciorek *m*, koralik *m*, kulka *f* (*naszyjnika*); **~s** *pl. rel.* różaniec *m*; korale *pl.*; **'~•y** (***-ier, -iest***) oczy jak koraliki *lub* paciorki
beak [biːk] dziób *m*; dzióbek *m* (*dzbanka*)
bea•ker ['biːkə] kubek *m*, kubeczek *m*
beam [biːm] **1.** belka *f*, dźwigar *m*; promień *m*; wiązka *f* (*światła, promieni*); **2.** promieniować, wysyłać wiązkę (*światła, promieni*); promienieć, rozpromienić się
bean [biːn] *bot.* fasolka *f*; ziarno (*fasoli*) *n*; ***be full of ~s*** F być pełnym wigoru
bear[1] [beə] *zo.* niedźwiedź *m*
bear[2] [beə] (***bore, borne*** *lub w str. biernej urodzić się*: ***born***) dźwigać, nieść; wydawać ⟨-dać⟩ na świat, ⟨u⟩rodzić; *zwłaszcza z przeczeniem*: znosić ⟨znieść⟩, wytrzymywać ⟨-mać⟩; ***~ out*** potwierdzać ⟨-dzić⟩; **~•a•ble** ['beərəbl] do zniesienia, znośny
beard [bɪəd] broda *f*; *bot.* wąs *m* kłosa; **'~•ed** brodaty
bear•er ['beərə] okaziciel(ka *f*) *m* (*dokumentu*); *econ.* posiadacz(ka *f*) *m*; doręczyciel(ka *f*) *m*
bear•ing ['beərɪŋ] podpora *f*; postawa *f*; *fig.* związek *m*, odniesienie *n*; namiar *m*; sytuacja *f*, położenie *n*; ***take one's ~s*** brać ⟨wziąć⟩ namiar; ***lose one's ~s*** stracić kierunek
beast [biːst] *dzikie* zwierzę *n*; bestia *f*; ***~ of 'prey*** drapieżnik *m*; **'~•ly** obrzydliwy, wstrętny
beat [biːt] **1.** (***beat, beaten*** *lub* ***beat***) ⟨po⟩bić; uderzać ⟨-rzyć⟩; ubijać ⟨ubić⟩; pokonywać ⟨-nać⟩; przewyższać ⟨-szyć⟩; ***~ it!*** F wynocha!; ***that ~s all!*** to już szczyty!; ***that ~s me*** to za trudne dla mnie; ***~ about the bush*** obwijać w bawełnę; ***~ down*** *econ. cenę* zniżać ⟨-niżyć⟩; ***~ up*** *kogoś* pobić doszczętnie; **2.** uderzenie *n*; *mus.* rytm *m*, takt *m*; (*w jazzie*): beat *m*, rytmika *f*; runda *f*; obchód *m*; **3.** (***dead***) **~** F całkiem wykończony; **~•en** ['biːtn] *p.p. od* ***beat*** 1; ***off the ~en track*** niezwykły
beau•ti•cian [bjuː'tɪʃn] (*zawód*) kosmetyczka *f*
beau•ti•ful ['bjuːtəfl] piękny; ***the ~ people*** *pl.* wyższe warstwy *pl.*
beaut•y ['bjuːtɪ] piękno *n*; ***Sleeping*** ♀ Śpiąca Królewna *f*; **'~ par•lo(u)r**, **'~ salon** salon *m* kosmetyczny
bea•ver ['biːvə] *zo.* bóbr
be•came [bɪ'keɪm] *pret. od* ***become***
be•cause [bɪ'kɒz] ponieważ; ***~ of*** z powodu (*G*)
beck•on ['bekən] przywoływać ⟨-łać⟩, skinąć na (*A*); ⚠ *nie* ***bekon***
be•come [bɪ'kʌm] (***-came, -come***) *v/i.* stawać się; *v/t. komuś* pasować, być do twarzy; **be'com•ing** pasujący, twarzowy; stosowny
bed [bed] **1.** łóżko *n*, tapczan *m*; legowisko *n* (*zwierzęcia*); *agr.* grzęda *f*, klomb *m*; dno *n*, (*rzeki*) koryto *n*; ściółka *f*; ***~ and breakfast*** pokój *m* ze śniadaniem; **2.** (***-dd-***): ***~ down*** ⟨przy⟩szykować sobie spanie; **'~•clothes** *pl.* bielizna *f* pościelowa; **'~•ding** posłanie *n*, pościel *f*
bed•lam ['bedləm] *fig.* dom *m* wariatów
'bed|•rid•den przykuty do łóżka; **'~•room** sypialnia *f*; **'~•side**: ***at the ~side*** przy łóżku (*chorego*); **~•side 'lamp** lampka *f* na stoliczku nocnym; **'~-sit** F, **~-'sit•ter, ~-'sit•ting room** *Brt.* kawalerka *f*; **'~•spread** narzuta *f* na łóżko; **'~•stead** łóżko *n* (*bez materacy*); **'~•time** czas zaśnięcia *lub* zasypiania
bee [biː] **1.** *zo.* pszczoła *f*; ***have a ~ in***

B

one's bonnet F mieć bzika; *attr.* pszczeli
beech [biːtʃ] *bot.* buk *m*; *attr.* bukowy; '**~·nut** bukiew *f* (*orzeszek buka*)
beef [biːf] wołowina *f*; '**~·bur·ger** *gastr. zwł. Brt.* hamburger *m* (*z wołowiny*); **~ 'tea** bulion *m*; '**~·y** (***-ier, -iest***) F muskularny
'**bee|·hive** ul *m*; '**~keep·er** pszczelarz *m*, pasiecznik *m*; '**~·line**: ***make a ~line for*** F iść ⟨pójść⟩ jak po sznurku *lub* prosto do (*G*)
been [biːn, bɪn] *p.p. od* ***be***
beep·er ['biːpə] *Am.* → ***bleeper***
beer [bɪə] piwo *n*
beet [biːt] *bot.* burak *m*; *Am.* burak *m* ćwikłowy
bee·tle ['biːtl] *zo.* żuk *m*, chrząszcz *m*
'**beet·root** *bot. Brt.* burak *m* ćwikłowy
be·fore [bɪ'fɔː] **1.** *adv.* (*w czasie*) przedtem, poprzednio, wcześniej; (*w przestrzeni*) przed, z przodu, na przedzie; **2.** *cj.* zanim, nim; **3.** *prp.* przed (*I*); **~·hand** wcześniej, uprzednio
be·friend [bɪ'frend] okazywać ⟨-zać⟩ przyjaźń, ⟨po⟩traktować jak przyjaciela
beg [beg] (***-gg-***) *v/t.* wypraszać ⟨-rosić⟩ (***from s.o.*** kogoś); upraszać ⟨uprosić⟩; wyżebrać; *v/i.* żebrać
be·gan [bɪ'gæn] *pret. od* ***begin***
be·get [bɪ'get] (***-tt-***; ***-got, -gotten***) ⟨s⟩płodzić
beg·gar ['begə] **1.** żebrak *m*, (-aczka *f*); F facet *m*, chłop *m*; **2.** ***it ~s all description*** nie da się opisać
be·gin [bɪ'gɪn] (***-nn-***; ***began, begun***) zaczynać ⟨-cząć⟩ (się), rozpoczynać⟨-cząć⟩ (się); **~·ner** początkujący *m* (-ca *f*); **~·ning** początek *m*, rozpoczęcie *n*
be·got [bɪ'gɒt] *pret. od* ***beget***; **~·ten** [bɪ'gɒtn] *p.p. od* ***beget***
be·grudge [bɪ'grʌdʒ] ⟨po⟩żałować, ⟨po⟩skąpić
be·guile [bɪ'gaɪl] łudzić, zwodzić ⟨zwieść⟩, ⟨o⟩mamić
be·gun [bɪ'gʌn] *p.p. od* ***begin***
be·half [bɪ'hɑːf]: ***on*** (*Am. też* ***in***) **~ *of*** w imieniu (*G*), na rzecz (*G*)
be·have [bɪ'heɪv] zachowywać ⟨-wać⟩ się
be·hav·io(u)r [bɪ'heɪvjə] zachowanie *n*, postępowanie *n*; **~·al** [bɪ'heɪvjərəl] *psych.* behawioralny
be·head [bɪ'hed] ścinać ⟨ściąć⟩ (głowę)
be·hind [bɪ'haɪnd] **1.** *adv.* z tyłu, w tyle; ***be ~ with*** zalegać z (*I*), opóźniać się (*I*); **2.** *prp.* za (*I*), z tyłu (*G*), poza (*I*); **3.** F tyłek *m*, pupa *f*
beige [beɪʒ] beż *m*; *attr.* beżowy
be·ing ['biːɪŋ] byt *m*, bycie *n*; istnienie *n*, stworzenie *n*; istota *f*, natura *f*
Belarus Białoruś *f*
be·lat·ed [bɪ'leɪtɪd] opóźniony
belch [beltʃ] **1.** F bekać ⟨beknąć⟩; ***she ~ed*** odbiło jej się, F beknęła; *też* **~ *out*** buchać ⟨-chnąć⟩ (*dymem itp.*), zionąć; **2.** odbicie *n* się, F beknięcie *n*
bel·fry ['belfrɪ] dzwonnica *f*
Bel·gium ['beldʒəm] Belgia *f*; **Bel·gian** ['beldʒən] **1.** belgijski; **2.** Belg(ijka *f*) *m*
Bel·grade Belgrad *m*
be·lief [bɪ'liːf] przekonanie *n*, wiara *f* (***in*** w *A*)
be·lie·va·ble [bɪ'liːvəbl] możliwy do uwierzenia, wiarygodny
be·lieve [bɪ'liːv] ⟨u⟩wierzyć (***in*** w *A*); sądzić (***that*** że), uważać; ***I couldn't ~ my eyes*** (***ears***) nie mogłem uwierzyć własnym oczom (uszom); **be'liev·er** *rel.* wierzący *m* (-ca *f*), wyznawca *m* (-czyni *f*)
be·lit·tle [bɪ'lɪtl] *fig.* pomniejszać ⟨-szyć⟩
bell [bel] dzwon *m*; dzwonek *m* (*do drzwi*); '**~·boy**, '**~·hop** *Am. hotelowy* boy *m*, goniec *m* hotelowy
-bel·lied [belɪd] (o *dużym itp.* brzuchu)
bel·lig·er·ent [bɪ'lɪdʒərənt] wojowniczy, bojowy, napastliwy
bel·low ['beləʊ] **1.** ⟨za⟩ryczeć; **2.** ryk *m*
bel·lows ['beləʊz] *pl., sg.* miech *m*, *zw. pl.*
bel·ly ['belɪ] **1.** brzuch *m*; **2. ~ *out*** wybrzuszać ⟨-szyć⟩ (się); '**~·ache** ból *m* brzucha
be·long [bɪ'lɒŋ] należeć; **~ *to*** należeć do (*G*); być na właściwym miejscu; **~·ings** *pl.* mienie *n*, rzeczy *pl.*
be·loved [bɪ'lʌvɪd] **1.** ukochany, umiłowany; **2.** ukochany *m* (-na *f*)
be·low [bɪ'ləʊ] **1.** *adv.* poniżej (*G*); **2.** pod (*I*), poniżej (*G*)
belt [belt] **1.** pas *m*; pasek *m*; strefa *f*, pas *m*; *tech.* taśma *f*; **2.** *też* **~ *up*** zapinać ⟨zapiąć⟩ pasek; **~ *up*** *mot.* zapinać ⟨zapiąć⟩ pas(y *pl.*) bezpieczeństwa; '**~·ed**

z paskiem, na pasek; '**~·way** *Am.* obwodnica *f*
be·moan [bɪ'məʊn] opłakiwać
bench [bentʃ] ławka *f*, ława *f*; warsztat *m*, stół *m* roboczy; ława *f* sędziowska, sąd *m*
bend [bend] **1.** zakręt *m*; zgięcie *n*, zagięcie *n*; ***drive s.o. round the ~*** F doprowadzać ⟨-dzić⟩ *kogoś* do obłędu; **2.** (***bent***) zginać ⟨zgiąć⟩ (się), wyginać ⟨wygiąć⟩ (się); *wysiłki* zwracać ⟨-cić⟩ (***to, on*** na *A*)
be·neath [bɪ'ni:θ] → ***below***
ben·e·dic·tion [benɪ'dɪkʃn] błogosławieństwo *n*
ben·e·fac·tor ['benɪfæktə] dobroczyńca *m*
be·nef·i·cent [bɪ'nefɪsnt] dobroczynny, zbawienny
ben·e·fi·cial [benɪ'fɪʃl] korzystny, pożyteczny
ben·e·fit ['benɪfɪt] **1.** korzyść *f*; zysk *m*; pożytek *m*; impreza *f* dobroczynna; *socjalne* świadczenie *n*, zapomoga *f*; *chorobowy* zasiłek; **2.** przynosić ⟨-nieść⟩ korzyść; ***~ by, ~ from*** odnosić ⟨odnieść⟩ korzyść z (*G*)
be·nev·o|·lence [bɪ'nevələns] życzliwość *f*, dobrodziejstwo *n*; **~·lent** życzliwy, dobroczynny
be·nign [bɪ'naɪn] *med.* łagodny, niezłośliwy
bent [bent] **1.** *pret. i p.p. od* ***bend*** 2; **2.** *fig.* skłonność *f*, upodobanie *n*, predyspozycja *f*
ben·zene ['benzi:n] *chem.* benzen *m*
be·queath [bɪ'kwi:ð] *jur.* pozostawiać ⟨-wić⟩ w spadku
be·quest [bɪ'kwest] *jur.* spadek *m*, spuścizna *f*
be·reave [bɪ'ri:v] (***bereaved*** *lub* ***bereft***) pozbawiać ⟨-wić⟩, osierocać ⟨cić⟩
be·reft [bɪ'reft] *pret. i p.p. od* ***bereave***
be·ret ['bereɪ] beret *m*
Ber·lin Berlin *m*
Bern Berno *n*
ber·ry ['berɪ] *bot.* jagoda *f*
berth [bɜ:θ] **1.** *naut.* miejsce *n* cumowania; *naut.* koja *f*; *rail.* miejsce *n* leżące, kuszetka *f*; **2.** ⟨przy⟩cumować, ⟨przy⟩bijać
be·seech [bɪ'si:tʃ] (***besought*** *lub* ***beseeched***) błagać
be·set [bɪ'set] (***-tt-***; ***beset***) dotykać ⟨dotknąć⟩, prześladować; ***~ with difficulties*** prześladowany przez trudności
be·side [bɪ'saɪd] *prp.* obok; przy; ***be ~ o.s.*** nie posiadać się (***with*** z *G*); ***be ~ the point, ~ the question*** nie mieć nic do rzeczy; **~s** [bɪ'saɪdz] **1.** *adv.* oprócz tego, poza tym; **2.** *prp.* poza (*I*), oprócz (*G*)
be·siege [bɪ'si:dʒ] oblegać ⟨oblec⟩
be·smear [bɪ'smɪə] obsmarowywać ⟨-ować⟩
be·sought [bɪ'sɔ:t] *pret. i p.p. od* ***beseech***
be·spat·ter [bɪ'spætə] opryskiwać ⟨-kać⟩
best [best] **1.** *adj.* (*sup. od* ***good*** 1) najlepszy; ***~ before ...*** należy spożyć (zużyć) do ...; **2.** (*sup. od* ***well***[1]) najlepiej; **3.** najlepszy *m*; ***all the ~!*** wszystkiego najlepszego!; ***to the ~ of...*** najlepiej jak...; ***make the ~ of*** wykorzystywać ⟨-stać⟩ (*A*) jak najlepiej; ***at ~*** w najlepszym wypadku; ***be at one's ~*** być w najlepszej formie; **~ be'fore date**, **~ 'by date** okres *m* przydatności do spożycia
bes·ti·al ['bestjəl] zwierzęcy, bestialski
best 'man (*pl.* ***-men***) drużba *m*
be·stow [bɪ'stəʊ] obdarzać ⟨-rzyć⟩, nadawać ⟨nadać⟩
bet [bet] **1.** zakład *m*; ***make a ~*** założyć się; **2.** (***-tt-***; ***bet*** *lub* ***betted***) zakładać ⟨założyć⟩ się; ***you ~!*** F no pewnie!, jeszcze jak!
Bethlehem Betlejem *m*
be·tray [bɪ'treɪ] zdradzać ⟨-dzić⟩ (*też fig.*); zawodzić ⟨-wieść⟩; **~·al** [bɪ'treɪəl] zdrada *f*; **~·er** zdrajca *m* (-czyni *f*)
bet·ter ['betə] **1.** *adj.* (*comp. od* ***good*** 1) lepszy; ***he is ~*** lepiej mu; **2.** ***get the ~ of*** brać ⟨wziąć⟩ górę nad (*I*); **3.** *adv.* (*comp. od* ***well***[1]) lepiej; bardziej; ***so much the ~*** tym lepiej; ***you had ~*** (*Am.* F ***you ~***) ***go*** lepiej już idź; **4.** *v/t.* polepszać ⟨-szyć⟩; *v/i.* polepszać ⟨-szyć⟩ się
be·tween [bɪ'twi:n] **1.** *adv.* pośrodku; ***few and far ~*** F co jakiś czas, sporadyczny; **2.** *prp.* pomiędzy (*I*), między (*I*); spośród (*G*); ***~ you and me*** tylko między nami
bev·el ['bevl] ukos *m*, skośna krawędź *f*
bev·er·age ['bevərɪdʒ] napój *m*
bev·y ['bevɪ] *zo.* stadko *n* (*przepiórek*);

B

gromadka *f* (*dziewcząt*)
be·ware [bɪ'weə] (**of**) wystrzegać się (*G*); strzec się (*G*); **~ of the dog!** uwaga zły pies!
be·wil·der [bɪ'wɪldə] oszałamiać ⟨-łomić⟩; zbijać ⟨zbić⟩ z tropu; **~·ment konsternacja** *f*
be·witch [bɪ'wɪtʃ] oczarowywać ⟨-ować⟩, urzekać ⟨urzec⟩
be·yond [bɪ'jɒnd] **1.** *adv.* dalej; więcej; powyżej; **2.** *prp.* poza (*I*), za (*I*); **~ remedy** nie do naprawienia
bi... [baɪ] bi..., dwu...
bi·as ['baɪəs] uprzedzenie *n*; skłonność *f*, przychylność *f*; '**~(s)ed** uprzedzony; *jur.* stronniczy
bi·ath|·lete [baɪ'æθliːt] (*w sporcie*) biatlonista *m* (-tka *f*); **~·lon** [baɪ'æθlən] (*w sporcie*) biatlon *m*
bib [bɪb] śliniaczek *m*; góra *f* (*fartucha*)
Bi·ble ['baɪbl] Biblia *f* (*też fig.*)
bib·li·cal ['bɪblɪkl] biblijny
bib·li·og·ra·phy [bɪblɪ'ɒgrəfɪ] bibliografia *f*
bi·car·bon·ate [baɪ'kɑːbənɪt] *też* **~ of soda** soda *f* oczyszczona, *tech.* wodorowęglan *m* sodu
bi·cen|·te·na·ry [baɪsen'tiːnərɪ], **~·ten·ni·al** [baɪsen'tenɪəl] *Am.* dwustulecie *n*
bi·ceps ['baɪseps] *anat.* biceps *m*, mięsień *m* dwugłowy
bick·er ['bɪkə] ⟨po⟩kłócić się, ⟨po⟩żreć się
bi·cy·cle ['baɪsɪkl] rower *m*
bid [bɪd] **1.** (**-dd-**; **bid** *lub* **bade, bid** *lub* **bidden**) (*na licytacji*) zgłaszać ⟨zgłosić⟩ ofertę *lub* cenę; (*w kartach*) ⟨za⟩licytować; **2.** *econ.* oferta *f*, cena *f*; (*w kartach*) (*odzywka*) *f*; **~·den** ['bɪdn] *p.p. od* **bid** 1
bi·en·ni·al [baɪ'enɪəl] *roślina*: dwuletni; (*odbywający się*) co dwa lata; **~·ly** co dwa lata
bier [bɪə] mary *pl.*
big [bɪg] (**-gg-**) duży, wielki; gruby; **talk ~** przechwalać się, chełpić się
big·a·my ['bɪgəmɪ] bigamia *f*
big|'busi·ness wielki interes *m*; '**~·head** F mądrala *m/f*; **~ 'shot** *osoba*: gruba ryba *f*
bike [baɪk] F rower *m*; motorower *m*; motor *m*; '**bik·er** rowerzysta *m*; motorowerzysta *m*; motocyklista *m*
bi·lat·er·al [baɪ'lætərəl] dwustronny
bile [baɪl] *anat.* żółć (*też fig.*)
bi·lin·gual [baɪ'lɪŋgwəl] dwujęzyczny; **~ 'sec·re·ta·ry** sekretarka *f* władająca obcym językiem
bill[1] [bɪl] dziób *m*
bill[2] [bɪl] faktura *f*; rachunek *m*; *econ.* weksel; *pol.* projekt *m* ustawy; *jur.* powództwo; afisz *m*, plakat *m*; *Am.* banknot *m*; **~ of de'liv·er·y** *econ.* pokwitowanie *n* dostawy; **~ of ex'change** *econ.* weksel *m*; **~ of 'sale** *jur.* akt *m* kupna-sprzedaży; '**~·board** *Am.* tablica *f* reklamowa, billboard *m*; '**~·fold** *Am.* portfel *m*
bil·li·ards ['bɪljədz] *sg.* bilard *m*
bil·li·on ['bɪljən] miliard *m*
bil·low ['bɪləʊ] **1.** kłąb *m*; **2.** *też* **~ out** wybrzuszać ⟨-szyć⟩ się; kłębić się
bil·ly goat ['bɪlɪgəʊt] *zo.* kozioł *m*
bin [bɪn] (duży) pojemnik *m* na śmieci
bi·na·ry ['baɪnərɪ] *math., phys. itp.* binarny, dwójkowy; **~ 'code** *komp.* kod *m* binarny; **~ 'num·ber** liczba *f* w zapisie dwójkowym
bind [baɪnd] (**bound**) *v/t.* ⟨za-, przy-, ob-, z⟩wiązywać ⟨-zać⟩; zobowiązywać ⟨-zać⟩; *książkę* oprawiać ⟨-wić⟩; *v/i.* wiązać; '**~·er** introligator *m*; segregator *m*, skoroszyt *m*; '**~·ing 1.** wiążący; zobowiązujący; **2.** oprawa *f*
bin·go ['bɪŋgəʊ] (*gra*) bingo *n*
bi·noc·u·lars [bɪ'nɒkjʊləz] *pl.* lornetka *f*
bi·o·chem·is·try [baɪəʊ'kemɪstrɪ] biochemia *f*
bi·o·de·gra·da·ble [baɪəʊdɪ'greɪdəbl] podlegający biodegradacji
bi·og·ra|·pher [baɪ'ɒgrəfə] biograf *m*; **~·phy** biografia *f*
bi·o·log·i·cal [baɪəʊ'lɒdʒɪkl] biologiczny; **bi·ol·o·gist** [baɪ'ɒlədʒɪst] biolog *m*; **bi·ol·o·gy** [baɪ'ɒlədʒɪ] biologia *f*
bi·o·rhyth·m ['baɪəʊrɪðəm] biorytm *m*
bi·o·tope ['baɪəʊtəʊp] biotop *m*
bi·ped ['baɪped] *zo.* dwónóg *m*, zwierzę *n* dwunożne
birch [bɜːtʃ] *bot.* brzoza *f*; *attr.* brzozowy
bird [bɜːd] ptak *m*; *attr.* ptasi; '**~·cage** klatka *f* na ptaki; **~ of 'pas·sage** ptak *m* przelotny *lub* wędrowny; **~ of 'prey** ptak *m* drapieżny; **~ 'sanc·tu·a·ry** rezerwat *m* ptaków; '**~·seed** pokarm *m* dla ptaków

bird's-eye 'view widok *m* z lotu ptaka

bi·ro ['baɪrəʊ] *TM Brt.* (*pl.* ***-ros***) długopis *m*

birth [bɜːθ] urodziny *pl.*; narodziny *pl.*; **'~ cer·tif·i·cate** metryka *f* (*urodzenia*); **'~ con·trol** antykoncepcja *f*; **~ con·trol 'pill** pigułka *f* antykoncepcyjna; **'~·day** urodziny *pl.*; *attr.* urodzinowy; **'~·mark** znamię *n* wrodzone; **'~·place** miejsce *n* urodzenia; **'~ rate** przyrost *m* naturalny

bis·cuit ['bɪskɪt] ciastko *n*, herbatnik *m*

bi·sex·u·al [baɪ'sekʃʊəl] obupłciowy, dwupłciowy; biseksualny

bish·op ['bɪʃəp] biskup *m*; (*w szachach*) goniec *m*, laufer *m*; **~·ric** ['bɪʃəprɪk] biskupstwo *n*

bi·son ['baɪsn] *zo.* bizon *m*; żubr *m*

bit [bɪt] **1.** kawałek *m*, odrobina *f*; wiertło *n*, świder *m*; wędzidło *n*; łopatka *f*, bródka *f* (*klucza*); *komp.* bit *m*; ***a ~*** trochę; ***a little ~*** odrobina; **2.** *pret. od* ***bite*** 2

bitch [bɪtʃ] *zo.* suka *f*; *pej.* dziwka *f*

'bit den·si·ty *komp.* gęstość *f* zapisu cyfrowego

bite [baɪt] **1.** ugryzienie *n*, ukąszenie *n*; kęs *m*, kąsek *m*; *tech.* chwyt *m*, zaciśnięcie *n* (*śruby itp.*); ***have a ~*** przekąsić coś; **2.** (***bit, bitten***) ⟨u⟩gryźć; kąsać ⟨ukąsić⟩ (*też o owadach, zimnie*); *paznokcie* gryźć ⟨obgryzać⟩; *pieprz*: ⟨za⟩piec; *dym*: ⟨za⟩szczypać; *tech.* chwytać ⟨chwycić⟩; *śrubę* zaciskać (się)

bit·ten ['bɪtn] *p.p. od* ***bite*** 2

bit·ter ['bɪtə] gorzki; *fig.* zgorzkniały

bit·ters ['bɪtəz] *pl.* (*lecznicza*) nalewka *f* gorzka

biz [bɪz] F → ***business***

black [blæk] **1.** czarny; ciemny; mroczny; ***have s.th. in ~ and white*** mieć coś czarno na białym; ***be ~ and blue*** być posiniaczonym; ***beat s.o. ~ and blue*** posiniaczyć kogoś; **2.** ⟨po⟩czernić; ***~ out*** chwilowo ⟨u⟩tracić przytomność; *okna* zaciemniać ⟨-nić⟩; **3.** czerń *f*, czarny kolor *m*; *człowiek*: czarnoskóry *m*, czarny *m*; **'~·ber·ry** *bot.* jeżyna *f*; **'~·bird** *zo.* kos *m*; **'~·board** tablica *f* (szkolna); **~ 'box** *aviat.* czarna skrzynka *f*; **~'cur·rant** *bot.* czarna porzeczka *f*; **'~·en** *v/t.* ⟨za⟩czernić; *fig.* oczerniać ⟨-nić⟩; *v/i.* ⟨s⟩czernieć; **~ 'eye** podbite oko *n*; **'~·head** *med.* zaskórnik *m*, wągier *m*; **~ 'ice** gołoledź *f*; **'~·ing** czarna pasta *f* do butów, czernidło *n*; **'~·leg** *Brt.* łamistrajk *m*; **'~·mail 1.** szantaż *m*; **2.** ⟨za⟩szantażować; **'~·mail·er** szantażysta *m* (-tka *f*); **~ 'mar·ket** czarny rynek *m*; **'~·ness** czerń *f*; **'~·out** zaciemnienie *n*; brak *m* energii (*prądu itp.*); **~ 'pud·ding** *gastr.* kaszanka *f*; **~ ' Sea** Morze Czarne; **~ 'sheep** (*pl.* ***-sheep***) *fig.* czarna owca *f*; **'~·smith** kowal *m*

blad·der ['blædə] *anat.* pęcherz *m* moczowy

blade [bleɪd] *bot.* źdźbło; łopatka *f* (*ramienia*); ostrze *n*, brzeszczot *m*; klinga *f*; łopata *f* (*śmigła*)

blame [bleɪm] **1.** wina *f*; odpowiedzialność *f*; **2.** obwiniać ⟨-nić⟩; ***be to ~ for*** ponosić ⟨-nieść⟩ winę za (*A*); **'~·less** bez winy, niewinny

blanch [blɑːntʃ] ⟨wy⟩bielić; *gastr.* ⟨z⟩blanszować; ⟨z⟩blednąć

blanc·mange [blə'mɒnʒ] *gastr.* budyń *m*

blank [blæŋk] **1.** pusty, czysty; nie zapełniony, nie wypełniony, nie zapisany; *econ.* in blanko, na okaziciela; **2.** puste miejsce *n*; luka *f*; formularz *m*, blankiet *m*, druk *m*; *los na loterii*: pusty; **~ 'car·tridge** ślepy nabój *m*; **~ 'cheque** (*Am.* ***'check***) *econ.* czek *m* na okaziciela

blan·ket ['blæŋkɪt] **1.** koc *m*; **2.** przykrywać ⟨-ryć⟩

blare [bleə] *radio*: ⟨za⟩ryczeć; *trąba*: ⟨za⟩grzmieć

blas|·pheme [blæs'fiːm] ⟨z⟩bluźnić; **~·phe·my** ['blæsfəmɪ] bluźnierstwo *n*

blast [blɑːst] **1.** (*wiatru*) podmuch *m*; wybuch *m*; fala *f* wybuchu; dźwięk *m* (*instrumentu dętego*); **2.** wysadzać ⟨-dzić⟩; *fig.* ⟨z⟩niszczyć, ⟨z⟩niweczyć; ***~ off*** (***into space***) wystrzelić w przestrzeń kosmiczną; *rakieta*: ⟨wy⟩startować; ***~!*** cholera!; ***~ you!*** szlag by cię trafił!; ***~ed*** cholerny; **'~ fur·nace** *tech.* wielki piec *m*; **'~-off** start *m* (*rakiety*)

bla·tant ['bleɪtənt] rażący; bezczelny

blaze [bleɪz] **1.** płomień *m*, ogień *m*; jaskrawe światło *n*, blask *m*; *fig.* wybuch *m*; **2.** ⟨s⟩płonąć, ⟨s⟩palić (się); błyszczeć ⟨błysnąć⟩; wybuchać ⟨-nąć⟩ płomieniami

blaz·er ['bleɪzə] blezer *m*

bla·zon ['bleɪzn] herb *m*

bleach [bliːtʃ] ⟨wy⟩bielić
bleak [bliːk] odludny, ogołocony, srogi; *fig.* ponury, posępny
blear·y ['blɪərɪ] (***-ier, iest***) mglisty, niewyraźny
bleat [bliːt] **1.** ⟨za⟩beczeć; **2.** beczenie *n*, bek *m*
bled [bled] *pret. i p.p. od* ***bleed***
bleed [bliːd] (***bled***) *v/i.* krwawić; *v/t. krew* puszczać ⟨puścić⟩; *fig.* F wyzyskiwać ⟨-skać⟩, ⟨wy⟩żyłować; **'~·ing 1.** *med.* krwawienie *n*, *med.* puszczanie *n* krwi; **2.** *sl.* cholerny, pieprzony
bleep [bliːp] **1.** krótki sygnał *m* (*jak w telefonie*), brzęk *n*; **2.** wzywać ⟨wezwać⟩ sygnałem (*pagera itp.*); **'~·er** *Brt.* F brzęczyk *m* (*w urządzeniu przyzywającym*)
blem·ish ['blemɪʃ] **1.** skaza *f* (*na urodzie*); brak *m*, skaza *f*; **2.** ⟨o⟩szpecić
blend [blend] **1.** ⟨z⟩mieszać (się); *wina* kupażować; **2.** mieszanka *f*; **'~·er** mikser *m*, malakser *m*
bless [bles] (***blessed*** *lub* ***blest***) ⟨po⟩błogosławić; ***be ~ed with*** być obdarzonym (*I*); (***God***) ***~ you!*** na zdrowie!; ***~ me, ~ my heart, ~my soul*** F Boże mój!; **'~·ed** błogosławiony, szczęśliwy; F przeklęty, cholerny; **'~·ing** błogosławieństwo *n*
blest [blest] *pret. i p.p. od* ***bless***
blew [bluː] *pret. od* ***blow***
blight [blaɪt] *bot.* rdza *f* zbożowa
blind [blaɪnd] **1.** niewidomy, ślepy (*fig.* ***to*** na *A*); *zakręt*: niewidoczny; **2.** żaluzja *f*, roleta *f*; ***the ~*** *pl.* niewidomi *pl.*, ślepi *pl.*; **3.** oślepiać ⟨-pić⟩; *fig.* zaślepiać ⟨-pić⟩, ⟨u⟩czynić ślepym (***to*** na *I*, wobec *G*); **~ 'al·ley** ślepa ulica *f*; **'~·ers** *pl. Am.* klapki *pl.* na oczy; **'~·fold 1.** z zawiązanymi oczyma; **2.** zawiązywać ⟨-zać⟩ oczy; **3.** przepaska *f* na oczy; **'~·ly** *fig.* ślepo, na ślepo; **'~·worm** *zo.* padalec *m*
blink [blɪŋk] **1.** mrugnięcie *n*; **2.** ⟨za⟩mrugać; ⟨za⟩migać; **'~·ers** *pl.* klapki *pl.* na oczy
bliss [blɪs] szczęśliwość *f*, rozkosz *f*
blis·ter ['blɪstə] **1.** *med.*, *tech.* pęcherz *m*; bąbel *m*; **2.** wywoływać ⟨-łać⟩ pęcherze; pokrywać ⟨-ryć⟩ (się) pęcherzami
blitz [blɪts] silny nalot *m* lotniczy; bombardowanie *n*; **2.** mocno ⟨z⟩bombardować
bliz·zard ['blɪzəd] zamieć *f* śnieżna
bloat|·ed ['bləʊtɪd] nadmuchany, wydęty; *fig.* nadęty, odęty; **'~·er** *gastr.* wędzony śledź *m* *lub* makrela *f*
blob [blɒb] kleks *m*
block [blɒk] **1.** blok *m*; klocek *m*; kloc *m*; blok, (pod)zespół; *tech.* blok budowlany, cegła *f*; *zwł. Am.* kwartał *m* (*domów*), działka *f*; korek; zator; *tech.* zatkanie *n* się; **~ (*of flats*)** *Brt. mieszkaniowy* blok *m*; **2.** *też* ***~ up*** zatykać ⟨-kać⟩, zapychać ⟨-chać⟩; ⟨za⟩blokować
block·ade [blɒ'keɪd] **1.** blokada *f*; **2.** ⟨za⟩blokować
block|·bust·er ['blɒkbʌstə] F szlagier *m*, hit *m*; **'~·head** F dureń *m*; **~ 'let·ters** *pl.* drukowane litery *pl.* *lub* pismo *n*
bloke [bləʊk] *Brt.* F facet *m*
blond [blɒnd] **1.** blondyn *m*; **2.** *adj.* blond; **~e** [blɒnd] **1.** blondynka *f*; **2.** *adj.* blond
blood [blʌd] krew; ***in cold ~*** z zimną krwią; **'~ bank** *med.* bank *m* krwi; **'~·cur·dling** ['blʌdkɜːdlɪŋ] mrożący krew w żyłach; **'~ do·nor** *med.* dawca *m* krwi; **'~ group** *med.* grupa *f* krwi; **'~·hound** *zo.* ogar *m*; **'~ pres·sure** *med.* ciśnienie *n* krwi; **'~·shed** rozlew *m* krwi; **'~·shot** nabiegły krwią; **'~·thirst·y** żądny krwi, krwiożerczy; **'~ ves·sel** *anat.* naczynie *n* krwionośne; **'~·y** (***-ier, -iest***) krwawy; *Brt.* F cholerny, pieprzony
bloom [bluːm] **1.** *poet.* kwiat *m*, kwiecie *n*; *fig.* rozkwit *m*; **2.** kwitnąć ⟨rozkwitać⟩; *fig.* kwitnąć, promienować
blos·som ['blɒsəm] **1.** kwiat *m*; **2.** kwitnąć ⟨rozkwitać⟩
blot [blɒt] **1.** kleks *m*; *fig.* skaza *f*, plama *f*; **2.** (***-tt-***) ⟨s-, po⟩plamić (się); osuszać ⟨-szyć⟩ (bibułą)
blotch [blɒtʃ] kleks *m*; plama *f* *lub* przebarwienie *n* na skórze; **'~·y** (***-ier, -iest***) *skóra*: plamisty
blot|·ter ['blɒtə] suszka *f*; **'~·ting pa·per** bibuła *f*
blouse [blaʊz] bluzka *f*
blow[1] [bləʊ] uderzenie *n*, cios *m*
blow[2] [bləʊ] (***blew, blown***) *v/i.* ⟨po⟩wiać, ⟨za⟩dąć; dmuchać ⟨-chnąć⟩; ⟨za⟩sapać; przedziurawiać ⟨-wić⟩ dętkę; *electr. bezpiecznik*: przepalać ⟨-lić⟩ się;

~ ***up*** wylatywać ⟨-lecieć⟩ w powietrze; *v/t.* ~ ***one's nose*** wydmuchiwać ⟨-chać⟩ nos; ~ ***one's top*** F dostawać ⟨dostać⟩ szału; ~ ***out*** zdmuchiwać ⟨-chnąć⟩; ~ ***up*** wysadzać ⟨-dzić⟩; *fotografię* powiększać ⟨-szyć⟩; '**~-dry** *włosy* ⟨wy⟩suszyć; '**~·fly** *zo.* (*mucha*) plujka *f*; **~n** [bləʊn] *p.p. od* ***blow***[2]; '**~·pipe** *tech.* palnik *m*, dmuchawka *f*; '**~-up** *phot.* powiększenie *n*

blud·geon ['blʌdʒən] pałka *f*

blue [bluː] **1.** niebieski, błękitny; melancholijny; **2.** błękit *m*, *kolor*: niebieski *m*; ***out of the*** ~ jak grom z jasnego nieba, nagle; '**~·ber·ry** *bot.* borówka *f* wysoka *lub* amerykańska; '**~·bot·tle** *zo.* (mucha) plujka *f*; **~-'col·lar work·er** pracownik *m* fizyczny

blues [bluːz] *pl. lub sg. mus.* blues *m* (*też fig.*); ***have the*** ~ F mieć chandrę

bluff[1] [blʌf] urwisko *n*, stromy brzeg *m*

bluff[2] [blʌf] **1.** blef *m*; **2.** ⟨za⟩blefować

blu·ish ['bluːɪʃ] niebieskawy

blun·der ['blʌndə] **1.** błąd *m*, F byk *m*; **2.** F strzelić byka, zrobić (*duży*) błąd; ⟨s⟩fuszerować, ⟨s⟩partaczyć

blunt [blʌnt] tępy; *fig.* bezceremonialny; '**~·ly** bez ceregieli *lub* ceremonii

blur [blɜː] (**-*rr*-**) *v/t.* zamazywać ⟨-zać⟩; *phot. TV* zniekształcać ⟨-cić⟩; *znaczenie* zamazywać ⟨-zać⟩; *v/i.* zamazywać ⟨-zać⟩się; *wspomnienia* zacierać ⟨zatrzeć⟩ się

blurt [blɜːt]: ~ ***out*** wyrzucać ⟨-cić⟩ z siebie

blush [blʌʃ] **1.** rumieniec *m*; zaczerwienienie *n* się; **2.** ⟨za⟩czerwienić się, ⟨za⟩rumienić się

blus·ter ['blʌstə] *wiatr*: ⟨za⟩huczeć; *fig.* wydzierać ⟨wydrzeć⟩ się; wychwalać się

Blvd *skrót pisany*: ***Boulevard*** bulwar

BMI [biː em 'waɪ] *skrót*: ***Body Mass Index*** wskaźnik masy ciała

BMX [biː em 'eks] *skrót*: ***bicycle motocross*** kros *m* rowerowy; rower *m* BMX; ~ **bike** rower *m* BMX

BO[biː 'əʊ] *skrót* → ***body odo(u)r***

boar [bɔː] *zo.* dzik *m*; knur *m*

board [bɔːd] **1.** deska *f*; tablica *f*; tektura *f*, karton *m*; plansza *f* (*do gry*); stół *m* konferencyjny; utrzymanie *n*, wyżywienie *n*; komisja *f*; zarząd *m*, dyrekcja *f*; (*w sporcie*) deska *f* (*surfingowa*); *naut.* burta *f*; **2.** *v/t.* wykładać ⟨wyłożyć⟩ deskami, ⟨o⟩szalować, ⟨o⟩deskować; wchodzić ⟨wejść⟩ na pokład (*G*); ⟨za⟩kwaterować, utrzymywać ⟨-mać⟩; ~ ***a train*** wsiadać ⟨wsiąść⟩ do pociągu; *v/i.* stołować się, mieszkać; '**~·er** gość *m* (*w pensjonacie itp.*), stołownik *m*; mieszkaniec *m* (-nka *f*) internatu; '**~ game** gra *f* planszowa; '**~·ing card** *aviat.* karta *f* wstępu (*do samolotu*); '**~·ing house** pensjonat *m*; '**~·ing school** internat *m*; ~ **of 'di·rec·tors** *econ.* dyrekcja *f*, rada *f* nadzorcza; **♀ of 'Trade** *Brt.* Ministerstwo *n* Handlu, *Am.* Izba *f* Handlowa; '**~·walk** *zwł. Am.* promenada *f* nad brzegiem

boast [bəʊst] **1.** przechwałki *pl.*, chełpliwość *f*; **2.** *v/i.* (***of, about***) chwalić się (*I*), przechwalać się (*I*); *v/t.* szczycić się, być dumnym z (*G*)

boat [bəʊt] łódź *f*, łódka *f*; szalupa *f*; statek *m*

bob [bɒb] **1.** dygnięcie *n*, dyg *m*; krótka fryzura *f*; *Brt. hist.* F szyling *m*; **2.** (**-*bb*-**) *v/t. włosy*: krótko obcinać ⟨obciąć⟩; *v/i.* dygać ⟨-gnąć⟩

bob·bin ['bɒbɪn] szpula *f*, szpulka *f*; *electr.* cewka *f*

bob·by ['bɒbɪ] *Brt.* F *policjant*: bobby *m*

bob·sleigh ['bɒbsleɪ] *sport*: bobslej *m*

bode [bəʊd] *pret. od* ***bide***

bod·ice ['bɒdɪs] stanik *m*; góra *f* (*sukni*)

bod·i·ly ['bɒdɪlɪ] cieleśnie

bod·y ['bɒdɪ] ciało *n*; zwłoki *pl.*; korpus *m*; organizacja *f*, stowarzyszenie *n*; gromada *f*, grupa *f*, ciało *n*; główna część *f*; *wodny* zbiornik *m*; *mot.* karoseria *f*, nadwozie *n*; '**~·guard** ochrona *f*, F ochroniarz *m*; '**~ o·do(u)r** (*skrót*: ***BO***) nieprzyjemny zapach *m* ciała; '**~ stock·ing** *ubiór*: body *n*; '**~·work** *mot.* karoseria *f*, nadwozie *n*

Boer ['bɔː] Bur *m*; *attr.* burski

bog [bɒg] bagno *n*, mokradło *n*

bo·gus ['bəʊgəs] fałszywy, podrabiany

boil[1] [bɔɪl] *med.* czyrak *m*, ropień *m*

boil[2] [bɔɪl] **1.** *v/t.* ⟨za-, u⟩gotować; *v/i.* ⟨za-, u⟩gotować się; ⟨za⟩wrzeć, ⟨za⟩kipieć; **2.** gotowanie *n* się, wrzenie *n*; '**~·er** bojler *m*, kocioł *m*; '**~·er suit** kombinezon *m*; '**~·ing point** punkt *m lub* temperatura *f* wrzenia; *fig.* punkt *m* krytyczny

bois·ter·ous ['bɔɪstərəs] hałaśliwy, ło-

B

buzerski, wrzaskliwy
bold [bəʊld] dzielny, śmiały; bezczelny; *kolory*: krzykliwy, rażący; *print.* wytłuszczony, pogrubiony; ***as ~ as brass*** F bezczelny na całego
bol·ster ['bəʊlstə] **1.** wałek *m* (*na tapczanie*); **2.** ***~ up*** podtrzymywać ⟨-mać⟩
bolt [bəʊlt] **1.** śruba *f*, sworzeń *m*; rygiel *m*; uderzenie *n* błyskawicy, błyskawica *f*; ***make a ~ for*** rzucić się do (*G*); **2.** *adv.* sztywno wyprostowany; **3.** ⟨za⟩ryglować, zamykać ⟨-knąć⟩; F *jedzenie* pochłaniać ⟨-łonąć⟩; *v/i.* uciekać ⟨uciec⟩, ⟨s⟩płoszyć się; *koń*: ponosić ⟨ponieść⟩
bomb [bɒm] **1.** bomba *f*; ***the ~*** bomba *f* atomowa; **2.** ⟨z⟩bombardować; **'~·er** *aviat.* bombowiec *m*
bom·bard [bɒm'bɑːd] ⟨z⟩bombardować
bomb|·proof ['bɒmpruːf] zabezpieczony przed bombami *lub* bombardowaniem; **'~·shell** bomba *f*; *fig.* zupełne zaskoczenie *n*
bond [bɒnd] wiązanie *n* (*też chem.*), więź *f*; *econ.* obligacja *f*, zobowiązanie *n* zapłaty; ***in ~*** w składzie wolnocłowym, pod zamknięciem celnym; **~·age** ['bɒndɪdʒ] niewola *f*, poddaństwo *n*
bonds [bɔndz] *pl.* więzy *pl.* (*przyjaźni*)
bone [bəʊn] kość *f*, ość *f*; ***bones*** *pl.* kości *pl.*, szczątki *pl.*; ***~ of contention*** kość *f* niezgody; ***have a ~ to pick with s.o.*** mieć z kimś do pomówienia; ***make no ~ about s.th.*** nie obwijać czegoś w bawełnę, nie robić tajemnicy z czegoś; **2.** usuwać ⟨-nąć⟩ kości *lub* ości
bon·fire ['bɒnfaɪə] ognisko *n*
bonk [bɒŋk] *Brt. sl.* (*mieć stosunek płciowy*) pieprzyć (się)
bon·net ['bɒnɪt] czepek *m*; *mot.* maska
bon·ny ['bɒnɪ] *zwł. Szkoc.* (***-ier, -iest***) śliczny, urodziwy; *dziecko*: zdrowe
bo·nus ['bəʊnəs] *econ.* premia *f*, gratyfikacja *f*
bon·y ['bəʊnɪ] (***-ier, -iest***) kościsty, ościsty
boo [buː] *int.* uu!; *theat.* ***~ off the stage***, (*w piłce nożnej*) ***~ off the park*** *kogoś* wygwizdać
boobs [buːbz] F *pl.* cycki *pl.*, cyce *pl.*
boo·by ['buːbɪ] F przygłup
book [bʊk] **1.** książka *f*, księga *f*; zeszyt *m*; wykaz *m*, lista *f*; ⟨za⟩rejestrować; ⟨za⟩księgować; *bilet* ⟨za⟩rezerwować; (*w sporcie*) dawać ⟨dać⟩ ostrzeżenie; ***~ in*** *zwł. Brt.* ⟨za⟩meldować się; ***~ in at*** zatrzymywać ⟨-mać⟩ się w (*L*); ***~ed up*** zarezerwowany, zajęty, wykupiony; **'~·case** biblioteczka *f*; **'~·ing** rezerwacja *f*; *sport*: ostrzeżenie *n*; **'~·ing clerk** pracownik *m* (-nica *f*) działu rezerwacji; **'~·ing of·fice** (*dział firmy*) rezerwacja *f*; kasa *f* (*biletowa*); **'~·keep·er** księgowy *m* (-wa *f*); **'~·keep·ing** księgowość *f*; **~·let** ['bʊklɪt] broszura *f*; **'~·mark(·er)** zakładka *f*; **'~·sell·er** księgarz *m*; **'~·shelf** (*pl.* ***-shelves***) regał *m* *lub* półka *f* na książki; **'~·shop**, *zwł. Brt.*, **'~·store** *Am.* księgarnia *f*
boom[1] [buːm] **1.** *econ.* boom *m*, prosperity *f*, świetność *f* gospodarcza, dobra koniunktura *f*; **2.** osiągać ⟨-gnąć⟩ okres boomu
boom[2] [buːm] *naut.* bom *m*; wysięgnik *m* (*też mikrofonowy itp.*)
boom[3] [buːm] ⟨za⟩huczeć, ⟨za⟩buczeć
boor [bʊə] cham(ka *f*) *m*, chamidło *n*; **~·ish** ['bʊərɪʃ] chamowaty, chamski
boost [buːst] **1.** zwiększać ⟨-szyć⟩, wzmagać ⟨wzmóc⟩; *napięcie prądu* wzmacniać ⟨-mocnić⟩; *fig.* pokrzepiać ⟨-pić⟩, dodawać ⟨dodać⟩ odwagi; **2.** pokrzepienie *n*; wzmocnienie *n*, zwiększenie *n*
boot[1] [buːt] but *m* (wysoki); *Brt. mot.* bagażnik *m*; **~·ee** ['buːtiː] but *m* (*zakrywający kostkę*); ⚠ *nie* ***but***
boot[2] [buːt]: ***~*** (***up***) *komp.* uruchamiać ⟨-chomić⟩ system
boot[3] [buːt]: ***to ~*** w dodatku, na dodatek
booth [buːð] budka *f*; stragan *m*; kabina *f*
'boot·lace sznurowadło *n*
boot·y ['buːtɪ] łup *m*
booze [buːz] F **1.** popijać ⟨popić⟩; **2.** popijawa *f*, pijatyka *f*; alkohol *m*, F wóda *f*
bor·der ['bɔːdə] **1.** obramowanie *n*, ramka *f*; lamówka *f*; granica *f*; rabat(k)a *f*; **2.** ogradzać ⟨ogrodzić⟩, opasywać ⟨-sać⟩, obramowywać ⟨-mować⟩; graniczyć (***on*** z *I*)
bore[1] [bɔː] **1.** średnica *f* otworu; *tech.* kaliber *m*; *mil.* przewód *m* lufy; **2.** wiercić, rozwiercać
bore[2] [bɔː] **1.** nudziarz *m* (-ara *f*); *zwł. Brt.* nudziarstwo *n*; **2.** nudzić, zanudzać ⟨-dzić⟩; ***be ~d*** nudzić się
bore[3] [bɔː] *pret. od* ***bear***

bore·dom ['bɔːdəm] nuda *f*
bor·ing ['bɔːrɪŋ] nudny
born [bɔːn] *p.p. od* ***bear²*** urodzony
borne [bɔːn] *p.p. od* ***bear²*** znosić
bo·rough ['bʌrə] dzielnica *f* (*miejska*); okręg *m* miejski (*Brt. wyborczy*)
bor·row ['bɒrəʊ] *od kogoś* pożyczać ⟨-czyć⟩, wypożyczać ⟨-czyć⟩
Bos·ni·a and Hercegovina Bośnia i Hercegowina
bos·om ['bʊzəm] piersi *pl.*; *fig.* łono *m*
boss [bɒs] F **1.** boss *m*, szef(owa *f*) *m*; **2.** *v/t.* rozkazywać ⟨-zać⟩; *v/i.* ***~ about, ~ around*** szarogęsić się, panoszyć się; **'~·y** F (***-ier, -iest***) apodyktyczny, despotyczny
bo·tan·i·cal [bə'tænɪkl] botaniczny; **bot·a·ny** ['bɒtənɪ] botanika *f*
botch [bɒtʃ] F **1.** *też* ***~-up*** knot *m*; chałtura *f*; **2.** ⟨s⟩knocić, ⟨s⟩paprać
both [bəʊθ] oba, obie, obaj, oboje; ***~ ... and ...*** zarówno ..., jak i ..., tak ..., jak ...
both·er ['bɒðə] **1.** kłopot *m*, przykrość *f*, nieprzyjemność *f*; **2.** *v/t.* kłopotać; niepokoić; przeszkadzać; *v/i.* naprzykrzać ⟨-rzyć⟩ się, sprawiać ⟨-wić⟩ kłopot; ***don't ~!*** nie sprawiaj sobie kłopotu!, nie zawracaj sobie głowy!
bot·tle ['bɒtl] **1.** butelka *f*, flaszka *f*; **2.** ⟨za⟩butelkować; **'~ bank** *Brt.* pojemnik *m* na szkło; **'~·neck** *fig.* wąskie gardło *n*
bot·tom ['bɒtəm] dno *n*; spód *m*; dół *m*; F siedzenie *n*, pupa *f*; ***be at the ~ of*** znajdować się na *lub* w dole (*G*); ***get to the ~ of s.th.*** docierać ⟨-trzeć⟩ do sedna sprawy
bough [baʊ] konar *m*, gałąź *f*
bought [bɔːt] *pret. i p.p. od* ***buy***
boul·der ['bəʊldə] głaz *m*, otoczak *m*
bounce [baʊns] **1.** odbijać ⟨-bić⟩ (się); podskakiwać ⟨-koczyć⟩, skakać ⟨skoczyć⟩; odskakiwać ⟨-koczyć⟩; F *czek*: nie mieć pokrycia, wrócić; **2.** odbicie się; podskok *m*, odskok *m*, skok *m*; **'bounc·ing** energiczny, *dziecko*: dziarski
bound¹ [baʊnd] **1.** *pret. i p.p. od* ***bind***; **2.** w drodze (***for*** do *G*), do (*G*)
bound² [baʊnd]: *zw.* ***~s*** granica *f*, limit *m*
bound³ [baʊnd] **1.** skok *m*, podskok *m*; **2.** odbijać ⟨-bić⟩ (się); podskakiwać ⟨-koczyć⟩, skakać ⟨-koczyć⟩
bound·a·ry ['baʊndərɪ] granica *f*
'bound·less bezgraniczny
boun|·te·ous ['baʊntɪəs], **~·ti·ful** ['baʊntɪfl] szczodrobliwy, hojny, szczodry
boun·ty ['baʊntɪ] szczodrobliwość *f*, hojność *f*, szczodrość *f*; premia *f*, nagroda *f*
bou·quet [bʊ'keɪ] bukiet *m* (*też wina*)
bout [baʊt] *boks*: starcie *n*, walka *f*
bou·tique [buː'tiːk] butik *m*, boutique *m*
bow¹ [baʊ] **1.** ukłon *m*, skłon *m*; **2.** *v/i.* kłaniać ⟨ukłonić⟩ się, skłaniać ⟨-łonić⟩ się (***to*** przed *I*); *fig.* chylić się, skłaniać się (***to*** przed *I*); *v/t.* wyginać ⟨-giąć⟩, ⟨wy⟩giąć
bow² [baʊ] *naut.* dziób *m*
bow³ [bəʊ] łuk *m*; *muz.* smyczek *m*; kokarda *f*
bow·els ['baʊəlz] *anat. pl.* jelita *pl.*, kiszki *pl.*
bowl¹ [bəʊl] miska *f* (*też klozetowa*), miseczka *f*; donica *f*; cukiernica *f*; miednica *f*; główka *f* (*fajki*); czarka *f* (*łyżki*)
bowl² [bəʊl] **1.** (*w grze w kręgle*) kula *f*; (*w grze w krykieta*) piłka *f*; **2.** rzucać ⟨-cić⟩ kulą *lub* piłką
bow-leg·ged ['bəʊlegd] krzywonogi, o kabłąkowatych nogach
'bowl·er gracz *m* w kręgle, kręglarz *m*; (*w grze w krykieta*) (*gracz rzucający piłkę*); **~ 'hat** melonik *m*
'bowl·ing (gra w) kręgle *pl.*
box¹ [bɒks] pudełko *n*, pudło *n*; karton *m*; kaseta *f*, szkatułka *f*; puszka *f*; skrzynka *f* (*pocztowa*); obudowa *f* (*maszynowa*); (*dla konia*) boks *m*; *Brt.* budka *f* (*telefoniczna*); *theat.* loża *f*; *jur.* ława *f* (*przysięgłych, oskarżonych*); (*dla samochodów*) koperta *f*
box² [bɒks] **1.** *sport*: boks; F ***~ s.o.'s ears*** natrzeć komuś uszu; **2.** F ***a ~ on the ear*** palnięcie *n* w ucho; **'~·er** bokser *m*; **'~·ing** boks *m*, boksowanie *n*; **'☊·ing Day** *Brt.* drugi dzień Bożego Narodzenia
box³ [bɒks] *bot.* bukszpan *m*; *attr.* bukszpanowy
'box| num·ber numer *m* oferty (*w gazecie*); numer *m* skrzynki pocztowej; **'~ of·fice** kasa *f* teatralna
boy [bɔɪ] chłopiec *m*
boy·cott ['bɔɪkɒt] **1.** ⟨z⟩bojkotować; **2.** bojkot *m*

B

'boy|·friend chłopiec *m*, sympatia *f*, przyjaciel *m*; **~·hood** ['bɔɪhʊd] chłopięctwo *n*; **'~·ish** chłopięcy; **'~ scout** skaut *m*, harcerz *m*
BPhil [biː 'fɪl] *skrót*: ***Bachelor of Philosophy*** (*niższy stopień naukowy*) licencjat *m*
BR [biː 'ɑː] *skrót*: ***British Rail*** (*brytyjskie koleje*)
bra [brɑː] stanik *m*, biustonosz *m*
brace [breɪs] **1.** *tech.* wspornik *m*, podpora *f*; aparat *m* korekcyjny (*na zęby*); nawias *m* kwadratowy; **2.** *tech.* usztywniać ⟨-nić⟩, wzmacniać ⟨wzmocnić⟩
brace·let ['breɪslɪt] bransoletka *f*
brac·es ['breɪsɪz] *pl. Brt.* szelki *pl.*
brack·et ['brækɪt] *tech.* wspornik *m*, podpora *f*; nawias *m*; *podatkowy* przedział *m*; ***lower income ~*** grupa *f* w przedziale o niższych dochodach
brack·ish ['brækɪʃ] słonawy
brag [bræg] (***-gg-***) chwalić się, przechwalać się (***about, of*** o *L*); **~·gart** ['brægət] samochwał *m*, pyszałek *m*
braid [breɪd] **1.** *zwł. Am.* warkocz *m*; galon *m*; **2.** *zwł. Am.* ⟨za⟩pleść, zaplatać ⟨zapleść⟩; obszywać ⟨-szyć⟩ galonem
brain [breɪn] *anat.* mózg *m*; *często* **~s** *fig.* umysł *m*, głowa *f*; **'~s trust** *Brt.*, **'~ trust** *Am.* grupa *f* ekspertów; **'~·wash** *komuś* ⟨z⟩robić pranie mózgu; **'~·wash·ing** pranie *n* mózgu; **'~wave** olśnienie *n*, oświecenie *n*; **'~·y** (***-ier, -iest***) F niegłupi, rozgarnięty
brake [breɪk] **1.** *tech.* hamulec *m*; **2.** ⟨za⟩hamować; **'~·light** *mot.* światło *n* hamowania
bram·ble ['bræmbl] *bot.* jeżyna *f*
bran [bræn] otręby *pl.*
branch [brɑːntʃ] **1.** gałąź *f*, konar *m*; dziedzina *f*; specjalizacja *f*; filia *f*, oddział *m*; **2.** rozgałęziać ⟨-zić⟩ się
brand [brænd] **1.** *econ.* marka *f*, gatunek *m*, rodzaj *m*; znak *m* towarowy; piętno *n*; **2.** ⟨na⟩piętnować; ⟨o⟩znakować
bran·dish ['brændɪʃ] wymachiwać, wywijać
'brand| name *econ.* znak *m* towarowy; nazwa *f* firmowa; **~'new** nowy jak spod igły
bran·dy ['brændɪ] brandy *n*, winiak *m*, koniak *m*
brass [brɑːs] mosiądz *m*; *mus.* instrumenty *pl.* dęte blaszane, F blacha *f*; F bezczelność *f*; **~ 'band** orkiestra *f* dęta
bras·sière ['bræsɪə] biustonosz *m*, stanik *m*
brat [bræt] *pej.* bachor *m*
Bratislava Bratysława *f*
brave [breɪv] **1.** (***-er, -est***) odważny, dzielny, nieustraszony; **2.** stawić czoło, przeciwstawiać się odważnie;
brav·er·y ['breɪvərɪ] odwaga *f*, śmiałość *f*, nieustraszoność *f*
brawl [brɔːl] **1.** bijatyka *f*; bójka *f*; **2.** wszczynać ⟨-cząć⟩ bójkę
brawn·y ['brɔːnɪ] (***-ier, -iest***) muskularny, atletyczny
bray [breɪ] **1.** ryk *m* (*osła*); **2.** ⟨za⟩ryczeć; *samochody*: hałasować
bra·zen ['breɪzn] bezwstydny, bezczelny
Bra·zil [brə'zɪl] Brazylia *f*; **Bra·zil·ian** [brə'zɪljən] **1.** brazylijski; **2.** Brazylijczyk *m* (-jka *f*)
breach [briːtʃ] **1.** wyłom *m*, luka *f*; *fig.* naruszenie *n*, zerwanie *n*; *mil.* przerwanie *n* (*frontu*); **2.** przerywać ⟨-rwać⟩ (front), dokonywać ⟨-nać⟩ wyłomu
bread [bred] chleb *m*; ***brown ~*** razowiec *m*; ***know which side one's ~ is buttered*** F wiedzieć, z czego można wyciągnąć korzyść
breadth [bredθ] szerokość *f*
break [breɪk] **1.** złamanie *n*; luka *f*; przerwa *f* (*Brt. też w szkole*), pauza *f*; zmiana *f*, przemiana *f*; świt *m*; ***bad ~*** F pech *m*; ***lucky ~*** F szczęście *n*, pomyślność *f*; ***give s.o. a ~*** F dawać ⟨dać⟩ komuś szansę; ***take a ~*** ⟨z⟩robić przerwę; ***without a ~*** bez przerwy; **2.** (***broke, broken***) *v/t.* ⟨z-, po-, ob-, wy⟩łamać; ⟨s-, po⟩tłuc; ⟨z⟩niszczyć, ⟨ze⟩psuć; *zwierzę* oswoić, obłaskawiać ⟨-wić⟩, *konia* ujeżdżać ⟨ujeździć⟩ (*też* ***~ in***); *prawo* naruszać ⟨-szyć⟩, *przepisy, szyfr itp.* ⟨z⟩łamać; *złą wiadomość* przekazywać ⟨-zać⟩; *v/i.* ⟨z-, po-, ob-, wy⟩łamać się; ⟨s-, po⟩tłuc się; ⟨z⟩niszczyć się, ⟨ze⟩psuć się; *pogoda*: zmieniać ⟨-nić⟩ się nagle; zalewać ⟨-lać⟩ się; ***~ away*** uciekać ⟨uciec⟩; odrywać ⟨oderwać⟩ się; ***~ down*** załamywać ⟨-mać⟩ (się); *drzwi* wyważać ⟨-żyć⟩; (*do domu*) włamywać ⟨-mać⟩ się; ⟨ze⟩psuć (się); *mot.* mieć awarię; *chemikalia* rozkładać ⟨rozłożyć⟩; ***~ in*** (*do domu*) włamywać ⟨-mać⟩ się; wtrącać ⟨wtrącić⟩ się; przyuczać ⟨-czyć⟩; ***~ off*** zrywać ⟨zerwać⟩;

przerywać ⟨-rwać⟩; odłamywać ⟨-mać⟩ (się); **~ out** wybuchać ⟨-chnąć⟩; *skóra*: pokrywać ⟨-kryć⟩ się; uciekać ⟨uciec⟩ (**of** z *G*); **~ through** przebijać ⟨-bić⟩ się; dokonywać ⟨-nać⟩ wyłomu; **~ up** rozbijać ⟨-bić⟩ (się); zakańczać ⟨-kończyć⟩; *małżeństwo itp.*: rozstawać ⟨-stać⟩ się; *Brt.* zaczynać ⟨-cząć⟩ wakacje; **'~·a·ble** łamliwy, kruchy; **~·age** ['breɪkɪdʒ] stłuczenie *n*, szkoda *f*, zniszczenie *n*; **'~·a·way** rozdzielenie *n*, separacja *f*, odłączenie *n*; *attr.* frakcyjny

'break·down załamanie *n* się (*też fig.*); *tech.* awaria *f*, uszkodzenie *n*, defekt *m*; **nervous ~** załamanie *n* nerwowe; **'~ lor·ry** *Brt. mot.* pojazd *m* pomocy drogowej; **'~ ser·vice** *mot.* pomoc *f* drogowa; **'~ truck** *Brt. mot.* pojazd *m* pomocy drogowej

break·fast ['brekfəst] śniadanie *f*; **have ~** → **have**; ⟨z⟩jeść śniadanie

'break|·through *fig.* przełom *m*, wyłom *m*; **'~·up** rozpad *m*, dezintegracja *f*

breast [brest] pierś *f*; *fig.* serce *n*; **make a clean ~ of s.th.** wyznawać ⟨-nać⟩ coś; **'~·stroke** (*w sporcie*) styl *m* klasyczny

breath [breθ] oddech *m*, dech *m*; **be out of ~** być bez tchu; **waste one's ~** mówić na próżno

breath·a|·lyse *Brt.*, **~·lyze** *Am.* ['breθəlaɪz] F dmuchać ⟨dmuchnąć⟩ w balonik; **'~·lys·er** *Brt.*; **'♀·lyz·er** *Am. TM* miernik *m* zawartości alkoholu we krwi, alkomat *m*, F balonik *m*

breathe [bri:ð] oddychać ⟨odetchnąć⟩

'breath|·less bez tchu, zadyszany; **'~·tak·ing** zapierający dech

bred [bred] *pret. i p.p. od* **breed**

breech·es ['brɪtʃɪz] *pl.* bryczesy *pl.*

breed [bri:d] **1.** rasa *f*, odmiana *f*; **2.** (**bred**) *v/t. rośliny, zwierzęta* hodować; *v/i.* rozmnażać ⟨-nożyć⟩ się; **'~·er** hodowca *m*; zwierzę *n* hodowlane; *phys.* reaktor *m* powielający; **'~·ing** rozmnażanie *n*; hodowla *f*; chów *m*

breeze [bri:z] wietrzyk *m*, bryza *f*

breth·ren ['breðrən] *zwł. rel., pl.* bracia *pl.*, *przest.* brać *f*

brew [bru:] *piwo* warzyć (się); *herbatę* parzyć (się), zaparzać (się); **'~·er** piwowar *m*; **~·er·y** ['brʊərɪ] browar *m*

bri·ar ['braɪə] → **brier**

bribe [braɪb] **1.** łapówka *f*; **2.** dawać ⟨dać⟩ łapówkę, przekupywać ⟨-pić⟩; **brib·er·y** ['braɪbərɪ] przekupstwo *n*, łapownictwo *n*

brick [brɪk] **1.** cegła *f*; *Brt.* klocek *m*; **'~·lay·er** murarz *m*; **'~·yard** cegielnia *f*

brid·al ['braɪdl] ślubny, małżeński, zaślubiony

bride [braɪd] panna *f* młoda; **~·groom** ['braɪdgrʊm] pan *m* młody; **~s·maid** ['braɪdzmeɪd] druhna *f*

bridge [brɪdʒ] **1.** most *m*, pomost *m*; *naut.*, *med.* mostek *m*; brydż *m*; **2.** kłaść ⟨położyć⟩ most nad (*I*); *fig.* pokonywać ⟨-nać⟩, przerzucić pomost nad (*I*)

bri·dle ['braɪdl] **1.** uzda *f*; **2.** zakładać ⟨założyć⟩ uzdę; *fig.* ⟨o⟩kiełznać; **'~ path** ścieżka *f* do jazdy konnej

brief [bri:f] **1.** zwięzły, krótki; **2.** ⟨po⟩instruować, ⟨po⟩informować; **'~·case** aktówka *f*

briefs [bri:fs] *pl.* majtki *pl.*, *męskie* slipy *pl.*, *damskie* figi *pl.*

bri·er ['braɪə] *bot.* dzika róża *f*, szypszyna *f*

bri·gade [brɪ'geɪd] *mil.* brygada

bright [braɪt] jasny, jaskrawy; błyszczący; żywy, pogodny; bystry; **~·en** ['braɪtn] *v/t. też* **~en up** rozjaśniać ⟨-śnić⟩; ożywiać ⟨-wić⟩; *v/i. też* **~en up** rozpogadzać ⟨-godzić⟩ się, rozjaśniać ⟨-śnić⟩ się; **'~·ness** jasność *f*, jaskrawość *f*, żywość *f*; pogoda *f*; bystrość *f*

bril|·liance, ~·lian·cy ['brɪljəns, -jənsɪ] blask *m*, połysk *m*; *fig.* błyskotliwość *f*, lotność *f*; **'~·liant** **1.** błyszczący; połyskujący; błyskotliwy, lotny; **2.** brylant *m*

brim [brɪm] **1.** brzeg *f*, krawędź *f*; rondo *n*; **2.** (**-mm-**) napełniać ⟨-nić⟩ po brzegi *lub* do pełna; **~·ful**(**l**) ['brɪmfʊl] pełny, napełniony po brzegi

brine [braɪn] solanka *f*

bring [brɪŋ] (**brought**) przyprowadzać ⟨-dzić⟩, przynosić ⟨-nieść⟩, przywozić ⟨-wieźć⟩; *kogoś* skłaniać ⟨skłonić⟩ (**to do s.th.** aby coś zrobił); *coś* doprowadzać (**to** do *G*); **~ about** ⟨s⟩powodować, wywoływać ⟨-łać⟩; **~ back** zwracać ⟨zwrócić⟩; oddawać ⟨oddać⟩; **~ forth** wydawać ⟨wydać⟩; **~ off** wykonywać ⟨-nać⟩; **~ on** ⟨s⟩powodować; **~ out** *produkt* wypuszczać ⟨-uścić⟩; *cechy* wywoływać ⟨-łać⟩, wyzwalać ⟨-wolić⟩; **~ round** ⟨o⟩cucić; przekonywać ⟨-nać⟩; **~ up** wychowywać ⟨-wać⟩; dawać dobre wyniki; wspominać⟨wspomnieć⟩; *zwł. Brt. jedzenie* zwracać ⟨zwrócić⟩

brink [brɪŋk] brzeg *f*; krawędź (*też fig.*)

brisk [brɪsk] energiczny, dynamiczny; *powietrze*: świeży

bris·tle ['brɪsl] **1.** szczecina *f*; szczeciniasty zarost *m*; **2.** *też* **~ up** ⟨z-, na⟩jeżyć się, ⟨na⟩stroszyć się; być najeżonym; tętnić; '**bris·tly** (**-*er*, -*iest***) szczeciniasty

Brit [brɪt] F Angol *m*

Brit·ain ['brɪtn] Brytania *f*

Brit·ish ['brɪtɪʃ] brytyjski; ***the* ~** *pl.* Brytyjczycy *pl.*; '**~ Isles** *pl.* Wyspy Brytyjskie *pl.*

Brit·on ['brɪtn] Brytyjczyk *m* (-jka *f*)

brit·tle ['brɪtl] kruchy, łamliwy, delikatny

broach [brəʊtʃ] *temat* poruszać ⟨-szyć⟩, omawiać ⟨-mówić⟩

broad [brɔːd] szeroki; *dzień*: biały; *mrugnięcie itp.*: wyraźny; *dowcip*: rubaszny; ogólny; rozległy, szeroki; liberalny; '**~·cast 1.** (***-cast*** *lub* ***-casted***) nadawać⟨-dać⟩, ⟨wy⟩emitować, przekazywać ⟨-zać⟩; **2.** (*w telewizji, radiu*) program *m*, audycja *f*; '**~·cast·er** spiker(ka *f*) *m*; **~·en** ['brɔːdn] rozszerzać ⟨-rzyć⟩ (się), poszerzać; ⟨-rzyć⟩ (się); '**~ jump** *Am.* (*w sporcie*) skok *m* w dal; **~'mind·ed** tolerancyjny, liberalny

bro·cade [brə'keɪd] brokat *m*

bro·chure ['brəʊʃə] broszura *f*, prospekt *m*, folder *m*

brogue [brəʊg] *mocny skórzany* but *m*; dialekt *m* (*zwł. irlandzki*)

broil [brɔɪl] *zwł. Am.* → ***grill*** 1

broke [brəʊk] **1.** *pret. od* ***break***; **2.** F bez grosza przy duszy, goły; **bro·ken** ['brəʊkən] **1.** *p.p. od* ***break***; **2.** złamany, stłuczony; zepsuty; rozbity (*też fig.*); *angielski itp.*: łamany; **brok·en·'heart·ed**: ***be* ~** mieć złamane serce

bro·ker ['brəʊkə] *econ.* makler *m*, broker *m*, agent *m*

bron·chi·tis [brɒŋ'kaɪtɪs] *med.* zapalenie *n* oskrzeli, bronchit *m*

bronze [brɒnz] **1.** (*metal*) brąz *m*; **2.** z brązu; w kolorze brązu, brązowy

brooch [brəʊtʃ] broszka *f*

brood [bruːd] **1.** wylęg *m*, lęg *m*; *attr.* lęgowy; **2.** wysiadywać (*jaja*) (*też fig.*)

brook [brʊk] strumień *m*

broom [bruːm, brʊm] miotła *f*; '**~·stick** kij *m* do miotły

Bros. [brɒs] *skrót*: ***brothers*** bracia *pl.* (*w nazwach firm*)

broth [brɒθ] bulion *m*, rosół *m*

broth·el ['brɒθl] burdel *m*, dom *m* publiczny

broth·er ['brʌðə] brat *m*; **~(*s*) *and sister*(*s*)** rodzeństwo *n*; **~·hood** *rel.* ['brʌðəhʊd] braterstwo *n*; **~-in-law** ['brʌðərɪnlɔː] (*pl.* ***brothers-in-law***) szwagier *m*; '**~·ly 1.** *adj.* braterski; **2.** *adv.* po bratersku

brought [brɔːt] *pret. i p.p. od* ***bring***

brow [braʊ] brew *f*; czoło *n*; grzbiet *m* (*wzgórza*); '**~·beat** (***browbeat, browbeaten***) zastraszać ⟨-szyć⟩, onieśmielać ⟨-lić⟩

brown [braʊn] **1.** brązowy; **2.** *kolor*: brąz *m*; **3.** ⟨z⟩brązowieć; ⟨pod-, przy⟩rumienić

browse [braʊz] przeglądać ⟨-dnąć⟩, ⟨po⟩szperać; *zwierzę*: ⟨po⟩skubać (*trawę*), paść się

bruise [bruːz] **1.** siniak *m*; obicie *n*; **2.** ⟨po⟩siniaczyć; *owoce* ⟨po⟩obijać

brunch [brʌntʃ] (*późne obfite śniadanie*)

brush [brʌʃ] **1.** szczotka *f*, szczoteczka *f*; pędzel *m*; *lisia* kita *f*, ogon *m*; scysja *f*, zwada *f*; otarcie *n* się; zarośla *pl.*; **2.** ⟨wy⟩szczotkować; zamiatać ⟨-mieść⟩; ocierać ⟨otrzeć⟩ się; **~ *against*** ocierać ⟨otrzeć⟩ się o (*A*); **~ *away*, ~ *off*** odrzucać ⟨-cić⟩; odsuwać ⟨-sunąć⟩ na bok; **~ *aside*, ~ *away*** ⟨z⟩ignorować; **~ *up*** *znajomość języka* ⟨pod⟩szlifować, odświeżać ⟨-żyć⟩; ***give one's English a* ~ *up*** podszlifować swój angielski; '**~·wood** chrust *m*, zarośla *pl.*

brusque [bruːsk] szorstki, opryskliwy

Brus·sels Bruksela *f*

Brus·sels sprouts [brʌsl'spraʊts] *bot. pl.* brukselka *f*

bru·tal ['bruːtl] brutalny; **~·i·ty** [bruː'tælətɪ] brutalność *f*

brute [bruːt] **1.** brutalny; **2.** zwierzę *n*, zwierz *m*, *fig.* F bydlę *n*, bydlak *m*

BS [biː 'es] *Brt. skrót*: ***British Standard*** Norma *f* Brytyjska; *Am.* → ***BSc***

BSc [biː es 'siː] *Brt. skrót*: ***Bachelor of Science*** licencjat *m* (*nauk przyrodniczych*)

BST [biː es 'tiː] *Brt. skrót*: ***British***

Summer Time czas letni w Wielkiej Brytanii
BT [biː 'tiː] *skrót*: ***British Telecom*** Brytyjski Telecom (*brytyjska firma telekomunikacyjna*)
BTA [biː tiː 'eɪ] *skrót*: ***British Tourist Authority*** (*brytyjski urząd ds. turystyki*)
bub·ble ['bʌbl] **1.** bańka *f*, pęcherzyk *m*; **2.** musować; ⟨za⟩kipieć; ⟨za⟩wrzeć, ⟨za⟩kipieć (*też fig.*)
buck[1] [bʌk] **1.** (*pl.* ***buck, bucks***) kozioł *m* (*antylopy, jelenia*); **2.** *v/i.* brykać ⟨bryknąć⟩, podskakiwać ⟨-koczyć⟩
buck[2] [bʌk] *Am.* (*dolar*) F dolec *m*, zielony *m*
buck·et ['bʌkɪt] kubeł *m*, wiadro *n*, ceber *m*; *tech.* czerpak *m*
buck·le ['bʌkl] **1.** klamra *f*; sprzączka *f*, zapinka *f*; **2.** *też* ~ ***up*** zapinać ⟨-piąć⟩ (*na klamrę lub sprzączkę*); ~ ***on*** przypinać ⟨-piąć⟩ (się)
'buck·skin zamsz *m*, ircha *f*
bud [bʌd] **1.** *bot.* pączek *m*, pąk *m*; *fig.* pączek *m*, zarodek *m*; **2.** (***-dd-***) puszczać ⟨puścić⟩ pączki
Bu·da·pest Budapeszt *m*
bud·dy ['bʌdɪ] *Am.* F koleś *m*, facet *m*
budge [bʌdʒ] *v/i.* ruszać ⟨ruszyć⟩ się (*z miejsca*); *v/t.* ruszać ⟨ruszyć⟩ (*z miejsca*)
bud·ger·i·gar ['bʌdʒərɪgɑː] *zo.* papużka *f* falista
bud·get ['bʌdʒɪt] budżet *m*, *parl.* plan *m* budżetowy
bud·gie ['bʌdʒɪ] *zo.* F → ***budgerigar***
buff [bʌf] F *w złożeniach*: entuzjasta *m* (-tka *f*) (*G*), znawca *m* (-czyni *f*) (*G*)
buf·fa·lo ['bʌfələʊ] (*pl.* ***-loes, -los***) bawół *m*; (*w USA*) bizon *m*
buff·er ['bʌfə] *tech.* bufor *m*; zderzak *m*
buf·fet[1] ['bʌfɪt] uderzać ⟨-rzyć⟩ o (*A*) *lub* w (*A*); ~ ***about*** obijać ⟨obić⟩ (się)
buf·fet[2] ['bʌfɪt] bufet *m*; kredens *m*
bug [bʌg] **1.** *zo.* pluskwa *f*; *Am. zo.* owad *m*, robak *m*; F (*ukryty mikrofon*) pluskwa *f*; *komp.* F (*błąd w programie*) pluskwa *f*; **2.** (***-gg-***) F zakładać ⟨-łożyć⟩ pluskwę (*podsłuch*); F wnerwiać ⟨-wić⟩; '~**·ging de·vice** F pluskwa *f*; urządzenie *n* podsłuchowe; '~**·ging op·e·ration** akcja *f* założenia podsłuchu
bug·gy ['bʌgɪ] *mot.* buggy *m* (*pojazd do jazdy po wydmach dla rozrywki*); *Am.* wózek *m* dziecięcy
bu·gle ['bjuːgl] trąbka *f* sygnałowa, sygnałówka *f*
build [bɪld] **1.** (***built***) ⟨z⟩budować; **2.** budowa *f* (*ciała*), figura *f*; '~**·er** budowniczy *m*, F budowlaniec *m*
build·ing ['bɪldɪŋ] budowa *f*, budowanie *n*; budynek *m*; *attr.* budowlany, ... budowy; '~ **site** plac *m* budowy
built [bɪlt] *pret. i p.p. od* ***build*** 1; ~-'**in** wbudowany; ~-'**up**: ***~-up area*** teren *m lub* obszar *m* zabudowany
bulb [bʌlb] *bot.* cebulka *f*, bulwa *f*; *electr.* żarówka *f*
Bul·gar·i·a Bułgaria *f*
bulge [bʌldʒ] **1.** wybrzuszenie *n*, wypukłość *f*; **2.** wybrzuszać ⟨-szyć⟩ (się); wypychać ⟨-pchać⟩
bulk [bʌlk] duża ilość *f*, masa *f*; większość *f*; *econ.* towar *m* masowy; ***in*** ~ *econ.* luzem, w całości; '~**·y** (***-ier, -iest***) zajmujący wiele miejsca; mało poręczny
bull [bʊl] *zo.* byk *m*, samiec *m* (*słonia*); '~**·dog** *zo.* buldog *m*
bull|·doze ['bʊldəʊz] ⟨z⟩niwelować; *fig.* ⟨z⟩równać; '~**·doz·er** *tech.* buldożer *m*, spycharka *f*
bul·let ['bʊlɪt] nabój *m*, kula *f*
bul·le·tin ['bʊlɪtɪn] biuletyn *m*; '~ **board** tablica *f* ogłoszeń
'bul·let-proof kuloodporny
bul·lion ['bʊljən] sztaby *pl.* kruszcu (*złota, srebra*)
bul·lock ['bʊlək] *zo.* wół *m*
'bull's-eye: ***hit the*** ~ trafić w dziesiątkę
bul·ly ['bʊlɪ] **1.** (*osoba znęcająca się nad słabszymi*); **2.** ⟨s⟩tyranizować
bul·wark ['bʊlwək] przedmurze *n* (*też fig.*); szaniec *m*; *naut.* nadburcie *n*
bum[1] [bʌm] *Am.* F **1.** włóczęga *m*, tramp *m*; nierób *m*, obibok *m*; **2.** włóczyć się; obijać się
bum[2] [bʌm] *Brt.* F zadek *m*, tyłek *m*
'bum·ble·bee *zo.* trzmiel *m*
bump [bʌmp] **1.** uderzenie *n*, stuknięcie *n*; guz *m* (*na kolanie itp.*); nierówność *f*, wybój *m*; **2.** *v/t.* uderzyć, stuknąć; *v/i.* podskakiwać; ~ ***into*** natykać ⟨-knąć⟩ się na (*A*)
'bump·er zderzak *m*; ~**-to-'**~ zderzak do zderzaka, zderzak w zderzak
'bump·y (***-ier, -est***) wyboisty

B

bun [bʌn] słodka bułka *f*; kok *m* (*na głowie*)
bunch [bʌntʃ] wiązka *f*, pęk *m*; wiązanka *f*, bukiet *m*; F paczka *f*, grupa *f*; ***a ~ of grapes*** kiść *f* winogron; ***~ of keys*** pęk *m* kluczy
bun·dle ['bʌndl] **1.** tłumok *m*, tobół *m*; wiązka *f* (*drew*); pakunek *m*; **2.** *v/t. lub* ***~ up*** ⟨z⟩wiązać razem
bun·ga·low ['bʌŋgələʊ] bungalow *m*, domek *m* parterowy
bun·gee [bən'dʒiː] lin(k)a *f* elastyczna; ***~ jumping*** (*skoki z bardzo dużej wysokości na elastycznej linie*)
bun·gle ['bʌŋgl] **1.** partanina *f*; **2.** ⟨s⟩partaczyć, ⟨s⟩paprać
bunk [bʌŋk] koja *f*; **'~ bed** łóżko *n* piętrowe
bun·ny ['bʌnɪ] króliczek *m*
buoy [bɔɪ] *naut.* **1.** boja *f*; **2.** ***~ up*** *fig.* wspierać ⟨wesprzeć⟩ duchowo
bur·den ['bɜːdn] **1.** ciężar *m*; obciążenie *n*; **2.** obciążać ⟨-żyć⟩, obarczać ⟨-czyć⟩ brzemieniem
bu·reau ['bjʊərəʊ] (*pl.* ***-reaux*** [-rəʊz], ***-reaus***) *Brt.* sekretarzyk *m*, biurko *n*; *Am.* komoda *f*, komódka *f* (*zwł. z lustrem*); biuro *n*, urząd *m*
bu·reauc·ra·cy [bjʊə'rɒkrəsɪ] biurokracja *f*
burg·er ['bɜːgə] *gastr.* hamburger *m*
bur|·glar ['bɜːglə] włamywacz *m* (-ka *f*); **~·glar·ize** ['bɜːgləraɪz] *Am.* → ***burgle***; **~·glar·y** ['bɜːglərɪ] włamanie *n*; **~·gle** ['bɜːgl] włamywać ⟨-mać⟩ się do (*G*)
bur·i·al ['berɪəl] pogrzeb *m*, pochówek *m*
bur·ly ['bɜːlɪ] (***-ier, -iest***) krzepki, zwalisty
burn [bɜːn] **1.** *med.* oparzenie *n*; przypalenie *n*; **2.** (***burnt*** *lub* ***burned***) ⟨po-, s⟩parzyć; ***~ down*** spalić (się); ***~ up*** spalić (się); rozpalać ⟨-lić⟩ (się); **'~·ing** płonący (*też fig.*)
burnt [bɜːnt] *pret. i p.p. od* ***burn*** 2
burp [bɜːp] F beknąć; ***she ~ed*** odbiło jej się, beknęła; ***he ~ed the baby*** sprawił, że dziecku odbiło się
bur·row ['bʌrəʊ] **1.** nora *f*; **2.** ⟨wy-, za⟩grzebać (się)
burst [bɜːst] **1.** pękanie *n*; pęknięcie *n*; rozrywanie *n* się; *fig.* wybuch *m*; **2.** (***burst***) *v/i.* pękać ⟨-knąć⟩; rozrywać ⟨-zerwać⟩ się; eksplodować; ***~ in on*** *lub* ***upon*** wpadać ⟨wpaść⟩ na (*A*); ***~ into tears*** wybuchać ⟨-nąć⟩ płaczem; ***~ out of*** *fig.* wypadać ⟨-paść⟩ z (*G*); *v/t.* przebijać ⟨-bić⟩
bur·y ['berɪ] *kogoś* ⟨po⟩grzebać, pochować; *coś* zakopywać ⟨-pać⟩
bus [bʌs] (*pl.* ***-es, -ses***) autobus *m*; **'~ driv·er** kierowca *m* autobusu
bush [bʊʃ] krzak *m*, krzew *m*
bush·el ['bʊʃl] buszel *m* (*Brt. 36,37 l, Am. 35,24 l*)
'bush·y (***-ier, -iest***) krzaczasty
busi·ness ['bɪznɪs] sprawa *f*; zadanie *n*; interes *m*, biznes *m*; działalność *f*; transakcja *f* handlowa; interesy *pl.*; przedsiębiorstwo *n*, firma *f*; branża *f*; *attr.* służbowy, handlowy, gospodarczy; ***~ of the day*** porządek *m* dnia; ***on ~*** służbowo; ***you have no ~ doing*** (*lub* ***to do***) ***that*** nie masz żadnego prawa tak robić; ***that's none of your ~*** to nie twoja sprawa; → ***mind*** 2; **'~ hours** *pl.* godziny *pl.* pracy; **'~·like** rzeczowy; **'~·man** (*pl.* ***-men***) biznesmen *m*; **'~ trip** podróż *f* służbowa; **'~·wom·an** (*pl.* ***-women***) kobieta *f* interesu, bizneswoman *f*
'bus stop przystanek *m* autobusowy
bust[1] [bʌst] biust *m*
bust[2] [bʌst] F: ***go ~*** ⟨s⟩plajtować
bus·tle ['bʌsl] **1.** ożywienie *n*, krzątanina *f*; **2.** ***~ about*** krzątać się, uwijać się
bus·y ['bɪzɪ] **1.** (***-ier, -iest***) zajęty (*też* ***at*** *I*); *ulica*: ruchliwy; *dzień*: pracowity *Am. tel.* zajęty; **2.** ***~ o.s. with*** zajmować się (*I*); **'~·bod·y** wścibski *m* (-ka *f*); **'~ sig·nal** *Am. tel.* sygnał *m* zajęty
but [bʌt, bət] **1.** *cj.* ale, lecz; ależ, jednak; ***~ then*** z drugiej strony; ***he could not ~ laugh*** musiał się wówczas roześmiać; **2.** *prp.* oprócz, prócz, poza; ***all ~ him*** wszyscy oprócz niego; ***the last ~ one*** przedostatni; ***nothing ~*** wyłącznie, jedynie; ***~ for*** gdyby nie; **3.** *adv.* tylko, dopiero; ***all ~*** prawie
butch·er ['bʊtʃə] **1.** rzeźnik *m*; **2.** ⟨za⟩szlachtować, zarzynać ⟨zarżnąć⟩ (*też fig.*)
but·ler ['bʌtlə] kamerdyner *m*
butt[1] [bʌt] **1.** kolba *f* (*broni*); uchwyt *m*; niedopałek *m*, F pet *m*; uderzenie *n* głową; **2.** uderzać ⟨-rzyć⟩ głową; ***~ in*** F ⟨w⟩mieszać się (***on*** do *G*)
butt[2] [bʌt] beczka *f*, baryłka *f*
but·ter ['bʌtə] **1.** masło *n*; **2.** ⟨po⟩sma-

rować masłem; '~·**cup** *bot.* jaskier *m*; '~·**fly** *zo.* motyl *m*

but·tocks ['bʌtəks] *pl.* pośladki *pl.*, F *lub zo.* zad *m*

but·ton ['bʌtn] **1.** guzik *m*; przycisk *m*; plakietka *f*, znaczek *m* (*z nazwiskiem*); **2.** *zw.* ~ ***up*** zapinać ⟨-piąć⟩ na guziki; '~·**hole** dziurka *f* (*od guzika*)

but·tress ['bʌtrɪs] *arch.* przypora *f*; ***flying*** ~ łuk *m* przyporowy

bux·om ['bʌksəm] dorodny, postawny

buy [baɪ] **1.** kupno *n*, nabytek *m*; **2.** (***bought***) *v/t.* kupować ⟨kupić⟩ (***of, from*** od *G*, z *G*, ***at*** u *G*), nabywać ⟨nabyć⟩; ~ ***out*** *lub* ***up*** wykupywać ⟨wykupić⟩; '~·**er** nabywca *m*, kupujący *m* (-ca *f*)

buzz [bʌz] **1.** brzęczenie *n*; szmer *m* (*głosów*); **2.** *v/i.* ⟨za⟩brzęczeć, ⟨za⟩szemrać; ~ ***off!*** *Brt.* F odwal się!

buz·zard ['bʌzəd] *zo.* myszołów *m*

buzz·er ['bʌzə] *electr.* brzęczyk *m*

by [baɪ] **1.** *prp. przestrzeń*: przy (*L*), u (*G*), obok (*G*); *czas*: do (*G*), aż do (*G*) (***be back by 9.30*** wróć do 9.30); *pora dnia*: za (*G*), w ciągu (*G*) (~ ***day*** w ciągu dnia); *przyczyna*: przez (*A*) (***done*** ~ ***Mary*** zrobione przez Mary); *środek transportu*: ~ ***bus*** autobusem; ~ ***rail*** koleją; ~ ***letter*** listownie; na (*A*) (~ ***the dozen*** na tuziny); na (*L*), według (*G*) (~ ***my watch*** na moim zegarku *lub* według mojego zegarka); z (~ ***nature*** z natury); *autor*: (napisane) przez (*G*) (***a play*** ~ ***Osborne*** sztuka Osborne'a); *porównania wielkości*: o (*A*) (~ ***an inch*** o cal); *math.* (pomnożone) przez (*A*), razy (***2*** ~ ***4*** 2 razy 4); *math.* (*podzielone*) przez (*A*) (***2*** ~ ***4*** 2 przez 4); **2.** *adv.* obok (*G*), w pobliżu (*G*) (***go*** ~ przechodzić obok (*G*), *czas*: przelatywać); na bok (***put*** ~ odłożyć na bok); ~ ***and large*** ogólnie, generalnie

by... [baɪ] uboczny, boczny

bye [baɪ] *int.* F: ~-'**bye** do widzenia!, cześć!

'**by|-e·lec·tion** wybory *pl.* uzupełniające; '~·**gone** **1.** miniony, były; **2.** ***let ~gones be ~gones*** co było, to było; '~·**pass** **1.** obwodnica *f*; *med.* bypass *m*, połączenie *n* omijające; **2.** omijać ⟨ominąć⟩; unikać ⟨-knąć⟩; '~-**prod·uct** produkt *m* uboczny; '~·**road** boczna droga *f*; '~·**stand·er** przechodzeń *m*, świadek *m*

byte [baɪt] *komp.* bajt *m*

'**by|·way** boczna droga *f*; '~·**word** symbol *m*, uosobienie *n*; ***be a ~word for*** uosabiać (*A*)

C

C *skrót pisany*: ***Celsius*** C, Celsjusza; ***centigrade*** w skali stustopniowej *lub* Celsjusza

c *skrót pisany*: ***cent*(*s*)** cent *m lub pl.*; ***century*** w., wiek(u); ***circa*** ca., ok., około; ***cubic*** sześcienny

cab [kæb] taksówka *f*; kabina *f* (*ciężarówki, dźwigu*); *rail.* przedział *m* maszynisty, budka *f* maszynisty; dorożka *f*

cab·a·ret ['kæbəreɪ] kabaret *m*

cab·bage ['kæbɪdʒ] *bot.* kapusta *f*

cab·in ['kæbɪn] *naut.*, *aviat.* kabina *f*; *naut.* kajuta *f*; chata *f*

cab·i·net ['kæbɪnɪt] szafka *f*, witryna *f*, gablota *f*; *pol.* gabinet *m*; '~-**mak·er** stolarz *m*; '~ **meet·ing** spotkanie *n* gabinetu

ca·ble ['keɪbl] **1.** *electr.* kabel *m*, przewód *m*; **2.** ⟨za-, prze⟩telegrafować; *pieniądze* przesyłać ⟨-słać⟩ telegraficznie; *TV* połączyć kablem; '~ **car** wagon (*kolejki linowej*) *m*; '~·**gram** telegram *m* (*zagraniczny*); '~ **rail·way** kolej *m* linowa; ~ '**tel·e·vi·sion**, ~ **TV** [- tiː 'viː] telewizja *f* kablowa

'**cab|rank**, '~·**stand** postój *m* taksówek *lub* dorożek

cack·le ['kækl] **1.** gdakanie *n*; *ludzki* rechot *m*; **2.** ⟨za⟩gdakać; ⟨za⟩rechotać

cac·tus ['kæktəs] *bot.* (*pl.* ***-tuses, -ti*** ['kæktaɪ]) kaktus *m*

CAD [siː eɪ 'diː, kæd] *skrót*: ***computer-aided design*** CAD (*projektowanie wspomagane komputerowo*)

ca·dence ['keɪdəns] *mus.* kadencja *f*; rytm *m* (*mowy*)

C

ca·det [kə'det] *mil.* kadet *m*
caf·é, caf·e ['kæfeɪ] kawiarnia *f*, kafejka *f*
caf·e·te·ri·a [kæfɪ'tɪərɪə] bar *m* samoobsługowy; bufet *m*; stołówka *f*
cage [keɪdʒ] **1.** klatka *f*; kabina *f* (*windy*); **2.** zamykać ⟨-knąć⟩ w klatce
Cai·ro Kair *m*
cake [keɪk] **1.** ciasto *n*, ciastko *n*, tort *m*; tabliczka *f* (*czekolady*), kostka *f* (*mydła*); **2.** *~d with mud* oblepiony błotem
CAL [kæl] *skrót*: ***computer-aided*** *lub* ***-assisted learning*** CAL (*nauczanie wspomagane komputerowo*)
ca·lam·i·ty [kə'læmɪtɪ] katastrofa *f*, klęska *f*, zguba *f*
cal·cu|·late ['kælkjʊleɪt] *v/t.* liczyć, ⟨ob-, wy⟩liczyć, kalkulować; *Am.* F przypuszczać ⟨-puścić⟩, sądzić; *v/i.* *~late on* liczyć na (*A*); **~·la·tion** [kælkjʊ'leɪʃn] obliczenie *n*, wyliczenie *n*, kalkulacja *f* (*też fig.*, *econ.*); namysł *m*; **~·la·tor** ['kælkjʊleɪtə] kalkulator *m*
cal·en·dar ['kælɪndə] kalendarz *m*
calf[1] [kɑːf] (*pl.* ***calves*** [kɑːvz]) łydka *f*
calf[2] [kɑːf] (*pl.* ***calves*** [kɑːvz]) cielę *n*; '**~·skin** skóra *f* cielęca
cal·i·bre *zwł. Brt.*, **cal·i·ber** *Am.* ['kælɪbə] kaliber *m*
Cal·i·for·nia Kalifornia *f*
call [kɔːl] **1.** wołanie *n*; *tel.* rozmowa *f*; głos *m*; wezwanie *n* (***to*** do *G*); powołanie *n* (***for*** na *A*); *krótka* wizyta *f* (***on s.o.*** u kogoś); *econ.* popyt *m*, zapotrzebowanie *n* (***for*** na *A*); potrzeba *f*; ***on ~*** na żądanie; ***be on ~*** *lekarz*: być dostępnym na wezwanie; ***make a ~*** ⟨za⟩dzwonić; składać ⟨złożyć⟩ wizytę (***on s.o.*** komuś); **2.** *v/t.* ⟨za⟩wołać, wzywać ⟨wezwać⟩; *tel.* ⟨za⟩dzwonić do (*G*); nazywać ⟨nazwać⟩; powoływać ⟨-łać⟩ (***to*** na *A*); *uwagę* ⟨s⟩kierować; ***be called*** nazywać się; ***~ s.o. names*** przezywać ⟨-zwać⟩ kogoś; *v/i.* wołać, wzywać ⟨wezwać⟩; *tel.* ⟨za⟩dzwonić; przybywać ⟨-być⟩ w odwiedziny (***on s.o.*** do kogoś, ***at s.o.'s*** [***house***] do czyjegoś domu); ***~ at a port*** zawijać ⟨zawinąć⟩ do portu; ***~ collect*** *Am. tel.* ⟨za⟩dzwonić na koszt odbiorcy; ***~ for*** wymagać, domagać się; *pomoc* wzywać ⟨wezwać⟩; *paczkę* zgłaszać ⟨zgłosić⟩ się po (*A*); ***~ on*** zwracać się do *kogoś* (***for*** o *A*), wzywać *kogoś* (***to do s.th.*** aby coś zrobił); ***~ on s.o.*** odwiedzać ⟨-wiedzić⟩ kogoś; '**~ box** *Brt.* budka *f* telefoniczna; '**~·er** telefonujący *m* (-ca *f*), rozmówca *m* (-czyni *f*); gość *m*; '**~ girl** (*prostytutka wzywana telefonicznie*) call girl *f*; '**~-in** *Am.* → ***phone-in***; '**~·ing** powołanie *n*; zawód *m*
cal·lous ['kæləs] *skóra*: zgrubiały; *fig.* gruboskórny
calm [kɑːm] **1.** spokojny; **2.** spokój *m*; cisza *f*; **3.** *często* ***~ down*** uspokajać ⟨-koić⟩ się
cal·o·rie ['kælərɪ] kaloria *f*; ***rich*** *lub* ***high in ~s*** *pred.* wysokokaloryczny; ***low in ~s*** *pred.* niskokaloryczny; → ***high-calorie, low-calorie***; '**~-con·scious** zwracający uwagę na ilość kalorii
calve [kɑːv] ⟨o⟩cielić się
calves [kɑːvz] *pl. od* ***calf***[2]
CAM [siː eɪ 'em, kæm] *skrót*: ***computer-aided manufacture*** (*produkcja wspomagana komputerowo*)
cam·cor·der ['kæmkɔːdə] (*kamera wideo zintegrowana z urządzeniem nagrywającym*) kamkorder *m*
came [keɪm] *pret. od* ***come***
cam·el ['kæml] *zo.* wielbłąd *m*
cam·e·o ['kæmɪəʊ] (*pl.* ***-os***) kamea *f*; *theat.*, *film*: krótka scenka *f* (*dla znanego aktora*)
cam·e·ra ['kæmərə] kamera *f*; aparat *m* fotograficzny
cam·o·mile ['kæməmaɪl] *bot.* rumianek *m*; *attr.* rumiankowy
cam·ou·flage ['kæmʊflɑːʒ] **1.** kamuflaż *m*; **2.** ⟨za⟩maskować
camp [kæmp] **1.** obóz *m*; **2.** obozować; ***~ out*** biwakować
cam·paign [kæm'peɪn] **1.** *mil.*, *fig.* kampania *f*; *pol.* walka *f* wyborcza; **2.** *fig.* prowadzić ⟨przeprowadzić⟩ kampanię (***for*** za *I*, ***against*** przeciwko *D*)
camp| 'bed *Brt.*, **~ 'cot** *Am.* łóżko *n* składane *lub* polowe; '**~er** (**van**) samochód *m* kempingowy; '**~·ground**, '**~·site** kemping *m*, pole *n* namiotowe
cam·pus ['kæmpəs] campus *m*, miasteczko *n* uniwersyteckie
can[1] [kæn, kən] *v/aux.* (*pret.* ***could***; *z przeczeniem*: ***cannot, can't***) móc; potrafić, umieć
can[2] [kæn, kən] **1.** puszka *f*; konserwa *f* (*w puszce*); kanister *m*; blaszanka *f*; **2.**

(**-nn-**) ⟨za⟩puszkować, ⟨za⟩konserwować

Can·a·da ['kænədə] Kanada *f*; **Ca·na·di·an** [kə'neɪdjən] **1.** kanadyjski; **2.** Kanadyjczyk *m* (-jka *f*)

ca·nal [kə'næl] kanał *m* (*też anat.*)

ca·nar·y [kə'neərɪ] *zo.* kanarek *m*

can·cel ['kænsl] (*zwł. Brt.* **-ll-**, *Am.* **-l-**) odwoływać ⟨-łać⟩; anulować, unieważniać ⟨-nić⟩; odmawiać ⟨odmówić⟩; ⟨s⟩kasować; ***be ~(l)ed*** nie odbywać ⟨odbyć⟩ się

can·cer ['kænsə] *med.* rak *m*; ♋ *znak Zodiaku*: Rak *m*; ***he/she is*** (***a***) ♋ on(a) jest spod znaku Raka; **~·ous** ['kænsərəs] rakowaty, rakowy

can·did ['kændɪd] szczery, otwarty

can·di·date ['kændɪdət] kandydat *m* (-ka *f*) (***for*** na *A*), ubiegający *m* się (-ca *f*) (***for*** o *A*)

can·died ['kændɪd] kandyzowany

can·dle ['kændl] świeca *f*; świeczka *f*; ***burn the ~ at both ends*** łapać wiele srok za ogon na raz; **'~·stick** lichtarz *m*, świecznik *m*

can·do(u)r ['kændə] szczerość *f*, otwartość *f*

C&W [siː ənd 'dʌbljuː] *skrót*: ***country and western*** (muzyka) country

can·dy ['kændɪ] **1.** cukier *m* gruboktystaliczny; *Am.* słodycze *pl.*; **2.** kandyzować; **'~floss** *Brt.* wata *f* cukrowa; **'~ store** sklep *m* ze słodyczami

cane [keɪn] *bot.* trzcina *f*

ca·nine ['keɪnaɪn] psi

canned [kænd] puszkowy, puszkowany; konserwowy, konserwowany; **~ 'fruit** konserwowane owoce *pl.*

can·ne·ry ['kænərɪ] *zwł. Am.* fabryka *f* konserw

can·ni·bal ['kænɪbl] kanibal *m*

can·non ['kænən] armata *f*, działo *n*; *mil.* lotnicze działko *f* szybkostrzelne

can·not ['kænɒt] → ***can***[1]

can·ny ['kænɪ] (***-ier, -iest***) przebiegły, sprytny

ca·noe [kə'nuː] **1.** kanoe *n*, canoe *n*, kajak *m*; **2.** pływać w kajaku *lub* kanoe

can·on ['kænən] kanon *m*

'can o·pen·er *Am.* otwieracz *m* do konserw

can·o·py ['kænəpɪ] baldachim *m*

cant [kænt] żargon *m*; frazesy *pl.*

can't [kɑːnt] *zamiast* ***cannot*** → ***can***[1]

can·tan·ker·ous [kæn'tæŋkərəs] zrzędliwy, gderliwy

can·teen [kæn'tiːn] *zwł. Brt.* stołówka; *mil.* kantyna *f*; *mil.* manierka; zestaw *pl.* sztućców

can·ter ['kæntə] **1.** kłus *m*; **2.** kłusować, iść kłusem

can·vas ['kænvəs] brezent *m*, płótno *n* żeglarskie; płótno *n*, obraz *m* na płótnie; *naut.* żagle *pl.*

can·vass ['kænvəs] **1.** *pol.* kampania *f* wyborcza; *econ.* akcja *f* reklamowa; akwizycja *f*; werbowanie *n*; **2.** *v/t. opinię* ⟨z⟩badać; ⟨z⟩werbować; *pol. głosy* zdobywać ⟨-być⟩; *v/i. pol.* ⟨prze⟩prowadzić kampanię wyborczą

can·yon ['kænjən] kanion *m*

cap [kæp] **1.** czapka *f*; *kąpielowy, pielęgniarski* czepek *m*; nasadka *f*; kapsel *m*, nakrętka *f*; **2.** (***-pp-***) nakrywać ⟨-ryć⟩, przykrywać ⟨-ryć⟩; *fig.* ⟨u⟩koronować; przewyższać ⟨-szyć⟩, przebijać ⟨-bić⟩

ca·pa|·bil·i·ty [keɪpə'bɪlətɪ] zdolność *f*; **~·ble** ['keɪpəbl] zdolny (***of*** do *G*); ***be ~ble of doing s.th.*** móc *lub* potrafić coś zrobić

ca·pac·i·ty [kə'pæsətɪ] pojemność *f*; możliwość *f*, zdolność *f*, zdatność *f*; *tech.* wydajność *f*, przepustowość *f*; ***in my ~ as*** w ramach moich obowiązków jako, jako

cape[1] [keɪp] przylądek *m*, cypel *m*

cape[2] [keɪp] peleryna *f*

Cape Town Kapsztad *m*

ca·per ['keɪpə] **1.** *bot.* kapar *m*; psota *f*, figlarny podskok *m* **2.** podskakiwać (*z radości*)

ca·pil·la·ry [kə'pɪlərɪ] *anat.* naczynie *n* włosowate

cap·i·tal ['kæpɪtl] **1.** stolica *f*; wersalik *m*, wielka litera *f*; **2.** główny, podstawowy, zasadniczy; *econ.* kapitałowy, inwestycyjny; *jur. przestępstwo*: karany śmiercią; **~ 'crime** przestępstwo *n* zagrożone karą śmierci

cap·i·tal|·is·m ['kæpɪtəlɪzəm] kapitalizm *m*; **~·ist** ['kæpɪtəlɪst] kapitalistyczny; **~·ize** ['kæpɪtəlaɪz] *econ.* ⟨z⟩kapitalizować, ⟨z⟩gromadzić kapitał; zaopatrywać ⟨-trzyć⟩ w kapitał; ***~ize on*** odcinać ⟨-ciąć⟩ kupony od (*G*)

cap·i·tal|'let·ter *print.* wielka litera *f*,

C

wersalik *m*; ~ **'pun·ish·ment** *jur.* kara *f* śmierci

ca·pit·u·late [kə'pɪtjʊleɪt] ⟨s⟩kapitulować (**to** przed *I*)

ca·pri·cious [kə'prɪʃəs] kapryśny

Cap·ri·corn ['kæprɪkɔːn] *znak Zodiaku:* Koziorożec *m*; **he/she is (a)** ~ on(a) jest spod znaku Koziorożca

cap·size [kæp'saɪz] przewracać ⟨-wrócić⟩ (się) do góry dnem

cap·sule ['kæpsjuːl] *pharm.* kapsułka *f*; *astr.* kapsuła *f*; kabina *f* (*statku kosmicznego*)

cap·tain ['kæptɪn] kapitan *m*; dowódca *m*

cap·tion ['kæpʃn] podpis *m* (*pod rysunkiem, zdjęciem*); napis *m* (*na filmie*)

cap|·ti·vate ['kæptɪveɪt] *fig.* porywać ⟨porwać⟩, urzekać ⟨urzec⟩; **~·tive** ['kæptɪv] **1.** pojmany, schwytany; zniewolony; *balon:* na uwięzi; **hold ~tive** pojmować ⟨pojmać⟩ do niewoli; **2.** jeniec *m*; **~·tiv·i·ty** [kæp'tɪvətɪ] niewola *f*

cap·ture ['kæptʃə] **1.** pojmanie *n*, schwytanie *n*, ujęcie *n*; **2.** pojmować ⟨-jąć⟩, schwytać, pojmować ⟨pojąć⟩; *naut.* ⟨s⟩kaperować

car [kɑː] samochód *m*, auto *n*; *tramwajowy, kolejowy* wagon *m*; gondola *f*, kosz *m*; kabina *f* (*windy*); **by ~** samochodem

car·a·mel ['kærəmel] (*cukier*) karmel *m*, cukier *m* palony; (*cukierek*) karmelek *m*

car·a·van ['kærəvæn] karawana *f*; *Brt.* przyczepa *f* kempingowa; ⚠ *nie* ***karawan***; **'~ site** pole *n* kempingowe (*dla przyczep*)

car·a·way ['kærəweɪ] *bot.* kminek *m*

car·bine ['kɑːbaɪn] *mil.* karabin *m*

car·bo·hy·drate [kɑːbəʊ'haɪdreɪt] *chem.* węglowodan *m*

'car bomb bomba *f* w samochodzie

car·bon ['kɑːbən] *chem.* węgiel *m*; ~ **'cop·y** kopia *f*, przebitka *f*; **'~ (pa·per)** kalka *f* (*maszynowa*)

car·bu·ret·(t)or [kɑːbə'retə] *tech.* gaźnik *m*

car·case *Brt.*, **car·cass** ['kɑːkəs] tusza *f* (*zwierzęcia*); resztki *pl.*

car·cin·o·genic [kɑːsɪnə'dʒenik] *med.* rakotwórczy

card [kɑːd] karta *f*; *pocztowa* kartka *f*; ***play ~s*** grać w karty; ***have a ~ up one's sleeve*** *fig.* trzymać asa w rękawie; **'~·board** tektura *f*, karton *m*; **'~·board box** pudełko *n* z tektury

car·di·ac ['kɑːdɪæk] *med.* sercowy; ~ **'pace·mak·er** *med.* stymulator *m* serca

car·di·gan ['kɑːdɪgən] *rozpinany* sweter *m*

car·di·nal ['kɑːdɪnl] **1.** główny; zasadniczy; kardynalny; szkarłatny; **2.** *rel.* kardynał *m*; ~ **'num·ber** *math.* liczba *f* kardynalna; liczebnik *m* główny

'card|·in·dex kartoteka *f*; **'~ phone** automat *m* telefoniczny na karty; **'~-sharp·er** szuler *m*, kanciarz *m*

'car dump złomowisko *n* samochodów, F szrot *m*

care [keə] **1.** troska *f*; ostrożność *f*; opieka *f*, nadzór *m*; ***medical ~*** opieka *f* medyczna; ***take ~ of*** ⟨za⟩troszczyć się o (*A*); uważać na (*A*); ***with ~!*** ostrożnie!; **2.** mieć ochotę; ~ ***about*** ⟨za⟩troszczyć się o (*A*); ~ ***for*** lubić; opiekować się; mieć ochotę; ***I don't ~*** F nie obchodzi mnie to; ***I couldn't ~ less*** wszystko mi jedno

ca·reer [kə'rɪə] **1.** kariera *f*; działalność *f* zawodowa; **2.** zawodowy; **3.** ⟨po⟩gnać, ⟨po⟩mknąć

ca'reers| ad·vice *Brt.* poradnictwo *n* zawodowe; ~ **ad·vi·sor** *Brt.* doradca *m* w sprawach zawodu; ~ **guid·ance** *Brt.* poradnictwo *n* zawodowe; ~ **of·fice** *Brt.* biuro *m* porad zawodowych; ~ **of·fic·er** *Brt.* doradca *m* w sprawach zawodu

'care|·free beztroski; **'~·ful** staranny; troskliwy, uważny; dokładny, skrupulatny; ***be ~ful!*** uważaj!; **'~·less** niedbały, niestaranny; nieostrożny, lekkomyślny

ca·ress [kə'res] **1.** pieszczota *f*; **2.** ⟨po⟩pieścić

'care|·tak·er dozorca *m* (-czyni *f*); **'~·worn** zatroskany, udręczony

'car|·fare *Am.* opłata *f* za przejazd (*autobusem*); **'~ fer·ry** prom *m* samochodowy

car·go ['kɑːgəʊ] (*pl.* **-goes,** *Am. też* **-gos**) ładunek *m*, *econ.* fracht *m*

'car hire *Brt.* wynajem *m* samochodów

Car·ib·be·an Sea Morze Karaibskie *n*

car·i·ca|·ture ['kærɪkətjʊə] **1.** karykatura *f*; **2.** ⟨s⟩karykaturować; **~·tur·ist**

['kærɪkətjʊərɪst] karykaturzysta *m* (-tka *f*)
car·ies ['keəriːz] *med. też* ***dental ~*** próchnica *m*
'car me·chan·ic mechanik *m* samochodowy
car·mine ['kɑːmaɪn] **1.** karminowy; **2.** karmin *m*
car·na·tion [kɑː'neɪʃn] *bot.* goździk *m*; ⚠ *nie* ***karnacja***
car·ni·val ['kɑːnɪvl] karnawał *m*
car·niv·o·rous [kɑː'nɪvərəs] mięsożerny
car·ol ['kærəl] kolęda *f*
carp [kɑːp] *zo.* (*pl.* ***carp*** *lub* **-s**) karp *m*
'car park *zwł. Brt.* parking *m* samochodowy
car·pen·ter ['kɑːpɪntə] cieśla *m*, stolarz *m*
car·pet ['kɑːpɪt] **1.** dywan *m*; wykładzina *f*; ***sweep s.th. under the ~*** tuszować coś, kryć coś w tajemnicy; **2.** wykładać ⟨wyłożyć⟩ dywanem
'car| phone telefon *m* w samochodzie; **'~ pool** (*grupa ludzi korzystająca przy dojazdach do pracy z jednego prywatnego samochodu*); **'~ pool(·ing) ser·vice** bank *m* przewozów; **'~·port** wiata *f* na samochód (*w funkcji garażu*); **'~ rent·al** *Am.* wynajem *m* samochodów; **'~ re·pair shop** warsztat *m* naprawy samochodów
car·riage ['kærɪdʒ] transport *m*, przewóz *m*; koszt *m* transportu; powóz *m*; *Brt. rail.* wagon *m* osobowy; postawa *f*; **'~·way** *Brt. mot.* jezdnia *f* (*o jednym kierunku ruchu*); pas *m* ruchu
car·ri·er ['kærɪə] przewoźnik *m*, spedytor *m*; bagażnik *m* rowerowy; *mil.* lotniskowiec *m*; **'~ bag** *Brt.* torba *f* (*na zakupy*)
car·ri·on ['kærɪən] padlina *f*, ścierwo *n*
car·rot ['kærət] *bot.* marchew *f*, marchewka *f*
car·ry ['kærɪ] *v/t.* nosić ⟨zanieść⟩; *ciężar* dźwigać; przewozić ⟨przewieźć⟩, ⟨prze⟩transportować; mieć *lub* nosić (*przy sobie*); *chorobę* przenosić ⟨-nieść⟩; *wniosek* przyjmować ⟨-jąć⟩, uchwalać ⟨-lić⟩; *korzyść* przynosić ⟨-nieść⟩; *artykuł* zamieszczać ⟨-mieścić⟩; *v/i. głos*: nieść się; *działo*: nieść; ***be carried*** zostawać ⟨-stać⟩ przyjętym *lub* uchwalonym; ***~ the day*** wygrywać ⟨-grać⟩; ***~ s.th. too far*** przesadzać ⟨-dzić⟩ z czymś; ***get carried away*** *fig.* dawać ⟨dać⟩ się ponieść; ***~ forward, over*** *econ.* sumę na następną stronę przenieść; ***~ on*** kontynuować; *biznes itp.* prowadzić; ***~ out, ~ through*** wykonywać ⟨-nać⟩, przeprowadzać ⟨-dzić⟩; **'~·cot** *Brt.* (*torba do noszenia dziecka*) nosidło *n*
cart [kɑːt] **1.** wózek *m*; wóz *m*; *Am.* wózek *m* na zakupy; ***put the ~ before the horse*** odwracać kota ogonem; **2.** przewozić ⟨-wieźć⟩ (*wozem, wózkiem*)
car·ti·lage ['kɑːtɪlɪdʒ] *ant.* chrząstka *f*
car·ton ['kɑːtən] karton *m*
car·toon [kɑː'tuːn] karykatura *f*; film *m* rysunkowy; **~·ist** [kɑː'tuːnɪst] karykaturzysta *m* (-tka *f*)
car·tridge ['kɑːtrɪdʒ] *mil.* nabój *m* (*też do pióra*); *phot.* kaseta; pojemnik *m* (*z tonerem lub tuszem*); wkładka *f* gramofonowa
'cart·wheel: ***turn ~s*** ⟨z⟩robić gwiazdę
carve [kɑːv] *mięso* ⟨po⟩kroić; ⟨wy⟩rzeźbić; wycinać ⟨-ciąć⟩; **'carv·er** snycerz *m*; rzeźbiarz *m*; nóż *m* do krojenia; **'carv·ing** snycerka *f*, rzeźbiarstwo *n*
'car wash myjnia *f* samochodów
cas·cade [kæ'skeɪd] kaskada *f*
case¹ [keɪs] **1.** pudełko *n*, pudło *n*; skrzynia *f*; futerał *m*, pokrowiec *m*; kaseta *f*; gablota *f*, witryna *f*; skrzynka *f* (*wina*); powłoczka *f*; *tech.* obudowa *f*; **2.** wkładać ⟨włożyć⟩ do pokrowca; *tech.* obudowywać ⟨-wać⟩, umieszczać ⟨umieścić⟩ w osłonie
case² [keɪs] przypadek (*też med., gr.*); *jur.* sprawa *f* (*sądowa*); stan *m*, sytuacja *f*; ***in ~ of*** w przypadku (*G*), w razie (*G*)
case·ment ['keɪsmənt] skrzydło *n* okienne; **~ 'win·dow** okno *n* skrzynkowe
cash [kæʃ] **1.** gotówka *f*; zapłata *f* gotówką; ***~ on delivery*** płatne gotówką przy odbiorze; **2.** *czek itp.* ⟨z⟩realizować; **'~·book** księga *f* kasowa; **'~ desk** (*w domu towarowym itp.*) kasa *f*; **'~ di·spens·er** *zwł. Brt.* bankomat *m*; **~·ier** [kæ'ʃɪə] kasjer(ka *f*) *m*; **'~·less** bezgotówkowy; **'~ ma·chine**, **'~·point** *Brt.* → ***~ dispenser***; **'~ re·gis·ter** kasa *f* rejestrująca
cas·ing ['keɪsɪŋ] obudowa *f*, osłona *f*; powłoka *f* (*kabla*)

C

cask [kɑːsk] beczka *f*, baryłka *f*
cas·ket ['kɑːskɪt] pudełko *n*, kasetka *f*; *Am.* trumna *f*
cas·se·role ['kæsərəʊl] naczynie *n* do zapiekanek; zapiekanka *f*
cas·sette [kə'set] kaseta *f*; **~ deck** magnetofon *m* kasetowy (*bez wzmacniacza*); **~ play·er** odtwarzacz *m* kasetowy; **~ ra·di·o**, **~ re·cord·er** magnetofon *m* kasetowy
cas·sock ['kæsək] *rel.* sutanna *f*
cast [kɑːst] **1.** rzut *m*; *tech.* odlew *m*; *theat.* obsada *f*; (*w wędkarstwie*) rzut *m*; *med.* opatrunek *m* gipsowy, gips *m*; typ *m*, rodzaj *m*; odcień *m*; **2.** (***cast***) *v/t.* *zarz*ucać ⟨-cić⟩, rzucać ⟨-cić⟩; *zo. skórę itp.* zrzucać ⟨-cić⟩; *zęby itp.* gubić; *pol.* rzucać ⟨-cić⟩ oddawać ⟨-dać⟩; ⟨u⟩kształtować; *tech.* odlewać ⟨-lać⟩; *też* ***~ up*** podliczać ⟨-czyć⟩, dodawać ⟨-dać⟩; *theat.* obsadzać ⟨-dzić⟩ w (*L*) (*sztuce itp.*); obsadzać w roli (*G*); ***~ lots*** rzucać ⟨rzucić⟩ losy (***for*** o *A*); ***~ away*** odrzucać ⟨-cić⟩; ***~ down*** przygnębiać ⟨-bić⟩; ***~ off*** *ubrania* pozbywać ⟨-być⟩ się; *przyjaciela itp.* odrzucać ⟨-cić⟩; *oczko* spuszczać ⟨spuścić⟩; *v/i.* ***~ about for***, ***~ around for*** szukać (*A*); *fig.* rozglądać się za (*I*)
cas·ta·net [kæstə'net] *mus.* kastaniet *m*
cast·a·way ['kɑːstəweɪ] *naut.* rozbitek *m*
caste [kɑːst] kasta *f* (*też fig.*)
cast·er ['kɑːstə] kółko *n* jezdne (*pod meblem*); *Brt.* dozownik *m* do cukru; *Brt.* solniczka *f*
cast·i·gate ['kæstɪgeɪt] surowo ⟨u⟩karać; ⟨s⟩krytykować
cast| 'i·ron żeliwo *n*, lane żelazo *n*; **~-'i·ron** żeliwny; *fig.* żelazny
cas·tle ['kɑːsl] (*rycerski*) zamek *m*; (*w szachach*) wieża *f*
cast·or ['kɑːstə] → ***caster***
cast·or oil [kɑːstə 'ɔɪl] olej *m* rycynowy
cas·trate [kæ'streɪt] ⟨wy⟩kastrować
cas·u·al ['kæʒʊəl] przypadkowy, niezamierzony; dorywczy; *ubranie*, *etc.*: swobodny, nieformalny; **~ 'wear** ubranie *n* codzienne
cas·u·al·ty ['kæʒʊəltɪ] nieszczęście *n*; ofiara *f*; ***casualties*** *pl.* ofiary *pl.*, *mil.* straty *pl.* w ludziach; **'~ (department)** (*w szpitalu*) oddział *m* urazowy; **'~ ward** (*w szpitalu*) stacja *f* pogotowia ratunkowego
cat [kæt] *zo.* kot *m*
cat·a·logue *zwł. Brt.*, **cat·a·log** *Am.* ['kætəlɒg] **1.** katalog *m*, spis *m*; **2.** ⟨s⟩katalogować
cat·a·lyt·ic con·ver·ter [kætəlɪtɪc kən'vɜːtə] *mot.* katalizator *m*
cat·a·pult ['kætəpʌlt] katapulta *f*; *Brt.* proca *f*
cat·a·ract ['kætərækt] katarakta *f*; *med.* katarakta *f*, zaćma *f*
ca·tarrh [kə'tɑː] *med.* katar *m*
ca·tas·tro·phe [kə'tæstrəfɪ] katastrofa *f*
catch [kætʃ] **1.** złapanie *n*, schwytanie *n*, pojmanie *n*; połów *m*, zdobycz *f*; zaczep *m*; zatrzask *m*; zaparcie *n* (*tchu*); *fig.* haczyk *m*; pułapka *f*; **2.** (***caught***) *v/t.* ⟨s⟩chwytać, ⟨z⟩łapać; pojmować ⟨-jąć⟩, ujmować ⟨-jąć⟩; zaskakiwać ⟨-koczyć⟩, ⟨z⟩łapać; *pociąg itp.* ⟨z⟩łapać, zdążyć na (*A*); pojmować ⟨-jąć⟩, ⟨z⟩łapać; zarażać ⟨-razić⟩ się, *chorobę itp.* ⟨z⟩łapać; *atmosferę itp.* chwytać ⟨uchwycić⟩; **~ (*a*) *cold*** przeziębiać ⟨-bić⟩ się; ***~ the eye*** wpadać ⟨wpaść⟩ w oko; ***~ s.o.'s eye*** przyciągać ⟨-gnąć⟩ czyjeś oko; ***~ s.o. up*** doganiać ⟨dogonić⟩ kogoś; ***be caught up in*** być zaplątanym w (*A*); *v/i.* złapać się, zaczepiać ⟨-pić⟩ się; ⟨z⟩łapać; sczepiać ⟨-pić⟩ się; *zamek itp.*: zatrzaskiwać ⟨-snąć⟩ się; ***~ up with*** doganiać ⟨dogonić⟩; **'~·er** osoba *f* łapiąca (*zwł. w sporcie*); **'~·ing** zaraźliwy; **'~·word** hasło *n*, hasło *n* słownikowe; **'~·y** (***-ier, -iest***) *melodia*: chwytliwy
cat·e·chis·m ['kætɪkɪzəm] *rel.* katechizm *m*
cat·e·go·ry ['kætɪgərɪ] kategoria *f*
ca·ter ['keɪtə] zaopatrywać (***for*** w); *fig.* ⟨za⟩troszczyć się o (*A*)
cat·er·pil·lar ['kætəpɪlə] *zo.* gąsienica *f* (*też tech.*); *TM* pojazd *m* gąsienicowy; **~ 'trac·tor** *TM* ciągnik *m* gąsienicowy
cat·gut ['kætgʌt] *med.* katgut *m*, nić *f* chirurgiczna
ca·the·dral [kə'θiːdrəl] katedra *f*
Cath·o·lic ['kæθəlɪk] *rel.* **1.** katolicki; **2.** katolik *m* (-iczka *f*)
cat·kin ['kætkɪn] *bot.* bazia *f* (*wierzby*)
cat·tle ['kætl] bydło *n*
Cau·ca·sus Kaukaz *m*

caught [kɔːt] *pret. i p.p. od* ***catch*** 2
ca(u)l·dron ['kɔːldrən] kocioł *m*
cau·li·flow·er ['kɒlɪflaʊə] *bot.* kalafior *m*
cause [kɔːz] **1.** przyczyna *f*, powód *m*; sprawa *f*; **2.** ⟨s⟩powodować, być przyczyną; sprawiać ⟨-wić⟩; '**~·less** bezpodstawny
cau·tion ['kɔːʃn] **1.** ostrożność *f*, przezorność *f*; ostrzeżenie *n*; ⚠ *nie* ***kaucja***; **2.** ostrzegać ⟨ostrzec⟩; udzielać ⟨-ić⟩ ostrzeżenia; *jur.* pouczać ⟨-czyć⟩
cau·tious ['kɔːʃəs] ostrożny, przezorny
cav·al·ry ['kævlrɪ] *mil.* kawaleria *f*
cave [keɪv] **1.** jaskinia *f*; **2.** *v/i.*: ***~ in*** zapadać ⟨-paść⟩ się
cav·ern ['kævən] jaskinia *f*, jama *f*
cav·i·ty ['kævətɪ] dziura *f*; *med.* ubytek *m* (*w zębie*), F dziura *f*
caw [kɔː] **1.** krakać; **2.** krakanie *n*
CB [siː 'biː] *skrót*: ***Citizens' Band*** radio *n* CB, CB *n*
CBS [siː biː 'es] *skrót*: ***Columbia Broadcasting System*** (*amerykańska firma fonograficzna, radiowa i TV*)
CD [siː 'diː] *skrót*: ***compact disc*** płyta *f* kompaktowa, kompakt *m*, CD *n*; **CD 'play·er** odtwarzacz *m* płyt kompaktowych; **CD-ROM** [siː diː 'rɒm] *skrót*: ***compact disc read-only memory*** CD-ROM *m*
cease [siːs] (za)przestawać, przerywać ⟨-rwać⟩; *spłaty itp.* zawieszać ⟨zawiesić⟩; '**~-fire** zawieszenie *n* broni, zaprzestanie *n* ognia; '**~·less** nieustanny
cei·ling ['siːlɪŋ] sufit *m*, strop *m*; *econ.*, *techn.* pułap *m*; *econ.* górna granica *f*
cel·e|·brate ['selɪbreɪt] celebrować, świętować ⟨święcić⟩, czcić; '**~·brat·ed** znany, sławny (***for*** z *G*); **~·bra·tion** [selɪ'breɪʃn] świętowanie *n*, obchody *pl.*
ce·leb·ri·ty [sɪ'lebrətɪ] (*osoba*) sława *f*
cel·e·riac [sə'lerɪæk] *bot.* seler *m* korzeniowy
cel·e·ry ['selərɪ] *bot.* seler *m* naciowy
ce·les·ti·al [sɪ'lestjəl] niebiański, niebieski
cel·i·ba·cy ['selɪbəsɪ] celibat *m*
cell [sel] komórka *f*; *electr. też* ogniwo *n*
cel·lar ['selar] piwnica *f*
cel|·list ['tʃelɪst] *mus.* wiolonczelista *m* (-tka *f*); **~·lo** ['tʃeləʊ] *mus.* (*pl.* **-los**) wiolonczela *f*
cel·lo·phane ['seləʊfeɪn] *TM* celofan *m*
cel·lu·lar ['seljʊlə] komórkowy; **~ 'phone** telefon *m* komórkowy
Cel·tic ['keltɪk] celtycki
ce·ment [sɪ'ment] **1.** cement *m*; klej *m*, kit *n*; **2.** ⟨s⟩cementować (*też fig.*); ⟨s⟩kleić
cem·e·tery ['semɪtrɪ] cmentarz *m*
cen·sor ['sensə] **1.** cenzor *m* (-ka *f*); **2.** ⟨o⟩cenzurować; '**~·ship** cenzura *f*
cen·sure ['senʃə] **1.** krytyka *f*, nagana *f*; ⚠ *nie* ***cenzura, cenzurka***; **2.** ⟨s⟩krytykować; ⟨z⟩ganić
cen·sus ['sensəs] spis *m* ludności; ⚠ *nie* ***cenzus***
cent [sent] cent *m* (*1/100 jednostki pieniężnej USA, etc.*); ***per ~*** procent *n*
cen·te·na·ry [sen'tiːnərɪ] stulecie *n*, setna rocznica *f*
cen·ten·ni·al [sen'tenjəl] **1.** stuletni; **2.** *Am.* → ***centenary***
cen·ti|·grade ['sentɪgreɪd]: ***10 degrees ~grade*** 10 stopni Celsjusza; '**~·me·tre**, *Brt.*; '**~·me·ter** *Am.* centymetr; **~pede** ['sentɪpiːd] *zo.* stonoga *f*
cen·tral ['sentrəl] centralny; główny; środkowy; ⚠ *nie* ***centrala***; **~ 'heating** ogrzewanie *n* centralne; **~·ize** ['sentrəlaɪz] ⟨s⟩centralizować; **~ 'locking** *mot.* zamek *m* centralny; **~ res·er'va·tion** *Brt.* pas *m* dzielący (*jezdnie na autostradzie*)
cen·tre *Brt.*; **cen·ter** *Am.* ['sentə] **1.** centrum *n*; środek *m*; ośrodek *m*; (*w piłce nożnej*) centra *f*, dośrodkowanie *n*; **2.** skupiać ⟨-pić⟩ (się); centrować, dośrodkowywać ⟨dośrodkować⟩; **~ 'back** (*w piłce nożnej*) stoper *m*; **~ 'for·ward** (*w piłkce nożnej*) środkowy napastnik *m*; **~ of 'grav·i·ty** *phys.* punkt *m* ciężkości
cen·tu·ry ['sentʃʊrɪ] wiek *m*, stulecie *n*
ce·ram·ics [sɪ'ræmɪks] *pl.* ceramika *f*, wyroby *pl.* ceramiczne
ce·re·al ['sɪərɪəl] **1.** zbożowy; **2.** zboże *n*, roślina *f* zbożowa; płatki *pl.* zbożowe; produkty *pl.* zbożowe (*na śniadanie*)
cer·e·bral ['serɪbrəl] *anat.* mózgowy
cer·e·mo|·ni·al [serɪ'məʊnjəl] **1.** ceremonialny, uroczysty; **2.** ceremonia *f*, uroczystość *f*; **~·ni·ous** [serɪ'məʊnjəs] ceremonialny, sztywny; **~·ny** ['serɪmənɪ] ceremonia *f*, uroczystość *f*; ceremoniał *m*

C

cer·tain ['sɜːtn] pewien, pewny; pewny, niejaki; niezawodny, pewny; '**~·ly** z pewnością, na pewno, niewątpliwie; (*w odpowiedzi*) oczywiście, naturalnie; '**~·ty** pewność *f*, przeświadczenie *n*; fakt *m* pewny

cer·tif·i·cate [sə'tɪfɪkət] świadectwo *n*; zaświadczenie *n*, metryka *f*; **~ *of* (*good*) *conduct*** zaświadczenie *n* moralności; ***General* ♀ *of Education advanced level* (*A level*)** *Brt. szkoła*: *jakby*: matura *f*, świadectwo *n* dojrzałości; ***General* ♀ *of Education ordinary level* (*O level*)** *Brt. hist. jakby*: mała matura *f*; ***medical* ~** świadectwo *n* lekarskie

cer·ti·fy ['sɜːtɪfaɪ] zaświadczać ⟨-czyć⟩; poświadczać ⟨-czyć⟩

cer·ti·tude ['sɜːtɪtjuːd] pewność *f*

CET [siː iː 'tiː] *skrót*: ***Central European Time*** czas *m* środkowoeuropejski

cf (*łacińskie* ***confer***) *skrót pisany*: ***compare*** por., porównaj

chafe [tʃeɪf] *v/t*. ocierać ⟨otrzeć⟩; *v/i*. trzeć; ocierać

chaff [tʃɑːf] sieczka *f*, plewy *pl*.

chaf·finch ['tʃæfɪntʃ] *zo*. zięba *f*

chag·rin ['ʃægrɪn] **1.** rozgoryczenie *n*, żal *m*, frustracja *f*; **2.** rozgoryczać ⟨-czyć⟩, ⟨s⟩frustrować

chain [tʃeɪn] **1.** łańcuch *m*; *fig*. okowy *pl*., pęta *pl*.; sieć *f* (*sklepów itp*.); **2.** przykuwać ⟨-kuć⟩ łańcuchem; wziąć na łańcuch; **~ re'ac·tion** reakcja *f* łańcuchowa; '**~-smok·er**: ***she*/*he is a ~-smoker*** pali jednego (*papierosa*) za drugim; '**~-smok·ing** palenie *n* jednego (*papierosa*) za drugim; '**~ store** sklep *m* firmowy

chair [tʃeə] krzesło *n*, fotel *m*; katedra *f*; przewodniczenie *n*; przewodniczący *m* (-ca *f*); ***be in the* ~** przewodniczyć; '**~ lift** wyciąg *m* krzesełkowy; '**~·man** (*pl*. **-men**) przewodniczący *m*; kierujący *m* dyskusją; '**~·man·ship** przewodniczenie *n*; '**~·wom·an** (*pl*. **-women**) przewodnicząca *f*; kierująca *f* dyskusją

chal·ice ['tʃælɪs] *mszalny* kielich *m*

chalk [tʃɔːk] **1.** kreda *f*; **2.** ⟨na⟩pisać kredą; zaznaczać ⟨-czyć⟩ kredą

chal|·lenge ['tʃælɪndʒ] **1.** wyzwanie *n*; kwestionowanie *n*; **2.** wyzywać ⟨-zwać⟩, rzucać ⟨-cić⟩ wyzwanie; ⟨za⟩kwestionować; '**~·len·ger** (*w sporcie*) pretendent *m*; ubiegający *m* (-ca *f*) się o tytuł

cham·ber ['tʃeɪmbə] *tech*. komora *f*; *parl*. izba *f*; *hist*. komnata *f*, sala *f*; '**~·maid** pokojówka *f*; **~ of 'com·merce** izba *f* handlowa

cham·ois ['ʃæmwɑː] *zo*. kozica *f*

cham·ois (leath·er) ['ʃæmɪ (leðə)] zamsz *m*

champ [tʃæmp] F → ***champion*** (*sport*)

cham·pagne [ʃæm'peɪn] szampan *m*

cham·pi·on ['tʃæmpjən] bojownik *m* (-iczka *f*) (***of*** o *A*), orędownik *m* (-iczka *f*); (*w sporcie*) mistrz(yni *f*) *m*; '**~·ship** mistrzostwa *pl*.

chance [tʃɑːns] **1.** przypadek *m*; okazja *f*, (korzystna) sposobność *f*; perspektywa *f*, możliwość *f*; ryzyko *n*; ***by* ~** przypadkiem; ***take a* ~** podejmować ⟨-djąć⟩ ryzyko; ***take no* ~*s*** nie ⟨za⟩ryzykować; **2.** przypadkowy; **2.** F ⟨za⟩ryzykować

chan·cel·lor ['tʃɑːnsələ] kanclerz *m*; *Brt*. rektor *m* (*honorowy uczelni*)

chan·de·lier [ʃændə'lɪə] kandelabr *m*, żyrandol *m*

change [tʃeɪndʒ] **1.** zmiana *f*, przemiana *f*, wymiana *f*, zamiana *f*; drobne *pl*. (pieniądze); reszta *f* (*z zapłaty*); ***for a* ~** dla odmiany; **~ *for the better* (*worse*)** *zmiana* na lepsze (gorsze); **2.** *v/t*. zmieniać ⟨-nić⟩, wymieniać ⟨-nić⟩ (***for*** na *A*); zamieniać ⟨-nić⟩; *tech. mot*. zmieniać ⟨-nić⟩ (*biegi*); **~ *over*** zmieniać ⟨-nić⟩, przechodzić ⟨przejść⟩ (***to*** na *A*); **~ *trains*** przesiadać się; *v/i*. zmieniać ⟨-nić⟩ się; ulegać ⟨ulec⟩ zmianie; zamieniać ⟨-nić⟩ się; '**~·a·ble** zmienny; '**~ ma·chine** automat *m* rozmieniający pieniądze; '**~·o·ver** zmiana *f*, przejście *n*

'chang·ing room (*w sporcie*) przebieralnia *f*, szatnia *f*

chan·nel ['tʃænl] **1.** kanał *m* (*też fig*.); *TV itp*. kanał *m*, program *m*; kanał *m*, sposób *m*, droga *f*; **2.** (*zwł. Brt*. **-ll-**, *Am*. **-l-**) *fig*. ⟨s⟩kierować; ♀ **' Is·lands** *pl*. Wyspy Normandzkie *pl*.; ♀ **'Tun·nel** tunel *m* pod kanałem La Manche

chant [tʃɑːnt] **1.** (*gregoriański itp*.) śpiew *m*; zaśpiew *m*; zawodzenie *n*, skandowanie *n*; **2.** ⟨za⟩śpiewać; *tłum itp*.: zawodzić, skandować

cha·os ['keɪɒs] chaos *m*

chap[1] [tʃæp] pęknięcie *n*

chap[2] [tʃæp] F facet *m*, gość *m*

chap·el ['tʃæpl] kaplica *f*

chap•lain ['tʃæplɪn] kapelan *m*
chap•ter ['tʃæptə] rozdział; *rel.* kapituła *f*
char [tʃɑː] (**-rr-**) zwęglać ⟨-lić⟩
char•ac•ter ['kærəktə] charakter *m*; reputacja *f*; (*drukarski, pisma itp.*) znak *m*, litera *f*; postać (*literacka itp.*) *f*; *theat.* rola *f*; **~•is•tic** [kærəktə'rɪstɪk] **1.** (**-ally**) charakterystyczny (**of** dla *G*); **2.** cecha *f* charakterystyczna; **~•ize** ['kærəktəraɪz] ⟨s⟩charakteryzować
char•coal ['tʃɑːkəʊl] węgiel *m* drzewny
charge [tʃɑːdʒ] **1.** *v/t. akumulator, broń itp.* ⟨na⟩ładować; zlecać ⟨-cić⟩; obciążać ⟨-żyć⟩; obwiniać ⟨-nić⟩, zarzucać ⟨-cić⟩ (*też jur.*); pobierać ⟨pobrać⟩, naliczać ⟨-czyć⟩ (**for** za *A*); *mil.* ⟨za⟩atakować, szturmować; **~ s.o. with s.th.** *econ.* zapisywać ⟨-sać⟩ coś na czyjś rachunek; *v/i.* **~ at s.o.** ⟨za⟩atakować kogoś, rzucać ⟨-cić⟩ się na kogoś; **2.** (*baterii, palny*) ładunek *m*; zlecenie *n*; odpowiedzialność *f*; zarzut *m* (*też jur.*), oskarżenie *n*; opłata *f*; atak *m*, szturm *m*; **~s** *pl.* koszty *pl.*, opłaty *pl.*, wydatki *pl.*; podopieczny *m* (-na *f*); ***free of ~*** bezpłatny; ***be in ~ of*** ponosić ⟨-nieść⟩ odpowiedzialność za (*A*), kierować; ***take ~ of*** przejmować ⟨-jąć⟩ kierownictwo (*G*)
char•i•ot ['tʃærɪət] *poet. lub hist.* rydwan *m*
cha•ris•ma [kə'rɪzmə] charyzmat *m*
char•i•ta•ble ['tʃærɪtəbl] dobroczynny
char•i•ty ['tʃærətɪ] dobroczynność *f*; pobłażliwość *f*, wyrozumiałość; instytucja *f* dobroczynna
char•la•tan ['ʃɑːlətən] szarlatan(ka *f*) *m*; znachor *m*
charm [tʃɑːm] **1.** czar *m*, urok *m*; wdzięk *m*, urok *m*; talizman *m*, amulet *m*; **2.** ⟨o⟩czarować; '**~•ing** czarujący
chart [tʃɑːt] mapa *f* (*morza, nieba, pogody*); diagram *m*, wykres *m*; **~s** *pl.* lista *f* przebojów
char•ter ['tʃɑːtə] **1.** statut *m*; *hist.* karta *f*, edykt *m*; czarter *m*; **2.** ⟨wy⟩czarterować, wynajmować ⟨-jąć⟩; '**~ flight** lot *m* czarterowy
char•wom•an ['tʃɑːwʊmən] (*pl.* **-women**) sprzątaczka *f*
chase [tʃeɪs] **1.** pościg *m*, pogoń *f*; **2.** ścigać, gonić; ⟨po⟩pędzić, ⟨po⟩gnać
chas•m ['kæzəm] otchłań *f*, czeluść *f*, przepaść *f*
chaste [tʃeɪst] czysty, cnotliwy
chas•tise [tʃæ'staɪz] ⟨u⟩karać (*bijąc*)
chas•ti•ty ['tʃæstətɪ] *płciowa* czystość *f*; cnotliwość *f*
chat [tʃæt] **1.** pogawędka *f*, pogaduszka *f*; gadanina *f*; **2.** ⟨po⟩gawędzić (*sobie*); '**~ show** *Brt. TV* talk-show *m*; **~-show 'host** prezenter(ka *f*) *m* talk-show
chat•tels ['tʃætlz] *pl. zw.*: ***goods and ~*** dobytek *m*, majątek *m* ruchomy
chat•ter ['tʃætə] **1.** paplać; *małpa, ptak itp.*: ⟨za⟩skrzeczeć; *zęby itp.*: ⟨za⟩szczękać; **2.** paplanina *f*; skrzeczenie *n*; szczękanie *n*; '**~•box** F gaduła *m*, *f*, papla *m*, *f*
chat•ty ['tʃætɪ] (**-ier, -iest**) gadatliwy
chauf•feur ['ʃəʊfə] szofer *m*, kierowca *m*
chau|•vinism ['ʃəʊvɪnɪzm] szowinizm *m*
chau•vin•ist ['ʃəʊvɪnɪst] szowinista *m* (-tka *f*); F ***male ~ pig*** męska szowinistyczna świnia *f*, męski szowinista *m*
cheap [tʃiːp] tani (*też fig.*); *fig.* podły; '**~•en** spadać ⟨spaść⟩ w cenie, zmniejszać ⟨-szyć⟩ wartość; *fig.* poniżać ⟨-żyć⟩ się
cheat [tʃiːt] **1.** oszust(ka *f*) *m*; szalbierz *m*; oszustwo *n*; **2.** oszukiwać ⟨-kać⟩
check [tʃek] **1.** sprawdzanie *n*, kontrola *f*; ograniczenie *n*, powstrzymanie *n*; odcinek *m* kontrolny, pokwitowanie *n*, kwit *m*; *Am.* żeton *m* (*do szatni, etc.*), numerek *m*; *Am.* czek *m*; *Am.* ptaszek *m*, znaczek *m* (*na pozycji listy*); *Am.* paragon *m*, wydruk *m* kasowy; (*w szachach*) szach *m*; kratka *f* (*na materiale*), materiał *m* w kratkę; ***keep s.th. in ~*** powstrzymywać ⟨-mać⟩ coś; **2.** *v/i.* zatrzymywać ⟨-mać⟩ się (*nagle*); **~ in** ⟨za⟩meldować się (*w hotelu itp.*) (**at** w *L*); *aviat.* zgłaszać ⟨zgłosić⟩ się do odprawy; **~ out** ⟨wy⟩meldować się (*z hotelu itp.*); **~ up** (**on**) F sprawdzać ⟨-dzić⟩, ⟨z⟩weryfikować; *v/t.* sprawdzać ⟨-dzić⟩, ⟨s⟩kontrolować; zatrzymywać ⟨-mać⟩, wstrzymywać ⟨-mać⟩, ⟨za⟩hamować; *Am.* zaznaczać ⟨-czyć⟩ (*na liście*); *Am.* zostawiać ⟨-wić⟩ (*w szatni itp.*); (*w szachach* ⟨za⟩szachować; '**~card** *Am.* gwarancyjna karta *f* czekowa (*określająca wysokość pokrycia czeku*); **~ed** [tʃekt]

C

kratkowany, w kratkę; **~·ers** *Am.* ['tʃekəz] *sg.* warcaby *pl.*; '**~-in** zameldowanie *n* się; *aviat.* odprawa *f*; '**~-in coun·ter** *aviat.*, '**~-in desk** *aviat.* miejsce *n* odpraw; '**~·ing ac·count** *Am. econ.* rachunek czekowy *m*, *jakby*: rachunek *m* oszczędnościowo-rozliczeniowy; '**~·list** lista *f* kontrolna; '**~·mate** **1.** (*w szachach*) szach-mat *m*; **2.** dawać ⟨dać⟩ mata; '**~-out** wymeldowanie *n* się (*z hotelu*); '**~-out coun·ter** kasa *f* (*zwł. w supermarkecie*); '**~·point** punkt *m* kontrolny; '**~·room** *Am.* garderoba *f*, szatnia *f*; przechowalnia *f* bagażu; '**~·up** sprawdzenie *n*, kontrola *f*; *med.* kontrola *f* lekarska

cheek [tʃiːk] policzek *m*; F czelność *f*; bezczelność; '**~·y** F (**-ier, -iest**) bezczelny

cheer [tʃɪə] **1.** wiwat *m*, aplauz *m*; otucha *f*, pociecha *f*; ***three ~s!*** trzy razy hura!; ***~s!*** na zdrowie!; **2.** *v/t.* wiwatować na cześć; *też* ***~ on*** kibicować; *też* ***~ up*** pocieszać ⟨-szyć⟩ dodawać ⟨dodać⟩ otuchy; *v/i.* wiwatować; cieszyć się; *też* ***~ up*** rozchmurzać ⟨-rzyć⟩ się; ***~ up!*** głowa do góry!; '**~·ful** wesoły, radosny, pogodny

cheer·i·o [tʃɪərɪ'əʊ] *int. Brt.* cześć!

'**cheer|·lead·er** organizator *m* wiwatów (*zwykle dziewczyna*); '**~·less** ponury; **~·y** ['tʃɪərɪ] (**-ier, -iest**) radosny

cheese [tʃiːz] ser *m*

chee·tah ['tʃiːtə] gepard *m*

chef [ʃef] szef *m* kuchni; ⚠ *nie* ***szef***

chem·i·cal ['kemɪkl] **1.** chemiczny; **2.** chemikalia *pl.*, środek *m* chemiczny

chem|·ist ['kemɪst] chemik *m* (-miczka *f*); aptekarz *m* (-arka *f*); pracownik *m* (-ica *f*) *lub* właściciel(ka *f*) *m* drogerii; **~·is·try** ['kemɪstrɪ] chemia *f*; '**~·ist's shop** apteka *f*; drogeria *f*

chem·o·ther·a·py [kiːməʊ'θerəpɪ] *med.* chemioterapia *f*

cheque [tʃek] *Brt. econ.* (*Am.* ***check***) czek *m*; ***crossed ~*** czek *m* zakreślony; '**~ ac·count** konto *n* czekowe; '**~ card** *Brt.* karta *f* czekowa (*określająca wysokość pokrycia czeku*)

cher·ry ['tʃerɪ] *bot.* wiśnia *f*; czereśnia *f*

chess [tʃes] szachy *pl.*; ***a game of ~*** partia *f* szachów; '**~·board** szachownica *f*; '**~·man** (*pl.* **-men**) bierka *f* szachowa; '**~ piece** figura *f*

chest [tʃest] *anat.* klatka *f* piersiowa, piersi *pl.*; skrzynia *f*, kufer *m*; ***get s.th. off one's ~*** zrzucić ten ciężar z serca

chest·nut ['tʃesnʌt] **1.** *bot.* kasztan *m*, kasztanowiec *m*; **2.** kasztanowy

chest of drawers [tʃest əv 'drɔːz] komoda *f*

chew [tʃuː] żuć, przeżuć ⟨-żuwać⟩; '**~·ing gum** guma *f* do żucia

chick [tʃɪk] pisklę *n*; F (*dziewczyna*) laska *f*

chick·en ['tʃɪkɪn] kurczę *n*, kurczak *m*; **~'heart·ed** tchórzliwy, strachliwy; **~ pox** ['tʃɪkɪnpɒks] *med.* ospa *f* wietrzna

chic·o·ry ['tʃɪkərɪ] *bot.* cykoria *f*

chief [tʃiːf] **1.** główny, naczelny, najważniejszy; **2.** kierownik *m* (-iczka *f*), szef(owa *f*) *m*; naczelnik *m*; wódz *m*; '**~·ly** głównie

chil·blain ['tʃɪlbleɪn] odmrożenie *n*

child [tʃaɪld] (*pl.* ***children***) dziecko *n*; ***from a ~*** od dziecka, od okresu dzieciństwa; ***with ~*** ciężarny; '**~ a·buse** znęcanie *n* się nad dziećmi; **~ 'ben·e·fit** *Brt.* zasiłek *f* rodzinny; '**~·birth** poród *m*; **~·hood** ['tʃaɪldhʊd] dzieciństwo *n*; '**~·ish** *fig.* dziecinny; '**~·like** dziecinny; dziecięcy; '**~·mind·er** opiekun(ka *f*) *m* do dzieci (*zwykle do południa, we własnym domu*)

chil·dren ['tʃɪldrən] *pl. od* ***child***

chill [tʃɪl] **1.** chłodny (*też fig.*); **2.** chłód *m* (*też fig.*); przeziębienie *n*; **3.** ⟨s⟩chłodzić, schładzać ⟨-dzić⟩; ⟨o⟩ziębić się; '**~·y** (**-ier, -iest**) chłodny (*też fig.*)

chime [tʃaɪm] **1.** kurant *m*; dźwięk *m lub* bicie *n* dzwonu; **2.** ⟨za⟩dzwonić

chim·ney ['tʃɪmnɪ] komin *m*; '**~-sweep** kominiarz *m*

chimp [tʃɪmp], **chim·pan·zee** [tʃɪmpən'ziː] *zo.* szympans *m*

chin [tʃɪn] broda *f*, podbródek *m*; ***~ up!*** głowa do góry!

chi·na ['tʃaɪnə] porcelana *f*

Chi·na ['tʃaɪnə] Chiny *pl.*; **Chi·nese** [tʃaɪ'niːz] **1.** chiński; **2.** Chińczyk *m*, Chinka *f*; język *m* chiński; ***the ~*** Chińczycy

chink [tʃɪŋk] szczelina *f*; *fig.* słaby punkt *m*; brzęczenie *n*

chip [tʃɪp] **1.** wiór *m*, drzazga *f*; okruch *m*, odłamek *m*; szczerba *f*, wyszczerbienie *n*; żeton *m*, szton *m*; *komp.* płytka *f*

półprzewodnika, F kość *f*; **2.** (**-pp-**) *v/t.* wyszczerbiać ⟨-bić⟩; ⟨wy⟩strugać; *v/i.* wyszczerbiać ⟨-bić⟩ się
chips [tʃɪps] *pl. Brt.* frytki *pl.*; *Am.* chipsy *pl.*, chrupki *pl.*
chi·rop·o·dist [kɪ'rɒpədɪst] specjalista *m* (-tka *f*) od chorób stóp; pedikurzysta *m* (-ka *f*)
chirp [tʃɜːp] ćwierkać; *owady*: cykać, brzęczeć
chis·el ['tʃɪzl] **1.** dłuto *n*; **2.** (*zwł. Brt.* **-ll-**, *Am.* **-l-**) ⟨wy⟩dłutować
chit-chat ['tʃɪttʃæt] pogaduszki *pl.*
chiv·al·rous ['ʃɪvlrəs] rycerski
chive [tʃaɪv(z)] (**-s** *pl.*) *bot.* szczypior *m*, F szczypiorek *m*
chlo·ri·nate ['klɔːrɪneɪt] chlorować; **chlo·rine** ['klɔːriːn] *chem.* chlor *m*
chlor·o·form ['klɒrəfɔːm] *chem.*, *med.* **1.** chloroform *m*; **2.** ⟨za⟩stosować chloroform
choc·o·late ['tʃɒkələt] czekolada *f*, czekoladka *f*, pralinka *f*; '**~s** *pl.* czekoladki *pl.*
choice [tʃɔɪs] **1.** wybór *m*; rzecz *f* wybrana, osoba *f* wybrana; **2.** pierwszej jakości; najlepszy; dobrany
choir ['kwaɪə] chór *m*
choke [tʃəʊk] **1.** ⟨za⟩dławić (się), dusić (się); **~ back** *gniew itp.* ⟨z⟩dusić, *łzy itp.* ⟨po⟩wstrzymywać; **~ down** *słowa* powstrzymywać; *też* **~ up** zatykać (się); **2.** *mot.* zasysacz *m*, F ssanie *n*
choose [tʃuːz] (**chose, chosen**) wybierać ⟨wybrać⟩; postanawiać ⟨postanowić⟩ (**to do s.th.** coś zrobić)
chop [tʃɒp] **1.** cios *m*; *gastr.* kotlet *m*; **2.** (**-pp-**) *v/t.* ⟨po⟩rąbać, ⟨po⟩siekać; **~ down** ⟨z⟩rąbać; *v/i.* rąbać; '**~·per** tasak *m*; F helikopter *m*; '**~·py** wzburzony; '**~·stick** pałeczka *f* (*do jedzenia*)
cho·ral ['kɔːrəl] chóralny
cho·rale [kɒ'rɑːl] chorał *m*
chord [kɔːd] *mus.* akord *m*
chore [tʃɔː] nieprzyjemna *lub* ciężka praca *f*; **~s** praca *f* domowa
cho·rus ['kɔːrəs] chór *m*; refren *m*; zespół *m* (*tancerzy lub śpiewaków*), zespół *m* towarzyszący
chose [tʃəʊz] *pret. od* **choose**; **cho·sen** ['tʃəʊzn] *p.p. od* **choose**
Christ [kraɪst] Chrystus *m*
chris·ten ['krɪsn] ⟨o⟩chrzcić; '**~·ing** chrzest *m*; *attr.* chrzestny
Chris·tian ['krɪstʃən] **1.** chrześcijański; **2.** chrześcijanin *m* (-anka *f*); **Chris·ti·an·i·ty** [krɪstɪ'ænətɪ] chrześcijaństwo *n*
'**Christian name** imię *n*
Christ·mas ['krɪsməs] Boże Narodzenie *n*; **at ~** na Boże Narodzenie, w ciągu Bożego Narodzenia; *attr.* bożonarodzeniowy; **~ 'Day** pierwszy dzień *m* Bożego Narodzenia; **~ 'Eve** wigilia *f* Bożego Narodzenia
chrome [krəʊm] *chem.* (*pierwiastek*) chrom *m*; **chro·mi·um** ['krəʊmjəm] (*pierwiastek*) chrom *m*
chron·ic ['krɒnɪk] (**~ally**) chroniczny, przewlekły
chron·i·cle ['krɒnɪkl] kronika *f*
chron·o·log·i·cal [krɒnə'lɒdʒɪkl] (**~ally**) chronologiczny; **chro·nol·o·gy** [krə'nɒlədʒɪ] chronologia *f*
chub·by ['tʃʌbɪ] F (**-ier, -est**) pyzaty, pucołowaty
chuck [tʃʌk] F **1.** rzucać ⟨-cić⟩; **~ out** wyrzucać ⟨-cić⟩; **~ up** *pracę itp.* rzucać ⟨-cić⟩; **2.** uchwyt *m* (*wiertła itp.*)
chuck·le ['tʃʌkl] **1.** ⟨za⟩chichotać; **2.** chichot *m*
chum [tʃʌm] kumpel F *m* (-ka *f*), przyjaciel *m* (-ciółka *f*); '**~·my** F (**-ier, -iest**) zaprzyjaźniony
chump [tʃʌmp] głuptas *m*
chunk [tʃʌŋk] kawał *m*, bryła *f*
Chun·nel ['tʃʌnl] F → ***Channel Tunnel***
church [tʃɜːtʃ] kościół *m*; *attr.* kościelny; '**~ ser·vice** nabożeństwo *n*; '**~·yard** cmentarz *m* (*przy kościele*)
churl·ish ['tʃɜːlɪʃ] arogancki, grubiański
churn [tʃɜːn] **1.** maselnica *f*; *Brt.* bańka *f* *lub* kanka *f* na mleko; **2.** ⟨z⟩robić masło (*w maselnicy*); *fig.* wzburzać ⟨-rzyć⟩ się
chute [ʃuːt] zjeżdżalnia *f*; zsyp *m* (*na śmieci*); *tech.* rynna *f* zsypowa; F spadochron *m*; próg *m* wodny
CIA [siː aɪ 'eɪ] *skrót*: ***Central Intelligence Agency*** CIA, Centralna Agencja *f* Wywiadowcza (*w USA*)
CID [siː aɪ 'diː] *skrót*: ***Criminal Investigation Department*** (*wydział policji kryminalnej w Wielkiej Brytanii*)
ci·der ['saɪdə] (*Am.* **hard ~**) jabłecznik *m*, wino *n* jabłkowe; (*Am.* **sweet ~**) sok *m* jabłkowy

C

cif [siː aɪ 'ef] *skrót*: ***cost, insurance, freight*** koszt, ubezpieczenie i fracht
ci·gar [sɪ'gɑː] cygaro *n*
cig·a·rette, cig·a·ret [sɪgə'ret] *Am*. papieros *m*
cinch [sɪntʃ] F (*łatwa rzecz*) małe piwo *n*, pestka *f*
cin·der ['sɪndə] żużel *m*; **~s** *pl*. popiół *m*
Cin·de·rel·la [sɪndə'relə] Kopciuszek *m*
'cin·der track (*w sporcie*) tor *m* żużlowy; żużel *m*
cin·e|·cam·e·ra ['sɪnɪkæmərə] kamera *f* filmowa (*na wąski film*); **'~·film** (wąska) taśma *f* filmowa
cin·e·ma ['sɪnəmə] *Brt*. kino *n*; kino *n*, film *m*, sztuka *f* filmowa
cin·na·mon ['sɪnəmən] cynamon *m*
ci·pher ['saɪfə] szyfr *m*, zero *n* (*też fig*.)
cir·cle ['sɜːkl] **1.** krąg *m*, koło *n*; *theat*. balkon *m*; *fig*. krąg *m*
cir·cuit ['sɜːkɪt] obieg *m*, okrążenie *n*; *electr*. obwód *m*, układ *m*; objazd *m*; *sport*: runda *f* spotkań; ***short ~*** *electr*. zwarcie *n*
cir·cu·i·tous [sə'kjuːɪtəs] okrężny
cir·cu·lar ['sɜːkjʊlə] **1.** kołowy, kolisty; okrężny; **2.** okólnik *m*, nota *f*; druk *m* reklamowy
cir·cu|·late ['sɜːkjʊleɪt] *v/i*. krążyć, wchodzić ⟨wejść⟩ w obieg; *v/t*. wprowadzać ⟨-dzić⟩ w obieg, rozprowadzać⟨-dzić⟩; **'~·lat·ing li·bra·ry** wypożyczalnia *f*; **~·la·tion** [sɜːkjʊ'leɪʃn] obieg *m*, krążenie *n* (*też anat*.); cyrkulacja *f*; *econ*. krążenie *n*; nakład *m* (*czasopisma*)
cir·cum·fer·ence [sə'kʌmfərəns] obwód *m*
cir·cum·nav·i·gate [sɜːkəm'nævɪgeɪt] okrążać ⟨-żyć⟩
cir·cum·scribe ['sɜːkəmskraɪb] *math*. opisywać ⟨-sać⟩; *fig*. ograniczać ⟨-czyć⟩
cir·cum·spect ['sɜːkəmspekt] ostrożny, przezorny
cir·cum·stance ['sɜːkəmstəns] okoliczność *f*; warunek *m*; **~s** *pl*. okoliczności *pl*.; ***in*** *lub* ***under no ~s*** w żadnym wypadku; ***in*** *lub* ***under the ~s*** w tej sytuacji
cir·cum·stan·tial [sɜːkəm'stænʃl] pośredni; szczegółowy; **~ evidence** dowody *pl*. poszlakowe
cir·cus ['sɜːkəs] cyrk *m*; *Brt*. plac *m*

CIS [siː aɪ 'es] *skrót*: ***Commonwealth of Independent States*** WNP, Wspólnota Niepodległych Państw
cis·tern ['sɪstən] cysterna *f*, zbiornik *m*; spłuczka *f*
ci·ta·tion [saɪ'teɪʃn] *jur*. wezwanie *n*; cytat *m*; **cite** [saɪt] *jur*. wzywać ⟨wezwać⟩, pozywać ⟨pozwać⟩; ⟨za⟩cytować
cit·i·zen ['sɪtɪzn] obywatel(ka *f*) *m*; **'~·ship** obywatelstwo *n*
cit·y ['sɪtɪ] **1.** (duże) miasto *n*; ***the*** ♀ City *n*; **2.** miejski; **~ 'cen·tre** *Brt*. centrum *n* miasta; **~ 'coun·cil·(l)or** *Am*. rajca *m* (-jczyni *f*); **~ 'hall** ratusz *m*; *zwł. Am*. zarząd *m* miasta; **~ 'slick·er** *często pej*. mieszczuch *m*; **~ 'va·grant** włóczęga *m*, tramp *m*
civ·ic ['sɪvɪk] obywatelski; miejski; **'~s** wychowanie *n* obywatelskie
civ·il ['sɪvl] cywilny (*też jur*.); obywatelski; społeczny; uprzejmy; ⚠ *nie* ***cywil***;
ci·vil·i·an [sɪ'vɪljən] cywil *m*
ci·vil·i·ty [sɪ'vɪlətɪ] uprzejmość *f*
civ·i·li|·za·tion [sɪvɪlaɪ'zeɪʃn] cywilizacja *f*; **~ze** ['sɪvɪlaɪz] ⟨u⟩cywilizować
civ·il 'rights *pl*. prawa *pl*. obywatelskie; **~ rights 'ac·tiv·ist** działacz(ka *f*) *m* ruchu obywatelskiego; **~ rights 'move·ment** ruch *m* obywatelski
civ·il| 'ser·vant urzędnik *m* (-iczka *f*) państwowy (-a); **~ 'ser·vice** administracja *f* państwowa; **~ 'war** wojna *f* domowa
CJD [siː dʒeɪ' diː] *skrót*: ***Creutzfeld(t)-Jakob disease*** choroba *f* Creutzfelda-Jakoba
clad [klæd] **1.** *pret. i p.p. od* ***clothe***; **2.** odziany, przyodziany
claim [kleɪm] **1.** żądanie *n*, roszczenie *n*; pretensja *f*; reklamacja *f*, zażalenie *n*; prawo *n*; *Am*. działka *f* górnicza; twierdzenie *n*; **2.** ⟨za⟩żądać, domagać się; twierdzić
clair·voy·ant [kleə'vɔɪənt] jasnowidz *m*
clam·ber ['klæmbə] ⟨wy⟩gramolić się, ⟨wy⟩leźć
clam·my ['klæmɪ] (***-ier, -iest***) lepki, kleisty
clam·o(u)r ['klæmə] **1.** wrzawa *f*, zgiełk *m*, larum *n*; **2.** domagać się (***for*** o *G*)
clamp [klæmp] *tech*. zacisk *m*, klamra *f*; *mot*. (*klamra blokująca*) klema *f*
clan [klæn] klan *m*

clan•des•tine [klæn'destɪn] potajemny, tajny
clang [klæŋ] ⟨za⟩dźwięczeć, ⟨za⟩brzęczeć
clank [klæŋk] **1.** brzęczenie *n*, łoskot *m*; **2.** ⟨za⟩brzęczeć, ⟨za⟩łoskotać
clap [klæp] **1.** łoskot *m*, grzmot *m*; aplauz *m*; klepnięcie *n*; **2.** (***-pp-***) ⟨za⟩-klaskać; klepnąć
clar•et ['klærət] czerwone wino *n*
clar•i•fy ['klærɪfaɪ] *v/t.* wyjaśniać ⟨-śnić⟩, ⟨wy⟩tłumaczyć; *v/i.* tłumaczyć się; *tłuszcz itp*.: ⟨wy⟩klarować się
clar•i•net [klærɪ'net] *muz.* klarnet *m*
clar•i•ty ['klærətɪ] jasność *f*
clash [klæʃ] **1.** zderzenie *n*; konflikt *m*; starcie *n*; szczęk *m*; **2.** zderzyć się; ścierać się; kolidować; nie pasować (***with*** do *G*)
clasp [klɑːsp] **1.** obejma *f*, klamra *f*; zatrzask *m*, zapięcie *n*; **2.** obejmować ⟨objąć⟩, ściskać ⟨ścisnąć⟩; zamykać ⟨zamknąć⟩; '**~ knife** (*pl.* ***-knives***) nóż *m* składany
class [klɑːs] **1.** klasa *f*; kurs *m*, zajęcia *pl.* (***in*** z *G*); *Am.* rocznik *m* (*absolwentów*); **2.** ⟨s-, za⟩klasyfikować
clas|•sic ['klæsɪk] **1.** klasyk *m*; **2.** (***-ally***) klasyczny; '**~•si•cal** klasyczny
clas•si|•fi•ca•tion [klæsɪfɪ'keɪʃn] klasyfikacja *f*; **~•fied** ['klæsɪfaɪd] zaklasyfikowany; *mil.*, *pol.* poufny; **~•fied 'ad** drobne ogłoszenie *n*; **~•fy** ['klæsɪfaɪ] ⟨za⟩klasyfikować, ⟨po⟩grupować
'**class|•mate** kolega *m* (-żanka *f*) z klasy; '**~•room** klasa *f*, pomieszczenie *n* szkolne
clat•ter ['klætə] **1.** stukot *m*, stukanie *n*; łomot *m*; **2.** ⟨za⟩stukać; ⟨za⟩łomotać
clause [klɔːz] *jur.* klauzula *f*, paragraf *m*; *gr.* zdanie *n* (składowe)
claw [klɔː] **1.** szpon *m*, pazur *m*; kleszcz *m* (*raka*); **2.** ⟨za-, po⟩drapać
clay [kleɪ] glina *f*, ił *m*
clean [kliːn] **1.** *adj.* czysty; porządny, równy; (*bez narkotyków*) *sl.* czysty; **2.** zupełnie, całkowicie, całkiem; **3.** ⟨wy⟩-czyścić, oczyszczać, ⟨wy⟩sprzątać; **~ *out*** ⟨wy⟩czyścić; **~ *up*** gruntownie ⟨wy⟩-czyścić; ⟨u⟩porządkować; '**~•er** sprzątaczka *f*; osoba *f* myjąca (*okna itp*.); środek *m* czyszczący; **~*s*** *pl.* pralnia *f* (*chemiczna*); ***take to the ~ers*** zanosić ⟨-nieść⟩ do pralni; F oskubać (*z pieniędzy*); '**~•ing**: ***do the ~ing*** sprzątać; → ***spring-cleaning***; **~•li•ness** ['klenlɪnɪs] czystość *f*, porządek *m*; **~•ly 1.** ['kliːnlɪ] *adv.* porządnie; **2.** ['klenlɪ] *adj.* (***-ier, -iest***) czysty, porządny
cleanse [klenz] ⟨o⟩czyścić, oczyszczać ⟨oczyścić⟩; '**cleans•er** środek *m* czyszczący
clear [klɪə] **1.** jasny; czysty; klarowny, przezroczysty; wyraźny; wolny (***of*** od *G*); *econ.* netto; **2.** *v/t.* oczyszczać ⟨oczyścić⟩; ⟨z⟩robić jasnym; usuwać ⟨usunąć⟩, sprzątać ⟨-tnąć⟩ (*też* **~ *away***); *las* ⟨wy⟩karczować; zaaprobować, udzielać ⟨-lić⟩ zezwolenia na (*A*); *przeszkodę itp.* pokonywać ⟨-nać⟩; *econ.* dokonywać ⟨-nać⟩ odprawy celnej; *dług* ⟨u⟩regulować; (*w sporcie*) wybijać ⟨-bić⟩ (*piłkę itp.*); *jur.* uniewinniać ⟨-nnić⟩; *v/i.* oczyszczać ⟨oczyścić⟩ się; *niebo itp*.: przejaśniać ⟨-śnić⟩ się; *fig.* rozchmurzać ⟨-rzyć⟩ się; przerzedzać ⟨-dzić⟩ się; **~ *out*** ⟨u-, s⟩przątać; F zmywać się; **~ *up*** ⟨z⟩robić porządek; uporać się; *zagadkę* rozwiązywać ⟨-zać⟩; *pogoda*: przejaśniać ⟨-śnić⟩ się; **~•ance** ['klɪərəns] oczyszczenie *n*; usunięcie *n*; *tech.* prześwit *m*, odstęp *m*; zwolnienie *n*; odprawa *f*; '**~•ance sale** wyprzedaż *f* (*likwidacyjna*); **~•ing** ['klɪə'rɪŋ] polana *f*
cleave [kliːv] (***cleaved*** *lub* ***cleft*** *lub* ***clove, cleaved*** *lub* ***cleft*** *lub* ***cloven***) rozszczepiać ⟨-pić⟩; '**cleav•er** tasak *m*
clef [klef] *mus.* klucz *m*
cleft [kleft] **1.** rozszczepienie *n*, szczelina *f*, szpara *f*; **2.** *pret. i p.p. od* ***cleave***
clem|•en•cy ['klemənsɪ] łaska *f*; pobłażliwość *f*, wyrozumiałość *f*; '**~•ent** łagodny
clench [klentʃ] *wargi, pięść itp.* zaciskać ⟨-snąć⟩
cler•gy ['klɜːdʒɪ] kler *m*, duchowieństwo *n*; '**~•man** (*pl.* ***-men***) duchowny *m*
clerk [klɑːk] urzędnik *m* (-iczka *f*); *Am.* sprzedawca *m* (-czyni *f*)
clev•er ['klevə] roztropny, mądry; sprytny
click [klɪk] **1.** pstryknięcie *n*, szczęknięcie *n*, stuknięcie *n*; *komp.* kliknięcie *n*; mlaśnięcie *n* (*językiem*); **2.** *v/i.*: **~ *shut*** zamknąć się ze szczękiem; *v/t.* pstrykać ⟨-knąć⟩, szczękać ⟨szczęknąć⟩, stukać ⟨-knąć⟩; *komp.* kliknąć na (*A*)

C

cli·ent ['klaɪənt] klient(ka *f*) *m*
cliff [klɪf] klif *m*
cli·mate ['klaɪmɪt] klimat *m* (*też fig.*)
cli·max ['klaɪmæks] punkt *m* kulminacyjny; klimaks *m*; szczytowanie *n*, orgazm *m*
climb [klaɪm] *v/i.* wspinać ⟨wspiąć⟩ się; iść ⟨pójść⟩ w górę; wchodzić ⟨wejść⟩, ⟨po⟩leźć; ***go ~ing*** uprawiać wspinaczkę; *v/t.* wspinać ⟨wspiąć⟩ się po (*I*); wchodzić ⟨wejść⟩ na (*A*) *lub* po (*I*); '**~·er** alpinista *m* (-tka *f*); *bot.* roślina *f* pnąca
clinch [klɪntʃ] **1.** *tech.* zaciskać ⟨-snąć⟩; (*w boksie*) wchodzić ⟨wejść⟩ w zwarcie, klinczować; rozstrzygać ⟨-gnąć⟩; ***that ~ed*** to było rozstrzygające; **2.** *tech.* zaciśnięcie; (*w boksie*) zwarcie *n*, klincz *m*
cling [klɪŋ] (***clung***) (***to***) przylegać ⟨-lec⟩ (do *G*); przytulać ⟨-lić⟩ się, przywrzeć ⟨-wierać⟩ (do *G*); '**~·film** samoprzylegająca folia *f* (*do żywności*)
clin|·ic ['klɪnɪk] klinika *f*; '**~·i·cal** kliniczny
clink [klɪŋk] **1.** brzęk *m*; **2.** ⟨za⟩brzęczeć, ⟨za⟩dzwonić (*łańcuchem*)
clip[1] [klɪp] **1.** (***-pp-***) przycinać ⟨-ciąć⟩, *owcę itp.* ⟨przy⟩strzyc; **2.** cięcie *n*, nacięcie *n*; *wideo itp.*: klip *m lub* clip *m*; urywek *m* (*filmu*)
clip[2] [klɪp] **1.** klamra *f*, spinacz *m*; zacisk *m*; klips *m*; magazynek *m* (*do broni*); **2.** (***-pp-***) spinać ⟨spiąć⟩; zaciskać ⟨zacisnąć⟩
clip|·per ['klɪpə]: (***a pair of***) ***~pers*** *pl.* nożyce *pl.*, sekator *m*; cążki *pl.*, obcinarka *f*; maszynka *f* do włosów; '**~·pings** *pl.* wycinki *pl.*; skrawki *pl.*, obcinki *pl.*
clit·o·ris ['klɪtərɪs] *anat.* łechtaczka *f*
cloak [kləʊk] **1.** peleryna *f*; **2.** *fig.* okrywać ⟨-ryć⟩; '**~·room** garderoba *f*; *Brt.* toaleta *f*
clock [klɒk] **1.** *ścienny, wieżowy* zegar *m*; ***9 o'~*** 9 godzina; licznik *m*; **2.** (*w sporcie*): ⟨z⟩mierzyć (czas); ***~ in***, ***~ on*** podbijać ⟨-bić⟩ kartę (*przychodząc*); ***~ out***, ***~ off*** podbijać ⟨-bić⟩ kartę (*wychodząc*); **~·wise** ['klɒkwaɪz] zgodnie z ruchem wskazówek zegara; '**~·work** werk *m*, mechanizm *m* zegarowy; ***like ~work*** jak w zegarku
clod [klɒd] gruda *f*, bryła *f*
clog [klɒg] **1.** chodak *m*, drewniak *m*; kłoda *f* (*też fig.*); **2.** (***-gg-***) *też* ***~ up*** zatykać ⟨zatkać⟩
clois·ter ['klɔɪstə] krużganek *m*; klasztor *m*
close 1. [kləʊs] *adj.* zamknięty; bliski; *tłumaczenie itp.*: dokładny; gęsty, ścisły, zwarty; *dzień itp.*: duszny; *przyjaciel itp.*: serdeczny, bliski; ***keep a ~ watch on*** dobrze pilnować (*A*); **2.** [kləʊs] *adv.* ściśle; dokładnie; blisko; gęsto; ***~ by*** tuż obok, w pobliżu; **3.** [kləʊz] koniec *m*, zakończenie *n*; zamknięcie *n*; ***come*** *lub* ***draw to a ~*** zbliżać się do końca; [kləʊs] *Brt.* mała zamknięta uliczka; **4.** [kləʊz] *v/t.* zamykać ⟨-knąć⟩; ⟨s-, za⟩kończyć; *v/i.* zamykać ⟨-knąć⟩ się; ⟨s-, za⟩kończyć się; ***~ down*** *program TV itp.* ⟨s-, za⟩kończyć (się); *fabrykę itp.* zamykać ⟨-knąć⟩ (się); ***~ in*** okrążać ⟨-żyć⟩; *fig.* nadchodzić ⟨nadejść⟩; ***~ up*** zamykać ⟨-knąć⟩ (się); *szeregi* zwierać ⟨zewrzeć⟩; **~d** zamknięty
clos·et ['klɒzɪt] szafa *f* ścienna; ⚠ *nie* ***klozet***
close-up ['kləʊsʌp] *phot.*, *film.* powiększenie *n*
clos·ing| date ['kləʊzɪŋdeɪt] termin *m* ostateczny, ostatni dzień *m*; '**~ time** godzina *f* zamknięcia;
clot [klɒt] **1.** bryła *f*, grudka *f*; ***~ of blood*** *med.* skrzep *m*; **2.** (***-tt-***) ⟨s⟩krzepnąć
cloth [klɒθ] (*pl.* ***cloths*** [klɒθs, klɒðz]) tkanina *f*, sukno *n*; ścierka *f*, ściereczka *f*; szmatka *f*; '**~·bound** oprawny w płótno
clothe [kləʊð] (***clothed*** *lub* ***clad***) ubierać ⟨ubrać⟩
clothes [kləʊðz] *pl.* ubranie *n*, ubrania *pl.*, odzież *f*; (*uprana bielizna*) pranie *n*; '**~ bas·ket** kosz *m* na pranie; '**~ horse** suszarka *f do rozwieszenia bielizny*; '**~ line** sznur *m* na bieliznę; '**~ peg** *Brt.*, '**~·pin** *Am.* klamerka *f* (*do bielizny*)
cloth·ing ['kləʊðɪŋ] ubranie *n*, odzież *f*
cloud [klaʊd] **1.** chmura *f*, obłok *m*; zachmurzenie *n*; *fig.* cień *m*; **2.** ⟨za⟩chmurzyć (się) (*też fig.*); '**~·burst** oberwanie *n* chmury; '**~·less** bezchmurny; '**~·y** (***-ier, -iest***) zachmurzony
clout [klaʊt] F cios *m*, F walnięcie *n*; *fig.* siła *f* przebicia, wpływ *m*;
clove[1] [kləʊv] *bot.*, *gastr.* goździk; ***a ~ of garlic*** ząbek *m* czosnku

C

clove[2] [kləʊv] *pret. od* ***cleave***; **clo•ven** ['kləʊvn] *pret. od* ***cleave***; **clo•ven 'hoof** (*pl.* ***- hoofs, - hooves***) *zo.* racica *f*
clo•ver ['kləʊvə] *bot.* koniczyna *f*
clown [klaʊn] klown *m*, *klaun m*
club [klʌb] **1.** pałka *f*, kij *m*; *sport*: kij *m*; klub *m*; **~s** *pl.* trefle *pl.*; **2.** (**-bb-**) obijać ⟨obić⟩ pałką; '**~•foot** (*pl.* ***-feet***) zdeformowana stopa *f*
cluck [klʌk] **1.** ⟨za⟩gdakać; **2.** gdakanie *n*
clue [kluː] wskazówka *f*, klucz *m*; (*w krzyżówce*) określenie *n*
clump [klʌmp] **1.** grupa *f*, kępa *f*; bryłka *f*, grud(k)a *f*; **2.** ciężko chodzić ⟨iść⟩
clum•sy ['klʌmzɪ] (***-ier, -iest***) niezgrabny, niezręczny
clung [klʌŋ] *pret. i p.p. od* ***cling***
clus•ter ['klʌstə] **1.** skupisko *n*, grupa *f*; *bot.* grono *n*, kiść *f*; **2.** skupiać ⟨-pić⟩ się
clutch [klʌtʃ] **1.** uścisk *m*; *tech.* sprzęgło *n*; *fig.* szpon *m*; **2.** ściskać ⟨ścisnąć⟩ (*mocno*)
CNN [siː en 'en] *skrót*: ***Cable News Network*** (*amerykańska telewizja kablowa, nadająca wiadomości ze świata*)
c/o [siː 'əʊ] *skrót*: ***care of*** na adres, pod adresem
Co[1] [kəʊ] *skrót*: ***company*** *econ.* spółka *f*
Co[2] *skrót pisany*: ***County*** *Brt.* hrabstwo *n*; *Am.* okręg *m* (*wyborczy*)
coach [kəʊtʃ] **1.** autobus *m* (*turystyczny*), autokar *m*; *Brt. rail.* wagon *m* osobowy; powóz *m*; *sport*: trener(ka *f*) *m*; korepetytor(ka *f*) *m*; **2.** *sport*: trenować; dawać ⟨dać⟩ korepetycje; '**~•man** (*pl.* ***-men***) trener *m*
co•ag•u•late [kəʊ'ægjʊleɪt] ⟨s⟩koagulować, ⟨s⟩krzepnąć
coal [kəʊl] węgiel *m*; ***carry ~s to Newcastle*** wozić drewno do lasu
co•a•li•tion [kəʊə'lɪʃn] *pol.* koalicja *f*; przymierze *n*
'**coal|•mine,** '**~•pit** kopalnia *f*
coarse [kɔːs] (***-r, -st***) gruby, chropowaty; surowy; grubiański
coast [kəʊst] **1.** brzeg *m*; **2.** *naut.* płynąć wzdłuż wybrzeża; jechać rozpędem (*samochodem, rowerem itp.*); *Am.* ślizgać się; '**~•guard** straż *f* przybrzeżna; '**~•line** linia *f* brzegowa
coat [kəʊt] **1.** płaszcz *m*; *zo.* sierść *f*; warstwa *f*, powłoka *f* (*farby itp.*); **2.** powlekać ⟨powlec⟩, pokrywać ⟨pokryć⟩, nakładać ⟨nałożyć⟩ powłokę; '**~ hang•er** → ***hanger***; '**~•ing** powłoka *f*; tkanina *f* płaszczowa
coat of 'arms herb *m*
coax [kəʊks] namawiać ⟨namówić⟩ (***into*** do *G*), przekonywać ⟨-nać⟩
cob [kɒb] kolba *f* (*kukurydzy*)
cob•bled ['kɒbld] wybrukowany
cob•bler ['kɒblə] szewc *m*
cob•web ['kɒbweb] pajęczyna *f*
co•caine [kəʊ'keɪn] kokaina *f*
cock [kɒk] **1.** *zo.* kogut *m*; V kutas *m*; zawór *m*, kurek *m*; **2.** naciągać ⟨naciągnąć⟩; **~ *one's ears*** nastawiać ⟨-wić⟩ uszu
cock•a•too [kɒkə'tuː] *zo.* kakadu *n*
cock•chaf•er ['kɒktʃeɪfə] *zo.* chrabąszcz *m*
cock'eyed F stuknięty; zezowaty
Cock•ney ['kɒknɪ] (*rodowity londyńczyk; dialekt Londynu*) cockney *m*
'**cock•pit** kokpit *m*
cock•roach ['kɒkrəʊtʃ] *zo.* karaluch *m*
cock'sure F pewny swego, arogancki
'**cock•tail** koktajl *m* alkoholowy
cock•y ['kɒkɪ] F (***-ier, -iest***) zarozumiały, zadufany
co•co ['kəʊkəʊ] *bot.* (*pl.* ***-cos***) palma *f* kokosowa
co•coa ['kəʊkəʊ] *gastr.* kakao *n*
co•co•nut ['kəʊkənʌt] *bot.* kokos *m*
co•coon [kə'kuːn] kokon *m*
cod [kɒd] *zo.* dorsz *m*, wątłusz *m*
COD [siː əʊ 'diː] *skrót*: ***cash*** (***Am. collect***) ***on delivery*** za zaliczeniem pocztowym
cod•dle ['kɒdl] rozpieszczać ⟨rozpieścić⟩
code [kəʊd] **1.** kod *m*; **2.** ⟨za⟩szyfrować, ⟨za⟩kodować
'**cod•fish** *zo.* → ***cod***
cod•ing ['kəʊdɪŋ] kodowanie *n*
cod-liv•er 'oil tran *m* (*z wątroby dorsza*)
co•ed•u•ca•tion [kəʊedjuː'keɪʃn] koedukacja *f*
co•ex•ist [kəʊɪg'zɪst] koegzystować, współżyć, współistnieć; **~•ence** koegzystencja *f*, współżycie *n*, współistnienie *n*
C of E [siː əv 'iː] *skrót*: ***Church of England*** Kościół *lub* kościół anglikański
cof•fee ['kɒfɪ] kawa *f*; '**~ bar** *Brt.* ka-

C

wiarnia *f*, bar *m* kawowy; '~ **bean** ziarno *n* kawy; '~ **pot** dzbanek *m do* kawy; '~ **set** serwis *m* do kawy; '~ **shop** *zwł. Am.* → ***coffee bar***; '~ **ta·ble** ława *f*, stolik *m*
cof·fin ['kɒfɪn] trumna *f*
cog [kɒg] *tech.* ząb *m* (*zębatki*); '~·**wheel** *tech.* zębatka *f*, koło *n* zębate
co·her|·ence, ~·en·cy [kəʊ'hɪərəns, -rənsɪ] spójność *f*, koherencja *f*; ~·**ent** spójny, koherentny
co·he|·sion [kəʊ'hiːʒn] zwartość *f*, spójność *f*; ~·**sive** [kəʊ'hiːsɪv] zwarty, spójny
coif·fure [kwɑː'fjʊə] fryzura *f*
coil [kɔɪl] **1.** *też* ~ ***up*** zwijać ⟨zwinąć⟩ (się); **2.** *tech.* zwój *m*, krąg *m*; spirala *f*
coin [kɔɪn] **1.** moneta *f*; **2.** ⟨u⟩kuć
co·in|·cide [kəʊɪn'saɪd] nakładać ⟨-łożyć⟩ się, zbiegać ⟨zbiec⟩ się; ~·**ci·dence** [kəʊ'ɪnsɪdəns] zbieg *m* okoliczności, przypadek *m*
'**coin-op·e·rat·ed**: ~ (***petrol,*** *Am.* ***gas***) ***pump*** automatyczny dystrybutor paliwa *m* na monety
coke [kəʊk] koks *m* (*też sl. kokaina*)
Coke *TM* [kəʊk] coca-cola *f*, koka-kola *f*
cold [kəʊld] **1.** zimny, chłodny; oziębły; **2.** chłód *m*, zimno *n*; przeziębienie *n*; ***catch*** (***a***) ~ przeziębić się; ***have a*** ~ być przeziębionym; ~-'**blood·ed** zimnokrwisty; ~-'**heart·ed** o twardym sercu; '~·**ness** zimno *n*; ~ '**war** *pol.* zimna wojna *f*
cole·slaw ['kəʊlslɔː] *gastr.* surówka *f* z kapusty
col·ic ['kɒlɪk] *med.* kolka *f*
col·lab·o|·rate [kə'læbəreɪt] współpracować; ~·**ra·tion** [kəlæbə'reɪʃn] współpraca *f*; ***in ~ration with*** wraz z (*I*)
col|·lapse [kə'læps] **1.** zawalać ⟨-lić⟩ się; rozpadać ⟨-paść⟩ się; załamać ⟨-mywać⟩ się; runąć; składać ⟨złożyć⟩ się; *fig.* rozpadać ⟨-paść⟩ się; załamać ⟨-mywać⟩ się; **2.** zawalenie *n* się, rozpad *m*, upadek *m*; ~'**lap·si·ble** składany, rozkładany
col·lar ['kɒlə] **1.** kołnierz *m*; obroża *f*; *rel.* koloratka *f*; **2.** ⟨z⟩łapać, ⟨s⟩chwytać, F capnąć; '~-**bone** *anat.* obojczyk *m*
col·league ['kɒliːg] kolega *m*, koleżanka *f*
col|·lect [kə'lekt] *v/t.* zbierać ⟨zebrać⟩; kolekcjonować; odbierać ⟨odebrać⟩; *pieniądze itp.* pobierać ⟨pobrać⟩; *v/i.* zbierać ⟨zebrać⟩ się; ~'**lect·ed** zebrany; *fig.* opanowany; ~'**lec·tion** zbieranie *n*; zbiór *m*; kolekcja *f*; *econ.* inkaso *n*; *rel.* kolekta *f*; odbiór *m*; ~'**lec·tive** zbiorowy, wspólny; ~'**lec·tive·ly** zbiorowo, wspólnie; ~'**lec·tor** kolekcjoner(ka *f*) *m*; inkasent(ka *f*) *m*; *rail.* kontroler(ka *f*) *m*; *electr.* kolektor *m*
col·lege ['kɒlɪdʒ] koledż *m*; wyższa szkoła *f*; szkoła *f* pomaturalna
col·lide [kə'laɪd] zderzać ⟨-rzyć⟩ się
col·lie·ry ['kɒljərɪ] kopalnia *f* węgla
col·li·sion [kə'lɪʒn] zderzenie *n*, kolizja *f*; → ***head-on ~, rear-end ~***
col·lo·qui·al [kə'ləʊkwɪəl] potoczny
co·lon ['kəʊlən] dwukropek *m*; *anat.* okrężnica *f*
colo·nel ['kɜːnl] *mil.* pułkownik *m*
co·lo·ni·al·is·m [kə'ləʊnjəlɪzəm] kolonializm *m*
col·o|·nize ['kɒlənaɪz] ⟨s⟩kolonizować, zasiedlać ⟨-dlić⟩; ~·**ny** ['kɒlənɪ] kolonia *f*
co·los·sal [kə'lɒsl] kolosalny
col·o(u)r ['kʌlə] **1.** kolor *m*, barwa *f*; ~**s** *pl. mil.* sztandar *m*, barwy *pl.*.; *naut.* bandera *m*; ***what ~ is ...?*** jakiego koloru jest ...?; ***with flying ~s*** triumfalnie, z wielkim sukcesem; **2.** *v/t.* ⟨za⟩barwić; ⟨za⟩farbować; *fig.* koloryzować; *v/i.* ⟨za⟩barwić się; ⟨za⟩czerwienić się; '~ **bar** segregacja *f* rasowa; '~-**blind** ślepy na kolory; '~**ed** kolorowy; '~·**fast** o trwałych kolorach; '~ **film** *phot.* film *m* kolorowy; '~·**ful** kolorowy; *fig.* barwny; ~·**ing** ['kʌlərɪŋ] barwnik *m*; cera *f*, karnacja *f*; '~·**less** bezbarwny; '~ **line** segregacja *f* rasowa; '~ **set** telewizor *m* kolorowy; '~ **tel·e·vi·sion** telewizja *f* kolorowa
colt [kəʊlt] źrebię *n*, źrebak *m*
col·umn ['kɒləm] kolumna *f* (*też mil.*); *print.* szpalta *f*; felieton *m*; ~·**ist** ['kɒləmnɪst] felietonista *m* (-tka *f*)
comb [kəʊm] **1.** grzebień *m*; **2.** *v/t.* ⟨wy-, roz⟩czesać
com|·bat ['kɒmbæt] **1.** walka *f*; ***single ~bat*** pojedynek *m*; *attr.* bojowy; **2.** (-***tt***-, *Am. też* -***t***-) zwalczać ⟨-czyć⟩; ~·**ba·tant** ['kɒmbətənt] walczący *m* (-ca *f*), żołnierz *m*; ⚠ *nie* ***kombatant***

com|·bi·na·tion [kɒmbɪ'neɪʃn] połączenie *n*, kombinacja *f*; **~·bine** [kəm'baɪn] **1.** łączyć (się), ⟨z⟩wiązać (się), zespalać ⟨zespolić⟩ (się); **2.** *econ.* koncern *m*; *agr. też* ***~bine harvester*** kombajn *m*

com·bus|·ti·ble [kəm'bʌstəbl] **1.** łatwopalny; **2.** materiał *m* łatwopalny; **~·tion** [kəm'bʌstʃən] spalanie *n*

come [kʌm] (***came, come***) przychodzić ⟨przyjść⟩, przyjeżdżać ⟨przyjechać⟩; ***to ~*** nadchodzący, w przyszłości; ***~ and go*** przychodzić i odchodzić; ***~ to see*** odwiedzać; ***~ about*** stać się, wydarzyć się; ***~ across*** natrafiać ⟨-fić⟩ na (*A*); ***~ along*** iść; nadchodzić ⟨-dejść⟩; ***~ apart*** rozpadać ⟨-paść⟩ się; ***~ away*** odchodzić ⟨-dejść⟩; ***~ back*** wracać ⟨wrócić⟩, powracać ⟨-wrócić⟩; ***~ by*** natrafiać ⟨-fić⟩ na (*A*); ***~ down*** schodzić ⟨zejść⟩; *cena*: spadać ⟨spaść⟩; runąć; ***~ down with*** F zachorować na (*A*); ***~ for*** przychodzić ⟨przyjść⟩ po (*A*); ⟨za⟩atakować (*A*); ***~ forwards*** zgłaszać ⟨zgłosić⟩ się; ***~ from*** pochodzić z (*G*); ***~ home*** przychodzić *lub* przyjeżdżać do domu; ***~ in*** wchodzić ⟨wejść⟩ do (*G*); *informacja*: nadchodzić ⟨nadejść⟩; *pociąg*: nadjeżdżać ⟨nadjechać⟩; ***~ in!*** proszę wejść!; ***~ loose*** obluzować się, poluzować się; ***~ off*** odpadać ⟨odpaść⟩, odrywać ⟨oderwać⟩ się; przechodzić ⟨przejść⟩; wypadać ⟨wypaść⟩; ***~ on!*** daj spokój!; dalej!; no już!; ***~ out*** *książka, sumowanie itp.*: wychodzić; *plama*: schodzić ⟨zejść⟩; ujawniać ⟨ujawnić⟩ się; ***~ over*** przyjeżdżać ⟨-jechać⟩, przychodzić ⟨przyjść⟩, przybywać ⟨przybyć⟩; ***~ round*** przyjeżdżać ⟨-jechać⟩, przychodzić ⟨przyjść⟩, przybywać ⟨przybyć⟩; przychodzić ⟨przyjść⟩ do siebie; ***~ through*** przechodzić ⟨przejść⟩; docierać ⟨dotrzeć⟩, *wiadomość itp.*: zostać ujawnionym; ***~ to*** wynosić ⟨-nieść⟩; dochodzić ⟨dojść⟩ do siebie; ***~ up to*** być równym, dorównywać ⟨-wnać⟩, odpowiadać; **'~·back** powrót *m*, comeback *m*

co·me·di·an [kə'miːdjən] komik *m*

com·e·dy ['kɒmədɪ] komedia *f*

come·ly ['kʌmlɪ] (***-ier, -iest***) atrakcyjny, dobrze wyglądający

com·fort ['kʌmfət] **1.** wygoda *f*, komfort *m*; pociecha *f*, otucha *f*; **2.** pocieszać ⟨-szyć⟩, dodawać ⟨-dać⟩ otuchy; **'com·for·ta·ble** wygodny; spokojny; nieskrępowany; dobrze sytuowany; ***be ~able*** być spokojnym; czuć się wygodnie; *chory itp.*: być w dobrym stanie; **'~·er** pocieszyciel(ka *f*) *m*; *zwł. Brt.* smoczek *m*; *Am.* kołdra *f* (*pikowana*); szalik *m* wełniany; **'~·less** niepocieszony, nieukojony; **'~ sta·tion** *Am.* toaleta *f* publiczna

com·ic ['kɒmɪk] (***~ally***) komiczny

com·i·cal ['kɒmɪkl] komiczny

com·ics ['kɒmɪks] *pl.* komiks *m*

com·ma ['kɒmə] przecinek *m*

com·mand [kə'mɑːnd] **1.** rozkaz *m*, komenda *f*; kierownictwo *n*; *mil.* dowództwo *n*, komenda *f*; **2.** rozkazywać ⟨-zać⟩; *mil.* dowodzić, komenderować; *poparcie itp.* uzyskiwać ⟨-skać⟩; panować nad (*I*) (*terenem itp.*); dysponować (*zasobami itp.*); **~·er** *mil.* dowódca *m*, dowodzący *m* (-ca *f*); **~·er in chief** *mil.* [kəmɑːndərɪn'tʃiːf] (*pl.* ***commanders in chief***) głównodowodzący *m*, wódz *m* naczelny; **~·ment** *rel.* przykazanie *n*; **~ mod·ule** (*w astronautyce*) człon *m* dowodzenia, kabina *f* załogi

com·man·do [kə'mɑːndəʊ] *mil.* (*pl.* ***-dos, -does***) jednostka *f* do zadań specjalnych; żołnierz *m* jednostki do zadań specjalnych, F komandos *m*

com·mem·o|·rate [kə'meməreɪt] upamiętniać ⟨upamiętnić⟩, ⟨u⟩czcić (*pamięć*); **~·ra·tion** [kəmemə'reɪʃn] uczczenie *n* (*pamięci*); ***in ~ration of*** dla uczczenia pamięci (*G*); **~·ra·tive** [kə'memərətɪv] upamiętniający, pamiątkowy

com|·ment ['kɒment] **1.** komentarz *m* (***on*** o *L*), uwaga *f* (o *L*); ***no ~ment!*** bez komentarza!; **2.** *v/i.* ***~ment on*** ⟨s⟩komentować (*A*); *v/t.* zauważać ⟨-żyć⟩ (***that*** że); **~·men·ta·ry** ['kɒməntərɪ] komentarz *m* (***on*** o *L*); **~·men·t-a·tor** ['kɒmənteɪtə] komentator *m* (-ka *f*); *radio, TV*: sprawozdawca *m*, reporter(ka *f*) *m*

com·merce ['kɒmɜːs] handel *m*

com·mer·cial [kə'mɜːʃl] **1.** handlowy, komercyjny; **2.** *radio, TV*: reklama *f*; **~ 'art** sztuka *f* użytkowa; **~ 'art·ist** grafik *m* użytkowy; **~·ize** [kə'mɜːʃəlaɪz] ⟨s⟩komercjalizować; **~ 'tel·e·vi·sion**

C

telewizja *f* komercyjna *lub* prywatna; ~ 'trav·el·ler → ***sales representative***

com·mis·e|·rate [kə'mɪzəreɪt]: ***~rate with*** współczuć (*D*); **~·ra·tion** [kəmɪzə'reɪʃn] współczucie *n* (***for*** dla *G*), wyrazy *pl.* współczucia

com·mis·sion [kə'mɪʃn] **1.** zlecenie *n*, zamówienie *n*; *econ.* prowizja *f*; komisja *f*; *jur.* popełnienie *n* (*wykroczenia itp.*); **2.** zlecać ⟨-cić⟩, zamawiać ⟨-mówić⟩; **~·er** pełnomocnik *m*; komisarz *m*

com·mit [kə'mɪt] (**-tt-**) *wykroczenie itp.* popełniać ⟨-nić⟩; powierzać ⟨-rzyć⟩, przeznaczać ⟨-czyć⟩; angażować (się); *kogoś* umieszczać; **~ *o.s.*** zobowiązywać się (***to*** do *G*); **~·ment** zobowiązanie *n*; zaangażowanie *n*, poświęcenie *n*; **~·tal** [kə'mɪtl] *jur.* uwięzienie *n*, przekazanie *n*; **~·tee** [kə'mɪtɪ] komitet *m*

com·mod·i·ty [kə'mɒdətɪ] *econ.* artykuł *m* handlowy; produkt *m*

com·mon ['kɒmən] **1.** wspólny; zwykły, zwyczajny, pospolity; powszechny, ogólny; *zwł. Brt.* pospolity, gminny; **2.** wspólna ziemia *f*; ***in ~*** wspólnie, razem (***with*** z *I*); '**~·er** człowiek *m* z gminu, F pospolitak *m*; **~ 'law** (*niepisane*) prawo *n* zwyczajowe; **2 'Mar·ket** *econ. pol.* Wspólny Rynek *m*; '**~·place 1.** banał *m*; **2.** zwykły, pospolity, powszedni; '**~s**: ***the 2s***, *lub* ***the House of 2s*** *Brt. parl.* Izba *f* Gmin; **~ 'sense** zdrowy rozsądek *m*; '**~·wealth**: ***the 2wealth (of Nations)*** Wspólnota *f* Narodów; ***the 2wealth of Independent States*** Wspólnota *f* Niepodległych Państw

com·mo·tion [kə'məʊʃn] zamieszanie *n*

com·mu·nal ['kɒmjʊnl] wspólny; ogólnodostępny

com·mune ['kɒmju:n] komuna *f*; wspólnota *f*; gmina *f*

com·mu·ni|·cate [kə'mju:nɪkeɪt] *v/t.* przekazywać ⟨-zać⟩, komunikować; *v/i.* porozumiewać ⟨-mieć⟩ się (***with*** z *I*); komunikować się; *pokoje itp.*: być połączonym; **~·ca·tion** [kəmju:nɪ'keɪʃn] porozumiewanie *n* się, komunikowanie *n* się; komunikacja *f*; przekazanie *n*

com·mu·ni·ca·tions [kəmju:nɪ'keɪʃnz] *pl.* połączenia *pl.*; komunikacja *f*, telekomunikacja *f*; *attr.* (tele)-komunikacyjny; **~ sat·el·lite** satelita *m* telekomunikacyjny

com·mu·ni·ca·tive [kə'mju:nɪkətɪv] komunikatywny, rozmowny

Com·mu·nion [kə'mju:njən] *rel. też* ***Holy ~*** Komunia *f* (*Święta*)

com·mu|·nis·m ['kɒmjʊnɪzəm] komunizm *m*; '**~·nist 1.** komunista *m* (-tka *f*); **2.** komunistyczny

com·mu·ni·ty [kə'mju:nətɪ] wspólnota *f*; społeczność *f*, społeczeństwo *n*

com|·mute [kə'mju:t] *rail.* dojeżdżać ⟨-jechać⟩ (*do pracy*); *jur.* ⟨z⟩łagodzić karę; **~'mut·er** dojeżdżający *m* (-ca *f*) do pracy; **~'mut·er train** pociąg *m* dla dojeżdżających do pracy

com·pact 1. ['kɒmpækt] puderniczka *f*; *Am.* niewielki samochód *m*, compact *m*; **2.** [kəm'pækt] *adj.* zwarty; niewielki; lapidarny; **~ car** [kɒmpækt 'kɑ:] *Am.* niewielki samochód *m*, compact *m*; **~ disc, ~ disk** [kɒmpækt 'dɪsk] (*skrót*: ***CD***) kompakt *m*, płyta *f* kompaktowa, CD *n*; **~ 'disk play·er** odtwarzacz *m* kompaktowy

com·pan·ion [kəm'pænjən] towarzysz(ka *f*) *m*; dama *f* do towarzystwa; encyklopedia *f*, podręcznik *m*; **~·ship** towarzystwo *n*

com·pa·ny ['kʌmpənɪ] towarzystwo *n*; *econ.* firma *f*, spółka *f*; *mil.* kompania *f*; *theat.* zespół; ***keep s.o. ~*** dotrzymywać komuś towarzystwa

com|·pa·ra·ble ['kɒmpərəbl] porównywalny, zbliżony; **~·par·a·tive** [kəm'pærətɪv] **1.** porównawczy; względny; **2.** *też* ***~parative degree*** *gr.* stopień *m* wyższy; **~·pare** [kəm'peə] **1.** *v/t.* porównywać ⟨-wnać⟩; ***~pared with*** w porównaniu z (*I*); *v/i.* wypadać ⟨-paść⟩ w porównaniu; **2. *beyond ~pare, without ~pare*** nie do opisania; **~·pa·ri·son** [kəm'pærɪsn] porównanie *n*

com·part·ment [kəm'pɑ:tmənt] przegródka *f*; *rail.* przedział *m*; komora *f*; schowek *m*

com·pass ['kʌmpəs] kompas *m*; ***a pair of ~es*** *pl.* cyrkiel *m*

com·pas·sion [kəm'pæʃn] współczucie *n*; **~·ate** [kəm'pæʃənət] współczujący; *urlop itp.*: okolicznościowy

com·pat·i·ble [kəm'pætəbl] zgodny; ***be ~*** (***with***) odpowiadać (*D*), *komp.*, *radio*: być kompatybilnym (z *I*)

C

com·pat·ri·ot [kəm'pætrɪət] rodak *m* (-aczka *f*)
com·pel [kəm'pel] (*-ll-*) nakłaniać ⟨-łonić⟩, zmuszać ⟨-sić⟩; **~·ling** nieodparty, ważny
com·pen|·sate ['kɒmpenseɪt] wynagradzać ⟨-grodzić⟩, rekompensować; stanowić kompensatę; wypłacać⟨-cić⟩ rekompensatę; **~·sa·tion** [kɒmpen'seɪʃn] rekompensata *f*; kompensata *f*, *jur.* wynagrodzenie *n*, odszkodowanie *n*
com·pere ['kɒmpeə] *Brt.* konferansjer *m*, prezenter(ka *f*) *m*
com·pete [kəm'piːt] współzawodniczyć (**for** o *A*), konkurować (**for** o *A*); (*w sporcie*) brać ⟨wziąć⟩ udział
com·pe|·tence ['kɒmpɪtəns] fachowość *f*, kompetencje *pl.*, kwalifikacje *pl.*; znajomość *f* (*języka obcego itp.*); '**~·tent** fachowy, kompetentny
com·pe·ti·tion [kɒmpɪ'tɪʃn] zawody *pl.*, konkurs *m*; rywalizacja *f*, współzawodnictwo *n*; konkurencja *f*
com·pet·i|·tive [kəm'petətɪv] konkurencyjny; **~·tor** [kəm'petɪtə] współzawodniczący *m* (-ca *f*), konkurent(ka *f*) *m*
com·pile [kəm'paɪl] ⟨s⟩kompilować, opracowywać ⟨-wać⟩, zbierać ⟨zebrać⟩
com·pla|·cence, ~·cen·cy [kəm'pleɪsns, -snsɪ] samozadowolenie *n*; **~·cent** [kəm'pleɪsnt] zadowolony z siebie, pełen samozadowolenia
com·plain [kəm'pleɪn] ⟨po⟩skarżyć się (**about** o *L*, **to** *D*), składać ⟨złożyć⟩ skargę *lub* zażalenie (**of** na *A*); **~t** skarga *f*; zażalenie *n*; *med.* dolegliwość *f*
com·ple|·ment 1. ['kɒmplɪmənt] uzupełnienie *n*, dopełnienie *n*; △ *nie* ***komplement***; **2.** ['kɒmplɪment] uzupełniać ⟨-nić⟩; **~·men·ta·ry** [kɒmplɪ'mentərɪ] uzupełniający, dopełniający; wzajemnie się dopełniający
com|·plete [kəm'pliːt] **1.** całkowity, kompletny; cały, zupełny; skończony; **2.** ⟨u-, za⟩kończyć; uzupełniać ⟨-nić⟩; *formularz itp.* wypełniać ⟨-nić⟩; **~·ple·tion** [kəm'pliːʃn] zakończenie *n*, uzupełnienie *n*
com·plex ['kɒmpleks] **1.** złożony, skomplikowany; **2.** kompleks *m* (*też psych.*)
com·plex·ion [kəm'plekʃn] cera *f*, karnacja *f*; *fig.* odmiana *f*
com·plex·i·ty [kəm'pleksətɪ] złożoność *f*, skomplikowanie *n*
com·pli|·ance [kəm'plaɪəns] zgodność *f*; stosowność *f*; uległość *f*; ***in ~ance with*** zgodnie z (*I*); **~·ant** uległy, ustępliwy
com·pli|·cate ['kɒmplɪkeɪt] ⟨s⟩komplikować; '**~·cat·ed** skomplikowany; **~·ca·tion** [kɒmplɪ'keɪʃn] komplikacja *f*, problem *m*; *med.* powikłanie *n*
com·plic·i·ty [kəm'plɪsətɪ] *jur.* współudział (**in** w *L*)
com·pli|·ment 1. ['kɒmplɪmənt] komplement *m*; ***~ments*** *pl.* pozdrowienia *pl.*; **2.** ['kɒmplɪment] *v/t.* prawić komplementy; ⟨po⟩gratulować; **~·men·ta·ry** [kɒmplɪ'mentərɪ] gratisowy, bezpłatny, okazowy
com·ply [kəm'plaɪ] zgadzać ⟨-zgodzić⟩ się (**with** z *I*); ⟨za⟩stosować się (do *G*) (*umowy itp.*)
com·po·nent [kəm'pəʊnənt] składnik *m*, część *f* składowa; *tech. electr.* podzespół *m*
com|·pose [kəm'pəʊz] składać ⟨złożyć⟩; *mus.* ⟨s⟩komponować; ***be ~posed of*** składać się z (*G*); ***~pose o.s.*** uspokajać ⟨-koić⟩ się; **~'posed** spokojny, opanowany; **~'pos·er** *mus.* kompozytor(ka *f*) *m*; **~·po·si·tion** [kɒmpə'zɪʃn] skład *m*; *mus.* kompozycja *f*, utwór *m*; *ped.* wypracowanie *n*; **~·posure** [kəm'pəʊʒə] opanowanie *n*, samokontrola *f*
com·pound[1] ['kɒmpaʊnd] *ogrodzony* teren *m*; obóz *m* dla jeńców *lub* więźniów; (*w zoo*) wybieg *m*
com·pound[2] **1.** ['kɒmpaʊnd] *chem.* związek *m*; *gr.* złożenie *n*; **2.** ['kɒmpaʊnd] złożony; ***~ interest*** *econ.* procent *m* składany; **3.** [kəm'paʊnd] *v/t.* składać ⟨złożyć⟩; zwiększać ⟨-szyć⟩, *zwł.* pogarszać ⟨pogorszyć⟩
com·pre·hend [kɒmprɪ'hend] ⟨z⟩rozumieć, pojmować ⟨pojąć⟩
com·pre·hen|·si·ble [kɒmprɪ'hensəbl] zrozumiały; **~·sion** [kɒmprɪ'henʃn] zrozumienie *n*, pojmowanie *n*; ***past ~sion*** nie do zrozumienia; **~·sive** [kɒmprɪ'hensɪv] **1.** ogólny; wszechstronny; zupełny; **2.** *też Brt.* średnia szkoła *f* ogólnokształcąca (*nie stosująca selekcji*)
com|·press [kəm'pres] ściskać ⟨ścisnąć⟩, sprężać ⟨-żyć⟩; ***~pressed air***

C

sprężone powietrze *n*; **~·pres·sion** [kəm'preʃn] *phys.* ściskanie *n*; *tech.* sprężanie *n*
com·prise [kəm'praɪz] zawierać ⟨zawrzeć⟩, obejmować ⟨objąć⟩; ***be ~d of*** składać się z (*G*)
com·pro·mise ['kɒmprəmaɪz] **1.** kompromis *m*; **2.** *v/t.* dochodzić ⟨dojść⟩ do porozumienia; ⟨s⟩kompromitować; *zasady itp.* zdradzać ⟨-dzić⟩; *v/i.* zawierać ⟨zawrzeć⟩ kompromis
com·pul|·sion [kəm'pʌlʃn] przymus *m*; *psych.* natręctwo; **~·sive** [kəm'pʌlsɪv] przymusowy; *psych.* nałogowy, poddany natręctwu; **~·so·ry** [kəm'pʌlsərɪ] obowiązkowy, obligatoryjny
com·punc·tion [kəm'pʌŋkʃn] skrupuły *pl.*, obiekcje *pl.*
com·pute [kəm'pjuːt] ⟨wy-, po⟩liczyć
com·put·er [kəm'pjuːtə] komputer *m*; **~-'aid·ed** wspomagany komputerowo; **~-con'trolled** sterowany komputerowo; **~ game** gra *f* komputerowa; **~ 'graph·ics** *pl.* grafika *f* komputerowa; **~·ize** [kəm'pjuːtəraɪz] ⟨s⟩komputeryzować (się); **~ pre'dic·tion** prognoza *f* komputerowa *lub* przewidywanie *n* komputerowe; **~ 'sci·ence** informatyka *f*; **~ 'sci·en·tist** informatyk *m*; **~ 'vi·rus** wirus *m* komputerowy
com·rade ['kɒmreɪd] towarzysz(ka *f*) *m*
con[1] [kɒn] *skrót:* → ***contra***
con[2] [kɒn] F (**-*nn*-**) oszwabiać ⟨-bić⟩, nabierać ⟨nabrać⟩
con·ceal [kən'siːl] ukrywać ⟨ukryć⟩, skrywać ⟨skryć⟩
con·cede [kən'siːd] przyznawać ⟨-znać⟩; przyznawać ⟨-znać⟩ rację; uznawać ⟨uznać⟩; ustępować ⟨ustąpić⟩
con·ceit [kən'siːt] zarozumiałość *f*; **~·ed** zarozumiały
con·cei|·va·ble [kən'siːvəbl] wyobrażalny; do pomyślenia; **~ve** [kən'siːv] *v/i.* zachodzić ⟨zajść⟩ w ciążę; *v/t. dziecko* począć; obmyślać ⟨-lić⟩
con·cen·trate ['kɒnsəntreɪt] ⟨s⟩koncentrować (się)
con·cept ['kɒnsept] pojęcie *n*
con·cep·tion [kən'sepʃn] pojęcie *n*, koncepcja *f*; *biol.* poczęcie *n*
con·cern [kən'sɜːn] **1.** sprawa *f*, rzecz *f*; zagadnienie *n*; zmartwienie *n*, niepokój *m*, troska *f*; *econ.* przedsiębiorstwo *n*, biznes *m*; **2.** dotyczyć (*G*); ⟨z⟩martwić, ⟨za⟩niepokoić; **~ed** zaniepokojony, zatroskany; zamieszany (***in*** w *L*); **~·ing** *prp.* odnośnie (*G*), dotyczący (*G*)
con·cert ['kɒnsət] *mus.* koncert *m*; koncertowy; **'~ hall** sala *f* koncertowa
con·ces·sion [kən'seʃn] ustępstwo *n*; koncesja *f*; ulga *f*, zwolnienie *n*
con·cil·i·a·to·ry [kən'sɪlɪətərɪ] pojednawczy, ugodowy
con·cise [kən'saɪs] zwięzły, krótki; **~·ness** zwięzłość *f*
con·clude [kən'kluːd] ⟨s-, za⟩kończyć, ⟨s⟩finalizować; *umowę itp.* zawierać ⟨zawrzeć⟩; wnioskować, dochodzić ⟨dojść⟩ do wniosku; ***to be ~d*** ciąg dalszy nastąpi
con·clu|·sion [kən'kluːʒn] wniosek *m*, konkluzja *f*; zakończenie *n*; podsumowanie *n*; zawarcie *n*; **~·sive** [kən'kluːsɪv] ostateczny, nieodparty
con|·coct [kən'kɒkt] ⟨s⟩preparować (*też fig.*); przygotowywać ⟨-tować⟩; **~·coc·tion** [kən'kɒkʃn] mikstura *f*; *fig.* mieszanina *f*
con·crete[1] ['kɒŋkriːt] konkretny
con·crete[2] ['kɒŋkriːt] **1.** beton *m*; *attr.* betonowy; **2.** ⟨za⟩betonować
con·cur [kən'kɜː] (**-*rr*-**) zgadzać ⟨-zgodzić⟩ się; współdziałać; zbiegać ⟨zbiec⟩ się; **~·rence** [kən'kʌrəns] zgodność *f*, zbieżność *f*, współdziałanie *n*; ⚠ *nie* ***konkurencja***
con·cus·sion [kən'kʌʃn] *med.* wstrząs *m* (*zwł. mózgu*)
con|·demn [kən'dem] potępiać ⟨-pić⟩; *jur.* skazywać ⟨-zać⟩; *budynek itp.* uznawać ⟨uznać⟩ za zagrożony; ***~demn to death*** skazywać na śmierć; **~·dem·na·tion** [kɒndem'neɪʃn] potępienie *n*; skazanie *n*
con|·den·sa·tion [kɒnden'seɪʃn] kondensacja *f*, skraplanie *n*; skroplona para *f*; zaparowanie *n*; **~·dense** [kən'dens] ⟨s⟩kondensować, skraplać ⟨-skroplić⟩; **~·densed 'milk** *słodzone* mleko *n* skondensowane; **~'dens·er** *tech.* kondensator *m*; skraplacz *m*
con·de·scend [kɒndɪ'send] zniżać ⟨zniżyć⟩ się; **~·ing** łaskawy, protekcjonalny
con·di·ment ['kɒndɪmənt] przyprawa *f*
con·di·tion [kən'dɪʃn] **1.** warunek *m*; stan *m*; kondycja *f*, forma *f*; *med.* dolegliwość *f*, schorzenie *n*; **~*s*** *pl.* warun-

ki *pl.*, okoliczności *pl.*, sytuacja *f*; ***on ~ that*** pod warunkiem że; ***be out of ~*** nie mieć kondycji; **2.** ⟨u⟩warunkować; ⟨na⟩uczyć; utrzymywać ⟨-mać⟩ w dobrej formie; **~·al** [kən'dɪʃənl] **1.** warunkowy; ***be ~al on*** *lub* ***upon*** być uzależnionym od (*G*); **2.** *też* ***~al clause*** *gr.* zdanie *n* warunkowe; *też* ***~al mood*** *gr.* tryb *m* warunkowy

con·do ['kɒndəʊ] *Am.* → ***condominium***

con|·dole [kən'dəʊl]: ***~dole with*** składać kondolencje (*D*); **~'do·lence** *zw. pl.* kondolencje *pl.*

con·dom ['kɒndəm] kondom *m*, prezerwatywa *f*

con·do·min·i·um [kɒndə'mɪnɪəm] *Am. jakby*: mieszkanie *m* własnościowe; *jakby*: budynek *m* z mieszkaniami własnościowymi

con·done [kən'dəʊn] wybaczać ⟨-czyć⟩, godzić się na (*A*)

con·du·cive [kən'dju:sɪv] sprzyjający (***to*** *D*), prowadzący (***to*** do *G*)

con|·duct **1.** ['kɒndʌkt] prowadzenie *n*; zachowanie *n* (się) **2.** [kən'dʌkt] prowadzić; kierować; zachowywać się; *phys.* przewodzić; *mus.* dyrygować; ***~ducted tour*** wycieczka *f* z przewodnikiem; **~·duc·tor** [kən'dʌktə] przewodnik *m*); (*w autobusie, tramwaju, Am. też pociągu*) konduktor(ka *f*) *m*; *mus.* dyrygent *m*; *phys.* przewodnik *m*; *electr.* piorunochron *m*, odgromnik *m*

cone [kəʊn] stożek *m*; wafel *m* (*na lody*), rożek *m*; *bot.* szyszka *f*

con·fec·tion [kən'fekʃn] wyrób *m* cukierniczy; ⚠ *nie* ***konfekcja***; **~·er** [kən'fekʃnə] cukiernik *m*; **~·e·ry** [kən'fekʃnərɪ] słodycze *pl.*, wyroby *pl.* cukiernicze; cukiernia *f*; ⚠ *nie* ***konfekcyjny***

con·fed·e|·ra·cy [kən'fedərəsɪ] konfederacja *f*; ***the* 𝔖*·ra·cy*** *Am. hist.* Konfederacja Południa; **~·rate** **1.** [kən'fedərət] skonfederowany, konfederacyjny; **2.** [kən'fedərət] konfederat *m*; **3.** [kən'fedəreɪt] konfederować (się); **~·ra·tion** [kənfedə'reɪʃn] konfederacja *f*

con·fer [kən'fɜ:] (***-tt-***) *v/t. tytuł itp.* nadawać ⟨-dać⟩; *v/i.* naradzać ⟨-dzić⟩ się

con·fe·rence ['kɒnfərəns] konferencja *f*

con|·fess [kən'fes] wyznawać ⟨-znać⟩; przyznawać się; spowiadać się; **~·fession** [kən'feʃən] wyznanie *n*; przyznanie *n* się; *rel.* spowiedź *f*; **~·fes·sion·al** [kən'feʃənl] *rel.* konfesjonał *m*; **~·fes·sor** [kən'fesə] *rel.* spowiednik *m*

con·fide [kən'faɪd]: ***~ s.th. to s.o.*** wyznawać coś komuś; ***~ in s.o.*** ufać komuś, zawierzyć komuś

con·fi·dence ['kɒnfɪdəns] zaufanie *n*; przekonanie *n*, wiara *f* (w siebie); **'~ man** (*pl.* ***-men***) → ***conman***; **'~ trick** szwindel *m*, oszustwo *n*

con·fi|·dent ['kɒnfɪdənt] ufny; pełen ufności; przekonany, pewny; ***be ~dent of*** być pewnym (*G*); **~·den·tial** [kɒnfɪ'denʃl] poufny, zaufany

con·fine [kən'faɪn] ograniczać ⟨-czyć⟩; ⟨u⟩więzić, odosobniać ⟨-nić⟩; ***be ~d to*** być odosobnionym w (*L*), być przykutym do (*G*; *łóżka itp.*); **~·ment** zamknięcie *n*; odosobnienie *n*; poród *m*

con|·firm [kən'fɜ:m] potwierdzać ⟨-dzić⟩, zatwierdzać; ***be ~firmed*** *rel.* być bierzmowanym; *rel.* otrzymywać ⟨-mać⟩ konfirmację; **~·fir·ma·tion** [kɒnfə'meɪʃn] potwierdzenie *n*, zatwierdzenie *n*; *rel.* bierzmowanie *n*; *rel.* konfirmacja *f*

con·fis|·cate ['kɒnfɪskeɪt] ⟨s⟩konfiskować; **~·ca·tion** [kɒnfɪ'skeɪʃn] konfiskata *f*

con·flict **1.** ['kɒnflɪkt] konflikt *m*; **2.** [kən'flɪkt] wchodzić ⟨wejść⟩ w konflikt; kolidować; **~·ing** [kən'flɪktɪŋ] kolidujący, sprzeczny

con·form [kən'fɔ:m] dostosowywać ⟨-wać⟩ się; być zgodnym (***to*** z *I*), zachowywać ⟨-wać⟩ się konformistycznie

con·found [kən'faʊnd] zmieszać, wprawiać ⟨-wić⟩ w zakłopotanie

con|·front [kən'frʌnt] stawać ⟨stanąć⟩ przed (*I*); natykać się na (*A*); stawiać czoło (*D*); ⟨s⟩konfrontować; **~·front·a·tion** [kɒnfrʌn'teɪʃn] konfrontacja *f*

con|·fuse [kən'fju:z] zmieszać, wprawiać ⟨-wić⟩ w zakłopotanie; pomieszać, pomylić; **~·fused** zmieszany; pomieszany; **~·fu·sion** [kən'fju:ʒn] zmieszanie *n*, zamieszanie *n*; pomieszanie *n*

con·geal [kən'dʒi:l] ⟨s⟩krzepnąć; ⟨z⟩gęstnieć

con|·gest·ed [kən'dʒestɪd] zatłoczony; zapchany; **~·ges·tion** [kən'dʒestʃən] *med.* przekrwienie *n*; *też* ***traffic ~gestion*** zator *m* drogowy

C

con·grat·u|·late [kən'grætjuleɪt] ⟨po⟩gratulować; **~·la·tion** [kəngrætjʊ'leɪʃn] gratulacje *pl.*; ***~lations!*** moje gratulacje!

con·gre|·gate ['kɒŋgrɪgeɪt] zbierać (się); **~·ga·tion** [kɒŋgrɪ'geɪʃn] *rel.* zebranie *n*; wierni *pl.*; kongregacja *f*

con·gress ['kɒŋgres] kongres *m*; ♀ *Am. parl.* Kongres *m*; '**♀·man** (*pl.* ***-men***) *Am. parl.* kongresman *m*; '**♀·wom·an** (*pl.* ***-women***) *Am. parl.* kobieta *f* kongresman

con|·ic ['kɒnɪk] *zwł. tech.*, '**~·i·cal** stożkowy

co·ni·fer ['kɒnɪfə] *bot.* drzewo *n* szpilkowe *lub* iglaste

con·jec·ture [kən'dʒektʃə] **1.** przypuszczenie *n*, domysł *m*; **2.** przypuszczać, wysuwać ⟨-sunąć⟩ przypuszczenie

con·ju·gal ['kɒndʒʊgl] małżeński

con·ju|·gate ['kɒndʒʊgeɪt] *gr.* odmieniać ⟨-nić⟩, koniugować; **~·ga·tion** [kɒndʒʊ'geɪʃn] *gr.* koniugacja *f*

con·junc·tion [kən'dʒʌŋkʃn] związek; *gr.* spójnik *m*; ***in ~ with*** wraz z (*I*)

con·junc·ti·vi·tis [kəndʒʌŋktɪ'vaɪtɪs] *med.* zapalenie *n* spojówek

con|·jure ['kʌndʒə] wyczarowywać ⟨-ować⟩; *diabła itp.* wywoływać ⟨-łać⟩; robić sztuczki magiczne; ***~jure up*** wyczarowywać ⟨-ować⟩, wywoływać ⟨-łać⟩ (*też fig.*); [kən'dʒʊə] *przest.* błagać; **~·jur·er** ['kʌndʒərə] *zwł. Brt.* sztukmistrz *m*, iluzjonista *m*; **~·jur·ing trick** ['kʌndʒərɪŋ -] sztuczka *f* magiczna; **~·jur·or** ['kʌndʒərə] → ***conjurer***

con·man ['kɒnmæn] (*pl.* ***-men***) hochsztapler *m*, oszust *m*

con|·nect [kə'nekt] ⟨po⟩łączyć; *electr.* przyłączać ⟨-czyć⟩, podłączać ⟨-czyć⟩; *rail., aviat itp.* mieć połączenie (***with*** z *I*); **~'nect·ed** połączony; spójny; **~·nec·tion**, **~·nex·ion** *Brt.* [kə'nekʃn] połączenie *n* (*też aviat., rail.*); przyłączenie *n*, podłączenie *n* (*też electr., tel.*); spójność *f*; *zwł.* ***~nections*** *pl.* stosunki *pl.*, związki *pl.*; krewni *pl.*

con·quer ['kɒŋkə] zdobywać ⟨-być⟩, pokonywać ⟨-nać⟩; **~·or** ['kɒŋkərə] zdobywca *m* (-wczyni *f*)

con·quest ['kɒŋkwest] podbój *m* (*też fig.*)

con·science ['kɒnʃəns] sumienie *n*

con·sci·en·tious [kɒnʃɪ'enʃəs] sumienny, staranny; **~·ness** sumienność *f*, staranność *f*; **~ ob'jec·tor** (*odmawiający pełnienia służby wojskowej ze względu na przekonania*)

con·scious ['kɒnʃəs] świadomy; przytomny; ***be ~ of*** zdawać sobie sprawę z (*I*); '**~·ness** świadomość *f*

con|·script **1.** *mil.* [kən'skrɪpt] powoływać ⟨-łać⟩; **2.** ['kɒnskrɪpt] poborowy *m*; **~·scrip·tion** [kən'skrɪpʃn] *mil.* pobór *m*

con·se|·crate ['kɒnsɪkreɪt] *rel.* poświęcać; **~·cra·tion** [kɒnsɪ'kreɪʃn] *rel.* poświęcenie *n*

con·sec·u·tive [kən'sekjʊtɪv] kolejny

con·sent [kən'sent] **1.** zgoda *f*; **2.** zgadzać się (***to*** na *A*)

con·se|·quence ['kɒnsɪkwəns] skutek *m*, konsekwencja *f*; znaczenie *n*; ***in ~quence of*** wskutek (*G*); '**~·quent·ly** w rezultacie, wreszcie; ⚠ *nie* ***konsekwentnie***

con·ser·va|·tion [kɒnsə'veɪʃn] konserwacja *f*; ochrona *f*; ochrona *f* przyrody; ***~tion area*** rezerwat *m* przyrody; **~·tion·ist** [kɒnsə'veɪʃnɪst] ekolog *m*; **~·tive** [kən'sɜːvətɪv] **1.** konserwatywny, zachowawczy; **2.** ***♀tive*** konserwatysta *m* (-stka *f*); **~·to·ry** [kɒn'sɜːvətrɪ] szklarnia *f*, cieplarnia *f*; **con·serve** [kən'sɜːv] zachowywać ⟨-wać⟩, oszczędzać; utrzymywać ⟨-mać⟩, *owoce itp.* ⟨za⟩konserwować

con·sid|·er [kən'sɪdə] *v/t.* rozważać ⟨-żyć⟩; rozpatrywać ⟨-trzyć⟩; zastanawiać ⟨-nowić⟩ się; uważać; brać ⟨wziąć⟩ pod uwagę; *v/i.* zastanawiać ⟨-nowić⟩ się'; **~·e·ra·ble** [kən'sɪdərəbl] znaczny; **~·e·ra·bly** [kən'sɪdərəblɪ] znacznie; **~·er·ate** [kən'sɪdərət] taktowny, grzeczny; **~·e·ra·tion** [kənsɪdə'reɪʃn] wzgląd *m*; rozwaga *f*; rozważanie *n*; zapłata *f*, rekompensata *f*; ***take into ~eration*** brać ⟨wziąć⟩ pod uwagę; ***under ~eration*** rozważany; **~·er·ing** [kən'sɪdərɪŋ] zważywszy (że)

con·sign [kən'saɪn] *econ.* przesyłać ⟨-słać⟩; **~·ment** *econ.* przesyłka *f*, partia *f*

con·sist [kən'sɪst]: ***~ in*** polegać na (*L*); ***~ of*** składać się z (*G*)

con·sis|·tence, **~·ten·cy** [kən'sɪstəns, -tənsɪ] konsystencja *f*, spoistość *f*; konsekwencja *f*, spójność *f*; **~·tent** [kən'sɪstənt] konsekwentny, spójny; zgodny (***with*** z *I*); stały

con|•so•la•tion [kɒnsə'leɪʃn] pociecha *f*; **~•sole** [kən'səʊl] pocieszać ⟨-szyć⟩

con•sol•i•date [kən'sɒlɪdeɪt] ⟨s⟩konsolidować; wzmacniać ⟨wzmocnić⟩

con•so•nant ['kɒnsənənt] *gr.* spółgłoska *f*

con•spic•u•ous [kən'spɪkjʊəs] *dobrze* widoczny, rzucający się w oczy

con|•spi•ra•cy [kən'spɪrəsɪ] konspiracja *f*; spisek *m*, zmowa *f*; **~•spi•ra•tor** [kən'spɪrətə] konspirator(ka *f*) *m*; spiskowiec *m*; **~•spire** [kən'spaɪə] zmawiać ⟨zmówić⟩ się, spiskować, konspirować

con•sta•ble ['kʌnstəbl] *Brt.* posterunkowy *m*

con•stant ['kɒnstənt] stały; niezmienny

con•ster•na•tion [kɒnstə'neɪʃn] konsternacja *f*, zakłopotanie *n*

con•sti|•pat•ed ['kɒnstɪpeɪtɪd] *med.*: ***be ~pated*** cierpieć na zatwardzenie; **~•pa•tion** [kɒnstɪ'peɪʃn] *med.* zatwardzenie *n*

con•sti•tu|•en•cy [kən'stɪtjʊənsɪ] okręg *m* wyborczy; **~•ent** część *f* składowa, składnik *m*; wyborca *m*

con•sti•tute ['kɒnstɪtjuːt] (u)stanowić; ⟨u⟩konstytuować; (u)stanowić, ⟨u⟩tworzyć

con•sti•tu•tion [kɒnstɪ'tjuːʃn] *pol.* konstytucja *f*; statut *m*; ustanowienie *n*, ukonstytuowanie *n*; skład *m*; kondycja *f* (*fizyczna*); **~•al** [kɒnstɪ'tjuːʃənl] konstytucyjny; *prawo itp.*: statutowy

con•strained [kən'streɪnd] wymuszony, nienaturalny

con|•strict [kən'strɪkt] zaciskać⟨-snąć⟩, ściskać ⟨-snąć⟩; **~•stric•tion** [kən'strɪkʃn] zaciśnięcie *n*, ściśnięcie *n*

con|•struct [kən'strʌkt] ⟨z⟩budować; ⟨s⟩konstruować; **~•struc•tion** [kən'strʌkʃn] konstrukcja *f*; budowa *f*; (*w przemyśle*) budownictwo *n*; ***under ~struction*** w trakcie budowy; **~'struc•tion site** plac *m* budowy; **~•struc•tive** [kən'strʌktɪv] konstruktywny; **~•struc•tor** [kən'strʌktə] konstruktor *m*, budowniczy *m*

con•sul ['kɒnsəl] konsul *m*; **con•su•late** ['kɒnsjʊlət] konsulat *m*; **con•su•late 'gen•e•ral** (*pl.* ***-s general***) konsulat *m* generalny; **con•sul 'gen•e•ral** (*pl.* ***-s general***) konsul *m* generalny

con•sult [kən'sʌlt] *v/t. coś* ⟨s⟩konsultować, zasięgnąć porady; ⟨po⟩radzić się; (*w książce*) sprawdzać ⟨-dzić⟩; *v/i.* udzielać ⟨-lić⟩ konsultacji; konsultować się (***with*** z *I*)

con•sul|•tant [kən'sʌltənt] konsultant(ka *f*) *m*; *Brt.* specjalista (*lekarz*) *m* (-tka *f*); **~•ta•tion** [kɒnsl'teɪʃn] konsultacja *f*; porada *f*; narada *f*

con•sult•ing [kən'sʌltɪŋ] udzielający konsultacji; *lekarz, adwokat itp.* z praktyką (*prywatną*); **~ hours** *pl.* godziny *pl.* przyjęć; **~ room** gabinet *m*

con|•sume [kən'sjuːm] *v/t.* ⟨s⟩konsumować, spożywać ⟨-żyć⟩; *paliwo itp.* zużywać ⟨-żyć⟩, *prąd itp.* pobierać ⟨pobrać⟩; ⟨s⟩trawić (*przez pożar, też fig.*); **~'sum•er** *econ.* konsument(ka *f*) *m*; **~'sum•er so•ci•e•ty** społeczeństwo *n* konsumpcyjne

con•sum•mate **1.** [kən'sʌmɪt] doskonały, wyśmienity; **2.** ['kɒnsəmeɪt] *wysiłki* ukoronować, zakończyć; *małżeństwo* skonsumować

con•sump•tion [kən'sʌmpʃn] zużycie *n* (*paliwa*), pobór *m* (*prądu*); *przest. med.* suchoty *pl.*, gruźlica *f*

cont *skrót pisany*: ***continued*** cd., ciąg dalszy

con•tact ['kɒntækt] **1.** kontakt *m*; styczność *m*, zetknięcie *n* się; osoba *f* kontaktowa; *med.* osoba *f* stykająca się z chorym; ***make ~s*** nawiązywać ⟨-zać⟩ kontakty; **2.** ⟨s⟩kontaktować się z (*I*); **'~ lens** szkło *f* kontaktowe

con•ta•gious [kən'teɪdʒəs] *med.* zakaźny; zaraźliwy (*też fig*)

con•tain [kən'teɪn] zawierać; *fig.* powstrzymywać ⟨-mać⟩, trzymać na wodzy; **~•er** pojemnik *m*; *econ.* kontener *m*; **~•er•ize** [kən'teɪnəraɪz] *econ.* ⟨s⟩konteneryzować

con•tam•i|•nate [kən'tæmɪneɪt] zanieczyszczać ⟨-czyścić⟩; skażać ⟨skazić⟩; **~•na•tion** [kəntæmɪ'neɪʃn] skażenie *n*; zanieczyszczenie *n*

contd *skrót pisany*: ***continued*** cd., ciąg dalszy

con•tem|•plate ['kɒntempleɪt] rozważać ⟨-żyć⟩; rozmyślać o (*L*); kontemplować; **~•pla•tion** [kɒntem'pleɪʃn] rozmyślanie *n*; kontemplacja *f*; **~•pla•tive** [kən'templətɪv, 'kɒntempleɪtɪv] kontemplacyjny, medytacyjny

con·tem·po·ra·ry [kən'tempərərɪ] **1.** współczesny; **2.** współczesny *m* (-na *f*)

con|·tempt [kən'tempt] pogarda *f*, wzgarda *f*; **~·temp·ti·ble** [kən'temptəbl] zasługujący na pogardę; **~·temp·tu·ous** [kən'temptʃʊəs] pogardliwy, lekceważący

con·tend [kən'tend] *v/t.* ⟨s⟩twierdzić, utrzymywać (***that*** że); *v/i.* walczyć (***for*** o *A*, ***with*** z *I*); rywalizować (***for*** o *A*); **~·er** *zwł. sport*: zawodnik *m* (-iczka *f*); rywal(ka *f*) *m*

con·tent[1] ['kɒntent] zawartość *f*; *książki itp.*: treść *f*; ***~s*** zawartość *f*; (***table of***) ***~s*** spis *m* treści

con·tent[2] [kən'tent] **1.** zadowolony; **2.** zadowalać ⟨-wolić⟩; **~ *o.s.*** zadowalać się, poprzestawać na (*I*); **~·ed** zadowolony; **~·ment** zadowolenie *n*

con|·test 1. ['kɒntest] współzawodnictwo *n*, rywalizacja *f*; konkurs *m*; **2.** [kən'test] rywalizować o (*A*), ubiegać się o (*A*); *też jur.* ⟨za⟩kwestionować, podawać ⟨-dać⟩ w wątpliwość; **~·testant** [kən'testənt] rywal(ka *f*) *m*, konkurent(ka *f*) *m*; *jur.* strona *f* w sporze

con·text ['kɒntekst] kontekst *m*

con·ti|·nent ['kɒntɪnənt] kontynent *m*; ***the* Ƨ*nent*** *Br.* Europa *f* (*bez Wlk. Brytanii*); **~·nen·tal** [kɒntɪ'nentl] kontynentalny

con·tin·gen|·cy [kən'tɪndʒənsɪ] ewentualność *f*, możliwość *f*; **~t 1.** ***be ~t on*** zależeć od (*G*); **2.** kontyngent *m*

con·tin|·u·al [kən'tɪnjʊəl] bezustanny, nieustający; **~·u·a·tion** [kəntɪnjʊ'eɪʃn] kontynuacja *f*; przedłużenie *n*; ciąg *m* dalszy; **~·ue** [kən'tɪnjuː] *v/t.* ciągnąć *coś* dalej, kontynuować; ***to be ~ued*** ciąg dalszy nastąpi; *v/i.* ciągnąć się dalej, trwać dalej; trwać nadal, utrzymywać się; **con·ti·nu·i·ty** [kɒntɪ'njuːətɪ] ciągłość *f*; **~·u·ous** [kən'tɪnjʊəs] nieprzerwany; **~·u·ous 'form** *gr.* forma *f* czasu ciągłego

con|·tort [kən'tɔːt] wykręcać (się), wykrzywiać (się), wyginać (się); **~·tortion** [kən'tɔːʃn] wygięcie *n* się, wykręcenie *n* się

con·tour ['kɒntʊə] kontur *m*; ***~s*** *pl.* zarys *m*; **con·tra** ['kɒntrə] przeciw, przeciwko

con·tra·band ['kɒntrəbænd] *econ.* kontrabanda *f*

con·tra·cep|·tion [kɒntrə'sepʃn] *med.* antykoncepcja *f*; zapobieganie *n* ciąży; **~·tive** [kɒntrə'septɪv] *med.* środek *m* antykoncepcyjny

con|·tract 1. ['kɒntrækt] kontrakt *m*, umowa *f*; **2.** [kən'trækt] ściągać (się), kurczyć (się); **~·trac·tion** [kən'trækʃn] skurcz *m*, skurczenie *n*; zwężenie *n*; **~·trac·tor** [kən'træktə]: ***building ~tractor*** przedsiębiorca *m* budowlany

con·tra|·dict [kɒntrə'dɪkt] zaprzeczać ⟨-czyć⟩ (*D*), zadawać ⟨zadać⟩ kłam; **~·dic·tion** [kɒntrə'dɪkʃn] sprzeczność *f*; zaprzeczenie *n*; **~·dic·to·ry** [kɒntrə'dɪktərɪ] sprzeczny

con·tra·ry ['kɒntrərɪ] **1.** przeciwstawny; **~ *to*** niezgodnie z (*I*), wbrew (*D*); **2.** przeciwieństwo *n*; ***on the ~*** przeciwnie

con·trast 1. ['kɒntrɑːst] kontrast *m*, przeciwstawienie *n*; **2.** [kən'trɑːst] *v/t.* przeciwstawiać ⟨-wić⟩, porównywać ⟨-nać⟩; *v/i.* odróżniać się (***with*** od *G*), stać w sprzeczności (***with*** z *I*)

con|·trib·ute [kən'trɪbjuːt] wnosić ⟨wnieść⟩ udział (***to*** do *G*), wpłacać ⟨-cić⟩; przyczyniać ⟨-nić⟩ się; pisywać ⟨pisać⟩; **~·tri·bu·tion** [kɒntrɪ'bjuːʃn] wkład *m*, udział *m*; przyczynek *m*; **~·trib·u·tor** [kən'trɪbjʊtə] ofiarodawca *m* (-czyni *f*); (*w czasopiśmie*) współpracownik *m* (-iczka *f*); **~·trib·u·to·ry** [kən'trɪbjʊtərɪ] przyczyniający się; ***~tributory cause*** przyczyna *f* sprawcza

con·trite ['kɒntraɪt] skruszony

con·trive [kən'traɪv] wymyślać ⟨-lić⟩; zdołać (zrobić), doprowadzć do (*G*)

con·trol [kən'trəʊl] **1.** panowanie *n*, władza *f*; kontrola *f*, sprawdzanie *n*; *tech.* regulator *m*, przełącznik *m*; ***~s*** *tech.* urządzenia *pl.* sterujące; ***bring*** (***get***) **~** opanować, wziąć pod kontrolę; ***have*** (***keep***) ***under ~*** kontrolować; ***get out of ~*** wymykać ⟨wymknąć⟩ się spod kontroli; ***lose ~ of*** stracić kontrolę nad (*I*); **2.** (***-ll-***) kontrolować; sprawdzać ⟨-dzić⟩; opanowywać ⟨-wać⟩; panować nad (*I*), sprawować władzę nad (*I*); *econ.* regulować, kontrolować; *tech.* regulować, sterować; **~ desk** *electr.* pulpit *m* sterowniczy; **~ pan·el** *electr.* tablica *m* sterownicza; **~ tow·er** *aviat.* wieża *f* kontroli lotów

con·tro·ver|·sial [kɒntrə'vɜːʃl] kontrowersyjny; **~·sy** ['kɒntrəvɜːsɪ] kon-

trowersja *f*; zatarg *m*
con·tuse [kən'tjuːz] *med.* kontuzjować, stłuc
con·va|·lesce [kɒnvə'les] odzyskiwać ⟨-skać⟩ zdrowie, powracać ⟨-rócić⟩ do zdrowia; **~·les·cence** [kɒnvə'lesns] rekonwalescencja *f*, zdrowienie *n*; **~'les·cent 1.** zdrowiejący; zdrowotny; **2.** rekonwalescent(ka *f*) *m*
con·vene [kən'viːn] *zebranie itp.* zwoływać ⟨-łać⟩; zbierać ⟨zebrać⟩ się
con·ve·ni|·ence [kən'viːnjəns] wygoda *f*, dogodność *f*; *Brt.* toaleta *f* (*publiczna*); ***all* (*modern*) *~ences*** z wszelkimi wygodami; ***at your earliest ~ence*** możliwie jak najszybciej; **~·ent** wygodny, dogodny
con·vent ['kɒnvənt] klasztor *m* (*żeński*)
con·ven·tion [kən'venʃn] konwencja *f*; zjazd *m*; umowa *f*; **~·al** [kən'venʃənl] konwencjonalny, umowny
con·verge [kən'vɜːdʒ] zbiegać ⟨zbiec⟩ się
con·ver·sa·tion [kɒnvə'seɪʃn] rozmowa *f*, konwersacja *f*; **~·al** [kɒnvə'seɪʃənl] potoczny; konwersacyjny; ***~al English*** potoczny angielski
con·verse [kən'vɜːs] rozmawiać, rozprawiać
con·ver·sion [kən'vɜːʃn] konwersja *f*, przeliczenie *n*; przekształcenie *n*; przebudowa *f*; *rel.* nawrócenie *n*; *econ.* przeliczenie *n*, wymiana *f*; **~ ta·ble** tabela *f* przeliczeniowa
con|·vert [kən'vɜːt] przeliczać ⟨-czyć⟩, wymieniać ⟨-nić⟩; przekształcać ⟨-cić⟩ (***into*** w *A*); *rel.* nawracać ⟨-wrócić⟩ (się); *math.* przeliczać ⟨-czyć⟩; **~'vert·er** *electr.* przetwornica *f*, przetwornik *m*; **~'ver·ti·ble 1.** zamienny; *econ.* wymienialny; **2.** *mot.* kabriolet *m*
con·vey [kən'veɪ] przewozić ⟨przewieźć⟩, ⟨prze⟩transportować; przekazywać ⟨-zać⟩; **~·ance** transport *m*, przewóz *m*; środek *m* transportu; przekazanie *n*; **~·er belt** przenośnik *m* transportowy
con|·vict 1. ['kɒnvɪkt] skazaniec *m*; więzień *m*, więźniarka *f*; **2.** [kən'vɪkt] *jur.* (***of***) uznawać ⟨-znać⟩ winnym (*G*), skazywać (na *A*); **~·vic·tion** [kən'vɪkʃn] *jur.* skazanie *n*; przekonanie *n*
con·vince [kən'vɪns] przekonywać ⟨-nać⟩
con·voy ['kɒnvɔɪ] **1.** konwój *m* (*też naut.*), eskorta *f*; **2.** konwojować, eskortować
con·vul|·sion [kən'vʌlʃn] *med. zw. pl.* konwulsje *pl.*, drgawki *pl.*; **~·sive** [kən'vʌlsɪv] konwulsyjny
coo [kuː] ⟨za⟩gruchać
cook [kʊk] **1.** kucharz *m* (-arka *f*); **2.** ⟨u⟩gotować (się); F *sprawozdanie itp.* ⟨s⟩fałszować; **~ *up*** F wymyślać ⟨-lić⟩; **'~·book** *Am.* książka *f* kucharska; **'~·er** *Brt.* kuchenka *f*; **~·e·ry** ['kʊkərɪ] kucharstwo *n*; **'~·e·ry book** *Brt.* książka *f* kucharska; **~·ie** ['kʊkɪ] *Am.* ciastko *n*, herbatnik *m*; **'~·ing** gotowanie (*umiejętność*) *n*; **~·y** ['kʊkɪ] *Am.* → ***cookie***
cool [kuːl] **1.** chłodny; *fig.* zimny, opanowany; obojętny; F świetny, kapitalny; **2.** chłód *m*, zimno *n*; F opanowanie *n*, spokój *m*; **3.** ⟨o⟩chłodzić (się); studzić (się); **~ *down*, ~ *off*** uspokajać ⟨-koić⟩ się
coon [kuːn] *zo.* F szop pracz *m*
coop [kuːp] **1.** klatka *f* (*dla królików itp.*); **2. ~ *up*, ~ *in*** wtłaczać ⟨-łoczyć⟩
co-op ['kəʊɒp] F spółdzielnia *f*, sklep *m* spółdzielczy
co·op·e|·rate [kəʊ'ɒpəreɪt] współpracować; kooperować; pomagać ⟨pomóc⟩; **~·ra·tion** [kəʊɒpə'reɪʃn] współpraca *f*; pomoc *f*; kooperacja *f*; **~·ra·tive** [kəʊ'ɒpərətɪv] **1.** wspólny; pomocny; *econ.* spółdzielczy; **2.** *też* ***~rative society*** spółdzielnia *f*; *też* ***~rative store*** sklep *m* spółdzielczy
co·or·di|·nate 1. [kəʊ'ɔːdɪneɪt] ⟨s⟩koordynować; **2.** [kəʊ'ɔːdɪnət] równorzędny; **~·na·tion** [kəʊɔːdɪ'neɪʃn] koordynacja *f*
cop [kɒp] F (*policjant*) glina *m* F
cope [kəʊp]: **~ *with*** dawać sobie radę z (*I*), radzić sobie z (*I*)
Co·pen·ha·gen Kopenhaga *f*
cop·i·er ['kɒpɪə] kopiarka *f*
co·pi·ous ['kəʊpjəs] obfity, duży
cop·per¹ ['kɒpə] **1.** *min.* miedź *f*; **2.** miedziany
cop·per² ['kɒpə] F (*policjant*) gliniarz *m*
cop·pice ['kɒpɪs], **copse** [kɒps] zagajnik *m*
cop·y ['kɒpɪ] **1.** kopia *f*; odpis *m*; reprodukcja *f*; egzemplarz *m* (*książki*); numer *m* (*czasopisma*); *print.* materiał *m*

C

do druku; ***fair*** ~ czystopis *m*; **2.** ⟨s⟩kopiować; przepisywać ⟨-sać⟩, sporządzać ⟨-dzić⟩ odpis; naśladować; '~**·book** notatnik *m*; '~**·ing** kopiujący; '~**·right** prawo *n* autorskie, copyright *m*

cor·al ['kɒrəl] *zo.* koral *m*; *attr.* koralowy

cord [kɔːd] **1.** sznur *m* (*też electr.*), linka *f*; sztruks; (***a pair of***) ~***s*** sztruksy *pl.*; **2.** zawiązywać ⟨-wiązać⟩ sznurem

cor·di·al¹ ['kɔːdjəl] sok *m* (skoncentrowany); *med.* lek wzmacniający

cor·di·al² ['kɔːdjəl] kordialny; ~**·i·ty** [kɔːdɪ'ælətɪ] kordialność *f*

'cord·less bezprzewodowy; '~ **phone** telefon bezprzewodowy

cor·don ['kɔːdn] **1.** kordon *m*; **2.** ~ ***off*** odgradzać ⟨-rodzić⟩ kordonem

cor·du·roy ['kɔːdərɔɪ] sztruks *m*; (***a pair of***) ~***s*** (*spodnie*) sztruksy *pl.*

core [kɔː] **1.** rdzeń *m*; jądro *n*; ogryzek *m*; *fig.* sedno *n*; '~ **time** *Brt.* (*okres, gdy większość pracujących w nienormowanym czasie pracy znajduje się w miejscu pracy*)

cork [kɔːk] **1.** korek *m*; **2.** *też* ~ ***up*** ⟨za⟩korkować; '~**·screw** korkociąg *m*

corn¹ [kɔːn] **1.** zboże *n*; ziarno *n*; *też* ***Indian*** ~ *Am.* kukurydza *f*; **2.** ⟨za⟩peklować

corn² [kɔːn] *med.* odcisk *m*

cor·ner ['kɔːnə] **1.** róg *m*; kąt *m*; *zwł. mot.* zakręt *m*; (*w piłce nożnej*) rzut *m* rożny, róg *m* F; *fig.* ciężka sytuacja *f*; **2.** rożny; **3.** przypierać ⟨-przeć⟩ do muru; '~**ed** ...rożny; '~ **kick** (*w piłce nożnej*) rzut *m* rożny, róg *m* F; '~ **shop** *Brt.* sklep *m* na rogu

cor·net ['kɔːnɪt] *mus.* kornet *m*; *Brt.* rożek *m* (*na lody*)

'corn·flakes *pl.* płatki *pl.* kukurydziane

cor·nice ['kɔːnɪs] *arch.* gzyms *m*

cor·o·na·ry ['kɒrənərɪ] **1.** *anat.* wieńcowy; **2.** *med.* zakrzepica *f* tętnicy wieńcowej; F zawał *m* serca

cor·o·na·tion [kɒrə'neɪʃn] koronacja *f*

cor·o·ner ['kɒrənə] *jur.* koroner *m* (*urzędnik badający przyczynę nagłego zgonu nie z przyczyn naturalnych*); ~**'s 'in·quest** śledztwo *n* (*przeprowadzone przez koronera*)

cor·o·net ['kɒrənɪt] (mała) korona *f*

cor·po·ral ['kɔːpərəl] *mil.* kapral *m*

cor·po·ral 'pun·ish·ment kara *f* cielesna

cor·po|·rate ['kɔːpərət] zbiorowy; korporacyjny; dotyczący firmy; ~**·ra·tion** [kɔːpə'reɪʃn] *jur.* korporacja *f*; władze *pl.* miasta; osoba *f* prawna; spółka *f*, *Am. też* spółka *f* akcyjna

corps [kɔː] (*pl.* ***corps*** [kɔːz]) korpus *m*

corpse [kɔːps] zwłoki *pl.*

cor·pu·lent ['kɔːpjʊlənt] korpulentny

cor·ral [kə'rɑːl, *Am.* kə'ræl] **1.** korral *m*, zagroda; **2.** *bydło* zaganiać ⟨-gonić⟩ do korralu

cor|·rect [kə'rekt] **1.** poprawny, prawidłowy; *też czas*: dokładny; **2.** poprawiać ⟨-wić⟩, ⟨s⟩korygować; ~**·rec·tion** [kə'rekʃn] poprawa *f*, poprawka *f*

cor·re|·spond [kɒrɪ'spɒnd] (***with, to***) odpowiadać (*D*); zgadzać się (z *I*); korespondować (***with*** z *I*); ~**'spon·dence** odpowiedniość *f*; korespondencja *f*; ~**'spon·dence course** kurs *m* korespondencyjny; ~**'spon·dent 1.** odpowiadający; **2.** korespondent(ka *f*) *m*; ~**'spon·ding** odpowiadający

cor·ri·dor ['kɒrɪdɔː] korytarz *m*

cor·rob·o·rate [kə'rɒbəreɪt] potwierdzać ⟨-dzić⟩, podtrzymywać ⟨-mać⟩

cor|·rode [kə'rəʊd] *chem., tech.* ⟨s⟩korodować, ⟨za⟩rdzewieć; ~**·ro·sion** [kə'rəʊʒn] *chem., tech.* korozja *f*, rdza *f*; ~**·ro·sive** [kə'rəʊsɪv] korodujący, korozyjny; *fig.* niszczący

cor·ru·gated ['kɒrʊgeɪtɪd] falisty; '~ **i·ron** blacha *f* falista

cor|·rupt [kə'rʌpt] **1.** skorumpowany; przekupny; *moralnie* zepsuty; **2.** ⟨s⟩korumpować; przekupić; *moralnie* ⟨ze⟩psuć, ⟨z⟩demoralizować; ~**'rupt·i·ble** przekupny, sprzedajny; ~**·ruption** [kə'rʌpʃn] korupcja *f*; sprzedajność *f*; *moralne* zepsucie *n*

cor·set ['kɔːsɪt] gorset *m*

cos|·met·ic [kɒz'metɪk] **1.** (***-ally***) kosmetyczny; **2.** kosmetyk *m*; ~**·me·ti·cian** [kɒzmə'tɪʃn] kosmetyczka *f*

cos·mo·naut ['kɒzmənɔːt] *astr.* kosmonauta *m*

cos·mo·pol·i·tan [kɒzmə'pɒlɪtən] **1.** kosmopolityczny; **2.** kosmopolita *m*, obywatel *m* świata

cost [kɒst] **1.** koszt *m*, koszty *pl.*; cena *f*; **2.** (***cost***) kosztować; '~**·ly** (***-ier, -iest***) drogi, kosztowny; ~ **of 'liv·ing** koszty *pl.* utrzymania

cos·tume ['kɒstjuːm] ubiór *m*, strój *m*;

'~ **jew·el(·le)ry** sztuczna biżuteria *f*
co·sy ['kəʊzɪ] **1.** (**-ier, -iest**) przytulny; **2.** → ***egg cosy, tea cosy***
cot [kɒt] łóżko *n* polowe; *Brt.* łóżeczko *n* dziecięce
cot·tage ['kɒtɪdʒ] chata *f*, chałupa *f*; *Am.* dom *m* letniskowy, dacza *f* F; ~ **'cheese** biały ser *m*
cot·ton ['kɒtn] **1.** bawełna *f*; przędza *f* bawełniana; *Am.* wata *f*; **2.** bawełniany; '~**·wood** *bot.* topola *f* kanadyjska; ~ **'wool** *Brt.* wata *f*
couch [kaʊtʃ] sofa *f*, leżanka *f*
cou·chette [ku:'ʃet] *rail.* kuszetka *f*, miejsce *n* do leżenia; *też* ~ ***coach*** wagon *m* z miejscami do leżenia
cou·gar ['ku:gə] *zo.* (*pl.* **-gars, -gar**) kuguar *m*, puma *f*
cough [kɒf] **1.** kaszel *m*; **2.** ⟨za⟩kaszleć
could [kʊd] *pret. od* **can**[1]
coun·cil ['kaʊnsl] rada *f*; '~ **house** *Brt. jakby*: mieszkanie *n* kwaterunkowe
coun·cil·(l)or ['kaʊnsələ] radny *m* (-na *f*), członek *m* (-kini *f*) rady
coun|·sel ['kaʊnsl] **1.** rada *f*, porada *f*; *Brt. jur.* adwokat *m*, obrońca *m*; ***~sel for the defense*** (*Am.* ***for the defence***) obrońca *m*; ***~sel for the prosecution*** oskarżyciel *m*; **2.** (*zwł. Brt.* **-ll-**, *Am.* **-l-**) doradzać ⟨-dzić⟩, ⟨po⟩radzić; udzielać ⟨-lić⟩ rady; ***~se(l)ling centre*** poradnia *f*; **~·sel·(l)or** ['kaʊnsələ] doradca *m*); *zwł. Am. jur.* adwokat *m*, obrońca *m*
count[1] [kaʊnt] hrabia *m* (*nie brytyjski*)
count[2] [kaʊnt] **1.** liczenie *n*, przeliczanie *n*; *jur.* punkt *m* (*oskarżenia*), zarzut *m*; **2.** *v/t.* ⟨po⟩liczyć, wyliczać ⟨-czyć⟩, obliczać ⟨-czyć⟩; ⟨po⟩rachować; liczyć do (*G*) (~ ***ten*** do dziesięciu); *fig.* uważać za (*A*); *v/i.* ⟨po⟩liczyć; liczyć się, mieć znaczenie; ~ ***down*** pieniądze podliczać ⟨-czyć⟩, odliczać wstecz (*przed startem rakiety*), wyczekiwać; ~ ***on*** liczyć na (*A*); spodziewać się; '~**·down** odliczanie *n* wstecz (*przed startem rakiety*); wyczekiwanie *n*
coun·te·nance ['kaʊntɪnəns] wyraz *m* twarzy, oblicze *n*; poparcie *n*
count·er[1] ['kaʊntə] *tech.* licznik *m*; pionek *m*
coun·ter[2] ['kaʊntə] lada *f*, kontuar *m*; okienko *n*
coun·ter[3] ['kaʊntə] **1.** przeciw, wbrew, na przekór; **2.** przeciwstawiać się, odparowywać ⟨-ować⟩, ⟨za⟩reagować
coun·ter·act [kaʊntər'ækt] przeciwdziałać; ⟨z⟩neutralizować
coun·ter·bal·ance 1. ['kaʊntəbæləns] przeciwwaga *f*; **2.** [kaʊntə'bæləns] ⟨z⟩równoważyć
coun·ter·clock·wise [kaʊntə'klɒkwaɪz] *Am.* → ***anticlockwise***
coun·ter·es·pi·o·nage ['kaʊntər'espɪənɑ:ʒ] kontrwywiad *m*
coun·ter·feit ['kaʊntəfɪt] **1.** fałszywy, sfałszowany; **2.** fałszerstwo *n*; **3.** *pieniądze, podpis itp.* ⟨s⟩fałszować; ~ **'mon·ey** fałszywe pieniądze *pl.*
coun·ter·foil ['kaʊntəfɔɪl] odcinek *m* (*kontrolny*), talon *m*
coun·ter·mand [kaʊntə'mɑ:nd] *rozkaz, zamówienie itp.* odwoływać ⟨-łać⟩, ⟨z⟩anulować
coun·ter·pane ['kaʊntəpeɪn] narzuta *f*; → ***bedspread***
coun·ter·part ['kaʊntəpɑ:t] odpowiednik *m*; kopia *f*, duplikat *m*
coun·ter·sign ['kaʊntəsaɪn] kontrasygnować
coun·tess ['kaʊntɪs] hrabina *f*
'count·less niezliczony
coun·try ['kʌntrɪ] **1.** kraj *m*, państwo *n*; wieś *f*; ***in the*** ~ na wsi; **2.** wiejski; '~**·man** (*pl.* **-men**) wieśniak *m*; *też* ***fellow ~man*** rodak *m*; '~ **road** droga *f* wiejska; '~**·side** wieś *f*; tereny *pl.* wiejskie; '~**·wom·an** (*pl.* **-women**) wieśniaczka *f*; *też* ***fellow ~woman*** rodaczka *f*
coun·ty ['kaʊntɪ] hrabstwo *n*; ~ **'seat** *Am.* siedziba *f* władz hrabstwa; ~ **'town** *Brt.* siedziba *f* władz hrabstwa
coup [ku:] znakomite posunięcie *n*; zamach *m* stanu, pucz *m*
cou·ple ['kʌpl] **1.** para *f*; ***a ~ of*** F trochę, kilka; **2.** ⟨z-, po⟩łączyć; *tech.* sprzęgać ⟨-gnąć⟩; *zo.* parzyć się
coup·ling ['kʌplɪŋ] *tech.* sprzęg *m*; łącznik *m*
cou·pon ['ku:pɒn] odcinek *m*, kupon *m*; talon *m*
cour·age ['kʌrɪdʒ] odwaga *f*; **cou·ra·geous** [kə'reɪdʒəs] odważny, śmiały
cou·ri·er ['kʊrɪə] kurier *m*; pilot *m* (*wycieczki*); *attr.* kurierski
course [kɔ:s] *naut., aviat., fig.* kurs *m*; (*w sporcie*) tor *m* wyścigowy, bieżnia

f, pole *n* golfowe; bieg *m*, przebieg *m*; ciąg *m*; seria *f*, cykl *m*; kurs *m*, zajęcia *pl*.; ***of ~*** oczywiście; ***in the ~ of events*** normalnym biegiem rzeczy; ***in due ~*** we właściwym czasie *lub* trybie;

court [kɔːt] **1.** dwór *m* (*króla itp.*); dziedziniec *m*; (*w nazwach*) plac *m*; (*w sporcie*): kort *m* tenisowy; *jur.* sąd *m*, trybunał *m*; **2.** zalecać się do (*G*); starać się o (*A*)

cour•te|•ous ['kɜːtjəs] uprzejmy; **~•sy** ['kɜːtɪsɪ] uprzejmość *f*; ***by ~sy of*** przez grzeczność (*G*), dzięki uprzejmości (*G*)

'court|•house *jur.* gmach *m* sądu; **~•ier** ['kɔːtjə] dworzanin *m*; **'~•ly** dworski; **~ 'mar•tial** (*pl.* ***courts martial, court martials***) *jur.* sąd *m* wojenny; **~-'mar•tial** (*zwł. Brt.* ***-ll-***, *Am.* ***-l-***) oddawać ⟨-dać⟩ pod sąd wojenny; **'~•room** *jur.* sala *f* rozpraw; **'~•ship** zalecanie *n* się; **'~•yard** podwórze *n*

cous•in ['kʌzn] kuzyn(ka *f*) *m*

cove [kəʊv] zatoczka *f*

cov•er ['kʌvə] **1.** pokrywa *f*, wieko *n*; pokrowiec *m*; okładka *f*, obwoluta *f*; powłoczka *f*, kapa *f*; schronienie *n*; *fig.* maska *f*, przykrywka *f*; nakrycie *n* stołowe; ubezpieczenie *n*; ***take ~*** schronić się; ***under plain ~*** jako zwykła przesyłka; ***under separate ~*** jako osobna przesyłka; **2.** przykrywać ⟨-ryć⟩, zakrywać ⟨-ryć⟩, pokrywać ⟨-ryć⟩; przebywać ⟨-być⟩, pokonywać ⟨-nać⟩; *obszar* zajmować ⟨-jąć⟩; rozciągać się na (*L*); *tematem* zajmować się (*I*); *przepis* ujmować ⟨ująć⟩; *econ.* pokrywać ⟨-ryć⟩; *econ.* ubezpieczać ⟨-czyć⟩; *TV, radio, prasa*: ⟨z⟩relacjonować, omawiać ⟨-mówić⟩; (*w sporcie*) *przeciwnika* kryć; ***~ up*** zakrywać ⟨-ryć⟩; okrywać ⟨-ryć⟩ się; *fig.* ⟨za⟩tuszować; ***~ up for s.o.*** kryć kogoś; **~•age** ['kʌvərɪdʒ] relacja *f* (***of*** z *G*), sprawozdanie *n*; **'~ girl** cover girl *f* (*zdjęcie atrakcyjnej dziewczyny na okładce czasopisma*); **~•ing** ['kʌvərɪŋ] pokrywa *f*, przykrywa *f*; warstwa *f*; **'~ sto•ry** relacja *f* tytułowa

cow[1] [kaʊ] *zo.* krowa *f* (*też fig.*)

cow[2] [kaʊ] zastraszać ⟨-szyć⟩

cow•ard ['kaʊəd] tchórz *m*; *attr.* tchórzliwy; **~•ice** ['kaʊədɪs] tchórzostwo *n*; **'~•ly** tchórzliwy

cow•boy ['kaʊbɔɪ] kowboj *m*

cow•er ['kaʊə] ⟨s⟩kulić się

'cow|•herd pastuch *m*; **'~•hide** skóra *f* bydlęca; **'~•house** obora *f*

cowl [kaʊl] habit *m* (*z kapturem*); kaptur *m*; *tech.* nasada *f* kominowa

'cow|•shed obora *f*; **'~•slip** *bot.* pierwiosnek *m*; *Am.* knieć *f* błotna

cox [kɒks], **~•swain** ['kɒksən, 'kɒksweɪn] sternik *m*

coy [kɔɪ] płochliwy, nieśmiały

coy•ote ['kɔɪəʊt] *zo.* kojot *m*

co•zy ['kəʊzɪ] *Am.* (***-ier, -iest***) → ***cosy***

CPU [siː piː 'juː] *skrót*: ***central processing unit*** *komp.* jednostka *f* centralna

crab [kræb] *zo.* krab *m*

crack [kræk] **1.** szczelina *f*, pęknięcie *n*; rysa *f*, zarysowanie *n*; trzask *m*, huk *m*; uderzenie *n*; **2.** *v/i.* pękać ⟨-knąć⟩, ⟨za⟩rysować się; *głos*: ⟨za⟩łamać się; *też* ***~ up*** *fig.* załamywać ⟨-mać⟩ się; ***get ~ing*** F brać ⟨wziąć⟩ się ostro do roboty; *v/t.* trzaskać ⟨-snąć⟩ (*batem, palcami*); ⟨s⟩tłuc, rozbijać ⟨-bić⟩, ⟨z⟩łamać; *orzech* łupać; *szyfr* F ⟨z⟩łamać; ***~ a joke*** F opowiadać kawał; **'~•er** krakers *m*; (*papierowy rulon z małą petardą w środku*); **~•le** ['krækl] trzaskać

Cracow Kraków *m*

cra•dle ['kreɪdl] **1.** kołyska *f*; **2.** kołysać, ⟨u⟩tulić

craft[1] [krɑːft] (*pl.* ***craft***) *naut.* statek *m*; *aviat.* samolot *m*; *astr.* pojazd *m* kosmiczny

craft[2] [krɑːft] rzemiosło *n*; umiejętność *f*, biegłość *f*; *fig.* sztuka *f*; podstęp *m*; **'~s•man** (*pl.* ***-men***) rzemieślnik *m*; **'~•y** (***-ier, -iest***) przebiegły, podstępny

crag [kræg] grań *f*, ostry występ *m* skalny

cram [kræm] (***-mm-***) wpychać ⟨wepchnąć⟩, wtykać ⟨wetknąć⟩; F wkuwać ⟨wkuć⟩, kuć (***for*** do *G*)

cramp [kræmp] **1.** *med.* kurcz *m*; *tech.* klamra *f*, zwora *f*; *fig.* więzy *pl.*; **2.** ⟨za⟩hamować, wstrzymywać ⟨-mać⟩

cran•ber•ry ['krænbərɪ] *bot.* żurawina *f*

crane[1] [kreɪn] *tech.* żuraw *m*, dźwig *m*

crane[2] [kreɪn] **1.** *zo.* żuraw *m*; **2.** ***~ forward, ~ out one's neck*** wyciągać ⟨-gnąć⟩ szyję

crank [kræŋk] **1.** *tech.* korba *f*; *tech.* wahacz *m*; F szajbus *m*; **2.** obracać ⟨-rócić⟩ korbą; **'~•shaft** wał *m* korbowy; **'~•y** (***-ier, -iest***) F szajbnięty; *Am.* marudny

cran•ny ['krænɪ] szczelina *f*

C

crap ['kræp] gówno *n*, bzdury *fpl*
crape [kreɪp] krepa *f*
crap·py ['kræpɪ] *sl.* (**-ier, -iest**) gówniany
craps [kræps] *Am. pl.* (*rodzaj gry w kości*)
crash [kræʃ] **1.** trzask *m*, grzmot *m*; *mot.* zderzenie *n*, katastrofa *f*; *aviat.* katastrofa *f*, runięcie *n*; *econ.* krach *m* (*na giełdzie*), załamanie *n*; **2.** *v/t.* rozbijać ⟨-bić⟩ (*mot.* **into** o *A*); *aviat.* rozbijać ⟨-bić⟩ przy lądowaniu; *v/i. zwł. mot.* rozbijać ⟨-bić⟩ się, zderzać ⟨-rzyć⟩ się; *zwł. econ.* załamywać ⟨-mać⟩ się; wjeżdżać ⟨wjechać⟩, wpadać ⟨wpaść⟩ (**against, into** w *A*); *mot.*, *aviat.* ulegać ⟨ulec⟩ katastrofie; **3.** intensywny, przyspieszony; '**~ bar·ri·er** bariera *f* ochronna; '**~ course** kurs *m* przyspieszony *lub* intensywny; '**~ di·et** intensywna dieta *f* (*odchudzająca*); '**~ hel·met** kask *m*; '**~-land** *aviat.* ⟨wy⟩lądować awaryjnie; **~'land·ing** *aviat.* awaryjne lądowanie *n*
crate [kreɪt] skrzynka *f*, kontener *m*
cra·ter ['kreɪtə] krater *m*; lej *m*
crave [kreɪv] mieć wielką ochotę (**for, after** na *A*), mieć zachcianki; '**crav·ing** wielka ochota *f*, zachcianka *f*
craw·fish ['krɔːfɪʃ] *zo.* (*pl.* **-fish, -fishes**) → **crayfish**
crawl [krɔːl] **1.** pełzanie *n*; *dziecko*: raczkowanie *n*; (*w sporcie*) kraul *m*; **2.** ⟨po⟩pełznąć, ⟨po⟩czołgać się, *dziecko*: raczkować; pływać kraulem; roić się (**with** od *G*); **it makes one's flesh ~** dostaje się gęsiej skórki od tego
cray·fish ['kreɪfɪʃ] *zo.* (*pl.* **-fish, -fishes**) rak *m*, langusta *f*
cray·on ['kreɪən] kredka *f* (*do rysowania*)
craze [kreɪz] *też fig.* szał *m*, szaleństwo *n*; **be the ~** być w modzie; '**cra·zy** (**-ier, -iest**) zwariowany (**about** na punkcie *G*)
creak [kriːk] ⟨za⟩skrzypieć
cream [kriːm] **1.** śmietan(k)a *f*; krem *m*; elita *f*, śmietanka *f*; **2.** kremowy, koloru kremowego; **~·e·ry** ['kriːmərɪ] mleczarnia *f*; '**~·y** (**-ier, -iest**) kremowy; śmietankowy; ze śmietanką
crease [kriːs] **1.** fałda *f*, zmarszczka *f*; (*w spodniach*) kant *m*; **2.** miąć (się), ⟨z-, po⟩gnieść (się); fałdować się, marszczyć się
cre|·ate [kriː'eɪt] ⟨s⟩tworzyć; **~·a·tion** [kriː'eɪʃn] tworzenie *n*; stworzenie *n* (*też* świata); **~'a·tive** twórczy; **~'a·tor** twórca *m*; stwórca *m*
crea·ture ['kriːtʃə] stworzenie *n*
crèche [kreɪʃ] żłobek *m*; *Am.* żłobek *lub* żłóbek *m*, szopka (*bożonarodzeniowa*)
cre·dence ['kriːdns]: **give ~ to** dawać wiarę w (*A*)
cre·den·tials [krɪ'denʃlz] *pl.* referencje *pl.*; listy *pl.* uwierzytelniające; dokumenty *pl.* tożsamości
cred·i·ble ['kredəbl] wiarygodny
cred|·it ['kredɪt] **1.** wiara *f*, zaufanie *n*; uznanie *n*; (*w szkole*) zaliczenie *n*; *econ.* kredyt *m*; **~it** (**side**) *econ.* strona „ma"; **on ~it** *econ.* na kredyt; *attr.* kredytowy; **2.** ⟨u⟩wierzyć, ⟨za⟩ufać; *econ.* zapisywać ⟨-sać⟩ (**to** na dobro *G*); **~it s.o. with s.th.** przypisywać ⟨-sać⟩ coś komuś; '**~·i·ta·ble** chlubny (**to** dla *G*); '**~it card** *econ.* karta *f* kredytowa; '**~·i·tor** *econ.* wierzyciel *m*; **~·u·lous** ['kredjʊləs] łatwowierny
creed [kriːd] wiara *f*, wyznanie *n*
creek [kriːk] *Brt.* zatoczka *f*; *Am.* strumień *m*, potok *m*
creep [kriːp] (**crept**) pełzać, ⟨po⟩pełznąć; skradać się; *roślina*: piąć się; **~ in** wkradać ⟨-raść⟩ się, zakradać ⟨-raść⟩ się; **it makes my flesh ~** dostaję gęsiej skórki od tego; '**~·er** *bot.* roślina *f* rozłogowa; **~s** *pl.*: F **the sight gave me the ~s** ten widok przyprawił mnie o gęsią skórkę
cre·mate [krɪ'meɪt] ⟨s⟩kremować, poddawać ⟨-dać⟩ kremacji
crept [krept] *pret. i p.p. od* **creep**
cres·cent ['kresnt] półksiężyc *m*
cress [kres] *bot.* rzeżucha *f*
crest [krest] *zo.* grzebień *m*, czub *m*; szczyt *m* (*górski*); wierzchołek *m*; pęk *m* piór, kita *f*; **family ~** herb *m* rodzinny; '**~·fal·len** przybity
cre·vasse [krɪ'væs] szczelina *f* (*lodowcowa*)
crev·ice ['krevɪs] szczelina *f*, pęknięcie *n*
crew[1] [kruː] obsada *f*, załoga *f*
crew[2] [kruː] *pret. od* **crow** 2
crib [krɪb] **1.** żłób *m*; *Am.* łóżeczko *n* dla dziecka; *zwł. Brt.* żłóbek *m*, *Boże Narodzenie*: szopka *f*; F (*w szkole*) ściąga *f*; **2.** (**-bb-**) F odpisywać ⟨-sać⟩, ściągać ⟨-gnąć⟩

C

crick [krɪk]: ***a ~ in one's back*** (***neck***) strzyknięcie *n* w plecach (*karku*)
crick·et[1] ['krɪkɪt] *zo.* świerszcz *m*
crick·et[2] ['krɪkɪt] (*w sporcie*) krykiet *m*
crime [kraɪm] *jur.* przestępstwo *n*, zbrodnia *f*, występek *m*;'**~ nov·el** (*powieść*) kryminał *m*
crim·i·nal ['krɪmɪnl] **1.** kryminalny, przestępczy, zbrodniczy; **2.** przestępca *m* (-czyni *f*), zbrodniarz *m* (-arka *f*), kryminalista *m* (-ka *f*)
crimp [krɪmp] *zwł. włosy* podkręcać ⟨-ręcić⟩
crim·son ['krɪmzn] karmazynowy
cringe [krɪndʒ] ⟨s⟩kulić się
crin·kle ['krɪŋkl] **1.** zagięcie *n*; zmarszczka *f*; **2.** ⟨po⟩miąć (się); ⟨z⟩marszczyć (się)
crip·ple ['krɪpl] **1.** kulawy *m* (-wa *f*), kaleka *m/f*; **2.** okulawiać ⟨-wić⟩; okaleczać ⟨-czyć⟩ (*też fig.*)
cri·sis ['kraɪsɪs] (*pl.* ***-ses*** [-siːz]) kryzys *m*
crisp [krɪsp] *chleb*: chrupiący; *warzywo*: kruchy, świeży; *powietrze*: świeży, ostry; *włosy*: kędzierzawy; '**~·bread** chleb *m* chrupki
crisps [krɪsps] *pl.*, *też* ***potato ~*** *Brt.* chrupki *pl.* (*ziemniaczane*)
criss-cross ['krɪskrɒs] **1.** kratkowany wzór *m*; **2.** krzyżować (się)
cri·te·ri·on [kraɪ'tɪərɪən](*pl.* ***-ria*** [-rɪə], ***-rions***) kryterium *n*
crit|·ic ['krɪtɪk] krytyk *m*;**~·i·cal** ['krɪtɪkl] krytyczny;**~·i·cis·m** ['krɪtɪsɪzəm] krytyka *f*;**~·i·cize** ['krɪtɪsaɪz] ⟨s⟩krytykować
cri·tique [krɪ'tiːk] krytyka *f*, omówienie *n*
croak [krəʊk] ⟨za⟩rechotać; ⟨za⟩skrzeczeć; ⟨za⟩chrypieć
Cro·a·tia Chorwacja *f*
cro·chet ['krəʊʃeɪ] **1.** szydełkowanie *n*; **2.** szydełkować
crock·e·ry ['krɒkərɪ] *niemetalowe* naczynia *pl.* stołowe
croc·o·dile ['krɒkədaɪl] *zo.* krokodyl *m*
cro·ny ['krəʊnɪ] F kumpel(ka *f*) *m*
crook [krʊk] **1.** zagięcie *n*, zgięcie *n*, zakrzywienie *n*; F oszust *m*; **2.** zakrzywiać ⟨-wić⟩(się), zaginać ⟨-giąć⟩ (się); **~·ed** ['krʊkɪd] zagięty, krzywy; F nieuczciwy, oszukańczy
croon [kruːn] ⟨za⟩nucić; śpiewać ckliwie;'**~·er** śpiewak *m* (-waczka *f*) (*ckliwych utworów*)
crop [krɒp] **1.** zbiór *m*, plon *m*; *zo.* wole *n*; krótka fryzura *f*; **2.** (**-pp-**) *trawę itp.* skubać; *włosy* przycinać ⟨-ciąć⟩ (*krótko*)
cross [krɒs] **1.** krzyż *m* (*też fig. ciężar*), krzyżyk *m*; skrzyżowanie *n*; *biol.* krzyżówka *f*; (*w piłce nożnej*) podanie *n* w poprzek; **2.** zły, rozzłoszczony; **3.** ⟨s⟩krzyżować (się); *ulicę* przecinać ⟨-ciąć⟩, przechodzić ⟨przejść⟩; *plan* ⟨po⟩krzyżować; *biol.* ⟨s⟩krzyżować; ***~ off***, ***~ out*** przekreślać ⟨-lić⟩, skreślać ⟨-lić⟩; ***~ o.s.*** ⟨prze⟩żegnać się; ***~ one's arms*** ⟨s⟩krzyżować ramiona; ***~ one's legs*** zakładać ⟨założyć⟩ nogę na nogę; ***keep one's fingers ~ed*** trzymać kciuki; '**~·bar** (*w sporcie*) poprzeczka *f*; '**~·breed** mieszaniec *m*; **~-'coun·try** przełajowy; ***~-country skiing*** narciarstwo *n* biegowe; **~-ex·am·i'na·tion** przesłuchiwanie *n* w formie pytań krzyżowych; **~-ex'am·ine** zadawać ⟨-dać⟩ pytania krzyżowe;'**~-eyed**: ***be ~-eyed*** zezować, mieć zeza;'**~·ing** skrzyżowanie *n*; przejazd *m* (*przez tory itp.*); *Brt.* przejście *n* dla pieszych; *naut.* przeprawa *f*;'**~·road** *Am.* droga *f* poprzeczna;'**~·roads** *pl. lub sg.* skrzyżowanie *n*; *fig.* rozstaje *pl.*, punkt *m* przełomowy;'**~-sec·tion** przekrój *m* poprzeczny; '**~·walk** *Am.* przejście *n* dla pieszych;'**~·wise** poprzecznie, w poprzek; '**~·word** (**puz·zle**) krzyżówka *f*
crotch [krɒtʃ] *anat.* krocze *n* (*też spodni*)
crouch [kraʊtʃ] **1.** kucać ⟨kucnąć⟩, przykucać ⟨-kucnąć⟩; **2.** przysiad *m*, kucnięcie *n*
crow [krəʊ] **1.** *zo.* wrona; **2.** (***crowed*** *lub* ***crew, crowed***) ⟨za⟩krakać
'**crow·bar** łom *m*
crowd [kraʊd] **1.** tłum *m*; masa *f*; **2.** tłoczyć się; *ulice* zatłaczać ⟨-tłoczyć⟩; '**~·ed** zatłoczony, przepełniony
crown [kraʊn] **1.** korona *f*; *med.* koronka *f*; **2.** ⟨u⟩koronować; nakładać ⟨nałożyć⟩ koronkę (*na ząb*); *fig.* ⟨s⟩koronować, ⟨u⟩wieńczyć
cru·cial ['kruːʃl] krytyczny, decydujący
cru·ci|·fix ['kruːsɪfɪks] krucyfiks *m*; **~·fix·ion** [kruːsɪ'fɪkʃn] ukrzyżowanie *n*;**~·fy** ['kruːsɪfaɪ] ⟨u⟩krzyżować

crude [kruːd] surowy, nieprzetworzony; *fig.* prymitywny; ~ (**'oil**) ropa *f* naftowa
cru·el [krʊəl] (**-ll-**) okrutny; '~**·ty** okrucieństwo *n*; ~***ty to animals*** (***children***) okrucieństwo *n* wobec zwierząt (dzieci); ***society for the prevention of ~ty to animals*** towarzystwo *n* zapobiegania okrucieństwu wobec zwierząt
cru·et ['kruːɪt] komplet *m* do przypraw; pojemnik *m* na ocet *lub* oliwę
cruise [kruːz] **1.** rejs *m*; wycieczka *f* morska; **2.** krążyć; odbywać ⟨-być⟩ rejs; *aviat.*, *mot.* lecieć *lub* jechać z prędkością podróżną; ~ **'mis·sile** *mil.* rakietowy pocisk *m* manewrujący, F rakieta *f* cruise; '**cruis·er** *mil. naut.* krążownik *m*; jacht *m* motorowy; *Am. policyjny* wóz *m* patrolowy
crumb [krʌm] okruch *m*, okruszek *m*
crum·ble ['krʌmbl] *v/t.* ⟨po⟩kruszyć; *v/i.* rozpadać ⟨-paść⟩ się
crum·ple ['krʌmpl] zgniatać ⟨zgnieść⟩, ⟨z⟩miąć (się); załamywać ⟨-mać⟩ (się); '~ **zone** *mot.* strefa *f* zgniecenia
crunch [krʌntʃ] ⟨za⟩chrzęścić; ⟨s⟩chrupać
cru·sade [kruː'seɪd] wyprawa *f* krzyżowa
crush [krʌʃ] **1.** tłok *m*, ścisk *m*; ***have a ~ on s.o.*** ⟨s⟩tracić głowę dla kogoś; **2.** *Brt.* sok *m* (*ze świeżych owoców*); ***orange ~*** sok ze świeżych pomarańczy; **3.** *v/t.* rozgniatać ⟨-nieść⟩, ⟨z⟩miażdżyć (*też fig.*); *tech.* rozdrabniać ⟨-drobnić⟩, ⟨s⟩kruszyć; *fig.* ⟨z⟩miażdżyć, ⟨z⟩dławić; *v/i.* tłoczyć się; '~ **bar·ri·er** bariera *f* ochronna
crust [krʌst] skórka *f* (*chleba*); skorupa *f*
crus·ta·cean [krʌ'steɪʃn] *zo.* skorupiak *m*
crust·y ['krʌstɪ] (***-ier, -iest***) chrupiący
crutch [krʌtʃ] kula *f*, szczudło *n*
cry [kraɪ] **1.** krzyk *m*, okrzyk *m*; głos *m* (*ptaka itp.*); płacz *m*; **2.** ⟨za⟩płakać; krzyczeć ⟨krzyknąć⟩; ⟨za⟩wołać (***for*** o *A*); wydawać ⟨-dać⟩ głos
crypt [krɪpt] krypta *f*
crys·tal ['krɪstl] kryształ *m*; *Am.* szkiełko *n* zegarka; *attr.* kryształowy; ~**·line** ['krɪstəlaɪn] krystaliczny; ~**·lize** ['krɪstəlaɪz] ⟨s⟩krystalizować
CST [siː es 'tiː] *skrót*: ***Central Standard Time*** (*amerykański czas standardowy*)
ct(**s**) *skrót pisany*: ***cent***(***s***) *pl.* cent *m*
cu *skrót pisany*: ***cubic*** sześcienny
cub [kʌb] młode *n* (*drapieżnika*); *jakby*: zuch *m*
cube [kjuːb] kostka *f*; *math.* sześcian *m*; *math.* sześcian *m*, trzecia potęga *f*; *phot.* kostka *f* lampy błyskowej; ~ **'root** *math.* pierwiastek *m* sześcienny *lub* trzeciego stopnia; '**cu·bic** (~***ally***), '**cu·bi·cal** sześcienny; trzeciego stopnia
cu·bi·cle ['kjuːbɪkl] kabina *f*
cuck·oo ['kʊkuː] *zo.* (*pl.* ***-oos***) kukułka *f*
cu·cum·ber ['kjuːkʌmbə] ogórek *m*; (***as***) ***cool as ~*** F niezwykle spokojny
cud [kʌd] (*u przeżuwaczy*) miazga *f* pokarmowa; ***chew the ~*** rozmyślać, dumać
cud·dle ['kʌdl] *v/t.* przytulać ⟨-tulić⟩do siebie, tulić; *v/i.* ~ ***up*** przytulać ⟨-tulić⟩ się (***to*** do *G*)
cud·gel ['kʌdʒəl] **1.** pałka *f*; **2.** (*zwł. Brt.* **-ll-** , *Am.* **-l-**) ⟨po⟩bić
cue[1] [kjuː] *theat.* replika *f*; *fig.* sygnał *m*, hasło *n*; rada *f*, wskazówka *f*
cue[2] [kjuː] *bilard*: kij *m* bilardowy
cuff[1] [kʌf] mankiet *m* (*Am. też u spodni*)
cuff[2] [kʌf] **1.** klaps *m*; **2.** dawać ⟨dać⟩ klapsa
'**cuff link** spinka *f* do mankietów
cui·sine [kwiː'ziːn] (*sztuka gotowania*) kuchnia *f*
cul·mi·nate ['kʌlmɪneɪt] ⟨za⟩kończyć się
cu·lottes [kjuː'lɒts] *pl.* spódnica *f*, *damskie* spodnie *pl.*
cul·prit ['kʌlprɪt] winowajca *m* (-jczyni *f*)
cul·ti|·vate ['kʌltɪveɪt] *agr.* uprawiać ⟨-wić⟩; kultywować, pielęgnować; '~**·vat·ed** *agr.* uprawny; *fig.* kulturalny; ~**·va·tion** [kʌltɪ'veɪʃn] *agr.* uprawa *f*, uprawianie *n*; *fig.* kultywowanie *n*
cul·tu·ral ['kʌltʃərəl] kulturalny
cul·ture ['kʌltʃə] kultura *f*; hodowla *f*; '~**d** kulturalny
cum·ber·some ['kʌmbəsəm] niezręczny, nieporęczny
cu·mu·la·tive ['kjuːmjʊlətɪv] kumulujący się; kumulacyjny
cun·ning ['kʌnɪŋ] **1.** przebiegły, sprytny; **2.** przebiegłość *f*, spryt *m*
cup [kʌp] **1.** filiżanka *f*; *sport*: puchar *m*;

kielich *m*; miseczka *f*; **2.** (**-pp-**) *dłoń* składać ⟨złożyć⟩; ujmować ⟨ująć⟩; ***she ~ped her chin in her hand*** objęła dłonią brodę; **~•board** ['kʌbəd] kredens *m*, szafka *f*; '**~•board bed** łóżko *n* składane; '**~ fi•nal** *sport*: finał *m* rozgrywek pucharowych

cu•po•la ['kjuːpələ] kopuła *f*

'**cup| tie** (*w sporcie*) rozgrywka *f* eliminacyjna (*w zawodach pucharowych*); '**~ win•ner** (*w sporcie*) zwycięzca *m* w zawodach pucharowych

cur [kɜː] *ostry* kundel *m*; *fig.* łotr *m*

cu•ra•ble ['kjʊərəbl] uleczalny

cu•rate ['kjʊərət] wikary *m* (*w kościele anglikańskim*)

curb [kɜːb] **1.** wędzidło *n* (*też fig.*); *zwł. Am.* → ***kerb***(***stone***); **2.** okiełznywać ⟨-znać⟩

curd [kɜːd] *też* ***~s*** *pl.* zsiadłe mleko *n*; twaróg *n*

cur•dle ['kɜːdl] *v/t. mleko* ⟨s⟩powodować zsiadanie się; *v/i.* zsiadać ⟨zsiąść⟩ się; ***the sight made my blood ~*** na ten widok krew zastygła mi w żyłach

cure [kjʊə] **1.** *med.* lekarstwo *n* (**for** na *A*), środek *m*; kuracja *f*; **2.** *med.* ⟨wy⟩leczyć; ⟨za⟩konserwować; ⟨u⟩wędzić; ⟨wy⟩suszyć

cur•few ['kɜːfjuː] *mil.* godzina *f* policyjna

cu•ri•o ['kjʊərɪəʊ] (*pl.* **-os**) kuriozum *n*, osobliwość *f*

cu•ri|•os•i•ty [kjʊərɪ'ɒsətɪ] ciekawość *f*; osobliwość *f*; **~•ous** ['kjʊərɪəs] ciekawy, ciekawski; żądny wiedzy; dziwny, osobliwy

curl [kɜːl] **1.** lok *m*; **2.** *v/t. włosy* podkręcać ⟨-ręcić⟩; *v/i.* kręcić się; zwijać się; '**~•er** lokówka *f*; '**~•y** (**-ier, -iest**) kręcony; skręcony; zakręcany

cur•rant ['kʌrənt] *bot.* czarna *lub* czerwona porzeczka *f*; rodzynka *f*

cur•ren|•cy ['kʌrənsɪ] *econ.* waluta *f*; ***foreign ~cy*** dewizy *pl.*; '**~t 1.** *miesiąc itp.*: bieżący; obecny, aktualny; *pogląd*: powszechny; ***~t events*** bieżące wydarzenia *pl.*; **2.** prąd *m*, nurt *m* (*oba też fig.*); *electr.* prąd *m* (*elektryczny*); '**~t account** *Brt. econ.* rachunek *m* bieżący

cur•ric•u•lum [kə'rɪkjʊləm] (*pl.* **-la** [-lə], **-lums**) program *m* zajęć; **~ vi•tae** [- 'vaɪtiː] życiorys *m*

cur•ry¹ ['kʌrɪ] curry *n*

cur•ry² ['kʌrɪ] czesać *konia* zgrzebłem

curse [kɜːs] **1.** klątwa *f*; przekleństwo *n*; **2.** wyklinać ⟨-kląć⟩; kląć, przeklinać ⟨-kląć⟩; **curs•ed** ['kɜːsɪd] przeklęty

cur•sor ['kɜːsə] *komp.* kursor *m*

cur•so•ry ['kɜːsərɪ] pobieżny, powierzchowny

curt [kɜːt] zwięzły; zdawkowy

cur•tail [kɜː'teɪl] skracać ⟨-rócić⟩; *prawa* ograniczać ⟨-czyć⟩

cur•tain ['kɜːtn] **1.** zasłona *f*, firanka *f*; kurtyna *n*; ***draw the ~s*** zasuwać *lub* odsuwać zasłony; **2.** **~ *off*** oddzielać ⟨-lić⟩ zasłoną

curt•s(e)y ['kɜːtsɪ] **1.** dygnięcie *n*; **2.** dygać ⟨dygnąć⟩ (***to*** przed *I*)

cur•va•ture ['kɜːvətʃə] krzywizna *f*, zakrzywienie *n*

curve [kɜːv] **1.** krzywa *f*; zagięcie *n*; łuk *m*, zakręt *m*; **2.** wyginać ⟨-giąć⟩ się (*w łuk*)

cush•ion ['kʊʃn] **1.** poduszka *f*; **2.** ⟨z⟩amortyzować; *uderzenie* osłabiać ⟨-bić⟩

cuss [kʌs] *sl.* **1.** przekleństwo *n*; **2.** przeklinać ⟨-kląć⟩

cus•tard ['kʌstəd] *zwł. Brt.* sos *m* waniliowy (*do deserów*)

cus•to•dy ['kʌstədɪ] *jur.* opieka *f*, nadzór *m*; areszt *m*

cus•tom ['kʌstəm] zwyczaj *m*, obyczaj *m*; '**~•a•ry** zwyczajowy, tradycyjny; zwykły, zwyczajny; **~-'built** zrobiony na życzenie *lub* zamówienie; '**~•er** klient(ka *f*) *m*; '**~ house** urząd *m* celny; **~-'made** zrobiony na życzenie *lub* zamówienie

cus•toms ['kʌstəmz] *pl.* cło *n*; '**~ clearance** odprawa *f* celna; '**~ of•fi•cer**, '**~ of•fi•cial** celnik *m* (-iczka *f*)

cut [kʌt] (***cut***) **1.** *v/t.* ⟨po⟩kroić, obcinać ⟨-ciąć⟩, przycinać ⟨-ciąć⟩; *cenę* obniżać ⟨-niżyć⟩; *karty* przełożyć; *v/i.* ciąć; ***~ one's finger*** skaleczyć się w palec; ***~ s.o. dead*** umyślnie kogoś nie dostrzegać; **2.** skaleczenie *n*; cięcie *n*; '**~•back** *roślinę* przycinać ⟨-ciąć⟩; *wydatki* ograniczyć

cute [kjuːt] F (***~r, ~st***) sprytny, zmyślny; *Am.* fajny

cu•ti•cle ['kjuːtɪkl] skórka *f* (*paznokcia*)

cut•le•ry ['kʌtlərɪ] sztućce *pl.*

cut•let ['kʌtlɪt] *gastr.* kotlet *m*; sznycel *m*

cut|-'price, **~-'rate** *econ.* obniżony,

przeceniony; '**~·ter** krajarka *f*, przecinarka *f*; szlifierz *m* (*diamentów, szkła*); *tech.* frez *m*, nóż *m*; *film*: ; *naut.* kuter *m*; '**~·throat 1.** morderca *m* (-czyni *f*); **2.** morderczy, bezlitosny; '**~·ting 1.** tnący; *tech.* skrawający; **2.** cięcie *n*, wycinanie *n*; *bot.* sadzonka *f*; *zwł. Brt.* wycinek *m*; '**~·tings** *pl.* wycinki *pl.*; wióry *pl.*

Cy·ber·space ['saɪbəspeɪs] → ***virtual reality***

cy·cle[1] ['saɪkl] cykl *m*; obieg *m*

cy·cle[2] ['saɪkl] rower *m*; *attr.* rowerowy; '**~ path** ścieżka *f* dla rowerów; '**cy·cling** cyklistyka *f*, jazda *m* na rowerze; kolarstwo *n*; '**cy·clist** rowerzysta *m* (-stka *f*), cyklista *m*; kolarz *m*

cy·clone ['saɪkləʊn] cyklon *m*; obszar *m* niskiego ciśnienia

cyl·in·der ['sɪlɪndə] cylinder *m*, *tech.* *też* walec *m*

cyn|·ic ['sɪnɪk] cynik *m*; '**~·i·cal** cyniczny

cy·press ['saɪprɪs] *bot.* cyprys *m*

Cy·prus Cypr *m*

cyst [sɪst] *med.* cysta *f*

czar [zɑː] → ***tsar***

Czech [tʃek] **1.** czeski; **~ *Republic*** Czechy *pl.*, Republika *f* Czeska; **2.** Czech *m*; Czeszka *f*; *ling.* język *m* czeski

D

D, d [diː] D, d *n*

d *skrót pisany*: ***died*** zm., zmarł(a)

DA [diː 'eɪ] *skrót*: ***District Attorney*** *Am.* prokurator *m* okręgowy

dab [dæb] **1.** pacnięcie *n*, pryśnięcie *n*, maźnięcie *n*; odrobina *f*; **2.** (***-bb-***) wycierać ⟨wytrzeć⟩; *krem itp.* nakładać ⟨-łożyć⟩

dab·ble ['dæbl] opryskiwać ⟨-skać⟩; **~ *at*, ~ *in*** imać się (*po amatorsku*) (*G.*)

dachs·hund ['dækshʊnd] *zo.* jamnik *m*

dad [dæd] F, **~·dy** ['dædɪ] tatuś *m*

dad·dy long·legs [dædɪ 'lɒŋlegz] (*pl.* ***daddy longlegs***) koziułka *f*, komarnica *f*; *Am.* kosarz *m*

daf·fo·dil ['dæfədɪl] *bot.* żonkil *m*

daft [dɑːft] F głupi

dag·ger ['dægə] sztylet *m*; ***be at ~s drawn with s.o.*** *fig.* być z kimś na noże

dai·ly ['deɪlɪ] **1.** dzienny, codzienny; ***the ~ grind*** *lub* ***rut*** codzienny mozół *m*; **2.** dziennik *m*; pomoc *f* domowa

dain·ty ['deɪntɪ] **1.** (***-ier, -iest***) delikatny, filigranowy; **2.** przysmak *m*

dair·y ['deərɪ] mleczarnia *f*; *attr.* mleczarski, mleczny

dai·sy ['deɪzɪ] *bot.* stokrotka *f*

dale [deɪl] *dial. lub poet.* dolina *f*, kotlina *f*

dal·ly ['dælɪ]: **~ *about*** guzdrać się

Dal·ma·tian [dæl'meɪʃn] *zo.* dalmatyńczyk *m*

dam [dæm] **1.** tama *f*, zapora *f*; **2.** (***-mm-***) *też* **~ *up*** ⟨za⟩tamować, stawiać ⟨postawić⟩ tamę

dam·age ['dæmɪdʒ] **1.** szkoda *f*, uszkodzenie *n*; ***~s*** *pl. jur.* odszkodowanie; **2.** uszkadzać ⟨-kodzić⟩

dam·ask ['dæməsk] adamaszek *m*

damn [dæm] **1.** potępiać ⟨-tępić⟩; **~ (*it*)!** F cholera!, niech to szlag (trafi)!; **2.** *adj i adv.* F → ***damned***; **3. *I don't care a ~*** F mało mnie to obchodzi; **~·a·tion** [dæm'neɪʃn] *rel.* potępienie *n*; **~ed** F [dæmd] cholerny; '**~·ing** potępiający; obciążający

damp [dæmp] **1.** wilgotny; **2.** wilgoć *f*; **3.** *też*; '**~·en** nawilżać ⟨-lżyć⟩; ⟨z⟩dławić; wygaszać ⟨-gasić⟩; '**~·ness** wilgotność *f*; wilgoć *f*

dance [dɑːns] **1.** taniec *m*; **2.** ⟨za⟩tańczyć; '**danc·er** tancerz *m* (-rka *f*); '**danc·ing** tańczenie *n*; taniec *m*; *attr.* taneczny

dan·de·li·on ['dændɪlaɪən] *bot.* mniszek *m* lekarski; F mlecz *m*, dmuchawiec *m*

dan·druff ['dændrʌf] łupież *m*

Dane [deɪn] Duńczyk *m*; Dunka *f*

dan·ger ['deɪndʒə] niebezpieczeństwo *n*; ***be out of ~*** być poza zasięgiem zagrożenia; '**~ ar·e·a** strefa *f* zagrożenia; **~·ous** ['deɪndʒərəs] niebezpieczny; '**~ zone** strefa *f* zagrożenia

dan·gle ['dæŋgl] ⟨po⟩majtać

D

Da·nish ['deɪnɪʃ] **1.** duński; **2.** *ling.* język *m* duński
dank [dæŋk] wilgotny
Dan·ube Dunaj *m*
dare [deə] *v/i.* mieć śmiałość, ważyć się; ***I ~ say*** sądzę, że; wprawdzie; ***how ~ you!*** jak śmiesz! *v/t. czemuś* stawić czoło; *kogoś* ⟨s⟩prowokować (***to do s.th.*** aby coś zrobił); '**~·dev·il** śmiałek *m*, chojrak *m*; *attr.* wyzywająco śmiały;
dar·ing ['deərɪŋ] **1.** śmiały, wyzywający; **2.** śmiałość *f*
dark [dɑːk] **1.** ciemny; mroczny; ciemnoskóry; *fig.* ponury; tajemniczy; **2.** ciemność *f*; zmrok *m*; ***before*** (***after***) **~** przed zmrokiem (po zmroku); ***keep s.o. in the ~ about s.th.*** nie wyjawiać ⟨-wić⟩ czegoś komuś; '**2 Ag·es** *pl.* Średniowiecze *n*; '**~·en** ściemniać (się); '**~·ness** ciemność *f*, zmrok *m*; '**~·room** *phot.* ciemnia *f*
dar·ling ['dɑːlɪŋ] **1.** kochanie *n*; **2.** kochany, ukochany
darn [dɑːn] ⟨za⟩cerować
dart [dɑːt] **1.** strzałka *f*; skok *m*; **~s** *sg.* (*gra*) strzałki *pl.*; **2.** *v/t.* rzucać ⟨-cić⟩; *v/i.* rzucać ⟨-cić⟩ się; '**~·board** tarcza *f* (*do gry w strzałki*)
dash [dæʃ] **1.** uderzenie *n*; łoskot *m* (*fal*); odrobina *f*, szczypta *f* (*soli*), domieszka *m* (*koloru*); *print.* myślnik *m*, pauza *f*; (*w sporcie*) sprint *m*; *fig.* szyk *m*; ***make a ~ for*** rzucać ⟨-cić⟩ się do (*G*); **2.** *v/t.* rzucać, ciskać; *nadzieje* unicestwiać ⟨-wić⟩; *v/i.* uderzać ⟨-rzyć⟩ (***against*** o *A*); **~ *off*** *list* naskrobać; '**~·board** *mot.* deska *f* rozdzielcza; '**~·ing** pełen fantazji
da·ta ['deɪtə] *pl.*, *sg.* dane *pl.* (*też komp.*); ⚠ *nie* ***data***; '**~ bank**, '**~·base** baza *f* danych; **~ 'cap·ture** pozyskiwanie *n* danych; **~ 'car·ri·er** nośnik *m* danych; **~ 'in·put** wprowadzanie *n* danych; **~ 'me·di·um** nośnik *m* danych; **~ 'mem·o·ry** pamięć *f* danych; **~ 'out·put** wyprowadzanie *n* danych; **~ 'pro·ces·s·ing** przetwarzanie *n* danych; **~ pro'tec·tion** zabezpieczanie *n* danych; **~ 'stor·age** przechowywanie *n* danych; **~ 'trans·fer** transfer *m lub* przesyłanie *n* danych; **~ 'typ·ist** osoba *f* wprowadzająca dane
date[1] [deɪt] *bot.* daktyl *m*
date[2] [deɪt] data *f*; dzień *m*; termin *m*; randka *f*; *Am.* F dziewczyna *f*, chłopak *m*; ***out of ~*** przeterminowany; ***up to ~*** nowoczesny, aktualny; **2.** datować; ustalać ⟨-lić⟩ datę; ⟨po⟩starzeć; *Am.* F iść ⟨pójść⟩ na randkę z (*I*), chodzić z (*I*); '**dat·ed** przestarzały
da·tive ['deɪtɪv] *gr. też* **~ *case*** celownik *m*
daub [dɔːb] ⟨za⟩smarować
daugh·ter ['dɔːtə] córka; **~·in-law** ['dɔːtərɪnlɔː] (*pl.* ***daughters-in-law***) synowa *f*
daunt [dɔːnt] onieśmielać ⟨-lić⟩; zniechęcać ⟨-cić⟩
daw [dɔː] *zo.* → ***jackdaw***
daw·dle ['dɔːdl] mitrężyć, guzdrać się
dawn [dɔːn] **1.** świt *m* (*też fig.*); ***at ~*** o świcie; **2.** ⟨za⟩świtać; **~ *on*** *fig. komuś* ⟨za⟩świtać
day [deɪ] dzień *m*; doba *f*; *często* **~s** *pl.* czas *m* życia; ***any ~*** kiedykolwiek; ***these ~s*** obecnie; ***the other ~*** niedawno; ***the ~ after tomorrow*** pojutrze; ***open all ~*** otwarty całą dobę; ***let's call it a ~!*** koniec na dzisiaj!; '**~·break** świt *m*; '**~ care cen·tre** (*Am.* **cen·ter**) → ***day nursery***; '**~·dream 1.** marzenie *n*, mrzonka *f*; **2.** (***dreamed*** *lub* ***dreamt***) marzyć, śnić na jawie; '**~·dream·er** marzyciel(ka *f*) *m*; '**~·light** światło *n* dzienne; ***in broad ~light*** w biały dzień; '**~ nur·se·ry** żłobek *m*; **~ 'off** (*pl.* ***days off***) dzień *m* wolnego, wolny dzień *m*; **~ re'turn** *Brt.* bilet *m* powrotny na jeden dzień; '**~·time**: ***in the ~time*** w ciągu dnia, za dnia
daze [deɪz] **1.** oszałamiać ⟨oszołomić⟩; **2.** ***in a ~*** oszołomiony, w stanie oszołomienia
DC [diː 'siː] *skrót*: ***direct current*** prąd *m* stały; ***District of Columbia*** Dystrykt *m* Kolumbii
DD [diː 'diː] *skrót*: ***double density*** podwójna gęstość *f* (*zapisu dyskietek komp.*)
dead [ded] **1.** martwy, nieżywy; *zwierzę*: zdechły, *ryba*: śnięty, *roślina*: zwiędły; obojętny (***to*** na *A*); *ręka*: zdrętwiały, bez czucia; *bateria*: wyładowany; nieczynny; *farba itp.*: matowy, bez połysku; *econ.* bez obrotów; *econ.* martwy, nie procentujący; **2.** *adv.* całkiem, zupełnie; od razu, bezpośrednio; **~ *slow*** *mot.* krok za krokiem; **~ *tired*** śmiertel-

nie zmęczony; **3. *the ~*** *pl.* martwi *pl.*, zmarli *pl.*; ***in the ~ of winter (night)*** w samym środku zimy (nocy); **~ 'bar·g·ain** niebywała okazja *m*, gratka; **~ 'centre,** (*Am.* **'cen·ter**) sam środek *m*; **'~·en** ⟨z⟩amortyzować, osłabiać ⟨-bić⟩; ⟨wy⟩tłumić; **~ 'end** ślepa ulica *f* (*też fig.*); **~ 'heat** *sport*: nierozstrzygnięty bieg *m*; **'~·line** termin ostateczny *m*; **'~·lock** *fig.* pat *m*, impas *m*; **'~·locked** w impasie; **~ 'loss** *econ.* czysta strata *f*; **'~·ly** (**-*ier, -iest***) śmiertelny

deaf [def] **1.** głuchy; ***~-mute, pej. ~-and dumb*** głuchoniemy; **2. *the ~*** *pl.* głusi *pl.*; **'~·en** osłabiać ⟨-bić⟩, zagłuszyć

deal [di:l] **1.** F interes *m*, transakcja *f*; postępowanie *n*; ***it's a ~!*** zgoda!; ***a good ~*** dużo, wiele; ***a great ~*** bardzo dużo, bardzo wiele; **2.** (***dealt***) *v/t.* rozdawać ⟨-dać⟩ (*też karty*); *uderzenie* wymierzać ⟨-rzyć⟩; *v/i.* handlować; *sl.* handlować narkotykami; *karty*: rozdawać ⟨-dać⟩; ***~ with*** zajmować się; poradzić sobie z (*I*); *econ.* mieć interesy z (*I*); **'~·er** *econ.* dealer *m* (*też narkotyków*), handlarz *m* (-rka *f*); **'~·ing** postępowanie *n*; *econ.* transakcja; **'~·ings** *pl.* stosunki *pl.* handlowe; interesy *pl.*; **~t** [delt] *pret. i p.p. od* ***deal*** 2

dean [di:n] dziekan *m*

dear [dɪə] **1.** *coś* drogi, kosztowny; *ktoś* drogi, szanowny; ***Ω Sir***, (*w listach*) Szanowny Panie; **2.** kochany *m* (-na *f*); kochanie *n*; ***my dear*** mój drogi *m*, moja droga *f*; **3.** (***oh***), ***~!, ~!, ~ me!*** F o Boże!; **'~·ly** gorąco, całym sercem; drogo

death [deθ] śmierć *f*; wypadek *m* śmiertelny, zgon *m*; **'~·bed** łoże *n* śmierci; **'~ cer·tif·i·cate** świadectwo *n* zgonu; **'~·ly** (**-*ier, -iest***) śmiertelny; **'~ war·rant** *jur.* wyrok *m* śmierci

de·bar [dɪ'bɑ:] (**-*rr-***): ***~ from doing s.th.*** kogoś powstrzymywać ⟨-mać⟩ przed zrobieniem czegoś

de·base [dɪ'beɪs] ⟨z⟩degradować; ⟨z⟩dewaluować, ⟨z⟩deprecjonować

de·ba·ta·ble [dɪ'beɪtəbl] dyskusyjny;

de·bate [dɪ'beɪt] **1.** dyskusja *f*, debata *f*; **2.** debatować (nad *I*), dyskutować

deb·it *econ.* ['debɪt] **1.** debet *m*; strona "winien" ***~ and credit*** przychód i rozchód; **2.** *kogoś, konto* obciążać ⟨-żyć⟩

deb·ris ['debri:] szczątki *pl.*, pozostałości *pl.*

debt [det] dług *m*; wierzytelność *f*; ***be in ~*** mieć dług; ***be out of ~*** nie mieć długu; **'~·or** dłużnik *m* (-iczka *f*), wierzyciel(ka *f*) *m*

de·bug [di:'bʌg] *tech.* (**-*gg-***) usuwać ⟨usunąć⟩ usterki (*zwł. programu*)

de·but ['deɪbju:] debiut *m*

Dec *skrót pisany*: ***December*** grudz., grudzień *m*

dec·ade ['dekeɪd] dekada *f*, dziesięciolecie *n*

dec·a·dent ['dekədənt] dekadencki

de·caf·fein·at·ed [di:'kæfɪneɪtɪd] bezkofeinowy

de·camp [dɪ'kæmp] F nawiewać ⟨-wiać⟩

de·cant [dɪ'kænt] przelewać ⟨-lać⟩; **~·er** karafka *f*

de·cath|·lete [dɪ'kæθli:t] (*w sporcie*) dziesięcioboista *m*; **~·lon** [dɪ'kæθlɒn] (*w sporcie*) dziesięciobój *m*

de·cay [dɪ'keɪ] **1.** *v/i.* ⟨ze⟩psuć się, ⟨z⟩gnić; rozkładać ⟨-łożyć⟩ się; upadać ⟨upaść⟩; *v/t.* rozkładać ⟨-łożyć⟩; **2.** rozkład *m*, rozpad *m*; upadek *m*

de·cease [dɪ'si:s] *zwł. jur.* śmierć *f*, zgon *m*; **~d** *zwł. jur.* **1. *the ~d*** zmarły *m* (-ła *f*), zmarli *pl.*; **2.** zmarły

de·ceit [dɪ'si:t] oszustwo *n*; fałsz *m*; **~·ful** oszukańczy; fałszywy

de·ceive [dɪ'si:v] oszukiwać ⟨-kać⟩; **de'ceiv·er** oszust(ka *f*) *m*

De·cem·ber [dɪ'sembə] (*skrót*: ***Dec***) grudzień *m*

de·cen|·cy ['di:snsɪ] przyzwoitość *f*; uczciwość *f*; **'~t** przyzwoity; uczciwy

de·cep|·tion [dɪ'sepʃn] oszustwo *n*; **~·tive**: ***be ~tive*** być podstępnym *lub* zwodniczym

de·cide [dɪ'saɪd] ⟨z⟩decydować się; ⟨za⟩decydować; rozstrzygać ⟨-gnąć⟩; **de'cid·ed** zdecydowany; wyraźny

dec·i·mal ['desɪml] **1.** dziesiętny; **2.** *też* ***~ fraction*** ułamek *m* dziesiętny

de·ci·pher [dɪ'saɪfə] odcyfrować; odszyfrować

de·ci|·sion [dɪ'sɪʒn] decyzja *f*; postanowienie *n*; stanowczość *f*; ***make (reach, come to) a ~sion*** podejmować ⟨-djąć⟩ decyzję; **~·sive** [dɪ'saɪsɪv] decydujący; zdecydowany

deck [dek] **1.** *naut.* pokład *m*; piętro *n* (*autobusu itp.*); *Am.* talia *f*; *tech.* deck *m*; **2. *~ out*** ⟨wy⟩stroić (się); **'~·chair** leżak *m*

dec·la·ra·tion [deklə'reɪʃn] deklaracja *f*; oświadczenie *n*; wypowiedzenie *n*; deklaracja *f* celna
de·clare [dɪ'kleə] zadeklarować, ogłaszać ⟨ogłosić⟩; zgłaszać ⟨zgłosić⟩ do oclenia; *wojnę* wypowiadać ⟨-wiedzieć⟩
de·clen·sion [dɪ'klenʃn] deklinacja *f*
de·cline [dɪ'klaɪn] **1.** odmawiać ⟨-mówić⟩, odmawiać ⟨-mówić⟩ przyjęcia; zmniejszać ⟨-szyć⟩ (się); chylić się do upadku; *ceny* spadać ⟨spaść⟩; *gr.* deklinować; **2.** upadek *m*; spadek *m*
de·cliv·i·ty [dɪ'klɪvətɪ] stok *m*, zbocze *n*
de·clutch [diː'klʌtʃ] *mot.* wyłączać ⟨-czyć⟩ sprzęgło
de·code [diː'kəʊd] dekodować
de·com·pose [diːkəm'pəʊz] rozkładać ⟨-łożyć⟩ (się)
de·con·tam·i|·nate [diːkən'tæmɪneɪt] odkażać ⟨odkazić⟩; **~'na·tion** odkażenie *n*; dekontaminacja *f*
dec·o|·rate ['dekəreɪt] ⟨u⟩dekorować, ozdabiać ⟨-dobić⟩; odnawiać ⟨-nowić⟩, ⟨od-, wy⟩malować, ⟨wy⟩tapetować; nadawać ⟨-dać⟩ odznaczenie; **~·ra·tion** [dekə'reɪʃn] dekoracja *f*; odnowienie *n*, wymalowanie *n*, wytapetowanie *n*; odznaczenie *n*; **~·ra·tive** ['dekərətɪv] dekoracyjny, ozdobny; **~·ra·tor** ['dekəreɪtə] dekorator *m*; malarz *m*, tapeciarz *m*
dec·o·rous ['dekərəs] przywoity; **de·co·rum** [dɪ'kɔːrəm] przywoitość *f*
de·coy 1. ['diːkɔɪ] przynęta *f*; **2.** [dɪ'kɔɪ] ⟨z⟩wabić (***into*** do *G*)
de·crease 1. ['diːkriːs] spadek *m*, zmniejszenie *n* się; **2.** [diː'kriːs] spadać ⟨spaść⟩, zmniejszać ⟨-szyć⟩ się
de·cree [dɪ'kriː] **1.** dekret *m*, rozporządzenie *n*; *zwł. Am. jur.* decyzja *f*, wyrok *m*; **2.** nakazywać ⟨-zać⟩
ded·i|·cate ['dedɪkeɪt] ⟨za⟩dedykować; **'~·cat·ed** wyspecjalizowany; **~·ca·tion** [dedɪ'keɪʃn] dedykacja *f*
de·duce [dɪ'djuːs] ⟨wy⟩dedukować; ⟨wy⟩wnioskować
de·duct [dɪ'dʌkt] odejmować ⟨-jąć⟩; *kwotę itp.* potrącać ⟨-cić⟩ (***from*** z *G*), odliczać ⟨-czyć⟩; **~·i·ble**: ***~ible from tax*** podlegający odpisaniu od podatku; **de·duc·tion** [dɪ'dʌkʃn] potrącenie *n* (*kwoty itp.*); odliczenie *n*, odpis *m*; wniosek *m*
deed [diːd] czyn *m*, uczynek *m*; wyczyn *m* (*bohaterski*); *jur.* dokument *m* (*prawny*)
deep [diːp] **1.** głęboki (*też fig.*); **2.** głębokość *f*; **'~·en** pogłębiać ⟨-bić⟩ (się) (*też fig.*); **~-'freeze 1.** (***-froze, -frozen***) zamrażać ⟨-mrozić⟩; **2.** zamrażarka *f*; **~-'fro·zen** zamrożony; **~-'fry** ⟨u⟩smażyć (*jak we frytkownicy*); **'~·ness** głębia *f*, głębokość *f*
deer [dɪə] *zo.* (*pl.* ***deer***) jeleń *m*, sarna *f*; zwierzyna *f* płowa
de·face [dɪ'feɪs] ⟨o⟩szpecić; zacierać ⟨zatrzeć⟩
def·a·ma·tion [defə'meɪʃn] zniesławienie *n*
de·fault [dɪ'fɔːlt] **1.** *jur.* niestawienie się (*przed sądem*); (*w sporcie*) niestawiennictwo *n*; *econ.* zwłoka; *komp. domyślna* wartość *f lub* nastawienie *n* domyślne; *attr.*, *komp.* domyślny, standardowy; **2.** *econ.* nie wywiązywać ⟨-wiązać⟩ się ze zobowiązania; *jur.* nie stawiać ⟨-wić⟩ się (przed sądem); (*w sporcie*) nie stawić się
de·feat [dɪ'fiːt] **1.** porażka *f*, klęska *f*; **2.** pobić; pokonywać ⟨-nać⟩; ⟨z⟩niweczyć
de·fect [dɪ'fekt] defekt *m*, wada *f*; **de'fec·tive** wadliwy
de·fence *Brt.*, **de·fense** *Am.* [dɪ'fens] obrona *f*; ***witness for the ~*** świadek *m* obrony; **~·less** bezbronny
de·fend [dɪ'fend] (***from, against***) bronić (się) (przed *I*); (*w sporcie*) ⟨o⟩bronić; **de'fen·dant** *jur.* pozwany *m* (-na *f*); oskarżony *m* (-na *f*); **de'fend·er** obrońca *m*
de·fen·sive [dɪ'fensɪv] **1.** defensywa *f*; ***on the ~*** w defensywie; **2.** defensywny, obronny
de·fer [dɪ'fɜː] (***-rr-***) odkładać ⟨-łożyć⟩, odraczać ⟨-roczyć⟩
de·fi|·ance [dɪ'faɪəns] wyzwanie *n*, bunt *m*; ***in ~ance of*** wbrew (*D*); **~·ant** wyzywający, buntowniczy
de·fi·cien|·cy [dɪ'fɪʃnsɪ] brak *m*, niedostatek *m*; niedobór *m*; **~t** brakujący, niedostateczny; ***~t in*** ubogi w (*A*), o niewystarczającej ilości (*G*)
def·i·cit ['defɪsɪt] *econ.* deficyt *m*, niedobór *m*
de·file[1] ['diːfaɪl] wąwóz *m*, przesmyk *m*
de·file[2] [dɪ'faɪl] ⟨z⟩bezcześcić, ⟨s⟩kalać
de·fine [dɪ'faɪn] ⟨z⟩definiować, określać ⟨-lić⟩; wyjaśniać ⟨-nić⟩; **def·i·nite**

['defɪnɪt] określony; jasny, sprecyzowany; **def·i·ni·tion** [defɪ'nɪʃn] definicja *f*; (*w TV, filmie*) rozdzielczość *f*; **de·fin·itive** [dɪ'fɪnɪtɪv] ostateczny, rozstrzygający; wzorcowy
de·flect [dɪ'flekt] *v/t.* odbijać ‹-bić›; *v/i.* zbaczać ‹zboczyć›, zmieniać ‹-nić› kierunek
de·form [dɪ'fɔːm] ‹z›deformować, zniekształcać ‹-cić›; **~ed** zdeformowany, zniekształcony; **de·for·mi·ty** [dɪ'fɔːmətɪ] deformacja *f*, zniekształcenie *n*
de·fraud [dɪ'frɔːd] ‹z›defraudować (***of*** na *A*), sprzeniewierzać ‹-rzyć›
de·frost [diː'frɒst] rozmrażać ‹-rozić› (się)
deft [deft] zręczny, zgrabny, zdolny
de·fy [dɪ'faɪ] wyzywać ‹-zwać›; przeciwstawiać ‹-wić› się (*D*); wzywać ‹wezwać›
de·gen·e·rate **1.** [dɪ'dʒenəreɪt] ‹z›degenerować się, ‹z›wyrodnieć; **2.** [dɪ'dʒenərət] zdegenerowany, zwyrodniały; **3.** degenerat *m*
deg·ra·da·tion [degrə'deɪʃn] poniżenie *n*; **de·grade** [dɪ'greɪd] *v/t.* poniżać ‹-żyć›
de·gree [dɪ'griː] stopień *m* (*też naukowy*); ***by ~s*** stopniowo; ***take one's ~*** otrzymywać ‹-mać› stopień naukowy (***in*** w zakresie *G*)
de·hy·drat·ed [diː'haɪdreɪtɪd] odwodniony, suszony
de·i·fy ['diːɪfaɪ] ubóstwiać ‹-wić›, deifikować
deign [deɪn] być łaskawym, raczyć
de·i·ty ['diːɪtɪ] bóstwo *n*
de·jec|·ted [dɪ'dʒektɪd] przygnębiony, przygaszony; **~·tion** [dɪ'dʒekʃn] przygnębienie *n*
de·lay [dɪ'leɪ] **1.** zwłoka *f*; *rail itp.* opóźnienie *n*; okres *m* opóźnienia; **2.** zwlekać ‹-wlec›; opóźniać ‹-nić›; odłożyć ‹odkładać›
del·e|·gate **1.** ['delɪgeɪt] *kogoś* ‹od›delegować; *uprawnienia itp.* przekazywać ‹-zać›, delegować; **2.** ['delɪgət] delegat *m*, wysłannik *m* (-iczka *f*); **~·ga·tion** [delɪ'geɪʃn] delegacja *f*; przekazanie *n*
de·lete [dɪ'liːt] wymazywać ‹-zać›; *komp.* ‹s›kasować
de·lib·e|·rate [dɪ'lɪbərət] umyślny; rozważny; **~·ra·tion** [dɪlɪbə'reɪʃn] zastanowienie *n*, rozwaga *f*; ***with ~·ra·tion*** z namaszczeniem
del·i|·ca·cy ['delɪkəsɪ] delikatność *f*; subtelność *f*; smakołyk *m*, przysmak *m*; **~·cate** ['delɪkət] delikatny; subtelny; **~·ca·tes·sen** [delɪkə'tesn] delikatesy *pl.*
de·li·cious [dɪ'lɪʃəs] smakowity
de·light [dɪ'laɪt] **1.** zachwyt *m*, przyjemność *f*; **2.** *v/t.* zabawiać; *v/i.* znajdować wielką przyjemność (***in*** w *L*); **~·ful** zachwycający
de·lin·quen|·cy [dɪ'lɪŋkwənsɪ] przestępczość *f*; **~t** **1.** winny przewinienia; **2.** przestępca *m* → ***juvenile delinquent***
de·lir·i|·ous [dɪ'lɪrɪəs] *med.* majaczący; **~·um** [dɪ'lɪrɪəm] majaczenie *n*; delirium *n*
de·liv·er [dɪ'lɪvə] dostarczać ‹-czyć›; *listy itp.* doręczać ‹-czyć›; *cios itp.* wymierzać ‹-czyć›; *wykład itp.* wygłaszać ‹-głosić›; uwalniać ‹-wolnić›; *med. dziecko itp.* odbierać ‹odebrać›; **~·ance** [dɪ'lɪvərəns] oswobodzenie *n*; **~·er** [dɪ'lɪvərə] oswobodziciel(ka *f*) *m*; **~·y** [dɪ'lɪvərɪ] dostarczenie *n*; doręczenie *n* (*poczty itp.*); wygłoszenie *n* (*mowy itp.*); odczyt *m*, referat *m*; *med.* poród *m*; **~·y van** furgonetka *f* dostawcza
dell [del] dolina *f*
de·lude [dɪ'luːd] łudzić
del·uge ['deljuːdʒ] potop *m*, *fig.* zalew *m*
de·lu·sion [dɪ'luːʒn] ułuda *f*, złudzenie *n*
de·mand [dɪ'mɑːnd] **1.** żądanie *n*; zapotrzebowanie *n*, popyt *m* (***for*** na *A*); obciążenie *n*; ***in ~*** na żądanie, w razie potrzeby; **2.** ‹za›żądać, domagać się; wymagać; **~·ing** wymagający
de·men·ted [dɪ'mentɪd] obłąkany; *med.* otępiały
dem·i... ['demɪ] pół..., demi...
de·mil·i·ta·rize [diː'mɪlɪtəraɪz] ‹z›demilitaryzować
dem·o ['deməʊ] F (*pl.* ***-os***) demo *n* (*wersja demonstracyjna*), demonstracja *f* (*uliczna*)
de·mo·bi·lize [diː'məʊbɪlaɪz] ‹z›demobilizować
de·moc·ra·cy [dɪ'mɒkrəsɪ] demokracja *f*
dem·o·crat ['deməkræt] demokrata *m*

(-tka *f*); **~·ic** [demə'krætɪk] demokratyczny
de·mol·ish [dɪ'mɒlɪʃ] ⟨z⟩burzyć; ⟨z⟩niszczyć, obalać ⟨-lić⟩; F *jedzenie* pochłaniać ⟨-łonąć⟩; **dem·o·li·tion** [demə'lɪʃn] (z)burzenie *n*; zniszczenie *n*, obalenie *n*
de·mon ['diːmən] demon *m*; czart *m*
dem·on|·strate ['demənstreɪt] ⟨za⟩demonstrować; wykazywać ⟨-zać⟩; dowodzić ⟨-wieść⟩; **~·stra·tion** [demən'streɪʃn] demonstracja *f*; dowód *m*; pokaz *m*; manifestacja *f*; **~·stra·tive** [dɪ'mɒnstrətɪv] *gr.* wskazujący; ***be ~strative*** być wylewnym; **~·stra·tor** ['demənstreɪtə] demonstrator(ka *f*) *m*
de·mor·al·ize [dɪ'mɒrəlaɪz] ⟨z⟩demoralizować; zniechęcać ⟨-cić⟩
de·mote [diː'məʊt] ⟨z⟩degradować
de·mure [dɪ'mjʊə] potulny, nieśmiały
den [den] jaskinia *f*, legowisko *n*; *fig.* własny kąt *m*
de·ni·al [dɪ'naɪəl] zaprzeczenie *n*; odmowa *f*; wyparcie *n* się; ***official ~*** dementi *n*
den·ims ['denɪmz] *pl.* dżinsy *pl.*
Den·mark ['denmɑːk] Dania *f*
de·nom·i·na·tion [dɪnɒmɪ'neɪʃn] *rel.* wyznanie *n*
de·note [dɪ'nəʊt] oznaczać, znaczyć
de·nounce [dɪ'naʊns] *kogoś* ⟨za⟩denuncjować; *coś* potępiać ⟨-pić⟩
dense [dens] (**-r, -st**) gęsty; *fig.* ciemny, przygłupi; **den·si·ty** ['densətɪ] gęstość *f*
dent [dent] **1.** wgniecenie *n*; **2.** wgniatać ⟨wgnieść⟩
den·tal ['dentl] zębny, nazębny; **~ 'plaque** osad *m* nazębny; **~ 'plate** proteza *f*; **~ 'sur·geon** dentysta *m* (-tka *f*), stomatolog *m*
den·tist ['dentɪst] dentysta *m* (-tka *f*), stomatolog *m*
den·tures ['dentʃəz] *med. pl.* proteza *f* dentystyczna
de·nun·ci·a|·tion [dɪnʌnsɪ'eɪʃn] potępienie *n*; denuncjacja *f*; **~·tor** [dɪ'nʌnsɪeɪtə] denuncjator(ka *f*) *m*
de·ny [dɪ'naɪ] zaprzeczać ⟨-czyć⟩; ⟨z⟩dementować; odmawiać ⟨-mówić⟩; wypierać ⟨-przeć⟩ się
de·o·do·rant [diː'əʊdərənt] dezodorant *m*
dep *skrót pisany*: ***depart*** odjeżdżać; ***departure*** odj., odjazd *m*
de·part [dɪ'pɑːt] odjeżdżać ⟨-jechać⟩; odejść ⟨odchodzić⟩ (***from*** od *G*), odstępować ⟨-stąpić⟩
de·part·ment [dɪ'pɑːtmənt] dział *m*; wydział *m*; *univ.* *też* zakład *m*, instytut *m*; *pol.* ministerstwo *n*; **≈ of De'fense**, *też* ***Defence*** *Am.* Ministerstwo *n* Obrony; **≈ of the En'vi·ron·ment** *Brt.* Ministerstwo *n* Ochrony Środowiska; **≈ of the In'te·ri·or** *Am.* Ministerstwo *n* Spraw Wewnętrznych; **≈ of 'State**, *też* ***State*** **≈** *Am. pol.* Departament *m* Stanu, Ministerstwo *n* Spraw Zagranicznych; **~ store** dom *m* towarowy
de·par·ture [dɪ'pɑːtʃə] *też rail.* odjazd *m*, *aviat.* odlot *m*; odejście *n* (od tematu); **~s** *pl.* odjazdy *pl.* (*w rozkładzie jazdy*); **~ gate** *aviat.* przejście *n* do samolotu; **~ lounge** *aviat.* hala *f* odlotów
de·pend [dɪ'pend]: **~ *on*** polegać na (*L*); liczyć na (*A*); zależeć od (*G*); ***that ~s*** to zależy
de·pen|·da·ble [dɪ'pendəbl] godny zaufania; **~·dant** osoba *f* na czyimś utrzymaniu; **~·dence** zależność *f*; zaufanie *n*; **~·dent** **1.** zależny (***on*** od *G*); **2.** → ***dependant***
de·plor|·a·ble [dɪ'plɔːrəbl] godny pożałowania; **~e** [dɪ'plɔː] ubolewać nad (*I*)
de·pop·u·late [diː'pɒpjʊleɪt] wyludniać ⟨-nić⟩
de·port [dɪ'pɔːt] deportować, wywozić ⟨-wieźć⟩; usuwać ⟨usunąć⟩
de·pose [dɪ'pəʊz] usuwać ⟨-nąć⟩ z urzędu; *jur.* zaświadczać ⟨-czyć⟩
de·pos|·it [dɪ'pɒzɪt] **1.** składać ⟨złożyć⟩; ⟨z⟩deponować; *geol.*, *chem.* osadzać ⟨-dzić⟩ (się); *econ.* *zaliczkę* uiszczać ⟨uiścić⟩; **2.** *chem.* osad *m*; *geol.* *też* złoże *n*; depozyt *m*; *econ.* wpłata *f*; kaucja *f*; ***make a ~it*** wpłacać ⟨-cić⟩ zaliczkę *lub* zadatek; **~it ac·count** *zwł. Brt.* rachunek *m* lokat okresowych; **~·i·tor** deponent(ka *f*) *m*
dep·ot ['depəʊ] skład *m*, magazyn *m*; *Am.* ['diːpəʊ] dworzec *m*
de·prave [dɪ'preɪv] *etycznie* ⟨z⟩deprawować
de·pre·ci·ate [dɪ'priːʃɪeɪt] ⟨z⟩deprecjonować, obniżać ⟨-żyć⟩ wartość
de·press [dɪ'pres] naciskać ⟨-cisnąć⟩; przygnębiać ⟨-bić⟩; ⟨z⟩tłumić, przygłu-

szać ⟨-szyć⟩; **~ed** w depresji; przygnębiony; *econ. rynek*: osłabiony; **~ed ar·e·a** obszar dotknięty depresją; **~·ing** deprymujący, przygnębiający; **de·pression** [dɪ'preʃn] depresja *f* (*też econ.*); przygnębienie *n*; obniżenie *n*; *meteor.* niskie ciśnienie *n*, obszar *m* niskiego ciśnienia

de·prive [dɪ'praɪv]: **~ *s.o. of s.th.*** pozbawiać ⟨-wić⟩ kogoś czegoś; **~d** nieuprzywilejowany

dept, **Dept** *skrót pisany*: ***Department*** dział, wydział

depth [depθ] głębokość *f*, głębia *f*

dep·u|·ta·tion [depjʊ'teɪʃn] delegacja *f*; **~·tize** ['depjʊtaɪz]: ***~tize for s.o.*** zastępować ⟨-stąpić⟩ kogoś; **~·ty** ['depjʊtɪ] zastępca *m* (-czyni *f*); *pol.* poseł *m* (-słanka *f*); *też* ***~ty sheriff*** zastępca *m* (-czyni *f*) szeryfa

de·rail [dɪ'reɪl] wykolejać; ***be ~ed*** wykoleić się

de·ranged [dɪ'reɪndʒd] obłąkany

der·e·lict ['derəlɪkt] opuszczony

de·ride [dɪ'raɪd] ⟨wy⟩szydzić; **de·ri·sion** [dɪ'rɪʒn] szyderstwo *n*; **de·ri·sive** [dɪ'raɪsɪv] szyderczy

de·rive [dɪ'raɪv] pochodzić (***from*** z *A*); wywodzić się (***from*** z *A*); ***~ pleasure from*** znajdować ⟨znaleźć⟩ przyjemność w (*L*)

der·ma·tol·o·gist [dɜːmə'tɒlədʒɪst] *med.* dermatolog *m*

de·rog·a·to·ry [dɪ'rɒgətərɪ] poniżający, uwłaczający, przynoszący ujmę

der·rick ['derɪk] *tech.* żuraw *m* masztowy; *naut.* żuraw *m* ładunkowy; wieża *f* wiertnicza

de·scend [dɪ'send] obniżać ⟨-żyć⟩ się, zniżać ⟨-żyć⟩ się; schodzić ⟨zejść⟩; *aviat.* wytracać ⟨-cić⟩ wysokość, schodzić ⟨zejść⟩ w dół; pochodzić, wywodzić się (***from*** z *G*); ***~ on*** zwalać ⟨-lić⟩ się na (*A*), ⟨za⟩atakować, napadać ⟨-paść⟩; **de'scen·dant** potomek *m*

de·scent [dɪ'sent] obniżanie *n* się; zniżanie *n* się; schodzenie *n*; *aviat.* wytracanie *n* wysokości; pochodzenie *n*; najście *n*, desant *m*

de·scribe [dɪ'skraɪb] opisywać ⟨-sać⟩

de·scrip|·tion [dɪ'skrɪpʃn] opis *m*; rodzaj *m*; **~·tive** [dɪ'skrɪptɪv] opisowy; obrazowy

des·e·crate ['desɪkreɪt] ⟨z⟩bezcześcić, ⟨s⟩profanować

de·seg·re|·gate [diː'segrɪgeɪt] znosić ⟨-nieść⟩ segregację rasową; **~·ga·tion** [diːsegrɪ'geɪʃn] znoszenie segregacji rasowej

des·ert[1] ['dezət] pustynia *f*; *attr.* pustynny

de·sert[2] [dɪ'zɜːt] *v/t.* opuszczać ⟨opuścić⟩, porzucać ⟨-cić⟩; *v/i. mil.* ⟨z⟩dezerterować; **~·er** *mil.* dezerter *m*; **de·ser·tion** [dɪ'zɜːʃn] (*jur. też złośliwe*) porzucenie *n*; dezercja *f*

de·serve [dɪ'zɜːv] zasługiwać ⟨-służyć⟩ na (*A*); **de·serv·ed·ly** [dɪ'zɜːvɪdlɪ] zasłużenie; **de·serv·ing** zasłużony

de·sign [dɪ'zaɪn] **1.** projekt *m*, plan *m*; *tech.* projekt *m*, rysunek *m* techniczny; wzór *m*, deseń *m*; zamiar *m*; **2.** ⟨za⟩projektować, ⟨za⟩planować; zamyślać ⟨-ślić⟩

des·ig·nate ['dezɪgneɪt] wyznaczać ⟨-czyć⟩

de·sign·er [dɪ'zaɪnə] konstruktor(ka *f*) *m*; projektant(ka *f*) *m*

de·sir|·a·ble [dɪ'zaɪərəbl] pożądany; **~e** [dɪ'zaɪə] **1.** chęć *f*, zamiar *m*; pożądanie *n* (***for*** *G*), chętka *f*; **2.** ⟨za⟩pragnąć, ⟨za⟩życzyć sobie; pożądać, mieć chęć

de·sist [dɪ'zɪst] zaprzestawać ⟨-tać⟩

desk [desk] biurko *n*; ławka *f*; recepcja *f*; punkt *m* informacyjny; **~·top com'put·er** komputer *m* biurkowy; **~·top 'pub·lish·ing** (*skrót*: ***DTP***) *komp.* DTP *n*, mała poligrafia *f*

des·o·late ['desələt] wyludniony, opuszczony

de·spair [dɪ'speə] **1.** rozpacz *f*; **2.** ⟨s⟩tracić nadzieję (***of*** na *A*); **~·ing** [dɪ'speərɪŋ] zrozpaczony

de·spatch [dɪ'spætʃ] → ***dispatch***

des·per|·ate ['despərət] zdesperowany; desperacki; F rozpaczliwy, beznadziejny; **~·a·tion** [despə'reɪʃn] desperacja *f*

des·pic·a·ble [dɪ'spɪkəbl] zasługujący na pogardę, nikczemny

de·spise [dɪ'spaɪz] ⟨po⟩gardzić, ⟨z⟩lekceważyć

de·spite [dɪ'spaɪt] (po)mimo (*G*)

de·spon·dent [dɪ'spɒndənt] pozbawiony nadziei, przygnębiony

des·pot 'despɒt] despota *m* (-tka *f*)

des·sert [dɪ'zɜːt] deser *m*

D

des|·ti·na·tion [destɪ'neɪʃn] przeznaczenie *n*, miejsce *n* przeznaczenia; **~·tined** ['destɪnd] przeznaczony; zdążający (***for*** do *G*); **~·ti·ny** ['destɪnɪ] przeznaczenie *n*
des·ti·tute ['destɪtjuːt] bez środków do życia
de·stroy [dɪ'strɔɪ] ⟨z⟩niszczyć; *zwierzęta* uśmiercać ⟨-cić⟩; **~·er** niszczyciel(ka *f*) *m*; *mil. naut.* niszczyciel *m*
de·struc|·tion [dɪ'strʌkʃn] zniszczenie *n*; **~·tive** [dɪ'strʌktɪv] niszczycielski, destruktywny
de·tach [dɪ'tætʃ] odczepiać ⟨-pić⟩, odłączać ⟨-czyć⟩; **~ed** oddzielny, osobny; *ktoś*: pełen dystansu; ***~ed house*** dom(ek) *m* wolnostojący; **~·ment** dystans *m*; *mil.* oddział *m* (*wydzielony*)
de·tail ['diːteɪl] **1.** szczegół *m*, detal *m*; *mil.* oddział *m* (*wydzielony*); ***in ~*** szczegółowo; **2.** wyszczególniać ⟨-nić⟩; *mil.* odkomenderować; **~ed** szczegółowy
de·tain [dɪ'teɪn] zatrzymywać ⟨-mać⟩; *jur.* ⟨za⟩aresztować
de·tect [dɪ'tekt] wykrywać ⟨-ryć⟩; wyczuwać ⟨-czuć⟩; **de·tec·tion** [dɪ'tekʃn] wykrycie *n*; **de·tec·tive** [dɪ'tektɪv] detektyw *m*, wywiadowca *m*; **de'tec·tive nov·el, de'tec·tive sto·ry** powieść *f* detektywistyczna
de·ten·tion [dɪ'tenʃn] zatrzymanie *n*; areszt *m*
de·ter [dɪ'tɜː] (***-rr-***) odstraszać ⟨-szyć⟩ (***from*** od *G*)
de·ter·gent [dɪ'tɜːdʒənt] detergent *m*; proszek *m* do prania; środek *m* do prania; *attr.* detergentowy
de·te·ri·o·rate [dɪ'tɪərɪəreɪt] podupadać ⟨-paść⟩; pogarszać ⟨-gorszyć⟩ się
de·ter|·mi·na·tion [dɪtɜːmɪ'neɪʃn] zdecydowanie *n*, stanowczość *f*; determinacja *f*; stwierdzenie *n*, ustalenie *n*; **~·mine** [dɪ'tɜːmɪn] postanawiać ⟨-nowić⟩, ⟨z⟩decydować się na (*A*); stwierdzać ⟨-dzić⟩, określać ⟨-lić⟩, ustalać ⟨-lić⟩; **~·mined** zdeterminowany, zdecydowany
de·ter|·rence [dɪ'terəns] odstraszanie *n*; **~·rent 1.** odstraszający; **2.** środek *m* odstraszający
de·test [dɪ'test] nie cierpieć
de·throne [dɪ'θrəʊn] ⟨z⟩detronizować
de·to·nate ['detəneɪt] *v/t.* ⟨z⟩detonować; **2.** wybuchać ⟨-chnąć⟩, eksplodować
de·tour ['diːtʊə] objazd *m*
de·tract [dɪ'trækt]: ***~ from*** zmniejszać ⟨-szyć⟩ (*A*)
de·tri·ment ['detrɪmənt] szkoda *f*, uszczerbek *m*
deuce [djuːs] (*w kartach*) dwa, dwójka *f*; (*w tenisie*) równowaga *f*
de·val·u|·a·tion [diːvælju'eɪʃn] dewaluacja *f*; **~e** [diː'] ⟨z⟩dewaluować
dev·a|·state ['devəsteɪt] ⟨z⟩dewastować, ⟨z⟩niszczyć; **'~·stat·ing** niszczycielski
de·vel·op [dɪ'veləp] rozwijać (się); *phot.* wywoływać ⟨-łać⟩; *teren budowlany* zagospodarowywać ⟨-ować⟩, rozbudowywać ⟨-ować⟩; *stare miasto*: dokonywać ⟨-konać⟩ sanacji; **~·er** *phot.* wywoływacz *m*; przedsiębiorca *m* budowlany; **~·ing** rozwijający (się); **~·ing 'coun·try, ~·ing 'na·tion** kraj *m* rozwijający się; **~·ment** rozwój *m*; zagospodarowanie *n*, sanacja *f*
de·vi|·ate ['diːvɪeɪt] zbaczać ⟨zboczyć⟩ (***from*** z *G*), odchodzić (***from*** od *G*); **~·a·tion** [diːvɪ'eɪʃn] zboczenie *n*; dewiacja *f*
de·vice [dɪ'vaɪs] urządzenie *n*, przyrząd *m*; plan *m*, pomysł *m*; *literacki* chwyt *m*; ***leave s.o. to his own ~s*** pozostawić kogoś samego
dev·il ['devl] czart *m*, diabeł *m*; **'~·ish** diabelski
de·vi·ous ['diːvjəs] *coś*: kręty; *ktoś*: pokrętny; ***~ route*** droga *f* okrężna
de·vise [dɪ'vaɪz] wymyślić
de·void [dɪ'vɔɪd]: ***~ of*** pozbawiony (*G*)
de·vote [dɪ'vəʊt] poświęcać ⟨-cić⟩; **de'vot·ed** poświęcony; oddany; **de·vo·tee** [devəʊ'tiː] wielbiciel(ka *f*) *m*; wyznawca *m* (-czyni *f*); **de·vo·tion** [dɪ'vəʊʃn] poświęcenie *n*; ofiarność *f*; oddanie *n*
de·vour [dɪ'vaʊə] pożerać ⟨-żreć⟩
de·vout [dɪ'vaʊt] pobożny; *nadzieja*: gorący
dew [djuː] rosa *f*; **'~·drop** kropla *f* rosy; **'~·y** (***-ier, -iest***) wilgotny
dex|·ter·i·ty [dek'sterətɪ] zręczność *f*, sprawność *f*; **~·ter·ous, ~·trous** ['dekstrəs] zręczny, sprawny
di·ag·|nose ['daɪəgnəʊz] ⟨z⟩diagnozować, stawiać ⟨postawić⟩ diagno-

zę; **~·no·sis** [daɪəg'nəʊsɪs] (*pl.* ***-ses*** [-siːz]) diagnoza *f*
di·ag·o·nal [daɪ'ægənl] **1.** przekątny, ukośny; **2.** przekątna *f*
di·a·gram ['daɪəgræm] diagram *m*, wykres *m*
di·al ['daɪəl] **1.** cyferblat *m*; *tel.* tarcza *f* (*telefonu*); *tech.* skala *f*; **2.** (*zwł. Brt.* ***-ll-***, *Am.* ***-l-***) *tel.* nakręcać ⟨-cić⟩, wybierać ⟨-brać⟩; ***~ direct*** wybierać bezpośredni numer (***to*** do *G*); ***direct ~(l)ing*** bezpośrednie połączenie *n*
di·a·lect ['daɪəlekt] dialekt *m*
'di·al·ling code *Brt. tel.* numer *m* kierunkowy
di·a·logue *Brt.*, **di·a·log** *Am.* ['daɪəlɒg] dialog *m*, rozmowa *f*
di·am·e·ter [daɪ'æmɪtə] średnica *f*; ***in ~*** średnicy
di·a·mond ['daɪəmənd] diament *m*, brylant *m*; romb *m*; (*w kartach*) karo *n*
di·a·per ['daɪəpə] *Am.* pielucha *f*, pieluszka *f*
di·a·phragm ['daɪəfræm] *anat.* przepona *f*; *opt.* przesłona *f*; *tel.* membrana *f*
di·ar·rh(o)e·a [daɪə'rɪə] *med.* biegunka *f*
di·a·ry ['daɪərɪ] pamiętnik *m*; kalendarzyk *m* kieszonkowy
dice [daɪs] **1.** *pl. od* ***die***[2]; kostka *f* do gry; kości (*gra*) *pl.*; **2.** *gastr.* ⟨po⟩kroić w kostkę; ⟨za-, po⟩grać w kości
dick [dɪk] *Am. sl.* (*prywatny detektyw*) glina *m*
dick·y·bird ['dɪkɪbɜːd] F ptaszek *m*; słówko *n*
dic|·tate [dɪk'teɪt] ⟨po⟩dyktować (*też fig.*); **~·ta·tion** [dɪk'teɪʃn] dyktowanie *n*; (*w szkole*) dyktando *n*
dic·ta·tor [dɪk'teɪtə] dyktator(ka *f*) *m*; **~·ship** dyktatura *f*
dic·tion ['dɪkʃn] wymowa *f*; styl *m*
dic·tion·a·ry ['dɪkʃnrɪ] słownik *m*
did [dɪd] *pret. od* → ***do***
die[1] [daɪ] umierać ⟨umrzeć⟩, ⟨z⟩ginąć; *zwierzęta*: zdychać ⟨zdechnąć⟩; ⟨u⟩schnąć; zamierać ⟨-mrzeć⟩, przestawać ⟨-stać⟩ pracować; ***~ of hunger*** (***thirst***) umierać ⟨umrzeć⟩ z głodu *lub* pragnienia; ***~ away*** *wiatr*, *dźwięk*: zanikać ⟨-niknąć⟩; ***~ down*** zamierać ⟨-mrzeć⟩; niknąć; ***~ out*** wymierać ⟨-mrzeć⟩ (*też fig.*)
die[2] [daɪ] *Am.* (*pl.* ***dice***) kostka *f*

di·et ['daɪət] **1.** dieta *f*; odżywianie *n* się; ***be on a ~*** być na diecie; **2.** być na diecie
dif·fer ['dɪfə] różnić się; być odmiennego zdania (***with, from*** od *G*);
dif·fe|·rence ['dɪfrəns] różnica *f*; różnica *f* zdań; **'~·rent** różny, odmienny (***from*** od *G*); różniący się; **~·ren·ti·ate** [dɪfə'renʃɪeɪt] rozróżniać, odróżniać
dif·fi|·cult ['dɪfɪkəlt] trudny; **'~·cul·ty** trudność *f*
dif·fi|·dence ['dɪfɪdəns] nieśmiałość *f*, rezerwa *f*; **'~·dent** nieśmiały, pełen rezerwy
dif|·fuse **1.** *fig.* [dɪ'fjuːz] rozpraszać ⟨-proszyć⟩; promieniować; **2.** [dɪ'fjuːs] rozproszony; *fig.* chaotyczny; **~·fu·sion** [dɪ'fjuːʒn] *chem.*, *phys.* rozproszenie *n*
dig [dɪg] **1.** (***-gg-***; ***dug***) kopać; ***~*** (***up***) wykopywać ⟨-pać⟩; ***~*** (***up*** *lub* ***out***) wykopywać ⟨-pać⟩; wygrzebywać ⟨-grzebać⟩ (*też fig.*); ***~ s.o. in the ribs*** szturchać ⟨-chnąć⟩ kogoś (*łokciem*); **2.** F szturchaniec *n*; ***~s*** *pl. Brt.* F (*wynajęte mieszkanie*) chata *f*
di·gest **1.** [dɪ'dʒest] ⟨s⟩trawić; ***~ well*** być lekkostrawnym; **2.** ['daɪdʒest] wyciąg *m*, przegląd *m*; **~·i·ble** [dɪ'dʒestəbl] strawny; **di·ges·tion** [dɪ'dʒestʃən] trawienie *n*; **di·ges·tive** [dɪ'dʒestɪv] trawienny
dig·ger ['dɪgə] poszukiwacz(ka *f*) *m* złota
di·git ['dɪdʒɪt] cyfra *f*; palec *m*; ***three-~ number*** liczba trzycyfrowa
di·gi·tal ['dɪdʒɪtl] cyfrowy; **~ 'clock**, **~ 'watch** zegar(ek) *m* cyfrowy
dig·ni|·fied ['dɪgnɪfaɪd] dystyngowany; pełen godności *lub* dostojeństwa; **~·ta·ry** ['dɪgnɪtərɪ] dygnitarz *m*; **~·ty** ['dɪgnɪtɪ] godność *f*; dostojeństwo *n*
di·gress [daɪ'gres] ⟨z⟩robić dygresję
dike[1] [daɪk] grobla *f*, wał *m*; rów *m*
dike[2] [daɪk] *sl.* lesbijka *f*
di·lap·i·dat·ed [dɪ'læpɪdeɪtɪd] zrujnowany, zdemolowany
di·late [daɪ'leɪt] rozszerzać ⟨-rzyć⟩ (się);
dil·a·to·ry ['dɪlətərɪ] opieszały
dil·i|·gence ['dɪlɪdʒəns] pilność *f*; **'~·gent** pilny
di·lute [daɪ'ljuːt] **1.** rozcieńczać ⟨-czyć⟩, rozrzedzać ⟨-dzić⟩; **2.** rozcieńczony, rozrzedzony

D

dim [dɪm] **1.** (**-*mm-***) ciemny; niewyraźny; *wzrok*: słaby; *światło*: nikły; *Brt.* tępy; **2.** przyciemniać ⟨-mnić⟩ (się); stawać ⟨stać⟩ się niewyraźnym; **~ *one's headlights*** *Am. mot.* włączać ⟨-czyć⟩ światła mijania
dime [daɪm] *Am.* dziesięciocentówka *f*
di·men·sion [dɪ'menʃn] wymiar *m*; aspekt *m*; **~*s*** *pl. też* wymiary *pl.*; **~·al** [dɪ'menʃənl]: ***three-~al*** trójwymiarowy
di·min·ish [dɪ'mɪnɪʃ] zmniejszać ⟨-szyć⟩ (się)
di·min·u·tive [dɪ'mɪnjʊtɪv] malutki, maluśki
dim·ple ['dɪmpl] dołek *m*
din [dɪn] hałas *m*, wrzawa *f*
dine [daɪn] ⟨z⟩jeść (*obiad*); **~ *in*** *lub* ***out*** jeść w domu *lub* na mieście; **'din·er** (*w restauracji*) gość *m*; *Am. rail.* wagon *m* restauracyjny; *Am.* restauracja *f*
din·ghy ['dɪŋgɪ] *naut.* ponton *m*
din·gy ['dɪndʒɪ] (**-*ier, -iest***) brudny
'din·ing| car *rail.* wagon *m* restauracyjny; **'~ room** jadalnia *f*; restauracja *f*
din·ner ['dɪnə] obiad *m*; *obfita* kolacja *f*; przyjęcie *n*; **'~ jack·et** smoking *m*; **'~ par·ty** przyjęcie *n*; **'~ ser·vice**, **'~ set** serwis *m* stołowy; **'~·time** obiad *m*
di·no ['daɪnəʊ] *zo. skrót*: **di·no·saur** ['daɪnəʊsɔː] dinozaur *m*
dip [dɪp] **1.** *v/t.* (**-*pp-***) zanurzać ⟨-rzyć⟩; **~ *one's headlights*** *Brt. mot.* włączać ⟨-czyć⟩ światła mijania; *v/i.* zanurzyć ⟨-rzać⟩ się; opadać ⟨opaść⟩, spadać ⟨spaść⟩; **2.** zanurzenie *n*; nachylenie *n*, pochylenie *n*; F *krótka* kąpiel *f*; sos *m*, dip *m*
diph·ther·i·a [dɪf'θɪərɪə] *med.* dyfteryt *m*, błonica *f*
di·plo·ma [dɪ'pləʊmə] dyplom *m*, zaświadczenie *n* ukończenia
di·plo·ma·cy [dɪ'pləʊməsɪ] dyplomacja *f*
dip·lo·mat ['dɪpləmæt] dyplomata *m*; **~·ic** [dɪplə'mætɪk] (**-*ally***) dyplomatyczny
dip·per ['dɪpə] chochla *f*, czerpak *m*
dire ['daɪə] (**-*r, -st***) okropny, skrajny
di·rect [dɪ'rekt] **1.** *adj.* bezpośredni; szczery; **2.** *adv.* bezpośrednio; szczerze; **3.** ⟨s⟩kierować; ⟨po⟩kierować; nakazywać ⟨-zać⟩; ⟨wy⟩reżyserować; *list* ⟨za⟩adresować; **~ 'cur·rent** *electr.* prąd *m* stały; **~ 'train** pociąg *m* bezpośredni
di·rec·tion [dɪ'rekʃn] kierunek *m*; kierownictwo *n*; reżyseria *f*; **~*s*** *pl.* wskazówki *pl.*; **~*s for use*** instrukcja *f* obsługi; ⚠ *nie* ***dyrekcja***; **~ find·er** namiernik *m*; **~ in·di·ca·tor** kierunkowskaz *m*, migacz *m*
di·rec·tive [dɪ'rektɪv] dyrektywa *f*, zarządzenie *n*
di·rect·ly [dɪ'rektlɪ] **1.** *adv.* bezpośrednio; **2.** *cj.* od razu, natychmiast
di·rec·tor [dɪ'rektə] dyrektor(ka *f*) *m*; reżyser *m* (*filmowy itp.*)
di·rec·to·ry [dɪ'rektərɪ] książka *f* z adresami; ***telephone* ~** książka *f* telefoniczna; *komp.* katalog *m*
dirt [dɜːt] brud *m*; *zbita* ziemia *f*; **~ 'cheap** F tani jak barszcz; **'~·y** **1.** (**-*ier, -iest***) brudny (*też fig.*), zabrudzony; **2.** ⟨za-, u⟩brudzić
dis·a·bil·i·ty [dɪsə'bɪlətɪ] kalectwo *n*; inwalidztwo *n*, niezdolność *f* do pracy
dis·a·bled [dɪs'eɪbld] **1.** niezdolny do pracy; *mil.* będący inwalidą w wyniku działań wojennych; kaleki, upośledzony; **2. *the* ~** *pl.* inwalidzi *pl.*
dis·ad·van|·tage [dɪsəd'vɑːntɪdʒ] wada *f*; strona *f* ujemna; **~·ta·geous** [dɪsædvɑːn'teɪdʒəs] ujemny, niekorzystny, niepomyślny
dis·a·gree [dɪsə'griː] nie zgadzać się, różnić się; *jedzenie*: szkodzić; **~·a·ble** nieprzyjemny, przykry; **~·ment** niezgoda *f*; rozbieżność *f*, niezgodność *f*; różnica *f* poglądów
dis·ap·pear [dɪsə'pɪə] znikać ⟨-knąć⟩; **~·ance** [dɪsə'pɪərəns] zniknięcie *n*
dis·ap·point [dɪsə'pɔɪnt] *kogoś* rozczarowywać ⟨-ować⟩; *plan itp.* ⟨po⟩krzyżować; **~·ing** rozczarowujący; **~·ment** rozczarowanie *n*
dis·ap·prov|·al [dɪsə'pruːvl] dezaprobata *f*; **~e** [dɪsə'pruːv] nie ⟨za⟩aprobować, nie pochwalać ⟨-lić⟩
dis|·arm [dɪs'ɑːm] rozbrajać ⟨-broić⟩ (się) (*też fig., mil., pol.*); **~·ar·ma·ment** [dɪs'ɑːməmənt] *mil., pol.* rozbrojenie *n*
dis·ar·range [dɪsə'reɪndʒ] ⟨z⟩robić bałagan, ⟨po⟩rozpraszać, ⟨po⟩rozstawiać
dis·ar·ray [dɪsə'reɪ] nieporządek *m*
di·sas·ter [dɪ'zɑːstə] katastrofa *f* (*też fig.*); klęska *f* (*żywiołowa*); **~ ar·e·a** obszar *m* klęski żywiołowej

di·sas·trous [dɪ'zɑːstrəs] katastrofalny
dis·be|·lief [dɪsbɪ'liːf] niedowierzanie *n*, niewiara *f*; wątpliwość (***in*** względem *G*); **~·lieve** [dɪsbɪ'liːv] nie wierzyć, nie dowierzać, wątpić w (*A*)
disc [dɪsk] *Brt.* tarcza *f*, krążek *m*; dysk *m*; płyta *f* (*gramofonowa*); (*okrągły wskaźnik czasu parkowania*); *anat.* chrząstka *f* międzykręgowa, F dysk *m*; *komp.* → ***disk***; ***slipped ~*** wypadnięcie *n* dysku
dis·card [dɪ'skɑːd] odrzucać ⟨-cić⟩; pozbywać ⟨-zbyć⟩ się; *karty* dokładać
di·scern [dɪ'sɜːn] dostrzegać ⟨-rzec⟩; rozróżniać ⟨-nić⟩; **~·ing** wybredny, wyrobiony; **~·ment** wybredność *f*, znawstwo *n*
dis·charge [dɪs'tʃɑːdʒ] **1.** *v/t.* zwalniać ⟨zwolnić⟩; rozładowywać ⟨-ować⟩; *baterię itp.* wyładowywać ⟨-ować⟩; ⟨wy⟩strzelić z (*G*) (*broni itp.*); wypływać ⟨-łynąć⟩, wylewać ⟨-lać⟩; ⟨wy⟩emitować; *obowiązek* spełniać ⟨-nić⟩; *gniew itp.* wyładowywać ⟨-ować⟩ (***on*** na *I*); *dług itp.* spłacać ⟨-cić⟩; *med.* wydzielać ⟨-lić⟩; *v/i. electr.* wyładowywać ⟨-ować⟩ się; *rzeka itp.*: wpływać, wpadać; *med.* ropieć; **2.** zwolnienie *n*; rozładunek *m* (*statku*); wystrzał *m* (*z broni*); *med.* wydzielina *f*, wydalina *f*; emisja *f*; *electr.* wyładowanie *n*; spełnienie *n* (*obowiązku*)
di·sci·ple [dɪ'saɪpl] uczeń *m* (-ennica *f*); *rel.* apostoł *m*
dis·ci·pline ['dɪsɪplɪn] **1.** dyscyplina *f*; **2.** wprowadzać ⟨-dzić⟩ dyscyplinę; ***well ~d*** zdyscyplinowany; ***badly ~d*** niezdyscyplinowany
'disc jock·ey dyskdżokej *m*
dis·claim [dɪs'kleɪm] zrzekać ⟨zrzec⟩ się; *jur.* wypierać ⟨-przeć⟩ się
dis|·close [dɪs'kləʊz] odsłaniać ⟨-łonić⟩, ujawniać ⟨-nić⟩; **~·clo·sure** [dɪs'kləʊʒə] odsłonięcie *n*, ujawnienie *n*
dis·co ['dɪskəʊ] F (*pl.* ***-cos***) disco *n*
dis·col·o(u)r [dɪs'kʌlə] zmieniać ⟨-nić⟩ barwę, odbarwiać ⟨-wić⟩ się
dis·com·fort [dɪs'kʌmfət] **1.** niewygoda *f*; dyskomfort *m*; zażenowanie *n*
dis·con·cert [dɪskən'sɜːt] zbijać ⟨-bić⟩ z tropu, ⟨z⟩deprymować
dis·con·nect [dɪskə'nekt] rozłączać ⟨-czyć⟩, odłączać ⟨-czyć⟩ (*też electr., tech.*); *prąd, gaz, telefon* wyłączać ⟨-czyć⟩; *tel. rozmowę* przerywać ⟨-rwać⟩; **~·ed** rozłączony
dis·con·so·late [dɪs'kɒnsələt] niepocieszony
dis·con·tent [dɪskən'tent] niezadowolenie *n*; **~·ed** niezadowolony
dis·con·tin·ue [dɪskən'tɪnjuː] przerywać ⟨-rwać⟩, zaprzestawać ⟨-stać⟩
dis·cord ['dɪskɔːd] niezgoda *f*; *mus.* dysonans *m*; **~·ant** [dɪ'skɔːdənt] niezgodny; *mus.* dysonansowy, nieharmonijny
dis·co·theque ['dɪskətek] dyskoteka *f*
dis·count ['dɪskaʊnt] *econ.* dyskonto *n*; *econ.* rabat *m*, bonifikata *f*;
dis·cour·age [dɪ'skʌrɪdʒ] zniechęcać ⟨-cić⟩, odradzać ⟨-dzić⟩; **~·ment** zniechęcanie *n*, odradzanie *n*
dis·course 1. ['dɪskɔːs] dyskusja *f*, dysputa *f*; wykład *m*, wywód *m*; dyskurs *m*; **2.** [dɪ'skɔːs] rozprawiać (***on*** o *L*)
dis·cour·te|·ous [dɪs'kɜːtjəs] niegrzeczny; **~·sy** [dɪs'kɜːtəsɪ] niegrzeczność *f*
dis·cov|·er [dɪ'skʌvə] odkrywać ⟨-ryć⟩, odnajdować ⟨-naleźć⟩; **~·e·ry** [dɪ'skʌvərɪ] odkrycie *n*
'disc park·ing *mot.* (*miejsce parkowania dla kierowców z wykupionym specjalnym krążkiem*)
dis·cred·it [dɪs'kredɪt] **1.** kompromitacja *f*, niesława *f*, hańba *f*; **2.** poddawać ⟨-dać⟩ w wątpliwość; ⟨z⟩dyskredytować; podważać ⟨-żyć⟩
di·screet [dɪ'skriːt] dyskretny; ostrożny, rozważny
di·screp·an·cy [dɪ'skrepənsɪ] rozbieżność *f*, rozdźwięk *m*
di·scre·tion [dɪ'skreʃn] dyskrecja *f*; (własne) uznanie *n*
di·scrim·i|·nate [dɪ'skrɪmɪneɪt] rozróżniać ⟨-nić⟩, odróżniać ⟨-nić⟩; ***~nate against*** ⟨z⟩dyskryminować (*A*); **~·nat·ing** wyrobiony; **~·na·tion** [dɪskrɪmɪ'neɪʃn] dyskryminacja *f*
dis·cus ['dɪskəs] (*w sporcie*) dysk *m*
di·scuss [dɪ'skʌs] ⟨prze⟩dyskutować, omawiać ⟨omówić⟩; **di·scus·sion** [dɪ'skʌʃn] dyskusja *f*; omówienie *n*
'dis·cus| throw *sport*: rzut *m* dyskiem; **'~ throw·er** dyskobol *m*
dis·ease [dɪ'ziːz] choroba *f*; **~d** chory
dis·em·bark [dɪsɪm'bɑːk] *v/i.* wysiadać ⟨-siąść⟩; *v/t.* wysadzać ⟨-dzić⟩, wyładowywać ⟨-ować⟩

D

dis·en·chant·ed [dɪsɪn'tʃɑːntɪd] rozczarowany; ***be ~ with*** nie łudzić się więcej (*I*)
dis·en·gage [dɪsɪn'geɪdʒ] rozłączać ⟨-czyć⟩; *sprzęgło* zwalniać ⟨zwolnić⟩
dis·en·tan·gle [dɪsɪn'tæŋgl] rozplątywać ⟨-tać⟩; wyplątywać ⟨-tać⟩ (się)
dis·fa·vo(u)r [dɪs'feɪvə] niechęć *f*; niełaska *f*
dis·fig·ure [dɪs'fɪgə] ⟨o⟩szpecić, zeszpecać ⟨-cić⟩
dis·grace [dɪs'greɪs] **1.** hańba *f*; niełaska *f*; **2.** sprowadzać ⟨-dzić⟩ hańbę na (*A*), przynosić *komuś* hańbę; **~·ful** haniebny
dis·guise [dɪs'gaɪz] **1.** przebierać ⟨-brać⟩ się (***as*** za *A*); *głos* zmieniać ⟨-nić⟩; *coś* ukrywać ⟨ukryć⟩; **2.** przebranie *n*; przemiana *f*, zmiana *f*; ukrycie *n*; ***in ~*** w przebraniu (*też fig.*); ***in the ~ of*** w przebraniu (*G*)
dis·gust [dɪs'gʌst] **1.** obrzydzenie *n*, wstręt *m*; **~·ing** obrzydliwy
dish [dɪʃ] **1.** talerz *m*; półmisek *m*; potrawa *f*, danie *n*; ***the ~es*** *pl. brudne* naczynia *pl.*; ***wash*** *lub* ***do the ~es*** ⟨z⟩myć naczynia; **2.** ***~ out*** F nakładać ⟨-łożyć⟩; *często* ***~ up*** *potrawy* nakładać ⟨-łożyć⟩; F *fakty*: podpicować; '**~·cloth** ścierka *f* do naczyń
dis·heart·en [dɪs'hɑːtn] zniechęcać ⟨-cić⟩
di·shev·el(l)ed [dɪ'ʃevld] rozczochrany, potargany
dis·hon·est [dɪs'ɒnɪst] nieuczciwy; **~·y** nieuczciwość *f*
dis·hon|·o(u)r [dɪs'ɒnə] **1.** hańba *f*; **2.** hańbić; *econ. weksla* nie honorować; **~·o(u)·ra·ble** [dɪs'ɒnərəbl] niehonorowy; haniebny
'**dish|·wash·er** zmywarka *f* do naczyń; '**~·wa·ter** pomyje *pl.*
dis·il·lu·sion [dɪsɪ'luːʒn] **1.** rozczarowanie *n*, zawód *m*; **2.** rozczarowywać ⟨-ować⟩, pozbawiać ⟨-wić⟩ złudzeń
dis·in·clined [dɪsɪn'klaɪnd] oporny, niechętny
dis·in|·fect [dɪsɪn'fekt] ⟨z⟩dezynfekować; **~'fec·tant** środek *m* dezynfekujący
dis·in·her·it [dɪsɪn'herɪt] wydziedziczać ⟨-czyć⟩
dis·in·te·grate [dɪs'ɪntɪgreɪt] rozpadać ⟨-aść⟩ (się)
dis·in·terest·ed [dɪs'ɪntrəstɪd] obiektywny, bezstronny; obojętny, niezainteresowany
disk [dɪsk] *zwł. Am.* → *Brt.* **disc**; *komp.* dysk *m*, dyskietka *f*; '**~ drive** *komp.* napęd *m lub* stacja *f* dyskietek
disk·ette [dɪ'sket, 'dɪsket] *komp.* dyskietka *f*
dis·like [dɪs'laɪk] **1.** niechęć *f*, awersja *f*; (***of, for*** do *G*); ***take a ~ to*** odczuwać ⟨-czuć⟩ niechęć do (*G*); **2.** nie lubić; ***he ~s this*** nie podoba mu się to
dis·lo·cate ['dɪsləkeɪt] *med.* zwichnąć
dis·loy·al [dɪs'lɔɪəl] nielojalny
dis·mal ['dɪzməl] ponury, przygnębiający
dis·man·tle [dɪs'mæntl] *tech.* rozbierać ⟨rozebrać⟩, ⟨z⟩demontować, rozmontowywać ⟨-ować⟩
dis·may [dɪs'meɪ] **1.** niepokój *m*, zaniepokojenie *n*, konsternacja *f*; ***in ~, with ~*** z przerażenia; ***to my ~*** ku mojej konsternacji; **2.** *v/t.* przestraszyć się
dis·miss [dɪs'mɪs] *v/t.* odprawiać ⟨-wić⟩, zwalniać ⟨zwolnić⟩; odrzucać ⟨-cić⟩; odstępować ⟨-tąpić⟩ (*od tematu*); *jur. skargę* oddalać ⟨-lić⟩; **~·al** [dɪs'mɪsl] zwolnienie *n*; *jur.* oddalenie *n*
dis·mount [dɪs'maʊnt] *v/t.* zsiadać ⟨zsiąść⟩ (***from*** z *konia, roweru itp.*); *v/t.* ⟨z⟩demontować; rozbierać ⟨-zebrać⟩
dis·o·be·di|·ence [dɪsə'biːdjəns] nieposłuszeństwo *n*; **~·ent** nieposłuszny
dis·o·bey [dɪsə'beɪ] nie ⟨po⟩słuchać, być nieposłusznym
dis·or·der [dɪs'ɔːdə] nieporządek *m*, bałagan *m*; wzburzenie *n*, zamieszki *pl.*; *med.* dolegliwość *f*; **~·ly** nieporządny; niespokojny; buntowniczy
dis·or·gan·ize [dɪs'ɔːgənaɪz] ⟨z⟩deorganizować
dis·own [dɪs'əʊn] nie uznawać; wypierać się
di·spar·age [dɪ'spærɪdʒ] ⟨z⟩dyskredytować, poniżać ⟨-żyć⟩
di·spar·i·ty [dɪ'spærətɪ] nierówność; ***~ of*** *lub* ***in age*** różnica *f* wieku
dis·pas·sion·ate [dɪ'spæʃnət] beznamiętny; obiektywny
di·spatch [dɪ'spætʃ] **1.** wysyłka *f*, przesyłka *f*; sprawność *f*, szybkość *f*; depesza *f*, doniesienie *n*; **2.** wysyłać ⟨-słać⟩, nadawać ⟨-dać⟩, ⟨wy⟩ekspediować

di·spel [dɪ'spel] (**-ll-**) rozwiewać ⟨-zwiać⟩, rozpraszać ⟨-proszyć⟩ (*też fig.*)
di·spen·sa|·ble [dɪ'spensəbl] zbyteczny, zbędny; **~·ry** [dɪ'spensərɪ] *szkolna, szpitalna* apteka *f*
dis·pen·sa·tion [dɪspen'seɪʃn] dyspensa *f*, zwolnienie *n*; *jur.* wymierzanie *n*
di·spense [dɪ'spens] wydawać ⟨-dać⟩; *sprawiedliwość* wymierzać ⟨-rzyć⟩; **~ *with*** obywać się bez (*G*); stawać się zbytecznym; **di'spens·er** automat *m*, maszyna *f* (*do znaczków itp.*); rolka *f* (*do taśmy samoprzylepnej*)
di·sperse [dɪ'spɜːs] rozpraszać (się)
di·spir·it·ed [dɪ'spɪrɪtɪd] przygnębiony, przybity
dis·place [dɪs'pleɪs] przemieszczać ⟨-eścić⟩; *kogoś* wysiedlać ⟨-dlić⟩, wypierać ⟨-przeć⟩
di·splay [dɪ'spleɪ] **1.** pokaz *m*; demonstracja *f*; *komp.* monitor *m*; *econ.* wystawa *f*, ekspozycja *f*; ***be on ~*** być wystawionym; **2.** pokazywać ⟨-zać⟩, ⟨za⟩demonstrować; wystawiać ⟨-wić⟩; wyświetlać ⟨-lić⟩
dis|·please [dɪs'pliːz] ⟨z⟩denerwować, ⟨z⟩irytować; **~'pleased** zdenerwowany, zirytowany; niezadowolony; **~·plea·sure** [dɪs'pleʒə] zdenerwowanie *n*, zirytowanie *n*; niezadowolenie *n*
dis|·po·sa·ble [dɪ'spəʊzəbl] *pojemnik itp.*: jednorazowy; **~·pos·al** [dɪ'spəʊzl] oczyszczanie *n*, wywóz *m* (*śmieci*); usuwanie *n*; rozmieszczenie *n* (*wojsk*); ***at s.o.'s ~posal*** do czyjejś dyspozycji; **~·pose** [dɪ'spəʊz] *v/t.* rozmieszczać ⟨-mieścić⟩, ⟨u⟩lokować; usposabiać ⟨-bić⟩; ***~pose of*** pozbywać ⟨-być⟩ się, usuwać ⟨-unąć⟩; dawać ⟨dać⟩ sobie radę; *econ.* odstępować ⟨-tąpić⟩; **~·posed** skłonny, chętny; **~·po·si·tion** [dɪspə'zɪʃn] usposobienie *n*; ⚠ *nie* ***dyspozycja***
dis·pos·sess [dɪspə'zes] pozbawiać ⟨-wić⟩; wywłaszczać ⟨-czyć⟩
dis·pro·por·tion·ate [dɪsprə'pɔːʃnət] nieproporcjonalny
dis·prove [dɪs'pruːv] obalać ⟨-lić⟩
di·spute [dɪ'spjuːt] **1.** kontrowersja *f*; polemika *f*, dysputa *f*; spór *m*; **2.** spierać się (o *A*); ⟨za⟩kwestionować
dis·qual·i·fy [dɪs'kwɒlɪfaɪ] ⟨z⟩dyskwalifikować; uznawać ⟨-nać⟩ za niezdolnego (***from*** do *G*)
dis·re·gard [dɪsrɪ'gɑːd] **1.** ignorowanie *n*, lekceważenie *n*; **2.** ⟨z⟩ignorować, ⟨z⟩lekceważyć
dis|·rep·u·ta·ble [dɪs'repjʊtəbl] naganny, o złej reputacji; **~·re·pute** [dɪsrɪ'pjuːt] zła reputacja *f*
dis·re·spect [dɪsrɪ'spekt] nieuprzejmość *f*, brak *m* respektu; **~·ful** nieuprzejmy
dis·rupt [dɪs'rʌpt] przerywać ⟨-rwać⟩
dis·sat·is|·fac·tion ['dɪssætɪs'fækʃn] niezadowolenie *n*; **~·fied** [dɪs'sætɪsfaɪd] niezadowolony (***with*** z *G*)
dis·sect [dɪ'sekt] rozcinać ⟨-ciąć⟩, ⟨wy-, s⟩preparować; ⟨z⟩analizować
dis·sen|·sion [dɪ'senʃn] niezgoda *f*; różnica *f* zdań; niejednomyślność *f*; **~t** [dɪ'sent] **1.** różnica *f* zdań; rozbieżność *f* poglądów; protest *m*; **2.** nie zgadzać się, być innego zdania (***from*** od *G*); **~t·er** *rel.* dysydent *m*, odszczepieniec *m*; osoba *f* o odmiennych poglądach
dis·si·dent ['dɪsɪdənt] osoba *f* o odmiennych poglądach; *pol.* dysydent *m*
dis·sim·i·lar [dɪ'sɪmɪlə] niepodobny (***to*** do *G*), odmienny (***to*** od *G*)
dis·sim·u·la·tion [dɪsɪmjʊ'leɪʃn] obłuda *f*, udawanie *n*
dis·si|·pate ['dɪsɪpeɪt] rozpraszać ⟨-roszyć⟩; ⟨s⟩trwonić; **'~·pat·ed** hulaszczy, rozwiązły
dis·so·ci·ate [dɪ'səʊʃɪeɪt] rozdzielać ⟨-lić⟩; **~ *o.s.*** odseparowywać ⟨-ować⟩ się, odcinać ⟨odciąć⟩ się
dis·so|·lute ['dɪsəluːt] → ***dissipated***; **~·lu·tion** [dɪsə'luːʃn] rozkład *m*, rozpad *m*
dis·solve [dɪ'zɒlv] rozpuszczać ⟨-uścić⟩ (się)
dis·suade [dɪ'sweɪd] wyperswadować (***s.o. from*** komuś *A*); odwodzić ⟨-wieść⟩ (***s.o. from*** kogoś *od G*)
dis·tance ['dɪstəns] **1.** odległość *f*; oddalenie *n*; dystans *m*; *fig.* odstęp *m*; ***at a ~*** z odległości; ***keep s.o. at a ~*** trzymać kogoś na dystans; **2.** odseparowywać ⟨-ować⟩ się, trzymać się na dystans; **'~ race** (*w sporcie*) bieg *m* długodystansowy; **'~ run·ner** biegacz *m* na długie dystanse
dis·tant [dɪs'tənt] dległy; chłodny, dystansujący się
dis·taste [dɪs'teɪst] niesmak *m*, niechęć

D

f, awersja *f*; **~·ful** nieprzyjemny, antypatyczny; ***be ~ful to s.o.*** być przykrym dla kogoś
dis·tem·per [dɪ'stempə] *zo.* nosówka *f*
dis·tend [dɪ'stend] rozszerzać (się); nadymać ⟨-dąć⟩ (się)
dis·til(l) [dɪ'stɪl] (**-*ll*-**) ⟨wy⟩destylować
dis|·tinct [dɪ'stɪŋkt] wyraźny; różny, odmienny; **~·tinc·tion** [dɪ'stɪŋkʃn] różnica *f*; odróżnienie *n*, wyróżnienie *n*; rozróżnienie *n*; **~·tinc·tive** [dɪ'stɪŋktɪv] wyróżniający się; odrębny
dis·tin·guish [dɪ'stɪŋgwɪʃ] rozróżniać ⟨-nić⟩; **~ *o.s.*** wyróżniać ⟨-nić⟩ się; **~ed** wyróżniający się; wybitny; znakomity
dis·tort [dɪ'stɔːt] zniekształcać ⟨-cić⟩; wykrzywiać ⟨-wić⟩
dis·tract [dɪ'strækt] rozpraszać ⟨-roszyć⟩; *uwagę* odrywać ⟨oderwać⟩; **~·ed** roztargniony, przejęty (***by, with*** *I*), zaniepokojony; **dis·trac·tion** [dɪ'strækʃn] rozproszenie *n*; zaniepokojenie *n*
dis·traught [dɪ'strɔːt] → ***distracted***
dis·tress [dɪ'stres] **1.** cierpienie *n*; troska *f*; trudna sytuacja *f*; niebezpieczeństwo *n*, stan *m* zagrożenia; **2.** ⟨s⟩powodować cierpienie; ⟨za⟩niepokoić się; **~ed** dotknięty nieszczęściem; bez środków do życia; **~ed ar·e·a** obszar *m* dotknięty klęską; **~·ing** niepokojący
dis|·trib·ute [dɪ'strɪbjuːt] rozprowadzać ⟨-dzić⟩, rozdzielać ⟨-lić⟩; *econ.* dystrybuować; *filmy* rozpowszechniać ⟨-nić⟩; **~·tri·bu·tion** [dɪstrɪ'bjuːʃn] rozdział *m*, rozprowadzenie *n*; dystrybucja *f*; rozpowszechnianie *n*
dis·trict ['dɪstrɪkt] dystrykt *m*, okręg *m*; dzielnica *f*
dis·trust [dɪs'trʌst] **1.** nieufność *f*, niedowierzanie *n*; **2.** nie ufać, nie mieć zaufania; niedowierzać; **~·ful** nieufny, niedowierzający
dis·turb [dɪ'stɜːb] zakłócać ⟨-cić⟩; niepokoić; przeszkadzać ⟨-szkodzić⟩; poruszać ⟨-szyć⟩; **~·ance** [dɪ'stɜːbəns] zakłócenie *n*, naruszenie *n*; niepokój *m*; ***~ances*** *pl.* zamieszki *pl.*, rozruchy *pl.*; ***~ance of the peace*** *jur.* naruszenie *n* spokoju; ***cause a ~ance*** spowodować naruszenie spokoju; **~ed** [dɪ'stɜːbd] niespokojny; niezrównoważony
dis·used [dɪs'juːzd] *maszyna*: nie będący w użyciu, *kopalnia*: nie eksploatowany
ditch [dɪtʃ] rów *m*
Div *skrót pisany*: ***division*** *sportowa* liga *f*
di·van [dɪ'væn, 'daɪvæn] kanapa *f*, sofa *f*; ⚠ *nie* ***dywan***; **~ bed** sofa *f*
dive [daɪv] **1.** (***dived*** *lub Am. też* ***dove, dived***) ⟨za⟩nurkować (*też aviat.*); (*z trampoliny*) skakać ⟨skoczyć⟩; skakać ⟨skoczyć⟩ do wody (*na głowę*); rzucać ⟨-cić⟩ się po (*A*); **2.** skok *m* (*do wody*); zanurkowanie *n*; (*w piłce nożnej*) (*upadek mający wymusić rzut karny*); *aviat.* lot *m* nurkowy; F knajpa *f*, speluna *f*; **'div·er** nurek *m*; (*w sporcie*) skoczek *m* (*do wody*)
di·verge [daɪ'vɜːdʒ] rozchodzić się; **di·ver·gence** [daɪ'vɜːdʒəns] rozbieżność *f*; **di'ver·gent** rozbieżny
di·verse [daɪ'vɜːs] różny; różnoraki, różnorodny; **di·ver·si·fy** [daɪ'vɜːsɪfaɪ] ⟨z⟩różnicować; **di·ver·sion** [daɪ'vɜːʃn] rozrywka *f*; objazd *m*; **di·ver·si·ty** [daɪ'vɜːsətɪ] różnorodność *f*, zróżnicowanie *n*
di·vert [daɪ'vɜːt] *uwagę* odwracać ⟨-rócić⟩; *kogoś* zabawiać ⟨-wić⟩; *w ruchu ulicznym* zmieniać ⟨-nić⟩ kierunek
di·vide [dɪ'vaɪd] **1.** *v/t.* ⟨po⟩dzielić (*też math.*), rozdzielać ⟨-lić⟩, oddzielać ⟨-lić⟩ (**by** przez *A*); *v/i.* ⟨po⟩dzielić się; *math.* dzielić się (**by** przez *A*); **2.** *geogr.* wododział *m*; **di'vid·ed** podzielony; **~ *highway*** *Am.* autostrada *f*
div·i·dend ['dɪvɪdend] *econ.* dywidenda *f*
di·vid·ers [dɪ'vaɪdəz] *pl.*: ***a pair of ~*** (*jeden*) cyrkiel *m* traserski, przenośnik *m*
di·vine [dɪ'vaɪn] (***-r, -st***) boski; **~ 'ser·vice** nabożeństwo *n*
div·ing ['daɪvɪŋ] nurkowanie *n*; (*w sporcie*) skoki *pl.* do wody; **'~·board** trampolina *f*; **'~·suit** skafander *m* do nurkowania
di·vin·i·ty [dɪ'vɪnətɪ] boskość *f*; bóstwo *n*; teologia *f*
di·vis·i·ble [dɪ'vɪzəbl] podzielny; **di·vi·sion** [dɪ'vɪʒn] podział *m*; dział *m*; *mil.* dywizja *f*; *math.* dzielenie *n*; *sport*: liga *f*
di·vorce [dɪ'vɔːs] **1.** rozwód *m*; ***get a ~*** rozwodzić ⟨-wieść⟩ się (***from*** z); **2.** *jur.* brać ⟨wziąć⟩ rozwód z (*I*); ***get ~d*** rozwodzić ⟨-wieść⟩ się; **di·vor·cee** [dɪvɔː'siː] rozwodnik *m* (-wódka *f*)

DIY *zwł. Brt.* [diː aɪ 'waɪ] → ***do-it-your-self***; ~ **store** sklep *m* z materiałami dla majsterkowiczów

diz·zy ['dɪzɪ] (***-ier, -iest***) cierpiący na zawroty głowy; zawrotny

DJ [diː 'dʒeɪ] *skrót*: ***disc jockey*** dyskdżokej *m*

do [duː] (***did, done***) *v/t.* ⟨z⟩robić; ⟨u⟩czynić; przygotowywać ⟨-ować⟩; *pokój* ⟨wy⟩sprzątać; *naczynia* ⟨wy⟩myć; *odcinek drogi* przebywać ⟨-być⟩; ***~ you know him ~?*** ***no, I don't*** znasz go? nie; ***what can I ~ for you?*** czym mogę służyć?; ***~ London*** F zaliczać ⟨-czyć⟩ Londyn; ***have one's hair done*** zrobić sobie fryzurę; ***have done reading*** skończyć czytać; *v/i.* ⟨z⟩robić; ⟨po⟩radzić sobie, dawać ⟨dać⟩ sobie radę; wystarczać ⟨-czyć⟩; dziać się; ***that will ~*** wystarczy; ***how ~ you ~?*** dzień dobry (*przy przedstawianiu*); ***~ be quick*** pospiesz się w miarę możności; ***~ you like Guildford? I ~*** czy podoba się Panu (Pani) Guildford? owszem; ***she works hard, doesn't she?*** ciężko pracuje, nieprawda?; ***~ well*** dobrze sobie ⟨po⟩radzić; ***~ away with*** *Am.* ⟨z⟩likwidować, usuwać ⟨-unąć⟩; ***I'm done in*** F jestem wykończony (-na); ***~ up*** *ubranie itp.* zapinać ⟨-piąć⟩; *dom itp.* ⟨wy⟩remontować; *paczkę itp.* ⟨za⟩pakować; ***~ o.s. up*** ⟨wy⟩stroić się; ***I could ~ with ...*** przydałby się ...; ***~ without*** obywać ⟨obyć⟩ się bez (*G*)

doc[1] [dɒk] F → (*lekarz*) ***doctor***

doc[2] [dɒk] *skrót*: ***document*** dokument *m*

do·cile ['dəʊsaɪl] potulny, uległy

dock[1] [dɒk] przycinać ⟨-ciąć⟩; *pensję* ⟨z⟩redukować, *pieniądze* potrącać ⟨-cić⟩

dock[2] [dɒk] **1.** *naut.* dok *m*; nabrzeże *n*; *jur.* ława *f* oskarżonych; **2.** *v/t. naut.* ⟨za⟩dokować, *statek* wprowadzać ⟨-dzić⟩ do doku; ⟨po⟩łączyć na orbicie; **'~·er** doker *m*; robotnik *m* portowy; **'~·ing** dokowanie *n*; połączenie *n*; **'~·yard** *naut.* stocznia *f*

doc·tor ['dɒktə] doktor *m*; lekarz *m* (-rka *f*); **~·al** ['dɒktərəl] doktorski

doc·trine ['dɒktrɪn] doktryna *f*, nauka *f*

doc·u·ment 1. ['dɒkjʊmənt] dokument *m*; **2.** ['dɒkjʊment] ⟨u⟩dokumentować

doc·u·men·ta·ry [dɒkjʊ'mentrɪ] **1.** dokumentalny; dokumentowy; **2.** film *m* dokumentalny

dodge [dɒdʒ] unikać ⟨-knąć⟩, uskakiwać ⟨uskoczyć⟩ przed (*I*); F uchylać ⟨-lić⟩ się przed (*I*); **'dodg·er**: ***tax dodger*** osoba *f* uchylająca się od płacenia podatków; ***draft dodger*** *Am.* osoba *f* odmawiająca przyjęcia karty poborowej; → ***fare dodger***

doe [dəʊ] *zo.* łania *f*; królica *f*; zajęczyca *f*

dog [dɒg] **1.** *zo.* pies *m*; **2.** (***-gg-***) chodzić krok w krok; prześladować; **'~-eared** *książka*: z oślimi uszami; **~·ged** ['dɒgɪd] uparty, zaparty

dog|·ma ['dɒgmə] dogmat *m*; prawda *f* wiary; **~·mat·ic** [dɒg'mætɪk] (***-ally***) dogmatyczny

dog-'tired F skonany, wykończony

do-it-your·self [duːɪtjɔː'self] **1.** majsterkowanie *n*; **2.** *attr.* dla majsterkowiczów; **~·er** majsterkowicz *m*

dole [dəʊl] **1.** datek *m*; *Brt.* F zasiłek *m* (*dla bezrobotnych*); ***go*** *lub* ***be on the ~*** *Brt.* F być na zasiłku; **2. ~ *out*** wydzielać ⟨-lić⟩ skąpo

dole·ful ['dəʊlfl] żałosny

doll [dɒl] lalka *f*

dol·lar ['dɒlə] dolar *m*

dol·phin ['dɒlfɪn] *zo.* delfin *m*

dome [dəʊm] kopuła *f*

do·mes·tic [də'mestɪk] **1.** (***~ally***) domowy; rodzinny; krajowy, rodzimy; *polityka itp.*: wewnętrzny; **2.** członek *m* rodziny; **~ 'an·i·mal** zwierzę *n* domowe *lub* udomowione; **do·mes·ti·cate** [də'mestɪkeɪt] udomawiać ⟨-mowić⟩; **~ 'flight** *aviat.* lot *m* krajowy; **~ 'market** rynek *m* wewnętrzny *lub* krajowy; **~ 'trade** handel *m* wewnętrzny; **~ 'vi·o·lence** przemoc *f* w obrębie rodziny (*wobec żony i dzieci*)

dom·i·cile ['dɒmɪsaɪl] miejsce *n* zamieszkania

dom·i|·nant ['dɒmɪnənt] dominujący, panujący; **~·nate** ['dɒmɪneɪt] ⟨z⟩dominować; **~·na·tion** [dɒmɪ'neɪʃn] dominacja *f*; **~·neer·ing** [dɒmɪ'nɪərɪŋ] apodyktyczny

do·nate [dəʊ'neɪt] ofiarowywać ⟨-ować⟩, przekazywać ⟨-zać⟩ (w darze); **do·na·tion** [dəʊ'neɪʃn] darowizna *f*, donacja *f*

done [dʌn] **1.** *p.p. od* **do**; **2.** *adj.* zrobio-

ny, wykonany; gotowy; *gastr.* przyrządzony → ***well-done***
don·key ['dɒŋkɪ] *zo.* osioł *m*
do·nor ['dəʊnə] *med*, dawca *m* (*zwł. krwi, organu*)
D
don't [dəʊnt] *zamiast*: ***do not*** → ***do***; *zamiast*: *Am.* F ***does not*** (*she don't*) → ***do***
doom [duːm] **1.** przeznaczenie *n*, zły los *m*; **2.** skazywać ⟨-zać⟩ (*na zgubę*); **~s·day** ['duːmzdeɪ]: ***till ~sday*** po wieczność, na zawsze
door [dɔː] drzwi *pl.*, drzwiczki *pl.*; brama *f*, furtka *f*; ***next ~*** obok, w sąsiedztwie; **'~·bell** dzwonek *m* do drzwi; **'~ han·dle** klamka *f*; **'~·keep·er** odźwierny *m*; **'~·knob** gałka *f* (*do drzwi*); **'~·mat** wycieraczka *f*; **'~·step** próg *m*; **'~·way** wejście *n*, drzwi *pl.*
dope [dəʊp] **1.** F narkotyk *m*; środek *m* odurzający; (*w sporcie*) środek *m* dopingujący; *sl.* dureń *m*; **2.** F ⟨z⟩narkotyzować; (*w sporcie*) podawać ⟨-dać⟩ środek dopingujący; **'~ test** kontrola *f* antydopingowa
dor·mant ['dɔːmənt] *zw. fig.* uśpiony, nieaktywny; *wulkan*: drzemiący
dor·mer (win·dow) ['dɔːmə (-)] okno *n* mansardowe
dor·mi·to·ry ['dɔːmətrɪ] sypialnia *f*; *zwł. Am.* akademik *m*, dom *m* akademicki
dor·mo·bile ['dɒːməbiːl] *TM* wóz *m* kempingowy
dor·mouse ['dɔːmaʊs] *zo.* (*pl.* ***-mice***) suseł *m*
DOS [dɒs] *skrót*: ***disk operating system*** DOS *m*, dyskowy system *m* operacyjny
dose [dəʊs] **1.** dawka *f*; doza *f*; **2.** dawkować; *lekarstwo* podawać ⟨-dać⟩ (*w dużych ilościach*)
dot [dɒt] **1.** punkt *m*, kropka *f*; plama *f*; ***on the ~*** F (*punktualnie*) co do sekundy; **2.** (***-tt-***) ⟨wy-, za⟩kropkować; rozrzucić ⟨-cać⟩; *czymś* zarzucać ⟨-cić⟩; ***~ted line*** kropkowana linia *f*
dote [dəʊt]: ***~ on*** bezgranicznie uwielbiać (*A*), świata nie widzieć poza (*I*); **dot·ing** ['dəʊtɪŋ] rozkochany
doub·le ['dʌbl] **1.** podwójny; dwu...; **2.** *adv.* podwójnie; **3.** sobowtór *m*; (*w filmie itp.*) dubler *m*; **4.** podwajać ⟨-woić⟩ (się); (*w filmie itp.*) dublować; *też* ***~ up*** składać się na dwoje; składać ⟨złożyć⟩; ***~ back*** zawracać ⟨-rócić⟩; ***~ up with*** zwijać ⟨-zwinąć⟩ się z (*G*), skręcać ⟨-ręcić⟩ się (*G*); **~-'breast·ed** *marynarka*: dwurzędowy; **~-'check** dokładnie sprawdzać ⟨-dzić⟩; **~ 'chin** podbródek *m*; **~-'cross** *v/t.* oszukiwać ⟨-kać⟩; **~-'deal·ing 1.** oszukańczy, krętacki; **2.** krętacz *m*, oszust(ka *f*) *m*; **~-'deck·er** autobus *m* dwupoziomowy, F piętrus *m*; **~ Dutch** *Brt.* F nierozumiałe słowa *pl.*, chińszczyzna *f*; **~-'edged** dwusieczny, obosieczny; **~-'en·try** *econ.* podwójny zapis *m*; **~ 'fea·ture** *filmowy* seans *m* z dwoma filmami pełnometrażowymi; **~-'park** *mot.* ⟨za⟩parkować w drugim rzędzie; **~-'quick** F w przyspieszonym tempie; **'~s** *sg.* (*zwł. w tenisie*) debel *m*; **~-'sid·ed** dwustronny
doubt [daʊt] **1.** *v/i.* wątpić w (*A*); *v/t.* ⟨z⟩wątpić w (*A*); mieć wątpliwości co do (*G*); nie wierzyć (*D*); **2.** wątpliwość *f*, zwątpienie *n*; **'~·ful** wątpliwy, niepewny; **'~·less** niewątpliwie, bez wątpliwości
douche [duːʃ] **1.** irygacja *f*; przemywanie *n*; tusz *m*, irygator *m*; **2.** *v/t.* przemywać ⟨-myć⟩; *v/i.* ⟨za⟩stosować irygację
dough [dəʊ] ciasto *n*; **'~·nut** *jakby*: pączek *m* (*do jedzenia*)
dove[1] [dʌv] *zo.* gołąb *m* (*mały, o długim ogonie*)
dove[2] [dəʊv] *Am. pret. od* ***dive*** 1
dow·dy ['daʊdɪ] nieelegancki, niegustowny
dow·el ['daʊəl] *tech.* kołek *m*
down[1] [daʊn] puch *m*, meszek *m*
down[2] [daʊn] **1.** *adv.* w dół, do dołu, na dół; **2.** *prp.* w dół (*G*); ***~ the river*** w dół rzeki; **3.** *adj.* przygnębiony, przybity; skierowany w dół; ***~ platform*** peron *m* dla odjeżdżających (*np. z Londynu*); ***~ train*** pociąg *m* (*odjeżdzający z Londynu*); **4.** *v/t. kogoś* powalić, obalać ⟨-lić⟩; *samolot* zestrzelać ⟨-lić⟩; F *napój* wychylać ⟨-lić⟩ duszkiem; ***~ tools*** przerywać ⟨-rwać⟩ pracę (*przy strajku*); **'~·cast** przybity, przygnębiony; **'~·fall** ulewa *f*; *fig.* upadek *m*; **~'heart·ed** przybity, przygnębiony; **~'hill 1.** *adv.* w dół (*zbocza*); **2.** *adj.* biegnący w dół zbocza; (*w narciarstwie*) zjazdowy; **3.** stok *m*, zbocze *n*; (*w narciarstwie*) zjazd *m*; **~ 'pay·ment** *econ.* zapłata *f* z góry; **'~·pour** ulewa *f*; **'~·right 1.** *adv.* zupeł-

nie, całkowicie; **2.** całkowity, zupełny; bezpośredni
downs [daʊnz] *pl.* pogórze *n* (*trawiaste, z wapieni*)
down|'stairs na dół; na dole; na parterze; **~'stream** w dole (*rzeki*); w dół (*rzeki*); **~-to-'earth** realistyczny, chodzący po ziemi; **~'town** *Am.* **1.** *adv.* w centrum; do centrum; **2.** *adj.* w centrum; **'~•town** *Am.* centrum *n*, śródmieście *n*; **~•ward(s)** ['daʊnwəd(z)] w dół, do dołu
down•y ['daʊnɪ] (***-ier, -iest***) puchaty, pokryty meszkiem
dow•ry ['daʊərɪ] posag *m*
doz. *skrót pisany*: ***dozen*** tuzin *m*
doze [dəʊz] **1.** ⟨po⟩drzemać; **2.** drzemka *f*
doz•en ['dʌzn] tuzin *m*
Dr *skrót pisany*: ***Doctor*** dr, doktor
drab [dræb] szary; ponury
draft [drɑːft] **1.** szkic *m*; projekt *m*; *econ.* trata *f*; *econ.* przekaz *m* bankowy; *Am. mil.* pobór *m*; **2.** ⟨na⟩szkicować; *list itp.* sporządzać ⟨-dzić⟩ pierwszą wersję; *Am. mil.* przeprowadzać ⟨-dzić⟩ pobór; **~•ee** [drɑːf'tiː] *Am. mil.* poborowy *m*; **'~s•man** *Am.* (*pl.* ***-men***), **'~s•wo•m•an** (*pl.* ***-women***) → ***draughtsman, draughtswoman***; **'~•y** *Am.* (***-ier, -iest***) → ***draughty***
drag [dræg] **1.** ciągnięcie *n*, wleczenie *n*; *fig.* przeszkoda *f*; F nudziarstwo *n*, nuda *f*; **2.** (***-gg-***) *v/t.* ⟨za⟩ciągnąć, ⟨za-, po⟩wlec; *v/i.* ciągnąć się, wlec się; *też* ***~ behind*** wlec się z tyłu, zostawać ⟨-tać⟩ z tyłu; ***~ on*** wlec się, ciągnąć się; **'~ lift** wyciąg *m* (*narciarski*)
drag•on ['drægən] smok *m*; **'~•fly** *zo.* ważka *f*
drain [dreɪn] **1.** ściek *m*, kratka *f* ściekowa; dren *m*; **2.** *v/t.* odprowadzać ⟨-dzić⟩ ścieki; ⟨z⟩drenować; odwadniać ⟨-wodnić⟩; opróżniać ⟨-nić⟩; odcedzać ⟨-dzić⟩; *fig. energię* wyczerpywać ⟨-pać⟩; *v/i.* ***~ away*** odprowadzać ⟨-dzić⟩, odpływać ⟨łynąć⟩; ***~ off*** odcedzać ⟨-dzić⟩; ociec; **~•age** ['dreɪnɪdʒ] drenaż *m*; odwadnianie *n*; odprowadzanie *n*; system *m* odwadniający; **'~•pipe** rura *f* spustowa *lub* odpływowa
drake [dreɪk] *zo.* kaczor *m*
dram [dræm] F łyczek *m*, kieliszeczek *m* (*alkoholu*)
dra•ma ['drɑːmə] dramat *m*; **dra•mat•ic** [drə'mætɪk] dramatyczny; **dram•a•tist** ['dræmətɪst] dramaturg *m*; **dram•a•t-ize** ['dræmətaɪz] ⟨u⟩dramatyzować
drank [dræŋk] *pret. od* ***drink*** **2.**
drape [dreɪp] **1.** ⟨u⟩drapować; **2.** *zw.* ***~s*** *pl. Am.* zasłony *pl.*; **drap•er•y** *Brt.* ['dreɪpərɪ] artykuły *pl.* tekstylne
dras•tic ['dræstɪk] (***~ally***) drastyczny
draught [drɑːft] (*Am.* ***draft***) przeciąg *m*, przewiew *m*; ciąg *m*; zanurzenie *n* (*statku*); ***beer on ~, ~ beer*** piwo *n* beczkowe, piwo *n* z beczki; **~s** *sg. Brt.* warcaby *pl.*; **'~s•man** (*pl.* ***-men***) *Brt. tech.* kreślarz *m*; **'~s•wom•an** (*pl.* ***-women***) *Brt. tech.* kreślarka *f*; **'~•y** (***-ier, -iest***) *Brt.* pełen przeciągów
draw [drɔː] **1.** (***drew, drawn***) *v/t.* ⟨po-, za⟩ciągnąć, wyciągać ⟨-gnąć⟩; *zasłony itp.* zaciągać ⟨-gnąć⟩; *oddech* wciągać ⟨-gnąć⟩; *fig. tłumy* przyciągać ⟨-gnąć⟩; ⟨na⟩rysować; *gotówkę* podejmować ⟨-djąć⟩; *czek* wystawiać ⟨-wić⟩; *v/i.* rysować; *komin*: ciągnąć; *herbata*: naciągać ⟨-gnąć⟩; (*w sporcie*) ⟨z⟩remisować; ***~ back*** cofać ⟨-fnąć⟩ się; ***~ near*** przysuwać ⟨-sunąć⟩ się; ***~ out*** *pieniądze* podejmować ⟨-djąć⟩; *fig.* ciągnąć się, przeciągać ⟨-gnąć⟩ się; ***~ up*** *tekst, listę itp.* przygotowywać ⟨-ować⟩; *pensję* pobierać ⟨-brać⟩; *samochód* zatrzymywać ⟨-mać⟩ się; podjeżdżać ⟨-jechać⟩; **2.** ciągnięcie *n*; (*na loterii*) losowanie *n*, ciągnienie *n*; (*w sporcie*) remis *m*; atrakcja *f*; **'~•back** wada *f*; **'~•bridge** most *m* zwodzony
draw•er[1] [drɔː] szuflada *f*
draw•er[2] ['drɔːə] rysownik *m*; *econ.* wystawca *m* (*czeku itp.*)
'draw•ing rysunek *m*; ciągnienie *n*, losowanie *n*; **'~ board** deska *f* kreślarska; rajzbret *m*; **'~ pin** *Brt.* pinezka *f*; pluskiewka *f*; **'~ room** → ***living room***; salon *m*
drawl [drɔːl] **1.** zaciągać (*przy mówieniu*); **2.** zaciąganie *n*
drawn [drɔːn] **1.** *p.p. od* ***draw*** 1; **2.** *adj.* (*w sporcie*) remisowy, nierozstrzygnięty; *twarz*: wyciągnięty
dread [dred] **1.** przerażenie *n*, strach *m*; **2.** bać się; **'~•ful** straszliwy, przerażający
dream [driːm] **1.** sen *m*, marzenie *n*; **2.** (***dreamed*** *lub* ***dreamt***) śnić, marzyć;

D

D

'~·er marzyciel(ka *f*) *m*; ~t [dremt] *pret. i p.p. od* **dream** 2; ~·y (**-ier, -iest**) marzycielski, rozmarzony
drear·y ['drɪərɪ] (**-ier, -iest**) ponury; nudny
dredge [dredʒ] **1.** pogłębiarka *f*; **2.** pogłębiać ⟨-bić⟩; '**dredg·er** pogłębiarka *f*
dregs [dregz] *pl.* fusy *pl.*; *fig.* męty *pl.*
drench [drentʃ] przemoczyć
dress [dres] **1.** ubranie *n*; suknia *f*, sukienka *f*; ⚠ *nie* **dres**; **2.** ubierać ⟨ubrać⟩ (się); ozdabiać ⟨-dobić⟩, przystrajać ⟨-roić⟩; poprawiać ⟨-wić⟩; *sałatkę* przybierać ⟨-brać⟩, *sałatę* przyprawiać ⟨-wić⟩; *drób* sprawiać ⟨-wić⟩; *ranę* opatrywać ⟨-trzyć⟩; *włosy* ⟨u⟩czesać; **get ~ed** ubrać się; **~ down** *kogoś* ⟨z⟩łajać; **~ up** ubierać ⟨-ubrać⟩ się (ładnie); przebierać ⟨-brać⟩ się; '~ **cir·cle** *theat.* pierwszy balkon *m*; '~ **de·sign·er** projektant(ka *f*) *m* mody; '~·**er** toaletka *f*; kredens *m*
'**dress·ing** ubieranie *n* (się); *med.* opatrunek *m*; sos *m* sałatkowy; *Am.* nadzienie *n*; ~ '**down** łajanie *n*; '~ **gown** szlafrok *m*; płaszcz *m* kąpielowy; '~ **room** garderoba *f*, szatnia *f*; '~ **ta·ble** toaletka *f*
'**dress·mak·er** krawiec *m* (-cowa *f*) (*dla kobiet*)
drew [druː] *pret. od* **draw** 1
drib·ble ['drɪbl] sączyć się; ⟨po⟩ciec kroplami; ślinić się; (*w piłce nożnej*) dryblować
dried [draɪd] suszony, wysuszony
dri·er ['draɪə] → **dryer**
drift [drɪft] **1.** prąd *m*, dryf *m*; zaspa *f*; sterta *f*, kupa *f*; *fig.* przesuwanie *n* się; **2.** ⟨z⟩dryfować, przesuwać ⟨-sunąć⟩ się; znosić ⟨znieść⟩, nanosić ⟨nanieść⟩; gromadzić (się)
drill [drɪl] **1.** *tech.* wiertarka *f*; wiertło *n*, świder *m*; *mil.* dryl *m* (*też fig.*), musztra *f*; **2.** ⟨na⟩wiercić; *mil.*, *fig.* musztrować; '~·**ing site** *tech.* teren *m* wiertniczy
drink [drɪŋk] **1.** napój *m*; **2.** (**drank, drunk**) ⟨wy⟩pić; **~ to s.o.** pić za kogoś; ~-'**driv·ing** *Brt.* prowadzenie *n* samochodu w stanie nietrzeźwym; '~·**er** pijąca osoba *f*; '~**s ma·chine** automat *m* z napojami
drip [drɪp] **1.** kapanie *n*; *med.* kroplówka *f*; **2.** (**-pp-**) ⟨na⟩kapać; ociekać ⟨-ciec⟩; ~-'**dry** nie wymagający prasowania; '~·**ping** tłuszcz *m* z pieczeni
driv|e [draɪv] **1.** jazda *f*, przejażdżka *f*; droga *f* dojazdowa; *prywatna* droga *f* *tech.* napęd *m*; *komp.* napęd *m*, stacja *f*; *psych.* popęd *m*; *fig.* kampania *f*, akcja *f*; *fig.* energia *f*, wigor *m*; *mot.* **left-hand ~e** lewostronny układ *m* kierowniczy; **2.** (**drove, driven**) *v/t.* ⟨po⟩jechać (*autem*), *auto itp.* prowadzić, ⟨po⟩kierować; ⟨po⟩jechać, ⟨za⟩wieźć (*samochodem*); doprowadzać ⟨-wić⟩ (*do szału itp.*); *bydło itp.* pędzić; *tech.* napędzać ⟨-dzić⟩; wbijać ⟨wbić⟩; **~e off** odjeżdżać ⟨-jechać⟩; **what are you ~ing at?** F o co ci chodzi?
'**drive-in 1.** auto...; dla zmotoryzowanych (*nie wysiadających z samochodu*); **~ cinema**, *Am.* **~ motion-picture theater** kino *n* dla zmotoryzowanych; **2.** kino *n* dla zmotoryzowanych; restauracja *f* dla zmotoryzowanych; *bankowy itp.* punkt *m* obsługi dla zmotoryzowanych
driv·el ['drɪvl] **1.** (*zwł. Brt.* **-ll-**, *Am.* **-l-**) brednie *pl.*, banialuki *pl.*; **2.** pleść brednie
driv·en ['drɪvn] *p.p. od* **drive** 2
driv·er ['draɪvə] *mot.* kierowca *m*; maszynista *m* (*lokomotywy*); *komp.* drajwer *m*, sterownik *m*; '~'**s li·cense** *Am.* prawo *n* jazdy
driv·ing ['draɪvɪŋ] *tech.* napędowy, napędzający; *mot.* **~ school** szkoła *f* nauki jazdy; '~ **li·cence** *Brt.* prawo *n* jazdy; '~ **test** egzamin *m* na prawo jazdy
driz·zle ['drɪzl] **1.** mżawka *f*, kapuśniak *m*; **2.** mżyć
drone [drəʊn] **1.** *zo.* truteń *m* (*też fig.*); **2.** ⟨za⟩brzęczeć, bzyczeć ⟨bzykać⟩
droop [druːp] opadać ⟨-paść⟩
drop [drɒp] **1.** kropla *f*; spadek *m*, upadek *m*; zmniejszanie *n* się; cukierek *m*; **fruit ~s** *pl.* drops *m*, *zw. pl.*; **2.** (**-pp-**) *v/t.* kapać; upuszczać ⟨-uścić⟩, spuszczać ⟨-uścić⟩; *temat itp.* zarzucać ⟨-cić⟩, zaniechać; **~ s.o. a postcard** F naskrobać kartkę do kogoś; *pasażera itp.* wysadzać ⟨-dzić⟩; *v/i.* kapać; spadać ⟨-aść⟩; opadać ⟨-aść⟩; **~ in** wpadać ⟨-aść⟩ (*z wizytą*); **~ off** spadać ⟨-aść⟩; F zdrzemnąć się; **~ out** wypadać ⟨-aść⟩; wysiadać ⟨-siąść⟩ (**of** z *G*); *też* **~ out of school** (**university**) rzucać

〈-cić〉 szkołę (uniwersytet); '~-**out** odszczepieniec *m*, outsider *m*; (*osoba, która porzuciła szkołę*)
drought [draʊt] susza *f*
drove [drəʊv] *pret. od* ***drive*** 2
drown [draʊn] *v/t.* 〈u〉topić; zatapiać 〈-topić〉; *fig.* zagłuszać 〈-szyć〉; *v/i.* 〈u〉tonąć, 〈u〉topić się
drow•sy ['draʊzɪ] (***-ier, -iest***) senny
drudge [drʌdʒ] harować; **drudg•e•ry** ['drʌdʒərɪ] harówka *f*
drug [drʌg] **1.** lekarstwo *n*, środek *m* farmaceutyczny; narkotyk *m*; ***be on ~s*** brać narkotyki; ***be off ~s*** nie brać narkotyków; **2.** (***-gg-***) podawać 〈-dać〉 lekarstwo *lub* narkotyk; dodawać 〈-dać〉 narkotyk *lub* środek odurzający do (*G*); *fig.* znieczulać 〈-lić〉, zobojętniać 〈-nić〉; '~ **a•buse** nadużywanie *n* narkotyków; '~ **ad•dict** narkoman(ka *f*) *m*; ***be a ~ addict*** brać narkotyki; ~•**gist** ['drʌgɪst] *Am.* aptekarz *m* (-arka *f*); właściciel(ka *f*) (*drugstore'u*); '~•**store** *Am.* drugstore *m*, *jakby*: apteka *f*, drogeria *f*; '~ **vic•tim** ofiara *f* zażywania narkotyków
drum [drʌm] **1.** *mus.* bęben(ek) *m*; *anat.* bębenek *m*; ~**s** *pl.* perkusja *f*; **2.** (***-mm-***) 〈za-, po〉bębnić; '~•**mer** *mus.* perkusista *m* (-tka *f*)
drunk [drʌŋk] **1.** *p.p. od* ***drink*** 2; **2.** *adj.* pijany; ***get ~*** upijać 〈upić〉 się; **3.** pijany *m*; pijak *m* (-aczka *f*); ~•**ard** ['drʌŋkəd] pijak *m* (-aczka *f*); '~•**en** pijany; ~•**en 'driv•ing** (*Am. też* ***drunk driving***) jazda po pijanemu (*samochodem*)
dry [draɪ] **1.** (***-ier, -iest***) suchy; wyschnięty; *wino*: wytrawny; bezdeszczowy; **2.** 〈wy〉suszyć; *też* ~ ***up*** wysychać 〈-schnąć〉; ~-'**clean** 〈wy〉czyścić chemicznie; ~ '**clean•er's** pralnia *f* chemiczna; '~•**er** (*też* ***drier***) suszarka *f*; '~ **goods** *pl. Am.* pasmanteria *f*
DTP [di: ti: 'pi:] *skrót*: ***desktop publishing*** *komp.* DTP *n*, mała poligrafia *f*
du•al ['dju:əl] podwójny; ~ '**car•riage•way** *Brt.* droga *f* szybkiego ruchu
dub [dʌb] (***-bb-***) (*w filmie*) podkładać 〈-dłożyć〉 dubbing
du•bi•ous ['dju:bjəs] wątpliwy
duch•ess ['dʌtʃɪs] księżna *f*
duck [dʌk] **1.** *zo.* kaczka *f*; ***my ~s*** F *Brt.* mój skarbie; **2.** uchylić (się); skrywać 〈-ryć〉 (się); '~•**ling** *zo.* kaczątko *n*
due [dju:] **1.** planowy; oczekiwany, spodziewany; należny; *econ.* przypadający do zapłaty; ~ ***to*** z powodu (*G*); ***be ~ to*** być spowodowanym (*I*); **2.** *adv.* bezpośrednio, prosto; dokładnie; ~ ***north*** dokładnie na północ
du•el ['dju:əl] pojedynek *m*
dues [dju:z] *pl.* należności *pl.*, opłaty *pl.*
du•et [dju:'et] *mus.* duet *m*
dug [dʌg] *pret. i p.p. od* ***dig*** 1
duke [dju:k] książę *m*
dull [dʌl] **1.** *kolor*: matowy; *dźwięk*: głuchy; *słuch*: przytępiony; *wzrok*: przygaszony; zachmurzony; nudny; tępy (*też fig.*); *econ.* mało aktywny, martwy; **2.** przytępić 〈-tępiać〉, osłabiać 〈-bić〉; stępiać 〈-pić〉
du•ly ['dju:lɪ] *adv.* należycie, właściwie; punktualnie, na czas
dumb [dʌm] niemy; *zwł. Am.* F durny; **dum(b)'found•ed** oniemiały
dum•my ['dʌmɪ] atrapa *f*, makieta *f*; manekin *m* (*też do testów*); *Brt.* smoczek *m*; (*w brydżu*) dziadek *m*
dump [dʌmp] **1.** *v/t.* rzucać 〈-cić〉, 〈z-, wy〉rzucać 〈-cić〉; porzucać 〈-cić〉; *śmieci* wysypywać 〈-pać〉; *nieczystości* pozbywać się, zrzucać; *econ. cenę* obniżać dumpingowo; **2.** wysypisko *n*; hałda *f*, zwał *m*; usypisko *n*; skład *m*; '~•**ing** *econ.* dumping *m*
dune [dju:n] wydma *f*
dung [dʌŋ] **1.** obornik *m*, gnój *f*; **2.** nawozić 〈-wieźć〉 (*obornikiem*)
dun•ga•rees [dʌŋgə'ri:z] *pl. Brt.* (***a pair of ~***) spodnie *pl.* robocze, kombinzeon *m*; (*spodnie*) rybaczki *pl.*
dun•geon ['dʌndʒən] loch *m*
dupe [dju:p] oszukiwać 〈-kać〉
du•plex ['dju:pleks] podwójny; '~ (**a•part•ment**) *Am.* mieszkanie *n* dwupoziomowe; '~ (**house**) *Am.* dom bliźniak
du•pli•cate **1.** ['dju:plɪkət] podwójny; ~ ***key*** drugi klucz *m*, duplikat *m*; **2.** ['dju:plɪkət] duplikat *m*, kopia *f*, odpis *m*; **3.** ['dju:plɪkeɪt] 〈z〉duplikować, 〈s〉kopiować, wykonywać 〈-nać〉 odpis
du•plic•i•ty [dju:'plɪsətɪ] dwulicowość *f*, obłuda *f*
dur•a•ble ['djʊərəbl] wytrzymały, trwa-

ły; do trwałego użytku; **du·ra·tion** [djʊə'reɪʃn] okres *m*, czas *m* trwania
du·ress [djʊə'res] przymus *m*
dur·ing ['djʊərɪŋ] *prp.* podczas (*G*)
dusk [dʌsk] zmierzch *m*; '**~·y** (**-ier, -iest**) mroczny (*też fig.*)
dust [dʌst] **1.** kurz *m*; pył *m*; **2.** *v/t.* odkurzać ⟨-rzyć⟩; posypywać ⟨-pać⟩; ⟨przy⟩pudrować; *tech.* opylać ⟨-lić⟩; *v/i.* ścierać ⟨zetrzeć⟩ kurz; ⟨przy⟩pudrować się; '**~·bin** *Brt.* kubeł *m lub* kosz *m* na śmieci; '**~·bin lin·er** jednorazowy worek *m* (*do kubła na śmieci*); '**~·cart** *Brt.* śmieciarka *f*; '**~·er** ścierka *f* (*do kurzu*); (*w szkole*) gąbka *f* do tablicy; '**~ cov·er**, '**~ jack·et** obwoluta *f*; '**~·man** (*pl.* **-men**) *Brt.* śmieciarz *m*; '**~·pan** śmietniczka *f*; '**~·y** (**-ier, -iest**) zakurzony, zapylony
Dutch [dʌtʃ] **1.** *adj.* holenderski; **2.** *adv.* **go ~** ⟨za⟩płacić składkowo; **2.** *ling.* holenderski; **the ~** *pl.* Holendrzy *pl.*; '**~·man** (*pl.* **-men**) Holender *m*; '**~·wo·m·an** (*pl.* **-women**) Holenderka *f*
du·ty ['dju:tɪ] obowiązek *m*, powinność *f*; *econ.* cło *n*; podatek *m*; **on ~** dyżurny; **be on ~** mieć dyżur *lub* służbę; **be off ~** być po dyżurze *lub* służbie; **~-'free** bezcłowy
dwarf [dwɔ:f] **1.** (*pl.* **dwarfs** [dwɔ:fs], **dwarves** [dwɔ:vz]) karzeł *m*; krasnal *m*, krasnoludek *m*; **2.** pomniejszać ⟨-szyć⟩, ⟨z⟩robić małym
dwell [dwel] (**dwelt** *lub* **dwelled**) mieszkać; *fig.* rozpamiętywać; '**~·ing** mieszkanie *n*
dwelt [dwelt] *pret. i p.p. od* **dwell**
dwin·dle ['dwɪndl] ⟨s⟩kurczyć się
dye [daɪ] **1.** farba *f*; barwnik *m*; **of the deepest ~** najgorszego rodzaju; **2.** ⟨za⟩farbować
dy·ing ['daɪɪŋ] **1.** umierający; **2.** umieranie *n*
dyke [daɪk] → **dike**[1, 2]
dy·nam·ic [daɪ'næmɪk] dynamiczny; **~s** *zw. sg.* dynamika *f*
dy·na·mite ['daɪnəmaɪt] **1.** dynamit *m*; **2.** wysadzać ⟨-dzić⟩ dynamitem
dys·en·te·ry ['dɪsntrɪ] *med.* czerwonka *f*, dyzenteria *f*
dys·pep·si·a [dɪs'pepsɪə] *med.* niestrawność *f*

E

E, **e** [i:] E, e *n*
E *skrót pisany*: **east** wsch., wschodni; **east(ern)** wschodni
each [i:tʃ] każdy; **~ other** siebie *lub* się nawzajem, wzajemnie; na osobę, na sztukę
ea·ger ['i:gə] chętny; gorliwy; '**~·ness** gorliwość *f*
ea·gle ['i:gl] *zo.* orzeł *m*; **~-'eyed** o ostrym wzroku, sokolooki
ear [ɪə] *anat.* ucho *n* (*też igielne, naczynia*); kłos *m*; **keep an ~ to the ground** słuchać co piszczy w trawie, mieć uszy otwarte; '**~·ache** ból *m* ucha; '**~·drum** *ant.* bębenek *m* uszny; **~ed**: **pink-eared** o różowych uszach
earl [ɜ:l] *angielski* hrabia *m*
'**ear·lobe** płatek *m* ucha
ear·ly ['ɜ:lɪ] wczesny; początkowy; **as ~ as May** już w maju; **as ~ as possible** najszybciej *lub* najwcześniej jak można; **~ 'bird** ranny ptaszek *m*; **~ 'warn·ing sys·tem** system *m* wczesnego ostrzegania
'**ear·mark** **1.** oznaczenie *n*, cecha *f*; **2.** oznaczać ⟨-czyć⟩; ⟨wy⟩asygnować (**for** na *A*), alokować
earn [ɜ:n] zarabiać ⟨-robić⟩; przynosić ⟨-nieść⟩
ear·nest ['ɜ:nɪst] **1.** poważny, zasadniczy; **2.** zadatek *m*; **in ~** na serio, na poważnie
earn·ings ['ɜ:nɪŋz] *pl.* wpływy *pl.*
'**ear|·phones** *pl.* słuchawki *pl.*; '**~·piece** *tel.* słuchawka *f*; '**~·ring** kolczyk *m*; '**~·shot**: **within** (**out of**) **~shot** w zasięgu (poza zasięgiem) słuchu
earth [ɜ:θ] **1.** ziemia *f*; Ziemia *f*; ląd *m*; **2.** *v/t. electr.* uziemiać ⟨-mić⟩; **~·en** ['ɜ:θn] gliniany; '**~·en·ware** wyroby *pl.* gliniane; '**~·ly** ziemski, doczesny; F możliwy; '**~·quake** trzęsienie *n* ziemi; '**~·worm** *zo.* dżdżownica *f*
ease [i:z] **1.** łatwość *f*; spokój *m*; beztro-

ska *f*; lekkość *f*; **at (one's) ~** spokojny, w spokoju; swobodny; **be** *lub* **feel ill at ~** nie czuć się swobodnie; **2.** *v/t.* ⟨z⟩łagodzić; ⟨o⟩słabnąć; *v/i. zwł.* **~ off, ~ up** ⟨z⟩łagodnieć, ⟨ze⟩lżeć; ⟨o⟩słabnąć

ea·sel ['iːzl] sztalugi *pl.*

east [iːst] **1.** wschód *m*; **2.** *adj.* wschodni; **3.** *adv.* na wschód

Eas·ter ['iːstə] Wielkanoc *f*; *attr.* wielkanocny; ~ **'bun·ny** króliczek *m* wielkanocny; '~ **egg** jajko *n* wielkanocne, pisanka *f*

eas·ter·ly ['iːstəlɪ] wschodni; **east·ern** ['iːstən] wschodni; **east·ward(s)** ['iːstwəd(z)] wschodni; na wschód

eas·y ['iːzɪ] (**-ier, -iest**) łatwy; nieskrępowany; beztroski; **go ~, take it ~** nie kłopotać się; **take it ~!** nie przejmuj się!; ~ **'chair** fotel *m*; ~**'go·ing** swobodny, nieskrępowany

eat [iːt] (**ate, eaten**) ⟨z⟩jeść; *rdza itp.*: zżerać ⟨zeżreć⟩; **~ out** jeść na mieście *lub* poza domem; **~ up** zjeść; '**~·a·ble** jadalny; **~·en** ['iːtn] *p.p. od* **eat** 1; '**~·er**: **he is a slow ~er** wolno je

eaves [iːvz] *pl.* okap *m*; '**~·drop** (**-pp-**) podsłuchiwać ⟨-chać⟩

ebb [eb] **1.** odpływ *m*; **2.** cofać ⟨-fnąć⟩ się; odpływać ⟨-łynąć⟩; **~ away** uchodzić ⟨ujść⟩, uciekać ⟨uciec⟩; ~ **'tide** odpływ *m*

eb·o·ny ['ebənɪ] heban *m*

ec *skrót pisany*: **Eurocheque** *Brt.* euroczek *m*

EC [iː 'siː] *skrót*: **European Community** Wspólnota *f* Europejska

ec·cen·tric [ɪk'sentrɪk] **1.** (**~ally**) ekscentryczny; **2.** ekscentryk *m* (-yczka *f*), oryginał *m*

ec·cle·si·as|·tic [ɪkliːzɪ'æstɪk] (**-ally**), **~·ti·cal** kościelny

ech·o ['ekəʊ] **1.** (*pl.***-oes**) echo *n*; **2.** *v/t.* powtarzać ⟨-tórzyć⟩; *fig. v/i.* odbijać ⟨-bić⟩ się, powtarzać ⟨-tórzyć⟩ jak echo

e·clipse *astr.* [ɪ'klɪps] zaćmienie *n* (*księżyca, słońca*)

e·co·cide ['iːkəsaɪd] niszczenie *n* przyrody

e·co·lo·gi·cal [iːkə'lɒdʒɪkl] ekologiczny

e·col·o|·gist [iː'kɒlədʒɪst] ekolog *m*; **~·gy** [iː'kɒlədʒɪ] ekologia *f*

ec·o·nom|·ic [iːkə'nɒmɪk] (**-ally**) ekonomiczny; gospodarczy; **~ic growth** rozwój *m* gospodarczy; **~·i·cal** ekonomiczny, gospodarczy; oszczędny; **~·ics** *sg.* ekonomia *f*, ekonomika *f*; gospodarka *f*

e·con·o|·mist [ɪ'kɒnəmɪst] ekonomista *m* (-tka *f*); **~·mize** [ɪ'kɒnəmaɪz] oszczędzać ⟨-dzić⟩; **~·my** [ɪ'kɒnəmɪ] **1.** gospodarka *f*; ekonomia *f*, ekonomika *f*; oszczędność *f*; **2.** dający oszczędności

e·co·sys·tem ['iːkəʊsɪstəm] ekosystem *m*

ec·sta|·sy ['ekstəsɪ] ekstaza *f*; **~t·ic** [ɪk'stætɪk] ekstatyczny

ECU ['ekjuː, eɪ'kuː] *skrót*: **European Currency Unit** ecu *n*

ed. [ed] *skrót*: **edited** red., redakcja *f*, redagował; **edition** wyd., wydanie *f*; **editor** red., redaktor *m*

ed·dy ['edɪ] **1.** wir *m*, zamęt *m*; **2.** ⟨za⟩wirować

edge [edʒ] **1.** brzeg *m*, skraj *m*; krawędź *f*, ostrze *n*; **be on ~** być poirytowanym; **have the ~ over** mieć przewagę nad (*I*); **2.** obszywać ⟨-szyć⟩; ⟨za-, na⟩ostrzyć; przysuwać (się); **~·ways** ['edʒweɪz], **~·wise** ['edʒwaɪz] bokiem, na boku

edg·ing ['edʒɪŋ] obramowanie *n*; obszycie *n*

edg·y ['edʒɪ] (**-ier, -iest**) ostry; F zirytowany

ed·i·ble ['edɪbl] jadalny

e·dict ['iːdɪkt] edykt *m*

ed·i·fice ['edɪfɪs] budynek *m*

Ed·in·burgh Edynburg *m*

ed·it ['edɪt] *tekst* ⟨z⟩redagować; *komp.* ⟨wy⟩edytować, ⟨na⟩pisać; *czasopisma* być wydawcą, wydawać; *film* ⟨z⟩montować; **e·di·tion** [ɪ'dɪʃn] wydanie *n*; **ed·i·tor** ['edɪtə] wydawca *m*; redaktor(ka *f*) *m*; **ed·i·to·ri·al** [edɪ'tɔːrɪəl] **1.** artykuł *m* wstępny; **2.** redakcyjny

EDP [iː diː 'piː] *skrót*: **electronic data processing** elektroniczne przetwarzanie *n* danych

ed·u|·cate ['edʒʊkeɪt] ⟨wy⟩kształcić; ⟨wy⟩edukować; '**~·cat·ed** wykształcony; **~·ca·tion** [edʒʊ'keɪʃn] wykształcenie *n*, edukacja *f*; kształcenie *n*, wychowanie *n*; **Ministry of** **℞cation** Ministerstwo *n* Oświaty; **~·ca·tion·al** [edʒʊ'keɪʃənl] edukacyjny; oświatowy

eel [iːl] *zo.* węgorz *m*

E

ef·fect [ɪ'fekt] rezultat *m*, skutek *m*; wynik *m*; wpływ *m*; efekt *m*; wrażenie *n*; **~s** *pl.*, *econ.* walory *pl.*; majątek *m* ruchomy; ***be in ~*** być w mocy; ***in ~*** faktycznie; ***take ~*** wchodzić ⟨wejść⟩ w życie; **ef'fec·tive** efektywny, skuteczny; faktyczny, realny; działający

E

ef·fem·i·nate [ɪ'femɪnət] zniewieściały
ef·fer|·vesce [efə'ves] musować; **~·vescent** [efə'vesnt] musujący
ef·fi·cien|·cy [ɪ'fɪʃənsɪ] skuteczność *f*; sprawność *f*; wydajność; ***~cy measure*** *econ.* środek *m* zwiększenia wydajności; **~t** skuteczny, sprawny; wydajny
ef·flu·ent ['eflʊənt] wyciek *m*; ścieki *pl.*
ef·fort ['efət] wysiłek *m*; staranie *n* (***at*** o *A*); ***without ~*** → **'~·less** bez wysiłku
ef·fron·te·ry [ɪ'frʌntərɪ] zuchwałość *f*, bezczelność *f*
ef·fu·sive [ɪ'fjuːsɪv] wylewny
EFTA ['eftə] *skrót*: ***European Free Trade Association*** EFTA, Europejskie Stowarzyszenie *n* Wolnego Handlu
e.g. [iː 'dʒiː] *skrót*: ***for example*** (*łacińskie* ***exempli gratia***) np., na przykład
egg¹ [eg] jajko; ***put all one's ~s in one basket*** postawić wszystko na jedną kartę
egg² [eg]: ***~ on*** podpuszczać ⟨-puścić⟩, podbechtywać ⟨-bechtać⟩
'egg| co·sy osłona *f* dla jaj; **'~·cup** kieliszek *m* dla jaj; **'~·head** (*intelektualista*) jajogłowy *m* (-wa *f*); **'~·plant** *bot.*, *zwł. Am.* bakłażan *m*; **'~·shell** skorupka *f* jajka; **'~ tim·er** minutnik *m*
e·go·is|·m ['egəʊɪzəm] egoizm *m*, samolubstwo *n*; **~t** ['egəʊɪst] egoista *m* (-tka *f*), samolub *m*
E·gypt ['iːdʒɪpt] Egipt *m*; **E·gyp·tian** [ɪ'dʒɪpʃn] **1.** egipski; **2.** Egipcjanin *m* (-anka *f*)
ei·der·down ['aɪdədaʊn] puch *m* (*edredona*); kołdra *f* puchowa
eight [eɪt] **1.** osiem; **2.** ósemka *f*; **eigh·teen** [eɪ'tiːn] osiemnaście; **eigh·teenth** [eɪ'tiːnθ] osiemnasty; **'~·fold** ośmiokrotny; **eighth** [eɪtθ] **1.** ósmy; **2.** jedna ósma; **'eighth·ly** po ósme; **eigh·ti·eth** ['eɪtɪɪθ] osiemdziesiąty; **'eigh·ty 1.** osiemdziesiąt; **2.** osiemdziesiątka *f*
Ei·re ['eərə] (*irlandzka nazwa Irlandii*)
ei·ther ['aɪðə, 'iːðə] którykolwiek, jakikolwiek (z dwóch); jeden (z dwóch); oba, obydwa; ***~ ... or ...*** albo ... albo ...; ***not ~*** też nie (*po zdaniu przeczącym*)
e·jac·u·late [ɪ'dʒækjʊleɪt] *v/t. physiol.* tryskać ⟨-snąć⟩ (*nasieniem*); wykrzyknąć; *v/i.* wytrysnąć, mieć wytrysk
e·ject [ɪ'dʒekt] ⟨wy⟩eksmitować; *tech.* wyrzucać ⟨-cić⟩, wypychać ⟨-pchnąć⟩
eke [iːk]: ***~ out*** *dochody* uzupełniać ⟨-nić⟩; *pieniądze* oszczędzać ⟨-dzić⟩; ***~ out a living*** ledwo zarabiać na życie
e·lab·o·rate 1. [ɪ'læbərət] skomplikowany, złożony; **2.** [ɪ'læbəreɪt] opracowywać ⟨-wać⟩, uzupełniać ⟨-nić⟩, ⟨s⟩konkretyzować
e·lapse [ɪ'læps] upływać ⟨-łynąć⟩, przechodzić ⟨przejść⟩
e·las|·tic [ɪ'læstɪk] **1.** (***-ally***) elastyczny, rozciągliwy: **2.** guma *f*, gumka *f*; **~·ti·ci·ty** [elæ'stɪsətɪ] elastyczność *f*
e·lat·ed [ɪ'leɪtɪd] zachwycony
Elbe Łaba *f*
el·bow ['elbəʊ] **1.** łokieć *m*; ostry zakręt *m*; *tech.* kolanko *n*; ***at one's ~*** pod ręką; **2.** *drogę* ⟨u⟩torować łokciami; ***~ one's way through*** przepychać ⟨-pchnąć⟩ się przez (*A*)
el·der¹ ['eldə] **1.** starszy; **2.** starszy *m*; **~s** starszyzna *f*; **'~·ly** starszy
el·der² *bot.* ['eldə] czarny bez *m*
el·dest ['eldɪst] najstarszy
e·lect [ɪ'lekt] **1.** elekt, wybrany; **2.** wybierać ⟨-brać⟩
e·lec|·tion [ɪ'lekʃn] **1.** wybory *pl.*; **2.** *pol.* wyborczy; **~·tor** [ɪ'lektə] wyborca *m*, *Am. pol.*, *hist.* elektor *m*; **~·to·ral** [ɪ'lektərəl] wyborczy; ***~toral college*** *Am. pol.* kolegium elektorskie; **~·to·rate** [ɪ'lektərət] *pol.* elektorat *m*
e·lec·tric [ɪ'lektrɪk] (***~ally***) elektryczny, elektro...
e·lec·tri·cal [ɪ'lektrɪkl] elektryczny, elektro...; **~ en·gi'neer** inżynier *m* elektryk; elektrotechnik *m*; **~ en·gi'neer·ing** elektrotechnika *f*
e·lec·tric 'chair krzesło *n* elektryczne
el·ec·tri·cian [ɪlek'trɪʃn] elektryk *m*
e·lec·tri·ci·ty [ɪlek'trɪsətɪ] elektryczność *f*
e·lec·tric 'ra·zor *elektryczna* maszynka *f* do golenia
e·lec·tri·fy [ɪ'lektrɪfaɪ] ⟨z⟩elektryzować (*też fig.*); ⟨z⟩elektryfikować
e·lec·tro·cute [ɪ'lektrəkjuːt] porażać

⟨-razić⟩ *kogoś* śmiertelnie prądem; wykonywać ⟨-nać⟩ *na kimś* wyrok śmierci na krześle elektrycznym

e·lec·tron [ɪ'lektrɒn] elektron *m*

el·ec·tron·ic [ɪlek'trɒnɪk] (**~ally**) elektroniczny; ~ **'da·ta pro·ces·sing** elektroniczne przetwarzanie *n* danych

el·ec·tron·ics [ɪlek'trɒnɪks] *sg.* elektronika *f*

el·e|·gance ['elɪgəns] elegancja *f*; **'~·gant** elegancki, wytworny

el·e|·ment ['elɪmənt] element *m*; składnik *m*; *chem.* pierwiastek *m*; **~ments** *pl.* elementy *pl.*, podstawy *pl.*; żywioły *pl.*; **~·men·tal** [elɪ'mentl] elementarny; istotny

el·e·men·ta·ry [elɪ'mentərɪ] elementarny, początkowy; **~ school** *Am.* szkoła *f* podstawowa

el·e·phant ['elɪfənt] *zo.* słoń

el·e|·vate ['elɪveɪt] podnosić ⟨-nieść⟩, podwyższać ⟨-szyć⟩; dawać ⟨dać⟩ awans; **'~·vat·ed** podniesiony, podwyższony; *fig.* wyniosły; **~·va·tion** [elɪ'veɪʃn] podniesienie *n*, podwyższenie *n*; wyniosłość *f*; awans *m*; wysokość *f*, wzniesienie *n*; **~·va·tor** *tech.* ['elɪveɪtə] *Am.* winda *f*; dźwig *m*

e·lev·en [ɪ'levn] **1.** jedenaście; **2.** jedenastka *f*; **~th** [ɪ'levnθ] **1.** jedenasty; **2.** jedna jedenasta

elf [elf] (*pl.* **elves**) elf *m*

e·li·cit [ɪ'lɪsɪt] wydobywać ⟨-być⟩ (**from** od *G*); wydostawać ⟨-tać⟩

el·i·gi·ble ['elɪdʒəbl] nadający się do (*G*) *lub* na (*A*); uprawniony (**for** do *G*); wolny

e·lim·i|·nate [ɪ'lɪmɪneɪt] ⟨wy⟩eliminować; usuwać ⟨usunąć⟩; **~·na·tion** [ɪlɪmɪ'neɪʃn] eliminacja *f*; wyeliminowanie *n*; usunięcie *n*

é·lite [eɪ'liːt] elita *f*

elk [elk] *zo.* łoś *m*; *Am.* wapiti *n*

el·lipse [ɪ'lɪps] *math.* elipsa *f*

elm [elm] *bot.* wiąz *m*

e·lon·gate ['iːlɒŋgeɪt] wydłużać ⟨-żyć⟩

e·lope [ɪ'ləʊp] uciekać ⟨-ciec⟩ (*z ukochanym lub ukochaną*)

e·lo|·quence ['eləkwəns] elokwencja *f*, łatwość *f* wysławiania się; **'~·quent** elokwentny

else [els] jeszcze; inny; **~'where** gdzie indziej

e·lude [ɪ'luːd] umykać ⟨-knąć⟩ (*przebiegle*) (*D*), unikać ⟨-knąć⟩ (*przebiegle*); nie przychodzić do głowy, umykać

e·lu·sive [ɪ'luːsɪv] nieuchwytny

elves [elvz] *pl. od* **elf**

e·ma·ci·ated [ɪ'meɪʃɪeɪtɪd] wychudzony, wymizerowany

em·a|·nate ['eməneɪt] wydobywać się, pochodzić (**from** z *G*); promieniować, emanować; **~·na·tion** [emə'neɪʃn] emanacja *f*; wydzielanie *n* się

e·man·ci|·pate [ɪ'mænsɪpeɪt] ⟨wy⟩emancypować; **~·pa·tion** [ɪmænsɪ'peɪʃn] emancypacja *f*

em·balm [ɪm'bɑːm] ⟨za⟩balsamować

em·bank·ment [ɪm'bæŋkmənt] nasyp *m*, wał *m*; nabrzeże *n*

em·bar·go [em'bɑːgəʊ] (*pl.* **-goes**) embargo *n*, ograniczenie *n*

em·bark [ɪm'bɑːk] *nat.*, *aviat.* ⟨za⟩ładować; przyjmować ⟨-jąć⟩ na pokład; *naut.* (*na statek*) wsiadać ⟨wsiąść⟩; **~ on** przedsiębrać ⟨-sięwziąć⟩ (*A*), podejmować ⟨-djąć⟩ (*A*)

em·bar·rass [ɪm'bærəs] ⟨za⟩kłopotać, wprawiać ⟨-wić⟩ w zakłopotanie; **~·ing** kłopotliwy, kłopoczący; **~·ment** zakłopotanie *n*, konsternacja *f*

em·bas·sy ['embəsɪ] *pol.* ambasada *f*

em·bed [ɪm'bed] (**-dd-**) osadzać ⟨-dzić⟩, zakleszczać ⟨-czyć⟩

em·bel·lish [ɪm'belɪʃ] upiększać ⟨-szyć⟩ (*też fig.*)

em·bers ['embəz] *pl.* żar *m*

em·bez·zle [ɪm'bezl] sprzeniewierzać ⟨-rzyć⟩, ⟨z⟩defraudować; **~·ment** sprzeniewierzenie *n*, defraudacja *f*

em·bit·ter [ɪm'bɪtə]: **be ~ed** być zgorzkniałym *lub* rozgoryczonym

em·blem ['embləm] emblemat *m*

em·bod·y [ɪm'bɒdɪ] ucieleśniać ⟨-nić⟩; zawierać ⟨-wrzeć⟩; włączać ⟨-czyć⟩

em·bo·lis·m ['embəlɪzəm] *med.* embolia *f*, zator *m*

em·brace [ɪm'breɪs] **1.** obejmować ⟨objąć⟩ (się), ⟨przy⟩tulić (się); uścisk *m*, obejmowanie *n* się

em·broi·der [ɪm'brɔɪdə] ⟨wy⟩haftować; *fig.* upiększać ⟨-szyć⟩, ubarwiać ⟨-wić⟩; **~·y** [ɪm'brɔɪdərɪ] haft *m*; *fig.* upiększanie *n*

em·broil [ɪm'brɔɪl] wciągać ⟨-gnąć⟩ (*w kłopoty itp.*), wplątywać ⟨-tać⟩

e·mend [ɪ'mend] poprawiać ⟨-wić⟩, wnosić ⟨wnieść⟩ poprawki

em·e·rald ['emərəld] **1.** szmaragd *m*; **2.** szmaragdowy

e·merge [ɪ'mɜːdʒ] wyłaniać ⟨-łonić⟩ się; ukazywać ⟨-zać⟩ się; wychodzić ⟨wyjść⟩ na jaw

e·mer·gen·cy [ɪ'mɜːdʒənsɪ] stan *m* wyjątkowy; wypadek *m*; awaria *f*; *pol.* ***state of ~*** stan *m* wyjątkowy; **~ brake** ręczny hamulec *m*; hamulec *m* bezpieczeństwa; **~ call** wezwanie *n* w razie nagłego wypadku; **~ exit** wyjście *n* bezpieczeństwa; **~ land·ing** lądowanie *n* awaryjne; **~ num·ber** numer *m* pogotowia (*ratunkowego, policji itp.*); **~ room** *Am.* izba *m* przyjęć (*na ostrym dyżurze*)

em·i|·grant ['emɪgrənt] emigrant(ka *f*) *m*; **~·grate** ['emɪgreɪt] ⟨wy⟩emigrować; **~·gra·tion** [emɪ'greɪʃn] emigracja *f*

em·i|·nence ['emɪnəns]; sława *f*; ***2nence*** *rel.* Eminencja *f*; **'~·nent** sławny; wybitny; **'~·nent·ly** wybitnie; bardzo

e·mis·sion [ɪ'mɪʃn] emisja *f*, promieniowanie *n*; **~-'free** nie wydzielający spalin

e·mit [ɪ'mɪt] ⟨wy⟩emitować, ⟨wy⟩promieniować; wydzielać ⟨-lić⟩

e·mo·tion [ɪ'məʊʃn] (***-tt-***) uczucie *n*, emocja *f*; **~·al** [ɪ'məʊʃənl] uczuciowy, emocjonalny; wzruszony; wzruszający; **~·al·ly** [ɪ'məʊʃnəlɪ] uczuciowo, emocjonalnie; wzruszająco; ***~ally disturbed*** mający zaburzenia emocjonalne; **~·less** nieczuły

em·pe·ror ['empərə] cesarz *m*, imperator *m*

em·pha|·sis ['emfəsɪs] (*pl.* ***-ses*** [-siːz]) nacisk *m*; **~·size** ['emfəsaɪz] podkreślać ⟨-lić⟩, ⟨za⟩akcentować; **~t·ic** [ɪm'fætɪk] (***-ally***) stanowczy, dobitny; wyraźny

em·pire ['empaɪə] cesarstwo *n*, imperium *n*

em·pir·i·cal [em'pɪrɪkl] empiryczny

em·ploy [ɪm'plɔɪ] **1.** zatrudniać ⟨-nić⟩; ⟨za⟩stosować, używać ⟨-żyć⟩; **2.** zatrudnienie *n*; ***in the ~ of*** zatrudniony u (*G*); **~·ee** [emplɔɪ'iː] pracownik *m* (-ica *f*); **~·er** [ɪm'plɔɪə] pracodawca *m*); **~·ment** [ɪm'plɔɪmənt] zatrudnienie *n*, praca *f*, użycie *n*; **~·ment ad** ogłoszenie *n* o możliwości zatrudnienia; **~·ment of·fice** urząd *m* zatrudnienia

em·pow·er [ɪm'paʊə] upoważniać ⟨-nić⟩, uprawniać ⟨-nić⟩

em·press ['emprɪs] cesarzowa *f*

emp|·ti·ness ['emptɪnɪs] pustka *f* (*też fig.*); **'~·ty 1.** (***-ier, -iest***) pusty (*też fig.*); **2.** opróżniać ⟨-nić⟩ (się); wysypywać ⟨-pać⟩; *rzeka*: uchodzić (***into*** do *G*)

em·u·late ['emjʊleɪt] naśladować; *komp.* emulować

e·mul·sion [ɪ'mʌlʃn] emulsja *f*

en·a·ble [ɪ'neɪbl] umożliwiać ⟨-wić⟩, dawać ⟨dać⟩ możność

en·act [ɪ'nækt] *prawo* ustanawiać ⟨-nowić⟩; nadawać ⟨-dać⟩ moc prawną

e·nam·el [ɪ'næml] **1.** emalia *f*; *anat.* szkliwo *n*; lakier *m*; lakier *m* do paznokci; **2.** (*zwł. Brt.* ***-ll-****, Am.* ***-l-***) ⟨po⟩emaliować; ⟨po⟩lakierować; szklić

en·am·o(u)red [ɪ'næməd]: ***~ of*** rozkochany w (*L*)

en·camp·ment [ɪn'kæmpmənt] *zwł. mil.* obóz *m*

en·cased [ɪn'keɪst]: ***~ in*** oprawny w (*A*), osadzony w (*A*), pokryty (*I*)

en·chant [ɪn'tʃɑːnt] oczarowywać ⟨-ować⟩; **~·ing** czarujący; **~·ment** oczarowanie *n*, czar *m*

en·cir·cle [ɪn'sɜːkl] okrążać ⟨-żyć⟩; otaczać ⟨otoczyć⟩; obejmować ⟨objąć⟩

encl *skrót pisany*: ***enclosed, enclosure*** zał., załącznik(i *pl.*) *m*

en·close [ɪn'kləʊz] otaczać ⟨otoczyć⟩; załączać ⟨-czyć⟩ (*do listu*); **en·clo·sure** [ɪn'kləʊʒə] zagroda *f*, ogrodzone miejsce *n*; załącznik *m*

en·code [en'kəʊd] ⟨za⟩kodować

en·com·pass [ɪn'kʌmpəs] obejmować ⟨-bjąć⟩

en·coun·ter [ɪn'kaʊntə] **1.** spotkanie *n*; potyczka *f*; **2.** spotykać ⟨-tkać⟩, napotykać ⟨-tkać⟩; natrafiać ⟨-fić⟩ na (*A*), napotykać ⟨-tkać⟩ na (*A*)

en·cour·age [ɪn'kʌrɪdʒ] zachęcać ⟨-cić⟩; popierać ⟨-przeć⟩; **~·ment** zachęta *f*; poparcie *n*

en·cour·ag·ing [ɪn'kʌrɪdʒɪŋ] zachęcający

en·croach [ɪn'krəʊtʃ] (***on***) *prawo, teren* naruszać; wkraczać ⟨-roczyć⟩, (*na teren*) wdzierać ⟨wedrzeć⟩ się; *czas* zabierać ⟨-brać⟩; **~·ment** naruszenie *n*; wkroczenie *n*, wtargnięcie *n*

en·cum|·ber [ɪn'kʌmbə] obarczać ⟨-czyć⟩, obciążać ⟨-żyć⟩; ⟨za⟩hamować; ~**·brance** [ɪn'kʌmbrəns] obciążenie *n*; przeszkoda *f*

en·cy·clo·p(a)e·di·a [ensaɪklə'piːdjə] encyklopedia *f*

end [end] **1.** koniec *m*, zakończenie *n*; cel *m*; ***no ~ of*** bez liku; ***at the ~ of May*** pod koniec maja; ***in the ~*** w końcu, wreszcie; ***on ~*** bez przerwy; ***stand on ~*** *włosy*: stawać ⟨-nąć⟩ dęba; ***to no ~*** na próżno; ***go off the deep ~*** ⟨s⟩tracić cierpliwość; ***make (both) ~s meet*** ⟨z⟩wiązać koniec z końcem; **2.** ⟨s⟩kończyć (się), ⟨za⟩kończyć (się)

en·dan·ger [ɪn'deɪndʒə] narażać ⟨-razić⟩, zagrażać ⟨-rozić⟩

en·dear [ɪn'dɪə] zdobywać ⟨-być⟩ popularność (***to s.o.*** wśród kogoś), przysparzać ⟨-porzyć⟩ popularności; ~**·ing** [ɪn'dɪərɪŋ] ujmujący, urzekający; ~**·ment**: ***words*** *pl.* ***of ~ment, ~ments*** *pl.* czułe słówka *pl.*, czułości *pl.*

en·deav·o(u)r [ɪn'devə] **1.** staranie *n*, usiłowanie *n*; **2.** ⟨po⟩starać się, dokładać ⟨-łożyć⟩ starań

end·ing ['endɪŋ] zakończenie *n*, koniec *m*; *gr.* końcówka *f*

en·dive ['endɪv, 'endaɪv] *pot.* cykoria *f*, endywia *f*

'end·less nie kończący się, nieskończony, niezmierzony; *tech.* bez końca

en·dorse [ɪn'dɔːs] *econ. czek* ⟨za⟩indosować, żyrować; umieszczać ⟨-eścić⟩ adnotację (***on*** na *odwrocie*); ⟨za⟩akceptować; ~**·ment** adnotacja *f*, uwaga *f*; *econ.* indosowanie *n*

en·dow [ɪn'daʊ] *fig.* wyposażać ⟨-żyć⟩, obdarowywać ⟨-ować⟩; dotować; ***~ s.o. with s.th.*** obdarzać ⟨-rzyć⟩ kogoś czymś; ~**·ment** dotacja *f*; ***~ments*** *pl.* talenty *pl.*, możliwości *pl.*

en·dur|·ance [ɪn'djʊərəns] wytrzymałość *f*; ***beyond ~ance, past ~ance*** nie do zniesienia; ~**e** [ɪn'djʊə] wytrzymywać ⟨-mać⟩, znosić ⟨znieść⟩

'end us·er użytkownik *m* końcowy, odbiorca *m*

en·e·my ['enəmɪ] **1.** wróg *m*, nieprzyjaciel *m*; **2.** wrogi, nieprzyjacielski

en·er·get·ic [enə'dʒetɪk] (***~ally***) energiczny

en·er·gy ['enədʒɪ] energia *f* (*też elektryczna*); '~ **cri·sis** kryzys *m* energetyczny; '~**-sav·ing** oszczędność *f* energii; '~ **sup·ply** dostawa *f* energii

en·fold [ɪn'fəʊld] otaczać ⟨-toczyć⟩ ramieniem; zawierać ⟨-wrzeć⟩

en·force [ɪn'fɔːs] wymuszać ⟨-musić⟩, ⟨wy⟩egzekwować; *prawo* wprowadzać ⟨-dzić⟩ w życie, nadawać ⟨-dać⟩ moc; ~**·ment** *econ.*, *jur.* narzucenie *n*; wprowadzenie *n* w życie

en·fran·chise [ɪn'fræntʃaɪz] *komuś* nadawać ⟨-dać⟩ prawo wyborcze

en·gage [ɪn'geɪdʒ] *v/t.* ⟨za⟩angażować, zatrudniać ⟨-nić⟩; *uwagę* przyciągać ⟨-gnąć⟩; *tech.* zaczepiać ⟨-pić⟩, sprzęgać ⟨-gnąć⟩; *mot.* włączać ⟨-czyć⟩ sprzęgło; *v/i. tech.* sczepiać ⟨-pić⟩ (się); ***~ in*** ⟨za⟩angażować się w (*L*); zajmować ⟨-jąć⟩ się (*I*); ~**d** zaręczony (***to*** z *I*); *toaleta*: *Brt.* zajęta; ***~d tone** lub **signal*** *Brt. tel.* zajęty sygnał *m*; ~**·ment** zaręczyny *pl.*; umowa *f*, zobowiązanie *n*; *mil.* potyczka *f*, starcie *n*; *tech.* włączenie *n*, zaczepienie *n*

en·gag·ing [ɪn'geɪdʒɪŋ] zajmujący; *uśmiech*: uroczy

en·gine ['endʒɪn] silnik *m*; *rail.* lokomotywa *f*; '~ **driv·er** *Brt. rail.* maszynista *m*

en·gi·neer [endʒɪ'nɪə] **1.** inżynier *m*, technik *m*, mechanik *m*; *Am. rail.* maszynista *m*; *mil.* saper *m*; **2.** ⟨wy⟩budować, ⟨za⟩projektować; *fig.* ukartować, ⟨u⟩knuć; ~**·ing** [endʒɪ'nɪərɪŋ] inżynieria *f*; technika *f*

Eng·land Anglia *f*

En·glish ['ɪŋglɪʃ] **1.** angielski; **2.** *ling.* angielski (*język*); ***the ~*** *pl.* Anglicy *pl.*; ***in plain ~*** prosto; '~ **Chan·nel** Kanał La Manche; '~**·man** (*pl.* ***-men***) Anglik *m*; '~**·wom·an** (*pl.* ***-women***) Angielka *f*

en·grave [ɪn'greɪv] ⟨wy⟩grawerować; rytować; *fig.* wyryć, zapadać ⟨-paść⟩; **en'grav·er** grawer *m*; rytownik *m*; **en'grav·ing** rycina *f*, sztych *m*; drzeworyt *m*

en·grossed [ɪn'grəʊst]: ***~ in*** pochłonięty (*I*)

en·hance [ɪn'hɑːns] wzmacniać ⟨-mocnić⟩, zwiększać ⟨-szyć⟩

e·nig·ma [ɪ'nɪgmə] zagadka *f*; **en·ig·mat·ic** [enɪg'mætɪk] (***~ally***) enigmatyczny, zagadkowy

en·joy [ɪn'dʒɔɪ] cieszyć się (*I*); lubić; ***did you ~ it?*** podobało ci się to?; ***~ o.s.*** bawić się; ***~ yourself!*** baw się dobrze!;

I ~ my dinner obiad mi odpowiada; **~·a·ble** miły, przyjemny; **~·ment** przyjemność *f*
en·large [ɪn'lɑːdʒ] powiększać ⟨-szyć⟩ (się); *phot.* powiększać ⟨-szyć⟩; ***~ on*** uszczegóławiać ⟨-łowić⟩ (*A*); rozprawiać nad (*I*); **~·ment** powiększenie *n* (*też phot.*)
en·light·en [ɪn'laɪtn] oświecać ⟨-cić⟩; **~·ment** oświecenie *n*
en·list [ɪn'lɪst] *mil. v/t.* ⟨z⟩werbować; *v/i.* wstępować ⟨wstąpić⟩ do wojska
en·liv·en [ɪn'laɪvn] ożywiać ⟨-wić⟩
en·mi·ty ['enmətɪ] wrogość *f*
en·no·ble [ɪ'nəʊbl] nobilitować
e·nor|·mi·ty [ɪ'nɔːmətɪ] ogrom *m*; potworność *f*, **~·mous** [ɪ'nɒːməs] ogromny
e·nough [ɪ'nʌf] wystarczający
en·quire [ɪn'kwaɪə], **en·qui·ry** [ɪn'kwaɪərɪ] → ***inquire, inquiry***
en·rage [ɪn'reɪdʒ] rozwścieczać ⟨-czyć⟩; **~d** rozwścieczony
en·rap·ture [ɪn'ræptʃə] wprawiać ⟨-wić⟩ w zachwyt; **~d** zachwycony
en·rich [ɪn'rɪtʃ] wzbogacać ⟨-cić⟩
en·rol(l) [ɪn'rəʊl] (***-ll-***) zapisywać ⟨-sać⟩ (się) (***for, in*** na *A*); (*na uniwersytet*) wstępować ⟨-tąpić⟩ (***at*** na *A*)
en·sign ['ensaɪn] *naut. zwł.* flaga *f*, bandera *f*; ['ensn] *Am.* podporucznik *m* marynarki
en·sue [ɪn'sjuː] następować ⟨-tąpić⟩
en·sure [ɪn'ʃʊə] zapewniać ⟨-nić⟩
en·tail [ɪn'teɪl] pociągać za sobą, wymagać
en·tan·gle [ɪn'tæŋgl] wplątywać ⟨-tać⟩
en·ter ['entə] *v/t.* wchodzić ⟨wejść⟩ do (*G*); wjeżdżać ⟨wjechać⟩ do (*G*); *naut.*, wpływać ⟨-łynąć⟩; wstępować ⟨-tąpić⟩ do (*G*); *nazwiska, dane* wprowadzać ⟨-dzić⟩; (*w sporcie*) przystępować ⟨-tąpić⟩ (***for*** do *G*); *v/i.* wchodzić ⟨wejść⟩; wjeżdżać ⟨wjechać⟩; *naut.*, wpływać ⟨-łynąć⟩ do portu; *theat.* wchodzić; zgłaszać ⟨-łosić⟩ się (***for*** do *G*) (*też w sporcie*); **'~ key** klawisz *m* Enter
en·ter|·prise ['entəpraɪz] przedsięwzięcie *n*; *econ.* przedsiębiorstwo *n*; przedsiębiorczość *f*; **'~·pris·ing** przedsiębiorczy
en·ter·tain [entə'teɪn] zabawiać ⟨-wić⟩; przyjmować ⟨-jąć⟩ (gości); **~·er** artysta *m* (-tka *f*) estradowy (-wa); **~·ment** rozrywka *f*; widowisko *n*; przyjmowanie *n* gości
en·thral(l) *fig.* [ɪn'θrɔːl] (***-ll-***) oczarowywać ⟨-wać⟩; ⟨za⟩fascynować
en·throne [ɪn'θrəʊn] intronizować
en·thu·si·as|·m [ɪn'θjuːzɪæzəm] entuzjazm *m*; **~t** [ɪn'θjuːzɪæst] entuzjasta *m* (-tka *f*); **~·tic** [ɪnθjuːzɪ'æstɪk] (***-ally***) entuzjastyczny
en·tice [ɪn'taɪs] ⟨z⟩nęcić, ⟨z⟩wabić; **~·ment** atrakcja *f*, powab *m*
en·tire [ɪn'taɪə] cały; niepodzielny, całkowity; **~·ly** całkowicie; w zupełności
en·ti·tle [ɪn'taɪtl] uprawniać ⟨-nić⟩ (***to*** do *G*)
en·ti·ty ['entətɪ] jednostka *f*
en·trails ['entreɪlz] *anat. pl.* wnętrzności *pl.*
en·trance ['entrəns] wejście *n*; pojawienie *n* się; wstęp *m*; ***make an ~*** zjawiać się; **'~ ex·am·(i·na·tion)** egzamin *m* wstępny; **'~ fee** opłata *f* za wejście; opłata *f* za wstęp
en·treat [ɪn'triːt] błagać; **en'trea·ty** błaganie *n*
en·trench [ɪn'trentʃ] *mil.* okopywać ⟨-pać⟩ się
en·trust [ɪn'trʌst] powierzać ⟨-rzyć⟩ (***s.th. to s.o.*** coś komuś)
en·try ['entrɪ] wejście *n*; wjazd *m*; wstęp *m* (***to*** do *G*); wjazd *m*, wlot *m*; (*w słowniku*) hasło *n*; (*w spisie*) pozycja *f*; (*w sporcie*) udział *m*; ***bookeeping by double (single) ~*** *econ.* podwójna (pojedyncza) księgowość *f*; ***no ~!*** wstęp wzbroniony; *mot.* brak wjazdu!; **'~ permit** pozwolenie *n* na wjazd; **'~·phone** domofon *m*; **'~ vi·sa** wiza *f* wjazdowa
en·twine [ɪn'twaɪn] oplatać ⟨-pleść⟩, splatać ⟨-pleść⟩
e·nu·me·rate [ɪ'njuːməreɪt] wyliczać ⟨-czyć⟩
en·vel·op [ɪn'veləp] owijać ⟨owinąć⟩, otaczać ⟨otoczyć⟩
en·ve·lope ['envələʊp] koperta *f*
en·vi|·a·ble ['envɪəbl] godny zazdrości; **'~·ous** zazdrosny
en·vi·ron·ment [ɪn'vaɪərənmənt] otoczenie *n*; środowisko *n*; środowisko *n* naturalne
en·vi·ron·men·tal [ɪnvaɪərən'mentl] środowiskowy; **~·ist** [ɪnvaɪərən'mentəlɪst] ekolog *m*; **~ 'law** prawo *n* ochrony środowiska; **~ pol'lu·tion** zanie-

czyszczanie *n* środowiska
en•vi•ron•ment 'friend•ly przyjazny dla środowiska
en•vi•rons ['envɪrənz] *pl.* okolice *pl.*
en•vis•age [ɪn'vɪzɪdʒ] przewidywać ⟨-idzieć⟩
en•voy ['envɔɪ] wysłannik *m* (-niczka *f*)
en•vy ['envɪ] **1.** zazdrość *f*; **2.** ⟨po⟩zazdrościć
ep•ic ['epɪk] **1.** epicki; **2.** epos *m*, epopeja *f*
ep•i•dem•ic [epɪ'demɪk] **1.** (**~*ally***) epidemiczny; **~ *disease*** → ***disease***; **2.** epidemia *f*, zaraza *f*
ep•i•der•mis [epɪ'dɜːmɪs] naskórek *m*
ep•i•lep•sy ['epɪlepsɪ] epilepsja *f*
ep•i•logue *zwł. Brt.*, **ep•i•log** *Am.* ['epɪlɔg] epilog *m*, posłowie *n*
e•pis•co•pal [ɪ'pɪskəpl] *rel.* biskupi
ep•i•sode ['epɪsəʊd] epizod *m*
ep•i•taph ['epɪtɑːf] epitafium *n*
e•poch ['iːpɒk] epoka *f*
eq•ua•ble ['ekwəbl] łagodny (*też klimat*)
e•qual ['iːkwəl] **1.** równy; jednakowy; ***be ~ to*** *fig.* móc podołać (*D*); **~ *rights*** *pl.* ***for women*** równe prawa *pl.* dla kobiet; **2.** równy *m*; **3.** (*zwł. Brt.* **-ll-**, *Am.* **-l-**) równać się z (*I*); **~•i•ty** [iː'kwɒlətɪ] równość *f*; **~•i•za•tion** [iːkwəlaɪ'zeɪʃn] wyrównywanie *n*; **~•ize** ['iːkwəlaɪz] wyrównywać ⟨-nać⟩, zrównywać ⟨-nać⟩; **'~•iz•er** gol *m* wyrównujący; *tech.* urządzenie *n* wyrównawcze
eq•ua•nim•i•ty [iːkwə'nɪmətɪ] równowaga *f*, opanowanie *n*
e•qua•tion [ɪ'kweɪʒn] *math.* równanie *n*
e•qua•tor [ɪ'kweɪtə] równik *m*
e•qui•lib•ri•um [iːkwɪ'lɪbrɪəm] równowaga *f*
e•quip [ɪ'kwɪp] (***-pp-***) wyposażać ⟨-żyć⟩; **~•ment** sprzęt *m*, wyposażenie *n*
e•quiv•a•lent [ɪ'kwɪvələnt] **1.** ekwiwalentny, równoważny; **2.** ekwiwalent *m*, odpowiednik *m*
e•ra ['ɪərə] era *f*
e•rad•i•cate [ɪ'rædɪkeɪt] wykorzeniać ⟨-nić⟩
e•rase [ɪ'reɪz] wymazywać ⟨-zać⟩; ⟨s⟩kasować (*też zapis magnetyczny*); *fig.* zmazywać ⟨-zać⟩; **e'ras•er** gumka *f*
e•rect [ɪ'rekt] **1.** wyprostowany; **2.** stawiać ⟨postawić⟩; *budynek* wznosić ⟨wznieść⟩; *maszynę itp.* ⟨z⟩montować;
e•rec•tion [ɪ'rekʃn] wznoszenie *n*; *physiol.* erekcja *f*, wzwód *m*
er•mine ['ɜːmɪn] *zo.* gronostaj *m*; *ubiór*: gronostaje *pl.*
e•rode [ɪ'rəʊd] *geol.* ⟨z⟩erodować;
e•ro•sion [ɪ'rəʊʒn] *geol.* erozja *f*
e•rot•ic [ɪ'rɒtɪk] (**~*ally***) erotyczny
err [ɜː] ⟨po⟩mylić (się)
er•rand ['erənd] zlecenie *n*, polecenie *n*; ***go on an ~, run an ~*** załatwiać sprawy; **'~ boy** chłopiec *m* na posyłki
er•rat•ic [ɪ'rætɪk] zmienny; *ruchy*: nieskoordynowany
er•ro•ne•ous [ɪ'rəʊnjəs] błędny
er•ror ['erə] błąd *m* (*też komp.*); ***~s excepted*** z zastrzeżeniem błędów; **'~ mes•sage** *komp.* komunikat *m* o błędzie
e•rupt [ɪ'rʌpt] *wulkan itp.*: wybuchać ⟨-chnąć⟩; *ząb*: wyrzynać ⟨-rżnąć⟩ się; **e•rup•tion** [ɪ'rʌpʃn] wybuch *m* (*wulkanu*); *med.* wyrzynanie *n* się (*zęba*)
ESA [iː es 'eɪ] *skrót*: ***European Space Agency*** Europejska Agencja *f* Przestrzeni Kosmicznej
es•ca|•late ['eskəleɪt] nasilać ⟨-lić⟩ (się); doprowadzać ⟨-dzić⟩ do eskalacji; **~•la•tion** [eskə'leɪʃn] eskalacja *f*
es•ca•la•tor ['eskəleɪtə] schody *pl.* ruchome
es•ca•lope ['eskələʊp] *gastr.* kotlet *m*, eskalopek *m* (*zwł. cielęcy*)
es•cape [ɪ'skeɪp] **1.** uciekać ⟨uciec⟩; zbiec; *gaz*: ulatniać ⟨-lotnić⟩ się; *woda itp.*: przeciekać ⟨-ciec⟩; unikać ⟨-knąć⟩; *komuś* umykać ⟨umknąć⟩; **2.** ucieczka *f*; ulatnianie *n* się; przeciek *m*; ***have a narrow ~*** ledwie ujść cało; **~ chute** *aviat.* ślizg *m* ratunkowy; **~ key** *komp.* klawisz *m* Escape
es•cort **1.** ['eskɔːt] *mil.* eskorta *f*; obstawa *f*; konwój *m*; osoba *f* towarzysząca; **2.** [ɪ'skɔːt] *mil.* eskortować; *aviat.*, *naut.* konwojować; towarzyszyć
es•cutch•eon [ɪ'skʌtʃən] tarcza *f* herbowa
esp. *skrót pisany*: ***especially*** zwł., zwłaszcza
es•pe•cial [ɪ'speʃl] szczególny; **~•ly** szczególnie
es•pi•o•nage [espɪə'nɑːʒ] szpiegostwo *n*
es•pla•nade [esplə'neɪd] promenada *f* (*zwł. nad brzegiem*)

E

es·say ['eseɪ] esej *m*; wypracowanie *n*
es·sence ['esns] istota *f*; esencja *f*
es·sen·tial [ɪ'senʃl] **1.** istotny; niezbędny; **2.** *zw.* **~s** *pl.* najistotniejsze rzeczy *pl.*; **~·ly** zasadniczo, właściwie
es·tab·lish [ɪ'stæblɪʃ] ustanawiać ⟨-nowić⟩; zakładać ⟨założyć⟩; **~ *o.s.*** osiedlać ⟨-lić⟩ się; obejmować ⟨objąć⟩ stanowisko; ustalać ⟨-lić⟩; **~·ment** założenie *n*, ustanowienie *n*; *econ.* przedsiębiorstwo *n*, firma *f*; ***the* ℒ*ment*** establishment *m*, warstwa *f* panująca
es·tate [ɪ'steɪt] posiadłość *f*, majątek *m* (*ziemski*); *jur.* majątek *m*, mienie *n*; ***housing* ~** *Brt.* osiedle *n* mieszkaniowe; ***industrial* ~** dzielnica *f* przemysłowa; ***real* ~** nieruchomości *pl.*; **~ a·gent** *Brt.* pośrednik *m* w handlu nieruchomościami; **~ car** *Brt. mot.* kombi *n*
es·teem [ɪ'sti:m] **1.** szacunek *m*, poważanie *n* (***with*** wśród *G*); **2.** poważać, darzyć szacunkiem
es·thet·ic(s) [es'θetɪk(s)] *Am.* → ***aesthetic*(*s*)**
es·ti|·mate 1. ['estɪmeɪt] oceniać ⟨-nić⟩, ⟨o⟩szacować; **2.** ['estɪmɪt] oszacowanie *n*; kosztorys *m*; **~·ma·tion** [estɪ'meɪʃn] zdanie *n*; oszacowanie *n*
Es·to·nia Estonia *f*
es·trange [ɪ'streɪndʒ] zrażać ⟨zrazić⟩
es·tu·a·ry ['estjʊərɪ] ujście *n*
etch [etʃ] rytować; wytrawiać ⟨-wić⟩; *fig.* ⟨wy⟩ryć; '**~·ing** rycina *f*; miedzioryt *m*
e·ter|·nal [ɪ'tɜ:nl] wieczny; **~·ni·ty** [ɪ'tɜ:nətɪ] wieczność *f*
e·ther ['i:θə] eter *m*; **e·the·re·al** [i:'θɪərɪəl] eteryczny (*też fig.*)
eth|·i·cal ['eθɪkl] etyczny; **~·ics** ['eθɪks] *sg.* etyka *f*
EU [i: 'ju:] *skrót*: ***European Union*** Unia *f* Europejska
Eu·ro... ['jʊərəʊ] Euro..., europejski; '**~·cheque** *Brt.* euroczek *m*
Eu·rope ['jʊərəp] Europa *f*; **Eu·ro·pe·an** [jʊərə'pi:ən] europejski *m*; **Eu·ro·pe·an Com'mu·ni·ty** (*skrót*: ***EC***) Wspólnota *f* Europejska
e·vac·u·ate [ɪ'vækjʊeɪt] ewakuować, dokonywać ⟨-nać⟩ ewakuacji
e·vade [ɪ'veɪd] unikać ⟨-knąć⟩; uchylać ⟨-lić⟩ się od (*G*); uchodzić ⟨ujść⟩ przed (*I*)
e·val·u·ate [ɪ'væljʊeɪt] oceniać ⟨-nić⟩; ⟨o⟩szacować
e·vap·o|·rate [ɪ'væpəreɪt] parować; odparowywać ⟨-ować⟩; znikać ⟨-knąć⟩; ***~rated milk*** mleko *n* skondensowane (*niesłodzone*); **~·ra·tion** [ɪvæpə'reɪʃn] parowanie *n*; odparowanie *n*
e·va|·sion [ɪ'veɪʒn] unikanie *n*, uchylanie się *n*; wymówka *f*; **~·sive** [ɪ'veɪsɪv] wymijający; ***be ~sive*** unikać ⟨-knąć⟩
eve [i:v] przeddzień *m*; wigilia *f*; ***on the ~ of*** w przededniu (*G*)
e·ven ['i:vn] **1.** *adj.* równy; gładki; *liczba*: parzysty; regularny, równomierny; ***get ~ with s.o.*** odpłacać się komuś; **2.** *adv.* nawet; ***not ~*** nawet nie; ***~ though, ~ if*** nawet jeśli; **3. *~ out*** zrównywać ⟨-wnać⟩, wyrównywać ⟨-wnać⟩ (się)
eve·ning ['i:vnɪŋ] wieczór *m*; ***in the ~*** wieczorem; '**~ class·es** *pl.* kurs *m* wieczorowy; '**~ dress** strój *m* wieczorowy; smoking *m*, frak *m*, suknia *f* wieczorowa
e·ven·song ['i:vnsɒŋ] nabożeństwo *n* wieczorne (*w kościele anglikańskim*)
e·vent [ɪ'vent] zdarzenie *n*, wydarzenie *n*; (*w sporcie*) konkurencja *f*, dyscyplina *f*; ***at all ~s*** w każdym razie; ***in the ~ of*** w przypadku (*G*); **~·ful** obfitujący w wydarzenia
e·ven·tu·al [ɪ'ventʃʊəl] ostateczny; ⚠ *nie* ***ewentualny***; **~·ly** ostatecznie
ev·er ['evə] zawsze; kiedykolwiek; ***~ after, ~ since*** od tego czasu; ***~ so*** F bardzo; ***for ~*** na zawsze; ***Yours ~, ..., ℒ yours ...*** (*w liście*) Pozdrowienia, Twój; Pański; ***have you ~ been to Poland?*** czy byłeś kiedyś w Polsce?; '**~·green 1.** wiecznozielony; zimozielony; nie do zdarcia, *zwł.* zawsze przyjemny do słuchania; **2.** roślina *f* zimozielona; **~'last·ing** wieczny; **~'more: (*for*) ~** na zawsze
ev·ery ['evrɪ] każdy; wszyscy *pl.*, wszystkie *pl.*; ***~ now and then*** od czasu do czasu; ***~ one of them*** każdy z nich; ***~ other day*** co drugi dzień; '**~·bod·y** każdy; '**~·day** codziennie; '**~·one** każdy, wszyscy *pl.*; '**~·thing** wszystko; '**~·where** wszędzie
e·vict [ɪ'vɪkt] *jur.* ⟨wy⟩eksmitować; *majątek* odzyskiwać ⟨-kać⟩
ev·i|·dence ['evɪdəns] dowód *m*, dowody *pl.*; zeznania *pl.*; ***give ~ence*** świadczyć; '**~·dent** oczywisty

e•vil ['iːvl] **1.** (*zwł. Brt.* **-ll-**, *Am.* **-l-**) zły, niedobry; paskudny; **2.** zło *n*; **~-'mind•ed** złośliwy
e•voke [ɪ'vəʊk] wywoływać ⟨-łać⟩
ev•o•lu•tion [iːvə'luːʃn] ewolucja *f*, rozwój *m*
e•volve [ɪ'vɒlv] rozwijać ⟨-winąć⟩ się
ewe [juː] *zo.* (*samica*) owca *f*
ex [eks] *prp. econ.* loco, loko; **~ *works*** loco fabryka
ex... [eks] eks..., były ...
ex•act [ɪg'zækt] **1.** dokładny, ścisły; **2.** wymuszać ⟨-music⟩, ⟨wy⟩egzekwować; **~•ing** wymagający; uciążliwy; **~•ly** dokładnie; (*w odpowiedzi*) właśnie (tak); **~•ness** dokładność *f*
ex•ag•ge|•rate [ɪg'zædʒəreɪt] przesadzać ⟨-dzić⟩; **~•ra•tion** [ɪgzædʒə'reɪʃn] przesada *f*
ex•am [ɪg'zæm] F egzamin *m*
ex•am|•i•na•tion [ɪgzæmɪ'neɪʃn] egzamin *m*; badanie *n*; *jur.* przesłuchanie *n*, śledztwo *n*; **~•ine** [ɪg'zæmɪn] badać; sprawdzać ⟨-dzić⟩; *szkoła itp.*: ⟨prze⟩egzaminować (***in, on*** w zakresie *G*); *jur.* przesłuchiwać ⟨-chać⟩, przeprowadzać ⟨-dzić⟩ śledztwo;
ex•am•ple [ɪg'zɑːmpl] przykład *m*; wzorzec *m*, wzór *m*; ***for ~*** dla przykładu, na przykład
ex•as•pe|•rate [ɪg'zæspəreɪt] doprowadzać ⟨-dzić⟩ do rozpaczy; **~•rat•ing** doprowadzający do rozpaczy
ex•ca•vate ['ekskəveɪt] *v/t.* wykopywać ⟨-pać⟩; *v/i.* prowadzić wykopaliska
ex•ceed [ɪk'siːd] przekraczać ⟨-roczyć⟩; przewyższać ⟨-szyć⟩; **~•ing** nadmierny; **~•ing•ly** nadmiernie
ex•cel [ɪk'sel] *v/t.* przewyższać ⟨-szyć⟩; *wyobrażenie itp.* przechodzić ⟨-ejść⟩; *v/i.* wyróżniać ⟨-nić⟩ się, celować; **~•lence** ['eksələns] doskonałość *f*, świetność *f*; **Ex•cel•lency** ['eksələnsɪ] ekscelencja *f/m*; **ex•cel•lent** ['eksələnt] doskonały, świetny
ex•cept [ɪk'sept] **1.** wykluczać ⟨-czyć⟩, wyłączyć ⟨-czać⟩; **2.** *prp.* oprócz, poza; **~ *for*** z wyjątkiem (*G*); **~•ing** z wyjątkiem, wyłączając
ex•cep•tion [ɪk'sepʃn] wyjątek *m*; uraza *f* (***to do*** *G*); ***make an ~*** robić wyjątek; ***take ~ to*** obruszać ⟨-szyć⟩ się na (*A*); ***without ~*** bez wyjątku; **~•al** [ɪk'sepʃənl] wyjątkowy; **~•al•ly** [ɪk'sepʃnəlɪ] wyjątkowo
ex•cerpt ['eksɜːpt] wyjątek *m*; urywek *m*
ex•cess [ɪk'ses] nadmiar *m*, nadwyżka *f*; dopłata *f*; **~ 'bag•gage** *aviat.* bagaż *m* dodatkowy; **~ 'fare** dopłata *f* za przejazd; **ex'ces•sive** nadmierny; **~ 'lug•gage** → ***excess baggage***; **~ 'post•age** dopłata *f*
ex•change [ɪks'tʃeɪndʒ] **1.** wymieniać ⟨-nić⟩ (***for*** za); **2.** wymiana *f* (*też pieniędzy*); ***bill of ~*** weksel *m*; giełda *f*; kantor *m* wymiany walut; centrala *f* telefoniczna; ***foreign ~*(*s*** *pl.*) dewizy *pl.*; ***rate of ~*** → ***exchange rate***; **~ of•fice** kantor *m* wymiany walut; **~ pu•pil** uczeń *m* (*uczennica f*) w ramach programu wymiany; **~ rate** kurs *m* wymiany; **~ stu•dent** student *m* (*studentka f*) w ramach programu wymiany; *Am.* uczeń *m* (*uczennica f*) w ramach programu wymiany
Ex•cheq•uer [ɪks'tʃekə]: ***Chancellor of the ~*** *Brt.* Minister Skarbu
ex•cise [ek'saɪz] akcyza *f*, opłata *f* akcyzowa
ex•ci•ta•ble [ɪk'saɪtəbl] łatwo się irytujący *lub* ekscytujący
ex•cite [ɪk'saɪt] ⟨pod⟩ekscytować; podniecać ⟨-cić⟩; pobudzać ⟨-dzić⟩; **ex'cit•ed** podekscytowany; podniecony; **ex'citement** ekscytacja *f*; podniecenie *n*; **ex'cit•ing** ekscytujący; podniecający
ex•claim [ɪk'skleɪm] wykrzykiwać ⟨-nąć⟩
ex•cla•ma•tion [eksklə'meɪʃn] wykrzyknięcie *n*, okrzyk *m*; **~ mark** *Brt.*, **~ point** *Am.* wykrzyknik *m*
ex•clude [ɪk'skluːd] wyłączać ⟨-czyć⟩; wykluczać ⟨-czyć⟩
ex•clu|•sion [ɪk'skluːʒn] wyłączenie *n*, wykluczenie *n*; **~•sive** [ɪk'skluːsɪv] wyłączny; ekskluzywny; ***~sive of*** z wyłączeniem (*G*)
ex•com•mu•ni|•cate [ekskə'mjuːnɪkeɪt] *rel.* ekskomunikować; **~•ca•tion** [ekskəmjuːnɪ'keɪʃn] *rel.* ekskomunika *f*
ex•cre•ment ['ekskrɪmənt] *physiol.* ekskrementy *pl.*, odchody *pl.*
ex•crete [ek'skriːt] *physiol.* wydzielać ⟨-lić⟩
ex•cur•sion [ɪk'skɜːʃn] wycieczka *f*, wyprawa *f*

E

E

ex•cu•sa•ble [ɪk'skju:zəbl] wybaczalny, do wybaczenia; **ex•cuse 1.** [ɪk'skju:z] ⟨wy⟩tłumaczyć; usprawiedliwiać ⟨-wić⟩; wybaczać ⟨-czyć⟩; przepraszać ⟨-rosić⟩; zwalniać ⟨zwolnić⟩ (***from*** z *I*); *~ **me*** przepraszam; **2.** [ɪk'skju:s] usprawiedliwienie *n*, wytłumaczenie *n*; wymówka *f*
ex-di•rec•to•ry num•ber [eksdɪ'rektərɪ -] *Brt. tel.* numer *m* zastrzeżony
ex•e|•cute ['eksɪkju:t] wykonywać ⟨-nać⟩; *skazańca* ⟨s⟩tracić; przeprowadzać ⟨-dzić⟩; **~•cu•tion** [eksɪ'kju:ʃn] wykonanie *n*; egzekucja *f*, stracenie *n*; *jur.* egzekucja *f* sądowa; ***put** lub **carry a plan into ~cution*** realizować *lub* wprowadzać w życie plan; **~•cu•tion•er** [eksɪ'kju:ʃnə] kat *m*
ex•ec•u•tive [ɪg'zekjʊtɪv] **1.** wykonawczy; *econ.* kierowniczy, dyrektorski; **2.** *pol.* egzekutywa *f*, organ *m* wykonawczy; *econ.* dyrektor *m*, kierownik *m*
ex•em•pla•ry [ɪg'zemplərɪ] przykładowy, wzorcowy
ex•em•pli•fy [ɪg'zemplɪfaɪ] służyć jako przykład, stanowić przykład; egzemplifikować
ex•empt [ɪg'zempt] **1.** wolny, zwolniony; **2.** uwalniać ⟨uwolnić⟩, zwalniać ⟨zwolnić⟩
ex•er•cise ['eksəsaɪz] **1.** ćwiczenie *n* (*też w szkole*); ćwiczenia *pl.* fizyczne, ruch *m*; *mil.* manewry *pl.*, ćwiczenia *pl.*; ***do one's ~s*** gimnastykować się; ***take ~*** zażywać ruchu, ruszać się; **2.** ćwiczyć; ruszać się; ⟨s⟩korzystać z (*G*); *mil.* przeprowadzać ⟨-dzić⟩ manewry; **'~ book** zeszyt *m*
ex•ert [ɪg'zɜ:t] *wpływ itp.* wywierać ⟨wywrzeć⟩; ***~ o.s.*** wysilać ⟨-lić⟩ się; **ex•er•tion** [ɪg'zɜ:ʃn] wywieranie *n* (*wpływu*); wysiłek *m*, trud *m*
ex•hale [eks'heɪl] wydychać; *dym* wydmuchiwać ⟨-chać⟩, wypuszczać ⟨-puścić⟩
ex•haust [ɪg'zɔ:st] **1.** wyczerpywać ⟨-pać⟩; **2.** *tech.* rura *f* wydechowa; *też **~ fumes*** *pl.* spaliny *pl.*; **~•ed** wyczerpany; zmęczony; **ex•haus•tion** [ɪg'zɔ:stʃən] wyczerpanie *n*; **ex•haus•tive** wyczerpujący; **~ pipe** rura *f* wydechowa
ex•hib•it [ɪg'zɪbɪt] **1.** wystawiać ⟨-wić⟩; *fig.* ukazywać ⟨-zać⟩; ⟨za⟩demonstrować; **2.** eksponat *m*; *jur.* dowód *m* rzeczowy; **ex•hi•bi•tion** [eksɪ'bɪʃn] wystawa *f*; demonstracja *f*
ex•hil•a•rat•ing [ɪg'zɪləreɪtɪŋ] radosny; *wiatr itp.*: odświeżający
ex•hort [ɪg'zɔ:t] nawoływać
ex•ile ['eksaɪl] **1.** wygnanie *n*; emigracja *f*; emigrant(ka *f*) *m*, wygnaniec *m*; ***in ~*** na emigracji *lub* wygnaniu; **2.** skazywać ⟨-zać⟩ na wygnanie
ex•ist [ɪg'zɪst] istnieć; egzystować, żyć; **~•ence** istnienie *n*; egzystencja *f*; **~•ent** istniejący
ex•it ['eksɪt] **1.** wyjście *n*; zjazd *m* (*z drogi*); **2.** *theat.* wychodzić
ex•o•dus ['eksədəs] exodus *m*; ***general ~*** ogólna ucieczka *f*
ex•on•e•rate [ɪg'zɒnəreɪt] uwalniać ⟨uwolnić⟩, zwalniać ⟨zwolnić⟩
ex•or•bi•tant [ɪg'zɔ:bɪtənt] wygórowany, nadmierny
ex•or•cize ['eksɔ:saɪz] wypędzać ⟨-dzić⟩ (***from*** z *G*); egzorcyzmować; uwalniać ⟨-wolnić⟩ (***of*** od *G*)
ex•ot•ic [ɪg'zɒtɪk] (***~ally***) egzotyczny
ex•pand [ɪk'spænd] rozszerzać ⟨-rzyć⟩ (się); omawiać ⟨-mówić⟩ szczegółowo; *econ.* powiększać ⟨-szyć⟩ (się), rozszerzać ⟨-rzyć⟩ (się); **ex•panse** [ɪk'spæns] przestrzeń *f*, przestwór *m*; **ex•pan•sion** [ɪk'spænʃn] ekspansja *f*; rozszerzanie *n* się; **ex•pan•sive** [ɪk'spænsɪv] ekspansywny
ex•pat•ri•ate [eks'pætrɪeɪt] **1.** emigrant(ka *f*) *m*; **2.** *kogoś* skazywać ⟨-zać⟩ na wygnanie; *kogoś* pozbawiać ⟨-wić⟩ obywatelstwa
ex•pect [ɪk'spekt] spodziewać się; oczekiwać, przypuszczać; ***be ~ing (a baby)*** spodziewać się dziecka; **ex•pec•tant** pełen oczekiwania; ***~ mother*** przyszła matka *f*; **ex•pec•ta•tion** [ekspek'teɪʃn] oczekiwanie *n*; nadzieja *f*
ex•pe•dient [ɪk'spi:djənt] **1.** celowy; **2.** sposób *m*, środek *m* (*zwł. doraźny*)
ex•pe•di|•tion [ekspɪ'dɪʃn] ekspedycja *f*, wyprawa *f*; **~•tious** [ekspɪ'dɪʃəs] szybki
ex•pel [ɪk'spel] (**-ll-**) (***from***) usuwać ⟨-sunąć⟩ (z *G*); wydalać ⟨-lić⟩ (z *G*); wyrzucać ⟨-cić⟩ (z *G*)
ex•pen•di•ture [ɪk'spendɪtʃə] wydatek *m*; *econ.* koszty *pl.*, wydatki *pl.*
ex•pense [ɪk'spens] wydatek *m*; ***at the ~ of*** na koszt (*G*); **ex'pen•ses** koszty

pl., wydatki *pl.*; **ex'pen•sive** drogi
ex•pe•ri•ence [ɪk'spɪərɪəns] **1.** doświadczenie *n*; przeżycie *n*; **2.** doświadczać ⟨-czyć⟩, przeżywać ⟨-żyć⟩; **~d** doświadczony
ex•per•i|•ment **1.** [ɪk'sperɪmənt] doświadczenie *n*; **2.** [ɪk'sperɪment] eksperymentować; **~•men•tal** [eksperɪ'mentl] eksperymentalny
ex•pert ['ekspɜːt] **1.** specjalistyczny; doświadczony; *komp.* ekspercki; **2.** ekspert *m*; specjalista *m* (-tka *f*)
ex•pi•ra•tion [ekspɪ'reɪʃn] upłynięcie *n*, koniec *m*; wygaśnięcie *n*; **ex•pire** [ɪk'spaɪə] upływać ⟨-łynąć⟩, ⟨s⟩kończyć się; wygasać ⟨-snąć⟩
ex•plain [ɪk'spleɪn] wyjaśniać ⟨-nić⟩; **ex•pla•na•tion** [ekspləˈneɪʃn] wyjaśnienie *n*
ex•pli•cit [ɪk'splɪsɪt] jasny; wyraźny; (***sexually***) **~** *film itp.*: (*pokazujący seks bez ogródek*)
ex•plode [ɪk'spləʊd] wybuchać ⟨-chnąć⟩, eksplodować; *bombę itp.* ⟨z⟩detonować; *fig.* wybuchać ⟨-chnąć⟩; *fig. teorię itp.* obalać ⟨-lić⟩; *fig.* rozwijać ⟨-winąć⟩ się gwałtownie
ex•ploit **1.** ['eksplɔɪt] wyczyn *m* (*bohaterski*); **2.** [ɪk'splɔɪt] ⟨wy⟩eksploatować; **ex•ploi•ta•tion** [eksplɔɪ'teɪʃn] eksploatacja *f*, wykorzystywanie *n*
ex•plo•ra•tion [ekspləˈreɪʃn] badanie *n*, eksploracja *f*; **ex•plore** [ɪk'splɔː] ⟨z⟩badać, eksplorować; **ex•plor•er** [ɪk'splɔːrə] eksplorator *m*, badacz(ka *f*) *m*
ex•plo|•sion [ɪk'spləʊʒn] eksplozja *f*, wybuch *m*; *fig.* wybuch *m*; *fig.* gwałtowny rozwój *m*; **~•sive** [ɪk'spləʊsɪv] **1.** wybuchowy (*też fig.*); rozwijający się gwałtownie; **2.** środek *m* wybuchowy
ex•po•nent [ek'spəʊnənt] *math.* wykładnik *m*, eksponent *m*
ex•port **1.** [ɪk'spɔːt] ⟨wy⟩eksportować; **2.** ['ekspɔːt] eksport *m*; artykuł *m* eksportowy; **ex•por•ta•tion** [ekspɔː'teɪʃn] eksport *m*; **ex•port•er** [ɪk'spɔːtə] eksporter *m*
ex•pose [ɪk'spəʊz] odsłaniać ⟨-łonić⟩; wystawiać ⟨-wić⟩; *phot.* naświetlać ⟨-lić⟩; *towary* ⟨wy⟩eksponować; *kogoś* ⟨z⟩demaskować; *coś* wyjawiać ⟨-wić⟩; **ex•po•si•tion** [ekspəˈzɪʃn] ekspozycja *f*; przedstawienie *n*
ex•po•sure [ɪk'spəʊʒə] odsłonięcie *n*; wystawienie *n* (*na czynniki zewnętrzne*) (***to*** na *A*); *phot.* naświetlanie *n*; *phot.* klatka *f*; ***die of ~*** umrzeć z zimna; **~ me•ter** *phot.* światłomierz *m*
ex•press [ɪk'spres] **1.** jawny, wyraźny; ekspresowy; **2.** ekspres *m*; ***go by ~*** jechać ekspresem **3.** *adv.* ekpresem; **4.** wyrażać ⟨-razić⟩; **ex•pres•sion** [ɪk'spreʃn] wyrażenie *n*; **ex'pres•sion•less** bez wyrazu; **ex•pres•sive** [ɪk'spresɪv] wyrazisty; ***be ~ of*** *coś* wyrażać ⟨-razić⟩; **ex•press 'let•ter** *Brt.* przesyłka *f* ekspresowa; **ex•press•ly** wyraźnie, jawnie; ekspres *m*; **ex•press•way** *zwł. Am.* droga *f* szybkiego ruchu
ex•pro•pri•ate *jur.* [eks'prəʊprɪeɪt] wywłaszczać ⟨-czyć⟩, ⟨s⟩konfiskować
ex•pul•sion [ɪk'spʌlʃn] (***from***) wypędzenie (z *G*), wydalenie (z *G*)
ex•pur•gate ['ekspɜːgeɪt] ⟨o⟩czyścić, usuwać ⟨usunąć⟩
ex•qui•site ['ekskwɪzɪt] wyborny; znakomity; wspaniały
ex•tant [ek'stænt] wciąż istniejący *lub* żyjący
ex•tend [ɪk'stend] *v/i.* rozciągać ⟨-nąć⟩ się; ciągnąć się; *v/t.* przedłużać ⟨-żyć⟩; *fabrykę* powiększać ⟨-szyć⟩; rozciągać ⟨-gnąć⟩; *rękę itp.* wyciągać ⟨-gnąć⟩; *podziękowania itp.* ⟨s⟩kierować; **~•ed 'fam•i•ly** wielopokoleniowa rodzina *f*
ex•ten|•sion [ɪk'stenʃn] przedłużenie *n*; powiększenie *n*; rozszerzenie *n*; *arch.* przybudówka *f*, rozbudowa *f*; *tel.* wewnętrzny (*numer*) *m*; telefon *m* wewnętrzny; *też* ***~sion lead*** (*Am.* ***cord***) *electr.* przedłużacz *m*; **~•sive** rozległy, obszerny
ex•tent [ɪk'stent] rozciągłość *f*; rozmiar *m*; zakres *m*; stopień *m*; ***to some ~, to a certain ~*** w pewnym stopniu; ***to such an ~ that*** do tego stopnia, że
ex•ten•u•ate [ek'stenjʊeɪt] ⟨z⟩łagodzić, zmniejszać ⟨-szyć⟩; ***extenuating circumstances*** *pl. jur.* okoliczności *pl.* łagodzące
ex•te•ri•or [ek'stɪərɪə] **1.** zewnętrzny; **2.** strona *f* zewnętrzna; powierzchowność *f*
ex•ter•mi•nate [ek'stɜːmɪneɪt] eksterminować; ⟨wy⟩tępić, ⟨wy⟩niszczyć
ex•ter•nal [ek'stɜːnl] zewnętrzny
ex•tinct [ɪk'stɪŋkt] wymarły; wygasły;

E

ex·tinc·tion [ɪk'stɪŋkʃn] wymarcie *n*; wyginięcie *n*; wygaśnięcie *n*
ex·tin·guish [ɪk'stɪŋgwɪʃ] ⟨u⟩gasić; *fig.* zagasić; ⟨wy⟩niszczyć; ~**·er** gaśnica *f*
ex·tort [ɪk'stɔːt] wymuszać ⟨-sić⟩
ex·tra ['ekstrə] **1.** *adj.* dodatkowy, ekstra; ***be ~*** być osobno liczonym; **2.** *adv.* ekstra, osobno; ***charge ~ for*** liczyć dodatkowo za (*A*); **3.** dopłata *f*; coś *n* ekstra; *zwł. mot.* dodatek *m*; *theat.*, (*w filmie*) statysta *m* (-tka *f*)
ex·tract 1. ['ekstrækt] ekstrakt *m*, wyciąg *m*; wyciąg *m*, wypis *m*; fragment *m*; **2.** [ɪk'strækt] wyciągać ⟨-gnąć⟩; *ząb itp.* usuwać ⟨-unąć⟩; uzyskiwać ⟨-skać⟩; *fig.* wydobywać ⟨-być⟩; *chem.* ekstrahować; **ex·trac·tion** [ɪk'strækʃn] wyciąganie *n*; ekstrakcja *f*, usuwanie *n*; ekstrahowanie *n*; wydobywanie *n*; pochodzenie *n*
ex·tra|·dite ['ekstrədaɪt] dokonywać ⟨-nać⟩ ekstradycji, wydalać ⟨-lić⟩; ~**·di·tion** [ekstrə'dɪʃn] ekstradycja *f*, wydalenie *n*
extra·or·di·na·ry [ɪk'strɔːdnrɪ] nadzwyczajny; niezwykły
ex·tra 'pay dodatek *m* (pieniężny)
ex·tra·ter·res·tri·al [ekstrətə'restrɪəl] pozaziemski
ex·tra 'time *sport*: dogrywka *f*
ex·trav·a|·gance [ɪk'strævəgəns] rozrzutność *f*, marnotrastwo *n*; ekstrawagancja *f*, ekscentryczność *f*; ~**·gant** rozrzutny, marnotrawny; ekstrawagancki, ekscentryczny
ex·treme [ɪk'striːm] **1.** skrajny; ekstremalny; najdalszy; największy; ***~ right*** skrajnie prawicowy; ***~ right wing*** skrajne skrzydło *n* prawicowe; **2.** skrajność *f*, krańcowość *f*; ostateczność *f*; ~**·ly** skrajnie, ekstremalnie; krańcowo
ex·trem|·is·m [ɪk'striːmɪzm] *zwł. pol.* ekstremizm *m*; ~**·ist** [ɪk'striːmɪst] ekstremista *m* (-tka *f*)
ex·trem·i·ties [ɪk'stremətɪz] *pl.* skrajności *pl.*; kończyny *pl.*
ex·trem·i·ty [ɪk'stremətɪ] skrajność *f*; ostateczność *f*; sytuacja *f* krytyczna
ex·tri·cate ['ekstrɪkeɪt] wyplątywać ⟨-tać⟩; oswobadzać ⟨-bodzić⟩
ex·tro·vert ['ekstrəʊvɜːt] ekstrawertyk *m* (-yczka *f*)
ex·u·be|·rance [ɪg'zjuːbərəns] euforia *f*; bujność *f*; ~**·rant** euforyczny, pełen euforii; bujny
ex·ult [ɪg'zʌlt] radować się (***at*** *I*)
eye [aɪ] oko *n*; oczko *n* (*na ziemniaku itp.*); ucho *n* (*igły*); uszko *n* (*w haftce*); ***see ~ to ~ with s.o.*** zgadzać się z kimś całkowicie; ***be up to the ~s in work*** mieć roboty po uszy; ***with an ~ to s.th.*** ze względu na coś; **2.** ⟨z⟩mierzyć wzrokiem; przypatrywać się (*D*); '~**·ball** gałka *f* oczna; '~**·brow** brew *f*; '~**-catch·ing** chwytający oko; ~**d** ...oczny; '~ **doc·tor** F okulista *m* (-tka *f*); '~**·glass·es** *pl.*, *też* ***a pair of ~glasses*** okulary *pl.*; '~**·lash** rzęsa *f*; '~**·lid** powieka *f*; '~**·lin·er** ołówek *m* do brwi; '~**-o·pen·er**: ***that was an ~opener to me*** to mi całkowicie oczy otworzyło; '~ **shad·ow** cień *m* do powiek; '~**·sight** wzrok *m*; '~**·sore** F okropieństwo *n*; ***be an ~sore*** kłuć w oczy; '~ **spe·cial·ist** okulista *m* (-tka *f*); '~**·strain** zmęczenie *n* oczu; '~**·wit·ness** naoczny świadek *m*

F

F, [ef] F, f *n*
F *skrót pisany*: ***Fahrenheit*** F, Fahrenheita (*skala termometru*)
FA [ef 'eɪ] *Brt. skrót*: ***Football Association*** Związek *m* Piłki Nożnej
fa·ble ['feɪbl] bajka *f*; legenda *f*
fab|·ric ['fæbrɪk] materiał *m*, tkanina *f*; struktura *f*; materia *f*; ⚠ *nie* ***fabryka***; ~**·ri·cate** ['fæbrɪkeɪt] ⟨s⟩fabrykować (*też fig.*)
fab·u·lous ['fæbjʊləs] kapitalny; bajeczny; bajkowy
fa·cade, fa·çade [fə'sɑːd] *arch.* fasada *f*
face [feɪs] **1.** twarz *f*; mina *f*; powierzchnia *f*; cyferblat *m*, tarcza *f*; front *m*, strona *f lub* ściana *f* przednia; ***~ to ~ with*** oko w oko z (*I*); ***save*** *lub* ***lose one's ~*** zachować *lub* stracić twarz; ***on the ~ of it*** na pierwszy rzut oka;

pull a long ~ zrobić cierpką minę; ***have the ~ to do s.th.*** mieć czelność coś zrobić; **2.** *v/t.* zwracać ⟨-rócić⟩ się przodem do (*G*); wychodzić na (*A*); stawiać ⟨-wić⟩ czoło (*D*); stawać ⟨stanąć⟩ wobec (*G*); *arch.* licować, okładać; *v/i.* ***~ about*** obracać ⟨-rócić⟩ się (*w tył*); **'~·cloth** ściereczka *f* do mycia twarzy; **~d**: ***stony-~d*** o kamiennej twarzy; **'~ flan·nel** *Brt.* → ***facecloth***; **~-lift** lifting *m*, face lifting *m*; *fig.* renowacja *f*, odnowienie *n*

fa·ce·tious [fə'siːʃəs] zabawny; dowcipny

fa·cial ['feɪʃl] **1.** *wyraz, rysy itp.*: twarzy; do twarzy; **2.** zabieg *m* kosmetyczny twarzy

fa·cile ['fæsaɪl] płytki; pusty

fa·cil·i·tate [fə'sɪlɪteɪt] ułatwiać ⟨-wić⟩

fa·cil·i·ty [fə'sɪlətɪ] łatwość *f*; łatwość *f* uczenia się; prostota *f*; opcja *f*, funkcja *f*; ***facilities*** *pl.* udogodnienia *pl.*, urządzenia *pl.*

fac·ing ['feisɪŋ] *tech.* okładzina *f*; lamówka *f* (*przy ubraniu*)

fact [fækt] fakt *m*; rzeczywistość *f*; ***in ~*** faktycznie, w rzeczywistości; ***~s*** *pl.*, *jur.* okoliczności *pl.*;

fac·tion ['fækʃn] *zwł. pol.* frakcja *f*, odłam *m*

fac·ti·tious [fæk'tɪʃəs] sztuczny

fac·tor ['fæktə] czynnik *m*; element *m*; *math.* współczynnik *m*

fac·to·ry ['fæktrɪ] fabryka *f*

fac·ul·ty ['fækəltɪ] zdolność *f*, umiejętność *f*; *fig.* dar *m*; *univ.* wydział *m*; *Am.* grono *n* nauczycielskie

fad [fæd] przelotna moda *f*

fade [feɪd] ⟨z⟩blaknąć; ⟨s⟩płowieć; ⟨z⟩więdnąć; niknąć, znikać; ***~ in*** *film itp.* rozjaśniać ⟨-nić⟩, wzmacniać ⟨-mocnić⟩; ***~ out*** ściemniać ⟨-nić⟩, wygaszać ⟨-gasić⟩; ***~d jeans*** *pl.* sprane dżinsy *pl.*

fag[1] [fæg] F męczarnia *f*, mordęga *f*; *Brt.* kot *m* (*uczeń, którym wysługują się starsi*)

fag[2] [fæg] *sl.*, *Brt.* (*papieros*) fajka *f*; *Am.* pedał *m*; **'~ end** *Brt.* F (*niedopałek*) pet *m*

fail [feɪl] **1.** *v/i.* zawodzić ⟨-wieść⟩; nie powodzić się; nie udać się; nie zdać (*egzaminu*); *biznes itp.*: załamywać się; pogarszać się; ***he ~ed*** nie udało mu się; ***~ to do s.th.*** nie zrobić czegoś, zaniedbać zrobienie czegoś; *v/t.* *kogoś* zawodzić ⟨-wieść⟩; (*na egzaminie*) *kogoś* oblewać ⟨-blać⟩; **2.** ***without ~*** na pewno, z pewnością; **~·ure** ['feɪljə] niepowodzenie *n*; fiasko *n*, porażka *f*; niedomoga *f*; nieurodzaj *m*; ***be a ~ure*** *ktoś*: nie mieć szczęścia

faint [feɪnt] **1.** słaby, nikły; **2.** ⟨ze⟩mdleć, ⟨za⟩słabnąć (***with*** od *G*); **3.** omdlenie *n*, zasłabnięcie *n*; **~-'heart·ed** małego serca; strachliwy

F

fair[1] [feə] uczciwy; szczery; sprawiedliwy; prawidłowy; niezły; spory; *skóra, włosy*: jasny; *pogoda*: ładny; *wiatr*: sprzyjający; ***play ~*** grać fair; *fig.* postępować ⟨-tąpić⟩ fair

fair[2] [feə] jarmark *m*, targ *m*; święto *n* ludowe; targi *pl.*

fair 'game gra *f* fair

'fair·ground wesołe miasteczko *n*

'fair|·ly sprawiedliwie; dość, prawie; **'~·ness** sprawiedliwość *f*; **~ 'play** fair play *f*

fai·ry ['feərɪ] wróżka *f*; elf *m*; *sl. Brt.* *pedał m*; **'~·land** kraina *f* czarów; **'~ sto·ry**, **'~ tale** baśń *f*, bajka *f*

faith [feɪθ] wiara *f*; zaufanie *n*; **'~·ful** wierny; ***Yours ~ly*** (*w liście*) Z poważaniem; **'~·less** niewierny

fake [feɪk] **1.** falsyfikat *m*; oszust(ka *f*) *m*; **2.** ⟨s⟩fałszować; podrabiać ⟨-robić⟩; symulować; **3.** podrabiany, sfałszowany

fal·con ['fɔːlkən] sokół *m*

fall [fɔːl] **1.** upadek *m* (*też fig.*); spadek *m*, zmniejszenie *n* się; opad *m*, opady *pl.*; *Am.* jesień *f*; *zw.* ***~s*** *pl.* wodospad *m*; **2.** (***fell, fallen***) upadać ⟨upaść⟩; spadać ⟨spaść⟩; *deszcz itp.*: padać, spadać ⟨spaść⟩; *wiatr, teren itp.*: opadać ⟨opaść⟩; *noc itp.*: zapadać ⟨zapaść⟩; *miasto itp.*: padać ⟨paść⟩; ***~ ill, ~ sick*** zachorować; ***~ in love with*** zakochać się w (*L*); ***~ short of*** *oczekiwań* nie spełniać ⟨-łnić⟩; ***~ back*** cofać ⟨-fnąć⟩ się; ***~ back on*** uciekać się do (*G*); ***~ for*** łapać się na (*A*); F zakochiwać ⟨-chać⟩ się w (*L*); ***~ off*** *popyt itp.*: spadać ⟨spaść⟩; zmniejszać ⟨-szyć⟩ się; ***~ on*** rzucać ⟨-cić⟩ się na (*A*); ***~ out*** ⟨po⟩sprzeczać się (***with*** z *I*); ***~ through*** nie dochodzić ⟨dojść⟩ do skutku; ***~ to*** zabrać się do (*G*); brać ⟨wziąć⟩ się do jedzenia

fal·la·cious [fə'leɪʃəs] błędny

fal·la·cy ['fæləsɪ] błąd *m*

fall·en ['fɔːlən] *p.p. od* ***fall*** 2
'fall guy *Am.* F kozioł *m* ofiarny
fal·li·ble ['fæləbl] omylny
fal·ling 'star gwiazda *f* spadająca
'fall·out opad *m* radioaktywny
fal·low ['fæləʊ] *zo.* jałowy; *agr.* jałowy, wyjałowiony
false [fɔːls] fałszywy; sztuczny; **~·hood** ['fɔːlshʊd], **'~·ness** fałsz *m*; **~ 'start** falstart *m*

F

fal·si|·fi·ca·tion [fɔːlsɪfɪ'keɪʃn] fałszerstwo *n*; **~·fy** ['fɔːlsɪfaɪ] ⟨s⟩fałszować, podrobić ⟨-rabiać⟩; **~·ty** ['fɔːlsɪtɪ] fałsz *m*
fal·ter ['fɔːltə] *v/i.* ⟨za⟩chwiać się; *głos* załamywać ⟨-mać⟩ się; ⟨za⟩wahać się; załamywać ⟨-mać⟩ się; *v/t. słowa* ⟨wy⟩bąkać
fame [feɪm] rozgłos *m*, sława *f*; **~d** słynny (***for*** ze względu na *A*)
fa·mil·i·ar [fə'mɪljə] znany; znajomy, bliski; poufały; **~·i·ty** [fəmɪlɪ'ærətɪ] znajomość *f*; obeznanie *n*; poufałość *f*; **~·ize** [fə'mɪljəraɪz] zaznajamiać ⟨-jomić⟩ się
fam·i·ly ['fæməlɪ] **1.** rodzina *f*; **2.** rodzinny; domowy; ***be in the ~ way*** F być w odmiennym stanie; **~ al'low·ance** → ***child allowance***; **'~ name** nazwisko *n* (*rodowe*); **~ 'plan·ning** planowanie *n* rodziny; **~ 'tree** drzewo *n* genealogiczne
fam|·ine ['fæmɪn] głód *m*; brak *m*; **'~·ished** wygłodzony; ***I'm ~ished*** F strasznie głodny jestem
fa·mous ['feɪməs] słynny, znany
fan[1] [fæn] **1.** wentylator *m*; wachlarz *m*; **2.** (**-*nn*-**) wachlować (się); *fig.* podsycać ⟨-cić⟩
fan[2] [fæn] kibic *m*, fan(ka *f*) *m*
fa·nat|·ic [fə'nætɪk] fanatyk *m* (-yczka *f*); **~·i·cal** [fə'nætɪkl] fanatyczny
'fan belt *tech.* pas klinowy
fan·ci·er ['fænsɪə] miłośnik *m* (-niczka *f*) (*zwierząt itp.*)
fan·ci·ful ['fænsɪfl] wymyślny; fantastyczny
fan·cy ['fænsɪ] **1.** fantazja *f*; upodobanie *n*, pociąg *m*; **2.** wymyślny; *cena itp.*: fantastyczny; **3.** mieć ochotę na (*A*); wyobrażać ⟨-razić⟩ sobie; ***I really ~ her*** naprawdę mi się podoba; ***~ that!*** no pomyśl tylko!; **~ 'ball** bal *m* kostiumowy; **~ 'dress** kostium *m*, przebranie *n*; **~-'free** całkiem wolny; **~ 'goods** *pl.* upominki *pl.*; **'~·work** haft *m*; wyszywanie *n*
fang [fæŋ] kieł *m*
'fan mail listy *pl.* od fanów
fan|·tas·tic [fæn'tæstɪk] (**-*ally***) fantastyczny; **~·ta·sy** ['fæntəsɪ] fantazja *f*; wyobraźnia *f*; (literatura) fantasy *f*
far [fɑː] (***farther, further, farthest, furthest***) **1.** *adj.* daleki, odległy; oddalony; **2.** *adv.* daleko; znacznie; ***as ~ as*** (aż) do; na ile; ***in so ~ as*** na ile; ***so ~*** dotąd; **~·a·way** ['fɑːrəweɪ] oddalony; odległy
fare [feə] **1.** opłata *f* za przejazd; pasażer(ka *f*) *m*; wyżywienie *n*, strawa *f*; **2.** radzić sobie; ***she ~d well*** dobrze jej poszło; **'~ dodg·er** pasażer(ka *f*) *m* na gapę; **~'well 1.** *int.* żegnaj!; **2.** pożegnanie *n*
far'fetched *fig.* przesadny, naciągany
farm [fɑːm] **1.** gospodarstwo *n* (*rolne*); ferma *f*; ***chicken ~*** ferma *f* kurza; **2.** uprawiać; **'~·er** rolnik *m*, gospodarz *m*; farmer *m*; **'~·hand** robotnik *m* rolny; **'~·house** budynek *m* wiejski; dom *m* (*w gospodarstwie*); **'~·ing 1.** rolny; wiejski; **2.** rolnictwo *n*; gospodarka *f* rolna; hodowla *f*; **'~·stead** budynek *m* wiejski; zabudowania *pl.* gospodarcze; **'~·yard** podwórze *n* (*w gospodarstwie rolnym*)
far|-off [fɑːr'ɒf] daleki, odległy; **~ 'right** *pol.* skrajnie prawicowy; **~'sight·ed** *zwł. Am.* dalekowzroczny
far|·ther ['fɑːðə] *comp. od* ***far***; **~·thest** ['fɑːðɪst] *sup. od* ***far***
fas·ci|·nate ['fæsɪneɪt] ⟨za⟩fascynować; **'~·nat·ing** fascynujący; **~·na·tion** [fæsɪ'neɪʃn] fascynacja *f*, zafascynowanie *n*
fas·cis|·m ['fæʃɪzəm] *pol.* faszyzm *m*; **~t** ['fæʃɪst] *pol.* faszysta *m* (-tka *f*)
fash·ion ['fæʃn] **1.** moda *f*; sposób *m*; ***be in ~*** być modnym; ***out of ~*** niemodny; **2.** ⟨u⟩kształtować; ⟨u⟩formować; **~·a·ble** ['fæʃnəbl] modny; **'~ pa·rade**, **'~ show** pokaz *m* mody
fast[1] [fɑːst] **1.** post *m*; **2.** pościć
fast[2] [fɑːst] szybki; trwały; mocno przymocowany; ***be ~*** *zegar:* spieszyć się; **'~·back** coupé *n*, fastback *m*; **~ 'breed·er, ~ breed·er re'ac·tor** *phys.* reaktor *m* powielający prędki

fas·ten ['fɑːsn] zapinać ⟨-piąć⟩ (się); umocowywać ⟨-wać⟩, przymocowywać ⟨-wać⟩; *spojrzenie itp.* ⟨s⟩kierować (***on*** na *A*); '**~·er** zamknięcie *n*

'**fast| food** dania *pl.* na szybko; **~-food** '**res·tau·rant** bar *m lub* restauracja *f* szybkiej obsługi

fas·tid·i·ous [fə'stɪdɪəs] wybredny

'**fast lane** *mot.* pas *m* szybkiego ruchu

fat [fæt] **1.** (**-*tt*-**) tłusty; otyły; gruby; **2.** tłuszcz *m*; ***low in ~*** o niskiej zawartości tłuszczu

fa·tal ['feɪtl] śmiertelny; zgubny (***to*** dla *G*); ⚠ *nie* ***fatalny***; **~·i·ty** [fə'tælətɪ] wypadek *m* śmiertelny; ofiara *f*

fate [feɪt] los *m*; przeznaczenie *n*

fa·ther ['fɑːðə] ojciec *m*; ♀ '**Christ·mas** *zwł. Brt. jakby*: Św. Mikołaj; '**~·hood** ojcostwo *n*; **~-in-law** ['fɑːðərɪnlɔː] (*pl.* ***fathers-in-law***) teść *m*; '**~·less** bez ojca; '**~·ly** ojcowski

fath·om ['fæðəm] **1.** *naut.* sążeń *m*; **2.** *naut.* sondować; *fig.* zgłębiać ⟨-bić⟩; '**~·less** bezdenny

fa·tigue [fə'tiːg] **1.** zmęczenie *n*; **2.** ⟨z⟩męczyć

fat|·ten ['fætn] ⟨u⟩tuczyć; '**~·ty** (**-*ier*, -*iest***) tłusty; otłuszczony

fau·cet ['fɔːsɪt] *Am.* kurek *m*, kran *m*

fault [fɔːlt] błąd *m*; wina *f*; skaza *f*; wada *f*; ***find ~ with*** ⟨s⟩krytykować (*A*); ***be at ~*** ponosić winę; '**~·less** bezbłędny; '**~·y** (**-*ier*, -*iest***) wadliwy, błędny

fa·vo(u)r ['feɪvə] **1.** uznanie *n*; przychylność *f*; faworyzowanie *n*; przysługa *f*; ***be in ~ of*** popierać (*A*); ***in ~ of*** na korzyść (*G*); ***do s.o. a ~*** wyświadczyć komuś przysługę; **2.** popierać ⟨-przeć⟩; faworyzować; sprzyjać; wyróżniać ⟨-nić⟩; **fa·vo(u)·ra·ble** ['feɪvərəbl] przychylny; sprzyjający; **fa·vo(u)·rite** ['feɪvərɪt] **1.** faworyt(ka *f*) *m*, ulubieniec *m* (-ica *f*); **2.** ulubiony

fawn[1] [fɔːn] **1.** *zo.* jelonek *m*; **2.** płowy

fawn[2] [fɔːn]: ***~ on*** *pies*: łasić się do (*G*); schlebiać ⟨-bić⟩ (*D*)

fax [fæks] **1.** faks *m*; **2.** ⟨prze⟩faksować; ***~ s.th.*** (***through***) ***to s.o.*** przefaksować coś do kogoś; '**~** (**ma·chine**) faks *m*, telefaks *m*

FBI [ef biː 'aɪ] *skrót*: ***Federal Bureau of Investigation*** FBI *n* (*federalny urząd śledczy w USA*)

fear [fɪə] **1.** strach *m* (***of*** przed *I*); lęk *m*; obawa *f*; **2.** bać się; lękać się; obawiać się (***for*** o *A*); '**~·ful** lękliwy; bojaźliwy; '**~·less** nieustraszony

fea·si·ble ['fiːzəbl] możliwy do wykonania, wykonalny

feast [fiːst] **1.** *rel.* święto *n*, dzień *m* świąteczny; uczta *f* (*też fig.*); **2.** *v/t.* podejmować ⟨-djąć⟩ uroczyście; *v/i.* cieszyć się

feat [fiːt] wyczyn *m* (*bohaterski*)

fea·ther ['feðə] **1.** pióro *n*; *też* ***~s*** upierzenie *n*; ***birds of a ~ flock together*** swój ciągnie do swego; ***that is a ~ in his cap*** to dla niego powód do dumy; **2.** wyściełać ⟨-ścielić⟩ piórami, przystrajać ⟨-roić⟩ w pióra; **~** '**bed** materac *m* puchowy, piernat *m*; '**~·bed** (**-*dd*-**) ⟨po⟩traktować ulgowo; '**~·brained** F o ptasim móżdżku; '**~ed** upierzony; '**~·weight** (*w sporcie*) waga *f* piórkowa; zawodnik *m* (-niczka *f*) wagi piórkowej; **~·y** ['feðərɪ] upierzony; lekki jak piórko

fea·ture ['fiːtʃə] **1.** rysa *f* (*twarzy*); *charakterystyczna* cecha *f*; *gazeta, TV*: reportaż *m* specjalny; film *m* pełnometrażowy; **2.** przedstawiać ⟨-wić⟩, pokazywać ⟨-zać⟩; pokazywać w głównej roli; '**~ film** film *m* fabularny; '**~s** *pl.* rysy *pl.* twarzy

Feb *skrót pisany*: ***February*** luty *m*

Feb·ru·a·ry ['februərɪ] (*skrót*: ***Feb***) luty *m*

fed [fed] *pret i p.p. od* ***feed*** 2

fed·e·ral ['fedərəl] *pol.* federalny; ♀ **Bu·reau of In·ves·ti'ga·tion** (*skrót*: ***FBI***) FBI *n*, federalny urząd *m* śledczy (*w USA*); ♀ **Re·pub·lic of** '**Ger·man·y** Federalna Republika Niemiec (*skrót*: ***RFN***)

fed·e·ra·tion [fedə'reɪʃn] *pol.* federacja *f*; stowarzyszenie *n*, związek *m*; *sport*: zrzeszenie *n*

fee [fiː] opłata *f*; honorarium *n*; składka *f* (*członkowska*); opłata *f* za wstęp

fee·ble ['fiːbl] (**-*r*, -*st***) wątły, mizerny

feed [fiːd] **1.** pokarm *m*; karma *f*, pasza *f*; *tech.* zasilanie *n*, podawanie *n*; **2.** (***fed***) *v/t.* ⟨na⟩karmić, żywić; *tech.* zasilać ⟨-lić⟩, podawać ⟨-dać⟩; *komp.* wprowadzać ⟨-dzić⟩, podawać ⟨-dać⟩; ***be fed up with s.th.*** mieć serdecznie dość czegoś; ***well fed*** dobrze odżywio-

ny; *v/i.* żywić się, odżywiać się; jeść; '~•**back** *electr.*, (*w cybernetyce*) feedback *m*, sprzężenie *n* zwrotne; reakcja *f* (**to** na *A*); '~•**er** *tech.* zasilacz *m*, podajnik *m*; ***be a noisy ~er*** jeść głośno; '~•**er road** droga *f* łącząca; '~•**ing bot•tle**butelka*f*zpokarmem(*dladzieci*)
feel [fiːl] **1.** (***felt***) czuć (się); odczuwać ⟨-czuć⟩; dotykać ⟨-tknąć⟩, macać; sądzić; ***he feels sorry for you*** żal mu ciebie; ***I ~ hot*** gorąco mi; ***~ like s.th.*** mieć ochotę na coś; **2.** uczucie *n* (*przy dotyku*); dotyk *m*; '~•**er** *zo.* czułek *m*; '~•**ing** uczucie *n*, odczucie *n*
feet [fiːt] *pl. od* ***foot*** 1
feign [feɪn] *chorobę, zainteresowanie itp.* udawać ⟨udać⟩
feint [feɪnt] zwód *m*
fell [fel] **1.** *pret. od* ***fall*** 2; **2.** zwalać ⟨-lić⟩; ścinać ⟨ściąć⟩
fel•low ['feləʊ] **1.** towarzysz(ka *f*) *m*, kolega *m*; F facet *m*, gość *m*; drugi *m* z pary; ***old ~*** stary *m*; **2.** współ...; ~ '**be•ing** bliźni *m*; ~ '**cit•i•zen** współobywatel(ka *f*) *m*; ~ '**coun•try•man** (*pl.* ***-men***) rodak *m*), '~•**ship** koleżeństwo *n*; związek *m*; ~ '**trav•el•(l)er** współtowarzysz(ka *f*) *m*
fel•o•ny ['felənɪ] *jur.* przestępstwo *n*, zbrodnia *f*
felt[1] [felt] *pret. i p.p. od* ***feel*** 1
felt[2] [felt] filc *m*; '~ **pen**, '~ **tip**, ~-**tip(ped)** '**pen** mazak *m*, flamaster *m*
fe•male ['fiːmeɪl] **1.** żeński; **2.** *pej.* kobieta *f*; *zo.* samica *f*
fem•i|•nine ['femɪnɪn] kobiecy; żeński; ~•**nis•m** ['femɪnɪzəm] feminizm *m*; ~•**nist** ['femɪnɪst] feminista *m* (-tka *f*)
fen [fen] tereny *pl.* podmokłe
fence [fens] **1.** płot *m*; *sl.* paser *m*; **2.** *v/t.* ***~ in*** ogradzać ⟨-rodzić⟩; ***~ off*** odgradzać ⟨-rodzić⟩; *v/i.* fechtować; (*w sporcie*) uprawiać szermierkę; '**fenc•er** (*w sporcie*) szermierz *m*; '**fenc•ing** ogrodzenie *n*; *sport:* szermierka *f*; *attr.* szermierczy
fend [fend]: ***~ off*** odparowywać ⟨-ować⟩; ***~ for o.s.*** radzić sobie samemu; '~•**er** ochraniacz *m*; *Am. mot.* błotnik *m*; osłona *f* (*przy kominku*)
fen•nel ['fenl] *bot.* koper *m* włoski
fer|•ment **1.** ['fɜːment] ferment *m*, wzburzenie *n*; **2.** [fə'ment] ⟨s⟩fermentować; ~•**men•ta•tion** [fɜːmen'teɪʃn] fermentacja *f*
fern [fɜːn] *bot.* paproć *f*
fe•ro|•cious [fə'rəʊʃəs] zaciekły; dziki; *fig.* wielki; ~•**ci•ty** [fə'rɒsətɪ] zaciekłość *f*; dzikość *f*
fer•ret ['ferɪt] **1.** *zo.* fretka *f*; *fig.* szperacz *m*; **2.** węszyć, myszkować; ***~ out*** wywęszyć, wymyszkować
fer•ry ['ferɪ] **1.** prom *m*; **2.** przewozić ⟨-wieźć⟩; '~•**boat** prom *m*; '~•**man** (*pl.* ***-men***) przewoźnik *m*
fer|•tile ['fɜːtaɪl] żyzny; płodny; ~•**til•i•ty** [fə'tɪlətɪ] żyzność *f*; płodność *f*; ~•**ti•lize** ['fɜːtɪlaɪz] zapładniać ⟨-łodnić⟩; nawozić ⟨-wieźć⟩; '~•**ti•liz•er** nawóz *m* (*zwł. sztuczny*)
fer•vent ['fɜːvənt] żarliwy
fer•vo(u)r ['fɜːvə] zapał *m*
fes•ter ['festə] jątrzyć się, zaogniać ⟨-nić⟩ się
fes|•ti•val ['festəvl] festiwal *m*; święto *n*; ~•**tive** ['festɪv] świąteczny; ~•**tiv•i•ties** [fe'stɪvətɪ] *pl.* uroczystości *pl.*
fes•toon [fe'stuːn] girlanda *f*
fetch [fetʃ] przynosić ⟨-nieść⟩; *ceny* osiągać ⟨-gnąć⟩; '~•**ing** F niebrzydki
fete, fête [feɪt] festyn *m*; ***village ~*** odpust *m*
fet•id ['fetɪd] cuchnący
fet•ter ['fetə] **1.** *też* ***~s*** *pl.* okowy *pl.*, pęta *pl.*; **2.** ⟨s⟩pętać
feud [fjuːd] zwada *f*; ~•**al** ['fjuːdl] feudalny; •**dal•is•m** ['fjuːdəlɪzəm] feudalizm *m*
fe•ver ['fiːvə] gorączka *f*; ~•**ish** ['fiːvərɪʃ] rozpalony; *fig.* rozgorączkowany, gorączkowy
few [fjuː] niewiele, niewielu; ***a ~*** kilka, kilku; ***no ~er than*** nie mniej niż; ***quite a ~, a good ~*** dość dużo
fi•an•cé [fɪ'ɑ̃ːŋseɪ] narzeczony *m*; ~**e** [fɪ'ɑ̃ːŋseɪ] narzeczona *f*
fib [fɪb] **1.** kłamstewko *n*, bujda *f*; **2.** (***-bb-***) bujać
fi•bre *Brt.*, **fi•ber** *Am.* ['faɪbə] włókno *n*; '~•**glass** włókno *n* szklane; **fi•brous** ['faɪbrəs] włóknisty
fick•le ['fɪkl] zmienny, niestały; '~•**ness** zmienność *f*, niestałość *f*
fic•tion ['fɪkʃn] fikcja *f*; (*proza*) literatura *f* piękna, beletrystyka *f*; ~•**al** ['fɪkʃnl] fikcyjny; beletrystyczny
fic•ti•tious [fɪk'tɪʃəs] fikcyjny, nieprawdziwy
fid•dle ['fɪdl] **1.** skrzypki *pl.*; ***play first***

(**_second_**) ~ *fig.* grać pierwsze (drugie) skrzypce; **_as fit as a_** ~ zdrów jak ryba; **2.** *mus.* ⟨za⟩grać na skrzypcach; *też* ~ **_about_** *lub* **_around_** (**_with_**) zabawiać się (*I*); '~**r** skrzypek *m* (-paczka *f*); '~**·sticks** *int.* bzdury!

fi·del·i·ty [fɪ'deləti] wierność *f*

fid·get ['fɪdʒɪt] F wiercić się; bawić się; '~**·y** nerwowy, wiercący się

field [fiːld] pole *n*; *sport*: boisko *n*; obszar *m* (*zainteresowań*); dziedzina *f*; '~ **e·vents** *pl.* (*w sporcie*) lekka atletyka *f*; '~ **glass·es** *pl.*, *też* **_a pair of ~glasses_** lornetka *f* polowa; '~ **mar·shal** *mil.* feldmarszałek *m*; '~ **sports** *pl.* sport *m* na powietrzu; '~**·work** praca *f* terenowa, zajęcia *pl.* terenowe; badania *pl.* terenowe

fiend [fiːnd] szatan *m*, diabeł *m*; F fanatyk *m* (-tyczka *f*); '~**·ish** szatański, diabelski

fierce [fɪəs] (**-_r_, -_st_**) zażarty; zaciekły; dziki; '~**·ness** zażartość *f*; zaciekłość *f*; dzikość *f*

fi·er·y ['faɪərɪ] (**-_ier_, -_iest_**) ognisty; zapalczywy

fif|·teen [fɪf'tiːn] **1.** piętnaście; **2.** piętnastka *f*; ~**·teenth** [fɪf'tiːnθ] piętnasty; ~**th** [fɪfθ] **1.** piąty; **2.** jedna *f* piąta; '~**th·ly** po piąte; ~**·ti·eth** ['fɪftɪɪθ] pięćdziesiąty; ~**·ty** ['fɪftɪ] **1.** pięćdziesiąt; **2.** pięćdziesiątka *f*; ~**·ty-'fif·ty** F fifty-fifty, po pół

fig [fɪg] *bot.* figa *f*

fight [faɪt] **1.** walka *f* (*też mil.*, *sport*); starcie *n*; kłótnia *f*, awantura *f*; **2.** (**_fought_**) *v/t.* bić się z (*I*) *lub* przeciw (*D*); walczyć z (*I*) *lub* przeciw (*D*); *walkę, pojedynek itp.*⟨s⟩toczyć, brać ⟨wziąć⟩ udział w (*L*) walce, pojedynku itp.; *grypę itp.* zwalczać ⟨-czyć⟩; *v/i.* bić się, walczyć; '~**·er** walczący *f* (-ca *f*); bojownik *m* (-iczka *f*); (*w sporcie*) bokser *m*; *też* **_~er plane_** *mil. myśliwski* samolot *m*; '~**·ing** walka *f*

fig·u·ra·tive ['fɪgjʊrətɪv] przenośny

fig·ure ['fɪgə] **1.** figura *f*, kształt *m*; postać *f*; cyfra *f*; liczba *f*; cena *f*; rycina *f*, rysunek *m*; **_be good at ~s_** dobrze liczyć; **2.** *v/t.* wyobrażać ⟨-razić⟩ (sobie); przedstawiać ⟨-wić⟩; *Am.* F sądzić; ~ **_out problem_** rozwiązywać ⟨-zać⟩; pojmować ⟨-jąć⟩; ~ **_up_** podliczać ⟨-czyć⟩; *v/i.* figurować, pojawiać ⟨-wić⟩ się; ~ **_on_** *zwł. Am.* liczyć się z (*I*); '~ **skat·er** *sport*: łyżwiarz *m* (-wiarka *f*) figurowy (-a); '~ **skat·ing** (*w sporcie*) łyżwiarstwo *n* figurowe

fil·a·ment ['fɪləmənt] *electr.* włókno *n*

filch [fɪltʃ] F podwędzić, zwinąć

file[1] [faɪl] **1.** kartoteka *f*; akta *pl.*; teczka *f*; *komp.* plik *m*, zbiór *m*; rząd *m*; *mil.* szereg *m*; **_on_** ~ w aktach; **2.** *v/t. listy itp.* wciągać ⟨-nąć⟩ do akt; wciągać ⟨-gnąć⟩ do ewidencji; *podanie, powództwo* wnosić ⟨wnieść⟩; *v/i.* iść ⟨pójść⟩ jeden za drugim

file[2] [faɪl] **1.** pilnik *m*; **2.** ⟨s⟩piłować (*pilnikiem*)

'file| man·age·ment *komp.* zarządzanie *n* plikami; '~ **pro·tec·tion** *komp.* ochrona *f* plików

fi·li·al ['fɪljəl]: ~ **_love_** miłość *f* dzieci

fil·ing ['faɪlɪŋ] wprowadzanie *n* do ewidencji; '~ **cab·i·net** szafka *f* na akta

fill [fɪl] **1.** napełniać ⟨-nić⟩ (się), zapełniać ⟨-nić⟩ (się), wypełniać ⟨-nić⟩(się); *ząb* wypełniać ⟨-nić⟩, ⟨za⟩plombować; ~ **_in_** zastępować ⟨-tąpić⟩; *formularz* wypełniać ⟨-nić⟩ (*Am. też* ~ **_out_**); ~ **_up_** napełniać ⟨-nić⟩ (się), wypełniać ⟨-nić⟩ (się); ~ **_her up!_** F *mot.* proszę do pełna!; **2.** wypełnienie *n*, napełnienie *n*; **_eat one's_** ~ najeść się do syta

fil·let *Brt.*, **fil·et** *Am.* ['fɪlɪt] filet *m*

fill·ing ['fɪlɪŋ] wypełnienie *n*; *med.* wypełnienie *n*, plomba *f*; '~ **sta·tion** stacja *f* benzynowa

fil·ly ['fɪlɪ] *zo. młoda* klacz *f*

film [fɪlm] **1.** warstwa *f*; błona *f*; *phot. zwł. Brt.* film *m kinowy*; folia *f*; zmętnienie *n* (*oka*); mgiełka *f*; **_make_** *lub* **_shoot a_** ~ ⟨na⟩kręcić film; **2.** ⟨s⟩filmować; '~ **star** *zwł. Brt.* gwiazda *f* filmowa

fil·ter ['fɪltə] **1.** filtr *m*; **2.** ⟨prze⟩filtrować; '~ **tip** filtr *m* (*papierosa*); ~**-'tipped**: **_~tipped cigarette_** papieros *m* z filtrem

filth [fɪlθ] brud *m*; '~**·y** (**-_ier_, -_iest_**) brudny; *fig.* plugawy

fin [fɪn] *zo.* płetwa *f* (*Am. też płetwonurka*)

fi·nal ['faɪnl] **1.** końcowy; finałowy; ostateczny; **2.** (*w sporcie*) finał *m*; *zw.* **_~s_** *pl.* egzaminy *pl.* końcowe; ~ **dis'pos·al** ostateczne usuwanie *n* (*odpadów radioaktywnych*); ~**·ist** ['faɪnəlɪst] (*w spor-*

F

cie) finalista *m* (-tka *f*); '**~·ly** ostatecznie; w końcu; **~ 'whis·tle** *sport*: gwizdek *m* końcowy
fi·nance [faɪ'næns] **1.** nauka *f* o finansach; **~s** *pl.* finanse *pl.*; **2.** ⟨s⟩finansować; **fi·nan·cial** [faɪ'nænʃl] finansowy; **fi·nan·cier** [faɪ'nænsɪə] finansista *m*
finch [fɪntʃ] *zo.* zięba *f*

F

find [faɪnd] **1.** (***found***) znajdować ⟨znaleźć⟩; odnajdować ⟨odnaleźć⟩; *pieniądze itp.* zdobywać ⟨-być⟩; stwierdzać ⟨-dzić⟩; *jur.* uznawać (*kogoś za* (*nie*)*winnego*); ***be found*** występować; **~ *out*** stwierdzać ⟨-dzić⟩; odkrywać ⟨-ryć⟩; dowiadywać ⟨-wiedzieć⟩ się; **2.** znalezisko *n*; odkrycie *n*; '**~·ings** *pl.* znalezisko *n*; *jur.* wnioski *pl.*
fine[1] [faɪn] **1.** *adj.* (***-r, -st***) świetny; wspaniały; znakomity; delikatny; cienki; drobny; subtelny; ***I'm ~*** świetnie mi idzie; świetnie się czuję; **2.** *adv.* F świetnie, znakomicie; drobno
fine[2] [faɪn] **1.** grzywna *f*, kara *f* pieniężna; **2.** nakładać ⟨-łożyć⟩ grzywnę
fin·ger ['fɪŋgə] **1.** palec *m* (*u ręki*); → ***cross*** 2; **2.** dotykać ⟨-tknąć⟩ palcami, obmacywać ⟨-cać⟩; '**~·nail** paznokieć *m*; '**~·print** odcisk *m* palca; '**~·tip** koniec *m* palca
fin·i·cky ['fɪnɪkɪ] pedantyczny; wybredny
fin·ish ['fɪnɪʃ] **1.** ⟨za-, s⟩kończyć (się); wykańczać ⟨-kończyć⟩; *też* **~ *off*** dokończyć, skończyć; *też* **~ *off*, ~ *up*** skończyć (*jeść, pić*); **2.** koniec *m*, zakończenie *n*; końcówka *f*; (*w sporcie*) finisz *m*, meta *f*; wykończenie *n*; '**~·ing line** meta *f*
Fin·land ['fɪnlənd] Finlandia *f*; **Finn** [fɪn] Fin(ka *f*) *m*; **'Finn·ish 1.** fiński; **2.** *ling.* język *m* fiński
fir [fɜː] *też* **~ *tree*** jodła *f*; '**~ cone** szyszka *f* jodły
fire ['faɪə] **1.** ogień *m* (*też mil.*); pożar *m*; ***be on ~*** palić się; ***catch ~*** zapalić się, zająć się ogniem; ***set on ~, set ~ to*** podpalać ⟨-lić⟩; **2.** *v/t.* podpalać ⟨-lić⟩; *fig.* rozpalać ⟨-lić⟩; *cegły itp.* wypalać ⟨-lić⟩; wystrzeliwać ⟨-lić⟩; strzelać ⟨-lić⟩ z (*I*); F *pracownika itp.* wylewać ⟨-lać⟩; *v/i.* strzelać ⟨-lić⟩; **~ a·larm** ['faɪərəlɑːm] alarm *m* pożarowy; **~·arms** ['faɪərɑːmz] *pl.* broń *f* palna; '**~ bri·gade** *Brt.* straż *f* pożarna; '**~·bug** F podpalacz(ka *f*) *m*; '**~·crack·er** petarda *f*; '**~ de·part·ment** *Am.* straż *f* pożarna; **~ en·gine** ['faɪərendʒɪn] wóz *m* strażacki; **~ es·cape** ['faɪərɪskeɪp] wyjście *n* pożarowe, schody *pl.* pożarowe; **~ ex·tin·guish·er** ['faɪərɪkstɪŋgwɪʃə] gaśnica *f*; '**~ fight·er** strażak *m*; '**~·guard** osłona *f* przy kominku; '**~ hydrant** *Brt.* hydrant *m* przeciwpożarowy; '**~·man** (*pl.* ***-men***) strażak *m*; '**~·place** kominek *m*; '**~·plug** *Am.* hydrant *m* przeciwpożarowy; '**~·proof** ognioodporny, ogniotrwały; '**~-rais·ing** *Brt.* podpalenie *n*; '**~·screen** *Am.* osłona *f* przy kominku; '**~·side** kominek *m*; '**~ sta·tion** remiza *f* straży pożarnej; '**~ truck** *Am.* wóz *m* strażacki; '**~·wood** drewno *n* na podpałkę; '**~·works** *pl.* fajerwerk *n*
fir·ing squad ['faɪərɪŋskwɒd] *mil.* pluton *m* egzekucyjny
firm[1] [fɜːm] twardy; mocny; *podstawa itp.*: solidny; *przekonanie*: niewzruszony; *oferta itp.*: wiążący; *głos itp.*: stanowczy
firm[2] [fɜːm] firma *f*
first [fɜːst] **1.** *adj.* pierwszy; najlepszy; **2.** *adv.* po pierwsze; najpierw; **~ *of all*** przede wszystkim; **3.** pierwszy *m* (-sza *f*); *mot.* jedynka *f*, pierwszy bieg *m*; ***at ~*** najpierw; ***from the ~*** od początku; **~ 'aid** pierwsza pomoc *f*; **~ 'aid box, ~ 'aid kit** apteczka *f*; '**~·born** pierworodny; **~ 'class** (*w pociągu itp.*) pierwsza klasa; **~-'class** znakomity, pierwszorzędny; **~ 'floor** *Brt.* pierwsze piętro *n*, *Am.* parter *m*; → ***second hand***; **~'hand** z pierwszej ręki; **~ 'leg** (*w sporcie*) pierwszy mecz *m*; '**~·ly** po pierwsze; '**~ name** imię *n*; **~-'rate** pierwszorzędny
firth [fɜːθ] odnoga *f* morska, fiord *m*
fish [fɪʃ] **1.** (*pl.* ***fish, fishes***) ryba *f*; **2.** łowić ryby; wędkować; '**~·bone** ość *f*
fish|·er·man ['fɪʃəmən] (*pl.* ***-men***) rybak *m*; **~·e·ry** ['fɪʃərɪ] rybołówstwo *n*; łowisko *n*
fish| 'fin·ger *zwł. Brt.* paluszek *m* rybny; '**~·hook** haczyk *m*
'fish·ing rybołówstwo *n*, wędkowanie *n*; '**~ line** linka *f* wędkarska, żyłka *f*; '**~ rod** wędka *f*; '**~ tack·le** sprzęt *m* wędkarski
'fish|·mon·ger *zwł. Brt.* handlarz *m* ryb;

~ 'stick *zwł. Am.* paluszek *m* rybny; '~·y (*-ier, -iest*) śliski, podejrzany
fis·sion ['fɪʃn] rozszczepienie *n*
fis·sure ['fɪʃə] szczelina *f*, pęknięcie *n*
fist [fɪst] pięść *f*
fit[1] [fɪt] **1.** (*-tt-*) odpowiedni; zdatny; przydatny; stosowny; (*w sporcie*) w dobrej kondycji; ***keep ~*** utrzymywać dobrą kondycję; **2.** (*-tt-*; ***fitted***, *Am. też* ***fit***) *v/t.* pasować na (*G*); pasować do (*G*); odpowiadać; dopasowywać ⟨-wać⟩; *tech.* ⟨za⟩montować; przytwierdzać ⟨-dzić⟩; czynić zdatnym (***for, to*** do *G*); ***~ in*** kogoś przyjmować ⟨-jąć⟩; robić miejsce (dla *kogoś*, na *coś*); *też* ***~ on*** przymierzać ⟨-rzyć⟩; *też* ***~ out*** wyposażać ⟨-żyć⟩ (***with*** w *A*), ⟨za⟩montować; *też* ***~ up*** zakładać ⟨założyć⟩, ⟨za⟩montować; przerabiać ⟨-robić⟩; *v/i.* pasować; *ubranie*: leżeć; **3.** ***be a beautiful ~*** pięknie leżeć
fit[2] [fɪt] atak *m*, napad *m*
'fit|·ful niespokojny, *sen itp.* przerywany; '**~·ness** zdatność *f*; (*w sporcie*) dobra kondycja *f*; '**~·ness cen·tre** (*Am.* **cen·ter**) siłownia *f*; '**~·ted** wyposażony; wbudowany; ***~ted carpet*** wykładzina *f* dywanowa; ***~ted kitchen*** zabudowana kuchnia *f*; '**~·ter** monter *m*; '**~·ting 1.** stosowny, właściwy; **2.** montaż *m*, instalacja *f*; ***~tings*** *pl.* wyposażenie *n*; armatura *f*
five [faɪv] **1.** pięć; **2.** piątka *f*
fix [fɪks] **1.** przymocowywać ⟨-ować⟩, przytwierdzać ⟨-dzić⟩ (***to*** do *G*); *cenę* ustalać ⟨-lić⟩, wyznaczać ⟨-czyć⟩; *oczy* wlepiać (***on*** w *A*); *bilety itp.* załatwiać ⟨-wić⟩; *zdjęcie* utrwalać ⟨-lić⟩; naprawiać ⟨-wić⟩; *zwł. Am. jedzenie* robić; *rezultaty* ⟨s⟩preparować; **2.** F trudna sytuacja *f*; **~ed** przytwierdzony, przymocowany; niewzruszony; '**~·ings** *pl. Am. gastr.* dodatki *pl.* (*do głównego dania*); **~·ture** ['fɪkstʃə] element *m* osprzętu; ***lighting ~ture*** oprawa *f* świetlna
fizz [fɪz] musować; perkotać, syczeć
fl *skrót pisany*: ***floor*** piętro
flab·ber·gast ['flæbəgɑːst] F zdumiewać ⟨-mieć⟩; ***be ~ed*** osłupieć
flab·by ['flæbɪ] (*-ier, -iest*) zwiotczały
flac·cid ['flæksɪd] sflaczały, zwiotczały
flag[1] [flæg] **1.** flaga *f*, sztandar *m*; **2.** (*-gg-*) oflagowywać ⟨-ować⟩; ***~ down*** zatrzymywać ⟨-mać⟩ (*taksówkę*)
flag[2] [flæg] **1.** płyta *f* (*kamienna lub chodnikowa*); **2.** wykładać (*płytami*)
flag[3] [flæg] ⟨o⟩słabnąć
'flag|·pole, '~·staff maszt *m* flagowy; '**~·stone** płyta *f* (*chodnikowa*)
flake [fleɪk] **1.** płatek *m*; **2.** *zw.* ***~ off*** łuszczyć się, złuszczać ⟨-czyć⟩ się; '**flak·y** (*-ier, -iest*) łuszczący się; ~ '**pas·try** ciasto *n* francuskie
flame [fleɪm] **1.** płomień *m* (*też fig.*); ***be in ~s*** stanąć w płomieniach; **2.** płonąć, rozpłomieniać ⟨-nić⟩ się
flam·ma·ble ['flæməbl] *Am. i tech.* → ***inflammable***
flan [flæn] tarta *f*
flank [flæŋk] **1.** bok *m*; *mil.* flanka *f*; **2.** otaczać ⟨otoczyć⟩
flan·nel ['flænl] flanela *f*; myjka *f*; ***~s*** *pl.* spodnie *pl.* flanelowe
flap [flæp] **1.** klapa *f*; (*w ubraniu*) patka *f*; płachta *f* (*namiotu*); uderzenie *n* (*skrzydeł*); **2.** (*-pp-*) ⟨za⟩łopotać (*skrzydłami*)
flare [fleə] **1.** ⟨za⟩migotać; *nozdrza*: rozszerzać się; ***~ up*** wybuchać ⟨-chnąć⟩; **2.** sygnał *m* świetlny; rakieta *f* świetlna
flash [flæʃ] **1.** błysk *m*, rozbłysk *m*; wiadomość *f* z ostatniej chwili; *phot.* F flesz *m*; *zwł. Am.* F latarka *f*; ***like a ~*** jak błyskawica; ***in a ~*** migiem; ***a ~ of lightning*** rozbłysk *m* błyskawicy; **2.** błyskać ⟨-snąć⟩, rozbłyskać ⟨-snąć⟩; przesyłać ⟨-słać⟩; ⟨po⟩mknąć; '**~·back** (*w filmie*) retrospekcja *f*; ~ '**freeze** *Am.* (***-froze, frozen***) → ***quick-freeze***; '**~·light** *phot.* lampa *f* błyskowa, flesz *m*; *zwł. Am.* latarka *f*; '**~·y** (*-ier, -iest*) krzykliwy, jaskrawy
flask [flɑːsk] piersiówka *f*; termos *m*
flat[1] [flæt] **1.** (*-tt-*) płaski, równy; *mot. dętka*: bez powietrza; *bateria*: wyładowany; zwietrzały, bez gazu; *econ.* apatyczny; *econ.* jednolity; **2.** *adv.* ***fall ~*** zawodzić ⟨-wieść⟩; ***sing ~*** ⟨za⟩śpiewać za nisko; **3.** płaska powierzchnia; płask *m*; równina *f*; *zwł. Am. mot.* F (*dętka bez powietrza*) guma *f*
flat[2] [flæt] *zwł. Brt.* mieszkanie *n*
flat|-'foot·ed z płaskostopiem; '**~·mate** *Brt.* współmieszkaniec *m*; **~·ten** ['flætn] spłaszczać ⟨-czyć⟩; przywierać ⟨-wrzeć⟩; *też* ***~ten out*** wyrównywać ⟨-wnać⟩ (*nad ziemią*)
flat·ter ['flætə] pochlebiać ⟨-bić⟩ (*D*);

F

~·**er** ['flætərə] pochlebca *m*; ~·**y** ['flætərɪ] pochlebstwo *n*
fla·vo(u)r ['fleɪvə] **1.** smak *m*, aromat *m*; *wina* bukiet *m*; przyprawa *f*; **2.** przyprawiać ⟨-wić⟩; ~·**ing** ['fleɪvərɪŋ] przyprawa *f*, aromat *m*
flaw [flɔː] skaza *f*; wada *f*; *tech. też* defekt *m*; '~·**less** nieskazitelny, nienaganny
flax [flæks] *bot. roślina*: len *m*
flea [fliː] *zo.* pchła *f*; '~ **mar·ket** pchli targ *m*
fleck [flek] plama *f*, plamka *f*
fled [fled] *pret. i p.p. od* ***flee***
fledg|ed [fledʒd] opierzony; ~**(e)·ling** ['fledʒlɪŋ] pisklę *n*; *fig.* żółtodziób *m*
flee [fliː] uciekać
fleece [fliːs] runo *n*, wełna *f*
fleet [fliːt] *naut.* flota *f*
'**Fleet Street** *fig.* prasa *f* brytyjska (*zwł. londyńska*)
flesh [fleʃ] ciało *n*; mięso *n* (*zwierzęcia*); miąższ *m* (*owocu*); '~·**y** (***-ier, -iest***) korpulentny
flew [fluː] *pret. od* ***fly***[3]
flex[1] [fleks] *zwł. anat.* zginać ⟨zgiąć⟩
flex[2] [fleks] *zwł. Brt. electr.* przedłużacz *m*, sznur *m*
flex·i·ble ['fleksəbl] elastyczny; giętki (*też fig.*); ~ ***working hours*** ruchomy czas *m* pracy
flex·i·time *Brt.* ['fleksɪtaɪm]; **flex·time** *Am.* ['flekstaɪm] ruchomy czas *m* pracy
flick [flɪk] **1.** strzepywać ⟨-pnąć⟩; machać ⟨-chnąć⟩; trzepać ⟨-pnąć⟩; **2.** strzepnięcie *n*; machnięcie *n*; trzepnięcie *n*
flick·er ['flɪkə] **1.** ⟨za⟩migotać; **2.** migotanie *n*
fli·er ['flaɪə] *aviat.* lotnik *m*; *reklamowy* folder *m*, ulotka *f*
flight [flaɪt] lot *m*; ucieczka *f*; stado *n* (*ptaków*); ***put to*** ~ zmuszać ⟨-sić⟩ do ucieczki; ***take*** (***to***) ~ rzucać ⟨-cić⟩ się do ucieczki; '~ **at·tend·ant** steward(essa *f*) *m*; '~·**less** nielotny; '~ **re·cord·er** *aviat.* rejestrator *m* przebiegu lotu, F czarna skrzynka *f*; '~·**y** (***-ier, -iest***) niestały, chimeryczny
flim·sy ['flɪmzɪ] (***-ier, -iest***) wątły, mizerny; cienki; *fig.* kiepski
flinch [flɪntʃ] wzdrygać ⟨-gnąć⟩ się; cofać ⟨-fnąć⟩ się (***from*** przed *I*)
fling [flɪŋ] **1.** (***flung***) rzucać, cisnąć ⟨-skać⟩; ~ ***o.s.*** rzucać ⟨-cić⟩ się; ~ ***open*** *lub* ***to*** *okno itp.* otwierać ⟨-worzyć⟩ *lub* zamykać ⟨-mknąć⟩ z rozmachem; **2.** ***have a*** ~ ⟨za⟩bawić się; ***have a*** ~ ***at*** flirtować z
flint [flɪnt] krzemień *m*; kamień *m* (*do zapalniczki*)
flip [flɪp] (***-pp-***) przerzucać ⟨-cić⟩, przewracać ⟨-rócić⟩; *monetę* rzucać ⟨-cić⟩
flip·pant ['flɪpənt] bezceremonialny, niepoważny
flip·per ['flɪpə] *zo.* płetwa *f* (*foki itp., też pływaka*)
flirt [flɜːt] **1.** ⟨po⟩flirtować; **2.** ***be a*** ~ chętnie flirtować; **flir·ta·tion** [flɜː'teɪʃn] flirt *m*
flit [flɪt] (***-tt-***) przelatywać ⟨-lecieć⟩, przemykać ⟨-mknąć⟩
float [fləʊt] **1.** *v/i.* pływać, unosić się; *też econ.* być w obiegu; *v/t.* spływać, przepływać; spławiać ⟨-wić⟩; *naut.* ⟨z⟩wodować; *econ.* puszczać w obieg; *econ.* upłynniać ⟨-nić⟩kurs walut; **2.** pływak *m*; spławik *m*; '~·**ing** **1.** pływający, unoszący się (*na wodzie*); *econ. pieniądz itp.*: w obiegu; *kurs*: płynny, zmienny; *kapitał*: obrotowy; **2.** kurs *m* zmienny; ~·**ing** '**vot·er** *pol.* niestały wyborca
flock [flɒk] **1.** stado *n* (*zwł. owiec i kóz*); trzoda *f* (*też rel.*); tłum *m*; **2.** *fig.* pchać się
floe [fləʊ] kra *f*
flog [flɒg] (***-gg-***) biczować, chłostać; '~·**ging** biczowanie *n*, chłosta *f*
flood [flʌd] **1.** *też* ~***-tide*** zalew (*też fig.*); powódź *f*, wylew *m*; **2.** wylewać ⟨-lać⟩, zalewać ⟨lać⟩; '~·**gate** śluza *f*; '~·**lights** *pl. electr.* reflektor *m*
floor [flɔː] **1.** podłoga *f*; strop *m*; piętro *n*, kondygnacja *f*; parkiet (*do tańczenia*); dno *n*; → ***first floor, second floor***; ***take the*** ~ zabierać ⟨-brać⟩ głos; **2.** kłaść podłogę; powalić na podłogę; F pokonać; '~·**board** deska *f* (*na podłodze*); '~ **cloth** ścierka *f* do podłogi; ~·**ing** ['flɔːrɪŋ] materiał *m* na podłogę; '~ **lamp** *Am.* lampa *f* stojąca; '~ **lead·er** *Am.* przewodniczący *m* klubu partyjnego; '~ **show** występ *m* w klubie nocnym; '~·**walk·er** *zwł. Am.* → ***shopwalker***
flop [flɒp] **1.** (***-pp-***) padać ⟨paść⟩, upadać ⟨upaść⟩; F ⟨z⟩robić klapę *lub* plajtę; **2.** F klapa *f*; plajta *f*; klapnięcie *n*;

'~·py, ~·py 'disk *komp.* dyskietka *f*
Flor·ence Florencja *f*
flor·id ['flɒrɪd] czerwony, rumiany
Flor·i·da Floryda *f*
flor·ist ['flɒrɪst] kwiaciarz *m* (-arka *f*)
floun·der[1] ['flaʊndə] *zo.* (*pl.* ***flounder, flounders***) flądra *f*, płastuga *f*
floun·der[2] ['flaʊndə] rzucać ⟨-cić⟩ się, trzepotać się; *fig.* plątać się
flour ['flaʊə] mąka *f*
flour·ish ['flʌrɪʃ] **1.** ozdobny gest *m*; ozdobnik *m*; *mus.* tusz *m*; **2.** *v/i.* rozwijać ⟨-winąć⟩ się, rozkwitać ⟨-tnąć⟩; *v/t.* wymachiwać
flow [fləʊ] **1.** ⟨po⟩płynąć, ⟨po-, wy⟩ciec; ⟨po⟩toczyć się; wzbierać ⟨wezbrać⟩; **2.** strumień *m*; wypływ *m*, wyciek *m*; przypływ *m*
flow·er ['flaʊə] **1.** kwiat *m* (*też fig*); **2.** kwitnąć, rozkwitać ⟨-tnąć⟩; **'~·bed** klomb *m*; **'~·pot** doniczka *f*
flown [fləʊn] *p.p. od* ***fly***[3]
fl. oz. *skrót pisany*: ***fluid ounce*** (*jednostka objętości*: *Brt.* *28,4 cm*^{3}, *Am.* *29,57 cm*^{3})
fluc·tu|·ate ['flʌktʃʊeɪt] podlegać fluktuacji, zmieniać ⟨-nić⟩ się; **~·a·tion** [flʌktʃʊ'eɪʃn] fluktuacja *f*
flu [fluː] F grypa *f*
flue [fluː] przewód *m* kominowy
flu·en|·cy ['fluːənsɪ] biegłość *f*, płynność *f*; potoczystość *f*; **'~t** biegły; płynny; potoczysty; *mówca*: wymowny
fluff [flʌf] **1.** puch *m*; włoski *pl.*, meszek *m*; **2.** *pióra* ⟨na⟩stroszyć; **'~·y** (***-ier, -iest***) puszysty
flu·id ['fluːɪd] **1.** płynny; ciekły; **2.** płyn *m*; ciecz *f*
flung [flʌŋ] *pret. i p.p. od* ***fling*** 1
flunk [flʌŋk] *Am.* F *egzamin* oblewać ⟨-lać⟩
flu·o·res·cent [flʊə'resnt] fluorescencyjny; jarzeniowy
flu·o·ride ['flɔːraɪd] *chem.* fluorek *m*
flu·o·rine ['flɔːriːn] *chem.* fluor *m*
flur·ry ['flʌrɪ] zawieja *f*; *fig.* poruszenie *n*, niepokój *m*
flush [flʌʃ] **1.** spłukanie *n* (*wodą*); zaczerwienienie *n*, wypieki *pl.*; **2.** *v/t.* *też* **~ *out*** przepłukiwać ⟨-kać⟩; **~ *down*** spłukiwać ⟨-kać⟩; **~ *the toilet*** spuszczać ⟨spuścić⟩ wodę; *v/i.* zaczerwieniać ⟨-nić⟩ się; spuszczać ⟨spuścić⟩ wodę
flus·ter ['flʌstə] **1.** denerwować (się); **2.** zdenerwowanie *n*
flute [fluːt] *mus.* **1.** flet *m*; **2.** ⟨za⟩grać na flecie
flut·ter ['flʌtə] **1.** ⟨za⟩trzepotać; **2.** trzepot *m*; *fig.* podniecenie *n*
flux [flʌks] *fig.* zmiana *f*, zmienianie *n* się
fly[1] [flaɪ] *zo.* mucha *f*
fly[2] [flaɪ] rozporek *m*;
fly[3] [flaɪ] (***flew, flown***) *v/i.* latać; lecieć; fruwać; uciekać ⟨-ciec⟩; *czas*: płynąć; **~ *at*** rzucać się na (*A*); **~ *into a passion*** *lub* ***rage*** wpadać ⟨-paść⟩ w pasję *lub* szał; *v/t.* pilotować; ⟨prze⟩transportować; *latawca* puszczać; **'~·er** → ***flier***
'fly·ing latający; **~'sau·cer** latający spodek *m*; **'~ squad** lotna brygada *f* (*policji*)
'fly|·o·ver *Brt.* estakada *f* (*dróg, kolejowa*); **'~·weight** *boks*: waga *f* musza; **'~·wheel** koło *n* zamachowe
FM [ef 'em] *skrót*: ***frequency modulation*** FM, UKF *m*, fale *pl.* utrakrótkie
foal [fəʊl] *zo.* źrebak *m*
foam [fəʊm] **1.** piana *f*; **2.** pienić się; **~ 'rub·ber** guma *f* piankowa, F pianka *f*; **'~·y** pienisty; spieniony
fo·cus ['fəʊkəs] **1.** (*pl.* ***-cuses, -ci*** [-saɪ]) ognisko *n* (*opt.*, *też fig.*); centrum *n*; *phot.* ostrość *f*; **2.** *opt.*, *phot.* nastawiać ⟨-wić⟩ ostrość; *fig.* skupiać ⟨-pić⟩ się (***on*** na *L*)
fod·der ['fɒdə] karma *f*, pasza *f*
foe [fəʊ] *poet.* wróg *m*, nieprzyjaciel *m*
fog [fɒg] mgła *f*; **'~·gy** (***-ier, -iest***) zamglony; *figt.* mglisty
foi·ble ['fɔɪbl] *fig.* słabość *f*
foil[1] [fɔɪl] folia *f*; *fig.* tło *n*
foil[2] [fɔɪl] ⟨po⟩krzyżować, udaremniać ⟨-nić⟩
foil[3] [fɔɪl] (*w szermierce*) floret *m*
fold[1] [fəʊld] **1.** fałda *f*; zagięcie *n*; **2.** składać ⟨złożyć⟩, zaginać ⟨-giąć⟩; *ramiona itp.* zakładać ⟨założyć⟩; zawijać ⟨-winąć⟩; *często* **~ *up*** składać ⟨złożyć⟩ się; ⟨za⟩kończyć się
fold[2] [fəʊld] okólnik *m*, zagroda *f*; *rel.* trzoda *f*, owczarnia *n*
'fold·er skoroszyt *m*, teczka *f*; folder *m*; broszura *f*
'fold·ing składany; **'~ bed** łóżko *n* składane *lub* polowe; **'~ bi·cy·cle** rower *m* składany, F składak *m*; **'~ boat** łódź *f* składana; **'~ chair** krzesło *n* składane;

'~ **door**(**s** *pl.*) drzwi *pl.* składane
fo·li·age ['fəʊlɪɪdʒ] liście *pl.*, listowie *f*
folk [fəʊk] *pl.* ludzie *pl.*; **~s** *pl.* F ludziska *pl.*; *attr.* ludowy; '**~·lore** folklor *m*;'~ **mu·sic** muzyka *f* ludowa;'~ **song** pieśń *f* ludowa
fol·low ['fɒləʊ] podążać ⟨-żyć⟩ za (*D*); iść ⟨pójść⟩ za (*I*); następować ⟨-tąpić⟩ po (*D*); śledzić; **~ *through*** *plan itp.* przeprowadzać ⟨-dzić⟩ do końca; **~ *up*** (za)stosować się do (*G*), *sugestię itp.* rozwijać ⟨-winąć⟩; ***as ~s*** jak następuje; '**~·er** zwolennik *m* (-iczka *f*); '**~·ing** **1.** uznanie *n*; zwolennicy *pl.*; ***the ~ing*** *osoby*: następujący *pl.*, *coś*: co następuje; **2.** następujący; następny; **3.** bezpośrednio po (*L*)
fol·ly ['fɒlɪ] szaleństwo *n*
fond [fɒnd] czuły; naiwny; ***be ~ of*** lubić (*A*)
fon·dle ['fɒndl] pieścić
'**fond·ness** czułość *f*
font [fɒnt] chrzcielnica *f*; *komp.* czcionka *f*
food [fuːd] jedzenie *n*; pożywienie *n*; żywność *f*
fool [fuːl] **1.** głupiec *m*, dureń *m*; ***make a ~ of s.o.*** robić z kogoś durnia; ***make a ~ of o.s.*** robić z siebie durnia; **2.** oszukiwać ⟨-kać⟩; wyłudzać ⟨-dzić⟩; *też* **~ *about*, ~ *around*** wygłupiać się; '**~·har·dy** ryzykowny, brawurowy; '**~·ish** głupi, durny; '**~·ish·ness** głupota *f*;'**~·proof** bezpieczny, nie do zepsucia
foot [fʊt] **1.** (*pl.* ***feet***) stopa *f*; (*pl.* F *też* ***foot***, *skrót*: ***ft***) stopa *f* (*=30,48 cm*); podstawa *f*; podnóże *n*; ***on ~*** pieszo; **2.** F *rachunek* pokrywać ⟨-ryć⟩; **~ *it*** iść ⟨pójść⟩ piechotą
'**foot·ball** piłka *f* nożna (*też gra*); *Am.* futbol *m*;'**foot·bal·ler** piłkarz *m*; *Am.* futbolista *m*; '~ **hoo·li·gan** pseudokibic *m*; '~ **play·er** piłkarz *m* (-arka *f*)
'**foot|·bridge** kładka *f* dla pieszych; '**~·fall** (*odgłos*) krok *m*;'**~·hold** mocne oparcie *n* (*dla stóp*)
'**foot·ing** oparcie *n*, podstawa *f*; ***be on a friendly ~ with s.o.*** mieć dobre stosunki z kimś; ***lose one's ~*** ⟨s⟩tracić oparcie *lub* równowagę
'**foot|·lights** *pl. theat.* światła *pl.* rampy; '**~·loose** nieskrępowany; ***~loose and fancy-free*** swobodny jak ptak; '**~·path** ścieżka *f*; '**~·print** odcisk *m* (*stopy*); ***~prints*** ślady *pl.*;'**~·sore** otarcie *n*; '**~·step** krok *m*; '**~·wear** obuwie *n*
fop [fɒp] strojniś *m*, elegancik *m*
for [fɔː, fə] **1.** *prp.* dla (*G*); *wymiana, przyczyna, cena, cel*: za (*I*); *tęsknić itp.*: za (*I*); *cel, przeznaczenie, kierunek*: do (*G*); *czekać, mieć nadzieję itp.*: na (*A*); *posyłać itp.* po (*A*); *popierać*: za (*I*); *okres czasu*: **~ *three days*** przez trzy dni, od trzech dni; **~ *tomorrow*** na jutro; *odległość*: ***I walked ~ a mile*** przeszedłem milę; ***I ~ one*** ja na przykład; **~ *sure*** na pewno, z pewnością; ***it is hard ~ him to do it*** ciężko jest mu to zrobić; **2.** *cj.* ponieważ
for·age ['fɒrɪdʒ] ⟨po⟩szukiwać; *też* **~ *about*** szperać (***in*** w *L*)
for·ay ['fɒreɪ] *mil.* wypad *m*; *fig.* wycieczka; **~ *into politics*** w dziedzinę polityki
for·bad(**e**) [fə'bæd] *pret. od* ***forbid***
for·bear ['fɔːbeə] → ***forebear***
for·bid [fə'bɪd] (***-dd-***; ***-bade*** *lub* ***-bad*** [-bæd], ***-bidden*** *lub* ***-bid***) zabraniać ⟨-ronić⟩; zakazywać ⟨-zać⟩;**~·ding** odpychający, przerażający
force [fɔːs] **1.** siła *f*; przemoc *f*; ***the*** (***police***) **~** policja *f*; (***armed***) **~s** siły *pl.* zbrojne; ***by ~*** siłą, przemocą; ***come*** *lub* ***put into ~*** wchodzić *lub* wprowadzać w życie; **2.** *kogoś* zmuszać ⟨-musić⟩; *coś* wymuszać ⟨-musić⟩; wpychać ⟨wepchnąć⟩ (*na siłę*); włamywać ⟨-mać⟩, wyłamywać ⟨-mać⟩; **~ *s.th. on s.o.*** wmuszać ⟨-sić⟩ coś komuś; **~ *o.s. on s.o.*** narzucać ⟨-cić⟩ się komuś; **~ *open*** otwierać ⟨-worzyć⟩ siłą; **~d** wymuszony; przymusowy; **~d 'land·ing** *aviat.* lądowanie *n* awaryjne; '**~·ful** energiczny, silny; mocny, dobitny
for·ceps ['fɔːseps] *med.* kleszcze *pl.*, szczypce *pl.*
for·ci·ble ['fɔːsəbl] dokonany siłą *lub* przemocą; potężny, dobitny
ford [fɔːd] **1.** bród *m*; **2.** przeprawiać ⟨-wić⟩ się w bród
fore [fɔː] **1.** przedni; dziobowy; **2.** przednia część *f*; ***come to the ~*** wyróżniać ⟨-nić⟩ się; **~·arm** ['fɔːrɑːm] przedramię *n*;'**~·bear**: *zw.* ***~bears*** przodkowie *pl.*; **~·bod·ing** [fɔː'bəʊdɪŋ] (*złe*) prze-

czucie *n*; '**~·cast** **1.** (**-*cast*** *lub* **-*casted***) przewidywać ⟨-widzieć⟩; prognozować; **2.** prognoza *f*; '**~·fa·ther** przodek *m*; '**~·fin·ger** palec *m* wskazujący; '**~·foot** (*pl.* ***feet***) *zo.* przednia łapa *f*; **~·gone con'clu·sion** sprawa *f* z góry przesądzona; '**~·ground** pierwszy plan *m*; '**~·hand** **1.** (*w sporcie*) forhend *m*; **2.** (*w sporcie*) z forhendu; **~·head** ['fɒrɪd] czoło *m*

for·eign ['fɒrən] zagraniczny; cudzoziemski; obcy; **~ af'fairs** *pl.* sprawy *pl.* zagraniczne; **~ 'aid** pomoc *f* z zagranicy; '**~·er** cudzoziemiec *m* (-mka *f*); **~ 'lan·guage** język *m* obcy; **~ 'min·is·ter** *pol.* minister *m* spraw zagranicznych; '**♀ Of·fice** *Brt. pol.* Ministerstwo *m* Spraw Zagranicznych; **~ 'pol·i·cy** polityka *f* zagraniczna; **♀ 'Sec·re·ta·ry** *Brt. pol.* minister *m* spraw zagranicznych; **~ 'trade** *econ.* handel *m* zagraniczny; **~ 'work·er** pracownik *m* cudzoziemski, gastarbeiter *m*

fore|'**knowl·edge** uprzednia wiedza *f*; '**~·leg** *zo.* noga *f* przednia; '**~·man** (*pl.* **-*men***) brygadzista *m*; *jur.* przewodniczący *m* (*ławy przysięgłych*); '**~·most** naczelny, najważniejszy; '**~·name** imię *n*

fo·ren·sic [fə'rensɪk] sądowy; **~ 'medi·cine** medycyna *f* sądowa

'**fore**|**·run·ner** prekursor *m*, poprzednik *m*; **~'see** (**-*saw*, -*seen***) przewidywać ⟨-widzieć⟩; **~'shad·ow** zapowiadać ⟨-wiedzieć⟩; '**~·sight** *fig.* przenikliwość *f*, dalekowzroczność *f*

for·est ['fɒrɪst] las *m* (*też fig.*)

fore·stall [fɔː'stɔːl] uprzedzać ⟨-dzić⟩, ubiegać ⟨ubiec⟩

for·est|**·er** ['fɒrɪstə] leśniczy *m*; **~·ry** ['fɒrɪstrɪ] leśnictwo *n*

'**fore**|**·taste** przedsmak *m*; **~'tell** (**-*told***) przepowiadać ⟨-wiedzieć⟩; '**~·thought** przezorność *f*, roztropność *f*

for·ev·er, for ev·er [fə'revə] na zawsze

'**fore**|**·wom·an** (*pl.* **-*women***) brygadzistka *f*; '**~·word** przedmowa *f*

for·feit ['fɔːfɪt] ⟨u-, s⟩tracić; być ⟨zostać⟩ pozbawionym

forge [fɔːdʒ] **1.** kuźnia *f*; **2.** ⟨s⟩fałszować; '**forg·er** fałszerz *m*; **·ge·ry** ['fɔːdʒərɪ] fałszerstwo *n*, falsyfikat *m*; '**for·ge·ry-proof** trudny do sfałszowania

for·get [fə'get] (**-*got*, *gotten***) zapominać ⟨-mnieć⟩; **~·ful** zapominalski; **~-me-not** *bot.* niezapominajka *f*

for·give [fə'gɪv] (**-*gave*, -*given***) wybaczać ⟨-czyć⟩, przebaczać ⟨-czyć⟩; **~·ness** wybaczenie *n*, przebaczenie *n*; **for·'giv·ing** wyrozumiały

fork [fɔːk] **1.** widelec *m*; widły *pl.*; rozwidlenie *n*; **2.** rozwidlać ⟨-lić⟩ (się); **~ed** rozwidlony; **~·lift 'truck** wózek *m* widłowy

form [fɔːm] **1.** forma *f*, kształt *m*; formularz *m*; *zwł. Brt.* klasa *f*; formalności *pl.*; kondycja *f*; ***in great ~*** w wielkiej formie; **2.** ⟨u⟩kształtować (się); ⟨u⟩formować (się); ⟨u⟩tworzyć (się); ustawiać ⟨-wić⟩ (się)

for|**m·al** ['fɔːml] formalny; oficjalny; uroczysty; **~·mal·i·ty** [fɔː'mælətɪ] formalność *f*, oficjalność *f*; uroczystość *f*

for·mat ['fɔːmæt] **1.** format *m*; forma *f*; **2.** (**-*tt*-**) *komp.* ⟨z⟩formatować

for·ma|**·tion** [fɔː'meɪʃn] tworzenie *n*, utworzenie *n*; formacja *f*, szyk *m*; **~·tive** ['fɔːmətɪv] tworzący, kształtujący; ***~tive years*** *pl.* okres *m* rozwoju osobowości

'**for·mat·ting** *komp.* formatowanie *n*

for·mer ['fɔːmə] **1.** były; wcześniejszy; **2.** ***the ~*** pierwszy (*z wymienionych*); '**~·ly** uprzednio, wcześniej

for·mi·da·ble ['fɔːmɪdəbl] straszny; wzbudzający respekt; *pytanie itp.*: trudny

'**form**| **mas·ter** wychowawca *m* (*klasy*); '**~ mis·tress** wychowawczyni *f* (*klasy*); '**~ teach·er** wychowawca *m* (-czyni *f*) (*klasy*)

for·mu|**·la** ['fɔːmjʊlə] *chem.*, *math.* wzór *m*; formuła *f*; recepta *f*; **~·late** ['fɔːmjʊleɪt] ⟨s⟩formułować

for|**·sake** [fə'seɪk] (**-*sook*, -*saken***) porzucać ⟨-cić⟩, opuszczać ⟨-uścić⟩; **~·sak·en** [fə'seɪkən] *p.p. od* ***forsake***; **~·sook** [fə'sʊk] *pret. od* ***forsake***; **~·swear** [fɔː'sweə] (**-*swore*, -*sworn***) wyrzekać ⟨-rzec⟩ się pod przysięgą

fort [fɔːt] *mil.* fort *m*, twierdza *f*

forth [fɔːθ] naprzód; dalej; ***and so ~*** i tak dalej; **~'com·ing** nadchodzący; przychylny; *książka*: mający się ukazać; ***be ~coming*** pojawiać się

for·ti·eth ['fɔːtɪɪθ] czterdziesty

for·ti|**·fi·ca·tion** [fɔːtɪfɪ'keɪʃn] *mil.* fortyfikacja *f*; **~·fy** ['fɔːtɪfaɪ] *mil.* ⟨u⟩fortyfikować; *fig.* wzmacniać ⟨-moc-

nić⟩; **~·tude** ['fɔːtɪtjuːd] hart *m* (ducha), męstwo *n*
fort·night ['fɔːtnaɪt] czternaście dni *pl.*, dwa tygodnie *pl.*
for·tress ['fɔːtrɪs] *mil.* forteca *f*
for·tu·i·tous [fɔː'tjuːɪtəs] nieprzewidziany, przypadkowy
for·tu·nate ['fɔːtʃnət] szczęśliwy; pomyślny; ***be ~*** mieć szczęście; **'~·ly** na szczęście
for·tune ['fɔːtʃn] fortuna *f*, majątek *m*; szczęście *n*; los *m*, pomyślność *f*; **'~-tell·er** wróżbita *m*, wróżka *f*
for·ty ['fɔːtɪ] **1.** czterdzieści; ***have ~ winks*** F uciąć ⟨-cinać⟩ sobie drzemkę; **2.** czterdziestka *f*
for·ward ['fɔːwəd] **1.** *adv.* naprzód, wprzód; **2.** *adj.* przedni; zdążający do przodu; zaawansowany; obcesowy; **3.** (*w piłce nożnej*) napastnik *m*; **4.** przesyłać ⟨-słać⟩, wysyłać ⟨-słać⟩; ⟨wy⟩ekspediować; wspierać ⟨wesprzeć⟩, popierać ⟨-przeć⟩; **'~·ing a·gent** spedytor *m*
fos·sil ['fɒsl] **1.** *geol.* skamielina *f*; *fig.* żywy relikt *m*; **2.** *adj.* kopalny; *paliwo*: z surowców kopalnych
fos·ter|-child ['fɒstətʃaɪld] (*pl.* ***-children***) wychowanek *m*; przybrane dziecko *n*; **'~-par·ents** *pl.* przybrani rodzice *pl.*
fought [fɔːt] *pret. i p.p. od* ***fight*** 2
foul [faʊl] **1.** okropny; *jedzenie*: cuchnący; *powietrze*, *jedzenie*: nieświeży; zanieczyszczony; *język*: plugawy; (*w sporcie*) nieprawidłowy; **2.** (*w sporcie*) faul *m*; ***vicious ~*** złośliwy faul *m*; **3.** (*w sporcie*) ⟨s⟩faulować; ⟨s⟩plugawić, ⟨za⟩brudzić
found[1] [faʊnd] *pret. i p.p. od* ***find*** 1
found[2] [faʊnd] zakładać ⟨założyć⟩; ⟨u⟩fundować
found[3] [faʊnd] *tech.* odlewać ⟨odlać⟩
foun·da·tion [faʊn'deɪʃn] *arch.* fundament *m*, podłoże *n*; założenie *n*; fundacja *f*; podstawa *f*
found·er[1] ['faʊndə] założyciel(ka *f*) *m*; fundator(ka *f*) *m*
foun·der[2] ['faʊndə] *naut.* ⟨za⟩tonąć
found·ling ['faʊndlɪŋ] podrzutek *m*
foun·dry ['faʊndrɪ] odlewnia *f*
foun·tain ['faʊntɪn] fontanna *f*; **'~ pen** pióro *n* wieczne
four [fɔː] **1.** cztery; **2.** czwórka *f* (*też w łodzi*); ***on all ~s*** na czworakach
'four|star *Brt.* F (*benzyna*) super; **~-star 'pet·rol** *Brt.* benzyna *f* super; **~-stroke 'en·gine** silnik *m* czterosuwowy
four|·teen [fɔː'tiːn] **1.** czternaście; **2.** czternastka *f*; **~·teenth** [fɔː'tiːnθ] czternasty; **~th** [fɔːθ] **1.** czwarty; **2.** jedna *f* czwarta; **'~th·ly** po czwarte
four-wheel 'drive *mot.* napęd *m* na cztery koła
fowl [faʊl] ptak *m*; drób *m*, ptactwo *n* (*domowe*)
fox [fɒks] *zo.* lis *m*; **'~·glove** *bot.* naparstnica *f*; **'~·y** (***-ier, -iest***) przebiegły, chytry
frac·tion ['frækʃn] ułamek *m* (*też math.*)
frac·ture ['fræktʃə] **1.** złamanie *n* (*zwł. kości*), pęknięcie; **2.** łamać (się); pękać
fra·gile ['frædʒaɪl] kruchy, łamliwy
frag·ment ['frægmənt] fragment *m*, kawałek *m*; urywek *m*
fra|·grance ['freɪgrəns] woń *f*, zapach *m*; **'~·grant** wonny, pachnący
frail [freɪl] kruchy; delikatny; *fig.* słaby; **'~·ty** kruchość *f*, delikatność *f*; słabość *f*
frame [freɪm] **1.** rama *f*, ramka *f*; oprawka *f* (*do okularów*); budowa *f* (*ciała*); *film*: kadr *m*; ***~ of mind*** usposobienie *n*, nastrój *m*; **2.** oprawiać ⟨-wić⟩; obramowywać ⟨-wać⟩; ⟨s⟩formułować; *też **~ up*** F *kogoś* wplątywać ⟨-tać⟩; **'~-up** F ukartowana gra *f*; intryga *f*; **'~·work** *tech.* szkielet *m* konstrukcji; *fig.* struktura *f*, system *m*, ramy *pl.*
franc [fræŋk] frank *m*
France [frɑːns] Francja *f*
fran·chise ['fræntʃaɪz] *pol.* prawo *n* wyborcze; koncesja *f*
frank [fræŋk] **1.** szczery, otwarty; **2.** *Brt.* ⟨o⟩frankować (*maszynowo*)
frank·fur·ter ['fræŋkfɜːtə] parówka *f*
'frank·ness szczerość *f*, otwartość *f*
fran·tic ['fræntɪk] (***~ally***) gorączkowy, rozgorączkowany; hektyczny
fra·ter|·nal [frə'tɜːnl] braterski; **~·ni·ty** [frə'tɜːnətɪ] braterstwo *n*; bractwo *n*; *Am. univ.* związek *m*
fraud [frɔːd] oszustwo *n*; F oszust(ka *f*) *m*; **~·u·lent** ['frɔːdjʊlənt] oszukańczy
fray [freɪ] ⟨po-, wy⟩strzępić (się)
freak [friːk] *też **~ of nature*** wybryk *m* (natury); dziwoląg *m*; potworek *m*; fanatyk *m* (-tyczka *f*); *attr.* dziwaczny; ***film ~*** maniak *m* (-aczka *f*) na punkcie filmów

freck·le ['frekl] pieg *m*; '~**d** piegowaty
free [fri:] **1.** (**-r, -st**) wolny, swobodny; darmowy, bezpłatny; ~ ***and easy*** beztroski; ***set*** ~ uwalniać ⟨uwolnić⟩; **2.** (***freed***) uwalniać ⟨uwolnić⟩, oswobadzać ⟨-bodzić⟩; ~**·dom** ['fri:dəm] wolność *f*, swoboda *f*; ~ '**fares** *pl.* przejazd *m* bezpłatny; ~**·lance** ['fri:lɑ:ns] *pisarz*: niezależny; '**2·ma·son** mason *m*; ~ '**skat·ing** (*w łyżwiarstwie*) jazda *f* dowolna; '~**·style** (*w sporcie*) styl *m* dowolny; ~ '**time** czas *m* wolny; ~ '**trade** wolny handel *m*; ~ **trade** '**ar·e·a** strefa *f* wolnego handlu; '~**·way** *Am.* droga *f* szybkiego ruchu; ~'**wheel** jechać na wolnym biegu
freeze [fri:z] **1.** (***froze, frozen***) *v/i.* zamarzać ⟨-marznąć⟩; ⟨za⟩krzepnąć; *v/t.* zamrażać ⟨-mrozić⟩ (*też ceny itp.*); **2.** mróz *m*; *econ.*, *pol.* zamrożenie *n*; ***wage*** ~, ~ ***on wages*** zamrożenie *n* płac; ~-'**dried** liofilizowany; ~-'**dry** liofilizować
'**freez·er** zamrażalnik *m*; (*też* ***deep freeze***) zamrażarka *f*
freeze-frame stop-klatka *f*
'**freez·ing** lodowaty; '~ **com·part·ment** zamrażalnik *m*; '~ **point** punkt *m* zamarzania
freight [freɪt] **1.** fracht *m*; ładunek *m*; *Am. attr.* towarowy; **2.** przesyłać ⟨-słać⟩ frachtem; ⟨za⟩frachtować; '~ **car** *Am. rail* wagon *m* towarowy; '~**·er** frachtowiec *m*; samolot *m* frachtowy; '~ **train** *Am.* pociąg *m* towarowy
French [frentʃ] **1.** francuski; **2.** *ling.* język *m* francuski; ***the*** ~ *pl.* Francuzi *pl.*; ~ '**doors** *pl. Am.* → ***French windows***; ~ '**fries** *pl. zwł. Am.* frytki *pl.*; '~**·man** (*pl.* **-*men***) Francuz *m*; ~ '**window(s** *pl.*) drzwi *pl.* balkonowe *lub* przeszklone; '~**·wom·an** (*pl.* ***-women***) Francuzka *f*
fren|·zied ['frenzɪd] rozgorączkowany; szalony; rozszalały; ~**·zy** ['frenzɪ] podniecenie *n*; rozgorączkowanie *n*; szaleństwo *n*
fre·quen|·cy ['fri:kwənsɪ] częstotliwość *f* (*też electr.*); ~**t** **1.** ['fri:kwənt] częsty; **2.** [frɪ'kwent] uczęszczać, odwiedzać ⟨-dzić⟩
fresh [freʃ] świeży; rześki; nowy; F obcesowy, chamski; ~**·en** ['freʃn] *wiatr*: przybierać ⟨-brać⟩ na sile; ~***en*** (***o.s.***) ***up*** odświeżać ⟨-żyć⟩ się; '~**·man** (*pl.* ***-men***) *univ.* student(ka *f*) *m* pierwszego roku; '~**·ness** świeżość *f*; ~ '**water** słodka woda *f*; '~**·wa·ter** słodkowodny
fret [fret] zamartwiać się; '~**·ful** kapryśny, płaczliwy, przykry
FRG [ef ɑ: 'dʒi:] *skrót*: ***Federal Republic of Germany*** RFN *f*
Fri *skrót pisany*: ***Friday*** piątek *m*
fri·ar ['fraɪə] mnich *m*
fric·tion ['frɪkʃn] tarcie *n* (*też fig.*)
Fri·day ['fraɪdɪ] (*skrót*: ***Fri***) piątek *m*; ***on*** ~ w piątek; ***on*** ~***s*** co piątek
fridge [frɪdʒ] F lodówka *f*
friend [frend] przyjaciel *m* (*przyjaciółka f*); znajomy *m* (-ma *f*); ***make*** ~***s with*** ⟨za⟩przyjaźnić się z (*I*), zawierać ⟨-wrzeć⟩ przyjaźń z (*I*); '~**·ly** **1.** przyjacielski; przyjazny; **2.** *zwł. Brt.* (*w sporcie*) spotkanie *n* towarzyskie; '~**·ship** przyjaźń *f*
fries [fraɪz] *zwł. Am. pl.* F frytki *pl.*
frig·ate ['frɪgɪt] *naut.* fregata *f*
fright [fraɪt] przerażenie *n*; ***look a*** ~ F okropnie wyglądać; ~**·en** ['fraɪtn] wystraszyć ⟨-szać⟩; ***be*** ~***ened*** wystraszyć się; '~**·ful** przerażający, straszliwy
fri·gid ['frɪdʒɪd] *psych.* oziębły; zimny
frill [frɪl] falbanka *f*; dodatek *m*
fringe [frɪndʒ] **1.** frędzle *pl.*; brzeg *m*, skraj *m*; grzywka *f*; **2.** otaczać ⟨otoczyć⟩, obramowywać ⟨-mować⟩; '~ **ben·e·fits** *pl.* świadczenia *pl.* dodatkowe; '~ **e·vent** impreza *f* dodatkowa; '~ **group** grupa *f* marginesowa
frisk [frɪsk] skakać, brykać; F *kogoś* przeszukiwać ⟨-kać⟩; '~**·y** (***-ier, -iest***) żywotny, dziarski
frit·ter ['frɪtə]: ~ ***away*** ⟨z⟩marnować
fri·vol·i·ty [frɪ'vɒlətɪ] brak *m* powagi; lekkomyślność *f*; **friv·o·lous** ['frɪvələs] niepoważny; lekkomyślny
friz·zle ['frɪzl] *gastr.* F przypalać się; ⟨za⟩skwierczeć
frizz·y ['frɪzɪ] (***-ier, -iest***) *włosy*: kręcony
fro [frəʊ]: ***to and*** ~ tam i z powrotem
frock [frɒk] sukienka *f*; habit *m*
frog [frɒg] żaba *f*; '~**·man** (*pl.* ***-men***) płetwonurek *m*
frol·ic ['frɒlɪk] **1.** zabawa *f*; figle *pl.*; **2.** (***-ck-***) brykać, ⟨po⟩skakać; '~**·some** rozbrykany, figlarny
from [frɒm, frəm] z; od (*G*); ***from ... to***

... od *lub* z ... do ...; ***where are you ~?*** skąd jesteś?
front [frʌnt] **1.** przód *m*; front *m* (*też mil.*); fasada *f*; ***at the ~, in ~*** z przodu, na przedzie; ***in ~ of*** *w przestrzeni*: przed (*I*); ***be in ~*** być na przedzie; **2.** przedni; **3.** *też ~* ***on, to(wards)*** wychodzić przodem na (*A*); **~·age** ['frʌntɪdʒ] elewacja *f*, fronton *m*; **'~ cov·er** strona *f* tytułowa; **~ 'door** przednie drzwi *pl.*; **~ 'en·trance** przednie wejście *n*
fron·tier ['frʌntɪə] granica *f* (*państwowa*); *Am. hist.* pogranicze *n* (*Dzikiego Zachodu*); *attr.* graniczny, przygraniczny
'front|-page F *wiadomości*: najnowszy; **~-wheel 'drive** *mot.* napęd *m* na przednie koła
frost [frɒst] **1.** mróz *m*; *też* ***hoar ~, white ~*** szron *m*; **2.** oszraniać ⟨-ronić⟩, pokrywać ⟨pokryć⟩ szronem; *szkło* ⟨za⟩matować; *gastr.*, *zwł. Am.* ⟨po⟩lukrować, posypywać ⟨-pać⟩ cukrem pudrem; ***~ed glass*** matowe *lub* mleczne szkło *n*; **'~·bite** odmrożenie *n*; **'~·bitten** odmrożony; **'~·y** (***-ier, -iest***) mroźny (*też fig.*); zaszroniony, oszroniony
froth [frɒθ] **1.** piana *f*; **2.** ⟨s⟩pienić (się); ⟨po⟩toczyć pianę; **'~·y** (***-ier, -iest***) spieniony, pienisty
frown [fraʊn] **1.** zmarszczenie *n* brwi; ***with a ~*** ze zmarszczonymi brwiami; **2.** ⟨z⟩marszczyć brew; ***~ (up)on s.th.*** ⟨s⟩krzywić się na coś
froze [frəʊz] *pret. od* **freeze** 1; **fro·zen** ['frəʊzn] **1.** *p.p. od* **freeze** 1; **2.** *adj.* zamarznięty; zamrożony; mrożony; **fro·zen 'foods** *pl.* mrożonki *pl.*
fru·gal ['fru:gl] oszczędny; skromny
fruit [fru:t] owoc *m*; owoce *pl.*; **~·er·er** ['fru:tərə] sklep *m* z owocami; handlarz *m* owocami; **'~·ful** owocny; **'~·less** bezowocny; **'~ juice** sok *m* owocowy; **'~·y** (***-ier, -iest***) owocowy; *głos*: donośny
frus|·trate [frʌ'streɪt] ⟨s⟩frustrować; udaremniać ⟨-mnić⟩, uniemożliwiać ⟨-wić⟩; **~·tra·tion** [frʌ'streɪʃn] frustracja *f*, uniemożliwienie *n*, udaremnienie *n*
fry [fraɪ] ⟨u⟩smażyć; ***fried eggs*** *pl.* jajka *pl.* sadzone; ***fried potatoes*** *pl.* smażone ziemniaki *pl.*; **~·ing pan** ['fraɪɪŋ -] patelnia *f*
ft *skrót pisany*: ***foot*** stopa *f lub pl.* (*30,48 cm*)
fuch·sia ['fju:ʃə] *bot.* fuksja *f*
fuck [fʌk] V pierdolić (się), jebać; ***~ off!*** odpierdol się!; **'~·ing** V pierdolony; ***~ing hell!*** kurwa (jego) mać!
fudge [fʌdʒ] (*cukierek*) krówka *f*
fu·el [fjʊəl] **1.** paliwo *n*; opał *m*; **2.** (*zwł. Brt.* ***-ll-***, *Am.* ***-l-***) *mot.*, *aviat.* ⟨za⟩tankować; **'~ in·jec·tion** *mot.* wtrysk *m* paliwa
fu·gi·tive ['fju:dʒɪtɪv] **1.** przelotny, ulotny; **2.** uciekinier(ka *f*) *m*
ful·fil *Brt.*, **full·fill** *Am.* [fʊl'fɪl] (***-ll-***) wypełniać ⟨-nić⟩, spełniać ⟨-nić⟩; wykonywać ⟨-nać⟩; **ful'fil(l)·ment** spełnienie *n*, wypełnienie *n*; wykonanie *n*
full [fʊl] **1.** pełny; ***~ of*** pełen (*G*); ***~ (up)*** wypełniony; F najedzony, napchany; ***house ~!*** *theat.* wolnych miejsc brak; ***~ of o.s.*** zarozumiały; **2.** *adv.* całkiem, zupełnie; **3.** ***in ~*** cały, w całości; ***write out in ~*** *zdanie itp.* zapisać całe; **~ 'board** pełne wyżywienie *n*; **~ 'dress** strój *m* wieczorowy; *attr.* wyjściowy; **~-'fledged** *Am.* → ***fully-fledged***; **~-'grown** dorosły; **~-'length** w całej postaci; *suknia*: długi; *film*: pełnometrażowy; **~ 'moon** pełnia *f*; **~ 'stop** *ling.* kropka *f*; **~ 'time** (*w sporcie*) koniec *m* gry; **~-'time** w pełnym wymiarze; **~-time 'job** praca *f* na pełen etat
ful·ly ['fʊlɪ] w pełni; całkowicie; **~-'fledged** opierzony; *fig.* samodzielny, wykwalifikowany; **~-'grown** *Brt.* → ***full-grown***
fum·ble ['fʌmbl] ⟨po⟩szukać po omacku; zabawiać ⟨-wić⟩ się (*I*); nieczysto zatrzymywać ⟨-mać⟩ piłkę
fume [fju:m] być wściekłym; wściekać się
fumes [fju:mz] *pl.* wyziewy *pl.*; spaliny *pl.*; opary *pl.*
fun [fʌn] radość *f*, zabawa *f*; ***for ~*** dla zabawy; ***make ~ of*** śmiać się z (*G*); ***have ~!*** baw(cie) się dobrze!
func·tion ['fʌŋkʃn] **1.** funkcja *f* (*też math.*); funkcjonowanie *n*; zadanie *n*; uroczystość *f*; **2.** funkcjonować; działać; **~·a·ry** ['fʌŋkʃnərɪ] funkcjonariusz(ka *f*) *m*; **'~ key** *komp.* klawisz *m* funkcyjny
fund [fʌnd] fundusz *m*; kapitał *m*; rezerwa *f*

fun·da·men·tal [fʌndə'mentl] **1.** fundamentalny; podstawowy; **2. ~s** *pl.* podstawy *pl.*; podstawowe zasady *pl.*; **~·ist** [fʌndə'mentəlɪst] fundamentalista *m*
fu·ne·ral ['fjuːnərəl] pogrzeb *m*; *attr.* pogrzebowy
'fun·fair ['fʌnfeə] wesołe miasteczko *n*
fun·gus ['fʌŋgəs] *bot.* (*pl.* **-gi** [-gaɪ], **-guses**) grzyb *m*
fu·nic·u·lar [fjuː'nɪkjʊlə] *też* **~ railway** kolejka *f* linowa
funk·y ['fʌŋkɪ] *zwł. Am.* F super (*o używanym przedmiocie*); *muz.* muzyka *f* funky
fun·nel ['fʌnl] lejek *m*; *naut.*, *rail.* komin *m* (*metalowy*)
fun·nies ['fʌnɪz] *Am.* F *pl.* komiks *m*
fun·ny ['fʌnɪ] (**-ier, -iest**) śmieszny, komiczny, zabawny; dziwny
fur [fɜː] futro *n*, sierść *f*; (*na języku*) nalot *m*; (*w czajniku*) kamień *m*
fu·ri·ous ['fjʊərɪəs] wściekły
furl [fɜːl] zwijać ⟨-winąć⟩; *parasol* składać ⟨złożyć⟩
fur·nace ['fɜːnɪs] piec *m*
fur·nish ['fɜːnɪʃ] ⟨u⟩meblować; zaopatrywać ⟨-trzyć⟩ (**with** w *A*); dostarczać ⟨-czyć⟩;
fur·ni·ture ['fɜːnɪtʃə] meble *pl.*; **a piece of ~** mebel *m*; **sectional ~** meble *pl.* w segmentach
furred [fɜːd] obłożony nalotem
fur·ri·er ['fʌrɪə] kuśnierz *m*
fur·row ['fʌrəʊ] **1.** bruzda *f*; rowek *m*; **2.** ⟨z⟩marszczyć; pomarszczyć
fur·ry ['fɜːrɪ] futrzany; puszysty
fur·ther ['fɜːðə] **1.** *comp. od* **far**; **2.** *fig.* dalej; **3.** wspierać ⟨wesprzeć⟩; **~ ed·u'ca·tion** *Brt.* edukacja *f* dla dorosłych; **~'more** *fig.* dodatkowo, poza tym; **'~·most** najdalszy
fur·thest ['fɜːðɪst] *sup. od* **far**
fur·tive ['fɜːtɪv] skryty
fu·ry ['fjʊərɪ] wściekłość *f*, furia *f*
fuse [fjuːz] **1.** *electr.* bezpiecznik *m*; lont *m*; **2.** *electr.* przepalać (się); ⟨s⟩topić (się); **'~ box** *electr.* skrzynka *f* bezpiecznikowa
fu·se·lage *aviat.* ['fjuːzɪlɑːʒ] kadłub *n*
fu·sion ['fjuːʒn] fuzja *f*, połączenie *n*; **nuclear ~** synteza *f* jądrowa
fuss [fʌs] **1.** zamieszanie *n*; histeria *f*; **2.** ⟨z⟩robić zamieszanie; niepotrzebnie się podniecać; **'~·y** (**-ier, -iest**) wybredny; przeładowany, przepełniony; rozgorączkowany, rozemocjonowany
fus·ty ['fʌstɪ] (**-ier, -iest**) zatęchły, zastały; *fig.* zaśniedziały
fu·tile ['fjuːtaɪl] daremny, nadaremny
fu·ture ['fjuːtʃə] **1.** przyszły; **2.** przyszłość *f*; *gr.* czas *m* przyszły; **in (the) ~** w przyszłości
fuzz[1] [fʌz] puszek *m*, meszek *m*
fuzz[2] [fʌz]: **the ~** *sg.*, *pl.* (*policja*) gliny *pl.*
fuzz·y ['fʌzɪ] F (**-ier, -iest**) nieostry, rozmyty; kędzierzawy; pokryty meszkiem

G

G, g [dʒiː] G, g *n*
gab [gæb] F gadanina *f*, trajkotanie *n*; **have the gift of the ~** mieć dar wymowy
gab·ar·dine ['gæbədiːn] gabardyna *f*
gab·ble ['gæbl] **1.** gadanina *f*, trajkotanie *n*; **2.** gadać, ⟨po⟩trajkotać
gab·er·dine ['gæbədiːn] *hist.* chałat *m* (*Żydów*); → **gabardine**
ga·ble ['geɪbl] *arch.* szczyt *m*
gad [gæd] F (**-dd-**): **~ about** włóczyć się
gad·fly ['gædflaɪ] *zo.* giez *m*
gad·get ['gædʒɪt] *tech.* urządzenie *n*, aparat *m*; *często pej.* zabawka *f* mechaniczna, gadżet *m*
gag [gæg] **1.** knebel (*też fig.*); F gag *m*; **2.** (**-gg-**) ⟨za⟩kneblować; *fig.* zamykać ⟨-mknąć⟩ usta
gage [geɪdʒ] *Am.* → **gauge**
gai·e·ty ['geɪətɪ] wesołość *f*, radość *f*
gai·ly ['geɪlɪ] *adv. od* **gay** 1
gain [geɪn] **1.** zyskiwać ⟨-skać⟩; odnosić ⟨-nieść⟩ korzyść; *wagę*, *szybkość* zwiększać; doganiać ⟨-gonić⟩; *zegarek*: spieszyć się; **~ 5 pounds** przybierać ⟨-brać⟩ pięć funtów; **~ in** zdobywać (*A*); **2.** zysk *m*, korzyść *f*; wzrost *m*, zwiększenie *n*

gait [geɪt] chód *m*; krok *m*
gai•ter ['geɪtə] kamasz *m*
gal [gæl] F dziewczyna *f*
ga•la ['gɑːlə] gala *f*; pokaz *m*, zawody *pl.*; *attr.* galowy
gal•ax•y ['gæləksɪ] *astr.* galaktyka *f*; ***the*** ♀ Droga *f* Mleczna
gale [geɪl] burza *f*, sztorm *m*
gall[1] [gɔːl] bezczelność *f*, czelność *f*
gall[2] [gɔːl] otarcie *n*, nadżerka *f*
gall[3] [gɔːl] ⟨roz⟩drażnić
gal|•lant ['gælənt] uprzejmy, grzeczny; odważny; **~•lan•try** ['gæləntrɪ] galanteria *f*, kultura *f*; odwaga *f*
'gall blad•der *anat.* woreczek *m* żółciowy
gal•le•ry ['gælərɪ] galeria *f*; empora *f*, balkon *m*
gal|•ley ['gælɪ] *naut.* kambuz *m*; *naut.* galera *f*; *też* **~ *proof*** *print.* odbitka *f* szczotkowa
gal•lon ['gælən] galon *m* (*Brt. 4,55 l, Am. 3,79 l*)
gal•lop ['gæləp] **1.** galop *m*; **2.** ⟨po⟩galopować; puścić galopem
gal•lows ['gæləʊz] *sg.* szubienica *f*; **'~ hu•mo(u)r** wisielczy humor *m*
ga•lore [gə'lɔː] w bród
gam•ble ['gæmbl] **1.** ⟨za⟩grać hazardowo; stawiać ⟨postawić⟩, ⟨za⟩ryzykować; **2.** gra *f* hazardowa; **'~r** hazardzista *m* (-tka *f*)
gam•bol ['gæmbl] **1.** skok *m*; **2.** (*zwł. Brt.* **-ll-**, *Am.* **-l-**) brykać, hasać
game [geɪm] gra *f*; mecz *m*; *hunt.* dzika zwierzyna *f*; dziczyzna *f*; **~*s*** *pl.* igrzyska *pl.*; *szkolne* zajęcia *pl.* sportowe; **'~•keep•er** leśniczy *m*; **'~ park** rezerwat *m* zwierząt; **'~ re•serve** rezerwat *m* zwierząt
gam•mon ['gæmən] *zwł. Brt.* szynka *f* wędzona
gan•der ['gændə] *zo.* gąsior *m*
gang [gæŋ] **1.** brygada *f* robocza, ekipa *f*; gang *m*, banda *f*; grupa *f*; **2. ~ *up*** F współdziałać; spiskować
gang•ster ['gæŋstə] gangster *m*
'gang| war, ~ war•fare [gæŋ'wɔːfeə] wojna *f* między gangami
gang•way ['gæŋweɪ] *naut.* trap *m*; *aviat.* przejście *n*
gaol [dʒeɪl], **'~•bird**, **'~•er** → ***jail*** *itp.*
gap [gæp] przerwa *f*; luka *f*; dziura *f*; przełęcz *f*
gape [geɪp] ziać; otwierać się; gapić się
gar•age ['gærɑːʒ] **1.** garaż *m*; warsztat *m* samochodowy; **2.** trzymać w garażu; wprowadzać ⟨-dzić⟩ do garażu
gar•bage ['gɑːbɪdʒ] *zwł. Am.* śmieci *pl.*; **'~ bag** *Am.* worek *m* na śmieci; **'~ can** *Am.* pojemnik *m* na śmieci, kubeł *m* na śmieci; **'~ truck** *Am.* śmieciarka *f*
gar•den ['gɑːdn] ogród *m*; **'~•er** ogrodnik *m*; **'~•ing** ogrodnictwo *n*
gar•gle ['gɑːgl] ⟨wy⟩płukać gardło
gar•ish ['geərɪʃ] jaskrawy, rażący
gar•land ['gɑːlənd] wieniec *m*, girlanda *f*
gar•lic ['gɑːlɪk] *bot.* czosnek *m*
gar•ment ['gɑːmənt] ubranie *n*
gar•nish ['gɑːnɪʃ] *gastr.* ⟨u⟩garnirować, przybierać ⟨-brać⟩
gar•ret ['gærət] pokój *m* na poddaszu
gar•ri•son ['gærɪsn] *mil.* garnizon *m*
gar•ter ['gɑːtə] podwiązka
gas [gæs] gaz; *Am.* F benzyna *f*; **~•e•ous** ['gæsjəs] gazowy
gash [gæʃ] *głębokie* cięcie *n*, nacięcie *n*
gas•ket ['gæskɪt] *tech.* uszczelnienie *n*, uszczelka *f*
'gas me•ter licznik *m* gazu
gas•o•lene, gas•o•line ['gæsəliːn] *Am.* benzyna *f*, etylina *f*; **'~ pump** dystrybutor *m* benzyny
gasp [gɑːsp] **1.** westchnięcie *n*, dyszenie *n*; **2.** ⟨z⟩łapać powietrze; **~ *for breath*** łapać powietrze (*z trudem*)
'gas| sta•tion *Am.* stacja *f* benzynowa; **'~ stove** kuchnia *f* gazowa; **'~•works** *sg.* gazownia *f*
gate [geɪt] brama *f*, bramka *f*; furtka *f*; szlaban *m*; *aviat.* przejście *n* do samolotu; **'~•crash** F wchodzić ⟨wejść⟩ bez zaproszenia; **'~•post** słupek *m*; **'~•way** przejście *m*, przejazd *m*; wjazd *m*; **'~•way drug**
gath•er ['gæðə] *v/t.* zbierać ⟨zebrać⟩; ⟨z⟩gromadzić (*zwł. informację*); *materiał itp.* zbierać ⟨zebrać⟩, ⟨z⟩marszczyć; *fig.* ⟨wy⟩wnioskować, sądzić (***from*** z *I*); **~ *speed*** nabierać ⟨-brać⟩ prędkości; *v/i.* zbierać ⟨zebrać⟩ się; ⟨z⟩gromadzić się; **~•ing** ['gæðərɪŋ] zebranie *n*, zgromadzenie *n*
GATT [gæt] *skrót*: ***General Agreement on Tariffs and Trade*** GATT *m*, Układ Ogólny w Sprawie Ceł i Handlu

gau·dy ['gɔːdɪ] (**-ier, -iest**) krzykliwy, krzyczący
gauge [geɪdʒ] **1.** miara *f*, skala *f*; *tech.* przyrząd *m* pomiarowy, wskaźnik *m*; *tech.* grubość *f* (*blachy lub drutu*); *rail.* szerokość *f* toru; **2.** *tech.* ⟨z⟩mierzyć, dokonywać ⟨-nać⟩ pomiaru
gaunt [gɔːnt] wynędzniały; ponury
gaunt·let ['gɔːntlɪt] rękawica *f* ochronna
gauze [gɔːz] gaza *f*; *Am.* bandaż *m*
gave [geɪv] *pret. od* **give**
gav·el ['gævl] młotek *m* (*licytatora, sędziego itp.*)
gaw·ky ['gɔːkɪ] (**-ier, -iest**) niezgrabny
gay [geɪ] **1.** wesoły; *kolor itp.*: żywy; radosny; F homoseksualny, dla homoseksualistów; **2.** F homoseksualista *m*, gej *m*
gaze [geɪz] **1.** *uporczywy* wzrok *m*, spojrzenie *n*; ⚠ *nie* **gaza**; **2.** wpatrywać się (**at** w *A*)
ga·zette [gə'zet] dziennik *m* urzędowy
ga·zelle [gə'zel] *zo.* (*pl.* **-zelles, -zelle**) gazela *f*
GB [dʒiː 'biː] *skrót*: **Great Britain** Wielka Brytania *f*
gear [gɪə] *tech.* koło *n* zębate, tryb *m*; *mot.* bieg *m*; *zwł. w złożeniach* sprzęt *m*, urządzenie *n*; F strój *m*, ubranie *n*; **change** (*zwł. Am.* **shift**) **~(s)** zmieniać bieg(i); **change** (*zwł. Am.* **shift**) **into second ~** wrzucić ⟨-cać⟩ drugi bieg; '**~·box** *mot.* skrzynia *f* biegów; '**~ lever** *Brt. mot.*, '**~ shift** *Am.*, '**~ stick** *Brt. mot.* drążek *m* zmiany biegów
geese [giːs] *pl. od* **goose**
Gei·ger count·er ['gaɪgə -] *phys.* licznik *m* Geigera-Müllera
geld·ing ['geldɪŋ] *zo.* wałach *m*
gem [dʒem] klejnot *m*, kamień *m* szlachetny
Gem·i·ni ['dʒemɪnaɪ] *astr.* Bliźnięta *pl.*; **he/she is (a) ~** on(a) jest spod znaku Bliźniąt
gen·der ['dʒendə] *gr.* rodzaj *m*
gene [dʒiːn] *biol.* gen *m*
gen·e·ral ['dʒenərəl] **1.** ogólny; generalny; **2.** generał *m*; **in ~** ogólnie rzecz biorąc; **~ de'liv·er·y**: (**in care of**) **~ delivery** *Am.* poste restante *n*; **~ e'lection** *Brt.* wybory *pl.* do parlamentu; **~ize** ['dʒenərəlaɪz] uogólniać ⟨-nić⟩; '**~ly** ogólnie, w ogólności; **~ prac'tition·er** (*skrót*: **GP**) lekarz *m* ogólny
gen·e|·rate ['dʒenəreɪt] wytwarzać ⟨-worzyć⟩; ⟨s⟩powodować; ⟨wy⟩generować; **~·ra·tion** [dʒenə'reɪʃn] wytwarzanie *n*; generowanie *n*; generacja *f*, pokolenie *n*; **~·ra·tor** ['dʒenəreɪtə] generator *m*; *Am. mot.* prądnica *f*
gen·e|·ros·i·ty [dʒenə'rɒsətɪ] hojność *f*, szczodrobliwość *f*; **~·rous** ['dʒenərəs] hojny, szczodrobliwy
ge·net·ic [dʒɪ'netɪk] (**~ally**) genetyczny; **~ 'code** kod *m* genetyczny; **~ engin'eer·ing** inżynieria *f* genetyczna; **~s** *sg.* genetyka *f*
ge·ni·al ['dʒiːnjəl] przyjazny; ⚠ *nie* **genialny**
gen·i·tive ['dʒenɪtɪv] *gr. też* **~ case** dopełniacz *m*
ge·ni·us ['dʒiːnjəs] geniusz *m*
gent [dʒent] F dżentelmen *m*; **~s** *sg. Brt.* F (*ubikacja*) dla panów
gen·tle ['dʒentl] (**-r, -st**) delikatny; łagodny; '**~·man** (*pl.* **-men**) dżentelmen *m*; '**~·man·ly** po dżentelmeńsku; '**~·ness** delikatność *f*; łagodność *f*
gen·try ['dʒentrɪ] *Brt.* wyższa warstwa *f*; *jakby*: ziemiaństwo *n*
gen·u·ine ['dʒenjʊɪn] prawdziwy
ge·og·ra·phy [dʒɪ'ɒgrəfɪ] geografia *f*
ge·ol·o·gy [dʒɪ'ɒlədʒɪ] geologia *f*
ge·om·e·try [dʒɪ'ɒmətrɪ] geometria *f*
Geor·gia Gruzja *f*
germ [dʒɜːm] *biol.* zarodek *m*, zalążek *m*; *bot.* kiełek *m*; *med.* zarazek *m*, bakteria *f*
Ger·man ['dʒɜːmən] **1.** niemiecki; **2.** Niemiec *m* (-mka *f*); *ling.* język *m* niemiecki; **~ 'shep·herd** *zwł. Am.* owczarek *m* niemiecki, wilczur *m*; '**German·y** Niemcy *pl.*
ger·mi·nate ['dʒɜːmɪneɪt] ⟨za⟩kiełkować
ger·und ['dʒerənd] *gr.* rzeczownik *m* odsłowny
ges·tic·u·late [dʒe'stɪkjʊleɪt] gestykulować
ges·ture ['dʒestʃə] gest *m*
get [get] (**-tt-**; **got, got** *lub* **gotten**) *v/t.* otrzymywać ⟨-mać⟩; dostawać ⟨-tać⟩; zdobywać, ⟨-być⟩; uzyskiwać ⟨-kać⟩; przynosić ⟨-nieść⟩, sprowadzać ⟨-dzić⟩; załatwiać ⟨-wić⟩; F ⟨z⟩łapać; F ⟨z⟩rozumieć, ⟨s⟩chwytać; wydostawać ⟨-tać⟩; *kogoś* nakłaniać (**to do**

G

do zrobienia); *tel.* połączyć się z (*I*); **~ *one's hair cut*** obcinać ⟨-ciąć⟩ sobie włosy; **~ *going*** uruchamiać ⟨-chomić⟩, *fig.* nabierać ⟨-brać⟩ rozpędu; **~ *s.th. by heart*** nauczyć się czegoś na pamięć; **~ *s.th. ready*** przygotować coś; ***have got*** mieć; ***have got to*** musieć; *v/i.* docierać, dostawać się, przyjeżdżać; *z p.p. lub adj.* stawać się; **~ *tired*** zmęczyć się; **~ *going*** uruchamiać ⟨-chomić⟩ się, działać; **~ *home*** jechać do domu; **~ *ready*** przygotowywać ⟨-wać⟩ się; **~ *to know s.th.*** poznawać ⟨-nać⟩ coś; **~ *about*** ruszać się (*z miejsca na miejsce*); *pogłoska itp.*: rozchodzić ⟨-zejść⟩ się; **~ *ahead of*** wyprzedzać ⟨-dzić⟩ (*A*); **~ *along*** iść naprzód; dawać sobie radę (***with*** z *I*); być w dobrych stosunkach (***with*** z *I*); **~ *at*** zbliżać się do (*G*), dosięgnąć ⟨-gać⟩; ***what is she getting at?*** o co jej chodzi?; **~ *away*** uciekać ⟨-ciec⟩; odchodzić ⟨odejść⟩; **~ *away with*** wychodzić ⟨wyjść⟩ obronną ręką z (*G*); **~ *back*** wracać ⟨wrócić⟩; *coś* odzyskiwać ⟨-kać⟩; **~ *in*** wchodzić ⟨wejść⟩, dostawać się (do *G*); wsiadać ⟨wsiąść⟩ do (*G*); **~ *off*** wysiadać ⟨-siąść⟩ z (*G*); wychodzić ⟨wyjść⟩ obronną ręką (***with*** z *G*); *coś* zdejmować ⟨zdjąć⟩; **~ *on*** wsiadać ⟨wsiąść⟩; → ***get along***; **~ *out*** wychodzić ⟨wyjść⟩ (***of*** z *G*); wysiadać ⟨-siąść⟩ (***of*** z *G*); wydostawać ⟨-tać⟩ się; **~ *over s.th.*** dochodzić ⟨dojść⟩ do siebie po (*L*); **~ *to*** dochodzić ⟨dojść⟩ do (*G*); **~ *together*** zbierać ⟨zebrać⟩ się; **~ *up*** wstawać ⟨-tać⟩; **'~·a·way** ucieczka *f*, zbiegnięcie *n*; **~ *car*** samochód *m* dla uciekających; **'~·up** *dziwaczne* ubranie *n*

gey·ser ['gaɪzə] gejzer *m*; ['giːzə] *Brt.* przepływowy grzejnik *m* wody

ghast·ly ['gɑːstlɪ] (**-*ier*, *-iest***) okropny, straszny; *wygląd itp.*: upiorny

gher·kin ['gɜːkɪn] ogórek *m* konserwowy, korniszon *m*

ghost [gəʊst] duch *m*; **'~·ly** (**-*ier*, *-iest***) upiorny

GI [dʒiː 'aɪ] (*żołnierz amerykański*)

gi·ant ['dʒaɪənt] **1.** gigant *m*; olbrzym *m*; **2.** gigantyczny

gib·ber·ish ['dʒɪbərɪʃ] bełkot *m*

gib·bet ['dʒɪbɪt] szubienica *f*

gibe [dʒaɪb] **1.** szydzić, drwić (***at*** z *G*); **2.** szyderstwo *n*

gib·lets ['dʒɪblɪts] *pl.* podroby *pl.* drobiowe

gid|·di·ness ['gɪdɪnɪs] *med.* zawroty *pl.* głowy; **~·dy** ['gɪdɪ] (**-*ier*, *-iest***) *wysokość itp.*: przyprawiający o zawrót głowy; ***I feel ~dy*** w głowie mi się kręci

gift [gɪft] dar *m*; talent *m*; **'~·ed** utalentowany

gig [gɪg] *mus.* F występ *m*, koncert *m*

gi·gan·tic [dʒaɪ'gæntɪk] (**~*ally***) gigantyczny, olbrzymi

gig·gle ['gɪgl] **1.** ⟨za⟩chichotać; **2.** chichot *m*

gild [gɪld] pozłacać, złocić

gill [gɪl] *zo.* skrzele *n*; *bot.* blaszka *f*

gim·mick ['gɪmɪk] F sztuczka *f*, trik *m*

gin [dʒɪn] dżin *m*, jałowcówka *f*

gin·ger ['dʒɪndʒə] **1.** imbir *m*; **2.** rudy, czerwony; **'~·bread** piernik *m*; **'~·ly** ostrożnie

gip·sy ['dʒɪpsɪ] Cygan(ka *f*) *m*

gi·raffe [dʒɪ'rɑːf] *zo.* (*pl.* ***-raffes, -raffe***) żyrafa *f*

gir·der ['gɜːdə] *tech.* dźwigar *m*

gir·dle ['gɜːdl] pas *m* elastyczny

girl [gɜːl] dziewczyna *f*, dziewczynka *f*; **'~·friend** dziewczyna *f*, sympatia *f*; **~ 'guide** *Brt.* harcerka *f*; **~·hood** ['gɜːlhʊd] lata *pl.* dziewczęce; młodość *f*; **'~·ish** dziewczęcy; **~ 'scout** *Am.* harcerka *f*

gi·ro ['dʒaɪrəʊ] *Brt.* pocztowy system *m* przelewowy; **'~ ac·count** *Brt.* pocztowy rachunek *m* rozliczeniowy; **'~ cheque** *Brt.* czek *m* przelewowy

girth [gɜːθ] obwód *m*; popręg *m*

gist [dʒɪst] sedno *n*, jądro *n*

give [gɪv] (***gave, given***) dawać ⟨dać⟩; *jako podarek* ⟨po⟩darować; *tytuł, prawo itp.* nadawać ⟨-dać⟩; *życie, pomoc* ofiarowywać ⟨-ować⟩; *pracę domową* zadawać ⟨-dać⟩; *pomoc, odpowiedź itp.* udzielać ⟨-lić⟩; *dotację itp.* przyznawać ⟨-nać⟩; *wykład* wygłaszać ⟨-łosić⟩; *radość* przysparzać ⟨-porzyć⟩; *sztukę* wystawiać ⟨-wić⟩; *pozdrowienia* przekazywać ⟨-zać⟩; **~ *her my love*** przekaż jej moje serdeczne pozdrowienia; **~ *birth to*** wydawać ⟨-dać⟩ (*A*) na świat; **~ *s.o. to understand that*** dać komuś do zrozumienia, że; **~ *way*** ustępować ⟨-tąpić⟩, *Brt. mot.* ustąpić pierwszeństwa przejazdu; **~ *away*** oddawać ⟨-dać⟩; rozdawać ⟨-dać⟩; *kogoś* zdradzać ⟨-dzić⟩; **~ back** zwracać ⟨zwrócić⟩; **~ in** *podanie itp.* składać ⟨złożyć⟩; *pracę, itp.* oddawać ⟨-dać⟩; poddawać ⟨-dać⟩ się; ustępować ⟨-tąpić⟩; **~ off** *zapach itp.* wydzielać ⟨-lić⟩; wydobywać ⟨-być⟩ się; **~ on(to)** wychodzić na (*A*); **~ out** rozdawać ⟨-dać⟩; wydawać ⟨-dać⟩; kończyć się; wyczerpywać ⟨-pać⟩ się; *zwł. Brt.* ogłaszać ⟨-łosić⟩; *silnik itp.*: F nawalać ⟨-lić⟩; **~ up** ⟨z⟩rezygnować, rzucać ⟨-cić⟩; poddawać ⟨-dać⟩ się; przestawać ⟨-tać⟩; *kogoś* wydawać ⟨-dać⟩; **~ o.s. up** oddawać się (**to the police** w ręce policji); **~-and-take** [gıvən'teık] wzajemne ustępstwa *pl.*, kompromis *m*; **giv·en** ['gıvn] **1.** *p.p. od* **give**; **2. be ~ to** mieć skłonności do (*G*); **'giv·en name** *zwł. Am.* imię *n*

gla·cial ['gleısjəl] lodowcowy; *fig.* lodowaty

gla·ci·er ['glæsjə] lodowiec *m*

glad [glæd] (**-dd-**) szczęśliwy, zadowolony; **be ~ of** być wdzięcznym za (*A*); **'~·ly** za radością, z przyjemnością

glam·o(u)r ['glæmə] urok *m*, splendor *m*, świetność *f*; **~·ous** ['glæmərəs] świetny, urokliwy, czarujący

glance [glɑːns] **1.** spojrzenie *n*, rzut *m* okiem (**at** na *A*); **at a ~** od razu; **2.** rzucać ⟨-cić⟩ okiem, spojrzeć (**at** na *A*)

gland [glænd] *anat.* gruczoł *m*

glare [gleə] **1.** ⟨za⟩świecić jaskrawo, oślepiać ⟨-pić⟩; być bardzo widocznym; **~ at s.o.** wpatrywać się ze wściekłością w kogoś; **2.** jaskrawe światło *n*; wściekłe spojrzenie *n*

glass [glɑːs] **1.** szkło *n*; szklanka *f*; kieliszek *m*; lornetka *f*; *Brt.* F lustro *n*; *Brt.* barometr *m*; (**a pair of**) **~es** *pl.* okulary *pl.*; **2.** szklany, ze szkład; **3. ~ in** *lub* **up** ⟨o⟩szklić; **'~ case** witryna *f*, gablota *f*; **'~·ful** szklanka *f*, kieliszek *m* (*miara*); **'~·house** szklarnia *f*; **'~·ware** wyroby *pl.* ze szkła; **'~·y** (**-ier, -iest**) szklany, zaszklony, szklisty

glaz|e [gleız] **1.** *v/t.* ⟨o⟩szklić; glazurować; *v/i. też* **~e over** *oczy*: szklić się; **2.** glazura *f*, szkliwo *n*; **~ier** ['gleızjə] szklarz *m*

gleam [gliːm] **1.** blask *m*, odblask *m*; **2.** błyszczeć ⟨błysnąć⟩

glean [gliːn] *v/t.* ⟨z⟩gromadzić; *v/i.* zbierać ⟨zebrać⟩ kłosy

glee [gliː] radość *f*; **'~·ful** radosny, szczęśliwy

glen [glen] (głęboka)dolina *f*

glib [glıb] (**-bb-**) wymowny, wygadany; natychmiastowy

glide [glaıd] **1.** ⟨po⟩szybować; sunąć, ślizgać się; **2.** *aviat.* szybowanie *n*, lot *m* ślizgowy; ślizg *m*; **'glid·er** *aviat.* szybowiec *m*; **'glid·ing** *aviat.* szybownictwo *n*

glim·mer ['glımə] **1.** ⟨za⟩migotać; **2.** migotanie *n*

glimpse [glımps] **1.** ujrzeć na chwilę; **2.** przelotne spojrzenie *n*

glint [glınt] **1.** ⟨za⟩skrzyć się; **2.** skrzenie *n* się; iskierka *f*

glis·ten ['glısn] ⟨za⟩skrzyć się

glit·ter ['glıtə] **1.** ⟨za⟩skrzyć się; ⟨za⟩migotać; **2.** skrzenie *n* się; migotanie *n*

gloat [gləʊt]: **~ over** upajać się, cieszyć się (*złośliwie lub ukradkiem*) (*A*); **'~·ing** cieszący się, zadowolony

glo·bal ['gləʊbl] globalny, światowy, ogólnoświatowy; **~ 'warm·ing** ogrzewanie *n* atmosfery ziemskiej

globe [gləʊb] kula *f*; kula *f* ziemska; globus *m*

gloom [gluːm] mrok *m*; ciemność *f*; ponurość *f*, przygnębienie *n*; **'~·y** (**-ier, -iest**) mroczny; ponury, przygnębiający

glo|·ri·fy ['glɔːrıfaı] gloryfikować, sławić; **~·ri·ous** ['glɔːrıəs] wspaniały, znakomity; **~·ry** ['glɔːrı] chwała *f*, świetność *f*

gloss [glɒs] **1.** połysk *m*; *ling.* glosa *f*; **2. ~ over** przemykać się nad (*I*)

glos·sa·ry ['glɒsərı] słowniczek *m*

gloss·y ['glɒsı] (**-ier, -iest**) połyskliwy, błyszczący

glove [glʌv] rękawiczka *f*; **it fits like a ~** leży jak ulał; **'~ com·part·ment** *mot.* schowek *m*

glow [gləʊ] **1.** żarzyć się; *fig.* promieniować, płonąć; **2.** żar *m*; promieniowanie *n*, płonięcie *n*

glow·er ['glaʊə] patrzeć się ze złością

'glow-worm *zo.* świetlik *m*

glu·cose ['gluːkəʊs] glukoza *f*

glue [gluː] **1.** klej *m*; **2.** ⟨s⟩kleić

glum [glʌm] (**-mm-**) przygnębiony

glut·ton ['glʌtn]: *fig.* **be a ~ for s.th.** strasznie coś lubić; **'~·ous** żarłoczny

GMT [dʒiː em 'tiː] *skrót*: **Greenwich**

G

G

Mean Time ['grenɪdʒ -] czas *m* Greenwich
gnarled [nɑːld] sękaty; powykrzywiany
gnash [næʃ] zgrzytać (*I*)
gnat [næt] *zo.* komar *m*
gnaw [nɔː] gryźć, wygryzać ⟨-ryźć⟩; *fig.* trapić
gnome [nəʊm] gnom *m*; krasnal *m* ogrodowy
go [gəʊ] **1.** (***went, gone***) iść ⟨pójść⟩, ⟨po⟩jechać (***to*** do *G*); odchodzić ⟨odejść⟩, odjeżdżać ⟨-jechać⟩; *ulica*: ⟨po⟩prowadzić (***to*** do *G*), rozciągać się; *autobus*: kursować, jeździć; *tech.* poruszać się, funkcjonować; *czas itp.*: przechodzić ⟨przejść⟩, upływać ⟨-łynąć⟩; *kapelusz*: pasować (***with*** do *G*); wchodzić ⟨wejść⟩; *żarówka itp.*: zepsuć się, nie działać; (*do szkoły*) uczęszczać; *praca itp.*: iść ⟨pójść⟩, wypadać; stawać się (***~ mad***; ***~ blind***); ***be ~ing to do s.th.*** zabierać się do zrobienia czegoś, mieć coś zrobić; ***~ shares*** ⟨po⟩dzielić się; ***~ swimming*** iść popływać; ***it is ~ing to rain*** będzie padało; ***I must be ~ing*** muszę już iść; ***~ for a walk*** iść na spacer; ***~ to bed*** iść do łóżka; ***~ to school*** chodzić do szkoły; ***~ to see*** iść z wizytą; ***let ~*** puszczać ⟨puścić⟩; ***~ after*** iść za (*I*); starać się o (*A*); ***~ ahead*** udawać ⟨udać⟩ się naprzód; iść ⟨pójść⟩ naprzód; ***~ ahead with*** zaczynać ⟨-cząć⟩ (*A*), przystępować ⟨-tąpić⟩ do (*G*); ***~ at*** zabierać ⟨-brać⟩ się do (*G*); ***~ away*** odchodzić ⟨odejść⟩, odjeżdżać ⟨-jechać⟩; ***~ between*** pośredniczyć między (*I*); ***~ by*** przejeżdżać ⟨-jechać⟩, przechodzić ⟨-ejść⟩; upływać ⟨-łynąć⟩; *fig.* kierować się, powodować się; ***~ down*** spadać ⟨-paść⟩; zachodzić ⟨zajść⟩; ***~ for*** udawać ⟨-dać⟩ się po (*A*); stosować się do (*G*); ***~ in*** wchodzić ⟨wejść⟩; ***~ in for an examination*** przystępować ⟨-tąpić⟩ do egzaminu; ***~ off*** wybuchać ⟨-chnąć⟩; uruchamiać ⟨-chomić⟩ się; ***~ on*** kontynuować (***doing*** robienie); nadal robić; mieć miejsce, dziać się; ***~ out*** wychodzić ⟨wyjść⟩; chodzić (***with*** z *I*); *światło*: ⟨z⟩gasnąć; ***~ through*** przechodzić (przez *A*), doświadczać; zużyć, wyczerpać; ***~ up*** wznosić ⟨-nieść⟩ się; iść ⟨pójść⟩ do góry; ***~ without*** obywać ⟨-być⟩ się; **2.** (*pl.* ***goes***) F witalność *f*, dynamizm *m*; *zwł.* *Brt.* F próba *f*; ***it's my ~*** *zwł. Brt.* F teraz moja kolej; ***on the ~*** w ruchu; ***in one ~*** za jednym razem; ***have a ~ at*** *Brt.* F spróbować (*G*)
goad [gəʊd] *fig.* podjudzać ⟨-dzić⟩
'go-a·head[1]: ***get the ~*** otrzymywać ⟨-mać⟩ zielone światło; ***give s.o. the ~*** zapalać ⟨-lić⟩ komuś zielone światło
'go-a·head[2] F postępowy, przodujący
goal [gəʊl] cel *m* (*też fig.*); (*w sporcie*) bramka *f*; ***score a ~*** zdobywać ⟨-być⟩ bramkę; ***consolation ~*** bramka *f* honorowa; ***own ~*** bramka *f* samobójcza; '**~·area** *sport*: pole *n* bramkowe; **~·ie**, F ['gəʊlɪ], '**~·keep·er** *sport*: bramkarz *m*; '**~ kick** (*w piłce nożnej*) wybicie *n* piłki od bramki; '**~ line** (*w sporcie*) linia *f* bramkowa; '**~·post** (*w sporcie*) słupek *m*
goat [gəʊt] *zo.* koza *f*; kozioł *m*
gob·ble ['gɒbl]: *zw.* ***~ up*** pochłaniać ⟨-łonąć⟩
'go-be·tween pośrednik *m* (-iczka *f*)
gob·lin ['gɒblɪn] chochlik *m*, diablik *m*
god [gɒd], *rel.* **♀** Bóg *m*; *fig.* bożek *m*; '**~·child** (*pl.* ***-children***) chrześniak *m*; **~·dess** ['gɒdɪs] bogini *f*; '**~·fa·ther** ojciec *m* chrzestny (*też fig.*); '**~·for·sak·en** *pej.* zapomniany, porzucony; '**~·less** bezbożny; '**~·like** podobny bogom; '**~·moth·er** matka *f* chrzestna; '**~·pa·rent** rodzic *m* chrzestny; '**~·send** dar *m* niebios
gog·gle ['gɒgl] gapić się; '**~ box** *Brt.* F *TV* telewizja *f*; '**~s** *pl.* gogle *pl.*
go·ings-on [gəʊɪŋz'ɒn] F *pl.* wydarzenia *pl.*
gold [gəʊld] **1.** złoto *n*; **2.** złoty; **~·en** *zw. fig.* ['gəʊldən] złoty, złocisty; '**~·finch** *zo.* szczygieł *m*; '**~·fish** *zo.* złota rybka *f*; '**~·smith** złotnik *m*
golf [gɒlf] **1.** golf *m*; *attr.* golfowy; **2.** ⟨za-, po⟩grać w golfa; '**~ club** kij *m* golfowy; klub *m* golfowy; '**~ course**, '**~ links** *pl. lub sg.* pole *n* golfowe
gon·do·la ['gɒndələ] gondola *f*
gone [gɒn] **1.** *p.p. od* ***go*** 1; **2.** *adj.* miniony; zużyty; F martwy; F upity
good [gʊd] **1.** (***better, best***) dobry; grzeczny; ***~ at*** dobry w (*L*); ***real ~*** F naprawdę dobry; **2.** dobro *n*; dobroć *f*; ***for ~*** na dobre; **~·by(e)** [gʊd'baɪ] **1.** ***wish s.o. ~bye, say ~bye to s.o.*** mówić ⟨powiedzieć⟩ komuś do widzenia; **2.** *int.* do widzenia!; **♀ 'Fri·day** Wielki

Piątek *m*; ~-'**hu·mo(u)red** dobrze usposobiony; dobroduszny; ~-'**look·ing** przystojny, atrakcyjny; ~-'**natured** o dobrym usposobieniu; '~·**ness** dobro; ***thank ~ness!*** dzięki Bogu!; (***my***) ***~ness!, ~ness gracious!*** Boże mój!; ***for ~ness' sake*** na litość Boską!; ***~ness knows*** Bóg jeden wie
goods [gʊdz] *econ., pl.* towary *pl.*
good'will dobra wola *f*; *econ.* wartość *f* przedsiębiorstwa
good·y ['gʊdɪ] F cukierek *m*
goose [gu:s] *zo.* (*pl.* ***geese***) gęś *f*
goose·ber·ry ['gʊzbərɪ] *bot.* agrest *m*
goose|·flesh ['gu:sfleʃ], '~**pim·ples** *pl.* gęsia skórka *f*
GOP [dʒi: əʊ 'pi:] *skrót*: ***Grand Old Party*** Partia Republikańska (*w USA*)
go·pher ['gəʊfə] *zo.* suseł *m* amerykański; wiewiórka *f ziemna*
gore [gɔ:] brać na rogi
gorge [gɔ:dʒ] **1.** wąwóz *m*; gardziel *f*; **2.** pochłaniać ⟨-łonąć⟩, napychać ⟨-pchać⟩ (się)
gor·geous ['gɔ:dʒəs] wspaniały
go·ril·la [gə'rɪlə] *zo.* goryl *m*
gor·y ['gɔ:rɪ] F (***-ier, -iest***) zakrwawiony; *fig.* krwawy
gosh [gɒʃ]: *int.* F ***by ~*** o Boże!
gos·ling ['gɒzlɪŋ] *zo.* gąsiątko *n*
go-slow [gəʊ'sləʊ] *Brt. econ.* strajk *m* włoski (*w którym pracownicy pracują bardzo mało wydajnie*)
Gos·pel ['gɒspəl] *rel.* ewangelia *f*
gos·sa·mer ['gɒsəmə] nić *f* pajęcza, pajęczyna *f*; *attr.* bardzo cienki
gos·sip ['gɒsɪp] **1.** plotka *f*; plotkarz *m* (-arka *f*); **2.** ⟨po⟩plotkować; '~·**y** plotkarski; *ktoś* rozplotkowany
got [gɒt] *pret. i p.p. od* ***get***
Goth·ic ['gɒθɪk] **1.** gotyk *m*; **2.** *adj.* gotycki; ***~ novel*** powieść *f* gotycka
got·ten ['gɒtn] *Am. p.p. od* ***get***
gourd [gʊəd] *bot.* tykwa *f*
gout [gaʊt] *med.* gościec *m*
gov·ern ['gʌvn] *v/t.* rządzić; kierować; *v/i.* sprawować władzę; '~·**ess** guwernantka *f*; '~·**ment** rząd *m*; rządzenie *n*; *attr.* rządowy; ~**or** ['gʌvənə] gubernator *m*; zarządca *m*; F *ojciec, szef*: stary *m*
gown [gaʊn] suknia *f*; toga *f*; szlafrok *m*
GP [dʒi: 'pi:] *skrót*: ***general practitioner*** *jakby*: lekarz *m* (-arka *f*) ogólny (-a), internista *m* (-tka *f*)
GPO *Brt.* [dʒi: pi: 'əʊ] *skrót*: ***General Post Office*** poczta *f* główna
grab [græb] **1.** (***-bb-***) ⟨s⟩chwytać, ⟨z⟩łapać; **2.** złapanie *n*, schwytanie *n*; *tech.* chwytak *m*
grace [greɪs] **1.** gracja *f*, wdzięk *m*; przyzwoitość *f*; *econ. ulga f*, prolongata *f*; *rel.* łaska *f*; *rel.* modlitwa *f* (*przy stole*); **2.** zaszczycać ⟨-cić⟩; '~·**ful** wdzięczny; pełen wdzięku; '~·**less** niewdzięczny
gra·cious ['greɪʃəs] łaskawy; miłosierny
gra·da·tion [grə'deɪʃn] stopniowanie *n*
grade [greɪd] **1.** ranga *f*; jakość *f*; gatunek *m*; → ***gradient***; *Am.* klasa (*w systemie edukacyjnym*) *f*; *zwł. Am.* stopień *m*, ocena *f*; **2.** ⟨po⟩sortować; oceniać ⟨-nić⟩; '~ **cross·ing** *Am.* jednopoziomowy przejazd *m* kolejowy; '~ **school** *Am.* szkoła *f* podstawowa
gra·di·ent ['greɪdjənt] *rail. itp.* nachylenie *n*, pochylenie *n*
grad·u|·al ['grædʒʊəl] stopniowy; '~·**al·ly** stopniowo; ~·**ate 1.** ['grædʒʊət] *univ.* absolwent(ka *f*) *m* (*szkoły wyższej*); *Am.* absolwent(ka *f*) *m*; **2.** ['grædjʊeɪt] skalować; stopniować; *univ.* studiować (***from*** na *L*); otrzymywać ⟨-mać⟩ dyplom uniwersytecki (***from*** na *L*); *Am.* ⟨s⟩kończyć; ~·**a·tion** [grædʒʊ'eɪʃn] podziałka *f*, skala *f*; *univ.* nadawanie *n* stopnia naukowego; *Am.* zakończenie *n*
graf·fi·ti [grə'fi:tɪ] *pl.* graffiti *pl.*, bazgroły *pl.* na ścianach
graft [grɑ:ft] **1.** *med.* przeszczep *m*; *agr.* szczep *m*; **2.** *med.* przeszczepiać ⟨-pić⟩, ⟨prze⟩transplantować; *agr.* ⟨za⟩szczepić
grain [greɪn] ziarno *n*; zboże *n*; ziarenko *n*; (*w drewnie*) włókno *n*; rysunek *m* słojów; ***go against the ~*** *fig.* postępować ⟨-tąpić⟩ niezgodnie z zasadami
gram [græm] gram *m*
gram·mar ['græmə] gramatyka *f*; '~ **school** *Brt. jakby*: liceum *n* (*ogólnokształcące*); *Am. jakby*: szkoła *f* podstawowa
gram·mat·i·cal [grə'mætɪkl] gramatyczny
gramme [græm] gram *m*
gra·na·ry ['grænərɪ] spichlerz *m*
grand [grænd] **1.** *fig.* wspaniały, zna-

G

komity; wyniosły; dostojny; ♀ ***Old Party*** Partia *f* Republikańska (*USA*); (*pl.* **grand**) F (*tysiąc dolarów lub funtów*) patyk *m*
grand|·child ['græntʃaɪld] (*pl.* ***-children***) wnuk *m*; **~·daugh·ter** ['grændɔːtə] wnuczka *f*
gran·deur ['grændʒə] wzniosłość *f*, dostojeństwo *n*; wielkość *f*
grand·fa·ther ['grændfɑːðə] dziadek *m*
gran·di·ose ['grændɪəʊs] wspaniały
grand|·moth·er ['grænmʌðə] babcia *f*; **~·par·ents** ['grænpeərənts] *pl.* dziadkowie *pl.*; **~·son** ['grænsʌn] wnuk *m*
grand·stand ['grændstænd] (*w sporcie*) trybuna *f* (*główna*)
gran·ny ['grænɪ] F babcia *f*
grant [grɑːnt] **1.** przyznawać ⟨-znać⟩; uznawać ⟨-nać⟩; *pozwolenia* udzielać ⟨-lić⟩; nadawać ⟨-dać⟩; *prośbę* spełniać ⟨-nić⟩; ***take s.th. for ~ed*** uznawać coś za oczywiste; **2.** stypendium *n*; grant *m*; dotacja *f*
gran|·u·lat·ed ['grænjʊleɪtɪd] granulowany; ***~ulated sugar*** cukier *m* kryształ; **~·ule** ['grænjuːl] granulka *f*, ziarno *n*
grape [greɪp] winogrono *n*; winorośl *f*; '**~·fruit** grapefruit *lub* grejpfrut *m*; '**~·vine** winorośl *f*
graph [græf] graf *m*, wykres *m*; **~·ic** ['græfɪk] (***-ally***) graficzny; *opis* plastyczny; ***~ic arts*** *pl.* grafika *f*; ***~ic artist*** artysta *m* grafik; '**·ics** *pl.* grafika *f*
grap·ple ['græpl]: **~ *with*** walczyć z (*I*), *fig.* borykać się z (*I*)
grasp [grɑːsp] **1.** ⟨s⟩chwytać, ⟨z⟩łapać; *fig.* ⟨z⟩rozumieć, ⟨z⟩łapać; **2.** uchwyt *m*; zasięg *m*; *fig.* pojmowanie *n*
grass [grɑːs] trawa *f*; *sl.* (*marihuana*) trawka *f*; **~·hop·per** ['grɑːshɒpə] *zo.* pasikonik *m*; **~ 'wid·ow** słomiana wdowa *f*; **~ 'wid·ow·er** słomiany wdowiec *m*; '**gras·sy** (***-ier, -iest***) trawiasty
grate [greɪt] **1.** krata *f*; *kominowy* ruszt *m*; **2.** ⟨u⟩trzeć; ⟨za⟩zgrzytać, ⟨za⟩skrzypieć; **~ *on s.o.'s nerves*** działać komuś na nerwy
grate·ful ['greɪtfl] wdzięczny
grat·er ['greɪtə] tarka *f*
grat·i|·fi·ca·tion [grætɪfɪ'keɪʃn] wynagrodzenie *n*, gratyfikacja *f*; satysfakcja *f*; **~·fy** ['grætɪfaɪ] dawać ⟨dać⟩ satysfakcję; ⟨u⟩cieszyć
grat·ing[1] ['greɪtɪŋ] zgrzytający, zgrzytliwy
grat·ing[2] ['greɪtɪŋ] krata *f*, okratowanie *n*
grat·i·tude ['grætɪtjuːd] wdzięczność *f*
gra·tu·i|·tous [grə'tjuːɪtəs] zbędny, niepotrzebny; dobrowolony; **~·ty** [grə'tjuːətɪ] napiwek *m*
grave[1] [greɪv] (***-r, -st***) poważny; stateczny
grave[2] [greɪv] grób *m*; '**~·dig·ger** grabarz *m*
grav·el ['grævl] **1.** żwir *m*; **2.** (*zwł. Brt.* ***-ll-***) ⟨po⟩żwirować
'**grave|·stone** nagrobek *m*, kamień *m* nagrobny; '**~·yard** cmentarz *m*
grav·i·ta·tion [grævɪ'teɪʃn] *phys.* grawitacja *f*, siła *f* ciężkości
grav·i·ty ['grævətɪ] siła *f* ciężkości; powaga *f*
gra·vy ['greɪvɪ] sos *m* (*z pieczeni*)
gray [greɪ] *zwł. Am.* → ***grey***
graze[1] [greɪz] *v/t.* pasać ⟨paść⟩; *v/i.* paść się
graze[2] [greɪz] **1.** ocierać ⟨otrzeć⟩ (się); **2.** otarcie *n*
grease 1. [griːs] tłuszcz *m*; *tech.* smar *m*; **2.** [griːz] natłuszczać ⟨-łuścić⟩; *tech.* ⟨na⟩smarować
greas·y ['griːzɪ] (***-ier, -iest***) tłusty, zatłuszczony; zabrudzony smarem
great [greɪt] wielki; F wspaniały, super; pra...
Great Brit·ain [greɪt'brɪtn] Wielka Brytania *f*
Great 'Dane *zo.* dog *m*
great|-'grand·child prawnuk *m*; **~-'grand·par·ents** *pl.* pradziadkowie *pl.*
'**great|·ly** wielce, bardzo; '**~·ness** wielkość *f*
Greece [griːs] Grecja *f*
greed [griːd] chciwość *f*, zachłanność *f*; '**~·y** (***-ier, -iest***) chciwy; zachłanny (***for*** na *A*)
Greek [griːk] **1.** grecki; **2.** Grek *m*, Greczynka *f*; *ling.* język *m* grecki
green [griːn] **1.** zielony; *fig.* zielony, niedojrzały; **2.** zieleń *f*; teren *m* zielony; ***~s*** *pl.* warzywa *pl.* (*zielone*); **~ belt** *zwł. Brt.* pas *m* zieleni; **~ 'card** *Am.* zielona karta *f* (*pozwalająca pracować*); '**~·gro·cer** *zwł. Brt.* sprzedawca *m*

(-czyni *f*) warzyw i owoców; sklep *m* warzywny; '~·**horn** żółtodziób *m*; '~·**house** cieplarnia *f*, szklarnia *f*; '~·**house ef·fect** efekt *m* cieplarniany; '~·**ish** zielonawy, zielonkawy
Green·land Grenlandia *f*
greet [griːt] ⟨po⟩witać; '~·**ing** powitanie *n*; pozdrowienie *n*; ***~ings*** *pl.* pozdrowienia *pl.*
gre·nade *mil.* [grɪ'neɪd] granat *m*
grew [gruː] *pret. od* ***grow***
grey [greɪ] **1.** szary; popielaty; *włosy*: siwy; szpakowaty; **2.** szarość *f*; szary *lub* popielaty kolor *m*; **3.** ⟨z⟩szarzeć; ⟨po⟩-siwieć; '~·**hound** *zo.* chart *m*
grid [grɪd] krata *f*; *electr. itp.* sieć *f*; *kartograficzna* siatka *f*; '~·**i·ron** ruszt *m*
grief [griːf] zmartwienie *n*
griev|·ance ['griːvns] skarga *f*; zażalenie *n*; **~e** [griːv] *v/t.* martwić; *v/i.* ⟨z⟩martwić się; ***~e for*** żałować (*G*); **~·ous** ['griːvəs] poważny
grill [grɪl] **1.** ⟨u⟩piec na grillu; **2.** grill *m*; ruszt *m*; pieczeń *f* z grilla
grim [grɪm] (***-mm-***) ponury; zacięty; F okropny
gri·mace [grɪ'meɪs] **1.** grymas *m*; **2.** ⟨z⟩robić grymas
grime [graɪm] brud *m*; '**grim·y** (***-ier, -iest***) zabrudzony
grin [grɪn] **1.** uśmiech *m* (*szyderczy*); **2.** (***-nn-***) uśmiechać ⟨-chnąć⟩ się (*szyderczo*)
grind [graɪnd] **1.** (***ground***) *v/t.* ⟨ze⟩mleć *lub* ⟨z⟩mielić; rozdrabniać ⟨-drobnić⟩; *noże itp.* ⟨na⟩ostrzyć; *soczewkę* ⟨o⟩szlifować; ***~ one's teeth*** ⟨za⟩zgrzytać zębami; *v/i.* harować; wkuwać ⟨-kuć⟩; **2.** harówka *f*; ***the daily ~*** codzienny znój *m*; '~·**er** szlifierz *m*; *tech.* szlifierka *f*; młynek *m*; '~·**stone** kamień *m* do ostrzenia
grip [grɪp] **1.** (***-pp-***) ⟨s⟩chwytać, ⟨z⟩łapać (*też fig.*); **2.** uścisk *m*; uchwyt *m*; rękojeść *f*; torba *f* podróżna; *fig.* władza *f*, moc *f*; ***come to ~s*** (***with s.th.***) zmierzyć się (z *I*)
gripes [graɪps] *pl.* kolka *f* (*jelitowa*)
gris·ly ['grɪzlɪ] (***-ier, -iest***) koszmarny, makabryczny
gris·tle ['grɪsl] chrząstka *f*
grit [grɪt] **1.** grys *m*, żwir *m*; *fig.* determinacja *f*; **2.** (***-tt-***): ***~ one's teeth*** zaciskać ⟨-snąć⟩ zęby
griz·zly (**bear**) *zo.* ['grɪzlɪ (-)] *niedźwiedź*: grizzly *m*
groan [grəʊn] **1.** jęczeć ⟨jęknąć⟩; **2.** jęk *m*
gro·cer ['grəʊsə] handlarz *m* (-rka *f*) artykułami spożywczymi; **~·ies** ['grəʊsərɪz] *pl.* artykuły *pl.* spożywcze; **~·y** ['grəʊsərɪ] sklep *m* z artykułami spożywczymi
grog·gy ['grɒgɪ] F (***-ier, -iest***) zamroczony, oszołomiony
groin *anat.* [grɔɪn] pachwina *f*
groom [grʊm] **1.** pan *m* młody; stajenny *m*; koniuszy *m*; **2.** *konie* oporządzać ⟨-dzić⟩, doglądać; ***well-groomed*** wypielęgnowany, zadbany
groove [gruːv] rowek *m*; żłobek *m*; bruzda *f*; '**groov·y** *sl.* (***-ier, -iest***) *przest.* bombowy, fajowy
grope [grəʊp] ⟨po⟩szukać (po omacku); *sl. dziewczynę* obmacywać ⟨-cać⟩
gross [grəʊs] **1.** *econ.* brutto; gruby, zwalisty; toporny; rażący; ordynarny; **2.** (*12 tuzinów*) gros *m*
gro·tesque [grəʊ'tesk] groteskowy
ground[1] [graʊnd] **1.** *pret. i p.p. od* ***grind*** 1; **2.** mielony; ***~ meat*** *mięso n* mielone
ground[2] [graʊnd] **1.** ziemia *f*; ląd *m*; teren *m*, miejsce *n*; (*w sporcie*) boisko *n*; tło *n*; *Am. electr.* uziemienie *n*; *fig.* motyw *m*, powód *m*; ***~s*** *pl.* osad *m*, fusy *pl.*; działka *f* (*gruntu*), teren *m*, park *m*; ***on the ~(s) of*** na podstawie (*G*); ***hold lub stand one's ~*** dotrzymywać ⟨-mać⟩ pola; **2.** *naut.* osiadać ⟨osiąść⟩ na mieliźnie; *Am. electr.* uziemiać ⟨-mić⟩; *fig.* opierać ⟨oprzeć⟩ się, polegać ⟨-lec⟩; '~ **crew** *aviat.* personel *m* naziemny; ~ '**floor** *zwł. Brt.* parter *m*; '~ **forc·es** *pl. mil.* siły *pl.* lądowe; '~·**hog** *zo.* świstak *m* amerykański; '~·**ing** *Am. electr.* uziemienie *n*; podstawy *pl.*; '~·**less** bezpodstawny; '~·**nut** *Brt. bot.* orzeszek *m* ziemny; '~·**s·man** (*pl.* ***-men***) (*w sporcie*) dozorca *m* obiektu sportowego; '~ **staff** *Brt. aviat.* personel *m* naziemny; '~ **sta·tion** (*w astronautyce*) stacja *f* naziemna; '~·**work** *fig.* fundament *m*
group [gruːp] **1.** grupa *f*; **2.** ⟨z⟩grupować (się)
group·ie ['gruːpɪ] F *natrętna* fanka *f*
group·ing ['gruːpɪŋ] zgrupowanie *n*
grove [grəʊv] gaj *m*, zagajnik *m*

grov·el ['grɒvl] (*zwł. Brt.* **-ll-**, *Am.* **-l-**) płaszczyć się, upokarzać ⟨-korzyć⟩ się
grow [grəʊ] (***grew, grown***) *v/i.* ⟨wy-, u⟩rosnąć; wzrastać ⟨-rosnąć⟩; **~ *up*** dorastać ⟨-rosnąć⟩; *v/t. bot.* ⟨wy⟩hodować; uprawiać; **~ *a beard*** zapuszczać ⟨-puścić⟩ brodę; '**~·er** hodowca *m*
growl [graʊl] ⟨za⟩warczeć
grown [grəʊn] **1.** *p.p. od* ***grow***; **2.** *adj.* dorosły; **~-up 1.** [grəʊn'ʌp] dorosły; **2.** ['grəʊnʌp] F dorosły *m* (-ła *f*)
growth [grəʊθ] wzrost *m*, rozrost *m*; *fig.* przyrost *m*; *med.* narośl *f*
grub [grʌb] **1.** *zo.* larwa *f*; F żarcie *n*; **2.** (**-*bb*-**) ⟨wy⟩ryć, ⟨wy⟩grzebać; '**~·by** (***-ier, -iest***) zabrudzony
grudge [grʌdʒ] **1.** ⟨po⟩żałować (***s.o. s.th.*** komuś czegoś); **2.** żal *m*, uraza *f*; '**grudg·ing·ly** niechętnie
gru·el [grʊəl] kleik *m*, papka *f* (*z owsa*)
gruff [grʌf] szorstki, opryskliwy
grum·ble ['grʌmbl] **1.** marudzić, narzekać; **2.** marudzenie *n*, narzekanie *n*; '**~r** *fig.* maruda *m lub f*
grump·y ['grʌmpɪ] F (***-ier, -iest***) marudny
grun·gy ['grʌndʒɪ] *Am. sl.* (***-ier, -iest***) zaniedbany; cuchnący; paskudny
grunt [grʌnt] **1.** chrząkać ⟨-knąć⟩; zrzędzić; **2.** chrząkanie *n*; zrzędzenie *n*
Gt *skrót pisany*: ***Great*** (*Gt Britain*)
guar·an|·tee [gærən'tiː] **1.** gwarancja *f*; *fig.* pewność *f*; **2.** ⟨za⟩gwarantować; ⟨po⟩ręczyć za (*A*); **~·tor** [gærən'tɔː] gwarant *m*, poręczyciel *m*; **~·ty** ['gærəntɪ] *jur.* gwarancja *f*, poręka *f*
guard [gɑːd] **1.** strażnik *m*, wartownik *m*; straż *f*, warta *f*; *Brt. rail.* konduktor(ka *f*) *m*; osłona *f*; garda *f*; ***be on ~*** trzymać straż; ***be on*** (***off***) ***one's ~*** (nie) mieć się na baczności; **2.** *v/t.* ⟨o⟩chronić, ⟨u⟩strzec (***from*** przed *I*); *v/i.* ⟨u⟩chronić się, wystrzegać się; '**~·ed** ostrożny; **~·i·an** ['gɑːdjən] *jur.* kurator(ka *f*) *m*, opiekun(ka *f*) *m*; '**~·i·an·ship** *jur.* kuratela *f*, ochrona *f*
gue(**r**)**·ril·la** [gə'rɪlə] *mil.* partyzant(ka *f*) *m*; **~ 'war·fare** partyzantka *f*
guess [ges] **1.** zgadywać ⟨-dnąć⟩, odgadywać ⟨-dnąć⟩; *Am.* sądzić, mniemać; **2.** odgadnięcie *n*; '**~·work** zgadywanka *f*, domysły *pl.*
guest [gest] gość *m*; '**~·house** pensjonat *m*; '**~·room** pokój *m* gościnny
guf·faw [gʌ'fɔː] **1.** *głośny, nieprzyjemny* śmiech *m*; **2.** *głośno, nieprzyjemnie* roześmiać (się)
guid·ance ['gaɪdns] prowadzenie *n*, kierowanie *n*
guide [gaɪd] **1.** przewodnik *m* (-niczka *f*); (*książka*) przewodnik *m* (***to*** po *L*); → ***girl guide***; **2.** ⟨po⟩prowadzić; oprowadzać ⟨-dzić⟩; kierować (się); '**~ book** (*książka*) przewodnik *m*; **~d 'tour** wycieczka *f* z przewodnikiem, oprowadzanie *n*; '**~·lines** *pl.* wytyczne *pl.* (***on*** w sprawie *G*)
guild [gɪld] *hist.* cech *m*
guile·less ['gaɪllɪs] prostoduszny, ufny
guilt [gɪlt] wina *f*; '**~·less** niewinny; '**~·y** (***-ier, -iest***) winny; czujący się winnym
guin·ea pig ['gɪnɪ -] *zo.* świnka *f* morska
guise [gaɪz] *fig.* przebranie *n*, płaszczyk *m*
gui·tar [gɪ'tɑː] *mus.* gitara *f*
gulch [gʌlʃ] *zwł. Am.* głęboki wąwóz *m*
gulf [gʌlf] zatoka *f*; *fig.* przepaść *f*
gull [gʌl] *zo.* mewa *f*
gul·let ['gʌlɪt] *anat.* przełyk *m*; gardło *n*
gulp [gʌlp] **1.** *duży* łyk *m*; **2.** *często* **~ *down*** łykać ⟨-knąć⟩ *szybko*
gum[1] [gʌm] *anat.*: *zw.* **~*s*** *pl.* dziąsła *pl.*
gum[2] [gʌm] **1.** guma *f*; klej *m*; guma *f* do żucia; żelatynka *f*; **2.** (**-*mm*-**) ⟨s⟩kleić
gun [gʌn] **1.** karabin *m*, strzelba *f*; działo *n*; pistolet *m*, rewolwer *m*; **2.** (**-*nn*-**): **~ *down*** zastrzelić; '**~·fight** *zwł. Am.* strzelanina *f*; '**~·fire** ogień *m* (*z broni palnej*); '**~ li·cence** (*Am.*; **li·cense**) zezwolenie *n* na broń; '**~·man** (*pl.* ***-men***) rewolwerowiec *m*; '**~·point**: ***at ~ point*** pod groźbą użycia broni; '**~·pow·der** proch *m* strzelniczy; '**~·run·ner** przemytnik *m* broni; '**~·run·ning** przemyt *m* broni; '**~·shot** strzał *m*; ***within*** (***out of***) **~*shot*** w zasięgu (poza zasięgiem) strzału
gur·gle ['gɜːgl] **1.** gaworzyć; ⟨za⟩gulgotać; **2.** gaworzenie *n*; gulgotanie *n*
gush [gʌʃ] **1.** tryskać ⟨trysnąć⟩ (***from*** z *G*); **2.** nagły wypływ *m*; wytrysk *m* (*też fig.*)
gust [gʌst] poryw *m* (*wiatru*), podmuch *m*
guts [gʌts] F *pl.* wnętrzności *pl.*; *fig.* odwaga *f*

gut·ter ['gʌtə] rynsztok *m* (*też fig.*); rynna *f*
guy [gaɪ] F facet *m*, gość *m*
guz·zle ['gʌzl] ⟨po⟩żreć; pochłaniać ⟨-łonąć⟩
gym [dʒɪm] F ośrodek *m* odnowy biologicznej; fitness center *m*; → ***gymnasium***; → ***gymnastics***; **~·na·sium** [dʒɪm'neɪzjəm] hala *f* sportowa; ⚠ *nie gimnazjum*; **~·nast** ['dʒɪmnæst] gimnastyk *m* (-tyczka *f*); **~·nas·tics** [dʒɪm'næstɪks] gimnastyka *f*
gy·n(a)e·col·o|·gist [gaɪnɪ'kɒlədʒɪst] ginekolog *m*; **~·gy** [gaɪnɪ'kɒlədʒɪ] ginekologia *f*
gyp·sy ['dʒɪpsɪ] *zwł. Am.* → ***gipsy***
gy·rate [dʒaɪə'reɪt] ⟨za⟩kręcić się, ⟨za⟩wirować

H

H, h [eɪtʃ] H, h *n*
hab·er·dash·er ['hæbədæʃə] *Brt.* sprzedawca *m* artykułów pasmanteryjnych; *Am.* sprzedawca *m* odzieży męskiej; **~·y** ['hæbədæʃərɪ] *Brt.* pasmanteria *f*, *Am.* odzież *f* męska; *Am.* sklep *m* z odzieżą męską
hab·it ['hæbɪt] przywyczajenie *n*, zwyczaj *m*; habit *m*; ***drink has become a ~ with him*** uzależnił się od alkoholu
ha·bit·u·al [hə'bɪtjʊəl] zwyczajowy; nałogowy
hack[1] [hæk] ⟨po⟩rąbać
hack[2] [hæk] pismak *m*
hack[3] [hæk] szkapa *f*
hack·er ['hækə] *komp.* haker *m*, maniak *m* komputerowy
hack·neyed ['hæknɪd] wytarty, wyświechtany
had [hæd] *pret. i p.p. od* ***have***
had·dock ['hædək] *zo.* (*pl.* ***-dock***) *ryba*: łupacz *m*
h(a)e·mor·rhage ['hemərɪdʒ] *med.* krwawienie *n*, krwotok *m*
hag [hæg] *fig.* jędza *f*, sekutnica *f*
hag·gard ['hægəd] wymizerowany, wynędzniały
hag·gle ['hægl] targować się
Hague: ***the ~*** Haga *f*
hail [heɪl] **1.** grad *m*; **2.** *grad*: padać; **'~·stone** (*kulka*) grad *m*; **'~·storm** burza *f* gradowa
hair [heə] *pojedynczy* włos *m*; *zbior.* włosy *pl.*; **'~·breadth** → ***hair's breadth***; **'~·brush** szczotka *f* do włosów; **'~·cut** strzyżenie *n*, obcięcie *n* włosów; **~·do** (*pl.* ***-dos***) F fryzura *f*; **'~·dress·er** fryzjer(ka *f*) *m*; **'~·dri·er**, **'~·dry·er** suszarka *f* do włosów; **'~·grip** *Brt.* klamra *f* do włosów; **'~·less** bezwłosy; **'~·pin** spinka *f* do włosów; **~·pin 'bend** ostry zakręt *m*; **~-rais·ing** ['heəreɪzɪŋ] podnoszący włosy na głowie; **'~'s breadth**: ***by a ~'s breadth*** o włos; **'~ slide** spinka *f* do włosów; **'~-split·ting** rozszczepianie *n* włosa; **'~·spray** lakier *m* do włosów; **'~·style** fryzura *f*; **'~ styl·ist** fryzjer(ka *f*) *m* damski (-*a*); **'~·y** (***-ier, -iest***) włochaty, owłosiony
half 1. [hɑːf] (*pl.* ***halves*** [hɑːvz]) połowa *f*; ***go halves*** ⟨po⟩dzielić się po połowie; **2.** pół; ***~ an hour*** pół godziny; ***~ a pound*** pół funta; ***~ past ten*** (w)pół do jedenastej; ***~ way up*** w połowie wysokości; **'~-breed** mieszaniec *m*; **'~-broth·er** brat *m* przyrodni; **'~-caste** mieszaniec *m*; **~-'heart·ed** bez przekonania; **~ 'time** *sport*: przerwa *f*; **~ time 'score** (*w sporcie*) rezultat *m* do przerwy; **~'way** w pół, w połowie; **~·way 'line linia** *f* środkowa; **~-'wit·ted** niedorozwinięty
hal·i·but ['hælɪbət] *zo.* (*pl.* ***-buts, but***) halibut *m*
hall [hɔːl] sala *f*, hala *f*; dwór *m*; przedpokój *m*, korytarz *m*; *univ.* ***~ of residence*** dom *m* akademicki
Hal·low·e'en [hæləʊ'iːn] dzień *m* przed dniem Wszystkich Świętych
hal·lu·ci·na·tion [həluːsɪ'neɪʃn] halucynacja *f*
'hall·way *zwł. Am.* przedpokój *m*, korytarz *m*
ha·lo ['heɪləʊ] (*pl.* ***-loes, los***) aureola *f* (*też astr.*)
halt [hɔːlt] **1.** zatrzymanie *n* się; **2.** zatrzymywać ⟨-mać⟩ (się)
hal·ter ['hɔːltə] stryczek *m*

halve [hɑːv] przepoławiać ⟨-łowić⟩; **~s** [hɑːvz] *pl. od* ***half*** 1
ham [hæm] szynka *f*; ***~ and eggs*** jajecznica *f* na szynce
ham·burg·er ['hæmbɜːgə] *gastr.* hamburger *m*; *Am.* mięso *n* mielone
ham·let ['hæmlɪt] *mała* wioska *f*
ham·mer ['hæmə] **1.** młotek *m*, młot *m*; **2.** walić (*młotkiem*); wbijać ⟨-bić⟩
ham·mock ['hæmək] hamak *m*
ham·per[1] ['hæmpə] kosz(yk) *m* z przykrywą
ham·per[2] ['hæmpə] przeszkadzać ⟨-kodzić⟩
ham·ster ['hæmstə] *zo.* chomik *m*
hand [hænd] **1.** ręka *f* (*też fig.*); pismo *n*; wskazówka *f* (*zegara*); *często w złoż.* pracownik *m*, robotnik *m*; ręka *f* (*karty trzymane przez gracza w jednym rozdaniu*); ***~ in glove*** w zmowie, ręka w rękę; ***change ~s*** przechodzić ⟨przejść⟩ z rąk do rąk; ***give*** *lub* ***lend a ~*** pomóc *komuś* (***with*** w *L*); ***shake ~s with s.o.*** ⟨u⟩ścisnąć komuś rękę; ***at ~*** pod ręką; ***at first ~*** z pierwszej ręki; ***by ~*** ręcznie; ***on the one ~*** z jednej strony; ***on the other ~*** z drugiej strony; ***on the right ~*** z prawej strony; ***~s off!*** ręce przy sobie!; **2.** wręczać ⟨-czyć⟩, dawać ⟨dać⟩, podawać ⟨-dać⟩; ***~ around*** rozdawać ⟨-dać⟩; ***~ down*** przekazywać ⟨-zać⟩; ***~ in*** *test itp.* oddawać ⟨-dać⟩; *sprawozdanie* składać ⟨złożyć⟩; ***~ on*** przekazywać ⟨-zać⟩; ***~ out*** rozdzielać ⟨-lić⟩, rozdawać ⟨-dać⟩; ***~ over*** przekazywać ⟨-zać⟩; ***~ up*** przekazywać ⟨-zać⟩; **'~·bag** torebka *f*; **'~·ball** piłka *f* ręczna; (*w piłce nożnej*) zagranie *n* ręką; **'~·bill** ulotka *f*; **'~·brake** *tech.* hamulec *m* ręczny; **'~·cuffs** *pl.* kajdanki *pl.*; **'~·ful** garść *f*, garstka *f*; F żywe srebro *n*
hand·i·cap ['hændɪkæp] **1.** ułomność *f*, *med. też* upośledzenie *n*; przeszkoda *f*; *sport*: handicap *m*, wyrównanie *n*; → ***mental***; → ***physical***; **2.** (***-pp-***) utrudniać ⟨-nić⟩; **'~ped 1.** upośledzony; niepełnosprawny; → ***mental***; → ***physical***; **2.** ***the ~ped*** *pl. med.* niepełnosprawni *pl.*
hand·ker·chief ['hæŋkətʃɪf] (*pl.* ***-chiefs***) chusteczka *f*, chustka *f*
han·dle ['hændl] **1.** uchwyt *m*, rączka *f*; rękojeść *f*; klamka *f*; ***fly off the ~*** F wściec się; **2.** dotykać ⟨-tknąć⟩ (*G*); obchodzić się z (*I*); ⟨po⟩radzić sobie z (*I*); prowadzić; handlować; **'~·bar(s** *pl.*) kierownica *f* (*roweru*)
'hand| lug·gage bagaż *m* ręczny; **~'made** ręcznie zrobione; **'~·out** datek *m*, darowizna *f*; konspekt *m*, tekst *m*; **'~·rail** poręcz *f*; **'~·shake** uściśnięcie *n* dłoni
hand·some ['hænsəm] (***-er, -est***) przystojny; *suma*: pokaźny
'hand|·writ·ing pismo *n*; **~'writ·ten** napisany ręcznie; **'~·y** (***-ier, -iest***) poręczny; przydatny; dogodnie położony; ***come in ~y*** przydawać ⟨-dać⟩ się
hang [hæŋ] (***hung***) *v/i.* wisieć; zwisać; *v/t.* wieszać, zawieszać ⟨-sić⟩; zwieszać ⟨-sić⟩; *tapetę* przyklejać ⟨-leić⟩; (*pret. i p.p.* ***hanged***) *kogoś* wieszać ⟨powiesić⟩; ***~ o.s.*** powiesić się; ***~ about, ~ around*** kręcić się, snuć się; ***~ on*** uczepiać ⟨-pić⟩ się; *tel.* nie odkładać słuchawki; ***~ up*** *tel.* rozłączać ⟨-czyć⟩ się; ***she hung up on me*** rozłączyła się ze mną
han·gar ['hæŋə] *aviat.* hangar *m*
hang·er ['hæŋə] wieszak *m*
hang|·glid·er ['hæŋglaɪdə] lotnia *f*; **'~ glid·ing** lotniarstwo *n*
hang·ing ['hæŋɪŋ] **1.** wiszący; **2.** wieszanie *n*; **'~s** *pl.* draperia *f*
'hang·man (*pl.* ***-men***) kat *m*
'hang·o·ver kociokwik *m*, kac *m*
han·ker ['hæŋkə] F tęsknić (***after, for*** do *G*)
han|·kie, ~·ky ['hæŋkɪ] F chustka *f*
hap·haz·ard [hæp'hæzəd] przypadkowy
hap·pen ['hæpən] zdarzać ⟨-rzyć⟩ się, wydarzać ⟨-rzyć⟩ się; ***~ to*** stać się (*D*), przytrafiać (*D*) się; ***he ~ed to be at home*** akurat był w domu; **~·ing** ['hæpnɪŋ] wydarzenie *n*; happening *m*
hap·pi|·ly ['hæpɪlɪ] szczęśliwie; **'~·ness** szczęście *n*
hap·py ['hæpɪ] (***-ier, -iest***) szczęśliwy; zadowolony; **~-go-'luck·y** beztroski
ha·rangue [hə'ræŋ] **1.** pouczenie *n*, kazanie *n*; **2.** pouczać ⟨-czyć⟩
har·ass ['hærəs] nękać, dręczyć; szykanować; **'~·ment** nękanie *n*; dręczenie *n*; szykany *pl.*; → ***sexual harassment***
har·bo(u)r ['hɑːbə] **1.** port *m*; przystań *f*; schronienie *n*; **2.** ofiarowywać

⟨-ować⟩ schronienie; *urazę itp.* żywić
hard [hɑːd] **1.** *adj.* twardy; *zadanie itp.*: trudny; silny; *życie*: ciężki; *zima, osoba itp.*: surowy; *pracodawca*: stanowczy; *dowód*: niezbity; *trunek*: mocny; *narkotyk*: niebezpieczny; **~ of hearing** niedosłyszący; **be ~ up** F być w ciężkiej sytuacji finansowej, odczuwać brak; **2.** *adv.* mocno; ciężko; ostro; **'~·back** książka *f* w twardej oprawie; **~-'boiled** ugotowany na twardo; *fig.* twardy, mało sentymentalny; **~ 'cash** gotówka *f*; **~ 'core** trzon *m*; *mus.* hardcore *m*; **~-'core** hard core; *pornografia*: *ostry*; **'~·cov·er** *print.* **1.** oprawny, oprawiony; **2.** twarda oprawa *f*; dzieło *n* oprawne; **~ 'disk** *komp.* twardy dysk *m*; **~·en** ['hɑːdn] ⟨s⟩twardnieć; utwardzać ⟨-dzić⟩; hartować; **'~ hat** kask *m*; **~'head·ed** wyrachowany; *zwł. Am.* twardogłowy; **~-'heart·ed** o twardym sercu, bezwzględny; **~ 'la·bo(u)r** *jur.* ciężkie roboty *pl.*; **~ 'line** *zwł. pol.* twardy kurs *m*; **~-'line** *zwł. pol.* twardy, dogmatyczny; **'~·ly** prawie (nie); ledwo, ledwie; **'~·ness** twardość *f*; **'~·ship** trudność *f*; **~ 'shoul·der** *Brt. mot.* pobocze *n* utwardzone; **'~·top** *mot.* dach *m* sztywny (*czasem zdejmowany*; *też typ samochodu*); **'~·ware** *komp.* sprzęt *m* komputerowy; wyroby *pl.* metalowe; towary *pl.* żelazne
har·dy ['hɑːdɪ] (**-ier, -iest**) mocny, wytrzymały; *roślina*: zimotrwały
hare [heə] *zo.* zając *m*; **'~·bell** *bot.* dzwonek *m*; **'~·brained** *osoba*, *plan*: zbzikowany; **~'lip** *anat.* warga *f* zajęcza
harm [hɑːm] **1.** szkoda *f*, krzywda *f*; **2.** ⟨s⟩krzywdzić, wyrządzać krzywdę; ⟨z⟩ranić; **'~·ful** szkodliwy; **'~·less** nieszkodliwy
har·mo|·ni·ous [hɑː'məʊnjəs] harmonijny; **~·nize** ['hɑːmənaɪz] harmonizować; współbrzmieć; **~·ny** ['hɑːmənɪ] harmonia *f*
har·ness ['hɑːnɪs] **1.** uprząż *f*; ***die in ~*** *fig.* umrzeć w kieracie; **2.** zaprzęgać ⟨-rząc⟩ (*też fig.*); wykorzystywać ⟨-tać⟩ (***to*** do *G*)
harp [hɑːp] **1.** *mus.* harfa *f*; **2.** *mus.* ⟨za⟩grać na harfie; **~ *on* (*about*)** *fig.* ględzić o (*L*)
har·poon [hɑː'puːn] **1.** harpun *m*; **2.** wbijać ⟨wbić⟩ harpun
har·row ['hærəʊ] *agr.* **1.** brona *f*; **2.** ⟨po⟩bronować
har·row·ing ['hærəʊɪŋ] wstrząsający, przygniatający
harsh [hɑːʃ] ostry; surowy
hart [hɑːt] *zo.* (*pl.* **harts, hart**) jeleń *m*
har·vest ['hɑːvɪst] **1.** żniwo *n*, *zw.* żniwa *pl.*; plon *m*, zbiory *pl.*; **2.** zbierać ⟨zebrać⟩; **'~·er** kombajn *m* żniwny
has [hæz] *on, ona, ono* ma
hash[1] [hæʃ] *gastr.* (*mięso krojone z warzywami w sosie*); ***make a ~ of s.th.*** *fig.* spartaczyć coś
hash[2] [hæʃ] F haszysz *m*
hash 'browns *pl. Am.* przysmażane kartofle *pl.*
hash·ish ['hæʃiːʃ] haszysz *m*
hasp [hɑːsp] klamra *f* zamka
haste [heɪst] pośpiech *m*; **has·ten** ['heɪsn] *kogoś* popędzać ⟨-dzić⟩; spieszyć się; *coś* przyspieszać ⟨-szyć⟩; **'hast·y** (**-ier, -iest**) pospieszny; pochopny
hat [hæt] kapelusz *m*
hatch[1] [hætʃ] *też* **~ *out*** wykluwać ⟨-luć⟩ się, wylęgać ⟨-lęgnąć⟩ się
hatch[2] [hætʃ] właz *m*; okienko *n*; **'~·back** (*typ samochodu i nadwozia*) hatchback *m*
hatch·et ['hætʃɪt] topór *m*; ***bury the ~*** zakopać topór wojenny
'hatch·way właz *m*, luk *m*
hate [heɪt] **1.** nienawiść *f*; **2.** ⟨z⟩nienawidzić; **'~·ful** okropny; pełen nienawiści; **ha·tred** ['heɪtrɪd] nienawiść *f*
haugh·ty ['hɔːtɪ] wyniosły
haul [hɔːl] **1.** ciągnąć, wyciągać ⟨-gnąć⟩; ⟨za⟩wlec; ⟨za⟩holować; ⟨prze⟩transportować, ⟨prze⟩wozić; **2.** ciągnienie *n*; połów *m*; łup *m*; transport *m*, przewóz *m*; **~·age** ['hɔːlɪdʒ] transport *m*, przewóz *m*; **~·er** ['hɔːlə] *Am.*, **~·i·er** ['hɔːljə] *Brt.* przewoźnik *m*
haunch [hɔːntʃ] pośladek *m*, biodro *n*; udo *n*
haunt [hɔːnt] **1.** nawiedzać ⟨-dzić⟩; często odwiedzać; prześladować; **2.** często odwiedzane miejsce *n*; kryjówka *f*; **'~·ing** dojmujący, dotkliwy
have [hæv] (***had***) *v/t.* mieć, posiadać; otrzymywać ⟨-mać⟩, dostawać ⟨-tać⟩; ⟨z⟩jeść, pić; **~ *breakfast*** ⟨z⟩jeść śniadanie; **~ *a cup of tea*** wypić filiżankę herbaty; *przed bezok.*: *musieć*; ***I ~ to***

H

go now muszę już iść; *z dopełnieniem i p.p.*: *kazać komuś coś* (*sobie*) *zrobić*; ***I had my hair cut*** obciąłem sobie włosy; ~ ***back*** dostawać ⟨-tać⟩ z powrotem; *ubranie*: ~ ***on*** mieć na sobie; *v/aux*. ***I ~ not finished yet*** jeszcze nie skończyłem; ~ ***you had your breakfast yet?*** czy już zjadłeś śniadanie?; ***I ~ come*** przyszedłem
ha·ven ['heɪvn] przystań *m* (*zwł. fig.*)
hav·oc ['hævək] zniszczenie *n*, spustoszenie *n*; ***play ~ with*** ⟨z⟩niszczyć, ⟨s⟩pustoszyć, *fig*. wprowadzać ⟨-dzić⟩ zamęt
Ha·wai·i [hə'waiiː] Hawaje *pl*.; **~·an** [hə'waɪɪən] **1.** hawajski; **2.** Hawajczyk *m* (-jka *f*); *ling*. język *m* hawajski
hawk¹ [hɔːk] *zo*. jastrząb *m* (*też fig*.)
hawk² [hɔːk] prowadzić sprzedaż domokrążną *lub* uliczną; '**~·er** domokrążca *m*; sprzedawca *m* uliczny; kolporter *m* (*subskrypcji prasy*)
haw·thorn ['hɔːθɔːn] *bot*. głóg *m*
hay [heɪ] siano *n*; '**~ fe·ver** katar *m* sienny; '**~·loft** stryszek *m* na siano; '**~·rick**, '**~·stack** stóg *m* siana
haz·ard ['hæzəd] zagrożenie *n*, niebezpieczeństwo *n*; '**~·ous** niebezpieczny, zagrażający życiu; **~·ous 'waste** niebezpieczne odpady *pl*.
haze [heɪz] mgła *f*
ha·zel ['heɪzl] **1.** *bot*. leszczyna *f*; **2.** orzechowy, brązowy; '**~·nut** orzech *m* laskowy
haz·y ['heɪzɪ] (***-ier, -iest***) mglisty (*też fig*.); zamglony
H-bomb ['eɪtʃbɒm] bomba *f* wodorowa
HD *skrót*: ***Hard Disk***
he [hiː] **1.** *pron*. on; **2.** *zo*. samiec *m*; **3.** *adj*.: *w złoż*. ***he-goat*** kozioł *m*
head [hed] **1.** głowa *f*; kierownik *m* (-niczka *f*), dyrektor(ka *f*) *m*; prowadzący *m* (-ca *f*); góra *f*, część *f* górna; reszka *f*; nagłówek *m*; głowica *f* (*w magnetofonie itp*.); łeb *m* (*śruby itp*.); główka *f* (*młotka, gwoździa itp*.); ***20 pounds a ~*** *lub* ***per ~*** po 20 funtów na głowę *lub* na osobę; ***40 ~*** *pl*. (***of cattle***) 40 sztuk *pl*. (bydła); ***~s or tails*** orzeł czy reszka?; ***at the ~ of*** na przedzie (*G*); ***~ over heels*** bez opamiętania; po uszy; ***bury one's ~ in the sand*** ⟨s⟩chować głowę w piasek; ***get it into one's ~ that...*** wbić sobie do głowy, że...; ***lose one's ~*** ⟨s⟩tracić głowę *lub* nerwy; **2.** główny, naczelny; najważniejszy; **3.** *v/t*. stać na czele; prowadzić; kierować; (*w piłce nożnej*) odbijać ⟨-bić⟩ głową; *v/i*. (***for***) kierować się (do *G*); *fig*. zmierzać (do *G*); trzymać kurs (na *A*); '**~·ache** ból *m* głowy; '**~·band** opaska *f* na głowę; '**~·dress** przybranie *n* głowy; '**~·er** odbicie *n* głową, F główka *f*; **~'first** głową wprzód; *fig*. bez opamiętania; '**~·gear** nakrycie *n* głowy; '**~·ing** nagłówek *m*, tytuł *m*; **~·land** ['hedlənd] przylądek *m*; '**~·light** *mot*. reflektor *m*; '**~·line** nagłówek *m*; ***news ~lines*** *pl*. *TV*, *radio*: skrót *m* najważniejszych wiadomości; '**~·long** głową naprzód; na łeb na szyję; **~'mas·ter** dyrektor *m* szkoły; **~'mis·tress** dyrektorka *f* szkoły; **~-'on** frontalny; czołowy; ***~on collision*** zderzenie czołowe; '**~·phones** *pl*. słuchawki *pl*.; '**~·quar·ters** *pl*. (*skrót*: ***HQ***) kwatera *f* główna; centrala *f*; '**~·rest** *Am*., '**~ re·straint** *Brt*. *mot*. zagłówek *m*; '**~·set** słuchawki *pl*.; **~ 'start** (*w sporcie*) przewaga *f*, fory *pl*.; '**~·strong** zawzięty, uparty; **~ 'teach·er** → ***headmaster***; → ***headmistress***; → *Am*. ***principal***; '**~·wa·ters** dopływy *pl*. w górnym biegu rzeki; '**~·way** *fig*. postęp(y *pl*.) *m*; ***make ~way*** iść ⟨pójść⟩ naprzód; '**~·word** (*w słowniku*) hasło *n*; '**~·y** (***-ier, -iest***) uderzający do głowy
heal [hiːl] ⟨wy⟩leczyć; ***~ over, ~ up*** ⟨za⟩goić się
health [helθ] zdrowie *n*; '**~ cer·tif·i·cate** świadectwo *n* zdrowia; '**~ club** ośrodek *m* odnowy biologicznej; '**~ food** zdrowa żywność *f*; '**~ food shop** *Brt*., '**~ food store** *zwł. Am*. sklep *m* ze zdrową żywnością; '**~·ful** zdrowy; dobrze wpływający na zdrowie; '**~ in·su·rance** ubezpieczenie *f* na wypadek choroby; '**~ re·sort** kurort *m*; '**~ ser·vice** służba *f* zdrowia; '**~·y** (***-ier, -iest***) zdrowy
heap [hiːp] **1.** kupa *f*, sterta *f*; stos *m*; **2.** *też* ***~ up*** składać ⟨złożyć⟩ na stos *lub* stertę; *fig*. *też* nagromadzać ⟨gromadzić⟩
hear [hɪə] (***heard***) ⟨u⟩słyszeć; ⟨wy⟩słuchać (*G*); ⟨po⟩słuchać; *świadka* przesłuchiwać ⟨-chać⟩; *jur*. sądzić; **~d** [hɜːd] *pret. i p.p. od* ***hear***; **~·er** ['hɪərə] słuchacz(ka *f*) *m*; **~·ing** ['hɪərɪŋ] słuch *m*; słyszalność *f*; *jur*. przesłuchanie *n*, rozprawa *f*; ***within*** (***out of***) ***~ing*** w zasięgu

(poza zasięgiem) słuchu; '**~·ing aid** aparat *m* słuchowy; '**~·say** pogłoska *f*; ***by ~say*** według pogłosek
hearse [hɜːs] karawan *m*
heart [hɑːt] *anat.* serce *n* (*też fig.*); centrum *n*, środek *m*; *gry w karty*: kier(y *pl.*) *m*; ***lose ~*** ⟨s⟩tracić serce; ***take ~*** nabierać ⟨-brać⟩ otuchy; ***take s.th. to ~*** brać ⟨wziąć⟩ coś do serca; ***with a heavy ~*** z ciężkim sercem; ***by ~*** na pamięć; '**~·ache** ból *m* serca; '**~ at·tack** atak *m* serca, zawał *m*; '**~·beat** bicie *n* serca; '**~·break** zawód *m* sercowy; rozczarowanie *n*; '**~·break·ing** rozdzierający serce; '**~·brok·en**: ***be ~broken*** mieć złamane serce; '**~·burn** zgaga *f*; **~en** ['hɑːtn] dodawać ⟨-dać⟩ otuchy; '**~ failure** *med.* niewydolność *f* serca; '**~·felt** z głębi serca, z wnętrza
hearth [hɑːθ] palenisko *n*, *fig.* ognisko *n* domowe
'**heart|·less** bez serca; '**~·rend·ing** rozdzierający serce; '**~ trans·plant** przeszczep *m lub* transplantacja *f* serca; '**~·y** (***-ier, -iest***) serdeczny; zdrowy
heat [hiːt] **1.** ciepło *n* (*też tech.*); upał *m*, gorąco *n*; zapał *m*; *zo.* ruja *f*; (*w sporcie*) bieg *m*; ***preliminary ~*** bieg *m* eliminacyjny; **2.** *v/t.* ogrzewać ⟨-rzać⟩; *też* ***~ up*** ⟨o⟩grzać, podgrzewać ⟨-rzać⟩; *v/i.* ogrzewać ⟨-rzać⟩ się (*też fig.*); '**~·ed** ogrzewany; podgrzewany; *rozmowa*: roznamiętniony, gorący; '**~·er** grzejnik *m*, grzałka *f*; podgrzewacz *m*, bojler *m*
heath [hiːθ] wrzosowisko *n*
hea·then ['hiːðn] **1.** poganin *m* (-anka *f*); **2.** pogański
heath·er ['heðə] *bot.* wrzosiec *m*, wrzos *m*
'**heat|·ing** ogrzewanie; *attr.* grzejny, grzewczy; '**~·proof**, '**~-re·sis·tant**, '**~-re·sist·ing** żaroodporny; '**~ shield** (*w astronautykce*) osłona *f* termiczna; '**~·stroke** *med.* porażenie *n* słoneczne; '**~ wave** fala *f* gorąca
heave [hiːv] (***heaved***, *zwł. naut.* ***hove***) *v/t.* dźwigać ⟨-gnąć⟩; miotać ⟨-tnąć⟩; *kotwicę* podnosić ⟨-nieść⟩; *westchnienie* wydawać ⟨-dać⟩; *v/i.* podnosić ⟨-nieść⟩ się; dźwigać ⟨-gnąć⟩ się
heav·en ['hevn] niebo *n*; '**~·ly** niebiański
heav·y ['hevɪ] (***-ier, -iest***) ciężki; *deszcz, opady, ruch*: silny; *palacz itp.*: nałogowy; *narzut, podatek itp.*: wysoki; *jedzenie*: ciężkostrawny; **~ 'cur·rent** *electr.* prąd *m* o dużym natężeniu; **~-'du·ty** *tech.* przewidziany do pracy o dużym obciążeniu; wytrzymały; **~-'hand·ed** surowy; mało taktowny; grubo ciosany; '**~·weight** (*w boksie*) waga *f* ciężka, zawodnik *m* wagi ciężkiej
He·brew ['hiːbruː] **1.** hebrajski; **2.** Hebrajczyk *m* (-jka *f*); *ling.* język *m* hebrajski
Heb·ri·des *pl.* Hebrydy *pl.*
heck·le ['hekl] *mówcy* przeszkadzać ⟨-kodzić⟩ (*uwagami*)
hec·tic ['hektɪk] (***~ally***) rozgorączkowany, gorączkowy
hedge [hedʒ] **1.** żywopłot *m*; **2.** *v/t.* *też* ***~ in*** ogradzać ⟨-rodzić⟩; *v/i. fig.* odpowiadać ⟨-wiedzieć⟩ wymijająco; '**~·hog** *zo.* jeż *m*; *Am.* jeżozwierz *m*; '**~·row** żywopłot *m*
heed [hiːd] **1.** brać ⟨wziąć⟩ pod uwagę; **2.** ***give*** *lub* ***pay ~ to, take ~ of*** zważać na; '**~·less**: ***be ~less of*** nie zważać na (*A*), nie mieć względu na (*A*)
heel [hiːl] **1.** *anat.* pięta *f* (*też w skarpecie itp.*); obcas *m*; ***down at ~*** wytarty, starty; *fig.* niechlujny, zaniedbany; **2.** dorabiać ⟨-robić⟩ obcasy do (*G*)
hef·ty ['heftɪ] (***-ier, -iest***) zwalisty; mocny, *uderzenie*: silny; *cena itp.*: wielki
heif·er ['hefə] *zo.* jałówka *f*
height [haɪt] wysokość *f*; *fig.* szczyt *m*, maksimum *n*; **~·en** ['haɪtn] podwyższać ⟨-szyć⟩; zwiększać ⟨-szyć⟩; wzmacniać ⟨-mocnić⟩
heir [eə] spadkobierca *m*, dziedzic *m*, następca *m*; ***~ to the throne*** następca *m* tronu; **~·ess** ['eərɪs] spadkobierczyni *f*, następczyni *f*; **~·loom** ['eəluːm] pamiątka *f* rodzinna
held [held] *pret. i p.p. od* ***hold*** 1
hel·i|·cop·ter *aviat.* ['helɪkɒptə] helikopter *m*, śmigłowiec *m*; '**~·port** *aviat.* lądowisko *n* helikopterów
hell [hel] **1.** piekło *n*; *attr.* piekielny; ***what the ~ ...?*** co u diabła ...?; ***raise ~*** F ⟨z⟩robić karczemną awanturę; **2.** *int.* F cholera!, szlag by to!; **~-'bent**: ***he is ~-bent on s.th.*** strasznie mu zależy na czymś; '**~·ish** piekielny
hel·lo [hə'ləʊ] *int.* cześć!
helm [helm] *naut.* ster *m*; ⚠ *nie* ***hełm***
hel·met ['helmɪt] hełm *m*; kask *m*

helms·man ['helmzmən] *naut.* (*pl.* ***-men***) sternik *m*
help [help] **1.** pomoc *f*; pomoc *f* domowa; ***a call*** *lub* ***cry for ~*** wołanie *n* o pomoc; **2.** pomagać ⟨-móc⟩; ***~ o.s.*** obsługiwać ⟨-łużyć⟩ się, poczęstować się; ***I cannot ~ it*** nie mogę nic na to poradzić; ***I could not ~ laughing*** nie mogłem się powstrzymać od śmiechu; **'~·er** pomocnik *m* (-ica *f*); **'~·ful** pomocny; użyteczny; **'~·ing** porcja *f*; **'~·less** bezradny; **'~·less·ness** bezradność *f*; **'~ men·u** *komp.* menu *n* pomocy
hel·ter-skel·ter [heltə'skeltə] **1.** *adv.* na łeb na szyję; **2.** *adj.* pospiesznie; **3.** *Brt.* zjeżdżalnia *f*
helve [helv] stylisko *n* (*topora*)
Hel·ve·tian [hel'vi:ʃjən] szwajcarski
hem [hem] **1.** obręb *m*, obwódka *f*; **2.** (***-mm-***) obrębiać ⟨-bić⟩; ***~ in*** zamykać ⟨-mknąć⟩
hem·i·sphere ['hemɪsfɪə] półkula *f*
'hem·line brzeg *m*
hem·lock ['hemlɒk] *bot.* cykuta *f*
hemp [hemp] *bot.* konopie *pl.*
'hem·stitch mereżka *f*
hen [hen] *zo.* kura *f* (*też samica różnych ptaków*); kwoka *f*
hence [hens] stąd, dlatego; ***a week ~*** za tydzień; **~'forth**, **~'for·ward** od teraz, odtąd
'hen|house kurnik *m*; **'~ pecked husband** mąż *m* pod pantoflem
her [hɜ:, hə] jej, niej; nią; niej
her·ald ['herəld] **1.** *hist.* herold *m*; **2.** zapowiadać ⟨-wiedzieć⟩, zwiastować; **~·ry** ['herəldrɪ] heraldyka *f*
herb [hɜ:b] *bot.* ziele *n*; **~·a·ceous** *bot.* [hɜ:'beɪʃəs] ziołowy, zielny; **~·al** ['hɜ:bəl] ziołowy; roślinny
her·bi·vore ['hɜ:bɪvɔ:] *zo.* roślinożerca
herd [hɜ:d] **1.** stado *n* (*też fig.*); **2.** *v/t.* *bydło* spędzać ⟨-dzić⟩; *v/i.* *też* ***~ together*** skupiać ⟨-pić⟩ się; **~s·man** ['hɜ:dzmən] (*pl.* ***-men***) pastuch *m*
here [hɪə] tu, tutaj; ***~ you are*** proszę (*przy dawaniu czegoś*); ***~'s to you!*** za pana (panią)!
here|·a·bout(s) ['hɪərəbaʊt(s)] gdzieś tu(taj), w pobliżu; **~·af·ter** [hɪər'ɑ:ftə] **1.** odtąd; **2.** zaświaty *pl.*; **~'by** niniejszym; przez to
he·red·i|·ta·ry [hɪ'redɪtərɪ] dziedziczny; **~·ty** [hɪ'redɪtɪ] dziedziczność *f*
here|·in [hɪər'ɪn] tu, tutaj, w niniejszym; **~·of** [hɪər'ɒv] niniejszego, tego
her·e|·sy ['herəsɪ] herezja *f*; **~·tic** ['herətɪk] heretyk *m* (-yczka *f*)
here|·up·on [hɪərə'pɒn] wówczas, wobec tego; **~'with** w załączeniu, z niniejszym
her·i·tage ['herɪtɪdʒ] dziedzictwo *n*
her·mit ['hɜ:mɪt] *rel.* pustelnik (-ica *f*) *m*
he·ro ['hɪərəʊ] (*pl.* ***-roes***) bohater *m*; **~·ic** [hɪ'rəʊɪk] (***-ally***) bohaterski
her·o·in ['herəʊɪn] heroina *f*
her·o|·ine ['herəʊɪn] bohaterka *f*; **~·is·m** ['herəʊɪzəm] bohaterstwo *n*
her·on ['herən] *zo.* (*pl.* ***-ons, -on***) czapla *f*
her·ring ['herɪŋ] *zo.* (*pl.* ***-rings, -ring***) śledź *m*
hers [hɜ:z] jej
her·self [hɜ:'self] się, sobie, siebie; sama; ***by ~*** przez siebie, bez pomocy
hes·i|·tant ['hezɪtənt] niezdecydowany, niepewny; **~·tate** ['hezɪteɪt] wahać się, zastanawiać się; **~·ta·tion** [hezɪ'teɪʃn] wahanie *n*, niepewność *f*, brak *m* zdecydowania; ***without ~tation*** bez zawahania
hew [hju:] (***hewed, hewed*** *lub* ***hewn***) ⟨po⟩rąbać, ⟨po⟩ciosać; ***~ down*** zrąbywać ⟨-bać⟩; **~n** [hju:n] *p.p. od* ***hew***
hey [heɪ] *int.* F hej!, halo!
hey·day ['heɪdeɪ] szczyt *m*, okres *m* rozkwitu
hi [haɪ] *int.* F halo! cześć!
hi·ber·nate ['haɪbəneɪt] *zo.* zapadać ⟨-paść⟩ w sen zimowy
hic|·cup, **~·cough** ['hɪkʌp] **1.** czkawka *f*; **2.** czkać
hid [hɪd] *pret. od* ***hide***[1]; **~·den** ['hɪdn] *p.p. od* ***hide***[1]
hide[1] [haɪd] (***hid, hidden***) ⟨s⟩chować się, ⟨s⟩kryć się; *coś* ukrywać ⟨-ryć⟩
hide[2] [haɪd] skóra *f* (zwierzęca)
hide|-and-seek [haɪdn'si:k] zabawa *f* w chowanego; **'~·a·way** F kryjówka *f*
hid·e·ous ['hɪdɪəs] okropny; ohydny, obrzydliwy
'hide·out kryjówka *f*
hid·ing[1] ['haɪdɪŋ] F lanie *n*, baty *pl.*
hid·ing[2] ['haɪdɪŋ]: ***be in ~*** ukrywać się; ***go into ~*** skryć się; **'~ place** kryjówka *f*
hi-fi ['haɪfaɪ] hi-fi *n*; sprzęt *m* hi-fi

high [haɪ] **1.** wysoki; *nadzieja*: duży; *mięso*: skruszały; F (*pijany*) zalany; F na haju (*narkotycznym*); ***be in ~ spirits*** być w świetnym humorze; **2.** *meteor.* wysokie ciśnienie *n*, wysoki poziom *m*; *Am.* F szkoła *f* średnia; **'~·brow** F **1.** intelektualista *m* (-tka *f*); **2.** intelektualny, przeintelektualizowany; **~-'cal·o·rie** o dużej kaloryczności; **~-'class** pierwszej klasy; **~·er ed·u'ca·tion** wyższe wykształcenie *n*; **~ fi'del·i·ty** hi-fi *n*, audiofilska jakość *f* (*dźwięku*); **~-'grade** wysokiej jakości; **~-'hand·ed** władczy, despotyczny; **~-'heeled** na wysokich obcasach; **'~ jump** (*w sporcie*) skok *m* wzwyż; **'~ jump·er** (*w sporcie*) skoczek *m* wzwyż; **~·land** ['haɪlənd] wyżyna *f*, pogórze *n*; **'~·light 1.** główna atrakcja *f*; punkt *m* kulminacyjny; **2.** podkreślać ⟨-lić⟩, uwypuklać ⟨-lić⟩; **'~·ly** wysoko; *fig.* dodatnio, pochlebnie; ***think ~ly of*** myśleć dobrze o (*L*); **~·ly-'strung** napięty, nerwowy; **'~·ness** *zw. fig.* wysokość *f*; ***Ꝣness*** (*tytuł*) Wysokość *f*; **~-'pitched** *ton*: ostry; *dach*: stromy; **~-'pow·ered** *tech.* o dużej mocy; *fig.* dynamiczny; **~-'pres·sure** *meteor.*, *tech.* wysokie ciśnienie *n*; **'~ rise** wysokościowiec *m*; **'~ road** *zwł. Brt.* droga *f* główna; **'~ school** *Am.* szkoła *f* średnia; **~ 'sea·son** szczyt *m* sezonu; **~ so'ci·e·ty** socjeta *f*, elita *f*; **'~ street** *Brt.* droga *f* główna; **~-'strung** → ***highly-strung***; **~ 'tea** *Brt.* wczesna kolacja *f*; **~ tech** [haɪ 'tek]: *też* ***hi-tech*** → **~ tech'nol·o·gy** najnowocześniejsza technologia *f*; *attr.* najnowocześniejszy; **~-'ten·sion** *electr.* wysokie napięcie *n*; **~ 'tide** przypływ *m*; **~ 'time**: ***it is ~time*** najwyższy czas; **~ 'wa·ter** wysoka woda *f* (*pływu*); **'~·way** *zwł. Am.* droga *f* główna, autostrada *f*; **Ꝣ·way 'Code** *Brt.* kodeks drogowy

hi·jack ['haɪdʒæk] **1.** *samolot*, *kogoś* porywać ⟨-rwać⟩; *transport* napadać ⟨-paść⟩; **2.** porwanie *n*; napad *m*; **'~·er** porywacz(ka *f*) *m*; rabuś *m*

hike [haɪk] **1.** wędrować; **2.** wędrówka *f*; **'hik·er** turysta *m* (-tka *f*); **'hik·ing** wycieczki *pl.*

hi·lar·i|·ous [hɪ'leərɪəs] przekomiczny, prześmieszny; **~·ty** [hɪ'lærətɪ] ogromna wesołość *f*

hill [hɪl] wzgórze *n*; **~·bil·ly** *Am.* ['hɪlbɪlɪ] nieokrzesany wieśniak *m* (*z górskich rejonów USA*); **~ music** (*odmiana muzyki country*); **~·ock** ['hɪlək] pagórek *m*; **'~·side** zbocze *n*, stok *m*; **'~·top** szczyt *m* wzgórza; **'~·y** (***-ier, -iest***) pagórkowaty

hilt [hɪlt] rękojeść *f*

him [hɪm] mu, jemu; go, jego; niego; nim; **~'self** [hɜː'self] się, sobie, siebie; sam; ***by ~self*** samodzielnie, bez pomocy

Hi·ma·la·ya Himalaje *pl.*

hind[1] [haɪnd] *zo.* (*pl.* ***hinds, hind***) łania *f*

hind[2] [haɪnd] tylny, zadni

hin·der ['hɪndə] przeszkadzać ⟨-kodzić⟩ (***from*** w *L*); utrudniać ⟨-nić⟩

hind·most ['haɪndməʊst] ostatni; najdalszy

hin·drance ['hɪndrəns] przeszkoda *f*, utrudnienie *n*

Hin·du [hɪn'duː] **1.** Hindus *m*; **2.** *adj.* hinduski; **~·is·m** ['hɪnduːɪzəm] hinduizm

hinge [hɪndʒ] **1.** zawias *m*; **2. ~ *on*** *fig.* zależeć od (*G*)

hint [hɪnt] **1.** aluzja *f*; sugestia *f*; wskazówka *f*, rada *f*; ***take a ~*** ⟨z⟩rozumieć sugestię; **2.** ⟨za⟩sugerować, ⟨z⟩robić aluzję; dawać ⟨dać⟩ do zrozumienia

hip [hɪp] *anat.* biodro *n*

hip·po ['hɪpəʊ] *zo.* F (*pl.* ***-pos***) hipcio *m*; **~·pot·a·mus** [hɪpə'pɒtəməs] *zo.* (*pl.* ***-muses, -mi*** [-maɪ]) hipopotam *m*

hire ['haɪə] **1.** *Brt. auto itp.* wynajmować ⟨-jąć⟩, *samolot*: ⟨wy⟩czarterować; *kogoś* zatrudniać ⟨-nić⟩, ⟨za⟩angażować, najmować ⟨-jąć⟩; **~ *out*** *Brt.* wynajmować ⟨-jąć⟩; **2.** wynajęcie *n*; najem *m*; ***for ~*** do wynajęcia; *taksówka*: wolny; **~ 'car** wynajęty samochód *m*; **~ 'purchase**: ***on ~purchase*** *Brt. econ.* na raty

his [hɪz] jego

hiss [hɪs] **1.** syczeć ⟨syknąć⟩; *kot*: prychać ⟨-chnąć⟩; wysyczeć; **2.** syk *m*; prychnięcie *n*

his|·to·ri·an [hɪ'stɔːrɪən] historyk *m* (-yczka *f*); **~·tor·ic** [hɪ'stɒrɪk] (***-ally***) historyczny, epokowy; **~·tor·i·cal** historyczny, odnoszący się do historii; ***~torical novel*** powieść historyczna; **~·to·ry** ['hɪstərɪ] historia *f*; ***~tory of civilization*** historia kultury *lub* cywilizacji; ***contemporary ~tory*** historia *f* najnowsza

hit [hɪt] **1.** (**-*tt*-**; ***hit***) uderzać ⟨-rzyć⟩; trafiać ⟨-fić⟩ (*też fig.*); *mot. itp. kogoś* potrącać ⟨-cić⟩, *coś* wjeżdżać ⟨-jechać⟩ w (*A*); **~ *it off with*** zaskarbić sobie sympatię (*G*); **~ *on*** natrafiać ⟨-fić⟩ na (*A*); **2.** uderzenie *n*; *fig.* trafienie *n*; (*piosenka, książka itp.*) hit *m*

hit-and-'run *kierowca*: zbiegły z miejsca wypadku; **~ *offence*** (*Am.* ***offense***) zbiegnięcie z miejsca wypadku

hitch [hɪtʃ] **1.** przytwierdzać ⟨-dzić⟩, przyczepiać ⟨-pić⟩, zaczepiać ⟨-pić⟩ (***to*** do *G*); **~ *up*** podciągać ⟨-gnąć⟩; **~ *a ride*** *lub* ***lift*** ⟨z⟩łapać okazję; F → ***hitchhike***; **2.** pociągnięcie *n*; trudność *f*, problem *m*; ***without a ~*** bez problemów; **'~·hike** ⟨po⟩jechać (auto)stopem; **'~·hik·er** autostopowicz(ka *f*) *m*

hi-tech [haɪ'tek] → ***high tech***

HIV [eɪtʃ aɪ 'viː]: **~ *carrier*** nosiciel(ka *f*) *m* wirusa HIV; **~ *negative*** (***positive***) o ujemnym (dodatnim) wyniku testu na nosicielstwo HIV

hive [haɪv] ul *m*, rój *m*

HM [eɪtʃ 'em] *skrót*: ***His/Her Majesty*** Jego/Jej Królewska Mość

HMS ['eɪtʃ em es] *skrót*: ***His/Her Majesty's Ship*** okręt Jego/Jej Królewskiej Mości

hoard [hɔːd] **1.** skarb *m*; **2.** *też* **~ *up*** ⟨na-, z⟩gromadzić

hoard·ing ['hɔːdɪŋ] ogrodzenie *n* (*na budowie*); *Brt.* billboard *m*

hoar·frost ['hɔːfrɒst] szron *m*

hoarse [hɔːs] (**-*r*, -*st***) ochrypły, zachrypnięty

hoax [həʊks] **1.** fałszywy alarm *m*; *głupi* kawał *m*; **2.** *kogoś* nabierać ⟨-brać⟩

hob·ble ['hɒbl] ⟨po⟩kuśtykać

hob·by ['hɒbɪ] hobby *n*, konik *m*, zainteresowania *pl.*; **'~·horse** konik *m*

hob·gob·lin ['hɒbgɒblɪn] kobold *m*, gnom *m*

ho·bo ['həʊbəʊ] *Am.* F (*pl.* **-*boes*, -*bos***) włóczęga *m*

hock[1] [hɒk] (*białe wino reńskie*) riesling *m*

hock[2] [hɒk] staw *m* skokowy (*konia*)

hock·ey ['hɒkɪ] *zwł. Brt.* hokej *m* (*na trawie*); *zwł. Am.* hokej *m* (*na lodzie*)

hoe [həʊ] *agr.* **1.** motyka *f*, graca *f*; **2.** okopywać ⟨-pać⟩ motyką, ⟨wy⟩gracować

hog [hɒg] świnia *f*

hoist [hɔɪst] **1.** podnosić ⟨-nieść⟩, wciągać ⟨-gnąć⟩; **2.** wyciąg *m*; podnośnik *m*

hold [həʊld] **1.** (***held***) trzymać; podtrzymywać ⟨-mać⟩, podpierać ⟨-deprzeć⟩; *ciężar* dźwigać; powstrzymywać ⟨-mać⟩, wstrzymywać ⟨-mać⟩ (***from*** przed *I*); *wybory*, *spotkanie* odbywać ⟨-być⟩; *pozycję*, *stanowisko* mieć, posiadać; *urząd* piastować; *miejsce* zajmować; (*w sporcie*) *mistrzostwo* utrzymywać ⟨-mać⟩; *rekord świata* utrzymywać, być zdobywcą; zawierać; utrzymywać, być zdania (***that*** że); mieć *kogoś* za (*A*); *uwagę* przykuwać ⟨-kuć⟩; być aktualnym, mieć ważność; obowiązywać; *pogoda*, *szczęście*: utrzymywać ⟨-mać⟩ się; **~ *one's ground*, ~ *one's own*** nie ulegać ⟨-lec⟩, nie poddawać ⟨-dać⟩ się; **~ *the line*** *tel.* nie rozłączać ⟨-czyć⟩ się; **~ *responsible*** czynić odpowiedzialnym; **~ *still*** nie ruszać się; **~ *s.th. against s.o.*** mieć coś przeciwko komuś; **~ *back*** powstrzymywać ⟨-mać⟩ (się), *fig.* nie wyjawiać; **~ *on*** trzymać się (***to*** *G*) mocno; zatrzymywać ⟨-mać⟩; *tel.* pozostawać ⟨-tać⟩ przy aparacie; **~ *out*** wyciągać ⟨-gnąć⟩; wytrzymywać ⟨-mać⟩; *zapasy*: wystarczać ⟨-czyć⟩; **~ *up*** unosić ⟨unieść⟩; wstrzymywać ⟨-mać⟩; *bank*, *kogoś* napadać ⟨-paść⟩ na (*A*); przedstawiać ⟨-wić⟩ (***as*** jako *przykład*); wspierać ⟨wesprzeć⟩, podtrzymywać ⟨-mać⟩; **2.** chwyt *m*; uchwyt *m*; władanie *n*, władza *f*; *naut.* ładownia *f*; ***catch*** (***get*, *take***) **~ *of s.th.*** chwycić (*A*); złapać za (*A*); **'~·er** oprawka *f*, uchwyt *m*; posiadacz *m*, okaziciel *m* (*zwł. econ.*); **'~·ing** udziały *pl.*, własność *f*; **'~ com·pa·ny** holding *m*, przedsiębiorstwo *n* holdingowe; **'~·up** zator *m*, korek *m*; napad *m* rabunkowy

hole [həʊl] **1.** dziura *f* (*też fig.*), otwór *m*; **2.** ⟨po⟩dziurawić, przedziurawiać ⟨-wić⟩

hol·i·day ['hɒlədɪ] święto *n*; dzień *m* wolny; *zwł. Brt. zw.* **~*s*** wakacje *pl.*, urlop *m*; ***be on ~*** być na wakacjach *lub* urlopie; **'~ home** dom *m* wczasowy; **'~·mak·er** urlopowicz(ka *f*) *m*

hol·i·ness ['həʊlɪnɪs] świętość *f*; ***His ~***

(*papież*) Jego Świątobliwość
Hol·land Holandia *f*
hol·ler ['hɒlə] *Am.* F wrzeszczeć ⟨wrzasnąć⟩
hol·low ['hɒləʊ] **1.** pusty, wydrążony; zapadnięty; głuchy; **2.** zagłębienie *n*, dziura *f*; **3.** ~ ***out*** wydrążać ⟨-żyć⟩
hol·ly ['hɒlɪ] *bot.* ostrokrzew *m*
hol·o·caust ['hɒləkɔːst] zagłada *f*, eksterminacja *f*; *hist.* ***the*** ≗ holocaust *m*
hol·ster ['həʊlstə] kabura *f*
ho·ly ['həʊlɪ] (**-*ier*, -*iest***) święty; ~ '**wa·ter** woda *f* święcona; '≗ **Week** Wielki Tydzień *m*
home [həʊm] **1.** dom *m*; mieszkanie *n*; kraj *m* ojczysty, ojczyzna *f*; ***at*** ~ w domu; w kraju; ***make oneself at*** ~ czuć się jak u siebie w domu; ***at*** ~ ***and abroad*** w kraju i za granicą; **2.** domowy; krajowy; ojczysty; (*w sporcie*) miejscowy; **3.** *adv.* w domu; do domu; *fig.* w celu *lub* dziesiątce; ***strike*** ~ trafiać ⟨-fić⟩ w sedno; ~ **ad'dress** adres *m* prywatny; ~ '**com·put·er** komputer *m* domowy; '~·**less** bezdomny; '~·**ly** (**-*ier*, -*iest***) zwykły, prosty; *Am.* nieatrakcyjny; ~'**made** domowego wyrobu; ~ '**mar·ket** rynek *m* wewnętrzny *lub* krajowy; '≗ **Of·fice** *Brt. pol.* Ministerstwo *n* Spraw Wewnętrznych; ≗ '**Sec·ret·a·ry** Minister *n* Spraw Wewnętrznych; '~·**sick**: ***be*** ~***sick*** cierpieć na nostalgię; '~·**sick·ness** nostalgia *f*; ~ '**team** (*w sporcie*) drużyna *f* miejscowa; ~·**ward** ['həʊmwəd] **1.** *adj.* powrotny (*w stronę domu*); **2.** *adv. Am.* w stronę domu; do domu; '~·**wards** w stronę domu; do domu; '~·**work** zadanie *n* domowe; ***do one's*** ~***work*** ⟨z⟩robić zadanie domowe (*też fig.*)
hom·i·cide ['hɒmɪsaɪd] *jur.* zabójstwo *n*; zabójca *m* (-czyni *f*); '~ **squad** wydział *m* zabójstw
ho·mo·ge·ne·ous [hɒmə'dʒiːnjəs] homogeniczny, jednolity
ho·mo·sex·u·al [hɒməʊ'sekʃʊəl] **1.** homoseksualny; **2.** homoseksualista *m* (-tka *f*)
hone [həʊn] *tech.* ⟨na-, wy⟩ostrzyć
hon|·est ['ɒnɪst] uczciwy; szczery; '~·**es·ty** uczciwość *f*; szczerość *f*
hon·ey ['hʌnɪ] miód *m*; *Am.* kochanie *n*, skarb *m*; ~·**comb** ['hʌnɪkəʊm] plaster *m* miodu; ~**ed** ['hʌnɪd] słodki (*jak miód*); '~·**moon** **1.** miesiąc *m* miodowy; podróż *f* poślubna; **2.** ***be*** ~***mooning*** być w podróży poślubnej
honk [hɒŋk] *mot.* ⟨za⟩trąbić
hon·ky-tonk ['hɒŋkɪtɒŋk] *Am.* speluna *f*
hon·or·ar·y ['ɒnərərɪ] honorowy
hon·o(u)r ['ɒnə] **1.** honor *m*; zaszczyt *m*; ~***s*** *pl.* wyróżnienie *n*; ***Your*** ≗ Wysoki Sądzie; **2.** zaszczycać ⟨-cić⟩; *econ. czek itp.* honorować, uznawać ⟨-nać⟩; ~·**a·ble** ['ɒnərəbl] honorowy; szanowany; szanowny
hood [hʊd] kaptur *m*; *mot.* dach *m* opuszczany; *mot. Am.* maska *f*; *tech.* pokrywa *f*, osłona *f*
hood·lum ['huːdləm] *sl.* chuligan *m*, zbir *m*
hood·wink ['hʊdwɪŋk] *kogoś* nabierać ⟨-brać⟩
hoof [huːf] (*pl.* ***hoofs*** [huːfs], ***hooves*** [huːvz]) kopyto *m*
hook [hʊk] **1.** hak *m*; haczyk *m*; ***by*** ~ ***or by crook*** F nie przebierając w środkach; **2.** przyczepiać ⟨-pić⟩ na haczyk, zahaczać ⟨-czyć⟩; ⟨z⟩łapać na haczyk (*też fig.*); ~**ed** [hʊkt] haczykowaty; zakrzywiony; F uzależniony (***on*** od *G*) (*też fig.*); '~·**y**: ***play*** ~***y*** *zwł. Am.* F wagarować
hoo·li·gan ['huːlɪgən] chuligan *m*; ~·**is·m** ['huːlɪgənɪzəm] chuligaństwo *n*
hoop [huːp] obręcz *f*, opaska *f*
hoot [huːt] **1.** pohukiwanie *n* (*sowy*); *mot.* klakson *m*, sygnał *m* dźwiękowy; *drwiący* okrzyk *m*; **2.** *v/i.* ⟨za⟩wyć; *mot.* ⟨za⟩trąbić; *sowa*: ⟨za⟩huczeć; *v/t.* ⟨za⟩trąbić (*I*)
Hoo·ver ['huːvə] *Brt. TM* **1.** odkurzacz *m*; **2.** *zw.* ≗ odkurzać ⟨-rzyć⟩
hooves [huːvz] *pl. od* ***hoof***
hop[1] [hɒp] **1.** (**-*pp*-**) skakać ⟨skoczyć⟩, podskakiwać ⟨-skoczyć⟩; przeskakiwać przez (*A*); ***be*** ~***ping mad*** F być w furii; **2.** podskok *m*
hop[2] [hɒp] *bot.* chmiel *m*; ~***s*** chmiel *m* (*szyszki*)
hope [həʊp] **1.** nadzieja *f*; **2.** mieć nadzieję; spodziewać się, wyczekiwać; ~ ***for the best*** być dobrej myśli; ***I*** ~ ***so, let's*** ~ ***so*** *odpowiadając* mam nadzieję; ***I*** (***sincerely***) ~ ***so*** mam nadzieję; '~·**ful**: ***be*** ~***ful that*** mieć nadzieję, że; '~·**ful·ly** z nadzieją, wyczekująco; ma-

H

m(y) nadzieję (że); '~·**less** beznadziejny; rozpaczliwy
hop·scotch ['hɒpskɒtʃ] gra *f* w klasy
ho·ri·zon [hə'raɪzn] horyzont *m*
hor·i·zon·tal [hɒrɪ'zɒntl] horyzontalny, poziomy
hor·mone ['hɔːməʊn] *biol.* hormon *m*
horn [hɔːn] róg *m*; *mot.* klakson *m*; **~s** *pl.* poroże *n*
hor·net ['hɔːnɪt] *zo.* szerszeń *m*
horn·y ['hɔːnɪ] (**-ier, -iest**) rogaty; V *mężczyzna*: podniecony, rozochocony
hor·o·scope ['hɒrəskəʊp] horoskop *m*
hor|·ri·ble ['hɒrəbl] straszny, przerażający, okropny; **~·rid** ['hɒrɪd] *zwł. Brt.* straszny, okropny; **~·rif·ic** [hɒ'rɪfɪk] (**-ally**) okropny, przerażający; **~·ri·fy** ['hɒrɪfaɪ] przerażać ⟨-razić⟩; **~·ror** ['hɒrə] przerażanie *n*; potworność *f*; F postrach *m*; '**~·ror film** horror *m*
horse [hɔːs] *zo.* koń *m*; (*w sporcie*) kozioł *m*, koń *m*; ***wild ~s couldn't drag me there*** szóstką wołów by mnie tam nie zaciągnęli; '**~·back**: ***on ~back*** wierzchem, konno; **~ 'chest·nut** *bot.* kasztanowiec *m*; '**~·hair** końskie włosie *n*; '**~·man** (*pl.* **-men**) jeździec *m*; '**~·pow·er** *phys.* koń *m* mechaniczny; (*jednostka anglosaska*) koń parowy (*1,0139 KM*); '**~ race** gonitwa *f* konna; '**~ rac·ing** wyścigi *pl.* konne; '**~·rad·ish** *bot.* chrzan *m*; '**~·shoe** podkowa *f*; '**~·wom·an** (*pl.* **-women**) *f*, amazonka *f*
hor·ti·cul·ture ['hɔːtɪkʌltʃə] ogrodnictwo *n*
hose[1] [həʊz] wąż *m*; szlauch *m*
hose[2] [həʊz] rajstopy *pl.*
ho·sier·y ['həʊzjərɪ] wyroby *pl.* pończosznicze
hos·pice ['hɒspɪs] hospicjum *n*
hos·pi·ta·ble ['hɒspɪtəbl] gościnny
hos·pi·tal ['hɒspɪtl] szpital *m*; ***in*** (*Am.* ***in the***) **~** w szpitalu
hos·pi·tal·i·ty [hɒspɪ'tælətɪ] gościnność *f*
hos·pi·tal·ize ['hɒspɪtəlaɪz] hospitalizować, umieszczać ⟨umieścić⟩ w szpitalu
host[1] [həʊst] **1.** gospodarz *m*; *biol.* żywiciel *m*; *radio, TV*: gospodarz *m* programu. prowadzący *m* program; ***your ~ was...*** audycję prowadził...; **2.** *radio, TV*: F *audycję* ⟨po⟩prowadzić
host[2] [həʊst] zastęp *m*, rzesza *f*
host[3] [həʊst] *rel. często* ♀ hostia *f*
hos·tage ['hɒstɪdʒ] zakładnik *m* (-niczka *f*); ***take s.o. ~*** brać ⟨wziąć⟩ kogoś jako zakładnika
hos·tel ['hɒstl] *zwł. Brt.* dom *m* (*studencki*); *zw.* ***youth ~*** schronisko *n* młodzieżowe
host·ess ['həʊstɪs] gospodyni *f*; *aviat.* stewardessa *f*; hostessa *f*
hos|·tile ['hɒstaɪl] wrogi; nieprzyjazny (***to*** wobec *G*); **~·til·i·ty** [hɒ'stɪlətɪ] wrogość *f* (***to*** wobec *G*)
hot [hɒt] (**-tt-**) gorący; *przyprawa*: ostry; *temperament*: zapalczywy; *wiadomości*: najnowszy; ***she is ~*** gorąco jej; ***it's ~*** gorąco (jest); '**~·bed** rozsadnik *m* (*też fig.*), *fig.* siedlisko *n*
hotch·potch ['hɒtʃpɒtʃ] miszmasz *m*
hot 'dog hot dog *m* (*bułka z parówką na gorąco*)
ho·tel [həʊ'tel] hotel *m*
'hot|·head zapalczywy człowiek *m*; '**~·house** inspekt *m*; '**~ line** *pol.* gorąca linia *f*; '**~ spot** *zwł. pol.* punkt *m* zapalny; **~-'wa·ter bot·tle** termofor *m*
hound [haʊnd] *zo.* pies *m* myśliwski
hour ['aʊə] godzina *f*; **~s** *pl.* godziny *pl.* (pracy); '**~·ly** **1.** *adj.* cogodzinny; godzinny; **2.** *adv.* co godzinę, na godzinę
house **1.** [haʊs] dom *m*; budynek *m*; *theat.* widownia *f*, publika *f*; **2.** [haʊz] ⟨z⟩mieścić, pomieścić; dawać ⟨dać⟩ mieszkanie; '**~·bound** *fig.* nie mogący wyjść z domu; '**~·break·ing** włamanie *n*; '**~·hold** gospodarstwo *n* domowe; dom *m*; rodzina *f*; '**~ hus·band** domator *m*; mężczyzna *m* prowadzący dom; '**~·keep·er** gosposia *f*; '**~·keep·ing** gospodarstwo *n*, gospodarowanie *n*; '**~·maid** pokojówka *f*; służąca *f*; '**~·man** (*pl.* **-men**) lekarz *m* stażysta; '**~·warm·ing** (**par·ty**) parapetówa *f*, oblewanie *n* nowego domu; '**~·wife** (*pl.* **-wives**) gospodyni *f* domowa; **~·work** prace *pl.* domowe
hous·ing ['haʊzɪŋ] budownictwo *n* mieszkaniowe; gospodarka *f* mieszkaniowa; *attr.* mieszkaniowy; '**~ de·vel·op·ment**, *Am.*; '**~ es·tate** *Brt.* dzielnica *f* mieszkaniowa
hove [həʊv] *pret. i p.p. od* **heave** 2
hov·er ['hɒvə] unosić się (*w powietrzu*); zawisnąć (*w powietrzu*); kręcić się; *fig.*

być zawieszonym; '~**·craft** (*pl.* ***-craft, -crafts***) poduszkowiec *m*
how [haʊ] jak; ~ ***are you?*** jak się masz?; ~ ***about...?*** a co z ...?; ~ ***do you do?*** *przy przedstawianiu* dzień dobry!; ~ ***much water?*** ile wody?; ~ ***many spoons?*** ile łyżeczek?
how·dy ['haʊdɪ] *Am. int.* F cześć!, siemanko!
how·ev·er [haʊ'evə] **1.** *adv.* jakkolwiek; **2.** jednak(że)
howl [haʊl] **1.** ⟨za⟩wyć; *wiatr, dziecko*: zawodzić; **2.** wycie *n*; zawodzenie *n*; '~**·er** F błąd *m*, byk *m*
HP [eɪtʃ 'piː] *skrót*: ***horsepower*** KM, koń *m* mechaniczny; *skrót*: ***hire purchase*** *Brt.* kupno *n* na raty
HQ [eɪtʃ 'kjuː] *skrót*: ***headquarters*** kwatera *f* główna
hr (*pl.* ***hrs***) *skrót pisany*: ***hour*** godz., godzina *f*
HRH [eɪtʃ ɑː(r) 'eɪtʃ] *skrót*: ***His/Her Royal Highness*** Jego/Jej Królewska Wysokość
hub [hʌb] piasta *f*; *fig.* ośrodek *m*, centrum *n*
hub·bub ['hʌbʌb] tumult *m*, rwetes *m*
hub·by ['hʌbɪ] F mężuś *m*
huck·le·ber·ry ['hʌklberɪ] *bot.* jagoda *f* amerykańska
huck·ster ['hʌkstə] domokrążca *m*, kramarz *m*
hud·dle ['hʌdl]: ~ ***together*** tulić (się); ~***d up*** pozwijany
hue[1] [hjuː] barwa *f*, kolor *m*; odcień *m*
hue[2] [hjuː]: ~ ***and cry*** *fig.* wrzawa *f* protestów
huff [hʌf]: ***in a*** ~ rozsierdzony
hug [hʌg] **1.** (***-gg-***) obejmować ⟨-bjąć⟩ (się); przytulać ⟨-lić⟩ się; **2.** objęcie *n*, uścisk *m*
huge [hjuːdʒ] wielki, ogromny
hulk [hʌlk] zawalidroga *m/f*; moloch *m*; kolos *m*
hull [hʌl] **1.** *bot.* łuska *f*, łupina *f*, szypułka *f*; *naut.* kadłub *m*; **2.** ⟨ob⟩łuskać, *truskawki* obierać ⟨-brać⟩
hul·la·ba·loo ['hʌləbə'luː] (*pl.* ***-loos***) wrzawa *f*, zgiełk *m*
hul·lo [hə'ləʊ] *int.* halo!, hej!
hum [hʌm] (***-mm-***) ⟨za⟩mruczeć, ⟨za⟩nucić
hu·man ['hjuːmən] **1.** ludzki; **2.** *też* ~ ***being*** człowiek *m*; ~**e** [hjuː'meɪn] ludzki, humanitarny; ~**·i·tar·i·an** [hjuːmænɪ'teərɪən] humanitarny; ~**·i·ty** [hjuː'mænətɪ] ludzkość *f*; humanitaryzm *m*; ***humanities*** *pl.* nauki *pl.* humanistyczne; '~**·ly**: ~***ly possible*** w ludzkiej mocy; ~ '**rights** *pl.* prawa *pl.* człowieka
hum·ble ['hʌmbl] **1.** (***-r, -st***) pokorny; skromny; uniżony; **2.** poniżać ⟨-żyć⟩; '~**·ness** uniżoność *f*; pokora *f*; skromność *f*
hum·drum ['hʌmdrʌm] monotonny, jednostajny
hu·mid ['hjuːmɪd] wilgotny; ~**·i·ty** [hjuː'mɪdətɪ] wilgotność *f*
hu·mil·i|·ate [hjuː'mɪlɪeɪt] poniżać ⟨-żyć⟩, upokarzać ⟨-korzyć⟩; ~**·a·tion** [hjuːmɪlɪ'eɪʃn] poniżenie *n*, upokorzenie *n*; ~**·ty** [hjuː'mɪlətɪ] pokora *f*
hum·ming·bird ['hʌmɪŋbɜːd] *zo.* koliber *m*
hu·mor·ous ['hjuːmərəs] humorystyczny, zabawny
hu·mo(u)r ['hjuːmə] **1.** humor *m*; komizm *m*; **2.** udobruchać; spełniać ⟨-nić⟩ (zachcianki)
hump [hʌmp] wybrzuszenie *n*; garb *m*; '~**·back(ed)** → ***hunchbacked***
hunch [hʌntʃ] **1.** → ***hump***; kawał *m*; przeczucie *n*; **2.** *też* ~ ***up*** krzywić się; ~ ***one's shoulders*** ⟨z⟩garbić się; '~**·back** garbus *m*; '~**·backed** garbaty
hun·dred ['hʌndrəd] **1.** sto; **2.** setka *f*; ~**th** ['hʌndrədθ] **1.** setny; **2.** jedna *f* setna; '~**·weight** *jakby*: cetnar (*=50,8 kg*)
hung [hʌŋ] *pret. i p.p. od* ***hang***[1]
Hun·ga·ri·an [hʌŋ'geərɪən] **1.** węgierski; **2.** Węgier(ka *f*) *m*; *ling.* język *m* węgierski; **Hun·ga·ry** ['hʌŋgərɪ] Węgry *pl.*
hun·ger ['hʌŋgə] **1.** głód, łaknienie *n*; **2.** *fig.* łaknąć; '~ **strike** strajk *m* głodowy
hun·gry ['hʌŋgrɪ] (***-ier, -iest***) głodny
hunk [hʌŋk] kawał *m*
hunt [hʌnt] **1.** polować na (*A*); poszukiwać ⟨-kać⟩, ⟨wy⟩tropić; ~ ***out***, ~ ***up*** wytropić (*A*); **2.** polowanie *n* (*też fig.*); tropienie *n*, poszukiwanie *n*; '~**·er** myśliwy *m*; '~**·ing** myślistwo *n*; '~**·ing ground** teren *m* łowiecki
hur·dle ['hɜːdl] *sport*: płotek *m* (*też fig.*); przeszkoda *f* (*też fig.*); '~**r** (*w sporcie*) płotkarz *m* (-rka *f*); '~ **race** (*w sporcie*) bieg *m* przez płotki

hurl [hɜːl] miotać ⟨-tnąć⟩; ~ ***abuse at s.o.*** obrzucać ⟨-cić⟩ kogoś wyzwiskami
hur|·rah [hʊ'rɑː] *int.*, ~**·ray** *int.* [hʊ'reɪ] hurra!
hur·ri·cane ['hʌrɪkən] huragan *m*, orkan *m*
hur·ried ['hʌrɪd] pospieszny
hur·ry ['hʌrɪ] **1.** *v/t.* przyspieszać ⟨-szyć⟩; *często* ~ ***up*** *kogoś* poganiać ⟨-gonić⟩, popędzać ⟨-dzić⟩; zwiększyć ⟨-szać⟩ tempo; *v/i.* ⟨po⟩śpieszyć się; ~ (***up***) śpieszyć się; ~ ***up!*** pośpiesz się!; **2.** pośpiech *m*; ***be in a*** ~ śpieszyć się
hurt [hɜːt] (***hurt***) ⟨z⟩ranić (*też fig.*); boleć; ⟨s⟩krzywdzić; '~**·ful** bolesny
hus·band ['hʌzbənd] mąż *m*
hush [hʌʃ] **1.** *int.* cicho!; **2.** cisza *f*; **3.** uciszać ⟨-szyć⟩; ~ **up** ⟨za⟩tuszować; '~ **mon·ey** pieniądze *pl.* (*na zatuszowanie czegoś*)
husk [hʌsk] *bot.* **1.** łuska *f*, plewa *f*, łupina *f*; **2.** ⟨ob⟩łuskać
'hus·ky (***-ier, -iest***) ochrypły; F silny, mocarny
hus·sy ['hʌsɪ] dziwka *f*
hus·tle ['hʌsl] **1.** *kogoś* poganiać ⟨-gonić⟩, popędzać ⟨-dzić⟩; wypychać ⟨-pchnąć⟩; nakłaniać ⟨-łonić⟩; spieszyć się; **2.** ~ ***and bustle*** wrzawa *f*, zamęt *m*, ruch *m*
hut [hʌt] chata *f*
hutch [hʌtʃ] klatka *f* (*zwł. dla królików*)
hy·a·cinth ['haɪəsɪnθ] *bot.* hiacynt *m*
hy·ae·na [haɪ'iːnə] *zo.* hiena *f*
hy·brid ['haɪbrɪd] *biol.* hybryda *f*, mieszaniec *m*
hy·drant ['haɪdrənt] hydrant *m*
hy·draul·ic [haɪ'drɔːlɪk] (~***ally***) hydrauliczny; ~**s** *sg.* hydraulika *f*
hy·dro... ['haɪdrə] hydro..., wodno...; ~**'car·bon** węglowodór *m*; ~**·chlor·ic ac·id** [haɪdrəklɒrɪk 'æsɪd] kwas *m* solny; '~**·foil** *naut.* wodolot *m*; ~**·gen** ['haɪdrədʒən] wodór *m*; '~**·gen bomb** bomba *f* wodorowa; '~**·plane** *aviat.* hydroplan *m*; *naut.* ślizgacz *m*; '~**·planing** *Am. mot.* akwaplaning *n*
hy·e·na [haɪ'iːnə] *zo.* hiena *f*
hy·giene ['haɪdʒiːn] higiena *f*; **hygien·ic** [haɪ'dʒiːnɪk] (~***ally***) higieniczny
hymn [hɪm] *kościelny* hymn *m*
hype [haɪp] F **1.** *też* ~ ***up*** nakręcać ⟨-cić⟩ reklamę; **2.** *nadmierna* reklama *f*; ***media*** ~ wrzawa *f* (*w gazetach*)
hy·per... ['haɪpə] hiper..., ponad..., nad...; '~**·mar·ket** *Brt.* (*duży supersam*) hipermarket *m*; ~**'sen·si·tive** nadpobudliwy (***to*** na *A*)
hy·phen ['haɪfn] łącznik *m*, tiret *n*; ~**·ate** ['haɪfəneɪt] wstawiać ⟨-wić⟩ łączniki
hyp·no·tize ['hɪpnətaɪz] ⟨za⟩hipnotyzować
hy·po·chon·dri·ac [haɪpə'kɒndrɪæk] hipochondryk *m*
hy·poc·ri·sy [hɪ'pɒkrəsɪ] hipokryzja *f*, obłuda *f*; **hyp·o·crite** ['hɪpəkrɪt] hipokryta *m* (-tka *f*), obłudnik *m* (-ica *f*); **hyp·o·crit·i·cal** [hɪpə'krɪtɪkl] obłudny
hy·poth·e·sis [haɪ'pɒθɪsɪs] (*pl.* ***-ses*** [-siːz]) hipoteza *f*
hys|·te·ri·a [hɪ'stɪərɪə] *med.* histeria *f*; ~**·ter·i·cal** [hɪ'sterɪkl] histeryczny, rozhisteryzowany; ~**·ter·ics** [hɪ'sterɪks] *pl.* histeria *f*; ***go into*** ~***terics*** dostawać ⟨-tać⟩ histerii; pękać ze śmiechu

I

I, i [aɪ] I, i *n*
I [aɪ] ja
IC [aɪ 'siː] *skrót*: ***integrated circuit*** obwód *m* zintegrowany
ice [aɪs] **1.** lód *m*; **2.** *napoje itp.* ⟨s⟩chłodzić w lodzie; *gastr.* ⟨po⟩lukrować; ~***d over*** *jezioro itp.*: zamarznięty; ~***d up*** *ulica itp.*: oblodzony; '~ **age** epoka *f* lodowcowa; ~**·berg** ['aɪsbɜːg] góra *f* lodowa; '~**·bound** przymarznięty; ~ **'cream** lody *pl.*; ~**-cream 'par·lo(u)r** lodziarnia *f*; '~ **cube** kostka *f* lodu; '~ **floe** kra *f*; ~**d** mrożony; schłodzony; '~ **hock·ey** (*w sporcie*) hokej *m* na lodzie; '~ **lol·ly** *Brt.* lody *pl.* na patyku; '~ **rink** *sztuczne* lodowisko *n*; '~ **skate** łyżwa *f*; '~**-skate** jeździć ⟨jechać⟩ na łyżwach; '~ **show** rewia *f* na lodzie

i·ci·cle ['aɪsɪkl] sopel *m* (*lodu*)
ic·ing ['aɪsɪŋ] lukier *m*
i·con ['aɪkɒn] ikona *f* (*też komp.*)
i·cy ['aɪsɪ] (**-ier, -iest**) lodowaty; oblodzony
ID [aɪ 'diː] *skrót*: ***identity*** tożsamość *f*; ***ID card*** dowód *m* tożsamości
i·dea [aɪ'dɪə] pomysł *m*; pojęcie *n*; idea *f*, pogląd *m*; zamiar *m*; ***have no ~*** nie mieć pojęcia
i·deal [aɪ'dɪəl] **1.** idealny; **2.** ideał *m*; **~·is·m** [aɪ'dɪəlɪzəm] idealizm *m*; **~·ize** [aɪ'dɪəlaɪz] ⟨wy⟩idealizować
i·den·ti·cal [aɪ'dentɪkl] identyczny (***to, with*** z *I*); **~ 'twins** *pl.* bliźnięta *pl.* jednojajowe
i·den·ti·fi·ca·tion [aɪdentɪfɪ'keɪʃn] identyfikacja *f*; **~ (pa·pers** *pl.*) dowód *m* tożsamości
i·den·ti·fy [aɪ'dentɪfaɪ] ⟨z⟩identyfikować; **~ *o.s.*** zidentyfikować się
i·den·ti·kit pic·ture [aɪ'dentɪkɪt -] portret *m* pamięciowy (*przestępcy*)
i·den·ti·ty [aɪ'dentətɪ] tożsamość *f*; **~ card** dowód *m* tożsamości
i·de|·o·log·i·cal [aɪdɪə'lɒdʒɪkl] ideologiczny; **~·ol·ogy** [aɪdɪ'ɒlədʒɪ] ideologia *f*
id·i|·om ['ɪdɪəm] idiom *m*, idiomatyzm *m*; **~·o·mat·ic** [ɪdɪə'mætɪk] idiomatyczny
id·i·ot ['ɪdɪət] idiota *m* (-tka *f*) (*też med.*); **~·ic** [ɪdɪ'ɒtɪk] idiotyczny
i·dle ['aɪdl] **1.** (**-r, -st**) bezczynny; bezproduktywny; próżniaczy; czczy, bezzasadny; *econ. pieniądze*: nieproduktywny, *wydajność*: niewykorzystany; *tech.* jałowy, nieobciążony; **2.** spędzać ⟨-dzić⟩ nieproduktywnie czas; chodzić ⟨iść⟩ na jałowym biegu; ***~ away*** *czas* ⟨z⟩marnować
i·dol ['aɪdl] idol *m*; bożek *m*; **~·ize** ['aɪdəlaɪz] ubóstwiać ⟨-wić⟩
i·dyl·lic [aɪ'dɪlɪk] (***~ally***) idylliczny
i.e. [aɪ 'iː] *skrót*: ***that is to say*** (*łacińskie **id est***) tj., to jest
if [ɪf] jeżeli, jeśli; gdyby; czy; ***~ I were you*** gdybym był na twoim miejscu
ig·loo ['ɪgluː] (*pl.* **-loos**) iglo *n*
ig·nite [ɪg'naɪt] zapalać ⟨-lić⟩ (się); *mot.* zapalać ⟨-lić⟩; **ig·ni·tion** [ɪg'nɪʃən] *tech.* zapłon; **~ key** kluczyk *m* zapłonu
ig·no·min·i·ous [ɪgnə'mɪnɪəs] haniebny, nikczemny
ig·no·rance ['ɪgnərəns] niewiedza *f*, ignorancja *f*; **'ig·no·rant**: ***be ~ of s.th.*** nie wiedzieć o czymś, nie mieć pojęcia o czymś; **ig·nore** [ɪg'nɔː] ⟨z⟩ignorować; pomijać ⟨-minąć⟩
ill [ɪl] **1.** (***worse, worst***) chory; zły, niedobry; ***fall ~, be taken ~*** zachorować; **2. *~s*** *pl.* problemy *pl.*; zło *n*; **~-ad'vised** nierozważny; **~-'bred** niewychowany
il·le·gal [ɪ'liːgl] nielegalny, bezprawny; ***~ parking*** niewłaściwe parkowanie *n*
il·le·gi·ble [ɪ'ledʒəbl] nieczytelny
il·le·git·i·mate [ɪlɪ'dʒɪtɪmət] nieślubny; bezprawny
ill|-'fat·ed fatalny; nieszczęśliwy; **~-'hu·mo(u)red** w złym humorze
il·li·cit [ɪ'lɪsɪt] zakazany, nielegalny
il·lit·e·rate [ɪ'lɪtərət] niepiśmienny
ill|-'man·nered niewychowany; **~-'na·tured** złośliwy
'ill·ness choroba *f*
ill|-'tem·pered w złym humorze; **~-'timed** w złą porę; **~-'treat** źle traktować; maltretować
il·lu·mi|·nate [ɪ'ljuːmɪneɪt] oświetlać ⟨-lić⟩, iluminować; oświecać ⟨-cić⟩; **~·nat·ing** pouczający; **~·na·tion** [ɪljuːmɪ'neɪʃn] oświetlenie *n*; ***~nations*** *pl.* iluminacja *f*
il·lu|·sion [ɪ'luːʒn] iluzja *f*, złudzenie *n*; **~·sive** [ɪ'luːsɪv], **~·so·ry** [ɪ'luːsərɪ] złudny, iluzoryczny
il·lus|·trate ['ɪləstreɪt] ⟨z⟩ilustrować; ⟨z⟩obrazować; **~·tra·tion** [ɪlə'streɪʃn] ilustracja *f*; obrazowanie *n*; **~·tra·tive** ['ɪləstrətɪv] ilustracyjny; obrazujący
il·lus·tri·ous [ɪ'lʌstrɪəs] znamienity
ill 'will wrogość *f*, nieprzyjazne uczucie *n*
im·age ['ɪmɪdʒ] wizerunek *m*, obraz *m*; odbicie *n*; metafora *f*, porównanie *n*; **im·ag·e·ry** ['ɪmɪdʒərɪ] symbolika *f*
i·ma·gi·na|·ble [ɪ'mædʒɪnəbl] wyobrażalny; **~·ry** [ɪ'mædʒɪnərɪ] urojony, zmyślony; **~·tion** [ɪmædʒɪ'neɪʃn] wyobraźnia *f*; **~·tive** [ɪ'mædʒɪnətɪv] o dużej wyobraźni, pełen fantazji, pomysłowy; **i·ma·gine** [ɪ'mædʒɪn] wyobrażać ⟨-razić⟩ sobie; sądzić
im·bal·ance [ɪm'bæləns] brak *m* równowagi

im·be·cile ['ɪmbɪsiːl] imbecyl *m*, kretyn(ka *f*) *m*
IMF [aɪ em 'ef] *skrót*: ***International Monetary Fund*** MFW, Międzynarodowy Fundusz *m* Walutowy
im·i|·tate ['ɪmɪteɪt] naśladować, imitować; **~·ta·tion** [ɪmɪ'teɪʃn] **1.** imitacja *f*, naśladownictwo *n*; naśladowanie *n*; **2.** sztuczny; ***~tation leather*** imitacja *f* skóry
im·mac·u·late [ɪ'mækjʊlət] *rel.* niepokalany; nieskazitelny
im·ma·te·ri·al [ɪmə'tɪərɪəl] nieistotny, bez znaczenia (***to*** dla *G*)
im·ma·ture [ɪmə'tjʊə] niedojrzały
im·mea·su·ra·ble [ɪ'meʒərəbl] niezmierzony, nieprzejrzany
im·me·di·ate [ɪ'miːdjət] bezpośredni; natychmiastowy, bezzwłoczny; *przyszłość, rodzina*: najbliższy; **~·ly** bezpośrednio; natychmiastowo, bezzwłocznie
im·mense [ɪ'mens] ogromny
im·merse [ɪ'mɜːs] zanurzać ⟨-rzyć⟩; **~ *o.s.*** in zagłębiać ⟨-bić⟩ się w (*L*); **im·mer·sion** [ɪ'mɜːʃn] zanurzenie *n*; **im'mer·sion heat·er** grzałka *f* (*nurkowa*)
im·mi|·grant ['ɪmɪgrənt] imigrant(ka *f*) *m*; **~·grate** ['ɪmɪgreɪt] imigrować (***into*** do *G*); **~·gra·tion** [ɪmɪ'greɪʃn] imigracja *f*
im·mi·nent ['ɪmɪnənt] zagrażający, nadchodzący; **~ *danger*** bezpośrednie zagrożenie
im·mo·bile [ɪ'məʊbaɪl] nieruchomy
im·mod·e·rate [ɪ'mɒdərət] nieumiarkowany
im·mod·est [ɪ'mɒdɪst] nieskromny
im·mor·al [ɪ'mɒrəl] niemoralny
im·mor·tal [ɪ'mɔːtl] **1.** nieśmiertelny; **2.** człowiek *m* nieśmiertelny; **~·i·ty** [ɪmɔː'tælətɪ] nieśmiertelność
im·mo·va·ble [ɪ'muːvəbl] nieruchomy, *fig.* niewzruszony
im·mune [ɪ'mjuːn] odporny (***to*** na *A*); nie podlegający; **im·mu·ni·ty** [ɪ'mjuːnətɪ] odporność *f*; niepodleganie *n*; immunitet *m*; **im·mu·nize** ['ɪmjuːnaɪz] immunizować, ⟨u⟩czynić odpornym (***against*** na *A*)
imp [ɪmp] chochlik *m*, diabełek *m*
im·pact ['ɪmpækt] zderzenie *n*, uderzenie *n*; *fig.* wpływ *m* (***on*** na *A*)
im·pair [ɪm'peə] osłabiać ⟨-bić⟩, pogarszać ⟨-gorszyć⟩
im·part [ɪm'pɑːt] (***to***) przekazywać ⟨-zać⟩ (*D*); nadawać (*D*)
im·par|·tial [ɪm'pɑːʃl] obiektywny, bezstronny; **~·ti·al·i·ty** [ɪmpɑːʃɪ'ælətɪ] obiektywność *f*, bezstronność *f*
im·pass·a·ble [ɪm'pɑːsəbl] nieprzejezdny, nie do przejścia
im·passe [æm'pɑːs] *fig.* impas *m*, ślepa uliczka *f*
im·pas·sioned [ɪm'pæʃnd] namiętny, żarliwy
im·pas·sive [ɪm'pæsɪv] beznamiętny, obojętny, bierny
im·pa|·tience [ɪm'peɪʃns] niecierpliwość *f*; **~·tient** niecierpliwy
im·peach [ɪm'piːtʃ] *jur.* pociągać ⟨-gnąć⟩ do odpowiedzialności (***for, of, with*** za *A*), oskarżać ⟨-rżyć⟩ (***for, of, with*** o *A*); ⟨za⟩kwestionować
im·pec·ca·ble [ɪm'pekəbl] nienaganny, bez zarzutu
im·pede [ɪm'piːd] przeszkadzać ⟨-kodzić⟩, utrudniać ⟨-nić⟩
im·ped·i·ment [ɪm'pedɪmənt] przeszkoda *f*; trudność *f* (***to*** przy *L*)
im·pel [ɪm'pel] (***-ll-***) nakłaniać ⟨-łonić⟩
im·pend·ing [ɪm'pendɪŋ] zagrażający, bliski
im·pen·e·tra·ble [ɪm'penɪtrəbl] niedostępny, nieprzenikniony (*też fig.*)
im·per·a·tive [ɪm'perətɪv] **1.** imperatywny; nakazujący; *gr.* rozkazujący; **2.** *też* **~ *mood*** *gr.* tryb *m* rozkazujący
im·per·cep·ti·ble [ɪmpə'septəbl] niedostrzegalny, niezauważalny
im·per·fect [ɪm'pɜːfɪkt] **1.** niedoskonały, nienajlepszy; **2.** *też* **~ *tense*** *gr.* czas przeszły niedokonany
im·pe·ri·al·is|·m [ɪm'pɪərɪəlɪzəm] *pol.* imperializm *m*; **~t** [ɪm'pɪərɪəlɪst] *pol.* imperialista *m*
im·per·il [ɪm'perəl] (*zwł. Brt.* ***-ll-*** , *Am.* ***-l-***) narażać ⟨-razić⟩
im·pe·ri·ous [ɪm'pɪərɪəs] władczy
im·per·me·a·ble [ɪm'pɜːmjəbl] nieprzepuszczalny
im·per·son·al [ɪm'pɜːsnl] bezosobowy
im·per·so·nate [ɪm'pɜːsəneɪt] podawać ⟨-dać⟩ się za (*A*); naśladować; *theat. itp.* odgrywać ⟨-degrać⟩
im·per·ti|·nence [ɪm'pɜːtɪnəns] bez-

czelność *f*, tupet *m*; **~·nent** impertynencki, bezczelny

im·per·tur·ba·ble [ɪmpə'tɜːbəbl] niewzruszony

im·per·vi·ous [ɪm'pɜːvjəs] nieprzepuszczalny; *fig.* niepodatny (***to*** na *A*)

im·pe·tu·ous [ɪm'petjʊəs] porywczy, impulsywny

im·pe·tus ['ɪmpɪtəs] rozpęd *m*, impet *m*

im·pi·e·ty [ɪm'paɪətɪ] bezbożność *f*; nieposzanowanie

im·pinge [ɪm'pɪndʒ]: **~ *on*** wpływać na (*A*), mieć wpływ na (*A*)

im·pi·ous ['ɪmpɪəs] bezbożny; nie szanujący

im·plac·a·ble [ɪm'plækəbl] nieubłagany, nieustępliwy

im·plant [ɪm'plɑːnt] *med.* wszczepiać ⟨-pić⟩; *fig.* zaszczepiać ⟨-pić⟩

im·ple·ment 1. ['ɪmplɪmənt] narzędzie *n*; **2.** ['ɪmplɪment] wprowadzać ⟨-dzić⟩ do użytku

im·pli|·cate ['ɪmplɪkeɪt] wplątywać ⟨-tać⟩ (***in*** do *G*), ⟨u⟩wikłać; **~·ca·tion** [ɪmplɪ'keɪʃn] wplątanie *n*, uwikłanie *n*, wmieszanie *n*

im·pli·cit [ɪm'plɪsɪt] domniemany, nie powiedziany otwarcie

im·plore [ɪm'plɔː] ⟨u⟩błagać

im·ply [ɪm'plaɪ] ⟨za⟩sugerować, dawać ⟨dać⟩ do zrozumienia; oznaczać; implikować

im·po·lite [ɪmpə'laɪt] nieuprzejmy

im·pol·i·tic [ɪm'pɒlɪtɪk] niezręczny; nierozsądny

im·port 1. [ɪm'pɔːt] importować, wwozić ⟨wwieźć⟩; **2.** ['ɪmpɔːt] import *m*; **~*s*** *pl.* towary *pl.* importowane

im·por|·tance [ɪm'pɔːtəns] ważność *f*, *duże* znaczenie *n*; **~·tant** ważny, *dużo* znaczący

im·por|·ta·tion [ɪmpɔː'teɪʃn] → ***import*** 2; **~·ter** [ɪm'pɔːtə] importer *m*

im·pose [ɪm'pəʊz] nakładać ⟨nałożyć⟩, narzucać ⟨-cić⟩ (***on s.o.*** na kogoś); **~ *o.s. on s.o.*** narzucać ⟨-cić⟩ się komuś; **im'pos·ing** imponujący, robiący *duże* wrażenie

im·pos·si|·bil·i·ty [ɪmpɒsə'bɪlətɪ] niemożliwość *f*; **~·ble** [ɪm'pɒsəbl] niemożliwy

im·pos·tor *Brt.*, **im·pos·ter** *Am.* [ɪm'pɒstə] oszust(ka *f*) *m*, szalbierz *m*

im·po|·tence ['ɪmpətəns] niemożność *f*, niemoc *f*; nieudolność *f*; *med.* impotencja *f*; '**~·tent** bezsilny, bezradny;

im·pov·e·rish [ɪm'pɒvərɪʃ] zubażać ⟨-bożyć⟩

im·prac·ti·ca·ble [ɪm'præktɪkəbl] niewykonalny

im·prac·ti·cal [ɪm'præktɪkl] niepraktyczny, mało praktyczny

im·preg·na·ble [ɪm'pregnəbl] *zamek itp.*: nie do zdobycia; niezbity

im·preg·nate ['ɪmpregneɪt] ⟨za⟩impregnować; zapładniać ⟨-łodnić⟩

im·press [ɪm'pres] *komuś* ⟨za⟩imponować; wywierać ⟨-wrzeć⟩ wrażenie; uzmysławiać ⟨-łowić⟩; *coś* odciskać ⟨-cisnąć⟩; **im·pres·sion** [ɪm'preʃn] wrażenie *n*; odcisk *m*; ***be under the ~ that*** mieć wrażenie, że; **im·pres·sive** [ɪm'presɪv] imponujący

im·print 1. [ɪm'prɪnt] odciskać ⟨-snąć⟩; **~ *s.th. on s.o.'s memory*** utrwalić coś w czyjejś pamięci; **2.** ['ɪmprɪnt] odcisk *m*; *print.* nazwa *f* (*wydawnictwa*), metryczka *f*

im·pris·on [ɪm'prɪzn] ⟨u⟩więzić; **~·ment** uwięzienie *n*

im·prob·a·ble [ɪm'prɒbəbl] nieprawdopodobny

im·prop·er [ɪm'prɒpə] niewłaściwy, niestosowny

im·pro·pri·e·ty [ɪmprə'praɪətɪ] niewłaściwość *f*, niestosowność *f*

im·prove [ɪm'pruːv] polepszać ⟨-szyć⟩ (się), ulepszać ⟨-szyć⟩ (się); *wartość itp.* zwiększać ⟨-szyć⟩ (się); **~ *on*** osiągać lepszy wynik od (*G*); poprawić wynik (*G*); **~·ment** polepszenie *n*, ulepszenie *n*; postęp *m* (***on*** względem *G*)

im·pro·vise ['ɪmprəvaɪz] ⟨za⟩improwizować

im·pru·dent [ɪm'pruːdənt] nieroztropny, nierozważny

im·pu|·dence ['ɪmpjʊdəns] czelność *f*, zuchwałość *f*; '**~·dent** zuchwały

im·pulse ['ɪmpʌls] impuls *m* (*też fig.*); bodziec *m*; **im·pul·sive** [ɪm'pʌlsɪv] impulsywny, zapalczywy

im·pu·ni·ty [ɪm'pjuːnətɪ]: ***with ~*** bezkarnie

im·pure [ɪm'pjʊə] nieczysty (*też rel., fig.*); zanieczyszczony

im·pute [ɪm'pjuːt]: **~ *s.th. to s.o.*** przypisywać ⟨-sać⟩ coś komuś

in[1] [ɪn] **1.** *prp. przestrzeń:* (*miejsce*) w (*L*),

I

na (*L*); ~ ***London*** w Londynie, ~ ***the street*** na ulicy; *ruch*: do (*G*); ***put it*** ~ ***your pocket*** włóż to do kieszeni; *czas*: w (*L*), w ciągu (*G*), w czasie (*G*), za (*G*); ~ ***1999*** w 1999 roku; ~ ***two hours*** za dwie godziny; ~ ***the morning*** rano; *stan, sposób*: po (*D*); na (*D*): ~ ***pencil*** ołówkiem; ~ ***writing*** na piśmie; ~ ***Polish*** po polsku; *stan, okoliczności*: przy (*L*), podczas (*G*); ~ ***crossing the street*** przechodząc przez ulicę; *materiał*: w (*A*), na; ***dressed*** ~ ***jeans*** (***blue***) ubrany w dżinsy (na niebiesko); *liczba, proporcja*: na (*A*), z (*G*); ***one*** ~ ***ten*** jeden na dziesięciu; ***three*** ~ ***all*** łącznie trzech; ***have confidence*** ~ ufać (*D*); ~ ***defence of*** w obronie (*G*); ~ ***my opinion*** w moim przekonaniu; **2.** *adv.* wewnątrz (*G*), do wewnątrz (*G*); w domu; w pracy; w modzie; **3.** *adj.* F modny

in² *skrót pisany*: ***inch***(***es***) cal *m* (*2,54 cm*)

in·a·bil·i·ty [ɪnəˈbɪlətɪ] niezdolność *f*

in·ac·ces·si·ble [ɪnækˈsesəbl] niedostępny (***to*** dla *G*)

in·ac·cu·rate [ɪnˈækjʊrət] niedokładny

in·ac|·tive [ɪnˈæktɪv] nieaktywny, bierny; ~**·tiv·i·ty** [ɪnækˈtɪvətɪ] bierność *f*, nieaktywność *f*

in·ad·e·quate [ɪnˈædɪkwət] niedostateczny; nieodpowiedni; nieadekwatny

in·ad·mis·si·ble [ɪnədˈmɪsəbl] niedopuszczalny, nie do przyjęcia

in·ad·ver·tent [ɪnədˈvɜːtənt] (~***ly***) nieumyślny, nierozmyślny

in·an·i·mate [ɪnˈænɪmət] nieożywiony

in·ap·pro·pri·ate [ɪnəˈprəʊprɪət] nieodpowiedni, niestosowny; niezdatny (***for*** dla *G*, ***to*** do *G*)

in·apt [ɪnˈæpt] nieodpowiedni, niestosowny

in·ar·tic·u·late [ɪnɑːˈtɪkjʊlət] niewyraźny, niezrozumiały; nie potrafiący się wysłowić

in·at·ten·tive [ɪnəˈtentɪv] nieuważny

in·au·di·ble [ɪnˈɔːdəbl] niesłyszalny

in·au·gu|·ral [ɪˈnɔːgjʊrəl] inauguracyjny; ~**·rate** [ɪˈnɔːgjʊreɪt] *kogoś* (*na stanowisko*) wprowadzać ⟨-dzić⟩ uroczyście; ⟨za⟩inaugurować, otwierać ⟨-worzyć⟩; rozpoczynać ⟨-cząć⟩; ~**·ra·tion** [ɪnɔːgjʊˈreɪʃn] inauguracja *f*; wprowadzenie *n*; otwarcie *n*; rozpoczęcie *n*; ***℞ration Day*** *Am.* dzień wprowadzenia prezydenta USA na urząd (*20 stycznia*)

in·born [ɪnˈbɔːn] wrodzony

Inc [ɪŋk] *skrót*: ***Incorporated*** posiadający osobowość prawną

in·cal·cu·la·ble [ɪnˈkælkjʊləbl] nieobliczalny

in·can·des·cent [ɪnkænˈdesnt] żarzący się; ~ ***lamp*** lampa *f* żarowa

in·ca·pa·ble [ɪnˈkeɪpəbl] niezdolny (***of*** do *G*), nie będący w stanie (***of doing s.th.*** zrobić czegoś)

in·ca·pa·ci|·tate [ɪnkəˈpæsɪteɪt] ⟨u⟩czynić niezdatnym *lub* niezdolnym; ~**·ty** [ɪnkəˈpæsətɪ] niezdolność *f*, niezdatność *f*

in·car·nate [ɪnˈkɑːnət] wcielony, ucieleśniony

in·cau·tious [ɪnˈkɔːʃəs] nieostrożny

in·cen·di·a·ry [ɪnˈsendjərɪ] zapalający, *fig.* zapalczywy

in·cense¹ [ˈɪnsens] kadzidło *n*

in·cense² [ɪnˈsens] rozwścieczać ⟨-czyć⟩

in·cen·tive [ɪnˈsentɪv] bodziec *m*, podnieta *f*, zachęta *f*

in·ces·sant [ɪnˈsesnt] nieprzerwany, ustawiczny

in·cest [ˈɪnsest] kazirodztwo *n*

inch [ɪntʃ] **1.** cal *m* (*=2,54 cm*) (*też fig.*); ***by*** ~***es***, ~ ***by*** ~ stopniowa, krok za krokiem; ***every*** ~ w każdym calu; **2.** posuwać się krok po kroku

in·ci|·dence [ˈɪnsɪdəns] rozmiar *m*, zasięg *m*, zakres *m* (*występowania*); ˈ~**·dent** incydent *m*, zajście *n*; ~**·den·tal** [ɪnsɪˈdentl] uboczny, marginesowy; ~ˈ**den·tal·ly** na marginesie, nawiasem mówiąc

in·cin·e|·rate [ɪnˈsɪnəreɪt] spalać ⟨-lić⟩ (*na popiół*); ~**·ra·tor** piec *m* do spalania śmieci

in·cise [ɪnˈsaɪz] nacinać ⟨-ciąć⟩, ⟨wy⟩ryć; **in·ci·sion** [ɪnˈsɪʒn] nacięcie *n*; **in·ci·sive** [ɪnˈsaɪsɪv] ostry, cięty; **in·ci·sor** [ɪnˈsaɪzə] *anat.* siekacz *m*

in·cite [ɪnˈsaɪt] podżegać, podburzać ⟨-rzyć⟩; ~**·ment** podżeganie *n*, podburzanie *n*

incl *skrót pisany*: ***including, inclusive*** wł., włącznie

in·clem·ent [ɪnˈklemənt] zły, *pogoda*: burzliwy

in·cli·na·tion [ɪnklɪˈneɪʃn] pochyłość *f*,

spadek *m*; *fig.* inklinacja *f*, skłonność *f*, upodobanie *n*; **in•cline** [ɪn'klaɪn] **1.** *v/i.* pochylać ⟨-lić⟩ się, nachylać ⟨-lić⟩ się (***to, towards*** w stronę *G*); *fig.* skłaniać ⟨-łonić⟩ się (***to, towards*** do *G*); *v/t.* nachylać; *fig.* nakłaniać ⟨-łonić⟩; **2.** zbocze *n*

in•close [ɪn'kləʊz], **in•clos•ure** [ɪn'kləʊʒə] → ***enclose, enclosure***

in•clude [ɪn'kluːd] włączać ⟨-czyć⟩; zawierać ⟨-wrzeć⟩, obejmować ⟨objąć⟩; ***tax ~d*** włącznie z podatkiem; **in'clud•ing** łącznie z (*I*); **in•clu•sion** [ɪn'kluːʒn] włączenie *n*; wliczenie *n*; **in•clu•sive** [ɪn'kluːsɪv] łączny, obejmujący (*wszystko*); włącznie (***of*** z *I*); ryczałtowy; ***be ~ of*** obejmować łącznie (*A*)

in•co•her•ent [ɪnkəʊ'hɪərənt] niespójny, niejasny

in•come ['ɪnkʌm] *econ.* dochód *m*, przychód *m*; **'~ tax** *econ.* podatek *m* dochodowy

in•com•ing ['ɪnkʌmɪŋ] nadchodzący; nowy, następujący; przybywający; ***~ mail*** poczta przychodząca

in•com•mu•ni•ca•tive [ɪnkə'mjuːnɪkətɪv] niekomunikatywny, mało rozmowny

in•com•pa•ra•ble [ɪn'kɒmpərəbl] nieporównany; nie do porównania

in•com•pat•i•ble [ɪnkəm'pætəbl] niedobrany, nieprzystający; niekompatybilny

in•com•pe|•tence [ɪn'kɒmpɪtəns] niekompetencja *f*, niefachowość *f*; **~•tent** niekompetentny, niefachowy

in•com•plete [ɪnkəm'pliːt] niekompletny; niedokończony

in•com•pre•hen|•si•ble [ɪnkɒmprɪ'hensəbl] niezrozumiały, niejasny; **~•sion** [ɪnkɒmprɪ'henʃn] niezrozumienie *n*

in•con•cei•va•ble [ɪnkən'siːvəbl] nie do pomyślenia, nie do pojęcia

in•con•clu•sive [ɪnkən'kluːsɪv] nieprzekonujący; bezowocny, nie zakończony pomyślnie; nie rozstrzygający

in•con•gru•ous [ɪn'kɒŋgrʊəs] nie na miejscu; nie pasujący (***to, with*** do *G*); niespójny

in•con•se•quen•tial [ɪnkɒnsɪ'kwenʃl] mało znaczący, nieważny

in•con•sid|•e•ra•ble [ɪnkən'sɪdərəbl] nieznaczny; **~•er•ate** [ɪnkən'sɪdərət] nieczuły, bezwzględny

in•con•sis•tent [ɪnkən'sɪstənt] niespójny, niekonsekwentny

in•con•so•la•ble [ɪnkən'səʊləbl] niepocieszony

in•con•spic•u•ous [ɪnkən'spɪkjʊəs] niepozorny

in•con•stant [ɪn'kɒnstənt] niestały, zmienny

in•con•ti•nent [ɪn'kɒntɪnənt] *med.* nie mogący utrzymać odchodów

in•con•ve•ni|•ence [ɪnkən'viːnjəns] **1.** niedogodność *f*; niewygoda *f*, kłopot *m*; **2.** sprawiać *komuś* kłopot; przysparzać kłopotów; **~•ent** niewygodny; niedogodny

in•cor•po|•rate [ɪn'kɔːpəreɪt] ⟨po-, z⟩łączyć się; włączać ⟨-czyć⟩, obejmować ⟨objąć⟩; uwzględniać ⟨-nić⟩; *econ., jur.* ⟨za⟩rejestrować; nadawać ⟨-dać⟩ osobowość prawną; **~•rat•ed 'com•pa•ny** *Am.* spółka *f* o osobowości prawnej; **~•ra•tion** [ɪnkɔːpə'reɪʃn] złączenie *n* (się); objęcie *n*; włączenie *n*; uwzględnienie *n*; rejestracja *f* (*firmy*); *Am.* nadanie *n* osobowości prawnej

in•cor•rect [ɪnkə'rekt] nieprawidłowy, niewłaściwy

in•cor•ri•gi•ble [ɪn'kɒrɪdʒəbl] niepoprawny

in•cor•rup•ti•ble [ɪnkə'rʌptəbl] nieprzekupny

in•crease 1. [ɪn'kriːs] wzrastać ⟨-rosnąć⟩; zwiększać ⟨-szyć⟩ (się); powiększać ⟨-szyć⟩ (się); **2.** ['ɪnkriːs] wzrost *m*; zwiększenie *n*; powiększenie *n*; podwyżka *f*; **in•creas•ing•ly** [ɪn'kriːsɪŋlɪ] wzrastająco, w coraz większym stopniu; ***~ difficult*** coraz trudniejszy

in•cred•i•ble [ɪn'kredəbl] niewiarygodny

in•cre•du•li•ty [ɪnkrɪ'djuːlətɪ] niedowierzanie *n*; **in•cred•u•lous** [ɪn'kredjʊləs] niedowierzający, sceptyczny

in•crim•i•nate [ɪn'krɪmɪneɪt] obwiniać ⟨-nić⟩

in•cu|•bate ['ɪnkjʊbeɪt] wysiadywać; wylęgać się; **'~•ba•tor** inkubator *m*; *agr.* wylęgarka *f*

in•cur [ɪn'kɜː] (***-rr-***) wywoływać ⟨-łać⟩; *koszty, szkody* ponosić ⟨-nieść⟩

in•cu•ra•ble [ɪn'kjʊərəbl] nieuleczalny

in•cu•ri•ous [ɪn'kjʊərɪəs] mało dociekliwy, mało ciekawy

in·cur·sion [ɪn'kɜːʃn] wtargnięcie *n*, najście *n*

in·debt·ed [ɪn'detɪd] zobowiązany; wdzięczny

in·de·cent [ɪn'diːsnt] nieprzyzwoity; *jur.* lubieżny; niemoralny; **~ assault** *jur.* czyn *m* lubieżny

in·de·ci|·sion [ɪndɪ'sɪʒn] niezdecydowanie *n*; **~·sive** [ɪndɪ'saɪsɪv] niezdecydowany; nie rozstrzygnięty, nie rozstrzygający

in·deed [ɪn'diːd] **1.** *adv.* rzeczywiście, faktycznie, naprawdę; ***thank you very much ~!*** serdecznie dziękuję; **2.** *int.* doprawdy?, naprawdę?

in·de·fat·i·ga·ble [ɪndɪ'fætɪgəbl] niestrudzony, niezmordowany

in·de·fen·si·ble [ɪndɪ'fensəbl] niewybaczalny

in·de·fi·na·ble [ɪndɪ'faɪnəbl] nieokreślony, nie ustalony

in·def·i·nite [ɪn'defɪnət] nieograniczony; niejasny; **~·ly** nieograniczenie *n*

in·del·i·ble [ɪn'delɪbl] nie do usunięcia, nie do zmazania (*też fig.*)

in·del·i·cate [ɪn'delɪkət] mało taktowny, nietaktowny; niedelikatny

in·dem·ni|·fy [ɪn'demnɪfaɪ] wynagradzać ⟨-rodzić⟩ straty (***for, against*** za *A*); zabezpieczać ⟨-czyć⟩ (***for***, za *A*); **~·ty** [ɪn'demnətɪ] wynagrodzenie *n* strat; zabezpieczenie *n*

in·dent [ɪn'dent] wgniatać ⟨-gnieść⟩; *print. wiersz* wcinać ⟨wciąć⟩

in·de·pen|·dence [ɪndɪ'pendəns] niepodległość *f*, niezależność *f*; ***♀dence Day*** *Am.* Dzień Niepodległości (*4 lipca*); **~·dent** niepodległy; niezależny

in·de·scri·ba·ble [ɪndɪ'skraɪbəbl] nieopisany, nie do opisania

in·de·struc·ti·ble [ɪndɪ'strʌktəbl] niezniszczalny; niespożyty

in·de·ter·mi·nate [ɪndɪ'tɜːmɪnət] nieokreślony; niejasny

in·dex ['ɪndeks] (*pl.* ***-dexes, -dices*** [-dɪsiːz]) indeks *m*, skorowidz *m*, wykaz *m*; wskaźnik *m*; ***cost of living ~*** wskaźnik *m* kosztów utrzymania; **'~ card** karta *f* kartotekowa; **'~ fin·ger** palec *m* wskazujący

In·di·a ['ɪndjə] Indie *pl.*; **In·di·an** ['ɪndjən] **1.** indyjski, hinduski; indiański; **2.** Hindus(ka *f*) *m*; *też* ***American ~*** Indianin *m* (-anka *f*)

In·di·an| 'corn *bot.* kukurydza *f*; **'~ file**: ***in ~ file*** gęsiego; **~ 'sum·mer** babie lato *n*

in·di·a 'rub·ber kauczuk *m* (*naturalny*)

in·di|·cate ['ɪndɪkeɪt] wskazywać ⟨-zać⟩ (*też tech.*); *mot.* wskazywać ⟨-zać⟩ (*kierunek ruchu*); *fig.* ⟨za⟩sygnalizować; **~·ca·tion** [ɪndɪ'keɪʃn] wskazywanie *n*; wskazanie *n*; oznaka *f*, zasygnalizowanie *n*; **in·dic·a·tive** [ɪn'dɪkətɪv] *też* ***~cative mood*** *gr.* tryb *m* oznajmujący; **~·cator** ['ɪndɪkeɪtə] *tech.* wskaźnik *m*; *mot.* kierunkowskaz *m*, migacz *m*

in·di·ces ['ɪndɪsiːz] *pl. od* ***index***

in·dict [ɪn'daɪt] *jur.* oskarżać ⟨-żyć⟩ (***for*** o *A*); **~·ment** oskarżenie *n*, stan *m* oskarżenia

in·dif·fer|·ence [ɪn'dɪfrəns] obojętność *f*; **~·ent** obojętny (***to*** wobec *G*)

in·di·gent ['ɪndɪdʒənt] ubogi

in·di·ges|·ti·ble [ɪndɪ'dʒestəbl] niestrawny; **~·tion** [ɪndɪ'dʒestʃən] niestrawność *f*

in·dig|·nant [ɪn'dɪgnənt] oburzony (***about, at, over*** na *A*); **~·na·tion** [ɪndɪg'neɪʃn] oburzenie *n* (***about, at, over*** na *A*); **~·ni·ty** [ɪn'dɪgnətɪ] upokorzenie *n*

in·di·rect [ɪndɪ'rekt] pośredni; okrężny; ***by ~ means*** *fig.* pośrednimi środkami

in·dis|·creet [ɪndɪ'skriːt] niedyskretny; nierozważny; **~·cre·tion** [ɪndɪ'skreʃn] niedyskrecja *f*; nierozwaga *f*

in·dis·crim·i·nate [ɪndɪ'skrɪmɪnət] niewybredny, bezkrytyczny; jak popadnie, na oślep

in·di·spen·sa·ble [ɪndɪ'spensəbl] nieodzowny

in·dis|·posed [ɪndɪ'spəʊzd] niedysponowany; **~·po·si·tion** [ɪndɪspə'zɪʃn] niedyspozycja *f*; niechęć *f* (***to*** do *G*)

in·dis·pu·ta·ble [ɪndɪ'spjuːtəbl] bezsporny

in·dis·tinct [ɪndɪ'stɪŋkt] niewyraźny

in·dis·tin·guish·a·ble [ɪndɪ'stɪŋgwɪʃəbl] nie do odróżnienia (***from*** od *G*)

in·di·vid·u·al [ɪndɪ'vɪdjʊəl] **1.** indywidualny; jednostkowy; poszczególny; pojedynczy; **2.** jednostka *f*; osoba *f*; osobnik *m*; **~·is·m** [ɪndɪ'vɪdjʊəlɪzəm] indywidualizm *m*; **~·ist** [ɪndɪ'vɪdjʊəlɪst] indywidualista *m* (-tka *f*); **~·i·ty** [ɪndɪvɪdjʊ'ælətɪ] indywidualność *f*; **~·ly**

[ɪndɪ'vɪdjʊəlɪ] indywiudalnie; pojedynczno
in·di·vis·i·ble [ɪndɪ'vɪzəbl] niepodzielny
in·dom·i·ta·ble [ɪn'dɒmɪtəbl] nieposkromiony
In·do·ne·sia Indonezja *f*
in·door ['ɪndɔː] wewnętrzny; domowy; *basen*: kryty; *sport*: halowy; **~s** [ɪn'dɔːz] wewnątrz; w domu; (*w sporcie*) w hali; do wnętrza, do środka
in·dorse [ɪn'dɔːs] → ***endorse***
in·duce [ɪn'djuːs] *kogoś* namawiać ⟨-mówić⟩, nakłaniać ⟨-łonić⟩; *coś* wywoływać ⟨-łać⟩, ⟨s⟩powodować; **~·ment** bodziec *m*, zachęta *f*
in·duct [ɪn'dʌkt] wprowadzać ⟨-dzić⟩ (na stanowisko); **in·duc·tion** [ɪn'dʌkʃn] wprowadzenie *n* na stanowisko; *electr.* indukcja *f*
in·dulge [ɪn'dʌldʒ] *komuś, sobie* pobłażać; spełniać ⟨-nić⟩ zachcianki; zaspokajać ⟨-koić⟩; **~ *in s.th.*** pozwalać sobie na (*A*), oddawać się (*D*); **in·dul·gence** [ɪn'dʌldʒəns] pobłażanie *n* (sobie); pobłażliwość *f*; słabość *f*; esktrawagancja *f*, luksus *m*; **in'dul·gent** pobłażliwy, wyrozumiały
in·dus·tri·al [ɪn'dʌstrɪəl] przemysłowy; industrialny; **~ 'ar·e·a** region *m* przemysłowy, zagłębie *n* przemysłowe; **~·ist** [ɪn'dʌstrɪəlɪst] *econ.* przemysłowiec *m*; **~·ize** [ɪn'dʌstrɪəlaɪz] *econ.* uprzemysławiać ⟨-łowić⟩, ⟨z⟩industrializować
in·dus·tri·ous [ɪn'dʌstrɪəs] pracowity, skrzętny
in·dus·try ['ɪndəstrɪ] *econ.* przemysł *m*; gałąź *f* przemysłu; pracowitość *f*
in·ed·i·ble [ɪn'edɪbl] niejadalny
in·ef·fec|·tive [ɪnɪ'fektɪv], **~·tu·al** [ɪnɪ'fektʃʊəl] bezskuteczny, nieskuteczny; nieefektywny
in·ef·fi·cient [ɪnɪ'fɪʃnt] niesprawny, nieskuteczny; nieudolny
in·el·e·gant [ɪn'elɪgənt] mało elegancki
in·eli·gi·ble [ɪn'elɪdʒəbl] niezdatny, nieodpowiedni; nie spełniający warunków
in·ept [ɪ'nept] niezręczny; niedorzeczny, nierozsądny
in·e·qual·i·ty [ɪnɪ'kwɒlətɪ] nierówność *f*
in·ert [ɪ'nɜːt] *phys.* bezwładny; inercyjny, nieaktywny; **in·er·tia** [ɪ'nɜːʃjə] inercja *f*, bezwład *m* (*też fig.*)
in·es·ca·pa·ble [ɪnɪ'skeɪpəbl] nieuniknione
in·es·sen·tial [ɪnɪ'senʃl] niepotrzebny, zbyteczny
in·es·ti·ma·ble [ɪn'estɪməbl] nieoszacowany, bezcenny
in·ev·i·ta·ble [ɪn'evɪtəbl] nieunikniony, nieuchronny
in·ex·act [ɪnɪg'zækt] niedokładny
in·ex·cu·sa·ble [ɪnɪ'skjuːzəbl] niewybaczalny
in·ex·haus·ti·ble [ɪnɪg'zɔːstəbl] niewyczerpany
in·ex·o·ra·ble [ɪn'eksərəbl] nieubłagany, nieprzejednany
in·ex·pe·di·ent [ɪnɪk'spiːdjənt] niecelowy, niepraktyczny
in·ex·pen·sive [ɪnɪk'spensɪv] niedrogi
in·ex·pe·ri·ence [ɪnɪk'spɪərɪəns] niedoświadczenie *n*, brak *m* doświadczenia; **~d** niedoświadczony
in·ex·pert [ɪn'ekspɜːt] nieudolny; niedoświadczony
in·ex·plic·a·ble [ɪnɪk'splɪkəbl] niepojęty, niewytłumaczalny
in·ex·pres|·si·ble [ɪnɪk'spresəbl] niewyrażalny, niewysłowiony, nieopisany; **~·sive** [ɪnɪk'spresɪv] beznamiętny, bez emocji
in·ex·tri·ca·ble [ɪn'ekstrɪkəbl] nieunikniony; zaplątany, zawiły
in·fal·li·ble [ɪn'fæləbl] nieomylny
in·fa|·mous ['ɪnfəməs] haniebny; niesławny; **'~·my** hańba *f*; niesława *f*, zła sława *f*
in·fan|·cy ['ɪnfənsɪ] wczesne dzieciństwo *n*; ***in its ~cy*** *fig.* w powijakach; **'~t** dziecko *n*, niemowlę *n*
in·fan·tile ['ɪnfəntaɪl] dziecinny; dziecięcy, niemowlęcy
in·fan·try ['ɪnfəntrɪ] *mil.* piechota *f*
in·fat·u·at·ed [ɪn'fætjʊeɪtɪd] zakochany, zadurzony (***with*** w *L*)
in·fect [ɪn'fekt] *med. kogoś* zarażać ⟨-razić⟩ (*też fig.*); *coś* zakażać ⟨-kazić⟩; **in·fec·tion** [ɪn'fekʃn] *med.* zakażenie *n*; zarażenie *n*; **in·fec·tious** [ɪn'fekʃəs] *med.* zakaźny; zaraźliwy (*też fig.*)
in·fer [ɪn'fɜː] (**-rr-**) ⟨wy⟩wnioskować (***from*** z *G*); wyciągać ⟨-gnąć⟩ wnioski;

~·ence ['ɪnfərəns] wniosek *m*; wnioskowanie *n*

in·fe·ri·or [ɪn'fɪərɪə] **1.** podległy (***to*** *D*), niższy (***to*** wobec *G*); pośledniejszy, gorszy (***to*** w stosunku do *G*); mniej wart (***to*** od *G*); ***be ~ to s.o.*** podlegać komuś (*służbowo*); **2.** podwładny *m* (-na *f*); **~·i·ty** [ɪnfɪərɪ'ɒrətɪ] niższość *f*; podrzędność *f*; **~·i·ty com·plex** kompleks *m* niższości

in·fer|·nal [ɪn'fɜːnl] piekielny; **~·no** [ɪn'fɜːnəʊ] (*pl.* ***-nos***) piekło *n*

in·fer·tile [ɪn'fɜːtaɪl] niepłodny

in·fest [ɪn'fest] zakażać ⟨-kazić⟩; ***be ~ed with*** być zaatakowanym przez (*A*)

in·fi·del·i·ty [ɪnfɪ'delətɪ] niewierność *f*, zdrada *f*

in·fil·trate ['ɪnfɪltreɪt] przesączać ⟨-czyć⟩ się przez (*A*); przenikać przez (*A*); *pol.* infiltrować

in·fi·nite ['ɪnfɪnət] nieskończony

in·fin·i·tive [ɪn'fɪnətɪv] *gr.* bezokolicznik *m*

in·fin·i·ty [ɪn'fɪnətɪ] nieskończoność *f*

in·firm [ɪn'fɜːm] słaby, niesprawny, wątły; **in·fir·ma·ry** [ɪn'fɜːmərɪ] szpital *m*; (*w szkole*) izolatka *f*; **in·fir·mi·ty** [ɪn'fɜːmətɪ] słabość *f*, niesprawność *f*, wątłość *f*

in·flame [ɪn'fleɪm] rozpalać ⟨-lić⟩ (*zw. fig.*) zapalać ⟨-lić⟩; ⟨s⟩powodować stan zapalny; ***become ~d*** *med.* zaognić się

in·flam·ma|·ble [ɪn'flæməbl] palny; zapalny; łatwopalny; **~·tion** [ɪnflə'meɪʃn] *med.* zapalenie *n*; **~·to·ry** [ɪn'flæmətərɪ] *med.* zapalny; *fig.* wzburzający

in·flate [ɪn'fleɪt] nadmuchiwać ⟨-chać⟩, nadymać ⟨-dąć⟩ (*też fig.*); ⟨na⟩pompować (powietrze); *econ. cenę* zawyżać ⟨-żyć⟩; **in·fla·tion** *econ.* [ɪn'fleɪʃn] inflacja *f*

in·flect [ɪn'flekt] *gr.* odmieniać ⟨-nić⟩; **in·flec·tion** [ɪn'flekʃn] *gr.* fleksja *f*, odmiana *f*

in·flex|·i·ble [ɪn'fleksəbl] sztywny (*też fig.*); nieelastyczny; **~·ion** *Brt. gr.* [ɪn'flekʃn] → ***inflection***

in·flict [ɪn'flɪkt] (***on***) *krzywdę* wyrządzać ⟨-dzić⟩; *rany* zadawać ⟨-dać⟩; *cierpienie* ⟨s⟩powodować; *karę* wymierzać ⟨-rzyć⟩; ***~ s.th. on s.o.*** narzucać coś komuś; **in·flic·tion** [ɪn'flɪkʃn] narzucenie *n*, spowodowanie *n*

in·flu|·ence ['ɪnflʊəns] **1.** wpływ *m*; **2.** wpływać ⟨-łynąć⟩ na (*A*); **~·en·tial** [ɪnflʊ'enʃl] wpływowy

in·flux ['ɪnflʌks] napływ *m*, przypływ *m*, dopływ *m*

in·form [ɪn'fɔːm] ⟨po⟩informować, zawiadamiać ⟨-domić⟩ (***of*** o *L*); ***~ against*** *lub* ***on s.o.*** donosić ⟨-nieść⟩ na kogoś, ⟨za⟩denuncjować kogoś

in·for·mal [ɪn'fɔːml] nieoficjalny; nieformalny; **~·i·ty** [ɪnfɔː'mælətɪ] nieoficjalność *f*; nieformalność *f*;

in·for·ma|·tion [ɪnfə'meɪʃn] informacja *f*; **~·tion (su·per·)'high·way** *komp.* autostrada *f* informatyczna; **~·tive** [ɪn'fɔːmətɪv] informacyjny, pouczający, kształcący

in·form·er [ɪn'fɔːmə] donosiciel(ka *f*) *m*; informator(ka *f*) *m*

in·fra·struc·ture ['ɪnfrəstrʌktʃə] infrastruktura *f*

in·fre·quent [ɪn'friːkwənt] rzadki, nieczęsty

in·fringe [ɪn'frɪndʒ] *też* ***~ on*** prawa, porozumienia naruszać ⟨-szyć⟩ (*A*), ⟨z⟩łamać (*A*)

in·fu·ri·ate [ɪn'fjʊərɪeɪt] rozwścieczać ⟨-czyć⟩

in·fuse [ɪn'fjuːz] *herbatę* zaparzać ⟨-rzyć⟩; **in·fu·sion** [ɪn'fjuːʒn] napar *m*; *med.* wlew *m*, infuzja *f*

in·ge|·ni·ous [ɪn'dʒiːnjəs] zmyślny, sprytny, pomysłowy; **~·nu·i·ty** [ɪndʒɪ'njuːətɪ] zmyślność *f*, sprytność *f*, pomysłowość *f*

in·gen·u·ous [ɪn'dʒenjʊəs] prostoduszny

in·got ['ɪŋgət] sztabka *f* (*złota itp.*), sztaba *f*

in·gra·ti·ate [ɪn'greɪʃɪeɪt]: ***~ o.s. with s.o.*** łasić się do kogoś, nadskakiwać komuś

in·grat·i·tude [ɪn'grætɪtjuːd] niewdzięczność *f*

in·gre·di·ent [ɪn'griːdjənt] składnik *m*

in·grow·ing ['ɪngrəʊɪŋ] wrastający

in·hab|·it [ɪn'hæbɪt] zamieszkiwać ⟨-szkać⟩; **~·it·a·ble** zdatny do zamieszkania; **~·i·tant** mieszkaniec *m*

in·hale [ɪn'heɪl] wdychać; zaciągać ⟨-gnąć⟩ się (*D*); *med.* wziewać

in·her·ent [ɪn'hɪərənt] (***in***) wrodzony; swoisty dla (*G*), właściwy dla (*G*); nieodłączny (od *G*)

in·her|·it [ɪn'herɪt] ⟨o⟩dziedziczyć

(***from*** *po L*); ~**·i·tance** dziedzictwo *n*, spadek *m*

in·hib·it [ɪn'hɪbɪt] ⟨za⟩hamować (*też psych.*), wstrzymywać ⟨-mać⟩ (***from*** przed *I*); ~**·ed** *psych.* zahamowany; **in·hi·bi·tion** [ɪnhɪ'bɪʃn] zahamowanie *n*

in·hos·pi·ta·ble [ɪn'hɒspɪtəbl] niegościnny; nieprzyjazny

in·hu·man [ɪn'hjuːmən] nieludzki; ~**e** [ɪnhjuː'meɪn] niehumanitarny, nieludzki

in·im·i·cal [ɪ'nɪmɪkl] wrogi, nieprzyjazny (***to*** *D*)

in·im·i·ta·ble [ɪ'nɪmɪtəbl] nie do podrobienia

i·ni|·tial [ɪ'nɪʃl] **1.** początkowy, wstępny; **2.** inicjał *m*; ~**·tial·ly** [ɪ'nɪʃəlɪ] początkowo; ~**·ti·ate** [ɪ'nɪʃɪeɪt] zaczynać ⟨-cząć⟩, zapoczątkowywać ⟨-wać⟩, ⟨za⟩inicjować; wprowadzać ⟨-dzić⟩ (***into*** do *G*); ~**·ti·a·tion** [ɪnɪʃɪ'eɪʃn] zapoczątkowanie *n*; wprowadzenie *n*; ~**·tiative** [ɪ'nɪʃɪətɪv] inicjatywa *f*; ***take the ~tiative*** podejmować ⟨-djąć⟩ inicjatywę; ***on one's own ~tiative*** z własnej inicjatywy

in·ject [ɪn'dʒekt] *med.* wstrzykiwać ⟨-knąć⟩; **in·jec·tion** [ɪn'dʒekʃn] *med.* wstrzyknięcie *n*, iniekcja *f*, zastrzyk *m*

in·ju·di·cious [ɪndʒuː'dɪʃəs] nierozsądny

in·junc·tion [ɪn'dʒʌnkʃn] *jur.* nakaz *m* sądowy

in·jure ['ɪndʒə] ⟨z⟩ranić; wyrządzać ⟨-dzić⟩ krzywdę (*D*); szkodzić (*D*); '~**d** zraniony, ranny; skrzywdzony, urażony; **in·ju·ri·ous** [ɪn'dʒʊərɪəs] szkodliwy; ***be ~ to*** ⟨za⟩szkodzić (*D*); ***be ~ to health*** szkodzić zdrowiu; **in·ju·ry** ['ɪndʒərɪ] *med.* zranienie *n*, obrażenie *n*; szkoda *f*; '**in·ju·ry time** *Brt.* (*zwł. w piłce nożnej*) doliczony czas *m* (*gry*)

in·jus·tice [ɪn'dʒʌstɪs] niesprawiedliwość *f*

ink [ɪŋk] **1.** tusz *m*, atrament *m*; **2.** ~**jet** ['ɪŋkdʒet] *drukarka*: atramentowy

ink·ling ['ɪŋklɪŋ] pojęcie *n*

'**ink|·pad** poduszka *f* do tuszu; '~**·y** (***-ier, -iest***) atramentowy; poplamiony atramentem

in·laid ['ɪnleɪd] inkrustowany; ~ ***work*** inkrustacja *f*

in·land 1. *adj.* ['ɪnlənd] lądowy, śródlądowy; krajowy; **2.** *adv.* [ɪn'lænd] w głąb kraju *lub* lądu; ♀ '**Rev·e·nue** *Brt.* urząd *m* skarbowy, fiskus *m*

in·lay ['ɪnleɪ] inkrustacja *f*; *med.* wypełnienie *n*, plomba

in·let ['ɪnlet] zatoczka *f*; *tech.* wlot *m*

in·mate ['ɪnmeɪt] współwięzień *m*; pacjent *m*

in·most ['ɪnməʊst] wewnętrzny, najgłębszy

inn [ɪn] gospoda *f*, zajazd *m*; *hist.* karczma *f*

in·nate [ɪ'neɪt] wrodzony

in·ner ['ɪnə] wewnętrzny; skryty; '~**·most** → ***inmost***

in·nings ['ɪnɪŋz] (*pl.* ***innings***) (*w krykiecie, baseballu*) runda *f*

'**inn·keep·er** właściciel(ka *f*) gospody *lub* zajazdu; *hist.* karczmarz *m*

in·no|·cence ['ɪnəsns] niewinność *f*; naiwność *f*; '~**·cent** niewinny; naiwny

in·noc·u·ous [ɪ'nɒkjʊəs] nieszkodliwy

in·no·va·tion [ɪnəʊ'veɪʃn] innowacja *f*, nowatorski pomysł *m*

in·nu·en·do [ɪnjuː'endəʊ] (*pl.* ***-does, -dos***) aluzja *f*, insynuacja *f*

in·nu·me·ra·ble [ɪ'njuːmərəbl] niezliczony

i·noc·u|·late [ɪ'nɒkjʊleɪt] *med.* ⟨za⟩szczepić; ~**·la·tion** [ɪnɒkjʊ'leɪʃn] *med.* szczepienie *n*, zaszczepienie *n*

in·of·fen·sive [ɪnə'fensɪv] nieszkodliwy

in·op·e·ra·ble [ɪn'ɒpərəbl] *med.* nieoperacyjny, nie nadający się do operowania; *plan*: nie dający się przeprowadzić

in·op·por·tune [ɪn'ɒpətjuːn] niefortunny, nie na miejscu, niestosowny

in·or·di·nate [ɪ'nɔːdɪnət] nieumiarkowany, niepohamowany; nadmierny, przesadny

'**in·pa·tient** *med.* pacjent(ka *f*) *m* hospitalizowany (-na)

in·put ['ɪnpʊt] wejście *n* (*też komp.*); wkład *m* (*pracy*); *komp.* dane *pl.* wejściowe, wprowadzanie *n* (*danych*)

in·quest ['ɪnkwest] *jur.* dochodzenie *n* sądowe; → ***coroner's inquest***

in·quire [ɪn'kwaɪə] ⟨za-, s⟩pytać (o *A*); ~ ***into*** ⟨z⟩badać; **in·quir·ing** [ɪn'kwaɪrɪŋ] dociekliwy, badawczy; **in·quir·y** [ɪn'kwaɪrɪ] dowiadywanie *n* się; badanie *n*, dochodzenie *n*

in·qui·si·tion [ɪnkwɪ'zɪʃn] przesłucha-

nie *n*, śledztwo *n*; ♀ *rel. hist.* Inkwizycja;
in·quis·i·tive [ɪn'kwɪzətɪv] badawczy, dociekliwy
in·roads ['ɪnrəʊdz] (***in, into, on***) najazd *m* (na *A*); ***make ~ into one's savings*** naruszać ⟨-szyć⟩ oszczędności
in·sane [ɪn'seɪn] szalony, pomylony
in·san·i·ta·ry [ɪn'sænɪtərɪ] niehigieniczny
in·san·i·ty [ɪn'sænətɪ] szaleństwo *n*, wariactwo *n*
in·sa·tia·ble [ɪn'seɪʃjəbl] niezaspokojony, nienasycony
in·scrip·tion [ɪn'skrɪpʃn] napis *m*; dedykacja *f*
in·scru·ta·ble [ɪn'skruːtəbl] niezbadany, nieprzenikniony
in·sect ['ɪnsekt] *zo.* owad *m*; **in·sec·ti·cide** [ɪn'sektɪsaɪd] środek *m* owadobójczy, insektycyd *m*
in·se·cure [ɪnsɪ'kjʊə] niepewny, niestabilny
in·sen·si·ble [ɪn'sensəbl] nieczuły, niewrażliwy (***to*** na *A*); nieprzytomny; nieświadomy
in·sen·si·tive [ɪn'sensətɪv] nieczuły, niewrażliwy
in·sep·a·ra·ble [ɪn'sepərəbl] nieodłączny, nierozłączny
in·ser|t 1. [ɪn'sɜːt] wstawiać ⟨-wić⟩, wkładać ⟨włożyć⟩; umieszczać ⟨-eścić⟩; **2.** ['ɪnsɜːt] wkładka *f* (*do gazety*); **~·tion** [ɪn'sɜːʃn] wstawienie *n*, zamieszczenie *n*; umieszczenie *n*; wstawka *f*, dopisek *m*; ogłoszenie *n*; **'~t key** *komp.* klawisz *m* "Insert" (*wstawiania*)
in·shore [ɪn'ʃɔː] przy *lub* do brzegu; przybrzeżny
in·side **1.** [ɪn'saɪd] wnętrze *n*, ***turn ~ out*** wywrócić do góry nogami, przenicować; **2.** ['ɪnsaɪd] *adj.* wewnętrzny; poufny; **3.** [ɪn'saɪd] *adv.* do wewnątrz *lub* środka; w środku, wewnątrz; ***~ of*** wewnątrz, w środku (*czegoś*) **4.** [ɪn'saɪd] *prp.* w ciągu (*G*); wewnątrz (*G*); **in·sid·er** [ɪn'saɪdə] osoba zaangażowana (*przy czymś*)
in·sid·i·ous [ɪn'sɪdɪəs] podstępny, skrycie działający
in·sight ['ɪnsaɪt] wgląd *m*, intuicja *f*
in·sig·ni·a [ɪn'sɪgnɪə] *pl.* insygnia *pl.*; atrybuty *pl.*, oznaki *pl.*
in·sig·nif·i·cant [ɪnsɪg'nɪfɪkənt] nieważki, nieważny, bez znaczenia
in·sin·cere [ɪnsɪn'sɪə] nieszczery
in·sin·u|·ate [ɪn'sɪnjʊeɪt] insynuować, imputować; **~·a·tion** [ɪnsɪnjʊ'eɪʃn] insynuacja *f*
in·sip·id [ɪn'sɪpɪd] bez smaku *lub* zapachu, mdły
in·sist [ɪn'sɪst] nalegać, upierać się (***on*** przy *D*); **in·sis·tence** [ɪn'sɪstəns] natarczywość *f*, uporczywość *f*; **in'sis·tent** uporczywy, natarczywy
in·sole ['ɪnsəʊl] podeszwa *f* wewnętrzna, brandzel *m*
in·so·lent ['ɪnsələnt] bezczelny
in·sol·u·ble [ɪn'sɒljʊbl] nierozpuszczalny
in·sol·vent [ɪn'sɒlvənt] niewypłacalny; w stanie upadłości, zbankrutowany
in·som·ni·a [ɪn'sɒmnɪə] bezsenność *f*
in·spect [ɪn'spekt] sprawdzać ⟨-dzić⟩, ⟨s⟩kontrolować; ⟨z⟩robić przegląd; **inspec·tion** [ɪn'spekʃn] sprawdzenie *n*; kontrola *f*; przegląd *m*; inspekcja *f*; **in'spec·tor** kontroler(ka *f*) *m*; inspektor *m*; *Brt.* wizytator(ka *f*) *m*
in·spi·ra·tion [ɪnspə'reɪʃn] inspiracja *f*, natchnienie *n*; **in·spire** [ɪn'spaɪə] ⟨za⟩inspirować, natchnąć; *otuchy* dodawać
in·stall [ɪn'stɔːl] *tech.* ⟨za⟩instalować, zakładać ⟨założyć⟩; (*na urząd*) wprowadzać ⟨-dzić⟩; **in·stal·la·tion** [ɪnstə'leɪʃn] *tech.* instalacja *f*, założenie *n*; wprowadzenie *n* (*na urząd*)
in·stal·ment *Brt.*, **in·stall·ment** *Am.* [ɪn'stɔːlmənt] *econ.* rata *f*, spłata *f* częściowa; kolejna część *f* (*książki*); odcinek *m* (*audycji radiowej lub telewizyjnej*)
in'stall·ment plan *Am.*: ***buy on the ~*** kupować ⟨-pić⟩ na raty
in·stance ['ɪnstəns] przykład *m*; przypadek *m*; *jur.* instancja *f*; ***for ~*** na przykład
in·stant ['ɪnstənt] **1.** moment *m*, chwila *f*; **2.** natychmiastowy; *kawa itp.*: rozpuszczalny; **~·a·ne·ous** [ɪnstən'teɪnjəs] natychmiastowy; **~ 'cam·e·ra** *phot.* polaroid *m TM*; **~ 'cof·fee** kawa *f* rozpuszczalna, neska *f*; **'~·ly** natychmiastowo, od razu
in·stead [ɪn'sted] zamiast tego; ***~ of*** zamiast (*G*)
'in·step podbicie *n*
in·sti|·gate ['ɪnstɪgeɪt] wszczynać ⟨-cząć⟩, ⟨za⟩inicjować; podburzać

⟨-rzyć⟩, podżegać; '~·**ga·tor** podżegacz(ka *f*) *m*

in·stil *Brt*., **in·still** *Am*. [ɪn'stɪl] (*-ll-*) *przekonania* wpajać ⟨wpoić⟩; *strach* wzbudzać ⟨-dzić⟩

in·stinct ['ɪnstɪŋkt] instynkt *m*; **in·stinc·tive** [ɪn'stɪŋktɪv] instynktowny

in·sti|·tute ['ɪnstɪtjuːt] instytut *m*; ~·**tu·tion** [ɪnstɪ'tjuːʃn] instytucja *f*, organizacja *f*; zakład *m*

in·struct [ɪn'strʌkt] nauczać ⟨-czyć⟩; ⟨wy⟩szkolić; ⟨po⟩instruować; ⟨po⟩informować; pouczać ⟨-czyć⟩; **in·struc·tion** [ɪn'strʌkʃn] nauczanie *n*, szkolenie *n*; instruktaż *n*; *komp*. rozkaz *m*; ~***s*** *pl*. ***for use*** instrukcja *f* użytkowania; ***operating*** ~***s*** *pl*. instrukcja *f* obsługi; **in·struc·tive** [ɪn'strʌktɪv] pouczający, kształcący; **in'struc·tor** instruktor *m*; **in'struc·tress** instruktorka *f*

in·stru|·ment ['ɪnstrʊmənt] instrument *m*; narzędzie *n* (*też fig*.); ~·**men·tal** [ɪnstrʊ'mentl] *mus*. instrumentalny; (bardzo) pomocny; ***be*** ~***mental in*** przyczyniać ⟨-nić⟩ się znacząco do (*G*)

in·sub·or·di|·nate [ɪnsə'bɔːdənət] niesubordynowany, niezdyscyplinowany; ~·**na·tion** [ɪnsəbɔːdɪ'neɪʃn] niesubordynacja *f*, brak *m* dyscypliny

in·suf·fe·ra·ble [ɪn'sʌfərəbl] nie do wytrzymania

in·suf·fi·cient [ɪnsə'fɪʃnt] niewystarczający, niedostateczny

in·su·lar ['ɪnsjʊlə] wyspiarski; *fig*. odizolowany

in·su|·late ['ɪnsjʊleɪt] ⟨za⟩izolować; ~·**la·tion** [ɪnsjʊ'leɪʃn] izolacja *f*

in·sult 1. ['ɪnsʌlt] obelga *f*, zniewaga *f*; **2.** [ɪn'sʌlt] ⟨ze⟩lżyć, znieważać ⟨-żyć⟩

in·sur|·ance [ɪn'ʃɔːrəns] ubezpieczenie *n*; ~**ance com·pa·ny** firma *f* ubezpieczeniowa; ~**ance pol·i·cy** polisa *f* ubezpieczeniowa; ~**e** [ɪn'ʃɔː] ubezpieczać ⟨-czyć⟩ (***against*** przeciwko *D*); ~**ed**: ***the*** ~***ed*** ubezpieczony *m* (-na *f*)

in·sur·gent [ɪn'sɜːdʒənt] **1.** powstańczy; **2.** powstaniec *m*

in·sur·moun·ta·ble [ɪnsə'maʊntəbl] niepokonany

in·sur·rec·tion [ɪnsə'rekʃn] powstanie *n*

in·tact [ɪn'tækt] nietknięty; nienaruszony

'**in·take** *tech*. wlot *m*; miejsce *n* poboru; pobór *m*; spożycie *n*, zużycie *n*; nabór *m*

in·te·gral ['ɪntɪgrəl] integralny, cały

in·te|·grate ['ɪntɪgreɪt] ⟨z⟩integrować (się); scalać ⟨-lić⟩, ⟨z-, po⟩łączyć w całość; ~***grated circuit*** układ *m* scalony; ~·**gra·tion** [ɪntɪ'greɪʃn] integracja *f*; scalenie *n*

in·teg·ri·ty [ɪn'tegrətɪ] integralność *f*; prawość *f*

in·tel|·lect ['ɪntəlekt] intelekt *m*, inteligencja *f*; ~·**lec·tual** [ɪntə'lektjʊəl] **1.** intelektualny; **2.** intelektualista *m* (-tka *f*)

in·tel·li|·gence [ɪn'telɪdʒəns] inteligencja *f*; *mil*. wywiad *m*; ~·**gent** inteligentny

in·tel·li·gi·ble [ɪn'telɪdʒəbl] zrozumiały (***to*** dla *G*)

in·tem·per·ate [ɪn'tempərət] nieumiarkowany

in·tend [ɪn'tend] zamierzać, planować, mieć zamiar; ~***ed for*** przeznaczony dla (*G*)

in·tense [ɪn'tens] intensywny, silny

in·ten·si|·fy [ɪn'tensɪfaɪ] ⟨z⟩intensyfikować; stawać się silniejszym; ~·**ty** [ɪn'tensətɪ] intensywność *f*

in·ten·sive [ɪn'tensɪv] intensywny; ~ '**care u·nit** oddział *m* intensywnej terapii

in·tent [ɪn'tent] **1.** zdeterminowany; ~ ***on doing s.th.*** zdecydowany na zrobienie czegoś; skoncentrowany; **2.** intencja *f*; **in·ten·tion** [ɪn'tenʃn] zamiar *m*; *jur*. intencja *f*, cel *m*; **in·ten·tion·al** [ɪn'tenʃənl] celowy, intencjonalny

in·ter [ɪn'tɜː] (*-rr-*) ⟨po⟩chować, ⟨po⟩grzebać

in·ter... ['ɪntə] inter..., między...

in·ter·act [ɪntər'ækt] współdziałać, wzajemnie oddziaływać; wchodzić ⟨wejść⟩ w interakcje

in·ter·cede [ɪntə'siːd] wstawiać ⟨-wić⟩ się (***with*** u *G*, ***for*** za *A*)

in·ter|·cept [ɪntə'sept] przechwytywać ⟨-wycić⟩; ~·**cep·tion** [ɪntə'sepʃn] przechwycenie *n*

in·ter·ces·sion [ɪntə'seʃn] wstawiennictwo *n*

in·ter·change 1. [ɪntə'tʃeɪndʒ] wymieniać ⟨-nić⟩ (się); **2.** ['ɪntətʃeɪndʒ] wymiana *f*; *mot.* (*na autostradzie*) skrzyżowanie *n*

in·ter·com ['ɪntəkɒm] interkom *m*; domofon *m*

in·ter·course ['ɪntəkɔːs] stosunek *m*; ***sexual ~*** stosunek *m* płciowy

in·terest ['ɪntrɪst] **1.** zainteresowanie *n*; interes *m*; korzyść *f*; znaczenie *n*, ważność *f*; *econ.* udział *m*; *econ.* odsetki *pl.*, procent *m*; ***take an ~ in*** zainteresować się (*D*); **2.** ⟨za⟩interesować się; **'~·ed** zainteresowany; ***be ~ed in*** interesować się (*D*); **'~·ing** interesujący; **'~ rate** *econ.* stopa *f* procentowa

in·ter·face ['ɪntəfeɪs] *komp.* interface *m lub* interfejs *m*

in·ter|·fere [ɪntə'fɪə] ⟨w⟩mieszać się, wtrącać ⟨-cić⟩ się (***with*** do *G*); ingerować; przeszkadzać; **~·fer·ence** [ɪntə'fɪərəns] wtrącanie *n* się; przeszkadzanie *n*; ingerencja *f*; *tech.* interferencja *f*

in·te·ri·or [ɪn'tɪərɪə] **1.** wewnętrzny; **2.** wnętrze *n*; wnętrze kraju; *pol.* sprawy *pl.* wewnętrzne; → ***Department of the*** ♀; **~ 'dec·o·ra·tor** architekt *m* wnętrz

in·ter|·ject [ɪntə'dʒekt] wykrzyknąć ⟨-rzyczeć⟩; **~·jec·tion** [ɪntə'dʒekʃn] wykrzyknięcie *n*; wtrącenie *n*; *ling.* wykrzyknik *m*

in·ter·lace [ɪntə'leɪs] przeplatać ⟨-leść⟩ (się)

in·ter·lock [ɪntə'lɒk] sczepiać ⟨-pić⟩ (się), łączyć (się)

in·ter·lop·er ['ɪntələʊpə] intruz *m*, natręt *m*

in·ter·lude ['ɪntəluːd] interludium *n*, intermedium *n*; przerwa *f* (*też fig.*), antrakt *m*

in·ter·me·di|·a·ry [ɪntə'miːdjərɪ] pośrednik *m* (-niczka *f*); **~·ate** [ɪntə'miːdjət] pośredni

in·ter·ment [ɪn'tɜːmənt] pochówek *m*, pogrzebanie *n*

in·ter·mi·na·ble [ɪn'tɜːmɪnəbl] niekończący się

in·ter·mis·sion [ɪntə'mɪʃn] przerwa *f* (*też Am. theat.*)

in·ter·mit·tent [ɪntə'mɪtənt] przerywany, periodyczny; **~ *fever*** *med.* gorączka *f* przerywana

in·tern[1] [ɪn'tɜːn] internować

in·tern[2] ['ɪntɜːn] *Am.* lekarz *m* (-arka *f*) stażysta (-tka)

in·ter·nal [ɪn'tɜːnl] wewnętrzny; krajowy; **~-com'bus·tion en·gine** silnik *m* spalinowy

in·ter·na·tion·al [ɪntə'næʃənl] **1.** międzynarodowy; **2.** (*w sporcie*) spotkanie *n* międzypaństwowe; **~ 'call** *tel.* rozmowa *f* międzynarodowa; **~ 'law** *jur.* prawo *n* międzynarodowe

in·ter|·pret [ɪn'tɜːprɪt] ⟨z⟩interpretować; wyjaśniać ⟨-nić⟩, ⟨wy⟩tłumaczyć; ⟨prze⟩tłumaczyć (*ustnie*); **~·pre·tation** [ɪntɜːprɪ'teɪʃn] interpretacja *f*; wytłumaczenie *n*; **~·pret·er** [ɪn'tɜːprɪtə] tłumacz *m* (*tekstów ustnych*)

in·ter·ro|·gate [ɪn'terəgeɪt] przesłuchiwać ⟨-chać⟩, indagować; **~·ga·tion** [ɪnterə'geɪʃn] przesłuchanie *n*; wypytywanie *n* się; **~'ga·tion mark** → ***question mark***

in·ter·rog·a·tive [ɪntə'rɒgətɪv] *gr.* pytajny

in·ter|·rupt [ɪntə'rʌpt] przerywać ⟨-rwać⟩; **~·rup·tion** [ɪntə'rʌpʃn] przerwanie *n*

in·ter|·sect [ɪntə'sekt] przecinać ⟨-ciąć⟩ się; **~·sec·tion** [ɪntə'sekʃn] przecięcie *n*; miejsce *n* przecięcia; skrzyżowanie *n*

in·ter·sperse [ɪntə'spɜːs] rozsiewać ⟨-siać⟩, rozrzucić ⟨-cać⟩ (***among*** pomiędzy *A*); przeplatać się (*o okresach pogody*)

in·ter·state [ɪntə'steɪt] *Am.* międzystanowy; **~ *highway*** autostrada *f* (*łącząca kilka stanów*)

in·ter·twine [ɪntə'twaɪn] ⟨s⟩platać (się)

in·ter·val ['ɪntəvl] przerwa *f*; odstęp *m* (czasu); interwał *m* (*też mus.*); *Brt.* antrakt *m*; ***at ~s of 5 inches, at 5-inch ~s*** co 5 cali; ***sunny ~*** przejaśnienie *n*

in·ter|·vene [ɪntə'viːn] ⟨za⟩interweniować, ⟨za⟩ingerować; stawać ⟨stanąć⟩ na przeszkodzie; **~·ven·tion** [ɪntə'venʃn] interwencja *f*, ingerencja *f*

in·ter·view ['ɪntəvjuː] **1.** wywiad *m*; rozmowa *f* (*zwł. kwalifikacyjna*); **2.** przeprowadzać ⟨-dzić⟩ wywiad *lub* rozmowę; **~·ee** [ɪntəvjuː'iː] osoba *f*, z którą przeprowadza się wywiad *lub* rozmowę; **~·er** ['ɪntəvjuːə] osoba *f* przeprowadzająca wywiad *lub* rozmowę

in·ter·weave [ɪntə'wiːv] (***-wove, -woven***) przeplatać ⟨-leść⟩ (się)

in·tes·tate [ɪn'testeɪt] *jur.*: ***die ~*** um-

rzeć bez pozostawienia testamentu
in·tes·tine [ɪn'testɪn] *anat.* jelito *n*; **~s** *pl.* wnętrzności *pl.*; ***large ~*** jelito *n* grube; ***small ~*** jelito *n* cienkie
in·ti·ma·cy ['ɪntɪməsɪ] poufałość *f*, bliskość *f*; stosunek *m* intymny
in·ti·mate ['ɪntɪmət] **1.** intymny; *przyjaciel*: bliski; kameralny; *wiedza*: gruntowny; **2.** powiernik *m* (-nica *f*), zausznik *m* (-iczka *f*)
in·tim·i|·date [ɪn'tɪmɪdeɪt] zastraszać ⟨-szyć⟩; **~·da·tion** [ɪntɪmɪ'deɪʃn] zastraszenie *n*
in·to ['ɪntʊ, 'ɪntə] do (*G*); w (*L*); *rozbić itp.* na (*A*); ***three ~ six is two*** sześć (*dzielone*) przez trzy to dwa
in·tol·e·ra·ble [ɪn'tɒlərəbl] nie do wytrzymania, nie do zniesienia
in·tol·e|·rance [ɪn'tɒlərəns] nietolerancja *f*, brak *m* tolerancji (***of*** na *A*); **~·rant** nietolerancyjny, nie tolerujący
in·to·na·tion [ɪntəʊ'neɪʃn] *mus.*, *gr.* intonacja *f*
in·tox·i|·cat·ed [ɪn'tɒksɪkeɪtɪd] nietrzeźwy; ***be ~cated*** być w stanie upojenia alkoholowego; **~·ca·tion** [ɪntɒksɪ'keɪʃn] nietrzeźwość *f*, rausz *m*; stan *m* upojenia alkoholowego; oszołomienie *n*, podniecenie *n* (*też fig.*)
in·trac·ta·ble [ɪn'træktəbl] nie do rozwiązania; nieustępliwy
in·tran·si·tive [ɪn'trænsətɪv] *gr.* nieprzechodni
in·tra·ve·nous [ɪntrə'viːnəs] *med.* dożylny
'in tray: ***in the ~*** w poczcie przychodzącej
in·trep·id [ɪn'trepɪd] nieustraszony, nieulękły
in·tri·cate ['ɪntrɪkət] zawiły, skomplikowany
in·trigue [ɪn'triːg] **1.** intryga *f*; **2.** ⟨za⟩intrygować, ⟨z⟩fascynować
in·tro|·duce [ɪntrə'djuːs] wprowadzać ⟨-dzić⟩ (***to*** do *G*); *kogoś* przedstawiać; **~·duc·tion** [ɪntrə'dʌkʃn] wprowadzenie *n*, przedstawienie *n*; ***letter of ~duction*** list *m* polecający; **~·duc·to·ry** [ɪntrə'dʌktərɪ] wstępny
in·tro·spec|·tion [ɪntrəʊ'spekʃn] introspekcja *f*, samoobserwacja *f*; **~·tive** [ɪntrəʊ'spektɪv] introspekcyjny
in·tro·vert ['ɪntrəʊvɜːt] *psych.* introwertyk *m* (-yczka *f*); '**~·ed** introwertyczny, introwersyjny, zamknięty w sobie
in·trude [ɪn'truːd] wtrącać ⟨-cić⟩ (się), przeszkadzać ⟨-kodzić⟩ (***on s.o.*** komuś); ***am I intruding?*** czy przeszkadzam?; **in'trud·er** intruz *m*, natręt *m*;
in·tru·sion [ɪn'truːʒn] najście *n*, wtargnięcie *n*; **in·tru·sive** [ɪn'truːsɪv] natrętny, niepożądany
in·tu·i|·tion [ɪntjuː'ɪʃn] intuicja *f*; **~·tive** [ɪn'tjuːɪtɪv] intuicyjny
in·un·date ['ɪnʌndeɪt] zalewać ⟨-lać⟩, zatapiać ⟨-topić⟩
in·vade [ɪn'veɪd] naruszać ⟨-szyć⟩, zakłócać ⟨-cić⟩; *mil.* najeżdżać ⟨-jechać⟩ na (*A*), dokonywać ⟨-nać⟩ inwazji (*G*); *fig.* nachodzić ⟨najść⟩, nękać; **~r** najeźdźca *m*
in·va·lid[1] ['ɪnvəlɪd] **1.** niesprawny, ułomny; **2.** inwalida *m* (-dka *f*); kaleka *m*/*f*
in·val·id[2] [ɪn'vælɪd] *jur.* nieprawomocny, nie posiadający mocy prawnej
in·val·u·a·ble [ɪn'væljʊəbl] nieoceniony
in·var·i·a|·ble [ɪn'veərɪəbl] niezmienny; **~·bly** niezmiennie; zawsze
in·va·sion [ɪn'veɪʒn] inwazja *f* (*też mil.*), wtargnięcie *n*, najazd *m*
in·vec·tive [ɪn'vektɪv] inwektywa *f*, obelga *f*
in·vent [ɪn'vent] wynajdywać ⟨-naleźć⟩; zmyślać ⟨-lić⟩; **in·ven·tion** [ɪn'venʃn] wynalazek *m*; **in·ven·tive** [ɪn'ventɪv] pomysłowy, pełen inwencji; **in·ven·tor** [ɪn'ventə] wynalazca *m*; **in·ven·tory** ['ɪnvəntrɪ] spis *m*, inwentarz *m*
in·verse [ɪn'vɜːs] **1.** odwrotny; **2.** odwrotność *f*, **in·ver·sion** [ɪn'vɜːʃn] odwrócenie *n*, inwersja *f*
in·vert [ɪn'vɜːt] odwracać ⟨-rócić⟩; **~·ed 'com·mas** *pl.* cudzysłów *m*
in·ver·te·brate [ɪn'vɜːtɪbrət] *zo.* **1.** bezkręgowy; **2.** bezkręgowiec *m*
in·vest [ɪn'vest] ⟨za⟩inwestować
in·ves·ti|·gate [ɪn'vestɪgeɪt] ⟨z⟩badać; ⟨po⟩prowadzić dochodzenie (***into*** w sprawie *G*); **~·ga·tion** [ɪnvestɪ'geɪʃn] dochodzenie *n*; **~·ga·tor** [ɪn'vestɪgeɪtə]: ***private ~gator*** prywatny detektyw *m*
in·vest·ment [ɪn'vestmənt] *econ.* inwestycja *f*; inwestowanie *n*; lokata *f*, nakład *m*; **in'ves·tor** *econ.* inwestor *m*

in·vet·e·rate [ɪn'vetərət] niepoprawny; uporczywy; zagorzały
in·vid·i·ous [ɪn'vɪdɪəs] krzywdzący; *zadanie*: niewdzięczny
in·vig·o·rate [ɪn'vɪgəreɪt] ożywiać ⟨-wić⟩, orzeźwiać ⟨-wić⟩
in·vin·ci·ble [ɪn'vɪnsəbl] niepokonany, niezwyciężony
in·vis·i·ble [ɪn'vɪzəbl] niewidzialny
in·vi·ta·tion [ɪnvɪ'teɪʃn] zaproszenie *n*; wezwanie *n*; **in·vite** [ɪn'vaɪt] zapraszać ⟨-rosić⟩; poprosić o (*A*); zachęcać do (*G*); **in'vit·ing** wabiący, kuszący
in·voice ['ɪnvɔɪs] *econ.* **1.** faktura *f*; **2.** wystawiać ⟨-wić⟩ fakturę; ⟨za⟩fakturować
in·voke [ɪn'vəʊk] wzywać; powoływać się na (*A*); przywoływać ⟨-łać⟩; błagać o (*A*)
in·vol·un·ta·ry [ɪn'vɒləntərɪ] mimowolny
in·volve [ɪn'vɒlv] *kogoś* uwikływać ⟨-kłać⟩, wplątywać ⟨-tać⟩ (***in*** w *L*); dotyczyć (*G*), tyczyć się (*G*); obejmować ⟨objąć⟩; odnosić się do (*G*); **~d** zawiły; ***be ~d with s.o.*** być związanym z kimś; **~·ment** wplątanie *n*, uwikłanie *n*; wmieszanie *n*; zaangażowanie *n*
in·vul·ne·ra·ble [ɪn'vʌlnərəbl] nie do zranienia; *fig* odporny
in·ward ['ɪnwəd] **1.** wewnętrzny, intymny; **2.** *adv.*: *zw.* **~s** do środka, do wewnątrz
I/O [aɪ 'əʊ] *skrót*: ***input/output*** *komp.* wejście/wyjście (*danych*)
IOC [aɪ əʊ 'siː] *skrót*: ***International Olympic Committee*** MKOl, Międzynarodowy Komitet *m* Olimpijski
i·o·dine ['aɪədiːn] *chem.* jod *m*; jodyna *f*
i·on ['aɪən] *phys.* jon *m*
IOU [aɪ əʊ 'juː] *skrót*: ***I owe you*** skrypt *m* dłużny
IQ [aɪ 'kjuː] *skrót*: ***intelligence quotient*** IQ, iloraz *m* inteligencji
IRA [aɪ ɑːr 'eɪ] *skrót*: ***Irish Republican Army*** IRA, Irlandzka Armia *f* Republikańska
I·ran [ɪ'rɑːn] Iran *m*; **I·ra·ni·an** [ɪ'reɪnjən] **1.** irański; **2.** Irańczyk *m* (*Iranka f*); *ling.* język *m* irański
I·raq [ɪ'rɑːk] Irak *m*; **I·ra·qi** [ɪ'rɑːkɪ] **1.** iracki; **2.** Irakijczyk *m* (-jka *f*)
i·ras·ci·ble [ɪ'ræsəbl] drażliwy, porywczy
i·rate [aɪ'reɪt] rozjątrzony
Ire·land ['aɪələnd] Irlandia *f*
ir·i·des·cent [ɪrɪ'desnt] opalizujący
i·ris ['aɪərɪs] *anat.* tęczówka *f*; *bot.* irys *m*, kosaciec *m*
I·rish ['aɪərɪʃ] irlandzki; ***the ~*** *pl.* Irlandczycy *pl.*; **'~·man** (*pl.* ***-men***) Irlandczyk *m*; **'~·wom·an** (*pl.* ***-women***) Irlandka *f*
irk·some ['ɜːksəm] drażniący
i·ron ['aɪən] **1.** żelazo *ni*; żelazko *n*; ***strike while the ~ is hot*** kuć żelazo, póki gorące; **2.** żelazny; **3.** ⟨u-, wy⟩prasować; **~ *out*** rozprasowywać ⟨-ować⟩; *fig.* rozwiązywać ⟨-zać⟩; ≗ **'Cur·tain** *pol. hist.* żelazna kurtyna *f*
i·ron·ic [aɪ'rɒnɪk] (**~*ally***), **i·ron·i·cal** [aɪ'rɒnɪkl] ironiczny
'i·ron·ing board deska *f* do prasowania
i·ron|'lung *med.* sztuczne płuca *pl.*; **~·mon·ger** *Brt.* ['aɪənmʌŋgə] handlarz *m* (-arka *f*) towarami żelaznymi, właściciel(ka *f*) *m* sklepu z towarami żelaznymi; **'~·works** *sg.* huta *f* żelaza
i·ron·y ['aɪərənɪ] ironia *f*
ir·ra·tion·al [ɪ'ræʃənl] irracjonalny, mało racjonalny
ir·rec·on·ci·la·ble [ɪ'rekənsaɪləbl] nie do pogodzenia; nieprzejednany
ir·re·cov·e·ra·ble [ɪrɪ'kʌvərəbl] nie do odzyskania; niepowetowany
ir·reg·u·lar [ɪ'regjʊlə] nieprawidłowy; nieregularny
ir·rel·e·vant [ɪ'reləvənt] nieistotny (***to*** dla *G*)
ir·rep·a·ra·ble [ɪ'repərəbl] nie do naprawienia; niepowetowany
ir·re·place·a·ble [ɪrɪ'pleɪsəbl] niezastąpiony
ir·re·pres·si·ble [ɪrɪ'presəbl] niepowstrzymany, niepohamowany, niekontrolowany
ir·re·proa·cha·ble [ɪrɪ'prəʊtʃəbl] nienaganny, bez zarzutu
ir·re·sis·ti·ble [ɪrɪ'zɪstəbl] nieodparty; fascynujący
ir·res·o·lute [ɪ'rezəluːt] niezdecydowany, niepewny
ir·re·spec·tive [ɪrɪ'spektɪv]: **~ *of*** niezależnie od (*G*), bez względu na (*A*)
ir·re·spon·si·ble [ɪrɪ'spɒnsəbl] nieodpowiedzialny; lekkomyślny
ir·re·trie·va·ble [ɪrɪ'triːvəbl] nie do odzyskania

ir·rev·e·rent [ɪ'revərənt] bez szacunku, lekceważący
ir·rev·o·ca·ble [ɪ'revəkəbl] nie do odwołania, nieodwołalny
ir·ri|·gate ['ɪrɪgeɪt] nawadniać ⟨-wodnić⟩, ⟨z⟩irygować; **~·ga·tion** [ɪrɪ'geɪʃn] nawodnienie *n*, irygacja *f* (*też med.*)
ir·ri|·ta·ble ['ɪrɪtəbl] drażliwy; **~·tant** ['ɪrɪtənt] środek *m* drażniący; **~·tate** ['ɪrɪteɪt] ⟨roz⟩drażnić; *med.* ⟨po⟩drażnić; **'~·tat·ing** drażniący; irytujący; **~·ta·tion** [ɪrɪ'teɪʃn] irytacja *f*, rozdrażnienie *n*; podrażnienie *n*; gniew *m* (**at** na *A*)
is [ɪz] *on, ona, ono* jest
ISBN [aɪ es biː 'en] *skrót*: ***International Standard Book Number*** ISBN, Międzynarodowy Standardowy Numer *m* Książki
Is·lam ['ɪzlɑːm] islam *m*
is·land ['aɪlənd] wyspa *f*; *też* ***traffic ~*** (*na ulicy*) wysepka *f*; **'~·er** wyspiarz *m*
isle [aɪl] *poet.* wyspa *f*, ostrów *m*
i·so|·late ['aɪsəleɪt] izolować; *kogoś* odizolowywać ⟨-wać⟩; *coś* wyizolowywać ⟨-wać⟩; **'~·lat·ed** osamotniony, odosobniony; ⚠ *nie* ***izolowany***; **~·lation** [aɪsə'leɪʃn] izolacja *f*, odseparowanie *n*; **~'la·tion ward** *med.* izolatka *f*
Is·rael ['ɪzreɪəl] Izrael *m*; **Is·rae·li** [ɪz'reɪlɪ] **1.** izraelski; *hist.* izraelicki; **2.** Izraelczyk (-ka *f*), *hist.* Izraelita *m* (-tka *f*)
is·sue ['ɪʃuː] **1.** zagadnienie *n*; sporna kwestia *f*; numer *m* (*czasopisma*); wydanie *n* (*czasopisma*); *jur.* spór *m*, zagadnienie *n*; potomstwo *n*; ***be at ~*** być przedmiotem sporu; ***point at ~*** kwestia *f* sporna; ***die without ~*** umrzeć bez potomstwa; **2.** *v/t. czasopismo, dokument* wydawać ⟨-dać⟩; *banknoty* ⟨wy⟩emitować; *v/i.* wynikać ⟨-knąć⟩; wypływać ⟨-łynąć⟩
it [ɪt] to; ono, jego, jemu
I·tal·i·an [ɪ'tæljən] **1.** włoski; **2.** Włoch *m*, Włoszka *f*; *ling.* język *m* włoski
i·tal·ics [ɪ'tælɪks] *print.* kursywa *f*
It·a·ly ['ɪtəlɪ] Włochy *pl.*
itch [ɪtʃ] **1.** swędzenie *n*; **2.** ⟨za⟩swędzieć; ***I ~ all over*** wszędzie mnie swędzi; ***be ~ing for s.th.*** F strasznie czegoś chcieć; ***be ~ing to do s.th.*** F mieć chęć coś zrobić; **'~·y** swędzący
i·tem ['aɪtəm] punkt *m* (*porządku dziennego*), (*na liście*) pozycja *f*; przedmiot *m*, rzecz *f*; wiadomość *f*; *prasowa* informacja *f*; *jur.* klauzula *f*, paragraf *m*; **~·ize** ['aɪtəmaɪz] wyszczególniać ⟨-nić⟩, wyliczać ⟨-czyć⟩
i·tin·e·ra·ry [aɪ'tɪnərərɪ] trasa *f* podróży, marszruta *f*, droga *f*
its [ɪts] jego
it's [ɪts] *skrót*: ***it is***; ***it has***
it·self [ɪt'self] się, sobie, siebie; ***by ~*** sam, bez pomocy; ***in ~*** samo w sobie
ITV [aɪ tiː 'viː] *skrót*: ***Independent Television*** ITV (*niezależna brytyjska komercyjna stacja TV*)
I've [aɪv] *skrót*: ***I have***
i·vo·ry ['aɪvərɪ] kość *f* słoniowa
i·vy ['aɪvɪ] *bot.* bluszcz *m*

J

J, j [dʒeɪ] J, j *n*
J *skrót pisany*: ***joule(s)*** J, dżul *m lub* joule *m*
jab [dʒæb] **1.** (***-bb-***) żgać ⟨żgnąć⟩, dźgać ⟨dźgnąć⟩; **2.** dźgnięcie *n*, żgnięcie *n*, pchnięcie *n*
jab·ber ['dʒæbə] paplać, trajkotać
jack [dʒæk] **1.** *tech.* podnośnik *m*; walet *m* (*w kartach*)
jack·al ['dʒækɔːl] *zo.* szakal *m*
jack|·ass ['dʒækæs] *zo.* osioł *m* (*też fig.*); **'~·boots** *pl.* wysokie buty *pl.* wojskowe; **'~·daw** *zo.* kawka *f*
jack·et ['dʒækɪt] marynarka *f*; kurtka *f*; żakiet *m*; *tech.* płaszcz *m*, osłona *f*; obwoluta *f*; *Am.* koperta *f* (*płyty*); ***~ potatoes*** *pl.*, ***potatoes (boiled) in their ~s*** *pl. Brt.* ziemniaki *pl.* w mundurkach
jack| knife ['dʒæknaɪf] **1.** (*pl.* ***-knives***) scyzoryk *m*; **2.** składać ⟨złożyć⟩ się (*jak scyzoryk*); **~-of-'all-trades** majster-klepka *m*; **'~·pot** główna wygrana *f*; ***hit the ~pot*** wygrać główną wy-

J

graną; *fig.* wygrać główny los na loterii, zgarnąć pulę
jag [dʒæg] szczerba *f*, wyszczerbienie *n*; **~·ged** ['dʒægɪd] wyszczerbiony; poszarpany
jag·u·ar ['dʒægjʊə] *zo.* jaguar *m*
jail [dʒeɪl] **1.** więzienie *n*; **2.** ⟨u⟩więzić; '**~·bird** F wyrokowiec *m*, kryminalista *m* (-tka *f*); '**~·er** strażnik *m* (-niczka *f*) więzienny (-a); '**~·house** *Am.* więzienie *n*
jam¹ [dʒæm] dżem *m*
jam² [dʒæm] **1.** (**-mm-**) *v/t.* ściskać ⟨-snąć⟩, wciskać ⟨-snąć⟩, wtłaczać ⟨-łoczyć⟩; *też ludzi* wpychać ⟨wepchnąć⟩; *też* **~ up** ⟨za⟩blokować, zatykać ⟨-tkać⟩; *radio* zagłuszać ⟨-szyć⟩; **~ on the brakes** *mot.* nagle zahamować; *v/i.* wtłaczać ⟨-łoczyć⟩ się, wpychać ⟨wepchać⟩ się; *tech.* zakleszczać ⟨-czyć⟩ się, ⟨za⟩-blokować się; **2.** tłok *m*, ścisk *m*; *tech.* blokada *f*, zakleszczenie *n*; zator *m*; **traffic ~** korek *m*; **be in a ~** F mieć kłopoty
Ja·mai·ca [dʒə'meɪkə] Jamajka *f*; **Jamai·can** [dʒə'meɪkən] **1.** *adj.* jamajski; **2.** Jamajczyk *m* (-jka *f*)
jamb [dʒæm] ościeże *n*
jam·bo·ree [dʒæmbə'riː] *mus.* jamboree *n*; mityng *m*
Jan *skrót pisany*: **January** stycz., styczeń *m*
jan·gle ['dʒæŋgl] ⟨za⟩brzęczeć; *fig.* zgrzytać ⟨-tnąć⟩
jan·i·tor ['dʒænɪtə] *Am.* dozorca *m* (-czyni *f*); (*w szkole*) woźny *m* (-na *f*)
Jan·u·a·ry ['dʒænjʊərɪ] (*skrót*: **Jan**) styczeń *m*; *attr.* styczniowy
Ja·pan [dʒə'pæn] Japonia *f*; **Jap·a·nese** [dʒæpə'niːz] **1.** japoński; **2.** Japończyk *m* (-onka *f*); *ling.* język *m* japoński; **the ~** *pl.* Japończycy *pl.*
jar¹ [dʒɑː] słój *m*, słoik *m*;
jar² [dʒɑː] (**-rr-**): **~ on** *barwa*: być krzykliwym; *zapach*: drażnić
jar·gon ['dʒɑːgən] żargon *m*, odmiana *f* środowiskowa
jaun·dice ['dʒɔːndɪs] *med.* żółtaczka *f*
jaunt [dʒɔːnt] **1.** wycieczka *f*, eskapada *f*; **2.** wyjeżdżać ⟨-jechać⟩ na wycieczkę
jaun·ty ['dʒɔːntɪ] (**-ier, -iest**) rzutki, żwawy
jav·e·lin ['dʒævlɪn] (*w sporcie*) oszczep *m*; **~ (throw), throwing the ~** rzut *m* oszczepem; **~ thrower** oszczepnik *m* (-niczka *f*)
jaw [dʒɔː] *anat.*, *tech.* szczęka *f*, **lower** (**upper**) **~** dolna (górna) szczęka *f*; **~s** *pl. zo.* pysk *m*, zęby *pl.*; '**~·bone** *anat.* kość *f* szczękowa
jay [dʒeɪ] *zo.* sójka *f*; '**~·walk** nieprawidłowo przechodzić ⟨przejść⟩ przez jezdnię; '**~·walk·er** osoba *f* nieprawidłowo przechodząca przez jezdnię
jazz [dʒæz] *mus.* jazz *m*
jeal·ous ['dʒeləs] zawistny (**of** o *A*); zazdrosny; '**~·y** zawiść *f*; zazdrość *f*
jeans [dʒiːnz] *pl.* dżinsy *pl.*
jeep [dʒiːp] *TM* dżip *m*, jeep *m*
jeer [dʒɪə] **1.** (**at**) wyśmiewać ⟨-miać⟩ się (z *A*); drwić (z *A*); szydzić (z *A*); **2.** szyderstwo *n*; drwina *f*
jel·lied ['dʒelɪd] w galarecie
jel·ly ['dʒelɪ] galareta *f*; galaretka *f*; '**~ ba·by** *Brt.* F cukierek *m* z żelatyny, żelatynka *f*; '**~ bean** cukierek *m* z żelatyny, żelatynka *f*; '**~·fish** *zo.* (*pl.* **-fish, -fishes**) meduza *f*
jeop·ar|·dize ['dʒepədaɪz] zagrażać ⟨-rozić⟩; narażać ⟨-razić⟩ na niebezpieczeństwo; '**~·dy** niebezpieczeństwo *n*, zagrożenie *n*
jerk [dʒɜːk] **1.** szarpać ⟨-pnąć⟩ (się); wzdrygnąć się; **2.** szarpnięcie *n*; *med.* odruch *m*; '**~·y** (**-ier, -iest**) szarpany; nierówny; trzęsący
Je·rusa·lem Jerozolima *f*
jer·sey ['dʒɜːzɪ] pulower *m*
jest [dʒest] **1.** żart *m*; **2.** ⟨za⟩żartować; '**~·er** *hist.* trefniś *m*, wesołek *m*
jet [dʒet] **1.** strumień *m*, struga *f*; *tech.* dysza *f*, rozpylacz *m*; *aviat.* odrzutowiec *m*; **2.** (**-tt-**) wytryskać ⟨-snąć⟩, tryskać ⟨-snąć⟩ strumieniem (**from** z *G*); *aviat.* F latać odrzutowcami; **~ 'en·gine** silnik *m* odrzutowy; '**~ lag** (*zaburzenia organizmu spowodowane nagłą zmianą rytmu dobowego po długiej podróży samolotem*); '**~ plane** odrzutowiec *m*; **~-pro'pelled** odrzutowy; napędzany silnikiem odrzutowym; **~ pro'pul·sion** napęd *m* odrzutowy; '**~ set** elita *f* towarzyska, high life *m*; '**~-set·ter** członek *m* elity towarzyskiej
jet·ty ['dʒetɪ] *naut.* nabrzeże *n*; pomost *m*, pirs *m*
Jew [dʒuː] Żyd *m*
jew·el ['dʒuːəl] klejnot *m*, kamień *m*

szlachetny; **'jew·eler** *Am.*, **'jew·el·ler** *Brt.* jubiler *m*; **jew·el·lery** *Brt.*, **jew·elry** *Am.* ['dʒuːəlrɪ] biżuteria *f*
Jew|·ess ['dʒuːɪs] Żydówka *f*; **'~·ish** żydowski
jif·fy ['dʒɪfɪ]: ***in a ~*** za chwileczkę
jig·saw ['dʒɪgsɔː] *tech.* wyrzynarka *f*, F piła *f* włosowa, laubzega *f*; → ***saw***; **'~ puz·zle** puzzle *m*, układanka *f*
jilt [dʒɪlt] porzucać ⟨-cić⟩
jin·gle ['dʒɪŋgl] **1.** podzwaniać, dzwonić; **2.** podzwanianie *n*, pobrzękiwanie *n*; melodyjka *f*
jit·ters ['dʒɪtəz] F *pl.*: ***the ~*** zdenerwowanie *n*, trema *f*
Jnr *skrót pisany*: ***Junior*** jr., junior; młodszy
job [dʒɒb] **1.** praca *f*; zajęcie *n*; miejsce *n* pracy; trudne zadanie *n*; *komp.* zadanie *n*; *też* ***~ work*** praca *f* na akord; ***by the ~*** na akord; ***out of a ~*** bez pracy; **2.** ***~ around*** szukać pracy; **'~ ad**, **~ ad'ver·tise·ment** ogłoszenie *n* o pracy; **'~·ber** *Brt.* makler *m*; spekulant *m* giełdowy; **'~ cen·tre** *Brt.* urząd *m* zatrudnienia; **'~ hop·ping** *Am.* częste zmiany *pl.* miejsca pracy; **'~·hunt·ing** poszukiwanie *n* pracy; **'~·less** bez pracy, bezrobotny; **'~·shar·ing** dzielenie *n* się etatem, podział *m* etatu (*między pracowników niepełnoetatowych*)
jock·ey ['dʒɒkɪ] dżokej *m*
jog [dʒɒg] **1.** potrącać ⟨-cić⟩; ***~ along, ~ on*** ⟨po⟩truchtać; biegać, biec; (*w sporcie*) uprawiać jogging; **2.** potrącenie *n*; bieg *m*; przebieżka *f*; **'~·ger** (*w sporcie*) osoba *f* uprawiająca jogging; **'~·ging** jogging *m*
join [dʒɔɪn] **1.** *v/t.* ⟨z-, po⟩łączyć; dołączać ⟨-czyć⟩, przyłączać ⟨-czyć⟩; dołączać ⟨-czyć⟩ się do (*G*), przyłączać ⟨-czyć⟩ się do (*G*); wstępować ⟨-tąpić⟩ do (*G*); łączyć się z (*I*); *v/i.* dołączać ⟨-czyć⟩, przyłączać ⟨-czyć⟩; łączyć się; ***~ in*** brać ⟨wziąć⟩ udział, przyłączać ⟨-czyć⟩; **2.** miejsce *n* złączenia; złączenie *n*; **'~·er** stolarz *m*
joint [dʒɔɪnt] **1.** miejsce *n* złączenia, połączenie *n*, spoina *f*; *anat.* staw *m*; *tech.* złącze *n*; *bot.* kolanko *n*; *Brt. gastr.* pieczeń *f*; *sl.* knajpa *f*, speluna *f*; *sl.* skręt *m* (*marihuany itp.*); ***out of ~*** zwichnięty; *fig.* wypaść z kolein; **2.** połączony; łączny; wspólny; współ...; **'~·ed** przegubowy; ruchomy; **~-'stock com·pa·ny** *Brt.* spółka *f* akcyjna; **~ 'ven·ture** *econ.* joint venture
joke [dʒəʊk] **1.** dowcip *m*, kawał *m*; żart *m*; ***practical ~*** kawał *m*, figiel *m*; ***play a ~ on s.o.*** zrobić komuś kawał; **2.** ⟨za⟩żartować; dowcipkować; **'jok·er** dowcipniś *m*, kawalarz *m*; (*w kartach*) dżoker *m*, joker *m*
jol·ly ['dʒɒlɪ] **1.** *adj.* (***-ier, -iest***) wesoły, radosny; **2.** *adv. Brt.* F okropnie, bardzo; ***~ good*** znakomicie
jolt [dʒəʊlt] **1.** potrząsnąć; trząść; *fig.* wstrząsnąć; **2.** trzęsienie *n*, wstrząsanie *n*; *fig.* szok *m*
jos·tle ['dʒɒsl] popychać ⟨-chnąć⟩, szarpać ⟨-pnąć⟩
jot [dʒɒt] **1.** ***not a ~*** ani krztyny; **2.** (***-tt-***): ***~ down*** ⟨za⟩notować
joule [dʒuːl] *phys.* dżul *m*
jour·nal ['dʒɜːnl] dziennik *m*; czasopismo *n*; **~·is·m** ['dʒɜːnəlɪzəm] dziennikarstwo *n*; **~·ist** ['dʒɜːnəlɪst] dziennikarz *m* (-arka *f*)
jour·ney ['dʒɜːnɪ] **1.** podróż *f*; **2.** podróżować; **'~·man** (*pl.* ***-men***) towarzysz(ka *f*) *m* podróży
joy [dʒɔɪ] radość *f*; ***for ~*** dla przyjemności; **'~·ful** radosny; rozradowany; **'~·less** ponury, smutny; **'~·ride** (***-rode, -ridden***) jeździć ⟨jechać⟩ skradzionym po to samochodem; **'~·stick** *aviat.* drążek sterowy; *komp.* joystick *m*, dżojstik *m*
Jr → ***Jnr***
jub·i·lant ['dʒuːbɪlənt] rozradowany, radosny
ju·bi·lee ['dʒuːbɪliː] jubileusz *m*
Ju·da·ism ['dʒuːdeɪɪzəm] *rel.* judaizm *m*
judge [dʒʌdʒ] **1.** *jur.* sędzia *m* (-ina *f*) (*też fig.*); juror *m* (-ka *f*); znawca *m* (-czyni *f*); **2.** *jur.* orzekać ⟨orzec⟩; wydawać ⟨-dać⟩ sąd
judg(e)·ment ['dʒʌdʒmənt] *jur.* orzeczenie *n*, wyrok *m*; sąd *m*, pogląd *m*; *rel.* dzień *m* sądu, sąd *m*; ***the Last* ♀** Sąd *m* Ostateczny; **'♀ Day**, *lub* ***Day of* ♀** dzień *m* Sądu Ostatecznego
ju·di·cial [dʒuː'dɪʃl] *jur.* sądowy; sędziowski
ju·di·cia·ry [dʒuː'dɪʃɪərɪ] *jur.* sądownictwo *n*; sędziowie *pl.*
ju·di·cious [dʒuː'dɪʃəs] rozumny, rozsądny
ju·do ['dʒuːdəʊ] judo *n lub* dżudo *n*

J

jug [dʒʌg] dzbanek *m*, dzban *m*
jug·gle ['dʒʌgl] żonglować (*I*); dopasować, dostosować; '**~r** żongler *m* (-ka *f*)
juice [dʒuːs] sok *m*; *sl. mot.* benzyna *f*; **juic·y** ['dʒuːsɪ] (**-ier, -iest**) soczysty; F pikantny
juke·box ['dʒuːkbɒks] szafa *f* grająca
Jul *skrót pisany*: ***July*** lipiec *m*
Ju·ly [dʒuː'laɪ] (*skrót*: ***Jul***) lipiec *m*
jum·ble ['dʒʌmbl] **1.** *też* **~ *together***, **~ *up*** ⟨z-, po⟩mieszać; ⟨po⟩rozrzucać; **2.** mieszanina *f*, mieszanka *f*; '**~ sale** *Brt.* wyprzedaż *f* (*rzeczy używanych*)
jum·bo ['dʒʌmbəʊ] **1.** ogromny, potężny; **2.** (*pl.* **-bos**) F → ***colossal***; '**~ jet** jumbo jet *m* (*wielki odrzutowiec pasażerski*); '**~-sized** ogromny
jump [dʒʌmp] **1.** *v/i.* skakać ⟨skoczyć⟩; podskakiwać ⟨-koczyć⟩; **~ *at*** rzucać się na (*A*); **~ *at the chance*** korzystać skwapliwie z okazji; **~ *to conclusions*** przedwcześnie wyciągać ⟨-gnąć⟩ wnioski; *v/t.* przeskakiwać ⟨-koczyć⟩; **~ *the queue*** *Brt.* wpychać ⟨wepchnąć⟩ się do kolejki; **~ *the lights*** przejeżdżać ⟨-jechać⟩ przez skrzyżowanie na czerwonym świetle; **2.** skok *m*; ***high*** (***long***) **~** (*w sporcie*) skok *m* wzwyż (w dal)
'**jump·er**[1] (*w sporcie*) skoczek *m*
'**jump·er**[2] *Brt.* pulower *m*; *Am.* fartuch *m*
'**jump|·ing jack** pajac *m*; '**~·y** (**-ier, -iest**) nerwowy
Jun *skrót pisany*: ***June*** czerwiec *m*; → ***Jnr***
junc|·tion ['dʒʌŋkʃn] skrzyżowanie *n*; *rail.* punkt *m* węzłowy; **~·ture** ['dʒʌŋktʃə]: ***at this ~ture*** w tym momencie
June [dʒuːn] (*skrót*: ***Jun***) czerwiec *m*
jun·gle ['dʒʌŋgl] dżungla *f*
ju·ni·or ['dʒuːnjə] **1.** junior; młodszy; podwładny; (*w sporcie*) w kategorii juniorów; **2.** junior *m*; młodszy *m*; podwładny *m*; **~ 'high (school)** *Am.* (*ostatnie klasy szkoły średniej*); '**~ school** *Brt.* szkoła *f* podstawowa (*dla dzieci od 7 do 11 roku życia*)
junk[1] [dʒʌŋk] *naut.* dżonka *f*
junk[2] [dʒʌŋk] F rupiecie *pl.*, graty *pl.*; odpadki *pl.*; *sl.* heroina *f*; '**~ food** złe jedzenie *n* (*wysokokaloryczne o niskiej wartości odżywczej*); **~·ie**, **~·y** ['dʒʌŋkɪ] *sl.* narkoman(ka *f*) *m*, ćpun(ka *f*) *m*; '**~·yard** *Am.* złomowisko *n*; ***auto ~yard*** złomowisko *n* samochodów, F szrot *m*
jur·is·dic·tion ['dʒʊərɪs'dɪkʃn] jurysdykcja *f*; kompetencja *f lub* właściwość *f* sądu
ju·ris·pru·dence ['dʒʊərɪs'pruːdəns] prawoznawstwo *f*
ju·ror ['dʒʊərə] *jur.* członek *m* sądu przysięgłych
ju·ry ['dʒʊərɪ] *jur.* sąd *m* przysięgłych; jury *n*; '**~·man** (*pl.* **-men**) *jur.* członek *m* sądu przysięgłych; '**~·wom·an** (*pl.* ***-women***) *jur.* członkini *f* sądu przysięgłych
just [dʒʌst] **1.** *adj.* sprawiedliwy, słuszny; zasłużony; **2.** *adv.* właśnie; zaledwie; tylko, jedynie; po prostu; **~ *about*** w przybliżeniu, prawie; **~ *like that*** po prostu tak; **~ *now*** właśnie teraz; dopiero co
jus·tice ['dʒʌstɪs] sprawiedliwość *f*; *jur.* sędzia *m*; **♎ *of the Peace*** sędzia *m* pokoju; ***court of ~*** (*budynek*) sąd *m*
jus·ti|·fi·ca·tion [dʒʌstɪfɪ'keɪʃn] usprawiedliwienie *n*; uzasadnienie *n*; **~·fy** ['dʒʌstɪfaɪ] usprawiedliwiać ⟨-wić⟩
just·ly ['dʒʌstlɪ] słusznie; sprawiedliwie
jut [dʒʌt] (**-tt-**): **~ *out*** wystawać, sterczeć
ju·ve·nile ['dʒuːvənaɪl] **1.** młodociany; nieletni; **2.** młodociany *m* (-na *f*); nieletni *m* (-nia *f*); **~ 'court** *jur.* sąd *m* dla nieletnich; **~ de'lin·quen·cy** *jur.* przestępczość *f* nieletnich; **~ de'lin·quent** młodociany przestępca *m*

K

K

K, k [keɪ] K, k *n*
kan·ga·roo [kæŋgə'ruː] *zo.* kangur *m*
ka·ra·te [kə'rɑːtɪ] karate *n*
KB [keɪ 'biː] *skrót*: ***kilobyte*** KB, kilobajt *m*
keel [kiːl] **1.** kil *m*, stępka *f*; **2.** **~ *over*** przewracać ⟨-rócić⟩ się
keen [kiːn] ostry (*też fig.*); *zimno*: przenikliwy; zapalony, gorliwy; ***be ~ on s.th.*** bardzo się czymś interesować; palić się do czegoś
keep [kiːp] **1.** (***kept***) trzymać; mieć;

zatrzymywać ⟨-mać⟩; przechowywać ⟨-wać⟩; *obietnicę, słowa* dotrzymywać ⟨-mać⟩; *porządek, pracę, rodzinę* utrzymywać; *dziennik, sklep* prowadzić; *zwierzęta* hodować; dochowywać ⟨-wać⟩ (*sekretu*); powstrzymywać ⟨-ymać⟩ (**from** przed *D*); **~ early hours** wcześnie chodzić spać; **~ one's temper** panować nad sobą; **~ s.o. company** dotrzymywać ⟨-mać⟩ komuś towarzystwa; **~ s.th. from s.o.** trzymać coś w sekrecie przed kimś; **~ time** dobrze pokazywać czas; trzymać rytm *lub* takt; *v/i.* trzymać się; *z ger.* wciąż, ciągle; **~ going** idź dalej; **~ smiling** zawsze się uśmiechaj!; **~ (on) talking** nadal mówić; **~ (on) trying** próbuj dalej; **~ s.o. waiting** kazać komuś czekać; **~ away** trzymać się z daleka (**from** od *G*); **~ back** wstrzymywać ⟨-mać⟩ się (*też fig.*); **~ from doing s.th.** nie robić czegoś; **~ in** *ucznia* zatrzymywać ⟨-mać⟩; **~ off** trzymać (się) z daleka; **~ off!** wstęp wzbroniony!; **~ on** *ubranie* nadal nosić; *światło* zostawiać ⟨-wić⟩ zapalone; nadal (**doing s.th.** robić coś); **~ out** trzymać z daleka; **~ out!** Wstęp wzbroniony!; **~ to** trzymać się (*G*); **~ up** zachowywać ⟨-wać⟩, utrzymywać ⟨-mać⟩; **~ it up** tylko tak dalej; **~ up with** dotrzymywać kroku (*D*); **~ up with the Joneses** nie odstawać od sąsiadów; **2.** utrzymanie *n*, koszty *pl.* utrzymania; **for ~s** F na zawsze

'keep|·er dozorca *m*; opiekun(ka *f*) *m*; *zwł. w złożeniach* właściciel(ka *f*) *m*; **'~·ing** nadzór *m*, dozór *m*; **be in (out of) ~ing with ...** (nie) pasować do (*G*); **~·sake** ['ki:pseɪk] pamiątka *f*

keg [keg] beczułka *f*

ken·nel ['kenl] buda *f*; **~s** *sg.* schronisko *n* dla psów

kept [kept] *pret. i p.p. od* **keep** 1

kerb [kɜ:b], **'~·stone** krawężnik *m*

ker·chief ['kɜ:tʃɪf] chustka *f* (*na głowę itp.*)

ker·nel ['kɜ:nl] jądro *n* (*też fig.*)

ket·tle ['ketl] czajnik *m*; **'~·drum** *mus.* kocioł *m*

key [ki:] **1.** klucz *m* (*też fig.*); klawisz *m*; *mus.* tonacja *f*; *attr.* kluczowy; **2.** dostosowywać ⟨-wać⟩ (**to** do *G*); *komp.* wpisywać ⟨-sać⟩, wprowadzać ⟨-dzić⟩; **~ed up** spięty; **'~·board** klawiatura *f*; **'~·hole** dziurka *f* od klucza; **'~·man** (*pl.* **-men**) kluczowa figura *f*; **'~·note** *mus.* tonika *f*, dźwięk centralny; *fig.* zasadnicza myśl *f*; **'~ ring** kółko *n* na klucze; **'~·stone** *arch.* zwornik *m*; *fig.* filar *m*; **'~ word** wyraz *m* kluczowy

kick [kɪk] **1.** kopać ⟨-pnąć⟩; (*w sporcie*) strzelać ⟨-lić⟩; *koń*: wierzgać ⟨-gnąć⟩; **~ off** rozpoczynać ⟨-cząć⟩ grę; **~ out** F wyrzucić, wykopać; **~ up** wybijać ⟨-bić⟩ kopnięciem; **~ up a fuss** *lub* **row** F wszcząć awanturę; **2.** kopnięcie *n*, kopniak *m*; wierzgnięcie *n*; (*w piłce nożnej*) rzut *m*, strzał *m*; **free ~** rzut *m* wolny; **for ~s** F dla draki; **they get a ~ out of it** strasznie ich to bawi; **'~·off** (*w piłce nożnej*) początek *m* gry

kid[1] [kɪd] koźlę *m*; skóra *f* koźlęcia; F dzieciak *m*; **~ brother** F młodszy brat *m*

kid[2] [kɪd] (**-dd-**) *v/t.* *kogoś* naciągać ⟨-gnąć⟩; **~ s.o.** oszukiwać ⟨-kać⟩ kogoś; *v/i.* ⟨za⟩żartować, robić żarty; **he is only ~ding** on tylko żartuje; **no ~ding!** słowo honoru!

kid 'gloves *pl.* rękawiczki *pl.* z koźlej skóry (*też fig.*)

kid·nap ['kɪdnæp] (**-pp-**, *Am. też* **-p-**) porywać ⟨-rwać⟩; **'kid·nap·(p)er** porywacz *m* (-ka *f*); **'kid·nap·(p)ing** porwanie *m*, kidnaperstwo *n*

kid·ney ['kɪdnɪ] *anat.* nerka *f*; **'~ bean** fasola *f*; **'~ ma·chine** *med.* sztuczna nerka *f*

Kiev Kijów *m*

kill [kɪl] zabijać ⟨-bić⟩, uśmiercać ⟨-cić⟩ (*też fig.*); *humor, nastrój* zwarzyć; *szanse* unicestwiać ⟨-wić⟩; **be ~ed in an accident** zostać zabitym w wypadku; **~ time** zabijać ⟨-bić⟩ czas; **'~·er** zabójca *m* (-czyni *n*); **'~·ing** morderczy

kiln [kɪln] piec *m* (*do wypalania*)

ki·lo ['ki:ləʊ] F (*pl.* **-los**) kilo *n*

kil·o|·gram(me) ['kɪləgræm] kilogram *m*; **'~·me·tre** *Brt.*, **'~·me·ter** *Am.* kilometr *m*

kilt [kɪlt] kilt *m*, spódniczka *f* szkocka

kin [kɪn] krewny

kind[1] [kaɪnd] uprzejmy, miły; grzeczny, życzliwy; serdeczny

kind[2] [kaɪnd] rodzaj *m*, typ *m*; gatunek *m*; odmiana *f*; **all ~s of** wszyscy, wszystkie; **nothing of the ~** nic w tym rodzaju; **~ of** F jakby; **in ~** w naturze; **this ~ of** tego rodzaju

K

kin·der·gar·ten ['kɪndəgɑːtn] przedszkole *n*
kind-'heart·ed dobry, o dobrym sercu
kin·dle ['kɪndl] rozpalać ⟨-lić⟩, zapalać ⟨-lić⟩ (się); *fig. zainteresowanie itp.* rozbudzać ⟨-dzić⟩
kind|·ly ['kaɪndlɪ] **1.** *adj.* (**-*ier*, -*iest***) przyjazny, przyjacielski; **2.** *adv.* uprzejmie; przyjaźnie, przyjacielsko; '**~·ness** uprzejmość *f*, serdeczność *f*, życzliwość *f*
kin·dred ['kɪndrɪd] pokrewny; **~ *spirits*** *pl.* pokrewne dusze *pl.*
king [kɪŋ] król *m* (*też fig. w szachach, grach*); **~·dom** ['kɪŋdəm] królestwo *n* (*też rel.*); ***animal*** (***vegetable***) **~*dom*** królestwo *n* zwierząt (roślin); '**~·ly** (**-*ier*, -*iest***) królewski; '**~-size**(**d**) ogromny
kink [kɪŋk] zapętlenie *n*, załamanie *n*; *fig.* dziwactwo *n*, perwersja *f*; '**~·y** (**-*ier*, -*iest***) dziwaczny, osobliwy; perwersyjny
ki·osk ['kiːɒsk] kiosk *m*; *Brt.* budka *f* telefoniczna
kip·per ['kɪpə] śledź *m* wędzony
kiss [kɪs] **1.** pocałunek *m*, całus *m*; **2.** ⟨po⟩całować
kit [kɪt] ekwipunek *m*; *Brt.* wyposażenie *n*; zestaw *m* (*przyborów*), komplet *m*; zestaw *m* (*do sklejenia*); → ***first-aid kit***; '**~ bag** worek *m* na wyposażenie
kitch·en ['kɪtʃɪn] kuchnia *f*; *attr.* kuchenny; **~·ette** [kɪtʃɪ'net] kuchenka *f*, wnęka *f* kuchenna; **~ 'gar·den** ogród *m* warzywny
kite [kaɪt] latawiec *m*; *zo.* kania *f*; ***fly a ~*** puszczać latawiec
kit·ten ['kɪtn] kociak *m*, kocię *n*
knack [næk] umiejętność *f*, zdolność *f*; talent *m*
knave [neɪv] łotr *m*, niegodziwiec *m*; (*w kartach*) *Brt.* walet *m*
knead [niːd] miesić; rozrabiać ⟨-robić⟩, gnieść
knee [niː] kolano *n*; *tech.* kolanko *n*; '**~·cap** *anat.* rzepka *f* (kolana); **~-'deep** po kolana; na głębokość kolan; '**~ joint** *anat.* połączenie *n* kolankowo-stawowe
kneel [niːl] (***knelt***, *Am. też* ***kneeled***) klękać ⟨-nąć⟩; uklęknąć (***to*** przed *I*)
'knee-length sukienka do kolan
knell [nel] dzwon *m* żałobny
knelt [nelt] *pret. i p.p. od* ***kneel***
knew [njuː] *pret. od* ***know***
knick·er·bock·ers ['nɪkəbɒkəz] *pl.* pludry *pl.*, pumpy *pl.*
knick·ers ['nɪkəz] *Brt.* F *pl.* figi *pl.*
knick-knack ['nɪknæk] drobiazg *m*, błahostka *f*, bibelot *m*
knife [naɪf] **1.** (*pl.* ***knives*** [naɪvz]) nóż *m*; **2.** dźgać ⟨-gnąć⟩ *nożem*
knight [naɪt] **1.** rycerz *m*; (*w szachach*) skoczek *m*, konik *m*; **2.** pasować na rycerza; nadawać ⟨-dać⟩ tytuł rycerski; **~·hood** ['naɪthʊd] tytuł *m lub* stan *m* rycerski
knit [nɪt] (**-*tt*-**; ***knit*** *lub* ***knitted***) *v/t.* ⟨z⟩robić na drutach; *też* **~ *together*** związywać ⟨-zać⟩, zespalać ⟨-polić⟩ (się); **~ *one's brows*** ⟨z⟩marszczyć brwi; *v/i.* ⟨z⟩robić na drutach; zespalać ⟨-polić⟩ się; *kości*: zrastać się; '**~·ting** robótka *f* na drutach; robienie *n* na drutach; '**~·ting nee·dle** drut *m* (*do robót dzianych*); '**~·wear** dzianina *f*, wyroby *pl.* z dzianiny
knives [naɪvz] *pl. od* ***knife*** 1
knob [nɒb] pokrętło *n*, gałka *f*; kulka *f* (*masła itp.*)
knock [nɒk] **1.** stukać ⟨-knąć⟩, pukać ⟨-knąć⟩; uderzać ⟨-rzyć⟩; **~ *at the door*** pukać do drzwi; **~ *about*, ~ *around*** obijać ⟨-bić⟩, ⟨s⟩tłuc; F włóczyć się, wędrować; F walać się; **~ *down*** *budynek itp.* ⟨z⟩burzyć; *przechodnia* potrącić, przejechać; *cenę* zbijać ⟨zbić⟩, obniżać ⟨-żyć⟩ ***be ~ed down*** zostać przejechanym; **~ *off*** *cenę* spuszczać ⟨-puścić⟩; F dawać sobie spokój (z *I*); F wyprodukować, wypuścić ⟨-puszczać⟩; F (*ukraść, zabić*) rąbnąć; *v/i* skończyć pracę; **~ *out*** powalić; pozbawiać ⟨-wić⟩ przytomności; *fajkę* wytrząsać ⟨-snąć⟩; (*w boksie*) ⟨z⟩nokautować; ⟨wy⟩eliminować; *fig.* F zwalać ⟨-lić⟩ z nóg; **~ *over*** przewracać ⟨-rócić⟩, powalić; ***be ~ed over*** zostać przejechanym; **2.** uderzenie *n*; pukanie *n*, stukanie *n*; ***there is a ~*** (***at*** [*Am.* ***on***] ***the door***) ktoś stuka; '**~·er** kołatka *f*; **~-'kneed** o krzywych nogach; z krzywymi nogami; '**~·out** *boks*: nokaut *m*
knoll [nəʊl] pagórek *m*
knot [nɒt] **1.** węzeł *m*, supeł *m*; sęk *m*; *naut.* węzeł *m*; **2.** (**-*tt*-**) wiązać, zawiązy-

wać ⟨-zać⟩; '~·ty (*-ier, -iest*) węzłowaty, węźlasty; *fig.* skomplikowany
know [nəʊ] (***knew, known***) wiedzieć; znać; poznać; umieć ~ ***how to do s.th.*** umieć coś zrobić; rozpoznawać ⟨-nać⟩; zapoznawać się (z *I*); ~ ***French*** umieć po francusku; ~ ***one's way around*** orientować się w (*L*); ~ ***all about it*** dobrze się znać na czymś; ***get to*** ~ poznawać ⟨-nać⟩; zapoznać się z (*I*); ~ ***one's business,*** ~ ***the ropes,*** ~ ***a thing or two,*** ~ ***what's what*** F orientować się w czymś; ***you*** ~ no wiesz; '~**-how** know-how *m*, wiedza *f* wyspecjalizowana, technologia *f*; '~**·ing** zorientowany, znający się na rzeczy; porozumiewawczy; '~**·ing·ly** świadomie, umyślnie; porozumiewawczo
knowl·edge ['nɒlɪdʒ] wiedza *f*, znajomość *f*; ***to my*** ~ o ile wiem; ***have a good*** ~ ***of*** dobrze znać (*A*), dobrze się znać na (*L*); '~**·a·ble**: ***be very*** ~***able about*** dobrze się znać na (*L*)
known [nəʊn] *p.p. od* **know**
knuck·le ['nʌkl] **1.** kostka *f* (*ręki*); **2.** ~ ***down to work*** zabierać ⟨-brać⟩ się ostro do pracy
KO [keɪ 'əʊ] *skrót*: ***knockout*** F nokaut *m*
Ko·re·a Korea *f*
Krem·lin ['kremlɪn]: ***the*** ~ Kreml *m*

L

L, l [el] L, l *n*
L [el] *skrót*: ***learner*** (***driver***) *Brt. mot.* nauka *f* jazdy; ***large*** (***size***) duży
l *skrót pisany*: ***left*** lewy, lewo; ***line*** linia *f*; ***litre***(***s***) l, litr *m*
£ *skrót pisany*: ***pound***(***s***) ***sterling*** GBP, funt *m* szterling
lab [læb] F laboratorium *n*
la·bel ['leɪbl] **1.** etykieta *f*, etykietka *f*; metka *f*; nalepka *f*; znak *m* wytwórni; ***on the X*** ~ na płytach wytwórni X; **2.** (*zwł. Brt.* **-ll-**, *Am.* **-l-**) etykietować, metkować; oznaczać ⟨-czyć⟩ etykietką *lub* metką; *fig.* określać ⟨-lić⟩, nadawać ⟨-dać⟩ miano
la·bor·a·to·ry [lə'bɒrətərɪ] laboratorium *n*; ~ **as'sis·tant** laborant(ka *f*) *m*
la·bo·ri·ous [lə'bɔːrɪəs] żmudny, ciężki
la·bor u·ni·on ['leɪbə -] *Am.* związek *m* zawodowy
la·bo(u)r ['leɪbə] **1.** *ciężka* praca *f*; trud *m*, wysiłek *m*; robocizna *f*; pracownicy *pl.* najemni, siła *f* robocza; *med.* poród *m*; ***Labour*** *pol.* Partia *f* Pracy; *attr.* laburzystowski; **2.** *ciężko* pracować; trudzić się; męczyć się, mozolić się; rozwodzić się (nad *I*); '~**ed** wysilony; ~**·er** ['leɪbərə] robotnik *m* (-nica *f*); **'labour ex·change** → ***job centre***; **'La·bour Par·ty** *pol.* Partia *f* Pracy
lace [leɪs] **1.** koronka *f*; sznurowadło *n*; **2.** ~ ***up*** ⟨za⟩sznurować; ~***d with brandy*** z dodatkiem brandy
la·ce·rate ['læsəreɪt] poszarpać, rozdzierać ⟨-zedrzeć⟩; *fig.* ⟨z⟩ranić
lack [læk] **1.** (***of***) brak *m*; niedostatek *m*; ⚠ *nie* ***lak*** ; **2.** *v/t.* nie mieć; ***he*** ~***s money*** brak mu pieniędzy; *v/i.* ***be*** ~***ing*** brakować; ***he is*** ~***ing in courage*** brakuje mu odwagi; ~**·lus·tre** *Brt.*, ~**·lus·ter** *Am.* ['læklʌstə] bezbarwny, bez wyrazu
la·con·ic [lə'kɒnɪk] (~***ally***) lakoniczny
lac·quer ['lækə] **1.** lakier *m* (*też do włosów*); **2.** ⟨po⟩lakierować
lad [læd] chłopiec *m*, chłopak *m*
lad·der ['lædə] drabina *f*; *Brt.* oczko *n* (*w rajstopach*); '~**·proof** z nielecącymi oczkami
la·den ['leɪdn] obładowany, objuczony
la·dle ['leɪdl] chochla *f*
la·dy ['leɪdɪ] pani *f*; dama *f*; ♀ lady *f*; ~ ***doctor*** lekarka *f*, kobieta *f* lekarz; ***Ladies***('), *Am.* ***Ladies' room*** toaleta damska; '~**·bird** *Brt.*, '~**·bug** *Am.* biedronka *f*; '~**·like** wytworny; jak dama
lag [læg] **1.** (***-gg-***): *zw.* ~ ***behind*** zostawać ⟨-tać⟩ w tyle; **2.** → ***time lag***
la·ger ['lɑːgə] piwo *n* jasne pełne
la·goon [lə'guːn] laguna *f*
laid [leɪd] *pret. i p.p. od* ***lay***[3]
lain [leɪn] *p.p. od* ***lie***[2]
lair [leə] legowisko *n*, łoże *n*; kryjówka *f*
la·i·ty ['leɪətɪ] laikat *m*
lake [leɪk] jezioro *n*
lamb [læm] **1.** jagnię *n*; *rel.* baranek *m*;

L

attr. mięso *n* z jagnięcia; **2.** *owca*: ⟨o⟩-kocić się
lame [leɪm] **1.** kulawy; *fig.* kulejący; **2.** kuleć, utykać
la·ment [lə'ment] **1.** lamentować, rozpaczać, biadać; **2.** lament *m*, biadanie *n*; **lam·en·ta·ble** ['læməntəbl] opłakany, tragiczny; żałosny; **lam·en·ta·tion** [læmən'teɪʃn] opłakiwanie *n*, biadanie *n*
lam·i·nat·ed ['læmɪneɪtɪd] laminowany; (wielo)warstwowy, laminatowy; ~ **'glass** szkło *n* wielowarstwowe
lamp [læmp] lampa *f*; latarnia *f* (*uliczna*); **'~·post** słup *m* latarni (*ulicznej*); **'~·shade** abażur *m*, klosz *m*
lance [lɑːns] lanca *f*
land [lænd] **1.** ziemia *f*; ląd *m*; *agr.* ziemia *f*, grunt *m*; ląd *m*, strona *f* świata; ***by ~*** lądem; **2.** ⟨wy⟩lądować; *ładunek* wyładowywać ⟨-ować⟩; *ludzi* wysadzać ⟨-dzić⟩ na ląd; **'~ a·gent** *Brt.* zarządca *m* majątku; **'~·ed** wyładowany; posiadający ziemię; ***~ed gentry*** ziemiaństwo *n*
land·ing ['lændɪŋ] lądowanie *n*; wyładunek *m*; podest *m*, podest *m*; **'~ field** *aviat.* lądowisko *n*; **'~ gear** *aviat.* podwozie *n* samolotu; **'~ stage** przystań *f*, miejsce *n* cumowania; **'~ strip** *aviat.* lądowisko *n*
land|·la·dy ['lænleɪdɪ] właścicielka *f*; gospodyni *f*; **~·lord** ['lænlɔːd] właściciel *m*; gospodarz *m*; **~·lub·ber** ['lændlʌbə] *naut. pej.* szczur *m* lądowy; **~·mark** ['lændmɑːk] punkt *m* charakterystyczny *lub* orientacyjny; *fig.* kamień *m* milowy; **~·own·er** ['lændəʊnə] właściciel(ka *f*) *m* ziemski (*-a*); **~ scape** ['lænskeɪp] krajobraz *m*; **~·slide** ['lændslaɪd] obsunięcie *n* się ziemi; osuwisko *n*; ***a ~slide victory*** *pol.* przygniatające zwycięstwo *n*; **~·slip** ['lændslɪp] osuwisko *n*
lane [leɪn] dróżka *f* (*polna*); uliczka *f*, alejka *f*; *aviat.* droga *f* powietrzna, trasa *f* lotnicza; (*w sporcie*) tor *m*; *mot.* pas *m* (*ruchu*); ***change ~s*** zmieniać ⟨-nić⟩ pas ruchu; ***get in ~*** *mot.* włączać ⟨-czyć⟩ się do ruchu
lan·guage ['læŋgwɪdʒ] język *m*; **'~ la·bor·a·to·ry** laboratorium *n* językowe
lan·guid ['læŋgwɪd] rozleniwiony; anemiczny, wątły
lank [læŋk] *włosy*: jak strąki, w strąkach; **'~·y** (***-ier, -iest***) tyczkowaty; szczudłowaty
lan·tern ['læntən] latarnia *f*
lap[1] [læp] łono *n* (*też fig.*), podołek *m*, kolana *pl.*
lap[2] [læp] **1.** (*w sporcie*) okrążenie *n*, etap *m*; ***~of hono(u)r*** runda *f* honorowa; **2.** (***-pp-***) (*w sporcie*) wykonać okrążenie; *przeciwnika* zdublować
lap[3] [læp] (***-pp-***): *v/t.* ***~ up*** wychłeptywać ⟨-tać⟩; *v/i.* chlupać ⟨-pnąć⟩, pluskać
la·pel [lə'pel] klapa *f* (*marynarki itp.*)
Lapland Laponia *f*
lapse [læps] **1.** upłynięcie *n* (*terminu, praw itp.*); błąd *m*, lapsus *m*; *jur.* wygaśnięcie *n*; ***he had a ~ of memory*** zawiodła go pamięć; **2.** upływać ⟨-łynąć⟩, wygasać ⟨-snąć⟩; *jur.* ulegać ⟨ulec⟩ przedawnieniu
lar·ce·ny ['lɑːsənɪ] *jur.* kradzież *f*, zabór *f* (*mienia*)
larch [lɑːtʃ] *bot.* modrzew *m*
lard [lɑːd] **1.** smalec *m*; **2.** *mięso* ⟨na⟩-szpikować; **lar·der** ['lɑːdə] spiżarnia *f*
large [lɑːdʒ] (***-r, -st***) duży, wielki; znaczny; ***at ~*** na wolności; ogół, wszyscy; **'~·ly** w dużej mierze; **~-'mind·ed** tolerancyjny, wielkoduszny; **'~·ness** wielkość *f*; znaczenie *n*
lar·i·at ['lærɪət] *zwł. Am.* lasso *n*
lark[1] [lɑːk] *zo.* skowronek *m*
lark[2] [lɑːk] F kawał *m*, szpas *m*
lar·va ['lɑːvə] *zo.* (*pl.* ***-vae*** [-viː]) larwa *f*
lar·yn·gi·tis [lærɪn'dʒaɪtɪs] *med.* zapalenie *n* krtani
lar·ynx ['lærɪŋks] *anat.* (*pl.* ***-ynges*** [lə'rɪndʒiːz], ***-ynxes***) krtań *f*
las·civ·i·ous [lə'sɪvɪəs] lubieżny, rozpustny
la·ser ['leɪzə] *phys.* laser *m*; **'~ beam** wiązka *f* lasera; **'~ print·er** drukarka *f* laserowa; **'~ tech·nol·o·gy** technika *f* laserowa
lash [læʃ] **1.** bicz *m*; uderzenie *n* (*biczem*); rzęsa *f*; **2.** biczować, chłostać (*też o wietrze*); ***~ out*** ⟨wy⟩smagać
lass [læs], **~·ie** ['læsɪ] dziewczyna *f*, dziewczę *n*
las·so [læ'suː] (*pl.* ***-sos, -soes***) lasso *n*
last[1] [lɑːst] **1.** *adj.* ostatni; ***~ but one*** przedostatni; ***~ night*** ostatniej *lub* poprzedniej nocy; **2.** *adv.* ostatnio, ostatnim razem; ***~ but not least*** wreszcie;

należy wspomnieć; **3.** ostatni *m*, końcowy *m*; ***at ~*** wreszcie; ***to the ~*** do końca
last² [lɑːst] trwać; wystarczać ⟨-czyć⟩
last³ [lɑːst] kopyto *n* szewskie
'last·ing trwały, stały
'last·ly wreszcie, w końcu
latch [lætʃ] **1.** zatrzask *m*; (*przy drzwiach*) haczyk *m*, zasuwa *f*; **2.** zatrzaskiwać ⟨-snąć⟩; **'~·key** klucz *m* do zamka
late [leɪt] (***-r, -st***) **1.** *adj*. późny; spóźniony; niedawny, były; zmarły; **2.** *adv*. późno; do późna; ***be ~*** spóźniać się; *pociąg itp*.: mieć opóźnienie; ***as ~ as*** dopiero; ***~r on*** później; **3.** ***of ~*** ostatnio; **'~·ly** ostatnio, niedawno
lath [lɑːθ] listwa *f*
lathe [leɪð] *tech*. tokarka *f*
la·ther ['lɑːðə] **1.** piana *f*; **2.** *v/t*. namydlać ⟨-lić⟩; *v/i*. ⟨s⟩pienić się
Lat·in ['lætɪn] **1.** *ling*. łaciński; latynoski; **2.** *ling*. łacina *f*; **~ A'mer·i·ca** Ameryka *f* Łacińska; **~ A'mer·i·can** **1.** latynoamerykański; **2.** Latynos *m*
lat·i·tude ['lætɪtjuːd] *geogr*. szerokość *f* (*geograficzna*)
lat·ter ['lætə] drugi, ostatni (*z dwóch*)
lat·tice ['lætɪs] kratownica *f*; krata *f*
Lat·via Łotwa *f*
lau·da·ble ['lɔːdəbl] chwalebny, godny pochwały; przynoszący zaszczyt
laugh [lɑːf] **1.** śmiać się (***at*** z *G*); ***~ at s.o.*** śmiać się z kogoś, wyśmiewać kogoś; **2.** śmiech *m*; dowcip *m*; **'~·a·ble** śmieszny; **~·ter** ['lɑːftə] śmiech *m*
launch¹ [lɔːntʃ] **1.** *statek* ⟨z⟩wodować; *pocisk* wyrzucać ⟨-cić⟩; *rakietę* wystrzeliwać ⟨-lić⟩; *projekt itp*. zaczynać ⟨-cząć⟩, rozpoczynać ⟨-cząć⟩; **2.** *naut*. szalupa *f*; start *m*, wystrzelenie *n*; zaczęcie *n*
launch² [lɔːntʃ] *naut*. barkas *m*
'launch·ing → ***launch¹***; **'~ pad** *też* ***launch pad*** płyta *f* wyrzutni; **'~ site** płyta *f* startowa
laun·der ['lɔːndə] ⟨wy⟩prać; F *pieniądze* prać
laun|·d(e)rette [lɔːn'dret] *Brt*., **~·dromat** ['lɔːndrəmæt] *TM zwł. Am*. pralnia *f* samoobsługowa; **~·dry** ['lɔːndrɪ] (*rzeczy prane*) pranie *n*
laur·el ['lɒrəl] *bot*. laur *m*, drzewo *n* laurowe, wawrzyn *m*; *attr*. laurowy
la·va ['lɑːvə] lawa *f*
lav·a·to·ry ['lævətərɪ] toaleta *f*, ubikacja *f*; ***public ~*** toaleta *f* publiczna
lav·en·der ['lævəndə] *bot*. lawenda *f*; *attr*. lawendowy
lav·ish ['lævɪʃ] **1.** szczodrobliwy; *nadmiernie* hojny, ***be ~ with s.th.*** nie żałować czegoś; **2.** ***~ s.th. on s.o.*** nie szczędzić komuś czegoś, obsypywać kogoś czymś
law [lɔː] prawo *n*; ustawa *f*; przepis(y *pl*.) *m*; reguła *f*; F gliniarze *pl*., glina *m*; ***~ and order*** prawo i porządek; **~-a·bid·ing** ['lɔːəbaɪdɪŋ] praworządny; **'~·court** sąd *m*; **'~·ful** legalny, zgodny z prawem; **'~·less** nielegalny, niezgodny z prawem
lawn [lɔːn] trawnik *m*; **'~·mow·er** kosiarka *f* (*do trawników*)
'law·suit proces *m* sądowy
law·yer ['lɔːjə] *jur*. prawnik *m* (-iczka *f*), adwokat *m*
lax [læks] rozluźniony; nie rygorystyczny, mało skrupulatny
lax·a·tive ['læksətɪv] *med*. **1.** rozwalniający; **2.** środek *m* rozwalniający
lay¹ [leɪ] *pret. od* ***lie²***
lay² [leɪ] *rel*. świecki, laicki
lay³ [leɪ] (***laid***) *v/t*. kłaść ⟨położyć⟩; wykładać ⟨wyłożyć⟩ (***with s.th.*** czymś); *stół* nakrywać ⟨-ryć⟩; *jaja* składać ⟨złożyć⟩; przedkładać ⟨-łożyć⟩ (***before*** przed *A*); *winę* składać ⟨złożyć⟩; *v/i*. *kura*: nieść się; ***~ aside*** odkładać ⟨-łożyć⟩; ***~ off*** *econ. pracowników* zwalniać ⟨zwolnić⟩ (*zwł. okresowo*); przestawać ⟨-stać⟩; F odczepić się, zostawić w spokoju; ***~ s.th. open*** coś otwierać ⟨-worzyć⟩; ***~ out*** rozkładać ⟨-złożyć⟩; *ogród itp*. ⟨za⟩projektować; *print*. ⟨z⟩robić skład; ***~ up*** odkładać ⟨-łożyć⟩; ***be laid up*** być przykutym do łóżka; **'~-by** (*pl*. ***-bys***) *Brt. mot*. zatoka *f* (*do parkowania lub zatrzymywania się*); **'~·er** warstwa *f*; *bot*. odkład *m*
'lay·man (*pl*. ***-men***) laik *m*
'lay|-off *econ*. zwolnienie *n* (*zwł. przejściowe*); **'~·out** układ *m*; rozkład *m*; *print*. projekt *m* graficzny
la·zy ['leɪzɪ] (***-ier, -iest***) leniwy
lb *skrót pisany*: ***pound*** (*łacińskie* ***libra***) funt (*453,59 g*)
LCD [el siː 'diː] *skrót*: ***liquid crystal display*** wyświetlacz *m* ciekłokrystaliczny
lead¹ [liːd] **1.** (***led***) *v/t*. ⟨za-, po⟩prowa-

dzić; ⟨po⟩kierować; skłaniać ⟨skłonić⟩ (***to do*** do zrobienia); *v/i.* prowadzić (*też w sporcie*); kierować; **~ *off*** rozpoczynać ⟨-cząć⟩; **~ *on*** *kogoś* nabierać ⟨-brać⟩; **~ *to*** *fig.* ⟨do⟩prowadzić do (*G*); **~ *up to*** *fig.* ⟨do⟩prowadzić do (*G*); **2.** prowadzenie *n* (*też w sporcie i fig.*), kierownictwo *n*; przewodnictwo *n*; czołowa pozycja *f*; przykład *m*, wzór *m*; przewaga *f*; *theat.* czołowa rola *f*; smycz *f*; sugestia *f*, trop *m*; ***be in the* ~** prowadzić; ***take the* ~** wychodzić ⟨wyjść⟩ na prowadzenie, obejmować ⟨objąć⟩ prowadzenie

lead[2] [led] *chem.* ołów *m*; *naut.* sonda *f*, ołowianka *f*; **~·ed** ['ledıd] *okno*: gomółkowy; *benzyna*: ołowiowy, etylizowany; **~·en** ['ledn] ołowiany (*też fig.*)

lead·er ['li:də] przywódca *m* (-dczyni *f*); lider *m*; *Brt.* artykuł *m* wiodący; **'~·ship** przewodnictwo *m*, prowadzenie *n*

lead-free ['ledfri:] bezołowiowy

lead·ing ['li:dıŋ] prowadzący; główny, przewodni

L

leaf [li:f] (*pl.* ***leaves*** [li:vz]) liść *m*; skrzydło *n* (*drzwi itp.*); (*składana część blatu*); **2. ~ *through*** kartkować, przekartkowywać ⟨-ować⟩; **~·let** ['li:flıt] ulotka *f*, folder *m*, prospekt *m*

league [li:g] liga *f*, związek *m*

leak [li:k] **1.** *woda*: przeciekać ⟨-ciec⟩; wyciekać ⟨-ciec⟩; *gaz*: ulatniać ⟨-lotnić⟩ się; *zbiornik*: przepuszczać ⟨-uścić⟩ *ciecz, gaz*; **~ *out*** wyciekać ⟨-ciec⟩; *fig.* przedostawać ⟨-stać⟩ się; **2.** przeciek *m* (*też fig.*), wyciek *m*, ulatnianie *n* się; **~·age** ['li:kıdʒ] wyciek *m*; **'~·y** (***-ier, -iest***) nieszczelny, przeciekający

lean[1] [li:n] (***leant*** *lub* ***leaned***) wychylać ⟨-lić⟩ się; pochylać ⟨-lić⟩ się; **~ *on*** opierać ⟨oprzeć⟩ się na (*L*)

lean[2] [li:n] **1.** chudy (*też fig.*), szczupły; **2.** chude mięso *n*

leant [lent] *pret. i p.p. od* ***lean***[1]

leap [li:p] **1.** (***leapt*** *lub* ***leaped***) skakać ⟨skoczyć⟩; **~ *at*** *fig.* rzucać się na (*A*); **2.** skok *m*; **'~·frog**: ***play ~frog*** skakać jeden przez drugiego; **~t** [lept] *pret. i p.p. od* ***leap*** 1; **'~ year** rok *m* przestępny

learn [lɜ:n] (***learned*** *lub* ***learnt***) ⟨na⟩uczyć się (*G*); dowiadywać ⟨-wiedzieć⟩ się; **~·ed** ['lɜ:nıd] uczony; **'~·er** uczący się *m*, ucząca się *f*; ***~er driver*** *Brt.* (*osoba ucząca się prowadzić samochód*); **'~·ing** wiedza *f*, uczoność *f*; **~t** [lɜ:nt] *pret. i p.p. od* ***learn***

lease [li:s] **1.** wynajem *m*, najem *m*, dzierżawa *f*; umowa *f* dzierżawy; **2.** najmować ⟨-jąć⟩, wynajmować ⟨-jąć⟩; ⟨wy⟩dzierżawić; brać ⟨wziąć⟩ w leasing; udzielać ⟨-lić⟩ leasingu; **~ *out*** wydzierżawiać ⟨-wić⟩

leash [li:ʃ] smycz *f*

least [li:st] **1.** *adj.* (*sup. od* ***little*** 1) najmniejszy; **2.** *adv.* (*sup. od* ***little*** 2) najmniej; **~ *of all*** szczególnie zaś; **3. *at* ~** przynajmniej; ***to say the* ~** mówiąc oględnie

leath·er ['leðə] **1.** skóra *f*; **2.** skórzany, ze skóry

leave [li:v] **1.** (***left***) *v/t.* ⟨po⟩zostawiać ⟨-wić⟩; porzucać ⟨-cić⟩; odjeżdżać ⟨-jechać⟩, odejść ⟨odchodzić⟩; wyjeżdżać ⟨-jechać⟩ (***for*** do *G*); wychodzić (z *G*); zwalniać się z (*G*); ***be left*** być zostawionym *lub* porzuconym; *v/i.* odchodzić ⟨odejść⟩; wyjeżdżać ⟨-jechać⟩; **~ *alone*** zostawiać ⟨-wić⟩ w spokoju; **~ *behind*** zostawiać ⟨-wić⟩; **~ *on*** pozostawiać ⟨-wić⟩; **~ *out*** pomijać ⟨-minąć⟩; wykluczać ⟨-czyć⟩; ⟨od⟩izolować; **2.** urlop *m*; przepustka *f*, zwolnienie *n*; ***on* ~** w czasie urlopu *lub* przepustki; pozwolenie *n*, zgoda *f*

leav·en ['levn] zakwas *m*, zaczyn *m*

leaves [li:vz] *pl. od* ***leaf*** 1; listowie *n*

leav·ings ['li:vıŋz] *pl.* pozostałości *pl.*, resztki *pl.*

lech·er·ous ['letʃərəs] lubieżny

lec|·ture ['lektʃə] **1.** *univ.* wykład *m*; referat *m*; *fig.* kazanie *n*; ⚠ *nie* ***lektura***; **2.** *v/i. univ.* wykładać, wygłaszać wykłady; *v/t. komuś* prawić kazanie; **~·tur·er** ['lektʃərə] wykładowca *m*; *univ.* docent *m*; mówca *m*

led [led] *pret. i p.p. od* ***lead***[1]

ledge [ledʒ] parapet *m*, półka *f*

leech [li:tʃ] *zo.* pijawka *f*

leek [li:k] *bot.* por *m*

leer [lıə] **1.** lubieżne spojrzenie *n*, lubieżny uśmiech *m*; **2.** lubieżnie się uśmiechać *lub* patrzeć (***at*** na *A*)

left[1] [left] *pret. i p.p. od* ***leave*** 1

left[2] [left] **1.** *adj.* lewy; lewostronny; **2.** *adv.* na lewo, w lewo; ***turn* ~** iść na lewo; **3.** lewa strona *f*; lewica *f* (*też pol.*); (*w boksie*) lewa *f*; ***on the* ~** z/po lewej; ***to the* ~** na lewo, w lewo; ***keep to the* ~**

trzymać się lewej; jechać po lewej; **~-'hand** lewostronny; **~-hand 'drive** *mot.* z lewostronnym układem kierowniczym; **~-'hand·ed** leworęczny; dla leworęcznych
left|'lug·gage of·fice *Brt. rail.* przechowalnia bagażu; **'~·o·vers** *pl.* resztki *pl.*; **~-'wing** *pol.* lewicowy, na lewicy
leg [leg] noga *f*; *barani* udziec *m*; *math.* ramię *n* (*cyrkla*); ***pull s.o.'s ~*** F naciągać kogoś; ***stretch one's ~s*** rozprostowywać ⟨-ować⟩ nogi
leg·a·cy ['legəsɪ] spadek *m*, dziedzictwo *n*
le·gal ['liːgl] legalny, prawny, zgodny z prawem
le·ga·tion [lɪ'geɪʃn] misja *f* poselska, legacja *f*
le·gend ['ledʒənd] legenda *f* (*też fig.*); **le·gen·da·ry** ['ledʒəndərɪ] legendarny
le·gi·ble ['ledʒəbl] czytelny
le·gis·la|·tion [ledʒɪs'leɪʃn] legislacja *f*, ustawodawstwo *n*, prawodawstwo *n*; **~·tive** ['ledʒɪslətɪv] *pol.* **1.** legislacyjny, ustawodawczy; **2.** legislatywa *f*, władza *f* ustawodawcza; **~·tor** ['ledʒɪsleɪtə] ustawodawca *m*
le·git·i·mate [lɪ'dʒɪtɪmət] prawowity, legalny
lei·sure ['leʒə] czas *m* wolny; odpoczynek *m*; ***at ~*** bez pośpiechu; **'~ cen·tre** *Am.* ośrodek *m* rekreacyjny; *Brt.* ośrodek *m* sportowy; **'~·ly** niespieszny; **'~ time** czas *m* wolny; **~time ac'tiv·i·ties** *pl.* rekreacja *f*; **'~·wear** ubranie *n* nieformalne
lem·on ['lemən] *bot.* cytryna *f*; *attr.* cytrynowy; **~·ade** [lemə'neɪd] lemoniada *f*
lend [lend] (***lent***) *komuś* pożyczać ⟨-czyć⟩
length [leŋθ] długość *f*; odcinek *m*; czas *m* trwania; ***at ~*** wreszcie; **~·en** ['leŋθən] wydłużać ⟨-żyć⟩ (się); przedłużać ⟨-żyć⟩ (się); **'~·ways, '~·wise** na długość; wzdłuż; **'~·y** (***-ier, -iest***) *zbyt* długi
le·ni·ent ['liːnjənt] wyrozumiały, łagodny; pobłażliwy
lens [lenz] *anat., phot., phys.* soczewka *f*; *phot.* obiektyw *m*
lent [lent] *pret. i p.p. od* **lend**
Lent [lent] *rel.* wielki post *m*
len·til ['lentɪl] *bot.* soczewica *f*
Le·o ['liːəʊ] *znak Zodiaku*: Lew *m*; ***he/she is (a) ~*** on(a) jest spod znaku Lwa
leop·ard ['lepəd] *zo.* leopard *m*; **~·ess** ['lepədes] *zo.* leopard *m* samica
le·o·tard ['liːəʊtɑːd] *gimnastyczny* trykot *m*
lep·ro·sy ['leprəsɪ] *med.* trąd *m*
les·bi·an ['lezbɪən] **1.** lesbijski; **2.** lesbijka *f*
less [les] **1.** *adj. i adv.* (*comp. od* **little** 1, 2) mniejszy; **2.** *prp.* mniej o (*A*), odjąć (*A*), minus (*A*)
less·en ['lesn] zmniejszać (się)
less·er ['lesə] mniejszy, pomniejszy
les·son ['lesn] lekcja *f*; *fig.* nauka *f*; **~s** *pl.* zajęcia *pl.*
let [let] (***let***) dawać, pozwalać; *zwł. Brt.* wynajmować ⟨-jąć⟩; ***~ alone*** zostawiać ⟨-wić⟩ w spokoju; ***~ down*** obniżać ⟨-żyć⟩, spuszczać ⟨-uścić⟩; *Am. ubrania* przedłużać ⟨-żyć⟩; zawodzić ⟨-wieść⟩; ***~ go*** puszczać ⟨puścić⟩; ***~ o.s. go*** zaniedbywać ⟨-bać⟩ się; F odpuszczać ⟨-uścić⟩ sobie; ***~'s go!*** chodźmy!; ***~ in*** wpuszczać ⟨-uścić⟩; ***~ s.o. in for s.th.*** dopuścić kogoś do czegoś
le·thal ['liːθl] śmiertelny, zabójczy, śmiercionośny
leth·ar·gy ['leθədʒɪ] letarg *m*
let·ter ['letə] litera *f*; *print.* czcionka *f*; list *m*, pismo *n*; **'~·box** *zwł. Brt.* skrzynka *f* na listy; **'~ car·ri·er** *Am.* listonosz(ka *f*) *m*, *pocztowy* (*-a*) doręczyciel(ka *f*) *m*
let·tuce ['letɪs] *bot.* sałata *f*
leu·k(a)e·mia [luː'kiːmɪə] *med.* białaczka *f*
lev·el ['levl] **1.** *adj.* poziomy; równy; ***be ~ with*** być na równej wysokości z (*N*); ***do one's ~ best*** F robić, co w czyjejś mocy; **2.** poziom *m* (*też fig.*); poziomica *f*; warstwa *f*; ***sea ~*** poziom *m* morza; ***on the ~*** F na poziomie; **3.** (*zwł. Brt.* ***-ll-***, *Am.* ***-l-***) równać, zrównywać ⟨-nać⟩; ***~ at*** *broń* ⟨s⟩kierować na (*A*); *oskarżenie* wymierzyć; **4.** *adv.*: ***~ with*** na wysokości (*G*); **~ 'cross·ing** *Brt.* jednopoziomowy przejazd *m* kolejowy; **~-'head·ed** zrównoważony
le·ver ['liːvə] dźwignia *f*
lev·y ['levɪ] **1.** podatek *m*, pobór *m* podatku; **2.** *podatki* nakładać ⟨-łożyć⟩, pobierać ⟨-brać⟩
lewd [ljuːd] obleśny, lubieżny

L

li·a·bil·i·ty [laɪə'bɪlətɪ] *econ., jur.* odpowiedzialność *f*, zobowiązanie *n*; *econ.* ***liabilities*** *pl.* pasywa *pl.*, należności *pl.*; obciążenie *n* (***to*** dla *G*), ciężar *m* (***to*** dla *G*)
li·a·ble ['laɪəbl] *econ., jur.* odpowiedzialny; ***be ~ for*** odpowiadać za (*A*); ***be ~ to*** być podatnym na (*A*)
li·ar ['laɪə] kłamca *m*
li·bel ['laɪbl] *jur.* **1.** (*na piśmie*) zniesławienie *n*, oszczerstwo *n*, potwarz *f*; **2.** (*zwł. Brt.* **-ll-**, *Am.* **-l-**) (*na piśmie*) zniesławiać ⟨-wić⟩
lib·e·ral ['lɪbərəl] **1.** liberalny (*też pol.*); tolerancyjny; szczodry, hojny; **2.** *pol.* liberał *m*
lib·e|·rate ['lɪbəreɪt] oswobadzać ⟨-bodzić⟩; **~·ra·tion** [lɪbə'reɪʃn] oswobodzenie *n*; **~·ra·tor** ['lɪbəreɪtə] oswobodziciel *m*
lib·er·ty ['lɪbətɪ] wolność *f*; ***take liberties with s.o.*** pozwalać sobie za dużo z kimś; ***take the ~ of*** pozwolić sobie na (*A*); ***at ~*** na wolności
Li·bra ['laɪbrə] *znak Zodiaku*: Waga *f*; ***he/she is*** (***a***) ~ on(a) jest spod znaku Wagi
li·brar·i·an [laɪ'breərɪən] bibliotekarz *m* (-arka *f*); **li·bra·ry** ['laɪbrərɪ] biblioteka *f*
lice [laɪs] *pl. od* ***louse***
li·cence *Brt.*, **li·cense** *Am.* ['laɪsəns] koncesja *f*, licencja *f*; zezwolenie *n*, pozwolenie *n*; **'li·cense plate** *Am. mot.* tablica *f* rejestracyjna
li·cense *Brt.*, **li·cence** *Am.* ['laɪsəns] udzielać ⟨-lić⟩ licencji *lub* koncesji; *urzędowo* zezwalać ⟨-wolić⟩
li·chen ['laɪkən] *bot.* porost *m*
lick [lɪk] **1.** liźnięcie *n*, polizanie *n*; lizawka *f* (*solna*); **2.** ⟨po⟩lizać, oblizywać ⟨-zać⟩; wylizywać ⟨-zać⟩; F pokonywać ⟨-nać⟩, przezwyciężać ⟨-żyć⟩
lic·o·rice ['lɪkərɪs] → ***liquorice***
lid [lɪd] **1.** pokrywka *f*; wieczko *n*; powieka *f*
lie[1] [laɪ] **1.** ⟨s⟩kłamać, okłamywać ⟨-mać⟩; ***~ to s.o.*** okłamywać ⟨-mać⟩ kogoś; **2.** kłamstwo *n*; ***tell a ~, tell ~s*** mówić kłamstwa; ***give the ~ to s.o.*** zadawać kłam komuś
lie[2] [laɪ] **1.** (***lay, lain***) leżeć; ***let sleeping dogs ~*** nie budzić licha; ***~ behind*** *fig.* leżeć u podstaw; ***~ down*** kłaść ⟨położyć⟩ się; **2.** położenie *n*, miejsce *n*; **'~-down** *Brt.* F drzemka; ***go for a ~-down*** *fig.* iść przyłożyć głowę do poduszki; **'~-in** *zwł.*: *Brt.* F ***have a ~-in*** długo nie wstawać z łóżka
lieu [lju:]: ***in ~ of*** w miejsce (*G*)
lieu·ten·ant [lef'tenənt, *Am.* lu:'tenənt] porucznik *m*
life [laɪf] (*pl.* ***lives*** [laɪvz]) życie *n*; *jur.* dożywocie *n*; ***all her ~*** przez jej całe życie; ***for ~*** na całe życie; *zwł. jur.* dożywotnio; **'~ as·sur·ance** ubezpieczenie *n* na życie; **'~ belt** pas *m* ratunkowy; koło *n* ratunkowe; **'~·boat** łódź *f* ratunkowa; **'~buoy** koło *n* ratunkowe; **'~·guard** (*na basenie*) ratownik *m*; **~ im'pris·on·ment** *jur.* kara *f* dożywotniego więzienia; **~ in·sur·ance** ubezpieczenie *n* na życie; **'~ jack·et** kamizelka *f* ratunkowa; **'~·less** bez życia; niemrawy; martwy; **'~·like** realistyczny; jak żywy; **'~·long** na całe życie; **'~ pre·serv·er** *zwł. Am.* kamizelka *f* ratunkowa; koło *n* ratunkowe; **~ 'sen·tence** *jur.* wyrok *m* dożywotniego więzienia; **'~·time** okres *m* życia; życie *n*
lift [lɪft] **1.** *v/t.* podnosić ⟨-nieść⟩; unosić ⟨unieść⟩; *zakaz itp.* znosić ⟨znieść⟩; *wzrok* unieść; F podprowadzić, zwędzić; *v/i.* unosić ⟨unieść⟩ się, podnosić ⟨-nieść⟩ się (*też o mgle*); ***~ off*** *rakieta*: ⟨wy⟩startować; *samolot*: unosić ⟨-nieść⟩ się w powietrze; **2.** podniesienie *n*; *aviat.* siła *f* nośna; *phys.* wypór *m*, siła *f* wyporu; *Brt.* winda *f*, dźwig *m*; ***give s.o. a ~*** podrzucać ⟨-cić⟩ kogoś (*samochodem*); F podnosić ⟨-nieść⟩ kogoś na duchu; **'~-off** start *m*; wzniesienie *n się* (*rakiety, samolotu*)
lig·a·ment ['lɪgəmənt] *anat.* wiązadło *n*
light[1] [laɪt] **1.** światło *n* (*też fig.*); oświetlenie *n*; blask *m* (*świecy*); ogień *m* (*dla papierosa*); *Brt. zw.* ***~s*** *pl. drogowe* światła *pl.*; ***have you got a ~, can you give me a ~?*** czy ma pan ogień?; **2.** (***lit*** *lub* ***lighted***) *v/t.* oświetlać ⟨-lić⟩; *też* ***~ up*** zapalać ⟨-lić⟩; *v/i.* zapalać ⟨-lić⟩ się; ***~ up*** *oczy itp.*: rozjarzać ⟨-rzyć⟩ się; **3.** jasny
light[2] [laɪt] lekki (*też fig.*); ***make ~ of*** coś lekko ⟨po⟩traktować (*A*), umniejszać ⟨-szyć⟩ (*A*)
light·en[1] ['laɪtn] rozjaśniać ⟨-nić⟩ (się), przejaśniać ⟨-nić⟩ (się)

L

light·en² ['laɪtn] zmniejszać ⟨-szyć⟩ (się)
'light·er zapalniczka *f*
light|-'head·ed lekkomyślny, niefrasobliwy; oszołomiony; **~-'heart·ed** beztroski; **'~·house** latarnia *f* morska; **'~·ing** oświetlenie *n*; **'~·ness** lekkość *f*
light·ning ['laɪtnɪŋ] błyskawica *f*; ***like ~*** jak błyskawica; **'~ con·duc·tor** *Brt.*, **'~ rod** *Am. electr* piorunochron *m*, odgromnik *m*
'light·weight *sport*: waga *f* lekka
like¹ [laɪk] **1.** *v/t.* ⟨po⟩lubić; ***I ~ it*** podoba mi się to; ***I ~ her*** lubię ją; ***how do you ~ it?*** jak ci się to podoba?; ***I should*** *lub* ***would ~ to know*** chciałbym wiedzieć; *v/i.* chcieć; **(*just*) *as you ~*** (tak) jak chcesz; ***if you ~*** jeżeli chcesz; **2. *~s*** *pl.* ***and dislikes*** *pl.* sympatie *pl.* i antypatie *pl.*
like² [laɪk] **1.** jak; ***~ that*** tak; ***feel ~*** mieć ochotę; ***what does it look ~?*** jak to wygląda?; ***what is he ~?*** jaki on jest?; ***that is just ~ him!*** to podobne do niego!; **2.** podobny; ***the ~ of him*** ktoś podobny do niego; ***the ~s of you*** ludzie podobni do was
like|·li·hood ['laɪklɪhʊd] prawdopodobieństwo *n*; **'~·ly 1.** *adj.* **(*-ier, -iest*)** prawdopodobny; **2.** *adv.* prawdopodobnie; ***not ~ly!*** z pewnością nie!
like|·ness ['laɪknɪs] podobieństwo *n*; **'~·wise** podobnie
lik·ing ['laɪkɪŋ] sympatia *f*
li·lac ['laɪlək] **1.** lila; **2.** *bot.* bez *m*
lil·y ['lɪlɪ] *bot.* lilia *f*; ***~ of the valley*** konwalia *f*
limb [lɪm] kończyna *f*, członek *m*; konar *m*
lime¹ [laɪm] wapno *n*
lime² [laɪm] *bot.* limona *f*
'lime·light światła *pl.* rampy; *fig.* centrum *n* uwagi
lim·it ['lɪmɪt] **1.** granica *f*; ***within ~s*** w pewnych granicach; ***off ~s*** *Am.* wstęp wzbroniony (***to*** do *G*); ***that is the ~!*** F to już szczyty!
lim·i·ta·tion [lɪmɪ'teɪʃn] ograniczenie *n*; *fig.* granica *f*
'lim·it|·ed ograniczony; ***~ed liability company*** *Brt.* spółka z ograniczoną odpowiedzialnością; **'~·less** nieograniczony; bezgraniczny
limp¹ [lɪmp] **1.** utykać, kuśtykać; **2.** utykanie *n*, kuśtykanie *n*
limp² [lɪmp] wiotki, zwiotczały
line¹ [laɪn] **1.** linia *f* (*też fig.*); kreska *f*; zmarszczka *f*; sznur *m*, linka *f*, żyłka *f* (*przy wędce, etc.*); kabel *m*, przewód *m*; *zwł. Am.* kolejka *f*, ogonek *m*; *autobusowa, telefoniczna itp.* linia *f*; rząd *m*, szereg *m*; branża *f*, dziedzina *f*, specjalność *f*; wiersz *m* (*tekstu*); *tel.* połączenie *n*; *fig.* granica *f*; *fig.* kurs *m*; ***~s*** *pl. theat.* rola *f*, kwestia *f*; ***the ~*** równik *m*; ***draw the ~*** ustalać ⟨-lić⟩ granice (***at s.th.*** czegoś); ***the ~ is busy*** *lub* ***engaged*** *tel.* linia jest zajęta; ***hold the ~*** *tel.* proszę nie odkładać słuchawki; ***stand in ~*** *Am.* stać w kolejce (***for*** za *I*); **2.** ⟨po⟩liniować; *twarz* ⟨z⟩marszczyć; *drzewa*: ⟨u⟩tworzyć szpaler, *ludzie*: wypełniać (*szeregami*); ***~ up*** ustawiać (się) w szeregu; (*w sporcie*) ustawiać ⟨-wić⟩ się; *zwł. Am.* stawać ⟨stanąć⟩ w kolejce (***for*** za *I*)
line² [laɪn] *ubranie* podbijać ⟨-bić⟩; wykładać ⟨wyłożyć⟩, wyścielać ⟨-lić⟩
lin·e·ar ['lɪnɪə] linearny, liniowy
lin·en ['lɪnɪn] **1.** *materiał*: len *m*; *pościelowa itp.* bielizna *f*; **2.** lniany; **'~ clos·et** *Am.*, **'~ cup·board** (*szafka*) bieliźniarka *f*
lin·er ['laɪnə] liniowiec *m*; samolot *m* kursowy; → ***eyeliner***
lines|·man ['laɪnzmən] (*pl.* ***-men***) (*w sporcie*) sędzia *m* liniowy; **'~·wom·an** (*pl.* ***-women***) (*w sporcie*) kobieta-sędzia *m* liniowy
'line·up (*w sporcie*) skład *m*; *zwł. Am.* rząd *m* ludzi
lin·ger ['lɪŋgə] zatrzymywać ⟨-mać⟩ się, zwlekać; ***~ on*** utrzymywać się, trwać; *fig.* wegetować
lin·ge·rie ['lɛ̃:nʒəri:] bielizna *f* damska
lin·i·ment ['lɪnɪmənt] *pharm.* środek *m* do nacierania, mazidło *n*
lin·ing ['laɪnɪŋ] wyściółka *f*; podszewka *f*, podpinka *f*; *tech.* okładzina *f*
link [lɪŋk] **1.** ogniwo *n* (*łańcucha też fig.*); spinka *f* (*do mankietów*); połączenie *n*; zależność *f*; **2.** *też* ***~ up*** ⟨po⟩łączyć się
links [lɪŋks] → ***golf links***
'link·up połączenie *n*
lin·seed ['lɪnsi:d] *bot.* siemię *n* lniane; **~ 'oil** olej *m* lniany
li·on ['laɪən] *zo.* lew *m*; **~·ess** *zo.* ['laɪənes] lwica *f*
lip [lɪp] *anat.* warga *f*; brzeg *m* (*filiżanki*

itp.); *sl.* czelność *f*; '**~·stick** szminka *f* (*do ust*)
liq·ue·fy ['lɪkwɪfaɪ] skraplać ⟨-roplić⟩ (się)
liq·uid ['lɪkwɪd] **1.** ciecz *f*; **2.** ciekły
liq·ui·date ['lɪkwɪdeɪt] ⟨z⟩likwidować; *dług* spłacać ⟨-cić⟩
liq·uid|·ize ['lɪkwɪdaɪz] ⟨z⟩miksować; rozdrabniać⟨-robnić⟩; '**~·iz·er** mikser *m*
liq·uor ['lɪkə] *zwł. Am.* silny napój alholowy; *Brt.* napój *m* alkoholowy, alkohol *m*; ⚠ *nie* ***likier***
liq·uo·rice ['lɪkərɪs] lukrecja *f*
Lis·bon Lizbona *f*
lisp [lɪsp] **1.** ⟨za⟩seplenić; **2.** seplenienie *n*
list [lɪst] **1.** lista *f*, spis *m*; **2.** umieszczać ⟨umieścić⟩ na liście; wypisywać ⟨-sać⟩
lis·ten ['lɪsn] słuchać; **~ *in*** ⟨wy⟩słuchać w radio (***to s.th.*** czegoś); **~ *in*** *rozmowę telefoniczną* podsłuchiwać ⟨-chać⟩; **~ *to*** ⟨po-, wy⟩słuchać (*G*); '**~·er** słuchacz(ka *f*) *m*
'**list·less** bierny, apatyczny
lit [lɪt] *pret. i p.p. od* ***light***[1]
lit·e·ral ['lɪtərəl] dosłowny, literalny
lit·e·ra|·ry ['lɪtərərɪ] literacki; **~·ture** ['lɪtərətʃə] literatura *f*
lithe [laɪð] gibki, sprężysty
Lith·u·a·nia Litwa *f*
li·tre *Brt.*, **li·ter** *Am.* ['liːtə] litr *m*
lit·ter ['lɪtə] **1.** (*zwł. papier*) śmieci *pl.*; podściółka *f*; *zo.* miot *m*; lektyka *f*; **2.** zaśmiecać ⟨-cić⟩; ***be ~ed with*** być zaśmieconym (*I*); '**~ bas·ket**, '**~ bin** kosz *m* na śmieci
lit·tle ['lɪtl] **1.** *adj.* (***less, least***) mały; ***the ~ ones*** *pl.* mali *pl.*; **2.** *adv.* (***less, least***) mało, niewiele; **3.** (za) mało; ***a ~*** trochę, nieco; ***~ by ~*** po trochę, stopniowo;
live[1] [lɪv] żyć (*też* ***with*** z *I*); mieszkać; ***~ to see*** dożyć; ***~ on*** trwać; utrzymywać się z (*I*); ***~ up to*** spełniać ⟨-nić⟩, *reputacji* sprostać
live[2] [laɪv] **1.** *adj.* żywy, żyjący; *electr.* pod napięciem; *amunicja*: uzbrojony; *transmisja*: na żywo; **2.** *adv.* na żywo, bezpośrednio
live|·li·hood ['laɪvlɪhʊd] środki *pl.* utrzymania; '**~·li·ness** żywość *f*, dynamizm *m*; '**~·ly** (***-ier, -iest***) żywy, żwawy, dynamiczny
liv·er ['lɪvə] *anat.* wątroba *f*; *gastr.* wątróbka *f*
liv·e·ry ['lɪvərɪ] liberia *n*
lives [laɪvz] *pl. od* ***life***
'**live·stock** inwentarz *m* żywy
liv·id ['lɪvɪd] siny; F rozwścieczony
liv·ing ['lɪvɪŋ] **1.** żywy, żyjący; ***the ~ image of*** dokładna podobizna *f* (*G*); **2.** środki *pl.* utrzymania; ***the ~*** *pl.* żywi *pl.*; ***standard of ~*** stopa *f* życiowa; ***earn*** *lub* ***make a ~*** zarabiać ⟨-robić⟩ na utrzymanie; '**~ room** salon *m*, pokój *m* dzienny
liz·ard ['lɪzəd] *zo.* jaszczurka *f*
load [ləʊd] **1.** ładunek *m*, obciążenie *n*; *fig.* ciężar *m*; **2.** obciążać ⟨-żyć⟩; *broń* ⟨za⟩ładować; ***~ a camera*** włożyć film do aparatu; *też* ***~ up*** załadowywać ⟨-ować⟩
loaf[1] [ləʊf] (*pl.* ***loaves*** [ləʊvz]) bochenek *m*
loaf[2] [ləʊf] *też* ***~ about, ~ around*** F próżnować; '**~·er** próżniak *m*
loam [ləʊm] glina *f* , ił *m*; '**~·y** (***-ier, -iest***) gliniasty, ilasty
loan [ləʊn] **1.** pożyczka *f*; *bankowy* kredyt *m*; wypożyczenie *n*; ***on ~*** wypożyczony; **2.** *zwł. Am. komuś* pożyczać ⟨-czyć⟩, wypożyczać ⟨-czyć⟩; udzielać ⟨-lić⟩ pożyczki; '**~ shark** *econ.* lichwiarz *m* (-arka *f*)
loath [ləʊθ]: ***be ~ to do s.th.*** nie chcieć zrobić czegoś
loathe [ləʊð] nienawidzić (*G*), nie cierpieć (*G*); '**loath·ing** obrzydzenie *n*, awersja *f*
loaves [ləʊvz] *pl. od* ***loaf***[1]
lob [lɒb] *zwł.* (*w tenisie*) lob *m*
lob·by ['lɒbɪ] **1.** przedsionek *m*, westybul *m*; *theat.* foyer *n*; kuluary *pl.*; *pol.* lobby *n*, grupa *f* nacisku; **2.** *pol.* wywierać ⟨-rzeć⟩ nacisk
lobe [ləʊb] *anat.*, *bot.* płat *m*, płatek *m*; → ***earlobe***
lob·ster ['lɒbstə] *zo.* homar *m*
lo·cal ['ləʊkl] **1.** lokalny, miejscowy; **2.** miejscowy *m* (-wa *f*); *Brt.* F stała knajpa *f* (*do której stale się chodzi*); ⚠ *nie* ***lokal***; **~ 'call** *tel.* rozmowa *f* miejscowa; **~ e'lec·tions** *pl.* wybory *pl.* komunalne *lub* do władz miejscowych; **~ 'gov·ern·ment** samorząd *m* terytorialny; '**~ time** czas *m* miejscowy; **~ 'traf·fic** ruch *m* (*uliczny*) miejscowy
lo·cate [ləʊ'keɪt] ⟨z⟩lokalizować, umiejscawiać ⟨-owić⟩; ***be ~d*** być położonym,

znajdować się; **lo·ca·tion** [ləʊ'keɪʃn] lokalizacja *f*, umiejscowienie *n*; miejsce (***for*** na *A*); *filmowy*: plener *m*; ***on ~*** w plenerze, poza studiem
loch [lɒk] jezioro *n*
lock[1] [lɒk] **1.** zamek *m* (*do drzwi, broni*); śluza *f*, komora *f* śluzowa; zamknięcie *n*; **2.** *v/t.* zamykać ⟨-mknąć⟩ (*na klucz*) (*też* ***~ up***); trzymać *kogoś* w uścisku; *tech.* unieruchamiać ⟨-chomić⟩, ⟨za⟩-blokować; *v/i.* zamykać ⟨-knąć⟩ się (na klucz); *mot. kierownica*: ⟨za⟩blokować się; ***~ away*** zamykać ⟨-mknąć⟩; ***~ in*** zamykać ⟨-mknąć⟩ (*w środku*); ***~ out*** ⟨za⟩stosować lokaut; ***~ up*** zamykać ⟨-mknąć⟩; ⟨u⟩więzić
lock[2] [lɒk] lok *m*
lock·er ['lɒkə] szafka *f* (*w szatni*); schowek *m* bagażu; **'~ room** *zwł.* (*w sporcie*) szatnia *f*, kabina *f* w szatni
lock·et ['lɒkɪt] medalion *m*
'lock|·out lokaut *m*; **'~·smith** ślusarz *m*; **'~·up** cela *f* w areszcie
lo·co·mo|·tion [ləʊkə'məʊʃn] zdolność *f* poruszania się, lokomocja *f*; **~·tive** ['ləʊkəməʊtɪv] lokomocyjny
lo·cust ['ləʊkəst] *zo.* szarańcza *f*
lodge [lɒdʒ] **1.** budka *f* stróża, stróżówka *f*; domek *m* (*myśliwski, narciarski*); altanka *f*; loża *f* (*masońska*); **2.** *v/i.* przebywać, ⟨za⟩mieszkać; *kul itp.*: utkwić; *v/t.* ⟨prze⟩nocować; *zażalenie itp.* składać ⟨złożyć⟩; **'lodg·er** lokator(ka *f*) *m*; **'lodg·ing** zamieszkanie *n*, mieszkanie *n*; ***~s*** *pl. zwł.* pokój *m* umeblowany
loft [lɒft] strych *m*, poddasze *n*; empora *f*; *Am.* piętro *n* w budynku niemieszkalnym; **'~·y** (***-ier, -iest***) wysoki; wzniosły; wyniosły
log [lɒg] kłoda *f*; ***sleep like a ~*** spać jak kamień; **'~·book** *naut.*, *aviat.* dziennik *m* okrętowy; *aviat.* dziennik *m* pokładowy; *mot.* książka *f* jazd; **~ 'cab·in** chata *f* zrębowa
log·ger·heads ['lɒgəhedz]: ***be at ~*** nie zgadzać się (***with*** z *I*)
lo·gic ['lɒdʒɪk] logika *f*; **'~·al** logiczny
loin [lɔɪn] *gastr.* polędwica *f*; ***~s*** *pl. anat.* lędźwie *pl.*
loi·ter ['lɔɪtə] pętać się, pałętać się; kręcić się
loll [lɒl] rozwalać ⟨-lić⟩ się, uwalić się; ***~ out*** zwieszać ⟨-sić⟩ się
lol·li·pop ['lɒlɪpɒp] lizak *m*; *zwł. Brt.* lody *pl.* na patyku; ***~ man, ~ woman, ~ lady*** *Brt.* (*osoba, pomagająca dzieciom przechodzić przez ulicę*)
Lon·don Londyn *m*
lone|·li·ness ['ləʊnlɪnɪs] samotność *f*; **'~·ly** (***-ier, -iest***), **'~·some** samotny
long[1] [lɒŋ] **1.** *adj.* długi; *odległość*: duży; **2.** *adv.* długo; ***as*** *lub* ***so ~ as*** jeżeli tylko; ***~ ago*** dawno temu; ***so ~!*** F cześć!; **3. *for ~*** na długo; ***take ~*** długo trwać *lub* wymagać dużo czasu
long[2] [lɒŋ] ⟨za⟩tęsknić (***for*** za *I*)
long-'dis·tance długodystansowy; zamiejscowy; **~ 'call** rozmowa *f* zamiejscowa; **~ 'run·ner** długodystansowiec
lon·gev·i·ty [lɒn'dʒevətɪ] długowieczność *f*
'long·hand pismo *n* ręczne
long·ing ['lɒŋɪŋ] **1.** tęskniący; **2.** tęsknota *f*
lon·gi·tude ['lɒndʒɪtjuːd] *geogr.* długość *f*
'long| jump (*w sporcie*) skok *m* w dal; **~-life 'milk** *zwł. Brt.* mleko *n* o przedłużonej trwałości; **~-'play·er**, **~-play·ing 'rec·ord** płyta *f* długogrająca; **~-'range** *mil.*, *aviat.* o dalekim zasięgu; długofalowy; **~·shore·man** ['lɒŋʃɔːmən] *zwł. Am.* (*pl.* ***-men***) doker *m*; **~'sight·ed** *zwł. Brt. fig.* dalekowzroczny; ***be ~sighted*** być dalekowidzem; **~-'stand·ing** dawny; **~-'term** długoterminowy; **~ 'wave** *radiowe* długie fale *pl.*; **~'wind·ed** rozwlekły, nużący
loo [luː] *Brt.* F ubikacja *f*
look [lʊk] **1.** ⟨po⟩patrzeć (***at*** na *A*); wyglądać (***happy*** na szczęśliwego; ***good*** dobrze); *okno*: wychodzić (***onto a street*** na ulicę), *dom*: być skierowanym (***west*** na zachód); ***~ here!*** posłuchaj!; ***~ like*** wyglądać jak; ***it ~s as if*** wygląda, jakby; ***~ after*** ⟨za⟩troszczyć się o (*A*), zajmować ⟨-jąć⟩ się (*I*); ***~ ahead*** patrzeć naprzód, *fig.* spoglądać w przyszłość; ***~ around*** rozglądać ⟨-zejrzeć⟩ się; ***~ at*** ⟨po⟩patrzeć na (*A*); ***~ back*** oglądać ⟨obejrzeć⟩ się; *fig.* spoglądać ⟨spojrzeć⟩ za siebie; ***~ down on*** patrzeć z góry na (*A*); ***~ for*** ⟨po⟩szukać (*G*); ***~ forward to*** wyczekiwać (*A*); ***~ in*** F wpadać ⟨wpaść⟩ z wizytą (***on s.o.*** do kogoś); ***~ onto*** wychodzić na (*A*); ***~ out*** wyglądać (***of*** z *G*); uważać; wypatrywać, wyszukiwać ⟨-kać⟩;

L

~ over *coś* przeglądać ⟨przejrzeć⟩; *kogoś* ⟨z⟩lustrować; **~ round** rozglądać ⟨-zejrzeć⟩ się; **~ through** *coś* przeglądać ⟨przejrzeć⟩; **~ up** podnosić ⟨-ieść⟩ wzrok na (*A*); *coś* ⟨po⟩szukać (*G*); *kogoś* odwiedzać ⟨-dzić⟩; **2.** spojrzenie *n*; wygląd *m*; (**good**) **~s** *pl.* uroda *f*; **have a ~ at s.th.** popatrzeć na coś; **I don't like the ~ of it** nie podoba mi się to; **'~·ing glass** lustro *n*; **'~·out** punkt *m* obserwacyjny; *naut.* wachta *f*; obserwator(ka *f*) *m*; *fig.* F perspektywa *f*; **be on the ~out for** rozglądać się za (*I*); **that's his ~out** *Brt.* F to jego sprawa

loom¹ [luːm] krosno *n*

loom² [luːm] *też* **~ up** wyłaniać ⟨-łonić⟩ się

loop [luːp] **1.** pętla *f* (*też naut., komp.*); *med. domaciczna* spirala *f*; **2.** owijać ⟨-winąć⟩ (się) dookoła, obwiązywać ⟨-zać⟩ dookoła; **'~·hole** otwór *m*; *mil.* otwór *m* strzelniczy; *fig.* furtka *f*; **a ~hole in the law** luka *f* prawna

loose [luːs] **1.** (**-r, -st**) luźny; ruszający się; *włosy*: rozpuszczony; wolny; **let ~** puszczać wolno; **2. be on the ~** znajdować się na wolności; **loos·en** ['luːsn] rozluźnić ⟨-niać⟩ (się) (*też fig.*); **~ up** (*w sporcie*) rozgrzewać ⟨-rzać⟩ się

loot [luːt] **1.** łup *m*; **2.** ⟨z⟩łupić, ⟨s⟩plądrować

lop [lɒp] (**-pp-**) obcinać ⟨-ciąć⟩; **~ off** obciosywać ⟨-sać⟩; **~-'sid·ed** krzywy

loq·ua·cious [ləʊ'kweɪʃəs] gadatliwy

lord [lɔːd] pan *m*; władca *m*; *Brt.* lord *m*, par *m*; **the ♀** Pan *m* Bóg; **the ♀'s Supper** Wieczerza *f* Pańska; **House of ♀s** *Brt.* Izba *f* Parów *lub* Lordów; **♀ 'Mayor** *Brt.* lord *m* burmistrz

lor·ry ['lɒrɪ] *Brt.* ciężarówka *f*

lose [luːz] (**lost**) ⟨s-, u⟩tracić; ⟨z⟩gubić; przegrywać ⟨-rać⟩; *zegarek*: późnić ⟨spóźniać⟩ się; **~ o.s.** ⟨z⟩gubić się; **'los·er** przegrywający *m* (-ca *f*); nieudacznik *m*, ofiara *f*

loss [lɒs] strata *f*, utrata *f*; zguba *f*; **at a ~** *econ.* ze stratą; **be at a ~** nie umieć znaleźć

lost [lɒst] **1.** *pret. i p.p. od* **lose**; **2.** *adj.* zagubiony; zaginiony; **be ~** zgubić się, pogubić się; **be ~ in thought** zatopić się w myślach; **get ~** ⟨z⟩gubić się; **get ~!** *sl.* spadaj!; **~-and-'found** (**office**) *Am.*, **~ 'prop·er·ty of·fice** *Brt.* biuro *n* rzeczy znalezionych

lot [lɒt] los *m*; parcela *f*, działka *f*; *econ.* partia *f*; zestaw *m*, grupa *f*; ⚠ *nie* **lot**; **the ~** wszystko; **a ~ of** F, **~s of** F dużo; **a bad ~** F niegodziwiec *m*; **cast** *lub* **draw ~s** rzucać ⟨-cić⟩ *lub* '0po⟩ciągnąć losy

loth [ləʊθ] → **loath**

lo·tion ['ləʊʃn] płyn *m* (*kosmetyczny*)

lot·te·ry ['lɒtərɪ] loteria *f*

loud [laʊd] **1.** *adj.* głośny; *fig. barwy* krzykliwy; **2.** *adv.* głośno; **~'speak·er** głośnik *m*

lounge [laʊndʒ] **1.** pokój *m* dzienny; salon *m*; (*w hotelu*) hall *m*; *aviat.* hala przylotów *lub* odlotów; **2. ~ about, ~ around** leniuchować; **'~ suit** *Brt.* garnitur *m*

louse [laʊs] *zo.* (*pl.* **lice** [laɪs]) wesz *f*; **lou·sy** ['laʊzɪ] (**-ier, -iest**) zawszony (*też fig.*); F podły, nędzny

lout [laʊt] ordynus *m*

lov·a·ble ['lʌvəbl] uroczy

love [lʌv] **1.** miłość *f* (**of, for, to, towards** do *G*); kochany *m* (-na *f*), skarb *m*; zamiłowanie *n*, pasja *f*; (*w tenisie*) zero *n*; **be in ~ with s.o.** kochać kogoś; **fall in ~ with s.o.** zakochać się w kimś; **make ~ with s.o.** kochać się z kimś; **give my ~ to her** proszę ją serdecznie pozdrowić ode mnie; **send one's ~ to** kogoś przekazać ⟨-zywać⟩ pozdrowienia; **~ from** serdeczne pozdrowienia od (*G*); **2.** ⟨po⟩kochać; **'~ af·fair** romans *m*; **'~·ly** (**-ier, -iest**) uroczy; wspaniały; **'lov·er** kochanek *m*; ukochany *m* (-na *f*); miłośnik *m* (-iczka *f*); **~s** *pl.* zakochani *pl.*

lov·ing ['lʌvɪŋ] kochający, pełen miłości

low [ləʊ] **1.** *adj.* niski (*też fig.*); głęboki (*też fig.*); cichy; przygnębiony; **2.** *adv.* nisko; cicho; **3.** *meteor.* niż *m*, obszar *m* niskiego ciśnienia; *fig.* niski poziom *m*; **'~·brow** F **1.** osoba *f* o niewyszukanych gustach; **2.** o niewyszukanym guście; **~-'cal·o·rie** niskokaloryczny; **~-e'mis·sion** o niskiej zawartości szkodliwych związków

low·er ['ləʊə] **1.** niższy; głębszy; dolny; **2.** obniżać ⟨-żyć⟩; opuszczać ⟨-puścić⟩; *oczy itp.* spuszczać ⟨-puścić⟩; *fig.* zniżać ⟨-żyć⟩

low|-'fat o niskiej zawartości tłuszczu;

~·**land** ['ləʊlənd] nizina *f*; '~·**ly** (**-ier, -iest**) niski; ~-'**necked** *suknia*: głęboko wycięty; ~-'**pitched** *mus.* głęboki, niski; ~-'**pres·sure** *meteor.* niskie ciśnienie *n*; '~-**rise** *zwł. Am.* niski (*budynek*); ~-'**spir·it·ed** przygnębiony

loy·al ['lɔɪəl] lojalny; '~·**ty** lojalność *f*

loz·enge ['lɒzɪndʒ] romb *m*; pastylka *f* (do ssania)

LP [el'piː] *skrót*: ***long-player, long-playing record*** LP *n*, płyta *f* długogrająca

Ltd *skrót pisany*: ***limited*** z o.o., z ograniczoną odpowiedzialnością

lu·bri|·cant ['luːbrɪkənt] środek do smarowania; smar *m*; ~·**cate** ['luːbrɪkeɪt] ⟨na⟩smarować; ~·**ca·tion** [luːbrɪ'keɪʃn] smarowanie *n*

lu·cid ['luːsɪd] klarowny

luck [lʌk] szczęście *n*; *pomyślny* los *m*; ***bad ~, hard ~, ill ~*** pech *m*; ***good ~*** szczęście *n*; ***good ~ !*** powodzenia!; ***be in ~*** mieć szczęście, ***be out of ~*** nie mieć szczęścia; ~·**i·ly** ['lʌkɪlɪ] na szczęście; '~·**y** (**-ier, -iest**) szczęśliwy, pomyślny; ***be ~y*** mieć szczęście; ***~y day*** szczęśliwy *lub* pomyślny dzień *m*; ***~y fellow*** szczęściarz *m*

lu·cra·tive ['luːkrətɪv] lukratywny, intratny

lu·di·crous ['luːdɪkrəs] śmieszny

lug [lʌg] (**-gg-**) ⟨za⟩taszczyć, ⟨za⟩tachać

luge [luːʒ] (*w sporcie*) sanki *pl.* sportowe; saneczkarstwo *n*

lug·gage ['lʌgɪdʒ] *zwł. Brt.* bagaż *m*; '~ **car·ri·er** bagażowy *m*; '~ **rack** *zwł. Brt.* półka *m* na bagaż; '~ **van** *Brt.* wagon *m* bagażowy

luke·warm ['luːkwɔːm] letni (*też fig.*)

lull [lʌl] **1.** uciszać ⟨-szyć⟩; *burza*: uspokajać ⟨-koić⟩ się; *zw.* ***~ to sleep*** ⟨u⟩kołysać do snu; **2.** okres *m* uspokojenia się (*też fig.*)

lul·la·by ['lʌləbaɪ] kołysanka *f*

lum·ba·go [lʌm'beɪgəʊ] *med.* postrzał *m*, lumbago *n*

lum·ber¹ ['lʌmbə] ⟨po⟩wlec się (*z wysiłkiem lub głośno*); ⟨po⟩telepać się

lum·ber² ['lʌmbə] **1.** *zwł. Am.* drewno *n* budowlane; tarcica *f*; *zwł. Brt.* rupiecie *pl.*; **2.** *v/t.*: ***~ s.o. with s.th.*** *Brt.* F obładować kogoś czymś; '~·**jack** *Am.* drwal *m*; '~ **mill** *Am.* tartak *m*; '~-**room** *zwł. Brt.* graciarnia *f*; '~·**yard** *Am.* skład *m* drzewny

lu·mi·na·ry *fig.* ['luːmɪnərɪ] luminarz *m*, koryfeusz *m*

lu·mi·nous ['luːmɪnəs] świecący; ~ **di's-play** tarcza *f* świecąca; ~ '**paint** fosforyzująca farba *f*

lump [lʌmp] **1.** gruda *f*, bryła *f*; kawał *m*; *med.* guz *m*; kostka *f*, kawałek *m* (*cukru*); ⚠ *nie* ***lump***; ***in the ~*** ryczałtem (*też econ.*); **2.** *v/t.* ***~ together*** *fig.* połączyć; *v/i. Am.* zbijać ⟨zbić⟩ się w grudy; ~ '**sug·ar** cukier *m* w kostkach; ~ '**sum** suma *f* ryczałtowa; '~·**y** (**-ier, -iest**) grudowaty, bryłowaty

lu·na·cy ['luːnəsɪ] szaleństwo *n*

lu·nar ['luːnə] księżycowy, lunarny; ~ '**mod·ule** (*w astronautyce*) lądownik *m* księżycowy

lu·na·tic ['luːnətɪk] **1.** szalony; *fig.* szaleńczy, wariacki; **2.** wariat(ka *f*) *m*, szaleniec *m* (*też fig.*); ⚠ *nie* ***lunatyk***

lunch [lʌntʃ], *dawniej* **lun·cheon** ['lʌntʃən] **1.** lunch *m*; **2.** ⟨z⟩jeść lunch; '**lunch hour**, '**lunch time** pora *f* lunchu *lub* obiadowa

lung [lʌŋ] *anat.* płuco *n*; ***the ~s*** *pl.* płuca *pl.*

lunge [lʌndʒ] rzucać ⟨-cić⟩ się (***at*** na *A*)

lurch [lɜːtʃ] **1.** zataczać się; *samochód*: szarpać ⟨-pnąć⟩; **2.** ***leave in the ~*** zostawiać ⟨-wić⟩ na łasce losu

lure [lʊə] **1.** przynęta *f*; *fig.* pokusa *f*; **2.** ⟨z⟩nęcić, ⟨z⟩wabić

lu·rid ['lʊərɪd] *kolor*: krzykliwy; odrażający, koszmarny

lurk [lɜːk] ⟨za⟩czaić się; ***~ about, ~ around*** czatować

lus·cious ['lʌʃəs] apetyczny (*też dziewczyna*)

lush [lʌʃ] bujny; *fig.* pełen przepychu

lust [lʌst] **1.** żądza *f*; **2.** ***~ after, ~ for*** pożądać (*G*)

lus·|tre *Brt.*, ~·**ter** *Am.* ['lʌstə] połysk *m*, blask *m*; ~·**trous** ['lʌstrəs] błyszczący, połyskliwy

lust·y ['lʌstɪ] (**-ier, -iest**) dziarski, witalny

lute [luːt] *mus.* lutnia *f*

Lu·ther·an ['luːθərən] **1.** *adj.* luterański; **2.** luteranin *m* (-anka *f*)

lux·u|·ri·ant [lʌg'ʒʊərɪənt] bujny; ~·**ri·ate** [lʌg'ʒʊərɪeɪt] upajać się; ~·**ri·ous** [lʌg'ʒʊərɪəs] luksusowy; ~·**ry** ['lʌkʃərɪ] luksus *m*; komfort *m*; *attr.* luksusowy

L

LV [el 'viː] *Brt. skrót*: ***lunch**(**eon**)* ***voucher*** bon *m* obiadowy

lye [laɪ] *chem.* ług *m*

ly·ing ['laɪɪŋ] **1.** *pret. i p.p. od* ***lie***[1] *i* ***lie***[2]; **2.** *adj.* kłamliwy, oszczerczy

lymph [lɪmf] *med.* limfa *f*

lynch [lɪntʃ] ⟨z⟩linczować; '**∼ law** prawo *n* linczu

lynx [lɪŋks] *zo.* ryś *m*

lyr|·ic ['lɪrɪk] **1.** *adj.* liryczny; **2.** liryka *f*; ***∼ics*** *pl.* słowa *pl.* (*piosenki*); '**∼·i·cal** liryczny, nastrojowy

M

M, m [em] M, m *n*

M [em] *skrót*: *Brt.* autostrada *f*; ***medium*** (***size***) o średnich rozmiarach

m *skrót pisany*: ***metre*** m, metr *m*; ***mile*** mila (*1,6 km*); ***married*** zam., zamężny; żon., żonaty; ***male, masculine*** męski

ma [mɑː] F mamusia *f*

MA [em 'eɪ] *skrót*: ***Master of Arts*** magister *m* nauk humanistycznych

ma'am [mæm] → ***madam***

mac [mæk] *Brt.* F → ***mackintosh***

ma·cad·am [mə'kædəm] *Am.* → ***tarmac***

mac·a·ro·ni [mækə'rəʊnɪ] *sg.* makaron *m* rurki

ma·chine [mə'ʃiːn] **1.** maszyna *f*; **2.** obrabiać ⟨-robić⟩ maszynowo; ⟨u⟩szyć na maszynie; **∼·gun** karabin *m* maszynowy; **∼-made** wytworzony maszynowo; **∼-'read·a·ble** *komp.* mogący być przetwarzany komputerowo

ma·chin|·e·ry [mə'ʃiːnərɪ] maszyneria *f*; maszyny *pl.*; **∼·ist** [mə'ʃiːnɪst] maszynista *m*; operator *m* obrabiarek

mach·o ['mætʃəʊ] *pej.* (*pl.* **-*os***) macho *m*, stuprocentowy mężczyzna *m*

mack [mæk] *Brt.* F → ***mackintosh***

mack·e·rel ['mækrəl] *zo.* (*pl.* ***mackerel*** *lub* ***mackerels***) makrela *f*

mack·in·tosh ['mækɪntɒʃ] *zwł. Brt.* płaszcz *m* przeciwdeszczowy

mac·ro... ['mækrəʊ] makro...

mad [mæd] szalony, zwariowany; *vet.* wściekły, chory na wściekliznę; *zwł. Am.* rozwścieczony; ***be ∼ about s.th.*** mieć bzika na punkcie czegoś, szaleć za czymś; ***drive s.o. ∼*** doprowadzać ⟨-dzić⟩ kogoś do szaleństwa; ***go ∼*** oszaleć; ***like ∼*** jak szalony

mad·am ['mædəm] pani *f*

'mad|·cap szalony; **∼·den** ['mædn] rozwścieczać ⟨-czyć⟩; **∼·den·ing** ['mædnɪŋ] rozwścieczający

made [meɪd] *pret. i p.p. od* ***make*** 1; ***∼ of gold*** zrobione ze złota

'mad|·house *fig.* F dom *m* wariatów; '**∼·ly** jak szalony; F nieprawdopodobnie, szalenie; '**∼·man** (*pl.* ***-men***) szaleniec *m*, wariat *m*; '**∼·ness** szaleństwo *n*, wariactwo *n*; '**∼·wom·an** (*pl.* ***-women***) wariatka *f*

Ma·drid Madryt *m*

mag·a·zine [mægə'ziːn] magazyn *m*, pismo *n*; magazynek *m* (*broni, aparatu itp.*); magazyn *m*, skład *m*

mag·got ['mægət] *zo.* czerw *m*, robak *m*

Ma·gi ['meɪdʒaɪ] *pl.*: ***the*** (***three***) **∼** Trzej Królowie *pl.*

ma·gic ['mædʒɪk] **1.** magia *f*, czary *pl.*; czar *m*; sztuczka *f* (*iluzjonisty*); **2.** (***∼ally***) *też* ***∼al*** magiczny, czarodziejski; **magi·cian** [mə'dʒɪʃn] czarodziej *m*; magik *m*, iluzjonista *m*

ma·gis·trate ['mædʒɪstreɪt] sędzia *m* pokoju, sędzia *m* policyjny; ⚠ *nie* ***magistrat***

mag|·na·nim·i·ty [mægnə'nɪmətɪ] wspaniałomyślność *f*; **∼·nan·i·mous** [mæg'nænɪməs] wspaniałomyślny

mag·net ['mægnɪt] magnes *m*; **∼·ic** [mæg'netɪk] (***∼ally***) magnetyczny

mag·nif·i·cent [mæg'nɪfɪsnt] wspaniały

mag·ni·fy ['mægnɪfaɪ] powiększać ⟨-szyć⟩; '**∼·ing glass** szkło *n* powiększające, lupa *f*

mag·ni·tude ['mægnɪtjuːd] wielkość *f*, rozmiar *m*

mag·pie ['mægpaɪ] *zo.* sroka *f*

ma·hog·a·ny [mə'hɒgənɪ] mahoń *m*; *attr.* mahoniowy

maid [meɪd] pokojówka *f*; pomoc *f* domowa; ***old ∼*** *przest.* stara panna *f*; ***∼ of***

all work *zwł. fig.* dziewczyna *f* do wszystkiego; **~ *of hono(u)r*** dama *f* dworu; *zwł. Am.* druhna *f*
maid•en ['meɪdn] panna *f*; dziewica *f*; *attr.* panieński; dziewiczy; **'~ name** nazwisko *n* panieńskie
mail [meɪl] **1.** poczta *f*; ***by ~*** *zwł. Am.* pocztą; **2.** *zwł. Am.* wysyłać ⟨-słać⟩ pocztą; *list* wrzucać ⟨-cić⟩; **'~•bag** torba *f* pocztowa; **'~•box** *Am.* skrzynka *f* pocztowa; **'~ car•ri•er** *Am.*, **'~•man** (*pl.* ***-men***) *Am.* listonosz(ka *f*) *m*, doręczyciel(ka *f*) *m* poczty; **~ 'or•der** zamówienie *n* pocztowe; **~-or•der 'firm, ~-or•der 'house** dom *m* sprzedaży wysyłkowej
maim [meɪm] okaleczać ⟨-czyć⟩
Main Men *m*
main [meɪn] **1.** główny, najważniejszy; **2.** *zw.* ***~s*** *gazowa, elektryczna itp.* sieć *f*; *gazowa, elektryczna itp.* magistrala *f*; ***in the ~*** przeważnie, na ogół; **'~•frame** *komp.* duży system *m* komputerowy, duży komputer *m* o wielkiej mocy; **~•land** ['meɪnlənd] ląd *m* stały; **'~•ly** głównie; **~ 'mem•o•ry** *komp.* pamięć *f* główna *lub* operacyjna; **~ 'men•u** *komp.* menu *n* główne; **~ 'road** droga *f* główna; **'~•spring** sprężyna *f* napędowa; *fig.* spiritus movens *m*; **'~•stay** *fig.* podstawa *f*; podpora *f*; **'~ street** *Am.* ulica *f* główna
main•tain [meɪn'teɪn] utrzymywać; ⟨s⟩twierdzić; zapewniać ⟨-nić⟩; ⟨za⟩konserwować; *życie* podtrzymywać ⟨-mać⟩
main•te•nance ['meɪntənəns] utrzymanie *n*; utrzymywanie *n* w dobrym stanie; konserwacja *f*; *jur.* alimenty *pl.*
maize [meɪz] *zwł. Brt.* kukurydza *f*
ma•jes|•tic [mə'dʒestɪk] (***-ally***) majestatyczny; **~•ty** ['mædʒəstɪ] majestat *m*
ma•jor ['meɪdʒə] **1.** większy; *fig.* ważny; *jur.* pełnoletni; ***C ~*** *mus.* C-dur; **2.** *mil.* major *m*; *jur.* osoba *f* pełnoletnia; *Am. univ.* główna specjalizacja *f*; *mus.* dur; **~ 'gen•e•ral** *mil.* generał *m* dywizji; **~•i•ty** [mə'dʒɒrətɪ] większość *f*; *jur.* pełnoletność *f*; *attr.* większościowy; większością; ***be in the ~ity*** stanowić większość; **~ 'league** *Am.* (*w baseballu*) pierwsza liga *f*; **~ 'road** droga *f* główna
make [meɪk] **1.** (***made***) ⟨z⟩robić; ⟨u⟩czynić; wytwarzać ⟨-worzyć⟩; wyrabiać ⟨-robić⟩, ⟨wy⟩produkować; *obiad* przyrządzić ⟨-dzać⟩; *pieniądze* zarabiać ⟨-robić⟩; *zysk, rezultat* osiągać ⟨-gnąć⟩; *mowę* wygłaszać ⟨-łosić⟩; *odległość* pokonywać ⟨-nać⟩; *sumę* stanowić; *podróż* odbywać ⟨-być⟩; *czas* ustalać ⟨-lić⟩; mianować, ustanawiać ⟨-nowić⟩; **~ *s.o. do s.th.*** nakłaniać ⟨-łonić⟩ *lub* zmuszać ⟨-sić⟩ kogoś do zrobienia czegoś; **~ *it*** zdążyć; mieć szczęście; **~ *do with s.th.*** zadowalać ⟨-wolić⟩ się czymś; ***what do you ~ of it?*** co o tym sądzisz?; ***will you ~ one of the party?*** dołączysz się do imprezy?; **~ *the bed*** ⟨po⟩ścielić łóżko; **~ *believe*** udawać; **~ *friends with s.o.*** zaprzyjaźnić się z kimś; **~ *good*** naprawiać ⟨-wić⟩, wyrównywać ⟨-nać⟩; dobrze ⟨z⟩robić; **~ *haste*** ⟨po⟩spieszyć się; **~ *way*** robić miejsce; **~ *for*** ⟨s⟩kierować się do (*G*); ułatwiać ⟨-wić⟩ (*A*); **~ *into*** przerabiać ⟨-robić⟩ w (*A*); **~ *off*** ulatniać ⟨ulotnić⟩ się; **~ *out*** *czek* wypisywać ⟨-sać⟩, *rachunek, dokument* sporządzać ⟨-dzić⟩, *formularz* wypełniać ⟨-nić⟩; ⟨z⟩rozumieć, pojmować ⟨-jąć⟩; udawać; **~ *over*** przekazywać ⟨-zać⟩; przerabiać ⟨-robić⟩; **~ *up*** sporządzać ⟨-dzić⟩, wykonywać ⟨-nać⟩; zestawiać ⟨-wić⟩; składać się; wynagradzać ⟨-rodzić⟩, ⟨z⟩rekompensować; zmyślać ⟨-lić⟩; nakładać ⟨-łożyć⟩ makijaż, ⟨u⟩malować się; **~ *it up*** ⟨po⟩godzić się (***with*** z *I*); **~ *up one's mind*** zdecydować się; ***be made up of*** być zrobionym z (*I*); **~ *up for*** nadrabiać ⟨-robić⟩ braki; **2.** marka *f*; **'~-be•lieve** iluzja *f*, pozory *pl.*; **'~r** wytwórca *m*; **Ꝝr** *Bóg*: Twórca *m*; **'~•shift 1.** prowizorka *f*; **2.** prowizoryczny, improwizowany; **'~-up** makijaż *m*; charakteryzacja *f*; szminka *f*, kosmetyki *pl.*; skład *m*, struktura *f*
mak•ing ['meɪkɪŋ] produkcja *f*; powstawanie *n*, tworzenie *n* się; ***in the ~*** w trakcie powstawania; ***have the ~s of*** mieć zadatki (*G*)
mal•ad•just•ed [mælə'dʒʌstɪd] źle przystosowany, niedostosowany
mal•ad•min•i•stra•tion [mælədmɪnɪ'streɪʃn] złe zarządzanie *n*, *pol.* niegospodarność *f*
mal•con•tent ['mælkəntent] **1.** niezadowolony; **2.** malkontent *m*
male [meɪl] **1.** męski; samczy; płci męskiej; **2.** mężczyzna *m*; *zo.* samiec *m*;

M

~ **'nurse** pielęgniarz *m*
mal·for·ma·tion [mælfɔː'meɪʃn] deformacja *f* (*zwł. wrodzona*)
mal·ice ['mælɪs] złośliwość *f*; *jur.* zła wola *f*
ma·li·cious [mə'lɪʃəs] złośliwy; *jur.* uczyniony w złej woli
ma·lign [mə'laɪn] **1.** *adj.* szkodliwy; **2.** ⟨o⟩szkalować; **ma·lig·nant** [mə'lɪgnənt] złośliwy (*też med.*)
mall [mɔːl, mæl] *Am.* centrum *n* handlowe
mal·le·a·ble ['mælɪəbl] *tech.* kowalny, ciągliwy; *fig.* plastyczny, podatny na wpływy
mal·let ['mælɪt] pobijak *m*; młotek *m* drewniany; (w grze w polo itp.) młotek *m*
mal·nu·tri·tion [mælnjuː'trɪʃn] złe odżywianie *n*, niedożywienie *n*
mal·o·dor·ous [mæl'əʊdərəs] o nieprzyjemnym zapachu
mal·prac·tice [mæl'præktɪs] zaniedbanie *n*; *med.* błąd *m* w sztuce lekarskiej
malt [mɔːlt] słód *m*; *attr.* słodowy

mal·treat [mæl'triːt] maltretować, znęcać się nad (*I*)
mam·mal ['mæml] *zo.* ssak *m*
mam·moth ['mæməθ] **1.** *zo.* mamut *m*; **2.** olbrzymi, kolosalny
mam·my ['mæmɪ] F mamusia *f*
man [mæn, *w złożeniach wymowa* -mən] (*pl.* ***men*** [men]) mężczyzna *m*; człowiek *m*; ludzkość *f*; F mąż *m*; F ukochany *m*, facet *m*; (*w szachach*) figura *f*; (*w grze w warcaby*) pionek *m*; ***the ~ in*** (*Am. też* ***on***) ***the street*** szary człowiek *m*; **2.** [mæn] (**-*nn*-**) *statek itp.* obsadzać ⟨-dzić⟩ załogą
man·age ['mænɪdʒ] *v/t. firmą* ⟨po⟩kierować (*I*); zarządzać (*I*); dawać sobie radę z (*I*); zdołać, podołać (***to do*** zrobić); umieć się obchodzić z (*I*); *v/i.* ⟨po⟩radzić sobie (***with*** z *I*, ***without*** bez *G*); dawać ⟨dać⟩ sobie radę; **'~·a·ble** możliwy do wykonania; **'~·ment** zarządzanie *n*, kierowanie *n*; *econ.* kierownictwo *n*, dyrekcja *f*
man·ag·er ['mænɪdʒə] kierownik *m* (-czka *f*), dyrektor(ka *f*) *m*; menedżer *m*; *sport:* trener *m*; **~·ess** [mænɪdʒə'res] kierowniczka *f*, dyrektorka *f*; kobieta menedżer *f*; (*w sporcie*) trenerka *f*
man·a·ge·ri·al [mænə'dʒɪərɪəl] *econ.* kierowniczy; ~ ***position*** kierownicze stanowisko; ~ ***staff*** kadra *f* kierownicza
man·ag·ing ['mænɪdʒɪŋ] *econ.* zarządzający, kierujący; ~ **di'rector** naczelny dyrektor *m*
man|·date ['mændeɪt] *pol.* mandat *m*; zadanie *n*, zlecenie *n*; **~·da·to·ry** ['mændətərɪ] obowiązkowy, obligatoryjny
mane [meɪn] grzywa *f*
ma·neu·ver [mə'nuːvə] *Am.* → ***manoeuvre***
man·ful ['mænfʊl] męski, mężny
mange [meɪndʒ] *vet.* świerzb *m*
manger ['meɪndʒə] żłób *m*
man·gle ['mæŋgl] **1.** magiel *m*; **2.** ⟨wy⟩maglować; ⟨z⟩deformować
mang·y ['meɪndʒɪ] (***-ier, -iest***) *vet.* chory na świerzb; *fig.* wyliniały
'man·hood wiek *m* męski, męskość *n*
ma·ni·a ['meɪnjə] mania *f*, ***have a ~ for*** być maniakiem na punkcie (*G*); **~c** ['meɪnɪæk] maniak *m*, szaleniec *m*; *fig.* fanatyk *m*
man·i·cure ['mænɪkjʊə] manicure *n*
man·i·fest ['mænɪfest] **1.** oczywisty, jawny; **2.** *v/t.* ⟨za⟩manifestować
man·i·fold ['mænɪfəʊld] różnorodny, różnoraki
ma·nip·u|·late [mə'nɪpjʊleɪt] manipulować (*I*); **~·la·tion** [mənɪpjʊ'leɪʃn] manipulacja *f*
man| 'jack F: ***every ~ jack*** każdy z osobna; **~'kind** ludzkość *f*; **'~·ly** (***-ier, -iest***) męski; **~-'made** sztuczny, wytworzony przez człowieka; ***~-made fibre*** (*Am.* ***fiber***) sztuczne włókno *n*
man·ner ['mænə] sposób *m*; styl *m*; postawa *f*; sposób *m* zachowania; (***good***) ***~s*** *pl. dobre* maniery *pl.*; zwyczaje *pl.*
ma·noeu·vre *Brt.*, **ma·neu·ver** *Am.* [mə'nuːvə] **1.** manewr *m* (*też fig.*); **2.** manewrować (*też fig.*)
man·or ['mænə] posiadłość *f* ziemska; **'~ house** dwór *m*
'man·pow·er siła *f* robocza; personel *m*, kadra *f*
man·sion ['mænʃn] rezydencja *f*
'man·slaugh·ter *jur.* nieumyślne zabójstwo *n*
man·tel|·piece ['mæntlpiːs], **'~·shelf** (*pl.* ***-shelves***) gzyms *m* kominka

man·u·al ['mænjʊəl] **1.** ręczny; fizyczny; **2.** podręcznik *m*

man·u·fac|·ture [mænjʊ'fæktʃə] **1.** wytwarzać ‹-worzyć›, ‹wy›produkować; **2.** produkcja *f*, wytwórstwo *n*, wytwarzanie *n*; **~tures** *pl.* produkty *pl.*; **~·tur·er** [mænjʊ'fæktʃərə] wytwórca *m*, producent *m*; **~·tur·ing** [mænjʊ'fæktʃərɪŋ] przemysł *m* (*wytwórczy*); wytwarzanie *n*; *attr.* wytwórczy

ma·nure [mə'njʊə] **1.** obornik *m*, gnój *m*, mierzwa *f*; **2.** nawozić ‹-wieźć›

man·u·script ['mænjʊskrɪpt] rękopis *m*; manuskrypt *m*

man·y ['menɪ] **1.** (***more, most***) wiele, wielu; **~ *a*** niejeden; **~ *times*** często; ***as* ~** równie często; **2.** wiele; ***a good* ~** dużo; ***a great* ~** bardzo dużo

map [mæp] **1.** mapa *f*, plan *m* (*miasta*); **2.** (**-*pp*-**) sporządzać ‹-dzić› mapę *lub* plan, nanosić ‹-nieść› na mapę *lub* plan; **~ *out*** *fig.* ‹za›planować

ma·ple ['meɪpl] *bot.* klon *m*

mar [mɑː] (**-*rr*-**) ‹ze›szpecić; ‹ze›psuć, ‹z›niszczyć

Mar *skrót pisany*: **March** marzec *m*

mar·a·thon ['mærəθn] **1.** *też* **~ *race*** maraton *m*, wyścig maratoński; **2.** maratoński; *fig.* forsowny

ma·raud [mə'rɔːd] ‹s›plądrować

mar·ble ['mɑːbl] **1.** marmur *m*; kulka *f* (do gry); **2.** marmurowy

march [mɑːtʃ] **1.** ‹po›maszerować; *fig.* iść ‹pójść› naprzód; ‹wy›prowadzić; **2.** marsz *m*; *fig.* postęp *m*; (*demonstracja*) pochód *m*; ***the* ~ *of time*** bieg *m* czasu

March [mɑːtʃ] (*skrót*: **Mar**) marzec *m*

'march·ing or·ders *pl.*: ***give s.o. his/her* ~** *Brt.* F posłać kogoś na zieloną trawkę

mare [meə] *zo.* klacz *f*, kobyła *f*

mar·ga·rine [mɑːdʒə'riːn], **marge** *Brt.* [mɑːdʒ] F margaryna *f*

mar·gin ['mɑːdʒɪn] margines *m* (*też fig.*); brzeg *m*, krawędź *f*; *fig.* dopuszczalny zakres *m*; rozpiętość *f*; *econ.* marża *f*; ***by a wide* ~** dużą przewagą; **'~·al** marginesowy; **~*al note*** notatka *f* na marginesie

mar·i·hua·na, mar·i·jua·na [mærjuː'ɑːnə] marihuana *f*

ma·ri·na [mə'riːnə] przystań *f* jachtowa

ma·rine [mə'riːn] **1.** *mil.* żołnierz *m* piechoty morskiej; ***merchant* ~** marynarka *f* handlowa; **2.** *adj.* morski

mar·i·ner ['mærɪnə] marynarz *m*

mar·i·tal ['mærɪtl] małżeński; **~ 'status** stan *m* cywilny

mar·i·time ['mærɪtaɪm] morski; żeglugowy

mark[1] [mɑːk] *econ.* marka *f*

mark[2] [mɑːk] **1.** znak *m*; plama *f*; ślad *m*; oznaka *f*; znamię *n*; cel *m*; cecha *f*, oznaczenie *n*; (*w szkole*) ocena *f*, stopień *m*; (*w sporcie*) linia startowa; *fig.* poziom *m*, jakość *f*, norma; *tech.* oznaczenie *n*; ***be up to the* ~** być na (odpowiednim) poziomie; *zdrowotnie* czuć się dobrze; ***be wide of the* ~** chybić celu, być chybionym; *fig.* nie być trafnym; ***hit the* ~** trafić (*do celu*); *fig.* trafić w dziesiątkę; ***miss the* ~** nie trafić (*do celu*), spudłować (*też fig.*); ⚠ *nie* ***marka***; **2.** zostawiać ‹-wić› ślady; ‹po›plamić; oznaczać ‹-czyć›; zaznaczać ‹-czyć›; cechować; oznaczać ‹-czyć›; upamiętniać ‹-nić›; *towar* ‹o›znakować; *cenę* ustalać ‹-lić›; (*w szkole*) sprawdzać ‹-dzić›, oceniać ‹-nić›; (*w sporcie*) *zawodnika* kryć; **~ *my words*** zważaj na moje słowa; ***to* ~ *the occasion*** w celu uświetnienia tej okazji; **~ *time*** iść w miejscu; *fig.* dreptać w miejscu; **~ *down*** odnotowywać ‹-ować›; *cenę* obniżać ‹-żyć›; **~ *out*** *linią* oznaczać ‹-czyć› (*I*); *kogoś* wyróżniać ‹-nić›, wyznaczać ‹-czyć› (***for*** do *G*); **~ *up*** *cenę* podwyższać ‹-szyć›; **~ed** wyraźny, dobitny; **'~·er** marker *m*, pisak *m*; zakładka *f*; znacznik *m*

mar·ket ['mɑːkɪt] **1.** rynek *m*; targ *m*; hala *f* targowa; *econ.* zbyt *m*; *econ.* popyt *m* (***for*** na *A*); ***on the* ~** na rynku, w handlu; ***put on the* ~** wprowadzać ‹-dzić› na rynek *lub* do handlu; *attr.* rynkowy; **2.** *v/t.* wprowadzać ‹-dzić›na rynek *lub* do handlu; zbywać ‹-być›, sprzedawać ‹-dać›; **~·a·ble** *econ.* nadający się do sprzedaży rynkowej; łatwo zbywalny; **~ 'gar·den** *Brt. econ.* zakład *m* ogrodniczy; **'~·ing** *econ.* marketing *m*

'mark·ing znak *m*, plama *f*; oznaczanie *n*, *zo.* cechowanie *n*; (*w sporcie*) krycie *n*

'marks·man (*pl.* **-*men***) dobry strzelec *m*; **'~·ship** umiejętność *f* strzelania

mar·ma·lade ['mɑːməleɪd] marmola-

M

da *f* (*zwł. z cytrusów*)
mar•mot ['mɑːmət] *zo.* świstak *m*
ma•roon [mə'ruːn] **1.** *adj.* bordo (*idkl.*); **2.** wyrzucać na ląd (*na wyspę*)
mar•quee [mɑː'kiː] duży namiot *m* (*używany na festynach itp.*)
mar•quis ['mɑːkwɪs] markiz *m*
mar•riage ['mærɪdʒ] małżeństwo (**to** z *I*); ślub *m*; ***civil ~*** ślub *m* cywilny; **'mar•ria•gea•ble** zdolny do zawarcia małżeństwa; **'~ cer•tif•i•cate** akt *m* ślubu
mar•ried ['mærɪd] *ktoś*: *mężczyzna*: żonaty, *kobieta*: zamężna; *coś*: ślubny, małżeński; ***~ couple*** małżeństwo *n*; ***~ life*** życie *n* małżeńskie
mar•row ['mærəʊ] *anat.* szpik *m* (*też fig.*); *fig.* sedno *n*; *też* ***vegetable ~*** *Brt. bot.* kabaczek *m*
mar•ry ['mærɪ] *v/t. para*: brać ⟨wziąć⟩ ślub; *mężczyzna*: ⟨o⟩żenić się z (*I*), *kobieta*: wychodzić ⟨wyjść⟩ za mąż za (*A*); ***be married*** mieć ślub (***to*** z *I*); ***get married*** *mężczyzna*: ⟨o⟩żenić się (***to*** z *I*), *kobieta*: wychodzić ⟨wyjść⟩ za mąż (***to*** za *A*); *v/i.* dawać ⟨dać⟩ ślub
marsh [mɑːʃ] mokradło *n*, moczary *pl.*
mar•shal ['mɑːʃl] **1.** *mil.* marszałek *m*; *Am.* naczelnik *m* (*okręgu policyjnego*); **2.** (*zwł. Brt.* **-ll-** , *Am.* **-l-**) ⟨z⟩organizować, układać ⟨ułożyć⟩; ⟨za⟩prowadzić, ⟨po⟩kierować
marsh•y ['mɑːʃɪ] podmokły, bagnisty
mar•ten ['mɑːtɪn] *zo.* kuna *f*
mar•tial ['mɑːʃl] wojskowy, wojenny; **~ 'arts** *pl.* wschodnie sztuki walki *pl.*; **~ 'law** prawo *n* wojenne; stan *m* wyjątkowy, stan *m* wojenny
mar•tyr ['mɑːtə] męczennik *m* (-ica *f*)
mar•vel ['mɑːvl] **1.** cud *m*; **2.** zadziwiać ⟨-wić⟩ się; **~•(l)ous** ['mɑːvələs] cudowny
mar•zi•pan [mɑːzɪ'pæn] marcepan *m*
mas•ca•ra [mæ'skɑːrə] tusz *m* do rzęs
mas•cot ['mæskət] maskotka *f*
mas•cu•line ['mæskjʊlɪn] męski; rodzaju męskiego
mash [mæʃ] **1.** ugniatać ⟨-nieść⟩; **2.** *Brt.* F purée *n* ziemniaczane; mieszanka *f* pastewna; **~ed po'ta•toes** *pl.* purée *n* ziemniaczane
mask [mɑːsk] **1.** maska *f*; **2.** ⟨za⟩maskować; *fig.* zakryć ⟨-ywać⟩; **~ed** zamaskowany; ***~ed ball*** bal *m* maskowy
ma•son ['meɪsn] murarz *m*; kamieniarz *m*; *zw.* ♀ wolnomularz *m*, mason *m* (-ka *f*); **~•ry** ['meɪsnrɪ] murarka *f*; kamieniarka *f*
masque [mɑːsk] *theat. hist.*: maska *f*
mas•que•rade [mæskə'reɪd] **1.** maskarada *f* (*też fig.*); przebranie *n*; **2.** *fig.* przebierać się (***as*** jako)
mass [mæs] **1.** masa *f* (*też fiz.*); kawał *m*; ogrom *m*; wielka ilość *f*; ***the ~es*** *pl.* szerokie masy *pl.*; **2.** zbierać ⟨zebrać⟩ się, ⟨z⟩gromadzić się; **3.** masowy
Mass [mæs] msza *f*
mas•sa•cre ['mæsəkə] **1.** masakra *f*; **2.** ⟨z⟩masakrować
mas•sage ['mæsɑːʒ] **1.** masaż *m*; **2.** ⟨roz-, po⟩masować
mas|•seur [mæ'sɜː] masażysta *m*; **~•seuse** [mæ'sɜːz] masażystka *f*
mas•sif ['mæsiːf] masyw *m* (*górski*)
mas•sive ['mæsɪv] masywny; rozległy
mass|'me•di•a *pl.* mass media *pl.*; **~-pro'duce** ⟨wy⟩produkować masowo; **~ pro'duc•tion** produkcja *f* masowa
mast [mɑːst] *naut.* maszt *m*
mas•ter ['mɑːstə] **1.** mistrz *m*; pan *m*; *zwł. Brt.* nauczyciel *m*; oryginał *m*; kapitan *m*; *univ.* magister *m*; ***♀ of Arts*** (*skrót*: ***MA***) magister *m* nauk humanistycznych; ***~ of ceremonies*** konferansjer *m*; **2.** mistrzowski, główny; ***~ copy*** oryginał *m*; ***~ tape*** *tech.* kopia-matka *f*; **3.** opanowywać ⟨-wać⟩; **'~ key** klucz *m* uniwersalny; **'~•ly** mistrzowski; **'~•piece** arcydzieło *n*; **~•y** ['mɑːstərɪ] opanowanie *n*, panowanie *n*
mas•tur•bate ['mæstəbeɪt] masturbować (się), onanizować (się)
Masuria Mazury *pl.*
mat[1] [mæt] **1.** mata *f*, podstawka *f*; **2.** (**-*tt*-**) sklejać ⟨-leić⟩ się; ⟨s⟩filcować się
mat[2] [mæt] matowy
match[1] [mætʃ] zapałka *f*
match[2] [mætʃ] **1.** para *f*, odpowiednik *m*; *w sporcie* mecz *m*, walka *f* (*bokserska*); *ktoś*: *dobra* partia *f*; ożenek *m*; ***be a ~ for s.o.*** dorównywać komuś; ***be no ~ for s.o.*** nie móc się równać z kimś; ***find*** *lub* ***meet one's ~*** spotkać sobie równego; **2.** *v/t.* dorównywać ⟨-nać⟩ (*D*); zestawiać ⟨-wić⟩, przeciwstawiać ⟨-wić⟩; dopasowywać ⟨-ować⟩, dobierać ⟨-brać⟩; *v/i.* pasować (*do siebie*), odpowiadać sobie; ***gloves to ~*** pasujące rękawiczki

'match·box pudełko *n* od zapałek
'match|·less nie do pary, niedopasowany; **'~·mak·er** swat(ka *f*) *m*; **~'point** (*w tenisie*) meczbol *m*
mate[1] [meɪt] → ***checkmate***
mate[2] [meɪt] **1.** towarzysz *m* (*pracy*); kolega *m*; partner *m* (*w parze zwierząt*); *naut.* oficer *m* pokładowy; **2.** parzyć (się), kojarzyć (się) (*w pary*)
ma·te·ri·al [mə'tɪərɪəl] **1.** materiał *m*; tworzywo *n*; ***writing ~s*** *pl.* materiały *pl.* piśmienne; **2.** materialny; materiałowy; znaczny, poważny
ma·ter·nal [mə'tɜːnl] matczyny, macierzyński; ze strony matki
ma·ter·ni·ty [mə'tɜːnətɪ] **1.** macierzyństwo *n*; **2.** położniczy; **~ *dress*** sukienka *f* ciążowa; **~ leave** urlop *m* macierzyński; **~ ward** oddział *m* położniczy
math [mæθ] *Am.* F matematyka *f*
math·e|·ma·ti·cian [mæθəmə'tɪʃn] matematyk *m* (-yczka *f*); **~·mat·ics** [mæθə'mætɪks] *zw. sg.* matematyka *f*
maths [mæθs] *Brt.* F matematyka *f*
mat·i·née ['mætɪneɪ] *theat. itp.* przedstawienie *n* popołudniowe
ma·tric·u·late [mə'trɪkjʊleɪt] immatrykulować (się)
mat·ri·mo|·ni·al [mætrɪ'məʊnjəl] małżeński; matrymonialny; **~·ny** ['mætrɪmənɪ] małżeństwo *n*, stan *m* małżeński
ma·trix *tech.* ['meɪtrɪks] (*pl.* ***-trices*** [-trɪsiːz], ***-trixes***) matryca *f*
ma·tron ['meɪtrən] *Brt.* siostra *f* przełożona; *Brt. jakby*: pielęgniarka *f* szkolna (*zajmująca się też opieką nad dziećmi*)
mat·ter ['mætə] **1.** materia *f* (*też phys.*), substancja *f*; sprawa *f*, kwestia *f*; przedmiot *m*; *med.* ropa *f*; ***printed ~*** *pocztowy* druk *m*; ***what's the ~ (with you)?*** co się z tobą dzieje?; ***no ~ who*** nieważne kto; ***for that ~*** jeśli o to chodzi; ***a ~ of course*** rzecz *f* oczywista; ***a ~ of fact*** fakt *m*; ***as a ~ of fact*** właściwie; ***a ~ of form*** zagadnienie *n* formalne; ***a ~ of time*** kwestia *f* czasu; **2.** mieć znaczenie (***to*** dla *G*); ***it doesn't ~*** nie szkodzi; **~-of-'fact** rzeczowy, praktyczny
mat·tress ['mætrɪs] materac *m*
ma·ture [mə'tjʊə] **1.** (***-r, -st***) dojrzały (*też fig.*); **2.** dojrzewać ⟨-rzeć⟩; **ma·tu·ri·ty** [mə'tjʊərətɪ] dojrzałość *f* (*też fig.*)
maud·lin ['mɔːdlɪn] ckliwy, rzewny
maul [mɔːl] ⟨po⟩kiereszować; *fig.* dobierać się do (*G*)
Maun·dy Thurs·day ['mɔːndɪ -] Wielki Czwartek *m*
mauve [məʊv] wrzosowy, jasnoliliowy
mawk·ish ['mɔːkɪʃ] czułostkowy, sentymentalny
max·i... ['mæksɪ] maksi...
max·im ['mæksɪm] maksyma *f*
max·i·mum ['mæksɪməm] **1.** (*pl.* ***-ma*** [-mə]) maksimum *n*; **2.** maksymalny, największy
May [meɪ] maj *m*
may [meɪ] *v/aux.* (*pret.* ***might***) móc
may·be ['meɪbiː] może
'May|-bee·tle *zo.*, **'~-bug** *zo.* chrabąszcz *m* majowy
'May Day 1 Maja; **mayday** (*międzynarodowe wołanie o pomoc, słowny odpowiednik SOS*)
may·on·naise [meɪə'neɪz] majonez *m*
mayor [meə] burmistrz *m*; ⚠ *nie* ***major***
'may·pole (*gałązka*) gaik *m*
maze [meɪz] labirynt *m* (*też fig.*)
Mazovia Mazowsze *n*
MB [em 'biː] *skrót*: ***megabyte*** MB, megabajt *m*
MCA [em siː 'eɪ] *Skrót*: ***maximum credible accident***
MD [em 'diː] *skrót*: ***Doctor of Medicine*** (*łacińskie* ***medicinae doctor***) dr n. med., doktor *m* nauk medycznych
me [miː] mnie, mi; F ja
mead·ow ['medəʊ] łąka *f*
mea·gre *Brt.*, **mea·ger** *Am.* ['miːgə] skąpy, niewielki
meal[1] [miːl] posiłek *m*; danie *n*
meal[2] [miːl] mąka *f* (*zwł. na paszę*)
mean[1] [miːn] skąpy, chytry; podły; nędzny
mean[2] [miːn] (***meant***) znaczyć; oznaczać; mieć na myśli; przywiązywać wagę; zamierzać, mieć zamiar (***to do s.th.*** zrobić coś); ***be ~t for*** być przeznaczonym dla (*G*); **~ *well* (*ill*)** mieć dobre (złe) intencje
mean[3] [miːn] **1.** średnia *f*, przeciętna *f*; środek *m*; **2.** średni, przeciętny
'mean·ing 1. znaczenie *n*, sens *m*; **2.** znaczący; **'~·ful** znaczący, sensowny; **'~·less** bez znaczenia, bezsensowny
means [miːnz] (*pl.* ***means***) środek *m*, środki *pl.*; środki *pl.* pieniężne; środki *pl.* do życia; ***by all ~*** ależ oczywiście; ***by***

no ~ w żaden sposób; ***by ~ of*** za pomocą (*G*)
meant [ment] *pret. i p.p. od* ***mean²***
'mean|•time *też* ***in the ~time*** tymczasem; **'~•while** tymczasem
mea•sles ['mi:zlz] *med. sg.* odra *f*; ***German ~*** różyczka *f*
mea•su•ra•ble ['meʒərəbl] mierzalny, wymierny
mea•sure ['meʒə] **1.** miara *f* (*też fig.*); rozmiar *m*, wymiar *m*; *mus.* takt *m*; krok *m*, środek *m*; ***beyond ~*** ponad miarę; ***in a great ~*** w dużej mierze; ***take ~s*** przedsiębrać ⟨-sięwziąć⟩ kroki; **2.** ⟨z-, po⟩mierzyć, dokonywać ⟨-nać⟩ pomiaru; ***~ up to*** znaleźć się na wysokości (*G*), spełniać oczekiwania (*G*); **~d** wymierzony; miarowy; ostrożny; **'~•ment** wymiar *m*; pomiar *m*; ***leg ~ment*** długość *f* nogawki
meas•ur•ing ['meʒərɪŋ] pomiarowy; **'~ tape** → ***tape measure***
meat [mi:t] mięso *n*; ***cold ~s*** *pl.* wędliny *pl.*; **' ~•ball** klops *m*
me•chan|•ic [mɪ'kænɪk] mechanik *m*; **~•i•cal** mechaniczny; **~•ics** *phys. zw. sg.* mechanika *f*
mech•a|•nis•m ['mekənɪzəm] mechanizm *m*; **~•nize** ['mekənaɪz] ⟨z⟩mechanizować
med•al ['medl] medal *m*; order *m*; **~•(l)ist** ['medlɪst] (*w sporcie*) medalista *m* (-tka *f*)
med•dle ['medl] ⟨w⟩mieszać się (***with, in*** do *A*); **'~•some** ciekawski
me•di•a ['mi:djə] *sg., pl.* media *pl.*, środki *pl.* masowego przekazu
med•i•ae•val [medɪ'i:vl] → ***medieval***
me•di•an ['mi:djn] *też* ***~ strip*** *Am.* (*na autostradzie*) pas *m* zieleni
me•di|•ate ['mi:dɪeɪt] pośredniczyć, być mediatorem; **~•a•tion** [mi:dɪ'eɪʃn] pośredniczenie *n*, mediacja *f*; **~•a•tor** ['mi:dɪeɪtə] mediator *m* (-ka *f*), rozjemca *m*
med•i•cal ['medɪkl] **1.** medyczny; **2.** badanie *n* lekarskie; **~ cer'tif•i•cate** zaświadczenie *n* lekarskie
med•i•cated ['medɪkeɪtɪd] leczniczy; ***~ soap*** mydło *n* lecznicze
me•di•ci•nal [me'dɪsɪnl] leczniczy, zdrowotny
medi•cine ['medsɪn] medycyna *f*; lekarstwo *n*
med•i•e•val [medɪ'i:vl] średniowieczny
me•di•o•cre [mi:dɪ'əʊkə] przeciętny
med•i|•tate ['medɪteɪt] *v/i.* medytować (***on*** nad *I*); rozmyślać (***on*** o *I*); **~•ta•tion** [medɪ'teɪʃn] medytacja *f*; rozmyślanie *n*; **~•ta•tive** ['medɪtətɪv] medytacyjny
Med•i•ter•ra•ne•an [medɪtə'reɪnjən] śródziemnomorski; ***~ Sea*** Morze Śródziemne
me•di•um ['mi:djəm] **1.** (*pl.* ***-dia*** [-djə], ***-diums***) środek *m*; środek *m* przekazu; środowisko *n*, ośrodek *m*; medium *n*; **2.** średni; pośredni; *gastr.* nie wysmażony
med•ley ['medlɪ] mieszanka; *mus.* potpourri *n*, wiązanka *f*, składanka *f*
meek [mi:k] potulny, uległy; **'~•ness** potulność *f*, uległość *f*
meet [mi:t] (***met***) *v/t.* spotykać ⟨-tkać⟩, spotkać ⟨-tykać⟩ się z (*I*); poznawać ⟨-nać⟩; wychodzić na spotkanie (*G*), wyjeżdżać na spotkanie (*G*); *oczekiwania, życzenia itp.* spełniać ⟨-nić⟩; *potrzeby itp.* zaspokajać ⟨-koić⟩; spłacać ⟨-cić⟩, pokrywać ⟨-ryć⟩; *terminu* dotrzymywać; *v/i.* spotykać ⟨-tkać⟩ się; poznawać się; zbierać ⟨zebrać⟩ się; schodzić ⟨zejść⟩ się; ***~ with*** napotykać ⟨-tkać⟩; spotykać ⟨-tkać⟩ się z (*I*); **'~•ing** spotkanie *n*; zebranie *n*, konferencja *f*; **'~ing place** miejsce *n* spotkania, miejsce *n* zebrania
mel•an•chol•y ['melənkəlɪ] **1.** melancholia *f*; **2.** melancholijny
mel•low ['meləʊ] **1.** łagodny; dojrzały (*też fig.*); *światło, kolor itp.*: ciepły
me•lo•di•ous [mɪ'ləʊdjəs] melodyjny
mel•o•dra•mat•ic [meləʊdrə'mætɪk] melodramatyczny
mel•o•dy ['melədɪ] melodia *f*
mel•on ['melən] *bot.* melon *m*
melt [melt] ⟨s⟩topnieć; ⟨s⟩topić (się); roztapiać ⟨-topić⟩ (się); ***~ down*** przetapiać ⟨-topić⟩
mem•ber ['membə] członek *m*; *anat.* członek *m* (*ciała*); ***♀ of Parliament*** *Brt. parl.* poseł *m* (-słanka *f*) do parlamentu; **'~•ship** członkostwo *n*
mem•brane ['membreɪn] błona *f*; membrana *f*
mem•o ['meməʊ] (*pl.* ***-os***) notka *f* służbowa, okólnik *m*
mem•oirs ['memwɑ:z] *pl.* pamiętniki *pl.*

mem•o•ra•ble ['memərəbl] pamiętny
me•mo•ri•al [mɪ'mɔːrɪəl] pomnik *m*, statua *f*; *attr.* pamiątkowy, upamiętniający
mem•o•rize ['meməraɪz] ⟨wy-, na⟩-uczyć się na pamięć
mem•o•ry ['memərɪ] pamięć *f* (*też komp.*); ***in ~ of*** ku pamięci (*G*); wspomnienie *n*; **~ ca'pac•i•ty** *komp.* pojemność *f* pamięci
men [men] *pl. od* ***man*** 1
men•ace ['menəs] **1.** zagrażać ⟨-rozić⟩; grozić; **2.** zagrożenie *n*; groźba *f*
mend [mend] **1.** *v/t.* naprawiać ⟨-wić⟩; ⟨z⟩reperować; ⟨za⟩cerować, zaszyć ⟨-ywać⟩; **~ *one's ways*** poprawiać ⟨-wić⟩ się; *v/i.* poprawiać ⟨-wić⟩ się; **2.** cera *f*, zaszyte miejsce *n*; ***on the ~*** dochodzący do siebie
men•di•cant ['mendɪkənt] **1.** żebrzący; **2.** zakonnik *m* żebrzący
me•ni•al ['miːnjəl] *praca*: podrzędny
men•in•gi•tis [menɪn'dʒaɪtɪs] *med.* zapalenie *n* opon mózgowych
men•o•pause ['menəupɔːz] menopauza *f*
men•stru|•ate ['menstrueɪt] miesiączkować, mieć miesiączkę; **~•a•tion** [menstru'eɪʃn] menstruacja *f*, miesiączka *f*
men•tal ['mentl] umysłowy, mentalny; psychiczny; **~ a'rith•me•tic** rachunek *m* pamięciowy; **~ 'hand•i•cap** upośledzenie *n* umysłowe; **~ 'hos•pi•tal** szpital *m* psychiatryczny; **~•i•ty** [men'tælətɪ] mentalność *f*; **~•ly** ['mentəlɪ] umysłowo; ***~ly handicapped*** upośledzony umysłowo; ***~ly ill*** chory umysłowo;
men•tion ['menʃn] **1.** wspominać ⟨-mnieć⟩; ***don't ~ it!*** nie ma za co!, proszę bardzo!; **2.** wspomnienie *n*
men•u ['menjuː] menu *n* (*też komp.*), karta *f*
MEP [em iː 'piː] *skrót*: ***Member of the European Parliament*** poseł do Parlamentu Europejskiego
mer•can•tile ['mɜːkəntaɪl] handlowy, kupiecki; merkantylny
mer•ce•na•ry ['mɜːsɪnərɪ] **1.** najemnik *m*; **2.** najemniczy
mer•chan•dise ['mɜːtʃəndaɪz] towar(y *pl.*) *m*
mer•chant ['mɜːtʃənt] **1.** kupiec *m*; **2.** handlowy
mer•ci|•ful ['mɜːsɪfl] litościwy, miłosierny; **'~•less** bezlitosny, niemiłosierny
mer•cu•ry ['mɜːkjurɪ] *chem.* rtęć *f*
mer•cy ['mɜːsɪ] litość *f*, miłosierdzie *n*
mere [mɪə] (**-*r*, -*st***), **'~•ly** tylko, jedynie
merge [mɜːdʒ] ⟨po⟩łączyć (***into, with*** z *I*) (się); *econ.* dokonywać fuzji; **'merg•er** *econ.* fuzja *f*
me•rid•i•an [mə'rɪdɪən] *geogr.* południk *m*; *fig.* szczyt *m*
mer•it ['merɪt] **1.** zasługa *f*; wartość *f*; zaleta *f*; **2.** zasługiwać ⟨-służyć⟩
mer•maid ['mɜːmeɪd] syrena *f*
mer•ri•ment ['merɪmənt] wesołość *f*
mer•ry ['merɪ] (**-*ier*, -*iest***) wesoły; ***♀ Christmas!*** Wesołych Świąt!; **'~-go--round** karuzela *f*
mesh [meʃ] **1.** oko *n*, oczko *f*; *fig. często* ***~es*** *pl.* siatka *f*; ***be in ~es*** *tech.* zazębiać ⟨-bić⟩ się; **2.** zazębiać ⟨-bić⟩ się; *fig.* pasować (***with*** do *G*)
mess [mes] **1.** bałagan *m*, nieporządek *m* (*też fig.*); brud *m*; paskudztwo *m*; łajno *n*; *mil.* kantyna *f*, kasyno *n*; (*na statku*) mesa *f*; ***make a ~ of*** F ⟨s⟩knocić (*A*); *plany* pokręcić (*A*); **2. *~ about, ~ around*** F obijać się; wygłupiać się (***with*** z *I*); ***~ up*** zrobić bałagan; F ⟨s⟩knocić; *plany* pokręcić
mes•sage ['mesɪdʒ] wiadomość *f*; informacja *f*; (*filmu itp.*) przesłanie *n*; ***can I take a ~?*** czy może coś powtórzyć? ***get the ~*** F ⟨po⟩kapować się
mes•sen•ger ['mesɪndʒə] posłaniec *m*
mess•y ['mesɪ] (**-*ier*, -*iest***) pobrudzony, zapaskudzony; *fig.* pogmatwany
met [met] *pret. i p.p. od* ***meet***
me•tab•o•lis•m [me'tæbəlɪzəm] *physiol.* metabolizm *m*
met•al ['metl] metal *m*; **me•tal•lic** [mɪ'tælɪk] (***~ally***) metaliczny; metalowy
met•a•mor•pho•sis [metə'mɔːfəsɪs] metamorfoza *f*, przekształcenie *n*
met•a•phor ['metəfə] metafora *f*
me•tas•ta•sis [mə'tæstəsɪs] *med.* (*pl.* **-*ses*** [-siːz]) metastaza *f*, przerzut *m*
me•te•or ['miːtɪɔː] meteor *m*
me•te•or•o•log•i•cal [miːtjərə'lɒdʒɪkl] meteorologiczny; pogodowy, synoptyczny; **~ 'of•fice** *lub* F ***met office*** stacja *f* meteorologiczna
me•te•o•rol•o•gy [miːtjə'rɒlədʒɪ] meteorologia *f*

M

me·ter ['miːtə] *tech.* miernik *m*, przyrząd *m* pomiarowy; ⚠ *Brt. nie* ***metr***
meth·od ['meθəd] metoda *f*; **me·thod·i·cal** [mɪ'θɒdɪkl] metodyczny
me·tic·u·lous [mɪ'tɪkjʊləs] drobiazgowy, skrupulatny
me·tre, *Brt.*, **me·ter** *Am.* ['miːtə] metr *m*
met·ric ['metrɪk] (**~*ally***) metryczny; '**~ sys·tem** system *m* metryczny
met·ro·pol·i·tan [metrə'pɒlɪtən] wielkomiejski, metropolitalny, stołeczny
met·tle ['metl]: ***show one's ~*** wykazać się owagę; ***try s.o.'s ~*** podawać ⟨-dać⟩ kogoś próbie
Mex·i·can ['meksɪkən] **1.** meksykański; **2.** Meksykanin *m* (-anka *f*)
Mex·i·co ['meksɪkəʊ] Meksyk *m*
mi·aow [miː'aʊ] ⟨za⟩miauczeć
mice [maɪs] *pl. od* ***mouse***
mi·cro... ['maɪkrəʊ] mikro...
mi·cro|·chip ['maɪkrəʊtʃɪp] układ *m* scalony; **~·com'put·er** mikrokomputer *m*
mi·cro·phone ['maɪkrəfəʊn] mikrofon *m*
mi·cro·pro·ces·sor [maɪkrəʊ'prəʊsesə] mikroprocesor *m*
mi·cro·scope ['maɪkrəskəʊp] mikroskop *m*
mi·cro·wave ['maɪkrəweɪv] mikrofala *f*; *attr.* mikrofalowy; → **~ 'ov·en** kuchenka *f* mikrofalowa
mid [mɪd] środkowy; **~'air**: ***in ~air*** w powietrzu; '**~·day** **1.** południe *n*; **2.** południowy
mid·dle ['mɪdl] **1.** środkowy; **2.** środek *m*; **~-'aged** w średnim wieku; **♀ 'Ag·es** średniowiecze *n*; **~ 'class**(**·es** *pl.*) klasa *f* średnia; '**~·man** (*pl.* ***-men***) *econ.* pośrednik *m*; **~ 'name** drugie imię *n*; **~-'sized** o średnim rozmiarze; '**~·weight** (*w boksie*) waga *f* średnia
mid·dling ['mɪdlɪŋ] F średni, przeciętny
'mid·field *zwł.* (*w piłce nożnej*) środek boiska *m*; '**~·er**, **~ 'play·er** (*w piłce nożnej*) pomocnik *m*
midge [mɪdʒ] *zo.* komar *m*
midg·et ['mɪdʒɪt] karzeł *m* (-rlica *f*), liliput *m*
'mid|·night północ *f*; ***at ~night*** o północy; **~st** [mɪdst]: ***in the ~st of*** w środku (*G*); '**~·sum·mer** środek *m* lata; *astr.* przesilenie *n* letnie; **~'way** w połowie drogi; '**~·wife** (*pl.* ***-wives***) położna *f*; **~'win·ter** środek *m* zimy; *astr.* przesilenie *n* zimowe
might [maɪt] **1.** *pret. od* ***may***; **2.** moc *f*, siła *f*; potęga *f*; '**~·y** (***-ier, -iest***) potężny
mi·grate [maɪ'greɪt] migrować (*też zo.*); ⟨wy⟩wędrować; **mi·gra·tion** [maɪ'greɪʃn] migracja *f*; wędrówka *f*; **mi·gra·to·ry** ['maɪgrətərɪ] wędrowny (*też zo.*); migracyjny
mike [maɪk] F mikrofon *m*
Mi·lan Mediolan *m*
mild [maɪld] łagodny
mil·dew ['mɪldjuː] *bot.* pleśń *f*
'mild·ness łagodność *f*
mile [maɪl] mila *f* (*1,6 km*)
mile·age ['maɪlɪdʒ] odległość *f lub* długość *f* w milach; *też* **~ *allowance*** zwrot *m* kosztów podróży
'mile·stone kamień *m* milowy (*też fig.*)
mil·i·tant ['mɪlɪtənt] bojowy, wojowniczy
mil·i·ta·ry ['mɪlɪtərɪ] **1.** militarny; wojskowy; **2.** ***the ~*** wojsko *n*; **~ 'gov·ern·ment** rząd *m* wojskowy; **~ po'lice** (*skrót*: ***MP***) żandarmeria *f lub* policja *f* wojskowa
mi·li·tia [mɪ'lɪʃə] straż *f* miejska
milk [mɪlk] **1.** mleko; *attr.* mleczny, z mleka; ***it's no use crying over spilt ~*** co się stało, to się nie odstanie; **2.** *v/t.* ⟨wy⟩doić; *v/i.* dawać ⟨dać⟩ mleko; **~·man** (*pl.* ***-men***) mleczarz *m*); **~ 'pow·der** mleko *n* w proszku; **~ 'shake** koktajl *m* mleczny; '**~·sop** maminsynek *m*; '**~ tooth** (*pl.* ***- teeth***) ząb *m* mleczny; '**~·y** (***-ier, -iest***) mleczny; **♀·y 'Way** *astr.* Droga *f* Mleczna
mill [mɪl] **1.** młyn *m*; młynek *m*; fabryka *f*, wytwórnia *f*; **2.** ⟨z⟩mielić *lub* ⟨ze⟩mleć; *metal* frezować; *monety* ⟨wy⟩tłoczyć; **~ *about*, ~ *around*** kotłować się
mil·le·pede ['mɪlɪpiːd] *zo.* → ***millipede***
'mill·er młynarz *m*
mil·let ['mɪlɪt] *bot.* proso *n*
mil·li·ner ['mɪlɪnə] modystka *f*
mil·lion ['mɪljən] milion *m*; **~·aire** [mɪljə'neə] milioner *m*; **~th** ['mɪljənθ] **1.** milionowy; **2.** jedna *f* milionowa
mil·li·pede ['mɪlɪpiːd] *zo.* stonoga *f*
'mill·stone kamień *m* młyński
milt [mɪlt] mlecz *m*
mime [maɪm] **1.** pantomima *f*; mim *m*;

migi *pl.*; **2.** pokazywać ⟨-zać⟩ na migi
mim·ic ['mɪmɪk] **1.** mimiczny; **2.** mimik *m*; imitator *m*; **3.** (*-ck-*) imitować, naśladować; **~·ry** ['mɪmɪkrɪ] mimikra *f*
mince [mɪns] **1.** *v/t.* ⟨po⟩siekać, ⟨z⟩mielić *lub* ⟨ze⟩mleć; ***he doesn't ~ matters*** *lub* ***his words*** mówi prosto z mostu; *v/i.* ⟨po⟩dreptać; **2.** *też* ***~d meat*** mięso *n* siekane; '**~·meat** *słodkie* nadzienie *n* do ciasta; **~ 'pie** ciasto *n* nadziewane bakaliami; '**minc·er** maszynka *f* do mięsa
mind [maɪnd] **1.** umysł *m*; rozum *m*; myśli *pl.*, głowa *f*; duch *m*; zdanie *n*; ***be out of one's ~*** nie być przy zdrowych zmysłach; ***bear*** *lub* ***keep in ~*** ⟨za⟩pamiętać, nie zapominać ⟨-mnieć⟩; ***change one's ~*** zmieniać ⟨-nić⟩ zdanie; ***come into sb's ~*** przychodzić ⟨-yjść⟩ komuś do głowy; ***give s.o. a piece of one's ~*** wygarnąć komuś; ***have a ~ to*** mieć chęć zrobić (*A*); ***have a half ~ to*** nie mieć zbytnio chęci zrobić (*A*); ***lose one's ~*** postradać zmysły; ***make up one's ~*** zdecydować się; ***to my ~*** według mnie; **2.** uważać (na *A*); mieć *coś* przeciwko (*D*), sprzeciwiać ⟨-wić⟩ się; ⟨za⟩troszczyć się o (*A*); ***~ the step!*** uwaga, stopień!; ***~ your own business!*** zajmij się swoimi sprawami!; ***do you ~ if I smoke?, do you ~ my smoking?*** czy będzie panu przeszkadzało, jak zapalę?; ***would you ~ opening the window?*** czy mógłby pan otworzyć okno?; ***would you ~ coming*** czy mógłby pan przyjechać?; **~** (***you***) proszę zauważyć; ***never ~!*** nie szkodzi!; ***I don't ~*** wszystko mi jedno; '**~·less** bezmyślny; ***~less of s.th.*** nie zważając na coś
mine[1] [maɪn] mój, moje; ***that's ~*** to moje
mine[2] [maɪn] **1.** kopalnia *f* (*też fig.*); *mil.* mina *f*; **2.** wydobywać ⟨-być⟩ (***for*** *A*), ⟨wy⟩eksploatować; *mil.* zaminowywać ⟨-ować⟩; '**min·er** górnik *m*
min·e·ral ['mɪnərəl] minerał *m*; *attr.* mineralny; ***~s*** *pl. Brt. słodkie* napoje *pl. gazowane*; '**~ oil** olej *m* mineralny; '**~ wa·ter** woda *f* mineralna
min·gle ['mɪŋgl] ⟨wy⟩mieszać (się); wmieszać się (***with*** do *G*)
min·i... ['mɪnɪ] mini...; → ***miniskirt***
min·i·a·ture ['mɪnətʃə] **1.** miniatura *f*; **2.** miniaturowy; **~ 'cam·e·ra** fotograficzny aparat *m* miniaturowy
min·i|·mize ['mɪnɪmaɪz] ⟨z⟩minimalizować; zmniejszać ⟨-szyć⟩, pomniejszać ⟨-szyć⟩, ⟨z⟩bagatelizować; **~·mum** ['mɪnɪməm] (*pl.* ***-ma*** [-mə], ***-mums***) **1.** minimum *n*; **2.** minimalny
min·ing ['maɪnɪŋ] górnictwo *n*; górniczy
min·i·on ['mɪnjən] *pej. fig.* sługus *m*, fagas *m*
'**min·i·skirt** minispódniczka *f*
min·is·ter ['mɪnɪstə] minister *m*; *rel.* duchowny *m*
min·is·try ['mɪnɪstrɪ] ministerstwo *n*; *rel.* urząd *m* duchowny
mink [mɪŋk] *zo.* (*pl.* ***mink***) norka *f*
mi·nor ['maɪnə] **1.** mniejszy, *fig.* nieznaczny, drobny; *jur.* niepełnoletni; ***A ~*** *mus.* a-moll *n*; **~ *key*** *mus.* tonacja *f* molowa; **2.** *jur.* niepełnoletni *m* (-nia *f*); *Am. univ.* specjalizacja *f* dodatkowa; *mus.* moll; **~·i·ty** [maɪ'nɒrətɪ] mniejszość *f*; *jur.* niepełnoletniość *f*
min·ster ['mɪnstə] kościół *m* opacki
mint[1] [mɪnt] **1.** mennica *f*; **2.** bić
mint[2] [mɪnt] *bot.* mięta *f*
min·u·et [mɪnjʊ'et] *mus.* menuet *m*
mi·nus ['maɪnəs] **1.** *prp.* odjąć; poniżej; F bez (*G*); **2.** *adj.* minusowy, ujemny; **3.** minus *m* (*też fig.*)
min·ute[1] ['mɪnɪt] minuta *f*; ***in a ~*** za chwilę; ***just a ~!*** chwileczkę!; ***~s*** *pl.* protokół *m*
mi·nute[2] mały, maleńki; drobiazgowy [maɪ'njuːt]
mir·a·cle ['mɪrəkl] cud *m*
mi·rac·u·lous [mɪ'rækjʊləs] cudowny; **~·ly** cudownie
mi·rage ['mɪrɑːʒ] miraż *m*, fatamorgana *f*
mire ['maɪə] szlam *m*; ***drag through the ~*** *fig.* obsmarowywać
mir·ror ['mɪrə] **1.** lustro *n*, zwierciadło *n*; **2.** odzwierciedlać ⟨-lić⟩
mirth [mɜːθ] wesołość *f*
mis... [mɪs] niewłaściwie ..., źle ...
mis·ad'ven·ture niepowodzenie *n*; *jur. Brt.* nieszczęśliwy wypadek *m*
mis·an|·thrope ['mɪzənθrəʊp], **~·thro·pist** [mɪ'zænθrəpɪst] mizantrop *m*
mis·ap'ply źle ⟨za⟩stosować
mis·ap·pre'hend źle ⟨z⟩rozumieć

M

mis·ap'pro·pri·ate sprzeniewierzać ⟨-rzyć⟩
mis·be'have niewłaściwie się zachowywać ⟨-wać⟩
mis'cal·cu·late przeliczyć się; źle obliczyć
mis'car|·riage *med.* poronienie *n*; błąd *m*, pomyłka *f*; **~riage of justice** *jur.* błąd *m* sądowy; **~·ry** *med.* poronić; popełniać ⟨-nić⟩ błąd
mis·cel·la|·ne·ous [mɪsɪ'leɪnjəs] różnoraki, różnorodny; **~·ny** [mɪ'selənɪ] różnorodność *f*; różnorakość *f*; zbiór *m*
mis·chief ['mɪstʃɪf] figlowanie *n*, dokazywanie *n*; figlarność *f*, psotliwość *f*; szkoda *f*; **'~-mak·er** figlarz *m*, psotnik *m* (-nica *f*)
mis·chie·vous ['mɪstʃɪvəs] figlarny, psotliwy; szelmowski
mis·con'ceive źle ⟨z⟩rozumieć, źle pojmować ⟨-jąć⟩
mis·con·duct 1. [mɪs'kɒndʌkt] złe zachowanie *n*; niewłaściwe prowadzenie się; **2.** [mɪskən'dʌkt] źle prowadzić; **~ o.s.** źle się prowadzić
mis·con·strue [mɪskən'struː] źle ⟨z⟩inerpretować
mis'deed zły czyn *m*, nieprawość *f*
mis·de·mea·no(u)r [mɪsdɪ'miːnə] *jur.* wykroczenie *n*, występek *m*
mis·di'rect źle ⟨s⟩kierować; *list itp.* źle ⟨za⟩adresować
mise-en-scène [miːzɑ̃ːn'seɪn] *theat.* inscenizacja *f*
mi·ser ['maɪzə] skąpiec *m*
mis·e·ra·ble ['mɪzərəbl] żałosny, nieszczęsny; nędzny
'mi·ser·ly skąpy; *fig.* nędzny
mis·e·ry ['mɪzərɪ] niedola *f*, nieszczęście *n*; ubóstwo *n*
mis'fire *broń* zawodzić ⟨-wieść⟩; *mot.* nie zapalać ⟨-lić⟩; *fig.* nawalać ⟨-lić⟩
'mis·fit człowiek *m* niedostosowany
mis'for·tune nieszczęście *n*
mis'giv·ing obawa *f*, niepokój *m*
mis'guided mylny, opaczny
mis·hap ['mɪshæp] nieszczęście *n*; **without ~** bez wypadku
mis·in'form źle ⟨po⟩informować
mis·in'ter·pret źle ⟨z⟩interpretować, mylnie ⟨wy⟩tłumaczyć
mis'lay (**-laid**) zagubić, podziać
mis'lead zwodzić ⟨zwieść⟩
mis'man·age źle zarządzać
mis'place kłaść ⟨położyć⟩ na niewłaściwym miejscu; **~d** *fig.* nie na miejscu, niestosowny
mis·print 1. [mɪs'prɪnt] źle ⟨wy⟩drukować; **2.** ['mɪsprɪnt] omyłka *f* w druku
mis'read (**-read** [-red]) źle odczytywać ⟨-tać⟩
mis·rep·re'sent błędnie przedstawiać ⟨-wić⟩, przekręcać ⟨-cić⟩
miss[1] [mɪs] **1.** *v/t.* chybiać ⟨-bić⟩ (*G*), nie trafiać ⟨-fić⟩ do (*G*); opuszczać ⟨opuścić⟩; spóźniać ⟨-nić⟩ się na (*A*); tęsknić za (*I*); *też* **~ out** pomijać ⟨-minąć⟩; *v/i.* chybiać ⟨-bić⟩, spóźniać ⟨-nić⟩ się; **~ out on** ⟨s⟩tracić na (*L*); **2.** chybienie *n*, niecelny strzał *m*
miss[2] [mɪs] (*z następującym nazwiskiem* ♀) panna *f*
mis'shap·en zniekształcony
mis·sile ['mɪsaɪl, *Am.* 'mɪsəl] pocisk *m*; *mil.* pocisk *m* rakietowy, rakieta *f*; *attr.* rakietowy
'miss·ing brakujący; **be ~** brakować; (*mil. też* **~ in action**) zaginiony; **be ~** *mil.* zaginąć
mis·sion ['mɪʃn] misja *f* (*też pol., rel.*); *mil.* zadanie *n*; *aviat., mil.* lot *m*; posłannictwo *n*; **~·a·ry** ['mɪʃənrɪ] **1.** misjonarz *m* (-arka *f*); **2.** *adj..* misyjny
Mis·sis·sip·pi Missisipi *n*
mis'spell (**-spelt** *lub* **-spelled**) źle (na)pisać
mis'spend (**-spent**) rozrzutnie wydawać ⟨-dać⟩
mist [mɪst] **1.** (lekka *lub* drobna) mgła *f*; **2. ~ over** zaparowywać ⟨-ować⟩; zachodzić ⟨zajść⟩ mgłą; **~ up** zaparowywać ⟨-ować⟩
mis|'take 1. (**-took, -taken**) wziąć (*kogoś* **for** za *A*); ⟨po⟩mylić (się); źle ⟨z⟩rozumieć; **2.** pomyłka *f*, błąd *m*; **by ~take** przez pomyłkę, pomyłkowo; **~'tak·en** pomyłkowy, błędny
mis·ter ['mɪstə] (*używa się jedynie jako skrótu przed nazwiskiem*) → **Mr**
mis·tle·toe ['mɪsltəʊ] *bot.* jemioła *f*
mis·tress ['mɪstrɪs] pani *f*; *zwł. Brt.* nauczycielka *f*; ukochana *f*, kochanka *f*
mis'trust 1. nie ufać (*D*), nie wierzyć (*D*); **2.** nieufność *f* (**of** wobec *G*); **~·ful** nieufny
mist·y ['mɪstɪ] (**-ier, -iest**) zamglony
mis·un·der'stand (**-stood**) źle ⟨z⟩rozumieć; **~·ing** nieporozumienie *n*;

niezrozumienie *n*
mis·use **1.** [mɪsˈjuːz] niewłaściwie używać ⟨-żyć⟩; nadużywać ⟨-żyć⟩; **2.** [mɪsˈjuːs] niewłaściwe użycie *n*; nadużycie
mite [maɪt] *zo.* roztocz *m*; *Brt.* F berbeć *m*; ***a ~*** F trochę, nieco
mi·tre *Brt.*, **mi·ter** *Am.* [ˈmaɪtə] mitra *f*, infuła *f*
mitt [mɪt] (*w baseballu*) rękawica *f* (*do łapania piłki*); *sl.* łapa *f*; → ***mitten***
mit·ten [ˈmɪtn] rękawiczka *f* (*z jednym palcem*)
mix [mɪks] **1.** ⟨z-, wy⟩mieszać (się); ⟨z⟩miksować (się); *drink itp.* ⟨z⟩robić; zadawać się (***with*** z *I*); ***~ well*** mieć łatwość nawiązywania kontaktów; ***~ up*** ⟨z⟩mieszać; ⟨po⟩mieszać; *kogoś* pomylić (***with*** z *I*); ***be ~ed up*** być wmieszanym (***in*** w *L*); być zmieszanym; **2.** mieszanka *f*; **~ed** wymieszany; zmieszany; pomieszany; **ˈ~·er** mikser *m*; *tech.* mieszarka *f*, mieszadło *n*; ***concrete ~er*** betoniarka *f*; ***be a bad ~er*** źle nawiązywać kontakty towarzyskie; **~·ture** [ˈmɪkstʃə] mieszanka *f*
MO [em ˈəʊ] *skrót*: ***money order*** przekaz *m* pieniężny, polecenie *n* wypłaty
moan [məʊn] **1.** jęczenie *n*, jęk *m*; **2.** ⟨za⟩jęczeć
moat [məʊt] fosa *f*
mob [mɒb] **1.** motłoch *m*, tłum *m*; zgraja *f*; **2.** (***-bb-***) otaczać ⟨otoczyć⟩, osaczać ⟨-czyć⟩
mo·bile [ˈməʊbaɪl] **1.** ruchomy, mobilny; przewoźny; *mil.* zmotoryzowany; **2.** → ***mobile telephone***; **~ ˈhome** przyczepa *f* mieszkalna; **~ ˈtel·e·phone**, **~ ˈphone** telefon *m* komórkowy, F komórka *f*
mo·bil·ize [ˈməʊbɪlaɪz] ⟨z⟩mobilizować; *mil.* przeprowadzać ⟨-dzić⟩ mobilizację
moc·ca·sin [ˈmɒkəsɪn] mokasyn *m*
mock [mɒk] **1.** *v/t.* naśmiewać się z (*A*); przedrzeźniać (*G*); *v/i.* ***~ at*** naśmiewać się z (*A*); **2.** niby-, quasi-; pseudo-; **~·e·ry** [ˈmɒkərɪ] kpina *f*, kpiny *pl.*; **ˈ~·ing·bird** *zo.* przedrzeźniacz *m*
mod cons [mɒd ˈkɒnz] *Brt.* F *pl.*: ***with all ~*** ze wszelkimi wygodami
mode [məʊd] tryb *m* (*pracy, życia*); sposób *m*; *tech.* mod *m*
mod·el [ˈmɒdl] **1.** model *m*; wzór *m*, wzorzec *m*; model(ka *f*) *m*; **2.** modelowy; wzorcowy; idealny; **3.** *v/t.* (*zwł. Brt.* ***-ll-***, *Am.* ***-l-***) ⟨wy⟩modelować, ⟨u⟩formować; budować model (*G*); *ubranie itp.* ⟨za⟩prezentować; *v/i.* pracować jako model(ka); pozować
mo·dem [ˈməʊdem] *komp.* modem *m*
mod·e|·rate **1.** [ˈmɒdərət] umiarkowany; *rozmiar, zdolności*: przeciętny; **2.** [ˈmɒdəreɪt] ⟨z⟩łagodzić; ⟨ze⟩lżeć; **~·ra·tion** [mɒdəˈreɪʃn] umiarkowanie *n*, złagodzenie *n*
mod·ern [ˈmɒdən] współczesny, nowy; nowoczesny **~·ize** [ˈmɒdənaɪz] ⟨z⟩modernizować
mod|·est [ˈmɒdɪst] skromny; **ˈ~·es·ty** skromność *f*
mod·i|·fi·ca·tion [mɒdɪfɪˈkeɪʃn] modyfikacja *f*; **~·fy** [ˈmɒdɪfaɪ] ⟨z⟩modyfikować
mod·u·late [ˈmɒdjʊleɪt] ⟨z⟩modulować
mod·ule [ˈmɒdjuːl] *tech.* moduł *m*; (*w astronautyce*) człon *m*
moist [mɔɪst] wilgotny; **~·en** [ˈmɔɪsn] *v/t.* zwilżać ⟨-żyć⟩; *v/i.* ⟨z⟩wilgotnieć; **mois·ture** [ˈmɔɪstʃə] wilgoć *m*
mo·lar [ˈməʊlə] *anat.* ząb *m* trzonowy
mo·las·ses [məˈlæsɪz] *Am. sg.* melasa *m*, syrop *m*
mole[1] [məʊl] *zo.* kret *m*
mole[2] [məʊl] pieprzyk *m*; myszka *f*
mole[3] [məʊl] molo *n*
mol·e·cule [ˈmɒlɪkjuːl] molekuła *f*
ˈmole·hill kretowisko *n*; ***make a mountain out of a ~*** robić z igły widły
mo·lest [məʊˈlest] napastować
mol·li·fy [ˈmɒlɪfaɪ] ⟨u⟩łagodzić, uspokajać ⟨-koić⟩ się
mol·ly·cod·dle [ˈmɒlɪkɒdl] F *dziecko* rozpuszczać ⟨-puścić⟩
mol·ten [ˈməʊltən] stopiony, roztopiony
mom [mɒm] F mamusia *f*
mo·ment [ˈməʊmənt] moment *m*, chwila *f*; znaczenie *n*; *phys.* moment *m*; **mo·men·ta·ry** [ˈməʊməntərɪ] chwilowy; **mo·men·tous** [məʊˈmentəs] znaczący, doniosły; **mo·men·tum** [məʊˈmentəm] (*pl.* ***-ta*** [-tə], ***-tums***) *phys.* moment *m*; rozmach *m*, impet *m*
Mon *skrót pisany*: ***Monday*** pon., poniedziałek *m*
mon|·arch [ˈmɒnək] monarcha *m*; **ˈ~·ar·chy** monarchia *f*

M

mon·as·tery ['mɒnəstrɪ] klasztor *m*
Mon·day ['mʌndɪ] poniedziałek *m*
mon·e·ta·ry ['mʌnɪtərɪ] monetarny; pieniężny; walutowy
mon·ey ['mʌnɪ] pieniądze *pl.*; *attr.* pieniężny; '**~·box** *Brt.* skarbonka *f*; '**~·chang·er** właściciel(ka *f*) *m* kantoru wymiany pieniędzy; *zwł. Am.* automat *m* do rozmieniania pieniędzy; '**~ or·der** przekaz *m* pieniężny
mon·ger ['mʌŋgə] *w złożeniach* handlarz *m*, kupiec *m*
mon·grel ['mʌŋgrəl] kundel *m*
mon·i·tor ['mɒnɪtə] **1.** monitor *m*; wskaźnik *m* kontrolny, ekran *m* kontrolny; **2.** monitorować; nadzorować; wsłuchiwać się w (*A*)
monk [mʌŋk] mnich *m*
mon·key ['mʌŋkɪ] **1.** *ogoniasta* małpa *f*; F psotnik *m*; ***make a ~ (out) of s.o.*** ⟨z⟩robić sobie żarty z kogoś; **2.** ***~ about, ~ around*** F wydurniać się; '**~ wrench** klucz *m* nastawny; ***throw a ~ wrench into s.th.*** *Am.* wsadzać kij w szprychy; '**~ busi·ness** ciemne interesy *pl.*
mon·o ['mɒnəʊ] **1.** (*pl.* ***-os***) *dźwięk* mono *n*; **2.** mono...
mon·o... ['mɒnəʊ] mono..., pojedynczy
mon·o·logue *zwł. Brt.*, **mon·o·log** *Am.* ['mɒnəlɒg] monolog *m*
mo·nop·o|·lize [mə'nɒpəlaɪz] ⟨z⟩monopolizować; ⟨z⟩dominować; **~·ly** monopol *m* (***of*** na *A*)
mo·not·o|·nous [mə'nɒtənəs] monotonny; **~·ny** monotonia *f*
mon·soon [mɒn'su:n] monsun *m*
mon·ster ['mɒnstə] monstrum *n*, potwór *m*; *attr.* monstrualny
mon|·stros·i·ty [mɒn'strɒsətɪ] monstrualność *f*; monstrum *n*; **~·strous** ['mɒnstrəs] powtorny, monstrualny
Montenegro Czarnogóra *f*
month [mʌnθ] miesiąc *m*; '**~·ly** **1.** miesięczny; **2.** miesięcznik *m*; F *zwł. Am.* miesiączka *f*
mon·u·ment ['mɒnjʊmənt] pomnik *m*, monument *m*; **~·al** [mɒnjʊ'mentl] monumentalny
moo [mu:] ⟨za⟩ryczeć
mood [mu:d] nastrój *m*, humor *m*; ***be in a good*** (***bad***) **~** być w dobrym (złym) nastroju; '**~·y** (***-ier, -iest***) humorzasty
moon [mu:n] **1.** księżyc *m*; ***once in a blue ~*** F od wielkiego dzwonu; **2.** ***~ about, ~ around*** F pętać się; F dumać; '**~·light** światło *n* księżycowe; '**~·lit** oświetlony księżycem; '**~·shine** *sl.* samogon *m*; '**~·struck** F trzepnięty
moor[1] [mʊə] wrzosowisko *n*
moor[2] [mʊə] *naut.* ⟨za-, przy⟩cumować; **~·ing** ['mʊərɪŋz] *naut.* cumowisko *n*; ***~ings*** *pl.* cumy *pl.*, liny *pl.* cumownicze
moose [mu:s] (*pl.* ***moose***) *północnoamerykański* łoś *m*
mop [mɒp] **1.** zmywak *m*, myjka *f*; grzywa *f*, kudły *pl.*; **2.** (***-pp-***) *też* ***~ up*** ścierać ⟨zetrzeć⟩, zmywać ⟨zmyć⟩
mope [məʊp] mieć chandrę, być w depresji
mo·ped ['məʊped] *Brt.* moped *m*
mor·al ['mɒrəl] **1.** moralny, prawy; **2.** morał *m*, nauka *f*; ***~s*** *pl.* moralność *f*; **mo·rale** [mɒ'rɑ:l] morale *n*; **mor·al·ize** ['mɒrəlaɪz] moralizować (***about, on*** na temat *G*)
mor·bid ['mɔ:bɪd] chorobliwy
more [mɔ:] **1.** *adj.* więcej; jeszcze (*więcej*); ***some ~ tea*** jeszcze trochę herbaty; **2.** *adv.* bardziej; jeszcze (*trochę*); ***~ and ~*** coraz bardziej; ***~ or less*** mniej lub bardziej; ***once ~*** jeszcze raz; ***the ~ so because*** tym bardziej, że; *przy tworzeniu comp.* ***~ important*** ważniejszy; ***~ often*** częściej; **3.** więcej (***of*** *G*, ***than*** niż); ***a little ~*** trochę więcej *lub* bardziej
mo·rel [mɒ'rel] *bot.* smardz *m*
more·o·ver [mɔ:'rəʊvə] ponadto, poza tym
morgue [mɔ:g] kostnica *f*
morn·ing ['mɔ:nɪŋ] rano *n*, poranek *m*; ***good ~!*** dzień dobry!; ***in the ~*** rano, ranem; przed południem; ***tomorrow ~*** jutro rano
mo·rose [mə'rəʊs] ponury
mor|·phi·a ['mɔ:fjə], **~·phine** ['mɔ:fi:n] morfina *f*
mor·sel ['mɔ:sl] kąsek *m*; ***a ~ of*** odrobina (*G*)
mor·tal ['mɔ:rtl] **1.** śmiertelny; **2.** śmiertelnik *m*; **~·i·ty** [mɔ:'tælətɪ] śmiertelność *f*
mor·tar[1] ['mɔ:tə] zaprawa *f* murarska
mor·tar[2] ['mɔ:tə] moździerz *m*
mort·gage ['mɔ:gɪdʒ] hipoteka *f*; dług *m* hipoteczny; wpis *m* hipoteczny; **2.** obciążać ⟨-żyć⟩ hipotekę

mor•ti•cian [mɔː'tɪʃn] *Am.* przedsiębiorca *m* pogrzebowy
mor•ti|•fi•ca•tion [mɔːtɪfɪ'keɪʃn] wstyd *n*; umartwianie *n* się; **~•fy** ['mɔːtɪfaɪ] zawstydzać ⟨-dzić⟩; umartwiać ⟨-twić⟩ się
mor•tu•a•ry ['mɔːtjʊərɪ] kostnica *f*
mo•sa•ic [mə'zeɪɪk] mozaika *f*; *attr.* mozaikowy
Mos•cow Moskwa *f*
Mos•lem ['mɒzləm] → ***Muslim***
mosque [mɒsk] meczet *m*
mos•qui•to [mə'skiːtəʊ] *zo.* (*pl.* ***-to(e)s***) moskit *m*
moss [mɒs] *bot.* mech *m*; '**~•y** *bot.* (***-ier, -iest***) omszały
most [məʊst] **1.** *adj.* najwięcej; większość; **~ *people*** *pl.* większość ludzi *pl.*; **2.** *adv.* najwięcej; **~ *of all*** najwięcej; *przed adj.* najbardziej; *też przy tworzeniu sup.* ***the ~ important*** najważniejszy; **3. *at (the) ~*** co najwyżej; ***make the ~ of s.th.*** wykorzystywać ⟨-tać⟩ coś do maksimum; '**~•ly** przeważnie, głównie
MOT [em əʊ 'tiː] *Brt.* F *też* **~ *test*** *jakby*: kontrola *f* sprawności pojazdu
mo•tel [məʊ'tel] motel *m*
moth [mɒθ] *zo.* ćma *f*; mól *m*; '**~-eat•en** zżarty przez mole
moth•er ['mʌðə] **1.** matka *f*; *attr.* ojczysty, rodzimy; krajowy; **2.** matkować (*D*); '**~coun•try** ojczyzna *f*; '**~•hood** macierzyństwo *n*; **~-in-law** ['mʌðərɪnlɔː] (*pl.* ***mothers-in-law***) teściowa *f*; '**~•ly** matczyny; macierzyński; **~-of-pearl** [mʌðərəv'pɜːl] macica *f* perłowa; **~ 'tongue** język *m* ojczysty
mo•tif [məʊ'tiːf] (*w sztuce, muzyce*) motyw *m*; deseń *m*
mo•tion ['məʊʃn] **1.** ruch *m*; *parl.* wniosek *m*; ***put*** *lub* ***set in ~*** wprawić w ruch; *fig.* nadawać *czemuś* bieg; **2.** *v/t.* skinąć na (*A*); wzywać ⟨wezwać⟩ gestem (*G*); *v/i.* skinąć, kiwnąć; '**~•less** nieruchomy; **~ 'pic•ture** *Am.* film *m*
mo•ti|•vate ['məʊtɪveɪt] nakłaniać ⟨-łonić⟩, zachęcać ⟨-cić⟩; ⟨s⟩powodować; **~•va•tion** [məʊtɪ'veɪʃn] motywacja *f*, pobudka *f*
mo•tive ['məʊtɪv] **1.** motyw *m*, pobudka *f*; **2.** napędowy (*też fig.*)
mot•ley ['mɒtlɪ] pstrokaty, różnoraki
mo•to•cross ['məʊtəʊkrɒs] (*w sporcie*) motokros *m*
mo•tor ['məʊtə] motor *m*, silnik *m*; siła *f* napędowa; *attr.* motoryzacyjny; '**~•bike** *Brt.* F motorower *m*; '**~•boat** motorówka *f*; **~•cade** ['məʊtəkeɪd] kolumna *f* samochodów; '**~•car** *Brt.* samochód *m*; '**~car•a•van** *Brt.* samochód *m* mieszkalny; '**~•cy•cle** motocykl *m*; '**~•cyc•list** motocyklista *m*; '**~ home** *Am.* samochód *m* mieszkalny; **~•ing** ['məʊtərɪŋ] jazda *f* samochodem; ***school of ~ing*** szkoła *f* nauki jazdy; *attr.* samochodowy; **~•ist** ['məʊtərɪst] kierowca *m*; **~•ize** ['məʊtəraɪz] ⟨z⟩motoryzować; '**~ launch** motorówka *f*; '**~•way** *Brt.* autostrada *f*
mot•tled ['mɒtld] cętkowany
mo(u)ld[1] [məʊld] pleśń *f*; próchnica *f*
mo(u)ld[2] [məʊld] **1.** *tech.* forma *f* odlewnicza; **2.** *tech.* odlewać ⟨-lać⟩
mo(u)l•der ['məʊldə] *też* **~ *away*** rozkładać ⟨-łożyć⟩ się
mo(u)ld•y ['məʊldɪ] (***-ier, -iest***) zapleśniały, spleśniały; stęchły, zatęchły
mo(u)lt [məʊlt] pierzyć się; *włosy* ⟨s⟩tracić
mound [maʊnd] wzgórek *m*; kopiec *m*
mount [maʊnt] **1.** *v/t.* dosiadać (-siąść) (*G*), *konia* wsiąść na (*A*); ⟨z⟩montować (*też fig.*); zamontowywać ⟨-ować⟩; wspinać ⟨-piąć⟩ się; *obraz itp.* oprawiać ⟨-wić⟩; *kamień szlachetny* oprawiać ⟨-wić⟩; ***~ed police*** policja *f* konna; *v/i.* dosiadać ⟨-siąść⟩ konia; wzrastać ⟨-rosnąć⟩; **~ *up*** ⟨na⟩gromadzić się; **2.** zawieszenie *n*, podstawa *f*; oprawa *f*; wierzchowiec *m*; (*w nazwach*) góra *f*
moun•tain ['maʊntɪn] **1.** góra *f*; **2.** górski; '**~ bike** rower *m* górski
moun•tain|•eer [maʊntɪ'nɪə] alpinista *m* (-tka *f*); **~•eer•ing** [maʊntɪ'nɪərɪŋ] alpinistyka *f*
moun•tain•ous ['maʊntɪnəs] górzysty
mourn [mɔːn] opłakiwać ⟨-kać⟩ (***for, over*** *A*), żałować; '**~•er** żałobnik *m* (-nica *f*); '**~•ful** żałobny; '**~•ing** żałoba *f*
mouse [maʊs] (*pl.* ***mice*** [maɪs]) mysz *f*; (*pl. też* ***mouses***) *komp.* mysz *f*
mous•tache [mə'stɑːʃ] *też* ***mustache*** wąsy *pl.*
mouth [maʊθ] (*pl.* ***mouths*** [maʊðz]) usta *pl.*; pysk *m* (*zwierzęcia*); ujście *n* (*rzeki*); otwór *m* (*pojemnika*); '**~•ful** kęs *m*; '**~ •or•gan** *ustna* harmonijka *f*, F organki *pl.*; '**~•piece** ustnik *m*; *fig.*

M

rzecznik *m* (-czka *f*); '**~·wash** płyn *m* do ust
mo·va·ble ['muːvəbl] ruchomy
move [muːv] **1.** *v/t.* ruszać ⟨-szyć⟩; poruszać ⟨-szyć⟩; przesuwać ⟨-unąć⟩; (*w szachach*) ⟨z⟩robić ruch (*D*); *parl.* stawiać ⟨postawić⟩ wniosek; wzruszać ⟨-szyć⟩; ***~ house*** przeprowadzać ⟨-dzić⟩ się; ***~ heaven and earth*** poruszyć niebo i ziemię; *v/i.* ruszać ⟨-szyć⟩ się; poruszać ⟨-szyć⟩ się; przesuwać ⟨-unąć⟩ się; przeprowadzać ⟨-dzić⟩ się, przenosić ⟨-nieść⟩ się (***to*** do *G*); (*w szachach*) robić ruch; ***~ away*** wyprowadzać ⟨-dzić⟩ się; ***~ in*** wprowadzać ⟨-dzić⟩ się; ***~ on*** iść ⟨pójść⟩ dalej; ***~ out*** wyprowadzać ⟨-dzić⟩ się; **2.** ruch *m*; *fig.* posunięcie *n*, krok *m*; (*w szachach*) ruch *m*, posunięcie *n*; przeprowadzka *f*; ***on the ~*** w ruchu; ***get a ~ on!*** F ruszaj się!; '**~·a·ble** → ***movable***; '**~·ment** ruch (*też fig.*); *mus.* część *f*; *tech.* mechanizm *m*
mov·ie ['muːvɪ] *zwł. Am.* film *m*; kino *n*; *attr.* filmowy, kinowy; '**~ cam·e·ra** kamera *f* filmowa; '**~ star** *Am.* gwiazda *f* filmowa; '**~ thea·ter** *Am.* kino *n*
mov·ing ['muːvɪŋ] ruszający się, ruchomy; *fig.* wzruszający; **~ 'stair·case** ruchome schody *pl.*; '**~ van** *Am.* samochód *m* do przeprowadzek
mow [məʊ] (***mowed, mowed*** *lub* ***mown***) ⟨s⟩kosić; '**~·er** kosiarka *f*; **~n** [məʊn] *p.p. od* ***mow***
MP [em 'piː] *skrót*: ***Member of Parliament*** *Brt.* poseł *m* (-słanka *f*); ***military police*** żandarmeria *f* wojskowa
mph *skrót pisany*: ***miles per hour*** mile na godzinę
Mr ['mɪstə] *skrót*: ***Mister*** pan *m*
Mrs ['mɪsɪz] *skrót*: ***Mistress*** pani *f*
MS *pl.* ***MSS*** *skrót pisany*: ***manuscript*** rękopis *m*
Ms [mɪz, məz] pani *f* (*neutralnie*)
Mt *skrót pisany*: ***Mount*** góra *f*
much [mʌtʃ] **1.** *adj.* (***more, most***) dużo; **2.** *adv.* bardzo; *w złożeniach* dużo; *przed comp.* znacznie; ***very ~*** bardzo; ***I thought as ~*** tak właśnie myślałem; **3.** ***nothing ~*** nic szczególnego; ***make ~ of*** wiele sobie robić z (*G*); ***think ~ of*** mieć dobrą opinię o (*L*); ***I am not ~ of a dancer*** F nie tańczę najlepiej
muck [mʌk] F łajno *n*, gnój *m*; paskudztwo *n*, brud *m*
mu·cus ['mjuːkəs] śluz *m*
mud [mʌd] błoto *n*; brud *m* (*też fig.*)
mud·dle ['mʌdl] **1.** rozgardiasz *m*; ***be in a ~*** być skołowanym; **2.** *też* ***~ up*** *kogoś* skołować; *coś* namieszać; ***~ through*** F przebrnąć przez (*A*)
mud|·dy ['mʌdɪ] (***-ier, -iest***) zabłocony; błotnisty, bagnisty; '**~·guard** błotnik *m*
mues·li ['mjuːzlɪ] muesli *n* (*śniadaniowa mieszanka zbożowa*)
muff [mʌf] mufka *f*
muf·fin ['mʌfɪn] bułeczka *f* (*jedzona na gorąco*)
muf·fle ['mʌfl] *dźwięk* ⟨s⟩tłumić; *często* ***~ up*** obwijać ⟨-inąć⟩, otulać ⟨-lić⟩; '**~r** (gruby) szalik *m*; *mot.* tłumik *m*
mug[1] [mʌg] kubek *m*, kufel *m*; *sl.* ryj *m*, morda *f*
mug[2] [mʌg] (***-gg-***) (*zwł. na ulicy*) napadać ⟨-paść⟩, ⟨z⟩rabować; '**~·ger** F rabuś *m*, napastnik *m*; '**~·ging** F rabunek *m*, napaść *m*
mug·gy ['mʌgɪ] parny, duszny
mul·ber·ry ['mʌlbərɪ] *bot.* morwa *f*
mule [mjuːl] *zo.* muł *m*
mulled [mʌld]: ***~ wine*** wino *n* grzane
mul·li·on ['mʌljən] *arch.* słupek *m* okienny
mul·ti... ['mʌltɪ] multi..., wielo...
mul·ti|·far·i·ous [mʌltɪ'feərɪəs] różnoraki, różnorodny; **~·lat·e·ral** [mʌltɪ'lætərəl] wielostronny
mul·ti·ple ['mʌltɪpl] **1.** wielokrotny; **2.** *math.* wielokrotność *f*; ***~'store*** *też* F ***multiple*** *zwł. Brt.* sklep *m* firmowy
mul·ti·pli·ca·tion [mʌltɪplɪ'keɪʃn] powielanie *n*; *math.* mnożenie *n*; ***~ table*** tabliczka *f* mnożenia
mul·ti·pli·ci·ty [mʌltɪ'plɪsətɪ] wielokrotność *f*; wielość *f*
mul·ti·ply ['mʌltɪplaɪ] powielać ⟨-lić⟩; rozmnażać ⟨-nożyć⟩ (się); *math.* ⟨po⟩mnożyć (***by*** przez *A*)
mul·ti|'pur·pose wielofunkcyjny; **~'sto·rey** *Brt.* wielopiętrowy; **~-sto·rey 'car park** *Brt.* parking *m* wielopiętrowy
mul·ti|·tude ['mʌltɪtjuːd] wielość *f*, mnogość *f*; **~·tu·di·nous** [mʌltɪ'tjuːdɪnəs] mnogi, liczny
mum[1] [mʌm] *Brt.* F mamusia *f*
mum[2] [mʌm] **1.** *int.*: ***~'s the word*** ani słowa o tym!, buzia na kłódkę; **2.** *adj.*: ***keep ~*** trzymać język za zębami

mum·ble ['mʌmbl] ⟨za-, wy⟩mamrotać
mum·mi·fy['mʌmɪfaɪ]⟨z⟩mumifikować
mum·my[1] ['mʌmɪ] mumia *f*
mum·my[2] ['mʌmɪ] *Brt.* F mamusia *f*
mumps [mʌmps] *med.* świnka *f*, nagminne zapalenie *n* przyuszniсy
munch [mʌntʃ] ⟨z⟩żuć z chrzęstem, ⟨s⟩chrupać
mun·dane [mʌn'deɪn] przyziemny
Mu·nich Monachium *n*
mu·ni·ci·pal [mjuː'nɪsɪpl] miejski; komunalny; **~ *council*** rada *f* miejska; **~·i·ty** [mjuːnɪsɪ'pælətɪ] gmina *f* miejska
mu·ral ['mjʊərəl] **1.** malowidło *n* ścienne; **2.** ścienny
mur·der ['mɜːdə] **1.** morderstwo *n*; **2.** ⟨za⟩mordować; *fig.* wykończyć ⟨-kańczać⟩; **~·er** ['mɜːdərə] morderca *m* (-czyni *f*); **~·ess** ['mɜːdərɪs] morderczyni *f*; **~·ous** ['mɜːdərəs] morderczy
murk·y ['mɜːkɪ] (***-ier, -iest***) mroczny, nieprzejrzysty
murmur ['mɜːmə] **1.** szmer *m*; szemranie *n*; **2.** szemrać, ⟨wy⟩mamrotać
mus|·cle ['mʌsl] mięsień *m*, muskuł *m*; **'~·cle-bound**: ***be ~cle-bound*** być nadmiernie umięśnionym; **~·cu·lar** ['mʌskjʊlə] muskularny, umięśniony
muse[1] [mjuːz] ⟨za⟩dumać (się), ⟨po⟩medytować (***on, over*** nad *I*)
muse[2] [mjuːz] *też* ♀ muza *f*
mu·se·um [mjuː'zɪəm] muzeum *n*
mush [mʌʃ] bryja *f*, breja *f*; *Am.* zupa *f* z kukurydzy
mush·room ['mʌʃrʊm] **1.** *bot.* grzyb *m*, *zwł.* pieczarka *f*; *attr.* grzybowy, pieczarkowy; **2.** *fig.* wyrastać ⟨-rosnąć⟩jak grzyby po deszczu
mu·sic ['mjuːzɪk] muzyka *f*; nuty *pl.*; ***it was put*** *lub* ***set to ~*** napisano do niego muzykę
'mu·sic·al **1.** muzyczny; muzykalny; melodyjny; **2.** musical *m*; **'~ box** *zwł. Brt.* pozytywka *f*; **~ 'in·stru·ment** instrument *m* muzyczny
'mu·sic| box *zwł. Am.* pozytywka *f*; **'~ cen·tre** (*Am.*; **cen·ter**) sprzęt *m* stereo, wieża *f* stereo; **'~ hall** *Brt.* teatr *m* rewiowy, music-hall *m*
mu·si·cian [mjuː'zɪʃn] muzyk *m*
'mu·sic stand pulpit *m*
musk [mʌsk] piżmo *n*; **'~ ox** (*pl.* ***- oxen***) wół *m* piżmowy, piżmowół *m*; **'~·rat** szczur *m* piżmowy, piżmak *m*
Mus·lim ['mʊslɪm] **1.** muzułmanin *m* (-anka *f*); **2.** muzułmański
mus·quash ['mʌskwɒʃ] szczur *m* piżmowy, piżmak *m*; futro *n* z piżmaków
mus·sel ['mʌsl] małż *m*, *zwł.* omułek *m*
must[1] [mʌst] **1.** *v/aux.* musieć; ***you must not*** (F ***mustn't***) nie wolno ci; **2.** konieczność *f*
must[2] [mʌst] moszcz *m*
mus·tache [mə'stɑːʃ] *Am.* wąsy *pl.*
mus·tard ['mʌstəd] musztarda *f*; *bot.* gorczyca *f*
mus·ter ['mʌstə] **1. ~ *up*** *siłę itp.* zbierać ⟨zebrać⟩; zdobywać ⟨-być⟩ się na (*A*) *odwagę*; **2. *pass ~*** *fig.* ⟨u⟩czynić zadość wymogom
must·y ['mʌstɪ] (***-ier, -iest***) zatęchły; stęchły
mu·ta·tion [mjuː'teɪʃn] mutacja *f* (*też bot.*)
mute [mjuːt] **1.** niemy; **2.** niemy *m*; niema *f*; *mus.* tłumik *m*
mu·ti·late ['mjuːtɪleɪt] okaleczać ⟨-czyć⟩, zniekształcać ⟨-cić⟩
mu·ti|·neer [mjuːtɪ'nɪə] rebeliant *m*, buntownik *m*; **~·nous** ['mjuːtɪnəs] rebeliancki, buntowniczy; **~·ny** ['mjuːtɪnɪ] rebelia *f*, bunt *m*
mut·ter ['mʌtə] **1.** ⟨wy⟩mamrotać; **2.** mamrotanie *n*, szemranie *n*
mut·ton ['mʌtn] *gastr.* baranina; ***leg of ~*** udziec *m* barani; **~ 'chop** kotlet *m* barani
mu·tu·al ['mjuːtʃʊəl] wzajemny, obopólny; wspólny
muz·zle ['mʌzl] **1.** *zo.* pysk *m*, morda *f*; wylot *m* (*lufy*); kaganiec *m*; **2.** zakładać ⟨założyć⟩ kaganiec (*D*); *fig.* zamykać ⟨-mknąć⟩ usta
my [maɪ] mój
myrrh [mɜː] *bot.* mirra *f*, mira *f*
myr·tle ['mɜːtl] *bot.* mirt *m*
my·self [maɪ'self] ja, mnie; się, sobie; ja sam; ***by ~*** samotnie
mys·te|·ri·ous [mɪ'stɪərɪəs] tajemniczy, zagadkowy; **~·ry** ['mɪstərɪ] tajemnica *f*; zagadka *f*; *rel.* misterium *n*; ***~ry tour*** podróż *f* w nieznane
mys|·tic ['mɪstɪk] **1.** mistyk *m* (-yczka *f*); **2.** *adj.* mistyczny; **'~·tic·al** mistyczny; **~·ti·fy** ['mɪstɪfaɪ] zwodzić ⟨zwieść⟩; oszałamiać ⟨oszołomić⟩
myth [mɪθ] mit *m*
my·thol·o·gy [mɪ'θɒlədʒɪ] mitologia *f*

N

N, n [en] N, n *n*

N *skrót pisany*: ***north*** płn., północ(ny); ***northern*** północny

nab [næb] F (***-bb-***) ⟨z⟩łapać, ⟨s⟩chwytać

na·dir ['neɪdɪə] *astr.* nadir *m*, *fig.* najniższy poziom *m*

nag[1] [næg] **1.** (***-gg-***) ⟨za-, u⟩dręczyć; zrzędzić (***at*** na *A*); **2.** F zrzęda *m/f*

nag[2] [næg] F szkapa *f*, chabeta *f*

nail [neɪl] **1.** *tech.* gwóźdź *m*; paznokieć *m*; **2.** przybijać ⟨-bić⟩ gwoździami (***to*** do *G*); '~ **pol·ish** lakier *m* do paznokci; '~ **scis·sors** *pl.* nożyczki *pl.* do paznokci; '~ **var·nish** lakier *m* do paznokci

na·ive, na·ïve [naɪ'iːv] naiwny; **na·iv·eté** [naɪ'iːvəti], **na·ive·ty** [naɪ'iːvɪti] naiwność *f*

na·ked ['neɪkɪd] nagi; odsłonięty; *fig.* nieosłonięty; '~**·ness** nagość *f*

name [neɪm] **1.** nazwa *f*; imię *n*; nazwisko *n*; ***by ~*** z imienia; ***by the ~ of ...*** imieniem ...; ***what's your ~?*** jak się pan(i) nazywa?; ***call s.o. ~s*** przezywać ⟨-zwać⟩ kogoś; **2.** nazywać ⟨-zwać⟩; dawać ⟨dać⟩ imię; dawać ⟨dać⟩ na imię; wymieniać ⟨-nić⟩ z imienia; '~**·less** bezimienny; nieznany; '~**·ly** mianowicie; '~**·plate** tabliczka *f* z nazwiskiem *lub* nazwą; '~**·sake** imiennik *m* (-iczka *f*); '~**-tag** (*na ubraniu*) naszywka *f* z nazwiskiem

nan·ny ['nænɪ] niania *f*; '~ **goat** *zo.* koza *f*

nap [næp]: **1.** drzemka *f*; ***have*** *lub* ***take a ~*** ucinać ⟨uciąć⟩ sobie drzemkę **2.** (***-pp-***) ucinać ⟨uciąć⟩ sobie drzemkę

nape [neɪp]: *zw.* ***~ of the neck*** kark *m*

nap·kin ['næpkɪn] serwetka *f*; *Brt.* → ***nappy***

Na·ples Neapol *m*

nap·py *Brt.* F pielucha *f*

nar·co·sis [nɑː'kəʊsɪs] *med.* (*pl.* ***-ses*** [-siːz]) narkoza *f*

nar·cot·ic [nɑː'kɒtɪk] **1.** (***~ally***) narkotyczny *m*; ***~ addiction*** uzależnienie n narkotyczne; **2.** narkotyk *m*; środek *m* odurzający; ***~s*** *pl.* narkotyki *pl.*; ***~s squad*** wydział służb *pl.* antynarkotykowych

nar|·rate [nə'reɪt] opowiadać ⟨-wiedzieć⟩; ⟨po⟩informować; **~·ra·tion** [nə'reɪʃn] narracja *f*; **~·ra·tive** ['nærətɪv] **1.** narracja *f*; relacja *f* (***of*** z *G*); **2.** narracyjny; **~·ra·tor** [nə'reɪtə] narrator(ka *f*) *m*

nar·row ['nærəʊ] **1.** wąski; nieznaczny; dokładny; *fig.* ograniczony; **2.** zwężać ⟨zwęzić⟩ (się); zmniejszać ⟨-szyć⟩ ;(się); ograniczać ⟨-czyć⟩; '~**·ly** ledwo; **~-'mind·ed** ograniczony; o wąskich horyzontach; '~**·ness** ograniczenie *n*

NASA ['næsə] *skrót*: ***National Aeronautics and Space Administration*** NASA *f*

na·sal [neɪzl] nosowy

nas·ty ['nɑːstɪ] (***-ier, -iest***) paskudny; *charakter itp.*: okropny; złośliwy, niedobry; *człowiek, zachowanie*: agresywny; *umysł*: plugawy

na·tal ['neɪtl] urodzeniowy

na·tion ['neɪʃn] naród *m*; państwo *n*

na·tion·al ['næʃənl] **1.** narodowy; państwowy; **2.** obywatel(ka *f*) *m* (*danego państwa*); ~ **'an·them** hymn *m* państwowy

na·tion·al|·i·ty [næʃə'nælətɪ] narodowość *f*; obywatelstwo *f*; **~·ize** ['næʃnəlaɪz] ⟨z⟩nacjonalizować, upaństwawiać ⟨-wowić⟩

na·tion·al| 'park park *m* narodowy; ~ **'team** (*w sporcie*) reprezentacja *f* kraju

'na·tion-wide ogólnokrajowy

na·tive ['neɪtɪv] **1.** rodzimy, ojczysty; krajowy, miejscowy; wrodzony; **2.** krajowiec *m*, tubylec *m*; ~ **'lan·guage** język *m* rodzimy *lub* ojczysty; ~ **'speak·er** rodzimy użytkownik (*języka*) *m*

Na·tiv·i·ty [nə'tɪvətɪ] narodzenie *n* Chrystusa; opowieść *f* o narodzeniu Chrystusa; jasełka *pl.*

NATO ['neɪtəʊ] *skrót*: ***North Atlantic Treaty Organization*** NATO *n*, Pakt *m* Północnoatlantycki

nat·u·ral ['nætʃrəl] naturalny, przyrodzony; urodzony, zawołany; przyrodniczy; ~ **'gas** gaz *m* ziemny; **~·ize** ['nætʃrəlaɪz] naturalizować (się); nada-

wać ⟨-dać⟩ obywatelstwo; '~·**ly** naturalnie; z natury; ~ **re'sourc·es** *pl.* bogactwa *pl.* naturalne; ~ **'sci·ence** nauka *f* przyrodnicza
na·ture ['neɪtʃə] przyroda *f*, natura *f*; '~ **con·ser·va·tion** ochrona *f* przyrody; '~ **re·serve** rezerwat *m* przyrodniczy; '~ **trail** szlak *m* przyrodoznawczy
naugh·ty ['nɔːtɪ] (***-ier, -iest***) niegrzeczny; *dowcip*: nieprzystojny
nau·se|·a ['nɔːsjə] nudności *pl.*, mdłości *pl.*; ~·**ate** ['nɔːsɪeɪt]: ~***ate s.o.*** doprowadzać ⟨-dzić⟩ kogoś do mdłości, przyprawiać ⟨-wić⟩ kogoś o mdłości; '~·**ating** przyprawiający o mdłości
nau·ti·cal ['nɔːtɪkl] morski, żeglarski
na·val ['neɪvl] morski; okrętowy; '~**base** baza *f* morska; '~ **of·fi·cer** oficer *m* marynarki wojennej; '~ **pow·er** potęga *f* morska
nave [neɪv] *arch.* nawa *f* główna
na·vel ['neɪvl] *anat.* pępek *m*
nav·i|·ga·ble ['nævɪgəbl] żeglowny; ~·**gate** ['nævɪgeɪt] *naut.* ⟨po⟩żeglować, pływać; nawigować; *fig.* pilotować; ~·**ga·tion** [nævɪ'geɪʃən] *naut.*, *aviat.* nawigacja *f*; pływanie *n*; *fig.* pilotowanie *n*; ~·**ga·tor** ['nævɪgeɪtə] *naut.*, *aviat.* nawigator *m*
na·vy ['neɪvɪ] marynarka *f* wojenna; ~ **'blue** *kolor*: granat *m*
nay *parl.* [neɪ] głos *m* przeciw
NBC [en biː 'siː] *skrót*: ***National Broadcasting Company*** (*amerykańska firma radiowa i TV*)
NE *skrót pisany*: ***northeast*** płn.-wsch., północny wschód; ***northeast*(*ern*)** płn.-wsch, północno-wschodni
near [nɪə] **1.** *adj.* bliski, niedaleki; *brzeg*: bliższy; ***it was a ~ miss*** ledwie brakowało (*do zderzenia itp.*); **2.** *adv.* blisko, niedaleko (*też* ***~ at hand***); prawie, niemal; **3.** *prp.* w pobliżu (*G*); **4.** zbliżać ⟨-żyć⟩ się; ~·**by 1.** *adj.* ['nɪəbaɪ] bliski, pobliski; **2.** [nɪə'baɪ] w pobliżu, blisko; '~·**ly** prawie, blisko; ~ **'sight·ed** *zwł. Am.* krótkowzroczny
neat [niːt] porządny; schludny; *rozwiązanie*: zgrabny; *wódka itp.*: czysty
neb·u·lous ['nebjʊləs] mglisty, mętny
ne·ces|·sar·i·ly ['nesəsərəlɪ] nieodzownie, koniecznie; ***not ~ sarily*** niekoniecznie; ~·**sa·ry** ['nesəsərɪ] nieodzowny, konieczny
ne·ces·si|·tate [nɪ'sesɪteɪt] wymagać (*G*), stwarzać ⟨stworzyć⟩ konieczność (*G*); ~·**ty** [nɪ'sesətɪ] konieczność *f*, potrzeba *f*
neck [nek] **1.** szyja *f*; szyjka *f*; kołnierzyk *m*; → ***neckline***; ***~ and ~*** F łeb w łeb; ***be up to one's ~ in debt*** F być po uszy w długach; **2.** F pieścić się
neck·er·chief ['nekətʃɪf] (*pl.* ***-chiefs, -chieves***) apaszka *f*
neck|·lace ['neklɪs] naszyjnik *m*; ~·**let** ['neklɪt] naszyjnik *m*; '~·**line** wycięcie *n* (*ubrania*); '~·**tie** *zwł. Am.* krawat *m*
née [neɪ]: ***~ Smith*** z domu Smith
need [niːd] **1.** potrzeba *f*; brak *m*; bieda *f*; ***be in ~ of s.th.*** potrzebować czegoś; ***in ~*** w potrzebie; ***be in ~ of help*** potrzebować pomocy; **2.** *v/t.* potrzebować (*G*); *v/aux.* potrzebować (*G*), musieć; ***it ~s to be done*** trzeba to zrobić
nee·dle ['niːdl] **1.** igła *f* (*też świerka itp.*); **2.** F *komuś* dawać się we znaki
'need·less niepotrzebny, zbyteczny
'nee·dle|·wom·an (*pl.* ***-women***) szwaczka *f*; '~·**work** robótki *pl.* ręczne
'need·y (***-ier, -iest***) potrzebujący, ubogi
ne·ga·tion [nɪ'geɪʃn] przeczenie *n*, negacja *f*; **neg·a·tive** ['negətɪv] **1.** negatywny; odmowny; przeczący; **2.** przeczenie *n*; *phot.* negatyw *m*; ***answer in the ~*** odpowiadać odmownie
ne·glect [nɪ'glekt] **1.** zaniedbywać ⟨-dbać⟩; zapominać ⟨-mnieć⟩ (***doing, to do*** zrobić); **2.** zaniedbanie *n*, niedbalstwo *n*
neg·li·gence ['neglɪdʒənts] zaniedbanie *n*, nieuwaga *f*; **neg·li·gent** ['neglɪdʒənt] niedbały
neg·li·gi·ble ['neglɪdʒəbl] bez znaczenia
ne·go·ti|·ate [nɪ'gəʊʃɪeɪt] ⟨wy⟩negocjować; ⟨po⟩prowadzić rozmowy, rokować; F *przeszkodę* pokonywać ⟨-nać⟩; *czek* ⟨z⟩realizować; ~·**a·tion** [nɪgəʊʃɪ'eɪʃn] negocjacje *pl.*; rokowania *pl.*; ~·**a·tor** [nɪ'gəʊʃɪeɪtə] negocjator *m* (-ka *f*)
neigh [neɪ] **1.** ⟨za⟩rżeć; **2.** rżenie *n*
neigh·bo(u)r ['neɪbə] sąsiad(ka *f*); *rel.* bliźni *m*; '~·**hood** sąsiedztwo *n*; najbliższa okolica *f*; ~·**ing** ['neɪbərɪŋ] sąsiedni, sąsiadujący; '~·**ly** życzliwy, przychylny
nei·ther ['naɪðə, 'niːðə] **1.** *adj.*, *pron.* żaden (z dwóch); **2.** ***~ ...nor...*** ani ... ani ...

N

ne·on ['ni:ən] *chem.* neon *m*; '**~ lamp** lampa *f* neonowa; '**~ sign** neon *m*
neph·ew ['nevju:] siostrzeniec *m*, bratanek *m*
nerd [nɜ:d] F ćwok *m*, żłób *m*
nerve [nɜ:v] nerw *m*; odwaga *f*, śmiałość *f*; F czelność *f*; ***get on s.o.'s ~s*** działać komuś na nerwy; ***he lost his ~*** nerwy go poniosły; ***you've got a ~!*** ty to masz tupet!; '**~·less** mało odważny
ner·vous ['nɜ:vəs] nerwowy; '**~·ness** nerwowość *f*
nest [nest] **1.** gniazdo *n*; **2.** gnieździć się
nes·tle ['nesl] ⟨przy⟩tulić się (***against, on*** do *G*); *też* ***~ down*** ⟨u⟩mościć się (***in*** w *L*)
net[1] [net] **1.** sieć *f*, siatka *f*; ***~ curtain*** firanka *f*; **2.** (**-*tt*-**) ⟨z⟩łowić *lub* ⟨s⟩chwytać siecią
net[2] [net] **1.** netto; na czysto; **2.** (**-*tt*-**) przynosić ⟨-nieść⟩ na czysto *lub* netto
Neth·er·lands ['neðələndz] *pl.* Holandia *pl.*
net·tle ['netl] *bot.* **1.** pokrzywa *f*; **2.** ⟨po⟩kłócić się
'**net·work** sieć *f* (*połączeń, komputerowa itp.*)
neu|·ro·sis [njʊə'rəʊsɪs] *med.* (*pl.* **-*ses*** [-si:z]) neuroza *f*, nerwica *f*; **~·rot·ic** [njʊə'rɒtɪk] neurotyk *m* (-yczka *f*)
neu·ter ['nju:tə] **1.** *gr.* nijaki; bezpłciowy; **2.** *gr.* rodzaj *m* nijaki; **3.** ⟨wy⟩trzebić, ⟨wy⟩kastrować
neu·tral ['nju:trəl] **1.** neutralny; obojętny; *electr.* zerowy; *mot.* jałowy; **2.** osoba *f* neutralna; państwo neutralne; *też* ***~ gear*** bieg *m* jałowy; **~·i·ty** [nju:'trælətɪ] neutralność *f*; **~·ize** ['nju:trəlaɪz] ⟨z⟩neutralizować
neu·tron ['nju:trɒn] *phys.* neutron *m*
nev·er ['nevə] nigdy; **~-'end·ing** nie kończący się; **~·the'less** pomimo to
new [nju:] nowy; *ziemniaki itp.*: młody; ***it's ~ to me*** to dla mnie nowość; '**~·born** nowo narodzony; '**~·com·er** przybysz *m*; nowy *m* (-wa *f*) ; nowy pracownik *m*; '**~·ly** nowo
New Or·leans Nowy Orlean *m*
news [nju:z] *sg.* wiadomości *pl.*, informacje *pl.*; '**~·a·gent** sprzedawca *m* (-czyni *f*) czasopism; '**~·boy** roznosiciel *m* gazet; '**~ bul·le·tin** skrót *m* wiadomości; '**~·cast** (*w radio, TV*) wiadomości *pl.*, dziennik *m*; '**~·cast·er** (*w radio, TV*) spiker(ka *f*) *m* (*prezentujący wiadomości w radio i w TV*); '**~ deal·er** → *Am.* ***newsagent***; '**~·flash** *TV*, (*w radio*) wiadomości *pl.* z ostatniej chwili; '**~·let·ter** biuletyn *m*; **~·mon·ger** ['nju:zmʌŋgə]; **~·pa·per** ['nju:speɪpə] gazeta *f*, dziennik *m*; *attr.* gazetowy; '**~·print** papier *m* gazetowy; '**~·read·er** *zwł. Brt.* → ***newscaster***; '**~·reel** kronika *f* filmowa; '**~·room** redakcja *f* dziennika; '**~·stand** kiosk *m*, stoisko *n* z gazetami; '**~·ven·dor** *zwł. Brt.* sprzedawca (-czyni *f*) gazet
new 'year nowy rok; ***New Year's Day*** Nowy Rok *m*; ***New Year's Eve*** Sylwester *m*
New York Nowy Jork *m*
New Zea·land Nowa Zelandia *f*
next [nekst] **1.** *adj.* następny; sąsiedni; (***the***) ***~ day*** następnego dnia; ***~ door*** sąsiedni; ***~ but one*** przedostatni; ***~ to*** obok (*G*); ***~ to nothing*** tyle co nic; **2.** *adv.* następnie; później; **3.** następny *m*; **~ -'door** obok (*G*); **~ of 'kin** najbliższy krewny
NHS [en eɪtʃ 'es] *Brt. skrót*: ***National Health Service*** Państwowa Służba *f* Zdrowia
nib·ble ['nɪbl] skubać ⟨-bnąć⟩ (***at*** *A*), ⟨wy⟩skubać
nice [naɪs] (**-*r*, -*st***) miły; przyjacielski; przyjemny; subtelny; '**~·ly** miło; przyjemnie; **ni·ce·ty** ['naɪsətɪ] subtelność *f*
niche [nɪtʃ] nisza *f*
nick [nɪk] **1.** zadraśnięcie *n*, zadrapanie *n*; ***in the ~ of time*** w ostatnim momencie; **2.** zadrasnąć (się); *Brt.* F (*ukraść*) gwizdnąć; *Brt.* F przymykać ⟨-mknąć⟩
nick·el ['nɪkl] **1.** *chem.* nikiel *m*; *Am.* moneta *m* pięciocentowa; **2.** (*zwł. Brt.* **-*ll*-** , *Am.* **-*l*-**) ⟨po⟩niklować; **~-'plate** ⟨po⟩niklować
nick-nack ['nɪknæk] → ***knick-knack***
nick·name ['nɪkneɪm] **1.** przezwisko *n*, przydomek *m*; **2.** przezywać ⟨-zwać⟩, nadawać ⟨-dać⟩ przydomek
niece [ni:s] siostrzenica *f*, bratanica *f*
nig·gard ['nɪgəd] skąpiec *m*; '**~·ly** skąpy, mało szczodry
night [naɪt] noc *f*; *późny* wieczór *m*; *attr.* nocny; ***at ~ , by ~ , in the ~*** nocą, w nocy; '**~·cap** kieliszek *m* przed zaśnięciem; '**~·club** klub *m* nocny; '**~·dress** koszula *f* nocna; '**~·fall**: ***at***

~fall o zmroku; **~·ie** F ['naɪtɪ] koszula *f* nocna

nigh·tin·gale ['naɪtɪŋgeɪl] *zo.* słowik *m*

'night|·ly nocny, wieczorny; co noc, co wieczór; **~·mare** ['naɪtmeə] koszmar *m* (*też fig.*); **'~ school** szkoła *f* wieczorowa; **'~ shift** zmiana *f* nocna; **'~·shirt** (*męska*) koszula *f* nocna; **'~·time**: ***in the ~time, at ~time*** nocą; **~ 'watch·man** (*pl.* **-men**) stróż *m* nocny; **' ~y** F → ***nightdress***

nil [nɪl] nic *n*, zero *n*; ***our team won two to ~*** *lub* ***by two goals to ~*** (**2-0**) nasz zespół wygrał dwa do zera (2-0)

nim·ble ['nɪmbl] (**-r, -st**) gibki; lotny

nine [naɪn] **1.** dziewięć; **~ *to five*** zwykłe godziny pracy (*od 9 do 17*); ***a ~-to-five job*** etat *m* o unormowanym czasie pracy; **2.** dziewiątka *f*; **'~·pins** kręgle *pl.*; **~·teen** [naɪn'tiːn] **1.** dziewiętnaście; **2.** dziewiętnastka *f*; **~·teenth** [naɪn'tiːnθ] dziewiętnasty; **~·ti·eth** ['naɪntɪɪθ] dziewięćdziesiąty; **~·ty** ['naɪntɪ] **1.** dziewięćdziesiąt; **2.** dziewięćdziesiątka *f*

nin·ny ['nɪnɪ] F głupiec *m*

ninth [naɪnθ] **1.** dziewiąty; **2.** jedna dziewiąta; **'~·ly** po dziewiąte

nip[1] [nɪp] **1.** (**-pp-**) szczypać ⟨-pnąć⟩; *rośliny* ścinać (*mróz*); F wyskakiwać ⟨-koczyć⟩; **~ *in the bud*** *fig.* ⟨z⟩niszczyć w zarodku; **2.** uszczypnięcie *n*; ***there's a ~ in the air today*** zimno już dzisiaj

nip[2] [nɪp] łyk *m* (*whisky itp.*)

nip·per ['nɪpə]: (***a pair of***) **~s** *pl.* szczypce *pl.*

nip·ple ['nɪpl] *anat.* sutek *m*; *Am.* smoczek *m* (*na butelkę*)

ni·tre *Brt.*, **ni·ter** *Am.* ['naɪtə] *chem.* saletra *f*

ni·tro·gen ['naɪtrədʒən] *chem.* azot *m*

no [nəʊ] **1.** *adv.* nie; **2.** *adj.* żaden; **~ *one*** nikt, żaden; ***in ~ time*** błyskawicznie

No., **no.** *skrót pisany*: ***number*** (*łacińskie* ***numero***) nr, numer

no·bil·i·ty [nəʊ'bɪlətɪ] szlachta *f*; szlachetność *f*

no·ble ['nəʊbl] (**-r, -st**) szlachetny; szlachecki; *budynek*: wyniosły; **'~·man** (*pl.* **-men**) szlachcic *m*; **'~·wom·an** (*pl.* **-women**) szlachcianka *f*

no·bod·y ['nəʊbədɪ] **1.** nikt; **2.** *fig.* nikt *m*

no-'cal·o·rie di·et dieta *f* niskokaloryczna

noc·tur·nal [nɒk'tɜːnl] nocny

nod [nɒd] **1.** (**-dd-**) kiwać ⟨-wnąć⟩; kłaniać ⟨ukłonić⟩ się; **~ *off*** odkłaniać ⟨-łonić⟩ się; ***have a ~ding acquaintance*** znać kogoś z widzenia; **2.** skinięcie *n* głową; ukłon *m*

node [nəʊd] węzeł *m* (*też med.*)

noise [nɔɪz] **1.** hałas *m*; dźwięk *m*; **2.** **~ *about*** (***abroad, around***) nagłaśniać ⟨-łośnić⟩; **'~·less** bezdźwięczny

nois·y ['nɔɪzɪ] (**-ier, -iest**) głośny

no·mad ['nəʊmæd] nomada *m*

nom·i|·nal ['nɒmɪnl] nominalny; ***~nal value*** *econ.* wartość *f* nominalna; **~·nate** ['nɒmɪneɪt] nominować, wyznaczać ⟨-czyć⟩; **~·na·tion** [nɒmɪ'neɪʃn] nominacja *f*

nom·i·na·tive ['nɒmɪnətɪv] *gr.* *też* **~ *case*** mianownik *m*

nom·i·nee [nɒmɪ'niː] kandydat(ka *f*) *m*

non... [nɒn] nie...

non·al·co'hol·ic bezalkoholowy

non·a'ligned *pol.* neutralny

non·com·mis·sioned 'of·fi·cer *mil.* podoficer *m*

non·com·mit·tal [nɒnkə'mɪtl] wymijający

non·con'duc·tor *electr.* nieprzewodnik *m*

non·de·script ['nɒndɪskrɪpt] nijaki, bez wyrazu

none [nʌn] **1.** *pron.* żaden (*zw. jako pl.*); nikt; nic; **~ *but*** tylko; **2.** *adv.* **~ *the...*** wcale nie...; ***I'm ~ the wiser*** nie jestem ani trochę mądrzejszy

non·en·ti·ty [nɒ'nentətɪ] osoba *f* bez znaczenia, miernota *f*

none·the'less mimo to

non·ex'ist|·ence brak *m* istnienia, nieistnienie *n*; **~·ent** nieistniejący

non'fic·tion książki *pl.* popularnonaukowe

non'flam·ma·ble, **non·in'flam·ma·ble** niepalny, ogniotrwały

non·in·ter'fer·ence, non·in·ter'ven·tion *pol.* nieinterweniowanie *n*

non-'i·ron non-iron, nie wymagający prasowania

no-'non·sense rzeczowy, realistyczny

non·par·ti·san [nɒnpɑːtɪ'zæn] *pol.* niezależny

non'pay·ment niezapłacenie *n*

non'plus (**-ss-**) ⟨s⟩konsternować

non·pol'lut·ing nie zanieczyszczający

non'prof·it *Am.*, **non-'prof·it-making** *Brt.* nie obliczony na zysk
non'res·i·dent **1.** zamiejscowy; *pacjent*: ambulatoryjny; **2.** osoba *f* zamiejscowa
non·re'turn·a·ble bezzwrotny; ~ **bot·tle** butelka *f* bez kaucji
non·sense ['nɒnsəns] nonsens *m*, bzdura *f*
non-'skid przeciwślizgowy
non'smok|·er osoba *f* niepaląca, niepalący *m* (-ca *f*); *Brt. rail.* wagon *m* dla niepalących; ~**·ing** dla niepalących
non'stick *jakby*: teflonowy
non'stop bez zatrzymania; nie zatrzymujący się; bezpośredni; ~ ***flight*** przelot *m* bezpośredni
non'u·ni·on niezrzeszony, nie należący do związków zawodowych
non'vi·o|·lence postawa *f* powstrzymania się od przemocy; ~**·lent** powstrzymujący się od przemocy
noo·dles ['nuːdl] *pl.* makaron *m*
nook [nʊk] zakątek *m*, zakamarek *m*
noon [nuːn] południe *n*; ***at*** ~ w południe
noose [nuːs] pętla *f*
nope F [nəʊp] nie
nor [nɔː] → ***neither***; też nie
norm [nɔːm] norma *f*; **nor·mal** ['nɔːml] normalny; **nor·mal·ize** ['nɔːməlaɪz] ⟨z⟩normalizować (się)
north [nɔːθ] **1.** północ *f*; **2.** *adj.* północny; **3.** *adv.* na północ; ~**'east** **1.** północny wschód; **2.** *adj.* północno-wschodni; **3.** *adv.* na północny wschód; ~**'east·ern** północno-wschodni
nor·ther·ly ['nɔːðəlɪ], **nor·thern** ['nɔːðn] północny
North 'Pole biegun *m* północny
north|·ward(s) ['nɔːθwəd(z)] *adv.* północny, na północ; ~**'west** **1.** północny zachód; **2.** *adj.* północno-zachodni; **3.** *adv.* na północny zachód; ~**'west·ern** północno-zachodni
Nor·way ['nɔːweɪ] Norwegia *f*
Nor·we·gian [nɔː'wiːdʒən] **1.** norweski; **2.** Norweg *m* (-weżka *f*); *ling.* język *m* norweski
nos. *skrót pisany*: ***numbers*** liczby *pl.*, numery *pl.*
nose [nəʊz] **1.** *anat.* nos *m*; *aviat.* nos *m*, dziób *m*; **2.** jechać ostrożnie (*samochodem*); *też* ~ ***about***, ~ ***around*** *fig.* F węszyć, myszkować; '~**·bleed** krwotok *m* z nosa; '~**·cone** stożek *m* ochronny rakiety; '~**·dive** *aviat.* nurkowanie *n*
nose·gay ['nəʊzgeɪ] bukiecik *m* (*przy ubraniu*)
nos·ey ['nəʊzɪ] → ***nosy***
nos·tal·gia [nɒ'stældʒɪə] nostalgia *f*
nos·tril ['nɒstrəl] dziurka *f* od nosa, nozdrze *n*
nos·y ['nəʊzɪ] F (***-ier, -iest***) wścibski; ~ **'park·er** *Brt.* F wścibska osoba *f*
not [nɒt] nie; ~ ***a*** żaden
no·ta·ble ['nəʊtəbl] godny uwagi
no·ta·ry ['nəʊtərɪ]: *zw.* ~ ***public*** notariusz *m*
notch [nɒtʃ] **1.** nacięcie *n*, karb *m*; *Am. geol.* przełęcz *f*; **2.** nacinać ⟨-ciąć⟩, wycinać ⟨-ciąć⟩
note [nəʊt] (*zw.* ~***s*** *pl.*) notatka *f*, uwaga *f*; przypis *m*; nota *f* dyplomatyczna; list *m*; banknot *m*, weksel *m*; *mus.* nuta *f*; *fig.* ton *m*; ***take*** ~***s*** (***of***) zanotowywać ⟨-ować⟩ (*A*); '~**·book** notes *m*; *komp.* notebook *m*, komputer *m* przenośny
not·ed ['nəʊtɪd] znany, notowany (***for*** z *G*)
'note|·pa·per papier *m* listowy; '~**·wor·thy** znaczący
noth·ing ['nʌθɪŋ] nic; ~ ***but*** nic prócz; ~ ***much*** F nic wielkiego; ***for*** ~ za nic; na nic; ***to say*** ~ ***of*** nie mówiąc już o (*L*); ***there is*** ~ ***like*** nie ma to jak
no·tice ['nəʊtɪs] **1.** zawiadomienie *n*; obwieszczenie *n*; ogłoszenie *n*, informacja *f*; wymówienie *n*, wypowiedzenie *n*; uwaga *f*, recenzja *f*; ***give*** *lub* ***hand in one's*** ~ składać ⟨złożyć⟩ wymówienie; ***give s.o.*** ~ dawać ⟨dać⟩ komuś wypowiedzenie; ***give s.o.*** (***his, etc.***) ~ wypowiedzieć komuś (*np. pokój*); ***at six months'*** ~ za sześciomiesięcznym wypowiedzeniem; ***take*** (***no***) ~ ***of*** zwracać uwagę (nie zwracać uwagi) na (*A*); ***at short*** ~ na krótki termin; ***until further*** ~ do odwołania; ***without*** ~ bezzwłocznie; **2.** zauważać ⟨-żyć⟩, spostrzegać ⟨-rzec⟩; zwracać uwagę na (*A*); ⚠ *nie* ***notować***; '~**·a·ble** zauważalny; godny uwagi; '~ **board** tablica *f* ogłoszeń
no·ti·fy ['nəʊtɪfaɪ] zawiadamiać ⟨-domić⟩, podawać ⟨-dać⟩ do wiadomości; ogłaszać ⟨-łosić⟩
no·tion ['nəʊʃn] pojęcie *n*; idea *f*
no·tions ['nəʊʃnz] *pl. zwł. Am.* pasmanteria *f*

no·to·ri·ous [nəʊ'tɔːrɪəs] notoryczny, o złej sławie (***for*** z powodu *G*)
not·with·stand·ing [nɒtwɪθ'stændɪŋ] jednak; pomimo
nought [nɔːt] *Brt.*: ***0.4*** (***~ point four***) 0,4 (zero przecinek cztery)
noun [naʊn] rzeczownik *m*
nour·ish ['nʌrɪʃ] żywić; karmić; odżywiać ⟨-wić⟩; **'~·ing** pożywny; **'~·ment** pokarm *m*
Nov *skrót pisany*: ***November*** listopad *m*
nov·el ['nɒvl] **1.** powieść *f*; ⚠ *nie* ***nowela*** ; **2.** nowatorski; **~·ist** ['nɒvəlɪst] powieściopisarz *m* (-arka *f*); **no·vel·la** [nəʊ'velə] (*pl.* ***-las, -le*** [-liː]) nowela *f*; **~·ty** ['nɒvltɪ] nowatorstwo *n*; nowość *f*
No·vem·ber [nəʊ'vembə] (*skrót*: ***Nov***) listopad *m*
nov·ice ['nɒvɪs] nowicjusz(ka *f*) *m* (*też rel.*)
now [naʊ] **1.** *adv.* teraz, obecnie; ***~ and again***, (***every***) ***~ and then*** od czasu do czasu; ***by ~*** teraz; ***from ~*** (***on***) od dzisiaj; ***just ~*** właśnie w tej chwili; przed chwilą; **2.** *cj. też* ***~ that*** teraz, gdy
now·a·days ['naʊədeɪz] obecnie
no·where ['nəʊweə] nigdzie
nox·ious ['nɒkʃəs] szkodliwy
noz·zle ['nɒzl] *tech.* wylot *m*; dysza *f*
NSPCC *Brt.* [en es piː siː 'siː] *skrót*: ***National Society for the Prevention of Cruelty to Children*** (*stowarzyszenie ochrony dzieci przed okrucieństwem*)
nu·ance ['njuːɑːns] niuans *m*
nub [nʌb] sedno *n*
nu·cle·ar ['njuːklɪə] nuklearny, jądrowy; atomowy; **~ 'en·er·gy** energia *f* nuklearna; **~ 'fam·i·ly** (*rodzina złożona tylko z rodziców i dzieci*); **~ 'fis·sion** rozszczepienie *n* jądra; **~-'free** pozbawiony broni nuklearnej; **~ 'fu·sion** synteza *f* jądrowa; **~ 'phys·ics** fizyka *f* nuklearna; **~ 'pow·er** potęga *f* atomowa; **~-'pow·ered** o napędzie atomowym; **~ 'pow·er plant** elektrownia *f* jądrowa; **~ re'ac·tor** reaktor *m* atomowy; **~ 'war** wojna *f* nuklearna; **~ 'war·head** głowica *f* jądrowa; **~ 'waste** odpady *pl.* radioaktywne; **~ 'weap·ons** *pl.* broń *f* jądrowa
nu·cle·us ['njuːklɪəs] (*pl.* ***-clei*** [-klɪaɪ]) jądro *n* (*też fig.*)
nude [njuːd] **1.** nagi; **2.** akt *m* (*sztuki*)
nudge [nʌdʒ] **1.** *kogoś* trącać ⟨-cić⟩, *kogoś* szturchnąć ⟨-chać⟩; 2. szturchnięcie *n*
nug·get ['nʌgɪt] bryłka *f* (*zwł. złota*)
nui·sance ['njuːsns] przykrość *f*; rzecz *f lub* osoba *f* dokuczliwa; ***what a ~!*** co za utrapienie!; ***be a ~ to s.o.*** naprzykrzać się komuś; ***make a ~ of o.s.*** działać komuś na nerwy
nukes [njuːks] F broń *f* jądrowa
null [nʌl] *zwł. jur.*: ***~ and void*** nieważny, bez mocy prawnej
numb [nʌm] **1.** odrętwiały, zdrętwiały; skostniały (***with*** z *I*); *fig.* odrętwiały (***with*** pod wpływem *G*); **2.** ⟨s⟩powodować zdrętwienie
num·ber ['nʌmbə] **1.** liczba *f*; ilość *f*; cyfra *f*; numer *m*; *ling.* liczba *f*; ***a ~ of*** kilka; ***sorry, wrong ~*** *tel.* pomyłka; **2.** ⟨po⟩numerować; wynosić ⟨-nieść⟩, liczyć; wyliczać ⟨-czyć⟩; policzyć; **'~·less** niezliczony; **'~·plate** *zwł. Brt. mot.* tablica *f* rejestracyjna
nu·me·ral ['njuːmərəl] cyfra *f*; *ling.* liczebnik *m*
nu·me·rous ['njuːmərəs] liczny
nun [nʌn] zakonnica *f*; **~·ne·ry** ['nʌnərɪ] klasztor *m* żeński
nurse [nɜːs] **1.** siostra *f*; pielęgniarka *f*, → ***male nurse***; *też* ***wet ~*** mamka *f*; opiekunka *f* do dzieci; **2.** pielęgnować; piastować, niańczyć; karmić piersią; pracować jako pielęgniarka; ***~ s.o. back to health*** otaczać ⟨otoczyć⟩ kogoś opieką do powrotu do zdrowia
nur·se·ry ['nɜːsərɪ] żłobek *m*; *przest.* pokój *m* dziecięcy; *agr.* szkółka *f*; **'~ rhyme** piosenka *f* dziecięca, wierszyk *m* dziecięcy; **'~ school** przedszkole *n*; **'~ slope** ośla łączka *f* (*dla narciarzy*)
nurs·ing ['nɜːsɪŋ] pielęgniarstwo *n*; opiekowanie *n* się; **'~ bot·tle** butelka *f* dla niemowląt; **'~ home** dom *m* opieki (*dla starszych*); *Brt.* prywatna klinika *f*
nut [nʌt] *bot.* orzech *m*; *tech.* nakrętka *f*; F dureń *m*; F łeb *m*; ***be off one's ~*** F dostać świra; **'~·crack·er**(**s** *pl.*) dziadek *m* do orzechów; **~·meg** ['nʌtmeg] *bot.* gałka *f* muszkatołowa
nu·tri·ent ['njuːtrɪənt] **1.** substancja *f* odżywcza; **2.** odżywczy
nu·tri|·tion [njuː'trɪʃn] odżywianie *n* się; **~·tious** [njuː'trɪʃəs] odżywczy; **~·tive** ['njuːtrɪtɪv] odżywczy

'nut|•shell skorupka *f* orzecha; (***to put it***) ***in a ~shell*** F w skrócie, jednym słowem; **~•ty** ['nʌtɪ] (***-ier, -iest***) orzechowy; *sl.* kopnięty
NW *skrót pisany*: ***northwest*** płn.-zach., północny-zachód; ***northwest***(***ern***) płn.-zach., północno-zachodni
NY *skrót pisany*: ***New York*** Nowy Jork
NYC *skrót pisany*: ***New York City*** (*miasto*) Nowy Jork
ny•lon ['naɪlɒn] nylon *m*; *attr.* nylonowy; ***~s*** *pl.* pończochy *pl.* nylonowe
nymph [nɪmf] nimfa *f*

O

O, o [əʊ] O, o *n*
o [əʊ] (*cyfra, też przy czytaniu numerów*) zero *n*
oaf [əʊf] gamoń *m*; fajtłapa *m*
oak [əʊk] dąb *m*
oar [ɔː] wiosło *n*; **~s•man** ['ɔːzmən] (*pl.* ***-men***) (*w sporcie*) wioślarz *m*; **'~s•wom•an** (*pl.* ***-women***) (*w sporcie*) wioślarka *f*
OAS [əʊ eɪ 'es] *skrót*: ***Organization of American States*** Organizacja *f* Państw Ameryki
o•a•sis [əʊ'eɪsɪs] (*pl.* ***-ses*** [-siːz]) oaza *f* (*też fig.*)
oath [əʊθ] (*pl.* ***oaths*** [əʊðz]) przysięga *f*; przekleństwo *n*; ***be on*** *lub* ***under ~*** być pod przysięgą; ***take the ~*** składać ⟨złożyć⟩ przysięgę
oat•meal ['əʊtmiːl] płatki *pl.* owsiane
oats [əʊts] *pl. bot.* owies *m*; ***sow one's wild ~*** wyszumieć się za młodu
o•be•di|•ence [ə'biːdjəns] posłuszeństwo *n*; **~•ent** posłuszny
o•bese [əʊ'biːs] otyły; **o•bes•i•ty** [əʊ'biːsətɪ] otyłość *f*
o•bey [ə'beɪ] być posłusznym (*D*), słuchać (*G*); *rozkazowi* podporządkowywać ⟨-wać⟩ się
o•bit•u•a•ry [ə'bɪtjʊərɪ] *też* ***~ notice*** nekrolog *m*; wspomnienie *n* pośmiertne
ob•ject 1. ['ɒbdʒɪkt] obiekt *m*, przedmiot *m*; cel *m*; *gr.* dopełnienie *n*; **2.** [əb'dʒekt] sprzeciwiać ⟨-wić⟩ się; mieć obiekcje; ⟨za⟩protestować
ob•jec|•tion [əb'dʒekʃn] sprzeciw *m* (***to*** wobec *G*); sprzeciw *m* (*też jur.*); **~•tio•na•ble** niewłaściwy, naganny
ob•jec•tive [əb'dʒektɪv] **1.** obiektywny; **2.** cel *m*; (*w mikroskopie*) obiektyw *m*
ob•li•ga•tion [ɒblɪ'geɪʃn] zobowiązanie *n*; ***be under an ~ to s.o.*** (***to do s.th.***) być zobowiązanym wobec kogoś (coś zrobić); **ob•lig•a•to•ry** [ə'blɪgətərɪ] obowiązkowy, obligatoryjny
o•blige [ə'blaɪdʒ] zobowiązywać ⟨-zać⟩ (się); ***~ s.o.*** wyświadczać ⟨-czyć⟩ komuś przysługę (*D*); ***much ~d*** wielce zobowiązany; **o'blig•ing** uczynny
o•blique [ə'bliːk] skośny, ukośny; *fig.* pośredni
o•blit•er•ate [ə'blɪtəreɪt] unicestwiać ⟨-wić⟩; przesłaniać ⟨-łonić⟩, zasłaniać ⟨-łonić⟩
o•bliv•i|•on [ə'blɪvɪən] zapomnienie *n*; stan *m* nieświadomości; **~•ous** [ə'blɪvɪəs]: ***be ~ous of*** *lub* ***to s.th.*** być nieświadomym czegoś
ob•long ['ɒblɒŋ] prostokątny
ob•nox•ious [əb'nɒkʃəs] obmierzły, okropny
ob•scene [əb'siːn] obsceniczny, nieprzyzwoity (*też fig.*)
ob•scure [əb'skjʊə] **1.** ciemny; niewyraźny, słabo widoczny; *fig.* ciemny, niejasny; ponury; nieznany; ⚠ *nie* ***obskurny***; **2.** zaciemniać ⟨-nić⟩; zasłaniać ⟨-łonić⟩; **ob•scu•ri•ty** [əb'skjʊərətɪ] niejasność *f*, zapomnienie *n*
ob•se•quies ['ɒbsɪkwɪz] *pl.* uroczystości *pl.* żałobne
ob•ser|•va•ble [əb'zɜːvəbl] zauważalny, dostrzegalny; **~•vance** [əb'zɜːvns] przestrzeganie *n*; **~•vant** [əb'zɜːvnt] spostrzegawczy; **~•va•tion** [ɒbzə'veɪʃn] obserwacja *f*; uwaga *f* (***on*** w sprawie *G*); **~•va•to•ry** [əb'zɜːvətrɪ] obserwatorium *n*
ob•serve [əb'zɜːv] ⟨za⟩obserwować; zauważyć, spostrzec; przestrzegać, stosować się do (*G*); **ob'serv•er** obserwator(ka *f*) *m*

ob·sess [əb'ses]: ***be ~ed by*** *lub* ***with*** mieć obsesję na punkcie czegoś; **ob·ses·sion** [əb'seʃn] obsesja *f*; idée fixe *f*; **ob·ses·sive** [əb'sesɪv] obsesyjny

ob·so·lete ['ɒbsəliːt] przestarzały

ob·sta·cle ['ɒbstəkl] przeszkoda *f*

ob·sti·nate ['ɒbstɪnət] uparty

ob·struct [əb'strʌkt] przeszkadzać ⟨-kodzić⟩; utrudniać ⟨-nić⟩; ⟨za⟩blokować, ⟨za⟩tarasować; **ob·struc·tion** [əb'strʌkʃn] przeszkoda *f*; zablokowanie *n*, zatarasowanie *n*; ⚠ *nie* ***obstrukcja*** (*w znaczeniu: zatwardzenie*); **ob·struc·tive** [əb'strʌktɪv] przeszkadzający, stwarzający trudności

ob·tain [əb'teɪn] uzyskiwać ⟨-kać⟩, otrzymywać ⟨-mać⟩; stosować się, obowiązywać; **~·a·ble** osiągalny

ob·tru·sive [əb'truːsɪv] natrętny, nieznośny

ob·tuse [əb'tjuːs] *kąt*: rozwarty

ob·vi·ous ['ɒbvɪəs] oczywisty, niewątpliwy

oc·ca·sion [ə'keɪʒn] okazja *f*, sposobność *f*; sytuacja *f*; powód *m*; ***on the ~ of*** przy okazji (*G*); **~·al** [ə'keɪʒənl] okazjonalny, okolicznościowy, przypadkowy

Oc·ci|·dent ['ɒksɪdənt] Zachód *m*; **♀·den·tal** [ɒksɪ'dentl] okcydentalny, zachodni

oc·cu|·pant ['ɒkjʊpənt] lokator(ka *f*) *m*, mieszkaniec *m* (-nka *f*); pasażer(ka *f*) *m*; **~·pa·tion** [ɒkjʊ'peɪʃn] zawód *m*; zajęcie *n*; *mil.*, *pol.* okupacja *f*, zajęcie *n*; **~·py** ['ɒkjʊpaɪ] zajmować ⟨-jąć⟩; *mil.*, *pol.* okupować; ***be occupied*** być zajętym, być zamieszkanym

oc·cur [ə'kɜː] (***-rr-***) zdarzać ⟨-rzyć⟩ się, wydarzać ⟨-rzyć⟩ się; występować; ***it ~red to me that*** przyszło mi do głowy, że; **~·rence** [ə'kʌrəns] występowanie *n*, pojawienie *n* się; wydarzenie *n*

o·cean ['əʊʃn] ocean *m*

o'clock [ə'klɒk] godzina (*przy podawaniu czasu*); (***at***) ***five ~*** o piątej (*godzinie*)

Oct *skrót pisany*: **October** październik *m*

Oc·to·ber [ɒk'təʊbə] (*skrót*: **Oct**) październik *m*

oc·u|·lar ['ɒkjʊlə] oczny; **~·list** ['ɒkjʊlɪst] okulista *m* (-tka *f*)

OD [əʊ 'diː] F *v/i.*: ***~ on heroin*** przedawkować heroinę

odd [ɒd] dziwny, osobliwy; nieparzysty; *rękawiczka itp.*: nie do pary, pojedynczy; dodatkowy; doraźny; ***30 ~*** ponad 30, trzydzieści kilka; ***~ jobs*** *pl.* doraźne zajęcia *pl.*

odds [ɒdz] *pl.* szanse *pl.*; ***the ~ are 10 to 1*** szanse są jak jeden do dziesięciu; ***the ~ are that*** bardzo prawdopodobne, że; ***against all ~*** wbrew oczekiwaniom; ***be at ~*** kłócić się (***with*** z *I*); ***~ and ends*** różności *pl.*, różne różności *pl.*; **~-'on** najprawdopodobniejszy

ode [əʊd] oda *f*

Oder Odra *f*

o·do(u)r ['əʊdə] nieprzyjemny zapach *m*

of [ɒv, əv] *prp. odpowiada dopełniaczowi* ***the leg ~ the table*** noga stołu; ***the works ~ Swift*** dzieła Swifta; z (*G*); ***~ wood*** z drewna; ***proud ~*** dumny z; ***your letter ~...*** pański list z...; na (*A*); ***die ~*** umrzeć na; o (*L*); ***speak ~*** mówić o; ***think ~*** myśleć o; ze strony (*G*); ***how kind ~ you*** jak miło z twojej strony; ***five minutes ~ twelve*** *Am.* za pięć dwunasta

off [ɒf] **1.** *adv.* z, od, w; z dala; od strony; spoza; w odległości; ***3 miles ~*** trzy mile od; ***I must be ~*** muszę już iść; ***~ with you!*** zabieraj się!; ***be ~*** być odwołanym; ***10% ~*** *econ.* 10% rabatu; ***~ and on*** czasami, od czasu do czasu; ***take a day ~*** wziąć dzień wolnego; ***s.o. is well*** (***badly***) ***~*** komuś się dobrze (źle) powodzi; **2.** *prp.* od (*G*); z (*G*); *naut.* tuż przy (*L*) (*brzegu*); ***be ~ duty*** nie być na służbie, nie mieć dyżuru; ***be ~ smoking*** przestać palić; **3.** *adj. światło*: wyłączony, zgaszony; *pokrętło*: zakręcony; *jedzenie*: nieświeży; wolny (*od pracy*); poza sezonem; *dzień*: niedobry

of·fal ['ɒfl] *Brt. gastr.* podroby *pl.*, podróbki *pl.*

of·fence *Brt.*, **of·fense** *Am.* [ə'fens] obraza *f* zniewaga *f*; *jur.* wykroczenie *n*, przestępstwo *n*; ***take ~*** obrażać ⟨-razić⟩ się (***at*** na *A*)

of·fend [ə'fend] obrażać ⟨-razić⟩, znieważać ⟨-żyć⟩; wykraczać ⟨-roczyć⟩ (***against*** przeciw(ko) *D*), naruszać; **~·er** przestępca *m* (-czyni *f*); ***first ~er***

O

jur. przestępca *m* (-czyni *f*) dotychczas nie karany (-a)
of·fen·sive [ə'fensɪv] **1.** obraźliwy; *zapach*: okropny; *działania*: ofensywny, zaczepny; **2.** ofensywa *f*
of·fer ['ɒfə] **1.** *v/t.* ⟨za⟩proponować, ⟨za⟩oferować (*też econ.*); *modlitwę* ⟨za⟩ofiarować; *opór* stawiać; ⟨za⟩proponować (***to do s.th.*** zrobienie czegoś); **2.** oferta *f*, propozycja *f*
off·hand [ɒf'hænd] bezceremonialny; bez przygotowania, improwizowany
of·fice ['ɒfɪs] biuro *n*; urząd *m*; kancelaria *f*; *zw.* ♀ *zwł. Brt.* ministerstwo *n*; stanowisko *n*, urząd *m*; '~ **hours** *pl.* godziny *pl.* urzędowania
of·fi·cer ['ɒfɪsə] oficer *m*; urzędnik *m* (-iczka *f*), funkcjonariusz *m*
of·fi·cial [ə'fɪʃl] **1.** urzędnik *m* (-iczka *f*), funkcjonariusz *m*; **2.** oficjalny, urzędowy, służbowy
of·fi·ci·ate [ə'fɪʃɪeɪt] urzędować
of·fi·cious [ə'fɪʃəs] nadgorliwy, namolny
'**off|-licence** *Brt.* sklep *m* z alkoholem; '**~·line** *komp.* autonomiczny, rozłączny; **~-'peak** *electr.* pozaszczytowy; ***~-peak hours*** *pl.* okres *m* poza godzinami szczytu; '**~ sea·son 1.** *adj.* poza okresem szczytu; **2.** okres *m* poza szczytem; '**~·set** ⟨z⟩rekompensować, kompensować; '**~·shoot** *bot.* pęd *m* boczny, odrośl *m*; **~'shore** przybrzeżny; **~'side** (*w sporcie*) ofsajd, spalony; ***~side position*** spalony; ***~side trap*** pułapka *f* ofsajdowa; '**~·spring** potomek *m*, potomstwo *n*; **~-the-'rec·ord** nieoficjalny
of·ten ['ɒfn] często
oh [əʊ] *int.* och, ach
oil [ɔɪl] **1.** oliwa *f*, olej *m*; ropa *f* naftowa; **2.** ⟨na⟩smarować; ⟨na⟩oleić, ⟨na⟩oliwić; '**~ change** *mot.* zmiana *f* oleju; '**~·cloth** cerata *f*; '**~·field** pole *n* naftowe; '**~ paint·ing** obraz *m* olejny; *olejne* malarstwo *n*; '**~ plat·form** → ***oil rig***; '**~ pol·lu·tion** zanieczyszczenie *n wody* olejami *lub* ropą naftową; '**~-pro·duc·ing coun·try** kraj-producent *m* ropy naftowej; '**~ re·fin·e·ry** rafineria *f* ropy naftowej; '**~ ·rig** platforma *f* wiertnicza; '**~·skin** tkanina *f* nieprzemakalna; ***~skins*** *pl.* ubranie *n* sztormowe; '**~ slick** plama *f* ropy naftowej; '**~ well** szyb *m* naftowy; '**~·y** (**-*ier*, -*iest***) oleisty, tłusty; *fig.* brudny, nieczysty
oint·ment ['ɔɪntmənt] maść *f*
OK, o·kay [əʊ'keɪ] **1.** *adj. i int.* OK, okay; w porządku; dobra; **2.** wyrażać ⟨-razić⟩ zgodę; **3.** zgoda *f*
old [əʊld] **1.** stary; **2.** ***the ~*** *pl.* starzy *pl.*; **~ 'age** wiek *m* podeszły, starość *f*; **~ age 'pen·sion** renta *f*, emerytura *f*; **~ age 'pen·sion·er** rencista *m* (-tka *f*), emeryt(ka *f*) *m*; **~-'fash·ioned** przestarzały; '**~·ish** starawy; **~ 'peo·ple's home** dom *m* starości
ol·ive ['ɒlɪv] *bot.* oliwka *f*; zieleń *f* oliwkowa
O·lym·pic Games [əlɪmpɪk 'geɪmz] *pl.* Igrzyska *pl.* Olimpijskie
om·i·nous ['ɒmɪnəs] złowieszczy
o·mis·sion [əʊ'mɪʃn] pominięcie *n*, opuszczenie *n*; zaniechanie *n*
o·mit [ə'mɪt] (**-*tt-***) pomijać ⟨-minąć⟩, opuszczać ⟨-puścić⟩; ***~ to do s.th.*** nie zrobić czegoś
om·nip·o·tent [ɒm'nɪpətənt] wszechmocny
om·nis·ci·ent [ɒm'nɪsɪənt] wszechwiedzący
on [ɒn] **1.** *prp.* na (*A lub L*); ***~ the table*** na stole; w (*L*); ***~ TV*** w telewizji; *okres czasu*: w (*A*); ***~ Sunday*** w niedzielę; *leżący, znajdujący się*: w (*L*); ***~ the committee*** w komisji; według (*G*); ***~ this model*** według tego modelu; z (*G*); ***live ~ s.th.*** żyć z kogoś; ***~ his arrival*** (zaraz) po jego przybyciu; ***~ duty*** na służbie; ***~ the street*** *Am.* na ulicy; ***~ the train*** *Am.* w pociągu; ***~ hearing it*** po usłyszeniu tego; ***have you any money ~ you?*** masz przy sobie jakieś pieniądze?; **2.** *adj. i adv. światło, urządzenie*: włączony; *pokrętło*: otwarty; ***have a coat ~*** mieć na sobie płaszcz; ***keep one's hat ~*** być w nakryciu głowy; ***and so ~*** i tak dalej; ***from this day ~*** od dzisiaj; ***be ~*** *theat.*, *TV* być granym, być w repertuarze; być transmitowanym (*w radio*); ***what's ~?*** co się dzieje?
once [wʌns] **1.** raz; jednokrotnie; ***~ again, ~ more*** jeszcze raz; ***~ in a while*** od czasu do czasu; ***~ and for all*** raz na zawsze; ***not ~*** ani razu; ***at ~*** od razu, natychmiast; jednocześnie; ***all at ~*** nagle; ***for ~*** choć raz; ***this ~*** ten jeden raz; **2.** skoro tylko

one [wʌn] **1.** *adj.* jeden; pewien; **~ *day*** pewnego dnia; **~ *Smith*** jakiś Smith; **2.** *pron.* jeden *m*; ten *m*; ***which ~?*** który?, która?, które?; **~'s** swój; **~ *should do ~'s duty*** należy wykonywać swoje obowiązki; **~ *another*** siebie, sobie; **3. ~ *by ~*, ~ *after ~*, ~ *after another*** jeden za drugim; ***I for ~*** ja na przykład; ***the little ~s*** *pl.* mali *pl.*; **~'self** się; siebie; sobie; (***all***) ***by ~self*** całkiem sam; ***to ~self*** dla siebie; **~-'sid·ed** jednostronny; **'~·time** były; **~-track 'mind**: ***have a one-track mind*** mieć w głowie tylko jedno; **~-'two** (*w piłce nożnej*) podwójne podanie *n*; **~-'way** jednokierunkowy; w jedną stronę; **~-way 'street** ulica *f* jednokierunkowa; **~-way 'tick·et** bilet *m* w jedną stronę; **~-way 'traf·fic** ruch *m* jednokierunkowy

on·ion ['ʌnjən] *bot.* cebula *f*

'on|·line *komp.* bezpośredni; **'~·look·er** widz *m*, przechodzień *m*

on·ly ['əʊnlɪ] **1.** *adj.* jedyny; **2.** *adv.* tylko, jedynie; **~ *yesterday*** dopiero wczoraj; **3.** *cj.* F tylko, jedynie

'on|·rush napływ *m*, przypływ *m*; napór *m*; **'~·set** *zimy* początek *m*; wybuch *m* (*choroby*); **~·slaught** ['ɒnslɔːt] szturm *m*

on·to ['ɒntʊ, 'ɒntə] na (*L*)

on·ward(s) ['ɒnwəd(z)] naprzód, wprzód; ***from now ~*** od dzisiaj

ooze [uːz] *v/i.* sączyć się; przesączać ⟨-czyć⟩ się; **~ *away*** *fig.* zanikać ⟨-knąć⟩; *v/t.* wydzielać; *fig.* promieniować

o·paque [əʊ'peɪk] (***-r, -st***) nieprzezroczysty; *fig.* niejasny

OPEC ['əʊpek] *skrót*: ***Organization of Petroleum Exporting Countries*** OPEC *f/m*, Organizacja *f* Krajów Eksportujących Ropę Naftową

o·pen ['əʊpən] **1.** otwarty (*też fig.*); dostępny, wolny; *fig.* dostępny, przystępny (***to*** dla *G*); **~ *all day*** otwarty całą dobę; ***in the ~ air*** na dworze; **2.** (*w golfie, tenisie*) zawody *pl.* open; ***in the ~*** na dworze; ***come out into the ~*** *fig.* wychodzić ⟨wyjść⟩ na jaw; **3.** *v/t.* otwierać ⟨-worzyć⟩ (się); rozpoczynać ⟨-cząć⟩ (się); **~ *into*** wychodzić na (*A*); **~ *onto*** wychodzić na (*A*); **~-'air** na wolnym powietrzu; *basen*: otwarty; **~-'end·ed** *dyskusja*: płynny; **~·er** ['əʊpnə] otwieracz *m*; **~-'eyed** zadziwiony; **~-'hand·ed** szczodry, hojny; **~·ing** ['əʊpnɪŋ] otwarcie *n*; *econ.* wakat *m*, wolne miejsce *n* (*pracy*); możliwość *f*; **~-'mind·ed** otwarty, przystępny; bez uprzedzeń

op·e·ra ['ɒpərə] opera *f*; **'~ glass·es** *pl.* lornetka *f* operowa; **'~ house** opera *f*, budynek *m* operowy

op·e·rate ['ɒpəreɪt] *v/i.* działać; *tech. maszyna, urządzenie*: pracować, chodzić; *med.* operować (**on s.o.** kogoś); *v/t.* *tech.* *urządzenie* obsługiwać; posługiwać się (*I*); *firmę* prowadzić

'op·e·rat·ing| room *Am.* sala *f* operacyjna; **'~ sys·tem** system *m* operacyjny; **'~ thea·tre** *Brt.* sala *f* operacyjna

op·e·ra|·tion [ɒpə'reɪʃn] operacja *f*; funkcjonowanie *n*, działanie *n* (*maszyny, firmy*); *tech.* obsługa *f*; ***in ~tion*** w działaniu; działający; **~·tive** ['ɒpərətɪv] skuteczny, operatywny; czynny, działający; *med.* operacyjny, chirurgiczny; **~·tor** ['ɒpəreɪtə] *tech.* operator *m*; *tel.* telefonista *m* (-tka *f*)

o·pin·ion [ə'pɪnjən] opinia *f*, zdanie *n*; mniemanie *n* (***on*** o *L*); ***in my ~*** moim zdaniem

op·po·nent [ə'pəʊnənt] przeciwnik *m* (-iczka *f*)

op·por|·tune ['ɒpətjuːn] dogodny; na czasie, we właściwym czasie; **~·tu·ni·ty** [ɒpə'tjuːnətɪ] sposobność *f*

op·pose [ə'pəʊz] przeciwstawiać ⟨-wić⟩ się (*D*), sprzeciwiać ⟨-wić⟩ się (*D*); **op·posed** przeciwny; ***be ~ to*** sprzeciwiać się (*D*); **op·po·site** ['ɒpəzɪt] **1.** przeciwieństwo *n*; **2.** *adj.* przeciwny; naprzeciwko; przeciwległy; **3.** *adv.* naprzeciwko; **4.** *prp.* naprzeciw; **op·po·si·tion** [ɒpə'zɪʃn] opozycja *f* (*też parl.*); opór *m*; przeciwstawianie *n* się

op·press [ə'pres] uciskać, ciemiężyć; **op·pres·sion** [ə'preʃn] ucisk *m*, ciemiężenie *n*; **op·pres·sive** [ə'presɪv] uciskający; uciążliwy; przygnębiający

op·tic ['ɒptɪk] optyczny; wzrokowy; **'op·ti·cal** optyczny; **op·ti·cian** [ɒp'tɪʃn] optyk *m* (-yczka *f*)

op·ti|·mis·m ['ɒptɪmɪzəm] optymizm *m*; **~·mist** ['ɒptɪmɪst] optymista *m* (-tka *f*); **~'mist·ic** (***-ally***) optymistyczny

op·tion ['ɒpʃn] wybór *m*; *econ.* opcja *f*, prawo *n* zakupu; *mot.* wyposażenie *n*

O

dodatkowe; **~·al** ['ɒpʃnl] nie obowiązkowy, wariantowy; *tech.* opcjonalny

or [ɔː] lub, albo; **~ *else*** bo inaczej

o·ral ['ɔːrəl] ustny; oralny

or·ange ['ɒrɪndʒ] **1.** *bot.* pomarańcza *f*; **2.** pomarańczowy; **~·ade** [ɒrɪndʒ'eɪd] oranżada *f*

o·ra·tion [ɔː'reɪʃn] przemowa *f*, oracja *f*; **or·a·tor** ['ɒrətə] mówca *m* (-czyni *f*), orator *m*

or·bit ['ɔːbɪt] **1.** orbita *f*; ***get*** *lub* ***put into ~*** umieszczać ⟨umieścić⟩ na orbicie; **2.** *v/t. Ziemię itp.* okrążać ⟨-żyć⟩; *v/t.* orbitować, krążyć po orbicie

or·chard ['ɔːtʃəd] sad *m*

or·ches·tra ['ɔːkɪstrə] *mus.* orkiestra *f*; *Am. theat.* parter *m*

or·chid ['ɔːkɪd] *bot.* orchidea *f*, storczyk *m*

or·dain [ɔː'deɪn]: **~ *s.o.*** (***priest***) wyświęcać ⟨-cić⟩ kogoś na księdza

or·deal [ɔː'diːl] udręka *f*, ciężkie przejście *n*

or·der ['ɔːdə] **1.** porządek *m* (*też parl.*); rząd *m* (*też biol.*); rozkaz *m*; *econ.* zamówienie *n*; *rel. itp.* zakon *m*; kolejność *f*; **~ *to pay*** *econ.* polecenie *n* zapłaty; ***in ~ to*** aby; ***out of ~*** nie w porządku; zepsuty; ***make to ~*** ⟨z⟩robić na zamówienie; **2.** *v/t. komuś* rozkazywać ⟨-zać⟩ (***to do s.th.*** coś zrobić); *coś* polecać ⟨-cić⟩; *med. komuś coś* zalecać ⟨-cić⟩; *econ.* zamawiać ⟨-mówić⟩ (*też w restauracji*); *fig.* ⟨u⟩porządkować; *v/i.* (*w restauracji*) zamawiać ⟨-mówić⟩; **'~·ly 1.** uporządkowany; *fig.* spokojny; **2.** *med.* sanitariusz(ka *f*) *m*

or·di·nal ['ɔːdɪnl] *math. też* **~ *number*** *math.* liczba *f* porządkowa

or·di·nary ['ɔːdnrɪ] zwyczajny, zwykły; ⚠ *nie* ***ordynarny***

ore [ɔː] ruda *f*

or·gan ['ɔːgən] *anat.* organ *m*, narząd *m* (*też fig.*); *mus.* organy *pl.*; **'~ grind·er** kataryniarz *m*; **~·ic** [ɔː'gænɪk] (***-ally***) organiczny; **~·is·m** ['ɔːgənɪzəm] organizm *m*; **~·i·za·tion** [ɔːgənaɪ'zeɪʃn] organizacja *f*; **~·ize** ['ɔːgənaɪz] ⟨z⟩organizować; *zwł. Am.* organizować się; **'~·iz·er** organizator(ka *f*) *m*

or·gas·m ['ɔːgæzəm] orgazm *m*, szczytowanie *m*

o·ri|·ent ['ɔːrɪənt] **1.** ♀ Wschód *m*, Orient *m*; **2.** orientować; zapoznawać ⟨-nać⟩; **~·en·tal** [ɔːrɪ'entl] **1.** orientalny, wschodni; **2.** ♀ człowiek *m* Wschodu; **~·en·tate** ['ɔːrɪənteɪt] → ***orient***

or·i·gin ['ɒrɪdʒɪn] pochodzenie *n*; początek *m*

o·rig·i·nal [ə'rɪdʒənl] **1.** oryginalny; początkowy; **2.** oryginał *m*; **~·i·ty** [ərɪdʒə'næləti] oryginalność *f*; **~·ly** [ə'rɪdʒənəlɪ] pierwotnie; oryginalnie

o·rig·i·nate [ə'rɪdʒəneɪt] *v/t.* dawać ⟨dać⟩ początek, zapoczątkowywać ⟨-ować⟩; *v/i.* brać ⟨wziąć⟩ początek, pochodzić

Ork·neys *pl.* Orkady *pl.*

or·na|·ment 1. ['ɔːnəmənt] ornament *m* (*też fig.*), ozdoba *f*; **2.** ['ɔːnəment] ozdabiać ⟨-dobić⟩; **~·men·tal** [ɔːnə'mentl] ozdobny, ornamentalny

or·nate [ɔː'neɪt] *fig. styl itp.* przeładowany, ciężki

or·phan ['ɔːfn] **1.** sierota *m/f*; **2. *be ~ed*** być osieroconym; **~·age** ['ɔːfənɪdʒ] sierociniec *m*

or·tho·dox ['ɔːθədɒks] ortodoksyjny

os·cil·late ['ɒsɪleɪt] *phys.* oscylować; *fig.* wahać się (***between*** między *I*)

os·ten·si·ble [ɒ'stensəbl] pozorny, rzekomy

os·ten·ta|·tion [ɒstən'teɪʃn] ostentacja *f*, demonstracja *f*; **~·tious** [ɒstən'teɪʃəs] ostentacyjny, demonstracyjny

os·tra·cize ['ɒstrəsaɪz] ostracyzować

os·trich ['ɒstrɪtʃ] *zo.* struś *m*

oth·er ['ʌðə] inny; ***the ~ day*** niedawno; ***every ~ day*** co drugi dzień; **'~·wise** inaczej; poza tym; w przeciwnym razie

ot·ter ['ɒtə] *zo.* wydra *f*

ought [ɔːt] *v/aux. ja*: powinienem, *ty*: powinieneś *itp.* (***to do*** zrobić); ***she ~ to have done it*** powinna była to zrobić

ounce [aʊns] uncja *f* (*28,35 g*)

our ['aʊə] nasz; **~s** ['aʊəz] nasz; **~·selves** [aʊə'selvz] się, sobie, siebie; my sami; ***by ~*** przez siebie, bez pomocy

oust [aʊst] wysiedlać ⟨-lić⟩, usuwać ⟨-sunąć⟩

out [aʊt] **1.** *adv. adj.* na zewnątrz, poza; na powietrzu, na powietrze; (*w sporcie*) na aut, na aucie; F niemodny; wygasły; rozkwitły; ***way ~*** wyjście *n*; **~ *of*** z (*G*); poza (*zasięgiem*); bez (*oddechu*); (*zrobiony*) z (*G*); ***be ~ of ...*** już ... nie mieć;

in nine ~ of ten cases na dziewięć przypadków z dziesięciu; **2.** *prp.* F przez (*A*); **3.** F wydawać 〈-dać〉

out|'bal·ance przeważać 〈-żyć〉; **~'bid** (**-*dd-***; ***-bid***) przelicytowywać 〈-ować〉; **~·board 'mo·tor** silnik *m* burtowy; **'~·break** wybuch *m* (*choroby itp.*); **'~·build·ing** dobudówka *f*; **'~·burst** wybuch *m* (*uczuć*); **'~·cast 1.** odrzucać 〈-cić〉; **2.** wyrzutek *m*; **'~·come** wynik *m*, rezultat *m*; **'~·cry** protest *m*, dezaprobata *f*; **~'dat·ed** przestarzały; **~'distance** prześcigać 〈-gnąć〉, zdystansować; **~'do** (***-did, -done***) przewyższać 〈-szyć〉, wyprzedzać 〈-dzić〉; **'~·door** *adj.* na dworze, na świeżym powietrzu; **~'doors** *adv.* na dwór

out·er ['aʊtə] zewnętrzny; **'~·most** najdalszy; **~ 'space** kosmos *m*, przestrzeń *f* kosmiczna

'out|·fit ubiór *m*, strój *m*; ekwipunek *m*; F zespół *m*, grupa *f*; **'~·fit·ter** dostawca *m*; ***sports ~fitters*** *pl.* artykuły *pl.* sportowe; **~'go·ing** wychodzący; **'~·goings** *pl. zwł. Brt.* wydatki *pl.*; **~'grow** (***-grew, -grown***) wyrastać 〈-rosnąć〉 z (*G*) *ubrania*); przerastać 〈-rosnąć〉; **'~·house** przybudówka *f*

out·ing ['aʊtɪŋ] wycieczka *f*

out|'land·ish dziwaczny; **~'last** przetrwać; przeżyć; **'~·law** *hist.* banita *m*; **'~·lay** *pl.* wydatki *pl.*; **'~·let** ujście *n*, wylot *m*; sklep *m*; *fig.* wentyl *m*; **'~·line 1.** zarys *m*; kontur *m*; szkic *m*; **2.** zarysowywać 〈-ować〉, 〈za-, na〉szkicować; **~'live** przeżywać 〈-żyć〉; **'~·look** widok *m*, perspektywa *f*; punkt *m* widzenia; **'~·ly·ing** oddalony, odległy; **~'num·ber** *kogoś liczebnie* przewyższać 〈-szyć〉; **~-of-'date** przestarzały; **~-of-the-'way** niedostępny; odległy; **'~·pa·tient** *ambulatoryjny* (*-a*) pacjent(ka *f*) *m*; **'~·post** placówka *f*; **'~·pour·ing** ulewa *f*; **'~·put** *econ.* wydajność *f*; moc *f* wyjściowa; produkcja *f*; *komp.* dane *pl.* wyjściowe; **'~·rage 1.** pogwałcenie *n*; gwałt *m*; przestępstwo *n*; zamach *m*; oburzenie *n*; **2.** zadawać 〈-dać〉 gwałt; wzburzać 〈-rzyć〉; **~·rageous** [aʊt'reɪdʒəs] skandaliczny, oburzający; horrendalny; **~·right 1.** *adj.* ['aʊtraɪt] całkowity; wyraźny, jawny; **2.** [aʊt'raɪt] *adv.* całkowicie; wyraźnie, jawnie; wprost; **~'run** (**-*nn-***; ***-ran, -run***) prześcigać 〈-gnąć〉; *fig.* przekraczać 〈-roczyć〉; **'~·set** początek *m*; **~'shine** (***-shone***) przewyższać 〈-szyć〉; przyćmiewać 〈-mić〉; **~'side 1.** zewnętrzna strona *f*; (*w sporcie*) napastnik *m* na skrzydle; ***at the*** (***very***) ***~side*** najdalej; najwyżej; ***left*** (***right***) **~** lewo-(prawo-)-skrzydłowy *m*; **2.** *adj.* zewnętrzny; **3.** *adv.* na zewnątrz; **4.** poza (*I*); za (*I*); pod (*I*); **~'sid·er** outsider *m*, autsajder *m*; osoba *f* postronna; **'~·size 1.** duży rozmiar *m*; **2.** o dużych rozmiarach; **'~·skirts** *pl.* przedmieścia *pl.*, peryferie *pl.*; **~'smart** → ***outwit***; **~'spo·ken** szczery, otwarty; **~'spread** rozciągnięty; **~'stand** wybitny; *econ. rachunek*: zaległy; *sprawa*: nie załatwiony; **~'stay** przebywać dłużej niż; → ***welcome*** 4; **~'stretched** rozpostarty; **~'strip**(***-pp-***) prześcigać 〈-gnąć〉; *fig.* zostawić w tyle; **'~tray**: ***in the ~tray*** w poczcie wychodzącej; **~'vote** przegłosowywać 〈-ować〉

out·ward ['aʊtwəd] **1.** zewnętrzny; **2.** *adv.*: *zw.* ***~s*** na zewnątrz; **'~·ly** zewnętrznie, na zewnątrz

out|'weigh *fig.* przeważać 〈-żyć〉; **~'wit** (***-tt-***) przechytrzać 〈-rzyć〉; **~'worn** zużyty, przestarzały

o·val ['əʊvl] **1.** owalny; **2.** owal *m*

o·va·tion [əʊ'veɪʃn] owacja *f*; ***give s.o. a standing ~*** oklaskiwać kogoś na stojąco

ov·en ['ʌvn] piec *m*; piekarnik *m*; **~-'read·y** gotowy do pieczenia

o·ver ['əʊvə] **1.** *prp.* nad (*I*), ponad (*I*); na (*L*); przez (*A*); po drugiej stronie (*G*); podczas (*G*); **2.** *adv.* na drugą stronę (*G*); więcej; zbytnio; **~ *here*** tutaj; (***all***) **~ *again*** jeszcze raz; ***all ~*** od nowa, od początku; **~ *and above*** oprócz (*G*); **~ *and* ~** (***again***) ciągle, nieustannie

o·ver|·act [əʊvər'ækt] przesadzać 〈-dzić〉 (*w grze*); **~·age** [əʊvər'eɪdʒ] ponad wymagany wiek; **~·all 1.** [əʊvər'ɔːl] całkowity, ogólny; **2.** ['əʊvərɔːl] *Brt.* fartuch *m*, kitel *m*; *Am.* kombinezon *m* roboczy; ***~s*** *pl. Brt.* kombinezon *m* roboczy; *Am.* spodnie *pl.* robocze; **~·awe** [əʊvər'ɔː] onieśmielać 〈-lić〉; **~'balance** 〈s〉tracić równowagę; **~'bearing** despotyczny; **'~·board** *naut.* za burtą, za burtę; **~'cast** zachmurzony;

~'charge przeciążać ⟨-żyć⟩ (*też electr.*); za dużo ⟨po⟩liczyć; '**~·coat** płaszcz *m*; **~'come** (***-came, -come***) przezwyciężać ⟨-żyć⟩; ***be ~come with emotion*** być ogarniętym uczuciem; **~'crowd·ed** zatłoczony; **~'do** (***-did, -done***) przesadzać ⟨-dzić⟩; *gastr.* smażyć *lub* gotować za długo; ***overdone*** *też* zbytnio wysmażony; '**~·dose** przedawkowanie *n*, nadmierna dawka *f*; '**~·draft** *econ.* przekroczenie *n* (*konta*); **~'draw** *econ. konto* przekraczać ⟨-roczyć⟩ (***by*** o *A*); **~'dress** ubierać ⟨ubrać⟩ się nadmiernie oficjalnie; ***~dressed*** ubrany oficjalnie; '**~·drive** *mot.* overdrive *m*, nadbieg *m*; **~'due** zaległy, przeterminowany; spóźniony; **~·eat** [əʊvər'iːt] (***-ate, -eaten***) ⟨prze⟩jeść się; **~·es·ti·mate** [əʊvər'estɪmeɪt] przeceniać ⟨-nić⟩, zbyt wysoko ⟨o⟩szacować; **~·ex·pose** *phot.* [əʊvərɪk'spəʊz] prześwietlać ⟨-lić⟩; **~·flow 1.** [əʊvə'fləʊ] *v/t.* przepełniać ⟨-nić⟩; *v/i.* przelewać ⟨-lać⟩ się; **2.** ['əʊvəfləʊ] przelew *m*; przelewanie *n* się; **~'grown** zarosły, zarośnięty; **~'hang** (***-hung***) *v/t.* nawisać nad; *v/i.* wystawać; **~'haul** przeglądać, poddawać generalnemu remontowi; **~'head 1.** *adv.* na górze; **2.** *adj.* górny; *econ.* ogólny; (*w sporcie*) (po)nad głową; ***~head kick*** strzał *m* przewrotką; '**~·head(s** *pl. Brt.*) *Am. econ.* koszty *pl.* bieżące; **~'hear** (***-heard***) podsłuchiwać ⟨-chać⟩; **~'heat·ed** przegrzany; **~'joyed** nadzwyczaj zadowolony; '**~kill** *mil.* możliwość *f* wielokrotnego unicestwienia; *fig.* przesada *f* (***of*** z *I*); **~'lap** (***-pp-***) nakładać ⟨-łożyć⟩ się; zachodzić na siebie; **~'leaf** na odwrocie strony; **~'load** przeciążać ⟨-żyć⟩ (*też electr.*); **~'look** wychodzić na (*A*); przeoczyć; nie dostrzegać ⟨-rzec⟩; **~'night 1.** przez noc; ***stay ~night*** pozostawać ⟨-tać⟩ na noc; **2.** podróżny; na noc; ***~night bag*** torba *f* podróżna; '**~pass** *zwł. Am.* kładka *f* (*nad ulicą*); **~'pay** (***-paid***) przepłacać ⟨-cić⟩; **~'pop·u·lat·ed** przeludniony; **~'pow·er** pokonywać, obezwładniać ⟨-nić⟩ (*też fig.*); **~'rate** przeceniać ⟨-nić⟩, oceniać ⟨-nić⟩ zbyt wysoko; **~'reach**: ***~reach o.s.*** przeliczyć się, przerachować się; **~·re'act** przesadnie ⟨za⟩reagować; **~·re'ac·tion** przesadna reakcja *f*; **~'ride** (***-rode, -ridden***) odsuwać ⟨-unąć⟩ na bok, anulować; **~'rule** unieważniać ⟨-nić⟩, uchylać ⟨-lić⟩; **~'run** (***-nn-***; ***-ran, -run***) ogarniać ⟨-nąć⟩; przekraczać ⟨-roczyć⟩ (ustalony czas); *sygnał* przejeżdżać ⟨-jechać⟩; ***be ~run with*** być ogarniętym (*D*); **~'seas 1.** *adj.* zagraniczny; zamorski; **2.** *adv.* za granicę; za granicą; **~'see** (***-saw, -seen***) nadzorować; '**~·seer** nadzorca *m*; **~'shad·ow** przyćmiewać ⟨-mić⟩; rzucać ⟨-cić⟩ cień na (*A*); '**~·sight** niedopatrzenie *n*; **~'size(d)** dużego rozmiaru; **~'sleep** (***-slept***) zaspać; **~'staffed** o nadmiernym zatrudnieniu; **~'state** wyolbrzymiać ⟨-mić⟩; przesadzać ⟨-dzić⟩; **~'state·ment** przesada *f*; wyolbrzymienie *n*; **~'stay** przebywać dłużej niż; → ***welcome*** 4; **~'step** *fig.* przekraczać ⟨-roczyć⟩; **~'take** (***-took, -taken***) mijać ⟨minąć⟩ wyprzedzać ⟨-dzić⟩; *fig.* zaskakiwać ⟨-skoczyć⟩; **~'tax** nakładać ⟨nałożyć⟩ zbyt wysoki podatek; *fig.* naruszać ⟨-szyć⟩; **~·throw 1.** [əʊvə'θrəʊ] (***-threw, -thrown***) *rząd itp.* obalać ⟨-lić⟩; **2.** ['əʊvəθrəʊ] obalenie *f*, przewrót *m*; '**~·time** *econ.* praca *f* nadliczbowa, F nadgodziny *pl.*; *Am.* (*w sporcie*) dogrywka *f*; ***be on ~time, do ~time, work ~time*** pracować w nadgodzinach

o·ver·ture ['əʊvətjʊə] *mus.* uwertura *f*

o·ver|'turn przewracać ⟨-rócić⟩; *rząd* obalać ⟨-lić⟩; *naut.* wywracać ⟨-rócić⟩ się; *jur.* anulować; '**~·view** *fig.* zarys *m*; **~·weight 1.** ['əʊvəweɪt] nadwaga *f*; **2.** [əʊvə'weɪt] z nadwagą; zbyt ciężki (***by*** o *A*); ***be five pounds ~weight*** mieć pięć funtów nadwagi; **~'whelm** przytłaczać ⟨-łoczyć⟩; zakrywać ⟨-ryć⟩; **~'whelm·ing** przytłaczający; **~'work** nadmiernie pracować, przepracowywać ⟨-ować⟩ się; **~'wrought** przewrażliwiony

owe [əʊ] *komuś coś* być winnym, być dłużnym; *coś* zawdzięczać

ow·ing ['əʊɪŋ]: **~ *to*** dzięki (*D*), na skutek (*G*)

owl [aʊl] *zo.* sowa *f*

own [əʊn] **1.** własny; ***my ~*** mój (*własny*); (***all***) ***on one's ~*** sam; **2.** posiadać; przyznawać się (***to*** do *G*)

own·er ['əʊnə] właściciel(ka *f*) *m*; posiadacz(ka *f*) *m*; **~-'oc·cu·pied** *zwł. Brt.* zajmowany przez właściciela;

'~**·ship** własność *f*, posiadanie *n*
ox [ɒks] *zo.* (*pl.* ***oxen*** ['ɒksn]) wół *m*
Ox·ford Oksford *m*
ox·ide ['ɒksaɪd] *chem.* tlenek *m*; **ox·i·dize** *chem.* ['ɒksɪdaɪz] utleniać ⟨-nić⟩ (się)
ox·y·gen ['ɒksɪdʒən] *chem.* tlen *m*
oy·ster ['ɔɪstə] *zo.* ostryga *f*
oz *skrót pisany*: ***ounce*(*s*** *pl.*) uncja *f* (uncje *pl.*) (*28,35 g*)
o·zone ['əuzəun] *chem.* ozon *m*; '~**-friend·ly** nie niszczący warstwy ozonu; '~ **hole** dziura *f* ozonowa; '~ **lay·er** warstwa *f* ozonu; '~ **lev·els** *pl.* poziom *m* zawartości ozonu; '~ **shield** osłona *f* ozonowa

P

P, p [piː] P, p *n*
p[1] *Brt.* [piː] *skrót*: ***penny*** (***pence*** *pl.*) pens(y *pl.*) *m*
p[2] (*pl.* ***pp***) *skrót pisany*: ***page*** s., str., strona *f*
pace [peɪs] **1.** tempo *n*, szybkość *f*; krok *m*; chód *m* (*konia*); **2.** *v/t.* chodzić po (*L*) (*pokoju itp.*); *też* ~ ***out*** ⟨z-, wy⟩mierzyć (*krokami*); *v/i.* kroczyć, chodzić; ~ ***up and down*** chodzić tam i z powrotem; '~**·mak·er** *med.* stymulator *m*; → '~**·set·ter** *Am.* (*w sporcie*) zając *m* (*zawodnik nadający tempo*)
Pa·cif·ic [pə'sɪfɪk] *też* ~ ***Ocean*** Pacyfik *m*, Ocean *m* Spokojny
pac·i|·fi·er ['pæsɪfaɪə] *Am.* smoczek *m*; ~**·fist** ['pæsɪfɪst] pacyfista *m* (-tka *f*); ~**·fy** ['pæsɪfaɪ] uspokajać ⟨-koić⟩
pack [pæk] **1.** paczka *f*, pakunek *m*; *Am.* paczka *f* (*papierosów*); stado *n*, wataha *f* (*wilków*); sfora *f*, zgraja *f* (*psów*); grupa *f*; *med. kosmetyczny* okład *m*; *med.* tampon *m*; talia *f* (*kart*); ***a*** ~ ***of lies*** stek *m* kłamstw; **2.** *v/t. też* ~ ***up*** ⟨s-, za⟩pakować; upychać ⟨upchać⟩; opakowywać ⟨-ować⟩; ~ ***off*** F odsyłać ⟨odesłać⟩; *v/i.* ⟨s-, za⟩pakować się; wpychać ⟨wepchnąć⟩ się (***into*** do *G*); ~ ***up*** zapakować się; ***send s.o.*** ~***ing*** odsyłać ⟨odesłać⟩ kogoś
pack·age ['pækɪdʒ] paczka *f*, pakiet *m*; ***software*** ~ *komp.* pakiet *m* oprogramowania; '~ **deal** F transakcja *f* wiązana; '~**hol·i·day** wczasy *pl.* zorganizowane; '~ **tour** wycieczka *f* zorganizowana *f*
'**pack·er** pakowacz(ka *f*) *m*; *Am.* producent *m* konserw
pack·et ['pækɪt] paczka *f*, pakiet *m*
'**pack·ing** opakowywanie *n*; opakowanie *n*
pact [pækt] pakt *m*, układ *m*
pad [pæd] **1.** poduszka *f* (*do ubrania, pieczątek*); (*w sporcie*) ochraniacz *m*; blok *m* (*papieru*); *zo.* poduszeczka *f*; płyta *f* (*wyrzutni*); tampon *m*; *Am.* podpaska *f*; **2.** (***-dd-***) wyściełać ⟨-elić⟩, watować; '~**·ding** wyściółka *f*, obicie *n*, watowanie *n*
pad·dle ['pædl] **1.** wiosło *n*; *naut.* łopatka *f* ; **2.** wiosłować; brodzić; '~ **wheel** *naut.* koło *n* łopatkowe
pad·dock ['pædək] padok *m*, wybieg *m*
pad·lock ['pædlɒk] kłódka *f*
pa·gan ['peɪgən] **1.** poganin *m* (-anka *f*); **2.** pogański
page[1] [peɪdʒ] **1.** strona *f*; **2.** numerować strony
page[2] [peɪdʒ] **1.** boy *m* hotelowy; **2.** wzywać ⟨wezwać⟩
pag·eant ['pædʒənt] widowisko *n* historyczne
pa·gin·ate ['pædʒɪneɪt] numerować strony
paid [peɪd] *pret. i p.p. od* ***pay*** 1
pail [peɪl] wiadro *n*, kubeł *m*
pain [peɪn] **1.** ból *m*; problem *m*; ~***s*** *pl.* starania *pl.*, fatyga *f*; ***be in*** (***great***) ~ mieć silne bóle; ***be a*** ~ (***in the neck***) F strasznie się naprzykrzać; ***take*** ~***s*** trudzić się; **2.** *zwł. fig.* czuć ból; boleć; '~**·ful** bolesny; '~**·kill·er** środek *m* uśmierzający ból; '~**·less** bezbolesny; ~**s·tak·ing** ['peɪnzteɪkɪŋ] drobiazgowy
paint [peɪnt] **1.** farba *f*; **2.** ⟨po⟩malować; *samochód itp.* ⟨po⟩lakierować; '~**·box** pudełko *n* na farby; '~**·brush** pędzel *m* malarski; '~**·er** malarz *m* (-arka *f*); '~**·ing** malowanie *n*; obraz *m*, malowidło *n*
pair [peə] **1.** para *f*; ***a*** ~ ***of*** para (*G*); ***a*** ~ ***of***

P

scissors nożyczki, para nożyc; **2.** *v/i. zo.* parzyć się; *też* **~ off, ~ up** ⟨u⟩tworzyć parę; *v/t.* **~ off, ~ up** dobierać ⟨-brać⟩ parami; **~ off** tworzyć parę z (*G*)
pa·ja·ma(s) [pəˈdʒɑːmə(z)] *Am.* → ***py-jama(s)***
pal [pæl] kolega *m*, koleżanka *f*, F kumpel *m*, kumpelka *f*
pal·ace [ˈpælɪs] pałac *m*
pal·a·ta·ble [ˈpælətəbl] do przełknięcia (*też fig.*)
pal·ate [ˈpælɪt] *anat.* podniebienie; *fig.* smak *m*
pale[1] [peɪl] **1.** (**-r, -st**) blady; *kolor*: jasny; **2.** ⟨z⟩blednąć; rozjaśniać ⟨-nić⟩ (się)
pale[2] [peɪl] pal *m*; *fig.* granica *f*
ˈpale·ness bladość *f*
Pal·es·tine Palestyna *f*
Pal·e·stin·i·an [pæləˈstɪnɪən] **1.** palestyński; **2.** Palestyńczyk (-tynka *f*)
pal·ings [ˈpeɪlɪŋz] częstokół *m*; pale *pl.*
pal·i·sade [pælɪˈseɪd] palisada *f*; *zwł. Am.* strome skały *pl.*
pal·let [ˈpælɪt] *tech.* paleta *f*
pal|·lid [ˈpælɪd] blady; **ˈ~·lor** bladość *f*
palm[1] [pɑːm] *bot. też* **~ tree** palma *f*
palm[2] [pɑːm] **1.** dłoń *f*; **2.** ⟨s⟩chować w dłoni; **~ *s.th.* off on *s.o.*** opychać ⟨-chnąć⟩ coś komuś
pal·pa·ble [ˈpælpəbl] wyczuwalny, namacalny
pal·pi|·tate [ˈpælpɪteɪt] *med. serce*: kołatać; **~·ta·tions** [pælpɪˈteɪʃnz] *pl.* palpitacje *pl.*, kołatanie *n*
pal·sy [ˈpɔːlzɪ] *med.* porażenie *n*
pal·try [ˈpɔːltrɪ] (***-ier, -iest***) marny, nędzny
pam·per [ˈpæmpə] dogadzać ⟨-godzić⟩; *dziecko itp.* rozpieszczać ⟨-pieścić⟩
pam·phlet [ˈpæmflɪt] broszura *f*; ⚠ *nie* ***pamflet***
pan [pæn] patelnia *f*
pan·a·ce·a [pænəˈsɪə] panaceum *m*
pan·cake [ˈpæŋkeɪk] naleśnik *m*
pan·da [ˈpændə] *zo.* panda *f*; **ˈ~ car** *Brt.* samochód *m* policyjny
pan·de·mo·ni·um [pændɪˈməʊnjəm] pandemonium *n*, zamieszanie *n*, chaos *m*
pan·der [ˈpændə] schlebiać (*gustom*)
pane [peɪn] szyba *f*
pan·el [ˈpænl] **1.** tafla *f*, płyta *f*, płycina *f*; *electr., tech.* tablica *f* (*rozdzielcza*); *jur.* lista *f* sędziów przysięgłych; panel *m*, grupa *f* (*ekspertów*); **2.** (*zwł. Brt.* **-ll-**, *Am.* **-l-**) wykładać ⟨-łożyć⟩ boazerią
pang [pæŋ] ukłucie *n* (bólu); **~s** *pl.* **of hunger** skurcze *pl.* głodowe; **~s** *pl.* **of conscience** wyrzuty *pl.* sumienia
ˈpan·han|·dle *Am.* żebrać; **ˈ~·dler** żebrak *m* (-aczka *f*)
pan·ic [ˈpænɪk] **1.** paniczny; **2.** panika *f*; **3.** (**-ck-**) panikować; wpadać ⟨wpaść⟩ w panikę
pan·sy [ˈpænzɪ] *bot.* bratek *m*, fiołek *m* trójbarwny; F pedał *m*
pant [pænt] dyszeć; ziajać
pan·ther [ˈpænθə] *zo.* (*pl.* **-thers, -ther**) pantera *f*; *Am.* puma *f*; *Am.* jaguar *m*
pan·ties [ˈpæntɪz] *pl.* majtki *pl.*, *kobiece* figi *pl.*
pan·to·mime [ˈpæntəmaɪm] *Brt.* F jasełka *pl.*; *theat.* pantomima *f*
pan·try [ˈpæntrɪ] spiżarnia *f*; *naut.* pentra *f*
pants [pænts] *pl. Brt.* majtki *pl.*; *zwł. Am.* spodnie *pl.*
ˈpant·suit *Am.* spodnium *m*
pan·ty| hose [ˈpæntɪhəʊz] *zwł. Am.* rajstopy *pl.*
pap [pæp] bryja *f*, ciapka *f*
pa·pal [ˈpeɪpl] papieski
pa·per [ˈpeɪpə] **1.** papier *m*; gazeta *f*, czasopismo *n*; praca *f* (pisemna *lub* semestralna); referat *m*; tapeta *f*; **~s** *pl.* papiery *pl.*, dowody *pl.* tożsamości; **2.** ⟨wy⟩tapetować; **ˈ~·back** książka *f* w miękkich okładkach; **ˈ~ bag** torba *f* papierowa; **ˈ~·boy** gazeciarz *m*; **ˈ~ clip** wycinek *m* prasowy; **ˈ~ cup** kubek *m* papierowy; **ˈ~·girl** gazeciarka *f*; **ˈ~·hang·er** tapeciarz *m*; **ˈ~ knife** (*pl.* ***knives***) *Brt.* nóż *m* do papieru; **ˈ~ mon·ey** pieniądz *m* papierowy; **ˈ~·weight** przycisk *m* do papieru
par [pɑː] *econ.* wartość *f* nominalna, nominał *m*; parytet *m* kurs *m* wymian; **at ~** na równi; według parytetu; ***on a ~ with*** na równi z (*I*)
par·a·ble [ˈpærəbl] przypowieść *f*
par·a|·chute [ˈpærəʃuːt] spadochron *m*; **ˈ~·chut·ist** spadochroniarz *m* (-arka *f*)
pa·rade [pəˈreɪd] **1.** parada *f*; pochód *m*; *fig.* pokaz *m*; ***make a ~ of*** *fig.* robić pokaz z (*G*); **2.** iść w pochodzie (***through*** przez *A*); *mil.* ⟨prze⟩defilować; ⟨po⟩prowadzić w paradzie; *fig.* ⟨za⟩prezentować (się)

P

par·a·dise ['pærədaɪs] raj *m*
par·a·glid|·er ['pærəglaɪdə] paralotnia *m*; lotniarz *m*; '**~·ing** lotniarstwo *n*
par·a·gon ['pærəgən] wzór *m*, wzorzec *m*
par·a·graph ['pærəgrɑːf] akapit *m*; paragraf *m*; notka *f* (*prasowa*)
par·al·lel ['pærəlel] **1.** równoległy (***to, with*** do *G*, z *I*); **2.** *math.* prosta *f* równoległa, równoległa *f* (*też fig.*); ***without ~*** bez analogii; *geogr.* równoleżnik *m*; **3.** (*zwł. Brt.* ***-ll-*** , *Am.* ***-l-***) odpowiadać (*D*), być podobnym do (*G*)
par·a·lyse *Brt.*, **par·a·lyze** *Am.* ['pærəlaɪz] *med.* ⟨s⟩paraliżować (*też fig.*); **pa·ral·y·sis** [pə'rælɪsɪs] (*pl.* ***-ses*** [-siːz]) *med.* paraliż *m* (*też fig.*)
par·a·mount ['pærəmaʊnt] nadrzędny, najważniejszy; ***of ~ importance*** najwyższego znaczenia
par·a·pet ['pærəpɪt] bariera *f*, balustrada *f*
par·a·pher·na·li·a [pærəfə'neɪljə] *pl.* parafernalia *pl.*, rzeczy *pl.* osobiste; *Brt.* zabiegi *pl.*, zachody *pl.*
par·a·site ['pærəsaɪt] pasożyt *m*
par·a·troop|·er ['pærətruːpə] *mil.* spadochroniarz *m*; '**~s** *pl.* wojska *pl.* spadochronowe
par·boil ['pɑːbɔɪl] obgotowywać ⟨-ować⟩
par·cel ['pɑːsl] **1.** paczka *f*; parcela *f*, działka *f*; **2.** (*zwł. Brt.* ***-ll-*** , *Am.* ***-l-***): ***~ out*** rozdzielać ⟨-lić⟩, rozparcelowywać ⟨-ować⟩; ***~ up*** zapakowywać ⟨-ować⟩ (*jako paczkę*)
parch [pɑːtʃ] wysychać ⟨-schnąć⟩; wysuszać ⟨-szyć⟩
parch·ment ['pɑːtʃmənt] pergamin *m*
par·don ['pɑːdn] **1.** *jur.* ułaskawienie *n*, darowanie *n* kary; ***I beg your ~!*** przepraszam!; *też* ***~?*** F słucham?; **2.** wybaczać ⟨-czyć⟩; darować; *jur.* ułaskawiać ⟨-wić⟩; ***~ me → I beg your ~***; *Am.* F słucham?; '**~·a·ble** wybaczalny
pare [peə] *paznokcie* obcinać ⟨-ciąć⟩; *jabłko* obierać ⟨-brać⟩
par·ent ['peərənt] rodzic *m*; matka *f*, ojciec *m*; **~s** *pl.* rodzice *pl.*; **~·age** ['peərəntɪdʒ] rodzicielstwo *n*; **pa·rental** [pə'rentl] rodzicielski
pa·ren·the·ses [pə'renθɪsiːz] *pl.* nawiasy *pl.* (*zwł. okrągłe*)
'**par·ents-in-law** *pl.* teściowie *pl.*
par·ent-'teach·er meet·ing wywiadówka *f*
par·ings ['peərɪŋz] *pl.* obierki *pl.*
Pa·ris Paryż *m*
par·ish ['pærɪʃ] parafia *f*; **pa·rish·io·ner** [pə'rɪʃənə] *rel.* parafianin *m* (-anka *f*)
park [pɑːk] **1.** park *m*; **2.** *mot.* ⟨za⟩parkować
par·ka ['pɑːkə] skafander *m*
'**park·ing** *mot.* parkowanie *n*; ***no ~*** zakaz *m* parkowania; '**~ disc** tarcza *f* czasu parkowania; '**~ fee** opłata *f* za parkowanie; '**~ ga·rage** *Am.* (*w budynku*) parking *m*; '**~ lot** *Am.* parking *m*; '**~ me·ter** parkometr *m*; '**~ space** miejsce *n* do (za)parkowania; '**~ tick·et** mandat *m* za nieprawidłowe parkowanie
par·ley ['pɑːlɪ] *zwł. mil. pokojowe* rokowania *pl.*
par·lia|·ment ['pɑːləmənt] parlament *m*; **~·men·tar·i·an** [pɑːləmen'teərɪən] parlamentarzysta *m*; **~·men·ta·ry** [pɑːlə'mentərɪ] parlamentarny
par·lo(u)r ['pɑːlə]: *zw. w złożeniach* ***beauty ~*** gabinet *m* kosmetyczny
pa·ro·chi·al [pə'rəʊkjəl] parafialny; zaściankowy
pa·role [pə'rəʊl] **1.** zwolnienie *n* warunkowe; ***he is out on ~*** jest na zwolnieniu warunkowym; **2.** **~ *s.o.*** zwolnić kogoś warunkowo
par·quet ['pɑːkeɪ] parkiet *m*; *Am. theat.* parter *m*; '**~ floor** parkiet *m*
par·rot ['pærət] **1.** *zo.* papuga *f* (*też fig.*); **2.** powtarzać (*jak papuga*)
par·ry ['pærɪ] ⟨od⟩parować, odbijać ⟨-bić⟩
par·si·mo·ni·ous [pɑːsɪ'məʊnjəs] skąpy
pars·ley ['pɑːslɪ] *bot.* pietruszka *f*
par·son ['pɑːsn] proboszcz *m*; **~·age** ['pɑːsnɪdʒ] probostwo *n*
part [pɑːt] **1.** część *f*; *tech.* element *m*, część *f*; udział *m*; strona *f*; *theat.*, *fig.* rola *f*; *mus.* głos *m*, partia *f*; odcinek *m* (*filmu*); *Am.* przedziałek *m*; ***for my ~*** z mojej strony; ***for the most ~*** w większości, przeważnie; ***in ~*** częściowo; ***on the ~ of*** ze strony (*G*); ***on my ~*** z mojej strony; ***take ~ in s.th.*** brać ⟨wziąć⟩ w czymś udział; ***take s.th. in good ~*** przyjmować ⟨-jąć⟩ coś w dobrej wierze;

2. *v/t.* ⟨po-, roz⟩dzielić; *włosy* ⟨u⟩czesać z przedziałkiem; ~ ***company*** rozstawać ⟨-tać⟩ się (***with*** z *I*); *v/i.* rozstawać ⟨-tać⟩ się (***with*** z *I*); **3.** *adj.* częściowy; **4.** *adv.* **~ ... ~ ...** częściowo ... a częściowo ...

par|·tial ['pɑːʃl] częściowy; stronniczy, tendencyjny (***to*** wobec *G*); **~·ti·al·i·ty** [pɑːʃɪ'ælətɪ] stronniczość *f*, tendencyjność *f* (***for*** wobec *G*); **~·tial·ly** ['pɑːʃəlɪ] stronniczo, tendencyjnie

par·tic·i|·pant [pɑː'tɪsɪpənt] uczestnik *m* (-iczka *f*); **~·pate** [pɑː'tɪsɪpeɪt] uczestniczyć, brać ⟨wziąć⟩ udział (***in*** w *L*); **~·pa·tion** [pɑːtɪsɪ'peɪʃn] uczestnictwo *n*

par·ti·ci·ple ['pɑːtɪsɪpl] *gr.* imiesłów *m*

par·ti·cle ['pɑːtɪkl] cząstka *f*

par·tic·u·lar [pə'tɪkjʊlə] **1.** szczególny; indywidualny; wybredny, wymagający; dokładny, drobiazgowy; **2.** szczegół *m*, detal *m*; **~s** *pl.* dane *pl.* szczegółowe; dane *pl.* osobiste; ***in*** ~ w szczególności; **~·ly** szczególnie

'part·ing **1.** rozstanie *n*, pożegnanie *n*; *zwł. Brt.* przedziałek *m*; **2.** pożegnalny

par·ti·san [pɑːtɪ'zæn] **1.** stronnik *m* (-iczka *f*); *mil.* partyzant *m*; **2.** stronniczy

par·ti·tion [pɑː'tɪʃn] **1.** podział *m*; rozbiór *m*; ścianka *f* działowa; przepierzenie *n*; **2.** ~ ***off*** oddzielać ⟨-lić⟩

'part·ly częściowo

P

part·ner ['pɑːtnə] partner(ka *f*) *m*; *econ.* wspólnik *m* (-iczka *f*); **'~·ship** partnerstwo *n*; *econ.* spółka *f*

part-'own·er współwłaściciel(ka *f*) *m*

par·tridge ['pɑːtrɪdʒ] *zo.* kuropatwa *f*

part|-'time **1.** *adj.* niepełnoetatowy; ~ ***worker*** → ***part-timer***; **2.** *adv.* na niepełny etat; na pół etatu; **~-'tim·er** pracownik *m* niepełnoetatowy *lub* na pół etatu

par·ty ['pɑːtɪ] partia *f*, stronnictwo *n*; grupa *f*, ekipa *f*; strona *f* (*umowy itp.*); *mil.* oddział *m*; uczestnik *m* (-iczka *f*); przyjęcie *n*, F impreza *f*; **'~ line** *pol.* linia *f* partyjna; ~ **'pol·i·tics** *sg. lub pl.* polityka *f* partyjna

pass [pɑːs] **1.** *v/i.* przechodzić ⟨-ejść⟩, przejeżdżać ⟨-jechać⟩ (***by*** koło *G*); przechodzić ⟨-ejść⟩ (***to*** do *G*); *ból, czas itp.*: przechodzić ⟨-ejść⟩, mijać ⟨minąć⟩; *egzamin itp.* zdawać ⟨-dać⟩ (*A*); (*w sporcie*) podawać ⟨-dać⟩ piłkę (***to*** do *G*); *parl.* uchwalać ⟨-lić⟩ ustawę; być uważanym (***as, for*** jako *A*); ***let s.o.*** ~ przepuszczać ⟨-puścić⟩ kogoś; ***let s.th.*** ~ puszczać ⟨puścić⟩ coś mimochodem; *v/t.* mijać ⟨minąć⟩; *czas* spędzać ⟨-dzić⟩; *egzamin itp.* zdawać ⟨-dać⟩; *pieprz, piłkę* podawać ⟨-dać⟩ (***to*** do *G*); sięgać ⟨-gnąć⟩ (***over*** do *G*); *parl.* uchwalać ⟨-lić⟩; *jur. wyrok* wydawać ⟨-dać⟩ (***on*** na *A*); *sąd* wygłaszać ⟨-łosić⟩; *fig.* przewyższać; ~ ***away*** umrzeć; ~ ***off*** zakończyć się (*dobrze itp.*); uchodzić (***as*** za *A*); ~ ***out*** ⟨ze⟩mdleć; **2.** przepustka *f*; zdanie *n* (*egzaminu*); (*w sporcie*) podanie *n*; przełęcz *f*; ***free*** ~ bilet *m* bezpłatny; ***make a*** ~ ***at*** F dobierać się do (*G*); **'~·a·ble** znośny; *droga*: przejezdny

pas·sage ['pæsɪdʒ] korytarz *m*, przejście *n*; przejazd *m*, rejs *m*; pasaż *m* (*też mus.*); passus *m*; ***bird of*** ~ ptak *m* wędrowny

'pass·book *zwł. Am.* książeczka *f* oszczędnościowa

pas·sen·ger ['pæsɪndʒə] pasażer(ka *f*) *m*

pass·er·by [pɑːsə'baɪ] (*pl.* ***passersby***) przechodzień *m*

pas·sion ['pæʃn] pasja *f*; namiętność *f*; zamiłowanie *n*; uczucie *n*; ♀ *rel.* pasja; **~·ate** ['pæʃənət] namiętny

pas·sive ['pæsɪv] bierny (*też gr.*), pasywny

pass·port ['pɑːspɔːt] paszport *m*

pass·word ['pɑːswɜːd] hasło *n*

past [pɑːst] **1.** *adj.* przeszły; wcześniejszy; *pred.* miniony, ubiegły; ***for some time*** ~ od jakiegoś czasu; ~ ***tense*** *gr.* czas przeszły; **2.** *adv.* obok (*G*), mimo (*G*); **3.** *prp. czas*: po (*D*); *miejsce*: obok (*G*), mimo (*G*); za (*D*); ***half*** ~ ***two*** (w)pół do trzeciej; ~ ***hope*** beznadziejny

pas·ta ['pæstə] *gastr.* makaron *m*; ⚠ *nie* ***pasta***

paste [peɪst] **1.** ciasto *n*; pasta *f*; klej *m*; klajster *m*; **2.** ⟨przy⟩kleić (***to*** do *G*, ***on*** na *A*); ~ ***up*** naklejać ⟨-leić⟩, przylepiać ⟨-pić⟩; **'~·board** karton *m*, tektura *f*

pas·tel [pæ'stel] **1.** pastel *m*; **2.** pastelowy

pas·teur·ize ['pɑːstʃəraɪz] pasteryzować

pas·time ['pɑːstaɪm] zajęcie *n* (*w wolnych chwilach*)

pas·tor ['pɑːstə] pastor *m*; **~·al** ['pɑːstərəl] *rel.* duszpasterski; idylliczny, bukoliczny

pas·try ['peɪstrɪ] ciasto *n*; ciastko *n*; '**~ cook** cukiernik *m*

pas·ture ['pɑːstʃə] **1.** pastwisko *n*; **2.** paść (się); wypasać

pas·ty[1] ['pæstɪ] *zwł. Brt.* pasztecik *m*

past·y[2] ['peɪstɪ] kredowobiały, blady

pat [pæt] **1.** klaps *m*, klepnięcie *n*; porcja *f* (*zwł. masła*); **2.** (**-tt-**) klepać ⟨-pnąć⟩, poklepywać ⟨-pać⟩

patch [pætʃ] **1.** plama *f*; miejsce *n*; łata *f*; działka *f*; przepaska *f* na oko; ***in ~es*** miejscami; **2.** ⟨za-, po⟩łatać; '**~·work** patchwork *m*

pa·tent ['peɪtənt] **1.** patentowy; opatentowany; oczywisty, ewidentny; **2.** patent *m*; **3.** *coś* ⟨o⟩patentować; **~·ee** [peɪtən'tiː] posiadacz(ka *f*) *m* patentu; **~ 'leath·er** skóra *f* lakierowana

pa·ter|·nal [pə'tɜːnl] ojcowski; **~·ni·ty** [pə'tɜːnətɪ] ojcostwo *n*

path [pɑːθ] (*pl.* ***paths*** [pɑːðz]) ścieżka *f*; trajektoria *f*, tor *m*

pa·thet·ic [pə'θetɪk] (**~*ally***) patetyczny; żałosny, pożałowania godny

pa·thos ['peɪθɒs] żałosność *f*, współczucie *n*

pa·tience ['peɪʃns] cierpliwość *f*; *zwł. Brt.* pasjans *m*

pa·tient[1] ['peɪʃnt] cierpliwy

pa·tient[2] ['peɪʃnt] pacjent(ka *f*) *m*

pat·i·o ['pætɪəʊ] (*pl.* **-*os***) patio *n*, dziedziniec *m*

pat·ri·ot ['pætrɪət] patriota *m* (-tka *f*); **~·ic** [pætrɪ'ɒtɪk] (**-*ally***) patriotyczny

pa·trol [pə'trəʊl] **1.** patrol *m*; ***on ~*** na patrolu; **2.** (**-*ll*-**) patrolować; **~ car** wóz *m* patrolowy; **~·man** (*pl.* **-*men***) *zwł. Am.* policjant(ka *f*) *m* na służbie patrolowej; *Brt.* (*osoba pomagająca zmotoryzowanym w razie awarii*)

pa·tron ['peɪtrən] mecenas *m*, sponsor *m*; patron(ka *f*) *m*; *stały* klient *m*, *stała* klientka *f* **pat·ron·age** ['pætrənɪdʒ] patronaż *m*; **pat·ron·ess** ['peɪtrənɪs] patronka *f*; *stała* klientka *f*; **pat·ron·ize** ['pætrənaɪz] ⟨po⟩traktować protekcjonalnie; być gościem (*G*); być patronem (*G*); **~ saint** [peɪtrən 'seɪnt] *rel.* patron(ka *f*) *m*

pat·ter ['pætə] *deszcz*: ⟨za⟩stukać; ⟨za⟩tupać

pat·tern ['pætən] **1.** wzór *m* (*też fig.*); **2.** wzorować się

paunch ['pɔːnʃ] brzuszysko *n*

pau·per ['pɔːpə] nędzarz *m* (-arka *f*)

pause [pɔːz] **1.** przerwa *f*; pauza *f*; **2.** zatrzymywać się; ⟨z⟩robić przerwę

pave [peɪv] ⟨wy⟩brukować; **~ *the way for*** *fig.* ⟨u⟩torować drogę do (*G*); '**~·ment** *Brt.* bruk *m*; *Am.* chodnik *m*

paw [pɔː] **1.** łapa *f* (*też fig.*); **2.** *v/t.* grzebać w (*ziemi itp*); ⟨za⟩skrobać do (*drzwi*); F macać, obmacywać ⟨-cać⟩; *v/i.* skrobać (***at*** po *L*)

pawn[1] [pɔːn] *szachowy* pionek *m* (*też fig.*)

pawn[2] [pɔːn] **1.** zastawiać ⟨-wić⟩; **2.** ***be in ~*** znajdować się w zastawie; '**~·broker** właściciel *m* lombardu; '**~·shop** lombard *m*

pay [peɪ] **1.** (***paid***) *v/t. coś* ⟨za⟩płacić (*też* za *A*); *komuś* ⟨za⟩płacić; *uwagę* poświęcać ⟨-cić⟩; *wizytę* składać ⟨złożyć⟩; *komplement* mówić ⟨powiedzieć⟩; **~ *attention*** zwracać ⟨-rócić⟩ uwagę (***to*** na *A*); **~ *cash*** ⟨za⟩płacić gotówką; *v/i.* ⟨za⟩płacić; *fig.* opłacać ⟨-cić⟩ się; **~ *for*** ⟨za⟩płacić za (*A*) (*też fig.*); **~ *in*** wpłacać ⟨-cić⟩; **~ *into*** wpłacać ⟨-cić⟩ na (*A*); **~ *off*** *coś* spłacać ⟨-cić⟩; opłacać ⟨-cić⟩ się; wypłacać ⟨-cić⟩ odprawę; **2.** zapłata *f*, wypłata *f*; płaca *f*, pobory *pl.*; '**~·a·ble** wypłacalny; '**~·day** dzień *m* wypłaty; **~·ee** [peɪ'iː] odbiorca *m* (*pieniędzy*); beneficjent *m*; '**~ en·ve·lope** *Am.* koperta *f* z wypłatą; '**~·ing** płatność *f*, wypłata *f*; **~·ing 'guest** gość *m* (*na kwaterze turystycznej*); podnajemca *m*, sublokator(ka *f*) *m*; '**~·ment** wypłata *f*; '**~ pack·et** *Brt.* koperta *f* z wypłatą; '**~ phone** *Brt.* automat *m* telefoniczny; '**~·roll** lista *f* płac; '**~·slip** odcinek *m* wypłaty

PC [piː 'siː] *skrót*: ***personal computer*** komputer osobisty *m*, F pecet *m*; **~ *user*** użytkownik *m* komputera osobistego

P.C., PC [piː 'siː] *Brt. skrót*: ***police constable*** policjant *m*

pd *skrót pisany*: ***paid*** zapł., zapłacony

pea [piː] *bot.* groszek *m*, groch *m*

peace [piːs] pokój *m jur.* spokój *m*; cisza *f*; ***at ~*** w spokoju; '**~·a·ble** pokojowy; '**~·ful** pokojowy; '**~·lov·ing** miłujący pokój; '**~ move·ment** ruch *m* obrony pokoju; '**~·time** pokój *m*

peach [piːtʃ] *bot.* brzoskwinia *f*

P

pea|·cock ['pi:kɒk] *zo.* paw *m*; '**~·hen** *zo.* pawica *f*

peak [pi:k] szczyt *m* (*też fig.*); wierzchołek *m*; daszek *m* (*czapki*); **~ed cap** [pi:kt 'kæp] czapka *f* z daszkiem; '**~ hours** *pl.* godziny *pl.* szczytu; *electr.* okres *m* szczytowego obciążenia; '**~ time** *też* ***peak viewing hours*** *pl. Brt. TV* okres *m* największej oglądalności

peal [pi:l] **1.** bicie *n* (*dzwonu lub dzwonów*); kurant *m*; grzmot *m* (*pioruna*); ***~ of laughter*** gromki śmiech *m*; **2.** *też* ***~ out*** rozbrzmiewać

pea·nut ['pi:nʌt] *bot.* orzeszek *m* ziemny, fistaszek *m*; ***~s*** *pl.* F śmieszna suma *f*

pear [peə] *bot.* gruszka *f*; grusza *f*

pearl [pɜ:l] perła *f*; *attr.* perłowy; '**~·y** (***-ier, -iest***) perłowy

peas·ant ['peznt] chłop *m*, wieśniak *m*

peat [pi:t] torf *m*; *attr.* torfowy

peb·ble ['pebl] kamień *m*, kamyk *m*, otoczak *m*

peck [pek] dziobać ⟨-bnąć⟩; cmokać ⟨-knąć⟩; ***~ at one's food*** przebierać ⟨-brać⟩ w jedzeniu

pe·cu·li·ar [pɪ'kju:ljə] szczególny, charakterystyczny; dziwny, osobliwy; **~·i·ty** [pɪkju:lɪ'ærətɪ] szczególność *f*; osobliwość *f*

pe·cu·ni·a·ry [pɪ'kju:njərɪ] pieniężny, finansowy

ped·a·go·gic [pedə'gɒdʒɪk] pedagogiczny

ped·al ['pedl] **1.** pedał *m*; **2.** (*zwł. Brt.* ***-ll-***, *Am.* ***-l-***) ⟨po⟩pedałować; ⟨po⟩jechać (*na rowerze*)

pe·dan·tic [pɪ'dæntɪk] (***~ally***) pedantyczny

ped·dle ['pedl] handlować (*I*); ***~ drugs*** handlować narkotykami; '**~r** → *Am.* ***pedlar***

ped·es·tal ['pedɪstl] piedestał *m* (*też fig.*)

pe·des·tri·an [pɪ'destrɪən] **1.** pieszy *m* (-sza *f*); **2.** pieszy; **~ 'cross·ing** przejście *n* dla pieszych; **~ 'mall** *Am.*, **~ 'pre·cinct** *zwł. Brt.* strefa *f* ruchu pieszego

ped·i·cure ['pedɪkjʊə] pedicure *m*

ped·i·gree ['pedɪgri:] rodowód *m*; *attr.* rodowodowy

ped·lar ['pedlə] handlarz *m* (-arka *f*)

pee [pi:] F **1.** siusiać; **2.** ***have*** (*lub* ***go for***) ***a ~*** wysiusiać się

peek [pi:k] **1.** zerkać ⟨-knąć⟩ (***at*** na *A*); **2.** ***have*** *lub* ***take a ~ at*** zerkać ⟨-knąć⟩ na (*A*)

peel [pi:l] **1.** *v/t.* obierać ⟨-brać⟩; *też* ***~ off*** *tapetę, ubranie itp.* zdzierać ⟨zedrzeć⟩; *v/i. też* ***~ off*** *tapeta*: odchodzić ⟨odejść⟩, *skóra, farba*: schodzić ⟨zejść⟩; **2.** skórka *f*

peep[1] [pi:p] **1.** zerkać ⟨-knąć⟩ (***at*** na *A*); **2.** ***take a ~ at*** zerkać ⟨-knąć⟩ na (*A*)

peep[2] [pi:p] **1.** pisk *m*, zabrzęczenie; **2.** ⟨za⟩piszczeć, ⟨za⟩brzęczeć

'peep·hole wizjer *m*, judasz *m*

peer [pɪə] **1.** przyglądać ⟨przyjrzeć⟩ się (***at*** *D*); **2.** równy *m* (-na *f*); *Brt.* par *m*, arystokrata *m*; '**~·less** niezrównany

peev·ish ['pi:vɪʃ] drażliwy, pobudliwy

peg [peg] **1.** kołek *m*; palik *m*; wieszak *m*; *Brt.* klamerka *f* do bielizny; śledź *m* (*do namiotu*)

Pe·king Pekin *m*

pel·i·can ['pelɪkən] *zo.* (*pl.* ***-can, -cans***) pelikan *m*; **~ 'cross·ing** *Brt.* przejście *n* dla pieszych (*na światłach*)

pel·let ['pelɪt] kulka *f* (*też śrutu*), grudka *f*

pelt[1] [pelt] *v/t.* obrzucać ⟨-cić⟩; *v/i.* ***it's ~ing*** (***down***), *zwł. Brt.* ***it's ~ing with rain*** leje jak z cebra

pelt[2] [pelt] skóra *f* (surowa)

pel·vis ['pelvɪs] *anat.* (*pl.* ***-vises, -ves*** [-vi:z]) miednica *f*

pen[1] [pen] pióro *n*, długopis *m*, pisak *m*

pen[2] [pen] **1.** zagroda; **2.** (***-nn-***): ***~in, ~up*** *zwierzęta, ludzi* zamykać ⟨-knąć⟩

pe·nal ['pi:nl] karny, karalny; '**~ code** kodeks *m* karny; **~·ize** ['pi:nəlaɪz] penalizować; ⟨u⟩karać

pen·al·ty ['penltɪ] kara *f*, grzywna *f*; (*w sporcie*) kara *f*, punkt *m* karny; (*w piłce nożnej*) rzut *m* karny; '**~ ar·e·a**, '**~ box** (*w piłce nożnej*) pole *n* karne; '**~ goal** (*w piłce nożnej*) bramka *f* z rzutu karnego; '**~ kick** (*w piłce nożnej*) rzut *m* karny; **~ 'shoot-out** (*w piłce nożnej*) strzały *pl.* z pola karnego (*dla rozstrzygnięcia meczu*); '**~ spot** (*w piłce nożnej*) punkt

pen·ance ['penəns] *rel.* pokuta *f*

pence [pens] (*skrót*: ***p***) *pl. od* ***penny***

pen·cil ['pensl] **1.** ołówek *m*; **2.** (*zwł. Brt.* ***-ll-***, *Am.* ***-l-***) zaznaczać ⟨-czyć⟩, zapisywać ⟨-sać⟩ (*ołówkiem*); '**~ case** piórnik *m*; '**~ sharp·en·er** temperówka *f*

P

pen·dant, pen·dent ['pendənt] wisiorek *m*
pend·ing ['pendıŋ] **1.** *prp.* w trakcie (*G*); **2.** *adj. zwł. jur.* *będący* w toku
pen·du·lum ['pendjʊləm] wahadło *n*
pen·e|·trate ['penıtreıt] przenikać ⟨-knąć⟩ do (*G*) *lub* przez (*A*), przenikać ⟨-knąć⟩ (***into*** do *G*, ***through*** przez *A*); '**~·trat·ing** przenikliwy; bystry; **~·tra·tion** [penı'treıʃn] przeniknięcie *n*, wniknięcie *n*; bystrość *f*
'pen friend (*osoba, z którą się koresponduje*)
pen·guin ['peŋgwın] *zo.* pingwin *m*
pe·nin·su·la [pə'nınsjʊlə] półwysep *m*
pe·nis ['pi:nıs] *anat.* penis *m*, członek *m*
pen·i|·tence ['penıtəns] skrucha *f*, żal *m* za grzechy; '**~·tent 1.** skruszony, żałujący za grzechy; **2.** *rel.* penitent *m*; **~·ten·tia·ry** [penı'tenʃərı] *Am.* zakład *m* karny
'pen|·knife (*pl.* ***-knives***) scyzoryk *m*; '**~ name** pseudonim *m* literacki
pen·nant ['penənt] wimpel *m*, proporczyk *m*
pen·ni·less ['penılıs] bez pieniędzy
pen·ny ['penı] (*skrót:* ***p***) (*pl.* ***-nies***, *coll.* ***pence***) *też* ***new ~*** *Brt.* pens *m*
'pen pal *zwł. Am.* → ***pen friend***
pen·sion ['penʃn] **1.** renta *f*, emerytura *f*; ⚠ *nie* ***pensja*** ; **2.** ***~ off*** przenosić ⟨-nieść⟩ w stan spoczynku; **~·er** ['penʃənə] rencista *m* (-tka *f*), emeryt(ka *f*) *m*
pen·sive ['pensıv] zadumany, zamyślony
pen·tath|·lete [pen'tæθli:t] (*w sporcie*) pięcioboista *m*; **~·lon** [pen'tæθlɒn] (*w sporcie*) pięciobój *m*
Pen·te·cost ['pentıkɒst] Zielone Świątki *pl.* Szawuot *m* (*w judaizmie*)
pent·house ['penthaʊs] penthouse *m* (*apartament na ostatnim piętrze wieżowca*)
pent-up [pent'ʌp] *uczucie itp.*: powstrzymywany
pe·o·ny ['pıənı] *bot.* piwonia *f*
peo·ple ['pi:pl] **1.** *pl.* ludzie *pl.*; ***the ~*** naród *m*; (*pl.* ***peoples***) lud *m*; **2.** zasiedlać ⟨-lić⟩; **~'s re'pub·lic** republika *f* ludowa
pep [pep] F **1.** ikra *f*, werwa *f*; **2.** (***-pp-***) uatrakcyjniać ⟨-nić⟩, pobudzać ⟨-dzić⟩
pep·per ['pepə] **1.** pieprz *m*; (*strąk*) papryka *f*; **2.** ⟨po⟩pieprzyć; '**~·mint** *bot.* mięta *f* (pieprzowa); miętus *m*; **~·y** ['pepərı] pieprzny; *fig.* drażliwy
'pep pill F środek *m* stymulujący
per [pɜ:] na (*A*); za (*A*); od (*A*); według (*A*)
per·am·bu·la·tor [pə'ræmbjʊleıtə] *zwł. Brt.* wózek *m* dziecięcy
per·ceive [pə'si:v] spostrzegać ⟨-ec⟩, dostrzegać ⟨-ec⟩
per cent, per·cent [pə'sent] procent *m*
per·cen·tage [pə'sentıdʒ] procent *m*; F zysk *m*, procenty *pl.*
per·cep|·ti·ble [pə'septəbl] dostrzegalny, zauważalny; **~·tion** [pə'sepʃn] percepcja *f*, dostrzeganie *n*
perch[1] [pɜ:tʃ] **1.** grzęda *f*; **2.** ***~ o.s.*** (***on***) ⟨u⟩sadowić się (na *L*)
perch[2] [pɜ:tʃ] *zo.* (*pl.* ***perch, perches***) okoń *m*
per·co|·late ['pɜ:kəleıt] *kawę itp.* zaparzać ⟨-rzyć⟩ (się); '**~·la·tor** ekspres *m* do kawy
per·cus·sion [pə'kʌʃn] uderzenie *n*; *mus.* instrumenty *pl.* perkusyjne; **~ in·stru·ment** *mus.* instrument *m* perkusyjny
pe·remp·to·ry [pə'remptərı] władczy, kategoryczny
pe·ren·ni·al [pə'renjəl] wieczny; *bot.* wieloletni, trwały
per|·fect 1. ['pɜ:fıkt] doskonały; perfekcyjny; zupełny, całkowity; wykończony; **2.** [pə'fekt] udoskonalać ⟨-lić⟩, ulepszać ⟨-szyć⟩; **3.** ['pɜ:fıkt] *też* ***~fect tense*** *gr.* czas *m* dokonany; **~·fec·tion** [pə'fekʃn] doskonałość *f*; perfekcja *f*; udoskonalenie *n*
per·fo·rate ['pɜ:fəreıt] ⟨prze⟩dziurawić, ⟨prze⟩dziurkować; perforować
per·form [pə'fɔ:m] *v/t.* wykonywać ⟨-nać⟩ (*też mus., theat.*); dokonywać ⟨-ać⟩; *theat.*, *mus.* grać; *v/i. theat. itp.* dawać ⟨dać⟩ przedstawienie, grać; *samochód*: sprawiać ⟨-wić⟩ się; **~·ance** wykonanie *n*; działanie *n*; osiągi *pl.*; *mus, theat.* występ *m*, przedstawienie *n*; **~·er** wykonawca *m* (-czyni *f*)
per·fume 1. ['pɜ:fju:m] perfumy *pl.*; **2.** [pə'fju:m] ⟨u⟩perfumować
per·haps [pə'hæps, præps] (być) może
per·il ['perəl] niebezpieczeństwo *n*; '**~·ous** niebezpieczny
pe·ri·od ['pıərıəd] okres *m*; lekcja *f*; *physiol.* okres *m* (*kobiety*); *gr. zwł. Am.*

kropka *f*; *attr.* stylowy, zabytkowy; **~·ic** [pɪərɪ'ɒdɪk] periodyczny, okresowy; **~·i·cal** [pɪərɪ'ɒdɪkl] **1.** periodyczny, okresowy; **2.** periodyk *m*

pe·riph·e·ral [pə'rɪfərəl] **1.** peryferyjny; **2.** *komp.* urządzenie *n* peryferyjne; **~ e'quip·ment** *komp.* urządzenia *pl.* peryferyjne

pe·riph·e·ry [pə'rɪfərɪ] obrzeże *n*, peryferia *pl.*

per·ish ['perɪʃ] ⟨z⟩ginąć; *Brt. gumę* rozłożyć; **'~·a·ble** *jedzenie itp.*: nietrwały; **'~·ing** *zwł. Brt.* F przenikliwy, przejmująco zimny

per|·jure ['pɜːdʒə]: ***~jure o.s.*** krzywoprzysięgać ⟨-gnąć⟩; **~·ju·ry** ['pɜːdʒərɪ] krzywoprzysięstwo *n*; ***commit ~jury*** popełniać ⟨-nić⟩ krzywoprzysięstwo *n*

perk [pɜːk]: ***~ up*** *v/i.* ożywiać ⟨-wić⟩ się; *v/t.* pobudzać ⟨-dzić⟩

perk·y ['pɜːkɪ] F (***-ier, -iest***) żywotny, rozradowany

perm [pɜːm] **1.** trwała *f*; **2.** ***get one's hair ~ed*** zrobić sobie trwałą

per·ma·nent ['pɜːmənənt] **1.** trwały; stały; **2.** *Am.* **~ 'wave** trwała *f*

per·me|·a·ble ['pɜːmjəbl] przepuszczalny (***to*** dla *G*); **~·ate** ['pɜːmɪeɪt] przenikać ⟨-knąć⟩ (***into*** do *A*, ***through*** przez *A*)

per·mis|·si·ble [pə'mɪsəbl] dozwolony, dopuszczalny; **~·sion** [pə'mɪʃn] pozwolenie *n*, zezwolenie *n*; **~·sive** [pə'mɪsɪv] przyzwalający, pobłażliwy; **~·sive so'ci·e·ty** społeczeństwo *n* przyzwalające

per·mit 1. [pə'mɪt] (***-tt-***) zezwalać ⟨-lić⟩, pozwalać ⟨-wolić⟩; **2.** ['pɜːmɪt] zezwolenie *n*; przepustka *f*

per·pen·dic·u·lar [pɜːpən'dɪkjʊlə] prostopadły

per·pet·u·al [pə'petʃʊəl] wieczny, trwały; dożywotni

per·plex [pə'pleks] ⟨za⟩kłopotać, ⟨z⟩mieszać, stropić; **~·i·ty** [pə'pleksətɪ] zakłopotanie *n*, stropienie *n*

per·se|·cute ['pɜːsɪkjuːt] prześladować, szykanować; ⟨u⟩karać; **~·cu·tion** [pɜːsɪ'kjuːʃn] prześladowanie *n*, szykanowanie *n*; **~·cu·tor** ['pɜːsɪkjuːtə] prześladowca *m*

per·se|·ver·ance [pɜːsɪ'vɪərəns] wytrwałość *f*; **~·vere** [pɜːsɪ'vɪə] wytrwać, nie poddawać się

per|·sist [pə'sɪst] trwać, utrzymywać się; ***~sist in doing s.th.*** nie zaprzestawać czegoś robić; **~'sis·tence** wytrzymałość *f*, uporczywość *f*; **~'sis·tent** uporczywy

per·son ['pɜːsn] osoba *f* (*też gr.*)

per·son·al ['pɜːsnl] osobisty, osobowy (*też gr.*); prywatny; **'~ col·umn** ogłoszenia *pl.* drobne; **~ com'pu·ter** (*skrót*: ***PC***) komputer *m* osobisty, F pecet *m*; **~ 'da·ta** *pl.* dane *pl.* osobiste

per·son·al·i·ty [pɜːsə'nælətɪ] osobowość *f*; ***personalities*** *pl.* uwagi *pl.* osobiste

per·son·al| 'or·ga·ni·zer (*notes, spis adresów*) kalendarz *m* biznesmena; **~ 'ster·e·o** walkman *m* (*TM*)

per·son·i·fy [pɜː'sɒnɪfaɪ] uosabiać ⟨-sobić⟩

per·son·nel [pɜːsə'nel] kadra *f*, personel *m*, załoga *f*; (*dział*) kadry *pl.*; **~ depart·ment** kadry *pl.*; **~ man·ag·er** dyrektor *m* do spraw osobowych

per·spec·tive [pə'spektɪv] perspektywa *f*; widok *m*; punkt *m* widzenia

per|·spi·ra·tion [pɜːspə'reɪʃn] pot *m*, pocenie *n* się; **~·spire** [pə'spaɪə] ⟨s⟩pocić się

per|·suade [pə'sweɪd] przekonywać ⟨-nać⟩; **~·sua·sion** [pə'sweɪʒn] przekonanie *n*; przekonywanie *n*, perswazja *f*; **~·sua·sive** [pə'sweɪsɪv] przekonujący

pert [pɜːt] *kapelusz*: szykowny; *dziewczyna*: czupurny

per·tain [pɜː'teɪn]: ***~ to s.th.*** odnosić się do czegoś

per·ti·nent ['pɜːtɪnənt] stosowny, właściwy

per·turb [pə'tɜːb] ⟨za⟩niepokoić

pe·ruse [pə'ruːz] przeglądać ⟨-dnąć⟩, ⟨z⟩badać

per·vade [pə'veɪd] przenikać ⟨-knąć⟩, wypełniać ⟨-nić⟩

per|·verse [pə'vɜːs] perwersyjny, zboczony; **~·ver·sion** [pə'vɜːʃn] perwersja *f*, zboczenie *n*; wypaczenie *n*, przekręcenie *n*; **~·ver·si·ty** [pə'vɜːsətɪ] perwersja *f*

per·vert 1. [pə'vɜːt] ⟨z⟩deprawować; przekręcać ⟨-cić⟩; **2.** ['pɜːvɜːt] zboczeniec *m*

pes·sa·ry ['pesərɪ] *med.* pesarium *n*, krążek *m* domaciczny

pes·si|·mis·m ['pesɪmɪzəm] pesymizm *m*; **~·mist** ['pesɪmɪst] pesymista *m* (-tka *f*); **~'mist·ic** (**-*ally***) pesymistyczny
pest [pest] szkodnik *m*; utrapienie *n*
pes·ter ['pestə] F ⟨z⟩nękać, dręczyć
pes·ti·cide ['pestɪsaɪd] pestycyd *m*
pet [pet] **1.** zwierzę *n* domowe; *często pej.* ulubieniec *m*; kochanie *n*; **2.** ulubiony, ukochany; pieszczotliwy; dla zwierząt domowych; **3.** (**-*tt*-**) pieścić (się)
pet·al ['petl] *bot.* płatek *m*
'pet food pokarm *m* dla zwierząt domowych
pe·ti·tion [pɪ'tɪʃn] **1.** petycja *f*, prośba *f*; skarga *f*; **2.** składać ⟨złożyć⟩ petycję (***for*** o *A*); ⟨po⟩prosić (***for*** o *A*)
'pet name pieszczotliwe przezwisko *n*
pet·ri·fy ['petrɪfaɪ] petryfikować, zmieniać w kamień; *fig.* ⟨s⟩paraliżować
pet·rol ['petrəl] etylina *f*, benzyna *f*
pe·tro·le·um [pə'trəʊljəm] ropa *f* naftowa
'pet·rol| pump dystrybutor *m* paliwa; pompa *f* paliwowa; **'~ sta·tion** stacja *f* benzynowa
'pet| shop; sklep *m* zoologiczny; **~ 'sub·ject** konik *m*
pet·ti·coat ['petɪkəʊt] półhalka *f*; halka *f*
pet·ting ['petɪŋ] F petting *m*
pet·tish ['petɪʃ] rozdrażniony, rozhisteryzowany
pet·ty ['petɪ] (**-*ier*, -*iest***) drobny, mały; nieznaczny; małostkowy; **~ 'cash** drobne *pl.*, podręczna gotówka *f*; **~ 'lar·ce·ny** *jur.* drobna kradzież *f*
pet·u·lant ['petjʊlənt] uprzykrzony
pew [pju:] ławka *f* (*w kościele*)
pew·ter ['pju:tə] cyna *f*; *też* **~ *ware*** naczynia *pl.* cynowe
phan·tom ['fæntəm] fantom *m*, zjawa *f*
phar·ma|·cist ['fɑ:məsɪst] aptekarz *m* (-arka *f*); **~·cy** ['fɑ:məsɪ] apteka *f*
phase [feɪz] faza *f*
PhD [pi: eɪtʃ 'di:] *skrót*: ***Doctor of Philosophy*** (*łacińskie* ***philosophiae doctor***) dr, doktor *m*; **~ 'the·sis** rozprawa *f* doktorska
pheas·ant ['feznt] *zo.* bażant *m*
phe·nom·e·non [fɪ'nɒmɪnən] (*pl.* **-*na*** [-nə]) zjawisko *n*
Phi·la·del·phia Filadelfia *f*
phi·lan·thro·pist [fɪ'lænθrəpɪst] filantrop *m*
Phil·ip·pines *pl.* Filipiny *pl.*
phi·lol·o|·gist [fɪ'lɒlədʒɪst] filolog *m*; **~·gy** [fɪ'lɒlədʒɪ] filologia *f*
phi·los·o|·pher [fɪ'lɒsəfə] filozof *m*; **~·phy** [fɪ'lɒsəfɪ] filozofia *f*
phlegm [flem] *med.* flegma *f* (*też fig.*); opanowanie *n*
phone [fəʊn] **1.** telefon *m*; ***answer the ~*** odbierać ⟨odebrać⟩ telefon; ***by ~*** telefonicznie, przez telefon; ***on the ~*** przy telefonie; ***be on the ~*** rozmawiać przez telefon; być przy telefonie; **2.** ⟨za⟩telefonować, ⟨za⟩dzwonić; **'~ book** książka telefoniczna *f*; **'~ booth** *Am.*, **'~ box** *Brt.* budka *f* telefoniczna; **'~ call** rozmowa *f* telefoniczna; **'~·card** karta *f* telefoniczna; **'~-in** *Brt.*: audycja (*radiowa lub telewizyjna*) *f* z telefonicznym udziałem odbiorców; **'~ num·ber** numer *m* telefoniczny
pho·net·ics [fə'netɪks] *sg.* fonetyka *f*
pho·n(e)y ['fəʊnɪ] F **1.** krętactwo *n*; krętacz *m*; **2.** (**-*ier*, -*iest***) fałszywy, udawany
phos·pho·rus ['fɒsfərəs] *chem.* fosfor *m*
pho·to ['fəʊtəʊ] F (*pl.* **-*tos***) fotografia *f*, zdjęcie *n*; ***in the ~*** na fotografii; ***take a ~*** zrobić zdjęcie; **'~·cop·i·er** fotokopiarka *f*; **'~·cop·y** fotokopia *f*
pho|·to·graph ['fəʊtəgrɑ:f] **1.** fotografia *f*, zdjęcie *n*; ⚠ *nie* ***fotograf***; **2.** ⟨s⟩fotografować; **~·tog·ra·pher** [fə'tɒgrəfə] fotograf *m*; **~·tog·ra·phy** [fə'tɒgrəfɪ] fotografia *f*
phras·al verb [freɪzl 'vɜ:b] czasownik *m* złożony
phrase [freɪz] zwrot *m*, wyrażenie *n*, idiom *m*; fraza *f*; **2.** wyrażać ⟨-razić⟩; **'~·book** rozmówki *pl.*
phys·i·cal ['fɪzɪkl] **1.** fizyczny; materialny; fizykalny; ***~ly handicapped*** upośledzony fizycznie; **2.** badanie *n* lekarskie; **~ ed·u'ca·tion** wychowanie *n* fizyczne; **~ ex·am·i'na·tion** badanie *n* lekarskie; **~ 'hand·i·cap** upośledzenie *n* fizyczne; **~ 'train·ing** wychowanie *n* fizyczne
phy·si·cian [fɪ'zɪʃn] lekarz *m* (-arka *f*); ⚠ *nie* ***fizyk***
phys|·i·cist ['fɪzɪsɪst] fizyk *m*; **~·ics** ['fɪzɪks] *sg.* fizyka *f*
phy·sique [fɪ'zi:k] budowa *f* ciała

P

pi·a·nist ['pɪənɪst] pianista *f* (-tka *f*)
pi·an·o [pɪ'ænəʊ] (*pl.* ***-os***) fortepian *m*, pianino *n*; *attr.* fortepianowy, na fortepian
pick [pɪk] **1.** wybierać ⟨-brać⟩; odrywać ⟨oderwać⟩, zrywać ⟨zerwać⟩; zbierać ⟨zebrać⟩; ⟨po⟩grzebać, ⟨po⟩dłubać; *zamek itp.* otwierać ⟨-worzyć⟩ wytrychem; *kłótnię itp.* ⟨s⟩prowokować; ~ ***one's nose*** (***teeth***) ‘0po⟩dłubać w nosie (zębach); ~ ***s.o.'s pocket*** okradać ⟨-raść⟩ kogoś; ***have a bone to ~ with s.o.*** mieć coś komuś do powiedzenia; ~ ***out*** wybierać ⟨-brać⟩; dostrzegać ⟨-rzec⟩, odróżniać ⟨-nić⟩; ~ ***up*** podnosić ⟨-nieść⟩ (się); zbierać ⟨zebrać⟩ (się); podejmować ⟨-djąć⟩; *kogoś, rzeczy itp.* odbierać ⟨-debrać⟩; *autostopowicza itp.* zabierać ⟨-brać⟩; F *dziewczynę itp.* poderwać ⟨-drywać⟩; *policja*: zatrzymywać ⟨-mać⟩; *sygnał itp.* odbierać ⟨-debrać⟩; *też* ~ ***up speed*** *mot.* zwiększać ⟨-szyć⟩ (prędkość); *choremu* pomagać ⟨-móc⟩; **2.** kilof *m*, oskard *m*; wybór *m*; ***take your*** ~ proszę sobie wybrać; **~-a-back** ['pɪkəbæk] na barana; '**~·axe** *Brt.*, **~·ax** *Am.* kilof *m*, oskard *m*
pick·et ['pɪkɪt] **1.** pikieta *f*; **2.** pikietować; '~ **fence** płot *m* ze sztachet; '~ **line** linia *f* pikietujących
pick·le ['pɪkl] **1.** zalewa *f* octowa; marynata *f*; *Am.* ogórki *pl.* konserwowe; *zw.* ~***s*** *pl. zwł. Brt.* pikle *pl.*; ***be in a*** (***pretty***) ~ F *fig.* narobić sobie bigosu; **2.** *gastr.* przyrządzać ⟨-dzić⟩ marynatę, ⟨za⟩marynować
'**pick**|**·lock** **1.** włamywacz(ka *f*) *m*; '**~·pock·et** kieszonkowiec *m*; '**~-up** *mot.* pickup *m*, pikap *m*; F zdobycz *f* (*poderwanie*)
pic·nic ['pɪknɪk] **1.** piknik *m*; **2.** (***-ck-***) ⟨z⟩robić piknik, piknikować
pic·ture ['pɪktʃə] **1.** obraz *m*, obrazek *m*; *phot.* zdjęcie *n*; film *m*; ~***s*** *pl. zwł. Brt.* kino *n*; **2.** przedstawiać ⟨-wić⟩ (sobie); wyobrażać sobie; '~ **book** książka *f* z obrazkami; ~ '**post·card** widokówka *f*
pic·tur·esque [pɪktʃə'resk] malowniczy
pie [paɪ] pasztecik *m*; ciasto *n*
piece [piːs] **1.** sztuka *f*; kawałek *m*; część *f* (*maszyny, serwisu itp.*); figura *f* (*szachowa*; pionek *m* (*do gry*); (*w gazecie*) artykuł *m*, notatka *f*; ***by the*** ~ na sztuki; ***a ~ of advice*** (***news***) rada *f*; ***a ~ of news*** informacja *f*, wiadomość *f*; ***give s.o. a ~ of one's mind*** nagadać komuś; ***go to ~s*** F załamywać ⟨-mać⟩ się; ***take to ~s*** rozbierać ⟨-zebrać⟩ na części; **2.** ~ ***together*** zestawiać ⟨-wić⟩ razem; ⟨po⟩składać; '**~·meal** kawałkami, po kawałku; '**~·work** praca *f* na akord; ***do ~work*** pracować na akord
pier [pɪə] pirs *m*, molo *n*
pierce [pɪəs] przedziurawić ⟨-wiać⟩, przebijać ⟨-bić⟩
pierc·ing ['pɪəsɪŋ] *zimno, ból, spojrzenie*: przenikliwy; *krzyk*: rozdzierający
pi·e·ty ['paɪətɪ] pobożność *f*
pig [pɪg] *zo.* świnia; *sl. pej.* gliniarz *m*
pi·geon ['pɪdʒɪn] (*pl.* ***-geons, -geon***) gołąb *m*; '**~·hole** **1.** przegródka *f*; **2.** odkładać ⟨odłożyć⟩; ⟨za⟩szufladkować
pig·gy ['pɪgɪ] F świnka *f* (*w języku dzieci*); '**~·back** na barana
pig|'**head·ed** durny; **~·let** ['pɪglɪt] prosiak *m*; '**~·sty** chlew *m* (*też fig.*); '**~·tail** warkoczyk *m*
pike[1] [paɪk] *zo.* (*pl.* ***pikes, pike***) szczupak *m*
pike[2] [paɪk] → ***turnpike***
pile[1] [paɪl] **1.** stos *m*, sterta *f*; F forsa *f*; **2.** ~ ***up*** układać ⟨ułożyć⟩ w stertę; ⟨na⟩gromadzić się; *mot.* F wpadać na siebie
pile[2] [paɪl] włos *n* (*dywanu*)
pile[3] [paɪl] pal *m*
piles [paɪlz] *med.* F *pl.* hemoroidy *pl.*
'**pile·up** *mot.* F masowy karambol *m*
pil·fer ['pɪlfə] ⟨u⟩kraść, F podwędzić
pil·grim ['pɪlgrɪm] pielgrzym *m*; **~·age** ['pɪlgrɪmɪdʒ] pielgrzymka *f*
pill [pɪl] pigułka *f*, tabletka *f*; ***the*** ~ pigułka *f* antykoncepcyjna; ***be on the*** ~ brać pigułkę antykoncepcyjną
pil·lar ['pɪlə] filar *m*, słup *m*; '~ **box** *Brt.* skrzynka *f* pocztowa
pil·li·on ['pɪljən] *mot.* siodełko *n* pasażera
pil·lo·ry ['pɪlərɪ] **1.** *hist.* pręgierz *m*; **2.** *fig.* stawiać pod pręgierzem
pil·low ['pɪləʊ] poduszka *f*; '**~·case**, '~ **slip** powłoczka *f* na poduszkę
pi·lot ['paɪlət] **1.** *aviat.*, *naut.* pilot *m*; *attr.* pilotażowy; **2.** pilotować; sterować; '~ **film** *TV* zapowiedź *f* filmu (*serialu itp.*); '~ **scheme** projekt *m* pilotażowy

P

pimp [pɪmp] alfons *m*, sutener *m*
pim·ple ['pɪmpl] krosta *f*, pryszcz *m*
pin [pɪn] **1.** szpilka *f*; spinka *f* (*do krawata, włosów*); *Am.* broszka *f*; *tech.* bolec *m*, sworzeń *m*, kołek *m*; kręgiel *m*; *Am.* klamerka *f* (*do bielizny*); *Brt.* pinezka *f*; **2.** (*-nn-*) przyszpilać ⟨-lić⟩, przypinać ⟨-piąć⟩ (***to*** do *G*); unieruchamiać ⟨-chomić⟩ (***against, to*** do *G*)
PIN [pɪn] *też* ***~ number*** *skrót*: ***personal identification number*** PIN, numer *m* PIN, osobisty numer *m* użytkownika
pin·a·fore ['pɪnəfɔː] bezrękawnik *m*, kamizelka *f*
'pin·ball (*automat*) bilard *m*; **'~ machine** automat *m* do gry w bilard; F fliper *m*
pin·cers ['pɪnsəz] *pl.* (*też* ***a pair of***) **~** szczypce *pl.*
pinch [pɪntʃ] **1.** *v/t.* szczypać ⟨-pnąć⟩; ściskać ⟨-snąć⟩ (*boleśnie*); zaciskać ⟨-snąć⟩; F (*ukraść*) zwinąć; *v/i. buty itp.*: cisnąć, uciskać; **2.** szczypta *f*; uszczypnięcie *n*; F trudne położenie *n*
'pin·cush·ion poduszka *f* do szpilek
pine¹ [paɪn] *bot. też* ***~ tree*** sosna *f*
pine² [paɪn] (bardzo) tęsknić (***for*** za *D*)
'pine|·ap·ple *bot.* ananas *m*; **'~ cone** *bot.* szyszka *f* sosny
pin·ion ['pɪnjən] *zo.* koło *n* zębate trzpieniowe
pink [pɪŋk] **1.** różowy; **2.** róż *m*; *bot.* goździk *m*
pint [paɪnt] pół kwarty *m* (*Brt. 0,57 l, Am. 0,47 l*); *Brt.* F duże piwo *n*
pi·o·neer [paɪə'nɪə] **1.** pionier *m* (-ka *f*); **2.** przecierać ⟨-trzeć⟩ szlak
pi·ous ['paɪəs] pobożny, nabożny
pip¹ [pɪp] pestka *f* (*jabłka, pomarańczy*)
pip³ [pɪp] (*w grze w karty*) oczko *n*; (*w grze w kości*) punkt *m*; *zwł. Brt. mil.* (*oznaka stopnia*) gwiazdka *f*
pipe [paɪp] **1.** rura *f*, przewód *m*; fajka *f*; *organowa* piszczałka *f*; fujarka *f*; **~s** *pl. Brt.* F dudy *pl.*; **2.** dostarczać ⟨-czyć⟩ przewodowo; ⟨za⟩grać na piszczałce; **'~·line** rurociąg *m*; **'~r** dudziarz *m*
pip·ing ['paɪpɪŋ] **1.** instalacja *f* rurowa *lub* przewodowa; **2.** ***~ hot*** wrzący, kipiący
pi·quant ['piːkənt] pikantny
pique [piːk] **1.** ***in a fit of ~*** w przypływie urazy; **2.** urażać ⟨urazić⟩; ***be ~d*** *też* ⟨po⟩czuć się urażonym
pi·rate ['paɪərət] **1.** pirat *m*; **2.** ⟨s⟩kopiować po piracku; **~ 'ra·di·o** radio *n* pirackie
Pis·ces ['paɪsiːz] *sg.* Ryby *pl.*; ***he/she is*** (***a***) **~** on/ona jest spod znaku Ryb
piss [pɪs] V szczać; ***~ off!*** odpieprz się!
pis·tol ['pɪstl] pistolet *m*
pis·ton ['pɪstən] *tech.* tłok *m*; **'~ rod** drążek *m* tłoka; **'~ stroke** skok *m* tłoka
pit¹ [pɪt] **1.** dół *m*, zagłębienie *n*, wżer *m*; wgłębienie *n*; jama *f* (*też anat.*); kopalnia *f*; *zwł. Brt. theat.* parter *m*; *też* ***orchestra ~*** *theat.* kanał *m*; **2.** (*-tt-*) ⟨z⟩robić zagłębienia
pit² [pɪt] *Am.* **1.** *bot.* pestka *f*; **2.** (*-tt-*) usuwać ⟨-unąć⟩ pestki
pitch¹ [pɪtʃ] **1.** *v/t. namiot, obóz itp.* rozbijać ⟨-bić⟩; rzucać ⟨-cić⟩, miotać ⟨-tnąć⟩; *mus.* ustawiać ⟨-wić⟩ wysokość (*dźwięku*); *v/i.* przewracać ⟨-rócić⟩ się; *naut. statek*: kołysać się; *dach itp.*: opadać; ***~ in*** F zabierać się do roboty *lub* jedzenia; **2.** *zwł. Brt.* boisko *n*; *mus.* strój *m*; *fig.* poziom *m*, stopień *m*; *zwł. Brt. miejsce n* na ulicy (*np. handlu*); *naut.* kołysanie *n*, kiwanie *n*; pochylenie *n* (*dachu itp.*); *mot.* kanał *m* (*sprawdzania pojazdów*)
pitch² [pɪtʃ] smoła *f*; **~-'black, ~-'dark** czarny jak smoła, kruczoczarny
pitch·er¹ ['pɪtʃə] dzbanek *m*
pitch·er² ['pɪtʃə] (*w baseballu*) zawodnik *m* rzucający piłkę
'pitch·fork widły *pl.*
pit·e·ous ['pɪtɪəs] żałosny
'pit·fall pułapka *f*, zasadzka *f*
pith [pɪθ] *bot.* rdzeń *m*; biała część skórki (*pomarańczy itp.*); *fig.* sedno *n*, jądro *n*; **'~·y** (***-ier, -iest***) treściwy, zwięzły
pit·i|·a·ble ['pɪtɪəbl] → ***pity***; **'~·ful** żałosny; **'~·less** bezlitosny
pits [pɪts] *pl.* (*w sportach motorowych*) miejsce *n* kontroli pojazdów
'pit stop (*w sportach motorowych*) kontrola *f* pojazdu
pit·tance ['pɪtəns] psi pieniądz *m*
pit·y ['pɪtɪ] **1.** litość *f*; współczucie *n* (***on*** do *G*); żal *m*; ***it is a*** (***great***) **~** *wielka* szkoda; ***what a ~!*** jaka szkoda!; **2.** współczuć, czuć litość
piv·ot ['pɪvət] **1.** *tech.* oś *f* (*przegubu*), czop *m*; *fig.* oś *f*, sedno *n*; **2.** obracać się; ***~ on*** *fig.* zależeć od (*G*)
pix·el ['pɪksəl] *komp.* piksel *m*

piz·za ['piːtsə] pizza *f*
plac·ard ['plækɑːd] **1.** plakat *m*; transparent *m*; **2.** ⟨o⟩plakatować
place [pleɪs] **1.** miejsce *n*; mieszkanie *n*, dom *m*; (*w pracy itp.*) pozycja *f*; posada *f*; okazja *f*; ***in the first ~*** przede wszystkim; ***in third ~*** (*w sporcie*) na trzecim miejscu; ***in ~ of*** na miejscu (*G*); zamiast (*G*); ***out of ~*** nie na swoim miejscu; ***take ~*** odbywać ⟨-być⟩ się; mieć miejsce; ⚠ *nie **zajmować miejsce***; ***take s.o.'s ~*** zajmować ⟨-jąć⟩ czyjeś miejsce; **2.** umieszczać ⟨umieścić⟩; *zamówienie itp.* składać ⟨złożyć⟩ (***with*** u *G*); stawiać ⟨-wić⟩ (*w sytuacji*); ***be ~ed*** (*w sporcie*) znaleźć się (***second*** na drugim miejscu)
pla·ce·bo [plə'siːbəʊ] *med.* (*pl.* ***-bos, -boes***) placebo *n*
'place| mat podkładka *f* pod naczynia; **'~·ment test** egzamin *m* wstępny; **'~ name** nazwa *f* miejscowości
plac·id ['plæsɪd] spokojny, cichy
pla·gia·rize ['pleɪdʒjəraɪz] popełniać ⟨-nić⟩ plagiat
plague [pleɪg] **1.** dżuma *f*; zaraza *f*; *fig.* plaga *f*; **2.** dręczyć
plaice [pleɪs] *zo.* (*pl.* ***plaice***) flądra *f*, płastuga *f*
plaid [plæd] pled *m*, koc *m*
plain [pleɪn] **1.** *adj.* zwykły; zwyczajny; nieozdobny, prosty; oczywisty, wyraźny; bezpośredni; szczery; **2.** *adv.* F po prostu; **3.** równina *f*; **~ 'choc·olate** czekolada *f* gorzka; **~-'clothes** w ubraniu cywilnym
plain|·tiff ['pleɪntɪf] powód *m*, strona *f* skarżąca; **~·tive** ['pleɪntɪv] żałosny
plait [plæt] *zwł. Brt.* **1.** warkocz *m*; **2.** zaplatać ⟨-leść⟩
plan [plæn] **1.** plan *m*; **2.** (***-nn-***) ⟨za⟩planować
plane¹ [pleɪn] samolot *m*; ***by ~*** samolotem; ***go by ~*** ⟨po⟩lecieć
plane² [pleɪn] **1.** równy, płaski; **2.** *math.* płaszczyzna *f*; *fig.* poziom *m*
plane³ [pleɪn] **1.** strug *m*, hebel *m*; **2.** ⟨ze⟩strugać, ⟨z⟩heblować
plan·et ['plænɪt] *astr.* planeta *f*
plank [plæŋk] deska *f*, listwa *f*; **'~·ing** deskowanie *n*, odeskowanie *n*; deski *pl.*, listwy *pl.*
plant [plɑːnt] **1.** *bot.* roślina; zakład *m*, fabryka *f*; elektrownia *f*; urządzenia *pl.* techniczne; *attr.* roślinny; **2.** ⟨ob-, po-, za⟩sadzić; *ogród* zakładać ⟨założyć⟩; umieszczać ⟨-mieścić⟩; wtykać ⟨wetknąć⟩; ***~ s.th. on s.o.*** F podkładać ⟨-dłożyć⟩ coś komuś;
plan·ta·tion [plæn'teɪʃn] plantacja *f*
plant·er ['plɑːntə] plantator *m*; sadzarka *f*
plaque [plɑːk] tablica *f* pamiątkowa, epitafium *n*; *med.* kamień *m* nazębny
plas·ter ['plɑːstə] **1.** zaprawa *f* tynkowa; tynk *m*; *med. plaster*; *med.* opatrunek *m* gipsowy; ***~ of Paris*** gips *m*; ***have one's leg in ~*** *med.* mieć nogę w gipsie; **2.** ⟨za-, o⟩tynkować; oklejać ⟨-eić⟩; **'~ cast** odlew *m* gipsowy; *med.* opatrunek *m* gipsowy
plas·tic ['plæstɪk] **1.** (***~ally***) plastyczny; plastikowy; **2.** plastik *m*, tworzywo *n* sztuczne; **~ 'mon·ey** F karty *pl.* kredytowe; **~ 'wrap** *Am.* samoprzylegająca folia *f* (*do żywności*)
plate [pleɪt] **1.** talerz *m*; płyta *f*; płytka *f* (*np. protezy*); tabliczka *f* (*z nazwiskiem*); tablica *f* (*rejestracyjna*); rycina *f*; (gruba) blacha *f*; (*w kościele*) taca *f*; *print.* klisza *f*; plater *m*; **2.** ***~d with gold, gold-~ed*** platerowany złotem
plat·form ['plætfɔːm] platforma *f*; *rail.* peron *m*; trybuna *f*, podium *n* (*mówcy*); *pol.* platforma *f*; ***party ~*** *pol.* program *m* partyjny; ***election ~*** *pol.* program *m* wyborczy
plat·i·num ['plætɪnəm] *chem.* platyna *f*
pla·toon [plə'tuːn] *mil.* pluton *m*
plat·ter ['plætə] taca *f*
plau·si·ble ['plɔːzəbl] wiarygodny, prawdopodobny
play [pleɪ] **1.** gra *f*; zabawa *f*; przedstawienie *n*, sztuka *f*; *tech.* luz *m*; *fig.* swoboda *f* działania; ***at ~*** przy zabawie; ***in ~*** żartem; w grze (*piłka*); ***out of ~*** na aucie; **2.** *v/i.* ⟨za⟩grać; ⟨po⟩bawić się; *v/t. sztukę itp.* ⟨za⟩grać; *rolę, itp.* odgrywać ⟨odegrać⟩; *w karty itp.* grać w (*A*); (*w sporcie*) *piłkę* ⟨s⟩kierować; ***~ s.o.*** (*w sporcie*) grać przeciwko komuś; ***~ the guitar*** ⟨za⟩grać na gitarze; ***~ a trick on s.o.*** ⟨z⟩robić komuś kawał; ***~ back*** *piłkę itp.* ⟨s⟩kierować z powrotem (***to*** do *G*); *kasetę* odtwarzać ⟨-worzyć⟩; ***~ off*** *fig.* wygrywać (***s.o. against*** kogoś przeciwko *D*); ***~ on*** *fig.* wykorzystywać ⟨-stać⟩; **'~·back** playback *m*; powtórka

f; '~·**boy** playboy *m*; '~·**er** (*w sporcie*) gracz *m*; *theat.* aktor(ka *f*) *m*; *mus.* instrumentalista *m* (-tka *f*); '~·**fel·low** *Brt.* → ***playmate***; '~·**ful** rozbawiony; żartobliwy; '~·**go·er** bywalec *m* teatralny; '~·**ground** plac *m* zabaw; podwórko *n* szkolne; '~·**group** *zwł. Brt.* (*rodzaj przedszkola*); '~·**house** *theat.* teatr *m*; domek *m* do zabawy

'**play·ing**| **card** karta *f* do gry; '~ **field** boisko *n*

'**play**|·**mate** towarzysz(ka *f*) *m* zabaw; '~·**pen** kojec *m* (*dla małych dzieci*); '~·**thing** zabawka *f* (*też fig.*); '~·**wright** dramaturg *m*

plc, PLC [piː el 'siː] *Brt. skrót*: ***public limited company*** S.A., spółka *f* akcyjna

plea [pliː] *jur.*: ***enter a ~ of*** (***not***) ***guilty*** (nie) przyznawać ⟨-nać⟩ się do winy

plead [pliːd] (***-ed***, *zwł. Szkoc., Am.* ***pled***) *v/i.* błagać (***for*** o *A*); ~ (***not***) ***guilty*** *jur.* (nie) przyznawać ⟨-nać⟩ się do winy; *v/t. jur. i ogóln.* odpowiadać ⟨-wiedzieć⟩ na zarzuty; ~ ***s.o.'s case*** bronić czyjejś sprawy (*też jur.*)

pleas·ant ['pleznt] przyjemny; przyjazny

please [pliːz] **1.** zadowalać ⟨-wolić⟩; sprawiać ⟨-wić⟩ przyjemność; ⟨ze⟩chcieć (*coś robić*); ***only to ~ you*** tylko by ci sprawić przyjemność; ~ ***o.s.*** robić co się chce; ~ ***yourself!*** wolna wola!; **2.** *int.* proszę; (***yes,***) ~ proszę (tak), z przyjemnością; ~ ***come in!*** proszę wejść!; ~**d** zadowolony; ***be ~d about*** cieszyć się z (*G*); ***be ~d with*** być zadowolonym z (*G*); ***I am ~d with it*** to mi się podoba; ***be ~d to do s.th.*** z przyjemnością coś ⟨z⟩robić; ***~d to meet you!*** bardzo mi miło

pleas·ing ['pliːzɪŋ] przyjemny

plea·sure ['pleʒə] przyjemność *f*; ***at*** (***one's***) ~ według czyjejś woli

pleat [pliːt] fałda *f*; '~·**ed skirt** spódnica *f* plisowana

pled [pled] *pret. i p.p. od* ***plead***

pledge [pledʒ] **1.** przyrzeczenie *n*; zastaw *m*; *fig.* oznaka *f*; **2.** przyrzekać ⟨-rzec⟩; zastawiać ⟨-wić⟩

plen·ti·ful ['plentɪfl] obfity

plen·ty ['plentɪ] **1.** obfitość *f*; ***in ~*** w obfitości; ~ ***of*** dużo; **2.** F zupełnie, całkowicie

pleu·ri·sy ['plʊərəsɪ] *med.* zapalenie *n* opłucnej, pleuritis *f*

pli|·**a·ble** ['plaɪəbl], ~·**ant** ['plaɪənt] plastyczny, giętki; *fig.* podatny; ugodowy

pli·ers ['plaɪəz] *pl.* (***a pair of ~***) szczypce *pl.*, kombinerki *pl.*

plight [plaɪt] ciężkie położenie *n*, opresja *f*

plim·soll ['plɪmsəl] *Brt.* tenisówka *f*

plod [plɒd] (***-dd-***) *też* ~ ***along*** wlec się; ~ ***away*** ⟨po⟩pracować

plop [plɒp] F **1.** plusk *m*; pluśnięcie *n*; **2.** (***-pp-***) plusnąć

plot [plɒt] **1.** działka *f*, parcela *f*; akcja *f*, fabuła *f* (*filmu itp.*); spisek *m*; intryga *f*; *tech.* wykres *m*; **2.** (***-tt-***) *v/i.* spiskować, ⟨u⟩knuć intrygę (***against*** przeciw *D*); *v/t.* ⟨za⟩planować; wykreślać ⟨-lić⟩; '~·**ter** ploter *m*

plough *Brt.*, **plow** *Am.* [plaʊ] **1.** pług *m*; **2.** ⟨za⟩orać; '~·**share** lemiesz *m*

pluck [plʌk] **1.** *v/t.* zbierać ⟨zebrać⟩; *mus. strunę* szarpać ⟨-pnąć⟩, uderzać ⟨-rzyć⟩ w (*A*); *ptaka* oskubywać ⟨-bać⟩; *zw.* ~ ***out*** wyskubywać ⟨-bać⟩; ~ ***up*** (***one's***) ***courage*** zebrać odwagę; *v/i.* szarpać ⟨-pnąć⟩ (***at*** za *A*); **2.** F odwaga *f*; '~·**y** F (***-ier, -iest***) odważny

plug [plʌg] **1.** korek *m*, zatyczka *f*; *electr.* wtyczka *f*; *electr.* wtyczka *f*; F *mot.* świeca *f* zapłonowa; **2.** (***-gg-***) *też* ~ ***up*** zatykać ⟨-tknąć⟩; ~ ***in*** *electr.* włączać ⟨-czyć⟩

plum [plʌm] *bot.* śliwka *f*; śliwa *f*

plum·age ['pluːmɪdʒ] upierzenie *n*

plumb [plʌm] **1.** ołowianka *f*, ciężarek *m* pionu; **2.** ⟨z⟩mierzyć głębokość; *fig.* zgłębiać ⟨-bić⟩; ~ ***in*** *zwł. Brt. pralkę* podłączać ⟨-czyć⟩ do odpływu; **3.** *adj.* pionowy; **4.** *adv.* F prosto; '~·**er** hydraulik *m*; '~·**ing** instalacja *f* wodociągowa

plume [pluːm] pióro *n*; pióropusz *m* (*też fig.*)

plump [plʌmp] **1.** pulchny, krągły; **2.** ~ ***down*** zwalić się

plum 'pud·ding pudding *m* śliwkowy

plun·der ['plʌndə] **1.** ⟨z⟩łupić, ⟨s⟩plądrować; **2.** łup *m*; łupienie *n*

plunge [plʌndʒ] **1.** zanurzać ⟨-rzyć⟩ (się); pogrążać ⟨-żyć⟩ (się) (***into*** w *L*); *ceny itp.*: spadać ⟨spaść⟩; **2.** (za)nurkowanie *n*; spadek *m* (*cen itp.*); ***take the ~*** *fig.* podejmować ⟨-djąć⟩ decydujący krok

P

plu·per·fect [plu:'pɜ:fɪkt] *gr.* *też* ~ ***tense*** czas *m* zaprzeszły
plu·ral ['plʊərəl] *gr.* liczba *f* mnoga
plus [plʌs] **1.** *prp.* plus (*N*), i, oraz; *econ.* z dodatkiem (*G*); **2.** *adj.* plusowy, dodatni; ~ ***sign*** znak *m* plusa; **3.** plus *m*, znak *m* plusa; *fig.* F plus *m*, zaleta *f*
plush [plʌʃ] plusz *m*
ply[1] [plaɪ] kursować (***between*** między *I*);
ply[2] [plaɪ] *zw. w złoż.* warstwa *f*; ***three-~*** trójwarstwowy; **'~·wood** sklejka *f*
pm, PM [pi: 'em] *skrót*: ***after noon*** (*łacińskie* ***post meridiem***) po poł., po południu
PM [pi: 'em] *zwł. Brt.* F *skrót*: ***Prime Minister*** premier *m*
pneu·mat·ic [nju:'mætɪk] (~***ally***) pneumatyczny; ~ **'drill** młot *m* pneumatyczny
pneu·mo·ni·a [nju:'məʊnjə] *med.* zapalenie *n* płuc
PO [pi: 'əʊ] *skrót*: ***post office*** urząd *m* pocztowy; ***postal order*** przekaz *m* pocztowy
poach[1] [pəʊtʃ] ⟨u⟩gotować *jajko* bez skorupki; ***~ed eggs*** *pl.* jajka *pl.* w koszulkach (*gotowane bez skorupki*)
poach[2] [pəʊtʃ] kłusować; **'~·er** kłusownik *m* (-iczka *f*)
POB [pi: əʊ 'bi:] *skrót*: ***post office box*** (***number***) skr. pocz., skrytka *f* pocztowa
PO Box [pi: əʊ 'bɒks] skrytka *f* pocztowa
pock [pɒk] *med.* krosta *f*
pock·et ['pɒkɪt] **1.** kieszeń *f*; *aviat.* → ***air pocket***; **2.** *adj.* kieszonkowy; **3.** wkładać ⟨włożyć⟩ do kieszeni; *fig.* przywłaszczać ⟨-czyć⟩ sobie; **'~·book** notes *m*; *Am.* teczka *f*; ~ **'cal·cu·la·tor** kalkulator *m* kieszonkowy; **'~·knife** (*pl.* ***-knives***) scyzoryk *m*; **'~ mon·ey** drobne *pl.*
pod [pɒd] *bot.* strączek *m*
po·em ['pəʊɪm] wiersz *m*
po·et ['pəʊɪt] poeta *m*; **~·ic** [pəʊ'etɪk] (***-ally***) poetyczny; **~·i·cal** poetyczny; **~·ic 'jus·tice** *fig.* symbol *m* sprawiedliwości; **~·ry** ['pəʊɪtrɪ] poezja *f*
poi·gnant ['pɔɪnjənt] *wspomnienie*: bolesny; przejmujący
point [pɔɪnt] **1.** punkt *m* (*też sport, math., phys.*); szpic *m*, koniuszek *m*; *math.* przecinek *m*; miejsce *n*; stopień *m* (*skali, kompasu itp.*); cel *m*; kwestia *f*; sens *m*; sprawa *f*; *geogr.* przylądek *m*; *electr.* gniazdko *n*; ***two ~ five*** (***2.5***) dwa przecinek pięć (2,5); ***~ of view*** punkt *m* widzenia; ***be on the ~ of doing s.th.*** (mieć) właśnie coś zrobić; ***be to the ~*** należeć do rzeczy; ***be beside the ~*** nie należeć do rzeczy; ***come to the ~*** przystępować ⟨-tąpić⟩ do rzeczy; ***that's not the ~*** to nie należy do rzeczy; ***what's the ~?*** jaki w tym sens?; ***win on ~s*** wygrywać ⟨-rać⟩ na punkty; ***winner on ~s*** zwycięzca *m* na punkty; **2.** wskazywać ⟨-zać⟩; *broń itp.* ⟨s⟩kierować (***at*** w stronę *G*); ***~ one's finger at s.o.*** wskazywać ⟨-zać⟩ (palcem) na kogoś; ***~ out*** wskazywać ⟨-zać⟩; *fig.* wykazywać ⟨-zać⟩; ***~ to*** wskazywać ⟨-zać⟩; *fig.* wskazywać ⟨-zać⟩ na (*A*); **'~·ed** zaostrzony; spiczasty; *fig.* uszczypliwy; *fig.* znaczący; **'~·er** wskaźnik *m*, wskazówka *f*; *zo.* pointer *m*; **'~·less** bezcelowy
points [pɔɪnts] *Brt. pl. rail.* zwrotnica *f*; *electr.* styki *pl.*
poise [pɔɪz] **1.** postawa *f*; *fig.* równowaga *f*; opanowanie *n*; **2.** stawiać ⟨postawić⟩ w równowadze; ***be ~d*** być w zawieszeniu; być gotowym
poi·son ['pɔɪzn] **1.** trucizna *f*; **2.** ⟨o⟩truć; **~·ous** ['pɔɪznəs] trujący (*też fig.*)
poke [pəʊk] **1.** *v/t.* szturchać ⟨-chnąć⟩; wtykać ⟨wetknąć⟩; *palenisko* przegarniać ⟨-nąć⟩; *v/i.* ***~ about, ~ around*** F ⟨po⟩szperać (***in*** w *L*); **2.** szturchaniec *m*; **'pok·er** pogrzebacz *m*
pok·y ['pəʊkɪ] F (***-ier, -iest***) przyciasny
Po·land ['pəʊlənd] Polska *f*
po·lar ['pəʊlə] polarny; ~ **'bear** *zo.* niedźwiedź *m* polarny
pole[1] [pəʊl] biegun *m*
pole[2] [pəʊl] drąg *m*, żerdź *f*, słup *m*; maszt *m*; (*w sporcie*) tyczka *f*
Pole [pəʊl] Polak *m* (-lka *f*)
'pole·cat *zo.* tchórz *m*; *Am.* skunks *m*
po·lem|·ic [pə'lemɪk], **~·i·cal** polemiczny
'pole star *astr.* gwiazda *f* polarna
'pole vault (*w sporcie*) skok *m* o tyczce
'pole-vault (*w sporcie*) skakać o tyczce; **'~·er** (*w sporcie*) tyczkarz *m*
po·lice [pə'li:s] **1.** policja *f*; **2.** patrolować, dozorować; ~ **car** wóz *m* policyjny; **~·man** (*pl.* ***-men***) policjant *m*; ~ **of·fi·cer** policjant *m*; ~ **sta·tion** komisa-

riat *m*; ~·**wom·an** (*pl.* ***-women***) policjantka *f*

pol·i·cy ['pɒləsɪ] polityka *f*; taktyka *f*; polisa *f* ubezpieczeniowa

po·li·o ['pəʊlɪəʊ] *med.* polio *n*, paraliż *m* dziecięcy, choroba *f* Heinego-Medina

pol·ish ['pɒlɪʃ] **1.** ⟨wy⟩polerować, ⟨wy⟩glansować, ⟨wy⟩froterować; *buty* czyścić; ~ **up** *fig.* podciągać ⟨-gnąć⟩; **2.** połysk *m*; środek *m* do nadawania połysku; pasta *f* (*do butów, podłogi*); *fig.* polor *m*

Pol·ish ['pəʊlɪʃ] **1.** polski; **2.** *ling.* język *m* polski

po·lite [pə'laɪt] (***-r, -st***) uprzejmy; ~·**ness** uprzejmość

po·lit·i·cal [pə'lɪtɪkl] polityczny; **pol·i·ti·cian** [pɒlɪ'tɪʃn] polityk *m*; **pol·i·tics** ['pɒlɪtɪks] *zw. sg.* polityka *f*

pol·ka ['pɒlkə] *mus.* polka *f*; '~**-dot** *materiał*: nakrapiany, cętkowany

poll [pəʊl] **1.** sondaż *m* opinii publicznej; głosowanie *n*; liczba *f* głosów; *też* ~**s** *pl.* wybory *pl.*; **2.** przeprowadzać ⟨-dzić⟩ sondaż; otrzymywać ⟨-mać⟩ liczbę głosów

pol·len ['pɒlən] *bot.* pyłek *m* kwiatowy

poll·ing ['pəʊlɪŋ] wybory *pl.*, głosowanie *n*; '~ **booth** *zwł. Brt.* kabina *f* dla głosujących; '~ **day** dzień *m* wyborów; '~ **place** *Am.*, '~ **sta·tion** *Brt.* lokal *m* wyborczy

polls [pəʊlz] *pl.* wybory *pl.*; *Am.* lokal *m* wyborczy

poll·ster ['pəʊlstə] ankieter(ka *f*) *m* opinii publicznej

pol|·lut·ant [pə'luːtənt] polutant *m*, środek *m* zanieczyszczający środowisko; ~·**lute** [pə'luːt] zanieczyszczać ⟨-czyścić⟩ środowisko; ~·**lut·er** [pə'luːtə] *też* ***environmental*** ~***luter*** zakład *m* zanieczyszczający środowisko; ~·**lu·tion** [pə'luːʃn] zanieczyszczenie *n* środowiska

po·lo ['pəʊləʊ] (*w sporcie*) polo *n*; '~ **neck** *zwł. Brt.* (*odzież*) golf *m*

pol·yp ['pɒlɪp] *zo.*, *med.* polip *m*

pol·y·sty·rene [pɒlɪ'staɪriːn] polistyren *m*; *attr.* polistyrenowy

pom·mel ['pʌml] łęk *m* (*siodła*)

pomp [pɒmp] pompa *f*, przepych *m*; ⚠ *nie* ***pompa*** (*do pompowania*)

pom·pous ['pɒmpəs] pompatyczny

pond [pɒnd] staw *m*

pon·der ['pɒndə] *v/i.* medytować, rozmyślać (***on, over*** o *L*); *v/t.* roztrząsać; ~·**ous** ['pɒndərəs] ociężały

pon·toon [pɒn'tuːn] ponton *m*; ~ **bridge** most *m* pontonowy

po·ny ['pəʊnɪ] kucyk *m*; '~·**tail** *fryzura*: kucyk *m*

poo·dle ['puːdl] *zo.* pudel *m*

pool[1] [puːl] staw *m*, sadzawka *f*; kałuża *f*; basen *m*;

pool[2] [puːl] **1.** grupa *f*, zespół *m*; park *m* samochodowy; wspólny *m* fundusz; *zwł. Am. econ.* kartel *m*; (*w kartach*) pula *f*; *Am.* bilard *m*; **2.** *pieniądze, siły itp.* zbierać ⟨zebrać⟩; '~ **hall** *Am.*, '~·**room** sala *f* bilardowa; ~**s** *pl. Brt też* ***football*** ~ *jakby*: totalizator *m* piłkarski

poor [pʊə] **1.** biedny, ubogi; marny, lichy, słaby; **2.** ***the*** ~ *pl.* biedni *pl.*; '~·**ly** **1.** *adj. zwł. Brt.* F niezdrowy; **2.** *adv.* biednie, ubogo; marnie, licho, słabo

pop[1] [pɒp] **1.** (***-pp-***) *v/t.* otwierać ⟨-worzyć⟩ z hukiem; wtykać ⟨wetknąć⟩; *v/i.* strzelić ⟨-lać⟩; ~ ***in*** wpadać ⟨wpaść⟩ na chwilę; ~ ***off*** F wykorkować; ~ ***up*** (*pojawiać się*) wyskoczyć; **2.** *dźwięk*: wystrzał *m*, trzask *m*; F oranżada *f*

pop[2] [pɒp] *mus.* pop *m*

pop[3] [pɒp] *zwł. Am.* tatuś *m*

pop[4] *skrót pisany*: ***population*** ludn., ludność *f*

'**pop con·cert** koncert *m* muzyki pop

'**pop·corn** popcorn *m*

pope [pəʊp] *rel.*: *zw.* ♀ papież *m*

pop-'eyed o wybałuszonych oczach

'**pop group** grupa *f* muzyki pop

pop·lar ['pɒplə] topola *f*

pop·py ['pɒpɪ] *bot.* mak *m*; *attr.* makowy; '~·**cock** F bzdury *pl.*

pop·u·lar ['pɒpjʊlə] popularny, ulubiony; powszechny; ~·**i·ty** [pɒpjʊ'lærətɪ] popularność *f*; powszechność *f*

pop·u|·late ['pɒpjʊleɪt] zasiedlać ⟨-lić⟩; zaludniać ⟨-nić⟩; ~·**la·tion** [pɒpjʊ'leɪʃn] ludność *f*, populacja *f*; ~·**lous** ['pɒpjʊləs] ludny

porce·lain ['pɔːslɪn] porcelana *f*; *attr.* porcelanowy

porch [pɔːtʃ] ganek *m*; *Am.* weranda *f*

por·cu·pine ['pɔːkjʊpaɪn] *zo.* jeżozwierz *m*

pore[1] [pɔː] *anat.* por *f*

pore[2] [pɔː]: ~ ***over*** ślęczeć nad (*I*)

P

pork [pɔːk] wieprzowina *f*
porn [pɔːn] F → ***porno*** F; **por·no** ['pɔːnəʊ] (*pl.* ***-nos***) porno *n*; pornos *m*; **por·nog·ra·phy** [pɔː'nɒgrəfɪ] pornografia *f*
po·rous ['pɔːrəs] porowaty
por·poise ['pɔːpəs] *zo.* morświn *m*
por·ridge ['pɒrɪdʒ] owsianka *f*
port[1] [pɔːt] port *m*; miasto *n* portowe
port[2] [pɔːt] *naut., aviat.* lewa burta *f*
port[3] [pɔːt] *komp.* port *m*
port[4] [pɔːt] portwajn *m*
por·ta·ble ['pɔːtəbl] przenośny
por·ter ['pɔːtə] bagażowy *m*; *zwł. Brt.* portier *m*; *Am. rail.* konduktor *m* wagonu sypialnego
'port·hole iluminator *m*
por·tion ['pɔːʃn] **1.** porcja *f*; część *f*; **2.** ~ ***out*** ⟨po⟩dzielić (***among, between*** pomiędzy *A*)
port·ly ['pɔːtlɪ] (***-ier, -iest***) korpulentny
por·trait ['pɔːtrɪt] portret *m*
por·tray [pɔː'treɪ] ⟨s⟩portretować; przedstawiać ⟨-wić⟩; **~·al** [pɔː'treɪəl] sportretowanie *n*, przedstawienie *n*
Por·tu·gal ['pɔːtʃʊgl] Portugalia *f*; **Por·tu·guese** [pɔːtʃʊ'giːz] **1.** portugalski; **2.** Portugalczyk *m* (-lka *f*); język *m* portugalski; ***the ~*** *pl.* Portugalczycy *pl.*
pose [pəʊz] **1.** *problem* przedstawiać ⟨-wić⟩; *pytanie* stawiać ⟨postawić⟩; pozować (*też jako model*); ***~ as s.o.*** udawać kogoś; **2.** poza *f*
posh [pɒʃ] *zwł. Brt.* F wyszukany, wytworny
po·si·tion [pə'zɪʃn] **1.** pozycja *f*, miejsce *n* (*też fig.*); właściwe miejsce *n*; miejsce *n* pracy, etat *m*; opinia *f*; **2.** ustawiać ⟨-wić⟩, umieszczać ⟨-eścić⟩
pos·i·tive ['pɒzətɪv] **1.** pozytywny; dodatni (*też math., electr.*); przekonany, pewny; konkretny; **2.** *phot.* pozytyw *m*; *gr.* stopień *m* równy
pos|·sess [pə'zes] posiadać; *fig. uczucie, itp.*: owładnąć, opętać; **~·sessed** [pə'zest] opętany; **~·ses·sion** [pə'zeʃn] posiadanie *n*; *fig.* opętanie *n*; **~·ses·sive** [pə'zesɪv] zachłanny; *gr.* dzierżawczy
pos·si|·bil·i·ty [pɒsə'bɪlətɪ] możliwość *f*; **~·ble** ['pɒsəbl] możliwy; **~·bly** ['pɒsəblɪ] możliwie; ***if I ~bly can*** jeżeli tylko mogę; ***I can't ~bly do this*** zupełnie nie mogę tego zrobić
post[1] [pəʊst] **1.** słupek *m*, kołek *m*; **2.** *też* ~ ***up*** *plakat itp.* przyklejać ⟨-leić⟩, wywieszać ⟨-esić⟩; ***be ~ed missing*** *naut., aviat.* zostać ogłoszonym za zaginionego
post[2] [pəʊst] *zwł. Brt.* **1.** poczta *f*; ***by ~*** pocztą; **2.** przesyłać ⟨-słać⟩ pocztą; *list* wrzucać ⟨-cić⟩
post[3] [pəʊst] **1.** miejsce *n*; praca *f*; placówka *f*, posterunek *m*; **2.** *posterunek itp.* wystawiać ⟨-wić⟩; *zwł. Brt.* ⟨od⟩delegować (***to*** do *G*); *mil.* odkomenderowywać ⟨-wać⟩
post... [pəʊst] po..., post...
post·age ['pəʊstɪdʒ] opłata *f* pocztowa, porto *n*; **'~ stamp** znaczek *m* pocztowy
post·al ['pəʊstl] pocztowy; **'~ or·der** *Brt.* przekaz *m* pocztowy; **'~ vote** *pol.* głos *m* oddany drogą pocztową
'post|·bag *zwł. Brt.* torba *f* listonosza; **'~·box** skrzynka *f* pocztowa; **'~·card** kartka *f* pocztowa; *też* ***picture ~card*** widokówka *f*; **'~·code** *Brt.* kod *m* pocztowy
post·er ['pəʊstə] plakat *m*
poste res·tante [pəʊst'restɑːnt] *Brt.* poste restante *n*
pos·te·ri·or [pɒ'stɪərɪə] *hum.* tyłek *m*, sempiterna *f*
pos·ter·i·ty [pɒ'sterətɪ] potomność *f*
post-'free *zwł. Brt.* wolny od opłaty pocztowej
post·grad·u·ate [pəʊst'grædjʊət] podyplomowy (*po licencjacie lub magisterium*)
post·hu·mous ['pɒstjʊməs] pośmiertny
'post|·man (*pl.* ***-men***) *zwł. Brt.* listonosz *m*; **'~·mark** **1.** stempel *m* pocztowy; **2.** ⟨o⟩stemplować (*pieczęcią pocztową*); **'~·mas·ter** naczelnik *m* urzędu pocztowego; ***℘master General*** *jakby*: Minister *m* Poczty; **'~ of·fice** urząd *m* pocztowy; **'~ of·fice box** → ***PO Box***; **~-'paid** *zwł. Am.* wolny od opłaty pocztowej
post·pone [pəʊst'pəʊn] odkładać ⟨odłożyć⟩; przekładać ⟨przełożyć⟩; **~·ment** odłożenie *n*
post·script ['pəʊsskrɪpt] dopisek *m*, postscriptum *n*, PS *n*
pos·ture ['pɒstʃə] **1.** postura *f*, postawa *f*; **2.** *fig.* pozować
post'war powojenny

P

'post·wom·an (*pl.* ***-women***) listonoszka *f*
po·sy ['pəʊzɪ] bukiecik *m*
pot [pɒt] **1.** garnek *m*; dzbanek *m*; słoik *m* (*dżemu*); doniczka *f*; nocnik *m*; *sport*: F puchar *m*; *sl.* (*marihuana*) trawka *f*; **2.** (***-tt-***) *rośliny* przesadzać ⟨-dzić⟩
po·ta·to [pə'teɪtəʊ] (*pl.* ***-toes***) ziemniak *m*, kartofel *m*; *attr.* ziemniaczany, kartoflany; → ***chips, crisps***
'pot·bel·ly duży brzuch *m*
po·ten|·cy ['pəʊtənsɪ] siła *f*, moc *f*; *physiol.* potencja *f*; **~t** ['pəʊtənt] silny, mocny; przekonujący; zdolny do życia płciowego; **~·tial** [pə'tenʃl] **1.** potencjalny; **2.** potencjał *m*, możliwości *pl.*
'pot·hole *mot.* wybój *m*
po·tion ['pəʊʃn] napój *m* (*leczniczy, trujący, magiczny*)
pot·ter¹ ['pɒtə]: **~ *about*** plątać się
pot·ter² ['pɒtə] garncarz *m*; **~·y** ['pɒtərɪ] garncarstwo *n*; wyroby *pl.* garncarskie
pouch [paʊtʃ] torba *f* (*też zo.*); *zo.* kieszeń *f*
poul·tice ['pəʊltɪs] *med.* kataplazm *m*
poul·try ['pəʊltrɪ] drób *m*, ptactwo *n*
pounce [paʊns] **1.** rzucać ⟨-cić⟩ się (***on*** na *A*); **2.** skok *m*
pound¹ [paʊnd] funt *m* (*453,59 g*); **~ (*sterling*)** funt *m* szterling
pound² [paʊnd] schronisko *n* dla zwierząt; (*miejsce odholowywania nieprawidłowo zaparkowanych samochodów*)
pound³ [paʊnd] *v/t.* ⟨u⟩tłuc; walić o (*A*); walić w (*A*); *v/i. serce*: walić; ⟨po⟩biec ciężko
pour [pɔː] *v/t.* nasypywać ⟨-pać⟩; nalewać ⟨-lać⟩; **~ *out*** rozlewać ⟨-lać⟩; *v/i.* lać się; wylewać ⟨-lać⟩ się; *deszcz*: lać
pout [paʊt] **1.** *v/t. usta* odymać ⟨odąć⟩; *v/i.* wydymać usta; **2.** odęte usta *pl.*
pov·er·ty ['pɒvətɪ] ubóstwo *n*
POW [piː əʊ 'dʌbljuː] *skrót*: ***prisoner of war*** jeniec *m* wojenny
pow·der ['paʊdə] **1.** proszek *m*; puder *m*; **2.** ⟨s⟩proszkować; pudrować (się); **'~ puff** puszek *m* do pudru; **'~ room** toaleta *f* damska
pow·er ['paʊə] **1.** moc *f*, siła *f*; potęga *f*; władza *f*; zdolność *f*; *jur.* pełnomocnictwo *n*, uprawnienie *n*; *jur.* moc *f* prawna; *math.* potęga *f*, wykładnik *m* potęgi; *electr.* energia *f*, prąd *m*; ***in* ~** przy władzy; **2.** *tech.* zasilać ⟨-lić⟩; **'~ cut** *electr.* przerwa *f* w dostawie energii elektrycznej; **'~ fail·ure** *electr.* przerwa *f* w dostawie energii elektrycznej; **'~·ful** mocny, silny; potężny; **'~·less** bezsilny; **'~ plant** *zwł. Am.* → ***power station***; **'~ pol·i·tics** *często sg.* polityka *f* siły; **'~ sta·tion** elektrownia *f*
pp *skrót pisany*: ***pages*** str., strony *pl.*
PR [piː 'ɑː] *skrót*: ***public relations*** służba *f* informacyjna
prac·ti|·ca·ble ['præktɪkəbl] możliwy do wykonania; **~·cal** ['præktɪkl] praktyczny; **~·cal 'joke** psota *f*, psikus *m*; **'~·cal·ly** praktycznie
prac·tice ['præktɪs] **1.** praktyka *f*; ćwiczenie *n*; doświadczenie *n*, wprawa *f*; zwyczaj *m*; ***it's common* ~** w powszechnym zwyczaju jest; ***put into* ~** wprowadzić w życie; **2.** *Am.* → ***practise***
prac·tise, *Brt.*, **prac·tice** *Am.* ['præktɪs] *v/t.* ćwiczyć; praktykować; (*w sporcie*) trenować; *zawód* praktykować; **~ *law* (*medicine*)** prowadzić praktykę prawniczą (lekarską); *v/i.* ćwiczyć; praktykować; **'~d** wyćwiczony (***in*** w *L*)
prac·ti·tion·er [præk'tɪʃnə]: ***general* ~** lekarz *m* rejonowy, lekarz *m* domowy
Prague Praga *f*
prai·rie ['preərɪ] preria *f*; *attr.* preriowy
praise [preɪz] **1.** chwalić, wychwalać; **2.** pochwała *f*; **'~·wor·thy** godny pochwały
pram [præm] *zwł. Brt.* F wózek *m* dziecięcy
prance [prɑːns] *koń*: tańczyć; *ludzie*: paradować, pysznić się
prank [præŋk] psikus *m*, figiel *m*
prat·tle ['prætl] F paplać
prawn [prɔːn] *zo.* krewetka *f*
pray [preɪ] modlić się (***to*** do *G*, ***for*** o *A*)
prayer [preə] modlitwa *f*; **'~ book** modlitewnik *m*
preach [priːtʃ] wygłaszać ⟨wygłosić⟩ (kazanie) (*też fig.*); głosić (*też fig.*); **'~·er** kaznodzieja *m*
pre·am·ble [priː'æmbl] preambuła *f*
pre·ar·range [priːə'reɪndʒ] ustalać ⟨-lić⟩ wcześniej
pre·car·i·ous [prɪ'keərɪəs] niebezpieczny, ryzykowny; niepewny
pre·cau·tion [prɪ'kɔːʃn] środek *n* ostrożności; **~·a·ry** [prɪ'kɔːʃnərɪ] zapo-

P

biegawczy, zabezpieczający
pre·cede [priːˈsiːd] poprzedzać ⟨-dzić⟩
pre·ce|·dence [ˈpresɪdəns] pierwszeństwo *n*; **~·dent** precedens *m*
pre·cept [ˈpriːsept] zasada *f*
pre·cinct [ˈpriːsɪŋkt] *zwł. Brt. handlowa* dzielnica *f*, rejon *m* (*ruchu pieszego*); *Am.* okręg *m* (*wyborczy*); *Am.* okręg *m* (*policyjny*); **~s** *pl.* teren *m*
pre·cious [ˈpreʃəs] **1.** *adj.* cenny; drogocenny; *kamień*: szlachetny; **2.** *adv.*: **~ *little*** F bardzo mało
pre·ci·pice [ˈpresɪpɪs] urwisko *n*
pre·cip·i|·tate 1. [prɪˈsɪpɪteɪt] *v/t.* przyspieszać ⟨-szyć⟩; wywracać się; *chem.* wytrącać ⟨-cić⟩; *fig.* popychać ⟨-pchnąć⟩ (***into*** do *G*); *v/i. chem.* wytrącać ⟨-cić⟩ się; **2.** [prɪˈsɪpɪtət] *adj.* pochopny; **3.** [prɪˈsɪpɪteɪt] *chem.* osad *m* wytrącony; **~·ta·tion** [prɪsɪpɪˈteɪʃn] *chem.* wytrącenie *n* (się); strącenie *n* (się); *meteor.* opad *m* atmosferyczny; *fig.* pośpiech *m*; **~·tous** [prɪˈsɪpɪtəs] stromy; *fig.* pochopny
pré·cis [ˈpreɪsiː] (*pl.* ***-cis*** [-siːz]) streszczenie *n*
pre|·cise [prɪˈsaɪs] dokładny; precyzyjny; **~·ci·sion** [prɪˈsɪʒn] dokładność *f*; precyzja *f*
pre·clude [prɪˈkluːd] wykluczać ⟨-czyć⟩
pre·co·cious [prɪˈkəʊʃəs] nad wiek rozwinięty, wcześnie dojrzały
pre·con|·ceived [priːkənˈsiːvd] uprzednio powzięty, z góry powzięty; **~·cep·tion** [priːkənˈsepʃn] uprzedzenie *n*; pogląd *m* przyjęty z góry
pre·cur·sor [priːˈkɜːsə] prekursor *m*, zwiastun *m*
pred·a·to·ry [ˈpredətərɪ] drapieżny
pre·de·ces·sor [ˈpriːdɪsesə] poprzednik *m* (-iczka *f*)
pre·des|·ti·na·tion [priːdestɪˈneɪʃn] predestynacja *f*, przeznaczenie *n*; **~·tined** [priːˈdestɪnd] przeznaczony, skazany (***to*** na *A*)
pre·de·ter·mine [priːdɪˈtɜːmɪn] ustalać ⟨-lić⟩ z góry
pre·dic·a·ment [prɪˈdɪkəmənt] opresja *f*, trudne położenie *n*
pred·i·cate [ˈpredɪkət] *gr.* predykat *m*, orzeczenie *n*; **pre·dic·a·tive** *gr.* [prɪˈdɪkətɪv] predykatywny
pre|·dict [prɪˈdɪkt] przewidywać ⟨-widzieć⟩, prognozować; **~·dic·tion** [prɪˈdɪkʃn] prognoza *f*, przewidywanie *n*
pre·dis|·pose [priːdɪˈspəʊz] usposabiać ⟨-sobić⟩; (***in favo(u)r of*** pozytywnie wobec *G*), sprzyjać; *med.* predysponować (***to*** do *G*); **~·po·si·tion** [priːdɪspəˈzɪʃn]: **~*position to*** skłonność *f* do (*G*), dyspozycja *f* (*G*), predyspozycja *f* do (*G*)
pre·dom·i|·nant [prɪˈdɒmɪnənt] dominujący; **~·nate** [prɪˈdɒmɪneɪt] dominować
pre·em·i·nent [priːˈemɪnənt] wyróżniający się
pre·emp·tive [priːˈemptɪv] uprzedzający; *mil.* wyprzedzający
preen [priːn] czyścić (*pióra*) (*ptaki*); *fig.* stroić się
pre·fab [ˈpriːfæb] F budynek *m* z prefabrykatów; **~·ri·cate** [priːˈfæbrɪkeɪt] prefabrykować; **~*ricated house*** budynek *m* z prefabrykatów
pref·ace [ˈprefɪs] **1.** przedmowa *f* (***to*** do *G*); **2.** *książkę itp.* poprzedzać ⟨-dzić⟩
pre·fect [ˈpriːfekt] *Brt.* (*starszy uczeń odpowiedzialny za młodszych chłopców*)
pre·fer [prɪˈfɜː] (***-rr-***) (***to***) woleć od (*G*), przedkładać nad (*A*), preferować
pref·e|·ra·ble [ˈprefərəbl]: ***be ~rable*** (***to***) być lepszym (niż *N*); **ˈ~·ra·bly** najlepiej, możliwie; **~·rence** [ˈprefərəns] preferencja *f*
pre·fix [ˈpriːfɪks] *gr.* przedrostek *m*, prefiks *m*
preg·nan|·cy [ˈpregnənsɪ] ciąża *f*; **~t** [ˈpregnənt] ciężarna, w ciąży
pre·heat [priːˈhiːt] *piekarnik itp.* wstępnie nagrzewać ⟨-rzać⟩
pre·judge [priːˈdʒʌdʒ] osądzać ⟨-dzić⟩ z góry
prej·u·dice [ˈpredʒʊdɪs] **1.** uprzedzenie *n*; *pozytywne* nastawienie *n*; ***to the ~ of*** ze szkodą dla (*G*); **2.** uprzedzać; **ˈ~d** uprzedzony; ***~d in favo(u)r*** z góry przychylnie nastawiony
pre·lim·i·na·ry [prɪˈlɪmɪnərɪ] **1.** wstępny; **2.** ***preliminaries*** *pl.* wstęp *m*, wprowadzenie *n*
prel·ude [ˈpreljuːd] *mus.* preludium *n*; *fig.* wstęp *m*, zapowiedź *f*
pre·mar·i·tal [priːˈmærɪtl] przedmałżeński
pre·ma·ture [ˈpremətjʊə] przedwczesny

P

pre·med·i|·tat·ed [priːˈmedɪteɪtɪd] rozmyślny, z premedytacją; **~·ta·tion** [priːmedɪˈteɪʃn]: ***with ~tation*** z premedytacją
prem·i·er [ˈpremjə] głowa *f* państwa
prem·i·ere, prem·i·ère [ˈpremɪeə] premiera *f*, prawykonanie *n*
prem·is·es [ˈpremɪsɪz] *pl.* teren *m*, siedziba *f*; lokal *m*; ***on the ~*** na miejscu
pre·mi·um [ˈpriːmjəm] premia *f*; składka *f* ubezpieczeniowa; **ˈ~ (gas·o·line)** *Am. mot.* (benzyna *f*) super
pre·mo·ni·tion [priːməˈnɪʃn] złe przeczucie *n*
pre·oc·cu|·pa·tion [priːɒkjʊˈpeɪʃn] zajęcie *n*, zaaferowanie *n*; **~·pied** [priːˈɒkjʊpaɪd] zajęty, zaaferowany; **~·py** [priːˈɒkjʊpaɪ] *bardzo* zajmować ⟨-jąć⟩
prep [prep] *Brt.* F zadanie *n* domowe
pre·packed [priːˈpækt], **pre·packaged** [priːˈpækɪdʒd] *pożywienie*: zapakowany
pre·paid [priːˈpeɪd] *poczta*: opłacony z góry; **~ envelope** ofrankowana koperta *f*, koperta *f* z opłaconym doręczeniem
prep·a·ra·tion [prepəˈreɪʃn] przygotowanie (***for*** do *G*); *chem.*, *med.* preparat *m*
pre·par·a·to·ry [prɪˈpærətərɪ] przygotowawczy, przygotowujący; **~ school** prywatna szkoła podstawowa
pre·pare [prɪˈpeə] *v/t.* przygotowywać ⟨-ować⟩; *jedzenie, etc.* przyrządzać ⟨-dzić⟩; *v/i.* ***~ for*** przygotowywać ⟨-ować⟩ się do (*G*) *lub* na (*A*), czynić przygotowania do (*G*); **~d** przygotowany
prep·o·si·tion [prepəˈzɪʃn] *gr.* przyimek *m*
pre·pos·sess·ing [priːpəˈzesɪŋ] pociągający, miły
pre·pos·ter·ous [prɪˈpɒstərəs] śmieszny, groteskowy
pre·pro·gram(me) [priːˈprəʊgræm] wstępnie zaprogramowywać ⟨-ować⟩
ˈprep school F → ***preparatory school***
pre·req·ui·site [priːˈrekwɪzɪt] warunek *m* wstępny
pre·rog·a·tive [prɪˈrɒgətɪv] prerogatywa *f*, przywilej *m*
pre·scribe [prɪˈskraɪb] *med.* przepisywać ⟨-sać⟩; zalecać
pre·scrip·tion [prɪˈskrɪpʃn] *med.* recepta *f*; zalecenie *n*; zarządzenie *n*
pres·ence [ˈprezns] obecność *f*; postawa *f*; **~ of ˈmind** przytomność *f* umysłu
pres·ent[1] [ˈpreznt] prezent *m*, podarunek *m*
pre·sent[2] [prɪˈzent] przedstawiać ⟨-wić⟩ (*też theat.*); ⟨za⟩prezentować; ⟨po⟩darować; wręczać ⟨-czyć⟩; *program* ⟨po⟩prowadzić
pres·ent[3] [ˈpreznt] **1.** obecny; aktualny; *rok, etc.*: bieżący; teraźniejszy; ***~ tense*** czas *m* teraźniejszy; **2.** teraźniejszość *f*; *gr.* czas *m* teraźniejszy; ***at ~*** obecnie; ***for the ~*** na razie
pre·sen·ta·tion [prezənˈteɪʃn] prezentacja *f*; wręczenie *n*; podarowanie *n*; przedstawienie *n*; wystąpienie *n*; prowadzenie *n* (*programu radiowego lub telewizyjnego*)
pres·ent-ˈday obecny, współczesny
pre·sent·er [prɪˈzentə] *radio, TV itp.*: prezenter(ka *f*) *m*
pre·sen·ti·ment [prɪˈzentɪmənt] (złe) przeczucie *n*
pres·ent·ly [ˈprezntlɪ] wkrótce; *zwł. Am.* obecnie
pres·er·va·tion [prezəˈveɪʃn] zachowanie *n*; konserwacja *f*; zabezpieczenie *n*; ochrona *f*
pre·ser·va·tive [prɪˈzɜːvətɪv] środek *m* konserwujący; ⚠ *nie* ***prezerwatywa***
pre·serve [prɪˈzɜːv] **1.** zachowywać ⟨-ować⟩; ⟨o⟩chronić; ⟨za⟩konserwować; **2.** rezerwat *m*; teren *m* myśliwski; *fig.* dziedzina *f*; *zw.* **~s** *pl.* przetwory *pl.*
pre·side [prɪˈzaɪd] przewodniczyć
pres·i|·den·cy [ˈprezɪdənsɪ] *pol.* prezydentura *f*; **~·dent** [ˈprezɪdənt] prezydent *m*; przewodniczący *m* (-ca *f*)
press [pres] **1.** *v/t.* naciskać ⟨-snąć⟩; przyciskać ⟨-snąć⟩; wciskać ⟨-snąć⟩; ściskać ⟨-snąć⟩; *owoce* wyciskać ⟨-snąć⟩; ⟨u⟩prasować; naciskać na (*A*); wywierać ⟨wywrzeć⟩ presję na (*A*); *v/i.* naciskać ⟨-nąć⟩; *czas*: naglić; wywierać ⟨wywrzeć⟩ presję; ***~ for*** nalegać na (*A*); ***~ on*** *dalej* podążać; **2.** nacisk *m* (*też fig.*); prasa *f* (*gazety itp.*); prasa *f* (*drukarska, do wina*); ***printing ~*** prasa *f* drukarska; **ˈ~ a·gen·cy** agencja *f* prasowa; **ˈ~ box** trybuna *f* dla prasy; **ˈ~·ing** pilny, naglący; **ˈ~ stud** *Brt.* (*zapięcie*) zatrzask *m*; **ˈ~-up** *zwł. Brt.* pompka *f*; ***do ten ~-ups*** zrobić dziesięć pompek

P

pres·sure ['preʃə] *phys., tech. itp.* ciśnienie *n* (*też fig.*); nacisk *m*; presja *f*; napięcie *n*; '**~ cook·er** szybkowar *m*

pres·tige [pre'stiːʒ] prestiż *m*, powaga *f*

pre|·su·ma·bly [prɪ'zjuːməblɪ] przypuszczalnie; **~·sume** [prɪ'zjuːm] *v/t.* mniemać, przypuszczać; *niewinność* domniemywać ⟨-mać⟩; *v/i.* ośmielać ⟨-lić⟩ się (***to do s.th.*** robić coś); **~*sume on*** wykorzystywać ⟨-tać⟩ niewłaściwie

pre·sump|·tion [prɪ'zʌmpʃn] przypuszczenie *n*, mniemanie *n*; domniemanie *n*; czelność *f*, arogancja *f*; **~·tu·ous** [prɪ'zʌmptʃʊəs] czelny, arogancki

pre·sup|·pose [priːsə'pəʊz] zakładać; **~·po·si·tion** [priːsʌpə'zɪʃn] założenie *n*

pre·tence *Brt.*, **pre·tense** *Am.* [prɪ'tens] pozór *m*, pretekst *m*; pretensja *f* (***to*** do *G*)

pre·tend [prɪ'tend] udawać ⟨udać⟩; rościć pretensje (***to*** do do *G*); **~·ed** udawany

pre·ten·sion [prɪ'tenʃn] pretensja *f* (***to*** do *G*); pretensjonalność *f*

pre·ter·it(e) ['pretərɪt] *gr.* czas *m* przeszły

pre·text ['priːtekst] pretekst *m*

pret·ty ['prɪtɪ] **1.** (***-ier, -iest***) ładny; **2.** *adv.* F całkiem, dość

pret·zel ['pretsl] precel *m*

pre·vail [prɪ'veɪl] zwyciężać ⟨-żyć⟩ (***over, against*** nad *D*); zapanowywać ⟨-ować⟩; przeważać; **~·ing** przeważający

pre|·vent [prɪ'vent] zapobiegać ⟨-biec⟩; uniemożliwiać ⟨-wić⟩; nie dawać możności; **~·ven·tion** [prɪ'venʃn] zapobieganie *n*; uniemożliwienie *n*; **~·ven·tive** [prɪ'ventɪv] zapobiegawczy; prewencyjny

pre·view ['priːvjuː] *film, TV*: pokaz *m* przedpremierowy

pre·vi·ous ['priːvjəs] poprzedni; uprzedni; **~ *to*** przed (*I*); '**~·ly** uprzednio

pre-war [priː'wɔː] przedwojenny

prey [preɪ] **1.** zdobycz *f*, łup *m*; ofiara *f*; ***of ~*** drapieżny; ***be easy ~ for*** *lub* ***to*** stanowić łatwy łup dla (*G*); **2. ~ *on*** *zo.* polować na (*A*); *fig.* dręczyć (*A*)

price [praɪs] **1.** cena *f*; **2.** ustalać ⟨-lić⟩ cenę (*G*), wyceniać ⟨-nić⟩ (***at*** na *L*); '**~·less** bezcenny; '**~tag** metka *f* (*z ceną*)

prick [prɪk] **1.** ukłucie *n*; V kutas *m*; **~*s*** *pl.* ***of conscience*** wyrzuty *pl.* sumienia; **2.** *v/t.* ⟨po-, na-, u⟩kłuć; ***her conscience ~ed her*** ⟨po⟩czuła wyrzuty sumienia; **~ *up one's ears*** nadstawiać ⟨-wić⟩ uszu

prick|·le ['prɪkl] kolec *m*; uczucie *n* kłucia; '**~·ly** (***-ier, -iest***) kolczasty, kłujący

pride [praɪd] **1.** duma *f*; pycha *f*; ***take*** (***a***) **~ *in*** szczycić się (*I*); **2. ~ *o.s. on*** szczycić się (*I*)

priest [priːst] ksiądz *m*, duchowny *m*

prig [prɪg] bigot *m*, świętoszek *m*; pedant *m*; '**~·gish** świętoszkowaty

prim [prɪm] (***-mm-***) pruderyjny, sztywny

pri·mae·val *zwł. Brt.* [praɪ'miːvl] → ***primeval***

pri·ma·ri·ly ['praɪmərəlɪ] przede wszystkim

pri·ma·ry ['praɪmərɪ] **1.** podstawowy; główny; pierwotny; **2.** *Am. pol.* wybory *pl.* wstępne; '**~ school** *Brt.* szkoła *f* podstawowa

prime [praɪm] **1.** *math.* liczba *f* pierwsza; *fig.* rozkwit *m*; ***in the ~ of life*** w kwiecie wieku; ***be past one's ~*** mieć już za sobą najlepsze lata; **2.** *adj.* pierwszy, początkowy; najważniejszy; główny; wyborowy, pierwszorzędny; **3.** *v/t.* *ścianę* ⟨za⟩gruntować; ⟨po⟩instruować, przygotowywać ⟨-ować⟩; **~ 'min·is·ter** premier *m*; **~ 'num·ber** *math.* liczba *f* pierwsza

prim·er ['praɪmə] elementarz *m*; środek *m* do gruntowania

'**prime time** *zwł. Am.* okres *m* największej oglądalności

pri·me·val [praɪ'miːvl] odwieczny; pierwotny; pradawny

prim·i·tive ['prɪmɪtɪv] prymitywny; pierwotny

prim·rose ['prɪmrəʊz] *bot.* pierwiosnek *m*, prymula *f*

prince [prɪns] książę *m*; **prin·cess** [prɪn'ses], (*przed nazwiskiem*) ['prɪnses] księżniczka *f*; księżna *f*

prin·ci·pal ['prɪnsəpl] **1.** główny; zasadniczy; ⚠ *nie* **pryncypialny**; **2.** *Am.* *szkoła*: dyrektor(ka *f*) *m*, kierownik *m* (-iczka *f*); *theat.* odtwórca *m* (-czyni *f*) głównej roli; *mus.* solista *m* (-tka *f*); *econ.* suma *f* nominalna

prin·ci·pal·i·ty [prɪnsɪ'pælətɪ] księstwo *n*

prin·ci·ple ['prɪnsəpl] zasada *f*; ***on ~*** z zasady

print [prɪnt] **1.** *print.* druk *m*; odcisk *m* (*palca*); *phot.* odbitka *f*; rycina *f*; tkanina *f* drukowana; ***in ~*** w druku; ***out of ~*** wyczerpany; **2.** *v/i.* drukować; *v/t.* ⟨wy-, za⟩drukować; odciskać ⟨-snąć⟩; ⟨na⟩pisać drukowanymi literami; *fig.* zapadać (***on*** w *A*); *też* ***~ off*** *phot.* odbijać ⟨-bić⟩; ***~ out*** *komp.* wydrukowywać ⟨-ować⟩; **'~ed mat·ter** druki *pl.* (*przesyłane pocztą*)
'print·er drukarz *m*; drukarka *f*; ***~'s error*** błąd *m* drukarski; ***~'s ink*** farba *f* drukarska
print·ing ['prɪntɪŋ] *print.* drukowanie *n*; **'~ ink** farba *f* drukarska; **'~ press** prasa *f* drukarska
'print·out *komp.* wydruk *m*
pri·or ['praɪə] wcześniejszy; uprzedni; priorytetowy; **~·i·ty** [praɪ'ɒrɪtɪ] priorytet *f*; *mot.* pierwszeństwo *n*
prise [praɪz] *zwł. Brt.* → ***prize²***
pris·m ['prɪzəm] pryzmat *m*; graniastosłup *m*
pris·on ['prɪzn] więzienie *n*; **'~·er** więzień *m* (-ęźniarka *f*); ***hold ~er, keep ~er*** więzić (*G*); ***take ~er*** uwięzić (*G*)
priv·a·cy ['prɪvəsɪ] prywatność *f*; sfera *f* osobista; odosobnienie *n*
pri·vate ['praɪvɪt] **1.** prywatny; odosobniony; *życie itp.*: osobisty; skryty, ukryty; ***~ parts*** *pl.* przyrodzenie *n*; **2.** *med.* szeregowy; ***in ~*** w cztery oczy, na osobności
pri·va·tion [praɪ'veɪʃn] prywacja *f*, wyrzeczenie *n*
priv·i·lege ['prɪvɪlɪdʒ] przywilej *m*; zaszczyt *m*; **'~d** uprzywilejowany
priv·y ['prɪvɪ] (***-ier, -iest***): ***be ~ to*** być wtajemniczonym w (*A*)
prize¹ [praɪz] **1.** nagroda *f*; premia *f*; wygrana *f*; **2.** nagrodzony; pierwszej jakości; **3.** wysoko cenić
prize² [praɪz]: ***~ open*** wyważać ⟨-żyć⟩
'prize·win·ner zdobywca *m* (-czyni *f*) pierwszej nagrody
pro¹ [prəʊ] F (*pl.* ***-s***) profesjonalista *m* (-tka *f*)
pro² [prəʊ] (*pl.* ***-s***): ***the ~s and cons*** *pl.* za i przeciw
prob|·a·bil·i·ty [prɒbə'bɪlətɪ] prawdopodobieństwo *n*; ***in all ~ability*** według wszelkiego prawdopodobieństwa; **~·a·ble** ['prɒbəbl] prawdopodobny; **'~·a·bly** prawdopodobnie
pro·ba·tion [prə'beɪʃn] próba *f*, okres *m* próbny, staż *m*; *jur.* dozór *m* kuratora sądowego; **~ of·fi·cer** *jur.* kurator *m* sądowy
probe [prəʊb] **1.** *med.*, *tech.* sonda *f*; *fig.* dochodzenie *n* (***into*** w *A*); ⚠ *nie* ***próba***; **2.** sondować; ⟨z⟩badać (*dokładnie*); ⚠ *nie* ***próbować***
prob·lem ['prɒbləm] problem *m*, zagadnienie *n*; *math. itp.* zadanie *n*; **~·at·ic** [prɒblə'mætɪk] (***-ally***); **~·at·i·cal** problematyczny
pro·ce·dure [prə'siːdʒə] procedura *f*
pro·ceed [prə'siːd] iść ⟨pójść⟩ dalej; podążać; postępować; przystępować ⟨-tąpić⟩ (***to*** do *G*); *fig.* kontynuować; ***~ from*** wynikać ⟨-knąć⟩, wypływać ⟨-łynąć⟩; ***~ to do s.th.*** przystępować ⟨-tąpić⟩ do robienia czegoś; **~·ing** *jur.* postępowanie *n* sądowe; **~·ings** *pl.* obrady *pl.*; sprawozdanie *n*; *jur.* proces *m* sądowy; ***start*** *lub* ***take*** (***legal***) ***~ings against*** *jur.* wszczynać ⟨-cząć⟩ postępowanie sądowe
pro·ceeds ['prəʊsiːdz] *pl.* wpływy *pl.*, przychód *m*
pro·cess ['prəʊses] **1.** proces *m*; tok *m*; *jur.* postępowanie *n* sądowe; ***in the ~*** w toku, w trakcie; ***be in ~*** toczyć się, zachodzić; ***in the ~ of construction*** w trakcie budowy, w budowie; **2.** *tech.* przetwarzać ⟨-worzyć⟩; *film* wywoływać ⟨-łać⟩
pro·ces·sion [prə'seʃn] procesja *f*; pochód *m*
pro·ces·sor ['prəʊsesə] *komp.* procesor *m*; procesor *m* tekstu; robot *m* kuchenny
pro·claim [prə'kleɪm] proklamować, ogłaszać ⟨-łosić⟩
proc·la·ma·tion [prɒklə'meɪʃn] proklamacja *f*, obwieszczenie *n*
pro·cure [prə'kjʊə] uzyskiwać ⟨-kać⟩, zdobywać ⟨-być⟩; stręczyć (*do nierządu*)
prod [prɒd] **1.** (***-dd-***) szturchać ⟨-chnąć⟩; dźgać ⟨-gnąć⟩, ⟨u⟩kłuć; pobudzać ⟨-dzić⟩ (***into*** do *G*); **2.** szturchnięcie *n*; dźgnięcie *n*
prod·i·gal ['prɒdɪgl] **1.** marnotrawny; **2.** F hulaka *m*
pro·di·gious [prə'dɪdʒəs] znakomity; monumentalny
prod·i·gy ['prɒdɪdʒɪ] cud *m*; ***child ~*** cudowne dziecko *n*

P

pro·duce[1] [prə'djuːs] tworzyć; *econ.* ⟨wy⟩produkować; wytwarzać ⟨-worzyć⟩; przedstawiać ⟨-wić⟩, okazywać ⟨-zać⟩ (***from*** z *G*); *econ. zysk itp.* przynosić ⟨-nieść⟩; być producentem (*filmu*); *sztukę* wystawiać ⟨-wić⟩; *fig.* dawać ⟨dać⟩

prod·uce[2] ['prɒdjuːs] *zwł. rolne* produkty *pl.*, płody *pl.*, wyroby *pl.*

pro·duc·er [prə'djuːsə] producent(ka *f*) *m*, wytwórca *m*; *film, TV*: producent *m*; *theat.* reżyser *m*

prod·uct ['prɒdʌkt] produkt *m*, wyrób *m*; iloczyn *m*

pro·duc|·tion [prə'dʌkʃn] *econ.* produkcja *f*; wytwórstwo *n*, wytwarzanie *n*; okazanie *n*; *theat.* wystawianie *n*, inscenizacja *f*; **~·tive** [prə'dʌktɪv] produktywny (*też fig.*); produkcyjny; owocny; *fig.* twórczy; **~·tiv·i·ty** [prɒdʌk'tɪvətɪ] produktywność *f*

prof [prɒf] F profesor *m*

pro|·fa·na·tion [prɒfə'neɪʃn] profanacja *f*, zbezczeszczenie *n*; **~·fane** [prə'feɪn] **1.** świecki; bluźnierczy; **2.** ⟨s⟩profanować; **~·fan·i·ty** [prə'fænətɪ]: ***profanities*** *pl.* bluźnierstwa *pl.*

pro·fess [prə'fes] wyrażać ⟨-razić⟩; utrzymywać; podawać się (***to be*** za); wyznawać; **~ed** [prə'fest] zdeklarowany, otwarty

pro·fes|·sion [prə'feʃn] zawód *m* (*zwł. lekarza, prawnika itp.*); ***the ~sions*** *pl.* wolne zawody *pl.*; **~·sion·al** [prə'feʃənl] **1.** profesjonalny, fachowy; zawodowy; **2.** profesjonalista *m* (-tka *f*); zawodowiec *m*; zawodowy sportowiec *m*; **~·sor** [prə'fesə] profesor *m*

P

pro·fi·cien|·cy [prə'fɪʃnsɪ] biegłość *f*; wprawa *f*; **~t** [prə'fɪʃnt] biegły; wprawny

pro·file ['prəʊfaɪl] profil *m*; zarys *m*; notka *f*, opis *m*

prof|·it ['prɒfɪt] **1.** zysk *m*, profit *m*; korzyść *f*; **2.** ***~it by, ~it from*** odnosić ⟨-nieść⟩ korzyść; **~·i·ta·ble** zyskowny, dochodowy; korzystny, pożyteczny; **~·i·teer** *pej.* [prɒfɪ'tɪə] spekulant *m*, paskarz *m*; '**~·it shar·ing** udział *m* w zyskach

prof·li·gate ['prɒflɪgət] marnotrawny, rozrzutny

pro·found [prə'faʊnd] głęboki

pro|·fuse [prə'fjuːs] obfity; *fig.* wylewny; **~·fu·sion** [prə'fjuːʒn] obfitość *f*; wylewność *f*; ***in ~fusion*** w obfitości

prog·e·ny ['prɒdʒənɪ] potomstwo *n*

prog·no·sis [prɒg'nəʊsɪs] *med.* (*pl.* ***-ses*** [-siːz]) prognoza *f*

pro·gram ['prəʊgræm] **1.** *komp.* program *m*; *Am.* → ***programme***; **2.** (***-mm-***) *komp.* ⟨za⟩programować; *Am.* → ***programme*** 2; '**~·er** → ***programmer***

pro·gramme *Brt.*; **pro·gram** *Am.* ['prəʊgræm] **1.** program *m*; transmisja *f* (*radiowa lub telewizyjna*); **2.** ⟨za⟩programować; ⟨za⟩planować; '**pro·gram·mer** *komp.* programista *m*

pro|·gress **1.** ['prəʊgres] postęp *m*; ***make slow ~gress*** wolno się rozwijać; ***be in ~gress*** być w toku; **2.** [prəʊ'gres] iść ⟨pójść⟩ dalej; ⟨z⟩robić postępy; **~·gres·sive** [prəʊ'gresɪv] postępowy, progresywny

pro|·hib·it [prə'hɪbɪt] zabraniać ⟨-ronić⟩, zakazywać ⟨-zać⟩; **~·hi·bi·tion** [prəʊɪ'bɪʃn] zakaz *m*; prohibicja *f*; **~·hib·i·tive** [prə'hɪbətɪv] nadmierny, przesadny

proj·ect[1] ['prɒdʒekt] projekt *m*, plan *m*; przedsięwzięcie *n*

pro·ject[2] [prə'dʒekt] *v/i.* wystawać, sterczeć; *v/t.* ⟨za⟩projektować, ⟨za⟩planować, prognozować; wyrzucać ⟨-cić⟩, wysuwać ⟨-sunąć⟩; wyświetlać ⟨-lić⟩

pro·jec·tile [prə'dʒektaɪl] pocisk *m*

pro·jec|·tion [prə'dʒekʃn] prognoza *f*, szacowanie *n*; projekcja *f*; występ *m* (*skalny, budowlany*); **~·tor** [prə'dʒektə] projektor *m*

pro·le·tar·i·an [prəʊlɪ'teərɪən] **1.** proletariacki, robotniczy; **2.** proletariusz (ka *f*) *m*

pro·lif·ic [prə'lɪfɪk] (***~ally***) płodny

pro·logue *zwł. Brt.*, **pro·log** *Am.* ['prəʊlɒg] prolog *m*

pro·long [prəʊ'lɒŋ] przedłużać ⟨-żyć⟩

prom·e·nade [prɒmə'nɑːd] **1.** *nadmorska* promenada *f*; **2.** przechadzać się

prom·i·nent ['prɒmɪnənt] wybitny, znakomity; prominentny

pro·mis·cu·ous [prə'mɪskjʊəs] rozwiązły

prom|·ise ['prɒmɪs] **1.** obietnica *f*, przyrzeczenie *n*; *fig.* zapowiedź *f*; **2.** obiecywać ⟨-cać⟩; '**~·is·ing** obiecujący

prom·on·to·ry ['prɒməntrɪ] przylądek *m*, cypel *m*
pro|·mote [prə'məʊt] *też* (*w wojsku, szkole*) promować, awansować; *produkt itp.* ⟨wy⟩promować; popierać ⟨-rzeć⟩; sponsorować; **~·mot·er** [prə'məʊtə] sponsor *m*; rzecznik *m* (-niczka *f*); **~·motion** [prə'məʊʃn] promocja *f*; awans *m*
prompt [prɒmpt] **1.** wywoływać ⟨-łać⟩, prowadzić do (*G*); zachęcać ⟨-cić⟩ (***to do*** do zrobienia *G*); *theat.* podpowiadać ⟨-wiedzieć⟩, suflerować; **2.** bezzwłoczny, niezwłoczny; punktualny, terminowy; '**~·er** sufler(ka *f*) *m*
prone [prəʊn] (**-r, -st**) leżący na brzuchu *lub* twarzą w dół; ***be ~ to*** *fig.* być skłonnym do (*G*), być podatnym na (*A*)
prong [prɒŋ] ząb *m* (*widelca, wideł*)
pro·noun ['prəʊnaʊn] *gr.* zaimek *m*
pro·nounce [prə'naʊns] wymawiać ⟨-mówić⟩; wypowiadać ⟨-wiedzieć⟩ się (***on*** o *L*); *jur. wyrok itp.* ogłaszać ⟨-łosić⟩
pron·to ['prɒntəʊ] F szybko, rączo
pro·nun·ci·a·tion [prənʌnsɪ'eɪʃn] wymowa *f*
proof [pruːf] **1.** dowód *m*, dowody *pl.*; próba *f*, sprawdzenie *n*; *print.* korekta *f*; *print., phot.* odbitka *f* próbna; stopień *m* zawartości alkoholu; **2.** *adj. w złoż.* odporny; → ***heatproof, soundproof, waterproof***; ***be ~ against*** być zabezpieczonym przed (*I*); **3.** ⟨za⟩impregnować; **~·read** ['pruːfriːd] (**-read** [-red]) ⟨z⟩robić korektę; '**~·read·er** korektor(ka *f*) *m*
prop [prɒp] **1.** podpora *f* (*też fig.*); **2.** (**-pp-**) *też* **~ up** podpierać ⟨-deprzeć⟩; *się lub coś* opierać (***against*** o *A*)
prop·a|·gate ['prɒpəgeɪt] *biol.* rozmnażać ⟨-nożyć⟩ (się); propagować, rozprzestrzeniać ⟨-nić⟩; **~·ga·tion** [prɒpə'geɪʃn] rozmnażanie *n*, propagacja *f*; propagowanie *n*
pro·pel [prə'pel] (**-ll-**) napędzać ⟨-dzić⟩, wprawiać ⟨-wić⟩ w ruch; **~·lant, ~·lent** gaz *m* pędny (*w aerozolu itp.*); paliwo *n* silnikowe, materiał *m* napędowy; **~·ler** *aviat.* śmigło *n*; *naut.* śruba *f* napędowa; **~·ling 'pen·cil** ołówek *m* automatyczny
pro·pen·si·ty [prə'pensətɪ] *fig.* skłonność *f*
prop·er ['prɒpə] właściwy, odpowiedni; stosowny; *zwł. Brt.* F straszny, całkowity; **~ 'name** imię *n* własne; **~ 'noun** rzeczownik *m* własny
prop·er·ty ['prɒpətɪ] własność *f*; nieruchomość *f*, posiadłość *f*; właściwość *f*, cecha *f*
proph|·e·cy ['prɒfɪsɪ] proroctwo *n*; **~·e·sy** ['prɒfɪsaɪ] ⟨wy⟩prorokować; **~·et** ['prɒfɪt] prorok *m*
pro·por·tion [prə'pɔːʃn] **1.** proporcja *f* (*też math.*); stosunek *m*; **~s** wielkość *f*, rozmiary *pl.*; udział *m*, część *f*, odsetek *m*; proporcjonalność *f*; ***in ~ to*** w proporcji do (*G*); **2.** (***to***) nadawać ⟨-dać⟩ *właściwe* proporcje (*D*); ⟨po⟩dzielić *właściwie*; **~·al** [prə'pɔːʃənl] stosunkowy; → **~·ate** [prə'pɔːʃnət] proporcjonalny (***to*** do *G*)
pro·pos|·al [prə'pəʊzl] propozycja *f*; oświadczyny *pl.*; **~e** [prə'pəʊz] *v/t.* ⟨za⟩proponować; przedstawiać ⟨-wić⟩; zamierzać (***to do s.th.*** coś zrobić); *toast itp.* wznosić ⟨-nieść⟩ (***to*** do *G*); ***~e s.o.'s health*** ⟨wy⟩pić za czyjeś zdrowie; *v/i.* ***~e to*** oświadczać ⟨-czyć⟩ się (*D*); **prop·o·si·tion** [prɒpə'zɪʃn] propozycja *f*; projekt *m*; *math.* twierdzenie *n*
pro·pri·e|·ta·ry [prə'praɪətərɪ] *econ.* prawnie zastrzeżony; opatentowany; *fig.* władczy; **~·tor** [prə'praɪətə] posiadacz *m*, właściciel *m*; **~·tress** [prə'praɪətrɪs] posiadaczka *f*, właścicielka *f*
pro·pri·e·ty [prə'praɪətɪ] stosowność *f*; właściwość *f*
pro·pul·sion [prə'pʌlʃn] *tech.* napęd *m*
pro·sa·ic [prəʊ'zeɪɪk] (***~ally***) prozaiczny; przyziemny
prose [prəʊz] proza *f*
pros·e|·cute ['prɒsɪkjuːt] *jur.* ścigać sądownie (***for*** za *A*), zaskarżać ⟨-żyć⟩; **~·cu·tion** *jur.* [prɒsɪ'kjuːʃn] dochodzenie *n* sądowe; ***the ~cution*** oskarżenie *n*, strona *f* oskarżająca; **~·cu·tor** *jur.* ['prɒsɪkjuːtə] *też* ***public ~cutor*** oskarżyciel *m* (*publiczny*)
pros·pect **1.** ['prɒspekt] widok *m* (*też fig.*), perspektywa *f* (*też fig.*); *econ.* potencjalny klient *m*; ⚠ *nie* ***prospekt***; **2.** [prə'spekt]: **~ for** (*w górnictwie*) prowadzić poszukiwania
pro·spec·tive [prə'spektɪv] potencjalny, ewentualny
pro·spec·tus [prə'spektəs] (*pl.* **-tuses**)

P

prospekt *m*, informator *m* (*o uczelni itp.*)

pros·per ['prɒspə] prosperować, pomyślnie się rozwijać; **~·i·ty** [prɒ'sperətɪ] dobra passa *f*, rozkwit *m*; dobra koniunktura *f*; **~·ous** ['prɒspərəs] rozkwitający, dobrze prosperujący

pros·ti·tute ['prɒstɪtjuːt] prostytutka *f*; ***male ~*** męska prostytutka *f*

pros|·trate 1. ['prɒstreɪt] leżący (*twarzą w dół*); *fig.* załamany; ***~trate with grief*** pogrążony w smutku; **2.** [prɒ'streɪt] padać ⟨paść⟩ na twarz (***before*** przed *I*); *fig.* załamywać ⟨-mać⟩się; **~·tra·tion** [prɒ'streɪʃn] padnięcie *n* na twarz; *fig.* załamanie *n* się

pros·y ['prəʊzɪ] (***-ier, -iest***) przegadany

pro·tag·o·nist [prəʊ'tægənɪst] bojownik *m* (***of*** o *A*); *theat.* bohater(ka *f*) *m*

pro·tect [prə'tekt] ochraniać ⟨ochronić⟩, chronić (***from, against*** przed *I*)

pro·tec·tion [prə'tekʃn] ochrona *f*; F opłata *f* za ochronę; ⚠ *nie* ***protekcja***; **~ mon·ey** opłata *f* za ochronę; **~ racket** F wyłudzanie *n* pieniędzy za ochronę

pro·tec·tive [prə'tektɪv] ochronny; dbały, troskliwy; **~ 'cloth·ing** ubranie *n* ochronne; **~ 'cus·to·dy** *jur.* areszt *m* zapobiegawczy; **~ 'du·ty, ~ 'tar·iff** *econ.* cła *pl.* ochronne

pro·tec·tor [prə'tektə] obrońca *m*; ochraniacz *m*; **~·ate** [prə'tektərət] protektorat *m*

pro·test 1. ['prəʊtest] protest *m*; sprzeciw *m*; **2.** [prə'test] *v/i.* ⟨za⟩protestować (***against*** przeciw *D*); *v/t. Am.* protestować przeciw (*D*); zapewniać o (*L*)

Prot·es·tant ['prɒtɪstənt] **1.** protestancki; **2.** protestant(ka *f*) *m*

prot·es·ta·tion [prɒte'steɪʃn] zapewnienie *n*; protest *m* (***against*** przeciw *D*)

pro·to·col ['prəʊtəkɒl] protokół *m*

pro·to·type ['prəʊtətaɪp] prototyp *m*

pro·tract [prə'trækt] przedłużać się, przewlekać się

pro|·trude [prə'truːd] wystawać, sterczeć (***from*** z *G*); **~'trud·ing** wystający, sterczący

proud [praʊd] dumny (***of*** z *G*)

prove [pruːv] (***proved, proved*** *lub zwł. Am.* ***proven***) *v/t.* udowadniać ⟨-wodnić⟩, wykazywać ⟨-zać⟩; *v/i.* **~** (***to be***) okazywać ⟨-zać⟩ się (*I*); **prov·en** ['pruːvən] **1.** *zwł. Am. p.p. od* ***prove***; **2.** udowodniony

prov·erb ['prɒvɜːb] przysłowie *n*

pro·vide [prə'vaɪd] *v/t.* dostarczać ⟨-czyć⟩ (***with*** *A*), zaopatrywać ⟨-trzyć⟩ (***with*** w *A*); postanawiać ⟨-nowić⟩ (***that*** że); *v/i.* **~ *against*** zabezpieczać ⟨-czyć⟩ się przeciwko (*I*); *prawo* zakazywać ⟨-zać⟩; **~ *for*** utrzymywać ⟨-mać⟩; przewidywać; uwzględniać ⟨-nić⟩; **pro'vid·ed**: ***~ed*** (***that***) pod warunkiem(, że), z zastrzeżeniem(, że)

prov·i·dent ['prɒvɪdənt] zapobiegliwy

pro·vid·er [prə'vaɪdə] dostawca *m*

prov·ince ['prɒvɪns] prowincja *f*; *fig.* kompetencja *f*; **pro·vin·cial** [prə'vɪnʃl] **1.** prowincjonalny; **2.** *pej.* prowincjusz(ka *f*) *m*

pro·vi·sion [prə'vɪʒn] zaopatrzenie *n* (***of*** w *A*); zabezpieczenie *n* się (***for*** na wypadek *G*, ***against*** przeciwko *D*); postanowienie *n*, klauzula *f*; ***with the ~ that*** pod warunkiem, że; ***~s*** *pl.* prowiant *m*, żywność *f*; ⚠ *nie* ***prowizja***; **~·al** [prə'vɪʒənl] tymczasowy, prowizoryczny

pro·vi·so [prə'vaɪzəʊ] (*pl.* ***-soes***) zastrzeżenie *n*, warunek *m*; ***with the ~ that*** pod warunkiem, że

prov·o·ca·tion [prɒvə'keɪʃn] prowokacja *f*; **pro·voc·a·tive** [prə'vɒkətɪv] prowokacyjny; wyzywający

pro·voke [prə'vəʊk] ⟨s⟩prowokować; wywoływać ⟨-łać⟩, ⟨s⟩powodować

prov·ost ['prɒvəst] rektor *m* (*w niektórych uczelniach*); *Szkoc.* burmistrz *m*

prowl [praʊl] **1.** *v/i. też* **~ *about,* ~ *around*** *banda*: grasować, buszować; *v/t.* grasować po (*L*), buszować po (*L*); **2.** grasowanie *n*, buszowanie *n*; **'~ car** *Am.* radiowóz *m*, wóz *m* patrolowy

prox·im·i·ty [prɒk'sɪmətɪ] bliskość *f*

prox·y ['prɒksɪ] pełnomocnictwo *n*, zastępstwo *n*; pełnomocnik *m*, zastępca *m*; ***by ~*** przez pełnomocnika

prude [pruːd]: ***be a ~*** być pruderyjnym

pru|·dence ['pruːdns] roztropność *f*, rozsądek *m*; **'~·dent** roztropny, rozsądny

'prud·ish pruderyjny

prune[1] [pruːn] *drzewa itp.* przycinać ⟨-ciąć⟩

prune[2] [pruːn] suszona śliwka *f*

P

pry[1] [praɪ] myszkować, wtrącać się; **~ *about*** węszyć wkoło; **~ *into*** wtykać nos w (*A*)
pry[2] [praɪ] *zwł. Am.* → ***prize***[2]
PS [piː 'es] *skrót*: ***postscript*** PS, postscriptum *n*, dopisek *m*
psalm [sɑːm] psalm *m*
pseu·do·nym ['sjuːdənɪm] pseudonim *m*, przydomek *m*
psy·chi·a|·trist [saɪ'kaɪətrɪst] psychiatra *m*; **~·try** [saɪ'kaɪətrɪ] psychiatria *f*
psy|·cho·log·i·cal [saɪkə'lɒdʒɪkl] psychologiczny; **~·chol·o·gist** [saɪ'kɒlədʒɪst] psycholog *m*; **~·chol·o·gy** [saɪ'kɒlədʒɪ] psychologia *f*; **~·cho·so·mat·ic** [saɪkəʊsəʊ'mætɪk] psychosomatyczny
pt *skrót pisany*: ***part*** cz., część *f*; ***pint*** kwarta *f* (*ok. 1/2 l*); *zw.* ***Pt***, *skrót*: ***port*** port *m*
PT [piː 'tiː] *zwł. Brt. skrót*: ***physical training*** wf., wychowanie *n* fizyczne
PTO, pto [piː tiː 'əʊ] *skrót*: ***please turn over*** verte
pub [pʌb] *Brt.* pub *m*
pu·ber·ty ['pjuːbətɪ] okres *m* dojrzewania, pokwitanie *n*
pu·bic ['pjuːbɪk] *anat.* łonowy; **~ 'bone** kość *f* łonowa; **~ 'hair** owłosienie *n* łonowe
pub·lic ['pʌblɪk] **1.** publiczny, ogólny, powszechny; *skandal*: jawny; **2.** ogół *m*; społeczeństwo *n*; publiczność *f*; ***in ~*** publicznie
pub·li·ca·tion [pʌblɪ'keɪʃn] publikacja *f*, wydanie *n*; opublikowanie *n*
pub·lic| con've·ni·ence *Brt.* toaleta *f* publiczna; **~ 'health** zdrowie *n* społeczeństwa; **~ 'hol·i·day** święto *n* państwowe; **~ 'house** *Brt.* → ***pub***
pub·lic·i·ty [pʌb'lɪsətɪ] reklama *f*; rozgłos *m*
pub·lic| 'li·bra·ry biblioteka *f* publiczna; **~ re'la·tions** (*skrót*: ***PR***) służba *f* informacyjna; **~ 'school** *Brt.* prywatna szkoła *f* (*dla zamożnych*); *Am.* szkoła *f* państwowa; **~ 'trans·port** *zwł. Brt. sg.*, **~ trans·por'ta·tion** *Am. sg.* komunikacja *f* publiczna
pub·lish ['pʌblɪʃ] ⟨o⟩publikować, wydawać ⟨-dać⟩; ogłaszać ⟨ogłosić⟩, ujawniać ⟨-nić⟩; **~·er** wydawca *m*; wydawnictwo *n*; **'~·er's, '~·ers** *pl.*, **'~·ing house** wydawnictwo *n*
puck·er ['pʌkə] *też* **~ *up*** *twarz, usta* krzywić, wykrzywiać ⟨-wić⟩; *czoło* ⟨z⟩marszczyć
pud·ding ['pʊdɪŋ] pudding *m*; *Brt.* deser *m*; *Am.* budyń *m*; ***black ~*** *Brt.* kaszanka *f*
pud·dle ['pʌdl] kałuża *f*
pu·er·ile ['pjʊəraɪl] dziecięcy, infantylny
puff [pʌf] **1.** *v/i.* sapać; *też* **~ *away*** *papieros itp.* pociągać (***at*** z *G*); *fajkę* pykać (***at*** z *G*); **~ *up*** nadymać (się), obrzęknąć ⟨-kać⟩; *v/t. dym* wydmuchiwać ⟨-chać⟩; **~ *out*** *świecę* zdmuchiwać ⟨-chnąć⟩; *policzki* wydymać ⟨-dąć⟩, *pierś* wypinać ⟨-piąć⟩; **2.** pociągnięcie *n*, zaciągnięcie się (*przy paleniu*); podmuch *m*, powiew *m* (*powietrza*); puszek *m* (*do pudru*); F dech *m*; **~ed 'sleeve** rękaw *m* z bufką; **~ 'pas·try** ciasto *n* francuskie; **'~ sleeve** rękaw *m* z bufką; **'~·y** (***-ier, -iest***) zasapany; obrzmiały
pug [pʌg] *zo. też* **~ *dog*** mops *m*
pug·na·cious [pʌg'neɪʃəs] bojowy, wojowniczy
puke [pjuːk] *sl.* rzygać ⟨-gnąć⟩, puszczać ⟨puścić⟩ pawia
pull [pʊl] **1.** ciągnięcie *n*, pociągnięcie *n*; przyciąganie *n*; podejście *n*; F wpływ *m*; **2.** ⟨po⟩ciągnąć; przyciągać ⟨-gnąć⟩ (*też fig.*); naciągać ⟨-gnąć⟩, wyciągać ⟨-gnąć⟩; rozciągać ⟨-gnąć⟩; *Brt. piwo* natoczyć, nalewać ⟨-lać⟩; **~ *ahead of*** wyprzedzać ⟨-dzić⟩; **~ *away*** odjeżdżać ⟨-jechać⟩; oddalać ⟨-lić⟩ się; **~ *down*** *budynek* ⟨z⟩burzyć; **~ *in*** *pociąg*: wjeżdżać ⟨-jechać⟩; podjeżdżać ⟨-jechać⟩; **~ *off*** F dokonywać ⟨-nać⟩; **~ *out*** wycofywać ⟨-fać⟩ się (***of*** z *G*); odjeżdżać ⟨-jechać⟩; oddalać ⟨-lić⟩ się; *stół* wyciągać ⟨-gnąć⟩; **~ *over*** zjeżdżać ⟨zjechać⟩ na bok; **~ *round*** ⟨wy⟩zdrowieć; **~ *through*** ⟨wy⟩zdrowieć; pokonywać ⟨-nać⟩ trudności; **~ *o.s. together*** brać ⟨wziąć⟩ się w garść; **~ *up*** zatrzymywać ⟨-mać⟩ się; wstrzymywać ⟨-mać⟩; **~ *up to*, ~ *up with*** (*w sporcie*) doganiać ⟨-gonić⟩ (*G*)
pul·ley ['pʊlɪ] *tech.* koło *n* pasowe
'pull|-in *Brt.* bar *m* przy szosie; **'~·o·ver** pulower *m*; **'~-up** *Brt.* (*na drążku*) podciągnięcie *n*; ***do a ~-up*** podciągać ⟨-gnąć⟩ się na drążku

P

pulp [pʌlp] miąższ *m* (*owocu*); miazga *f* (*też anat.*); lichota *f*; **~ novel** brukowa literatura *f*
pul·pit ['pʊlpɪt] ambona *f*
pulp·y ['pʌlpɪ] (**-ier, -iest**) miazgowaty
pul·sate [pʌl'seɪt] pulsować, tętnić
pulse [pʌls] puls *m*, tętno *n*
pul·ver·ize ['pʌlvəraɪz] rozdrabniać ⟨-drobnić⟩, ⟨s⟩proszkować
pu·ma ['pju:mə] *zo.* puma *f*
pum·mel ['pʌml] (*zwł. Brt.* **-ll-**, *Am.* **-l-**) okładać kułakami
pump [pʌmp] **1.** pompa *f*, pompka *f*; dystrybutor *m* (*paliwa*); **2.** ⟨na⟩pompować; tłoczyć; *pieniądze itp.* wtłaczać ⟨-tłoczyć⟩; tryskać; F ciągnąć za język; '**~ at·tend·ant** operator *m* dystrybutora paliwa
pump·kin ['pʌmpkɪn] *bot.* dynia *f*
pun [pʌn] **1.** gra *f* słów; kalambur *m*; **2.** (**-nn-**) ⟨u⟩tworzyć kalambury
punch¹ [pʌntʃ] **1.** uderzać ⟨-rzyć⟩ (*pięścią*); **2.** uderzenie *n* (*pięścią*)
punch² [pʌntʃ] **1.** ⟨prze⟩dziurkować; *dziurkę* ⟨z⟩robić; *bilet* ⟨s⟩kasować; **~ in** *zwł. Am.* podbijać ⟨-bić⟩ kartę przy przyjściu do pracy; **~ out** *zwł. Am.* podbijać ⟨-bić⟩ kartę przy wychodzeniu z pracy; **2.** dziurkarka *f*; dziurkacz *m*; *tech.* przebijak *m*; stempel *m*
punch³ [pʌntʃ] poncz *m*
Punch [pʌntʃ] Punch *m* (*okrutna postać teatru kukiełkowego*); **be as pleased** *lub* **proud as ~** cieszyć się jak dziecko; **~ and Ju·dy show** [pʌntʃ ən 'dʒu:dɪ ʃəʊ] Punch i Judy (*postacie teatru kukiełkowego*)
'**punch card, punched 'card** karta *f* perforowana
punc·tu·al ['pʌŋktʃʊəl] punktualny
punc·tu|·ate ['pʌŋktʃʊeɪt] wstawiać ⟨-wić⟩ znaki przestankowe; **~·a·tion** [pʌŋktʃʊ'eɪʃn] interpunkcja *f*; **~'a·tion mark** znak *m* przestankowy
punc·ture ['pʌŋktʃə] **1.** dziura *f*; przedziurawienie *n*; *mot.* przebicie *n* dętki, F guma *f*; **2.** ⟨prze⟩dziurawić; ⟨prze⟩dziurawić dętkę; F ⟨z⟩łapać gumę
pun·gent ['pʌndʒənt] ostry (*też fig.*); dotkliwy
pun·ish ['pʌnɪʃ] ⟨u⟩karać; '**~a·ble** karalny, podlegający karze; '**~·ment** kara *f*; ukaranie *n*
punk [pʌŋk] punk *m*; *attr.* punkowy; **~ 'rock** punk-rock *m*
pu·ny ['pju:nɪ] (**-ier, -iest**) wątły
pup [pʌp] *zo.* szczeniak *m*, szczenię *n*
pu·pa ['pju:pə] *zo.* (*pl.* **-pae** [-pi:], **-pas**) poczwarka *f*; ⚠ *nie* **pupa**
pu·pil¹ ['pju:pl] uczeń *m* (uczennica); ⚠ *nie* **pupil**
pu·pil² ['pju:pl] *anat.* źrenica *f*
pup·pet ['pʌpɪt] lalka *f*; *fig.* marionetka *f*; *attr.* marionetkowy; '**~ show** teatr *m* lalek; **pup·pe·teer** [pʌpɪ'tɪə] lalkarz *m*
pup·py ['pʌpɪ] *zo.* szczeniak *m*, szczenię *n*
pur|·chase ['pɜ:tʃəs] **1.** kupować⟨-pić⟩, nabywać ⟨-być⟩; **2.** nabytek *m*; **make ~chases** kupować; '**~·chas·er** kupujący *m* (-ca *f*), nabywca
pure [pjʊə] (**-r, -st**) czysty; '**~·bred** czystej krwi
pur·ga·tive ['pɜ:gətɪv] *med.* **1.** przeczyszczający; **2.** środek *m* przeczyszczający
pur·ga·to·ry ['pɜ:gətərɪ] *rel.* czyściec *m*
purge [pɜ:dʒ] **1.** *w partii itp.* ⟨z⟩robić czystkę; oczyszczać ⟨-yścić⟩ (**of** z *G*); **2.** czystka *f*
pu·ri·fy ['pjʊərɪfaɪ] oczyszczać ⟨-yścić⟩
pu·ri·tan ['pjʊərɪtən] **1.** purytanin *m* (-anka *f*); **2.** purytański
pu·ri·ty ['pjʊərətɪ] czystość *f*
purl [pɜ:l] **1.** lewe oczko *n*; **2.** wyrabiać ⟨-robić⟩ lewe oczko
pur·loin [pɜ:'lɔɪn] przywłaszczać ⟨-czyć⟩ sobie
pur·ple ['pɜ:pl] fioletowy; purpurowy
pur·pose ['pɜ:pəs] **1.** cel *m*; zdecydowanie *n*; **on ~** celowo; **to no ~** bezskutecznie, daremnie; **2.** zamierzać, mieć zamiar; '**~·ful** celowy, rozmyślny; '**~·less** bezcelowo, daremnie; '**~·ly** celowo
purr [pɜ:] *kot, silnik*: ⟨za⟩mruczeć
purse¹ [pɜ:s] portmonetka *f*; *Am.* torebka *f* (*damska*); pieniądze *pl.*, fundusz *m*
purse² [pɜ:s]: **~ (up) one's lips** zaciskać ⟨-snąć⟩ usta
pur·su·ance [pə'sju:əns]: **in (the) ~ of his duty** w trakcie wykonywania swoich obowiązków
pur|·sue [pə'sju:] ścigać; *studia itp.* kontynuować; *zawód* wykonywać; dążyć do (*G*) (*celu*); *fig.* prześladować;

~'su·er prześladowca *m* ścigający *m* (-ca *f*); **~·suit** [pə'sjuːt] pościg *m*; zajęcie *n*

pur·vey [pə'veɪ] *żywność* dostarczać ⟨-czyć⟩; **~·or** dostawca *m*

pus [pʌs] *med.* ropa *m*

push [pʊʃ] **1.** pchać, popychać ⟨-pchnąć⟩; *guzik itp.* naciskać ⟨-snąć⟩; ⟨za-, roz⟩reklamować; *narkotykami itp.* handlować; *fig.* naciskać ⟨-snąć⟩ (***to do s.th.*** aby coś zrobić); **~ *one's way*** przepychać ⟨-pchnąć⟩ się (***through*** przez *A*); **~ *ahead with*** zamierzenie kontynuować; **~ *along*** F jechać, iść; **~ *around*** F pomiatać (*I*); **~ *for*** domagać się (*G*); **~ *forward with*** → ***push ahead with***; **~ *o.s. forward*** *fig.* pchać się do przodu; **~ *in*** F wpychać ⟨wepchnąć⟩ się; **~ *off!*** F spływaj!; **~ *on with*** → ***push ahead with***; **~ *out*** *fig.* wyrzucać ⟨-cić⟩; **~ *through*** *fig.* przepychać ⟨-pchnąć⟩; **~ *up*** *cenę* ⟨wy⟩windować; **2.** pchnięcie *n*; popchnięcie *n*; naciśnięcie *n*; akcja *f* reklamowa; F energia *f*, zapał *m*; '**~ but·ton** guzik *m*, przycisk *m*, klawisz *m*; '**~-but·ton** *tech.* na guziki, na klawisze; **~*-button*** (***tele***)***phone*** telefon *m* na klawisze; '**~·chair** *Brt.* wózek *m* spacerowy; '**~·er** *pej.* handlarz *m* narkotykami; '**~·o·ver** F dziecinna zabawka *f*, łatwizna *f*; '**~-up** *Am.* → ***press-up***

puss [pʊs] F kicia *f*

'**pus·sy** *też* **~ *cat*** kiciuś *m*; V cipa *f*; '**~·foot** F: **~*foot about***/***around*** postępować ⟨-tąpić⟩ ostrożnie

put [pʊt] (***-tt-***; ***put***) kłaść ⟨położyć⟩; umieszczać ⟨-mieścić⟩; odkładać ⟨odłożyć⟩; stosować; *na rynek, do obrotu itp.* wprowadzać ⟨-dzić⟩; *na miejsce* stawiać ⟨-wić⟩, kłaść ⟨położyć⟩; *porządek* zaprowadzać ⟨-dzić⟩; *uczucia* wkładać ⟨włożyć⟩; (*w sporcie*) *kulę* pchać; *słowami* wyrażać ⟨-razić⟩; *kłopoty* przysparzać ⟨-porzyć⟩; *pytania* przedstawiać ⟨-wić⟩; przekładać ⟨przełożyć⟩ (***into Polish*** na polski); *winę* składać ⟨złożyć⟩; **~ *right*** ⟨u⟩porządkować; **~ *s.th. before s.o.*** *fig.* przedstawiać ⟨-wić⟩ coś komuś; **~ *to bed*** kłaść ⟨położyć⟩ do łóżka; **~ *about*** *plotki* rozgłaszać; **~ *across*** przekazywać ⟨-zać⟩, ⟨u⟩czynić zrozumiałym; **~ *ahead*** wychodzić na prowadzenie; **~ *aside*** odkładać ⟨odłożyć⟩; nie zwracać uwagi na (*A*); **~ *away*** odkładać ⟨odłożyć⟩ (*z powrotem*); **~ *back*** (*na miejsce*) odkładać ⟨odłożyć⟩; przekładać ⟨przełożyć⟩; *wskazówki zegara* cofać ⟨-fnąć⟩ (***by*** o *A*); **~ *by*** *pieniądze* odkładać ⟨odłożyć⟩; **~ *down*** *v/t.* odkładać ⟨odłożyć⟩; kłaść ⟨położyć⟩; *kogoś* poniżać ⟨-żyć⟩; (*z samochodu*) wysadzać ⟨-dzić⟩; *bunt* ⟨s⟩tłumić, zdusić; zapisywać ⟨-sać⟩; *zwierzę* usypiać ⟨uśpić⟩; (*też v/i.*) *aviat.* ⟨wy⟩lądować; **~ *down to*** przypisywać ⟨-sać⟩; **~ *forward*** *plan itp.* przedstawiać ⟨-wić⟩; *wskazówki zegara* przesuwać ⟨-sunąć⟩ do przodu (***by*** o *A*); przesuwać ⟨-sunąć⟩ (***two days*** o dwa dni; ***to*** na *A*); **~ *in*** *v/t.* wkładać ⟨włożyć⟩, umieszczać ⟨-mieścić⟩ w (*L*); *rośliny* ⟨po⟩sadzić; *sprzęt* ⟨za⟩instalować; *żądanie, dokument, rachunek itp.* przedstawiać ⟨-wić⟩; *pieniądze* wpłacać ⟨-cić⟩; ⟨za⟩inwestować; *czas, pracę* wkładać ⟨włożyć⟩ (***on*** przy *L*); *v/i. naut.* wchodzić ⟨wejść⟩ do portu (***to*** do *G*); **~ *off*** odkładać ⟨odłożyć⟩ (***until*** do *G*); *kogoś* zwodzić ⟨zwieść⟩; ⟨z⟩deprymować; rozpraszać ⟨-roszyć⟩; **~ *on*** *ubranie, czapkę itp.* wkładać ⟨włożyć⟩ (na siebie), nakładać ⟨nałożyć⟩; *światło, radio* włączać ⟨-czyć⟩; *dodatkowy pociąg* podstawiać ⟨-wić⟩; *theat. sztukę* przedstawiać ⟨-wić⟩; F nabierać ⟨-brać⟩; *cenę* zwiększać ⟨-szyć⟩; **~ *on airs*** wywyższać się; **~ *on weight*** przybierać ⟨-brać⟩ na wadze; **~ *out*** *v/t.* wyjmować ⟨-jąć⟩; ⟨z⟩gasić; *przed dom* wystawiać ⟨-wić⟩; *kota* wypuszczać ⟨-puścić⟩; *rękę* wyciągać ⟨-gnąć⟩; *język* wystawiać ⟨-wić⟩; nadawać ⟨-dać⟩ (*program*); *oświadczenie* wydawać ⟨-dać⟩; *kogoś* ⟨z⟩denerwować; *komuś* sprawiać kłopot; *ramię* zwichnąć, naciągnąć; *v/i. naut.* wypływać ⟨-łynąć⟩; **~ *over*** → ***put across***; **~ *through*** *tel.* ⟨po⟩łączyć (***to*** z *I*); przeprowadzać ⟨-dzić⟩; **~ *together*** składać ⟨złożyć⟩; zestawiać ⟨-wić⟩; **~ *up*** *v/t. rękę, cenę* podnosić ⟨-nieść⟩; *namiot* stawiać ⟨postawić⟩; *budynek* wznosić ⟨wznieść⟩; *obraz* zawieszać ⟨-wiesić⟩; *plakat* wywieszać ⟨-wiesić⟩; *parasol* rozkładać ⟨-złożyć⟩; *na noc* ⟨u⟩lokować; *na sprzedaż* wystawiać ⟨-wić⟩; *pieniądze* zbierać ⟨zebrać⟩; *opór* stawiać ⟨-wić⟩; *obóz* rozkładać ⟨-złożyć⟩;

P

~ up with znosić ⟨znieść⟩
pu·tre·fy ['pju:trɪfaɪ] powodować gnicie
pu·trid ['pju:trɪd] gnijący; F okropny
put·ty ['pʌtɪ] **1.** kit *m*; **2.** ⟨za⟩kitować
'put-up job F ukartowana gra *f*
puz·zle ['pʌzl] **1.** zagadka *f*, łamigłówka *f*; → ***jigsaw*** (***puzzle***); **2.** *v/t.* stanowić zagadkę; ***be ~d*** być zaskoczonym; ***~ out*** rozwiązanie wymyślić, znaleźć; *v/i.* łamać sobie głowę (***about, over*** nad *I*)
PX [pi: 'eks] *TM* (*pl.* **-s** [- 'eksɪz]) *skrót*: ***post exchange*** (*kasyno dla członków sił zbrojnych USA*)
pyg·my ['pɪgmɪ] Pigmej(ka *f*) *m*; karzeł *m*; *attr.* karłowaty
py·ja·mas [pə'dʒɑ:məz] *Brt. pl.* (***a pair of ~***) piżama *f*
py·lon ['paɪlən] pylon *m*; słup *m* wysokiego napięcia
pyr·a·mid ['pɪrəmɪd] piramida *f*
pyre ['paɪə] stos *m* pogrzebowy
py·thon ['paɪθn] *zo.* (*pl.* **-thons, -thon**) pyton *m*
pyx [pɪks] *rel.* puszka *f* na komunikanty

Q

Q, q [kju:] Q, q *n*
qt *skrót pisany*: ***quart*** kwarta *f* (*Brt. 1,14 l, Am. 0,95 l*)
quack[1] [kwæk] **1.** ⟨za⟩kwakać, kwaknąć; **2.** kwaknięcie *n*
quack[2] [kwæk] *też* ***~ doctor*** szarlatan *m*; *Brt.* konował *m*; **~·er·y** ['kwækərɪ] szarlatańststwo *n*
quad·ran|·gle ['kwɒdræŋgl] czworokąt *m*; **~·gu·lar** [kwɒ'dræŋgjʊlə] czworokątny
quad·ra·phon·ic [kwɒdrə'fɒnɪk] (***~ally***) kwadrofoniczny
quad·ri·lat·er·al [kwɒdrɪ'lætərəl] **1.** czworobok *m*; **2.** czworoboczny
quad·ro·phon·ic [kwɒdrə'fɒnɪk] kwadrofoniczny
quad·ru·ped ['kwɒdrʊped] *zo.* czworonóg *m*
quad·ru|·ple ['kwɒdrʊpl] **1.** poczwórny; czterokrotny; **2.** zwiększać (się) czterokrotnie *lub* poczwórnie; **~·plets** ['kwɒdrʊplɪts] *pl.* czworaczki *pl.*
quads [kwɒdz] F *pl.* czworaczki *pl.*
quag·mire ['kwægmaɪə] bagno *n*, trzęsawisko *n* (*też fig.*)
quail [kweɪl] *zo.* (*pl.* ***quail, quails***) przepiórka *f*
quaint [kweɪnt] osobliwy, niespotykany
quake [kweɪk] **1.** trząść się (***with, for*** z *D*, ***at*** na *A*); **2.** F trzęsienie *n* ziemi
Quak·er ['kweɪkə] *rel.* kwakier(ka *f*) *m*
qual·i|·fi·ca·tion [kwɒlɪfɪ'keɪʃn] kwalifikacje *pl.*, predyspozycje *pl.* (***for*** do *G*); zastrzeżenie *n*; **~·fied** ['kwɒlɪfaɪd] wykwalifikowany; dyplomowany; ***be ~fied to*** mieć kwalifikacje do (*G*); z zastrzeżeniami; **~·fy** ['kwɒlɪfaɪ] *v/t.* ⟨za⟩kwalifikować (***for*** do *G*); nadawać ⟨-dać⟩ kwalifikacje (***to do*** do wykonywania); ⟨z⟩modyfikować; *v/i.* kwalifikować się (***for*** do *G*); nabywać ⟨-być⟩ kwalifikacji; nabywać prawa (***for*** do *G*); *sport*: ⟨za⟩kwalifikować się (***for*** do *G*); **~·ty** ['kwɒlətɪ] jakość *f*; właściwość *f*, cecha *f*
qualms [kwɑ:mz] *pl.* skrupuły *pl.*, obiekcje *pl.*
quan·da·ry ['kwɒndərɪ]: ***be in a ~ about what to do*** nie wiedzieć, co robić
quan·ti·ty ['kwɒntətɪ] ilość *f*
quan·tum ['kwɒntəm] *phys.* (*pl.* **-ta** [-tə]) kwant *m*; *attr.* kwantowy
quar·an·tine ['kwɒrənti:n] **1.** kwarantanna *f*; **2.** poddawać ⟨-dać⟩ kwarantannie
quar·rel ['kwɒrəl] **1.** kłótnia *f*, sprzeczka *f*; spór *m*; **2.** (*zwł. Brt.* **-ll-**, *Am.* **-l-**) kłócić się; ⟨s⟩kłócić; **'~·some** kłótliwy
quar·ry[1] ['kwɒrɪ] kamieniołom *m*
quar·ry[2] ['kwɒrɪ] *hunt.* zdobycz *f*; *fig.* ofiara *f*
quart [kwɔ:t] kwarta *f* (*skrót*: ***qt***) (*Brt. 1,14 l, Am. 0,95 l*)
quar·ter ['kwɔ:tə] **1.** ćwierć *f*, ćwiartka *f*; kwartał *m*; kwadrans *m*; ćwierć *f* funta; ćwierć *f* dolara; (*w sporcie*) kwarta *f*; (*księżyca*) kwadra *f*; dzielnica *f*; strona *f* (*świata*); ćwierćtusza *f*; ***~s*** *pl.* za-

kwaterowanie *n*; *mil.* kwatera *f*; ***a ~ of an hour*** kwadrans *m*; ***a ~ to*** (*Am.* ***of***) ***five*** za kwadrans piąta; ***a ~ past*** (*Am.* ***after***) ***five*** piętnaście po piątej; ***at close ~s*** z bliska; ***from official ~s*** ze strony urzędu; **2.** ⟨po⟩ćwiartować; *zwł. mil.* zakwaterować (***on*** u *A*); **'~·deck** achterdek *m*, pokład *m* rufowy; **~'fi·nals** *pl.* ćwierćfinały *pl.*; **'~·ly 1.** kwartalnie; **2.** kwartalnik *m*

quar·tet(te) [kwɔː'tet] *mus.* kwartet *m*

quartz [kwɔːts] *mins.* kwarc *m*; *attr.* kwarcowy; **'~ clock** zegar *m* kwarcowy; **'~ watch** naręczny zegarek *m* kwarcowy

qua·ver ['kweɪvə] **1.** *głos*: ⟨za⟩drżeć; mówić ⟨powiedzieć⟩ drżącym głosem; **2.** drżenie *n*; *mus.* ósemka *f*

quay [kiː] *naut.* nabrzeże *n*, keja *f*

quea·sy ['kwiːzɪ] (**-ier, -iest**): ***I feel ~*** niedobrze mi, mdli mnie

queen [kwiːn] królowa *f*; (*w kartach*) dama *f*; (*w grze w warcaby*) damka *f*; (*w szachach*) królowa *f*, hetman *m*; *sl.* pedał *m*, homo *m*; **~ 'bee** (*w ulu*) matka *f*; **'~·ly** królewski, jak królowa

queer [kwɪə] **1.** dziwaczny; F pedałowaty, pedalski; **2.** F pedał *m*

quench [kwentʃ] *pragnienie* ugasić

quer·u·lous ['kwerʊləs] marudny

que·ry ['kwɪərɪ] **1.** pytanie *n*, zapytanie *n*; wątpliwość *f*; **2.** zapytywać ⟨-tać⟩, dowiadywać się

quest [kwest] **1.** poszukiwanie *n*; ***in ~ of*** w poszukiwaniu (*G*); **2.** poszukiwać

ques·tion ['kwestʃən] **1.** pytanie *n*; problem *m*, zagadnienie *n*; kwestia *f*; wątpliwość *f*; ***only a ~ of time*** tylko kwestia czasu; ***this is not the point in ~*** to nie o to chodzi; ***there is no ~ that, it is beyond ~ that*** nie ulega kwestii, że; ***there is no ~ about this*** co do tego nie ma żadnych wątpliwości; ***be out of the ~*** być wykluczonym; **2.** ⟨za⟩pytać (***about*** o *A*); *jur.* pytać (***about*** o *A*); ⟨za⟩kwestionować; **'~·a·ble** wątpliwy, sporny; **'~·er** osoba *f* zadająca pytanie; **'~ mark** znak *m* zapytania; **'~ mas·ter** *zwł. Brt.* osoba *f* prowadząca kwiz

ques·tion·naire [kwestʃə'neə] kwestionariusz *m*

queue *zwł. Brt.* [kjuː] **1.** ogonek *m*, kolejka *f*; **2.** *zw.* ***~ up*** stawać ⟨stanąć⟩ do kolejki, ustawiać ⟨-wić⟩ się w kolejce

quib·ble ['kwɪbl] ⟨po⟩sprzeczać się (***with*** z *I*, ***about, over*** o *A*)

quick [kwɪk] **1.** *adj.* szybki, prędki; zapalczywy; ***be ~!*** pospiesz się!; **2.** *adv.* szybko, prędko; **3.** ***cut s.o. to the ~*** dotknąć kogoś do żywego; **'~·en** przyspieszać ⟨-szyć⟩; **'~-freeze** (***-froze, -frozen***) *żywność* szybko zamrażać ⟨-rozić⟩; **~·ie** ['kwɪkɪ] F (*coś krótkiego, naprędce, np.*) krótkie pytanie *n*; **'~·ly** szybko, prędko; **'~·sand** lotne piaski *pl.*, kurzawka *f*; **~-'tem·pered** zapalczywy; **~-'wit·ted** lotny

quid *Brt. sl.* [kwɪd] (*pl.* ***quid***) *pieniądze*: funt *m*

qui·et ['kwaɪət] **1.** cichy; spokojny; ***~, please*** proszę o ciszę; ***be ~!*** siedź cicho!; **2.** cisza *f*, spokój *m*; ***on the ~*** F cichaczem; **3.** *zwł. Am.* → **~·en** *zwł. Brt.* ['kwaɪətn] *też* ***~en down*** uciszać ⟨-szyć⟩ (się); uspokajać ⟨-koić⟩ (się); **'~·ness** cisza *f* spokój *m*

quill [kwɪl] *zo. długie* pióro *n*; kolec *m*; **~ ('pen)** gęsie pióro *n* (*do pisania*)

quilt [kwɪlt] kołdra *f*; narzuta *f*, kapa *f*; **'~·ed** pikowany

quince [kwɪns] *bot.* pigwa *f*

quin·ine [kwɪ'niːn] *pharm.* chinina *f*

quins [kwɪnz] *Brt.* F *pl.* pięcioraczki *pl.*

quin·tes·sence [kwɪn'tesns] kwintesencja *f*, esencja *f*

quin·tet(te) [kwɪn'tet] *mus.* kwintet *m*

quints [kwɪnts] *Am.* F *pl.* pięcioraczki *pl.*

quin·tu|·ple ['kwɪntjʊpl] **1.** pięciokrotny; **2.** zwiększać (się) pięciokrotnie; **~·plets** ['kwɪntjʊplɪts] pięcioraczki *pl.*

quip [kwɪp] **1.** dowcipna uwaga *f*; **2.** (***-pp-***) zrobić dowcipną uwagę

quirk [kwɜːk] osobliwość *f*; ***by some ~ of fate*** jakimś zrządzeniem losu

quit [kwɪt] F (***-tt-***; *Brt.* **~** *lub* ***~ted***, *Am. zwł.* **~**) *v/t.* opuszczać; przestawać ⟨-tać⟩; ***~ one's job*** porzucać ⟨-cić⟩ pracę; *v/i.* odchodzić ⟨odejść⟩

quite [kwaɪt] całkiem, zupełnie; dość; ***~ a few*** dość dużo; ***~ nice*** całkiem przyjemny; **~ (*so*)*!*** *zwł. Brt.* ano właśnie!; ***be ~ right*** mieć zupełnie rację; ***she's ~ a beauty*** z niej jest całkiem piękna dziewczyna

quits [kwɪts] F kwita (***with*** z *I*); ***call it ~*** to kwita

Q

quit·ter ['kwɪtə] F: ***be a ~*** łatwo się poddawać ⟨-ddać⟩
quiv·er[1] ['kwɪvə] ⟨za⟩drżeć (***with*** z *G*; ***at*** na *A*)
quiv·er[2] ['kwɪvə] kołczan *m*
quiz [kwɪz] **1.** (*pl.* ***quizzes***) kwiz *m*, quiz *m*; *zwł. Am.* test *m*, sprawdzian *m*; **2.** (***-zz-***) wypytywać ⟨-tać⟩, rozpytywać ⟨-tać⟩ (***about*** o *L*); **'~·mas·ter** *zwł. Am.* prowadzący *m* (-ca *f*) kwiz; **~·zi·cal** ['kwɪzɪkl] *spojrzenie*: zagadkowy
quo·ta ['kwəʊtə] limit *m*, dopuszczalna ilość *f*; kontyngent *m*
quo·ta·tion [kwəʊ'teɪʃn] cytat *m*; *econ.* oferta *f*; *econ.* stawka *f*, *econ. giełdowe* notowanie *n*; **~ marks** *pl.* cudzysłów *m*
quote [kwəʊt] ⟨za⟩cytować, *przykład* przytaczać ⟨-toczyć⟩; *econ. cenę* podawać ⟨-dać⟩; ***be ~d at*** *econ.* być notowanym na (*L*); → ***unquote***
quo·tient ['kwəʊʃnt] *math.* iloraz *m*

R

R, **r** [ɑː] R, r *n*
rab·bi ['ræbaɪ] *rel.* rabin *m*; *tytuł*: rabbi *m*
rab·bit ['ræbɪt] *zo.* królik *m*
rab·ble ['ræbl] hołota *f*, motłoch *m*; **~-rous·ing** ['ræblraʊzɪŋ] podżegający, judzący
rab·id ['ræbɪd] *vet.* wściekły; *fig.* fanatyczny
ra·bies ['reɪbiːz] *vet.* wścieklizna *f*
rac·coon [rə'kuːn] *zo.* szop *m* pracz
race[1] [reɪs] rasa *f*
race[2] [reɪs] **1.** wyścig *m*; **2.** *v/i.* ścigać się; brać ⟨wziąć⟩ udział w wyścigu; ⟨po⟩pędzić, ⟨po⟩mknąć; *serce*: walić; *v/t.* ścigać się z (*I*); *konia* wystawiać ⟨-wić⟩ w wyścigach; *silnik*: pracować na przyspieszonych obrotach; **'~ car** *zwł. Am.* samochód *m* wyścigowy; **'~·course** *sport konny*: tor *m* wyścigowy; hipodrom *m*; **'~·horse** koń *m* wyścigowy; **'rac·er** koń *m* wyścigowy; rower *m* wyścigowy; samochód *m* wyścigowy; **'~·track** (*w sporcie*) tor *m* wyścigowy; bieżnia *f*
ra·cial ['reɪʃl] rasowy
rac·ing ['reɪsɪŋ] wyścigowy; **'~ car** *zwł. Brt.* samochód *m* wyścigowy
ra|·cis·m ['reɪsɪzəm] rasizm *m*; **~·cist** ['reɪsɪst] **1.** rasista *m* (-tka *f*); **2.** rasistowski
rack [ræk] **1.** stojak *m*; suszarka *f* (*na naczynia*); stelaż *m* (*na gazety*); *rail.* półka *f*; *mot.* bagażnik *m* (*dachowy*); **2.** ***be ~ed by*** *lub* ***with*** być dręczonym (*I*); ***~ one's brains*** łamać sobie głowę
rack·et[1] ['rækɪt] *tenisowa* rakieta *f*
rack|·et[2] ['rækɪt] harmider *m*, rejwach *m*; oszustwo *n*; wymuszenie *n*, szantaż *m*; **~·e·teer** [rækə'tɪə] szantażysta *m* (-tka *f*)
ra·coon [rə'kuːn] *zo.* → ***raccoon***
rac·y ['reɪsɪ] (***-ier, -iest***) *opowiadanie*: pikantny
ra·dar ['reɪdə] radar *m*; *attr.* radarowy; **'~ screen** ekran *m* radaru; **~ 'speed check** kontrola *f* radarowa; **'~ sta·tion** stacja *f* radarowa; **'~ trap** *mot.* kontrola *f* radarowa
ra·di·al ['reɪdjəl] **1.** radialny; promieniowy; **2.** opona *f* radialna; **~ 'tire** *Am.*, **~ 'tyre** *Brt.* → ***radial*** 2
ra·di·ant ['reɪdjənt] promienisty; *fig.* promienny, rozpromieniony (***with*** z powodu *G*)
ra·di|·ate ['reɪdɪeɪt] promieniować; rozchodzić się promieniowo (***from*** z *G*); **~·a·tion** [reɪdɪ'eɪʃn] radiacja *f*, promieniowanie *n*; **~·a·tor** ['reɪdɪeɪtə] grzejnik *m*, kaloryfer *m*; *mot.* chłodnica *f*
rad·i·cal ['rædɪkl] **1.** radykalny (*też pol.*); *math.* pierwiastkowy; **2.** radykał *m*; *math.* pierwiastek *m*, znak *m* pierwiastka
ra·di·o ['reɪdɪəʊ] **1.** (*pl.* ***-os***) radio *m*; radioodbiornik *m*; *attr.* radiowy; ***by ~*** radiem, drogą radiową; ***on the ~*** w radiu; **2.** przekazywać ⟨-zać⟩ drogą radiową; **~'ac·tive** radioaktywny, promieniotwórczy; ***~active waste*** odpady *pl.* promieniotwórcze; **~·ac'tiv·i·ty** radioaktywność *f*, promieniotwórczość *f*; **'~ ham** radioamator *m*; **'~ play** słuchowisko *m*; **'~ set** odbiornik *m* radiowy;

R

'~ **sta·tion** stacja *f* radiowa; ~'**ther·a·py** *med.* radioterapia *f*; ~ '**tow·er** wieża *f* radiowa

rad·ish ['rædɪʃ] *bot.* rzodkiew(ka) *f*

ra·di·us ['reɪdjəs] (*pl.* ***-dii*** [-dɪaɪ]) promień *m*

RAF [ɑːr eɪ 'ef, ræf] *skrót*: ***Royal Air Force*** RAF *m*

raf·fle ['ræfl] **1.** loteria *f* fantowa, tombola *f*; **2.** *też* ~ ***off*** dawać ⟨dać⟩ w nagrodę

raft [rɑːft] tratwa *f*

raf·ter ['rɑːftə] krokiew *f*

rag [ræg] szmata *f*; ścierka *f*; łach *m*; ***in ~s*** w łachmanach; ~**-and-'bone man** (*pl.* ***-men***) *zwł. Brt.* szmaciarz *m* (-ciarka *f*), handlarz *m* (-arka *f*) starzyzną

rage [reɪdʒ] **1.** wściekłość *f*, szał *m*; ***fly into a ~*** wpaść we wściekłość *f*; ***the latest ~*** F najnowsza moda *f*; ***be all the ~*** być ostatnim krzykiem *m* mody; **2.** wściekać się (***against, at*** na *A*); *choroba*: szaleć

rag·ged ['rægɪd] obszarpany; obdarty; *broda, linia*: nierówny

raid [reɪd] **1.** (***on***) napad (na *A*); *mil. też* nalot *m* (na *A*), wypad *m* (na *A*); obława *f* (na *A*); **2.** napadać ⟨-paść⟩, najeżdżać ⟨-jechać⟩; ⟨z⟩robić obławę

rail [reɪl] **1.** poręcz *f*; barierka *f*; wieszak *m* (*na ręczniki*); szyna *f*; *rail.* kolej *f*; ~***s*** *pl. też* tory *pl.*; ***by ~*** koleją, pociągiem; **2.** ~ ***off*** odgradzać ⟨-rodzić⟩; '~**·ing**, *często* ~***s*** *pl.* balustrada *f*, ogrodzenie *n*

'**rail·road** *Am.* → ***railway***

'**rail·way** *zwł. Brt.* kolej *f*; '~ **line** *Brt.* linia *f* kolejowa; '~**·man** (*pl.* ***-men***) kolejarz *m*; '~ **sta·tion** *Brt.* dworzec *m*, stacja *f* kolejowa

rain [reɪn] **1.** deszcz *m*; ~***s*** *pl.* opady *pl.* deszczu; ***the ~s*** pora *f* deszczowa; (***come***) ~ ***or shine*** bez względu na pogodę; **2.** *deszcz*: padać; ***it is ~ing*** (deszcz) pada; ***it is ~ing cats and dogs*** F leje jak z cebra; ***it never ~s but pours*** nieszczęścia chodzą parami; '~**·bow** tęcza *f*; '~**·coat** płaszcz *m* przeciwdeszczowy; '~**·fall** opady *pl.* deszczu; '~ **for·est** *bot.* wilgotny las równikowy, selwa *f*; '~**·proof** wodoodporny; '~**·y** (***-ier, -iest***) deszczowy; ***save s.th. for a ~y day*** odkładać ⟨odłożyć⟩ coś na czarną godzinę

raise [reɪz] **1.** podnosić ⟨-nieść⟩; *budynek* wznosić ⟨-nieść⟩; unosić ⟨unieść⟩; uprawiać, hodować; wychowywać ⟨-wać⟩; *pieniądze* zdobywać ⟨-być⟩; zbierać ⟨zebrać⟩; *zagadnienie* poruszać ⟨-szyć⟩; *blokadę, zakaz* znosić ⟨znieść⟩; **2.** *Am.* podwyżka *f* (*płacy*)

rai·sin ['reɪzn] rodzynka *f*, rodzynek *m*

rake [reɪk] **1.** grabie *pl.*; **2.** *v/t.*: ~ (***up***) grabić, zagrabiać ⟨-bić⟩, zgrabiać ⟨-bić⟩; *v/i.* ~ ***about***, ~ ***around*** przetrząsnąć

rak·ish ['reɪkɪʃ] hulaszczy; zawadiacki

ral·ly ['rælɪ] **1.** zbierać ⟨zebrać⟩ się; poprawiać ⟨-wić⟩ się, ożywiać ⟨-wić⟩ się (*też econ.*); ~ ***round*** skupiać ⟨-pić⟩ się wokół (*G*); **2.** wiec *m*, zgromadzenie *n*; *mot.* rajd *m*; (*w tenisie itp.*) wymiana *f* piłek

ram [ræm] **1.** *zo.* baran *m*, tryk *m*; *tech.* kafar *m*; bijak *m*; **2.** (***-mm-***) ⟨s⟩taranować; ubijać ⟨ubić⟩; wbijać ⟨wbić⟩, zasuwać ⟨-unąć⟩; ~ ***s.th. down s.o.'s throat*** wciskać coś komuś na siłę

RAM [ræm] *skrót*: ***random access memory*** *komp.* RAM *m*, pamięć *f* o swobodnym dostępie

ram|·ble ['ræmbl] **1.** wędrować, włóczyć się; ględzić (chaotycznie); płozić się, rozrastać ⟨-rosnąć⟩ się; **2.** wędrówka *f*; '~**·bler** wędrowiec *m*; *bot.* pnącze *n*; '~**·bling** chaotyczny, bez ładu i składu; chaotycznie zbudowany; *bot.* pnący

ram·i·fy ['ræmɪfaɪ] rozwidlać ⟨-lić⟩ się

ramp [ræmp] rampa *f*, pochylnia *f*; *Am.* → ***slip road***

ram·page [ræm'peɪdʒ] **1.** ~ ***through*** przejść tratując przez (*A*); **2.** ***go on the ~ through*** przejść niszcząc przez (*A*)

ram·pant ['ræmpənt]: ***be ~*** szerzyć się; rozrastać się

ram·shack·le ['ræmʃækl] rozklekotany; rozwalający się

ran [ræn] *pret. od* ***run***

ranch [rɑːntʃ, *Am.* ræntʃ] ranczo *n*, rancho *n*; *Am.* ferma *f* (*drobiu itp.*); '~**·er** ranczer *m*; farmer *m*, hodowca *m*

ran·cid ['rænsɪd] zjełczały

ran·co(u)r ['ræŋkə] nienawiść *f*, wrogość *f*

ran·dom ['rændəm] **1.** *adj.* przypadkowy; losowy; ~ ***sample*** próba *f* losowa; **2.** ***at ~*** przypadkowo, na oślep

rang [ræŋ] *pret. od* ***ring***²

range [reɪndʒ] **1.** zakres *m*; przedział *m* (cenowy), rozpiętość *f*; zasięg *m*; donośność *f*; *econ.* asortyment *m*, wybór *m*; łańcuch *m* (*górski*); strzelnica *f*, poligon *m*; *Am.* kuchenka *f*; piec *m* (*kuchenny*); pastwisko *n*; ***at close ~*** z bliska; ***within ~ of vision*** w zasięgu wzroku; ***a wide ~ of ...*** szeroki asortyment (*G*); **2.** *v/i.* **~ ... to ..., ~ between ...and...** *ceny*: wahać się od ... do ...; *v/t.* ⟨u⟩szeregować; **'~ find·er** *phot.* dalmierz *m*; **'rang·er** leśniczy *m*, strażnik *m* leśny; *Am.* komandos *m*

rank[1] [ræŋk] **1.** ranga *f* (*też mil.*), stanowisko *n*; *mil.* stopień *m*; pozycja *f*; rząd *m*, szereg *m*; postój *m* taksówek; ***of the first ~*** *fig.* pierwszorzędny; ***the ~ and file*** szeregowi członkowie *pl.*; doły *pl.* (*partyjne*); ***the ~s*** *pl. fig.* szeregi *pl.*, masy *pl.*; **2.** zaliczać (się) (***among*** pomiędzy *A*); zajmować miejsce (*G*); ⟨za⟩klasyfikować (się) (***as*** jako)

rank[2] [ræŋk] *trawa*: rozrosły; cuchnący, obrzydliwy; *nowicjusz*: zupełny, całkowity

ran·kle ['ræŋkl] *fig.* napełniać ⟨-nić⟩ goryczą, rozgoryczać

ran·sack ['rænsæk] przewrócić wszystko do góry nogami; ⟨s⟩plądrować

ran·som ['rænsəm] **1.** okup *m*; **2.** ⟨za⟩płacić okup

rant [rænt]: **~ (*on*) *about*, ~ *and rave about*** rozprawiać o (*L*), perorować o (*L*)

rap [ræp] **1.** uderzenie *n*, stukanie *n*; *mus.* rap *m*; **2.** (**-*pp*-**) uderzać ⟨-rzyć⟩, stukać ⟨-knąć⟩

ra·pa·cious [rə'peɪʃəs] łapczywy, zachłanny

rape[1] [reɪp] **1.** ⟨z⟩gwałcić; **2.** gwałt *m*

rape[2] [reɪp] *bot.* rzepak *m*; *attr.* rzepakowy

rap·id ['ræpɪd] prędki, bystry; **ra·pid·i·ty** [rə'pɪdətɪ] prędkość *f*; **rap·ids** ['ræpɪdz] *pl.* progi *pl.* rzeczne

rapt [ræpt]: ***with ~ attention*** z niesłabnącą uwagą; **rap·ture** ['ræptʃə] zachwyt *m*; ***go into ~s*** unosić się z zachwytu

rare[1] [reə] (***-r, -st***) rzadki; *światło*: wątły

rare[2] [reə] *gastr.* (***-r, -st***) *befsztyk*: krwisty, niedosmażony

rare·bit ['reəbɪt] *gastr.* → ***Welsh rarebit***

rar·e·fied ['reərɪfaɪd] rozrzedzony

rar·i·ty ['reərətɪ] rzadkość *f*

ras·cal ['rɑːskəl] łajdak *m*; *hum.* łobuziak *m*

rash[1] [ræʃ] pochopny, nieprzemyślany

rash[2] [ræʃ] *med.* wysypka *f*

rash·er ['ræʃə] (cienki) plasterek *m* (*bekonu itp.*)

rasp [rɑːsp] **1.** ⟨wy⟩chrypieć; ⟨o⟩trzeć; **2.** tarnik *m*, raszpla *f*; chrypienie *n*, zgrzyt *m*, zgrzytanie *n*

rasp·ber·ry ['rɑːzbərɪ] *bot.* malina *m*; *attr.* malinowy

rat [ræt] *zo.* szczur *m* (*też pej.*); ***smell a ~*** *fig.* ⟨wy⟩czuć coś (niedobrego); ***~s!*** F cholera!

rate [reɪt] **1.** stopa *f*, stawka *f*; *econ.* cena *f*, kurs *m* (*walut itp.*); tempo *n*, szybkość *f*; ⚠ *nie* **rata** (**instal[l]ment**); ***at any ~*** w każdym bądź razie; **2.** ⟨o⟩szacować (***as*** jako *A*), oceniać ⟨-nić⟩; *na pochwałę* zasłużyć; ***be ~d as*** być uważanym za (*A*); **~ of ex'change** kurs *m* wymiany; **~ of 'in·ter·est** stopa *f* procentowa

ra·ther ['rɑːðə] raczej; dosyć, dość; ***I would*** *lub* ***had ~ go*** chciał(a)bym już pójść

rat·i·fy ['rætɪfaɪ] *pol.* ratyfikować

rat·ing ['reɪtɪŋ] oszacowanie *n*, ocena *f*; klasyfikacja filmu (*dla dzieci, dorosłych itp.*); **~s** *pl. radio*, *TV*: klasyfikacja *f*, lista *f* (*oglądalności*)

ra·ti·o ['reɪʃɪəʊ] *math.* (*pl.* **-*os***) stosunek *m*, proporcja *f*

ra·tion ['ræʃn] **1.** racja *f* (*żywności itp.*); **2.** racjonować; ***~ out*** wydzielać ⟨-lić⟩

ra·tion·al ['ræʃənl] racjonalny, rozsądny; **~·i·ty** [ræʃə'nælətɪ] racjonalność *f*, rozsądek *m*; **~·ize** ['ræʃnəlaɪz] ⟨z⟩racjonalizować; *econ. zwł. Brt.* usprawniać ⟨-nić⟩

'rat race F wyścig *m* szczurów (*niekończące się konkurowanie*)

rat·tle ['rætl] **1.** stukać (*I*); ⟨za⟩grzechotać (*I*); ⟨za⟩terkotać; ⟨za⟩turkotać; *pociąg*: łoskotać, stukotać; F zdeprymować (się), speszyć (się); ***~ at ~ off*** F odklepywać ⟨-pać⟩; ***~ on*** F trajkotać (***about*** o *L*); ***~ through*** F odbębnić (*A*); **2.** stukot *m*, grzechot *m*, terkotanie; grzechotka *f*; **'~·snake** *zo.* grzechotnik *m*

rau·cous ['rɔːkəs] jazgotliwy

rav·age ['rævɪdʒ] ⟨z⟩dewastować, ⟨s⟩pustoszyć; **'~s** *pl.* spustoszenia *pl.*

rave [reɪv] majaczyć, bredzić (***about*** o *L*); pomstować (***against*** przeciw *D*);

piać z zachwytu (***about*** nad *I*)
rav•el ['rævl] (*zwł. Brt.* **-ll-**, *Am.* **-l-**) rozplątywać ⟨-tać⟩ (się); plątać (się); → ***unravel***
ra•ven ['reɪvn] *zo.* kruk *m*
rav•e•nous ['rævənəs] wygłodniały; nienasycony
ra•vine [rə'viːn] wąwóz *m*
rav•ings ['reɪvɪŋz] *pl.* majaczenia *pl.*
rav•ish ['rævɪʃ] zniewalać ⟨-wolić⟩; '**~•ing** zniewalający
raw [rɔː] surowy (*też fig.*); *econ., tech. też* nieprzetworzony; *skóra*: zaczerwieniony; *wiatr*: lodowaty; niedoświadczony; **~ *vegetables and fruit*** *pl.* surówka *f*; **~ *materials*** *pl.* surowce *pl.*; '**~•hide** skóra *f* surowa
ray [reɪ] promień *m*, *fig.* promyk *m*
ray•on ['reɪɒn] sztuczny jedwab *m*
ra•zor ['reɪzə] brzytwa *f*; maszynka *f* do golenia; golarka *f*; ***electric* ~** elektryczna maszynka *f* do golenia; '**~ blade** żyletka *f*; **~('s) 'edge**: ***be on a ~ edge*** *fig.* wisieć na włosku, stać na skraju przepaści
RC [ɑː 'siː] *skrót*: ***Roman Catholic*** rzym.-kat., rzymsko-katolicki
Rd *skrót pisany*: ***Road*** ul., ulica *f*
re [riː]: **~ *your letter of ...*** odnośnie Pańskiego listu z dnia ...
re... [riː] re..., ponownie, powtórnie
reach [riːtʃ] **1.** *v/t.* sięgać ⟨-gnąć⟩ (*G*); dosięgać ⟨-gnąć⟩ (*G*); osiągać ⟨-gnąć⟩; docierać ⟨dotrzeć⟩ do (*G*); dochodzić ⟨dojść⟩ do (*G*); **~ *down to*** dochodzić do (*G*); **~ *out*** sięgać ⟨-gnąć⟩ (***for*** po *A*); *ramię* wyciągać ⟨-gnąć⟩; **2.** zasięg *m*; zakres *m*; ***within* ~** w zasięgu, ***out of* ~** poza zasięgiem; ***within easy* ~** w pobliżu
re•act [rɪ'ækt] ⟨za⟩reagować (***to*** na *A*, *chem.* ***with*** z *I*); **~ *against*** występować przeciwko (*D*); **re•ac•tion** [rɪ'ækʃn] reakcja *f* (*też chem., pol.*)
re•ac•tor [rɪ'æktə] *phys.* reaktor *m*
read 1. [riːd] (***read*** [red]) ⟨prze⟩czytać; *termometr itp.*: odczytywać (-tać); *univ.* studiować (*też* ***for*** *A*); ⟨z⟩rozumieć (***as*** jako); czytać się dobrze; brzmieć; **~ (*s.th.*) *to s.o.*** komuś coś ⟨prze⟩czytać; **~ *medicine*** studiować medycynę; **2.** [red] *pret. i p.p. od* ***read*** 1; **'rea•da•ble** do czytania (*nadający się*); **'read•er** czytelnik *m* (-iczka *f*); lektor *m* (-ka *f*), starszy *m* wykładowca; czytanka *f*
read•i|•ly ['redɪlɪ] łatwo; bez przeszkód; '**~•ness** gotowość *f*
read•ing ['riːdɪŋ] czytanie *n* (*też parl.*); *tech.* wskazanie *n*; odczyt (*termometru*) *m*; rozumienie *n*
re•ad•just [riːə'dʒʌst] *tech.* dostrajać ⟨-roić⟩, ⟨s⟩korygować; **~ (*o.s.*) *to*** przystosowywać ⟨-ować⟩ się do (*G*)
read•y ['redɪ] (***-ier, -iest***) gotowy, gotów; zakończony; ***be* ~ *to do*** być bliskim zrobienia czegoś; **~ *for use*** gotowy do użycia; ***get* ~** przygotowywać ⟨-wać⟩ (się); **~ 'cash** → ***ready money***; **~-'made** konfekcyjny; **~*-made clothes*** *pl.* konfekcja *f*; **~ 'meal** wyrób *m* garmażeryjny; **~ 'mon•ey** F gotówka *f*
real [rɪəl] prawdziwy; rzeczywisty; ***for* ~** *zwł. Am.* F naprawdę; '**~ es•tate** nieruchomość *f*; '**~ es•tate a•gent** pośrednik *m* handlu nieruchomościami
re•a•lis|•m ['rɪəlɪzəm] realizm *m*; **~t** ['rɪəlɪst] realista *m* (-tka *f*); **~•tic** [rɪə'lɪstɪk] (***-ally***) realistyczny
re•al•i•ty [rɪ'ælətɪ] rzeczywistość *f*; **~ show, ~ TV** F reality show
re•a|•li•za•tion [rɪəlaɪ'zeɪʃn] realizacja *f*, urzeczywistnienie *n*; uprzytomnienie *n* sobie, zrozumienie *n*; *econ.* sprzedaż *f*; **~•lize** ['rɪəlaɪz] ⟨z⟩realizować, urzeczywistnić; zdawać ⟨zdać⟩ sobie sprawę, uświadamiać ⟨-domić⟩ sobie; sprzedawać ⟨-dać⟩, spieniężać ⟨-żyć⟩
real•ly ['rɪəlɪ] naprawdę, faktycznie, rzeczywiście
realm [relm] królestwo *n*; *fig.* domena *f*
real•tor ['rɪəltə] *Am.* pośrednik *m* handlu nieruchomościami
reap [riːp] *zboże* żąć, zżynać ⟨zżąć⟩; *plony* zbierać ⟨zebrać⟩ (*też fig.*)
re•ap•pear [riːə'pɪə] ponownie się pojawiać ⟨-wić⟩
rear [rɪə] **1.** *v/t. dziecko* wychowywać ⟨-wać⟩, *zwierzę* ⟨wy⟩hodować; *głowę* podnosić ⟨-nieść⟩; *v/i. koń*: stawać ⟨stanąć⟩ dęba; **2.** tył *m*; tyłek *m*; ***at*** (*Am.* ***in the***) **~** z tyłu, w tyle; ***bring up the* ~** zamykać ⟨-mknąć⟩ pochód; **3.** tylny; '**~•guard** *mil.* ariergarda *f*, straż *f* tylna; '**~ light** *mot.* światło *n* tylne
re•arm [riː'ɑːm] *mil.* ponownie uzbrajać ⟨-roić⟩; **re•ar•ma•ment** *mil.* [riː'ɑːməmənt] ponowne uzbrajanie *n* (się)

R

'rear·|most położony najdalej z tyłu; **~·view 'mir·ror** lusterko *n* wsteczne; **~·ward** ['rɪəwəd] **1.** *adj.* tylny; **2.** *adv.* *też* ***~wards*** do tyłu, w tył; **~-wheel 'drive** *mot.* napęd *m* na tylne koła; **'~ win·dow** *mot.* szyba *f* tylna

rea·son ['riːzn] **1.** powód *m*, przyczyna *f*; rozsądek *m*; rozum *m*; ***by ~ of*** z powodu (*G*); ***for this ~*** z tego powodu; ***listen to ~*** słuchać głosu rozsądku; ***it stands to ~ that*** jest to oczywiste, że; **2.** *v/i.* rozumować; przemawiać ⟨-mówić⟩ do rozsądku; *v/t.* ⟨wy⟩wnioskować (***that*** że); ***~ s.o. into/out of s.th.*** namówić kogoś, by coś zrobił, wyperswadować komuś, by czegoś nie robił; **'rea·so·na·ble** rozsądny; należyty; *cena itp.*: umiarkowany

re·as·sure [riːə'ʃɔː] uspokajać ⟨-koić⟩

re·bate ['riːbeɪt] *econ.* rabat *m*, bonifikata *f*; zapłata *f* zwrotna

reb·el[1] ['rebl] **1.** buntownik *m* (-iczka *f*), rebeliant *m*; **2.** rebeliancki, buntowniczy

re·bel[2] [rɪ'bel] ⟨z⟩buntować się, powstawać ⟨-tać⟩ (***against*** przeciwko *D*); **~·lion** [rɪ'beljən] bunt *m*, rebelia *f*; **~·lious** [rɪ'beljəs] buntowniczy, rebeliancki

re·birth [riː'bɜːθ] ponowne narodziny *pl.*

re·bound 1. [rɪ'baʊnd] odbijać ⟨-bić⟩ się (***from*** z/od *G*); *fig.* opadać ⟨-paść⟩ z powrotem; **2.** ['riːbaʊnd] (*w sporcie*) odbicie *n* się

re·buff [rɪ'bʌf] **1.** (ostra) odmowa *f*, odprawa *f*; **2.** odtrącać ⟨-cić⟩

re·build [riː'bɪld] (***-built***) odbudowywać ⟨-ować⟩ (*też fig.*)

re·buke [rɪ'bjuːk] **1.** upominać ⟨-mnieć⟩, strofować; **2.** upomnienie *n*, strofowanie *n*

re·call [rɪ'kɔːl] **1.** odwoływać ⟨-łać⟩, wycofywać ⟨-fać⟩; przypominać ⟨-mnieć⟩ (sobie); **2.** odwołanie *n*, wycofanie *n*; przypomnienie *n*

re·ca·pit·u·late [riːkə'pɪtjʊleɪt] ⟨z⟩rekapitulować, podsumowywać ⟨-ować⟩

re·cap·ture [riː'kæptʃə] ponownie ⟨s⟩chwytać; *mil.* odbijać ⟨-bić⟩; *fig.* oddawać ⟨oddać⟩, uchwycić

re·cast [riː'kɑːst] (***-cast***) *tech.* przetapiać ⟨-topić⟩; przerabiać ⟨-robić⟩; *theat.* obsadzać ⟨-dzić⟩ na nowo

re·cede [rɪ'siːd] cofać się, wycofywać ⟨-fać⟩ się; *fig.* zamierać ⟨zamrzeć⟩; ***receding*** *broda, czoło*: cofnięty

re·ceipt [rɪ'siːt] *zwł. econ.* przyjęcie *n*, odebranie *n*; rachunek *m*, pokwitowanie *n*; ***~s*** *pl.* wpływy *pl.*; ⚠ *nie* ***recepta***

re·ceive [rɪ'siːv] otrzymywać ⟨-mać⟩; przyjmować ⟨-jąć⟩ (*też* ***into*** do *G*); odbierać ⟨odebrać⟩ (*TV itp.*); **re'ceiv·er** odbiornik *m*; *tel.* słuchawka *f*; *też* ***official ~*** *Brt.* syndyk *m* masy upadłościowej

re·cent ['riːsnt] niedawny, ostatni; **'~·ly** niedawno, ostatnio

re·cep·tion [rɪ'sepʃn] odbiór *m* (*też radiowy lub telewizyjny*); przyjęcie *n* (***into*** do *G*); *też* ***~ desk*** (*hotelu*) recepcja *f*; **~·ist** [rɪ'sepʃənɪst] recepcjonista *m* (-tka *f*); *med.* rejestrator(ka *f*) *m*

re·cep·tive [rɪ'septɪv] *umysł*: chłonny; otwarty (***to*** na *A*)

re·cess [rɪ'ses] przerwa *f* (*Am. też między lekcjami*); *parl.* przerwa *f*; nisza *f*, wnęka *f*

re·ces·sion [rɪ'seʃn] *econ.* recesja *f*

re·ci·pe ['resɪpɪ] przepis *m* (*kulinarny*)

re·cip·i·ent [rɪ'sɪpɪənt] odbiorca *m* (-czyni *f*)

re·cip·ro|·cal [rɪ'sɪprəkl] wzajemny; **~·cate** [rɪ'sɪprəkeɪt] *v/i.* poruszać się ruchem postępowo-zwrotnym; odwzajemniać ⟨-nić⟩ się; *v/t.* *zaproszenie* odwzajemniać ⟨-nić⟩

re·cit·al [rɪ'saɪtl] recital *m*; **re·ci·ta·tion** [resɪ'teɪʃn] recytacja *f*; **re·cite** [rɪ'saɪt] ⟨za-, wy⟩recytować; wyliczać ⟨-czyć⟩, wymieniać ⟨-nić⟩

reck·less ['reklɪs] nieostrożny; lekkomyślny

reck·on ['rekən] *v/t.* obliczać ⟨-czyć⟩; ⟨o⟩szacować; sądzić; zaliczać (***among*** do *G*, ***as*** jako); *też* ***~ up*** wyliczać ⟨-czyć⟩; *v/i.* ***~ on*** liczyć na (*A*); ***~ with*** liczyć się z (*I*); ***~ without*** nie przewidywać ⟨-widzieć⟩ (*G*); **~·ing** ['reknɪŋ] obliczenie *n*, rachunek *m*; ***be out in one's ~ing*** pomylić się w liczeniu

re·claim [rɪ'kleɪm] odbierać ⟨odebrać⟩; ⟨z⟩rekultywować, ⟨z⟩meliorować; *tech.* odzyskiwać ⟨-skać⟩; *przestępcę* nawracać ⟨-wrócić⟩; ⚠ *nie* ***reklamować***

re·cline [rɪ'klaɪn] leżeć, w pół leżeć

re·cluse [rɪ'kluːs] odludek *m*

rec·og|·ni·tion [rekəg'nɪʃn] rozpoznanie *n*; uznanie *n*; **~·nize** ['rekəgnaɪz] rozpoznawać ⟨-nać⟩; uznawać ⟨-nać⟩

re·coil 1. [rɪ'kɔɪl] odskakiwać ⟨-koczyć⟩ (*z przestrachu*) (***from*** przed *I*); *fig.* uchylać ⟨-lić⟩ się (***from*** od *G*); **2.** ['riː-kɔɪl] odrzut *m*, odskok *m*

rec·ol|·lect [rekə'lekt] przypominać ⟨-mnieć⟩ (sobie); **~·lec·tion** [rekə'lekʃn] przypomnienie *n* sobie (***of*** *G*), wspomnienie *n*

rec·om|·mend [rekə'mend] ⟨za⟩rekomendować, polecać ⟨-cić⟩ (***as*** jako, ***for*** na *A*); **~·men·da·tion** [rekəmen'deɪʃn] rekomendacja *f*

rec·om·pense ['rekəmpens] **1.** ⟨z⟩rekompensować, wynagradzać ⟨-rodzić⟩ (***for*** za *A*); **2.** rekompensata *f*, wynagrodzenie *n*

rec·on|·cile ['rekənsaɪl] ⟨po⟩godzić; doprowadzać ⟨-dzić⟩ do zgody (***with*** z *I*); **~·cil·i·a·tion** [rekənsɪlɪ'eɪʃn] pogodzenie *n*; pojednanie *n* (***between*** pomiędzy *I*, ***with*** z *I*)

re·con·di·tion [riːkən'dɪʃn] przeprowadzać ⟨-dzić⟩ generalny remont, przywracać ⟨-rócić⟩ do stanu użytkowego

re·con|·nais·sance [rɪ'kɒnɪsəns] *mil.* rekonesans *m*, rozpoznanie *n*, zwiad *m*; **~·noi·tre** *Brt.*, **~·noi·ter** [rekə'nɔɪtə] *Am. mil.* przeprowadzać ⟨-dzić⟩ rekonesans

re·con·sid·er [riːkən'sɪdə] ponownie rozważyć

re·con|·struct [riːkən'strʌkt] ⟨z⟩rekonstruować, odbudowywać, ⟨-ować⟩ (*też fig.*); **~·struc·tion** [riːkən'strʌkʃn] rekonstrukcja *f*, odbudowa *f*

rec·ord[1] ['rekɔːd] zapis *m*; *jur.* protokół *m*; rejestr *m*; akta *pl.*; płyta *f* (*winylowa*); *sport*, *komp*. rekord *m*; ***off the ~*** F nie do protokołu, nieoficjalnie; ***have a criminal ~*** mieć kryminalną przeszłość; *attr.* rekordowy

re·cord[2] [rɪ'kɔːd] zapisywać ⟨-sać⟩; ⟨za⟩rejestrować; *jur.* ⟨za⟩protokołować; *na taśmie itp*. zapisywać ⟨-sać⟩, nagrywać ⟨-rać⟩; **~·er magnetofon** *m*; *mus.* flet *m* prosty; **~·ing** nagranie *n*

rec·ord play·er ['rekɔːd-] gramofon *m* (*do płyt winylowych*)

re·count [rɪ'kaʊnt] przeliczać ⟨-czyć⟩

re·cov·er [rɪ'kʌvə] *v/t.* odzyskiwać ⟨-kać⟩; ***~ o.s.*** odzyskiwać ⟨-kać⟩ równowagę (*też fig.*); ⟨z⟩rekompensować; wyciągać ⟨-gnąć⟩; *v/i.* dochodzić ⟨dojść⟩ do siebie (***from*** po *L*); **~·y** [rɪ'kʌvərɪ] wyzdrowienie *n*; powrót *m* do normy; odzyskanie *n*; rekompensata *f*

rec·re·a·tion [rekrɪ'eɪʃn] odpoczynek *m*; rekreacja *f*

re·cruit [rɪ'kruːt] **1.** *mil.* rekrut *m*; nowy członek *m*, nowy *m* (nowa *f*); **2.** *też mil.* rekrutować, ⟨z⟩werbować; zatrudniać ⟨-nić⟩

rec·tan|·gle ['rektæŋgl] *math.* prostokąt *m*; **~·gu·lar** [rek'tæŋgjʊlə] prostokątny

rec·ti·fy ['rektɪfaɪ] prostować (*też prąd*)

rec|·tor ['rektə] proboszcz *m*; (*na uniwersytecie*) rektor *m*; **~·to·ry** ['rektərɪ] probostwo *n*

re·cu·pe·rate [rɪ'kjuːpəreɪt] odzyskiwać ⟨-kać⟩ (*zdrowie*), *econ.* wyrównywać ⟨-nać⟩

re·cur [rɪ'kɜː] (**-rr-**) powracać ⟨-rócić⟩; wracać ⟨wrócić⟩; powtarzać ⟨-tórzyć⟩ się; **~·rence** [rɪ'kʌrəns] powrót *m*, nawrót *m* (*choroby*); powtarzanie *n* się; **~·rent** [rɪ'kʌrənt] powracający, nawracający

re·cy|·cle [riː'saɪkl] *odpadki* ⟨z⟩utylizować, przetwarzać ⟨-worzyć⟩; ***~cled paper*** papier z surowców wtórnych; **~·cla·ble** [riː'saɪkləbəl] nadający się do utylizacji; **~·cling** [riː'saɪklɪŋ] recykling *m*, utylizacja *f*

red [red] **1.** czerwony; **2.** czerwień *f*; ***be in the ~*** *econ.* mieć debet *m lub* deficyt *m*; **'~·breast** *zo.* → ***robin***; **≗ 'Crescent** Czerwony Półksiężyc *m*; **≗ 'Cross** Czerwony Krzyż *m*; **~'cur·rant** *bot.* czerwona porzeczka *f*; **~·den** ['redn] ⟨za⟩czerwienić (się), poczerwienieć; **~·dish** ['redɪʃ] czerwonawy

re·dec·o·rate [riː'dekəreɪt] *pokój* ⟨wy⟩remontować, odmalowywać ⟨-ować⟩

re·deem [rɪ'diːm] *zastaw itp.* wykupywać ⟨-kupić⟩; *rel.* odkupywać ⟨-pić⟩; **≗·er** *rel.* Odkupiciel *m*

re·demp·tion [rɪ'dempʃn] wykupienie *n*; *rel.* odkupienie *n*

re·de·vel·op [riːdɪ'veləp] ⟨z⟩modernizować

red|-'faced poczerwieniony, spąsowiały; **~-'hand·ed**: ***catch s.o. ~-handed*** ⟨s⟩chwytać kogoś na gorącym uczynku; **'~·head** F rudzielec *m*; **~-'head·ed** rudy; **~ 'her·ring** *fig.* fałszywy trop *m*; **~-'hot** rozgrzany do czerwoności; *fig.* rozpłomieniony; **≗ 'In·di·an** V czerwo-

R

noskóry *m*; **~-'let·ter day** święto *n*; **'~·ness** czerwień *f*
re·dou·ble [riː'dʌbl] *zwł. aktywność* zdwajać ⟨-woić⟩
red 'tape biurokratyzm *f*, formalizm *m*
re·duce [rɪ'djuːs] zmniejszać ⟨-szyć⟩, ⟨z⟩redukować; *cenę itp.* obniżać ⟨-żyć⟩; zmniejszyć ⟨-szać⟩ ilość; doprowadzać ⟨-dzić⟩ (***to*** do *G*), zmieniać ⟨-nić⟩ (***to*** w *A*), nakłaniać ⟨-łonić⟩; **re·duc·tion** [rɪ'dʌkʃn] zmniejszenie *n*; redukcja *f*; obniżka *f*
re·dun·dant [rɪ'dʌndənt] nadmierny; zbyteczny
reed [riːd] *bot.* trzcina *f*
re·ed·u|·cate [riː'edʒʊkeɪt] reedukować; **~·ca·tion** ['riːedʒʊ'keɪʃn] reedukacja *f*
reef [riːf] rafa *f*
reek [riːk] **1.** smród *m*, odór *m*; **2.** cuchnąć
reel[1] [riːl] **1.** szpula *f*, szpulka *f*, rolka *f*; (*skoczny taniec szkocki*); **2.** ***~ off*** odwijać ⟨-winąć⟩ ze szpul(k)i; *fig.* ⟨wy⟩recytować
reel[2] [riːl] zataczać ⟨-toczyć⟩ się; ⟨za⟩wirować; ***my head ~ed*** w głowie mi się kręciło
re-e·lect [riːɪ'lekt] ponownie wybierać ⟨-brać⟩
re-en|·ter [riː'entə] ponownie wchodzić ⟨wejść⟩; (*w astronautyce*) wchodzić ⟨wejść⟩ (*w atmosferę*); **~·try** [riː'entrɪ] ponowne wejście *n*; (*w astronautyce*) wejście *n* w atmosferę
ref[1] [ref] F (*w sporcie*) sędzia *f*
ref.[2] *skrót pisany*: ***reference*** odesłanie *n*
re·fer [rɪ'fɜː]: ***~ to*** odnosić się do (*G*); powoływać się na (*A*), wspominać ⟨-mnieć⟩ o (*L*); odsyłać ⟨odesłać⟩ do (*G*); ⟨s⟩kierować do (*G*); ⟨s⟩korzystać (*z notatek*)
ref·er·ee [refə'riː] (*w sporcie*) sędzia *m*; osoba *f* polecająca
ref·er·ence ['refrəns] odniesienie *n* (***to*** do *G*); odesłanie *n* (***to*** do *G*); powołanie *n* się (***to*** na *A*), wzmianka *f* (***to o*** *L*); referencje *pl.*; ***list of ~s*** bibliografia *f*; ***with ~ to*** w odniesieniu do (*G*); **'~ book** poradnik *m*, encyklopedia *f*, słownik *m*; **'~ li·bra·ry** biblioteka *f* podręczna; **'~ num·ber** numer *m* akt
ref·e·ren·dum [refə'rendəm] (*pl.* ***-da*** [-də], ***-dums***) referendum *n*
re·fill 1. [riː'fɪl] ponownie napełniać ⟨-nić⟩; **2.** ['riːfɪl] wkład *m* (*do długopisu*), nabój *m* (*do pióra*); dolewka *f*
re·fine [rɪ'faɪn] *tech.* rafinować, oczyszczać ⟨oczyścić⟩; *fig.* udoskonalać ⟨-lić⟩; **~d** rafinowany, oczyszczony; *fig.* wyrafinowany; **~·ment** *tech.* rafinacja *f*; wyrafinowanie *n*; **re·fin·e·ry** [rɪ'faɪnərɪ] *tech.* rafineria *f*
re·flect [rɪ'flekt] *v/t.* odbijać ⟨-bić⟩; odzwierciedlać ⟨-lić⟩; ***be ~ed in*** odbijać się w (*L*); *v/i.* przemyśleć; ***~ (badly) on*** rzucać (złe) światło na (*A*); **re·flec·tion** [rɪ'flekʃn] odbicie *n*; odzwierciedlenie *n* (*też fig.*); refleksja *f*, namysł *m*; **re·flec·tive** [rɪ'flektɪv] refleksyjny; odblaskowy
re·flex ['riːfleks] refleks *m*; odruch *m*; **'~ ac·tion** odruch *m* bezwarunkowy; **'~ cam·e·ra** *phot.* lustrzanka *f*
re·flex·ive [rɪ'fleksɪv] *gr.* zwrotny
re·form [rɪ'fɔːm] **1.** ⟨z⟩reformować, ulepszać ⟨-szyć⟩; poprawiać ⟨-wić⟩ (się); **2.** reforma *f*; poprawa *f*; **ref·or·ma·tion** [refə'meɪʃn] poprawa *f*; ***the*** **♀** Reformacja *f*; **~·er** [rɪ'fɔːmə] reformator *m*
re·fract [rɪ'frækt] *światło* załamywać ⟨-mać⟩ (się); **re·frac·tion** [rɪ'frækʃn] załamanie *n*, refrakcja *f*
re·frain[1] [rɪ'freɪn]: ***~ from*** powstrzymywać ⟨-mać⟩ się od (*G*)
re·frain[2] [rɪ'freɪn] refren *m*
re·fresh [rɪ'freʃ] (***o.s.*** się) odświeżać ⟨-żyć⟩ (*też pamięć*); **~·ing** odświeżający (*też fig.*); **~·ment** odświeżenie *n*, napój *m* odświeżający
re·fri·ge|·rate [rɪ'frɪdʒəreɪt] ⟨s⟩chłodzić; **~·ra·tor** lodówka *f*
re·fu·el [riː'fjʊəl] (*zwł. Brt.* ***-ll-***, *Am.* ***-l-***) ⟨za⟩tankować
ref·uge ['refjuːdʒ] schronienie *n*; *Brt.* (*na jezdni*) wysepka *f*
ref·u·gee [refjʊ'dʒiː] uchodźca; **~ camp** obóz *m* dla uchodźców
re·fund 1. ['riːfʌnd] spłata *f*, zwrot *m*; **2.** [riː'fʌnd] spłacać ⟨-cić⟩, zwracać ⟨zwrócić⟩
re·fur·bish [riː'fɜːbɪʃ] przeprowadzać ⟨-dzić⟩ renowację (*G*), *fig.* odświeżać ⟨-żyć⟩
re·fus·al [rɪ'fjuːzl] odmowa *f*
re·fuse[1] [rɪ'fjuːz] *v/t.* odmawiać ⟨-mówić⟩ (*też* ***to do s.th.*** zrobienia czegoś);

R

ofertę itp. odrzucać ⟨-cić⟩; *v/i.* odmawiać ⟨-mówić⟩
ref·use² ['refju:s] odpadki *pl.*, śmieci *pl.*; **'~ dump** wysypisko *n* śmieci
re·fute [rɪ'fju:t] obalać ⟨-lić⟩
re·gain [rɪ'geɪn] odzyskiwać ⟨-kać⟩
re·gale [rɪ'geɪl]: **~ *s.o. with s.th.*** zabawiać ⟨-wić⟩ kogoś czymś
re·gard [rɪ'gɑ:d] **1.** szacunek *m*, poważanie *n*; wzgląd *m*; ***in this ~*** w tym względzie; ***with ~ to*** w odniesieniu do (*G*); **~s** *pl.* (*w listach*) pozdrowienia *pl.*; **2.** uważać; patrzeć na (*A*); ***~ as*** uważać za (*A*); ***as ~s*** co się tyczy (*G*); **~·ing** odnośnie (*G*); **~·less**: ***~less of*** niezależnie od (*G*), bez względu na (*A*)
regd *skrót pisany*: ***registered*** *econ.* zarejestrowany; *przesyłka*: polecony
re·gen·e·rate [rɪ'dʒenəreɪt] ⟨z⟩regenerować (się); odradzać ⟨-rodzić⟩ (się)
re·gent ['ri:dʒənt] regent(ka *f*) *m*
re·gi·ment 1. ['redʒɪmənt] *mil.* pułk *m*; *fig.* zastępy *pl.*; **2.** ['redʒɪment] sprawować ścisłą kontrolę nad (*I*)
re·gion ['ri:dʒən] region *m*; rejon *m*; obszar *m*; **'~·al** regionalny
re·gis·ter ['redʒɪstə] **1.** rejestr *m*; spis *m*, lista *f*; dziennik *m* lekcyjny; **2.** *v/t.* ⟨za⟩rejestrować, zapisywać ⟨-sać⟩; *uczucia, wartość* pokazywać ⟨-zać⟩; *list itp.* nadawać ⟨-dać⟩ (*jako polecony*); *v/i.* wpisywać ⟨-sać⟩ się; **~ed 'let·ter** list *m* polecony
re·gis·tra·tion [redʒɪ'streɪʃn] rejestracja *f*, zarejestrowanie *n*; wpis *m*; **~ fee** opłata *f* rejstracyjna; wpisowe *n*; **~ num·ber** *mot.* numer *m* rejestracyjny
re·gis·try ['redʒɪstrɪ] miejsce *n* przechowywania akt stanu cywilnego; **'~ of·fice** *zwł. Brt.* urząd *m* stanu cywilnego
re·gret [rɪ'gret] **1.** (**-*tt-***) żałować; ⟨po⟩informować z przykrością; **2.** żal *m*; ubolewanie *n*; **~·ful·ly** z żalem, z ubolewaniem; **~·ta·ble** godny ubolewania
reg·u·lar ['regjʊlə] **1.** regularny; miarowy; stały; prawidłowy; *zwł. Am.* zwykły, normalny; *mil.* zawodowy; **2.** F stały (-a) klient(ka *f*), *m* stały bywalec; gość *m*; *mil.* żołnierz *m* zawodowy; *Am. mot.* zwykła benzyna *f*; **~·i·ty** [regjʊ'lærətɪ] regularność *f*
reg·u|·late ['regjʊleɪt] regulować, kontrolować; *tech.* ⟨wy-, na-, u⟩regulować; **~·la·tion** [regjʊ'leɪʃn] przepis *m*, zarządzenie *n*; kontrola *f*; regulacja *f*; **~·la·tor** ['regjʊleɪtə] *tech.* regulator *m*, stabilizator *m*
re·hears|·al [rɪ'hɜ:sl] *mus., theat.* próba *f*; **~e** [rɪ'hɜ:s] *mus., theat.* ⟨z⟩robić próbę
reign [reɪn] **1.** panowanie *n*, władanie *n* (*też fig.*); **2.** panować, władać
re·im·burse [ri:ɪm'bɜ:s] *wydatki* zwracać ⟨-rócić⟩
rein [reɪn] **1.** *zwł. pl.* cugle *pl.*; **2. *~ in*** *konia itp.* wziąć ⟨brać⟩ w cugle (*też fig.*)
rein·deer ['reɪndɪə] *zo.* (*pl.* ***reindeer***) renifer *m*
re·in·force [ri:ɪn'fɔ:s] wzmacniać ⟨-mocnić⟩; **~·ment** wzmocnienie *n*; ***~ments*** *pl. mil.* posiłki *pl.*
re·in·state [ri:ɪn'steɪt] przywracać ⟨-rócić⟩ (***as*** jako, ***in*** na *A*)
re·in·sure [ri:ɪn'ʃɔ:] reasekurować
re·it·e·rate [ri:'ɪtəreɪt] powtarzać
re·ject [rɪ'dʒekt] odrzucać ⟨-cić⟩; nie przyjmować ⟨-jąć⟩; **re·jec·tion** [rɪ'dʒekʃn] odrzucenie *n*
re·joice [rɪ'dʒɔɪs] radować się (***at, over*** *I lub* z *G*); **re'joic·ing**(**s** *pl.*) radowanie *n* się
re·join¹ [ri:'dʒɔɪn] wstąpić ⟨wstępować⟩ powtórnie
re·join² [rɪ'dʒɔɪn] odpowiadać ⟨-wiedzieć⟩
re·ju·ve·nate [rɪ'dʒu:vɪneɪt] ożywiać ⟨-wić⟩
re·kin·dle [ri:'kɪndl] *ogień* rozpalać ⟨-lić⟩ ponownie
re·lapse [rɪ'læps] **1.** popaść ponownie (***into*** w *A*); *med.* mieć nawrót; **2.** nawrót *m*
re·late [rɪ'leɪt] *v/t.* ⟨z⟩relacjonować, zdawać ⟨zdać⟩ sprawę; ⟨po⟩wiązać, ⟨po⟩łączyć (***to*** z *G*); *v/i.* ***~ to*** odnosić się do (*G*); **re·lat·ed** powiązany (***to*** z *G*)
re·la·tion [rɪ'leɪʃn] krewny *m* (-na *f*); związek *m*, relacja *f* (***between*** (po)między *I*, ***to*** do *G*); ***in** lub **with ~ to*** w odniesieniu do (*G*); **~s** *pl. dyplomatyczne itp.* stosunki *pl.*; **~·ship** związek *m*; stosunek *m*; relacja *f*
rel·a·tive¹ ['relətɪv] krewny *m* (-na *f*)
rel·a·tive² ['relətɪv] relatywny, stosunkowy; odnoszący się (***to*** do *G*); *gr.* względny; **~ 'pro·noun** *gr.* zaimek *m* względny

R

re•lax [rɪ'læks] *v/t.* rozluźniać ⟨-nić⟩; *fig.* ⟨z⟩łagodzić; *v/i.* rozluźniać ⟨-nić⟩ się; odprężać ⟨-żyć⟩ się; ulegać ⟨-lec⟩ złagodzeniu; **~•a•tion** [riːlæk'seɪʃn] rozluźnienie *n*; odprężenie *n*; złagodzenie *n*; **~ed** rozluźniony; odprężony;

re•lay¹ **1.** ['riːleɪ] zmiana *f*; (*w sporcie*) sztafeta *f*; przekaźnik *m* (*radiowy lub telewizyjny*); [*też* riː'leɪ] **2.** [riː'leɪ] przekazywać ⟨-zać⟩, ⟨prze⟩transmitować

re•lay² [riː'leɪ] (**-laid**) *kabel*, *dywan* kłaść ⟨położyć⟩ na nowo

re•lay race ['riːleɪreɪs] (*w sporcie*) bieg *m* sztafetowy, sztafeta *f*

re•lease [rɪ'liːs] **1.** *ptaka*, *płytę*, *gaz itp.* wypuszczać ⟨-puścić⟩; *gaz* spuszczać ⟨spuścić⟩; *więźnia*, *hamulec* zwalniać ⟨zwolnić⟩; ⟨o⟩publikować; **2.** wypuszczenie *n*; spuszczenie *n*; zwolnienie *n*; *tech.*, zwalniacz *m*; *phot.* wyzwalacz *m*; udostępnienie *n*; wydanie *n*; film *m*

rel•e•gate ['relɪgeɪt] przenosić ⟨-nieść⟩ (*na gorsze miejsce*); (*w sporcie*) przesuwać ⟨-nąć⟩ (**to** do *G*)

re•lent [rɪ'lent] okazywać ⟨-zać⟩ litość; *fig.* ⟨z⟩łagodnieć; **~•less** bezlitosny, nieustępliwy

rel•e•vant ['reləvənt] istotny (**to** dla *G*), ważny; właściwy; **be ~ to** mieć znaczenie dla (*G*)

re•li|•a•bil•i•ty [rɪlaɪə'bɪlətɪ] wiarygodność *f*; niezawodność *f*; **~•a•ble** [rɪ'laɪəbl] wiarygodny; niezawodny; **~•ance** [rɪ'laɪəns] zaufanie *n*; uzależnienie *n*, zależność *f* (**on** od *G*)

rel•ic ['relɪk] relikt *m*; *rel.* relikwia *f*; *attr.* reliktowy

re•lief [rɪ'liːf] ulga *f*; ulżenie *n*; pomoc *f* (*materialna*); *Am.* zapomoga *f*; relief *m*; płaskorzeźba *f*

re•lieve [rɪ'liːv] *ból itp.* ⟨z⟩łagodzić; *wartownika itp.* zmieniać ⟨-nić⟩; *nudę itp.* zmniejszać ⟨-szyć⟩; **~ s.o. of s.th.** odejmować ⟨odjąć⟩ komuś czegoś

re•li|•gion [rɪ'lɪdʒən] religia *f*; **~•gious** religijny

rel•ish ['relɪʃ] **1.** *fig.* smak *m*, upodobanie *n* (**for** do *G*); *gastr.* przyprawa *f*; **with ~** z przyjemnością; **2.** delektować się (*I*), unosić się nad (*I*); znajdować ⟨znaleźć⟩ upodobanie w (*L*)

re•luc|•tance [rɪ'lʌktəns] niechęć *f*; **with ~tance** niechętnie; **~•tant** niechętny; **be ~tant to do s.th.** nie mieć chęci czegoś zrobić

re•ly [rɪ'laɪ]: **~ on** polegać na (*L*); zależeć od (*G*)

re•main [rɪ'meɪn] **1.** pozostawać ⟨-tać⟩, zostawać ⟨-tać⟩; **2. ~s** *pl.* resztki *pl.*, pozostałości *pl.*; **~•der** [rɪ'meɪndə] pozostałość *f*, reszta *f*

re•make **1.** [riː'meɪk] (**-made**) ⟨z⟩robić powtórnie *lub* ponownie; **2.** ['riːmeɪk] nowa wersja *f* filmu, remake *m*

re•mand [rɪ'mɑːnd] *jur.* **1. be ~ed in custody** być odesłanym do aresztu śledczego; **2. be on ~** pozostawać w areszcie śledczym

re•mark [rɪ'mɑːk] **1.** *v/t.* zauważać ⟨-żyć⟩; *v/i.* **~ on** ⟨s⟩komentować (*A*); **2.** uwaga *f*; **re'mar•ka•ble** godny uwagi

rem•e•dy ['remədɪ] **1.** środek *m* (*leczniczy*, *zapobiegawczy*); **2.** *szkodę* naprawiać ⟨-wić⟩; *złu* zaradzać ⟨-dzić⟩ (*D*)

re•mem|•ber [rɪ'membə] ⟨za⟩pamiętać; przypominać ⟨-mnieć⟩ sobie; **please ~ber me to her** proszę przekazać jej moje pozdrowienia; **~•brance** [rɪ'membrəns] pamiętanie *n*; pamięć *f*; **in ~brance of** ku pamięci (*G*)

re•mind [rɪ'maɪnd] przypominać ⟨-mnieć⟩ (**of** o *L*); **~•er** przypomnienie *n*; upomnienie *n*

rem•i•nis|•cences [remɪ'nɪsnsɪz] *pl.* wspomnienia *pl.* (**of** o *L*); **~•cent**: **be ~cent of** przypominać o (*L*)

re•mit [rɪ'mɪt] (**-tt-**) *grzechy* odpuszczać ⟨-puścić⟩, przebaczać ⟨-czyć⟩; *winy* darować; *pieniądze* przekazywać ⟨-zać⟩, przesyłać ⟨-słać⟩; **~•tance** przekaz *m* (*pieniężny*) (**to** dla *G*)

rem•nant ['remnənt] pozostałość *f*

re•mod•el [riː'mɒdl] (*zwł. Brt.* **-ll-**, *Am.* **-l-**) przemodelować, przekształcać ⟨-cić⟩

re•mon•strance [rɪ'mɒnstrəns] protest *m*; upomnienie *n*; **rem•on•strate** ['remənstreɪt] ⟨za⟩protestować (**against** przeciw *D*); czynić zarzuty (**with** *D*, **about** w sprawie *G*)

re•morse [rɪ'mɔːs] wyrzuty *pl.* sumienia; **~•less** niemiłosierny

re•mote [rɪ'məʊt] (**-r**, **-st**) odległy, oddalony; *ktoś* pełen rezerwy; *szansa*: niewielki; **~ con'trol** *tech.* zdalne sterowanie *n*; *radio*, *TV*: pilot *m*

re•mov•al [rɪ'muːvl] usuwanie *n*; usunięcie *n*; przeprowadzka *f*; ~ **van** wóz *m* meblowy

re·move [rɪ'muːv] *v/t.* usuwać ⟨usunąć⟩; zdejmować ⟨zdjąć⟩; *z drogi itp.* zabierać ⟨zabrać⟩; *v/i.* przenosić ⟨-nieść⟩ się (***from ... to ...*** z *G* ... do *G* ...); **re'mov·er** środek *m* do usuwania (plam)

Re·nais·sance [rə'neɪsəns] renesans *m lub* Renesans *m*

ren·der ['rendə] *możliwym, trudnym itp.* ⟨u⟩czynić; *przysługę* oddawać ⟨-dać⟩; *sprawozdanie* zdawać ⟨zdać⟩; *mus.* ⟨z⟩interpretować; przekładać ⟨-łożyć⟩ (***into*** na *A*); **~·ing** *zwł. Brt.* ['rendərɪŋ] → ***rendition***

ren·di·tion [ren'dɪʃn] interpretacja *f*; tłumaczenie *n*

re·new [rɪ'njuː] odnawiać ⟨-nowić⟩; *rozmowę itp.* wznawiać ⟨-nowić⟩; *atak* ponawiać ⟨-nowić⟩; przedłużać ⟨-żyć⟩; *siły* ⟨z⟩regenerować; **~·al** odnowienie *n*; wznowienie *n*; ponowienie *n*; przedłużenie *n*

re·nounce [rɪ'naʊns] wyrzekać ⟨-rzec⟩ się; zrzekać ⟨zrzec⟩ się (*G*); wypierać ⟨-przeć⟩ się

ren·o·vate ['renəʊveɪt] odnawiać ⟨-nowić⟩, ⟨wy⟩remontować

re·nown [rɪ'naʊn] sława *f*; **~ed** sławny, słynny (***as*** jako, ***for*** z *G*)

rent[1] [rent] **1.** czynsz *m*, komorne *n*; *zwł. Am.* opłata *f* za wypożyczenie; ***for ~*** *zwł. Am.* do wynajęcia; ⚠ *nie* ***renta***; **2.** wynajmować ⟨-jąć⟩ (***from*** od *G*, ***to*** *D*); ***~ out*** *zwł. Am.* wynajmować ⟨-jąć⟩

rent[2] [rent] rozdarcie *n*

'Rent-a-... wynajem (*G*)

rent|·al ['rentl] czynsz *m*; *zwł. Am.* opłata *f* za wynajęcie; *zwł. Am.* → **~·ed 'car** wynajęty samochód *m*

re·nun·ci·a·tion [rɪnʌnsɪ'eɪʃn] wyrzeczenie *n* się; zrzeczenie *n* się

re·pair [rɪ'peə] **1.** naprawiać ⟨-wić⟩, ⟨z⟩reperować, ⟨wy⟩remontować; *fig.* naprawiać ⟨-wić⟩, ⟨s⟩korygować; **2.** naprawianie *n*, reperowanie *n*, remontowanie *n*; ***~s*** *pl.* naprawa *f*, reperacja *f*, remont *m*; ***beyond ~*** nie do naprawienia; ***in good/bad ~*** w dobrym/złym stanie; ***be under ~*** być w naprawie

rep·a·ra·tion [repə'reɪʃn] odszkodowanie *n*; ***~s*** *pl.* odszkodowania *pl.* wojenne, reparacje *pl.*

rep·ar·tee [repɑː'tiː] cięta odpowiedź *f*; błyskotliwość *f*

re·pay [riː'peɪ] (***-paid***) zapłacić (***to*** *D*), spłacać ⟨-cić⟩; odpłacać ⟨-cić⟩ za (*A*); **~·ment** spłata *f*

re·peal [rɪ'piːl] uchylać ⟨-lić⟩, unieważniać ⟨-nić⟩

re·peat [rɪ'piːt] **1.** *v/t.* powtarzać ⟨-tórzyć⟩; *zamówienie* ponawiać ⟨-nowić⟩; ***~ o.s.*** powtarzać ⟨-tórzyć⟩ się; *v/i.* F *potrawa*: przypominać się, odbijać się (***on*** *D*); **2.** powtórka *f* (*programu*); *mus.* znak *m* powtórzenia; **~·ed** powtórzony, powtórny

re·pel [rɪ'pel] (***-ll-***) odpierać ⟨odeprzeć⟩; odpychać ⟨odepchnąć⟩ (*też fig.*); **~·lent** [rɪ'pelənt] **1.** *adj.* odpychający, odstręczający; **2.** środek *m* odstraszający owady

re·pent [rɪ'pent] żałować; **re'pent·ance** żal *m*, skrucha *f*; **re'pen·tant** żałujący; skruszony

re·per·cus·sion [riːpə'kʌʃn]: *zw.* ***~s*** *pl.* reperkusje *pl.*

rep·er·toire ['repətwɑː] *theat.* repertuar *m*

rep·er·to·ry thea·tre ['repətərɪ -] (*teatr, w którym grane są różne sztuki*)

rep·e·ti·tion [repɪ'tɪʃn] powtórzenie *n*

re·place [rɪ'pleɪs] zastępować ⟨-tąpić⟩; wymieniać ⟨-nić⟩; (*na miejsce*) odkładać ⟨odłożyć⟩; **~·ment** zastępstwo *n*; wymiana *f*; odłożenie *n* na miejsce

re·plant [riː'plɑːnt] przesadzać ⟨-dzić⟩

re·play 1. [riː'pleɪ] (*w sporcie*) *mecz* powtarzać ⟨-tórzyć⟩; *kasetę* odtwarzać ⟨-worzyć⟩; **2.** ['riːpleɪ] powtórny mecz *m*, *Brt.* ***action ~*** , *Am.* ***instant ~*** replay *m*

re·plen·ish [rɪ'plenɪʃ] dopełniać ⟨-nić⟩; uzupełniać ⟨-nić⟩

re·plete [rɪ'pliːt] nasycony; pełny; całkowicie wyposażony (***with*** w *A*)

rep·li·ca ['replɪkə] replika *f*; kopia *f*

re·ply [rɪ'plaɪ] **1.** odpowiadać ⟨-wiedzieć⟩ (***to*** na *A*); **2.** odpowiedź *f* (***to*** na *A*); replika *f*; ***in ~ to*** w odpowiedzi na (*A*); **~ 'cou·pon** (*kupon pokrywający koszt znaczka na odpowiedź*); **~-paid 'en·ve·lope** koperta *f* z opłaconą odpowiedzią

re·port [rɪ'pɔːt] **1.** sprawozdanie *n*; relacja *f*; raport *m*; meldunek *m*; *Brt.* (*Am.* ***~ card***) świadectwo *n* szkolne; pogłos *m* (*strzału*); **2.** składać ⟨złożyć⟩ sprawozdanie; ⟨z⟩relacjonować, ⟨po⟩informować; donosić ⟨-nieść⟩; zgłaszać ⟨zgłosić⟩ (się), ⟨za⟩meldować (się); donosić ⟨-nieść⟩; na (*A*); ***it is ~ed that*** mówi się, że; ***~ed speech*** *gr.* mowa *f* zależna; **~·er** reporter(ka *f*) *m*, korespondent(ka *f*) *m*

re·pose [rɪ'pəʊz] spokój *m*; spoczynek *m*

re·pos·i·to·ry [rɪ'pɒzɪtərɪ] skład *m*, magazyn *m*; *fig.* źródło *n*, skarbnica *f*

rep·re|·sent [reprɪ'zent] reprezentować; przedstawiać ⟨-wić⟩ (*też* ***as, to be*** jako); stanowić; **~·sen·ta·tion** [reprɪzen'teɪʃn] reprezentacja *f*; przedstawienie *n*; *jur.* zastępstwo *n* prawne; **~·sen·ta·tive** [reprɪ'zentətɪv] **1.** reprezentatywny, typowy (***of*** dla *G*); **2.** przedstawiciel(ka *f*) *m* (*też handl., pol.*); *parl.* deputowany *m* (-na *f*); ***House of ♀sentative*** *Am.* Izba *f* Reprezentantów

re·press [rɪ'pres] ⟨s⟩tłumić, zduszać ⟨zdusić⟩; *psych.* hamować; **repres·sion** [rɪ'preʃn] (s)tłumienie *n*; *psych.* (za)hamowanie *n*

re·prieve [rɪ'priːv] **1.** ***he was ~d*** odroczono *lub* zawieszono mu wykonywanie kary; **2.** (*kary*) odroczenie *n*; zawieszenie *n*

rep·ri·mand ['reprɪmɑːnd] **1.** udzielać ⟨-lić⟩ nagany (***for*** za *A*); **2.** nagana *f*, upomnienie *n*, reprymenda *f*

re·print 1. [riː'prɪnt] przedrukowywać ⟨-ować⟩; *książkę* wznawiać ⟨wznowić⟩; **2.** ['riːprɪnt] przedruk *m*, wznowienie *n*; reprint *m*

re·pri·sal [rɪ'praɪzl] odwet *m*, środek odwetowy; *jur.* retorsja *f*

re·proach [rɪ'prəʊtʃ] **1.** wyrzut *m*; zarzut *m*; **2.** zarzucać ⟨-cić⟩ (***s.o. with s.th.*** coś komuś); ⟨z⟩robić wyrzuty (***for*** za *A*); **~·ful** pełny wyrzutu

rep·ro·bate ['reprəbeɪt] ladaco *m*; rozpustnik *m* (-nica *f*)

re·pro·cess [riː'prəʊses] *paliwo nuklearne* przetwarzać ⟨-worzyć⟩; **~·ing plant** zakład *m* przetwarzania paliwa nuklearnego

re·pro|·duce [riːprə'djuːs] *v/t.* powtórzyć; ⟨z⟩reprodukować; ⟨s⟩kopiować; ***~duce o.s.*** *v/i. biol.* rozmnażać ⟨-nożyć⟩ się; **~·duc·tion** [riːprə'dʌkʃn] *biol.* rozmnażanie *m* (się); reprodukcja *f*, reprodukowanie *n*; kopia *f*; **~·duc·tive** *biol.* [riːprə'dʌktɪv] rozrodczy

re·proof [rɪ'pruːf] wyrzut *m*, zarzut *m*

re·prove [rɪ'pruːv] zarzucać ⟨-cić⟩

rep·tile ['reptaɪl] *zo.* gad *m*

re·pub|·lic [rɪ'pʌblɪk] republika *f*; **~·lican** [rɪ'pʌblɪkən] **1.** republikański; **2.** republikanin *m*

re·pu·di·ate [rɪ'pjuːdɪeɪt] odrzucać ⟨-cić⟩; *econ. zapłaty* odmawiać ⟨-mówić⟩

re·pug|·nance [rɪ'pʌgnəns]: ***in ~nance, with ~nance*** z odrazą, ze wstrętem; **~·nant** odrażający, wstrętny

re·pulse [rɪ'pʌls] **1.** odpychać ⟨odepchnąć⟩; ⟨z⟩mierzić; *mil. atak* odpierać ⟨odeprzeć⟩; **2.** odepchnięcie *n*; odparcie *n*

re·pul|·sion [rɪ'pʌlʃn] wstręt *m*; niechęć *f*; *phys.* odpychanie *n*; **~·sive** [rɪ'pʌlsɪv] wstrętny; *phys.* odpychający

rep·u·ta|·ble ['repjʊtəbl] szanowany, szanowny; **~·tion** [repjʊ'teɪʃn] reputacja *f*

re·pute [rɪ'pjuːt] renoma *f*; **re'put·ed** renomowany

re·quest [rɪ'kwest] **1.** (***for***) prośba *f* (o *A*), życzenie *n*; ***at the ~ of s.o., at s.o.'s ~*** na czyjeś życzenie; ***on ~*** na życzenie; **2.** prosić o (*A*); ***be ~ed to do s.th.*** być proszonym o zrobienie czegoś; **~ stop** *Brt.* przystanek *m* na żądanie

re·quire [rɪ'kwaɪə] wymagać, potrzebować (*G*); **~·ment** wymóg *m*, potrzeba *f*; żądanie *n*

req·ui·site ['rekwɪzɪt] **1.** niezbędny, wymagany; **2.** *zw.* ***~s*** *pl.* artykuły *pl.*, przybory *pl.*; ***toilet ~s*** *pl.* przybory *pl.* toaletowe; ⚠ *nie* ***rekwizyt***

req·ui·si·tion [rekwɪ'zɪʃn] **1.** zapotrzebowanie *n*, zamówienie *n*; *mil.* rekwizycja *f*; ***make a ~*** coś zgłaszać ⟨zgłosić⟩ zapotrzebowanie na (*A*); **2.** zgłaszać ⟨zgłosić⟩ zapotrzebowanie na (*A*); *mil.* ⟨za⟩rekwirować

re·sale ['riːseɪl] odprzedaż *f*, odsprzedaż *f*

re·scind *jur.* [rɪ'sɪnd] unieważniać ⟨-nić⟩; anulować; odwoływać ⟨-łać⟩

res·cue ['reskjuː] **1.** ⟨wy-, u⟩ratować (***from*** z *G*, od *G*); **2.** ratunek *m*; pomoc *f*

re·search [rɪ'sɜːtʃ] **1.** badanie *n* naukowe; **2.** *v/i.* prowadzić badania naukowe;

v/t. ⟨z⟩badać; ~**·er** naukowiec *m*, badacz(ka *f*) *m*
re·sem|·blance [rɪ'zembləns] podobieństwo *n* (***to*** do *G*, ***among*** między *I*); ~**·ble** [rɪ'zembl] przypominać; być podobnym do (*G*)
re·sent [rɪ'zent] nie cierpieć (*G*), nie znosić (*G*); czuć urazę do (*G*); ~**·ful** urażony, dotknięty; ~**·ment** uraza *f* (***against, at*** wobec *G*); niechęć *f*
res·er·va·tion [rezə'veɪʃn] rezerwacja *f*; zastrzeżenie *n*; rezerwat *m* (*dla Indian, Am. przyrodniczy*); → ***central reservation***
re·serve [rɪ'zɜːv] **1.** przeznaczać ⟨-czyć⟩ (***for*** na *A*); zastrzegać ⟨-rzec⟩; ⟨za⟩rezerwować; **2.** rezerwa *f* (*też mil., fig.*); zapas *m*; powściągliwość *f*; rezerwat *m* (*przyrody*); (*w sporcie*) gracz *m* rezerwowy; ~**d** zarezerwowany
res·er·voir ['rezəvwɑː] rezerwuar *m*, zbiornik *m*; *fig.* źródło *n*
re·set [riː'set] (**-*tt*-**; **-*set***) *zegar, miernik* przestawiać ⟨-wić⟩; *med. kość* zestawiać ⟨-wić⟩ na nowo; *komp.* ⟨z⟩resetować
re·set·tle [riː'setl] przesiedlać ⟨-lić⟩ się
re·side [rɪ'zaɪd] mieszkać, rezydować
res·i·dence ['rezɪdəns] miejsce *n* zamieszkania; zamieszkanie *n*; rezydencja *f*; siedziba *f*; '~ **per·mit** zezwolenie *n* na zamieszkanie
res·i·dent ['rezɪdənt] **1.** zamieszkały (na stałe); miejscowy; **2.** mieszkaniec *m* (-nka *f*); *hotelowy* gość *m*
res·i·den·tial [rezɪ'denʃl] *dzielnica*: mieszkaniowy; *konferencja*: poza miejscem zamieszkania; ~ **'ar·e·a** dzielnica *f* mieszkaniowa
re·sid·u·al [rɪ'zɪdjʊəl] szczątkowy; resztkowy; ~ **pol'lu·tion** zanieczyszczenia *pl*; **res·i·due** ['rezɪdjuː] pozostałość *f*; *chem.* residuum *n*
re·sign [rɪ'zaɪn] *v/i.* ⟨z⟩rezygnować (***from*** z *G*); ustępować ⟨-tąpić⟩; *v/t.* ustępować ⟨-tąpić⟩ z (*G*) (*stanowiska*); zrzekać ⟨-rzec⟩ się (*G*); ~ ***o.s. to*** pogodzić się z (*I*); **res·ig·na·tion** [rezɪg'neɪʃn] rezygnacja *f*; ustąpienie *n*; zrzeczenie się *n*; pogodzenie się *n*; ~**ed** [rɪ'zaɪnd] zrezygnowany
re·sil·i|·ence [rɪ'zɪlɪəns] elastyczność *f*, sprężystość *f*; *fig.* odporność *f*; ~**·ent** sprężysty, elastyczny; *fig.* odporny
res·in ['rezɪn] żywica *f*
re·sist [rɪ'zɪst] opierać ⟨oprzeć⟩ się (*D*); przeciwstawiać ⟨-wić⟩ się; ~**·ance** opór *m*; odporność *f*; *electr.* rezystancja *f*; ***line of least*** ~***ance*** droga *f* najmniejszego oporu; **re·sis·tant** oporny (***to*** na *A*)
res·o|·lute ['rezəluːt] zdecydowany, zdeterminowany; ~**·lu·tion** [rezə'luːʃn] *pol.* rezolucja *f*; uchwała *f*, postanowienie *n*; zdecydowanie *n*; *komp.* rozdzielczość *f*
re·solve [rɪ'zɒlv] **1.** *problem itp.* rozwiązywać ⟨-zać⟩; postanawiać ⟨-nowić⟩; ~ ***on doing s.th.*** ⟨z⟩decydować się coś zrobić; **2.** postanowienie *n*; zdecydowanie *n*
res·o|·nance ['rezənəns] pogłos *m*, rezonans *m*; '~**·nant** *pokój itp.*: o dużym pogłosie; *głos*: głęboki, dźwięczny
re·sort [rɪ'zɔːt] **1.** uzdrowisko *n*, kurort *m*, miejscowość *f* wypoczynkowa; → ***health*** (***seaside, summer***) ***resort***; **2.** ~ ***to*** uciekać ⟨-ciec⟩ się do (*G*)
re·sound [rɪ'zaʊnd] rozbrzmiewać ⟨-mieć⟩
re·source [rɪ'sɔːs] zasób *m*; rozwiązanie *n*; pociecha *f*, schronienie *n*; pomysłowość *f*; ~***s*** *pl.* środki *pl.*; zasoby *pl.*, bogactwa *pl.* naturalne; ~**·ful** pomysłowy
re·spect [rɪ'spekt] **1.** szacunek *m*, poważanie *n*; respekt *m* (***for*** dla *G*); wzgląd (***for*** dla *G*); ***with*** ~ ***to*** odnośnie (*G*); ***in this*** ~ pod tym względem; ***give my*** ~***s to*** proszę przekazać pozdrowienia (*D*); **2.** *v/t.* szanować, poważać; respektować, przestrzegać (*G*); **re'spec·ta·ble** szanowny, szacowny; ~**·ful** pełen szacunku
re·spect·ive [rɪ'spektɪv] odnośny, właściwy; ***we went to our*** ~ ***places*** każdy udał się na swoje miejsce; ~**·ly** właściwie, odpowiednio
res·pi·ra|·tion [respə'reɪʃn] oddychanie *n*; ~**·tor** ['respəreɪtə] respirator *m*
re·spite ['respaɪt] wytchnienie *n*, spoczynek *m*; ***without*** ~ bez wytchnienia
re·splen·dent [rɪ'splendənt] olśniewający
re·spond [rɪ'spɒnd] odpowiadać ⟨-wiedzieć⟩ (***to*** na *A*, ***that*** że); ⟨za⟩reagować (***to*** na *A*)

R

re·sponse [rɪ'spɒns] odpowiedź *f*; odzew *m*, reakcja *f* (***to*** na *A*)
re·spon|·si·bil·i·ty [rɪspɒnsə'bɪlətɪ] odpowiedzialność *f*; ***on one's own ~sibility*** na własną odpowiedzialność; ***sense of ~sibility*** poczucie *n* odpowiedzialności; ***take*** (***full***) ***~ sibility for*** przyjmować ⟨-jąć⟩ *pełną* odpowiedzialność za (*A*); **~·si·ble** [rɪ'spɒnsəbl] odpowiedzialny
rest[1] [rest] **1.** odpoczynek *m*, spoczynek *m*; *tech.* oparcie *n*; *tel.* widełki *pl.*; ***have*** *lub* ***take a ~*** odpoczywać ⟨-cząć⟩; ***set s.o.'s mind at ~*** uspokoić kogoś; **2.** *v/i.* odpoczywać ⟨-cząć⟩; spoczywać ⟨-cząć⟩; opierać ⟨oprzeć⟩ się (***against, on*** o *A*); ***let s.th. ~*** zostawiać ⟨-wić⟩ coś w spokoju; ***~ on*** spoczywać ⟨-cząć⟩ na (*L*) (*też fig. spojrzenie*); *v/t.* opierać ⟨-przeć⟩ (***against, on*** o *A*); dawać ⟨dać⟩ odpocząć
rest[2] [rest] reszta *f*; ***all the ~ of them*** wszyscy pozostali; ***for the ~*** co do reszty
res·tau·rant ['restərɒnt, 'restərənt, 'restərɔ̃:ŋ] restauracja *f*
'rest|·ful spokojny; uspokajający; **'~ home** *jakby*: dom *m* spokojnej starość
res·ti·tu·tion [restɪ'tju:ʃn] przywrócenie *n*, restytucja *f*
res·tive ['restɪv] niespokojny, zaniepokojony
'rest·less niespokojny
res·to·ra·tion [restə'reɪʃn] przywrócenie *n*, zwrot *m*, restytucja *f*; odbudowa *f*, restauracja *f*;
re·store [rɪ'stɔ:] przywracać ⟨-rócić⟩; zwracać ⟨-rócić⟩; ⟨od⟩restaurować, odbudowywać ⟨-ować⟩; ***be ~d to health*** wrócić do zdrowia
re·strain [rɪ'streɪn] (***from***) powstrzymywać ⟨-mać⟩ przed (*I*); ***I had to ~ myself*** musiałem się powstrzymywać (***from doing s.th.*** przed zrobieniem czegoś); **~ed** [rɪ'streɪnd] powściągliwy, opanowany; *kolor itp.*: stonowany; **~t** [rɪ'streɪnt] opanowanie *n*, powściągliwość *f*
re·strict [rɪ'strɪkt] ograniczać ⟨-czyć⟩ (***to*** do *G*); **re·stric·tion** [rɪ'strɪkʃn] ograniczenie *n*; ***without ~s*** bez ograniczeń
'rest room *Am.* (*w hotelu itp.*) toaleta *f*
re·sult [rɪ'zʌlt] **1.** wynik *m*, rezultat *m*; skutek *m*, efekt *m*; ***as a ~ of*** na skutek *G*, w wyniku *G*; ***without ~*** bez wyniku, bezskutecznie; **2.** wynikać ⟨-knąć⟩ (***from*** z *G*); ***~ in*** dawać ⟨dać⟩ w wyniku (*A*)
re·sume [rɪ'zju:m] podejmować ⟨-djąć⟩, wznawiać ⟨wznowić⟩; *miejsce* zajmować ⟨-jąć⟩ ponownie; **re·sumption** [rɪ'zʌmpʃn] podjęcie *n* (*na nowo*); wznowienie *n*
Res·ur·rec·tion [rezə'rekʃn] Zmartwychwstanie *n*
re·sus·ci|·tate [rɪ'sʌsɪteɪt] *med.* reanimować; ocucić; **~·ta·tion** *med.* [rɪsʌsɪ'teɪʃn] reanimacja *f*
re·tail **1.** ['ri:teɪl] handel *m* detaliczny; detal *m*; ***by ~*** detalicznie; **2.** ['ri:teɪl] *adv.* detalicznie; **3.** [ri:'teɪl] *v/t.* sprzedawać ⟨-dać⟩ detalicznie (***at, for*** za *A*); *v/i.* być sprzedawanym detalicznie (***at, for*** za *A*); **~·er** [ri:'teɪlə] detalista *m*
re·tain [rɪ'teɪn] zatrzymywać ⟨-mać⟩; zachowywać ⟨-ować⟩
re·tal·i|·ate [rɪ'tælɪeɪt] odwzajemniać ⟨-mnić⟩ się; ⟨za⟩stosować odwet; **~·a·tion** [rɪtælɪ'eɪʃn] odwet *m*, retorsja *f*
re·tard [rɪ'tɑ:d] opóźniać ⟨-nić⟩; wstrzymywać ⟨-mać⟩; (***mentally***) ***~ed*** opóźniony umysłowo
retch [retʃ] *med.* mieć odruchy wymiotne
re·tell [ri:'tel] (***-told***) opowiadać ⟨-wiedzieć⟩ na nowo
re·think [ri:'θɪŋk] (***-thought***) przemyśleć
re·ti·cent ['retɪsənt] milczący, milkliwy
ret·i·nue ['retɪnju:] świta *f*, orszak *m*
re·tire [rɪ'taɪə] *v/i.* przechodzić ⟨przejść⟩ na rentę *lub* emeryturę; wycofywać ⟨-fać⟩ się; *v/t.* przenosić ⟨przenieść⟩ na rentę *lub* emeryturę; **~d** emerytowany, w stanie spoczynku; ***be ~d*** być na rencie *lub* emeryturze; **~·ment** emerytura *f*, stan *m* spoczynku; **re·tir·ing** [rɪ'taɪərɪŋ] płochliwy
re·tort [rɪ'tɔ:t] **1.** odpowiadać ⟨-wiedzieć⟩ ostro; **2.** ostra odpowiedź *f*
re·touch [ri:'tʌtʃ] *phot.* ⟨wy⟩retuszować
re·trace [rɪ'treɪs] ⟨z⟩rekonstruować; ***~ one's steps*** wracać ⟨-rócić⟩ po własnych śladach

re·tract [rɪ'trækt] *v/t.* wycofywać ⟨-fać⟩, odwoływać ⟨-łać⟩; wciągać ⟨-gnąć⟩, ⟨s⟩chować
re·train [riː'treɪn] przeszkalać ⟨-kolić⟩; zmieniać ⟨-nić⟩ kwalifikacje
re·tread **1.** [riː'tred] *oponę* bieżnikować; **2.** ['riːtred] bieżnikowana opona *f*
re·treat [rɪ'triːt] **1.** odwrót *m*; wycofanie *n* się; ***beat a (hasty) ~*** pospiesznie się wycofywać ⟨-fać⟩; **2.** wycofywać ⟨-fać⟩ się (***from*** z *G*)
ret·ri·bu·tion [retrɪ'bjuːʃn] odpłata *f*, odwet *m*
re·trieve [rɪ'triːv] odzyskiwać ⟨-skać⟩; *błąd* naprawiać ⟨-wić⟩; *komp.* uzyskiwać dostęp; *hunt.* aportować
ret·ro|·ac·tive [retrəʊ'æktɪv] *jur.* działający wstecz; **~·grade** ['retrəʊgreɪd] wsteczny, regresywny; **~·spect** ['retrəʊspekt]: ***in ~spect*** z perspektywy (*lat lub czasu*); **~·spec·tive** [retrəʊ'spektɪv] retrospektywny; *jur.* działający wstecz
re·try [riː'traɪ] *jur. przypadek* ponownie sądzić
re·turn [rɪ'tɜːn] **1.** *v/i.* wracać ⟨wrócić⟩, powracać ⟨-rócić⟩; **~ *to*** powracać ⟨-rócić⟩ do (*G*); *v/t.* oddawać ⟨-dać⟩; zwracać ⟨-rócić⟩; odsyłać ⟨odesłać⟩; *zysk* przynosić ⟨-nieść⟩, dawać ⟨dać⟩; odwzajemniać ⟨-nić⟩; (*w sprawozdaniu*) zgłaszać ⟨-łosić⟩; → ***verdict***; **2.** powrót *m*; zwrot *m*, zwrócenie *n*; odesłanie *n*; sprawozdanie *n*; *podatkowa* deklaracja *n*; (*w tenisie*) odbicie *n*; *też* **~s** zysk *m*, dochód *m*, wpływy *pl.*; ***many happy ~s (of the day)*** wszystkiego najlepszego z okazji urodzin; ***by ~ (of post)*** *Brt.* odwrotną pocztą; ***in ~ for*** (*w zamian*) za (*A*); **3.** *adj.* powrotny; zwrotny; **re'tur·na·ble** do zwrotu; **~ *bottle*** butelka *f* z kaucją
re·turn| 'key *komp.* klawisz *m* powrotu karetki; klawisz *m* Enter; **~ 'game**, **~ 'match** *sport*: mecz *m* rewanżowy; **~ 'tick·et** *Brt.* bilet *m* powrotny
re·u·ni·fi·ca·tion [riːjuːnɪfɪ'keɪʃn] *pol.* zjednoczenie *n*
re·u·nion [riː'juːnjən] zjazd *m*; zejście *n* się
re·us·a·ble [riː'juːzəbl] zdatny do ponownego użytku
rev [rev] F *mot.* **1.** obroty *pl.*; **~ *counter*** obrotomierz *m*; **2.** (**-vv-**) *też.* **~ *up*** zwiększać ⟨-szyć⟩ obroty (*silnika*)
Rev *skrót pisany*: ***Reverend*** *rel.* wielebny (*tytuł i zwrot*)
re·val·ue [riː'væljuː] *econ.* przeszacować ⟨-wywać⟩
re·veal [rɪ'viːl] odsłaniać ⟨-łonić⟩; ujawniać ⟨-nić⟩; **~·ing** *sukienka itp.*: mało osłaniający; *fig. uwaga itp.*: dużo odkrywający
rev·el ['revl] (*zwł. Brt.* **-ll-** , *Am.* **-l-**): **~ *in*** lubować się (w *L*), rozkoszować się (*I*)
rev·e·la·tion [revə'leɪʃn] rewelacja *f*; ujawnienie *n*; *rel.* objawienie *n*
re·venge [rɪ'vendʒ] **1.** zemsta *f*; rewanż *m*; ***in ~ for*** z zemsty za (*A*); **2.** ⟨po⟩mścić; **~ *o.s. on*** mścić się na (*L*); **~·ful** mściwy
rev·e·nue ['revənjuː] *rel.* dochody *pl.*, wpływy *pl.*
re·ver·be·rate [rɪ'vɜːbəreɪt] rozlegać ⟨-lec⟩ się; rozbrzmiewać ⟨-mieć⟩
re·vere [rɪ'vɪə] czcić
rev·e|·rence ['revərəns] cześć *f*, szacunek *m* (***for*** dla *G*); **♀·rend** ['revərənd] *rel.* wielebny; **~·rent** ['revərənt] pełen atencji
rev·er·ie ['revərɪ] marzenia *pl.*
re·vers·al [rɪ'vɜːsl] odwrócenie *n*; anulowanie *n*, uchylenie *n*
re·verse [rɪ'vɜːs] **1.** *adj.* odwrotny, przeciwny; *bieg*: wsteczny; ***in ~ order*** w odwrotnym kierunku; **2.** *samochód*: cofać ⟨-fnąć⟩ (się); wycofywać ⟨-fać⟩; *porządek* odwracać ⟨-rócić⟩; *decyzję* uchylać ⟨-lić⟩; **~ *the charges*** *Brt. tel.* ⟨za⟩dzwonić na koszt odbiorcy; **3.** odwrotność *f*; odwrócenie *n*; *mot.* cofanie *n*; strona *f* odwrotna; rewers *m* (*monety*); **~ 'gear** *mot.* bieg *m* wsteczny; **~ 'side** lewa strona *f* (*materiału itp.*)
re·vers·i·ble [rɪ'vɜːsəbl] odwracalny; odwołalny
re·vert [rɪ'vɜːt]: **~ *to*** powracać ⟨-rócić⟩ do (*G*); cofać ⟨-nąć⟩ się (*w rozwoju*)
re·view [rɪ'vjuː] **1.** przegląd *m*; rewizja *f*, badanie *n*; krytyka *f*, recenzja *f*, omówienie *n*; *mil.* defilada *f*; *Am. ped.* powtórka *f* (*materiału*) (***for*** do *G*); **2.** dokonywać ⟨-nać⟩ przeglądu; poddawać ⟨-dać⟩ rewizji; ⟨z⟩badać; omawiać ⟨omówić⟩; ⟨z⟩recenzować; *Am. ped.* po-

R

wtarzać ⟨-tórzyć⟩ (*materiał*) (**for** do *G*); **~·er** recenzent(ka *f*) *m*, krytyk *m*

re·vise [rɪ'vaɪz] ⟨z⟩rewidować; *opinię* ⟨s⟩korygować; *książkę* poprawiać ⟨-wić⟩, ⟨s⟩korygować; *Brt. ped.* powtarzać ⟨-tórzyć⟩ (*materiał*) (**for** do *G*); **re·vi·sion** [rɪ'vɪʒn] rewizja *f*; korekta *f*; zmiana *f*; *Brt. ped.* powtórka *f* (*materiału*) (**for** do *G*)

re·viv·al [rɪ'vaɪvl] odrodzenie *n*; ożywienie *n*; wznowienie *n* (*sztuki*); **revive** [rɪ'vaɪv] odradzać ⟨-rodzić⟩; ożywiać ⟨-wić⟩; wznawiać ⟨-nowić⟩

re·voke [rɪ'vəʊk] cofać ⟨-fnąć⟩; odwoływać ⟨-łać⟩; anulować

re·volt [rɪ'vəʊlt] **1.** *v/i.* ⟨z⟩buntować się, burzyć się (**against** przeciwko *D*); wzbudzać ⟨-dzić⟩ odrazę (**against, at, from** przeciwko *D*); *v/t.* napełniać ⟨-nić⟩ odrazą; **2.** bunt *m*, rewolta *f*; **~·ing** wzbudzający odrazę

rev·o·lu·tion [revə'luːʃn] rewolucja (*też pol.*), przewrót *m*; *astr., tech.* obrót *m*; **number of ~s** *tech.* liczba *f* obrotów; **~ counter** *mot.* obrotomierz *m*; **~·ar·y** [revə'luːʃnərɪ] **1.** rewolucyjny; **2.** *pol.* rewolucjonista *m* (-tka *f*); **~·ize** *fig.* [revə'luːʃnaɪz] ⟨z⟩rewolucjonizować

re·volve [rɪ'vɒlv] obracać się (**on, round** wokół *G*); **~ around** *fig.* obracać się wokół (*G*); **re'volv·er** rewolwer *m*; **re'volv·ing** obrotowy; **~ door**(**s** *pl.*) drzwi *pl.* obrotowe, turnikiet *m*

re·vue [rɪ'vjuː] *theat.* rewia *f*

re·vul·sion [rɪ'vʌlʃn] wstręt *m*, odraza *f*

re·ward [rɪ'wɔːd] **1.** nagroda *f*; **2.** nagradzać ⟨-rodzić⟩; **~·ing** zyskowny; dający satysfakcję, satysfakcjonujący

R

re·write [riː'raɪt] (**-wrote, -written**) *tekst* przerabiać ⟨-robić⟩; ⟨na⟩pisać na nowo

rhap·so·dy ['ræpsədɪ] *mus.* rapsodia *f*

rhe·to·ric ['retərɪk] retoryka *f*

rheu·ma·tism *med.* ['ruːmətɪzəm] reumatyzm *m*

Rhine Ren *m*

rhi·no ['raɪnəʊ] *zo.* F (*pl.* **-nos**), **rhi·no·ce·ros** [raɪ'nɒsərəs] *zo.* (*pl.* **-ros** [-sɪz], **-roses**) nosorożec *m*

rhu·barb ['ruːbɑːb] *bot.* rabarbar *m*; *attr.* rabarbarowy

rhyme [raɪm] **1.** rym *m*; wiersz *m*; **without ~ or reason** bez ładu i składu; **2.** rymować (się)

rhyth|·m ['rɪðəm] rytm *m*; **~·mic** ['rɪðmɪk] (**-ally**), **~·mi·cal** rytmiczny

rib [rɪb] *anat.* żebro *n*

rib·bon ['rɪbən] wstążka *f*; taśma *f* (*maszyny do pisania*)

'rib cage *anat.* klatka *f* piersiowa

rice [raɪs] *bot.* ryż *m*; *attr.* ryżowy; **~ 'pud·ding** pudding *m* ryżowy

rich [rɪtʃ] **1.** bogaty (*też* **in** w *A*); kosztowny, wystawny; *jedzenie*: ciężki, tłusty; *ziemia*: tłusty, żyzny; *ton*: pełny; *ton*: głęboki; **~** (**in calories**) wysokokaloryczny; **2. the ~** *pl.* bogaci *pl.*

rick [rɪk] stóg *m*

rick·ets ['rɪkɪts] *med.* krzywica *f*

rick·et·y ['rɪkətɪ] F chwiejny, kiwający się

rid [rɪd] (**-dd-**; **rid**) uwalniać ⟨uwolnić⟩ (**of** od *G*); **get ~ of** pozbywać ⟨-być⟩ się (*G*)

rid·dance F ['rɪdəns]: **good ~!** krzyżyk na drogę!

rid·den ['rɪdn] **1.** *p.p. od* **ride** 1; **2.** *w złoż.* nękany

rid·dle[1] ['rɪdl] zagadka *f*

rid·dle[2] ['rɪdl] **1.** rzeszoto *n*; **2.** ⟨po⟩dziurawić (**with I**) (*jak rzeszoto*)

ride [raɪd] **1.** (**rode, ridden**) *v/i.* ⟨po⟩jechać (**on** na *rowerze*, **in** *lub Am.* **on** w *autobusie itp.*); ⟨po⟩jechać (*konno*); *v/t.* jeździć na (*L*) (*koniu, rowerze*); ⟨po⟩jechać (*I*) (*samochodem itp.*); **2.** jazda *f*, przejażdżka *f*; **'rid·er** jeździec *m*; rowerzysta *m* (-tka *f*); motocyklista *m* (-tka *f*)

ridge [rɪdʒ] (*górski*) grzebień *m*; (*dachu*) kalenica *f*

rid·i·cule ['rɪdɪkjuːl] **1.** szyderstwo *n*, drwina *f*; **2.** drwić z (*G*); szydzić z (*G*), kpić z (*G*); **ri·dic·u·lous** [rɪ'dɪkjʊləs] śmieszny, groteskowy

rid·ing ['raɪdɪŋ] jeździecki

riff-raff ['rɪfræf] *pej.* motłoch *m*, hołota *f*

ri·fle[1] ['raɪfl] karabin *m*, strzelba *f*

ri·fle[2] ['raɪfl] ⟨s⟩plądrować

rift [rɪft] szczelina *f* (*też fig.*); pęknięcie *n*

rig [rɪg] **1.** (**-gg-**) *statek* ⟨o⟩taklować; **~ out** kogoś ⟨wy⟩stroić; **~ up** F ⟨s⟩klecić, ⟨z⟩montować (**from** z *G*); **2.** *naut.* takielunek *m*; *tech.* urządzenie wiertnicze; F ciuchy *pl.*; **'~·ging** *naut.* takielunek *m*

right [raɪt] **1.** *adj.* prawy; dobry, poprawny; właściwy, prawidłowy; *pol.* prawicowy; ***all ~!*** w porządku!, dobrze!; ***that's all ~!*** nie ma za co!, proszę!; ***that's ~!*** dobrze!, zgoda!; ***be ~*** mieć rację; ***put ~, set ~*** ⟨u⟩porządkować, naprawiać ⟨-wić⟩; **2.** *adv.* na prawo, w prawo; dobrze, poprawnie, właściwie, prawidłowo; bezpośrednio, wprost; ***~ away*** od razu; ***~ now*** obecnie; ***~ on*** prosto; ***turn ~*** skręcić w prawo; **3.** prawa strona *f*; *pol.* prawica *f*; ***on the ~*** z prawej; ***to the ~*** na prawo; ***keep to the ~*** trzymać się prawej; jechać z prawej strony; **4.** ⟨wy⟩prostować; *coś* ⟨s⟩prostować; ⟨s⟩korygować; **'~ an•gle** kąt *m* prosty; **'~-an•gled** *math.* pod kątem prostym; **~•eous** ['raɪtʃəs] *człowiek*: prawy; *oburzenie*: słuszny; **'~•ful** legalny; słuszny; **~-'hand** prawostronny; **~-hand 'drive** z prawostronnym układem kierowniczym; **~-'hand•ed** praworęczny; **'~•ly** słusznie; **~ of 'way** *mot.* pierwszeństwo przejazdu *n*; **~-'wing** *pol.* prawicowy

rig•id ['rɪdʒɪd] sztywny; *fig.* nieugięty

rig•ma•role ['rɪgmərəʊl] F ceregiele *pl.*

rig•or•ous ['rɪgərəs] rygorystyczny; surowy

rig•o(u)r ['rɪgə] surowość *f*; ostrość *f*; rygor *m*

rile [raɪl] F ⟨z⟩denerwować, ⟨z⟩irytować

rim [rɪm] brzeg *m*, krawędź *f*; obrzeże *n*; obwódka *f*; *tech.* obręcz *f*; **'~•less** *okulary*: bezobwódkowy; **'~med** z obwódką

rind [raɪnd] skórka *f* (*cytryny, sera itp.*)

ring[1] [rɪŋ] **1.** pierścień *m*; kółko *n*; obrączka *f*, pierścionek *m*; krążek *m*; (*w boksie*) ring *m*; arena *f*; *przestępcza* siatka *f*; **2.** otaczać ⟨-toczyć⟩; okrążać ⟨-żyć⟩; *ptaki* ⟨za⟩obrączkować

ring[2] [rɪŋ] **1.** (***rang, rung***) ⟨za⟩dzwonić; ⟨za⟩brzmieć, rozbrzmiewać ⟨-mieć⟩; *zwł. Brt. tel.* ⟨za⟩telefonować, ⟨za⟩dzwonić; ***the bell is ~ing*** dzwoni; ***~ the bell*** zadzwonić; ***~ back*** oddzwaniać ⟨-wonić⟩; ***~ for*** ⟨za⟩dzwonić po (*A*); ***~ off*** *zwł. Brt. tel.* odkładać ⟨odłożyć⟩ słuchawkę; ***~ s.o. (up)*** ⟨za⟩dzwonić do kogoś; **2.** dzwonienie *n*; dzwonek *m*; dźwięk *m*; brzmienie *n*; ***give s.o. a ~*** ⟨za⟩dzwonić do kogoś

'ring| bind•er kołonotatnik *m*; **'~•lead•er** przywódca *m* (*szajki itp.*); **'~•mas•ter** dyrektor *m* cyrku; **'~ road** *Brt.* obwodnica *f*; **'~•side**: ***at the ~side*** ***boks*** przy ringu

rink [rɪŋk] *sztuczne* lodowisko *n*; tor *m* wrotkarski

rinse [rɪns] *też* ***~ out*** ⟨wy⟩płukać

ri•ot ['raɪət] **1.** zamieszki *pl.*, rozruchy *pl.*; ***run ~*** rozszaleć się; ***~ police*** oddziały *pl.* prewencji; **2.** wszczynać ⟨-cząć⟩ rozruchy; **'~•er** uczestnik *m* zamieszek; **'~•ous** rozszalały, wzburzony

rip [rɪp] **1.** (***-pp-***) *też* ***~ up*** ⟨po⟩drzeć; ***~ open*** rozdzierać ⟨-zedrzeć⟩; **2.** rozdarcie *n*

ripe [raɪp] dojrzały; **rip•en** ['raɪpən] dojrzewać ⟨-jrzeć⟩

rip•ple ['rɪpl] **1.** ⟨z⟩marszczyć się; rozchodzić ⟨-zejść⟩ się falą; **2.** zmarszczka *f*; fala *f*

rise [raɪz] **1.** (***rose, risen***) wstawać ⟨-tać⟩ (*też rano*); podnosić ⟨-nieść⟩ się; *dym*: unosić ⟨unieść⟩ się; *ciasto*: ⟨u⟩rosnąć; *nastrój*: poprawiać ⟨-wić⟩ się; *temperatura itp.*: wzrastać ⟨-rosnąć⟩; *wiatr*: wzmagać ⟨wzmóc⟩ się; wschodzić ⟨wzejść⟩; *drzewa, góry itp.*: wznosić się; *fig.* ⟨z⟩rodzić się (***from, out of*** z *G*); *też* ***~ up*** powstawać ⟨-tać⟩ (***against*** przeciw *D*); ***~ to the occasion*** stawać ⟨stanąć⟩ na wysokości zadania; **2.** wzrost *m*; podniesienie *n* się; zwyżka *f*; podwyżka *f* (*Brt. też płacy*); rośnięcie *n*; *astr.* wschód *m*; wzniesienie *n* się; *fig.* rozrost *m*; ***give ~ to*** prowadzić do (*G*); **ris•en** ['rɪzn] *p.p. od* ***rise*** 1; **ris•er** ['raɪzə]: ***be an early riser*** wcześnie wstawać (*z łóżka*); **ris•ing** ['raɪzɪŋ] **1.** powstanie *n*; **2.** *fig.* wschodzący

risk [rɪsk] **1.** ryzyko *n*; ***at one's own ~*** na własną odpowiedzialność; ***at the ~ of*** (*ger.*) ryzykując, że; ***be at ~*** być zagrożonym; ***run the ~ of doing s.th.*** narażać ⟨-razić⟩ się na zrobienie czegoś; ***run a ~, take a ~*** podejmować ⟨-djąć⟩ ryzyko; **2.** ⟨za⟩ryzykować; **'~•y** (***-ier, -iest***) ryzykowny, niebezpieczny

rite [raɪt] obrządek *m*, obrzęd *m*, ceremoniał *m*; **rit•u•al** ['rɪtʃʊəl] **1.** rytualny; **2.** ryt *m*, rytuał *m*

ri•val ['raɪvl] **1.** rywal(ka *f*) *m*; konkurent(ka *f*) *m*; **2.** rywalizujący, konkurencyjny; **3.** (*zwł. Brt.* **-ll-**, *Am.* **-l-**) ry-

R

walizować z (*I*), konkurować z (*I*), współzawodniczyć z (*I*); **~·ry** ['raɪvlrɪ] rywalizacja *f*, współzawodnictwo *n*

riv·er ['rɪvə] rzeka *f*; *attr.* rzeczny; '**~·side** brzeg *m*; ***by the ~side*** nad rzeką

riv·et ['rɪvɪt] **1.** *tech.* nit *m*; **2.** *tech.* ⟨przy⟩nitować; spojrzenie utkwić (***on*** w *A*); *uwagę* przykuwać ⟨-kuć⟩ (***on*** do *G*)

RN [ɑːr 'en] *skrót*: ***Royal Navy*** *Brt.* Marynarka *f* Królewska

road [rəʊd] droga *f* (*też fig.*); szosa *f*; ***on the ~*** w drodze; na drodze (***to*** do *G*); na tourn(e); *attr.* drogowy; '**~ ac·ci·dent** wypadek *m* drogowy; '**~·block** korek *m* uliczny; '**~ map** mapa *f* drogowa; **~ 'safe·ty** bezpieczeństwo *n* drogowe; '**~·side** pobocze *n*; '**~ toll** myto *n*, opłata *f* za korzystanie z drogi; '**~·way** jezdnia *f*; '**~ works** *pl.* prace *pl.* na drodze; '**~·wor·thy** nadający się do poruszania po drogach

roam [rəʊm] *v/i.* błąkać się, wędrować; *v/t.* błąkać się po (*L*), wędrować po (*L*)

roar [rɔː] **1.** ryk *m*; ***~s** pl. **of laughter*** ryk *pl.* śmiechu; **2.** ryczeć ⟨ryknąć⟩, zaryczeć

roast [rəʊst] **1.** *v/t. mięso* ⟨u⟩piec; *kawę itp.* palić; **2.** pieczeń *f*; **3.** *adj.* pieczony; **~ 'beef** rostbef *m*, pieczeń *f* wołowa

rob [rɒb] (***-bb-***) okradać ⟨okraść⟩, obrabowywać ⟨-ować⟩; **~·ber** ['rɒbə] rabuś *m*; **~·ber·y** ['rɒbərɪ] rabunek *m*; obrabowanie *n*

robe [rəʊb] *też* ***~s*** *pl.* toga *f*; *zwł. Am.* szlafrok *m*

rob·in ['rɒbɪn] *zo.* (*w Europie*) rudzik *m*; (*w Ameryce*) drozd *m* wędrowny

ro·bot ['rəʊbɒt] robot *m*

ro·bust [rə'bʌst] czerstwy, kwitnący

rock[1] [rɒk] **1.** kołysać (się); ⟨za-, po⟩kiwać, ⟨po⟩bujać; wstrząsać ⟨-snąć⟩ (*I*) (*też fig.*)

rock[2] [rɒk] skała *f*; głaz *m*; *Am.* kamień *m*; *Brt. długi, twardy, jaskrawy* cukierek *m*; ***~s*** *pl.* rafy *pl.*; ***on the ~s*** *firma* w opałach; *małżeństwo*: w rozpadzie; *whisky*: z lodem

rock[3] [rɒk] *też* ***~ music*** rock *m*; → ***rock'n'roll***

'**rock·er** fotel *m* bujany; płoza *f*; ***off one's ~*** F zbzikowany

rock·et ['rɒkɪt] **1.** rakieta *f*; **2.** *też* ***~ up*** wystrzelić w górę; pędzić, przemykać ⟨-mknąć⟩

'**rock·ing| chair** fotel *m* bujany; '**~ horse** koń *m* na biegunach

rock 'n' roll [rɒkən'rəʊl] rock and roll *m*

'**rock·y** (***-ier, -iest***) skalisty, kamienisty; twardy jak kamień

Rock·y Moun·tains *pl.* Góry Skaliste *pl.*

rod [rɒd] *tech.* pręt *m*, drąg *m*

rode [rəʊd] *pret. od* ***ride*** 1

ro·dent ['rəʊdənt] *zo.* gryzoń *m*

ro·de·o [rəʊ'deɪəʊ, 'rəʊdɪəʊ] (*pl.* ***-os***) rodeo *n*

roe [rəʊ] *zo. też* ***hard ~*** ikra *f*; ***soft ~*** mlecz *m*

roe|·buck ['rəʊbʌk] *zo.* (*pl.* ***-bucks, -buck***) kozioł *m* (*sarny*); '**~ deer** sarna *f*

rogue [rəʊg] łobuz *m*; drań *m*; **ro·guish** ['rəʊgɪʃ] łobuzerski

role [rəʊl] *theat. itp.* rola *f* (*też fig.*)

roll [rəʊl] **1.** *v/i.* ⟨po⟩toczyć się; *naut.* przechylać ⟨-lić⟩ się; ⟨za⟩kołysać się; *grzmot*: przetaczać ⟨-toczyć⟩ się; *v/t.* ⟨po⟩toczyć; przetaczać ⟨-toczyć⟩; *papierosa* zwijać ⟨zwinąć⟩; ***~ down*** *rękaw* odwijać ⟨-winąć⟩; *mot. okno* otwierać ⟨-worzyć⟩ (*korbką*); ***~ out*** rozwijać ⟨-winąć⟩; ***~ up*** podwijać ⟨-winąć⟩; zwijać ⟨-zwinąć⟩; *mot. okno* zamykać ⟨-mknąć⟩ (*korbką*); **2.** rolka *f*, wałek *m*; zwój *m*, zwitek *m*; bułka *f*; lista *f* (*nazwisk*); pomruk *m* (*grzmotu*); werbel *m*; *naut.* kołysanie *n*; '**~ call** odczytanie *n* listy obecności

'**roll·er** *tech.* wałek *m*; krążek *m*; rolka *f*; walec *m*; lokówka *f*; '**~·blades** *pl.* łyżworolki *pl.*; '**~ coast·er** kolejka *f* górska (*w wesołym miasteczku*); '**~ skate** wrotka *f*; '**~-skate** jeździć na wrotkach; '**~-skat·ing** jazda *f* na wrotkach; '**~ tow·el** ręcznik *m* na wałku

'**roll·ing pin** wałek *m* (*do ciasta*)

'**roll-on** dezodorant *m* z kulką

ROM [rɒm] *skrót*: ***read only memory*** ROM *m*

Ro·man ['rəʊmən] **1.** rzymski; romański; **2.** Rzymianin *m* (-anka *f*)

ro·mance [rəʊ'mæns] romans *m*; przygoda *f*

Ro·mance [rəʊ'mæns] język romański

Ro·ma·ni·a [ruː'meɪnjə] Rumunia *f*;

Ro•ma•ni•an [ruː'meɪnjən] **1.** rumuński; **2.** Rumun(ka *f*) *m*; *ling.* język *m* rumuński
ro•man|•tic [rəʊ'mæntɪk] **1.** romantyczny; **2.** romantyk *m* (-yczka *f*); **~•ticism** [rəʊ'mæntɪsɪzəm] romantyzm *m*
Rome Rzym *m*
romp [rɒmp] *też* **~ *about*, ~ *around*** dokazywać; '**~•ers** *pl.* śpiochy *pl.*
roof [ruːf] **1.** dach *m*; **2.** przykrywać ⟨-ryć⟩ dachem; **~ *in*, ~ *over*** zadaszać ⟨-szyć⟩; '**~•ing felt** papa *f*; '**~ rack** bagażnik *m* dachowy
rook[1] [rʊk] *zo.* gawron *m*
rook[2] [rʊk] (*w szachach*) wieża *f*
rook[3] [rʊk] F oszwabiać ⟨-bić⟩
room [ruːm, *w złoż.*rʊm] **1.** pokój *m*; pomieszczenie *n*, izba *f*; sala *f*; miejsce *n*; wolne miejsce *n*; **2.** *Am.* mieszkać; '**~•er** *zwł. Am.* sublokator(ka *f*) *m*; '**~•ing-house** *Am. mieszkalny* blok *m*; '**~•mate** współlokator(ka *f*) *m*; '**~ service** dostarczanie *n* posiłków do pokoju; '**~•y** (***-ier, -iest***) przestronny
roost [ruːst] **1.** grzęda *f*; **2.** siedzieć *lub* spać na grzędzie; '**~•er** *zwł. Am. zo.* kogut *m*
root [ruːt] **1.** korzeń *m*; *fig.* źródło *n*, przyczyna *f*; *math.* pierwiastek *m*; **2.** *v/i.* zakorzeniać ⟨-nić⟩ się; ryć (***for*** w poszukiwaniu *G*); **~ *about*** grzebać (***among*** wśród *G*); *v/t.* **~ *out*** *fig.* wykorzeniać ⟨-nić⟩; **~ *up*** wyrywać ⟨-rwać⟩ z korzeniami; '**~•ed**: ***deeply ~ed*** *fig.* głęboko zakorzeniony; ***stand ~ed to the spot*** stać jak wryty w miejscu
rope [rəʊp] **1.** lina *f*, powróz *m*; *naut.* cuma *f*; sznur *m* (*pereł itp.*); ***give s.o. plenty of ~*** dawać ⟨dać⟩ komuś dużo swobody; ***know the ~s*** F dobrze się orientować; ***show s.o. the ~s*** F wprowadzać ⟨-dzić⟩ kogoś; **2.** przywiązywać ⟨-zać⟩ (***to*** do *G*); **~ *off*** odgradzać ⟨-grodzić⟩ (*linami*); '**~ lad•der** drabinka *f* sznurowa
ro•sa•ry ['rəʊzərɪ] *rel.* różaniec *m*
rose[1] [rəʊz] *pret. od* **rise** 1
rose[2] [rəʊz] **1.** *bot.* róża *f*; (*w konewce itp.*) sitko *n*; **2.** różowy
ros•trum ['rɒstrəm] (*pl.* ***-tra*** [-trə], ***-trums***) podium *n*
ros•y ['rəʊzɪ] (***-ier, -iest***) różowy (*też fig.*)
rot [rɒt] **1.** (***-tt-***) ⟨ze⟩psuć (*też fig.*); *v/i. też* **~ *away*** ⟨ze⟩psuć się, ⟨z⟩gnić; ⟨s⟩próchnieć, ⟨z⟩murszeć, ⟨z⟩butwieć; **2.** gnicie *n*, butwienie *n*
ro•ta•ry ['rəʊtərɪ] obrotowy, rotacyjny
ro•tate [rəʊ'teɪt] obracać (się); wirować; **ro•ta•tion** [rəʊ'teɪʃn] ruch *m* obrotowy, obrót *m*; rotacja *f*
ro•tor ['rəʊtə] *tech.*, *aviat.* wirnik *m*
rot•ten ['rɒtn] zgniły, zepsuty; *drewno*: zmurszały, spróchniały; zbutwiały; kiepski, podły; ***feel ~*** F czuć się okropnie
ro•tund [rəʊ'tʌnd] okrągły, korpulentny
rough [rʌf] **1.** *adj.* szorstki; chropowaty; *ulica itp.*: nierówny; *morze*: wzburzony; *pogoda*: burzliwy; obcesowy, grubiański; *pomiar*: niedokładny, przybliżony; *warunki, przejścia*: ciężki, męczący; *jedzenie*: prosty; *warunki*: prymitywny; **2.** *adv.* ***sleep ~*** spać pod gołym niebem; ***play ~*** (*w sporcie*) ⟨za⟩grać brutalnie; **3.** (*w golfie*) zarośla *pl.*, krzaki *pl.*; ***write it out in ~ first*** napisać najpierw na brudno; **4.** **~ *it*** F żyć w prymitywnych warunkach; **~ *out*** ⟨na⟩szkicować; **~•age** ['rʌfɪdʒ] *biol.* nietrawiona część *f* pożywienia; '**~•cast** *arch.* tynk *m* kamyczkowy; **~ 'cop•y** brudnopis *m*; **~ 'draft** brudnopis *m*, szkic *m*; **~•en** ['rʌfn] czynić szorstkim; *skóra*: ⟨z⟩grubieć; '**~•ly** szorstko; *fig.* w przybliżeniu, orientacyjnie; '**~•neck** naftowiec *m*; *Am.* F grubianin *m*; '**~•shod**: ***ride ~shod over*** ⟨z⟩ranić, dotykać ⟨-tknąć⟩
round [raʊnd] **1.** *adj.* okrągły; ***a ~ dozen*** okrągły tuzin; ***in ~ figures*** w zaokrągleniu; **2.** *adv.* wokoło, dookoła; ***turn ~*** obracać ⟨-rócić⟩ się dookoła; ***invite s.o. ~*** zapraszać ⟨-rosić⟩ kogoś do siebie; **~ *about*** F coś koło; ***all*** (***the***) ***year ~*** okrągły rok; ***the other way ~*** na odwrót; **3.** *prp.* wokół (*G*), dookoła (*G*); po (*L*); za (*I*); ***trip ~ the world*** podróż dookoła świata; **4.** runda *f* (*też sportowa*); tura *f*; obchód *m* (*też med.*); kolejka *f* (*piwa itp.*); ładunek *m*, nabój *m*; (*w sporcie*) partia *f* (*golfa*); *mus.* kanon *m*; **5.** okrążać ⟨-żyć⟩; zaokrąglać ⟨-lić⟩; *zakręt* brać ⟨wziąć⟩; **~ *down*** *liczbę* zaokrąglać ⟨-lić⟩ (***to*** do *G*); **~ *off*** *posiłek* zakończyć, ukoronować; *liczbę* zaokrąglać ⟨-lić⟩ (***to*** do *G*); **~ *up*** *bydło* zaganiać ⟨-gonić⟩; *ludzi* spędzać ⟨-dzić⟩; *liczbę* zaokrąglać ⟨-lić⟩ (***to*** do

R

G); '~·**a·bout 1.** *Brt.* skrzyżowanie *n* okrężne, rondo *n*; *Brt.* karuzela *f*; **2.** ***take a ~about route*** ⟨po⟩jechać okrężną drogą; ***in a ~about way*** *fig.* w zawoalowany sposób; ~ **'trip** podróż *f* tam i z powrotem; ~**-trip 'tick·et** bilet *m* tam i z powrotem
rouse [raʊz] *kogoś* ⟨o⟩budzić; *fig. kogoś* pobudzać ⟨-dzić⟩
route [ruːt] droga *f*, trasa *f*; *autobusowa* linia *f*; szlak *m*
rou·tine [ruːˈtiːn] **1.** procedura *f*, tok *m*; ***the same old*** (***daily***) ~ codzienne obowiązki *pl.*; rutyna *f*; **2.** rutynowy, utarty
rove [rəʊv] wędrować (*też* po *L*)
row¹ [rəʊ] rząd *m*, szereg *m*
row² [rəʊ] **1.** wiosłować; **2.** przejażdżka *f* (*łodzią*)
row³ [raʊ] *Brt.* F **1.** awantura *f*; rejwach *m*; **2.** kłócić się
row|·boat [ˈrəʊbəʊt] *Am.* łódź *f* wiosłowa; '~·**er** wioślarz *m* (-arka *f*)
row house [ˈrəʊhaʊs] *Am.* domek *m* szeregowy
row·ing boat [ˈrəʊɪŋ bəʊt] *zwł. Brt.* łódź *f* wiosłowa
roy·al [ˈrɔɪəl] królewski; ~·**ty** [ˈrɔɪəltɪ] rodzina *f* królewska; tantiemy *pl.* (***on*** od *G*)
RSPCA [ɑːr es piː siː ˈeɪ] *skrót*: ***Royal Society for the Prevention of Cruelty to Animals*** (*towarzystwo opieki nad zwierzętami*)
RSVP [ɑːr es viː ˈpiː] *skrót*: ***please reply*** (*francuskie* ***répondez s'il vous plaît***) proszę o odpowiedź
rub [rʌb] **1.** (***-bb-***) *v/t.* trzeć, nacierać ⟨natrzeć⟩; wcierać ⟨wetrzeć⟩; pocierać ⟨potrzeć⟩; ~ ***dry*** wycierać ⟨wytrzeć⟩ do sucha; ~ ***it in*** *fig.* F wytykać ⟨-tknąć⟩ coś, odgrzebywać bez przerwy coś; ~ ***shoulders with*** F zadawać się z (*I*), stykać się z (*I*); *v/i.* trzeć; ocierać ⟨otrzeć⟩ (***against, on*** o *A*); ~ ***down*** wycierać ⟨wytrzeć⟩; wygładzać ⟨-ładzić⟩; ~ ***off*** ścierać ⟨zetrzeć⟩ się; *farba*: odchodzić ⟨odejść⟩; ~ ***off on***(***to***) *fig.* przenosić ⟨-nieść⟩ się na (*A*); ~ ***out*** *Brt.* wycierać ⟨wytrzeć⟩ (*gumką*); **2.** ***give s.o. a*** ~ natrzeć coś, wytrzeć coś
rub·ber [ˈrʌbə] guma *f*; *zwł. Brt.* gumka *f* (*do wycierania*); gąbka *f* (*do tablicy*); F (*prezerwatywa*) kondom *m*; ~ **'band** gumka *f* (*aptekarska*), recepturka *f*; ~ **'din·ghy** dingi *n*; '~·**neck** *Am.* F **1.** gapić się; **2.** *też* ***rubbernecker*** ciekawski *m* (-ka *f*); ~·**y** [ˈrʌbərɪ] gumowy; *mięso*: gumowaty, jak guma
rub·bish [ˈrʌbɪʃ] śmieci *pl.*, odpadki *pl.*; *fig.* bzdury *pl.*; barachło *n*; '~ **bin** *Brt.* kubeł *m* na śmieci; '~ **chute** zsyp *m* na śmieci
rub·ble [ˈrʌbl] gruz *m*, rumowisko *n*, gruzy *pl.*
ru·by [ˈruːbɪ] rubin *m*; *attr.* rubinowy
ruck·sack [ˈrʌksæk] plecak *m*
rud·der [ˈrʌdə] *naut.*, *aviat.* ster *m*
rud·dy [ˈrʌdɪ] (***-ier, -iest***) czerstwy, rumiany; rdzawy
rude [ruːd] (***-r, -st***) niegrzeczny, nietaktowny; *dowcip*: brzydki; *szok*: silny
ru·di|·men·ta·ry [ruːdɪˈmentərɪ] rudymentarny, elementarny; ~·**ments** [ˈruːdɪmənts] *pl.* podstawy *pl.*
rue·ful [ˈruːfʊl] zafrasowany
ruff [rʌf] kreza *f*; *zo.* pióra *pl.* (*wokół szyi*)
ruf·fle [ˈrʌfl] **1.** ⟨z⟩wichrzyć; *włosy* ⟨po⟩czochrać; ~ ***s.o.'s composure*** zirytować kogoś; **2.** falbanka *f*
rug [rʌg] dywanik *m*; *zwł. Brt.* pled *m*
rug·by [ˈrʌgbɪ] *też* ~ ***football*** (*w sporcie*) rugby *n*
rug·ged [ˈrʌgɪd] wytrzymały; *okolica*: surowy; *rysy*: gruby
ru·in [ˈrʊɪn] **1.** ruina *f*; *zw.* ~***s*** *pl.* ruiny *pl.*; **2.** ⟨z⟩rujnować, ⟨z⟩niszczyć; '~·**ous** zrujnowany
rule [ruːl] **1.** reguła *f*, zasada *f*, przepis *m*; panowanie *n*, rządy *pl.*; linijka *f*, przymiar *m*; ***against the ~s*** wbrew przepisom, niezgodnie z regułami; ***as a*** ~ z reguły; ***as a ~ of thumb*** jako praktyczna zasada; ***work to*** ~ pracować zgodnie z przepisami; **2.** *v/t.* panować (*I*), rządzić (*I*); *zwł. jur.* orzekać; *papier* ⟨po⟩liniować; *linię* ⟨po⟩ciągnąć; ***be ~d by*** *fig.* rządzić się (*I*); ~ ***out*** coś wykluczać ⟨-czyć⟩; *v/i.* panować (***over*** nad *I*); *zwł. jur.* postanawiać ⟨-nowić⟩; **'rul·er** władca *m*; linijka *f*, przymiar *m*
rum [rʌm] rum *m*
rum·ble [ˈrʌmbl] ⟨za⟩łoskotać, ⟨za⟩dudnić; *żołądek*: ⟨za⟩burczeć
ru·mi|·nant [ˈruːmɪnənt] *zo.* przeżuwacz *m*; ~·**nate** [ˈruːmɪneɪt] przeżuwać ⟨-żuć⟩

R

rum·mage ['rʌmɪdʒ] F **1.** *też* ~ ***about*** ⟨po⟩grzebać, ⟨po⟩gmerać (***among, in, through*** w *L*); **2.** *zwł. Am.* rzeczy *pl.* używane; '~ **sale** *Am.* wyprzedaż *f* rzeczy używanych

ru·mo(u)r ['ruːmə] **1.** pogłoska *f*, plotka *f*; ~ ***has it that*** wieść niesie, że; ***he is ~ed to be*** mówi się, że on; ⚠ *nie* ***rumor***

rump [rʌmp] zad *m*; *fig.* pozostałości *pl.*, niedobitki *pl.*

rum·ple ['rʌmpl] ⟨po⟩gnieść, ⟨z⟩gnieść

run [rʌn] **1.** (***-nn-***; ***ran, run***) *v/i.* ⟨po⟩biec, ⟨po⟩biegnąć, (*w sporcie*) biegać; *pojazd*: ⟨po⟩jechać; *autobus*, *pociąg*: kursować; spływać ⟨-łynąć⟩; *kolory*: puszczać ⟨puścić⟩; *tech. silnik*: chodzić, pracować; być w ruchu; *ulica*: biec; *zwł. jur.* obowiązywać (***for one year*** przez jeden rok); *theat. sztuka*: iść; *tekst*, *melodia*: brzmieć; *zwł. Am. pol.* kandydować; ~ ***dry*** wysychać ⟨-schnąć⟩; ~ ***low*** wyczerpywać ⟨-pać⟩ się; ~ ***short*** wyczerpywać ⟨-pać⟩ się; ~ ***short of petrol*** nie mieć już benzyny; *v/t. odległość* ⟨prze⟩biec, przebiegać ⟨-biec⟩; *pociągiem*, *autobusem* ⟨po⟩kierować; *tech. maszynę* uruchamiać ⟨-chomić⟩; *wodę* puszczać; *firmę*, *hotel* ⟨po⟩prowadzić; *artykuł* ⟨o⟩publikować, zamieszczać ⟨-mieścić⟩; ~ ***s.o. home*** F zawozić ⟨-wieźć⟩ kogoś do domu; ***be ~ning a temperature*** mieć temperaturę; → ***errands***; ~ ***across*** *kogoś* spotykać ⟨-tkać⟩ przypadkiem; ~ ***after*** pogonić ⟨-gnać⟩ za (*I*); narzucać się (*D*); ~ ***along!*** F uciekaj!; ~ ***away*** uciekać ⟨uciec⟩; ~ ***away with*** uciekać ⟨uciec⟩ z (*I*); dawać ⟨dać⟩ się ponieść (*D*); ~ ***down*** *mot.* potrącać ⟨-ącić⟩; F obmawiać ⟨-mówić⟩; wyszukiwać ⟨-kać⟩; *czas*: upływać ⟨-łynąć⟩; *bateria*: wyczerpywać ⟨-pać⟩ się; ~ ***in*** *samochód itp.* docierać ⟨dotrzeć⟩; F ⟨s⟩chwytać; ~ ***into*** zderzać ⟨zderzyć⟩ się (*I*); *kogoś* spotykać ⟨-tkać⟩ przypadkiem; *fig.* wpadać ⟨wpaść⟩ w (*A*) (*kłopoty*); *fig.* wynosić ⟨-nieść⟩ (*A*); ~ ***off with*** → ***run away with***; ~ ***on*** przeciągać ⟨-gnąć⟩ się (***until*** do *G*); F ględzić (***about*** o *L*); ~ ***out*** *jedzenie*: wyczerpywać ⟨-pać⟩ się; *czas*: uciekać; ~ ***out of sugar*** nie mieć już cukru; ~ ***over*** *mot.* przejechać; przelewać ⟨-lać⟩ się; ~ ***through*** powtarzać ⟨-tórzyć⟩; przelatywać ⟨-lecieć⟩ (wzrokiem); zużywać ⟨-żyć⟩; ~ ***up*** *flagę* podnosić ⟨-nieść⟩; *dług* zaciągnąć ⟨-gać⟩; ~ ***up against*** napotykać ⟨-tkać⟩; **2.** bieg *m*; kurs *m*; przejazd *m*, wycieczka *f*; tok *m*, przebieg *m*; okres *m*; *econ.* run *m*, popyt *m* (***on*** na *A*); *theat. itp.* okres *m* wystawiania; *Am.* oczko *n* (*w rajstopach itp.*); zagroda *f*, kojec *m*; wybieg *m*; (*w sporcie*) tor *m*; ~ ***of good*** (***bad***) ***luck*** pasmo *n* (nie)powodzeń; ***in the long ~*** na dłuższą metę; ***in the short ~*** na krótszą metę; ***on the ~*** uciekający

'run|·a·bout F *mot.* mały samochód *m*, samochód *m* miejski; '**~·a·way** zbieg *m*

rung[1] [rʌŋ] *p.p. od* ***ring***[2]

rung[2] [rʌŋ] szczebel *m*

run·ner ['rʌnə] (*w sporcie*) biegacz(ka *f*) *m*; koń *m* wyścigowy; *zw. w złoż.* szmugler *m*; płoza *f*, prowadnica *f*; *bot.* pęd *m* rozłogowy; ~ **'bean** *Brt. bot.* fasolka *f* szparagowa; **~-up** [rʌnər'ʌp] (*pl.* ***runners-up***) (*w sporcie*) drugi *m* (-ga *f*), zdobywca *m* (-czyni *f*) drugiego miejsca

run·ning ['rʌnɪŋ] **1.** bieganie *n*; prowadzenie *n*, kierowanie *n*; bieg *m*, praca *f*; **2.** *woda* bieżący; ciągły; (*w sporcie*) *buty*: do biegania; ***two days ~*** dwa dni pod rząd; '**~ costs** *pl.* koszty *pl.* bieżące

run·ny ['rʌnɪ] F *nos* cieknący; *oczy* łzawiący

'run·way *aviat.* pas *m* startowy

rup·ture ['rʌptʃə] **1.** pęknięcie *n*, rozerwanie *n*; *med.* przepuklina *f*; **2.** pękać ⟨-knąć⟩, rozrywać ⟨-zerwać⟩; ~ ***o.s.*** dostawać ⟨-tać⟩ przepukliny

ru·ral ['rʊərəl] wiejski

ruse [ruːz] trik *m*, sztuczka *f*

rush[1] [rʌʃ] **1.** *v/i.* ⟨po⟩pędzić, ⟨po⟩gnać, ⟨po⟩biec, ⟨prze-, po⟩mknąć (***to*** do *G*, ***towards*** w stronę *G*); spieszyć się; ~ ***into*** spieszyć się do (*G*); *v/t.* szybko przewozić ⟨-wieźć⟩; szybko przesyłać ⟨-słać⟩; spieszyć się z (*I*); popędzać, poganiać; ***don't ~ it*** nie spiesz się z tym; ⟨s⟩forsować; **2.** pośpiech *m*; gonitwa *f*, pogoń *f*; pęd *m*; gorączka *f* (*złota*); *econ.* ogromny popyt *m*; ***what's all the ~?*** po co ten pośpiech?

rush[2] [rʌʃ] *bot.* sit *m*

'rush| hour godzina *f* szczytu; **~-hour**

'**traf•fic** ruch *m* uliczny w godzinie szczytu
rusk [rʌsk] *zwł. Brt.* sucharek *m*
Rus•sia ['rʌʃə] Rosja *f*; **Rus•sian** ['rʌʃn] **1.** rosyjski; **2.** Rosjanin *m* (-anka *f*); *ling.* język *m* rosyjski
rust [rʌst] **1.** rdza *f*, korozja *f*; **2.** ⟨za⟩rdzewieć, ⟨s⟩korodować
rus•tic ['rʌstɪk] (*~ally*) chłopski, wieśniaczy; rustykalny
rus•tle ['rʌsl] **1.** szeleścić; *Am. bydło* ⟨u⟩kraść; **2.** szelest *m*
'**rust|•proof** nierdzewny; '**~•y** (**-ier, -iest**) zardzewiały (*też fig.*), *fig.* mało używany
rut[1] [rʌt] **1.** koleina *f*; *fig.* sztampa *f*, rutyna *f*; ***the daily ~*** codzienna rutyna *f*
rut[2] *zo.* [rʌt] ruja *f*, okres *m* godowy
ruth•less ['ru:θlɪs] bezlitosny, nielitościwy, bez skrupułów
rye [raɪ] *bot.* żyto *m*; *attr.* żytni

S

S, s [es] S, s *n*
S *skrót pisany*: ***South*** płd., południe *n*, południowy; ***south(ern)*** południowy; ***small (size)*** mały, eska *f*
$ *skrót pisany*: ***dollar(s pl.)*** USD, $, dolar(y *pl.*) *m*
sa•ble ['seɪbl] *zo.* soból *m*; *futro*: sobole *pl.*
sab•o•tage ['sæbətɑ:ʒ] **1.** sabotaż *m*; **2.** ⟨za⟩sabotować
sa•bre *Brt.*, **sa•ber** *Am.* ['seɪbə] szabla *f*
sack [sæk] **1.** worek *m*; ***get the ~*** F (*być zwolnionym*) dostawać ⟨-tać⟩ kopa; ***give s.o. the ~*** F wywalić kogoś; ***hit the ~*** F walnąć się do wyra; **2.** ⟨za⟩pakować do worka; F wywalać ⟨-lić⟩ kogoś; '**~•cloth**, '**~•ing** tkanina *f* workowa
sac•ra•ment ['sækrəmənt] *rel.* sakrament *m*
sa•cred ['seɪkrɪd] sakralny; święty
sac•ri•fice ['sækrɪfaɪs] **1.** ofiara *f*; poświęcenie *n*; **2.** ofiarować; poświęcać ⟨-cić⟩
sac•ri•lege ['sækrɪlɪdʒ] świętokradztwo *n*
sad [sæd] smutny
sad•dle ['sædl] siodło *n*
sa•dis|•m ['seɪdɪzəm] sadyzm *m*; **~t** ['seɪdɪst] sadysta *m* (-tka *f*); **~•tic** [sə'dɪstɪk] sadystyczny
'**sad•ness** smutek *m*
sa•fa•ri [sə'fɑ:rɪ] safari *n*; **~ park** park *m* safari
safe [seɪf] **1.** (**-r, -st**) bezpieczny; **2.** sejf *m*; skarbiec *m*; **~ 'con•duct** gwarancja *f* bezpieczeństwa, glejt *m*; '**~•guard** **1.** zabezpieczenie *n* (***against*** przeciw *D*); **2.** zabezpieczać ⟨-czyć⟩ (***against*** przeciw *D*); **~'keep•ing** ochrona *f*, bezpieczne przechowywanie *n*
safe•ty ['seɪftɪ] bezpieczeństwo *n*; *attr.* zabezpieczający; '**~ belt** → ***seat belt***; '**~ catch** bezpiecznik *m*; '**~ is•land** *Am.* (*na jezdni*) wysepka *f*; '**~ mea•sure** środek *m* bezpieczeństwa; '**~ pin** agrafka *f*; '**~ ra•zor** *nieelektryczna* maszynka *f* do golenia
sag [sæg] (**-gg-**) obwisać ⟨-snąć⟩; *policzki*: zapadać ⟨-paść⟩ się; *wartość*: spadać ⟨spaść⟩; *popyt*: zmniejszać ⟨-szyć⟩ się; *książka*: nużyć
sa•ga|•cious [sə'geɪʃəs] bystry, roztropny; **~•ci•ty** [sə'gæsətɪ] bystrość *f*, roztropność *f*
sage [seɪdʒ] *bot.* szałwia *f*
Sa•git•tar•i•us [sædʒɪ'teərɪəs] *znak Zodiaku*: Strzelec *m*; ***he/she is (a) ~*** on(a) jest spod znaku Strzelca
said [sed] *pret. i p.p. od* ***say***
sail [seɪl] **1.** żagiel *m*; przejażdżka *f* łodzią; śmigło *n* (*wiatraka*); ***set ~*** wypływać (***for*** do *G*); ***go for a ~*** iść ⟨pójść⟩ popływać łodzią; *attr.* żaglowy; **2.** *v/i. naut.* ⟨po⟩żeglować, pływać; przepłynąć przez (*A*); *naut.* wypływać ⟨-łynąć⟩ (***for*** do *G*); *ktoś*: wpływać ⟨-łynąć⟩, *coś*: szybować; ***go ~ing*** iść ⟨pójść⟩ na żagle; *v/t. naut.* przepływać ⟨-łynąć⟩; *łódką* żeglować; *statek* ⟨po⟩prowadzić; '**~•board** deska *f* surfingowa; '**~•boat** *Am.* żaglówka *f*, łódź *f* żaglowa
'**sail•ing** żeglarstwo *n*, rejs *m*; ***when is the next ~ to ?*** kiedy będzie następny

S

rejs do (*G*)?; '~ **boat** *zwł. Brt.* żaglówka *f*; łódź *f* żaglowa; '~ **ship** żaglowiec *m*
'sail·or żeglarz *m*; ***be a good*** (***bad***) **~** dobrze (źle) czuć się na morzu
saint [seɪnt] święty *m*; *przed imionami* ♀ [snt] (*skrót*: ***St***): ***St George*** święty Jerzy; '~·**ly** święty
sake [seɪk]: ***for the ~ of*** ze względu na (*A*); ***for my ~*** ze względu na mnie; ***for God's ~*** F na litość boską
sa·la·ble ['seɪləbl] pokupny; sprzedażny
sal·ad ['sæləd] sałatka *f*; ⚠ *nie* ***sałata*** (*zielona*); '~ **dress·ing** przybranie *n* do sałatki, sos *m*
sal·a·ried ['sælərɪd]: **~** ***employee*** (*pracownik m* (*-nica f*) *otrzymujący* (*-a*) *pensję co miesiąc*)
sal·a·ry ['sælərɪ] pensja *f*
sale [seɪl] sprzedaż *f*; wyprzedaż *f*; aukcja *f*; ***for ~*** na sprzedaż; ***not for ~*** nie na sprzedaż; ***be on ~*** być na sprzedaż; **~s** *pl.* obroty *pl* **sale·a·ble** ['seɪləbl] → ***salable***
sales|·clerk ['seɪlzklɑːk] *Am.* sprzedawca *m* (-czyni *f*); '~·**girl** sprzedawczyni *f*; '~·**man** (*pl.* ***-men***) sprzedawca *m*; akwizytor *m*; '~ **rep·re·sen·ta·tive** przedstawiciel(ka *f*) *m* handlowy (-wa *f*); '~·**wom·an** (*pl.* ***-women***) sprzedawczyni *f*; akwizytorka *f*
sa·line ['seɪlaɪn] słony, zasolony
sa·li·va [sə'laɪvə] ślina *f*
sal·low ['sæləʊ] *skóra*: zżółkły, żółtawy
salm·on ['sæmən] *zo.* (*pl.* ***-on, -ons***) łosoś *m*
sal·on ['sælɔ̃ːŋ, 'sælɒn] *kosmetyczny itp.* salon *m*
sa·loon [sə'luːn] *Brt. mot.* sedan *m*; *Am. hist.* saloon *m*, bar *m*; *naut.* salon *m*; → **~ bar** *Brt.* (*elegancka część pubu*); **~ car** *Brt. mot.* sedan *m*
salt [sɔːlt] sól *f*; **2.** ⟨po⟩solić; zasalać ⟨-solić⟩ (*też* ***~ down***); *ulicę* posypywać ⟨-pać⟩ solą; **3.** słony; solny; solony; '~·**cel·lar** solniczka *f*; **~·pe·tre** *zwł. Brt.*, **~·pe·ter** *Am.* [sɔːlt'piːtə] *chem.* saletra *f* potasowa; '~·**wa·ter** solanka *f*; '~·**y** (***-ier, -iest***) słony
sal·u·ta·tion [sæljuː'teɪʃn] pozdrowienie *n*; początek *m* (*listu*)
sa·lute [sə'luːt] **1.** *mil.* ⟨za⟩salutować; oddawać ⟨-dać⟩ honory (*D*); pozdrawiać ⟨-rowić⟩; **2.** *mil.* oddanie *n* honorów; honory *pl.*; salut *m* (armatni); pozdrowienie *n*
sal·vage ['sælvɪdʒ] **1.** ratowanie *n* mienia; akcja *f* ratownicza; uratowane mienie *n*; **2.** ⟨u⟩ratować (***from*** od *G*)
sal·va·tion [sæl'veɪʃn] *rel.* zbawienie *n*; wybawienie *n*; ♀ ***Army*** Armia *f* Zbawienia
salve [sælv] maść *f*
same [seɪm]: ***the ~*** ten sam, ta sama, to samo; ***all the ~*** mimo wszystko; ***it is all the ~ to me*** wszystko mi jedno
sam·ple ['sɑːmpl] **1.** próbka *f*; **2.** pobierać ⟨-brać⟩ próbkę; ⟨s⟩próbować
san·a·to·ri·um [sænə'tɔːrɪəm] (*pl.* ***-riums, -ria*** [-rɪə]) sanatorium *n*
sanc·ti·fy ['sæŋktɪfaɪ] uświęcać ⟨-cić⟩
sanc·tion ['sæŋkʃn] **1.** aprobata *f*; *zw.* **~s** *pl.* sankcje *pl.*; **2.** ⟨za⟩aprobować, ⟨u⟩sankcjonować
sanc·ti·ty ['sæŋktətɪ] świętość *f*
sanc·tu·a·ry ['sæŋktʃʊərɪ] rezerwat *m*; azyl *m*, schronienie *n*
sand [sænd] **1.** piasek *m*; **~s** *pl.* piaski *pl.*; **2.** ⟨prze⟩szlifować papierem ściernym; posypywać ⟨-pać⟩ piaskiem
san·dal ['sændl] sandał *m*
'sand|·bag worek *m* z piaskiem; '~·**bank** piaszczysty brzeg *m*; '~·**box** *Am.* piaskownica *f*; '~·**cas·tle** zamek *m* z piasku; '~·**pa·per** papier *m* ścierny; '~·**pip·er** *zo.* siewka *f*, biegus *m*; '~·**pit** *Brt.* piaskownica *f*; '~·**stone** *geol.* piaskowiec *m*; '~·**storm** burza *f* piaskowa
sand·wich ['sænwɪdʒ] **1.** kanapka *f*; **2.** ***be ~ed between*** być wciśniętym pomiędzy (*A*); ***~ s.th. in between*** wciskać ⟨-snąć⟩ coś pomiędzy (*A*)
sand·y ['sændɪ] (***-ier, -iest***) piaszczysty; rudoblond
sane [seɪn] (***-r, -st***) zdrowy na umyśle; rozsądny, sensowny
sang [sæŋ] *pret. od* ***sing***
san·i·tar·i·um [sænɪ'teərɪəm] *Am.* → ***sanatorium***
san·i·ta·ry ['sænɪtərɪ] higieniczny; '~ **nap·kin** *Am.*, '~ **tow·el** *Brt.* podpaska *f*
san·i·ta·tion [sænɪ'teɪʃn] urządzenia *pl.* sanitarne; kanalizacja *f*
san·i·ty ['sænətɪ] zdrowie *n* psychiczne; rozsądek *m*
sank [sæŋk] *pret. od* ***sink*** 1

San·ta Claus ['sæntəklɔːz] Święty Mikołaj
sap[1] [sæp] *bot.* sok *m* (*np. brzozy*)
sap[2] [sæp] (**-pp-**) *zdrowie* nadwątlać ⟨-lić⟩
sap·phire ['sæfaɪə] szafir *m*; szafirowy
sar·cas|·m ['sɑːkæzəm] sarkazm *m*; **~·tic** [sɑː'kæstɪk] sarkastyczny
sar·dine [sɑː'diːn] *zo.* sardynka *f*
SASE [es eɪ es 'iː] *Am. skrót*: ***self-addressed, stamped envelope*** koperta *f* zwrotna ze znaczkiem
sash[1] [sæʃ] szarfa *f*
sash[2] [sæʃ] skrzydło *n* okienne; rama *f* okienna; '**~ win·dow** okno *n* otwierane pionowo (*z przesuwanymi do góry skrzydłami*)
sat [sæt] *pret. i p.p. od* **sit**
Sat *skrót pisany*: ***Saturday*** sob., sobota *f*
Sa·tan ['seɪtən] *rel.* szatan *m*
satch·el ['sætʃəl] tornister *m*
sat·el·lite ['sætəlaɪt] satelita *m*; *attr.* satelitarny
sat·in ['sætɪn] satyna *f*; atłas *m*; *attr.* satynowy
sat|·ire ['sætaɪə] satyra *f*; **~·ir·ist** ['sætərɪst] satyryk *m*; **~·ir·ize** ['sætəraɪz] satyryzować, przedstawiać ⟨-wić⟩ satyrycznie
sat·is·fac|·tion [sætɪs'fækʃn] satysfakcja *f*, zadowolenie *n*; spełnienie *n*; zadośćuczynienie *n*; **~·to·ry** [sætɪs'fæktərɪ] zadowalający; dostateczny
sat·is·fy ['sætɪsfaɪ] zadowalać ⟨-lić⟩; zaspokajać ⟨-koić⟩, zadośćuczynić; ***be satisfied that*** być przekonanym, że
sat·u·rate ['sætʃəreɪt] nasycać ⟨-cić⟩; *chem.* wysycać ⟨-cić⟩
Sat·ur·day ['sætədɪ] sobota *f*; ***on ~*** w sobotę; ***on ~s*** sobotami, co sobotę
S
sauce [sɔːs] sos *m*; '**~·pan** rondel *m*
sau·cer ['sɔːsə] spodek *m*
sauc·y ['sɔːsɪ] F (***-ier, -iest***) zadziorny, z tupetem
saun·ter ['sɔːntə] kroczyć, przechadzać się
saus·age ['sɒsɪdʒ] kiełbasa *f*; *też* ***small ~*** parówka *f*
sav|·age ['sævɪdʒ] **1.** dziki; niecywilizowany; bestialski; **2.** dzikus *m*; **~·ag·e·ry** ['sævɪdʒərɪ] bestialstwo *n*, okrucieństwo *n*
save [seɪv] **1.** ⟨u⟩ratować (***from*** z *G*); *życie* ocalać ⟨-lić⟩; *pieniądze itp.* oszczędzać ⟨-dzić⟩, zaoszczędzać ⟨-dzić⟩; *coś* zachowywać ⟨-wać⟩ (***for*** na *A*); *komp.* zapisywać ⟨-sać⟩; (*w sporcie*) *strzał* ⟨o⟩bronić; **2.** (*w sporcie*) parada *f*, obrona *f*
sav·er ['seɪvə] ratownik *m* (-niczka *f*); *Brt.* oszczędzający *m* (-ca *f*); ***it is a time-~*** to bardzo oszczędza czas
sav·ings ['seɪvɪŋz] *pl.* oszczędności *pl.*; '**~ ac·count** konto *n* oszczędności; '**~ bank** kasa *f* oszczędności; '**~ de·pos·it** wkład *m* oszczędnościowy
sa·vio(u)r ['seɪvjə] zbawca *m*; ***the*** ♀ *rel.* Zbawiciel *m*
sa·vo(u)r ['seɪvə] ⟨z⟩jeść *lub* ⟨wy⟩pić ze smakiem, rozkoszować się; ***~ of*** *fig.* smakować (*I*); **~·y** ['seɪvərɪ] smakowity; pikantny, nie słodki
saw[1] [sɔː] *pret. od* **see**[1]
saw[2] [sɔː] **1.** piła *f*; **2.** (***~ed, ~n*** *lub zwł. Am.* ***~ed***) ⟨s-, u⟩piłować; '**~·dust** trociny *pl.*; '**~·mill** tartak *m*; **~n** [sɔːn] *p.p. od* **saw**[2]
Sax·on ['sæksn] **1.** Anglosas *m*; **2.** (anglo)saski
say [seɪ] **1.** (***said***) mówić ⟨powiedzieć⟩; *pacierz* odmawiać ⟨-mówić⟩; ***what does your watch ~?*** która godzina na twoim zegarku?; ***he is said to be ...*** podobno jest...; ***it ~s*** napisane jest; ***it ~s here*** tu jest napisane; ***it goes without ~ing*** to rozumie się samo przez siebie; ***no sooner said than done*** zostało wykonane od razu; ***that is to ~*** to znaczy; (***and***) ***that's ~ing s.th.*** a to coś mówi; ***you said it*** to ty tak powiedziałeś; ***you can ~ that again!*** szczera prawda!; ***you don't ~*** (***so***)***!*** niemożliwe!; nie mów!; ***I ~*** *Brt.* przepraszam; ***not to ~ no to*** nie odmawiać (*G*); **2.** prawo *n* głosu; głos *m* (***in*** w *L*); ***have one's ~*** wypowiadać ⟨-wiedzieć⟩ się; ***he always has to have his ~*** on zawsze musi coś powiedzieć; '**~·ing** porzekadło *n*, powiedzenie *n*; ***as the ~ing goes*** jak to mówią
scab [skæb] *med.* strup *m*; *vet.* świerzb *m*; *sl.* łamistrajk *m*
scaf·fold ['skæfəld] rusztowanie *n*; szafot *m*; '**~·ing** rusztowanie *n*
scald [skɔːld] **1.** oparzać ⟨-rzyć⟩, sparzyć; **2.** ***~ing hot*** gorący jak ukrop; **2.** sparzenie *n*; poparzenie *n*
scale[1] [skeɪl] **1.** *tech., math., też fig.* skala *f*; podziałka *f* (*math., też mapy*); *zwł.*

Am. waga *f*; *mus.* gama *f*; ***to ~*** w skali; **2.** sporządzać ⟨-dzić⟩ w skali; ***~ down*** *fig.* ⟨z⟩redukować; ***~ up*** *fig.* zwiększać ⟨-szyć⟩; wspinać ⟨-piąć⟩ się
scale[2] [skeıl] szala *f* wagi; (***a pair of***) ***~s*** *pl.* waga *f*
scale[3] [skeıl] **1.** łuska *f*; kamień *m* (*w czajniku*); ***the ~s fell from my eyes*** łuski mi spadły z oczu; **2.** *rybę* ⟨o⟩-skrobać
scal·lop ['skɒləp] *zo.* (*małż*) przegrzebek *m*
scalp [skælp] **1.** skóra *f* głowy; skalp *m*; **2.** ⟨o⟩skalpować
scal·y ['skeılı] (***-ier, -iest***) łuskowaty
scamp [skæmp] F urwis *m*, huncwot *m*
scam·per ['skæmpə] pierzchać ⟨-chnąć⟩; smyknąć
scan [skæn] **1.** (***-nn-***) przeszukiwać ⟨-kać⟩; *gazetę* przeglądać ⟨-dnąć⟩; *komp.* ⟨ze⟩skanować; przeszukiwać zakres *radio*; *telewizyjny obraz* ⟨prze-, z⟩-analizować, składać ⟨złożyć⟩; **2.** *med. itp.* skaning *m*
scan·dal ['skændl] skandal *m*; słuchy *pl.*; **~·ize** ['skændəlaız]: ***be ~ized at s.th.*** ⟨z⟩gorszyć się czymś; **~·ous** ['skændələs] skandaliczny; ***it's ~ous that*** to skandal, że
Scan·di·na·vi·a [skændı'neıvjə] Skandynawia *f*; **Scan·di·na·vi·an** [skændı'neıvjən] skandynawski
scan·ner ['skænə] *tech.* skaner *m*
scant [skænt] skąpy, niewielki, mały; '**~·y** (***-ier, -iest***) skąpy, niewielki, mały
scape·goat ['skeıpgəʊt] kozioł *m* ofiarny
scar [skɑː] **1.** blizna *f*; **2.** (***-rr-***) pokrywać ⟨-ryć⟩ bliznami; pozostawiać ⟨-wić⟩ uraz; ***~ over*** zabliźniać ⟨-nić⟩ się
scarce [skeəs] (***-r, -st***) rzadki, mało dostępny; '**~·ly** ledwo, ledwie; **scar·ci·ty** ['skeəsətı] skąpość *f*, mała dostępność *f*
scare [skeə] **1.** ⟨wy⟩straszyć; ***be ~d*** bać się; ***~ away, ~ off*** odstraszać ⟨-szyć⟩; **2.** strach *m*; panika *f*; ***bomb ~*** alarm *m* bombowy; '**~·crow** strach *m* na wróble
scarf [skɑːf] (*pl.* ***scarfs*** [skɑːfs], ***scarves*** [skɑːvz]) szal *m*, szalik *m*; chusta *f* (*na głowę, ramię itp.*)
scar·let ['skɑːlət] pąsowy; **~ 'fe·ver** *med.* szkarlatyna *f*, płonica *f*; **~ 'run·ner** *bot.* fasola *f* wielokwiatowa
scarred [skɑːd] pokryty bliznami, zbliznowaciały
scarves [skɑːvz] *pl. od* ***scarf***
scath·ing ['skeıðıŋ] *krytyka*: niszczący, zjadliwy
scat·ter ['skætə] rozpraszać ⟨-roszyć⟩ (się); rozbiegać ⟨-biec⟩ się; rozrzucać ⟨-cić⟩; '**~·brained** F roztrzepany, roztargniony; '**~ed** rozproszony
scav·enge ['skævındʒ]: ***~ on*** *zo.* żerować na (*L*); ***~ for*** wyszukiwać ⟨-kać⟩
sce·na·ri·o [sı'nɑːrıəʊ] (*pl.* ***-os***) scenariusz *m* (*filmowy, telewizyjny, też fig.*)
scene [siːn] scena *f*; ***behind the ~s*** za kulisami; **sce·ne·ry** ['siːnərı] sceneria *f*; krajobraz *m*
scent [sent] **1.** zapach *m*, aromat *m*; *zwł. Brt.* perfumy *pl.*; *hunt.* wiatr *m*, zapach *m*; trop *m*, ślad *m*; **2.** ⟨z⟩wietrzyć, wyczuwać ⟨-czuć⟩ (*też fig.*); *zwł. Brt.* ⟨u⟩-perfumować; napełniać ⟨-nić⟩ aromatem; '**~·less** bezwonny, bezzapachowy
scep|·tic ['skeptık] *Brt.* sceptyk *m*; '**~·ti·cal** *Brt.* sceptyczny
scep·tre *Brt.*, **scep·ter** *Am.* ['septə] berło *n*
sched·ule ['ʃedjuːl, *Am.* 'skedʒʊl] **1.** harmonogram *m*, plan *m*; wykaz *m*, spis *m*; taryfa *f*; *zwł. Am.* rozkład *m* jazdy; ***ahead of ~*** przed terminem; ***be behind ~*** mieć opóźnienie, z opóźnieniem; ***on ~*** w terminie, zgodnie z planem; **2.** ⟨za⟩planować; wstawiać do rozkładu; ***the meeting is ~d for Monday*** spotkanie zostało zaplanowane na poniedziałek; ***it is ~d to take place tomorrow*** zostało zaplanowane na jutro; **~d de'par·ture** planowy odjazd *m*; **~d 'flight** rejsowy lot *m*
scheme [skiːm] **1.** *zwł. Brt.* program *m*, projekt *m*; schemat *m*; intryga *f*, spisek *m*; **2.** ⟨u⟩knuć intrygę; ⟨u⟩knuć
schnit·zel ['ʃnıtsl] *gastr.* sznycel *m*
schol·ar ['skɒlə] uczony *m* (*-a f*); *univ.* stypendysta *m* (-tka *f*); **~·ly** uczony; naukowy; '**~·ship** uczoność *f*, (duża) wiedza *f*; *univ.* stypendium
school[1] [skuːl] **1.** szkoła (*też fig.*); *univ.* fakultet *m*; *Am.* uczelnia *f*, szkoła *f* wyższa; ***at ~*** w szkole; ***go to ~*** chodzić ⟨pójść⟩ do szkoły; *attr.* szkolny; **2.** ⟨wy⟩szkolić; *zwierzę* ⟨wy⟩tresować
school[2] [skuːl] *zo.* ławica *f* (*ryb*); stado *n* (*wielorybów*)

S

'school|·bag torba *f*; **'~·boy** uczeń *m*; **'~·child** (*pl.* ***-children***) uczeń *m*; **'~·fellow** → ***schoolmate***; **'~·girl** uczennica *f*; **'~·ing** szkolenie *n*, nauka *f* szkolna; **'~·mate** kolega *m* (-leżanka *f*) szkolny (-na); **'~·teach·er** nauczyciel(ka *f*) *m*; **'~·yard** podwórko *n* szkolne
schoo·ner ['skuːnə] *naut.* szkuner *m*
sci·ence ['saɪəns] *przyrodnicza* nauka *f*; ***natural ~s*** *pl.* przyrodnicze nauki *pl.*; **~ 'fic·tion** (*skrót:* ***SF***) science-fiction *n*
sci·en·tif·ic [saɪən'tɪfɪk] (***~ally***) naukowy
sci·en·tist ['saɪəntɪst] naukowiec *m*, uczony *m* (-na *f*)
sci-fi [saɪ'faɪ] F science-fiction *n*
scin·til·lat·ing ['sɪntɪleɪtɪŋ] błyskotliwy, efektowny
scis·sors ['sɪzəz] *pl.* (***a pair of ~***) nożyce *pl.*, nożyczki *pl.*
scoff [skɒf] **1.** natrząsać się (***at*** z *G*); **2.** szyderstwo *n*, kpina *f*
scold [skəʊld] strofować
scol·lop ['skɒləp] *zo.* → ***scallop***
scone [skɒn] *zwł. Brt.* bułka *f* słodka (*jedzona z masłem*)
scoop [skuːp] **1.** szufla *f*, szufelka *f*; łopatka *f*; łyżka *f* (*koparki, do lodów*); gałka *f* (*lodów*); sensacyjna wiadomość *f*, scoop *m*; **2.** nabierać ⟨-brać⟩, czerpać ⟨zaczerpnąć⟩; ***~ down*** wybierać ⟨-brać⟩; ***~ up*** podnosić ⟨-nieść⟩
scoot·er ['skuːtə] hulajnoga *f*; skuter *m*
scope [skəʊp] zakres *m*, zasięg *m*; pole *n* widzenia; pole *n* działania;
scorch [skɔːtʃ] *v/t.* przypalać ⟨-lić⟩, przypiekać ⟨-piec⟩; *v/i. Brt.* (*jechać*) *mot.* grzać
score [skɔː] **1.** wynik *m* (*gry*); punkt *m*; *mus.* partytura *f*; muzyka *f* filmowa; dwudziestka *n*; *też* ***~ mark*** karb *m*, nacięcie *n*; ***what is the ~?*** jaki wynik?; ***the ~ stood at*** *lub* ***was 3-2*** w grze było 3-2; ***keep*** (***the***) ***~*** zapisywać ⟨-sać⟩ punkty; ***~s*** *pl.* ***of*** dziesiątki *pl.* (*G*); ***four ~ and ten*** dziewięćdziesiąt; ***on that ~*** pod tym względem; ***have a ~ to settle with s.o.*** mieć z kimś porachunki do załatwienia; **2.** *v/t.* (*w sporcie*) *punkty* zdobywać ⟨-być⟩, *bramkę* strzelać ⟨-lić⟩; *zwycięstwo* odnosić ⟨-nieść⟩; *mus.* ⟨z⟩instrumentować; ⟨na⟩pisać muzykę do (*G*); ⟨wy⟩karbować, nacinać ⟨-ciąć⟩; *v/i.* (*w sporcie*) zdobywać ⟨-być⟩ punkty, strzelać ⟨-lić⟩ bramkę; odnosić ⟨-nieść⟩ sukces; **'~·board** *v/i.* (*w sporcie*) tablica *f* wyników; **scor·er** ['skɔːrə] *v/i.* (*w sporcie*) strzelec *m*, zdobywca *m* (-czyni *f*) punktu; *v/i.* (*w sporcie*) (*osoba zapisująca punktację, wyniki*)
scorn [skɔːn] pogarda *f*; **'~·ful** pogardliwy
Scor·pi·o ['skɔːpɪəʊ] *znak Zodiaku:* Skorpion *m*; ***he/she is*** (***a***) **~** on(a) jest spod znaku Skorpiona
Scot [skɒt] Szkot(ka *f*) *m*
Scotch [skɒtʃ] **1.** *whisky itp.*: szkocki; **2.** *whisky*: szkocka *f*
scot-free [skɒt'friː] F: ***he got off ~*** uszło mu na sucho
Scot·land ['skɒtlənd] Szkocja *f*
Scots [skɒts] szkocki (*o osobach*); **'~·man** (*pl.* ***-men***) Szkot *m*; **'~·wom·an** (*pl.* ***-women***) Szkotka *f*
Scot·tish ['skɒtɪʃ] szkocki
scoun·drel ['skaʊndrəl] łajdak *m*
scour[1] ['skaʊə] ⟨wy⟩szorować, ⟨o⟩skrobać
scour[2] ['skaʊə] przeszukiwać ⟨-kać⟩
scourge [skɜːdʒ] **1.** plaga *f*; bicz *m* (*też fig.*); **2.** biczować; ⟨z⟩nękać
scout [skaʊt] **1.** *zwł. mil.* zwiadowca *m*; *Brt.* (*osoba pomagająca zmotoryzowanym w razie awarii*); *też* ***boy ~*** skaut ***m***; *też* ***girl ~*** skautka *f*; *też* ***talent ~*** poszukiwacz(ka *f*) *m* talentów; **2.** ***~ about, ~ around*** rozglądać się (***for*** za *I*); *też* ***~ out*** *mil.* wynajdywać ⟨-naleźć⟩
scowl [skaʊl] **1.** ponura mina *f*; **2.** ⟨s⟩krzywić się (*też* ***at*** na *A*)
scram·ble ['skræmbl] **1.** wdrapywać ⟨-pać⟩ się; pchać się (***for*** do *G*); *tech.* ⟨za⟩kodować; **2.** wdrapywanie *n* się; przepychanka *f*, szarpanina *f*; ***~d 'eggs*** *gastr. pl.* jajecznica *f*
scrap[1] [skræp] **1.** strzęp *m*, skrawek *m*; złom *m*; ***~s*** *pl.* odpadki *pl.*, resztki *pl.* (*jedzenia*); **2.** (***-pp-***) *plan itp.* porzucać ⟨-cić⟩, odrzucać ⟨-cić⟩; ⟨ze⟩złomować
scrap[2] F [skræp] **1.** scysja *f*, zatarg *m*; **2.** ⟨po⟩kłócić się, wszczynać ⟨-cząć⟩ sprzeczkę
'scrap·book album *m* z wycinkami
scrape [skreɪp] **1.** skrobać, zeskrobywać ⟨-bać⟩; *kolano itp.* ocierać ⟨otrzeć⟩; *samochód* zarysowywać ⟨-ować⟩; trzeć,

S

pocierać ⟨potrzeć⟩ (***against*** o *A*); **2.** otarcie *n*, zarysowanie *n*
'**scrap**| **heap** kupa *f* złomu; '**~ met•al** złom *m*; '**~ pa•per** *zwł. Brt.* makulatura *f*; '**~ val•ue** wartość *f* złomowa; '**~•yard** złomowisko *n*
scratch [skrætʃ] **1.** ⟨po-, za-, wy⟩drapać; *plan* porzucać ⟨-cić⟩; ⟨po⟩drapać (się); **2.** zadrapanie *n*, rysa *f*; podrapanie *n*, zadraśnięcie *n*; ***from ~*** F od zera; **3.** prowizoryczny, zrobiony na łapu capu; '**~•pad** *zwł. Am.* notatnik *m*; '**~ pa•per** *Am.* papier *m* do pisania na brudno
scrawl [skrɔːl] **1.** ⟨na⟩bazgrać; **2.** bazgroły *pl.*
scraw•ny ['skrɔːnɪ] (***-ier, -iest***) kościsty
scream [skriːm] **1.** krzyczeć ⟨-yknąć⟩ (***with*** z *G*); *też* ***~ out*** wrzasnąć; ***~ with laughter*** zanosić się ze śmiechu; **2.** krzyk *m*; ***~s*** *pl.* ***of laughter*** rozgłośny śmiech *m*; ***he is a ~*** F przy nim można pęknąć ze śmiechu
screech [skriːtʃ] **1.** wydzierać ⟨-drzeć⟩ się (*piszcząco*); ⟨za⟩piszczeć; **2.** pisk *m*
screen [skriːn] **1.** ekran *m*; parawan *m*; zasłona *f*, szpaler *m* (*drzew*); **2.** osłaniać ⟨-łonić⟩ (*też fig.*), zasłaniać ⟨-łonić⟩; *kandydatów* przesiewać ⟨-siać⟩, odsiewać ⟨-siać⟩ (*G*); *film* wyświetlać ⟨-lić⟩, pokazywać ⟨-zać⟩; ***~ off*** przedzielać ⟨-lić⟩ (*parawanem*); '**~•play** scenariusz *m*; '**~ sav•er** *komp.* (*program oszczędzający ekran komputerowy*)
screw [skruː] **1.** *tech.* wkręt *m*, śruba *f*; ***he has a loose ~*** F szajba mu odbiła; **2.** wkręcać ⟨-cić⟩, przyśrubowywać ⟨-wać⟩; V ⟨wy⟩dupczyć; ***~ up*** *twarz* wykrzywiać ⟨-wić⟩; *oczy* ⟨z⟩mrużyć; ***~ up one's courage*** zdobyć się na odwagę; '**~•ball** *zwł. Am.* F szajbus *m*; '**~•driv•er** śrubokręt *m*, wkrętak *m*; **~ 'top** nakrętka *f*
scrib•ble ['skrɪbl] **1.** ⟨na⟩bazgrać, ⟨na⟩gryzmolić; ; **2.** bazgroły *pl.*, gryzmoły *pl.*
scrimp [skrɪmp]: ***~ and save*** liczyć każdy grosik
script [skrɪpt] manuskrypt *m*; tekst *m* (*też theat.*); scenariusz *m* (*filmowy lub telewizyjny*); pismo *n*; *Brt. univ.* test *m*
Scrip•ture ['skrɪptʃə] *też* ***the ~s*** *pl.* Pismo *n* Święte
scroll [skrəʊl] **1.** zwój *m*, rulon *m* (*pergaminu itp.*); **2.** ***~ down/up*** *obraz na ekranie* przewijać ⟨-winąć⟩, przesuwać ⟨-sunąć⟩
scro•tum *anat.* ['skrəʊtəm] (*pl.* ***-ta*** [-tə], ***-tums***) moszna *f*
scrub[1] [skrʌb] **1.** (***-bb-***) ⟨wy⟩szorować; **2.** (wy)szorowanie *n*
scrub[2] [skrʌb] skrub *m*, busz *m* australijski
scru|**•ple** ['skruːpl] **1.** skrupuł *m*; wątpliwość *f*; **2.** mieć skrupuły; **~•pu•lous** ['skruːpjʊləs] skrupulatny
scru•ti|**•nize** ['skruːtɪnaɪz] dokładnie ⟨z⟩badać; **~•ny** ['skruːtɪnɪ] dokładne badanie *n*, analiza *f*
scu•ba ['skuːbə] akwalung *m*; '**~ div•ing** nurkowanie *n* swobodne
scud [skʌd] (***-dd-***) sunąć szybko, ⟨po⟩szybować
scuf•fle ['skʌfl] **1.** bójka *f*; **2.** wszczynać ⟨-szcząć⟩ bójkę
scull [skʌl] **1.** *jednopiórowe* krótkie wiosło *n*; skul *m*, jedynka *f*; **2.** wiosłować
scul•le•ry ['skʌlərɪ] zmywalnia *f*, pomywalnia *f*
sculp|**•tor** ['skʌlptə] rzeźbiarz *m* (-arka *f*); **~•ture** ['skʌlptʃə] **1.** rzeźba *f*; **2.** ⟨wy⟩rzeźbić; ⟨u⟩kształtować
scum [skʌm] piana *f*; szumowiny *pl.* (*też fig.*)
scurf [skɜːf] łupież *m*
scur•ri•lous ['skʌrɪləs] obelżywy, nie przebierający w słowach
scur•ry ['skʌrɪ] przemykać ⟨-mknąć⟩; ⟨po⟩tuptać
scur•vy ['skɜːvɪ] *med.* szkorbut *m*, gnilec *m*
scut•tle ['skʌtl]: ***~ away, ~ off*** uciekać ⟨-ciec⟩ drobnymi kroczkami
scythe [saɪð] kosa *f*
SE *skrót pisany:* ***southeast*** płd.-wsch., południowy wschód *m*; ***southeast(ern)*** płd.-wsch., południowo-wschodni
sea [siː] morze *n* (*też fig.*); ***at ~*** na morzu; ***be all*** *lub* ***completely at ~*** *fig.* F pogubić się; ***by ~*** morzem, drogą morską; ***by the ~*** nad morzem; *attr.* morski; nadmorski; '**~•food** owoce *pl.* morza; '**~•gull** *zo.* mewa *f*
seal[1] [siːl] *zo.* (*pl.* ***seals, seal***) foka *f*
seal[2] [siːl] **1.** pieczęć *f*; *tech.* uszczelka *f*; **2.** ⟨o-, za⟩pieczętować; zamykać

⟨-mknąć⟩, zaklejać ⟨-leić⟩; *tech.* uszczelniać ⟨-nić⟩; *fig.* przypieczętowywać ⟨-ować⟩; **~ed envelope** zamknięta koperta *f*; **~ off** *dostęp* zamykać ⟨-mknąć⟩

'sea lev·el: **above ~** nad poziomem morza; **below ~** poniżej poziomu morza

'seal·ing wax lak *m* (*do pieczętowania*)

seam [siːm] szew *m*; połączenie *n*; *geol.* pokład *m*

'sea·man (*pl.* **-men**) żeglarz *m*

seam·stress ['semstrɪs] krawcowa *f*

'sea|·plane wodnosamolot *m*, hydroplan *m*, wodnopłat *m*; **'~·port** port *m* morski; miasto *n* portowe; **'~ pow·er** potęga *f* morska

sear [sɪə] wypalać ⟨-lić⟩ (*też fig.*); palić, piec (w *A*); *mięso* obsmażać ⟨-żyć⟩

search [sɜːtʃ] **1.** *v/i.* szukać (**for** *G*), poszukiwać ⟨-kać⟩ (**for** *A*); **~ through** przeszukiwać ⟨-kać⟩; *v/t.* szukać; przeszukiwać ⟨-kać⟩; ⟨z⟩rewidować; **~ me!** F nie mam pojęcia!; **2.** poszukiwanie *n* (**for** *G*); szukanie *n*; rewizja *f*; **'~·ing** *spojrzenie*: badawczy; *przegląd*: wnikliwy; **'~·light** (*reflektor*) szperacz *m*; **'~ par·ty** wyprawa *f* poszukiwawcza; **'~ war·rant** nakaz *m* rewizji

'sea|·shore brzeg *m* morza; **'~·sick**: **be ~sick** cierpieć na chorobę morską; **'~·side**: **at** *lub* **by the ~side** nad morzem; **go to the ~side** ⟨po⟩jechać nad morze; **~·side re'sort** uzdrowisko *n* nadmorskie

sea·son¹ ['siːzn] pora *f* roku; sezon *m* (*też theat.*); *myśliwski, urlopowy* okres *m*; **in ~** w sezonie, **out of ~** poza sezonem; **cherries are now in ~** teraz jest sezon na czereśnie; **ꭥ!** Wesołych Świąt (*Bożego Narodzenia*)!; **with the compliments of the ~** najlepsze życzenia z okazji świąt

sea·son² ['siːzn] przyprawiać ⟨-wić⟩, doprawiać ⟨-wić⟩; *drewno* sezonować

sea·son·al ['siːzənl] sezonowy; okresowy

sea·son·ing ['siːznɪŋ] przyprawa *f*

'sea·son tick·et *rail.* bilet *m* okresowy; *theat.* abonament *m*

seat [siːt] **1.** miejsce *n*; siedzenie *n*; siedziba *f*; **take one's/a ~** zajmować ⟨-jąć⟩ miejsce; **2.** *kogoś* sadzać ⟨posadzić⟩; *sala*: ⟨po⟩mieścić; *uszczelkę* osadzać ⟨-dzić⟩; **be ~ed** siedzieć; **please be ~ed** proszę usiąść; **remain ~ed** pozostawać na swoim miejscu; **'~ belt** *aviat.*, *mot.* pas *m* bezpieczeństwa; **fasten one's ~belt** zapinać ⟨-piąć⟩ pas bezpieczeństwa; **'...-seat·er**: **forty-seater** o 40 miejscach

sea| ur·chin ['siːɜːtʃɪn] *zo.* jeżowiec *m*; **~·ward(s)** ['siːwəd(z)] w stronę morza; **'~·weed** *bot.* wodorost *m* morski; **'~·wor·thy** zdatny do żeglugi

sec [sek] *zwł. Brt.* F *fig.* chwileczka *f*, sekunda *f*; **just a ~** sekundeczka *f*

se·cede [sɪ'siːd] odłączać ⟨-czyć⟩ się (**from** od *G*); **se·ces·sion** [sɪ'seʃn] secesja *f*, odłączenie *n* się

se·clud·ed [sɪ'kluːdɪd] *dom*: odosobniony; *życie*: samotniczy; **se·clu·sion** [sɪ'kluːʒn] odosobnienie *n*; samotnictwo *n*

sec·ond¹ ['sekənd] **1.** *adj.* drugi; **every ~ day** co drugi dzień; **~ to none** nie ustępujący nikomu; **but on ~ thoughts** (*Am.* **thought**) jednak po namyśle; **2.** *adv.* jako drugi; **3.** drugi *m*, druga *f*, drugie *n*; *mot.* drugi bieg *m*; sekundant *m*; **~s** *pl.* F *econ.* drugi wybór *m*, resztki *pl.*; **4.** *wniosek itp.* popierać ⟨poprzeć⟩

sec·ond² ['sekənd] sekunda *f*; *fig.* sekunda *f*, chwila *f*; **just a ~** (za) chwilkę

sec·ond·a·ry ['sekəndərɪ] drugorzędny, wtórny, uboczny; *ped. szkoła itp.* średni

sec·ond|-'best drugiej jakości; na drugim miejscu; **~ 'class** *rail.* druga klasa *f*; **~-'class** drugiej klasy; **~ 'floor** *Brt.* drugie piętro; *Am.* pierwsze piętro; **~-'hand** używany; antykwaryczny; **'~ hand** sekundnik *m*; **'~·ly** po drugie; **~-'rate** drugiego gatunku

se·cre·cy ['siːkrɪsɪ] tajemnica *f*; dyskrecja *f*

se·cret ['siːkrɪt] **1.** tajny, poufny; sekretny; **2.** sekret *m*; tajemnica *f*; **in ~** skrycie, w tajemnicy; **keep s.th. a ~** zachowywać ⟨-ować⟩ coś w sekrecie; **can you keep a ~?** umiesz dotrzymywać tajemnicy?; **~ 'a·gent** tajny (-a) agent(ka *f*) *m*

sec·re·ta·ry ['sekrətrɪ] sekretarz *m* (-arka *f*); **ꭥ of 'State** *Brt.* Minister *m*; *Am.* Sekretarz *m* Stanu

se·crete [sɪ'kriːt] *physiol.* wydzielać ⟨-lić⟩; **se·cre·tion** [sɪ'kriːʃn] *physiol.* wydzielina *f*

S

se•cre•tive ['si:krətɪv] skryty
se•cret•ly ['si:krɪtlɪ] potajemnie, w tajemnicy
se•cret 'ser•vice tajna służba *f*
sec•tion ['sekʃn] część *f*; sekcja *f*; *jur.* paragraf *m*; część *f*; *tech.* przekrój *m*; *math.* odcinek *m*
sec•u•lar ['sekjʊlə] świecki
se•cure [sɪ'kjʊə] **1.** bezpieczny; zabezpieczony (***against, from*** przed *I*); **2.** *drzwi itp.* umocowywać ⟨-ować⟩; zabezpieczać ⟨-czyć⟩ (***against, from*** przed *I*)
se•cu•ri•ty [sɪ'kjʊərətɪ] bezpieczeństwo *n*, zabezpieczenie *n*; ***securities*** *pl.* papiery *pl.* wartościowe; **~ check** kontrola *f* bezpieczeństwa; **~ mea•sure** środek *m* bezpieczeństwa; **~ risk** zagrożenie *n* bezpieczeństwa
se•dan [sɪ'dæn] *Am. mot.* sedan *m*
se•date [sɪ'deɪt] **1.** stateczny; **2.** podawać ⟨dać⟩ środki uspokajające
sed•a•tive ['sedətɪv] środek *m* uspokajający
sed•i•ment ['sedɪmənt] osad *m*
se•duce [sɪ'dju:s] uwodzić ⟨uwieść⟩; **se•duc•er** [sɪ'dju:sə] uwodziciel(ka *f*) *m*; **se•duc•tion** [sɪ'dʌkʃn] uwiedzenie *n*; **se•duc•tive** [sɪ'dʌktɪv] uwodzicielski
see[1] [si:] (***saw, seen***) *v/i.* widzieć; zobaczyć; ⟨z⟩rozumieć; ***I ~!*** rozumiem!; ach tak!; ***you ~*** widzisz; ***let me ~*** pozwól mi się zastanowić; ***we'll ~*** zobaczymy; *v/t.* widzieć; zauważać ⟨-żyć⟩; wybierać się ⟨-brać się⟩ do (*G*), ⟨s⟩konsultować się z (*I*); **~ *s.o. home*** odprowadzać ⟨-dzić⟩ kogoś do domu; **~ *you!*** cześć!; na razie!; **~ *about*** zajmować ⟨-jąć⟩ się; zobaczyć; **~ *off*** odprowadzać ⟨-dzić⟩ (***at*** na *L*); **~ *out*** towarzyszyć; odprowadzać ⟨-dzić⟩; **~ *through*** przejrzeć *kogoś* na wskroś; pomagać ⟨-móc⟩ *komuś* przetrwać; **~ *to it that*** dopilnować, że
see[2] [si:] biskupstwo *n*, diecezja *f*; ***Holy*** ♀ Stolica *f* Święta
seed [si:d] **1.** *bot.* nasienie *n*; ziarno *n* (*też fig.*); *Am.* (*jabłka itp.*) pestka *f*; (*w sporcie*) rozstawiony (-a) zawodnik *m* (-niczka *f*); ***go*** *lub* ***run to ~*** wydawać ⟨-dać⟩ nasiona; *fig.* F ⟨s⟩kapcanieć; **2.** *v/t.* wysiewać ⟨-siać⟩; siać, obsiewać ⟨-siać⟩; ⟨wy⟩drylować; (*w sporcie*) rozstawiać ⟨-wić⟩; *v/i. bot.* wysiewać⟨-siać⟩ się; **'~•less** bezpestkowy; **'~•y** F (***-ier, -iest***) zapuszczony, zaniedbany
seek [si:k] (***sought***) szukać, poszukiwać ⟨-kać⟩
seem [si:m] wydawać ⟨-dać⟩ się, zdawać ⟨zdać⟩ się; **'~•ing** pozorny
seen [si:n] *p.p. od* ***see***[1]
seep [si:p] przeciekać ⟨-ciec⟩, przesączać ⟨-czyć⟩ się
see•saw ['si:sɔ:] huśtawka *f*
seethe [si:ð] gotować się, kipieć (*też fig.*)
'see-through przezroczysty, przeświecający
seg•ment ['segmənt] *math.* odcinek *m*; segment *m*, cząstka *f*; przekrój *m*
seg•re|•gate ['segrɪgeɪt] ⟨po⟩segregować; rozdzielać ⟨-lić⟩; **~•ga•tion** [segrɪ'geɪʃn] segregacja *f*; rozdział *m*
Seine Sekwana *f*
seize [si:z] ⟨s⟩chwytać, ⟨z⟩łapać; *władzę itp.* przechwytywać ⟨-wycić⟩; *uczucia*: owładnąć; **sei•zure** ['si:ʒə] przechwycenie *n* władzy; zajęcie *n* (*majątku*); *med.* atak *m*, napad *m*
sel•dom ['seldəm] *adv.* rzadko
se•lect [sɪ'lekt] **1.** wybierać ⟨-brać⟩; ⟨wy⟩selekcjonować; **2.** wyselekcjonowany; ekskluzywny; **se•lec•tion** [sɪ'lekʃn] wybór *m*; dobór *m*
self [self] (*pl.* ***selves*** [selvz]) ja *m*, ego *n*; **~-as'sured** pewny siebie; **~-'cen•tred** *Brt.*, **~-'cen•tered** *Am.* egocentryczny; **~-'col•o(u)red** jednobarwny, jednokolorowy; **~-'con•fi•dence** pewność *f* siebie; **~-'con•fi•dent** pewny siebie; **~-'con•scious** niepewny (*siebie*), skrępowany; **~-con'tained** samodzielny, odrębny; zamknięty w sobie; **~-con'trol** samoopanowanie *n*; **~-de'fence** *Brt.*, **~-de'fense** *Am.* samoobrona *f*; ***in ~-defence/-defense*** w obronie własnej; **~-de•ter•mi'na•tion** *pol.* samostanowienie *n*; **~-em'ployed** na własnym rozrachunku; **~-es'teem** poczucie *n* własnej wartości; **~-'ev•i•dent** oczywisty; **~-'gov•ern•ment** samorząd *m*; **~-'help** samopomoc *f*; **~-im'por•tant** zarozumiały; **~-in'dulgent** folgujący swoim zachciankom; **~-'in•terest** własny interes *m*; **'~•ish** egoistyczny, sobkowski; **~-made 'man** (*pl.* ***-men***) self-made man *m* (*człowiek wszystko zawdzięczający tylko sobie*); **~-'pit•y** roztkliwianie *n* się nad sobą; **~-pos'sessed**

S

opanowany; ~-**pos'ses'sion** opanowanie *n*; ~-**re·li·ant** [selfrɪ'laɪənt] niezależny, samodzielny; ~-**re'spect** poważanie *m* dla siebie samego; ~-'**right·eous**, faryzejski, świętoszkowaty; ~-'**sat·is·fied** zadowolony z siebie; ~-'**serv·ice** **1.** samoobsługowy; **2.** samoobsługa *f*; ~-**suf'ficient** samowystarczalny; ~-**sup'porting** niezależny materialnie; ~-'**willed** krnąbrny

sell [sel] (***sold***) sprzedawać ⟨-dać⟩; sprzedawać ⟨-dać⟩ się (***at, for*** za *A*); iść (dobrze); ~ ***by...*** okres przydatności do ...; ~ ***off*** wyprzedawać ⟨-dać⟩ (*zwł. tanio*); ~ ***out*** wyprzedać; ***be sold out*** zostać wyprzedanym; ~ ***up*** *zwł. Brt.* rozprzedawać ⟨-dać⟩ (*swój majątek*); '~-**by date** data *f* przydatności do spożycia; '~·**er** sprzedawca *m* (-czyni *f*), zbywający *m* (-ca *f*); ***good*** ~***er*** artykuł dobrze się sprzedający

selves [selvz] *pl. od* ***self***

sem·blance ['sembləns] pozór *m*

se·men ['siːmen] *physiol.* nasienie *n*, sperma *f*

se·mes·ter [sɪ'mestə] *univ.* semestr *m*

sem·i... ['semɪ] pół..., semi...

'**sem·i**|·**cir·cle** półokrąg *m*; ~'**co·lon** średnik *m*; ~·**de'tached** (**house**) (*dom*) bliźniak *m*; ~'**fi·nals** *pl.* (*w sporcie*) półfinały *pl.*

sem·i·nar·y ['semɪnərɪ] seminarium *n*

Sen → ***Snr***

sen|·**ate** ['senɪt] senat *m*; ~·**a·tor** ['senətə] senator *m*

send [send] (***sent***) wysyłać ⟨-słać⟩, posyłać (***to*** do *G*); *pomoc* nadsyłać ⟨-desłać⟩ (***to*** do *G*); *pozdrowienia, towary itp.* przesyłać ⟨-słać⟩ (***to*** do *G*); *list, program itp.* nadawać ⟨-nadać⟩; *z adj. i p.pr.* czynić; ~ ***s.o. mad*** *Brt.* doprowadzać kogoś do szaleństwa; ~ ***word to s.o.*** przesyłać ⟨-łać⟩ komuś wiadomości; ~ ***away*** odsyłać ⟨odesłać⟩; odprawiać ⟨-wić⟩; ~ ***down*** *Brt.* relegować z uczelni; *fig. cenę* obniżać ⟨-żyć⟩; ~ ***for*** posyłać ⟨-słać⟩ po (*A*); wzywać ⟨wezwać⟩ (*G*); zamawiać ⟨-mówić⟩; ~ ***in*** nadsyłać ⟨-desłać⟩; ~ ***off*** odsyłać ⟨odesłać⟩; wysyłać ⟨-słać⟩; (*w sporcie*) usunąć z boiska; ~ ***on*** przesyłać ⟨-słać⟩ (***to*** na *nowy adres*); *bagaże* przesyłać ⟨-słać⟩ wcześniej; ~ ***out*** rozsyłać ⟨-zesłać⟩; wysyłać ⟨-słać⟩; ~ ***up*** *fig. cenę itp.* podwyższać ⟨-szyć⟩; '~·**er** nadawca *m*

se·nile ['siːnaɪl] zniedołężniały (*ze starości*); **se·nil·i·ty** [sɪ'nɪlətɪ] zniedołężnienie *m* (*starcze*)

se·ni·or ['siːnjə] **1.** senior (*po nazwisku*); starszy (***to*** od *G*); starszy rangą; **2.** starszy *m* (-sza *f*); *Am.* student(ka *f*) *m* ostatniego roku; ***he is my ~ by a year*** jest ode mnie starszy o rok; ~ '**cit·i·zens** *pl.* emeryci *pl.*; ~·**i·ty** [siːnɪ'ɒrətɪ] starszeństwo *n*; wysługa *f* lat, staż *m* pracy; ~ '**part·ner** *econ. główny* wspólnik *m*

sen·sa·tion [sen'seɪʃn] odczucie *n*; uczucie *n*; czucie *n*; sensacja *f*; ~·**al** [sen'seɪʃənl] F sensacyjny; rewelacyjny

sense [sens] **1.** sens *m*; znaczenie *n*; rozsądek *m*; zmysł *m*; poczucie *n*, uczucie *n*; ***bring s.o. to his ~s*** przywrócić komuś poczucie rzeczywistości; ***come to one's ~s*** opamiętać się; ***in a ~*** w pewnym stopniu; ***make ~*** mieć sens; ***~ of duty*** poczucie *n* obowiązku; ***~ of security*** poczucie *n* bezpieczeństwa; **2.** odczuwać ⟨-czuć⟩; wyczuwać ⟨-czuć⟩; '~·**less** bezsensowny

sen·si·bil·i·ty [sensɪ'bɪlətɪ] wrażliwość *f*; *też* ***sensibilities*** uczucia *pl.*

sen·si·ble ['sensəbl] rozsądny; praktyczny;

sen·si·tive ['sensɪtɪv] wrażliwy; *aparat:* czuły

sen·sor ['sensə] *tech.* czujnik *m*; sensor *m*

sen·su·al ['sensjʊəl] zmysłowy

sen·su·ous ['sensjʊəs] zmysłowy

sent [sent] *pret. i p.p. od* ***send***

sen·tence ['sentəns] **1.** *gr.* zdanie *n*; *jur.* wyrok *m*; ***pass*** *lub* ***pronounce ~*** ogłaszać ⟨-łosić⟩ wyrok, skazywać ⟨-zać⟩; **2.** *jur.* skazywać ⟨-zać⟩ (***to*** na *A*)

sen·ti|·**ment** ['sentɪmənt] uczucie *n*; nastrój *m*; sentyment *m*; ~·**ment·al** [sentɪ'mentl] sentymentalny; ~·**men·tal·i·ty** [sentɪmen'tælətɪ] sentymentalność *f*, sentymentalizm *m*

sen·try ['sentrɪ] *mil.* wartownik *m*; warta *f*

Seoul Seul *m*

sep·a|·**ra·ble** ['sepərəbl] rozdzielny, rozłączny; ~·**rate** **1.** ['sepəreɪt] rozdzielać ⟨-lić⟩ (się); oddzielać ⟨-lić⟩ (się); ⟨po⟩dzielić (się) (***into*** na *A*); **2.** ['seprət] oddzielny; odrębny; osobny; ~·**ra**-

S

tion [sepə'reɪʃn] oddzielenie *n*; rozłąka *f*; separacja *f*; rozdzielanie *n*
Sept *skrót pisany*: ***September*** wrzes., wrzesień *m*
Sep·tem·ber [sep'tembə] wrzesień *m*
sep·tic ['septɪk] *med.* (***~ally***) septyczny, zakaźny
se·quel ['siːkwəl] ciąg *m* dalszy; następstwo *n*
se·quence ['siːkwəns] kolejność *f*; następstwo *n*; ciąg *m*; sekwencja *f* (*w filmie, TV*); ***~ of tenses*** *gr.* następstwo *n* czasów
Ser·bi·a Serbia *f*
ser·e·nade [serə'neɪd] *mus.* **1.** serenada *f*; **2.** ⟨za⟩grać *lub* ⟨za⟩śpiewać serenadę
se·rene [sɪ'riːn] spokojny; jasny, bezchmurny
ser·geant ['sɑːdʒənt] sierżant *m*
se·ri·al ['sɪərɪəl] **1.** serial *m*; powieść *f* w odcinkach; **2.** seryjny; w odcinkach; *komp.* szeregowy
se·ries ['sɪəriːz] (*pl.* ***-ries***) seria *f*, szereg *m*; seria *f* (*wydawnicza*); ciąg *m*
se·ri·ous ['sɪərɪəs] poważny; ***be ~*** zachowywać się poważnie; '***~·ness*** powaga
ser·mon ['sɜːmən] *rel.* kazanie *n* (*też fig.*)
ser·pen·tine ['sɜːpəntaɪn] powykręcany; *droga*: serpentynowy
se·rum ['sɪərəm] (*pl.* ***-rums, -ra*** [-rə]) serum *n*, surowica *f*
ser·vant ['sɜːvənt] służący *m* (-ca *f*) (*też fig.*); *fig.* sługa *m*; → ***civil servant***
serve [sɜːv] **1.** *v/t. komuś, krajowi, celowi itp.* służyć (*D*); *praktykę itp.* odbywać ⟨-być⟩; ⟨s⟩pełnić obowiązki; pracować dla (*G*); zaopatrywać ⟨-trzyć⟩ (***with*** w *A*); *jedzenie* podawać ⟨-dać⟩; *kogoś* obsługiwać ⟨-łużyć⟩; *jur. karę* odbywać ⟨-być⟩; *jur. wezwanie* doręczać ⟨-czyć⟩ (***on s.o.*** komuś); (*w tenisie*) ⟨za⟩serwować; ***are you being ~d?*** czy jest już Pan obsługiwany?; (***it***) ***~s him right*** F dobrze mu tak; *v/i. zwł. mil.* odbywać ⟨-być⟩ służbę; służyć (***as, for*** jako); ⟨s⟩pełnić funkcję; (*w tenisie*) ⟨za⟩serwować; podawać ⟨-dać⟩; ***XY to ~*** (*w tenisie*) serw XY; ***~ on a committee*** być członkiem komitetu; **2.** (*w tenisie itp.*) serw *m*, serwis *m*; '**serv·er** (*w tenisie itp.*) serwujący *m* (-ca *f*); łyżka *f* (*do nakładania*); *komp.* serwer *m*

ser|·vice ['sɜːvɪs] **1.** służba *f* (***to*** dla *G*) (*też fig.*); służba *f* publiczna; *pocztowe, transportowe itp.* usługi *pl.*; połączenie *n*, *kolejowa itp.* komunikacja *f*; serwis *m*; obsługa *f*; *rel.* nabożeństwo *n*; usługa *f*, przysługa *f*; *jur.* doręczenie *n* (*wezwania*); (*w tenisie itp.*) serw *m*, serwis *m*; ***~vices*** *mil. pl.* siły *pl.* zbrojne; **2.** *tech.* obsługiwać ⟨-łużyć⟩; ***~·vi·cea·ble*** ['sɜːvɪsəbl] zdatny do użytku; przydatny; '***~vice ar·e·a*** *Brt.* usługi *pl.* dla zmotoryzowanych (*przy autostradzie*); '***~vice charge*** dodatek *m* za obsługę; '***~vice sta·tion*** stacja *f* benzynowa; warsztat *m* naprawy samochodów
ser·vi·ette [sɜːvɪ'et] *zwł. Brt.* serwetka *f*
ser·vile ['sɜːvaɪl] służalczy; niewolniczy
serv·ing ['sɜːvɪŋ] porcja *f*
ser·vi·tude ['sɜːvɪtjuːd] służalczość *f*
ses·sion ['seʃn] sesja *f*, zebranie *n*; posiedzenie *n* (*sądu itp.*); ***be in ~*** *jur., parl.* odbywać ⟨-być⟩ sesję
set [set] **1.** (***-tt-***; ***set***) *v/t.* ustawiać ⟨-wić⟩, stawiać ⟨postawić⟩; umieszczać ⟨-mieścić⟩; przykładać ⟨-łożyć⟩; *zegar, urządzenie, kość itp.* nastawiać ⟨-wić⟩; *stół* nakrywać ⟨-ryć⟩; *cenę, termin* ustalać ⟨-lić⟩; *rekord* ustanawiać ⟨-nowić⟩; *klejnot* oprawiać ⟨-wić⟩ (***in*** *w A lub L*), osadzać ⟨-dzić⟩; *galaretę* zestalać ⟨-lić⟩; *włosy* układać ⟨ułożyć⟩; *mus. print.* składać ⟨złożyć⟩; *pytanie, zadanie* zadawać ⟨-dać⟩; *hunt.* wystawiać ⟨-wić⟩; ***~ s.o. at ease*** uspokajać ⟨-koić⟩ kogoś; ***~ an example*** ustanawiać ⟨-nowić⟩ przykład; ***~ s.o. free*** uwalniać ⟨-wolnić⟩ kogoś; ***~ s.th. going*** uruchamiać ⟨-mić⟩ coś; ***~ s.o. thinking*** dawać ⟨dać⟩ komuś do myślenia; ***~ one's hopes on s.th.*** wiązać z czymś nadzieję; ***~ s.o.'s mind at rest*** uspokajać ⟨-koić⟩ kogoś; ***~ s.th. to music*** napisać muzykę do czegoś; ***~ great*** (***little***) ***store by*** przykładać wielką (małą) wagę do czegoś; ***the novel is ~ in*** akcja powieści dzieje się w (*L*); *v/i. słońce*: zachodzić ⟨zajść⟩; *galareta*: ⟨za⟩stygnąć, zestalać ⟨-lić⟩ się; *hunt.* wystawiać ⟨-wić⟩ zwierzynę; ***~ about doing s.th.*** zabrać się do czegoś; ***~ about s.o.*** F rzucać ⟨-cić⟩ się na kogoś; ***~ aside*** odkładać ⟨odłożyć⟩; *jur. wyrok* uchylać ⟨-lić⟩; ***~ back*** opóźniać ⟨-nić⟩ (***by two months*** o dwa miesiące); ***be set back***

S

być cofniętym (***from*** od *G*); ***~ in*** *pogoda*: nastawać ⟨-tać⟩; ***~ off*** wyruszać ⟨-szyć⟩; ⟨z⟩detonować, odpalać ⟨-lić⟩; wywoływać ⟨-łać⟩; uwydatniać ⟨-nić⟩, podkreślać ⟨-lić⟩; ***~ out*** ustawiać ⟨-wić⟩; wyruszać ⟨-szyć⟩; wyjaśniać ⟨-nić⟩; ***~ out to do s.th.*** zabierać ⟨-brać⟩ się do zrobienia czegoś, podejmować ⟨-djąć⟩ się zrobienia czegoś; ***~ up*** wznosić ⟨-nieść⟩; *urządzenie itp.* ⟨z⟩montować; *komitet, firmę itp.* ⟨z⟩organizować; zaopatrywać (***with*** w *A*); *problemy itp.* stwarzać ⟨-worzyć⟩; ***~ o.s. up*** urządzać ⟨-dzić⟩ się (***as*** w charakterze *G*); **2.** *adj.* położony; osadzony; *godziny*: ustalony; *lektura*: obowiązkowy; gotowy; *miód*: zestalony; ***~ lunch*** *Brt.* obiad *m* firmowy; ***~ phrase*** utarty zwrot *m*, fraza *f*; ***be ~ on doing s.th.*** być zdecydowanym coś zrobić; ***be ~ against s.th.*** być nastawionym przeciw czemuś; ***be all ~*** F być gotowym; **3.** zestaw *m* (*narzędzi itp.*); komplet *m* (*narzędzi, mebli itp.*); aparat *m*, *telewizyjny, radiowy* odbiornik *m*; *theat.* scenografia *f*; plan *m* filmowy; (*w tenisie*) set *m*; grupa *f* (*ludzi*); modelowanie *n* (*włosów*); *math.* zbiór *m*; *poet.* zachód *m*; ***have a shampoo and ~*** umyć i ułożyć sobie włosy; **'~·back** porażka *f*, zahamowanie *n*; **'~·square** *Brt.* ekierka *f*

set·tee [se'tiː] sofa *f*

'set the·o·ry *math.* teoria *f* zbiorów

set·ting ['setɪŋ] zachód *m* (*słońca itp.*); *tech.* nastawienie *n*; oprawa *f* (*klejnotu*); usytuowanie *n* (*budynku*), miejsce *n*; **'~ lo·tion** lakier *m* do włosów

set·tle ['setl] *v/i.* osiadać ⟨osiąść⟩ (***on*** na *L*); osiadać, osiedlać ⟨-lić⟩ się (***in*** w *mieście*); usadawiać ⟨-dowić⟩ się; *płyn*: ⟨wy⟩klarować się; uspokajać ⟨-koić⟩ się; zabierać ⟨-brać⟩ się (***to*** do *G*) (*też* ***~down***); układać ⟨ułożyć⟩ się; *v/t. problem* załatwiać ⟨-wić⟩; *sprawy* ⟨u⟩regulować; *spór* rozstrzygać ⟨-gnąć⟩; *rachunek* ⟨u⟩regulować; *kogoś* usadawiać ⟨-dowić⟩; *teren* zasiedlać ⟨-lić⟩; ***~ o.s.*** ⟨u⟩sadowić się (***on*** na *L*); ***that ~s it*** to przesądza sprawę; ***that's ~d then*** wszystko więc jasne; ***~ down*** → *v/i.*; ***~ for*** zadowalać się (*D*); ***~ in*** przywyknąć (do *G*), wrosnąć w (*A*); ***~ on*** ugodzić się co do (*G*); ***~ up*** rozliczać ⟨-czyć⟩ się (***with*** z *I*); **'~d** ustalony (*też pogoda*); *życie* uregulowany; **'~·ment** osiedle *n*; uregulowanie *n*; ustalenie *n*; ułożenie *n* się; rozstrzygnięcie *n*; porozumienie *n*, ugoda *f*; zapłata *f*; rozliczenie *n*; ***reach a ~ment*** dochodzić ⟨dojść⟩ do porozumienia; **'~r** osadnik *m* (-iczka *f*)

sev·en ['sevn] **1.** siedem; **2.** siódemka *f*; **~·teen** [sevn'tiːn] **1.** siedemnaście; **2.** siedemnastka *f*; **~·teenth** [sevn'tiːnθ] **1.** siedemnasty; **2.** siedemnasta część *f*; **~th** ['sevnθ] **1.** siódmy; **2.** siódma część *f*; **'~th·ly** po siódme; **~·ti·eth** ['sevntɪɪθ] siedemdziesiąty; **~·ty** ['sevntɪ] **1.** siedemdziesiąt; **2.** siedemdziesiątka *f*

sev·er ['sevə] przerywać ⟨-rwać⟩; *znajomość itp.* zrywać ⟨zerwać⟩

sev·e·ral ['sevrəl] kilka; kilku; **'~·ly** osobno, pojedynczo

se·vere [sɪ'vɪə] (***-r, -st***) *zima, człowiek*: surowy; *choroba itp.*: poważny; *ból*: silny; *krytyka*: ostry; **se·ver·i·ty** [sɪ'verətɪ] surowość *f*; ostrość *f*; powaga *f*; duża siła *f*

sew [səʊ] (***sewed, sewn*** *lub* ***sewed***) szyć

sew·age ['suːɪdʒ] ścieki *pl.*; **'~ works** *sg.* oczyszczalnia *f* ścieków

sew·er [sʊə] ściek *m*; **~·age** ['sʊərɪdʒ] kanalizacja *f*

sew·ing ['səʊɪŋ] szycie *n*; **'~ ma·chine** maszyna *f* do szycia

sewn [səʊn] *p.p. od* ***sew***

sex [seks] płeć *f*; seksualność *f*; seks *m*; stosunek *m* płciowy

sex|·is·m ['seksɪzəm] seksizm *m*; **'~·ist** **1.** seksistowski; **2.** seksista *m*

sex·ton ['sekstən] zakrystian *m*, kościelny *m*

sex·u·al ['sekʃʊəl] płciowy; seksualny; **~ 'har·ass·ment** prześladowanie *n* na tle seksualnym; **~ 'in·ter·course** stosunek *m* płciowy; **~·i·ty** [sekʃʊ'ælətɪ] płciowość *f*

sex·y ['seksɪ] F sexy, seksowny

SF [es 'ef] *skrót*: ***science fiction*** science fiction *n*

shab·by ['ʃæbɪ] (***-ier, -iest***) niechlujny, zaniedbany

shack [ʃæk] buda *f*, szopa *f*

shack·les ['ʃæklz] *pl.* okowy *pl.* (*też fig.*), kajdany *pl.*

shade [ʃeɪd] **1.** cień *m* (*też fig.*); osłona *f*;

odcień *m* (*koloru, znaczenia*); *Am.* żaluzja *f*, roleta *f*; ***a ~*** *fig.* trochę, nieco; **2.** osłaniać ⟨-łonić⟩ (***from*** przed *I*); ocieniać ⟨-nić⟩; *kolory*: przechodzić ⟨przejść⟩ (***off/into*** w *A*); **~s** *pl.* F okulary *pl.* przeciwsłoneczne

shad·ow ['ʃædəʊ] **1.** cień *m* (*też fig.*); ***there's not a*** *lub* ***the ~ of a doubt*** nie ma nawet cienia wątpliwości; **2.** *kogoś* ocieniać ⟨-nić⟩; '**~·y** (***-ier, -iest***) zacieniony, ciemny; nieokreślony

shad·y ['ʃeɪdɪ] (***-ier, -iest***) zacieniony, ciemny; F ciemny, podejrzany

shaft [ʃɑːft] trzonek *m*; drzewce *n* (*strzały*); wał *m* (*samochodu*); szyb *m* (*kopalni*); promień *m* (*słońca*); dyszel *m*

shag·gy ['ʃægɪ] (***-ier, -iest***) *pies*: kudłaty; *broda*: nastroszony; *płaszcz*: kosmaty

shake [ʃeɪk] **1.** (***shook, shaken***) *v/t.* trząść (*I*), potrząsać ⟨-nąć⟩ (*I*); otrząsać ⟨-snąć⟩; *koktajl* ⟨z⟩robić (*mieszając*); ***~ hands*** ściskać ⟨ścisnąć⟩ *czyjąś* dłoń; *v/i.* trząść się (***with*** z *G*); otrząsać ⟨-snąć⟩ się; ***~ down*** *Brt.* przespać się; *Brt.* przywykać ⟨-knąć⟩; ***~ off*** strząsać ⟨-snąć⟩; *choroby* pozbywać ⟨-być⟩ się; ***~ up*** *poduszki* wzruszać ⟨-szyć⟩; *napój* wymieszać; *fig.* wstrząsać ⟨-snąć⟩; **2.** potrząśniecie *n*, wstrząśniecie *n*; otrząśnięcie *n* (się); *Am.* F koktajl *m* mleczny; '**~·down** F **1.** *Am.* szantaż *m*, wymuszenie *n*; *Am.* rewizja *f*, przeszukanie *n*; *tymczasowe* miejsce *n* noclegu; ostateczny test *m*; **2.** *adj. lot, podróż*: testowy; **shak·en** ['ʃeɪkən] **1.** *p.p.* od ***shake*** 1; **2.** *adj. też* ***~ up*** wstrząśnięty

shak·y ['ʃeɪkɪ] (***-ier, -iest***) trzęsący się; *fig.* słaby

shall *v/aux.* [ʃæl] (*pret.* ***should***) ***I ~ be*** będę; ***we ~ be*** będziemy; ***you ~ do it*** masz to zrobić, powinieneś to zrobić; *w pytaniach*: ***~ we go?*** może byśmy poszli?

shal·low ['ʃæləʊ] płytki (*też fig.*); *fig.* powierzchowny; '**~s** *pl.* mielizna *f*, płycizna *f*

sham [ʃæm] **1.** fikcja *f*; pozór *m*; **2.** fikcyjny, pozorny; fałszywy, udawany; **3.** (***-mm-***) *v/t. współczucie* pozorować; *chorobę* symulować; *v/i.* udawać ⟨-dać⟩, symulować

sham·bles ['ʃæmblz] *sg.* F bałagan *m*, chaos *m*

shame [ʃeɪm] **1.** wstyd *m*; hańba *f*; ***~ !*** hańba!; ***~ on you!*** ale wstyd!; ***put to ~*** *kogoś* zawstydzać ⟨-dzić⟩ **2.** zawstydzać ⟨-dzić⟩; przynosić ⟨-nieść⟩ *komuś* wstyd; przewyższać ⟨-szyć⟩; **~'faced** zawstydzony; '**~·ful** haniebny; '**~·less** bezwstydny

sham·poo [ʃæm'puː] **1.** (*pl.* ***-poos***) szampon; → ***set*** 3; **2.** *włosy* ⟨u⟩myć; *dywan* ⟨wy⟩prać

sham·rock ['ʃæmrɒk] koniczyna *f* drobnogłówkowa

shank [ʃæŋk] *tech.* trzon(ek) *m*; goleń *f*

shan't [ʃɑːnt] = ***shall not***

shan·ty[1] ['ʃæntɪ] buda *f*, szopa *f*

shan·ty[2] ['ʃæntɪ] szanta *f*

shape [ʃeɪp] **1.** kształt *m*; forma *f*; stan *m* (*budynku itp.*); **2.** *v/t.* ⟨u⟩kształtować; ⟨u⟩formować; *v/i.* ***~ up*** dawać ⟨dać⟩ sobie radę; brać ⟨wziąć⟩ się w garść; *zwł. Am.* ⟨u⟩formować się; **~d** uformowany; '**~·less** bezkształtny, bezforemny; '**~·ly** (***-ier, -iest***) kształtny

share [ʃeə] **1.** udział *m* (***in*** w *L*, ***of*** *G*); część *f*; *zwł. Brt. econ.* akcja *f*; ***go ~*** ⟨po⟩dzielić się (*kosztami itp.*); ***have a ~ in*** mieć w (*L*) udział; ***have no ~ in*** nie mieć w (*L*) udziału; **2.** *v/t.* ⟨po⟩dzielić się (***with*** z *I*); dzielić; *też* ***~ out*** rozdzielać ⟨-lić⟩ (***among, between*** (po)między *A*); *v/i.* dzielić się; ***~ in*** brać ⟨wziąć⟩ udział w (*L*); **~·hold·er** *zwł. Brt.* udziałowiec *m*, akcjonariusz *m*

shark [ʃɑːk] (*pl.* ***shark, sharks***) *zo.* rekin *m*; F *finansowy* rekin *m*

sharp [ʃɑːp] **1.** *adj.* ostry (*też fig.*); *umysł*: lotny; *mus.* (*o pół tonu*) podwyższony; ***C ~*** *mus.* Cis *lub* cis ; **2.** *adv.* ostro; nagle; *mus.* za wysoko; punktualnie, dokładnie; ***at eight o'clock ~*** punkt o ósmej; ***look ~*** F ⟨po⟩spieszyć się; ***look ~!*** F tempo!; uwaga!; **~·en** ['ʃɑːpən] ⟨na-, za⟩ostrzyć; *ołówek też* ⟨za⟩temperować; **~·en·er** ['ʃɑːpnə] ostrzałka *f*, przyrząd *m* do ostrzenia; temperówka *f*; '**~·ness** ostrość *f* (*też fig.*); '**~·shoot·er** snajper *m*, strzelec *m* wyborowy; **~-'sight·ed** o ostrym wzroku

shat·ter ['ʃætə] *v/t.* ⟨s⟩trzaskać; rozbijać ⟨-bić⟩; *nadzieje* rozwiewać ⟨-wiać⟩; *v/i.* roztrzaskać się, rozbijać ⟨-bić⟩ się

shave [ʃeɪv] **1.** ⟨o⟩golić (się); zgolić; zeskrobywać ⟨-bać⟩; **2.** ogolenie *n*, ostrzyżenie *n*; ***have a ~*** ⟨o⟩golić się; ***that***

S

was a close ~ niewiele brakowało; **shav·en** ['ʃeɪvn] ogolony; **shav·er** ['ʃeɪvə] *elektryczna* golarka *f*, maszynka *f* do golenia; **shav·ing** ['ʃeɪvɪŋ] **1.** golenie *n*; **~s** *pl.* wióry *pl.*; **2.** do golenia
shawl [ʃɔːl] chusta *m* (*na głowę itp.*)
she [ʃiː] **1.** *pron.* ona; **2.** *zo.* samica *m*; **3.** *adj. w złoż.* ***she-bear*** niedźwiedzica *f*
sheaf [ʃiːf] (*pl.* ***sheaves***) *agr.* snop *m*; plik *m* (*papierów*)
shear [ʃɪə] **1.** (***sheared, sheared*** *lub* ***shorn***) ⟨o⟩strzyc; **2.** (***a pair of***) **~s** *pl.* nożyce *pl.*
sheath [ʃiːθ] (*pl.* ***sheaths*** [ʃiːðz]) pochwa *f* (*na miecz itp.*); *Brt.* prezerwatywa *f*; *tech.* osłona *f*, pokrowiec *m*; **~e** [ʃiːð] ⟨s⟩chować do pochwy; *tech.* osłaniać ⟨-nić⟩
sheaves [ʃiːvz] *pl. od* ***sheaf***
shed[1] [ʃed] szopa *f*
shed[2] [ʃed] (***-dd-***; ***shed***) *łzy* wylewać ⟨-lać⟩; *liście, skórę* zrzucać ⟨-cić⟩; *krew* przelewać ⟨-lać⟩; *fig.* pozbywać ⟨-być⟩ się; ***~ a few pounds*** zrzucać ⟨-cić⟩ kilka funtów
sheen [ʃiːn] połysk *m*
sheep [ʃiːp] *zo.* (*pl.* ***sheep***) owca *f*; **'~·dog** owczarek *m*; **'~ farm·ing** owczarstwo *n*; **'~·fold** okólnik *m*, zagroda *f* dla owiec; **'~·ish** zbaraniały; głupkowaty; **~·skin** kożuch *m*
sheer [ʃɪə] czysty, sam; *brzeg*: pionowy; *materiał*: przejrzysty
sheet [ʃiːt] prześcieradło *n*; arkusz *m* (*papieru, blachy*); kartka *f*; płyta *f* (*szkła*); tafla *f* (*szkła, lodu itp.*); ***the rain was coming down in ~s*** lało strumieniami; **~ light·ning** błyskawica *f* (*rozświetlająca całe niebo*)
shelf [ʃelf] (*pl.* ***shelves***) półka *f* (*też skalna*); ***shelves*** *pl.* regał *m*
shell [ʃel] **1.** skorup(k)a *f* (*jaja, orzecha, ślimaka itp.*); łupina *f*; muszla *f*; *zo.* pancerz *m*; *mil.* pocisk *m* artyleryjski; szkielet *m* (*budynku, też fig.*); **2.** łuskać; obierać ⟨obrać⟩; *mil.* ostrzeliwać ⟨-lać⟩; **'~·fire** ostrzał *m* artyleryjski; **'~·fish** *zo.* (*pl.* ***-fish***) skorupiak *m*
shel·ter ['ʃeltə] **1.** schronienie *n*; *mil.* schron *m*, bunkier *m*; (*na przystanku*) wiata *f*; osłona *f*; ***run for ~*** ⟨po⟩szukać schronienia; ***take ~*** ⟨s⟩chronić się (***under*** pod *I*); **2.** *v/t.* osłaniać ⟨-łonić⟩ (***from*** przed *I*); *v/i.* ⟨s⟩chronić się
shelve [ʃelv] *v/t. książki* ustawiać ⟨-wić⟩; *fig. plan* odkładać ⟨odłożyć⟩ na półkę, zaniechać; *v/i.* opadać ⟨opaść⟩
shelves [ʃelvz] *pl. od* ***shelf***
she·nan·i·gans [ʃɪ'nænɪgənz] F *pl.* nonsens *m*; manipulacje *pl.*
shep·herd ['ʃepəd] **1.** pasterz *m*; **2.** ⟨po⟩prowadzić
sher·iff ['ʃerɪf] *Am.* szeryf *m*
Shet·land Is·lands *pl.* Szetlandy *pl.*
shield [ʃiːld] **1.** tarcza *f*; osłona *f*; *tech.* ekran *m*; **2.** osłaniać ⟨-łonić⟩ (***from*** przed *I*); ekranować
shift [ʃɪft] **1.** *v/t. coś* przesuwać ⟨-sunąć⟩, przemieszczać ⟨-mieścić⟩; *winę itp.* przerzucać ⟨-cić⟩ (***on***(***to***) na *A*); *koszt itp.* przenosić ⟨-nieść⟩; *plamy* usuwać ⟨usunąć⟩; ***~ gear***(***s***) *zwł. Am. mot.* zmieniać ⟨-nić⟩ bieg(i); *v/i.* przesuwać ⟨-sunąć⟩ się; *wiatr*: zmieniać ⟨-nić⟩ się; *Am.* zmieniać ⟨-nić⟩ bieg(i) ((***in***)***to*** na *A*); ***~ from one foot to another*** przestępować z nogi na nogę; ***~ on one's chair*** kręcić się na krześle; **2.** *fig.* przesunięcie *n*, zmiana *f*; *econ.* zmiana *f* (*pracowników, czasu*); **'~ key** klawisz *m* "shift" (*zmieniający małe litery na duże*); **'~ work·er** pracownik *m* (-nica *f*) zmianowy (-wa); **'~·y** (***-ier, -iest***) F *oczy*: rozbiegany; kombinatorski
shil·ling ['ʃɪlɪŋ] *Brt. hist.* szyling *m*
shim·mer ['ʃɪmə] ⟨za⟩migotać; *powietrze*: drgać
shin [ʃɪn] **1.** *też* ***~bone*** *anat.* goleń *f*; **2.** (***-nn-***): ***~ up*** wspinać ⟨-piąć⟩ się na (*A*) (*drzewo*)
shine [ʃaɪn] **1.** *v/i.* (***shone***) błyszczeć ⟨błysnąć⟩; świecić (się); *v/t.* (***shined***) *buty* ⟨wy⟩polerować, ⟨wy⟩glansować; **2.** połysk *m*
shin·gle[1] ['ʃɪŋgl] otoczak *m*, kamień *m*
shin·gle[2] ['ʃɪŋgl] gont *m* (*na dachu*)
shin·gles ['ʃɪŋglz] *med. sg.* półpasiec *m*
shin·y ['ʃaɪnɪ] (***-ier, -iest***) błyszczący, wyglansowany
ship [ʃɪp] **1.** statek *m*, okręt *m*; **2.** (***-pp-***) przewozić ⟨-wieźć⟩ drogą morską; przesyłać ⟨-słać⟩; ⟨prze⟩transportować; **'~·board**: ***on ~board*** na pokładzie; **'~·ment** przesyłka *f*; **'~·own·er** właściciel(ka *f*) statku; **'~·ping** *handlowa* żegluga *f*; flota *f* (*danego kraju*); przesyłka *f*, ekspedycja *f*; **'~·wreck** rozbicie *n* statku; wrak *m* statku; **'~·wrecked 1.**

be ~wrecked przejść rozbicie statku; **2.** ocalały z katastrofy morskiej; **'~·yard** stocznia *f*

shire ['ʃaɪə, ʃə] *w złoż., przest.* hrabstwo *n*

shirk [ʃɜːk] uchylać ⟨-lić⟩ się przed (*I*); **'~·er** dekownik *m*, lawirant *m*

shirt [ʃɜːt] koszula *f*; **'~·sleeve 1.** rękaw *m* (*koszuli*); ***in (one's) ~s*** w samej koszuli; **2.** w (*samej*) koszuli

shit [ʃɪt] V **1.** gówno *n* (*też fig.*); **2.** (***-tt-***; ***shit*** *lub* ***shat***) srać

shiv·er ['ʃɪvə] **1.** ⟨za⟩drżeć (***with*** z *G*); **2.** drżenie *n*; ***~s*** *pl.* F dreszcze *pl.*

shoal[1] [ʃəʊl] mielizna *f*, płycizna *f*

shoal[2] [ʃəʊl] ławica *f*

shock[1] [ʃɒk] **1.** szok *m*; wstrząs *m*; uderzenie *n*; porażenie *n* (*prądem*); **2.** wstrząsać ⟨-snąć⟩; ⟨za⟩szokować; porażać ⟨-razić⟩ (*prądem*)

shock[2] [ʃɒk] (***~ of hair***) czupryna *f*, szopa *f* (*włosów*)

'shock| ab·sorb·er *tech.* amortyzator *m*; **'~·ing** szokujący

shod [ʃɒd] *pret. i p.p. od* ***shoe*** 2

shod·dy ['ʃɒdɪ] (***-ier, -iest***) niskiej jakości; podły

shoe [ʃuː] **1.** but *m*; podkowa *f*; **2.** (***shod***) *konia* podkuwać ⟨-kuć⟩; **'~·horn** łyżka *f* do butów; **'~·lace** sznurowadło *n*; **'~·mak·er** szewc *m*; **'~·shine** czyszczenie *n* butów; **'~·shine boy** czyścibut *m*; **'~·string** sznurowadło *n*

shone [ʃɒn, *Am.* ʃəʊn] *pret. i p.p. od* ***shine*** 1

shook [ʃʊk] *pret. od* ***shake*** 1

shoot [ʃuːt] **1.** (***shot***) *v/t.* zastrzelić; zabijać ⟨-bić⟩ (*strzelając*); rozstrzelać; postrzelić; wystrzelić; strzelać ⟨-lić⟩ z (*G*); *hunt.* polować na (*A*); *kogoś* ⟨s⟩fotografować; *film* ⟨na⟩kręcić; *pytanie, spojrzenie* miotać; *narkotyk* wstrzykiwać ⟨-knąć⟩; ***~ the lights*** przejechać na czerwonym świetle; *v/i.* strzelać ⟨-lić⟩ (***at*** do *G*); polować; przemykać ⟨-mknąć⟩; filmować; fotografować; *bot.* ⟨za-, wy⟩kiełkować; wyrastać ⟨-rosnąć⟩; **2.** *bot.* kiełek *m*; pęd *m*; polowanie *n*; teren *m* myśliwski; **'~·er** *zwł. Brt. sl.* (*broń*) gnat *m*

'shoot·ing 1. strzelanie *n*, strzelanina *f*; postrzelenie *n*; zastrzelenie *n*; polowanie *n*; kręcenie *n* (*filmu, programu*), filmowanie *n*; **2.** *ból* rwący; **'~ gal·le·ry** (*pomieszczenie*) strzelnica *f*; **'~ range** (*teren*) strzelnica *f*; **~ 'star** spadająca gwiazda *f*

shop [ʃɒp] **1.** sklep *m*; zakład *m*; warsztat *m*; ***talk ~*** rozmawiać na tematy zawodowe; **2.** (***-pp-***): *zw.* ***go ~ping*** chodzić ⟨iść⟩ na zakupy; **'~ as·sis·tant** ekspedient(ka *f*) *m*; **'~·keep·er** sklepikarz *m* (-rka *f*); **'~·lift·er** *sklepowy* (*-a*) złodziej(ka *f*) *m*; **'~·lift·ing** kradzież *f* w sklepie; **'~·per** klient(ka *f*) *m*, kupujący *m* (-ca *f*)

shop·ping ['ʃɒpɪŋ] **1.** kupowanie *n*; zakupy *pl.*; ***do one's ~*** robić zakupy; **2.** handlowy; na zakupy; **'~ bag** torba *f* na zakupy; **'~ cart** (*w sklepie*) wózek *m*; **'~ cen·tre** *Brt.*, (*Am.* ***center***) centrum *f* handlowe; **'~ list** lista *f* zakupów; **'~ mall** *Am.* centrum *f* handlowe; **'~ street** ulica *f* handlowa

shop| 'stew·ard mąż *m* zaufania; **'~·walk·er** *Brt.* osoba *f* oglądająca towary; **'~ win·dow** witryna *f*, wystawa *f*, okno *n* wystawowe

shore[1] [ʃɔː] brzeg *m*; wybrzeże *n*; ***on ~*** na lądzie; *attr.* brzegowy, przybrzeżny

shore[2] [ʃɔː]: ***~ up*** podeprzeć ⟨-dpierać⟩

shorn [ʃɔːn] *p.p. od* ***shear*** 1

short [ʃɔːt] **1.** *adj.* krótki; *ktoś*: niski; skrócony; opryskliwy (***with*** wobec *G*); *ciasto*: kruchy; ***be ~ for*** być skrótem (*G*); ***be ~ of ...*** nie mieć wystarczająco ...; **2.** *adv.* nagle; ***~ of*** z wyjątkiem (*G*); ***cut ~*** przerywać ⟨-rwać⟩ nagle; ***fall ~ of*** nie osiągać ⟨-gnąć⟩ (*G*); ***stop ~*** przerywać ⟨-rwać⟩ nagle; ***stop ~ of*** powstrzymywać się przed (*I*); → ***run*** 1; **3.** F krótkometrażówka *f*; *electr.* spięcie *n*; ***for ~*** w skrócie; ***in ~*** w skrócie; **~·age** ['ʃɔːtɪdʒ] niedostatek *m*, niedobór *m*, brak *m*; **'~·com·ings** *pl.* niedostatki *pl.*, braki *pl.*; **'~ cut** skrót *m*; ***take a ~ cut*** iść ⟨pójść⟩ na skróty; **~·en** ['ʃɔːtn] *v/t.* skracać ⟨skrócić⟩; *v/i.* ⟨s⟩kurczyć się

short·en·ing ['ʃɔːtnɪŋ] tłuszcz *m* do pieczenia

'short|·hand stenografia *f*; **~·hand 'typ·ist** stenografista *m* (-tka *f*); **'~·ly** niebawem, wkrótce; opryskliwie; lakonicznie; **~s** *pl. też* ***a pair of ~s*** szorty *pl.*; *zwł. Am. krótkie* kalesony; **~'sight·ed** krótkowzroczny; **~ 'sto·ry** opowiadanie *n*, nowela *f*; **~-'term** *econ.* krótkoterminowy; **~ 'time** *econ.* niepeł-

S

ny wymiar *m* (*pracy*); ~ **'wave** *zw.* fale *pl.* krótkie; ~**-'wind·ed** łatwo tracący oddech

shot [ʃɒt] **1.** *pret. i p.p. od* ***shoot*** 1; **2.** strzał *m*, wystrzał *m*; śrut *m*; śrucina *f*; kula *f*; strzelec *m*; (*w tenisie, golfie*) uderzenie *n*; (*w fotografii, filmie, TV*) F zdjęcie *n*, ujęcie *n*; *med.* F zastrzyk *m*; *fig.* F próba *f*; ~ ***in the dark*** strzał *m* na oślep; ***I'll have a ~ at it*** spróbuję jednak; ***not by a long ~*** *zwł. Am.* F wcale nie; → ***big shot***; **'~·gun** strzelba *f*; **~·gun 'wed·ding** F przyspieszone małżeństwo *n*; **'~ put** *sport*: pchnięcie *n* kulą; **'~ put·ter** *sport*: miotacz *m* kulą

should [ʃʊd] *pret. od* ***shall***

shoul·der ['ʃəʊldə] **1.** ramię *n* (*też fig.*), bark *m*; *Am. mot.* pobocze *n* utwardzone; **2.** brać ⟨wziąć⟩ na ramię; *koszty itp.* brać ⟨wziąć⟩ na *swoje* barki; **'~ bag** torba *f* na ramię; **'~ blade** *anat.* łopatka *f*; **'~ strap** ramiączko *n*; pasek *m* (*torby*)

shout [ʃaʊt] **1.** *v/i.* krzyczeć (***to*** do *G*, ***at*** na *A*); wołać (***for*** o *A*); **2.** *v/t.* krzyczeć, wykrzykiwać ⟨-rzyczeć⟩; **2.** krzyk *m*; wołanie *n*

shove [ʃʌv] **1.** pchać ⟨pchnąć⟩; *coś* wpychać ⟨wepchnąć⟩; **2.** pchnięcie *n*, popchnięcie *n*; wepchnięcie *n*

shov·el ['ʃʌvl] **1.** łopata *f*, szufla *f*; **2.** (*zwł. Brt.* **-ll-**, *Am.* **-l-**) zgarniać ⟨-nąć⟩; ⟨s⟩kopać

show [ʃəʊ] **1.** (***showed, shown*** *lub* ***showed***) *v/t.* pokazywać ⟨-zać⟩; ukazywać ⟨-zać⟩; okazywać ⟨-zać⟩; (*w galerii*) wystawiać ⟨-wić⟩; ⟨za⟩prowadzić (***to*** do *G*); *v/i.* być widocznym; ***be ~ing***: iść, być wyświetlanym; ~ ***around*** oprowadzać ⟨-dzić⟩; ~ ***in*** wprowadzać ⟨-dzić⟩; ~ ***off*** popisywać ⟨-sać⟩ się (*I*); ⟨po⟩chwalić się (*I*); ~ ***out*** wyprowadzać ⟨-dzić⟩; ~ ***round*** oprowadzać ⟨-dzić⟩; ~ ***up*** *v/t.* wykazywać ⟨-zać⟩; odsłaniać ⟨-łonić⟩; kłopotać, przynosić ⟨-nieść⟩ *komuś* wstyd; **2.** być widocznym; F zjawiać ⟨-wić⟩ się; **2.** *theat.* przedstawienie *n*, spektakl *m*; show *m*; seans *m*; pokaz *m*; wystawa *f*; pozór *m*, pretekst *m*; ***be on ~*** być pokazywanym; ***steal the ~*** przyćmić wszystkich; ***make a ~ of*** ⟨za⟩demonstrować (*A*); ***put up a poor ~*** F nie popisać się; ***be in charge of the ~*** F kierować interesem; **3.** wzorcowy; ~ ***flat*** mieszkanie *n* wzorcowe; **'~·biz** F, **'~ busi·ness** show-biznes *m*; **'~·case** witryna *f*, okno *n* wystawowe; **'~·down** ostateczna rozgrywka *f*

show·er ['ʃaʊə] **1.** przelotny opad *m*; *fig.* grad *m*, deszcz *m*; prysznic *m*, natrysk *m*; ***have*** *lub* ***take a ~*** brać ⟨wziąć⟩ prysznic; **2.** *v/t. kogoś* zasypywać ⟨-pać⟩ (*I*); opryskiwać ⟨-kać⟩ (*I*); *v/i.* brać ⟨wziąć⟩ prysznic; padać; ~ ***down*** opadać ⟨opaść⟩

'show| jump·er (*w sporcie*) jeździec *m*; **'~ jump·ing** (*w sporcie*) konkurs *m* hippiczny; **~n** [ʃəʊn] *p.p. od* ***show*** 1; **'~-off** F pokaz *m*; popis *m*; **~·room** salon *f* wystawowy; **'~·y** (**-*ier*, -*iest***) krzykliwy, wyzywający

shrank [ʃræŋk] *pret. od* ***shrink*** 1

shred [ʃred] **1.** strzęp *m*; *fig.* odrobina *f*; **2.** (**-*dd*-**) ⟨po⟩drzeć (*na strzępy*); *gastr.* ⟨po⟩szatkować; *dokumenty* ⟨z⟩niszczyć; **'~·der** niszczarka *f*, szatkownica *f*

shrew [ʃruː] *zo.* ryjówka *f*; sekutnica *f*, jędza *f*

shrewd [ʃruːd] chytry, sprytny

shriek [ʃriːk] **1.** wykrzykiwać ⟨-knąć⟩, zakrzyczeć ⟨-knąć⟩; ~ ***with laughter*** ⟨za⟩rechotać ze śmiechu; **2.** *przenikliwy* krzyk *m*

shrill [ʃrɪl] ostry (*też fig.*)

shrimp [ʃrɪmp] *zo.* krewetka *f*; F karzełek *m*

shrine [ʃraɪn] sanktuarium *n*, przybytek *m* święty

shrink [ʃrɪŋk] **1.** (***shrank, shrunk***) ⟨s⟩kurczyć się; *tkanina itp.*: zbiegać ⟨zbiec⟩ się; zmniejszać ⟨-szyć⟩ się; **2.** F (*psychiatra*) lekarz *m* od czubków; **~·age** ['ʃrɪŋkɪdʒ] (s)kurczenie *n* się, zbiegnięcie *n* się, zmniejszenie *n* się; ubytek *m*; **'~-wrap** (**-*pp*-**) pakować w folię

shriv·el ['ʃrɪvl] (*zwł. Brt.* **-ll-** , *Am.* **-l-**) wysuszać ⟨-suszyć⟩; zsychać ⟨zeschnąć⟩ (się)

shroud [ʃraʊd] **1.** całun *m*; **2.** *fig.* okrywać ⟨-ryć⟩

Shrove Tues·day [ʃrəʊv 'tjuːzdɪ] ostatki *pl.*

shrub [ʃrʌb] krzew *m*; **~·be·ry** ['ʃrʌbərɪ] krzewy *pl.*

shrug [ʃrʌg] **1.** (**-*gg*-**) *też* ~ ***one's shoulders*** wzruszać ⟨-szyć⟩ ramionami; **2.** wzruszenie *n* (*ramion*)

S

shrunk [ʃrʌŋk] *p.p. od* ***shrink*** 1
shuck *zwł. Am.* [ʃʌk] **1.** łuska *f*, łupina *f*; **2.** łuskać, obierać ⟨-brać⟩
shud·der ['ʃʌdə] **1.** wzdrygać ⟨-gnąć⟩ się, ⟨za⟩drżeć; **2.** wzdrygnięcie *n*, dreszcz *m*
shuf·fle ['ʃʌfl] **1.** *v/t. karty* ⟨po⟩tasować; *papiery* przekładać ⟨-łożyć⟩; ~ ***one's feet*** powłóczyć nogami; *v/i.* przekładać ⟨-ełożyć⟩; **2.** tasowanie *n* (*kart*)
shun [ʃʌn] (***-nn-***) odrzucać ⟨-cić⟩, unikać ⟨-knąć⟩
shunt [ʃʌnt] *pociąg itp.* przetaczać ⟨-toczyć⟩, manewrować; *też* ~ ***off*** F *kogoś* odstawiać ⟨-wić⟩ na bok
shut [ʃʌt] (***-tt-***; ***shut***) zamykać ⟨-mknąć⟩; ~ ***down*** zamykać ⟨-mknąć⟩ *fabrykę itp.*; ~ ***off*** *wodę, gaz itp.* odcinać ⟨-ciąć⟩; *maszynę* wyłączać ⟨-czyć⟩; ~ ***up*** zamykać ⟨-mknąć⟩ się; zamykać ⟨-mknąć⟩ (*w pokoju, itp., zakład*); ~ ***up!*** zamknij się!; '~**·ter** okiennica *f*; *phot.* migawka *f*; '~**·ter speed** *phot.* czas *m* naświetlania
shut·tle ['ʃʌtl] **1.** samolot *m*, autobus *m itp.*, wahadłowy; prom *m* kosmiczny, wahadłowiec *m*; *tech.* czółenko *n*; **2.** kursować tam i z powrotem; '~**·cock** (*w sporcie*) lotka *f*; '~ **di·plo·ma·cy** *pol.* dyplomacja *f* wahadłowa; '~ **service** połączenie *n* wahadłowe
shy [ʃaɪ] **1.** nieśmiały; lękliwy, płochliwy; **2.** ⟨s⟩płoszyć się (*zwł. koń*); ~ ***away from*** *fig.* wycofywać ⟨-fać⟩ się; '~**·ness** nieśmałość *f*, płochliwość *f*
Si·be·ri·a Syberia *f*
Sic·i·ly Sycylia *f*
sick [sɪk] **1.** chory; ***be*** ~ *zwł. Brt.* ⟨z⟩wymiotować; ***she was*** *lub* ***felt*** ~ ⟨po⟩czuła się źle; ***fall*** ~ zachorować; ***be off*** ~ być na zwolnieniu, F być na chorobowym; ***report*** ~ zgłaszać, że się jest chorym; ***be*** ~ ***of s.th.*** F mieć czegoś serdecznie dość; ***it makes me*** ~ F niedobrze mi się od tego robi; **2.** ***the*** ~ *pl.* chorzy *pl.*; ~**·en** *v/t.* napełniać ⟨-nić⟩ obrzydzeniem, przyprawiać ⟨-wić⟩ kogoś o mdłości; *v/i.* ⟨za⟩chorować
sick·le ['sɪkl] sierp *m*
'**sick**| **leave**: ***be on*** ~ ***leave*** być na zwolnieniu, F być na chorobowym; '~**·ly** (***-ier, -iest***) chorobliwy; chorowity; *zapach*: mdlący; '~**·ness** choroba *f*; mdłości *pl.*; '~**·ness ben·e·fit** *Brt.* zasiłek *m* chorobowy
side [saɪd] **1.** strona *f*; bok *m*; *zwł. Brt.* zespół *m*; stok *m*; ~ ***by*** ~ obok siebie; ***take*** ~***s with s.o.*** stawać ⟨stanąć⟩ po czyjejś stronie; **2.** boczny; *efekt*: uboczny; **3.** ~ ***with s.o.*** stawać ⟨stanąć⟩ po czyjejś stronie; '~**·board** (*kredens*) pomocnik *m*; '~**·car** *mot. boczny* wózek *m* (*motocykla*); '~ **dish** *gastr.* przystawka *f*; '~**·long** z boku, boczny; '~ **street** ulica *f* boczna; '~**·stroke** (*w sporcie*) pływanie *n* na boku; '~**·track** zbaczać ⟨zboczyć⟩ z tematu; *Am. pociąg* przetaczać ⟨-toczyć⟩, manewrować; '~**·walk** *zwł. Am.* chodnik *m*; '~**·ways** z boku; bokiem; na bok
sid·ing ['saɪdɪŋ] *rail.* bocznica *f*
si·dle ['saɪdl]: ~ ***up to s.o.*** przysuwać ⟨-unąć⟩ się do kogoś
siege [siːdʒ] oblężenie *n*; ***lay*** ~ ***to*** oblegać ⟨-ec⟩ (*A*)
sieve [sɪv] **1.** sito *n*; **2.** ⟨prze⟩siewać ⟨-siać⟩
sift [sɪft] ⟨prze⟩siewać ⟨-siać⟩; *też* ~ ***through*** *fig.* ⟨prze⟩studiować, przeszukiwać ⟨-kać⟩
sigh [saɪ] **1.** wzdychać ⟨westchnąć⟩; **2.** westchnięcie *n*
sight [saɪt] **1.** wzrok *m*; widok *m*; ~***s*** *pl.* przyrząd *m* celowniczy; wizjer *m*; osobliwość *f*, *turystyczna* atrakcja *f*; ***at*** ~, ***on*** ~ natychmiast; ***at*** ~ *econ.* za okazaniem; ***at the*** ~ ***of*** na widok (*G*); ***at first*** ~ na pierwszy rzut oka; ***catch*** ~ ***of*** ujrzeć (*A*); ***know by*** ~ znać *kogoś* z widzenia; ***lose*** ~ ***of*** ⟨s⟩tracić *kogoś* z oczu; ***be*** (***with***)***in*** ~ być w zasięgu wzroku (*też fig.*); **2.** dojrzeć, spostrzegać ⟨-rzec⟩; '~**·ed** widzący; '~**-read** *mus.* czytać a (prima) vista (*nuty*); ~**·see·ing** zwiedzanie *n*; ***go*** ~***seeing*** iść ⟨pójść⟩ na zwiedzanie; '~**·see·ing tour** wycieczka *f* (*na zwiedzanie*); '~**·se·er** turysta *m* (-tka *f*)
sign [saɪn] **1.** znak *m*; gest *m*; napis *m*, wywieszka *f*; *fig.* oznaka *f*, objaw *m*; **2.** podpisywać ⟨-sać⟩; ~ ***in*** wpisywać ⟨-sać⟩ się; ~ ***out*** wypisywać ⟨-sać⟩ się
sig·nal ['sɪgnl] **1.** sygnał *m* (*też fig.*); sygnalizator *m*; znak *m* (*też fig.*); **2.** (*zwł. Brt.* ***-ll-***, *Am.* ***-l-***) ⟨za⟩sygnalizować; dawać ⟨dać⟩ sygnał(y) (*D*)
sig·na·to·ry ['sɪgnətərɪ] sygnatariusz *m*

S

sig·na·ture ['sɪgnətʃə] podpis *m*; '~ **tune** *radio, TV*: sygnał (*muzyczny*) *m* audycji (*radiowej lub telewizyjnej*)
'sign|·board szyld *m*; '~**·er** niżej podpisany *m* (-na *f*)
sig·net ring ['sɪgnɪt] sygnet *m*
sig·nif·i|·cance [sɪg'nɪfɪkəns] znaczenie *n*; doniosłość *f*; ~**·cant** znaczący, ważny, doniosły
sig·ni·fy ['sɪgnɪfaɪ] oznaczać, znaczyć
'sign·post drogowskaz *m*
si·lence ['saɪləns] **1.** cisza *f*; spokój *m*; ~**!** spokój!; ***in*** ~ w milczeniu; ***reduce to*** ~ *kogoś* uciszać **2.** uciszać ⟨-szyć⟩; **'si·lenc·er** *tech.* tłumik *m*
si·lent ['saɪlənt] cichy; milczący; bezgłośny; *film*: niemy; ~ **'part·ner** cichy (-a) wspólnik *m* (-iczka *f*)
Si·le·sia Śląsk *m*
sil·i|·con ['sɪlɪkən] *chem.* krzem *m*; *attr.* krzemowy; ~**·cone** ['sɪlɪkəʊn] *chem.* silikon *m*; *attr.* silikonowy
silk [sɪlk] jedwab *m*; *attr.* jedwabny; '~**·worm** *zo.* jedwabnik *m*; '~**·y** (***-ier, -iest***) jedwabny; jedwabisty
sill [sɪl] parapet *m* (*okienny*)
sil·ly ['sɪlɪ] (***-ier, -iest***) głupi; **2.** głuptas *m*
sil·ver ['sɪlvə] **1.** *chem.* srebro; **2.** srebrny; **3.** ⟨po⟩srebrzyć; ~**-'plat·ed** posrebrzany; '~**·ware** naczynia *pl.* ze srebra; ~**·y** ['sɪlvərɪ] *fig.* srebrzysty
sim·i·lar ['sɪmɪlə] podobny (***to*** do *G*); ~**·i·ty** [sɪmɪ'lærətɪ] podobieństwo *n*
sim·i·le ['sɪmɪlɪ] porównanie *n*
sim·mer ['sɪmə] ⟨u⟩gotować (się) na wolnym ogniu; ~ ***with*** *fig.* kipieć z (*złości itp.*); ~ ***down*** F ochłonąć
sim·per ['sɪmpə] uśmiechać ⟨-chnąć⟩ się głupawo
sim·ple ['sɪmpl] (***-r, -st***) prosty, nieskomplikowany; naiwny; ~**-'mind·ed** naiwny
sim·pli|·ci·ty [sɪm'plɪsətɪ] prostota *f*; naiwność *f*; ~**·fi·ca·tion** [sɪmplɪfɪ'keɪʃn] uproszczenie *n*; ~**·fy** ['sɪmplɪfaɪ] upraszczać ⟨-rościć⟩
sim·ply ['sɪmplɪ] po prostu; prosto
sim·u·late ['sɪmjʊleɪt] naśladować; *mil., tech.* przeprowadzać ⟨-dzić⟩ symulację
sim·ul·ta·ne·ous [sɪməl'teɪnjəs] równoczesny, jednoczesny
sin [sɪn] **1.** grzech *m*; **2.** (***-nn-***) ⟨z⟩grzeszyć
since [sɪns] **1.** *adv.* też ***ever*** ~ od tego czasu; **2.** *prp.* od (*G*); **3.** *cj.* ponieważ; odkąd
sin·cere [sɪn'sɪə] szczery; ***Yours*** ~***ly***, ♀ ***yours*** Z poważaniem (*w zakończeniu listu*); **sin·cer·i·ty** [sɪn'serətɪ] szczerość *f*
sin·ew ['sɪnjuː] *anat.* ścięgno *n*; '~**·y** *mięso*: żylasty; *fig.* muskularny
'sin·ful grzeszny
sing [sɪŋ] (***sang, sung***) ⟨za⟩śpiewać; ~ ***s.th. to s.o.*** zaśpiewać coś komuś
singe [sɪndʒ] przypalać ⟨-lić⟩ (się)
sing|·er ['sɪŋə] śpiewak *m* (-aczka *f*); pieśniarz *m* (-arka *f*); ~**·ing** ['sɪŋɪŋ] śpiewanie *n*
sin·gle ['sɪŋgl] **1.** pojedynczy; jeden; ***in*** ~ ***file*** gęsiego; **2.** *Brt.* bilet *m* w jedną stronę (*też* ~ ***ticket***); (*płyta*) singel *m*; osoba *f* stanu wolnego; **3.** ~ ***out*** wyróżniać ⟨-nić⟩, wybierać ⟨-brać⟩; ~**-'breast·ed** *marynarka*: jednorzędowy; ~**-'en·gined** *aviat.* jednosilnikowy; ~ **entry** *econ.* pojedynczy zapis *m*; ~ **fam·i·ly 'home** dom *m* jednorodzinny; ~ **'fa·ther** samotny ojciec *m*; ~**-'hand·ed** samotnie, samodzielnie; ~**-'lane** *mot.* jednopasmowy; ~**-'mind·ed** silnie zdeterminowany; ~ **'moth·er** samotna matka *f*; ~ **'pa·rent** samotny rodzic *m*; ~ **'room** pojedynczy pokój *m*; '~**s** *sg.* (*zwł. w tenisie*) gra *f* pojedyncza, gra *f* singlowa
sin·glet ['sɪŋglɪt] *Brt.* podkoszulek *m*
'sin·gle-track jednotorowy, jednopasmowy
sin·gu·lar ['sɪŋgjʊlə] **1.** wyjątkowy, jedyny; **2.** *gr.* liczba *f* pojedyncza
sin·is·ter ['sɪnɪstə] złowieszczy; złowrogi
sink [sɪŋk] **1.** (***sank, sunk***) *v/i.* ⟨za-, u⟩tonąć; opadać ⟨-paść⟩; *wartość*: spadać ⟨spaść⟩; pogrążać ⟨-żyć⟩ się; ~ ***in*** docierać ⟨dotrzeć⟩ do (*G*); *v/t.* ⟨za⟩topić; *studnię* ⟨wy⟩wiercić, ⟨wy⟩kopać; obniżać ⟨-żyć⟩; *pieniądze* ⟨w⟩pakować; *zęby* zatapiać ⟨-topić⟩ (***into*** w *A*); **2.** zlew *m*, zlewozmywak *m*; *Am.* umywalka *f*
sin·ner ['sɪnə] grzesznik *m* (-ica *f*)
Sioux [suː] (*pl.* ***Sioux*** [suːz]) Siuks *m*
sip [sɪp] **1.** łyk *m*; **2.** (***-pp-***) *napój itp.* sączyć, popijać
sir [sɜː] pan (*przy zwracaniu się*); (*w li-*

S

ście) ***Dear*** ~ Szanowny Panie; ~ *Brt.* (*tytuł szlachecki)* sir *m*
sire ['saɪə] ojciec
si·ren ['saɪərən] syrena *f*
sir·loin ['sɜːlɔɪn] *gastr.*: ~ **'steak** pieczeń *f* z polędwicy
sis·sy ['sɪsɪ] F baba *f*, maminsynek *m*
sis·ter ['sɪstə] siostra *f* (*też rel.*); *Brt. med.* siostra *f*, pielęgniarka *f*; ~**-in--law** ['sɪstərɪnlɔː] (*pl.* ***sisters-in-law***) szwagierka *f*; '~**·ly** siostrzany
sit [sɪt] (**-*tt*-**; sat) *v/i.* siedzieć ⟨siąść⟩; siadać ⟨usiąść⟩; *komisja itp.*: obradować; *książka, wioska, garnitur itp.*: leżeć; *v/t. kogoś* sadzać ⟨posadzić⟩; *zwł. Brt. egzamin* zdawać; ~ ***down*** siadać ⟨usiąść⟩; ~ ***for*** *Brt.* pozować do (*G*); *egzamin* zdawać; ~ ***in for*** zastępować ⟨-tąpić⟩; ~ ***in on*** uczestniczyć w (*L*); ~ ***on*** *w komisji* zasiadać⟨-siąść⟩; ~ ***out*** *taniec* przesiedzieć; dotrwać do końca; *kryzys* przeczekiwać ⟨-kać⟩; ~ ***up*** *prosto* siadać ⟨siąść⟩; (*w łóżku itp.*) sadzać ⟨posadzić⟩; nie kłaść się spać
sit·com ['sɪtkɒm] → ***situation comedy***
'sit-down *też* ~ ***strike*** strajk *m* okupacyjny; ~ ***demonstration*** blokada *f* (*przez siedzących ludzi*)
site [saɪt] miejsce *n*; teren *m* (*wykopalisk itp.*); plac *m* budowy
'sit-in strajk *m* okupacyjny
sit·ting ['sɪtɪŋ] sesja *f*; tura *f* (*przy stole*); ***in a single*** ~ nie wstając; '~ **room** *zwł. Brt.* pokój *m* dzienny
sit·u·at·ed ['sɪtjʊeɪtɪd]: ***be*** ~ być położonym
sit·u·a·tion [sɪtjʊ'eɪʃn] sytuacja *f*; położenie *n*; posada *f*, praca *f*; ~ **'come·dy** komedia *f* sytuacyjna, sitcom *m* (*seria odcinków komediowych o tych samych postaciach*)
six [sɪks] **1.** sześć; **2.** szóstka *f*; ~**·teen** [sɪks'tiːn] **1.** szesnaście; **2.** szesnastka *f*; ~**·teenth** [sɪks'tiːnθ] szesnasty; ~**th** [sɪksθ] **1.** szósty; **2.** jedna *f* szósta; '~**th·ly** po szóste; ~**·ti·eth** ['sɪkstɪɪθ] sześćdziesiąty; ~**·ty** ['sɪkstɪ] **1.** sześćdziesiąt; **2.** sześćdziesiątka *f*
size [saɪz] **1.** rozmiar *m*; wielkość *f*; wymiar *m*, format *m*; **2.** ~ ***up*** F oceniać ⟨-nić⟩, ⟨z⟩mierzyć (*wzrokiem*)
siz(e)·a·ble ['saɪzəbl] duży
siz·zle ['sɪzl] ⟨za⟩skwierczeć
skate[1] [skeɪt] **1.** łyżwa *f*; łyżworolka *f*; wrotka *f*; **2.** ślizgać się (*na łyżwach*); jeździć na wrotkach; '~**·board** skateboard *m*; **'skat·er** łyżwiarz *m* (-arka *f*), wrotkarz *m* (-arka *f*)
skate[2] [skeɪt] *zo.* płaszczka *f*, raja *f*
skat·ing ['skeɪtɪŋ] łyżwiarstwo *n*; wrotkarstwo *n*; ***free*** ~ jazda *f* dowolna na łyżwach; '~ **rink** lodowisko *n*; tor *m* wrotkarski
skel·e·ton ['skelɪtn] szkielet *m* (*też konstrukcji*); szkic *m*, plan *m*; '~ **key** klucz *m* główny (*do wszystkich drzwi budynku*)
skep·tic ['skeptɪk] *itp. zwł. Am.* → ***sceptic***
sketch [sketʃ] **1.** szkic *m*; *theat. itp.* skecz *m*; **2.** ⟨na⟩szkicować
ski [skiː] **1.** narta *f*; *attr.* narciarski; **2.** jeździć na nartach
skid [skɪd] **1.** (**-*dd*-**) *mot.* wpadać ⟨wpaść⟩ w poślizg; **2.** *mot.* poślizg *m*; *aviat.* płoza *f*; '~ **mark(s** *pl.*) *mot.* ślady *pl.* poślizgu
ski|·er ['skiːə] narciarz *m* (-arka *f*); '~**·ing** narciarstwo *n*; '~ **jump** skocznia *f*; '~ **jump·er** (*w sporcie*) skoczek *m*; '~ **jump·ing** (*w sporcie*) skoki *pl.* narciarskie
skil·ful ['skɪlfl] zręczny, wprawny
'ski lift wyciąg *m* narciarski
skill [skɪl] umiejętność *f*; wprawa *f*, zręczność *f*; ~**ed** wprawny; wykwalifikowany (***at, in*** w *L*); ~**ed 'work·er** pracownik *m* wykwalifikowany
'skill·ful *Am.* → ***skilful***
skim [skɪm] (**-*mm*-**) *tłuszcz itp.* zbierać ⟨zebrać⟩ (*też* ~ ***off***); *mleko* odtłuszczać ⟨-łuścić⟩; *też* ~ ***over***, ~ ***through*** przebiegać ⟨-biec⟩ wzrokiem; ślizgać się nad (*I*); ~**(med) 'milk** mleko *n* odtłuszczone
skimp [skɪmp] *też* ~ ***on*** skąpić (*G*); '~**·y** (**-*ier*, -*iest***) skąpy
skin [skɪn] **1.** skóra *f*; łupina *f* (*owocu*); kożuch *m* (*na mleku itp.*); **2.** (**-*nn*-**) *zwierzę* oskórować, obdzierać ⟨obedrzeć⟩ ze skóry; *łupinę* zdejmować ⟨zdjąć⟩, obierać ⟨obrać⟩; *kolano itp.* otrzeć; ~**-'deep** powierzchowny; '~**-dive** nurkować swobodnie; '~ **diving** *swobodne* nurkowanie *n*; '~**·flint** sknera *f/m*; '~**·ny** (**-*ier*, -*iest***) kościsty, chudy; '~**·ny-dip** F ⟨wy⟩kąpać się nago
skip [skɪp] **1.** (**-*pp*-**) *v/i.* podskakiwać; skakać, przeskakiwać; uciekać ⟨-ciec⟩; skakać przez skakankę; *v/t.* opuszczać

⟨-uścić⟩, pomijać ⟨-minąć⟩; **2.** podskok *n*; '**~p•ing rope** *Brt.* skakanka *f*
skip•per ['skɪpə] *naut.*, kapitan *m* (*drużyny sportowej*)
skir•mish ['skɜːmɪʃ] potyczka *f*; scysja *f*
skirt [skɜːt] **1.** spódnica *f*, spódniczka *f*; **2.** *też* **~ (*a*)*round*** obchodzić ⟨-bejść⟩; *fig. problem itp.*: unikać; '**~•ing board** *Brt.* listwa *f* przypodłogowa
'**ski| run** nartostrada *f*; '**~ tow** wyciąg *m* orczykowy
skit•tle ['skɪtl] kręgiel *m*
skulk [skʌlk] ⟨s⟩kryć się
skull [skʌl] *anat.* czaszka *f*
skul(l)•dug•ge•ry [skʌl'dʌgərɪ] F kombinatorstwo *n*
skunk [skʌŋk] *zo.* skunks *m*
sky [skaɪ] *też* ***skies*** *pl.* niebo *n*; '**~•jack** *samolot* porywać ⟨-rwać⟩; '**~•jack•er** porywacz(ka *f*) *m*; '**~•lark** *zo.* skowronek *m*; '**~•light** (*okno*) świetlik *m*; '**~•line** sylwetka *f*; linia *f* (*horyzontu*); '**~•rock•et** F (*ceny itp.*) strzelać ⟨-lić⟩ w górę; '**~•scrap•er** drapacz *m* chmur
slab [slæb] *kamienna itp.* płyta *f*; kawał *m* (*ciasta itp.*)
slack [slæk] **1.** zwisający, obwisły; *dyscyplina*: luźny; *econ. popyt*: słaby; *sezon*: martwy; niestaranny; **2.** *też* **~ *off*** obijać się; '**~•en** *v/t.* zmniejszać ⟨-szyć⟩ (się); ⟨o⟩słabnąć; ⟨po⟩luzować; **~s** *pl. zwł. Am.* F spodnie *pl.*
slag [slæg] żużel *m*
slain [sleɪn] *p.p. od* ***slay***
sla•lom ['slɑːləm] (*w sporcie*) slalom *m*
slam [slæm] **1.** (***-mm-***) *też* **~ *shut*** zatrzaskiwać ⟨-snąć⟩; *też* **~ *down*** F zwalać ⟨-lić⟩; **~ *on the brakes*** *mot.* gwałtownie zahamować; **2.** trzaśnięcie *n*; zatrzaśnięcie *n*
slan•der ['slɑːndə] **1.** zniesławienie *n*; potwarz *f*; **2.** zniesławiać ⟨-wić⟩; spotwarzać ⟨-rzyć⟩; **~•ous** ['slɑːndərəs] oszczerczy, zniesławiający
slang [slæŋ] **1.** slang *m*; *gr.* gwara *f* środowiskowa; **2.** *zwł. Brt.* F przeklinać, kląć
slant [slɑːnt] **1.** nachylać ⟨-lić⟩ (się), pochylać ⟨-lić⟩ (się); być stronniczym; **2.** pochyłość *f*, nachylenie *n*; *fig.* perspektywa *f*; ***at*** *lub* ***on a*** **~** pod kątem, nachylony; '**~•ing** pochyły
slap [slæp] **1.** klaps *m*; **2.** (***-pp-***) klepać ⟨-nąć⟩; dawać ⟨dać⟩ klapsa; zwalić (***down on*** na *A*); pacnąć; **~•stick** *theat.* slapstick *m*, farsa *f*; '**~•stick com•e•dy** komedia *f* slapstickowa
slash [slæʃ] **1.** ciąć; przecinać ⟨-ciąć⟩; rozcinać ⟨-ciąć⟩; *deszcz*: zacinać (***against*** o *A*); *wydatki* obcinać ⟨-ciąć⟩; **2.** cięcie *n*; nacięcie *n*, rozcięcie *n*
slate [sleɪt] **1.** łupek *m*, *zw.* łupki *pl.*; łupek *m* dachówkowy; *Am. pol.* lista *f* kandydatów; **2.** ⟨po⟩kryć łupkiem; *Am.* wybierać ⟨-brać⟩; *Am.* ⟨za⟩planować
slaugh•ter ['slɔːtə] **1.** rzeź *f* (*też fig.*); masakra *f*; ubój *m*; **2.** ⟨za⟩szlachtować, ubić; urządzać ⟨-dzić⟩ masakrę *lub* rzeź; '**~•house** rzeźnia *f*
Slav [slɑːv] **1.** Słowianin *m* (-anka *f*); **2.** słowiański
slave [sleɪv] **1.** niewolnik *m* (-nica *f*) (*też fig.*); **2.** *też* **~ *away*** zaharowywać ⟨-ować⟩ się
slav•er ['slævə] ślinić się
sla•ve•ry ['sleɪvərɪ] niewolnictwo *n* (*też fig.*)
Slavic ['slævɪk] słowiański
slav•ish ['slævɪʃ] niewolniczy
Sla•von•ic [slə'vɒnɪk] słowiański
slay [sleɪ] (***slew, slain***) ⟨za⟩mordować, zabijać ⟨-bić⟩
sleaze [sliːz] flejtuch *m*; plugawość *f*;
slea•zy ['sliːzɪ] odrażający; flejtuchowaty
sled [sled] *Am.* → ***sledge***
sledge [sledʒ] **1.** sanie *pl.*, sanki *pl.*; **2.** jeździć saniami, ⟨po⟩jechać saniami
'**sledge•ham•mer** młot *m* dwuręczny
sleek [sliːk] **1.** lśniący, błyszczący; *samochód itp.*: wytworny; **2.** nabłyszczać ⟨-czyć⟩
sleep [sliːp] **1.** sen *m*; ***I couldn't get to* ~** nie mogłem zasnąć; ***go to* ~** iść ⟨pójść⟩ spać; *ramię*: ⟨z⟩drętwieć; ***put to* ~** *zwierzę* usypiać ⟨uśpić⟩; **2.** (***slept***) *v/i.* spać; **~ *late*** spać do późna; **~ *on*** *podjęcie decyzji* przeczekać przez noc; **~ *with s.o.*** spać z kimś; *v/t.* przenocowywać ⟨-ować⟩; '**~•er** śpiący *m* (-ca *f*); *Brt. rail.* podkład *m*; *rail.* wagon *m* sypialny
'**sleep•ing| bag** śpiwór *m*; ♀ '**Beau•ty** Śpiąca Królewna *f*; '**~ car** *rail.* wagon *m* sypialny; **~ 'part•ner** *Brt. econ.* cichy (-a) wspólnik *m* (-iczka *f*)
'**sleep|•less** bezsenny; '**~•walk•er** luna-

S

tyk *m* (-yczka *f*); '~·**y** (**-ier, -iest**) śpiący; senny

sleet [sli:t] **1.** śnieg *m* z deszczem, chlapawica *f*, **2.** ***it's ~ing*** pada deszcz ze śniegiem

sleeve [sli:v] rękaw *m*; *tech.* tuleja *f*; *zwł. Brt.* okładka *f* (*płyty*)

sleigh [sleɪ] sanie *pl.* (*zwł. konne*)

sleight of hand [slaɪt əv 'hænd] zręczny gest *m*; *fig.* trik *m*

slen·der ['slendə] smukły, wysmukły; szczupły; *fig.* niewielki, znikomy

slept [slept] *pret. i p.p. od* **sleep** 2

sleuth F [slu:θ] detektyw *m*

slew [slu:] *pret. od* **slay**

slice [slaɪs] **1.** plasterek *m*; kromka *f*; kawałek *m* (*tortu*); łopatka *f* (*do nabierania*); *fig.* część *f*; **2.** *też* **~ up** ⟨po⟩kroić na plasterki *lub* kromki; **~ off** odcinać ⟨-ciąć⟩

slick [slɪk] **1.** gładki; *człowiek*: ulizany; dobrze zrobiony; *droga*: śliski; **2.** F plama *f* ropy naftowej; **3. ~down** włosy nabłyszczać ⟨-czyć⟩; '~·**er** *Am.* płaszcz *m* przeciwdeszczowy; F cwaniak *m*

slid [slɪd] *pret. i p.p. od* **slide** 1

slide [slaɪd] **1.** (**slid**) ślizgać się; prześlizgiwać ⟨-gnąć⟩ się; przesuwać ⟨-sunąć⟩; wysuwać ⟨-sunąć⟩ się; spadać ⟨spaść⟩; ***let things ~*** machnąć na wszystko ręką; **2.** zsunięcie *n* się; poślizg *m*; ześlizg *m*; zjazd *m*; spadek *m*; zjeżdżalnia *f*; *phot.* przezrocze *n*, slajd *m*, diapozytyw *m*; preparat *m* mikroskopowy; *Brt.* spinka *f* (*do włosów*); *tech.* suwak *m*; '**~ rule** suwak *m* logarytmiczny; '**~ tack·le** *piłka nożna*: wślizg *m*

slid·ing door [slaɪdɪŋ 'dɔ:] przesuwane drzwi *pl.*

slight [slaɪt] **1.** lekki; nieznaczny; drobny; **2.** ubliżać ⟨-żyć⟩, znieważać ⟨-żyć⟩; **2.** zniewaga *f*; ubliżenie *n*

slim [slɪm] (**-mm-**) **1.** szczupły; *fig.* mały, niewielki; **2.** *też* ***be ~ming, be on a ~ming diet*** odchudzać się

slime [slaɪm] śluz *m*

slim·y ['slaɪmɪ] (**-ier, -iest**) ośliz(g)ły, śliski (*też fig.*)

sling [slɪŋ] **1.** (**slung**) zawieszać ⟨-sić⟩; F rzucać ⟨-cić⟩, ciskać ⟨-snąć⟩; **2.** temblak *m*; proca *f*; pętla *f*; nosidełko *n* (*dla dziecka*)

slink [slɪŋk] (**slunk**) wycofywać ⟨-wać⟩ się

slip[1] [slɪp] **1.** (**-pp-**) *v/i.* pośliz(g)nąć się; wślizgiwać ⟨-z(g)nąć⟩ się, wyślizgiwać ⟨-z(g)nąć⟩ się; pomylić się; spadać ⟨spaść⟩; *v/t.* wsuwać ⟨wsunąć⟩; wysuwać ⟨-sunąć⟩ się z (*G*); ***~ s.th. into s.o.'s hand*** wsuwać ⟨wsunąć⟩ coś do czyjejś ręki; ***~ s.o.'s attention*** umykać ⟨-knąć⟩ czyjejś uwadze; ***~ s.o.'s mind*** nie przychodzić ⟨-yjść⟩ do głowy; ***she has ~ped a disc*** *med.* dysk jej wypadł; ***~ by, ~ past*** *czas*: przelatywać; **~ off** *ubranie* zrzucać ⟨-cić⟩; **~ on** *ubranie* narzucać ⟨-cić⟩; **2.** poślizgnięcie *n*; pomyłka *f*, błąd *m*; halka *f*; poszewka *f*; ***~ of the tongue*** lapsus *m*; ***give s.o. the ~*** F nawiać komuś

slip[2] [slɪp] *też* ***~ of paper*** kawałek *m* papieru

'**slip**|·**case** pudełko *n* (*na książkę*); '**~-on 1.** *adj.*: ***~-on shoe*** niesznurowany but **2.** but *m* niesznurowany; **~ped 'disc** *med.* wypadnięty dysk *m*; '**~·per** pantofel *m*, kapeć *m*; **~·per·y** ['slɪpərɪ] (**-ier, -iest**) śliski; '**~ road** *Brt.* wjazd *m* (*na autostradę*), zjazd *m* (*z autostrady*); '**~·shod** byle jaki

slit [slɪt] **1.** nacięcie *n*, rozcięcie *n*; szczelina *f*, szpara *f*; **2.** (**-tt-**; **slit**) nacinać ⟨-ciąć⟩; **~ open** rozcinać ⟨-ciąć⟩

slith·er ['slɪðə] wić się, pełznąć; ślizgać się

sliv·er ['slɪvə] odłamek *m* (*szkła itp.*); drzazga *f*

slob·ber ['slɒbə] ślinić się

slo·gan ['sləʊgən] slogan *m*

sloop [slu:p] *naut.* szalupa *f*

slop [slɒp] **1.** (**-pp-**) *v/t.* rozlewać ⟨-lać⟩; *v/i.* wylewać ⟨-lać⟩ się, przelewać ⟨-lać⟩ się (**over** nad *A*); **2.** *też* **~s** *pl.* pomyje *pl.*; fusy *pl.*, resztki *pl.*; *Brt.* F lura *f*, siki *pl.*

slope [sləʊp] **1.** zbocze *n*, stok *m*; nachylenie *n*, pochylenie *n*; **2.** opadać ⟨opaść⟩

slop·py ['slɒpɪ] (**-ier, -iest**) niechlujny; F *ubranie*: znoszony; F ckliwy

slot [slɒt] szczelina *f*, szpara *f*, otwór *m* (*podłużny*); *komp.* miejsce *n* (*na kartę itp.*); czas *m* emisji (*programu radiowego lub telewizyjnego*)

sloth [sləʊθ] *zo.* leniwiec *m*

'**slot ma·chine** automat *m* wrzutowy (*do biletów itp.*)

slouch [slaʊtʃ] **1.** przygarbienie *n*; skulona postawa *f*; F leniuch *m*; **2.** ⟨z⟩gar-

S

bić się, ⟨s⟩kulić się; ~ ***around*** łazić
slough[1] [slʌf]: ~ ***off*** *skórę* zrzucać ⟨-cić⟩
slough[2] [slaʊ] bagno *n*, trzęsawisko *n*
Slo·vak ['sləʊvæk] **1.** słowacki; **2.** Słowak *m* (-aczka *f*); *ling.* język *m* słowacki; **Slo·va·ki·a** [sləʊ'vækɪə] Słowacja *f*
Slo·ve·ni·a Słowenia *f*
slov·en·ly ['slʌvnlɪ] niechlujny, niestaranny
slow [sləʊ] **1.** *adj.* wolny, powolny; leniwy; opieszały (*też econ.*); ***be*** (***ten***) ***minutes*** ~ spóźniać się (10) minut; **2.** wolno, powoli; **3.** *v/t.* *często* ~ ***down,*** ~ ***up*** spowalniać ⟨-wolnić⟩, zwalniać ⟨zwolnić⟩; *v/i.* *często* ~ ***down,*** ~ ***up*** zwalniać ⟨zwolnić⟩; '~**·coach** *Brt.* guzdrała *f/m*; '~**·down** *Am. econ.* strajk *m* włoski; '~ **lane** *mot.* pasmo *n* wolnego ruchu; ~ '**mo·tion** *phot.* zwolnione tempo *n*; '~**-mov·ing** *samochód*: wolno poruszający się; '~**·poke** *Am.* → ***slowcoach***; '~**·worm** *zo.* padalec *m*
sludge [slʌdʒ] szlam *m*; osad *m* kanalizacyjny
slug[1] [slʌg] *zo.* ślimak *m* nagi
slug[2] [slʌg] *zwł. Am.* F kula *f*, pocisk *m*; łyczek *m* (*wódki itp.*)
slug[3] [slʌg] *zwł. Am.* F (**-gg-**) *komuś* przywalić
slug·gish ['slʌgɪʃ] leniwy, powolny; *econ.* w okresie zastoju
sluice [slu:s] *tech.* śluza *f*, upust *m*
slum [slʌm] *też* ~**s** slumsy *pl.*
slum·ber ['slʌmbə] *lit.* **1.** spać; **2.** sen *m*
slump [slʌmp] **1.** *econ.* załamywać ⟨-mać⟩ się (*gwałtownie*); ***sit*** ~***ed over*** siedzieć bezwładnie nad (*I*); ~ ***into a chair*** opadać ⟨-paść⟩ na krzesło; **2.** *econ.* załamanie *n* się
slung [slʌŋ] *pret. i p.p. od* ***sling*** 1
slunk [slʌŋk] *pret. i p.p. od* ***slink***
slur[1] [slɜ:] **1.** (**-rr-**) *mus.* ⟨za⟩grać legato; ~ ***one's speech*** ⟨za⟩bełkotać; **2.** bełkot *m*
slur[2] [slɜ:] **1.** (**-rr-**) oczerniać ⟨-nić⟩; **2.** potwarz *f*
slurp [slɜ:p] F siorbać ⟨-bnąć⟩
slush [slʌʃ] błoto *n* (*ze śniegu*)
slut [slʌt] V dziwka *f*
sly [slaɪ] (**-er, -est**) skryty; przebiegły, chytry; ***on the*** ~ skrycie, po kryjomu
smack[1] [smæk] **1.** klepać ⟨-pnąć⟩; dawać ⟨dać⟩ klapsa; ~ ***one's lips*** cmokać ⟨-knąć⟩; ~ ***down*** plaskać ⟨-snąć⟩ (*I*); **2.** klepnięcie *n*; (*całus*) cmoknięcie *n*; klaps *m*
smack[2] [smæk]: ~ ***of*** *fig.* trącić *lub* pachnieć (*I*), przypominać (*A*)
small [smɔ:l] **1.** *adj.* mały, niewielki; drobny; ~ ***wonder*** (***that***) nic dziwnego(, że); ***feel*** ~ czuć się niepozornym; **2.** *adv.* mało; **3.** ~ ***of the back*** *anat.* krzyż *m*; '~ **ad** ogłoszenie drobne *n*; '~ **arms** *pl.* broń *f* palna ręczna; ~ '**change** *monety*: reszta *f*, drobne *pl.*; '~ **hours** *pl.*: ***in the*** ~ ***hours*** nad ranem; ~-'**mind·ed** o ciasnych horyzontach; małostkowy; ~**·pox** ['smɔ:lpɒks] *med.* ospa *f*; '~ **print** *fig.* informacje *pl.* szczegółowe; '~ **talk** zdawkowa rozmowa *f*, rozmowa *f* towarzyska; ~-'**time** F nieznaczący; ~ '**town** małe miasto *n*
smart [smɑ:t] **1.** elegancki; *zwł. Brt.* wytworny; *zwł. Am.* bystry; szybki; *wzrok*: ostry; **2.** ⟨za⟩boleć, ⟨za⟩piec; cierpieć (***from, over*** z powodu *G*); **3.** piekący ból *m*; ~ **aleck** ['smɑ:t ælɪk] F spryciarz *m*; '~**·ness** elegancja *f*; wytworność *f*
smash [smæʃ] **1.** *v/t.* rozbijać ⟨-bić⟩ (*też* ~ ***up***); *pięścią itp.* walić ⟨-lnąć⟩; *rekord* pobić; (*w tenisie*) ścinać ⟨ściąć⟩; *v/i.* roztrzaskiwać ⟨-kać⟩ się; ~ ***into*** zderzać ⟨-rzyć⟩ się z (*I*); **2.** cios *n*; trzask *m*; (*w tenisie*) smecz *m*, ścięcie *n*; → ~ ***hit,*** ~ ***up***; ~ '**hit** hit *m*; '~**·ing** *zwł. Brt.* F niesamowity, kapitalny; '~**-up** *mot.*, kraksa *f*; *rail.* katastrofa *f*
smat·ter·ing ['smætərɪŋ]: ***a*** ~ ***of English*** bardzo ograniczona znajomość *f* angielskiego
smear [smɪə] **1.** plama *f* (*też fig.*); *med.* wymaz *m*; **2.** ⟨po⟩mazać (się); ⟨za⟩smarować (się); *wydruk itp.*: zamazywać ⟨-zać⟩ (się); *fig.* obsmarować
smell [smel] **1.** (***smelt*** *lub* ***smelled***) *v/i.* czuć zapach; pachnieć, *zwł.* śmierdzieć; *v/t.* ⟨po⟩wąchać; ⟨po⟩czuć; *fig.* wyczuwać, przeczuwać; **2.** zapach *m*; woń *f*; smród *m*; węch *m*; '~**·y** (**-ier, -iest**) śmierdzący, cuchnący
smelt[1] [smelt] *pret. i p.p. od* ***smell*** 1
smelt[2] [smelt] *metal* wytapiać ⟨-topić⟩
smile [smaɪl] **1.** uśmiech *m*; **2.** uśmiechać ⟨-chnąć⟩ się; ~ ***at*** wyśmiewać się z (*G*)
smirk [smɜ:k] uśmieszek *m*
smith [smɪθ] kowal *m*

S

smith•e•reens [smɪðə'ri:nz] F *pl.*: ***smash s.th. (in)to ~*** rozbić ⟨-bijać⟩ coś w drobny mak
smith•y ['smɪðɪ] kuźnia *f*
smit•ten ['smɪtn] *zwł. humor.* rozmiłowany, rozkochany (***with, by*** w *L*)
smock [smɒk] bluzka *f* (*tunika, ciążowa*); fartuch *m*, kitel *m*
smog [smɒg] smog *m*
smoke [sməʊk] **1.** dym *m*; ***have a ~*** zapalić papierosa; **2.** dymić (się); ⟨za-, wy⟩palić; '**smok•er** palacz(ka *f*) *m*; *rail.* wagon *m* dla palących; '**smoke•stack** komin *m*
smok•ing ['sməʊkɪŋ] palenie *n*; ***no ~*** palenie *n* wzbronione; ⚠ *nie* ***smoking***; **~ com'part•ment** *rail.* przedział *m* dla palących
smok•y ['sməʊkɪ] (**-ier, -iest**) zadymiony; przydymiony; koloru dymu
smooth [smu:ð] **1.** gładki (*też fig.*); *ciasto itp.*: jednolity; *ruch, smak itp.*: łagodny; uprzedzająco grzeczny; **2.** *też* ***~ out*** wygładzać ⟨-dzić⟩; ***~ away*** wygładzać; *trudności* usuwać ⟨usunąć⟩; ***~ down*** włosy przygładzać ⟨-dzić⟩
smoth•er ['smʌðə] ⟨s⟩tłumić; ⟨u⟩dusić
smo(u)l•der ['sməʊldə] żarzyć się, tlić się
smudge [smʌdʒ] **1.** plama *f* (*też fig.*); **2.** ⟨za⟩plamić; rozmazywać ⟨-zać⟩ (się)
smug [smʌg] (**-gg-**) zadowolony z siebie
smug•gle ['smʌgl] ⟨prze⟩szmuglować, przemycać ⟨-cić⟩ (***into*** do *G*); '**~r** szmugler *m*, przemytnik *m* (-niczka *f*)
smut [smʌt] płatek *m* sadzy; brud *m*; *fig.* plugastwo *n*; '**~•ty** (**-ier, -iest**) *fig.* plugawy
snack [snæk] przekąska *f*; ***have a ~*** ⟨z⟩jeść coś; '**~ bar** snack-bar *m*
snag [snæg] **1.** *fig.* problem *m*; zadzior *m*; **2.** (**-gg-**) *czymś* zaczepiać ⟨-pić⟩ (*o coś*), coś zadzierać ⟨-drzeć⟩
snail [sneɪl] *zo. skorupkowy* ślimak *m*
snake [sneɪk] *zo.* wąż *m*
snap [snæp] **1.** (**-pp-**) *v/i.* ⟨z⟩łamać się, trzasnąć; *też* ***~ shut*** zatrzaskiwać ⟨-snąć⟩ się; ***~ at*** warczeć ⟨-rknąć⟩ na (*A*), drzeć się na (*A*); *pies*: kłapać zębami na (*A*); ***~ out of it!*** F głowa do góry!; ***~ to it!*** F pospiesz się! *v/t.* ⟨z⟩łamać; *phot.* F zdjęcie pstrykać ⟨-knąć⟩; ***~ one's fingers*** strzelać ⟨-lić⟩ palcami; ***~ one's fingers at*** *fig.* lekceważyć (*A*); ***~ off*** odłamywać ⟨-mać⟩; ***~ up*** *coś* kupować ⟨-pić⟩; **2.** *phot.* zdjęcie *n*; *Am.* zatrzask *m*; *fig.* F (*energia*) ikra *f*; ***cold ~*** *krótkotrwałe* nagłe ochłodzenie *n*; '**~ fas•ten•er** *Am.* zatrzask *m*; '**~•pish** *fig.* wściekły; '**~•py** (**-ier, -iest**) szykowny; ***make it ~py!*** *Brt. też* ***look ~py!*** pospiesz się!; '**~•shot** *phot.* zdjęcie *n*
snare [sneə] **1.** sidła *pl.*; *fig.* pułapka *f*; **2.** ⟨s⟩chwytać w sidła; F ⟨s⟩chwytać w pułapkę
snarl [snɑ:l] **1.** warczeć ⟨-rknąć⟩; ⟨za⟩burczeć (***at*** na *A*); **2.** warknięcie *n*, burknięcie *n*
snatch [snætʃ] **1.** *v/t. coś* ⟨s⟩chwytać, ⟨z⟩łapać (*też* ***~ at***); *kogoś, coś* porywać ⟨-rwać⟩; *ze sposobności* ⟨s⟩korzystać (*też* ***~ at***); ***~ s.o.'s handbag*** wyrywać ⟨-rwać⟩ komuś torebkę; ***~ an hour's sleep*** zdołać przespać się godzinę; **2.** ***make a ~*** ⟨s⟩chwytać (*A*); ***~ of conversation*** urywek *m* rozmowy
sneak [sni:k] **1.** *v/i.* przekradać ⟨-raść⟩ się, wkradać ⟨-raść⟩ się (***into*** do *G*); *Brt.* F donosić ⟨-nieść⟩; *v/t.* F podkradać ⟨-raść⟩; ***~ a look*** ukradkiem rzucić spojrzenie; **2.** *Brt.* F donosiciel(ka *f*) *m*; '**~•er** *Am.* adidas *m*, tenisówka *f*
sneer [snɪə] **1.** uśmiechać ⟨-chnąć⟩ się drwiąco; ⟨za⟩drwić (***at*** z *G*); **2.** drwiący uśmieszek *m*; drwiąca uwaga *f*, drwina *f*
sneeze [sni:z] **1.** kichać ⟨-chnąć⟩; **2.** kichnięcie *n*
snick•er ['snɪkə] *zwł. Am.* → ***snigger***
sniff [snɪf] **1.** *v/i.* pociągać ⟨-gnąć⟩ nosem; ⟨po⟩wąchać; ***~ at*** *fig.* krzywić nos na (*A*); *v/t. narkotyk* wdychać; **2.** pociągnięcie *n* nosem
snif•fle ['snɪfl] **1.** pociągać ⟨-gnąć⟩ nosem; **2.** pociągnięcie *n* nosem; ***she's got the ~s*** F ona ma zatkany nos
snig•ger *zwł. Brt.* ['snɪgə] podśmiewać się (***at*** z *G*)
snip [snɪp] **1.** cięcie *n*; **2.** (**-pp-**) przecinać ⟨-ciąć⟩; ***~ off*** odcinać ⟨-ciąć⟩
snipe[1] [snaɪp] *zo.* kszyk *m*
snipe[2] [snaɪp] strzelać ⟨-lić⟩ z ukrycia (***at*** do *G*); '**snip•er** snajper *m*, strzelec *m* wyborowy
sniv•el ['snɪvl] (*zwł. Brt.* **-ll-** , *Am.* **-l-**) chlipać, labiedzić
snob [snɒb] snob *m*; '**~•bish** snobistyczny

S

snoop [snu:p]: **~ about, ~ around** F myszkować, węszyć; '**~·er** wścibski *m* (-ka *f*)
snooze [snu:z] F **1.** drzemka *f*; **2.** drzemać
snore [snɔ:] **1.** chrapać; **2.** chrapanie *n*
snor·kel ['snɔ:kl] **1.** fajka *f* (*do nurkowanie*); *naut.* chrapy *pl.* (*okrętu podwodnego*); **2.** nurkować z fajką
snort [snɔ:t] **1.** parskać ⟨-knąć⟩; *narkotyk* wdychać; **2.** parsknięcie *n*
snout [snaʊt] pysk *m*
snow [snəʊ] **1.** śnieg *m*; F (*kokaina*) koka *f*; **2.** śnieżyć; *śnieg*: padać ⟨spaść⟩; ***be ~ed in*** *lub* ***up*** być przysypanym śniegiem; '**~·ball** kula *f* śniegowa; **~·ball 'fight** bitwa na kule śniegowe; '**~·bound** zaśnieżony, pokryty śniegiem; '**~·drift** zaspa *f* (*śniegu*); '**~·drop** *bot.* przebiśnieg *m*; '**~·fall** opady *pl.* śniegu; '**~·flake** płatek *m* śniegu; '**~·man** (*pl.* ***-men***) bałwan *m* śniegowy; '**~·plough** *Brt.*, '**~·plow** *Am.* pług *m* śnieżny; '**~·storm** burza *f* śniegowa, śnieżyca *f*; **~-'white** śnieżnobiały; '**~ White** Królewna *f* Śnieżka; '**~·y** (***-ier, -iest***) zaśnieżony; śnieżny; ośnieżony
Snr *skrót pisany*: ***Senior*** sen., senior *m*
snub [snʌb] **1.** (***-bb-***) ⟨po⟩traktować lekceważąco; **2.** leceważenie *n*; '**~ nose** zadarty nos *m*; **~-'nosed** z zadartym nosem
snuff[1] [snʌf] tabaka *f*
snuff[2] [snʌf] *świecę* ⟨z⟩gasić; **~ *out*** *życie* przerwać
snuf·fle ['snʌfl] obwąchiwać ⟨-chać⟩
snug [snʌg] (***-gg-***) przytulny, zaciszny; *ubranie*: dobrze leżący; przyciasny
snug·gle ['snʌgl]: **~ *up to s.o.*** przytulać ⟨-lić⟩ się do kogoś; **~ *down in bed*** wtulać ⟨-lić⟩ się do łóżka
so [səʊ] **1.** *adv.* tak, w ten sposób; także; → ***hope*** 2, ***think***; ***is that ~?*** naprawdę?; ***an hour or ~*** coś koło godziny; ***she is tired – ~ am I*** ona jest zmęczona – ja też; **~ *far*** dotąd, dotychczas; **2.** *cj.* tak więc, więc; aby
soak [səʊk] *v/t.* ⟨za⟩moczyć (***in*** w *L*); **~ *up*** *gąbka, gałgan*: wchłaniać ⟨wchłonąć⟩; *v/i.* przemoczyć; ***leave the dirty clothes to ~*** namocz brudne rzeczy
soap [səʊp] **1.** mydło *n*; F → ***soap opera***; **2.** namydlać ⟨-lić⟩ (się); '**~ ope·ra** opera *f* mydlana (*radiowa lub telewizyjna*) '**~·y** (***-ier, -iest***) mydlany; *fig.* F wazeliniarski
soar [sɔ:] ⟨po⟩szybować; wzbijać ⟨-bić⟩ się, wznosić ⟨-nieść⟩ się; iść ⟨pójść⟩ w górę
sob [sɒb] **1.** (***-bb-***) szlochać; **2.** szloch *m*
so·ber ['səʊbə] **1.** trzeźwy (*też fig.*); **2.** ⟨wy⟩trzeźwieć; **~ *up*** otrzeźwiać ⟨-wić⟩
so-'called tak zwany
soc·cer ['sɒkə] piłka *f* nożna; '**~ hoo·li·gan** pseudokibic *m*
so·cia·ble ['səʊʃəbl] towarzyski
so·cial ['səʊʃl] społeczny; socjalny; towarzyski; **~ 'dem·o·crat** socjaldemokrata *m* (-tka *f*); **~ in'sur·ance** ubezpieczenie *n* społeczne
so·cial|·is·m ['səʊʃəlɪzəm] socjalizm *m*; '**~·ist 1.** socjalista *m* (-tka *f*); **2.** socjalistyczny
so·cial·ize ['səʊʃəlaɪz] utrzymywać kontakty towarzyskie (***with*** z *I*)
so·cial| 'sci·ence nauka *f* społeczna; **~ se'cu·ri·ty** *Brt.* pomoc *f* społeczna; ***be on ~ security*** otrzymywać zasiłek z pomocy społecznej; **~ 'serv·i·ces** *pl. zwł. Brt.* opieka *f* społeczna; '**~ work** praca *f* społeczna; '**~ work·er** pracownik *m* (-nica *f*) opieki społecznej
so·ci·e·ty [sə'saɪətɪ] społeczeństwo *n*; towarzystwo *n*
so·ci·ol·o·gy [səʊsɪ'ɒlədʒɪ] socjologia *f*
sock [sɒk] skarpetka *f*
sock·et ['sɒkɪt] *electr.* gniazdko *n*; *electr.* oprawka *f* (*żarówki*); *anat.* oczodół *m*
sod [sɒd] *Brt.* V kutas *m*, ciul *m*
so·da ['səʊdə] woda *f* sodowa; *zwł. Am.* napój *m* gazowany *f*
sod·den ['sɒdn] przemoczony, nasiąknięty wodą
so·fa ['səʊfə] sofa *f*, kanapa *f*
soft [sɒft] miękki; delikatny; *głos*: cichy; *światło*: łagodny; *napój*: bezalkoholowy; *narkotyk*: nie powodujący uzależnienia; *też* **~ *in the head*** F przygłupiasty; ***a ~ job*** F łatwa (prosta, spokojna) praca; '**~ drink** napój *m* bezalkoholowy
soft·en ['sɒfn] *v/t.* zmiękczać ⟨-czyć⟩; *ton, światło* ⟨z⟩łagodzić; **~ *up*** F *kogoś* zmiękczać (-czyć); *v/i.* ⟨z⟩mięknąć; ⟨z⟩łagodnieć
soft|-'head·ed przygłupi; **~'heart·ed** dobroduszny, o miękkim sercu; **~ 'land-**

S

ing (*w astronautyce*) miękkie lądowanie *f*; '**~·ware** *komp.* software *n*, oprogramowanie *n*; **~·ware 'pack·age** *komp.* pakiet *m* oprogramowania; '**~·y** F (*osoba*) mięczak *m*
sog·gy ['sɒgɪ] (**-ier, -iest**) namiękły, rozmokły
soil¹ [sɔɪl] gleba *f*, ziemia *f*
soil² [sɔɪl] ⟨u-, za⟩brudzić
sol·ace ['sɒləs] pociecha *f*, pocieszenie *n*
so·lar ['səʊlə] słoneczny; **~ 'en·er·gy** energia *f* słoneczna; **~ 'pan·el** bateria *f* słoneczna; '**~ sys·tem** układ *m* słoneczny
sold [səʊld] *pret. i p.p. od* **sell**
sol·der ['sɒldə] ⟨z-, przy⟩lutować
sol·dier ['səʊldʒə] żołnierz *m*
sole¹ [səʊl] **1.** podeszwa *f*; **2.** ⟨pod⟩zelować
sole² [səʊl] *zo.* (*pl.* **sole, soles**) sola *f*
sole³ [səʊl] jedyny; wyłączny; '**~·ly** jedynie; wyłącznie
sol·emn ['sɒləm] poważny; uroczysty
so·li·cit [sə'lɪsɪt] ⟨po⟩prosić
so·lic·i·tor [sə'lɪsɪtə] *Brt. jur.* adwokat *m* (*uprawniony do występowania w sądach niższej instancji*); doradca *m* prawny
so·lic·i·tous [sə'lɪsɪtəs] troskliwy; uczynny
sol·id ['sɒlɪd] **1.** stały; pełny, lity; solidny; *ściana itp.*: masywny; *math. geometria*: przestrzenny; *Brt. protest*: solidarny; *okres czasu*: bity; **2.** *math.* bryła; *phys.* ciało *n* stałe
sol·i·dar·i·ty [sɒlɪ'dærətɪ] solidarność *f*
so·lid·i·fy [sə'lɪdɪfaɪ] zestalać się; zastygać ⟨-gnąć⟩; ⟨s⟩krzepnąć
so·lil·o·quy [sə'lɪləkwɪ] *theat.* monolog *m*
sol·i·taire [sɒlɪ'teə] *Am.* pasjans *m*; (*gra*) samotnik *m*
sol·i·ta·ry ['sɒlɪtərɪ] samotny, pojedynczy; odludny, odosobniony; **~ con'fine·ment** *jur.* kara *f* izolatki
so·lo ['səʊləʊ] (*pl.* **-los**) *mus.* solo *n*; *aviat.* samotny lot *m*; *attr.* solowy; samotny; '**~·ist** *mus.* solista *m* (-tka *f*)
sol·u·ble ['sɒljʊbl] rozpuszczalny; *fig.* do rozwiązania; **so·lu·tion** [sə'luːʃn] roztwór *m*; rozwiązanie *n*
solve [sɒlv] rozwiązywać ⟨-zać⟩; **sol·vent** ['sɒlvənt] **1.** *econ.* wypłacalny; **2.** *chem.* rozpuszczalnik *m*
som·bre *Brt.*, **som·ber** *Am.* ['sɒmbə] poważny, smutny; *fig.* ponury
some [sʌm] jakiś; *przed pl.*: trochę (*G*); kilka (*G*); nieco (*G*); niektórzy; **~ 20 miles** jakieś 20 mil; **~ more cake** jeszcze trochę ciasta; **to ~ extent** w pewnej mierze; **~·bod·y** ['sʌmbədɪ] ktoś; '**~·day** kiedyś; '**~·how** jakoś; '**~·one** ktoś; '**~·place** *zwł. Am.* → **somewhere**
som·er·sault ['sʌməsɔːlt] **1.** salto *n*; przewrót *m* w przód; **turn a ~** ⟨z⟩robić przewrót *m* w przód; **2.** ⟨z⟩robić salto; wykonać przewrót w przód
'**some|·thing** coś; **~thing like** coś jakby; '**~·time** kiedyś; '**~·times** czasami; '**~·what** trochę (*G*), nieco (*G*); '**~·where** gdzieś
son [sʌn] syn *m*; **~ of a bitch** *zwł. Am.* V sukinsyn *m*
song [sɒŋ] pieśń *f*, piosenka *f*; **for a ~** F za Bóg zapłać; '**~·bird** ptak *m* śpiewający
son·ic ['sɒnɪk] dźwiękowy; **~ 'bang** *Brt.*, **~ 'boom** *aviat.* uderzenie *n* dźwiękowe (*przy przekraczaniu prędkości dźwięku*)
son-in-law ['sʌnɪnlɔː] (*pl.* **sons-in-law**) zięć *m*
son·net ['sɒnɪt] sonet *m*
so·nor·ous [sə'nɔːrəs] donośny, dźwięczny
soon [suːn] wkrótce, niebawem; **as ~ as** skoro tylko; **as ~ as possible** jak najszybciej można; '**~·er** prędzej, wcześniej; **~er or later** wcześniej lub później; **the ~er the better** im szybciej, tym lepiej; **no ~er... than** nie szybciej niż ...; **no ~er said than done** od razu zrobione
soot [sʊt] sadza *f*
soothe [suːð] ⟨u⟩koić, uspokajać ⟨-koić⟩ (*też* **down**); ⟨za-, u⟩łagodzić; *ból itp.* uśmierzać ⟨-rzyć⟩; **sooth·ing** ['suːðɪŋ] kojący, uśmierzający
soot·y ['sʊtɪ] (**-ier, -iest**) czarny (*od sadzy*)
sop¹ [sɒp] (*rzecz dana lub zrobiona na odczepnego*)
sop² [sɒp] (**-pp-**): **~ up** *ścierka, gałgan*: wchłaniać ⟨wchłonąć⟩ (*płyn*)
so·phis·ti·cat·ed [sə'fɪstɪkeɪtɪd] wyrafinowany; obyty; *tech.* wysoko rozwinięty
soph·o·more ['sɒfəmɔː] *Am.* student(ka *f*) *m* drugiego roku

sop·o·rif·ic [sɒpə'rɪfɪk] (***-ally***) usypiający; nasenny
sop·ping ['sɒpɪŋ]: **~ *wet*** F ociekający wodą
sor·cer|·er ['sɔːsərə] czarownik *m*, czarodziej *m*, czarnoksiężnik *m*; **~·ess** ['sɔːsərɪs] czarownica *f*, czarodziejka *f*; **~·y** ['sɔːsərɪ] czarodziejstwo *n*
sor·did ['sɔːdɪd] nędzny, brudny; nikczemny
sore [sɔː] **1.** (***-r, -st***) obolały; bolący; *fig.* bolesny; punkt czuły; *zwł. Am.* F *fig.* wściekły (***at*** na *A*); ***I'm ~ all over*** wszystko mnie boli; **~ *throat*** zapalenie *n* gardła; ***I have a ~ finger*** palec mnie boli; **2.** rana *f*, owrzodzenie *n*
sor·rel¹ ['sɒrəl] *bot.* szczaw *m*; *attr.* szczawiowy
sor·rel² ['sɒrəl] *koń* kasztanowy
sor·row ['sɒrəʊ] smutek *m*, żal *m*; **'~·ful** smutny, przygnębiony
sor·ry ['sɒrɪ] **1.** *adj.* (***-ier, -iest***) smutny; przygnębiony; ***be** lub **feel ~ for s.o.*** współczuć komuś; ***I'm ~ for her*** żal mi jej; ***I am ~ to say*** z przykrością muszę powiedzieć **2.** *int.* przepraszam!; **~?** *zwł. Brt.* słucham?
sort [sɔːt] **1.** rodzaj *m*, gatunek *m*; **~ *of*** F jakby, jakoś; ***of a ~, of ~s*** F coś w rodzaju; ***all ~s of things*** najróżniejsze rzeczy; ***nothing of the ~*** nic podobnego; ***what ~ of (a) man is he?*** jaki on jest?; ***be out of ~s*** F być nie w sosie; ***be completely out of ~s*** (*w sporcie*) kompletnie nie mieć formy; **2.** ⟨po⟩sortować, ⟨po⟩układać; **~ *out*** oddzielać ⟨-lić⟩; *problem itp.* rozwiązywać ⟨-zać⟩; **'~·er** sortownik *m*; klasyfikator(ka *f*) *m*
SOS [es əʊ 'es] SOS *n*; ***send an ~*** wysyłać ⟨-słać⟩ sygnał SOS; **~ *call** lub **message*** wezwanie *n* SOS
sought [sɔːt] *pret. i p.p. od* ***seek***
soul [səʊl] dusza *f* (*też fig.*); *mus.* soul *m*
sound¹ [saʊnd] **1.** dźwięk *m*; odgłos *m*; (*w głośniku radiowym lub telewizyjnym*) głos *m*, fonia *f*; *gr.* głoska *f*; *med.* szmer *m*, ton *m*; *attr.* dźwiękowy; **2.** *v/i.* ⟨za⟩brzmieć; ⟨za⟩dźwięczeć; *v/t. alarm* włączać ⟨-czyć⟩; **~ *the bell*** bić w dzwon; *ling.* wypowiadać ⟨-wiedzieć⟩; *naut.* sondować; **~ *one's horn*** *mot.* dawać ⟨dać⟩ sygnał (*klaksonem*), ⟨za⟩trąbić
sound² [saʊnd] zdrowy; w dobrym stanie; rozsądny; *przeszkolenie*: dogłębny; solidny; *sen*: głęboki
'sound| bar·ri·er bariera *f* dźwiękowa; **'~ film** film *m* dźwiękowy; **'~·less** bezgłośny; **'~·proof** dźwiękoszczelny; **'~·track** ścieżka *f* dźwiękowa; **'~ wave** fala *f* dźwiękowa
soup [suːp] **1.** zupa *f*; **2. ~ *up*** *mot.* F *silnik* podrasowywać ⟨-ować⟩
sour ['saʊə] **1.** kwaśny; skwaśniały; *mleko*: zsiadły; *fig.* cierpki; **2.** ⟨s⟩kwaśnieć, zsiadać ⟨zsiąść⟩ się
source [sɔːs] źródło *n* (*też fig.*)
south [saʊθ] **1.** południe *n*; **2.** *adj.* południowy; **3.** *adv.* na południe
South Af·ri·ca Republika *f* Południowej Afryki
south east [saʊθ iːst] **1.** południowy wschód *m*; **2.** *adj.* południowo-wschodni; **3.** *adv.* na południowy wschód; **~'east·ern** południowo-wschodni
south|·er·ly ['sʌðəlɪ], **~·ern** ['sʌðən] południowy; **'~·ern·most** wysunięty najbardziej na południe
South 'Pole biegun *m* południowy
south|·ward(s) ['saʊθwəd(z)] na południe; **~'west 1.** południowy zachód *m*; **2.** *adj.* południowo-zachodni; **3.** *adv.* na południowy zachód; **~'west·ern** południowo-zachodni
sou·ve·nir [suːvə'nɪə] pamiątka *f*
sove·reign ['sɒvrɪn] **1.** monarcha *m*, władca *m*; **2.** *państwo itp.*: suwerenny; **~·ty** ['sɒvrəntɪ] suwerenność *f*
So·vi·et ['səʊvɪət] *hist.* radziecki, sowiecki
sow¹ [səʊ] (***sowed, sown** lub **sowed***) ⟨za⟩siać
sow² [saʊ] *zo.* maciora *f*
sown [səʊn] *p.p. od* ***sow¹***
spa [spɑː] uzdrowisko *n*, kurort *m*
space [speɪs] **1.** miejsce *n*; obszar *m*; przestrzeń *f*; kosmos *m*; **2.** *też* **~ *out*** rozstawiać ⟨-wić⟩; *print.* rozstrzeliwać ⟨-lać⟩; **'~ age** era *f* kosmiczna; **'~ bar** klawisz *m* spacji; **'~ cap·sule** kapsuła *f*, kabina *f* (*statku kosmicznego*); **'~ cen·tre** centrum *n* lotów kosmicznych; **'~·craft** (*pl.* ***-craft***) statek *m* kosmiczny; **'~ flight** lot *m* kosmiczny; **'~·lab** laboratorium *n* kosmiczne; **'~·man** (*pl.* ***-men***) F astronauta *m*, kosmonauta *m*; **'~ probe** sonda *f* kosmiczna; **'~ research** badanie *n* przestrzeni

S

kosmicznej; '~·**ship** statek *m* kosmiczny; '~ **shut·tle** prom *m* kosmiczny; '~ **sta·tion** stacja *f* kosmiczna; '~·**suit** skafander *m* kosmiczny; '~ **walk** spacer *m* w przestrzeni kosmicznej; '~·**wom·an** (*pl.* ***-women***) astronautka *f*, kosmonautka *f*

spa·cious ['speɪʃəs] przestrzenny

spade [speɪd] szpadel *m*; (*w kartach*) pik *m*; ***king of ~s*** król *m* pik; ***call a ~*** nazywać rzeczy po imieniu

Spain [speɪn] Hiszpania *f*

span [spæn] **1.** rozpiętość *f*; okres *m* czasu; **2.** (***-nn-***) spinać ⟨spiąć⟩ brzegi; obejmować ⟨objąć⟩

span·gle ['spæŋgl] **1.** cekin *m*; **2.** naszywać ⟨-szyć⟩ cekiny

Span·iard ['spænjəd] Hiszpan *m* (-nka *f*)

span·iel ['spænjəl] *zo.* spaniel *m*

Span·ish ['spænɪʃ] **1.** hiszpański; **2.** *ling.* język *m* hiszpański; ***the ~*** *pl.* Hiszpanie *pl.*

spank [spæŋk] dawać ⟨dać⟩ klapsa (*D*); '~·**ing 1.** *adj.* szybki; prędki; **2.** *adv.* ***~ing clean*** czyściutki; ***~ing new*** nowiutki; **3.** lanie *n*

span·ner ['spænə] *zwł. Brt.* klucz *m* (maszynowy); ***put*** *lub* ***throw a ~ in the works*** F wsadzać kij między szprychy

spar [spɑː] (***-rr-***) (*w boksie*) odbywać ⟨-być⟩ sparing (***with*** z *I*); przeprowadzać ⟨-dzić⟩ pojedynek na słowa (***with*** z *I*)

spare [speə] **1.** przeznaczać ⟨-czyć⟩, *kogoś* wyznaczać ⟨-czyć⟩; *pieniądze, czas itp.* oszczędzać ⟨-dzić⟩; ***~ no expenses*** nie szczędzić wydatków; ***~ s.o. s.th.*** oszczędzać coś komuś; ***can you ~ me a minute?*** czy może mi pan poświęcić minutę?; ***to ~*** do dyspozycji; **2.** zapasowy; *czas*: wolny; **3.** część *f* zapasowa; opona *f* zapasowa; ~ '**part** *mot.* część *f* zapasowa; ~ '**room** pokój *m* gościnny; ~ '**time** wolny czas *m*

spar·ing ['speərɪŋ] oszczędny

spark [spɑːk] **1.** iskra *f* (*też fig.*); **2.** ⟨za⟩iskrzyć; '~**ing plug** *Brt. mot.* → ***spark plug***

spar·kle ['spɑːkl] **1.** skrzyć się; błyszczeć ⟨błysnąć⟩ (***with*** od *G*); *napój*: musować; **2.** migotanie *n*; połysk *m*; **spark·ling** ['spɑːklɪŋ] migocący; *fig.* błyskotliwy; ~ ***wine*** wino *n* musujące

'**spark plug** *mot.* świeca *f* zapłonowa

spar·row ['spærəʊ] *zo.* wróbel *m*; '~·**hawk** krogulec *m*

sparse [spɑːs] rzadki, przerzedzony

spas·m ['spæzəm] *med.* skurcz *m*, spazm *m*; *med.* atak *m*; **spas·mod·ic** [spæz'mɒdɪk] (***~ally***) *med.* spazmodyczny, spazmatyczny; *fig.* sporadyczny

spas·tic ['spæstɪk] *med.* **1.** (***~ally***) spastyczny, kurczowy; **2.** osoba *f* z porażeniem spastycznym

spat [spæt] *pret. i p.p. od* ***spit***[1]

spa·tial ['speɪʃl] przestrzenny

spat·ter ['spætə] obryzgiwać ⟨-gać⟩; opryskiwać ⟨-kać⟩; posypywać ⟨-pać⟩

spawn [spɔːn] **1.** *zo.* składać ⟨złożyć⟩ skrzek *lub* ikrę; *fig.* ⟨s⟩płodzić, ⟨z⟩rodzić; **2.** *zo.* skrzek *m*; ikra *f*

speak [spiːk] (***spoke, spoken***) *v/i.* mówić ⟨powiedzieć⟩; ⟨po⟩rozmawiać (***to, with*** do *G*, ***about*** o *L*); ***so to ~*** że tak powiem; ***~ing!*** *teleph.* przy aparacie!; ***~ up*** mówić głośniej; *v/t.* mówić; ***~ Polish*** mówić po polsku; '~·**er** mówca *m* (-czyni *f*); ♀ *parl. Brt., Am.* speaker *m* (*w niższej izbie parlamentu*)

spear [spɪə] **1.** oszczep *m*; włócznia *f*; **2.** nabijać ⟨-bić⟩, przeszywać ⟨-szyć⟩ oszczepem; '~·**head** grot *m*; *mil.* szpica *f*, czołówka *f* (*też fig.*); '~·**mint** *bot.* mięta *f* zielona

spe·cial ['speʃl] **1.** specjalny; szczególny; nadzwyczajny; dodatkowy; **2.** pociąg *m lub* autobus *m* specjalny *lub* dodatkowy; audycja *f* specjalna (*radiowa lub telewizyjna*); *Am. econ.* okazja *f*; ***be on ~*** *Am. econ.* F być dostępnym po obniżonej cenie; **spe·cial·ist** ['speʃəlɪst] specjalista *m* (-tka *f*); *med.* lekarz *m* specjalista (***in*** w zakresie *G*); *attr.* specjalistyczny; **spe·ci·al·i·ty** [speʃɪ'ælətɪ] specjalność *f*; **spe·cial·ize** ['speʃəlaɪz] ⟨wy⟩specjalizować się; **spe·cial·ty** *Am.* ['speʃltɪ] → ***speciality***

spe·cies ['spiːʃiːz] (*pl.* ***-cies***) gatunek *m*

spe|·cif·ic [spɪ'sɪfɪk] (***-ally***) konkretny; szczegółowy; właściwy; specyficzny, swoisty (***to*** dla *G*); **~·ci·fy** ['spesɪfaɪ] określać ⟨-lić⟩; wyszczególniać ⟨-nić⟩

spe·ci·men ['spesɪmən] okaz *m*; próbka *f*

speck [spek] plamka *f*; cętka *f*; *fig.* kropka *f*;

speck·led ['spekld] plamiasty

spec·ta·cle ['spektəkl] przedstawienie

S

n (*też fig.*); spektakl *m*; (***a pair of***) **~s** *pl.* okulary *pl.*
spec·tac·u·lar [spek'tækjʊlə] **1.** spektakularny; widowiskowy; **2.** uroczystość *f*, gala *f*
spec·ta·tor [spek'teɪtə] widz *m*
spec|·tral ['spektrəl] widmowy (*też phys.*); *phys.* spektralny; **~·tre** *Brt.*, **~·ter** *Am.* ['spektə] widmo *n*, zjawa *f*; **~·trum** ['spektrəm] *phys.* widmo *n*, spektrum *n*
spec·u|·late ['spekjʊleɪt] rozważać ⟨-żyć⟩ (***about, on*** *A*), spekulować (***about, on*** nad *A*); *econ.* spekulować, dokonywać ⟨-nać⟩ spekulacji; **~·la·tion** [spekjʊ'leɪʃn] domysł *m*; *econ.* spekulacja *f*; **~·la·tive** ['spekjʊlətɪv] spekulatywny; *econ.* spekulacyjny; **~·la·tor** ['spekjʊleɪtə] *econ.* spekulator *m*
sped [sped] *pret. i p.p. od* ***speed*** 2
speech [spiːtʃ] mowa *f*; przemówienie *n*, przemowa *f*; ***make a ~*** przemawiać ⟨-mówić⟩; '**~ day** *Brt.* (*w szkole*) *m* rozdania nagród; '**~·less** oniemiały; ***be ~less with*** oniemieć od (*G*)
speed [spiːd] **1.** prędkość *f*, szybkość *f*; *phot.* czułość *f*; *sl.* (*narkotyk amfetamina*) speed *m*; bieg *m* (*roweru itp.*); ***five-~ gearbox*** pięciobiegowa skrzynia *f* biegów; ***at a ~ of*** z prędkością (*G*); ***at full*** *lub* ***top ~*** z pełną prędkością; **2.** (***sped***) *v/i.* ⟨po⟩pędzić, ⟨po⟩mknąć; ***be ~ing*** *mot.* przekraczać ⟨-roczyć⟩ dozwoloną prędkość; ***~ up*** (*pret. i p.p.* ***speeded***) przyspieszać ⟨-szyć⟩; '**~·boat** *naut.* ślizgacz *m*; '**~·ing** *mot.* przekraczanie *n* właściwej prędkości; '**~ lim·it** *mot.* ograniczenie *n* prędkości
spee·do ['spiːdəʊ] *Brt. mot.* F licznik *m*, prędkościomierz *m*
speed·om·e·ter [spɪ'dɒmɪtə] *mot.* licznik *m*, prędkościomierz *m*
'**speed trap** pułapka *f* radarowa (*miejsce kontroli prędkości*)
'**speed·y** (***-ier, -iest***) prędki
spell[1] [spel] (***spelt*** *lub zwł. Am.* ***spelled***) *też* ***~ out*** ⟨prze⟩literować; ⟨na⟩pisać ortograficznie
spell[2] [spel] okres *m*; atak *m*; ***a ~ of fine weather*** okres *m* pięknej pogody; ***hot ~*** fala *f* upałów
spell[3] [spel] czar *m*, urok *m*; '**~·bound** zauroczony
'**spell|·er** *komp.* program *m* sprawdzania pisowni; ***be a good*** (***bad***) ***~er*** umieć (nie umieć) pisać ortograficznie; '**~·ing** pisownia *f*; '**~·ing mis·take** błąd *m* ortograficzny
spelt [spelt] *pret. i p.p. od* ***spell***[1]
spend [spend] (***spent***) *pieniądze* wydawać ⟨-dać⟩; *urlop itp.* spędzać ⟨-dzić⟩; '**~·ing** wydatki *pl.*; '**~·thrift** marnotrawca *m*
spent [spent] **1.** *pret. i p.p. od* ***spend***; **2.** *adj.* wyczerpany
sperm [spɜːm] sperma *f*, nasienie *n*; plemnik *m*
SPF [es piː 'ef] *skrót*: ***Sun Protection Factor*** faktor ochronny IP (*przed słońcem*)
sphere [sfɪə] kula *f*; *fig.* sfera *f*; **spher·i·cal** ['sferɪkl] kulisty, sferyczny
spice [spaɪs] **1.** przyprawa *f*; *fig.* pikanteria *f*; **2.** doprawiać ⟨-wić⟩, przyprawiać ⟨-wić⟩
spick-and-span [spɪkən'spæn] lśniący od czystości
spic·y ['spaɪsɪ] (***-ier, -iest***) doprawiony, przyprawiony; *fig.* pikantny
spi·der ['spaɪdə] *zo.* pająk *m*
spike [spaɪk] **1.** ostrze *n*; kolec *m*; szpic *m*; **~s** *pl.* (*w sporcie*) kolce *pl.*; **2.** wbijać ⟨wbić⟩ kolce
spill [spɪl] **1.** (***spilt*** *lub zwł. Am.* ***spilled***) *v/t.* rozlewać ⟨-lać⟩; ***~ the beans*** F wyśpiewać wszystko; → ***milk*** 1; *v/i.* rozlewać ⟨-lać⟩ się; *fig.* ogarniać ⟨-nąć⟩; **2.** F upadek *m*
spilt [spɪlt] *pret. i p.p. od* ***spill*** 1
spin [spɪn] **1.** (***-nn-***; spun) *v/t.* obracać ⟨-rócić⟩; *pranie* odwirowywać ⟨-ować⟩; *monetą* rzucać ⟨-cić⟩; *przędzę itp.* ⟨u⟩prząść; ***~ out*** *pracę* przeciągać ⟨-gnąć⟩; *pieniądze* oszczędzać ⟨-dzić⟩; *v/i.* obracać ⟨-rócić⟩ się; wirować; ⟨u⟩prząść; ***my head was ~ning*** kręciło mi się w głowie; ***~ along*** *mot.* F ⟨po⟩mknąć; ***~ round*** obracać ⟨-rócić⟩ się; **2.** wirowanie *n*; obrót *m*; (*w sporcie*) podkręcenie *n*; odwirowanie *n* (*prania*); *aviat.* korkociąg *m*; *mot.* F przejażdżka *f*; ***be in a*** (***flat***) ***~*** *zwł. Brt.* F wpadać ⟨wpaść⟩ w popłoch; ***go for a ~*** *mot.* F wyruszyć na przejażdżkę
spin·ach ['spɪnɪdʒ] *bot.* szpinak *m*; *attr.* szpinakowy
spin·al ['spaɪnl] *anat.* kręgowy; **~ 'col·umn** *anat.* kręgosłup *m*; **~ 'cord**, **~ 'mar·row** *anat.* rdzeń *m* kręgowy

S

spin·dle ['spɪndl] wrzeciono *n*
spin|-'dri·er wirówka *f*; **~-'dry** *pranie* ⟨od⟩wirować; **~-'dry·er** wirówka *f*
spine [spaɪn] *anat.* kręgosłup *m*; *zo.*, *bot.* kolec *m*; grzbiet *m* (*książki*)
'spin·ning| mill przędzalnia *f*; **'~ top** (*zabawka*) bąk *m*; **'~ wheel** kołowrotek *m*
spin·ster ['spɪnstə] stara panna *f*
spin·y ['spaɪnɪ] (**-*ier*, -*iest***) *zo.*, *bot.* kolczasty
spi·ral ['spaɪərəl] **1.** spiralny; **2.** spirala *f*; **~ 'stair·case** schody *pl.* kręte
spire ['spaɪə] iglica *f*, stromy hełm *m* (*na wieży*)
spir·it ['spɪrɪt] dusza *f*; duch *m*; nastrój *m*, humor *m*; zaangażowanie *n*, determinacja *f*; *chem.* spirytus *m*; *zw.* **~*s*** *pl.* napoje *pl.* alkoholowe; ***Holy*** **♀** Duch *m* Święty; **'~·ed** energiczny; zaangażowany; dynamiczny; *koń* ognisty; **'~·less** bez temperamentu
spir·its ['spɪrɪts] *pl.* nastrój *m*; ***be in high*** (***low***) **~** być w znakomitym (podłym) nastroju
spir·i·tu·al ['spɪrɪtʃʊəl] **1.** duchowy; **2.** *mus.* spirituals *pl.*
spit[1] [spɪt] **1.** (**-*tt-***; ***spat*** *lub zwł. Am.* ***spit***) pluć; spluwać ⟨-lunąć⟩; *ogień*: trzaskać ⟨-snąć⟩; *tłuszcz itp.*: ⟨za⟩skwierczeć; *też* **~ *out*** wypluwać ⟨-luć⟩; **~ *at s.o.*** opluwać ⟨-luć⟩ kogoś; ***it is ~ting*** (***with rain***) siąpi; **2.** plwocina *f*
spit[2] [spɪt] rożen *m*; *geogr.* cypel *m*
spite [spaɪt] **1.** złośliwość *f*; ***out of* ~** *lub* ***from pure* ~** z czystej złośliwości; ***in* ~ *of*** mimo, pomimo (*G*); **2.** *komuś* ⟨z⟩robić na złość; **'~·ful** złośliwy
spit·ting 'im·age: ***be the* ~ *of s.o.*** być kubek w kubek jak ktoś
spit·tle ['spɪtl] plwocina *f*, ślina *f*
splash [splæʃ] **1.** opryskiwać ⟨-kać⟩, ochlapywać ⟨-pać⟩; *dywan* zachlapać ⟨-pywać⟩; *wodę* rozbryzgiwać ⟨-gać⟩; chlapać się; **~ *down*** *statek kosmiczny* wodować; **2.** pochlapanie *n*, chlapnięcie *n*; plusk *m*, pluśnięcie *n*; plama *f*; rozbryzg *m* (*koloru*); *zwł. Brt.* dodatek *m* (*wody sodowej*); **'~·down** wodowanie *n* (*statku kosmicznego*)
splay [spleɪ] *też* **~ *out*** *palce itp.* rozpościerać ⟨-postrzeć⟩
spleen [spliːn] *anat.* śledziona *f*
splen|·did ['splendɪd] znakomity, wspaniały; doskonały; **'~·do(u)r** przepych *m*, świetność *f*
splice [splaɪs] *sznur* ⟨z-, po⟩łączyć, *taśmę fot. itp.* ⟨s⟩kleić
splint [splɪnt] *med.* szyna *f*, *zw.* łubki *pl.*; ***put in a* ~, *put in* ~** zakładać ⟨założyć⟩ szynę
splin·ter ['splɪntə] **1.** drzazga *f*, odprysk *m*, odłamek *m*; **2.** rozszczepiać ⟨-pić⟩; rozłupywać ⟨-pać⟩; **~ *off*** odseparowywać ⟨-ować⟩ się (***from*** od *G*)
split [splɪt] **1.** (**-*tt-***; ***split***) *v/t.* rozszczepiać ⟨-pić⟩ (*też phys.*), rozłupywać ⟨-pać⟩; *też* **~ *up*** ⟨po⟩dzielić (***into*** na *A*); **~ *hairs*** dzielić włos na czworo; **~ *one's sides*** F zrywać boki ze śmiechu; *v/i.* pękać ⟨-knąć⟩; rozszczepiać ⟨-pić⟩ się; *też* **~ *up*** ⟨po⟩dzielić się (***into*** na *A*); *też* **~ *up*** (***with***) rozstawać ⟨-tać⟩ się z (*I*); **2.** pęknięcie *n*, szczelina *f*; podział *m*; *fig.* rozłam *m*; **'~·ting** *ból*: rozsadzający
splut·ter ['splʌtə] krztusić się (*też mot.*); *płomień*: syczeć
spoil [spɔɪl] **1.** (***spoilt*** *lub* ***spoiled***) *v/t.* ⟨ze-, po⟩psuć; ⟨z⟩niszczyć; ⟨ze⟩psuć, rozpieszczać ⟨-pieścić⟩ (*też dziecko*); *v/i.* ⟨ze-, po⟩psuć się; ⟨z⟩niszczyć się; **2.** *zw.* **~*s*** *pl.* łupy *pl.*
'spoil·er *mot.* spoiler *m*
'spoil·sport F (*osoba psująca innym zabawę*)
spoilt [spɔɪlt] *pret. i p.p. od* ***spoil*** 1
spoke[1] [spəʊk] *pret. od* ***speak***
spoke[2] [spəʊk] szprycha *f*
spok·en ['spəʊkən] *p.p. od* ***speak***
spokes|·man ['spəʊksmən] (*pl.* **-*men***) rzecznik *m*; **'~·person** rzecznik *m* (*-niczka f*); **'~·wom·an** (*pl.* **-*women***) rzeczniczka *f*
sponge [spʌndʒ] **1.** gąbka *f* (*też zo.*); *fig.* pasożyt *m*; *Brt.* → ***sponge cake***; **2.** *v/t.* *też* **~ *down***, obmywać ⟨-myć⟩ (*gąbką*); **~ *off*, ~ *down*** zmywać ⟨-myć⟩; **~*up*** *płyn* zbierać ⟨zebrać⟩; *fig.* F ciągnąć (***from*, *off*, *on*** z *G*) (*zyski itp.*); **'~ cake** biszkopt *m*; **'spong·er** *fig.* pasożyt *m*; **'spong·y** (**-*ier*, -*iest***) gąbczasty
spon·sor ['spɒnsə] **1.** sponsor *m*; projektodawca *m* (*-czyni f*), inicjator(ka *f*) *m* (*ustawy itp.*); **2.** ⟨za⟩sponsorować, wspierać ⟨wesprzeć⟩ finansowo; *projekt itp.* ⟨za⟩inicjować
spon·ta·ne·ous [spɒn'teɪnjəs] spontaniczny; samoistny; samorzutny

S

spook [spuːk] F duch *m*, widmo *n*; '**~·y** (**-ier, -iest**) F niesamowity, widmowy
spool [spuːl] szpula *f*, rolka *f*
spoon [spuːn] **1.** łyżka *f*, łyżeczka *f*; **2.** nabierać ⟨-brać⟩ łyżką; '**~-feed** *dziecko* ⟨na⟩karmić łyżką *lub* łyżeczką; '**~·ful** (*ilość*) łyżka *f*, łyżeczka *f*
spo·rad·ic [spəˈrædɪk] (**-ally**) sporadyczny, jednostkowy
spore [spɔː] *bot.* spora *f*, zarodnik *m*
sport [spɔːt] **1.** sport *m*; F kumpel(ka *f*) *m*; **~s** *pl.* sport(y *pl.*) *m*; **2.** ⟨za⟩demonstrować, ⟨za⟩prezentować
sports [spɔːts] sportowy; '**~ car** samochód *m* sportowy; '**~ cen·tre** (*Am.* **center**) centrum *n* sportowe; '**~·man** (*pl.* **-men**) sportowiec *m*, zawodnik *m*; '**~·wear** odzież *f* sportowa; '**~·wom·an** (*pl.* **-women**) sportsmenka *f*; zawodniczka *f*
spot [spɒt] **1.** punkt *m*; plamka *f*, plama *f* (*też med., anat.*); cętka *f*, kropka *f*; skaza *f*, znamię *n*; miejsce *n*; spot *m* reklamowy; F reflektor *m* punktowy; **a ~ of** *Brt.* F trochę, nieco; **on the ~** na miejscu; od razu; w miejscu (*biec*); **be in a ~** F być w tarapatach; **soft ~** słabość *f* (**for** dla *G*); **tender ~** czułe miejsce *n*; **weak ~** słabe miejsce *n*; **2.** (**-tt-**) dostrzegać ⟨-rzec⟩, zauważać ⟨-żyć⟩; ⟨po-, s⟩plamić; **~ 'check** próba *f* losowa, kontrola *f* losowa; '**~·less** nieskazitelny (*też fig.*); '**~·light** reflektor *m* punktowy; '**~·ted** cętkowany, nakrapiany; plamiasty, nakrapiany; '**~·ter** obserwator *m*; '**~·ty** (**-ier, -iest**) krostowaty
spouse [spaʊz] małżonek *m*
spout [spaʊt] **1.** tryskać ⟨-snąć⟩ (**from** z *G*); *fig.* F chlustać ⟨-snąć⟩; **2.** dziobek *m*; struga *f* (*płynu*)
sprain [spreɪn] *med.* **1.** *nogę itp.* skręcić; **2.** skręcenie *n*
sprang [spræŋ] *pret. od* **spring** 1
sprat [spræt] *zo.* szprot *m*
sprawl [sprɔːl] rozciągać ⟨-gnąć⟩ się; (*też* **~ out**) rozwalać ⟨-lić⟩ się
spray [spreɪ] **1.** rozpylać ⟨-lić⟩, rozpryskiwać ⟨-kać⟩; opryskiwać ⟨-kać⟩; *włosy* ⟨s⟩pryskać (*lakierem*); **2.** pył *m* wodny; spray *m*; rozpylacz *m*; → **sprayer**; '**~ can** → '**~·er** pojemnik *m* ciśnieniowy, spray *m*, aerozol *m*
spread [spred] **1.** (**spread**) *v/t.* rozkładać ⟨-złożyć⟩; *ramiona itp.* rozpościerać ⟨-postrzeć⟩; *masło itp.* rozsmarowywać ⟨-ować⟩; *chleb itp.* ⟨po⟩smarować; *chorobę itp.* roznosić ⟨-nieść⟩; *wiadomość itp.* rozpowszechniać ⟨-nić⟩; *v/i.* rozciągać ⟨-gnąć⟩ się (*też* **~ out**); rozchodzić ⟨-zejść⟩ się; *wiadomość itp.* roznosić ⟨-nieść⟩ się; **2.** rozszerzanie *n* się; rozpiętość *f*; zasięg *m*; rozprzestrzenianie *n* się; pasta *f* (*do chleba*); *w gazecie* rozkładówka *f*; '**~·sheet** *komputer:* arkusz *m* kalkulacyjny
spree [spriː] F: **go** (**out**) **on a ~** wypuszczać ⟨-puścić⟩ się na balangę; **go on a buying** (*lub* **shopping, spending**) **~** kupować bez opamiętania
Spree Sprewa *f*
sprig [sprɪg] *bot.* gałązka *f*
spright·ly [ˈspraɪtlɪ] (**-ier, -iest**) *taniec:* skoczny; *starsza osoba:* żwawy, dziarski
spring [sprɪŋ] **1.** (**sprang** *lub Am.* **sprung, sprung**) *v/i.* skakać ⟨skoczyć⟩; **~ from** wynikać ⟨-knąć⟩ z (*G*); pojawiać ⟨-wić⟩ się; **~ up** *wiatr:* zrywać ⟨zerwać⟩ się; wyrastać ⟨-rosnąć⟩, zjawiać ⟨-wić⟩ się (*też fig.*); *v/t.* **~ a leak** zaczynać ⟨-cząć⟩ przeciekać; **~ a surprise on s.o.** zaskakiwać ⟨-skoczyć⟩ kogoś; **2.** wiosna *f*; źródło *n*; sprężyna *f*; sprężystość *f*; żwawość *f*; skok *m*; **in** (**the**) **~** na wiosnę, wiosną; '**~·board** trampolina *f*; odskocznia *f* (*też fig.*); **~-'clean** przeprowadzać ⟨-dzić⟩ gruntowne *lub* wiosenne porządki (w *L*); '**~-clean** *Brt.*, '**~-clean·ing** *Am.* gruntowne *lub* wiosenne porządki *pl.*; **~ 'tide**; '**~·time** wiosna *f*; **~·y** [ˈsprɪŋɪ] (**-ier, -iest**) elastyczny, sprężysty
sprin|·kle [ˈsprɪŋkl] **1.** *wodą* ⟨po⟩kropić, skrapiać ⟨-ropić⟩; *solą itp.* posypywać ⟨-pać⟩; **it is sprinkling** (*deszcz*) kropi; **2.** (*deszcz*) kapuśniaczek *m*; posypanie *n*; pokropienie *n*; '**~·kler** zraszacz *m*; *przeciwpożarowe* urządzenie *n* tryskaczowe; '**~·kling**: **a ~kling of** trochę (*G*), nieco (*G*)
sprint [sprɪnt] (*w sporcie*) **1.** ⟨po⟩biec sprintem; **2.** sprint *m*; '**~·er** (*w sporcie*) sprinter(ka *f*) *m*
sprite [spraɪt] duszek *m*; *fig.* chochlik *m*
sprout [spraʊt] **1.** ⟨wy⟩kiełkować; ⟨wy⟩rosnąć; **~ a beard** zapuszczać ⟨-puścić⟩ brodę; **2.** *bot.* kiełek *m*, pęd *m*; odrost *m*; (**Brussels**) **~s** *pl. bot.* brukselka *f*
spruce[1] [spruːs] *bot.* świerk *m*

S

spruce² [spruːs] wytworny
sprung [sprʌŋ] *pret. i p.p. od* **spring** 1
spry [spraɪ] *starsza osoba*: żwawy, dziarski
spun [spʌn] *pret. i p.p. od* **spin** 1
spur [spɜː] **1.** ostroga *f*; *fig.* bodziec *m*; ***on the ~ of the moment*** pod wpływem chwili; **2.** (**-rr-**) *konia* spinać ⟨spiąć⟩ ostrogami; *często* **~ on** *fig.* zachęcać ⟨-cić⟩
spurt¹ [spɜːt] **1.** ⟨po⟩mknąć; **2.** zryw *m*, przypływ *m* energii
spurt² [spɜːt] **1.** tryskać ⟨-snąć⟩ (***from*** z *G*); **2.** struga *f*, strumień *m* (*pary*)
sput·ter ['spʌtə] krztusić się (*też mot.*); *płomień*: syczeć
spy [spaɪ] **1.** szpieg *m*; **2.** szpiegować; **~ *into*** *fig.* wnikać ⟨-knąć⟩ w (*A*); **'~·hole** judasz *m*, wizjer *m*
Sq *skrót pisany*: ***Square*** pl., plac *m*
sq *skrót pisany*: ***square*** *kw.*, *kwadratowy*
squab·ble ['skwɒbl] ⟨po⟩spierać się
squad [skwɒd] grupa *f*; ekipa *f*; oddział *m* (*policji itp.*); **'~ car** *zwł. Am.* radiowóz *m*
squad·ron ['skwɒdrən] *mil.* szwadron *m*; *naut.* eskadra *f*; *aviat.* dywizjon *m*
squal·id ['skwɒlɪd] zapuszczony, zaniedbany; nędzny
squall [skwɔːl] szkwał *m*
squan·der ['skwɒndə] *pieniądze* ⟨z⟩marnotrawić; *szansę* zaprzepaszczać ⟨-paścić⟩
square [skweə] **1.** kwadrat *m*; czworokąt *m*; plac *m*, skwer *m*; *math.* kwadrat *m* (*liczby*); pole *n* (*szachownicy*); (*w krzyżówce*) kratka *f*; *tech.* kątownik *m*; **2.** kwadratowy; czworokątny; prostopadły; *math.* kwadratowy, do kwadratu; rzetelny; rozliczony; **be (*all*) ~** być kwita; **3.** nadawać ⟨-dać⟩ kwadratowy kształt; ustawiać ⟨-wić⟩ pod kątem prostym (*też* ***~ off, up***); ⟨po⟩kratkować (*też* ***~ off***); *math.* podnosić ⟨-nieść⟩ do kwadratu; *należności* uregulowywać ⟨-ować⟩, wyrównywać ⟨-nać⟩; *rachunki* uzgadniać ⟨-godnić⟩; ***~ with*** *fig.* pasować do (*G*), dopasowywać ⟨-ować⟩ do (*G*); wyjaśniać ⟨-nić⟩; ***~ up*** *v/i.* F rozliczać ⟨-czyć⟩ się; ***~ up to*** stawiać ⟨-wić⟩ czoło (*D*); **~d 'pa·per** kratkowany papier *m*; **~ 'root** *math.* pierwiastek *m* kwadratowy
squash¹ [skwɒʃ] **1.** ⟨z⟩miażdżyć, zgniatać ⟨zgnieść⟩; wtłaczać ⟨-łoczyć⟩ (się) (***into*** do *G*); ***~ flat*** zgniatać ⟨zgnieść⟩ na miazgę; **2.** ścisk *m*; (*w sporcie*) squash *m*; ***lemon*** *lub* ***orange ~*** sok *m* pitny cytrynowy *lub* pomarańczowy
squash² [skwɒʃ] *zwł. Am. bot.* kabaczek *m*
squat [skwɒt] **1.** (**-tt-**) kucać ⟨-cnąć⟩, przykucać ⟨-cnąć⟩ (*też* ***~ down***); *mieszkanie* zamieszkiwać ⟨-kać⟩ nielegalnie; **2.** krępy; **'~·ter** dziki lokator(ka *f*) *m*
squaw [skwɔː] squaw *f*
squawk [skwɔːk] **1.** ⟨za⟩skrzeczeć; F ⟨za⟩protestować (***about*** w sprawie *G*)
squeak [skwiːk] **1.** *mysz itp.*: ⟨za⟩piszczeć; *drzwi*: ⟨za⟩skrzypieć; **2.** pisk *m*; skrzypienie *n*; **'~·y** (***-ier, -iest***) *głos*: piskliwy; *drzwi*: skrzypiący
squeal [skwiːl] **1.** ⟨za⟩piszczeć (***with*** z *G*); ***~ on s.o.*** *sl.* donosić ⟨-nieść⟩ na kogoś; **2.** pisk *m*
squeam·ish ['skwiːmɪʃ] drażliwy, czuły
squeeze [skwiːz] **1.** ściskać ⟨-snąć⟩; wyciskać ⟨-snąć⟩; zgniatać ⟨-nieść⟩; wciskać ⟨-snąć⟩ (się) (***into*** do *G*); przepychać ⟨-pchnąć⟩ się; **2.** uścisk *m*, ściśnięcie *n*; odrobina *f* (*soku itp.*); ścisk *m*, tłok *m*; **'squeez·er** wyciskarka *f* do soku
squid [skwɪd] *zo.* (*pl.* ***squids, squid***) mątwa *f*, kałamarnica *f*, kalmar *m*
squint [skwɪnt] **1.** zezować; ⟨po⟩patrzeć przez zmrużone oczy; **2.** zez *m*
squirm [skwɜːm] wiercić się; zwijać się
squir·rel ['skwɪrəl] *zo.* wiewiórka *f*
squirt [skwɜːt] **1.** strzykać ⟨-knąć⟩; tryskać ⟨-snąć⟩; **2.** strzyknięcie *n*; tryśnięcie *n*
Sr → ***Snr***
SS ['es es] *skrót*: ***steamship*** SS, statek *m* parowy
St *skrót pisany*: ***Saint ...*** św. ..., święty ... *m* (-ta *f*); ***Street*** ul., ulica *f*
st *skrót pisany*: ***stone*** *Brt.* (*jednostka masy = 6,35 kg*)
Sta *skrót pisany*: ***Station*** st., stacja *f* (*zwł. na mapach*)
stab [stæb] **1.** (***-bb-***) *v/t.* pchnąć (*nożem itp.*); dźgać ⟨dźgnąć⟩; ***be ~bed in the arm*** otrzymać pchnięcie w ramię; *v/i.* dźgać ⟨dźgnąć⟩; **2.** pchnięcie *n*; dźgnięcie *n*
sta·bil|·i·ty [stə'bɪlətɪ] stabilizacja *f*;

ustabilizowanie *n*; **~·ize** ['steıbəlaız] ⟨u⟩stabilizować (się)
sta·ble[1] ['steıbl] ustabilizowany; stały
sta·ble[2] ['steıbl] stajnia *f*
stack [stæk] **1.** stos *m*, sterta *f*; **~s of, a ~ of** F kupa (*roboty itp.*); → **haystack**; **2.** układać ⟨ułożyć⟩ w stos; zastawiać ⟨-wić⟩; **~ up** *zwł. Am.* porównywać
sta·di·um ['steıdjəm] (*w sporcie*) stadion *m*
staff [stɑːf] **1.** personel *m*, pracownicy *pl.*; (*w szkole*) grono *n* pedagogiczne, nauczyciele *pl.*; *mil.* sztab *m*; kij *m*, laska *f*; **2.** obsadzać ⟨-dzić⟩ (*personelem*); '**~ room** pokój *m* nauczycielski
stag [stæg] *zo.* (*pl.* **stags, stag**) jeleń *m*
stage [steıdʒ] **1.** *theat.* scena *f* (*też fig.*); podium *n*; stadium *n*; etap *m* (*też fig.*); odcinek *m* (*podróży*); *Brt. biletowa* strefa *f*; *tech.* człon *m* (*rakiety*); **2.** *theat.* ⟨za⟩inscenizować, wystawiać ⟨-wić⟩; ⟨z⟩organizować; '**~·coach** *hist.* dyliżans *m*; '**~ di·rec·tion**; '**~ fright** trema *f*; '**~ man·ag·er** inspicjent *m*
stag·ger ['stægə] **1.** *v/i.* zataczać ⟨-toczyć⟩ się (**towards** w stronę *G*); iść ⟨pójść⟩ zataczając się; *v/t.* wstrząsać ⟨-snąć⟩; zamykać ⟨-mknąć⟩ usta; **~ imagination** przerastać ⟨-rosnąć⟩ wyobraźnię; *czas pracy* układać ⟨ułożyć⟩ przemiennie
stag|·nant ['stægnənt] *woda*: stojący; *zwł. econ.* (będący) w zastoju; **~·nate** *zwł. econ.* [stæg'neıt] trwać w stagnacji
stain [steın] **1.** *v/t.* ⟨po⟩plamić; ⟨za⟩barwić, ⟨za⟩farbować; *drewno itp.* ⟨za⟩bejcować; *v/i.* ulegać ⟨-lec⟩ zaplamieniu; **2.** plama *f* (*też fig.*); zabarwienie *n*, zafarbowanie *n*; bejca *f*; **~ed 'glass** szkło *n* witrażowe; **~ed glass 'window** witraż *m*; '**~·less** nierdzewny
stair [steə] stopień *m*; **~s** *pl.* schody *pl.*; '**~·case**, '**~·way** klatka *f* schodowa
stake[1] [steık] **1.** pal *m*, słup *m*; *hist.* stos *m*, słup męczeński; **2. ~ off, ~ out** ogradzać ⟨-rodzić⟩
stake[2] [steık] **1.** udział *m* (**in** w *L*) (*też econ.*); stawka *f*; **be at ~** *fig.* wchodzić w grę; **2.** *pieniądze itp.* stawiać ⟨postawić⟩ (**on** na *A*); *pieniądze, reputację itp.* ⟨za⟩ryzykować
stale [steıl] (**-r, -st**) *chleb*: czerstwy; *jedzenie*: nieświeży; *piwo*: zwietrzały; *powietrze*: stęchły
stalk[1] [stɔːk] *bot.* łodyga *f*
stalk[2] [stɔːk] *v/t.* ⟨wy⟩tropić, ⟨wy⟩śledzić; *v/i.* kroczyć, stąpać
stall[1] [stɔːl] **1.** stragan *m*, stoisko *n*; (*w stajni*) boks *m*; **~s** *rel. pl.* stalle *pl.*; *Brt. theat.* parter *m*; **2.** *v/t. silnik* ⟨s⟩powodować zgaśnięcie; *v/i.* zgasnąć
stall[2] [stɔːl] *v/i.* zwlekać ⟨-lec⟩; *v/t. kogoś* wstrzymywać ⟨-mać⟩; zwodzić ⟨zwieść⟩
stal·li·on ['stæljən] *zo.* ogier *m*
stal·wart ['stɔːlwət] wierny, oddany
stam·i·na ['stæmınə] wytrwałość *f*, hart *m*
stam·mer ['stæmə] **1.** jąkać się; **2.** jąkanie *n* się
stamp [stæmp] **1.** *v/i.* tupać; nadeptywać ⟨-pnąć⟩; *v/t.* ⟨o⟩stemplować, ⟨przy-, o⟩pieczętować; naklejać ⟨-leić⟩ znaczek na (*A*) (*list*); *fig. kogoś* określać ⟨-lić⟩ (**as** jako *A*); **~ out** ogień ⟨s⟩tłumić; *tech.* ⟨wy⟩tłoczyć; **2.** znaczek *m* (*na list*); stempel *m*, pieczątka *f*; **~ed (addressed) envelope** zaadresowana koperta z naklejonym znaczkiem
stam·pede [stæm'piːd] **1.** popłoch *m*, panika *f*; paniczna ucieczka *f* (*zwierząt*); gonitwa *f*, pogoń *f* (**for** za *I*); **2.** ⟨s⟩płoszyć (się)
stanch [stɑːntʃ] *Am.* → **staunch**
stand [stænd] **1.** (**stood**) *v/i.* stać; wstawać ⟨wstać⟩; *wartość*: utrzymywać się; *fig.* pozostawać ⟨-stać⟩ w mocy *lub* ważnym; **~ still** stać bez ruchu; *v/t.* stawiać ⟨postawić⟩ (**on** na *L*); znosić ⟨znieść⟩; *test* wytrzymywać ⟨-mać⟩; *szansę itp.* mieć; *drinka itp.* stawiać ⟨postawić⟩ (*D*); *sprawy*: wyglądać, przedstawiać się; **I can't ~ him** nie mogę go znieść; **~ aside** odchodzić ⟨odejść⟩ na bok; **~ back** cofać ⟨-fnąć⟩ się; **~ by** stać bezczynnie; *fig.* stać przy *kimś*; dotrzymywać ⟨-mać⟩ (*obietnicy itp.*); stać w pogotowiu; **~ down** ustępować ⟨-tąpić⟩ (*ze stanowiska*); **~ for** oznaczać; znosić ⟨znieść⟩; reprezentować; *zwł. Brt.* kandydować na (*A*); **~ in** zastępować ⟨-tąpić⟩; **~ out** rzucać się w oczy, odznaczać się; wyróżniać się (**against** wśród *G*); **~ over** stać nad (*I*); **~ together** trzymać się razem; **~ up** wstawać ⟨-tać⟩, powstawać ⟨-tać⟩; **~ up for** ⟨o⟩bronić, popierać ⟨poprzeć⟩; **~ up to** przeciwstawiać ⟨-wić⟩ się; stawiać *komuś* czoło; **2.** stoisko *n*, stragan *m*; stojak *m*, podstaw-

S

ka *f*; (*w sporcie*) trybuna *f*; postój *m* (*taksówek*); *Am. jur.* miejsce *n* dla świadka; ***take a ~*** *fig.* zajmować ⟨-jąć⟩ stanowisko

stan·dard[1] ['stændəd] **1.** standard *m*; norma *f*; miara *f*; ***~ of living, living ~*** poziom *m* życia, stopa *f* życiowa; **2.** standardowy. normalny; typowy

stan·dard[2] ['stændəd] sztandar *m*

stan·dard·ize ['stændədaɪz] standaryzować, ujednolicać ⟨-cić⟩

'stan·dard lamp *Brt.* lampa *f* stojąca

'stand|·by 1. (*pl.* ***-bys***) rezerwa *f*; *aviat.* stand-by (*tańszy bilet tuż przed wyjazdem*); ***be on ~by*** być w pogotowiu; **2.** rezerwowy; awaryjny; *aviat.* stand-by; **'~-in** (*w filmie*, *telewizjii*) dubler(ka *f*) *m*; zastępca *m* (-czyni *f*)

stand·ing ['stændɪŋ] **1.** stojący; *fig.* stały; → ***ovation***; **2.** pozycja *f*, ranga *f*; ***of long ~*** znany od dawna; długotrwały; **~ 'or·der** *econ.* zamówienie *n* stałe; **'~ room**: ***~ room only*** brak miejsc siedzących

stand|·off·ish [stænd'ɒfɪʃ] F oficjalny, sztywny; **'~·point** *fig.* punkt *m* widzenia; **'~·still** bezruch *m*; ***be at a ~still*** nie ruszać się; *produkcja*: być w zastoju; ***bring to a ~still*** *auto* zatrzymywać; doprowadzać produkcję do zastoju; **'~-up** *posiłek*: na stojąco

stank [stæŋk] *pret. of* ***stink***

stan·za ['stænzə] strofa *f*, zwrotka *f*

sta·ple[1] ['steɪpl] **1.** główny typ pożywienia; główny produkt *m*; **2.** główny

sta·ple[2] ['steɪpl] **1.** zszywka *f*; **2.** zszywać⟨zszyć⟩; **'~r** zszywacz *m* (*do papieru*)

star [stɑː] **1.** gwiazda *f*; *print.* gwiazdka *f*; (*w filmie*, *telewizji*, *sporcie*) gwiazda *f*; **2.** (***-rr-***) *v/t.* oznaczać ⟨-czyć⟩ gwiazdką; ***~ring ...*** w roli głównej występuje ...; ***a film ~ring ...*** film z ... w roli głównej; *v/i.* grać rolę główną (***in*** w *L*)

star·board ['stɑːbəd] *naut.* (*prawa strona*) sterburta *f*

starch [stɑːtʃ] **1.** krochmal *m*; skrobia *f*; **2.** *pranie* ⟨na⟩krochmalić

stare [steə] **1.** wpatrywać ⟨-trzyć⟩ się (***at*** w *A*); gapić się (***at*** w *A*); **2.** *uporczywe* spojrzenie *n*

stark [stɑːk] **1.** *adj.* surowy; ponury; ***be in ~ contrast to*** różnić się krańcowo od (*G*); **2.** *adv.* F ***~ naked*** całkiem goły; ***~ raving mad*** zupełnie stuknięty

'star·light światło *n* gwiazd

star·ling ['stɑːlɪŋ] *zo.* szpak *m*

star·lit ['stɑːlɪt] rozświetlony gwiazdami

star·ry ['stɑːrɪ] (***-ier, -iest***) gwiaździsty, rozgwieżdżony; **~-'eyed** F naiwny

Stars and 'Stripes *flaga USA*

Star-Span·gled Ban·ner [stɑː-spæŋgld 'bænə] (*hymn narodowy USA*)

start [stɑːt] **1.** *v/i.* zaczynać ⟨-cząć⟩ (też ***~ off***); rozpoczynać ⟨-cząć⟩; wyruszać ⟨-szyć⟩ (***for*** do *G*) (*też* ***~ off, ~ out***); *autobus itp.*: odjeżdżać ⟨-jechać⟩, *statek*: odpływać ⟨-łynąć⟩; *aviat.* ⟨wy⟩startować; *silnik*: zaskoczyć; *maszynę* uruchamiać ⟨-chomić⟩ się; (*w sporcie*) ⟨wy-⟩startować; wzdrygać ⟨-gnąć⟩ się (***at*** z powodu *G*); ***to ~ with*** na początek; najpierw; ***~ from scratch*** zaczynać ⟨-cząć⟩ od zera; *v/t.* zaczynać ⟨-cząć⟩ (też ***~ off***); rozpoczynać ⟨-cząć⟩; *silnik*, *maszynę* uruchamiać ⟨-chomić⟩; *firmę* zakładać ⟨założyć⟩; *produkcję* uruchamiać ⟨-chomić⟩; **2.** początek *m*; (*zwł. sport*, *aviat.*) start *m*; odjazd *m*, odpłynięcie *n*; wzdrygnięcie *n* się; przewaga *f* (***on, over*** nad *I*); ***at the ~*** na początku; *sport*: na starcie; ***for a ~*** na początek, najpierw; ***from ~ to finish*** od początku do końca; **'~·er** (*w sporcie*) starter *m*; *mot.* rozrusznik *m*, starter *m*; zawodnik *m* (-niczka *f*); *zwł. Brt.* przystawka *f* (*do posiłku*); ***for ~s*** F na dobry początek

start·le ['stɑːtl] *kogoś* zaskakiwać ⟨-koczyć⟩, wystraszać ⟨-szyć⟩

starv|·a·tion [stɑː'veɪʃn] głód *n*; ***die of ~ation*** umrzeć z głodu; ***~ation diet*** F dieta *f* zerowa; **~e** [stɑːv] *v/i.* głodować; ***~e (to death)*** zagłodzić się; ***I'm starving!*** *Brt.*, ***I'm ~ed!*** umieram z głodu!; *v/t.* ⟨za⟩głodzić

state [steɪt] **1.** stan *m* (*też pol.*); państwo *n*; ***be in a ~*** być zdenerwowanym; **2.** państwowy; stanowy; **3.** określać ⟨-lić⟩; stwierdzać ⟨-dzić⟩; **'♀ De·part·ment** *Am. pol.* Departament *m* Stanu, Ministerstwo *n* Spraw Zagranicznych; **'~·ly** (***-ier, -iest***) uroczysty; majestatyczny, wyniosły; **'~·ment** stwierdzenie *n*; określenie *n*; *jur.* oświadczenie *n*; *econ.* wyciąg *m* (*z konta*); ***make a ~ment*** oświadczać ⟨-czyć⟩; **~-of-the-'art** *adj.* nowoczesny; **'~·room** *naut.* *luksusowa* kabina *f* jednoosobowa;

'~·**side** *Am.* F w Stanach, do Stanów; ~**s·man** *pol.* ['steɪtsmən] (*pl.* ***-men***) mąż *m* stanu
stat·ic ['stætɪk] (~***ally***) statyczny
sta·tion ['steɪʃn] **1.** *badawcza, benzynowa* stacja *f*; *autobusowy* dworzec *m*; remiza *f* (*straży pożarnej*); komisariat *m*; *pol.* lokal *m* wyborczy; **2.** *wojsko*: stacjonować; *posterunki* ustawiać ⟨-wić⟩
sta·tion·a·ry ['steɪʃnərɪ] stacjonarny
sta·tion·er ['steɪʃnə] sprzedawca *m* (-czyni *f*) artykułów piśmiennych; '~'**s (shop)** sklep *m* z artykułami piśmiennymi; ~·**y** ['steɪʃnərɪ] artykuły *pl.* piśmienne
'**sta·tion**|·**mas·ter** *rail.* naczelnik *m* stacji; '~ **wag·on** *Am. mot.* kombi *n*
sta·tis|**ti·cal** [stə'tɪstɪkəl] statystyczny; ~·**tics** [stə'tɪstɪks] *pl. i sg.* statystyka *f*
stat·ue ['stætʃuː] pomnik *m*, posąg *m*
sta·tus ['steɪtəs] status *m*; pozycja *f*; stan *m*; stan *m* cywilny; '~ **line** *komp.* wiersz *m* stanu
stat·ute ['stætjuːt] ustawa *f*; ~***s*** *pl.* statut *m*
staunch[1] [stɔːntʃ] lojalny, oddany
staunch[2] [stɔːntʃ] *krwotok* ⟨za⟩tamować
stay [steɪ] **1.** pozostawać ⟨-tać⟩; przebywać (***at*** w *L*, ***with*** u *G*); ~ ***away*** trzymać się z daleka (***from*** od *G*); ~ ***put*** F pozostawać na miejscu; ~ ***up*** nie kłaść się (*spać*); **2.** pobyt *m*; *jur.* odroczenie *n*
stead·fast ['stedfɑːst] *przyjaciel*: oddany; *wzrok*: nieruchomy
stead·y ['stedɪ] **1.** *adj.* (***-ier, -iest***) stały; niezmienny; regularny; solidny; *ręka*: pewny; *nerwy*: dobry; **2.** ⟨u⟩stabilizować (się); wyrównywać ⟨-nać⟩; *nerwy* uspokajać ⟨-koić⟩; **3.** *int. też* ~ ***on!*** *Brt.* F uwaga!; **4.** *adv. Am.*: ***go*** ~ ***with s.o.*** chodzić z kimś na poważnie; **5.** *Am.* stały chłopak *m*, stała dziewczyna *f*
steak [steɪk] stek *m*, zraz *m*; filet *m*
steal [stiːl] (***stole, stolen***) ⟨u⟩kraść (*też fig.*); skradać się; wymykać ⟨-mknąć⟩ się (***out of*** z *G*)
stealth [stelθ]: ***by*** ~ ukradkiem; '~·**y** (***-ier, -iest***) ukradkowy
steam [stiːm] **1.** para *f* (*wodna*); *attr.* parowy; ***let off*** ~ spuszczać ⟨spuścić⟩ parę; *fig.* ulżyć sobie; **2.** *v/i.* parować; ~ ***up*** *szkło*: zaparować się; *v/t. gastr.* ⟨u⟩gotować na parze; '~·**boat** *naut.* łódź *m* parowa; '~·**er** *naut.* parowiec *m*; szybkowar *m*; '~·**ship** *naut.* parowiec *m*
steel [stiːl] **1.** stal *f*; *attr.* stalowy; **2.** ~ ***o.s. for*** przygotować się na (*A*); '~·**works** *sg.* stalownia *f*
steep[1] [stiːp] stromy; *wzrost*: ostry, gwałtowny; F *cena*: nadmierny
steep[2] [stiːp] *pranie* namaczać ⟨-moczyć⟩ (***in*** w *L*); zanurzać ⟨-rzyć⟩ (***in*** w *L*)
stee·ple ['stiːpl] wieża *f* kościelna; '~·**chase** (*w sportach konnych*) steeplechase *m* (*wyścig z przeszkodami*); (*w lekkiej atletyce*) steeplechase *m* (*bieg z przeszkodami*)
steer[1] [stɪə] *zo. młody* wół *m*
steer[2] [stɪə] ⟨po⟩sterować, ⟨po⟩kierować; ~·**ing col·umn** *mot.* ['stɪərɪŋkɒləm] kolumna *f* kierownicy; ~·**ing wheel** ['stɪərɪŋwiːl] *mot.* koło *n* kierownicy; *naut. też* koło *n* sterowe
stein [staɪn] kufel *m*
stem [stem] **1.** *bot.* łodyga *f*; ogonek *m*; nóżka *f* (*kieliszka*); *ling.* rdzeń *m*; **2.** (***-mm-***): ~ ***from*** wynikać ⟨-knąć⟩ z (*G*)
stench [stentʃ] odór *m*, smród *m*
sten·cil ['stensl] szablon *m*; *print.* matryca *f*
ste·nog·ra·pher [ste'nɒgrəfə] *Am.* stenograf(ka *f*) *m*
step [step] **1.** krok *m* (*też fig.*); stopień *m*; (***a pair of***) ~***s*** *pl.* składana drabina *f*; ***mind the*** ~***!*** uwaga na stopień!; ~ ***by*** ~ krok za krokiem; ***take*** ~***s*** podejmować ⟨-djąć⟩ kroki; **2.** (***-pp-***) iść ⟨pójść⟩; następować ⟨-tąpić⟩ (***on*** na *A*); wdeptywać ⟨-pnąć⟩ (***in*** w *A*); ~ ***on it***, ~ ***on the gas*** *mot.* F dodaj gazu!; ~ ***aside*** odstępować ⟨-tąpić⟩; *fig.* ustępować ⟨-tąpić⟩ miejsca; ~ ***down*** schodzić ⟨zejść⟩; *fig.* ustępować ⟨-tąpić⟩ miejsca; ~ ***up*** *produkcję* zwiększać ⟨-szyć⟩
'**step·broth·er** brat *m* przyrodni
step-by-'step *fig.* stopniowo
'**step·daugh·ter** pasierbica *f*
'**step·fa·ther** ojczym *m*
'**step·lad·der** składana drabina *f*
'**step·moth·er** macocha *f*
'**step·sis·ter** siostra *f* przyrodnia
'**step·son** pasierb *m*
steppe [steps] *geogr.* step *m*
step·ping-stone *fig.* ['stepɪŋstəʊn] odskocznia *f*
ster·e·o ['sterɪəʊ] (*pl.* ***-os***) stereo *n*; zestaw *m* stereo; sprzęt *m* elektronicz-

S

ny; *attr.* stereo; '~ **sys•tem** *Am. mus.* zestaw *m* stereo

ster•ile ['steraɪl] sterylny (*też fig.*); wyjałowiony; niepłodny, bezpłodny; *fig.* jałowy; **ste•ril•i•ty** [ste'rɪlətɪ] sterylność *f*; jałowość *f*; bezpłodność *f*; **ster•il•ize** ['sterəlaɪz] ⟨wy⟩sterylizować

ster•ling ['stɜːlɪŋ] funt *m* szterling

stern¹ [stɜːn] surowy

stern² [stɜːn] *naut.* rufa *f*

stew [stjuː] *gastr.* **1.** *mięso itp.* ⟨u⟩dusić, *owoce* ⟨u⟩gotować; ~***ed apples*** kompot *m* z jabłek; **2.** potrawka *f*; ***be in a*** ~ być w tarapatach

stew•ard [stjʊəd] *naut.*, *aviat.* steward *m*; gospodarz *m* (*imprezy*); ~**•ess** ['stjʊədɪs] *naut.*, *aviat.* stewardesa *f*

stick¹ [stɪk] patyk *m*; kij *m* (*też do hokeja itp.*); laska *f*; *aviat.* drążek *m* sterowy; laska *f* (*warzywa, dynamitu itp.*); kredka *f* (*do ust*)

stick² [stɪk] (***stuck***) *v/t.* wbijać ⟨wbić⟩ (***into*** w *A*); przebijać ⟨-bić⟩; przyklejać ⟨-kleić⟩ (***on*** do *G*); sklejać ⟨skleić⟩ (***with*** z *I*); F wtykać ⟨wetknąć⟩; ***I can't*** ~ ***him*** *zwł. Brt.* F nie mogę go znieść; *v/i.* przywierać ⟨-wrzeć⟩ (***to*** do *G*); przyklejać ⟨-leić⟩ się (***to*** do *G*); utykać ⟨utknąć⟩, ⟨u⟩więznąć; ~ ***at nothing*** nie cofać ⟨-fnąć⟩ się przed niczym; ~ ***by*** F trwać przy (*L*); stosować się do (*G*); ~ ***out*** wystawać; *język itp.* wysuwać ⟨-nąć⟩; przetrwać *coś*; ~ ***to*** trwać przy (*L*); '~**•er** naklejka *f*; ~**•ing plas•ter** *Brt.* przylepiec *m*; '~**•y** (***-ier, -iest***) lepki; kleisty (***with*** od *G*); F *położenie itp.*: niezręczny

stiff [stɪf] **1.** *adj.* sztywny; F *alkohol, lekarstwo*: mocny; *zadanie*: trudny, ciężki; *konkurencja*: silny; *wyrok*: surowy; *opór*: twardy; F *cena*: wygórowany; ***keep a*** ~ ***upper lip*** *fig.* nie okazywać ⟨-zać⟩ emocji; **2.** *adv.* bardzo; ***be bored*** ~ F być śmiertelnie znudzonym; ***frozen*** ~ zamarznięty na kość; **3.** *sl.* truposz *m*; ~**•en** ['stɪfn] *coś* usztywniać ⟨-nić⟩; ⟨ze⟩sztywnieć; *fig.* wzmacniać ⟨-mocnić⟩ (się)

sti•fle ['staɪfl] dusić (się); *fig.* ⟨s⟩tłumić

stile [staɪl] przełaz *m*

sti•let•to [stɪ'letəʊ] (*pl.* ***-tos***) sztylet *m*; ~ **'heels** *pl.* szpilki *pl.* (*buty, też obcasy*)

still¹ [stɪl] **1.** *adv.* wciąż, jeszcze; ~ ***higher*** jeszcze wyższy; **2.** *cj.* jednak, mimo to

still² [stɪl] **1.** *adj.* spokojny; nieruchomy; cichy; *napój*: niegazowany; **2.** fotos *m*; '~**•born** *płód n*: martwo urodzony; ~ **'life** (*pl.* ***- lifes***) martwa natura *f*

stilt [stɪlt] szczudło *n*; pal *m*; '~**•ed** *styl*: zmanierowany

stim•u|•lant ['stɪmjʊlənt] *med.* środek *m* stymulujący *lub* pobudzający; używka *f*; impuls *m*, bodziec *m* (***to*** do *G*); ~**•late** ['stɪmjʊleɪt] *med.* stymulować (*też fig.*); pobudzać ⟨-dzić⟩; ~**•lus** ['stɪmjʊləs] (*pl.* ***-li*** [-laɪ]) bodziec *m* (*też fig.*); *fig.* zachęta *f* (***for*** do *G*)

sting [stɪŋ] **1.** (***stung***) *v/t.* ⟨u⟩ciąć, ⟨u⟩kłuć, ⟨u⟩kąsić; *pszczoła itp.*: ⟨u⟩żądlić; piec w (*A*); F oszukać, naciągnąć; *fig.* dotykać ⟨-tknąć⟩; *v/i.* ⟨za⟩piec, szczypać; *roślina itp.*: parzyć; **2.** żądło *n*; włosek *m* parzący (*rośliny*); oparzenie *n*; użądlenie *n*; ukąszenie *n*; pieczenie *n*, szczypanie *n*

stin•gy ['stɪndʒɪ] F (***-ier, -iest***) *osoba*: chciwy; *posiłek*: lichy, nędzny

stink [stɪŋk] **1.** (***stank*** *lub* ***stunk, stunk***) śmierdzieć, cuchnąć; **2.** smród *m*

stint [stɪnt]: ~ ***o.s.*** (***of s.th.***) odmawiać sobie (*G*); ~ (***on***) ***s.th.*** skąpić (*G*)

stip•u|•late ['stɪpjʊleɪt] postanawiać ⟨-nowić⟩; przewidywać ⟨-dzieć⟩; ~**•la•tion** [stɪpjʊ'leɪʃn] postanowienie *n*; warunek *m*

stir [stɜː] **1.** (***-rr-***) *v/t.* ⟨po-, za⟩mieszać; poruszać ⟨-szyć⟩ (*też fig.*); *fig.* wywoływać ⟨-łać⟩; ~ ***up*** *kłopoty itp.* wywoływać ⟨-łać⟩; *kogoś* poruszać ⟨-szyć⟩; *v/i.* ruszać się (*z domu itp.*); ⟨po⟩ruszać się (*we śnie*); **2.** ***give s.th. a*** ~ zamieszać coś; ***cause a*** ~, ***create a*** ~ wywoływać ⟨-łać⟩ poruszenie

stir•rup ['stɪrəp] strzemię *n*

stitch [stɪtʃ] **1.** *szycie*: ścieg *m*; *wydziergane* oczko *n*; *med.* szew *m*; kolka *f* (*w boku*); **2.** zszywać ⟨-szyć⟩, przyszywać ⟨-szyć⟩ (***on*** do *G*); ~ ***up*** *fig.* dopinać na ostatni guzik

stock [stɒk] **1.** zapas *m*; zasób *m*; *gastr.* bulion *m*, wywar *m*; *też* ***live*** ~ inwentarz *m* żywy; kolba *f* (*karabinu*); *fig.* ród *m*; *zwł. Am. econ.* akcja *f*; ~***s*** *pl. econ.* papiery *pl.* wartościowe; ***have s.th. in*** ~ *econ.* mieć coś na stanie; ***take*** ~ *econ.* przeprowadzać ⟨-dzić⟩ spis *lub* inwentaryzację; ***take*** ~ ***of*** *fig.* oceniać ⟨-nić⟩ (*G*); **2.** *econ.* *towar* mieć na składzie, prowadzić; **~ up** zaopatrywać ⟨-trzyć⟩ się (**on, with** w *A*); **3.** *wyrażenie itp.*: oklepany, wyświechtany; seryjny; *rozmiar itp.*: standardowy; '**~·breed·er** hodowca *m* bydła; '**~·brok·er** *econ.* broker *m*, makler *m*; '**~ ex·change** *econ.* giełda *f* pieniężna; '**~·hold·er** *zwł. Am. econ.* akcjonariusz(ka *f*) *m*

Stock·holm Sztokholm *m*

stock·ing ['stɒkɪŋ] pończocha *f*

'**stock| mar·ket** *econ.* giełda *f* walorów; '**~·pile 1.** zapas *m*; **2.** ⟨z⟩gromadzić zapasy (*G*); **~-'still** bez ruchu; '**~·tak·ing** *econ.* inwentaryzacja *f*, spis *m*; *fig.* ocena *f*

stock·y ['stɒkɪ] (**-ier, -iest**) przysadzisty

stole [stəʊl] *pret. od* **steal**; **sto·len** ['stəʊlən] *p.p. od* **steal**

stol·id ['stɒlɪd] bezwolny, bierny

stom·ach ['stʌmək] **1.** żołądek *m*; *fig.* apetyt *m* (**for** na *A*); **2.** ⟨s⟩trawić (*też fig.*); '**~·ache** ból *m* brzucha; '**~ up·set** rozstrój *m* żołądkowy

stone [stəʊn] **1.** kamień *m* (*też med.*); *bot.* pestka *f*; kulka *f* (*gradu*); (*pl.* **stone(s)**; skrót: **st**) *Brt.* jednostka wagi (= *6,35 kg*); **2.** ⟨u⟩kamienować; ⟨ob⟩rzucać kamieniami; usuwać ⟨usunąć⟩ pestki z (*G*); **~-'dead** martwy na amen; **~-'deaf** głuchy jak pień; '**~·ma·son** kamieniarz *m*; '**~·ware** naczynia *pl.* z kamionki

ston·y ['stəʊnɪ] (**-ier, -iest**) kamienny (*też fig.*); *fig. spojrzenie itp.*: niewzruszony

stood [stʊd] *pret. i p.p. od* **stand** 1

stool [stuːl] stołek *m*, taboret *m*; *med.* stolec *m*; '**~·pi·geon** F szpicel *m*

stoop [stuːp] **1.** *v/i.* schylać ⟨-lić⟩ się (*też* **~ down**); ⟨z⟩garbić się; **~ to** *fig.* posuwać ⟨-sunąć⟩ się do (*G*), nie cofać ⟨-fnąć⟩ się przed (*I*); **2.** garbienie *n* się

stop [stɒp] **1.** (**-pp-**) *v/i.* zatrzymywać ⟨-mać⟩ się; stawać ⟨stanąć⟩ (*też zegar*); przerywać ⟨-rwać⟩; *Brt.* pozostawać ⟨-tać⟩; **~ dead** zatrzymywać ⟨-mać⟩ się jak wryty; **~ at nothing** nie cofać ⟨-fnąć⟩ się przed niczym; **~ short of doing, ~ short at s.th.** powstrzymywać ⟨-mać⟩ się przed (*I*); *v/t.* zatrzymywać ⟨-mać⟩; powstrzymywać ⟨-mać⟩ (**from** przed *I*); przerywać ⟨-rwać⟩; *krwawienie* ⟨za⟩tamować; *rurę* zatykać ⟨-tknąć⟩ (*też* **~ up**); *dziurę* wypełniać ⟨-nić⟩; *wypłatę itp.* wstrzymywać ⟨-mać⟩; **~ by** wpadać ⟨wpaść⟩ (*z wizytą*); **~ in** wpadać ⟨wpaść⟩ (**at** do *G*) (*z wizytą*); **~ off** F zatrzymywać ⟨-mać⟩ się; **~ over** przerywać ⟨-rwać⟩ podróż; **2.** postój *m*; przystanek *m* (*autobusu*); *phot.* otwór *m* przesłony; *zw.* **full ~** kropka *f*; '**~·gap** rozwiązanie *n* tymczasowe; *attr.* tymczasowy, prowizoryczny; '**~·light** *mot.* światło *n* stopu; *zwł. Am. zw.* **~lights** *pl.* światła *pl.* sygnalizacyjne; '**~·o·ver** przerwa *f* w podróży; *aviat.* lądowanie *n* pośrednie; **~·page** ['stɒpɪdʒ] zatrzymanie *n* (*pracy itp.*), wstrzymanie *n*; przerwa *f*, postój *m*; *zwł. Brt.* potrącenie *n* (*z pensji*); blokada *f*, zatkanie *n*; '**~·per** zatyczka *f*, korek *m*; '**~ sign** *mot.* znak *m* zatrzymania się; '**~·watch** stoper *m*

stor·age ['stɔːrɪdʒ] składowanie *n*, magazynowanie *n*; skład *m*; *komp.* pamięć *f*

store [stɔː] **1.** ⟨z⟩gromadzić (*też dane*); ⟨z⟩magazynować; *też* **~ up** *fig.* zachowywać ⟨-ować⟩; **2.** zapas *m*, zasób *m*; magazyn *m*, skład *m*; *zwł. Brt.* dom *m* towarowy; *zwł. Am.* sklep *m*; ⚠ *nie* **stora**; '**~·house** magazyn *m*, skład *m*; *fig.* kopalnia *f*, skarbnica *f*; '**~·keep·er** *zwł. Am.* sklepikarz *m* (-arka *f*), właściciel(ka *f*) *m* sklepu; '**~·room** schowek *m*

sto·rey *Brt.*, **sto·ry** *Am.* ['stɔːrɪ] piętro *n*

...sto·reyed *Brt.*, **...sto·ried** *Am.* ['stɔːrɪd] ...piętrowy, o ... piętrach

stork [stɔːk] *zo.* bocian *m*

storm [stɔːm] **1.** burza *f* (*też fig.*), sztorm *m*; **2.** *v/t. mil.* szturmować; *v/i.* wypadać ⟨-paść⟩ jak burza; '**~·y** (**-ier, -iest**) burzliwy

sto·ry[1] ['stɔːrɪ] opowiadanie *n*; historia *f*; fabuła *f*; *gazeta itp.* artykuł *m*, relacja *f* (**on** z *G*)

sto·ry[2] *Am.* ['stɔːrɪ] → **storey**

stout [staʊt] **1.** korpulentny, otyły; *fig.* zagorzały, zapalony; **2.** porter *m*

stove [stəʊv] piec *m*; kuchenka *f*

stow [stəʊ] *też* **~ away** umieszczać ⟨-mieścić⟩, składać ⟨złożyć⟩; '**~·a·way** pasażer(ka *f*) *m* na gapę

strad·dle ['strædl] siedzieć ⟨usiąść⟩ okrakiem na (*I*)

strag|·gle ['strægl] słać się; *domy*: być rozrzuconym; *ludzie*: ⟨po⟩dzielić się na grupki; '**~·gler** maruder *m*; '**~·gly** (*-ier, -iest*) *włosy*: nastroszony; *bot.* płożący się
straight [streɪt] **1.** *adj.* prosty; *whisky*: czysty; porządny, uporządkowany; szczery; prosty; jasny; *koncert*: bez przerwy; *sl.* (*nie homoseksualny*) normalny; (*nie narkoman*) czysty; ***put ~*** uporządkowywać ⟨-ować⟩; **2.** *adv.* prosto; natychmiast, od razu; szczerze; porządnie; wyraźnie (*myśleć, widzieć*); ***~ ahead*** prosto; ***~ off*** F od razu; ***~ on*** prosto; ***~ out*** F wyraźnie; **3.** (*w sporcie*) prosta *f*; '**~·en** *v/t.* ⟨wy⟩prostować (się); poprawiać ⟨-wić⟩; ***~en out*** doprowadzać ⟨-dzić⟩ do porządku, uporządkowywać ⟨-ować⟩; *v/i. też* ***~en out*** *ulicę itp.* ⟨wy⟩prostować; ***~en up*** wyprostowywać ⟨-ować⟩ się; **~'for·ward** prosty; nieskomplikowany
strain [streɪn] **1.** *v/t. linę itp.* naprężać ⟨-żyć⟩; *oczy itp.* wytężać ⟨-żyć⟩; wytężać ⟨-żyć⟩ się; *mięsień* nadwerężać ⟨-żyć⟩; *herbatę itp.* cedzić, przecedzać ⟨-dzić⟩; *v/i.* wytężać ⟨-żyć⟩ się; ***~ at*** napinać ⟨-piąć⟩ (*A*); **2.** napięcie *n* (*też fig.*); nadwerężenie *n*; przeciążenie *n*; odmiana *f* (*zwierzęcia, rośliny*); **~ed** przeciążony; *śmiech*: wysilony; *relacje*: napięty; ***look ~ed*** wyglądać na spiętego; '**~·er** sitko *n*, sito *n*
strait [streɪt] (*w nazwach własnych* ***♀s*** *pl.*) cieśnina *f*; ***~s*** *pl.* tarapaty *pl.*; ***♀ of Dover*** Cieśnina *f* Kaletańska
strait|·ened ['streɪtnd]: ***live in ~ened circumstances*** żyć w trudnych warunkach (*finansowych*); '**~·jack·et** *med.* kaftan *m* bezpieczeństwa
strand [strænd] pasmo *n* (*włóczki, włosów; też fig.*); żyła *f* (*kabla*); plaża *f*, brzeg *m*
strand·ed ['strændɪd]: ***be ~*** *naut.* osiadać ⟨-siąść⟩ na mieliźnie; ***be*** (***left***) ***~*** *fig.* zostać osamotnionym (*w kłopotach*)
strange [streɪndʒ] (*-r, -st*) dziwny; obcy; nieznajomy; '**strang·er** obcy *m* (-ca *f*); nieznajomy (-ma *f*)
stran·gle ['stræŋgl] ⟨u⟩dusić; *fig.* zduszać ⟨zdusić⟩
strap [stræp] **1.** pasek *m*; ramiączko *n*; **2.** (*-pp-*) przypinać ⟨-piąć⟩
stra·te·gic [strə'tiːdʒɪk] (*-ally*) strategiczny; **strat·e·gy** ['strætɪdʒɪ] strategia *f*
stra·tum ['strɑːtəm] *geol.* (*pl.* ***-ta*** [-tə]) warstwa *f*
straw [strɔː] słoma *f*; słomka *f* (*do picia*); **~·ber·ry** ['strɔːbərɪ] *bot.* truskawka *f*
stray [streɪ] **1.** odchodzić ⟨odejść⟩; zabłądzić, zabłąkać się; *fig.* odbiegać ⟨-biec⟩ (***from*** od *G*); **2.** zabłąkane zwierzę *n*; **3.** zabłąkany; *przykład*: przypadkowy
streak [striːk] **1.** pasmo *n*; smuga *f* (*światła*); cecha *f*; ***a ~ of lightning*** błyskawica *f*; ***lucky ~*** dobra passa *f*; **2.** przemykać ⟨-mknąć⟩; pokrywać ⟨-ryć⟩ pasmami; '**~·y** (*-ier, -iest*) w pasmach; *bekon*: tłusty
stream [striːm] **1.** strumień *m*; potok *m*; *fig.* prąd *m*; **2.** ⟨po⟩płynąć strumieniami; wypływać ⟨-łynąć⟩; '**~·er** serpentyna *f*; proporzec *m*; *komp.* streamer *m*
street [striːt] **1.** ulica *f*; *attr.* uliczny; ***in*** (*zwł. Am.* ***on***) ***the ~*** na ulicy; '**~·car** *Am.* tramwaj *m*
strength [streŋθ] **1.** siła *f* (*też fig.*); silny punkt *m*; *tech.* wytrzymałość *f*; '**~·en** *v/t.* wzmacniać ⟨-mocnić⟩; *v/i.* umacniać ⟨-mocnić⟩ się
stren·u·ous ['strenjʊəs] wyczerpujący, forsowny
stress [stres] **1.** *fig.* stres *m*; *phys., tech.* naprężenie *n*, nacisk *m*; *ling.* przycisk *m*, akcent *m*; *fig.* nacisk *m*; **2.** ⟨za⟩akcentować; '**~·ful** stresujący
stretch [stretʃ] **1.** *v/t.* rozciągać ⟨-gnąć⟩; ***~ out*** wyciągać ⟨-gnąć⟩; *fig. fakty* naciągać; *v/i.* rozciągać ⟨-gnąć⟩ się; wyciągać ⟨-gnąć⟩ się; ciągnąć się; ***~ out*** *ktoś*: przeciągać ⟨-gnąć⟩ się; **2.** rozciągnięcie *n*; naprężenie *n*; elastyczność *f*; odcinek *m* (*też czasu*); okres *m*; ***have a ~*** przeciągnąć się; '**~·er** nosze *pl.*
strick·en ['strɪkən] udręczony, umęczony; ***~ with*** dotknięty (*I*)
strict [strɪkt] ścisły; surowy, srogi; ***~ly speaking*** dokładnie rzecz biorąc
strid·den ['strɪdn] *p.p.* ***stride*** 1
stride [straɪd] **1.** (***strode, stridden***) kroczyć (*dużymi krokami*); **2.** duży krok *m*
strife [straɪf] walka *f*
strike [straɪk] **1.** (***struck***) *v/t.* uderzać ⟨-rzyć⟩; ⟨z⟩bić; ⟨za⟩atakować; *zapałkę*

pocierać ⟨potrzeć⟩; natrafiać ⟨-fić⟩ na (*ropę, złoto*); *godzinę* wybijać ⟨-bić⟩; *monety* bić; *obóz* rozbijać ⟨-bić⟩; *flagę, żagiel* zwijać ⟨zwinąć⟩; *równowagę itp.* osiągać ⟨-gnąć⟩; *transakcję* zawierać ⟨-wrzeć⟩; wykreślać ⟨-lić⟩ (***from, off*** z *listy*); ~ ***out*** przekreślać ⟨-lić⟩; ~ ***up*** *melodię* rozpoczynać ⟨-cząć⟩; *przyjaźń itp.* zawierać ⟨-wrzeć⟩; *v/i. econ.* ⟨za⟩strajkować; wydarzać się; wybijać ⟨-bić⟩ godzinę; ⟨za⟩atakować; uderzać ⟨-rzyć⟩; ~ (***out***) ***at s.o.*** ⟨za⟩atakować kogoś; uderzać ⟨-rzyć⟩ na kogoś; **2.** *econ.* strajk *m*; odkrycie *n* (*ropy, złota*); *mil.* uderzenie *n*; ***be on*** ~ strajkować; ***go on*** ~ zastrajkować; ***a lucky*** ~ szczęśliwe odkrycie; **'strik·er** *econ.* strajkujący *m* (-ca *f*); (*w piłce nożnej*) napastnik *m* (-niczka *f*); **'strik·ing** uderzający; zachwycający

string [strɪŋ] **1.** sznurek *m*; sznur *m* (*też fig.*); nić *f*, drut *m* (*do marionetki*); struna *f* (*skrzypiec, rakiety tenisowej itp.*); cięciwa *f* (*łuku*); włókno *n*, łyko *n* (*fasoli itp.*); *komp.* ciąg *m*; ***the*** **~*s*** *pl. mus.* smyczki *pl.*, instrumenty *pl.* smyczkowe; ***pull*** **~*s*** *fig.* pociągać za sznurki; ***with no ~s attached*** *fig.* bez dodatkowych warunków; **2.** (***strung***) *paciorki itp.* ⟨na⟩nizać na (*sznur*); zakładać ⟨założyć⟩ strunę; usuwać ⟨-sunąć⟩ łyko z (*fasoli itp.*); **3.** *mus.* smyczkowy; ~ **'bean** *zwł. Am.* fasolka *f* szparagowa

strin·gent ['strɪndʒənt] ostry

string·y ['strɪŋɪ] (***-ier, -iest***) łykowaty

strip [strɪp] **1.** (***-pp-***) *v/i. też* ~ ***off*** rozbierać ⟨-zebrać⟩ się (***to*** do *G*); *v/t. ubranie, farbę itp.*. ściągać ⟨-gnąć⟩; rozbierać ⟨-zebrać⟩; *tapetę* zrywać ⟨zerwać⟩ (***from, off*** z *G*); *też* ~ ***down*** *tech.* ⟨z⟩demontować, rozmontowywać ⟨-tować⟩; ~ ***s.o. of s.th.*** pozbawiać ⟨-wić⟩ kogoś czegoś; **2.** pasek *m*; pas *m* (*wody itp.*); striptiz *m*

stripe [straɪp] pasek *m*; prążek *m*; **~d** prążkowany

strode [strəʊd] *pret. od* ***stride*** 1

stroke [strəʊk] **1.** ⟨po⟩głaskać; ⟨po⟩gładzić; **2.** uderzenie *n* (*zegara, batem, w grze itp.*); pociągnięcie *n* (*pędzlem*); *med.* udar *m*, porażenie *n*; (*w pływaniu*) ruch *m*; *tech.* suw *m*, skok *m*; ***four-~ engine*** silnik *m* czterosuwowy; ~ ***of luck*** *fig.* szczęśliwy traf *m*

stroll [strəʊl] **1.** przechadzać się; spacerować; **2.** przechadzka *f*; spacer *m*; **'~·er** ['strəʊlə] spacerowicz(ka *f*) *m*; *Am.* wózek *m* spacerowy

strong [strɒŋ] silny, mocny; *kraj*: potężny; *wyrażenie*: dosadny; ***70*** ~ w liczbie 70; **'~·box** sejf *m*, kasa *f*; **'~·hold** twierdza *f*; warownia *f*; *fig.* bastion *m*; **~-'mind·ed** przekonany; **'~ room** skarbiec *m*

struck [strʌk] *pret. i p.p. od* ***strike*** 1

struc·ture ['strʌktʃə] struktura *f*; budowa *f*; budowla *f*; konstrukcja *f*

strug·gle ['strʌgl] **1.** walczyć, zmagać się (***with*** z *I*, ***for*** za *A*); **2.** walka *f*, zmaganie *n* się

strum [strʌm] (***-mm-***) uderzać w (*struny*), brzdąkać ⟨-knąć⟩ na (*instrumencie*)

strung [strʌŋ] *pret. i p.p. od* ***string*** 2

strut[1] [strʌt] (***-tt-***) dumnie kroczyć

strut[2] [strʌt] *tech.* rozpórka *f*; zastrzał *m*

stub [stʌb] **1.** ogryzek *m* (*ołówka*); niedopałek *m* (*papierosa*); odcinek *m* kontrolny; **2.** (***-bb-***) uderzyć się w (*palec stopy*); ~ ***out*** *papierosa* ⟨z⟩gasić

stub·ble ['stʌbl] ściernisko *n*; (*broda*) szczecina *f*

stub·born ['stʌbən] uparty; zawzięty; *plama*: oporny

stuck [stʌk] *pret. i p.p. od* ***stick*** 2; **~-'up** F wynoszący się, nadęty

stud[1] [stʌd] **1.** nit *m* (*na ubraniu*); zatrzask *m*; spinka *f* (*do kołnierzyka itp.*); korek *m* (*na bucie*); **~*s*** *pl. mot.* kolce *pl.*; **2.** ***be ~ed with*** być nabijanym (*I*); być usianym (*I*); ***~ed tyres*** (*Am.* ***tires***) *pl.* opony *pl.* z kolcami

stud[2] [stʌd] stadnina *f*

stu·dent ['stju:dnt] student(ka *f*) *m*; *zwł. Am. ogólnie* uczeń *m*; uczennica *f*

'stud| farm stadnina *f*; **'~ horse** ogier *m* rozpłodowy

stud·ied ['stʌdɪd] wystudiowany

stu·di·o ['stju:dɪəʊ] (*pl.* ***-os***) studio *n*, atelier *n*; *też* ~ ***flat*** *Brt.*, ~ ***apartment*** *zwł. Am.* kawalerka *f*

stu·di·ous ['stju:djəs] staranny, obowiązkowy

stud·y ['stʌdɪ] **1.** studium *n*; nauka *f*; gabinet *m*; ***studies*** *pl.* studia *pl.*; **2.** studiować (***for*** do *G*); uczyć się (*G*)

stuff [stʌf] **1.** rzecz *f*; rzeczy *pl.*; coś; **2.** wypychać ⟨-pchać⟩; wpychać ⟨wep-

S

chnąć⟩ (***into*** do *G*); *gastr.* nadziewać ⟨-dziać⟩, ⟨na⟩faszerować; ~ ***o.s.*** F napychać ⟨-pchać⟩ się; '**~·ing** *gastr.* nadzienie *n*, farsz *m*; (*pierze itp.*) wypełnienie *n*; '**~·y** (***-ier, -iest***) duszny; staromodny

stum·ble ['stʌmbl] **1.** potykać ⟨-tknąć⟩ się (***on, over***, *fig.* ***at, over*** o *A*); ~ ***across***, ~ ***on*** natykać ⟨-tknąć⟩ się na (*A*); **2.** potknięcie *n* się

stump [stʌmp] **1.** kikut *m*; pieniek *m*; **2.** chodzić ⟨iść⟩ ciężkim krokiem; wprawiać w zakłopotanie; '**~·y** (***-ier, -iest***) F kikutowaty

stun [stʌn] (***-nn-***) ogłuszać ⟨-szyć⟩; oszałamiać ⟨-szołomić⟩

stung [stʌŋ] *pret. i p.p. od* ***sting*** 1

stunk [stʌŋk] *pret. i p.p. od* ***stink*** 1

stun·ning ['stʌnɪŋ] fantastyczny; oszałamiający

stunt[1] [stʌnt] ⟨za⟩hamować; ***~ed*** skarlały

stunt[2] [stʌnt] wyczyn *m* (*akrobatyczny*); wyczyn *m* kaskaderski; *reklamowa* akcja *f*; '~ **man** (*pl.* ***-men***) kaskader *m*; '~ **wom·an** (*pl.* ***-women***) kaskaderka *f*

stu·pid ['stjuːpɪd] głupi, durny; **~·i·ty** [stjuː'pɪdətɪ] głupota *f*, durnota *f*

stu·por ['stjuːpə] stupor *m*; osłupienie *n*; ***in a drunken*** ~ w otępieniu pijackim

stur·dy ['stɜːdɪ] (***-ier, -iest***) krzepki; wytrzymały; *fig.* zacięty

stut·ter ['stʌtə] **1.** ⟨za⟩krztusić się; jąkać się; **2.** jąkanie *n* się

sty[1] [staɪ] → ***pigsty***

sty[2], **stye** [staɪ] *med.* jęczmień *m*

style [staɪl] **1.** styl *m*; rodzaj *m*; moda *f*; *bot.* słupek *m*; **2.** stylizować; ⟨u⟩kształtować

styl|·ish ['staɪlɪʃ] elegancki; pełen stylu; '**~·ist** fryzjer(ka *f*) *m*; stylista *m*

sty·lus ['staɪləs] *gramofonowa* igła *f*

sty·ro·foam ['staɪərəfəʊm] *TM zwł. Am.* styropian *m*

suave [swɑːv] naskakujący

sub·di·vi·sion ['sʌbdɪvɪʒn] podział *m* wtórny

sub·due [səb'djuː] opanowywać ⟨-nować⟩; **~d** *ktoś, coś*: przygaszony; *głos*: przytłumiony

sub|·ject **1.** ['sʌbdʒɪkt] temat *m*; *ped.*, *univ.* przedmiot *m*; *gr.* podmiot *m*; poddany *m* (-na *f*); **2.** ['sʌbdʒɪkt] *adj.* ***~ject to*** podlegający (*D*), za zastrzeżeniem (*G*); ***be ~ject to*** podlegać (*D*); być podatnym na (*A*); ***prices ~ject to change*** ceny mogą ulec zmianie; **3.** [səb'dʒekt] poddawać ⟨-ddać⟩ (*D*); **~·jec·tion** [səb'dʒekʃn] poddanie *n*, podporządkowanie *n*

sub·ju·gate ['sʌbdʒʊgeɪt] podporządkowywać ⟨-ować⟩

sub·junc·tive [səb'dʒʌŋktɪv] *gr. też* ~ ***mood*** tryb *m* łączący, koniunktyw *m*

sub|·lease [sʌb'liːs], ~'**let** (***-tt-. -let***) podwynajmować ⟨-jąć⟩

sub·lime wzniosły

sub·ma·chine gun [sʌbmə'ʃiːn -] pistolet *m* maszynowy

sub·ma·rine [sʌbmə'riːn] **1.** podwodny; **2.** okręt *m* podwodny

sub·merge [səb'mɜːdʒ] zanurzać ⟨-rzyć⟩ się (***in*** w *I*)

sub·mis|·sion [səb'mɪʃn] poddanie *n* się, podporządkowanie *n* się; składanie *n*, złożenie *n*; zgłoszenie *n*; **~·sive** [səb'mɪsɪv] uległy, podporządkowany

sub·mit [səb'mɪt] (***-tt-***) przedstawiać ⟨-wić⟩; poddawać ⟨-ddać⟩ się; (*D*)

sub·or·di·nate **1.** [sə'bɔːdnət] podporządkowany, podległy; **2.** [sə'bɔːdnət] podwładny *m* (-na *f*); **3.** [sə'bɔːdɪneɪt]: ~ ***to*** podporządkowywać ⟨-ować⟩ (*D*); ~ '**clause** *gr.* zdanie *n* podrzędne

sub|·scribe [səb'skraɪb] *v/t. pieniądze* ofiarowywać ⟨-ować⟩; *v/i.* ***~scribe to*** prenumerować (*A*); składać ⟨złożyć⟩ pieniądze na (*A*); *idee itp.* popierać ⟨-przeć⟩ (*A*); ~'**scrib·er** prenumerator(ka *f*) *m*; *tel.* abonent *m*

sub·scrip·tion [səb'skrɪpʃn] prenumerata *f*, subskrypcja *f*; abonament *m*

sub·se·quent ['sʌbsɪkwənt] następujący, późniejszy

sub·side [səb'saɪd] *ulica, budynek*: zapadać ⟨-paść⟩ się; *wiatr itp.*: uspokajać ⟨-koić⟩ się

sub·sid·i·a·ry [səb'sɪdjərɪ] **1.** pomocniczy; ~ ***question*** pytanie *n* dodatkowe; **2.** *econ.* przedsiębiorstwo *n* zależne, filia *f*

sub·si|·dize ['sʌbsɪdaɪz] subsydiować; **~·dy** ['sʌbsɪdɪ] subsydium *n*, subwencja *f*

sub|·sist [səb'sɪst] utrzymywać się, żyć (***on*** z *G*); ~'**sis·tence** egzystencja *f*

sub·stance ['sʌbstəns] substancja *f* (*też fig.*); *fig.* istota *f*

S

sub·stan·dard [sʌb'stændəd] gorszego gatunku
sub·stan·tial [səb'stænʃl] *mebel*: solidny; *ilość*: znaczny; *zmiany*: poważny
sub·stan·ti·ate [səb'stænʃɪeɪt] popierać ⟨poprzeć⟩, udowadniać ⟨-wodnić⟩
sub·stan·tive ['sʌbstəntɪv] *gr.* rzeczownik *m*
sub·sti|·tute ['sʌbstɪtjuːt] **1.** substytut *m*; surogat *m*, namiastka *f*; zastępca *m* (-czyni *f*); (*w sporcie*) zmiennik *m* (-niczka *f*); *attr.* zastępczy; rezerwowy; **2.** ***~tute s.th. for s.th.*** zastępować ⟨-tąpić⟩ coś czymś; **~·tu·tion** [sʌbstɪ'tjuːʃn] zamiana *f*; (*w sporcie*) zmiana *f*
sub·ter·fuge ['sʌbtəfjuːdʒ] podstęp *m*, wybieg *m*
sub·ter·ra·ne·an [sʌbtə'reɪnjən] podziemny
sub·ti·tle ['sʌbtaɪtl] (*na filmie*) napis *m*
sub·tle ['sʌtl] (***-r, -st***) subtelny; delikatny; zmyślny
sub|·tract [səb'trækt] *math.* odejmować ⟨-djąć⟩ (***from*** od *G*); **~·trac·tion** [səb'trækʃn] *math.* odejmowanie *n*
sub·trop·i·cal [sʌb'trɒpɪkl] subtropikalny, podzwrotnikowy
sub|·urb ['sʌbɜːb] przedmieście *n*; **~·ur·ban** [sə'bɜːbən] podmiejski
sub·ver·sive [səb'vɜːsɪv] wywrotowy
sub·way ['sʌbweɪ] *Brt.* przejście *n* podziemne; *Am.* metro *n*
suc·ceed [sək'siːd] *v/i.* odnosić ⟨-nieść⟩ sukces (*in* w *L*); powodzić ⟨-wieść⟩ się; ***~ to*** *urząd itp.* przejmować ⟨-jąć⟩; ***~ to the throne*** ⟨o⟩dziedziczyć tron; *v/t.* ***~ s.o. as*** być czyimś następcą w (*L*)
suc·cess [sək'ses] sukces *m*, powodzenie *n*; **~·ful** udany, pomyślny
suc·ces|·sion [sək'seʃn] następstwo *n*; szereg *m*; dziedziczenie *n*, sukcesja *f*; ***five times in ~sion*** pięć razy pod rząd; ***in quick ~sion*** szybko jeden za drugim; **~·sive** [sək'sesɪv] sukcesywny, kolejny, stopniowy; **~·sor** [sək'sesə] następca *f* (-czyni *f*)
suc·cu·lent ['sʌkjʊlənt] *mięso itp.*: soczysty
such [sʌtʃ] taki *m*, taka *m*
suck [sʌk] **1.** ssać ((***at***) ***s.th.*** coś); wysysać ⟨wessać⟩, zasysać ⟨zassać⟩; **2.** ***have*** *lub* ***take a ~ at*** possać (*A*); '**~·er** *zo.* ssawka *f*; *tech.*, *zo.* przyssawka *f*; *bot.* odrost *m*; F frajer *m*, jeleń *m*; *Am.* lizak *m*; **~·le** ['sʌkl] *pierś* ssać; karmić piersią
suc·tion ['sʌkʃn] ssanie *n*, zasysanie *n*; '**~ pump** *tech.* pompa *f* ssąca
sud·den ['sʌdn] nagły; ***all of a ~*** F nagle, znienacka; '**~·ly** nagle
suds [sʌdz] *pl.* mydliny *pl.*
sue [suː] *jur. kogoś* pozywać ⟨-zwać⟩, zaskarżać ⟨-żyć⟩ (*do sądu*) (***for*** za *A*); wnosić (***for*** o *A*)
suede, **suède** [sweɪd] zamsz *m*; *attr.* zamszowy
su·et ['suɪt] sadło *n*
suf·fer ['sʌfə] *v/i.* ⟨u-, wy⟩cierpieć (***for*** za *A*); doznawać ⟨-nać⟩ uszczerbku; ***~ from*** cierpieć na (*A*); *v/t. konsekwencje*, *straty* ponosić ⟨-nieść⟩; doznawać ⟨-nać⟩; doświadczać ⟨-czyć⟩ (*upokorzenia*); **~·er** ['sʌfərə] cierpiący *m* (-ca *f*); poszkodowany *m* (-na *f*); **~·ing** ['sʌfərɪŋ] cierpienie *n*
suf·fice [sə'faɪs] wystarczać ⟨-czyć⟩ (***for*** na *A*)
suf·fi·cient [sə'fɪʃnt] wystarczający, dostateczny; ***be ~*** wystarczać ⟨-czyć⟩
suf·fix ['sʌfɪks] *gr.* przyrostek *m*, sufiks *m*
suf·fo·cate ['sʌfəkeɪt] ⟨u⟩dusić się
suf·frage ['sʌfrɪdʒ] *pol.* prawo *n* głosowania
suf·fuse [sə'fjuːz] zalewać ⟨-lać⟩ (*światłem*)
sug·ar ['ʃʊgə] **1.** cukier *m*; *attr.* cukrowy; **2.** ⟨po⟩słodzić; '**~ bowl** cukiernica *f*; '**~·cane** trzcina *f* cukrowa; **~·y** ['ʃʊgərɪ] cukrowy; słodki; *fig.* przesłodzony, ckliwy
sug|·gest [sə'dʒest] ⟨za⟩proponować; ⟨za⟩sugerować; wskazywać; podsuwać ⟨-sunąć⟩ (*myśl*); **~·ges·tion** [sə'dʒestʃən] sugestia *f*, wskazówka *f*, propozycja *f*; **~·ges·tive** [sə'dʒestɪv] niedwuznaczny; *spojrzenie itp.*: wiele mówiący
su·i·cide ['sjʊɪsaɪd] samobójstwo *n*; ***commit ~*** popełnić samobójstwo
suit [suːt] **1.** garnitur *m*; *kąpielowy* kostium *m*; (*w kartach*) kolor *m*; *jur.* proces *m*; ***follow ~*** *fig.* iść ⟨pójść⟩ za przykładem; **2.** *v/t. komuś* odpowiadać (*termin itp.*); pasować do (*G*); ***~ s.th., be ~ed to s.th.*** pasować do czegoś, nadawać się do czegoś; ***~ yourself!*** rób jak chcesz!; '**sui·ta·ble** odpowiedni, właś-

S

ciwy, stosowny (***for, to*** do *G*); '**~·case** walizka *f*
suite [swi:t] komplet *m* (*mebli*); zestaw *m*; apartament *m*; świta *f*; *mus.* suita *f*
sul·fur ['sʌlfə] *Am.* → ***sulphur***
sulk [sʌlk] ⟨na⟩dąsać się, boczyć się; **~s** *pl.*: ***have the ~s*** dąsać się
sulk·y¹ ['sʌlkɪ] (***-ier, -iest***) dąsający się; nadąsany
sulk·y² ['sʌlkɪ] (*w wyścigach konnych*) sulki *pl.*
sul·len ['sʌlən] ponury
sul|·phur ['sʌlfə] *chem.* siarka *f*; **~·phu·ric ac·id** [sʌlfjʊərɪk 'æsɪd] *chem.* kwas *m* siarkowy
sul·try ['sʌltrɪ] (***-ier, -iest***) duszny; *głos, spojrzenie*: zmysłowy
sum [sʌm] **1.** suma *f*; kwota *f*; ***do ~s*** ⟨wy⟩liczyć; **2.** (***-mm-***): ***~ up*** podsumowywać ⟨-mować⟩; dokonywać ⟨-nać⟩ podsumowania; *fig.* oceniać ⟨-nić⟩
sum|·mar·ize ['sʌməraɪz] streszczać ⟨-reścić⟩; **~·ma·ry** ['sʌmərɪ] streszczenie *n*
sum·mer ['sʌmə] lato; ***in*** (***the***) **~** latem, w lecie; '**~ camp** kolonia *f* (*dla dzieci*); **~ 'hol·i·days** *pl.* wakacje *pl.* letnie; **~ re'sort** (*miejscowość*) letnisko *n*; '**~ school** szkoła *f* letnia; '**~·time** lato *n*; ***in*** (***the***) ***~time*** latem, w lecie; '**~ time** *zwł. Brt.* czas *m* letni; **~ va'ca·tion** *zwł. Am.* wakacje *pl.* letnie; **~·y** ['sʌmərɪ] letni
sum·mit ['sʌmɪt] wierzchołek *m*; szczyt *m* (*też econ., pol., fig.*); '**~** (**con·fe·rence**) konferencja *f* na szczycie; '**~** (**meet·ing**) spotkanie *n* na szczycie
sum·mon ['sʌmən] wzywać ⟨wezwać⟩, zwoływać ⟨-łać⟩; *jur.* pozywać ⟨-zwać⟩; ***~ up*** *siłę, męstwo itp.* zbierać ⟨zebrać⟩; **~s** ['sʌmənz] *jur.* wezwanie *n*
sump·tu·ous ['sʌmptʃʊəs] wystawny, okazały
sun [sʌn] **1.** słońce *n*; *attr.* słoneczny; **2.** (***-nn-***): ***~ o.s.*** opalać się
Sun *skrót pisany*: ***Sunday*** niedz., niedziela *f*
'**sun|·bathe** brać ⟨wziąć⟩ kąpiele słoneczne; '**~·beam** promień *m* słońca; '**~·bed** (*urządzenie*) solarium *n*; '**~·burn** oparzenie *n* słoneczne
sun·dae ['sʌndeɪ] puchar *m* lodowy
Sun·day ['sʌndɪ] (*skrót*: ***Sun***) niedziela *f*; ***on ~*** w niedzielę; ***on ~s*** co niedzielę
'**sun|·dial** ['sʌndaɪəl] zegar *m* słoneczny; '**~·down** → ***sunset***
sun|·dries ['sʌndrɪz] *pl.* różności *pl.*; **~·dry** ['sʌndrɪ] różny, rozmaity
sung [sʌŋ] *p.p. od* ***sing***
'**sun·glass·es** (***a pair of ~***) *pl.* okulary *pl.* słoneczne
sunk [sʌŋk] *pret. i p.p. od* ***sink*** 1
sunk·en ['sʌŋkən] *policzki*: zapadnięty; *statek itp.*: zatopiony; *ogród itp.*: wgłębiony
'**sun|·light** światło *n* słoneczne; '**~·lit** oświetlony słońcem
sun·ny ['sʌnɪ] (***-ier, -iest***) słoneczny
'**sun|·rise** wschód *m* słońca; '**~·roof** taras *m*; *mot.* (*dachowe okno uchylne*) szyberdach *m*; '**~·set** zachód *m* słońca; '**~·shade** parasol *m* przeciwsłoneczny; parasolka *f* przeciwsłoneczna; osłona *f* od słońca; '**~·shine** światło *n* słońca; '**~·stroke** porażenie *n* słoneczne; '**~·tan** opalenizna *f*
su·per ['su:pə] F super
su·per... ['su:pə] nad...
su·per|·a·bun·dance [su:pərə'bʌndəns] nadmiar *m*; **~·an·nu·at·ed** [su:pə'rænjʊeɪtɪd] emerytowany, w stanie spoczynku
su·perb [su:'pɜ:b] znakomity
'**su·per|·charg·er** *mot.* sprężarka *f* doładowująca; **~·cil·i·ous** [su:pə'sɪlɪəs] wyniosły; **~·fi·cial** [su:pə'fɪʃl] powierzchowny; **~·flu·ous** [su:'pɜ:flʊəs] nadmierny; zbyteczny; **~'hu·man** nadludzki; **~·im·pose** [su:pərɪm'pəʊz] nakładać ⟨nałożyć⟩; **~·in·tend** [su:pərɪn'tend] nadzorować; ⟨s⟩kontrolować; **~·in·tend·ent** [su:pərɪn'tendənt] nadzorca *m* (-rczyni *f*); *Brt.* inspektor *m*
su·pe·ri·or [su:'pɪərɪə] **1.** zwierzchni, przełożony; starszy (*rangą*); lepszy; ***Father*** ♀ Ojciec Przełożony; ***Mother*** ♀ Matka Przełożona; **2.** zwierzchnik *m* (-niczka *f*), przełożony *m* (-na *f*); **~·i·ty** [su:pɪərɪ'ɒrətɪ] starszeństwo *n*, wyższość *f*, przewaga *f* (***over*** nad *I*)
su·per·la·tive [su:'pɜ:lətɪv] **1.** doskonały, znakomity; **2.** *też* ***~ degree*** *gr.* stopień *m* najwyższy
'**su·per|·mar·ket** supermarket *m*; **~'nat·u·ral** nadprzyrodzony; **~·nu·me·ra·ry** [su:pə'nju:mərərɪ] nadliczbowy; **~·sede** [su:pə'si:d] zastępować ⟨-tąpić⟩; **~'son·ic** *aviat., phys.* nad-

dźwiękowy; **~·sti·tion** [suːpə'stɪʃn] zabobon *m*; **~·sti·tious** [suːpə'stɪʃəs] zabobonny; **'~·store** megasam *m*; **~·vene** [suːpə'viːn] zachodzić ⟨-zajść⟩; **~·vise** ['suːpəvaɪz] nadzorować; **~·vi·sion** [suːpə'vɪʒn] nadzór *m*, dozór *m*; ***under s.o.'s ~vision*** pod czyimś nadzorem *lub* kierownictwem; **~·vi·sor** ['suːpəvaɪzə] nadzorca *m* (-czyni *f*), kontroler(ka *f*) *m*

sup·per ['sʌpə] kolacja *f*; ***have ~*** ⟨z⟩jeść kolację; → ***lord***

sup·plant [sə'plɑːnt] zastępować ⟨-tąpić⟩; wypierać ⟨-przeć⟩

sup·ple ['sʌpl] (***-er, -est***) giętki, elastyczny

sup·ple|·ment **1.** ['sʌplɪmənt] dodatek *m*; uzupełnienie *n*; suplement *m*; **2.** ['sʌplɪment] dodawać ⟨-dać⟩, uzupełniać ⟨-nić⟩; **~·men·ta·ry** [sʌplɪ'mentərɪ] uzupełniający, dodatkowy

sup·pli·er [sə'plaɪə] dostawca *m*; *też* ***~s*** *pl.* firma *f* dostawcza, dostawcy *pl.*

sup·ply [sə'plaɪ] **1.** dostarczać ⟨-czyć⟩; *econ.* zaopatrywać ⟨-trzyć⟩ (***with*** w *A*); *potrzebę* zaspokajać ⟨-koić⟩; **2.** dostawa *f*; dostarczenie *n*; *econ.* zaopatrzenie *n*; *zw.* **supplies** *pl.* rezerwy *pl.*, zapasy *pl.*; prowiant *m*, ***school ~*** *pl.* materiały *pl.* szkolne; ***~ and demand*** podaż i popyt

sup·port [sə'pɔːt] **1.** podpierać ⟨-deprzeć⟩; podtrzymywać ⟨-mać⟩; *ciężar* wytrzymywać ⟨-mać⟩; wspierać ⟨wesprzeć⟩ (*finansowo*); *żądania itp.* popierać ⟨-przeć⟩; *rodzinę itp.* utrzymywać ⟨-mać⟩; **2.** podpora *f* (*też fig.*); oparcie *n*; wsparcie *n*; utrzymanie *n*; **~·er** poplecznik *m*, stronnik *m*; *sportowy* kibic *m*

sup|·pose [sə'pəʊz] **1.** sądzić; przypuszczać; ***be ~posed to ...*** mieć *inf.*; ***what is that ~posed to mean?*** co to ma znaczyć?; ***I ~pose so*** tak mi się wydaje; **2.** *cj.* przypuśćmy że; jeżeli; a może; **~'posed** domniemany; **~'pos·ing** → ***suppose*** 2; **~·po·si·tion** [sʌpə'zɪʃn] przypuszczenie *n*

sup|·press [sə'pres] ⟨s⟩tłumić; ⟨po⟩hamować; skrywać ⟨-ryć⟩; zakazywać ⟨-zać⟩ publikacji (*G*); **~·pres·sion** [sə'preʃn] stłumienie *n*; pohamowanie *n*; skrycie *n*; zakaz *m* publikacji

sup·pu·rate ['sʌpjʊəreɪt] *med.* ⟨z⟩ropieć

su·prem·a·cy [sʊ'preməsɪ] wyższość *f*; supremacja *f*; dominacja *f*

su·preme [suː'priːm] naczelny; najwyższy; krańcowy

sur·charge **1.** [sɜː'tʃɑːdʒ] obciążać ⟨-żyć⟩ dodatkową opłatą; **2.** ['sɜːtʃɑːdʒ] dopłata *f*

sure [ʃɔː] **1.** *adj.* (***-r, -st***) pewny; ***~ of s.o.*** pewny czegoś; ***~ of winning*** przekonany o swej wygranej; ***~ thing!*** *zwł. Am.* F oczywiście!; ***be*** *lub* ***feel ~*** czuć się pewnie; ***be ~ to ....*** nie zapomnieć ...; ***for ~*** na pewno, z pewnością; ***make ~ that*** upewniać ⟨-nić⟩ się, że; ***to be ~*** dla pewności; **2.** *adv.* F z pewnością, na pewno; ***~ enough*** oczywiście; faktycznie; **'~·ly** z pewnością; pewnie; zapewne; **sur·e·ty** ['ʃɔːrətɪ] przekonanie *n*, pewność *f*; poręka *f*; ***stand ~ for s.o.*** poręczyć za kogoś

surf [sɜːf] **1.** przybój *m*; **2.** uprawiać surfing

sur·face ['sɜːfɪs] **1.** powierzchnia *f*; nawierzchnia *f* (*ulicy itp.*); tafla *f* (*jeziora itp.*); **2.** wychodzić ⟨wyjść⟩ na powierzchnię; wynurzać ⟨-rzyć⟩ się; *ulicę* pokrywać ⟨-ryć⟩ nawierzchnią; **3.** powierzchniowy; **'~ mail** poczta *f* naziemna

'surf|·board *sport*: deska *f* surfingowa; **'~·er** (*osoba uprawiająca surfing*); **'~·ing** surfing *m*

surge [sɜːdʒ] **1.** *fig.* fala *f*, napływ *m* (*uczuć*); przypływ *m*; **2.** napływać ⟨-łynąć⟩; przepływać ⟨-łynąć⟩; *też* ***~ up*** wzbierać ⟨wezbrać⟩

sur·geon ['sɜːdʒən] *med.* chirurg *m*

sur·ge·ry ['sɜːdʒərɪ] *med.* chirurgia *f*; operacja *f*; *Brt.* gabinet *m* lekarski; *Brt.* godziny *pl.* przyjęć; *też* ***doctor's ~*** praktyka *f* lekarska; **'~ hours** *pl. Brt.* godziny *pl.* przyjęć

sur·gi·cal ['sɜːdʒɪkl] *med.* chirurgiczny

sur·ly ['sɜːlɪ] (***-ier, -iest***) gburowaty, mrukliwy

sur·name ['sɜːneɪm] nazwisko *n*

sur·pass [sə'pɑːs] *oczekiwania itp.* przewyższać ⟨-szyć⟩

sur·plus ['sɜːpləs] **1.** nadwyżka *f*; **2.** dodatkowy

sur·prise [sə'praɪz] **1.** niespodzianka *f*; ***take s.o. by ~*** brać ⟨wziąć⟩ kogoś przez zaskoczenie; **2.** zaskakiwać ⟨-koczyć⟩; ***be ~d at*** *lub* ***by*** być zaskoczonym (*I*)

sur·ren·der [sə'rendə] **1.** **~ to** *mil.*, *też fig.* poddawać ⟨-dać⟩ (się) (*D*), kapitulować przed (*I*); **~ (o.s.) *to the police*** oddawać ⟨-dać⟩ się w ręce policji; zrzekać ⟨zrzec⟩ się (*G*); **2.** *mil.* kapitulacja *f* (*też fig.*); poddanie *n* się; zrzeczenie *n* się

sur·ro·gate ['sʌrəgeɪt] surogat *m*, substytut *m*; **~ 'moth·er** zastępcza matka *f*

sur·round [sə'raʊnd] otaczać ⟨otoczyć⟩; **~·ing** otaczający; **~·ings** *pl.* otoczenie *n*

sur·vey **1.** [sə'veɪ] oglądać ⟨-dnąć⟩, poddawać ⟨-dać⟩ oględzinom; dokonywać ⟨-nać⟩ przeglądu (*budynku*); *ziemię* ⟨z⟩mierzyć; *opinię* ⟨z⟩badać; **2.** ['sɜːveɪ] badanie *n* (*opinii itp.*); przegląd *m*; zbadanie *n*, oględziny *pl.*; **~·or** [sə'veɪə] geodeta *m*, mierniczy *m*

sur·viv·al [sə'vaɪvl] przeżycie *n*; przetrwanie *n*; **~ kit** zestaw *m* ratunkowy; **~ train·ing** szkoła *f* przetrwania

sur|·vive [sə'vaɪv] przetrwać; przeżyć; **~'vi·vor** ocalały *m* (-ła *f*) (***from***, *od* z *G*)

sus·cep·ti·ble [sə'septəbl] podatny (***to*** na *A*)

sus·pect **1.** [sə'spekt] podejrzewać (***of*** o *A*); nie dowierzać (*D*); obawiać się; **2.** ['sʌspekt] podejrzany *m* (-na *f*); **3.** ['sʌspekt] podejrzany; niepewny

sus·pend [sə'spend] zawieszać ⟨-wiesić⟩; *coś* wstrzymywać ⟨-mać⟩; wykluczać ⟨-czyć⟩ (***from*** z *G*); **~·er** *Brt.* podwiązka *f*; (*też* ***a pair of***) **~ers** *pl. Am.* szelki *pl.*

sus·pense [sə'spens] napięcie *n*

sus·pen·sion [sə'spenʃn] zawieszenie *n* (*też mot.*); wykluczenie *n*; wstrzymanie *n*; zawiesina *f*; **~ bridge** most *m* wiszący

sus·pi|·cion [sə'spɪʃn] podejrzenie *n*; podejrzliwość *f*; **~·cious** podejrzliwy; podejrzany

sus·tain [sə'steɪn] utrzymywać ⟨-mać⟩; utrzymywać *kogoś* na siłach; *zainteresowanie itp.* podtrzymywać ⟨-mać⟩; *obrażenia itp.* ponosić ⟨-nieść⟩; *uszkodzenia itp.* doznawać ⟨-nać⟩

SW *skrót pisany*: ***southwest*** płd.-zach.; południowy zachód *m*; ***southwest*(*ern*)** południowo-zachodni

swab *med.* [swɒb] **1.** wacik *m*, gazik *m*; wymaz *m*; **2.** (**-*bb*-**) oczyszczać ⟨-yścić⟩ wacikiem

swad·dle ['swɒdl] *niemowlę* opatulać ⟨-lić⟩

swag·ger ['swægə] chodzić ⟨iść⟩ kołyszącym się krokiem

swal·low[1] ['swɒləʊ] **1.** łykać; połykać ⟨-łknąć⟩ (*tez fig.*); przełykać ⟨-łknąć⟩; *fig.* pochłonąć; **~ *one's pride*** ⟨s⟩chować dumę do kieszeni; **2.** łyk *m*

swal·low[2] ['swɒləʊ] *zo.* jaskółka *f*

swam [swæm] *pret. od* ***swim*** 1

swamp [swɒmp] **1.** bagnisko *n*; **2.** zalewać ⟨-lać⟩ (*też fig.*); ***be ~ed with*** *fig.* być zasypanym (*I*); **'~·y** (**-*ier*, -*iest***) bagnisty

swan [swɒn] *zo.* łabędź *m*

swank [swæŋk] F *zwł. Brt.* **1.** przechwalać się; **2.** przechwałki *pl.*; chwalipięta *m*; **'~·y** (**-*ier*, -*iest***) F chełpliwy

swap [swɒp] F **1.** (**-*pp*-**) wymieniać ⟨-nić⟩ (się), zamieniać ⟨-nić⟩ (się); **2.** wymiana *f*, zamiana *f*

swarm [swɔːm] **1.** chmara *f* (*owadów, turystów*); rój *m* (*pszczół*); **2.** *pszczoły, ludzie*: ⟨wy⟩roić się

swar·thy ['swɔːðɪ] (**-*ier*, -*iest***) *cera*: śniady, smagły

swat [swɒt] (**-*tt*-**) *muchę* pacnąć

sway [sweɪ] **1.** *v/i.* kołysać się, chwiać się; **~ *between*** *fig.* wahać się między (*I*); *v/t.* kołysać; wpływać ⟨-łynąć⟩; **2.** kołysanie *n*, kiwanie *n*

swear [sweə] (***swore*, *sworn***) przysięgać ⟨-siąc⟩; przeklinać ⟨-ląć⟩; ⟨za⟩kląć; **~ *at s.o.*** kląć na kogoś; **~ *by*** *fig.* F kląć się na (*A*); **~ *s.o. in*** zaprzysięgać ⟨-siąc⟩ kogoś

sweat [swet] **1.** (***sweated***, *Am. też* ***sweat***) ⟨s⟩pocić się (***with*** od *G lub* z *G*); *v/t.* **~ *out*** wypacać ⟨-pocić⟩ (*w chorobie*); **~ *blood*** F naharować się jak wół; **2.** pot *m*; ***get into a ~ about*** F podniecać ⟨-cić⟩ się (*I*); **'~·er** sweter *m*; **'~·shirt** bluza *f*; **'~·y** (**-*ier*, -*iest***) spocony; przepocony

Swede [swiːd] Szwed(ka *f*) *m*; **Swe·den** ['swiːdn] Szwecja *f*; **Swe·dish** ['swiːdɪʃ] **1.** szwedzki; **2.** *ling.* język *m* szwedzki

sweep [swiːp] **1.** (***swept***) zamiatać ⟨-mieść⟩; zmiatać ⟨-mieść⟩; *horyzont* omiatać ⟨-mieść⟩ (***for*** w poszukiwaniu

S

G); *v/i.* przelatywać ⟨-lecieć⟩; przemykać ⟨-mknąć⟩; rozciągać ⟨-gnąć⟩ się; **2.** zamiecenie *n*; półkolisty ruch *m*; półkolista linia *f*; cios *m*; ***give the floor a good ~*** zamieść dobrze podłogę; ***make a clean ~*** dokonać daleko idących zmian *f*; (*w sporcie*) osiągnąć całkowite zwycięstwo; **'~·er** zamiatacz *m*; (*maszyna*) zamiatarka *f*; (*w sporcie*) libero *m*; **'~·ing** zamaszysty; daleko idący; **'~·ings** *pl.* zmiotki *pl.*

sweet [swi:t] **1.** słodki (*też fig.*); ***~ nothings*** *pl.* czułości *pl.*; ***have a ~ tooth*** lubić słodycze; **2.** *Brt.* słodycze *pl.*, cukierek *m*; *Brt.* deser *m*; **'~ corn** *zwł. Brt. bot.* kukurydza *f* cukrowa; **'~·en** ⟨po⟩słodzić; **'~·heart** (*ktoś*) skarb *m*; **~ 'pea** *bot.* groszek *m* pachnący; **'~ shop** *zwł. Brt.* sklep *m* ze słodyczami

swell [swel] **1.** (***swelled, swollen*** *lub* ***swelled***) *v/i. też* ***~ up*** *med.* ⟨s⟩puchnąć; *też* ***~ out*** wydymać ⟨-dąć⟩ się, nadymać ⟨-dąć⟩ się; *v/t. fig. liczba itp.*: rozdymać ⟨-dąć⟩; *też* ***~ out*** *żagiel* wydymać ⟨-dąć⟩; **2.** *naut.* fala *f* martwa; **'~·ing** spuchnięcie *n*

swel·ter ['sweltə] *człowiek*: prażyć się

swept [swept] *pret. i p.p. od* ***sweep*** 1

swerve [swɜːv] **1.** skręcać ⟨-cić⟩ ostro (***to the left*** na lewo); *fig.* odchodzić ⟨odejść⟩ (***from*** od *G*); **2.** skręcenie *n*, skręt *m*; odchylenie *n* się

swift [swɪft] **1.** szybki, prędki; **2.** *zo.* jerzyk *m*

swim [swɪm] **1.** (***-mm-; swam, swum***) *v/i.* pływać; płynąć; *fig.* kręcić się; ***my head was ~ming*** kręciło mi się w głowie; *v/t.* przepływać ⟨-łynąć⟩; *kraulem* pływać; **2.** kąpiel *f*; **'~·mer** pływak *m* (-waczka *f*)

'swim·ming pływanie *n*; **'~ bath(s** *pl.*) *Brt.* pływalnia *f*; **'~ cap** czepek *m* kąpielowy; **'~ cos·tume** kostium *m* kąpielowy; **'~ pool** basen *m* kąpielowy; **'~ trunks** *pl.* kąpielówki *pl.*

'swim·suit kostium *m* kąpielowy

swin·dle ['swɪndl] **1.** wyłudzać ⟨-dzić⟩ (***s.o. out of s.th.*** coś od kogoś); **2.** wyłudzenie *n*

swine [swaɪn] (*pl. zo.* ***swine***, *sl. pej. też* ***swines***) świnia *f*

swing [swɪŋ] **1.** (***swung***) *v/i.* ⟨po-, za⟩huśtać się; ⟨za⟩kołysać się; wjeżdżać ⟨wjechać⟩ łukiem (***into*** do *G*); *mus.* swingować; ***~ round*** obrócić się; ***~ shut*** zatrzasnąć się; *v/t.* machać (*ramionami itp.*); **2.** huśtawka *f* (*też fig.*); zamachnięcie *n*; zmiana *f*; *mus.* swing *m*; ***in full ~*** w pełni, na cały gaz; **~ 'door** drzwi *pl.* wahadłowe

swin·ish ['swaɪnɪʃ] świński

swipe [swaɪp] **1.** uderzenie *n*; **2.** uderzać ⟨-rzyć⟩ (***at*** w *A*)

swirl [swɜːl] **1.** ⟨za⟩wirować; **2.** wir *m*

swish[1] [swɪʃ] **1.** *v/i. bat, ogon*: świstać ⟨-snąć⟩; *jedwab*: ⟨za⟩szeleścić; *v/t.* machać ⟨-chnąć⟩ ze świstem; **2.** świst *m*; szelest *m*; machnięcie *n*

swish[2] [swɪʃ] F szykowny

Swiss [swɪs] **1.** szwajcarski; **2.** Szwajcar(ka *f*) *m*; ***the ~*** *pl.* Szwajcarzy *pl.*

switch [swɪtʃ] **1.** *electr., tech.* przełącznik *m* , wyłącznik *m*; *Am. rail.* zwrotnica *f*; gałązka *f*; *fig.* diametralna zmiana *f*; **2.** *electr., tech.* przełączać ⟨-czyć⟩ (*też* ***~ over***) (***to*** na *A*); *Am. rail.* manewrować, przetaczać ⟨-toczyć⟩; zmieniać ⟨-nić⟩ (***to*** na *A*); ***~ off*** wyłączać ⟨-czyć⟩; ***~ on*** włączać ⟨-czyć⟩; **'~·board** *electr.* tablica *f* rozdzielcza; *tel.* centralka *f*

Swit·zer·land ['swɪtsələnd] Szwajcaria *f*

swiv·el ['swɪvl] (*zwł. Brt.* ***-ll-*** , *Am.* ***-l-***) obracać (się); **'~ chair** krzesło *n* obrotowe

swol·len ['swəʊlən] *p.p. od* ***swell*** 1

swoon [swuːn] ⟨ze-, o⟩mdleć

swoop [swuːp] **1.** *fig.* F *policja*: ⟨z⟩robić nalot; *też* ***~ down*** *ptak drapieżny*: spadać ⟨-paść⟩ (***on*** na *A*); **2.** nalot *m*

swop [swɒp] F → ***swap***

sword [sɔːd] miecz *m*

swore [swɔː] *pret. od* ***swear***

sworn [swɔːn] *p.p. od* ***swear***

swum [swʌm] *p.p. od* ***swim*** 1

swung [swʌŋ] *pret. i p.p. od* ***swing*** 1

syc·a·more ['sɪkəmɔː] *bot.* jawor *m*; *Am.* platan *m*; sykomora *f*

syl·la·ble ['sɪləbl] *gr.* sylaba *f*

syl·la·bus *pred. univ.* ['sɪləbəs] (*pl.* ***-buses, -bi*** [-baɪ]) program *m* nauczania

sym·bol ['sɪmbl] symbol *m*; **~·ic** [sɪm'bɒlɪk] symboliczny; **~·ism** ['sɪmbəlɪzəm] symbolizm *m*; **~·ize** ['sɪmbəlaɪz] symbolizować

S

sym|·met·ri·cal [sɪ'metrɪkl] symetryczny; **~·me·try** ['sɪmɪtrɪ] symetria *f*
sym·pa|·thet·ic [sɪmpə'θetɪk] (**-*ally***) współczujący; rozumiejący; życzliwy; **~·thize** ['sɪmpəθaɪz] współczuć; **~·thy** ['sɪmpəθɪ] współczucie *n*
sym·pho·ny ['sɪmfənɪ] *mus.* symfonia *f*; *attr.* symfoniczny
symp·tom ['sɪmptəm] symptom *m*, oznaka *f*
syn·chro|·nize ['sɪŋkrənaɪz] *v/t.* ⟨z⟩synchronizować; *zegarki itp.* uzgadniać ⟨-godnić⟩; *v/i.* być zsynchronizowanym
syn·o·nym ['sɪnənɪm] synonim *m*; **sy·non·y·mous** [sɪ'nɒnɪməs] synonimiczny
syn·tax ['sɪntæks] *gr.* składnia *f*
syn·the·sis ['sɪnθəsɪs] (*pl.* **-*ses*** [-siːz]) synteza *f*
syn·thet·ic [sɪn'θetɪk] (***~ally***) syntetyczny; **~ 'fi·bre** *Brt.*, (*Am.*; **fi·ber**) włókno *n* syntetyczne
sy·ringe ['sɪrɪndʒ] *med.* strzykawka *f*
syr·up ['sɪrəp] syrop *m*
sys·tem ['sɪstəm] system *m*; *uliczna* sieć *f*; organizm *m*
sys·te·mat·ic [sɪstə'mætɪk] (***~ally***) systematyczny
'sys·tem er·ror *komp.* błąd *m* systemu

T

T, t [tiː] T, t
t *skrót pisany*: ***ton*(*s*)** tona *f* (-ny *pl.*) (*Brt.* =*1016 kg*, *Am.* = *907,18 kg*)
ta *Brt. int.* F [tɑː] dzięki
tab [tæb] etykietka *f*; wieszak *m*; konik *m*, (*w kartotece*) nalepka *f*; F rachunek *m*
ta·ble ['teɪbl] **1.** stół *m*, stolik *m*; tabela *f*; zestawienie *n*; *math.* tablica *f*; *attr.* stołowy; ***at ~*** przy stole; ***be on the ~*** *fig.* być na tapecie; ***turn the ~s* (*on s.o.*)** *fig.* odwracać ⟨-rócić⟩ role; **2.** *fig.* przedstawiać ⟨-wić⟩ (*do rozpatrzenia*); *zwł. Am. fig.* odkładać ⟨odłożyć⟩; **'~·cloth** obrus *m*; **'~·land** plateau *n*, płaskowyż *m*; **'~ lin·en** bielizna *f* stołowa; **'~·mat** podkładka *f* (*pod talerz*); **'~·spoon** duża łyżka *f* stołowa (*do nabierania potraw*)
tab·let ['tæblɪt] tabletka *f*; *kamienna* tablica *f*; kostka *f* (*mydła*)
'table| ten·nis (*w sporcie*) tenis *m* stołowy; **'~ ·top** blat *m*; **'~·ware** naczynia *pl.* stołowe
tab·loid ['tæblɔɪd] gazeta *f* bulwarowa; **'~ press** prasa *f* bulwarowa
ta·boo [tə'buː] **1.** tabu; **2.** (*pl.* **-*boos***) tabu *n*
tab·u|·lar ['tæbjʊlə] tabelaryczny; **~·late** ['tæbjʊleɪt] układać ⟨ułożyć⟩ tabelarycznie; **'~·la·tor** tabulator *m*
tach·o·graph ['tækəʊgrɑːf] *mot.* tachograf *m*, tachometr *m* piszący
ta·chom·e·ter [tæ'kɒmɪtə] *mot.* obrotomierz *m*, tachometr *m*
ta·cit ['tæsɪt] milczący; **ta·ci·turn** ['tæsɪtɜːn] małomówny
tack [tæk] **1.** gwóźdź *m* (*tapicerski*); pinezka *f*; fastryga *f*; *naut.* hals *m*; **2.** ⟨przy⟩fastrygować (***to do*** *G*); **~ *on*** doklejać ⟨-kleić⟩, doczepiać ⟨-czepić⟩ (***to*** do *G*)
tack·le ['tækl] **1.** *problem itp.* zabierać ⟨-brać⟩ się do (*G*); (*w piłce nożnej*) przeciwnika ⟨za⟩atakować; dawać ⟨dać⟩ znać (*D*); **2.** *tech.* wielokrążek *m*; sprzęt *m* (*wędkarski itp.*)
tack·y ['tækɪ] (**-*ier*, -*iest***) kleisty, lepki; *zwł. Am.* F tandetny
tact [tækt] takt *m*; **'~·ful** taktowny
tac·tics ['tæktɪks] *pl. i sg.* taktyka *f*
'tact·less nietaktowny
tad·pole ['tædpəʊl] *zo.* kijanka *f*
taf·fe·ta ['tæfɪtə] tafta *m*
taf·fy ['tæfɪ] *Am.* → ***toffee***
tag [tæg] **1.** etykieta *f*; metka *f*; plakietka *f* (*z nazwiskiem*); skuwka *f* (*na sznurowadl itp.*); *też* ***question ~*** pytanie *n* ucięte; **2.** (**-*gg-***) etykietować, przyczepiać ⟨-pić⟩ etykietę do (*G*); ***~ along*** F przyklejać ⟨-leić⟩ się; ***~ along behind s.o.*** ciągnąć się za kimś
tail [teɪl] **1.** ogon *m* (*też aviat.*); tylna część *f*; F (*osoba śledząca*) ogon *m*; ***put a ~ on*** śledzić (*A*); ***turn ~*** *fig.* dawać ⟨-dać⟩ nogę; ***with one's ~ between***

one's legs *fig.* z podkulonym ogonem; **~*s*** *pl.* odwrotna strona *f* (*monety*); frak *m*; **2.** F *kogoś* śledzić; **~ *back*** *zwł. Brt. mot.* ciągnąć się (***to*** do *G*); **~ *off*** zmniejszać ⟨-szyć⟩ się; **'~·back** *zwł. Brt. mot.* korek *m*; **~'coat** frak *m*; **~ 'end** koniec *m*, tył *m*; **'~·light** *mot.* światło *n* tylne

tai·lor ['teɪlə] **1.** krawiec *m* (*męski*); **2.** ⟨u⟩szyć, ⟨s⟩kroić; *fig.* dopasowywać ⟨-sować⟩; **~-'made** szyte na miarę

'tail| pipe *Am. tech.* rura *f* wydechowa; **'~·wind** tylny wiatr *m*

taint·ed ['teɪntɪd] *zwł. Am. mięso*: zepsuty; *fig.* splamiony

take [teɪk] **1.** (***took, taken***) *v/t.* brać ⟨wziąć⟩ (*też mil. itp.*); przyjmować ⟨-jąć⟩; (*w szachach*) *figurę* zbijać ⟨zbić⟩; *egzamin* zdawać ⟨-dać⟩; *univ. specjalność* studiować; *nagrodę itp.* zdobywać ⟨-być⟩; *czek, odpowiedzialność itp.* przyjmować ⟨-jąć⟩; *miejsce itp.* zajmować ⟨-jąć⟩; *phot.* ⟨z⟩robić; *temperaturę itp.* ⟨z⟩mierzyć; *kąpiel* brać ⟨wziąć⟩; *autobusem itp.* jeździć, pojechać; *drogą itp.* ⟨po⟩jechać; *samolotem* polecieć; korzystać z(e) (*G*) (*sposobności itp.*); *odwagę* zbierać ⟨zebrać⟩; *czas* zabierać ⟨-brać⟩; *gazety* ⟨za⟩prenumerować; *kroki* podejmować ⟨-djąć⟩; ***it took him four hours*** zajęło mu to cztery godziny; ***I ~ it that*** sądzę, że; **~ *it or leave*** F rób co chcesz; ***be ~n*** *miejsce*: być zajętym; ***be ~n by*** *lub* ***with*** zachwycony (*D*); ***be ~n ill*** *lub* ***sick*** zachorować; **~ *to bits*** *lub* ***pieces*** rozbierać ⟨-zebrać⟩; **~ *the blame*** przyjmować ⟨-jąć⟩ winę; **~ *care*** ⟨za⟩opiekować się, ⟨za⟩troszczyć się; **~ *care!*** F trzymaj się!; → ***care*** 1; **~ *hold of*** ⟨s⟩chwytać; **~ *part*** brać ⟨wziąć⟩ udział; → ***part*** 1; **~ *pity on*** żałować (*G*); **~ *a walk*** iść ⟨pójść⟩ na spacer; **~ *my word for it*** daję ci słowo; → ***advice***, ***bath***, ***break***, ***lead***[1]; ***message***, ***oath***, ***place***, ***prisoner***, ***risk***, ***seat***, ***step***, ***trouble*** *itp.*; *v/i. med.* ⟨po⟩działać; **~ *after*** być podobnym do (*G*); **~ *along*** brać ⟨wziąć⟩ ze sobą (*A*); **~ *apart*** rozbierać ⟨-zebrać⟩ (*na części*); **~ *away*** umniejszać ⟨-szyć⟩; ***...to ~ away*** *Brt.* ...na wynos; **~ *back*** odbierać ⟨-debrać⟩; *słowa* cofać ⟨-fnąć⟩; przywracać ⟨-rócić⟩ (*do łas itp.*); ⟨o⟩budzić *czyjeś* wspomnienia; **~ *down*** ⟨za⟩notować; rozbierać ⟨-zebrać⟩; *ubranie itp.* ściągać ⟨-gnąć⟩ do dołu; **~ *for*** brać ⟨wziąć⟩ za (*A*); **~ *from*** przejmować ⟨-jąć⟩ *coś* od *kogoś*; *math.* odejmować ⟨-djąć⟩ (od *G*); **~ *in*** przyjmować ⟨-jąć⟩ (*u siebie*); *fig.* obejmować ⟨-bjąć⟩; *ubranie* zwężać ⟨zwęzić⟩; *coś* ⟨z⟩rozumieć; *kogoś* oszukiwać ⟨-kać⟩; **~ *off*** zdejmować ⟨zdjąć⟩; *aviat.*, (*w sporcie*) ⟨wy⟩startować (*też fig.*); F odjeżdżać ⟨odjechać⟩; **~ *a day off*** brać ⟨wziąć⟩ dzień wolnego; **~ *on*** przyjąć *kogoś* (do pracy); *odpowiedzialność* brać ⟨wziąć⟩; *kolor* przybierać ⟨-brać⟩; podejmować ⟨-djąć⟩ się (*pracy*); przeciwstawiać ⟨-wić⟩ się; **~ *out*** wyjmować ⟨-jąć⟩; wychodzić ⟨wyjść⟩ z (*I*) (***to*** *do* (*kina itp.*); *ząb* usuwać ⟨-sunąć⟩; *polisę itp.* uzyskiwać ⟨-kać⟩; **~ *out on*** wyżywać ⟨-żyć⟩ się na (*I*); **~ *over*** *władzę itp.* przejmować ⟨-jąć⟩; przyjmować ⟨-jąć⟩ obowiązki; **~ *to*** polubić (od razu); **~ *to doing s.th.*** zaczynać ⟨-cząć⟩ coś robić; **~ *up*** zainteresować się (*I*); *kwestię* podejmować ⟨-djąć⟩; zajmować ⟨-jąć⟩; *opowieść* kontynuować; **~ *up doing s.th.*** zabierać ⟨-brać⟩ się do (robienia) czegoś; podnosić; **~ *up with*** zajmować się (*I*); **2.** *film, TV*: ujęcie *n*; F wpływ *m*

'take·a·way *Brt.* posiłki *pl.* na wynos; restauracja *f* z posiłkami na wynos

tak·en ['teɪkən] *p.p. od* **take** 1

'take·off start *m* (*samolotu*)

tak·ings ['teɪkɪŋz] *pl.* wpływy *pl.*, dochód *m*

tale [teɪl] opowieść *f*; baśń *f*; ***tell ~s*** puszczać ⟨puścić⟩ plotki

tal·ent ['tælənt] talent *m*; powołanie *n*; **'~·ed** utalentowany

tal·is·man ['tælɪzmən] talizman *m*

talk [tɔːk] **1.** *v/i.* mówić; rozmawiać (***to, with*** do *G*, ***about*** o *L*); ***s.o. to ~ to*** osoba, z którą można porozmawiać; *v/t. bzdury* mówić, wygadywać; mówić o (*L*) (*interesach itp.*); **~ *s.o. into s.th.*** namawiać ⟨-mówić⟩ kogoś do czegoś; **~ *s.o. out of s.th.*** wyperswadować komuś coś; **~ *s.th. over*** *problem itp.* omawiać ⟨-mówić⟩ (***with*** z *I*); **~ *round*** *kogoś* namówić (***to*** do *G*); **2.** rozmowa *f* (***with*** z *I*, ***about*** o *L*); pogadanka *f*, prelekcja *f*; mowa *f* (*dziecka itp.*); gadanina *f*; ***give a ~*** wygłaszać ⟨-łosić⟩ pogadan-

kę (***to*** *D*, ***about, on*** o *L*); ***be the ~ of the town*** być na językach wszystkich; ***baby ~*** mowa *f* dziecka; → ***small talk***
talk|·a·tive ['tɔːkətɪv] gadatliwy; '**~·er**: ***be a good ~er*** umieć dobrze mówić; '**~·ing-to** (*pl.* ***-tos***) F bura *f*; ***give s.o. a good ~ing-to*** nagadać komuś; '**~ show** *zwł. Am.* talkshow *m*; **~-show 'host** *zwł. Am.* prowadzący *m* (-ca *f*) talkshow
tall [tɔːl] wysoki; ***be 5 feet ~*** mieć 5 stóp wzrostu
tal·low ['tæləʊ] łój *m*
tal·ly¹ ['tælɪ] *econ.*, (*w sporcie*) wynik *m*; liczenie *n*; ***keep a ~ of*** prowadzić rejestr (*G*)
tal·ly² ['tælɪ] zgadzać ⟨zgodzić⟩ się (***with*** z *I*); *też* ***~ up*** podliczać ⟨-czyć⟩
tal·on ['tælən] *zo.* szpon *m*
tame [teɪm] **1.** (***-r, -st***) *zo.* oswojony; łagodny; **2.** *zwierzę* oswajać ⟨-woić⟩
tam·per ['tæmpə]: ***~ with*** manipulować (*I*), dokonywać manipulacji z (*I*)
tam·pon ['tæmpən] tampon *m*
tan [tæn] **1.** (***-nn-***) opalać ⟨-lić⟩ się; *skórę* ⟨wy⟩garbować; **2.** opalenizna *f*; jasny brąz *m*; **3.** jasnobrązowy
tang [tæŋ] ostry smak *m lub* zapach *m*
tan·gent ['tændʒənt] *math.* tangens *m*; ***fly*** *lub* ***go off at a ~*** zbaczać ⟨zboczyć⟩ z tematu
tan·ge·rine [tændʒə'riːn] *bot.* mandarynka *f*
tan·gi·ble ['tændʒəbl] dotykalny; *fig.* namacalny
tan·gle ['tæŋgl] **1.** ⟨za⟩plątać się; *włosy* ⟨z⟩mierzwić; **2.** plątanina *f*; bałagan *m*
tank [tæŋk] *mot. itp.* zbiornik *m*; *mil.* czołg *m*
tank·ard ['tæŋkəd] kufel *m* (*do piwa*)
tank·er ['tæŋkə] *naut.* zbiornikowiec *m*; *aviat.* samolot *m* cysterna; *mot.* (*samochód*) cysterna *f*
tan|·ner ['tænə] garbarz *m*; **~·ne·ry** ['tænərɪ] garbarnia *f*
tan·ta|·lize ['tæntəlaɪz] dręczyć (*I*); '**~·liz·ing** dręczący
tan·ta·mount ['tæntəmaʊnt]: ***be ~ to*** być równoznacznym z (*I*)
tan·trum ['tæntrəm] *fig.* histeria *f*
tap¹ [tæp] **1.** kran *m*; *tech.* kurek *m*; zawór *m*; ***beer on ~*** piwo *n* z beczki; **2.** (***-pp-***) *zasoby* wykorzystywać ⟨-tać⟩, eksploatować; zakładać ⟨założyć⟩ podsłuch; podsłuchiwać ⟨-chać⟩; ⟨na⟩czerpać (*z beczki*)
tap² [tæp] **1.** (***-pp-***) *palcami* pukać, stukać (***on*** o *A*); ***~ s.o. on the shoulder*** ⟨po⟩klepać kogoś po ramieniu; ***~ on*** ⟨za⟩stukać w (*A*); **2.** (lekkie) uderzenie *n*; klaps *m*; '**~ dance** stepowanie *n*
tape [teɪp] **1.** taśma *f*; tasiemka *f*; taśma *f* klejąca; *TV, video, magnetofonowa itp.* kaseta *f*; → ***red tape***; *TV* zapis *m*; **2.** zapisywać ⟨-sać⟩ na taśmie; *też* ***~ up*** zaklejać ⟨-leić⟩ taśmą; '**~ deck** deck *m* magnetofonowy; '**~ meas·ure** taśma *f* krawiecka, przymiar *m*
ta·per ['teɪpə] *też* ***~ off*** zwężać się (*do dołu*); *fig.* zmniejszać ⟨-szyć⟩ się
'tape| re·cord·er magnetofon *m*; '**~ re·cord·ing** nagranie *n* magnetofonowe
ta·pes·try ['tæpɪstrɪ] gobelin *m*
'tape·worm *zo.* tasiemiec *m*
taps [tæps] *zwł. Am. pl.* (*sygnał*) capstrzyk *m*
'tap water woda *f* bieżąca
tar [tɑː] **1.** smoła *f*; (*w papierosie*) substancja *f* smolista; **2.** (***-rr-***) ⟨na⟩smołować
tare [teə] *econ.* tara *f*
tar·get ['tɑːgɪt] cel *m* (*też mil., fig.*); *mil.* zadanie *n*; tarcza *f* strzelnicza; *attr.* docelowy; '**~ ar·e·a** *mil.* rejon *m* celu; '**~ group** *reklamy*: grupa *f* odbiorców; '**~ lan·guage** język *m* docelowy; '**~ prac·tice** ćwiczenia *pl.* w strzelaniu do tarczy
tar·iff ['tærɪf] taryfa *f*; taryfa *f* celna; *zwł. Brt.* stawki *pl.*
tar·mac ['tɑːmæk] asfalt *m*; *aviat.* pas *m* startowy
tar·nish ['tɑːnɪʃ] ⟨z⟩matowieć, ⟨s⟩tracić połysk; *fig. reputację* ⟨s⟩plamić
tart¹ [tɑːt] *zwł. Brt.* placek *m lub* ciastko *n* z owocami; F dziwka *f*, puszczalska *f*
tart² [tɑːt] ostry; cierpki (*też fig.*)
tar·tan ['tɑːtn] tartan *m*
tar·tar ['tɑːtə] osad *m* nazębny; *chem.* kamień *m* winny
task [tɑːsk] zadanie *n*; ***take s.o. to ~*** *fig.* udzielać ⟨-lić⟩ komuś reprymendy (***for*** za *A*); '**~ force** *mil.* oddział *m* specjalny (*wojska, policji*)
tas·sel ['tæsl] frędzel *m*
taste [teɪst] **1.** smak *m* (*też fig.*); gust *m*; posmak *m*; zamiłowanie (***for*** do *G*);

2. *v/i.* ⟨s⟩próbować, ⟨s⟩kosztować; *v/t.* smakować (***of*** *I*), mieć smak; '**~·ful** gustowny; '**~·less** niesmaczny (*też fig.*); niegustowny
tast·y ['teɪstɪ] (***-ier, -iest***) smaczny
ta-ta [tæ'tɑː] *int. Brt.* F cześć!
Tatra Mountains *pl.* Tatry *pl.*
tat·tered ['tætəd] obszarpany
tat·tle ['tætl] plotkować
tat·too¹ [tə'tuː] **1.** (*pl.* ***-toos***) tatuaż *m*; **2.** ⟨wy⟩tatuować
tat·too² [tə'tuː] *mil.* (*pl.* ***-toos***) capstrzyk *m*
taught [tɔːt] *pret. i p.p. od* ***teach***
taunt [tɔːnt] **1.** ⟨za⟩drwić z (*I*); **2.** drwina *f*
Tau·rus ['tɔːrəs] *znak Zodiaku*: Byk *m*; (***s***)***he is*** (***a***) **~** on(a) jest spod znaku Byka
taut [tɔːt] napięty (*też fig.*), naprężony
taw·dry ['tɔːdrɪ] (***-ier, -iest***) (tani i) tandetny
taw·ny ['tɔːnɪ] (***-ier, -iest***) płowy
tax [tæks] **1.** podatek *m* (***on*** od *G*); **2.** opodatkowywać ⟨-ować⟩; *cierpliwość* wystawiać ⟨-wić⟩ na ciężką próbę; **~·a·tion** [tæk'seɪʃn] opodatkowanie *n*
tax·i ['tæksɪ] **1.** taksówka *f*; **2.** *aviat.* kołować; '**~ driv·er** taksówkarz *m*; '**~ rank**, '**~ stand** postój *m* taksówek
'**tax**|**·pay·er** podatnik *m*; '**~ re·turn** deklaracja *f* podatkowa
T-bar ['tiːbɑː] teownik *m*; *też* **~ *lift*** wyciąg *m*
tea [tiː] herbata *f*; ***have a cup of* ~** wypić filiżankę herbaty; ***make some* ~** zaparzyć herbatę; → ***high tea***; '**~·bag** herbata *f* ekspresowa
teach [tiːtʃ] (***taught***) uczyć, nauczać ⟨-czyć⟩ (*G*); '**~·er** nauczyciel(ka *f*) *m*
'**tea**| **co·sy** kapturek *m* (*na naczynie z herbatą*); '**~·cup** filiżanka *f* do herbaty
team [tiːm] zespół *m*; (*w sporcie*) drużyna *f*; zespół *m*; **~·ster** *Am.* ['tiːmstə] kierowca *m* ciężarówki; '**~·work** praca *f* zespołowa
'**tea·pot** czajniczek *m*
tear¹ [tɪə] łza *f*; ***in* ~*s*** we łzach;
tear² [teə] **1.** (***tore, torn***) *v/t.* rozdzierać ⟨-zedrzeć⟩; *też* **~ *up*** ⟨po⟩drzeć (***into*** na *A*); wydzierać ⟨-drzeć⟩; odrywać ⟨oderwać⟩ (***from*** od *G*); *drzewo, kartkę itp.* wyrywać ⟨-rwać⟩ (***from, out of*** z *G*); *dach itp.* zrywać ⟨zerwać⟩; *v/i.* ⟨po⟩rwać się; F ⟨po⟩gnać, ⟨po⟩mknąć; **~ *down*** *plakat itp.* zrywać ⟨zerwać⟩; *dom* ⟨z⟩burzyć; **~ *off*** *ubranie* zrywać z siebie; **2.** rozdarcie *n*
'**tear**|**·drop** łza *f*; '**~·ful** łzawy; zapłakany
'**tea·room** herbaciarnia *f*
tease [tiːz] dokuczać ⟨-czyć⟩; dręczyć
'**tea·spoon** łyżeczka *f* do herbaty
teat [tiːt] *zo.* cycek *m*, sutek *m*; *Brt.* smoczek *m* (*na butelkę*)
tech·ni·cal ['teknɪkl] techniczny; fachowy; *jur.* formalny; **~·i·ty** [teknɪ'kælətɪ] szczegół *m* techniczny; *jur.* kwestia *f* formalna
tech·ni·cian [tek'nɪʃn] technik *m*
tech·nique [tek'niːk] technika *f* (*sposób wykonywania)*; ⚠ *nie* ***technika*** (*przemysłowa*)
tech·nol·o·gy [tek'nɒlədʒɪ] technologia *f*
ted·dy bear ['tedɪ -] miś *m* pluszowy
te·di·ous ['tiːdjəs] nużący
teem [tiːm]: **~ *with*** roić się od (*G*), mrowić się od (*G*)
teen|**-age**(**d**) ['tiːneɪdʒ(d)] nastoletni; '**~·ag·er** nastolatek *m* (-tka *f*)
teens [tiːnz] *pl.*: ***be in one's* ~** mieć kilkanaście lat
tee·ny ['tiːnɪ], **~-wee·ny** [tiːnɪ'wiːnɪ] (***-ier, -iest***) malutki, maluśki
tee shirt ['tiːʃɜːt] → ***T-shirt***
teeth [tiːθ] *pl. od* ***tooth***
teethe [tiːð] ząbkować
tee·to·tal·(l)er [tiː'təʊtlə] abstynent(ka *f*) *m*
tel·e·cast ['telɪkɑːst] transmisja *f* telewizyjna
tel·e·com·mu·ni·ca·tions [telɪkəmjuːnɪ'keɪʃnz] *pl.* telekomunikacja *f*
tel·e·gram ['telɪgræm] telegram *m*
tel·e·graph ['telɪgrɑːf] **1.** telegraf *m*; ***by* ~** telegraficznie; **2.** ⟨za⟩telegrafować; **~·ic** [telɪ'græfɪk] (***-ally***) telegraficzny
te·leg·ra·phy [tɪ'legrəfɪ] telegrafia *f*
tel·e·phone ['telɪfəʊn] (*też* ***phone*** 1, 2) **1.** telefon *m*; **2.** ⟨za⟩telefonować; '**~ booth** *zwł. Am.*, '**~ box** *Brt.* budka *f* telefoniczna; '**~ call** rozmowa *f* telefoniczna; '**~ di·rec·to·ry** → ***phone book***; '**~ ex·change** centrala *f* telefoniczna; '**~ num·ber** numer *m* telefoniczny

T

te·leph·o·nist [tɪ'lefənɪst] *zwł. Brt.* telefonista *m* (-tka *f*)
tel·e·pho·to lens [telɪfəʊtəʊ 'lenz] *phot.* teleobiektyw *m*
tel·e·print·er ['telɪprɪntə] dalekopis *m*
tel·e·scope ['telɪskəʊp] teleskop *m*
tel·e·text ['telɪtekst] teletekst *m*, telegazeta *f*
tel·e·type·writ·er [telɪ'taɪpraɪtə] *zwł. Am.* dalekopis *m*
tel·e·vise ['telɪvaɪz] *TV* transmitować
tel·e·vi·sion ['telɪvɪʒn] telewizja *f*; *attr.* telewizyjny; ***on ~*** w telewizji; ***watch ~*** oglądać telewizję; *też* ***~ set*** telewizor *m*
tel·ex ['teleks] **1.** teleks *m*, dalekopis *m*; **2.** ⟨za⟩teleksować (***to*** do *G*)
tell [tel] (***told***) *v/t.* mówić ⟨powiedzieć⟩; opowiadać ⟨-wiedzieć⟩ (***about, of*** o *L*); *wskaźnik*: wskazywać ⟨-zać⟩; polecać ⟨-cić⟩ (***to do*** zrobić); odróżniać ⟨-nić⟩ (***from*** od *G*); ***I can't ~ them apart*** nie mogę ich odróżnić; *v/i.* dawać znać (***on*** po *L*); ***who can ~?*** kto wie?; ***you can never ~, you never can ~*** nigdy nie wiadomo; ***~ against*** świadczyć przeciwko (*D*); *v/t.* ***~ off*** F ⟨z⟩rugać (*A*); *v/i.* ***~ on s.o.*** ⟨na⟩skarżyć na kogoś; **'~·er** *zwł. Am.* (*w banku*) kasjer(ka *f*) *m*; **'~·ing** znaczący, wymowny; **'~·tale 1.** niedwuznaczny, wymowny; **2.** F skarżypyta *m*, *f*
tel·ly ['telɪ] *Brt.* F telewizor *m*
te·mer·i·ty [tɪ'merətɪ] czelność *f*
tem·per ['tempə] **1.** temperament *m*; humor *m*, nastrój *m*; *tech.* stopień *m* twardości (*stali*); ***keep one's ~*** nie dawać ⟨dać⟩ się ponieść; ***lose one's ~*** ⟨s⟩tracić panowanie nad sobą; **2.** *stal* ⟨za⟩hartować
tem·pe|·ra·ment ['tempərəmənt] temperament *m*; usposobienie *n*; **~·ra·men·tal** [tempərə'mentl] porywczy, o żywym temperamencie; kapryśny
tem·pe·rate ['tempərət] *klimat itp.*: umiarkowany
tem·pe·ra·ture ['temprətʃə] temperatura *f*; ***have*** *lub* ***be running a ~*** mieć podwyższoną temperaturę
tem·pest ['tempɪst] *poet.* burza *f*
tem·ple¹ ['templ] świątynia *f*
tem·ple² ['templ] *anat.* skroń *f*
tem·po|·ral ['tempərəl] doczesny; *gr.* (*dotyczący czasów*), czasowy; **~·ra·ry** ['tempərərɪ] prowizoryczny, tymczasowy
tempt [tempt] ⟨s⟩kusić (*też rel.*); ⟨z⟩wabić (***to*** do *G*); **temp·ta·tion** [temp'teɪʃn] kuszenie *n* (*też rel.*); wabienie *n*; **'~·ing** kuszący
ten [ten] **1.** dziesięć; **2.** dziesiątka *f*
ten·a·ble ['tenəbl] (*argument dający się obronić*)
te·na·cious [tɪ'neɪʃəs] uporczywy, wytrwały
ten·ant ['tenənt] lokator(ka *f*) *m*
tend [tend] mieć tendencję (***to*** do *G*); skłaniać się (***towards*** w stronę *G*); ***~ to do s.th.*** zwykle coś robić; ***~ upwards*** mieć tendencje zwyżkowe; **ten·den·cy** ['tendənsɪ] tendencja *f*
ten·der¹ ['tendə] czuły; tkliwy, bolesny; *pieczeń itp.*: miękki
ten·der² ['tendə] *rail.*, *naut.* tender *m*
ten·der³ ['tendə] *econ.* **1.** oferta *f*; ***legal ~*** prawny środek *m* płatniczy; **2.** przedstawiać ⟨-wić⟩ ofertę (***for*** na *A*)
'ten·der|·foot (*pl.* ***-foots, -feet***) *Am.* F nowicjusz(ka *f*) *m*; **'~·loin** polędwica *f*; **'~·ness** czułość *f*; tkliwość *f*, obolałość *f*
ten·don ['tendən] *anat.* ścięgno *n*
ten·dril ['tendrɪl] *bot.* wąs *m* pnącza
ten·e·ment ['tenɪmənt] dom *m* czynszowy
ten·nis ['tenɪs] (*w sporcie*) tenis *m*; **'~ court** kort *m* tenisowy; **'~ play·er** tenisista *m* (-tka *f*)
ten·or ['tenə] *mus.* tenor *m*; wydźwięk *m*, brzmienie *n*
tense¹ [tens] *gr.* czas *m*
tense² [tens] (***-r, -st***) *ktoś, coś* napięty; *ktoś* spięty; *żagiel* naprężony; **ten·sion** ['tenʃn] napięcie *n*
tent [tent] namiot *m*
ten·ta·cle ['tentəkl] *zo.* macka *f*; czułek *m*
ten·ta·tive ['tentətɪv] próbny; nie ostateczny
ten·ter·hooks ['tentəhʊks]: ***be on ~*** siedzieć jak na szpilkach
tenth [tenθ] **1.** dziesiąty; **2.** dziesiątka *f*; **'~·ly** po dziesiąte
ten·u·ous ['tenjʊəs] *fig.* nieznaczny, niepozorny
ten·ure ['tenjʊə] posiadanie *n*; okres *m* posiadania; ***~ of office*** piastowanie *n* urzędu

T

tep·id ['tepɪd] letni

term [tɜːm] **1.** termin *m*, okres *m*; kadencja *f*; *zwł. Brt. ped., univ.* trymestr *m*, *Am.* semestr *m*; określenie *n*, wyrażenie *n*; **~ *of office*** kadencja *f*; **~s** *pl.* warunki *pl.*; ***be on good*** (***bad***) **~ *with*** być z *kimś* w dobrych (złych) stosunkach; ***they are not on speaking* ~s** nie rozmawiają ze sobą; ***come to* ~s *with*** ⟨po⟩godzić się z (*I*); **2.** nazywać ⟨-zwać⟩, określać ⟨-lić⟩

ter·mi|·nal ['tɜːmɪnl] **1.** końcowy; *med.* terminalny; krańcowy; **~*ally ill*** śmiertelnie chory; **2.** *rail. itp.* stacja *f* końcowa; terminal *m*; → ***air terminal***; *electr.* zacisk *m*, przyłącze *n*; *komp.* terminal *m*; **~·nate** ['tɜːmɪneɪt] *v/t.* ⟨za⟩kończyć; *umowę* rozwiązywać ⟨-zać⟩; *ciążę* przerywać ⟨-rwać⟩; *v/i.* ⟨za⟩kończyć się; wygasać ⟨-snąć⟩; **~·na·tion** [tɜːmɪ'neɪʃn] zakończenie *n*; rozwiązanie *n*; przerwanie *n*; upłynięcie *n*

ter·mi·nus ['tɜːmɪnəs] (*pl.* **-*ni*** [-naɪ], **-*nuses***) *rail. itp.* stacja *f* końcowa

ter·race ['terəs] taras *m*; szereg *m* domów; *zw.* **~s** *pl. zwł. Brt.* (*na trybunie sportowej*) miejsca *pl.* stojące; **~d 'house** dom *m* szeregowy

ter·res·tri·al [tə'restrɪəl] ziemski; *zwł. zo., bot.* lądowy

ter·ri·ble ['terəbl] straszny

ter·rif·ic [tə'rɪfɪk] (**~*ally***) fantastyczny, wspaniały; *prędkość* straszny

ter·ri·fy ['terɪfaɪ] przerażać ⟨-razić⟩

ter·ri·to|·ri·al [terə'tɔːrɪəl] terytorialny; **~·ry** ['terətərɪ] terytorium *n*, obszar *m*

ter·ror ['terə] terror *m*; przerażenie *n*; **~·is·m** ['terərɪzm] terroryzm *m*; **~·ist** ['terərɪst] terrorysta *m* (-tka *f*); **~·ize** ['terəraɪz] ⟨s⟩terroryzować

terse [tɜːs] (**-*r*, -*st***) zwięzły

test [test] **1.** test *m*, sprawdzian *m*; egzamin *m*; badanie *n*; próba *f*; **2.** ⟨prze⟩testować; sprawdzać ⟨-dzić⟩; ⟨z⟩badać; poddawać ⟨-ddać⟩ próbie

tes·ta·ment ['testəmənt] testament *m* (*też rel.*); ***last will and* ~** ostatnia wola *f*

'test| card *TV* obraz *m* kontrolny; **'~ drive** *mot.* jazda *f* próbna

tes·ti·cle ['testɪkl] *anat.* jądro *n*

tes·ti·fy ['testɪfaɪ] *jur.* świadczyć, zeznawać ⟨-nać⟩

tes·ti·mo|·ni·al [testɪ'məʊnjəl] referencja *f*; **~·ny** ['testɪmənɪ] *jur.* świadectwo *n*, zaświadczenie *n*

'test| pi·lot *aviat.* oblatywacz *m*; **'~ tube** probówka *f*; **'~-tube ba·by** *med.* dziecko *n* z probówki

tes·ty ['testɪ] (**-*ier*, -*iest***) drażliwy

tet·a·nus ['tetənəs] *med.* tężec *m*

teth·er ['teðə] **1.** *zw.* więzy *pl.*; ***at the end of one's* ~** u kresu wytrzymałości; **2.** *zwierzę* przywiązywać ⟨-zać⟩

Texas Teksas *m*

text [tekst] tekst *m*; **'~·book** podręcznik *m*

tex·tile ['tekstaɪl] tekstylny; **~s** *pl.* artykuły *pl.* tekstylne

tex·ture ['tekstʃə] faktura *f*; budowa *f*, struktura *f*

Thames Tamiza *f*

than [ðæn, ðən] niż

thank [θæŋk] **1.** *komuś* ⟨po⟩dziękować (***for*** za *A*); **~ *you*** (***very much***) dziękuję (bardzo); ***no,* ~ *you*** nie, dziękuję; (***yes,***) **~ *you*** tak, proszę; **2. ~s** *pl.* podziękowania *pl.*; **~*s!*** dzięki!; ***no,* ~s** nie, dziękuję; **~*s to*** dzięki (*D*); **'~·ful** wdzięczny; **'~·less** niewdzięczny

'Thanks·giv·ing (**Day**) *Am.* Dzień *m* Dziękczynienia

that [ðæt, ðət] **1.** *pron. i adj.* (*pl.* ***those*** [ðəʊz]) ten *m*; tamten *m*; to, tamto; **2.** *relative pron.* (*pl.* ***that***) kiedy; gdy; **3.** *cj.* że; **4.** *adv.* F tak; ***it's* ~ *simple*** to takie proste

thatch [θætʃ] **1.** ⟨po⟩kryć strzechą; **2.** strzecha *f*

thaw [θɔː] **1.** ⟨od⟩tajać; **2.** odwilż *f* (*też fig.*)

the [ðə, *przed samogłoskami* ðɪ, *akcentowane* ðiː] **1.** *rodzajnik określony*: (*najczęściej nie tłumaczony*); **~ *horse*** koń *m*; **2.** *adv.* **~ ... ~ ...** im ..., tym ...; **~ *sooner* ~ *better*** im szybciej, tym lepiej

the·a·tre *Brt.*, **the·a·ter** *Am.* ['θɪətə] teatr *m*; sala *f* wykładowa; *Brt. med.* sala *f* operacyjna; *mil.* teatr *m* działań wojennych; **'~·go·er** teatroman(ka *f*) *m*; **the·at·ri·cal** [θɪ'ætrɪkl] teatralny; *fig.* kabotyński

theft [θeft] kradzież *f*

their [ðeə] *pl.* ich; **~s** [ðeəz] ich

them [ðem, ðəm] ich (*G, A*) *pl.*; im (*D*) *pl.*

theme [θiːm] temat *m*
them·selves [ðəm'selvz] się; sobie; sami; ***by ~*** przez siebie, bez pomocy
then [ðen] **1.** *adv.* wtedy; wówczas; ***by ~*** do tego czasu; ***from ~ on*** od tego czasu; → ***every, now*** 1, ***there***; **2.** *adj. zwł.* ***the ~*** ówczesny
the·o·lo·gian [θɪə'ləʊdʒən] teolog *m*;
the·ol·o·gy [θɪ'ɒlədʒɪ] teologia *f*
the·o|·ret·i·cal [θɪə'retɪkl] teoretyczny; **~·ry** ['θɪərɪ] teoria *f*
ther·a|·peu·tic [θerə'pjuːtɪk] terapeutyczny; **~·pist** ['θerəpɪst] terapeuta *m* (-tka *f*); **~·py** ['θerəpɪ] terapia *f*
there [ðeə] **1.** tam; ***~ is*** jest; ***~ are*** *pl.* są; ***~ isn't, aren't*** nie ma; ***~ and then*** na miejscu; ***~ you are*** proszę; ano właśnie!; **2.** *int.* no; ***~, ~*** no już dobrze; **~·a·bout(s)** ['ðeərəbaʊt(s)] coś koło tego; **~·aft·er** [ðeər'ɑːftə] następnie, później; **~·by** [ðeə'baɪ] poprzez to; **~·fore** ['ðeəfɔː] dlatego; **~·up·on** [ðeərə'pɒn] następnie
ther·mal ['θɜːml] **1.** termiczny; cieplny; *odzież*: ocieplany; termo...; **2.** prąd *m* termiczny
ther·mom·e·ter [θə'mɒmɪtə] termometr *m*
ther·mos ['θɜːmɒs] *TM* termos *m*
these [ðiːz] *pl. od* **this**
the·sis ['θiːsɪs] (*pl.* ***-ses*** [-siːz]) teza *f*; *univ.* rozprawa *f*, praca *f* doktorska
they [ðeɪ] oni *pl.*, one *pl.*
thick [θɪk] **1.** *adj.* gruby; *mgła, zupa itp.*: gęsty; F głupi; *akcent*: ciężki; *głos*: ochrypły; ***be ~ with*** roić się od (*G*); ***that's a bit ~!*** *zwł. Brt.* F tego już za dużo; **2.** *adv.* grubo; gęsto; ***lay it on ~*** F przesadzać (***about*** z *I*); **3.** ***in the ~ of*** w środku (*G*); ***through ~ and thin*** na dobre i na złe; **'~·en** zagęszczać ⟨-ęścić⟩; ⟨z⟩gęstnieć; **~·et** ['θɪkɪt] gąszcz *m*; **~'head·ed** F tępy; **'~·ness** grubość *f*; **~'set** krępy; **~-'skinned** *fig.* gruboskóry
thief [θiːf] (*pl.* ***thieves*** [θiːvz]) złodziej(ka *f*) *m*
thigh [θaɪ] *anat.* udo *m*
thim·ble ['θɪmbl] naparstek *m*
thin [θɪn] **1.** *adj.* (***-nn-***) cienki; chudy; rzadki; rozrzedzony; *głos, wymówka itp.*: słaby; **2.** *adv.* cienko; **3.** (***-nn-***) rozrzedzać ⟨-dzić⟩ (się); *rośliny*: przerzedzać ⟨-dzić⟩; rzednąć
thing [θɪŋ] rzecz *f*; przedmiot *m*, obiekt *m*; coś *n*; ***I couldn't see a ~*** nie widziałem niczego; ***another ~*** coś innego; ***the right ~*** właściwa rzecz *f*; ***~s*** *pl.* rzeczy *pl.*; sprawy *pl.*
thing·a·ma·jig F ['θɪŋəmɪdʒɪg] wihajster *m*, dings *m*
think [θɪŋk] *v/i.* (***thought***) ⟨po⟩myśleć (***about*** o *L*); zastanawiać ⟨-nowić⟩ się (***of*** nad *I*); rozważać ⟨-żyć⟩; sądzić, przypuszczać (***that*** że); ***I ~ so*** tak sądzę; ***I'll ~ about it*** zastanowię się nad tym; ***~ of*** przypominać ⟨-mnieć⟩ sobie o (*L*); ***~ of doing s.th.*** zastanawiać się nad zrobieniem czegoś; ***what do you ~ of...*** *lub* ***about...?*** co myślisz o ...?; *v/t.* ⟨po⟩myśleć; rozważać ⟨-żyć⟩; uważać (się) za (*A*); ***~ over*** zastanowić się nad (*I*), przemyśleć; ***~ up*** wymyślać ⟨-lić⟩; **'~ tank** grupa *lub* komisja *f* ekspertów
third [θɜːd] **1.** trzeci; **2.** trzecia część *f*; **'~·ly** po trzecie; **~-'rate** trzeciorzędny; ♀ **'World** Trzeci Świat *m*
thirst [θɜːst] pragnienie *n*; **'~·y** (***-ier, -iest***) spragniony; ***he's ~y*** pić mu się chce
thir|·teen [θɜː'tiːn] **1.** trzynaście; **2.** trzynastka *f*; **~·teenth** [θɜː'tiːnθ] trzynasty; **~·ti·eth** ['θɜːtɪɪθ] trzydziesty; **~·ty** ['θɜːtɪ] **1.** trzydzieści; **2.** trzydziestka *f*
this [ðɪs] (*pl.* ***these*** [ðiːz]) to, ten; ***~ morning*** dzisiejszego ranka; ***~ is John speaking*** John przy telefonie
this·tle ['θɪsl] *bot.* oset *m*
thong [θɒŋ] rzemień *m*, rzemyk *m*
thorn [θɔːn] cierń *m*, kolec *m*; **'~·y** (***-ier, -iest***) ciernisty, kolczasty; *fig.* trudny
thor·ough ['θʌrə] dokładny, gruntowny; całkowity; drobiazgowy; **'~·bred** *zo.* koń *m* pełnej krwi; **'~·fare** magistrala *f*, arteria *f*
those [ðəʊz] *pl. od* **that** 1
though [ðəʊ] **1.** *cj.* chociaż, choć; ***as ~*** jakby; **2.** *adv.* jednak
thought [θɔːt] **1.** *pret. i p.p. od* **think**; **2.** myśl *f*; zastanowienie *n* się; ***on second ~s*** po zastanowieniu się; **'~·ful** zamyślony; troskliwy; **'~·less** bezmyślny
thou·sand ['θaʊznd] **1.** tysiąc; **2.** tysiąc *m*; **~th** ['θaʊzntθ] **1.** tysięczny; **2.** tysięczna część *f*
thrash [θræʃ] *kogoś* ⟨wy⟩młócić; (*w grze*) pobić; ***~ about, ~ around*** rzu-

cać ⟨-cić⟩ się; ~ ***out*** *problem* przedyskutować; '~•**ing** młócka *f*; lanie *n*
thread [θred] **1.** nić *f* (*też fig.*); wątek *m* (*też fig.*); *tech.* gwint *m*; **2.** *igłę* nawlekać ⟨-leć⟩; ⟨na⟩gwintować; '~•**bare** wytarty; *fig.* oklepany
threat [θret] groźba *f*; zagrożenie *n* (***to*** dla *G*); ~•**en** ['θretn] zagrażać ⟨-rozić⟩; '~•**en•ing** zagrażający
three [θriː] **1.** trzy; **2.** trójka *f*; '~•**fold** trzykrotny, potrójny; '~-**ply** → ***ply***[4]; '~•**score** sześćdziesiąt; '~-**stage** trójstopniowy
thresh [θreʃ] *agr.* ⟨wy⟩młócić; '~•**ing ma•chine** młockarnia *f*
thresh•old ['θreʃhəʊld] próg *m* (*też fig.*)
threw [θruː] *pret. od* ***throw*** 1
thrift [θrɪft] oszczędność *f*; gospodarność *f*; '~•**y** (***-ier, -iest***) oszczędny; gospodarny
thrill [θrɪl] **1.** dreszcz *m* (*zwł. emocji*); przeżycie *n*; **2.** *v/t.* ***be ~ed*** być podekscytowanym (***at, about*** z powodu *G*); '~•**er** dreszczowiec *m*, kryminał *m*; '~•**ing** ekscytujący
thrive [θraɪv] (***thrived*** *lub* ***throve***) dobrze się rozwijać; *fig.* rozkwitać ⟨-tnąć⟩
throat [θrəʊt] gardło *n*; ***clear one's ~*** odchrząkiwać ⟨-knąć⟩; → ***sore*** 1
throb [θrɒb] **1.** (***-bb-***) *puls*: tętnić; *ból*: pulsować; *serce*: walić; *silnik*: dudnić; **2.** tętnienie *n*; pulsowanie *n*; walenie *n*
throm•bo•sis [θrɒm'bəʊsɪs] *med.* (*pl.* ***-ses*** [-siːz]) zakrzepica *f*
throne [θrəʊn] tron *m* (*też fig.*)
throng [θrɒŋ] **1.** tłum *m*, ciżba *f*; **2.** tłoczyć się; cisnąć się; zatłaczać
throt•tle ['θrɒtl] **1.** ⟨z-, za⟩dusić; ~ ***down*** ⟨z⟩dławić; *mot.*, *tech.* ⟨z⟩dławić; **2.** *tech.* przepustnica *f*
through [θruː] **1.** *prp.* przez (*A*), poprzez (*A*); *Am.* do (*G*) (*włącznie*); ***Monday ~ Friday*** *Am.* od poniedziału do piątku (włącznie); **2.** *adv.* całkiem, zupełnie; prosto; ***~ and ~*** całkowicie; ***put s.o. ~ to*** *tel.* połączyć kogoś z (*I*); ***wet ~*** całkiem mokry; **3.** *adj. pociąg*: przelotowy; ~'**out 1.** *prp.* przez (*A*); ~ ***the night*** przez (całą) noc; **2.** *adv.* całkowicie; zupełnie; '~ **traf•fic** ruch *m* przelotowy; '~•**way** *Am.* → ***thruway***
throve [θrəʊv] *pret. od* ***thrive***
throw [θrəʊ] **1.** (***threw, thrown***) rzucać ⟨-cić⟩, ciskać ⟨-snąć⟩; *przełącznik* przerzucać ⟨-cić⟩; F *imprezę* urządzać ⟨-dzić⟩; ~ ***a four*** wyrzucić cztery punkty; ~ ***off*** *ubranie* zrzucać ⟨-cić⟩; pozbywać ⟨-być⟩ się (*choroby, prześladowców*); ~ ***out*** *kogoś* wyrzucać ⟨-cić⟩; ~ ***up*** *v/t.* podrzucać ⟨-cić⟩; F *pracę* porzucać ⟨-cić⟩; F zwracać ⟨-rócić⟩; *v/i.* F ⟨z⟩wymiotować; **2.** rzucenie *n*; '~•**a•way** jednorazowy; *uwaga*: rzucony niedbale; '~•**a•way pack** opakowanie *n* jednorazowe; '~-**in** (*w piłce nożnej*) wrzut *m* z autu; ~**n** [θrəʊn] *p.p. od* ***throw*** 1
thru [θruː] *Am.* → ***through***; '~•**way** *Am.* droga *f* przelotowa
thrum [θrʌm] (***-mm-***) → ***strum***
thrush [θrʌʃ] *zo.* drozd *m*
thrust [θrʌst] **1.** (***thrust***) wpychać ⟨wepchnąć⟩ (***into*** w *A*); wbijać ⟨wbić⟩ (***into*** w *A*); ~ ***at*** pchnąć (*A*); ~ ***upon s.o.*** narzucać ⟨-cić⟩ komuś; **2.** pchnięcie *n*; *tech.* ciąg *m*, siła *f* ciągu; *mil.* wypad *m*
thud [θʌd] **1.** głuche uderzenie *n*; **2.** (***-dd-***) uderzyć głucho
thug [θʌg] kryminalista *m*
thumb [θʌm] **1.** *anat.* kciuk *m*; **2.** ~ ***a lift*** *lub* ***ride*** zatrzymywać ⟨-mać⟩ samochody na (auto)stopie (***to*** w kierunku *G*); ~ ***through a book*** przekartkowywać ⟨-wać⟩ książkę; ***well-~ed*** zaczytany; '~•**tack** *Am.* pinezka *f lub* pineska *f*
thump [θʌmp] **1.** *v/t. kogoś* palnąć, walnąć; ~ ***out*** *melodię* ⟨wy⟩bębnić (***on the piano*** na fortepianie); *v/i.* walić, łomotać; **2.** walnięcie *n*; walenie *n*, łomot *m*
thun•der ['θʌndə] **1.** grzmot *m*; piorun *m*; **2.** ⟨za⟩grzmieć (*też fig.*); '~•**bolt** błyskawica *f*; '~•**clap** uderzenie *n* pioruna; '~•**cloud** chmura *f* burzowa; ~•**ous** ['θʌndərəs] *oklaski*: burzliwy; '~•**storm** burza *f* z piorunami; '~•**struck** (jak) rażony piorunem
Thur(s) *skrót pisany*: ***Thursday*** czw., czwartek *m*
Thurs•day ['θɜːzdɪ] (*skrót*: ***Thur, Thurs***) czwartek *m*; ***on ~*** w czwartek; ***on ~s*** w czwartki
thus [ðʌs] tak; w ten sposób; ~ ***far*** jak dotąd
thwart [θwɔːt] udaremniać ⟨-nić⟩, ⟨po⟩krzyżować

T

thyme [taɪm] *bot.* tymianek *m*
thy·roid (gland) ['θaɪrɔid (-)] *anat.* tarczyca *f*
tick[1] [tɪk] **1.** tykanie *n*; znaczek *m*, ptaszek *m*; **2.** *v/i.* tykać; *v/t. zw.* ~ ***off*** odfajkowywać ⟨-ować⟩, odhaczać ⟨-czyć⟩
tick[2] [tɪk] *zo.* kleszcz *m*
tick[3] [tɪk]: ***on*** ~ *Brt.* F na kredyt
tick·er·tape ['tɪkəteɪp] taśma *f* perforowana; *jakby*: serpentyna *f*; ~ **pa'rade** ceremonia *f* (*z rzucaniem serpentyn*)
tick·et ['tɪkɪt] **1.** bilet *m*; (*w sklepie*) metka *f*; mandat *m*; kwit *m* (*do przechowalni itp.*); etykietka *f*; paragon *m*; *Am. pol.* mandat *m*; '~-**can·cel·(l)ing ma·chine** kasownik *m*; '~ **col·lec·tor** konduktor(ka *f*) *m*; '~ **ma·chine** automat *m* do biletów; '~ **of·fice** *rail.* kasa *f* biletowa
tick·ing ['tɪkɪŋ] płótno *n* pościelowe
tick|·le ['tɪkl] ⟨po⟩łaskotać; ~·**lish** ['tɪklɪʃ] łaskotliwy
tid·al ['taɪdl]: ~ ***wave*** fala *f* pływu
tid·bit ['tɪdbɪt] *Am.* → ***titbit***
tide [taɪd] **1.** pływ *m*, odpływ *m* morza; *fig.* napływ *m*; ***high*** ~ przypływ *m*; ***low*** ~ odpływ *m*; **2.** ~ ***over*** *fig.* pomagać ⟨-móc⟩ przetrwać
ti·dy ['taɪdɪ] **1.** (***-ier, -iest***) schludny; porządny (*też fig.*); F *suma*: niezły; **2.** *też* ~ ***up*** uporządkowywać ⟨-ować⟩; doprowadzać ⟨-dzić⟩ do porządku; ⟨po⟩sprzątać; ~ ***away*** uprzątać, ⟨-tnąć⟩
tie [taɪ] **1.** krawat *m*; sznur *m*; (*w sporcie*) remis *m*; (*w sporcie*) mecz *m* (*w rozgrywkach pucharowych*); *Am. rail.* podkład *m*; *zw.* ~***s*** *pl.* więzy *pl.*; **2.** *v/t.* ⟨za⟩wiązać, zawiązać ⟨-zywać⟩; powiązać; (***to*** z *I*); ***the game was*** ~***d*** (*w sporcie*) mecz zakończył się wynikiem remisowym; *v/i.* ***they*** ~***d for second place*** (*w sporcie*) zdobyli ex aequo drugie miejsce; ~ ***down*** *fig.* '0z⟩wiązać ręce; wiązać ⟨związywać⟩ terminem (***to*** do *G*); ~ ***in with*** odpowiadać (*D*), zgadzać się z (*I*), korelować z (*I*); ~ ***up*** *pieniądze* związywać ⟨-zać⟩, unieruchamiać ⟨-chomić⟩; powiązywać ⟨-zać⟩; *ruch* unieruchamiać ⟨-chomić⟩; '~·**break(·er)** (*w tenisie*) tie-break *m*; '~-**in** powiązanie *n*; *econ.* sprzedaż *f* wiązana; ***a*** ~***-in with his latest movie*** *jakby*: książka *f* oparta na fabule jego najnowszego filmu; '~-**on** przywiązywany
tier [tɪə] rząd *m*; poziom *m* (*też fig.*); warstwa *f*
'tie-up powiązanie *n*; związek *m*; *econ.* fuzja *f*
ti·ger ['taɪgə] *zo.* tygrys *m*
tight [taɪt] **1.** *adj.* szczelny; *żagiel itp.*: napięty; (za) ciasny, *ubranie itp.*: opięty; *econ. pieniądz*: ograniczony; F (*pijany*) wstawiony; *w złoż.* ...szczelny; ***be in a*** ~ ***corner*** F być w trudnej sytuacji; **2.** *adv.* mocno; F dobrze; ***sleep*** ~***!*** F śpij dobrze; ~·**en** ['taɪtn] zaciskać ⟨-snąć⟩; napinać ⟨-piąć⟩; ~***en one's belt*** *fig.* zaciskać ⟨-snąć⟩ pasa; ~***en up*** (***on***) *prawa* zaostrzać ⟨-rzyć⟩; ~'**fist·ed** F skąpy; ~***s*** *pl.* trykot *m*; *zwł. Brt.* rajstopy *pl.*
ti·gress ['taɪgrɪs] *zo.* tygrysica *f*
tile [taɪl] **1.** dachówka *f*; kafel(ek) *m*; **2.** pokrywać ⟨-ryć⟩ dachówka; wykładać ⟨wyłożyć⟩ kaflami; '**til·er** dekarz *m*; kafelkarz *m*
till[1] [tɪl] → ***until***
till[2] [tɪl] kasa *f*
tilt [tɪlt] **1.** przechylać ⟨-lić⟩ (się); nachylać ⟨-lić⟩ (się); **2.** nachylenie *n*; pochylenie *n*; ***at a*** ~ przechylony; (***at***) ***full*** ~ F na całego (*jechać itp.*)
tim·ber ['tɪmbə] *Brt.* drewno *n* budowlane; budulec *m*; belka *f*
time [taɪm] **1.** czas *m*; godzina *f*; pora *m*; raz *m*; *mus.* takt *m*; ~ ***after*** ~, ~ ***and again*** ciągle; ***every*** ~ ***he*** ...za każdym razem, gdy on; ***how many*** ~***s?*** ile razy?; ***next*** ~ następnym razem; ***this*** ~ tym razem; ***three*** ~***s*** trzy razy; ***three*** ~***s four equals*** *lub* ***is twelve*** trzy razy cztery równa się dwanaście; ***what's the*** ~***?*** która godzina?; ***all the*** ~ cały czas; ***at all*** ~***s, at any*** ~ za każdym razem; ***at the same*** ~ w tym samym czasie; ***at*** ~***s*** czasami; ***by the*** ~ do czasu gdy; ***for a*** ~ na jakiś czas; ***for the*** ~ ***being*** na razie; ***from*** ~ ***to*** ~ od czasu do czasu; ***have a good*** ~ dobrze się bawić; ***in*** ~ punktualnie, na czas; ***in no*** ~ (***at all***) szybko; wkrótce; ***on*** ~ punktualnie; ***some*** ~ ***ago*** jakiś czas temu; ***take one's*** ~ nie spieszyć się (***to do s.th.*** ze zrobieniem czegoś); **2.** mierzyć czas (*G*) (*też w sporcie*); ustalać ⟨-lić⟩ czas (*G*); wyliczyć ⟨-czać⟩ czas; '~ **card** *Am.* karta *f* kontrolna; '~ **clock** zegar *m* kontrolny; '~ **lag** różnica *f* czasowa; '~-**lapse**: ~ ***photography*** (*w fil-*

T

mie) zdjęcia *pl.* poklatkowe; '**~·less** bezczasowy; wieczny; '**~ lim·it** limit *m*; '**~·ly** (**-*ier*, -*iest***) terminowy, planowy; **~ sheet** karta *f* kontrolna; '**~ sig·nal** *radiowy* sygnał *m* czasu; '**~·ta·ble** rozkład *m* jazdy *lub* lotów; program *m*; *szkolny* rozkład *m* zajęć
tim·id ['tɪmɪd] nieśmiały, płochliwy
tim·ing ['taɪmɪŋ] timing *m*; wybór *m* najwłaściwszego momentu
tin [tɪn] **1.** cyna *f*; *Brt. blaszana, konserwowa* puszka *f*; **2.** (**-*nn*-**) ⟨po⟩cynować; *Brt.* ⟨za⟩konserwować, ⟨za⟩puszkować
tinc·ture ['tɪŋktʃə] tynktura *f*
'**tin·foil** folia *f* aluminiowa, staniol *m*
tinge [tɪndʒ] **1.** nadawać odcień; ***be ~d with*** być zabarwionym (*I*); **2.** odcień *m*; *fig.* odrobina *f*
tin·gle ['tɪŋgl] mrowić, szczypać, kłuć
tink·er ['tɪŋkə] grzebać się (***with*** przy *L*)
tin·kle ['tɪŋkl] ⟨za⟩dźwięczeć; ⟨za⟩dzwonić
tinned [tɪnd] *Brt.* puszkowany; konserwowy; **~ 'fruit** owoce *pl.* w puszkach
'**tin o·pen·er** *Brt.* otwieracz *m* do konserw
tin·sel ['tɪnsl] lameta *f*
tint [tɪnt] **1.** barwa *f*; zabarwienie *n*; **2.** zabarwiać ⟨-wić⟩
ti·ny ['taɪnɪ] (**-*ier*, -*iest***) malutki, drobny
tip[1] [tɪp] **1.** szpic *m*, koniuszek *m*, wierzchołek *m*; filtr *m* (*papierosa*); ***it's on the ~ of my tongue*** mam to na końcu języka; **2.** (**-*pp*-**) zakańczać ⟨-kończyć⟩ szpicem
tip[2] [tɪp] **1.** (**-*pp*-**) *zwł. Brt.* wysypywać ⟨-pać⟩; przechylać ⟨-lić⟩; ***~ over*** przewracać ⟨-rócić⟩; **2.** *zwł. Brt.* wysypisko *n*; *Brt. fig.* F chlew *m*
tip[3] [tɪp] **1.** napiwek *m*; **2.** (**-*pp*-**) dawać ⟨dać⟩ napiwek (*D*)
tip[4] [tɪp] **1.** porada *f*, rada *f*; **2.** (**-*pp*-**) ⟨po⟩radzić; ⟨po⟩stawiać (***for*** na *A*); typować (***as*** jako *A*); ***~ off*** dawać ⟨dać⟩ znać (*D*)
tip·sy ['tɪpsɪ] (**-*ier*, -*iest***) wstawiony, podpity
'**tip·toe 1.** ***on ~*** na palcach; **2.** iść na końcach palców
tire[1] ['taɪə] *Am.* → ***tyre***
tire[2] ['taɪə] ⟨z⟩męczyć (się); '**~d** zmęczony; ***be ~d of*** być zmęczonym (*I*); '**~·less** niestrudzony, niezmordowany; '**~·some** męczący; uciążliwy
Ti·rol [tɪ'rəʊl, 'tɪrəl] Tyrol *m*
tis·sue ['tɪʃuː] *biol.* tkanka *f*; chusteczka *f* higieniczna; '**~ pa·per** bibułka *f*
tit[1] [tɪt] *sl.* cycek *m*
tit[2] [tɪt] *zo.* sikor(k)a *f*
tit·bit ['tɪtbɪt] *zwł. Brt.* smakołyk *m*
tit·il·late ['tɪtɪleɪt] *kogoś (seksualnie)* podniecać ⟨-cić⟩
ti·tle ['taɪtl] tytuł *m*; nagłówek *m*; *jur.* tytuł *m* prawny (***to*** do *G*); '**~ page** strona *f* tytułowa
tit·mouse ['tɪtmaʊs] *zo.* (*pl.* **-*mice***) sikor(k)a *f*
tit·ter ['tɪtə] **1.** ⟨za⟩chichotać; **2.** chichot *m*
TM *skrót pisany*: ***trademark*** znak *m* towarowy
tn *Am.* → ***t***
to [tuː, tʊ, tə] **1.** *prp.* do (*G*); na (*A*); przy (*I*); dla (*G*); w relacji do, w stosunku do (*G*); ku (*D*) (*zdumieniu itp.*); *w określeniach czasu* za (*A*); ***~ me*** mnie *lub* mi *itp.*; ***from Monday ~ Friday*** od poniedziału do piątku; ***a quarter to ~ one*** za kwadrans pierwsza; ***go ~ Poland*** jechać do Polski; ***go ~ school*** chodzić do szkoły; ***have you ever been ~ London?*** czy byłeś kiedyś w Londynie?; ***here's ~ you!*** za twoje zdrowie!; ***~ the left*** na lewo; ***~ my regret*** ku mojemu żalowi; **2.** *adv.* ***pull ~*** zamykać ⟨-mknąć⟩; ***come ~*** przyjść do siebie; ***~ and fro*** tam i z powrotem; **3.** *z bezokolicznikiem*: ***~ go*** iść ⟨pójść⟩; *cel*: w celu, żeby; ***easy ~ learn*** łatwy do nauczenia się; **... *~ earn money*** ... aby zarabiać pieniądze
toad [təʊd] *zo.* ropucha *f*; **~·stool** *bot.* ['təʊdstuːl] muchomor *m*
toad·y ['təʊdɪ] **1.** pochlebca *m*; **2.** przypochlebiać się
toast[1] [təʊst] **1.** tost *m*, grzanka *f*; **2.** przypiekać ⟨-piec⟩; ⟨z⟩robić grzanki
toast[2] [təʊst] **1.** toast *m*; **2.** wznosić ⟨-nieść⟩ toast
toast·er ['təʊstə] opiekacz *m* do grzanek, toster *m*
to·bac·co [tə'bækəʊ] (*pl.* **-*cos***) tytoń *m*; *attr.* tytoniowy; ⚠ *nie* ***tabaka***; **~·nist** [tə'bækənɪst] właściciel(ka *f*) *m* sklepu z wyrobami tytoniowymi
to·bog·gan [tə'bɒgən] **1.** sanki *pl.*; tobogan *m*; **2.** zjeżdżać ⟨zjechać⟩ na sankach

to·day [tə'deɪ] **1.** *adv.* dzisiaj; dziś; ***a week ~, ~ week*** od dzisiaj za tydzień; **2.** dzisiejszy; ***of ~, ~'s*** z dnia dzisiejszego, dzisiejszy
tod·dle ['tɒdl] ⟨po⟩dreptać (*zwł. małe dziecko*)
tod·dy ['tɒdɪ] grog *m* (*z whisky*)
to-do [tə'duː] F *fig.* (*pl.* ***-dos***) zamieszanie *n*, rejwach *m*
toe [təʊ] *anat.* palec *m* nogi; czubek *m* (*buta*); '**~·nail** paznokieć *m* palc u nogi
tof |**·fee, ~·fy** ['tɒfɪ] toffi *n*
to·geth·er [tə'geðə] razem; wspólnie; ***~ with*** wraz z (*I*)
toi·let ['tɔɪlɪt] toaleta *f*; '**~ pa·per** papier *m* toaletowy; '**~ roll** *zwł. Brt.* rolka *f* papieru toaletowego
to·ken ['təʊkən] **1.** znak *m*; żeton *m*; ***as a ~, in ~ of*** na znak (*G*); ***by the same ~*** tym samym; **2.** *adj.* zdawkowy; symboliczny
told [təʊld] *pret. i p.p. od* ***tell***
tol·e|**·ra·ble** ['tɒlərəbl] znośny; **~·rance** ['tɒlərəns] tolerancja *f*; **~·rant** ['tɒlərənt] tolerancyjny (***of, towards*** względem *G*); **~·rate** ['tɒləreɪt] tolerować, znosić ⟨-nieść⟩
toll[1] [təʊl] opłata *f* (*portowa, za przejazd itp.*); cło *n*; ***heavy death ~*** duża liczba ofiar śmiertelnych; ***take its ~*** (***on***) *fig.* wyciskać swoje piętno (na *I*)
toll[2] [təʊl] *dzwony*: ⟨za⟩dzwonić
toll|**-'free** *Am. tel.* wolny od opłaty drogowej; '**~ road** droga *f* płatna
to·ma·to [tə'mɑːtəʊ, tə'meɪtəʊ] *bot.* (*pl.* ***-toes***) pomidor *m*
tomb [tuːm] grobowiec *m*
tom·boy ['tɒmbɔɪ] chłopczyca *f*
'**tomb·stone** nagrobek *m*, kamień *m* nagrobny
tom·cat ['tɒmkæt] *zo. też* F kocur *m*
tom·fool·e·ry [tɒm'fuːlərɪ] błazenada *f*
to·mor·row [tə'mɒrəʊ] **1.** *adv.* jutro; ***a week ~, ~ week*** od jutra za tydzień; ***~ morning*** jutro rano; ***~ night*** jutro wieczorem; **2.** ***the day after ~*** pojutrze; ***of ~, ~'s*** jutrzejszy
ton [tʌn] (*skrót*: ***t, tn***) (*waga*) tona; ⚠ *nie* ***ton***
tone [təʊn] **1.** ton *m*, dźwięk *m*; brzmienie *n*; *Am. mus.* nuta *f*; *med.* tonus *m*; *fig.* poziom *m*; **2.** ***~ down*** osłabiać ⟨-bić⟩; ***~ up*** wzmacniać ⟨-mocnić⟩
tongs [tɒŋz] *pl.* (***a pair of ~***) szczypce *pl.*
tongue [tʌŋ] *anat.* język *m* (*też w bucie*); ozór *m* (*zwierzęcia*); *gastr.* ozorek *m*; mowa *f*, język *m*; ***hold one's ~*** trzymać język za zębami
ton·ic ['tɒnɪk] tonik *m*; *med.* lek *m* tonizujący; *mus.* tonika *f*
to·night [tə'naɪt] dzisiaj w nocy, dzisiejszej nocy
ton·sil ['tɒnsl] *anat.* migdał *m*; **~·li·tis** *med.* [tɒnsɪ'laɪtɪs] zapalenie *n* migdałków; angina *f*
too [tuː] też, także; zbyt, zbytnio
took [tʊk] *pret. od* ***take*** 1
tool [tuːl] narzędzie *n*; '**~ bag** torba *f* na narzędzia; '**~ box** skrzynka *f* na narzędzia; '**~ kit** zestaw *m* narzędzi; '**~·shed** szopa *f* na narzędzia
toot [tuːt] ⟨za⟩trąbić
tooth [tuːθ] (*pl.* ***teeth***) ząb *m*; '**~·ache** ból *m* zęba; '**~·brush** szczotka *f* do zębów; '**~·less** bezzębny; '**~·paste** pasta *f* do zębów; '**~·pick** wykałaczka *f*
top[1] [tɒp] **1.** góra *f*; wierzch *m*; szczyt *m* (*góry*); wierzchołek *m*; czubek *m*; korona *f* (*drzewa*); zakrętka *f* (*butelki, tubki itp.*); *mot.* (*składany*) dach *m*; *mot.* najwyższy bieg *m*; ***at the ~ of the page*** na górze strony; ***at the ~ of one's voice*** na całe gardło; ***on ~*** na wierzchu; ***on ~ of*** na (*L*); **2.** górny; szczytowy; maksymalny; **3.** (***-pp-***) przykrywać ⟨-ryć⟩; *fig.* przewyższać ⟨-szyć⟩, przekraczać, ⟨-roczyć⟩; ***~ up*** *zbiornik* dopełniać ⟨-nić⟩; F uzupełniać ⟨-nić⟩
top[2] [tɒp] (*zabawka*) bąk *m*
top| '**hat** cylinder *m*; **~-'heav·y** przeładowany u góry; *fig.* o zbyt dużej górze
top·ic ['tɒpɪk] temat *m*; '**~·al** aktualny
top·ple ['tɒpl]: *zw.* ***~ over*** przewracać ⟨-rócić⟩ się; *fig. rząd itp.* obalać ⟨-lić⟩
top·sy-tur·vy [tɒpsɪ'tɜːvɪ] postawiony do góry nogami
torch [tɔːtʃ] *Brt.* latarka *f*; pochodnia *f*; '**~·light** światło *n* pochodni
tore [tɔː] *pret. od* ***tear***[2]
tor·ment **1.** ['tɔːment] męczarnia *f*; **2.** [tɔː'ment] dręczyć; znęcać się nad (*I*)
torn [tɔːn] *p.p. od* ***tear***[2]
tor·na·do [tɔː'neɪdəʊ] (*pl.* ***-does, -dos***) tornado *n*
tor·pe·do [tɔː'piːdəʊ] (*pl.* ***-does***) torpeda *f*

T

tor|·rent ['tɒrənt] *wartki* strumień *m*, potok *m* (*też fig.*); **~·ren·tial** [tə'renʃl]: **~*rential rain*** ulewny deszcz *m*
tor·toise ['tɔːtəs] *zo.* żółw *m*
tor·tu·ous ['tɔːtʃʊəs] kręty; zawikłany
tor·ture ['tɔːtʃə] **1.** tortura *f* (*też fig.*); **2.** torturować
toss [tɒs] **1.** *v/t.* rzucać ⟨-cić⟩ (*też monetą*); *naleśnik* przewracać ⟨-rócić⟩; *v/i. też* ***~ about, ~ and turn*** rzucać się (*we śnie*); ***~ for s.th.*** rzucać ⟨-cić⟩ monetą o coś; ***~ off*** *drinka* strzelić sobie; *szkic itp.* machnąć; **2.** rzut *m* (*też monetą*); podrzucenie *n*; szarpnięcie *n* (*głową*)
tot [tɒt] F berbeć *m*
to·tal ['təʊtl] **1.** całkowity; ogólny; całkowity; totalny; **2.** suma *f* (*całkowita*); liczba *f* całkowita *lub* ogólna; **3.** (*zwł. Brt.* **-ll-**, *Am.* **-l-**) wynosić ⟨-nieść⟩ ogółem; ***~ up*** podsumowywać ⟨-ować⟩
tot·ter ['tɒtə] chwiać się; iść ⟨pójść⟩ chwiejnie
touch [tʌtʃ] **1.** dotykać ⟨-tknąć⟩ (się); zbliżać ⟨-żyć⟩ się do (*G*) (*standardu itp.*); wzruszać ⟨-szyć⟩ (się); ***~ wood!*** odpukaj w niemalowane!; ***~ down*** *aviat.* ⟨wy⟩lądować; ***~ up*** ulepszać ⟨-szyć⟩; *phot.* ⟨z⟩retuszować; **2.** dotyk *m*; dotknięcie *n*; ślad *m* (*pędzla itp.*); kontakt *m*; ***a ~ of flu*** lekka grypa *f*; ***get in ~ with s.o.*** wchodzić ⟨wejść⟩ z kimś w kontakt; ***a personal ~*** akcent *m* osobisty; **~-and-go** [tʌtʃən'gəʊ] *sytuacja*: niepewny; ***it was ~-and-go whether*** wcale nie było pewne, czy; **'~·down** *aviat.* lądowanie *n*; **~ed** wzruszony; **'~·ing** wzruszający; **'~·line** (*w piłce nożnej*) linia *f* autowa; **'~·stone** probierz *m*; **'~·y** (***-ier, -iest***) drażliwy
tough [tʌf] wytrzymały; twardy; *negocjacje*: nieustępliwy; ciężki; *problem*: trudny; *okolica*: niebezpieczny; **~·en** ['tʌfn] *też* ***~en up*** ⟨s⟩twardnieć; utwardzać ⟨-dzić⟩
tour [tʊə] **1.** podróż *f* ((***a***)***round*** wokół *G*); wycieczka *f*; zwiedzanie *n*; obchód *m*; *theat.* tourn(e) *n* (***of*** po *L*); → ***conduct***; **2.** objeżdżać ⟨-jechać⟩; zwiedzać ⟨-dzić⟩
tour·is·m ['tʊərɪzəm] turystyka *f*, ruch *m* turystyczny
tour·ist ['tʊərɪst] turysta *m* (-tka *f*); *attr.* turystyczny; **'~ class** *aviat.*, *naut.* klasa *f* turystyczna; **'~ in·dus·try** przemysł *m* turystyczny; **~ in·for'ma·tion of·fice**, **'~ of·fice** biuro *n* turystyczne; **'~ season** sezon *m* turystyczny
tour·na·ment ['tʊənəmənt] turniej *m*
tou·sled ['taʊzld] *włosy*: zmierzwiony
tow [təʊ] **1.** *łódź, samochód* holować; **2.** hol *m*; ***give s.o. a ~*** poholować kogoś; ***take in ~*** brać ⟨wziąć⟩ na hol
to·ward *zwł. Am.*, **to·wards** *zwł. Brt.* [tə'wɔːd(z)] do (*G*), w stronę (*G*); w kierunku (*G*); *czas*: pod (*A*); w odniesieniu do (*G*); na (*A*)
tow·el ['taʊəl] **1.** ręcznik *m*; **2.** (*zwł. Brt.* **-ll-**, *Am.* **-l-**) wycierać ⟨wytrzeć⟩ (się) (*ręcznikiem*)
tow·er ['taʊə] **1.** wieża *f*; **2.** ***~ above, ~ over*** górować nad (*I*); **'~ block** *Brt.* wieżowiec *m*; **~·ing** ['taʊərɪŋ] wyniosły; *fig.* niebotyczny
town [taʊn] miasto *n*; **~ 'cen·tre** *Brt.* centrum *n* miasta; **~ 'coun·cil** rada *f* miejska; **~ 'coun·ci(l)·lor** radny *m* (-dna *f*); **~ 'hall** ratusz *m*; **~s·peo·ple** ['taʊnzpiːpl] *pl.* mieszkańcy *pl.* miasta
'tow·rope *mot.* lina *f* holownicza
tox·ic ['tɒksɪk] (***~ally***) toksyczny; **~ 'waste** odpadki *pl.* toksyczne; **~ waste 'dump** składowisko *n* odpadków toksycznych
tox·in ['tɒksɪn] *biol.* toksyna *f*
toy [tɔɪ] **1.** zabawka *f*; **~s** *pl.* zabawki *pl.*, *econ.* wyroby *pl.* zabawkarskie; **2.** zabawkowy; miniaturowy; mały; **3.** ***~ with*** bawić się (*I*); *fig.* igrać z (*I*)
trace [treɪs] **1.** ⟨prze-, wy⟩śledzić; odnajdować ⟨-naleźć⟩; *też* ***~ back*** wywodzić się (***to*** od *G*); ***~ s.th. to*** odnajdować ⟨-naleźć⟩ źródło (*G*); odkalkowywać ⟨-kować⟩
track [træk] **1.** ślad *m* (*też fig.*); trop *m*; szlak *m*, droga *f*; tor *m*, bieżnia *f*; *rail.* tor *m*; *dźwiękowa* ścieżka *f*; *tech.* gąsienica *f*; **2.** ⟨wy⟩tropić; ***~ down*** ⟨wy⟩śledzić; **~ and 'field** *zwł. Am.* (*w sporcie*) lekkoatletyczny; **'~ e·vent** (*w sporcie*) bieg *m* lekkoatletyczny; **'~·ing sta·tion** (*w astronautyce*) stacja *f* naziemna; **'~·suit** dres *m*
tract [trækt] przestrzeń *f*, obszar *m*; *anat.* przewód *m*; traktat *m*, rozprawa *f*
tra·c·tion ['trækʃn] trakcja *f*; **'~ engine** lokomobila *f*
trac·tor ['træktə] traktor *m*

T

trade [treɪd] **1.** handel *m*; branża *f*, gałąź *f*; zawód *m*, fach *m*; **2.** handlować (*I*), prowadzić handel (*I*); **~ on** żerować na (*L*); '**~·mark** (*skrót*: ***TM***) znak *m* towarowy; '**~ name** nazwa *f* handlowa, marka *f*; '**~ price** cena *f* hurtowa; '**trad·er** hurtownik *m*; **~s·man** ['treɪdzmən] (*pl.* ***-men***) detalista *m*; właściciel(ka *f*) sklepu; **~(s) 'un·i·on** związek *m* zawodowy; **~(s) 'un·i·on·ist** działacz(ka *f*) *m* związkowy (-a)

tra·di·tion [trə'dɪʃn] tradycja *f*; **~·al** [trə'dɪʃənl] tradycyjny

traf·fic ['træfɪk] **1.** ruch *m*; (*zwł. nielegalny*) handel *m*; **2.** (***-ck-***) (*zwł. nielegalnie*) handlować; '**~ cir·cle** *Am.* rondo *n*; '**~ is·land** wysepka *f* drogowa; '**~ jam** zator *m lub* korek *m* drogowy; '**~ lights** *pl.* światła *pl.* drogowe; '**~ offence** (*Am.* ***offense***) *jur.* wykroczenie *n* drogowe; '**~ of·fend·er** *jur.* osoba *f* popełniająca wykroczenie drogowe; '**~ reg·u·la·tions** *pl.* przepisy *pl.* ruchu drogowego; '**~ sign** znak *m* drogowy; '**~ sig·nal** → ***traffic lights***; '**~ war·den** *Brt.* (*kontroler prawidłowości parkowania pojazdów*)

tra|·ge·dy ['trædʒɪdɪ] tragedia *f*; **~·gic** ['trædʒɪk] (***-ally***) tragiczny

trail [treɪl] **1.** *v/t.* ⟨po⟩ciągnąć; ⟨po⟩wlec; (*w sporcie*) przegrywać ⟨rać⟩ z (*I*) (**by** *I*); *v/i. też* **~ *along*** (***behind***) ciągnąć się; wlec się; (*w sporcie*) przegrywać; **2.** trop *m*, ślad *m*; szlak *m*; smuga *f*; **~ *of blood*** ślad *m* krwi; **~ *of dust*** pióropusz *m* pyłu; '**~·er** *mot.* przyczepa *f*; *Am. mot.* przyczepa *f* kempingowa; *TV* zwiastun *m* (*filmu*); '**~·er park** parking *m* dla przyczep

train [treɪn] **1.** *rail.* pociąg *m*; kolumna *f*, szereg *m*; tren *m*; *fig.* ciąg *m*; **by ~** pociągiem, koleją; **~ *of thought*** bieg *m* myśli; **2.** *v/t. kogoś* ⟨wy⟩szkolić (**as** jako *G*); (*w sporcie*) ⟨wy⟩trenować; *zwierzę* ⟨wy⟩tresować; *kamerę* ⟨s⟩kierować (**on** na *A*); *v/i.* ⟨wy⟩szkolić się (**as** na *A*); *sport*: trenować (**for** do); **~·ee** [treɪ'niː] praktykant(ka *f*) *m*; '**~·er** trener(ka *f*) *m*; treser(ka *f*) *m*; '**~·ing** szkolenie *n*; *sport*: trening *n*; tresura *f*

trait [treɪ, treɪt] cecha *f* (*charakterystyczna*)

trai·tor ['treɪtə] zdrajca *m* (-czyni *f*)

tram [træm] *Brt.* tramwaj *m*; '**~·car** *Brt.* wóz *m* tramwajowy

tramp [træmp] **1.** stąpać; ⟨z⟩deptać; **2.** włóczęga *m*, tramp *m*; wędrówka *f*; *zwł. Am.* dziwka *f*

tram·ple ['træmpl] ⟨z-, po⟩deptać

trance [trɑːns] trans *m*

tran·quil ['træŋkwɪl] spokojny, cichy; **~·(l)i·ty** [træŋ'kwɪlətɪ] spokój *m*, cisza *f*; **~·(l)ize** ['træŋkwɪlaɪz] uspokajać ⟨-koić⟩; **~·(l)iz·er** *med.* ['træŋkwɪlaɪzə] środek *m* uspokajający, trankwilizator *m*

trans|·act [træn'zækt] *interesy, handel* ⟨po⟩prowadzić; **~·ac·tion** [træn'zækʃn] transakcja *f*, interes *m*

trans·at·lan·tic [trænzət'læntɪk] transatlantycki

tran·scribe [træn'skraɪb] ⟨prze⟩transkrybować; *mus.* dokonywać ⟨-nać⟩ transkrypcji

tran|·script ['trænskrɪpt] zapis *m*; **~·scrip·tion** [træn'skrɪpʃn] transkrypcja *f*

trans·fer **1.** [træns'fɜː] (***-rr-***) *v/t.* (**to**) *pracownika, produkcję* przenosić ⟨-nieść⟩ (do *G*); (*w sporcie*) *zawodnika* dokonywać ⟨-nać⟩ transferu (do *G*); *pieniądze* przekazywać ⟨-zać⟩, przelewać ⟨-lać⟩ (na *A*); *jur. prawo* ⟨s⟩cedować (na *A*), odstępować ⟨-tąpić⟩ (*D*); *v/i.* (*w sporcie*) *zawodnik*: przechodzić ⟨-ejść⟩ (**to** do *G*); przesiadać ⟨-siąść⟩ się (**from ... to ...** z ... na ...); **2.** ['trænsfɜː] przeniesienie *n*; (*w sporcie*) transfer *m*; przelew *m*; przekazanie *n*; *jur.* cesja *f*; *zwł. Am.* bilet *m* na połączenie z przesiadkami; **~·a·ble** [træns'fɜːrəbl] dający się przekazać *lub* odstąpić innej osobie

trans·fixed [træns'fɪkst] *fig.* sparaliżowany

trans|·form [træns'fɔːm] przekształcać ⟨-cić⟩, ⟨prze⟩transformować; **~·for·ma·tion** [trænsfə'meɪʃn] przekształcenie *n*; transformacja *f*

trans·fu·sion [træns'fjuːʒn] *med.* transfuzja *f*, przetoczenie *n* krwi

trans·gress [træns'gres] *termin* przekraczać ⟨-roczyć⟩; *prawo* naruszać ⟨-szyć⟩

tran·sient ['trænzɪənt] ulotny, przelotny

tran·sis·tor [træn'sɪstə] tranzystor *m*

tran·sit ['trænsɪt] tranzyt *m*; *econ.* przewóz *m*, transport *m*; *attr.* tranzytowy;

T

in ~ w trakcie tranzytu, w tranzycie
tran·si·tion [træn'sɪʒn] przejście *n*
tran·si·tive ['trænsɪtɪv] *gr. czasownik*: przechodni
tran·si·to·ry ['trænsɪtərɪ] → ***transient***
trans|·late [træns'leɪt] ⟨prze⟩tłumaczyć, przekładać ⟨-ełożyć⟩ (***from English into Polish*** z angielskiego na polski); **~·la·tion** [træns'leɪʃn] tłumaczenie *n*, przekład *m*; **~·la·tor** [træns'leɪtə] tłumacz(ka *f*) *m*
trans·lu·cent [trænz'luːsnt] półprzezroczysty
trans·mis·sion [trænz'mɪʃn] przenoszenie *n* (*choroby*); transmisja *f*; *mot.* przekładnia *f*, napęd *m*
trans·mit [trænz'mɪt] (***-tt-***) *sygnał* wysyłać ⟨-słać⟩; transmitować, nadawać ⟨-dać⟩; *chorobę* przenosić ⟨-nieść⟩; *światło* przepuszczać ⟨-puścić⟩; **~·ter** transmiter *m*, nadajnik *m*
trans·par|·en·cy [træns'pærənsɪ] przezroczystość *f* (*też fig.*); przezrocze *n*, slajd *m*; folia *f* (*do wyświetlania*); **~·ent** przezroczysty; *fig.* ewidentny
tran·spire [træn'spaɪə] ⟨s⟩pocić się; *fig.* okazywać ⟨-zać⟩ się; F zdarzać ⟨-rzyć⟩ się
trans·plant **1.** [træns'plɑːnt] przesadzać ⟨-dzić⟩; przenosić ⟨-nieść⟩; *med.* przeszczepiać ⟨-pić⟩; **2.** ['trænsplɑːnt] *med.* przeszczep *m*
trans|·port **1.** ['trænspɔːt] transport *m*, przewóz *m*; środek *m* transportu; *mil.* transportowiec *m*; **2.** [træns'pɔːt] przewozić ⟨-wieźć⟩, ⟨prze⟩transportować; **~·por·ta·tion** [trænspɔː'teɪʃn] transport *m*, przewóz *m*
trap [træp] **1.** pułapka *f* (*też fig.*); ***set a ~ for s.o.*** zastawiać ⟨-wić⟩ pułapkę na kogoś; ***shut one's ~, keep one's ~ shut*** *sl.* zamknąć japę; **2.** (***-pp-***) ⟨z⟩łapać w pułapkę (*też fig.*); ***be ~ped*** być uwięzionym (*jak w pułapce*); '**~·door** klapa *f* w podłodze; *theat.* zapadnia *f*
tra·peze [trə'piːz] trapez *m* (*w cyrku*)
trap·per ['træpə] traper *m*
trap·pings ['træpɪŋz] *pl.* atrybuty *pl.*, *fig.* insygnia *pl.*
trash [træʃ] szmira *f*; bzdura *f*; *Am.* śmieci *pl.*; *zwł. Am.* hołota *f*; '**~·can** *Am.* kosz *m* na śmieci; kubeł *m* na śmieci; '**~·y** (***-ier, -iest***) kiczowaty
trav·el ['trævl] **1.** (*zwł. Brt.* ***-ll-***, *Am.* ***-l-***) *v/i.* jeździć, podróżować; *tech.* przesuwać ⟨-sunąć⟩ się; *światło itp.*: poruszać się; *dźwięk*: rozchodzić ⟨-zejść⟩ się; *fig.* ⟨po⟩wędrować; *v/t.* objeżdżać ⟨-jechać⟩; *drogę* przejeżdzać ⟨-jechać⟩; **2.** podróż *f*; *attr.* podróżny; '**~ a·gen·cy** biuro *n* podróży; '**~ a·gent** właściciel(ka *f*) *m* biura podróży; '**~ a·gent's**, '**~ bu·reau** (*pl.* ***-reaux*** [-rəʊz], ***-reaus***) biuro *n* podróży; '**~·(l)er** podróżnik *m* (-niczka *f*), podróżny *m* (-na *f*); '**~·(l)er's cheque** (*Am.* ***check***) czek *m* podróżny; '**~·sick** chory *m* (-na *f*) na chorobę lokomocyjną; '**~·sick·ness** choroba *f* lokomocyjna
trav·es·ty ['trævɪstɪ] trawestacja *f*
trawl [trɔːl] **1.** niewód *m*; **2.** ⟨z⟩łowić niewodem, ⟨wy⟩trałować; '**~·er** *naut.* trawler *m*
tray [treɪ] taca *f*; *tech.* paleta *f*
treach·er|·ous ['tretʃərəs] zdradziecki; **~·y** ['tretʃərɪ] zdrada *f*
trea·cle ['triːkl] *zwł. Brt.* syrop *m*
tread [tred] **1.** (***trod, trodden*** *lub* ***trod***) deptać; nadeptywać ⟨-pnąć⟩ (***on*** na *A*); *ścieżkę* wydeptywać ⟨-ptać⟩; **2.** stąpanie *n*; *mot.* bieżnik *m*; stopień *m* (*na schodach*); '**~·mill** kierat *m* (*też fig.*)
trea·son ['triːzn] zdrada *f* stanu
trea|·sure ['treʒə] **1.** skarb *m*; **2.** cenić; **~·sur·er** ['treʒərə] skarbnik *m* (-niczka *f*)
trea·sure trove [treʒə 'trəʊv] ukryty skarb *m*
Trea·su·ry ['treʒərɪ] *Brt.*, '**~ De·part·ment** *Am.* Ministerstwo *n* Skarbu, Skarb *m* Państwa
treat [triːt] **1.** ⟨po⟩traktować (***as*** jako *A*); obchodzić się z (*I*); traktować; *med.* ⟨wy⟩leczyć (***for*** z *G*), leczyć (***for*** na *A*); *komuś* ⟨za⟩fundować; ***~ s.o. to s.th.*** *też* stawiać ⟨postawić⟩ komuś coś; ***~ o.s. to s.th.*** ⟨po⟩częstować się czymś; ***be ~ed for*** być leczonym na (*A*); **2.** uczta *f*; poczęstunek *m*; ***this is my ~*** ja stawiam
trea·tise ['triːtɪz] rozprawa *f*
treat·ment ['triːtmənt] traktowanie *n*
treat·y ['triːtɪ] układ *m*
tre·ble[1] ['trebl] **1.** potrójny; **2.** ⟨po⟩troić (się)
tre·ble[2] ['trebl] *mus.* dyszkant *m*; wysokie dźwięki *pl.* (*radiowe*)
tree [triː] drzewo *n*

tre•foil ['trefɔɪl] *bot.* koniczyna *f*
trel•lis ['trelɪs] ażurowa krata *f*, treliaż *m*
trem•ble ['trembl] trząść się (***with*** od *G*)
tre•men•dous [trɪ'mendəs] ogromny; F wspaniały
trem•or ['tremə] drżenie *n*, dreszcz *m*
trench [trentʃ] rów *m*; *mil.* okop *m*
trend [trend] trend *m*, tendencja *f*; moda *f*; '**~•y** F **1.** (**-*ier, -iest***) modny; ***be ~y*** być szykownym; **2.** *zwł. Brt. pej.* modniś *m* (-nisia *f*)
tres•pass ['trespəs] **1.** ***~ on*** *ląd* wkraczać ⟨-roczyć⟩ *nielegalnie* na (*A*); *prawa* naruszać ⟨-szyć⟩ (*A*); *hojność* nadużywać ⟨-żyć⟩; ***no ~ing*** wstęp wzbroniony!; **2.** przekroczenie *n*; naruszenie *n*; nadużycie *n*; '**~•er**: ***~ers will be prosecuted*** Wstęp pod karą wzbroniony!
tres•tle ['tresl] stojak *m*, kozioł *m*
tri•al ['traɪəl] *jur.* rozprawa *f* sądowa, proces *m*; próba *f*; test *m*; *fig.* utrapienie *n*; *attr.* próbny; ***on ~*** na próbę, na okres próbny; wypróbowywany; ***be on ~, stand ~*** *jur.* stawać ⟨stanąć⟩ przed sądem
tri•an|•gle ['traɪæŋgl] trójkąt *m*; *Am.* ekierka *f*; *mus.* triangel *m*, trójkąt *m*; **~•gu•lar** [traɪ'æŋgjʊlə] trójkątny
tri•ath•lon [traɪ'æθlɒn] (*w sporcie*) trójbój *m*
trib|•al ['traɪbl] szczepowy; **~e** [traɪb] szczep *m*
tri•bu•nal [traɪ'bjuːnl] *jur.* trybunał *m*, sąd *m*
trib•u•ta•ry ['trɪbjʊtərɪ] dopływ *m*
trib•ute ['trɪbjuːt] danina *f*; ***be a ~ to*** dawać ⟨dać⟩ dowód (*D*); ***to pay ~ to*** składać ⟨złożyć⟩ hołd (*D*)
trice [traɪs] *zwł. Brt.*: ***in a ~*** w mig
trick [trɪk] **1.** sztuczka *f*; trick *m*; podstęp *m*; figiel *m*; (*w grze w karty*) lewa *f*; zwyczaj *m*; ***play a ~ on s.o.*** ⟨s⟩płatać komuś psikusa; **2.** podstępny; ***~ question*** podstępne pytanie *n*; **3.** *kogoś* podchodzić ⟨-dejść⟩, oszukiwać ⟨-kać⟩; **~•e•ry** ['trɪkərɪ] podstęp *m*, oszustwo *n*
trick•le ['trɪkl] **1.** sączyć się, kapać; przeciekać ⟨-ciec⟩; **2.** strużka *f*
trick|•ster ['trɪkstə] oszust(ka *f*) *m*; **~•y** ['trɪkɪ] (**-*ier, -iest***) podstępny; trudny, skomplikowany
tri•cy•cle ['traɪsɪkl] rowe(ek) *m* trójkołowy
tri•dent ['traɪdənt] trójząb *m*
tri|•fle ['traɪfl] **1.** drobiazg *m*; błahostka *f*; ***a ~fle*** trochę, nieco; **2.** ***~fle with*** *fig.* zabawiać ⟨-wić⟩ się; ***he is not to be ~fled with*** z nim nie ma żartów; **~•fling** ['traɪflɪŋ] błahy, drobny
trig•ger ['trɪgə] **1.** język *m* spustowy, cyngiel *m*; ***pull the ~*** pociągać za cyngiel; **2.** ***~ off*** wywoływać ⟨-łać⟩; '**~-hap•py** z lubością sięgający po broń
trill [trɪl] **1.** (*śpiew*) tryl *m*, trele *pl.* (*ptaków*); **2.** używać ⟨-żyć⟩ trylu; *ptaki*: wywodzić ⟨-wieść⟩ trele
trim [trɪm] **1.** (**-*mm-***) przycinać ⟨-ciąć⟩; *ubranie* ozdabiać ⟨-dobić⟩; ***~med with fur*** podbity futrem; ***~ off*** odcinać ⟨-ciąć⟩; **2.** przycięcie *n*; ***give s.th. a ~*** przycinać ⟨-ciąć⟩ coś; ***in ~*** F w dobrej formie; **3.** (**-*mm-***) schludny; '**~•ming**: ***~s*** *pl.* ścinki *pl.*; *gastr.* dodatki *pl.*
Trin•i•ty ['trɪnɪtɪ] *rel.* Trójca *f*
trin•ket ['trɪŋkɪt] ozdóbka *f* (*zwł. tania*)
trip [trɪp] **1.** (**-*pp-***) *v/i.* potykać ⟨-tknąć⟩ się (***over*** o *A*); *v/t. też* ***~ up*** podstawiać ⟨-wić⟩ nogę (*D*); ⟨z⟩mieszać; **2.** wycieczka *f*, *krótka* podróż *f*; potknięcie *n* się; *sl.* trip *m*, odlot *m*
tripe [traɪp] *gastr.* flaki *pl.*
trip•le ['trɪpl] potrójny; '**~ jump** (*w sporcie*) trójskok *m*
trip•lets ['trɪplɪts] *pl.* trojaczki *pl.*
trip•li•cate ['trɪplɪkɪt] **1.** potrójny; **2.** ***in ~*** w trzech egzemplarzach
tri•pod ['traɪpɒd] *phot.* statyw *m*
trip•per ['trɪpə] *zwł. Brt.* (*zwł. na jedne dzień*) podróżny *m* (-na *f*)
trite [traɪt] banalny, trywialny
tri|•umph ['traɪəmf] **1.** triumf *m*; *fig.* zwycięstwo *n* (***over*** nad *I*); **2.** ⟨za⟩triumfować (***over*** nad *I*); **~•um•phal** [traɪ'ʌmfl] triumfalny; **~•um•phant** [traɪ'ʌmfənt] triumfujący
triv•i•al ['trɪvɪəl] trywialny; błahy
trod [trɒd] *pret. i p.p. od* ***tread*** 1; **~•den** ['trɒdn] *p.p. od* ***tread*** 1
trol•ley ['trɒlɪ] *zwł. Brt.* wózek *m* (*na zakupy itp.*); stolik *m* na kółkach; '**~•bus** trolejbus *m*
trom•bone [trɒm'bəʊn] *mus.* puzon *m*
troop [truːp] **1.** gromada *f*; oddział *m*; ***~s*** *mil.* wojska *pl.*, oddziały *pl.*; **2.** iść ⟨pójść⟩ gromadą; ***~ out*** wychodzić ⟨wyjść⟩ gromadą; '**~•er** *mil.* kawalerzysta *m*; (*w kawalerii*) szeregowy *m*; *Am. federalny* policjant *m*

T

tro·phy ['trəʊfɪ] trofeum *n*
trop·ic ['trɒpɪk] *astr., geogr.* zwrotnik *m*; ***the ~ of Cancer*** Zwrotnik *m* Raka; ***the ~ of Capricorn*** Zwrotnik *m* Koziorożca
trop·i·cal ['trɒpɪkl] tropikalny; (pod)zwrotnikowy
trop·ics ['trɒpɪks] *pl.* tropiki *pl.*
trot [trɒt] **1.** kłus *m* (*konia*); trucht *m*; **2.** ⟨po⟩kłusować; ⟨po⟩truchtać
trou·ble ['trʌbl] **1.** kłopot *m*, zmartwienie *n*; niedogodność *f*; zagrożenie *n*; *med.* dolegliwość *f*; ***~s*** *pl.* zamieszki *pl.*, niepokoje *pl.*; ***be in ~*** mieć kłopoty; ***get into ~*** napytać *sobie lub komuś* kłopotów; ***get*** *lub* ***run into ~*** mieć kłopoty *lub* problemy; ***put s.o. to ~*** narobić komuś kłopotów; ***take the ~ to do s.th.*** podejmować ⟨-djąć⟩ fatygę zrobienia czegoś; **2.** *v/t.* kłopotać; ⟨z⟩martwić; niepokoić; prosić (***for*** o *A*, ***to do s.th.*** o zrobienie czegoś); ***s.o. is ~d by s.th.*** coś dokucza komuś; *v/i.* zadawać ⟨-dać⟩ sobie trud (***to do s.th.*** zrobienia czegoś); '**~·mak·er** wichrzyciel(ka *f*) *m*; '**~·some** dokuczliwy
trough [trɒf] koryto *n*
trounce [traʊns] (*w sporcie*) sprawić lanie (*D*)
troupe [tru:p] *theat.* trupa *f*, zespół *m* teatralny
trou·ser ['traʊzə]: (***a pair of***) ***~s*** *pl.* spodnie *pl.*; ***~ leg*** nogawka *f* spodni; '**~ suit** *Brt.* spodnium *n*
trous·seau ['tru:səʊ] (*pl.* ***-seaux*** [-səʊz], ***-seaus***) *ślubna* wyprawa *f*
trout [traʊt] *zo.* (*pl.* ***trout, trouts***) pstrąg *m*
trow·el ['traʊəl] kielnia *f*
tru·ant ['tru:ənt] *Brt.* wagarowicz *m*; ***play ~*** iść na wagary
truce [tru:s] zawieszenie *n* broni
truck[1] [trʌk] **1.** *mot.* ciężarówka *f*; *Brt. rail. towarowa* platforma *f*; **2.** *zwł. Am.* ⟨prze⟩transportować samochodami ciężarowymi
truck[2] [trʌk] *Am.* warzywa *pl.*, owoce *pl.* (*na sprzedaż*)
'**truck| driv·er**, '**~·er** *zwł. Am.* kierowca *m* ciężarówki
'**truck farm** *Am. econ.* gospodarstwo *n* warzywnicze *lub* owocowe
trudge [trʌdʒ] stąpać ciężko
true [tru:] (***-r, -st***) prawdziwy; rzeczywisty; *przyjaciel*: wierny; wierny; ***be ~*** mieć rację; ***come ~*** spełniać ⟨-nić⟩ się; ***~ to life*** wiernie oddający rzeczywistość
tru·ly ['tru:lɪ] faktycznie; rzeczywiście; szczerze; ***Yours ~*** *zwł. Am.* Z poważaniem (*na zakończenie listu*)
trump [trʌmp] **1.** atut *m* (*też fig.*); karta *f* atutowa; **2.** bić atutem
trum·pet ['trʌmpɪt] **1.** *mus.* trąbka *f*; **2.** ⟨za⟩trąbić; *fig.* roztrąbiać ⟨-bić⟩
trun·cheon ['trʌntʃən] *policyjna* pałka *f*
trun·dle ['trʌndl] *wózek* popychać ⟨-pchać⟩
trunk [trʌŋk] pień *m*; *anat.* tułów *m*; waliza *f*, skrzynia *f*; *zo.* trąba *f* (*słonia*); *Am. mot.* bagażnik *m*; '**~ road** *Brt.* droga *f* główna, szosa *f*
trunks [trʌŋks] *pl.* (***a pair of ~***) kąpielówki *pl.*; szorty *pl.*, spodenki *pl.*
truss [trʌs] **1.** *też* ***~ up*** ⟨z⟩wiązać; *gastr. kurczaka* związywać ⟨-zać⟩; **2.** *med.* pas *m* przepuklinowy
trust [trʌst] **1.** zaufanie *n* (***in*** do *G*); *jur.* powiernictwo *n*; *econ.* trust *m*; ***hold s.th. in ~*** mieć coś w zarządzie powierniczym (***for*** dla *G*); ***place s.th. in s.o.'s ~*** powierzać ⟨-rzyć⟩ coś komuś; **2.** *v/t.* ⟨za⟩ufać (*D*); **~·ee** [trʌs'ti:] powiernik *m*; zarządca *m*; '**~·ful**, '**~·ing** ufny; '**~·wor·thy** godny zaufania, solidny
truth [tru:θ] (*pl.* ***-s*** [tru:ðz, tru:θs]) prawda *f*; '**~·ful** prawdziwy
try [traɪ] **1.** *v/t.* ⟨s⟩próbować; ⟨po⟩próbować; *jur.* sądzić; *jur.* ubiegać się (***for*** o *A*); *cierpliwość* wystawiać ⟨-wić⟩ na próbę; ***~ s.th. on*** przymierzać ⟨-rzyć⟩; ***~ s.th. out*** wypróbowywać ⟨-ować⟩; ***~ for*** *Brt.*, ***~ out for*** *Am.* starać się o (*A*); **2.** próba *f*; '**~·ing** dokuczliwy, męczący
tsar [zɑ:] *hist.* car *m*
T-shirt ['ti:ʃɜ:t] koszulka *f lub* podkoszulek *m* (*z krótkim rękawem*), T-shirt *m*
TU [ti: 'ju:] *skrót*: ***trade union*** związek *m* zawodowy
tub [tʌb] kadź *f*; F wanna *f*
tube [tju:b] rura *f*, przewód *m*; tubka *f* (*pasty, etc.*); *anat.* ***bronchial ~s*** *pl.* oskrzela *pl.*; *Brt.* F metro *n* (*w Londynie*); dętka *f*; *Am.* F telewizja *f*; '**~·less** bezdętkowy *m*
tu·ber ['tju:bə] *bot.* bulwa *f*
tu·ber·cu·lo·sis [tju:bɜ:kjʊ'ləʊsɪs] *med.* gruźlica *f*

T

tu·bu·lar ['tju:bjʊlə] cylindryczny; rurowy

TUC [ti: ju: 'si:] *Brt. skrót*: ***Trades Union Congress*** TUC *m*, Kongres Związków Zawodowych (*w Wielkiej Brytanii*)

tuck [tʌk] **1.** zakładać ⟨założyć⟩; ~ ***away*** F odkładać ⟨odłożyć⟩; ~ ***in*** *zwł. Brt.* F *jedzenie*: wcinać; ~ ***up*** (***in bed***) *dziecko* otulać ⟨-lić⟩ (w łóżku); **2.** zakładka *f*, fałda *f*

Tue(s) *skrót pisany*: wt., wtorek *m*

Tues·day ['tju:zdɪ] (*skrót*: ***Tue***) wtorek *m*; ***on*** ~ we wtorek; ***on*** ~***s*** we wtorki

tuft [tʌft] kępka *f* (*włosów, trawy*)

tug [tʌg] **1.** (***-gg-***) ⟨po⟩ciągnąć; szarpać ⟨-pnąć⟩ (***at*** za *A*); **2. *give s.th. a*** ~ pociągnąć coś; ~**-of-'war** przeciąganie *n* liny

tu·i·tion [tju:'ɪʃn] nauka *f*; nauczanie *n*; opłata *f* za naukę, czesne *n*

tu·lip ['tju:lɪp] *bot.* tulipan *m*

tum·ble ['tʌmbl] **1.** spadać ⟨spaść⟩ (*też ceny*); upadać ⟨upaść⟩; staczać ⟨stoczyć⟩ się; **2.** spadek *m*, upadek *m*; '~**·down** walący się

tum·bler ['tʌmblə] szklanka *f*

tu·mid ['tju:mɪd] *med.* obrzmiały

tum·my ['tʌmɪ] F brzuszek *m*, brzusio *n*

tu·mo(u)r ['tju:mə] *med.* nowotwór *m*

tu·mult ['tju:mʌlt] zgiełk *m*, hałas *m*; **tu·mul·tu·ous** [tju:'mʌltjʊəs] zgiełkliwy, hałaśliwy

tu·na ['tu:nə] *zo.* (*pl.* ***-na, -nas***) tuńczyk *m*

tune [tju:n] **1.** melodia *f*; ***be out of*** ~ *mus.* fałszować; *fortepian itp.*: nie być nastrojonym; **2.** *v/t.*: *zw.* ~ ***in*** *radio* dostrajać ⟨-roić⟩ (***to*** do *G*); *też* ~ ***up*** *mus.* ⟨na⟩stroić; *mot. silnik* ⟨wy⟩regulować; *v/i.* ~ ***in*** dostrajać ⟨-roić⟩ radio; ~ ***up*** brzmieć prawidłowo; '~**·ful** melodyjny; '~**·less** niemelodyjny

tun·er ['tju:nə] *TV* tuner *m*

tun·nel ['tʌnl] **1.** tunel *m*; **2.** (*zwł. Brt.* ***-ll-***, *Am.* ***-l-***) ⟨wy⟩drążyć tunel; *górę* przebijać ⟨-ebić⟩ tunelem

tun·ny ['tʌnɪ] *zo.* (*pl.* ***-ny, -nies***) tuńczyk *m*

tur·ban ['tɜ:bən] turban *m*

tur·bid ['tɜ:bɪd] *płyn itp.*: mętny (*też fig.*); *dym itp.*: gęsty

tur·bine ['tɜ:baɪn] *tech.* turbina *f*

tur·bo ['tɜ:bəʊ] F *mot.* (*pl.* ***-bos***), ~**·charg·er** ['tɜ:bəʊtʃɑ:dʒə] turbosprężarka *f* doładowująca

tur·bot ['tɜ:bət] *zo.* (*pl.* ***-bot, -bots***) turbot *m*

tur·bu·lent ['tɜ:bjʊlənt] wzburzony, burzliwy

tu·reen [tə'ri:n] waza *f*

turf [tɜ:f] **1.** (*pl.* ***turfs, turves*** [tɜ:vz]) darń *f*; bryła *f* (*ziemi*), gruda *f*; ***the*** ~ tor *m* wyścigów konnych; **2.** pokrywać ⟨-ryć⟩ darnią

tur·gid ['tɜ:dʒɪd] *med.* obrzmiały, nabrzmiały

Turk [tɜ:k] Turek *m* (-rczynka *f*)

Tur·key ['tɜ:kɪ] Turcja *f*

tur·key ['tɜ:kɪ] *zo.* indyk *m* (-dyczka *f*); ***talk*** ~ *zwł. Am.* F wykładać ⟨wyłożyć⟩ kawę na ławę

Turk·ish ['tɜ:kɪʃ] **1.** turecki; **2.** *ling.* język *m* turecki

tur·moil ['tɜ:mɔɪl] wzburzenie *n*, zamieszanie *n*

turn [tɜ:n] **1.** *v/t.* obracać ⟨-rócić⟩; *klucz itp.* ⟨prze⟩kręcić; *stronę, naleśnik* przewracać ⟨-rócić⟩, ⟨s⟩kierować (***on*** na *A*, ***towards*** w stronę *A*); zwracać ⟨-rócić⟩ się (***to*** do *G*); zmieniać ⟨-nić⟩ (***into*** w *A*); *liście* ⟨za⟩barwić; *mleko* ⟨z⟩warzyć; *tech.* ⟨wy⟩toczyć (*na obrabiarce itp.*); ~ ***the corner*** zakręcać ⟨-cić⟩ na rogu; ~ ***loose*** zwalniać ⟨-wolnić⟩, wypuszczać ⟨-puścić⟩; ***s.th.*** ~***s s.o.'s stomach*** od czegoś wywraca się komuś w żołądku; → ***inside, upside down, somersault***; *v/i.* obracać ⟨-rócić⟩ się; ⟨prze⟩kręcić się, skręcać ⟨-cić⟩ (***into, onto*** w *A*); odwracać ⟨-rócić⟩ się; *kwaśnym, siwym* stawać ⟨stać⟩ się, ⟨z⟩robić się; *fig.* zmieniać się (***into*** w *A*); → ***left***², ***right***²; ~ ***against*** zwracać ⟨-rócić⟩ się przeciw(ko) (*D*); ~ ***away*** odwracać ⟨-rócić⟩ się (***from*** od *G*); *kogoś* odsyłać ⟨odesłać⟩ (*G*) z niczym; ~ ***back*** zawracać ⟨-rócić⟩; cofać ⟨-fnąć⟩; ~ ***down*** *radio* ściszać ⟨-szyć⟩; *gaz itp.* przykręcać ⟨-cić⟩; *ogrzewanie* zmniejszać ⟨-szyć⟩; *prośbę itp.* odrzucać ⟨-cić⟩; *kołdrę* zawijać ⟨-winąć⟩; *kołnierzyk itp.* odwijać ⟨-winąć⟩; ~ ***in*** *v/t.* zwracać ⟨-rócić⟩; *zyski* uzyskiwać ⟨-skać⟩; *zwł. Am. pracę* przedstawiać ⟨-wić⟩, oddawać ⟨-dać⟩; *w ręce policji* oddawać ⟨-dać⟩ (***o.s.*** się); *v/t.* F iść ⟨pójść⟩ spać; ~ ***off*** *v/t. gas, wodę itp.*

T

zakręcać ⟨-cić⟩; *światło*, ⟨z⟩gasić; *silnik* wyłączać ⟨-czyć⟩; F wzbudzać ⟨-dzić⟩ obrzydzenie; *v/i.* skręcać ⟨-cić⟩; **~ on** odkręcać ⟨-cić⟩; włączać ⟨-czyć⟩; F podniecać ⟨-cić⟩; **~ out** *v/t. światło* ⟨z⟩gasić; *kogoś* wyrzucać ⟨-cić⟩ (**of** z *G*); *econ.* F ⟨wy⟩produkować; *kieszeń* wywracać ⟨-rócić⟩; opróżniać ⟨-nić⟩; *v/i.* przychodzić ⟨-yjść⟩ (**for** na *A*); okazywać ⟨-zać⟩ się; układać ⟨ułożyć⟩ się; **~ over** *v/i.* obracać ⟨-rócić⟩ się; odwracać ⟨-rócić⟩ się; *v/t.* przewracać ⟨-rócić⟩; odwracać ⟨-rócić⟩ na drugą stronę; rozważać, przemyśliwać; zwracać ⟨-rócić⟩; przekazywać ⟨-zać⟩; *econ.* mieć obroty (rzędu *G*); **~ round** obracać (się); odwracać (się); **~ one's car round** zawracać ⟨-rócić⟩; **~ to** zwracać ⟨-rócić⟩ się do (*G*); przechodzić ⟨-ejść⟩ na (*stronę itp.*); **~ up** *v/t.* podnosić ⟨-nieść⟩; *radio* ⟨z⟩robić głośniej; *natężenie* zwiększać ⟨-szyć⟩; podwijać ⟨-winąć⟩; odkrywać ⟨-ryć⟩; *v/i.* przybywać ⟨-być⟩, zjawiać ⟨-wić⟩ się; zdarzać ⟨-rzyć⟩ się; **2.** obrót *m*; zakręt *m*, skręt *m*; kolej *f*, kolejność *f*; skłonność *f*, zdolność *f*; *fig.* zwrot *m*, zmiana *f*; **at every ~** na każdym kroku; **by ~s** na zmianę; **in ~** kolejno; **out of ~** poza kolejnością; **it's my ~** to moja kolej; **make a left ~** skręcać ⟨-cić⟩ w lewo; **take ~s** zmieniać ⟨-nić⟩ się (**at** przy *L*); **take a ~ for the better/worse** zmieniać ⟨-nić⟩ się na lepsze/gorsze; **do s.o. a good/bad ~** wyrządzać ⟨-dzić⟩ komuś dobrą/złą przysługę; **at the ~ of the 20th century** na przełomie XX i XXI wieku; **'~·coat** zdrajca *m* (-czyni *f*); **'~·er** tokarz *m*

'turn·ing *zwł. Brt.* zakręt *m*; **'~ cir·cle** *mot.* promień *m* skrętu; **'~ point** *fig.* punkt *m* zwrotny

tur·nip ['tɜːnɪp] *bot.* rzepa *f*

'turn|-off zakręt *m*; **'~·out** frekwencja *f*; wydajność *f*; F ubiór *m*; **'~·o·ver** *econ.* obrót *m*; zmiana *f*; fluktuacja *f*; **'~·pike** *Am.*, **~·pike 'road** *Am.* płatna autostrada *f*; **'~·stile** kołowrót *m*; **'~·ta·ble** talerz *m* (*gramofonu itp.*); **'~-up** *Brt.* mankiet *m* (*spodni*)

tur·pen·tine ['tɜːpəntaɪn] *chem.* terpentyna

tur·quoise ['tɜːkwɔɪz] *min.* turkus *m*; *attr.* turkusowy

tur·ret ['tʌrɪt] *mil.*, *arch.* wieżyczka *f*; *naut.* kiosk *m* (*okrętu podwodnego*)

tur·tle ['tɜːtl] *zo.* żółw *m*; *attr.* żółwiowy; **'~·dove** *zo.* sierpówka *f*, synogarlica *f*; **'~·neck** *zwł. Am.* golf *m*

Tus·ca·ny Toskania *f*

tusk [tʌsk] kieł *m* (*słonia, morsa*)

tus·sle ['tʌsl] F bójka *f*

tus·sock ['tʌsək] kępa *f* trawy

tu·te·lage ['tjuːtɪlɪdʒ] prowadzenie *n*, kierownictwo *n*; *jur.* kuratela *f*, opieka *f*

tu·tor ['tjuːtə] korepetytor(ka *f*) *m*; *Brt. univ.* tutor *m*, prowadzący *m* (-ca *f*) (*grupę studentów*)

tu·to·ri·al [tjuː'tɔːrɪəl] *Brt. univ.* zajęcia *pl.* pod opieką tutora

tux·e·do [tʌk'siːdəʊ] *Am.* (*pl.* **-dos**) smoking *m*

TV [tiː'viː] TV *f*, telewizja *f*; *attr.* telewizyjny; **on ~** w telewizji; **watch ~** oglądać telewizję

twang [twæŋ] **1.** brzęk *m*, brzęknięcie *n*; *zw.* **nasal ~** wymowa *f* nosowa; **2.** brzęczeć ⟨brzęknąć⟩

tweak [twiːk] F ⟨po⟩ciągnąć za (*A*)

tweet [twiːt] ⟨za⟩ćwierkać

tweez·ers ['twiːzəz] *pl.* (**a pair of ~**) pinceta *f*

twelfth [twelfθ] **1.** dwunasty; **2.** jedna *f* dwunasta

twelve [twelv] **1.** dwanaście; **2.** dwunastka *f*

twen|·ti·eth ['twentɪɪθ] **1.** dwudziesty; **2.** jedna *f* dwudziesta; **~·ty** ['twentɪ] **1.** dwudziesty; **2.** dwudziestka *f*

twice [twaɪs] dwa razy

twid·dle ['twɪdl] bawić się; **~ one's thumbs** *fig.* marnować czas

twig [twɪg] gałązka *f*

twi·light ['twaɪlaɪt] zmrok *m*, zmierzch *m*; półmrok *m*

twin [twɪn] **1.** bliźniak *m* (-niaczka *f*); **~s** *pl.* bliźniaki *pl.*; **2.** bliźniaczy; podwójny; **3.** (**-nn-**): **be ~ned with** mieć partnerstwo z (*I*); **~-bed·ded 'room** pokój *m* z dwoma łóżkami; **~ 'beds** *pl.* dwa pojedyncze łóżka *pl.*; **~ 'broth·er** bliźniak *m*

twine [twaɪn] **1.** sznurek *m*, szpagat *m*; **2.** owijać ⟨owinąć⟩ (się) (**round** wokół *G*); *też* **~ together** splatać ⟨spleść⟩

twin-'en·gined *aviat.* dwusilnikowy

twinge [twɪndʒ] ukłucie *n* (*bólu*); **a ~ of conscience** wyrzut *m* sumienia

T

twin·kle ['twɪŋkl] **1.** ⟨za⟩migotać; błyszczeć ⟨-łysnąć⟩ (***with*** od *G*); **2.** migotanie *n*; błysk *m* (*też oka*)

twin| 'sis·ter bliźniaczka *f*; ~ **'town** miasto *n* siostrzane

twirl [twɜːl] **1.** kręcić (***round*** wokół); ⟨za⟩wirować; **2.** (za)kręcenie *n*; wirowanie *n*

twist [twɪst] **1.** *v/t.* skręcać ⟨-cić⟩; okręcać ⟨-cić⟩ (***round*** wokół *G*); obracać ⟨-rócić⟩; *kostkę itp.* wykręcać ⟨-cić⟩; *pranie* wyżymać ⟨-żąć⟩; *słowa* przekręcać ⟨-cić⟩; ~ ***off*** odkręcać ⟨-cić⟩; ~ ***on*** zakręcać ⟨-cić⟩; ***her face was ~ed with pain*** twarz miała wykrzywioną z bólu; *v/i.* wić się; skręcać ⟨-cić⟩ się (*z bólu itp.*); **2.** skręt *m*; skręcenie *n*; zakręt *m*; wykręcenie *n*; *fig.* zwrot *m*; *mus.* twist *m*

twitch [twɪtʃ] **1.** *v/i.* drgać; ⟨s⟩krzywić się (***with*** od *G*); *v/t.* szarpać ⟨-pnąć⟩; **2.** drgnięcie *n*; drganie *n*; szarpnięcie *n*, tik *m*

twit·ter ['twɪtə] **1.** ćwierkać ⟨-knąć⟩; **2.** ćwierkanie *n*; świergot *m*; ***be all of a ~*** F być rozgorączkowanym

two [tuː] **1.** dwa; ***the ~ cars*** oba samochody; ***the ~ of us*** my obaj *m lub* obie *f lub* oboje; ***in ~s*** dwójkami; ***cut in ~*** przecinać ⟨-ciąć⟩ na dwoje; ***put ~ and ~ together*** ⟨s⟩kojarzyć fakty; **2.** dwójka *f*; **~-'edged** obosieczny (*też fig.*); **~-'faced** dwulicowy; **'~·fold** dwojaki; **~·pence** ['tʌpəns] *Brt.* dwa pensy *pl.*; **~·pen·ny** ['tʌpnɪ] *Brt.* F za dwa pensy; **~-'piece** dwuczęściowy; **~-'seat·er** *mot.* samochód *m* dwumiejscowy; *aviat.* samolot *m* dwumiejscowy; **'~-stroke** *tech.* **1.** dwutaktowy; **2.** *też* ***~-stroke engine*** silnik *m* dwutaktowy; **~-'way** dwustronny; **~-way 'traf·fic** ruch *m* dwukierunkowy

ty·coon [taɪ'kuːn] *przemysłowy* magnat *m*

type [taɪp] **1.** typ *m*; rodzaj *m*; *print.* czcionka *f*; druk *m*, rodzaj *m* druku; **2.** *v/t.* *coś* ⟨na⟩pisać na maszynie, ⟨na⟩pisać (przy użyciu klawiatury); *v/i.* ⟨na⟩pisać na maszynie, ⟨na⟩pisać (*przy użyciu klawiatury*); **'~·writ·er** maszyna *f* do pisania; **'~·writ·ten** napisany na maszynie

ty·phoid ['taɪfɔɪd] *med.*, ~ **'fe·ver** dur *m lub* tyfus *m* brzuszny

ty·phoon [taɪ'fuːn] tajfun *m*

ty·phus ['taɪfəs] *med.* dur *m lub* tyfus *m* plamisty

typ·i|·cal ['tɪpɪkl] typowy (***of*** dla *G*); **~·fy** ['tɪpɪfaɪ] być typowym dla (*G*)

typ·ing| er·ror ['taɪpɪŋ -] błąd *m* maszynowy; **'~ pool** hala *m* maszyn

typ·ist ['taɪpɪst] maszynistka *f*

ty·ran·ni·cal [tɪ'rænɪkl] tyrański

tyr·an|·nize ['tɪrənaɪz] ⟨s⟩tyranizować; **~·ny** ['tɪrənɪ] tyrania *f*

ty·rant ['taɪərənt] tyran *m*

tyre ['taɪə] *Brt.* opona *f*

tzar [zɑː] *hist.* → ***tsar***

U

U, u [juː] U, u *n*

ud·der ['ʌdə] *zo.* wymię *n*

UEFA [juː'iːfə] *skrót:* ***Union of European Football Associations*** UEFA *n*

UFO ['juːfəʊ, juː ef 'əʊ] (*pl.* ***-os***) *skrót:* ***unidentified flying object*** UFO *n*

ug·ly ['ʌglɪ] (***-ier, -iest***) brzydki (*też fig.*); *rana:* paskudny

UHF [juː eɪtʃ 'ef] *skrót:* ***ultrahigh frequency*** UHF *n*, fale *pl.* ultrakrótkie

UK [juː 'keɪ] *skrót:* ***United Kingdom*** Zjednoczone Królestwo *n* (*Wielkiej Brytanii i płn. Irlandii*)

U·kraine Ukraina *f*

ul·cer ['ʌlsə] *med.* wrzód *m*

ul·te·ri·or [ʌl'tɪərɪə]: ~ ***motive*** ukryty motyw *lub* pobudka *f*

ul·ti·mate ['ʌltɪmət] ostateczny; końcowy; krańcowy; **'~·ly** ostatecznie; w końcu

ul·ti·ma·tum [ʌltɪ'meɪtəm] (*pl.* ***-tums, -ta*** [-tə]) ultimatum *n*

ul·tra|·high fre·quen·cy [ʌltrəhaɪ 'friːkwənsɪ] fale *pl.* ultrakrótkie; **~·ma'rine** ultramaryna *f*; **~'son·ic** ponaddźwiękowy; **'~·sound** ultradźwięk *m*; **~'vi·o·let** ultrafioletowy, nadfioletowy

U

um·bil·i·cal cord [ʌmbɪlɪkl 'kɔːd] *anat.* pępowina *f*

um·brel·la [ʌm'brelə] parasol *m* (*przeciwdeszczowy*); *fig.* osłona *f*

um·pire ['ʌmpaɪə] (*w sporcie*) **1.** sędzia *m*; **2.** sędziować

UN [juː 'en] *skrót*: ***United Nations*** *pl.* ONZ *m*, Narody *pl.* Zjednoczone

un·a·bashed [ʌnə'bæʃt] nie zbity z tropu

un·a·bat·ed [ʌnə'beɪtɪd] nie zmniejszony, nie obniżony

un·a·ble [ʌn'eɪbl]: ***be ~ to do s.th.*** nie być w stanie czegoś zrobić

un·ac·coun·ta·ble [ʌnə'kaʊntəbl] niewytłumaczalny

un·ac·cus·tomed [ʌnə'kʌstəmd] nieprzyzwyczajony

un·ac·quaint·ed [ʌnə'kweɪntɪd]: ***be ~ with s.th.*** nie być zaznajomionym z czymś

un·ad·vised [ʌnəd'vaɪzd] nierozsądny; niecelowy

un·af·fect·ed [ʌnə'fektɪd] naturalny, niewymuszony; ***be ~ by s.th.*** nie ulegać ⟨ulec⟩ wpływowi czegoś

un·aid·ed [ʌn'eɪdɪd] samodzielnie, bez pomocy

un·al·ter·a·ble [ʌn'ɔːltərəbl] niezmienny

u·nan·i·mous [juː'nænɪməs] jednogłośny

un·an·nounced [ʌnə'naʊnst] niezapowiedziany

un·an·swer·a·ble [ʌn'ɑːnsərəbl] niepodważalny, nie do obalenia

un·ap·proach·a·ble [ʌnə'prəʊtʃəbl] niedostępny; nieprzystępny

un·armed [ʌn'ɑːmd] nieuzbrojony

un·asked [ʌn'ɑːskt] *ktoś*: nie pytany; *pytanie*: nie zadany

un·as·sist·ed [ʌnə'sɪstɪd] bez pomocy, samodzielnie, nie wspomagany

un·as·sum·ing [ʌnə'sjuːmɪŋ] bezpretensjonalny

un·at·tached [ʌnə'tætʃt] niezwiązany, wolny

un·at·tend·ed [ʌnə'tendɪd] działający *lub* pozostawiony bez opieki

un·at·trac·tive [ʌnə'træktɪv] nieatrakcyjny

un·au·thor·ized [ʌn'ɔːθəraɪzd] nieupoważniony; nie uprawniony; nie autoryzowany

un·a·void·a·ble [ʌnə'vɔɪdəbl] nieunikniony

un·a·ware [ʌnə'weə]: ***be ~ of s.th.*** nie zdawać ⟨-zdać⟩ sobie sprawy z czegoś; **~s** [ʌnə'weəz] niespodzianie, niespodziewanie; ***catch*** *lub* ***take s.o. ~*** zaskoczyć kogoś

un·bal·ance [ʌn'bæləns] wyprowadzać ⟨-dzić⟩ z równowagi; **~d** niezrównoważony

un·bar [ʌn'bɑː] otwierać ⟨-worzyć⟩

un·bear·a·ble [ʌn'beərəbl] nie do zniesienia

un·beat·a·ble [ʌn'biːtəbl] bezkonkurencyjny; **un·beat·en** [ʌn'biːtn] niepokonany; nie przetarty

un·be·known(st) [ʌnbɪ'nəʊn(st)]: ***~ to s.o.*** bez czyjejś wiedzy

un·be·lie·va·ble [ʌnbɪ'liːvəbl] nie do uwierzenia

un·bend [ʌn'bend] (***-bent***) rozluźniać ⟨-nić⟩ się; odprężać ⟨-żyć⟩ się, ⟨wy⟩prostować; **~·ing** nieugięty

un·bi·as(s)ed [ʌn'baɪəst] nieuprzedzony, bezstronny

un·bind [ʌn'baɪnd] (***-bound***) rozwiązywać ⟨-zać⟩

un·blem·ished [ʌn'blemɪʃt] niesplamiony, nieskalany

un·born [ʌn'bɔːn] nienarodzony

un·break·a·ble [ʌn'breɪkəbl] nietłukący (się)

un·bri·dled [ʌn'braɪdld] nieokiełznany; rozpasany

un·bro·ken [ʌn'brəʊkən] nie zbity, nie uszkodzony; *rekord itp.*: nie pobity; *koń*: nieujeżdżony

un·buck·le [ʌn'bʌkl] rozpinać ⟨-piąć⟩

un·bur·den [ʌn'bɜːdn]: ***~ o.s. to s.o.*** zwierzać ⟨-rzyć⟩ się komuś

un·but·ton [ʌn'bʌtn] *guziki* rozpinać ⟨-piąć⟩

un·called-for [ʌn'kɔːldfɔː] nie na miejscu; niepożądany

un·can·ny [ʌn'kænɪ] (***-ier, -iest***) niesamowity

un·cared-for [ʌn'keədfɔː] zaniedbany, zapuszczony

un·ceas·ing [ʌn'siːsɪŋ] nieustanny

un·ce·re·mo·ni·ous [ʌnserɪ'məʊnjəs] bezceremonialny

un·cer·tain [ʌn'sɜːtn] niepewny; wątpliwy; ***be ~ of*** nie być pewnym (*G*); **~·ty** [ʌn'sɜːtntɪ] niepewność *f*; wątpliwość *f*

U

un·chain [ʌn'tʃeɪn] rozkuwać ⟨-kuć⟩
un·changed [ʌn'tʃeɪndʒd] nie zmieniony; **un·chang·ing** [ʌn'tʃeɪndʒɪŋ] niezmienny, nie zmieniający się
un·char·i·ta·ble [ʌn'tʃærɪtəbl] nieżyczliwy
un·checked [ʌn'tʃekt] nie sprawdzony; nie kontrolowany
un·chris·tian [ʌn'krɪstʃən] niechrześcijański
un·civ·il [ʌn'sɪvl] niegrzeczny, nieuprzejmy; **un·civ·i·lized** [ʌn'sɪvlaɪzd] niecywilizowany; barbarzyński
un·cle ['ʌŋkl] wuj(ek) *m*, stryj(ek) *m*
un·com·for·ta·ble [ʌn'kʌmfətəbl] niewygodny; ***feel ~*** ⟨po⟩czuć się niezręcznie
un·com·mon [ʌn'kɒmən] niepowszedni, rzadki
un·com·mu·ni·ca·tive [ʌnkə'mjuːnɪkətɪv] mało komunikatywny, niekomunikatywny
un·com·pro·mis·ing [ʌn'kɒmprəmaɪzɪŋ] bezkompromisowy
un·con·cerned [ʌnkən'sɜːnd]: ***be ~ about*** nie przejmować się (*I*); ***be ~ with*** nie być zainteresowanym (*I*)
un·con·di·tion·al [ʌnkən'dɪʃənl] bezwarunkowy
un·con·firmed [ʌnkən'fɜːmd] nie potwierdzony
un·con·scious [ʌn'kɒnʃəs] *med*. nieprzytomny; nieświadomy (*też* ***of*** *G*); ***be ~ of s.th.*** nie zdawać sobie sprawy z czegoś; **~·ness** nieprzytomność *f*; nieświadomość *f*
un·con·sti·tu·tion·al [ʌnkɒnstɪ'tjuːʃənl] niekonstytucjonalny
un·con·trol·la·ble [ʌnkən'trəʊləbl] nie do opanowania; nieopanowany; rozjuszony; **un·con·trolled** [ʌnkən'trəʊld] niekontrolowany
un·con·ven·tion·al [ʌnkən'venʃənl] niekonwencjonalny
un·con·vinced [ʌnkən'vɪnst]: ***be ~ about*** nie być przekonanym o (*L*); **un·con'vinc·ing** nieprzekonujący
un·cooked [ʌn'kʊkt] nie gotowany, surowy
un·cork [ʌn'kɔːk] odkorkowywać ⟨-ować⟩
un·count·a·ble [ʌn'kaʊntəbl] niepoliczalny
un·coup·le [ʌn'kʌpl] *wagony* rozłączać ⟨-czyć⟩
un·couth [ʌn'kuːθ] nieokrzesany
un·cov·er [ʌn'kʌvə] odsłaniać ⟨-łonić⟩; odkrywać ⟨-ryć⟩
un·crit·i·cal [ʌn'krɪtɪkl] bezkrytyczny; ***be ~ of s.th.*** nie być krytycznym względem czegoś
unc|·tion ['ʌŋkʃn] *rel*. namaszczenie *n*; **~·tu·ous** ['ʌŋktjʊəs] obłudny
un·cut [ʌn'kʌt] *film*, *powieść*: nieokrojony; *diament*: nieoszlifowany
un·dam·aged [ʌn'dæmɪdʒd] nieuszkodzony
un·dat·ed [ʌn'deɪtɪd] nie datowany, bez daty
un·daunt·ed [ʌn'dɔːntɪd] nieustraszony
un·de·cid·ed [ʌndɪ'saɪdɪd] niezdecydowany
un·de·mon·stra·tive [ʌndɪ'mɒnstrətɪv] opanowany, powściągliwy
un·de·ni·a·ble [ʌndɪ'naɪəbl] niezaprzeczalny
un·der ['ʌndə] **1.** *prp*. pod (*I*, *A*); pod kierownictwem *lub* rozkazami (*G*); zgodnie z (*I*); **2.** *adv*. pod spodem; **~·age** [ʌndər'eɪdʒ] niepełnoletni; **~'bid** (***-dd-***; ***-bid***) ⟨za⟩oferować lepsze warunki; przelicytowywać ⟨-ować⟩; **'~·brush** *zwł. Am.* → ***undergrowth***; **'~·car·riage** *aviat*. podwozie *n*; **~'charge** ⟨po⟩liczyć za mało; **~·clothes** ['ʌndəkləʊðz] *pl*., **~·cloth·ing** ['ʌndəkləʊðɪŋ] → ***undewear***; **'~·coat** podkład *m*; **~'cov·er**: ***~cover agent*** tajny agent *m*; **~'cut** (***-tt-***; ***-cut***) konkurować ceną z (*I*); **~·de'vel·oped** zacofany, nierozwinięty; **'~·dog** strona *f* słabsza; słabszy człowiek *m*; **~'done** niedosmażony, niedogotowany; **~·es·ti·mate** [ʌndər'estɪmeɪt] nie doceniać ⟨-nić⟩ (*też fig*.); **~·ex·pose** [ʌndərɪk'spəʊz] niedoświetlać ⟨-lić⟩; **~'fed** niedożywiony; **~'go** (***-went, -gone***) przechodzić ⟨przejść⟩; ulegać ⟨-lec⟩; **~·grad** F ['ʌndəgræd], **~·grad·u·ate** [ʌndə'grædʒʊət] student(ka *f*) *m* (*niższych lat*); **~·ground 1.** *adv*. [ʌndə'graʊnd] pod ziemią; **2.** *adj*. ['ʌndəgraʊnd] podziemny; *fig*. undergroundowy, niekomercyjny; **3.** ['ʌndəgraʊnd] *zwł. Brt.* metro *n*; ***by ~ground*** metrem; **'~·growth** poszycie *n*; **~'hand**, **~'hand·ed** za-

kulisowy; ~'**lie** (***-lay, -lain***) znajdować się u podstaw (*G*); ~'**line** podkreślać ⟨-lić⟩; '~·**ling** *pej*. podwładny *m* (-na *f*); ~'**ly·ing** leżący u podstaw; ~'**mine** podminowywać ⟨-ować⟩; *fig*. podkopywać ⟨-pać⟩; ~·**neath** [ʌndə'ni:θ] **1.** *prp*. pod (*I*); **2.** *adv*. pod spodem; ~'**nour·ished** niedożywiony; '~·**pants** *pl*. kalesony *pl*.; '~·**pass** *Brt*. przejście *n* podziemne; przejazd *m* podziemny; ~'**pay** (***-paid***) niedopłacać ⟨-cić⟩; ~'**priv·i·leged** upośledzony (*pod względem statusu społecznego*); biedny; ~'**rate** niedoceniać⟨-nić⟩; ~'**sec·re·ta·ry** *pol*. podsekretarz *m*; ~'**sell** (***-sold***) *econ*. sprzedawać⟨-dać⟩ poniżej wartości; ***~sell o.s.*** *fig*. źle się sprzedać; '~·**shirt** *Am*. podkoszulek *m*; '~·**side** spód *m*; '~·**signed 1.** podpisany; **2.** ***the ~signed*** niżej podpisany *m* (-na *f*) *lub* podpisani *pl*. *m* (-ne *pl*. *f*); ~'**size(d)** za mały; ~'**staffed** o niedostatecznej ilości personelu; ~'**stand** (***-stood***) ⟨z⟩rozumieć; pojmować ⟨-jąć⟩; ***make o.s. ~stood*** dogadywać ⟨-dać⟩ się; ***am I to ~stand that*** czy mam to zrozumieć, że; ~'**stand·able** zrozumiały; ~'**stand·ing 1.** rozumienie *n*; zrozumienie *n*; porozumienie *n*; ***come to an ~standing*** dochodzić ⟨dojść⟩ do porozumienia (***with*** z *I*); ***on the ~standing that*** pod warunkiem, że; **2.** zrozumiały; ~'**state** umniejszać ⟨-szyć⟩, pomniejszać ⟨-szyć⟩; ~'**state·ment** pomniejszanie *n*, umniejszanie *n*; niedopowiedzenie *n*; ~'**take** (***-took, -taken***) podejmować ⟨-djąć⟩ się (*G*) (***to do s.th.*** zrobienia); przedsiębrać ⟨-wziąć⟩; zobowiązywać ⟨-zać⟩ się; '~·**tak·er** przedsiębiorca *m* pogrzebowy; ~'**tak·ing** przedsięwzięcie *n*; zobowiązanie *n*; '~·**tone** *fig*. zabarwienie *n* (*głosu*); ~'**val·ue** nie doceniać ⟨-nić⟩; ~'**wa·ter 1.** *adj*. podwodny; **2.** *adv*. pod wodą; '~·**wear** bielizna *f*; ~·**weight 1.** ['ʌndəweɪt] niedowaga *f*; **2.** [ʌndə'weɪt] z niedowagą; zbyt lekki (***by*** o *G*); ***be five pounds ~weight*** mieć pięć funtów niedowagi; '~·**world** środowisko *n* przestępcze, świat *m* przestępczy

un·de·served [ʌndɪ'zɜ:vd] niezasłużony

un·de·si·ra·ble [ʌndɪ'zaɪərəbl] niepożądany

un·de·vel·oped [ʌndɪ'veləpt] nierozwinięty

un·dies ['ʌndɪz] F *pl*. bielizna *f* damska

un·dig·ni·fied [ʌn'dɪgnɪfaɪd] mało dystyngowany

un·dis·ci·plined [ʌn'dɪsɪplɪnd] niezdyscyplinowany

un·dis·cov·ered [ʌndɪ'skʌvəd] nie odkryty

un·dis·put·ed [ʌndɪ'spju:tɪd] bezdyskusyjny

un·dis·turbed [ʌndɪ'stɜ:bd] niezakłócony

un·di·vid·ed [ʌndɪ'vaɪdɪd] niepodzielony

un·do [ʌn'du:] (***-did, -done***) rozpinać ⟨-piąć⟩; rozwiązywać ⟨-zać⟩; *fig*. ⟨z⟩niweczyć; **un'do·ing**: ***be s.o.'s ~*** stawać się czyjąć ruiną; **un'done** rozwiązany, rozpięty; ***come ~*** rozwiązywać ⟨-zać⟩ się, rozpinać ⟨-piąć⟩ się

un·doubt·ed [ʌn'daʊtɪd] niewątpliwy; ~·**ly** niewątpliwie

un·dreamed-of [ʌn'dri:mdɒv], **un·dreamt-of** [ʌn'dremtɒv] niesłychany

un·dress [ʌn'dres] rozbierać ⟨-zebrać⟩ (się)

un·due [ʌn'dju:] nadmierny, przesadny

un·du·lat·ing ['ʌndjʊleɪtɪŋ] falujący

un·dy·ing [ʌn'daɪɪŋ] nieśmiertelny; dozgonny

un·earned [ʌn'ɜ:nd] *fig*. niezasłużony

un·earth [ʌn'ɜ:θ] wykopywać ⟨-pać⟩; *fig*. wygrzebywać ⟨-bać⟩, wydobywać ⟨-być ⟩na światło dzienne; ~·**ly** niesamowity; ***at an ~ly hour*** o nieludzkiej porze

un·eas|·i·ness [ʌn'i:zɪnɪs] niepokój *m*; zaniepokojenie *n*; ~·**y** [ʌn'i:zɪ] (***-ier, -iest***) *sen*: niespokojny; niepewny; niepokojący; zaniepokojony; ***feel ~y*** czuć się nieswojo; ***I'm ~y about*** jestem niespokojny co do (*G*)

un·e·co·nom·ic ['ʌni:kə'nɒmɪk] nieekonomiczny, niepopłatny

un·ed·u·cat·ed [ʌn'edjʊkeɪtɪd] niewykształcony

un·e·mo·tion·al [ʌnɪ'məʊʃənl] beznamiętny, chłodny; racjonalny

un·em·ployed [ʌnɪm'plɔɪd] **1.** niezatrudniony, bezrobotny; **2.** ***the ~*** *pl*. bezrobotni *pl*.

un·em·ploy·ment [ʌnɪm'plɔɪmənt] bezrobocie *n*; ~ **ben·e·fit** *Brt*., ~ **com-**

U

pen·sa·tion *Am.* zasiłek *m* dla bezrobotnych
un·end·ing [ʌn'endɪŋ] niekończący się
un·en·dur·a·ble [ʌnɪn'djʊərəbl] nie do wytrzymania
un·en·vi·a·ble [ʌn'envɪəbl] nie do pozazdroszczenia
un·e·qual [ʌn'iːkwəl] nierówny; ***be ~ to*** nie potrafić sprostać (*D*); **~(l)ed** niezrównany
un·er·ring [ʌn'ɜːrɪŋ] nieomylny
UNESCO [juː'neskəʊ] *skrót*: ***United Nations Educational, Scientific and Cultural Organization*** UNESCO *n*, Organizacja Narodów Zjednoczonych do Spraw Oświaty, Nauki i Kultury
un·e·ven [ʌn'iːvn] nierówny; *liczba*: nieparzysty
un·e·vent·ful [ʌnɪ'ventfl] bez zakłóceń, spokojny
un·ex·am·pled [ʌnɪg'zɑːmpld] bezprzykładny
un·ex·pec·ted [ʌnɪk'spektɪd] niespodziewany
un·ex·posed [ʌnɪk'spəʊzd] *phot.* niewywołany
un·fail·ing [ʌn'feɪlɪŋ] niezawodny, pewny
un·fair [ʌn'feə] nie fair, nieprzepisowy; niesprawidliwy, nieuczciwy
un·faith·ful [ʌn'feɪθfl] niewierny (***to*** wobec *G*)
un·fa·mil·i·ar [ʌnfə'mɪljə] nieznany; nie obeznany (***with*** z *I*)
un·fas·ten [ʌn'fɑːsn] rozpinać ⟨-piąć⟩, otwierać ⟨-worzyć⟩
un·fa·vo(u)·ra·ble [ʌn'feɪvərəbl] nieprzychylny (***to*** wobec *G*); niesprzyjający; niepomyślny
un·feel·ing [ʌn'fiːlɪŋ] nieczuły, nieludzki
un·fin·ished [ʌn'fɪnɪʃt] niezakończony, nieukończony
un·fit [ʌn'fɪt] nie w formie; nieodpowiedni, niezdatny; niezdolny (***for*** do *G*, ***to do*** do zrobienia)
un·flag·ging [ʌn'flægɪŋ] nie słabnący
un·flap·pa·ble [ʌn'flæpəbl] F niewzruszony
un·fold [ʌn'fəʊld] rozwijać ⟨-winąć⟩ (się)
un·fore·seen [ʌnfɔː'siːn] nieprzewidziany
un·for·get·ta·ble [ʌnfə'getəbl] niezapomniany, pamiętny
un·for·got·ten [ʌnfə'gɒtn] nie zapomniany, pamiętany
un·for·mat·ted [ʌn'fɔmæɪd] *komp.* niesformatowany
un·for·tu·nate [ʌn'fɔːtʃnət] nieszczęsny; niefortunny; pechowy; **~·ly** niestety
un·found·ed [ʌn'faʊndɪd] nieuzasadniony, bezpodstawny
un·friend·ly [ʌn'frendlɪ] (***-ier, -iest***) nieprzyjazny (***to, towards*** wobec *G*)
un·furl [ʌn'fɜːl] *sztandar* rozpościerać ⟨-postrzeć⟩; *żagiel* rozwijać ⟨-winąć⟩
un·fur·nished [ʌn'fɜːnɪʃt] nie umeblowany
un·gain·ly [ʌn'geɪnlɪ] niezgrabny, niezdarny
un·god·ly [ʌn'gɒdlɪ] bezbożny; ***at an ~ hour*** o nieprzyzwoitej godzinie
un·gra·cious [ʌn'greɪʃəs] niewdzięczny
un·grate·ful [ʌn'greɪtfl] niewdzięczny
un·guard·ed [ʌn'gɑːdɪd] niebaczny, nieostrożny
un·hap·pi·ly [ʌn'hæpɪlɪ] nieszczęśliwie, pechowo; **un·hap·py** [ʌn'hæpɪ] (***-ier, -iest***) nieszczęśliwy, pechowy
un·harmed [ʌn'hɑːmd] nietknięty, cały
un·health·y [ʌn'helθɪ] niezdrowy; *pej.* chorobliwy
un·heard [ʌn'hɜːd]: ***go ~*** nie znajdować ⟨-naleźć⟩ posłuchu; **~-of** [ʌn'hɜːdɒv] niesłychany, bezprzykładny
un·hinge [ʌn'hɪndʒ]: ***~ s.o.('s mind)*** pozbawiać ⟨-wić⟩ rozumu
un·ho·ly [ʌn'həʊlɪ] F (***-ier, -iest***) nieprawdopodobny, nieslychany
un·hoped-for [ʌn'həʊptfɔː] nieoczekiwany
un·hurt [ʌn'hɜːt] cało, bez szwanku
UNICEF ['juːnɪsef] *skrót*: ***United Nations International Children's Fund*** UNICEF *m*, Fundusz Narodów Zjednoczonych Pomocy Dzieciom
u·ni·corn ['juːnɪkɔːn] jednorożec *m*
un·i·den·ti·fied [ʌnaɪ'dentɪfaɪd] niezidentyfikowany
u·ni·fi·ca·tion [juːnɪfɪ'keɪʃn] zjednoczenie *n*
u·ni·form ['juːnɪfɔːm] **1.** uniform *m*; mundur *m*; **2.** jednolity; jednaki; **~·i·ty** [juːnɪ'fɔːmətɪ] jednorodność *f*; jednolitość *f*

U

u·ni·fy ['juːnɪfaɪ] ⟨z⟩jednoczyć; ⟨z⟩unifikować; ⟨s⟩konsolidować
u·ni·lat·e·ral [juːnɪ'lætərəl] *fig.* jednostronny
un·i·ma·gi·na·ble [ʌnɪ'mædʒɪnəbl] niewyobrażalny; **un·i·ma·gi·na·tive** [ʌnɪ'mædʒɪnətɪv] bez wyobraźni, pozbawiony wyobraźni
un·im·por·tant [ʌnɪm'pɔːtənt] nieważny
un·im·pressed [ʌnɪm'prest] nieporuszony (***by*** przez *A*)
un·in·formed [ʌnɪn'fɔːmd] nie poinformowany, nieświadomy
un·in·hab·i·ta·ble [ʌnɪn'hæbɪtəbl] niezdatny do zamieszkania; **un·in·hab·it·ed** [ʌnɪn'hæbɪtɪd] niezamieszkały, bezludny
un·in·jured [ʌn'ɪndʒəd] cały, bez szwanku
un·in·tel·li·gi·ble [ʌnɪn'telɪdʒəbl] niezrozumiały
un·in·ten·tion·al [ʌnɪn'tenʃənl] nieumyślny
un·in·terest·ed [ʌn'ɪntrɪstɪd] nie zainteresowany; ***be ~ in*** *też* nie interesować się (*I*); **un·in·te·rest·ing** [ʌn'ɪntrɪstɪŋ] nieinteresujący
un·in·ter·rupt·ed ['ʌnɪntə'rʌptɪd] nieprzerwany
u·nion ['juːnjən] unia *f*; połączenie *n*; związek *m*; **~·ist** ['juːnjənɪst] związkowiec *m*; **~·ize** ['juːnjənaɪz] zrzeszać się (*w związek*), przyłączać ⟨-czyć⟩ się do związku; **♀ 'Jack** (*brytyjska flaga narodowa*) Union Jack *m*
u·nique [juː'niːk] unikalny, unikatowy; wyjątkowy; niespotykany
u·ni·son ['juːnɪzn]: ***in ~*** zgodnie; *mus.* unisono
u·nit ['juːnɪt] jednostka *f*; *ped.* godzina *f* nauczania; *math.* jednostka *f*, jedność *f*; *tech.* element *m*, moduł *m*; ***sink ~*** szafka *f* pod zlewozmywak
u·nite [juː'naɪt] ⟨z⟩jednoczyć (się), ⟨z⟩łączyć (się); **u'nit·ed** zjednoczony
U·nit·ed 'King·dom (*skrót*: ***UK***) Zjednoczone Królestwo *n* (*Anglia, Szkocja i płn. Irlandia*)
U·nit·ed 'Na·tions *pl.* (*skrót*: ***UN***) Narody *pl.* Zjednoczone, ONZ *m*
U·nit·ed States of A'mer·i·ca *pl.* (*skrót*: ***USA***) Stany *pl.* Zjednoczone Ameryki, USA *pl.*

U

u·ni·ty ['juːnətɪ] jedność *f*
u·ni·ver·sal [juːnɪ'vɜːsl] uniwersalny, powszechny; ogólny
u·ni·verse ['juːnɪvɜːs] wszechświat *m*
u·ni·ver·si·ty [juːnɪ'vɜːsətɪ] uniwersytet *m*, wyższa uczelnia *f*; **~ 'grad·u·ate** absolwent *m* szkoły wyższej
un·just [ʌn'dʒʌst] niesprawiedliwy
un·kempt [ʌn'kempt] *włosy*: rozczochrany; *ubranie*: zaniedbany
un·kind [ʌn'kaɪnd] nieprzyjazny, nieżyczliwy
un·known [ʌn'nəʊn] **1.** nieznany (***to*** *D*); niewiadomy; **2.** niewiadoma *f* (*też math.*); **~ 'quan·ti·ty** wielkość *f* nieznana
un·law·ful [ʌn'lɔːfl] bezprawny, nielegalny
un·lead·ed [ʌn'ledɪd] *benzyna*: bezołowiowy
un·learn [ʌn'lɜːn] (***-ed*** *lub* ***-learnt***) oduczać ⟨-czyć⟩ się
un·less [ən'les] jeżeli nie, o ile nie
un·like [ʌn'laɪk] *prp.* niepodobny do (*G*), mało podobny do (*G*); ***he is very ~ his father*** jest bardzo niepodobny do swego ojca; ***that is very ~ him*** to do niego zupełnie niepodobne; **~·ly** mało prawdopodobny; ***she's ~ly to be there*** mało prawdopodobne, by tam była
un·lim·it·ed [ʌn'lɪmɪtɪd] nieograniczony
un·list·ed [ʌn'lɪstɪd] *Am. tel. numer*: zastrzeżony; **~ 'num·ber** numer *m* zastrzeżony
un·load [ʌn'ləʊd] wyładowywać ⟨-ować⟩, rozładowywać ⟨-ować⟩
un·lock [ʌn'lɒk] otwierać ⟨-worzyć⟩
un·loos·en [ʌn'luːsn] rozwiązywać ⟨-zać⟩; rozluźniać ⟨-nić⟩
un·loved [ʌn'lʌvd] niekochany
un·luck·y [ʌn'lʌkɪ] (***-ier, -iest***) nieszczęśliwy, pechowy; ***be ~*** mieć pecha
un·made [ʌn'meɪd] nie pościelony
un·manned [ʌn'mænd] bezzałogowy
un·marked nie oznaczony; bez skazy; *sport*: nie kryty
un·mar·ried [ʌn'mærɪd] *kobieta*: niezamężny; *mężczyzna*: nieżonaty
un·mask [ʌn'mɑːsk] *fig.* ⟨z⟩demaskować
un·matched [ʌn'mætʃt] niezrównany
un·men·tio·na·ble [ʌn'menʃnəbl] tabu; ***be ~*** być tabu

un·mis·ta·ka·ble [ʌnmɪ'steɪkəbl] niewątpliwy, jednoznaczny
un·moved [ʌn'muːvd] nieporuszony; ***she remained ~ by it*** nie poruszyło jej to
un·mu·si·cal [ʌn'mjuːzɪkl] mało muzykalny, niemuzykalny
un·named [ʌn'neɪmd] nienazwany
un·nat·u·ral [ʌn'nætʃrəl] nienaturalny, wbrew naturze
un·ne·ces·sa·ry [ʌn'nesəsərɪ] niepotrzebny
un·nerve [ʌn'nɜːv] wytrącać ⟨-cić⟩ z równowagi
un·no·ticed [ʌn'nəʊtɪst] niezauważony
un·num·bered [ʌn'nʌmbəd] nienumerowany
UNO ['juːnəʊ] *skrót*: ***United Nations Organization*** ONZ *n*
un·ob·tru·sive [ʌnəb'truːsɪv] nie rzucający się w oczy
un·oc·cu·pied [ʌn'ɒkjʊpaɪd] nie zajęty; niezamieszkały
un·of·fi·cial [ʌnə'fɪʃl] nieoficjalny
un·pack [ʌn'pæk] rozpakowywać ⟨-ować⟩ (się)
un·paid [ʌn'peɪd] nie zapłacony; nie opłacany, nie wynagradzany
un·par·al·leled [ʌn'pærəleld] niezrównany, bezprzykładny
un·par·don·a·ble [ʌn'pɑːdnəbl] niewybaczalny
un·per·turbed [ʌnpə'tɜːbd] niewzruszony
un·pick [ʌn'pɪk] rozpruwać ⟨-ruć⟩
un·placed [ʌn'pleɪst]: ***be ~*** (*w sporcie*) nie zająć miejsca medalowego
un·play·a·ble [ʌn'pleɪəbl] (*w sporcie*) nie nadający się do rozgrywek
un·pleas·ant [ʌn'pleznt] nieprzyjemny, przykry
un·plug [ʌn'plʌg] odłączać ⟨-czyć⟩ od sieci
un·pol·ished [ʌn'pɒlɪʃt] nie oszlifowany; nie polerowany *fig.* bez polotu
un·pol·lut·ed [ʌnpə'luːtɪd] nie zanieczyszczony
un·pop·u·lar [ʌn'pɒpjʊlə] mało popularny, niepopularny; **~·i·ty** ['ʌnpɒpjʊ'lærətɪ] niepopularność *f*
un·prac·ti·cal [ʌn'præktɪkl] niepraktyczny, mało praktyczny
un·prac·tised *Brt.*, **un·prac·ticed** *Am.* [ʌn'præktɪst] nie przećwiczony
un·pre·ce·dent·ed [ʌn'presɪdentɪd] bezprecedensowy
un·pre·dict·a·ble [ʌnprɪ'dɪktəbl] nieprzewidywalny; nie dający się przewidzieć
un·prej·u·diced [ʌn'predʒʊdɪst] nie uprzedzony, bezstronny
un·pre·med·i·tat·ed [ʌnpriː'medɪteɪtɪd] nieumyślny, nierozmyślny
un·pre·pared [ʌnprɪ'peəd] nie przygotowany
un·pre·ten·tious [ʌnprɪ'tenʃəs] bezpretensjonalny
un·prin·ci·pled [ʌn'prɪnsəpld] bez skrupułów, pozbawiony skrupułów
un·prin·ta·ble [un'prɪntəbl] nie nadający się do druku
un·pro·duc·tive [ʌnprə'dʌktɪv] nieproduktywny, mało produktywny
un·pro·fes·sion·al [ʌnprə'feʃənl] nieprofesjonalny, mało profesjonalny
un·prof·i·ta·ble [ʌn'prɒfɪtəbl] nierentowny
un·pro·nounce·a·ble [ʌnprə'naʊnsəbl] nie do wymówienia
un·pro·tect·ed [ʌnprə'tektɪd] nieosłonięty
un·proved [ʌn'pruːvd], **un·prov·en** [ʌn'pruːvn] nie udowodniony
un·pro·voked [ʌnprə'vəʊkt] nie sprowokowany
un·pun·ished [ʌn'pʌnɪʃt] bezkarny, nie karany
un·qual·i·fied [ʌn'kwɒlɪfaɪd] niewykwalifikowany, bez kwalifikacji; nie nadający się (***for*** do *G*); *odmowa*: kategoryczny
un·ques·tio·na·ble [ʌn'kwestʃənəbl] bezsporny, bezsprzeczny; **un·ques·tion·ing** [ʌn'kwestʃənɪŋ] zupełny, absolutny
un·quote [ʌn'kwəʊt]: ***quote ... ~*** cytuję ... koniec cytatu
un·rav·el [ʌn'rævl] (*zwł. Brt.* **-ll-**, *Am.* **-l-**) rozplątywać ⟨-tać⟩; *sweter itp.*: ⟨s⟩pruć (się); *zagadkę* rozwiązać
un·rea·da·ble [ʌn'riːdəbl] nieczytelny, nie do przeczytania
un·re·al [ʌn'rɪəl] nierzeczywisty; **un·re·a·lis·tic** [ʌnrɪə'lɪstɪk] (***~ally***) nierealistyczny
un·rea·so·na·ble [ʌn'riːznəbl] nierozsądny; nadmierny; *cena*: wygórowany

un·rec·og·niz·a·ble [ʌn'rekəgnaɪzəbl] nie do rozpoznania
un·re·lat·ed [ʌnrɪ'leɪtɪd]: ***be ~ to*** nie mieć odniesienia do (*G*)
un·re·lent·ing [ʌnrɪ'lentɪŋ] nie słabnący; bezlitosny
un·rel·i·a·ble [ʌnrɪ'laɪəbl] niepewny; nierzetelny
un·re·lieved [ʌnrɪ'liːvd] nieprzerwany, nieustający
un·re·mit·ting [ʌnrɪ'mɪtɪŋ] nieustanny
un·re·quit·ed [ʌnrɪ'kwaɪtɪd] nie wynagrodzony
un·re·served [ʌnrɪ'zɜːvd] bezwarunkowy; *miejsce*: nie zarezerwowany
un·rest [ʌn'rest] *pol. itp.* niepokój *m*
un·re·strained [ʌnrɪ'streɪnd] nieskrępowany
un·re·strict·ed [ʌnrɪ'strɪktɪd] nieograniczony
un·ripe [ʌn'raɪp] niedojrzały
un·ri·val(l)ed [ʌn'raɪvld] niezrównany, niedościgniony
un·roll [ʌn'rəʊl] rozwijać ⟨-winąć⟩
un·ruf·fled [ʌn'rʌfld] spokojny; nieporuszony
un·ru·ly [ʌn'ruːlɪ] (***-ier, -iest***) niesforny, krnąbrny
un·sad·dle [ʌn'sædl] *konia* rozsiodływać ⟨-łać⟩; zsiadać ⟨zsiąść⟩ z (*G*)
un·safe [ʌn'seɪf] niebezpieczny; niepewny, ryzykowny
un·said [ʌn'sed] niewypowiedziany
un·sal(e)·a·ble [ʌn'seɪləbl] niepokupny
un·salt·ed [ʌn'sɔːltɪd] nie solony, niesłony
un·san·i·tar·y [ʌn'sænɪtərɪ] niehigieniczny
un·sat·is·fac·to·ry ['ʌnsætɪs'fæktərɪ] niezadowalający
un·sat·u·rat·ed [ʌn'sætʃəreɪtɪd] *chem.* nienasycony
un·sa·vo(u)r·y [ʌn'seɪvərɪ] podejrzany, mętny
un·scathed [ʌn'skeɪðd] nietknięty
un·screw [ʌn'skruː] odkręcać ⟨-cić⟩
un·scru·pu·lous [ʌn'skruːpjʊləs] bez skrupułów
un·seat [ʌn'siːt] *jeźdźca* wysadzać ⟨-dzić⟩ z siodła; usuwać ⟨-nąć⟩ (*ze stanowiska*)
un·seem·ly [ʌn'siːmlɪ] niewłaściwy, niestosowny
un·self·ish [ʌn'selfɪʃ] bezinteresowny; **~·ness** bezinteresowność *f*
un·set·tle [ʌn'setl] zaburzać ⟨-rzyć⟩ spokój, pozbawiać ⟨-wić⟩ spokoju; **~d** niespokojny; nierozstrzygnięty; *pogoda*: zmienny
un·sha·k(e)a·ble [ʌn'ʃeɪkəbl] niewzruszony, niezachwiany
un·shav·en [ʌn'ʃeɪvn] nieogolony
un·shrink·a·ble [ʌn'ʃrɪŋkəbl] niekurczliwy
un·sight·ly [ʌn'saɪtlɪ] okropny, paskudny
un·skilled [ʌn'skɪld] niewykwalifikowany
un·so·cia·ble [ʌn'səʊʃəbl] mało towarzyski, nietowarzyski
un·so·cial [ʌn'səʊʃl]: ***work ~ hours*** pracować poza normalnymi godzinami pracy
un·so·lic·it·ed [ʌnsə'lɪsɪtɪd] nie zamawiany; nieproszony
un·solved [ʌn'sɒlvd] nie rozwiązany
un·so·phis·ti·cat·ed [ʌnsə'fɪstɪkeɪtɪd] mało wyrafinowany
un·sound [ʌn'saʊnd] niezdrowy; *budynek*: zagrożony; *towar*: wadliwy; *argument*: mało rozsądny; ***of ~ mind*** *jur.* o zaburzonych władzach umysłowych
un·spar·ing [ʌn'speərɪŋ] hojny, szczodry
un·spea·ka·ble [ʌn'spiːkəbl] niewypowiedziany; okropny
un·spoiled [ʌn'spɔɪld], **un·spoilt** [ʌn'spɔɪlt] nie zepsuty; nietknięty
un·sta·ble [ʌn'steɪbl] chwiejny; niepewny; *człowiek*: niezrównoważony
un·stead·y [ʌn'stedɪ] (***-ier, -iest***) niestały, chwiejny; niepewny
un·stop [ʌn'stɒp] (***-pp-***) *butelkę* odkorkowywać ⟨-ować⟩; odblokowywać ⟨-kować⟩
un·stressed [ʌn'strest] *ling.* nieakcentowany
un·stuck [ʌn'stʌk]: ***come ~*** odchodzić ⟨-dejść⟩, odklejać ⟨-kleić⟩ się; *fig.* zawodzić ⟨-wieść⟩
un·stud·ied [ʌn'stʌdɪd] niewymuszony
un·suc·cess·ful [ʌnsək'sesfl] nieudany; nie mający szczęścia; nie mający powodzenia
un·suit·a·ble [ʌn'sjuːtəbl] nieodpowiedni (***for*** do *G*)
un·sure [ʌn'ʃɔː] (***-r, -st***) niepewny; ***be ~***

of o.s. nie być pewnym siebie
un·sur·passed [ʌnsə'pɑːst] nieprześcigniony
un·sus·pect|·ed [ʌnsə'spektɪd] nie podejrzewany; **~·ing** niczego nie podejrzewający
un·sus·pi·cious [ʌnsə'spɪʃəs] niczego nie podejrzewający
un·sweet·ened [ʌn'swiːtnd] niesłodzony
un·swerv·ing [ʌn'swɜːvɪŋ] niezachwiany
un·tan·gle [ʌn'tæŋgl] rozplątywać ⟨-tać⟩ (*też fig.*)
un·tapped [ʌn'tæpt] *surowce itp.*: nie wykorzystany
un·teach·a·ble [ʌn'tiːtʃəbl] niewyuczalny
un·ten·a·ble [ʌn'tenəbl] *teoria itp.*: nie do utrzymania
un·think|·a·ble [ʌn'θɪŋkəbl] nie do pomyślenia; **~·ing** bezmyślny
un·ti·dy [ʌn'taɪdɪ] (***-ier, -iest***) nieporządny
un·tie [ʌn'taɪ] rozwiązywać ⟨-zać⟩; odwiązywać ⟨-zać⟩
un·til [ən'tɪl] *prp., cj.* aż do (*G*), do (*G*); ***not ~*** dopóki nie
un·time·ly [ʌn'taɪmlɪ] przedwczesny; nie w porę; niewczesny
un·tir·ing [ʌn'taɪərɪŋ] niezmordowany
un·told [ʌn'təʊld] niewypowiedziany, nieopisany; przemilczany
un·touched [ʌn'tʌtʃt] nietknięty
un·true [ʌn'truː] nieprawdziwy
un·trust·wor·thy [ʌn'trʌstwɜːðɪ] niegodny zaufania; wątpliwy
un·used¹ [ʌn'juːzd] nie używany; nie wykorzystany
un·used² [ʌn'juːst]: ***be ~ to (doing) s.th.*** nie być przyzwyczajonym do (robienia) czegoś
un·u·su·al [ʌn'juːʒʊəl] niezwykły
un·var·nished [ʌn'vɑːnɪʃt] nie ozdobiony; nie upiększony; *prawda*: nagi
un·var·y·ing [ʌn'veərɪɪŋ] niezmienny
un·veil [ʌn'veɪl] *pomnik itp.* odsłaniać ⟨-łonić⟩
un·versed [ʌn'vɜːst] nie zaznajomiony (***in*** z *I*)
un·voiced [ʌn'vɔɪst] niewypowiedziany
un·want·ed [ʌn'wɒntɪd] niechciany
un·war·rant·ed [ʌn'wɒrəntɪd] nie zagwarantowany; bezpodstawny
un·washed [ʌn'wɒʃt] nie umyty
un·wel·come [ʌn'welkəm] niechciany
un·well [ʌn'wel]: ***be*** *lub* ***feel ~*** źle się czuć
un·whole·some [ʌn'həʊlsəm] niezdrowy; niedobry
un·wield·y [ʌn'wiːldɪ] nieporęczny
un·will·ing [ʌn'wɪlɪŋ] niechętny; ***be ~ to do s.th.*** nie chcieć czegoś robić
un·wind [ʌn'waɪnd] (***-wound***) odwijać ⟨-winąć⟩, rozwijać ⟨-winąć⟩
un·wise [ʌn'waɪz] niemądry
un·wit·ting [ʌn'wɪtɪŋ] nieświadomy, niezamierzony
un·wor·thy [ʌn'wɜːðɪ] niegodny; ***he is ~ of it*** on nie jest godzien tego
un·wrap [ʌn'ræp] rozwijać ⟨-winąć⟩
un·writ·ten [ʌn'rɪtn] niepisany; **~ 'law** *jur* prawo *n* niepisane
un·yield·ing [ʌn'jiːldɪŋ] nieugięty, nieustępliwy
un·zip [ʌn'zɪp] rozpinać ⟨-piąć⟩ (*zamek błyskawiczny*)
up [ʌp] *adv.* w górę, do góry; w górze; ***~ there*** tam w górze; ***jump ~ and down*** skakać w górę i w dół; ***walk ~ and down*** chodzić tam i z powrotem; ***~ to*** aż do (*G*); ***be ~ to s.th.*** F kombinować coś; ***not to be ~ to s.th.*** nie spełniać ⟨-nić⟩ czegoś; ***it's ~ to you*** to zależy od ciebie; **2.** *prp.* w górę (*G*); ***~ the river*** w górę rzeki; **3.** *adj.* idący *lub* skierowany w górę; *okres czasu*: zakończony; ***the ~ train*** pociąg do *Londynu* (*do stolicy itp.*); ***be ~ and about*** ruszać się (już); ***what's ~?*** co się dzieje?; ***road ~*** *mot.* roboty *pl.* drogowe; **4.** (***-pp-***) F *v/t. cenę itp.* podwyższać ⟨-szyć⟩; **5. *the ~s and downs*** *pl.* wzloty i upadki *pl.*
up-and-com·ing [ʌpən'kʌmɪŋ] dobrze się zapowiadający
up·bring·ing ['ʌpbrɪŋɪŋ] wychowanie *n*
up·com·ing ['ʌpkʌmɪŋ] nadchodzący
up·coun·try [ʌp'kʌntrɪ] **1.** *adv.* w głąb kraju; **2.** *adj.* w głębi kraju
up·date [ʌp'deɪt] ⟨z⟩aktualizować, ⟨z⟩modernizować
up·end [ʌp'end] stawiać ⟨postawić⟩ pionowo
up·grade [ʌp'greɪd] **1.** przenosić ⟨-nieść⟩ do wyższej grupy; ulepszyć ⟨-szać⟩; ⟨z⟩aktualizować; **2.** *komp.* nowa wersja *f* programu, upgrade *m*

up·heav·al *fig.* [ʌp'hiːvl] wstrząs *m*
up·hill [ʌp'hɪl] pod górę; *fig.* mozolny
up·hold [ʌp'həʊld] (*-held*) podtrzymywać ⟨-ymać⟩; *jur.* utrzymywać ⟨-mać⟩ w mocy
up|·hol·ster [ʌp'həʊlstə] *meble* pokrywać ⟨-ryć⟩; **~·hol·ster·er** [ʌp'həʊlstərə] tapicer *m*; **~·hol·ster·y** [ʌp'həʊlstərɪ] tapicerka *f*, obicie *n*
UPI [juː piː 'aɪ] *skrót*: ***United Press International*** UPI *n*
up·keep ['ʌpkiːp] utrzymanie *n*
up·land ['ʌplənd]: *zw.* ***~s*** *pl.* pogórze *n*
up·lift 1. [ʌp'lɪft] podnosić ⟨-nieść⟩ na duchu; **2.** ['ʌplɪft] podniesienie *n* na duchu
up·on [ə'pɒn] → ***on***; ***once ~ a time*** pewnego razu
up·per ['ʌpə] górny; wierzchni; **'~·most 1.** *adj.* najwyższy; najważniejszy; ***be ~most*** być na górze; stać na pierwszym miejscu; **2.** *adv.* najwyżej
up·right ['ʌpraɪt] **1.** *adj.* pionowy, prosty; *fig.* uczciwy, prawy; **2.** *adv.* pionowo, prosto
up·ris·ing ['ʌpraɪzɪŋ] powstanie *n*, insurekcja *f*
up·roar ['ʌprɔː] hałas *m*, zamieszanie *n*; **~·i·ous** [ʌp'rɔːrɪəs] *śmiech*: grzmiący
up·root [ʌp'ruːt] wyrywać z korzeniami; *fig.* przenosić ⟨-nieść⟩
UPS [juː piː 'es] *Am. skrót*: ***United Parcel Service*** (*firma przesyłająca paczki*)
up·set [ʌp'set] (*-set*) przewracać ⟨-rócić⟩, wywracać ⟨-rócić⟩; *fig. plany itp.* ⟨po⟩krzyżować; *fig.* ⟨z⟩denerwować, ***the fish has ~ me*** *lub* ***my stomach*** po tej rybie dostałem rozstroju żołądka; ***be ~*** być zdenerwowanym
up·shot ['ʌpʃɒt] rezultat *m*, wynik *m*
up·side down [ʌpsaɪd'daʊn] do góry nogami
up·stairs [ʌp'steəz] **1.** na górze (*domu itp.*); na górę; w górę; **2.** *adj.* górny, na górze
up·start ['ʌpstɑːt] karierowicz(ka *f*) *m*
up·state [ʌp'steɪt] *Am.* na północy (*stanu*)
up·stream [ʌp'striːm] pod prąd
up·take ['ʌpteɪk] F: ***be quick on the ~*** pojmować w lot, ***be slow on the ~*** mieć ciężki pomyślunek
up-to-date [ʌptə'deɪt] aktualny; nowoczesny
up·town [ʌp'taʊn] *Am.* w dzielnicach mieszkaniowych, do dzielnic mieszkaniowych (*poza centrum miasta*)
up·turn ['ʌptɜːn] poprawa *f*
up·ward(s) ['ʌpwəd(z)] w górę
u·ra·ni·um [jʊ'reɪnɪəm] *chem.* uran *m*
ur·ban ['ɜːbən] miejski
ur·chin ['ɜːtʃɪn] łobuz *m*
urge [ɜːdʒ] **1.** nastawać, nalegać (***to do s.th.*** na zrobienie czegoś); *też* ***~ on*** zalecać ⟨-cić⟩; popędzać ⟨-dzić⟩; **2.** pragnienie *n*, chęć *f*; **ur·gen·cy** ['ɜːdʒənsɪ] nagła potrzeba *f*; **ur·gent** ['ɜːdʒənt] pilny, naglący
u·ri|·nal ['jʊərɪnl] pisuar *m*; **~·nate** ['jʊərɪneɪt] oddawać ⟨-ddać⟩ mocz; **u·rine** ['jʊərɪn] mocz *m*, uryna *f*
urn [ɜːn] urna *f*; duży termos *m*
us [ʌs, əs] nas, nam, nami; ***all of ~*** my wszyscy; ***both of ~*** my obaj
US [juː 'es] *skrót*: ***United States*** USA *pl.*, Stany *pl.* Zjednoczone
USA [juː es 'eɪ] *skrót*: ***United States of America*** USA *pl.*, Stany *pl.* Zjednoczone Ameryki
USAF [juː es eɪ 'ef] *skrót*: ***United States Air Force*** lotnictwo *n* USA
us·age ['juːzɪdʒ] użycie *n*; zwyczaj *m*; stosowana praktyka *f*; *gr.* uzus *m*, użycie *n* języka
use 1. [juːz] *v/t.* używać ⟨użyć⟩; ⟨wy⟩korzystać; ***~ up*** zużywać ⟨-żyć⟩; **2.** [juːs] użycie *n*; wykorzystanie *n*; użytek *m*; korzyść *f*; pożytek *f*; ***be of ~*** być przydatnym (***to*** do *G*); ***it's no ~ ...*** nie ma sensu ...; → ***milk*** 1
used[1] [juːst]: ***I ~ to live here*** kiedyś tu mieszkałem; ***be ~ to do*** (***doing***) ***s.th.*** być przyzwyczajonym do (robienia) czegoś
used[2] [juːzd] użyty, zużyty; używany; **~ 'car** używany samochód *m*; **~ car 'deal·er** sprzedawca *m* (-wczyni *f*) używanych samochodów
use|·ful ['juːsfl] użyteczny; **'~·less** bezużyteczny
us·er ['juːzə] użytkownik *m* (-niczka *f*); posługujący *m* (-ca *f*) się; **~-'friend·ly** przyjazny dla użytkownika; **~ 'in·ter·face** *komp.* interfejs *m* użytkownika
ush·er ['ʌʃə] **1.** bileter *m*; *jur.* woźny *m* sądowy; **2.** wprowadzać ⟨-dzić⟩ (***into*** do *G*), ⟨za⟩prowadzić (***into*** do *G*); **~·ette** [ʌʃə'ret] bileterka *f*

USN [juː es 'en] *skrót*: ***United States Navy*** marynarka *f* Stanów Zjednoczonych
USS [juː es 'es] *skrót*: ***United States Ship*** okręt Stanów Zjednoczonych
USSR [juː es es 'ɑː] *hist. skrót*: ***Union of Socialist Soviet Republics*** ZSRR *n*, Związek *m* Socjalistycznych Republik Radzieckich
u·su·al ['juːʒl] zwykły; ***as ~*** jak zwykle; **~·ly** ['juːʒəlɪ] zwykle
u·sur·er ['juːʒərə] lichwiarz *m* (-rka *f*)
u·su·ry ['juːʒʊrɪ] lichwiarstwo *n*
u·ten·sil [juː'tensl] przybór *m*, urządzenie *n*
u·te·rus ['juːtərəs] (*pl.* ***-ri*** [-raɪ], ***-ruses***) *anat.* macica *f*
u·til·i·ty [juː'tɪlətɪ] użyteczność *f*; ***utilities*** *pl.* usługi *pl.* komunalne
u·til·ize ['juːtɪlaɪz] używać ⟨-żyć⟩, ⟨s⟩pożytkować, wykorzystywać ⟨-tać⟩
ut·most ['ʌtməʊst] najwyższy
U·to·pi·an [juː'təʊpjən] utopijny
ut·ter[1] ['ʌtə] całkowity, zupełny
ut·ter[2] ['ʌtə] wypowiadać ⟨-wiedzieć⟩; *dźwięki* wydawać ⟨-dać⟩ (z siebie)
U-turn ['juːtɜːn] *mot.* zawrócenie *n*; *fig.* zwrot *m* o 180 stopni
UV [juː 'viː] *skrót*: ***ultraviolet*** nadfiolet *m*
u·vu·la ['juːvjʊlə] *anat.* (*pl.* ***-las, -lae*** [-liː]) języczek *m*

V

V, v [viː] V, v *n*
v. *Brt. skrót pisany*: ***against*** (*łacińskie* ***versus***) *zwł. sport, jur.*: przeciw
va|·can·cy ['veɪkənsɪ] wolne miejsce *n*; wakat *m*; ***vacancies*** wolne miejsca; ***no vacancies*** brak wolnych miejsc; '**~·cant** próżny, pusty; wolny; *miejsce*: wakujący; *fig. wyraz twarzy*: nieobecny
va·cate [və'keɪt] *pokój, etat itp.* zwalniać ⟨zwolnić⟩; *miejsce* opuszczać ⟨opuścić⟩
va·ca·tion [və'keɪʃn] **1.** *zwł. Am.* wakacje *pl.*; urlop *m*; *zwł. Brt. univ.* ferie *pl.*; *jur.* wakacje *pl.* sądowe; ***be on ~*** *zwł. Am.* być na urlopie, mieć urlop; **2.** *zwł. Am.* urlopować; odbywać wakacje *lub* urlop; **~·er** [və'keɪʃnə], **~·ist** [və'keɪʃənɪst] *zwł. Am.* urlopowicz(ka *f*) *m*; wczasowicz(ka *f*) *m*
vac|·cin·ate ['væksɪneɪt] zaszczepiać ⟨-pić⟩; **~·cin·a·tion** [væksɪ'neɪʃn] szczepienie *n*; **~·cine** ['væksiːn] szczepionka *f*
vac·il·late ['væsɪleɪt] *fig.* wahać się
vac·u·um ['vækjʊəm] **1.** *phys.* próżnia *f*; **2.** F *dywan, pokój itp.* odkurzać ⟨-rzyć⟩; '**~ bot·tle** *Am.* termos *m*; '**~ clean·er** odkurzacz *m*; '**~ flask** *Brt.* termos *m*; '**~-packed** (za)pakowane próżniowo
vag·a·bond ['vægəbɒnd] włóczęga *m*, wagabunda *m*
va·ga·ry ['veɪgərɪ]: *zw.* ***vagaries*** *pl.* fanaberie *pl.*
va·gi|·na [və'dʒaɪnə] *anat.* pochwa *f*; **~·nal** [və'dʒaɪnl] *anat.* pochwowy; dopochwowy
va·grant ['veɪgrənt] włóczęga *m*
vague [veɪg] (***-r, -st***) niewyraźny; *fig.* mglisty; *fig.* mętny
vain [veɪn] próżny; bezskuteczny; *pogróżka itp.*: czczy; ***in ~*** na próżno
vale [veɪl] *poet. lub w nazwach*: dolina *f*
val·en·tine ['væləntaɪn] walentynka *f*; (*osoba, do której wysyła się walentynkę*)
va·le·ri·an. [və'lɪərɪən] *bot., pharm.* waleriana *f*
val·et ['vælɪt] kamerdyner *m*; '**~ service** (*w hotelu*) czyszczenie *n* odzieży
val·id ['vælɪd] ważny (***for two weeks*** na dwa tygodnie); uzasadniony; przekonujący; ***be ~*** *też* być ważny; **va·lid·i·ty** [və'lɪdətɪ] ważność *f*; *jur.* legalność *f*
va·lise [və'liːz] walizka *f*
val·ley ['vælɪ] dolina *f*
val·u·a·ble ['væljʊəbl] **1.** wartościowy; **2. ~s** *pl.* przedmioty *pl.* wartościowe
val·u·a·tion [væljʊ'eɪʃn] ocena *f*, oszacowanie *n*
val·ue ['væljuː] **1.** wartość *f*; ***be of ~*** mieć wartość (***to*** dla *G*); ***get ~ for money*** nie przepłacić; **2.** *dom itp.* ⟨o⟩sza-

cować, wyceniać ⟨-nić⟩; *radę itp.* doceniać ⟨-nić⟩; **~-ad·ded 'tax** *Brt. econ.* (*skrót*: ***VAT***) podatek *m* od wartości dodanej, VAT *m*; **'~·less** bezwartościowy
valve [vælv] *tech.* zawór *m*; *anat.* zastawka *f*; *mus.* wentyl *m*
vam·pire ['væmpaɪə] wampir *m*
van [væn] furgonetka *f*; *Brt. rail. zamknięty* wagon *m* towarowy
van·dal ['vændl] wandal *m*; **~·is·m** ['vændəlɪzəm] wandalizm *m*; **~·ize** ['vændəlaɪz] ⟨z⟩demolować
vane [veɪn] łopata *f* (*śmigła*); chorągiewka *f* kierunkowa
van·guard ['vængɑːd] *mil.* straż *f* przednia
va·nil·la [və'nɪlə] wanilia *f*; *attr.* waniliowy
van·ish ['vænɪʃ] znikać ⟨-knąć⟩
van·i·ty ['vænətɪ] próżność *f*; **'~ bag, '~ case** kosmetyczka *f*
van·tage·point ['vɑːntɪdʒpɔɪnt] punkt *m* widzenia
va·por·ize ['veɪpəraɪz] odparowywać ⟨-ować⟩; parować
va·po(u)r ['veɪpə] para *f* (*wodna*); **'~ trail** *aviat.* smuga *f* kondensacyjna
var·i|·a·ble ['veərɪəbl] **1.** zmienny; *fig.* nierówny; **2.** *math., phys.* zmienna *f* (*też fig.*); **~·ance** ['veərɪəns]: ***be at ~ance with*** znajdować się w sprzeczności; **~·ant** ['veərɪənt] **1.** odmienny; zmienny; **2.** wariant *m*; **~·a·tion** [veərɪ'eɪʃn] zmiana *f*; zmienność *f*, wahania *pl.*; *mus.* wariacja *f*
var·i·cose veins [værɪkəus 'veɪnz] *med. pl.* żylaki *pl.*
var·ied ['veərɪd] zróżnicowany
va·ri·e·ty [və'raɪətɪ] różnorodność *f*; *bot.* odmiana *f*; *econ.* wybór *m*; ***for a ~ of reasons*** dla licznych powodów; **~ show** przedstawienie *n* teatru rozmaitości; vari(t)s *n*; **~ thea·tre** teatr *m* rozmaitości; vari(t)s *n*
var·i·ous ['veərɪəs] różny
var·nish ['vɑːnɪʃ] **1.** lakier *m*; **2.** ⟨po⟩lakierować
var·si·ty team ['vɑːsətɪ -] *Am.* (*w sporcie*) drużyna *f* uniwersytecka *lub* szkolna
var·y ['veərɪ] *v/i.* różnić się; zmieniać ⟨-nić⟩ się; ***~ in size*** różnić się wielkością; *v/t.* zmieniać ⟨-nić⟩; ⟨z⟩różnicować
vase [vɑːz, *Am.* veɪs, veɪz] wazon *m*

V

vast [vɑːst] ogromny; rozległy; **'~·ly** niezmiernie
vat [væt] kadź *f*
VAT [viː eɪ 'tiː, væt] *skrót*: ***value-added tax*** VAT *m*, podatek *m* od wartości dodanej
Vat·i·can Cit·y Watykan *m*
vau·de·ville ['vɔːdəvɪl] *Am.* wodewil *m*; *attr.* wodewilowy
vault[1] [vɔːlt] *arch.* sklepienie *n*; *też* **~s** *pl.* skarbiec *m*; krypta *f*; piwnica *f* (*na wino*)
vault[2] [vɔːlt] **1. ~** (***over***) przeskakiwać ⟨-skoczyć⟩ nad (*I*); **2.** *zwł.* (*w sporcie*) skok *m*; **'~·ing horse** koń *m* (*do skoków*); **'~·ing pole** tyczka *f* (*do skoku o tyczce*)
VCR [viː siː 'ɑː] *skrót*: ***video cassette recorder*** magnetowid *m*
VDU [viː diː 'juː] *skrót*: ***visual display unit*** *komp.* monitor *m*, wyświetlacz *m*
veal [viːl] cielęcina *f*; *attr.* cielęcy; ***~ chop*** kotlet *m* cielęcy; ***roast ~*** pieczona cielęcina *f*
veer [vɪə] skręcać ⟨-cić⟩ nagle
vege·ta·ble ['vedʒtəbl] **1.** *zw.* **~s** *pl.* warzywo *n*, jarzyna *f*; **2.** warzywny; jarzynowy; roślinny
ve·ge·tar·i·an [vedʒɪ'teərɪən] **1.** wegetarianin *m* (-anka *f*), jarosz *m*; **2.** wegetariański; jarski
ve·ge|·tate ['vedʒɪteɪt] wegetować; **~·ta·tion** [vedʒɪ'teɪʃn] wegetacja *f*
ve·he|·mence ['viːɪməns] zawziętość *f*; gwałtowność *f*; **'~·ment** zawzięty, gwałtowny
ve·hi·cle ['viːɪkl] pojazd *m*; *fig.* medium *n*
veil [veɪl] **1.** welon *m*; woalka *f*; *fig.* zasłona *f*; **2.** skrywać ⟨-ryć⟩
vein [veɪn] *anat., geol.* żyła *f*; *bot.* żyłka *f*; *fig.* ton *m*
ve·loc·i·ty [vɪ'lɒsətɪ] prędkość *f*, szybkość *f*
ve·lour(s) [və'lʊə] welur *m*
vel·vet ['velvɪt] aksamit; **~·y** aksamitny
vend|·er ['vendə] → ***vendor***; **'~·ing machine** automat *m* (*do sprzedaży*); **'~·or** sprzedawca *m* (-wczyni *f*) uliczny (-na)
ve·neer [və'nɪə] **1.** fornir *m*; *fig.* fasada *f*; **2.** fornirować
ven·e|·ra·ble ['venərəbl] czcigodny; **~·rate** ['venəreɪt] poważać; **~·ra·tion** [venə'reɪʃn] cześć *f*, poważanie *n*, głęboki szacunek *m*

ve·ne·re·al dis·ease [vɪnɪərɪəl dɪ'ziːz] *med.* choroba *f* weneryczna
Ve·ne·tian [vɪ'niːʃn] **1.** wenecjanin *m* (-janka *f*); **2.** wenecki; ≈ **'blind** żaluzja *f*
ven·geance ['vendʒəns] zemsta *f*; ***take ~ on*** ⟨ze⟩mścić się na (*L*); ***with a ~*** F zajadle
ve·ni·al ['viːnjəl] *grzech itp.*: lekki
Ven·ice Wenecja *f*
ven·i·son ['venɪzn] dziczyzna *f*
ven·om ['venəm] *zo.* jad *m* (*też fig.*); **'~·ous** jadowity (*też fig.*)
ve·nous *med.* ['viːnəs] żylny
vent [vent] **1.** *v/t. fig. gniew itp.* wyładowywać ⟨-ować⟩ (***on*** na *L*); **2.** otwór *m* wentylacyjny; (*w ubraniu*) rozcięcie *n*; ***give ~ to*** gniew wyładowywać ⟨-ować⟩ (*A*)
ven·ti|·late ['ventɪleɪt] wentylować; przewietrzać ⟨-rzyć⟩; **~·la·tion** [ventɪ'leɪʃn] wentylacja *f*; **~·la·tor** ['ventɪleɪtə] wywietrznik *m*
ven·tri·cle ['ventrɪkl] *anat.* komora *f* serca
ven·tril·o·quist [ven'trɪləkwɪst] brzuchomówca *m*
ven·ture ['ventʃə] **1.** *zwł. econ.* przedsięwzięcie *n*; *econ.* ryzyko *n*; → ***joint venture***; **2.** przedsiębrać ⟨-ęwziąć⟩; ⟨za⟩ryzykować
verb [vɜːb] *gr.* czasownik *m*; **~·al** ['vɜːbl] czasownikowy; werbalny
ver·dict ['vɜːdɪkt] *jur.* werdykt *m*, wyrok *m*; *fig.* sąd *m*; ***bring in** lub **return a ~ of*** (***not***) ***guilty*** wydawać ⟨-dać⟩ werdykt o winie (niewinności)
ver·di·gris ['vɜːdɪgrɪs] grynszpan *m*
verge [vɜːdʒ] **1.** brzeg *m*, krawędź *f* (*też fig.*); ***be on the ~ of*** być prawie gotowym na (*A*); ***be on the ~ of despair*** (***tears***) być na krawędzi rozpaczy (łez); **2. ~ *on*** *fig.* graniczyć z (*I*)
ver·i·fy ['verɪfaɪ] ⟨z⟩weryfikować; sprawdzać ⟨-dzić⟩, ⟨s⟩kontrolować
ver·i·ta·ble ['verɪtəbl] *święto, triumf itp.*: prawdziwy
ver·mi·cel·li [vɜːmɪ'selɪ] makaron *m* nitki
ver·mi·form ap·pen·dix [vɜːmɪfɔːm ə'pendɪks] *anat.* wyrostek *m* robaczkowy
ver·mil·i·on [və'mɪljən] **1.** cynobrowy; **2.** cynober *m*
ver·min ['vɜːmɪn] robactwo *n*; szkodniki *pl.*; **'~·ous** rojący się od robactwa
ver·nac·u·lar [və'nækjʊlə] język *m* miejscowy
ver·sa·tile ['vɜːsətaɪl] wszechstronny; uniwersalny
verse [vɜːs] wiersz *m*; wers *m*; strofa *f*
versed [vɜːst]: ***be*** (***well***) ***~ in*** być dobrze zaznajomionym z (*I*)
ver·sion ['vɜːʃn] wersja *f*
ver·sus ['vɜːsəs] (*skrót*: **v., vs.**) *sport, jur.*: (na)przeciw (*G*)
ver·te|·bra ['vɜːtɪbrə] *anat.* (*pl.* **-brae** [-riː]) krąg *m*; **~·brate** ['vɜːtɪbreɪt] *zo.* kręgowiec *m*
ver·ti·cal ['vɜːtɪkl] pionowy, wertykalny
ver·ti·go ['vɜːtɪgəʊ] *med.* zawroty *pl.* głowy; ***suffer from ~*** cierpieć na zawroty głowy
verve [vɜːv] werwa *f*
ver·y ['verɪ] **1.** *adv.* bardzo; ***I ~ much hope that*** mam wielką nadzieję, że; ***the ~ best things*** same najlepsze rzeczy; **2.** *adj.* ***the ~*** właśnie ten; sam; ***the ~ opposite*** dokładne przeciwieństwo; ***the ~ thing*** właśnie to; ***the ~ thought of*** sama myśl o (*L*)
ves·i·cle ['vesɪkl] *med.* pęcherzyk *m*
ves·sel ['vesl] *anat., bot.* naczynie *n*; statek *m*
vest [vest] *Brt.* podkoszulka *f*, podkoszulek *m*; kamizelka *f* kuloodporna; *Am.* kamizelka *f*
ves·ti·bule ['vestɪbjuːl] westybul *m*, kruchta *f*
ves·tige ['vestɪdʒ] *fig.* ślad *m*
vest·ment ['vestmənt] ornat *m*
ves·try ['vestrɪ] *rel.* zakrystia *f*
vet[1] [vet] F weterynarz *m*
vet[2] [vet] *zwł. Brt.* F ⟨z⟩badać
vet[3] [vet] *Am. mil.* kombatant *m*
vet·e·ran ['vetərən] **1.** *mil.* kombatant(ka *f*) *m*; weteran(ka *f*) *m*; **2.** zaprawiony; doświadczony; **'~ car** *Brt. mot.* stary samochód *m* (*sprzed 1919 roku*)
vet·e·ri·nar·i·an [vetərɪ'neərɪən] *Am.* weterynarz *m*
vet·e·ri·na·ry ['vetərɪnərɪ] weterynaryjny; **~ 'sur·geon** *Brt.* weterynarz *m*
ve·to ['viːtəʊ] **1.** (*pl.* **-toes**) weto *n*; **2.** ⟨za⟩wetować
vexed ques·tion [vekst 'kwestʃən] pytanie *n* pozostające bez odpowiedzi

VHF [viː eɪtʃ 'ef] *skrót*: ***very high frequency*** UKF *m*, fale *pl*. ultrakrótkie
vi·a ['vaɪə] poprzez (*A*)
vi·a·duct ['vaɪədʌkt] wiadukt *m*
vi·al ['vaɪəl] próbówka *f*
vibes [vaɪbz] F *pl*. wibracje *pl*., atmosfera *f* (*miejsca*)
vi·brant ['vaɪbrənt] *barwa*: żywy; energiczny; *głos*: donośny; rozedrgany (***with*** od *G*)
vi·brate [vaɪ'breɪt] *v/i*. wibrować; *powietrze*: drżeć; *fig*. tętnić; *v/t*. wprawiać ⟨-wić⟩ w drganie; **vi·bra·tion** [vaɪ'breɪʃn] wibracja *f*; drganie *n*; **~s** *pl*. F atmosfera *f* (*miejsca*)
vic·ar ['vɪkə] *rel*. (*w kościele protestanckim*) pastor *m*; (*w kościele protestanckim*) wikariusz *m*; **~·age** ['vɪkərɪdʒ] plebania *f*
vice[1] [vaɪs] przywara *f*, wada *f*
vice[2] [vaɪs] *zwł. Brt. tech*. imadło *n*
vi·ce... [vaɪs] wice..., zastępca (*G*)
'vice squad wydział *m* obyczajowy (*policji*); wydział *m* służb antynarkotykowych
vi·ce ver·sa [vaɪsɪ'vɜːsə]: ***and ~*** i vice versa; i na odwrót
vi·cin·i·ty [vɪ'sɪnətɪ] bliskość *f*; pobliże *n*
vi·cious ['vɪʃəs] brutalny; zły
vi·cis·si·tudes [vɪ'sɪsɪtjuːdz] *pl*. koleje *pl*. losu
vic·tim ['vɪktɪm] ofiara *f*; **~·ize** ['vɪktɪmaɪz] dyskryminować
vic·to|·ri·ous [vɪk'tɔːrɪəs] zwycięski; **~·ry** ['vɪktərɪ] zwycięstwo *n*
vid·e·o ['vɪdɪəʊ] **1.** (*pl*. ***-os***) wideo *n*; kaseta *f* wideo; F taśma *f* wideo; *zwł. Brt*. wideo *n*, magnetowid *m*; ***on ~*** na wideo; **2.** *zwł. Brt*. nakręcać ⟨-cić⟩ na wideo; **'~ cam·e·ra** kamera *f* wideo; **~ cas'sette** kaseta *f* wideo; **~ cas'sette re·cor·der** → ***video recorder***; **'~ clip** wideoklip *m*, teledysk *m*; **~·disc** płyta *f* wizyjna; **'~ game** gra *f* wideo; **'~ li·bra·ry** wideoteka *f*; **'~ re·cord·er** magnetowid *m*, wideo *n*; **'~ re·cord·ing** nagranie *n* wideo; **'~ shop** *Brt*.; **'~ store** *Am*. sklep z kasetami wideo; **~·tape 1.** kaseta *f* wideo; taśma *f* wideo; **2.** nagrywać ⟨-rać⟩ na wideo; **'~·text** *Am*. teletekst *m*
vie [vaɪ] rywalizować (***with*** z *I*)
Vi·en·na Wiedeń *m*
Vi·en·nese [vɪə'niːz] **1.** wiedeńczyk *m* (-denka *f*); **2.** wiedeński
view [vjuː] **1.** widok *m*; spojrzenie *n* (***of*** na *A*); pogląd *m* (***about, on*** w sprawie *G*); *fig*. orientacja *f*; ***a room with a ~*** pokój z (*dobrym*) widokiem; ***be on ~*** być wystawionym na pokaz; ***be hidden from ~*** nie być widocznym; ***come into ~*** stać się widocznym; ***in full ~ of*** *fig*. na oczach *G*; ***in ~ of*** *fig*. ze względu na (*A*); ***in my ~*** moim zdaniem; ***keep in ~*** *coś* mieć na uwadze; ***with a ~ to*** *fig*. z zamiarem (*G*); **2.** *v/t*. *dom itp*. oglądać ⟨obejrzeć⟩; *fig*. oceniać⟨-nić⟩ (***as*** jako); zapatrywać się na (*A*) (***with*** z *I*); *v/i*. oglądać telewizję; **'~ da·ta** *pl*. teletekst *m*, telegazeta *f*; **'~·er** widz *m*; **'~·find·er** dalmierz *m*; **'~·point** punkt *m* widzenia
vig|·il ['vɪdʒɪl] *nocne* czuwanie *n*; **~·i·lance** ['vɪdʒɪləns] czujność *f*; **'~·i·lant** czujny
vig|·or·ous ['vɪgərəs] energiczny; pełen wigoru; **~·o(u)r** ['vɪgə] wigor *m*; sprawność *f*
Vi·king ['vaɪkɪŋ] wiking *m*
vile [vaɪl] nikczemny, niegodziwy; F okropny
vil|·lage ['vɪlɪdʒ] wieś *m*, wioska *f*; *attr*. wiejski; **~ 'lage green** *Brt*. łąka *f* (*wspólna dla całej wioski*); **'~·lag·er** mieszkaniec *m* (-nka *f*) wsi
vil·lain ['vɪlən] łotr *m*, niegodziwiec *m*; czarny charakter *m*; *Brt*. F złoczyńca *m*
vin·di·cate ['vɪndɪkeɪt] ⟨z⟩rehabilitować
vin·dic·tive [vɪn'dɪktɪv] mściwy
vine [vaɪn] *bot*. winorośl *f*; ⚠ *nie* ***wino***
vin·e·gar ['vɪnɪgə] ocet *m*
'vine|·grow·er hodowca *m* winorośli; **~·yard** ['vɪnjəd] winnica *f*
vin·tage ['vɪntɪdʒ] **1.** rocznik *m* (*wina*); winobranie *n*; **2.** *wino*: z dobrego rocznika; *film*: klasyczny; *okres*: znakomity; ***a 1994 ~*** rocznik 1994; **'~ car** *zwł. Brt. mot*. stary samochód *m* (*produkcja 1919-1930*)
vi·o·la [vɪ'əʊlə] *mus*. altówka *f*
vi·o|·late ['vaɪəleɪt] *umowę itp*. pogwałcić, ⟨z⟩łamać; *grób* ⟨z⟩bezcześcić; *ciszę* zakłócać ⟨-cić⟩; *granice itp*. naruszać ⟨-szyć⟩; **~·la·tion** [vaɪə'leɪʃn] naruszenie *n*; pogwałcenie *n*; zbezczeszczenie *n*

vi•o|•lence ['vaɪələns] gwałtowność *f*; przemoc *f*, gwałt *m*; '**~•lent** gwałtowny
vi•o•let ['vaɪələt] **1.** *bot.* fiołek *m*; **2.** fioletowy
vi•o•lin [vaɪə'lɪn] *mus.* skrzypce *pl.*; **~•ist** [vaɪə'lɪnɪst] *mus.* skrzypek *m* (-paczka *f*)
VIP [viː aɪ 'piː] *skrót*: ***very important person*** VIP *m*, *ważna* osobistość *f*; **~ lounge** pomieszczenie *n* dla ważnych osobistości
vi•per ['vaɪpə] *zo.* żmija *f*
vir•gin ['vɜːdʒɪn] **1.** dziewica *f*; **2.** dziewiczy; **~•i•ty** [və'dʒɪnətɪ] dziewictwo *n*
Vir•go ['vɜːgəʊ] (*pl.* ***-gos***) *znak Zodiaku*: Panna *f*; ***he/she is (a) ~*** on(a) jest spod znaku Panny
vir•ile ['vɪraɪl] męski; **vi•ril•i•ty** [vɪ'rɪlətɪ] męskość *f*
vir•tu•al ['vɜːtʃʊəl] faktyczny; *komp.* wirtualny; '**~•ly** faktycznie, praktycznie; **~ re'al•i•ty** rzeczywistość *f* wirtualna
vir|•tue ['vɜːtʃuː] cnota *f*; zaleta; ***by** lub **in ~tue of*** z mocy (*G*), z tytułu (*G*); ***make a ~tue of necessity*** robić cnotę z konieczności; **~•tu•ous** ['vɜːtʃʊəs] cnotliwy
vir•u•lent ['vɪrʊlənt] *med.* zjadliwy (*też fig.*)
vi•rus ['vaɪərəs] wirus *m*; *attr.* wirusowy
vi•sa ['viːzə] wiza *f*; **~ed** ['viːzəd] opatrzony wizą
vis•cose ['vɪskəʊz, 'vɪskəʊs] wiskoza *f*; *attr.* wiskozowy
vis•cous ['vɪskəs] lepki
vise [vaɪs] *Am. tech.* imadło *n*
vis•i|•bil•i•ty [vɪzɪ'bɪlətɪ] widoczność *f*; **~•ble** ['vɪzəbl] widoczny; wyraźny
vi•sion ['vɪʒn] wizja *f*; wzrok *m*; widzenie *n*; **~•a•ry** ['vɪʒnrɪ] **1.** wizjonerski; **2.** wizjoner(ka *f*) *m*
vis•it ['vɪzɪt] **1.** *v/t.* odwiedzać ⟨-dzić⟩; *zabytek* zwiedzać ⟨-dzić⟩; wizytować; *v/i.* ***be ~ing*** być z wizytą (*Am.*: ***with*** u *G*); **~ *with*** *Am.* ucinać ⟨-ciąć⟩ pogawędkę; **2.** odwiedziny *pl.*, wizyta *f* (***to*** w *L*); *Am.* pogawędka *f*; ***for** lub **on a ~*** z wizytą; ***have a ~ from*** mieć wizytę ze strony (*G*); ***pay a ~ to*** składać ⟨złożyć⟩ wizytę (*D*); ⚠ *nie* ***odwiedziny w szpitalu***
vis•i•ta•tion [vɪzɪ'teɪʃn] wizytacja *f*; inspekcja *f*
'**vis•it•ing hours** *pl.* godziny *pl.* odwiedzin
'**vis•it•or** gość *m*, odwiedzający *m* (-ca *f*)
vi•sor ['vaɪzə] osłona *f* (*hełmu*); *mot.* osłona *f* przeciwsłoneczna; przyłbica *f*
vis•u•al ['vɪʒʊəl] wizualny; wzrokowy; **~ 'aids** *pl.*: wizualne pomoce *pl.* naukowe; **~ dis'play u•nit** *komp.* monitor *m*; **~ in'struc•tion** (*nauka z wykorzystaniem wizualnych pomocy naukowych*); **~•ize** ['vɪʒʊəlaɪz] przedstawiać sobie, wyobrażać ⟨-zić⟩ sobie
vi•tal ['vaɪtl] istotny, zasadniczy; życiowy; *organ*: ważny dla życia; *ktoś*: żywotny, pełen życia; ***of ~ importance*** o zasadniczym znaczeniu; **~•i•ty** [vaɪ'tælətɪ] witalność *f*
vit•a•min ['vɪtəmɪn] witamina *f*; *attr.* witaminowy; **~ de'fi•cien•cy** niedobór *m* witamin
vit•re•ous ['vɪtrɪəs] szklisty
vi•va•cious [vɪ'veɪʃəs] pełen temperamentu, żywiołowy
viv•id ['vɪvɪd] *światło, kolor*: jaskrawy; *opis*: żywy; *wyobraźnia*: bujny
vix•en ['vɪksn] *zo.* lisica *f*
viz. [vɪz] *skrót*: ***namely*** (*łacińskie* ***videlicet***) mianowicie
V-neck ['viːnek] (*wycięcie ubrania*) szpic *m*; '**V-necked** wycięty w szpic
vo•cab•u•la•ry [və'kæbjʊlərɪ] słownictwo *n*
vo•cal ['vəʊkl] *mus.* wokalny; głosowy; F donośny; '**~ cords** *anat. pl.* struny *pl.* głosowe; **~•ist** ['vəʊkəlɪst] wokalista *m* (-tka *f*); '**~s: ~ *XY*** śpiew XY
vo•ca•tion [vəʊ'keɪʃn] powołanie *n* (***for*** do *G*)
vo•ca•tion•al [vəʊ'keɪʃənl] zawodowy; **~ ed•u'ca•tion** wykształcenie *n* zawodowe; **~ 'guid•ance** poradnictwo *n* zawodowe; **~ 'train•ing** szkolenie *n* zawodowe
vogue [vəʊg] moda *f*; ***be in ~*** być modnym, być w modzie
voice [vɔɪs] **1.** głos *m*; ***active ~*** *gr.* strona *f* czynna; ***passive ~*** *gr.* strona *f* bierna; **2.** wygłaszać ⟨-łosić⟩, wyrażać ⟨-razić⟩; **~d** *ling.* dźwięczny; '**~•less** *ling.* bezdźwięczny
void [vɔɪd] **1.** pusty; pozbawiony; *jur.* nieważny; **2.** pustka *f*
vol [vɒl] (*pl.* ***vols***) *skrót*: ***volume*** vol., wolumin *m*, tom *m*

V

vol·a·tile ['vɒlətaɪl] pobudliwy, choleryczny; *chem.* ulotny
vol·ca·no [vɒl'keɪnəʊ] (*pl.* ***-noes, -nos***) wulkan *n*
Vol·ga Wołga *f*
vol·ley ['vɒlɪ] **1.** salwa *f*; *fig.* (*wyzwisk*) grad *m*; (*w tenisie, piłce nożnej*) wolej *m*; **2.** *piłkę* odbijać ⟨-bić⟩ wolejem *lub* z woleja (***into the net*** w siatkę); **'~·ball** (*w sporcie*) siatkówka *f*
volt [vəʊlt] *electr.* wolt *m*; **~·age** ['vəʊltɪdʒ] *electr.* napięcie *n*
vol·u·ble ['vɒljʊbl] gadatliwy; *wymówka itp.*: przegadany
vol·ume ['vɒljuːm] objętość *f*; wolumen *m* (*handlu itp.*); wolumin *m*, tom *m*; głośność *f*, głos *m*; **vo·lu·mi·nous** [və'luːmɪnəs] *ubranie*: obszerny; *walizka*: pakowny; *pisarz*: płodny
vol·un·ta·ry ['vɒləntərɪ] ochotniczy
vol·un·teer [vɒlən'tɪə] **1.** *v/i.* zgłaszać ⟨-łosić⟩ się na ochotnika (***for*** do *G*); *v/t. pomoc itp.* zgłaszać ⟨-łosić⟩ dobrowolnie; **2.** ochotnik *m* (-niczka *f*)
vo·lup·tu·ous [və'lʌptʃʊəs] *usta*: zmysłowy; *kształt*: pełny, krągły
vom·it ['vɒmɪt] **1.** ⟨z⟩wymiotować; **2.** wymiociny *pl.*
vo·ra·cious [və'reɪʃəs] *apetyt*: nienasycony
vote [vəʊt] **1.** głosowanie *n* (***about, on*** na *A*); głos *m*; *też* **~s** prawo *n* głosowania; **~ *of no confidence*** wotum *n* nieufności; ***take a ~ on s.th.*** poddawać ⟨-ddać⟩ coś głosowaniu; **2.** *v/i.* głosować (***for*** na *A*, ***against*** przeciw *D*); **~ *on*** poddawać ⟨-ddać⟩ coś głosowaniu; *v/t.* wybierać ⟨-brać⟩; **~ *out of office*** pozbawiać ⟨-wić⟩ urzędu przez głosowanie; **'vot·er** wyborca *m*; **'vot·ing booth** kabina *f* wyborcza
vouch [vaʊtʃ]: **~ *for*** ⟨za⟩ręczyć za (*A*); **'~·er** kupon *m*, talon *m*; kwit *m*, rachunek *m*
vow [vaʊ] **1.** przyrzeczenie *n*; ***take a ~, make a ~*** przyrzekać ⟨-rzec⟩; **2.** przyrzekać ⟨-rzec⟩ (***to do s.th.*** zrobić coś)
vow·el ['vaʊəl] *gr.* samogłoska *f*
voy·age ['vɔɪɪdʒ] podróż *f*, rejs *m*
vs. *Am. skrót pisany*: **against** (*łacińskie* **versus**) *zwł. sport, jur.*: przeciw(ko)
vul·gar ['vʌlgə] wulgarny; ordynarny; pospolity
vul·ne·ra·ble ['vʌlnərəbl] *fig.* łatwy do zranienia; wrażliwy; nieodporny (***to*** na *A*)
vul·ture ['vʌltʃə] *zo.* sęp *m*
vy·ing ['vaɪɪŋ] → ***vie***

W

W, w ['dʌbljuː] W, w *n*
W *skrót pisany*: **west** zach., zachód *m*, zachodni; **west(ern)** zachodni; **watt(s)** W, wat(y *pl.*) *m*
wad [wɒd] tampon *m* (*waty*); zwitek *m* (*banknotów*); zwój *m* (*papieru*); **~·ding** ['wɒdɪŋ] wyściółka *f*; *med.* podściółka *f*
wad·dle ['wɒdl] człapać
wade [weɪd] *v/i.* brodzić; **~ *through*** przechodzić ⟨-ejść⟩ w bród; F ⟨prze⟩brnąć; *v/t.* przechodzić ⟨-ejść⟩ w bród
wa·fer ['weɪfə] wafel *m* (*zwł. do lodów*); *rel.* opłatek *m*
waf·fle¹ ['wɒfl] wafel *m*
waf·fle² ['wɒfl] *Brt.* F nudzić
waft [wɑːft] *v/i.* unosić się; *v/t.* unosić ⟨unieść⟩
wag [wæg] **1.** (**-gg-**) ⟨po⟩machać; ⟨za⟩merdać; **2. *with a ~ of its tail*** machnięciem ogona
wage¹ [weɪdʒ]: *zw.* **~s** *pl.* pensja *f*, wypłata *f* (*zwł. robotnika*)
wage² [weɪdʒ]: **~ (*a*) *war against*** *lub* ***on*** *mil.* toczyć wojnę przeciw (*D*) *lub* wobec (*G*) (*też fig.*)
'wage| earn·er żywiciel(ka *f*) rodziny; **'~ freeze** zamrożenie *n* płac; **'~ ne·go·ti·a·tions** *pl.* negocjacje *pl.* płacowe; **'~ pack·et** wypłata *f*; **'~ rise** podwyżka *f* pensji
wa·ger ['weɪdʒə] zakład *m*
wag·gle ['wægl] F ruszać (się)
wag·gon *Brt.*, **wag·on** *Am.* ['wægən] wóz *m*; *Brt. rail.* otwarty wagon *m* towarowy; *Am.* wózek *m* (*z napojami*

itp.); ⚠ *nie* ***wagon***
wag·tail ['wægteɪl] *zo.* pliszka *f*
wail [weɪl] **1.** *ktoś, wiatr:* zawodzić; *syrena:* ⟨za⟩wyć; **2.** zawodzenie *n*; wycie *n*
wain·scot ['weɪnskət] boazeria *f*
waist [weɪst] talia *f*, kibić *f*; **~·coat** *zwł. Brt.* ['weɪskəʊt] kamizelka *f*; '**~·line** talia *f*
wait [weɪt] **1.** *v/i.* ⟨po⟩czekać (***for*** na *A*), oczekiwać (***for*** *G lub* na *A*); ***keep s.o. ~ing*** kazać komuś czekać; ***~ and see!*** tylko poczekaj!; ***~ at*** (*Am.* ***on***) ***table*** podawać ⟨-dać⟩ do stołu; ***~ on s.o.*** obsługiwać ⟨-łużyć⟩ kogoś; ***~ up*** F nie kłaść ⟨położyć⟩ się spać; *v/t.* ***~ one's chance*** czekać na swoją szansę (***to do s.th.*** zrobienia czegoś); ***~ one's turn*** czekać na swoją kolej; **2.** oczekiwanie *n*; ***have a long ~*** musieć długo czekać; ***lie in ~ for s.o.*** czekać w zasadzce na kogoś; '**~·er** kelner *m*; ***~er, the bill*** (*Am.* ***check***)***!*** proszę o rachunek!
'**wait·ing** oczekiwanie *n*; ***no ~*** (*na znaku*) zakaz postoju; '**~ list** lista *f* oczekujących; '**~ room** poczekalnia *f*
wait·ress ['weɪtrɪs] kelnerka *f*; ***~, the bill*** (*Am.* ***check***)***!*** proszę o rachunek!
wake[1] [weɪk] (***woke*** *lub* ***waked, woken*** *lub* ***waked***) *v/i. też* ***~ up*** ⟨o⟩budzić się; *v/t.* ***~ up*** ⟨o⟩budzić
wake[2] [weɪk] *naut.* kilwater *m*; ***follow in the ~ of*** *fig.* podążać ⟨-żyć⟩ czyimś śladem
wake·ful ['weɪkfl] bezsenny; mało śpiący
wak·en ['weɪkən] *v/i. też* ***~ up*** ⟨o⟩budzić się; *v/t.* ***~ up*** ⟨o⟩budzić
Wales Walia *f*
walk [wɔːk] **1.** *v/i.* iść; chodzić ⟨pójść⟩; spacerować; *v/t.* chodzić po (*L*) (*ulicach*); przechodzić ⟨przejść⟩ piechotą; odprowadzać ⟨-dzić⟩ (***to*** do *G*, ***home*** do domu); *psa* wyprowadzać ⟨-dzić⟩ (*na spacer*); ***~ away*** → ***~ off***; ***~ off*** odchodzić ⟨odejść⟩; ***~ off with*** F buchnąć; F *nagrodę* łatwo zdobywać ⟨-być⟩; ***~ out*** wychodzić ⟨wyjść⟩; opuszczać ⟨opuścić⟩ salę (*na znak protestu*); *econ.* ⟨za⟩strajkować; ***~ out on s.o.*** F porzucać ⟨-cić⟩ kogoś; ***~ up*** podchodzić ⟨-dejść⟩; **2.** chód *m*; spacer *m*; przechadzka *f*; trasa *f* spacerowa; ścieżka *f*; przejście *n*; ***go for a ~, take a ~*** iść ⟨pójść⟩ na spacer; ***it's half an hour's ~ from here*** stąd jest pół godziny spacerem; ***from all ~s*** (*lub* ***every ~***) ***of life*** *ludzie:* z wszystkich grup społecznych; '**~·er** spacerowicz *m*; (*w sporcie*) chodziarz *m*; ***be a good ~er*** być dobrym piechurem
walk·ie-talk·ie [wɔːkɪ'tɔːkɪ] walkie-talkie *n*, krótkofalówka *f*
'**walk·ing** chodzenie *n*; spacery *pl.*; wycieczki *pl.*; '**~ pa·pers** *pl.*: ***give s.o. his/her ~ papers*** *Am.* F posłać kogoś na zieloną trawkę; '**~ shoes** *pl.* buty *pl.* turystyczne; '**~ stick** laska *f*; '**~ tour** wycieczka *f* piesza
'**Walk·man** *TM* (*pl.* ***-mans***) walkman *m TM*
'**walk|·out** demonstracyjne opuszczenie *n* konferencji; *econ.* strajk *m*; '**~·over** *sport:* walkower *m*; F łatwe zwycięstwo *n*; '**~-up** *Am.* F budynek *m* bez windy
wall [wɔːl] **1.** ściana *f*; mur *m*; **2.** *też* ***~ in*** otaczać ⟨-toczyć⟩ murem; ***~ up*** zamurowywać ⟨-ować⟩; '**~·chart** plansza *f* ścienna
wal·let ['wɒlɪt] portfel *m*
'**wall·flow·er** *fig.* F osoba *f* nie uczestnicząca w tańcach
wal·lop ['wɒləp] F ⟨przy⟩lać; (*w sporcie*) położyć na obie łopatki, pobić (***at*** w *L*)
wal·low ['wɒləʊ] ⟨wy⟩tarzać się; *fig.* pogrążać ⟨-żyć⟩ się (***in*** w *L*)
'**wall|·pa·per** **1.** tapeta *f*; **2.** ⟨wy⟩tapetować; **~-to-'~**: ***~to-wall carpet***(***ing***) wykładzina *f* podłogowa
wal·nut ['wɔːlnʌt] *bot.* orzech *m* włoski
wal·rus ['wɔːlrəs] *zo.* (*pl.* ***-ruses, -rus***) mors *m*
waltz [wɔːls] **1.** walc *m*; **2.** ⟨za⟩tańczyć walca, walcować
wand [wɒnd] pałeczka *f* czarodziejska, różdżka *f*
wan·der ['wɒndə] wędrować, ⟨za⟩błąkać się; zbaczać ⟨-boczyć⟩; *fig.* fantazjować
wane [weɪn] **1.** ⟨z⟩maleć, zmniejszać się; zanikać ⟨-knąć⟩; ubywać (*o księżycu*); **2.** ***be on the ~*** maleć
wan·gle ['wæŋgl] F wydostawać ⟨-tać⟩; ***~ s.th. out of s.o.*** wycisnąć coś z kogoś; ***~ one's way out of*** wykręcać ⟨-cić⟩ się z (*G*)
want [wɒnt] **1.** *v/t.* chcieć (*G*); potrzebować; F wymagać; ***be ~ed*** być poszukiwanym (***for*** za *A*) (*przez policję*); *v/i.*

W

he does not ~ for anything nie brak mu niczego; **2.** brak *m*; potrzeba *f*; niedostatek *m*; ***be in ~ of*** wymagać (*G*); **'~ ad** *zwł. Am.* drobne ogłoszenie *n*; **'~·ed** poszukiwany

wan·ton ['wɒntən] lubieżny, rozpustny

war [wɔː] wojna *f* (*też fig.*); *fig.* walka *f* (***against*** przeciwko *D*)

war·ble ['wɔːbl] ⟨za⟩ćwierkać

ward [wɔːd] **1.** *med.* oddział *m*; *Brt. pol.* okręg *m* policyjny; *jur.* podopieczny *m* (-na *f*) (*pod kuratelą*); **2. ~ *off*** *uderzenie* odpierać ⟨-deprzeć⟩; *chorobie itp.* zapobiegać ⟨-biec⟩; *duchy itp.* odganiać ⟨-gonić⟩; **war·den** ['wɔːdn] opiekun(ka *f*) *m*; nadzorca *f*; kustosz *m*; kurator *m*; *Am.* naczelnik *m* więzienia; **~·er** *Brt.* ['wɔːdə] strażnik *m* (-niczka *f*) więzienny (-na)

war·drobe ['wɔːdrəʊb] szafa *f*; garderoba *f*

ware [weə] *w złożeniach* naczynia *pl.*, wyroby *pl.*

'ware·house skład *m* (*hurtowy*)

war|·fare ['wɔːfeə] wojna *f*, działania *pl.* wojenne; **'~·head** *mil.* głowica *f* bojowa; **'~·like** bojowy

warm [wɔːm] **1.** *adj.* ciepły (*też fig. barwy, głos, przyjęcie*); ***I am ~, I feel ~*** ciepło mi; **2.** *też* **~ *up*** ogrzewać ⟨-rzać⟩ (się); **3.** ***come into the ~!*** *zwł. Brt.* chodź do ciepła!; **~th** [wɔːmθ] ciepło *n*; **'~-up** (*w sporcie*) rozgrzewka *f*

warn [wɔːn] ostrzegać ⟨-rzec⟩ (***against, of*** przeciwko *D*); **'~·ing** ostrzeżenie *n* (***of*** o *L*); **'~·ing sig·nal** sygnał *m* ostrzegawczy

warp [wɔːp] ⟨wy-, s⟩paczyć się

war·rant ['wɒrənt] **1.** *jur. sądowy* nakaz *m* (*rewizji itp.*); → ***death ~***; **2.** uzasadniać ⟨-nić⟩, usprawiedliwiać; **~ of ar'rest** *jur.* nakaz *m* aresztowania

war·ran·ty ['wɒrəntɪ] *econ.* gwarancja *f*; ***it's still under ~*** nadal jest na gwarancji

war·ri·or ['wɒrɪə] wojownik *m* (-niczka *f*)

War·saw Warszawa *f*

'war·ship okręt *m*

wart [wɔːt] brodawka *f*

war·y ['weərɪ] (***-ier, -iest***) nieufny

was [wɒz, wəz] *ja* byłem, *ja* byłam, *on* był, *ona* była, *ono* było

wash [wɒʃɪ] **1.** *v/t.* ⟨u⟩myć; ⟨wy⟩prać; *v/i.* ⟨u⟩myć się; **~ *up*** *v/i. Brt.* zmywać ⟨-myć⟩ naczynia; *v/t.* wyrzucać ⟨-cić⟩ *coś* na brzeg; **2.** umycie *n*; pranie *n*; ***be in the ~*** być w praniu; ***give s.th. a ~*** wyprać coś, umyć coś; ***have a ~*** ⟨u⟩myć się; **'~·a·ble** mogący być prany; zmywalny; **~-and-'wear** nie wymagający prasowania; **'~·ba·sin**, **'~·bowl** *Am.* umywalka *f*; **'~·cloth** *Am.* myjka *f*; **'~·er** *Am.* pralka *f*; → ***dishwasher***; *tech.* podkładka *f*; *tech.* uszczelka *f*; **'~·ing** pranie *n*; mycie *n*; **'~·ing machine** pralka *f*; **'~·ing pow·der** proszek *m* do prania

Wash·ing·ton Waszyngton *m*

wash·ing-'up [wɒʃɪŋʌp] *Brt.* zmywanie *n* naczyń; ***do the ~*** zmywać naczynia; **'~·rag** *Am.* ścierka *f* do zmywania; **'~·room** *Am.* toaleta *f*

wasp [wɒsp] *zo.* osa *f*

WASP [wɒsp] *skrót*: ***White Anglo-Saxon Protestant*** (*biały Amerykanin, protestant, pochodzenia anglosaskiego*)

waste [weɪst] **1.** marnotrawstwo *n*; marnowanie *n*; strata *f*; odpady *pl.*, odpadki *pl.*; **~ *of time*** strata *f* czasu; ***hazardous ~*** niebezpieczne odpady *pl.*; **2.** *v/t.* ⟨z⟩marnować, ⟨s⟩tracić; *ciało itp.* wyniszczać ⟨-czyć⟩; *v/i.* **~ *away*** ⟨z⟩marnieć; **3.** *produkt*: odpadowy; *ziemia*: jałowy, leżący odłogiem; ***lay ~*** ⟨s⟩pustoszyć; **'~ dis·pos·al** usuwanie *n* odpadków; **~ dis·pos·al 'site** składowisko *n* śmieci; **'~·ful** marnotrawny; rozrzutny; **'~ gas** *zw.* gazy *pl.* odlotowe; **~ 'pa·per** makulatura *f*; **~'pa·per bas·ket** kosz *m* na śmieci; **'~ pipe** rura *f* ściekowa

watch [wɒtʃ] **1.** *v/i.* patrzeć, przyglądać się, obserwować; **~ *for*** oczekiwać (*G*); ***~ out!*** uwaga!; ***~ out for*** uważać na (*A*); wyglądać (*G*); *v/t.* oglądać ⟨obejrzeć⟩; przyglądać się; → ***television***; **2.** zegarek *m* (*naręczny*); wachta *f*; ***be on the ~ for*** mieć się na baczności przed (*I*); ***keep*** (***a***) ***careful*** *lub* ***close ~ on*** obserwować bacznie (*A*); **'~·dog** pies *m* podwórzowy; **'~·ful** baczny; **'~·ma·k·er** zegarmistrz *m*; **'~·man** (*pl.* **-*men***) dozorca *m* (-czyni *f*)

wa·ter ['wɔːtə] **1.** woda *f*; **2.** *v/t. kwiaty* podlewać ⟨-lać⟩; *bydło* ⟨na⟩poić; ***~ down*** rozwadniać ⟨-wodnić⟩ (*też fig.*); ***make s.o.'s mouth ~*** sprawiać, że

W

komuś ślinka cieknie; '~ **bird** *zo.* ptak *m* wodny; '~**·col·o(u)r** akwarela *f*; '~**·course** tor *m* wodny; '~**·cress** *bot.* rzeżucha *f*; '~**·fall** wodospad *m*; '~**·front** nabrzeże *n*; '~**·hole** wodopój *m*

wa·ter·ing can ['wɔːtərɪŋ -] konewka *f*

'wa·ter| jump (*w sporcie*) przeszkoda *f* wodna; '~ **lev·el** poziom *m* wody; '~ **lil·y** *bot.* lilia *f* wodna; '~**·mark** znak *m* wodny; '~**·mel·on** *bot.* arbuz *m*; '~ **pol·lu·tion** zanieczyszczenie *n* wody; '~ **po·lo** (*w sporcie*) piłka *f* wodna; '~**·proof 1.** wodoszczelny; **2.** *Brt.* płaszcz *m* przeciwdeszczowy; **3.** ⟨za⟩impregnować; '~**s** *pl.* wody *pl.*; woda *f*; '~**·shed** *geogr.* dział *m* wodny; *fig.* punkt *m* zwrotny; '~**·side** nabrzeże *n*; '~ **ski·ing** *sport:* narciarstwo *n* wodne; '~**·tight** wodoszczelny; *fig.* niepodważalny; '~**·way** magistrala *f* wodna; '~**·works** *często sg.* wodociąg *m*; ~**·y** ['wɔːtərɪ] wodnisty, rozwodniony

watt [wɒt] *electr.* (*skrót:* ***W***) wat *m*

wave [weɪv] **1.** *v/t.* ⟨po⟩machać (*I*); *flagą* powiewać (*I*); *włosy* ⟨za⟩kręcić; ~ ***one's hand*** pomachać ręką; ~ ***s.o. goodbye*** pomachać na pożegnanie; *v/i.* falować; *włosy:* kręcić się; ~ ***at s.o.***, ~ ***to s.o.*** ⟨po⟩machać do kogoś; **2.** fala *f* (*też fig.*); pomachanie *n*; '~**·length** *phys.* długość *f* fali

wa·ver ['weɪvə] ⟨za⟩wahać się; *płomień:* ⟨za⟩migotać; *głos:* ⟨za⟩drżeć

wav·y ['weɪvɪ] (***-ier, -iest***) falisty, pofalowany

wax[1] [wæks] **1.** wosk *m*; woskowina *f*; **2.** ⟨na⟩woskować; ⟨wy⟩pastować

wax[2] [wæks] *księżyc:* przybywać

wax|·en ['wæksən] woskowy; nawoskowany; biały, blady; '~**·works** *sg.* gabinet *m* figur woskowych; ~**·y** ['wæksɪ] (***-ier, -iest***) blady, biały

way [weɪ] **1.** droga *f*; trasa *f*; kierunek *m*; przejście *n*; przejazd *m*; sposób *m*; zwyczaj *m*; ~***s and means*** *pl.* środki *pl.*, sposoby *pl.*; ~ ***back*** droga *f* powrotna; ~ ***home*** droga *f* do domu; ~ ***in*** wejście *n*; ~ ***out*** wyjście *n*; ***be on the*** ~ ***to, be on one's*** ~ ***to*** być w drodze do (*G*); ***by*** ~ ***of*** przez (*A*); *Brt.* zamiast (*G*); ***by the*** ~ przy sposobności; ***give*** ~ ustępować ⟨-tąpić⟩ drogi; ***in a*** ~ w jakiś sposób; ***in no*** ~ w żaden sposób; ***lead the*** ~ prowadzić; ***let s.o. have his/her (own)*** ~ dawać komuś postępować według jego woli; ***lose one's*** ~ ⟨z⟩gubić się; ***make*** ~ ustępować ⟨-tąpić⟩ miejsca; ***no*** ~ F ależ skąd; w ogóle nie; ***out of the*** ~ niezwykły, niespotykany; ***this*** ~ tędy; **2.** *adv.* daleko; '~**·bill** list *m* przewozowy; ~**'lay** (***-laid***) zasadzać się ⟨-dzić⟩ się (***s.o.*** na kogoś); ~**·ward** ['weɪwəd] samowolny

we [wiː, wɪ] my *pl.*

weak [wiːk] słaby (*też* ***at, in*** w *L*); '~**·en** *v/t.* osłabiać ⟨-bić⟩ (*też fig.*); *v/i.* ⟨o⟩słabnąć; ustępować ⟨-tąpić⟩; '~**·ling** słabeusz *m*; '~**·ness** słabość *f*

weal [wiːl] ślad *m* (*jak po uderzeniu batem*)

wealth [welθ] bogactwo *n*, majątek *m*; *fig.* obfitość *f*; '~**·y** (***-ier, -iest***) bogaty, majętny

wean [wiːn] *dziecko* odstawiać ⟨-wić⟩ od piersi; ~ ***s.o. from*** *lub* ***off s.th.*** odzwyczajać ⟨-czaić⟩ kogoś od czegoś

weap·on ['wepən] broń *f*

wear [weə] **1.** (***wore, worn***) *v/t.* nosić; mieć na sobie; ubierać się w (*A*); wycierać ⟨wytrzeć⟩; ~ ***the trousers*** (*Am.* ***pants***) F być głową rodziny; ~ ***an angry expression*** przybrać gniewny wyraz twarzy; *v/i.* wycierać ⟨wytrzeć⟩ się; zużywać ⟨zużyć⟩ się; trzymać się (*dobrze itp.*); ***s.th. to*** ~ coś do ubrania; ~ ***away*** wycierać ⟨wytrzeć⟩ się; ~ ***down*** ścierać ⟨zetrzeć⟩; *opór itp.* ⟨z⟩łamać; ~ ***off*** ⟨ze⟩lżeć; ~ ***on*** ciągnąć się (***all day*** cały dzień); ~ ***out*** zużywać ⟨-żyć⟩ się; wyczerpywać ⟨-pać⟩; **2.** *często w złożeniach* ubranie *n*, strój *m*; ~ ***and tear*** zużycie *n*; ***the worse for*** ~ zużyty; F *osoba:* wyczerpany

wear|·i·some ['wɪərɪsəm] męczący; ~**·y** ['wɪərɪ] (***-ier, -iest***) zmęczony, znużony; F męczący

wea·sel ['wiːzl] *zo.* łasica *f*

weath·er ['weðə] **1.** pogoda *f*; **2.** *v/t.* poddawać ⟨-ddać⟩ działaniu czynników atmosferycznych; *kryzys* przetrwać; *v/i.* ⟨z⟩wietrzeć; '~**-beat·en** osmagany wiatrem, ogorzały; '~ **chart** mapa *f* pogody; '~ **fore·cast** prognoza *f* pogody; '~**·man** (*pl.* ***-men***) synoptyk *m* dyżurny (*radiowy lub telewizyjny*); '~**·proof 1.** odporny na działanie czynników atmosferycznych; nieprzemakalny; **2.** ⟨za⟩impregnować; '~ **re·port** komunikat *m*

W

meteorologiczny; '~ **sta·tion** stacja *f* meteorologiczna; '~ **vane** kurek *m* na dachu
weave [wiːv] (***wove, woven***) ⟨u⟩tkać; *sieć* pleść, zaplatać ⟨-pleść⟩; *kosz* wyplatać ⟨-pleść⟩; (*pret. i pp.* ***weaved***): ***~one's way through*** prześliz(g)nąć się przez (*A*); '**weav·er** tkacz(ka *f*) *m*
web [web] pajęczyna *f* (*też fig.*); sieć *f* (*też komp.*); *zo.* błona *f* pławna; '~**·bing** gurt *m*, taśma *f* tapicerska
wed [wed] (***-dd-***; ***wedded*** *lub rzadko* ***wed***) poślubiać ⟨-bić⟩
Wed(s) *skrót pisany:* ***Wednesday*** śr., środa *f*
wed·ding ['wedɪŋ] ślub *m*; wesele *f*; *attr.* weselny; '~ **ring** obrączka *f* ślubna
wedge [wedʒ] **1.** klin *m*; kawałek *m* (*klinowaty*); **2.** ⟨za⟩klinować
wed·lock ['wedlɒk]: ***born in*** (***out of***) ~ (nie)ślubny
Wednes·day ['wenzdɪ] środa *f*
wee[1] [wiː] F maluśki; ***a ~ bit*** malusieńki kawałek
wee[2] [wiː] F **1.** siusiać; **2.** ***do*** *lub* ***have a ~*** wysiusiać się
weed [wiːd] **1.** chwast *m*; **2.** ⟨wy⟩pielić; ***~ out*** *fig.* wykluczać ⟨-czyć⟩ (***from*** z *G*); '~**·kill·er** środek *m* chwastobójczy; '~**·y** (***-ier, -iest***) zachwaszczony; F słabowity; F słaby
week [wiːk] tydzień; ***~ after ~*** tydzień za tygodniem; ***a ~ today, today ~*** od dzisiaj za tydzień; ***every other ~*** co drugi tydzień; ***for ~s*** przez całe tygodnie; ***four times a ~*** cztery razy na tydzień; ***in a ~('s time)*** za tydzień; '~**·day** dzień *m* tygodnia; ~**·end** [wiːk'end] koniec *m* tygodnia; weekend *m*; ***at*** (*Am.* ***on***) ***the ~end*** w ciągu weekendu; ~'**end·er** (*osoba udająca się poza miasto na weekend*); '~**·ly 1.** tygodniowy; **2.** tygodnik *m*
weep [wiːp] (***wept***) płakać (***for*** za *I*, ***over*** nad *I*); ***the wound is ~ing*** sączy się z rany; ~**·ing 'wil·low** *bot.* wierzba *f* płacząca; '~**·y** (***-ier, -iest***) F płaczliwy; rzewny, ckliwy
wee-wee ['wiːwiː] F → ***wee***[2]
weigh [weɪ] *v/t.* ważyć; *fig.* rozważać ⟨-żyć⟩; ~ ***anchor*** *naut.* *podnosić* ⟨-nieść⟩ kotwicę; ***be ~ed down with*** *fig.* być przybitym (*I*); ***~ on*** *fig.* ciążyć (*D*)
weight [weɪt] **1.** waga *f* (*też fig.*); ciężar *m* (*tech., fig.*); ***gain ~, put on ~*** przybierać ⟨-brać⟩ na wadze; ***lose ~*** ⟨s⟩tracić na wadze; **2.** obciążać ⟨-żyć⟩; '~**·less** nieważki; '~**·less·ness** nieważkość; '~ **lift·er** (*w sporcie*) ciężarowiec *m*; '~ **lift·ing** (*w sporcie*) podnoszenie *n* ciężarów; '~**·y** (***-ier, -iest***) ciężki; *fig.* doniosły, ważki
weir [wɪə] jaz *m*
weird [wɪəd] niesamowity; F nie z tej ziemi
wel·come ['welkəm] **1.** *int.* ***~ back!, ~ home!*** witaj w domu!; ***~ to England!*** witamy w Anglii!; **2.** *v/t.* ⟨po⟩witać; ⟨za⟩akceptować; **3.** *adj.* mile widziany; ***you are ~ to do it*** oczywiście możesz to zrobić; ***you're ~!*** *Am.* nie ma za co!; **4.** powitanie *n*; ***outstay*** *lub* ***overstay one's ~*** zbyt długo u kogoś gościć
weld *tech.* [weld] ⟨ze⟩spawać
wel·fare ['welfeə] dobro *n*, interes *m*; *Am.* opieka *f* społeczna; ***be on ~*** być na zasiłku z opieki społecznej; ~ '**state** państwo *n* opiekuńcze; ~ '**work** praca *f* w opiece społecznej; ~ '**work·er** pracownik *m* (-nica *f*) opieki społecznej
well[1] [wel] **1.** *adv.* (***better, best***) dobrze; ***as ~*** również, też; ***... as ~ as ...*** tak ... jak ..., zarówno ... jak i ...; ***very ~*** bardzo dobrze; ***~ done!*** brawo!; → ***off*** 1; **2.** *int.* no; więc; ***~, ~!*** no, no!; **3.** *adj.* zdrowy; ***feel ~*** dobrze się czuć
well[2] [wel] **1.** studnia *f*; szyb *m*; **2.** *też* ***~ out*** tryskać ⟨trysnąć⟩; ***tears ~ed*** (***up***) ***in their eyes*** ich oczy wezbrały łzami
well|-'**bal·anced** zrównoważony; ~'**be·ing** dobre samopoczucie *n*; ~-'**done** dobrze wysmażony; ~-'**earned** należny; ~-'**found·ed** *w pełni* uzasadniony; ~-**in'formed** dobrze poinformowany; ~-'**known** dobrze znany; ~-'**mean·ing** w dobrej wierze; mający dobre intencje; ~-'**meant** w dobrej wierze; ~-'**off 1.** (***better-off, best-off***) zamożny; **2.** ***the ~-off*** *pl.* bogaci *pl.*, zamożni *pl.*; ~-'**read** oczytany; ~-'**timed** w porę (*zrobiony*); ~-**to-'do** F → ***well-odd***; ~-'**worn** zużyty, wytarty
Welsh [welʃ] **1.** walijski; **2.** *ling.* język *m* walijski; ***the ~*** *pl.* Walijczycy *pl.*; ~**man** (***-men***) Walijczyk *m*; ~ '**rab·bit**, ~ '**rare·bit** *gastr. jakby:* grzanka *f* z serem
welt [welt] wypustka *f*, lamówka *f*
wel·ter ['weltə] stos *m*, góra *f*
went [went] *pret. od* ***go*** 1
wept [wept] *pret. i p.p. od* ***weep***

W

were [wɜː, wə] *ty* byłeś *lub* byłaś, *my* byliśmy *lub* byłyśmy, *oni* byli, *one* były, *wy* byliście *lub* byłyście

west [west] **1.** zachód *m*; ***the*** ♀ *pol.* Zachód *m*; *Am.* Zachód *m*; **2.** *adj.* zachodni; **3.** *adv.* na zachód, ku zachodowi; **~·er·ly** ['westəlɪ] zachodni; **~·ern** ['westən] **1.** zachodni; **2.** western *m*; **~·ward(s)** ['westwəd(z)] na zachód, zachodni

wet [wet] **1.** mokry; wilgotny; **2.** wilgoć *f*; **3.** (***-tt-***; ***wet*** *lub* ***wetted***) zwilżać ⟨-żyć⟩; ⟨z⟩moczyć (się)

weth·er ['weðə] *zo.* skop *m*, kastrowany baran *m*

'wet nurse mamka *f*

whack [wæk] *głośne* uderzenie *n*; F udział *m*, dola *f*; ***have a ~ at*** spróbować (*G*); **~ed** F wykończony; **'~·ing 1.** F kobylasty; **2.** lanie *n*

whale [weɪl] *zo.* wieloryb *m*

wharf [wɔːf] (*pl.* ***-wharfs, wharves*** [wɔːvz]) nabrzeże *n*

what [wɒt] **1.** *pron.* co; ***~ about...?*** a co z ...?; ***~ for*** po co?; ***so ~?*** to co?; ***know ~'s ~*** F wiedzieć, co jest co; **2.** *adj.* jaki *m*, jaka *m*, jakie *n*; **~·cha·ma·call·it** F ['wɒtʃəməkɔːlɪt] → ***whatsit***; **~'ev·er 1.** *pron.* cokolwiek; jakikolwiek; cóż; **2.** *adj.* ***no ... ~ever*** w ogóle ...

whats·it ['wɒtsɪt] F wihajster *m*, dings *m*

what·so'ev·er → ***whatever***

wheat [wiːt] *bot.* pszenica *f*; *attr.* pszeniczny, z pszenicy

whee·dle ['wiːdl] skłaniać; ***~ s.o. out of s.th.*** wyłudzać ⟨-dzić⟩ coś od kogoś

wheel [wiːl] **1.** koło *n*; *mot.*, kierownica *f*; *naut.* koło *n* sterowe; **2.** *wózek* pchać; *ptaki*: krążyć; ***~ about,*** (***a***)***round*** odwracać ⟨-rócić⟩ się; **'~·bar·row** taczka *f*; **'~·chair** wózek *m* inwalidzki; **'~ clamp** *mot.* blokada *f* koła; **'~ed** kołowy

wheeze [wiːz] *ktoś*: sapać; *silnik*: rzęzić

whelp [welp] *zo.* szczeniak *m*, młode *n*

when [wen] kiedy; gdy; ***since ~?*** od kiedy?

when'ev·er kiedykolwiek

where [weə] gdzie; dokąd; **~ ... (*from*)?** skąd ...; **~ ... (*to*)?** dokąd?; **~·a·bouts 1.** *adv.* [weərə'baʊts] gdzie; **2.** *sg.*, *pl.* ['weərəbaʊts] miejsce *n* przebywania; **~·as** [weər'æz] podczas gdy; **~·by** [weə'baɪ] dzięki któremu; **~·u·pon** [weərə'pɒn] na co; po czym

wher·ev·er [weər'evə] gdziekolwiek; skądżeż

whet [wet] (***-tt-***) *noże itp.* ⟨na⟩ostrzyć; *apetyt fig.* zaostrzać ⟨-rzyć⟩

wheth·er ['weðə] czy

whey [weɪ] serwatka *f*

which [wɪtʃ] który; *w odniesieniu do poprzedzającego zdania* co; ***~ of you?*** który z was?; **~'ev·er** którykolwiek; jakikolwiek

whiff [wɪf] zapaszek *m* (*też fig.* ***of*** *G*); haust *m* (*powietrza itp.*)

while [waɪl] **1.** chwila *f*; ***for a ~*** na chwilę; **2.** *cj.* podczas, w czasie; **3.** *zw.* ***~ away*** skracać ⟨-rócić⟩ *sobie* czas (***by doing s.th.*** robiąc coś)

whim [wɪm] zachcianka *f*

whim·per ['wɪmpə] **1.** ⟨za⟩jęczeć, ⟨za⟩chlipać; *pies*: ⟨za⟩skomleć; **2.** jęczenie *n*, chlipanie *n*; skomlenie *n*

whim|·si·cal ['wɪmzɪkl] chimeryczny; kapryśny; **~·sy** ['wɪmzɪ] kaprys *m*

whine [waɪn] **1.** *pies*: ⟨za⟩skomleć; ⟨za⟩jęczeć; **2.** skomlenie *n*; jęczenie *n*

whin·ny ['wɪnɪ] **1.** ⟨za⟩rżeć; **2.** rżenie *n*

whip [wɪp] **1.** bicz *m*, pejcz *m*; *gastr.* krem *m*; **2.** (***-pp-***) *v/t.* ⟨wy⟩chłostać, ⟨o⟩bić; *jajka*, *śmietanę* ubijać ⟨-bić⟩; *v/i. wiatr*: zacinać; ***~ s.th. out*** wyciągać ⟨-gnąć⟩ coś (*nagle*); **'~ped cream** bita śmietana *f*; **'~ped eggs** *pl.* piana *f* z białek

whip·ping ['wɪpɪŋ] bicie *n*; chłosta *f*; **'~ boy** chłopiec *m* do bicia; **'~ cream** bita śmietana *f*

whir [wɜː] *zwł. Am.* → ***whirr***

whirl [wɜːl] **1.** ⟨za⟩wirować; kręcić się; ***my head is ~ing*** w głowie mi wiruje; **2.** wirowanie *n* (*też fig.*); kręcenie *n* się; ***my head's in a ~*** w głowie mi wiruje; **'~·pool** wir *m* (*w rzece itp.*); **'~·wind** trąba *f* powietrzna

whirr [wɜː] (***-rr-***) ⟨za⟩warczeć

whisk [wɪsk] **1.** machnięcie *n*; *gastr.* trzepaczka *f* do piany; **2.** *pianę* ubijać ⟨ubić⟩; ***~ one's tail*** *koń*: machnąć ogonem; ***~ away*** *muchy* odganiać ⟨-gonić⟩; szybko *kogoś* zabierać ⟨-brać⟩

whis·kers ['wɪskəz] baczki *pl.*; wąsy (*kota itp.*)

whis·key ['wɪskɪ] (*amerykańska lub irlandzka*) whisky *f*

whis·ky ['wɪskɪ] *zwł. szkocka*: whisky *f*
whis·per ['wɪspə] **1.** ⟨za⟩szeptać; **2.** szept *m*; ***to say s.th. in a ~*** wyszeptać coś
whis·tle ['wɪsl] **1.** gwizdek *m*; gwizd *m*; **2.** ⟨za⟩gwizdać
white [waɪt] **1.** (***-r, -st***) biały; **2.** biel *f*; biały kolor *m*; *człowiek*: biały *m* (-ła *f*); białko *n* (*jajka, oka*); ~ **'bread** biały chleb *m*; ~ **'cof·fee** kawa *f* z mlekiem, kawa *f* mleczna; **~-'col·lar work·er** pracownik *m* biurowy; ~ **'lie** niewinne kłamstwo *n*, kłamstewko *n*; **whit·en** ['waɪtn] ⟨z⟩bieleć; pobielić; **'~·wash** **1.** wapno *n* (*do malowania*); *tech.* mleko *n* wapienne; **2.** ⟨po⟩bielić (*wapnem*)
whit·ish ['waɪtɪʃ] białawy
Whit·sun ['wɪtsn] Zielone Świątki *pl.*; **Whit Sunday** [wɪt 'sʌndɪ] niedziela *f* Zielonych Świątek; **'Whit·sun·tide** okres *m* Zielonych Świątek
whit·tle ['wɪtl] ⟨po⟩rąbać; *też* ***~ away, ~ down*** zmniejszać ⟨-szyć⟩
whiz(z) [wɪz] F **1.** (***-zz-***): ***~ by*** *lub* ***past*** przelatywać ⟨-lecieć⟩ obok (*G*), przemykać ⟨-mknąć⟩ obok (*G*); **2.** wizg *m*; geniusz *m* (***at s.th.*** w czymś); **'~ kid** F mały geniusz *m*
who [huː] kto; który
WHO [dʌbljuː eɪtʃ 'əʊ] *skrót*: ***World Health Organization*** WHO *n*, Światowa Organizacja *f* Zdrowia
who·dun·(n)it [huː'dʌnɪt] F (*książka*) kryminał *m*
who'ev·er ktokolwiek; którykolwiek
whole [həʊl] **1.** *adj.* cały; **2.** całość *f*; ***the ~ of London*** cały Londyn; ***on the ~*** w ogóle; **~-'heart·ed** stuprocentowy, zupełny; **~-'heart·ed·ly** stuprocentowo, całkowicie; **'~·meal** pełne ziarno *n*; ***~meal bread*** chleb *m* z pełnego ziarna
'whole·sale *econ.* **1.** handel *m* hurtowy; **2.** hurtowy; **'~ mar·ket** *econ.* rynek *m* hurtowy; **'whole·sal·er** *econ.* hurtownik *m*
'whole|·some zdrowy; **'~ wheat** → ***wholemeal***
whol·ly ['həʊllɪ] *adv.* całkowicie, zupełnie
whom [huːm] *formy zależne od* **who**
whoop [huːp] **1.** wrzeszczeć ⟨wrzasnąć⟩ (*z radości*); ***~ it up*** F cieszyć się; **2.** okrzyk *m*
whoop·ing cough ['huːpɪŋkɒf] *med.* koklusz *m*
whore [hɔː] kurwa *f*
whose [huːz] *G od* **who**
why [waɪ] dlaczego; ***that's ~*** dlatego
wick [wɪk] knot *m*
wick·ed ['wɪkɪd] nikczemny; haniebny
wick·er ['wɪkə] wiklinowy; **'~ bas·ket** kosz *m* wiklinowy; **'~·work** wyroby *pl.* wiklinowe
wick·et ['wɪkɪt] (*w grze w krykieta*) bramka *f*
wide [waɪd] **1.** *adj.* szeroki; *oczy*: szeroko otwarty; *fig. zainteresowania*: rozległy; **2.** *adv.* szeroko; ***go ~ (of the goal)*** (*w sporcie*) przechodzić ⟨przejść⟩ (z daleka od celu); **~-a'wake** rozbudzony (*też fig.*); **~-'eyed** o wielkich *lub* szeroko otwartych oczach; *fig.* naiwny
wid·en ['waɪdn] poszerzać ⟨-szyć⟩, rozszerzać ⟨-rzyć⟩
wide|-'o·pen *oczy*: szeroko otwarty; **'~·spread** rozpowszechniony, powszechny
wid·ow ['wɪdəʊ] wdowa *f*; **'~ed** owdowiały; **'~·er** wdowiec *m*
width [wɪdθ] szerokość *f*
wield [wiːld] *władzę* dzierżyć; *głosy, wpływy* posiadać; władać (*mieczem*)
wife [waɪf] (*pl.* ***wives*** [waɪvz]) żona *f*
wig [wɪg] peruka *f*
wild [waɪld] **1.** *adj.* dziki; *aplauz, pogoda*: burzliwy; oszalały (**with** z *gniewu*); *pomysł*: szalony; ***make a ~ guess*** zgadywać w ciemno; ***be ~ about*** przepadać za (*I*); **2.** *adv.* ***go ~*** oszaleć; wściec się; ***let one's children run ~*** pozwolić dzieciom robić, co chcą; **3.** ***in the ~*** na wolności; ***the ~s*** *pl.* pustkowie *n*; **'~·cat** *zo.* żbik *m*; **~·cat 'strike** dziki strajk *m*
wil·der·ness ['wɪldənɪs] pustkowie *n*
'wild|·fire: ***spread like a ~fire*** rozchodzić się błyskawicznie; **'~·life** przyroda *f* w stanie naturalnym
wil·ful ['wɪlfl] krnąbrny, uparty, samowolny; *zwł. jur.* rozmyślny, z premedytacją
will[1] [wɪl] *v/aux.* (*pret.* ***would***; *przeczenie* ***~ not, won't***): ***~ be*** *ja* będę, *ty* będziesz, *on, ona, ono* będzie, *my* będziemy, *wy* będziecie, *oni* będą
will[2] [wɪl] wola *f*; testament *m*; ***of one's own free ~*** z własnej nieprzymuszonej woli

W

will³ [wɪl] ⟨ze⟩chcieć; *jur.* pozostawiać ⟨-wić⟩ w testamencie
'will·ful → ***wilful***
'will·ing chętny (***to do s.th.*** do zrobienia czegoś); chcący
will-o'-the-wisp [wɪləðə'wɪsp] błędny ognik *m*
wil·low ['wɪləʊ] *bot.* wierzba *f*; **'~·y** *fig.* wysmukły
'will·pow·er siła *f* woli
wil·ly-nil·ly [wɪlɪ'nɪlɪ] chcąc niechcąc
wilt [wɪlt] usychać ⟨-schnąć⟩, ⟨z⟩więdnąć
wi·ly ['waɪlɪ] (***-ier, -iest***) zmyślny, przebiegły
win [wɪn] **1.** (***-nn-***; ***won***) *v/t.* zwyciężać ⟨-żyć⟩, wygrywać ⟨-rać⟩; ***~ s.o. over*** *lub* ***round to*** zdobywać ⟨-być⟩ czyjeś poparcie co do (*G*); ***OK, you ~*** dobra, wygrałeś; **2.** (*zwł. w sporcie*) wygrana *f*, zwycięstwo *n*
wince [wɪns] ⟨s⟩krzywić się
winch [wɪntʃ] *tech.* wyciąg *m*, wciągarka *f*
wind¹ [wɪnd] **1.** wiatr *m*; dech *m*; *med.* wzdęcie, wiatry *pl.*; ***the ~s*** *sg. lub pl. mus.* instrumenty *pl.* dęte; **2.** pozbawiać ⟨-wić⟩ tchu
wind² [waɪnd] **1.** (***wound***) *v/t. zegarek itp.* nakręcać ⟨-cić⟩; nawijać ⟨-winąć⟩, zwijać ⟨zwinąć⟩; owijać ⟨owinąć⟩ (***round*** wokół *G*); *v/i. ścieżka itp.*: wić się; ***~ back*** *film itp.* przewijać ⟨-winąć⟩ do tyłu; ***~ down*** *okno w samochodzie* otwierać ⟨-worzyć⟩; *produkcję* zwijać ⟨zwinąć⟩; ***~ forward*** *film itp.* przewijać ⟨-winąć⟩ do przodu; ***~ up*** *v/t. okno w samochodzie* zamykać ⟨-knąć⟩; *zegarek itp.* nakręcać ⟨-cić⟩; *zebranie* ⟨za⟩kończyć (*też* ***with*** *I*); *firmę* zamykać ⟨-knąć⟩; *v/i.* F ⟨za⟩kończyć (***by saying*** mówiąc); **2.** obrót *m*
'wind|·bag F gaduła *m/f*; **'~·fall** (*owoc*) spad *m*; szczęśliwa gratka *f*
wind·ing ['waɪndɪŋ] kręty, wijący się; **'~ stairs** *pl.* schody *pl.* kręte
wind in·stru·ment ['wɪnd ɪnstrʊmənt] *mus.* instrument *m* dęty
wind·lass ['wɪndləs] *tech.* kołowrót *m*
wind·mill ['wɪnmɪl] wiatrak *m*
win·dow ['wɪndəʊ] okno *n*; okno *n* wystawowe; okienko *n* (*w instytucji itp.*); **'~ clean·er** osoba *f* myjąca okna; **'~ dres·ser** dekorator *m* wystaw; **'~ dress·ing** dekoracja *f* wystawy; F mamienie *n* oczu; **'~·pane** szyba *f*; **'~ seat** siedzenie *n* przy oknie; **'~ shade** *Am.* roleta *f*; **'~-shop** (***-pp-***): ***go ~-shopping*** iść ⟨pójść⟩ pooglądać wystawy sklepowe; **'~·sill** parapet *m*
wind|·pipe ['wɪndpaɪp] *anat.* tchawica *f*; **'~·screen** *Brt. mot.* szyba *f* przednia; **'~·screen wip·er** *mot.* wycieraczka *f*; **'~·shield** *Am.* → ***windscreen***; **'~·shield wip·er** → ***windscreen wiper***; **'~·surf·ing** windsurfing *m*
wind·y ['wɪndɪ] (***-ier, -iest***) wietrzny; *med.* wywołujący wzdęcia, cierpiący na wzdęcia
wine [waɪn] wino *n*
wing [wɪŋ] skrzydło *n*; *Brt. mot.* błotnik *m*; *theat.* ***~s*** *pl.* kulisy *pl.* (*też fig.*); **'~·er** (*w sporcie*) skrzydłowy *m* (-wa *f*)
wink [wɪŋk] **1.** mrugać ⟨-gnąć⟩ (***at*** do *G*); ***~ one's lights*** *Brt. mot.* ⟨za⟩mrugać światłami; **2.** mrugnięcie *n*; ***I didn't get a ~ of sleep last night*** zeszłej nocy nawet nie zmrużyłem oka
win|·ner ['wɪnə] zwycięzca *m* (-zczyni *f*); **'~·ning 1.** zwycięski; **2.** ***~nings*** *pl.* wygrana *f*
win·ter ['wɪntə] **1.** zima *f*; ***in*** (***the***) ***~*** w zimie, zimą; **2.** ⟨prze⟩zimować; **~ 'sports** *pl.* sporty *pl.* zimowe; **'~·time** zima *f*, okres *m* zimowy; ***in*** (***the***) ***~time*** w zimie, zimą
win·try ['wɪntrɪ] zimowy; *fig.* lodowaty
wipe [waɪp] wycierać ⟨wytrzeć⟩, ***~ off*** ścierać ⟨zetrzeć⟩; ***~ out*** wymazywać ⟨-zać⟩ z powierzchni ziemi; ***~ up*** wycierać ⟨wytrzeć⟩, **'wip·er** *mot.* wycieraczka *f* (*do szyby*)
wire ['waɪə] **1.** drut *m*; *electr.* przewód *m*; *Am.* telegram *m*; **2.** podłączać ⟨-czyć⟩ (*też* ***~ up***); *Am.* ⟨za⟩telegrafować do (*G*); przesyłać ⟨-słać⟩ telegraficznie; **'~·less** bezprzewodowy; **~ net·ting** [waɪə 'netɪŋ] siatka *f* metalowa; **'~-tap** (***-pp-***) *rozmowy telefoniczne* podsłuchiwać ⟨-chać⟩
wir·y ['waɪərɪ] (***-ier, -iest***) *postać*: żylasty
wis·dom ['wɪzdəm] mądrość *f*; **'~ tooth** (*pl.* ***teeth***) ząb *m* mądrości
wise¹ [waɪz] (***-r, -st***) mądry
wise² [waɪz] *przest.* sposób *m*
'wise|·crack F **1.** wic *m*, dowcipna uwaga *f*; **2.** dowcipkować; **'~guy** F mądrala *m*

wish [wɪʃ] **1.** życzyć (sobie), chcieć; *~ **s.o. well*** życzyć komuś wszystkiego dobrego; ***if you ~ (to)*** jeżeli sobie tak życzysz; *~ **for s.th.*** pragnąć czegoś; **2.** życzenie *n*, pragnienie *n*; **(*with*) *best ~es*** (*zakończenie listu*) serdeczne pozdrowienia; **~·ful 'think·ing** pobożne życzenia *pl.*
wish·y-wash·y ['wɪʃɪwɒʃɪ] *zupa itp.*: rozwodniony; *osoba, poglądy*: bezbarwny
wisp [wɪsp] kosmyk *m* (*włosów itp.*)
wist·ful ['wɪstfl] nostalgiczny
wit [wɪt] dowcip *m*; inteligencja *f*; kpiarz *m*; *też* **~s** *pl.* rozsądek *m*; ***be at one's ~s' end*** nie wiedzieć, co ⟨z⟩robić; ***keep one's ~s about one*** zachowywać ⟨-ować⟩ rozsądek
witch [wɪtʃ] czarownica *f*; **'~·craft** czary *pl.*; **'~-hunt** *pol.* polowanie *n* na czarownice
with [wɪð] z (*I*); u (*G*) (***stay***); z (*G*)
with·draw [wɪð'drɔː] (***-drew***, ***-drawn***) *v/t.* cofać ⟨-fnąć⟩; *pieniądze* podejmować ⟨-djąć⟩ (***from*** z *G*); *mil. oddziały* wycofywać ⟨-fać⟩; *v/i.* cofać ⟨-fnąć⟩ się; wycofywać ⟨-fać⟩ się (***from*** z *G*)
with·draw·al [wɪð'drɔːəl] wycofanie *n* (się) (*też mil.*); cofanie *n* (się); odwołanie *n*; *mil.* odwrót *m*; *med.* wycofanie *n* (leku); ***make a ~*** wycofać się (***from*** z *G*); **~ cure** *med.* leczenie *n* objawów abstynencji; **~ symp·toms** *pl. med.* (*przykre objawy towarzyszące kuracji odwywkowej*)
with·er ['wɪðə] usychać ⟨uschnąć⟩, ⟨z⟩więdnąć
with'hold (***-held***) wstrzymywać ⟨-mać⟩; ***~ s.th. from s.o.*** powstrzymywać ⟨-mać⟩ kogoś przed zrobieniem czegoś
with|·in [wɪ'ðɪn] wewnątrz (*G*), w środku (*G*); w zakresie (*G*); w przedziale (*G*); w ciągu (*G*); **~·out** [wɪ'ðaʊt] bez (*G*)
with'stand (***-stood***) wytrzymywać ⟨-mać⟩; powstrzymywać ⟨-mać⟩
wit·ness ['wɪtnɪs] **1.** świadek *m*; ***~ for the defence*** (*Am.* ***defense***) *jur.* świadek *m* obrony; ***~ for the prosecution*** *jur.* świadek *m* oskarżenia; **2.** być świadkiem (*G*); świadczyć o (*L*); **'~ box** *Brt.*, **'~ stand** *Am.* miejsce *n* dla świadka (*do składania zeznań w sądzie*)

wit|·ti·cis·m ['wɪtɪsɪzəm] żart *m*, dowcipne powiedzenie *n*; **~·ty** ['wɪtɪ] (***-ier, -iest***) dowcipny
wives [waɪvz] *pl. od* **wife**
wiz·ard ['wɪzəd] czarodziej *m*, czarnoksiężnik *m*; *fig.* geniusz *m* (***at*** w *L*)
wiz·ened ['wɪznd] pomarszczony
wob·ble ['wɒbl] *v/i. stół*: chwiać się; *głos*: drgać ⟨drżeć⟩; *galareta*: ⟨za⟩trząść się; *mot. koła*: bić; *v/t.* chwiać; trząść
woe [wəʊ] żal *m*, żałość *f*; **'~·ful** żałosny
woke [wəʊk] *pret. od* **wake**¹; **wok·en** ['wəʊkən] *p.p. od* **wake**¹
wold [wəʊld] pogórze *n*
wolf [wʊlf] **1.** *zo.* wilk *m*; ***lone ~*** *fig.* samotnik *m*; **2.** *też* ***~ down*** F *fig.* pochłaniać ⟨-chłonąć⟩
wolves [wʊlvz] *pl. od* **wolf** 1
wom·an ['wʊmən] (*pl.* ***women*** ['wɪmɪn]) kobieta *f*; **~ 'doc·tor** lekarka *f*; **~ 'driv·er** kobieta *f* kierowca; **~·ish** kobiecy; zniewieściały; **'~·ly** kobiecy
womb [wuːm] *anat.*macica *f*; *fig.* łono *n*
wom·en ['wɪmɪn] *pl. od* ***woman***
women's| lib [wɪmɪnz 'lɪb] F ruch *m* feministyczny; **~ 'lib·ber** F feministka *f*; **'~ move·ment** ruch *m* feministyczny; **'~ ref·uge** *Brt.*, **'~ shel·ter** *Am.* dom *m* kobiet
won [wʌn] *pret. i p.p. od* **win** 1
won·der ['wʌndə] **1.** dziwić się; zastanawiać się (***about*** nad *I*, ***if, whether*** czy); ***I ~ if you could help me*** czy mógłbyś mi może pomóc?; **2.** podziw *m*, zadziwienie *n*; cud *m*; ***do*** *lub* ***work ~s*** czynić cuda; ***no ~ that*** nic dziwnego, że; ***it's a ~ that*** to zadziwiające, że; **'~·ful** cudowny
wont [wəʊnt] **1.** ***s.o. is ~ to do s.th.*** ktoś zwykł coś robić; **2.** ***as was his ~*** jak to było w jego zwyczaju
won't [wəʊnt] *zamiast* ***will not*** → ***will***¹
woo [wuː] zalecać się do (*G*); starać się o (*A*) (*też fig.*); ubiegać się o (*A*)
wood [wʊd] drewno *n*; *też* **~s** *pl.* las(y *pl.*) *m*; ***touch ~*** odpukaj w niemalowane!; ***he can't see the ~ for the trees*** im dalej w las, tym więcej drzew; **'~·cut** drzeworyt *m*; **'~·cut·ter** drzeworytnik *m*; **'~·ed** zalesiony; **'~·en** drewniany (*też fig.*), z drewna; **~·peck·er** *zo.* ['wʊdpekə] dzięcioł *m*; **~·wind** *mus.* ['wʊdwɪnd] **1.** ***the ~*** *sg. lub pl.* instrumenty *m* dęte drewniane; **2.** *adj.* dęty

W

drewniany; '~•**work** stolarka *f*; '~•**y** (**-ier, -iest**) lesisty
wool [wʊl] wełna *f*; ~•(**l**)**en** ['wʊlən] **1.** wełniany; **2.** ~(**l**)**ens** *pl.* odzież *f* wełniana; '~•(**l**)**y** **1.** (**-ier, -iest**) wełniany; *fig.* mętny; **2.** **wool**(**l**)**ies** *pl.* F odzież *f* wełniana
Worces•ter sauce [wʊstə 'sɔːs] sos *m* Worcester
word [wɜːd] **1.** wyraz *m*, słowo *n*; wieść *f*; *też* ~**s** *pl.* słówko *n*, rozmowa *f*; ~**s** *pl.* słowa *f* (*piosenki itp.*); **have a** ~ *lub* **a few** ~**s with** odbyć z kimś rozmowę; **2.** wyrażać ⟨-razić⟩, ⟨s⟩formułować; '~•**ing** sformułowanie *n*; '~ **or•der** *gr.* szyk *m* wyrazów; '~ **pro•cess•ing** *komp.* przetwarzanie *n* tekstów; '~ **pro•ces•sor** *komp.* procesor *m* tekstów, edytor *m*
'**word•y** (**-ier, -iest**) przegadany, wielosłowny
wore [wɔː] *pret. od* **wear** 1
work [wɜːk] **1.** praca *f*; dzieło *n*; ~**s** *pl.* *tech.* zakład *m*, fabryka *f*; **at** ~ przy pracy; **be in** ~ mieć pracę; **be out of** ~ nie mieć pracy; **set to** ~ wziąć się do pracy; **2.** *v/i.* pracować (**at, on** nad *I*); działać, funkcjonować; ~ **to rule** pracować (wyłącznie) zgodnie z przepisami; *v/t.* obciążać ⟨-żyć⟩ pracą; *maszynę itp.* obsługiwać ⟨-łużyć⟩; *materiał itp.* obrabiać; *kopalnię itp.* eksploatować; *cuda itp.* sprawiać ⟨-wić⟩; przepracować, zapracować; sprawiać ⟨-wić⟩, ⟨s⟩powodować; ~ **one's way** ⟨u⟩torować sobie drogę; ~ **off** *długi* odpracowywać ⟨-ować⟩; *gniew* odreagowywać⟨-ować⟩; ~ **out** *v/t.* wypracowywać ⟨-ować⟩; *plan itp.* opracowywać ⟨-ować⟩; *wynik* znajdować ⟨znaleźć⟩; stwierdzać ⟨-dzić⟩; *problem* rozwiązywać ⟨-ować⟩; *v/i.* układać ⟨ułożyć⟩ się; *liczenie*: wychodzić ⟨wyjść⟩; F (*w sporcie*) trenować; ~ **up** *słuchaczy itp.* pobudzać ⟨-dzić⟩; wprawiać ⟨-wić⟩ się (**into** w *A*); opracowywać ⟨-ować⟩; **be** ~**ed up** być podekscytowanym (**about** w sprawie *G*)
work|•a•ble ['wɜːkəbl] plastyczny; *fig.* wykonalny; ~•**a•day** ['wɜːkədeɪ] powszedni; ~•**a•hol•ic** [wɜːkə'hɒlɪk] pracoholik *m* (-liczka *f*); '~•**bench** *tech.* stół *m* warsztatowy; '~•**book** zeszyt *m* do ćwiczeń; '~•**day** dzień *m* roboczy; **on** ~**days** w dnie robocze; '~•**er** robotnik *m* (-nica *f*), pracownik *m* (-nica *f*); '~ **ex•pe•ri•ence** uprzednie doświadczenie *n*
'**work•ing** roboczy; praktyczny; pracujący; ~ **knowledge** znajomość *f* praktyczna; **in** ~ **order** działający; ~ '**class**- (**•es** *pl.*) klasa *f* pracująca; ~ '**day** → **workday**; ~ '**hours** *pl.* godziny *pl.* pracy; **reduced** ~ **hours** *pl.* skrócony dzień *m* pracy; '~**s** *pl.* działanie *n*
'**work•man** (*pl.* **-men**) robotnik *m*; '~•**like**; '~•**ship** fachowość *f*
work| of 'art (*pl.* **works of art**) dzieło *n* sztuki; '~•**out** F (*w sporcie*) trening *m*; '~•**place** miejsce *n* pracy, stanowisko *n* robocze; '~**s coun•cil** *zwł. Brt.* rada *f* pracownicza *lub* zakładowa; '~•**sheet** arkusz *m* roboczy; '~•**shop** warsztat *m*; '~•**shy** stroniący od pracy; '~•**sta•tion** *komp.* stacja *f* robocza; ~-**to-'rule** *Brt.* praca *f* (*wyłącznie*) zgodnie z przepisamu
world [wɜːld] **1.** świat *m*; **all over the** ~ na całym świecie; **bring into the** ~ wydawać ⟨-dać⟩ na świat; **do s.o. a** *lub* **the** ~ **of good** bardzo dobrze komuś zrobić; **mean all the** ~ **to s.o.** wszystko znaczyć dla kogoś; **they are** ~**s apart** są diametralnie różni; **think the** ~ **of s.o.** mieć o kimś dobre mniemanie; **what in the** ~**...?** co u licha ...?; **2.** światowy; ♀ '**Cup** Puchar *m* Świata
'**world•ly** (**-ier, -iest**) światowy, bywały; doczesny, ziemski; ~-'**wise** światowo
world| 'pow•er *pol.* mocarstwo *n* światowe; ~•'**wide** ogólnoświatowy
worm [wɜːm] **1.** *zo.* robak *m*; **2.** *psa itp.* odrobaczać ⟨-czyć⟩; ~ **one's way through** przeciskać ⟨-cisnąć⟩ się przez (*G*); ~ **o.s. into s.o.'s confidence** wkradać ⟨-raść⟩ się w czyjeś zaufanie; ~ **s.th. out of s.o.** wyciągać ⟨-ciągnąć⟩ coś z czegoś; '~-**eat•en** zżarty prze korniki; ~'**s-eye 'view** perspektywa *f* żabia
worn [wɔːn] *p.p.* *od* **wear** 1; ~-'**out** zużyty; wyczerpany
wor•ried ['wʌrɪd] zmartwiony
wor•ry ['wʌrɪ] **1.** *v/t.* ⟨z⟩martwić; ⟨za⟩niepokoić; *v/i.* ⟨z⟩martwić się, ⟨za⟩niepokoić się; **don't** ~**!** nie przejmuj się!; **2.** zmartwienie *n*, niepokój *m*
worse [wɜːs] (*comp. od* **bad**) gorszy; ~ **still** co gorsze; **to make matters** ~ na domiar złego; **wors•en** ['wɜːsn] po-

garszać ⟨-gorszyć⟩ (się)

wor·ship ['wɜːʃɪp] **1.** cześć *f* (*religijna*); nabożeństwo *n*; **2.** (*zwł. Brt.* **-pp-**, *Am.* **-p-**) *v/t.* czcić; *v/i.* oddawać ⟨-dać⟩ cześć; uczęszczać na nabożeństwa; '**~·(p)er** czciciel(ka *f*) *m*, wyznawca (-wczyni *f*) *m*

worst [wɜːst] **1.** *adj.* (*sup. od* ***bad***) najgorszy; **2.** *adv.* (*sup. od* ***badly***) najgorzej; **3.** najgorsze *n*; ***at*** (***the***) **~** w najgorszym razie

wor·sted ['wʊstɪd] wełna *f* czesankowa

worth [wɜːθ] **1.** warty; **~ *reading*** wart przeczytania; **2.** wartość *f*; ***20 pounds' ~ of groceries*** artykuły spożywcze o wartości 20 funtów; '**~·less** bezwartościowy; **~'while** opłacający się, wart zachodu; ***be ~while*** opłacać się; **~·y** ['wɜːðɪ] (***-ier, -iest***) godny, godzien; szanowany

would [wʊd] *pret. od* ***will***[1]; ***would you like ...?*** czy chciał(a)byś ...?; '**~-be** niedoszły

wound[1] [waʊnd] *pret. i p.p. od* ***wind***[2]

wound[2] [wuːnd] **1.** rana *f*; **2.** ⟨z⟩ranić

wove [wəʊv] *pret. od* ***weave***; **wov·en** ['wəʊvən] *p.p. od* ***weave***

wow [waʊ] *int.* F no, no!

WP [dʌbljuː 'piː] *skrót*: ***word processing*** *komp.* przetwarzanie *n* tekstów; ***word processor*** *komp.* procesor *m* tekstów, edytor *m*

wran·gle ['ræŋgl] **1.** kłócić się; **2.** kłótnia *f*

wrap [ræp] **1.** (**-pp-**) *v/t. też* **~ *up*** ⟨za⟩pakować, opakowywać ⟨-ować⟩ (***in*** w *A*); owijać ⟨owinąć⟩ ([***a***]***round*** wokół *G*); *v/i.* **~ *up*** ubierać ⟨-brać⟩ się ciepło; **2.** *zwł. Am.* szal *m*; '**~·per** obwoluta *f*; '**~·ping** opakowanie *n*; '**~·ping paper** papier *m* pakowy

wrath [rɒθ] *lit.* gniew *m*

wreath [riːθ] (*pl.* ***wreaths*** [riːðz]) wieniec *m*

wreck [rek] **1.** *naut.* wrak *m* (*też człowieka*); **2.** *plany* unicestwiać ⟨-wić⟩; ***be ~ed*** *naut.* rozbić się; **~·age** ['rekɪdʒ] szczątki *pl.*; '**~·er** *Am. mot.* samochód *m* pomocy drogowej; '**~·ing com·pa·ny** *Am.* (*firma*) pomoc *f* drogowa; '**~·ing ser·vice** *Am. mot.* pomoc *f* drogowa

wren *zo.* [ren] strzyżyk *m*

wrench [rentʃ] **1.** *med. ramię itp.* skręcić; **~ *s.th. from*** *lub* ***out of s.o.'s hands*** wyrwać *lub* wyszarpnąć coś komuś z rąk; **~ *off*** coś oderwać; **~ *open*** szarpnięciem *coś* otworzyć; **2.** szarpnięcie *n*; *med.* skręcenie *n*; *Brt. tech.* klucz *m* nastawny *lub* francuski; *Am. tech. nienastawny* klucz *m*

wrest [rest]: **~ *s.th. from*** *lub* ***out of s.o.'s hands*** wyszarpnąć coś komuś

wres|·tle ['resl] *v/t.* mocować się (***with*** z *I*); *fig.* zmagać się (***with*** z *I*); *v/t.* (*w sporcie*) uprawiać zapasy; '**~·tler** (*w sporcie*) zapaśnik *m* (-niczka *f*); '**~·tling** (*w sporcie*) zapasy *pl.*

wretch [retʃ] *często humor.* szelma *m/f*; *też* ***poor ~*** biedak *m* (-aczka *f*), nieborak *m* (-aczka *f*); '**~·ed** [retʃɪd] *pogoda, ból*: paskudny; przeklęty

wrig·gle ['rɪgl] *v/i.* wiercić się; **~ *out of*** *fig.* F wywinąć się z (*G*); *v/t.* ⟨po⟩machać (*I*)

wring [rɪŋ] (***wrung***) ukręcać ⟨-cić⟩; *rękę* ściskać ⟨-snąć⟩; **~ *hands*** załamywać ręce (*ze smutku*); **~ *out*** *pranie* wykręcać ⟨-cić⟩, wyżymać ⟨-żąć⟩; **~ *s.o.'s heart*** złamać komuś serce

wrin·kle ['rɪŋkl] **1.** zmarszczka *f*; **2.** *v/i.* pomarszczyć się; *v/t. nos* zmarszczyć

wrist [rɪst] nadgarstek *m*, przegub *m*; '**~·band** pasek *m*, bransoleta *f* (*do zegarka itp.*); mankiet *m* (*koszuli*); '**~·watch** zegarek *m* (*naręczny*)

writ [rɪt] *jur.* pismo *n* urzędowe; nakaz *m*

write [raɪt] **1.** (***wrote, written***) ⟨na⟩pisać; **~ *down*** zapisywać ⟨-sać⟩; **~ *off*** *econ.* odpisywać ⟨-sać⟩; **~ *out*** *nazwiska itp.* wypisywać ⟨-sać⟩; *rachunek itp.* wystawiać ⟨-wić⟩; '**~ pro·tec·tion** *komp.* zabezpieczenie *n* przed zapisaniem; '**writ·er** pisarz *m* (-rka *f*); autor(ka *f*) *m*

writhe [raɪð] wić się

writ·ing ['raɪtɪŋ] pisanie *n*; pismo *n*; *attr.* pisemny, piśmienny; ***in ~*** na piśmie; **~*s*** *pl.* dzieła *pl.*; '**~ case** teczka *f*; '**~ desk** biurko *m*; '**~ pad** notes *m*, blok *m* papieru; '**~ pa·per** papier *m* listowy

writ·ten ['rɪtn] **1.** *p.p. od* ***write***; **2.** *adj.* napisany

wrong [rɒŋ] **1.** *adj.* zły; nieprawidłowy; ***be ~*** nie mieć racji; *zegar*: źle chodzić; ***be on the ~ side of forty*** przekroczyć czterdziestkę; ***is anything ~?*** czy coś nie w porządku?; ***what's ~ with her?*** co się z nią dzieje?; **2.** *adv.* źle; nieprawidłowo; ***get ~*** źle zrozumieć; ***go ~*** popełnić błąd; iść źle; zepsuć się; **3.** zło *n*; ***be in the ~*** nie mieć racji; **4.** ⟨s⟩krzywdzić; **~'do•er** sprawca *m* (-czyni *f*) szkody; **~'do•ing** przestępstwo *n*; bezprawie *n*; **'~•ful** zły; krzywdzący; bezprawny

wrote [rəʊt] *pret. od **write***

wrought| **'i•ron** kute żelazo *n*; **~-'i•ron** z kutego żelaza

wrung [rʌŋ] *pret. i p.p. od **wring***

wry [raɪ] (***-ier, -iest***) *uśmiech, humor*: cierpki

wt *skrót pisany*: ***weight*** waga *f*

WTO [dʌblju: ti: 'əʊ] *skrót*: ***World Trade Organization*** WTO *n/f*, Światowa Organizacja *f* Handlu

WWF [dʌblju: dʌblju: 'ef] *skrót*: ***World Wide Fund for Nature*** (*towarzystwo ochrony przyrody*)

wwoofer ['wu:fə]

WYSIWYG ['wɪzɪwɪg] *skrót*: ***what you see is what you get*** WYSIWYG *m*, to się ma, co się widzi (*identyczność graficznej reprezentacji tekstu na ekranie i wydruku*)

X

X, x [eks] X, x *n*

xen•o•pho•bi•a [zenə'fəʊbjə] ksenofobia *f*

XL [eks 'el] *skrót*: ***extra large*** (***size***) bardzo duży (rozmiar)

X•mas ['krɪsməs, 'eksməs] → ***Christmas***

X-ray ['eksreɪ] **1.** prześwietlać ⟨-lić⟩ (*aparatem rentgenowskim*); **2.** promień *m* rentgenowski; zdjęcie *n* rentgenowskie; badanie *n* rentgenowskie

xy•lo•phone ['zaɪləfəʊn] *mus.* ksylofon *m*

Y

Y, y [waɪ] Y, y *n*

yacht [jɒt] **1.** (*w sporcie*) jacht *m*; **2.** ⟨po⟩żeglować; ***go ~ing*** iść na żagle; **'~ club** klub *m* jachtowy; **'~•ing** żeglarstwo *n*

Yan•kee ['jæŋkɪ] F **1.** Jankes *m*; **2.** jankeski

yap [jæp] (***-pp-***) ujadać

yard[1] [jɑ:d] (*skrót*: ***yd***) jard *m* (*=91,44 cm*)

yard[2] [jɑ:d] podwórko *n*; plac *m* (*budowy itp.*); *Am.* ogród *m*

'yard•stick *fig.* miara *f*

yarn [jɑ:n] przędza *f*; ***spin s.o. a ~ about*** komuś sprzedawać dzikie opowieści o (*I*)

yawn [jɔ:n] **1.** ziewać ⟨-wnąć⟩; **2.** ziewnięcie *n*

yd *skrót pisany*: ***yard***(***s***) jard(y *pl.*) *m*

yeah [jeə] F tak

year [jɪə, jɜ:] rok *m*; ***all the ~ round*** (*przez*) okrągły rok; ***~ after ~*** rok po roku; ***~ in, ~ out*** z roku na rok; ***this ~*** tego roku, w tym roku; ***this ~'s*** tegoroczny; **'~•ly** coroczny, doroczny

yearn [jɜ:n] tęsknić (***for*** za *I*), ***to do*** do tego, by *coś* zrobić; **'~•ing** tęsknota *f*

yeast [ji:st] drożdże *pl.*

yell [jel] **1.** wrzeszczeć (***with*** od *G*, ***~ at*** na *A*); ***~*** (***out***) wykrzykiwać ⟨-knąć⟩; **2.** wrzask *m*

yel•low ['jeləʊ] **1.** żółty; F tchórzliwy; **2.** żółć *f*; ***at ~*** *Am. mot.* na żółtym świetle; **3.** ⟨z⟩żółknąć; **~ 'fe•ver** *med.* żółta febra *f*; **'~•ish** żółtawy; **~ 'Pag•es** *pl. TM tel.* (*spis instytucji*) żółte strony *pl.*; **~ 'press** prasa *f* brukowa

yelp [jelp] **1.** *pies*: skowyczeć ⟨zaskowytać⟩; ⟨wy⟩krzyknąć; **2.** skowyt *m*; krzyk *m*

yes [jes] tak

yes•ter•day ['jestədɪ] wczoraj; ***~ afternoon/morning*** wczoraj wieczorem/rano; ***the day before ~*** przedwczoraj

yet [jet] **1.** *adv.* jeszcze; już; ***as ~*** jak dotąd; ***not ~*** jeszcze nie; **2.** *cj.* ale, mimo to

yew [juː] *bot.* cis *m*
yield [jiːld] **1.** *v/t. owoce, zysk* dawać ⟨dać⟩; *korzyści* przynosić ⟨-nieść⟩; *v/i.* ustępować ⟨-tąpić⟩; ⟨z⟩rezygnować; *~ to Am. mot.* ustępować ⟨-tąpić⟩ pierwszeństwa przejazdu; **2.** wydajność *f*; plon *m*; dochód *m*
yip·pee [jɪ'piː] *int.* F hurra!
YMCA [waɪ em siː 'eɪ] *skrót*: ***Young Men's Christian Association*** YMCA *f*, Chrześcijańskie Stowarzyszenie *n* Młodzieży Męskiej
yo·del ['jəʊdl] **1.** (*zwł. Brt.* **-ll-**, *Am.* **-l-**) ⟨za⟩jodlować; **2.** jodlowanie *n*
yo·ga ['jəʊgə] joga *f*
yog·h(o)urt, yog·urt ['jɒgət] jogurt *m*
yoke [jəʊk] jarzmo *n* (*też fig.*)
yolk [jəʊk] żółtko *n*
you [juː, jʊ] ty; wy; pan(i); państwo; (*G*) ciebie, was *pl.*; (*D*) tobie, ci, wam *pl.*; (*A*) ciebie, cię, was *pl.*; (*I*) tobą, wami *pl.*; (*L*) tobie, was *pl.*; ***~ cannot buy it in Poland*** tego nie da się kupić w Polsce
young [jʌŋ] **1.** młody; **2.** *zo.* młode *pl.*; ***the ~*** *pl.* młodzi *pl.*, młodzież *f*; **~·ster** ['jʌŋstə] młodzieniec *m*; dziewczyna *f*, chłopak *m*
your [jɔː] twój, wasz *pl.*; państwa *pl.*; **~s** [jɔːz] twój, wasz *pl.*; państwa *pl.*; ***a friend of ~s*** twój przyjaciel; ♀***, Bill*** (*zakończenie listu*) Twój Bill; **~·self** [jɔː'self] (*pl.* ***yourselves*** [jɔː'selvz]) się, sobie, siebie; sam; ***by ~self*** samodzielnie, bez pomocy
youth [juːθ] (*pl.* **-s** [juːðz]) młodość *f*; młodzieniec *m*; '**~ club** klub *m* młodzieżowy; '**~·ful** młodzieńczy; '**~ hostel** schronisko *n* młodzieżowe
yuck·y ['jʌkɪ] F *cont.* (**-ier, -iest**) paskudny
Yu·go·slav [juːgəʊ'slɑːv] **1.** jugosłowiański; **2.** Jugosłowianin *m* (*-anka*) *f*; **Yu·go·sla·vi·a** [juːgəʊ'slɑːvjə] Jugosławia *f*
yule·tide ['juːltaɪd] *zwł. poet.* Boże Narodzenie *n*
yup·pie, yup·py ['jʌpɪ] (*ze skrótu*) ***young upwardly-mobile*** *lub* ***urban professional*** (*młody wielkomiejski przedstawiciel wolnego zawodu*), yuppie *m*; F japiszon *m*
YWCA [waɪ dʌbljuː siː 'eɪ] *skrót*: ***Young Women's Christian Association*** YWCA *f*, Chrześcijańskie Stowarzyszenie *n* Młodzieży Żeńskiej

Z

Z, z [zed, *Am.* ziː] Z, z *n*
Zagreb Zagrzeb *m*
zap [zæp] F (**-pp-**) *zwł. komp.* wykańczać ⟨-kończyć⟩; usuwać ⟨-sunąć⟩; *samochód* rozpędzać ⟨-dzić⟩; przełączać ⟨-czyć⟩ (*kanały pilotem*); '**~·per** *Am.* F *TV* pilot *m*
zap·py ['zæpɪ] (**-ier, -iest**) energiczny
zeal [ziːl] zapał *m*; **~·ot** ['zelət] fanatyk *m* (-tyczka *f*), gorliwiec *m*; **~·ous** ['zeləs] gorliwy, pełen zapału
ze·bra ['zebrə, 'ziːbrə] *zo.* (*pl.* **-bra, -bras**) zebra *f*; **~ 'cross·ing** *Brt.* zebra *f lub* przejście *n* dla pieszych
zen·ith ['zenɪθ] zenit *m* (*też fig.*)
ze·ro ['zɪərəʊ] (*pl.* **-ros, -roes**) zero *n*; *attr.* zerowy; ***20 degrees below ~*** 20 stopni poniżej zera; **~ 'growth** wzrost *m* zerowy; **~ 'in·terest**: ***have ~ interest in s.th.*** wykazywać zero zainteresowania czymś; **~ 'op·tion** *pol.* opcja *f* zerowa
zest [zest] *fig.* zapał *m*, entuzjazm *m*; ***~ for life*** radość *f* z życia
zig·zag ['zɪgzæg] **1.** zygzak *m*; *attr.* zygzakowy; **2.** (**-gg-**) ⟨po⟩jechać zygzakiem; *droga*: iść zygzakami
zinc [zɪŋk] *chem.* cynk *m*; *attr.* cynkowy
zip¹ [zɪp] **1.** zamek *m* błyskawiczny; **2.** (**-pp-**): ***~ the bag open/shut*** otworzyć/zamknąć zamek błyskawiczny w torbie; ***~ s.o. up*** zapinać ⟨-piąć⟩ komuś zamek błyskawiczny (*w ubraniu*)
zip² [zɪp] **1.** świst *m*; F energia *f*; **2.** świsnąć; ***~ by, ~ past*** przemykać ⟨-knąć⟩ ze świstem obok (*G*)
'zip| code *Am.* kod *m* pocztowy;

~ **'fas·ten·er** *Brt.* **'~·per** *Am.* zamek *m* błyskawiczny

zo·di·ac ['zəʊdɪæk] *astr.* zodiak *m*; ***signs*** *pl.* ***of the ~*** znaki *pl.* zodiaku

zone [zəʊn] strefa *f*

zoo [zuː] (*pl.* ***zoos***) zoo *n*; ogród *m* zoologiczny

zo·o·log·i·cal [zəʊə'lɒdʒɪkl] zoologiczny; ~ **gar·dens** [zʊlɒdʒɪkl 'gɑːdnz] *pl.* ogród *m* zoologiczny

zo·ol·o|·gist [zəʊ'ɒlədʒɪst] zoolog *m*; **~·gy** [zəʊ'ɒlədʒɪ] zoologia *f*

zoom [zuːm] **1.** przemykać ⟨-mknąć⟩; F ⟨po⟩szybować w górę; ***~ by, ~ past*** przemykać ⟨-mknąć⟩ obok; ***~ in on*** *phot.* najeżdżać na (*A*); **2.** warkot *m* (*samochodu itp.*); *też* ***~ lens*** *phot.* obiektyw *m* z zoomem *lub* transfokatorem

Zu·rich Zurych *m*

Summary of Polish Grammar

A. Declension

Declension is the inflection of nouns, adjectives, numerals, pronouns and adjectival participles by using endings that indicate case, number and gender. Note: nouns and substantival pronouns are not inflected according to gender. They appear in a specified gender: masculine, feminine or neuter.

The Declension of Nouns

The following declensions are distinguished according to the kind of noun: masculine, feminine or neuter.

The Masculine Declension

I. The table below shows the declension of masculine nouns whose stem ends in a hard consonant: *-b, -d, -f, -ł, -t, -m, -n, -p, -r, -s, -t, -w, -z.*

		N	G	D	A	I	L	V
sg.	*anim.*	syn-ϕ	syn-a	syn-owi	= G	syn-em	syn-u	= L
	inanim.	sen-ϕ	sn-u	sn-owi	= N	sn-em	śn(i)-e	= L
	inanim.	dom-ϕ	dom-u	dom-owi	= N	dom-em	dom-u	= L
pl.	*anim.*	syn-owie	syn-ów	syn-om	= G	syn-ami	syn-ach	= N
	inanim.	sn-y	sn-ów	sn-om	= N	sn-ami	sn-ach	= N
	inanim.	dom-y	dom-ów	dom-om	= N	dom-ami	dom-ach	= N

II. The table below shows the declension of masculine nouns whose stem ends in a soft consonant: *-ć, -dź, -j, -l, -ń, -ś,* or a functionally soft consonant: *-c, -cz, -dz, -dź, -rz, -sz, -ż* and *-g, -ch, -k.*

		N	G	D	A	I	L	V
sg.	*anim.*	harcerz-ϕ	harcerz-a	harcerz-owi	= G	harcerz-em	harcerz-u	= L
	anim.	dziadek-ϕ	dziadk-a	dziadk-owi	= G	dziadk-iem	dziadk-u	= L
	inanim.	ból-ϕ	ból-u	ból-owi	= N	ból-em	ból-u	= L
pl.	*anim.*	harcerz-e	harcerz-y	harcerz-om	= G	harcerz-ami	harcerz-ach	= N
	anim.	dziadk-owie	dziadk-ów	dziadk-om	= G	dziadk-ami	dziadk-ach	= N
	inanim.	ból-e	ból-ów	ból-om	= N	ból-ami	ból-ach	= N

III. List of endings of the masculine declension

	sg.	*pl.*
N	-ϕ, -o	-owie, -i, -y, -e
G	-a, -u	-ów, -i, -y
D	-a, -owi	-om
A	-a, -ϕ	-ów, -i, -y, -e
I	-em	-ami, -mi
L	-e, -u	-ach
V	-e, -u	-owie, -i, -y, -e

IV. Summary of noun inflectional endings: masculine declension

1. Nominative sg.: ***-ϕ***, *syn-ϕ, ból-ϕ* (diminutive forms are exceptions, e.g. *Józi-o, dziadzi-o,* which end in ***-o***).
2. Genetive sg.: ***-a*** for animate nouns, e.g. *harcerz-a, ps-a* and for nouns denoting the names of tools and parts of the body, e.g. *talerz-a, kolan-a*; ***-u*** for inanimate nouns, e.g. *ból-u, dom-u, sn-u.*
3. Locative sg.: ***-e*** for hard-stemmed nouns, e.g. *śni-e*, (exceptions: *dom-u, syn-u*); ***-u*** for soft-stemmed nouns and for those whose stem ends in *-k, -g, -ch,* np. *chłopc-u, ból-u.*
4. Vocative sg. has the same endings as locative sg. Exception: nouns that end in *-ec*, e.g. *chłopiec – chłopcz-e*!
5. Nominative pl.: ***-e*** for soft-stemmed and for functionally soft-stemmed nouns, e.g.: *harcerz-e, ból-e*; ***-y, -i*** for hard-stemmed nouns, but ***-y*** is characteristic of inanimate nouns: *dom-y, sn-y,* ***-i*** for animate nouns: *chłop-i*, (exception: nouns which end in *-k, -g, -ch,* and *-ec*, e.g.: *Polak – Polac-y, Norweg – Norwedz-y, chłopiec – chłopc-y*); ***-owie*** for words which denote the names of degrees of relationships; e.g.: *sędzi-owie, syn-owie.*
6. Genetive pl.: ***-ów*** for nouns ending in a hard stem, e.g.: *syn-ów, dom-ów*; ***-i, -y*** for soft-stemmed and for functionally soft nouns, e.g.: *harcerz-y*; ***-ϕ*** is rare, e.g. *mieszczan-ϕ.*
7. Accusative pl. for animate nouns A = G pl., e.g. *harcerz-y, chłopc-ów*; for inanimate nouns A = N pl., e.g.: *sn-y, ból-e.*

The Feminine Declension

I. The table below shows the declension of feminine nouns whose stem ends in a hard consonant: *-ba, -cha, -da, -fa, -ła, -ta, -ma, -na, -pa, -ra, -sa, -ta, -wa, -za.*

	N	G	D	A	I	L	V
sg.	wdow-a	wdow-y	wdow(i)-e	wdow-ę	wdow-ą	wdow(i)-e	wdow-o!
	wizyt-a	wizyt-y	wizyc(i)-e	wizyt-ę	wizyt-ą	wizyc(i)-e	wizyt-o!
pl.	wdow-y	wdów-ϕ	wdow-om	= N	wdow-ami	wdow-ach	= N
	wizyt-y	wizyt-ϕ	wizyt-om	= N	wizyt-ami	wizyt-ach	= N

II. The table below shows the declension of feminine nouns whose stem ends in a soft consonant or a functionally soft consonant or *-k, -g, -ch*. They end as follows: *-ca, -cza, -dza, -dża, -rza, -sza, -ża, -la, -bia, -cia, -dzi1a, -fia, -gia, -ja, -kia, -lia, -mia, -nia, -pia, -ria, -sia, -tia, -wia, -zia.*

	N	G	D	A	I	L	V
sg.	niani- a	nian-i	nian-i	niani-ę	niani-ą	nian-i	niani-u!
	wież-a	wież-y	wież-y	wież-ę	wież-ą	wież-y	wież-o!
pl.	niani-e	niań-ϕ	niani-om	= N	niani-ami	niani-ach	= N
	wież-e	wież-ϕ	wież-om	= N	wież-ami	wież-ach	= N

III. The table below shows the declension of feminine nouns that end in a consonant in the nominative sg.

	N	G	D	A	I	L	V
sg.	brew-ϕ	brw-i	brw-i	= N	brwi-ą	brw-i	= G
	noc-ϕ	noc-y	noc-y	= N	noc-ą	noc-y	= G
pl.	brw-i	brw-i	brwi-om	= N	brwi-ami	brwi-ach	= N
	noc-e	noc-y	noc-om	= N	noc-ami	noc-ach	= N

IV. List of endings of the feminine declension

	sg.	*pl.*
N	-a, -i, -ϕ	-y, -i, -e
G	-y, -i	-ϕ, -i, -y
D	-e, -i, -y	-om
A	-ę, -ϕ	= N
I	-ą	-ami,-mi
L	= G	-ach
V	-o, -i, -y	= N

V. Summary of noun inflectional endings: feminine declension

1. Nominative sg.: ***-a*** for nouns with a hard stem, e.g.: *wdow-a*; ***-i*** for nouns with a soft stem, e.g.: *pan-i*; ***-ϕ*** for nouns ending in a consonant, e.g.: *noc-ϕ*.
2. Genitive sg.: ***-y*** for nouns with a hard stem, e.g.: *wizyt-y*; ***-i*** for nouns ending in *-k*, *-g*, e.g. *matk-i*, *nog-i*; and such nouns whose stem ends in a soft consonant: nominative sg. *dłoń*-ϕ, genitive sg. *dłon-i*.
3. Accusative sg.: ***-ę***, e.g. *matk-ę,* apart from nouns ending in a consonant in the nominative sg., e.g.: *noc-ϕ* (A sg. = N sg.). Exception: ***-ą***, *pani-ą.*
4. In the genitive pl. most nouns take the form of the stem, e.g.: *wdów*-ϕ, *niań*-ϕ. Nouns which end in: *-alnia*, *-arnia*, *-ernia*, *-ja* have the ending ***-i***, e.g. *księgarnia – księgarn-i, cukiernia – cukiern-i, transmisja – transmisj-i*. Nouns that end in a consonant in the nominative sg. take the following endings: ***-y***, ***-i,*** e.g. *noc – noc-y*, *dłoń – dłon-i*.
5. Instrumental pl.: ***-ami,*** e.g.: *wdow-ami*, *noc-ami,* with the exception of nouns with the suffix *-ość* which take the ending ***-mi***, e.g.: *kość – kość-mi.*

The Neuter Declension

I. The table below shows the declension of neuter nouns with the ending *-o* in the nominative sg.

	N	G	D	A	I	L	V
sg.	okn-o	okn-a	okn-u	= N	okn-em	okni-e	= N
	lat-o	lat-a	lat-u	= N	lat-em	leci-e	= N
pl.	okn-a	okien-ϕ	okn-om	= N	okn-ami	okn-ach	= N
	lat-a	lat-ϕ	lat-om	= N	lat-ami	lat-ach	= N

II. The table below shows the declension of neuter nouns with the ending *-e* in the nominative sg.

	N	G	D	A	I	L	V
sg.	pol-e	pol-a	pol-u	= N	pol-em	pol-u	= N
	zboże	zboż-a	zboż-u	= N	zboż-em	zboż-u	= N
pl.	pol-a	pól-ϕ	pol-om	= N	pol-ami	pol-ach	= N
	zboż-a	zbóż-ϕ	zboż-om	= N	zboż-ami	zboż-ach	= N

III. The table below shows the declension of neuter nouns with the ending *-ę* in the nominative sg.

	N	G	D	A	I	L	V
sg.	ciel-ę	ciel-ęci-a	ciel-ęci-u	= N	ciel-ęci-em	ciel-ęci-u	= N
	źrebi-ę	źrebi-ęci-a	źrebi-ęci-u	= N	źrebi-ęci-em	źrebi-ęci-u	= N
pl.	ciel-ę-ta	ciel-ąt-ϕ	ciel-ęt-om	= N	ciel-ęt-ami	ciel-ęt-ach	= N
	źrebi-ęt-a	źrebi-ąt-ϕ	źrebi-ęt-om	= N	źrebi-ęt-ami	źrebi-ęt-ach	= N

IV. List of endings of neuter declension

	sg.	*pl.*
N	-o, -e, -ę	-a
G	-a	-ϕ, -i, -y
D	-u	-om
A	= N	= N
I	-em	-ami
L	-e, -u	-ach
V	= N	= N

V. Summary of noun inflectional endings: neuter declension

1. Genitive pl.: ***-ϕ***, e.g.: *okien-ϕ, pól-ϕ, cieląt-ϕ,* but nouns ending in *-e* in the nominative sg. have the genitive pl. ***-i, -y***, e.g. *narzędzie – narzędz-i, wybrzeże – wybrzeż-y.*
2. The nouns which end in *-um* in the nominative sg. are indeclinable in the singular and declined as follows in the plural:

	N	G	D	A	I	L	V
pl.	lice-a	lice-ów	lice-om	= N	lice-ami	lice-ach	= N

Declension of Nouns – Some Peculiarities

1. Masculine nouns ending in *-a* (*poeta, znawca*) decline in the singular like feminine nouns, and in the plural like masculine nouns.

2. The following nouns are indeclinable: *kakao, boa, menu, salami, jury, alibi*
3. Plural nouns, e.g. *rodzice, państwo, usta, drzwi, nożyce, okulary, fusy, imieniny, perfumy* are declined as follows:

	N	G	D	A	I	L	V
pl.	skrzypc-e	skrzypc-ów	skrzypc-om	skrzypc-e	skrzypc-ami	skrzypc-ach	skrzypc-e!
pl.	obcęg-i	obcęg-ów	obcęg-om	obcęg-i	obcęg-ami	obcęg-ach	obcęg-i!

The Declension of Adjectives

Adjectives are declined by using endings that indicate case, number and gender. In the singular, they occur in three forms e.g. *zdrow-y, zdrow-a, zdrow-e*. In the plural adjectives have two forms: masculine, which describes masculine nouns, e.g.: *zdrow-i mężczyźni, zdrow-i uczniowie*; and non-masculine, which describes feminine, neuter and inanimate masculine nouns, e.g.: *zdrow-e kobiety, zdrow-e cielęta, zdrow-e owoce.*

I. The table below shows the declension of adjectives.

	sg.	*sg.*	*sg.*	*pl.*	*pl.*
	masculine	*feminine*	*neuter*	*masculine*	*non-masculine*
N	tan-i mił-y	tani-a mił-a	tani-e mił-e	tan-i mil-i	tani-e mił-e
G	tani-ego mił-ego	tani-ej mił-ej	tani-ego mił-ego	tan-ich mił-ych	tan-ich mił-ych
D	tani-emu mił-emu	tani-ej mił-ej	tani-emu mił-emu	tan-im mił-ym	tan-im mił-ym
A	tan-i mił-ego	tani-ą mił-ą	tani-e mił-e	tan-ich mił-ych	tani-e mił-e
I	tan-im mił-ym	tani-ą mił-ą	tan-im mił-ym	tan-imi mił-ymi	tan-imi mił-ymi
L	tan-im mił-ym	tani-ej mił-ej	tan-im mił-ym	tan-ich mił-ych	tan-ich mił-ych
V	tan-i! mił-y!	tani-a! mił-a!	tani-e! mił-e!	tan-i! mil-i!	tani-e! mił-e!

II. List of endings of the adjective declension

	sg.	*sg.*	*sg.*	*pl.*	*pl.*
	masculine	*feminine*	*neuter*	*masculine*	*non-masculine*
N	-y, -i	-a	-e	-i, -y	-e
G	-ego	-ej	-ego	-ich, -ych	-ich, -ych
D	-emu	-ej	-emu	-im, -ym	-im, -ym
A	-y, -i, -ego	-ą	-e	-ich, -ych	-e
I	-im, -ym	-ą	-im, -ym	-imi, -ymi	-imi, -ymi
L	-im, -ym	-ej	-im, -ym	-ich, -ych	-ich, -ych
V	= N	= N	= N	= N	= N

III. Summary of inflectional endings of adjectives

1. The differentiation between endings of the same case (e.g. locative sg. masc. has parallel endings ***-im, -ym***), depends on the stem of the adjective. An adjective whose stem ends in a soft consonant has ***-i*** in its ending and ***-y*** if it ends in a hard consonant.
2. The nominative sg. masc. has the following endings: ***-i*** for adjectives whose stem ends in a soft consonant *-k*, *-g*, *-ch*, e.g.: *tan-i*, *dług-i;* ***-y*** for adjectives whose stem ends in a hard consonant e.g.: *chciw-y.*
3. The accusative sg. of adjectives denoting animate nouns is the same as the genitive e.g. *dobr-ego człowieka*, The accusative sg. of adjectives denoting inanimate nouns is the same as the nominative, e.g. *now-y samochód.*
4. In the nominative pl. masculine, hard consonants change into soft ones: ***-py*** – ***-pi***, ***-by*** – ***-bi***, ***-wy*** – ***-wi***, ***-ny*** – ***-ni***, ***-dy*** – ***-dzi***, ***-ty*** – ***-ci***, e.g.: *równy – równi, garbaty – garbaci.* Additionally, the following consonants change: ***-k*** – ***-c***, ***-g*** – ***-dz***, ***-ch*** – ***-s***, e.g.: *wysoki – wysocy, ubogi – ubodzy, cichy – cisi.*
5. Simple adjectives: *zdrów-ϕ, wesół-ϕ, ciekaw-ϕ, pewien-ϕ, gotów-ϕ,* take only the masculine form of the nominative sg., e.g. *Chłopiec jest zdrów.*

IV. Degrees of comparison in adjectives

The comparative is formed by adding the endings ***-szy, -si*** to the stem of the basic form of the adjective, e.g. sg. *młod-y – młod-szy,* pl. *młodz-i – młod-si.* The superlative is formed by adding the prefix *naj-* to the comparative form of the adjective, e.g.: *młodszy – naj-młodszy.*

V. Irregular adjectives:

duży – większy – największy
mały – mniejszy – najmniejszy
dobry – lepszy – najlepszy
zły – gorszy – najgorszy

The Declension of Pronouns

I. The declension of personal pronouns

In the declension of personal pronouns, oblique cases are not formed by using the nominative stem. Within the same case there are variant forms (stressed – longer, and unstressed – shorter), e.g. in the nominative sg. *mnie – mi, tobie – ci.*

N	ja	ty
G	mnie	ciebie
D	mnie, mi	tobie, ci
A	mnie, mię	ciebie, cię
I	mną	tobą
L	mnie	tobie

II. The declension of possessive pronouns

Possessive pronouns e.g. *mój, twój, nasz, wasz* are declined in the same way as adjectives. Oblique cases are not formed by using the nominative stem. Variant forms also occur.

	sg.	*sg.*	*sg.*	*pl.*	*pl.*
	masculine	*feminine*	*neuter*	*masculine*	*non-masculine*
N	on	ona	ono	oni	one
G	jego, go, niego	jej, niej	jego, go, niego	ich, nich	ich, nich
D	jemu, mu, niemu	jej, niej	jemu, mu, niemu	im, nim	im, nim
A	jego, go, niego	ją, nią	je, nie	ich, nich	je, nie
I	nim	nią	nim	nimi	nimi
L	nim	niej	nim	nich	nich

The Declension of Numerals

I. The numeral *jeden* has the same forms as the personal pronoun *on*. It is declined in the same way as adjectives e.g.: *jeden uczeń, jedna uczennica, jedno dziecko, jedni uczniowie, jedne uczennice.*

II. The numeral *dwa* occurs in three forms: masculine (*dwaj uczniowie*), feminine (*dwie uczennice*) and non-masculine and neuter (*dwa zeszyty*).

III. The numerals from *trzech* to *tysiąc* have only two forms: masculine (*trzej uczniowie*) and non-masculine (*trzy uczennice, trzy zeszyty*).

IV. Collective numerals, e.g. *dwoje, troje, czworo*, etc. are declined in the same way as neuter nouns in the singular, e.g.: *troj-e ludzi, trojg-a ludzi, trojg-u ludziom, trojgi-em ludzi.*

V. Ordinal numbers, e.g. *pierwszy, drugi, trzeci*, etc. are declined in the same way as adjectives, e.g. *pierwszy uczeń, pierwszego ucznia, pierwszemu uczniowi*, etc.

B. Conjugation

Polish verbs fall into 11 conjugations according to thematic suffixes.

Group I verbs with the thematic suffix ***-a-***
e.g. *kochać, biegać, czytać*, the ending of the infinitive is ***-ać,***

infinitive	*1st pers., sg., present tense*	*3rd pers., sg., present tense*	*3rd pers., pl., present tense*	*imperative*	*3rd pers., sg., m, f, n, past tense*	*adverbial simultaneous participle*
czyt-a-ć	czyt-a-m	czyt-a	czyt-aj-ą	czyt-a-j!	czyt-a-ł(a, -o)	czyt-aj-ąc

In the third person plural present tense, the imperative and the simultaneous participle, the suffix ***-a-*** undergoes extension to ***-aj-***, e.g. *czyt-aj-ą*.

Group II verbs with the thematic suffix ***-e-***
e.g. *umieć, rozumieć*, the ending of the infinitive is ***-eć***

infinitive	*1st pers., sg., present tense*	*3rd pers., sg., present tense*	*3rd pers., pl., present tense*	*impera-tive*	*3rd pers., sg., m, f, n, past tense*	*adverbial simulta-neous participle*
umi-e-ć	umi-e-m	umie	umi-ej-ą	umi-ej!	umi-a-ł(a, -o)	umi-ej-ąc

In the third person plural present tense, the imperative and the simultaneous participle, the suffix ***-e-*** undergoes extension to ***-ej-***, e.g. *umi-ej-ą*.

Group III verbs with the thematic suffix ***-eje-***
e.g. *szaleć, maleć, posmutnieć*, the ending of the infinitive is ***-eć***

infinitive	*1st pers., sg., present tense*	*3rd pers., sg., present tense*	*3rd pers., pl., present tense*	*impera-tive*	*3rd pers., sg., m, f, n, past tense*	*adverbial simulta-neous participle*
mal-e-ć	mal-ej-ę	mal-ej-e	mal-ej-ą	mal-ej!	mal-a-ł(a, -o)	mal-ej-ąc

The thematic suffix ***-eje-*** shortens to ***-ej-*** before vowels, e.g. (*on*) *mal-ej-e*; before consonants it takes the following form: ***-eje-*** e.g. (*ty*) *mal-eje-sz*, (*my*) *mal--eje-my*.

Group IV verbs with the thematic suffix ***-uje-***
e.g. *pracować, malować*, the ending of the infinitive is ***-ować***

infinitive	*1st pers., sg., present tense*	*3rd pers., sg., present tense*	*3rd pers., pl., present tense*	*impera-tive*	*3rd pers., sg., m, f, n, past tense*	*adverbial simulta-neous participle*
prac-owa-ć	prac-uj-ę	prac-uj-e	prac-uj-ą	prac-uj!	prac-owa-ł(a, -o)	prac-uj-ąc

The thematic suffix ***-uje-*** gets shortened to ***-uj-*** before vowels, e.g. (*on*) *prac--uj-e*.

Group V verbs with the thematic suffix: ***-nie-***, ***-nę-*** or ***-ną-***
e.g. *puchnąć, chudnąć, sunąć*, the ending of the infinitive is ***-nąć***

infinitive	*1st pers., sg., present tense*	*3rd pers., sg., present tense*	*3rd pers., pl., present tense*	*impera-tive*	*3rd pers., sg., m, f, n, past tense*	*adverbial simulta-neous participle*
ciąg-ną-ć	ciąg-n-ę	ciąg-nie	ciąg-n-ą	ciąg-nij!	ciąg-ną-ł (-ęła, -ęło)	ciąg-n-ąc
su-ną-ć	su-n-ę	su-nie	su-n-ą	su-ń!	su-ną-ł (-ęła, -ęło)	su-n-ąc
gi-ną-ć	gi-n-ę	gi-nie	gi-n-ą	gi-ń!	gi-ną-ł (-ęła, -ęło)	gi-nąc

Group VI verbs with the thematic suffix: ***-i-*** or ***-y-***
e.g. *topić, mierzyć*, the ending of the infinitive is ***-ić, -yć***

infinitive	*1st pers., sg., present tense*	*3rd pers., sg., present tense*	*3rd pers., pl., present tense*	*impera-tive*	*3rd pers., sg., m, f, n, past tense*	*adverbial simulta-neous participle*
top-i-ć	top-i-ę	top-i	top-i-ą	top!	top-i-ł(a, -o)	top-i-ąc
mierz-y-ć	mierz-ę	mierz-y	mierz-ą	mierz!	mierz-y-ł(a, -o)	mierz-ąc

Group VII verbs with the thematic suffix: ***-e*** in the infinitive, ***-i-*** or ***-y-*** in the present tense
e.g. *myśleć, usłyszeć*, the ending of the infinitive is ***-ić, -yć***

infinitive	*1st pers., sg., present tense*	*3rd pers., sg., present tense*	*3rd pers., pl., present tense*	*impera-tive*	*3rd pers., sg., m, f, n, past tense*	*adverbial simulta-neous participle*
myśl-e-ć	myśl-ę	myśl-i	myśl-ą	myśl!	myśl-a-ł(a, -o)	myśl-ąc
usłysz-e-ć	usłysz-ę*	usłysz-y*	usłysz-ą*	usłysz!	usłysz-a-ł(a, -o)	–

* forms of the future simple tense

Group VIII verbs with the thematic suffix: ***-ywa-, -iwa-***
e.g. *widywać, wymachiwać,* the ending of the infinitive is ***-ywać*** or ***-iwać***,

infinitive	*1st pers., sg., present tense*	*3rd pers., sg., present tense*	*3rd pers., pl., present tense*	*impera-tive*	*3rd pers., sg., m, f, n, past tense*	*adverbial simulta-neous participle*
wid-ywa-ć	wid-uj-ę	wid-uj-e	wid-uj-ą	widuj!	wid-ywa-ł(a, -o)	wid-uj-ąc
wymach-iwa-ć	wymach-uj-ę	wymach-uj-e	wymach-uj-ą	wymach-uj!	wymach-iwa-ł(a,-o)	wymach-uj-ąc

In the present tense verbs have the following suffix ***-uje-***, e.g. (*ja*) *wymach-uj-ę*, (*ty*) *wymach-uje-sz*.

Group IX verbs with the thematic suffix: ***-a-*** in the infinitive, ***-e-*** in the present tense e.g. *łapać, pisać, chrapać*, the ending of the infinitive is ***-ać***

infinitive	*1st pers., sg., present tense*	*3rd pers., sg., present tense*	*3rd pers., pl., present tense*	*impera-tive*	*3rd pers., sg., m, f, n, past tense*	*adverbial simulta-neous participle*
łap-a-ć	łapi-ę	łapi-e	łapi-ą	łap!	łap-a-ł(a, -o)	łapi-ąc

Group X comprises various verbs: with the thematic suffix: ***-a-*** in the infinitive, ***-e-*** in the present tense:
Xa – the stem of the verbs ends in ***-i, -y, -u***;
Xb – they have the thematic suffix ***-eje-*** in the present tense, ***-a-*** in the past tense and in the infinitive;
Xc – there is a change in the stem from ***-n-, -m-*** into ***-ą-*** e.g. *dąć – dmie, tchnąć – tchnie.*

infinitive	*1st pers., sg., present tense*	*3rd pers., sg., present tense*	*3rd pers., pl., present tense*	*impera-tive*	*3rd pers., sg., m, f, n, past tense*	*adverbial simulta-neous participle*
ży-ć	żyj-ę	żyj-e	żyj-ą	żyj!	żył(a, -o)	żyj-ąc
grz-a-ć	grz-ej-ę	grz-ej-e	grz-ej-ą	grzej!	grzał(a, -o)	grz-ej-ąc
dą-ć	dm-ę	dmi-e	dm-ą	dmij!	dął (-ęła, -ęło)	dmi-ąc

Group XI verbs with the thematic suffix: ***-e-*** in the present tense (*wiezi-e-sz, tłucz-e-my).*
There is no suffix in the infinitive.

infinitive	*1st pers., sg., present tense*	*3rd pers., sg., present tense*	*3rd pers., pl., present tense*	*impera-tive*	*3rd pers., sg., m, f, n, past tense*	*adverbial simulta-neous participle*
wieś-ć	wioz-ę	wiezi-e	wioz-ą	wieź!	wiózł(a, -o)	wioz-ąc
tłuc	tłuk-ę	tłucz-e	tłuk-ą	tłucz!	tłukł(a, -o)	tłuk-ąc

Rules for Forming Conjugations

The Past Simple Tense (the forms are based on the stem of the verb in the past tense)

sg. m, f, n
1. czytał-em, -am
2. czytał-eś, -aś
3. czytał-ϕ, -a, -o

pl. m, non-m
1. czytali-śmy, czytały-śmy
2. czytali-ście, czytały-ście
3. czytali-ϕ, czytały-ϕ

The Present Simple Tense (only imperfect verbs; the forms are based on the stem of the verb in the present tense)

sg.	*pl.*
1. czyta-m	1. czyta-my
2. czyta-sz	2. czyta-cie
3. czyta-ϕ	3. czyta-ją

The Future Simple Tense (only perfect verbs; the forms are based on the stem of the verb in the present tense)

sg.	*pl.*
1. przeczyta-m	1. przeczyta-my
2. przeczyta-sz	2. przeczyta-cie
3. przeczyta-ϕ	3. przeczyta-ją

The Future Tense type I (only imperfect verbs; the forms are based on the stem of the verb in the past tense)

sg.	*pl.*
1. będ-ę czytać	1. będzie-my czytać
2. będzie-sz czytać	2. będzie-cie czytać
3. będzie-ϕ czytać	3. będ-ą czytać

The Future Tense type II

sg. m, f, n	*pl. m, non-m*
1. będę pisał, -a	1. będziemy pisali, będziemy pisały
2. będziesz pisał, -a	2. będziecie pisali, będziecie pisały
3. będzie pisał, -a, -o	3. będą pisali, będą pisały

Declensional forms of the verb

1. Active and passive participles are declined according to the adjectival declension.
   a) The active participle is formed by adding the following to the stem of the verb in the third person plural of the present tense: the suffix ***-ąc-*** and the appropriate case ending, e.g. N sg. *czytaj-ąc-a kobieta, czytaj-ąc-y chłopiec*, G sg. *czytaj-ąc-ej kobiety, czytaj-ąc-ego chłopca*, etc.
   b) The passive participle is formed by adding the following to the stem of the verb in the past tense: the suffix ***-n-***, ***-on-***, ***-t-*** and the appropriate case ending, e.g. N sg. *czyta-n-a książka*, G sg. *czyta-n-ej książki*, etc.
2. Gerunds are declined according to the noun declension. They are formed by adding the following to the stem: the suffixes ***-nie***, **-(*i*)*enie***, ***-cie***, **-(*i*)*ęcie***, **-(*ie*)*nie*** and the appropriate case ending, e.g. *czyta-nie*, *macha-nie*, *widywa-nie*, *d-ęcie.*

Indeclinable forms of the verb

1. Infinitives
2. Adverbial participles
   a) Simultaneous participle – is formed by adding the suffix ***-ąc*** to the stem of the verb in the 3rd person plural in the present tense, e.g. *czytaj-ąc, widz-ąc*
   b) Anticipatory participle – is formed by adding the following suffixes to the stem of the verb in the past tense: ***-łszy*** (if the stem ends in a consonant), e.g. *zjad-łszy, podniósłszy*; or ***-wszy*** (if the stem ends in a vowel), e.g. *dojecha-wszy, przeczyta-wszy.*
3. Modal verbs, e.g.: *trzeba*, *warto*, *można, wolno.*

Liczebniki – Numerals

Liczebniki główne – Cardinal Numerals

0 *nought*, zero
telefon: *O*, zero
1 *one* jeden, jedna, jedno
2 *two* dwa, dwie
3 *three* trzy
4 *four* cztery
5 *five* pięć
6 *six* sześć
7 *seven* siedem
8 *eight* osiem
9 *nine* dziewięć
10 *ten* dziesięć
11 *eleven* jedenaście
12 *twelve* dwanaście
13 *thirteen* trzynaście
14 *fourteen* czternaście
15 *fifteen* piętnaście
16 *sixteen* szesnaście
17 *seventeen* siedemnaście
18 *eighteen* osiemnaście
19 *nineteen* dziewiętnaście
20 *twenty* dwadzieścia
21 *twenty-one* dwadzieścia jeden
22 *twenty-two* dwadzieścia dwa
30 *thirty* trzydzieści
31 *thirty-one* trzydzieści jeden
40 *forty* czterdzieści
41 *forty-one* czterdzieści jeden
50 *fifty* pięćdziesiąt
51 *fifty-one* pięćdziesiąt jeden
60 *sixty* sześćdziesiąt
61 *sixty-one* sześćdziesiąt jeden
70 *seventy* siedemdziesiąt
71 *seventy-one* siedemdziesiąt jeden
80 *eighty* osiemdziesiąt
81 *eighty-one* osiemdziesiąt jeden
90 *ninety* dziewięćdziesiąt
91 *ninety-one* dziewięćdziesiąt jeden
100 *a hundred, one hundred* sto
101 *a/one hundred and one* sto jeden
200 *two hundred* dwieście
300 *three hundred* trzysta
572 *five hundred and seventy-two* pięćset siedemdziesiąt dwa
1000 *a thousand, one thousand* tysiąc
2000 *two thousand* dwa tysiące
5000 *five thousand* pięć tysięcy
1,000,000 *a million, one million* milion
2,000,000 *two million* dwa miliony
1,000,000,000 *a billion, one billion* miliard

Liczebniki porządkowe – Ordinal Numerals

1st *first* pierwszy
2nd *second* drugi
3rd *third* trzeci
4th *fourth* czwarty
5th *fifth* piąty
6th *sixth* szósty
7th *seventh* siódmy
8th *eighth* ósmy
9th *ninth* dziewiąty
10th *tenth* dziesiąty
11th *eleventh* jedenasty
12th *twelfth* dwunasty
13th *thirteenth* trzynasty
14th *fourteenth* czternasty
15th *fifteenth* piętnasty
16th *sixteenth* szesnasty
17th *seventeenth* siedemnasty
18th *eighteenth* osiemnasty
19th *nineteenth* dziewiętnasty
20th *twentieth* dwudziesty
21st *twenty-first* dwudziesty pierwszy
22nd *twenty-second* dwudziesty drugi
23rd *twenty-third* dwudziesty trzeci
30th *thirtieth* trzydziesty
31st *thirty-first* trzydziesty pierwszy
40th *fortieth* czterdziesty
41st *forty-first* czterdziesty pierwszy
50th *fiftieth* pięćdziesiąty
51st *fifty-first* pięćdziesiąty pierwszy
60th *sixtieth* sześćdziesiąty
61st *sixty-first* sześćdziesiąty pierwszy
70th *seventieth* siedemdziesiąty
71st *seventy-first* siedemdziesiąty pierwszy
80th *eightieth* osiemdziesiąty
81st *eighty-first* osiemdziesiąty pierwszy
90th *ninetieth* dziewięćdziesiąty
100th (*one*) *hundredth* setny
101st *hundred and first* sto pierwszy
200th *two hundredth* dwusetny *lub* dwóchsetny
300th *three hundredth* trzechsetny
572nd *five hundred and seventy-second* pięćset siedemdziesiąty drugi
1000th (*one*) *thousandth* tysięczny
1950th *nineteen hundred and fiftieth* tysiąc dziewięćset pięćdziesiąty
2000th *two thousandth* dwutysięczny
1,000,000th *millionth* milionowy
2,000,000th *two millionth* dwumilionowy

Ułamki – Fractions

$^1/_2$ *one half* lub *a half* pół *lub* jedna druga
$1^1/_2$ *one and a half* półtora *lub* jeden i jedna druga
$2^1/_2$ *two and a half* dwa i pół *lub* dwa i jedna druga
$^1/_3$ *one third, a third* jedna trzecia
$^2/_3$ *two thirds* dwie trzecie
$^1/_4$ *one a quarter, one fourth* ćwierć *lub* jedna czwarta
$^3/_4$ *three quarters, three fourths* trzy czwarte
$^1/_5$ *one fifth lub a fifth* jedna piąta
$3^4/_5$ *three and four fifths* trzy (całe) i cztery piąte
$^5/_8$ *five eighths* pięć ósmych
0.45 (*nought*) *point four five* zero przecinek czterdzieści pięć *lub* czterdzieści pięć setnych
2.5 *two point five* dwa przecinek pięć *lub* dwa i pięć dziesiątych *lub* dwa i pół

once raz
twice dwa razy
three times trzy razy
four times cztery razy
twice as much dwa razy tyle (*przy rzeczownikach niepoliczalnych*)
twice as many dwa razy tyle (*przy rzeczownikach policzalnych*)
firstly, in the first place po pierwsze
secondly, in the second place po drugie
thirdly, in the third place po trzecie

Wykaz angielskich czasowników nieregularnych

Poniższe zestawienie zawiera listę najważniejszych czasowników nieregularnych. W pierwszej kolumnie podano bezokolicznik (infinitive), w drugiej znaczenie (meaning), w trzeciej formę czasu przeszłego (past tense) a w czwartej imiesłów bierny (past participle).

Infinitive	Meaning	Past tense	Past participle
arise	*powstawać*	arose	arisen
awake	*budzić (się)*	awoke	awoken
be	*być*	was *albo* were	been
bear	*nosić/rodzić*	bore	borne/born
beat	*bić*	beat beaten	
become	*stawać się*	became	become
beget	*począć*	begot	begotten
begin	*zaczynać*	began	begun
bend	*zginać (się)*	bent	bent
bet	*zakładać się*	bet *lub* betted	bet *lub* betted
bid[1]	*oferować*	bid	bid
bid[2]	*mówić*	bade *lub* bid	bidden
bind	*wiązać*	bound	bound
bite	*gryźć*	bit	bitten
bleed	*krwawić*	bled	bled
blow	*wiać/dmuchać*	blew	blown
break	*łamać*	broke	broken
breed	*hodować*	bred	bred
bring	*przynosić*	brought	brought
broadcast	*radio i TV: nadawać*	broadcast	broadcast
build	*budować*	built	built
burn	*palić (się)/oparzyć (się)*	burnt *lub* burned	burnt *lub* burned
burst	*pękać*	burst	burst
buy	*kupować*	bought	bought
can	*móc, umieć*	could	–
cast	*rzucać*	cast	cast
catch	*łapać*	caught	caught
choose	*wybierać*	chose	chosen
cling	*przywierać*	clung	clung
come	*przychodzić*	came	come
cost	*kosztować*	cost	cost
creep	*skradać się/pełzać*	crept	crept
cut	*ciąć*	cut	cut
deal	*handlować/zajmować się*	dealt	dealt
dig	*kopać*	dug	dug
dive	*skakać/nurkować*	dived, *AE* dove	dived
do	*robić*	did	done
draw	*ciągnąć/rysować*	drew	drawn
dream	*śnić/marzyć*	dreamt *lub* dreamed	dreamt *lub* dreamed
drink	*pić*	drank	drunk
drive	*prowadzić (pojazd)*	drove	driven
dwell	*mieszkać*	dwelt *lub* dwelled	dwelt *lub* dwelled
eat	*jeść*	ate	eaten
fall	*padać*	fell	fallen
feed	*karmić*	fed	fed
feel	*czuć*	felt	felt
fight	*walczyć*	fought	fought
find	*znajdować*	found	found

fit	*pasować*	fitted, *AE też* fit	fitted, *AE też* fit
flee	*uciekać*	fled	fled
fling	*rzucać*	flung	flung
fly	*latać*	flew	flown
forbid	*zakazywać*	forbade *lub* forbad	forbidden
forecast	*prognozować*	forecast	forecast
foresee	*przewidywać*	foresaw	foreseen
forget	*zapominać*	forgot	forgotten
forgive	*wybaczać*	forgave	forgiven
freeze	*zamarzać/zamrażać*	froze	frozen
get	*dostawać*	got	got, *AE też* gotten
give	*dać/dawać*	gave	given
go	*iść/jechać*	went	gone
grind	*mielić/ostrzyć*	ground	ground
grow	*rosnąć/uprawiać*	grew	grown
hang[1]	*wisieć/wieszać*	hung	hung
hang[1]	*powiesić (człowieka)*	hanged	hanged
have	*mieć*	had	had
hear	*słyszeć*	heard	heard
hide	*ukrywać (się)*	hid	hidden
hit	*uderzać/trafić*	hit	hit
hold	*trzymać*	held	held
hurt	*boleć/ranić*	hurt	hurt
keep	*trzymać*	kept	kept
kneel	*klęczeć*	knelt, *AM* kneeled	knelt, *AM* kneeled
knit	*robić na drutach*	knitted, knit	knitted, knit
know	*wiedzieć/znać*	knew	known
lay	*kłaść/znosić (jajka)*	laid	laid
lead	*prowadzić*	led	led
lean	*opierać (się)*	leaned, leant	leaned, leant
leap	*skakać*	leapt, *AM* leaped	leapt, *AM* leaped
learn	*uczyć się*	learned, learnt	learned, learnt
leave	*wyjeżdżać/zostawiać*	left	left
lend	*pożyczać (komuś)*	lent	lent
let	*pozwalać*	let	let
lie	*leżeć*	lay	lain
light	*oświetlić/zapalić (się)*	lit, lighted	lit, lighted
lose	*zgubić/przegrać*	lost	lost
make	*robić*	made	made
mean	*znaczyć*	meant	meant
meet	*spotykać (się)*	met	met
mislead	*wprowadzać w błąd*	misled	misled
mistake	*pomylić*	mistook	mistaken
misunder-stand	*źle zrozumieć*	misunderstood	misunderstood
mow	*kosić*	mowed	mown, mowed
outdo	*przewyższać*	outdid	outdone
outgrow	*wyrastać*	outgrew	outgrown
overcome	*pokonać*	overcame	overcome
overdo	*przesadzać (z czymś)*	overdid	overdone
overhear	*przypadkowo usłyszeć*	overheard	overheard
oversleep	*zaspać*	overslept	overslept
overtake	*wyprzedzać*	overtook	overtaken
pay	*płacić*	paid	paid
plead	*błagać*	pleaded, *AM* pled	pleaded, *AM* pled
prove	*udowodnić*	proved	proved, *AM* proven
put	*kłaść/stawiać*	put	put
read	*czytać*	read	read

resit	*ponownie zdawać*	resat	resat
rewind	*przewijać*	rewound	rewound
ride	*jeździć/jechać*	rode	ridden
ring	*dzwonić/telefonować*	rang	rung
rise	*wzrastać/wschodzić*	rose	risen
run	*biec*	ran	run
saw	*piłować*	sawed	sawn, sawed
say	*powiedzieć/mówić*	said	said
see	*widzieć/zobaczyć*	saw	seen
seek	*szukać*	sought	sought
sell	*sprzedawać (się)*	sold	sold
send	*wysyłać*	sent	sent
set	*umieścić/nastawić*	set	set
sew	*szyć/przyszyć*	sewed	sewn, sewed
shake	*trząść (się)*	shook	shaken
shine	*świecić/polerować*	shone, shined	shone, shined
shoot	*strzelać*	shot	shot
show	*pokazywać*	showed	shown
shrink	*kurczyć się*	shrank, shrunk	shrunk
shut	*zamykać (się)*	shut	shut
sing	*śpiewać*	sang	sung
sink	*tonąć/zatopić*	sank	sunk
sit	*siedzieć*	sat	sat
sleep	*spać*	slept	slept
slide	*ślizgać się/przesuwać*	slid	slid
smell	*pachnieć/wąchać*	smelt, *AM* smelled	smelt, *AM* smelled
sow	*siać*	sowed	sown, sowed
speak	*mówić/rozmawiać*	spoke	spoken
spell	*pisać/literować*	spelt, spelled	spelt, spelled
spill	*rozlać (się)*	spilt, *AM* spilled	spilt, *AM* spilled
spin	*wirować/obracać*	spun, span	spun
spit	*pluć*	spat, *AM* spit	spat, *AM* spit
split	*rozczepiać (się)*	split	split
spoil	*psuć/niszczyć/ rozpieszczać*	spoilt, *AM* spoiled	spoilt, *AM* spoiled
spread	*rozkładać/rozpościerać*	spread	spread
spring	*skoczyć*	sprang, *AM* sprung	sprung
stand	*stać/stawiać*	stood	stood
steal	*kraść*	stole	stolen
stick	*wbijać/przyklejać (się)*	stuck	stuck
sting	*żądlić*	stung	stung
stink	*śmierdzieć*	stank, stunk	stunk
strike	*atakować/uderzać*	struck	struck
strive	*dokładać starań*	strove, strived	striven, strived
swear	*kląć/przysięgać*	swore	sworn
sweep	*zamiatać/zgarniać*	swept	swept
swell	*powiększać (się)/puchnąć*	swelled	swollen, swelled
swim	*płynąć*	swam	swum
swing	*hustać się/kołysać się*	swung	swung
take	*brać/przyjmować*	took	taken
teach	*uczyć/nauczać*	taught	taught
tear	*rwać/odrywać*	tore	torn
tell	*powiedzieć/opowiadać*	told	told
think	*myśleć*	thought	thought
throw	*rzucać*	threw	thrown
tread	*kroczyć*	trod	trodden, trod
understand	*rozumieć*	understood	understood
undertake	*podejmować się*	undertook	undertaken

undo	*rozpinać*	undid	undone
upset	*sprawić przykrość*	upset	upset
wake	*budzić (się)*	woke, waked	woken, waked
wear	*nosić (ubranie)*	wore	worn
weave	*tkać/wyplatać*	wove	woven
wed	*poślubić*	wedded, wed	wedded, wed
weep	*płakać/łkać*	wept	wept
win	*wygrać/zwyciężyć*	won	won
wind	*nawijać/wić się*	wound	wound
withdraw	*wycofać się*	withdrew	withdrawn
wring	*wykręcać*	wrung	wrung
write	*pisać*	wrote	written

Headword in **blue**

a·board [ə'bɔːd] na pokładzie; ***all ~!*** *naut.* wszyscy na pokład!, *rail.* proszę wsiadać!; ***~ a bus*** w autobusie; ***go ~ a train*** wsiadać ⟨wsiąść⟩ do pociągu

Translation in normal characters

a·bridge [ə'brɪdʒ] skracać ⟨-rócić⟩; **a'bridg(e)·ment** skrót *m*

International Phonetic Alphabet

hop² [hɒp] *bot.* chmiel *m*; **~s** chmiel *m* (*szyszki*)

Swung dash replaces the headword or the part of it

ac·ces|·si·ble [ək'sesəbl] *łatwo* dostępny; **~·sion** [ək'seʃn] objęcie *n* (*urzędu*); ***~sion to power*** przejęcie *n* władzy; ***~sion to the throne*** objęcie *n* tronu

Examples and phrases in ***bold italics***

ab·di|·cate ['æbdɪkeɪt] *prawo, władza itp.*: zrzekać ⟨-ec⟩ się; ***~cate from (the) throne*** abdykować; **~·ca·tion** [æbdɪ'keɪʃn] zrzeczenie się *n*, abdykacja *f*

Homonyms marked with superscript numerals

Co¹ [kəʊ] *skrót*: ***company*** *econ.* spółka *f*
Co² *skrót pisany*: ***County*** *Brt.* hrabstwo *n*; *Am.* okręg *m* (*wyborczy*)